MW01030885

OLD TESTAMENT

WILLIAM MACDONALD
Edited with Introductions by Arthur Farstad

THOMAS NELSON PUBLISHERS
Nashville

Library of Congress Catalog Card Number: 87-073458
ISBN: 0-8407-6810-9

Some of the materials in this volume were previously published by Harold Shaw Publishers and Walterick Publishers, and used with their permission. However, they have been revised, expanded, and considerably edited.

Library of Congress Cataloging-in-Publication Data

MacDonald, William, 1917–
Believer's Bible commentary. Old Testament / William MacDonald ; edited with introductions by Arthur Farstad.
p. cm.
Includes bibliographical references.
ISBN 0-8407-6810-9
1. Bible. O.T.—Commentaries. I. Farstad, Arthur L. II. Title.
BS1151.2.M33 1992
221.7—-dc20 91-39765
CIP

1 2 3 4 5 — 96 95 94 93 92

CONTENTS

Author's Preface

The purpose of the *Believer's Bible Commentary (BBC)* is to give the average Christian reader a basic knowledge of what the Old Testament (OT) is all about.

The *BBC* is also intended to stimulate such a love and taste for these neglected books that the believer will want to delve more deeply into their inexhaustible treasures. While scholars will hopefully find food for their souls, they will be considerate in understanding that the book was not designed primarily for them.

With the exception of Psalms, Proverbs, and Ecclesiastes, the exposition of the OT is generally presented in paragraph-by-paragraph rather than in verse-by-verse form. The comments on the text are augmented by practical applications of spiritual truths and by a study of typology, where appropriate.

Passages that point forward to the coming Redeemer are highlighted and handled in greater detail.

The Books of Psalms, Proverbs, and Ecclesiastes are handled verse by verse, either because they do not lend themselves to condensation, or because most believers desire to study them in greater depth.

We have tried to face problem texts and to give alternative explanations where possible. Many passages are the despair of commentators, and we must confess that on these we still "see in a mirror, dimly."

More important than any commentary is *the Word of God itself,* as illuminated by the Holy Spirit of God. Without it there is no life, growth, holiness, or acceptable service. We should read it, study it, memorize it, meditate on it, and above all obey it. As someone has said, "Obedience is the organ of spiritual knowledge."

Editor's Introduction

"Don't despise the commentaries." This was the advice of a Bible teacher to his class at Emmaus Bible School (now College) in the late 1950's. At least one student remembered those words through three decades. The teacher was William MacDonald, the author of *Believer's Bible Commentary*. The student was the editor, Arthur Farstad, at that time a callow freshman. He had only read one commentary in his life—*In the Heavenlies* (Ephesians) by Harry A. Ironside. Reading the commentary every night one summer as a teenager, Art Farstad found out what a commentary is.

What a Commentary Is

Exactly what is a commentary and why should we not despise one? Recently a prominent Christian publisher listed *fifteen* types of Bible-related books. If some people don't know exactly how a commentary differs from a study Bible, e.g., or even from a concordance, an atlas, an interlinear, a Bible dictionary—to name five—it should be no surprise.

A commentary comments, or makes (hopefully) helpful remarks on the text, either verse by verse or paragraph by paragraph. Some Christians sneer at commentaries and say, "I only want to hear the spoken word and read the Bible itself!" Sounds pious, but it is not. A commentary merely puts in print the best (and hardest!) type of Bible exposition—the verse by verse teaching and preaching of the Word of God. Some commentaries (such as Ironside's) are quite literally sermons put into print. What's more, the greatest Bible expositions of all ages and tongues are available in English. Unfortunately many are so long, so dated, and so difficult that the ordinary Christian gets discouraged, not to say overwhelmed. Hence, *Believer's Bible Commentary (BBC)*.

Kinds of Commentaries

Theoretically, anyone interested in the Bible could write a commentary. For this reason they range from extremely liberal to very conservative—with every shade of thought in between. The *BBC* is a very conservative one, accepting the Bible as the inspired and flawless Word of God, totally sufficient for faith and practice.

A commentary can range all the way from highly technical (minute details of Greek and Hebrew syntax, e.g.) to a very breezy sketch. The *BBC* is somewhere in between. What technicalities are needed are largely relegated to the endnotes, but a serious interaction with the details of the text is given with no dodging of difficult passages or convicting applications. Mr. MacDonald's writing is rich in exposition. It's aim is to help produce, not merely garden-variety, lowest-common-denominator Christians, but disciples.

Commentaries also differ as to theological camp—conservative or liberal, Protestant or Roman Catholic, premillennial or amillennial. The *BBC* is conservative, Protestant, and premillennial.

How to Use This Book

There are several approaches to the *BBC*. We suggest the following, pretty much in this order:

Browsing—If you like or love the Bible you will enjoy leafing through this book, reading bits and pieces here and there to get the flavor of the whole work.

Specific Passage—You may have a question on a verse or paragraph that you need help on. Look it up in the appropriate place in context and you will surely find good material.

A Doctrine—If you are studying creation, the Sabbath, the covenants, the dispensations, or the angel of the Lord, look up the passages that deal with those subjects. The Table of Contents lists essays[1] on a number of these topics. Use a concordance to help locate key words to guide to central passages for topics other than the ones listed.

Bible Book—Perhaps your Sunday school class or congregation is going through a book of the Old Testament. You will greatly enrich yourself (and have something to contribute, if there is a discussion) if you read ahead each week the passage to be covered. (Of course, if the leader is also using the *BBC* as a main study help, you may want to have two different commentaries!)

The Whole Book—Eventually every Christian should read through the entire Bible. There are hard texts scattered throughout, and a careful, conservative book like the *BBC* will greatly enhance your study.

Bible study may start out in the "shredded wheat" stage—"nutritious but dry," but as you progress it will become "chocolate pie"!

Mr. MacDonald's advice to me thirty years ago was, "Don't despise the commentaries." Having studied his Commentaries on the Old and New Testaments[2] with great care while editing them for the New King James text, I can go a step further. My advice: "Enjoy!"

ENDNOTES

[1]Technically a discussion in a commentary that expands on some subject touched upon in the text is called an *excursus*.

[2]It was my privilege to edit the New Testament volume of the *BBC*, released in 1990 by Thomas Nelson Publishers.

Illustrations and Tables

Figures

Tables

Maps

Abbreviations

Abbreviations of Books of the Bible

Old Testament Books

Gen.	Genesis	2 Chron.	2 Chronicles	Dan.	Daniel
Ex.	Exodus	Ezra	Ezra	Hos.	Hosea
Lev.	Leviticus	Neh.	Nehemiah	Joel	Joel
Num.	Numbers	Est.	Esther	Amos	Amos
Deut.	Deuteronomy	Job	Job	Obad.	Obadiah
Josh.	Joshua	Ps.(Pss.)	Psalm(s)	Jon.	Jonah
Judg.	Judges	Prov.	Proverbs	Mic.	Micah
Ruth	Ruth	Eccl.	Ecclesiastes	Nah.	Nahum
1 Sam.	1 Samuel	Song	Song of Solomon	Hab.	Habakkuk
2 Sam.	2 Samuel	Isa.	Isaiah	Zeph.	Zephaniah
1 Kgs.	1 Kings	Jer.	Jeremiah	Hag.	Haggai
2 Kgs.	2 Kings	Lam.	Lamentations	Zech.	Zechariah
1 Chron.	1 Chronicles	Ezek.	Ezekiel	Mal.	Malachi

New Testament Books

Matt.	Matthew	Eph.	Ephesians	Heb.	Hebrews
Mark	Mark	Phil.	Philippians	Jas.	James
Luke	Luke	Col.	Colossians	1 Pet.	1 Peter
John	John	1 Thess.	1 Thessalonians	2 Pet.	2 Peter
Acts	Acts	2 Thess.	2 Thessalonians	1 Jn.	1 John
Rom.	Romans	1 Tim.	1 Timothy	2 Jn.	2 John
1 Cor.	1 Corinthians	2 Tim.	2 Timothy	3 Jn.	3 John
2 Cor.	2 Corinthians	Tit.	Titus	Jude	Jude
Gal.	Galatians	Phmn.	Philemon	Rev.	Revelation

Abbreviations of Bible Versions, Translations, and Paraphrases

ASV	American Standard Version	NEB	New English Bible
FWG	F. W. Grant's *Numerical Bible*	NIV	New International Version
JND	John Nelson Darby's New Translation	NKJV	New King James Version
KJV	King James Version	NRSV	New Revised Standard Version
—	Knox Version	RSV	Revised Standard Version
LB	Living Bible	RV	Revised Version (England)
—	Moffatt Translation	—	*The Holy Scriptures* (Jewish Publication Society)
NASB	New American Standard Bible		

Other Abbreviations

A.D.	*Anno Domini*, in the year of our Lord marginal reading
Aram.	Aramaic
BBC	*Believer's Bible Commentary*
B.C.	Before Christ
c.	*circa*, about
cf.	*confer*, compare
chap.	chapter
chaps.	chapters
ed.	edited, edition, editor
eds.	editors
e.g.	*exempli gratia*, for example
et al.	*et alii*, and others
fem.	feminine
Gk.	Greek
Heb.	Hebrew
ICC	*International Critical Commentary*
ibid.	*ibidem*, in the same place
i.e.	*id est*, that is
lit.	literal, literally
LXX	Septuagint (ancient Gk. version of the OT)
marg.	margin, marginal reading
masc.	masculine
ms., mss.	manuscript(s)
M	Majority Text
MT	Masoretic text
n.d.	no date
NIC	*New International Commentary*
n.p.	no publisher, no place of publication
NT	New Testament
NU	Nestle-Aland/United Bible Societies Greek NT
OT	Old Testament
p., pp.	page(s)
trans.	translation, translator translated
vol(s).	volume(s)
v., vv.	verse(s)
vs.	versus

Transliteration of Hebrew Words

The Believer's Bible Commentary, being tailor-made for the ordinary Christian who has studied no Hebrew, uses only a handful of Hebrew words in the text, and a few more in the endnotes.

The Hebrew Alphabet

Form	*Final Form*	*Transliterated by*	*Name*	*Pronunciation*
א		'	'Aleph	(silent)
בּ (ב)		b (v)	Bêth	B in boy (v in very)
גּ (ג)		g	Gîmel	G in go
דּ (ד)		d	Dāleth	D in day (th in them)[1]
ה		h	Hê	H in hat
ו		w	Wāw	W in way[2]
ז		z	Zayin	Z in zeal
ח		ḥ	Ḥêth	CH in Scottish "loch"
ט		t	Têth	T in toy
י		y	Yôd	Y in yet
כּ (כ)	ך	k (kh)	Kaph	K in kick
ל		l	Lāmed	L in let
מ	ם	m	Mêm	M in met
נ	ן	n	Nûn	N in net
ס		s	Sāmekh	S in set
ע		'	'Ayin	(silent)[3]
פּ (פ)	ף	p (ph)	Pê	P in pet (ph in phone)
צ	ץ	ts	TSādhê	TS in hits
ק		q	Qôph	Q in Iraq (=k)
ר		r	Rêsh	R in run
שׂ		s	Sîn	S in so
שׁ		sh	SHîn	SH in she
תּ (ת)		t (th)	Tāw	T in tin (th in thin)[4]

The Consonants

OT Hebrew has twenty-two letters, all consonants; the early biblical scrolls did not contain vowels. These vowel "points," as they are called, were invented and inserted during the seventh century A.D. Hebrew words are written from right to left, just the opposite from English writing.

We have used a somewhat simplified system of transliteration (similar to what is used in popular transliterations from Israel).

For example, when a *bêth* is pronounced "v" we put a v in the transliteration, not a *b* with a line under it (*nevî'îm,* not *nebî'îm.* Because the difference in sound between *hê* (=h) and *ḥêth* (=guttural h) is strong, we have put a dot under the *h* when it represents *ḥêth* (=ḥ).[5]

We have not, however, put marks on English *s's* or *t's* to differentiate minor differences that are too subtle for popular usage.

Names that have become anglicized by frequent usage, such as *Elohim*, are not usually marked with diacritical marks over the English vowels.

The Vowels

Here are a few pointers on how to pronounce the vowels:

The *unmarked* vowels are short: a, e, i, o, u, are pronounced as in c*a*t, p*e*t, k*i*d, d*o*ll, p*u*t.

The vowels marked with either a long mark (ˉ) or a circumflex accent (ˆ) are pronounced as follows:

ā or â as in f*a*ther (e.g. *Tôrāh*)
ē or ê as in th*ey* (e.g. *'āmēn*)
î as in pol*i*ce (e.g.: *'Elōhîm*)
ō or ô as in g*o*ld (e.g.: *shālôm*)
ū or û as in tr*u*th (e.g.: *hallēlû Yāh*)

ENDNOTES

[1]In modern (Israeli) Hebrew the letter is always pronounced as a "d."

[2]In modern Hebrew this letter is called *vav* and pronounced as "v."

[3]In biblical times *'ayin* had a guttural sound. For example the Hebrew original of the name *Gaza* began with this letter; apparently it was close enough to a hard "g" sound to make the Hellenists transliterate it here with a *gamma*.

[4]In modern Hebrew this letter is called *tav* and always pronounced as a "t."

[5]This is usually done in scholarly journals and other more technical works.

INTRODUCTION TO THE OLD TESTAMENT

"For us the supreme sanction of the Old Testament is that which it derived from Christ Himself. . . . What was indispensable to the Redeemer must always be indispensable to the redeemed."

—Professor G. A. Smith

I. The Name "Old Testament"

Before launching out into the deep seas of OT studies, or even the comparatively small area of studying a particular book, it will prove helpful to outline briefly some general facts about the Sacred Book we call "The Old Testament."

Our word "covenant" translates the Hebrew word *berîth*.[1] In the NT *covenant* and *testament* both translate the same Greek word (*diathēkē*). In the title of the Scriptures the *meaning* "covenant" seems definitely preferable because the Book constitutes a pact, alliance, or *covenant* between God and His people.

It is called the *Old* Testament (or Covenant) to contrast it with the "New" one, although "Older Covenant" might be a better title, since *Old* to some people suggests that it is not worth learning. This would be a deadly error from a spiritual, historical, or cultural viewpoint. Both Testaments are inspired by God and therefore profitable for all Christians. While the believer in Christ frequently turns to that part of the Bible that specifically tells of our Lord, His church, and how He wishes His disciples to live, the importance of the OT for a fully-furnished believer cannot be overstressed.

The relationship between the OT and the NT was nicely expressed by Augustine:

> The New is in the Old concealed;
> The Old is in the New revealed.[2]

II. The OT Canon

The word *canon* (Gk. *kanōn*) refers to a "rule" by which something is measured or evaluated. The OT Canon is that collection of divinely inspired, and hence authoritative, books recognized by the spiritual leaders of Israel in ancient times. How do we know that these are the *only* books that should be in the canon or that *all* of these thirty-nine writings should be there? Since there were other religious writings (including heretical ones) from early days, how can we be sure that these are the right ones?

It is often said that a Jewish council drew up the canonical list in the late first century of our era. Actually, the books were *canonical* as soon as they were written. Godly and discerning Jews recognized inspired Scriptures from the start. However, there was a dispute for a time over some of the books (Esther, Ecclesiastes, Song of Songs, e.g.) in some quarters.

The Jews divide the OT into three parts: The Torah, the Prophets (Former and Latter), and the Writings.[3]

There are several theories as to why, for example, the Book of Daniel, a prophecy, should be among the Writings, and not among the Prophets. A common liberal view is that Daniel was written too late to get into the second section, which they see as already "closed" when Daniel wrote (See Introduction to Daniel.) A conservative view sees Daniel in the third section because he was not a prophet by *office*, but a statesman used by God to write a prophecy. Dr. Merrill F. Unger taught that the three-fold division is determined by the position of the writers[4]:

> This is the conservative and (we believe) the correct view. The Old Testament books were written with the definite purpose of being held sacred and divinely authoritative. Therefore, they possessed the stamp of canonicity from the moment of their appearance. The three-fold division is due to the official position and status of the writers and not to degrees of inspiration, differences of content or chronology.[5]

The council that officially recognized our canon was actually *confirming* what had been generally accepted for centuries. The council drew up not an *inspired list* of books, but a list of *inspired books*.

Even more important for Christians is the fact that our Lord Himself quoted frequently and treated as authoritative books from the three sections of the Hebrew OT. See, for example, Luke 24:27 and 44; endnote 4. Furthermore, Christ never quoted from the so-called apocryphal books.

III. The Apocrypha

Eastern Orthodox, Roman Catholic, and Protestant Bible students all agree on the twenty-seven-book NT Canon, generally[6] in the same order, with the exact same 260 chapters. The situation with the OT is a little more complex.

Protestants and Jews agree on the content of the OT, but the Eastern Orthodox and Roman Catholics[7] accept several Jewish books of history and poetry which they call "deuterocanonical" (Gk. for secondary canon) and Protestants and Jews call "apocryphal" (Gk. for "hidden"[8]).

The thirty-nine books of the *current* King James,[9] New King James, and other truly Protestant versions constitute the exact same materials as the twenty-four books of the Hebrew Bible. The difference in number is because of several combinations in the Jewish editions. For example, the six books of Samuel, Kings, and Chronicles are considered to be just three books, and the Minor Prophets, called "The Book of the Twelve," are seen as just one book.

The Jews wrote many other religious books, often not even in Hebrew, that they did not consider inspired and authoritative. Some, such as 1 and 2 Maccabees, are valuable for inter-testamental history. Others, such as "Bel and the Dragon," need only to be read by the discerning to reveal their non-canonical status.

The least valuable of these Jewish books are called *Pseudepigrapha* (Gk. for "false writings") and the better ones are called *Apocrypha*.

Some ancient Jews and Christians, but especially the Gnostics of Egypt, accepted a larger canon, including some of these books.

When scholarly St. Jerome was asked to translate the apocryphal books into Latin by Damasus, the Bishop of Rome, he did so only *under protest*. This was because he knew his *Hebrew* text well and also that they were not authentic parts of the Jewish Canon. Hence, although Jerome could discern their (at best) secondary status, he did translate these books for the Latin Vulgate. Today they also appear in Roman Catholic versions such as the New American Bible and the Jerusalem Bible, and usually in such ecumenical versions as the New English Bible, the Revised English Bible, and the New Revised Standard Version.

Even the Roman Catholic Church did not *officially* recognize the Apocrypha as canonical until the Counter-Reformation Period (1500's).[10] One reason that the Vatican did this was that a few of her teachings, such as praying for the dead, are found in the Apocrypha. Actually, the Apocrypha is largely *Jewish* literature and history, and not directly relevant to Christian doctrine. While not inspired, some of these books are worth reading from a cultural and historical viewpoint, after one has a firm grip on the inspired books of the Hebrew Canon.

IV. Authorship

The Divine Author of the OT is the Holy Spirit. He moved Moses, Ezra, Isaiah, and the anonymous authors to write under His guidance. The best and correct understanding of this question of how the OT books were produced is called *dual authorship*. The OT is not partly human and partly divine, but totally human and totally divine at the same time. The divine element kept the human element from making any errors. The result is an inerrant or flawless book in the original manuscripts.

A helpful analogy to the *written* Word is the dual nature of the *Living* Word, our Lord Jesus Christ. He is not partly human and partly divine (like some Greek myth) but completely human and completely divine at the same time. The divine nature made it impossible for the human to err or sin in any way.

V. Dates

Unlike the NT, which took only half a century to write (about A.D. 50–100), the OT took at least a millennium to complete (about 1400–400 B.C.).[11] The first books written were either the Pentateuch (about 1400 B.C.) or Job (date unknown, but the contents suggest an era before the law was given).

Other books followed that were written *before* the exile (about 600 B.C.), such as Joshua through Samuel, *during* the exile (such as Lamentations and Ezekiel), or *after* the exile, such as Chronicles, Haggai, Zechariah, and Malachi (about 400 B.C.).

VI. Contents

The contents of the OT, presented in the order of the Protestant versions, may be summarized concisely as follows:

Pentateuch
Genesis through Deuteronomy
Historical[12]
Joshua through Esther
Poetic
Job through Song of Solomon
Prophetic
Isaiah through Malachi

Separate introductions to these four main sections of the OT will be found in the *Believers Bible Commentary* at the appropriate places.

A Christian who gets a good grasp of these books, along with the later and fuller revelation of the NT, will be "thoroughly furnished for every good work."

It is our prayer that the BBC will greatly aid many believers to be just that.

VII. Languages

1. Hebrew

Except for a few sections in Aramaic, a related Semitic[13] tongue, the OT was originally written in the Hebrew language.

Believers are not surprised that God used a thoroughly suitable vehicle for the earlier portion of His Word, an expressive language rich in color and idiom, well adapted to the inspired narratives, poetry, and laws that constitute the OT. Hebrew is one of the *ancient* languages—but it is the only one that (almost miraculously) has been revived as the *modern*[14] everyday speech of a nation—Israel.

Hebrew is written from right to left, originally in consonants only. The person reading aloud supplied the proper vowel sounds from his knowledge of the language. Providentially, this made it possible for the Hebrew text to remain readable for many centuries, since it is chiefly the vowel sounds that change from century to century, from country to country, and from region to region.[15]

Sometimes what was *written* (called *kethîv*), such as the name of God,[16] was thought too sacred to pronounce and so a marginal note told what to *read aloud* (*qerē*). This was also the case for copyists' errors and for words that, over the centuries, had come to be considered vulgar.

In the earlier Christian centuries Jewish scholars called Masoretes (from the Hebrew word for *tradition*) arose. Seeing that Hebrew was becoming an obsolete language, and desiring to preserve the correct reading of the sacred OT text, they devised a sophisticated phonetic system of dots and dashes above, and in, but chiefly below, the twenty-two Hebrew consonants to indicate the accepted vocalization of the words. Even today this ancient "vowel pointing," as it is called, is more scientific and precise than English, French, or *even* German spelling!

The consonantal text is also the source of disputed readings, since a set of consonants at times can be read with different *vowels*, and therefore different *meanings*. Usually the context will determine which is original, but not always. The variant spellings of names in Chronicles (see commentary there) that differ from Genesis, e.g., are partly due to this phenomenon.

By and large, however, the traditional, or Masoretic Text, is remarkably well-preserved. It is a living witness to the Jews' great reverence for God's Word. Often the ancient versions (Targums, Septuagint, and Vulgate) help us to choose the correct variant where a problem exists. Since the mid-twentieth century the Dead Sea Scrolls have given added information on the Hebrew text—chiefly as a confirmation of the accuracy of the Masoretic Text.

Fortunately for us who read the OT in an English translation, Hebrew translates very nicely into English—much better than it does into Latin, for example, as the great sixteenth century Reformation translator William Tyndale pointed out.

The version on which the BBC is based is a direct descendant of Tyndale's beginnings in the OT. He managed to complete Genesis through Chronicles and some poetic and prophetic sections before the Inquisition had him burned at the stake for his efforts (1536). His OT work was completed by others and updated in the King James Version of 1611 and more recently in the New King James Version of 1982.

2. Aramaic

Like Hebrew, Aramaic is a Semitic language, but a Gentile one, spoken widely in the ancient world for very many centuries. As Hebrew became a dead language for the Jews, the OT had to be interpreted for them into Aramaic, the closely related, but different, language that they had come to adopt. The script that we associate with Hebrew was probably borrowed from Aramaic about 400 B.C. and developed into the artistic square letters that are familiar to Hebrew students today.[17]

Most of the above facts concerning Hebrew are also true for the Aramaic portions of the OT. These passages are few, and understandably, chiefly concern Israel's contacts with her Gentile neighbors, such as in the Babylonian Exile and afterward.[18]

VIII. Translation

English is blessed with many translations (perhaps too many). There are, however, far fewer translations of the OT than of the NT. These translations fall into four general types:

1. Very Literal

J. N. Darby's "New" Translation of 1882 (NT much earlier), the English Revised Version of 1881 and its U.S. variant, the American Standard Version of 1901, are extremely literal. This makes them helpful for careful study but weak for worship, public reading, and memorization. The masses of believers have never abandoned the majesty and beauty of the Tyndale—King James tradition for these useful—but rather wooden—versions.

2. Optimum Equivalence

Versions that are quite literal and follow the Hebrew or Greek closely when English allows it, yet still permit a freer translation where good style and idiom demand it, include the KJV, the RSV, the NASB, and the NKJV. Unfortunately, the RSV, while generally reliable in the NT, is wedded to an OT that plays down many Messianic prophecies. This dangerous trend is seen today even among some previously sound scholars. The BBC was edited to conform to the NKJV as the most viable position between the beautiful (but archaic) KJV and today's usage, yet without using any *thee's* and *thou's*.[19]

3. Dynamic Equivalence

This type of translation is freer than the complete—equivalence type, and sometimes resorts to paraphrase, a valid technique as long as the reader is made aware of it. The NEB, NIV, and the Jerusalem Bible all fall into this category. An attempt is made to put whole thoughts into the structure that Moses and Isaiah might have used if they were writing today—and in English. When done conservatively, this methodology can be a helpful tool. The danger lies in the theological looseness of many translators who use this method.

4. Paraphrase

A paraphrase seeks to transmit the text thought by thought, yet it often takes great liberties in *adding* material. Since it is far removed from the original text in wording there is always the danger of *too much interpre-*

tation. The Living Bible, e.g., while evangelical, makes many interpretive decisions that are *at best* debatable.

It is good to have a Bible from at least three of these categories for purposes of comparison. However, we believe that the complete, or optimum-equivalence translation is safest for the type of detailed Bible study presented in the BBC.

IX. Inspiration

Amid all this welter of historical and technical details we do well to consider the words of the great English Baptist preacher, Charles Haddon Spurgeon:

> This volume is the writing of the living God: each letter was penned with an Almighty finger; each word in it dropped from the everlasting lips; each sentence was dictated by the Holy Spirit. Albeit, that Moses was employed to write his histories with his fiery pen, God guided that pen. It may be that David touched his harp, and let sweet Psalms of melody drop from his fingers; but God moved his hands over the living strings of his golden harp. It may be that Solomon sang canticles of love, or gave forth words of consummate wisdom, but God directed his lips, and made the preacher eloquent. If I follow the thundering Nahum, when his horses plow the waters, or Habakkuk, when he sees the tents of Cushan in affliction; if I read Malachi, when the earth is burning like an oven; . . . it is God's voice, not man's; the words are God's words, the words of the Eternal, the Invisible, the Almighty, the Jehovah of this earth.[20]

ENDNOTES

[1]It appears in the name of the Jewish organization called "B'nai B'rith" ("Sons of the Covenant").

[2]His words (in Latin) have also been translated:

> The New is in the Old contained;
> The Old is in the New explained.

[3]The order of the twenty-four OT books as found in a Hebrew Bible or a Jewish translation is as follows:

I. The Law *(Tôrāh)*
   Genesis
   Exodus
   Leviticus
   Numbers
   Deuteronomy
II. The Prophets *(Nevî'îm)*
   1. *The Former Prophets*
      Joshua
      Judges
      Samuel
      Kings
   2. *The Latter Prophets*
      Isaiah
      Jeremiah
      Ezekiel
      The Book of the Twelve (Hosea through Malachi)
III. The Writings *(Ketûvîm)*
   Psalms
   Job
   Proverbs
   Ruth
   Song of Songs
   Ecclesiastes
   Lamentations
   Esther
   Daniel
   Ezra-Nehemiah
   Chronicles

[4]Merrill F. Unger, *Introductory Guide to the Old Testament*, p. 59.

[5]*Ibid*.

[6]However, the Russian NT has a somewhat different order after the Gospels, for example.

[7]See the Introduction to the New Revised Standard Version with Apocrypha for books added to the Canon by these groups. (They do not agree

among themselves on all books, either.)

[8]The idea of "spurious" has become associated with this word.

[9]Early editions of the KJV in the seventeenth century contained the Apocrypha, but sandwiched *in between* the OT and NT to indicate their inferior status. It shocks many people who look on the KJV as the only true Bible when (and if) they find out that it actually once contained *whole books* that are not of divine origin!

[10]At the Council of Trent, held between 1545 and 1563 (with intermissions) at Trento, Italy.

[11]Less conservative scholars move the dates later but end up with a similar period of time.

[12]Many Bible students prefer to put these two together (Genesis through Esther) and label them *historical*.

[13]Semitic (or Shemitic) are languages which were or are spoken largely by the descendants of *Shem*. They include Arabic, Phoenician, and Akkadian, as well as Hebrew.

[14]Language experts, using French, English, and freshly-coined words based on ancient Hebrew roots, as well as new constructions, helped to bring this ancient tongue into the twentieth century.

[15]For example, an English-speaking person is aware of the different sounds in a word such as *past*, as pronounced at Oxford, Boston, Dallas, and Brooklyn. The consonant sounds remain the same, but the "a" is pronounced *quite* differently in each city!

[16]For example, where the KJV/NKJV reads *Lord* (all capitals, representing the publicly *read* Hebrew word *Adōnai*), the *written* form is actually the sacred "tetragrammaton" (four letters, YHWH) that spell the covenant name of God, *Yahweh*, or in English tradition, *Jehovah*.

[17]Unger, *Introduction*, p. 124.

[18]The Aramaic portions are: Ezra 4:8—6:18; 7:12–26; Jeremiah 10:11; Daniel 2:4—7:28.

[19]For example, the similar (but less literary) NASB retains *thee's* and *thou's* in prayer and in some poetry.

[20]Charles Haddon Spurgeon, *Spurgeon's Sermons*, I:28. The word "dictated" should not be taken in the modern secretarial sense. As the rest of the quotation shows, Spurgeon believed in the orthodox teaching of inspiration—dual authorship (human and divine) of each book.

INTRODUCTION TO THE PENTATEUCH

"Modern criticism has ventured to undermine and assail almost all the books of holy scripture, but none with such boldness as the Pentateuch, unless it be the prophecy of Daniel. . . . Let us take our stand on the fact, broad, deep, and conclusive, that the authority of Christ has decided the question for all who own Him to be God as well as man."

—William Kelly

"The Pentateuch is an essential introduction to the entire word of God. It opens up that which is afterwards unfolded, and ever leads us on in hope to a consummation which, though distant, is certain."

—Samuel Ridout

Before commenting on the individual Books of Moses, since this is such a basic part of biblical revelation, we would like to present a few facts on the Pentateuch as a whole.

I. Titles of the Pentateuch

The first five books of the Bible are commonly called "the Pentateuch." In ancient times books were in the form of scrolls rather than bound as pages of a "codex" (book form). These scrolls, called *teuchoi*[1] in Greek, were stored in sheathlike containers. The Greek word for "five-roll" is *pentateuchos,* whence our word "Pentateuch."

Jews refer to the Pentateuch as "the Torah" (Heb. *tôrâ,* "law" or "instruction"), and treat it as the most important part of their Bible.

A third common title of these volumes is "the Books of Moses." It is ironical that the Bibles of certain northern European countries that most widely reject the Mosaic authorship of the Pentateuch label these books not as "Genesis, Exodus," etc., but as "First Book of *Moses,*" "Second Book of *Moses,*" etc.

Except for *Numbers,* whose name is the English translation of the Greek *Arithmoi* and the Latin *Numeri,* we retain the Greek LXX (Septuagint) titles of these five books, but anglicize the spelling and pronunciation. (See the individual books in the Believers Bible Commentary for their meanings.)

The Jews often call the books by their first few words in the Hebrew text. Thus Genesis is called *Berēshîth* ("In the beginning").

II. Contents of the Pentateuch

The usage of our English word *law* is more restricted than the Hebrew meanings of *tôrâ,* hence the term "Pentateuch" is ideal for Christian usage to express the great importance of this five-volume set.

A. Genesis

Genesis is well-named, as it is the Greek word for *beginning*. The first book of the Bible traces the origins of the universe, the earth, man, marriage, sin, true religion, the nations, diverse languages, and the chosen people. The first eleven chapters recount the broad sweep of human history, but chapters twelve through fifty narrow the story down to the family of Abraham, Isaac, Jacob, and his sons.

B. Exodus

Exodus, Greek for *the way out*, narrates how in four hundred years the family of Abraham grew to a nation under the forced labor of the Pharaohs in Egypt, and their redemption from bondage under Moses. The Law of Moses and the detailed description of the tabernacle make up the rest of the book.

C. Leviticus

Leviticus is a manual for the Levites, hence the name. It describes the rituals necessary for sinful men of that era to have fellowship with a holy God. The book contains pictures and types of the sacrifice of Christ.

D. Numbers

Numbers, as the name suggests, includes a numbering of the people, or census—one at the beginning and another at the end of the book. The Hebrew title for the book, "in the desert" (*Bemidbār*), is more expressive, since Numbers recounts the historical events experienced by the Israelites in their wilderness wanderings.

E. Deuteronomy

Deuteronomy, Greek for *second law*, is more than a mere re-telling of the law to a new generation, though it is that. It is the link with the historical books that follow, since it recounts the death of Moses, and his replacement by Joshua, his successor.

Griffith Thomas, in his usual lucid and concise style, summarizes the contents of the Books of Moses as follows:

> The five books of the Pentateuch record the introduction of the Divine religion into the world. Each book gives one phase of God's plan, and together they constitute a real unity. Genesis speaks of the origin of the religion, and of the people chosen by God as its medium. Exodus records the formation of the people into a nation, and the establishment of God's relationship with it. Leviticus shows the various ways in which this relationship was maintained. Numbers shows how the people were organized for the purpose of commencing the life of the Divine religion in the Promised Land. This book also tells of the nation's failure and the consequent delay, with re-organization. Then Deuteronomy shows how the people were prepared, while on the border of the Promised Land, for the entry which was soon to follow.[2]

III. Importance of the Pentateuch

Since the whole OT, in fact the whole Bible, is based on these first five books, the importance of the Pentateuch for revealed religion can hardly be overstated. If rationalistic, unbelieving scholars can undermine faith in the integrity and authenticity of *these* books, the origins of Judaism become lost in a sea of uncertainty. Christians should not think that *our* faith is unaffected by such attacks either, since the NT and our Lord Himself also quote the Books of Moses as true and trustworthy.

Dr. Merrill Unger put the case very bluntly:

> The foundation of all revealed truth and of God's redemptive plan is based on the Pentateuch. If this foundation is unreliable, the whole Bible is unreliable.[3]

IV. Authorship of the Pentateuch

Except for some who in early Christian times opted for Ezra[4] as the author of the Torah, by and large, Judeo-Christian orthodoxy has maintained Mosaic authorship through the centuries—and still does.

A. Mosaic Authorship

Before examining briefly the documentary theory, which largely *denies* Mosaic authorship, let us note the positive evidence *for* it.

1. *Moses' Qualifications*

The nineteenth century German critic Hartmann denied Mosaic authorship on the grounds that it was quite literally impossible—writing not having yet been invented. (Or, so many thought then!) Archaeology has shown that Moses could have written in early Hebrew script, Egyptian hieroglyphics, or Accadian cuneiform. Of course Acts 7:22 told believers long before archaeology confirmed it, that Moses was educated "in all the learning of the Egyptians." When we say Moses "wrote" the Pentateuch, this allows for his using previous documents in Genesis. It also allows for inspired editorial updatings as Hebrew script changed through the centuries. Of course, the fact that Moses *could have written* the Pentateuch doesn't prove that he *did*. However, as the father of the Jewish faith it is inevitable that he would make a permanent record of God's revelation for future generations. And so God had commanded him.

2. *Pentateuchal Claims*

The text of the Torah says specifically that Moses *did* write down at God's command on occasion. See, e.g., Exodus 17:14; 24:4; 34:27; Numbers 33:2; Deuteronomy 31:19.

3. *Later Biblical Claims*

The rest of God's Word accepts Mosaic authorship as well. See, e.g., Joshua 1:7 and 1 Kings 2:3; and in the NT, Luke 24:44 and 1 Corinthians 9:9.

4. *The Witness of Christ*

For Christians the fact that our Lord Himself accepted Mosaic authorship should settle the matter. The notion that in His humanity Jesus was ignorant of science and history, or that He knew better but accommodated Himself to the ignorance and prejudice of His countrymen is unworthy of a believer's consideration.

5. *Archaeology and the Pentateuch*

Many customs, words, names, and historical and cultural details that liberal critics once said were "too late" to be Mosaic have now been found to *predate* Moses by centuries. While this doesn't "prove" Mosaic authorship, it tallies much better with the traditional view than it does with the theory that "redactors" or editors living many centuries later knew all these (by then largely lost) details and pieced them together so nicely.

B. The Documentary Hypothesis

In 1753 Jean Astruc, a French doctor, set forth the theory that Moses compiled Genesis from two documents. Those passages that used the name *Jehovah* for God came from one source, he wrote, and those using *Elohim* another. These supposed sources he labeled "J" and "E" respectively.

Later, liberal scholars developed the theory much further, eventually putting all their supposed sources much later than Moses. Other proposed documents were "D" ("Deuteronomic") and "P" ("Priestly"). The Pentateuch was viewed as a patchwork of sources built up between the ninth and sixth centuries B.C. Popularly, the hypothesis became known as the "JEDP theory."

Several things made the hypothesis attractive to nineteenth-century scholars. First of all it fitted in well with Darwin's theory of evolution, which was being applied to many fields other than just to biology. Next, the anti-supernaturalistic spirit of the day found delight in trying to put the Bible down on a merely human level. Thirdly, the humanistic trends that replaced divine revelation with man's efforts dovetailed with this theory.

In 1878 Julius Wellhausen popularized the documentary hypothesis in a clever and deceptively plausible way.

In this short Introduction we can only mention a few of the main points against the theory.[5]

Serious problems with the theory include the following:

1. *Lack of Manuscript Evidence*

There is no manuscript evidence that any of the editorial work proposed in the "JEDP" theory ever occurred.

2. *Conflicting and Subjective Fragmentation*

Scholars divide the Pentateuch up into fragments quite differently, which exposes the extreme, personal viewpoints and lack of concrete, objective evidence for the theory.

3. *Archaeology*

Archaeology has tended to support the writing, customs, religious knowledge, etc., of the Pentateuch as being very ancient, and definitely *not* from the much later period of composition proposed by the Wellhausen theory.

4. *Linguistics*

Supposedly "late" language forms and personal names found in the Pentateuch have been found in sources well before the time of Moses. An example is the recently unearthed "Ebla tablets," which contain many Pentateuchal names.

5. *Unity of the Pentateuch*

Editorially, the five books of Moses hold together very well and exhibit a unity and coherence that is most difficult to reconcile with the alleged evolutionary "scissors and paste" origins of these books.

6. *Spiritual Bankruptcy*

Finally, from a spiritual viewpoint, the documentary theories, even as modified by archaeology and other similar theories, are unworthy of the great and beautiful truths enshrined in these books. If these theories were true, the Pentateuch would be, in the words of Dr. Unger, "unauthentic, unhistorical, and unreliable, a fabrication of men, not the work of God."[6]

V. Date of the Pentateuch

The contents of the Pentateuch take us back to creation, but the actual writing, of course, was thousands of years later. Obviously the date for the writing that we choose is dependent upon *who* wrote it.

Liberal scholars date the various theorized stages of the work largely as follows: The so-called "J document" is dated about 850 B.C.; the "E document" about 750 B.C.; the "D document" about 621 B.C.;[7] and the "P document" about 500 B.C.

Conservative scholars generally date the Pentateuch around the time of the Exodus, in the fifteenth century B.C. Some prefer a date for this event of about a century and half later.

Probably the best date to fit all the biblical data is sometime between 1450–1410 B.C. See the individual books in the BBC for more details.

VI. Conclusion

We conclude our Introduction to the Pentateuch with the words of Canada's foremost OT scholar:

> The Pentateuch is a homogeneous composition in five volumes, and not an agglomeration of separate and perhaps only rather casually related works. It described, against an accredited historical background, the manner in which God revealed Himself to men and chose the Israelites for special service and witness in the world and in the course of human history. The role of Moses in the formulation of this literary corpus appears pre-eminent, and it is not without good reason that he should be accorded a place of high honor in the growth of the epic of Israelite nationhood, and be venerated by Jews and Christians alike as the great mediator of the ancient Law.[8]

ENDNOTES

[1]The word *teuchos* originally meant a tool or implement, and then a roll of material to write on.

[2]W. H. Griffith Thomas, *The Pentateuch*, p. 25.

[3]Merrill F. Unger, *Unger's Bible Handbook*, p. 35.

[4]The Jewish philosopher Spinoza also chose Ezra as the author.

[5]A Christian approach can be found in R. K. Harrison, *Introduction to the Old Testament* (Grand Rapids: Wm. B. Eerdmans Publishing Co., 1966). The Jewish American novelist Hermann Wouk exposes the theory in *This Is My God* (Garden City, NY: Doubleday & Co., 1959).

[6]Unger, *Handbook*, p. 35.

[7]Many liberals posit such a specific date from the mistaken belief that Josiah conveniently "found" (fabricated) what is now called Deuteronomy in order to promote a central sanctuary in his capital, Jerusalem.

[8]Harrison, *Introduction*, p. 541.

GENESIS

Introduction

"The first book of the Bible is for several reasons one of the most interesting and fascinating portions of Scripture. Its place in the Canon, its relation to the rest of the Bible, and the varied and striking character of its contents combine to make it one of the most prominent in Holy Writ. It is with a real spiritual insight, therefore, that the people of God in all ages have fastened upon this book, and given it their earnest attention."

—W. H. Griffith Thomas

I. Unique Place in the Canon

Genesis (Greek for "Beginning"), called *Bereshîth* by the Jews (Hebrew for "In the beginning"), is well named. This exciting volume gives the only true account of creation by the only One who was there—the Creator!

Through His servant Moses, the Holy Spirit traces the beginnings of man, woman, marriage, the home, sin, sacrifices, cities, trade, agriculture, music, worship, languages, and the races and nations of the world. All this in the first eleven chapters.

Then, from chapters 12—50 we see the beginnings of Israel, God's "test-tube nation," to be a spiritual microcosm of all the peoples of the world. The lives of the patriarchs Abraham, Isaac, Jacob, and his twelve sons—especially the attractively devout Joseph, have inspired untold millions, from young children to advanced OT scholars.

A solid grasp of Genesis is necessary for an understanding of the rest of the sixty-five books of the Bible. They all build on its beautifully proportioned literary base.

II. Authorship

We accept the ancient Jewish and Christian teaching that Genesis was written and compiled by Moses the man of God and Lawgiver of Israel. Since all the events in Genesis are pre-Mosaic it is virtually certain that Moses used ancient documents and perhaps oral accounts as he was guided by the Holy Spirit. See *Introduction to the Pentateuch* for a discussion of Mosaic authorship.

III. Date

The most conservative scholars generally date the Exodus about 1445 B.C. Hence Genesis would probably have been written between this date and Moses' death about forty years later. It is always possible, of course, that this one book of the Pentateuch was written *before* the Exodus, since all the events in Genesis predate that great event.

See *Introduction to the Pentateuch* for further details.

IV. Background and Themes

Except for those who are extremely biased against the Bible, Judaism, or Christianity, nearly everyone agrees that Genesis is a fascinating account of very ancient times and contains narratives of great beauty, such as the story of Joseph.

But just what is the *background* of this first book of the Bible. In short, what *is* it?

Those who reject a personal God have tended to class Genesis as a collection of *myths* adapted from pagan Mesopotamian myths and "cleaned up" from their worst polytheistic elements for monotheistic Hebrew edification.

Others, not quite as skeptical, see Genesis as a collection of *sagas* or *legends*, with some historical value.

Yet others see the stories as explanations of the origins of things in nature and culture (technically called *etiologies*). There *are* etiologies in the OT, especially in this book of beginnings (the origin of sin, the rainbow, the Hebrew people, e.g.) but this by no means makes the explanations unhistorical.

Genesis is *history*. Like all history, it is interpretive. It is *theological* history, or facts narrated in a framework of the divine plan. It has been well said that "history is His story."

Though Genesis is the first book of the "law" there is very little *legal* material in it. It is *"Law"* (*Torah*, Heb. for instruction) in that it lays the foundation for Exodus through Deuteronomy and God's giving of the Law through Moses. In fact, it lays the foundation of all Bible history—yes, of history itself.

The twin *themes* of blessing and cursing are carefully woven throughout the fabric of Genesis, and indeed, the whole word of God. Obedience brings enrichment of blessing, and disobedience the opposite.

The great *curses* are the penalties of the Fall, the universal Flood, and the confusion of tongues at Babel.

The great *blessings* are the promise of a Redeemer, the salvation of a remnant through the Flood, and the choice of a special nation to be a channel of God's grace, Israel.

If Genesis is factual history, how could Moses have known all the ancient genealogies, conversations, events and correct interpretation of these events?

First, let it be said, that archaeology has supported (not "proved" but confirmed and illustrated) the Genesis account in many areas, especially regarding the patriarchs and their customs.

Some nineteenth century liberals, such as Hartmann,[1] taught that Moses could not have written the Pentateuch because writing had not yet been invented! Now we know that Moses could have written in any one of several ancient scripts, being learned in all the lore of Egypt.

Moses no doubt used accounts left by Joseph, and the tablets, parchments, and oral translations brought from ancient Mesopotamia by Abraham and his descendants. These would include the genealogies, the major sections, known as "the generations of Adam," etc.

In the final analysis this is still not enough. The Holy Spirit of God inspired Moses to choose exactly the right materials and to ignore the rest. He probably supplied details of conversations and other things by direct revelation.

It comes down to a matter of *faith*. Either God is capable of producing such a work through His servants or He is not. Believers of all generations from primeval times to today have set their seal that God is true.

Archaeology can help us reconstruct the culture of the patriarchs to make the Bible accounts more vivid,[2] but only the Holy Spirit can illuminate the truth of Genesis to our hearts and daily lives.

As you read the *Believers Bible Commentary* on Genesis—or any of the OT books—you must be dependent on the Spirit's illumination of the *Holy Word itself* to really benefit from the comments. A true commentary is not an independent means, but an arrow, pointing to a "thus says the Lord."

OUTLINE

I. EARTH'S EARLIEST AGES (Chaps. 1—11)
  A. The Creation (Chaps. 1, 2)
  B. The Temptation and Fall (Chap. 3)
  C. Cain and Abel (Chap. 4)
  D. Seth and His Descendants (Chap. 5)
  E. Widespread Sin and the Universal Flood (Chaps. 6—8)
  F. Noah after the Flood (Chap. 9)
  G. The Table of Nations (Chap. 10)
  H. The Tower of Babel (Chap. 11)

II. THE PATRIARCHS OF ISRAEL (Chaps. 12—50)
  A. Abraham (12:1—25:18)
    1. The Call of Abraham (12:1–9)
    2. To Egypt and Back (12:10—13:4)
    3. Experiences with Lot and Abimelech (13:5—14:24)
    4. Abraham's Promised Heir (Chap. 15)
    5. Ishmael, Son of the Flesh (Chaps. 16, 17)
    6. Sodom and Gomorrah (Chaps. 18, 19)
    7. Abraham and Abimelech (Chap. 20)
    8. Isaac, Son of the Promise (Chap. 21)
    9. The Offering of Isaac (Chap. 22)
    10. The Family Burial Place (Chap. 23)
    11. A Bride for Isaac (Chap. 24)
    12. Abraham's Descendants (25:1–18)
  B. Isaac (25:19—26:35)
    1. Isaac's Family (25:19–34)
    2. Isaac and Abimelech (Chap. 26)
  C. Jacob (27:1—36:43)
    1. Jacob Cheats Esau (Chap. 27)
    2. Jacob's Flight to Haran (Chap. 28)
    3. Jacob, His Wives, and His Offspring (29:1—30:24)
    4. Jacob Outwits Laban (30:25–43)

5. Jacob's Return to Canaan (Chap. 31)
6. Jacob and Esau Reconciled (Chaps. 32, 33)
7. Sins at Shechem (Chap. 34)
8. The Return to Bethel (Chap. 35)
9. The Descendants of Jacob's Brother Esau (Chap. 36)

D. Joseph (37:1—50:26)

1. Joseph Sold into Slavery (Chap. 37)
2. Judah and Tamar (Chap. 38)
3. Joseph's Test and Triumph (Chap. 39)
4. Joseph Interpreting the Butler's and Baker's Dreams (Chap. 40)
5. Joseph Interpreting Pharaoh's Dreams (Chap. 41)
6. Joseph's Brothers in Egypt (Chaps. 42—44)
7. Joseph Reveals Himself to His Brothers (Chap. 45)
8. Joseph's Reunion with His Family (Chap. 46)
9. Joseph's Family in Egypt (Chap. 47)
10. Jacob's Blessing of Joseph's Sons (Chap. 48)
11. Jacob's Prophecy Concerning His Sons (Chap. 49)
12. Death of Jacob and then of Joseph in Egypt (Chap. 50)

Commentary

I. EARTH'S EARLIEST AGES (Chaps. 1—11)

A. The Creation (Chaps. 1, 2)

1:1 "In the beginning God. . . ." These first four words of the Bible form the foundation for faith. Believe these words, and you can believe all that follows in the Bible. Genesis provides the only authoritative account of creation, meaningful for people of all ages but exhaustible by no one. The divine record assumes the existence of God rather than seeking to prove it. The Bible has a special name for those who choose to deny the fact of God. That name is *fool* (Ps. 14:1 and 53:1). Just as the Bible begins with God, so He should be first in our lives.

1:2 One of several conservative interpretations of the Genesis account of creation, the creation-reconstruction view, says that between verses 1 and 2 a great catastrophe occurred, perhaps the fall of Satan (see Ezek. 28:11–19).[3] This caused God's original, perfect creation to become **without form and void** (*tōhû wāvōhû*). Since God didn't *create* the earth waste and empty (see Isa. 45:18), only a mighty cataclysm could explain the chaotic condition of verse 2. Proponents of this view point out that the word translated **was** (*hāyethā*) could also be translated "had become."[4] Thus the earth "had become waste and empty."

The Spirit of God was hovering over the face of the waters, preparatory to the great creative and reconstructive acts to follow. The remaining verses describe the six days of creation and reconstruction which prepared the earth for human habitation.

1:3–5 On **the first day God** commanded **light** to shine out of **darkness** and established the **Day** and **Night**

cycle. This act is not to be confused with the establishment of the sun, moon, and stars on the fourth day. In 2 Corinthians 4:6 the Apostle Paul draws a parallel between the original separation of light from darkness and the conversion of a sinner.

1:6–8 Prior to **the second day**, it seems that the earth was completely surrounded by a thick layer of water, perhaps in the form of a heavy vapor. On **the second day** God divided this layer, part covering the earth with water and part forming clouds, with the atmospheric layers (**firmament** or "dome") between. **God called the firmament Heaven**—that is, the expanse of space immediately above the earth (not the stellar heavens, nor the third heaven, where God dwells). Verse 20 makes it clear that the heaven here is the sphere where the birds fly.

1:9–13 Then God caused **the dry land** to **appear** out of the **waters** that covered the face of the planet. Thus were born the **Earth** and the **Seas**. Also on **the third day** He caused vegetation and trees of all kinds to spring up in the earth.

1:14–19 It was not until **the fourth day** that the Lord set the sun, moon, and **stars** in **the heavens** as lightbearers and as means for establishing a calendar.

1:20–23 The fifth day saw **the waters** stocked with fish and the earth stocked with bird-life and insects. The word translated **birds** means "flying ones" and includes bats and probably flying insects.

1:24, 25 On **the sixth day** God first created animals and reptiles. The law of reproduction is repeatedly given in the words **according to its kind**. There are significant variations within "kinds" of biological life, but there is no passing from one kind to another.

1:26–28 The crown of God's work was the creation of **man in** His **image and according to** His **likeness**. This means that man was placed on earth as God's representative, and that He resembles God in certain ways. Just as God is a Trinity (Father, Son, and Holy Spirit), so man is a tripartite being (spirit, soul, and body). Like God, man has intellect, a moral nature, the power to communicate with others, and an emotional nature that transcends instinct. There is no thought of physical likeness here. In contrast to animals, man is a worshiper, an articulate communicator, and a creator.

There is an allowance for or even an intimation of the Trinity in verse 26: **Then God** [*Elohim*, plural] **said** [singular verb in Hebrew], **"Let Us** [plural] **make man in Our image . . . ."**

The Bible describes the origin of the sexes as a creative act of God. Evolution has never been able to explain how the sexes began. Humanity was commanded to **be fruitful and multiply**.

God gave man a mandate to **subdue** creation and **have dominion over** it—to use it but not abuse it. The modern crises in the earth's environment are due to man's greed, selfishness, and carelessness.

1:29, 30 It is clear from these verses that animals were originally herbivorous and that man was vegetarian. This was changed after the Flood (see 9:1–7).

Were the six days of creation literal 24-hour days, or were they geological ages? Or were they days of "dramatic vision" during which the creation account was *revealed* to Moses? No scientific evidence has ever refuted the concept that they were literal solar days. The expression "the evening and the morning" points to 24-hour days. Everywhere else in the

OT these words mean normal days. Adam lived through the seventh day and died in his 930th year, so the seventh day could not have been a geological age. Wherever the "day" is used with a number in the OT ("first day," etc.) it means a literal day. When God commanded Israel to rest on the Sabbath day, He based the command on the fact that He had rested on the seventh day, after six days of labor (Ex. 20:8–11). Consistent interpretation here requires the same meaning of the word "day."

A difficulty, however, is that the solar day as we know it may not have begun until the fourth day (vv. 14–19).

As far as the Bible is concerned, the creation of the heavens and the earth is undated. The creation of man is undated also. However, genealogies are given, and, even allowing for possible gaps in the genealogies, man could not have been on the earth for the millions of years demanded by evolutionists.

We learn from John 1:1, 14, Colossians 1:16, and Hebrews 1:2 that the Lord Jesus was the active Agent in creation. For the inexhaustible wonders of His creation, He is worthy of endless worship.

1:31 At the end of the six days of creation **God saw everything that He had made, and indeed it was very good.**

2:1–3 God **rested** from His creative activity **on the seventh day**. This is not the rest that follows weariness but the rest of satisfaction and completion of a job well done. Although God did not command man to keep the Sabbath at this time, He taught the principle of one day of rest in seven.

2:4–6 The name **LORD God** (*Jehovah [Yahweh] Elohim*) appears for the first time in verse 4, but only after the creation of man (1:27). As Elohim, God is the Creator. As Jehovah, He is in covenant relation with man. Failing to see this, some Bible critics have concluded that these different names for God can only be explained by a change in authorship.

This is the history (v. 4) refers to the beginnings described in chapter 1. Verse 5, which reads, **"before any plant of the field was in the earth and before any herb of the field had grown,"** describes conditions on the earth in 1:10, when the dry land appeared but before vegetation appeared. **The earth** was watered by **a mist** rather than by **rain**.

2:7 A fuller account of the creation of **man** is now given. **God formed** his body from **the dust of the ground**, but only the impartation of **the breath** of God made him **a living being**. Adam ("red" or "ground") was named after the red earth from which he was made.

2:8–14 The **garden** that **God planted in Eden** was toward the east, i.e., east of Palestine, the point of reference for Bible directions. It was located in the region of Mesopotamia, near the **Hiddekel** (Tigris) and **Euphrates** Rivers. **The tree of the knowledge of good and evil** provided a test of man's obedience. The only reason it was wrong to eat of that fruit was because God had said so. In different forms, that fruit is *still with us today*.

2:15–23 The penalty for violating the commandment was death (v. 17)—instant spiritual death and progressive physical death. In the process of naming the animals and birds, Adam would have noticed that there were males and females. Each one had a mate that was similar to itself, yet different. This prepared Adam for **a helper** who would be **comparable to**

himself. His bride was formed from **one of his ribs**, taken from his side as **he slept**. So from Christ's side, His Bride was secured as He shed His life's blood in untold agony. **Woman** was taken not from Adam's head to dominate him, nor from his feet to be trodden down, but from under his arm to be protected, and from near his heart to be loved.

God gave headship to man before sin entered. Paul argues this fact from the order of creation (man was created first) and the purpose of creation (woman was made for the man) (1 Cor. 11:8, 9). Also, although it was Eve who sinned first, it is by Adam, the head, that sin is said to have entered the world. He had the position of head and was thus responsible.

Verse 19 is clearer with the English pluperfect tense[5]: **"The Lord God** *had* **formed . . . every beast,"** i.e., before He made man.

2:24 With the words of verse 24 God instituted monogamous marriage. Like all divine institutions, it was established for man's good and cannot be violated with impunity. The marriage bond illustrates the relationship that exists between Christ and the church (Eph. 5:22–32).

2:25 Although Adam and Eve lived in the Garden of Eden without any clothes, they **were not ashamed**.

B. The Temptation and Fall (Chap. 3)

3:1–6 The serpent that appeared to Eve is later revealed to be none other than Satan himself (see Rev. 12:9). Those who seek to "demythologize" the Bible believe that this account of the fall is allegorical and not literal. They cite the talking serpent as proof. Can the story of the serpent's deceiving Eve be accepted as factual? The Apostle Paul thought so (2 Cor. 11:3). So did the Apostle John (Rev. 12:9; 20:2). Nor is this the only instance of a talking animal in Scripture. God gave a voice to Balaam's donkey to restrain the madness of the prophet (Num. 22), and the Apostle Peter accepted this as literal (2 Pet. 2:16). These three apostles were inspired by the Holy Spirit to write as they did. Thus to reject the account of the fall as literal is to reject the inspiration of Holy Scripture. There are allegories in the Bible, but this is not one of them.

Notice the steps that plunged the human race into sin. First Satan insinuated doubt about the Word of God: **"Has God indeed said?"** He misrepresented God as forbidding Adam and Eve to **eat of every tree**. Next, Eve said that they were **not** to **eat** or **"touch the fruit of the tree which is in the midst of the garden."** But God had said nothing about *touching* the tree. Then Satan flatly contradicted God about the inevitability of judgment on those who disobeyed, just as his followers still deny the facts of hell and eternal punishment. Satan misrepresented God as seeking to withhold from Adam and Eve something that would have been beneficial to them. Eve yielded to the threefold temptation: the lust of the flesh (**good for food**), the lust of the eyes (**pleasant to the eyes**), and the pride of life (**a tree desirable to make one wise**). In doing so, she acted independently of Adam, her head. She should have consulted him instead of usurping his authority. In the words **"she took of its fruit and ate"** lie the explanation of all the sickness, sorrow, suffering, fear, guilt, and death that have plagued the human race ever since that time. Someone has said, "The wreckage of earth and a million billion graves attest that God is true and

Satan is the liar." Eve was deceived (1 Tim. 2:14), but Adam acted willfully and in deliberate rebellion against God.

Secular humanism perpetuates Satan's lie, "You will be like God."

3:7–13 The first result of sin was a sense of shame and fear. The aprons of **fig leaves** speak of man's attempt to save himself by a bloodless religion of good works. When called to account by God, sinners excuse themselves. Adam said, **"The woman whom You gave to be with me . . ."** as if blaming God (see Prov. 19:3). Eve said, **"The serpent . . ."** (v. 13).

In love and mercy God searched after His fallen creatures with the question **"Where are you?"** This question proved two things—that man was lost and that God had come to seek. It proved man's sin and God's grace.[6] God takes the initiative in salvation, demonstrating the very thing Satan got Eve to doubt—His love.

3:14 The LORD God cursed the **serpent** to degradation, disgrace, and defeat. The fact that the serpent is **cursed more than all cattle** or any **other beast of the field** suggests that reptiles are primarily in view here rather than Satan.

3:15 But verse 15 switches to the Devil himself. This verse is known as the *protevangelium*, meaning "The First Gospel." It predicts the perpetual hostility **between** Satan **and the woman** (representing all mankind), **and between** Satan's **seed** (his agents) **and her Seed** (the Messiah). The woman's **Seed** would crush the Devil's **head**, a mortal wound spelling utter defeat. This wound was administered at Calvary when the Savior decisively triumphed over the Devil. Satan, in turn, would **bruise** the Messiah's **heel**. The **heel** wound here speaks of suffering and even of physical death, but not of ultimate defeat. So Christ suffered on the cross, and even died, but He arose from the dead, victorious over sin, hell, and Satan. The fact that He is called the *woman's* **Seed** may contain a suggestion of His virgin birth. Note the kindness of God in promising the Messiah before pronouncing sentence in the following verses.

3:16–19 Sin has inevitable consequences. **The woman** was sentenced to suffering in childbirth. She would be subject to her **husband**. The man was sentenced to earn his livelihood from **ground** that was **cursed** with **thorns and thistles**. It would mean **toil** and **sweat** for him. Then at the end of life, he himself would **return** to **dust**. It should be noted here that work itself is *not* a curse; it is more often a blessing. It is the sorrow, toil, frustration, perspiration, and weariness connected with work that are the curse.

3:20, 21 Adam displayed faith in calling **his wife's name Eve . . . the mother of all living**, since no baby had ever been born up to this time. Then **tunics of skin** were provided by God through the death of an animal. This pictures the robe of righteousness which is provided for guilty sinners through the shed blood of the Lamb of God, made available to us on the basis of faith.

3:22–24 There was a shade of truth in Satan's lie that Eve would become like God (v. 5). But she and Adam learned by the hard way of experience to discern between **good and evil**. If they had then eaten of the tree of life, they would have lived forever in bodies subject to sickness, degeneration, and infirmity. Thus it was God's mercy that prevented them from returning to Eden. **Cherubim** are celestial creatures whose function is to "vindicate the holiness of God against the presumptuous pride of fallen man."[7]

Adam and Eve had to decide whether God or Satan was lying. They decided that God was. "Without faith it is impossible to please God." Thus their names are missing from the Honor Roll of Faith in Hebrews 11.

The ideal environment of Eden did not prevent the entrance of sin. A favorable environment is not the answer to man's problems.

C. Cain and Abel (Chap. 4)

4:1 Adam knew Eve his wife in the sense that he had sexual relations with her. When **Cain** was born, she acknowledged that this birth was only by the Lord's enablement. In naming him **Cain** ("acquisition"), Eve may have thought that she had given birth to the Promised Seed.

4:2–6 The process of time mentioned in verse 3a allows for a considerable increase in the world's population. There must have been a time when **Cain** and **Abel** were instructed that sinful man can approach the holy God only on the ground of the blood of a substitutionary sacrifice. Cain rejected this revelation and came with a bloodless offering of fruits and vegetables. Abel believed the divine decree and offered slain animals, thus demonstrating his faith and his justification by God (Heb. 11:4). He brought **the firstborn of his flock**, saying in effect that **the Lord** deserves the best. Abel's offering points forward to the substitutionary death of the Lamb of God, who takes away the sin of the world.

4:7 Because Cain's jealous anger was incipient murder, God spoke to him in loving warning. Verse 7 may be understood in several ways:

1. "**If you do well** [by repenting], you will be able to look up again in freedom from anger and guilt. **If you do not do well** [by continuing to hate Abel], **sin** is crouching **at** your **door**, ready to destroy you. His [Abel's] **desire is for you** [i.e., he will acknowledge your leadership] and **you** will **rule over** him" [i.e., if you do well].

2. "**If you do well** (or, as the Septuagint reads it, "If you offer correctly") will you not be accepted?" The well-doing had reference to the offering. Abel did well by hiding himself behind an acceptable sacrifice. Cain did badly by bringing an offering without blood, and all his after-conduct was but the legitimate result of this false worship.[8]

3. The RSV says, "If you do well, will you not be accepted? And if you do not do well, sin is crouching at the door; its desire is for you, but you must master it."

4. F. W. Grant says in his *Numerical Bible*, "If you do not well, a sin-offering croucheth or lieth at the door."[9] In other words, provision was made if he wanted it.

4:8–12 Cain's evil attitude of jealous rage was soon translated into evil action, the murder of **his brother**. Though Abel is dead, he still witnesses to us that the life of faith is the life that counts (Heb. 11:4). When the Lord's loving question was met by an unrepentant, insolent reply, He pronounced Cain's judgment—he would no longer be able to make a living from the soil, but would wander as **a fugitive** in the desert.

4:13–16 Cain's whimpering complaint reveals remorse for the consequences of his sin rather than for its guilt. But even then the Lord allayed the fugitive's fears for his life by putting a protective **mark on Cain** and a curse on anyone who killed him. **Cain went out from the presence of the Lord**, the saddest of all departures.

4:17–24 Cain married his sister or other blood relative. As mentioned, Genesis 4:3 allows time for a population increase, and Genesis 5:4 specifically states that Adam had sons and daughters. Marriage of close relatives was not forbidden then (nor was it genetically risky).

Verses 17–24 list Cain's posterity, and a series of firsts: the first **city**, named **Enoch**; the first case of polygamy; the beginning of organized animal husbandry; the beginning of the art of music and of metalcrafts; the first song, concerning violence and bloodshed. In the song, **Lamech** explains **to his wives** that he **killed . . . a young man** in self-defense, but that because it wasn't premeditated, like Cain's murder of his brother, Lamech would be much more immune from reprisal.

4:25, 26 Now in striking relief, the godly line of **Seth** is introduced. It was through this line that the Messiah would eventually be born. When **Enosh** (meaning "frail" or "mortal") was born, men began to use **the name of the Lord** (Jehovah) for God, or perhaps **to call on the name of** Jehovah in public worship.

D. Seth and His Descendants (Chap. 5)

Chapter 5 has been called "The Tolling of the Death Bells" because of the oft-repeated expression "and he died." It records the bloodline of the Messiah from Adam to Noah's son, Shem (compare Luke 3:36–38).

5:1–17 **Adam** was created **in the likeness of God**. **Seth** was born in the **image** of **Adam**. In between, the Fall took place and the image of God in man became marred by sin. Verse 5 records the *physical* fulfillment of what God said would happen in 2:17; the *spiritual* fulfillment took place the day Adam sinned.

5:18–24 The **Enoch** and Lamech mentioned here should not be confused with those in chapter 4. The **Enoch** in verse 18 is the seventh from Adam (Jude 14), not the third. By faith **Enoch walked with God** for 300 years and pleased the Lord (Heb. 11:5). It seems that the birth of his son had a sanctifying, ennobling influence on his life (v. 22a). It is good to start well, but it is even better to continue steadfastly to the end. The word *walk* implies a steady, progressive relationship and not just a casual acquaintance. To walk **with God** is the business of a lifetime, and not just the performance of an hour. **Enoch** was transported to heaven prior to the flood just as the church will be raptured to heaven before the Tribulation begins (1 Thess. 4:13–18; Rev. 3:10).

5:25–32 **Methuselah lived** longer than any other man (**nine hundred and sixty-nine years**). If, as Williams says, the name **Methuselah** means "it shall be sent,"[10] it may be a prophecy, because the flood came in the year of his death. Perhaps Lamech's prediction when he named **Noah** looked forward to the comfort that would come to the world through Noah's greater Son, the Lord Jesus Christ. Noah's name means "rest." As the years passed, man's life expectancy decreased. Psalm 90:10 speaks of seventy years as normal.

An artist's conception of Noah's ark, based on information from an explorer who claimed he saw the ark on Mt. Ararat in 1908.

E. Widespread Sin and the Universal Flood (Chaps. 6—8)

6:1, 2 There are two principal interpretations of verse 2. One is that **the sons of God** were angels who left their proper sphere (Jude 6) and intermarried with women on earth, a form of sexual disorder that was most hateful to God. Those who hold this view point out that the expression "sons of God" in Job 1:6 and 2:1 means angels who had access to the presence of God. Also, "the sons of God" as a term for angels is a standard Semitic expression. The passage in Jude 6, 7 suggests that the angels who left their own abode were guilty of vile sexual behavior. Notice the words "as Sodom and Gomorrah" at the beginning of verse 7, immediately after the description of the fallen angels.

The main objection to this view is that angels don't reproduce sexually, as far as we know. Matthew 22:30 is used to prove that Jesus taught that the angels don't marry. What the verse actually says, however, is that the angels *in heaven* neither marry nor are given in marriage. Angels appeared in human form to Abraham (Gen. 18:1–5), and it seems from the text that the two who went to Sodom had human parts and emotions.

The other view is that **the sons of God** were the godly descendants of Seth, and **the daughters of men** were the wicked posterity of Cain. The argument is as follows: The preceding context deals with the descendants of Cain (chap. 4) and the descendants of Seth (chap. 5). Genesis 6:1–4 describes the intermarriage of these two lines. The word *angels* is not found in the context. Verses 3 and 5 speak of the wickedness of *man*. If it was the *angels* who sinned, why was the race of *man* to be destroyed? Godly men are called "sons of God," though not in exactly the same Hebrew wording as in Genesis

6:2 (see Deut. 14:1; Ps. 82:6; Hos. 1:10; Matt. 5:9).

There are several problems with this view. Why were all the Sethite *men* godly and all the *women* of Cain's lineage ungodly? Also, there is no indication that Seth's line *stayed* godly. If they did, why should they be destroyed? Also, why should such a union between godly men and ungodly women produce giants?

6:3 **The LORD** warned that His **Spirit** would not **strive with man forever**, but that there would be a delay of **one hundred and twenty years** before the judgment of the flood would occur. God is longsuffering, not willing that any should perish, but there is a limit. Peter tells us that it was Christ who was preaching through Noah to the antediluvians by the Holy Spirit (1 Pet. 3:18–20; 2 Pet. 2:5). They rejected the message and are now imprisoned.

6:4, 5 Regarding the **giants** (Heb. *nephilim*, "fallen ones") Unger explains:

> The Nephilim are considered by many as giant demigods, the unnatural offspring of "the daughters of men" (mortal women) in cohabitation with "the sons of God" (angels). This utterly unnatural union, violating God's created orders of being, was such a shocking abnormality as to necessitate the worldwide judgment of the Flood.[11]

6:6, 7 The Lord's sorrow does not indicate an arbitrary change of mind, though it seems that way to man. Rather, it indicates a different attitude on God's part in response to some change in man's behavior. Because He is holy, He must react against sin.

6:8–22 **Noah found grace in the eyes of the LORD** and was forewarned to build **an ark**. The measurements are given in **cubits** (1 cubit = 18 inches). Thus the ark was 450 feet long, 75 feet wide, and 45 feet high. It had three decks. The **window** in verse 16 was literally "a place of light," probably an opening for light and air which extended the full length of the ark.

Noah was saved by **grace**, an act of divine sovereignty. His response was to do **all that God** had **commanded** (v. 22), an act of human responsibility. Noah built the ark to save his family, but it was *God* who shut and sealed the door. Divine sovereignty and human responsibility are not mutually exclusive, but are complementary.

Noah (v. 9) and Enoch (5:22) are the only men in Scripture who are said to have **walked with God**. If Enoch is a symbol of the church raptured to heaven, Noah symbolizes the faithful Jewish remnant preserved through the Tribulation to live on the millennial earth.

Verse 18 gives the first mention of **covenant** in the Bible. Scofield lists eight covenants: Edenic (Gen. 2:16); Adamic (Gen. 3:15); Noahic (Gen. 9:16); Abrahamic (Gen. 12:2); Mosaic (Ex. 19:5); Palestinian (Deut. 30:3); Davidic (2 Sam. 7:16); and the New Covenant (Heb. 8:8). These eight, plus the Solomonic Covenant, are covered in the following essay. Needless to say, a subject as complex as the covenants has been interpreted differently by various schools of theology. The treatment presented here is in the premillennial and dispensational tradition.

THE MAJOR COVENANTS OF SCRIPTURE

The Edenic Covenant (Gen. 1:28–30; 2:16, 17)

The Edenic Covenant made man, in his innocence, responsible to multiply, populate the earth, and subdue it. He was given authority over all animal life. He was to cultivate the garden and eat of all its produce except the fruit of the tree of the knowledge of good and evil. Disobedience to this latter command would bring death.

The Adamic Covenant (Gen. 3:14–19)

After the fall of man, God cursed the serpent and predicted enmity between the serpent and the woman, and between Satan and Christ. Satan would injure Christ, but Christ would destroy Satan. Woman would experience pain in childbirth and would be under the authority of her husband. The ground was cursed. Man would have to contend with thorns and thistles in cultivating it. His work would involve sweat and weariness, and he would eventually return to dust, from which he came.

The Noahic Covenant (Gen. 8:20—9:27)

God promised Noah that He would not curse the ground again or destroy the entire earth with a flood. He gave the rainbow as a pledge of this. But the covenant also includes the establishment of human government, with the power of capital punishment. God guaranteed the regularity of time periods and seasons, directed man to repopulate the earth, and reaffirmed his dominion over lower creatures. Man could now add meat to his previous vegetarian diet. Concerning Noah's descendants, God cursed Ham's son, Canaan, to be a servant to Shem and Japheth. He gave Shem a place of favor, which we know includes being in the line of the Messiah. Japheth would enjoy great expansion, and would dwell in the tents of Shem.

The Abrahamic Covenant (Gen. 12:1–3; 13:14–17; 15:1–8; 17:1–8)

The Abrahamic Covenant is unconditional. Only God, manifesting Himself as "a smoking oven and a burning torch," passed through the two pieces of the sacrificed animal in Genesis 15:12–21. This is quite significant. When two people made (Heb., "cut") a covenant, they would *both* walk together between the two pieces to show they would abide by the conditions of the covenant. God put no conditions on Abraham; hence the provisions listed below will (and have) come to pass no matter how faithful Abraham's descendants might prove.

Those who see no future for God's ancient people often try to make this covenant appear to be conditional, at least regarding the land. Then they lay claim to all the blessings for the church, leaving Israel with little or nothing.

The covenant includes the following promises to Abraham and his descendants: a great nation (Israel); personal blessings to Abraham; a name of renown; being a source of blessing to others (12:2); divine favor to his friends and a curse on his enemies; blessing to all nations—fulfilled through Christ—(12:3); everlasting possession of the land known as Canaan and later as Israel and Palestine (13:14, 15, 17); numerous posterity, natural and spiritual (13:16; 15:5); a fatherhood of many nations and kings—through Ishmael and Isaac—(17:4, 6); special relationship to God (17:7b).

The Mosaic Covenant (Ex. 19:5; 20:1–31:18)

In its broadest sense, the Mosaic Covenant includes the Ten Commandments, describing duties to God and to one's neighbor (Ex. 20:1–26); numerous regulations concerning the social life of Israel (Ex. 21:1—24:11); and detailed ordinances dealing with religious life (Ex. 24:12—31:18). It was given to the nation of Israel, not to the Gentiles. It was a conditional covenant, requiring man's obedience, and therefore it was "weak through the flesh" (Rom. 8:3a). The Decalogue was never intended to provide salvation, but rather to produce conviction of sin and failure. Nine of the Ten Commandments are repeated in the NT (the Sabbath excepted), not as law with penalty attached, but as behavior suitable for those who have been saved by grace. The Christian is under grace, not law, but he is enlawed to Christ (1 Cor. 9:21), a higher motivation.

The Palestinian Covenant (Deut. 30:1–9)

This covenant has to do with the still-future occupation of the land which God promised to Abraham "from the river of Egypt [i.e., the Brook of Egypt, not the Nile] to the great river, the River Euphrates" (Gen. 15:18). Israel has never fully occupied the land. During Solomon's reign, countries in the eastern portion paid tribute (1 Kgs. 4:21, 24), but that cannot be counted as possession or occupation.

The Palestinian Covenant foresees the dispersion of Israel among the nations because of disobedience, their return to the Lord, the Lord's Second Advent, their regathering to the land, their prosperity in the land, their change of heart (to love and obey the Lord), and the punishment of their enemies.

The Davidic Covenant (2 Sam. 7:5–19)

God promised David not only that his kingdom would endure forever, but that he would always have a lineal descendant to sit on the throne. It was an unconditional covenant, not dependent in any way on David's obedience or righteousness. Christ is the legal heir to the throne of David through Solomon, as is seen in Joseph's genealogy (Matt. 1).

He is a lineal descendant of David through Nathan, as is seen in Mary's genealogy (Luke 3). Because He lives forever, His kingdom is everlasting. His one-thousand-year reign on earth will merge into the eternal kingdom.

The Solomonic Covenant (2 Sam. 7:12–15; 1 Kgs. 8:4, 5; 2 Chron. 7:11–22)

The covenant with Solomon was unconditional as far as the everlasting kingdom was concerned, but conditional as far as Solomon's descendants sitting on the throne (1 Kgs. 8:4, 5; 2 Chron. 7:17, 18). One of Solomon's descendants, Coniah (also called Jeconiah), was barred from having any physical descendant sit on David's throne (Jer. 22:30). Jesus is not a descendant of Solomon, as pointed out above. Otherwise He would come under the curse of Coniah.

The New Covenant (Jer. 31:31–34; Heb. 8:7–12; Luke 22:20)

The New Covenant is clearly made with the house of Israel and the house of Judah (Jer. 31:31). It was future when Jeremiah wrote (Jer. 31:31a). It is not a conditional covenant, like the Mosaic Covenant, which Israel broke

(Jer. 31:32). In it God unconditionally promises (note the repetition of "I will"): Israel's regeneration (Ezek. 35:25); the indwelling of the Holy Spirit (Ezek. 36:27); a heart that is favorably disposed to do the will of God (Jer. 31:33a); a unique relationship between God and His people (Jer. 31:33b); universal knowledge of the Lord in Israel (Jer. 31:34a); sins both forgiven and forgotten (Jer. 31:34b); and the continuance of the nation forever (Jer. 31:35–37).

Israel as a nation has not as yet received the benefits of the New Covenant, but will at the Lord's Second Advent. In the meantime, true believers do share some of the blessings of the covenant. The fact that the church is related to the New Covenant is seen in the Lord's Supper, where the cup represents the covenant and the blood by which it was ratified (Luke 22:20; 1 Cor. 11:25). Also Paul spoke of himself and the other apostles as ministers of a New Covenant (2 Cor. 3:6).‡

A pair of every living creature was to be brought into the ark, as well as food. Critics claim that the ark was not big enough to hold all the species of animals and enough food for one year and seventeen days. But it is likely that the ark contained only the basic kinds of animal and bird life, and that many variations have resulted since then. The ark was more than large enough for this.

7:1 The word **"come"** appears for the first time in verse 1—a gracious gospel invitation: **"Come into the ark** of safety."

7:2–18 No reason is given why Noah was commanded to **take seven** pairs of **clean** animals into the ark, but only one pair of **unclean**. Perhaps it was for food and in anticipation of the **clean** animals' being needed for sacrifice (see 8:20). The ark was filled with its inhabitants for **seven days** before the **rain** began and the underground reserves of water gushed out. The torrent continued for **forty days and forty nights**; **forty** is the number of probation or testing in the Bible.

7:19–24 Was this a local flood, as some allege? Consider the following: **All the high hills under the whole heaven were covered** (v. 19). God need not have told Noah to build an **ark** equivalent to 1½ football fields in length and 800 railroad cars in volume to escape a local flood. He could easily have moved eight people and the animals to a different location. Traditions of a universal flood have come from all parts of the world. The mountains of Ararat range up to 17,000 feet. The flood was **fifteen cubits** higher (vv. 19, 20). By what sort of miracle was this water kept in a localized area? In Genesis 9:15 God promised that the water would never again become a flood to destroy **all** flesh. There have been many local floods since then, but never a universal flood. If the flood was local, then God's promise has been broken—an impossible conclusion. Peter uses the destruction of the world by water as a symbol of a still future destruction of the earth by fire (2 Pet. 3:6).

The ark is a picture of Christ. The waters depict God's judgment. The Lord Jesus went under the waters of divine wrath at Calvary. Those who are in Christ are saved. Those who are outside are doomed (see 1 Pet. 3:21).

8:1–19 The chronology of the Flood is as follows:

1. 7 days—from the time Noah entered the ark until the Flood began (7:10).

2. 40 days and nights—duration of the rain (7:12).
3. 150 days—from the time the rain began until **the waters decreased** (8:3) and **the ark rested** on Mount **Ararat** (compare 7:11 and 8:4).
4. 224 days—from the beginning of the Flood until the mountaintops reappeared (compare 7:11 and 8:5).
5. 40 days—from the time the mountaintops were seen until Noah **sent out a raven** (8:7).
6. 7 days—from the sending of the raven to the first sending forth of **a dove** (8:6–10; v. 10, **"yet another seven days"**).
7. 7 more days—until **the dove** was sent forth a second time (8:10).
8. 7 more days—until the final sending forth of the dove.
9. 314 days—from the beginning of the Flood until **Noah removed the covering** from **the ark** (compare 7:11 and 8:13).
10. 371 days—from the beginning of the Flood until **the earth was dried** (compare 7:11 and 8:14). At this time, Noah was commanded to **go out of the ark** (v. 16)

The unclean **raven** (v. 7) and the clean **dove** (v. 8) are good illustrations of the believer's old and new natures. The old nature loves to feed on garbage and carrion whereas the new nature cannot find satisfaction in a scene of death and judgment. It finds no rest until it sets its feet on resurrection ground.

8:20–22 Noah responded to God's saving grace by building **an altar**. Those of us who have been saved from the wrath to come should likewise bring to God our heartfelt worship. It is as acceptable and pleasing today as it was in Noah's day. **The** **Lord** made a covenant that He would **never again curse the ground** or **destroy every living thing, as** He had **done**; also, He would provide regular seasons as long as the **earth** endured.

In 6:5 and here in verse 21, God speaks of the intense evil of man's heart. In the first instance, there was *no* sacrifice, and judgment ensued. Here there *is* a sacrifice; and God acts in mercy.

F. Noah after the Flood (Chap. 9)

9:1–7 Verse 3 suggests that after the Flood people were permitted to eat meat for the first time. Eating of **blood** was forbidden, however, because the **blood** is the **life** of the **flesh**, and the life belongs to God.

The institution of capital punishment presupposes the establishment of governmental authority. It would be chaos if anyone and everyone avenged a murder. Only duly appointed governments may do so. The NT perpetuates capital punishment when it says concerning the government, ". . . he does not bear the sword in vain" (Rom. 13:4).

9:8–17 The rainbow was given as a pledge that God would **never again destroy the earth** with **a flood**.

9:18–23 In spite of God's grace to Noah, he sinned by becoming **drunk** and then lying naked **in his tent**. When **Ham** saw him and reported the matter to **his brothers**, they **covered** their father's shame without looking on his naked body.

9:24, 25 When he **awoke, Noah** pronounced a curse on **Canaan**. The question arises, "Why did the curse fall on **Canaan** instead of **Ham**?" One possible explanation is that the evil tendency which was manifested in

Ham was even more pronounced in **Canaan**. The curse was thus a prophecy of his immoral conduct and its fitting punishment. Another explanation is that Canaan himself committed some vulgar act against his grandfather, and that Noah later became aware of it. Noah **knew what his younger son had done to him**. It may be that verse 24 refers to Canaan as Noah's *youngest grandson,* rather than to Ham as his *younger son*. In the Bible, "son" often means "grandson" or other descendant. In this event, **Canaan** was not **cursed** for his father's sin, but for his own. Yet another possibility is that God's grace allowed Noah to curse only a small segment of Ham's descendants and not a possible third of the human race.

9:26–29 Canaan was cursed to serve **Shem** and **Japheth**. The Canaanites' servitude to the Israelites may be seen in Joshua 9:23 and Judges 1:28. This passage has been used to suggest the slavery of the black people, but there is absolutely no support for this view. Canaan was the ancestor of the Canaanites, who dwelt in the Holy Land before Israel arrived. There is no evidence that they were black people. **Shem** and **Japheth** were blessed with dominion. Verse 27 may suggest Japheth's sharing in spiritual blessings through Shem's descendants, the Israelites.

There is a dispute as to whether Shem or Japheth was the oldest son of Noah. Chapter 10:21 may read "Shem . . . the brother of Japheth the elder" or "Shem . . . the older brother of Japheth" (NKJV marg.) The latter is the preferred reading. Shem appears first in the genealogies of Genesis 5:32 and 1 Chronicles 1:4.

G. The Table of Nations (Chap. 10)

10:1–32 Shem, Ham, and Japheth became the fathers of the nations.

Shem: The Semitic peoples—Jews, Arabs, Babylonians, Assyrians, Arameans, Phoenicians.

Ham: The Hamitic peoples—Ethiopians, Egyptians, Canaanites, Philistines, possibly the African and Oriental peoples, though many scholars view the Orientals as Japhetic.

Japheth: The Japhetic peoples—the Medes, Greeks, Cypriots, etc. Probably the Caucasian people of Europe and of northern Asia. Many scholars would also include the Orientals here.

The order in this chapter is **the sons of Japheth** (vv. 2–5), **the sons of Ham** (vv. 6–20), and **the sons of Shem** (vv. 21–31). The Spirit of God is going to center on Shem and his descendants during the rest of the OT. The different languages of verse 5 probably look forward to the time after the tower of Babel (11:1–9).

Notice three references in this chapter to the division of the people. Verse 5 describes the division of the Japhetic tribes into their different areas. Verse 25 tells us that the division of the earth (at Babel) took place in the days of **Peleg**. Verse 32 serves as an introduction to the Tower of Babel in chapter 11, when **the families of the** sons of Noah were divided into different **nations** with different languages.

Nimrod (vv. 8–10) means *rebel*. He appears as the first **"mighty one on the earth"** after the flood (v. 8) and as the first to establish a **kingdom** (v.

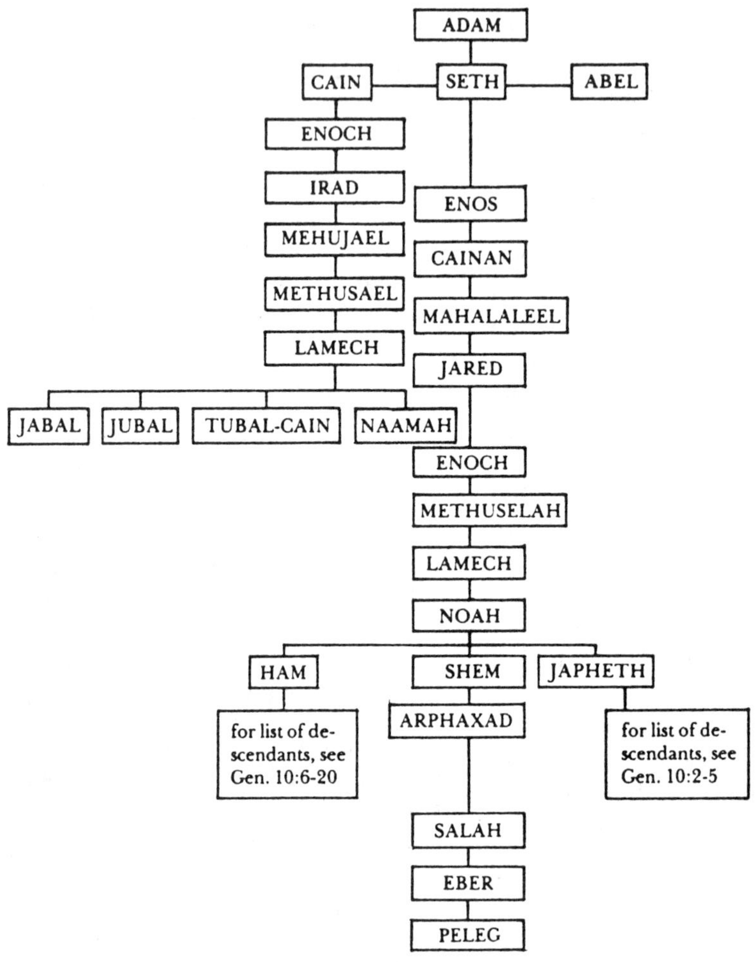

Descendants of Adam

10). He built **Babel** (Babylon) in rebellion against God, and also **Nineveh** in **Assyria** (see v. 11), another inveterate enemy of God's people.

As already mentioned, verse 21 lists **Shem** as the *older* **brother of Japheth**.

It is impossible to identify with certainty the places where the various people settled, but the following will prove helpful in later studies.

Tarshish (v. 4) — Spain
Kittim (v. 4) — Cyprus
Cush (v. 6) — Ethiopia
Mizraim (v. 6) — Egypt
Put or Phut (v. 6) — Libya
Canaan (v. 6) — Palestine
Asshur (v. 11, KJV)— Assyria
Elam (v. 22) — Persia
Aram (v. 22) — Syria and Mesopotamia

H. The Tower of Babel (Chap. 11)

11:1–4 In chapter 10, which *chronologically* comes *after* chapter 11, mankind was divided according to languages (vv. 5, 20, 31). Now we learn the cause of the divisions. Instead of dispersing over the earth, as God, intended, men built **a city and a tower** in **Shinar** (Babylon). **They said to one another, "Come, let us build ourselves a city, and a tower whose**

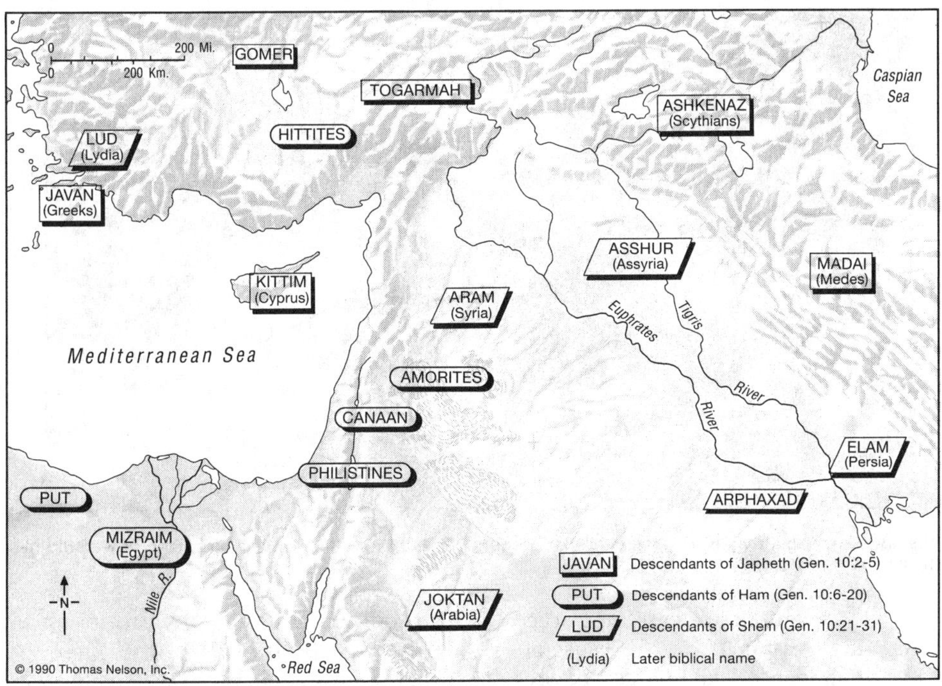

The Nations of Genesis 10

top is in the heavens; let us make us a name for ourselves, lest we be scattered abroad over the face of the whole earth." So it was a policy of pride (to **make a name for** themselves) and defiance (to avoid being **scattered**). To us the **tower** may also picture fallen man's ceaseless effort to reach heaven by his own works instead of receiving salvation as a free gift of grace.

11:5–9 The Lord judged the people by confounding **their language**. This was the beginning of the many different languages which we have in the world today. Pentecost (Acts 2:1–11) was the reverse of Babel in the sense that every man heard the wonderful works of God in his own language. Babel means *confusion*, the inevitable result of any union that leaves God out or is not according to God.

11:10–25 These verses trace the line of **Shem** to **Abram**. Thus the historical record narrows from the human race to one branch of that race (the Semites) and then to one man (**Abram**), who becomes the head of the Hebrew nation. The rest of the OT is largely a history of this nation.

11:26–32 Abram was a mighty man of faith and one of the most important men in history. Three world religions— Judaism, Christianity, and Islam—venerate him. He is mentioned in sixteen books of the OT and eleven books of the NT. His name means "exalted father" or, as changed to Abraham, "father of a multitude."

There is a mathematical problem in this passage. Derek Kidner explains:

> Terah's age at death presents a difficulty, since it makes his eldest son 135 years old (26), whereas Abram was only 75 (12:4, with Acts 7:4). One solution is to suppose Abram to have been the youngest son, born

The Tower of Babel may have been similar to ziggurats built by the Babylonians as places of worship of their chief god Marduk.

sixty years after the eldest but placed first in the list in 11:26, 27 because of his prominence (like Ephraim before Manasseh). Another is to follow the Samaritan text, which gives Terah's age as 145 at death. This seems preferable, if only because Abram would scarcely have made the exclamation of 17:17 had his own father begotten him at 130.[12]

Ur of the Chaldeans (v. 31), in Mesopotamia, was a center of pagan idolatry. Terah and his family traveled northwest to **Haran**, en route **to the land of Canaan**.

II. THE PATRIARCHS OF ISRAEL (Chaps. 12—50)

A. Abraham (12:1—25:18)

1. *The Call of Abraham (12:1–9)*

12:1–3 The call of **the LORD** had come to **Abram** when he was still in Ur (compare v. 1 with Acts 7:1,2). Abram was called to leave his **country**, his **family**, and his **father's house**, and to embark on a life of pilgrimage (Heb. 11:9). God made a marvelous covenant with him which included the following significant promises: **a land**—that is, the **land** of Canaan; **a great nation**—namely, the Jewish people; material and spiritual prosperity for Abram and his seed; a **great name** for Abram and his posterity; they would be a channel of **blessing** to others; friends of Israel would be **blessed** and anti-Semites would be cursed; **all the families of the earth** would be **blessed in** Abram, pointing forward to the Lord Jesus Christ, who would be a descendant of Abram. This covenant was renewed and enlarged in 13:14–17; 15:4–6; 17:10–14; and 22:15–18.

12:4–9 After what have been called "the wasted years in Haran," that is, years without progress, Abram moved to Canaan with **his wife Sarai**, his nephew **Lot**, other relatives, and **possessions**. They came first to **Shechem**, where Abram **built an altar to the LORD**. The presence of hostile **Canaanites** was no obstacle to a man who was walking by faith. Abram next relocated between **Bethel** (*house of God*) and **Ai**. True to form, **he** not only **pitched** a **tent** for himself but

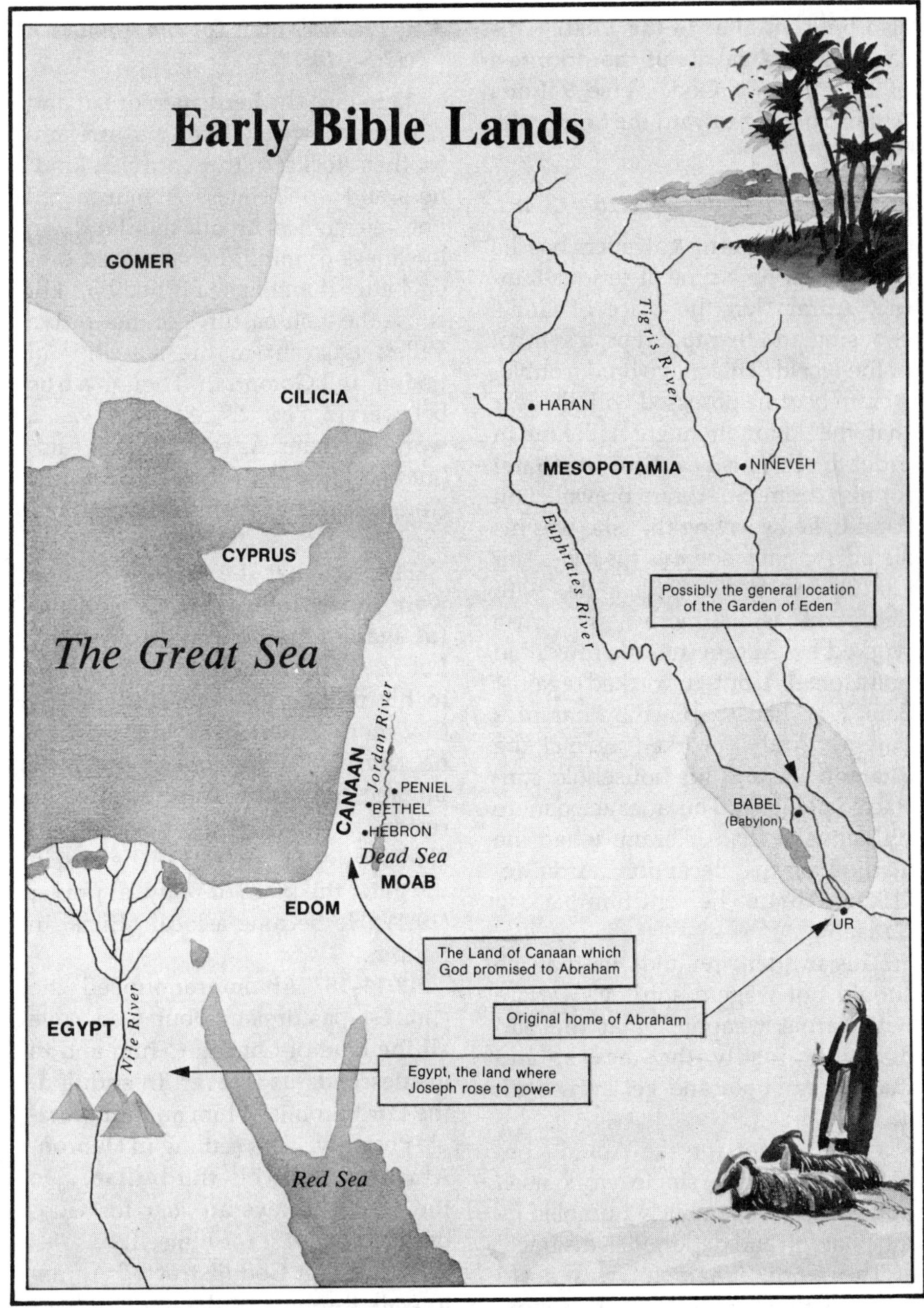

Early Bible Lands

also built **an altar to the** LORD. This says a great deal about the priorities of this man of God. Verse 9 finds **Abram** moving **toward the South** (the Negev).

2. *To Egypt and Back (12:10—13:4)*

12:10–20 Faith, however, has its lapses. During a time of serious **famine**, **Abram** left the place of God's choosing and fled **to Egypt**, a symbol of the world. This move bred trouble. Abram became obsessed with the fear that the Pharaoh might kill him in order to seize his **beautiful** wife **Sarai** for his harem. So Abram prevailed on Sarai to lie by saying that she was his **sister**. Actually she *was* his *half*-sister (20:12), but it was still a lie, with deception as its motive. The ruse worked for Abram (he was rewarded handsomely) but it worked against Sarai (she had to join the **Pharaoh's** harem). And it worked against the **Pharaoh** (he and **his** household contracted **plagues**). The latter acted more righteously than Abram when he learned of the deception. After rebuking **Abram**, he sent him back to Canaan.

This incident reminds us that we should not wage a spiritual warfare with carnal weapons, that the end does not justify the means, and that we can't sin and get away with it.

God did not forsake Abram, but He did allow the sin to work itself out. Abram was publicly humbled by the Pharaoh and deported in disgrace.

The word "**Pharaoh**" was not a proper name but a title, such as king, emperor, president, etc.

13:1–4 Underlying Abram's return to **Bethel . . . from Egypt** was a return to fellowship with God. "Back to Bethel" is the rallying cry for all who have wandered from the Lord.

3. *Experiences with Lot and Abimelech (13:5—14:24)*

13:5–13 The **herdsmen** of **Lot** and **Abram** quarreled over pastureland for their **flocks**. In true courtesy, kindness, and unselfishness, Abram offered Lot his choice of **all** the **land**. In lowliness of mind, he esteemed others better than himself (Phil. 2:3). Lot chose the lush pastures of the **Jordan** Valley, adjacent to the sin-cities of **Sodom and Gomorrah**. Though a true believer (2 Pet. 2:7, 8), Lot was a world-borderer. As someone has said, "he got grass for his cattle while Abram got grace for his children" (vv. 15, 16).

The fact that **the men of Sodom were exceedingly wicked and sinful against the** LORD didn't restrain Lot in his choice. Notice the steps in his plunge into worldliness: He (his men) experienced **strife** (v. 7); he **saw** (v. 10); he **chose** (v. 11); he **pitched his tent** toward (v. 12); he resided away from the place where God's priest was (14:12); he sat in the gate, the place of political power (19:1). He became a local official in Sodom.

13:14–18 Abram renounced the choicest pastureland, but God gave **all the land** of Canaan to him and **to** his **descendants forever**. In addition, the Lord promised him an innumerable posterity. After settling **in Hebron, Abram . . . built** his third **altar . . . to the** LORD—always an *altar* for God, but never a *house* for himself!

Notice that God instructed Abram to walk throughout the land and see his possession. So we are to appropriate God's promises by faith.

14:1–12 Thirteen years before the main events of this chapter, **Chedorlaomer, king of Elam** (Persia), had conquered various kings in the plains

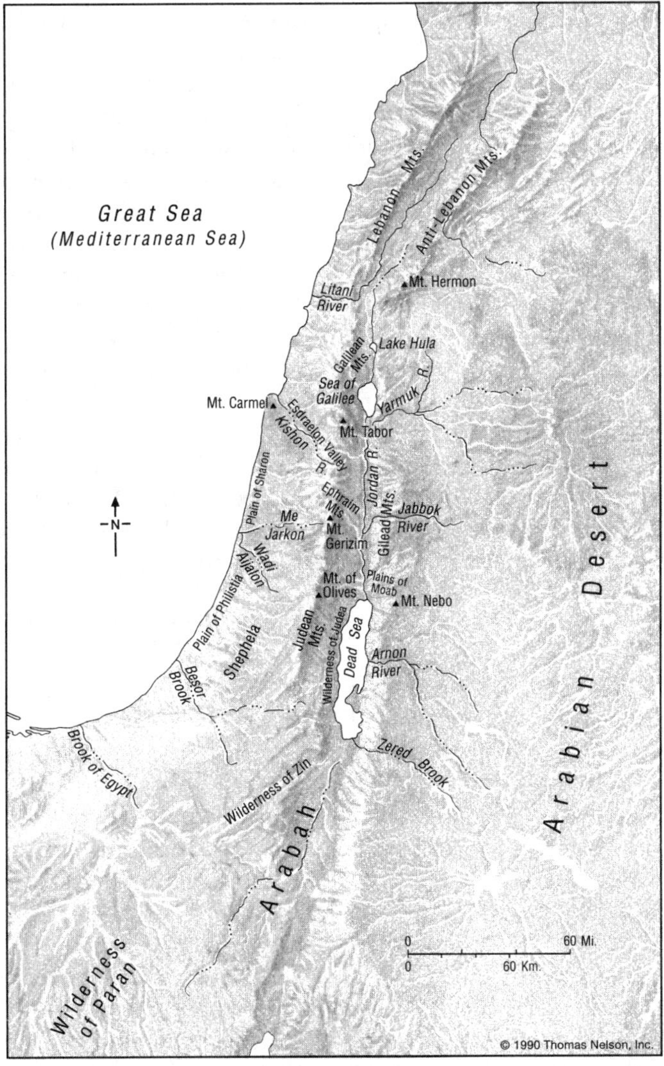

The Promised Land

adjacent to the Dead (**Salt**) **Sea**. **In the thirteenth year**, the five captive kings **rebelled** against Chedorlaomer. So he allied himself with three other kings from the region of Babylon, marched south along the eastern side of the Dead Sea, then north on the western side to **Sodom**, **Gomorrah**, and the other cities of the plain. The battle took place **in the Valley of Siddim**, which **was full of asphalt pits**. The invaders defeated the rebels and marched north with their booty and captives—including **Lot**, Abram's backslidden nephew.

14:13–16 When **Abram** received the news, he assembled a fighting force of **three hundred and eighteen trained** men and pursued the victors to **Dan**, in the north. He finally defeated them near **Damascus**, in Syria, and rescued **Lot and** all the spoils. Backsliders bring not only misery on themselves but trouble on others. Here Abram delivered Lot by the sword. Later he delivers him through intercessory prayer (chaps. 18, 19).

14:17, 18 As Abram was returning home, **the king of Sodom went out to meet him**, just as Satan often tempts the believer after a great spiritual victory. But **Melchizedek**, **king of Salem** and **priest of God Most High**, was on hand with **bread and wine** to strengthen Abram. We cannot read this first mention of **bread and wine** without thinking of these symbols of our Savior's passion. When we consider the price He paid to save us from sin, we are strengthened to resist every sinful temptation.

Names in Scripture have meanings. **Melchizedek** means *king of righteousness* and **Salem** (short for Jerusalem) means *peace*. So he was king of righteousness and king of peace. He is a symbol of Christ, true King of righteousness and peace, and our Great High Priest. When it says in Hebrews 7:3 that Melchizedek was "without father, without mother, without genealogy, having neither beginning of days nor end of life," this is to be understood *only in connection with his priesthood*. Most priests inherited their office and served for a limited tenure. But the priesthood of Melchizedek was unique in that, as far as the record is concerned, it wasn't passed on to him from his parents, and it did not have a beginning or an end. Christ's priesthood is "according to the order of Melchizedek" (Ps. 110:4; Heb. 7:17).

14:19, 20 Melchizedek **blessed** Abram, and Abram in turn **gave** to this priest of God **a tithe of all** his captured prizes. In Hebrews 7 we learn that there was a deep spiritual significance to these actions. Because Abram was the progenitor of Aaron, he is seen as representing the Aaronic priesthood. The fact that Melchizedek **blessed** Abram means that Melchizedek's priesthood is greater than Aaron's, because the one who blesses is superior to the one who is blessed. The fact that Abram paid tithes to Melchizedek is seen as a picture of the Aaronic priesthood acknowledging the superiority of Melchizedek's priesthood, because the lesser pays tithes to the greater.

14:21–24 **The king of Sodom said**, in effect, "**Give me the persons**; you **take the** material things." So Satan still tempts us to be occupied with toys of dust while people around us are perishing. Abram replied that he wouldn't take anything **from a thread to a sandal strap**.

4. Abraham's Promised Heir (Chap. 15)

15:1 The first verse is closely linked with the last part of chapter 14. Because the patriarch refused the rewards of the king of Sodom, Jehovah said to him, **"Do not be afraid, Abram. I am your shield, your exceedingly great reward,"** thus making Abram both protected and fabulously wealthy.

15:2–6 Being **childless**, **Abram** feared that their servant, **Eliezer of Damascus**, would be their **heir**, since that was the law at that time. But God promised him a son and **descendants** as numerous as **the stars**. Humanly speaking this was impossible, since Sarai had passed the time when she could bear a child. But Abram **believed** God's promise, and God declared him to be righteous. The truth of justification by faith enunciated here is repeated in Romans 4:3, Galatians 3:6, and James 2:23. In 13:16 God had promised **descendants** as numerous as the dust, and here in 15:5 as numerous as the stars. The *dust* pictures Abram's natural posterity—

those who are Jews by birth. The *stars* depict his spiritual seed—those who are justified by faith (see Gal. 3:7).

15:7–21 To confirm the promise of a seed (vv. 1–6) and of a land (vv. 7, 8, 18–21), God acted out a strange and significant symbolism (vv. 9–21). David Baron explains:

> According to the ancient Eastern manner of making a covenant, both the contracting parties passed through the divided pieces of the slain animals, thus symbolically attesting that they pledged their very lives to the fulfillment of the engagement they made (see Jer. 34:18, 19). Now in Genesis 15, God alone, whose presence was symbolized by the smoking furnace and lamp of fire, passed through the midst of the pieces of the slain animals, while Abram was simply a spectator of this wonderful exhibition of God's free grace.[13]

This signified that it was an *unconditional* **covenant**, dependent for fulfillment on God alone.

According to another view of this passage, the sacrificial **pieces** represent the nation of Israel. The **vultures** speak of the Gentile nations. The **land that is not theirs**, of course, is Egypt. Israel would be delivered from Egyptian bondage and return to Canaan **in the fourth generation**. The **smoking oven** and the **burning torch** describe the national destiny of Israel—suffering and witness-bearing.

Israel's deliverance would not come until **the iniquity of the Amorites** was **complete**. These pagan inhabitants of Canaan must eventually be exterminated. But God often allows evil to run its course, sometimes to the seeming detriment of His people, before He judges it. He is longsuffering, not willing that any should perish—even the depraved **Amorites** (2 Pet. 3:9). He also allows evil to come to fruition so that the awful consequences of wickedness can be clear to all. Thus His wrath is demonstrated to be completely righteous.

Verses 13 and 14 pose a chronological problem. They predict that Abram's people would be in harsh servitude in a foreign **land** for *400* **years**, and that they would leave at the end of that time, carrying **great** wealth with them. In Acts 7:6 this figure of 400 years is repeated.

In Exodus 12:40, 41 we read that the children of Israel, who dwelt in Egypt, were sojourners for *430* years, to the very day.

Then in Galatians 3:17 Paul says that the period from the confirming of the Abrahamic Covenant until the giving of the Law was *430* years.

How can these figures be reconciled?

The *400* years mentioned in Genesis 15:13, 14 and in Acts 7:6 refer to the time of Israel's *harsh affliction* in Egypt. Jacob and his family were not in bondage when they first came to Egypt. On the contrary, they were treated quite royally.

The *430* years in Exodus 12:40, 41 refer to the total time the people of Israel spent in Egypt—to the very day. This is an exact figure.

The 430 years in Galatians 3:17 cover *approximately* the same period as Exodus 12:40, 41. They are reckoned from the time that God confirmed the Abrahamic Covenant to Jacob, just as Jacob was preparing to enter Egypt (Gen. 46:14), and they extend to the giving of the Law, about three months after the Exodus.

The four generations of Genesis 15:16 can be seen in Exodus 6:16–20: Levi, Kohath, Amram, Moses. Israel has not yet occupied the land promised in verses 18–21. Solomon had dominion over it (1 Kgs. 4:21, 24), as over vassal states, but his people did not occupy it. The covenant will be fulfilled when Christ returns to reign. Nothing can stop its fulfillment. What God has promised is as sure as if it had already occurred!

The river of Egypt (v. 18) is generally believed to be a small stream south of Gaza now known as Wadi el Arish, and not the Nile.

5. Ishmael, Son of the Flesh (Chaps. 16, 17)

16:1–6 The restlessness of the sin nature is seen here. Instead of waiting on God, **Sarai** persuaded **Abram** to obtain a child **by** her **maid, Hagar,** who was probably acquired during the ill-fated sojourn in Egypt. God is faithful in recording the marital irregularities of His people, even if He never approved them. When **Hagar** became pregnant, she looked down in disdain on **her mistress**. **Sarai** responded by blaming Abram, then driving Hagar out of the house. This illustrates the conflict between law and grace. They cannot cohabit (Gal. 4:21–31). While some of the behavior in this section may have been culturally acceptable then, it is certainly irregular from a Christian standpoint.

16:7–15 While **Hagar** was in the desert at **Shur**, on the way to Egypt, **the Angel of the LORD** came to her. This was the Lord Jesus in one of His preincarnate appearances, known as a Christophany. (See Judges 6 for an essay on the Angel of the LORD.) He counseled her to **return** and **submit** to Sarai, and promised that her **son** would become head of a great nation. That promise, of course, is fulfilled in the Arab people. The words **"Return . . . and submit"** have marked great turning points in the lives of many who have had dealings with God.

Hagar's exclamation in verse 13 might be paraphrased, "You are a God who may be seen," for she said, **"Have I also here seen Him who sees me?"** She named the **well "Beer Lahai Roi"** (literally, *well of the One who lives and sees me*).[14]

16:16 Abram was eighty-six when **Ishmael** was born to **Hagar**. The name **Ishmael** means *God hears*. In this case He heard Hagar's misery. We should remember throughout this narrative that Hagar represents law whereas Sarai represents grace (see Gal. 4).

17:1–14 God's words to Abram in verse 1 may have been a veiled way of saying that he should stop trying to work things out in his own strength and let **Almighty God** work for him. Immediately afterward God renewed His **covenant** and changed the patriarch's **name** from **Abram** (*exalted father*) to **Abraham** (*father of a multitude*). Circumcision was then instituted as a sign of the covenant. This surgical operation, performed on the **male child**, was a physical **sign** that the person belonged to God's chosen earthly people. Although it was already practiced in the Middle East at this time, it took on new meaning for Abraham and his family. Every male in Abraham's house was **circumcised**, and thereafter every male baby was to be circumcised when he was **eight days old** or else **be cut off from his people**—that is, put away from the congregation of Israel (vv. 9–14). The expression "cut off" sometimes means to put to death, as in Exodus 31:14,15. In other places, as here, it seems to mean to ban or ostracize.

The Apostle Paul is careful to point out that Abraham was justified (15:6) *before* he was circumcised. His circumcision was "a seal of the righteousness of the faith which he had while still uncircumcised" (Rom. 4:11).

Believers today are not sealed with a physical mark; they receive the Holy Spirit as a seal at the time of their conversion (Eph. 4:30).

THE SIGN OF CIRCUMCISION

Circumcision was adopted by God as a physical sign of the covenant between Him and His people (Gen. 17:10–14). Thus all descendants of Abraham became known as "the circumcision" (Acts 10:45) and Gentiles were called the "uncircumcision" (Eph. 2:11). It is also the sign and seal of the righteousness which Abraham had by faith (Rom. 4:5).

But then the words "circumcision" and "circumcised" took on a variety of meanings. "Uncircumcised lips" (Ex. 6:12) signified a lack of skill in public speaking. "Uncircumcised ears" and "uncircumcised hearts" spoke of failure to hear, love, and obey the Lord (Lev. 26:41; Deut. 10:16; 30:6; Jer. 6:10; Acts 7:51). "Uncircumcised in flesh" (Ezek. 44:7) meant unclean.

In the NT, "the circumcision of Christ" (Col. 2:11) refers to His death on the cross. Believers are circumcised through their identification with Christ; Paul speaks of it as "the circumcision made without hands, in putting off the body of the sins of the flesh" (Col. 2:11). This circumcision speaks of death to the fleshly nature. It is true positionally of every believer, but should be followed by a practical mortifying of the sinful deeds of the flesh (Col. 3:5). The apostle speaks of believers as the true circumcision (Phil. 3:3), in contrast to a party of Jewish legalists known as "the circumcision" (Gal. 2:12).

In addition to their symbolism, some of God's kindly laws were designed to save His people from the diseases of the Gentiles. Many medical authorities today believe that circumcision tends to prevent certain forms of cancer in both the man and his wife.‡

17:15–17 **God** changed Sarai's **name** to **Sarah** (*princess*) and promised Abraham that his ninety-year-old wife would have a son. The patriarch **laughed**, but in joyful wonder, not in unbelief. His faith did not waver (Rom. 4:18–21).

17:18–27 When **Abraham** pled that **Ishmael** might have favor **before** God, he was told that the **covenant** would be fulfilled through his son, **Isaac**. However, **Ishmael** would be **fruitful**, would **multiply**, and would become **a great nation**. **Isaac** was a symbol of Christ, through whom the **covenant** receives its ultimate fulfillment.

Notice the promptness of Abraham's obedience: **That very same day Abraham was circumcised, and his son Ishmael**.

6. Sodom and Gomorrah (Chaps. 18, 19)

18:1–15 Shortly after the events of chapter 17, **three men** appeared to Abraham. Actually two of them were angels and the other was the LORD Himself. With typical Middle Eastern hospitality, **Abraham** and **Sarah** entertained the angels unawares (Heb. 13:2) and One who was greater than angels. When **Sarah** overheard the Lord say that she would have a child within a year, her laughter betrayed her unbelief. She was rebuked with the searching question, **"Is anything too hard for the LORD?"** But the promise was repeated in spite of her doubting (vv. 9–15). Hebrews 11:11 indicates that Sarah was basically a woman of faith in spite of this momentary lapse.

18:16–33 After the LORD revealed to **Abraham** that He was going to destroy **Sodom**, and while the two angels were walking toward that city, Abraham's great intercessory countdown began—**fifty . . . forty-five . . . forty . . . thirty . . . twenty . . . ten.** Even for **ten righteous** people the Lord would **not destroy Sodom!** Abraham's prayer is a wonderful example of effectual intercession. It was based on the righteous character of the Judge of all the earth (v. 25) and evidenced that boldness, yet deep humility which only an intimate knowledge of God can give. Only when Abraham stopped pleading did the Lord close the matter and depart (v. 33). There are many mysteries in life for which the truth of verse 25 is the only satisfying answer.

Don't miss the tribute God paid to Abraham as an outstanding family man (v. 19). Something worth coveting!

19:1–11 The name of **Sodom** has become synonymous with the sin of homosexuality or sodomy. But sexual perversion was not the only cause of the city's fall. In Ezekiel 16:49, 50, the Lord describes the sin of Sodom as "pride, fullness of food, and abundance of idleness."

Lot received the **two angels** and insisted that they **spend the night** in his home, knowing all too well the danger that would face them otherwise. Even then **the men of Sodom** sought to commit homosexual rape against these heavenly visitors. In a desperate effort to save his guests, Lot shamelessly offered his **two daughters**. Only a miracle saved the day; the angels struck the Sodomites **with** a temporary, confusing **blindness**.

HOMOSEXUALITY

Both in the OT (Gen. 19:1–26; Lev. 18:22; 20:13) and in the NT (Rom. 1:18–32; 1 Cor. 6:9; 1 Tim. 1:10), God condemns the sin of homosexuality. He showed His wrath against it by destroying the cities of Sodom and Gomorrah. Under the law of Moses, sodomy was punishable by death. No practicing homosexual will inherit the kingdom of God.

So-called "gays" pay a high price for their immoral lifestyle. Paul says that they receive in themselves "the penalty of their error which was due" (Rom. 1:27b). This includes venereal diseases, pneumocystis, Kaposi's sarcoma (a form of cancer) and AIDS. It also includes haunting guilt, mental and emotional disturbances, and abnormal personality changes.

Like all other sinners, a homosexual or lesbian can be saved if he or she repents of sin and receives the Lord Jesus Christ as personal Savior. God loves the gay person and the lesbian even if He hates their sin.

There is a difference between being a *practicing* homosexual and having a homosexual *tendency*. It is the practice that the Bible condemns, not the orientation. There are many who have an attraction to their own sex but refuse to give in to it. By the power of the Spirit, they have disciplined themselves to resist the temptation and to live in purity. Many Christian persons of homosexual orientation

> . . . have regarded their condition with sorrow and contrition, but, unable to change, have drawn on the Spirit for the power of forbearance and chastity, which is sanctification indeed . . . . In commitment to Christ, [they] have offered an enduring inner blemish for God's use that divine power may be perfected in human weakness.[15]

Some blame God that they were born with this tendency, but the fault does not lie with God but with human sinfulness. Every fallen child of Adam has evil tendencies. Some have a weakness in one area, some in another. The sin is not in being tempted, but in yielding to the temptation.

There is deliverance from homosexuality or lesbianism, as there is from any form of lust. However, ongoing godly counseling assistance is very important in nearly every case.

Christians should accept gays and lesbians as persons without approving their lifestyle. Because they are people for whom Christ died, believers should seek in every possible way to win them to a life of "holiness, without which no one will see the Lord" (Heb. 12:14).‡

19:12–29 The angels insisted that Lot and his family leave the city. But when he tried to persuade **his sons-in-law** (or perhaps prospective sons-in-law—see RSV), they thought he was **joking**. His backslidden life nullified his testimony when the crisis came. **When the morning dawned, the angels** escorted **Lot**, his **wife**, and **daughters** out of Sodom. Even then Lot temporized, preferring to stay in **Zoar**, one of the satellite sin cities. Not even ten righteous men were found in the city of Sodom, so God destroyed it. But Abraham's prayer was not unanswered, for **God remembered Abraham, and sent Lot out of the midst of the overthrow**.

Though Lot's **wife** left the city, her heart was still in it, and she fell under the judgment of God. In the words "Remember Lot's wife" (Luke 17:32), Christ held her up as a warning to all who trifle with His offer of salvation.

19:30–38 Leaving **Zoar**, Lot fled to a mountain **cave**. There **his daughters made** him drunk and enticed him to commit incest with them. The older daughter subsequently **bore a son** named **Moab**, and the **younger... bore a son, Ben-Ammi**. Thus began the **Moabites** and Ammonites, who became recurring thorns in Israel's side. It was Moabite women who later seduced the men of Israel to commit immorality (Num. 25:1–3) and Ammonites who taught Israel the worship of Molech, including the sacrifice of children (1 Kgs. 11:33; Jer. 32:35). We know from 2 Peter 2:7, 8 that Lot was a just man, but because of his worldliness he lost his testimony (v. 14), his wife (v. 26), his sons-in-law, his friends, his communion (there was none in Sodom), his property (he went in rich but came out poor), his character (v. 35), his life's work, and nearly his life (v. 22). The depraved behavior of his daughters shows that they had been influenced by Sodom's vile standards. There is no escape (Heb. 2:3).

7. *Abraham and Abimelech (Chap. 20)*

20:1–18 It seems incredible to us that **Abraham** would again try to pass off **Sarah** as his **sister** within twenty years of the same blunder with Pharaoh—incredible, that is, until we remember our *own* perpetual proneness to sin! The incident with **Abimelech** in **Gerar** is almost a replay of Abraham's duplicity in Egypt (12:10–17). God intervened to work out His purposes in the birth of Isaac, which might otherwise have been frustrated. He threatened **Abimelech** with death. He is more than just a spectator on the sidelines of history. He can overrule the evil of His people, even through the lives of the unregenerate. The pagan **Abimelech** acted more righteously in this incident than Abraham, the "friend of God." (*Abimelech* is a title, and not a proper name.) It is shameful when a believer has to be justly rebuked by a man of the world! When a half-truth is presented as the whole truth, it is an untruth. Abraham even tried to shift some of the blame onto God for making him **wander** in the first place. He would have been wiser to humbly acknowledge his guilt. Nevertheless, he was still God's man. And so the Lord sent Abimelech to him so that Abraham would pray that his household be healed of its barrenness.

The expression **"this vindicates you"** (v. 16) is literally "it is a covering of the eyes," meaning a gift given for the purpose of appeasing. Thus it might read, "It is given to you as a payment in satisfaction as evidence to all who are with you and to all men that the wrong has been righted."

8. Isaac, Son of the Promise (Chap. 21)

21:1–10 When the promised son was born to **Abraham** and **Sarah**, the ecstatic parents named him **Isaac** ("laughter"), as commanded by God (17:19, 21). This expressed their own delight and the delight of all who would hear the news. **Isaac** was probably from two to five years old when he **was weaned**. Ishmael would have been between thirteen and seventeen. When **Sarah saw** Ishmael mocking Isaac at the weaning party, she ordered Abraham to **cast out** Hagar **and her son**. Paul interprets this action as evidence that law persecutes grace, that law and grace cannot be mixed, and that spiritual blessings cannot be obtained on the legal principle (Gal. 4:29).

21:11–13 Abraham was grieved to lose Hagar and Ishmael, **but God** consoled him with the promise that Ishmael would become the father of **a** great **nation**. And yet the Lord made it clear that Isaac was the promised son through whom the covenant would be carried out.

21:14–21 When **Hagar** and **the boy** almost perished from thirst in the desert south of Canaan, God caused them to find a **well**, and they were spared. Ishmael was in his teens at this time; therefore, verse 15 probably means that Hagar pushed him **under one of the shrubs** in his weakness. Ishmael's name, "God hears," is found twice in verse 17—**"God heard"** and **"God has heard."** Children and young people should be encouraged to pray. God hears and answers!

21:22–34 The **Abimelech** in verse 22 is not necessarily the same one as in chapter 20. This chieftain's **servants** had taken a **well of water** from Abraham's men. When **Abimelech** and **Abraham** made a treaty of friendship, the patriarch told Abimelech about the **well** that had been **seized**. The result was a **covenant** granting the well to Abraham. He promptly named it **Beersheba** ("well of the oath"). The place later became a city, marking the southernmost boundary of the land. **Abraham planted a tamarisk tree** as a memorial.

9. The Offering of Isaac (Chap. 22)

22:1–10 Perhaps no scene in the Bible except Calvary itself is more poignant than this one, and none gives a clearer foreshadowing of the death of God's only, well-beloved Son on the cross. The supreme test of Abraham's faith came when God ordered him to **offer up** Isaac **as a burnt offering** in **the land of Moriah**. Actually God had no intention of allowing Abraham to go through with it; He has always been opposed to human sacrifice. **Moriah** is the mountain range where Jerusalem is situated (2 Chron. 3:1) and also where Calvary stood. God's words, **"your only son Isaac, whom you love,"** must have pierced

Abraham's heart like ever-deepening wounds. Isaac was Abraham's **only son** in the sense that he was the **only son** of promise—the unique son, the son of miraculous birth.

The first occurrence of a word in the Bible often sets the pattern for its usage throughout Scripture. **Love** (v. 2) and "worship" (v. 5) are first found here. Abraham's **love** for his **son** is a faint picture of God's love for the Lord Jesus. The sacrifice of Isaac was a picture of the greatest act of worship—the Savior's self-sacrifice to accomplish the will of God.

22:11, 12 **"Abraham, Abraham"** is the first of ten name duplications found in the Bible. Seven are spoken by God to man (Gen. 22:11; 46:2; Ex. 3:4; 1 Sam. 3:10; Luke 10:41; 22:31; Acts 9:4). The other three are Matthew 7:21, 22; 23:37; Mark 15:34. They introduce matters of special importance. **The Angel of the LORD** (v. 11) was **God** (v. 12).

22:13–15 To offer Isaac was surely the supreme test of Abraham's faith. God had promised to give Abraham a numberless posterity through his son. Isaac could have been as much as twenty-five at this time, and he was unmarried. If Abraham slew him, how could the promise be fulfilled? According to Hebrews 11:19, Abraham believed that even if he slew his son, God would raise him from the dead. This faith was remarkable because there was no recorded case of resurrection up to this time in the world's history. Notice his faith also in 22:5: "the lad and I will go yonder and worship, and we will come back to you." Abraham was first justified by faith (15:6), then justified (vindicated) by works here (see James 2:21). His faith was the means of his salvation, while his works were the proof of the reality of his faith. When Isaac asked, **"Where is the lamb?"**, his father replied, **"God will provide for Himself the lamb."** This promise was not ultimately fulfilled by the **ram** of verse 13 but by the Lamb of God (John 1:29).

There are two outstanding symbols of Christ in this chapter. Isaac is the first: an **only son**, loved by his father, willing to do his father's will, received back from the dead in a figure. The **ram** is the second: an innocent victim died as a substitute for another, its blood was shed, and it was a **burnt offering** wholly consumed for God. Someone has said that, in providing the **ram** as a substitute for Isaac, "God spared Abraham's heart a pang He would not spare His own." **The Angel of the LORD** in verses 11 and 15, as in all the OT, is the Lord Jesus Christ. Abraham named the place **The-LORD-Will-Provide** (Jehovah-jireh) (v. 14). This is one of the seven compound names for God in the OT. The others are:

- Jehovah-Ropheka—"The LORD who heals you" (Ex. 15:26).
- Jehovah-Nissi—"The LORD my banner" (Ex. 17:8–15).
- Jehovah-Shalom—"The LORD our peace" (Judg. 6:24).
- Jehovah-Roi—"The LORD my Shepherd" (Ps. 23:1).
- Jehovah-Tsidkenu—"The LORD our righteousness" (Jer. 23:6).
- Jehovah-Shammah—"The LORD is present" (Ezek. 48:35).

22:16–19 **The LORD** swore by Himself because He couldn't swear by anyone greater (Heb. 6:13). God's promise here, confirmed by His oath, includes the blessing of the Gentile nations through Christ (see Gal. 3:16). In verse 17c God adds to the already vast blessing promised: Abraham's seed would **possess the gate of** his

enemies. This means that his descendants would "occupy the place of authority over those who would oppose them. The capture of the city gate meant the fall of the city itself."[16]

22:20–24 Abraham's **brother Nahor** had twelve sons, whereas Abraham had only two—Ishmael and Isaac. How this must have tested Abraham's faith concerning God's promise of descendants as the stars of the sky! It may have prompted him to send Eliezer in search of a wife for Isaac (chap. 24). Notice the name **Rebekah** in 22:23.

10. The Family Burial Place (Chap. 23)

23:1–16 When **Sarah died** at **one hundred and twenty-seven years**, Abraham bargained with the Hittite inhabitants of **Hebron** for the purchase of **the cave of Machpelah** as a **burial place**—his only purchase of real estate during his long life of pilgrimage. The passage gives a priceless description of the bargaining that is so typical in Eastern lands. At first, the Hittites suggested that Abraham choose any one of their **burial places**. With overflowing courtesy, Abraham refused and insisted on paying full price for a cave owned by **Ephron**. At first **Ephron** offered not just the **cave** but the entire **field** as an outright gift, but Abraham understood that this was just a polite gesture. The owner really had no intention of giving it away. When Abraham countered by insisting on his desire to purchase it, Ephron suggested a price of **four hundred shekels of silver**, pretending that this was a great bargain. Actually it was an extortionate price, and ordinarily the buyer would have continued to haggle. So it was a surprise to everyone when Abraham agreed to Ephron's first asking price. Abraham didn't want to be indebted to an unbeliever, and neither should we.

23:17–20 **The cave of Machpelah** later became the **burial place** of Abraham, Isaac, Rebekah, Jacob, and Leah. The traditional location is now the site of a Moslem mosque.

11. A Bride for Isaac (Chap. 24)

24:1–9 Abraham bound his **oldest servant** by an **oath** that in seeking a bride for **Isaac**, he would not allow him to marry a Canaanite or to live in Mesopotamia. The ancient form of oath described in verses 2–4 and 9 is explained by Charles F. Pfeiffer:

> According to Biblical idiom, children are said to issue from the "thigh" or "loins" of their father (cf. Gen. 46:26). Placing the hand on the thigh signified that, in the event that an oath were violated, the children who had issued, or might issue from the "thigh" would avenge the act of disloyalty. This has been called a "swearing by posterity" and is particularly applicable here, because the servant's mission is to insure a posterity for Abraham through Isaac.[17]

24:10–14 **The servant** is a type (symbol) of the Holy Spirit sent by the Father to win a bride for the "heavenly Isaac," the Lord Jesus. The narrative carefully records the preparation for the journey, the gifts carried by the servant, and the sign by which he would know the Lord's chosen woman. Murdoch Campbell elaborates:

> It was a sign that was calculated to throw much light on the character and disposition of the girl worthy of his master's son. He was merely to ask her for "a sip"—as the Hebrew word may be rendered—of water for himself; but the one whom God had chosen to be the mother of a great

people and a remote ancestress of Jesus Christ would reveal her generous nature and her willingness to serve others by offering him not a mere "sip" of water but an abundant "drink." To this she was also to add the astonishing offer of drawing water for the camels also. Now when we consider that these ten beasts, after the toil of the long desert, were prepared to empty at least four barrels of water in all, the spontaneous willingness of the girl of his prayers to serve man and beast would point to a kindly and unselfish disposition and also to a character of the highest order.[18]

24:15–52 It was lovely **Rebekah**, of course, who fulfilled the conditions and who therefore received the servant's gifts. As she led him to her father's home, Abraham's servant knew that his search had ended. When Rebekah explained the situation to her brother, **Laban**, he welcomed the entourage graciously, then heard **the servant** present his request for **Rebekah** as a bride for Isaac. The marvelous convergence of circumstances in answer to the servant's prayer convinced **Laban** and **Bethuel**, Rebekah's father, that **the Lord** had arranged it all.

24:53–61 **The servant** then brought out gifts for **Rebekah**, Laban, and her **mother**, sealing the engagement. In the morning, the family wanted to delay her departure, but Rebekah's willingness to go settled the matter, and she left with their blessing.

24:62–67 The first time we see **Isaac** after his experience on Mount Moriah is when he **went** out to meet Rebekah. So the first time we will see the Savior after His death, burial, resurrection, and ascension is when He returns to claim His chosen bride (1 Thess. 4:13–18). Isaac's meeting with Rebekah is one of tender beauty. Without ever having seen her before, he married her and **loved her**, and, unlike other patriarchs, he had no other wife besides her.

12. Abraham's Descendants (25:1–18)

25:1–6 In 1 Chronicles 1:32 **Keturah** is called Abraham's concubine. Verse 6 seems to confirm this. Thus she was a *lesser* **wife**, one who did not enjoy the full privileges of a wife in the home. Once again God records marital irregularities that He never approved.

25:7–18 **Abraham breathed his last** at **one hundred and seventy-five years** of age and became the second person to be **buried in the cave** at Hebron. The twelve **sons of Ishmael** listed in verses 12–16 fulfilled God's promise to Abraham: "He shall beget twelve princes" (17:20). With the death of **Ishmael**, **Isaac** moves to center stage in the narrative.

B. Isaac (25:19—26:35)

1. Isaac's Family (25:19–34)

25:19–26 For almost twenty years after her marriage, **Rebekah . . . was barren**. Then, in answer to Isaac's prayer, she **conceived**. The struggle of two sons **within her** perplexed her until she was told that her sons would become the heads of **two** rival **nations** (Israel and Edom). The firstborn twin was named **Esau** (*hairy*). The other was named **Jacob** (*supplanter*). Even at birth, Jacob tried to gain advantage over his brother by grabbing **hold of Esau's heel**! **Isaac was sixty** when his twin boys were born.

25:27, 28 As **the boys grew** up, Esau turned into an outdoorsman and **a skillful hunter**. Jacob on the other hand was a **mild**, indoor type, **dwelling in tents**. **Isaac loved Esau**

best, **but Rebekah loved Jacob**. Perhaps he was a "mama's boy."

25:29–34 As the firstborn, **Esau** was entitled to a double portion of his father's possessions—that is, twice as much as any other son might inherit. He also became the tribal or family head. This was known as the **birthright**. In Esau's case, it would also have included being the ancestor of the Messiah. One day, as Esau was returning from a hunting trip, he saw Jacob cooking some **red stew**. He asked for some of the red stuff so imploringly that he got the nickname "Red" (**Edom**), and it stuck to him and to his posterity, the Edomites. When Jacob offered some soup in exchange for Esau's **birthright**, Esau foolishly agreed. "No food except the forbidden fruit was as dearly bought as this broth."[19] The prophecy of verse 23 is partially fulfilled in verses 29–34. God does not condone Jacob's wheeling and dealing, but one thing is apparent—Jacob valued the **birthright** and a place in the godly line, while Esau preferred the gratification of his physical appetite to spiritual blessings.

The chapter closes by emphasizing Esau's treatment of **his birthright** rather than Jacob's treatment of his brother. Esau's descendants were bitter foes of Israel. Their final doom is pronounced in Obadiah.

2. Isaac and Abimelech (Chap. 26)

26:1–6 **Isaac** reacted to **famine** as his father had done (chaps. 12 and 20). As he journeyed south, the Lord appeared to him at **Gerar** and warned him not to go to Egypt. **Gerar** was sort of a halfway house on the route to Egypt. God told Isaac to stay temporarily[20] in Gerar but instead Isaac **dwelt** there. God also reconfirmed to him the unconditional covenant that He had made with **Abraham**.

26:7–17 **Isaac** reacted to fear as his father had done. He misrepresented his **wife** as his **sister** to the **men of** Gerar. It is the sad story of a father's weakness being repeated in his son. When the deceit was exposed and rebuked, Isaac confessed. Confession leads to blessing. Isaac became wealthy in Gerar—so wealthy that the Abimelech who was then reigning asked him to leave. So Isaac moved from Gerar to the **Valley of Gerar**, not far away.

26:18–25 **The Philistines** had **stopped up** the **wells** which Abraham **had dug**—an unfriendly act signifying that the newcomers were not welcome. Isaac cleaned out the wells. Strife ensued with the Philistines at **Esek** (*contention*) and **Sitnah** (*enmity*). Finally Isaac moved away from the Philistines. This time there was no strife when he **dug** a **well**, so he called it **Rehoboth** (*broad places* or *room*). **He went from there to Beersheba**, where the LORD reassured him with the promise of blessing, and where Isaac **built an altar** (worship), **pitched a tent** (abiding), and **dug a well** (refreshment). Just as water is a basic essential in the physical realm, so is the water of the Word in the spiritual.

26:26–33 Concerning verses 26–31, Williams says:

> It is when Isaac definitely separates himself from the men of Gerar that they come to him seeking blessing from God. . . . The Christian best helps the world when living in separation from it. . . . [21]

Isaac's servants . . . found water the same day that Isaac made a nonaggression pact with **Abimelech**. Abraham had previously named the place

Beersheba because he made a covenant there with his contemporary, **Abimelech** (21:31). Now, under similar circumstances, **Isaac** renames it **Shebah** or **Beersheba**.

26:34, 35 Esau's marriage to **Judith** and **Basemath**, two pagan women, caused **grief** to his parents, as have many other unequal yokes since then. It also brought out further his unfitness for the birthright.

C. Jacob (27:1—36:43)

1. Jacob Cheats Esau (Chap. 27)

27:1–22 Approximately thirty-seven years have passed since the events of the previous chapter. **Isaac** is now 137, his sight has failed, and he thinks he is about to die, perhaps because his brother Ishmael had died at that age (Gen. 25:17). But he will live forty-three more years.

When **Isaac** craved some venison from **Esau**, promising a blessing in return, **Rebekah** plotted to deceive her husband and to get the blessing for **Jacob**, whom she loved. Her trickery was unnecessary because God had already promised the blessing to Jacob (25:23b). She cooked goat's meat so that it tasted like **savory** venison, and put the goat's **skins** on Jacob's arms to impersonate the **hairy** Esau. Isaac made the mistake of trusting his feelings; the hairy arm "felt" like Esau's. We should not trust our emotional feelings in spiritual matters. As Martin Luther observed:

> Feelings come and feelings go, and
> feelings are deceiving;
> Our warrant is the Word of God;
> naught else is worth believing.[22]

Although Rebekah planned the deception, Jacob was equally guilty for carrying it out. And he reaped what he sowed. C. H. Mackintosh observed that:

> . . . whoever observes Jacob's life, after he had surreptitiously obtained his father's blessing, will perceive that he enjoyed very little worldly felicity. His brother sought to murder him, to avoid which he was forced to flee from his father's house; his uncle Laban deceived him. . . . He was obliged to leave him in a clandestine manner. . . . He experienced the baseness of his son Reuben . . . the treachery and cruelty of Simeon and Levi towards the Shechemites; then he had to feel the loss of his beloved wife . . . the supposed untimely end of Joseph; and to complete all, he was forced by famine to go into Egypt, and there died in a strange land. . . .[23]

27:23–29 Isaac **blessed** Jacob with prosperity, dominion, and protection. It is interesting that the blessings spoken by the patriarchs were prophetic; they came to pass literally because, in a real sense, these men spoke by inspiration.

27:30–40 When Esau returned and learned of the deception, he sought the **blessing** tearfully. But the blessing had been granted to **Jacob** and it couldn't be retracted (Heb. 12:16, 17). However, Isaac did have a word for Esau, as follows:

> Far from rich soil on earth shall you live, far from the dew of heaven on high; you shall live by the sword and serve your brother; but when you grow restive, his yoke you shall break (vv. 39, 40—Moffatt).

This suggests that the Edomites would live in desert places, would be warriors, would be subject to the Israelites, but would one day rebel against this rule. This latter prophecy was fulfilled in the reign of Joram, King of Judah (2 Kgs. 8:20–22).

27:41–46 **Esau** planned to **kill** his **brother Jacob** as soon as his father would die and the period **of mourning** would end. When **Rebekah** learned of this, she told Jacob to head for her brother Laban's home **in Haran**. She feared not only that Jacob would be killed but that Esau would run away or be killed in a blood feud, and she would lose two sons at once. However, to explain Jacob's departure to Isaac, she said she was afraid Jacob might marry a Hittite, as Esau had done. Jacob expected to return soon, but it was not to be for more than twenty years. His father would still be living, but his mother would have passed on.

2. Jacob's Flight to Haran (Chap. 28)

28:1–9 **Isaac called Jacob** and **blessed him**, and sent him to **Paddan Aram**, a district of Mesopotamia, so that he would find a wife among his **mother's** people rather than among the Canaanites. This inspired Esau to try to regain his father's blessing by marrying a **daughter of Ishmael**. It was a case of doing evil (multiplying **wives**) that good might come.

28:10–19 At **Bethel**, **Jacob** had a wonderful dream in which he saw a **ladder** or staircase extending from earth to heaven. This suggested "the fact of a real, uninterrupted, and close communion between heaven and earth, and in particular between God in His glory and man in his solitude."[24] In His encounter with Nathanael, the Lord Jesus made an apparent reference to this incident and connected it with His Second Advent and millennial glory (John 1:51). But believers even now can enjoy moment-by-moment fellowship with the Lord. At this time when Jacob's heart was probably filled with regret for the past, loneliness in the present, and uncertainty about the future, God graciously made a covenant with him as He had with Abraham and Isaac. Notice the promise of *companionship:* **"I am with you"**; *safety:* "I **will keep you wherever you go"**; *guidance:* **"and will bring you back to this land"**; and *personal guarantee:* **"I will not leave you until I have done what I have spoken to you."** Conscious that he had met God there, Jacob changed the name of the place from **Luz** (*separation*) to **Bethel** (*house of God*).

"Prior to Bethel, where Jacob was 'surprised by joy' and 'transfixed by awe,' he had had no personal contact with God. Everything had come to him second-hand" (*Daily Notes of the Scripture Union*).

28:20–22 Next Jacob seems to be bargaining with God. He was actually bargaining for *less* than God had promised (v. 14). His faith was not strong enough to take God at His word, so he had to make his tithe conditional on God's performance of His part of the agreement, Another interpretation, however, is that the **"if"** is simply an inherent part of all Hebrew oaths and that Jacob was binding himself to give a tenth unconditionally (see Num. 21:2; Judg. 11:30,31; 1 Sam. 1:11 for similar Hebrew oaths).

3. Jacob, His Wives, and His Offspring (29:1—30:24)

29:1–14 Jacob was seventy-seven when he left Beersheba for Haran. He would spend twenty years serving his uncle Laban, thirty-three years back in Canaan, and the last seventeen years of his life in Egypt. Arriving in Paddan Aram, he was guided to the very **field** where some shepherds **from Haran** were tending their **flocks**. So perfect was God's timing that **Rachel** was just arriving with her flock when Jacob was talking with the shepherds. Being a good shepherd, Jacob wondered why they were all waiting at the well when there was still daylight for feeding the sheep. They explained that they did not remove the cover from the well until all the herds had arrived. It was an emotion-packed moment for Jacob when he met his cousin Rachel, and for **Laban** a short while later when he met his nephew Jacob.

29:15–35 **Laban** agreed to give Rachel to Jacob in exchange for **seven years** of service. The years **seemed** to Jacob but **a few days because of the love he had for her**. That is how it should be in our service for the Lord.

Leah was weak-eyed and not attractive. **Rachel was beautiful**.

According to custom, it was arranged that the bride should go in to the groom on the wedding night, veiled and perhaps when the room was in darkness. You can imagine how irate Jacob was in the morning when he found that his bride was **Leah**! Laban had tricked him, but excused the trick on the ground that the older daughter should be married first according to the local custom. Then Laban said, **"Fulfill her week** (that is, carry through on the marriage to Leah) **and we will give you this one also** (Rachel) **for the service which you will serve with me still another seven years."** At the end of the week-long wedding feast, Jacob also married Rachel, then served **seven** more **years** for her. Jacob had sown deceit, and now he was reaping it! When the Lord saw that Leah was hated (that is, loved less than Rachel) He compensated for this by giving her children. This law of divine compensation still operates: People who lack in one area are given extra in another. Leah acknowledged the Lord when she named her children (vv. 32, 33, 35). From her comes the priesthood (**Levi**), the royal line (**Judah**), and ultimately the Christ. In this chapter we have the first four of the sons of Jacob. The complete list of Jacob's sons is as follows:

The sons born to Leah:

> **Reuben**—(*see, a son*) (29:32)
> **Simeon**—(*hearing*) (29:33)
> **Levi**—(*joined*) (29:34)
> **Judah**—(*praise*) (29:35)
> Issachar—(*hire*) (30:18)
> Zebulun—(*dwelling*) (30:20)

The sons born to Bilhah, the handmaid of Rachel:

> Dan—(*judge*) (30:6)
> Naphtali—(*wrestling*) (30:8)

The sons born to Zilpah, handmaid of Leah:

> Gad—(*a troop* or *good fortune*) (30:11)
> Asher—(*happy*) (30:13)

The sons born to Rachel:

> Joseph—(*adding*) (30:24)
> Benjamin—(*son of the right hand*) (35:18)

30:1–13 In desperation to have a child playing on her knees, **Rachel** gave **her maid, Bilhah,** to Jacob as a wife or concubine. Even though such arrangements were common in those days, they were contrary to God's will. **Bilhah bore** two sons, **Dan** and **Naphtali**. Not to be outdone by Rachel, **Leah** gave **her maid, Zilpah,** to Jacob, and two more sons were born, **Gad** and **Asher**.

30:14–24 The **mandrakes** which **Reuben found** were a sort of love-apple, believed by the superstitious to impart fertility. Since Rachel was barren, she was anxious to have **some** of the **mandrakes**. In exchange, she agreed to let Leah live as wife with Jacob. (For some unexplained reason, Leah had apparently lost her privileges as wife.) After this, two more sons were born to Leah—**Issachar** and **Zebulun**—and also **a daughter, Dinah**. At last Rachel bore her first **son** and named him **Joseph**, expressing faith that God would give her still **another son**.

4. Jacob Outwits Laban (30:25–43)

30:25–36 When **Jacob** told **Laban** that he wanted to return home to Canaan, his uncle urged him to **stay**. Laban said he had learned by **experience** that the LORD had **blessed** him because of Jacob, and he would meet his wage demands if he would stay. Jacob agreed to continue serving if Laban would give him **all the speckled and spotted sheep** and **goats** and all the dark **lambs**. All other animals in the flock would be acknowledged as Laban's. The latter agreed to the pact, saying, **"Oh, that it were according to your word."** Laban took most of the animals designated for Jacob and gave them to his sons to shepherd, realizing that they would probably reproduce with markings that identified them as belonging to Jacob. Then he entrusted his own animals to Jacob, separated from his own sons by a three-day journey. This made it impossible for the marked animals in the herds tended by Laban's sons to breed with Laban's unmarked animals that were tended by Jacob.

30:37–43 When breeding Laban's herd, Jacob put **rods that he had peeled** in front of them, whether they were of solid color or marked. The lambs or kids were born **streaked, speckled, and spotted**. This, of course, meant that they belonged to Jacob. Did these **rods** actually determine the markings on the animals? There may or may not have been a scientific basis to the method. (New genetic evidence suggests that there might have been.) How else might the animals have been born with the markings Jacob desired?

First of all, it may have been a miracle (see 31:12).

Or it may have been a clever trick on Jacob's part. There are indications in the narrative that he knew the science of selective breeding. By careful breeding, he not only produced animals with the markings he desired, but he was also able to produce **stronger** animals for himself and **feeble** ones for Laban. Perhaps the peeled rods were just a trick to hide his breeding secrets from others. Whatever the explanation, Jacob's wealth increased during his final six years of serving Laban.

5. Jacob's Return to Canaan (Chap. 31)

31:1–18 After **Jacob** discovered that **Laban** and his **sons** were growing jealous and resentful, the LORD told him that the time had come to **return to** Canaan. First he **called Rachel and Leah** and discussed the matter, rehearsing how Laban had cheated him and **changed** his **wages ten times**, how God had overruled so that the flocks always bred in his favor, how God had reminded him of the vow he had made twenty years earlier (28:20–22), and how the Lord had told him to **return to** Canaan. His wives agreed that their father had not dealt honestly and that they should leave.

Griffith Thomas points out several interesting principles for discerning God's guidance here. First, Jacob had a *desire* (30:25). Secondly, *circumstances* necessitated a change of some sort. Thirdly, *God's word* came strongly to him. And finally, there was *confirming support* from his wives, despite their natural ties to Laban. . . . [25] Note that the Angel of God (v. 11) is the God of Bethel (v. 13).

31:19–21 Before the secret departure, **Rachel** stole her father's **household idols** and hid them in her camel's saddle. Possession of these household gods implied leadership of the family, and, in the case of a married daughter, assured her husband the right of the father's property.[26] Since Laban had sons of his own when Jacob fled to Canaan, they alone had the right to their father's *teraphim*. Rachel's theft was therefore a serious matter, aimed at preserving for her husband the chief title to Laban's estate.

31:22–30 When **Laban** learned of their departure, he and his men **pursued** them **for seven days' journey**, but the Lord warned him **in a dream** not to trouble **Jacob** and his caravan. When he finally overtook them, he only complained that he had been denied the privilege of giving them a royal send-off and that his idols had been stolen.

31:31–35 To the first complaint **Jacob answered** that he left secretly for fear that Laban would **take** his **daughters** (Rachel and Leah) **from** him **by force**. To the second complaint, he denied having stolen the **gods** and rashly decreed death for the culprit. Laban made a thorough search of the caravan, but in vain. **Rachel** was sitting **on them** and excused herself for not getting off the camel's saddle to honor her father because it was her menstrual period—or so she said.

31:36–42 Now it was Jacob's turn to be **angry**. He denounced Laban for accusing him of theft and for treating him so unfairly for **twenty years**, in spite of Jacob's faithful and generous service. This passage reveals that Jacob was a hard worker and that the blessing of the Lord was upon him in all that he did. Are we faithful to our employers? Does the blessing of God rest upon our work?

31:43–50 **Laban** avoided the issue by lamely protesting that he would not harm his own **daughters**, grandchildren, or cattle, then suggested that they should make a pact. It was *not* a gracious, friendly **covenant**, asking the Lord to watch over them while they were separated. Rather, it was a compact between two cheats, asking the Lord to make sure that they did what was right when they were out of sight from one another! It was, in effect, a nonaggression treaty, but it also charged Jacob not to treat Laban's daughters harshly nor to marry other wives. Laban called the **pillar** of **stones** marking the pact **Jegar Sahadutha**, an Aramaic expression. **Jacob called it Galeed**, a Hebrew word. Both words mean "the **heap** of **witness**." Neither man was to pass the stone-heap to attack the other.

31:51–55 **Laban** swore by the **God of Abraham, the God of Nahor, and the God of their father**, Terah. The capitalization of *God* in the NKJV (also Moffatt, NIV, etc.) indicates that the translators felt Laban was referring to the one true God that Abraham came to know. However, since the Hebrew does not have upper and lower case letters, we can't tell if Laban might have been referring to the pagan gods which these men had worshiped in Ur. **Jacob swore by the Fear of his father Isaac**—that is, the God whom Isaac feared. Isaac had never been an idolater. **Jacob** first **offered a sacrifice**, then made a banquet for all those present and camped **all** that **night on the mountain**.

Early in the morning, Laban kissed his grandchildren and **daughters** good-bye and left for home.

6. Jacob and Esau Reconciled (Chaps. 32, 33)

32:1–8 En route to Canaan, Jacob met a band of **angels** and called the place **Mahanaim** (*two hosts* or *double camp*). The two camps may be God's army (v. 2) and Jacob's entourage. Or two hosts may be a figurative expression for a great multitude (v. 10). As Jacob neared the land, he remembered his **brother Esau** and feared revenge. Would Esau still be angry at the way he had been cheated out of the blessing? First, **Jacob sent messengers . . . to Esau** with greetings of peace. Then when he heard that Esau was **coming to meet** him with a band of **four hundred men**, he was so terrified that **he divided** his family **into two companies**, so that if the first group was destroyed, the second could flee.

32:9–12 Jacob's prayer was born out of a desperate sense of need for divine protection. It was based on the ground of covenant relationship which the Lord had established with him and his forefathers, and it was prayed in humility of spirit. He based his plea on the word of the Lord and claimed the promises of God.

The best prayer comes from a strong inward necessity. By human security systems, we often protect ourselves from a dynamic prayer life. Why do we do ourselves this wrong?

32:13–21 Jacob next sent three **successive droves** of animals totaling 580 head as gifts for Esau, hoping to **appease him**. Esau would get the gift in three installments. Jacob's maneuvers manifested his unbelief or at least a mixture of faith and unbelief.

32:22–32 After sending his immediate family across the stream **Jabbok** (*he will empty*), Jacob spent the **night** alone at Peniel for what was to be one of the great experiences of his life. **A Man wrestled with him**. That Man was an angel (Hos. 12:4), the Angel of Jehovah, the Lord Himself. The Lord put **the socket of Jacob's hip . . . out of joint**, causing him to walk with a limp the rest of his life. Although Jacob lost the encounter physically, he won a great spiritual victory. He learned to triumph through defeat and to be strong through weakness. Emptied of self and of confidence in his own cleverness, he confessed he was **Jacob**, a supplanter, a "con man." God then changed his **name** to **Israel** (variously translated as "God rules," "one who strives with God," or "a prince of God"). Jacob called the name of the place **Peniel** (*the face of God*) because he realized he had **seen** the Lord. Pfeiffer points out that verse 32 is still true among Jews today:

> The sciatic nerve, or thigh vein, must be removed from the slaughtered animal before that portion of the animal may be prepared for consumption by orthodox Jews.[27]

33:1–11 As **Esau** drew near, Jacob lapsed back into fearfulness and merely natural behavior, arranging his household in such a way as to afford maximum protection for those he loved most. Jacob **bowed himself to the ground seven times** as he approached **his brother**. **Esau**, by comparison, was relaxed, warm, and effusive as he met Jacob first, then Jacob's wives and **children**. He protested mildly against the extravagant gift of livestock but finally consented to accept it. Jacob seems to have shown undue servility to his brother, speaking of himself as his **servant**. Some think that he resorted to flattery and exaggeration in telling Esau that seeing his **face** was like seeing **God**. Others think that **the face of God** here means a reconciled face.

33:12–17 When **Esau** suggested that they travel back together, Jacob pretended that this would be impossible because of the slow pace required by the **children** and young animals. Jacob promised to meet Esau **in Seir** (Edom), although he had no intention of doing so. Even when Esau tried to leave behind **some of** his men to travel with Jacob's household, the latter refused the offer without revealing the real reasons—fear and suspicion.

33:18–20 Instead of traveling south to Mount Seir, Jacob went northwest. At length he arrived at **Shechem** and settled there, erecting **an altar** which he (perhaps presumptuously) called **El Elohe Israel** (*God, the God of Israel*). Twenty years earlier, when God had appeared to him at Bethel, Jacob had vowed that the Lord would be his God, that he would give a tenth of his wealth to the Lord, and that he would establish Bethel as God's house (28:20–22). Now, instead of returning to Bethel, he settles thirty miles away in the fertile area of Shechem, probably for the sake of his livestock. (Shechem represents the world.) God does not speak directly to him until several years later, when He calls on Jacob to fulfill his vow (chap. 35). In the meantime, the tragic events of chapter 34 take place.

7. *Sins at Shechem (Chap. 34)*

34:1–12 The name of God is not mentioned in this chapter. While Jacob and his family were living in Shechem, **Dinah his daughter** mingled socially with the heathen women, a breach of proper separation from the ungodly. On one such occasion, **Shechem, the son of Hamor,** sexually assaulted her, then greatly desired to marry her. Realizing that Jacob and his sons were enraged, **Hamor** proposed a peaceful solution: intermarriage between the Israelites and Canaanites, and full rights for the Israelites as citizens of the land. (Verse 9 can be seen as one of many Satanic attempts to pollute the godly line.) Shechem also offered to pay whatever **dowry and gift** was requested.

34:13–24 **The sons of Jacob** had no intention of giving **Dinah** to Shechem, but they lied that they would do so if the men of the city would be **circumcised**. The sacred sign of God's covenant was to be used wickedly. In good faith, **Hamor, Shechem, and all** the men **of** their **city** met the condition.

34:25–31 But while the Shechemites were recovering from the surgery, Simeon and Levi treacherously murdered them and **plundered** their wealth. When Jacob administered a mild rebuke, **Simeon and Levi** answered that their **sister** should not have been treated **like a harlot**. Actually Jacob seemed to be more concerned about his own welfare than the horrible injustice that had been done to the men of Shechem. Notice his eight uses of the first-person pronoun in verse 30.

8. *The Return to Bethel (Chap. 35)*

35:1–8 Chapter 35 opens with God's command to Jacob to fulfill the vow made about thirty years earlier (28:20–22). The Lord used the tragic events of the previous chapter to prepare the patriarch to do it. Notice that God is referred to about twenty times in this chapter, in contrast to no references in chapter 34. Before obeying God's command to return **to Bethel**, Jacob first ordered his family to **put away the foreign** household

gods and to put on clean clothes. As soon as they did this, they became a **terror** to their heathen neighbors. It was appropriate that Jacob should build an altar at **"El Bethel"** and worship the God who had protected him from his brother, Esau.

35:9–15 Once again God stated that Jacob's **name** was now **Israel** and renewed the covenant He had made with Abraham and Isaac. The patriarch marked the sacred spot with a **pillar** and once again named the place **Bethel**.

35:16–20 As Jacob's family **journeyed** south **from Bethel, . . . Rachel died** in childbirth. She had named the child **Ben-Oni** (*son of my sorrow*), but Jacob named this twelfth son **Benjamin** (*son of my right hand*). These two names pre-picture the sufferings of Christ and the glories that would follow. The traditional (but probably not authentic) site of **Rachel's grave** may still be seen on the road from Jerusalem to **Bethlehem**. Why was she not buried with Abraham, Sarah, and Rebekah in the cave of Hebron? Perhaps it was because she had brought idols into the family.

35:21–29 A brief mention is made of Reuben's sin **with Bilhah his father's concubine**, a sin by which he forfeited the birthright (49:3, 4). The last sentence in verse 22 begins a new paragraph: **Now the sons of Jacob were twelve.** The next two verses list the twelve **sons**. Though it says in verse 26 that these sons were born to Jacob in **Paddan Aram, Benjamin** (v. 24) is excepted. He was born in Canaan (vv. 16–19). Jacob returned to **Hebron** in time to see **his father Isaac** before he **died**. His mother, Rebekah, had died some years earlier. Three funerals are recorded in this chapter: that of Deborah, Rebekah's nurse (v. 8); of Rachel (v. 19); and of **Isaac** (v. 29).

9. The Descendants of Jacob's Brother Esau (Chap. 36)

36:1–30 Chapter 36 is devoted to the descendants **of Esau,** who dwelt in the land of **Edom**, southeast of the Dead Sea. **The genealogy** represents the fulfillment of the promise that Esau would be the head of a nation (25:23). Esau had three or possibly four wives, depending on whether some of the women had two names (compare 26:34; 28:9; 36:2, 3). In verse 24 **Anah** found **water** (or "hot springs," NASB).

36:31–43 Moses, the author of Genesis, knew by divine revelation (see 35:11) that Israel would eventually have **a king**. As seven generations of the ungodly line of Cain were given in chapter 4, so seven generations of kings in the ungodly line of Esau are mentioned here in verses 33–39. Seven, the number of completeness, probably indicates the entire line. Not one of Esau's descendants is mentioned in God's registry of the faithful; all are lost in the obscurity of those who depart from the living God. They had temporary riches and the passing fame of this world, but nothing for eternity.

D. Joseph (37:1—50:26)

1. Joseph Sold into Slavery (Chap. 37)

37:1–17 The words **"This is the history of Jacob"** seem abrupt. Jacob's history (chaps. 25—35) is interrupted by the generations of Esau (chap. 36), then continued from chapter 37 to the end of the book, with emphasis on Jacob's son, Joseph.

Joseph is one of the most beautiful types (symbols) of the Lord Jesus Christ in the OT, though the Bible

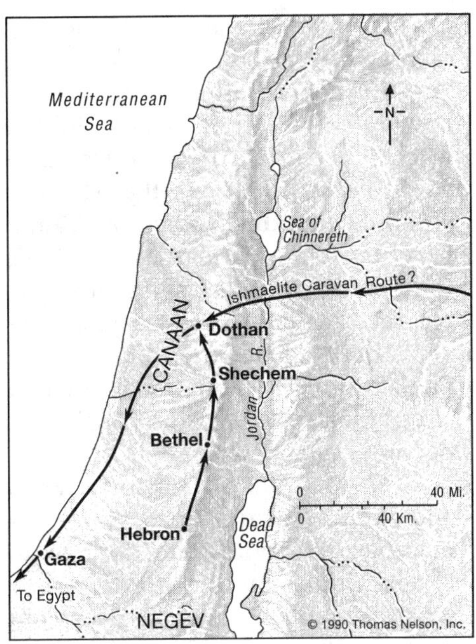

Joseph's Journey into Egypt

never labels him as a type. A. W. Pink lists 101 correspondences between Joseph and Jesus,[28] and Ada Habershon lists 121. For example, Joseph was **loved** by his father (v. 3); he rebuked the sin of his brothers (v. 2); he was **hated** by **his brothers** and sold into the hands of enemies (vv. 4, 26–28); he was punished unjustly (chap. 39); he was exalted and became the savior of the world, for all the world had to come to him for bread (41:57); he received a Gentile bride during his rejection by his brethren (41:45).

The **tunic of many colors** (or a long robe with sleeves, RSV) was a sign of his father's special affection, and it stirred up the jealous hatred of his brothers. In Joseph's first **dream**, ele ven **sheaves** of grain **bowed down to** the twelfth **sheaf**, a prophecy that his brothers would one day bow down to him. In the next **dream, the sun, moon, and the eleven stars bowed down to** Joseph. The **sun** and **moon** represented Jacob and Leah (Rachel had died), and **the eleven stars** were Joseph's **brothers** (vv. 9–11).

37:18–28 When Joseph was sent on an errand to his brothers, they **conspired . . . to kill him**, but at Reuben's suggestion they agreed to **cast him into a pit** near Dothan. As they sat down to eat, they saw **a company of Ishmaelites** bound for **Egypt**, and at Judah's suggestion decided to sell him. In this passage, the Ishmaelites are also called Midianites, as in Judges 8:22–24. As the **Midianite traders passed by**, Joseph's brothers brought Joseph **out of the pit and sold him to the** traders.

37:29–36 **Reuben** was absent when all this was taking place. When he **returned** he was terrified, since he would be responsible to explain Joseph's absence to his father. So the brothers **dipped** Joseph's **tunic in the blood** of a goat and then callously returned it to Jacob, who naturally assumed that Joseph had been killed. Jacob had once deceived his father with a goat, using the skin to impersonate his brother's hairy arms (27:16–23). Now he himself was cruelly deceived by the blood of a goat on Joseph's coat. "The pain of deceit is learned once again." **The Midianites** unwittingly fulfilled God's purposes by providing free transportation for Joseph to Egypt and selling him **to Potiphar, an officer of Pharaoh**. Thus God makes man's wrath to praise Him, and what will not praise Him, He restrains (see Ps. 76:10).

2. *Judah and Tamar (Chap. 38)*

38:1–11 The sordid story of Judah's sin with **Tamar** serves to magnify the grace of God when we remember that the Lord Jesus was descended from **Judah** (Luke 3:33). **Tamar** is one of five women mentioned in the genealogy in Matthew 1; three of them were guilty of immorality—Tamar, Rahab (v. 5), and Bathsheba (v. 6). The others are Ruth, a Gentile (v. 5) and Mary, a godly virgin (v. 16). Pink notes deeper meanings to this story of moral failure:

> Genesis 37 closes with an account of Jacob's sons selling their brother Joseph unto the Midianites, and they in turn selling him into Egypt. This speaks, in type, of Christ being rejected by Israel and delivered unto the Gentiles. From the time that the Jewish leaders delivered their Messiah into the hands of Pilate, they have as a nation had no further dealings with Him; and God, too, has turned from them to the Gentiles. Hence it is that there is an important turn in our type at this stage. Joseph is now seen *in the hands of the Gentiles*. But before we are told what happened to Joseph in Egypt, the Holy Spirit traces for us, in typical outline, the history of the Jews, while the antitypical Joseph is *absent from the land*.[29]

It is no accident that the story of Joseph is interrupted by chapter 38. The disreputable behavior of other members of Joseph's family makes his conduct, by contrast, shine like a bright light in a sordid world.

Judah's first mistake was in marrying a Canaanite woman, the **daughter of . . . Shua**. She bore him three sons—**Er, Onan,** and **Shelah**. **Er** married a Canaanite woman named **Tamar**, but was slain by **the Lord** for some unspecified wickedness. It was the custom at that time for a brother or other near relative to marry the widow and raise children for the one who had died. **Onan** refused to do this because the first child born as a result would be the legal **heir** of Er, not his own legal child. His sin was not so much sexual as it was selfish. It was not a single act but, as the Hebrew reveals, a persistent refusal. And the refusal affected the genealogy by which Christ would inherit legal right to the throne of David. It so displeased **the Lord** that **He** slew **Onan**. Seeing this, **Judah** told **Tamar** to return to her father's house till his third son, **Shelah**, was of marriageable age. Actually this was just a diversionary tactic. He didn't want **Shelah** to marry Tamar at all; he had already lost two sons and considered her an "unlucky woman."

38:12–23 When Shelah grew up and Judah still did not arrange his marriage to **Tamar**, she decided to "hook" Judah by laying a trap. She dressed as a **harlot** and **sat in an open place** on the road **to Timnah**, where Judah was going to join his **sheep-shearers**. Sure enough, he went in and had illicit relations with her, not knowing it **was his** own **daughter-in-law**. The agreed fee was **a young goat from the flock**, but until he could send it to her, the "harlot" demanded Judah's **signet, cord, and staff**. The **cord** may have been the string by which the seal-ring was suspended. When Judah tried to deliver the kid and have the pledges returned, he couldn't find the "harlot."

38:24–26 Three months later, **Tamar** was accused of playing the **harlot** because she, a widow, was **with child**. **Judah** ordered her to be **burned**. At this point she returned the pledges with the announcement that their owner was the father of her expected **child**. They furnished positive proof that Judah had had sex with her. Walter C. Wright describes the scene vividly:

> The companions of Judah bring him word that his daughter-in-law, Tamar, has played the harlot. His judgment

is quick and decisive: let her be burned. There is neither hesitation nor compromise. As he utters this fearful sentence, we cannot detect even a tremor in his voice. The Israelitish society must be preserved from such folly and wickedness. The word goes out; the day is fixed; the preparations go forward; the stake is planted; the pile is arranged; the procession forms; the crowd gathers; the woman walks to her apparent doom. But she bears in her hands the tokens; the pledges are with her; she carries the staff and the ring. And the staff is the staff of Judah, and the ring is his ring! The pledges become the accusation of her judge. What weight will his sentence have now?[30]

38:27–30 When Tamar **was giving birth** and a baby's hand emerged, **the midwife** tied **a scarlet thread** on it, thinking that it would be born **first**. But the **hand** withdrew and another baby was the first to come forth. She named the firstborn **Perez** (*breakthrough*) and the other **Zerah**. Both **twins** are mentioned in Matthew 1:3, though the Messianic line goes through **Perez**. **Zerah** was an ancestor of Achan (Josh. 7:1). "It is simply astonishing" comments Griffith Thomas, "that God could take up the threads of this very tangled skein, and weave them into His own pattern."[31]

Judah's marriage to the Canaanite woman (v. 2) was a first step in the intermingling of God's people with a race that was proverbial for its gross immorality. Israel would become contaminated by the unspeakable enormities of lewd nature worship. God is a God of separation; when we fraternize with the world, we pay an awful price.

3. *Joseph's Test and Triumph (Chap. 39)*

39:1–19 The story now returns **to Egypt**, where **Joseph** was appointed **overseer** in the **house** of **Potiphar, . . . captain of the guard** in Pharaoh's palace. **The Lord was with** him and he became **a successful man** (Tyndale, in 1534, translated it, he was "a lucky fellow," v. 2). Potiphar's **wife** tried repeatedly to seduce Joseph, but he steadfastly **refused**. He would not betray his master's confidence or sin against his God. One day **she caught him by his garment**. He squirmed out of it **and fled,** leaving **her** holding it. He lost his coat but saved his character and eventually gained a crown. She used the coat as "evidence" that Joseph had attempted to rape her.

Believers are taught to flee fornication, idolatry, and youthful lusts. Better to flee than to fall.

39:20–23 Without proper investigation, **Joseph's master** ordered **him** to **prison**; but even there Joseph was blessed by the Lord and was given a position of responsibility. The fact that Joseph was not executed may indicate that Potiphar did not entirely believe his wife; he couldn't help knowing her true character. The truth of Romans 8:28 is wonderfully displayed in this chapter. God was working behind the scenes for Joseph. The latter resisted temptation and sought to avoid occasions for sin (vv. 8–10). Despite this, his would be seducer framed him. And so for a second time Joseph found himself in chains (Ps. 105:17–19). Under the circumstances he should have been upset. But he was not "under the circumstances"; he was above them and saw God's hand in them. His time in prison was "training time for reigning time." So things that were meant by others for evil turned out to be for good.

4. *Joseph Interpreting the Butler's and Baker's Dreams (Chap. 40)*

40:1–19 Among Joseph's fellow-prisoners were **the butler** (cupbearer) **and the baker of the king of Egypt** (vv. 1–4). When they each **had a dream, Joseph** offered to interpret them (vv. 5–8). The butler's **dream** of the **vine** meant that **Pharaoh** would **lift up** his **head** to a position of favor **in three days** (vv. 9–15). But the baker's **dream** of the **three white** cake **baskets** indicated that **within three days Pharaoh** would **lift off** his **head**—by hanging him (vv. 16–19).

Notice that Joseph did not wait for his circumstances to change. He glorified God and served others in the circumstances.

40:20–23 When **the chief butler** was released, he failed to intercede for Joseph, as he had promised (v. 23). But the Lord did not forget. "Remember me, when it is well with you" (v. 14). The Savior spoke similar words on the night of His betrayal, words which we can obey by taking the symbolic bread and wine.

5. *Joseph Interpreting Pharaoh's Dreams (Chap. 41)*

41:1–13 When none of **the magicians of Egypt** could interpret Pharaoh's **dreams** of the **seven fat** and **seven ugly and gaunt cows,** of the **seven plump and good ears** and **seven thin heads of grain, then the chief butler** remembered Joseph and his ability to interpret **dreams**. The **two full years** mentioned in verse 1 may refer either to the time of Joseph's imprisonment or the time since the chief butler's release.

41:14–32 Called before **Pharaoh, Joseph** explained that there would be **seven years of great plenty** in **Egypt**, followed by **seven years of famine** which would devastate the land. The repetition or duplication of Pharaoh's **dream** meant that it was **established by God and** that He would **shortly bring it to pass**. We see this also in Joseph's two dreams concerning his future (37:6–9) and in the similar visions of Daniel 2 and 7. In the Bible, *two* is the number of witness. Joseph gave the same reply to Pharaoh in the royal hall as he gave to his servants in the prison house. **"It is not in me; God will give . . . an answer of peace"** (v. 16; cf. 40:8). It is this humility that made it possible for the Lord to entrust Joseph with tremendous responsibility without fear that it would corrupt him.

41:33–36 Joseph counseled **Pharaoh** to set aside reserves of grain during the years of plenty so that there would be sufficient **during the famine** years. His plan was what has since been called "the ever-normal granaries."

41:37–46 Pharaoh was so pleased that he made Joseph second in command, appointed him to administer the program (v. 40), assured him that **without** his **consent** no one would do anything (v. 44), and gave him a new name, **Zaphnath-Paaneah** (v. 45a). The meaning of the name is uncertain. Some suggest *Savior of the world;* others say it probably means *God speaks and He lives*. He also gave **Asenath**, a Gentile, to be Joseph's **wife** (v. 45). How could Pharaoh set a Hebrew prisoner over the land of Egypt on the basis of a dream's interpretation without waiting to see if it was true? The answer is in Proverbs 21:1: "The king's heart is in the hand of the Lord." Cream rises to the surface. Joseph was the first of many godly Jews to rise to prominence in Gentile governments. He **was thirty years old when he** began this ministry (v.

46); it was thirteen years since he was sold by his brothers (cf. 37:2).

41:47–52 The abundance of the first **seven years** was so great that it was impossible to keep an accurate record. It was during those years that **two sons** were born to **Joseph—Manasseh** (*making to forget*) and **Ephraim** (*fruitful*). Forgetting the wrongs committed against him, Joseph became fruitful.

41:53–57 When **the seven years of famine came**, the starving people of **Egypt** and of **all the countries came to Joseph . . . to buy grain**. Here Joseph is a type (symbol) of Christ, through whom all the blessings of God are dispensed to the hungering people of this earth. It was the providence of God that brought Joseph to Egypt to save his people from famine, but it was also to isolate them from the moral pollution of the land of Canaan. Chapter 38 illustrates what was happening to the children of Israel in Canaan. God's remedy was to remove them to Egypt, where they would be virtually cut off from the heathen (43:32).

6. *Joseph's Brothers in Egypt (Chaps. 42—44)*

42:1–5 The scene switches back to **Jacob** in Canaan, where the famine was very severe. Hearing **that there was** plenty of food (**grain**) in **Egypt**, but knowing nothing of Joseph's being there, Jacob sent ten of **his sons** for supplies. Only **Benjamin** remained at home. So far as Jacob knew, Benjamin was the only living son of his beloved Rachel.

42:6–25 When **Joseph's brothers** appeared before him, he treated them **roughly**, accusing them of being **spies**, putting them **in prison**, then demanding that their **youngest brother**, Benjamin, be brought to him. At last, **Simeon** was kept as a hostage in prison while the nine others returned to Canaan for Benjamin, well supplied with **grain**, with **provisions**, and with their **money** refunded secretly in the bags. Shining through the narrative we see Joseph's underlying love and compassion for his brothers (vv. 24a, 25) and their growing conviction of sin for what they had done to their "missing" brother over twenty years earlier (vv. 21, 22). Joseph, of course, was seeking to get them to confess their guilt.

We believe that Joseph is a *type* of Christ dealing with His Jewish brethren during the coming Tribulation Period. The events leading up to the reconciliation of Joseph's brothers form one of the most moving portions in the Bible. Almost no other story is as intimate, detailed, or complete a picture of Christ.

TYPOLOGY

Certain persons, events, and things in the OT are clearly identified as "types" (from the Gk. *tupoi*) or symbols in the NT. Thus, Adam is said to be a type of Christ (Rom. 5:14). Others are not specifically referred to as types, yet the parallels are too many and too obvious to be denied. Joseph, for instance, is never referred to as a type of the Lord Jesus, yet there are *over one hundred* correspondences between Jesus and Joseph.

When the Lord Jesus talked to the two sorrowing disciples on the road to Emmaus, "He expounded to them *in all the Scriptures* [emphasis supplied] the things concerning Himself" (Luke 24:27). The incarnate Christ said, "In the volume of the book it is written of Me. . . ." (Heb. 10:7). Therefore we are justified in looking for Christ in all the Scriptures.

Regarding Israel's experiences in

the OT, Paul tells us that "all these things happened to them as examples (Gk., *tupoi*), and they were written for our admonition, upon whom the ends of the ages have come" (1 Cor. 10:11). This would strongly support the view that not just specifically named types are valid, but many more as well.

Paul reminded Timothy that all Scripture is profitable (2 Tim. 3:16). There are spiritual lessons to be learned, if only we have eyes to see them.

Large sections of the Book of Hebrews are an explanation of the typology of the tabernacle and its furnishings. While it is true that a too narrow view of typology will restrict a believer's spiritual enjoyment of much of the OT, the other extreme of making virtually *everything* a type, or even turning all history into allegory, is to be avoided as well.

Strained or fanciful explanations of the types have brought disrepute on the subject. We should not allow extremism to rob us of the spiritual wealth in the OT. If an interpretation exalts Christ, and/or edifies His people, and/or conveys the gospel to the lost, and is consistent with the entire teaching of the Word, it is at the very least a valid *application* of the truth.‡

42:26–28 On the way home, one of the brothers found his **money** in **his sack**. This threw them into panic, making them fear they might be accused of theft (vv. 26–28).

42:29–38 When they got home and told their story, the rest of them also found their **money**, and their fears multiplied. Jacob was inconsolable. In spite of Reuben's offering the lives of his **two sons** as a guarantee, the patriarch feared to allow **Benjamin** to go to Egypt lest harm **befall him**.

43:1–15 Finally Jacob was forced by the severity of **the famine** to take action. The brothers could not return without Benjamin—that was the condition laid down by the governor, Joseph. So **Judah** agreed to serve as **surety** for Benjamin, and Jacob accepted the offer. In this one respect at least, Judah here reminds us of his descendant, the Lord Jesus, who became our Surety at the cross of Calvary. Jacob sent a **present** to the governor of Egypt, consisting of **balm, honey, gum, spices, myrrh, pistachio nuts, and almonds**—items not affected by the famine. He also insisted they take **double** the amount of **money** in case the refunded money was an **oversight**.

43:16–25 Joseph was deeply moved when he saw his brothers again, but he still did not reveal his identity. He ordered his servants to prepare a banquet. When his brothers were brought to Joseph's **house**, they thought they were on the carpet **because of the money** they found **in** their **sacks**. They made a complete explanation to the chief **steward**, and he in turn assured them there was nothing to worry about. His records showed that they had paid in full. **Simeon** was released from prison and joined them in preparation for the banquet. They got their father's **present ready** to give to Joseph when he arrived **at noon**.

If we ask whether the replaced money was in truth discovered *on the way back to Canaan* (42:27; 43:21) or *when they had arrived* in the presence of Jacob (42:35), the answer is *both*. The discovery was in two stages. One brother discovered his plight *en route*, the others *on arriving home*. It is understandable that in relating the events to Joseph's steward (43:21), a compressed account was given (*Daily Notes of the Scripture Union*).

43:26–34 **When Joseph** arrived, his brothers **bowed down before him** in fulfillment of his dream (37:7). He was overcome with emotion as he asked for the family and met **Benjamin**. At the banquet, he ate **by himself**; the eleven brothers were served separately; and the **Egyptians** likewise ate **by themselves**. The astonishment of the brothers was caused by their being seated **according to** their ages. How could anyone in Egypt know their order of birth? Special favor was shown to **Benjamin**, Joseph's own full brother.

44:1–13 When the brothers were leaving to return to Canaan, Joseph **commanded** his **silver cup** to be hidden in Benjamin's **sack**. It was not only the **cup** from which he drank, but also the one which he used in **divination**—probably referring to his interpretation of dreams.

Later God's people were forbidden to practice divination (Deut. 18:10–12). But even at this early date, it is unlikely that Joseph practiced the Egyptian forms of fortune-telling. His intuition and foresight came from the Lord, but perhaps by using the cup as a prop, he wished to confirm in his brothers' minds that he was an Egyptian.

Afterwards, when Joseph's brothers were accused of stealing the cup, they protested their innocence, rashly offering the life of anyone who was found with it. Joseph's steward agreed that the guilty one would be his slave. When the cup was found in **Benjamin's sack**, the brothers were crushed and **returned to the city**.

44:14–17 After Joseph had reproached them, **Judah** suggested that they all become his slaves, but Joseph said that Benjamin would do and the rest could return home. His action in hiding the silver cup in Benjamin's sack and in detaining Benjamin was purposely designed to bring his brothers to acknowledge their bloodguiltiness. George Williams writes:

> He acted so as to bring their sin to remembrance, to make them confess it with their own lips . . . . His detention of Simeon, and afterwards of Benjamin, was skillfully designed so as to find out if they were still indifferent to the cries of a captive brother and the tears of a bereaved father. His plan succeeded admirably; his sternness and his kindness both conspired to disquiet them; and his goodness helped to lead them to repentance.[32]

The whole scene foreshadows that coming day when the remnant of Israel will confess its guilt in connection with the death of the Messiah and will mourn for Him as one mourns for an only son (Zech. 12:10).

44:18–34 **Judah** stood **near** Joseph and gave a detailed review of Benjamin's involvement—how Joseph had demanded the presence of the youngest son, how their father, still grieving over the loss of one son, had protested against Benjamin's going to Egypt and how Judah had offered himself as **surety** for Benjamin's safety. Judah said that their **father** would **die** if the brothers went back without Benjamin, so he offered to stay in Egypt and serve **as a slave** in the place of Benjamin.

What a change had been worked in Judah! In chapter 37 he ruthlessly sold Joseph for profit, without concern for his father's heartbreak. In chapter 38 he was involved in deception and immorality. But God was working in his heart, so that in chapter 43 he became surety for Benjamin. Now in chapter 44 he pours out his heart in intercession before Joseph, offering himself as a slave so as not to bring upon his father the crushing sorrow of losing Benjamin. From selling his own brother into slavery to becoming a slave in his brother's stead; from callousness toward his father to sacrificial concern for his well-being—this is the progress of the grace of God in the life of Judah!

7. *Joseph Reveals Himself to His Brothers (Chap. 45)*

45:1–8 In one of the most moving scenes in all the Bible, Joseph ordered his staff to **go out** of the room while, with an enormous emotional release, he revealed his identity **to his brothers**. He told them not to grieve for the way they had treated him, because **God** had overruled it for good.

45:9–15 They were to **bring** their **father**, their households, and their possessions to **Goshen** in Egypt for the remaining **five years of famine**. **"Tell my father of all my glory in Egypt"**—a command we too can obey when we rehearse before God the glories of His beloved Son. The fountains of the great deep were broken up as **Joseph** embraced **Benjamin** and then **kissed all his brothers**.

This is a happy preview of the joy that awaits the people of Israel when the Christ of Calvary appears to them and reveals Himself as their Messiah-King.

45:16–24 When Pharaoh heard what was going on, he told **Joseph's brothers** to **bring** their **father** and families from Canaan, but not to bother bringing their heavy furniture and **goods** because he would provide everything they needed. So they went back to Canaan with wagons provided by Pharaoh, and with beautiful **garments**, animals, and provisions from Joseph. **Benjamin** got a gift of money and a special wardrobe. Fearing that his brothers might accuse each other for their guilt in mistreating him years earlier, Joseph warned them not to quarrel on their homeward journey.

45:25–28 On reaching home, they broke the news **to Jacob**. At first it was too much for him. But when he heard the full story and saw the loaded **carts**, he knew it was true—**Joseph** was **still alive** and they would meet again!

Joseph mentions his father five times in this chapter. This reveals his Christlikeness in addition to the free forgiveness he extended to his brothers. It was our Lord's love for His Father and His desire to do the Father's will that brought Him into the world to redeem fallen man. Joseph's love for Jacob is but a faint shadow of that love.

8. *Joseph's Reunion with His Family (Chap. 46)*

46:1-7 On the way to Egypt, **Israel** stopped the caravan at historic **Beersheba** to worship **the God of his father Isaac**. This was the place where God appeared to Abraham in connection with the offering of Isaac (21:31—22:2). It was also the place where the Lord appeared to Isaac (26:23, 24). Now He appears to **Jacob** to encourage him. This is the last of the Lord's seven appearances to him. The second promise of verse 4 seems to indicate that Jacob would return to Canaan. Actually, of course, he died in Egypt. But the promise was fulfilled in two ways. His body was taken back to Canaan for burial, and, in a sense, he also returned when his descendants went back in the days of

Joshua. The expression **"Joseph will put his hand on your eyes"** predicted a peaceful death. Atkinson explains the idiom beautifully:

> ...Joseph would close his father's eyes at the time of his death. Joseph would be with him when he died. Notice the personal promise graciously made to Jacob, which would compensate him for the long years of sorrow and mourning for Joseph. God cares for the personal needs of His servants (1 Pet. 5:7).[33]

And so **Jacob** reached **Egypt** with **all his descendants**, his **livestock**, and his personal **goods**.

46:8–27 In verses 8–27 we have the family register of **Jacob and his sons**. There were **sixty-six** family members (v. 26) who came **with Jacob to Egypt**. There are admitted difficulties in reconciling this figure with the **seventy** of verse 27 and of Exodus 1:5 and the seventy-five of Acts 7:14. The most obvious explanation is that the numbers expand from direct descendants to wider circles of relatives.

46:28–34 The epic meeting between **Israel** and **Joseph** took place in **Goshen**, the most fertile section of Egypt, near the delta of the Nile. Jacob and his sons preferred to stay there, since it provided the best pasture for their herds. It was agreed that they would **tell Pharaoh** that they were **shepherds**. Since shepherds were despised by **the Egyptians**, Pharaoh would let them live **in the land of Goshen**, far away from the royal palace. There in Goshen they were isolated from social intercourse with the Egyptians, first because of their nationality (43:32) and then because of their **occupation**. God left them in this incubator until they were a strong nation, able to possess the land that He promised to their forefathers.

9. Joseph's Family in Egypt (Chap. 47)

47:1–6 When **five** of Joseph's **brothers** told **Pharaoh** that they were **shepherds**, he responded, as expected, by telling them to settle in the lush pasturelands **of Goshen**. He also asked Joseph to find some **competent** men from among his relatives to tend the royal herds.

47:7–12 **Joseph** arranged for **his father**, then **one hundred and thirty**, to be presented to **Pharaoh**. The fact that **Jacob blessed Pharaoh** means that this aged, obscure Jew was greater than the potentate of Egypt, because the lesser is blessed by the greater (Heb. 7:7). Jacob said that his days had been **few and evil**. Actually he had brought *most* of the evil upon himself! **Joseph** settled his family in the best part of Egypt, and provided all they needed. Theirs was truly the more abundant life.

47:13–26 When the people **of Egypt** and Canaan had spent **all** their **money** for food, Joseph accepted their **livestock** in payment. Then later he **bought all the land**, except that belonging to the Egyptian **priests**, gave the people **seed** with which to plant crops, and charged them **one-fifth** of the crop for **land** rental, a very fair arrangement.

47:27–31 As **Israel** neared the end of his life, he made **Joseph** promise to **bury** him in Canaan. Then he bowed himself **on the head of** his **bed** (or "on the top of his staff," Heb. 11:21). Actually the same Hebrew consonants can be read either "bed" or "staff," depending on which vowels are supplied. The traditional Hebrew text reads **bed**, but here the Septuagint, quoted in the Hebrews passage, reads "staff." Kidner comments:

> While both versions have "bed" at 48:2, the present occasion tells of Jacob before his last illness (*cf.* 48:1), and "staff" may well be the right meaning. It would be an appropriate object to mention as the symbol of his pilgrimage (*cf.* his grateful words in 32:10), worthy of the prominence it receives in the New Testament passage.[34]

And thus the ex-supplanter was to end his life in an act of worship. He is the only hero of faith of Hebrews 11 to be commended as a worshiper. He had come a long way by the grace of God, and would soon go out in a blaze of glory.

10. Jacob's Blessing of Joseph's Sons (Chap. 48)

48:1–7 When **Joseph was told** that his **father** was **sick**, he hurried to his bedside with **Ephraim** and **Manasseh**. The dying patriarch **sat up on the bed** and adopted his **two** grandsons as his own. By doing this he arranged that the tribe of Joseph would receive a double portion of the land of Canaan when it would be divided among the tribes years later. Joseph thus received the birthright as far as territory was concerned. Any **offspring** born to Joseph **after them** would be Joseph's, not Jacob's, and would dwell in the territories allotted to Ephraim or Manasseh. Verse 7 explains why Jacob wanted to adopt Joseph's sons as his own. They were his grandsons by his beloved wife, **Rachel**, who he felt had died so prematurely.

48:8–22 Then Jacob **blessed** the grandsons, giving the birthright to **Ephraim**, who was the younger. **Joseph** tried to correct this in favor of **Manasseh, the firstborn,** but Jacob said that he had done this intentionally. What memories must have gone through his mind as he, by faith, gave the blessing to the **younger**. Years earlier his own father had unknowingly blessed him, the younger. But now he was blessing the younger, not through ignorance, but because he was in touch with the God who holds the future. Israel had faith that his descendants would one day return to the Promised **land**. Jacob gave Joseph a mountain slope which he captured from **the Amorites**. Perhaps this refers to the area containing the well that came to be known as "Jacob's well" (John 4:5).

11. Jacob's Prophecy Concerning His Sons (Chap. 49)

49:1, 2 Jacob's last words were both a *prophecy* (v. 1) and a *blessing* (v. 28).

49:3, 4 Reuben, as the **firstborn** son, represented the primacy of his father's manly **strength** in procreation, and held the place of **power** and **dignity**. The birthright, with its double portion, belonged to him. But he forfeited his preeminence because he boiled over with dark passion and sinned with Bilhah, his **father's** concubine (35:22).

49:5–7 Because these **brothers** had cruelly killed the men of Shechem and **hamstrung an ox, Simeon and Levi** would be dispersed **in Jacob** and scattered **in Israel**. By the time of the second census (Num. 26), these were the two smallest tribes. This was also fulfilled when the tribe of Simeon was largely absorbed by Judah (Josh. 19:1–9), and the tribe of Levi was assigned to forty-eight cities throughout the land. Jacob **cursed** their **cruel** deception but not the people of these two tribes themselves.

49:8–12 Judah (meaning **praise**) would be praised and respected by his **brothers** because of his victories over his **enemies**. He is likened to **a**

lion that goes forth to capture **prey**, then returns to well-deserved rest that no one dares disturb. Just as Joseph inherited the birthright with regard to territory, so Judah inherited it with regard to government. Rulership would continue in this tribe till **Shiloh** (the Messiah) came, and in **Him** it would remain forever. His **people** would give Him willing **obedience** in the day of His power. The meaning of the name **"Shiloh"** is obscure. Some suggested meanings are: *Prince of peace, tranquil, seed* (of Judah), *his descendant, whose it is* (cf. Ezek. 21:27).

49:13 **Zebulun** would enjoy prosperity from maritime commerce. Since this tribe's territory in OT times was landlocked, this prophecy may look forward to the Millennium.

49:14, 15 **Issachar** is likened to **a strong donkey**, so content to **rest** in **pleasant** pastoral surroundings that it had no will to fight for independence and so became subject to the enemy's yoke.

49:16–18 **Dan,** true to the tribe's name, would concern itself with judging the **people**. Verse 17 is difficult. It may allude to Dan's introducing the idolatry which caused the nation's **fall** (Judg. 18:30, 31). Many think that it is a veiled reference to the Antichrist's springing from **Dan**, and that this is why this tribe goes unmentioned in 1 Chronicles 2:3; 8:40 and Revelation 7:3–8. In verse 18, Jacob injects a prayer for the final deliverance of his people from their foes or for his own deliverance.

49:19 **Gad,** unprotected in its territory east of the Jordan, would be subjected to frequent enemy raids. But the tribe would trample the troops of its foes.

49:20 Happily for **Asher** (*happy*), this tribe would have fertile agricultural land, producing delicacies fit for a king.

49:21 **Naphtali** is likened to a doe that has been released from confinement. It springs forth with tremendous speed to carry good news. All the disciples except the traitor came from the territory of **Naphtali**, and much of the Lord's ministry was there (Mark 4:13–16).

49:22–26 Compassing the territories of Ephraim and Manasseh, **Joseph is a fruitful bough,** sending out blessing far beyond his own borders. He was the object of bitter hostility but he did not yield, because he was strengthened by **the Mighty God of Jacob**—the One from whom **the Shepherd, the Stone of Israel** (that is, the Messiah) comes forth. God blesses Joseph with rain in abundance, wells and gushing springs, and numerous progeny. Jacob humbly felt that he had been blessed more richly than his **ancestors**. Now he wishes that such **blessings** might come to **Joseph**, the one **who was separate from his brothers**.

49:27 **Benjamin,** a tribe of fighters, would continually conquer and **divide the spoil**. Someone has said that Benjamin proved himself the most spirited and warlike of all the tribes.

49:28–33 In closing, Jacob instructed his sons to **bury** him in the **cave . . . of Machpelah**, near his home in Hebron the burial place of **Abraham and Sarah, Isaac and Rebekah,** and **Leah**. Then **he drew** himself back **into the bed and breathed his last**.

12. Death of Jacob and Then of Joseph in Egypt (Chap. 50)

50:1–14 Even **the Egyptians mourned for . . . seventy days** when Jacob died. His body was **embalmed** by the palace **physicians**. Then **Pharaoh** gave Joseph permission to accompany the body back to Canaan, with a great procession of officials, relatives, and servants. They stopped east of **the Jordan** and mourned for **seven days** so deeply that **the Canaanites . . . called** the place **Abel Mizraim**, the meadow (or **mourning**) of Egypt. Following the burial in the **cave . . . of Machpelah** at Hebron, **Joseph and his** entourage **returned to Egypt**.

50:15–21 Now that Jacob **was dead**, **Joseph's brothers** feared that he might seek vengeance on them, **They sent** word **to** him, claiming that their **father** Jacob had left word that **Joseph** should **forgive** them. Joseph disclaimed any intent to seek revenge or to judge, since that was God's prerogative. He further relieved their fears with the memorable words, **"You meant evil against me, but God meant it for good. . . ."**

50:22–26 **Joseph** was apparently the first of the twelve sons of Jacob to die. This was fifty-four years after his father's death. His faith that God would take the people of Israel back to Canaan is eulogized in Hebrews 11:22. He gave instructions that his **bones** be buried in that land.

It has been pointed out that Genesis opens with God's perfect creation and closes with **a coffin in Egypt**. It is a book of biographies. Whereas two chapters are devoted to an account of the creation of the heavens and earth, forty-eight chapters are largely concerned with the lives of men and women. God is interested primarily in people. What a comfort and challenge to those who know Him!

ENDNOTES

[1](Intro) Anton Hartmann (1831). See Merrill F. Unger, *Introductory Guide to the Old Testament*, p. 244.

[2](Intro) See, e.g., Gleason Archer, *Archaeology and the Old Testament*.

[3](1:2) Others put the catastrophe *before* v. 1 and see v. 1 as a summary statement.

[4](1:2) However, the Hebrew verb *hayah* usually is followed by the preposition *le* when it means "become," and that is not the case here.

[5](2:15–23) Hebrew has only two tenses (plus participles): perfect and imperfect. Context determines the precise verb form that is best in translating into English.

[6](3:7–13) C. H. Mackintosh, *Genesis to Deuteronomy*, p. 33.

[7](3:22–24) Merrill F. Unger, *Unger's Bible Dictionary*, p. 192.

[8](4:7) Mackintosh, *Genesis to Deuteronomy*, p. 42.

[9](4:7) F. W. Grant, "Genesis," *The Numerical Bible*, I:38.

[10](5:25–32) George Williams, *The Student's Commentary on the Holy Scriptures*, p. 12.

[11](6:4, 5) Unger, *Bible Dictionary*, p. 788.

[12](11:26–32) Derek Kidner, *Genesis*, p. 112.

[13](15:7–21) David Baron, further documentation unavailable.

[14](16:7–15) F. Davidson, *The New Bible Commentary*, p. 90.

[15](Excursus) Bennett J. Sims, "Sex and Homosexuality," *Christianity Today*, February 24, 1978, p. 29.

[16](22:16–19) Charles F. Pfeiffer, *The Book of Genesis*, p. 6.

[17](24:1–9) *Ibid.*, p. 62.

[18](24:10–14) Murdoch Campbell, *The Loveliest Story Ever Told*, p. 9.

[19](25:29–34) D. L. Moody, *Notes From My Bible*, p. 23.

[20](26:1–6) The word *dwell* in v. 3 is a different verb in Hebrew from that in verse 6 and suggests a less settled stay.

[21](26:26–33) Williams, *Student's Commentary*, p. 31.

[22](27:1–22) Martin Luther, further documentation unavailable.

[23](27:1–22) Mackintosh, *Genesis to Deuteronomy*, p. 114.

[24](28:10–19) H. D. M. Spence and J. S. Exell, "Genesis," in *The Pulpit Commentary*, pp. 349–50.

[25](31:1–18) W. H. Griffith Thomas, *Genesis: A Devotional Commentary*, p. 288.

[26](31:19–21) Unger, *Bible Dictionary*, p. 550.

[27](32:22–32) Pfeiffer, *Genesis*, p. 80.

[28](37:1–17) Arthur W. Pink, *Gleanings in Genesis*, pp. 343–408.

[29](38:1–11) Ibid., pp. 343–408.

[30](38:24–26) Walter C. Wright, *Psalms*, II:27.

[31](38:27–30) Griffith Thomas, *Genesis*, p. 366.

[32](44:14–17) Williams, *Student's Commentary*, p. 39.

[33](46:1–7) Basil F. C. Atkinson, *The Pocket Commentary of the Bible, The Book of Genesis*, p. 405.

[34](47:27–31) Kidner, *Genesis*, p. 212.

BIBLIOGRAPHY

Atkinson, Basil F. C. *The Pocket Commentary of the Bible. The Book of Genesis*. Chicago: Moody Press, 1957.

Campbell, Murdoch. *The Loveliest Story Ever Told*. Inverness: Highland Printers Ltd., 1962.

Grant, F. W. *Genesis in the Light of the New Testament*. New York: Loizeaux Bros. Inc., n.d.

———. "Genesis." In *The Numerical Bible*, Vol. 1. Neptune, NJ: Loizeaux Brothers, 1977.

Keil, C. F. and Delitzsch, F. "Genesis." In *Biblical Commentary on the Old Testament*, Vol. 3. Grand Rapids: Wm. B. Eerdmans Publishing Company, 1971.

Kidner, Derek. *Genesis*. The Tyndale Old Testament Commentaries. Downers Grove, IL: InterVarsity Press, 1973.

Pfeiffer, Charles F. *The Book of Genesis*. Grand Rapids: Baker Book House, 1976.

Pink, Arthur W. *Gleanings in Genesis*. Chicago: Moody Press, 1922.

Ross, Allen P. "Genesis." In *The Bible Knowledge Commentary*. Wheaton: Victor Books, 1985.

Spence, H. D. M., and Exell, J. S. "Genesis." In *The Pulpit Commentary, Genesis*. New York: Funk and Wagnalls, n.d.

Thomas, W. H. Griffith. *Genesis: A Devotional Commentary*. Grand Rapids: Wm. B. Eerdmans Publishing Co., 1973.

Yates, Kyle M., Sr. "Genesis." In *The Wycliffe Bible Commentary*. Chicago: Moody Press, 1968.

EXODUS

Introduction

"To those who see theology as essentially the recital of the saving acts of God, Exodus 1—15 gives the supreme example, around which the rest of the biblical narrative can be assembled. To those who see the Old Testament as the product of the worshipping life of the community, at the heart of the book of Exodus lies the account of the institution of the passover, greatest and most characteristic of Israel's festivals . . . To those who see God's tôrâ, His law, as central to the life and thinking of later Israel, Exodus enshrines the law giving and contains the very kernel of the law in the form of the ten commandments."

—R. Alan Cole

I. Unique Place in the Canon

Exodus (*the way out* in Greek) picks up the narrative of the Israelites after the death of Joseph. The foundations of the Jewish religion in the Passover are rooted in Israel's escape from four centuries of slavery in Egypt—but only after stubborn Pharaoh has defied the God of the Hebrews and has had to suffer ten dreadful plagues on his nation, the Bible's picture of the world.

The narrative of the Red Sea crossing, many other marvelous miracles, the giving of the law on Mount Sinai, and the detailed instructions for the tabernacle complete this wonderful book.

II. Authorship

We hold to the traditional Jewish and Christian view that The Second Book of Moses, like the rest of the Pentateuch, is actually by Moses. For a defense of this position see Introduction to the Pentateuch.

III. Date

Bible scholars have set the date of the Exodus from Egypt as early as 1580 B.C. and as late as 1230 B.C. First Kings 6:1 says that the Exodus took place 480 years previous to Solomon's starting to build the temple. Since this was about 960 B.C. it would place the Exodus at 1440 B.C., the more conservative date. Many scholars maintain that archaeology better supports a later date (c. 1290 B.C.) but other archaeological finds seem to fit the early date. We cannot be sure of the exact date, of course, but all things considered, the early date of 1440 for the Exodus event, and the somewhat later date for the Book of Exodus, seems best.

IV. Background and Theme

As Exodus opens we find the Israelites in Egypt where we left them at the end of Genesis. But the *background* has changed completely. It is over four centuries later; the once-favored Hebrews are now slaves, making bricks for Pharaoh's vast building programs.

The *themes* of Exodus are *redemption* and the founding of *the nation of Israel*. For over 3,400 years Jews the world over have celebrated this event—the escape from Egypt by power and by blood, and the beginnings of the people of Israel as an actual nation—in the Passover.

The Christian Lord's Supper, also celebrating the redemption of God's people by power and blood, grows out of the Passover, both historically and theologically. To a certain extent, the bread and wine of the communion hark back to the same elements in the Passover ritual.

After the Exodus from Egypt, the scene changes to the wilderness, where Moses receives God's Law for His people. Nearly half of the book concerns the tabernacle and its priesthood (chaps. 25—40). These details are not merely historical.

To really enjoy the book of Exodus, we need to look for Christ in it. Moses, the Passover lamb, the rock, and the tabernacle are only a few of the types (symbols) of the Lord Jesus, many of which are referred to elsewhere in Scripture (see, for example, 1 Cor. 5:7; 10:4; Heb. chaps. 3—10). May the Lord do for us what He did for the two disciples on the road to Emmaus—interpret to us "in all the Scriptures the things concerning Himself" (Luke 24:27).

OUTLINE

I. ISRAEL'S BONDAGE IN EGYPT (Chap. 1)

II. THE BIRTH, RESCUE, AND TRAINING OF MOSES (Chap. 2)

III. THE CALL OF MOSES (Chaps. 3, 4)
   A. The Revelation of Jehovah to Moses (Chap. 3)
   B. The Reluctance of Moses (4:1–17)
   C. The Return of Moses to Egypt (4:18–31)

IV. MOSES' CONFRONTATIONS WITH PHARAOH (5:1—7:13)
   A. The First Confrontation (5:1—7:6)
   B. The Second Confrontation (7:7–13)

V. THE FIRST NINE PLAGUES (7:14—10:29)
   A. The First Plague—The Nile Turned to Blood (7:14–25)
   B. The Second Plague—Frogs (8:1–15)
   C. The Third Plague—Lice (8:16–19)
   D. The Fourth Plague—Flies (8:20–32)
   E. The Fifth Plague—Pestilence on Livestock (9:1–7)
   F. The Sixth Plague—Boils (9:8–12)
   G. The Seventh Plague—Hail and Fire (9:13–35)
   H. The Eighth Plague—Locusts (10:1–20)
   I. The Ninth Plague—Three Days of Darkness (10:21–29)

VI. THE PASSOVER AND THE DEATH OF THE FIRSTBORN (11:1—12:30)

VII. THE EXODUS FROM EGYPT (12:31—15:21)
- A. Flight toward the Sea (12:31—13:22)
- B. Crossing the Red Sea (Chap. 14)
- C. The Song of Moses (15:1–21)

VIII. THE JOURNEY TO SINAI (15:22—18:27)
- A. The Wilderness of Shur (15:22–27)
- B. The Wilderness of Sin (Chap. 16)
- C. Rephidim (Chap. 17)
- D. Moses and Jethro (Chap. 18)

IX. THE GIVING OF THE LAW (Chaps. 19—24)
- A. Preparation for Revelation (Chap. 19)
- B. The Ten Commandments (Chap. 20)
- C. Miscellaneous Laws (Chaps. 21—24)
  1. Laws Regarding Slaves (21:1–11)
  2. Laws Regarding Personal Injury (21:12–36)
  3. Laws Regarding Stealing and Property Damage (22:1–6)
  4. Laws Regarding Dishonesty (22:7–15)
  5. Laws Regarding Seduction (22:16, 17)
  6. Laws Regarding Civil and Religious Obligations (22:18—23:19)
  7. Laws Regarding Conquest (23:20–33)
  8. Ratification of the Covenant (24:1–8)
  9. Revelation of God's Glory (24:9–18)

X. THE TABERNACLE AND THE PRIESTHOOD (Chaps. 25—40)
- A. Instructions for Building the Tabernacle (Chaps. 25—27)
  1. The Collection of Materials (25:1–9)
  2. The Ark of the Covenant (25:10–16)
  3. The Mercy Seat (25:17–22)
  4. The Table of Showbread (25:23–30)
  5. The Golden Lampstand and Its Accessories (25:31–40)
  6. The Tabernacle Itself (Chap. 26)
  7. The Bronze Altar of Burnt Offering (27:1–8)
  8. The Outer Court, Pillars, and Screen (27:9–19)
  9. The Anointing Oil (27:20, 21)
- B. The Priesthood (Chaps. 28, 29)
  1. The Garments of the Priests (Chap. 28)
  2. The Consecration of the Priests (Chap. 29)
- C. Further Instructions Concerning the Tabernacle (Chaps. 30, 31)
  1. The Altar of Incense (30:1–10)
  2. The Redemption Money (30:11–16)
  3. The Laver (30:17–21)
  4. The Anointing Oil (30:22–33)
  5. The Incense (30:34–38)

6. The Gifted Artisans (31:1–11)
7. The Sign of the Sabbath (31:12–18)

D. An Outbreak of Idolatry (Chaps. 32, 33)
1. The Golden Calf (32:1–10)
2. The Intercession and Anger of Moses (32:11–35)
3. The Repentance of the People (33:1–6)
4. Moses' Tent of Meeting (33:7–11)
5. The Prayer of Moses (33:12–23)

E. The Covenant Renewed (34:1—35:3)

F. Preparation of the Tabernacle Furnishings (35:4—38:31)
1. The People's Gifts and the Gifted People (35:4—36:7)
2. The Curtains Covering the Tabernacle (36:8–19)
3. The Boards for the Three Sides (36:20–30)
4. The Bars Which Held the Boards Together (36:31–34)
5. The Veil Leading to the Most Holy Place (36:35, 36)
6. The Screen Leading to the Holy Place (36:37, 38)
7. The Ark of the Covenant (37:1–5)
8. The Mercy Seat (37:6–9)
9. The Table of Showbread (37:10–16)
10. The Golden Lampstand and Its Accessories (37:17–24)
11. The Altar of Incense (37:25–28)
12. The Anointing Oil and the Incense (37:29)
13. The Altar of Burnt Offering (38:1–7)
14. The Laver (38:8)
15. The Outer Court, Pillars, and Screen (38:9–31)

G. Preparation of the Priests' Garments (Chap. 39)

H. Erection of the Tabernacle (Chap. 40)

Commentary

I. ISRAEL'S BONDAGE IN EGYPT (Chap. 1)

1:1–8 The first words of the book, **"Now these are the names"** (Heb., *weēlleh shemôth*), constitute the title of Exodus in the Jewish tradition. How personal God is! Not numbers or notches in a computer card, but **names**. Jesus said of the Good Shepherd, "He calls his own sheep by name and leads them out" (John 10:3). This is very fitting here. The Israelites came down to Egypt as shepherds—but now they are slaves. But God, the Good Shepherd, has plans "to lead them out."

For explanations of the **seventy persons who were descendants of Jacob**, see the notes on Genesis 46:8–27. The **seventy** people had multiplied to a few million, including 603,550 men of war, by the time the Jewish people were ready to leave Sinai for Canaan (Num. 1:46). Verses 6 and 7 indicate that many years elapsed between the end of Genesis and the events of Exodus. The meaning of verse 8 is that **a new king . . . arose** who **did not** *look with approval on* the descendants of **Joseph**; Joseph himself was already dead, of course.

1:9–10 The Israelites had so increased in number and in power that the Pharaoh thought they would pose a threat in time of war, so he decided to make slaves of the people and to destroy every male child and thus eventually wipe out the Hebrew race. Three evil rulers in Scripture ordered the slaughter of innocent children: Pharaoh, Athaliah (2 Kgs. 11), and Herod (Matt. 2). These satanically inspired atrocities were aimed at the extinction of the messianic line. Satan had never forgotten God's promise in Genesis 3:15.

1:11–14 **Pharaoh** used the enslaved Jews to build the **supply cities** of **Pithom and Raamses**. But instead of being wiped out by his repression, **they multiplied** all the more! Pharaoh meant the **hard bondage** for evil, but God meant it for good. It helped prepare the Jews for their arduous journey from Egypt to the Promised Land.

1:15–19 When **Shiphrah and . . . Puah**, who were probably the chief **Hebrew midwives**, saw the Jewish mothers bearing children **on the birthstools**, they did not kill the male children, as **Pharaoh** had ordered. They excused their inaction by explaining that the **Hebrew** children were usually born too quickly—that is, **before the midwives could** get to the mothers. This assertion probably had some truth to it.

1:20–22 *The Daily Notes of the Scripture Union* comment on the midwives:

> The reward given to the midwives in terms of a flourishing family life (v. 21) was granted them not for their falsehood but for their humanity. This is not to say that the end justified the means, still less that there are no absolute standards of morality. But in a world as charged with sin and its effects as ours has become, it may be that obedience to greater duties is possible only at the cost of obedience to lesser ones. In this as in all else, "the fear of the Lord is the beginning of wisdom."

Foiled by the Hebrew midwives, **Pharaoh** now **commanded his** own **people** to enforce the decree.

II. THE BIRTH, RESCUE, AND TRAINING OF MOSES (Chap. 2)

2:1, 2 The **man of the house of Levi** in verse 1 was Amram, and the **daughter of Levi** was Jochebed (6:20). Thus both of Moses' parents were of the priestly tribe of **Levi**. By faith Moses' parents **hid him** for **three months** (Heb. 11:23). This must mean that they received some revelation that he was a child of destiny, because faith must be based on some revealed word of God.

2:3–8 Jochebed's **ark**, like Noah's, is a picture of Christ. Moses' **sister** was Miriam (Num. 26:59). This chapter is full of seeming coincidences. For example, why did Pharaoh's **daughter** happen to **bathe** right where the ark was floating? Why did **the baby** happen to cry and thus draw out her **compassion**? Why was Moses' **mother** accepted by **Pharaoh's daughter** as his **nurse**?

2:9, 10 Christian parents should take the words of verse 9 as a sacred charge and an unfailing promise. In Egyptian, **"Moses,"** the **name** given

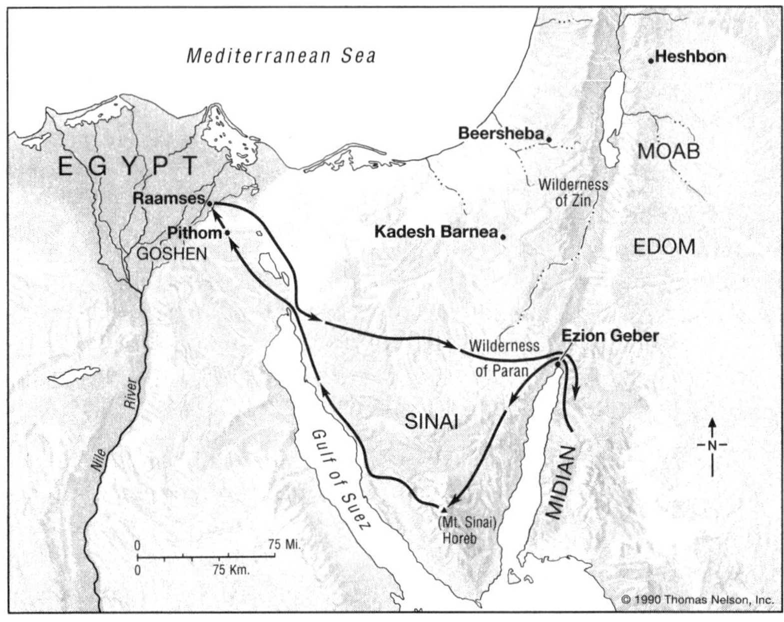

Moses' Flight & Return to Egypt

by **Pharaoh's daughter**, probably means *child* or *son*. In Hebrew the same name means *drawn out*—i.e., drawn out of the water.[1] Mackintosh remarks with his usual insight:

> The devil was foiled by his own weapon, inasmuch as Pharaoh, whom he was using to frustrate the purpose of God, is used of God to nourish and bring up Moses, who was to be His instrument in confounding the power of Satan.[2]

2:11, 12 We know from Acts 7:23 that **Moses** was forty years old when he visited **his** own people. His killing **the Egyptian** was ill-advised; his zeal outran his discretion. God would one day use Moses to deliver his people from the Egyptians, but the time had not yet come. First he must spend forty years on the back side of the desert, learning in the school of God. God had predicted that His people would be in the land of Egypt as slaves for 400 years (Gen. 15:13), so Moses' actions were forty years premature. He needed more training in the solitude of the desert. And the people needed more training in the brickkiln. The Lord orders all things according to His infinite wisdom. He is not in a hurry, but neither will He leave His people in affliction one moment longer than necessary.

2:13–15a When he went out the second day Moses tried to break up a fight between **two Hebrew men**, but they rejected his leadership, as the Hebrews were later to reject One greater than Moses. When he found out they knew he had **killed the Egyptian**, Moses panicked. **When Pharoah heard** about the killing, he sought to kill Moses, so **Moses fled** to **the land of Midian**—that is, Arabia or the Sinai area.

2:15b–22 At a well in Midian, **Moses helped the seven daughters** of the **priest of Midian** against some surly **shepherds**, and watered their flocks. This **priest of Midian** is given two names—Jethro (3:1) and **Reuel**

(v. 18), which is the same as Raguel (Num. 10:29; NKJV marg.; LXX). The Midianites were distant relatives of the Hebrews (Gen. 25:2). Jethro's **daughter, Zipporah,** became Moses' wife, and **a son, . . . Gershom** (meaning *stranger there*), was born to them.

2:23–25 **God** was not oblivious to the plight of His people. When a new **king** ascended to the throne, **God heard** and **remembered** and **looked upon the children of Israel** and **acknowledged** their condition. His response was to bring His servant back to Egypt (chap. 3) to lead His people out of that land in the mightiest display of power since the creation of the world.

III. THE CALL OF MOSES (Chaps. 3, 4)

A. The Revelation of Jehovah to Moses (Chap. 3)

3:1–4 In **tending the flock of Jethro, Moses** learned valuable lessons about leading God's people. When he went to **Horeb** (Mount Sinai), the Lord appeared to him in **a bush** that burned **with fire but . . . was not consumed**. The **bush** suggests the glory of God, before which he was told to stand with unshod **feet**. It might also foreshadow Jehovah's dwelling in the midst of His people without their being consumed. And some have even seen in it the destiny of Israel, tried in the fires of affliction but **not consumed**. We should all be like the **burning . . . bush**—burning for God, yet **not consumed.**[3]

3:5 The Lord promised Moses that He would deliver His people from Egypt and bring them into a land of abundance—that is, Canaan—inhabited by the six heathen nations listed in verse 8. The word **"holy"** occurs here for the first time in the Bible. By removing his **sandals**, Moses acknowledged that **the place** was **holy**.

3:6 God reassures Moses that He is the **God** of his forefathers—**Abraham** and **Isaac** and **Jacob**. Cole shows the importance of this revelation:

> Moses brings no new or unknown god to his people, but a fuller revelation of the One whom they have known. Not even Paul's words to the Athenians on the Areopagus are a fair parallel here (Acts 17:23). The only true parallel is the continuing Self-revelation made by God in later centuries, culminating in the coming of Christ. Yet in its day the Mosaic revelation, while a fulfilment of patriarchal promises, was as new and shattering to Israel as the coming of the Messiah was later to prove to be.[4]

3:7–12 Moses protested God's sending him **to Pharaoh**, citing his own inadequacy. But the Lord assured Moses of His presence and promised that he would yet **serve God on this mountain** (Mount Sinai) with a liberated people. J. Oswald Sanders remarks:

> His inventory of disqualifications covered lack of capability (3:11), lack of message (3:13), lack of authority (4:1), lack of eloquence (4:10), lack of special adaptation (4:13), lack of previous success (5:23), and lack of previous acceptance (6:12). A more complete list of disabilities would be difficult to conjure up. But instead of pleasing God, his seeming humility and reluctance stirred His anger. "The anger of the Lord was kindled against Moses" (4:14). In point of fact, the excuses Moses advanced to show his incapacity were the very reasons for God's selection of him for the task.[5]

3:13, 14 Moses anticipated questions from the children of Israel when he returned **to them** as the Lord's spokesman, and he wanted to be able to tell them who sent him. It was at this point that God first revealed Himself as Jehovah, the great **I AM.** Jehovah (more precisely Yahweh) comes from the Hebrew verb "to be," *hāyāh*. This sacred name is known as the *tetragrammaton* ("four letters"). English *Jehovah* comes from the Hebrew *YHWH*, with vowel markings supplied from Elohim and Adonai, other names of God. No one knows for sure the true pronunciation of *YHWH* because the ancient Hebrew spelling used no actual vowels in its alphabet. However, the pronunciation "Yahweh" is probably correct. The Jews consider *YHWH* too sacred to utter. The name proclaims God as self-existent, self-sufficient, eternal,[6] and sovereign. The fuller name **I AM WHO I AM** may mean I AM BECAUSE I AM or I WILL BE THAT I WILL BE.

3:15–22 Fortified by this revelation that God was really present and ready to come to His people's aid, Moses was told to announce to the people of Israel that they would soon be free. Also, he was to test Pharaoh by requesting that the Israelites be allowed to travel **three days' journey** to **sacrifice to the LORD.** This was not an attempt to deceive but a minimal test of Pharaoh's willingness. It would also prevent the Egyptians from witnessing the slaying of animals that were sacred to them. God knew that Pharaoh wouldn't yield until compelled by divine power. The **wonders** of verse 20 are the plagues that God sent on **Egypt**. By the time God was finished with them, the Egyptians would be glad to give the Jewish women anything they asked! The wealth thus accumulated would only be just compensation for all the slave labor of the Jews under the taskmasters of Egypt. The Israelites did not "borrow" jewels and clothing (as in the KJV); they "asked" for them (NKJV). No deceit was involved—only the just payment of wages.

B. The Reluctance of Moses (4:1–17)

4:1–9 Moses continued to doubt that the people would accept him as a spokesman of God. Maybe the disillusionment of 2:11–15 had eaten deep into his soul. Therefore God gave him three signs, or miracles, to confirm his divine commission. (1) His **rod**, thrown on the ground, **became a serpent**. Taken **by the tail**, the serpent **became a rod again**. (2) **His hand**, placed **in his bosom**, became **leprous**. The same **hand**, placed **in his bosom again**, became free of leprosy. (3) **Water** of the Nile, poured out on the land, became **blood**.

These signs were designed to convince the people of Israel that Moses was sent by God. They spoke of God's power over Satan (i.e., the **serpent**), and sin (pictured by the **leprosy**) and of the fact that Israel would be redeemed from both of these through **blood**.

4:10–17 Moses was still reluctant to obey **the LORD**, excusing himself because he was **not eloquent**. After reminding Moses that the Lord **made man's mouth**, and therefore could make him eloquent, God appointed **Aaron**, Moses' **brother**, to **speak** for him. Moses should have obeyed the Lord in simple dependence, knowing that His commands are His enablements. God never asks us to do anything without giving us the power to do it. Because Moses was not satisfied with God's best, he had to take God's second best—that is, having Aaron as his spokesman. Moses thought that Aaron would be a help, but he later proved to be a hindrance in leading the people to worship the golden calf (chap. 32).

C. The Return of Moses to Egypt (4:18–31)

4:18–23 Forty years after fleeing to Midian, Moses returned to Egypt at God's command and with Jethro's blessing. His wife and sons were **Zipporah**, **Gershom**, and Eliezer (18:2–4). The staff in verse 2 becomes **the rod of God** in verse 20. The Lord uses ordinary objects to do extraordinary things so that it can be plainly seen that the power is from God. The **wonders** which God commanded Moses to perform **before Pharaoh** were the plagues that followed. God hardened Pharaoh's **heart**, but only after that despotic ruler had first hardened his own heart. **"Firstborn"** sometimes refers to the order in physical birth, but here it means a position of honor normally held by the firstborn son, the inheritor of the birthright. Pharaoh was forewarned that if he did not obey, God would slay his **son**.

4:24–26 But before Moses could deliver the message, he had to learn obedience himself. He had failed to circumcise his own son (Gershom or Eliezer), possibly because of Zipporah's opposition. When God threatened **to kill** Moses, perhaps by serious illness, Zipporah angrily circumcised the son and secured her husband's release. She called him a **"husband** (or "bridegroom," NASB) **of blood."** This incident, plus Zipporah's apparent lack of faith in the Lord, may have been the reason why Moses sent Zipporah home to her father with her two sons (18:2, 3).

4:27–31 **Aaron** came out to meet Moses as he returned to Egypt. They both stood before the people of Israel, delivered the Lord's message, and confirmed it with the three **signs** which the Lord had given. **So the people believed** and **worshiped** the Lord.

IV. MOSES' CONFRONTATIONS WITH PHARAOH (5:1—7:13)

A. The First Confrontation (5:1–7:6)

5:1 In 3:18 God had told Moses to take the elders when he went before Pharaoh. In the meantime, the Lord had appointed Aaron as Moses' spokesman (4:14–16). So **Aaron went** with **Moses** in place of the elders. The LORD's message was unequivocal: **"Let My people go."**

5:2–14 When Moses and Aaron delivered their first ultimatum to Pharaoh, he accused them of distracting **the people from their work**. Also, he changed their work load by insisting that henceforth they would have to **gather** their own **straw** for making **bricks**, yet produce the same **quota** as **before**. Pharaoh was making an impossible situation for the Jews, reminding one of the Nazi treatment of the Jews in the concentration camps. They had to go **throughout all the land of Egypt to gather stubble instead of straw**. The Hebrew text indicates the contempt with which these repressed people were treated. Cole points out that stubble is a poor substitute for straw since it is rough and uneven.[7]

5:15–23 Until now the straw had been provided for the Israelites. It was used to reinforce the bricks, and to keep them from sticking to the forms in which they were made. When the Jewish foremen were **beaten**, they protested **to Pharaoh** but received no consideration. Then they blamed **Moses and Aaron**, and Moses in turn blamed **the LORD**. Opposition from *within* the ranks of God's people is often harder to bear than persecution from *without*.

6:1–12 **The LORD** graciously answered Moses' petulant speech first by assuring him that **Pharaoh** would **let** the Israelites **go** because he would be compelled by God's **strong hand**. Then He reminded Moses that He had revealed Himself to the patriarchs as El-Shaddai or **God Almighty**, not primarily as Jehovah (*NKJV* "LORD"), the personal name of the covenant-keeping God. The thought here seems to be that He would now reveal Himself as Lord in a new way—that is, in new power in delivering His people. He had made a covenant and was about to fulfill it by freeing the Israelites from Egypt and bringing them **into the** Promised Land. Notice the seven "I will's" in verses 6–8. The name "Jehovah" (or "LORD") had been used before, but now it took on new significance. Notice twenty-five personal pronouns used by God in these verses, emphasizing what He had done, was doing, and would do. Moses seems to have missed the point, being still occupied with his own inadequacy. After further reassurance, he did obey the word of the Lord (chap. 7). **"Uncircumcised lips"** in verse 12 and 30 means faltering speech. Moses did not consider himself a great speaker.

6:13–30 The genealogies in verses 14–25 are limited to **Reuben**, **Simeon**, and **Levi**, the first three sons born to Jacob. The author did not want to give a complete genealogy but only to trace the line to **Moses and Aaron**. So he quickly passed over Reuben and Simeon to come to the priestly tribe.

7:1–5 At the close of chapter 6, Moses wondered why the mighty Pharaoh would listen to such a poor speaker as he. The Lord's answer was that Moses stood before **Pharaoh** as a representative of **God**. Moses would speak to Aaron, and **Aaron** would convey the message to **Pharaoh**. **Pharaoh** would **not heed**, but God would deliver His people anyway!

7:6 **Moses** and **Aaron** were **eighty** and **eighty-three years old** respectively when their great ministry of deliverance began. Even in what today would be called "old age," God can use men and women for His glory.

B. The Second Confrontation (7:7–13)

Pharaoh was forewarned of coming trouble. When **Aaron cast down his rod** and it became **a serpent**, Pharaoh's **magicians and sorcerers** were able to duplicate the miracle through demonic powers. We learn from 2 Timothy 3:8 that the magicians of Egypt were Jannes and Jambres. They resisted Moses by imitating him and Aaron, but **Aaron's rod swallowed up their rods**. God hardened **Pharaoh's heart**, not arbitrarily, but in response to his stubbornness. It was now time for the first plague.

V. THE FIRST NINE PLAGUES (7:14—10:29)

A. The First Plague—The Nile Turned to Blood (7:14–25)

7:14–18 **The LORD** told Moses to have a personal confrontation with **Pharaoh** down by the riverside when his majesty went out **to the water**. (He was probably bathing in the "sacred" Nile.) Moses was to warn the king that the **fish** would **die**, the **river** would **stink** and become loathsome to **the Egyptians** after it was **turned to blood by the rod** in Moses' **hand**.

7:19–25 Moses and Aaron did as God commanded. They stretched out the **rod over the waters of Egypt**. The **waters** of the Nile and of **the land of Egypt** were **turned to blood**, **the fish . . . died**, and **the river stank**. The magicians duplicated this miracle with water found elsewhere than in the Nile. This probably encouraged Pharaoh to resist Moses' demands to let the people go. During the **seven days** when the Nile was polluted, the people obtained water by digging wells.

B. The Second Plague—Frogs (8:1–15)

The plague of **frogs** which covered **the land of Egypt** was so distressing that Pharaoh seemed to relent. When he asked Moses to have the plague lifted, Moses said, **"Accept the honor of saying when I shall intercede for you, for your servants, and for your people, to destroy the frogs from you and your houses, that they may remain in the river only." The magicians** were able to produce **frogs** also—as if there weren't enough already! They probably did this by demonic power, but they dared not *destroy* the frogs because the frog was worshiped as the god of fertility! When the frogs died the next day, there was a tremendous stench from their dead bodies. **Pharaoh** once again **hardened his heart**.

C. The Third Plague—Lice (8:16–19)

In the third plague **the dust of the earth** changed into gnats or **lice**. This time **the magicians**, unable to produce **lice**, warned **Pharaoh** that a power greater than theirs was at work, but the king was obdurate. The more he hardened his **heart**, the more it was hardened by God.

D. The Fourth Plague—Flies (8:20–32)

8:20–24 So God sent the fourth plague—**swarms** ***of flies***. As the italics in the NKJV indicate, the Hebrew literally means **swarms** (or "mixed"), and the specific insect (**flies**) is supplied by the translators. Perhaps the **swarms** were a mixture of many species. Since most or all of the plagues were aimed at the false gods of Egypt (the Nile, and virtually every creature was a deity in Egypt!), it is possible that the beetle is meant. This would be an attack against Khepri, the god of the sacred beetle.[8]

8:25–32 Pharaoh buckled to the extent of allowing the Israelites to **sacrifice to** God **in the land** of Egypt. But this wouldn't do because they would be sacrificing animals worshiped by **the Egyptians** and thus incite a riot. Pharaoh made a further concession: The Jews could go into **the wilderness** to sacrifice but they must **not go . . . far**. This too was unsatisfactory because God had commanded them to go three days' journey. As soon as Egypt got relief from the plague, Pharaoh changed his mind and forbade **the people** to **go**.

E. The Fifth Plague—Pestilence on Livestock (9:1–7)

After **Pharaoh** had been warned, God sent a **pestilence**, possibly anthrax, that killed **all** the Egyptians' **livestock . . . in the field**. The animals belonging to the Israelites were not affected. So it was a discriminating judgment that cannot be explained by natural phenomena. All attempts to explain the plagues on naturalistic grounds dash themselves against the rocks. Not all the animals of the Egyptians were destroyed, since some are referred to in verse 19 and some were later killed on the Passover night (12:29b). Some fled into the houses (v. 20). So the **"all"** of verse 6a means "all in the field" or "all kinds." The ram, the goat, and the bull were sacred animals in Egypt. Now their decomposing carcasses were polluting the environment.

F. The Sixth Plague—Boils (9:8–12)

When **Pharaoh** steeled himself still further, God caused **ashes** to be turned into **boils** on the men and animals **of Egypt**. Even **the magicians** were affected. The more Pharaoh hardened his heart, the more it became judicially **hardened** by God.

G. The Seventh Plague—Hail and Fire (9:13–35)

"All My plagues" probably indicates the full force of God's plagues. The Lord reminds Pharaoh that He could have destroyed him and the Egyptians with the preceding **pestilence**, but instead He had spared Pharaoh in order to demonstrate His **power** and spread His fame. There is no thought in verse 16 that Pharaoh was predestined to be damned. Reprobation is not a Bible doctrine. The Lord used Pharaoh as an example of what happens to a person who is determined to resist the power of God (see also Rom. 9:16,17).

The next plague consisted of **hail** and lightning or **fire**, accompanied by **thunder**. It destroyed men, beasts, and **the flax and . . . barley**, that were ready for harvest (cf. vv. 31, 32); **but the wheat and the spelt were not struck, for they are late crops**. The Israelites, dwelling in **Goshen**, were untouched. In response to Pharaoh's plea, Moses prayed and the plague stopped. But, as **Moses** expected, **Pharaoh** became even more adamant against letting the Hebrews leave.

H. The Eighth Plague—Locusts (10:1–20)

Moses and Aaron warned Pharaoh of an impending locust plague, but he would agree to **let** only **the men go** to hold a feast to **the LORD**. The women and children had to stay behind. But God would not have the men in the wilderness while their families were still in Egypt. The plague was of unprecedented severity, with **locusts** covering **the land** and eating everything edible. This showed that the god Serapis was powerless to protect from **locusts**. **Pharaoh** seemed willing to yield, but **he** would **not let the children of Israel go**.

I. The Ninth Plague—Three Days of Darkness (10:21–29)

10:21–28 The ninth plague was **three days** of **darkness which** could **be felt**. Only **the children of Israel had light in their dwellings**, an obvious miracle. The Egyptian sun god, Ra, was unmasked as impotent. Pharaoh told Moses to **go** to the wilderness with the women and children but to leave the **flocks and . . . herds** behind. He thought this would guarantee their return. (Perhaps he also wanted to replenish his own herds.) But in that case, there would be nothing to sacrifice to Jehovah, and **sacrifice** was the reason for their departure from Egypt. When Moses was unwilling to make the demanded compromise, Pharaoh ordered him banished from his presence forever.

10:29 Moses' strong statement, **"You have spoken well. I will never see your face again,"** seems contradicted by 11:8, where it says that Moses "went out from Pharaoh in great anger." Matthew Henry suggests that **"never . . . again"** means "after this time," and 11:8 is included in the same "conference." He writes:

> So that, after this interview, Moses came no more, till he was sent for. Note, when men drive God's word from them he justly permits their delusions, and answers them according to the multitude of their idols. When the Gadarenes desired Christ to depart, he presently left them.[9]

VI. THE PASSOVER AND THE DEATH OF THE FIRSTBORN (11:1—12:30)

11:1–10 Moses had not yet departed from Pharaoh's presence. In verses 4–8 he is still speaking to the ruler. The first three verses may be thought of as a parenthesis. In view of the tenth and final plague, God told Moses to have the Israelites **ask** (not "borrow," as in KJV) for **gold** and **silver articles** from **the Egyptians**. Moses warned Pharaoh that **all the firstborn . . . of Egypt** would be slain at **midnight** of the appointed date (see 12:6), that the Israelites would not be affected by the slaughter, and that Pharaoh's officials would **bow down**, begging the Hebrews to leave at once and en masse. **Then** Moses left the potentate in **great anger**. The warning fell on deaf ears, and **the LORD hardened Pharaoh's heart** still more.

12:1–10 **The LORD** gave detailed instructions to **Moses and Aaron** on how to prepare for the primary **Passover**. The **lamb**, of course, is a type of the Lord Jesus Christ (1 Cor. 5:7). It was to be **without blemish**, speaking of the sinlessness of Christ; **a male of the first year**, perhaps suggesting our Lord's being cut off in the prime of life; kept **until the fourteenth day of the . . . month**, pointing forward to the Savior's thirty years of private life in Nazareth, during which He was tested by God, then publicly for three years by the full scrutiny of man; killed by **the congregation of Israel**, as Christ was taken by wicked hands and slain (Acts 2:23); killed **at twilight**, between the ninth and eleventh hours, as Jesus was killed at the ninth hour (Matt. 27:45–50). Its **blood** was to be applied to the door, bringing salvation from the destroyer (v. 7), just as the blood of Christ, appropriated by faith, brings salvation from sin, self, and Satan. **The flesh** was to be **roasted** with **fire**, picturing Christ enduring God's wrath against our sins. It was to be eaten **with unleavened bread and with bitter herbs**, symbolizing Christ as the food of His people. We should live lives of sincerity and truth, without the leaven of malice and wickedness, and with true repentance, always remembering the bitterness of Christ's suffering. Not a bone of the lamb was to be broken (v. 46), a stipulation that was literally fulfilled in the case of our Lord (John 19:36).

12:11–20 The first **Passover** was to be observed by a people ready to travel, a reminder to us that pilgrims on a long journey should travel light. The **Passover** was so named because the Lord *passed over* the houses where the blood was applied. The expression "passover" does not mean "pass by." Cole explains:

> Whether it was correct etymology or a pun, *pesah* to Israel meant "a passing-over" or "a leaping over" and was applied to God's act in history on this occasion, in sparing Israel.[10]

The **Passover** was **on the fourteenth day** of Israel's religious calendar year (v. 2). Closely connected with the Passover was **the Feast of Unleavened Bread**. On that first Passover night, the people left Egypt in such a hurry that there was no time for the dough to become leavened (vv. 34, 39). Thereafter, in keeping the Feast **for seven days**, they would be reminded of the speed of their exodus. But since leaven speaks of sin, they would also be reminded that those who have been redeemed by blood should leave sin and the world (Egypt) behind them. **Whoever** ate **leavened** bread would be **cut off**—that is, excluded from the camp and its privileges. In some contexts, the expression "cut off" means condemned to death.

12:21–27 Next we hear **Moses** passing on the instructions to **the elders of** the people. Further details are given about how to sprinkle **the blood** on **the door**. The **hyssop** may picture faith, which makes a personal application of **the blood** of Christ. The **Passover** would provide a springboard for teaching future generations the story of redemption when they would ask the meaning of the ceremony.

12:28–30 **At midnight** the blow finally fell as threatened. **There was a great cry in Egypt, for there was not a house where there was not one dead.** The Israelites were at last permitted to leave.

VII. THE EXODUS FROM EGYPT (12:31—15:21)

A. Flight toward the Sea (12:31—13:22)

12:31–37 Verse 31 does not necessarily mean that **Moses** met **Pharaoh** face-to-face (see 10:29). What a servant says or does is often ascribed to his master. Moses had predicted that Pharaoh's servants would beg the Israelites to go (11:8).

The Israelites **journeyed . . . to Succoth**, a district in Egypt, not to be confused with the town of that name in Palestine (Gen. 33:17). **The Egyptians** were only too glad to give their wealth to the Israelites and be rid of them. For the Hebrews, it was only just recompense for all the labor they had given to Pharaoh. It provided them with equipment for the journey and materials for the service of God. **About six hundred thousand men** left Egypt, in addition to women and **children**. The exact number of men was 603,550 (38:26). The total number of Israelites was about two million.

12:38, 39 There is considerable dispute concerning the date of the Exodus. A commonly accepted conservative date is c. 1440 B.C. Other scholars place it at 1290 B.C. or even later (see Introduction). **A mixed multitude** (that is, including foreigners) tagged along with the Israelites when they left Egypt. They are referred to as "rabble" in Numbers 11:4 (NASB), where they are seen complaining against the Lord despite His goodness to them.

12:40–42 Concerning the chronology in verse 40, see the commentary on Genesis 15:13, 14. The **four hundred and thirty years** mentioned here cover the total time that the Israelites spent in Egypt. It is an exact figure, to the **very . . . day**. The important thing to see is that the Lord did not forget the promise He had made centuries earlier. In bringing His people out, He fulfilled His Word. God is not slack concerning the promise of *our* redemption either (2 Pet. 3:9). In a coming day, Moses' "antitype," the Lord Jesus, will lead His people out of this world to the eternal Promised Land.

12:43–51 The ordinance of **the** permanent **Passover** specified that only **circumcised** men were allowed to participate, whether aliens, neighbors, or servants. **No foreigner shall eat it . . . a sojourner and a hired servant shall not eat it.**

13:1–15 God had saved **the firstborn** of the Israelites from death in Egypt; therefore, **the firstborn** of humans and of animals were to be **consecrated** to God, as belonging to Him. The firstborn sons became priests

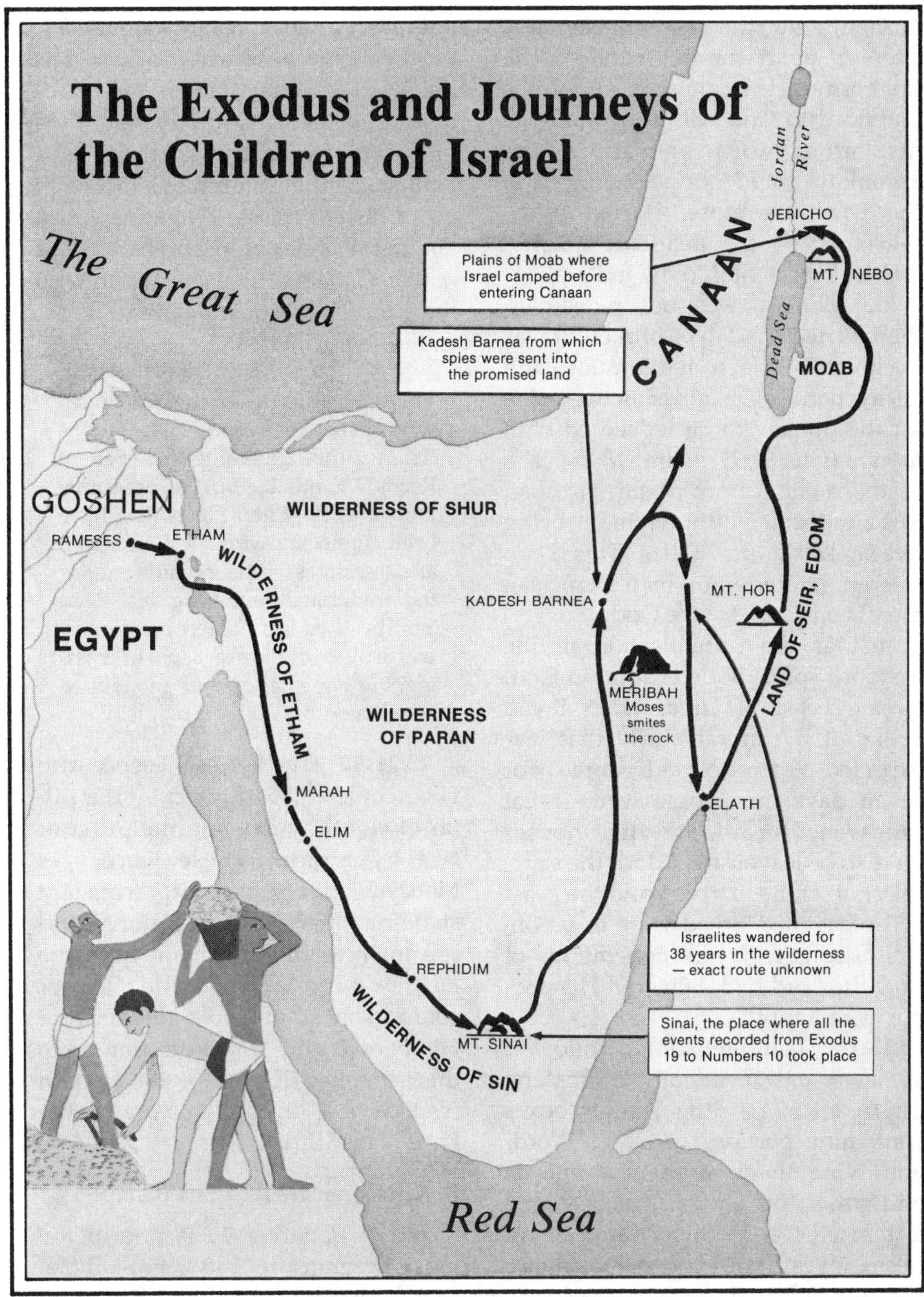

The Exodus and Journeys of the Children of Israel

of God, until the tribe of Levi was later set apart for this service. The firstborn of clean animals were to be sacrificed to God within a year. The firstborn of unclean animals, such as **a donkey**, could not be sacrificed to the Lord; therefore, **it** had to be redeemed by the death of **a lamb**; that is, a lamb had to die in its place. If the donkey was not redeemed, then **its neck** had to be broken. It was a choice between redemption and destruction. Later, provision was made for the donkey to be redeemed with money (Lev. 27:27; Num. 18:15). The firstborn child, born in sin, also had to be redeemed, the payment being five shekels (Num. 18:16). This was a solemn reminder of man's unclean moral condition before God.

Just as the sanctification of the firstborn spoke of dedication to God, so the Feast of Unleavened Bread spoke of the moral purity that was expected of a redeemed people. For **seven days** the people were to **eat unleavened bread**, and their houses were to be leaven-free. Both the sanctification of the firstborn and the Feast of Unleavened Bread were to be object lessons to future generations of how the Lord had delivered His people from Egypt.

13:16 The Jews later followed verses 9 and 16 literally by making phylacteries, or little leather boxes containing portions of God's Word, and tying them to their foreheads and wrists. But the *spiritual* meaning is that all we do (**hand**) and all we desire (**eyes**) should be in accordance with God's Word.

13:17–20 The most direct route from Egypt to Canaan would have been through Philistine country, a trip of about two weeks along the coastal road known as "The Way of Horus." But this was a busy thoroughfare, under constant surveillance by the Egyptian army. To save His people from attack and consequent discouragement, **God led** them by a more southerly route through the Sinai Peninsula. The children of Israel went up **in orderly ranks.** They were also taking the bones of Joseph back to his native Canaan, in accordance with their ancestors' solemn oath to do so. C. F. Pfeiffer writes:

> The Biblical term for the sea which was opened before the Israelites is "Yam Suph," literally the "Sea of Reeds" (Exod. 13:18). The area now known as the Bitter Lakes may have been connected with the Red Sea in ancient times, thus accounting for the traditional rendering of "Reed Sea" by "Red Sea." There are numerous theories of the exact spot of crossing, but none has gained unqualified acceptance.[11]

13:21, 22 The Lord's presence with His people was indicated by **the pillar of cloud by day** and **the pillar of fire by night**. "These were," as Matthew Henry puts it, "constant standing miracles."[12] This glory cloud is known as the Shekinah, from the Hebrew word for *dwell*. The pillar (or column) spoke of God's guidance for His people and His protection from their enemies (Ex. 14:19, 20). In both respects it is a good picture of the Lord Jesus Christ.

B. Crossing the Red Sea (Chap. 14)

14:1–9 Chapter 14 is one of the most dramatic in the whole Bible. **The Lord** directed **the children of Israel** southward to **Pi Hahiroth**, somewhere west of the Red Sea. This made escape seem impossible, but made the subsequent miracle more marvelous. Pharaoh thought they were trapped and set out after them with his army of **six hundred choice chariots, and all the chariots of Egypt with captains over every one of them**. Pharaoh's overtaking the two million apparently helpless Israelites **camping by the sea** and shut in between the two is probably the origin of the popular idiom for a terrible dilemma: "Between the devil (Pharaoh) and the deep blue (Red!) sea."

14:10–14 When **the children of Israel** raised **their eyes** and saw the Egyptian army marching **after them** they were naturally petrified, but wisely **cried out to the LORD**. Yet they quickly complained to the Lord's leader, Moses, as they had once before (5:21), saying **it would have been better for** them **to serve the Egyptians than** to **die in the wilderness**. This was sheer unbelief on their part, and not the last instance, by any means. No longer timid, Moses told them to **"stand still and see the salvation of the LORD."**

14:15–18 One of the greatest miracles in all history was about to occur:

> **The LORD** instructed **Moses, . . . "Tell the children of Israel to go forward. But lift up your rod, and stretch out your hand over the sea and divide it. And the children of Israel shall go on dry ground through the midst of the sea."**

Regarding God's hardening of **the hearts of the Egyptians**, and gaining **honor over Pharaoh and over all his** military might, Matthew Henry writes:

> It is a righteous thing with God to put those under the impressions of his wrath who have long resisted the influences of his grace. It is spoken in a way of triumph over this obstinate and presumptuous rebel.[13]

14:19–28 The Angel of God (Christ, see Judges 6 for discussion) took His place as a **pillar of cloud** at the rear of the host of Israel, protecting them from **the Egyptians**. **The pillar of cloud** provided **light** for the Israelites **and darkness** for **the Egyptians**. At Moses' bidding the Red Sea parted, forming two walls of water with a path of **dry land** between. The Israelites passed through safely, but when **Pharaoh's** army tried to follow, **the LORD . . . troubled** them and disabled their chariots **so that they drove them with difficulty**. Before they could retreat, **the sea** closed in on them at Moses' command. **Not so much as one of them remained**. The same faith that opened up the Red Sea enables us to do the impossible when we are moving forward in the will of God.

14:29–31 The crossing of the Red Sea is set forth as the greatest display of God's power *in the OT*, but the greatest power *of all time* is that which raised Christ from the dead.

C. The Song of Moses (15:1–21)

Just as the Passover speaks of redemption by *blood*, the Red Sea tells of redemption by *power*. The song of Moses celebrates the latter. Dr. H. C. Woodring outlined it as follows:[14]

Prelude (v. 1)—The triumph of Jehovah.
Stanza #1 (vv. 2,3)—What *He is:* **strength, song, salvation**.
Stanza #2 (vv. 4–13)—What *He has done:* victory over past enemies, deliverance of His people from Egypt.
Stanza #3 (vv. 14–18)—What *He will do:* victory over future enemies; bring His people into their inheritance.
Postlude (v. 19)—Contrast of the defeat of Egypt and the deliverance of Israel.
Antiphonal response by **Miriam** and **all the women** (vv. 20, 21).

Nearly three centuries ago the English commentator Matthew Henry expressed his appreciation and understanding of this great spiritual ode as follows:

> We may observe respecting this song, that it is, (1.) An ancient song, the most ancient that we know of. (2.) A most admirable composition, the style lofty and magnificent, the images lively and proper, and the whole very moving. (3.) It is a holy song, consecrated to the honour of God, and intended to exalt his name and celebrate his praise, and his only, not in the least to magnify any man: holiness to the Lord is engraven on it, and to him they made melody in the singing of it. (4.) It is a typical song. The triumphs of the gospel church, in the downfall of its enemies, are expressed in the song of Moses and the song of the Lamb put together, which are said to be sung upon a sea of glass, as this was upon the Red Sea, Rev xv. 2, 3.[15]

VIII. THE JOURNEY TO SINAI (15:22—18:27)

A. The Wilderness of Shur (15:22–27)

Verse 22 begins the record of the journey **from the Red Sea** to Mount Sinai. Each step is filled with spiritual lessons for believers of every age. **Marah**, which means *bitter*, for instance, speaks of the bitter experiences of life. The tree suggests the cross of Calvary, which transmutes the bitter things of life into sweetness. At **Marah** the Lord revealed Himself as *"the Lord who heals you"* (*YHWH Rōphekā*). He promised to deliver Israel from **the diseases** that afflicted the Egyptians. **Elim**, with its **twelve wells of water** and **seventy palm trees**, suggests the rest and refreshment which are ours after we have been to the cross.

B. The Wilderness of Sin (Chap. 16)

16:1–19 Journeying to the southeast, the people **came to the Wilderness of Sin.**[16] There they **complained** bitterly about the lack of food and sighed for the food **of Egypt**, seemingly forgetful of the terrible slavery that accompanied the food. God graciously responded by supplying plenty of **quails** at night and manna **in the morning**. The quails were provided only twice, here and in Numbers 11:31, whereas the manna was provided continuously. "Manna" means **"What is it?"** It was food miraculously provided by God; no attempts to explain it on a natural basis succeed. Manna was **small, round**, white, and sweet (v. 31), picturing the humility, perfection, purity, and sweetness of Christ, the Bread of God (John 6:48–51). Its arrival was somehow connected with the **morning dew**, reminding us that it is the Holy Spirit who ministers Christ to our souls. The Israelites were allowed to **gather . . . one omer** (about three pints) per person. No matter how much or how little they gathered, seeking to approximate an omer, they always had enough and never too much. This suggests the sufficiency of Christ to meet every need of all His people, and the results achieved when Christians share with those who are in need (2 Cor. 8:15). The manna had to be gathered early in the **morning**, before the **sun . . . melted** it. So we should feed on Christ at the start of each day, before the pressures of life crowd in on us. It had to be gathered daily, just as we must feed daily on the Lord. It was to be gathered on the first six days of the week; none was provided on the seventh.

16:20–31 **On the sixth day** the people were ordered to gather **twice**

as much as on the other days, to tide them over the **Sabbath**. If they **left part of it** on any other day, the manna **bred worms and stank. Manna was like white coriander seed, and the taste of it was like wafers made with honey.** It could be baked or cooked. Moses rebuked those who went out to gather it on the Sabbath.

16:32–34 Some of the **manna** was placed in a golden urn and **kept** as a memorial, later to be placed in the Ark of the Covenant (Heb. 9:4). God rested on the seventh day at creation (Gen. 2:2), but He did not command man to do so at that time. But now He gave the law of the Sabbath to the nation of Israel. Later it became one of the Ten Commandments (20:9–11). It was a sign of the covenant made with Israel at Mount Sinai (31:13) and a weekly reminder of their deliverance from Egyptian bondage (Deut. 5:15). Gentiles were never commanded to keep the Sabbath. Nine of the Ten Commandments are repeated in the NT as instructions in righteousness for the church. The only one that is *not* repeated is the law of the Sabbath. Yet there is a *principle* of one day of rest in seven for all mankind. For the Christian, that day is the first day of the week, the Lord's Day. It is not a day of legal responsibility but a day of gracious privilege, when, released from secular activities, we can give ourselves more wholly to the worship and service of the Lord.

The "Testimony," meaning the "Ark" of the Covenant, is mentioned here before it ever existed. This is an illustration of the law of prior mention. **The "Testimony"** can also mean the Ten Commandments, depending on the context.

16:35, 36 Eating manna for **forty years** is a prediction of the time the Israelites would wander in the wilderness. The manna ceased when they reached Gilgal, just inside **the border of the land of Canaan** (Josh. 5:12).

C. Rephidim (Chap. 17)

17:1–7 At **Rephidim** the people **contended with Moses** because of a shortage of **water**. The Lord instructed Moses to proceed to the general area known as **Horeb** (meaning *the desolate place*) and to **strike the rock** with his **rod**. When he did, water flowed from the rock—a picture of the Holy Spirit, who was given on the day of Pentecost as the fruit of Christ's being struck on Calvary. **Massah** (*tempting* or *testing*) was where they tried or tested God. **Meribah** (*chiding* or *strife*) was where they strove with Moses.

17:8–16 **Joshua** (*Jehovah is salvation*) now comes on the stage for the first time. As the servant of Moses, he **fought** against **Amalek** in Rephidim. As long as **Moses held up his hand** in intercession and in dependance on God, the Israelites had the margin of victory. But when Moses' hand sagged, Amalek gained the ascendancy. **Amalek**, a descendant of Esau, is a type of the flesh—that is, the evil, corrupt, Adamic nature of man. Observe the following parallels between the flesh and Amalek: (1) It presents itself after the Holy Spirit is given at conversion to fight against the Spirit; (2) **The Lord will have war with** the flesh from generation to generation; (3) It is never eradicated from the believer till death or the Rapture of the church. (4) Two means of triumph over the flesh are suggested—prayer and the Word.

According to the ancient Jewish historian Josephus, **Hur** was the husband of Miriam, Moses' sister. This same Hur was later left with **Aaron** to supervise the people while Moses was on Mount Sinai (24:14).

The-LORD-Is-My-Banner (Heb. *YHWH Nissî*) is a compound name of Jehovah.

D. Moses and Jethro (Chap. 18)

18:1–12 Chapter 18 marks a distinct division in the book of Exodus. Until now we have had the manna, the stricken rock, and the stream—speaking of Christ's incarnation, His death, and the giving of the Holy Spirit. Now we seem to have a foregleam of Christ's future glory. **Moses** is a type of Christ reigning over the earth. We also see the Jews, represented by his **sons**; the Gentiles, pictured by **Jethro**; and the church, typified by Moses' Gentile bride, **Zipporah**. All these will enjoy the blessings of the Millennial Kingdom—the Jews and Gentiles as subjects in it, and the Church reigning with Christ over the earth.

The events are not in chronological order. Jethro is described as coming to Moses at Mount Sinai in verse 5, but the Israelites did not arrive at Mount Sinai until 19:2. One commentator suggests that this arrangement is to clear the way for an uninterrupted account of the meeting with Jehovah and the giving of the Law. Moses had probably left his wife and two sons in Midian when he went back to Egypt. Now **Jethro** brings **Zipporah, Gershom** and **Eliezer** (*my God is help*) to Moses for a joyous reunion. It appears that Jethro had become a convert to the one true **God** here, though some scholars believe he had already been a worshiper of Jehovah.

18:13–27 When Jethro saw the tremendous task that fell to **Moses** in judging **the people**, he advised his son-in-law to **select men** of high character, **such as fear God, men of truth, hating covetousness**, to assist him. Jethro's suggestion included **rulers of thousands, rulers of hundreds, rulers of fifties, and rulers of tens**. This would ease the **burden** on Moses and enable the work to be handled more quickly. Some think that Jethro's counsel was divinely given, that it urged a sensible delegation of authority to others. Others remind us, however, that God never assigns tasks without giving grace for them. Up to this time God had been speaking to Moses as a man speaks with a friend, and had not been using a go-between. Therefore Moses should have carried on until God Himself made other arrangements.

IX. THE GIVING OF THE LAW (Chaps. 19—24)

A. Preparation for Revelation (Chap. 19)

19:1–9 The children of Israel have now arrived at Mount **Sinai**. The rest of the book of Exodus, the entire book of Leviticus, and the first nine chapters of Numbers record events that took place here.

From Adam until this time, there had been no direct law of God. The Lord's dealings with His people had been predominantly in grace. Now He offered them a conditional covenant of law: **If you will indeed obey My voice and keep My covenant, then you shall be a special treasure to Me above all people; . . . you shall be to Me a kingdom of priests and a holy nation.** If they would **obey**, He would bless. Not realizing their own sinfulness and helplessness, the people readily agreed. D. L. Moody comments:

> "All that the Lord has spoken we will do." Bold and self-confident language. The golden calf, the broken tablets, the neglected ordinances, the stoned messengers, the rejected and crucified Christ, are overwhelming evidences of man's dishonored vows.[17]

THE DISPENSATIONS

There is a very major break here in the history of God's dealings with mankind, especially with His chosen nation Israel. The change in the Divine ordering of human affairs here and elsewhere indicates a change in *dispensations* or administrations.

Augustine once said, "Distinguish the ages and the Scriptures harmonize." God has divided human history into ages: ". . . by whom also he made the ages" (Heb. 1:2 RV, marg.). These ages may be long or short. What distinguishes them is not their length but the way God deals with mankind in them.

While God *Himself* never changes, His *methods* do. He works in different ways at different times. We call the way God administers His affairs with man during a particular era a *dispensation*. Technically, a dispensation does not mean an age but rather an administration, a stewardship, an order, or an *economy* (our word "economy" comes from *oikonomia*, the NT Greek word for "dispensation" or "administration"). But it is difficult to think of a dispensation without thinking of time. For example, the history of the United States government has been divided into administrations. We speak of the Kennedy administration or the Bush administration. We mean, of course, the way the government was operated while those presidents were in office. The important point is the policies that were followed, but we necessarily link those policies with a particular period of time.

Therefore, we think of *a dispensation as the way God deals with people during any period of history*. God's dispensational dealings may be compared to the way a home is run. When there are only a husband and wife in the home, a certain program is followed. But when there are young children, an entirely new set of policies is introduced. As the children mature, the affairs of the home are handled differently again. We see this same pattern in God's dealings with the human race (Gal. 4:1–5).

For example, when Cain killed his brother Abel, God set a mark on him, so that anyone finding him would not kill him (Gen. 4:15). Yet after the Flood God instituted capital punishment, decreeing that "Whoever sheds man's blood, by man his blood shall be shed" (Gen. 9:6). The difference is due to the change in dispensations.

Another example is Psalm 137:8, 9, where the writer calls down severe judgment on Babylon: "O daughter of Babylon, who are to be destroyed, happy the one who repays you as you have served us! Happy the one who takes and dashes your little ones against the rock!"

Still later the Lord taught His people: "Love your enemies, bless those who curse you, do good to those who hate you, and pray for those who spitefully use you and persecute you" (Matt. 5:44).

It seems clear that language suitable for the psalmist living under law would no longer be suitable for a Christian living under grace.

In Leviticus 11 *certain foods* were designated as *unclean*. But in Mark 7:19b Jesus declared *all foods* to be *clean*.

In Ezra 10:3 the Jews were told to *put away* their foreign wives and children. In the NT, believers are instructed *not* to put them away (1 Cor. 7:12–16).

Under the law *only the high priest* could enter the presence of God (Heb. 9:7). Under grace *all believers* have access into the Most Holy Place (Heb. 10:19–22).

These changes clearly show that there has been a change of dispensations.

Not all Christians are agreed on the number of dispensations or the names that should be given to them. In fact, not all Christians accept dispensations at all.

But we can demonstrate the existence of dispensations as follows. First of all, there are at least two dispensations—law and grace: "For the law was given through Moses, but grace and truth came through Jesus Christ" (John 1:17). The fact that our Bibles are divided into Old and New Testaments indicates that a change of administrations occurred. Further proof is given by the fact that believers in this age are not required to offer animal sacrifices. This too shows that God has introduced a new order. Hardly any Christians fail to see this major break between the Testaments.

But if we agree that there are *two* dispensations, we are forced to believe that there are *three*, because the Dispensation of Law was not introduced until here in Exodus 19, hundreds of years after Creation. So there must have been at least one dispensation before the law (see Rom. 5:14). That makes three.

And then we should be able to agree on a *fourth* dispensation, because the Scriptures speak of "the age to come" (Heb. 6:5). This is the time when the Lord Jesus Christ will return to reign over the earth, otherwise known as the Millennium.

Paul also distinguishes between the *present age* and *an age to come*. First he speaks of a dispensation that was committed to him in connection with the truth of the gospel and the church (1 Cor. 9:17; Eph. 3:2; Col. 1:25). That is the present age. But then he also points forward to a future age when (Eph. 1:10) he refers to "the dispensation of the fullness of times." It is apparent from his description of it that it has not yet arrived.

So we know that we are not living in the final age of the world's history.

Dr. C. I. Scofield lists seven dispensations, as follows:

1. Innocence (Gen. 1:28). From Adam's creation up to his fall.
2. Conscience or Moral Responsibility (Gen. 3:7). From the fall to the end of the Flood.
3. Human Government (Gen. 8:15). From the end of the Flood to the call of Abraham.
4. Promise (Gen. 12:1). From the call of Abraham to the giving of the Law.
5. Law (Ex. 19:1). From the giving of the Law to the Day of Pentecost.
6. Church (Acts 2:1). From the Day of Pentecost to the Rapture.
7. Kingdom (Rev. 20:4). The thousand-year reign of Christ.[18]

While it is not important to agree on the exact details, it is very helpful to see that there are different dispensations. The distinction between law and grace is especially important. Otherwise we will take portions of Scripture that apply to other ages and refer them to ourselves. While all Scriptures are *profitable for us* (2 Tim. 3:16), not all were written directly *to us*. Passages dealing with other ages have applications for us, but their primary interpretation is for the age for which they were written. We have already noted the dietary restrictions of Leviticus 11. While this prohibition is not binding on Christians today (Mark 7:18, 19), the underlying principle remains—that we should avoid moral and spiritual uncleanness.

God promised the people of Israel that if they obeyed Him, He would make them materially prosperous (Deut. 28:1–6). The emphasis then was on material blessings in earthly places. But this is not true today. God does not promise that He will reward our obedience with financial prosperity. Instead, the blessings of this dispensation are spiritual blessings in the heavenly places (Eph. 1:3).

While there are differences among the various ages, there is one thing that never changes, and that is the gospel. Salvation always has been, is now, and always will be by faith in the Lord. And the basis of salvation for every age is the finished work of Christ on the cross.[19] People in the OT were saved by believing whatever revelation the Lord gave them. Abraham, for example, was saved by believing God when He said that the patriarch's seed would be as numerous as the stars (Gen. 15:5, 6). Abraham probably did not know much, if anything, about what would take place at Calvary centuries later. But the Lord knew. And when Abraham believed God, He put to Abraham's account all the value of the future work of Christ at Calvary.

As someone has said, the OT saints were saved "on credit." That is, they were saved on the basis of the price that the Lord Jesus would pay many years later (that is the meaning of Romans 3:25). We are saved on the basis of the work which Christ accomplished over 1900 years ago. But in both cases salvation is by faith in the Lord.

We must guard against any idea that people in the Dispensation of Law were saved by keeping the law or even by offering animal sacrifices. The law can only condemn; it cannot save (Rom. 3:20). And the blood of bulls and goats cannot put away a single sin (Heb. 10:4). No, God's way of salvation is by faith and faith alone! (See Rom. 5:1.)

Another good point to remember is this: When we speak of the present Church Age as the Age of Grace, we don't imply that God wasn't gracious in past dispensations. We simply mean that God is now testing man under grace rather than under law.

It is also important to realize that the ages do not close with split-second precision. Often there is an overlapping or a transition period. We see this in Acts, for instance. It took time for the new church to throw off some of the trappings of the previous dispensation. And it's possible that there will be a period of time between the Rapture and the Tribulation during which the Man of Sin will be manifested and the temple will be built in Jerusalem.

One final word. Like all good things, the study of dispensations can be abused. There are some Christians who carry dispensationalism to such an extreme that they accept only Paul's Prison Epistles as applicable for the church today! As a result they don't accept baptism or the Lord's Supper,[20] since these are not found in the Prison Epistles. They also teach that Peter's gospel message was not the same as Paul's. (See Gal. 1:8, 9 for a refutation of this.) These people are sometimes called ultradispensationalists or Bullingerites (after a teacher named E. W. Bullinger). Their extreme view of dispensations should be rejected.‡

19:10–20 The people were told to prepare for a revelation from God by washing **their clothes** and refraining from sexual intercourse. This was designed to teach them the necessity for purity in the presence of God. **Mount Sinai** was a forbidding place. Neither mankind nor animals were to **touch** it on penalty of **death**. A transgressor was not to be followed onto the mount but was to be **shot** through **with an arrow** or **stoned** from a distance. Only Moses and Aaron were allowed to ascend (v. 24), and then only **when the** ram's horn sounded. The mount was covered with **a thick cloud; there were thunderings and lightnings, fire** and **smoke; the whole mountain quaked greatly**. All this spoke of the terrors of meeting God, especially on the basis of lawkeeping.

19:21–25 The LORD repeated His warning **to Moses** that the people should not touch the mount. Moses at first thought it unnecessary to remind the people but later obeyed. **The priests** in verses 22 and 24 were probably the firstborn sons.

B. The Ten Commandments (Chap. 20)

The Ten Commandments were divided by the Lord Jesus into two sections, one covering love to God and the other covering love to one's neighbor (Matt. 22:37–40). Some suggest that the first four commandments teach love to God, while others add the fifth. The expression "The LORD your God" is found in the first five commandments.

I.

20:1–3 Have no other gods. This is a prohibition against the worship of many gods (polytheism) or against the worship of any other god except Jehovah.

II.

20:4–6 Use no **carved image**. Not only the worship of idols but their manufacture is forbidden. This includes pictures, images, and statues used in worship. It does not, however, include all pictures or statues, since the tabernacle contained carved cherubim. Also, God told Moses to make a serpent of brass (Num. 21:8).

Mount Sinai. Viewed from a trail leading to its summit, Jebel Musa (right) is traditionally considered to be the biblical Mount Horeb, or Sinai. It is located on the southern portion of the Sinai Peninsula between the Red Sea and the Gulf of Aqaba.

The commandment undoubtedly refers to pictures or images of deity.

God is **a jealous God**—that is, jealous of the worship and love of His people. He visits **the iniquity of the fathers upon the children to the third and fourth generations**, through inherited weaknesses, poverty, diseases, and shortened lifespan. But God's **mercy** endures **to thousands** (of generations) of **those who love** Him **and keep** His **commandments**.

III.

20:7 Taking God's **name . . . in vain** is forbidden. This means to swear by God's name that a false statement is actually true. It could also include profanity, cursing, minced oaths, or swearing to a promise and failing to fulfill it.

IV.

20:8–11 Remember the Sabbath day. First mentioned in Genesis 2:1–3, and enjoined in connection with the gathering of manna (Ex. 16), the Sabbath was now formally given to the nation of Israel for strict observance. It was a picture of the rest which believers now enjoy in Christ and which a redeemed creation will enjoy in the Millennium. The Sabbath is the seventh day of the week, from sundown on Friday to sundown on Saturday. Nowhere in the NT are Christians commanded to keep the Sabbath.

V.

20:12 Honor **father** and **mother**. To honor here means to obey. The verse teaches that a life of obedience to parents is the type of life which, in general, insures length of days. A life of disobedience and sin often leads to premature death. This is the first commandment with a promise attached (Eph. 6:2). It teaches respect for authority.

VI.

20:13 You shall not murder. This refers specifically to murder and not to capital punishment or to manslaughter. The command teaches respect for human life.

VII.

20:14 You shall not commit adultery. This prohibition teaches respect for marriage, and warns against exploiting another person's body. It *may* cover all forms of unlawful sexual behavior.

VIII.

20:15 You shall not steal. This refers to any act by which a person wrongfully deprives another person of his property. It teaches respect for private property.

IX.

20:16 You shall not bear false witness. This commandment forbids damaging the character of another person by making statements which are not true, and thus possibly causing him to be punished or even executed. It teaches respect for a person's reputation.

X.

20:17 You shall not covet. The tenth commandment passes from acts to thoughts, and it shows that it is sinful to lust after anything that God never intended one to have. Paul states that this commandment produced deep conviction of sin in his life (Rom. 7:7).

20:18–21 After the Ten Commandments were given, **the people** were terrified by the manifestations of the divine Presence. They were afraid they would die if God spoke to them directly, so **Moses** became their mediator.

20:22–26 The purpose of the Law of Moses was to show the people their sinfulness. Next, God graciously gave instructions for the erection of **an altar**, reminding the people that sinners can approach God only on the ground of shed blood. The altar speaks of Christ as the way of approach to God. Man could contribute nothing to the perfection of Christ, either by the tools of personal effort or the steps of human achievement. Priests ascending **steps** in long, flowing garments might accidentally expose themselves in a manner that would be inappropriate for such a solemn occasion.

C. Miscellaneous Laws (Chaps. 21—24)

1. Laws Regarding Slaves (21:1–11)

21:1–6 Following the giving of the Ten Commandments, God delivered many other miscellaneous laws for the conduct of the children of Israel.

A Hebrew could become a slave to pay off a debt, to make restitution for a theft, or by being born to Hebrew slaves. **A Hebrew servant** could be required to work for **six years**, but **in the seventh** year **he** had to be set **free**. **If he** was **married** when he became a slave, **then his wife** was freed with him. But if he married during his servitude, then **the wife and her children** were the **master's** property. In such a case, he could choose to remain a slave by having his ear bored to the doorpost, thus voluntarily identifying himself with his master's house. Henceforth he was "earmarked." This is a beautiful picture of Christ, the perfect Servant, who so loved us that He would not go out free, but rather went to the cross of Calvary. In view of what the Savior has done for us, we should be His willing bondslaves, saying in the words of Bishop Moule:

> My Master, lead me to the door;
> Pierce this now-willing ear once more.
> Thy bonds are freedom; let me stay
> With Thee to toil, endure, obey.[21]

21:7–11 In the case of **a female** slave, she could **not go out** free in the seventh year if her master had taken her as a wife or concubine and was willing to fulfill his responsibilities to her. If he was not willing, she had to **be redeemed**, but not sold to Gentiles. If he wanted her as a wife for **his son**, then he had to treat her as he would any daughter-in-law. If the master took **another wife**, he was still responsible to provide for the slave girl and to give **her** full **marriage rights**. The latter probably means nothing more than living accomodations. Otherwise, she must be freed **without paying money**. The fact that God gave legislation concerning slavery does not mean that He approved it. He was only protecting the civil rights of the enslaved.

2. Laws Regarding Personal Injury (21:12–36)

21:12–14 Verse 12 states the general rule that to kill another person brings the sentence of **death** upon the offender. An exception is provided in the case of manslaughter; if the death was involuntary, the manslayer could **flee** to the altar of God, or later to special cities of refuge. But in cases of willful murder, the **altar** of God provided no safety for the offender.

21:15–17 Parenthood was especially protected by making the striking of one's **father or . . . mother** a crime punishable by **death**. Kidnapping and cursing one's parents were also capital crimes.

21:18, 19 If a man injured another in a quarrel, he was responsible to pay his **loss of . . . time** at work and also his medical expenses.

21:20, 21 A master could punish a slave, but he did not have the right to kill him. If a servant died immediately after a beating, the master was guilty; but if the slave lived **a day or two**, the master was not punishable because he obviously did not intend to kill a slave who was worth money to him.

21:22 If a pregnant woman was hit as a result of a **fight** between two **men** and **she** gave **birth prematurely**, though there was no serious injury, then her **husband** named the amount of the fine and **the judges** arbitrated the case.

21:23–25 The general rule concerning personal injury was **life for life, eye for eye, tooth for tooth,** etc. *The penalty should suit the crime,* avoiding excessive leniency or extreme severity. In practice, all cases except murder could be settled by paying a fine (see Num. 35:31).

21:26–36 If a man injured his slave's **eye** or **tooth**, the slave was allowed to **go free. If an ox** unexpectedly killed a person, the **ox** was to **be stoned**, and his **flesh** could **not be eaten**. If the **owner** knew that **the ox** was vicious and had been informed of it, then he too was to be **put to death**. But provision was made for the owner to pay a fine in lieu of **his life**. The fine would be the same for the death of **a son or . . . a daughter**. For the death of a **servant**, the fine was **thirty shekels of silver**, and **the ox** was to **be stoned**. Note: Judas betrayed Jesus for the same cost that was claimed for a slave killed by an ox, thus pricing Him at the value of a dead slave. **If a man** left **a pit** uncovered, he was responsible for any loss incurred by animals falling into it. **If one man's ox** killed another man's ox, the value of both animals was divided equally. If the owner of the offending animal knew of its dangerous habits, then he had to **pay** for the slain animal, but he himself could take **the dead animal**.

3. *Laws Regarding Stealing and Property Damage (22:1–6)*

A **thief** had to **make full restitution** for what he had stolen, the amount depending on the nature of the theft. **If a thief** was slain while **breaking in** at night, his killer was not accountable; he had no way of knowing whether the motive was theft or murder. But to kill a thief during daylight hours brought guilt on the killer. If the thief of verse 1 could not make **restitution**, then he was **sold** as a slave. If a stolen animal was **found alive**, the thief had to **restore double**. If a farmer allowed an **animal** to stray into a neighbor's grain **field**, he had to restore the same amount that was **grazed from the best of his own field** or **vineyard**. Anyone who carelessly started a **fire** that destroyed crops had to **make restitution**.

4. *Laws Regarding Dishonesty (22:7–15)*

22:7–13 Verses 7–9 deal with the theft of **money** or property that was being kept in trust by one person for another. The one who stole it had to **pay double. If the thief** could **not** be **found**, the one holding the money in safekeeping had to appear before **the judges** to see if he himself was the guilty one. In any case of breach of trust, the judges decided whether the accused or accuser was guilty, then required **double** payment. If an **animal**

died, was **hurt**, **or** was **driven away** while being held in trust, and if the trustee swore **an oath** before **the Lord** that what had happened was beyond his power to prevent, no restitution was necessary. **If** the animal was **stolen** through the trustee's lack of watchfulness, he had to **make restitution**. No restitution was required for a mauled animal if the carcass was produced **as evidence**.

22:14, 15 If a borrowed animal was **injured** or killed, the borrower had to **make it good**. But **if** the **owner was** present when it happened, and was therefore able to protect it, no restitution was necessary. No restitution was necessary in the case of a **hired** animal, since the risk of loss was included in the price.

5. Laws Regarding Seduction (22:16, 17)

If a man seduced an unengaged **virgin** to sin with him, he was obligated to marry her and to **pay the** regular dowry. **If** the **father** refused **to give** his daughter in marriage, the man still had to pay the **"bride-price"** to the father, since the possibility that the daughter would ever marry was now greatly reduced.

6. Laws Regarding Civil and Religious Obligations (22:18–23:19)

22:18–20 Three capital crimes in addition to murder were sorcery or witchcraft, sexual intercourse **with an animal**, and idolatry.

22:21–24 The Jews were to be compassionate toward strangers in their land, because they too had been **strangers in** a foreign **land**. Humane treatment was also to be accorded to widows and **fatherless** children. The Lord took it upon Himself to enforce this commandment. Men were appointed to punish most other violations, but in this case, God would punish directly. He hasn't changed in His attitude toward the defenseless. He still cares for **widows** and orphans, and we as believers should do the same.

22:25–27 No interest was to be charged on **money** lent to an Israelite, though it could be charged to Gentiles (Deut. 23:20). Clothing taken **as a pledge** had to be returned **before** nightfall, since the cloak was used as a blanket.

22:28–31 It was forbidden to **revile God** or **curse a ruler** (cf. Acts 23:5). The Lord was to receive His portion, whether of crops or **sons** or animals. **Firstborn** animals were to be offered **on the eighth day**. It was forbidden to **eat meat** that had been **torn by beasts**. In such a case, the blood would not have been drained immediately, and to eat blood was a violation of God's law (Lev. 17). Also, there was the danger of infection from various diseases spread by animals (such as rabies), from which God was protecting His people.

23:1–12 In judicial matters, it was forbidden to **circulate a false report**, to conspire **with the wicked** to defend the guilty, to take sides with an evil **crowd**, or to **show partiality to** the **poor**. No spite was to be shown to an animal belonging to an enemy. If it was lost, it should be returned to its owner; and if it had fallen down with a heavy load, it should be assisted to its feet. Justice was to be shown to the **poor**, and **the innocent and righteous** were not to be condemned through **wicked** legal tricks. It was forbidden to take a **bribe**, or to **oppress** strangers. **The seventh year** was a sabbath, during which **land** was to **lie fallow** (idle). **The poor** were allowed to take what grew by itself that year. **The seventh day** was also to provide **rest** for master, **servant**, and animal. Note that the God of the OT was merciful and just, in spite of the charges made against Him by unbelieving modern critics.

23:13–17 Jews were forbidden to **mention . . . other gods** (idols) except perhaps by way of condemning them, as the prophets did. Three great feasts were to be kept to Jehovah: (1) **The Feast of Unleavened Bread**. It was held at the beginning of the year, immediately after the Passover Feast. It speaks of the importance of purging our lives from malice and wickedness. (2) **The Feast of Harvest**, also called Pentecost and the Feast of Weeks. It speaks of the coming of the Holy Spirit on the Day of Pentecost and the formation of the church. (3) **The Feast of Ingathering**, also called the Feast of Tabernacles. It typifies Israel dwelling securely in the land during the Millennium. Adult **males** were *required* to attend these feasts; for others it was *voluntary*. In the NT we see not only Joseph, but Mary and Jesus the Boy also going up annually to Jerusalem for the Passover Feast (Luke 2:41).

23:18, 19 **Leavened bread** (leaven symbolizes sin) was not to be used in connection with **the blood of** God's **sacrifice**, i.e., the Passover. **The fat** of an offering was the Lord's because it signified the best part; it was **not** to be left **until** the **morning**, but probably was to be burned. The best of **the firstfruits** were to be brought to **the house of the LORD**. An animal was not to be cooked **in its mother's milk**. This was probably aimed against fertility rites practiced by idolaters. Strict Jews today refrain from cooking meat and milk dishes in the same pan. Also, they refrain from eating meats in cream sauces, etc.[22]

7. Laws Regarding Conquest (23:20–33)

Here God promised to **send . . . an Angel** (the Lord Himself) **before** the Israelites, to lead them to the Promised Land and to **drive out** the heathen inhabitants. If the Jews refrained from idolatry and obeyed the Lord, He would do great things for them. Regarding the warning against disobedience, Henry writes:

> We do well to take heed of provoking our protector and benefactor, because if our defence depart from us, and the streams of his goodness be cut off, we are undone.[2,3]

Their land would extend **from the Red Sea to the sea** of the Philistines (the Mediterranean Sea) and **from the desert** (the Negev south of Canaan) **to the River** (Euphrates).

Notice the command to **drive . . . out** the inhabitants of the land. There were to be **no** treaties, no idolatry, no intermingling. God had already promised to destroy the wicked Canaanites, but Israel had to cooperate. This enshrines an important spiritual principle: God will give us victory over our enemies (the world, the flesh, and the devil), but He expects us to fight the good fight of faith.

Verse 33 finds its counterpart in 2 Corinthians 6:14–18. Separation from the world has always been God's will for His people. Israel's failure to obey this command led to her downfall. It is still true that "bad company corrupts good morals."

8. Ratification of the Covenant (24:1–8)

24:1, 2 Moses was on Mount Sinai when God spoke to him the laws and ordinances contained in Exodus 20–23. Before Moses left the top of the mountain, God told him to return with **Aaron** and his two sons, **Nadab and Abihu, and** with **seventy of the elders**. However, only **Moses** was to draw **near** to **the Lord**; the others were to remain at a distance. Under law, distance must be maintained between the sinner and God. Under grace we have "boldness to enter the Holiest by the blood of Jesus" (Heb. 10:19). Law says, "They shall not come near." Grace says, "Let us draw near" (Heb. 10:22).

24:3–8 **Moses** then descended to **the people** and delivered the law to them. They immediately agreed to keep it, little realizing their powerlessness to do so. To ratify this conditional covenant between God and Israel, Moses first **built an altar** with **twelve pillars** (for the twelve tribes of Israel). He then **took . . . blood** from the offerings and **sprinkled . . . half . . . on the altar** (representing God's part in the covenant) and half **on the people** (signifying their determination to keep their part of the agreement).

9. Revelation of God's Glory (24:9–18)

24:9–11 Following this, **Moses** and the others **went back up** on Mount Sinai, as instructed in verses 1 and 2. There **they saw . . . God** in His glory. Ordinarily, to see God would be sufficient to kill a person, but it was not so here. They were not destroyed; **they saw God, and they ate and drank.** In other words, they saw God and lived to eat the peace offering.

There is a seeming paradox in the Bible with regard to the matter of seeing God. On the one hand, there are verses which indicate that it is impossible to see God (Ex. 33:20; John 1:18; 1 Jn. 4:12). On the other hand, there are passages which speak of men seeing God, such as Genesis 32:30; Exodus 24:10; 33:23. The explanation is that while God in His unveiled glory is a consuming fire which would vaporize anyone looking at Him, yet He can reveal Himself in the form of a man, an angel, or a glory cloud (Deut. 5:24) which a person could see and still live.

24:12–18 A different ascent to Mount Sinai is apparently described here. This time **Joshua** accompanied Moses for part of the distance. In his absence, he delegated **Aaron and Hur** to serve as judges for the people. For **six days** Moses waited on the side of the mountain while the glory **cloud covered** the summit. Then, at God's invitation, he climbed up to the top and entered **the cloud**, where he was to remain for the next **forty days and forty nights**. Forty is the number of testing or probation. Here the testing was for the people rather than for Moses. They failed the test by plunging into sin. Thus the Lord revealed through the law what was in the heart of man.

The instructions Moses received during this time are recorded up to 31:18.

X. THE TABERNACLE AND THE PRIESTHOOD (Chaps. 25—40)

The next seven chapters deal with instructions for building the tabernacle, setting up the priesthood, and related legislation. Fully fifty chapters in the Bible are devoted to the tabernacle, showing its importance in God's sight.

The tabernacle was a tentlike structure which was to be God's dwelling place among His people. Each part of the tabernacle teaches us spiritual lessons concerning the Person and work of Christ and the way of approach to God. The priesthood reminded the people that sin had created distance between God and themselves, and that they could draw near to Him only through these representatives appointed and made fit by Him.

A. Instructions for Building the Tabernacle (Chaps. 25—27)

1. The Collection of Materials (25:1–9)

Moses was told to take from the people **an offering** of the materials that would be needed in erecting the **tabernacle** (sanctuary). The precious metals, fine fabrics, skins, **oil**, spices, and precious **stones** were no doubt the payment the Israelites received from the Egyptians when they left Egypt. They had worked—yes, slaved—for these things. Now they were giving them sacrificially. God insisted that **the tabernacle** be made strictly according to the divine pattern. If this is true of a physical building, how much more important to build up Christ's congregations (the people) according to the divine NT pattern!

2. The Ark of the Covenant (25:10–16)

The **ark** was a wooden chest, covered **inside and out . . . with pure gold**. On each side were **rings of gold** through which **poles** were placed for carrying it. The ark was to contain **the Testimony**—that is, the two tablets of the Law (v. 16) and later Aaron's rod and a jar of manna (Heb. 9:4).

3. The Mercy Seat (25:17–22)

The lid of the ark was called the **mercy seat**. It was a solid **gold** platform supporting two angel-like figures. These **cherubim**[24] faced **one another** and had **their wings** spread upward to meet each other. God manifested Himself in the glory cloud **between the two cherubim** and **above the mercy seat**. Cherubim are mentioned in at least thirteen books of the Bible. They are connected primarily with the holiness and righteousness of Jehovah, and are often mentioned in association with the throne of God. They are described in Ezekiel chapters 1 and 10.

4. The Table of Showbread (25:23–30)

The **table** of **showbread** was a wooden table covered **with pure gold**. It had an ornamental **molding** around the top (a crown), and **a handbreadth-**wide rim or **frame** with a second ornamental **gold molding**. Like the ark, **the table** was **carried** by **poles** placed through **rings . . . at** the lower **corners that are at its four legs**. On top of the table were placed twelve loaves (v. 30) for the twelve tribes of Israel. Also, there were various **dishes, pans, pitchers, and . . . bowls for pouring**.

5. The Golden Lampstand and Its Accessories (25:31–40)

25:31–39 The **lampstand** was made of solid **gold**. It had seven **branches** or arms at the top, each one holding a small lamp on a swivel with a wick for burning oil. In connection with the **lampstand**, there were **wick-trimmers** and **trays** for holding the pieces that were trimmed off (vv. 38, 39).

25:40 The great single requirement in making these objects was to follow the **pattern** which God gave **on the mountain**. There was no room for human improvising. So it is with all spiritual matters: We must follow divine directives and not deviate from **the pattern** that the Lord in His wisdom has given.

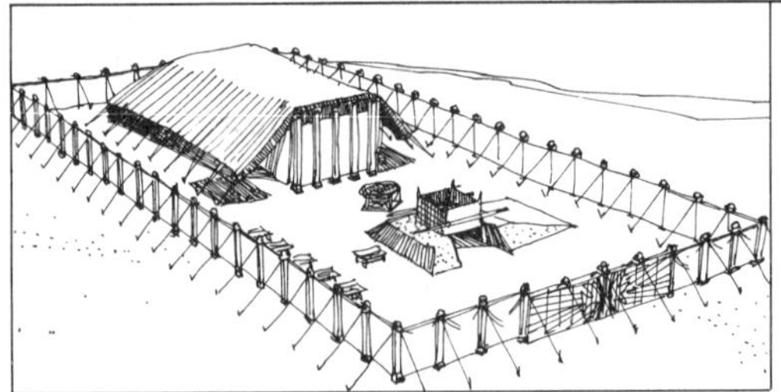

The tabernacle was to provide a place where God might dwell among His people. The term *tabernacle* sometimes refers to the tent, including the holy place and the Most Holy, which was covered with embroidered curtains. But in other places it refers to the entire complex, including the curtained court in which the tent stood.

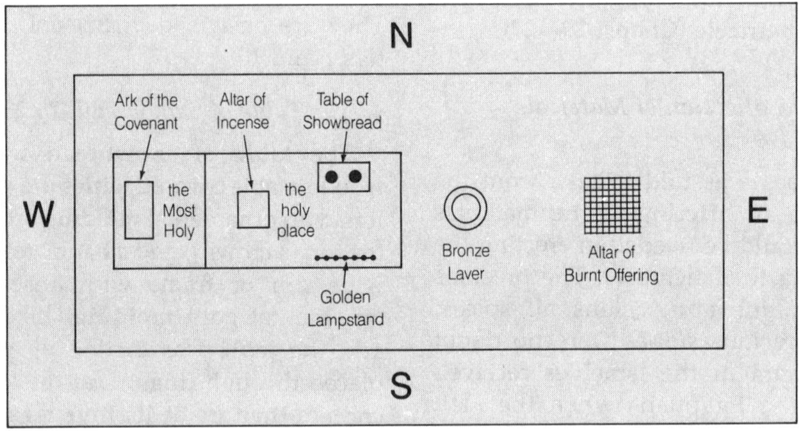

This illustration shows the relative positions of the tabernacle furniture used in Israelite worship. The tabernacle is enlarged for clarity.

The Plan of the Tabernacle

All the furniture of the tabernacle spoke of Christ in glory: the ark symbolized His deity (gold) and humanity (wood). The mercy seat pictured Christ as our mercy seat, or propitiation (Rom. 3:25). The table of showbread represented Christ as the Bread of life. The candlestick portrayed Christ as the Light of the world. The bronze altar (chap. 27) typified Christ as the Burnt Offering, wholly consumed for God. The altar of incense or the golden altar (chap. 30) pictured the fragrance of Christ to God. The laver (chap. 30) symbolized Christ cleansing His people by the washing of water by the Word (cf. Tit. 3:5; John 13:10; Eph. 5:26).

6. The Tabernacle Itself (Chap. 26)

26:1–6 Chapter 26 describes the tabernacle itself. It measured approximately forty-five feet long, fifteen feet wide, and fifteen feet high (assuming a cubit of about 18 inches). The two sides and one end consisted of upright boards, set in sockets and joined together. The other end (the entrance) had pillars.

The first covering, here called the tabernacle, was made of **fine woven linen, with artistic designs of cherubim** embroidered in **blue, purple, and scarlet**. It consisted of two sets of **five curtains . . . coupled** together. These two sets were joined by **clasps of gold** that were apparently attached to **fifty . . . loops of blue**. The total covering measured forty-two by sixty feet. It formed the ceiling and covered the sides to within eighteen inches from the ground.

26:7–13 The next covering, called **the tent**, was made **of goats' hair**. A set of **five curtains** was joined to a set of **six curtains** by **bronze clasps** that were connected to **fifty loops**. The total covering, measuring forty-five by sixty-six feet, overlapped all sides of the tabernacle except the front. There a section was folded back.

26:14 The third **covering** was made **of rams' skins**, and the fourth was made **of badger skins** (also translated seal, porpoise, or dolphin skins).[25] No measurements are given; these coverings were probably the same size as the goats' hair covering.

26:15–30 The **upright . . . boards** that formed three sides of the tabernacle are described in verses 15–25. Each **board** was fifteen by two-and-one-quarter feet. It was made **of acacia wood** covered with gold and had **two tenons** at the bottom to fit into **sockets**. There were **twenty boards** on each **side** and **six boards** on the rear. **Two** special **boards** were made for the **back corners**. The **boards** were kept in place by wooden **bars**, covered **with gold**, that passed through **gold rings** on **the boards**. **The middle bar** was one continuous piece. Two shorter **bars** of varying lengths may have been joined together to form one bar at the top, and two others joined to form one bar at the bottom. Some think that the boards were trellised frames.

26:31–37 The tabernacle itself was divided into two rooms—first **the holy place**, measuring thirty feet by fifteen feet, and then **the Most Holy** place (the Holy of Holies), measuring fifteen feet by fifteen feet. These two rooms were separated by **a veil** made **of fine woven linen** and embroidered with **cherubim**. The **veil** was hung on **four pillars**. The **ark** and the **mercy seat** were to be put **in the Most Holy** place, whereas **the table** of showbread and the golden **lampstand** were to be put in the holy place. The altar of incense (chap. 30) was the only other furniture in the holy place; it was placed in front of the veil. The **lampstand** was on **the south** side of the holy place **and the table on the north side**. The door of the tabernacle was a woven **screen**, similar to the veil, but hung on **five pillars of acacia wood** covered **with gold**, and standing on bronze bases.

7. The Bronze Altar of Burnt Offering (27:1–8)

The altar of burnt offering, also known as the bronze altar, was made **of acacia wood** covered with **bronze**. It measured seven-and-a-half feet square and four-and-a-half feet high. **Horns** protruded from each of **its four corners**. It was carried by **poles** attached to the lower **sides**.

8. The Outer Court, Pillars, and Screen (27:9–19)

Surrounding the tabernacle itself was a large area known as **the court**. This was enclosed by **woven linen . . . hangings** stretched between **bronze pillars**. The enclosure measured 150 feet long, 75 feet wide, and 7.5 feet high. The **gate** at the east end was thirty feet wide. It had a **screen** of embroidered linen, similar to the curtains of the tabernacle. Unless otherwise designated, **all the utensils of the tabernacle** were to be made **of bronze**.

9. The Anointing Oil (27:20, 21)

Oil for the lampstand was to be **pure oil of pressed olives**, a symbol of the Holy Spirit. It was **to burn continually**—that is, every evening, **"from evening until morning."** The expression **"the tabernacle of meeting"** or "the tent of meeting" (NASB) is used here of the tent that would be

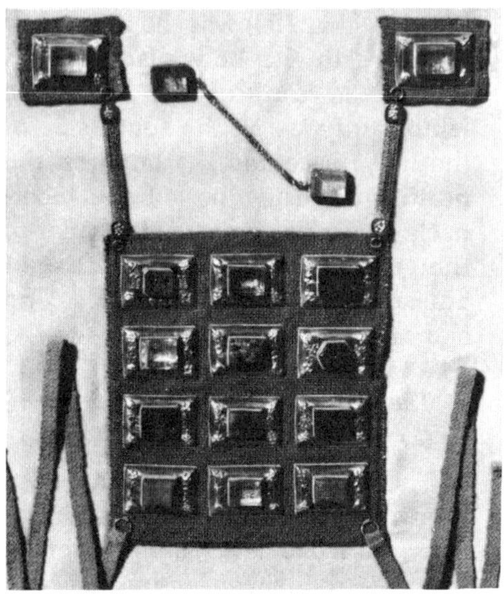

This replica of the high priest's breastplate is set with stones representing the 12 tribes of Israel. On each stone the name of one tribe is engraved.

God's dwelling place, but it is used in chapter 33:7 of a provisional tent erected by Moses.

B. The Priesthood (Chaps. 28, 29)

1. *The Garments of the Priests (Chap. 28)*

28:1, 2 Chapter 28 deals with the **garments** of the high **priest** and of his **sons**. These garments, their colors, the jewels, etc., all speak of the various glories of Christ, our Great High Priest. The family of **Aaron** was the priestly family.

28:3–29 The high **priest** had two sets of **garments**: (1) garments of glory and beauty, richly colored and intricately embroidered; (2) plain white linen garments. The former are described here (vv. 2–4). **The ephod** (vv. 6,7) was similar to an apron, with **two** sections **joined** at the shoulders and open at the sides. **The intricately woven band** (v. 8) was a belt which went around the waist just above the hem of the ephod. The **settings** (v. 13) were **of gold** filigree to hold precious stones. On each shoulder was placed an **onyx** stone engraved with **the names of . . . six** of the tribes **of Israel** (vv. 9–12). On the front of the ephod rested **the breastplate**, containing twelve precious **stones, each one** bearing the **name** of a tribe. The breastplate was attached to the ephod by gold **chains** (vv. 13–28). Thus the high priest carried the tribes **of Israel** before God on his **shoulders** (v. 12—the place of strength) and **over his heart** (the place of affection; v. 29).

28:30 The breastplate is called **the breastplate of judgment** (vv. 15, 19, 30), probably because **the Urim and Thummim** were in it and were used to determine the judgments of the Lord (Num. 27:21).

The expression **"Urim and Thummim"** means *lights* and *perfections*. We do not know exactly what these were, but we do know (as explained above) that they were connected with the breastplate and that they were used to obtain guidance from the Lord (1 Sam. 28:6).

28:31–35 The robe of the ephod was a **blue** garment worn underneath the ephod. It extended below the knees. On the **hem** were small **bells** and **pomegranates**, speaking of testimony and fruit. The **sound** of the bells had to **be heard** when **Aaron** entered or left **the holy place**.

28:36–38 On the headcovering, or **turban**, the high priest wore a golden **plate** or miter bearing the words **"HOLINESS TO THE LORD,"** which was **always** to **be on his forehead**. It was for **the iniquity of the holy things**, a reminder that even our most sacred acts are stained with sin. As Archbishop Beveridge once said, "I cannot pray but I sin. . . . My repentance needs to be repented of and my tears need to be washed with the blood of my Redeemer."[26]

28:39–43 The woven **tunic** of checkered work was a **linen** coat which the high priest wore underneath the blue robe. This had a **woven . . . sash**. Aaron's sons wore plain white **tunics**, **sashes**, and **hats . . . for glory and beauty** (v. 40). As underclothing, they wore **linen trousers**. They were clothed from head to ankles, but there was no covering on their feet. This is because they were on holy ground when they ministered to the Lord (3:5). The word rendered **"consecrate"** (v. 41) literally means *to fill the hand* (that is, with offerings).

2. *The Consecration of the Priests (Chap. 29)*

29:1–9 God ordained Aaron and his sons as the first priests. After that the only way to become a priest was by being born into the priestly tribe and family. In the church the only way to become a priest is by the *new birth* (Rev. 1:5,6). For man to ordain priests is sheer human presumption.

The ritual described here was carried out in Leviticus 8. The consecration of the priests is somewhat similar to the cleansing of lepers (Lev. 14). In both cases, sacrificial blood was applied to the person himself, teaching the necessity for expiation before sinful man can approach God.

The materials for the offerings are introduced in verses 1–3; detailed instructions are given later concerning their use. The first step in the consecration of the priests was the washing of **Aaron and his sons . . . with water** at **the door of the tabernacle** (v. 4). Second, **Aaron** was clothed with the **garments** described in the previous chapter (vv. 5, 6). Then he was anointed with **oil** (v. 7). Next, the **sons** were clothed in their priestly **tunics** (vv. 8, 9).

29:10–21 Three offerings followed: a **bull** for **a sin offering** (vv. 10–14); a **ram** for **a burnt offering** (vv. 15–18); another **ram of consecration** (vv. 19–21). Laying **hands on the head of** a sacrificial victim signified identification with it and indicated that the animal was to die in place of the offerer (v. 10). **The blood**, of course, was a picture of the blood of Christ, shed for the forgiveness of sins. **The fat** was considered the choicest part of the animal and was therefore offered to the Lord (v. 13). The first **ram** was completely burned on the altar (vv. 15–18). This speaks of Christ's complete devotion to God and His being completely offered up to God. The **blood** of the second **ram** (the **ram of consecration**) was to be **put . . . on the tip of the right ear of Aaron . . . and . . . his sons, on the thumb of their right hand**, upon the **big toe of their right foot** (v. 20), and sprinkled on their **garments** (v. 21). This signified the need of cleansing from sin in every area of human life—the **ear** for obedience to God's Word, the **hand** for action or service, and the **foot** for walk or deportment. It might seem strange that the priests' beautiful **garments** should be sprinkled with blood; atoning blood might not seem attractive in man's eyes, but it is absolutely necessary in the sight of God.

29:22–34 Next, Moses was ordered to fill the priests' **hands** with the materials necessary for sacrifice and thus authorize them to sacrifice (vv. 22–28). The first offering (vv. 22–25) was to be waved **before the Lord** and then burned **on the altar** of **burnt offering. The breast of the ram** was waved **before the Lord**, perhaps horizontally, and the shoulder or **thigh**

was heaved before the Lord, doubtless vertically. These two portions were then given to the priests for food (vv. 26–28). The waved breast speaks of God's affection for us, and the heaved shoulder symbolizes His power stretched forth in our behalf. Aaron's **garments** became the property of **his sons after him**, since the priesthood was handed down from father to son (vv. 29, 30). The food of the priests and how it was prepared is described in verses 31–34.

29:35–46 The consecration ceremony lasted **seven days**, with the sacrifices repeated **every day** and **the altar** cleansed by blood and anointed with oil (vv. 35–37). From then on, the priests were required to **offer on the altar** of burnt offering **two lambs** which were one **year** old—**one lamb . . . in the morning** and the **other** in the evening of every day **at twilight** (vv. 38–42). God then promised to meet with the people **at the . . . tabernacle**, to **dwell among** them and to **be their God** (vv. 43–46).

C. Further Instructions Concerning the Tabernacle (Chaps. 30, 31)

1. *The Altar of Incense (30:1–10)*

The **altar** of **incense** was a **gold**-plated wooden **altar** which stood in the holy place. It was eighteen inches square and three feet high. It was also known as the golden altar. On this altar, **incense** was burned both **morning** and evening, picturing the intercessory work of Christ on our behalf. Although this altar was in the holy place, it was so intimately connected with the Holy of Holies that the writer to the Hebrews possibly mentions it as being behind the second veil (Heb. 9:4, KJV), although the word in Hebrews can also be translated *censer* (NKJV).[27] The altar was carried on **poles** that were placed through **rings** that were **under the molding** on opposite **sides**.

2. *The Redemption Money (30:11–16)*

God ordered every male Israelite **twenty years old and above** to pay **half a shekel** as **a ransom for himself**. This payment, the same for **rich** and **poor**, was levied whenever there was a **census** and was used to finance **the service of the tabernacle**. It guaranteed protection against plague (v. 12). At the outset it was used to make silver sockets to support the boards of the tabernacle. Silver speaks of redemption, which is the foundation of our faith. Redemption is needed by all and is available to all on the same terms.

3. *The Laver (30:17–21)*

The **laver of bronze** stood **between** the entrance to **the tabernacle of meeting and the altar**. It was a basin where the priests could **wash their hands and their feet**. It was made of the bronze mirrors donated by the women (38:8). No dimensions are given. Any priest who handled holy things before washing was sentenced to death. This is a solemn reminder that we must be spiritually and morally clean before entering any service for the Lord (see Heb. 10:22).

4. *The Anointing Oil (30:22–33)*

A holy anointing oil was used to **anoint the tabernacle**, its furniture, and the priests themselves. It was not to be used for any other purpose. **Oil** in Scripture is often a *type of the Holy Spirit*. The anointing of the priests signifies the necessity for enduement of the Spirit in all divine service.

5. *The Incense (30:34–38)*

The **incense** was a perfume made of various **spices** that was burned on the golden altar of incense morning and evening. Like the oil, it was not to be imitated or used elsewhere.

6. *The Gifted Artisans (31:1–11)*

God appointed **gifted artisans, Bezalel**[28] and **Aholiab**, to construct **the tabernacle . . . and all** its **furniture**. They supervised other workers in this holy task (v. 6b). The repetition of **"I"** in this paragraph shows that with the divine command there is divine enablement. The Lord appoints His workers, endows them with ability and talent, and gives them a work to do for His glory (v. 6). The work is all the Lord's, but He accomplishes it through human instrumentality, then rewards His agents.

7. *The Sign of the Sabbath (31:12–18)*

31:12–17 Keeping the **Sabbath** was to be **a sign between** God and Israel. No **work** was to be done **on the seventh day**, not even the building of the tabernacle. Disobedience was punishable by **death**.

31:18 At this point the Lord **gave Moses two tablets of . . . stone** inscribed with the Law **of God**—that is, the Ten Commandments (cf. Deut. 10:4).

THE TABERNACLE: GOD'S PICTURE OF CHRIST

Basically the tabernacle speaks of Christ, the Word who became flesh and "tabernacled" among us (John 1:14, Greek).[29]

It can also be used as picturing God's way of salvation and the subsequent life and ministry of the believer.

But although it pictures the way of salvation, it was given to a people who were already in covenant relationship with God. Rather than providing a way of salvation, the tabernacle offered the means by which the people could be cleansed from outward, ritual defilement and thus be able to approach God in worship.

The tabernacle and the services connected with it were copies of things in the heavens (Heb. 8:5; 9:23, 24). This does not mean that there must be a structural or architectural likeness in heaven, but that the tabernacle pictures spiritual realities in heaven. Notice these correspondences:

The earthly sanctuary (Heb. 9:1–5)	The heavenly sanctuary (Heb. 8:2; 9:11–15)
The Holiest of all (Heb. 9:3b)	The Holiest, God's presence (Heb. 10:19)
The veil (Heb. 9:3a)	The veil, Christ's body (Heb. 10:20)
The blood of animals (Heb. 9:13)	The blood of Christ (Heb. 9:14)
The altar (Heb. 7:13; Ex. 27:1–8)	Christ, our altar (Heb. 13:10)
The high priest (Heb. 5:1–4)	Christ our Great High Priest (Heb. 4:14, 15; 5:5–10; 7:20–28; 8:1; 10:21)
The sacrifices (Heb. 10:1–4, 11)	Christ, our sacrifice (Heb. 9:23–28; 10:12)
The ark (Heb. 9:4)	The throne of grace (Heb. 4:16)
The altar of incense (Heb. 9:4, KJV)	The altar of incense in heaven (Rev. 8:3)

The Linen Curtains Forming the Outer Court (150 ft. x 75 ft.)

The curtains were made of white, fine-twined linen, symbolizing the perfect righteousness of God. They were 7½ feet high, forming a barrier that prevented man from seeing over them. This suggests man's failure to reach God's standard of righteousness (Rom. 3:23) and the sinner's inability to see or understand the things of God (1 Cor. 2:14). The curtains were held upright by 56 pillars that stood in bronze sockets and had silver hooks and bands.

The Gate

To enter the court, a person had to go through the door or gate. There was only one way of entrance, just as Christ is the only way to God (John 14:6; Acts 4:12). The gate was 30 feet wide, picturing the sufficiency of Christ for all mankind (John 6:37; Heb. 25).

The curtains forming the gate were made of white linen, embroidered with blue, purple, and scarlet. This typifies Christ as presented in the four Gospels:

Purple	Matthew	The King (Matt. 2:2)
Scarlet	Mark	The lowly Servant, suffering for sins, that are likened to scarlet in Isaiah 1:18
White	Luke	The perfect Man (Luke 3:22)
Blue	John	The heavenly One (John 3:13)

The Bronze Altar of Burnt Offering (7½ ft. sq., 4½ ft. high)

The first object in the inner court was the altar. This was the place of sacrifice. It speaks of the cross of Christ at Calvary (Heb. 9:14, 22). This is where the sinner must begin in approaching God. The altar was made of bronze and acacia wood, the incorruptible wood of the wilderness. Bronze speaks of judgment and the wood pictures Christ's sinless, incorruptible humanity. He who knew no sin bore God's judgment against our sins (2 Cor. 5:21).

The altar was hollow, with a grating halfway down, on which the animal was placed. There were four horns overlaid with bronze, one at each corner (Ex. 27:2). Apparently the sacrifice was tied to these horns (Ps. 118:27b). It was not cords or even nails that bound our Savior to the cross, but His everlasting love for us.

When an Israelite brought a burnt offering, he laid his hand on the head of the victim, identifying himself with it, and saying in this way that the animal would die in his place. It would be a substitutionary sacrifice. The animal was slain and its blood poured out, pointing forward to the blood of Christ, without which there is no forgiveness of sins (Heb. 9:22).

All except the skin was burned on the altar. Here, as so often, the type breaks down because Christ was *totally* devoted to the Father's will at Calvary.

It was a sweet aroma offering, reminding us of God's complete satisfaction with the work of Christ. And it made atonement for the offerer.

The Laver

The laver was made of bronze from the mirrors of the women (Ex. 38:3). J. H. Brown remarks: "They handed over those things that were used for self-gratification, those things that in some measure ministered to the gratification of the flesh." Self-judgment must precede worship (1 Cor. 11:31).

The laver was for the priests. It spoke of the necessity of cleansing for service (Isa. 52:11). The priests were bathed once on entering their office (Lev. 8:6). After that, they were required to wash their hands and feet regularly. One bath—many cleansings. Today all believers are priests (1 Pet. 2:5, 9). We need the bath of regeneration only once (John 3:5; 13:10; Tit. 3:5). But we need to constantly wash our hands (for service) and our feet (for the godly walk) (John 13:10). We do this with the water of the Word (Ps. 119:9–11; John 15:3; Eph. 5:26).

The laver may have had an upper basin for washing the hands and a lower one for washing the feet. The Bible does not describe the exact form or size of the laver.

The Tabernacle Itself (15 ft. x 45 ft.)

The structure itself was outwardly plain but inwardly beautiful. Everything inside was covered with gold or was embroidered work. It suggests Christ, who tabernacled among us (John 1:14); He had no beauty outwardly that we should desire Him (Isa. 53:2b), but inwardly He is altogether lovely.

There were four coverings in the following order from the inside out:

Fine embroidered linen	The righteousness and beauty of Christ.
Goat's hair	The atonement of Christ, who became our Scapegoat (cf. Lev. 16).
Ram's skins, dyed red	The consecration of Christ (cf. the ram of consecration, Ex. 29:19–22).
Badger skins	These are also translated porpoise skins, dolphin skins, and hides of sea cows. They protected the tabernacle from the elements, suggesting Christ's guarding His people from outward evil.

The Boards

Some think these were lattice frames rather than solid boards. In any case, they picture believers, forming a unified habitation of God in the Spirit (Eph. 2:22). They were made of acacia wood overlaid with gold, representing our humanity and our position in Christ. God sees us in Him. The boards were 15 feet high and were joined together by five horizontal bars covered with gold (Ex. 26:26–28). The middle one went through the boards, perhaps a type of the Holy Spirit. Each board was held in place by tenons in two silver sockets. Silver speaks of redemption (cf. Ex. 30:15 where the silver shekel was the atonement money). The believer's foundation is the redemptive work of Christ (1 Pet. 1:18, 19).

The Holy Place

The veil leading to the holy place suggests Christ as the way to communion with God (Eph. 2:18; 3:12). There was no chair in the holy place because the priests' work was never completed. Contrast the once-for-all work of Christ (Heb. 10:12).

The Table of Showbread (36 in. long, 18 in. wide, 27 in. high; on the north side)

The table was made of acacia wood overlaid with gold, picturing the humanity and deity of our Lord. There were twelve unleavened loaves on the table, symbolizing God's people as they appear before God in association with Christ. The bread was surrounded by two crowns of gold, just as we are kept secure by the crowned, glorified Christ.

The Lampstand (Weighed 75 lbs. No dimensions given; on the south side)

Made of beaten gold, it had a base and a stem rising from it, out from which rose seven arms with an oil lamp on top of each. It was the only source of light in the tabernacle. It may picture the Holy Spirit in His ministry of glorifying Christ (John 16:14) or it may speak of Christ as the One who is the light of heaven (Rev. 21:23) and the source of all spiritual light (John 8:12). The pure gold speaks of deity.

The lamps burned from evening until morning (Ex. 27:21; 1 Sam. 3:3).

The Altar of Incense (18 in. sq. and 36 in. high; before the veil in the center)

It was made of acacia wood and gold, typifying the humanity and deity of Christ. It pictures the glorified Christ interceding for His people (Heb. 7:24–26; Rev. 8:3, 4). The incense speaks of the fragrance of His Person and work. The fire had to come from the altar of burnt offering, the fragrance of Christ's offering of Himself without spot to God.

The incense was made of stacte, onycha, galbanum, and frankincense—all combining to make one fragrance—the sweet aroma of Christ (Eph. 5:2).

The Most Holy Place

The veil leading to the Most Holy Place speaks of the flesh of Christ (Heb. 10:19–22), rent in death at Calvary (Luke 23:45). Whereas only the priests could enter the holy place, and only the high priest could enter the Holiest on only one day of the year, believers now have access to God's presence at any and all times (Heb. 10:19–22).

The Ark (3¾ ft. long, 2¼ ft. wide and high)

This was a chest of acacia wood plated with gold. It spoke of the throne of God. There are two ways of thinking of its contents, one man-centered and somewhat negative, and one Christ-centered, and very positive:

First, it contained three memorials of rebellion (manna, Ex. 16:2, 3; the law, Ex. 32:19; Aaron's rod, Num. 17:1–13) and thus may picture Christ bearing the curse because of our rebellion.

Or the manna may picture *Christ* as the Bread of God; the law as that expression of God's holiness which the Lord magnified and made glorious; and Aaron's rod as Christ in resurrection, a Priest of God's own choosing.

The Mercy Seat

The mercy seat was a lid for the ark. On top were two cherubim, made of beaten gold, guardians of God's throne and defenders of His righteousness. They looked down on the blood that was sprinkled before the ark and on the mercy seat. The blood of Christ satisfies God's righteousness and hides all our transgressions from view. Thus a judgment seat becomes a mercy seat. Christ is our Mercy Seat (same word as *propitiation*, 1 Jn. 2:2). God meets the sinner in Christ.

The Glory Cloud

When the tabernacle was completed, the Lord appeared on the mercy seat in a glory cloud, also known as the *Shekinah*; from the Hebrew word for *dwell*. This was a visible symbol of His glory.‡

D. An Outbreak of Idolatry (Chaps. 32, 33)

1. The Golden Calf (32:1–10)

Impatient at Moses' delay in returning to them, **the people** asked **Aaron** to **make** an idol for them. He meekly complied by converting their **golden earrings** into a golden **molded calf**, an act that was expressly forbidden (Ex. 20:4). Then they broke out in revelry, worshiping the idol and eating, drinking, and playing immorally. They professed to be worshiping **the Lord** (v. 5), but by means of the calf. God had blessed His people with gold when they left Egypt (12:35, 36), but the blessing turned into a curse through the sinful hearts of the people. God informed **Moses** what was going on at the foot of the mountain (vv. 7, 8) and threatened to destroy **this people** (vv. 9, 10).

2. The Intercession and Anger of Moses (32:11–35)

32:11–13 In his reply, **Moses** stands out as one of the great intercessors of the Bible. Notice the strong arguments he uses: The people were the Lord's **people** (vv. 11, 12). God had cared for them enough to deliver them from **Egypt** (v. 11). **The Egyptians** would gloat if God did to His people what the Egyptians had been unable to do (v. 12). God must be true to the covenants He made with the patriarchs (v. 13).

32:14 "So the LORD relented of the harm . . ." (v. 14). The word *harm* means punishment in this context. In response to the intercession of Moses, the Lord turned away from the punishment which He otherwise **would** have inflicted on **His people**.

32:15–20 Moses descended the mountain with **the two tablets of the Testimony**, met **Joshua** on the way, and **came** to the people as they were carrying on their sensual, idolatrous feast. In righteous **anger, he . . . broke** the tablets of the law as a witness of what the people had already done. He then **ground** the golden **calf . . . to powder, scattered it on the water and made the** people **drink it** (v. 20)—perhaps a suggestion that our sins return to us as a bitter potion.

32:21–24 When **Moses** asked Aaron **what** the **people** had done to deserve this treatment, Aaron explained to him what had happened, implying that the golden **calf** had come **out** of **the fire** rather mysteriously (v. 24). It was only because of the intercession of Moses that the Lord did not kill Aaron (Deut. 9:19, 20).

32:25–29 Some of **the people** were still carrying on without restraint. When Moses called for loyal followers, the tribe of **Levi** responded and proceeded to slay with **the sword** those who were "out of control" (NASB). Even close relatives were not spared (vv. 25–29). Here the broken law brought death to **three thousand . . . people**. At Pentecost the gospel of grace brought salvation to 3,000 people. The heroic loyalty of the Levites may be why theirs was chosen to be the priestly tribe (see v. 29).

32:30–35 Moses returned up the mountain to meet **the LORD**, thinking that he might **make atonement for** the people's **sin** (vv. 30–32). The Lord's answer was twofold: First, He would punish the people who made the calf (He did this by sending a plague—v. 35); second, He would send His **Angel** to **go before** Moses as he led **the people to the** Promised Land. The character of Moses shines out in verse 32—he was willing to die for his people. **"Blot me out of Your book"** is a figurative way of saying "end my life."[30] God spared Moses but He did not spare His beloved Son. How like our Lord who died, the Just for the unjust!

3. *The Repentance of the People (33:1–6)*

The Lord refused to accompany the sinful Israelites on their journey to Canaan, **lest** He be compelled to destroy them **on the way**. Instead, He would send an **Angel** as His representative. **When the people heard this bad news, they mourned** and **stripped themselves of their ornaments**, such as had been used to make the golden calf, and never wore them from **Mount Horeb** onward.

4. *Moses' Tent of Meeting (33:7–11)*

The **tent** mentioned in verse 7 was *not* the tabernacle, which had not yet been erected, but a provisional tent **pitched** by **Moses** and called here **"the tabernacle** (tent) **of meeting."** Individuals who desired to seek the Lord could go there, **outside the camp**. The camp itself had been defiled by the sin of the people, so the tent was situated **outside**. When **Moses entered the** tent, the pillar of cloud descended, indicating God's presence. Verse 11 cannot mean that Moses saw God in His essential being. It simply means that he had direct, **face to face**, unhindered communion with God. It is worth noting that *Joshua*, then **a young man**, did **not depart from** the **tabernacle**. Perhaps this was the secret of his later spiritual success.

5. The Prayer of Moses (33:12–23)

33:12–17 Moses asked for God's presence to lead His **people** to Canaan. Then the Lord graciously promised that His **Presence** would **go with** them. Moses insisted that nothing short of this would do. Like Noah, Moses had **found grace in** the Lord's **sight** and received his request. "Safety does not consist in the absence of danger but in the presence of God."

33:18–23 Next Moses asked for a sight of God's **glory**. God replied by promising to reveal Himself as a God of grace and **compassion** (see Ex. 34:6, 7). Moses could not **see** God's **face . . . and live**, but he would be permitted to **stand on** a **rock** while God's **glory** passed **by**, and he would see an appearance of God's **back**. This is figurative language, of course, since God does not have a body (John 4:24). As Hywel Jones put it, "Moses is to see the afterglow which is a reliable indication of what the full splendor is to be."[31]

No one can see God's face and live (v. 20). This means that no one can look upon the unveiled glory of God; He dwells "in unapproachable light, whom no man has seen or can see" (1 Tim. 6:16). In that sense, no one has seen God at any time (1 Jn. 4:12). How then do we explain passages in the Bible where people saw God and did not die? For example, Hagar (Gen. 16:13); Jacob (Gen. 32:30); Moses, Aaron, Nadab, Abihu, and seventy of the elders of Israel (Ex. 24:9–11); Gideon (Judg. 6:22,23); Manoah and his wife (Judg. 13:22); Isaiah (Isa. 6:1); Ezekiel (Ezek. 1:26, cf. 10:20); John (Rev. 1:17).

The answer is that these people saw God as represented by the Lord Jesus Christ. Sometimes He appeared as the Angel of the LORD (see Judges 6 for a discussion of this doctrine), sometimes as a Man, and once manifested Himself as a Voice (Ex. 24:9–11; cf. Deut. 4:12). The only begotten Son, who is in the bosom of the Father, has fully declared God (John 1:18). Christ is the brightness of God's glory and the express image of His Person (Heb. 1:3). That is why He could say, "He who has seen Me has seen the Father" (John 14:9).

E. The Covenant Renewed (34:1—35:3)

34:1–9 Again **Moses** alone was called **up . . . to Mount Sinai**, this time with **two tablets of stone** which he himself had prepared. There the Lord revealed Himself as a **merciful and gracious** God, **longsuffering, and abounding in goodness and truth** (vv. 6, 7).

Three different words are used in verse 7 for wrongdoing. **Iniquity** has to do with perverting the ways of the Lord. **Transgression** means rebellion against God. **Sin** is literally "offense," primarily by missing the mark which God has set. They all convey the idea of falling short of the glory of God (Rom. 3:23). The Israelites should all have died for having broken the law of God, but God spared them in **mercy**. Moses **worshiped** the Lord and pled for His presence and **grace** on the basis of His people's unworthiness (vv. 8, 9).

34:10–17 God then renewed the **covenant**, promising to do marvels for Israel in **driving out** the inhabitants of Canaan. He cautioned them against intermingling with the heathen or adopting their idolatrous practices. Asherim were obscene images, or phallic idols, symbols of fertility.

Because God had made a **covenant** with His people, they were not to **make a covenant with the inhabitants of the land**. It is impossible to be joined to God and to idols at the same time (see 1 Cor. 10:21).

34:18–27 God then repeated instructions concerning **the Feast of Unleavened Bread** (v. 18); the consecration of **the firstborn** (vv. 19, 20); the Sabbath (v. 21); the **Feast of Weeks** and the **Feast of Ingathering** (v. 22). **All** males were to **appear before the Lord** for the **three** annual feasts mentioned in 23:14–17 (vv. 23,24). Note in verse 24 that God promised to control the wills of the Canaanites so that they would not try to seize the property of the Jewish men when the latter went to Jerusalem **three times** a **year**. After repeating other rules (vv. 25, 26), **the Lord** ordered Moses to **write** down the **words** He had just spoken in verses 11–26 (v. 27). Then the Lord Himself **wrote . . . the Ten Commandments . . . on the tablets of stone** (v. 28; cf. v. 1 and Deut. 10:1–4).

34:28–35 After **forty days and forty nights** on the mountain, **Moses came down** with the **two tablets in** his **hand** (vv. 28, 29a). He was unaware that **his face** was shining as a result of being in the Lord's presence (vv. 29b, 30). People **were afraid to come near him**. After delivering the **commandments** of the Lord to **Israel, he put a veil on his face** (vv. 31–33). Verse 33 (NKJV) reads **"And when Moses had finished speaking . . ."** instead of "Till . . ." (KJV). Paul explains in 2 Corinthians 3:13 that Moses veiled his face so the people would not see the fading glory of the law, the legal dispensation.

35:1–3 Then Moses gathered all the congregation . . . together and repeated the law of the **Sabbath** to them.

F. Preparation of the Tabernacle Furnishings (35:4—38:31)

1. The People's Gifts and the Gifted People (35:4—36:7)

35:4–20 Moses gave instructions for a free-will **offering to the Lord** consisting of materials for the building of **the tabernacle** (vv. 4–9). He also called for **gifted artisans** to make the various parts (vv. 10–19). God had two buildings for worship, the tabernacle and the temple. Both were paid for in advance. God moved the hearts of His people to supply what was needed (vv. 5, 21, 22, 26, 29). Our giving and service should likewise be voluntary and ungrudging.

35:21—36:1 Many of the people responded generously with the treasures they had brought from Egypt (vv. 21–29). Those who had given gold for the calf lost it all. Those who invested in the tabernacle had the joy of seeing their wealth used for the glory of Jehovah.

Moses publicly named **Bezalel** and **Aholiab** as the ones whom God had appointed **to work in all manner of artistic workmanship**. They also had **the ability to teach** others (35:30—36:1).

36:2–7 The skilled workers began the task of **making the sanctuary**, but the people brought so much material **each morning** that Moses had to restrain them **from bringing** more.

From verse 8 of chapter 36 to the end of chapter 39 we find a detailed account of the construction of the tabernacle and its furnishings. The repetition of so much detail reminds us that God never tires of those things which speak to Him about His beloved Son.

2. The Curtains Covering the Tabernacle (36:8–19)

The inner **curtains**, made **of fine linen**, were called **"the tabernacle"**

Ark of the Covenant
(Ex. 25:10–22)
The ark was most sacred of all the furniture in the tabernacle. Here the Hebrews kept a copy of the Ten Commandments, which summarized the whole covenant.

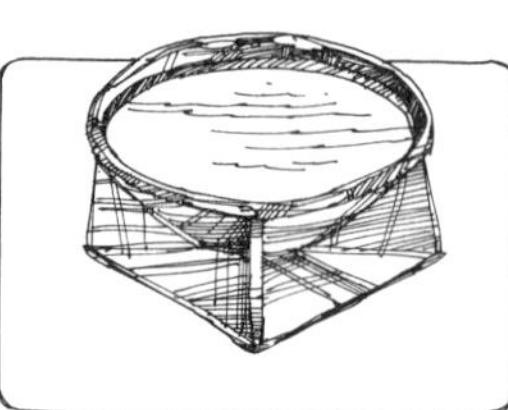

Bronze Laver
(Ex. 30:17–21)
It was to the laver of bronze that the priests would come for cleansing. They must be pure to enter the presence of God.

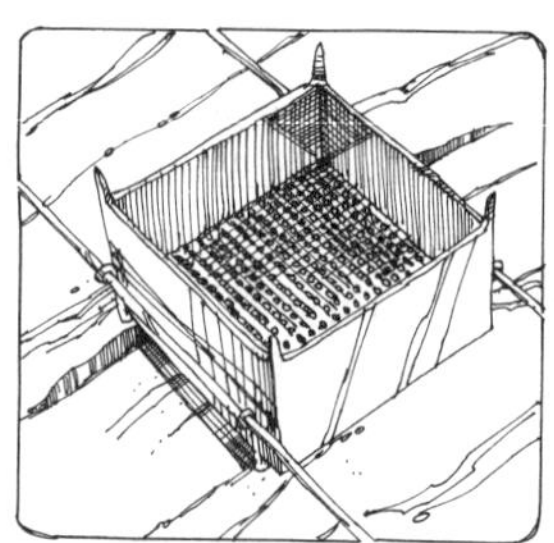

Altar of Burnt Offering
(Ex. 27:1–8)
Animal sacrifices were offered on this altar, located in the court in front of the tabernacle. The blood of the sacrifice was sprinkled on the four horns of the altar.

Golden Lampstand
(Ex. 25:31–40)
The gold lampstand stood in the holy place, opposite the table of showbread. It held seven lamps, flat bowls in which a wick lay with one end in the oil of the bowl and the lighted end hanging out.

Table of Showbread
(Ex. 25:23–30)
The table of showbread was a stand on which the offerings were placed. Always in God's presence on the table were the 12 loaves of bread representing the 12 tribes.

Altar of Incense
(Ex. 30:1–10)
The altar of incense inside the tabernacle was much smaller than the altar of burnt offering outside. The incense burned on the altar was a perfume of a sweet smelling aroma.

The Furniture of the Tabernacle

(v. 8). Next were **curtains of goats' hair, "the tent"** (v. 14). The curtains **of ram skins** and **badger** skins (or possibly seal or porpoise skins) were called "the **covering**" (v. 19).

3. The Boards for the Three Sides (36:20–30)

These **boards** were made **of acacia wood**, the only kind of wood used in the tabernacle. Acacia trees flourished in dry places, were very beautiful, and produced wood that was practically indestructible. Likewise, the Lord Jesus was a root out of dry ground (Isa. 53:2), was morally beautiful, and is the Eternal One.

4. The Bars Which Held the Boards Together (36:31–34)

Four of the **bars** were visible, one invisible because it passed **through the** center of the **boards**. The invisible bar is a good picture of the Holy

Spirit, binding believers together into "a holy temple in the Lord" (Eph. 2:21, 22). The four other bars may suggest the life, love, position, and confession that are common to all God's people.

5. The Veil Leading to the Most Holy Place (36:35, 36)

This **veil** represents the flesh of the Lord Jesus (Heb. 10:20), torn on Calvary in order to open the way of approach to God for us. The **cherubim** on the veil are thought to represent guardians of the righteous throne of God.

6. The Screen Leading to the Holy Place (36:37, 38)

This **screen** was made of the same material as the gate of the court and the veil mentioned above, and pictures Christ as the way to God.

7. The Ark of the Covenant (37:1–5)

The ark was a chest made **of acacia wood . . . overlaid . . . with pure gold**. It pointed to the humanity and deity of our Lord. It contained the tablets of the Law, a golden jar of manna, and Aaron's rod that budded. If applied to Christ, these things speak of Him as the One who said, "Your law is within my heart" (Ps. 40:8b); as the bread of God come down from heaven (John 6:33); and as the Priest of God's choosing, risen from the dead (Heb. 7:24–26). If applied to the people of Israel, they were all memorials of failure and rebellion.

8. The Mercy Seat (37:6–9)

The **mercy seat** was God's throne, the place of His dwelling on earth. As the golden **cherubim** looked down upon it, they did not see the Law (which Israel had broken) or the jar of manna and Aaron's rod, both of which were associated with rebellions by Israel. Rather, they saw the sprinkled blood, which enabled God to be merciful to rebellious sinners. The mercy seat typifies Christ as the One "whom God set forth as a *mercy seat*" (Rom. 3:25, lit.).[32] . . . The mercy seat was the lid of the ark.

9. The Table of Showbread (37:10–16)

The **table** of showbread held twelve loaves, "typical of Israel's place before God in the acceptability of Christ, who as the true Aaron maintains them even now before God."[33] The loaves may also speak of God's provision for each of the twelve tribes.

10. The Golden Lampstand and Its Accessories (37:17–24)

Some see the **lampstand of pure gold** as a type of Christ, the true Light of the world (John 8:12). Others prefer to view it as picturing the Holy Spirit, whose mission is to glorify Christ, since it illuminates all that speaks of Christ in the holy place. Still others see it as typifying Christ in union with believers. The middle **shaft** is unique because the other **six branches** come out of it, **three branches** on each side; yet they are all made of one piece of gold.

11. The Altar of Incense (37:25–28)

The **altar** of **incense** speaks of Christ being a perpetual sweet aroma of God. It also suggests the present ministry of the Lord Jesus, interceding for us in heaven.

12. The Anointing Oil and the Incense (37:29)

Oil typifies the Holy Spirit, and the **incense** speaks of the ever-fragrant perfections of our Lord, bringing delight to His Father.

13. *The Altar of Burnt Offering (38:1–7)*

The altar of burnt offering represents the cross, where the Lord Jesus offered Himself to God as a complete sacrifice. There can be no access to God apart from His sacrificial death.

14. *The Laver (38:8)*

The laver speaks of the present ministry of Christ, cleansing His people by the washing of water with the Word (Eph. 5:26). The priests were required to wash their hands and feet before performing any service. So our actions and our walk must be clean before we can serve the Lord effectively. The laver was made from the bronze mirrors of the serving women. Glorification of self gave way to service for God.

15. *The Outer Court, Pillars, and Screen (38:9–31)*

38:9–20 The outer **court** around the tabernacle consisted of white **linen hangings**, fifty-six **pillars** with **bronze sockets** and **silver hooks**, and an embroidered **screen** at the **gate**. The white linen speaks of the righteousness which bars the unbelieving sinner from approaching God, but which also separates and protects the believer inside. The only entrance to the court was the **gate**, made of **fine woven linen** and embroidered with **blue, purple, and scarlet thread**. This suggests Christ ("I am the door," John 10:9) here as the only way of approach to God. The fine linen is a picture of His spotless purity; the blue, of His heavenly origin; the purple, of His regal glory; the scarlet, of His suffering for sin.

38:21–23 The names of the skilled workers are repeated. Whenever God has a task to do, He raises up people to do it. For the tabernacle He called and equipped **Bezalel** and **Aholiab**. For the building of the temple He used Hiram to supply materials. For the building of the church, he used His chosen workmen, Peter and Paul.

38:24–31 The materials used in building the tabernacle are carefully tabulated. They would be valued in the millions of dollars in today's currency. We too can dedicate our possessions to the work of the Lord, saying in effect, "Take my silver and my gold; not a mite would I withhold."[34]

G. Preparation of the Priests' Garments (Chap. 39)

39:1–7 Now we come to the preparation of the priests' **garments**. We are struck at the outset by the repetition of the four colors. Some see them as representing the manifold glories of Christ as seen in the four Gospels: **purple**—Matthew—the King; **scarlet**—Mark—the Suffering Servant; **white**—Luke—the sinless Man; **blue**—John—the Son of God come down from heaven. The **gold** threads in the ephod speak of Christ's deity (v. 3). On each shoulder-strap of the **ephod** was an **onyx** stone engraved with the names of six of the tribes of Israel.

39:8–21 The **breastplate** held **twelve** precious **stones**, one for **each** of the **twelve tribes** (vv. 10–14). So it is with our Great High Priest. The gospel preacher Peter Pell expressed it beautifully. "The strength of His shoulders and the love of His heart are thus bearing the names of God's people before the presence of God."

39:22–26 **The robe of the ephod** was a **blue** garment worn under the ephod. **On** its **hem** were **bells of pure gold** and **pomegranates of blue, purple, and scarlet**. These speak of spiritual fruit and testimony as they are found in our Great High Priest and as they should be reproduced in us.

39:27–29 The linen **tunics** were the first garments that the priests put on (Lev. 8:7). Then came the garments of glory. God first clothes the repentant sinner with His own righteousness (2 Cor. 5:21). When the Lord Jesus returns, He will clothe His own people in garments of glory (Phil. 3:20, 21). Righteousness must precede glorification.

39:30, 31 The gold **plate** on the high priest's turban was engraved like **a signet** with the words **"HOLINESS TO THE LORD"** so that he might bear the iniquity of the holy things (Ex. 28:38). All that we do is stained with sin, but our worship and service are purged from all imperfection by our Great High Priest before they reach the Father.

39:32–43 When the people **finished** the work **and brought** the parts of **the tabernacle** to Moses, he inspected them and found that **all the work** had been made exactly according to God's specifications. **And Moses blessed** the people.

H. Erection of the Tabernacle (Chap. 40)

40:1–8 God commanded that **the tabernacle** be **set up** on the first day of the year (vv. 1, 2); this was about a year after the Exodus and eight and a half months after Israel's arrival at Sinai. He also described where each piece of furniture should be placed, (see Figure 4 at Ex. 26).

40:9–17 In verses 9–15, instructions were repeated for **anointing . . . the tabernacle**, its furnishings, and the high priest **and his sons**. The instructions were carried out on the first day of the first month, almost one year after the Israelites had left Egypt (vv. 16, 17).

40:18–33 So Moses raised up the tabernacle . . . This paragraph tells how the great lawgiver carried out all the detailed instructions **as the LORD had commanded Moses** for each part of the structure itself, as well as for each item of furniture.

Last of all Moses **raised up the court all around the tabernacle**. Then come the climactic words of completion of an important task well done: **So Moses finished the work.**

40:34–38 The glory **cloud** descended on and filled **the tabernacle** so that **Moses was not able to enter**. This cloud was to accompany the people on their journeys. They were to move only when **the cloud** moved. When it stopped, they were to stop also (vv. 34–38). As a member of the tribe of Levi, Moses was apparently qualified to perform priestly functions until Aaron and his sons were invested with this responsibility (Lev. 8).

And so Exodus is the history of God's people during the year between their deliverance from Egypt and the erection of the tabernacle at Mount Sinai. The book is filled with beautiful pictures of Christ and His moral perfections. It is our responsibility to worship this Christ of glory and to live in the light of His holiness.

ENDNOTES

[1] (2:9, 10) The Hebrew *māshāh*, "draw out" may be actually a bilingual play on words. The Hebrews used puns even in serious situations, such as the naming of children. (See, for example, the naming of Jacob's sons in Genesis 29, 30.)

[2] (2:9, 10) C. H. Mackintosh, *Genesis to Deuteronomy*, p. 144.

[3] (3:1–4) Appropriately, the Scottish Covenanters adopted the burning bush

as their emblem, with the Latin motto below: *"Nec consummaretur"* ("Yet it was not consumed").

[4] (3:6) R. Alan Cole, *Exodus: An Introduction and Commentary*, p. 66.

[5] (3:7–12) J. Oswald Sanders, further documentation unavailable.

[6] (3:13, 14) Some Bibles, such as the Moffatt Version, translate the name by "the Eternal" (cf. also Louis Segond's French version: "l' éternel").

[7] (5:2–14) Cole, *Exodus*, p. 82. The author attempts to reproduce the contemptuous attitude of the taskmasters in English by the translation "stub themselves stubble" (v. 12).

[8] (8:20–24) The Septuagint, which was produced in Egypt and may reflect local knowledge and Jewish tradition, translates by *dog-fly* (*kynomuia*), a gadfly with a painful bite. See Cole, *Exodus*, pp. 93, 94, for more details.

[9] (10:29) Matthew Henry, "Exodus," in *Matthew Henry's Commentary on the Whole Bible*, I:314.

[10] (12:11–20) Cole, *Exodus*, p. 108.

[11] (13:17–20) C. F. Pfeiffer, *Baker's Bible Atlas*, pp. 73, 74.

[12] (13:21, 22) Henry, "Exodus," I:328.

[13] (14:15–18) Henry, "Exodus," I:332.

[14] (15:1–21) Dr. H. C. Woodring, unpublished notes, Emmaus Bible School.

[15] (15:1–21) Henry, "Exodus," I:335, 336.

[16] (16:1–19) The name is not related to the English word *sin*.

[17] (19:1–9) D. L. Moody, *Notes From My Bible*, pp. 33, 34.

[18] (Essay) *The New Scofield Study Bible, New King James Version*, p. 4.

[19] (Essay) The old charge that dispensationalists believe in "seven different ways to get saved" is totally false.

[20] (Essay) Some do accept one of the ordinances.

[21] (21:1–6) This is the second stanza of Bishop Handley C. G. Moule's hymn, "My Glorious Victor, Prince Divine," *Hymns of Truth and Praise*, #535.

[22] (23:18, 19) Orthodox Jews have two complete sets of china: one for meat products and one for milk products. To discourage Jews from eating meat and milk products in the same meal some cafeterias in Israel force one to go through two lines to have both. One Jerusalem cafeteria visited by the editor of this volume actually had the meat and milk lines on separate floors!

[23] (23:20–33) Henry, "Exodus," I:376.

[24] (25:17–22) The word *cherub* may come from a Semitic root meaning "bless," "praise," or "adore," but it is more commonly held to be from the Hebrew *kārav, draw near*. Thus cherubim are "covering ones" or those who draw near as protectors.

[25] (26:14) The reason for the variety of translations is that we do not know for sure which animal skin the Hebrew word refers to.

[26] (28:36–38) Archbishop Beveridge, further documentation unavailable.

[27] (30:1–10) The Greek word *thumiatērion* literally means "place (or thing) for incense." Hence it could refer to the incense altar or to the censer which was taken behind the veil on the Day of Atonement, filled with incense from the altar.

[28] (31:1–11) It is noteworthy that the national art academy in modern Israel is named after Bezalel.

[29] (Essay) The typology of the tabernacle is widely held among evangelical believers, though obviously there is not complete agreement on all details. Some Christians accept only those types that are mentioned specifically in the NT, chiefly in Hebrews. See Genesis 42 for a brief discussion of typology.

[30] (32:30–35) Some believe that, like Paul fifteen centuries later, Moses was willing to be accursed and lost if it would save his fellow Israelites.

[31] (33:18–23) Hywel R. Jones, further documentation unavailable.

[32] (37:6–9) The same Greek word, *hilastērion*, means both *propitiation (satisfaction by sacrifice)* and *place of propitiation* (i.e., the mercy seat).

[33] (37:10–16) G. Morrish, *New and Concise Bible Dictionary*, p. 754.

[34] (38:24–31) It is much easier to *sing* this line from Frances Ridley Havergal's great spiritual hymn, "Take My Life and Let It Be," than it is to *practice* it!

BIBLIOGRAPHY

Borland, James A. "Exodus." In *Liberty Bible Commentary*. Lynchburg, VA: The Old-Time Gospel Hour, 1982.

Cole, R. Alan. *Exodus: An Introduction and Commentary*. The Tyndale Old Testament Commentaries. Downers Grove, IL: InterVarsity Press, 1973.

Dennett, Edward. *Typical Teachings of Exodus*. Reprint. Denver: Wilson Foundation, n.d.

Henry, Matthew. "Exodus." In *Matthew Henry's Commentary on the Whole Bible*. Vol. 1. *Genesis to Deuteronomy*. McLean, VA: MacDonald Publishing Company, n.d.

Keil, C. F. and Delitzsch, F. "Exodus." In *Biblical Commentary on the Old Testament*. Vols. 1, 2. Grand Rapids: Wm. B. Eerdmans Publishing Co., 1971.

Lange, John Peter. "Exodus." In *Commentary on the Holy Scriptures, Critical, Doctrinal and Homiletical*. Vol. 2. Reprint (24 vols. in 12). Grand Rapids: Zondervan Publishing House, 1980.

Pell, Peter, Jr. *The Tabernacle* (Correspondence Course). Oak Park, IL: Emmaus Bible School, 1957.

Ridout, Samuel. *Lectures on the Tabernacle*. New York: Loizeaux Brothers, Inc., 1973.

Rosen, Moishe and Ceil. *Christ in the Passover*. Chicago: Moody Press, n.d.

LEVITICUS

Introduction

"There is no book, in the whole compass of that inspired Volume which the Holy Ghost has given us, that contains more of the very words of God than Leviticus. *It is God that is the direct speaker on almost every page; His gracious words are recorded in the form wherein they were uttered. This consideration cannot fail to send us to the study of it with singular interest and attention."*

—Andrew Bonar

I. Unique Place in the Canon

J. N. Darby once warned of the dire results if believers grow bored with holiness. Holiness is the main theme of Leviticus, and this book certainly is the hardest one for many Christians to read. Of course, if the instructions are merely taken as details of ancient Jewish sacrificial rituals and laws to maintain holiness in everyday life and separation from pagan peoples, the blessing will be limited. Once see, however, that every detail of the sacrifices pictures the perfection of Christ's person and work, and there is much to meditate upon. Further blessing comes from correlating Leviticus with its NT counterpart, The Epistle to the Hebrews.

II. Authorship

Twenty of the twenty-seven chapters in Leviticus and about thirty-five other paragraphs start with "And the Lord spoke to Moses, saying . . ." or a similar, equivalent expression. Until fairly modern times most people who professed Judaism or Christianity accepted these words at face value. Our Lord Himself refers to Leviticus 13:49—a leper showing himself to the priest and making an offering—as "those things which Moses commanded" (Mark 1:44). Today, however, it is fashionable in many circles to deny or at least to question Mosaic authorship, not only of Leviticus, but of the whole Pentateuch.

Since we believe the traditional view is not only true but important as well, the issue is taken up in some detail in our Introduction to the Pentateuch, which should be read carefully.

III. Date

Accepting the Mosaic authorship of Leviticus and the evidence within the Pentateuch, we suggest that the book was revealed to Moses during the fifty-day period after the tabernacle was set up (Ex. 40:17), and before the Israelites left Sinai (Num. 10:11). The exact year of writing is unknown, but somewhere between 1450 and 1410 B.C. is indicated.

IV. Background and Theme

An easy way to remember the contents of Leviticus is to associate its name with the word "Levites" or "priests," and then realize that the book is a manual for the priests. Exodus ended with the setting up of the tabernacle in the wilderness. Now the priests and Levites need instruction on how to carry out the sacrifices associated with that structure and with some other rituals as well (e.g., cleansing "leprous" houses).

In Exodus we saw Israel delivered from Egypt and set apart as God's special possession. In Leviticus we see how they are to be separated from sin and uncleanness in order to approach God in the sanctuary. Holiness becomes the rule of the camp. Both in the OT and the NT God demands that His people be holy because He is holy. This poses a serious problem, since man by nature and by practice is unholy. The solution lies in blood atonement (Lev. 17:11). In the OT there were animal sacrifices that looked forward to the once-for-all sacrifice of the Lamb of God, as revealed in the NT, especially in Hebrews.

OUTLINE

I. TYPES OF OFFERINGS (1:1—6:7)
  A. The Burnt Offering (Chap. 1)
  B. The Grain Offering (Chap. 2)
  C. The Peace Offering (Chap. 3)
  D. The Sin Offering (4:1—5:13)
  E. The Trespass Offering (5:14—6:7)

II. LAWS OF THE OFFERINGS (6:8—7:38)

III. CONSECRATION OF THE PRIESTS (Chaps. 8—10)
  A. Investiture of the Priests by Moses (Chap. 8)
  B. Offerings Presented by Aaron (Chap. 9)
  C. Nadab and Abihu's Sacrilege (Chap. 10)

IV. THE CLEAN AND THE UNCLEAN (Chaps. 11—15)
  A. Clean and Unclean Foods (Chap. 11)
  B. Purification after Childbirth (Chap. 12)
  C. The Diagnosis of Leprosy (Chap. 13)
  D. The Cleansing of Leprosy (Chap. 14)
  E. Purification after Bodily Secretions (Chap. 15)

V. THE DAY OF ATONEMENT (Chap. 16)

VI. LAWS CONCERNING SACRIFICE (Chap. 17)

VII. LAWS CONCERNING PERSONAL CONDUCT (Chaps. 18—22)
  A. Laws of Sexual Purity (Chap. 18)
  B. Laws of Everyday Life (Chap. 19)
  C. Punishment for Gross Offenses (Chap. 20)
  D. Conduct of the Priests (Chaps. 21, 22)

VIII. THE FEASTS OF THE LORD (Chap. 23)
  A. The Sabbath (23:1–3)
  B. The Passover (23:4, 5)

C. The Feast of Unleavened Bread (23:6–8)
D. The Feast of Firstfruits (23:9–14)
E. The Feast of Weeks (23:15–22)
F. The Feast of Trumpets (23:23–25)
G. The Day of Atonement (23:26–32)
H. The Feast of Tabernacles (23:33-44)

IX. CEREMONIAL AND MORAL LEGISLATION (Chap. 24)

X. THE SABBATICAL YEAR AND THE YEAR OF JUBILEE (Chap. 25)

XI. BLESSINGS AND CURSINGS (Chap. 26)
A. The Blessings for Obedience to God (26:1–13)
B. The Curses for Disobedience to God (26:14–39)
C. Restoration through Confession and Repentance (26:40-46)

XII. VOWS AND TITHES (Chap. 27)

Commentary

I. TYPES OF OFFERINGS (1:1—6:7)

A. The Burnt Offering (Chap. 1)

Leviticus opens with **the Lord** calling **to Moses**, speaking **to him from** the **tabernacle of meeting**. As Bonar said in our opening quotation, no other book "contains more of the very words of God than Leviticus," which should show that we should study it "with singular interest and attention." At the outset the Lord prescribes the five offerings—burnt, meal, peace, sin, and trespass. The first three were known as sweet-savor offerings, the last two as sin offerings. The first three were voluntary, the last two compulsory.

The first message God has for **the children of Israel** is that they should **bring** their **offerings to the Lord** from their **livestock**—both from the **herd and** from **the flock**.

Chapter 1 deals with the **burnt sacrifice** (Heb. *'ōlāh*[1]). There were three grades, depending on what the offerer could afford: a **bull** from **the herd** (v. 3; cf. v. 5), a **male without blemish**; a sheep or a goat from the flock (v. 10), **a male without blemish**; **turtledoves or young pigeons** (v. 14). All were peaceful creatures; nothing wild was offered on the altar of the Lord.

Peter Pell suggests that the bull speaks of our Lord as the patient, unwearied Laborer, always doing the Father's will in a life of perfect service and a death of perfect sacrifice. The sheep represents the Lord as the meek and lowly One, submissive to God's will in unresisting self-surrender. The goat speaks of Christ as our Substitute. The turtledove points to Him as the heavenly One, and also as the Man of sorrows (mourning dove).[2]

Behold! a spotless Victim dies,
My Surety on the tree;
The Lamb of God, the Sacrifice,
He gave Himself for me!
—*Author unknown*

Duties of the offerer: He brought the offering to **the door of the tabernacle**, near the bronze altar (v. 3); **he put his** hand on the head of the victim (v. 4) (or, "he leaned his hand as if in reliance"); **he** killed **the bull** (v. 5) or the sheep or goat (v. 11); **he** skinned the animal **and cut it into its pieces** (vv. 6, 12); **he** washed the **entrails and legs with water** (vv. 9, 13). In verse 3, the expression **"of his own free will"** is translated in some versions "to be accepted." Note verse 4.

Duties of the priests: They sprinkled **the blood** of the animal **all around on the altar** (vv. 5, 11); they **put** the **fire** and **the wood on the altar** (v. 7) and then placed the parts of the animal **in order on the wood** (vv. 8, 12). Everything was burned on the altar except the skin (v. 13; 7:8); in the case of the **birds**, the priest wrung **off its head**, pressed out **its blood at the side of the altar**, put **the crop** (gullet) **with its feathers on the east side** of **the altar**, opened the body of the bird without cutting it in pieces, and burned it **on the altar**. The word for *burn* is the one used for burning incense; a different word is used in connection with the sin offerings.

Distribution of the offering: All that was burned on the altar belonged to God; the skin was given to the priests (7:8); the offerer received no part of this particular offering.

The person bringing a burnt offering was expressing his complete surrender and devotion to the Lord. We learn elsewhere that this offering was presented on many different occasions. (See a Bible dictionary for details.)

Typically, the burnt offering pictures the offering of Christ without spot to God. On Calvary's altar the Lamb of God was totally consumed by the flames of divine justice. Amelia M. Hull's hymn captures the spirit of this:

> I have been at the altar and
> witnessed the Lamb
> Burnt wholly to ashes for me;
> And watched its sweet savour
> ascending on high,
> Accepted, O Father, by Thee.

B. The Grain Offering (Chap. 2)

The **grain offering** (Heb. *minḥāh*) was of meal flour, or grain.[3]

The offering itself: There were various types of **grain** offerings, as follows: **fine flour**, with **oil** and **frankincense** poured **on it** (v. 1). This was not cooked, but a **handful** of it was burned **on the altar** (v. 2). There were three different types of bread or cakes: (a) **baked in the oven** (v. 4); (b) **baked** in a flat **pan** (v. 5); (c) cooked **in a covered pan** (v. 7; the KJV and RSV say "frying pan," but some believe this offering was boiled in water, like a dumpling). There were also kernels of **grain** representing **firstfruits** of harvest, **roasted** in fire (v. 14). Verse 12 refers to a special meal offering (23:15–21) which was **not to be burned on the altar** because it contained leaven.

No **leaven** or **honey** was to be used in any of these meal offerings (v. 11). These implied fermentation and natural sweetness. But **salt** was to be added, as a sign of the covenant between God and Israel. It was called the **salt of the covenant** (v. 13), signifying that the covenant was unbreakable. See Numbers 18:19; 2 Chronicles 13:5; Ezekiel 43:24 for other references to "the covenant of salt."

Duties of the offerer: He prepared the offering at home and brought it to **the priests** (vv. 2, 8).

Duties of the priest: The priest presented the offering at the altar (6:14); he then took a **handful of** the offering and burned this **memorial** handful **on the altar** (vv. 2, 9).

Distribution of the offering: The "memorial handful," burned on the altar with *all* the frankincense, was the Lord's; the priests were permitted to take all the rest of the offering as food (vv. 3, 10). The officiating priest was entitled to whatever was baked in the oven or cooked in a pot or pan (7:9). Everything mixed with oil and everything dry was to belong to the rest of the priests (7:10); the offerer received no part of this offering.

The person who brought the meal offering acknowledged the bounty of God in providing the good things of life, represented by flour, frankincense, oil (and wine in the case of the drink offering).

Symbolically this offering speaks of the moral perfection of the life of our Savior (fine flour), untainted by evil (no leaven), fragrant to God (frankincense), and filled with the Holy Spirit (oil). The hymn writer expresses it beautifully:

> Life, life of love poured out fragrant
> and holy!
> Life, 'mid rude thorns of earth,
> stainless and sweet!
> Life, whence God's face of love,
> glorious but lowly,
> Shines forth to bow us, Lord, low
> at Thy feet!
>
> —*F. Allaben*

C. The Peace Offering (Chap. 3)

3:1–15 The **peace** or fellowship **offering** (Heb. *shelem*[4]) celebrated peace with God that was established on the basis of the efficacy of the atoning blood. It was a feast of joy, love, and communion.

The offering itself: There were three grades of this offering also: an animal from **the herd** (oxen or cattle), **male or female** (vv. 1–5); a **lamb** from **the flock, male or female** (vv. 6–11); a goat from the flock, male or female (vv. 12–17).

Duties of the offerer: He presented the animal **before the LORD** at the gate of the court (vv. 1,6,12); he laid **his hand on the head of** the victim (vv. 2, 8, 13); he killed it at the **door of the tabernacle** (vv. 2, 8, 13); he removed certain portions of the animal—**the fat, the kidneys, the whole fat tail,** and **the fatty lobe attached to the liver**—to be burned on the altar (vv. 3, 4, 9, 10, 14, 15).

Duties of the priests: They sprinkled **the blood all around on the altar** (vv. 2, 8, 13); they burned the Lord's portion (the fat, etc.) on top of **the burnt sacrifice** (v. 5).

Distribution of the offering: The Lord's portion, *called* the **food** of the **offering made by fire** (v. 11), was the fat, the kidneys, the caul, and the fat tail; in Leviticus 7:32, 33 we learn that the officiating priest received the right thigh after it had been first presented as a heave offering; the other priests received the animal's breast (7:31). This was first presented as a wave offering before the Lord; the offerer received all the rest (7:15–21). This is the only offering in which the offerer received a portion. He probably made a feast for his family and friends as a kind of fellowship meal. Thus the offering promoted peace between fellow Israelites within the covenant.

The person bringing this offering was expressing his joyful gratitude for the peace he enjoyed in fellowship with Jehovah. A person might also present the peace offering in connection with some vow he was making to the Lord, or in thanksgiving for some special favor.

As to its typical (symbolic) meaning, Peter Pell comments:

> The finished work of Christ in relation to the believer is seen in the peace offering. The Lord Jesus is our

> peace (Eph. 2:14), having made peace through the blood of His cross (Col. 1:20). He preached this peace to those who were afar off and to those who were near (Eph. 2:17), thus breaking down the middle wall of partition between Jew and Gentile. In Christ, God and the sinner meet in peace; the enmity that was ours is gone. God is propitiated, the sinner is reconciled, and both alike are satisfied with Christ and with what He has done.[5]

Lord Adalbert Cecil's hymn exults in what Christ has done for us:

> Oh, the peace forever flowing
> From God's thoughts of His own
> Son!
> Oh, the peace of simply knowing
> On the cross that all was done.
> Peace with God! the blood in heaven
> Speaks of pardon now to me:
> Peace with God! the Lord is ris'n!
> Righteousness now counts me free.

3:16, 17 The people of Israel were forbidden to eat **fat** or **blood**, since both belonged to the Lord. In addition to its symbolic meaning, this regulation concerning fat was an early form of preventive medicine. Today doctors recommend a reduction in fat intake to reduce the incidence of hypertension, heart disease, strokes, diabetes, and lung disease.

These first three offerings—burnt, meal, and peace—had a place in the public worship of the nation, but they could also be brought to the Lord by an individual at any time on a voluntary basis. The next two offerings were commanded to be brought when someone had sinned. Thus we have the twin concepts of *voluntary worship* and *compulsory atonement* set forth in the offerings.

D. The Sin Offering (4:1—5:13)

Chap. 4 The **sin offering** (Heb., *hattā'th*[6]) was appointed for a redeemed people. It does not speak of a sinner coming to the Lord for *salvation*, but of an Israelite, in covenant relationship with the Lord, seeking *forgiveness*. It has to do with sins committed unconsciously or unintentionally.

The offering itself: There were different grades of offerings, depending upon the person who sinned: **The anointed priest**—that is, the high priest, if he by sinning brought **guilt on the people** (v. 3)—brought **a young bull without blemish**; **the whole congregation** (v. 13) brought **a young bull** also; **a ruler** (v. 22) brought **a kid of the goats, a male without blemish**; an ordinary person (v. 27) brought a **female** goat, **without blemish** (v. 28), or a **female** sheep, **without blemish** (v. 32). (The Hebrew wording here indicates full-grown animals.)

Duties of the offerer(s): In general, the offerer brought the animal to the gate of the tabernacle court, presented it to the Lord, laid his hand on its head, killed it, and removed the fat, the kidneys, and the fatty lobe above the liver. **The elders** acted for **the congregation** (v. 15). The victim's death was regarded symbolically as the sinner's death.

Duties of the priest: For himself and for the congregation, the high priest carried the blood of the sacrifice into the holy place of the tabernacle, sprinkled it seven times before the veil (vv. 5, 6, 16, 17) and on the horns of the golden altar of incense (vv. 7, 18). Then he poured the rest of the blood at the base of the altar of burnt offering (vv. 7, 18). For a ruler and for common people, a priest sprinkled the blood on the horns of the altar of burnt offering and poured the rest of the blood at the bottom of the altar

(vv. 25, 30, 34). For all classes, he burned the fat, kidneys, fatty lobe above the liver, and fat tail on the altar of burnt offering (vv. 8–10, 19, 26, 31). In the case of the offering for the high priest or for the whole congregation, all the rest of the animal was taken outside the camp and burned (vv. 11, 12, 21).

Distribution of the offering: The Lord's share was the portion that was burned upon the altar—the fat, kidneys, fatty lobe above the liver, etc. The priest was allowed to eat the flesh of the offerings of a ruler or of a commoner because the blood of these offerings was not taken into the sanctuary (7:30), as in the case of the offerings of the high priest and the congregation (4:5, 6, 16, 17). He could also eat the offerings described in 5:6, 7, 11 for the same reason. No part of the above offerings was set aside for the offerer.

The body of any sin offering whose blood was taken into the holy place was burned outside the camp. So our Lord, through His own blood, entered the holy place once for all (Heb. 9:12) after He had suffered outside the city of Jerusalem. We are admonished to "go forth to Him outside the camp, bearing His reproach" (Heb. 13:13).

Note: The expression "sin through ignorance" seems to mean more than lack of knowledge of the sin. It probably means that the sin was not willful, deliberate, or done in defiance or rebellion. There was no sacrifice for willful sin; the death penalty had to be exacted (Num. 15:30).

The person who brought a sin offering was acknowledging that he had sinned unintentionally through weakness or negligence. He sought forgiveness of sins and ceremonial cleansing.

The sin offering points symbolically to Christ, who was "made sin" for us, though He knew no sin, that we might be made the righteousness of God in Him. Some suggest that the sin offering speaks of Christ dealing with *what we are,* whereas the trespass offering pictures Him dealing with *what we have done.*

The Holy One who knew no sin,
God made Him sin for us;
The Savior died our souls to win,
Upon the shameful cross.
His precious blood alone availed
To wash our sins away;
Through weakness He o'er hell
  prevailed,
Through death He won the day.
—Hannah K. Burlingham

5:1–13 The first 13 verses of chapter 5 seem to describe the trespass offering (see v. 6), but it is generally agreed that these verses have to do with two additional grades of sin offering. The reason for not treating them with the trespass offering is that there is no mention of restitution, which was an important part of the trespass offering. (However, it is freely admitted that verses 1–13 are closely linked to both the sin and trespass offerings.)

Instead of dealing with various classes of people, these offerings have to do with differing types of sins: Verse 1 describes a man who has knowledge of a crime, and yet refuses to testify after hearing the high priest or judge put him under **oath**. As a Jew living under the Law, Jesus testified when the chief priest put Him under oath (Matt. 26:63, 64). Verse 2 deals with the defilement which a Jew contracted by touching a dead body, even if he did not know it at the time. Verse 3 describes the uncleanness contracted by touching a person with leprosy, a running sore, etc. Verse 4 has to do with the making of rash oaths or promises which one later finds he cannot fulfill.

The offering itself: There were three types of offerings for these sins, depending upon the ability of the offerer to pay: a **female** lamb or goat—**as a sin offering** (v. 6); **two turtledoves or two young pigeons—one as a sin offering and the other as a burnt offering** (v. 7); the **tenth** part **of an ephah of fine flour** with **no oil** or **frankincense** (v. 11). This put the sin offering within reach of the poorest person. Likewise, no one is excluded from forgiveness through Christ. The question arises in verses 11–13, "How can a meal offering serve as a sin offering to make atonement for sin when we know that without the shedding of blood there is no remission" (Heb. 9:22)? The answer is that it was offered *on top of* a fire offering on the altar (which did have blood), and this gave the meal offering the value of a blood sacrifice.

Duties of the offerer: He first of all confessed his guilt (v. 5), then brought his offering **to the priest** (v. 8).

Duties of the priest: In the case of the female lamb or goat, he offered it in accordance with the instructions for a sin offering in chapter 4. If the offering was two birds, he first offered one bird as a **sin offering**, wringing **its neck**, sprinkling some blood on the side of the altar, and draining out the rest **at the base of the altar** (vv. 8, 9). He next offered the **second** bird **as a burnt offering**, burning it completely on the bronze altar (v. 10). If the offering was **fine flour**, the priest took a **handful of** it and burned it on the altar of burnt offering. He burned it over other offerings involving the shedding of blood, thus giving it the character of a sin offering (v. 12).

Distribution of the offering: The Lord's portion consisted of whatever was burned on the altar. The priest was entitled to whatever was left (v. 13).

E. The Trespass Offering (5:14—6:7)

The **trespass offering** (Heb., *'āshām*[7]) is taken up in 5:14—6:7. The distinctive feature of this offering is that **restitution** had to be made for the sin committed *before* the offering was presented (5:16).

There were several types of sin for which an offering had to be made. *Trespass against God:* Withholding from the Lord that which rightly belonged to Him—tithes and offerings, consecration of firstfruits or of the firstborn, etc. (5:14). Unwittingly committing some act forbidden by the Lord (5:17), and presumably an act that required restitution. "In cases where it was not possible to know whether another had been wronged, the scrupulously devout Israelite would still offer a guilt offering by itself" (*Daily Notes of the Scripture Union*).

Trespass against man: Dealing falsely with one's neighbor in a matter of deposit or bargain or robbery or oppression (6:2). Finding a lost article and swearing to a lie about it (6:3). A trespass offering was also required in the case of immorality with a slave girl who was engaged (19:20–22), the cleansing of a leper (14:10–14), and the defilement of a Nazirite (Num. 6:6–12).

The offering itself: A ram without blemish (5:15, 18; 6:6) or a male lamb in the case of a leper (14:12) or a Nazirite (Num. 6:12).

Duties of the offerer: In the case of a trespass against God, he first brought the restitution to the priest, with twenty percent added. Then he brought the animal to the priest at the entrance to the tabernacle court, presented it to the Lord, placed his hand on its head, and killed it. He also removed the fat, fat tail, kidneys, and fatty lobe above the liver. The procedure was the same in the case of a trespass against a neighbor. In both instances, the offerer had to pay the twenty percent penalty, reminding him that sin is unprofitable and costly.

Duties of the priest: He sprinkled the blood around the bronze altar (7:2); he then burned the fat, the fat tail (rump), the kidneys, and the fatty lobe above the liver on the altar (7:3, 4).

Distribution of the offering: The Lord's portion was that which was burned on the altar (7:5). The officiating priest received the skin of the ram (7:8). All the priests shared the meat of the animal as food (7:6). The offerer had no part in the sin or trespass offerings.

As has been mentioned, the person bringing a trespass offering was seeking to make amends for some action of his that had caused loss or damage to someone else.

Symbolically, the trespass offering points to that aspect of the work of Christ by which He restored that which He took not away (Ps. 69:4b). Through man's sin, God was robbed of service, worship, obedience, and glory. And man himself was robbed of life, peace, gladness, and fellowship with God. As our trespass offering, the Lord Jesus not only restored what had been stolen through man's sin, but He added more. *For God has received more glory through the finished work of Christ than if sin had never entered the world.* And we are better off in Christ than we ever could have been in unfallen Adam.

Aside He threw His most divine array,
And veiled His Godhead in a robe of clay;
And in that garb did wondrous love display,
Restoring what He never took away.
—*Author unknown*

II. LAWS OF THE OFFERINGS (6:8—7:38)

The section from 6:8 to 7:38 presents "the law of the offerings." In many ways, it is very similar to what has gone before. However, it is addressed to the priests whereas the previous instructions were for the children of Israel (1:2).

6:8–13 *The law of the burnt offering:* Additional details are given here concerning the **garments** worn by **the priest**, the manner in which he disposed of **the ashes** from **the burnt offering**, and the care he must exercise to see that **the fire on the altar** never went **out**. The ashes were first placed at the east side of the altar, and then carried **outside the camp to a clean place**.

6:14–17 *The law of the grain offering:* Here we learn that the priests had to **eat** their portion of the offering within **the court of the tabernacle**, and that it was **not** to be leavened because **it** was **most holy** to the Lord.

6:18 Any male **children of Aaron** could **eat** the grain offering, but they **must be holy**, that is, ceremonially clean. These priests did not become holy by touching the offerings. Holiness was not imparted by touch, but defilement was (Hag. 2:11–13).[8]

6:19–23 These verses describe a special **grain offering** which the high **priest** had to offer **morning** and evening continually. It was **wholly burned** by fire.

6:24–30 ***The law of the sin offering***: As explained previously, **the priest** was allowed to **eat** portions of certain sin offerings (those described in Lev. 4:22—5:13, where **the blood** was not carried into the sanctuary). The offerings had to **be eaten . . . in the court of the tabernacle**. Notice that this offering was **most holy**. If a layman touched the **flesh** of the offering, he **must be** holy or consecrated and had to cleanse himself from ceremonial defilement just as the priests did, though he could not exercise priestly functions. If any of the **blood** was **sprinkled on** a **garment**, the garment had to be washed—not because it was unclean but so that the most holy blood might not be carried out of the sanctuary into everyday life, and thus be profaned. An **earthen vessel** used to cook the meat of the sin offering had to **be broken** because the earthenware, being porous, absorbed some of the blood and might later be used for profane purposes. A **bronze pot** had to **be both scoured and rinsed in water** to prevent any portion of the most holy sin offering from ever coming in contact with anything that was common or unclean. **The sin offering**, like the guilt offering, was to be slain **in the place where the burnt offering is killed**. This was the north side of the altar (1:11), the place of shadows.

7:1–7 The first seven verses of chapter 7 review **the law of the trespass offering**, most of which has already been covered in 5:14—6:7.

7:8 Verse 8 refers to the **burnt offering** and provides that the officiating **priest** was entitled to **the skin** of the animal.

7:9, 10 Verse 9 indicates the portion of the **grain offering** that was to go to the *officiating* **priest**, and verse 10 what was to go to the *rest* of the priests.

7:11–18 **The law of** the **peace** offering is given in 7:11–21. There were three types of **peace offerings**, depending on the motive or purpose of the offering: **for . . . thanksgiving** (v. 12), praising God for some special blessing; for **a vow** (that is, a votive **offering**) (v. 16), "in fulfillment of a promise or pledge made to God for the granting of some special request in prayer; for example, preservation on a hazardous journey"[9]; **voluntary** or freewill (vv. 16, 17), "This would appear to be in the nature of a spontaneous expression of praise to God in appreciation of what He has revealed Himself to be."[10] The **peace offering** itself was a sacrificial animal (chap. 3), but here we learn that it was accompanied by certain **cakes** or breads. The **cakes** that were required with a thank offering are listed in verses 12 and 13. The offerer was to bring **one** of **each** for **a heave offering**, and this was given to **the** officiating **priest** (v. 14). **The flesh of the . . . thanksgiving** offering was to be eaten **the same day** (v. 15), whereas the votive offering and the freewill offering could be eaten on the first or second **day** (v. 16). Anything remaining after two days had to be **burned** (v. 17); to eat such meat would cause the person to be **"cut off,"** meaning excommunicated or removed from the privileges of the people of Israel. "This shows," John Reid writes, "that communion with God must be fresh and not too far removed from the work of the altar."[11]

7:19–21 If **the flesh** touched **any unclean thing**, it could **not** be **eaten** but had to **be burned**. Only persons **who** were ceremonially **clean** could **eat** the **clean flesh**. Any **person who** was ceremonially **unclean** and who ate **of the peace offering** would **be cut off**.

The fact that different portions of the peace offering were designated for the Lord, the priests, and the offerer indicates that it was a time of fellowship. But since God can have no fellowship with sin or uncleanness, those who partook of this festive meal had to be clean.

7:22–27 **The fat**, considered the best portion, belonged **to the Lord**. It was burned for Him on the altar, and it was not to be eaten (vv. 22–25). Likewise, the **blood**, being the life of the flesh, belonged to God and was not to be eaten (vv. 26, 27). Today many Jews still seek to comply with these dietary laws. In order for meat to be fit for their consumption, or "kosher," the blood must be removed. In avoiding the consumption of fat, many Jewish households will not use soaps which contain animal fats. They believe that even to use such products in washing dishes would be to make the dishes non-kosher. Besides the spiritual reason for not eating fat there is also a medical reason, as Dr. S. I. McMillen points out:

> In the past few years medical science has awakened to the fact that the eating of animal fat is an important cause of arteriosclerosis. This fat forms the tiny, fatty, cholesterol tumors within the walls of the arteries, which hinder the flow of blood. Now, in this decade, magazines, radio and T.V. are broadcasting the good news that we can reduce the ravages from man's greatest killer by cutting down our intake of animal fats. Happy as we are with the fact that medical science has arrived, we may be amazed to discover that our ultramodern research is about thirty-five hundred years behind the Book of books.[12]

7:28–34 The offerer waved **the breast** of the peace offerings **before the Lord**, and it then became the portion of the priests. **The right thigh** was heaved before the Lord, and then was given to the officiating **priest** as food for himself and his family.

7:35, 36 These verses repeat that the breast and right thigh were the **portion** of **Aaron and his sons** from the day that God first anointed them **as priests**. As previously suggested, the breast speaks of divine affection and the thigh of divine power.

7:37, 38 This paragraph concludes the section on the laws of the offerings, which began in 6:8. God has devoted much space in His Word to the offerings and their ordinances because they are important to Him. Here in beautiful imagery the Person and work of His Son can be seen in minute detail. Like the different facets of a diamond, these types all reflect the resplendent glory of Him "who through the eternal Spirit offered Himself without spot to God" (Heb. 9:14). Miss F. T. Wigram expresses her praise in a hymn:

> The person of the Christ,
> Enfolding every grace,
> Once slain, but now alive again,
> In heaven demands our praise.

III. CONSECRATION OF THE PRIESTS (Chap. 8—10)

A. Investiture of the Priests by Moses (Chap. 8)

8:1–5 In Exodus 28 and 29, God gave Moses elaborate instructions for consecrating Aaron and his sons as priests. Now, in Leviticus 8–10, we read how Moses carried out these instructions. He called together the assembly—priests and people—**at the door of the tabernacle**. It was a very public investiture service.

8:6–9 **Moses washed** both **Aaron and his sons with water**. Next **Moses** dressed **Aaron** in the complete vestments of the high priest: **the tunic**,

the sash, the robe, the **ephod**, the **band of the ephod, the breastplate, the Urim and the Thummim, the turban** and **the holy crown**. It must have been an impressive sight.

8:10–13 Then Moses . . . anointed the tabernacle and all its contents, and sanctified them.

The fact that **he poured** (not sprinkled) **on Aaron's** head is a lovely picture of the Holy Spirit being poured out without measure on the Lord Jesus, our Great High Priest.

Next **Moses put tunics** and **sashes**, as well as **hats** (or head-pieces), on **Aaron's sons**.

8:14–17 As **Aaron and his sons laid their hands on the head of the bull for the sin offering, . . . Moses killed it**. Even the highest religious leaders (then as well as now) are merely sinners who need God's atoning sacrifice as well as the least important member of the community.

8:18–21 Moses likewise brought a ram for a **burnt offering** for **Aaron and his sons** and carried out the prescribed rites.

8:22–29 The **consecration** offering for **Aaron and his sons** was also called **the ram of consecration** (or, more literally the ram of the "fill offering"). It differed from the customary peace offerings as to the application of the **blood** (vv. 23, 24), and also as to the burning of the **right thigh** and bread cakes, which ordinarily would have been eaten. Since he officiated, **Moses** received **the breast** as his **part**.

The **blood** was placed **on . . . the ear, . . . hand, and . . . foot** of Aaron and his sons, reminding us that Christ's blood should affect our *obedience, service*, and *walk*.

8:30–36 Moses . . . sprinkled . . . Aaron and **his sons** with **some of the blood** and **some of the anointing oil** from the sacrifice. The priests were instructed to eat of the **flesh** of the peace offering along **with the bread**.

The above **consecration** ritual was repeated **for seven days**, during which they were not allowed **to go outside the door of the tabernacle**.

In commenting on this chapter, Matthew Henry discerns the one thing that is missing:

> But after all the ceremonies that were used in their consecration, there was one point of ratification which was reserved to be the honour and establishment of Christ's priesthood, which was this, that they were *made priests without an oath, but Christ with an oath* (Heb. vii.21), for neither such priests nor their priesthood could continue, but Christ's is a perpetual and unchangeable priesthood.[13]

B. Offerings Presented by Aaron (Chap. 9)

9:1-4 Aaron and his sons took up their official duties **on the eighth day**. First, they were to offer for themselves a **young bull** for **a sin offering and a ram** for **a burnt offering**. Then they were to offer for the people: a he-goat for **a sin offering; a** yearling **calf** and **a lamb** for **a burnt offering; a bull and a ram** for **peace offerings; a grain offering**.

9:5–23 All the congregation drew near to the Lord's presence in front of **the tabernacle**. When **Aaron** had fully complied with all the instructions of Moses regarding **the sin offering, the burnt offering**, the **people's offering**, the **grain offering**, the **peace offerings**, and **the wave offering** (vv. 5–20), he **lifted his hand** and **blessed** the **people** (vv. 22, 23).

9:24 Then a **fire came out from**

the Most Holy place of the tabernacle **and consumed the burnt offering** which was upon the bronze **altar**. This indicated God's acceptance of the offering. This fire of the Lord was to be kept burning continually on the altar of burnt offering.

C. Nadab and Abihu's Sacrilege (Chap. 10)

10:1–3 Nadab and Abihu, the sons of Aaron, each burned **incense . . . before the LORD** with **profane fire**, perhaps **fire** that was not taken off the brazen altar. Since the altar speaks of Calvary, it was as if they tried to approach God in some way other than through the atoning work of Christ. **Fire went out from** the Most Holy Place and **devoured them** as they stood by the golden altar in the holy place. Moses warned Aaron, in effect, that any complaint would be rebellion against God's righteous dealings.

10:4–7 After **Mishael and Elzaphan** had **carried** the corpses from in front of the tabernacle to a place outside **the camp**, Moses told Aaron and his two remaining sons that they must not mourn but remain within **the tabernacle** while the **the whole house of Israel** mourned the flaring forth of God's wrath.

10:8–11 Some have inferred from the injunction against drinking **wine or intoxicating drink** in **the tabernacle** that Nadab and Abihu may have been drunk when they offered the strange fire.

10:12–18 **Moses** commanded **Aaron and Eleazar and Ithamar, his** remaining **sons**, to **eat . . . the grain offering** (vv. 12, 13) and the **breast of the wave offering** (vv. 14, 15). When he looked for **the goat** that had been used as a **sin offering** for the people, he found that **Eleazar and Ithamar, . . . sons of Aaron,** had **burned** the sacrifice instead of eating it **in a holy place**. (Perhaps they feared God's wrath which had just fallen on their brothers.) The rule was that if the **blood** of the sin offering was **brought** into **the holy place**, then the sacrifice was to be burned (6:30). But if not, it was to be eaten (6:26). Moses reminded them that, in this case, the **blood** had **not** been **brought inside the holy place**; therefore, they should **have . . . eaten** the meat (vv. 16–18).

10:19, 20 In reply to Moses' reprimand, **Aaron** explained that they had carried out the **sin** and **burnt** offerings, as required, but, in view of the Lord's severe chastisement on Nadab and Abihu, he wondered if his eating **the sin offering would have been accepted** by **the LORD. Moses** accepted the excuse.

Chapter 10 concludes the section on the priesthood.

IV. THE CLEAN AND THE UNCLEAN (Chaps. 11—15)

The next five chapters deal with matters of ceremonial cleanness and uncleanness. For the Jews there were acts that were not morally wrong but nevertheless barred them from participating in the rituals of Judaism. Those who became defiled were ritually unfit until they were cleansed. A holy people must be holy in every area of life. God used even food to illustrate the difference between what is clean and unclean.

A. Clean and Unclean Foods (Chap. 11)

11:1–8 A *clean* animal was one which had **hooves** that were completely **cloven** and which chewed **the cud**. The expression **"whatever divides the hoof, having cloven hooves"**

seems to say the same thing in two different ways. But the words mean that the **hoof** must be *completely* divided. Clean animals were oxen, cattle, sheep, goats, deer, etc. **Unclean** animals were pigs, camels, rock badgers (hyraxes), rabbits, etc. The spiritual application is that Christians should meditate on the Word of God (chew the cud) and have a separated walk (the cloven hoof).

But God was also protecting the health of His people by prohibiting meat that was likely to transmit disease in days when there was little or no refrigeration and the use of antibiotics in animal husbandry was unknown.

11:9–12 A clean fish was one that had both **fins and scales**. Fish such as mackerel, eels, and shellfish were unclean. Scales are often taken to picture the Christian's armor, protecting him in a hostile world, while the fins typify the divine power which enables him to navigate through the world without being overcome by it.

11:13–19 **Birds** which preyed on other creatures were unclean—e.g., eagles, hawks, vultures, bats. (Bats are not birds, but the Hebrew word translated *birds* is broader than the English word, meaning "flying thing.")

11:20–23 Verses 20–23 deal with certain forms of **flying insects**. Only those which had jointed legs above their feet were clean—namely, locusts, **destroying** locusts, crickets, and grasshoppers.

11:24–28 Touching **the carcass of any** of the foregoing unclean creatures rendered a person **unclean until evening**. Special mention is made of animals which walk **on . . . paws**, such as cats, dogs, lions, tigers, bears, etc.

11:29–38 Other creeping animals are described next—**the mole, the mouse,** the **large lizard, . . . the gecko,** the **monitor lizard, the sand reptile, the sand lizard, and the chameleon**. A person touching their carcasses became **unclean until evening**. If the **dead** body of one of these creatures fell on any **vessel**, the utensil had to be washed **in water**, and it was **unclean until evening**, except that an **earthen vessel** had to be broken. **Any edible food** in the **earthen vessel** became **unclean** and could not be eaten. Two exceptions are given—**a spring** of running water did not become unclean through contact with the body of one of these animals, nor did **planting seed** used for sowing, if it had not been soaked in **water**.

11:39, 40 Human contact with the carcass of a clean **animal** which had died (rather than being slaughtered) or eating such meat unintentionally made a person **unclean until evening. His clothes** had to be washed.

11:41-47 Verses 41–43 refer to worms, snakes, rodents, and insects. Anyone eating them became ritually **unclean**. In giving this law concerning clean and unclean creatures, God was teaching lessons concerning His holiness and the necessity for His people to **be holy** as well (vv. 4–47).

In Mark 7:18, 19, the Lord Jesus declared all foods to be ceremonially clean. And Paul taught that no food should be refused if it is received with thanksgiving (1 Tim. 4:1–5). However, even that would not include foods that are contaminated, culturally unacceptable, or digestively disagreeable to a person.

B. Purification after Childbirth (Chap. 12)

12:1-4 Chapter 12 deals with uncleanness connected with childbirth. A woman giving birth to a boy was **unclean** for **seven days**, just as the days of the **impurity** of her menstruation. **On the eighth day**, the boy was **circumcised** (v. 3). The eighth day was the safest as far as blood clotting was concerned. Today the blood clotting problem is solved by injections of vitamin K. She then remained at home for an additional **thirty-three days** so as **not** to **touch any hallowed thing** or enter **the sanctuary**—i.e., the court surrounding the tabernacle.

12:5 In the case of a baby girl, the mother was **unclean** for **two weeks**, and then remained home for an additional **sixty-six days**.

12:6–8 At the end of the time of **purification**, the mother was commanded to **bring a** yearling **lamb** for **a burnt offering** and **a young pigeon or a turtledove** for **a sin offering**. If she was too poor to afford the **lamb**, **she** could **bring two turtledoves or two young pigeons—one** for the **burnt offering** and **the other** for the **sin offering**. The mother of our Lord brought two birds (Luke 2:22–24), an indication of the poverty into which Jesus was born.

It may seem strange that uncleanness is connected with the birth of a baby, since marriage was instituted before sin entered the world, since the Scriptures teach that marriage is holy, and since God commanded men to reproduce. The uncleanness is probably a reminder that, with the exception of our Lord, we are all brought forth in iniquity and conceived in sin (Ps. 51:5). The extended time of uncleanness in the case of a baby girl was perhaps an intended reminder that man was created before woman, that the woman was created for the man, that the woman is given a place of positional submission (not intrinsic inferiority) to the man, and that the woman was the first to sin.

Williams sees in this legislation the tender care of God in protecting the mother from visitors during a time when her weakness and the danger of infection were greatest.[14]

C. The Diagnosis of Leprosy (Chap. 13)

Chapter 13 has to do with the diagnosis of leprosy, and chapter 14 with its cleansing. Opinion is divided as to the nature of biblical leprosy. Bible lepers were usually mobile, were not deformed, were harmless when completely leprous, and were sometimes cured.

In some ways the priest filled the role of physician, perhaps a subtle reminder of the close connection between the spiritual and the physical. Man is a tripartite being, and what affects one part affects all.

Chapter 13 is admittedly difficult, dealing as it does with technical descriptions of leprous and non-leprous diseases and with "leprosy" in houses and garments. Dr. R. K. Harrison, who has medical training as well as being a Hebrew scholar, points out that there is "no translation that is satisfactory for all the conditions covered by the Hebrew word, but that it should be broad enough to include the disease we call Hansen's disease."[15]

He summarizes the known facts about the Hebrew term and its Greek translation (whence our English terms *leprosy, leper, leprous*):

> The Hebrew term *sāra'at* comes from a root meaning "to become diseased in the skin," and is a generic rather than a specific description. In Old Testament usage it was extended to include mould or mildew in fabrics, as well as mineral eruptions on the walls of buildings, and possibly dry rot in the fabric of such structures.

In the LXX the Hebrew was rendered by the Greek word *lepra*, which itself appears to have been rather indefinite in nature and meaning. The Greek medical authors used the word to describe a disease that made the surface of the skin flaky or scaly, while Herodotus mentioned it in connection with an affliction known as *leukē*, a type of cutaneous eruption which seems to have been the same as the Greek *elephantiasis*, and thus similar to modern clinical leprosy (Hansen's disease).[16]

13:1–3 The opening paragraph describes **the priest** inspecting **a man** for the symptoms of biblical leprosy.

13:4–8 Next the proper procedure in questionable cases is detailed. The person was confined for **seven days. If the . . . spot** had **not spread**, then he was confined for **another seven** more **days**. Then if the disease seemed to be checked, **the priest** pronounced the person **clean**. If the eruption in the skin had spread after the second examination, then the priest declared him to be **unclean**.

13:9–11 When the **leprosy** was **old** or chronic, **the priest** pronounced the leper unclean.

13:12, 13 Strangely, when a person had turned **white** all over, the disease was no longer active, and **the priest** pronounced the leper **clean**.

13:14, 15 When **raw flesh** appeared on a person, **the priest** pronounced him **unclean. It** was **leprosy**.

13:16, 17 In a case of leprosy where the **raw flesh** had healed and **turned white**, here again the person was **clean**.

13:18–23 Three possible diagnoses regarding a **boil** are next presented. When it is obvious to **the priest** that the boil is **deeper than the skin, and its hair has turned white**, he must **pronounce** the patient unclean (vv. 18–20). When in quarantine the sore **spread** during a seven-day test period, it was **leprous** (vv. 21, 22). When it did **not** spread, the person was pronounced **clean** (v. 23).

13:24–28 The case of a possibly leprous **burn** is described. When from its symptoms it was obviously **leprous, the priest** would **pronounce** the person **unclean** (vv. 24, 25). A seven-day period of testing would reveal the condition to be spreading and therefore **leprous** (vv. 26, 27). Where it is merely **a swelling from the burn** it was not leprous (v. 28).

13:29–37 The case of a **scale** of the head or beard is considered next. Where **a man or a woman** obviously had **leprosy** from his or her symptoms, the person had to be declared **unclean** (vv. 29, 30). Where it was not clearly known (vv. 31–37), the person was confined for **seven days**. If the condition had **not spread**, the person shaved off his hair and waited for **another seven days**. If the **scale** had **spread**, the person was **unclean. If the scale** had been checked, the person was **clean**.

13:38, 39 **A man or a woman** with **white bright spots on the skin of the body** was declared ceremonially **clean**. According to Harrison's semi-technical translation, it was "a mottling that has arisen in the skin."[17]

13:40-44 Ordinary baldness (alopecia) is differentiated from that which was caused by **leprosy**.

13:45, 46 A **leper** was a miserable person. He was put **outside the camp** of Israel and had to wear **torn . . . clothes** and let his **head** be **bare**. Whenever people approached, he had to **cover his** upper lip or **mustache and cry, "Unclean! Unclean!"** Again we have an early example of preventive medicine. Isolation is an accepted medical procedure to prevent the spread of infection.

13:47–59 The case of "leprosy" in a **garment** probably refers to some type of mold or mildew on a **wool or linen** cloth or **leather** garment. Harrison explains the wisdom of destroying garments so tainted:

> Moulds are fungous growths on dead or decomposing animal or vegetable matter, and occur in patches of various shades.[18]

He goes on to make a spiritual application:

> The fungous growth affects the entire article by its presence, just as the taint of original sin reaches all areas of the human personality.[19]

Jehovah's people must be pure and clean externally as well as internally:

> Oh, for a heart to praise my God,
> A heart from sin set free;
> A heart that's trusting in the blood
> So freely shed for me.
>
> A humble, lowly, contrite heart,
> Believing, true, and clean,
> Which neither death nor life can part
> From Him that dwells within.
>
> —*Charles Wesley*

D. The Cleansing of Leprosy (Chap. 14)

14:1–7 Here is given the ritual for cleansing a leper after he had been **healed**: First he was inspected by the **priest** outside **the camp**. If healed, he offered **two living and clean birds**, with **cedar wood, scarlet, and hyssop**. The **cedar wood** and the **hyssop**, coming from a lofty tree and a lowly plant, picture the judgment of God on all men and on all that the world contains, from the highest to the lowest things. **Scarlet** is associated with sins in Isaiah 1:18, so the thought here may be of God's judgment on sins. **One** bird was **killed . . . over running water**, and the other with the **cedar wood and the scarlet and the hyssop** was dipped **in the blood of the** slain bird. The cleansed leper was sprinkled with the blood **seven times** and pronounced **clean**. Then the **living bird** was allowed to go free.

In many ways, **leprosy** is a type of sin. It rendered a man unclean, it excluded him from the camp of God and the people of God, it made the victim miserable, etc. This is why there needed to be an application of **blood** (the blood of Christ) and the **running water** (the Holy Spirit's regenerating work) in the cleansing of a leper. When a sinner turns to the Lord in repentance and faith today, the death and resurrection of Christ (pictured by the two birds) is reckoned to his account. The **blood** is applied through the power of the Spirit and, in God's sight, the person is **clean**.

> Rock of Ages, cleft for me,
> Let me hide myself in Thee;
> Let the water and the blood,
> From Thy riven side which flowed,
> Be of sin the double cure,
> Cleanse me from its guilt and power.
>
> —*Augustus M. Toplady*

14:8–20 The **cleansed** leper washed **his clothes**, shaved **off all his hair, and** washed his body (v. 8). Then he was allowed to enter **the camp**, but he could not enter **his** own **tent** for **seven** more **days**. Seven days later he again washed and shaved and was pronounced **clean** (v. 9). **On the eighth day**, he brought offerings to **the LORD** (vv. 10, 11): **a trespass offering** (vv. 12–18); a **sin offering** (v. 19); a **burnt**

offering (v. 20). **The priest** applied **the blood** to the leper's **ear, hand,** and **foot** (v. 14). This speaks of *hearing* God's Word, of *doing* God's will, and of *walking* in God's ways.

14:21–32 If the cleansed leper was too **poor** to bring all the required animals, then he was permitted to bring **two turtledoves or two young pigeons, one** for **a sin offering and the other** for **a burnt offering**, but he still had to bring **the lamb** for the **trespass offering**.

A **grain offering** accompanied the trespass, sin, and burnt offerings in each instance.

14:33–53 Finally, laws for the detection of **leprosy... in a house** are given. These would apply when the people finally reached **Canaan** and dwelt in permanent houses rather than in tents. "Leprosy" in a house was probably some sort of fungus, mildew, or dry rot. The Lord made provision for **the house** to be emptied **before the priest** went **in** so that the contents need **not** become **unclean** or be quarantined (vv. 36, 38). At first only the affected **stones** in a house were removed. But if the leprosy continued to break out, the house was torn down (vv. 39–45). In the event that the leprosy was arrested in the house, the priest followed a ritual of cleansing similar to that for a leper (vv. 48–53).

14:54–57 This paragraph is a summary of chapters 13 and 14.

E. Purification after Bodily Secretions (Chap. 15)

15:1–18 Chapter 15 deals with the **uncleanness** arising from discharges from the human body, either natural or diseased. Verses 1–12 seem to refer to a running **discharge** from a **man**, resulting from disease, such as gonorrhea. The ritual for **cleansing** is given in verses 13–15. Verses 16–18 refer to the **emission of semen**, involuntary (vv. 16, 17) and voluntary (v. 18).

15:19–33 Verses 19–24 deal with a woman's normal menstrual cycle. This required no offerings. Verses 25–30 describe **a discharge of blood** from **a woman**, but not connected with menstruation—therefore abnormal. Verses 31–33 summarize the chapter.

V. THE DAY OF ATONEMENT (Chap. 16)

The greatest day on the Jewish calendar was the Day of Atonement (Heb., *Yôm Kippur*), when the high priest went into the Most Holy Place with sacrificial blood to make atonement for himself and for the people. It fell on the tenth day of the seventh month, five days before the Feast of Tabernacles. Although the Day of Atcnement is usually listed along with the *feasts* of Jehovah, it was actually a time of *fasting* and solemnity (23:27–32).

It will be helpful to remember that in this chapter the Most Holy Place (the "Holy of Holies") is called the Holy Place, and the Holy Place is called the tabernacle of meeting.

16:1–3 The sacrilege of **the two sons of Aaron**, Nadab and Abihu, forms the backdrop for these instructions. A fate similar to theirs would befall the high priest if he entered the Most **Holy Place** on **any** day other than the Day of Atonement. And on that day he must carry **the blood of a young bull** for **a sin offering and of a ram as a burnt offering**.

16:4–10 The order of events is not easy to follow, but the following is a general outline of the ritual. First the high priest bathed and dressed in white **linen... garments** (v. 4). By way of preliminaries, he brought a bullock and a ram to the tabernacle. He would offer these **for himself and for his** family, the bull for **a sin offering** and the ram for a burnt offering (v. 3). He brought **two . . . goats and one ram** which he would offer for the people, the **goats** for **a sin offering** and the **ram** for **a burnt offering** (v. 5). He presented **the two goats** before **the door of the tabernacle** and **cast lots—one for the LORD** and **the other lot** as **a scapegoat** (vv. 7, 8). The word translated "scapegoat" is *azazel,* meaning "goat of departure."

16:11–22 Then he killed the **bull as the sin offering . . . for himself and for his house** (v. 11). Next **he** took **a censer . . . of burning coals with his hands full of sweet incense** and carried them into the Most Holy Place. There he poured **the incense** over the live coals, causing a **cloud of incense** to **cover the mercy seat** (vv. 12, 13). He returned to the altar of burnt offering for some **blood of the bull,** took it into the Most Holy Place, and sprinkled it **on** top of **the mercy seat** and in front of it **seven times** (v. 14). He killed **the goat** chosen for a **sin offering** (v. 8), and sprinkled **its blood,** as he did the blood of the bull, before and on the **mercy seat** (vv. 9, 15). This made **atonement for the Most Holy Place because of the uncleanness of the children of Israel** (v. 16). By the sprinkling of blood he also made **atonement . . . for the tabernacle** and **for** the **altar** of burnt offering (vv. 18, 19), though the details here are not clear. Atonement started with the Most Holy place, then worked outward to the holy place and finally to the bronze altar (vv. 15–19). After he **laid both his hands on the head of** the scapegoat (v. 8) and confessed the sins of the people (vv. 10, 20, 21), **a** chosen **man** led the **goat** into **the wilderness** (vv. 21, 22). The two goats symbolized two different aspects of atonement: "that which meets the character and holiness of God, and that which meets the need of the sinner as to the removal of his sins."[20] Aaron's laying his hands on the head of the live goat pictures the placing of the sins of Israel (and of ourselves) on Christ, to be taken away forever (v. 21).

The hymnwriter has expressed it thus:

My sins were laid on Jesus,
The spotless Lamb of God;
He bore them all and freed me
From the accursed load.
My guilt was borne by Jesus;
He cleansed the crimson stains
In His own blood most precious
And not a spot remains.
—*Horatius Bonar, alt.*

16:23–33 The high priest bathed **in a holy place,** perhaps at the laver, then **put on his garments** of glory and beauty (vv. 23, 24a). Jewish tradition says that the white linen garments were never worn again. The high priest next offered two rams as **burnt** offerings, one **for himself** and the other **for the people** (v. 24b). He burned **the fat of the** two **sin** offerings **on the altar** while **their skins, their flesh, and their offal** were being burned **outside the camp** (vv. 25, 27). Even the skin of the burnt offering, which usually went to the priest (7:8), was to be burned. According to the Jewish Talmud, the high priest went into the Holy of Holies after the evening sacrifice to bring out the censer. In the ritual of atonement, the people confessed their sins and refrained from work (v. 29).

From the above it will be seen that the high priest entered the Most Holy Place at least four times. This does not contradict Hebrews 9:7–12, where the thought is that there was only *one day* in the year when the high priest could enter.

16:34 Despite the solemn ceremonies of this day, its failure to adequately deal with sins was written across it in the words **"once a year."** "For it is not possible that the blood of bulls and goats could take away sins" (Heb. 10:4). In vivid contrast is the work of Christ, by which human sins are totally removed instead of being merely covered for a year! Isaac Watts expressed it this way:

Not all the blood of beasts
On Jewish altars slain,
Could give the guilty conscience peace,
Or wash away its stain.

But Christ, the heavenly Lamb
Took all our sins away,
A sacrifice of nobler name
And richer blood than they.

VI. LAWS CONCERNING SACRIFICE (Chap. 17)

17:1–9 Commentators hold differing views on verses 1–9. (1) The passage prohibited the killing of any animals, even for food, without offering them at the tabernacle. (2) It forbade the offering of sacrificial animals in the fields or in any place other than the tabernacle. (3) It prohibited the slaughter of sacrificial animals for food as long as the people were in the wilderness. This was changed when the people reached the Promised Land (Deut. 12:15). Morgan explains:

> The Hebrew word [translated 'devils' in KJV and 'goatdemons' in ASV] is literally 'hairy ones.' In Isaiah 13:21 and 34:14 it is rendered 'satyr' in the Authorized Version and 'wild-goats' in the American Standard Version. The satyr was an imaginary being, half-goat, half-man, of demon nature. In Egypt the goat-man, Pan, was worshiped. It would seem as though this word recognized the fact that these people had in Egypt probably worshiped the false god.[21]

17:10–14 The eating of **blood** was likewise forbidden. The blood was for **atonement**, not for nourishment. **"The life of the flesh is in the blood"** (v. 11). The principle behind atonement is life for life. Since the wages of sin is death, symbolized by the shedding of blood, so "without the shedding of blood is no remission." Forgiveness does not come because the penalty of sin is *excused*, but because it is *transferred* to a sacrifice whose lifeblood is poured out. Verse 11 is one of the key verses in Leviticus and should be memorized. When an animal was slaughtered, its blood was drained immediately. An animal that died accidentally was unclean if its blood was not drained right away.

17:15, 16 This refers to a **person who** ignorantly ate the meat of an animal that had not been bled. Provision was made for his cleansing. But if he refused this provision, he was to be punished.

VII. LAWS CONCERNING PERSONAL CONDUCT (Chaps. 18—22)

A. Laws of Sexual Purity (Chap. 18)

18:1–5 Chapter 18 deals with various forms of unlawful marriages with which the Israelites had become familiar in **Egypt** but which they were to completely renounce in **the land of Canaan.**

18:6–18 The expression **"to uncover the nakedness"** here means to have sexual intercourse. Verse 6 states the general principle. Marriage with a close relative was forbidden, whether **mother** (v. 7); stepmother (v. 8); **sister** or half-sister (v. 9); granddaughter (v. 10); the **daughter of** a stepmother (v. 11); aunt (vv. 12, 13); uncle (v. 14a). Modern medicine confirms that in marriages of blood relatives, the physical or mental weaknesses of the parents are sometimes magnified in the children. But the prohibition extended to in-laws and other relatives-by-marriage as well (vv. 14b–16), sometimes known as relationships of affinity. A reason sometimes given for this latter code is that the term "one flesh" in Genesis 2:24 describes a family relationship that is so close and permanent that even the union of relatives-by-marriage is considered to be incest. A man must not marry a **daughter-in-law** or step-granddaughter (v. 17) or take a woman as a rival to her sister (v. 18), as in the case of Hannah and Peninnah (1 Sam. 1:1–8). Verse 16 was later amended by Deuteronomy 25:5: If a man died childless, his brother was obliged to marry the widow. This was known as *levirate* marriage.

18:19–21 Intercourse with **a woman** was forbidden during menstruation. Adultery with a **neighbor's wife** was prohibited. Also banned were the terrible practices sometimes connected with the worship of the idol **Molech**, causing newborn babies to **pass through . . . fire** (2 Kgs. 23:10; Jer. 32:35). Molech was the god of the Ammonites: His idol-image was in the Valley of Hinnom. Francis Schaeffer describes the ritual:

> According to one tradition there was an opening at the back of the brazen idol, and after a fire was made within it, each parent had to come and with his own hands place his firstborn child in the white-hot, outstretched arms of Molech. According to this tradition, the parent was not allowed to show emotion, and drums were beaten so that the baby's cries could not be heard as the baby died in the arms of Molech.[22]

18:22, 23 Sodomy or homosexuality was forbidden, as well as sexual intercourse with **an animal**. In legislating against homosexuality, God may also have been anticipating the modern AIDS epidemic and seeking to save people from it.

18:24–30 Verses 1–23 tell the people *what* not to do; verses 24–30 tell them *why* not to do it. It is no accident that impurity and idolatry are found together in the same chapter (see also chap. 20). A person's morality is the fruit of his theology, his concept of God. The Canaanites were a graphic illustration of the degradation that idolatry produces (vv. 24–27). When the children of Israel took possession of the land, they killed thousands of these people at Jehovah's command. When we consider the moral degradation of the Canaanites, as described in verses 24–30, we can understand why God dealt so harshly with them.

B. Laws of Everyday Life (Chap. 19)

19:1–25 The basis of all holiness is found in the words **"I the LORD your God am holy"** (v. 2). Various laws for the conduct of the people are here laid down, as follows:

> **Mother and father** were to be revered (v. 3)—the fifth commandment.
>
> God's **Sabbaths** were to be observed (v. 3)—the fourth commandment.
>
> Idolatry was prohibited (v. 4)—the second commandment.
>
> Eating of the peace offering on

the third day was forbidden (vv. 5–8).

In harvesting a **field**, the owner was to **leave** some grain in the corners **for the poor and** strangers (vv. 9, 10). Field crops and grapes are mentioned as examples, not as a complete list.

Stealing, cheating, and lying were forbidden (v. 11)—the eighth commandment.

Swearing **by the Name of . . . God** to a false statement was outlawed (v. 12)—the third commandment.

Defrauding, robbing, or withholding wages were prohibited (v. 13).

Cursing **the deaf** or causing **the blind** to stumble were condemned (v. 14). The people were to express their reverence for Jehovah by their respect for one another (25:17). The handicapped (v. 14), the aged (v. 32), and the poor (25:26, 43) were all to be treated with kindness by those who feared the Lord.

Showing partiality **in judgment** was forbidden (v. 15).

Slander and plotting **against the life of** a **neighbor** were prohibited (v. 16).

Hatred of one's **brother** was forbidden: **"You shall surely rebuke your neighbor, and not bear sin because of him"** (v. 17). Matters should be dealt with openly and frankly lest they become the cause of inward animosity leading to outward sin.

Vengeance or bearing of grudges was prohibited (v. 18). The second part of verse 18, loving **your neighbor as yourself**, is the summation of the whole law (Gal. 5:14). Jesus said it was the second-greatest command (Mark 12:31). The greatest command is found in Deuteronomy 6:4, 5.

Verse 19 is generally understood to forbid the interbreeding of animals that results in mules. **Livestock** here means beasts in general.

Also, sowing a **field** with different kinds of **seed**, or wearing a **garment of mixed linen and wool** was forbidden. God is a God of separation, and in these physical examples He was teaching His people to separate themselves from sin and defilement.

If a man had illicit relations with a slave-girl **betrothed to** another **man**, both were scourged and he was required to **bring** a **trespass offering** (vv. 20–22).

When settled in Canaan, the Israelites were not to pick the **fruit** of their **trees** for **three years**. The **fruit** of **the fourth year** was to be offered **to the Lord**, and **in the fifth year** the **fruit** could be eaten (vv. 23–25). Perhaps the fruit of the fourth year went to the Levites or, as one commentator suggests, was eaten before the Lord as part of the second tithe.

19:26–37 Other forbidden practices were: eating of flesh from which the **blood** had not been drained (v. 26a); practicing witchcraft (v. 26b); trimming the hair in accordance with idolatrous practices (v. 27); making **cuttings in** one's **flesh** as an expression of mourning **for the dead** (v. 28a); making **marks on** the body as the heathen did (v. 28b); making one's **daughter** become a **prostitute**, as was common in pagan worship (v. 29); breaking of the Sabbath (v. 30); consulting **mediums** or **familiar spirits** (v. 31). **Honor** was to be shown to the aged (v. 32), and strangers were to be treated with kindness and hospitality (vv. 33, 34). **Honest** business practices were enjoined (vv. 35–37).

C. Punishment for Gross Offenses (Chap. 20)

This chapter gives the punishments for some of the offenses listed in chapters 18 and 19. The person who caused a child to go through the fire in an offering **to Molech** was to be stoned **to death** (vv. 1–3). **If the people** failed to kill him, God would destroy **him** and **his family** (vv. 4, 5). The death penalty was also pronounced against one who consulted **mediums** and **familiar spirits** (v. 6); one who cursed **his father or his mother** (v. 9); an **adulterer** and an **adulteress** (v. 10); one who committed incest **with his father's wife** (v. 11) or **daughter-in-law** (v. 12); and a sodomite (v. 13). (Both parties were to be killed in these cases of unlawful intercourse.) In the case of a man having unlawful sexual intercourse with a **mother** and her daughter, all three offenders were to **be burned** (v. 14). Sexual perversion between humans and animals was a capital crime; both man and beast were to be slain (vv. 15, 16). The death penalty (or, as some think, excommunication) was pronounced against intercourse with a **sister** or half-sister (v. 17) or with a menstruous **woman** (v. 18). Intercourse with an aunt called forth the judgment, **"they shall bear their guilt,"** but no details were given (v. 19). Some think it means that they would die childless, as in verse 20, where a man had intercourse with his uncle's wife, and in verse 21, where the offense was with a sister-in-law.

Verse 21 applied only as long as the brother was alive. If he died without leaving a son to carry on his name, his brother was commanded to marry the widow and name the first son after the deceased (Deut. 25:5). Such unions were known as *levirate* marriages.

The longing of God's heart was to have a holy people, separated from the abominations of the Gentiles and enjoying the blessings of the Promised Land (vv. 22–26). Mediums and people with **familiar spirits** were to be exterminated by stoning (v. 27).

D. Conduct of the Priests (Chaps. 21, 22)

Chapters 21 and 22, along with 16 and 17, are addressed to Aaron and his sons.

21:1–4 **Priests** were not to **defile** themselves by touching **the dead . . . except** in the case of **nearest relatives**. Even entering the tent of the dead defiled a person for seven days (Num. 19:14). This would disqualify a priest from serving the Lord during that time, so he was forbidden to make himself unclean for any but his **nearest relatives**. Verse 4 probably means that, because of his high rank, he must **not defile himself** for any reason except those listed in verses 2 and 3.

21:5–9 Practices of the heathen in defacing their bodies with signs of mourning for the dead were forbidden. The priest was not permitted to marry a woman profaned by harlotry or a **divorced . . . woman**. However, he could marry a widow. A priest's **daughter** who became a **harlot** was to **be burned** to death.

21:10–15 A **high priest** was not permitted to mourn in the customary ways or leave the **sanctuary** to show honor to the dead. He was to **marry** an Israelite **virgin**, and his married life was to be above reproach.

21:16–24 A physical **defect** barred a man from the service of the priesthood—blindness, lameness, facial deformities, a deformed limb, foot or hand injuries, hunchbackedness, dwarfism, defective eyes, itching diseases, scabs, or injured reproductive organs. Any son **of Aaron** who was defective in any of these ways could share the food of the priests, but he could not actively serve as a priest before the Lord (vv. 22, 23). The **holy** food was the priests' share of the peace offerings. The **most holy** food was their share of other offerings. The priests who offered the sacrifices must be without **defect** because they portrayed Christ as our unblemished High Priest.

22:1–9 If a priest was ceremonially unclean through leprosy, a running **discharge**, contact with something defiled by a dead body, eating meat that had not been drained of its blood, or for any other reason, he was not to partake of the food of the priests. That is what is meant by **"separate themselves from the holy things"** (v. 2). If the priest was a leper or had a running sore, the disqualification probably lasted for a long time. In the other cases mentioned, the following ritual prevailed for the priest: First, he must bathe himself, then wait until the evening, at which time he would **be clean** again.

22:10–13 In general, strangers, visitors, and hired servants were not permitted to **eat** the **holy** food. But a slave who had been purchased by the **priest**, as well as the slave's children, could **eat** it. **If the priest's daughter** got **married** to **an outsider, she** was **not** permitted to **eat** it, but if she were widowed **or divorced** and childless, and living with her father, then she could share the food of the priests.

22:14–16 **If a man** ate some of **the holy** food **unintentionally**, he could make restitution by replacing it and adding **one-fifth**, as in the case of the trespass offering.

22:17–30 **Offerings** brought **to the Lord** had to be **without blemish** (v. 19), whether for **burnt** offerings (vv. 18–20) or **peace** offerings (v. 21). Diseased, disabled, or disfigured animals were forbidden (v. 22). **A bull or a lamb** with an overgrown **limb** or a stunted **limb** could be presented for **a freewill offering** but not for a votive offering (v. 23). Castrated animals or those with damaged reproductive organs were not acceptable (v. 24). Israelites were not to accept any of the above defective animals as an offering from a stranger (v. 25). A sacrificial animal could not be offered until it was at least eight days old (vv. 26, 27). A mother animal and **her young** were **not** to be killed on **the same day** (v. 28). The meat of a **thanksgiving** offering was to **be eaten . . . on the same day** that it was offered (vv. 29, 30).

22:31–33 The final paragraph explains why the Israelites were to **keep** and **perform** all these **commandments of the Lord**. It was because the God **who** had **brought** them **out of the land of Egypt** is holy. Several expressions in this short section stress the message of Leviticus as a whole: **"not profane," "holy name," "I will be hallowed,"** and **"I am the Lord who sanctifies."**

VIII. THE FEASTS OF THE LORD (Chap. 23)

A. The Sabbath (23:1–3)

The religious calendar of Israel now becomes the subject of God's legislation. **The Lord** told the **children of Israel** through **Moses** to proclaim **the feasts of the Lord** as **holy convocations**.

After **six days** of labor, **the seventh day**, or **Sabbath**, was to be a day of **rest** from **work**. This was the only weekly holy day.

B. The Passover (23:4, 5)

The LORD's Passover was held **on the fourteenth day of the first month** (Nisan, or Abib). It commemorated Israel's redemption from slavery in Egypt. The **Passover** lamb was a type of Christ, the Lamb of God, our Passover (1 Cor. 5:7), whose blood was shed to redeem us from slavery to sin. He did not die at Creation but in the fullness of time (Gal. 4:4–6).

C. The Feast of Unleavened Bread (23:6–8)

The Feast of Unleavened Bread occurred in connection with the Passover. It extended over a period of **seven days**, beginning with the day after Passover—i.e., from **the fifteenth day of** Nisan to the twenty-first. The names of these two feasts are often used interchangeably. During this time the Jews were required to put away all leaven from their households. In Scripture, leaven speaks of sin. The feast pictures a life from which the leaven of malice and wickedness has been put away, and a life which is characterized by "the unleavened bread of sincerity and truth" (1 Cor. 5:8). There was no lapse between the **Passover** (our redemption) and the **Feast of Unleavened Bread** (our obligation to walk in holiness) . . . Even today the Jews eat unleavened bread during this feast. The bread is called matzo. The preparation of matzo involves piercing the bread, and in the *baking process* it becomes striped. This **unleavened bread** clearly reminds us of the sinless Messiah. He was pierced for us, and by His stripes we are healed.

D. The Feast of Firstfruits (23:9–14)

The presentation of a **wave . . . sheaf** of barley took place the second day of the Feast of Unleavened Bread (**on the day after the Sabbath**—i.e., the first day of the week). This is known as the Feast of **Firstfruits**. It marked the beginning of the barley **harvest**, the first grain of the year. A **sheaf** of barley was waved **before the LORD** in thanksgiving for the **harvest**. **A burnt offering** and **a grain offering** were also presented. This first harvest was viewed as the promise of the larger harvest to come. This pictures Christ in resurrection—"Christ . . . the firstfruits of those who have fallen asleep" (1 Cor. 15:20). His resurrection is the guarantee that all who put their faith in Him will also gain immortality through resurrection.

E. The Feast of Weeks (23:15–22)

23:15–22 The Feast of Weeks (Heb., *Shāvûôt*) or Pentecost (Gk. for "fifty") was held **fifty days . . . after the** Passover **Sabbath**. It was a **harvest** festival thanking God for the beginning of the wheat harvest. The **firstfruits** of the wheat harvest were presented at this time, along with **a burnt offering**, **a new grain offering**, **drink offerings**, and a **peace offering**. According to Jewish tradition, Moses received the law on this day of the year. The Feast is typical of the descent of the Holy Spirit on the Day of Pentecost, when the church was brought into existence. The **wave offering** consisted of **two . . . loaves** of bread made from the freshly reaped **fine flour**. (This was the only offering that was made **with leaven**.) These loaves represent, in type, the Jews and the Gentiles made into "one new man in [Christ]" (Eph. 2:15).

After Pentecost there was a long interval, about four months, before there was another feast. This span of time may picture the present church age, in which we eagerly await the return of our Savior.

F. The Feast of Trumpets (23:23–25)

The Feast of **Trumpets** took place on the **first day of the . . . seventh month**. The blowing of trumpets called the sons of Israel together for a solemn **holy convocation**. At this time there was a period of ten days for self-examination and repentance, leading up to the Day of Atonement. It typifies the time when Israel will be regathered to the land prior to her national repentance. This was the first day of the civil year, today called Rosh Hashanah (Heb. *head of the year*). Some see this feast as picturing another gathering as well—that is, the gathering of the saints to meet the Lord in the air at the Rapture.

G. The Day of Atonement (23:26–32)

The Day of Atonement (Heb., *Yôm Kippur*), occurring on **the tenth day of** the **seventh month**, has been described in detail in chapter 16. It prefigures the national repentance of Israel, when a believing remnant will turn to the Messiah and be forgiven (Zech. 12:10; 13:1). In almost every verse dealing with the Day of Atonement, God repeats the command to **do no work**. The only person who was to be active on this day was the high priest. The Lord reinforced the charge by threatening to **destroy** any **person** who violated it. This is because the salvation which our High Priest obtained for us was "not on the basis of deeds which we have done" (Titus 3:5). There can be no human works involved in the business of removing our sins. Christ's work and His alone is the source of eternal salvation. To **"afflict your souls"** (vv. 27, 29) means to fast. Even today religious Jews observe the day as a time for fasting and prayer. Although the **Day of Atonement** is listed among the feasts of Jehovah, it was actually a time for *fasting* rather than *feasting*. However, after the sin question was settled, there came a time of rejoicing in the Feast of Tabernacles.

H. The Feast of Tabernacles (23:33–44)

The Feast of Tabernacles (Heb., *Sukkôth*, "booths") began on **the fifteenth day of** the **seventh month. For seven days** the Israelites dwelt **in booths** (v. 42). It pictured the final rest and final harvest, when Israel will be dwelling securely in the land during the Millennium. This feast is also called the Feast of Ingathering (Ex. 23:16). It was associated with harvesting. In fact several of the feasts mentioned in this chapter have to do with harvesting. The two **Sabbaths** may picture the Millennium and the Eternal Rest. Moishe and Ceil Rosen describe the tradition:

> The Jewish people built booth-like structures and lived in them during this feast as a reminder of the temporary dwellings the Israelites had in the wilderness. Even today many Jewish people build open-roofed, three-sided huts for this festival. They decorate them with tree boughs and autumn fruits to remind them of harvest.
>
> Everyone who was able came up to Jerusalem for this harvest festival every year. The Temple worship for the holiday included the ritual pouring of water from the Pool of Siloam, symbolic of the prayers for the winter rains. It was at this time that Jesus cried out, ". . . If any man thirst, let him come to Me and drink" (John 7:37–38).
>
> After Israel's final Day of Atonement, the Feast of Booths will be celebrated again in Jerusalem (Zech. 14:16).[23]

One of the things the Lord sought to teach His people through the feasts was the close association between the spiritual and the physical aspects of life. Times of bounty and blessing were to be times of rejoicing **before the Lord**. The Lord was portrayed to them as the One who abundantly provided for their daily needs. Their response as a nation to His goodness found expression in the festivals connected with the harvest.

Notice the repetition of the commandment that the Israelites were to do **no** servile or **customary work** on these solemn occasions (vv. 3, 7, 8, 21, 25, 28, 30, 31, 35, 36).

A definite chronological progression can be traced in the Feasts of Jehovah. The Sabbath takes us back to God's rest after creation. The Passover and the Feast of Unleavened Bread speak to us of Calvary. Next comes the Feast of Firstfruits, pointing to the resurrection of Christ. The Feast of Pentecost typifies the coming of the Holy Spirit. Then looking to the future, the Feast of Trumpets pictures the regathering of Israel. The Day of Atonement foreshadows the time when a remnant of Israel will repent and acknowledge Jesus as Messiah. Finally the Feast of Tabernacles sees Israel enjoying the millennial reign of Christ.

IX. CEREMONIAL AND MORAL LEGISLATION (Chap. 24)

In chapter 23 the yearly feasts were dealt with. Now the daily and weekly ministries before the Lord are taken up.

24:1–9 Pure **oil of pressed olives** was to be burned in the **gold lampstand before the Lord continually**. The **twelve cakes** were to be **set** in **two rows** or piles on the **table** of showbread, and replaced each Sabbath. The **frankincense** mentioned in verse 7 belonged **to the Lord**. It was offered to Jehovah when the old bread was removed and given to the priests for food.

24:10–23 Then there is the abrupt account of **a son of an Israelite woman, whose father was an Egyptian**, who was **stoned** to death for cursing God (vv. 10–16, 23). The incident shows that the law was the same for anyone who lived in the camp of Israel, whether he was a fullblooded Jew or not (v. 22). It shows that blasphemy, like murder, was punishable by **death** (vv. 14, 16, 17, 23). (Verse 16 was probably the law against blasphemy, which the Jews referred to when they said, "We have a law, and according to our law He [the Lord Jesus] ought to die, because He made Himself the Son of God" [John 19:7].) It shows that compensation could be made for some other crimes (vv. 18, 21). Finally the incident shows that:

> . . . retribution was a basic principle of law; wrongs had to be righted. Softness brought the law into disrepute. The law of retaliation is scoffed at today in the Western world, but thoughtful people will not dismiss it. (a) In ancient society, punishment was often out of all proportion with the wrong done. Retaliatory punishment was thus a great step toward true justice. (b) Furthermore, rehabilitative punishment—the alternative most frequently suggested—suffers from subjectivism. Who is to decide when a man is rehabilitated, ready to rejoin society? The terms may be lenient today, but what of tomorrow? True justice is an eye (and not more) for an eye. (*Daily Notes of the Scripture Union*)

In verses 1–9 we see a picture of Israel as God intended. In verses 10–16 the cursing man pictures Israel as it actually became, blaspheming the Name and cursing ("His blood be on us, and on our children").

X. THE SABBATICAL YEAR AND THE YEAR OF JUBILEE (Chap. 25)

The legislation in chapters 25—27 was given **to Moses on Mount Sinai** and not from within the tabernacle (25:1; 26:46; 27:34).

25:1–7 Every **seventh year** was to be observed as **a sabbath**. **The land** was to lie fallow (uncultivated). **Food** for the people would be provided from the crop that grew **of its own accord**. The owner was not to harvest it, but leave it for free use by the people.

25:8–17 **The fiftieth year** was also a sabbath, known as **the Year of Jubilee**. It began **on the Day of Atonement** following **seven** sabbatic-year cycles (**forty-nine years**). Slaves were to be set free, the **land** was to lie fallow, and was to revert to its original owner. **The price** of a slave or a piece of land decreased as the Year of Jubilee approached (vv. 15–17), and all business transactions were supposed to take this fact into account. The words "Proclaim liberty throughout all the land unto all the inhabitants thereof" (v. 10 KJV) are inscribed on the United States Liberty Bell. Believers today may liken the **Year of Jubilee** to the coming of the Lord. As we get closer to His coming, our material wealth decreases in value. The moment He comes, our money, real estate, and investments will be worthless to us. The moral is to put these things to work for Him *today!*

25:18–22 With regard to the sabbatic year, the people might wonder how they would have enough food to eat that year and the following year. God promised them that if they were obedient, He would give them sufficient crops during the sixth year to last **for three years**.

Once every fifty years, there would be two successive years when there would be no sowing or harvesting, that is, when the regular sabbatic year would be followed by the year of jubilee. Presumably the Lord gave enough crops in the forty-eighth year to last for four years.

Some scholars believe that, by inclusive reckoning, the fiftieth year was actually the forty-ninth. At any rate, this is an ancient example of good ecology: conserving the land's fertility by enforced rest. In modern times man has become concerned about preserving our planet's resources. As so often, God's Word is centuries ahead of the times.

25:23–28 **Land** could **be sold**, but not **permanently**, because Jehovah is the Owner. There were three ways in which land could be "redeemed" (revert to its original Jewish owner): The nearest **relative** could buy it back for the seller (v. 25); the seller (original owner), if he regained financial solvency, could redeem it, paying the purchaser for the years remaining until the Year of Jubilee (vv. 26, 27); otherwise, the land automatically reverted to the original owner in **the Year of Jubilee** (v. 28).

25:29–34 **A house in a walled city** was subject to redemption for one **year**; after that, it became the property of the new owner **permanently**. **Houses** in unwalled **villages** were **counted** as part of the land and therefore reverted to the original owner in **the Year of Jubilee**. **Houses** owned by **the Levites** in the special **cities** assigned to them were always subject to being bought back by the Levites. The **field** assigned to **the Levites** for **common-land** was **not** to be **sold**.

25:35–38 If an Israelite fell **into** debt and **poverty**, his Jewish creditors were not to oppress him. They were not to charge him **interest** on money or demand additional food for **food** that was lent.

25:39-46 If an impoverished Israelite sold **himself** to a Jewish creditor for nonpayment of debt, he was not to be treated **as a slave** but **as a hired servant**, and was to be released in the **Year of Jubilee**, if this came before the end of his six years of service. The Jews were permitted to have slaves from the Gentile nations, and these were considered their own property, to be handed down to their descendants. But Jewish people were **not** to be **slaves** themselves.

25:47–54 If a Jew **sold** himself to a Gentile who happened to be living in the land, the Jew could always be bought back and set free. The redemption **price** was determined by **the number of years** remaining **until the Year of Jubilee**. The relative redeeming the Jew could use him as **a hired servant** until the **Jubilee**. If no relative **redeemed** him, then he automatically went free in **the Year of Jubilee**.

25:55 This verse is a vivid reminder that the Israelites and their land (v. 23) belonged to **the Lord** and that He should be recognized as rightful Owner. Neither God's people nor God's land could be sold permanently.

XI. BLESSINGS AND CURSINGS (Chap. 26)

A. The Blessings for Obedience to God (26:1–13)

Twice as much space is devoted to warning as to blessing in this chapter. Adversity, the promised fruit of disobedience, is a tool which God uses, not to inflict revenge but to lead His people to repentance (vv. 40–42). National chastisement would be increasingly severe until the people confessed their iniquity. Notice the progression in verses 14, 18, 21, 24, and 28.

After warnings against idolatry (v. 1), sabbath-breaking, and irreverence (v. 2), the Lord promised the following blessings to the nation if it would keep His commandments: **rain**, fertility (v. 4), productivity, security (v. 5), **peace**, safety (v. 6), victory over **enemies** (vv. 7, 8), fruitfulness, and the presence of the Lord (vv. 9–13). Knox's version of verse 13 is especially graphic: "Was it not I . . . that . . . struck the chains from your necks, and gave you the upright carriage of free men?"

B. The Curses for Disobedience to God (26:14–39)

26:14–33 Disobedience would result in **terror**, **disease**, conquest by **enemies**, drought, barrenness, **wild beasts**, **pestilence**, invasion, and captivity.

Verse 26 describes famine conditions. **Bread** would be so scarce that **ten women** would be able to **bake** their supply **in one oven**, ordinarily big enough for only one family's use. Even more severe famine is pictured in verse 29, where cannibalism prevails (see 2 Kgs. 6:29 and Lam. 4:10 for the historical fulfillment of this warning).

26:34–39 Persistent disobedience on Israel's part would result in their being taken captive by a foreign power. The **land** of Israel would **enjoy** a period of **rest** equal to the number of sabbatic years which the people disregarded. This is what happened in the Babylonian captivity. During the years from Saul to the captivity the people had failed to keep the sabbatic years. Thus they spent seventy years in exile, and the land enjoyed its rest (2 Chron. 36:20, 21).

C. Restoration through Confession and Repentance (26:40–46)

The final section of chapter 26 provided a way of recovery through confession and repentance for the disobedient nation. God would not completely forsake His people but would **remember** His **covenant** promises to **their ancestors**.

XII. VOWS AND TITHES (Chap. 27)

The last chapter of Leviticus deals with voluntary vows made to the Lord. It seems that in gratitude to the Lord for some blessing, a man could vow to the Lord a person (himself or a member of his family), an animal, a house, or a field. The things vowed were given to the priests (Num. 18:14). Since these gifts were not always of use to the priests, provision was made that the person making the vow could give the priest a sum of money in lieu of the thing vowed.

27:1, 2 A **vow** of consecration was very special.

27:3–7 If a person was vowed to the Lord, then the redemption price to be paid to the priest was as follows:

A man **from** 20–60 **years old**	50 **shekels**
A woman **from** 20–60 years old	30 **shekels**
A male from 5–20 **years old**	20 **shekels**
A female from 5–20 years old	10 **shekels**
A male from 1 **month to** 5 **years old**	5 **shekels**
A female from 1 month to 5 years old	3 **shekels**
A male 60 **years old and above**	15 **shekels**
A female 60 years old and above	10 **shekels**

27:8 If a man was **too poor** to redeem his vow according to this chart, then the **priest** determined some figure **according to** his **ability**.

27:9–13 If the vow was an animal, the following rules applied: A clean **animal**, suitable for sacrifice, could not be redeemed (v. 9). It was to be offered to the Lord upon the altar (Num. 18:17); nothing could be gained by exchanging one **animal** for another, because both would then become the Lord's (vv. 10, 33); an unclean animal could be redeemed by paying the **value** placed on it by **the priest**, plus **one-fifth** (vv. 11–13).

27:14, 15 If **a man** dedicated **his house to . . . the LORD**, he could change his mind and buy it back by paying the priest's estimate of its value, plus **one-fifth**.

27:16–18 Appraising the value of **a field** was complicated by the fact that it reverted to the original owner **in the Year of Jubilee**.

If it was dedicated by its original owner, that is, if he inherited it, then the rules in verses 16–21 applied. It was valued **according to the seed** sown in it. For example, if a **homer of barley seed** were sown in it, it would be valued **at fifty shekels of silver**.

If the **field** was vowed near or at the **Year of Jubilee**, then the above appraisal was effective. **But if** it was dedicated some years **after the** Year of **Jubilee**, then the value of the field decreased accordingly. In other words, the field would be worth only 30 shekels if it was vowed 20 years after the Year of Jubilee.

27:19–21 If **the field** was redeemed, then an added payment of **one-fifth** was required.

If, after giving the land to the Lord, the owner did **not . . . redeem** it before the Year of Jubilee, or if he secretly **sold** it to someone else, it could no longer **be redeemed** but became the **possession of the priest** at **the** Year of **Jubilee**. The land was then **"devoted"** or **"holy" to the LORD**.

27:22–25 If **a field** was dedicated by someone who was not its original owner, that is, by someone who bought it, then verses 22–25 applied. **The priest** set a value on the property, depending on how many crops could be raised on it before the Year of Jubilee. In that year, **the field** went back to its original owner.

27:26, 27 The **firstborn** of a sacrificial animal could not be dedicated to the Lord, because it belonged to Him anyway. The firstborn of **an unclean animal** could be redeemed by paying the priest's **valuation** of it, plus **one-fifth**. Otherwise the priest could sell it.

27:28, 29 Nothing that was under sentence of **death** or **destruction** could **be redeemed**. This is what was meant by a **devoted** or proscribed thing. Thus a son who cursed his parents could not **be redeemed** but must **be put to death**.

It should be noted that there is an important distinction in this chapter between what is consecrated (NASB) or sanctified (KJV) and what is proscribed (NASB) or devoted (NKJV, KJV). Things sanctified by vow—that is, set apart for divine use—could be redeemed. Devoted things were given completely and finally, and could not be redeemed.

27:30, 31 A **tithe** or tenth of the grain and **fruit** belonged to the Lord. If the offerer wanted to keep it, he could pay its value plus **one-fifth**.

27:32, 33 The expression **"whatever passes under the rod"** refers to the practice of numbering sheep or goats by causing them to pass under the shepherd's rod. Leslie Flynn comments:

> With rod in hand, he [the shepherd] would touch every tenth one. He could in no way contrive to change their order so that a good animal would escape tenth place. If he tried to alter the order, both the real tenth and the attempted switch would be the Lord's.[24]

This first **tithe** was called the levitical tithe, because it was paid to the Levites (Num. 18:21–24). A second tithe, which apparently is a different one, is prescribed in Deuteronomy 14:22–29.

27:34 The commandments which the LORD commanded Moses in the last verse of Leviticus probably refer to the whole book. After studying the multitude of detailed rituals and blood sacrifices, we can rejoice with Matthew Henry that

> We are not under the *dark shadows* of the law, but enjoy the clear light of the gospel, . . . that we are not under the *heavy yoke* of the law, and the carnal ordinances of it . . . , but under the sweet and easy institutions of the gospel, which pronounces those the *true worshippers that worship the Father in spirit and truth,* by Christ only, and in his name, who is our priest, temple, altar, sacrifice, purification, and all. Let us not therefore think that because we are not tied to the ceremonial cleansings, feasts, and oblations, a little care, time, and expense, will serve to honour God with. No, but rather have our hearts more enlarged with free-will offerings to his praise, more inflamed with holy love and joy, and more engaged in seriousness of thought and sincerity of intention. *Having boldness to enter into the holiest by the blood of Jesus, let us draw near with a true heart, and in full assurance of faith,* worshipping God with so much the more cheerfulness and humble confidence, still saying, *Blessed be God for Jesus Christ!*[25]

ENDNOTES

[1] (Chap. 1) The word *'ōlāh* comes from the root word meaning "to go up." The idea is that the whole animal is brought up to God's altar and offered up as a gift in its entirety.

[2] (Chap. 1) Peter Pell, *The Tabernacle*, pp. 102, 103.

[3] (Chap. 2) The translation "meat" in the KJV meant solid food as opposed to liquid in 1611. What we call *meat* today was called *flesh* in the seventeenth century. Some scholars derive the word *minḥāh* from a root meaning "lead" or "guide." Most suggest a root meaning "gift."

[4] (3:1–15) This word, almost always in the plural form *shelāmîm*, is related to the well-known Hebrew word *shālôm*. The Hebrew concept is broader than merely absence of hostility, but includes prosperity and wholeness as well as peace with God. A second meaning of this word is a sacrifice of communion in God's presence. Usually, though not here, the peace offering is last in order, and some scholars derive the word from the rare meaning "to complete." Carr makes a nice application: "If this sense is correct, the NT references to Christ our Peace (e.g., Eph 2:14) become more meaningful, as he is the final sacrifice for us (cf. Heb. 9:27; 10:12)." G. Lloyd Carr, *"Shelem," Theological Wordbook of the Old Testament*, III:932.

[5] (Chap. 3) Pell, *Tabernacle*, p. 92.

[6] (Chap. 4) Strangely enough to us, this same Hebrew word, occurring almost 300 times in the OT, can mean either "sin" or "sin offering."

[7] (5:14—6:7) The RSV and NEB translate by "guilt offering," but the traditional translation is preferable.

[8] (6:18) Keil and Delitzsch interpret the latter part of this verse to mean that "every layman who touched these most holy things became holy through the contact, so that henceforth he had to guard against defilement in the same manner as the sanctified priests." C. F. Keil and Franz Delitzsch, "Leviticus," in *Biblical Commentary on the Old Testament*, II:319.

[9] (7:11–18) A. G. Clarke, *Precious Seed Magazine*, No. 2, Vol. 11, March-April 1960, p. 49.

[10] (7:11–18) *Ibid*.

[11] (7:11–18) John Reid, *The Chief Meeting of the Church*, p. 58.

[12] (7:22–27) Dr. S. I. McMillen, *None of These Diseases*, p. 84.

[13] (Chap. 8) Matthew Henry, *Matthew Henry's Commentary on the Whole Bible*, I:474.

[14] (Chap. 12) George Williams, *The Student's Commentary on the Holy Scriptures*, p. 71.

[15] (13:Intro) Harrison, *Leviticus*, p. 137. In Appendix A, p. 241 of his commentary he gives a semi-technical translation of chapter 13 that proves helpful for those who are interested in the medical aspects of the conditions mentioned.

[16] (13:Intro) *Ibid*., pp. 136, 137.

[17] (13:38, 39) *Ibid*., p. 245.

[18] (13:47–59) *Ibid*., p. 146.

[19] (13:47–59) *Ibid*.

[20] (16:11–22) G. Morrish, publisher, *New and Concise Bible Dictionary*, p. 91.

[21] (17:1–9) G. Campbell Morgan, *Searchlights from the Word*, p. 38.

[22] (18:19–21) Francis A. Schaeffer, *The Church at the End of the 20th Century*, p. 126.

[23] (23:33–44) Moishe and Ceil Rosen, *Christ in the Passover*, pagination unavailable.

[24] (27:32, 33) Leslie B. Flynn, *Your God and Your Gold*, pp. 30, 31.

[25] (27:34) Henry, "Leviticus," I:562.

BIBLIOGRAPHY

Bonar, Andrew. *A Commentary on the Book of Leviticus*. 1852. Reprint. Grand Rapids: Baker Book House, 1978.

Borland, James A. "Leviticus." In *Liberty Bible Commentary*. Lynchburg, VA: The Old-Time Gospel Hour, 1982.

Coleman, Robert O. "Leviticus." In *Wycliffe Bible Commentary*. Chicago: Moody Press, 1962.

Harrison, R. K. *Leviticus: An Introduction and Commentary*. The Tyndale Old Testament Commentaries. Downers Grove, IL: InterVarsity Press, 1980.

Henry, Matthew. "Leviticus." In *Matthew Henry's Commentary on the Whole Bible*. Vol. 1. McLean, VA: MacDonald Publishing Company, n.d.

Jukes, Andrew. *The Law of the Offerings*. London: The Lamp Press, 1954.

Keil, C. F., and Delitzsch, F. "Leviticus." In *Biblical Commentary on the Old Testament. The Pentateuch, Vol. 4*. Grand Rapids: Wm. B. Eerdmans Publishing Co., 1971.

Lindsey, F. Duane. "Leviticus." In *The Bible Knowledge Commentary*. Wheaton, IL: Victor Books, 1985.

Smith, Arthur E. *Leviticus for Lambs*. Privately Printed, n.d.

Periodicals

Clarke, A. G. "The Levitical Offerings," *Precious Seed Magazine*, 1960.

NUMBERS

Introduction

"Numbers has a unique contribution to the life of the Christian when the broad sequence of its historical setting is seen as a parallel situation to Christian living. The writer of the Epistle to the Hebrews makes this significant application, devoting two chapters to it (Heb. 3 and 4)."

—Irving L. Jensen

I. Unique Place in the Canon

The English name of the fourth book of Moses is a translation of the Septuagint's title, *Arithmoi,* and obviously is so-called because of the census in chapter 1 and again in chapter 26, as well as the many other numerical data given throughout.

The Hebrew title is much more descriptive of the book as a whole: "In the Wilderness" (*Bemidbār*). The narrative of forty years in the wilderness is full of interesting and well-known stories: the spies visiting Canaan, Korah's rebellion, Aaron's rod that budded, the brass serpent, Balaam and his donkey, and other lesser known events.

It should not be thought that this is merely "Hebrew history." All of these things happened for our spiritual edification. We are to learn from the mistakes of the children of Israel, not repeat them. Consequently Numbers is a very important book.

II. Authorship

According to Jewish and Christian teaching, Numbers was written by the great law-giver, Moses. This is widely discounted in liberal circles, but see Introduction to the Pentateuch for a concise defense of the Mosaic authorship.

III. Date

Rationalistic scholars put the Pentateuch very late in Jewish history, but a date of about 1406 B.C. is compatible with conservative and believing scholarship. (See Introduction to the Pentateuch for details.)

IV. Background and Theme

The historical backdrop for the Book of Numbers, as its Hebrew title suggests, is the wilderness. The journeys and wanderings depicted here cover about thirty-eight years, from Israel's departure from Mount Sinai till they reached the Plains of Moab, opposite the Promised Land. The wanderings were due to unbelief, hence God gives no itinerary of them. As Scroggie remarks, "The movements of God's people out of His will are not on His calendar."[1]

As Leviticus stresses worship and spiritual position, the theme of Numbers is *walk* and spiritual *progress* (or lack of it!). Christians should not think that this book is a dry Jewish history book! It is full of applications to modern Christian experience. It would be pleasant to think that all (or most) Christians advance swiftly from salvation to a full entering into God's promises of victory; observation and experience, however, show how much *we* resem ble the ancient Israelites in complaining, backsliding, and rank unbelief.

The good news is that we do not need to repeat the wanderings of Israel in our spiritual pilgrimage. God has made full provision for spiritual success through faith. (See *Believers Bible Commentary, New Testament*, especially Romans 6—8.)

OUTLINE

I. THE LAST DAYS AT SINAI (1:1—10:10)
   A. The Census and Arrangement of the Tribes (Chaps. 1, 2)
   B. The Number and Duties of the Levites (Chaps. 3, 4)
   C. Cleanliness and Confession (5:1–10)
   D. The Law of Jealousy (5:11–31)
   E. The Law of the Nazirite (Chap. 6)
   F. The Offering of the Princes (Chap. 7)
   G. The Services of the Tabernacle (Chap. 8)
   H. The Passover, the Cloud, and the Silver Trumpets (9:1—10:10)

II. FROM SINAI TO THE PLAINS OF MOAB (10:11—22:1)
   A. Setting out from the Sinai Wilderness (10:11–36)
   B. Rebellion in the Camp (Chap. 11)
   C. Rebellion of Aaron and Miriam (Chap. 12)
   D. Spying out the Promised Land (Chaps. 13, 14)
   E. Various Legislation (Chap. 15)
   F. Korah's Rebellion (Chaps. 16, 17)
   G. Instructions to the Levites (Chaps. 18, 19)
   H. The Sin of Moses (20:1–13)
   I. The Death of Aaron (20:14–29)
   J. The Bronze Serpent (21:1—22:1)

III. EVENTS ON THE PLAINS OF MOAB (22:23—6:13)
   A. The Prophet Balaam (22:2—25:18)
      1. Balaam Summoned by Balak (22:2–40)
      2. Balaam's Oracles (22:41—24:25)
      3. Balaam's Corruption of Israel (Chap. 25)
   B. The Second Census (Chap. 26)
   C. Inheritance Rights of Daughters (27:1–11)
   D. Joshua, Moses' Successor (27:12–23)
   E. Offering and Vows (Chaps. 28—30)
   F. Destruction of the Midianites (Chap. 31)

G. The Inheritance of Reuben, Gad, and Half of Manasseh (Chap. 32)
H. Review of the Israelite Encampments (Chap. 33)
I. Boundaries of the Promised Land (Chap. 34)
J. Cities of the Levites (35:1–5)
K. Cities of Refuge and Capital Punishment (35:6–34)
L. The Inheritance of Daughters Who Marry (Chap. 36)

Commentary

I. THE LAST DAYS AT SINAI (1:1—10:10)

A. The Census and Arrangement of the Tribes (Chaps. 1, 2)

1:1 As the book of Numbers opens, it is one year and one month after the children of Israel left **Egypt** and one month after the **tabernacle** was erected (Ex. 40:17). As noted, the book received its name because the people are numbered twice (chaps. 1, 26). The census mentioned here is not the same as the one recorded in Exodus 30:11–16. They were taken at different times and for different purposes. The second census (Num. 1) was probably based on the earlier census; hence the similar totals.

1:2, 3 The people of Israel were soon to begin their journey from Mount Sinai to the Promised Land. It was essential that they be arranged as orderly marching **armies**, and for this purpose God commanded that **a census** should be taken. The census would include all men **twenty years old and above—all who were able to go to war**.

1:4–17 One **man** was appointed **from every tribe** to assist Moses with the census. Their names are given in verses 5–16. Verse 17 reads, **"Then Moses and Aaron took these men who had been mentioned by name."**

1:18–46 The results of the census were as follows:

TRIBE	REFERENCE	NUMBER
Reuben	vv. 20, 21	46,500
Simeon	vv. 22, 23	59,300
Gad	vv. 24, 25	45,650
Judah	vv. 26, 27	74,600
Issachar	vv. 28, 29	54,400
Zebulun	vv. 30, 31	57,400
Ephraim	vv. 32, 33	40,500
Manasseh	vv. 34, 35	32,200
Benjamin	vv. 36, 37	35,400
Dan	vv. 38, 39	62,700
Asher	vv. 40, 41	41,500
Naphtali	vv. 42, 43	53,400
TOTAL		603,550

Notice that **Ephraim** is larger than **Manasseh**. This is in accordance with the blessing of Jacob in Genesis 48:19, 20. The tribes are listed beginning with **Reuben**, the firstborn, and his camp (south), then **Judah** and his camp (east), then **Dan** and his camp (north), and finally **Ephraim** and his camp (west).

1:47–54 **The Levites were not numbered among** the men of Israel who were to be warriors (v. 47). They were charged with the setting **up** and taking **down** of the **tabernacle** and with the ministry connected with it. By positioning themselves around the tabernacle, they protected it from desecration and thus protected the people from punishment (v. 53).

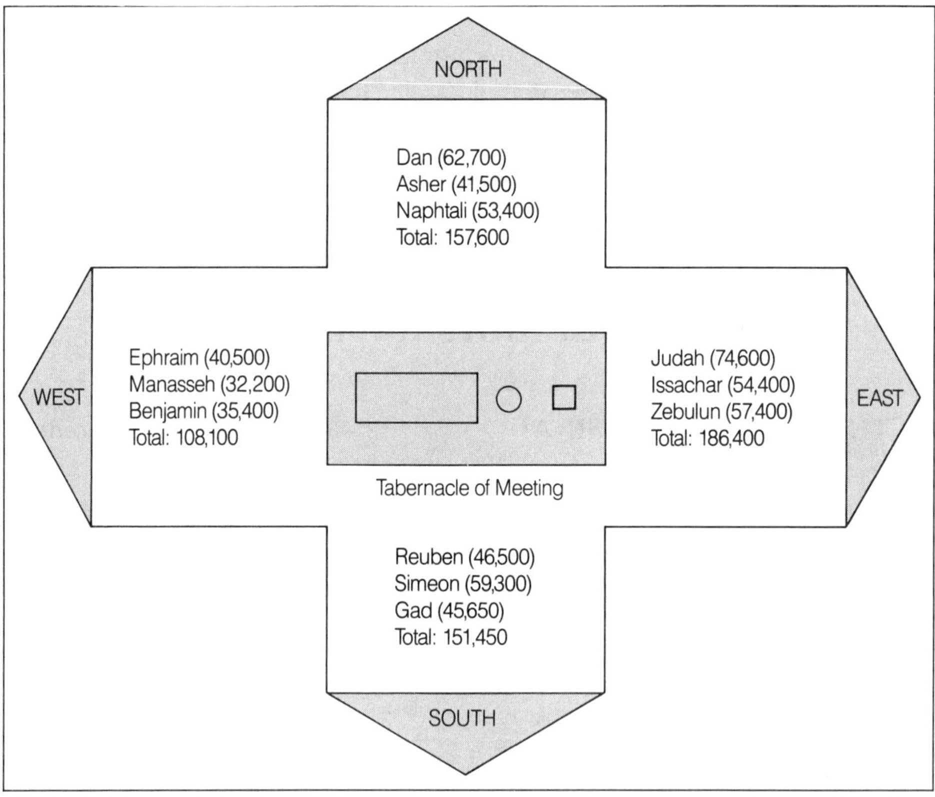

Placement of the Tribes in the Israelite Encampment

2:1, 2 The tribes of Israel were commanded to pitch their tents in the area around **the tabernacle** (see diagram), three tribes on each side

2:3–16 On the east side, under the flag of **Judah**, were **Judah, Issachar,** and **Zebulun** (vv. 3–9). Each tribe had its own military **leader**. These tribes totaled **one hundred and eighty-six thousand four hundred. On the south side**, under the flag of **Reuben**, were **Reuben, Simeon,** and **Gad** (vv. 10–16). The camp of Reuben totaled **one hundred and fifty-one thousand four hundred and fifty**.

2:17–31 On the west side, under the flag of **Ephraim**, were **Ephraim, Manasseh,** and **Benjamin** (vv. 18–24). This camp numbered **one hundred and eight thousand one hundred**. **On the north side**, under the flag of **Dan**, were **Dan, Asher,** and **Naphtali** (vv. 25–31). These totaled **one hundred and fifty-seven thousand six hundred**. The tribes were to march in the order given—the camp of **Judah** first, etc. **The Levites** marched after **Gad** and before **Ephraim** (v. 17).

2:32–34 The total number of men of war was **six hundred and three thousand five hundred and fifty** (v. 32). The total manpower, including the Levites (3:39), was 625,550. Assuming the men to be a third of the nation, then the total population must have been at least 1,876,650. The number of warriors is a better index of the strength of a church than the number of pewsitters!

B. The Number and Duties of the Levites (Chaps. 3, 4)

Chapters 3 and 4 have to do with the service of the Levites, who were not included in the census of chapters 1 and 2. The tribe of Levi was set aside by God for the service of the sanctuary. Originally, He had selected the firstborn sons to belong to Himself, but later He selected the tribe of Levi in their place for divine service (vv. 12, 13). Levi had three sons—Gershon, Kohath, and Merari. Their descendants were charged with the care of the tabernacle and its fixtures.

3:1–10a The family of **Aaron** (descended from Kohath) was the priestly family (v. 9). All other **Levites** served in connection with the **tabernacle** but were not priests. (The expression "the priests the Levites," found later in the Pentateuch, means the Levitical priests. It does not mean that all Levites were priests but that all priests were descended from **Levi**.) The priestly family is described in verses 1–4. After Nadab and Abihu had been slain for their sacrilege, Aaron was left with two sons—Eleazar and Ithamar. The Levites were servants of the priests (vv. 5–9). No one but **Aaron and his descendants** were to serve in **the priesthood** (v. 10a).

3:10b–13 The mediation of the OT priests could not bring the individual sinner into close communion with God. He had to stay away from the holy things under pain of **death** (v. 10b). But now the mediation of the Lord Jesus Christ, our Great High Priest, gives us not only access to God but also boldness to enter into His very presence (Heb. 4:16). This drastic change stems from that great event which lies between Numbers and Hebrews—the miracle of Calvary.

3:14–39 The Levites were **numbered**, not as warriors but as worshipers (v. 15). Each son of Levi was charged with responsibility for certain parts of the tabernacle:

TRIBE	CHARGE	REFERENCE	NUMBER
Gershon	All the curtains, coverings, and **hangings** of **the tabernacle** and outer **court**, except the "veil" which was wrapped around the ark.	vv. 18–26	7500
Kohath	The most holy things—**the ark, the table** of showbread, **the utensils, the screen, the altars, the** golden **lampstand**, etc.	vv. 27–32	8600
Merari	**The boards**, the **bars**, the **pillars**, the **sockets**, the **pegs, and** the **cords**.	vv. 33–37	6200

The Levites were to pitch their tents immediately outside the tabernacle enclosure, with the **Gershonites** on the west (v. 23), the **Kohathites** on the south (v. 29), and **the families of Merari** on the north (v. 35). **Moses** and **Aaron** and **sons were to camp . . . on the east**, at the entrance to the tabernacle (vv. 38, 39). (See diagram.)

Levi was the smallest tribe in Israel. The total number of Levites a month old and upward was **twenty-two thousand** (v. 39). However, the figures recorded in verses 22, 28, and 34 total 22,300. Various explanations of this discrepancy have been given. Williams suggests that the additional 300 were firstborn sons, born since the Exodus, who would naturally be omitted when the Levites were chosen to replace the firstborn of the other tribes.[2]

3:40–51 The meaning of this passage is as follows: the **Levites** were chosen by God to be His own, **instead of all the firstborn** sons. There were 22,000 Levites and 22,273 firstborn sons (vv. 39, 43). Thus there weren't enough Levites to compensate for all the firstborn of Israel who would have served under the original plan. The Lord commanded that the additional **two hundred and seventy-three** firstborn sons could be redeemed (bought back) by the payment of **five shekels . . . each**. This redemption money (273 x 5 = 1365 shekels) was paid to Aaron and his sons (v. 51). It should be noted that the **firstborn** mentioned in verse 43 might include only those born since the Exodus from Egypt.

4:1–3 The numbering in chapter 4 was to determine the number of Levites who were available for active **service** in connection with **the tabernacle**. These were the men **from thirty . . . to fifty years** of age.

4:4–20 Exodus 25:15 says, "The poles shall be in the rings of the ark; they shall not be taken from it." But verse 6 says that the priests **"shall insert its poles."** A possible solution suggested in Keil and Delitzsch's commentary is that verse 6 might be translated, "adjust its bearing poles."[3]

The duties of **the Kohathites** are taken up first (vv. 4–20). Aaron and his sons were designated to pack the **tabernacle** and the sacred **vessels** (vv. 5–13). **The ark** (vv. 5, 6), **the table of showbread** (vv. 7, 8), the golden **lampstand** (vv. 9, 10), **the golden altar** (v. 11), **the utensils** (v. 12), and the **bronze altar** (vv. 13, 14) were to be draped with **a covering of badger skins**. The other **sons of Kohath** were then appointed to **carry** these covered articles. (The laver isn't mentioned here but they must have carried it also.) They were **not** allowed to **touch** or even look on them uncovered, lest they die (vv. 15, 17–20). **Eleazar the son of Aaron** was placed in charge of the **tabernacle** and its sacred **furnishings** (v. 16).

The **veil** between the Holiest and the holy place always hid the ark from view (v. 5). Even when Israel was on the move, the ark was covered by this same veil, which pictured the body of our Lord Jesus Christ. No one except the high priest could look upon the throne of God above the ark until Calvary, when the veil was forever torn in two.

4:21–28 **The Gershonites** were to carry **the curtains of the tabernacle**, the **tabernacle of meeting**, **the hangings of the court**, and the screens. **Ithamar the son of Aaron** was in charge of the Gershonites.

4:29–33 **The families of the sons of Merari** were appointed to **carry** the **boards, bars, pillars, sockets, pegs, and cords**.

4:3–49 The results of the census were as follows:

Kohathites	2750
Gershonites	2630
Merarites	3200
TOTAL number of **Levites** from ages 30–50	8580

C. Cleanliness and Confession (5:1–10)

This section deals with precautions the Israelites were to take to keep the camp free from defilement. The reason for the command in verse 3 can be found in Deuteronomy 23:14: God was walking in the midst of the camp.

5:1-4 Lepers, people with running sores, and those who had touched a dead body were to be **put . . . outside the camp**. The camp was composed of the tabernacle area plus that space around it occupied by the tents of Israel.

5:5–10 When a man or woman . . . committed **any sin** against another, he or she was required to **confess** the **sin**, to offer a trespass **offering**, to **make restitution**, and to add **one-fifth** part. If the person who was wronged had died or could not be located, and if **no** near **relatives** were available, then payment was to be made to **the priest**.

D. The Law of Jealousy (5:11–31)

5:11–15 This passage describes a lie-detecting ritual known as the trial of **jealousy**. The purpose of this ceremony was to determine the **guilt** or innocence of **a woman** who was suspected of being unfaithful to **her husband**. The woman was required to **drink . . . water** mixed with **dust** from **the floor of the tabernacle**. If she was guilty, it would prove a **curse** to her, causing swelling of the **stomach** and rotting of the **thigh**. If she was innocent, no ill effects would follow. It is obvious from verses 12–14 that the **husband** did not know whether his wife had been unfaithful. He first was required to **bring his wife to the priest**, together with **a grain offering**.

5:16–31 The **priest** prepared the mixture of **water** and **dust . . . in an earthen vessel**. He brought her to the altar **before the Lord**, unbound the hair of her **head**, and **put** the meal **offering . . . in her hands**. Then he made her agree to an **oath** whereby she would be cursed if guilty. After writing **the curses in a book** and scraping **them off into the bitter water**, he waved the **grain offering before the Lord**, burned **a handful of** it **on the altar**, and then made **the woman drink the water**. The statement in verse 24 that he caused the woman to drink the water is repeated in verse 26. She drank only once. If she was guilty, the threatened judgments came upon her, including sterility. If innocent, then she was pronounced **clean**, was **free** from punishment, and was able to live a normal married life, bearing **children**. Verses 29–31 summarize the trial of jealousy.

Jealousy can destroy a marriage, whether it has justifiable grounds or not. This ritual provided a way to settle the issue once for all. The judgment of God would be upon the guilty, and the innocent would be freed from the suspicion of her partner.

Some Bible students believe that this section will have a special application in a coming day, when the nation of Israel will be tried for its unfaithfulness to Jehovah.

E. The Law of the Nazirite (Chap. 6)

6:1–8 The word "Nazirite" comes from a root meaning **"to separate." The vow of a Nazirite** was a voluntary vow which **a man or woman** could make for a specified period of time. The Mishna states that a Nazirite **vow** could last as long as 100 days, but the usual length was thirty days. In some rare cases, people were Nazirites for life—e.g., Samuel, Samson, John the Baptist. The vow contained three provisions: (1) He would **neither . . . eat** nor **drink** of the fruit of the **grapevine**—including **vinegar, wine, grape juice, grapes or raisins** (vv. 2–4); (2) he would not cut his hair (v. 5); (3) he would **not go near a dead body** (vv. 6–8).

Wine speaks of human joy. Long hair, being a shame for a man, is a sign of humiliation. A **dead body** causes defilement.

> Thus the Nazirite was, and is, an enigma to the children of this world. To be joyful, he withdrew from joy; to be strong, he became weak; and in

order to love his relatives, he 'hated' them (Luke 14:26).[4]

6:9–12 This paragraph describes the procedure to be used when a man broke a vow through unintentional contact with a dead body. First he had to go through the seven-day **cleansing** process described in Numbers 19. **On the seventh day he** shaved **his head**, and on the following day he offered **two turtledoves or two young pigeons, one** for **a sin offering and the other** for **a burnt offering**. He also brought a yearling **lamb** for **a trespass offering**. In spite of all the offerings, **the days of his** original **separation** were **lost**, and he had to begin all over again. Thus although a defiled Nazirite could be reconsecrated, the days of his defilement were lost. For us, this means that a backslidden believer can be restored but the time spent out of fellowship with God is wasted.

6:13–21 Here we have the ceremony required when a man came to the close of the time of his vow. Four offerings were brought—**burnt, sin, peace**, and **meal** (vv. 14, 15). **The Nazirite** shaved **his . . . head** and burned **the hair** in **the fire . . . under . . . the peace offering** (v. 18). The priest's part in the ritual is given in verses 16, 17, 19, and 20. Verse 21 refers to a freewill **offering** which the **Nazirite** could offer upon completion of his vow.

6:22–27 The closing verses of chapter 6 give the lovely and familiar blessing with which **Aaron and his sons** were to **bless** the people. The great evangelist D. L. Moody appreciated it very much:

> Here is a benediction that can go all the world over, and can give all the time without being impoverished. Every heart may utter it: it is the speech of God: every letter may conclude with it; every day may begin with it; every night may be sanctified by it. Here is blessing—keeping—shining—the uplifting upon our poor life of all heaven's glad morning. It is the Lord himself who brings this bar of music from heaven's infinite anthems.[5]

F. The Offering of the Princes (Chap. 7)

7:1–9 This chapter takes us back to Exodus 40:17, when the **tabernacle** had been set up. The **leaders of Israel** were **the heads of** the various **tribes**. Their names were already given in Numbers 1:5–16 and in Numbers 2. They first of all brought an offering of **six covered carts and twelve oxen** (v. 3). **Moses** distributed **two carts and four oxen . . . to the sons of Gershon**, and **four carts and eight oxen . . . to the** Merarites to be used in carrying their share of the tabernacle fixtures. No wagons or oxen were given to the Kohathites because they bore the precious burden of the sacred vessels **on their shoulders**.

7:10–83 The tribal **leaders** brought offerings on twelve consecutive days for **the dedication of the altar**. These offerings are described in minute detail, as follows:

Day	Name of Prince	Tribe	Reference
1	Nahshon	Judah	vv. 12–17
2	Nethanel	Issachar	vv. 18–23
3	Eliab	Zebulun	vv. 24–29
4	Elizur	Reuben	vv. 30–35
5	Shelumiel	Simeon	vv. 36-41
6	Eliasaph	Gad	vv. 42-47
7	Elishama	Ephraim	vv. 48–53
8	Gamaliel	Manasseh	vv. 54–59
9	Abidan	Benjamin	vv. 60–65
10	Ahiezer	Dan	vv. 66–71
11	Pagiel	Asher	vv. 72–77
12	Ahira	Naphtali	vv. 78–83

7:84–89 The total of all the gifts is given in verses 84–88. God doesn't forget any service that is done for

Him. He keeps a careful record. At the close of the **offering, Moses went into the** Most Holy Place and **heard the voice of** God **speaking to him from above the mercy seat**, perhaps expressing satisfaction with the gifts of the leaders (v. 89). Although Moses was of the tribe of Levi, he was not a priest. Yet God made an exception in his case, not only authorizing him to enter the Most Holy Place but commanding him to do so (Ex. 25:21, 22).

G. The Services of the Tabernacle (Chap. 8)

8:1–4 **Aaron** was instructed to **arrange the lamps** on the golden **lampstand** in such a way that the light would be cast **in front of the lampstand**. If the light speaks of the testimony of the Holy Spirit and the lampstand speaks of Christ, then it is a reminder that the Spirit's ministry is to glorify Christ.

8:5–13 The consecration of **the Levites** is described next. They were first cleansed by sprinkling with the **water of purification** (explained in Num. 19), by shaving their bodies with a razor, and by washing **their clothes and . . . themselves** (v. 7). Representatives of the people laid **their hands on the** heads of the **Levites** at the door of the tabernacle, **and Aaron** offered **the Levites before the LORD like a wave offering**. This reminds us of Romans 12:1, 2, where today's believers are to present their bodies as a living sacrifice to God. Moses then offered **a burnt offering** and **a sin offering**.

8:14–22 God repeats that He had chosen the **Levites** to belong to Himself **instead of . . . the firstborn** whom He had claimed as His own after the Exodus. The **Levites** were appointed to serve the priests. The consecration of **the Levites** took place as commanded, and they took up their **service** in connection with **the tabernacle.**

8:23–26 **The Levites** were to serve from **twenty-five years** of age to **fifty** (v. 24). In Numbers 4:3, the beginning age was said to be thirty years. Some take the reference in chapter 4 to apply to those who carried the tabernacle through the wilderness. They understand the lower age in chapter 8 to refer to service at the tabernacle after it had been set up in the Promised Land. Others understand the additional five years to be a sort of apprenticeship. Those retiring at **fifty years** of age no longer did heavy **work** but were allowed to continue in a kind of supervisory capacity (vv. 25, 26). These verses distinguish between **"work"** and ministry or attending **to needs**. The former is heavy work; the latter is overseeing.

Someone has pointed out that the Levites are pictures of Christians, who are redeemed, cleansed, and set apart to serve the Lord, having no inheritance on earth.

H. The Passover, the Cloud, and the Silver Trumpets (9:1—10:10)

9:1–14 God's instructions to **keep the Passover** (v. 1) preceded the events in chapter 1. Not all the events in Numbers are chronological. The Passover was kept **on the fourteenth day of** the first **month**. Special provision was made for those who were ceremonially **defiled** (perhaps involuntarily), through contact with **a human corpse**, or were away on a journey, to keep the Passover one month later—**on the fourteenth day of the second month** (vv. 6–12). But anyone else who failed to keep the Passover was **cut off from among his people** (v. 13). **A stranger** (Gentile) was permitted **to keep the LORD's Passover** if he so desired, but on the same terms as the Jews (v. 14).

9:15–23 These verses anticipate the next chapters. They describe the glory **cloud** which **covered the tabernacle—the cloud . . . by day** and **the appearance of fire by night. Whenever the cloud** lifted off **the tabernacle**, the people **of Israel** were to break camp and march forward. When **the cloud settled**, the people were to stop and **pitch their tents**. The cloud was, of course, a symbol of God guiding His people. Although the Lord does not lead in such a visible way today—we walk by *faith*, not by *sight*—the principle is still valid. Move when the Lord moves, and not before, because "darkness about going is light about staying."

10:1–10 **Moses** was instructed to **make two silver trumpets**. These were to be used to: (a) assemble **the congregation . . . at the door of the tabernacle of meeting** (vv. 3, 7); (b) give the signal for marching forward; (c) assemble the **leaders** (**only one** trumpet was used for this) (v. 4); (d) **sound an alarm** in time of **war** (v. 9); (e) announce certain special days, such as feast days (v. 10).

Different trumpet calls were used for these different purposes. Sounding **the advance** in verse 5 was the signal to march. The tribes **on the east side** of the tabernacle set out first. **The second sound** of **advance** was the signal for those **on the south side** to start. Presumably those on the west and north followed in that order. The **trumpets** were not only for the wilderness march, but were to be used in the land as well (v. 9). Note the words **"in your land."** God would fulfill His promise made to Abraham. His descendants *would* be given a land, but their disobedience and faithlessness would *delay* their entrance for forty years.

II. FROM SINAI TO THE PLAINS OF MOAB (10:11—22:1)

A. Setting out from the Sinai Wilderness (10:11–36)

10:11 Verse 11 marks a definite division in the book. Up to this point, the people had camped at Mount Sinai. From verse 11 to 22:1 is the record of the journey from Mount Sinai to the plains of Moab, just outside the Promised Land. This journey covered a period of almost forty years. They did not start until **the twentieth day** because of the celebration of the second Passover (see Num. 9:10, 11).

10:12, 13 The first section of the journey was from Mount **Sinai** to **the Wilderness of Paran**. However, there were three stops before they reached this wilderness—Taberah, Kibroth Hattaavah, and Hazeroth. They actually reached the Wilderness of Paran in Numbers 12:16.

10:14–28 The order in which the tribes marched is given next. The leader of each tribe was at its head. The order is the same as in chapter 2, with one exception: in 2:17, it seems that the Levites marched after Gad and before Ephraim. In 10:17, the Gershonites and Merarites are listed after Zebulun, and the Kohathites after Gad. Apparently the Gershonites and Merarites moved on ahead with their equipment so they could have it all set up at the camping site when the Kohathites arrived with the sacred vessels.

10:29–32 **Hobab** was Moses' brother-in-law. **Raguel** (same as Reuel and Jethro) was Hobab's father and therefore **Moses' father-in-law**. Being a **Midianite**, Hobab was probably very familiar with **the wilderness**. Perhaps that is why Moses invited him to accompany the Israelites—**"You**

can be our eyes." Many Bible interpreters believe that this invitation showed a lack of faith on Moses' part, since God had already promised to guide.

Another view is held by Kurtz, who suggests,

> The pillar of cloud determined the general route to be taken, the place of encampment, and the length of tarry in each location; yet human prudence was by no means precluded with respect to arranging the encampment so as to combine most advantageously the circumstances of water, pasture, shelter, supply of fuel. In all these particulars, Hobab's experience, and knowledge of the desert, would be exceedingly useful as supplementary to the guidance of the cloud.[6]

10:33, 34 The ark of the covenant was wrapped in the veil that separated the holy place from the Most Holy (Num. 4:5), and was carried by the Kohathites at the front of the procession. The trip from Sinai to Kadesh Barnea lasted three days. The glory **cloud** overshadowed the people as the Lord searched out **a resting place for them**.

10:35, 36 We are not told whether Hobab actually did accompany the Israelites. However, it appears from Judges 1:16 and 4:11 that he did, since his descendants are found among the Israelites. **Whenever the ark set out** in the morning, **Moses** called on the **LORD** for victory. And when at evening **it rested**, he prayed for **the LORD** to **return to** the people **of Israel**.

B. Rebellion in the Camp (Chap. 11)

11:1–3 The reader is startled by the readiness of **the people** to complain against God after all He had done for them. A clue to the discontent is found in verse 1—**"consumed some in the outskirts of the camp."** The malcontents were at a distance from the ark. **Fire** from God **"consumed" in the** extremity **of the camp**, giving the name **Taberah** ("burning") to the place. The King James and New King James Versions read that the fire **consumed some** of the complainers. The ASV states only that the fire devoured in the uttermost part of the camp. Either way it was a merciful warning to the people as a whole of a judgment that would be severe.

11:4–9 The second complaining took place right in the midst of the camp, but this time the reason can be found in the expression **the mixed multitude** or "rabble." Some unbelievers had come out of **Egypt** with the Israelites, and this **mixed multitude** was a source of continual grief to the Israelites. Their disaffection spread to the Israelites, causing them to long with **intense craving** for the food of **Egypt** and to despise the **manna**. See Psalm 78:17–33 for God's commentary on this.

> How strange that souls whom Jesus feeds
> With manna from above
> Should grieve Him by their evil deeds,
> And sin against His love.
>
> But 'tis a greater marvel still
> That He from whom they stray
> Should bear with their rebellious will,
> And wash their sins away.

11:10–15 Moses first cried **to the LORD** concerning his own inability to take care of such a people **alone**; then he described the utter impossibility of providing **meat** for such a multitude. Finally, he asked for death as an escape from such problems.

11:16, 17 The Lord's first reply

was to provide for the appointment of **seventy... elders** to share **the burden of the people** with Moses. Many Bible students question whether this was God's best for Moses. They reason that because God gives strength to do whatever He orders, Moses suffered a decrease of divine enablement when his responsibilities decreased.[7] Earlier, Moses had appointed men to act as civil authorities according to his father-in-law's advice (Ex. 18:25; Deut. 1:9–15). Possibly the **seventy** chosen here were to help bear the *spiritual* burden. These two distinct appointments should not be confused.

11:18–23 As for the people, God said that they would have plenty of **meat to eat**. He would send them enough **meat** to make them sick of it. They would have it **for a whole month**. Moses questioned the possibility of such an event, but the Lord promised to bring it to pass. On the way to Mount Sinai, God had miraculously provided meat for the children of Israel (Ex. 16:13). Moses should have remembered this and not questioned the ability of the Lord. How quickly we forget the Lord's past mercies when circumstances close in around us!

11:24–30 When the **seventy** elders were officially installed, **the Spirit** of **the LORD came... upon them** and **they prophesied**; that is, they spoke direct revelations from God. Even **two** of the **men** who **had remained in the camp... prophesied**. **Joshua** apparently thought that this miracle posed a threat to Moses' leadership and sought to restrain them. But **Moses** showed his largeness of spirit by his noble answer in verse 29.

11:31–35 The promised meat came in the form of a swarm of **quail**. Verse 31 may mean that the quail flew two cubits off the ground or were piled **two cubits** deep on **the ground**. The latter is not impossible; quail that were exhausted by migration have been known to land on a ship in sufficient quantity to sink it.[8] The people went forth to feast on the meat, but many were soon struck by a terrible **plague**. The place was called **Kibroth Hattaavah** ("the graves of lust") because the people's **craving** brought them to the grave. **Hazeroth** is listed as the next place of encampment (v. 35).

C. Rebellion of Aaron and Miriam (Chap. 12)

12:1, 2 The next sad chapter in the history of Israel concerns two of the leaders of the people, **Miriam and Aaron**. Though they were Moses' sister and brother, they spoke against him for marrying **an Ethiopian woman**. At least that was their pretext. But the real reason seems to be given in verse 2: they resented Moses' leadership and wanted to share it—they were jealous. At this time there was no law against marrying **an Ethiopian**, though when they came to the land, the Israelites were forbidden to marry a non-Jew.

12:3 Moses did not try to vindicate himself but trusted God, who had placed him in the position of leadership. His family (chap. 12), the leaders (chap. 16), and ultimately the whole congregation (16:41, 42) disputed his authority. Yet when the judgment of God fell upon his adversaries, Moses did not gloat but interceded for them. He was indeed **very humble, more than all men who were on the face of the earth**. The fact that he wrote this about himself does not deny his humility; rather it illustrates 2 Peter 1:21b; he wrote as he was moved by the Holy Spirit.[9]

12:4–8 God summoned **Moses, Aaron, and Miriam** to the door of **the tabernacle of meeting**, rebuked Miriam and Aaron, and reminded them that **Moses** held a position of nearness to God that no other prophet ever held. He might speak to others indirectly, by visions and dreams, but He spoke to Moses directly, **face to face**. (The word **plainly** in v. 8 means "directly," i.e., without a go-between.) **The form of the Lord** means some manifestation or visible representation. Although **Miriam** herself was a prophetess (Ex. 15:20), the Lord made clear the difference between His relationship with Moses and other prophets. The only other thing recorded about Miriam after this incident is her death (Num. 20:1).

12:9, 10 **The Lord** was angry with **them**, and **He departed**. As punishment for her rebellion, **Miriam** was smitten with leprosy. Since **Aaron** was not punished, some suggest that Miriam was the ringleader. They point out that the verb in verse 1 is feminine singular. Others believe that Aaron's punishment was to see his sister become **a leper**. Aaron was the high priest, and he would have been unable to function on behalf of the people if he had been made leprous. His position might have saved him from the humiliation that Miriam had to go through.

12:11–16 **Aaron** confessed his **sin** to **Moses** and asked that Miriam should not be "like a stillborn child, which comes into the world half decomposed."[10] In response to Moses' intercession, God healed Miriam of the leprosy but insisted that she should go through the usual seven-day period for the cleansing of a leper. The Lord reminded Moses that she would have been barred from **the camp** as unclean **if her father had but spit in her face**.

D. Spying out the Promised Land (Chaps. 13, 14)

13:1–20 In this chapter sending out the spies was ordered by **the Lord**. In Deuteronomy 1:19–22 it was suggested by the people. Doubtless God's instruction was in response to the people's request, even if their attitude was one of unbelief. The names of the twelve spies are given in verses 4–15. Notice particularly **Caleb** (v. 6) and **Hoshea** (v. 8). **Moses called Hoshea** by the name **Joshua** (v. 16). Moses asked the twelve spies to bring back a complete report concerning the land and its inhabitants (vv. 17–20). First they were to go to the Negev in **the South**, then to the hill country in the central part of the land.

13:21–29 The spies searched **the land from the Wilderness of Zin** in the south to **Rehob** in the north (v. 21). Verses 22–24 describe the spying operation in **the South**. At **Hebron** they saw three sons **of Anak**, who were giants, according to Deuteronomy 2:10, 11. Near Hebron they came to a valley of vineyards. They cut down a large **cluster of grapes** and, suspending it **on a pole . . . between two** men, carried it back to the camp of Israel, together with **pomegranates and figs. The place was called the Valley of Eshcol**, meaning **"cluster."** The majority report of the spies pictured a beautiful **land** with dangerous inhabitants. The spies doubted the ability of Israel to conquer the inhabitants (in spite of God's promise to drive them out).

13:30–32 Reference to Nephilim (v. 33, Heb.) does not mean that these **giants** survived the Flood. The Israelites had heard about the Nephilim that lived before the Flood, and they identified these giants with them. **Caleb** (speaking for Joshua and him-

The Arabah. Derived from a Hebrew word meaning "steppe" or "desert," *Arabah* is the name given to the southern extension of the Jordan Valley. This depression extends more than 160 km. (100 mi.) from the Dead Sea to the Gulf of Aqaba.

self) expressed confidence that Israel would be victorious. But the others flatly denied this. The expression **"a land that devours its inhabitants"** means that the present inhabitants would destroy any others who tried to settle there.

13:33 Ten of the spies had the wrong perspective. They saw themselves as the inhabitants of Canaan saw them (**like grasshoppers**). Joshua and Caleb saw Israel from God's point of view, **well able to** conquer the land. To the ten unbelieving spies the problem of **giants** was insurmountable. To the two believing spies the presence of giants was insignificant.

14:1–10 **All the congregation** broke out into bitter complaint **against Moses and Aaron**, accused the Lord of delivering them from **Egypt** so they would be slain in the Promised Land, and proposed a new **leader** who would take them back **to Egypt** (vv. 1–3). When **Joshua . . . and Caleb** sought to assure the people that they would be victorious against the enemy, the Israelites conspired to **stone them** (vv. 6–10).

Verses 3 and 4 demonstrate graphically the stupidity of unbelief. **Return to Egypt**! Return to a land devastated by their God! Return to a land still mourning for its firstborn sons! Return to the land they had plundered on the eve of their exodus! Return by the Red Sea where the Egyptian army had been drowned, pursuing them! And what kind of welcome would Pharaoh give them? Yet this seemed safer than to believe that God would lead them to victory in Canaan. Jehovah had struck Egypt, parted the sea, fed them with bread from heaven, and led them through the wilderness, yet they still could not trust His power to prevail over a few giants! Their actions revealed clearly what they thought about God. They doubted His power; was the Lord really a match for the giants? They had failed to grasp what had been so manifestly revealed to them the past year—namely, the nature and ways of Jehovah. A low concept of God can ruin a person or an entire nation, as is here so painfully illustrated.

14:11–19 The Lord threatened to abandon the Jews and raise up a new **nation** from Moses' descendants (vv. 11, 12). But Moses interceded for them by reminding the Lord that the Gentile nations would then say that **the LORD was not able to bring** His **people** into the Promised Land (vv. 13–19). The honor of God was at stake, and Moses pled that argument with tremendous forcefulness. In Exodus 34:6, 7 the Lord had revealed Himself to Moses. In verse 18 Moses repeats almost verbatim God's description of Himself as the basis of his prayer. How different is the theology of Moses from the theology of the people! His is based on divine revelation; theirs is based on human imagination.

14:20–35 Although God replied that He would not destroy the people, He decreed that of all the men **twenty years** of age or older who came out of Egypt and who were able to go to war (Num. 26:64, 65; Deut. 2:14), only **Joshua** and **Caleb** would **enter** the Promised Land. The people would wander **in the wilderness** for **forty years, until** the unbelieving generation died. The sons had to **bear the brunt of** their fathers' **infidelity** (v. 33). However, they would be permitted after forty years to enter the Promised Land. **Forty years** were specified because the spies had spent **forty days in the land** on their expedition (v. 34). Forty years here is a round number; it was actually about thirty-eight years. It was forty years from the time Israel left Egypt till they reached Canaan. The people refused the good the Lord wanted to give them, so they had to suffer the evil they chose instead. However, the fact that they were excluded from the land does not mean that they were eternally lost. Many of them were saved through faith in the Lord, even though they suffered His governmental punishment in this life because of their disobedience.

There is a great deal of obscurity concerning the exact route followed by the Israelites during their wilderness wanderings. There is also uncertainty concerning how long they stayed in each place. Some believe, for example, that over thirty-seven years were spent at Kadesh and that one year was spent on a journey south to the shore of the Red Sea, now known as the Gulf of Aqaba. Many of the place names on the route between Sinai and the Plains of Moab are no longer identifiable.

The glory of the LORD in verse 21 refers to His glory as righteous Judge, punishing the disobedient people of Israel. The Israelites had tempted God **ten times** (v. 22). These temptings were as follows: at **the Red Sea** (Ex. 14:11, 12), at Marah (Ex. 15:23), in the Wilderness of Sin (Ex. 16:2), two rebellions concerning the manna (Ex. 16:20, 27), at Rephidim (Ex. 17:1), at Horeb (Ex. 32:7), at Taberah (Num. 11:1), at Kibroth Hattaavah (Num. 11:4 ff.), and at Kadesh (the murmuring at the spies' report—Num. 14).

Of the 603,550 men of war who came out of Egypt, only **Joshua** and **Caleb** entered the land (vv. 29, 30; Deut. 2:14).

14:36–38 The ten unbelieving spies **who brought the evil report** were killed **by a plague, but Joshua** and **Caleb** escaped it.

14:39–45 Hearing the doom pronounced upon them, **the people** told

Moses that they would obey God and go into the land, probably meaning directly north from Kadesh Barnea (v. 40). But Moses told them that it was too late, that the Lord had departed from them, and that they would be **defeated** in the attempt. Disregarding Moses' advice, they advanced **to the mountaintop** and were **attacked** and driven **back** by some of the heathen inhabitants of the land (v. 45).

E. Various Legislation (Chap. 15)

15:1, 2 We don't know how much time elapsed between chapters 14 and 15, but the contrast is striking. "... they certainly shall not see the land" (14:23). **"When you have come into the land"** (15:2). God's purposes, though sometimes hindered by sin, are never thwarted. He promised the land of Canaan to Abraham, and if one generation of his descendants was too faithless to receive it, He would give it to the next.

15:3–29 The first 29 verses of this chapter describe offerings which were to be brought by the children of Israel when they were settled in the land. Most of these offerings have already been described in minute detail. Special emphasis is given here to **unintentional** sins **committed** by **the congregation** (vv. 22–26) or by an individual (vv. 27–29). Verse 24 mentions two offerings for the congregation, a **bull** and a goat. However, Leviticus 4 states that the congregation was only to bring a bullock. But Leviticus 4 also says that a leader, when he sinned, was to bring a goat. Possibly the account here in Numbers mentions these offerings together, whereas in Leviticus they are mentioned separately. In verses 20 and 21 we find an oft-repeated command in Scripture: **"Of the first . . . to the Lord."** Whether the firstborn or the firstfruits, the Lord was to have the best of everything. This also served as a reminder to the people that everything they possessed came from, and ultimately belonged to, Jehovah.

15:30–36 There was no offering for the sin of presumption—that is, for willful, defiant rebellion against the word of the Lord. All who committed such a sin were to be **cut off** (vv. 30, 31). An example of presumptuous sin is given in verses 32–36. **A man** was **found . . . gathering sticks on the Sabbath** in clear violation of the Law. It was known that he should **be put to death** (Ex. 31:15), but the mode of execution had never been stated. The Lord now declared that he should be **stoned . . . to death outside the camp**.

15:37-41 The Jews were commanded **to make tassels on the corners of their garments** and **to put a blue thread in the tassels of the corners. Blue** is the heavenly color, and it was intended to speak to them of the holiness and obedience which suited them as children of **God**.

F. Korah's Rebellion (Chaps. 16, 17)

16:1–3 Korah, a cousin of Aaron (Ex. 6:18–21), was a Levite but not a priest. He apparently resented the fact that the family of Aaron should have exclusive right to the priesthood. **Dathan**, **Abiram**, and **On** were of the tribe of **Reuben**, and they resented Moses' leadership over them. **On** is not mentioned after verse 1, and it is impossible to know if he shared the doom of the others. **Two hundred and fifty** of the princes—**leaders** of Israel—joined in the rebellion against the priesthood and the civil authority (v. 2). They argued that **all** the people were **holy** and should not be excluded from offering sacrifices (v. 3).

16:4–11 To settle the matter, **Moses** ordered **Korah** and his rebels to appear the following day with **censers** (vv. 6, 7). The burning of **incense** was a priestly function; if God did not recognize them as priests, He would show His displeasure.

16:12–15 Dathan and Abiram refused to leave their tents when called by **Moses** but scolded him for his leadership. These men were referring to the earlier promise (Ex. 3:8) that God would bring them into a "a land flowing with milk and honey," and they were complaining here (with sarcasm) that Moses had instead brought them **out of a land flowing with milk and honey** (Egypt) and had **brought** them into a land *not* **flowing with milk and honey** (the desert).

The thought of verse 14 may be that, having failed to fulfill his promise, Moses was now trying to blind the people to his failure or to his true intentions. Moses reminded the Lord that he had not demanded tribute from the people, as rulers usually do.

16:16–22 The following day, **Korah, Aaron**, and the **two hundred and fifty** rebels appeared before the tabernacle with censers. The congregation of Israel also assembled, perhaps in sympathy with Korah. **Then the glory of the LORD appeared to the** whole **congregation. And the LORD** told **Moses and Aaron** to **separate** themselves **from** the **congregation** before He destroyed them. Because Moses and Aaron interceded, the judgment was not executed.

16:23–35 The scene now changes to **the tents** where **Korah, Dathan, and Abiram** lived (v. 24). Moses warned the rest of the people to move away from the vicinity of those tents. Then Moses announced that **if these men** died a natural death, **or** were **visited by the common fate of all men, then** Moses himself would be discredited. **But if the LORD** miraculously caused the earth to swallow **them up, then** the people would know **that these men** had been guilty of rebellion (v. 30). No sooner had he uttered **these words** than **the earth opened** up **and swallowed** Dathan and Abiram and their families [**households**], who must have joined in their rebellion (vv. 32, 33). There is considerable question as to when **Korah** died. Some believe that he was swallowed by the earth with Dathan and Abiram (vv. 32, 33). Others suggest that he was destroyed by the same **fire** that killed the **two hundred and fifty** rebels (v. 35). It seems from Numbers 26:10 that he was swallowed up along with Dathan and Abiram. Verse 11 of the same chapter shows that his sons were spared. Israel's next great prophet, Samuel, was a descendant of Korah (1 Chron. 6:22–23, 28). . . . In verse 30 pit (Heb. *Sheol*) means the grave, but it can also mean the disembodied state.

At certain times in history, God has shown His extreme displeasure at certain sins by judging them instantly. He judged Sodom and Gomorrah (Gen. 19:24, 25); Nadab and Abihu (Lev. 10:1, 2); Miriam (Num. 12:10); Korah, Dathan, and Abiram, plus 250 leaders (this chapter); Ananias and Sapphira (Acts 5:5, 10). Clearly He does not do this every time these sins are committed, but He does break in on history on selected occasions as a warning to future generations.

The men with Korah (v. 32) might mean his servants or his followers.

16:36-40 The **holy . . . censers** used by the sinners were converted into **hammered plates** to cover **the altar** of burnt offering. These were a reminder that only the family of **Aaron** had priestly privileges. **The fire** in the censers was scattered abroad.

16:41–50 On the day following these solemn events, the people accused **Moses and Aaron** of killing God's **people**. The Lord, in wrath, threatened to destroy them, but **Moses and Aaron** went **before** the **tabernacle of meeting**, no doubt to intercede for them. The Lord then struck the people with a dreadful **plague**. Only when Aaron rushed **into the midst of** the congregation with **incense** and **made atonement for the people** was the **plague . . . stopped**. But even by then, **fourteen thousand seven hundred** had perished. The leaders, along with the congregation, had challenged the priesthood of **Aaron**. Now it was the priestly intercession of **Aaron** which **stopped** the **plague**. Moses and Aaron were not the ones who killed the Lord's people, but the ones who saved them!

17:1–9 In order to emphasize to the people that the priesthood was committed only to the family of Aaron, God commanded that **a rod** for **each** tribe of Israel be placed **in the tabernacle** overnight. **The rod of Levi** had **Aaron's name on** it. The right to the priesthood belonged to the **rod** that blossomed. In the morning, when the rods were examined, it was found that Aaron's **rod . . . had sprouted** with **buds, had produced blossoms, and yielded ripe almonds**. Aaron's rod pictures the resurrected Christ as the Priest of God's choosing. Just as the almond tree is the first to blossom in the spring, so Christ is the firstfruits of resurrection (1 Cor. 15:20, 23). The golden lampstand in the holy place was "made like almond blossoms, each with its ornamental knob and flower" (Ex. 25:33, 34). It was a priestly function to take care of the lampstand daily. Aaron's rod corresponded in design and fruit to the lampstand, thus signifying that the household of Aaron had been divinely chosen to minister as priests.

17:10–13 From now on, **Aaron's rod** was **to be kept** in the ark of the covenant **as a** token **sign against the rebels**. After this, the people were seized with terror and feared to go into the general vicinity of **the tabernacle**.

G. Instructions to the Levites (Chaps. 18, 19)

18:1–7 Chapter 18 is closely linked to the last two verses of the preceding chapter. In order to allay the fears of the people, the Lord repeated the instructions about service at the tabernacle. If these instructions were obeyed, there need be no fear of His wrath. Verse 1 is in two parts. **"You and your sons and your father's house with you"** refers to all the Levites, including the priests. **"You and your sons"** refers to the priests alone. The former bore **the iniquity related to the sanctuary**; the latter bore the **iniquity associated with** their **priesthood**. To **"bear the iniquity"** means to be responsible for any neglect or failure to comply with sacred **duties**. The Levites were assistants to the priests but were not to enter the **tabernacle** on priestly **service . . . lest they die**.

18:8–20 The priests were permitted a certain **portion** of various **offerings** as compensation (vv. 8–11). They were also entitled to the **firstfruits** of **oil, wine, grain**, and **fruit** (vv. 12, 13), to things devoted **to the LORD** (v. 14), and to the **firstborn**. In the case of **firstborn** sons and **unclean animals**, the priests received the redemption money in place of the sons or animals. In the case of sacrificial animals, the **firstborn** was sacrificed **to the LORD**, and the priests received their portion (vv. 17–19). **A covenant of salt** (v. 19) means one that is inviolable and permanent. The priests did not receive any **land** because the Lord was to be their special **portion** and **inheritance** (v. 20).

18:21–32 The **Levites** received **tithes** from the people, but they in turn were responsible to give **a tenth** to the priests. This tenth was offered as **a heave offering . . . to the LORD**.

19:1–10 Chapter 19 deals with one of the strongest symbols of cleansing in the OT, the use of the **ashes of** a **red heifer**. This offering had to do particularly with removing defilement caused by coming in contact with a dead person. The children of Israel had just rebelled against the Lord at Kadesh. They were now being sent out into the wilderness to die because of their unbelief. Over 600,000 people would die in a thirty-eight year period, or over forty people a day. One can see the need for the ashes of the red heifer, for who could avoid contact with death on such a journey?

The **heifer** was taken **outside the camp** and **slaughtered** (v. 3). **Eleazar the priest** sprinkled **its blood seven times** before **the tabernacle**, and **then the heifer** was **burned**, skin and all, together with **cedar wood**, **hyssop** and **scarlet**. These same materials were used in the cleansing of lepers (Lev. 14:4, 6). **The priest** and the man who burned the heifer were **unclean until evening**. **Then a man who** was **clean** carefully gathered **up the ashes** and stored **them outside the camp** for future use (v. 9); then he was **unclean until evening**.

19:11–19 This paragraph tells how the ashes were to be used. If a person had become ceremonially **unclean** through touching a **dead body** or through being **in a tent** where someone had died, a **clean person** took **some of the ashes** and mixed them with **running water**. The clean person sprinkled **the water** with **hyssop . . . on the** unclean person or thing **on the third day** and **on the seventh day**. **On the seventh day** the unclean man washed **his clothes**, bathed himself, and was **clean** that **evening** (v. 19).

Williams suggests that the red heifer symbolized Christ: spotless externally and without blemish internally; free from any bondage to sin; and robed with the red earth of manhood.[11] But we must be careful not to press the type too far.

The one historical record of the use of the ashes of a heifer is in Numbers 31. Mantle says that:

> . . . the ashes were regarded as a concentration of the essential properties of the sin offering, and could be resorted to at all times with comparatively little trouble and no loss of time. One red heifer availed for centuries. Only six are said to have been required during the whole of Jewish history; for the smallest quantity of the ashes availed to impart the cleansing virtue of the pure spring water.[12]

The writer of the Epistle to the Hebrews argues that whereas the ashes of a red heifer could do no more than set a person apart from outward, ceremonial defilement, the blood of Christ has infinite power to produce an inward cleansing of the conscience from dead works (Heb. 9:13, 14). An unknown author comments:

> The red heifer is God's provision for inevitable, unavoidable contact with the spiritual death that is around us. It probably has special reference to Israel's bloodguiltiness in connection with the Messiah. It resembles the trespass offering but does not displace it.

Old Testament regulations concerning washing with water, sometimes with running water (Lev. 15:13), are now an accepted medical technique for disinfection.

19:20–22 Punishment was inevitable for an unclean person who did not use **the water of purification**. Also, God decreed that anyone who touched or sprinkled the water was **unclean until evening**, and anyone he touched was also **unclean** for the remainder of the day.

H. The Sin of Moses (20:1–13)

20:1 As this chapter opens, it is forty years since the Israelites left Egypt and thirty-eight years since they sent the spies into the land. The people had wandered for thirty-eight years and had now come back to **Kadesh**, in **the Wilderness of Zin**—the very place from which they had sent the spies. They were no closer to the Promised Land than they had been thirty-eight years earlier! Here **Miriam died . . . and was buried**. Over 600,000 people had died during the wasted years between chapters 19 and 20. The bitter fruit of unbelief was harvested in silence for an entire generation.

20:2–9 The people who complained to **Moses and Aaron** about the lack of **water** were a new generation, but they acted like their fathers (vv. 2–5). **The Lord** told **Moses** to *speak* to the rock, and **it** would **yield water**. He was to **take the rod** of Aaron which had been deposited in the tabernacle (v. 9; cf. 17:10), though it is **"his rod"** in verse 11. Aaron's rod was the rod of the priesthood; Moses' rod was the rod of judgment and power.

20:10–13 Once before, at a place called Massah (and Meribah), the people had murmured for water. At that time, the Lord told Moses to *strike* the rock (Ex. 17:1–7). But now Moses' patience was exhausted. First, he spoke unadvisedly with his lips, calling the people **rebels** (v. 10). Secondly, he **struck the rock twice** instead of speaking to it. The rock smitten in Exodus 17 was a type of Christ, stricken at Calvary. But Christ was only to be struck once. After His death, the Holy Spirit would be given, of which the water in verse 11 is a type. Because of the sin of **Moses and Aaron** in this matter, God decreed that they would not enter the Promised Land. He called the place **Meribah**, but it is not the same Meribah as in Exodus 17. This is sometimes known as Meribah-Kadesh. G. Campbell Morgan comments:

> By this manifestation of anger, which as we have said was so very natural, the servant of God misrepresented God to the people. His failure was due to the fact that for the moment his faith failed to reach the highest level of activity. He still believed in God, and in His power: but he did not believe in Him *to sanctify Him in the eyes of His people*. The lesson is indeed a very searching one. Right things may be done in so wrong a way as to produce evil results. There is a hymn in which we may miss the deep meaning, if we are not thoughtful—
>
> Lord, speak to me that I may speak
> In living echoes of Thy tone.
>
> That is far more than a prayer that we may be able to deliver the Lord's message. It is rather that we may do so in His tone, with His temper. That is where Moses failed, and for this failure he was excluded from the Land.[13]

I. The Death of Aaron (20:14–29)

20:14–21 The plan for entering the land was not to go directly north from the wilderness but to travel east through the territory of the Edomites, and then north along the east coast of the Dead Sea. The people would then cross the Jordan. But **the king of Edom . . . refused** safe **passage** to the people of **Israel**—and this in spite of assurances that the Jews would not eat, **drink**, or damage any of Edom's supplies. Later in history, Israel under Saul fought against and defeated the Edomites, descendants of Jacob's brother, Esau.

20:22–29 When the people had **journeyed from Kadesh . . . to Mount Hor**, near **the border of . . . Edom, . . . Aaron died** and was replaced by **Eleazar his son** (vv. 22–29). Matthew Henry writes:

> Aaron, though he dies for his transgression, is not put to death as a malefactor, by a plague, or fire from heaven, but dies with ease and in honour. He is not *cut off from his people*, as the expression usually is concerning those that die by the hand of divine justice, but he is *gathered to his people*, as one that died in the arms of divine grace. . . . Moses, whose hands had first clothed Aaron with his priestly garments, now strips him of them; for, in reverence to the priesthood, it was not fit that he should die in them.[14]

J. The Bronze Serpent (21:1—22:1)

21:1–3 **The king of Arad** lived in the southern portion of the land of promise. When he **heard that** the Israelites were encamped in the wilderness and were planning to invade the land, he attacked but was defeated at a **place . . . called Hormah** (vv. 1–3).

21:4–9 **The Red Sea** (v. 4) does not mean the gulf that the Israelites crossed in their escape from Egypt but the portion of the Red Sea which we know as the Gulf of Aqaba. **The Way of the Red Sea**, however, may be a route name; the Israelites might not have gone to the Gulf of Aqaba at this time.

Once again the people complained about their living conditions, with the result that God **sent fiery serpents among** them. **Many of the people . . . died**, and many more were dying. In answer to the intercession of Moses, God commanded that a **bronze serpent** be lifted **on a pole** and promised that whoever **looked at the bronze serpent** would be healed of the snakebite. This incident was used by the Lord Jesus to teach Nicodemus that Christ must be lifted up on a pole (the cross), so that sinners looking to Him by faith might have everlasting life (John 3:1–16).

The serpent later became a stumbling block to the nation and was finally destroyed in the days of Hezekiah (2 Kgs. 18:4).

21:10–20 The journeys of the children of Israel from Mount Hor to the Plains of Moab can no longer be traced exactly. However, the stops are listed in Numbers 21:10 to 22:1. **The book of the wars of the Lord** (v. 14) was probably a historical record of the early wars of Israel. It is no longer available. At **Beer** (vv. 16–18) the Lord miraculously provided **water** when the princes **dug . . . with their staves** in the arid desert.

21:21–26 When Israel came near the country of **the Amorites**, they sought permission to **pass through** but were refused. In fact, **Sihon, king of the Amorites**, declared war on **Israel** but was thoroughly defeated. This Amorite king, like Pharaoh before him, was hardened by the Lord in order that he and his people might be defeated in battle by Israel (Deut.

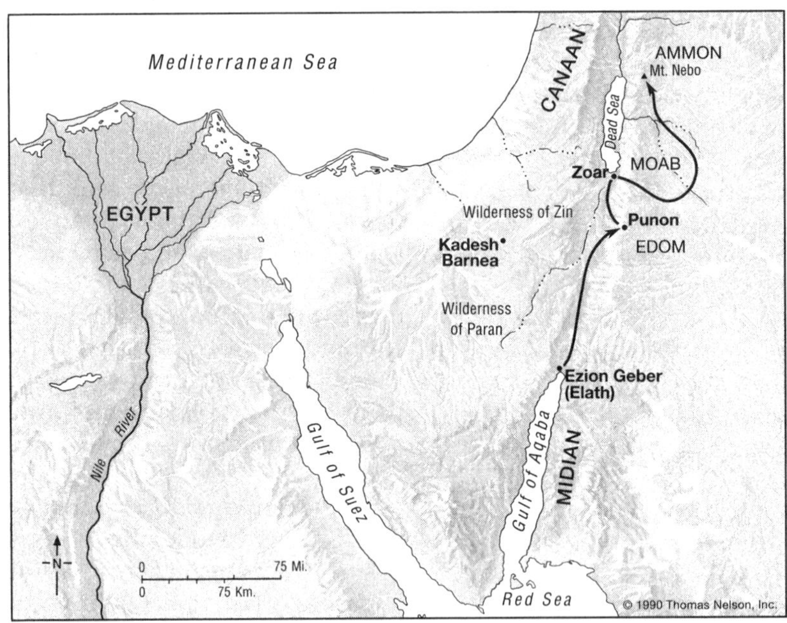

From the Wilderness to Canaan

2:30). "The iniquity of the Amorites" (Gen. 15:16) was complete, and Israel was the instrument of the judgment by Jehovah.

21:27–30 The proverbial song of verses 27–30 seems to say this: **Heshbon** had only recently been captured from the Moabites by the **Amorites**. Now **Heshbon** has fallen to the people of Israel. If those who conquered this city of Moab have themselves been conquered, then **Moab** must be a third-class power. Also, this proverb is probably quoted as evidence that the land was fully in the possession of the Amorite king, Sihon, and no longer a Moabite territory. This fact was important to establish because Israel was forbidden to take any land from **Moab** (Deut. 2:9).

21:31—22:1 The exact route of the Israelites is difficult to reconstruct. It is suggested that they basically moved east from Mount Hor, then north outside the western boundary of Edom to the River Zered. They followed the Zered eastward between Edom and Moab, then north along Moab's eastern boundary to the Arnon, then west to the King's Highway. They conquered Sihon, King of the Amorites, then pushed north to conquer **Bashan**, the Kingdom of **Og**. **Bashan** was rich pastureland east of the Jordan and north of the place where Israel would cross the Jordan into the land. Having conquered **Bashan**, the Israelites returned to **the plains of Moab . . . and camped** there **across from Jericho** (v. 1). These **plains** had been taken from Moab by the Amorites (Num. 21:26), but the name of **Moab** lingered on.

III. EVENTS ON THE PLAINS OF MOAB (22:2—36:13)

A. The Prophet Balaam (22:2—25:18)

1. Balaam Summoned by Balak (22:2–40)

22:2–14 When **the Moabites**, to the south, heard how the Amorites had been conquered, they became terrified (unnecessarily, see Deut. 2:9). Therefore **Balak**, the **king**, sought to hire the prophet **Balaam** to **curse** Israel. Though a heathen prophet, Balaam seems to have had some knowledge of the true God. The Lord used him to reveal His mind concerning Israel's separation, justification, beauty, and glory. The first attempt to get **Balaam** to **curse** is recorded in verses 7–14. The messengers of **Balak** came to Balaam with the rewards of **divination**—that is, with rewards for him if he would successfully pronounce a curse on Israel. But **God** told him that he must **not curse the people** because the Lord had **blessed** them. Balak means "waster." Balaam means "swallower of the people" or "confuser of the people."

22:15–21 Balaam's second try is recorded next. **Balaam** knew what God's will was, yet he dared to go before the Lord, perhaps in hopes that there would be a change of mind. The Lord told Balaam to **go with** Balak's **men** but to do only what the Lord told him. Balaam's reason for going is clearly pointed out in 2 Peter 2:15, 16. He was motivated by his love of "the wages of unrighteousness." He is typical of the "hireling prophet" who prostitutes his God-given ability for money.

22:22–27 **The "Angel of the Lord"** (v. 22) was Christ in a preincarnate appearance. **Three times** He **stood** before **Balaam** and his **donkey** to hinder him, because He knew his motives. The first time the **donkey saw the Angel** and detoured **into a field**. For this, the poor animal was **struck** by **Balaam**. The second time the **Angel stood in a narrow path between the vineyards**. The terrified **donkey crushed Balaam's foot against the wall** and again was abused. The third time **the Angel** confronted them **in a narrow** pass. The frustrated **donkey lay down** on the ground and received a third thrashing from Balaam. Even a **donkey**, the symbol of stubbornness, knew when to quit, but not the stubborn, willful prophet!

22:28-40 The **donkey** was given the power to speak **to Balaam**, rebuking him for his inhumane treatment (vv. 28–30). Then Balaam **saw the Angel of the Lord with His drawn sword** and heard Him explain His mission to hinder Balaam in his disobedience (vv. 31–35). The Angel then permitted the prophet to go to Balak but to **speak . . . only the word that** God gave him (v. 35). After meeting Balaam, **Balak offered** sacrifices to his god.

2. Balaam's Oracles (22:41—24:25)

22:41—23:12 **The next day Balak** took Balaam into a **high** mountain (Pisgah) where he would look down over the tents of Israel. Later, from this same mountain, Moses would take his only look at the Promised Land, and then die (Deut. 34:1, 5). This chapter and the next chapter contain four memorable utterances by Balaam concerning Israel. The first three were preceded by the offering of **seven bulls and seven rams** as **burnt** offerings. The first **oracle** expressed Balaam's inability to **curse** a people **whom God** had **not cursed**. It predicted for Israel a life of separation from the Gentile nations and a numberless posterity. It pictured Israel as a righteous nation whose eventual destiny was something to be coveted (vv. 7–10). Balak's protest against this blessing availed nothing. The prophet had to speak the word of **the LORD**.

23:13–15 Balak then took Balaam to a different vantage point in hopes that the prophet would see them in a less favorable light (vv. 13, 14).

23:16–26 The second **oracle** assured **Balak** that God's original blessing on Israel was unchanged (vv. 18–20). The first part of verse 21 describes the nation's position, not its practice. The people were reckoned righteous through faith. So believers today stand before God in all the perfections of His beloved Son. The Lord was with Israel, and the people could **shout** because He reigned as **King** in their midst (v. 21b). He had delivered them from **Egypt** and given them **strength**. No evil pronouncement against them would come to pass. Instead, the victories Israel would soon win would cause the nations to say, **"Oh, what God has done!"** (vv. 22–24). Since **Balaam** refused to **curse** the people, **Balak** ordered him not to **bless them** either (v. 25), but the prophet protested that he could only do what **the LORD** said.

23:27–30 A third time **Balak** tried to wring a **curse** out of **Balaam**, this time from **the top of** Mount **Peor**.

24:1, 2 Realizing that God was determined **to bless Israel**, Balaam did not **seek to** get a message of cursing. He simply looked down over the camp of **Israel**, and **the Spirit of God came upon him**, causing him to say things beyond his own wisdom and will.

24:3–9 The third message spoke of the beauty of the **tents** of **Israel** and predicted tremendous fruitfulness, widespread prosperity, a glorious **kingdom**, and crushing power over all foes. **Agag** (v. 7) was probably a name common to many Amalekites. None would dare to **rouse** this crouching **lion** (v. 9). Those who blessed Israel would be **blessed**, and a curse would only bring cursing. Balaam's prophecy here echoes the covenant given to Abraham: "I will bless them that bless you, and curse him who curses you" (Gen. 12:3).

24:10–14 Thoroughly frustrated by now, **Balak** denounced **Balaam** for his failure to cooperate. But the prophet reminded him that from the beginning he had said that he could only **speak . . . the word of the LORD**. Before leaving Balak to return to his own home, Balaam offered to tell the king what Israel would **do to** the Moabite **people** in **days** to come.

24:15–19 The fourth **oracle** concerns a king (**"Star"** or **"Scepter"**) who would **rise** in **Israel** to conquer **Moab** and **all the sons of tumult** (v. 17; cf. Jer. 48:45). **Edom** also would be subjugated by this ruler. This prophecy was partially fulfilled by King David, but will enjoy its complete fulfillment at the Second Coming of Christ.

24:20–25 Similar promises of doom were uttered by Balaam concerning the Amalekites, **the Kenites**, Assyria (**Asshur**), and the people of **Eber** (vv. 20–24). The Amalekites would be utterly destroyed. The Kenites would be gradually depleted in number until the Assyrians would finally take them captive. Even the Assyrians would be captured by armed forces from **Cyprus** (Heb. *Kittim*, which generally means **Cyprus**, but probably represents Greece here and the forces of Alexander the Great). **Eber** probably means the non-Jewish descendants of this postdiluvian patriarch.

Before Balaam left Balak, he set the

wheels in motion for the tragic events of chapter 25.

3. Balaam's Corruption of Israel (Chap. 25)

25:1–3 Although Balaam's name is not mentioned in this chapter, we learn in Numbers 31:16 that he was responsible for the terrible corruption of the children of Israel that is described here. All of Balak's rewards could not induce Balaam to curse Israel, but they finally did persuade him to corrupt **Israel** by causing some of the people to **commit harlotry** and idolatry **with the women of Moab**. Often when Satan cannot succeed in a direct attack, he will succeed in an indirect one.

Balaam's true character emerges here. Up to this point we might think of him as a godly prophet who was loyal to the word of God and an admirer of the people of God. But from Numbers 31:16 and 2 Peter 2:15, 16 we learn that he was a wicked apostate who loved the wages of unrighteousness. Balaam advised Balak how to make the Israelites stumble: get them "to eat things sacrificed to idols, and to commit sexual immorality" (Rev. 2:14). His advice was heeded. This led to gross idolatry at the shrine of **Baal of Peor**.

25:4–8a God commanded that **all the** guilty **leaders** should be hanged **out in the sun**. Before the sentence was carried out, a leader of the tribe of Simeon brought a **Midianite woman** into the camp **of Israel**, to take her **into** his **tent** (v. 14). **Phinehas, the son of** the high priest (**Eleazar**), killed both man and woman with his **javelin**. Samuel Ridout comments:

> Phinehas, "a mouth of brass," is singularly appropriate to him who was so unyieldingly faithful to God, and by his relentless judgment of sin secured an abiding priesthood for himself and family.[15]

25:8b–13 God sent a **plague** into the camp **of Israel**, killing a total of **twenty-four thousand** of the offenders during the course of the plague (23,000 in one day—1 Cor. 10:8). It was Phinehas' heroic action that **stopped . . . the plague**. Because **he was zealous for his God**, the LORD decreed that **an everlasting priesthood** would continue in the family of **Phinehas**.

25:14, 15 Zimri's position of prominence in his tribe and the fact that the woman was a **daughter of** a **Midianite** chief might have stopped the judges from executing judgment upon him, but it did not stop Phinehas. He was jealous for Jehovah's sake.

25:16–18 **The LORD** ordered **Moses to** war against **the Midianites** (who were mingled with the Moabites at this time). This command was carried out in chapter 31.

B. The Second Census (Chap. 26)

26:1–51 Again **Moses** was instructed to **take a census . . . of the children of Israel**, since they were about to enter the land to war against its inhabitants and to receive their share of the inheritance. There was a decrease of 1,820 people from the first census, as seen in the following numbers:

Tribe	Census (Chap. 1)	Census (Chap. 26)
Reuben (vv. 5–11)	46,500	43,730
Simeon (vv. 12–14)	59,300	22,200
Gad (vv. 15–18)	45,650	40,500
Judah (vv. 19–22)	74,600	76,500
Issachar (vv. 23–25)	54,400	64,300
Zebulun (vv. 26, 27)	57,400	60,500
Joseph (vv. 28–37):		
–Manasseh (v. 34)	32,200	52,700
–Ephraim (v. 37)	40,500	32,500
Benjamin (vv. 38–41)	35,400	45,600
Dan (vv. 42, 43)	62,700	64,400

Tribe (*cont'd*)	Census (Chap. 1)	Census (Chap. 26)
Asher (vv. 44–47)	41,500	53,400
Naphtali (vv. 48–51)	53,400	45,400
TOTAL	603,550	601,730

Noting the decrease in numbers over the long period of time between the 603,550 of chapter 1 and the 601,730 **children of Israel** here, Moody comments:

> Israel's growth ceased for forty years. So it may be with us as churches, and so forth, if we are unbelieving.[16]

The most striking decrease is seen in the Simeonites, who diminished by almost 37,000. The tribe of Simeon was chiefly involved in the incident at Peor in the previous chapter (Zimri was a leader in that tribe), and perhaps most of the slain were Simeonites. Verse 11 tells us that the sons of Korah did not die with their father.

26:52–56 **The land** was to **be divided** according to the **number of** people in each tribe, and yet according to **lot**. This can only mean that the *size* of the tribal territory was determined by the **number** in the tribe, but the *location* of the land was determined by lot.

26:57–65 **The Levites** were **numbered** separately at **twenty-three thousand**. Only **Joshua** and **Caleb** were included in both censuses. All the other men of war listed in the first census had by now perished in the wilderness. Verses 64 and 65 refer to the men who were able to go to war. Levites and women are excluded, though some of these did die during the thirty-eight year journey.

C. Inheritance Rights of Daughters (27:1–11)

The five **daughters of Zelophehad**, of the tribe of **Manasseh**, **came** to Moses to request property in the distribution of the land even though they had no male in the numbered of Israel, among whom Canaan was to be divided (26:53). Their **father** had **died**, but **not** as one of the guilty companions of **Korah**. **The Lord** answered that they should inherit **their father's** portion. In general, it was God's will that the land be inherited by sons, then daughters, brothers, uncles, or nearest relatives. In this way it would be permanently kept in a family (vv. 1–11).

D. Joshua, Moses' Successor (27:12–23)

27:12–14 God forewarned **Moses** that he would die soon, and He instructed Moses to **go up** to **Mount Abarim** (actually a chain of mountains east of the Dead Sea). Mount Nebo, where Moses died, was a part of this chain [range].

27:15–23 Moses unselfishly thought of a successor to lead the people, and **Joshua the son of Nun** was named in his place. The priesthood and later the kingship in Israel was usually passed on from one generation to the next within the same family. However, Moses' successor was not his son but his servant (Ex. 24:13).

E. Offering and Vows (Chaps. 28—30)

Chaps. 28, 29 In these chapters, the people are reminded of the offerings and feasts which were to be observed in the land.

Daily offerings:

Continual **burnt offering, morning** and **evening**, with a **grain offering** and **drink offering** included (28:3–8).

Every **day** in life, so long as the temple stood, the following sacrifices had to be carried out both **morning** and **evening** (Num. 28:3–8).

Every morning and every evening a one-year-old male **lamb . . . without** spot or **blemish** was offered **as a *burnt offering*.** Along with it there was offered **a *grain offering***, which consisted of **one-tenth of an ephah of fine flour . . . mixed with** a quarter **of a hin** of pure **oil**. Also there was a ***drink offering***, which consisted of a quarter **of a hin** of wine.

There was an offering of incense before these offerings in the morning, and after them in the evening. Ever since there was a Jewish temple, and so long as the temple continued to exist, this routine of sacrifice went on. There was a kind of priestly treadmill of sacrifice. Moffatt speaks of "the levitical drudges" who, day in and day out, kept offering these sacrifices. There was no end to this process, and when all was said and done, it still left men conscious of their sin and alienation from God.

Weekly offerings:

Weekly **burnt offering**, **on** each **Sabbath**, with **grain offering** and **drink offering** (28:9,10).

Monthly offerings:

Burnt offering on the first day of each month, with **grain offering** and **drink offering** (28:11–14).

Sin offering (28:15).

Feasts of Jehovah:

Passover—fourteenth day of first month (28:16).

Feast of **Unleavened Bread—fifteenth day** to twenty-first day of first **month** (28:17–25).

Feast of weeks (28:26–31).

Note: **The** *day* of the firstfruits (v. 26) should not be confused with the *Feast* of Firstfruits (Lev. 23:9–14).

Feast of **Trumpets—first day of seventh month** (29:1–6).

Day of Atonement—**tenth day of seventh month** (29:7–11).

Feast of Tabernacles—**fifteenth day** through twenty-first day **of the seventh month** (29:12–34). There was a special Sabbath observance **on the eighth day** (29:35–39).

30:1–5 Chapter 30 contains special instructions about **vows**. A man making **a vow to the Lord** must carry it out without fail. **If a** young **woman**, still under **her father's** care, made **a vow**, and **her father** heard **her**, he could speak out against the vow—i.e., forbid it—**on the** first **day**, and it would be canceled. If he waited until after the first day or if he did not say anything, the vow was effective and had to be carried out.

30:6–16 Verses 6–8 seem to describe a vow made by a woman before her marriage. Although her husband would not, of course, have heard it on the day it was made, he could **overrule** it **on the day** when he first heard about it. Vows made by **a widow or a divorced woman** were binding (v. 9). Vows made by a married woman could be canceled by the **husband . . . on the** first **day** (vv. 10–15). This maintained the headship of the husband. If a husband canceled her vow after the first day, **he** had to **bear her guilt**—that is, bring the required sacrifice or be punished by the Lord (v. 15).

F. Destruction of the Midianites (Chap. 31)

31:1–11 God commanded **Moses** to destroy **the Midianites** for corrupting His people through fornication and idolatry at Baal of Peor. **Twelve thousand** Israelites marched against the enemy **and they killed all the males. Phinehas** went to war (v. 6) rather than his father the high priest, possibly because Phinehas had been the one to turn away the wrath of Jehovah by killing Zimri and the Midianite woman (chap. 25). Now he was to lead the armies of the living God to complete the judgment of the Lord on Midian. **"All the males"** (v. 7) refers to all the Midianite soldiers, and not to all the Midianites in existence, because in the days of Gideon they again become a menace to Israel (Judges 6). **Zur** (v. 8) was probably the father of Cozbi, the Midianite woman slain in the camp of Israel (25:15). (Either **Balaam** never made it all the way back to his home or else he had returned to Midian for some reason, for he too was **killed**.)

31:12–18 Though they had killed all the Midianite soldiers, the children of Israel spared **the women** and children and proudly **brought** them back **to the camp** with a great quantity of **spoil**. Moses was **angry** that they would have spared the very ones who caused Israel to sin and commanded that the **male** children and **every woman who** had lain with **a man** should be slain. The **young girls** were spared, probably for domestic service. This punishment was righteous and necessary to preserve Israel from further corruption.

31:19–54 The warriors and captives were required to undergo the customary **seven days** of purification (v. 19). Also, the spoil had to be cleansed, either by **fire** or by washing with **water** (vv. 21–24). The **spoil** was divided among the warriors and the whole **congregation** (vv. 25–47). **The men of war** were so thankful that **not** one of their number had perished that they brought a large gift to **the Lord** (vv. 48–54).

G. The Inheritance of Reuben, Gad, and Half of Manasseh (Chap. 32)

32:1–15 When the children of **Reuben** and **Gad . . . saw the** rich pasture **land** east of the **Jordan** River, they petitioned that they might settle there permanently (vv. 1–5). **Moses** thought this meant that they did not intend to cross the Jordan and fight against the heathen inhabitants of Canaan with their brethren (vv. 6–15). Their **fathers** had **discouraged** the Israelites at **Kadesh Barnea** from entering the land.

32:16-42 But when Reuben and Gad the two tribes assured him three times that they intended to fight for the land west of **the Jordan** (vv. 16–32 16–32), Moses granted permission. **Gad, Reuben**, and **half the tribe of Manasseh the son of Joseph** acquired **the kingdom of Sihon king of the Amorite and the kingdom of Og king of Bashan**. They **built fortified cities** and sheepfolds and also took over **small towns** and **villages** (vv. 33–42).

Many feel that Reuben and Gad made an unwise choice because, although the land was fertile, the area was exposed to enemy attack. They did not have the protection of the Jordan River. The tribes of **Reuben** and **Gad** (and **half the tribe of Manasseh** which joined them) were the first to be conquered in later years and carried off into captivity. On the other hand, what was to be done with the land east of the Jordan River if none of the children of Israel were to settle in it? God had given this land to them and told them to possess it (Deut. 2:24, 31; 3:2).

H. Review of the Israelite Encampments (Chap. 33)

33:1–49 The journeys of the children of Israel from **Egypt** to **the plains of Moab** are summarized in this chap-

Central Canaan's Surroundings

ter. As mentioned previously, it is impossible to locate all the cities with accuracy today. The chapter may be divided as follows: from **Egypt** to Mount **Sinai** (vv. 5–15); from Mount **Sinai** to **Kadesh** Barnea (vv. 16–36); from **Kadesh** Barnea to **Mount Hor** (vv. 37–40); from **Mount Hor** to **the plains of Moab** (vv. 41–49). This list is not complete, as can be seen by comparing it with other lists of camping spots, as in chapter 21.

33:50–56 God's order to the invading army was to completely exterminate **the inhabitants** of **Canaan**. This may seem cruel to people today, but actually these people were among the most corrupt, immoral, depraved creatures whom the world has ever known. God patiently dealt with them for over 400 years without any change on their part. He knew that if His people did not kill them, Israel would become infected by their immorality and idolatry. Not only were the Israelites to kill the people, but they were to **destroy** every trace of idolatry (v. 52).

I. Boundaries of the Promised Land (Chap. 34)

34:1–15 The **boundaries** of **the land** which God promised to Israel are given in verses 1–15. In general, the southern boundary extended from the southern tip of the **Salt** (Dead) **Sea** to **the Brook** (not River) **of Egypt** and to **the** Mediterranean **Sea** (vv. 3–5). The **western border** was the **Great** (Mediterranean) **Sea** (v. 6). The **northern border** stretched from the Mediterranean **Sea to Mount Hor** (not the one mentioned in the journeys of Israel) **to the entrance of Hamath** and **Hazar Enan** (vv. 7–9). The **eastern border** extended from **Hazar Enan** south **to the Sea of Chinnereth**[17] (Galilee), **down . . . the Jordan** River to the **Salt** (Dead) **Sea** (vv. 10–12). The **nine** and one-half **tribes** were to inherit the above land, since the **two** and one-half **tribes** had already been promised the land east of the Jordan (vv. 13–15).

34:16–29 The **names of the men who** were appointed to **divide the land** are given in verses 16–29.

J. Cities of the Levites (35:1–5)

Since the tribe of Levi did not inherit with the other tribes, God decreed that forty-eight **cities** should be set apart for the **Levites**. It is difficult to understand the measurements given in verses 4 and 5, but it is at least clear that the cities were surrounded by **common-land**[18] for grazing the livestock. (Perhaps the **two thousand cubits** mentioned in verse 5 were inclusive of the one **thousand cubits** already mentioned in verse 4.)

K. Cities of Refuge and Capital Punishment (35:6–34)

35:6–8 Six of the Levite **cities** were to be designated as **cities of refuge**. A person who had *accidentally* killed another could **flee** to one of these cities and be safe to stand trial. Those tribes which had much territory would donate **cities** for the **Levites** accordingly. Those which had little were not expected to give as many cities.

35:9–21 Of the **cities of refuge, three** were to be on each **side of the Jordan** River. A manslayer would ordinarily be pursued by a near relative of the victim, known as **the avenger.** If the **manslayer** reached a city of refuge, he was safe there until his case came up for trial (v. 12). The cities of refuge did not provide sanctuary for a **murderer** (vv. 16–19). Crimes committed through **hatred** or **enmity** were punishable by **death** (vv. 20, 21).

35:22–28 If the homicide appeared to be a case of manslaughter, the man would be tried by **the congregation** (vv. 22–24). If acquitted, the **manslayer** had to stay **in the city of refuge . . . until the death of the high priest**. He was then allowed to **return** home (v. 28). If he ventured **outside . . . the city** before the death of the high priest, the **avenger of blood** could slay him without incurring guilt (vv. 26–28).

The death of the high priest brought freedom to those who had escaped to the cities of refuge. They could no longer be harmed by the avenger of blood. The death of our Great High Priest frees us from the condemning demands of the Law. How foolish this stipulation would be if one failed to see in it a symbol of the work of our Lord at the Cross!

Unger relates some traditional details:

> According to the rabbis, in order to aid the fugitive it was the business of the Sanhedrin to keep the roads leading to the cities of refuge in the best possible repair. No hills were left, every river was bridged, and the road itself was to be at least thirty-two cubits broad. At every turn were guideposts bearing the word Refuge; and two students of the law were appointed to accompany the fleeing man, to pacify, if possible, the avenger, should he overtake the fugitive.[19]

As for the symbolic teaching, the people of Israel are the manslayer, having put the Messiah to death. Yet they did it ignorantly (Acts 3:17). The Lord Jesus prayed, ". . . they know not what they do" (Luke 23:34). Just as the manslayer was displaced from his own home and had to live in the city of refuge, so Israel has been living in exile ever since. The nation's complete restoration to its possession will take place, not at the death of the Great High Priest (for He can never die), but when He comes to reign.

35:29–34 Capital punishment was decreed for murderers; there was no escape or satisfaction (vv. 30, 31). A manslayer could not purchase release from a **city of refuge** (v. 32). **Blood** that was **shed** in murder defiled **the land**, and such blood demanded the death of the murderer (vv. 33, 34). Think of this in connection with the death of Christ!

L. The Inheritance of Daughters Who Marry (Chap. 36)

Representatives of the half-tribe of **Manasseh** who settled in **Gilead**, east of the Jordan, came to Moses with a problem (see Num. 27:1–11). If the **daughters of Zelophehad . . . married** men belonging to another **tribe**, their property would pass to the other **tribe**. The Year of **Jubilee** would finalize the transfer to the other tribe (v. 4). The solution was that those women who inherited land should **marry** in their own **tribe**, and thus there would be no transfers of land from one tribe to another (vv. 5–11). The **daughters of Zelophehad** obeyed by marrying in the tribe **of Manasseh** (vv. 10–12). Verse 13 summarizes the section from chapter 26.

Three things stand out in the book of Numbers:

1. The consistent wickedness and unbelief of the human heart.
2. The holiness of Jehovah, tempered with His mercy.
3. The man of God (Moses) who stands as a mediator and intercessor between the sinful people and a holy God.

The human heart has not changed since Numbers was written. Neither has the holiness or mercy of God. But Moses has been replaced by his Antitype, the Lord Jesus Christ. In Him we have strength to avoid the sins that characterized Israel, and thus avoid the displeasure of God which they incurred. In order to profit from what we have studied we must realize that "these things happened to them as examples, and they were written for our admonition" (1 Cor. 10:11).

ENDNOTES

[1](Intro) W. Graham Scroggie, *Know Your Bible, Vol. 1, The Old Testament*, p. 35.

[2](3:14–39) George Williams, *The Student's Commentary on the Holy Scriptures*, p. 80.

[3](4:4–20) C. F. Keil and F. Delitzsch, "Numbers," in *Biblical Commentary on the Old Testament*, III:25.

[4](6:1–8) Williams, *Student's Commentary*, p. 82.

[5](6:24–26) D. L. Moody, *Notes from My Bible*, p. 41.

[6](10:29–32) Quoted by John W. Haley, *Alleged Discrepancies of the Bible*, p. 431.

[7](11:16, 17) In Moses' defense the following points are worth noting: (1) God does not rebuke Moses; (2) God rather encourages Moses, promising him that after the seventy were endued with His Spirit, they would share his burden; (3) God Himself answers his need; (4) Moses was leading up to 2,000,000 complaining and unspiritual people; (5) Verse 17 does not indicate a decrease in Moses' enduement with the Spirit, but rather a distribution of the same Spirit to the seventy.

[8](11:31–35) See *International Standard Bible Encyclopedia* under "Quails," IV:2512.

[9](12:3) It is always possible that an inspired editor (such as Joshua) added these words later.

[10](12:11–16) Keil and Delitzsch, "Numbers," III:81.

[11](19:11–19) Williams, *Student's Commentary*, p. 88.

[12](19:11–19) J. G. Mantle, *Better Things*, p. 109.

[13](20:10–13) G. Campbell Morgan, *Searchlights from the Word*, pp. 47-48.

[14](20:22–29) Matthew Henry, "Numbers," in *Matthew Henry's Commentary on the Whole Bible*, I:662.

[15](25:4–8a) Samuel Ridout, further documentation unavailable.

[16](26:1–51) Moody, *Notes*, p. 43.

[17](34:1–15) Chinnereth (pronounced Kin–) is Hebrew for *harp*, named from the shape of the Sea of Galilee.

[18](35:1–5) Colonial New England towns sometimes had "commonlands" too, such as Boston Common.

[19] (35:22–28) Merrill F. Unger, *Unger's Bible Dictionary*, p. 208.

BIBLIOGRAPHY

Harrison, R. K. "Numbers." In the *Introduction to the Old Testament*.

Grand Rapids: Wm. B. Eerdmans Publishing Co., 1969.

Henry, Matthew. "Numbers." In *Matthew Henry's Commentary on the Whole Bible*. Vol. I. McLean, VA: MacDonald Publishing Company, n.d.

Jensen, Irving L. *Numbers*. Chicago: Moody Press, 1964.

Keil, C. F. and Delitzsch, F. "Numbers." In *Biblical Commentary on the Old Testament. The Pentateuch*. Vol. 3. Grand Rapids: Wm. B. Eerdmans Publishing Co., 1971.

Lange, John Peter. "Numbers." In *Commentary on the Holy Scriptures, Critical, Doctrinal and Homiletical*. Vol. 3. Translated by Philip Schaff. Reprint. Grand Rapids: Zondervan Publishing House, 1980.

Merrill, Eugene H. "Numbers." In the *Bible Knowledge Commentary*. Wheaton: Victor Books, 1985.

Wenham, Gordon J. *Numbers: An Introduction and Commentary*. Downers Grove, IL: InterVarsity Press, 1981.

DEUTERONOMY

Introduction

"Deuteronomy is one of the greatest books of the Old Testament. Its influence on the domestic and personal religion of all ages has not been surpassed by any other book in the Bible. It is quoted over eighty times in the New Testament and thus it belongs to a small group of four Old Testament books [Genesis, Deuteronomy, Psalms, and Isaiah] to which the early Christians made frequent reference."

—J. A. Thompson

I. Unique Place in the Canon

Our Lord Jesus Christ was tempted by Satan for forty days and nights in the wilderness. Three of these temptations are specifically recounted in the Gospels for our spiritual benefit. Not only did Christ use the OT "sword of the Spirit" three times, but each time He used the same part of the "blade"—Deuteronomy! It is likely that this book was one of Jesus' favorites—and it should be one of ours as well. Deuteronomy has been sadly neglected in many quarters, perhaps due to its somewhat inappropriate title in English, which is from the Greek Septuagint. Its meaning, "Second Law," has given some the false idea that the book is merely a recapitulation of material already presented in Exodus through Numbers. God never repeats just to repeat— there is always a different emphasis or new details. So also with Deuteronomy, a marvelous book worthy of careful study.

II. Authorship

Moses is the author of Deuteronomy as a whole, though the Lord may have used inspired editors to recount and update some details. The last chapter, which records his death, could have been written by him prophetically, or may have been added by Joshua or someone else.

Liberal criticism says confidently that Deuteronomy is the "Book of the Law" that was found in Josiah's time (c. 620 B.C.). They maintain that it was actually a "pious fraud" written at that time *as if by Moses* to unify Jewish worship around a central Jerusalem sanctuary.

Actually there is no such category as a "pious fraud"; if it's a fraud it's not pious, and if it's pious, it's no fraud.

There is also no indication that "the Book of the Law" in 2 Kings 22 does not refer to the *whole Pentateuch*. Josiah's predecessors, Manasseh and Amon, were both wicked kings. They actually perpetuated idolatry in the very temple of Jehovah where the Law of Moses had apparently been hidden by some godly person or persons.

The rediscovery of God's Word and submission to it always bring revival and recovery, as in the great Protestant Reformation.

For a concise defense of Mosaic authorship, see Introduction to the Pentateuch.

III. Date

Deuteronomy was written largely by 1406 B.C., but some material, equally inspired, may have been added after Moses' death, as was noted.

For a more detailed discussion of dating see Introduction to the Pentateuch.

IV. Background and Theme

Deuteronomy is a *re-statement* (not merely a repetition) of the law for the new generation that had arisen during the wilderness journey. They were about to enter the Promised Land. In order to enjoy God's blessing there, they must know the law and obey it.

The book consists first of all of a spiritual interpretation of Israel's history from Sinai onward (chaps. 1–3). The thought is that those who refuse to learn from history are doomed to relive it. The main section is a review of important features of God's legislation for His people (chaps. 4–26). Then follows a preview of God's purposes of grace and government from Israel's entrance into the land until the second advent of the Messiah (chaps. 27–33). The book closes with the death of Moses and the appointment of Joshua as his successor (chap. 34).

The Apostle Paul reminds us that the book has a message for us as well as for Israel. In commenting on Deuteronomy 25:4, he says that it was written "altogether for our sakes" (1 Cor. 9:10).

The book is rich in exhortation, which can be summed up in the verbs of Deuteronomy 5:1: "Hear . . . learn . . . keep and do."

OUTLINE

I. MOSES' FIRST DISCOURSE—APPROACHING THE LAND (Chaps. 1—4)
   A. Introduction (1:1–5)
   B. From Horeb to Kadesh (1:6–46)
   C. From Kadesh to Heshbon (Chap. 2)
   D. Trans-Jordan Secured (Chap. 3)
   E. Exhortation to Obedience (Chap. 4)

II. MOSES' SECOND DISCOURSE—PURITY IN THE LAND (Chaps. 5—28)
   A. Review of the Sinai Covenant (Chap. 5)
   B. Warnings Against Disobedience (Chap. 6)
   C. Instructions on Dealing with Idolatrous Nations (Chap. 7)
   D. Lessons from the Past (8:1—11:7)
   E. Rewards for Obedience (11:8—32)
   F. Statutes for Worship (Chap. 12)
   G. Punishment of False Prophets and Idolaters (Chap. 13)

H. Clean and Unclean Foods (14:1–21)
I. Tithing (14:22–29)
J. Treatment of Debtors and Slaves (Chap. 15)
K. Three Appointed Feasts (Chap. 16)
L. Judges and Kings (Chap. 17)
M. Priests, Levites, and Prophets (Chap. 18)
N. Criminal Laws (Chap. 19)
O. Laws Concerning Warfare (Chap. 20)
P. Various Laws (Chaps. 21—25)
   1. Expiation for Unsolved Murder (21:1–9)
   2. Female Prisoners of War (21:10–14)
   3. Rights of the Firstborn (21:15–17)
   4. Stubborn and Rebellious Sons (21:18–21)
   5. The Bodies of Hanged Criminals (21:22–23)
   6. Nine Laws of Behavior (22:1–22)
   7. Offenses Against Chastity (22:13–30)
   8. Those Barred from Entering the Assembly (23:1–8)
   9. Cleanliness in the Camp (23:9–14)
   10. Social and Religious Laws (23:15–25)
   11. Divorce and Remarriage (24:1–4)
   12. Various Social Laws (24:5—25:5)
   13. Law of Levirate Marriage (25:5–10)
   14. Three Distinct Laws (25:11–19)
Q. Rituals and Ratifications (Chap. 26)
   1. The Ritual for Firstfruits (26:1–11)
   2. The Ritual for the Third Year Tithe (26:12–15)
   3. Ratification of the Covenant (26:16–19)
R. Curses and Blessings (Chaps. 27, 28)

III. MOSES' THIRD DISCOURSE—COVENANT FOR THE LAND (Chaps. 29, 30)
A. The Covenant Made in Moab (29:1–21)
B. Punishment for Breaking the Covenant (29:22–29)
C. Restoration for Returning to the Covenant (Chap. 30)

IV. MOSES' LAST DAYS—DEATH OUTSIDE THE LAND (Chaps. 31—34)
A. Moses' Replacement (Chap. 31)
B. Moses' Song (Chap. 32)
C. Moses' Blessing (Chap. 33)
D. Moses' Death (Chap. 34)

Commentary

I. MOSES' FIRST DISCOURSE—APPROACHING THE LAND (Chaps. 1—4)

A. Introduction (1:1–5)

1:1, 2 As the Book of Deuteronomy opens, the children of Israel are camped on the plains **of Moab**, which they had reached in Numbers 22:1. In Deuteronomy 1:1 their location is said to be **in the plain opposite Suph**. This means that the wilderness, of which the plains of Moab were an extension, stretched southward to that portion of the Red Sea known as the Gulf of Aqaba. The journey from **Horeb** (Sinai) by way of **Mount Seir to Kadesh Barnea**, on the threshold of Canaan, required only *eleven days*, but now *thirty-eight years* had passed before the Israelites were ready to enter the Promised Land!

1:3–5 Moses delivered his subsequent discourse **to the children of Israel**, preparatory to their entering Canaan **in the fortieth year** after they left Egypt. It was **after** both **Sihon king of the Amorites** and **Og king of Bashan** had been slain (Num. 21).

B. From Horeb to Kadesh (1:6–46)

From Deuteronomy 1:6—3:28 we have a review of the period from Mount Sinai to the plains of Moab. Since most of this has already been covered in Numbers, we shall simply summarize it here: God's command to march to the Promised Land and **possess** it (vv. 6–8); the appointment of **judges** over civil matters (vv. 9–18); the journey from Sinai **to Kadesh Barnea** (vv. 19–21); the sending of the spies and the subsequent rebellion (vv. 22–46). With the exception of **Joshua** and **Caleb**, no soldier who had left Egypt was allowed to enter the **land** (vv. 34–38).

C. From Kadesh to Heshbon (Chap. 2)

2:1–23 The journey from **Kadesh Barnea** to the borders of Edom (vv. 1–7) avoided conflict with the Edomites. The journey from the borders of Edom to the **Valley of Zered** (vv. 8–15) avoided conflict with the Moabites. **The LORD** commanded the Israelites **not to meddle with** the Ammonites because He had **given** this **land to** these **descendants of Lot as a possession** (vv. 16–19). God had already **dispossessed** certain **giants**[1] whom the Ammonites called **Zamzummim, just as He had done for the descendants of Esau** by destroying **the Horites**, the **Avim**, and **the Caphtorim** (vv. 20–23).

2:24–37 The rest of chapter 2 details the smashing defeat of **Sihon the Amorite**, the **king of Heshbon**. Verse 29a indicates that the **descendants** of **Esau**, the Edomites, sold **food** and **water** to the Israelites as the latter skirted the country of Edom. But the record in Numbers 20:14–22 suggests that the king of Edom was completely uncooperative. He was staunch in his refusal to assist Israel, but it seems that some of his people sold **food** and water to the Jews, though this is uncertain. Verses 10–12 and 20–23 were probably added by someone later than Moses, but are nonetheless inspired Scripture.

D. Trans-Jordan Secured (Chap. 3)

3:1–11 Og king of Bashan had **sixty cities**, all **fortified with high walls, gates, and bars**, as well as

many rural towns. The LORD God also delivered these enemies into the **hands** of His people. **Og** is remembered as a **giant**, with a huge **iron bedstead** that was **nine cubits** long and **four cubits** wide (about thirteen or fourteen feet by six feet). Thompson says this **"bedstead"** was his final resting place, not his regular bed:

> On his death he was buried in a massive sarcophagus (lit. *bedstead*, "resting place") made of basalt, called *iron* here because of its colour. . . . According to the record here the sarcophagus could be seen in Rabbah Ammon (the modern Amman) at the time Deuteronomy was committed to writing.[2]

3:12–20 The captured **land** east **of the Jordan** was distributed **to the Reubenites**, the **Gadites**, and **to half the tribe of Manasseh** (vv. 12–17). Moses **commanded** their **men of valor to cross over armed** to **aid their brethren** conquer the territory west of the Jordan. Then they could **return** to their own **possession** and their **wives**, **little ones**, **livestock**, and the **cities** they had taken over.

3:21–29 Moses also commanded **Joshua** to remember past victories and trust God for future ones (vv. 21, 22).

But the LORD was angry with Moses for his disobedience regarding the children of Israel and would not let him cross over Jordan. He did, however, let him view the Promised Land in every direction from the **top of** Mount **Pisgah** (vv. 23–29).

E. Exhortation to Obedience (Chap. 4)

Chapter 4 introduces Moses' rehearsal of the law. Here he dealt particularly with the worship of the one true God and with the penalties that would follow any turning to idolatry.

4:1–24 Israel was commanded to obey **the statutes and the judgments of the LORD God** when they entered Canaan (v. 1). They were **not** to **add to** it **nor take from** it (v. 2). God's punishment of the idolatry practiced at **Beth Peor** should serve as a constant warning (vv. 3, 4). (Perhaps this particular incident of divine wrath against idolatry is mentioned here because it had taken place just a short time earlier and would be fresh in their minds.) Obedience to the **law** would cause Israel to be admired as a **great nation** by the Gentiles (vv. 5–8). Israel should remember from past experiences the blessings of following the Lord (v. 8). They were especially instructed to remember the giving of **the Ten Commandments** at Mount Sinai (**Horeb**) (vv. 9–13). At that time, they did not see the form of God; that is, although they might have seen a manifestation of God, they did not see a physical **form** which could be reproduced by an image or an idol. They were forbidden to **make** an **image** of any kind to represent God, or to worship **the sun**, **the moon**, or **the stars** (vv. 14–19). The Israelites were reminded of their deliverance from **Egypt**, of Moses' disobedience and consequent judgment, and of God's wrath against idolatry (vv. 20–24). **"Only take heed to yourself . . . lest you forget"** (v. 9); **"Take careful heed to yourselves . . . lest you act corruptly"** (vv. 15, 16); **"Take heed to yourselves, lest you forget"** (v. 23). Moses knew only too well the natural tendency of the human heart, and so he earnestly charged the people to pay close attention.

4:25–40 If the nation in later years should turn to idols, it would be sent away into captivity (vv. 25–28). But even then, if the people repented and turned to **the LORD with all** their **heart**, He would restore them (vv. 29–31). No nation had ever had the privileges of Israel, particularly the miracles connected with the deliverance from **Egypt** (vv. 32–38). Therefore they should be obedient to Him and thus enjoy His continued blessing (vv. 39, 40). It is a sad fact of Jewish history that the nation was subjected to a purging captivity because of their disobedience and failure to take the warning of Jehovah seriously. God's warnings are not idle words. No man and no nation can set them aside with impunity.

4:41–43 **Moses set apart three cities** of refuge on the east **side of the Jordan—Bezer**, **Ramoth**-Gilead, **and Golan** (vv. 41–43).

4:4–49 Here begins Moses' second discourse, delivered on the plains of Moab, **east . . . of the Jordan**. Verse 48 is the only instance where Mount **Hermon** is called **Mount Sion**.[3]

II. MOSES' SECOND DISCOURSE—PURITY IN THE LAND (Chaps. 5—28)

A. Review of the Sinai Covenant (Chap. 5)

5:1–6 Chapter 5 reviews the giving of the Ten Commandments at Mount Sinai (**Horeb**). In verse 3, supply the word "only" after "fathers." The covenant *was* made with the **fathers**, but it was intended for *future* generations of Israelites as well.

5:7–21 The Ten Commandments

1. **No other gods** were to be worshiped (v. 7).
2. No **carved image** was to be made or worshiped (vv. 8–10). This commandment does not repeat the first. People might worship mythical beings, or the sun and moon, without the use of idols. **Children** who thus hate God will suffer the same punishment as their fathers (v. 9).
3. **The name of the LORD** was **not** to be taken **in vain** (v. 11).
4. The **Sabbath** was to be kept **holy** (vv. 12–15). A different reason for keeping the **Sabbath** is given here from the one given in Exodus 20:8–11 (God's rest in Creation). The Jews were to remember that they were slaves in Egypt (v. 15). These two reasons are complementary, not contradictory.
5. Parents were to be honored (v. 16).
6. **Murder** was prohibited (v. 17).
7. **Adultery** was prohibited (v. 18).
8. Stealing was prohibited (v. 19).
9. Bearing **false witness against** a **neighbor** was prohibited (v. 20).
10. Coveting was prohibited (v. 21).

5:22 J. A. Thompson comments on this verse:

> The expression *and He added no more* is unusual and may indicate that these commandments were such a complete summary of the fundamental requirements of the covenant that no other law needed to be added. All other law was a mere interpretation and expansion of these basic principles. Alternatively, the expression may refer to a particular occasion when the Lord made known precisely these ten laws. Other laws must have been given on other occasions, since the total volume of law known in Israel and originating from God was considerable.[4]

5:23–33 When the law was given, the people were terrified by the manifestations of the divine Presence and feared for their lives. They sent Moses to speak to the Lord and to assure Him that they would **do** whatever He said. (They did not realize their own sinfulness and powerlessness when they made such a rash vow.) Consequently the rest of the laws and ordinances were given through Moses the mediator. The Ten Words or Ten **Commandments** appear to have been spoken verbally to the whole nation when they were at Mount Sinai (vv. 30, 31).

In verse 28, **the Lord** is not commending them for their promise to keep the law, but rather for their expressions of fear and awe (compare 18:16–18). God knew that they did not have **a heart** to **keep** His **commandments**. He wished that they did, so that He could bless them abundantly (vv. 28–33).

B. Warnings Against Disobedience (Chap. 6)

6:1–9 When the people would enter the Promised Land, God wanted them to be in a right moral condition. In order to enjoy the land as He intended, they must be an obedient people. Therefore, Moses gave them practical instruction to fit them for life in Canaan (vv. 1, 2). The Israelites were to bear testimony to the truth that God is the only true **God** (vv. 3, 4). They were to **love** Him supremely and keep His Word (vv. 5, 6). The commandments of the Lord were to be taught **diligently to** their **children** and to guide them in every department of their lives.

Many Christian parents take this passage as a mandate to teach their own children, not only the faith, but also other so-called secular subjects, rather than sending them to humanistic schools.

In the days of Christ, the Jews actually bound portions of the law to their hands and suspended them **between** their **eyes** (v. 8). But doubtless the Lord intended rather that their actions (**hand**) and desires (**eyes**) should be controlled by the law.

Verses 4–9 are known as the "Shema" (Heb. for "hear") and were recited daily as a creed by devout Jews along with 11:13–21 and Numbers 15:37–41.

> The Hebrew word for "one" in verse 4 is significant, viewed in the light of the fuller revelation of the New Testament. It stands, not for absolute unity, but for compound unity, and is thus consistent with both the names of God used in this verse. Jehovah (Lord) emphasizes His oneness. Elohim (God) emphasizes His three persons. The same mysterious hints of trinity in unity occur in the very first verse of the Bible, where "Elohim" is followed by a singular verb (created) and in Genesis 1:26, where the plural pronouns *us* and *our* are followed by the singular nouns *image* and *likeness*. (*Daily Notes of the Scripture Union*)

6:10–15 When the people would enter **the land** and enjoy its great prosperity, there was a danger that they would **forget** the One who gave the law to them or that they would **go after other gods**. Obedience to the law was not so much a means of *gaining favor* with Jehovah as it was of *showing love* to Him. Biblical love is not a warm sentimentality but a calculated pattern of conformity to the revealed will of God. Love is not an option but a necessity for wellbeing. God's jealousy (zeal for His own glory) would **destroy** the people if they broke His covenant through disobedience.

6:16 The Lord Jesus quoted this verse in Matthew 4:7 and Luke 4:12 to answer the tempter's suggestion that He throw Himself down from the pinnacle of the temple. At **Massah**, there was not enough water to drink, and the people questioned that Jehovah was with them (Ex. 17). To doubt God's care and goodness is to **tempt** Him.

6:17–25 Obedience would bring victory over Israel's foes (vv. 17–19). Future generations were to be instructed in God's deliverance of the people from **Egypt** and of His giving of the law **for** their **good** and blessing (vv. 20–25). Compare verse 25 with Romans 3:21, 22. The law says, **"if we are careful to observe"**; grace says, "to all and on all those who *believe.*" Today believers are clothed with the righteousness on which the law was based, the righteousness of God (2 Cor. 5:21), and this according to faith, not works (Rom. 4:5).

C. Instructions on Dealing with Idolatrous Nations (Chap. 7)

7:1–5 The people of Israel were strongly warned against mixing with the heathen, idolatrous **nations** which were then inhabiting Canaan. To punish these **seven nations—the Hittites, Girgashites, Amorites, Canaanites, Perizzites, Hivites, and Jebusites**—for their unspeakable sin and to preserve Israel from contamination, God decreed that these Gentiles should be **utterly** exterminated and that every trace of idolatry should be destroyed. Perhaps verse 3 anticipates the failure of the Jews to obey verse 2, because if they destroyed all the inhabitants of the land, obviously there would be no threat of intermarriage.

7:6–11 **God** had **chosen** Israel **to be a people** who were separated to Himself. He did not want them to be like the other nations. He **did not . . . choose** them because of their superior numbers (they were the fewest **of all peoples**). He chose them simply because He loved them, and He wanted them to obey Him in all things. **A thousand generations** means forever. The Lord hated the Canaanite nations because of their evil deeds. He loved the nation of Israel not because of any good but simply because He loved them and **would keep the oath which He swore to** their forefathers. Who can understand the electing grace of a sovereign God!

7:12–26 If God's people would be faithful to Him **in the land**, He would **bless** them with numerous children, abundant crops, large herds, health, and victory over their enemies (vv. 12–16). If they were ever tempted to fear their enemies, they should **remember** God's mighty deliverances in the past, especially the deliverance from **Egypt** (vv. 17–19). As He had done in the past, He would do for them again, sending the **hornet** to **destroy** their foes. **The hornet** may be literal or a figure of speech for a conquering army (vv. 20–24). He would not destroy their enemies all at once lest the land be overrun with wild **beasts** (v. 22). (Unpopulated areas become breeding grounds for wild animals, whereas urban areas serve to control their numbers.) Another reason victory was not to be immediate can be found in Judges 2:21–23: God would use the remaining heathen to test Israel. All idols were to be utterly **destroyed** lest they become a temptation to Israel (vv. 25, 26). The most serious threat to Israel was not the people of Canaan but their idols and the gross immorality associated with these idols. The battles which they needed to prepare for most were spiritual, not physical.

D. Lessons from the Past (8:1—11:7)

Concerning chapters 8 and 9, J. A. Thompson succinctly points out:

> Two important lessons from the past are now referred to. First, the experience of God's care in the wilderness period, when the people of Israel were unable to help themselves, taught them the lesson of humility through the Lord's providential discipline. The memory of that experience should keep them from pride in their own achievements amid the security and prosperity of the new land (8:1–20). Secondly, any success they might enjoy in the coming conquest was not to be interpreted as a mark of divine approval for their own righteousness (9:1–6). In fact, both in the incident of the golden calf (9:7–21) and a number of other incidents (9:22–29), Israel had proved herself stubborn and rebellious.[5]

8:1–5 Again Moses urged the people to obey God, using the loving, preserving care of God as a motive. The Lord had allowed trials to come into their lives **to humble** them, prove them, and **test** their obedience. But He also **fed** them with **manna** from heaven, and provided clothes that **did not wear out** and shoes which kept their feet from swelling during the **forty years** of wilderness wanderings.

God knew **what was in** the hearts of the people. He was not trying to learn something by testing Israel **in the wilderness** (v. 2), but He was manifesting to the people themselves their own rebellious nature so that they might more fully appreciate His mercy and grace. Another lesson they were to learn through their wanderings was to fear the Lord.

8:6–20 Moses pled his case not only on the basis of what God had done but on what He was about to do (vv. 6, 7). The blessings of **the good land** of Canaan are described in detail (vv. 7–9). Prosperity might lead to forgetfulness and forgetfulness to disobedience, so the people were to watch against these perils (vv. 10–20). Faithfulness on God's part was to be met by a corresponding faithfulness on the part of Israel. God was keeping His **covenant** with the patriarchs (v. 18); the people needed to keep their word to God in return (Ex. 19:8). **If** the people forgot God's mighty acts on their behalf and attributed their wealth to their own power, Jehovah would destroy them as He destroyed the Gentile **nations** in Canaan.

9:1–3 Chapter 9 opens with a description of the **nations** which **Israel** was soon to face in battle. Israel was not to be afraid, as they had been forty years earlier, because God would fight for them. "*He* will destroy them . . . so *you* shall drive them out and destroy them quickly." Notice the complementary working of divine sovereignty and human agency. Both were essential for securing the Promised Land.

9:4–7 **After . . . God** had defeated the Canaanite inhabitants of the land, the Israelites were not to boast. Three times the people are warned about attributing success to their own **righteousness** (vv. 4–6). God would give them the **land . . . because of the wickedness of** the present inhabitants (v. 4), because of His oath to **Abraham, Isaac, and Jacob** (v. 5), and not because of any merit in them. The truth of the matter is that they were **stiff-necked** (stubborn) (v. 6) as well as provocative and **rebellious** (v. 7).

9:8–23 Moses cites as an example the people's behavior at Mount **Horeb**

(Sinai) (vv. 8–21). Verses 22 and 23 mention other places where the people sinned: **Taberah** (Num. 11:3); **Massah** (Ex. 17:7); **Kibroth Hattaavah** (Num. 11:34); **Kadesh Barnea** (Num. 13:31–33). Note how the golden **calf** was destroyed beyond recovery (v. 21).

9:24–29 At Mount Sinai the intercession of Moses was the only thing that saved the people from the wrath of Jehovah. He did not base his plea on the righteousness of the people (which further shows that they had none) but on *possession:* "Your people and Your inheritance" (v. 26); *promise:* "Remember Your servants, Abraham, Isaac, and Jacob" (v. 27); *power* (God's power would be ridiculed by the Egyptians): **"lest the land from which You brought us should say, 'Because the LORD was not able' "** (v. 28).

In verse 1 of chapter 10, the narrative goes back to the events at Mount Sinai and therefore follows verse 29 of chapter 9. The Bible is not always chronological; often the order of events has a spiritual or moral order that is more important than the mere chronological order. A more appropriate place for the chapter division[6] would seem to be after verse 11, because the first 11 verses deal with events at Mount Sinai (the theme taken up in 10:8) while verses 12 and following are an exhortation to obedience based on God's gracious mercy.

10:1–5 This paragraph records the second giving of the law and the deposit of the **two tablets** in the **ark**. Verse 3 doesn't mean that Moses personally made the ark, but only that he had it made. A person is often said to do what he orders to be done.

10:6–9 Verses 6 and 7 seem to be an abrupt change at this point. Actually they are a parenthesis, recording events that took place at a later date, as the NKJV indicates. But they bring the reader up to the death of **Aaron**. (The NKJV puts vv. 6–9 in parentheses, which makes the passage easier to understand.)

Moserah was probably a district where Mount Hor was located, since that is the mountain **where Aaron died** (Num. 20:25–28). The exact location of Moserah is unknown today. Perhaps this mention of the death of **Aaron** caused Moses to think of the priesthood, and so he reverted to the choosing of **Levi** as the priestly **tribe** (vv. 8, 9). The threefold function of the priesthood is given in verse 8: (1) **to bear the ark of the covenant**; (2) **to stand before the LORD to minister to Him**; (3) **to bless in His name**. Instructions about the priesthood were important for this generation which was about to enter Canaan.

10:10, 11 Moses again reminded them of his second stay on Sinai when for **forty days and forty nights** he interceded for them. God heard, withheld judgment, and told them to **go in and possess the land**.

10:12–22 Jehovah's desire for His people was summed up in the words **"to fear . . . to walk . . . to love . . . to serve . . . to keep"** (vv. 12, 13). All of God's **commandments** were designed **for** their **good** (v. 13b). Moses encouraged them to obey God because of His greatness (v. 14), His sovereign choice of Israel as His special people (v. 15), His righteousness and **justice** (vv. 17–20), and His past favors to the nation (vv. 21, 22). A circumcised **heart** (v. 16) is one that obeys.

11:1–7 Once more Moses reviewed the past history of Israel in order to draw spiritual lessons from it. In verse 2, Moses is speaking to survivors of the older generation as distinguished from those who were born in the desert. Soldiers who were over twenty when they left Egypt were excluded from entering Canaan (2:14; Josh. 5:6). God delivered His people from Egypt and led them through **the wilderness**, but He would not tolerate the rebellion of **Dathan and Abiram**. God's judgment of the idolatrous Egyptians and His vigorous judgment on rebels within the nation itself should serve as lessons on the folly of incurring His displeasure.

E. Rewards for Obedience (11:8–32)

11:8–17 Conversely, the way to **prolong** their **days in the land** (v. 9) was to **keep every commandment** (v. 8). The land which they would enjoy, if obedient, is described in verses 10–12. The expression **"watered it by foot"** may refer to the use of some pedal device for pumping water or perhaps to the opening of sluices with the foot. **Egypt** was a barren land made fruitful by irrigation, but the Promised Land enjoyed the special favor of the God of nature (vv. 11, 12). Abundant **rain** and plentiful harvests would be the reward of obedience (vv. 13–15), but forgetfulness of God or idolatry would be followed by drought and barrenness.

11:18–21 The Word of God was to be the subject of household conversation. It was to be loved and lived. The reward for practicing the Word was that their **days** would **be multiplied in the land**, and also **like the days of the heavens above the earth** (v. 21).

> Latterday Jews took 18b literally, and so wore small pouches with portions of Scripture on their foreheads, and put them on their doorposts (as some still do). But verse 19a suggests the truth intended—the Word on the hand means a pair of hands that will not lend themselves to shoddy or unworthy workmanship; the Word between our eyes represents the control of God over our vision—where we look, and what we covet; the Word on the doorpost signifies home and family life under the constraint of responsibility to God, especially for any young lives entrusted to our care. (*Daily Notes of the Scripture Union*)

11:22–25 Those who walked in the ways of the Lord would **drive out** the heathen Canaanites and possess all the land their feet walked on. The rule of possession is given in verse 24. All the land was theirs by promise, but they had to go in and make it their own, just as we have to appropriate the promises of God. The boundaries given in verse 24 have never been realized historically by Israel. It is true that Solomon's kingdom extended from the river (Euphrates) to the border of Egypt (1 Kgs. 4:21), but the Israelites did not actually possess all that territory. Rather, it included states that *paid tribute* to Solomon but maintained their own internal government. Verse 24, along with many others, will find its fulfillment in the Millennial Reign of the Lord Jesus Christ.

11:26–32 So it was to be **a blessing** or **a curse** for Israel—**a blessing** in the event of obedience, and **a curse** for disobedience. Two mountains in Canaan represented this truth—**Mount Gerizim** stood for the **blessing**, and **Mount Ebal** for the **curse**. These two mountains, located near Shechem, had a small valley between them. Half of the tribes were supposed to stand on **Gerizim** while the priests would pronounce the blessings that would follow obedience. The other six tribes were to stand on **Mount Ebal** while the priests recited the curses that would flow from disobedience. In each case, the people were to say "Amen!" See Deuteronomy 27:11–26 for details concerning the significance of these two mountains.

The terebinth trees of Moreh are probably those mentioned in Genesis 35:1–4. There, several centuries earlier, Jacob had purged his house of idolatry. Perhaps this reference was intended to impart not only geographical guidance but spiritual guidance as well.

F. Statutes for Worship (Chap. 12)

12:1–3 When they entered **the land**, the people of God were to **destroy all** idols and idol shrines, all places where a false worship had been carried on. The wooden images (Heb. *ashērîm*) were symbols of a female deity. The **pillars** were symbolic of Baal, the male deity.

12:4–14 God would set apart a place for **worship**, a place where **sacrifices** and **offerings** should be brought. This place was where the tabernacle was pitched at first (Shiloh—Josh. 18:1) and later where the temple was erected (Jerusalem). Only in this appointed place was worship approved. The Christian's center of worship is a Person, the Lord Jesus Christ, the visible manifestation of the invisible Godhead. . . . God had overlooked certain irregularities in the wilderness that must not be practiced in the land of Canaan (vv. 8, 9).

12:15–28 In Leviticus 17:3, 4, God had commanded that when any sacrificial animal such as an ox, sheep, or goat was slain, it had to be brought to the tabernacle. Now that the people were about to settle in Canaan, the law must be changed. Henceforth the Jews could kill and eat domestic animals commonly used for sacrifices, just as they would eat the **gazelle** and the **deer** (clean animals that were not used for sacrifices). This permission was granted to those who were ceremonially **unclean** as well as to those who were **clean**. However, they were repeatedly warned **not** to **eat the blood**, because **the blood is the life** of the flesh, and **the life** belongs to God.

12:29–32 The Israelites were solemnly warned not even to investigate the idolatrous practices of the heathen, lest they be tempted to introduce these wicked practices into the **worship** of the true **God**. Verse 31 refers to the horrible practices associated with the worship of Molech and Chemosh. In the NT, Paul tells us that the motivating force behind idolatry is demonic (1 Cor. 10:20). Should we marvel at the cruelty and degradation of idolatry when we realize its true nature? That the human heart gravitates toward this kind of darkness more readily than it seeks the light of the true God is illustrated by the nation to whom Deuteronomy is addressed. Solomon, Israel's third king, actually did build an altar for Chemosh and Molech right in Jerusalem, the city where the Lord had put His Name (1 Kgs. 11:7).

G. Punishment of False Prophets and Idolaters (Chap. 13)

Individuals or groups which might tempt God's people to practice idolatry were to be stoned **to death**, whether a **prophet** (vv. 1–5), a near relative (vv. 6–11), or a community (vv. 12–18). A prophet who encouraged people into idolatry was not to be followed, even if some miracle he predicted came **to pass**. Such a person was a false **prophet**, and he must be put **to death**. Even if a close relative enticed his family to practice idolatry, he too was to be slain.

The **corrupt men** of verse 13 were

base fellows, or "sons of worthlessness" (Heb. *belîyya'al*). Any such gang which led the people **of their city** away from God to idols should be killed, together with **the inhabitants of that city**, and **the city** should be burned.

The same treatment was to be meted out to an idolatrous Israelite **city** as to the Canaanite cities—namely, total destruction. God is not partial; He will deal severely with sin, even among His chosen people. But His motives are different. In the case involving a Jewish city His motive would be fatherly discipline, with a view to correction of the nation as a whole.

H. Clean and Unclean Foods (14:1–21)

14:1, 2 These two verses prohibit the idolatrous practice of disfiguring the body in mourning **for the dead**. The Jews had a higher regard for the body as God's creation than did the Gentiles.

14:3–21a This paragraph reviews the subject of **clean** and **unclean** foods, whether **animals** (vv. 4–8), fishes (vv. 9, 10), flying insects (v. 19), or **birds** (vv. 11–18, 20). (For exceptions to verse 19, see Lev. 11:21, 22.) A similar list is given in Leviticus 11. The two lists are not identical in every detail, nor are they intended to be. Some **animals** were **unclean** for hygienic reasons, and some because they were used in idolatrous rites or venerated by the heathen.

The NT principle concerning foods can be found in Mark 7:15, Romans 14:14, and 1 Timothy 4:3b–5. Gentiles were permitted to eat the flesh of an animal that died by **itself**, whereas Jews were **not** (v. 21a). To do so would violate Deuteronomy 12:23 because the blood had not been properly removed from the animal.

14:21b A **goat** was **not** to be **boiled** in the same pan with **milk** from its mother (v. 21b). (This appears to have been a Canaanite practice. It is forbidden three times in the Pentateuch.) From a natural standpoint, this rule would save the people from the poisoning that is so common when creamed meat dishes spoil. In addition, there is evidence that the calcium value is canceled when both are eaten together. From this restriction the elaborate rabbinical rules about having different sets of dishes for meat and dairy products have evolved.

I. Tithing (14:22–29)

14:22–27 Verses 22–29 deal with the subject of tithes. Some commentators feel that this section does not refer to the first **tithe** (Lev. 27:30–33), which belonged to God alone, was given to the Levites, and was not to be eaten by the Israelites. Rather it may refer to a secondary **tithe**, called the festival tithe, part of which the offerer himself ate. Generally speaking, these secondary tithes were to be brought to **the place** which **God** appointed as the center for worship. However, if the offerer lived so **far from . . . the place** where God placed **His name** that he was **not able to carry** his **tithe** there, he could **exchange** the produce **for money**, carry **the money** to God's sanctuary, and buy food and **drink** there to be enjoyed **before the LORD**. Notice in verse 26 that the Bible does not teach total abstinence. But it does teach moderation, self-control, non-addiction, and abstinence from anything that would cause offense to another. The difference between wine and strong drink is that wine is made from grapes, and strong drink is made from grain, fruit, or honey. For two years the offerer was required to go up with either the tithe or its monetary equivalent.

14:28, 29 In the **third year** he used **the tithe** at home to feed **the Levite, the stranger, the fatherless,** and **the widow**. Once again we see that the poor and needy are a high priority as far as **the LORD** is concerned. "He who has pity on the poor lends to the LORD, and He will pay back what he has given" (Prov. 19:17).

J. Treatment of Debtors and Slaves (Chap. 15)

15:1–3 At the end of every seven years, all **debts** among the children of Israel were to be canceled. The seventh year probably coincided with the sabbatic year. The Jews were not required to cancel debts owed to them by foreigners; this law applied only to debts incurred between Jews. Matthew Henry comments:

> Every seventh year was a year of release, in which the ground rested from being tilled and servants were discharged from their services; and, among other acts of grace, this was one that those who had borrowed money, and had not been able to pay it before, should this year be released from it; and though, if they were able, they were afterwards bound in conscience to repay it, yet thenceforth the creditor should never recover it by law.[7]

Seven is the number of fullness or completeness in Scripture. In the fullness of time, God sent forth His Son and through Him proclaimed remission of sins—a "year of release" not only for the Jews (v. 3) but for all men.

15:4–6 Verse 4 seems to conflict with verse 11. Verse 4 suggests a time when there would be **no poor** people **in the land,** whereas verse 11 says that there will always be poor people. Bullinger's note is helpful on this. He suggests that verse 4 means "that there be no poor among you."[8] In other words, they should release their brethren in debt every seven years *so that* there would be no people in continual poverty. The creditor would not suffer because God would richly **bless** him. The thought in verse 11 is that there will always be poor people, partly as punishment and partly to teach others compassion in sharing.

15:7–11 The fact that all debts were canceled in the seventh year should not cause a person to refuse to **lend** money to **a poor** Israelite as **the year of release** drew near. To refuse is the base or **wicked thought** of verse 9. In this connection, the Jewish people have been deservedly well known for caring for their own throughout history. Paul says the same thing in 2 Corinthians 9:7 that Moses says in verse 10: "God loves a cheerful giver." This verse is not only a command but a promise, for God is no man's debtor. "The generous soul will be made rich, and he who waters will also be watered himself" (Prov. 11:25).

15:12–15 A Hebrew slave was also to be released during **the seventh year** (vv. 12–18). But he was **not** to be sent **away** without first providing for **him liberally**. God provided abundantly for His people when He brought them out of slavery in **Egypt** (Ex. 12:35, 36), and for this reason a freed slave should **not . . . go** out **empty-handed**. The Lord's desire is for His people to follow His example or, to rephrase the golden rule, "Do unto your brother as the Lord has done unto you."

15:16–18 On the other hand, the slave could refuse freedom and choose to become "a perpetual love **servant**." He indicated this by having his **ear** pierced with **an awl . . . to the door** of his master's house. A bondservant was **worth** twice as much as a **hired servant**.

15:19–23 Beginning with verse 19 and continuing through 16:17, we have regulations about certain functions which were to be carried out in the place where Jehovah had placed His name:

1. The setting apart of the firstborn animals (15:19–23).
2. The Passover and the Feast of Unleavened Bread (16:18).
3. The Feast of Weeks, or Pentecost (16:9–12).
4. The Feast of Tabernacles (16:13–17).

The firstborn of clean animals were to be offered **to the Lord**, and the people were allowed to **eat** their share but not the **blood**. The animals had to be without spot or **defect**—nothing but the best for God.

K. Three Apointed Feasts (Chap. 16)

16:1–8 Chapter 16 reviews the three feasts for which the men in Israel were to go to the central sanctuary each year. As to their purpose, Moody writes,

The holy feasts were (in general) appointed for these ends and uses:—

1. To distinguish the people of God from other nations.
2. To keep afoot the remembrance of the benefits already received.
3. To be a type and figure of benefits yet further to be conferred upon them by Christ.
4. To unite God's people in holy worship.
5. To preserve purity in holy worship prescribed by God.[9]

The Passover and Feast of **Unleavened Bread** were closely connected. **The Passover** is described in verses 1, 2, 5–7; the Feast of **Unleavened Bread** in verses 3, 4, and 8. These feasts were to remind God's people of His redemptive work on their behalf. The Lord's Supper is a weekly remembrance feast for the NT believer, a memorial of Christ our Passover sacrificed for us. The Feast of **Unleavened Bread** pictures the kind of lives the redeemed should live—full of praise "according to the blessing of the Lord your God" (v. 17) and free from malice and wickedness (1 Cor. 5:8).

The details given concerning the Passover here are different in several respects from the details given in Exodus 12 and 13. For example, what could be offered and where it could be offered are different in each passage.

16:9–12 **The Feast of Weeks** (Pentecost) began with the firstfruits of the wheat harvest, and is a symbol of the gift of the Holy Spirit. It is not to be confused with the Feast of Firstfruits (barley), which was held on the second day of the Feast of Unleavened Bread. The **freewill offering**, as in 2 Corinthians 8 and 9, was to be proportionate to the Lord's blessing on the individual's endeavors, in this case his crops.

16:13–15 **The Feast of Tabernacles** was at the end of the harvest season and looks forward to the time when Israel will be regathered in the land under the rule of Christ.

16:16, 17 **Three times a year all** the Israelite males were to **appear before the Lord** with a gift according to each one's ability. Moody indicates the spiritual meaning of the three feasts they had to attend:

The Passover, Pentecost, and Feast of Tabernacles typify a completed redemption:

1. By the passion of the cross: Suffering.

2. By the coming of the Holy Spirit: Grace.
3. By the final triumph of the coming King: Glory.[10]

16:18–20 **Judges** must be honest, **righteous**, and impartial. They should not accept **a bribe** because a bribe makes a man incapable of judging fairly.

16:21, 22 The **wooden image** (Heb. *'ashērāh*) was a pole made from a tree, and represented a pagan goddess. Eventually **the altar** of the Lord would rest in the temple in Jerusalem, where no trees could easily be planted but where an idolatrous symbol could be, and ultimately was, set up (2 Kgs. 23:6).

L. Judges and Kings (Chap. 17)

17:1 Sacrificial animals were to be without **blemish**. They were a symbol of the sinless, spotless Lamb of God.

17:2–7 A person suspected of idolatry was to be tried. **The testimony of two or three witnesses** was required. If convicted, he was to be stoned **to death**.

17:8–13 If legal problems arose which were **too hard** to be handled by the elders of a city, they were to be taken to **the judge**. By comparing 17:9 with 17:12 and 19:17, it appears that there was a group of **priests** and a group of judges who heard these difficult cases. The high **priest** and the chief **judge** were the respective leaders, this being implied by the definite articles used in verse 12. This tribunal met at **the place** where God's sanctuary was located. The decision of this tribunal was final; it was the Supreme Court of Israel. If the accused refused to **heed the priest . . . or the judge**, he was to **die** (vv. 12, 13).

17:14–20 God anticipated the desire of the people for **a king** by about 400 years, and He stated the qualifications for such a ruler, as follows: (1) He must be the man of God's choice (v. 15). (2) He must be an Israelite—**from among your brethren** (v. 15). (3) He must **not multiply horses**—that is, depend on such natural means for victory over his foes (v. 16). His trust must be in the Lord. (4) He must not **cause the people to return to Egypt**, thinking that the **horses** they could get there would save them (v. 16). (5) He must not **multiply wives** (v. 17). This is not only a prohibition against polygamy and a warning against the danger of wives who would lead him off into idolatry, but also a ban on marriages designed to form political alliances (v. 17). (6) He must not **greatly multiply silver and gold**, since these might lure him away from dependence on the Lord (v. 17). (7) He must **write**, **read**, and obey the **law** of the Lord, lest he become proud and willful (vv. 18–20). By continually spending time in the law the king was to become a model for the people. (8) He must not be **lifted up** with pride (v. 20).

Solomon, who ruled Israel in her golden days, violated almost every one of these injunctions—to his own destruction and the ruin of his kingdom (1 Kgs. 10:14–11:10).

M. Priests, Levites, and Prophets (Chap. 18)

18:1–8 Again God's care for **the priests** and **Levites** is seen. Because they did not receive a tribal **inheritance** of land, they were to be supported by the people. Their part in the offerings was **the shoulder**, the two **cheeks** (jawbones), **the stomach**, and **the firstfruits** of **grain**, **wine**, **oil**, and **fleece**. Verses 6–8 describe **a Levite** who sold his home and moved **to the**

place where God had placed His name to **serve** Him. He was to share in the offerings with the other Levites, and this was in addition to whatever he received **from the sale of his inheritance**. (Levites could own property even though they did not inherit a tribal possession.)

18:9–14 The Israelites were forbidden to have any contact with anyone who claimed to communicate with the unseen world. Eight means of communication with the spirit world are given. They are called **abominations** by God. They include: **one who practices witchcraft** (a witch or a warlock), **. . . a soothsayer** (a seer; a false prophet), **. . . one who interprets omens** (a palm-reader; a fortune-teller; an astrologer), **. . . a sorcerer** (a witch-doctor), **. . . one who conjures spells** (a wizard), **. . . a medium** (spirit medium), **. . . a spiritist** (a séance leader), **. . . one who calls up the dead** (a necromancer). Some of these "professions" overlap.

Tragically, this nearly 3,400 year-old prohibition is just as much needed in "enlightened" modern times as it was long ago. Henry G. Bosch writes:

> Satanism, demons, and the occult are dark, sinister realities, not tricks. One of the signs that we are nearing the close of this age is the widespread interest in witchcraft, astrology, and other forms of the occult. . . . Thousands consult their horoscope each day, attend séances, or seek to communicate with deceased loved ones. There's also a great interest in Satanism and demons. The Bible repeatedly warns against such practices (Lev. 19:31; 20:27; 2 Chron. 33:6; Jer. 10:2; Gal. 5:19, 20).
>
> How urgent and up-to-date are the warnings of Scripture! Let's not play around with something that could become a kiss of death.[11]

To **be blameless** (v. 13) in regard to these forbidden "communications" means to listen to God's voice alone.

18:15–19 In sharp contrast to the evils of the leaders of the occult, verse 15 presents a beautiful prophecy about Christ, the true **Prophet** of God (Acts 3:22, 23). Notice the description in verses 15, 18, and 19: (1) **a Prophet**—that is, one who speaks God's word; (2) **from your midst**—i.e., truly human; (3) **from your brethren**—i.e., an Israelite; (4) **like me**—i.e., like Moses in the sense of being raised up by God; (5) **I . . . will put My words in His mouth**—fullness of inspiration; (6) **He shall speak to them all that I command Him**—fullness of revelation; (7) all are responsible to listen to Him and obey Him.

This section also teaches that this **Prophet** would serve as a Mediator between God and man. The people had been so terrified at Mount Sinai that they asked that God would not speak to them directly anymore and that they might not see the fire anymore lest they die. In response to that request, God promised Christ as the Mediator. That this passage held Messianic hope for the Jews can be seen clearly in the Gospels (John 6:14; 7:40).

18:20–22 False prophets could be detected in various ways. We have previously learned that they were false if they sought to lead the people away from the worship of the true God (13:1–5). Here is another means of detection: If a prediction failed to come to pass, **that prophet** should be put to death, and no one need fear any curse he might pronounce.

N. Criminal Laws (Chap. 19)

19:1–10 Three cities of refuge had already been set up east of the Jordan River. Here Moses reminded the people to set up **three cities** on the other side, conveniently located so that a **manslayer** could **flee there** from **the avenger of blood** (vv. 1–7). To the previous instruction on this subject is added the provision for **three** additional **cities** of refuge, if the people ever possessed the full **territory** originally promised to them (vv. 8–10). No further mention is made of these three extra cities because Israel has never occupied all the land promised in Genesis 15:18. The **three cities** *west* of the Jordan were Kedesh, Hebron, and Shechem (Josh. 20:7).

19:11–13 The **city** of refuge did not provide safety for a murderer. Even though he fled **to one of these cities**, **the elders** were to weigh the evidence and **deliver him . . . to . . . the avenger** if he was found guilty.

19:14 A **landmark** was a stone placed in a field to indicate the boundary of one's land. These could be moved secretly at night to expand one's own farm, at the same time cheating one's neighbor. Why this one verse is placed in the midst of a passage dealing with judicial practice—i.e., cities of refuge and witnesses false and true—is difficult to say, but its position does not obscure its teaching.

19:15–21 The **witness** of **one** person was not enough in a legal case. There had to be **two or three witnesses**. **A false witness** was to be tried by **the priests and the judges** (17:8, 9) and punished with the penalty of the crime with which he accused the defendant (vv. 16–21).

The **"eye for eye"** and **"tooth for tooth"** principle is called the *Lex talionis* in Western culture (Latin for "law of retaliation"). It is commonly misrepresented as vindictive, but it is not. This law is not a *license* for cruelty, but a *limit* to it. In the context it refers to what kind of penalty could be inflicted upon a false witness.

O. Laws Concerning Warfare (Chap. 20)

20:1–8 Chapter 20 is a manual on warfare for God's people. The priests were charged with encouraging the people as they battled **against** the enemy. Various classes were exempt from military service: (1) those who had just **built a new house**; (2) those who had just **planted a vineyard** and had never partaken of the fruit; (3) those whose marriage had not been consummated; (4) those **who** were **fearful and fainthearted**.

> The Jewish writers agree that this liberty to return was allowed only in those wars which they made voluntarily . . . not those which were made by the divine command against Amalek and the Canaanites, in which every man was bound to fight.[12]

20:9 Since in any good army there must be organization and rank, the officers appointed **captains of the armies** to **lead the people**.

20:10–20 Unlike other nations, Israel was to make distinctions in her warfare under Jehovah's direction. These distinctions were a further reflection of Israel as a holy people under a loving God. War was necessary, but the Lord would control the evil it caused. One has only to study the cruel practices of other nations, such as the Assyrians,[13] to appreciate these guidelines. Instructions are given as to how war was to be waged. Notice the following distinctions:

1. Cities . . . near and far (10–18). The cities in the land were an immediate danger, totally reprobate and fit for destruction. Cities outside the land but within the

rest of the area promised to Abraham were to be approached first with terms of peace. If they refused, only the men were to be killed; the women and children were to be spared. These cities did not pose so great a threat to contaminate Israel as did the ones within Israel's borders.

2. Fruitful and unfruitful trees (19, 20). The principle here is that Israel was not to practice "desolation warfare." They were to preserve what was useful instead of engaging in wholesale destruction of the land.

P. Various Laws (Chaps. 21—25)

1. *Expiation for Unsolved Murder (21:1–9)*

If a man was **found slain . . . in the land**, and the slayer could not be located, **the elders of the . . . nearest . . . city** were required to make **atonement**. They brought **a heifer . . . to a valley with flowing water** and killed it **there**. Washing **their hands over the heifer**, they protested their innocence of the crime and asked that no guilt of bloodshed should attach to them. Even when individual **guilt** could not be ascertained, there was still a corporate **guilt** that needed to be taken care of; the land had to be cleansed from the defilement of **blood**. This became the responsibility of the **nearest . . . city**.

Someone has called verses 1–9 "God's Great Inquest Over His Son." Israel is bloodguilty in connection with Christ's death and must be cleansed in a righteous way.

2. *Female Prisoners of War (21:10–14)*

An Israelite was permitted to marry **a beautiful woman** captured in **war** after she went through a ceremonial cleansing and separation. (But the passage does *not* apply to female inhabitants of the land of Canaan.) The marriage was of a probationary nature; he could subsequently let her leave him if he was not pleased with her. However, he could **not sell her** or **treat her brutally**.

3. *Rights of the Firstborn (21:15–17)*

The son of an **unloved** wife could not be deprived of the birthright, if he was **the firstborn**. These verses do not prove that God ever approved of bigamy, but simply that He guarded **the right of the firstborn** even in the case of multiple marriages. Sometimes God sovereignly set aside the firstborn of a family to bless the younger—e.g., Jacob and Esau, Ephraim and Manasseh. However, this was the exception, based on the selective choosing of God, and not the rule, which is stated here.

4. *Stubborn and Rebellious Sons (21:18–21)*

A **rebellious son** was to be stoned **to death**, after having been found guilty by **the elders of** the **city**. Compare this with the reception given to the repentant prodigal son in Luke 15.

5. *The Bodies of Hanged Criminals (21:22, 23)*

This text definitely points forward to Christ. Though innocent Himself, He was hanged **on a tree**. He was bearing the curse that *we* deserved. **His body** was not allowed to remain **on the** cross **overnight** (see John 19:31).

> To Him who suffered on the tree
> Our souls at His soul's price to gain,
> Blessing and praise and glory be;
> Worthy the Lamb, for He was slain!
>
> To Him enthroned by filial right,
> All power in heaven and earth proclaim,
> Honor, and majesty, and might;
> Worthy the Lamb, for He was slain!
>
> —*James Montgomery*

6. Nine Laws of Behavior (22:1–12)

22:1–3 Chapter 22 expands upon Leviticus 19:18, describing the general command to "Love your neighbor." Even a man's enemies were to be treated with neighborly concern (Ex. 23:4, 5). An Israelite was not allowed to act indifferently toward anything lost by his neighbor (**brother**). Whether it was an animal, a **garment**, or anything else, he was obligated to take **it to** his **own house** and keep it until it was claimed.

22:4 Israelites were also obligated to assist a neighbor's animal which had fallen.

22:5 Men were not to wear women's clothing, or vice versa. God hates transvestism.

22:6, 7 Young birds could be taken from **a bird's nest**, but **the mother** had to be freed, probably so that she could continue reproducing.

22:8 **A parapet** or railing had to be built around the flat **roof** of a house to prevent people from falling off. The roof was the place of fellowship. It is important to guard the communion, especially of the young and careless.

22:9–11 The Jews were forbidden to: (1) **sow** a **vineyard** with **different kinds of seed**; (2) **plow with an ox** (clean) **and a donkey** (unclean) yoked **together**; (3) wear clothes made of a mixture of **wool and linen**. The first prohibition suggests adding to the pure teaching of the Word of God. The second describes the unequal yoke in service. The third speaks of the mixture of righteousness and unrighteousness in the practical life of the believer.

22:12 Jews were supposed to wear **tassels** on the **four corners** of their garments as constant reminders to obey the Lord (Num. 15:37–41). The reason for these **tassels** is given in Numbers 15:37 and following.

7. Offenses Against Chastity (22:13–30)

22:13–21 This paragraph deals with a **man** who married a girl and then suspected that **she was not a virgin**. **Evidence of . . . virginity** probably consisted of marks on the linen of the marriage bed after a woman's first sexual experience.[14] If **the father and mother** could produce evidence of the **young woman's virginity**, the overly suspicious husband was chastised, fined **one hundred shekels of silver**, and required to live with her. If, however, **the young woman** had been immoral before her marriage, then she was to be stoned **to death**.

22:22–30 The remaining verses of this chapter deal with various types of sexual immorality: (1) Both **man** and **woman . . . found** in the act of adultery were to be put to death. (2) If **a man** raped a **betrothed . . . woman . . . in the city**, and **she did not cry out** for help, then both were guilty of adultery and were to be put **to death**. (3) **If a man** raped **a betrothed woman** in a field, where her cries for help could not be heard, then **the man** was to be killed, but **the woman** was innocent. (4) A **man who** had sexual relations with **a virgin** was required to pay **fifty shekels of silver** to her **father** and also to marry her. (5) Verse 30 forbids incest—i.e., sexual relations with a member of the family.

8. Those Barred from Entering the Assembly (23:1–8)

Various persons were barred from entering the **assembly of the LORD**, that is, from full rights as citizens and worshipers: (1) a man whose reproductive organs were damaged or missing; (2) an **illegitimate** person—i.e., one born out of wedlock[15]; (3) **an Ammonite or Moabite**; (4) **an Edomite** or **Egyptian**. Verse 4 says that Moab did not "meet the Israelites with food and drink," whereas Deuteronomy 2:29 implies that certain Moabites sold food supplies to the Jews. "To **meet . . . with bread and water**" is an idiomatic expression meaning to give a hospitable reception. This the Moabites did not do.

The eunuch was excluded from the congregation. The illegitimate person, the **Moabite**, and the **Ammonite** were barred from **the assembly . . . to the tenth generation**. The **Edomite** and the **Egyptian** could enter after three generations. However, there were exceptions to these general rules when individuals sought Jehovah. Among David's mighty men could be found both an Ammonite and a Moabite (1 Chron. 11:39, 46). Some think that the rules of exclusion applied only to males and therefore did not apply to Ruth, for example. Some think that **"the tenth generation"** is an idiom that means indefinitely.

9. Cleanliness in the Camp (23:9–14)

Verse 9 warns against the temptations that face men who are away from home in military service. (Or perhaps it serves as an introduction to verses 10–14.)

The law on nocturnal emissions shows the sacredness with which the reproduction of life was regarded.

Each soldier was required to carry a shovel with his weapons for sanitation of the camp. All excrement was to be covered immediately with dirt. If all armies down through history had followed this simple regulation, they would have avoided the spread of plagues many times.

10. Social and Religious Laws (23:15–25)

23:15, 16 A foreign **slave** who had **escaped** to freedom was not to be delivered up **to his master**. Thus Israel was to be an asylum for the oppressed.

23:17, 18 Male or female prostitution was not to be tolerated in the land, and money derived from such immoral traffic should never be brought **to the house of the LORD** in payment of a vow. A **"dog"** means a male prostitute.

23:19, 20 Jews were **not** to **charge interest** on **anything** they lent to another Jew, though it was permitted for them to **charge interest . . . to a foreigner**. This is a further expansion of the principle already given in Exodus 22:25, which prohibited exacting usury from the poor.

23:21–23 Vows were voluntary. A man did not have to make **a vow to the LORD**, but once he made it, he was obligated to **pay it**.

23:24, 25 Travelers were allowed to help themselves to **grapes** for their current needs, but they were **not** allowed to **put any** in a **container**. Likewise, they were allowed to take **grain** from a field, but only what they could pick with their hands, not with **a sickle**. In our Lord's day, His twelve disciples made use of this privilege (Mark 2:23).

11. Divorce and Remarriage (24:1–4)

A man could **divorce** his **wife** for **uncleanness** by writing **her a certificate of divorce** and giving it to her. She was then free to marry someone else. But **if** her second **husband** died or divorced **her**, the first **husband** was not allowed to marry her again. Jehovah gave Israel a certificate of divorce (Jer. 3:1–8); yet in a future day

He will take her to Himself again, having purged her of her unfaithfulness. Oh, the depths of the riches of the love of God; how low He stoops to love the unlovable!

12. Various Social Laws (24:5—25:4)

24:5 A man who was newly married was **not** required to **go out to war** for the first **year**. This gave him time to cultivate and strengthen the marriage bond and to start a family. If he had to go to war and was killed, his name would be cut off from Israel unless his redeeming relative raised up descendants for him. This "kinsman redeemer"[16] was the nearest relative who was able and willing to marry the widow. The first male born to such a union became the heir of the former husband. This continued the family name and kept the land in the family.

24:6 Since a **millstone** was a person's means of livelihood, it could not be required as a **pledge** in a business transaction. To take either **the lower or the upper millstone** would deprive one of the means of grinding grain.

24:7 A **kidnapper** or a slave trader was to be put to death.

24:8, 9 Special precautions were to be observed in the event of **an outbreak of leprosy**, following previous instructions given **to the Levites**. **Miriam** is cited as a warning.

24:10–13 A man's **house** could not be invaded to obtain a **pledge** from him. If the **man** was so **poor** that he gave his clothing as a **pledge**, it was to be returned to him each night so **that he** could **sleep in** it.

24:14, 15 The **wages** of **a hired servant** should be paid promptly.

24:16 No man was to **be put to death for** another person's sin.

24:17–22 **Justice** was to be shown to **the stranger**, **the fatherless**, and **the widow**. A **field** was not to be completely harvested. Gleanings were to be left for the poor and the helpless. The same applied to the harvesting of **olive trees** and **grapes**. Ronald Sider comments:

> The memory of their own poverty and oppression in Egypt was to prompt them to leave generous gleanings for the poor sojourner, the widow, and the fatherless.[17]

When John Newton was born again, he printed verse 22 in large letters and hung it over his mantlepiece, where he would be constantly reminded of it.

25:1–3 When an offender was found guilty and was sentenced **to be beaten**, he was not to receive more than **forty blows**. The Jews commonly inflicted thirty-nine blows or stripes, lest they miscount and thus transgress this regulation (see 2 Cor. 11:24).

25:4 The **ox** that trod **out the grain** was **not** to be muzzled but rather to be allowed to eat some of the grain. Paul uses this verse in 1 Corinthians 9:9–11 to teach that the man who labors in spiritual things should be taken care of in material things. Thus Paul shows us that there is a spiritual aspect to the law. This does not minimize the literal meaning; it only shows that many times there is a spiritual lesson under the surface. The diligent student will look for and heed this important spiritual lesson.

13. Law of Levirate Marriage (25:5–10)

If an Israelite died and left his **widow** without a **son**, there was the danger that his name might perish and his property pass out of the family. Therefore, a **brother** of the dead man was supposed to marry the widow. This practice of "Levirate" marriages existed in many ancient nations. **If the** brother would not agree to do this, then the widow went **to the elders** of the city and announced this fact. He was called before **the elders** and given an opportunity to confirm his unwillingness. If he persisted in his refusal, the widow removed one of his sandals and spat **in his face**. From then on he was known by a name of reproach because of his unwillingness to perpetuate his brother's house.

Leviticus 20:21 *prohibited* a man from marrying his brother's wife; here he is *commanded* to marry her. The passage in Leviticus no doubt applied when the husband was still living, while Deuteronomy refers to a time when the husband is dead, having left behind no male heir.

14. *Three Distinct Laws (25:11–19)*

25:11, 12 If a woman interfered by seizing a man immodestly in a fight in which **her husband** was involved, **her** offending **hand** was to be **cut off**. Her actions might endanger the man's having an heir; thus the severe penalty.

25:13–16 Honest **weights** and **measures** were required. Often men had one set of scales for buying and another for selling. This was **an abomination to the LORD**.

25:17–19 The descendants of **Amalek** were to be utterly destroyed because of his treachery and cruelty (Ex. 17:8–16). Israel is told **not** to **forget** to destroy the Amalekites, but it appears that they did forget. Saul disobeyed the Lord in not exterminating them in his day (1 Sam. 15). In fact, it was not until the days of Hezekiah that "they defeated the rest of the Amalekites who had escaped" (1 Chron. 4:43).

Q. Rituals and Ratifications (Chap. 26)

1. *The Ritual for Firstfruits (26:1–11)*

After the people were settled in **the land**, they were supposed to **go to** God's sanctuary and present the **first of all the produce** to the **priest** in joyful recognition of what God had done. Then they were to rehearse the Lord's gracious dealings with them, beginning with their ancestor, Jacob (a wandering **Syrian**), going on to the slavery in **Egypt**, God's **mighty** deliverance, and concluding with their possession of the **land flowing with milk and honey**. Phillip Keller explains this colorful term:

> In the Scriptures the picture portrayed of the Promised Land, to which God tried so hard to lead Israel from Egypt, was that of a "land flowing with milk and honey." Not only is this figurative language but also essentially scientific terminology. In agricultural terms we speak of a "milk flow" and a "honey flow." By this we mean the peak season of spring and summer, when pastures are at their most productive stages. The livestock that feed on the forage and the bees that visit the blossoms are said to be producing a corresponding "flow" of milk or honey. So a land flowing with milk and honey is a land of rich, green, luxuriant pastures. And when God spoke of such a land for Israel He also foresaw such an abundant life of joy and victory and contentment for His people.[18]

2. *The Ritual for the Third Year Tithe (26:12–15)*

In addition to the above firstfruits, the Jews were to offer a second tithe, called the festival tithe, which was to be shared with **the Levite, the stranger, the fatherless, and the widow** every

third year. This tithe was to be distributed to the needy in their own towns. The people then had to testify **before the LORD** that they had **obeyed . . . all** of the commands concerning the tithe.

3. Ratification of the Covenant (26:16–19)

Because the people had agreed to **walk in** the **ways** of the Lord, He in turn acknowledged them as **His** own **special people** and promised to exalt them **above all** other **nations**. They were **a holy people** because God had set them apart from the other **nations**—not because of any intrinsic merit. They were different from any other nation on earth, being the peculiar treasure of Jehovah. Their response to such an honor was supposed to be obedience to His **commands**.

R. Curses and Blessings (Chaps. 27, 28)

27:1–8 After they crossed **the Jordan** River into the Promised Land, the Israelites were to raise up a large monument of **stones, whitewash** it, and **write all the words of** the **law** on it. This monument was to be erected on **Mount Ebal**, together with **an altar** which was to be made with uncut **stones**.

27:9, 10 The Jews had been God's people by His choice for some time, but now that they were about to enter the land, they became His **people** in a special sense. The favor He was showing to them called for loving obedience on their part.

27:11–13 Six tribes were appointed to **stand on Mount Gerizim** in order to "Amen" the blessings. These six tribes were descendants of Leah and Rachel. The other tribes were to **stand on Mount Ebal** to confirm the curses. Notice that Ephraim and Manasseh aren't mentioned separately, but instead the tribe of Joseph is listed. Reuben, Israel's firstborn (who lost his birthright), and Zebulun, Leah's youngest, were on Mount Ebal with the sons of the handmaids. The favored tribes were on Mount Gerizim.

27:14–26 The Levites (see v. 9) were to stand in the valley between the two mountains. As they pronounced the curses or blessings, the people were to answer **"Amen!"** The curses are given in verses 15–26. They have to do with idolatry; disrespect of parents (v. 16); dishonesty in removing boundary lines (v. 17); deceiving **the blind** (v. 18); taking advantage of the poor and defenseless (v. 19); various forms of incest (vv. 20, 22, 23); bestiality (v. 21); secret murder of one's **neighbor**; murder of the **innocent** for a **bribe** (v. 25); and disobedience to the **law** of God (v. 26). The historical account of this ceremony can be found in Joshua 8:30 and following. Notice how closely Joshua follows the instructions given by Moses.

It is significant that only the curses are given in Chapter 27. It could not be otherwise because, as Paul reminds us, "For as many as are of the works of the law are under the curse" (Gal. 3:10). It was not merely that the Israelites would *transgress* the law, but that they were under the law *as a principle*.

28:1–14 Verse 1 refers to the end of chapter 26 with the words, **"God will set you high above."** This gives chapter 27 the appearance of being parenthetical. Many Bible students feel that the blessings pronounced in verses 3–6 were not those addressed to the six tribes on Mount Gerizim, but that this entire chapter is a statement by Moses as to what lay ahead for the children of Israel. The first fourteen verses speak of the blessings that would follow obedience, whereas the last fifty-four verses describe the curses that would fall upon the people if they forsook the Lord. The blessings promised include preeminence among **the nations**, material prosperity, fruitfulness, fertility, abundance of crops, victory in battle, and success in international trade.

28:15–37 The curses included scarcity, barrenness, crop failure, pestilence, disease, blight, drought, defeat in battle, madness, fright, adversity, calamity, and powerlessness (vv. 15–32). Verses 33–37 predict captivity in a foreign land, and this was fulfilled by the Assyrian and Babylonian captivities.

Israel would **become an astonishment, a proverb, and a byword** among all **nations**.

28:38-46 The Jews would be cursed with failed crops, **vineyards**, and **olive trees**. Their children would **go into captivity** and **locusts** would **consume** their **trees** and **produce**. The **alien** would **rise higher and higher** and the Israelites would go **down lower and lower**. There is no contradiction between verses 12 and 44. If obedient, the Jews would become international lenders. If disobedient, they would have to borrow from strangers.

28:47–57 The horrors of a **siege** by a foreign invader are described in verses 49–57—so fierce that the people would **eat** one another. This came to pass when Jerusalem was beseiged by the Babylonians and later by the Romans. At both times, cannibalism was widespread. People who were normally refined and **sensitive** became **hostile** and cannibalistic.

28:58–68 Plagues and **diseases** would greatly reduce the population of Israel. The survivors would be scattered throughout **the earth**, and there they would live in constant **fear** of persecution. God would even **take** His people **back to Egypt in ships**. According to Josephus, the prophecy that Israel would go **to Egypt** again was partially fulfilled in the time of Titus, when Jews were taken there by ship and sold as **slaves**. But the name **"Egypt"** here may mean servitude in general. God had delivered Israel from literal Egyptian slavery in the past, but if she would not love Him and acknowledge His sovereign right to her obedience, if she would not keep herself pure as His wife, if she would not be His peculiar treasure, choosing instead to be like the other nations, then she would be sold back into slavery. But by then she would be so crushed that **no** one would want her even as a slave.

"To whom much is given, from him much will be required" (Luke 12:48). Israel had been given privileges above all other nations, and therefore her accountability was greater and her punishment more severe.

To meditate on these curses leaves one amazed at the outpouring of Jehovah's wrath. No words are minced, no details are left to the imagination. Moses paints the picture with bold, stark realism. Israel must know what disobedience will bring in order that she may learn to fear **this glorious and awesome name, THE LORD YOUR GOD**.

III. MOSES' THIRD DISCOURSE—COVENANT FOR THE LAND (Chaps. 29, 30)

A. The Covenant Made in Moab (29:1–21)

29:1 The first verse of chapter 29 may logically belong to the previous chapter, as in the Hebrew Bible. Keil and Delitzsch, however, see it as a "heading" for the addresses of chapters 29 and 30.[19]

29:2–9 The people had broken the covenant which God made with them at Mount Sinai. Now **Moses** called on them to ratify the **covenant** contained here in the book of Deuteronomy made on the plains of Moab, just prior to their entrance into the land. The people lacked an understanding of the Lord and His purposes for them. Jehovah longed to give them a **heart to perceive, eyes to see and ears to hear**, but they rendered themselves unfit to receive these things through their continual unbelief and disobedience. Israel had enjoyed manna from heaven and water from the rock; she did not depend on the things manufactured by man for her survival (i.e., bread, wine, strong drink). This was in order that she might come to know the Lord her God in all of His faithfulness and love.

As an incentive to keep **this covenant**, Moses once again reviewed the goodness of God to Israel—the miracles in **Egypt**, the mighty deliverance, the **forty years in the wilderness**, the defeat of **Sihon . . . and Og**, and the distribution of the trans-Jordanian **land** to Reuben, Gad, and the half-tribe **of Manasseh**.

29:10–21 Moses called on all the people to **enter into** the sworn **covenant with the Lord** (vv. 10–13) and reminded them that the **covenant** applied to their posterity as well (vv. 14, 15). Failure to keep the covenant would result in bitter punishment. Rebels should beware of any temptation to **serve** the **idols** of the Gentile **nations** or to think that they would escape God's **anger** if they did so (vv. 16–21). Verse 19 in the RSV reads: "One who, when he hears the words of this sworn covenant, blesses himself in his heart saying, 'I shall be safe, though I walk in the stubbornness of my heart.' This would lead to the sweeping away of moist and dry alike." No one would escape.

B. Punishment for Breaking the Covenant (29:22–29)

29:22–28 Generations to come, and foreign nations as well, would be amazed at the desolation of Israel and would ask the reason why the **land** should have been treated **like the** cities of the plain—**Sodom and Gomorrah, Admah, and Zeboiim**. The answer would be given, **"Because they have forsaken the covenant of the Lord God of their fathers . . . and served other gods."**

29:29 While there are certain **secret things** that **belong to the Lord**, especially matters concerning His judgments, Moses reminded the people that their responsibility was clearly revealed—to keep the covenant of the Lord. What this is saying is that revelation brings responsibility. Men are accountable to obey, not to sit in judgment on the word of the Lord. This principle can be found many times in the NT also. "To him who knows to do good [revelation] and does not do it [responsibility], to him it is sin" (Jas. 4:17).

C. Restoration for Returning to the Covenant (Chap. 30)

30:1–10 Chapter 30 anticipates that the people would break the covenant and be carried away into exile. This, of course, is exactly what happened. Even then, God would **have compassion** and **restore them if they would turn to** Him in repentance. He would **bring** them back **to the land**. In addition to this physical restoration, there would be a spiritual renewal (**"the**

LORD your God will circumcise your heart"—v. 6). The people would then enjoy the blessings of obedience, whereas their **enemies** would be cursed. The counsels of the Most High will not fail, even though the *objects* of those counsels *do* fail. God would fulfill His word to the patriarchs and give their **descendants... the land** forever. After the exile, which He knew was inevitable, He would restore them and change them. Such is the working of the unconditional love of the great Lover! Verse 6 touches on a theme developed hundreds of years later by the prophets—namely, the New Covenant (Jer. 32:39ff; Ezek. 36:24ff). This covenant, although revealed in the OT, was not ratified until the death of Christ, for His was the blood of the New Covenant (Luke 22:20).

30:11–14 Moses reminded the people that the covenant was not too hard for them to understand (**mysterious**), **nor** was **it far off** (inaccessible). They were not required to do the impossible to find it. The Lord had brought it to them, and their responsibility was to obey it. These verses are used by Paul in Romans 10:5–8 and are applied to Christ and the gospel. The covenant was not easy to keep, but God had made provision in case of failure. The people were then required to repent and to bring the appointed sacrifices. Since the sacrifices were types of Christ, the lesson is that those who sin should repent and put their faith in the Lord Jesus Christ.

30:15–20 The people were called on to choose between **life and good** on the one hand, and **death and evil** on the other—**life** for obedience, but **death** for disobedience. Moses strongly pleaded with them to choose **life and... blessing**. The desired response brought good results, including **length of... days** and abundant spiritual **life**, implied by the words **"that you may cling to Him."** The only alternative was one of **cursing**.

IV. MOSES' LAST DAYS—DEATH OUTSIDE THE LAND (Chaps. 31—34)

A. Moses' Replacement (Chap. 31)

31:1–8 Moses was now **one hundred and twenty years old**. He knew God's decree stating that he would **not** be allowed to **cross** the **Jordan** with the people, but he reminded the people that **the LORD** would go **with** them, that **Joshua** would be their captain, and that victory over their enemies was assured. **Moses** next encouraged **Joshua** publicly concerning his new appointment and assured him of the Lord's presence (vv. 7, 8).

31:9–13 The written **law** was entrusted to the Levites. It was to be kept beside **the ark**. The two tablets of the Decalogue were placed *inside* the ark (Ex. 25:16; Heb. 9:4). This copy of the law was placed *beside* the ark. **Every seven years** the **law** was to be **read** in the presence of **all Israel**.

The reading of Holy Scripture is sadly neglected even in doctrinally conservative circles today. The following extended but valuable words from C. H. Mackintosh are unfortunately much more true today than a century ago when they were written:

> The Word of God is not loved and studied, either privately or publicly. Trashy literature is devoured in private, and music, ritualistic services, and imposing ceremonies are eagerly sought after in public. Thousands will flock to hear music, and pay for admission, but how few care for a meeting to read the holy Scriptures!

These are facts, and facts are powerful arguments. We cannot get over them. There is a growing thirst for religious excitement, and a growing distaste for the calm study of holy Scripture and the spiritual exercises of the Christian assembly. It is perfectly useless to deny it. We cannot shut our eyes to it. The evidence of it meets us on every hand.

Thank God, there are a few, here and there, who really love the Word of God, and delight to meet, in holy fellowship, for the study of its precious truths. May the Lord increase the number of such, and bless them, "till traveling days are done."[20]

31:14–18 As Moses' death drew near, God called him and **Joshua** to **the tabernacle of meeting** and **appeared** before them in a **pillar of cloud**. He first revealed **to Moses** that the Israelites would soon give themselves over to idolatry and suffer God's **anger**.

31:19–22 Then He commanded Moses to **write down** a **song** and **teach it to the children of Israel** as **a witness . . . against** them in days to come.

31:23 God personally **inaugurated Joshua** to lead His people **into the** Promised Land and encouraged him to **be** brave and **strong**. Joshua must have been strengthened by these words from Jehovah. He had just heard God speak of a coming national apostasy (v. 16), and he needed to be reassured, rather than discouraged, for the task ahead.

31:24–27 The **Book of the Law**, i.e., Deuteronomy, committed to the Levites, would also serve as **a witness against** the Israelites when they forsook the Lord.

31:28–30 **Then Moses** delivered the following **song** to the **elders of** their **tribes, and** the **officers**, as God had commanded him.

B. Moses' Song (Chap. 32)

32:1–3 The song may be summarized as follows: The universe is summoned to **hear** the word of the Lord. It is refreshing and nourishing, like **the rain** and **the dew**. In verse 3 (which could serve as a title to the song) Moses speaks of ascribing **greatness to** their **God**. The song reveals God's **greatness** in the context of His historical dealings with His people.

32:4–9 In spite of God's greatness, justice, faithfulness, and holiness, the people of Israel forsook Him and sinned against Him. The glory of Jehovah's attributes are displayed here against the dark backdrop of Israel's **perverse** wickedness. It was small thanks He received for being their **Father** and Creator. **When the Most High divided** the earth among **the** Gentile **nations**, He first provided for the needs of His own people. Such was His love and care for them.

32:10–14 The birth and childhood of the nation of Israel are described in verse 10. After the Exodus from Egypt, God guided, **instructed**, and preserved His people with the love of a mother **eagle** (v. 11). **There was no foreign god** who had a part in Israel's preservation. Why then should the nation turn to idolatry and ascribe the goodness of Jehovah to another? Beginning in verse 13, the song is prophetic. He brought them into the blessings of the Promised Land.

32:15–20 **But Jeshurun** (a poetic name for the people of Israel meaning "upright people") rebelled against Jehovah by turning to idols. They chose to sacrifice **to demons**, many times offering up their own children. They even sank to the stupidity of worshiping **new gods**. Thus they neglected their true **Rock**; they forgot their true Father. As a result, **the**

LORD hid His **face from them**. This hiding of His face was fulfilled in their being sold into captivity.

32:21–33 After setting Israel aside, God acted in grace toward the Gentiles, seeking to **provoke** Israel **to jealousy** (as in the present Church Age). Israel in the meantime would be scattered and persecuted. The people would not be totally destroyed, though, because Jehovah did not want Israel's enemies to misinterpret the nation's downfall. It was not that **their** enemies' **rock** was stronger, but that Israel's **Rock had surrendered them** to slaughter because of their wickedness.

32:34–43 This section has to do with God's **vengeance** upon the nations that were used to punish Israel. **Vengeance** (v. 35) and vindication (v. 36) belong to the Lord. He has sworn by Himself (for there is no one greater) to deal with His **adversaries**. Notice how completely this judgment will be carried out (vv. 41, 42). As a result, God's people and all the nations are to rejoice, because God has avenged Himself and made **atonement for His land and His people**.

32:44–47 The song thus gives a historical and prophetical outline of the nation of **Israel**. Having read the song, Moses solemnly urged the people to follow the Lord with the words: **"For it is not a futile thing for you, because it is your life. . . ."**

32:48–52 **Then the LORD** called **Moses** to the top of **Mount Nebo**, where he would be allowed to **see the land**. He would not be allowed to enter **Canaan** because of his sin at **Meribah Kadesh**, but would **die on . . . Mount Nebo** and be buried in a valley in Moab (cf. 34:6).

C. Moses' Blessing (Chap. 33)

The Hebrew wording in this chapter is obscure in many places; thus there are various opinions and interpretations offered by different commentators. It is not within the scope of this work to go into detail as to the possible Hebrew renderings; we just suggest a short, prophetical view of each blessing.

33:1–5 As his final official act, **Moses** the **man of God** pronounced a **blessing** on the tribes **of Israel**. Verses 2–5 celebrate God's loving care for His own people. At **Sinai** He gave the **law**. **Seir** and **Mount Paran** were on the route from Sinai to Canaan. In poetic language, Moses describes the Lord as **King in Jeshurun** leading His people on to victory. Then follow the individual blessings:

33:6 *Reuben*. Situated east of the Jordan River and immediately north of Moab, Reuben would be vulnerable to attack; hence the prayer that the tribe would not become extinct but would be populous.

Simeon is not mentioned. It became closely associated with Judah and may be included in that blessing.

33:7 *Judah*. This tribe would be a leader in the conquest of Canaan. The Lord is asked to **help** the warriors and **bring** them back safely to their **people**.

33:8–11 *Levi*. God's **Thummim and** His **Urim** belonged to **Levi**, the tribe criticized by the people at **Massah** and **the waters of Meribah**. Levi was also the tribe that took sides with God against its own people when the latter worshiped the golden calf. Levi was set apart to **teach** the people and to present sacrifices. Moses prays that the LORD will **bless his substance**, find pleasure in his service, and destroy **those who hate him**.

33:12 *Benjamin*. The temple, God's dwelling place on earth, would be located in Benjamin's territory, surrounded by shouldering hills. Therefore **Benjamin** is pictured as a **beloved** tribe, enjoying intimate communion with the Lord.

33:13–17 *Joseph*. The territory of the sons of Joseph would be watered by **dew** from above and springs from **beneath**. It would be unusually fruitful, enjoying the goodwill of the One who revealed Himself **in the** burning **bush**. Majestic and powerful, Joseph's two sons would conquer nations. **Ephraim** got the birthright and is therefore assigned **ten thousands** whereas **Manasseh** is credited with only **thousands**.

33:18, 19 *Zebulun and Issachar*. Successful at home and abroad, they would lead nations to worship at Jerusalem, **the mountain** of the Lord. These tribes would feast on **the abundance of the seas** and of the land. Since there is no record of their leading nations to worship, and since both tribes were landlocked in the past, this blessing must look forward to the Millennium.

33:20, 21 *Gad*. God gave this tribe a large territory east of the Jordan. **Gad** fought like **a lion** to capture and preserve it. It was choice pastureland that he chose for himself—a leader's **portion**. But he also joined **with the heads of the people** to conquer the land west of the Jordan, thus carrying out the Lord's righteous will.

33:22 *Dan* is compared to **a lion's whelp**, ferocious and strong, striking suddenly from ambush. Dan's original territory was in the southwest of Canaan, but the Danites migrated to the northeast and seized additional land adjoining **Bashan**.

33:23 *Naphtali* was located in northeast Canaan and extended **south** to the Sea of Galilee. The tribe was honored with the **favor** and **blessing of the Lord**.

33:24, 25 *Asher* was to be blessed with a numerous posterity, good relations with the other tribes, and a land flowing with olive **oil. Iron and bronze** seem to be strange materials for **sandals**—even in highly poetic passages such as this. F. W. Grant suggests an interesting alternative translation here:

> The moderns against the ancients read "rest" instead of "strength." In these two there would be doubly expressed their abiding security: and though we may not be willing to give up what we are so familiar with, that "as thy days thy strength shall be," it is certainly not unsuited as the close of this wonderful blessing to have "as thy days shall be thy *rest*."[21]

33:26–29 The closing verses celebrate the greatness of God as He acts in behalf of His people. The **God of Jeshurun** is unique **in the heavens to help**. Millions have been fortified by the words in verse 27: **"The eternal God is your refuge, and underneath are the everlasting arms."**

God's future destruction of Israel's enemies and the promise of safety, peace, prosperity, and victory close the Song of Moses.

D. Moses' Death (Chap. 34)

34:1–8 Even if the death of **Moses** here was recorded by someone else, this does not affect the fact that the rest of the Pentateuch was written by Moses.[22] After **Moses** had seen **the land**, he died on **Mount Nebo** and was **buried** by **the Lord** in a secret **grave**. Doubtless the reason for the secrecy was to prevent men from making a shrine at the lawgiver's tomb and worshiping him there. **Moses was one hundred and twenty years old** at the time of his death, but he was still strong, alert, and keen. This statement is not in contradiction with 31:2. The reason Moses could no longer lead the people was not physical but spiritual. God had told him that because of his sin he would not lead the people into Canaan (31:2), even though physically he was able to do so.

34:9 **Joshua** then assumed his duties as commander-in-chief. **Moses had** confirmed Joshua as his successor according to the word of the Lord in Numbers 27:18–23. Thus his servant became his successor, a further testimony to Moses' humility.

34:10–12 Of few men could the tribute paid to Moses ever be spoken. Of course, when these closing verses were written, the Messiah had not yet appeared. Verse 10 was true only up to the time of Christ's First Advent.

"And Moses indeed was faithful in all His house as a *servant*" (Heb. 3:5). Because of his sin he died; his burial place is unknown. But his antitype, the Lord Jesus, "was faithful . . . , as a *Son* over His own house" (Heb. 3:5, 6). It was for *our* sins that *He* died; His burial place is empty because He has ascended to the right hand of the Father in heaven. "Therefore, holy brethren, partakers of the heavenly calling, *consider the Apostle and High Priest of our confession, Christ Jesus*. . . . For this One has been counted worthy of more glory than Moses, inasmuch as He who built the house has more honor than the house" (Heb. 3:1, 3).

ENDNOTES

[1](2:1–23) "Giants" (transliterated *rephā'îm*), were an ancient race of giants from whom Og was descended. The word Rephaim came to mean any people of large stature.

[2](3:1–11) J. A. Thompson, *Deuteronomy: An Introduction and Commentary*, p. 93.

[3](4:4–49) The Syriac Version reads *Sirion*.

[4](5:22) Thompson, *Deuteronomy*, p. 119.

[5](8:Intro) *Ibid.*, p. 134.

[6](10:Intro) The chapter and verse divisions in the Bible were made centuries after the originals were written.

[7](15:1–3) Matthew Henry, "Deuteronomy," *Matthew Henry's Commentary on the Whole Bible*, I:786.

[8](15:4–6) E. W. Bullinger, *The Companion Bible*, p. 259.

[9](16:1–8) D. L. Moody, *Notes from My Bible*, pp. 44, 45.

[10](16:16, 17) *Ibid.*, p. 45.

[11](18:9–14) Henry G. Bosch, *Our Daily Bread*, Grand Rapids: Radio Bible Class, June-July-August 1989, August 31.

[12](20:1–8) Henry, "Deuteronomy," I:806.

[13](20:10–20) See Introduction to Jonah for some details.

[14](22:13–21) Another possible meaning is that "tokens of virginity" should be translated "tokens of adolescence," that is, "that the girl was menstruating regularly. A man who married such a girl would expect to have evidence of this after his marriage unless, of course, she became pregnant by him at once. What was needed was evidence that at the time of marriage the girl was not pregnant and was menstruating. If she had been guilty of sexual misconduct after betrothal, any pregnancy before marriage would eventually show up and a child would be born before nine months had elapsed. The law of verses 13–21 might therefore be concerned with the bride's conduct during her betrothal period prior to marriage and the 'tokens of adolescence' might have been a pregnancy test." (Thompson,

Deuteronomy, p. 236. See also discussion on p. 235.)

[15](23:1–8) The category may refer specifically to offspring of incestuous relations among Jews, or of mixed relations with pagans.

[16](24:5) "Kinsman redeemer" is the older term from the KJV.

[17](24:17–22) Ronald Sider, *Rich Christians in an Age of Hunger*, p. 92.

[18](26:1–11) Phillip Keller, *A Shepherd Looks at Psalm 23*, pp. 46, 47.

[19](29:1) C. F. Keil and F. Delitzsch, "Deuteronomy." In *Biblical Commentary on the Old Testament*, III:446.

[20](31:9–13) C. H. Mackintosh, "Deuteronomy," in *Notes on the Pentateuch*, p. 895.

[21](33:24, 25) F. W. Grant, "Deuteronomy," in *The Numerical Bible*, I:622.

[22](34:1–8) See "Introduction to the Pentateuch" for a defense of the Mosaic authorship of the Pentateuch.

BIBLIOGRAPHY

Grant, F. W. "Deuteronomy." In *The Numerical Bible*. Vol. I. Neptune, NJ: Loizeaux Brothers, 1977.

Henry, Matthew. "Deuteronomy." In *Matthew Henry's Commentary on the Whole Bible*. Vol. I. MacLean, VA: MacDonald Publishing Company, n.d.

Keil, C. F. and Delitzsch, F. "Deuteronomy." In *Biblical Commentary on the Old Testament. The Pentateuch*, Vol. III. Grand Rapids: Wm. B. Eerdmans Publishing Co., 1971.

Kline, Meredith G. "Deuteronomy." In *The Wycliffe Bible Commentary*. Chicago: Moody Press, 1962.

Mackintosh, C. H. "Deuteronomy." In *Notes on the Pentateuch*. Neptune, NJ: Loizeaux Brothers, 1972.

Shultz, Samuel J. *Deuteronomy: The Gospel of Love*. Everyman's Bible Commentary. Chicago: Moody Press, 1971.

Thompson, J. A. *Deuteronomy: An Introduction and Commentary*. The Tyndale Old Testament Commentaries. Downers Grove, IL: Inter-Varsity Press, 1974.

Towns, Elmer L. "Deuteronomy." In the *Liberty Bible Commentary*. Lynchburg, VA: The Old-Time Gospel Hour, 1982.

INTRODUCTION TO THE HISTORICAL BOOKS

For the millions of people who love a good story, especially a *true* story, the second main division of the OT is unusually captivating. It picks up the story of God's people where Deuteronomy left off and takes it forward a thousand years to the end of OT history. (The poetical and prophetic books fit into this same framework but they do not advance the *story* any.)

For those who do *not* like "history" (by nature or by faulty exposure to dull history teachers) we can only say that *this* history is unique. First of all Bible history is truly, to use an old saying, "His story" in every sense of the word. It is not a complete account of any period of Hebrew history, but a divinely selected continuous story. Secondly, it is history with a *purpose*—not merely to instruct or entertain, but to make us better believers. To use the Apostle Paul's words in the NT, these things "were written for our learning" (Rom. 15:4).

While all of these events really occurred, the selection and presentation by God's human writers under His Spirit's inspiration was to make it easy for the meditative reader to see the lessons that God wants us to learn, e.g., from David's life, from the division of the Kingdom, or from the return of the Jewish remnant after the Exile.

I. Chronology

The historical books extend from about 1400 B.C. to about 400 B.C., or a full millennium of Hebrew history. This long period divides naturally into three main eras: The Theocratic Period (1405–1043 B.C.), the Monarchical Period (1043–586 B.C. or from Saul to the destruction of Jerusalem), and the Restoration Period (536 to 420 B.C.).

II. The Theocratic Books

Just as a *democracy* (Greek for *people-rule*) is supposed to be a government run by the people, so a *theocracy* is supposed to be a government directly ruled by God. Ancient Israel from Joshua to Saul (1405–1043 B.C.) was such a rule by God.[1]

Three books cover the theocratic era: Joshua, Judges, and Ruth.

A. Joshua

This book continues from the death of Moses and his replacement by Joshua, a military leader who was also a spiritual one. Joshua goes on to challenge the Israelites not only to conquer Palestine but also to follow the Lord. The first half of the book recounts the conquest of the Promised Land and the second half details the division of that land among the twelve tribes of Israel.

B. Judges

Because the Israelites were disobedient to God's orders and left pockets of pagans scattered throughout Palestine, they subsequently experienced wave after wave of Gentile oppressors—seven in all.

The Book of Judges contains some fairly grim—and one or two grisly—stories illustrating what disobedience to God's Word can bring.

C. Ruth

This charming little book does not take place after the time of the book of Judges but during that spiritually dark era, showing that even at a time of great spiritual decline, the godly remnant can serve God in a beautiful and acceptable way.

III. The Monarchical Books

There are also three books covering the era of the monarchy (1043–586 B.C.), but they have been divided into six books for convenience in all modern versions.

A. Samuel

First and Second Samuel can be summarized in three names: Samuel, Saul, and David. They are named after *Samuel*, the prophet who anointed Israel's first king, *Saul*, and also his successor, *David*, whose trials and successes are recounted in some detail.

B. Kings

Solomon, David's son, though a wise and splendid ruler, lost his spiritual power by marrying hosts of pagan women. His son Rehoboam caused the split of the kingdom into Judah in the south (which had good and evil rulers), and Israel in the north (which had only evil rulers). In 722 B.C. the Northern Kingdom went into captivity, and between 605 and 586 the Southern Kingdom was taken captive.

C. Chronicles

In the Hebrew Bible this is the last book, recounting Jewish history from Adam (merely by genealogies) through the downfall of the Southern Kingdom. Since it is a spiritual retelling of Hebrew history, it stresses positive elements (even omitting David's great sin and totally ignoring the rebellious Northern Kingdom).

IV. The Restoration Books

After the seventy-year exile in Babylon, the nation that was once a *theocracy*, then a *monarchy*, became a mere *province* of world Gentile powers—first of Persia, then of Greece, then of Rome. The period covered is 536–420 B.C.

A. Ezra

In 536 B.C. King Cyrus issued a decree allowing the Jews to return to their homeland. About 50,000 Jews (a very small minority) went back under Zerubbabel to rebuild the temple. Ezra the priest took about 2,000 Jews with him in 458 B.C.

B. Nehemiah

In 444 B.C. Nehemiah obtained permission from the king of Persia to rebuild the walls of Jerusalem around the reconstructed temple. When the walls were finished, Ezra and Nehemiah led a reformation and revival in the Jewish state.

C. Esther

This book is not the last of the three Restoration books chronologically, since the events take place in Persia, between chapters 6 and 7 of Ezra. Perhaps the book is put last because it recounts the lives of those who did not bother to return to the Holy Land when they could have done so. Esther illustrates God working behind the scenes (His name is not even mentioned once) to protect His ancient people from antisemitic persecution, indeed from genocide. The instruments that He used were a beautiful and heroic Jewish queen and her shrewd cousin, Mordecai.

ENDNOTES

[1]Calvin's Geneva (1500's) and Puritan New England (1600's) were basically Reformed Protestant attempts at theocracy.

JOSHUA

Introduction

"The sacred canon here presents us with a book of history and historical art, such as our generation, prolific in writing on history, but nevertheless poor in historical feeling and perception, stands in pressing need of."

—Paulus Cassel

I. Unique Place in the Canon

Joshua is an indispensable bridge between the Books of Moses and the history of Israel in the land of Canaan. Both in the Hebrew book order and the modern Christian order Joshua is the fifth book of the OT. To Christians it is the first of the twelve "historical books" (Joshua through Esther); to Jews it is the first of what they call "the Former Prophets" (Joshua through Ezra-Nehemiah, putting Ruth and Chronicles in the "writings" at the end of the Hebrew OT).

Jensen stresses the book's importance in these words:

> In a real sense Joshua is the *climax* of a progressive history as well as the *commencement* of a new experience for Israel. Thus its historical nexus gives it a strategic place in the Old Testament Scriptures.[1]

II. Authorship

While the book is anonymous, the ancient tradition that it is largely by Joshua himself, completed after his death by Eleazar the high priest and his son Phinehas, has much to commend it. Joshua contains vivid material, suggesting that the author was an eyewitness. There are also passages in the first person ("I," "we"), such as 5:1, 6. Also the book specifically records that Joshua had some documents written (18:9; 24:26). The fact that Rahab was still alive (6:25) at the time of composition fits well with Joshua's being the main author.

III. Date

The date of Joshua is partly dependent on the date of the Exodus (15th or 13th century B.C.). The facts fit better with the early, more conservative date of the mid–1400's B.C. A date for Joshua between 1400 and 1350 B.C. seems likely for the following reasons: The book has to be earlier than Solomon (cf. 16:10 with 1 Kgs. 9:16) and also before his father David (cf. 15:63 with 2 Sam. 5:5–9). Since Joshua 13:4–6 calls the Phoenicians "Sidonians," it must be before the 1100's B.C. when Tyre subjugated Sidon, and before 1200 B.C. because the Philistines invaded Palestine after that time, yet they are not a problem in Joshua's time.

IV. Background and Theme

Just as Exodus is the story of God leading His people out of Egypt, so Joshua is the story of God leading His people into the Promised Land. He would complete the good work He began despite the unbelief of the nation. As we will see, the people hadn't changed; they were still faithless. Nevertheless, the Word of the Lord would be fulfilled and the seed of Abraham would be planted in the covenant land (Gen. 15:13–16) to take root and grow.

The events of this book follow those recorded in the last chapter of Deuteronomy. The people of Israel were encamped on the plains of Moab, east of the Jordan River. Moses had died, and Joshua had become commander-in-chief. He was about to lead the people across the Jordan and into the Promised Land. Law, as represented by Moses, cannot lead God's people into their inheritance. Only Christ in resurrection, pictured by Joshua, can do that.

We should pause to review some important facts about Joshua. Moses had changed his name from Hoshea to Joshua (Num. 13:16). He was an Ephraimite (Num. 13:8) and Moses' personal servant (Joshua 1:1). He was early a man engaged in fighting the Lord's battles. He led the Israelites in their first combat against the Amalekites (Ex. 17) and was the only general they had known since Egypt. But what equipped Joshua to replace Moses at the head of the nation was not his military prowess but his spiritual vitality and faith. As a young man he constantly attended the tent of the Lord (Ex. 33:11). He had been on Mount Sinai with Moses (Ex. 32:17). He and Caleb were the only ones who saw the Promised Land with believing eyes when the people had been at Kadesh Barnea thirty-eight years earlier (Num. 14:6–10). Trained by Moses, he was now commissioned by Jehovah, although he was over ninety years of age.

OUTLINE

I. THE OCCUPATION OF THE PROMISED LAND (Chaps. 1–12)
- A. Preparations for Crossing the Jordan (Chap. 1)
- B. The Spies at Jericho (Chap. 2)
- C. Crossing the Jordan (3:1—5:1)
- D. Ceremonies at Gilgal (5:2–12)
- E. The Conquest of Jericho (5:13—6:27)
- F. The Campaign at Ai (7:1—8:29)
- G. The Confirmation of the Covenant at Shechem (8:30–35)
- H. The Treaty with the Gibeonites (Chap. 9)
- I. The Southern Campaign (Chap. 10)
- J. The Northern Campaign (Chap. 11)
- K. Summary of Conquests (Chap. 12)

II. THE SETTLEMENT OF THE PROMISED LAND (Chaps. 13—21)
- A. The Lands Yet to Be Possessed (13:1–7)
- B. The Allotment of the Land (13:8—19:51)

1. The Allotment to Reuben, Gad, and Half of Manasseh (13:8–33)
2. The Allotment to Judah (Chaps. 14, 15)
3. The Allotment to Joseph (Chaps. 16, 17)
4. The Allotment to the Rest of the Tribes (Chaps. 18, 19)

C. The Cities of Refuge (Chap. 20)
Excursus on the Cities of Refuge

D. The Levitical Cities (Chap. 21)

E. The Altar East of the Jordan (Chap. 22)

F. Joshua's Farewell Address to the Leaders of Israel (Chap. 23)

G. Joshua's Farewell Address to the People of Israel (24:1–15)

H. The Covenant Renewed at Shechem (24:16–28)

I. The Death of Joshua (24:29–33)

Commentary

I. THE OCCUPATION OF THE PROMISED LAND (Chaps. 1—12)

A. Preparations for Crossing the Jordan (Chap. 1)

1:1–9 The LORD first delivered a solemn charge to **Joshua the son of Nun** concerning the task ahead of him. **The land** had been promised to **Israel**, but they must possess it, from the Negev at the south to **Lebanon** in the north, and from the Mediterranean on the west to **the River Euphrates** on the east (see vv. 3, 4). Joshua must **be strong, very courageous**, and obedient. Now, as then, we are assured of **good success** when we fill our hearts and minds with God's Word and obey it (v. 8).

Three times Joshua is told by the Lord to **be strong and very courageous** (vv. 6, 7, 9). The size and duration of the task ahead, the pressures of leading such an obstinate people, and the absence of his spiritual mentor, Moses, were perhaps heavy on Joshua's mind at this time. But the Lord was not calling him without enabling him. There were good reasons for Joshua to **be strong**: *God's promise* (vv. 5, 6), a sure victory; *God's Word* (vv. 7, 8), a safe guide; *God's presence* (v. 9), a sustaining power.

T. Austin Sparks writes:

> The real battle of faith is joined here. Not what we are, but what He is! Not what we feel, but His facts.[2]

1:10–18 **The people** were to **prepare provisions** for their journey into **the land** of Canaan. As for the two and a half tribes which were settling east of the Jordan, the men were reminded by Joshua that they must help in the conquest of the land; **then** they could **return to** their families (vv. 12–15). To this they readily agreed (vv. 16–18). Any who turned back would **be put to death**.

In some hymns, crossing the Jordan

is likened to death and the land of Canaan pictures heaven. But there was conflict in Canaan, whereas there is no conflict in heaven. Actually the land of Canaan pictures our present spiritual inheritance. It is all ours, but we must possess it by obeying the Word, claiming the promises, and fighting the good fight of faith.

B. The Spies at Jericho (Chap. 2)

2:1a In preparation for the invasion, **Joshua the son of Nun sent out two** spies **from Acacia Grove** to **Jericho**. This was not an indication of lack of faith on his part; rather, it was a matter of military strategy. They were not **to spy** out the whole **land**, as had been done years earlier, but only to look ahead one step at a time.

2:1b–24 The spies found shelter in **the house of a harlot named Rahab**. As Keil and Delitzsch point out, "Their entering the house of such a person would not excite so much suspicion."[3] It is clear from the narrative that **Rahab** had **heard** of the marvelous victories which **the LORD** had **given** to the Jewish people (vv. 8–11). She concluded that their **God** must be the true **God**, and so she trusted in Him, becoming a true convert. She proved the reality of her faith by protecting the spies, even though it meant betraying her country.

The spies promised to spare Rahab and her family if she hung a **scarlet cord in the window** of her **home** and if the **household** remained indoors during the attack against Jericho (vv. 6–21). The **scarlet cord** makes us think of a house protected by the blood, as at the original Passover (Ex. 12).

When messengers from **the king of Jericho** asked **Rahab** where the spies were, she told them they had already left the city (v. 5). While **the men** of Jericho searched for **them** on **the road to the Jordan**, Rahab sent the spies westward **to the mountain**. After hiding there for **three days**, the spies escaped across the Jordan, carrying a confident report **to Joshua** (vv. 22–24).

Rahab's "works" and not her "words" justified her (Jas. 2:25). The Bible does not commend her deceit (vv. 4, 5) but it does commend her faith (Heb. 11:31). James also calls her deed a work of faith (Jas. 2:25). She risked her life to save the lives of the spies because she believed in the power and sovereignty of their God. So in our Lord's day some outside the commonwealth of Israel showed more faith than those who were eyewitnesses of His glory (Luke 7:2–9). Great faith, wherever it is found, is always rewarded (see chap. 6), for it is pleasing to God (Heb. 11:6).

C. Crossing the Jordan (3:1—5:1)

3:1–13 The time had come to **cross . . . the Jordan** River, which was now in flood stage. **The priests** were instructed to go forth, carrying **the ark of the covenant**. (The Kohathites usually carried the ark, as in Numbers 4:1–15, but **the priests** were to carry it on this special occasion.) **The people** were ordered to follow the ark at a distance, but always keeping it in view. The ark speaks of Christ. We should maintain a respectful distance by not irreverently trying to solve mysteries concerning His Person that are too deep for the human mind. Some of the worst heresies in Christian history have arisen because of brazen attempts to do this. But we should always keep Christ in view. This assures us of victory.

3:14–17 When the priests' **feet** touched **the water** of **the Jordan**, a miracle occurred. The river was stopped at **the city** of **Adam**, some

The Jordan River is neither large nor impressive, but it has become the most famous river in the world because of scriptural events associated with it. This is one of the myriad of bends in the Jordan's path from the Sea of Galilee to the Dead Sea. (Photo by Willem Van Gemeren)

miles to the north. **The waters** piled up there **in a heap**, and whatever water was left in the bed of the river below that point drained into **the Salt** (Dead) **Sea**.

Similar stoppages of the Jordan near where Adam no doubt was located took place in 1267, when the river was dammed for ten hours, and in 1927 for twenty-one hours. Both *times it was due to earthquakes.*[4] However, D. K. Campbell argues that there is much here to suggest not merely perfect timing, but a special miracle:

> Many supernatural elements were brought together: (1) The event came to pass as predicted (3:13, 15). (2) The timing was exact (v. 15). (3) The event took place when the river was at flood stage (v. 15). (4) The wall of water was held in place for many hours, possibly an entire day (v. 16). (5) The soft, wet river bottom became **dry** at once (v. 17). (6) The water returned immediately as soon as the people had crossed over and **the priests** came up out of the river (4:18). Centuries later the Prophets Elijah and Elisha crossed the same river on dry ground to the east (2 Kgs. 2:8). Soon thereafter Elisha crossed back over the river on dry ground. If a natural phenomenon is necessary to explain the Israelites' crossing under Joshua, then one would have to conclude that two earthquakes occurred in quick sequence for Elijah and Elisha, which seems a bit presumptuous.[5]

God, represented by the ark, led the people into the Jordan even as He would lead them to victory west of the Jordan. He was demonstrating that His presence, which caused the waters to flee before Israel, was their hope of triumph, and not anything in themselves.

The priests walked to the middle of the riverbed and stayed there while **all Israel crossed over on dry ground**.

4:1–24 **The Lord** directed that **twelve men** (**one man from every tribe**) should **carry** one **stone** apiece **out of the** bed **of the Jordan** and erect **a memorial** marker where **Israel** first camped west of the Jordan. Accordingly, the monument was **set up** at **Gilgal** as a permanent reminder to future generations of God's miraculous stopping of the Jordan so that the Israelites could cross **over . . . on dry land**.

The tribes that received their inheritance east of Jordan—**Reuben, Gad, and half the tribe of Manasseh**—sent **armed** warriors over to help their brethren occupy the land of Canaan. Although the combined strength of the two and a half tribes was over 100,000 men (see Num. 26), only **forty thousand . . . crossed** the Jordan; the rest probably stayed behind to secure their land and protect their families.

After all the people had crossed over, including the men of the two and a half tribes, and after the **twelve stones** had been taken out of the Jordan, **Joshua set up twelve stones in the midst of the Jordan, where the . . . priests** were standing. Then as soon as **the priests** marched to the west bank with the ark of the covenant, **the waters of the Jordan** flowed down again in flood tide.

The stones in the riverbed speak of identification with Christ *in death*. Those on the west bank speak of identification with Christ *in resurrection*.

By cutting off the waters of the Jordan, **the Lord exalted Joshua in the sight of all Israel** as He had earlier exalted Moses. Up to now, Joshua had been a servant, humbly serving in Moses' shadow, learning the ways of God. Now was the time of his exaltation, for "he who humbles himself will be exalted" (Luke 14:11).

The people crossed **the Jordan on the tenth day of the first month**, five days short of a full forty years since the Exodus from Egypt, and just in time to prepare for the Passover (see Ex. 12:2, 3).

5:1 The heathen inhabitants of Canaan were seized with panic when they **heard** of the miraculous crossing of the Jordan by the Hebrew army.

D. Ceremonies at Gilgal (5:2–12)

5:2–9 This chapter tells about the events that took place **at Gilgal**, the first encampment Israel made in Canaan. There **the men** were **circumcised** (vv. 2–9). There they kept the Passover, the first in Canaan (v. 10). There the manna ceased (vv. 11, 12), and there Joshua met the Commander-in-chief of the host of the Lord's army, Jesus Christ (vv. 13–15).

The Lord directed **Joshua** to renew the rite of circumcision at this time. All the men **who came out of Egypt . . . had been circumcised**, but **the men of war had** all **died** in the meantime (Deut. 2:16). For **forty years** there had been no circumcision. A new generation had arisen during the **forty years** of wandering, and they now had to undergo this ceremony as a sign of their restoration to the full enjoyment of their covenant blessings. As long as they wandered in the desert, they were ridiculed by the Egyptians for not gaining the Promised Land. But now that they were in the land, **the reproach** was **rolled away** (v. 9). **The "second time"** (v. 2) means the second time that circumcision was practiced by the nation.

5:10 **The Passover** was **kept** four days after the Jordan was crossed (**on the fourteenth day of the month**). Notice Joshua's faith: Although he was in enemy territory, he obeyed God by circumcising his soldiers and by keeping the Passover. These have been called "most unmilitary acts."

Through circumcision and the Passover the Lord was calling His people back to the basics of their relationship with Him. Both of these rites had been neglected in the wilderness.

Circumcision was a sign of the covenant between God and Abraham, and God in His faithfulness was keeping His unconditional promise by giving them the land (Gen. 15:18–21). It was also a picture of self-judgment and putting away the filth of the flesh, vitally necessary to victory. The Passover was a reminder of their redemption. Jehovah had bought them and freed them from slavery in Egypt. In observing the Passover the Jews were obeying the word of the Lord given through Moses at the time of the first Passover forty years earlier (Ex. 13:5). Grace was His motive in calling His people and bringing them out. Faithfulness was His guarantee that He would bring them in.

5:11, 12 **The manna** speaks of Christ in His Incarnation, the bread that came down from heaven as a provision for our wilderness needs. **The produce of the land** illustrates Christ in Resurrection, after entering into the blessings of Canaan. We feed on both. **The manna ceased on** the morning **after they** first ate the **parched grain**. "What a wonderful Time-keeper and Supplier God is!"

E. The Conquest of Jericho (5:13—6:27)

5:13, 14a The **"Man"** in verse 13 was the Angel of Jehovah—the Lord Jesus in one of His preincarnate appearances. He introduced Himself **as Commander of the army of the Lord**. Christ does not come merely to help

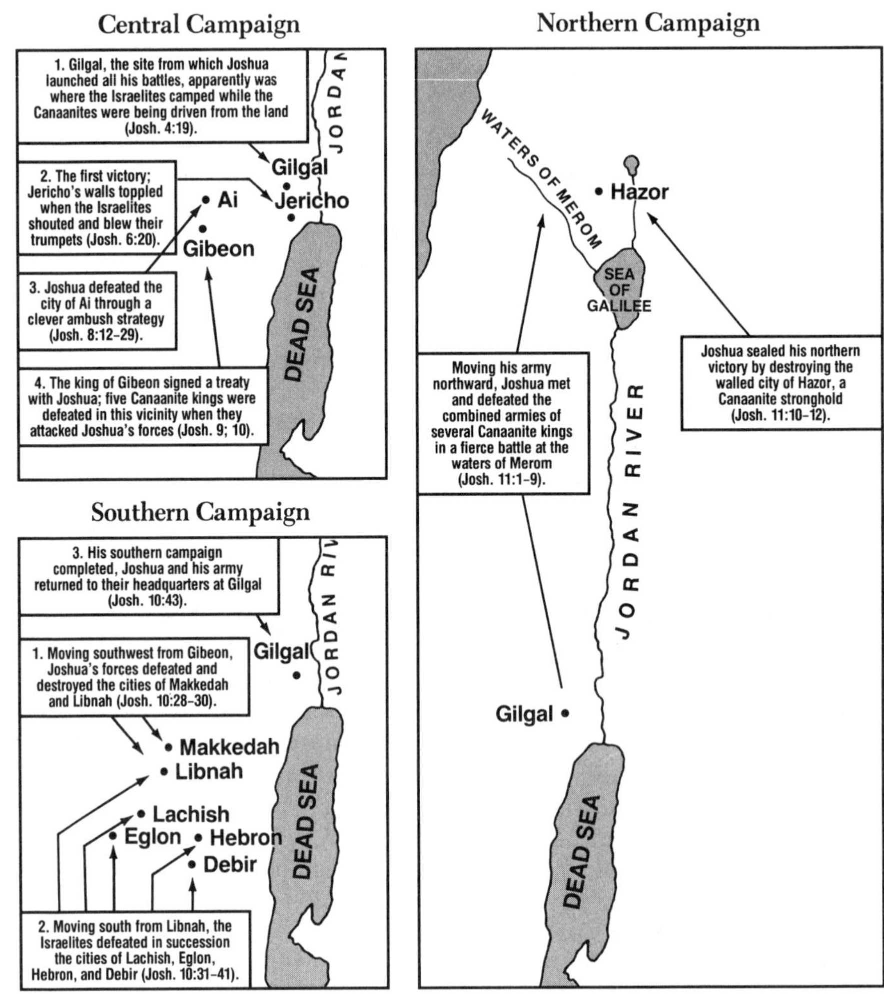

Joshua's Conquest

us, and certainly not to harm us; He comes to take full control.

5:14b, 15 Here is conclusive proof that **Joshua** was in the presence of God, and knew it. Mere angels never accepted worship, but here the Angel of the Lord *commands* worship, thereby proving His divine nature. Joshua must learn firsthand what Moses had to learn at the beginning of his ministry (Ex. 3)—the holiness and supremacy of the Lord.

6:1–21 The conquest of Canaan was accomplished by three military campaigns—central, southern, and northern. The central campaign, designed to divide and conquer, consisted of two major engagements, one at Jericho and the other at Ai.

Jericho was a fortified **city**, but her walls and gates served only to keep her inhabitants inside for judgment; they certainly didn't keep Israel out. It was a low city topographically (over 800 feet below sea level) and morally. It was a doomed city because it stood on God's land and its rightful tenants had come to claim their property. Many things in our lives loom out as Jerichos, impeding our progress in possessing our possessions. Perhaps we've been discouraged with the sheer immensity of our trials. If we will only claim the victory the Lord gives and move ahead in faith, with eyes fixed upon God for success, we too will see miracles.

Fear of the Jews had caused Jericho to be barricaded before the invaders arrived. For **six days** the Israelites **marched around the city, once** each day, returning at night to Gilgal. **On the seventh day . . . they marched around** it **seven times. When the priests blew the** rams' horns (**trumpets**), the Israelites let out a great shout. **The** walls **fell down flat**, and **the people** of God were able to enter **the city**.

Some Bible students think that the walls descended into the ground like an elevator, allowing the Israelites to walk across the top of the walls into the city. However it happened, it resulted from the faith of God's people (Heb. 11:30). Notice that **the ark** is mentioned seven times between verses 6 and 12.

Everything in **the city** was "accursed"—that is, **doomed by the Lord to destruction** as the firstfruits of Canaan. The inhabitants (except for **Rahab** and her family) and the livestock were to be **destroyed**, but the **silver, gold, bronze, and iron** were to be put **into the treasury of the Lord**. No one could take anything for himself.

When one realizes the moral perversity of the Canaanites, it is easy to see why God ordered the complete destruction of life within Jericho. Rather than criticize the Lord for administering deserved judgment to the wicked, we should marvel at His grace which preserved Rahab and her family from the same.

6:22–27 The faith that brought the walls down (Heb. 11:30) also **brought . . . Rahab** and **her relatives out** (Heb. 11:31). The grace of God not only made provision for her safety but also elevated her to a place in the ancestry of David and ultimately of the Lord Jesus Christ (Matt. 1:5, 6). Grace not only saves us from destruction but also guarantees our exaltation (Rom. 8:29, 30). Faith is the hand that takes hold of grace.

After **Rahab** and her family were escorted out safely, **the city** was **burned. Joshua** pronounced a curse on anyone who sought to rebuild Jericho as a fortress, prophesying that the man's oldest son would die when the **foundation** was laid and **his youngest** son would die when **its gates** were erected. See 1 Kings 16:34 for the fulfillment of this curse.

F. The Campaign at Ai (7:1—8:29)

Chapter 7 deals with the sin question in Canaan. Even though the people had crossed the Jordan, they were still prone to sin. Here is the story of Israel's *defeat* at Ai and Israel's *victory* over sin at Achor.

7:1–5 When **Joshua sent** spies **to Ai, they returned** with the confident report that the city was poorly defended and that it would not be necessary to send more than **two or three thousand** soldiers against it. But when an army of **about three thousand men** marched on Ai, they met defeat rather than victory.

7:6–10 Many times defeat comes after victory; that's when we least expect it. That's when we feel strongest in ourselves. The people didn't pray before going against Ai, nor did the Lord command them to go, as He had commanded them to take Jericho. Consequently, they learned painfully that all was not well; something had changed. **The Canaanites** were not any stronger, but Israel was weaker, and the reason was that sin had entered the camp. Although only one man was at fault, the whole nation was guilty (v. 11) and thirty-six men died (v. 5). **The LORD** told **Joshua** that this wasn't a time for prayer but a time for action (v. 10).

7:11–26 Joshua learned that the defeat was caused by sin in the camp. Someone had disobeyed the Lord in the conquest of Jericho by looting. We are not told what method was used to find the culprit; perhaps it was by casting lots. At any rate, the field was narrowed first to **the tribe**, then to **the family**, then to **the household**, and then to **the man—Achan**. He confessed to stealing a **Babylonian garment, two hundred shekels of silver,** and **a wedge of gold**. He also admitted to burying them **in the** floor of his **tent.**

"When I saw . . . I coveted . . . and took" (v. 21). The story of Achan provides a vivid illustration of James 1:14, 15: "But each one is tempted when he is drawn away by his own desires and enticed. Then, when desire has conceived, it gives birth to sin; and sin, when it is full-grown, brings forth death."

Achan, by taking something that was under the ban, became accursed himself (Deut. 7:26). It may seem harsh that all of Achan's family shared in his fate, but sin is a serious matter. Rahab's faith saved her entire household. Achan's sin condemned his. Besides, they must have been aware of his activities, since the stolen goods were buried under their tent. Perhaps his children even participated in his sin. The lesson God was teaching His people was clear: Sin defiles the whole camp, and it must be totally eradicated whenever it surfaces.

As punishment for his crime, **Achan** and his household were **stoned** to death and then **burned**. Also burned were all his possessions, as well as the stolen goods. H. J. Blair comments:

> By Achan's death, the act of sacrilege was expiated, and the scene of the tragedy, the valley of Achor, became a door of hope as the people set their faces once more to the advance.[6]

8:1–29 On the second attempt, Joshua and his army captured **Ai** by the strategy of **ambush.** Although the details of the **ambush** are difficult to understand clearly, the general plan seems to have been as follows: A company of Israelites went past Ai under cover of darkness and hid **on the west side of the city**. In the morning, the rest of the soldiers attacked the city from the north. When the men of Ai counterattacked, Joshua and his men purposely retreated, drawing the inhabitants away from their city. Then **Joshua** stretched **out** his **spear;** that was the signal for the men lying in ambush to enter **the city** and **set** it **on fire**. Seeing their city on fire, **the men of Ai** panicked. It was then easy for the Israelites to trap Ai's soldiers on both sides, and destroy them.

Verse 3 says that **thirty thousand . . . men** were sent to **ambush . . . the city**, while verse 12 speaks of **five thousand.** There may have been two ambushes. But **thirty thousand** seems an unnecessarily large number for an ambush. Some believe that thirty **thousand** should read **thirty** *captains*, since the Hebrew word for thousand can also be translated chief. Others believe that **thirty thousand** is a copyist's error for **five thousand**. The

five thousand men (v. 12) may have been sent to repel any possible attack by the men of **Bethel**, two miles west of **Ai**.

The Jews were allowed to keep the **livestock and the spoil . . . for themselves** in this particular engagement. If Achan had only waited, he might have gotten his booty without losing his life over it!

Israel lost thirty-six men in the first battle; this time they lost none as far as the biblical record mentions. Having purged themselves of defilement, they were once again safe in the midst of war. Victory in the Christian life is not the *absence of* conflict but the presence and protection of God *in the midst of* conflict.

G. The Confirmation of the Covenant at Shechem (8:30–35)

8:30–35 In obedience to the Word of God (Deut. 27:2–6), **Joshua built an altar** on **Mount Ebal** and inscribed upon **stones a copy of the Law of Moses**. The tribes were assembled, **half . . . in front of Mount Gerizim, and half . . . in front of Mount Ebal**. Joshua stood in the valley between them, and he either **read . . . the blessings and the cursings** that are found **written in the Book of the Law** of **Moses** or else instructed the Levites to read them (Deut. 27:14). "Persons are often said in Scripture to do that which they only command to be done."[7]

H. The Treaty with the Gibeonites (Chap. 9)

9:1–27 News of the military successes of Israel caused **all the kings** in Canaan to unite against **Joshua and Israel** (vv. 1, 2). But **the inhabitants of** the city of **Gibeon** and three other cities, **Chephirah, Beeroth, and Kirjath Jearim** (vv. 3, 17) decided that it was futile to oppose the invaders. They knew that the Israelites had been ordered **to destroy all the** heathen **inhabitants of the land**. But they also knew that no such orders had been issued concerning nations outside Canaan (Deut. 20:10, 15). If they could persuade Joshua and his army that they had come on a **long journey . . . from a** distant **country**, they would not be killed.

So they disguised themselves in tattered **old garments** and **patched sandals**. Also, they brought with them **dry and moldy bread** and **torn . . . wineskins**. They told Joshua they had **come . . . from a very far country**, and everything about them seemed to support the statement.

The Israelites **did not ask counsel of the LORD** about the matter, but **made a covenant with** the Gibeonites. Three days later the scheme was exposed, and there was agitation among the Jews to kill the tricksters. But **the rulers** decided to honor the treaty by sparing the Gibeonites. However, they would henceforth serve **the congregation** as **woodcutters and water carriers** in connection with the service of **the altar of the Lord**.

Joshua and the princes were wise in keeping their oath, even though they had been **deceived** in the matter. Later Saul tried to exterminate the Gibeonites and was punished for it (2 Sam. 21).

I. The Southern Campaign (Chap. 10)

10:1–6 Chapter 10 records the southern campaign. When the **kings** of five Canaanite **cities . . . heard** that the Gibeonites had defected to the Israelites, they realized that this made the central hilly district vulnerable, and so they decided to **attack Gibeon**.

The Gibeonites **sent** an appeal for military assistance **to Joshua**.

10:7, 8 Once again **Joshua** heard those comforting words from the mouth of **the LORD, "Do not fear them."** He had heard them before the victory at Jericho and before the successful ambush of Ai. They guaranteed triumph despite the size of the opposition.

10:9–11 Assured of victory by the Lord, **Joshua** engaged the enemy's forces **at Gibeon**, causing them to flee. Two miracles occurred in the destruction of the enemy. First there was a tremendous hailstorm, which killed **more** men **than** the Israelites had slain. But note that they were discriminating **hailstones**—they killed only the enemies.

10:12–15 Then, at the request of **Joshua**, the **sun** and **moon** "stood **still**" (or "tarried"), prolonging the hours that the Israelites could continue to pursue and destroy the foe before they could escape to the security of their walled cities. It is literally descriptive language to say that the sun and the moon stood still. We use such language when we say that the sun rose or set. Various natural explanations have been given as to what actually happened at this time.[8] But it is enough to know that it was a miracle which resulted in an extended day for fighting. Spurgeon says,

> How He did it is no question for us. . . . It is not ours to try and soften down miracles, but to glorify God in them.[9]

The Book of Jasher (v. 13) may mean "The Book of the Upright." No book of that name can be identified today, and it certainly was not inspired.

The battle was a tremendous undertaking for Israel. They had marched all night and then fought through the longest day in history. They exerted themselves beyond ordinary limits, but still the victory was the Lord's (vv. 10, 11). With his usual insight Matthew Henry observes:

> But why needed Joshua to put himself and his men so much to the stretch? Had not God promised him that without fail He would *deliver the enemies into his hand?* It is true He had; but God's promises are intended, not to slacken and supersede, but to quicken and encourage our endeavours.[10]

10:16–27 The five kings were trapped **in a cave at Makkedah**, then slain and hung **on five trees**, and finally buried in **the cave**.

10:28–39 Following this, Joshua conquered the Canaanite cities of **Makkedah** (v. 28), **Libnah** (vv. 29, 30), **Lachish** (vv. 31, 32), **Gezer** (v. 33), **Eglon** (vv. 34, 35), **Hebron** (vv. 36, 37), and **Debir** (vv. 38, 39). The **king** of **Hebron** in verse 37 was a successor to the one slain in verse 26.

10:40–43 This paragraph summarizes the southern campaign.

The destruction referred to in this chapter must be taken generally, as noted by Haley:

> . . . Joshua swept over this region in too rapid a manner to depopulate it entirely. . . . All whom he pursued he destroyed; but he did not stop to search into every possible hiding place. This was left to be done by each tribe in its own inheritance.[11]

J. The Northern Campaign (Chap. 11)

11:1–9 News of Israel's mounting triumphs caused **the kings** of **the north** to confederate. They gathered **together at the waters of Merom**, north of the Sea of Galilee. **Joshua**

and his army **attacked** and defeated them. Then, in obedience to the Lord, Joshua **hamstrung their horses and burned their chariots**. To hamstring means to cut a tendon in the leg, disabling the horse.

11:10–15 The capital city of **Hazor** was **burned**; the other **cities that stood on their mounds** were **destroyed** but not **burned**. Perhaps Joshua felt that the cities standing on mounds would be useful to the Israelites who would settle there. The inhabitants of all the cities were killed, **and all the spoil** was taken by **the Israelites**. Complete obedience brings complete victory (v. 15).

11:16–20 These verses review Joshua's conquest of the land from Edom (**Seir**) in **the South** to **Mount Hermon** in the northeast and **the Valley of Lebanon** in the northwest. **Gibeon** escaped destruction. Jerusalem remained unconquered until the time of David. (The **Goshen** mentioned in verse 16 was not in Egypt but was an area to the south of Palestine.)

11:21–23 Special mention is made of the fact that the **Anakim** were **destroyed** in all the **cities** except **in Gaza, in Gath, and in Ashdod. "The land rested from war"** (v. 23) in the sense that the major battles were fought, though there was still a great deal of "mopping up" to be done.

K. Summary of Conquests (Chap. 12)

12:1–6 The first six verses take us back to the victory that God gave Moses over **Sihon, king of the Amorites**, and **Og, king of Bashan**. These victories are considered as part of the total conquest, since the territory was occupied by the two and a half tribes east of the Jordan River.

12:7–24 God had made a promise earlier to Israel before they crossed the Jordan: "He will deliver their kings into your hand, and you will destroy their name from under heaven; no one shall be able to stand against you until you have destroyed them" (Deut. 7:24). Here are **thirty-one** instances of God's faithfulness (vv. 7–24); **Joshua** defeated **thirty-one . . . kings** on the west side of the **Jordan**.

II. THE SETTLEMENT OF THE PROMISED LAND (Chaps. 13—21)

A. The Lands Yet to Be Possessed (13:1–7)

13:1–6 Joshua was now an **old** man, and the entire **land** promised to the Israelites had not as yet been occupied by them. Verses 2–6 describe portions in the southwest and in the northeast that were still inhabited by the heathen. We know also that the land eastward to the Euphrates had been promised to the Jews, but it has never yet been occupied by them.[12]

13:7 The Lord instructed Joshua to **divide** the **land** which had already been conquered among **the nine tribes and half the tribe of Manasseh**.

B. The Allotment of the Land (13:8—19:51)

1. *The Allotment to Reuben, Gad, and Half of Manasseh*

13:8–33 Two and a half tribes had already been assigned land on the east side of **the Jordan** River as follows: the entire territory occupied by the two and a half tribes (vv. 8–13); **Reuben** (vv. 15–23); **Gad** (vv. 24–28); and **half the tribe of Manasseh** (vv. 29–31).

Levi did not receive a tribal **inheritance** (v. 14), since that was the priestly tribe, and **the Lord** was its **inheritance** in a special way (v. 33).

Dropping Levi from the tribes leaves

only eleven tribes. But Joseph's two sons, Ephraim and Manasseh, are included in Joseph's place, and that raises the number to twelve again. The reason Joseph's sons are included is that they were adopted by Jacob as his own sons before his death (Gen. 48:5).

Special mention is made of the fact that **Balaam** was among those slain in Transjordan (v. 22). The Lord had not forgotten the terrible calamity that this wicked prophet caused His people (see Num. 23–25). "Be sure your sin will find you out" (Num. 32:23).

An interesting problem arises in verse 25. The tribe of **Gad** possessed some of **the land of the Ammonites**, which was forbidden in Deuteronomy 2:19. But this land had earlier been taken from the Ammonites by Sihon, king of the Amorites, and made part of his kingdom. So by the time Israel took the land from Sihon, it no longer belonged to the Ammonites.

The **Debir** mentioned in verse 26 is not the same city mentioned in the previous chapter. This city was east of the Jordan, while the one Joshua conquered was west of the river.

2. *The Allotment to Judah (Chaps. 14, 15)*

14:1–5 This chapter begins the distribution of the land on the west side of Jordan to **the nine tribes and the half-tribe. The Lord had commanded . . . Moses** that the distribution be made **by lot**. This probably means that the general location of the tribal portion was determined by lot, but the size of the territory was according to the population of the tribe (Num. 26:53–56).

14:6–15 First in the list of tribes is **Judah** (14:6—15:63). The men of **Judah** led the armies of Israel (see Num. 10:14) and were the largest and most powerful tribe, boasting over 76,000 warriors.

Before giving the territorial boundaries, the Spirit of God records the noble request of **Caleb** for the city of **Hebron**. Though he was then **eighty-five years old**, his faith, courage, and **strength** were unabated. He longed for more spiritual conquests and received **Hebron** for his **inheritance**.

Hebron meant not only the city but the country around it as well (v. 12). The city had been conquered earlier by Joshua (10:36, 37). It later was given to the priests, but **Caleb** kept the surrounding region for his **inheritance**.

Caleb had been spared from the plague that took the lives of the unbelieving spies **forty-five years** earlier (Num. 14:36–38). He had been preserved during the wilderness wanderings. He had survived several years of war in Canaan. He knew that God would not have **kept** him **alive**, promising him a reward for his faith, only to give him over to the **Anakim**. So what if they were giants? They were on his land, and he would **drive them out** by the strength of God. He still saw things through the eyes of faith and not as they appeared outwardly. This was the secret of his abiding **strength** and amazing success. He was not about to retire (although **eighty-five years old**) until he possessed his possessions.

15:1–12 The boundaries of **Judah** are described in verses 1–12. It is almost impossible to trace them with exactness at the present time. This may cause some to wonder why all these details are included in the Bible. The answer is, of course, that these details are important in the sight of God. They are inspired and profitable, full of rich spiritual lessons.

15:13–20 Caleb's conquest of

Hebron is recorded in verse 14. He offered his **daughter**, **Achsah**, to whoever would capture **Kirjath Sepher** (Debir) (v. 16). Caleb's nephew, **Othniel**, was the one who **took** the city and gained the bride (v. 17). He later became the first judge in Israel (Judg. 3:9). **Achsah . . . persuaded** Othniel **to ask her father for a field** (v. 18). Her words **"since you have given me land"** imply that Othniel had done this and obtained **the field**. Then Achsah requested **upper** and **lower springs** to **water** the land.

Some cities, like **Debir** and **Hebron**, had to be taken more than once because of the guerrilla warfare of the Canaanites (see notes on chap. 10). It should also be noted that there was more than one city with the same name (e.g., Debir).

15:21–63 The cities of Judah's territory are listed in verses 21–63. Some of these cities should be familiar to us from our study of the patriarchs: **Hebron** (v. 54) (also called **Kirjath Arba** and Mamre) was familiar to Abraham, Isaac, and Jacob (Gen. 13:18; 35:27), and they were all buried there (Gen. 23:17–20). Perhaps this is what made it so precious to the spiritually discerning Caleb. **Beersheba** (v. 28) means "the well of the oath"; the patriarchs spent much time there. It was a place of renewal, refreshment, and rest (Gen. 21:31; 26:33; 46:1). **Jerusalem** (v. 63) was held by **the Jebusites**. It was not until the time of David that they were finally driven out of Jerusalem (2 Sam. 5:6, 7).

These cities provided a rich heritage for Judah and a powerful stimulus to strengthen their faith. The God of Abraham, Isaac, and Jacob was in the midst of their children to perform His ancient promise.

When we count the cities in verses 21–32, we find that there are thirty-eight, although verse 32 says there are only twenty-nine. Nine of these cities belonged to Simeon, whose inheritance was within the borders of Judah (19:1–9). That leaves **twenty-nine . . . cities** belonging to Judah. There is a similar problem in numbering in verses 33–36; fifteen cities are enumerated, but perhaps **Gederah and Gederothaim** are two names for the same city, leaving the total of **fourteen cities** mentioned in verse 36.[13]

Note the last verse especially. The upper part of the city, Mount Zion, was not taken until the time of David. The lower city, **Jerusalem**, was taken by Judah (Judg. 1:8), then later recaptured by **the Jebusites** (Judg. 1:21). **Jerusalem** is listed as belonging to Benjamin (18:28) as well as to **Judah**; it was located on the border between these two tribes.

3. *The Allotment to Joseph (Chaps. 16, 17)*

16:1-4 **The tribe of Joseph** is taken up next. To **Joseph** had been given the birthright (i.e., the double portion, 1 Chron. 5:1) which Reuben had forfeited (Gen. 49:4). The general boundaries of Joseph's territory are given in verses 1–4. This was, of course, divided between **Ephraim** and half of the tribe of **Manasseh** which settled west of the **Jordan**.

16:5–10 Ephraim's boundaries are described in verses 5–10. Pay particular attention to verse 10. Failure to **drive out the Canaanites** brought grief to the Israelites in their later history.

17:1–13 The inheritance of **Manasseh** was partly in **Gilead and Bashan**, on the east side of the Jordan (v. 1), and partly on the west side (vv. 7–11). The territory west of the Jordan was flanked **on the north** by six Canaanite fortresses—**Beth Shean**,

Ibleam, Dor, En Dor, Taanach, and Megiddo (vv. 11, 12).

Some of the **cities of Ephraim** were in the territory **of Manasseh**, and some of **Manasseh's towns** were in the territory of **Asher . . . and Issachar** (vv. 7–12).

The **daughters** of **Zelophehad** inherited with the **sons** of **Manasseh**, as God had **commanded Moses** (vv. 3, 4) (Num. 27:1–7). This was done to insure that the house of Zelophehad would have a portion even though there were no male heirs. **The daughters** had to marry within their own tribe so that the land which belonged to Manasseh would not be absorbed by another tribe through intermarriage (Num. 36:1–13).

17:14–18 After Ephraim and Manasseh had received their adjoining allotments west of the Jordan, they complained that they had **only one lot** (v. 14) and that they were hemmed in by fortresses on the north (v. 16). Joshua turned all their arguments against them. When they said they needed more land because they were a numerous **people** (v. 14), he told them to use their manpower to **clear** out **the forest** in their territory and settle there (v. 15). When they complained that there were **Canaanites** within their borders who had **chariots of iron** (v. 16), he assured them that they had superior power to **drive out the Canaanites** (v. 18). The **"one lot"** of verse 14 means the combined territories of Ephraim and Manasseh west of the Jordan. When Joshua said, **"You shall not have only one lot"** (v. 17b), he didn't mean that they would get additional land but that they must occupy all the land that had been given to them.

4. The Allotment to the Rest of the Tribes (Chaps. 18, 19)

18:1 The encampment of **Israel** now changes from Gilgal to **Shiloh**. Here **the tabernacle** is **set up**, and here it remains until the days of Samuel. The division of the land continues here.

18:2–10 **Judah** and **Joseph** had received their inheritance by casting of **lots**, but there were still **seven tribes** west of the Jordan **which had not** been assigned **their inheritance**. Therefore, **Joshua** sent a group of **men**, **three** from **each tribe**, to **survey** the remaining **seven** tribes by lot.

18:11–28 Benjamin's boundaries are given in verses 11–20, and **the cities** in verses 21–28. Benjamin's portion was small, but it was choice. It occupied the heart of the land and possessed within its borders the firstfruits of Israel's labors in Canaan.

Gilgal was in Benjamin's territory, the first campsite west of the Jordan. The memorial stones were there to bear witness to the miraculous crossing of the Jordan. There the people kept the first Passover in Canaan, and began feeding on the produce of the land. There the nation was once again circumcised and the reproach of Egypt was rolled away. There was hardly a more historically significant spot in all of Canaan, because no other place taught so many spiritual lessons.

The ruins of **Jericho** were still visible in Benjamin's land. Her walls, once thought invincible, were now laid low. The portion belonging to Rahab's house remained standing as a testimony to the grace of God, which always responds to faith. A Benjamite could always visit here whenever he needed a fresh reminder that the battle was the Lord's.

Bethel (*the house of God*) caused the Benjamites to remember the faith of their fathers and the faithfulness of Israel's divine Deliverer (Gen. 28:18–22; 35:1–15).

Jerusalem was destined to be the capital city, but it was not until the son of Jesse came that the Jebusites would be driven from their mountain fortress.

Benjamin's land encompassed many evidences and signs of past, present, and future blessings. What a rich lot fell to Jacob's youngest son!

19:1–9 Simeon's inheritance was in the midst of **the inheritance of** the tribe of **Judah**. It seems that Judah's land was so **large** that the tribe could not occupy its portion, so some was assigned to **Simeon**. This is a fulfillment of Jacob's prophetic word concerning Simeon, "I will divide them in Jacob, and scatter them in Israel" (Gen. 49:7).

Beersheba and **Sheba** (v. 2) probably refer to the same place; hence a total of only **thirteen cities** as mentioned in verse 6. Some cities were listed in detailing the borders of individual portions although they were not within the land, so sometimes the number of cities given doesn't match the number stated in the text (e.g., vv. 15, 30, 38).

19:10–39 The borders of the remaining six tribes are given next: **Zebulun** (vv. 10–16); **Issachar** (vv. 17–23); **Asher** (vv. 24–31); **Naphtali** (vv. 32–39); and **Dan** (vv. 40–48). Dan received some of Judah's cities (cf. v. 41 with 15:33).

19:40-48 The original territory allotted to **Dan** was in the southwest, bordering on the Mediterranean Sea, and included the cities of **Joppa** and **Ekron** (vv. 40–46). Later, when this territory proved too small, some of the tribe migrated to Laish (**Leshem**) in the northeast and changed the name of the city to **Dan** (vv. 47, 48; cf. Judg. 18).

19:49–51 Verse 51 brings to **an end** the division of **the country**. The cities of refuge had to be set apart (chap. 20) and the Levitical cities had yet to be appointed (chap. 21), but Joshua's work was almost done. He received **Timnath Serah**, **according to the word of the Lord** (v. 50).

C. The Cities of Refuge (Chap. 20)

The next step was to set apart six **cities of refuge**, three **on** each **side of the Jordan** River, where a manslayer might **flee** from **the avenger of blood**. A manslayer was someone who **accidentally** killed another **person**. The **avenger of blood** was usually a close relative of the slain person who sought to avenge the dead. If the manslayer could flee to a city of refuge, he found sanctuary there **until the death of the . . . high priest**. **Then** he could **return . . . to his** native **city** in safety.

THE CITIES OF REFUGE

The cities of refuge are interesting and of theological importance. MacLear gives traditional details about the cities:

> Jewish commentators tell us how in later times, in order that the asylum offered to the involuntary homicide might be more secure—(a) the roads leading to the cities of refuge were always kept in thorough repair, and required to be about 32 cubits (about 48 feet) broad; (b) all obstructions were removed that might stay the flier's foot or hinder his speed; (c) no hillock was left, no river was allowed over which there was not a bridge;

(d) at every turning there were posts erected bearing the words 'Refuge,' to guide the unhappy man in his flight; (e) when once settled in such a city the manslayer had a convenient habitation assigned to him, and the citizens were to teach him some trade that he might support himself.[14]

These cities picture the nation of Israel and its guilt in connection with the slaying of the Messiah. Christ is the City of Refuge to whom penitent Israel may flee for sanctuary. D. L. Moody noted that "the cities of refuge are a type of Christ, and their names are significant in that connection."[15]

The cities of refuge and the meaning of the names are as follows:

West of Jordan
Kedesh—Holiness
Shechem—Strength
Kirjath-Arba or Hebron—Fellowship

East of Jordan
Ramoth-Gilead—Uplifting
Golan—Happiness
Bezer—Safety

Thus Christ provides every blessing suggested by the names of these cities. A glance at the map will show that the cities of refuge were strategically located so that no point in the land was more than thirty miles from one of them. Moody makes the application:

> As the cities of refuge were so situated as to be accessible from every part of the land, so Christ is very accessible to needy sinners (1 John 2:1, 2).[16]

Notice the parallels between the temporal salvation offered the manslayer in the cities of refuge and the eternal salvation offered the sinner in Christ. The roads to the city were clear and well-marked, just like the way of salvation, so that none would make a mistake and lose his life. The cities were spread throughout the land and easily accessible to all, even as Christ is accessible to all men. Crisis drove people to the city of refuge, and many times a crisis is needed to drive people to the Lord Jesus for refuge. There was no neutral ground for the guilty person—he was either safe in the city or subject to the wrath of the blood avenger. Each individual is either safe in Christ or under the judgment of God (John 3:36).‡

D. The Levitical Cities (Chap. 21)

21:1–42 Forty-eight cities (v. 41) with their common-lands for pasture, including the cities of refuge, were assigned to **the Levites** as the Lord had commanded (Num. 35:2–8).

Kohathites:
(a) The sons **of Aaron** (i.e., the priests)—**thirteen cities** out of **Judah, . . . Simeon, and . . . Benjamin**.
(b) **The rest of the** Kohathites—**ten cities** out of **Ephraim, . . . Dan, and . . . the half-tribe of Manasseh**.

Gershonites: **thirteen cities** out of **Issachar, . . . Asher, . . . Naphtali, and . . . the half-tribe of Manasseh**.

Merarites: **twelve cities** out of **Reuben, . . . Gad, and . . . Zebulun**.

Every tribe gave four cities except Judah and Simeon, which gave nine cities between them, and Naphtali, which gave three cities.

The cities **of refuge**, being cities of **the Levites** (vv. 13, 21, 27, 32, 36, 38), were scattered throughout all the tribes of Israel to fulfill the prophecy of

Jacob (Gen. 49:5–7) and to better facilitate their teaching ministry to the nation.

21:43 This verse must be read in the light of other Scripture. It does not mean that Israel occupied **all the land** from the river of Egypt to the Euphrates; instead, it means that the **land** which Joshua divided was in fulfillment of God's promise that He would give them every place that the sole of their feet walked upon (Josh. 1:3).

21:44 Likewise, verse 44 must be interpreted carefully. There were still **enemies** within the land; not all the Canaanites had been destroyed. But that was not God's fault; He fulfilled His promise by defeating every foe against which the Israelites fought. If there were still undefeated foes and pockets of resistance, it was because Israel did not claim God's promise.

21:45 Note verse 45. **The LORD** had fulfilled every promise. **Not** one **word failed.** What a tribute to God's faithfulness! But Israel did not appropriate every promise.

E. The Altar East of the Jordan (Chap. 22)

22:1–9 When the land west of the Jordan had been divided, **Joshua** permitted **the Reubenites, the Gadites, and half the tribe of Manasseh** to **return** to their territory east **of the Jordan**, as originally agreed. He also told them to take with them their share of **the spoil** from the battles they had fought.

It was over seven years since they had left their loved ones to fight the Canaanites. They endured the hardships of combat until the land was secured. We too are called upon by our Commander to endure hardships and fight the good fight of faith to further the kingdom of God on earth (1 Tim. 6:12; 2 Tim. 2:3). This kind of sacrifice is not easy, but it is an essential ingredient in the life that pleases God. Men with fiery zeal are needed on the battlefield today:

> Must I be carried to the skies on
> flowery beds of ease,
> While others fought to win the prize,
> and sailed through bloody seas?
>
> Sure I must fight if I would reign;
> increase my courage, Lord;
> I'll bear the toil, endure the pain,
> supported by Thy Word.
>
> —*Isaac Watts*

22:10, 11 On the way home these men decided to erect **an altar** near the banks of **the Jordan**. When the other nine and a half tribes heard about it, they were highly incensed. They feared that it was a rival altar to the one at Shiloh. They feared too that it might become an idolatrous altar in time to come and that God would punish the entire nation because of it.

22:12–20 Before declaring **war** on the tribes east of the Jordan, **the children of Israel sent** a delegation to interview them and offered them land west of the Jordan if they considered their own territory **unclean** (v. 19).

In dealing with the men who built the altar, **Phinehas** and the others recalled how Israel had suffered because of **the iniquity of Peor** (v. 17; cf. Num. 25) and **the trespass** of **Achan** (v. 20; cf. chap. 7).

They saw this altar as another threat to their welfare; hence their strong reaction to it. As a people they had learned that sin defiled the whole camp, and that God held the nation responsible for the behavior of its individuals.

22:21–29 Then the men **of Reuben, . . . Gad, and half the tribe of Manasseh** explained that this was

not an altar of **sacrifice** at all. It was simply a memorial **altar**, testifying to future generations that the tribes east of the Jordan were indeed a part of the nation of Israel.

22:30–34 The other tribes were **pleased** by this explanation, and war was averted. The eastern tribes **called the altar** *Witness*, meaning that it was **a witness between** the tribes on both sides of the Jordan **that the LORD is** the true **God**.

F. Joshua's Farewell Address to the Leaders of Israel (Chap. 23)

This is the first of two farewell addresses by **Joshua**. Here he spoke to the leadership of Israel.

Joshua's command to be both courageous and scriptural (v. 6) echo the words of the Lord to him years earlier (1:7). He had since proven the veracity of them in the crucible of life and was now able to confidently pass them on to the following generation.

He reminded them of the faithfulness of God in fulfilling His promises concerning the land and concerning its heathen inhabitants. God would continue to **drive . . . out** the enemy, but the people would have to be obedient to Him. Above all, they should keep themselves free from the idolatry of the nations or from intermarrying with the Canaanites. Otherwise these pagans would be a continual source of trouble to Israel.

None of God's words had **failed** (v. 14). This does not mean that all of the land was as yet in Jewish hands, for the Lord Himself had said that He would not drive out the inhabitants all at once but gradually (Deut. 7:22). The fact that not one promise of the Lord's had yet failed was the strong encouragement that Joshua was using to urge the leaders to finish the job he had started. To this exhortation he attached a warning (vv. 5, 16) that Jehovah would be just as faithful in destroying them **from** off **the good land** as He would be in destroying the Canaanites, if they forgot their covenant and turned to idols.

The NT parallel to this chapter is 2 Corinthians 6:14–18. Separation is vital for the man of God. We cannot cleave to the Lord and be bound to His enemies at the same time.

G. Joshua's Farewell Address to the People of Israel (24:1–15)

24:1–14 The second farewell message, this one to the people, was delivered at **Shechem**.

Joshua reviewed the history of the people of God, beginning with **Terah** and continuing on through the time of **Abraham**, **Isaac**, and **Jacob**. He reminded the people of the mighty deliverance from Egypt, the wilderness wandering, and the victory over the Moabites on the east side of Jordan. Then he recounted their entrance into the Promised Land, their victory at **Jericho**, and their destruction of **kings** in Canaan (vv. 2–13). The **darkness** in verse 7 points back to Exodus 14:19, 20, where the cloud produced light for the Israelites and darkness for the Egyptians.

In this succinct summary of history from Genesis to Joshua, one outstanding fact is evident: the sovereignty of God. Notice how He tells the story: **I took** (v. 3), **I gave** (v. 4), **I sent** (v. 5), **I brought** (vv. 6–8), **I would not listen** (v. 10), **I delivered** (v. 11), **I sent** (v. 12), **I have given** (v. 13). Jehovah works according to His eternal purposes, and who can stay His hand? Such a God is to be feared and obeyed (v. 14).

24:15 The choice here was not between **the LORD** and idols: Joshua assumed that the people had *already* decided *against* serving God. So he challenged them to **choose** between **the gods** which their ancestors had served in Mesopotamia and **the gods of the Amorites** that they had found in Canaan. Joshua's noble decision for himself and his household has been an inspiration to succeeding generations of believers: **"But as for me and my house, we will serve the LORD."**

H. The Covenant Renewed at Shechem

24:16–28 When the people promised to **serve** Jehovah, **Joshua** said, **"You cannot serve the LORD"** (v. 19). This means that they could not serve Jehovah and worship idols too. Joshua doubtless realized that the people would drift into idolatry, because even then they had **foreign gods** in their tents (v. 23). **The people** persisted in promising allegiance to their **God**, so **Joshua** erected **a large stone** marker **under the oak** as **a witness** of the **covenant** made by Israel. (The **sanctuary of the LORD** mentioned in verse 26 does not refer to the tabernacle, which was at Shiloh, but simply to a holy place.)

Regarding the problem of idols, Carl Armerding writes:

> Idolatry seems to have been one of Israel's besetting sins. Their earliest ancestors served other gods, as we have seen (v. 2). When Jacob and his family left Laban, it was Rachel who carried off her father's gods (Gen. 31:30–34). But when they arrived in the land, Jacob ordered his household to put away these "strange gods," and he hid them under an oak tree that was by Shechem (Gen. 35:2, 4). And in the same place Joshua urged his generation to put away the gods which their fathers served (v. 14).[17]

I. The Death of Joshua

24:29–33 Joshua . . . died at the age of **one hundred and ten years** and was **buried** in the city **of his inheritance**. The people of **Israel** remained true to **the LORD** as long as the men of Joshua's generation lived. We do not know who penned the last verses of the book, nor is such knowledge necessary, or else it surely would have been included.

The bones of Joseph, which had been carried **out of Egypt** by his request, were now **buried at Shechem** (Gen. 50:24; Ex. 13:19).

Finally, **Eleazar the son of Aaron died** and was **buried in the mountains of Ephraim**.

Three burials are mentioned in the last five verses of this book: Joshua's (vv. 29–31), Joseph's (v. 32), and Eleazar's (v. 33). All three were buried in Joseph's territory. All three had served their God and their country well. Joshua and Joseph were great deliverers during their lives, and Eleazar was a deliverer in his death, for he was the high priest and his death set free all who had fled to a city of refuge (20:6). Like the books of Genesis and Deuteronomy, Joshua closes with the toll of the death bell over great and godly men. "God buries His workmen but continues His work."

ENDNOTES

[1](Intro) Irving L. Jensen, *Joshua, Rest-Land Won*, p. 14.

[2](1:1–9) T. Austin Sparks, *What Is Man?* p. 104.

[3](2:1) C. F. Keil and Franz Delitzsch, "Joshua," in *Biblical Commentary on the Old Testament*, VI:34.

[4](3:14–17) Donald K. Campbell, "Joshua," in *The Bible Knowledge Commentary*, I:335.

[5](3:14–17) *Ibid.*

[6](7:11–26) Hugh J. Blair, "Joshua," *The New Bible Commentary*, p. 229.

[7](8:30–35) R. Jamieson, A. R. Fausset, and D. Brown, *Critical and Experimental Commentary*, II:23.

[8](10:12–15) Three views that recognize that a unique miracle took place and explain (rather than explain away) the text are as follows:

1. That God actually restrained (or halted) the earth's rotation while the sun was above Joshua, making the rotation last forty-eight hours. There are parallels in other ancient cultures that speak of "a long day," which may well have been Joshua's long day.
2. Translating "stand still" (Heb. *dōm*) as "leave off" or "cease" (as in 2 Kgs. 4:6 and Lam. 2:18), some see this as a prayer for relief from the blazing sun on Joshua's troops, the very long hailstorm being God's answer to Joshua's prayer.
3. Since Joshua attacked in the early morning, some believe he was praying for the sun to "hold off" and for semi-darkness to continue. The hailstorm would then have been God's answer to prayer.

The first view seems to fit in best with the text: "So the sun stood still in the midst of heaven, and did not hasten to go down for about a whole day" (v. 13b).

[9](10:12–15) C. H. Spurgeon, *Spurgeon's Devotional Bible*, p. 168. For a brief but helpful treatment of the scientific aspects of the text see Chapter X of *Difficulties in the Bible* by R. A. Torrey (Chicago: Moody Press, 1907).

[10](10:12–15) Matthew Henry, *Matthew Henry's Commentary on the Whole Bible*, II:59.

[11](10:40–43) John Haley, *Alleged Discrepancies of the Bible*, p. 324.

[12](13:1–6) Under Solomon the kingdom did reach to that part of the Euphrates River in the northwest as far as lands under tribute were concerned, but if the entire river is meant as an eastern boundary it must still be a future event.

[13](15:21–63) Keil and Delitzsch maintain that these and similar numerical problems in the OT are simply copyists' errors ("Joshua," pp. 163–64). For further discussion on apparent discrepancies, see the Commentary on 2 Chronicles.

[14](Essay) MacLear, further documentation unavailable.

[15](Essay) D. L. Moody, *Notes from My Bible*, pp. 48, 49.

[16](Essay) *Ibid.*, p. 49.

[17](24:16–28) Carl Armerding, *The Fight for Palestine*, p. 149.

BIBLIOGRAPHY

Blair, Hugh J. "Joshua." In *The New Bible Commentary*. Grand Rapids: Wm. B. Eerdmans Publishing Company, 1953.

Campbell, Donald K. "Joshua." In *The Bible Knowledge Commentary*. Wheaton, IL: Victor Books, 1985.

Freedman, H. "Joshua." In *Soncino Books of the Bible*, Vol. 2. London: The Soncino Press, 1967.

Grant, F. W. "Joshua." In *The Numerical Bible*, Vol. 2. Neptune, N.J.: Loizeaux Bros., 1977.

Henry, Matthew. "Joshua." In *Matthew Henry's Commentary on the Whole Bible*. Vol. 2. McLean, VA: MacDonald Publishing Company, n.d.

Jensen, Irving L. *Joshua: Rest-Land Won*. Everyman's Bible Commentary. Chicago: Moody Press, 1966.

Keil, C. F., and Franz Delitzsch. "Joshua." In *Biblical Commentary on the Old Testament*. Vol. 6. Grand

Rapids: Wm. B. Eerdmans Publishing Company, 1971.

Kroll, Woodrow Michael. "Joshua." In the *Liberty Bible Commentary. Old Testament*. Lynchburg, VA: The Old Time Gospel Hour, 1982.

Pink, Arthur W. *Gleanings in Joshua*. Chicago: Moody Press, 1964.

JUDGES

Introduction

"There is much in Judges to sadden the heart of the reader; perhaps no book in the Bible witnesses so clearly to our human frailty. But there are also unmistakable signs of the divine compassion and long-suffering.... As the lives of these lesser-saviours are considered, there may be a realization of the need in modern times of a greater Saviour, of unblemished life, who is able to effect a perfect deliverance, not only in time but for eternity."

—Arthur E. Cundall

I. Unique Place in the Canon

God bringing strength out of human weakness is uniquely chronicled in this fascinating book. In fact, in a sense, the book of Judges is a commentary on the three verses, "But God has chosen the foolish things of the world to put to shame the wise, and God has chosen the weak things of the world to put to shame the things which are mighty; and the base things of the world and the things which are despised God has chosen, and the things that are not, to bring to nothing the things that are, that no flesh should glory in His presence" (1 Cor. 1:27–29). For example, Ehud was a left-handed Benjamite (3:12–30), the left hand being thought of as weaker than the right. Shamgar used an oxgoad, a rather disreputable weapon, with which to slay 600 enemies (3:31). Deborah was a member of the "weaker sex" (though she herself was not weak!) (4:1—5:31). Barak's 10,000 foot-soldiers were a poor match, humanly speaking, for Sisera's 900 iron chariots (4:10, 13). Jael, also a member of the weaker sex, killed Sisera by driving a tent pin through his skull (4:21). She held the pin with her left hand (5:26, Septuagint). Gideon marched against the enemy with an army which the Lord had reduced from 32,000 to 300 (7:1–8). Barley bread, the food of the poor, suggests poverty and feebleness (7:13). The unconventional weapons of Gideon's army were earthenware pitchers, torches, and trumpets (7:16), and the pitchers had to be smashed (7:19). Abimelech was felled by a woman's hand hurling a piece of millstone (9:53). The name "Tola" means worm (10:1). When we meet Samson's mother, she is a nameless, barren woman (13:2). And Samson killed 1000 Philistines with the jawbone of a donkey (15:15).

II. Authorship

Although Judges is anonymous, the Jewish Talmud and early Christian tradition say that Judges, Ruth, and Samuel were all written by Samuel. This view may be supported by 1 Samuel 10:25, which indicates the prophet was a writer. Also the internal indications of date of writing fit in with Samuel's *time* at the very least.

III. Date

Judges is best dated in the first half-century of the monarchy (1050–1000 B.C.) for the following reasons:

First of all, the repeated phrase "in those days there was no king in Israel" (17:6; 18:1; 19:1; 21:25) suggests that there *was* a king at the time of writing.

Second, since 1:21 shows the Jebusites were still in Jerusalem, a date before David captured that city is needed. Finally, Gezer, mentioned in 1:29, was later given to Solomon by Pharaoh as a wedding present, implying a date before that event. Thus Saul's reign or the early years of David's rule seem very likely.

IV. Background and Theme

The book of Judges takes up the history of the nation of Israel after Joshua's generation had died. The people had failed to drive out the heathen inhabitants of Canaan completely. In fact, they had mingled with the pagans and were practicing idolatry. As a result, God repeatedly delivered His people into the hands of Gentile oppressors. This servitude brought the Jews to the place of repentance and contrition. When they cried out to the Lord to deliver them, He raised up judges. It is from these leaders that the book gets its name.

The events in the book span about 325 years, from Othniel to Samson.

The judges were military leaders rather than simply jurists. By heroic deeds of faith they executed God's judgment or overthrew their oppressors, thereby restoring a measure of peace and freedom to the people. Twelve judges were raised up to deliver Israel. Some are given extensive coverage in the book while others are mentioned in only one or two verses. They came from nine different tribes and delivered their people from the Mesopotamians, Moabites, Philistines, Canaanites, Midianites, and Ammonites. No judge ruled over the entire nation until Samuel.

The book of Judges is not strictly chronological. The first two chapters contain introductory material, both historical and prophetical. The record of the judges themselves (chaps. 3—16) is not necessarily chronological. Some of the judges may have been conquering their enemies at the same time but in different sections of the land. This is important to remember, since the number of years mentioned in the book, if added consecutively, totals over 400, which is more time than the Bible allots for this period (Acts 13:19, 20; 1 Kgs. 6:1).

The closing chapters (17—21) record events that took place during the time of the judges, but they are placed at the end of the book to give a picture of the religious, moral, and civil corruption in Israel during this period. The character of the times is well-described in the key verse (17:6): "In those days there was no king in Israel, everyone did what was right in his own eyes."

If we believe that every word of God is pure and that all Scripture is profitable, then it follows that Judges contains important spiritual themes and lessons for us. Some of these lessons are hidden in the names of the Gentile oppressors and the judges

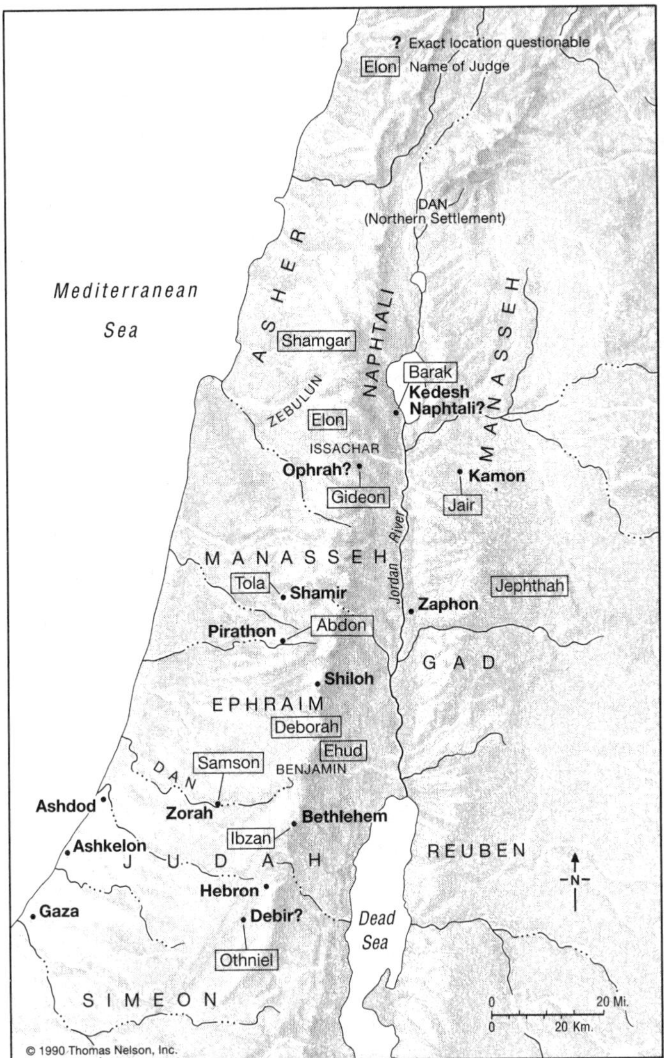

The Judges of Israel

who delivered Israel. The oppressors picture the powers of this world that seek to bring God's people into bondage. The judges symbolize the means by which we fight the spiritual warfare.

In our comments we have included some practical applications, many taken from old classic works.[1]

There is always a danger of taking the study of types or figures to an extreme. We have tried to avoid any interpretations that are strained or fanciful. Also, it must be admitted that the meanings of some of the names are uncertain. We have given alternate meanings where such are possible.

OUTLINE

I. REVIEW AND PREVIEW (1:1—3:6)
   A. Looking Back (1:1—2:10)
   B. Looking Forward (2:11—3:6)

II. THE TIMES OF THE JUDGES (3:7—16:31)
   A. Othniel (3:7–11)
   B. Ehud (3:12–30)
   C. Shamgar (3:31)
   D. Deborah and Barak (Chaps. 4, 5)
      1. Their Story in Prose (Chap. 4)
      2. Their Story in Song (Chap. 5)
   E. Gideon (6:1—8:32)
      1. Gideon's Call to Service (Chap. 6)
      2. Gideon's Three Hundred (Chap. 7)
      3. Gideon's Victory over the Philistines (8:1–32)
   F. Abimelech's Usurpation (8:33—9:57)
   G. Tola and Jair (10:1–5)
   H. Jephthah (10:6—12:7)
      1. Israel's Misery (10:6–18)
      2. Jephthah's Defense of Israel (11:1–28)
      3. Jephthah's Vow (11:29–40)
      4. Jephthah Slays the Ephraimites (12:1–7)
   I. Ibzan, Elon, and Abdon (12:8–15)
   J. Samson (Chaps. 13—16)
      1. Samson's Godly Heritage (Chap. 13)
      2. Samson's Feast and Riddle (Chap. 14)
      3. Samson's Reprisals (Chap. 15)
      4. Samson Duped by Delilah (Chap. 16)

III. RELIGIOUS, MORAL, AND POLITICAL DECAY (Chaps. 17—21)
   A. Micah's Religious Establishment (Chap. 17)
   B. Micah and the Danites (Chap. 18)
   C. The Levite and His Concubine (Chap. 19)
   D. The War with Benjamin (Chaps. 20, 21)

Commentary

I. REVIEW AND PREVIEW (1:1—3:6)

A. Looking Back (1:1—2:10)

1:1–3 After the death of Joshua (cf. 2:8), the tribe of **Judah** took the leadership in warring **against the Canaanites** in the south. In spite of God's promise of victory, **Judah** sought the assistance of the tribe of **Simeon**, showing that their faith lacked complete dependence on God's Word.

1:4–7 Their first victory was over the inhabitants of **Bezek**. After slaying **ten thousand men**, they **cut off** the **thumbs and big toes** of the king, as he had done to his foes. He should have been put to death, as the Lord had commanded (Deut. 7:24), but instead he was only maimed. Then he was taken to Jerusalem, where he later died. This foreshadowed Israel's disobedience in dealing with the heathen in their land. Rather than completely crushing them, the Israelites only crippled them. Such partial obedience was disobedience and would cost the Jews dearly in the days ahead.

1:8 **Judah** had a measure of success **against Jerusalem**, putting **the city** to the torch. But neither Judah nor Benjamin could drive the Jebusites out of their fortress (see commentary on Josh. 15:21–63). This was not done until the time of David (2 Sam. 5:6, 7).

1:9–15 The capture of **Hebron** is here credited to **Judah**; Joshua 14 and 15 tell us that Caleb was the one responsible for the conquest of this city. There is no discrepancy here, since **Caleb** was from the tribe of Judah. These verses (9, 10) probably refer to Caleb's conquest of the city (cf. v. 20) and not to a subsequent expedition after Joshua's death, even as the capture of **Kirjath Sepher** by **Othniel** is repeated in verses 11–15, although it took place previously (Josh. 15:16–19).

1:16 The Kenites continued to dwell **with the children of Judah**, though they never were truly converted.

1:17–21 Other conquests of **Judah** include **Hormah**, **Gaza**, **Ashkelon**, **and Ekron**, but the victories were not complete. **The inhabitants of the lowland—elhad chariots of iron**, and Judah did not have the faith to launch an attack against them. They were unwilling to persevere in difficult circumstances. Verse 21 indicates that Judges was written before David took Jerusalem.

1:22–26 Only the two tribes of **Joseph** are credited with other victories. (These verses perhaps refer to the conquest of **Bethel** while Joshua was still living [Josh. 12:16], just as the previous verses concerning Hebron and Kirjath Sepher hark back to the days of that great general.) They attacked **the city** of **Bethel**, **formerly** called **Luz**, and destroyed it. But their mistake was in promising safety to a collaborator. He promptly started building another **city** by the **name** of **Luz** in **the land of the Hittites**. Unjudged sin survives and has to be met later.

1:27–36 In the rest of the chapter, seven central and northern tribes are named as having failed to **drive . . . the Canaanites** from their territory: **Benjamin** (v. 21), **Manasseh** (vv. 27, 28), **Ephraim** (v. 29), **Zebulun** (v. 30),

Asher (vv. 31, 32), **Naphtali** (v. 33), and **Dan** (vv. 34–36).

2:1–5 **The Angel of the LORD** (the Lord Jesus) rebuked the people at **Bochim** (weepers) for their disobedience. Verse 1 says that He **came up from Gilgal** (the place of blessing) **to Bochim** (the place of weeping). Israel had gone from the place of victory to the place of mourning. They had failed to drive out the Canaanites and to destroy their idolatrous altars. Therefore the Lord would refuse to **drive . . . out . . . the inhabitants of** the **land**, but would instead allow them to harass the Israelites. Verses 1–5 thus give the underlying reason for the oppression which followed. No wonder **the people . . . wept** and **called the . . . place Bochim**!

2:6–10 Verses 6–10 review the close of Joshua's life and the generation that outlived him. In Deuteronomy 6 the Lord gave some specific commands to His people. Failure to obey them led to the sad state of affairs described in verse 10, where a lack of spiritual leadership is seen to result in a corresponding lack of obedience on the part of God's people. The previous **generation** had not taught their children to fear **the LORD** and to keep His commandments. The neglect of the fathers led to the apostasy of their sons.

B. Looking Forward (2:11—3:6)

2:11–19 The remaining verses, on the other hand, give a preview of the entire period of the judges. They trace the fourfold cycle which characterized that time:

Sin (vv. 11–13)
Servitude (14, 15)
Supplication (not stated here, but see 3:9; 3:15; 4:3; etc.)
Salvation (vv. 16–18)

This pattern of behavior has also been described as:

Rebellion
Retribution
Repentance
Rest

This synopsis of Judges (vv. 11–19), as Jensen points out, brings into focus the two divergent truths evident throughout the book:

> (1) the desperate wickedness of the human heart, revealing its ingratitude, stubbornness, rebellion, and folly; (2) God's longsuffering, patience, love and mercy. No book in the Bible brings these two truths into sharper contrast—the utter failure of Israel and the persistent grace of Jehovah![2]

2:20–23 Because Israel persisted in disobedience, God decided to allow the nations to remain in the land as chastisement upon His people (vv. 20–23). Punishment for disobedience was not the only reason the Lord did not drive out all the Canaanites. He left them *to* **test** Israel (v. 22; 3:4) and *to train* succeeding generations for war (3:1, 2). We can gain insight from this as to why the Lord allows believers to go through problems and trials. He wants to know if **"they will keep the ways of the LORD . . . or not"** (v. 22).

3:1–4 **The nations** that were **left** as a trial to Israel are listed in verse 3: **five lords of the Philistines, all the Canaanites, the Sidonians, and the Hivites who dwelt in Mt. Lebanon**.

Now the first cycle begins: sin (vv. 5–7); servitude (v. 8); supplication (v. 9a); salvation (vv. 9b–11).

3:5, 6 Six of the seven pagan nations among whom the Israelites lived are given. To the nations listed in verse 3, **the Hittites, the Amorites, the Perizzites, the Hivites, and the**

Jebusites are added here.The seventh was the Girgashites (Josh. 3:10; 24:11).

Dr. Cohen pinpoints the beginning of each downward cycle concisely:

> The Israelites ignored the warning of Moses (Deut. vii. 3f.) and intermarried with the natives, the consequence being the adoption of their seductive cults.[3]

II. THE TIMES OF THE JUDGES (3:7—16:31)

A. Othniel (3:7–11)

3:7, 8 The people **did evil in the sight of the Lord** by marrying the heathen and then worshiping their idols. Impurity and immorality (v. 6) lead to idolatry (v. 7). God had warned them earlier of the grave consequences of mingling with the inhabitants of Canaan. They were a holy people and must remain separate from defilement if they would know the blessing of God (Deut. 7:3–6). God punished Israel by delivering the nation **into the hand of Chushan-Rishathaim, king of Mesopotamia,** for **eight years**. His name means *Cush, man of double wickedness*.

3:9–11 In response to the penitent cry of His people, **the LORD** then **raised up . . . Othniel**, a nephew of Caleb, to deliver them from their enemy and to usher in **forty years** of peace. **Othniel** (*lion of God*) had previously taken Kirjath Sepher (*city of the book*), turning it into Debir (*a living oracle*). This is what faith does with God's Word.

B. Ehud (3:12–30)

3:12–14 In the second cycle, Israel was subjugated by **Eglon**, the **king of Moab**, for **eighteen years**.

3:15–30 The military leader whom God gave to Israel at this time was **Ehud, . . .** a left-handed man of the tribe of Benjamin. He was commissioned by the people to take a gift as **tribute to** King **Eglon**. He also hid **a double-edged . . . dagger . . . under his clothes**. After the gift had been delivered, the king probably felt at ease concerning the attitude of his Jewish subjects. Then **Ehud** asked for a private audience to discuss **a secret message**. When **all** the attendants had been sent away, **Ehud** assassinated the king and fled. By the time the deed was discovered, Ehud had assembled the men of Israel, marched against Moab, and **killed about ten thousand** retreating soldiers. Israel then enjoyed **rest for eighty years**.

When *meditation* (Gera, v. 15) gives birth to *praise* (Ehud), the *world ruler* (Eglon), is doomed by the sharp, two-edged *sword* (the Bible), even when the Word is used by a left-handed man.

Othniel was from Judah, the mightiest tribe in Israel. Ehud was from Benjamin, now the smallest tribe. God can use the great or the small to gain the victory, since the power is from Him anyway. Men are simply the agents of deliverance, not the originators of it.

C. Shamgar (3:31)

3:31 Only one verse is devoted to this judge. He slew **six hundred men of the Philistines with an oxgoad** (a sharp, pointed instrument used to prod oxen). This is another of the instances in Judges where God used a "weak thing" to accomplish a mighty victory. A *pilgrim* (**Shamgar**) wielding the *Word of God* (**oxgoad**—see Eccl. 12:11) can put to rout wanderers (**Philistines**) among God's people.

CHART OF THE JUDGES

Oppressor	*Meaning or Type*	*Years of Oppression*	*Deliverer*	*Meaning*	*Years of Rest*	*Ref.*
Chushan-Rishathaim King of Mesopotamia	Cush—man of double wickedness Self-exaltation, pride	8	Othniel	Lion of God (The power of God)	40	3:7–11
Eglon King of Moab	Circle Worldly profession	18	Ehud	Majesty	80	3:12–30
Philistines	Wanderers among God's people or carnal religion		Shamgar	Stranger or pilgrim		3:31
Jabin King of Hazor in Canaan	Understanding or human intellect Settlement	20	Deborah	Honeybee	40	4:1—5:31
Commander-in-Chief Sisera	Battle array Meaning unknown		Barak	Lightning		
Midianites	Contention, strife, the world	7	Gideon (Jerubbaal)	The cutter down Let Baal plead for himself or Baal-fighter	40	6:1—8:35
			Abimelech a Usurper	My father was king	3	9:1–57
			Tola	A worm	23	10:1, 2
			Jair	Light-giver	22	10:3–5
Ammonites	Rationalism or false doctrine	18	Jephthah	He will open	6	10:6—12:7
			Ibzan	Meaning uncertain	7	12:8–15
			Elon	Meaning uncertain	10	
			Abdon	Service	8	
Philistines	Carnal religion	40	Samson	Little sun	20	13:1—16:31

D. Deborah and Barak (Chaps. 4, 5)

1. *Their Story in Prose (Chap. 4)*

4:1–3 The next oppressor was **Jabin, king of** the Canaanite stronghold of **Hazor. The commander of his army was Sisera**. With his boasted **nine hundred chariots of** war he held the Israelites under his domination **for twenty years.**

4:4–9 God did not raise up a man this time. He raised up a member of the "weaker sex," **a prophetess** named **Deborah**. (It is not the norm for a woman to occupy such a place of spiritual authority, but this was a time of declension. She should not be used as an example of the woman's role in the church today, since she is the exception and not the rule. Also, this was Israel, not the church.) Deborah commissioned **Barak** to **go** north and attack Sisera's forces, but he refused to go unless she accompanied him. Because of his reluctance to lead he was told that the victory over **Sisera** would be given to **a woman** rather than to him.

4:10–16 Deborah took the initiative in calling Barak and ordering him to engage Sisera in battle, as the Lord had commanded. But **Barak**, not Deborah, is commended for his faith in Hebrews 11:32. Though somewhat hesitant at first, he obeyed the Lord by faith and delivered Israel. (According to the NIV, **Hobab** in verse 11 should be listed as *the "brother-in-law* **of Moses**," not **father-in-law**, as in the NKJV.)

> Barak openly showed his force of 10,000 on the southern slopes of Mount Tabor. Sisera rose to the bait. He and his chariots crossed the dry Kishon riverbed at the ford just south of Harosheth. They raced southeast along the ancient highway toward Taanach. Israelites from the south, from Ephraim, entered the valley at Jenin (5:14) and joined forces with Barak and his northern troops in the valley below Taanach, south of the Kishon. Deborah called for the attack (14). Footmen against chariots! At the critical moment rain fell, turning the plain into mire, utterly confounding the chariots and horses (5:4). The advantage was now fully with the infantry. ... Barak pressed the attack. Sisera was separated from his men and fled. The leaderless troops, not used to fighting on foot, ran for their base. The rains continued and the Kishon rose to a torrent. Those who were not slain by the Israelites in pursuit were swept away by the Kishon as they tried to cross the ford to Harosheth ... [vv. 10–16; cf. 5:20, 21].—*(Daily Notes of the Scripture Union)*

4:17–24 Seeking refuge in **the tent of Jael**, a **Kenite**, **Sisera** was given food and lodging. While he slept, **Jael** hammered **a tent peg . . . into his temple**. As **Barak** passed by in pursuit, **Jael** invited him in to see the corpse of his enemy. Thus was Deborah's prophecy of verse 9 fulfilled. God used a mere honeybee (Deborah) to cast down human reason (**Jabin**), when it exalted itself against the knowledge of God. The judgment came upon the foe like lightning (**Barak**). **Jael** (climber) used **a tent peg** (the witness of her pilgrim life) to bring down the pretensions of the mighty. The **hammer** speaks of the Word (Jer. 23:29).

2. *Their Story in Song (Chap. 5)*

5:1–5 The song of **Deborah and Barak** is a classic of inspired literature. After opening with **praise to the Lord**, Deborah recalled the Lord's triumphant march when the Israelites left the borders **of Edom** to move toward the Promised Land. All opposition melted **before** the majesty of **the Lord God of Israel**.

5:6, 7 Then she described conditions **in the days of Shamgar**. The dangers were such that **the highways were deserted**. **Travelers** used less direct routes in order to avoid robber bands. The villagers dared not venture out of their homes—that is, **until . . . Deborah arose**.

5:8 Because the people had turned to idols, the land was given over to **war** and bloodshed, and **Israel** did not have weapons with which to fight.

5:9–15 But when God raised up **Deborah** and **Barak**, some of the rulers of Israel and some of the people stepped forward gallantly to help. There were men **from Ephraim**, men from **Benjamin**, men **from Machir** (the tribe of Manasseh), and men **from Zebulun** and **Issachar**.

5:16, 17 And then Deborah remembered those who did *not* come to help. **Reuben** had **great searchings of heart** but stayed **among the sheepfolds**. **Gilead** (Gad) did not cross **the Jordan** to join in the battle. **Dan** remained **in ships**, and **Asher** sat idly **at the seashore**.

Scripture notes carefully those who fought in the battle and those who stood passively by, unwilling to risk their safety in Jehovah's cause. And so it is today: The Lord knows who is actively confronting the world and the devil and who is sitting back and simply watching. There is a time of reward coming, but it is also a time of loss (1 Cor. 3:10–15).

5:18–22 **Zebulun** and **Naphtali** were outstanding, risking their lives for Jehovah without pay (**they took no spoils of silver**). They were in the thick of the battle against **the kings of Canaan**. The forces of nature were on their side because they were on the Lord's side.

5:23–27 **Meroz** was singled out for a **curse** for failing to **come to** Jehovah's **help**. The men of this city remained neutral when help was needed against the foe. But **Jael**, living in a tent, was **blessed** for her bravery and cunning in destroying **Sisera**. Our Lord's mother is the only other woman who is specifically called blessed among women (Luke 1:42).

5:28–31 Sisera's **mother**, in the meantime, was looking out **the window**, waiting for her son to return with the spoils of victory. She could not understand his delay. **Her wisest ladies** assured her that he must be **dividing the** booty with his men. But **Sisera** would never return. And let his fate be the same for **all . . . enemies** of Jehovah.

On the other hand, may **those who love** the Lord be as the rising **sun**. The chapter closes with the statement that **the land had rest for forty years** after Sisera's death.

E. Gideon (6:1—8:32)

1. Gideon's Call to Service (Chap. 6)

6:1–6 In the next cycle, the Israelites were oppressed by **the Midianites**. These were marauding Bedouin bands who conducted raids on Israel's crops, stripping **the land** like **locusts** and stealing the **livestock**. Israel's backsliding resulted in poverty, slavery, and fear. Those whom Israel had once conquered were now her masters. When we turn from the Lord as Christians, old habits enslave and impoverish us as well.

6:7–16 When **Israel cried out to the Lord** for help, **a prophet** was first **sent** to remind them of their idolatry. Then **the Angel of the Lord**, whom we believe to be the preincarnate Christ (see essay below), **appeared to** a man of Manasseh named **Gideon** as he was secretly threshing **wheat in a winepress . . . to hide it from the Midianites. The Angel** told this **"mighty man of valor"** that God would use him to deliver **Israel from** Midian. Despite Gideon's protests, the Angel repeated his call to this important task.

THE ANGEL OF THE LORD

The Angel of the Lord (Jehovah) is the Lord Jesus Christ in a preincarnate appearance. A study of the passages in which He is mentioned makes it clear that He is God, and that He is the Second Person of the Trinity.

First, the Scriptures show that He is God. When He appeared to Hagar, she recognized that she was in the presence of God; she referred to Him as "the-God-Who-Sees" (Gen. 16:13). Speaking to Abraham on Mount Moriah, the Angel identified Himself as "the LORD" (Heb. YHWH, or Jehovah; Gen. 22:16). Jacob heard the Angel introduce Himself as the God of Bethel (Gen. 31:11–13). When blessing Joseph, Israel used the names "God" and "the Angel" interchangeably (Gen. 48:15, 16). At the burning bush, it was the Angel of the LORD" who appeared (Ex. 3:2), but Moses "hid his face, for he was afraid to look upon God" (Ex. 3:6). The Lord who went before Israel in a pillar of cloud (Ex. 13:21) was none other than "the Angel of God" (Ex. 14:19). Gideon feared that he would die because, in seeing the Angel of the LORD, he had seen God (Judg. 6:22, 23). The Angel of the LORD told Manoah that His name was Wonderful (Judg. 13:18), one of the names of God (Isa. 9:6). When Jacob struggled with the Angel, he struggled with God (Hos. 12:3, 4). These are convincing proofs that when the Angel of the LORD is referred to in the OT, the reference is to Deity.

John F. Walvoord (as quoted by Chafer) gives four arguments to support this:

> "(a) The Second Person is the Visible God of the New Testament. (b) The Angel of Jehovah of the Old Testament No Longer Appears after the Incarnation of Christ. (c) Both the Angel of Jehovah and Christ Are Sent by the Father. (d) The Angel of Jehovah Could Not Be Either the Father Or the Holy Spirit."[4] As for the fourth evidence, Walvoord goes on to explain that the Father and the Spirit are invisible to man and both have the attribute of immateriality. He concludes, "There is not a single valid reason to deny that the Angel of Jehovah is the Second Person, every known fact pointing to His identification as the Christ of the New Testament."

As the Angel of Jehovah, Christ is distinguished from other angels in that He is uncreated. The words translated *Angel*[5] in both Testaments mean "messenger"; He is the *Messenger* of Jehovah. Thus, as Chafer says, He is an "angel" only by office.[6]‡

6:17–24 Sensing that he was talking to the Lord, **Gideon** asked for **a sign**. Then he **prepared** an **offering** of **a young goat** and of **unleavened bread**. When **the Angel . . . touched** the offering with his **staff** and it was **consumed** by **fire**, Gideon knew he was in the Lord's presence and feared he would **die**. But **the LORD** assured him with the words **"Peace be with you,"** and **Gideon** thereupon **built an altar** and named the place Jehovah-Shalom (**The-Lord-Is-Peace**).

6:25–32 That **night**, in obedience to **the Lord**, **Gideon** destroyed an **altar** which his **father** had erected to **Baal** and **the wooden image . . . beside it**, and instead erected another **altar to** Jehovah. **In the morning . . . the men of the city** were ready to kill him for this bold act. But his father, **Joash**, intervened, saying that if **Baal** were truly **a god**, he should be able to defend himself. **Joash** decreed that anyone who espoused Baal's cause would be executed. Gideon was nicknamed **Jerubbaal**, meaning **"Let Baal plead** (for himself)**."**

Some people might fault Gideon for tearing down the altar at **night** because of fear. But we must not lose sight of the fact that he did obey **the LORD**. His fear did not stop him from being obedient. All of us have fear, and fear in and of itself is not necessarily wrong. But when it keeps us from obeying the Lord, it has become an obstacle to faith and is sin.

6:33–35 At this time **the Midianites**, the **Amalekites** and **the people of the East gathered together** to make war on Israel as they **crossed** the Jordan **and encamped in the Valley of Jezreel. The Spirit of the LORD came upon Gideon** and he assembled an army from the tribes of **Manasseh, Asher, Zebulun, and Naphtali**. Abiezer (v. 34) was an ancestor of Gideon. His name is used here (Hebrew text) as a family name (the Abiezrites, NKJV) for his living descendants. See also 8:2.

6:36–40 Before **Gideon** went into battle, he desired a pledge of victory from **God**. The first pledge came when **dew** fell **on** his **fleece of wool** but not on **the ground** around it. The second came the following night, when the **dew** fell **on . . . the ground** but not on **the fleece**.

Gideon's fleece is often misunderstood by Christians. There are two things about this incident that we should keep in mind: Gideon was not looking to the fleece for *guidance* but for *confirmation*. God had already told him what he was to do. Gideon was just seeking assurance of success. People who talk about putting out a fleece to find the will of the Lord in a certain matter are misapplying the passage. Secondly, Gideon had asked for a *supernatural* sign, not a natural one. Naturally speaking, what Gideon asked for would never have happened without the direct intervention of God. Today people use things as a "fleece" that could happen naturally, without divine intervention. This, too, is a wrong way to use the story. What we see here is God condescending to a man of weak faith to assure him of victory. God can, and does, give such assurances today in answer to prayer.

2. *Gideon's Three Hundred (Chap. 7)*

7:1–3 In order that victory against Midian might be clearly divine, the Lord first reduced Gideon's army from 32,000 to **ten thousand** by sending the **fearful and** fainthearted home, as the law commanded (Deut. 20:8).

7:4–8 In order to reduce the army still further, God tested the soldiers at the river. Those who took time to get **down on** their **knees** for a **drink** of **water** were eliminated. Those, on the other hand, who lapped up water like **a dog** and quickly moved on were kept in the army. These numbered **three hundred men**.

7:9–14 **The Lord** then directed **Gideon** to visit the outskirts of **the camp** of **the Midianites** by **night**. Accompanied by **Purah his servant**, Gideon went to the outermost part of the enemy's encampment. There he heard a Midianite **telling** his friend of **a dream** he had had in which **a loaf** of barley bread rolled over a Midianite **tent**, crushing it. The friend understood the dream as meaning that the Israelites would defeat **Midian. Barley bread** was the food of the common farming people and represented Israel. The **tent** typified the armies of the Midianites.

7:15–20 Perhaps the thought of his diminishing army rekindled Gideon's fears, and justifiably so. God was asking him to face an army of 135,000 with a force of 300 (8:10)! But this word from the mouth of his enemies strengthened his faith. In response, **he** first *worshiped* (v. 15), then *warred*.

Thus assured of victory, Gideon **returned to the camp of Israel** and summoned his men to war. After dividing the army **into three companies** of one hundred each, he armed each man with **a trumpet** and an earthenware pitcher with a lamp or torch **inside**. They marched to the fringe of **the camp** of the Midianites, and then at the appointed signal they all **blew the trumpets, broke the** earthenware **pitchers** so that the light of the lamps would be visible, and cried, **"The sword of the Lord and of Gideon!"**

The divine interpretation of this incident is given in 2 Corinthians 4:7. Our bodies are the earthen vessels. It is only as we are constantly delivered unto death for Jesus' sake that the light of the knowledge of the glory of God in the face of Jesus Christ shines forth to others.

7:21–25 In confusion and panic, the Midianites began attacking one another, then **fled**. At first they were chased by men from the tribes of **Naphtali, Asher, and all Manasseh**. But **then all the men of Ephraim** were summoned to join in by taking the fords of **Jordan** and destroying the foe as they sought to escape across the river. The Ephraimites succeeded in capturing and killing **two** of the **princes of** Midian: **Oreb** (*raven*) and **Zeeb** (*wolf*).

There are lessons we can learn about leadership in Gideon's actions. The leader must be thoroughly convinced about what he is doing before he can lead others. He must be a worshiper first of all, giving God His rightful place (v. 15). He must lead by example (v. 17). He must be careful that the credit goes where it belongs—to God first, then to the instruments of His choosing (v. 18).

3. *Gideon's Victory over the Philistines (8:1–32)*

8:1–3 At first **the men of Ephraim** were angry with Gideon that they had not been invited to help sooner. But when Gideon reminded them that their capture of the two **princes** was more illustrious than anything he had done, they were pacified. As explained previously, **Abiezer** (v. 2) refers to Gideon and his men.

8:4–7 The Jews **of Succoth refused to give food to Gideon** and his hungry **three hundred** because they feared reprisal from the Midianites if he were defeated. Gideon threatened to **tear** (Heb. *thresh*) their **flesh** with **thorns** and **briers** when **the LORD** had **delivered Zebah and Zalmunna into** his **hand**.

8:8, 9 **The men of Penuel** answered Gideon's request for food in the negative also. His threat to them was that **when** he came **back in peace** he would **tear down** their **tower**.

8:10–17 Gideon kept his word. He captured the two Midianite kings and **routed the whole army**. With the help of **a young** informer's written list, Gideon **taught** a lesson to the **seventy seven** leading **men of Succoth**. Cohen says:

> This form of punishment "is described in Plato's *Republic* as one inflicted upon the worst offenders."[7]

The learned Rabbis Kimchi and Rashi saw this as an idiom meaning "strike with violence."

> Others explain that he [Gideon] threatened to throw them naked into a bed of thorns and trample them together, like grain on the threshing-floor.[8]

As for **Penuel**, Gideon did tear **down** its **tower** and he also **killed the men of the city**.

"A soft answer turns away wrath, but a harsh word stirs up anger" (Prov. 15:1). The first truth is illustrated in verses 1–3 by Gideon's answer to the Ephraimites. The second truth is illustrated in verses 4–17 by the words of the men of Succoth and Penuel.

8:18–21 **Zebah and Zalmunna had killed** some of Gideon's **brothers** at **Tabor**, so he ordered his oldest son, **Jether**, to slay them. He **was afraid** to **because he was still a youth, . . . so Gideon** finished the job himself.

8:22, 23 **The men of Israel** asked **Gideon** to be their king, so impressed were they by his military exploits.

They gave the glory to man instead of to God (cf. 7:2). But Gideon nobly refused for himself and his sons, pointing out that **the Lord** alone had the right to **rule over** them.

8:24–27 But, after resisting one temptation, Gideon fell into another. He asked for the **golden earrings** which the Israelites had taken from the Midianites (also known as Ishmaelites; cf. Ex. 32:1–6). With these **Gideon made . . . an ephod**, the apron-like vestment of the priest. When this was **set . . . up** in **Ophrah**, **it became** an object of idolatrous worship and thus **a snare** to Israel, drawing them away from Shiloh and the tabernacle. "He refused the kingship but wanted the priesthood."

8:28–32 After the conquest of the Midianites, **Israel** enjoyed **quiet for forty years**.

Special mention is made of the fact that **Gideon . . . had many wives**, and these bore him **seventy sons.** Also, he had a **concubine . . . in Shechem** who **bore him a son** by the name of **Abimelech.**

Two more characteristics of Gideon's multifaceted personality show themselves in this chapter. His relentless pursuit of the Midianites displayed a thoroughness and completeness in carrying out his orders. Even though he was tired, even though he had already done a great deal, and even though no one would help him, he pressed on until the Ishmaelites were destroyed and their kings were dead at his feet. The Apostle Paul had a similar drive, only it showed itself in spiritual warfare (Phil. 3:12–14).

The second characteristic is a negative one: he requested and accepted **golden earrings from** the **plunder** as a reward for defeating the Ishmaelites (v. 24), and this **became a snare to Gideon,** his family, and his country. Contrast this with Abraham's behavior in Gen. 14:21–24. We should strive under God to emulate Gideon's virtues and avoid his vices.

F. Abimelech's Usurpation (8:33—9:57)

8:33–35 No sooner had **Gideon** died than **Israel** turned aside to worship of **the Baals**. How quickly the Israelites forgot Gideon's heroic national exploits, even to the point of mistreating his descendants and forgetting God's deliverance! But are we much better at remembering the blessings we have received from the Lord or even from our fellow men? To our shame we tend to forget them.

9:1–6 **Abimelech** (*my father was king*), a **son of** Gideon, was not a judge of Israel but a usurper—one who sought to rule Israel without proper authority. To eliminate any threats to his rule, he murdered all **his brothers** except **Jotham, the youngest**. Working through **worthless and reckless** relatives in **Shechem,** he persuaded the people of that area to recognize him as **king**. Since Gideon had **seventy . . . sons** (v. 2), and not all were slain, the **seventy** of verse 5 must be a round number.

9:7–15 The Gospels contain many parables, or stories with a deeper meaning. Here is one of the few OT parables. Jensen comments on it as follows:

> When Jotham heard of Abimelech's coronation, he hurried to the top of Mount Gerizim at a time when the people were gathered in the valley below. From that vantage point his voice could be heard across the valley, and the people listened intently to the strange parable he related. Using the figure of a republic of trees electing a king, he pictured Israel's conduct. He spoke of Gideon and his

sons as the olive tree, the fig tree, and the vine, who wisely refused to leave their God-appointed places of usefulness in order to go and reign over the trees. But he likened Abimelech to a bramble, who not only eagerly accepted the invitation but warned that he would destroy the cedars of Lebanon if the trees did not elect him king.[9]

9:16–21 Jotham then announced boldly to the people that if they had **done** right in destroying his brothers, **then** they could **rejoice in** their new ruler. **But if not, the men of Shechem** and **Abimelech** would become embroiled in civil war and destroy each other.

9:22–33 This is exactly what happened. **Three years** later **God sent a spirit of ill will between Abimelech and the men of Shechem**. God is not the author of evil, but He does allow evil, and even uses it to accomplish His purposes with evil men (cf. 1 Sam. 16:14; 1 Kgs. 22:19–23). **The men of Shechem . . . robbed** those who traveled the trade routes near Shechem, thus depriving Abimelech of the taxes he would ordinarily collect (v. 25). **Gaal the son of Ebed** used the harvest festival as the occasion to call for a rebellion against Abimelech, saying, **"Who is Abimelech, and who** are we of **Shechem, that we should serve him?" Zebul**, Abimelech's puppet-governor of Shechem, secretly notified **Abimelech** of the conspiracy and advised him to march against the **city . . . in the morning**.

9:34–40 When Gaal . . . went . . . to the city gate in the morning, he thought he saw **people** moving **down from the tops of the mountains**. At first **Zebul** pretended that what he saw were just **shadows**, hoping to gain time for **Abimelech**. Finally **Gaal** realized that it was actually **people**, with a second **company . . . coming from** a different direction. **Then Zebul** challenged him to **go out . . . and fight** the one whose rule he had **despised**. When **Gaal** and his band of outlaws engaged the foe, **many** of his men **fell** and he was soon chased back into the city.

9:41–44 With **Abimelech** camped at nearby **Arumah**, **Zebul** expelled **Gaal and his brothers** from **Shechem**. **The next day . . . people** from Shechem went out into **the field** to work, or perhaps to take spoil from the fallen men. When **Abimelech** heard of this, **he . . . divided** his men **into three companies** and set an ambush. **Two companies** were to rush **upon** them and another was to cut off any retreat back into **the city**. The ambush was successful.

9:45 After a day of fighting, **the city** fell. **The people** were all slain and their **city** was **demolished** and sown . . . **with salt**. (Sowing **with salt** makes the ground sterile. Here it was a symbolic action on the part of Abimelech, expressing his determination that the place be forever a barren salt waste.)

9:46–49 Nearby was **the tower of Shechem**, where there was a **temple of the god Berith**. **The** people **of the tower** hid in a large room of the temple. **Abimelech** and his men took boughs from the forest of nearby **Mount Zalmon** and made a huge **fire** over **the stronghold**. **About a thousand men and women** perished in the inferno.

9:50–57 In capturing **Thebez**, **Abimelech** met his downfall. As he attacked **a . . . tower** where many of **the people** had sought refuge, **a . . . woman dropped an upper millstone on Abimelech's head**. Seriously injured, he asked one of his own men to slay him rather than have it said he was slain by **a woman**. Thus the bramble was devoured, as **Jotham** had predicted.

Justice has its own way of suiting the punishment to the crime. Abimelech had slain his brothers on a stone (v. 5), and a stone crushed his own proud head. Those who live by violence will die by the same.

G. Tola and Jair (10:1–5)

Tola, of the tribe **of Issachar, judged Israel** for **twenty-three years. He** lived **in the mountains of Ephraim**.

The next judge was **Jair, a Gileadite,** who ruled for **twenty-two years** over **Israel**. Mention is made in passing of his **thirty sons**, who ruled over **thirty towns**.

H. Jephthah (10:6—12:7)

1. Israel's Misery (10:6–18)

10:6–9 Again we read the dreary account of how **the children of Israel . . . forsook the Lord** and turned to idolatry. Service to idols brought Israel into slavery to idolaters. **The Philistines** and Ammonites fought **against** the Jews who were **on the** east **side of the Jordan**, and the Ammonites also **crossed over the Jordan to fight against Judah, . . . Benjamin, and . . . Ephraim**.

Israel was powerless before the Philistines and the Ammonites because they abandoned the worship of Jehovah and **served the . . . gods of** these heathen (v. 6).

10:10–16 When the Israelites **cried out to the Lord**, He refused their pleas at first. He cited several instances of past deliverances and reminded them that after each deliverance they had turned away from Him (v. 13). But when they continued to pray and after **they put away** their idols, God listened to their cry. Verse 16 gives us some insight into the Lord's great heart of tenderness. Like a father, He was moved by the plight of His wayward children. Their **misery** called forth His mercy.

10:17, 18 As the chapter closes, the armies **of Ammon** were camped **in Gilead**, and **Israel** had **assembled . . . in Mizpah**. The men of Gilead were seeking a military leader (vv. 17, 18).

2. Jephthah's Defense of Israel (11:1–28)

11:1–3 The man of the hour was **Jephthah**. He is described as a **Gileadite, a mighty man of valor**, and **the son of a harlot**. Having been rejected by his own countrymen, he had wandered off to **the land of Tob** (probably in Syria), where he became the leader of a band of desperadoes or outlaws.

11:4–11 **The elders of Gilead** now asked **Jephthah** to lead the armies of Israel against the Ammonites, promising to recognize him as their **head** if he defeated the foe.

In some ways Jephthah reminds us of the Lord Jesus: There was a shadow over his birth and he was rejected by his brethren. When they got into bondage they remembered him and called upon him as their savior; and in agreeing to help the Gileadites, Jephthah agreed to be their savior but insisted on being their lord as well.

11:12–28 Jephthah's first action was to send **messengers to the king of . . . Ammon**, giving him an opportunity to explain his aggression. **The king** complained that **Israel** had stolen his **land** from him **when** the nation marched from **Egypt** to Canaan. Jephthah explained clearly that this was not so. The Lord had instructed His people not to meddle with the Edomites (Deut. 2:4, 5), the Moabites

(Deut. 2:9), or the Ammonites (Deut. 2:19)—all distant relatives of the Jews. Therefore, the Israelites **bypassed the land of Edom and the land of Moab**. However, when they came to the territory of the Ammonites, it had already been captured by **the Amorites**, whose **king** was **Sihon**. **Israel** took **possession of** this **land** by defeating **the Amorites.**

When **the king of . . . Ammon** refused to withdraw his claim to the land, **Jephthah** prepared for war.

3. *Jephthah's Vow (11:29–40)*

Before going into battle, **Jephthah made a** rash **vow** that he would devote to the Lord **whatever** first came **out of** his **doors . . . to meet** him if he returned home victorious. **The Lord** gave him victory over the Ammonites, and as he returned to his house **his daughter** came out to meet him. Jephthah therefore offered her to the Lord.

There is considerable disagreement as to what Jephthah actually did to his daughter. One view is that he killed her and offered her as a burnt offering to the Lord. This is perhaps the most obvious meaning of the text, even though the idea of human sacrifice is repulsive and was never approved by God (Deut. 18:9–14). Only animals were sacrificed; human beings were dedicated, then redeemed by money (Ex. 13:12, 13; Lev. 27:1–8).

The other common view is that Jephthah gave his daughter to be a perpetual virgin in the service of Jehovah. Those holding this viewpoint state that Jephthah's **vow** was that **whatever** came forth from **the doors of** his **house . . . "shall surely be the Lord's,** or I will offer it up for a burnt offering" (v. 31). The idea of perpetual **virginity** is strongly supported by verses 37–39. In any case, *the lesson* is that we should not make rash promises.

4. *Jephthah Slays the Ephraimites (12:1–7)*

12:1–4 The men of Ephraim were jealous of Jephthah's victory, complaining that they had not been allowed to share in it. **Jephthah** reminded them that he had appealed to them in vain for help. The Ephraimites mocked Jephthah's people, the **Gileadites**, saying that they were nothing but **fugitives** from **Ephraim**. (The Ephraimites were troublemakers. They took issue with Gideon when he defeated the Midianites (chap. 8) and now they quarreled with Jephthah without just cause.)

12:5, 6 Jephthah and his **men** attacked the Ephraimites and cut off their way of escape at **the fords of the Jordan**. Before anyone was allowed to **cross** the Jordan, he was forced to say the password, **"Shibboleth"** (lit. *a flowing stream*). The Ephraimites **could not pronounce** this word correctly; they betrayed their identity by saying **"Sibboleth."**[10] **Jephthah** killed **forty-two thousand** men of Ephraim **at . . . the Jordan**—a frightful slaughter of his own countrymen.

This type of infighting among the people of God is a distressing thing to see. The blood of the Ephraimites was now mingled with the blood of the Ammonites. Even the bright spots in Judges are smudged with calamity. Ridout makes a sad observation:

> Is it not a fact that . . . those who have met and overthrown heresy are those who have then crossed swords with their brethren, and fought over things that were not a vital question of truth?[11]

12:7 Jephthah's service as a judge lasted for **six years**; **then** he **died and**

was buried in **Gilead**. Jephthah is cited in Hebrews 11:32 along with Gideon, Barak, and Samson. All these men had their faults, but they all, at one time or another, demonstrated great faith.

I. Ibzan, Elon, and Abdon (12:8–15)

12:8–10 Ibzan . . . judged Israel for seven years. All we know of him is that he was a native **of Bethlehem** who **had thirty sons**, all of whom obtained wives **from elsewhere** (that is, outside his clan).

12:11, 12 Elon was of the tribe **of Zebulun**. His work as judge lasted for **ten years**. He was **buried at Aijalon**.

12:13–15 Abdon the son of Hillel came from the city of **Pirathon . . . in the mountains of the Amalekites, in the land of Ephraim. He judged Israel** for **eight years**. Special mention is made of his **forty sons and thirty grandsons**.

J. Samson (Chaps. 13—16)

1. Samson's Godly Heritage (Chap. 13)

13:1–3 For the seventh time in Judges we read: **"Again the children of Israel did evil in the sight of the LORD."** The cycle begins again; this time **the Philistines** enslaved Israel **for forty years**. This was the longest oppression the nation had yet undergone. While the Israelites were being oppressed by the Philistines, **the Angel of the LORD** (Christ) **appeared to** the wife of **Manoah**, of the tribe of Dan, and announced that, though she had been **barren**, she would become the mother of **a son**. The barren womb is often a starting place in the purposes of God. He calls life out of death and uses the things that "are not" to confound the things that are.

13:4–7 This son was to **be a Nazirite** from his mother's **womb to the day of his death**. He was not to **drink . . . wine** or eat grapes or raisins, nor was his hair to be cut. The mother herself was to abstain from **wine or similar drink** and from **anything unclean**.

For the scriptural background of the Nazirite vow, see Numbers 6:2. Ordinarily, Naziriteship was a vow which a person made of his own will. But in Samson's case Naziriteship was to extend from his birth to his death.

13:8–14 Manoah prayed for another visit from **the Angel of the LORD** and for further instructions. **The Angel** appeared **to the woman again**, and she hurriedly brought **her husband** out to meet this heavenly Visitor. No further instructions were given by the Angel at this time, however.

13:15–18 Then Manoah offered to **prepare** a meal for **the Angel**, thinking that he was a mere man. **The Angel** refused to **eat** with **Manoah** merely as one of equal rank. He proposed instead that a kid be offered as **a burnt offering . . . to the LORD**. When **Manoah** asked the Angel's **name**, he was told it was *Wonderful*—one of the names given to the Lord Jesus in Isaiah 9:6.

13:19–23 Then **Manoah** offered **the young goat to the LORD. The Angel ascended** to heaven **in the flame of the altar**, showing clearly that this was an appearance **of the LORD** Himself. **Manoah and his wife** then worshiped by falling **on their faces**—an act that would have been improper if the Angel were less than God. They had seen **the LORD**, but they would not **die** as a result, since God had received **a burnt offering and a grain offering** from them.

13:24, 25 After this the **son** was born and named **Samson** (*little sun*).

It soon became obvious that **the Spirit of the Lord** was working powerfully in his life.

Few men in the Bible exhibit such a contrast of strength and weakness. When we think of Samson, we ordinarily think of *his strengths*. He killed a lion with his bare hands (Judg. 14:6). He killed thirty Philistines single-handed (14:19). He broke the cords with which the men of Judah had bound him, and slew 1000 Philistines with the jawbone of a donkey (15:14–16). In escaping from a trap which the Philistines had laid for him, he walked away with the gates of Gaza (16:3). Three times he escaped the treachery of Delilah—once by breaking the seven fresh bowstrings that bound him, once by snapping the new ropes as if they were a thread, and once by pulling out the pin that fastened the seven locks of his hair to a loom (16:6–14). Finally, he pulled down the pillars of the house in which the Philistines were being amused by him, killing more in his death than he did in his life (16:30).

But Samson's *weaknesses* were even more apparent. He had a weakness for women, and was willing to disobey God in order to get a woman who pleased him (14:1–7). He also disobeyed his parents (14:3). He practiced deceit (14:9; 16:7, 11, 13b). He fraternized with thirty Philistines, the enemies of God's people (14:11–18). He gave way to temper and vindictiveness (14:19b; 15:4, 5). He had a cruel streak in his nature (15:4, 5). He consorted with a harlot (16:1, 2). He dallied with evil (16:6–14). He revealed the secret of his strength to the enemy (16:17, 18). He was too cocky and self-confident (16:20b). Last, but not least, he broke his Nazirite vow (14:9).

2. *Samson's Feast and Riddle (Chap. 14)*

14:1-4 Samson's willfulness soon appeared in his determination to marry **a** Philistine **woman**—one of the enemies of Israel. **His father and mother** sought to dissuade him, but he insisted. Verse 4 does not mean that **the Lord** approved of Samson's disobedience, but that He permitted it and planned to overrule it for Israel's welfare and for the punishment of the enemy.

14:5–7 En route **to Timnah** (a Philistine city) **with his** parents, Samson was threatened by **a young lion. The Spirit of the Lord came mightily upon him** and enabled him to kill **the lion** unaided. Presumably arrangements for the marriage were made at this time.

14:8, 9 Later, when **Samson** was returning to Timnath to claim his bride, he found **honey... in the carcass of the lion** he had slain and shared it with **his father and mother**. He didn't tell them that the honey was defiled by contact with a dead body (As a Nazirite he broke part of his vow by touching the dead animal.)

14:10–14 At Timnah, **a** great wedding **feast** was arranged, and **Samson** gave **a riddle**, offering each of his **thirty companions** a complete outfit if they could explain it. If not, they would have to give him **thirty linen garments and thirty changes of clothing**. The riddle was:

> **Out of the eater came something to eat,**
> **And out of the strong came something sweet.**

It referred, of course, to his killing of the lion and to his finding the honey in its carcass.

14:15–18 When the men failed to guess the answer, they persuaded **Samson's wife** with threats to obtain the answer from him. **She** did this and **explained** it to the thirty young men. They came to Samson with the answer and demanded the clothing. Samson then realized that they had collaborated with his wife.

14:19, 20 In order to get the clothing to pay the men, Samson angrily **killed thirty... men** of **Ashkelon** and **took their apparel**. On the seventh day, when the marriage should have been consummated, he returned home. His **wife was given to his companion, his best man.**

3. Samson's Reprisals (Chap. 15)

15:1–6 When his father-in-law refused to let Samson have his **wife**, Samson took personal revenge by tying the **tails** of **three hundred foxes** in pairs, putting **a** lighted **torch between each pair of tails**, and releasing the animals in the **grain** fields, **vineyards, and olive groves**. The Philistines learned the cause of this cruel and wasteful act and retaliated by burning to death Samson's wife **and her father**.

15:7–13 Samson's answer was to slay a **great** multitude of Philistines; then he retired to **the cleft of the rock of Etam** in the territory of Judah. But violence triggers more violence. When **the Philistines** marched after him, **the men of Judah** slavishly reminded him that **the Philistines** were their rulers. To save their own skin they agreed to **tie** Samson **securely** and turn him over to the enemy. Samson agreed to this as long as his own countrymen did **not** attempt to **kill** him. They had sunk to a vassal mentality, and chose to betray their own countryman and remain loyal to their oppressors rather than to befriend Samson and rid themselves of their chains.

15:14–17 Then follows one of the glorious moments of Samson's career. When he was brought out bound, **the Spirit of the LORD came mightily upon him. With the jawbone of a donkey** he proceeded to slay **a thousand** Philistines. He named the **place Ramath Lehi** (*Jawbone Heights*, NKJV marg.). There is a play on words in verse 16, as if to say, "With the jawbone of an ass I have ass-ass-inated them," or "With the jawbone of an ass I have piled them in a mass! With the jawbone of an ass I have assailed assailants" (Moffatt).

One wonders why the Lord gave such a great victory through such an unlikely weapon. Samson was forbidden to touch anything that was unclean, and the jawbone was certainly that, being part of a dead animal. But this unusual weapon made it all the more evident that the victory was a supernatural one, given by God through base means. This is an example of the Lord allowing irregularities during a time of extreme crisis which ordinarily would not be permitted.

15:18–20 In response to Samson's prayer for **water**, **God** miraculously provided a spring out of "Jawbone Heights." This place was named **En Hakkore**, *Spring of the Caller* (NKJV marg.).

It is at this illustrious period in Samson's career that the Spirit of God records his judging of **Israel** for **twenty years**.

4. Samson Duped by Delilah (Chap. 16)

16:1–3 Toward the end of his rule, Samson's unbridled lust led him to the house of **a harlot** in the Philistine city of **Gaza**. The men of the city thought that at last they had trapped their enemy. But **Samson . . . arose at midnight** and carried off **the doors of the gate of the city**, as well as the **two gateposts, to the top of the hill that faces Hebron**, a distance of almost forty miles.

16:4–10 Next **Samson** fell in love with a Philistine **woman** named **Delilah**. When this became known, **the lords of the Philistines** offered her great reward if she would lure Samson into revealing the secret of **his great strength**.

On her first attempt, Samson said that if he were bound with **seven fresh bowstrings**, he would **become weak**. She thereupon tied **him with . . . seven fresh bowstrings** and suggested that **the Philistines** were about to pounce on him. But Samson broke the cords as if they were **a strand of yarn**.

16:11, 12 On the second attempt, **Delilah** followed Samson's suggestion by binding him **with new ropes** and warning him that **the Philistines** were closing in for the kill. But again Samson **broke** his bonds as if they were **thread**.

16:13, 14 Still playing with fire, Samson told Delilah that he would be helpless if she wove **the seven locks of** his hair and then fastened them **into the web of the loom**. When she woke him up with the warning that **the Philistines** were about to seize him, he left with **the batten and the web**.

16:15–20 Finally Samson broke down and revealed to **Delilah** the secret of his **strength**. His long hair, while not the source of his power, was the outward indication of his being **a Nazirite**—his separation to God. It was his relationship **to God** that made him strong, not his hair. But if his hair were cut off, he would be powerless. Delilah knew now that she had his secret. When he was asleep **on her knees**, she called in **the Philistines**. One of them shaved his head, and **his strength left him**.

C. H. Mackintosh observes:

> The lap of Delilah proved too strong for the heart of Samson, and what a thousand Philistines could not do was done by the ensnaring influence of a single woman.[12]

When **Samson . . . awoke**, he tried to summon his strength, **not** knowing that **the LORD had departed from him**.

16:21, 22 The Philistines . . . put out Samson's **eyes** and imprisoned him in **Gaza**, where he was forced to grind grain. Someone has described this threefold degradation as the "binding, blinding, grinding bondage of sin." But slowly his **hair . . . began to grow again**.

16:23–31 When **the lords of the Philistines** held **a great sacrifice** in celebration of **their god, Dagon**, they brought **Samson** forth as an exhibit of what **their god** had done for them. Also, they compelled him to entertain them with his feats. During the feast, **Samson took hold of the two middle pillars** supporting **the temple, called to the Lord** for strength, and then **pushed** down the pillars and demolished the building. **All the people** were **killed**. The melancholy record is that Samson **killed** more in **his death . . . than he had killed in his life**.

Because he consorted with the Philistines so often in his life and found their women irresistible, Samson is *now* found with the Philistines in his death, a corpse among corpses in the rubble of Dagon's temple. Separation would have earned for him a nobler death. Here we are taught a sober lesson, one we should not take lightly.

Loss of separation (sanctification) leads to loss of power and eventual ruin. To yield our members to sin is to pursue self-destruction. Samson's body was removed to the territory of Dan by his relatives and was **buried** there.

III. RELIGIOUS, MORAL, AND POLITICAL DECAY (Chaps. 17—21)

This last section of Judges is almost like an appendix to the book. As far as time is concerned chapters 17—21 do not advance the narrative. Rather, they give frightening glimpses of the low religious, moral, and political state to which Israel had sunk during the period of the judges. The little book of Ruth likewise does not advance the history of the judges in time but, by way of contrast, does give a charming glimpse of the godly remnant during this dark era in Hebrew history.

A. Micah's Religious Establishment (Chap. 17)

17:1–4 The first narrative is one of religious corruption. **Micah**, a man **of Ephraim**, had stolen **eleven hundred shekels of silver** from **his mother**. She in turn had cursed the thief, not knowing that it was her own son. Apparently he feared the results of the **curse**, so **he returned the silver** to her. She then lifted the curse and **blessed** her son for returning the **silver**. Now she could use it for its intended purpose. She **took two hundred shekels of silver and** ordered two idols to be **made** from them. One was **a** graven **image . . . carved** from wood and overlaid with silver. The **molded image** was made entirely of silver.

17:5, 6 Micah put the **idols** in **a shrine** with his **household** gods (*teraphim*). He also decided to set up a priesthood for his family, so he **made an ephod** (priestly garment) and **consecrated one of his sons** to be **his priest**. This, of course, was contrary to God's law, which forbade an Ephraimite from being a **priest**. In fact, the whole procedure was contrary to the Mosaic Law.

17:7–13 Sometime later **a Levite** who lived in **Bethlehem**, among the people **of Judah**, went into the hill country **of Ephraim** looking for **a place** to stay. (He should have been employed in the service of Jehovah and supported by the tithes of the nation. But since the law was not obeyed he was forced to seek out his own placement.) **Micah** offered him a position as **priest** in his family. Though this man was **a Levite**, he was not of the family of Aaron and therefore not eligible to serve as **a priest**. However, **Micah** offered him a salary, food, and clothing, and the Levite agreed to serve. The Levite should have confronted Micah with the fact that all these arrangements were contrary to God's order. Instead, he gave tacit assent by accepting the salary and other fringe benefits, thereby effectively sealing his lips from declaring the full counsels of God.

The word to describe the state of affairs in this chapter is "confusion": Stolen money is used for idols, and the Lord is invoked to bless the thief (v. 2); individual shrines replace worship at the tabernacle; Levites and common people are consecrated as priests; idols are used in the worship of Jehovah. And Micah supposed the Lord would bless him in all of this (v. 13)! This confusion stemmed from the heart of man (v. 6). If the law of

God had been observed at this time in Israel, none of these things would have happened. "There is a way that seems right to a man, but its end is the way of death" (Prov. 14:12), as we shall see in the next chapter.

B. Micah and the Danites (Chap. 18)

18:1–6 At about this same time, the people of **the tribe of the Danites** decided to look for additional territory in which **to dwell**.

(When verse 1 says that Dan did not have **an inheritance**, it does not mean that they weren't given any land when Canaan was originally divided [Josh. 19:40–48], but rather that their portion, the smallest of the twelve, was too little for them.) When some of their spies came **to the house of Micah** in the hill country **of Ephraim, they recognized the voice of the young Levite** and asked him for assurance of the divine blessing on their plans.

18:7–13 Five men of Dan spied out the northern town of **Laish**, finding it **quiet and secure**. What is more, **the town had no ties with anyone**, that is, they were a peace-loving community with "no treaty of mutual aid with any neighbouring people."[13]

Taking their unprotected condition as a gift from **God, six hundred** fully **armed Danites** set out for Laish.

18:14–26 Later, when **the five men** of Dan were marching north to capture **Laish**, they entered **the house of Micah** and seized all **the idols**. After a mild protest, the Levite gladly obeyed their order to serve the tribe of Dan as a priest rather than to serve just the house of Micah. When Micah and some of his townsmen went out to the Danites to protest this theft of his **gods**, he was told to keep quiet and was sent home empty-handed.

18:27–31 The Danites then **struck** the peaceful town of **Laish** and changed **the name of the city** to **Dan**. They set up **the carved image** there and appointed **Jonathan the son of Gershom, the son of** *Moses* (NKJV marg.) **and his sons** as **priests**.

> It is generally admitted that, in Judges, for 'Manasseh' (KJV, NASB) we should read 'Moses'—the name having been disguised by Jewish copyists to prevent supposed disgrace to Moses resulting from the idolatry of his grandson.[14]

Presumably, **Jonathan** is the name of the Levite previously mentioned. The city of **Dan** became an idolatrous city from this time onward. It was here that Jeroboam later set up one of the golden calves. It is not known whether the captivity mentioned in verse 30 refers to a Philistine captivity of that area (e.g., 1 Sam. 4:11) or the Assyrian captivity (2 Kgs. 15:29).

Not all the Danites went to **Laish** (v. 11) or sank into idolatry. Some stayed in their land, between Judah and Ephraim. Samson, the most famous member of this tribe, was from this latter group of Danites.

C. The Levite and His Concubine (Chap. 19)

19:1–12 We now come to a story of incredible moral corruption—the account of the **Levite** and **his concubine**. This particular Levite had a concubine who had come **from Bethlehem in Judah**. She forsook him to return to her home and live as a **harlot**. He **went** to her father's house to get her and was entertained there day after day. Each time he tried to leave with **his concubine**, her **father** prevailed on him to stay a little longer. Finally he left, on the evening of the fifth day, with **his servant**, his **two saddled donkeys**, and **his concubine**.

It was late afternoon when they came to **Jebus (that is, Jerusalem)**, but they did not stop because that city was still inhabited by the heathen Jebusites. George Williams observes:

> It would have been better for the Levite to have spent the night with the heathen than with the professed children of God, for the latter had already become viler than the former.[15]

19:13–21 At sunset they came to **Gibeah**, in the territory of Benjamin. No one offered to provide lodging for the caravan, so the Levite relaxed temporarily in the street. Then **an old** Ephraimite **man** who was living **in Gibeah** offered to take the party to his home, and the offer was accepted.

19:22–24 That evening a band of sexual perverts **surrounded the house** and demanded that the visiting Levite be brought **out** to them. The only other time we read of such debauched behavior is in the days of Lot (Gen. 19). Unfortunately for the young woman, there were no guardian angels present at Gibeah, as there were in Sodom. Both incidents brought severe consequences on the offenders. The Lord abhors homosexuality. Human depravity can hardly sink lower. The owner sought to satisfy these wicked Benjamites by offering his **virgin daughter and** the Levite's **concubine**. Arthur Cundall comments on their conduct as follows:

> In his concern for the accepted conventions of hospitality the old man was willing to shatter a code which, to the modern reader, appears of infinitely more importance, namely, the care and protection of the weak and helpless. Womanhood was but lightly esteemed in the ancient world; indeed it is largely due to the precepts of the Jewish faith, and particularly the enlightenment which has come through the Christian faith, that women enjoy their present position. The old man was willing to sacrifice his own virgin daughter and the Levite's concubine to the distorted lusts of the besiegers, rather than allow any harm to befall his principal guest.[16]

19:25–30 Finally, fearing for his own skin, the cowardly Levite sent his **concubine** out **to them**. As a result of their vile and harrowing abuse of her, she died during the night. Without excusing the Benjamites, we might point out that if she hadn't given herself to harlotry beforehand (v. 2) she would not have suffered a harlot's death. Sin mercilessly rewards its followers. The Levite found her body at the doorstep in the morning. He was so enraged that such grossness should be practiced in Israel that he cut her body into **twelve pieces . . . and sent** one part to each of the twelve tribes with an account of what had happened.

The nation of Israel was stunned!

D. The War with Benjamin (Chaps. 20, 21)

20:1–14 Chosen warriors from **the tribes of Israel** (except Benjamin) gathered together at **Mizpah** and heard **the Levite** tell what had happened. They decided to fight against **Gibeah**, but first they gave the Benjamites an opportunity to **deliver up** the guilty **perverted men** to them for punishment. When the Benjamites refused, civil war broke out.

20:15–48 This incident took place not long after the death of Joshua and his generation, for **Phinehas** was the high priest at the time (v. 28). The tribe of Benjamin had only 26,700 soldiers, against **four hundred thousand** from the other tribes (vv. 15–17). Yet in the first battle, Benjamin killed

twenty-two thousand men (vv. 18–21). In the second encounter, **eighteen thousand** men of **Israel** were slain (vv. 22–25). The reason Israel had such a hard time of it, even though their cause was just, was because they themselves were not walking close to the Lord. In verses 18, 23, and 26–28 we can see the nation being forced to humble itself before the Lord until finally success was promised. In the third engagement, the Israelites used the strategy of **ambush**. They drew the men of Benjamin away from the city of Gibeah, set the city on fire, and then **destroyed** a total of **twenty-five thousand one hundred Benjamites** as they fled to **the wilderness**. Then they burned all of Benjamin's **cities** and killed the women and children (vv. 29–48).

In three battles Benjamin lost 26,100 men (cf. vv. 15, 47). (We must conclude that they lost 1000 in the first two days.) The slain in verses 35 and 44–46 refer to the casualties in the last battle only. **Six hundred** survivors took refuge in **the rock of Rimmon for four months** (v. 47). Were it not for this remnant, the tribe would have been completely wiped out.

21:1–15 Now the eleven tribes of Israel were seized with regret that the tribe of **Benjamin** was almost annihilated. They did not want this tribe to die out. Yet they had made a rash vow in **Mizpah** that they would not give their daughters as wives **to** the men of **Benjamin**. Their first solution was to fight against **Jabesh Gilead**, east of Jordan, because its inhabitants had not helped in the war against Benjamin. All the people were killed except **four hundred young virgins**. These were then taken and given to the men of **Benjamin**.

21:16–24 But it was evident that further provision must be made if the tribe was to prosper. The men of Israel had vowed that they would not give their daughters to Benjamin, and they would not go back on the vow. So they hit on a scheme to allow **the survivors of Benjamin** to take wives for themselves from the young women who danced at an annual feast (perhaps the Feast of Tabernacles) in **Shiloh**. When the men of Shiloh complained, the other tribes explained to them that this was necessary to prevent the loss of one of the tribes of Israel. So Benjamin went back to his land to rebuild for the future.

These last few chapters have given us an intimate look at two tribes in Israel during the early period of the judges. One can imagine what went on unrecorded in the other tribes! And we know that things got worse as time went on! These gruesome stories show how far a people can wander from the Lord. Here we see enough of the fruit of apostasy to revolt us. Better still if what we have read would turn our hearts to seek the Lord our God and to serve Him faithfully all our days.

21:25 Judges closes with the sad theme ringing in our ears: **"In those days there was no king in Israel; everyone did what was right in his own eyes."**

There is one wholesome episode from this dark period, but it is set off by itself so as not to be defiled by too close association with the depravity of Judges. We now turn our attention to the chaste story of Ruth.

ENDNOTES

[1](Intro) These are largely adapted from Grant, Jennings, and Ridout (see Bibliography).

[2](2:11–19) Irving L. Jensen, *Judges/Ruth*, p. 12.

[3](3:5, 6) A. Cohen, "Joshua • Judges", pp. 176, 177.

[4](Essay) Quoted by Lewis Sperry Chafer in *Systematic Theology*, V:32.

[5](Essay) In Hebrew *mal'āk*, in Greek *angelos* (whence our English word *angel*).

[6](Essay) Chafer, *Systematic Theology*, I:328.

[7](8:10–17) Cohen, "Joshua • Judges", p. 227.

[8](8:10–17) *Ibid.*, p. 225.

[9](9:7–15) Jensen, *Judges/Ruth*, p. 49.

[10](12:5, 6) Some languages (including Greek and Latin) do not have the "sh" sound. Apparently one dialect of Hebrew either couldn't *pronounce* "sh" or couldn't *distinguish* between "s" and "sh," in this word at least. A similar situation existed in World War II when American soldiers in the South Seas chose "lalapalooza" as a password. The Japanese had trouble differentiating between the "l" and "r," and tended to say "raraparooza."

[11](12:5, 6) Samuel Ridout, *Lectures on the Books of Judges and Ruth*, p. 177.

[12](16:15–20) C. H. Mackintosh, further documentation unavailable.

[13](18:7–13) Cohen, "Joshua • Judges", p. 291.

[14](18:27–31) John Haley, *Alleged Discrepancies of the Bible*, p. 338. In Hebrew the consonants spelling *Moses* and *Manasseh* are nearly the same (*Mshh* and *Mnshh*), so it could be simply a copyist's error.

[15](19:1–12) George Williams, *The Student's Commentary on the Holy Scriptures*, p. 132.

[16](19:22–24) Arthur E. Cundall, *Judges and Ruth*, p. 197.

BIBLIOGRAPHY (Judges and Ruth)

Atkinson, David. *The Message of Ruth: The Wings of Refuge*. Downers Grove, IL: InterVarsity Press, 1983.

Barber, Cyril J. *Ruth: An Expositional Commentary*. Chicago: Moody Press, 1983.

Campbell, Donald K. *No Time for Neutrality*. Wheaton, IL: Scripture Press Publications, Victor Books, 1981.

Cohen, A. "Joshua • Judges." *Soncino Books of the Bible*. London: The Soncino Press, 1967.

Cundall, Arthur E. and Leon Morris. *Judges and Ruth*. The Tyndale Old Testament Commentaries. Downers Grove, IL: InterVarsity Press, 1968.

Fausset, A. R. *A Critical and Expository Commentary on the Book of Judges*. London: James Nisbet & Co., 1885.

Grant, F. W. "Judges" and "Ruth." In *The Numerical Bible, Vol. 3, Joshua to 2 Samuel*. Neptune, NJ: Loizeaux Brothers, 1977.

Jennings, F. C. *Judges and Ruth*. New York: Gospel Publishing House, 1905.

Jensen, Irving L. *Judges/Ruth*. Chicago: Moody Press, 1968.

McGee, J. Vernon. *Ruth and Esther: Women of Faith*. Nashville: Thomas Nelson Publishers, 1988.

Ridout, Samuel. *Lectures on the Books of Judges and Ruth*. New York: Loizeaux Bros., 1958.

RUTH

Introduction

"The little Book of Ruth, the exposition of which usually follows that of the Book of Judges, consists of only eighty-five verses; but these inclose a garden of roses, as fragrant and full of mystic calyxes, as those which the modern traveller still finds blooming and twining about the solitary ruins of Israel and Moab, this side of Jordan and beyond. The significance and beauty of the brief narrative cannot be highly enough estimated, whether regard be had to the thought that fills it, the historical value which marks it, or the pure and charming form in which it is set forth."

—Paulus Cassel

I. Unique Place in the Canon

It is noteworthy that of the two books in the Bible named after women, one was a Jewish girl who married a prominent Gentile (Esther and King Ahasuerus) and the other was a Gentile woman who married a prominent Hebrew (Ruth and Boaz). Another significant thing these two women have in common is that both were part of God's redemptive history. God used Esther to save His people from physical destruction and He used Ruth as an important genealogical link in the messianic line, first to David and ultimately to Christ, who would save His people from their sins. We are told in Matthew 1:5 that Boaz was a descendant of the Gentile Rahab, almost certainly the Rahab of Jericho. Now Ruth, another Gentile, enters the lineage of Christ as Boaz's wife. Both Rahab and Ruth picture God's grace, since both would have been excluded from the commonwealth of Israel because of their ethnic origin.

"The Book of Ruth," as McGee notes, "is essentially a woman's story, and God has set His seal of approval upon it by its inclusion in the divine library."[1]

The charm and beauty of the book is well illustrated in an incident involving Benjamin Franklin, the American statesman and inventor. When serving at the French court he heard some of the aristocrats "putting down" the Bible as being unworthy of reading, lacking in style, and so forth. Though not personally a believer himself, his youth in the American colonies had exposed him to the excellence of the Bible as literature. So he decided to play a little trick on the French. He wrote out Ruth longhand, *changing all the proper names to French names*. Then he read his manuscript to the assembled elite of France. They all exclaimed on the elegance and simplicity of style of this touching story.

"*Charmant!* But where did you find this gem of literature, Monsieur Franklin?"

"It comes from that Book you so despise," he answered—*"la sainte Bible!"* There were some red faces in Paris that night, just as there should be in our own biblically illiterate culture today for neglecting God's Word.

II. Authorship

Jewish tradition says that Samuel is the author of Ruth, though the book is anonymous. Since the book ends with David, the author cannot have been written before his time. Samuel, who anointed David as king, may well have provided the book to show the new monarch's pedigree.

III. Date

Since David's name occurs in 4:17, 22 as the culmination towards which the history of Ruth is leading, it is likely that it was written during or soon after his reign (c. 1011–970 B.C.), or at least after Samuel anointed him king.

Jensen writes:

> It was probably written before Solomon, David's successor on the throne, or the writer probably would have included Solomon's name in the genealogy. So the author was a contemporary of David.[2]

Some, however, have preferred a little later date, partly since a need was felt by the author to explain the custom of removing the sandal in a business transaction (4:7). This suggests a certain time lapse between this practice and the writing of the book of Ruth.

IV. Background and Theme

The events in the book of Ruth took place during the time of Judges (1:1). While most of the nation of Israel was wandering away from the Lord, there was a Gentile maiden named Ruth whose faith shone out with brilliance.

The key word of the book is *redeem*. Another key word is *kinsman* (KJV) or *relative* (NKJV), occurring twelve times. Boaz is a redeeming relative who buys back the land which belonged to Elimelech and raises up posterity to continue the family name. He is a type of Christ, the true Redeeming Relative. Ruth, the Moabitess, pictures the church as the bride of Christ, redeemed by His wonderful grace.

OUTLINE

I. RESIDING IN MOAB (1:1–5)

II. RETURN TO BETHLEHEM (1:6–22)

III. RUTH IN THE FIELDS OF BOAZ (Chap. 2)

IV. RUTH'S REDEEMING RELATIVE (Chap. 3)

V. REDEMPTION BY BOAZ (4:1–12)

VI. ROYAL GENEALOGY OF DAVID TRACED BACK TO OBED (4:13–22)

Commentary

I. RESIDING IN MOAB (1:1–5)

1:1, 2 As the book opens we meet a Jewish family which left **Bethlehem** (*house of bread*) of **Judah** (*praise*) because of **famine**, and settled in the land **of Moab**, southeast of the Dead Sea. The parents were **Elimelech** (*my God is King*) and **Naomi** (*my pleasant one*). The sons were **Mahlon** (*sickly*) and **Chilion** (*pining*). It would have been better to stay in the land and trust God than to emigrate to **Moab**. *Ephrata* (root of **Ephrathites**), the ancient name of **Bethlehem**, means fruitfulness.

The time of the **judges** was characterized by moral decline. So it is not surprising to find the land undergoing **famine**, God's promised chastisement for disobedience. **Elimelech** should not have left the Promised Land, least of all to settle in **Moab**. Had he never read Deuteronomy 23:3–6? Why not settle with his Jewish brethren east of the Jordan River? He led his family from the land of the living to the place of death and barrenness (neither **Mahlon** nor **Chilion** fathered children).

1:3–5 After **Elimelech . . . died**, his **sons** married Moabite wives. **Mahlon** married **Ruth** (4:10) and **Chilion** married **Orpah**. Although Moabites were not specifically named in Deuteronomy 7:1–3 as people whom Israelites should not marry, it is clear from later references that they were included by the law (Ezra 9:1, 2; Neh. 13:23–25). The law also specified that Moabites were not allowed to be received into the congregation of the Lord to the tenth generation (Deut. 23:3). Grace overruled in Ruth's case, as we shall see, permitting her descendant, David, to become the king of Israel.

After **ten years, Mahlon and Chilion...died**, leaving Naomi with two foreign daughters-in-law, **Orpah** and **Ruth**.

II. RETURN TO BETHLEHEM (1:6–22)

1:6–15 Naomi decided to move back to Judah when she heard that there was plenty of food there. **Her two daughters-in-law** started to accompany **her**. But when she urged them to **return . . . to** their homes in Moab, reminding them that she had no more sons to offer to them as husbands, **Orpah kissed her mother-in-law** and went back.

Notice the different attitudes of the three widows: **Naomi** was a *grieving* widow, stripped of the earthly joys of husband and family by divine judgment. **Orpah**, having soberly considered the words of her mother-in-law, proved to be a *leaving* widow, choosing the easiest and most convenient course. But **Ruth** was a *cleaving* widow, clinging to Naomi in spite of the latter's discouragements. When Ruth chose a new life with Naomi, she knew that it wouldn't be easy. There was hard work and poverty ahead since they were without a male provider. There was separation from home and loved ones, too.

1:16, 17 **Ruth**, however, would **not leave** Naomi. In one of the noblest utterances by a Gentile in the OT, she showed that she was making a total commitment (to **Naomi**). She chose Naomi's destination, her dwelling, her **people**, her **God**, and even her burial place.

1:18–22 By divine coincidence, it

was **the beginning of the barley harvest**, the season of firstfruits (typifying Christ's Resurrection), when Naomi and Ruth arrived back in **Bethlehem**. **All the city was excited** to see **Naomi** once again and greeted her cordially by name.

She said to them, "Do not call me Naomi (*Pleasant*); **call me Mara** (*Bitter*), **for the Almighty has dealt very bitterly with me."** She had gone **out full** (i.e., with her husband and sons), but the Lord had **brought** her back **empty** (i.e., a widow and childless). So it is with us—we can go out by ourselves into paths of backsliding, but the Lord will bring us back empty, and usually through bitter chastening.

III. RUTH IN THE FIELDS OF BOAZ (Chap. 2)

2:1–3 Under the law, Israelites were not allowed to strip the fields clean when harvesting. Instead, they were to leave some of the grain as gleanings for the needy, for strangers, for the fatherless, and for widows (Lev. 19:9; 23:22; Deut. 24:19).

Ruth decided to take advantage of this law by going out to the barley fields to gather up some of these gleanings. It was not good luck but divine arrangement that led her **to the field** owned by **Boaz** (*in him is strength*), a wealthy **relative** of her dead father-in-law.

2:4–12 When **Boaz** arrived **from Bethlehem**, he asked the identity of the **young woman**. Learning that she was Naomi's daughter-in-law, he cordially invited her to continue gleaning in his fields and to share the water provided for his workers. In praising her for the loyal and selfless step that she had taken, Boaz concluded with a little prayer for her:

> The LORD repay your work, and a full reward be given you by the LORD God of Israel, under whose wings you have come for refuge (v. 12).

Leon Morris comments:

> In due course, the prayer was answered through him who uttered it. He recognizes the religious aspect of Ruth's change of country by saying that she has *come to trust* (AV) under Yahweh's wings. The imagery is probably that of a tiny bird struggling under the wings of a foster-mother. It gives a vivid picture of trust and security. . . .[3]

She marveled that he, a Jew, should show such undeserved favor to a Gentile. But there was a reason! **Boaz** had, of course, heard of the kindness which Ruth had shown to Naomi, and how she had become a convert to the Jewish faith.

2:13–16 He was so impressed with her that he invited her to **eat** with his workers, and instructed **the reapers** to leave extra **grain** for her on purpose.

2:17 At the end of the day, she **beat out what she had gleaned**, and **she had about an ephah of barley**, which was a very generous amount. We must do this in our study of the Word; that is, we must appropriate the precious truths for ourselves and put them into practice.

In Boaz we see illustrated many of the excellencies of Christ. Boaz was a man of great wealth (v. 1). He was compassionate to the stranger, who had no claim on his favors (vv. 8, 9). He knew all about Ruth, even before she met him (v. 11), even as the Lord knows all about us even before we come to know Him. He served Ruth graciously, and all her needs were satisfied (v. 14). He granted her protection and prosperity for the future (vv. 15, 16). In these acts of grace we see a foreshadowing of our blessed

Redeeming Relative's mercies to us.

2:18–23 When Ruth **brought** the grain home and told Naomi all that had happened, the wise old Jewess knew that the Lord's program was unfolding satisfactorily. She knew that Boaz was a close relative of her dead husband and sensed that the Lord was going to work wonderfully for Ruth and for herself. Therefore she encouraged Ruth to continue to **glean** in the **field** of **Boaz**.

Naomi's counsel to stay in the fields of Boaz was prudent. Since he had shown himself gracious, why should Ruth insult him or spurn his protection by going into another's **field**? We too should not wander from the Lord's promised provision and protection into the fields of worldly pleasures.

IV. RUTH'S REDEEMING RELATIVE (Chap. 3)

3:1–5 Naomi was anxious that Ruth should find **security**—that is, a husband and a home. She therefore relinquished her own prior claim to marriage and property, and instead advised Ruth to **go down to the threshing floor** one night when **Boaz** was **winnowing barley**.

> Ruth, being a stranger to Israelite customs, had to be told in detail how she was to make the customary appeal to her kinsman for protection and levirate marriage (*Daily Notes of the Scripture Union*).

3:6, 7 So **after Boaz had** finished his work, **eaten** his meal, and retired, Ruth **lay** . . . at his feet under a corner of his blanket. This may seem very irregular to us in our culture, but actually it was the accepted practice in that day (see Ezek. 16:8), and there was nothing evil or suggestive about it.

3:8–11 Awakened **at midnight**, Boaz found Ruth **at his feet**. Far from rebuking her, he **blessed** her after she had asked him to act as her redeeming relative. The word *wings* in 2:12 is the plural of the same word here translated **"wing."** Boaz had commended Ruth for seeking refuge in Jehovah; how could he refuse her the refuge she sought from him according to Jehovah's laws? Besides, she was **a virtuous woman**, one of those whose worth is far above jewels (Prov. 31:10). He commended her for her loyalty, saying that her latter **kindness** (her personal devotion to him) was better than her first (her leaving home and family to be with Naomi).

The Law of Moses required that when a man died childless, a close relative should marry the widow (Deut. 25:5–10), thus perpetuating the family name and keeping the land in the family. It was especially important that when a man died without a son, someone should marry his widow so that a son would be born and the name carried on.

Now Ruth, of course, had been left childless. Since Boaz was a relative of Elimelech, he was eligible to serve as redeeming relative by marrying her. And not only was he eligible; he was willing.

3:12, 13 But there was a legal complication: There was a **relative closer** than he, and this man had prior claim. If this **closer relative** did not wish to serve as redeeming relative, then Boaz would. The matter would be settled in the **morning**.

3:14–18 Ruth stayed **at his feet** till just before dawn. Boaz filled her **shawl** with **six ephahs of barley**. This assured Ruth of his deep love and gave evidence to Naomi that he would follow through on the matter without delay.

Ruth was a noble woman, intrinsically worthy of Boaz's kindnesses. But we were unworthy sinners. Yet the Lord spread His covering over us and took us as we were. He has loaded us with gifts and encouraged us with His promised return to consummate the marriage. Our salvation is settled, a finished work. But entrance into the full bliss of our union awaits the Bridegroom's return.

When Naomi heard all that had taken place, she told Ruth to **sit still** and wait for the outcome of this complex sequence of events.

> This is often the most difficult part of faith—when no more action can be taken and nothing remains but to wait patiently for God to work out His will. It is at this moment that doubts arise and anxiety creeps in (*Daily Notes of the Scripture Union*).

V. REDEMPTION BY BOAZ (4:1–12)

4:1–6 In the morning **Boaz went up to the gate** of the city, where the elders **sat** and where legal matters were settled. It so "happened' '—another designed coincidence—that the **close relative** walked **by** at that very moment. Addressing him as **"friend,"**[4] and asking him to stop for a while, Boaz stood before the **ten . . . elders** and told the story of **Naomi** and Ruth. Then he gave **the close relative** the chance to **buy** back the **land** belonging to **Elimelech**, which had probably been mortgaged when Elimelech went to Moab. Up to this point, the unnamed relative was willing. However, when Boaz told him that whoever bought the land must also marry **Ruth the Moabitess**, he backed away, explaining that this would **ruin** his **inheritance**.

> He would have to devote time and energy to looking after Ruth's property, thus possibly having to neglect his own. Ultimately, the land would go to Ruth's heirs, not his own.[5]

Commenting on the omission of the nearer relative's name, Matthew Poole writes:

> Doubtless Boaz knew his name, and called him by it; but it is omitted by the holy writer, partly because it was unnecessary to know it; and principally in way of contempt, as is usual, and as a just punishment upon him, that he who would not preserve his brother's name might lose his own.[6]

The closer relative is widely taken to typify the law. Ten witnesses (the Ten Commandments) confirm its inability to redeem the sinner. "The law can't redeem those whom it condemns. It would be against its own purpose."[7] The law could not redeem because it was weak through the flesh (Rom. 8:3).

The refusal of the closer relative freed Boaz, who was next in line, to marry Ruth.

4:7, 8 In those days, all transactions concerning redemption and exchange were confirmed by one of the parties taking **off his sandal** and handing it to the other. The law actually specified that the widow should take off the sandal of the refusing kinsman and spit in his face (Deut. 25:9). In this case **the closer relative** simply **took off his sandal and gave it to** Boaz.

4:9–12 As soon as **Boaz** received the sandal, he announced that he would purchase **Elimelech's** property and marry **Ruth the Moabitess**. The crowd blessed Boaz, wishing him a posterity as numerous as that of **Rachel and Leah**. The mention of **Perez**, the offspring of **Tamar** by **Judah**, overlooks the sordid aspects of that story and concentrates on the fact that it was another case of levirate marriage involving an Israelite and a foreigner.

VI. THE ROYAL GENEALOGY OF DAVID TRACED BACK TO OBED (4:13–22)

4:13–16 **Boaz** married **Ruth**, and **she bore** him **a son** named Obed (*servant*). **Naomi** took the baby as her own and **became a nurse to him**.

4:17–22 **Obed** later became **the** ancestor **of Jesse**, **the father of David**. Thus the book closes with a short genealogy of **David** (*beloved*) which was to become part of a greater genealogy—that of David's great Son, the Lord Jesus Christ (Matt. 1). This genealogy is not intended to be complete. **Salmon** lived at the beginning of the period of the judges, and David was not born until the beginning of the period of the kings, a span of almost 400 years. Names are often deliberately omitted in biblical genealogies.

With this little genealogy ending with David, the reader is prepared for the monarchy and the next books in biblical order, 1 and 2 Samuel.

ENDNOTES

[1](Intro) J. Vernon McGee, *Ruth and Esther: Women of Faith*, p. 15.

[2](Intro) Irving L. Jensen, *Judges/Ruth*, p. 80.

[3](2:4–12) Leon Morris (with Arthur E. Cundall), *Judges and Ruth*, pp. 276, 277.

[4](4:1–6) The Hebrew here is colorful. Instead of giving the man's name the text calls him *so and so* (*peloni almoni*, NKJV marg.).

[5](4:1–6) Source unknown.

[6](4:1–6) Matthew Poole, *Matthew Poole's Commentary on the Holy Bible*, p. 511.

[7](4:1–6) Source unknown.

BIBLIOGRAPHY

For Bibliography see Judges.

FIRST SAMUEL

Introduction

"For sheer interest, I Samuel is unsurpassed. Not only does it recount eventful history; it is eventful history interwoven with the biographies of three colourful personalities—Samuel, Saul, David: and it is around these three that the chapters are grouped."

—J. Sidlow Baxter

I. Unique Place in the Canon

Without 1 and 2 Samuel there would be a gaping hole in the OT Canon. Originally one book, Samuel was first divided into two in the Septuagint translation for convenience. Every version of the OT, including printed Hebrew Bibles, has followed suit ever since.

Untold millions of Jewish and Christian children have been charmed and edified by the stories of Samuel, David and Goliath, David and Jonathan, David's flight from Saul, his kindness to Mephibosheth, and his sorrow over his son Absalom's rebellion and death.

On a more doctrinal level, more mature readers have studied the Davidic Covenant and the dreadful parallels to David's sin with Bathsheba that cropped up among his own children.

First and Second Samuel bridge the gap between the judges and the full establishment of the royal line of David. They hold a unique place in the history of Israel.

II. Authorship

While Jewish tradition makes Samuel the author of the book that is now divided into 1 and 2 Samuel, this authorship can only apply to the events *during* his own lifetime (1:1—25:1).[1] Much of the material in these books takes place *after* the prophet's demise.

It is possible that one of the young prophets who studied under Samuel wrote the book, incorporating writings of his teacher. Another possibility is that Abiathar, a priest who would be accustomed to keeping close records, compiled the book. He was closely associated with David's career and even spent time in exile with him.

III. Date

The date of the books of Samuel is impossible to pinpoint. The early part may date from about 1000 B.C. The fact that no reference is made to the captivity of Israel (722 B.C.) certainly demands a date before that event. Some believe that references to "Israel" and "Judah" demand a date after 931 B.C., when the monarchy split into these two parts. Such terms could easily have been used before the political split, however, somewhat as in American history the terms "Yankees" and "Southrons" were used before the secession of 1861.

IV. Background and Theme

First and Second Samuel trace God's dealings with Israel from the twelfth to the early tenth centuries B.C. *Samuel* (the prophet-judge), *Saul* (the rejected king), and *David* (the shepherd-king) are the main characters around which the narrative is framed.

Samuel was raised up by God to end the period of the judges and to inaugurate the era of the kings. He lived in a day that saw the failure of the priesthood (represented by Eli and his sons) and the introduction of the prophetic ministry. Samuel himself was the last of the judges, the first of the prophets of this period (not the first prophet in Scripture—Gen. 20:7), and the man to anoint the first kings of Israel. Although a Levite, he was not of the family of Aaron; yet he served as a priest, apparently with God's approval. His heart was pure and devoted; Eli's was polluted and disobedient.

The theme of Samuel is how God, Israel's true King, at the people's request delegated royal sovereignty first to Saul, and then to David and his lineage. Eugene Merrill ties the books in nicely with the theme of the whole Bible:

> Also through David's royal house his greater Son, Jesus Christ, eventually became incarnate. Christ perfectly exercised kingship in His own life, and provided in His death and resurrection the basis on which all people who believe can reign with and through Him (2 Sam. 7:12–16; Ps. 89:36–37; Isa. 9:7).[2]

OUTLINE

I. SAMUEL'S MINISTRY UNTIL THE ANOINTING OF SAUL (Chaps. 1—9)
- A. Samuel's Birth and Childhood (Chap. 1)
- B. Hannah's Song (2:1–10)
- C. Eli and His Wicked Sons (2:11–36)
- D. Samuel's Call (Chap. 3)
- E. The Ark of God (Chaps. 4—7)
  1. The Ark Captured (Chap. 4)
  2. The Ark's Power (Chap. 5)
  3. The Ark Restored (Chaps. 6, 7)
- F. A King Demanded and Chosen (Chaps. 8, 9)

II. SAUL'S REIGN UNTIL HIS REJECTION (Chaps. 10—15)
- A. Anointing and Confirmation (Chaps. 10, 11)
- B. Rebuke and Charge to the People (Chap. 12)
- C. Disobedience and Rejection (Chaps. 13—15)
  1. Saul's Sinful Sacrifice (Chap. 13)
  2. Saul's Rash Vows (Chap. 14)
  3. Saul's Incomplete Obedience (Chap. 15)

III. DAVID'S LIFE UNTIL THE DEATH OF SAUL (Chaps. 16—30)
- A. Anointing by Samuel (16:1–13)
- B. Ministering to Saul (16:14–23)

C. Defeating Goliath (Chap. 17)
D. Marrying Michal (Chap. 18)
E. Fleeing from Saul (Chaps. 19—26)
  1. Jonathan's Loyalty (Chaps. 19, 20)
  2. Ahimelech's Kindness to David (Chap. 21)
  3. David's Escape and Saul's Slaughter of the Priests (Chap. 22)
  4. Keilah's Betrayal (Chap. 23)
  5. Saul Spared (Chap. 24)
  6. Nabal's Folly (Chap. 25)
  7. Saul Spared a Second Time (Chap. 26)
F. Living in Philistia (Chaps. 27—30)
  1. Ziklag Acquired (Chap. 27)
  2. Saul's Doom Foretold (Chap. 28)
  3. David Discharged by Achish (Chap. 29)
  4. Amalekites Defeated (Chap. 30)

IV. SAUL'S DEATH (Chap. 31)

Commentary

I. SAMUEL'S MINISTRY UNTIL THE ANOINTING OF SAUL (Chaps. 1—9)

A. Samuel's Birth and Childhood (Chap. 1)

1:1–10 First Samuel opens by introducing us to **Elkanah** and his **two wives**, **Hannah** (*grace*) and **Peninnah** (*pearl*). He was a Levite from **Ramathaim Zophim** in **Ephraim**; hence the designation **Ephraimite** in verse 1 (cf. 1 Chron. 6:22–28). As a faithful historical record, the Bible notes the practice of polygamy but never approves it. As was the case with Leah and Rachel, one wife was fruitful while the other was barren. This caused rivalry in the the home because, although **Hannah** was childless, she was more **loved** by her husband. When the family traveled to **Shiloh . . . yearly** to celebrate one of the feasts, Hannah would receive **a double portion** of the peace **offering** (vv. 3–5). But this drew forth stinging taunts from Peninnah. Year after year her barbs cut deeper and deeper, until finally, in desperation, Hannah took the matter before the **Lord** at the **tabernacle**.

1:11–18 Hannah vowed that if God would **give** her **a male child**, she would **give him** back **to the Lord**. He would be a Nazirite from birth. Bishop Hall counsels:

> The way to obtain any benefit is to devote it in our hearts to the glory of that God of whom we ask it; by this means shall God both please his servant and honor Himself.[3]

The old priest, **Eli**, saw Hannah's **lips** moving and supposed her to be **drunk**. But as soon as she had explained her actions, he perceived her seriousness, blessed her, and sent her on her way **in peace**. Hannah was concerned about her *physical* barrenness. We should mourn our *spiritual* barrenness.

1:19–28 When Hannah's prayer was answered, she named her baby **Samuel** (*heard of God*),[4] because he was **"asked . . . from the LORD." When** Samuel was **weaned**, she **took him . . . to the house of the LORD** and **lent him to the LORD** in a once-for-all act of dedication. From the outset the boy assisted the priests and ministered before the Lord. The last phrase in verse 28 includes Samuel: He was a worshiper, although very young, because his life was devoted to the service of **the LORD**.

B. Hannah's Song (2:1–10)

The devotedness of Elkanah's wife and son stands out against the depravity of Eli's family. After giving her son to the Lord, **Hannah** poured out her heart in thanksgiving. Her words reveal an in-depth knowledge of God, His character, and His deeds. The prayer seems to rebuke Peninnah for the many spiteful things she had said to Hannah, but it prophetically goes beyond this domestic squabble to the triumph of Israel over her foes and to the eventual reign of Christ. Mary's song, often called the *Magnificat* (Luke 1:46–55), was obviously influenced by her knowledge of Hannah's song.

C. Eli and His Wicked Sons (2:11–36)

2:11–17 The narrative now turns to Eli's wicked **sons**. They **did not know the LORD** in the sense that they had not been saved by faith. Three sins are charged to them: They robbed **the people** of their share of the peace offering, not being satisfied with just the breast and thigh (cf. Lev. 7:28–34). They demanded **meat** before the **fat** had been offered to God, thus shirking the law. Third, they wanted to roast the **meat** instead of boiling it, putting their own carnal appetites first. If anyone tried to protest, they took the **meat . . . by force**. Their **sin . . . was very great** because they treated the Lord's offering with contempt.

2:18–21 In contrast to their wickedness was the devotedness of the child **Samuel**, and the faithfulness of Samuel's parents to the **yearly** feasts. Since the firstfruits of Hannah's womb had been dedicated to the Lord, she was blessed with **three sons and two daughters**. It is a good illustration of our Lord's promise: "Give, and it shall be given to you."

2:22–26 It wasn't until **Eli** heard reports of immorality that he finally reproved **his sons**. But it was far too late for his mild verbal reproof to have any effect. They hardened their hearts and so were judicially hardened, like Pharaoh of old, for God had determined to destroy them. During this time **Samuel** was quietly growing, his purity and goodness pleasing **both . . . the LORD and men**. If we remember that these events took place during the time of the judges, it is not surprising that the priesthood failed to escape the moral decadence of the period.

2:27–36 The Lord's rebuke of Eli was as harsh as Eli's rebuke of his sons had been soft. An unnamed **man of God** appeared and announced the doom of Eli's **priestly . . . house**. The prophet began by reviewing God's call to Aaron's family to be His **priest**, and His generous allowance of sacrificial meats for their sustenance. He then rebuked **Eli** for allowing his sons' appetites to have priority over the claims of God (v. 29). The Lord's previous promise of the perpetuity of the priesthood assumed that the priests would be men of good character. But because of the wickedness of Eli and his **house**, they would no longer be allowed to function in the priestly service; no member of his family would reach old age; the sanctuary at Shiloh would fall into decay; and Eli's posterity would be a grief and a shame. Furthermore, **both . . . Hophni and Phinehas** would **die** on the same **day** as **a sign** that all these judgments would come to pass.

The doom of Eli's house was fulfilled in: The murder of Ahimelech and all his sons (except Abiathar) by Saul (v. 31; 22:16–20); the expulsion of Abiathar from the priesthood by Solomon (vv. 32, 33; 1 Kgs. 2:27); and the death of **Hophni and Phinehas** (v. 34; 4:11). Eli was from the house of Ithamar, and when Abiathar was later removed by Solomon, the priesthood was restored to the house of Eleazar, where it should have been all along. **Phinehas**, the son of Eli, is not to be confused with Phinehas, the grandson of Aaron (Num. 25:7, 8).

The **faithful priest** promised in verse 35 is Zadok, of the house of Eleazar, who ministered in the days of David and Solomon. His priesthood will endure, even during the Millennial Reign of Christ (Ezek. 44:15). But the descendants of Eli would desire the priest's office not in order to serve the Lord, but simply to get something to eat (v. 36). Many see a messianic allusion in the **faithful priest** of verse 35, partly in light of the word **forever**.

D. Samuel's Call (Chap. 3)

3:1–3 At the time that **Samuel** was serving **the LORD** in **the tabernacle** at Shiloh, **the word of the LORD was rare**; that is, the Lord very seldom spoke in visions to men. Williams sees in the first three verses a picture of Israel's moral condition.

> Night reigned; the lamp of God was going out in the Temple; the High Priest's eyes were grown dim so that he could not clearly see; and both he and Samuel were asleep.[5]

The lamp of God refers to the lampstand, whose light was extinguished at sunrise.

3:4–9 One night, shortly before morning, **Samuel** heard a voice calling him. He thought it was **Eli**, but the priest had not called. **Samuel did not yet know the LORD** in the sense that he had never previously received a direct, personal revelation from Him (v. 7). After Samuel heard the voice two more times, Eli realized that **the LORD** was calling Samuel. The old priest told the boy to say, **"Speak, LORD, for Your servant hears,"** if he heard the voice again.

3:10–14 When **the LORD . . . called** the fourth time, Samuel replied, **"Speak, for Your servant hears,"** apparently leaving out the word "Lord." The Lord's message confirmed the judgment spoken earlier **against Eli** and **his house**, and the judgment may have included the defeat of Israel and the capture of the ark. The father was as much to blame as the **sons**, because **he did not restrain them** or turn them from their sins. They should have been put to death for their sacrilege instead of just being scolded. **Sacrifice** could not atone for their **iniquity**; their doom was sealed and was confirmed to Eli in the mouth of two witnesses: The man of God (chap. 2) and the boy prophet, Samuel (v. 14).

3:15–18 At first **Samuel was afraid to tell Eli** what the Lord had said, but under a solemn oath he revealed to the priest the impending judgment. Eli took the news submissively. Surely he realized God's justice in the sentence. Could God have struck down the sons of Aaron for their impiety

(Lev. 10) but leave Hophni and Phinehas unjudged?

3:19–21 It soon became known in **all Israel from Dan to Beersheba** that **the LORD was with . . . Samuel**, and all Israel recognized in the young lad **a** true **prophet of the LORD**.

E. The Ark of God (Chaps. 4—7)

1. The Ark Captured (Chap. 4)

4:1–4 The next three chapters follow the **ark of the covenant of the LORD** on a journey into and back out of enemy territory. God would defend His honor in the midst of **the Philistines** (chap. 5), but He would not defend the Israelites when He was in their midst because they had ceased to honor Him. When they **went out to battle against the Philistines** at **Ebenezer**, they lost **four thousand men**. In an effort to turn the tide, the elders had **the ark of the covenant** brought from **Shiloh . . . into the camp**.

4:5–11 The Israelites rejoiced greatly **when** they saw **the ark**, and **the Philistines** feared greatly because they knew the reputation of Jehovah. But they encouraged themselves and drew near to the battle once more. To their amazement, **Israel . . . fled, thirty thousand foot soldiers** were slain, the priests **Hophni and Phinehas** were killed, and **the ark** itself **was captured**!

4:12–22 When a runner went back **to Shiloh** and informed **Eli** that **the ark** had **been captured**, the old priest **fell . . . backward . . . off** his magistrate's **seat**, broke **his neck**, and **died**. The bad news caused **Phinehas' wife** to go into **labor**, and she died in childbirth. Hearing of the death of **her father-in-law and her husband** did not seem to affect her as much as the news that **the ark** had fallen into the hands of the Philistines. As she died, **she named** her son **Ichabod**, (*inglorious*), **saying, "The glory has departed."**

2. The Ark's Power (Chap. 5)

5:1–5 The Philistines . . . brought . . . the ark of God . . . from Ebenezer to Ashdod and **set it** in the temple of **Dagon**, the national god of the Philistines. **Dagon** was supposed to be the father of Baal, another idol we meet often in Scripture. **The Philistines . . . set . . . the ark** beside the image of **Dagon**, thinking them equal. But when they returned to the temple **in the morning** they found that the Lord had caused Dagon to topple to the foot **of the ark**. Not perceiving the significance of this event, they once again **set** up Dagon by the ark. But **the next morning** there was no doubt as to who was the stronger, for Dagon's **head** and **hands** had been **broken off**. If Dagon were a real god, he could have defended himself. His followers should have faced the facts. Instead, they made a superstitious rule about walking **on the threshold**. Dagon did not fare well in confrontation with the God of Israel. Samson had destroyed his temple in Gaza, God giving him the strength to pull the entire building down on the noblemen of Philistia (Judg. 16). Now Jehovah Himself maimed the image of Dagon, demonstrating that there is no wisdom (**head**) or power (**hands**) to be found in idols.

5:6–9 Not only their idol but **the people of Ashdod** themselves began to feel the displeasure **of the LORD**, suffering confusion, swellings or **tumors**, and death. In desperation the Philistines decided to move **the ark . . . to Gath**, another of their great cities. Here again the men were struck with **tumors**.

5:10–12 When **the ark** was **sent**

. . . to Ekron, the people were extremely frightened, their fears being justified by a **deadly destruction** that killed many. **The men who did not die** broke out with **tumors**. They begged that **the ark** be sent **back to** Israel.

3. *The Ark Restored (Chaps. 6, 7)*

6:1–6 In **seven** short **months . . . the Philistines** had gained a proper fear of **the ark**. They wanted to **return it** to Israel, but in the proper way so as to avoid further judgment. The heathen **priests and . . . diviners** were consulted. They suggested returning the ark with a guilt or **trespass offering** of **five golden tumors** and **five golden rats**. It was common among these people to appease their gods and make indemnity with an offering of whatever had caused destruction among them. The reference to **rats** leads Bible students to think that **the plague** that afflicted the cities was **the** bubonic **plague** carried by fleas on **rats**. The priests further reminded them of Egypt's fate at the hands of Jehovah, and urged them not to **harden** their **hearts as the Egyptians and Pharaoh hardened** theirs, but to make every effort to return **the ark . . . to its** proper **place**.

6:7–12 To make sure that the things which had happened to them were judgments of Jehovah, and not mere **chance**, the Philistine priests arranged the details of the return trip in a way that would evidence divine intervention. The **two milk cows** that were used to pull **the cart** had young **calves** and it would violate all natural instincts if they left their calves behind. **The cows** had **never been yoked**, yet they pulled well in a yoke together, turning aside neither **to the right hand** nor **the left**. Without being guided, **the cows headed straight** toward **Beth Shemesh**, in the territory of Judah!

6:13–18 **The men of Beth Shemesh were reaping** when **the ark** drew near. What a sight—two unattended cows bringing the ark of God back to Israel! Great rejoicing broke out. **The cart** was used to make a fire, and **the cows** were **offered as a burnt offering to the LORD**. **The ark** and **the chest** containing the **trespass offering** were placed **on** top of a **large stone**.

There is a *spiritual parallel* in the story of **the cows** of **Beth Shemesh**. Christian missionaries leave home and family and carry the message of the Lord to wherever the Lord guides them, turning neither to the right nor to the left. They cause people to rejoice when they see the Lord by faith. They are prepared for service or for sacrifice.

6:19–21 But **the men of Beth Shemesh** did not treat **the ark of the LORD** as holy; **they had looked into the ark**. As a result, God **struck fifty thousand and seventy of** them. Fearful of having the ark remain in their midst, the people **sent messengers to** the men of **Kirjath Jearim**, and asked them to **take the ark**. (It is doubtful that there were 50,070 men at Beth Shemesh. Josephus,[6] Keil and Delitzsch[7] and many other authorities say that the text should simply read seventy men, since the 50,000 is lacking in many Hebrew manuscripts.)

7:1–6 **The ark** was **brought** to **the house of Abinadab** in **Kirjath Jearim**, where it **remained** for **twenty years**. Then **Samuel** came forward and urged the people to **return to the LORD** so that God could **deliver** them **from** their Philistine oppressors. Idols were thrown **away** and the nation **gathered** to Samuel **at Mizpah**. There they **fasted** and repented before Jehovah. Their repentance was symbolized by pouring **out . . . water** on the ground.

7:7–14 Hearing that the Israelites were **at Mizpah**, and supposing that a revolt was in the making, **the Philistines** attacked. The Hebrews, unprepared for war, were terrified. When they pleaded with **Samuel** to intercede for them, he offered **a whole burnt offering** (which it seems Levites could do—1 Chron. 23:26–31), and prayed. God subsequently routed the enemy miraculously with **loud thunder**, and Israel won the day. In gratitude **Samuel . . . set . . . up . . . a stone** as a monument and named it **"Ebenezer"** (*stone of help*). Verse 13 refers only to a temporary victory, as is clear from the last part of the verse and from 9:16. Some land was also recovered at this time, and **Israel** enjoyed **peace** with her neighbors for a while.

7:15–17 After this, **Samuel** became a **circuit** judge, traveling through the cities of **Israel** and administering justice according to the law of the Lord. He lived in **Ramah**, **his** father's **home**, and **built an altar . . . there**. We aren't told why he didn't return to the Lord's altar, now at Nob, nor why he allowed the ark to remain in Abinadab's house. But these were days of irregularities, many things being practiced which God allowed even though they weren't according to His original design.

Chapter 7 is a study in revival. God first raised up a man, Samuel, who called the people to repentance, confession, and cleansing. Intercession was made through the blood of a lamb (a type of Calvary's Lamb), and then there was victory. These are the steps to individual as well as national revival.

F. A King Demanded and Chosen (Chaps. 8, 9)

8:1–5 In his **old** age, **Samuel** tried to have **his** two **sons** succeed him as **judges**. But they were wicked men who accepted **bribes** and **perverted justice**. Like Eli before him, Samuel did not turn his sons from their evil ways, and so his house was rejected also. **The elders of Israel** refused to accept **Joel** and **Abijah**; they wanted **a king** instead, like **the** other **nations**.

8:6–18 It was God's intention, of course, that He Himself should be the King of Israel. His people were to be holy, and not like any other nation on earth. But they didn't *want* to be different; they wanted to conform to the world. Samuel was grieved by such a request, but **the Lord** told him to do as they said. After all, **they** had **not rejected** the prophet, but the Lord. In agreeing to their wishes, Samuel was to protest **solemnly** and to **forewarn them** as to **the behavior of the king** they would get. In brief, the king would enrich *himself* by impoverishing the people, would draft their young men and women for military and domestic duties, and would make virtual slaves of them. It was true that God had made provisions for the rule of kings in the law (Deut. 17:14–20), but His perfect will was that He Himself should be their King (8:7; 12:12). These laws in Deuteronomy were meant to curb the evil that was sure to follow.

8:19–22 When **the people** persisted in their demand, despite the warning, the Lord again told Samuel to do as they asked **and make them a king.** The prophet then sent the people home. Soon they would have their king.

9:1–14 Now **Saul**, the **son** of **Kish** (**a Benjamite**), enters the picture. While searching for his father's **donkeys**, he and **his servant** decided to inquire as to the animals' whereabouts from **a man of God** in a nearby **city**. With a small gift in hand, they approached

the city and found out from **some young women** that **the seer** they were looking for would make an appearance that very day at a religious festival. As they hurried along, they met the man they sought. Little did **Saul** realize that the prophet was also looking for him!

9:15–21 On the preceding day **the LORD had** promised to direct **Samuel** to the **man** who was to be king. Now it was revealed to him that **Saul** was **the man**. But the prophet did not tell Saul immediately. First he invited him to a feast. **The high place** (i.e., a place set apart for worship) was usually connected with the worship of idols, but in this case it was for the worship of Jehovah. Samuel then told the tall, handsome Benjamite that he would have some important news for him in the morning. Apparently without being told of Saul's mission, Samuel told him that the **donkeys** had **been found**, and that he was **not** to **be anxious**. What were a few **donkeys**, anyway? He was soon to possess "all that is desirable in Israel." Saul took this statement with apparent modesty. **Benjamin** was certainly **the smallest . . . tribe** in **Israel**. In the past their numbers had been reduced to 600 because of their wickedness (Judg. 20).

9:22–27 At the banquet **Saul** was given **the place of honor** and was served the choicest cut of meat. In the evening Samuel had a long talk with him. The next day **Samuel** detained **Saul** as he was leaving **the city** and revealed **the word of God** to him.

II. SAUL'S REIGN UNTIL HIS REJECTION (Chaps. 10—15)

A. Anointing and Confirmation (Chaps. 10, 11)

10:1–6 Privately **Samuel** anointed Saul as ruler of Israel by pouring **oil . . . on his head**. The priesthood had been inaugurated with anointing (Lev. 8:12), and now the first king was **anointed** in the same manner. A public ceremony would follow later. Three signs were then given to confirm the word of the Lord to Saul: (1) **Two men** would meet him at **Rachel's tomb** and tell him that his father's **donkeys** had **been found**; (2) **three men** would **meet** him at the oak **of Tabor**, en route to **Bethel**, and would **give** him **two loaves of bread**; (3) when he would **come to "the hill of God"** and would **meet a group of prophets**, **the Spirit of the LORD** would **come upon** him and he would **prophesy**.

10:7–9 After all **these signs** occurred, Saul was to go **to Gilgal** and wait seven days for Samuel to come and to offer sacrifices. All the signs in verses 2–6 took place that same day; the events in Gilgal occurred later (13:7–15).

It should not be concluded from verse 9 that Saul was genuinely converted. Actually, he was a man after the flesh, as his later history so evidently demonstrates. He was equipped for his official position as ruler of God's people by the Spirit even though he did not know God in a personal, saving way. In other words, he was God's man *officially* even though we believe he was not a true believer.[8]

10:10–16 The **prophets** were dedicated and zealous men, and it surprised **the people** to see Saul **prophesying . . . among them**. This gave rise to the **proverb: "Is Saul also among the prophets?"** It became a common saying expressing surprise that Saul should engage in an activity that was so out-of-character for him. **Saul's uncle** (not his father, as we would expect) quizzed him about his discussion with Samuel. **Saul** mentioned his visit with **Samuel** but did not disclose that he had been privately anointed as king.

10:17–19 Meanwhile, **Samuel** assembled **the people . . . at Mizpah** to announce the appointment of **a king**. Before making the actual announcement, he once again reminded them that their demand for **a king** was a rejection of the **God** who **brought** them **out of Egypt** and into the Promised Land. When Saul was selected he was hiding either because of modesty or fear. Matthew Henry gives four reasons why Saul might have been afraid:

> (1) Because he was conscious to himself of unfitness for so great a trust. . . . (2) Because it would expose him to the envy of his neighbors that were ill-affected towards him. (3) Because he understood, by what Samuel had said, that the people sinned in asking a king, and it was in anger that God granted their request. (4) Because the affairs of Israel were at this time in a bad posture; the Philistines were strong, the Ammonites threatening: and he must be bold indeed that will set sail in a storm.[9]

10:20–27 **Saul** was brought forth and presented to the people as their **king**. A better physical specimen could scarcely be found in all Israel. Several **valiant men** attached themselves to Saul and accompanied him to his **home** in **Gibeah**, but not everyone was solidly behind the new monarch. Saul wisely **held his peace** in front of these **rebels** who **despised him**.

11:1–5 Jabesh Gilead was a city on the east side of the Jordan River in the **territory** belonging to Gad. When the Ammonites, the neighbors to the southeast, besieged the city, the inhabitants asked for terms of surrender. But **Nahash** wanted to maim them and make them a **reproach** in **Israel** by gouging out their **right eyes**. Surprisingly, the Ammonites allowed **the elders of Jabesh** to **send** for help. Perhaps **Nahash** was not fully prepared, or was not afraid that the rest of Israel would help Jabesh. **Messengers** were sent **to Gibeah**, where **Saul** was still working in **the field**. It was high time to assert himself as Israel's new king!

11:6–11 With the vividly threatening object lesson of a chopped up yoke of oxen, Saul summoned the nation to arms. **The fear of the Lord** came **on the people**. **Israel** and **Judah** combined mustered 330,000 strong at **Bezek** and marched all night to **Jabesh**, where they thoroughly routed **the Ammonites**.

11:12–15 Flushed with victory, **the people** wanted to kill those who formerly had not accepted Saul's rule. But **Saul** wisely stopped them. The fact that **the Lord** had given the victory was enough for him. **Samuel** then called a solemn assembly at **Gilgal**, and Saul's **kingdom** was renewed on a nationwide scale. There was no opposition this time. Gilgal speaks of spiritual renewal (Josh. 5:9).

B. Rebuke and Charge to the People (Chap. 12)

12:1–13 After the ceremony to renew the kingdom at Gilgal, **Samuel** spoke to **all Israel**. He first of all reminded them of his righteous rule as judge. No one could charge him with injustice. But in asking for a king, Israel had rejected this rule and God's sway over them. The Lord had been gracious in the past, raising up deliverers when they were needed. **"Bedan"** in verse 11 probably refers to Barak (NKJV marg., LXX and Syriac versions).[10] **Samuel** placed himself in the line of deliverers that began with

Moses. But Israel was ungrateful for these past mercies and **cried** out for **a king**. The Lord working through His judges wasn't enough for them, so He gave them Saul.

12:14–18 In demanding a king, they committed a great sin. But **if** they would **obey... the LORD**, even now He would bless them. **If... not**, they would experience His wrath. As solemn proof, **Samuel** prayed down a great thunderstorm, an obvious sign from God because such a storm was unseasonal **during the wheat harvest** and too well-timed to be a fluke of nature.

12:19–25 Stark **fear** gripped **the people** and they implored **Samuel** to **pray for** them. His prayer had brought down judgment; it could also bring down mercy. To this he replied with another appeal to follow **the LORD**; that was the way to avoid judgment. As for him, he couldn't stop praying for them; to do so would have been **sin**. This important statement shows that prayerlessness is *sin* and not just carelessness.

C. Disobedience and Rejection (Chaps. 13—15)

1. Saul's Sinful Sacrifice (Chap. 13)

13:1 There are obvious difficulties with verse 1, as can readily be seen by reading the verse in different versions. The KJV and NKJV read: **"Saul reigned *one* year; and when he had reigned *two* years over Israel..."** The ERV says: "Saul was *thirty* years old when he began to reign, and he reigned two years over Israel..." The RSV states: "Saul was... years old when he began to reign, and he reigned... two years over Israel." The NASB: "Saul was *forty* years old when he began to reign, and he reigned *thirty-two* years over Israel." Some manuscripts of the Septuagint simply omit the problem verse altogether! The most likely explanation for this confusion is that some letters were dropped out of the Hebrew text by careless copyists in later centuries.[11] We do know that Saul was a mature man when he came to power because his son Jonathan was old enough to go to war.

13:2–5 Saul had established a standing army of **three thousand men**. **Jonathan** took his detachment and successfully **attacked** the Philistine **garrison... in Geba**, north of Jerusalem. This incited the Philistines to prepare a huge army for all-out war. (Some translations, following the Syriac and some manuscripts of the Septuagint, read 3,000 chariots in verse 5, a more likely number to accommodate the **six thousand horsemen**.)[12]

13:6–9 The Hebrews responded to the challenge with great cowardice; some even fled across **the Jordan**. They had been under the yoke for so long that breaking free seemed almost impossible; the Philistines possessed every advantage. As **Saul** waited for **Samuel** at **Gilgal** (see 10:8), more and more men were missing at each roll call. The seventh day began, **but** still **Samuel** failed to appear. With his forces diminishing and with war impending, Saul was moved by expediency to offer **the burnt offering** himself, even though he had no authority to do so, not being a Levite. Even if Samuel was late, that did not justify Saul's intruding into the priestly office.

13:10–14 Arriving immediately afterward, **Samuel** realized what **Saul** had **done**. What appeared to be valid excuses did not change the fact that Saul had disobeyed God. For this he would lose the **kingdom**. God had already found another **man**, one **after**

His own heart. This was the first of several sins in Saul's life which resulted in his losing the throne of Israel. The others were: his rash vow (chap. 14); sparing Agag and the best of the spoil in the battle with the Amalekites (chap. 15); the murder of Ahimelech and eighty-four other priests (chap. 22); his repeated attempts on David's life (chaps. 18–26); and consulting the witch at En Dor (chap. 28).

13:15–23 **Saul** took his **six hundred men** and joined **Jonathan** at **Gibeah. The Philistines, encamped** a short distance away at **Michmash,** began sending out **raiders** to the north, west, and east, and Israel seemed helpless to halt them. The Philistines had been in such complete control for so long that they had removed every **blacksmith** from **Israel.** The Hebrews had to come to them to get their farm implements sharpened. Only a few men had **swords.** Things looked grim indeed.

2. *Saul's Rash Vows (Chap. 14)*

14:1–15 Seeing his father's inactivity, **Jonathan** slipped away with **his armorbearer** to attack **the Philistines.** This was not a brash stunt or a foolish suicide mission. Jonathan was looking to God to provide a great victory. It did not matter that there were only two of them. Jonathan's confidence was: **"For nothing restrains the LORD from saving by many or by few."** Jonathan's faith would be rewarded. God showed him that he would have success when the Philistines would invite him up, perhaps thinking he was a deserter. As soon as the Philistines said **"Come up to us," . . . Jonathan climbed up** to their **garrison,** and soon laid **twenty** of their number in the dust. As the survivors fled, God sent an earthquake which caused great confusion in the Philistine camp. The *faith* evidenced by **Jonathan** (v. 6) and **his armorbearer** (v. 7) was all God needed to deal with the Philistines. Too bad that Saul's *foolishness* lessened the fruits of victory!

14:16–23 Saul's **watchmen** noticed the confusion and reported it to him. When **the roll** was **called, Jonathan and his armorbearer were** missing. **Saul** promptly called for **Ahijah** the priest to **bring the ark** so that he could inquire of the Lord. (The NKJV margin, following the Septuagint, reads *ephod* for *ark.*[13] The ark was probably still at Kirjath Jearim.) But Saul quickly changed his mind when the tumultuous **noise** among the enemy increased; he told **the priest** to **withdraw** his **hand**—i.e., to stop seeking the Lord's will (v. 19). He rallied his forces, convinced that he did not need divine guidance to know that the Lord was delivering the Philistines into his hands. Others also noticed that God was fighting for Israel. Those **Hebrews** who had previously defected turned on their Philistine masters, and even **the men . . . who had** been hiding **in the mountains of Ephraim** found new courage to join the battle. Everyone wants to fight when victory is almost won, but where are the Jonathans to make the initial confrontation?

14:24–30 To ensure speedy success, **Saul had** rashly forbidden his soldiers **under oath** to eat anything **until evening,** when the battle was over. He sealed his order with a curse. Hunger caused his men to become fatigued and thus put them at a disadvantage. Not knowing of his father's edict, **Jonathan** ate some **honey** to regain his strength. When he was told about the curse, he mourned that Israel's triumph was to be hindered by such a stupid order.

14:31–42 Saul's restriction not only angered Jonathan, but it endangered the people as well. When the fighting was over, they **rushed on the spoil**, killed the livestock, and **ate** it without draining **the blood**, in violation of Leviticus 17:10–14 and Deuteronomy 12:23–25. When **Saul** heard this, he rebuked them and set up **a large stone** where animals were to be **brought** and slain properly. He also **built an altar**, his **first**. In his zeal, Saul wanted to pursue **the Philistines** into the **night**, so he again talked to **the priest** about consulting **God**. But God **did not answer him**. This led Saul to believe that there was **sin** in the camp. As was done in such cases, the lot was brought out, and to Saul's surprise, **Jonathan was taken**, that is, shown to be the guilty one by the way the lot came out.

14:43–46 **Jonathan** explained what had happened, and Saul, to save face, ordered him put to death. **But the people** showed more sense than did their king. Hadn't **Jonathan . . . worked with God** to bring this great victory? How could God be displeased with him for breaking Saul's curse, when He had used him so mightily in battle? No, Jonathan would **not die**. Thus the hero was spared an undeserved death. But while Saul was engaged in such unnecessary nonsense, **the Philistines** fled. For the second time his lack of wisdom had diminished his victory.

14:47–52 Verses 47 and 48 summarize some of Saul's military victories. The next three verses give details concerning his family. The last verse is a fulfillment of Samuel's prediction that the king would draft Israel's valiant sons into military service (1 Sam. 8:11).

3. Saul's Incomplete Obedience (Chap. 15)

15:1–3 Saul was on a downward slide and accelerating as he neared the bottom. No matter what he was given to do, he came short of complete obedience. In this chapter he was commanded by God to destroy the Amalekites—the nation that had mercilessly **ambushed** the Hebrew stragglers when they had left **Egypt . . . on the way** to Canaan (Deut. 25:17–19). The order was very clear; everything that breathed was to be destroyed; it was devoted to God. God's longsuffering had put up with the people of **Amalek** for years, but His word against them had not changed (Ex. 17:14–16; Num. 24:20). They were to be blotted out as punishment for their sin.

15:4–12 **Saul gathered** an army and marched south **to a city of Amalek**. Before attacking, he warned **the Kenites** to escape because these nomadic Midianites had shown **kindness to . . . Israel** during the Exodus. This action showed that **Saul** was not just interested in carnage; rather, he was executing the vengeance of the Lord on a wicked people. He thoroughly defeated **the Amalekites** and put everything to **the sword** *except* the **king** and **the best of the** spoil. (A remnant, probably living elsewhere, also survived—see 30:1–6; 2 Sam. 8:12; 1 Chron. 4:43.) Miles away, **the Lord** informed **Samuel** of Saul's disobedience. This greatly disturbed Samuel and drove him to spend the **night** in prayer. By **morning** it was clear what he must do.

15:13–35 On the way **to Gilgal**, Saul stopped and built **a monument**, celebrating his victory. But **Samuel** saw things differently and challenged **Saul** for disobeying. Saul was never short of excuses, but the noise of his failure reached the prophet's ears and left Saul's excuses hanging in midair. *Rejected!* Saul had heard that before (13:14). It came again with stunning force. Saul was constantly redefining the Lord's commands, doing what seemed best to him rather than what God said was best. He made a show of repentance and pleaded with Samuel not to abandon him. He even **tore** the prophet's **robe** when he tried to leave. This too was a sign that **the kingdom** would be **torn . . . from** Saul and **given . . . to** another man.

After accompanying Saul to **worship the LORD, Samuel** called for **Agag** to be brought forth. Thinking that he might be spared, **Agag came to him cautiously** saying, **"Surely the bitterness of death is past"** (v. 32). **Samuel** then **hacked** him **in pieces** with the sword. The aged judge carried a burden the rest of his life because of Saul's failure. In one sense even God **regretted that He had made Saul king over Israel**.

We should memorize verse 22. It is one of the classics in the Word of God. Obedience first, last, and always. It is the watchword of those who would serve and please the Lord. Erdmann comments:

> In the following words: **To obey is better than sacrifice**, the thought takes a new turn: apart from what alone is well-pleasing to God, only an obedient disposition of mind is in itself something good, the offering, without such a disposition, is not a good thing, has no moral value. . . . So disobedience and the thence-resulting rebellion and defiant self-dependence is similar in essence to, stands on the same moral plane with the outward wickedness of *witchcraft*, that is, "divination in the service of anti-godly demonic powers" (Keil), and of idolatry.[14]

Verses 29 and 35 seem to be contradictory. The first says that God does not change His mind or **relent**, while the second says that He **regretted** making **Saul king**. Verse 29 describes God in His *essential character*. He is unchanging and unchangeable, the immutable One. Verse 35 means that a change in Saul's *conduct* required a corresponding change in God's *plans and purposes* for him. To be consistent with His attributes, God must bless obedience and punish disobedience.

III. DAVID'S LIFE UNTIL THE DEATH OF SAUL (Chaps. 16—30)

A. Anointing by Samuel (16:1–13)

16:1–3 While **Samuel** was still grieving over **Saul, the LORD** told him bluntly to face the fact that Saul was **rejected**; God had chosen another man to rule His people. **Samuel** was to go to Bethlehem and **anoint . . . one** of the **sons** of **Jesse** to be **king**. Secrecy is not the same as deceit. God was not telling Samuel to lie about his intentions in **Bethlehem**; he really did offer a **sacrifice** there. But the anointing of the new king was a secret affair, not to be made public for many years.

16:4–13 When **Samuel** came **to Bethlehem, the elders . . . trembled**. After inviting **Jesse and his sons . . . to the** sacrificial feast, he looked over the men one by one, confident that the next king was before him. But none was the Lord's choice. **Samuel** should have learned from his experience with Saul that **the outward** man is not nearly as important as the inner man (13:14). God judges **the heart** (v. 7). The principle of verse 7 has always been true: People do judge by looks, dress, and outward things. But today the mass media encourage this faulty outlook by using glamorous people in advertisements, television, and printed matter to such an extent that ordinary-looking people don't seem as satisfactory as they should. Saul was tall, dark, and handsome. Actually, David was **good-looking**, too (v. 12), but still looked too young for major service. Unfortunately the church, especially on television, has often emphasized, not spirituality, but superficial glamor—with disastrous results when these TV idols fall.

David had to be **brought** to the feast. He was so insignificant in his father's eyes that **Jesse** was sure the prophet wouldn't be interested in him. But **the LORD** was very interested in the shepherd boy, and **Samuel**, obeying God's voice, **anointed . . . David**. **From that** point onward **the Spirit of the LORD came** powerfully **upon David** and left Saul. It would be years before David wore Saul's crown, but from this **day forward** the kingdom was secure for David.

B. Ministering to Saul (16:14–23)

About this time Saul became afflicted with a form of mental disorder caused by an evil spirit. The expression **"a distressing spirit from the LORD"** is explained by the fact that what God *permits* He is often said to *do*. Dr. Rendle Short analyzes the king's problem as follows:

> King Saul would now be diagnosed as a typical example of manic-depressive insanity. The periods of intense gloom with occasional outbreaks of homicidal violence for no particular reason, the delusion that people were plotting against him . . . are unmistakable.[15]

Saul's servants suggested that the king find someone gifted in music to calm him. David's name was suggested, and Saul sent for him. Verse 18 shows that David had already made quite a name for himself, even before he faced Goliath. Now his music seemed to lift the king out of his depression. Saul liked him so well that he made David **his** personal **armorbearer**.

C. Defeating Goliath (Chap. 17)

17:1–11 The Philistines gathered their armies for **battle** near **the Valley of Elah**, southwest of Jerusalem and not far **from Gath**. **Saul and** his army assembled nearby, with **the Valley of Elah** between them. **A champion** by the name of **Goliath** came out of the Philistine camp daily for forty days, defying **the armies of Israel** to send him a worthy opponent. There were no volunteers. This giant was about nine feet nine inches tall and wore at least 175 pounds of armor. **His iron spearhead** alone weighed over fifteen pounds. The heavy weapons were no problem for Goliath, since he himself must have weighed somewhere between 600 and 750 pounds (possibly more, depending on his build). This gave him many times the strength of a normal man.

17:12–30 On one occasion, when **David** was bringing supplies to his three oldest **brothers at the** battlefront, he heard the taunts of the giant and saw the fear on the faces of the Hebrew soldiers. He asked **what** would **be done for the man who** silenced this swaggering brute. **Eliab, his oldest brother,** rebuked him, probably to mask his own cowardice, but David persisted in checking into the prizes that awaited **the man who** would kill the giant.

17:31–40 Saul soon got word that a young man had been found to fight for Israel, and **David** was brought before him. When Saul saw David, he had understandable doubts about the lad's ability. But David had known the power of God working through him when he defended his flock against the **lion** and the **bear**. He had proved God in private; now he could rely on God in public. Seeing his courage and determination, **Saul** gave him **his** own **armor**, but **David** discarded it because it was a hindrance to him. Instead, he went forth armed with **five smooth stones**, a **sling**, a **staff**, and the power of **the living God**!

17:41–54 When Goliath saw **David**, who was probably around twenty at this time, he was incensed that Israel should insult him by sending out what in his eyes was a mere child to fight him. But David had no trace of fear as he responded to the giant's curses. He had complete faith that the Lord would give him the victory. As Goliath moved toward him, **David . . . slung** the first **stone**, hitting him **in his forehead**. The giant **fell** forward **on his face**. David then used the Philistine's own **sword** to kill him and **cut off his head**. **When the Philistines saw** this, **they fled**, with **Israel** in hot pursuit.

17:55–58 These verses[16] seem to present a problem: It is strange that Saul did not recognize David when he had already appointed him as his armorbearer (16:21). However, it should be noted that it does not say that Saul did not know who this young hero *was*; it simply says that he asked, **"Whose son is this?"** Saul could have easily forgotten David's family background. Williams comments:

> Saul, having promised exemption of taxation to the family of the victor, and the hand of his daughter in marriage with a handsome dowry, naturally asks Abner for information respecting David's father and his position in society. . . .[17]

This seems to be confirmed by the fact that David later expressed his unworthiness to be the king's son-in-law (18:18). Michael Griffiths makes a good application:

> Both Jonathan (chap. 14) and David initiated action on a small front just where they were, but what they did led to great victories. There is a need for us alike to take the field locally. We cannot hope to take on the whole of the enemy force, but we do not have to do so. There is a work for Jesus ready at your "front." We are called to be bold and to take the initiative where we are. God will take care of the rest when, as a result of our action, the battle spreads along the whole front.[18]

D. Marrying Michal (Chap. 18)

18:1–5 A deep and lasting friendship sprang up between **Jonathan** and **David**. They were kindred souls, each possessing that rare quality of true courage. **Jonathan** was the legitimate successor to his father's throne, but in giving **his robe . . . to David** he indicated that he was willing to forgo his right in order to see David crowned instead.

18:6–16 As **David** continued to win battle after battle, **Saul** became extremely jealous. When he heard the songs of **the women** ascribing to **David** greater exploits than to himself, he became livid with rage. God sometimes uses evil to chastise evil; that is why he allowed Saul to be tormented by **a distressing spirit** (v. 10). **Twice** the king tried to personally kill **David**, **but** both times **David escaped**. Then Saul **made him . . . captain over a thousand** soldiers, perhaps hoping that David would be killed while fighting the Philistines. (It appears that he had formerly held a larger command.) But **the LORD was**

with David, and his exploits attracted the attention of **all Israel**.

18:17–30 The king's **daughter** had been promised to the man who would kill the Philistine giant, so **Merab**, Saul's **older daughter**, was offered to David. However, more victories would have to be won first. **Saul** hoped David would be killed in the process. When David expressed his social unworthiness to be a **son-in-law to the king, Merab . . . was given to** another man, which was perhaps Saul's way of trying to humiliate David. But **Saul's** younger **daughter, Michal, loved David,** and **Saul** agreed to give her to him, provided he produced a **dowry** of **one hundred** Philistine **foreskins**. Again Saul hoped to kill **David by the hand of the Philistines**. But David was not to be eliminated so easily. He returned with the bizarre **dowry** in double measure and won **Michal** as his bride. As continual military success made it clear that **the LORD was with David**, Saul's hatred and fear of him continued to grow.

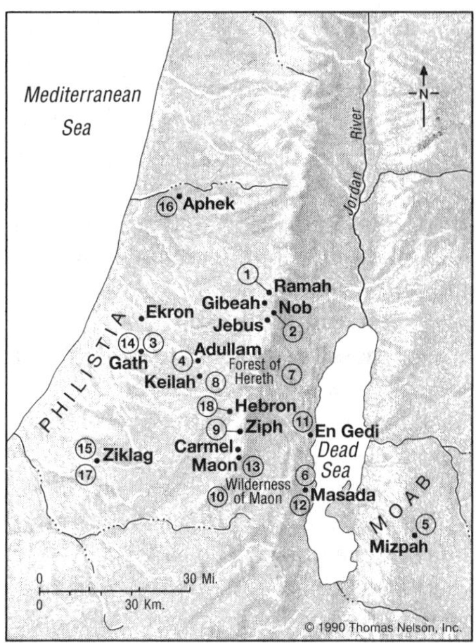

Saul's Pursuit of David

1. David flees Gibeah to Samuel at Ramah (1 Sam. 19:18)
2. David travels to Nob (1 Sam. 21:1-9)
3. David goes to Gath (1 Sam. 21:10)
4. David flees Philistines to Adullam (1 Sam. 22:1)
5. David takes his family to safety in Moab (1 Sam. 22:3)
6. David goes to Moab (1 Sam. 22:4)
7. David moves to the Forest of Hereth (1 Sam. 22:5)
8. David and his men attack Philistines plundering Keilah (1 Sam. 23:5)
9. David retreats to the Wilderness of Ziph (1 Sam. 23:14)
10. David withdraws to the Wilderness of Maon (1 Sam. 23:24)
11. Saul's pursuit drives David to Engedi (1 Sam. 23:29)
12. Sparing Saul's life, David returns to Moab (1 Sam. 24:22)
13. David returns to Carmel Maon, marries Abigail (1 Sam. 25)
14. Sparing Saul's life again, David returns to Gath (1 Sam. 26:1 — 27:2)
15. David is given Ziklag by Achish, Philistine King of Gath (1 Sam. 27)
16. David and his men go to Aphek, joining Philistine forces (1 Sam. 29:1-3)
17. Opposition to David from Philistine commanders forces his return to Ziklag (1 Sam. 30)
18. After Saul's death, David returns to Hebron, where he is crowned King (2 Sam. 1-2).

E. Fleeing from Saul (Chaps. 19—26)

1. Jonathan's Loyalty (Chaps. 19, 20)

19:1–7 When **Jonathan** realized that his **father** intended to murder David, he advised David to **hide . . . in the field** while he sought to pacify the king. In reasoning with **Saul** about **David, Jonathan** reminded him of David's bravery, loyalty, and success against Israel's enemy. He had done nothing worthy of death. Saul was temporarily conciliated and David was restored to his position in the royal court.

19:8–10 But when **war** broke out again **David** once more distinguished himself, and Saul's jealousy was kindled afresh. **The distressing spirit** returned and **Saul sought to pin David to the wall with** his **spear**. This was the third time Saul missed. **David** barely **escaped** with his life.

19:11–17 That same night King Saul **sent messengers** to **kill** David at his **house**. **Michal** knew of the plot and helped him escape by putting the household **image in** his **bed**. (The idol probably belonged to her, since David was never an idolater.) **When Saul sent** the men **to** seize **David**, her subterfuge was discovered.

19:18–23 But by then **David** had **escaped**. He **fled** to **Ramah** to see **Samuel**. Men of God go to other men of God in time of trouble. Three times Saul's **messengers** failed to catch David because, **when they** came near the **prophets** who were with **Samuel**, **they** themselves began to prophesy under the control of **the Spirit of God**. Later, when Saul himself **went** after **David**, he too was gripped by the power of God. This divine overpowering, however, was not the same thing as conversion.

19:24 Once again the people repeated the proverb about **Saul** being **among the prophets** (10:11, 12). His fluctuating behavior must have been puzzling to them. The word **"naked"** does not mean absolutely nude. It simply means that Saul took off his outer garments, the symbol of his royalty. While **God** held Saul prostrate on the ground **all that day and all that night**, David escaped (20:1).

Verse 24 does not contradict 15:34, 35, which says, "Samuel came no more to see Saul." Here it was *Saul who came to the prophet*, and that unintentionally and quite unexpectedly.

20:1–3 After leaving **Naioth**, **David** came **to Jonathan** and tried to find out why Saul was so intent on his destruction. Apparently Jonathan knew nothing of his father's continued attempts on David's life. David explained that the king would not share his plans with Jonathan because of the friendship that existed between him and David.

20:4–9 A test was proposed that would make it plain whether **David** was in danger or not. Instead of taking his place at the royal table for the monthly feast, David would remain absent. If Saul inquired as to his absence, **Jonathan** would explain that he had gone to the **yearly sacrifice** at **Bethlehem**. (This might have been true, even though the trip is not recorded in Scripture. If it was a lie, it is simply recorded as a fact that is not approved by God.) **If** Saul didn't object, this would show that David was **safe**; **but if** the king became **angry** because David had once again slipped out of his hands, then Jonathan would know that David was in grave peril.

20:10–17 **Jonathan** promised to **go . . . into the field** on **the third day** and let **David** know how things had gone by means of a prearranged sign. Perhaps sensing what the outcome would be, Jonathan asked David to **show** the loyal love of **the LORD** to him and to his **house** when he rose to power. It is clear from verses 14–17 that Jonathan believed that David would yet be king; but he reaffirmed his love to David even though he realized the throne rights, vested in him, would be David's. What unselfish devotion!

20:18–23 These verses detail the sign by which David would be notified as to the king's attitude. **Jonathan** would come to the field and **shoot** some **arrows** near a rock where **David** would be hiding. The directions he called **to the lad** who would fetch the **arrows** would tell David to flee for his life or to return to the court in **safety**. We might wonder why Jonathan arranged all this play-acting to communicate with David when he later went and talked with David directly anyway. At this time, however, he might not have known that he would be able to contact David without being seen.

20:24–34 On the first night of **the feast, Saul** said nothing about David's absence, reasoning to himself that David was probably ceremonially **unclean**. But on **the second day**, when he quizzed **Jonathan** about David's whereabouts and found that he had gone **to Bethlehem**, Saul flew into a rage, accusing Jonathan of befriending the man who would rob him and his mother of honor. His language was rough and his manner even rougher as he tried to pin his own son to the wall, transferring his hatred for David momentarily to Jonathan.

20:35–42 On **the morning** of the third day, the appropriate sign was given and David's fears were confirmed. The men **wept** in each other's arms; they must now travel separate paths, no longer to enjoy each other's companionship. David went into hiding, a necessary part of God's plan to prepare him for the throne. **Jonathan went** back to the royal court, remaining loyal to his father, yet knowing deep inside that he would not be Israel's next king. Should he have gone with David? Was he right in remaining loyal to his father, even though the Lord had rejected Saul from being king?

2. *Ahimelech's Kindness to David (Chap. 21)*

Even great men have feet of clay. David is no exception. This sad chapter records his lies before the tabernacle, now situated in Nob (vv. 1–9), and his pretended lunacy before the Philistines (vv. 10–15).

21:1–6 David had gone to Samuel (chap. 19) and to Jonathan (chap. 20), and now he comes to the high **priest** in his flight from Saul. **Ahimelech was afraid** of David, and wondered why he was traveling alone. (He did have a few companions with him who were waiting elsewhere—v. 2; Matt. 12:3.) David lied by saying that he was on a secret mission for **the king**. Then David asked for some **bread**. But all that was available was showbread, the **holy bread** used in the tabernacle for worship. **The priest** offered it to David, provided that his men were not ceremonially unclean through having sexual relations within the past few days. David said that his **men** were not only clean, but that they were **holy** (set apart) by virtue of their special mission. Shakespeare was right: "Oh what a tangled web we weave when first we practice to deceive!" **The showbread** that **had** just **been taken from** the holy place was given to David.

In Matthew 12:3, 4 the Lord Jesus approved this unlawful use of the showbread, presumably because there was sin in Israel and David represented the cause of righteousness. If David had had his rightful place on the throne, there would have been no need for him to be begging bread. The law, which forbade the profane use of the bread, was not intended to forbid a work of mercy such as this.

21:7–9 **Doeg**, a servant **of Saul**, was detained **before the LORD** in Nob at the time. Though **an Edomite**, he had converted to the Hebrew religion, and was detained by a vow, by uncleanness, or by some other ceremonial requirement. He naturally observed Ahimelech's collaboration with David and carried the report back to Saul. Meanwhile, David made a second request, this time for **weapons**. Again he lied, saying that he was on an urgent mission for the king. Goliath's **sword** was produced and David eagerly took it, exclaiming that there was **none** other **like it**. He had trusted in the Lord to slay the giant, only to lapse into confidence in the **sword** of his slain enemy.

21:10–15 Then David left Israel and **fled** to the city **of Gath**, Goliath's hometown. Here he, the anointed king of Israel, sought refuge among the enemies of God's people. When the Philistines became suspicious of him, he was forced to act the **madman** to save his life. DeRothschild notes that David knew well "that the insane were held inviolable, as smitten but protected by the Deity."[19] And so the psalmist of Israel stood drooling in **his beard** as he scribbled **on the doors of the gate**. Because of the callousness of God's people and David's own lapse of faith, he was reduced to this disgraceful behavior.

But David learned some valuable lessons through this ordeal. Before going on to the next chapter, read Psalm 34, which was written about this time. In this psalm we gain new insight into David's character. He possessed a remarkable resilience which enabled him to grow in his knowledge of God despite his failures.

3. *David's Escape and Saul's Slaughter of the Priests (Chap. 22)*

22:1, 2 When **David** returned to Israel, he found shelter in **the cave of Adullam**, in the territory **of Judah**, southwest of Bethlehem. This became a place for all who were **distressed**, **discontented**, and **in debt**. David here is a type of Christ in His present rejection, calling the downhearted to Himself for salvation. In a short time, a small army of **about four hundred men** had gathered at Adullam; later it would expand to six hundred men. In the world these men were misfits, but under David they became mighty men of valor (2 Sam. 23).

22:3–5 David's parents had joined him too. Because of concern for their welfare, he traveled **to . . . Moab** to make arrangements for them to stay there while he was in hiding. Though David was a descendant of Ruth, a Moabitess (Ruth 4:17), he was wrong in putting confidence in the Lord's enemies. (Tradition says that the Moabites eventually killed David's parents.) Soon after David returned, **the prophet Gad** told him to leave Adullam, so he **went** to **the forest of Hereth**, also in **Judah**.

22:6–8 In Gibeah, in the land of Benjamin, **Saul** was ranting to the **Benjamites** and **to his servants** against David. He asked them if David would reward them as generously as he had done. David, after all, was not from their tribe. Saul accused them of concealing from him plots **against** his life. By now he was completely paranoid and irrational. He saw everyone as being against him, even his own **son**.

22:9–15 Doeg the Edomite, wanting to make the most of his opportunity to impress the king, told Saul how **Ahimelech** the priest had helped David by giving **him provisions** and inquiring **of the Lord for him. The priest** and his family were promptly summoned to **the king** and charged with treason. In reply, **Ahimelech** cited David's loyalty to the king and his own innocence in helping a man whom he believed to be **faithful** to Saul. He pointed out that this was not the first time he had inquired of the Lord for David. As for Saul's accusation that David was rebelling against him and lying in wait for him, Ahimelech said he **knew nothing** at all about it.

22:16–19 Saul's actions prove that he was quite insane by now. When his **guards** refused to **kill the priests of the Lord, Doeg**, a Gentile "dog" in the true sense of the word, fell on them swiftly, little caring that they were **priests**, and slew **eighty-five** of them. As if that was not enough, he **also** attacked **Nob**, Ahimelech's **city**, and killed all the inhabitants and livestock.

22:20–23 Only **Abiathar** survived; he **fled** to **David** and **told** him what had taken place. Then he stayed with David and served as high priest until he was justly removed from office by Solomon (1 Kgs. 2:27). In one sense **the death** of the priests was the result of David's lying and scheming (v. 22). In another sense it was the judgment of God upon the house of Eli (2:31–36; 3:11–14). But Saul himself must bear the major share of the blame for the massacre, since he ordered it.

Prophet (Gad), priest (Abiathar), and King (David), all in exile together, picture Christ today as He waits until His enemies are made His footstool and His throne is set up on earth.

4. *Keilah's Betrayal (Chap. 23)*

23:1–5 News came to **David** that the city of **Keilah**, south of Adullam, was under attack by **the Philistines**. Guided by **the Lord**, he fought against the enemy, **saved** the town, and captured a large amount of **livestock**.

23:6–12 When **Saul** heard that **David** was in **Keilah**, he decided to trap him there. But David found out about the plot and asked **the Lord** for guidance as to his next move. Would he be safe in Keilah? Would the inhabitants turn him over to **Saul** despite the favor he had shown them? Through the ephod which Abiathar had brought, and more particularly through the Urim and Thummim, God revealed that when Saul would **come**, the ungrateful people would indeed betray David.

23:13–18 **So David and his men** fled to **the Wilderness of Ziph**, southeast of Hebron. But even there they were relentlessly pursued. It was there that **Jonathan** found **David** and encouraged him in the Lord. What a needed ministry today! The church would greatly benefit if there were more encouragers around. Only those who have experienced the power of a strengthening word spoken in season know the blessing it brings to the soul. Jonathan's love for David was self-abasing. He reassured David that God would fulfill His purpose for him, despite Saul. A man who has a friend like Jonathan is fortunate. Why he failed to stay with David, and always returned home, is an enigma.[20]

23:19–29 **The Ziphites** also betrayed **David**, sending news **to Saul** as to his whereabouts and promising **to deliver** the fugitive **into the king's hand**. When David heard that Saul was coming, he fled to **the Wilderness of Maon** with Saul in hot pursuit. Just when it seemed that he would be surrounded, **the Philistines** attacked Israel and Saul was forced to abandon the chase. Unwittingly, Israel's enemy served as an ally to Israel's rejected king. The son of Jesse then traveled to **En Gedi**, on the western shore of the Dead Sea.

5. *Saul Spared (Chap. 24)*

24:1–7 After the Philistine threat had been dealt with, **Saul . . . returned** to hunt for **David**. He traced him to the rocky cliffs at **En Gedi**. While there, the king entered one of the caves for a rest stop. The **cave** he chose was not empty. Farther in, the man he ruthlessly hunted was restraining **his men** from taking the monarch's life! They thought God had delivered Saul over to them. But David knew of no command from

God to take the kingdom by force. He was content to await God's time and method. Even when he **cut off a corner of** the king's **robe**, his conscience bothered him. He did not take lightly the fact that Saul had been **anointed** as Israel's king. God must remove this king; David was to respect him until the Lord removed him.

24:8–15 After **Saul** left, **David . . . went out of the cave and called** after him. Bowing to **the king**, David told him that the slanderous reports to which he had listened were untrue. That very day David could have taken his life, but he did not because Saul was **the LORD's anointed**. The portion of the **robe in** David's **hand** was evidence of his kindness. A **wicked** man might want to avenge himself, but David had no such desire. He asked Saul why he should conduct such a relentless campaign against one who was as harmless and insignificant as **a dead dog** and **a flea**.

24:16–22 Temporarily moved to tears by David's words, Saul acknowledged the righteousness of David's behavior and his own wickedness. Surprisingly, he admitted that David would one day **be king** in **Israel**, and he made David take a solemn oath that he would deal kindly with his family. Then Saul left peaceably. But the respite David enjoyed was short. Saul soon forgot his kindness.

In David's words to Saul, he twice called on **the LORD** to act as **Judge**. He was content to leave his case in the hands of God rather than do what might seem right to the natural man. One of the things Peter remembered about our Lord was that "when He was reviled, [He] did not revile in return; when He suffered, He did not threaten, but committed Himself to Him who judges righteously" (1 Pet. 2:23). May God enable us to be as trustingly calm in the face of adversity!

6. Nabal's Folly (Chap. 25)

25:1–9 The death of **Samuel** brought to a close the period of the judges. The nation had now become a monarchy. David's descendants would occupy Israel's throne forever, Christ being the fulfillment of the promise. The deep respect in which Samuel was held is indicated by the grief that swept across the nation when he died.

After the prophet's death, **David . . . went down to the Wilderness of Paran**, in the southern part of Judah, perhaps to get further away from Saul and his murderous schemes. The **Carmel** mentioned in verse 2 was not the *Mount* Carmel which is in the north, but *a town* near **Maon**. **Nabal was shearing his sheep** there, and **David**, according to custom, **sent** some **young men** to ask for a gift in return for the protection he had provided for Nabal's flocks.

25:10–13 But **Nabal answered David's servants** in such a selfish and rude manner that David became enraged and started toward Carmel with **about four hundred men** to punish Nabal and his household.

25:14–22 **Nabal's** beautiful and discerning **wife, Abigail,** learned of the danger that her husband's ill-advised behavior had brought upon them. She quickly gathered a large supply of foodstuffs and went out to meet David. As **David** approached Carmel, he was rehearsing to himself the **good** he had shown Nabal and the contempt Nabal had shown him.

25:23–31 **When Abigail** met **David, she** prostrated herself at his feet and delivered a masterful and successful plea. She first admitted that her husband was true to his name (**Nabal** means *fool* or *cad*). When David's men had come earlier, she had not known about it. As she asked for forgiveness, she reminded him that **the Lord** had restrained him **from . . . bloodshed** and that God would punish his **enemies**—even **Nabal**. She had real spiritual insight into who David was, the anointed of the Lord, and praised him sincerely for fighting **the battles of the Lord**. How much better it would be when he became king if he did not have to look back on a time when he had stretched out his own hand and **avenged himself** instead of leaving his enemies to the vengeance of the Lord!

25:32–35 **David** was deeply impressed by these words of diplomacy and thanked her for preventing him from destroying **Nabal**. The Lord knows how to bring the right people into our lives to direct us and warn us. We should be thankful that He does. Abigail's **advice** was effective; her generous gift was accepted. David left Nabal with the Lord. God wasn't long in acting. Some might argue that Abigail violated God's order by not consulting her husband and by usurping authority over him. Yet the Bible does not suggest that she acted wrongly. On the contrary, she probably saved Nabal and his household from destruction by her emergency action.

25:36–44 When **Abigail** returned home, **Nabal . . . was very drunk**. She waited until the next day to tell him what had happened. When he heard the news, he was probably seized with paralysis, a stroke, or a **heart** attack. **Ten days** later **he died**, leaving behind all the possessions he had selfishly hoarded to himself. Hearing of Nabal's death, **David** soon **sent** a proposal of marriage **to Abigail**, which she accepted with great humility. David had also acquired another wife, **Ahinoam**, since he had gone into hiding. Meanwhile, **Michal**, his first wife, **had** been **given** to another man.

In this story we see afresh that whoever exalts himself will be humbled (Nabal was killed by God), and she who humbles herself will be exalted (Abigail became the wife of the king) (Luke 14:11).

7. Saul Spared a Second Time (Chap. 26)

26:1–4 Once again **the Ziphites** reported David's whereabouts **to Saul** (cf. 23:19). Saul promptly gathered a force five times larger than David's meager band **and went down to the Wilderness of Ziph**. We are not told what happened to incite Saul anew. When the two men had last parted, they seemed somewhat reconciled (chap. 24). Maybe evil men had stirred up the king's hatred afresh (see v. 19).

26:5–12 **David** spied out Saul's camp, and in the evening he and his relative, **Abishai**, penetrated the camp and came to where Saul was sleeping. An unnatural slumber from the Lord made this possible. **Abishai** wanted to **strike** the king with a quick blow, but David forbade any such action because, although Saul was a wicked man, he was **the Lord's anointed**. It was the Lord's responsibility to deal with him. **David took** Saul's **spear** and **jug of water** and left.

26:13–16 When **David** was safely outside the camp, he raised his voice and taunted **Abner** for his carelessness in guarding **the king**. Such negligence was worthy of death. The **jug** and **spear** which David had taken told of Saul's second deliverance from death at his hand.

26:17–20 What still puzzled David was **why** King **Saul** pursued him so untiringly when he had proven that he meant him no harm. **If the Lord** had **stirred . . . up** Saul **against** David, then David could satisfy Him by presenting a sacrificial **offering. But if . . . men** had incited Saul's hostility, then **they** should **be cursed** because they were driving David away from the only sanctuary where he could worship God. The expression **"Go, serve other gods"** (v. 19b) was what these evil men were saying by their actions, if not by their words. David asked that he might not die "away from the presence of the Lord," i.e., in a foreign land (v. 20, NASB). Saul was hunting **a flea as . . . one hunts a partridge in the mountains**.

26:21–25 Saul apparently repented when he realized that David had spared his **life** again. He acknowledged that David was more righteous than he, for he sought David's life without cause, whereas David spared his life, though he could have killed the king in self-defense. David made a final appeal to **the Lord** to take note of his **righteousness. Then Saul** responded **to David** with a blessing and a prophecy of future greatness for his **"son David."**[21] **David went on his way, and Saul returned to his** city.

F. Living in Philistia (Chaps. 27—30)

1. Ziklag Acquired (Chap. 27)

27:1–4 The pressure of constantly running from place to place one step ahead of death finally took its toll on **David**. In spite of the Lord's miraculous care for him, David's faith wavered. He lost sight of the fact that he was the anointed king of Israel. Would God appoint him king and then allow him to be killed before he could reign? Would God deliver him from the hand of Goliath only to deliver him into **the hand of Saul**? No, but circumstances have a way of distorting one's outlook. Present danger often obscures the promises of God. David fled **to the land of the Philistines** again and contacted **Achish, . . . king of Gath**. It had been a long time since he was here last, and Achish was probably aware that he was a fugitive. This heathen **king** welcomed him warmly, seeing in him a valiant warrior and an ally against Israel. This is not necessarily the same Achish that David met in 21:10, since "Achish" was a royal name among the Philistines.[22] When **Saul** heard **that David had fled** the country, he stopped hunting for him.

27:5–7 The last time David had been in Gath (chap. 21), the servants of Achish had been suspicious of him and had tried to have him killed. David had not forgotten this. With a show of modesty, he now refused to **dwell** in the capital city and asked for a city of his own. He was given **Ziklag**, a city close to Israel's border that originally **belonged to . . . Judah** (Josh. 15:31).

27:8–12 During his sixteen-month stay with **the Philistines, David** made raids against **the Geshurites, the Girzites, and the Amalekites**. These people were heathen inhabitants of Canaan whose destruction had been ordered by God (Ex. 17:14; Josh. 13:13; 1 Sam. 15:2, 3). Even in exile, David was fighting the Lord's battles. This presents quite a paradox: He could trust the Lord to preserve him for victory over Israel's enemies, but he could not trust Him for protection from Saul!

2. Saul's Doom Foretold (Chap. 28)

28:1, 2 Now David's position became extremely difficult. **The**

Philistines were going to war against Israel, and **David** was ordered by the king to join them. To this he seemed to agree, although his words in verse 2 are capable of two meanings—**"You** will **know what your servant can do** to assist you" or "You will know what your servant can do to double-cross you!" Achish chose the first meaning and made David a member of his personal bodyguard.

28:3–8 The rival armies gathered in the northwest of Israel at the plain of Esdraelon (the valley of Armageddon). **The Philistines encamped . . . at Shunem**, and **Israel . . . at Gilboa**. When Saul failed to get any response from **the Lord, either by dreams or by Urim or by the prophets**, he sought out **a** spirit **medium**. Earlier he **had** ordered all **the mediums** in Israel killed or exiled, according to the law. Now when **a medium** was located in the nearby town of **En Dor**, **Saul disguised himself and . . . went to** her to seek counsel from the dead.

28:9, 10 The medium's first concern was for her own safety. She reminded her visitor of the king's edict against **mediums and . . . spiritists**. How **Saul** could promise protection in the name of **the Lord**, who had decreed the death of such persons, or how the medium could be assured of safety by an oath sworn to that God, is an enigma.

28:11–14 Commentators are disagreed as to what actually happened next. Some feel that an evil spirit *impersonated* **Samuel**, while others believe that God interrupted the séance unexpectedly by allowing the *real* **Samuel** to appear. The latter is preferred for the following reasons: The medium was startled by the sudden appearance of Samuel in place of the familiar spirits with whom she was used to dealing. Also, the text specifies that **it was Samuel**. Finally, the **spirit** prophesied accurately what would happen the following day.

28:15–19 **Saul** told **Samuel** why he had summoned him from the realm of the dead. Samuel's rebuke must have cut the king deeply. Did he think Samuel could help him when the *God* whom Samuel served remained silent? Instead, Samuel confirmed Saul's deepest fears. **The kingdom** would be taken from him and **given to** David, as he had been told earlier. **The Philistines** would defeat **Israel** the next day, and **Saul . . . and** his **sons** would join Samuel in death. This does not mean that they shared the same eternal destiny. If we judge them by their fruits, it would appear that Saul was an unbeliever whereas Jonathan was a man of faith.

28:20–25 All Saul's sins would be visited on him before another nightfall. With difficulty he was prevailed upon to **eat** something before he went **on** his **way**. The **fatted calf** was killed, but not for the purpose of celebrating. Shrouded in gloomy silence, the condemned man **ate** his final meal before disappearing into the night.

3. *David Discharged by Achish (Chap. 29)*

29:1–5 As **the Philistines gathered together** for battle, **David and his men** joined them, marching **with Achish . . . at the rear** of the column. Some of **the princes of the Philistines** wisely objected to David's presence. They realized that he might turn on them during the battle. How could he better reconcile himself to King Saul than by producing a row of Philistine heads? Was **this not** the **David** who had been praised as the killer of more Philistines than **Saul** himself?

29:6–11 Their arguments were reasonable, so **Achish** requested **David** to **return** to Ziklag. David's answer seems unworthy of a man of God. He protested that he should be allowed to enter the **fight against "the enemies of my lord the king"**—even though these enemies were his own people. David had lied to Achish before (chap. 27), and this was probably another attempt to deceive the Philistines. If, as seems unlikely, he actually intended to fight against Israel, God prevented it and saved him from the shame of killing his fellow Israelites and strengthening the arm of the Philistines against them. David would not be allowed to use Goliath's sword against Israel.

4. *Amalekites Defeated (Chap. 30)*

30:1–6 While David had been marching north with the armies of Achish, **the Amalekites had** raided **Ziklag** and **taken . . . the women and** children **captive**. Thus when **David** returned he found only the smoldering remains of his city. Was this possibly a judgment of God upon him for joining the Philistines? If so, David showed his great insight into the character of God, because he went to Him for comfort when everything and everyone was against him. He knew there was no one to turn to for strength in such an overwhelming crisis except **the Lord**, of whom it is said, "He has torn, but He will heal us; He has stricken, but He will bind us up" (Hos. 6:1).

30:7–15 After inquiring **of the Lord, David went** out after the Amalekites, assured of success. **Two hundred** of his **men** (one third) **could** travel no farther than **the Brook Besor** because they were emotionally drained from their recent loss and physically exhausted from their three-day march to **Ziklag**. David left them there and went south with the remaining **four hundred men**, tired yet pursuing. In a short while **they found** an ailing **Egyptian in the field** who had been **left . . . behind** by his **Amalekite . . . master** to die. He was given food and water and soon regained a measure of **strength**. In return for promised safety, he led David to the Amalekite camp.

30:16–25 The last thing the drunken **Amalekites** expected was a surprise guest at their victory celebration. **David** sprang like a leopard on the revelers and completely overpowered the much larger force. Only **four hundred young men . . . escaped** the sword, riding off **on camels**. The Hebrew captives were freed unharmed and an immense amount of **spoil** was taken, all in less than twenty-four hours. **David** was given the sheep and cattle captured from the Amalekites as his portion; but some of his men didn't want to **share** the rest of the **spoil** with their comrades who had stayed behind at **Besor**. David **made . . . an ordinance** that those who "stayed by the stuff" would **share** equally with those who went out **to the battle** (see also Num. 31:27).

30:26–31 **David** divided his **spoil** into gifts for various friends back in **Judah**. These presents were sent **to all the places where** he was **accustomed to rove**. They evidenced that God had prospered him against his enemies. He might also have been trying to cement his friendships to gain support in his struggle against Saul, not realizing that Saul was now dead.

IV. SAUL'S DEATH (Chap. 31)

31:1–6 Whereas David enjoyed success in battle, **Saul** met defeat.

The Israelites were pushed back and the king's three **sons** were slain. Saul himself was **severely wounded by the archers**. As he lay dying on **Mount Gilboa**, he begged **his armorbearer** to kill him, lest the Philistines find him alive and **abuse** him. But the man **was . . . afraid** to strike the king, so **Saul** took his own life, falling **on . . . a sword**. Shortly thereafter, **his armorbearer** did the same.

31:7–13 Israel now became totally demoralized, and they retreated before the invading army. When **the Philistines came to strip** the dead and **found Saul and his three sons** among the **fallen, they cut off** Saul's **head** and sent **word throughout** their **land. His body** and **the bodies of his sons** were taken to **Beth Shan** and hung on the city's **wall. When the** men **of Jabesh Gilead heard** of this, they marched the ten miles to recover **the bodies**. The remains were given a proper burial **under the tamarisk tree at Jabesh**. These men had not forgotten how Saul had saved them from the Ammonites in his first major battle as king (chap. 11). Cremation was not generally practiced in Israel. Perhaps it was used here because the bodies had been so mutilated. Also, it would prevent the Philistines from the possibility of ever dishonoring the bodies still further.

God's judgment on Saul was now complete (see notes on 1 Chron. 10). Many times Saul had tried to arrange for David to be killed by the Philistines, but he himself was the one to eventually fall before them. David received the throne as appointed by God. Saul received the just recompense of his deeds, according to the justice of the Lord to which David often committed him.

ENDNOTES

[1](Intro) The Jewish scholar Abarbanel explained the tradition this way: "All the contents of both books may in a certain sense be referred to Samuel, even the deeds of Saul and David because both, having been anointed by Samuel, were, so to speak, the work of his hands" (quoted by Erdmann, "The Books of Samuel," Lange's *Commentary on the Holy Scriptures*, p. 1).

[2](Intro) Eugene H. Merrill, "1 Samuel," *The Bible Knowledge Commentary*," p. 432.

[3](1:11–18) Bishop Hall, quoted in *Spurgeon's Devotional Bible*, p. 222.

[4](1:19–28) Gesenius and other Hebrew scholars believed the name means *name (Shem) of God*.

[5](3:1–3) George Williams, *The Student's Commentary on the Holy Scriptures*, p. 140.

[6](6:19–21) Flavius Josephus, *The Works of Flavius Josephus (Ant. vi 1:4)*, p. 178.

[7](6:19–21) C. F. Keil and F. Delitzsch, "The Books of Samuel," *Biblical Commentary on the Old Testament*, VII:68.

[8](10:7–9) Some Evangelical scholars consider Saul a believer, but one who became terribly backslidden and then mentally deranged. They argue that it is improbable that God would choose an unregenerate person to be the first king of His chosen people.

[9](10:17–19) Matthew Henry, "I Samuel," in *Matthew Henry's Commentary on the Whole Bible*, II:334, 35.

[10](12:1–13) The names *Bedan* and *Barak* look much alike in the ancient texts. Hebrew "d" (*dalet*) and "r" (*resh*) are often confused in copying, as well as the final forms of "n" (*nun*) and "k" (*kaph*).

[11](13:1) A large part of OT ms.

problems have to do with the Hebrew system of numbers, which were easy to mis-copy. See commentary on Chronicles for more details on this.

[12](13:2–5) See previous note.

[13](14:16–23) The old ERV of 1885 reads: "Bring hither the Ephod: for he wore the Ephod at that time before Israel."

[14](15:13–35) Christian F. Erdmann, "The Books of Samuel," in Lange's *Commentary on the Holy Scriptures, Critical, Doctrinal and Homiletical*, III:209.

[15](16:14–23) Dr. Rendle Short, further documentation unavailable.

[16](17:55–58) The Septuagint omits these verses.

[17](17:55–58) Williams, *Student's Commentary*, p. 152.

[18](17:55–58) Michael Griffiths, *Take My Life*, p. 128.

[19](21:10–15) DeRothschild, further documentation unavailable.

[20](23:13–18) Perhaps he felt a loyalty to his father's *position* even though he knew that he was *personally* in the wrong.

[21](26:21–25) These may have been mere words. On the other hand, if Saul was sincere it could be an argument that in spite of his sin and his paranoia he did have faith in God.

[22](27:1–4) Keil and Delitzsch, suggesting a fifty-year reign as "not impossible," believe the same Achish is mentioned in both texts, as well as in 1 Kgs. 2:39 ("Samuel," VII:255).

BIBLIOGRAPHY
(1 and 2 Samuel)

Blaikie, William Garden. "The First Book of Samuel." In *The Expositor's Bible*. London: Hodder and Stoughton, 1909.

——. "The Second Book of Samuel." In *The Expositor's Bible*. London: Hodder and Stoughton, 1909.

Erdmann, Christian F. "The Books of Samuel." In Lange's *Commentary on the Holy Scriptures, Critical, Doctrinal and Homiletical*. Vol. 3. Grand Rapids: Zondervan Publishing House, 1960.

Grant, F. W. "Samuel." In *The Numerical Bible*. Vol. 2. New York: Loizeaux Brothers, 1904.

Henry, Matthew. "The Books of Samuel." In *Matthew Henry's Commentary on the Whole Bible*. Vol. 2, Joshua to Esther. McLean, VA: MacDonald Publishing Company, n.d.

Jensen, Irving L. *I & II Samuel*. Chicago: Moody Press, 1968.

Keil, C. F., and Delitzsch, F. "The Books of Samuel." In *Biblical Commentary on the Old Testament*. Vol. 7. Grand Rapids: Wm. B. Eerdmans Publishing Co., 1971.

Laney, J. Carl. *First and Second Samuel*. Everyman's Bible Commentary. Chicago: Moody Press, 1982.

Merrill, Eugene H. "1 and 2 Samuel." In *The Bible Knowledge Commentary. Old Testament*. Wheaton, IL: Victor Books, 1985.

Meyer, F. B. *Samuel*. Chicago: Fleming H. Revell Co., n.d. Reprint. Fort Washington, PA: Christian Literature Crusade, 1978.

SECOND SAMUEL

"David the king is the great figure of this Book; and, when walking in the Light, presents a rich type of Messiah the King. The first part of the Book records the victories which accompanied his life of faith and conflict; the second part relates the defeats he suffered when prosperity had seduced him from the path of faith and had opened the door to self-will."

—George Williams

For Introduction see 1 Samuel.

OUTLINE

I. DAVID'S RISE TO POWER (Chaps. 1—10)
   A. Lament over Saul and Jonathan (Chap. 1)
   B. Coronation as King of Judah (2:1–7)
   C. Conflict with Saul's House (2:8—4:12)
   D. Coronation as King over All Israel (Chap. 5)
   E. The Ark Brought to Jerusalem (Chap. 6)
   F. God's Covenant with David (Chap. 7)
   G. Defeat of Israel's Enemies (Chap. 8)
   H. Compassion Shown to Mephibosheth (Chap. 9)
   I. Further Conquests (Chap. 10)

II. DAVID'S FALL (Chaps. 11, 12)
   A. Crimes Against Bathsheba and Uriah (Chap. 11)
   B. Confession to the Lord (Chap. 12)

III. DAVID'S TROUBLES (Chaps. 13—20)
   A. Rape of Tamar by Amnon (13:1–19)
   B. Absalom's Revenge on Amnon, and Absalom's Flight (13:20–39)
   C. Absalom's Return to Jerusalem (Chap. 14)
   D. Absalom's Revolt and David's Flight (15:1–18)
   E. David's Friends and Foes (15:19—16:14)
   F. Absalom's Counselors (16:15—17:23)
   G. Absalom's Death and David's Lament (17:24—19:8)
   H. David's Return from Exile (19:9–43)
   I. Sheba's Rebellion and Death (Chap. 20)

Commentary

I. DAVID'S RISE TO POWER (Chaps. 1—10)

A. Lament over Saul and Jonathan (Chap. 1)

1:1–16 First Samuel 29 records how the Lord kept **David** out of the battle in which Saul and Jonathan lost their lives. Instead, he was busy fighting **the Amalekites**, who had raided Ziklag (1 Sam. 30). After he **had returned** to **Ziklag**, a messenger **came to** him **from** the north with news of Saul's death. The messenger wore **torn . . . clothes** and had **dust on his head**—symbols of mourning. He told how he had found **Saul, leaning** wounded **on his spear** as the enemy's forces drew near. He said that Saul asked him, **an Amalekite**, to administer the death blow, and that he complied with the king's request. This account of Saul's death is obviously in conflict with the one in 1 Samuel 31, where Saul is said to have committed suicide. The most reasonable explanation is that the Amalekite's account was a lie. He thought that David would be pleased to meet Saul's slayer and would reward him handsomely. Instead, David **mourned** deeply all that day, and then at **evening** he ordered the execution of the Amalekite because he had slain the Lord's anointed.

The Amalekites were the inveterate enemies of Israel (Ex. 17). One reason Saul lost the kingdom was because he had failed to thoroughly execute the Lord's wrath on them (1 Sam. 15). Some Amalekites had recently been killed by David and his men for their plunder of Ziklag. So when this Amalekite arrived in camp and announced that he had killed Saul, it is little wonder that he received the sword and not a reward.

1:17, 18 It was surely a mark of greatness on David's part that instead of rejoicing over Saul's death, he wept bitterly.

O. von Gerlach sees a parallel between David and Christ here:

> The only deep mourning for Saul, with the exception of that of the Jabeshites (1 Sam. xxxi. 11), proceeded from the man whom he had hated and persecuted for so many years even to the time of his death; just as David's successor wept over the fall of Jerusalem, even when it was about to destroy Himself.[1]

David also composed a moving **lamentation** entitled **"The Song of the Bow." The Book of Jasher**, or the "Book of the Upright," was probably a collection of poems concerning great men of the nation of Israel (see also Josh. 10:13). As far as is known, it is no longer in existence and certainly is not part of inspired Scripture.

1:19–27 David's stirring ode laments the death of **Saul** and **Jonathan—the beauty of Israel**. In majestic poetry, it cautions against letting the cities **of the Philistines** know of the death of the king and his sons **lest** they **rejoice**. The **mountains of Gilboa**, where Saul died, are called upon to suffer drought and barrenness. There **the shield of Saul** was cast down unanointed **with oil** (v. 21); that is, it was discarded and no longer oiled for battle. Tribute is paid to the bravery **of Saul** and **of Jonathan** (v. 22) and their personal virtues. They were together **in their death** as they had been **in their lives** (v. 23), but this should not be pressed to include their eternal destiny. Those who benefited from Saul's reign are called on to **weep** (v. 24). The poem closes with a loving eulogy of **Jonathan**, David's close friend. The refrain "How the mighty have fallen" (vv. 19, 25, 27) has become part of our language.

B. Coronation as King of Judah (2:1–7)

2:1–7 With Saul dead and Israel without a king, **David** sought guidance from **the Lord** and was directed to go **to Hebron**, one **of the cities of Judah**. There **the men of Judah . . . anointed** him as their **king**. When they informed him how **the men of Jabesh Gilead** had kindly **buried Saul**, David immediately sent a message of thanks to them and rather indirectly invited them to recognize him as **king**, as the men **of Judah** had done.

C. Conflict with Saul's House (2:8—4:12)

2:8–11 **But** not all the tribes of Israel wanted to recognize David as their monarch. **Abner**, the **commander**-in-chief of the late Saul and also his uncle, **took** Saul's only surviving son, **Ishbosheth**, and proclaimed **him king**. For **seven years and six months . . . David** reigned **over** the lone tribe of **Judah**, with **Hebron** as his capital. However, it was for only **two** of these **years** that **Ishbosheth . . . reigned** over the other eleven tribes. It may have taken Abner five years to push the Philistines back out of Israel and establish Ishbosheth on his father's throne.

David had never asserted his right to the throne. Neither did he do so now. Rather, he chose to leave the matter in the hands of the Lord. If Jehovah had anointed him as king, Jehovah would subdue his enemies and bring him into the possession of his kingdom. The Lord Jesus similarly awaits the Father's timing to reign over the entire globe. His dominion is recognized only by a minority of mankind now, but there is an appointed day in which every knee will bow and every tongue will confess that Jesus Christ is Lord (Phil. 2:10, 11).

2:12–17 In the course of time, **Abner, the son of Ner,** the captain of the army of Israel (the 11 tribes) met **Joab, the son of Zeruiah**, the military leader of David's soldiers at **Gibeon**. Seated at opposite sides of a pool, they decided to **let** some of their **young men** engage in a contest to determine who was militarily superior. When **Abner** suggested that **the young men** should **arise** and hold a contest, he did not expect that they would play. It was a military engagement. The **twelve** Benjamites fought the **twelve** men of Judah, and they destroyed each other. Since the result was inconclusive, a **very fierce battle** broke out between the rest of **the men**, with the result that Abner's **men . . . were beaten** and fled in disarray.

2:18–23 One of Joab's brothers, the swift-footed **Asahel**, chased **Abner** with the intent to kill him. At first Abner tried to persuade Asahel to be satisfied with capturing **one of the young men**. It seems that **Abner** realized that he could easily kill **Asahel**, but he did not want to do it because it would further antagonize **Joab**. When Asahel would not listen to Abner's second plea to stop pursuing him, Abner turned on him in self-defense and killed him **with the blunt end of** his **spear**.

2:24–32 **Joab and** his other brother, **Abishai**, continued to chase until they came to **the hill of Ammah**. There Abner pled with Joab to stop this needless civil war. Joab's reply may be understood in two ways. First, it may mean that if Abner had not issued the original challenge (in verse 14), then the young men would have gone home peaceably. Or it may mean, as in the NIV, that if Abner had not called for a truce, then the young men would have continued chasing **their brethren** until **morning**. In any case, Joab agreed to stop fighting. **Abner and his men . . . crossed over . . . to Mahanaim**, on the east side of **the Jordan** River where Ishbosheth had his capital. He had lost **three hundred and sixty men**. **Joab** and his soldiers **returned** to Hebron, with only **nineteen men . . . missing**.

3:1–5 During David's seven-and-a-half years at Hebron, his kingdom **grew stronger** while Saul's **house**, ruled by Ishbosheth, **grew weaker**. David's family also grew larger. When he first came to **Hebron**, he had two wives, **Ahinoam** and **Abigail**. Contrary to God's will, he married four more—**Maacah, Haggith, Abital,** and **Eglah**. By these six wives he had six sons, three of whom were to be a grief to him—**Amnon, Absalom**, and **Adonijah**. (He had other sons later.)

3:6–11 While professedly serving Ishbosheth, **Abner was** actually **strengthening his** own political position because he saw the balance of power shifting to **David**. **Ishbosheth** accused **Abner** of having relations with **Rizpah**, a **concubine** of **Saul**, and probably interpreted this as an indication that Abner wanted to seize control of the eleven tribes. Whether Abner was guilty of this we do not know; he denied it vigorously and disrespectfully, and announced that he would **transfer** his allegiance and that of the tribes of **Israel** to **David**. **Ishbosheth** was powerless to resist. **"Am I a dog's head that belongs to Judah?"** (v. 8) means "Am I a worthless, contemptible traitor who has been loyal to Judah in the past?"

3:12–16 **Abner** now **sent messengers . . . to David**, offering to turn over **all Israel to** him. Before **David** would agree to Abner's proposal, he demanded that **Michal, Saul's daughter,** be returned to him, hoping thereby to strengthen his claim to Saul's kingdom. **Ishbosheth** meekly assented and **Michal** was brought to **David**—to the great grief of **her husband, Paltiel**. David's personal life thus became further entangled, and another dark chapter was written in his biography.

3:17–21 **Abner** then went to the tribe of **Benjamin** and to the other tribes that had followed Ishbosheth and told them that **David** was God's promised means of saving them **from the** oppression **of the Philistines**. Since their response was apparently favorable, he visited **David** and expressed his readiness to **gather all Israel** together in a great expression of allegiance.

3:22–30 While Abner was leaving David to carry out this plan, **Joab** returned to the royal house and heard of the day's events. After rebuking **the king** for so foolishly entertaining a spy, he secretly **sent** out soldiers to bring Abner **back**. As soon as **Abner . . . returned to Hebron, Joab** pretended he wanted a private interview near **the gate**, but his real purpose was to kill Abner in revenge, which he did by stabbing **him in the stomach**, thus avenging **his brother** Asahel's death and eliminating a potential rival as commander-in-chief. Joab seemed unconcerned that Hebron was a city of refuge, where Abner was at least entitled to a trial (Num. 35:22–25). The expression **"one . . . who leans on a staff"** (v. 29) may mean a cripple. In the NASB it is rendered "one who takes hold of a distaff" (that is, an effeminate man). The RSV similarly translates "one who holds a spindle," meaning unfit for war or heavy work.

3:31–39 David proclaimed a great time of mourning **for Abner** but took no action against **Joab** for murdering him. It grieved the king that Abner should have died so ingloriously, since his courage and power deserved a more honorable death. The thought in verse 33 may be, "Did Abner die like an inexperienced fool, who knew not how to defend himself?" And the intended answer is "No, he fell victim to a deceitful, wicked plot."[2] The people knew by the king's sorrow that Joab had acted independently. In fact, David publicly expressed his displeasure at the cruelty of **the sons of Zeruiah** (Joab and Abishai) and called on the Lord to punish them. In chapter 3 we have seen God using the sin and intrigue of men to give the united kingdom to David. He makes even the wrath of men to praise Him (Ps. 76:10).

4:1–7 Abner's death weakened the kingdom of Ishbosheth still further. As soon as the army had lost its powerful leader, **two** rebels rose up—**Baanah and . . . Rechab**—and assassinated the king. They were able to do this by entering **the house** while **Ishbosheth** was taking his siesta. They pretended that they had come to pick up some **wheat**. The RSV of verse 6, following the Septuagint, reads, "And behold, the doorkeeper of the house had been cleaning wheat, but she grew drowsy and slept; so Rechab and Baanah his brother slipped in." This left only one male heir to the throne of Saul, a crippled lad by the **name** of **Mephibosheth**.

4:8–12 Rechab and Baanah brought the head of Ishbosheth to David in hopes of winning his favor. These **wicked men** tried to suggest that **the Lord** had prompted their action. But **David** knew better than that! God would not lead men to break His law in order to enthrone His king. God was well able to fulfill His promises to David without enlisting the aid of murderers. David told them that they were **more** guilty than the one who claimed to have murdered **Saul**, and ordered them to be slain immediately. Their bodies were exposed to the shame of public display, while **the head of Ishbosheth** was honorably **buried in the tomb of Abner**.

D. Coronation as King over All Israel (Chap. 5)

5:1–5 With words of loyalty and allegiance, the eleven **tribes of Israel** now joined Judah in acknowledging **David** as rightful king. Those who came are enumerated in 1 Chronicles 12:23–40. Thus **began** a **reign** over the united nation that was to last **thirty-three years**. In all, David's reign lasted **forty years**.

Verse 3 records David's third

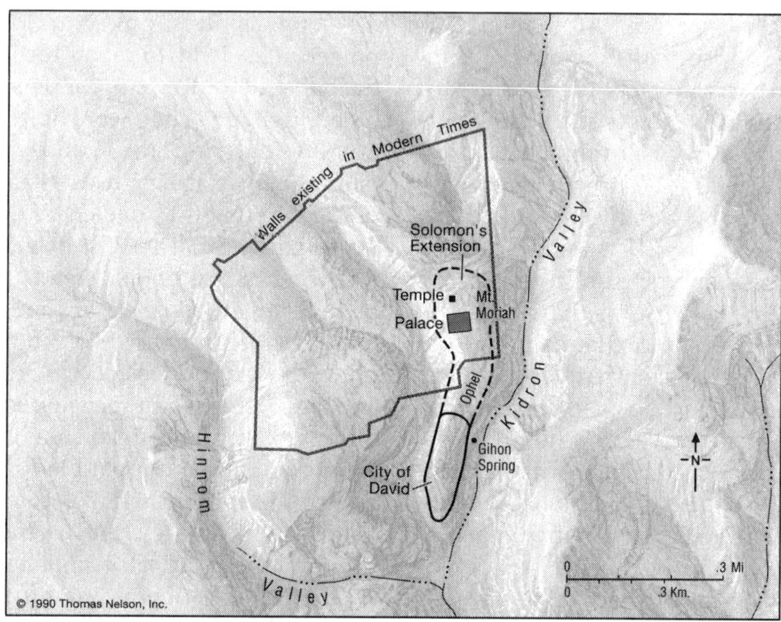

Jerusalem: David's City. David took the fortress called Jebus and renamed it the "City of David." This established his kingship militarily and politically. He then established his religious leadership by moving the ark of the covenant to the City of David. Solomon later expanded northward to Mt. Moriah and built the temple and the royal place.

anointing. He was first anointed by the prophet Samuel (1 Sam. 16:13). Then he was anointed as king over the house of Judah in Hebron (2:4). Now he was finally **anointed** as rightful **king** by the entire nation.

5:6–10 One of King David's first military acts was to capture the fortress on Mount **Zion** from **the Jebusites**. These heathen warriors considered their city so invincible that it could be defended by **the lame and the blind**. David detected a weak point in the city's **water** system; he ordered his men to climb up through an underground watercourse which the Jebusites used to bring water to the city from a fountain below. The strategy was successful, and Jebus became **Jerusalem**, also called **the City of David**, the capital of the nation of Israel. The latter part of verse 8 looks back to the Jebusite taunt in verse 6, which later became a common saying: **"The blind and the lame shall not come into the house." The Millo** was a part of the fortification of the ancient city. (The parallel account in 1 Chronicles 11 reveals that Joab led the successful attack on the city and thus secured his place as commander of David's forces.)

5:11–16 **Hiram,** the Gentile **king of Tyre, sent** materials and workmen to build a palace for David in Jerusalem. **David took more concubines and wives** while at **Jerusalem**, in violation of Deuteronomy 17:17, and additional **sons and daughters were born to** him. The royal line of the Messiah is traced through **Solomon**. There are two other lists of the sons born to David **in Jerusalem** (1 Chron. 3:5–8; 14:3–7), with minor variations (mostly in spelling) among the three lists.

5:17–21 Disturbed by news of Israel's unity and strong central government, **the Philistines** decided to attack. They gathered their forces at

the Valley of Rephaim, south of Jerusalem. Assured of victory by the Lord, **David** attacked the foe and defeated them. **He called** the **place Baal Perazim**, meaning *Baal is broken* or *the master of breakthrough* (NASB and NKJV marg.). The Lord had made breaches in the ranks of the enemy there. The **images** which the Philistines abandoned were seized by **David** (v. 21) and burned (1 Chron. 14:12) so as not to become stumbling blocks to future generations.

5:22–25 Sometime later, **the Philistines** returned to this same **Valley of Rephaim** and threatened Israel. This time **the LORD** told **David** to **circle around behind** the enemy forces, opposite some **mulberry trees**. When he heard **the sound of marching in the tops of the mulberry trees**, he would know that **the LORD** was marching against **the Philistines**. The result was that David destroyed the foe **from Geba** to **Gezer**. **Geba** probably should read *Gibeon* (NKJV marg., LXX, and 1 Chron. 14:16.)[3] Note that David did not assume that God's guidance for one battle (v. 19) would be the same for the next (v. 23). We must constantly seek God's will in everything. God's strategy in the first battle was direct assault; in the second, ambush.

E. The Ark Brought to Jerusalem (Chap. 6)

The events in chapter 6 did not take place immediately after those recorded in chapter 5. Second Samuel does not always follow a strict chronological order.

6:1–7 The last time we read about **the ark of God** was in 1 Samuel 7:1, 2. It had been sent back by the Philistines and was placed in **the house of Abinadab** in Kirjath Jearim. Many years passed. Then **David** decided to bring it to Jerusalem, in order that the city might be the *religious* as well as the *political* capital. So he took **thirty thousand . . . men . . . of Israel** to **Baale Judah** (the same as Kirjath Jearim) to get it. God had instructed that the ark was to be carried on poles, supported on the shoulders of the Kohathites (Num. 7:9). Instead, **David** made **a new cart** and with great jubilation **brought . . . the ark . . . to** the **threshing floor** of Nachon (called Chidon in 1 Chron. 13:9). There **the oxen stumbled**, and the ark was in danger of falling off the cart. So **Uzzah**, a son of **Abinadab**, steadied **the ark** with **his hand**. Since it was forbidden for even the priests to touch the ark (Num. 4:15), **Uzzah** was instantly struck dead by the Lord.

It has frequently been asked why God struck Uzzah for touching the ark when the Philistines often touched it without being destroyed. The answer seems to be that "the nearer a man is to God, the more solemnly and speedily he will be judged for any evil." Judgment must begin at the house of God.

> Was God's action too severe? We feel free to judge God because we lack a sense of His awesome holiness and majesty. The Ark was as close to a visible representation of God Himself as men would see until Jesus. Uzzah disregarded this. His death was a lasting lesson to the Israelites to take seriously the glory of their God. Do our language and our actions demonstrate that we mean it when we pray "Hallowed be Thy Name"? (*Daily Notes of the Scripture Union*).

6:8–11 **David** protested to **the LORD** against this solemn judgment and temporarily abandoned his plan to bring **the ark . . . into the City**. Rather, he had it placed in **the house of Obed Edom**, probably near Jerusalem.

The LORD greatly **blessed** the **household** of **Obed-Edom** during the **three months . . . the ark** was **in** his **house**.

6:12–15 Hearing of this blessing, **King David** decided to bring **the ark of God to** Jerusalem. The account in 1 Chronicles 15:13–15 tells us that during these three months David investigated the Scriptures to see how the ark was to be transported. The new cart was abandoned and the Levites carried the ark on their shoulders. After the bearers moved forward cautiously for **six paces** to make sure the Lord wasn't still displeased, David **sacrificed oxen and fatted sheep**. Then, with dancing in the streets, the ark was brought to a temporary tent in **the City of David**. (It is likely that Psalm 68 was written at this time.) The king himself was so elated that he **danced before the LORD with all his might. David was wearing a linen ephod** instead of his customary royal clothes.

6:16–23 His wife, **Michal, looked through a window and saw** him dressed in an ephod, acting in a manner which she considered unworthy of a king. When he **returned** home, she falsely accused him of indecently dancing in public. (**"Uncovering"** in verse 20 must be understood in the light of verse 14.) He answered that his dancing was an expression of his joy in the Lord and intimated that he did not intend to stifle his enthusiasm for the things of God. He would let himself be even more despised by men and **humble in** his **own sight**, but he would **be held in honor** by the "slave girls" **Michal** had **spoken** of. Because of her critical attitude, **Michal** suffered the reproach of bearing **no children to the day of her death**. This is a needed reminder that a critical spirit stifles fruitfulness.

F. God's Covenant with David (Chap. 7)

7:1–5 **David** felt that it was unsuitable for him to be **dwelling in his** fine home while **the ark of God** was kept **inside tent curtains**. So he notified **Nathan the prophet** of his intention to **build a house** for the ark. Nathan at first approved, apparently because he acted without consulting the Lord. Then **the word of the LORD came to** him, informing him that David would not be allowed to build a temple for Jehovah.

7:6–11 **The LORD** reminded **Nathan** that He had **dwelt in a tent** from **the time** of the Exodus **from Egypt**. The **tent** was suitable for the people of Israel as long as they were on the **move**. The **time** had now come for a settled temple.

7:12–15 Then **the LORD** revealed to Nathan an unconditional covenant which He would make with **David**. This covenant promised that David would have a son (Solomon) who would **build** the temple; that this son's **throne** would be established **forever**; that when he would sin, God would correct **him**, but His **mercy** would **not** cease.

7:16, 17 It further promised that David's **house**, his **kingdom**, and his **throne** would **be established forever**, and that his own descendants would sit upon the **throne**. David's dynasty has been interrupted since the Babylonian captivity, but it will be restored when Christ, the Seed of David, returns to reign over all the earth. Jensen elaborates:

> David wanted to build a temple for God, but Solomon was given the privilege. Undoubtedly the character of David's life work for God was fighting, not building. But even by this fighting he was clearing the way

for another to lay the foundation of that house of worship which his heart had so fondly desired to build. After the warring was over, Solomon erected the temple from materials which David had prepared. David represents Christ in His suffering and victory over the great enemy. Solomon represents Christ in His glory after the suffering and the conflicts are finished. The church, which is the true temple of God, having Christ for its chief cornerstone, will be manifested in the last day. Now in the church's days of suffering and conflict the materials are being prepared for this glorious building for God.[4]

7:18–29 Deeply moved by God's covenant of grace, **David went in** the temporary tent and offered the prayer of thanksgiving recorded here. In it, says Blaikie,

> He expresses wonder at the past, at God's selecting one obscure in family and obscure in person; he wonders at the present: How is it Thou hast brought me thus far? and still more he wonders at the future, the provision made for the stability of his house in all time coming.[5]

"And this is the custom ('law' in margin) of man, O Lord God" (v. 19b NASB) means that God had treated David with the same love and condescension that He commanded men to show to one another.

G. Defeat of Israel's Enemies (Chap. 8)

8:1, 2 David's policy as king was to purge out of the kingdom the heathen inhabitants who rebelled against his rule. This policy resulted in the enlargement of the territory of Israel.

For example, **he defeated . . . the Philistines** and seized **Metheg Ammah**—i.e., Gath (1 Chron. 18:1). He had once played the part of a *madman* in Gath (1 Sam. 21:10–15); now he would serve as *king* there. Also, he conquered **the Moabites** and used a measuring **line** to select two-thirds **to be put to death**. Moab must have shown treachery to Israel.

8:3–8 David's next victory was in the area of Syria. He defeated **Hadadezer, king of** a country named **Zobah**, between Hamath and **Damascus**, capturing **one thousand chariots, seven hundred horsemen**, and **twenty thousand foot soldiers**.

David also hamstrung all of **the chariot horses, except . . . enough of them for one hundred chariots.**[6] This means that a tendon in the leg was cut, making the animals unfit for warfare. **When the Syrians of Damascus came to help Hadadezer, . . . David** destroyed **twenty-two thousand of** them and made **the Syrians** his vassals. Then **David** returned to Jerusalem with **the shields of gold** and **bronze** which he had captured from **Hadadezer**.

8:9–12 **Toi**, the neighboring **king of Hamath** congratulated **David** for his military triumph over **Hadadezer** and **sent** gifts **of silver, . . . gold, and . . . bronze**. These precious metals, together **with** all the other **silver and gold** David had won in his wars, were **dedicated . . . to the Lord** and later used in the temple.

8:13 There is an apparent discrepancy here. It says that *David* killed **eighteen thousand** *Syrians* in the Valley of Salt. But 1 Chronicles 18:12 says that *Abishai* killed eighteen thousand *Edomites* in the Valley of Salt. It is true that in some Hebrew manuscripts, as well as in the ancient LXX and Syriac versions, "Edomites" is also found here in 2 Samuel 8:13.[7]

But the fact that **David made him-**

self a name from the victory in 2 Samuel and Abishai is credited with the glory in 1 Chronicles is unusual. Second Chronicles is usually very laudatory of David. Perhaps, as so often happens in war, the "top brass," in this case David, got credit for the victory as "commander-in-chief." But the actual direct leading of the battle was under Abishai, and even the chronicler, who seeks to emphasize the Davidic line, was led of the Holy Spirit to draw attention to the leader in the field. To further complicate things, the superscription to Psalm 60 states that "*Joab* [Abishai's brother] killed twelve thousand Edomites in the Valley of Salt."[8]

Eugene Merrill makes the following suggestion:

> Perhaps this difference is explainable by noting that the entire campaign was under Abishai's direct command, and that Joab was responsible (with the soldiers in his contingency) for killing two thirds of the Edomites.[9]

8:14 The fact that David **put garrisons throughout all Edom** and made **all the Edomites** become his **servants** probably is further support for the marginal reading "Edomites" in verse 13, and all manuscripts of the parallel passage in Chronicles.

8:15–18 So David's kingdom and power were greatly enlarged, and he ruled with **justice** and equity. Some of his chief officers are listed in verses 16–18: **Joab**—commander-in-chief of **the army**; **Jehoshaphat—recorder**; **Zadok** and **Ahimelech** (perhaps a copyist's error for **Abiathar**, see below) —**priests**; **Seraiah—scribe** or secretary; **Benaiah**—in charge of David's bodyguards; **David's sons—chief ministers**. There is a textual problem in verse 17. There and in 1 Chronicles 18:16 and 24:6 **Ahimelech** is listed as **the son of Abiathar**, but in 1 Samuel 22:20 **Abiathar** is said to be "the son of Ahimelech." The simplest solution is that in the verses listing Ahimelech as the son of Abiathar, a copyist may have transposed the names.

However, there is another possibility based on an OT custom by which every other generation had the same name, that is, grandsons were named after their grandfathers. Thus, at any given time the priestly colleague of Zadok would be either Abiathar or Ahimelech. Abiathar and Ahimelech functioned as fellow-priests as Annas and Caiaphas apparently did in the time of our Lord (Luke 3:2).

When Saul killed **Ahimelech** and his sons at Nob, **Abiathar** was the only survivor. When David became king, he appointed **Abiathar** as high priest but did not depose **Zadok**.

H. Compassion Shown to Mephibosheth (Chap. 9)

9:1–13 David remembered his covenant with Jonathan (1 Sam. 20:14–17) to **show him kindness** and wanted some opportunity to fulfill it. **Ziba, a servant of** the late King **Saul**, reported that a crippled **son of Jonathan** was living **in Lo Debar**, on the east side of the Jordan River. **David** had him **brought** to Jerusalem, ordered that the family property be returned to him, and arranged for him to **eat** at the royal **table**. **Ziba** and his **sons** were appointed to serve **Mephibosheth**.

Mephibosheth is a picture of an unconverted soul living in a barren land (**Lo Debar** may mean *no pasture*[10]) and sold under sin (**Machir** means *sold*—v. 4). He was an outcast from **the** fallen **house of Saul**. He was unable to come to the king to beg for mercy, being **lame in both his feet**. But the gracious sovereign sought him out in order to bless him. Once found, Mephibosheth was given great riches and a place of fellowship at the king's table. The parallels to salvation are obvious. Like Mephibosheth, we were *helpless* (unable to come to God); our condition was *hopeless* (being part of a fallen race). But by grace we became objects of divine favor. We have been elevated to a place in the family of God and made joint-heirs with Christ.

> Love so amazing, so divine,
> Demands my heart, my life, my all!
> —*Isaac Watts*

I. Further Conquests (Chap. 10)

10:1–5 Apparently **Nahash, the king of** the Ammonites, had done David a favor at one time. This was the same Nahash whom Saul defeated early in his reign (1 Sam. 11). **Nahash** might have helped David when he was a fugitive, since Saul was their mutual enemy for a time. Now **David** desired to repay that loyalty, so he **sent** messengers **to Hanun the son of Nahash,** who was crowned king when his father **died**. **The princes of . . . Ammon** suspected David's men of being spies, and so **Hanun** ordered them to be subjected to personal insults and indignities. David was angered when he saw his humiliated messengers.

10:6–8 As soon as the Ammonites learned of this, they prepared for war against Israel by hiring **the Syrians** from the north (see 1 Chron. 19). Thus David's men, under **Joab**, faced two armies—**the Syrians** and the Ammonites.

John Haley gives the following explanation of the apparent inconsistencies between verse 6 and 1 Chronicles 19:6, 7:

> Bethrehob was one of the little kingdoms of Mesopotamia, as also were Maacah, Zobah, and Tob petty monarchies of Syria. Thus the names and numbers agree as follows:[11]

2 Samuel	
Syrians of Beth Rehob and Zobah	20,000
Syrians of Tob	12,000
Syrians of Maacah	1,000
TOTAL	33,000

1 Chronicles	
Syrians from Zobah, etc.	32,000
Syrians of Maacah (number not given)	[1,000]
TOTAL	33,000

10:9–14 **Joab** divided his men into two groups. He himself commanded **some of Israel's best** soldiers in a drive **against the Syrians. His brother . . . Abishai** led the **rest** of the Israelites **against . . . Ammon**. Both generals agreed to send help should the other be threatened. **The Syrians . . . fled** as **Joab and** his men attacked in the open field. Then the frightened Ammonites retreated into their **city** (probably Rabbah).

10:15–19 Shortly thereafter **the Syrians** reorganized their forces and solicited aid from other Syrian states. They marched as far as **Helam**, east of the Jordan (exact location unknown), where David's army met and defeated them. The Israelites destroyed **seven hundred charioteers and forty thousand horsemen**. (In 1 Chron. 19:18 the losses are stated as "seven thousand charioteers and forty thousand foot soldiers." Williams suggests that there was a cavalry brigade of 40,000 men with 700 light chariots, and an infantry brigade of 40,000 with 7,000 heavy chariots.)[12] This battle convinced the Syrians of David's power, so **they made peace with Israel** and refused **to help the** Ammonites **anymore**.

II. DAVID'S FALL (Chaps. 11, 12)

A. Crimes Against Bathsheba and Uriah (Chap. 11)

11:1–5 David's notorious moral lapse was occasioned, writes the venerable commentator Matthew Henry, by three things: (1) "Neglect of his business"; (2) "Love of ease and the indulgence of a slothful temper"; (3) "A wandering eye."[13] Instead of going **to battle** against the Ammonites **in the spring of the year, . . . David sent Joab** against them while he himself **remained** idly at home. Times of idleness are often times of greatest temptation. **One evening . . . he** looked out **from the roof of** his palace and saw **a . . . beautiful . . . woman bathing.** Inquiry revealed that she was **Bathsheba, . . . the wife of Uriah,** one of David's mighty warriors. **David sent** for her and committed adultery **with her**. She purified herself **from her** ceremonial defilement, then **returned to her house**. When she found out she was pregnant, **she sent** the news to **David**.

11:6–13 The king then plotted to hide his sin. First he called **Uriah** back from **the war**, pretending that he wanted to hear of the progress of **Joab** and the army. After **Uriah** had answered his questions, **David** instructed him to return home, hoping that he would have intercourse with Bathsheba. Then when the baby was born, Uriah would think that it was his own child. But Uriah upset David's plans. Instead of returning home, he **slept at the door of the king's house**; he did not feel he could enjoy the comforts of home as long as his nation was at war. In desperation **David . . . made** Uriah **drunk**, but the faithful soldier still refused to **go** home. Uriah's loyalty and faithfulness stand in marked contrast to the king's treachery.

11:14–17 Then **David** stooped to his lowest act of infamy. He ordered **Uriah** to carry **a letter to Joab**—a letter which contained Uriah's death sentence. The king ordered Joab to put **Uriah in the forefront of the hottest battle**, where death would be inevitable. Then Uriah would not be alive to disown the baby that would be born. Joab directed the battle so that Uriah would be sure to be killed. He ordered his troops to advance, then called both flanks to withdraw. As Uriah and his men in the center moved forward, they were easy targets for the Ammonites on the wall. Militarily it was ridiculous, but it succeeded in eliminating **Uriah** as well as many other loyal **servants of David**.

11:18–21 When **Joab sent** news back to **David**, he knew **the king** would be angered by the military defeat. David would say, "**Why did you approach so near to the city**? Didn't you remember how **Abimelech, the son of** Gideon (**Jerubbesheth**) was killed when he did this very thing?" (see Judg. 9:50–55.) So Joab instructed **the messenger** to forestall **the king's wrath** by adding, **"Your servant Uriah the Hittite is dead also."** This would make David forget about the military reverses of the day.

11:22–25 **The messenger** reported to **David** as instructed. Then he was told to carry back a message **to Joab**, saying that military reverses are inevitable and that Uriah's death should not cause grief because in warfare **the sword devours** indiscriminately. Thus David hypocritically tried to hide his deep guilt "with a fatalistic comment about the inevitability and capriciousness of death."

After the customary time of **mourn-**

ing, David sent for Bathsheba to become **his wife**. Sometime later, the baby was born.

> That the Scriptures report this incident from the life of David is an indicator of their faithfulness. They give us an honest and uncut view of God's people the way they really were, warts and all (*Daily Notes of the Scripture Union*).

B. Confession to the Lord (Chap. 12)

12:1–9 It is generally believed that about a year elapsed between chapters 11 and 12. During that time the hand of **the Lord** was heavy upon David; his spiritual struggle is described in Psalms 32 and 51. The prophet **Nathan . . . came to him** with this parable, asking David's judgment on the matter: "A rich man with many sheep was unwilling to use any of his own animals as food when a visitor called on him. Instead, he took the one little ewe lamb belonging to a poor man and slaughtered it. David could judge sin in others more easily than in himself. He angrily declared that the man should restore fourfold and deserved to die for his sin." **Nathan** fearlessly pointed the accusing finger at David, saying, in effect, "You are the man who did it. God dealt graciously with you, making you king, enriching you, giving you everything that your heart could desire. But you took Bathsheba from her husband and then killed him to cover your crime."

12:10–14 The king's solemn sentence was then pronounced: His children would be a grief to him. His family would be torn by bloody conflict. His **wives** would be stolen from him and violated publicly (see 2 Sam. 16:22). His sinful **deed** would become a matter of general knowledge. David then came to the place of repentance and confessed his sin as being **against the Lord**. Morgan comments:

> Note the "also" in verse 13. A man puts away his own sin when in sincerity he confesses it. That makes it possible for God also to put it away.[14]

Nathan immediately assured him that the *penalty* of his **sin** was remitted—he would **not die**. But the *consequences* of his sin would follow him. Actually, he would have to restore fourfold (Ex. 22:1), as he himself had decreed concerning the rich man in the parable: The baby would **die**; Amnon would be murdered (chap. 13); Absalom would be slain (chap. 18); Adonijah would be executed (1 Kgs. 2).

12:15–23 When the baby **became ill, David** prostrated himself in prayer and fasting. He was deeply grieved. But **when** he learned that the baby had **died**, he **arose and ate**, explaining that the baby could not return, but that he, David, would one day join the baby when he died. Verse 23 has been a source of great comfort to believing parents who have lost infants and young children.

Matthew Henry comments:

> Godly parents have great reason to hope concerning their children that die in infancy that it is well with their souls in the other world; for *the promise is to us and to our seed*, which shall be performed to those that do not put a bar in their own door, as infants do not.[15]

We can be confident that children who die before they reach the age of accountability go to heaven because Jesus said, "Of such is the kingdom of heaven" (Matt. 19:14).

That David possessed a deep understanding of God's character is evident by the way he responded to God's judgment. Before the blow fell he prayed, knowing that Jehovah was *a God of mercy*. After the blow fell he worshiped, knowing that Jehovah was *a God of righteousness*. He forgot the things that were behind, accepted the divine discipline, and looked ahead to the future. He did not despair because he knew that God would yet bless him. He was right.

12:24, 25 **Bathsheba** gave birth to another **son**, **Solomon**, who was destined to succeed his father as king. Through the prophet **Nathan**, God gave the child the additional **name** of **Jedidiah** (*beloved of Jehovah*).

12:26–30 Now the narrative returns to the attack **against Rabbah** interrupted at 11:1 by David's sin. It seems that **Joab** had captured all but one portion of the city, perhaps the fortress on the top. (Josephus[16] and the NKJV say that Joab captured **the city's water supply**, making surrender imminent.) Then he called for **David** to come and finish the job, thus giving him complete credit for the victory. It was a striking act of selflessness on Joab's part. Joab was at best an unpredictable person. At times he seemed to show a real strength of character. But his overall behavior was that of a clever, ruthless, wicked schemer. David succeeded in capturing **Rabbah** and was rewarded with a **crown . . . of gold** weighing **a talent**, plus much other booty.

12:31 Bible scholars are disagreed as to whether the last verse describes cruel punishment to which David subjected **the people of Ammon** (KJV rendering)[17] or whether it simply describes menial agricultural work or industrial servitude (NKJV rendering). The latter seems more typical of David's way of dealing with his enemies.

III. DAVID'S TROUBLES (Chaps. 13—20)

A. Rape of Tamar by Amnon (13:1–19)

13:1–14 **Absalom** was David's **son** by Maacah, whereas **Amnon** was a son by Ahinoam; thus they were half-brothers. **Amnon** lusted after **Tamar**, the **lovely** full **sister** of Absalom, and therefore his own half-sister. He did not see how he could get near her because of her secluded life and her purity. Then **Jonadab** (David's nephew—v. 3) suggested a solution. By pretending sickness, Amnon lured her into his bedroom to nurse him and then forcibly raped her.

13:15–19 After the crime was committed, **he hated her** more **than . . . he had** ever **loved her**, as is so often the case. Lust and hatred are closely related. He tried to get rid of her, but she would not leave. So he finally had her expelled by force, hoping that "out of sight" would be "out of mind." She wore the symbol of mourning, and this alerted Absalom to what had happened.

B. Absalom's Revenge on Amnon, and Absalom's Flight (13:20–39)

13:20 **Absalom** comforted **Tamar** as if he did not think it was very serious, but actually he was already plotting revenge against Amnon.

Disgraced and unwanted for marriage, through no fault of her own, **Tamar remained desolate in her brother Absalom's house**. This probably means that she lived and died unwed. Lust hurts the innocent as well as the guilty.

13:21 Though David **was very angry**, he did not punish Amnon as he should have done—probably because his own sin was so fresh in everyone's mind.

> He knew his duty, but his hands were tied. This is what willful sin does in robbing us of moral freedom, liberty of speech and testimony (*Daily Notes of the Scripture Union*).

The fact that Amnon was his firstborn (1 Chron. 3:1) and the natural successor to the throne might also have influenced David.

13:22–29 **Absalom** waited his time for vengeance. It came **after two full years**. A great celebration was planned, as always, at the time of sheepshearing near Bethel. Absalom's urgent invitation failed to attract his father, probably because David wanted to spare his son heavy expense. But it did succeed in bringing **all the king's sons**, and most important of all, **Amnon**, who as the eldest son represented his absent father. At a predetermined signal, Absalom's **servants** killed **Amnon**. The rest of the princes **fled** back toward Jerusalem in panic.

13:30–36 In the meantime, **news** reached **David** that **Absalom** had **killed all** of his **sons**! Again David was plunged into mourning. **Jonadab** corrected the false report with the information that it was **only Amnon** who was **dead**, and that **Absalom** had plotted his death since the day that **Tamar** was violated. Shortly thereafter David's **sons** returned to Jerusalem with great lamentation, confirming Jonadab's report that they were still alive.

13:37–39 **Absalom fled** for his life to **Geshur**, in Syria, where his mother had lived, and where **Talmai**, his maternal grandfather, was **king**. Absalom lived in Geshur for **three years**. Amnon was older than Absalom and until his death was next in line to the throne. With Amnon dead, Absalom had visions of *himself* on the throne. **King David longed to** see **Absalom** again, after his grief over Amnon's death had subsided with the passing of time.

C. Absalom's Return to Jerusalem (Chap. 14)

14:1 **Joab** realized **that the** king longed to have **Absalom** back in Jerusalem. But the people knew that **Absalom** was guilty of murder and should be executed. Thus the fear of public disapproval kept David from bringing Absalom back.

14:2–7 So **Joab** sent a **woman** from **Tekoa** (near Bethlehem) to David with a family situation similar to David's. Pretending to be in deep mourning, she told how one of her **sons** had **killed** the other. Now her **family** was demanding the death of her only heir. This would completely wipe out the family **name** from **the earth**.

14:8–13 At first **the king** told her to return home and await an answer, hoping perhaps to avoid guilt in exonerating the murderer. But she wanted an answer immediately so she could trap David by his own decision. She offered to assume any guilt which his decision might involve. King David made another general statement, promising her security. Then she asked him pointblank for assurance that her son would not be killed. As soon as he gave this, she had him trapped. If **the king** would grant this pardon to her son, why would he not restore his own **banished** son, Absalom?

> The woman's pretended situation is roughly analogous to David's. One son is dead, and his relatives are calling for the death of the guilty one, as retributive revenge (v. 7). David's decision showed mercy and suspended the usual blood-vengeance that often, in the Middle East, con-

tinued through many generations. But the woman presses on to apply the story to David and Absalom, and again, as with Nathan, David is caught in the web of his own moral wisdom. He is bound to restore, with protection, the banished and fearful Absalom (*Daily Notes of the Scripture Union*).

14:14 The woman apparently meant to suggest that, **like water spilled on the ground**, what was past (i.e., the death of Amnon) could not **be gathered up again**, so why dwell on that. Possibly also, that life is too short to be wasted in a prolonged quarrel.[18] The last part of verse 14 seems to mean that **God does not** immediately destroy an offender (as David should well know) **but . . . devises means** by which the sinner might be forgiven and restored. If God acts in this manner, why should not the king do so too?

14:15–23 The woman said that she came to **the king** expecting such God-like clemency. She had obtained it for her own **son**, and now she was pleading for his **son**. **The king** suspected that **Joab** had engineered the plot, and **the woman** freely admitted it. King David weakly ordered Joab to **bring** Absalom **back** to Jerusalem in spite of the fact that Absalom was unrepentant. It was most unrighteous for David to do this, and he was to pay for it dearly.

14:24–33 For **two full years . . . Absalom** lived **in Jerusalem** without being permitted into his father's presence. (His natural **good looks** and luxurious growth of **hair** are mentioned as factors that would aid him in stealing the hearts of the people of Israel.) After two years Absalom tried to contact Joab for permission to see the king. **Joab** refused to come to him twice, so **Absalom** ordered his **field** of **barley** to be burned. This brought Joab to his door quickly! Absalom's request for an audience with his father was granted, and the two were reunited.

It had been seven years since Tamar had been raped and five years since the murder of Amnon. For five years Absalom had not seen his father. Though David had forgiven him and brought him back to Jerusalem instead of executing him, he had refused to forget what had happened. But when the two men finally met, Absalom received a complete pardon. He then took the favor his father had shown him and used it as a platform from which to launch a revolution (chaps. 15—18). David spared his son's life, but in response Absalom schemed his father's death.

Joab's actions in all this seemed designed to obtain David's favor and also the favor of Absalom, who was next in line as king.

D. Absalom's Revolt and David's Flight (15:1–18)

15:1–6 Up to this point **Absalom** had concealed his desire to be king. But now he traveled about with an impressive entourage. Also he went boldly up **to the** city **gate** (where legal matters were settled) and acted as if he were the only one in **Israel** who was genuinely interested in the welfare of the people. He practically accused his father of failure to provide adequate legal aid and said that if he were king, the people would receive the **justice** they deserved. He courted the favor of people from the various cities **of Israel**.

15:7–12 After four **years**[19] (according to LXX mss., Syriac, Josephus, NKJV marg.) **Absalom** received permission to **go to Hebron**, ostensibly to fulfill a **vow** he had **made** while in exile. **Hebron** was probably disaffected because David had moved his capital from there to Jerusalem. Also, Hebron was the place of Absalom's birth. The **two hundred men** who accompanied **Absalom** did not know that his real purpose was to announce the formation of a new government, with himself as king! **Ahithophel**, one of David's counselors and Bathsheba's grandfather (cf. 11:3 with 23:34), defected to **Absalom**, and many of **the people** joined Absalom in his **conspiracy** to usurp the throne. Perhaps Ahithophel wanted to get even with David for the latter's sin with his granddaughter.

15:13–18 On hearing the news, **David** decided that the situation was serious and that he should abandon **Jerusalem**, so he gathered **his household** together immediately and fled to **the outskirts** of the city. **But the king left ten . . . concubines** behind **to keep the house**.

E. David's Friends and Foes (15:19—16:14)

15:19–22 Among those who went with David was a group of Philistines who had left **Gath** with him. One of these was **Ittai the Gittite**. When he started out to follow, the king urged him to return. After all, he was not a Jew; he was an exile; he had only recently joined the ranks; and David's cause was at best uncertain. But **Ittai** would not be dissuaded. He resolutely determined to accompany the king, no matter what the cost might be. David rewarded the loyalty of this Gentile by permitting him and his followers to accompany him into exile. **Ittai . . . said: ". . . surely in whatever place my lord the king shall be, whether in death or life, even there also your servant will be."** Believers should have the same devotion to the King of kings during His rejection as Ittai had to David in his.

15:23 They **crossed over the Brook Kidron**, east of Jerusalem, and headed for the Jordan Valley. Nearly a thousand years later David's Greater Son would retrace his steps, Himself a rejected King (John 18:1). David **crossed** the **Kidron** and fled to *save* his life. Jesus crossed the valley and prayed in Gethsemane, en route to *giving* His life a ransom for many.

15:24–29 **Zadok** and **Abiathar**, the priests, came out of **the city** with **the ark**, intending to follow David into exile. But he sent them **back** with the hope that **the Lord** would allow him to return. Also, he told the priests that they could be more help to him right in **Jerusalem** (as a sort of fifth-column among Absalom's men). He would go as far as the west bank of the Jordan and await **word . . . from** them as to the progress of Absalom's rebellion.

Rather than becoming bitter at his enforced exile, David submitted meekly to what God had allowed. According to its title, Psalm 3 was composed at this time. In this psalm we find that David's trust in the Lord was unshaken as the storm broke over him.

15:30–37 **David** ascended **the Mount of Olives** with his faithful followers in deep mourning, praying that God would **defeat** whatever **counsel** that **Ahithophel** might give to **Absalom**. At the summit of the Mount of Olives, the king was met by **Hushai the Archite**. David asked him to **return to** Jerusalem and pretend loyalty **to Absalom**. In this way he might be able to counteract whatever advice **Ahithophel** might offer. He could relay any important news to **Zadok and Abiathar the priests,** who in turn would send **their two sons** with reports to David. **Hushai** reached **Jerusalem** just as **Absalom** was arriving to take over the government.

16:1–4 After **David** passed the summit of Olivet, **Ziba the servant of Mephibosheth . . . met him with** a large supply of food and **wine**, plus two **donkeys**. When David asked about Mephibosheth, Ziba falsely reported (see 19:27) that the son of Jonathan had stayed **in Jerusalem** in hopes that **the kingdom** would return to **the house of** Saul and thus to him as the next in line. David believed this lie and ordered that Mephibosheth's property should become Ziba's.

16:5–14 At **Bahurim**, on the road to Jericho, a descendant **of Saul** named **Shimei** came out and cursed **David** fiercely, charging him with **the blood of** Saul's **house**. **Abishai**, one of David's officers, wanted to kill **Shimei** on the spot, but the king would not allow it. He suggested that **the Lord** may have **ordered him** to **curse**. He pointed out that, after all, a member of Saul's house had **more** cause to seek his **life** than his own **son**, Absalom. Also, perhaps David remembered the death of Uriah and realized that Shimei's accusations were not entirely without foundation. And David hoped that Shimei's excessive hostility might move God to have mercy. As David and his men headed for the Jordan, **Shimei** followed them, cursing and throwing **dust** and **stones**. Finally **the** exiled **king** reached the river, where he and his party **refreshed themselves**.

F. Absalom's Counselors (16:15—17:23)

16:15–19 The scene now switches back **to Jerusalem**, where **Absalom** had just arrived. **Hushai** made a loud and vigorous display of loyalty **to Absalom**. At first he was suspected, but finally he was accepted by the usurper.

16:20–23 Ahithophel's first counsel to **Absalom** was that he should **go in to** the ten **concubines** David had **left** behind in Jerusalem. Such an act, disgraceful in itself, would be an unspeakable insult to David, would make reconciliation out of the question, and would constitute a direct claim to the throne. Absalom accepted the **advice** by going in to the royal harem, **in the sight of all Israel**, thus fulfilling Nathan's prophecy in 12:11, 12.

Ahithophel's counsel was highly respected in those days. **Absalom** followed it unquestioningly, as his father had done. But when we remember that Ahithophel was Bathsheba's grandfather, we can see how the desire for revenge might determine his particular counsel.

17:1–4 Having been successful in his first counsel, **Ahithophel** next advised **Absalom** to muster **twelve thousand men**, overtake **David**, kill him unexpectedly, and **bring** his followers **back to Jerusalem**.

17:5–14 **Absalom** was pleased but decided to **call Hushai** for his advice. This was the opportunity **Hushai** had been waiting for. He said that this second bit of **advice** by **Ahithophel** was **not good "at this time."** After all, David **and his men** were **enraged** by the insurrection, and they would fight fiercely. And David was too wise to spend the night with his troops; he would be hiding in a cave somewhere. If Ahithophel's first attack was not successful, then panic would spread throughout the nation, and Absalom's cause would be lost. **Hushai** had an alternative plan, which seemed to indicate his loyalty to Absalom but which in reality was designed to provide additional time for David to escape and to include the possibility of Absalom's death. He suggested a general mobilization of **all** the armies of **Israel**, led by Absalom. Such an army would be invincible. David would be attacked, and escape would be impossible. Absalom decided that Hushai's advice was best, so he rejected Ahithophel's plan, as David had prayed (15:31).

17:15–17 Hushai immediately sent word **to Zadok and Abiathar the priests**, and instructed them to notify David to **cross** the Jordan and escape to safety. The priests sent the message by **a female servant** to their sons who were waiting **at En Rogel**, at the outskirts of **the city**.

17:18–22 Nevertheless a lad saw this secret meeting and reported the spies to **Absalom**. Accordingly, the two sons of the priests, **Jonathan and Ahimaaz**, hid in **a well** (dry cistern) at **Bahurim** until the search parties had passed. Then they escaped and carried the news to **David**. David **crossed . . . the Jordan**, putting this natural barrier between his forces and those of Absalom. Then David marched to **Mahanaim**, a city in the land of Gilead.

17:23 Ahithophel became despondent because his **advice** had been rejected, and because he perceived that David would be victorious. He returned **to his house**, set his **household in order, and hanged himself**. Both in life and in death he was a "type" of Judas Iscariot.

G. Absalom's Death and David's Lament (17:24—19:8)

17:24–26 Absalom pursued his father across **the Jordan** to Gilead, having appointed **Amasa** as commander of his forces. Amasa's father was an Ishmaelite by birth (1 Chron. 2:17) but **an Israelite** by religion. He was David's nephew and a first cousin of Joab.

17:27–29 While **David** was encamped at **Mahanaim**, three men came to him with necessary, nonperishable provisions **for** him **and** his **people**; they were **Shobi**, **Machir**, and **Barzillai**.

Shobi was a **son of Nahash**, the deceased king of the Ammonites. His brother Hanun had rejected David's goodwill and suffered for it (chap. 10). But **Shobi**, although by birth an alien, cared more for Israel's king than most of the Jews did. Likewise, many Gentiles have received Him who was rejected by "His own" (John 1:11).

Machir had cared for Mephibosheth for many years, until David brought the latter to Jerusalem (9:3–5). He ministered to those in need, whether a lame prince or a dethroned king. Those who give of their substance to aid the cause of Christ through hospitality will have their kindnesses returned a hundredfold when He returns in glory.

Barzillai helped sustain David the entire time he stayed in **Mahanaim**. He was a very wealthy man and his support meant a lot to the king (19:31–39). On his deathbed, David told Solomon to elevate the sons of Barzillai to places in the royal court (1 Kgs. 2:7). Christ won't forget those who have ministered to Him; they will be given positions of honor in His kingdom.

18:1–5 David divided his army into three companies, with **Joab**, **Abishai**, and **Ittai** as the three generals. The king wanted to participate in the coming battle, but **the people** persuaded him to remain **in the city** and send **help** if needed. As the soldiers marched out of the city, David gave public orders to his generals to **deal gently for** his **sake with . . . Absalom**.

18:6–9 The battle was fought **in the woods of Ephraim**, east of the Jordan and near Mahanaim. There were **twenty thousand** fatalities that day among Absalom's troops, largely the result of the dense forest which trapped the soldiers. David's army was victorious. As **Absalom** was fleeing through the forest, he was **caught** by **his head** in **a** huge **terebinth tree, . . . and the mule . . . went on** without him. It is a sort of poetic justice that the same part of his body of which he was so proud became the means of his downfall.

18:10–15 The messenger who reported Absalom's helpless position **to Joab** was rebuked for not killing the rebel. He carefully explained that no amount of money would induce him to violate **the king's** instructions. Besides, if he killed Absalom, the news would get back to the king, and Joab would not come to his defense. **Joab** considered all this talk a waste of time. He plunged **three spears through Absalom's heart**, then let his **ten** armorbearers administer the *coup de grâce*. All this was against the king's command, but it was best for the kingdom. David had consistently refused to punish his sons for their crimes, so the task fell to someone else.

18:16–18 As soon as the deed was done, **Joab** wisely called a halt to the fighting, since his major objective had been accomplished. Absalom's body was thrown **into a large pit** and covered with **a very large heap of stones**. This was in marked contrast to the monument which he had erected **for himself** in **the King's Valley**, probably near Jerusalem. Absalom had three sons (14:27), but they must have died young and left him without an heir. Consequently, he had built **Absalom's monument** to preserve his **name** for posterity.

18:19–23 Ahimaaz wanted to carry **the news to** David, but **Joab** did **not** want him to. It seems that Ahimaaz had a reputation for being a bearer of good news (v. 27b), and it would have been out of character for him to bring the news of Absalom's death. So Joab sent a **Cushite** as the official messenger. But after he left, **Ahimaaz** persuaded **Joab** to **let** him go also, even if he would receive no reward for the errand. He succeeded in overtaking **the Cushite** by taking a quicker route.

18:24–30 David was on the lookout for **news** from the battle. **The watchman** reported one runner approaching, then **another**. When David heard that **the first** resembled **Ahimaaz**, he prepared himself for **good news** because Ahimaaz had always brought welcome messages in the past. Drawing near, **Ahimaaz** ceremoniously announced that **the LORD** had smitten the rebel army. But when David asked about **Absalom**, Ahimaaz's courage failed, and he gave a vague answer about seeing **a great tumult** but not knowing the details.

18:31–33 By then **the Cushite** had arrived. He announced that David's enemies had been defeated. The inevitable question from the king about Absalom brought the blunt reply that **all** David's **enemies** should **be like that young man**—in other words, *dead*. This news plunged David into very deep mourning. His pathetic lament is recorded in verse 33. This was one of the greatest griefs of his life, and it is doubtful that he ever forgave Joab for it.

19:1–8 So great was the king's sorrow that the people felt ashamed and guilty. They acted as if they were victims rather than victors. **Joab** was impatient with all this and delivered a stern rebuke to the king. He complained that David seemed more interested in his **enemies** than in his faithful followers, and that he was ungrateful to those who had **saved** his **life**. He warned that **if** David did **not** immediately show a kindly interest in his people, they would forsake him that **night**. David complied by taking a position by **the gate** of the city and talking to the people.

H. David's Return from Exile (19:9–43)

19:9, 10 In the meantime confusion reigned in the land of **Israel**. **All the people** were quarreling among themselves. King David, who had **saved** them **from . . . the Philistines**, was in exile, they reasoned, and **Absalom**, their self-appointed ruler, was dead. A movement thus began to restore David to his throne. **"Why do you say nothing about bringing back the king?"** is an appropriate question for a sleeping church today.

19:11–15 When **David** heard that the ten tribes of **Israel** were talking about restoring him to the throne, he **sent** two priests **to the elders of Judah**, asking **why** they, his blood relatives, were **the last to bring** him **back** as **king**. **Judah** had supported Absalom heavily in the rebellion, and doubtless some resentment or fear lingered.

David decided to remove **Joab** as **commander** in chief (probably because Joab had killed Absalom) and to appoint **Amasa** to take his **place**. **Amasa**, a nephew of David, had only recently been Absalom's general. To outsiders it must have looked like David punished loyalty and rewarded rebellion, a government policy unlikely to produce political stability. But these moves won **the hearts of all the men of Judah** over to David's side, and they sent a unanimous "welcome home" message to him.

19:16–23 **Shimei**, who had **cursed** David previously, **and Ziba**, who had slandered Mephibosheth, **came** rushing down **to the Jordan** River to meet the returning monarch. Shimei's profuse apology was probably insincere; his great desire was to escape punishment now that David was in power again. In the enthusiasm of the moment, the king overruled Abishai's desire to kill Shimei, and instead promised him amnesty. But **David** did not forget Shimei's curses. He later ordered Solomon to deal ruthlessly with the foulmouthed Benjamite (1 Kgs. 2:8, 9).

19:24–30 **Mephibosheth** also **came . . . to meet the king**. It was obvious from his appearance that he had mourned David's exile from the day it began. He had been truly loyal to the king, in spite of Ziba's false charges against him. The king spoke rather roughly to him for not accompanying him into exile. Mephibosheth explained that he had asked his servant Ziba to **saddle a donkey**, and when Ziba had failed to do it, Mephibosheth was helpless, being a cripple. He stated frankly that Ziba had **slandered** him but that injustice did not matter as long as **the king** had returned. When David rather unfairly ruled that **Ziba** and Mephibosheth should **divide the land** between them, the crippled son of Jonathan revealed the true loyalty of his heart: **"Rather, let him take it all, inasmuch as my lord the king has come back in peace to his own house."**

19:31–39 **Barzillai**, the **eighty**-year-**old . . . Gileadite**, was another true friend to David. **He had provided** the king **with supplies at Mahanaim**. Now he accompanied him to **the Jordan**. David invited him to go with him to **Jerusalem**, promising him that he would be well cared for. **But Barzillai** refused to go on the grounds of his short life expectancy, his inability to **discern between** what was pleasant and unpleasant, his loss of **taste**, and his deafness. He would only **be a further burden to . . . the king** if he went. So he agreed to accompany David **a little way** past **the Jordan** and then return **to** his **own city**. His suggestion that **Chimham** (perhaps his son) should go **with** David was readily accepted.

19:40–43 By now a great procession had formed—**all the people of Judah . . . and half the** men of the other tribes—to bring **the king** back to Jerusalem.

Internal strife broke out because **Judah** had taken such a prominent place in the restoration of the king (i.e., bringing him **across the Jordan**) without inviting the ten tribes to participate. **Judah** explained that David was their **close relative** and that they had not profited in any way above the others by taking the lead. The ten tribes argued that they had **ten** times as much right to participate as Judah. The fierceness of Judah's **words** was an indication of the serious *trouble* that lay ahead.

I. Sheba's Rebellion and Death (Chap. 20)

20:1, 2 A wicked **rebel** named **Sheba**, of the tribe of Benjamin (and possibly related to Saul), took the words **of Judah** (19:42) and turned them into the basis for a rebellion. **The men of Judah** had claimed **David** as their own. **Sheba** now defiantly announced that the ten tribes had **no** part **in David** and were seceding. Only the tribe **of Judah** was left to David. Later events indicate that Sheba had a relatively small following. The expression **"every man of Israel"** must be understood in a restricted sense, involving only the dissident men of the ten tribes.

20:3 On reaching **Jerusalem, the king** found the **ten . . . concubines whom he had left** there, who had been dishonorably treated by Absalom. David arranged for them to be kept in a house **in seclusion** for the rest of their lives, as if **in widowhood**.

20:4–7 By now Joab had been demoted, and **Amasa**, Absalom's rebel commander, was in charge of David's army. **The king** ordered him to **assemble the** soldiers **of Judah . . . within three days** to **pursue** and capture the rebel leader, **Sheba**. For some unexplained reason, **Amasa** did not complete the job within the **time** given, so **David** ordered **Abishai** to take command and set out with chosen **men** to prevent **Sheba** from getting established in **fortified cities**. Joab was among those who went with Abishai.

20:8–10a As they reached a **large stone** marker in **Gibeon**, **Amasa came** to meet them. **Joab, . . . dressed in** a soldier's **battle armor**, advanced to meet Amasa, and as he did so his **sword** dropped to the ground. It seems that he did this purposefully. He then picked up his **sword** and moved toward his unsuspecting cousin. With a great show of friendliness, **Joab** grabbed Amasa's **beard** as if **to kiss him**, then killed him with one thrust of the sword.

20:10b–13 When **Joab and Abishai** began to pursue **Sheba**, their followers were immobilized by the sight of **Amasa** wallowing **in his blood** on **the highway**. Not until his body was **removed** did Joab's men follow him.

20:14–22 The hunt for Sheba led

to the far north, to the city of **Abel of Beth Maachah**. This was located north of the waters of Merom. It was a city famous for its **wise** people. As Joab laid **siege** to the city, **a wise woman** called down to him and asked him why he was going **to destroy a mother . . . city in Israel** (i.e., an important city) that had always been proverbial for its wisdom. When **Joab** explained that he was simply after the rebel leader, **Sheba**, who was hiding inside, she agreed to have him killed and **his head . . . thrown over the wall** as proof that he was dead. As soon as this was done, Joab **blew** the **trumpet** and **returned to . . . Jerusalem**, his mission accomplished. Sheba's revolt probably did not last more than a week.

20:23–26 David had demoted **Joab**, appointing first Amasa (19:13) and then Abishai (20:6) in his place. But Joab had regained his position as commander-in-chief.

The list of the king's important officials in verses 23–26 is largely the same as that in 8:15–18. **Joab** headed **the army**; **Benaiah** was in charge of David's bodyguard; **Jehoshaphat . . . was** the **recorder**; **Sheva** (same as Seraiah) **was** the **scribe** or stenographer; **Zadok and Abiathar were the priests**. (**Zadok and** Ahimelech were the priests in the earlier list.) The only other differences were that **Adoram was in charge of revenue** and **Ira the Jairite was** David's priest (or **chief minister**), whereas David's sons had been mentioned in chapter 8.

IV. APPENDIX (Chaps. 21—24)

The remainder of 2 Samuel is really an appendix highlighting various incidents in the reign of David, though not in chronological order. (The chronological order continues again in 1 Kings 1.)

A. The Famine and Its Termination (Chap. 21)

21:1 The first event was the **famine**, which lasted **for three years**. When **David inquired of the Lord** as to the cause, he was told that it was **because . . . Saul** had broken the covenant with **the Gibeonites**. These heathen inhabitants of the land had tricked Joshua into making a treaty with them. **Saul** had broken the treaty by trying to destroy **the Gibeonites**, a fact not mentioned previously in the OT. The term **"bloodthirsty house"** may imply that Saul's descendants had an active part in the slaughter of the Gibeonites, in which case their punishment (vv. 2–9) was just. It may seem harsh that the nation should suffer for the crime of a man now dead, but centuries earlier Israel had sworn a solemn oath to the Gibeonites (Josh. 9:19, 20), and the famine came because that oath had been broken. Time does not dull God's memory or His sense of justice.

21:2–9 David approached **the Gibeonites** to find out what they would accept as satisfaction for Saul's offense. They explained that they didn't want any of Saul's **silver or gold**, and that they had no right to put **any man** to death **in Israel**. Nothing would do but the execution of **seven** of Saul's male descendants, and David consented to this. The seven sons were: **the two sons of Rizpah—Armoni and Mephibosheth** (not Mephibosheth the son of Jonathan)—and **the five sons of** Saul's daughter **Merab** (v. 8, NKJV marg.). Two reasons for rejecting **"Michal"** as the proper reading here are that Michal was married to Palti, not **Adriel** (see 1 Sam. 25:44), and she was childless (2 Sam. 6:23). The **Barzillai** mentioned here is not the same man

The Davidic Kingdom. David's military exploits successfully incorporated into the Israelite kingdom the powers of Edom, Moab, Ammon, and Zobah.

who later helped David when he fled from Absalom (17:27).

21:10 Rizpah, Saul's loyal concubine, set up a watch by the bodies, day and night, so that neither vultures nor wild **beasts** could touch them. She kept this vigil **from the beginning of harvest until** God sent rain and thus ended the famine which had led to these deaths.

21:11–14 When **David** heard of her devotion, he took steps to give decent burial to these seven bodies and also to the **bones of Saul** and **of Jonathan**, which had been buried in **Jabesh Gilead**. **The bones of Saul** and **Jonathan** were laid to rest **in the tomb of Kish** in **Benjamin**.

21:15–22 This passage describes various battles against Philistine giants. In the first one, **David** was almost slain by **Ishbi-Benob**, but **Abishai** rescued him and **killed . . . the Philistine**. From then on the people would not let **David . . . go out with** them **to battle**. In the second battle, **at Gob** (or Gezer), another son of a giant was slain by **Sibbechai**. In the third battle, **Elhanan . . . killed the brother of Goliath the Gittite** and his brother—cf. 1 Chron. 20:5. The fourth battle resulted in the death of a giant **who had six fingers on each hand and six toes on each foot**. Pliny mentions certain six-fingered (*sedigiti*) Romans, and this peculiarity is hereditary in some families.[20]

B. David's Thanksgiving Psalm (Chap. 22)

22:1–51 With **the words of this song David** praises **the Lord** for deliverance from his **enemies** and for the innumerable blessings which had been showered upon him. It was probably penned after David had firmly established himself on the throne. Saul was dead, the kingdom was united under his leadership, and Israel's foes were beaten back. The words are found, with some variations, in Psalm 18 and are quoted in the NT as applying to the Messiah (v. 3, "in whom I will trust," cf. Heb. 2:13; v. 50, cf. Rom. 15:9).

Looking at it as a Messianic psalm, we may outline it as follows:

1. Praise to God for hearing and answering prayer (vv. 2–4)
2. Death closing in on the Savior (vv. 5–7a).
3. God warring against the hosts of hell as they seek unsuccessfully to prevent the Resurrection (vv. 7b–20).
4. Reasons why God raised Messiah from the dead (vv. 21–30).
5. The Messiah's Second Advent, in which He destroys His enemies (vv. 31–43).
6. The glorious kingdom of the Messiah (vv. 44–51).

For a detailed exposition see commentary on Psalm 18.

C. David's Mighty Men (Chap. 23)

23:1–7 The first seven verses give **the** very beautiful **last words of David**—that is, his last inspired utterance in song. He describes the ideal ruler, the Messiah, whose reign shall be a glorious dawn, **a morning without clouds** after a long stormy night.[21] David realized that he did not fit the description, but he took comfort in the fact that God's covenant assured him that the Messiah would be descended from him. Verses 6 and 7 describe Christ's judgment on **the sons of rebellion** when He returns to set up His kingdom.

23:8–12 A catalog of David's mighty men is given in verses 8–39. It is significant that Joab is not honored in this list, probably because he killed Absalom (not to mention Abner and Amasa!). This register is near the end of David's reign, while the parallel list in 1 Chronicles 11:11–47 is placed at the beginning. Although not identical, there are great similarities between the two rosters. More information about these men and their exploits can be found in the commentary on 1 Chronicles 11.

The first three **mighty men** were:

1. **Josheb-Basshebeth**, also **called Adino the Eznite—he** slew **eight hundred men at one time**. (1 Chron. says three hundred, but that number is probably a copyist's error.)
2. **Eleazar**—he fought off the Philistines when his fellow soldiers had retreated. They returned only to strip the slain. When the battle was over, **his hand was** so **weary** (probably cramped) that he could not unclasp his fingers from **the sword**.

3. **Shammah**—he stood alone against **the Philistines** when the men of Israel had **fled**. Standing **in** a **field . . . of lentils**, he fought off the enemy and gained **a great victory**.

23:13–17 The **three** unnamed mighty **men** referred to here **came to David** when he was in **the cave of Adullam**, and when **Bethlehem** was in the hands of **the Philistines**. **David** expressed a **longing** for **a drink of the water from the well of Bethlehem**. At the risk of their lives, these **men broke through** the lines **of the Philistines** and **brought** some **water** back **to David**. He was so overcome by this sacrifice that he **poured it out** as an offering **to the Lord**; he did **not** feel that he could **drink it**. Williams comments:

> Those who live close to Jesus hear the longings of His heart for draughts of love from Africa and India and China; and, like these mighty men, they turn their backs on home and wealth, and risk or lay down their lives to win for Christ the affection and service of nations held as hopelessly in the power of Satan as the well of Bethlehem was in the hand of the Philistine.[22]

23:18–23 Two more of David's illustrious heroes were:

1. **Abishai**—he **killed three hundred men** and was commander **of** the **three** mentioned in verse 16, though not one of them.
2. **Benaiah**—he **killed two lion-like heroes of Moab. He also . . . killed a lion in . . . a pit on a snowy day**, and **an Egyptian** who was better-armed than he.

23:24–39 The final mighty men of David—**the thirty** (or **thirty-seven**) are given in verses 24–39.

Some numbers in this chapter need to be explained, such as **the thirty** chiefs (vv. 13, 24), the **thirty-seven** (v. 39), etc. **The thirty** may have been an elite military group, but counting all those who had served in it at one time or another, the total was **thirty-seven**. There were three in the first group: Josheb-Basshebeth (or Adino), Eleazar, and Shammah (vv. 8–12). Two were in the second group: Abishai and Benaiah (vv. 18–23). In the third group (vv. 24–39), the number "thirty" may have been a technical term, like "the twelve" for the apostles, even if one or more were not always there. It could also be quite literal, but the extra men beyond thirty may have been replacements for those who died in battle, such as **Uriah the Hittite**, the last valiant man in the list and Bathsheba's husband.

The Lord Jesus has His mighty men (and women!) too. He takes note of them just as surely as David took note of those who valiantly served him. Whatever our rank, let us fight the good fight of faith:

> Soldiers of Christ, arise,
> And put your armor on,
> Strong in the strength which God supplies,
> Through His eternal Son.
>
> Stand, then, in His great might,
> With all His strength endued;
> But take, to arm you for the fight,
> The panoply of God.
>
> —*Charles Wesley*

D. David's Census and Its Consequences (Chap. 24)

William D. Crockett suggests that the events recorded here took place some time after David captured Jerusalem (chap. 5) but before he brought the ark into the holy city (chap. 6).[23]

24:1 It would appear that God in His **anger** told **David** to take a census of **Israel and Judah**. But we learn from 1 Chronicles 21:1 that it was *Satan* who moved David to do this. Satan *precipitated* it, David *performed* it (because of the pride of his heart), and God *permitted* it. The Septuagint rendering of verse 1 reads "and Satan moved David" rather than **"and He moved David."**

24:2–9 When **the king** ordered **Joab** to begin the numbering, his military **commander** demonstrated better judgment than **David**. He realized that the purpose of the census was to cater to David's pride, and he urged **the king** to desist, but in vain. Obedient to David, Joab and his men went throughout the land, numbering the people; they found that there were **eight hundred thousand** soldiers **in Israel** and **five hundred thousand** in **Judah**.

Exodus 30:12, 13 commanded that a half-shekel ransom be collected when a census was taken. There is no record of David's doing so. Pride motivated him to number the people. The census might cause him to depend on the size of his army and not on the arm of the Lord.

24:10–14 **After** the census was finished, the king was convicted of his sin, and cried out **to the LORD** for forgiveness. God sent **the prophet Gad** to him, offering any one of three punishments: (1) **seven years of famine . . . in the land**; (2) **three months** of pursuit by his **enemies**; (3) **three days** of pestilence or **plague**. **David** chose to **fall into the hand of the LORD**, and not into man's.

24:15–25 **The LORD sent** three days of **plague**, killing **seventy thousand men**. **The** destroying **angel** was about to **destroy** the city of **Jerusalem** when God stopped him at **the threshing floor of Araunah** (also called Ornan). David asked the Lord why He was destroying the people of Israel when it was David and his house who were guilty. God's reply, given through **Gad**, was for David to build **an altar . . . on the threshing floor of Araunah**. **So David** the king immediately began to arrange with **Araunah the Jebusite** for the purchase of the site. Although he was a Gentile, Araunah offered not only **the threshing floor** without charge but also **oxen** for sacrifices and the **threshing implements** for firewood. The king's noble answer was, **"nor will I offer burnt offerings to the LORD my God with that which costs me nothing."**

Finally **David bought the threshing floor and the oxen for fifty shekels of silver.** (1 Chron. 21:25 says that David paid 600 shekels of gold for the place, but this undoubtedly included the property surrounding the threshing floor.) **The plague** stopped when **burnt offerings** were offered on the altar (v. 25).

The threshing floor of Araunah, on Mount Moriah, was probably the very same spot where Abraham offered Isaac. It later became the site of Solomon's temple and then of Herod's temple in the time of Christ. Today it is occupied by a Moslem shrine—the Dome of the Rock. It will probably be the location of the temple in the Tribulation and finally of the millennial temple.

The Scriptures are completely honest in their treatment of the heroes of the faith. David had his *faults* and they are mentioned alongside *his faith*. We have followed David from the flock through exile into exaltation. Few men walked closer to God; few men fell deeper into sin. But through it all he was sustained by the Lord. We have all benefited from the experiences that David passed through, because he recorded them in his psalms.

Matthew Henry remarks on David as he appears in Samuel and how he appears in Psalms:

> Many things in his history are very instructive; but for the hero who is the subject of it, though in many instances he appears here very great, and very good, and very much the favourite of heaven; yet it must be confessed that his honour shines brighter in his Psalms than in his Annals.[24]

The words of Psalm 40 fitly summarize David's life:

> I waited patiently for the LORD, and He inclined to me, and heard my cry. He also brought me up out of a horrible pit, out of the miry clay, and He set my feet upon a rock, and established my steps. He has put a new song in my mouth—praise to our God; many will see it and fear, and will trust in the LORD (Ps. 40:1–3).

ENDNOTES

[1](1:17, 18) Quoted by Keil and Delitzsch, "The Books of Samuel," in *Biblical Commentary on the Old Testament*," VII: 286, 87.

[2](3:31–39) William Hoste and William Rodgers, *Bible Problems and Answers*, p. 214.

[3](5:22–25) Keil and Delitzsch maintain that Gibeon "is unquestionably the true reading, and *Geba* an error of the pen," because Geba is in the wrong place for this account ("Samuel," VII:326).

[4](7:16, 17) Irving L. Jensen, *I and II Samuel*, p. 92.

[5](7:18–29) William Garden Blaikie, "The Second Book of Samuel," in the *Expositor's Bible*, p. 105.

[6](8:3–8) There is some confusion when we compare v. 4 with 1 Chronicles 18. Verse 4 says that one thousand chariots (the word *chariots* is supplied by the translators), seven *hundred* horsemen were captured, while 1 Chronicles 18:4 says that seven *thousand* horsemen were taken. The number in 2 Samuel may be from one battle, while the number in 1 Chronicles may be the total taken throughout the conflict. Or this may simply be a copyist's error.

[7](8:13) If "Syrians" (Heb. Aram) is correct here it could mean that the Edomites (Heb. Edom) sought help from them. However, since *Aram* and *Edom* are spelled nearly alike in the Hebrew consonantal text ("r" and "d" being often confused in copying) it is more likely a copyist's error.

[8](8:13) Not all conservative commentators believe the superscriptions of the Psalms are original, but the author and editor of the *BBC* do so.

[9](8:13) Eugene H. Merrill, "2 Chronicles," in *The Bible Knowledge Commentary*, p. 608.

[10](9:1–13) However, while "Lo" definitely means "no," the standard vowels for "pasture" are *d***ō***b***e***r*, not *d***e***b***a***r*. The consonants *dbr* can mean "word" or "thing" in Hebrew. A possible rendering could thus be "no thing" or "nothing."

[11](10:6–8) John Haley, *Alleged Discrepancies of the Bible*, p. 321.

[12](10:15–19) George Williams, *The Student's Commentary on the Holy Scriptures*, p. 166.

[13](11:1–5) Matthew Henry, "The Books of Samuel," *Matthew Henry's Commentary on the Whole Bible*, II:494.

[14](12:10–14) G. Campbell Morgan, *Searchlights from the Word*, p. 91.

[15](12:15–23) Henry, "Samuel," II:504.

[16](12:26–30) Flavius Josephus, *The Works of Josephus*, Peabody, MA: Hendrickson Publishers, 1987, p. 193.

[17](12:31) Keil and Delitzsch believe that the more cruel meaning is correct and that the facts should not be softened by re-translating. However, they see the punishment as meted out either only on the fighting men taken prisoners or referring "at the most to the male population of the acropolis of Rabbah" ("Samuel," VII:396).

[18](14:14) Hoste and Rodgers, *Bible Problems*, p. 215.

[19](15:7–12) Since David's *entire reign* was forty years long the traditional reading here (*forty*) is doubtless a copyist's error. Numbers were especially hard to copy perfectly in ancient Hebrew manuscripts.

[20](21:15–22) Cited by Keil and Delitzsch, "Samuel," VII:446.

[21](23:1–7) A marvelous musical setting of verses 3b and 4 was made by one of America's earliest composers, Richard Billings.

[22](23:13–17) Williams, *Student's Commentary*, p. 309.

[23](Chap. 24: Intro) William D. Crockett, *A Harmony of Samuel, Kings and Chronicles*, pp. 138–40.

[24](24:15–25) Henry, "Samuel," II:446.

BIBLIOGRAPHY

For Bibliography see 1 Samuel.

FIRST KINGS

Introduction

"The history of the nation is recorded from the close of the reign of David to the middle of the reign of Ahaziah. In its highest glory under Solomon, the kingdom foreshadows the millennial kingdom of our Lord. The prosperity of the nation rises or falls according to the character of the ruler and his people, illustrating for us the important principle that obedience is the condition of blessing."

—F. B. Meyer

I. Unique Place in the Canon

The importance of Kings, which was originally only one book, can be seen from a historical perspective in that it spans 400 years of the history of Israel, from the reign of Solomon to the Babylonian Captivity. It records the reigns, not only of Judah (as does Chronicles), but also of the apostate nation called "Israel" or "Ephraim" in the North. However, it is not a mere history book; Kings gives a spiritual analysis of the kings as to whether they served the Lord or idols—or were half-hearted in their loyalty to God.

Perhaps most helpful of all to most Bible readers are the exciting yet edifying ministries of the Prophets Elijah and his successor Elisha.

An important lesson of Kings is that God rewards loyalty and punishes apostasy. Hezekiah and Josiah are the clearest examples of the former (2 Kgs. 18:3; 22:2). The obvious examples of the latter—on a national scale—are the exiles, first of the Northern Kingdom (722 B.C.) and then of the Southern (586 B.C.).

II. Authorship

The human author of Kings is unknown. A great deal of the book is apparently compiled from records, but with the guidance of the Holy Spirit. Some have suggested a priestly author, but one wonders what suitable priestly writers would have been available in the apostate Northern Kingdom. A prophetic author seems more likely. The final editor of the book is thought possibly to be Ezra if it was a priest and Ezekiel or Jeremiah if it was a prophet.

III. Date

Second Kings ends on the positive conciliatory note of Babylonian King Evil-Merodach's kindly elevation of King Jehoiachin of Judah after thirty-seven years of prison (c. 560 B.C.). An even more encouraging historical event that is conspicuous by its *absence* is the beginning of the return of the Jews to Palestine (536 B.C.). Since it is unlikely that such a patriotic writer as the author of Kings would neglect to mention this return if it had already started, it seems that the date Kings was finished would be between 560 and 536 B.C.

IV. Background and Themes

The two prominent groups mentioned in Kings are the kings and the prophets. The judgment passed on a king stemmed directly from his obedience or disobedience to the Lord. The prophet's ministry was always one of calling the wandering nation back to Jehovah.

O. J. Gibson summarizes the book as follows:

> Two chronological lines of kings are interwoven in the account. Israel, with ten tribes, is sometimes called the northern kingdom because its land was to the north of Jerusalem. From its first ruler, Jeroboam, to its destruction and captivity by Assyria, it was continuously in disobedience and idolatry before God. The so-called southern kingdom of Judah, centering in Jerusalem, was far from faithful to God, but yet maintained a semblance of obedience among a faithful minority. The most glorious period of the time was that of Solomon's reign. The building of the Temple and its dedication receive more attention than any other period, indicating its importance in God's eyes. Solomon's reign, ending with departure and judgment, is a solemn warning of what will happen when divine privileges and honor are abused and His Word flouted. Only when every appeal of grace had been exhausted by persistent disobedience did God, not heathendom, destroy first the northern and then the southern kingdom.[1]

OUTLINE

- I. THE LAST DAYS OF DAVID (1:1—2:11)
  - A. Adonijah's Attempt to Seize the Throne (1:1–38)
  - B. Solomon's Anointing at Gihon (1:39–53)
  - C. David's Final Charge to Solomon (2:1–11)
- II. THE GOLDEN REIGN OF KING SOLOMON (2:12—11:43)
  - A. Solomon's Purge of the Opposition (2:12–46)
  - B. The Wisdom of Solomon (Chap. 3)
  - C. Solomon's Administrators (4:1–19)
  - D. Solomon in All His Splendor (4:20–34)
  - E. Solomon's Temple (Chaps. 5—7)
    - 1. Solomon's Agreement with King Hiram (Chap. 5)
    - 2. Description and Construction of the Temple (Chap. 6)
    - 3. The Construction of Other Buildings (7:1–12)
    - 4. Furnishings of the Temple (7:13–51)
  - F. Dedication of the Temple (Chap. 8)
  - G. Solomon's Fame (Chaps. 9, 10)
    - 1. His Covenant from God (9:1–9)
    - 2. His Gifts to Hiram (9:10–14)
    - 3. His Subjects and Sacrifices (9:15–25)
    - 4. His Navy (9:26–28)

5. His Visit from the Queen of Sheba (10:1–13)
6. His Riches (10:14–29)

H. Solomon's Apostasy and Death (Chap. 11)

III. THE DIVIDED KINGDOM (Chaps. 12—22)

A. King Rehoboam of Judah (12:1–24)

B. King Jeroboam of Israel (12:25—14:20)
1. Jeroboam's False Religious Centers (12:25–33)
2. Jeroboam and the Man of God (13:1–32)
3. Jeroboam's False Priesthood (13:33, 34)
4. Death of Jeroboam's Son (14:1–20)

C. King Rehoboam of Judah (cont'd) (14:21–31)

D. King Abijam of Judah (15:1–8)

E. King Asa of Judah (15:9–24)

F. King Nadab of Israel (15:25–27)

G. King Baasha of Israel (15:28—16:7)

H. King Elah of Israel (16:8–10)

I. King Zimri of Israel (16:11–20)

J. King Tibni of Israel (16:21, 22)

K. King Omri of Israel (16:23–28)

L. King Ahab of Israel and the Prophet Elijah (16:29—22:40)
1. The Sins of Ahab (16:29–34)
2. Elijah and the Drought (17:1–7)
3. Elijah and the Widow of Zarephath (17:8–24)
4. Elijah's Challenge to the Priests of Baal (18:1–19)
5. Elijah's Victory over the Priests of Baal (18:20–40)
6. Elijah's Prayer for Rain (18:41–46)
7. Elijah's Flight to Horeb (19:1–18)
8. Elijah's Appointment of Elisha (19:19–21)
9. Ahab's First Victory over Syria (20:1–22)
10. Ahab's Second Victory over Syria (20:23–34)
11. Ahab's Disobedience (20:35–43)
12. Ahab's Crimes against Naboth (Chap. 21)
13. Ahab's Last Battle (22:1–40)

M. King Jehoshaphat of Judah (22:41–50)

N. King Ahaziah of Israel (22:51–53)

Commentary

I. THE LAST DAYS OF DAVID (1:1—2:11)

A. Adonijah's Attempt to Seize the Throne (1:1–38)

1:1–4 **David was** now seventy years **old** and in declining health. He was about to pass off the stage of history. The proposal of **his servants** in verse 2 seems at first glance both puzzling and shocking. However, this practice was accepted at that time as being of value in the case of an illness like David's. It was not an act of doubtful morality and would not create a public scandal. One thing we can be sure of is that David **did not "know"** (in the sense of having sexual intercourse with) **Abishag** (v. 4b). And it seems probable from chapter 2 that she was considered a legal wife of David because Solomon interpreted Adonijah's later request for her as a claim to the throne (2:21, 22).

1:5–10 **Adonijah** was apparently David's oldest surviving **son** (2:22) and thus considered himself next in line for the throne. Amnon and **Absalom** were both dead. Chileab was probably dead as well (2 Sam. 3:2–4). Before his father died, Adonijah proclaimed himself as **king**, prepared a great entourage, and enlisted the support of **Joab** and **Abiathar**. Being a **very good-looking** man, he won a great following. Verse 6a indicates that David was an indulgent **father** and Adonijah a spoiled son. When **Adonijah . . . sacrificed** a great many animals near **En Rogel, he . . . invited** to the feast **all** except those whom he knew to be loyal to his father—**Nathan the prophet, Benaiah, the mighty men** of David, and **Solomon**.

1:11–38 God had told David before Solomon was born that Solomon would be Israel's next king (1 Chron. 22:9). **Nathan** had a desire to see the word of the Lord fulfilled. Being concerned about the threat of **Adonijah,** he skillfully brought the issue to David's attention. Coached by **Nathan, Bathsheba** appeared before **the** ailing **king** and notified him of the plot. She also reminded him of a promise he had previously made (though unrecorded) that **Solomon**, her **son**, would be the next king. Just as she finished requesting that he publicly announce Solomon as his successor, **Nathan** arrived and **Bathsheba** withdrew. **Nathan** repeated the news concerning Adonijah's plot to seize the kingdom and asked if this was the king's desire. When **David** called for **Bathsheba**, Nathan withdrew. **David** reassured **Bathsheba** that **Solomon** would indeed be his successor. Then he instructed **Zadok the priest, Nathan the prophet, and Benaiah** to **take . . . Solomon . . . to Gihon,** a spring located outside the city, on the king's **own mule** and to **anoint him** as **king**.

B. Solomon's Anointing at Gihon (1:39–53)

Since it is widely held that Solomon had a two-year co-regency with his father, for which he would have had to be anointed, this was a second anointing that recognized him as sole ruler. This public anointing by **Zadok the priest** caused **great** rejoicing among David's followers, but consternation among **Adonijah and** those **who were** feasting **with him**. When the latter heard that **Solomon** was now sitting **on the** royal **throne** and that David was grateful to the Lord for this, they realized that Adonijah's plot was a failure. **Adonijah** fled to the tabernacle and **took hold of the horns of the altar**, an act which was supposed to grant him safety from punishment. Solomon decreed that Adonijah would be spared if found **worthy**, but punished if caught in any future wickedness. Then he sent Adonijah home.

C. David's Final Charge to Solomon (2:1–11)

If David in exile typifies Christ in His rejection during this age of grace, Solomon typifies Him as the King reigning in millennial glory. When He returns to set up His kingdom, His first act will be to destroy His foes and to purge out of His kingdom everything that offends. We see this pictured in chapter 2.

Just before his death, **David** delivered a solemn charge to **Solomon**, urging him to be obedient to **the LORD** and instructing him to take appropriate action concerning certain men: **Joab** should be slain for murdering **Abner . . . and Amasa**; **the sons of Barzillai** should be shown **kindness** because of their father's kindness to David when he was fleeing **from Absalom**; **Shimei** should be slain eventually because he cursed David, but Solomon could work out the details. The expression **". . . shed the blood of war in peacetime"** (v. 5b) reads in the NIV, "shedding their blood in peacetime as if in battle."

After a reign of **forty years**, **David** died and was **buried in** Jerusalem.

II. THE GOLDEN REIGN OF KING SOLOMON (2:12—11:43)

A. Solomon's Purge of the Opposition (2:12–46)

2:12–25 Solomon sat on the throne, and **his kingdom was firmly established**. **Adonijah** was grieved that he had been deprived of the throne, although he had to admit that it was Solomon's by the will of God (v. 15b). Whether innocently or insidiously, he made a **petition** of **King Solomon** through **Bathsheba** that **Abishag**, David's nurse, might be given to him for a **wife**. **Solomon** looked upon this as being the next thing to asking **for . . . the kingdom** itself, so he ordered **Benaiah** to execute **Adonijah**.

2:26–34 The king also expelled **Abiathar** from the priesthood, doubtless because he had supported Adonijah in his abortive plot. This was in partial fulfillment of God's judgment on **the house of Eli** (see 1 Sam. 2:31–35). When **Joab** heard of Abiathar's dismissal, he **fled to the . . . horns of the altar** for refuge. **Benaiah** ordered him to leave the altar, but Joab refused, expressing the determination to **die** there. Benaiah executed him quickly and had him **buried in his own house in the wilderness**. The deaths of **Abner** and **Amasa** were finally avenged. **The altar** of God gave no protection to anyone who broke the law of God.

2:35 Benaiah was appointed commander of **the army**, and **Zadok** succeeded **Abiathar** as **priest**. **Benaiah** had served David since the days of Saul. He was a man of great valor and the captain of David's personal bodyguard (2 Sam. 20:23). His unfailing courage was surpassed only by his undying loyalty to the house of David. Courage and loyalty should also characterize those who serve David's greater Son, the Lord Jesus Christ.

2:36–46 Solomon did not order Shimei's execution immediately. Rather, he put him under a sort of **house** arrest, forbidding him to leave the city. After **three years . . . Shimei** left **Jerusalem . . . to seek . . . two** escaped **slaves . . . in Gath**. In so doing he broke **the oath** that Solomon had made him **swear** earlier, and he demonstrated that he was no more faithful to Solomon than he had been to David. When he returned, **the king commanded Benaiah** to put **him** to death.

Thus **Solomon** made his **kingdom** secure by aggressively removing all whose hearts were not with him. Thereafter his reign was one of peace. The Christian will know the peace of God as he puts out of his life the things which oppose the reign of Christ within.

B. The Wisdom of Solomon (Chap. 3)

3:1 Solomon married the **daughter** of the **Pharaoh** who was then in power in **Egypt**. Perhaps this shows that his trust was in political alliances. The marriage, although politically expedient, was spiritually disastrous as well as forbidden by the law. From this point onward, Solomon's harem grew until it contained hundreds of foreign women. Solomon thus linked himself with many foreign powers but alienated himself from the Lord (11:1–8).

3:2–4 High places were here used for the worship of **the LORD**. This was not strictly in accordance with the law; God was supposed to be worshiped only in the place which He designated. But it is here excused on the ground that **there was no** official **house**, since Shiloh had been destroyed by the Philistines about 1050 B.C. when the ark was carried away (1 Sam. 4). After the temple was built, **high places** continued to be used, but for idolatrous worship. Although the ark was in Jerusalem at this time, the tabernacle was in **Gibeon** (1 Chron. 21:29), about six miles away. It was there that the king **offered a thousand burnt offerings**, probably at the outset of his reign.

3:5–15 God **appeared to Solomon . . . at Gibeon** and asked him what he would like most of all. The king requested **an understanding heart** for the great task of judging and ruling **the people** of Israel. The request **pleased the LORD**, and it was granted—together with **riches and honor**, and also long life, if Solomon would **walk in** obedience to God. Today God offers to everyone the greatest gift for which one could possibly ask—the Lord Jesus Christ, "in whom are hidden all the treasures of wisdom and knowledge" (Col. 2:3).

3:16–28 The remainder of chapter 3 gives an example of the king's great wisdom. **Two . . . harlots** were quarreling over which one was the **mother** of a baby. When Solomon threatened to **divide** the baby with a **sword** into **two** equal parts, the true **mother** was revealed by her desire to spare the **child** even if she didn't get the baby for herself. Such **wisdom** caused Solomon to be greatly **feared** and respected in all Israel.

C. Solomon's Administrators (4:1–19)

4:1–6 These verses list Solomon's high **officials**, or cabinet: **Azariah**, a grandson **of Zadok**, who seems to have succeeded him as high priest; **Elihoreph and Ahijah**, secretaries of state; **Jehoshaphat, recorder** or chronicler; **Benaiah**, commander of **the army**; **Zadok and Abiathar, the priests**; **Azariah— over the officers**; **Zabud**—the **friend** of Solomon; **Ahishar**, in charge of the palace; **Adoniram**, in charge of the **labor force** (tribute). The name **"Abiathar"** in verse 4 presents a difficulty if it is the same one

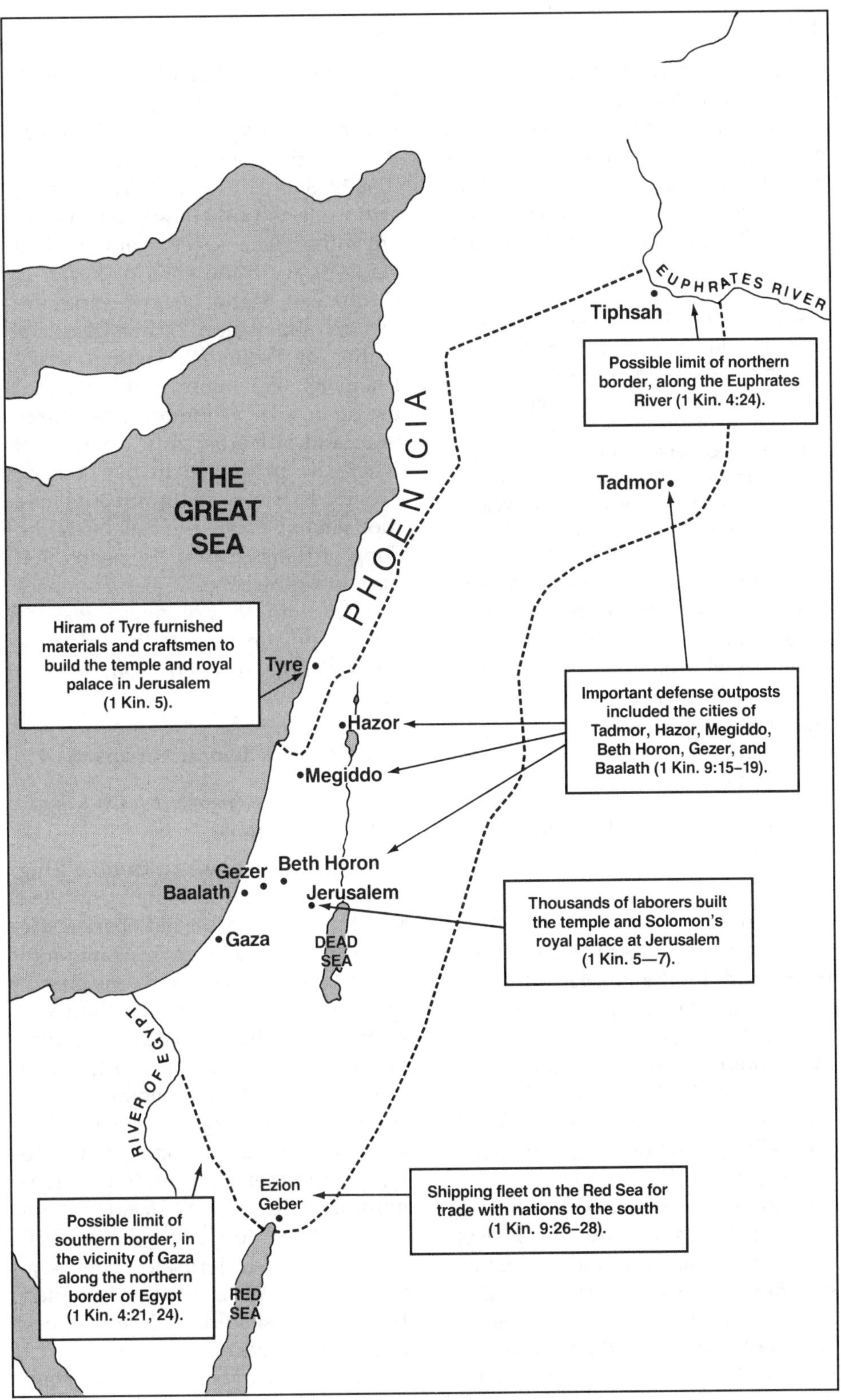

Solomon's Empire: The Twelve Districts

Solomon dismissed in 2:27. Perhaps he was dismissed after this period. Or perhaps he still retained the title of priest though no longer exercising priestly functions. It may, however, have been another Abiathar (see 2 Sam. 8:15–18). Matthew Poole comments:

> Some say that here is mention made of all Solomon's chief officers, both such as now were, and such as had been, and such as were afterwards, as they gather from verses 11 and 15, where two persons are named who married two of Solomon's daughters, which could not be till many years after this time.[2]

4:7–19 **Solomon** divided the land of Israel into **twelve** sections and put a governor in charge of each area to collect **food** from the people. Each division of the land with its officer in charge was responsible for supplying the royal board **one month** out **of the year**. Judah is not mentioned.

D. Solomon in All His Splendor (4:20–34)

4:20, 21 The kingdom under **Solomon** reached out to **the River** Euphrates, **to the land of the Philistines**, and to **the border of Egypt** (vv.21, 24). Much of this territory consisted of **kingdoms** that paid **tribute** to **Solomon** but were not considered part of Israel. Therefore Solomon's kingdom was not the complete fulfillment of the Palestinian covenant (Gen. 15:18–21).

4:22–28 The magnificence of Solomon's reign is described: his vast food supply, his thousands of **horses**, etc. But we must remember that in order to support such lavishness, it was necessary to tax the people very heavily. Also, we need to remember that Solomon's accumulation of **horses** was a violation of God's order (Deut. 17:16). (On the apparent contradiction between verse 26 and 2 Chron. 9:25, see the notes on that chapter.)

4:29–34 The king's **wisdom** is again referred to. **He was wiser than** any other. The sages mentioned in verse 31 were the sons of Zerah (1 Chron. 2:6), **Mahol** (*dancer*) being simply an appellation. **Ethan** was the author of Psalm 89; **Heman** wrote Psalm 88. We know nothing about the other men. Solomon **spoke three thousand proverbs**, only a portion of which are preserved in the book of Proverbs. **His songs** numbered **one thousand and five**, the best being the Song of Songs. Verse 33 means that his wide knowledge of many sciences enabled him to use object lessons from nature in expounding his wisdom. People traveled from afar to hear him.

E. Solomon's Temple (Chaps. 5—7)

1. Solomon's Agreement with King Hiram (Chap. 5)

5:1–12 **Hiram** was a Gentile **king of Tyre**, and as such he controlled vast **timber** resources in Lebanon. He had been very friendly to **David** and now wished to show that same friendliness to **Solomon**. It was therefore arranged that he should provide lumber with which Solomon could **build** a temple for **the LORD**. Solomon would send workers north to Lebanon to assist in the cutting operation. The **logs** would then be taken to the Mediterranean **Sea**, floated **in rafts** down to a point near Joppa, and then transported inland to Jerusalem. As payment for the timber, **Solomon** provided Hiram's **household** with food supplies **year by year**.

5:13–18 In order to obtain the manpower for this gigantic task of cutting lumber, **Solomon** drafted **thirty thousand men** of **Israel**, requiring them to go **to Lebanon . . . in shifts** of **ten thousand** each **month**. In addition to these men, **the king** had **eighty thousand** Canaanite slaves (**Gebalites**) working in the quarries of Israel, preparing **stones** for **the temple** (cf. v. 15; 2 Chron. 2:17, 18). **He** also **had seventy thousand who carried burdens**.

> Solomon's massive building operations involved a great force of slave labor (cf. 9:15–22). But even this proved inadequate, and he was compelled to draft native Israelites (probably excluding Judah), not as slave laborers but as forced laborers. The Israelites, with their tradition for sturdy independence, bitterly resented this, and it became a major cause of the division of the kingdom (12:4). How necessary it is to have divine wisdom in all matters, and not to ride roughshod over the sensitivities and welfare of others! (*Daily Notes of the Scripture Union*).

(See the notes on problems in 2 Chron. 2 for an explanation of the numerical discrepancies between these two chapters.)

2. *Description and Construction of the Temple (Chap. 6)*

6:1 In verse 1, the work of building the temple is said to have been started 480 years after the exodus from **Egypt**. If Solomon began the construction in 967/66 B.C., this would date the exodus at 1446/47 B.C. It is not possible, however, to fix these dates with absolute certainty. There is much dispute among scholars on this subject, but 1446 B.C. is very close to the early date of the exodus.

6:2–6 Details concerning the plan of **the temple** are given in chapter 6. They are at times technical and involved, making it difficult to get the exact picture. However, we do know that the temple was built somewhat as follows. It was 90 feet long, 30 feet wide, and 45 feet high (v. 2). It was divided into two rooms. The first room was the **sanctuary**, measuring 60 feet long by 30 feet wide by 45 feet high (vv. 2, 17). Latticed **windows**, probably near the top, provided light and an escape for smoke (v. 4). The second room was **the inner sanctuary**, 30 feet long by 30 feet wide by 30 feet high. The **vestibule** added 30 more feet to the length at the east or front end and was elevated 15 feet above ground level. On the north, west, and south sides of the temple were three stories of **side chambers**, or rooms, for the priests. These were **against the wall of the temple** but were not an integral part of it.

6:7–10 All the lumber and **stone** for the temple was **finished at the quarry** to exact specifications so that when brought to Jerusalem, the pieces could be fitted together without **iron** tools (v. 7). Thus **the temple** was erected silently, just as the living temple of God is **being built** today. Verses 8 and 10 describe the **doorway** to the side chambers and the height of each story (7½ feet). Verse 9 describes the roof of the whole temple.

6:11–22 The word of the LORD graciously **came to Solomon** during the construction, promising to confirm the Davidic covenant and that God would **dwell** in the temple **among the children of Israel if** the king would be obedient (vv. 11–13). The interior of the building was lined **with cedar boards**, completely **overlaid . . . with pure gold**; **no stone** was **seen**. These stones, so skillfully and precisely cut, were not even visible. Spurgeon makes a spiritual application:

> Even the foundation stones were not rugged and rough, but hewn and costly. God would have everything which is done for him done well. He careth not so much for that which meets the eye of man, he delights himself with the beauty of those living stones of his spiritual temple which are hidden away from observation.[3]

6:23–28 Standing on either side of the ark, **in the inner sanctuary,** were **two** carved **cherubim, overlaid . . . with gold**. Their outstretched **wings** reached from **one wall** to **the other**. These are not the same as the cherubim on the mercy seat (Ex. 25:18; 37:9).

6:29, 30 Nothing but **gold** was visible inside the temple.

6:31–35 The **folding** or sliding **doors** leading to **the inner sanctuary** are described in verses 31 and 32. The rooms were also separated by a veil which hung inside the doors of the inner sanctuary—2 Chron. 3:14. The main **doors** leading to the **sanctuary** are described in verses 33–35.

6:36 In front of the temple was **the inner court** of the priests. There was a low wall between it and the outer court. This wall consisted of **three rows of hewn stone** and **a row of cedar beams**.

In the inner court were a huge brazen altar for sacrifices, a huge laver used by the priests for cleansing, and ten smaller lavers (chap. 7). The outer court was for the people of Israel.

6:37, 38 The temple was begun **in the fourth year** of Solomon's reign and **was finished . . . seven years** later.

3. *The Construction of Other Buildings (7:1–12)*

7:1 The narrative now turns to the construction of Solomon's **own house** and other royal buildings included in the great court.

Solomon's **house**, or the royal palace, took **thirteen years to build**. It was located slightly southeast of the temple and just outside the wall of the inner court. Some think that the fact that it took six years longer to build the palace than the temple indicates a greater concern for Solomon's ego than for God's glory. On the other hand, perhaps the temple took only seven years because of Solomon's zeal for God to be given a place, and his thousands of laborers built a "holy temple" (for the LORD) at a greater speed.

7:2–12 The House of the Forest of Lebanon (vv. 2–5) was at the southern portion of the great court. Its outstanding feature was the large number of **cedar pillars** in it. Perhaps this accounted for its name. We do not know definitely the function of this building, but we surmise from 1 Kings 10:17 that it was an armory. Immediately north of the House of the Forest of Lebanon was **the Hall** (or Porch) **of Pillars** (v. 6). It was probably the entrance to **the Hall of Judgment** and **the throne** room (v. 7). Adjoining the royal palace was the House of **Pharaoh's daughter**, where it is likely that the royal harem lived (v. 8). **All** the buildings **were** made **of costly** stone blocks **cut to** exact measurements. Also, the wall around the great court was made of **three rows of** stone blocks covered by **cedar beams**.

Another perspective of these verses sees **the House of the Forest of Lebanon, the Hall of Pillars**, and the Hall of the Throne (**the Hall of Judgment**) as all part of the palace. The **hall** made **for Pharaoh's daughter** adjoined the royal residence.

4. *Furnishings of the Temple (7:13–51)*

7:13, 14 Huram (spelled *Hiram* in Heb. and KJV) was not the same as the king of Tyre. He was a master workman of Jewish lineage who lived in **Tyre**.

7:15–22 Next **two** huge **pillars of bronze** which stood at the entrance of the temple are described. One was named **Jachin** (*He shall establish*) and the other **Boaz** (*in Him is strength*). At the top of each pillar was a bowl-like **capital**, highly ornamental. Although the physical details of these **pillars** are given, we are not told the spiritual significance behind them. Someone has well observed that the **pillars** of God's living temple today are believers of holy character (Gal. 2:9). Revelation 3:12 is God's promise that those who overcome will be made **pillars** in His heavenly temple for all eternity.

7:23–26 The **Sea of cast bronze** was the huge laver which stood in the inner court. It was a large basin, supported by **twelve** bronze **oxen** and placed between the temple and the altar, but to the south (2 Chron. 4:10). It supplied water for the priests to wash their hands and feet.

7:27–39 In addition to the large laver, there were **ten** smaller **lavers** resting on **four**-wheeled **carts** or stands. No mention is made of the bronze altar until 8:64, although it too was in the inner court.

7:40–47 Huram supervised the construction of all the **burnished bronze** work in connection with the temple area, including **the pots, the shovels, and the bowls** of the temple itself. The **bronze articles** were cast in clay, in much the same manner as is done today (v. 46).

7:48–50 The **furnishings** of the holy place included **the** golden **altar of** incense, **the table of gold**, ten golden tables of showbread (2 Chron. 4:8), ten golden **lampstands of pure gold**, and the golden utensils.

7:51 David had made elaborate preparations for the temple that he was not allowed to build. **Solomon brought** these treasures into the temple for use and safekeeping.

Differences between this chapter and 2 Chronicles 2—4 are discussed in the notes on 2 Chronicles.

F. Dedication of the Temple (Chap. 8)

8:1–5 With the temple completed, the next step was to **bring . . . the ark of the covenant from** the section of Jerusalem known as **the City of David**, or **Zion**, to the temple on Mount Moriah. This probably took place almost a year after the building was completed (cf. v. 2 with 1 Kgs. 6:37, 38).

Just before the Feast of Tabernacles, a great national holiday took place, and **the ark**, **the tabernacle**, and **the holy furnishings** were **brought** to the temple by **the priests and the Levites**. This was accompanied by the sacrifice of a great number of **sheep and oxen**.

8:6–9 The ark was put in **the Most Holy Place**. In some way that we do not understand, **the ends of the poles** were visible **from the holy place, but they could not be seen from outside**, on the porch. The **poles** were not removed, as stated in the KJV (v. 8). At this time the only items in **the ark** were **the two tablets of stone**, containing the Ten Commandments. We are not told what happened to the pot of manna or to Aaron's rod that budded (Heb. 9:4).

8:10, 11 As soon as the ark (typical of Christ) was given its proper place, the glory **cloud**, signifying the divine Presence, **filled the** temple. **The priests** were **not** able to carry on their duties because **the glory of the Lord filled the house**.

8:12, 13 When all was finished, **Solomon** addressed **the Lord**. God had said that **He would dwell in** thick darkness. Now Solomon had **built** Him **an exalted house** with a Most Holy Place that had no illumination except the glory of God Himself.

With his usual spiritual insight, Matthew Henry comments:

> He showed himself ready to hear the prayer Solomon was now about to make; and not only so, but took up his residence in this house, that all his praying people might there be encouraged to make their applications to him. But the glory of God appeared in a cloud, a dark cloud, to signify, (1.) The darkness of that dispensation in comparison with the light of the gospel, by which, *with open face, we behold, as in a glass, the glory of the Lord*. (2.) The darkness of our present state in comparison with the vision of God, which will be the happiness of heaven, where the divine glory is unveiled. Now we only say what he is not, but then we shall see him as he is.[4]

8:14–21 Next **the king turned** to the people in blessing. He traced the fulfillment of God's promise to **David** concerning the **temple** and expressed his satisfaction that **the ark** of **the covenant** now had a settled abode.

8:22–26 The prayer of dedication is recorded in verses 22–53. After extolling God for keeping His **covenant** with **David** concerning the temple, he asked Him to fulfill another covenant that He had made with David—the promise that there would never **fail to** be a descendant of David to **sit . . . on the throne**.

8:27–30 Although Solomon realized that no temple on earth was adequate to **contain** the great **God**, yet he asked that the **Lord** might recognize **this temple** and that when he or any of the **people** of **Israel** addressed God there, He might **hear** and **forgive**.

8:31–53 Then the king listed various specific cases in which the Lord's answer was especially desired.

1. In lawsuits where oaths were taken, presumably because no definite evidence was available, God was asked to punish the guilty and reward the innocent (vv. 31, 32).
2. When defeat came to Israel's army **because** of **sin**, God was asked to **forgive** and restore them **to** their **land** when they confessed their **sin** (vv. 33, 34).
3. In times of drought, God was asked to **send rain . . . when** the **people** humbled themselves before Him in repentance (vv. 35, 36).
4. If **famine** or **pestilence, or blight or mildew**, or insect plagues, or **enemy** siege, or any other calamity should befall them, God was requested to honor any prayers that were **made** to Him **toward** the **temple** and to **forgive . . . the land** (vv. 37–40).
5. If a Gentile converted to Judaism and prayed to God, then He was asked to answer the prayer of such a proselyte (vv. 41–43).
6. Prayers for victory in **battle** were anticipated by Solomon, and he asked the Lord to be mindful of all such supplications (vv. 44, 45).
7. Speaking prophetically, Solomon next envisioned the time when Israel might be carried into cap-

tivity because of **sin**. He asked the Lord to listen to their prayer of repentance and cause their captors to be merciful to them; after all, the Israelites were His **people**, whom He had delivered **out of Egypt**. These verses found fulfillment in the Babylonian captivity and in the subsequent return under the decree of Cyrus (vv. 46–53).

8:54–61 After **praying** to God, **Solomon . . . blessed** the people by pouring out an eloquent request for God's presence, and for power to be **loyal to** Him and to be a witness for Him among the nations **of the earth**.

> Solomon's benediction, like the rest of his prayer, shows an immense appreciation of great spiritual truths: 1. *God is utterly reliable.* "Not one word has failed" (56)—what a testimony! 2. *The past guarantees the future* (57). Since God is unchanging (cf. Heb. 13:8), we can build upon the fact that what He has shown Himself to be in times past He will be to us (cf. Josh. 1:5). 3. *Man needs God's help in the life of discipleship* (58), a truth which Jeremiah knew and for which he gave the reason (see Jer. 10:23; 17:9). Even the impulse of man's free will comes from God—a paradox indeed! Compare the activity of the Holy Spirit in John 16:8–11. 4. *We stand in daily need of the assistance of God* ("as each day requires," 59). But then, He neither slumbers nor sleeps (Psa. 121:4)! 5. *God's care for His children is never for their selfish enjoyment, but that others might come to know Him* (60). 6. In view of all this, *can we give less than our absolute loyalty and obedience to Him* (61)? (*Daily Notes of the Scripture Union*)

This prayer is also recorded in 2 Chronicles 6 (see notes), with the only differences being: In 2 Chronicles Solomon ended his prayer with three requests (2 Chron. 6:40–42), omitted in 1 Kings; in 1 Kings Solomon blessed the people (vv. 54–61). This is omitted in 2 Chronicles.

8:62–65 Of the great number of animals that were sacrificed, some were used as food for the huge throng that had assembled (v. 65). Since **the bronze altar** was not large enough **to receive** all **the burnt offerings**, etc., Solomon **consecrated** a place in **the middle of the court** where the rest could be **offered** to the Lord. This great celebration was characterized by joy and worship and thanksgiving. Of the thousands of animals slain, not one was offered as a sin or trespass offering.

At this same **time**, **Solomon held** the Feast of Tabernacles with Israelites who had come **from** as far as **the entrance of Hamath**, near Dan, in the north and from **the Brook of Egypt** in the south. The Feast of Dedication and the Feast of Tabernacles together lasted for **fourteen days**.

8:66 Then **the people** returned to their homes **joyful and glad of heart**. Second Chronicles 7:9 says that a solemn assembly was held on the "eighth day," while verse 66 says that the people were sent away on the "eighth day." John Haley harmonizes these two accounts as follows:

> The feast of tabernacles began on the fifteenth and ended on the twenty-second of the month, closing with a "holy convocation" on the "eighth day" (Lev. 23:33–39), at the end of which Solomon dismissed the people; the dismissal taking effect the next morning, the twenty-third (2 Chron. 7:10).[5]

G. Solomon's Fame (Chaps. 9, 10)

1. *His Covenant from God (9:1–9)*

9:1–5 God's answer to Solomon's **prayer** was that He would accept the temple as His **house** and would **put** His **name there forever**. Although Solomon's temple has long since ceased to exist, God will yet dwell in a temple in Jerusalem when the Lord Jesus returns to set up His worldwide kingdom. In the meantime, God dwells in the temple of the believer's body and of the church.

9:6–9 As for Solomon's family, God promised that Solomon and his sons would always have descendants to sit **on the throne** if they would be obedient. **But if** they departed **from** the living God and turned to idolatry, **then** He would send the people into exile, destroy the temple, and make **Israel . . . a proverb and a byword among** the Gentiles. The temple would become a heap of ruins, and visitors would **be astonished** at its desolation.

2. *His Gifts to Hiram (9:10–14)*

With regard to this paragraph, some commentators suggest that Solomon had borrowed **one hundred and twenty talents of gold** from **Hiram** (v. 14) in order to finance his elaborate building program, and had given **twenty cities . . . of Galilee** to **Hiram** as security. It was because of Hiram's previous help (v. 11a) that Solomon felt free to request the loan. When **Hiram** saw **the cities**, he was dissatisfied and **called them the land of Cabul** (meaning *displeasing*, *dirty*, or *rubbish*; lit. *Good for Nothing*, NKJV marg.). It appears from 2 Chronicles 8:2 that Solomon may have redeemed the **cities** by paying off the loan.

3. *His Subjects and Sacrifices (9:15–25)*

9:15–23 Verses 15–22 give the account (rather than **"reason,"** as in KJV and NKJV) of the **forced labor** which **Solomon** used in his construction program. **Hazor, Megiddo, and Gezer** were three cities which Solomon fortified for defense purposes. **Hazor** was in the north and protected the northern door to Palestine. **Megiddo** was:

> . . . an important city of north-central Palestine, overlooking the Plain of Esdraelon. It dominated the intersection of important trade routes and served as the key to the defense of the Jordan Valley (from the south) and the Central Plain (from the north).[6]

Gezer was situated west of Jerusalem on a main trade route from the interior to the coastal land of Philistia. **All the** Gentile captives listed in verse 20 were **forced laborers**. **The children of Israel** were not reduced to bondage. There were **five hundred and fifty** supervisors established **over Solomon's work.**

9:24 The "Millo" which Solomon **built** was some type of fortification for Jerusalem. It was undertaken after the palace for **Pharaoh's daughter** was completed.

9:25 Solomon sacrificed **to the Lord . . . three times a year** at the three major feasts: Unleavened Bread, Weeks (Pentecost), and Tabernacles (2 Chron. 8:13).

4. *His Navy (9:26–28)*

King Solomon had **a fleet of ships at Ezion Geber, . . . on the** Gulf of Aqaba, **near Elath. Hiram sent** some of **his servants with the fleet . . . to Ophir** (exact location unknown—some say southern Arabia, some India, and others Africa). **They . . . brought . . . four hundred and twenty talents of gold . . . to King Solomon**.

5. His Visit from the Queen of Sheba (10:1–13)

The purpose of chapter 10 is to emphasize Solomon's glory. From drinking vessels to sailing vessels, from an ivory throne to handcrafted chariots, he possessed everything the human heart could desire in quantities that stagger the imagination. **The queen of Sheba**, that daughter of opulence, was completely overwhelmed by Solomon's **wisdom** and by the splendor of his kingdom. This was in fulfillment of the Lord's promise, to which Solomon owed everything (3:11–13).

The queen of Sheba (probably Saba, in the southern Arabian peninsula) **came . . . to test** Solomon's wisdom by plying him **with hard questions**, but he was able to answer them **all** (v. 3a). **When** she saw the magnificence of his kingdom, she had to acknowledge that the glowing reports she had heard were only partial. She presented him with gifts of **gold** and **spices in great . . . abundance** and then received gifts from him in return before going back **to her own country**.

6. His Riches (10:14–29)

10:14, 15 Hiram's help brought not only **gold** from Ophir for **Solomon** but also great amounts of almug wood and precious stones. Solomon was a genius in trade relationships.

10:16–22 **Gold** was so plentiful that **Solomon** even used it for making **shields** to hang **in the House of the Forest of Lebanon**. His **ivory . . . throne** was **overlaid . . . with pure gold**. At each **side** of **the throne** was a large carved lion. Also **on each side of the six steps** leading to the throne was a lion. **Silver** was considered as of relatively minor value **in the days of Solomon**. Solomon's **merchant ships** brought not only **gold** and **silver,** but such exotic items as **ivory, apes, and monkeys**.[7]

10:23–25 Solomon's **riches and wisdom** brought him worldwide fame, and gifts poured in to him from admirers who came to visit him.

10:26–29 Mention is made of the fact that Solomon invested heavily in **horses** and **chariots**. **Keveh**[8] (probably Cilicia) was famous for its **horses**. Solomon not only acquired **chariots and horsemen** and **horses** for national defense but also **exported them to** other countries.

Although not mentioned here, the luxury of Solomon's reign required heavy taxation to support it. This was to lead to the disruption of the kingdom (12:3–15).

"The taxation," writes J. R. Lumly, "must have been crushing, and with all this oriental splendor and luxury, there was rottenness within. Solomon was the Jewish Louis XIV."[9]

This multiplication of riches and horses violated God's Word (Deut. 17:16, 17).

H. Solomon's Apostasy and Death (Chap. 11)

11:1–3 Deuteronomy 17:17 forbade the king of Israel to marry heathen wives. The extent to which Solomon disobeyed this important command is shocking. The result was exactly as predicted: **His wives turned** him to idolatry.

11:4–8 Verse 4 means that King David's **heart** had been wholly true **to the LORD his God** as far as keeping himself from idolatry was concerned, but **Solomon** did not follow **his father** in this matter. He **built** idolatrous shrines on the Mount of Olives, **east of Jerusalem**.

11:9–13 God **had appeared to** Solomon **twice**—in Gibeon (3:5) and in Jerusalem at the dedication of the temple (9:2). Now He announced that, because of Solomon's idolatry, **the kingdom** would be torn **away from** him and given **to** one of **his** servants. However, it would not happen during Solomon's lifetime, and not all twelve tribes would be taken from the house of **David**. **One tribe** (Benjamin; Judah is taken for granted—12:23) would be given to Solomon's **son**.

11:14–22 Three of Solomon's adversaries are now described. The first was **Hadad**, an **Edomite** prince who had escaped **to Egypt** as **a little child** when **Joab** was killing all the males **in Edom**. He was treated well by the **Pharaoh** and was even given **the sister of Queen Tahpenes as** his **wife**. **When Hadad heard . . . that David . . . and Joab** were **dead**, he obtained the Pharaoh's reluctant permission to return to Edom. From there he began military operations against Solomon from the south.

11:23–25 The second **adversary** was **Rezon, who had** escaped **when David killed those of Zobah**. **He** then **became** the leader of **a band of raiders**. Later he set up an independent kingdom at **Damascus**, and became a military peril to **Solomon** from the north. **Damascus** had worn the yoke of Israel ever since David had captured the city and stationed troops there (2 Sam. 8:5, 6).

Losing Damascus, Syria's chief city-state, was especially significant because the kingdom of Syria would prove to be a thorn in Israel's flesh for centuries to come.

11:26–28 The third adversary was the **servant** of Solomon whom God had mentioned in verse 11: **Jeroboam the son of Nebat**, of the tribe of Ephraim. **Solomon** had given him a position of responsibility in the building of **the Millo**. Perhaps this power gave Jeroboam the desire to reign over all Israel.

11:29–39 One day **Jeroboam** met a **prophet** named **Ahijah**. When they **were alone in the field**, **Ahijah took hold of** his own **new garment . . . and tore it into twelve pieces**. He gave **ten pieces . . . to Jeroboam** as a sign that **God** would **give** him command over **ten tribes** of Israel. He also explained to Jeroboam that **one tribe** (Benjamin) would be left for Solomon's **son** (Judah understood—12:23) and that **the kingdom** would not be divided until after Solomon's death. **If** Jeroboam would obey the Lord, he would be assured of the Lord's blessing and help. Notice the limitations which God put on Jeroboam: He was to have **ten tribes**, ***not* the whole kingdom**; he was to come to power *only after Solomon's death*; God would make him **an enduring house** *only **if*** he would obey the Lord and wholly follow Him.

11:40 Apparently **Jeroboam** rebelled while **Solomon** was still alive, so he had to flee **to Egypt** to escape the king's wrath. He remained there **until** Solomon's **death**. Instead of facing his sin and repenting, Solomon tried to thwart the word of God by doing away with Jeroboam. It was foolish to fight against Jeroboam, though, since he was now the divinely appointed heir of the northern tribes. Saul had been unsuccessful in his attempts to kill his successor, David. Solomon was likewise unsuccessful in his attempts to murder Jeroboam.

The tribes over which Jeroboam would rule would be: Reuben, Dan, Naphtali, Gad, Asher, Issachar,

Zebulun, Ephraim, Manasseh, and portions of Levi and Simeon. The tribes over which Solomon's son would reign would be: Judah, Benjamin, and portions of Levi and Simeon. For the most part Levi (2 Chron. 11:13–16) and Simeon were loyal to Judah.

11:41 The book of the acts of Solomon was probably the official chronicle of his reign, but certainly not an inspired part of Scripture.

11:42, 43 After reigning for **forty years, Solomon** died **and was buried in** Jerusalem. **Rehoboam his son** succeeded him. Solomon's beginning was better than his ending. A good start does not guarantee a good finish. He had been raised to the pinnacle of greatness, but he plunged off into the abyss of moral degradation and idolatry. If only the king had practiced what he preached in Ecclesiastes 12:13, 14:

> Let us hear the conclusion of the whole matter: Fear God and keep His commandments, for this is man's all. For God will bring every work into judgment, including every secret thing, whether good or evil.

III. THE DIVIDED KINGDOM (Chaps. 12—22)

A. King Rehoboam of Judah (12:1–24)

Rehoboam the son of Solomon ruled **in Judah** for **seventeen years** (931/30–913 B.C.; 1 Kgs. 12:20–24; 2 Chron. 11 and 12).

12:1–11 Rehoboam went to Shechem to be acknowledged as **king.** Having **heard** of the death of Solomon, **Jeroboam** returned from **Egypt** and also went to Shechem, along with **the whole assembly of** men **of Israel.** The Israelites delivered an ultimatum **to Rehoboam—"Lighten the burdensome service of your father, and his heavy yoke which he put on us, and we will serve you."** To maintain the oriental opulence of his court Solomon had used forced labor and taxed heavily. So they were saying in effect: "Lower the taxes with which your father oppressed us, and we will serve you. Otherwise we will revolt." Rehoboam asked **for three days** to think it over. During that time he first **consulted** his older counselors. **They** advised **him** to treat the people kindly and **be a servant to** them. His younger advisers, however, suggested the very opposite—they told him to threaten the people with *still* heavier demands! In that sense, Rehoboam's **little finger** would **be thicker than** Solomon's **waist**. If Solomon **chastised** them **with whips**, then Rehoboam would use **scourges** (probably meaning whips with sharp points).

12:12–20 When **Jeroboam and** the congregation of Israel returned for the decision on **the third day**, they were **answered . . . according to the advice of the young men**. Verse 15 points out that this was a **turn of events** brought about by **the LORD** to **fulfill His word . . . spoken** through **Ahijah the Shilonite** (11:30–39). At this point the people of **Israel** revolted against **Rehoboam**, although some of them were still living in the territory **of Judah**. **Rehoboam sent Adoram**, his unpopular taskmaster over forced labor, to bring these latter Israelites under subjection, but they **stoned** Adoram to death. Then the people of **Israel... made...Jeroboam** their **king**. Although it says in verse 20 that **only . . . the tribe of Judah . . . followed** Rehoboam, we must remember that Benjamin (v. 21), Simeon (Josh. 19:1b), and most of Levi *belonged to* **Judah**.

12:21–24 Rehoboam planned to

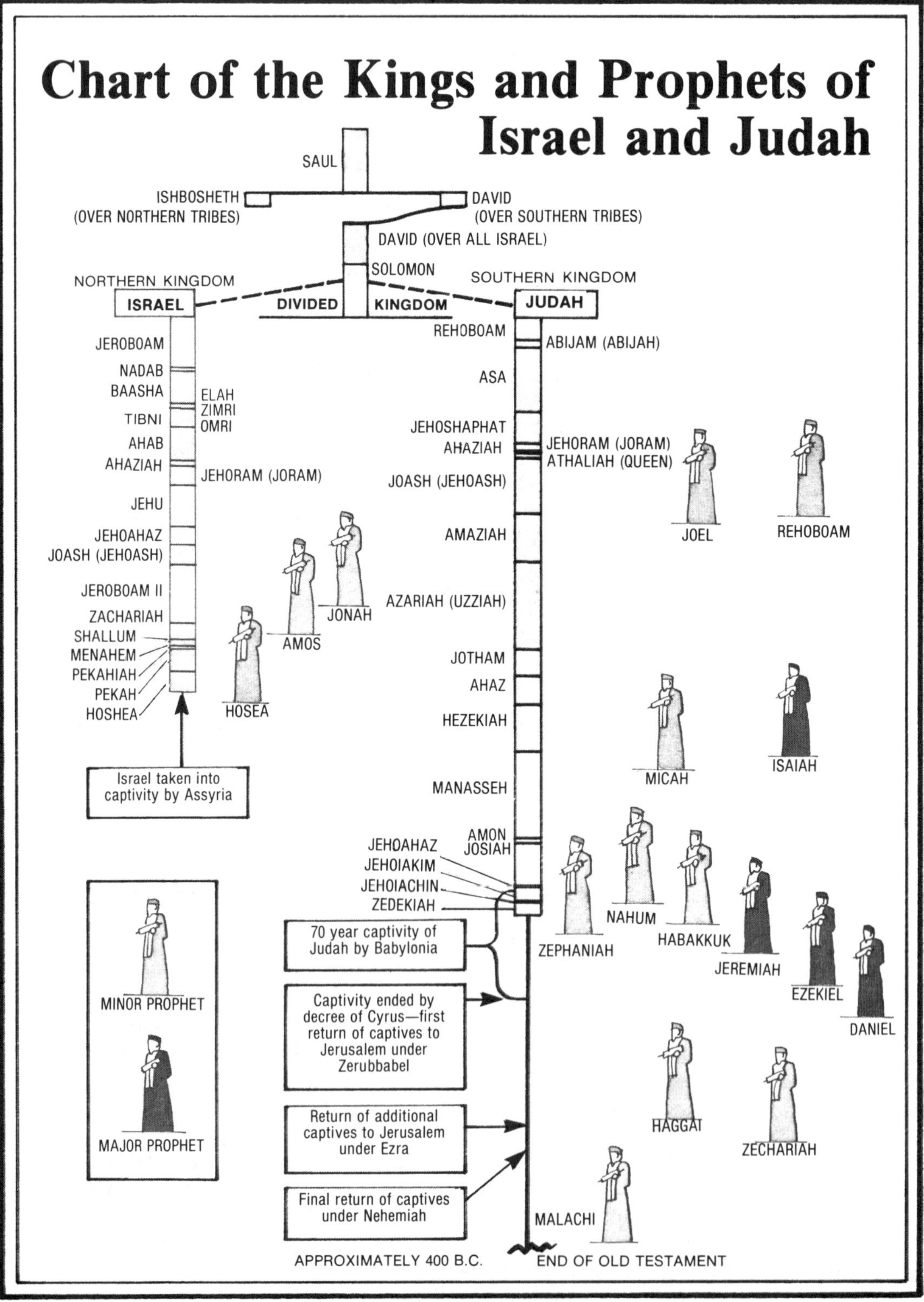

The Kings and Prophets of Israel and Judah

thwart this by declaring war on Israel, but he canceled his plan as a result of a divine command. Having earlier ignored the counsel of his elders, **Rehoboam** now heeded the counsel of **the LORD** and spared the lives of many Israelites. The word of the Lord decreed the split, and the word of the Lord ensured that the division was without bloodshed.

The Division of the Kingdom

The history of the divided kingdom begins here and continues through 2 Kings. Jeroboam reigned over the northern ten tribes, usually known as "Israel" and sometimes referred to in the prophets as "Ephraim." This kingdom had a succession of *nine* dynasties, and *all* the kings were wicked.

Rehoboam reigned over the southern kingdom, known as "Judah." This kingdom had only *one* dynasty. Every king was a descendant of David. It was through this kingdom that Christ's legal title to the throne of David is traced through Joseph His foster father (see genealogy in Matthew 1). He was also physically a Son of David through the Virgin Mary, who was herself a descendant of David's own son Nathan (see genealogy in Luke 3). A few of these kings were outstanding reformers, though most of them were wicked.

The Kings of Israel and Judah

Dynasty	Israel	Dynasty	Judah—
1	Jeroboam	1	Rehoboam
	Nadab		Abijam (Abijah)
2	Baasha		Asa [good]
	Elah		Jehoshaphat [good]
3	Zimri		Jehoram (Joram)
4	Omri-Tibni		Ahaziah
	Ahab		Athaliah—usurper
	Ahaziah		Jehoash (Joash) [good]
	Joram (Jehoram)		Amaziah [good]
5	Jehu		Uzziah (Azariah) [good]
	Jehoahaz		Jotham [good]
	Joash (Jehoash)		Ahaz
	Jeroboam II		Hezekiah [good]
	Zachariah (Zechariah)		Manasseh
6	Shallum		Amon
7	Menahem		Josiah [good]
	Pekahiah		Jehoahaz (Shallum)
8	Pekah		Jehoiakim (Eliakim)
9	Hoshea		Jehoiachin (Jeconiah, Coniah)
			Zedekiah (Mattaniah)

The history of the divided kingdom can be divided into four phases. *First,* there was a time of open conflict, extending from Jeroboam (1 Kgs. 12:1) to Omri (1 Kgs. 16:28). *Secondly,* the two kingdoms settled down to a period of detente, from Omri (1 Kgs. 16:29) to Jehu (2 Kgs. 8). *The third phase,* from Jehu to the captivity of Israel by Assyria (722 B.C.), was one of relative independence (2 Kgs. 9—17). *Finally,* Judah was left as the surviving kingdom, until it was taken into captivity by the Babylonians in 586 B.C. (2 Kgs. 18—25).

The kingdom of Israel never returned to the land as a nation. Judah remained in captivity for seventy years, and then groups returned to Jerusalem in significant numbers, as recorded in Ezra and Nehemiah. The southern tribes thus came back to the land, under Gentile rule, approximately 500 years before the birth of Christ.

At the close of OT history, the Jews in the land were subject to the king of Persia. Later, Persia was conquered by Greece, and the Jews were ruled by this world power. Finally, the Greeks were subjugated by the Roman Empire; it was this empire that was in power when the Lord Jesus appeared.

In studying the divided kingdom, the student frequently comes across seeming contradictions in the dates given. Most of these chronological difficulties can be accounted for by the fact that different methods were used in calculating the length of reigns in Israel and in Judah. Another important factor is that oftentimes two kings served as coregents for a while. The whole subject of the chronology of the kings has been treated capably and in great detail in *The Mysterious Numbers of the Hebrew Kings*, by Edwin R. Thiele.[10]

We shall study the divided kingdom in the order in which the kings are listed, giving the important events in the reign of each. The dates are taken from Thiele's book mentioned above.‡

B. King Jeroboam of Israel (12:25—14:20)

Jeroboam the son of Nebat, of the tribe of Ephraim, was king of Israel for twenty-two years (931/30—910/09 B.C.).

1. Jeroboam's False Religious Centers (12:25–33)

12:25–30 Israel's first king made **Shechem** his capital at the outset, then **built Penuel**, across the Jordan River. Fearing that the **people** of Israel would return to **Jerusalem** to worship on the feast days and then transfer their loyalty **back to** the **king of Judah**, he set up his own system of religion: He established **Dan** and **Bethel** as new centers of **worship**, setting up a golden calf in each place and declaring *these idols* to be the **gods** which delivered Israel **from the land of Egypt**!

12:31–33 Jeroboam **made** idolatrous **shrines on the high places**. He established a new priesthood from among all the **people—not** necessarily from the tribe **of Levi**, as God had ordained. He set up a new religious calendar, with **a** great **feast on the fifteenth day of the eighth month**, replacing the Feast of Tabernacles, which was in the seventh month. He himself usurped the office of the priest by offering sacrifices **on the altar which he had made at Bethel**.

That many of the people of Israel accepted these changes reveals that their hearts were far from the Lord. Their fathers had worshiped a calf before and were punished for it (Ex. 32). Solomon had erected high places and lost most of his kingdom for it (chap. 11). Korah and his followers had tried to usurp the priesthood and lost their lives for it (Num. 16). These innovations by which Jeroboam sought to secure his kingdom only ensured its eventual downfall. Those who had a heart for God fled to Judah (2 Chron. 11:14–16), leaving their brethren to the conveniences—and consequences—of man-made religion. It has been well said that "Jeroboam did not deserve so good a post [as king], but Israel deserved so bad a prince."

2. Jeroboam and the Man of God (13:1–32)

13:1–3 While Jeroboam was offering incense at the altar in Bethel, **a man of God** was sent **from Judah** to denounce the idolatrous **altar**. He predicted that a king named **Josiah** would arise in Judah and would burn **the** idolatrous **priests** on the altar. The fulfillment of the prophecy in verse 2 is found in 2 Kings 23:15, 16. Over 300 years elapsed between the prophecy and its fulfillment. As a token of the certainty of the prophecy, he said that **the altar** would be **split apart** and **the ashes . . . poured out**.

13:4–6 As **Jeroboam** pointed to the prophet and ordered him to be apprehended, the king's **hand** became **withered**. Also, **the altar was split apart and the ashes** spilled **out**—an omen of doom for Jeroboam's religion. In answer to the prophet's gracious prayer, the withered **hand . . . was restored to** normal.

13:7–10 If **the king** could not silence the prophet by threats, he would try by gaining his fellowship. God had issued strict instructions to the prophet that he was to do nothing to indicate the slightest tolerance of Jeroboam's evil reign. Thus, in accordance with the instructions of the Lord, the prophet refused to **eat** or **drink** with Jeroboam. Also, **he** took a different route home from **Bethel**.

13:11–19 On the way he was intercepted by **an old prophet** of **Bethel**. At first **the man of God** refused the hospitality of the **old prophet** lest he show the slightest sympathy with what was going on at **Bethel**. But then the old man said that **an angel** had told him to entertain **the man of God**, and this lie succeeded in persuading the latter to accept the proffered hospitality.

13:20–25 While they were eating together, **the LORD** spoke to the old **prophet** of Bethel, and he in turn delivered the message to the man of God. Because of his disobedience, the man of God would die and would not be buried with his family. If this seems harsh or severe, we should remember that God deals more strictly with those He loves, with those who are His spokesmen, and with those who are greatly privileged. On his way home, the man of God was **killed** by a **lion**. Contrary to all the laws of nature, **the lion** and the prophet's **donkey stood** watch together over his **corpse on the road**.

13:26–32 **When the** old **prophet . . . heard** the news, **he** immediately realized that it was the Lord's judgment against disobedience. **He went** to the scene of the tragedy, **brought** the body **back** to Bethel, and buried it in his own tomb. He then instructed **his sons** that he desired to be **buried . . . beside . . . the man of God**; he realized that the idolatrous system of which he was a part was doomed to destruction by God.

3. Jeroboam's False Priesthood (13:33, 34)

King **Jeroboam** persisted in his evil, making **priests from every class of people** and serving as a priest himself. Such **sin** was the eventual cause of destruction to the dynasty **of Jeroboam**.

Irving L. Jensen notes:

> King Jeroboam ought to have seen a picture of himself and his own fate if he did not repent, by the fate of the prophet from Judah. Jeroboam, like the prophet, had been chosen by God for a high position. Also like the prophet, he knew perfectly well what God would have him do. But like the prophet, he had disobeyed the word of God.[11]

4. Death of Jeroboam's Son (14:1–20)

14:1–4 When **Abijah the son of Jeroboam became sick**, the king sent **his wife** to **the prophet . . . Ahijah**—

the man of God who had previously told Jeroboam that he **would be king over** the ten northern tribes.

The queen disguised herself, perhaps for several reasons. First, to visit the man of God openly would betray a lack of faith in the idols at Dan and Bethel. Second, Jeroboam realized that Ahijah was opposed to idolatry and would not speak favorable things to her if he knew her identity. Third, perhaps the king thought that by fooling the prophet he might even fool the Lord.

14:5–13 The LORD forewarned the blind prophet of the queen's approach. As soon as she arrived, the prophet exposed her disguise and then sent her back to Jeroboam with a message of doom. Because of the king's diso-

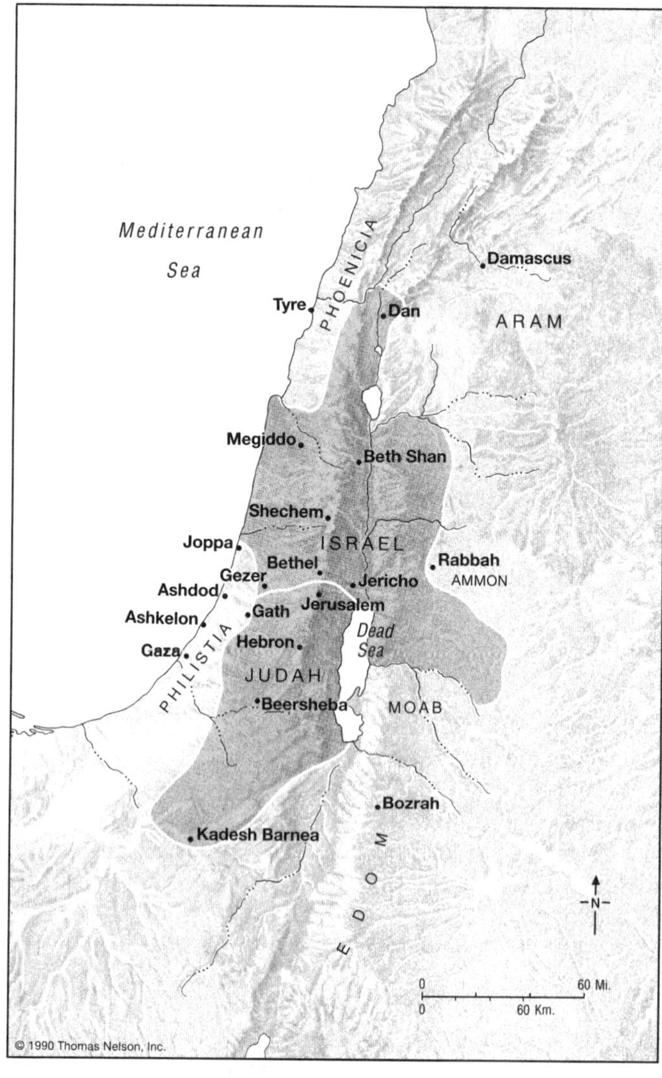

A Kingdom Divided. The glory of the united kingdom began to fade at the death of Solomon when his son Rehoboam spoke harshly to Jeroboam and those following him. Their response: "Every man to your tents, O Israel! Now, see to your own house, O David!" Rehoboam reigned over Judah to the south, and Jeroboam became king of Israel to the north.

bedience and idolatry, the Lord would **cut off from** him **every male in Israel**, both **bond and free**, and would utterly consume his house. None of his family would have a decent burial, except the ailing son, Abijah—who would **die** as soon as the queen entered **the city**.

14:14–16 God would **raise up** another **king** (Baasha), who would destroy Jeroboam's family. Eventually the nation of Israel would be led into captivity because **Jeroboam** had inaugurated the worship of Asherim.[12] The Asherim were carved **wooden images** symbolizing fertility.

14:17, 18 It appears from verse 17 that **Tirzah** was now the capital of Israel. As soon as the queen returned there, her son **died**. Israel **buried him** and **mourned**, as predicted by **the prophet**.

14:19, 20 After reigning for **twenty-two years**, **Jeroboam** died and was succeeded by **his son . . . Nadab**. **The book of the chronicles of the kings of Israel** does not refer to the book of Chronicles in the Bible but to the official record **of the kings** which was kept as a public national history.

The scene now switches to the kingdom of Judah.

C. King Rehoboam of Judah (cont'd) (14:21–31)

14:21–24 We have already studied the first part of Rehoboam's reign in chapter 12. This section summarizes the significant features of his reign. The fact that the queen mother is mentioned twice as **an Ammonitess** (vv. 21, 31) may be designed to call the reader's attention to an underlying reason for the failure of Rehoboam's rule—his father, Solomon, had married foreign wives, who led him and his family into idolatry. Idolatry was prevalent in **Judah**, and male cult prostitutes (**perverted persons**) carried on their abominable practices at the shrines.

14:25–28 **Jerusalem** was attacked and plundered by **Shishak, king of Egypt**. **Treasures** were stolen from the temple and the royal palace. **Rehoboam** ordered **bronze shields** to be made **in . . . place** of the **gold** ones that were taken.

Isn't it ironic that Solomon had sought to protect himself from Egypt by marrying Pharaoh's daughter, but within a short time after his death Shishak of Egypt walked off with much of the glitter of Solomon's golden city!

14:29–31 This was a period of warfare between Judah and Israel. It continued for fifty-seven years, through the reign of Asa in Judah and Omri in Israel. The Lord prevented an all-out war between Judah and Israel (12:24), but the sister kingdoms were constantly skirmishing with each other. **Rehoboam** died at the age of fifty-seven, and **his son . . . Abijam** became king in his place.

D. King Abijam of Judah (15:1–8)

Abijam the son of Rehoboam was king of Judah for **three years** (913—911/10 B.C.; 2 Chron. 13:1—14:la).

15:1 Verse 1 contains a formula that is frequently repeated in the books of Kings. This formula describes the beginning of one reign by naming the king who was reigning in the *other kingdom* and telling how long he had been reigning. Thus this verse explains that **Abijam** began to reign **over Judah** during **the eighteenth year of** Jeroboam's reign over Israel. He is also called Abijah (1 Chron. 3:10; 2 Chron. 12:16).

15:2 Here Abijam's mother is listed as **Maachah the granddaughter of Abishalom**; in 2 Chronicles 11:21 it is

Maachah the daughter of Absalom; in 2 Chronicles 13:2 it is Michaiah the daughter of Uriel. It is possible that his mother had two names, and that she was the daughter of Uriel and the **granddaughter** of Absalom (same as **Abishalom**). ("Son" or "daughter" often simply designates a *descendant* in biblical usage.)

15:3–8 **Abijam** followed **his father** as an idolater and thus failed to follow **David**, who was **loyal** in the sense that he refrained from the worship of carved images. Verses 4 and 5 imply that God would have destroyed the house of Abijam had it not been for His covenant with **David**. Notice at the end of verse 5 how an otherwise exemplary life can be marred by a moment of passion! The **war** with Israel that began in Rehoboam's reign continued through Abijam's reign. In verse 6 **Rehoboam** and **Jeroboam** stand for Judah and Israel. **There was war between** these two kingdoms throughout Abijam's life. He tried to bring Israel back both by persuasion and by force of arms, killing 500,000 Israelites in the attempt (2 Chron. 13:1–20).

E. King Asa of Judah (15:9–24)

Asa the son of Abijam was king of Judah for **forty-one years** (911/10—870/69 B.C.; cf. 2 Chron. 14:1b—16:14).

15:9–15 **Asa** was one of the few good kings of **Judah**. He removed the sodomites (idolatrous homosexuals) from the land and destroyed **all the idols that his fathers had made** (v. 12; cf. 2 Chron. 14:3–5). He deposed **Maachah his grandmother** and destroyed her **obscene image**, though **not . . . the high places** associated with this idol. He enriched the temple with gifts from **his father** and from **himself**.

15:16–22 When **Baasha, king of Israel**, began to fortify **Ramah**, a few miles north of Jerusalem, **Asa** realized that his capital was in peril. However, instead of turning to the Lord, he sought the assistance of **Ben-Hadad, . . . king of Syria**. By making a liberal payment to this foreign monarch, he persuaded him to attack Israel from the north in the region of Galilee. This drew Baasha's forces to the north and enabled **Asa** to disassemble **Ramah** and to build the fortified cities of **Geba** and **Mizpah** along his northern border.

The silver and gold that Asa brought to the temple had been given to the Lord. But when **Baasha** threatened his kingdom, Asa **took all the** treasures and gave them to a heathen king, defrauding God and enriching **Syria**. Christians need to be careful not to take what belongs to God (i.e., their time, money, resources, etc.) and give it to someone else.

15:23, 24 The fact that he was stricken with a disease of the **feet** may be mentioned to indicate God's displeasure that **Asa** had trusted in the king of Syria to deliver him. During his last three or four years, Asa's **son . . . Jehoshaphat** probably **reigned** with him.

F. King Nadab of Israel (15:25–27)

Nadab the son of Jeroboam, of the tribe of Ephraim, was **king** of **Israel** for **two years** (910/09—909/08 B.C.).

Nadab followed **his father** in the practice of idolatry. One of his subjects, **Baasha, conspired against him** and **killed him**. At the same time **Baasha killed all** the remaining members of **the house of Jeroboam**, in fulfillment of the prophecy of **Ahijah** (14:10, 14).

G. King Baasha of Israel (15:28—16:7)

Baasha the son of Ahijah, of the tribe of Issachar, was king of Israel for

twenty-four years (909/08—886/85 B.C.).

15:28–34 Baasha's reign marks the beginning of the second dynasty in the kingdom of Israel. Conflict between **Judah** and **Israel** continued throughout Baasha's reign. With **Tirzah** as his capital, he continued the idolatrous worship that **Jeroboam** had instituted.

16:1–7 A prophet named **Jehu** announced to **Baasha** that because he followed Jeroboam's idolatry, his **posterity** would suffer a similar fate. They would not be given the customary burial but would be eaten by **dogs** or **birds**. Another reason for Baasha's doom is given at the end of verse 7—**he killed . . . the house of Jeroboam**. Either he was not the one whom God intended to do this or he did it in a cruel and vengeful manner, contrary to God's will.

H. King Elah of Israel (16:8–10)

Elah the son of Baasha, of the tribe of Issachar, was king of Israel for **two years** (886/85—885/84 B.C.).

Elah was a wicked **king**, given over to idolatry and drunkenness. After he had **reigned two years**, he was assassinated by **Zimri, commander of half his chariots**. Also slain were all the rest of Baasha's family, in fulfillment of Jehu's prophecy (16:3). Elah's death ended the second dynasty in Israel.

I. King Zimri of Israel (16:11–20)

Zimri was king of Israel for **seven days**, (885/84 B.C.).

Zimri's wicked reign was the shortest of all the kings, lasting only **seven days**. When he usurped the throne, the army of Israel was trying to capture the city of **Gibbethon** from **the Philistines**. The army proclaimed its **commander**, **Omri**, to be **king**. He promptly marched against **Tirzah**, the capital, to seize the reins of government. **Zimri** retreated **into the citadel of the** royal palace, set it on **fire**, and perished in the flames.

J. King Tibni of Israel (16:21, 22)

Tibni the son of Ginath was king of Israel for four years (885/84—881/80 B.C.)

Although Israel made Omri, the commander of the army, king over Israel (v. 16), he had a rival in Tibni, and there was civil war for four or five years (cf. v. 15 with v. 23). Half of the Northern Kingdom followed Tibni until his death.

K. King Omri of Israel (16:23–28)

Omri was king of Israel for **twelve years** (885/84—874/73 B.C.).

Omri's reign began the fourth dynasty in the northern kingdom. **Tibni** was defeated in 880 B.C., **and Omri** became the undisputed king. For the first **six years he reigned in Tirzah**. Then he purchased **the hill of Samaria . . . for two talents of silver** and moved his capital there. The **evil** character of his reign is emphasized in verses 25 and 26.

Omri's chronology is somewhat complex. He was proclaimed king in the twenty-seventh year of Asa (with only **half of the people** behind him), after the death of Zimri (v. 15). After the four years of civil war, he became undisputed king over the northern kingdom in Asa's **thirty-first year** (v. 23). He died in the thirty-eighth year of Asa (v. 29). Thus he had about four years of internal strife and about eight years of relative peace.

Omri was a progressive king and brought a measure of peace and prosperity to Israel. Extrabiblical sources mention Omri as the conqueror of Moab. So prominent was he in the view of the Assyrians that they called Israel "the House of Omri" or "the Land of Omri." Archaeologists have found what they believe was Omri's palace in Samaria.

L. King Ahab of Israel and the Prophet Elijah (16:29—22:40)

Ahab the son of Omri was **king** of **Israel** for **twenty-two years** (874/73–853 B.C.).

1. The Sins of Ahab (16:29–34)

Ahab was an exceedingly **evil king**, not only because he followed **Jeroboam** in idolatry, but also because he married **Jezebel**, a **daughter of** the **king of the Sidonians**. This villainous woman was a Baal-worshiper who succeeded in influencing **Ahab** to promote Baal-worship in Israel by building **a temple**, **an altar**, and **a wooden image**. The godlessness of the times is witnessed by the brazen attempt by **Hiel of Bethel** to rebuild **Jericho** in defiance of God's curse (Josh. 6:26). When **he laid** the **foundation**, his oldest son, **Abiram**, died. As the **gates** were erected, **his youngest son**, **Segub**, died.

2. Elijah and the Drought (17:1–7)

17:1 In chapter 17 we are introduced to the prophet **Elijah**. His ministry extends through 2 Kings 2:11. God spoke to His people through prophets during times of sin and declension. These prophets were really mouthpieces for Jehovah. They fearlessly cried out against idolatry, immorality, and all other forms of iniquity. They urged the people to repent and return to the Lord, and then warned of dire consequences if they failed to do so. Some prophets ministered primarily to Israel, some to Judah, and some to both. Since Israel was the more wicked of the two kingdoms, God accompanied the prophet's messages to Israel with miracles and wonders. This left Israel without excuse.

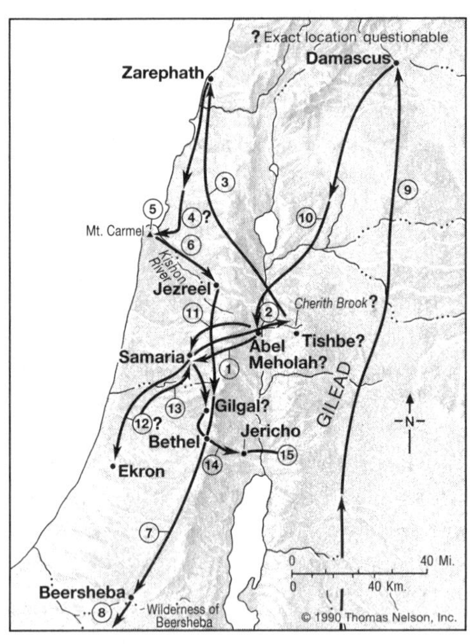

Life of Elijah

1. Elijah the Tishbite Prophesies to Ahab.
2. Elijah hides by the Brook Cherith.
3. Elijah goes to Zarephath.
4. En route to Ahab, Elijah meets Obadiah.
5. Ahab agrees to meet Elijah on Mt. Carmel.
6. Elijah outpaces Ahab to Jezreel.
7. Fearing Jezebel, Elijah goes to Beersheba.
8. Elijah departs into the Wilderness of Beersheba; from there he goes South all the way to Mt. Sinai.
9. Elijah journeys to Damascus by way of the desert to anoint Hazael King of Syria.
10. Elijah finds Elisha.
11. Elijah condemns Ahab's murder of Naboth.
12. Elijah confronts Ahaziah's servants en route to Ekron.
13. Elijah prophesies Ahaziah's death.
14. Elijah and Elisha's last journey.
15. Elijah taken to heaven by a whirlwind.

Elijah is mentioned in the Gospels in connection with the ministry of John the Baptist. John came in the spirit and power of Elijah (Luke 1:17).

Elijah came from Tishbe in **Gilead**, east of the Jordan River, and was thus called a **Tishbite**. His history is recorded only in Kings. We are told nothing about his background, family, or call to the prophetic ministry. But that he was a man sent from God no one could deny. He was God's chosen instrument to bring adulterous and haughty Israel to her knees. His prayers could bring down blessing (rain) or wrath (drought and fire). He served his generation as a fearless, embodied conscience. His first recorded act was to announce **to Ahab** that the land would suffer a drought. This was obviously a divine judgment against idolatry. God chose to use a severe drought to get the people's attention. They did not care that idolatry had brought a spiritual drought upon the land, but they could not ignore the physical drought that typified it.

17:2–7 In obedience to **the Lord**, Elijah went **from** Samaria to **the Brook Cherith**, east of **the Jordan**. There he was sustained by water **from the brook** and by food which was miraculously brought to him morning and evening by **ravens**. **After a while**, however, due to the drought **the brook dried up**.

3. *Elijah and the Widow of Zarephath (17:8–24)*

17:8–16 In obedience to **the word of the Lord**, Elijah journeyed **to Zarephath**, on the Mediterranean coast between Tyre and Sidon. There God had arranged that **a** Gentile **widow** would feed him. At first she hesitated because she had only enough meal **for** her **son** and herself. However, the prophet ordered her to **make . . . a small cake for** him **first**. By doing this she was, in effect, giving God the first place. When she obeyed, she learned the precious lesson that those who put God first never lack the necessities of life. Her **bin of flour** and **jar of oil** never failed. Jesus made note of the fact that Elijah was sent to a *Gentile* **widow** and not to any of the numerous *Israelite* widows (Luke 4:26).

During the drought Jehovah provided for His prophet in most humbling ways—first through unclean birds and then through a Gentile woman, and a poor widow at that. The king in his palace was hard-pressed, but Elijah had all he needed. God's man, obeying God's voice, will always have his needs met, despite the conditions that prevail around him.

17:17–24 Later **the son of the woman** was stricken with a **serious sickness** and died. Immediately the mother suspected that **Elijah** had ordered his death because of some **sin** she had committed. The prophet **took** the lad up to his bedroom, **stretched himself out on the child three times, and cried out to the Lord**. The boy **revived** and was taken **down . . . to his mother** in normal health. This convinced **the woman** that **Elijah** was **a man of God** and that the Lord's **word** was **the truth**. As a Gentile, she showed faith in the God of Israel.

4. *Elijah's Challenge to the Priests of Baal (18:1–19)*

18:1–6 Three years after Elijah left Israel, and three and a half years after the drought had begun (Luke 4:25), the prophet was instructed to appear before **Ahab**—an action that, humanly speaking, was extremely dangerous. So **severe** was the **famine** that **Ahab** and his steward, **Obadiah** (not the prophet who wrote the book of Obadiah), had searched **the land** for **grass** to feed the animals. (It was this **Obadiah** who had saved **one hundred . . . prophets** of the Lord **when Jezebel** had murdered some and was seeking to exterminate others.)

18:7–15 While **Obadiah was on his** search for grass, **Elijah met him**

and ordered him to notify **Ahab** of Elijah's whereabouts. Obadiah feared that this would result in his death, since Ahab had been searching relentlessly for Elijah in order to silence him once and for all. If Obadiah revealed Elijah's presence, the king would undoubtedly respond. But by then **the Spirit of the LORD** might have carried Elijah away. Then Ahab would **kill** Obadiah for his "false" report. And besides all this, Obadiah's position in the royal court was already precarious because he had protected **the LORD's prophets**. Elijah promised that he would not leave the place, and a meeting was then arranged.

18:16–19 King Ahab went to meet Elijah and accused him of being a **troubler of Israel**, not realizing that the man of God was one of the best friends **Israel** ever had. Not fearing for his own life, Elijah answered Ahab fearlessly and accusingly. He blamed the king for mixing the worship of Jehovah with **Baal**-worship and challenged him to assemble his idolatrous **prophets** for a contest **on Mount Carmel** to determine who was the true God. (**The four hundred and fifty prophets of Baal** went to **Carmel**, but **the four hundred prophets of Asherah** did not; cf. vv. 19, 22.)

5. *Elijah's Victory over the Priests of Baal (18:20–40)*

18:20–25 Addressing the assembled representatives of Israel, Elijah accused them of wavering between two opinions; they should choose either **the LORD** or **Baal**. Then the contest began. **Two bulls** were to be killed and laid **on** kindling **wood**. **Elijah** would represent **the LORD**, whereas **four hundred and fifty** of Ahab's **prophets** would represent **Baal**. **The God who** answered **by fire** would be acknowledged as the true **God**.

18:26–29 The prophets of Baal cried out to their god and hopped around **the altar from morning . . . till noon. Elijah mocked them** with "helpful" excuses for Baal's failure to answer. "Perhaps he was such a small, weak god that he could not do two things at once." In desperation, **they . . . cut themselves** (**as was their custom**) with **knives and lances** and raved on **until the time . . . of the evening sacrifice. But there was no voice; no one answered, no one paid attention.**

18:30–35 Then Elijah . . . built an altar of **twelve stones in the name of the LORD**, representing the twelve **tribes of** Israel. Then, to eliminate any possibility that the altar might be ignited in any way other than by a miracle, he saturated the oxen and the wood with twelve barrels of **water** (**four waterpots** emptied three times).

Some wonder how Elijah obtained so much water during a time of drought. But this is not a real difficulty. Twelve barrels of water is not an impossible amount during drought time. The drought had affected farmlands, but drinking water must have been obtainable or else everyone would have died. Another explanation is that this water could have come from the Mediterranean Sea, a few miles away. Williams says:

> The Kishon (v. 40), the sea (v. 43), and a well which still exists could severally or collectively supply the water needed to fill the trench (v. 35).[13]

18:36–40 At the time of . . . the evening sacrifice, . . . Elijah prayed that God would reveal himself by sending fire from heaven. Immediately **the fire of the LORD fell from heaven,** consuming not only the **sacrifice** but also **the wood and the stones and the dust, and... the water... in the trench** around the altar. **The people** were thus compelled to acknowledge **the Lord** as the real **God**. Then they obeyed Elijah's order to slay **the** wicked **prophets of Baal**. Only after the people *acknowledged* that Jehovah was God and *executed*—elthe prophets of Baal could the rain come. Confession of sin and obedience to the Word of God are the steps to blessing.

6. Elijah's Prayer for Rain (18:41–46)

The prophet advised **Ahab** to **eat** a meal because he would soon have to leave Mount Carmel to escape the oncoming **rain**. While **Ahab** sat down **to eat, Elijah** rose up to pray. He ascended **to the top of** Mount **Carmel, bowed down on the ground** with **his face between his knees**, and fervently asked the Lord to fulfill His word by sending rain. He continued in prayer until **his servant** reported a tiny **cloud** on the horizon. That was enough for Elijah. He immediately sent word **to Ahab** to make haste for **Jezreel**, a city in Issachar where the royal family lived at times (21:1). As a loyal subject and faithful servant, the prophet **ran** before Ahab's chariot in **a** drenching **rain** twenty miles **to Jezreel**.

7. Elijah's Flight to Horeb (19:1–18)

19:1–4 When **Ahab told Jezebel** of the defeat and death of **the prophets** of Baal on Mount Carmel, she swore that she would slay **Elijah** within a day. Then the prophet whose faith had gained such a mighty victory the previous day lost courage. He **ran for his life** from Jezreel, south across the land **to Beersheba**, about one hundred miles away, at the southern boundary of **Judah**. Leaving **his servant** at **Beersheba**, Elijah continued south **a day's journey into the wilderness**. At length he rested **under a broom tree**, despondent, defeated, and depressed.

19:5–8 It is interesting to notice God's treatment for this severe depression: rest; food and drink; more rest; more food and drink. Thus fortified, the prophet traveled **in the strength of that food** 200 miles in **forty days and... nights** to Mount **Horeb** (Sinai), where God had given the law to Moses.

19:9–14 There in **a cave... the Lord** dealt with him. In a self-righteous spirit, Elijah protested his own faithfulness and denounced **the children of Israel**. He said in effect that he was the only one who had remained true to the Lord. God then commanded him to **stand on the mountain** of the law, but Elijah did not obey. We know this because later (v. 13) **he went out and stood in the entrance of the cave**. In rapid succession **the mountains** were visited by **a great... wind, an earthquake**, and **a fire**. These violent storms must have reminded Elijah of his harsh, censorious spirit. None of them brought him out of the cave. Finally, **after the fire** the prophet heard **a still, small voice**. It was this gracious voice of the Lord which brought him to **the entrance of the cave**. There he again exalted himself as God's sole remaining witness. George Williams comments:

> Had his heart not been occupied with self, he would have learned that tempests, earthquakes and fires cannot accomplish what the gentle voice of love can. He should have recognized that there was no difference between his heart and that of the nation; and, that as coercion failed to make him leave his cave, so it failed, and must fail, to compel men to leave their sins.[14]

19:15–18 It seems that Elijah's usefulness as a servant of God suffered when he adopted this attitude of self-importance. God told him to return north **to the Wilderness of Damascus**, where he would conduct three anointings: (1) He would **anoint Hazael** to be **king over Syria**. The disobedient nation of Israel would be punished by this king. (2) He would **anoint Jehu** to be **king over Israel**. Jehu would execute God's judgment on the house of Ahab. (3) He would **anoint . . . Elisha** as his own successor.[15] This would teach him that he was not indispensable. These three men would execute God's judgment on idolaters in Israel (v. 17), but the Lord would leave **seven thousand** who had **not bowed** the knee **to Baal** or **kissed him**.

8. Elijah's Appointment of Elisha (19:19–21)

19:19 Elijah traveled north to Abel Meholah, in the Jordan Valley near Beth Shean. There he **found Elisha**, a farmer **plowing** in the field. The fact that Elisha had **twelve yoke of oxen** indicates that he was not poor. He was probably plowing with one yoke and his servants with the other eleven. **Elijah threw his mantel on** Elisha, a sign that Elisha was to be his successor.

19:20, 21 Elisha asked permission to return home and make a farewell feast for his family. Elijah gave consent but warned him not to forget what had just happened to him—i.e., how Elijah had anointed him. After a sumptuous feast, Elisha **arose and followed Elijah and became his** personal **servant**.

Elisha's request to say goodbye to his parents sounds dangerously like that of a would-be disciple whom Jesus pronounced unfit for the kingdom (Luke 9:61, 62). The difference is that in Elisha's case it was a no-nonsense decision to sever ties immediately, whereas in the other case it was a delaying tactic and an excuse.

9. Ahab's First Victory over Syria (20:1–22)

20:1–6 Ben-Hadad, the king of Syria, was formerly thought to be the son of the Ben-Hadad mentioned in 15:18, 20. But later research has raised the possibility that he was the same person. He formed an alliance of **thirty-two** Aramean **kings** and marched against **Samaria with horses and chariots**. When the city was in a state of siege, he sent surrender terms to Ahab—**"Your silver . . . your gold . . . your loveliest wives and children."** Ahab meekly and weakly agreed. Not satisfied with Ahab's capitulation to his first terms, **Ben-Hadad** next demanded right of entry for his **servants** and the right to seize anything they wanted.

20:7–12 The elders of Israel were indignant at this second demand and urged noncompliance. When **Ben-Hadad** was notified of Israel's refusal, he flew into a rage, boasting that he would strip Samaria so bare that there wouldn't be **a handful** of **dust . . . for each of** his soldiers. To this, Ahab replied that a soldier putting **on his armor** should not **boast** as if the victory were already won. This taunt stirred the carousing Syrian and his confederates to action.

20:13–15 At this point **a prophet** of the Lord **approached Ahab**, assuring him of victory. God used a small force of **two hundred and thirty-two** servants of the governors of the districts, followed by **seven thousand** of the people **of Israel**, to defeat the assembled armies from the north. The phrase **"all the children of Israel"** (v. 15b) means all the soldiers in

Samaria. A small number of young servants was chosen to begin the battle, to make it all the more apparent that victory was *from the Lord* and not from the arm of the flesh.

20:16–22 Ahab attacked **at noon**, when **Ben-Hadad and** his allies **were getting drunk**. When Ben-Hadad heard that the 232 men of Israel were advancing, he ordered that they be taken **alive**. This, of course, gave a military advantage to the Israelites and resulted in **a great slaughter** of **the Syrians**. The survivors retreated to their homeland. **The prophet** of the Lord warned Ahab that the Syrian army would return **in the spring**.

10. Ahab's Second Victory over Syria (20:23–34)

20:23–25 Ben-Hadad's **servants** attributed their shameful defeat to two factors: (1) The Israelites had won the battle in hill country. Doubtless **their gods** were **gods of the hills**. But they would be impotent on the plains. So the Syrians should engage them the next time on the plains. (2) The thirty-two kings who fought against Ahab had apparently proved themselves unskilled in warfare. Ben-Hadad's **servants** advised that they be replaced by professional **captains**.

20:26–30a In the spring, . . . Ben-Hadad marched **against Israel** again. The army of Israel looked like **two little flocks of goats** compared to the host of Syria. **A man of God** told Ahab that **the LORD** would show Ben-Hadad that He was the **God of the valleys** as well as **of the hills**. In the battle, **Israel killed one hundred thousand foot soldiers**. **The Syrians** who escaped tried to take up positions on the walls of the city of **Aphek**, but the walls collapsed, killing **twenty-seven thousand** of them.

20:30b–34 Ben-Hadad hid in **an inner chamber** of Aphek. **His servants** persuaded him to **let** them **go out to** Ahab, clothed with symbols of surrender and mourning, and to plead for mercy. In the interview, Ahab stupidly referred to the king as his **"brother."** The men of Syria quickly caught that word and said, "Yes, **your brother Ben-Hadad!"** Ahab ordered that the king of Syria be brought to him. Ben-Hadad promised to **restore the cities** which had been taken from Ahab's predecessor (15:20) and to allow Israel to establish **marketplaces in Damascus** (v. 34). **Ahab** made **a treaty** on these terms and let Ben-Hadad escape instead of killing him, as he should have done.

11. Ahab's Disobedience (20:35–43)

20:35, 36 Ahab wanted a strong Syria as a buffer between Israel and the growing menace of Assyria. The incident that follows was an object lesson, acted out by the prophet, to illustrate the folly of Ahab's action.

One **of the sons of the prophets** ordered his fellow **by the word of the LORD** to **strike** him. **The man** disobeyed him and therefore disobeyed **the LORD**. For his failure to obey the Lord's voice, he was destroyed by **a lion**.

> If a good prophet were thus punished for sparing his friend and God's, when God said *Smite*, of much sorer punishment should a wicked king be thought worthy, who spared his enemy and God's, when God said *Smite*.[16]

20:37–43 The prophet **found another man** who obeyed him by striking and wounding him. Then **the prophet . . . disguised himself with a bandage over his eyes** and **waited for** King Ahab. When **the king** was passing by, the prophet told of being in the battle and of being charged with the custody of an enemy prisoner. He had been warned that if the prisoner escaped, he would have to pay either with **his** own **life** or with the exorbitant figure of one **talent of silver**. The disguised prophet told how he had become preoccupied with other things and how the prisoner had escaped. **The king** showed no leniency; he insisted that the original terms of punishment be carried out. Then the prophet sprang the trap. He removed his bandage to reveal himself as a prophet known by Ahab. **Ahab** had had an enemy prisoner, **Ben-Hadad**, in his grasp. Obedience to the Lord required that the Syrian king be killed. For his disobedience Ahab would be slain. Campbell Morgan explains:

> This was the meaning of the parable: Ahab had one thing to do by the command of God, and while he did a hundred things, he neglected the one. What a revelation of a perpetual reason and method of failure! We are given some one responsibility by God, some central, definite thing to do. We start to do it with all good intentions, and then other things, not necessarily wrong in themselves, come in our way. We get "busy here and there" doing many things and we neglect the one central thing.[17]

Like King David before him, Ahab condemned himself by his own words. But unlike David, who repented, Ahab became **sullen** and stormed off to his palace to pout. Instead of asking the Lord for mercy, he continued to incite the Lord to wrath, as we read in the remaining chapters of 1 Kings.

12. Ahab's Crimes against Naboth (Chap. 21)

21:1–4 Chapter 21 traces the events leading up to Ahab's death. The scene is **in Jezreel**, where **Ahab** and Jezebel had a **palace**. Adjoining the palace was **a vineyard** owned by **Naboth the Jezreelite**. **Ahab** desired to annex the **vineyard** so he could plant **a vegetable garden** there. **Naboth** refused to sell or exchange his land, since the law of Israel decreed that property should remain in the family to which it was originally assigned (Lev. 25:23–28; Num. 36:7; Ezek. 46:18).

21:5–16 When **Jezebel** found her husband vexed and **sullen** and learned of Naboth's refusal to sell his **vineyard**, she assured Ahab that the vineyard would soon be his. **She** ordered **a fast** and a court of inquiry. **Two** evil **men** were appointed to charge Naboth with blasphemy against **God and the king**. Accordingly, **Naboth** was taken **outside** the city and **stoned** to death.

The treacherous Jezebel thus framed Naboth so that it would appear he was being executed for breaking the law of Jehovah. Since the property would pass on to Naboth's sons after his death, Jezebel had them murdered as well (2 Kgs. 9:26). The iniquitous queen was as thorough as she was wicked.

21:17–26 When **Ahab** was on his way **to take possession of the vineyard, Elijah** met him and condemned him for murder and theft. Elijah predicted that **Ahab** himself would be slain, that his **male** descendants would be slain, ending his dynasty, that the body of **Jezebel** would be eaten by **dogs** in **Jezreel**, and that Ahab's descendants would not be given a decent burial (v. 24). The severity of Ahab's punishment is explained by the extremes to which he went in idolatry—**"there was no one like Ahab who sold himself to do wickedness."**

21:27–29 When Ahab heard his doom, he **humbled himself before** the Lord. For this, the Lord decreed that the judgments on his wife and family would not take place until after Ahab's death.

If we learn anything from these verses, it is that God is a God of grace and mercy. " 'As I live,' says the Lord GOD, 'I have no pleasure in the death of the wicked, but that the wicked turn from his way and live. Turn, turn from your evil ways! For why should you die?' " (Ezek. 33:11). Even Ahab's superficial repentance brought a respite. But the next chapter proves that his heart was unchanged. Grace was met by pride, so the Lord handed Ahab over to the angel of death, and Jehu was appointed to carry out the bloody decree against the rest of his house according to the prophecy of Elijah (2 Kgs. 9, 10).

13. Ahab's Last Battle (22:1–40)

22:1–6 After **three years** of peace **between Syria and Israel**, Ahab conceived the idea of recapturing **Ramoth Gilead**, on the east of the Jordan, from the Syrians. Ben-Hadad had promised to return Israel's cities when he received amnesty from Ahab (20:34), but he apparently had failed to do so. **Jehoshaphat**, king of Judah, happened to be visiting Ahab at the time and expressed willingness to cooperate in the military venture. But first **Jehoshaphat** suggested that they **inquire** of **the LORD** through **the prophets**. **Four hundred** prophets in Ahab's court advised in favor of the plan and promised victory. These may well have been the 400 prophets who did not go to Mount Carmel for the showdown with Elijah (18:19, 22).

22:7–12 Jehoshaphat must have felt uneasy because he asked if there were **a prophet of the LORD** who could be consulted. This brought to the fore **Micaiah**, a fearless prophet who was hated by Ahab because of his uncompromising messages. At the time Micaiah was summoned, the 400 prophets were unanimously urging the kings of **Israel** and **Judah** to march against Syria. One of them, **Zedekiah**, **made horns of iron** to depict the irresistible power of Ahab and Jehoshaphat against **the Syrians**.

22:13–17 Micaiah was informed that his message should agree with that of **the** other **prophets**, but the advice was wasted on him. When Ahab asked if the campaign **against Ramoth Gilead** should be undertaken, Micaiah first said the same thing as the prophets: **"Go and prosper, for the LORD will deliver it into the hand of the king!"** But it is probable that he said it in a mocking manner. The tone of his voice must have dripped with irony and sarcasm.

Ahab sensed this and put Micaiah under oath to **tell . . . the truth** (Lev. 5:1). The prophet then related a vision in which **Israel** was **scattered** because they had **no shepherd**, intimating that Ahab would be killed and his army dispersed.

22:18–23 King Ahab presented this **to Jehoshaphat** as evidence that Micaiah could speak nothing but evil against him. Then the brave prophet spoke up again. He related a vision in which **a lying spirit**, appearing before **the LORD**, agreed to trick Ahab into going against **Ramoth Gilead** and be slain. The **lying spirit** would put this advice into **the mouth of all** the king's **prophets**. This is an example of how God, while not the author of evil, uses it to achieve His ultimate ends. He sent the **lying spirit** only in the sense that He permitted it.

22:24, 25 The point of this parable was not lost upon **Zedekiah**. Realizing that he and the other prophets were being accused of lying, he **struck Micaiah** and asked, **"Which way did**

the spirit from the Lord go from me to speak to you?" In other words, Zedekiah was saying:

> I spoke by the Spirit of God when I advised Ahab to go against Ramoth Gilead. Now you profess to speak by the Spirit, yet you advise the very opposite. How did the Spirit go from me to you?

Micaiah answered calmly that Zedekiah would know the truth when he would **hide** in terror in a secret place—evidently when Ahab's death would expose Zedekiah to the fate of a false prophet.

22:26–30 The infuriated **king of Israel** ordered that **Micaiah** be **put . . . in prison and** fed **with bread . . . and water, until** he (Ahab) returned **in peace** from Ramoth Gilead. Micaiah's parting salute was, **"If you ever return in peace, the LORD has not spoken by me."** Ahab decided to **disguise** himself before going **into battle**, hoping in this way to avoid the disaster predicted by Micaiah. **Jehoshaphat**, on the other hand, would wear his kingly **robes**, exposing himself to the very danger that Ahab was trying to escape. Ahab thus attempted to fool the Lord and the king of Syria, but "God is not mocked; for whatever a man sows, that he will also reap" (Gal. 6:7). Ahab was *slain*, but Jehoshaphat was *saved*.

22:31–36 The Syrians had been ordered to kill **the king of Israel**; this was their prime military objective. At first they mistook **Jehoshaphat** for Ahab. The king of Judah **cried out** in terror, perhaps revealing his true identity in this way. Then Ahab was **struck between the joints of his armor** by a **random** arrow and was removed from the active fighting. He **was propped up in his chariot** so that his army would not lose heart. When he **died at** sunset, the fact became known, and his soldiers retreated to their homes.

22:37–40 Ahab's body was taken back **to Samaria** and **buried**. His bloodstained **chariot** was **washed** beside **a pool in Samaria, . . . while the harlots bathed**. This was only a partial fulfillment of Elijah's prophecy (21:19); it took place **in Samaria** rather than in Jezreel. Because Ahab had humbled himself (21:29), God compassionately deferred the complete fulfillment to the king's son, Joram (2 Kgs. 9:25, 26).

Ahab received three separate prophetic warnings of his death. One was pronounced by an unnamed prophet when Ahab spared Ben-Hadad (20:42); one was given by Elijah when Ahab took the vineyard of Naboth (21:19); and the third prophecy was uttered by Micaiah on the eve of the eventful battle (vv. 17–23).

M. King Jehoshaphat of Judah (22:41–50)

Jehoshaphat the **son of Asa** was king of Judah for **twenty-five years** (873/72–848 B.C.).

For the first three or four years, **Jehoshaphat** co-reigned with his father **Asa**. We have already been introduced to Jehoshaphat in verses 2–4, where he made a shameful alliance with the wicked king of Israel and nearly lost his life as a result. In general, however, his reign was good. The following are significant features of Jehoshaphat's administration.

1. He followed his father's example in combating idolatry, though he was not successful in eradicating it completely (v. 43).
2. He reigned jointly with **his father Asa**.
3. He **made peace with** Ahab, king of Israel (v. 44).

4. He expelled the male cult prostitutes **from the land** (v. 46).
5. His kingdom included the land of **Edom** (2 Sam. 8:14), where he was represented by **a deputy** (v. 47). His son Jehoram later lost Edom through a revolution (2 Kgs. 8:20).
6. He allied himself with **Ahaziah**, Ahab's son, in a shipbuilding project at **Ezion Geber** (2 Chron. 20:35, 36). Their plan was to send the **ships . . . to Ophir for gold**. But **the ships were wrecked** before they ever left port (v. 48), no doubt by a windstorm. The prophet Eliezer told Jehoshaphat that this was because the Lord disapproved of the unholy alliance with Ahaziah (2 Chron. 20:37). When **Ahaziah** suggested renewing the project, **Jehoshaphat** declined (v. 49).

N. King Ahaziah of Israel (22:51–53)

Ahaziah the son of Ahab was **king** of **Israel**, for **two years** (853—852 B.C.; cf. 2 Kgs. 1:1–18).

The reign of **Ahaziah** was one of gross idolatry and wickedness. His mother, Jezebel, no doubt urged him on in ungodliness even as she had pushed **his father**. **He** worshiped **Baal . . . and provoked the Lord God of Israel to anger**. Like father, like son. There is no formal close to 1 Kings, since 1 and 2 Kings were originally one book, and the break was made strictly for convenience. Second Kings continues the narrative from this point.

ENDNOTES

[1](Intro) O. J. Gibson, unpublished notes.

[2](4:1–6) Matthew Poole, *Matthew Poole's Commentary on the Holy Bible*, p. 657.

[3](6:11–22) C. H. Spurgeon, *Spurgeon's Devotional Bible*, p. 305.

[4](8:12, 13) Matthew Henry, "1 Kings," in *Matthew Henry's Commentary on the Whole Bible*, II:614.

[5](8:66) John Haley, *Alleged Discrepancies of the Bible*, p. 223.

[6](9:15–23) *Baker's Bible Atlas*, p. 309.

[7](10:16–22) The word rendered "peacocks" in the KJV is now generally translated *monkeys* (NKJV) or *baboons* (NIV). Ancient kings did indeed favor peacocks, and so that translation (probably a guess) was made by Jerome in the Latin Vulgate.

[8](10:26–29) *Keveh* (also transliterated *Kue*) was translated "linen yarn" in KJV because they did not know in the seventeenth century that it was a place name.

[9](10:26–29) J. R. Lumly, further documentation unavailable.

[10](Essay) See the Bibliography for details.

[11](13:33, 34) Irving L. Jensen, *I Kings with Chronicles*, pp. 80–81.

[12](14:14–16) The word translated *groves* in the KJV is the Hebrew word properly transliterated *Asherim*.

[13](18:30–35) George Williams, *The Student's Commentary on the Holy Scriptures*, p. 195.

[14](19:9–14) *Ibid.*, p. 196.

[15](19:15–18) Elijah must have directed his successor, Elisha, to fulfill the Lord's command to anoint Hazael and Jehu, since these anointings took place after Elijah's homecall (2 Kgs. 8:7ff; 9:1ff). Elisha was the only one of the three whom Elijah would personally anoint.

[16](20:35, 36) Henry, "1 Kings," II:692–93.

[17](20:37–43) G. Campbell Morgan, *Searchlights from the Word*, p. 100.

BIBLIOGRAPHY

Gates, John T. "1 Kings." In *The Wycliffe Bible Commentary*. Chicago: Moody Press, 1962.

Henry, Matthew. "1 and 2 Kings." In *Matthew Henry's Commentary on the Whole Bible*. Vol. 2.

Jamieson, Robert. "I and II Kings." In *A Commentary, Critical, Experimental and Practical on the Old and New Testaments*. 3rd ed. Grand Rapids: Zondervan Publishing House, 1983.

Jensen, Irving L. *I Kings with Chronicles*. Chicago: Moody Press, 1968.

Keil, C. F. "The Books of Kings." In *Biblical Commentary on the Old Testament*. Vol. 8. Grand Rapids: Wm. B. Eerdmans Publishing Co., 1971.

McNeely, Richard I. *First & Second Kings. Everyman's Bible Commentary*. Chicago: Moody Press, 1978.

Stigers, Harold. "II Kings." In *The Wycliffe Bible Commentary*. Chicago: Moody Press, 1962.

Thiele, Edwin R. *A Chronology of the Hebrew Kings*. Grand Rapids: Zondervan Publishing House, 1977.

——. *The Mysterious Numbers of the Hebrew Kings*. Rev. ed. Chicago: University of Chicago Press, 1983.

Whitcomb, J. C., Jr. *Solomon to the Exile*. Grand Rapids: Baker Book House, 1975.

SECOND KINGS

Introduction

"The history of the Kings is one of downward progress; things get darker and darker until there is no remedy. . . . The ten tribes are first carried away captive, then the two tribes."

—Samuel Ridout

See 1 Kings for Introduction to both books.

OUTLINE

I. THE DIVIDED KINGDOM (Cont'd. from 1 Kings) (Chaps. 1—17)

A. King Ahaziah of Israel and the Ministry of Elijah (Chap. 1)

B. The Translation of Elijah (2:1–12a)

C. The Beginning of Elisha's Ministry (2:12b–25)

D. King Jehoram (Joram) of Israel (Chap. 3)

E. The Miraculous Ministry of Elisha (4:1—8:15)
1. Miraculous Provision of Oil (4:1–7)
2. Miraculous Birth (4:8–17)
3. Raising the Shunammite's Son to Life (4:18–37)
4. Detoxifying the Poisonous Stew (4:38–41)
5. Miraculous Provision of Bread (4:42–44)
6. Miraculous Cleansing of Naaman the Leper (5:1–19)
7. The Greed of Gehazi (5:20–27)
8. Miraculous Recovery of an Axhead (6:1–7)
9. Miraculous Military Maneuvers (6:8–23)
10. The Famine in Samaria (6:24—7:20)
11. Restoration of the Shunammite's Property (8:1–6)
12. Elisha's Prophecy of Hazael's Reign (8:7–15)

F. King Jehoram (Joram) of Judah (8:16–24)

G. King Ahaziah of Judah (8:25–29)

H. King Jehu of Israel and Elisha's Ministry (Chaps. 9, 10)
1. Jehu's Anointing (9:1–10)
2. Jehu's Executions (9:11—10:17)
3. Jehu's Purge of the Baal-Worshipers (10:18–36)

I. Queen Athaliah's Usurpation in Judah (Chap. 11)
J. King Jehoash (Joash) of Judah (Chap. 12)
K. King Jehoahaz of Israel (13:1–9)
L. King Jehoash (Joash) of Israel (13:10–13)
M. The Close of Elisha's Ministry (13:14–25)
N. King Amaziah of Judah (14:1–20)
O. King Azariah (Uzziah) of Judah (14:21, 22)
P. King Jeroboam II of Israel (14:23–29)
Q. King Azariah (Uzziah) of Judah, Cont'd (15:1–7)
R. King Zechariah of Israel (15:8–12)
S. King Shallum of Israel (15:13–15)
T. King Menahem of Israel (15:16–22)
U. King Pekahiah of Israel (15:23–26)
V. King Pekah of Israel (15:27–31)
W. King Jotham of Judah (15:32–38)
X. King Ahaz of Judah (Chap. 16)
Y. King Hoshea of Israel (17:1–6)
Z. The Fall of the Northern Kingdom (17:7–41)

II. THE KINGDOM OF JUDAH TO THE CAPTIVITY (Chaps. 18—25)
A. King Hezekiah (Chaps. 18—20)
1. Hezekiah's Righteous Reign (18:1–8)
2. The Capture of Samaria (18:9–12)
3. Sennacherib's First Invasion of Judah (18:13–16)
4. Sennacherib's Second Invasion of Judah (18:17—19:34)
5. Sennacherib's Defeat and Death (19:35–37)
6. Hezekiah's Sickness and Recovery (20:1–11)
7. Hezekiah's Foolish Pride (20:12–21)
B. King Manasseh (21:1–18)
C. King Amon (21:19–26)
D. King Josiah (22:1—23:30)
1. Josiah's Repairs of the Temple (22:1–7)
2. Josiah's Recovery of the Book of the Law (22:8–20)
3. Josiah's Renewal of the Covenant (23:1–3)
4. Josiah's Reforms (23:4–30)
E. King Jehoahaz (23:31–33)
F. King Jehoiakim (23:34—24:7)
G. King Jehoiachin (24:8–16)
H. King Zedekiah (24:17—25:7)
I. The Fall of Jerusalem (25:8–21)
J. Gedaliah's Governorship (25:22–26)
K. King Jehoiachin (25:27–30)

Commentary

I. THE DIVIDED KINGDOM (Cont'd. from 1 Kings) (Chaps. 1— 17)

A. King Ahaziah of Israel and the Ministry of Elijah (Chap. 1)

1:1 **Moab** had been subjugated by David (2 Sam. 8:2). When Solomon's kingdom was divided into Israel and Judah, Moab came under Israel's sway. **After** Ahab's **death**, the Moabites **rebelled** and won their independence.

1:2 King **Ahaziah fell through the lattice** on the roof of his palace **in Samaria** and **was** seriously **injured**. Instead of appealing to the Lord for healing, **he sent messengers** to **Baal-Zebub, the god of Ekron**, to see if he would **recover**. John C. Whitcomb identifies the pagan god as follows:

> The real name of this Syrian deity was Baal-zebul ('Lord of life'), but the Jews called him Baal-zebub ('Lord of flies') in derision. By the time of Christ, this deity had become a symbol of Satan.[1]

It is pathetic that a king whose name means "whom Jehovah sustains" should turn to Baal for healing!

1:3–8 **A hairy man wearing a leather belt**, **Elijah** met **the messengers** and sent them back to Ahaziah with a stern rebuke for inquiring **of Baal-Zebub** and with the announcement that his illness would be fatal.

1:9–12 Ahaziah responded by sending **a captain . . . with . . . fifty men** to order **Elijah** to appear before him immediately. When the captain deliv ered the insolent demand, God vindicated Elijah by causing **fire . . . from heaven** to destroy the captain and his **fifty men**. A second **captain . . . with . . . fifty men** ordered Elijah to **"Come down quickly!"** but they met the same fate. With **fire . . . from heaven** God had previously discredited Baal and his priests (1 Kgs. 18). Now that same heavenly flame destroyed the soldiers of Baal who sought to lay unholy hands on Elijah. The prophet took his orders from Israel's true King, not from an idolatrous usurper. We are not told specifically why the two captains and their men were killed; perhaps they shared Ahaziah's determination to destroy Elijah.

1:13–16 Only when the **third captain** humbly acknowledged Elijah's power and **pleaded** for mercy was the prophet instructed by **the angel of the Lord** (Christ in preincarnate appearance) to go and speak with Ahaziah. **Elijah** fearlessly told **the king** that he would **not** recover because he had treated the Lord with contempt by consulting **Baal-Zebub**.

1:17, 18 When **Ahaziah died**, he was succeeded by his brother, **Jehoram** (later referred to as Joram), **because he had no son** to wear the crown. Judah at this time had a co-regency composed of Jehoshaphat (3:1) and his son, who was also named **Jehoram**.

B. The Translation of Elijah (2:1–12a)

This chapter opens with the saintly Elijah being "taken up" (vv. 1–11) and closes with the hooligans of Bethel being "torn up" (vv. 23–25).

2:1–6 The time had now come for **Elijah** to finish his ministry and for **Elisha** to succeed him. But first **Elijah** must visit **Bethel**, **Jericho**, and **Jordan**. Elisha faithfully insisted on going with him to these places. In **Bethel** and **Jericho**, **the sons of the prophets** told **Elisha** that **the Lord** was going to **take** Elijah **"away from** his head" that day. This refers to the practice of a disciple sitting at his master's feet; in such an arrangement, the master was at the disciple's head, of course. Elisha already knew this and told the prophets to **"keep silent!"** The matter was too sad and sacred to discuss.

2:7–9 From Jericho, Elijah and Elisha went down **to the Jordan** River, followed **at a distance** by **fifty of the . . . prophets**. When **Elijah . . . struck the Jordan** with **his mantle**, the waters **divided** and the two men **crossed over on dry land**. Elijah had come from Gilead, east of the Jordan, during the reign of Ahab, to begin his prophetic work (1 Kgs. 17:1). Now at the close of his ministry he crossed back over Jordan to be taken up into heaven. Encouraged by the departing prophet to make a request, Elisha asked for **a double portion of** his **spirit**. The **double portion** is the right of the firstborn son and may simply mean here that Elisha wanted to be his worthy successor. George Williams says that the fulfillment of the request is seen in the fact that, whereas Elijah performed eight recorded miracles, Elisha performed sixteen.[2]

2:10–12a Elijah said that it was not in his power to grant the request, then added a condition that was also beyond his control: **If** Elisha would **see** him depart, then his request would be granted. **As they** walked **on and talked**, they were **separated** by **a chariot of fire . . . with horses of fire**. Then **a whirlwind** caught **Elijah . . . up . . . into heaven** in full view of Elisha. **Elisha . . . cried out, "My father, my father, the chariot of Israel and its horsemen!"** This may indicate that Elijah was the strongest weapon of God's power and the best defense of Israel.

C. The Beginning of Elisha's Ministry (2:12b–25)

2:12b–14 After tearing apart **his own clothes** in grief, Elisha returned to the east **bank of the Jordan, struck the water** with Elijah's **mantle, and said, "Where is the LORD God of Elijah?"** This question did not express doubt or unbelief but merely afforded opportunity for God to show that He was with **Elisha** as He had been with Elijah. The waters **divided**, permitting the prophet to return to the west bank of the river, where the **fifty** sons of the prophets had been waiting and watching.

2:15–18 After seeing the parting of the Jordan, they acknowledged that **Elisha** was truly the successor of **Elijah**. Against Elisha's better judgment they insisted on sending out a party to **search for** Elijah, but the trip was in vain, of course, as Elisha had warned. Either they had not witnessed Elijah's translation, or, if they had, they thought his absence was temporary.

2:19–22 The ministry of Elisha from this point to 13:20 consists of a series of miracles designed to turn the nation of Israel away from idolatry to the true and living God. The incidents are not necessarily in chronological order. The first of these miracles occurred when **Elisha** threw **salt** into the brackish **water** in the fountain at Jericho; never again did it cause **death or barrenness**.

2:23, 24 En route from Jericho **to Bethel**, one of the centers of calf worship, Elisha was met by some rowdy **youths** who called him a **baldhead** and mockingly challenged him to **go up** to heaven as Elijah had done. After he cursed them **in the name of the LORD, two female bears came out of the woods and mauled forty-two of** them. An insult to God's messenger is an insult to God Himself.

2:25 Elisha retraced Elijah's steps, going to the schools of the prophets in Jericho and Bethel before traveling

to Mount Carmel and **Samaria**. At Jericho the people treated him respectfully and received a blessing. Because of their irreverence for Jehovah, the young people at Bethel treated him shamefully, for which they received a curse.

D. King Jehoram (Joram) of Israel (Chap. 3)

Jehoram the son of Ahab was **king** of **Israel** for **twelve years** (852–841 B.C.; 2 Kgs. 3:1—9:29).

3:1–3 When **Jehoram the son of Ahab** began to reign as **king over Israel**, there was a co-regency in **Judah** (**Jehoshaphat** and his son Jehoram). That explains how **Jehoram, king** of **Israel**, began to reign **in the eighteenth year of Jehoshaphat** and in the second year of Jehoram, king of Judah (2 Kgs. 1:17).

Jehoram (same name as Joram) was **not** as evil as his parents; **he put away the . . . pillar of Baal** which Ahab had erected. However, he clung to the golden-calf-worship instituted by **Jeroboam the son of Nebat**.

3:4–9 Under Ahab's reign, the **king of Moab** had been required to pay annual tribute to **Israel**. **When Ahab died**, King **Mesha** decided that it was a strategic time to rebel. The famous Moabite Stone, discovered by a German missionary in 1868, mentions Israel's subjugation of Moab and Mesha's successful rebellion.[3]

Ahaziah had done nothing about Moab's rebellion. However, when his successor Jehoram came to power he immediately sought to bring Moab back under his control, not wanting to lose her sizable tribute. **Jehoram** asked **Jehoshaphat** to join with him in the battle, and once again Jehoshaphat foolishly agreed. (See 1 Kgs. 22, where Jehoshaphat almost lost his life by allying himself with Israel.) They decided to march down the west side of the Dead Sea, east through **Edom**, and north to Moab. Since **the king of Edom** was a vassal of Jehoshaphat at this time, his help was enlisted in the war.

3:10–12 As they approached Moab, **the army** ran out of **water**. The insolence of Jehoram in blaming **the Lord** was answered by Jehoshaphat's suggestion that **a prophet of the Lord** be consulted. When it became known that **Elisha**, the servant **of Elijah**, was nearby, the three kings **went down to him**.

3:13–19 At first **Elisha** protested that he had nothing **to do with** the idolatrous king of Israel and suggested that he **go to the** idolatrous **prophets of** his **father**. Jehoram's reply may have suggested that it wasn't the idols but **the Lord** who was causing the problem. In deference to **Jehoshaphat**, Elisha agreed to seek the mind of the Lord. As a **musician played,** the power of God **came upon** Elisha and he predicted that the **valley** would be full of pools not caused by **rain**, and that **the Moabites** would be defeated.

3:20–25 The next **morning, water** flowed in the valley, coming from the direction **of Edom**. In the light of the sunrise, the **water** looked like **blood** to **the Moabites**, and they decided that **the kings** of Israel, Judah, and Edom had fought among themselves. As they hurried **to the camp of Israel** for **the spoil**, they met a devastating attack. The Israelites **filled** the arable **land** with stones, **stopped up** the wells, **and cut down all the good trees**.

3:26, 27 The king of Moab, embittered at his former allies, the Edomites, and suspecting that their king would not fight as wholeheartedly as Israel and Judah, sought **to break**

through the lines **of Edom**. When this strategem failed, he offered **his eldest son** as a sacrifice on **the wall** of the city to appease his gods, to incite his men to fiercer battle, and to frighten the enemy. Israel was stunned by this human sacrifice, which was, of course, an abomination. Smitten directly by God or by their own consciences, they withdrew without bringing Moab back into subjection. Harold Stigers comments:

> The author seems to be asking: If Israel was so deeply moved in this case, why was she not shocked enough to forsake her own idolatry? But idolatry continued in Israel and in Judah.[4]

E. The Miraculous Ministry of Elisha (4:1—8:15)

1. *Miraculous Provision of Oil (4:1–7)*

An impoverished widow of one of **the** godly **prophets** was in danger of losing her sons to slavery because of unpaid debts. She was miraculously supplied with **oil**, the only limit being the number of **vessels** she could borrow to receive it. By selling **the oil** she was able to **pay** her **debt** and support her family. This event illustrates grace for the debtor, enough to meet present needs and to provide for future sustenance. God's grace to needy sinners sets us free from debt and slavery and provides all we need for a new life.

2. *Miraculous Birth (4:8–17)*

A prominent **woman** of **Shunem** had shown unusual hospitality to **Elisha**, even fitting out **a small upper room** for him in her home. When she was offered a position or favor from **the king** through Elisha's intercession, she humbly expressed her satisfaction at dwelling simply **among** her **own people**. **Gehazi**, the **servant** of the prophet, suggested that she might like a **son**, and this suggestion became a reality at the word of the prophet. The following spring she bore **a son**. Out of death (the barren womb) the Lord brought life, a picture of the spiritual birth of every child of God (Eph. 2:1–10).

3. *Raising the Shunammite's Son (4:18–37)*

4:18–25a Years later the lad suffered a stroke of some kind while out in the field. He was carried back **to his mother** and **died** in her arms at **noon**. She put his body in the prophet's chamber. **Then**, without revealing the reason, she told **her husband** that she wanted to visit **the man of God** on **Mount Carmel**. He thought it strange to visit the prophet when it was not a religious holiday, but he made the necessary arrangements for transportation. With great speed she rode from Shunem, in the plain of Esdraelon, to Mount Carmel.

4:25b–28 Seeing her approach, Elisha sent **Gehazi** to **meet her** and to inquire as to her welfare. She did not tell Gehazi the purpose of her visit. In fact, she deceived him by saying that all was **well** with herself, her **husband**, and her **son**. She preferred to present her case directly to the prophet. The woman met Elisha with an emotional outburst and would have been dismissed by **Gehazi** if the prophet had not sensed her **deep distress** and permitted her to speak. **The Lord** had **not** revealed to Elisha the purpose of her visit, and neither did she. But she gave a hint when she said, **"Did I ask a son of my**

lord? Did I not say, 'Do not deceive me'?" In other words, "I do not want to be deceived by being given a son and then having him taken away from me." Perhaps Elisha surmised from this that the son was seriously ill.

4:29–31 At first the prophet sent **Gehazi** to **lay** his **staff on the** dead **child**, telling him to avoid the usual prolonged Eastern greetings en route. The woman sensed that this would not do and insisted that Elisha himself return with her. As they approached Shunem, **Gehazi** met them with the news that the lad had **not awakened**.

4:32–37 Elisha then went **into** the room where the body lay, closed **the door**, **prayed**, and **stretched himself out on the child—mouth** to **mouth**, **eyes** to **eyes**, and **hands** to **hands**. The prophet got up, **walked back and forth**, and then **stretched himself out on** the boy again. This time the lad **sneezed seven times and . . . opened his eyes**. The thankful mother received her son back to life again. In raising the child, Elisha fully identified with the dead youth: mouth to mouth, eye to eye, hand to hand. His staff had effected no change, but when he put himself on the boy and breathed his own life into him, the lad came alive.

4. *Detoxifying the Poisonous Stew (4:38–41)*

The next recorded miracle took place at **Gilgal**. During a time of **famine** (perhaps the seven-year famine mentioned in chap. 8), Elisha ordered **his servant** to cook some **stew for the sons of the prophets**. By mistake some poisonous **gourds** were put **into the pot**. When the mistake was detected, Elisha threw **some flour into the pot** and in this way made it safe to **eat**.

5. *Miraculous Provision of Bread (4:42–44)*

At another time Elisha fed **one hundred men** with **twenty** small, round, flat **loaves of barley bread** and some fresh ears of **grain**. There was enough and to spare, as the Lord had promised there would be. Elisha unselfishly gave to others what rightfully belonged to him. When we share with others and leave the consequences with God, He is able to meet our needs and the needs of others, and to even leave a surplus (Prov. 11:24, 25).

6. *Miraculous Cleansing of Naaman the Leper (5:1–19)*

5:1–4 Elisha's miracle-working power extended even to the army of the Syrians. A captive Jewish **girl** was a servant in the home of **Naaman**, the **commander of the** Syrian **army**. Knowing that **he was . . . a leper**, she suggested that the prophet Elisha **in Samaria** could **heal him**. This girl illustrates how a person of no importance in the eyes of the world, by being in a key place and showing loyalty to God, can influence the course of the history of salvation. D. L. Moody comments:

> A little maid said a few words that made a commotion in two kingdoms. God honored her faith by doing for Naaman, the idolater, what he had not done for any in Israel. See Luke 4:24. How often has the finger of childhood pointed grown-up persons in the right direction. The maid boasted of God that he would do for Naaman what he had not done for any in Israel; and God honored her faith.[5]

5:5–7 Naaman obtained **a letter** of introduction from Ben-Hadad, **king of Syria**, to Joram, **king of Israel**, and also took gifts of money and **clothing** with him. Apparently the letter did not mention Elisha but simply requested healing for **Naaman**. **The king of Israel** was infuriated by such an unreasonable request and suspected that the Syrian king was looking for an excuse to attack Israel.

5:8–12 **Elisha** received word of the king's predicament and asked for Naaman to be sent to him. There was no power in the palace, for they were all idolaters there; but there was **a prophet** of God **in Israel** who had power to cleanse a man and make him whole. Elisha didn't talk to Naaman personally; his word was enough if acted upon by faith. **Elisha sent** word to Naaman to **wash in the Jordan** River **seven times**. Naaman had expected some more dramatic and colorful mode of healing than this, and he protested **in a rage** that **the waters of** his native **Damascus** were superior to the Jordan.

5:13, 14 D. L. Moody analyzed the problem accurately:

> Naaman had two diseases—pride and leprosy. The first needed curing as much as the second. Naaman had to get down from his chariot of pride; afterwards, to wash according to the prescribed way.[6]

Finally **his servants** persuaded him to obey the prophet in such a simple matter, and he was thoroughly healed. As has been well said, "He swallowed his pride and lost his leprosy."

5:15–19 Naaman became a convert to the **God** of **Israel** and sought to reward Elisha, but the prophet would accept **nothing** from him. The Syrian general then obtained permission to take **two mule-loads of earth** back home with him so he could worship the true God on the displaced soil of Israel. He explained that his official duties might require him to go to the **temple of** the idol **Rimmon** with his **master** and even **bow down**, but he hoped that **the Lord** would **pardon** him for **this**. Elisha neither approved nor disapproved this, but simply sent him on his way.

In the story of Naaman we find a classic illustration of the gospel of grace. He was an *enemy* of God, being the captain of the Syrian army. Humanly speaking, his condition was *helpless* and *hopeless*, since he was a leper (cf. Rom. 5:6–10). Being a Gentile, he was a *stranger* to the promises and covenants of God and had no claim on His blessing (Eph. 2:11, 12). But God's grace reached out to touch human need. All Naaman had to do was to humble himself and obey the word of the Lord. He eventually washed himself in obedience to God's word and came up a new man, with new skin and a new heart.

> Marvelous grace of our loving Lord,
> Grace that exceeds our sin and our guilt,
> Yonder on Calvary's mount outpoured,
> There where the blood of the Lamb was spilt.
>
> —*Julia H. Johnston*

7. The Greed of Gehazi (5:20–27)

But Gehazi coveted the gifts from **Naaman** which Elisha had refused. He told the **Syrian** that Elisha had sent him to collect the gifts for **two young... prophets** who had just **come to** him **from the mountains of Ephraim**. Then he took the money and the garments to his own home. As a prophet, Elisha often received special revelations from the Lord. Now he was informed as to what his servant had done, and when Gehazi arrived, Elisha exposed him. He reminded the greedy servant that it was no **time to receive money and** garments or other things that could be bought with money. Gehazi was struck with **the leprosy of Naaman**. He had sinned greatly in giving the Syrians occasion to think that God's free gift of grace was not free at all.

8. Miraculous Recovery of an Axhead (6:1–7)

Some of **the sons of the prophets** were dissatisfied with the cramped quarters where they lived with **Elisha**, probably in Jericho or Gilgal. Therefore they gained the prophet's permission to move near **the Jordan** and build **a place** there. In the process of building, one of the men lost a borrowed **axhead** in the Jordan. Elisha responded to his distressed plea by casting **a stick** into the river. The **axhead** floated and was retrieved by the grateful builder.

9. Miraculous Military Maneuvers (6:8–23)

Another evidence of Elisha's miraculous powers concerned his knowledge of highly confidential military moves in the **camp** of the enemy. **The** Syrian **king** was nonplussed because all his secret plans repeatedly became known **to the king of Israel**; he suspected that one of his men was a spy for **Israel**. When he learned that the Prophet **Elisha** was revealing his plans to **the king of Israel**, he determined to capture Elisha at all costs. Hearing that **the prophet** was **in Dothan**, a city not far north of Samaria, he sent a band of marauders to surround **the city . . . by night**. In the morning Elisha's servant was terrified when he saw the enemy host surrounding the city. But in answer to the prophet's prayer, the servant was given miraculous power to **see** a protective host of **horses and chariots of fire** sent by God to guard His people.

Elisha asked **the LORD** to **strike** the Syrians **with blindness**. The prophet was then able to lead them from Dothan **to Samaria** without a struggle. **When the king of Israel** suggested killing them, Elisha reminded him that he **would** not **kill** the captives **whom** he had **taken . . . with . . . sword and bow**, so why kill these who were delivered into his hands without any effort on his part? Instead, the king was ordered to feed them and send them home. By this humane treatment he overcame evil with good. Such marauding **bands** conducted no more raids on **Israel**. Verse 16 reminds us of 1 John 4:4b—". . . He who is in you is greater than he who is in the world." In our spiritual battle with the forces of evil, we have protection and power given us by our omnipotent Ally. Through the prayer of faith the Lord can open the eyes of our hearts to the reassuring fact that He is defending us and frustrating Satan's destructive intentions.

10. The Famine in Samaria (6:24—7:20)

6:24–31 The incident beginning here is not necessarily in chronological order. **Ben-Hadad, king of Syria, besieged Samaria** so successfully that **famine** conditions prevailed **in** the city. (If this siege took place *after* the seven-year famine mentioned in 8:1–2, as some suggest, we can understand how serious the situation really was.) People had to pay exorbitant prices for ceremonially unclean foods (**a donkey's head**) and for herbs or grain. **"Dove droppings"**[7] was the name of a plant with an edible bulb. The plant bears the name "Star of Bethlehem" today. **The king of Israel** acknowledged that no one but **the LORD** could **help**, and he mourned greatly when he found cannibalism being practiced by the people. Blaming **Elisha** for the terrible conditions and for failing to do anything to relieve the situation, he vowed to kill him before the day was over.

6:32, 33 But Elisha received divine information about the king's intentions and told **the elders** that a **messenger** from **the king** was on the way, followed by the king himself. He ordered them to refuse entrance to **the messenger** until the king himself arrived. Almost immediately the messenger arrived, and then the king. He felt there was nothing to do but surrender to Syria. **Then the king said, "Surely this calamity is from the LORD; why should I wait for the LORD any longer?"** The incident reminds us that "The king's heart is in the hand of the LORD, like the rivers of water; He turns it wherever He wishes" (Prov. 21:1).

The king of Israel is not mentioned by name here; in fact, the name of the king is not given in any of the incidents recorded in chapters 4—8. Many commentators hold that Jehoram (Joram) was king during the siege, but it is impossible to be certain since Elisha's ministry, which stretched over half a century under four different kings, is not recorded in chronological order.

7:1, 2 Elisha then made a remarkable prediction to the king. He promised that the next day **fine flour and . . . barley** would **be sold** at very low prices **at the gate of Samaria**. When the king's skeptical aide questioned the likelihood of such incredible plenty, Elisha added that he would **see it with** his **eyes, but** would **not eat of it**. "If you would believe," writes Moody, "you must crucify the question, 'how?' "[8] (cf. our Lord's disciples before the feeding of the 4000 in Mark 8:4).

7:3–7 That evening **four leprous men** who sat **at the . . . gate** of Samaria decided in desperation to desert to the camp of **the Syrians** in hope of getting food. When they arrived, **the Syrian camp** was abandoned—**the LORD had caused the** enemy forces **to hear the noise** of a mighty onrushing army. Supposing it to be **Hittites** and Egyptian soldiers **hired** by **the king of Israel**, they retreated in pandemonium. Matthew Henry comments:

> The Syrians that besieged Dothan had their *sight* imposed upon, *ch.* vi.18. These had their *hearing* imposed upon. . . . Whether the noise was really made in the air by the ministry of angels, or whether it was only a sound in their ears, is not certain; which soever it was, it was from God.[9]

7:8–16 At first the **lepers** helped themselves liberally to food, money, and clothing. But realizing that the people would soon find out that the Syrians were gone and would punish them for their silence, they decided to notify the king. He immediately suspected **the Syrians** of laying an ambush for the Israelites. But a servant suggested sending a few **men** as scouts, reasoning that if they weren't killed by the Syrians, they would die of starvation anyway like the rest of Israel. The scouts found that **the Syrians** had actually fled, leaving a trail of abandoned spoil. So **the people** of Israel **plundered the tents of the Syrians**, and the famine was over.

7:17–20 In accordance with the prophecy of Elisha, **fine flour** and

barley . . . sold at very low prices that day. The king's **officer** who had doubted the prediction saw this, but he did not enjoy it because he was **trampled** to death by the jubilant throng at the city gate. Verses 18–20 reemphasize that the man died according to the word of the Lord because of his unbelief. Unbelief robs its victims of blessing and rewards them with death.

The memorable words of the lepers, **"We are not doing right. This day is a day of good news, and we remain silent"** (v. 9), are a constant challenge to those of us who are entrusted with the gospel of redeeming grace.

11. Restoration of the Shunammite's Property (8:1–6)

Before a seven-year **famine** came to **the land** (perhaps the famine of 4:38), **Elisha** warned **the** Shunammite **woman** (of chap. 4) to leave with her family, including the **son** whom **he had restored to life**. **She went** to **the land of the Philistines** and then **returned** when the famine had ended. At this time **Gehazi** was in the court of **the king** of Israel, a place that would ordinarily have been forbidden to a leper. Just **as he was** relating to **the king how** Elisha **had restored** a lad **to life, the woman** arrived to petition that her property be restored to her. **The king** ordered both the property and the produce which had grown on it during the seven years of her absence to be restored to her.

12. Elisha's Prophecy of Hazael's Reign (8:7–15)

8:7–12 When the ailing **Ben-Hadad, king of Syria**, heard that **Elisha** had **come . . . to Damascus**, he sent an officer, **Hazael**, with a large gift to **inquire** if he would **recover**. Since Naaman was captain of the Syrian army under Ben-Hadad, the king would have been aware of Elisha's healing power (chap. 5). Perhaps the prophet would heal him as well. The prophet's vague answer to **Hazael** was, **"Go, say to him, 'You shall certainly recover.' However the LORD has shown me that he will really die."** This meant that the illness itself was not necessarily fatal, but that Ben-Hadad would not recover from it because Hazael was going to murder him. Elisha gazed so intently on Hazael that the latter became **ashamed**. Elisha also foresaw that Hazael would inflict terrible loss and suffering on **the children of Israel**—so terrible that the thought of it caused him to weep.

8:13–15 **Hazael** answered that he was but **a dog**; how could he be expected to do such a **gross thing**? Williams paraphrases it:

> Can it be that I, who am only a dog, should mount the throne of Syria and accomplish such great deeds![10]

But **Elisha** had been told by **the LORD** that Hazael would be **king** of **Syria**. Following this announcement, Hazael returned to Ben-Hadad, told him that he **would . . . recover**, and then treacherously smothered him with **a thick cloth** soaked **in water**.

The following quotation succinctly tells how accurate Elisha's prophecy was:

> Soon after [the murder of Ben-Hadad], Hazael fought against the combined forces of Jehoram and Ahaziah at Ramoth-gilead (8:28, 29; 9:14, 15). He frequently defeated Jehu in battle, devastating all his country east of the Jordan from the Arnon in the south to Bashan in the north (10:32, 33). During the reign of Jehoahaz, Jehu's successor, he repeatedly encroached

upon the territory of Israel, which was kept from complete destruction only by God's mercy (13:3, 22, 23). Hazael also moved into southwest Palestine, taking Gath; he compelled the king of Judah to pay a heavy bribe for sparing Jerusalem (12:17, 18; 2 Chron. 24:23, 24). It was not until the death of Hazael that Israel was able to successfully check the aggression of Syria under Ben-Hadad III, the son of Hazael (2 Kgs. 13:24, 25).[11]

F. King Jehoram (Joram) of Judah (8:16–24)

Jehoram (Joram) **the son of Jehoshaphat** was **king of Judah** for **eight years** (853–841 B.C.; cf. 2 Chron. 21:4–20).

8:16, 17 The chronology in verse 16 needs to be reconciled with that in 1 Kings 22:42, 51; 2 Kings 3:1; and 2 Kings 8:25. One explanation is that **Jehoram** was coregent with his father, **Jehoshaphat**, for five years. Another is that Jehoshaphat shared part of his reign with Asa and that the reigns of Ahaziah and Jehoram are dated from the beginning of Jehoshaphat's sole regency.

8:18, 19 Jehoram had married Athaliah, a **daughter of Ahab** and Jezebel. This marriage had doubtless been engineered by his father, Jehoshaphat, as part of his policy of conciliation with Israel. The result of it, however, was to lead the kingdom of **Judah** farther into the idolatrous ways of the northern kingdom. Because of this apostasy, **the Lord** would have destroyed **Judah** had it not been for his promise to **David** (2 Sam. 7:12–16).

8:20–24 During Joram's reign, **Edom revolted against** him. To quell the rebellion, he marched with his army **to Zair** (Edom), south of the Dead Sea. **The Edomites . . . surrounded him**, forcing him to break through their lines to safety. His army **fled** home. From that time, **Edom** was not in complete subjection to Judah. It may have been during the reign of Jehoram that the prophet Obadiah spoke his oracle against Edom.

Mention is made that **Libnah**, near Philistia, also **revolted**, thus calling attention to the inherent weakness of the kingdom of Judah during the evil reign of **Joram**. **Libnah** was a Levitical city. The reason for her revolt is given in 2 Chronicles 21:10, 11. Judah evidently regained control of the city at a later time (19:8).

G. King Ahaziah of Judah (8:25–29)

Ahaziah the son of Jehoram was **king of Judah** for **one year** (841 B.C., cf. 2 Chron. 22:1–9).

8:25–27 Ahaziah is spoken of in verse 26 as the son of **Athaliah, the granddaughter of Omri. Ahaziah** is the same as Jehoahaz in 2 Chronicles 21 and is also called Azariah in 2 Chronicles 22:6. Ahaziah was a nephew of Joram, king of Israel. His mother, **Athaliah**, was the daughter of Ahab and the sister of *Israel's* Joram. The names get a bit confusing at this particular point in history! Ahab, king of Israel, had two sons who came to the throne successively, Ahaziah and Jehoram (Joram). Jehoshaphat, king of Judah, had a son named Jehoram who reigned after him. This **Jehoram** was followed on the throne by his **son . . . Ahaziah**. Thus Ahaziah and Jehoram ruled in Israel while **Jehoram** and **Ahaziah** ruled in Judah.

ISRAEL	*JUDAH*
Ahaziah	Jehoram
Jehoram	Ahaziah

Here **Ahaziah, . . . king of Judah**, is said to have been **twenty-two years** old when he **began to reign**; in 2 Chronicles 22:2 his age is given as forty-two years. Most evidence points to **twenty-two** as the correct age. The other figure is probably a copyist's error.

8:28, 29 **Ahaziah** joined his uncle **Joram**, king of Israel, in a **war against... Syria at Ramoth Gilead. King Joram** was wounded in battle and taken **to Jezreel... to recover. Ahaziah** visited him there while he was recovering. Joram's father, Ahab, lost his life at Ramoth Gilead (1 Kgs. 22). Ahaziah's grandfather, Jehoshaphat, had unwisely joined Ahab there and was almost killed as a result. But Ahaziah did not heed history's warning (about allying himself with Israel) and was later killed as a result (chap. 9).

H. King Jehu of Israel and Elisha's Ministry (Chaps. 9, 10)

1. *Jehu's Anointing (9:1–10)*

Elisha directed **one of the sons of the prophets** to **go to Ramoth Gilead** and secretly anoint **Jehu** as **king** of **Israel** to succeed Joram. **Jehu** was **the son of Jehoshaphat, the son of Nimshi** (v. 2), *not* the son of Jehoshaphat, king of Judah. **Jehu** was **commander** of Joram's **army** and had been stationed at **Ramoth Gilead** to hold back the Syrians. In anointing him, the prophet commissioned him to destroy **the house of Ahab**, in accordance with the prophecy of Elijah (1 Kgs. 21:21–24). Elijah had been told to anoint Jehu (1 Kgs. 19:16), but it appears that he passed this responsibility on to his successor, Elisha, who in turn sent an unknown prophet to Ramoth Gilead that the anointing might be carried out in secret. This secrecy gave **Jehu** the element of surprise, which he skillfully used in seizing the throne.

2. *Jehu's Executions (9:11—10:17)*

9:11–13 When Jehu emerged from the **inner room**, his fellow officers wanted to know what the **"madman of a prophet"** had said to him. Jehu first tried to evade the question by suggesting that they already knew. Perhaps he suspected that they had sent the prophet to anoint him in order to overthrow Joram. But at their insistence, he revealed that he had just been **anointed... king**. In haste, his men covered **the steps** with their garments and publicly proclaimed him as **king** of Israel.

Jehu the son of Jehoshaphat was king of Israel for twenty-eight years (841–814/13 B.C.; 2 Kgs. 9:14—10:36).

9:14–26 Jehu's reign began the fifth dynasty of the northern kingdom. Before news of his anointing could get to **Jezreel**, Jehu hurried there to kill **Joram. A watchman... saw** the approach of Jehu's **company** and notified Joram. Messengers were sent out twice to learn the identity of the approaching company, but **Jehu** prevented them from returning. By then the watchmen notified the king that the furious **driving** resembled that of **Jehu, the "son"** (grandson) **of Nimshi. Joram** then went forth in his royal **chariot**, accompanied by his nephew **Ahaziah, king of Judah**, supposing that there was important news about Ramoth Gilead. He greeted Jehu with **"Is it peace** (*shālôm*), **Jehu?"**, but received warlike words in reply. Sensing **treachery**, **Joram** tried to flee but was killed by Jehu's **arrow**. In literal fulfillment of Elijah's prophecy (1 Kgs. 21:19), his body was cast to the **ground** in Naboth's vineyard.

9:27–29 **Ahaziah** also tried to escape, but he too was hit by an arrow and died at **Megiddo**. By fraternizing with the house of Ahab, he fell under the divine curse that Jehu had been commissioned to carry out. His body was then returned **to Jerusalem** for burial. Second Chronicles 22:9 says that he died in Samaria, but this could refer to either the kingdom of Samaria or the region. Verse 29 is not in chronological order, being a repetition of 8:25. The discrepancy between the years mentioned (**eleventh** and twelfth) is probably due to different methods of reckoning.

9:30–37 When Jehu reached the city of **Jezreel** itself, **Jezebel** mocked him, shouting, **"Is it peace, Zimri, murderer of your master?" Zimri** too had become king of Israel by murdering his master, but he enjoyed anything but peace. His abortive *coup d'état* lasted only seven days (1 Kgs. 16:9–19). **Jezebel** was intimating to **Jehu** that he would not prosper in his rebellion. **Two eunuchs** in the palace proved their loyalty to Jehu by throwing Jezebel out the window. **Her blood spattered on the wall and on the horses**, and her body was eaten by the **dogs** of **Jezreel** in fulfillment of 1 Kings 21:23—all except **the skull and the feet and the palms of her hands**. Campbell Morgan remarks:

> The very dogs turned from the skull and hands and feet that had designed and executed such abominations; and no tomb but infamy perpetuates her memory.[12]

10:1–11 Jehu's next step was to slay **seventy** descendants (**"sons"**) of **Ahab** who were living **in Samaria**. He first gave their guardians an ultimatum—**choose the best qualified of** Ahab's descendants as kings **and fight** against Jehu and his men. But they remembered how **two kings** (Joram and Ahaziah) had been powerless against **Jehu** at Jezreel, so they **sent** back word that they would be obedient **servants**. He wrote back that they could demonstrate their loyalty to him by delivering **the heads of** Ahab's seventy male descendants to **Jezreel** the next day. They agreed to this. In the morning Jehu went out to see **the heads**, lying **in two heaps at the entrance of the gate**. Perhaps the assembled people expected him to be angry at this wholesale destruction, not knowing that he had ordered it. Quickly he set their minds at ease, saying in effect:

> You are innocent of this deed. I am innocent too. It is true that I killed my master, Joram, but who killed these? It must have been God, fulfilling what He predicted to His servant Elijah.

In further fulfillment of Elijah's prophecy, **Jehu** proceeded to kill **all** of Ahab's relatives, **great men, close acquaintances, and his priests** in Jezreel.

10:12–14 On the way to the capital, **Samaria, Jehu met . . . forty-two** of Ahaziah's relatives. **"Brothers"** (v. 13) means cousins, nephews, etc., since Ahaziah's brothers had been slain (2 Chron. 21:17). These people had come from Judah to visit the royal family of Israel. Realizing that they had ties with the house of Ahab, Jehu ordered them to be killed **at the well of Beth Eked**.

10:15–17 Jehu also **met Jehonadab** (also called Jonadab), a Rechabite. On the assurance that **Jehonadab** was loyal to him, Jehu invited him to **ride to Samaria** and witness his **zeal for the Lord**. Jeremiah 35 tells us a little more about Jehonadab. He ordered his descendants to return to the early lifestyle that Israel had known under Moses and Joshua, in an attempt to keep them from following the kingdom into apostasy, the national sin of Israel. Upon hearing of Jehu's purge, he went with the new king, who immediately welcomed him as a great ally in the fight against Baalism. **In Samaria, Jehu** slew all the remaining relatives of **Ahab**. Morgan warns:

> He [Jehu] was proud of his own zeal. How subtle the peril! And it is a peril. Wherever it exists it leads to other evil things. While this man was carrying out the judgments of God upon Israel, he was in his own life corrupt.[13]

3. *Jehu's Purge of the Baal-Worshipers (10:18–36)*

10:18–28 The new king's next assault was aimed at the worshipers **of Baal**. In order to identify them, he ordered **a great** holiday in honor of **Baal. The temple of Baal** was filled with **worshipers** from **all** parts of **Israel**, wearing special identifying **vestments**. Care was taken to see that no worshipers of Jehovah were present. **As soon as** Jehu had offered **the burnt offering**, he gave the signal for his **guard and . . . captains** to **kill** all the idolaters. **Eighty men** were stationed **outside** to prevent anyone from escaping. Jehu's men **went into the inner room of the temple of Baal**, removed the **sacred pillars** that were there, **and burned them. They tore down the temple of Baal**, converting it into a latrine or **refuse dump**.

10:29, 30 In many ways Jehu was one of the best, perhaps *the* best of the kings of Israel. He executed God's judgment on **the house of Ahab** and purged the land of Baal-worshipers. The Lord rewarded what was praiseworthy by promising that his dynasty would continue **to the fourth generation** (i.e., Jehoahaz, Joash, Jeroboam II, and Zechariah).

10:31–36 However, Jehu continued to promote the worship of **the golden calves**, which **Jeroboam** had inaugurated. Also, he is condemned in Hosea 1:4 for his extreme cruelty in exterminating the house of Ahab. As a result of his failures, **the LORD began to cut off parts of Israel. Hazael**, the king of Syria, captured the land east of **the Jordan** that had originally been occupied by the tribes of **Reuben** and **Gad** and the half-tribe of **Manasseh**. Elisha had foreseen the activity of **Hazael** (8:12). The Syrian king was carrying out the judgment of the Lord on the house of Israel even as Jehu had executed judgment on the house of Ahab. Behind the activities of these wicked kings the spiritual eye can see the sovereign hand of Jehovah making the wrath of man accomplish His purposes.

I. Queen Athaliah's Usurpation in Judah (Chap. 11)

Athaliah, the daughter of Ahab, was queen of Judah for six years (841–835 B.C.; 2 Chron. 22:10—23:21).

11:1 The scene now changes from Israel to Judah. **Athaliah** seized control when her son **Ahaziah** was slain by Jehu. To prevent any threat to her rule, **she** ordered the deaths of **all** (or so she thought)—**elthe sons** of Ahaziah. That **Athaliah** could cold-bloodedly order the execution of her own grandchildren shows just how much like her mother (Jezebel) she was. She was also unwittingly carrying out the curse pronounced on the descendants of Ahab, her father (1 Kgs. 21:21, 22).

11:2, 3 Jehosheba, the wife of Jehoiada (2 Chron. 22:11) and an aunt of **the** doomed **sons**, courageously entered the royal house **and stole** a lad named **Joash** (same as Jehoash) **from among the . . . sons who were being murdered. Athaliah** would have cut off the royal line, but the Lord preserved **Joash** because of the Davidic covenant. The long-range consequences of what she tried to do are staggering. This was a satanic attempt to break the royal Messianic line. Joash was hidden with **his nurse in the bedroom** of the unused temple. He remained there **for six years, while Athaliah reigned over the land**.

11:4–11 In the seventh year, Jehoiada the high **priest** called **the captains of hundreds—of the bodyguards and the escorts**, showed them the heir to the throne, and **made a covenant with them** to overthrow Athaliah and crown Joash as king. Williams comments:

> The steps taken by Jehoiada to bring about the royal revolution (vv. 4–11) may be thus paraphrased. He sent for the officers of the royal bodyguard. One regiment was ordered to surround the king's house, and the two remaining regiments to parade in front of the temple. Any person attempting to force his way through the troops was to be put to death. The guard relieved on that morning (v. 9) was not to return to barracks, but to fall in with the relieving guard and join the main body in defense of the king.[14]

11:12 Then Joash was **brought out** to the people. A **crown** was placed **on** his head and a copy of **the Testimony** (the law) was handed to him. The shout went up from the people, **"Long live the king!"**

11:13–16 When Athaliah was attracted by **the noise** to the court of **the temple** and saw what was going on, she cried, **"Treason! Treason!"** Because **Jehoiada** did not want **her** to **be killed in the** environs of the temple, he ordered that she be taken **outside** between ranks of soldiers and **killed** at **the horses' entrance**.

11:17–21 A covenant was then **made between the LORD, the** new **king, and the people, that they** would serve the Lord. In demonstration of this, the people sacked **the temple of Baal**, which Athaliah had promoted, **and killed Mattan the priest of Baal.** The king was escorted to the royal palace in a great precession. **The people of the land rejoiced, and the city was quiet** after **Athaliah** had been executed.

J. King Jehoash (Joash) of Judah (Chap. 12)

Jehoash (Joash), the son of Ahaziah, **king** of Judah, reigned for **forty years** (835–796 B.C.; cf. 2 Chron. 23:1—24:27).

12:1–5 John C. Whitcomb comments on the reign of Jehoash:

> The forty-year reign of Joash may be divided into two parts—before and after the death of his spiritual guardian, Jehoiada. The statement that "Joash did that which was right in the eyes of Jehovah *all the days of Jehoiada the priest*" is ominous. Without the moral and spiritual courage of this high priest, Joash was as unstable as Lot without Abram. Therefore, God showed His mercy to the people of Judah by extending Jehoiada's life to an amazing 130 years (2 Chron. 24:15)! Thus Jehoiada lived longer than anyone on record during the previous thousand years, since Amram, an ancestor of Moses, died at 137 (Ex. 6:20).[15]

In general, the reign of **Jehoash** was commendable. However, he failed to stop **the people** from worshiping at **the high places**. His major contribution was his undertaking to **repair . . . the temple**. To do this he issued instructions **to the priests** that certain funds should be laid aside for the purpose of restoring **the house of the**

Lord. According to Williams, these were: (1) the money of everyone who passed the account—that is, the **census** tax of Exodus 30:12; (2) the money that every man is set at—that is, the **assessment money** of Leviticus 27; (3) **all the money that a man** desired **to bring**—that is, the ordinary freewill offerings legislated for in Leviticus.[16]

12:6–16 When no repairs had been made **by the twenty-third year of** the reign of **King Jehoash**, the king **called Jehoiada . . . and the other priests** and announced a new plan for collecting the money and repairing the temple. The priests would no longer collect the funds directly, nor would they supervise the repairs on the temple (v. 7). Instead, **a chest** with **a hole in its lid** was to be placed at **the right side** of **the altar** to receive **money** for the restoration of the temple. **The king's scribe and the high priest** added up the funds and distributed them to **the workmen**. The overseers were honest, so it was not necessary to demand a public accounting of the funds. Verse 13 seems to contradict 2 Chronicles 24:14; however, verse 13 means that these funds were not used to purchase utensils for the temple while it was being restored, whereas 2 Chronicles 12:14 means that after the work on the temple was completed, the surplus funds were used for this purpose. In obedience to God's Word (Lev. 5:16; Num. 5:8, 9), **the money from the sin** and **trespass offerings** continued to be given **to the priests**.

12:17, 18 At this time **Hazael, king of Syria**, captured **Gath** and marched toward **Jerusalem**. **Jehoash** gave him **sacred things** from the temple and from the **king's house** to dissuade him from attacking the capital of Judah.

12:19–21 After the death of Jehoiada, the princes of Judah turned their king to idolatry. When Zechariah, a son (or grandson) of the high priest, tried to call the people back to the worship of Jehovah, King Jehoash ordered him to be stoned to death (2 Chron. 24).

Jehoash's own **servants** conspired against him **and killed** him **in the house of Millo**. This was God's judgment on him for the murder of Zechariah.

Jesus referred to the death of Zechariah when He reproved the lawyers (Luke 11:51). He said that the blood of all the prophets, from the blood of Abel to that of Zechariah, would be required of that generation. Thus He included the blood of all martyrs in the OT period, from that of Abel in Genesis to that of Zechariah here and in 2 Chronicles, the last book of the Hebrew Bible. (The Hebrew Bible contains the same books as our OT but in a different order.)

Jehoiada was a godly man who devoted himself to the service of the kingdom and the temple. He received two blessings in return: His son Zechariah followed in his steps, and he was buried with the kings of Judah, a great honor indeed for one born outside the royal family. Joash, on the other hand, got progressively worse after the death of Jehoiada. He plundered the temple he had once repaired and robbed the royal treasury to buy off the Syrians. He was not buried in the tomb of the kings because he died under divine judgment for the murder of Zechariah. It is vital that we persevere in godliness lest we hinder the kingdom of God. Jehoiada, a shining example! Joash, a solemn warning!

K. King Jehoahaz of Israel (13:1–9)

Jehoahaz the son of Jehu was **king** of **Israel** for **seventeen years** (814/13–798 B.C.).

Jehoahaz followed **Jeroboam** in the mixed worship of Jehovah and the Asherah (v. 6). God punished him by sending the Syrians against **Israel**. They reduced Jehoahaz's forces to **only fifty horsemen, ten chariots, and ten thousand foot soldiers**. When **Jehoahaz pleaded with the LORD**, He raised up **a deliverer** who rescued Israel **from . . . the hand of the Syrians**. The deliverer might have been Adad-nirari III, king of Assyria, who late in the reign of Jehoahaz caused more and more trouble for Syria, leaving her little time to bother Israel. Some commentators suggest that Elisha was the deliverer. Others say that verse 5 refers to either Jehoash (v. 25) or Jeroboam II (14:26, 27). Verse 23 explains why God answered Jehoahaz's prayer: It was because of His covenant with Abraham, Isaac, and Jacob.

Notice that verses 5 and 6 are a parenthesis. The parenthesis is one of grace. Before another century passed, Israel would be swept off the promised land because of her persistence in the sins of Jeroboam. By providing **a deliverer** for the nation, the Lord was seeking to turn her from her destructive course before the final stroke of judgment fell. However, **they did not depart from the sins of the house of Jeroboam . . . but walked in them.**

L. King Jehoash (Joash) of Israel (13:10–13)

Jehoash (Joash) the son of Jehoahaz was **king** of **Israel** for **sixteen years** (798–782/81 B.C.; 2 Kgs. 13:10—14:16).

13:10–13 This King **Jehoash** is to be differentiated from the king of Judah with the same name who was reigning at this time. The reign of this Jehoash was wicked, patterned after that of **Jeroboam the son of Nebat**. These verses give a condensed account of his reign: **He became king; he did evil in the sight of the LORD;** he **rested with his fathers**. His dealings with Amaziah of Judah are recorded in 14:8–16.

M. The Close of Elisha's Ministry (13:14–25)

13:14–19 Verses 14–25 tell of the prophecy and death of **Elisha**, which took place during the rule of Jehoash. When the prophet Elisha was dying, **Joash** (Jehoash) visited him **and wept over** him, saying, **"O my father, my father, the chariots of Israel and their horsemen!"** He meant that men of Elisha's caliber were the truest and best defense of the people of Israel. Elisha had used the same words to lament the passing of Elijah (2:12). He realized that the death of the prophet would be a great loss to the kingdom. From his sickbed, **Elisha** directed Joash to **take a bow and some arrows**, to **shoot** one arrow eastward, and then to **strike the ground** with **the arrows**. The arrow that shot eastward signified victory over the Syrians, who had occupied Israel's land east of the Jordan. Because Joash had **struck** the ground only **three times**, he would strike down **Syria . . . only three times**. If he had **struck five or six times**, the threat of **Syria** would have been eliminated. But he lacked perseverance and endurance. Victory over enemies depends on the measure of obedience. Joash must have known the significance of what he was doing, or else he would not have been held responsible. Elisha's death spelled no good for the northern kingdom.

13:20, 21 In the spring of each **year**, marauding **bands** of Moabites **invaded the land**. One day as some men of Israel were taking out a corpse to be buried, they saw one of these marauding bands approaching. Hurriedly they opened **the tomb of Elisha** and threw the corpse in. As soon as **the man . . . touched the bones of Elisha, he revived and stood on his feet**.

13:22–25 Scripture tells us nothing of the last forty-five years of Elisha's ministry, from the anointing of Jehu, in 841 B.C. (chap. 9), until his death in about 795 B.C. His final prophecy (from his deathbed) was one of victory (v. 17). His final miracle (accomplished long after his death—v. 21) was a validation of his message and ministry to Israel and her king. In fulfillment of Elisha's prophecy, **Jehoash . . . recaptured . . . the cities which . . . Hazael . . . had taken** from **Israel**. This was accomplished by **three** successive victories.

N. King Amaziah of Judah (14:1–20)

Amaziah the son of Joash was **king of Judah** for **twenty-nine years** (796–767 B.C.; 2 Chron. 25).

14:1–7 Amaziah's reign, though good, lacked the excellence of David's reign. It was more like his father's (**Joash**) in that both failed to abolish **the high places**. One of Amaziah's first acts was to kill the conspirators **who had murdered his father** (12:20, 21). However, he spared **the children of** these men, in obedience to Deuteronomy 24:16. Also, he led a brilliant campaign against Edom, killing **ten thousand** of its inhabitants and capturing the rock city of **Selah** (probably the same as Petra). Unfortunately, he brought back Edomite gods and began to worship them (2 Chron. 25:14).

14:8–14 Inflated with pride, **Amaziah** foolishly invited **Jehoash, king of Israel**, to a show of strength. **Jehoash** answered by a parable in which **the thistle** (Judah) said **to the cedar** (Israel), **"Give your daughter to my son as wife"** (a weed making an impertinent request to a mighty tree). **A wild beast** (the army of Israel) **trampled** down **the thistle** (Judah). Amaziah should be satisfied with his victory over **Edom** and not invite disaster by antagonizing Israel. When **Amaziah** refused to listen, **Jehoash** marched against **Judah, broke down the wall of Jerusalem**, and carried away some of its treasures.

14:15–20 The antagonism between Judah and Israel which began at this time continued until the fall of Israel in 722 B.C. **Amaziah . . . fled to Lachish** to escape **a conspiracy but** he was followed **and** slain **there**.

O. King Azariah (Uzziah) of Judah (14:21, 22)

Azariah (same as Uzziah) **the son of Amaziah** was king of Judah for **fifty-two years** (792/91–740/39 B.C.; cf. 15:1–7; 2 Chron. 26).

The ministry of Isaiah, Amos, and Hosea began at this time in OT history (Isa. 1:1; Hos. 1:1; Amos 1:1). The books of Amos and Hosea reveal the social and religious conditions prevalent in Israel. Through these prophets the Lord constantly warned of coming disaster while trying to woo His people back from the precipice of judgment.

Azariah was coregent with his father for the first twenty-four years. **He built Elath**, at the north of the Gulf of Aqaba. A fuller record of his reign is given in chapter 15 and in 2 Chronicles 26.

P. King Jeroboam II of Israel (14:23–29)

Jeroboam II the **son of Jehoash** was **king** of **Israel** for **forty-one years** (793/92–753 B.C.).

The first twelve years of Jeroboam's reign overlapped with that of his father, **Joash** (Jehoash). As to his religious policy, this king followed the idolatry of his namesake, **Jeroboam the son of Nebat**. Politically, he recovered for **Israel** the land **from the entrance of Hamath** (Galilee) **to the Sea of the Arabah** (Transjordan), as **Jonah** had prophesied. This particular prophecy is not recorded in the Bible. (Verse 25 pinpoints the time of Jonah's ministry, which is important in studying the book bearing his name. It is startling to realize that the Assyrians carried Israel into captivity only forty to seventy years after the repentance of Nineveh occasioned by Jonah's preaching!) **Jeroboam** II may be the deliverer mentioned in 13:5 (cf. 14:26, 27). Verses 26 and 27 give deep insight into the tender love and patience of **the Lord**. Verse 27 must be understood in context; **Israel**, and later Judah, were subsequently blotted out for a time, but, according to God's promise to the Jewish fathers, the nation will be regathered and replanted in the land.

Q. King Azariah (Uzziah) of Judah, Cont'd (15:1–7)

In general **Azariah** was a good **king**. Part of his failure was his permitting **the high places** to continue in **Judah**. When he insisted on intruding into the priest's office by offering incense in the temple, despite the protests of the priests, he was **struck** with leprosy and had to dwell **in an isolated house** to **the day of his death** (cf. 2 Chron. 26:16–21).

The ministry of Amos ended at this period.

R. King Zechariah of Israel (15:8–12)

Zechariah the son of Jeroboam II reigned over Israel for **six months** (753–752 B.C.).

Like his predecessors, **Zechariah** walked in the steps of **Jeroboam** I, worshiping the golden calves at Dan and Bethel. After a brief reign of **six months**, he was assassinated by **Shallum**. The RSV, following the LXX, says he was killed at Ibleam, a town in the Jezreel Valley close to where Ahaziah had been killed by Jehu (9:27). His death marked the end of the **Jehu** dynasty, **Zechariah** being **the fourth generation** which God had promised Jehu would **sit on the throne of Israel** (v. 12; cf. 10:30).

S. King Shallum of Israel (15:13–15)

Shallum the **son of Jabesh** was **king** of **Israel** for **one month** (752 B.C.).

Little is recorded about this king. His was the only reign in the sixth dynasty of the ten tribes. **Shallum** had gained the throne by assassination and now lost it the same way one **month** later. He was assassinated by **Menahem**.

T. King Menahem of Israel (15:16–22)

Menahem the son of Gadi was **king** of **Israel** for **ten years** (752–742/41 B.C.).

Menahem proceeded to sack **Tiphsah**—not the city of Tiphsah on the Euphrates but the one near **Tirzah**. When the city refused to **surrender,** he cruelly massacred the people, including the pregnant **women**.

At this time the Syrian kingdom had declined, and Assyria had become Israel's chief enemy. During the reign of Menahem, **Pul**, the **king of Assyria**, invaded **Israel**. **Menahem gave** him **a thousand talents of silver** to appease him and to enlist Pul's support in confirming Menahem's uncertain power. The king of Israel raised this money by taxing all the wealthy men **fifty shekels of silver** apiece

(v. 20). The price of a slave in Assyria at this time was **fifty shekels of silver**. Menahem was voluntarily submitting to the yoke of Assyria because he felt it was to his personal advantage to do so. **Pul** is generally considered to be the same as Tiglath-Pileser III (v. 29).

U. King Pekahiah of Israel (15:23–26)

Pekahiah the son of Menahem was **king** of **Israel** for **two years** (742/41–740/39 B.C.).

All that we know of this king is that his reign was brief and **evil** and that he was slain by **Pekah** and **fifty** Gileadites **in Samaria**. His reign ended the seventh dynasty of Israel. He was the only one of Israel's latter kings who did not take the crown by force, but it wasn't long before it was forcibly taken from him by one of his officials.

V. King Pekah of Israel (15:27–31)

Pekah the **son of Remaliah** was **king** of **Israel** for **twenty years** (752–732/31 B.C.).

Pekah was captain to Pekahiah, whom he killed. From other Scriptures we learn that he invaded Judah and then enlisted Syrian aid against Judah. But Ahaz, king of Judah, called Assyria to aid him. The king of Assyria first killed Rezin, king of Syria, and then attacked Israel. He conquered the two and a half tribes east of the Jordan and the territory of Galilee, carrying the inhabitants into captivity. This was the first phase of the Assyrian captivity. Pekah's power as captain overlapped with Menahem's (ten years) and Pekahiah's (two years). Supported by Assyria, **Hoshea** seized the throne of Israel by conspiring **against Pekah** and killing him. This ended Israel's eighth dynasty.

W. King Jotham of Judah (15:32–38)

Jotham the **son of Uzziah** was **king** of **Judah** for a total of twenty **years**, including four years of co-regency with Uzziah (750–732/31 B.C.; cf. 2 Chron. 27).

The first part of Jotham's reign was spent in a coregency with his father Uzziah, the last part with Ahaz. His official reign lasted **sixteen years**. **Jotham** was one of the better kings of Judah, even though he did not abolish **the high places. He built the Upper Gate of the house of the Lord** and sponsored other construction projects in the land. Just before his death, **Rezin** and **Pekah** began their joint attack **against Judah**. The prophet Micah began his ministry during the reign of Jotham.

Second Chronicles 27:6 includes the following editorial comment praising Jotham: "So Jotham became mighty, because he prepared his ways before the Lord his God." This is in stark contrast to the kings of Israel, who ordered their ways after Jeroboam.

Josephus also makes mention of Jotham's godliness.[17]

X. King Ahaz of Judah (Chap. 16)

Ahaz the son of Jotham was **king** of **Judah** for twenty **years** (735–716/15 B.C.; cf. 2 Chron. 28).

16:1–4 Ahaz was coregent with his father for perhaps twelve years. The name Ahaz is a contraction for Jehoahaz. It is by the latter name that the king is known on Assyrian inscriptions. The prefix "Jeho-" stands for Jehovah, and doubtless the Holy Spirit omitted it purposely because Ahaz was an apostate. He followed **the kings of Israel** in his idolatry, even making **his son pass through the fire**. In the worship of Molech, it is believed that children were passed between the red-hot arms of the brass idol, signifying cleansing from evil and dedication to the god. Sometimes the children were actually killed and burned (Jer. 7:31; Ezek. 16:21).

16:5–9 In order to force Judah to join them against Assyria, and to install a vassal king on the throne of Judah (Isa. 7:6), **Syria** and **Israel** united to attack **Jerusalem**. At the same time **Syria captured Elath** and planted a colony of Syrians there. In his distress, **Ahaz** sent a call for help to **Assyria**, accompanying it with **silver and gold** treasures from the temple and the palace. **Tiglath-Pileser** complied by capturing **Damascus** and killing the king of Syria. This was in fulfillment of the prophecy of Isaiah. But God would make the Assyrians a curse to Judah (Isa. 7:17–25).

16:10–16 On a trip **to Damascus to** visit **Tiglath-Pileser, Ahaz . . . saw** a heathen **altar** and decided to build one like it in Jerusalem. So he sent a model of it **to Urijah the priest**, and **Urijah** in turn had the **altar . . . built . . . before King Ahaz** returned. **Ahaz** offered various **offerings on** his new altar (all but sin and trespass-offerings) and then **commanded Urijah** to use it henceforth instead of **the bronze altar**. The last clause in verse 15 seems to suggest that Ahaz would use the **bronze altar** for divination. However, it may also be understood to mean, "As for the bronze altar, it will be for me to enquire (or consider) what I shall do with it."[18] **Urijah the priest** sinfully obeyed **King Ahaz** in his sacrilege instead of fearlessly rebuking him. Uriah (the same as Urijah) is mentioned favorably in Isaiah 8:2, but this was before the attack on Jerusalem. His wicked acquiescence to the demand of Ahaz to build the altar took place at a later date.

16:17–20 Ahaz . . . removed certain furnishings from **the temple** area, perhaps for fear that the king of Assyria might take them if he ever captured Jerusalem. Some think he used them to pay tribute. Second Chronicles 28:24 tells how Ahaz closed the temple entirely toward the end of his reign. Like other apostate kings before him, Ahaz was not buried in the royal tombs (2 Chron. 28:27) but **was buried with his fathers in the City of David.**

Y. King Hoshea of Israel (17:1–6)

Hoshea the son of Elah was **king** of **Israel** for **nine years** (732/31–723/22 B.C.).

17:1, 2 We come now to the final king and the ninth and final dynasty of Israel. **Hoshea** killed Pekah (cf. 15:30), perhaps because of his inability to resist Assyria's inroads into Israel, and took the reins of government. He was not as wicked as his predecessors, but the nation had gone too far—his improvements were too late.

17:3–6 Shalmaneser, king of Assyria, marched **against** Samaria and made **Hoshea** pay **tribute**. Hoshea conspired with the **king of Egypt** against **Assyria** and reneged on his payment of **tribute**. Therefore **the king of Assyria** (either Shalmaneser or Sargon, his successor) imprisoned Hoshea, **besieged . . . Samaria . . . for three years, and carried** some of the people into captivity. We are not told Hoshea's fate; he simply disappears into an Assyrian **prison**, leaving Samaria without a king during her last days. The final fall of Israel took place in 723 or 722 B.C.

Z. The Fall of the Northern Kingdom (17:7–41)

17:7–23 These verses explain the underlying reasons why **God** was displeased with Israel and allowed the nation to be conquered and exiled. **They had feared other gods, walked in the** customs **of the nations, built for themselves high places, sacred pillars**, and **wooden images** (Asherim) everywhere, and multiplied their idolatry. They refused to listen to **His prophets** but **stiffened their necks** and refused to **believe** the word of **the LORD their God**. They turned their backs on God's **commandments** and adopted the man-made religion of their neighbors. They were zealous in their pursuit of **evil**, offering **their sons and daughters** to false gods.

17:24, 25 The king of Assyria carried the ten northern tribes of Israel away to Mesopotamia and Media. Also, he **brought people from** five other nations which he had conquered and **placed them in the** land of Israel. Earlier, when Israel obeyed the Lord, He drove out the heathen nations and settled His people in Canaan by the hand of Joshua. When they stopped listening to Jehovah, He drove them out and brought the nations back in by the hand of the king of Assyria. These pagan people worshiped their own heathen deities and thus brought themselves under God's displeasure, especially since they were now living in Immanuel's land. The Lord's anger was revealed when He **sent lions among them** which roamed through the land, killing **some of** the people.

17:26–28 Someone notified **the king of Assyria** that the plague of **lions** was caused by the presence of these foreigners who did **not know** the law of **the God of** Israel. **The king of Assyria** then ordered an Israelite **priest** to be returned from captivity for the purpose of instructing the heathen colonists how they should fear the Lord. The priest who returned was likely one of the idolatrous priests of Israel, not a true priest of Jehovah. He went to Bethel, the seat of calf-worship (although the calf was no longer there), and taught the new inhabitants the polluted religion of Jeroboam, which included, but was in no way limited to, the worship of Jehovah. These foreign colonists intermarried with the Israelites in the land, and this produced the people known as Samaritans—a mixed ethnic group with its own religion and customs.

17:29–34a These verses seem to describe the foreign settlers in the land. Each nationality had **its own . . . gods** and **appointed . . . priests** from among its own people. They also adopted the worship of Jehovah, and the result was a mixed religion, which was worse than out-and-out paganism.[19]

17:34b–40 The section from verse 34b ("**they do not fear the LORD . . .**") through verse 40 seems to describe the Israelites who remained in the land. They did not heed the repeated warnings of the Lord against idolatry but continued to worship the golden calves.

17:41 This refers back to the foreign settlers in the land. They appeared to be less guilty than Israel. With what little light they had, they **feared the LORD** after a fashion; but the ten tribes, with all the light they had, did **not fear the LORD** (v. 34b).

As far as we know the ten tribes never returned to the land.[20] They are scattered throughout the world. Perhaps they include the black Falasha Jews of Ethiopia, the Chinese Jews of Kaifeng-Fu, and the Cochin Jews of India. Their identity is not hidden from God; He will bring them back to Israel in a coming day.

The prophet Hosea's ministry probably ended at this time—that is, with the fall of Samaria and the captivity of Israel.

II. THE KINGDOM OF JUDAH TO THE CAPTIVITY (Chaps. 18—25)

A. King Hezekiah (Chaps. 18—20)

Hezekiah the son of Ahaz was **king** of **Judah** for **twenty-nine years** (716/15–687/86 B.C.; cf. 2 Chron. 29—32; Isa. 36—39). He is believed to have had a co-regency with Ahaz before that from 729/28 to 716/15.

1. Hezekiah's Righteous Reign (18:1–8)

18:1–6 More space is devoted to **Hezekiah** in Holy Scripture than to almost any king since the time of Solomon. The parallel accounts in 2 Chronicles 29—32 and Isaiah 36—39 should be read to better understand the spiritual and political victories that Hezekiah gained through his faith in God.

When **Hezekiah** came to power, Judah was virtually a vassal state under Assyria. His reign was one of great reform. He conducted a campaign against all forms of idolatry, destroying even **the high places** and the **bronze serpent** of Numbers 21 (because the **children of Israel burned incense to it**). He **called it Nehushtan**, meaning literally *"a bronze thing"* (NKJV marg.). As far as his trust **in the Lord God** was concerned, Hezekiah was the greatest of **the kings of Judah**. Josiah was the greatest of the kings as far as thoroughness in expelling evildoers from the land was concerned (23:24, 25).

18:7, 8 Eventually Hezekiah **rebelled against** the Assyrian yoke, perhaps because of his military success in driving **the Philistines** out of the land **from watchtower** (country places) **to fortified city** (thickly inhabited and well-defended places).

2. The Capture of Samaria (18:9–12)

This paragraph reviews the capture of **Samaria** by the Assyrians, and is perhaps introduced here to emphasize the seriousness of the threat which faced **Hezekiah** at this time. The seeming contradiction between the dates in verses 9 and 10 is explained by the fact that in Jewish reckoning a part of a year is counted as a year. The siege of **Samaria** began during the latter part of **the fourth year of** Hezekiah's reign, continued during the fifth year, and ended in the first part of **the sixth year**—therefore **"three years."** This would have been 725–722 B.C., during the co-regency mentioned above.

3. Sennacherib's First Invasion of Judah (18:13–16)

Assyria had been having troubles of her own at this time; Sargon II had died and Babylon was in rebellion. It wasn't until 701 B.C. that **Sennacherib,** Sargon's successor, was able to march on Palestine and Phoenicia. In his annals Sennacherib claimed to have taken forty-six **fortified cities** and 200,000 captives from **Judah**. **Hezekiah . . . sent** a servile message to him acknowledging that he had been **wrong** in rebelling. He abjectly paid **three hundred talents of silver and thirty talents of gold** (a huge sum) to prevent an attack on Jerusalem. At the time, **Sennacherib** was in **Lachish,** southwest of Jerusalem, on the way to Egypt.

4. Sennacherib's Second Invasion of Judah (18:17—19:34)

18:17–19 Hezekiah then began to fortify Jerusalem (2 Chron. 32:5). Perhaps it was news of this that caused **the king of Assyria** at a later date to dispatch his army officials to Jerusalem, demanding unconditional surrender. Three Jewish officials went **out to** meet the Assyrian emissaries and to hear their demands. The NIV renders the terms as "supreme commander," "chief officer," and "field commander." The NKJV labels these officials by their original military titles: **the Tartan, the Rabsaris, and the Rabshakeh**. These terms are not proper names.[21]

18:20–25 The Rabshakeh spoke insultingly **to them . . . in** their own **Hebrew** (lit. "Judean") tongue. First, he mocked Hezekiah's **trust** in the fortifications of Jerusalem. Then he revealed his knowledge that **Hezekiah** had sought the help **of Egypt** against Assyria, and ridiculed **Egypt** as a **broken reed** (v. 21). Third, he said that **Judah** could not **trust in the LORD** because **Hezekiah** had destroyed all the **high places and . . . altars. Rabshakeh** did not realize that these were *heathen* shrines and not places where the Lord was worshiped! Next he suggested a bet—he would **give . . . two thousand horses** to Judah if Hezekiah could find that number of horsemen. Judah did not have that many cavalrymen, he taunted, and so had to depend on **Egypt for chariots and horsemen**. Finally, **the Rabshakeh** claimed that **the LORD** had sent Assyria to **destroy** Judah.

18:26, 27 The Jewish officials quickly suggested **to the Rabshakeh** that all further discussions be carried on **in Aramaic**, the language of diplomacy, rather than **in Hebrew**. They were secretly fearful that such arrogant talk might be destructive to the morale of **the** Jewish **people** listening **on the wall**. But the Rabshakeh countered that he wanted the people to hear and understand their coming starvation and doom.

18:28–37 Addressing the people directly, **the Rabshakeh** warned them **not** to **let Hezekiah deceive** them into trusting **in the LORD** for deliverance. If they would surrender, they would be granted the privilege of living in Jerusalem temporarily. Then when **the king of Assyria** returned from the Egyptian campaign, he would **take** them to Assyria, **"a land like your own."** No other tribal deities had been able to deliver nations **from . . . Assyria**; how could they expect their God to do it? **The people** on the wall remained silent while the three Jewish officials returned **to Hezekiah**, thoroughly disheartened.

19:1–7 Hezekiah was greatly distressed when he heard of the Rabshakeh's taunt. **He sent** messengers **to Isaiah the prophet**, saying that Judah was powerless when it needed strength the most. Further, he asked Isaiah to pray **for the remnant** of Judah and Jerusalem. **Isaiah** sent word back to Hezekiah that he didn't need to fear **the** Assyrian **king**, that God would put **a spirit** of fear **upon him** and cause him to **hear a rumor and** to **return to his own land**, where he would be slain.

19:8–13 When the **Rabshakeh returned to** Lachish, he **found** that Sennacherib had transferred his assault to the neighboring fortress of **Libnah**.

Sennacherib **heard** that **Tirhakah, king of Ethiopia** in upper (i.e., southern) Egypt, was advancing to attack him. He immediately tried to frighten Jerusalem into quick surrender by sending a blasphemous letter. Some scholars think that the rumor mentioned in verse 7 is explained in verse 9—namely, the rumor of the approach of the Egyptians. Others say that it was a report that the Babylonians were rebelling.

19:14–20 **Hezekiah** wisely took **the letter . . . to the** temple and **spread it before the LORD**. His prayer was a revelation of his deep trust in Jehovah. In reply, God sent **Hezekiah** a twofold answer by way of **Isaiah**.

19:21–28 Verses 21–28 are addressed to Sennacherib. Verses 29–34 are addressed to Hezekiah. The prophecy of **Isaiah** is a taunt song **against . . . Assyria**. It pictures Jerusalem, **the virgin daughter of Zion**, as laughing at Assyria's threats. It denounces Sennacherib for blaspheming God's holy name, and for boasting that he would invade Judah (**Lebanon**), destroy her rulers and great men (**tall cedars and cypress trees**), and enter the palaces of **Mount Zion** (lodging place and **forest**). Sennacherib also boasted of other foreign conquests, including his victory over Egypt. What he didn't realize was that all he had done was what God had already determined to be done. God knew him inside and out and would break his towering arrogance, sending back to Assyria the remnants of his shattered army.

19:29–34 Then, turning to Hezekiah,the Lord gave **a sign** that the Assyrian would not conquer Jerusalem. For two years the people of Judah would not be able to raise normal crops because of the Assyrian presence, but would **eat** things that grew without cultivation. Then, **in the third year**, they would be safe enough from the threat of assault that they could carry on their normal activities. Not only would the people of Jerusalem survive, but **the king of Assyria** would not even be allowed to **come into** the **city** or to **shoot an arrow there**.

5. Sennacherib's Defeat and Death (19:35–37)

That **night . . . the angel of the Lord**[22] visited the encampment of Assyria **and killed one hundred and eighty-five thousand** soldiers. **When** men **arose early in the morning, the Assyrians** were **corpses**.

Sennacherib returned to his capital, **Nineveh**, where he was slain twenty years later (681 B.C.). (He actually outlived Hezekiah by five years.) Isaiah's prophecy (v. 7) was fulfilled when **two** of Sennacherib's own **sons** murdered him and a third, **Esarhaddon, reigned in his place**.

6. Hezekiah's Sickness and Recovery (20:1–11)

20:1–7 The events of chapter 20 are generally believed to have taken place earlier, probably in the early part of chapter 18, during the first invasion of Sennacherib (see v. 6). When **Hezekiah was** taken seriously ill, **Isaiah** told him to **set** his **house in order** because death was imminent. The king **prayed** earnestly for recovery and was granted **fifteen** additional **years** of life. Whitcomb comments:

> What would I do with the remainder of my life if God told me that I had

Hezekiah's Tunnel was dug through solid rock from the Pool of Siloam to Jerusalem in order to insure a supply of water for the city in case of an Assyrian attack.

just 15 years to live? What did Hezekiah do with those years? The Bible does not say, for the last event recorded of his reign was the destruction of Sennacherib's army, in 701 B.C. (which probably occurred less than a year after his sickness). It has been suggested that one reason why God prolonged his life was that he had no male heir to the throne (2 Kings 21:1 states that Manasseh was only twelve when he began to reign). However, it is probable that Manasseh was a coregent with his father for nearly ten years, because otherwise it would be impossible to fit the 55 years of his reign into this period of Judah's history, working back from the fixed dates of the Babylonian Captivity.[23]

20:8–11 As a **sign** that Hezekiah would be healed and would return to the temple to worship, God caused **the shadow . . . on the sundial** (or steps, NASB) **of Ahaz** to go back **ten degrees**. (Chronologically, verse 7 follows verses 8–11.)

From 2 Chronicles 32:31 we conclude that it was a supernatural event, the news of which reached as far as Babylon. The Babylonians worshiped the heavenly bodies and they would certainly notice any irregularities. Word spread quickly that it was on Hezekiah's behalf that this great miracle had taken place.

7. Hezekiah's Foolish Pride (20:12–21)

20:12–18 The **king of Babylon, Berodach-Baladan**, sent congratulations **to Hezekiah** on his recovery. Doubtless his real purpose was to strengthen his ties with Judah against Assyria. **Hezekiah** foolishly **showed** the messengers from Babylon **all . . . his treasures**. (From 2 Chron. 32:31 we learn that God was testing him through this situation to know what was in his heart. The answer: PRIDE!) **Isaiah** rebuked him for this and prophesied that Judah would be taken into captivity by **Babylon** and that **some** of Hezekiah's own **sons** would **be eunuchs** (officials, NASB) **in the palace of the** Babylonian **king**. Before these treasures ended up in Babylon,

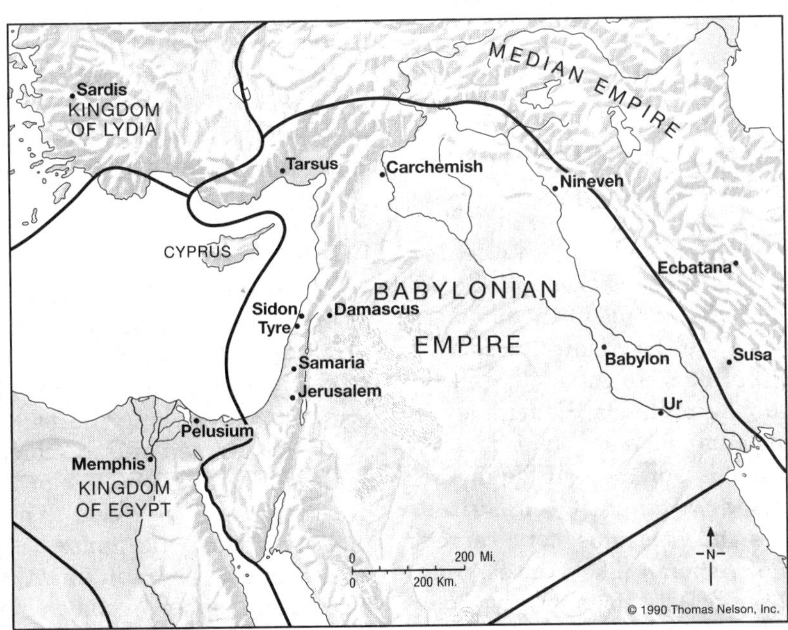

The Babylonian Empire, c. 560 B.C.

many of them would first go to Assyria as part of the tribute that Hezekiah paid to Sennacherib when the Assyrians invaded Palestine shortly after Hezekiah's recovery (18:13–16).

20:19 Hezekiah submitted to God's decree and acknowledged its leniency. "For he said, 'Why not, if there will be peace and security in my days?' " (RSV).

20:20, 21 Hezekiah built **a pool and a tunnel** by which **water** could be **brought . . . into** Jerusalem from a well outside the city. Such a hidden source would be especially valuable in a time of siege. It is still possible to wade through Hezekiah's tunnel from the Spring of Gihon to the Pool of Siloam.

In 1880 an inscription made by Hezekiah's workers in the ancient prong-shaped Semitic script was found. It was removed to a museum in Turkey, which was then ruling Palestine as part of the old Ottoman Empire.[24]

The ministry of Micah ended at this time.

B. King Manasseh (21:1–18)

Manasseh the son of Hezekiah was **king** of **Judah** for **fifty-five years** (697/96–643/42 B.C.; cf. 2 Chron. 33:1–20).

21:1–9 Manasseh's reign was the longest and most wicked of all the kings of Judah. Some of the blots on his record are: He reintroduced the worship of **Baal**, of Asherah, and of the stars; he profaned the temple by building **altars** there for star worship; **he made his son pass through the fire; used witchcraft; consulted spiritists and mediums; set a carved image of Asherah** (likely an obscene sexual symbol) in the temple of God. The Spirit of God dwells on the seriousness of this act by rehearsing God's promise to His people in connection with the temple (1 Kgs. 8:29; 9:3).

21:10–15 Manasseh led the people into worse **abominations . . . than** those of **the Amorites**. As a result, God said that He would punish **Judah** as He punished **Samaria** and **the house of Ahab**. **The measuring line . . . and the plummet** (v. 13) symbolize judgment. Also, He would empty **Jerusalem . . . as** a man empties **a dish** by **turning it upside down** and wiping it out. His people would be led away into captivity because they had provoked the Lord so grievously.

21:16–18 In addition to his idolatry, **Manasseh shed very much innocent blood**. According to "*The Assumption of Isaiah*," a noncanonical book, Manasseh had the prophet Isaiah sawn in two (cf. Heb. 11:37).

From 2 Chronicles 33 we learn that Manasseh was taken into captivity in Babylon by the king of Assyria (Ashurbanipal). There, while in prison, he repented and turned to the Lord. After this he was permitted to return to Jerusalem and resume his reign—a fitting proof of the grace, love, and mercy of the Lord. He tried to undo the damage he had done, but it was too late. The people, including his son, followed his earlier example (2 Chron. 33:14–23).

C. King Amon (21:19–26)

Amon the son of Manasseh was **king** of Judah for **two years** (642–639 B.C.; cf. 2 Chron. 33:21–25).

Amon was notorious for his idolatry and for forsaking the true **God**. Some of his **servants . . . conspired against him and killed** him after a brief reign of **two years**. **The people . . . executed** the guilty assassins and them **made his son Joiah king in his place.** Neither Amon nor his father was **buried** in the tombs of the kings of Judah.

D. King Josiah (22:1—23:30)

Josiah the son of Amon was **king** of **Judah** for **thirty-one years** (641–609 B.C.; cf. 2 Chron. 34—35).

1. *Josiah's Repairs of the Temple (22:1–7)*

Zephaniah (Zeph. 1:1) and Jeremiah (Jer. 25:3) began their prophetic ministries at about this time. Habakkuk may have ministered toward the end of Josiah's time. Josiah's reign was the last era of reform in the kingdom of Judah. He took resolute action against idolatry and encouraged the people to return to the Lord. **In the eighteenth year of** his reign, when he was twenty-six, he instituted a program for the **repair** of the temple. **Money** that had been collected at the temple was turned over to workmen for labor and materials. Because of their honesty, **no accounting** was asked for **the money** which was turned over to them.

2. *Josiah's Recovery of the Book of the Law (22:8–20)*

22:8–10 While the repairs were going on, **Hilkiah the high priest . . . found** a copy of **the Book of the Law**, perhaps the entire Pentateuch or the book of Deuteronomy. This was taken to King Josiah and **read . . . before** him.

22:11–13 When the king heard the Word of God and realized how far the nation had wandered from Him, **he tore his clothes** in penitence. Then he sent five of his officials to **inquire of the Lord**, realizing that **the wrath of** God must be hovering over Judah for its sins.

22:14–20 The officials **went to Huldah, a prophetess** who **dwelt in Jerusalem in the Second Quarter**, a district or suburb of the city. They did not go directly to either Jeremiah or Zephaniah. Huldah was probably Jeremiah's aunt (v. 14; cf. Jer. 32:7). She confirmed Josiah's fears that God was going to punish **Judah** soon because of the corruption of the people. But she added that it would not happen during Josiah's lifetime because he had **humbled** himself and was penitent.

The fact that Josiah later died in battle (23:29) does not contradict verse 20. **"You shall be gathered to your grave in peace"** may mean "before the promised catastrophe of the Babylonian captivity." Or it may mean that Josiah would die at **peace** with God (he certainly did not die at peace with man).

3. *Josiah's Renewal of the Covenant (23:1–3)*

The king now held a holy convocation at the temple and **read the words of the Book of the Covenant** to all the people. Standing **by** the **pillar, he made a covenant** to obey all the words of the law. **The people** also entered into **the covenant** with **the Lord**.

4. *Josiah's Reforms (23:4–30)*

23:4–9 Then follows a list of the many reforms which Josiah undertook. He cleansed **the temple** of **all the articles** used in idolatry, **burned them**, and took the **ashes to Bethel** (to defile the shrine there). He deposed and probably killed **the idolatrous priests**. He took **the wooden image** (Asherah) out of the temple, **burned it**, and scattered the **ashes on the graves of the common people**. **He tore down the ritual booths** of the male cult prostitutes (sodomites) in the temple area, **where the women wove hangings** for the Asherah **image**. He **defiled the high places**. This means that he desecrated them in such a way that they would not be used again. **He brought all the priests** out of **the cities of Judah, where** they had offered to Jehovah on **the high places**. God had designated Jerusalem as the place where these offerings should be made. Josiah barred these **priests** from further service in the temple, but gave them a share of the **unleavened bread**.

23:10–12 **He** desecrated and ruined **Topheth**, the heathen shrine **in the Valley of the Son of Hinnom**, where child sacrifices had been offered **to Molech**. **He removed the horses . . . dedicated to the sun** and **burned the chariots of the sun . . . that the kings of Judah had** used in connection with **sun** worship. He destroyed idolatrous **altars** erected by **Ahaz** and **Manasseh**. Manasseh himself had removed these altars after his conversion (2 Chron. 33:15), but they were undoubtedly pressed back into service by idolatrous Amon. Josiah made sure they would never be used again.

23:13, 14 He **defiled the high places** at the southern end of the Mount of Olives (**Mount of Corruption**), dating from the time of **Solomon**. **He broke** down **the** idolatrous **sacred pillars and cut down the wooden images** (Asherim), and then defiled their locations **with the bones of men**.

23:15–18 He destroyed **the altar that was at Bethel . . . and burned the high place**. Then **he took the bones** from nearby **tombs** and **burned them on** the remains of **the altar**. ("Both Israelites and heathen regarded dead men's bones as a perpetual defilement.")[25] All of this was in fulfillment of the prophecy uttered over 300 years previously by the man of God to **Jeroboam**. Josiah is one of the few men in Scripture named before his birth (1 Kgs. 13:2). He was a chosen vessel, foreordained to fulfill the oracle of the unnamed prophet against **the altar . . . at Bethel**.

When King Josiah saw the **gravestone** of **the man of God who** had testified **against the altar of Bethel**, he ordered that **no one** should **move . . . the bones of the prophet**. So they were permitted to remain there **with** the **bones** of the unnamed **prophet who came** out of **Samaria** (cf. 1 Kgs. 13:30, 31).

23:19, 20 The king's reforms even extended into **Samaria**. Apparently he had won control over this area, largely because the power of Assyria was declining. He destroyed **the high places** and **executed the** idolatrous **priests . . . on the altars** where they had offered sacrifices. Also, he defiled these places with the ashes of **men's bones**.

23:21–23 On his return to Jerusalem, Josiah reinstituted **the Passover**, according to the Word of the Lord which he had read (see 2 Chron. 35:1–19 for more details). It was the greatest such observance **since the days of the judges**. Other Passovers had been larger and more elaborate, but this one was particularly pleasing to **the Lord**. Scripture makes mention of only three Passovers during the kingdom years: Solomon's (2 Chron. 8), Hezekiah's (2 Chron. 30), and Josiah's.

23:24 **Josiah** also cleansed the land of **those who consulted mediums and spiritists,** fortune-tellers, and other wizards.

23:25–27 As to the thoroughness of his reforms, he was the greatest of the kings of Judah. Hezekiah held the same honor as far as trust in God was concerned (18:5, 6). Yet in spite of Josiah's good reign, **the Lord did not** change His plan to punish **Judah** by sending the people into captivity and by destroying Jerusalem.

23:28–30 In 609 B.C. **Pharaoh Necho . . . of Egypt** marched north along the coast of Palestine **to . . . aid** the Assyrians in their struggle against Babylon. For political reasons **Josiah** decided to resist Necho's advance and as a result was mortally wounded at **Megiddo. His servants** transported him **to Jerusalem**, where he died and was **buried** (cf. 2 Chron. 35:20–24). **Necho** advanced **to the River Euphrates**, where four years later the Babylonians defeated him in the battle of Carchemish (Jer. 46:2).

E. King Jehoahaz (23:31–33)

Jehoahaz (also called Shallum) the son of Josiah was **king** of Judah for only **three months** (609 B.C.; cf. 2 Chron. 36:1–4).

Jehoahaz disregarded his father's reforms and allowed the people to return to idolatry. **Pharaoh Necho**, king of Egypt, summoned him to **Riblah**, in **Hamath**, a region of Syria where the Egyptians had encamped, and there he put Judah under **tribute**. Later he carried **Jehoahaz** off **to Egypt**, where **he died** (Jer. 22:11, 12).

F. King Jehoiakim (23:34—24:7)

Jehoiakim the son of Josiah was **king** of Judah for eleven **years** (609–598 B.C.; cf. 2 Chron. 36:5–8; Jer. 22:18, 19; 26:21–23; 36:9–32).

23:34–37 Pharaoh Necho made Eliakim, Jehoahaz's brother, **king in** Josiah's **place** and **changed** Eliakim's **name to Jehoiakim. Jehoiakim** was the eldest surviving son of Josiah (cf. vv. 31, 36), but the people had originally placed **Jehoahaz** on the throne instead. **Necho** reversed this and appointed **Jehoiakim** as a vassal king. He was more faithful **to Pharaoh** than he was to Jehovah.

24:1–4 Egypt was defeated by **Babylon** at Carchemish in 605 B.C., and Judah came under the control of the Babylonians.

Jehoiakim put Urijah the prophet to death (Jer. 26:23) and burned the Word of God which Jeremiah had written concerning Judah and Israel (Jer. 36:23). He tried to arrest Jeremiah and also Baruch, his scribe, but the Lord hid them (Jer. 36:26). In the third year of Jehoiakim's reign, **Nebuchadnezzar . . . came . . . against** Jerusalem (v. 1), carried some of the inhabitants (including Daniel) to Babylon, and also took some of the vessels from the temple (2 Chron. 36:7; Dan. 1:1, 2). He also bound Jehoiakim in chains to bring him to Babylon. Either he changed his mind or returned the king of Judah to Jerusalem because Jehoiakim subsequently rebelled against the Babylonians (24:1). Whitcomb describes the situation as follows:

> The Chronicler says that Nebuchadnezzar "bound him in fetters to carry him to Babylon" (2 Chron. 36:6); but before the plan was fulfilled something of urgent importance happened that caused Nebuchadnezzar to change his mind. He received word that his father Nabopolassar had died in Babylon on August 15. Realizing that the throne was now in jeopardy, he forced Jehoiakim to promise loyalty as a vassal, then took the short route across the Arabian desert to Babylon.[26]

God sent invasion armies from four nations against **Judah** because of Manasseh's **sins**.

24:5–7 The Lord decreed that the king would have the burial of a donkey—that is, his body would be drawn outside the city and left exposed to the elements and to the creatures of prey (Jer. 22:19). No details of his death are given.

G. King Jehoiachin (24:8–16)

Jehoiachin, also called Jeconiah and Coniah, son of Jehoiakim, was **king** of Judah for **three months** (598–597 B.C.; cf. 25:27–30; 2 Chron. 36:9, 10).

During the short reign of this wicked king, **Nebuchadnezzar . . . besieged** the city of **Jerusalem** and **carried** away a second group of **captives**. Ezekiel was taken to Babylon in this deportation. Also included were the royal family, 7000 soldiers, and the trained **craftsmen**. In fact, only **the poorest people of the land** were left. **Nebuchadnezzar** also took **treasures** from the temple and from **the king's** palace. Verse 14 says that there were **ten thousand captives** in all. Jeremiah says that 4600 captives were taken (Jer. 52:28–30). The number in Kings may include captives taken on other occasions as well. After Jehoiachin had been in captivity for thirty-seven years, Evil-Merodach, the king of Babylon, freed him from prison, set him above the other captive kings, gave him a position of honor in the court, and provided liberally for him (25:27–30).

The prophet Ezekiel began his ministry at this period.

H. King Zedekiah (24:17—25:7)

Zedekiah, Jehoiachin's uncle, was **king** of Judah for **eleven years** (597–586 B.C.; cf. 2 Chron. 36:11–21; Jer. 52:1–30).

24:17–20 The king of Babylon appointed **Mattaniah**, an **uncle** of Jehoiachin, as **king in his place**. The king of Babylon **changed** Mattaniah's **name to Zedekiah**. Zedekiah made a treaty with Nebuchadnezzar, agreeing to serve as his puppet. But then he broke the agreement, **rebelled against the king of Babylon**, and sought the help of Egypt. Zedekiah's treachery in breaking his oath and God's subsequent judgment upon him are recorded in Ezekiel 17:11–21.

25:1–7 Zedekiah's intrigue with Egypt brought the final blow on the city of **Jerusalem**. **Nebuchadnezzar . . . besieged** it for eighteen months, causing severe **famine** conditions within the walls. **Zedekiah** and his **men of war** tried to escape from the city **at night** and to flee to the wilderness near the Dead Sea. **The Chaldeans** captured **the king** and **brought him . . . to** Nebuchadnezzar **at Riblah** (in Hamath of Syria). After slaying his **sons . . . before his eyes**, the king of Babylon ordered that his **eyes** should be **put out** and that he should be carried in **bronze fetters to Babylon.** This fulfilled two remarkable prophecies: Jeremiah had predicted that Zedekiah would see the king of Babylon face to face (Jer. 32:4; 34:3). This was fulfilled **at Riblah**. Ezekiel had also prophesied that he would be brought to Babylon but would not see it and would die there (Ezek. 12:13). Zedekiah's **eyes** were **put out** before he ever got **to Babylon**. He died in Babylon.

I. The Fall of Jerusalem (25:8–21)

25:8–12 The final destruction of Jerusalem took place in 586 B.C. by **Nebuzaradan, captain of the** Babylonian **guard. He burned the** temple, the royal palace, and all the great buildings. He **broke down the walls** and **carried** into exile all but the poorest people **of the land**.

25:13–17 These verses describe the wholesale looting of the temple treasures. Those things which were too big to be carried away were cut up into smaller **pieces. The bronze** which was seized **was beyond measure**. In addition, **the Chaldeans . . . took** all **the solid gold and solid silver** they could find.

25:18–21 Nebuzaradan . . . took

about seventy-two of the leading citizens of Jerusalem to King Nebuchadnezzar in **Riblah**, where they were summarily executed.[27]

J. Gedaliah's Governorship (25:22–26)

The king of Babylon appointed **Gedaliah** to be **governor over the people** remaining **in . . . Judah**. **When** four army **captains . . . heard** this, **they came to** him **at Mizpeh**, perhaps to recommend that the people flee to Egypt. **Gedaliah** counseled them to submit to the Babylonian yoke and that all would **be well**. Later **Ishmael**, a member **of the royal family**, attacked **and killed Gedaliah** and his associates. The people were thus left without organized government and fled **to Egypt**.

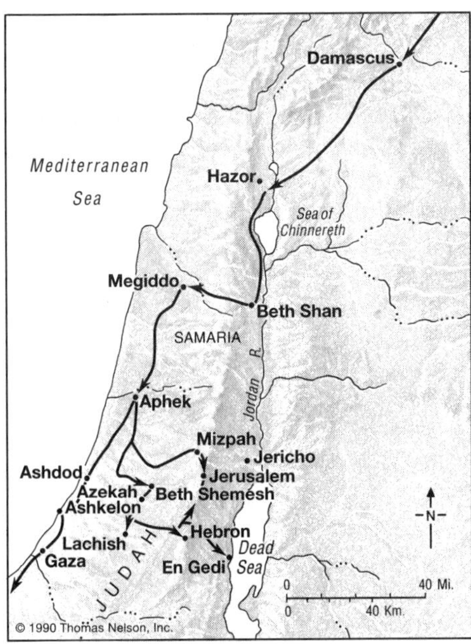

Nebuchadnezzar's Campaigns Against Judah. From 605 to 586 B.C. Judah suffered repeated Babylonian invasions. The final blow came from the southern approach to Jerusalem.

K. King Jehoiachin (25:27–30)

The book closes on an encouraging note. Second Kings and Jeremiah have identical endings (cf. 25:27–30; Jer. 52:31–34). In his **thirty-seventh year** of exile, **Jehoiachin** was afforded honorable treatment **by the king of Babylon**. This gave hope that the rigors of the exile would be eased and later ended completely.

First Kings opens with David's death and 2 Kings closes with Judah's destruction. The nation had failed under Moses, had failed under the judges, and now had failed under the kings. The people refused to listen to God's Word. They refused to be moved by the tears of the prophets. They hardened their hearts and stiffened their necks until God appointed the Assyrians and the Babylonians to teach them that the wages of sin is death. The captivity served its purpose well: It purged the heart of God's chosen people of idolatry.

ENDNOTES

[1](1:2) John C. Whitcomb, Jr., *Solomon to the Exile*, p. 64. *Baal-zebul* is translated "exalted Baal" by many scholars.

[2](2:7–9) George Williams, *The Student's Commentary on the Holy Scriptures*, p. 200.

[3](3:4–9) See *Unger's Bible Dictionary*, pp. 217, 226, 227.

[4](3:26, 27) Harold Stigers, "II Kings," in *The Wycliffe Bible Commentary*, p. 344.

[5](5:1–4) D. L. Moody, *Notes from My Bible*, p. 58.

[6](5:13, 14) *Ibid*.

[7](6:24–31) Some take this to be literal bird excrement, but used for fuel.

[8](7:1, 2) Moody, *Notes*, p. 58.

[9](7:3–7) Matthew Henry, "2 Kings," in *Matthew Henry's Commentary on the Whole Bible*, II:745, 746.

[10](8:13–15) Williams, *Commentary*, p. 207.

[11](8:13–15) Merrill C. Tenney, *The Zondervan Pictorial Encyclopedia of the Bible*, III:49.

[12](9:30–37) G. Campbell Morgan, *Searchlights from the Word*, p. 209.

[13](10:15–17) *Ibid.*, p. 104.

[14](11:4–11) Williams, *Commentary*, p. 210.

[15](12:1–5) Whitcomb, *Solomon*, p. 103.

[16](12:1–5) Williams, *Commentary*, p. 211.

[17](15:32–38) Flavius Josephus, summarized by Matthew Henry, "2 Kings," *Matthew Henry's Commentary*, II:785.

[18](16:10–16) F. C. Cook, ed., *Barnes' Notes on the Old and New Testaments, I Samuel—Esther*, p. 273.

[19](17:29–34a) Such a mixed religion is called "syncretistic."

[20](17:41) However, Luke 2:36 mentions that the prophetess Anna was "of the tribe of Asher," one of the ten tribes. Apparently some from those tribes did return. Also, James sent his Epistle "to the twelve tribes which are scattered abroad" (1:1), so the ten tribes were not totally "lost" from sight even in the early Christian era.

[21](18:17–19) By omitting the definite articles, the KJV gives the impression that these are proper names.

[22](19:35–37) He is widely believed to be the pre-incarnate Christ (the NKJV footnote with capitalized *Angel* suggests this view).

[23](20:1–7) Whitcomb, *Solomon*, p. 127.

[24](20:20, 21) The text of the inscription can be found in *Unger's Bible Dictionary*, pp. 481, 482, and in *First and Second Kings*, by Richard I. McNeely, p. 145.

[25](23:15–18) Williams, *Commentary*, p. 221.

[26](24:1–4) Whitcomb, *Solomon*, p. 146.

[27](25:18–21) There are three numerical problems in chapter 25, all of them probably copyists' errors, either here in 2 Kings or else in the corresponding verses in 1 Kings and Jeremiah. The accurate copying of numbers in ancient manuscripts posed special problems. (See 2 Chronicles for more details on this type of problem.) The difficulties are: the date Jerusalem was burned (v. 8 says the seventh of the month while Jer. 52:12 says the tenth); the height of the capitals on the pillars (v. 17 says three cubits but 1 Kgs. 7:16 says five cubits); the number of advisors slain (vv. 19–21 say five were killed; Jer. 52:25 says seven were put to death).

BIBLIOGRAPHY

See Bibliography at the end of 1 Kings.

FIRST CHRONICLES

Introduction

"Chronicles has a character and beauty of its own, and a moral propriety, beyond anything, because it takes up and shows that in the ruin of all else the purpose of God stands fast. That is what we have to comfort ourselves with at this present time. There is a ruined state in Christendom; but God's purposes never fail, and those who have faith settle themselves and find their comfort in the sure standing of the purpose of God."

—William Kelly

I. Unique Place in the Canon

Chronicles, originally one large book, occupies the last position in the Hebrew Bible.[1] The Hebrew title means "Journals," or more literally, "Words of the Days." The title in the Greek translation (LXX) is "Omissions" (*Paralipomena*), an unfortunate and misleading title.[2] Our excellent English title traces back to Jerome's Latin Vulgate.

Since at first glance, 1 Chronicles seems to repeat 1 and 2 Samuel, and 2 Chronicles seems to cover the same material as 1 and 2 Kings, what unique contribution does Chonicles make? Chronicles shows marked differences from Samuel and Kings. Those books emphasize the *historical* side of things whereas Chronicles emphasizes the *spiritual*. Thus Chronicles concentrates on the reign of David and his successors, and on the temple and its worship. It gives details not previously found concerning the priests, Levites, musicians, singers, and doorkeepers. It elaborates on the transporting of the ark to Jerusalem, on preparation for building the temple, and on reforms under some of the good kings of Judah. The northern kingdom is mentioned only in its dealings with David's dynasty. The chronicler even passes over the tragic stories of Amnon, Absalom, and Adonijah, and the faithlessness of Solomon. So the books of Chronicles are by no means an unnecessary repetition. Rather, they are a spiritual interpretation of the history in the preceding books.

The affairs of each king's reign were regularly recorded in a book (1 Kgs. 14:29; 15:7; etc.). No doubt it was from this common source that the passages in Samuel and Kings which are identical with those in Chronicles were derived.

Some have criticized Chronicles for not being more complete and well-rounded, for not including important history of the period covered.[3] However, with his usual spiritual perception, William Kelly shows how Chronicles, like all inspired books, reflects just what the Holy Spirit desires:

> These collections of testimonies of God that are brought together in the books of Chronicles . . . are frag-

> mentary; they are meant to be fragmentary. God could have given a completeness to them if He pleased, but it would have been out of His order. God Himself has deigned and been pleased to mark His sense of the ruin of Israel by giving only fragmentary pieces of information here and there. There is nothing really complete. The two books of Chronicles savor of this very principle. This is often a great perplexity to men of learning, because they, looking upon it merely with a natural eye, cannot understand it. They fancy it altogether corrupted. Not so. It was written, advisedly and deliberately so, by the Spirit of God.[4]

Kelly makes a pertinent application of the situation in Israel to the modern divided and chaotic state of professing Christendom:

> So, I am persuaded, the provision by the grace of God for His people at this present time looks very feeble, looks very disorderly, to a man with a natural eye; but when you look into it, you will find that it is according to the mind of God, and that the pretension of having all complete would put us out of communion with His mind—would make us content with ourselves instead of feeling with Him for the broken state of His Church.[5]

First and Second Chronicles are not dull history books. They are a priestly interpretation of sacred history from Adam through Israel's return from the Babylonian Captivity. They are written for us believers and apply to our daily life.

II. Authorship

Most commentators suggest Ezra as the author or compiler of Chronicles. The last two verses of 2 Chronicles are the same as the first two of the book of Ezra, and there are many stylistic similarities. The inspired editor drew on a number of contemporary works for his information, as can be seen from the following list of reference works which he mentions:

1. The book of Samuel the seer (1 Chron. 29:29)
2. The book of Nathan the prophet (1 Chron. 29:29)
3. The book of Gad the seer (1 Chron. 29:29)
4. The prophecy of Ahijah the Shilonite (2 Chron. 9:29)
5. The visions of Iddo the seer (2 Chron. 9:29)
6. The book of Shemaiah the prophet (2 Chron. 12:15)
7. The book of Iddo the seer (2 Chron. 12:15)
8. The annals of the prophet Iddo (2 Chron. 13:22)
9. The book of the kings of Israel and Judah (2 Chron. 20:34; 27:7; 32:32)
10. The story of the book of the kings (2 Chron. 24:27)
11. The vision of Isaiah the prophet (2 Chron. 26:22; 32:32)
12. The sayings of Hozai[6] (2 Chron. 33:19)

III. Date

Chronicles was written after the captivity (2 Chron. 36:22, 23). By using the genealogies we can pinpoint the date more closely. The last person in the Davidic genealogy, Anani (1 Chron. 3:24), is eight generations later than King Jehoiachin (also called Jeconiah [v. 17] or Coniah [v. 17, NKJV marg.]). This was about 600 B.C. Allowing an average of twenty-five years per generation, this brings us up to about 400 B.C. at the earliest. Chronicles can scarcely be much *later* than that, either, since a writer as dedicated to David's line as was the Chronicler would have included any later descendants of the king.

Thus we see that Chronicles is one of the last OT books written, near the time of Malachi.

IV. Background and Theme

The late date of Chronicles also helps us understand its emphasis. The monarchy is no more, but the royal lineage is still traced as far as it has gone, in preparation for the Son of David, the Messiah, who was yet to come.

Although the monarchy no longer exists, the temple services are still central to the spiritual life of the nation. W. Graham Scroggie writes:

> Then, again, all that pertains to worship is here emphasised; the Temple and its services, priests, Levites, singers, and the hatefulness of idolatry. It is shown that the troubles of the nation were due to their disregard of the claims of Jehovah, and their prosperity was due to their return to Him. The KINGS are political and royal, but the CHRONICLES are sacred and ecclesiastical.[7]

It is worth noting that both of these themes—the Messiah and worship—are fundamental to present-day believers as well.

Second Chronicles takes up where 1 Chronicles leaves off. In 1 Chronicles 29 David established Solomon as his successor. Second Chronicles traces the Davidic line from Solomon to the return of the Jewish remnant from the Babylonian Captivity. First and Second Kings cover basically the same time period, but the emphasis in Kings is more on Israel, while in Chronicles the emphasis is on Judah, as we noted earlier. The kings of Israel are mentioned only as they relate to the history of Judah. Although much of the material is the same in both books, Chronicles sometimes contains details not found in Kings, Chronicles having been written at a later date and for a different purpose. We will comment on some of the differences between the two books, but it will be impossible to go into depth about all of them. Other books have been written for this purpose.

OUTLINE

I. THE GENEALOGIES (Chaps. 1—9)
   A. From Adam to Abraham (1:1–27)
   B. From Abraham to Israel (1:28–54)
   C. Descendants of Israel (Chaps. 2—8)
      1. Judah (2:1—4:23)
      2. Simeon (4:24–43)
      3. Reuben, Gad, and the Half-tribe of Manasseh East of the Jordan (Chap. 5)
      4. Levi (Chap. 6)
      5. Issachar (7:1–5)
      6. Benjamin (7:6–12)

7. Naphtali (7:13)
8. Half-tribe of Manasseh West of the Jordan (7:14–19)
9. Ephraim (7:20–29)
10. Asher (7:30–40)
11. Benjamin (Chap. 8)

D. Those who Returned from Captivity (9:1–34)
E. The Genealogy of Saul (9:35–44)

II. THE DEATH OF SAUL (Chap. 10)

III. THE REIGN OF DAVID (Chaps. 11—29)

A. David's Army (Chaps. 11, 12)
1. David's Valiant Warriors (Chap. 11)
2. David's Loyal Followers (Chap. 12)

B. David Brings the Ark to Jerusalem (Chaps. 13—16)
C. David's Desire to Build the Temple and God's Response (Chap. 17)
D. David's Victories (Chaps. 18—20)
E. The Census and the Plague (Chap. 21)
F. Preparations for the Temple (Chaps. 22—26)
1. Materials, Men, and Motivation (Chap. 22)
2. Divisions and Duties of the Levites (Chaps. 23—26)

G. Military and Governmental Leaders (Chap. 27)
H. David's Last Days (Chaps. 28, 29)

Commentary

I. THE GENEALOGIES (Chaps. 1—9)

The first nine chapters of 1 Chronicles contain genealogical tables, or "family trees," as we like to call them. Genealogies were very important to the Jews in seeking to maintain their tribal distinctions. After the confusion of the captivity, it was also important to establish the kingly and priestly lines once more.

There are several instances in these chapters where names differ from the names given in other parts of the Bible. There are different reasons for these apparent inconsistencies. Sometimes a man had more than one name. It should not surprise us that some names changed in spelling over the centuries. After all, there is a whole millennium between some of the genealogies in Genesis and their counterparts here in Chronicles (1400–400 B.C.). Many cases are copyists' errors. A look at the Hebrew language will show just how easily this could have happened. These "discrepancies" do not stumble the serious student, since most did not exist in the original documents and in no way affect any major doctrine of the faith.[8]

A. From Adam to Abraham (1:1–27)

The book of Genesis appears to have been the source of these genealogies. Verses 1–4 go back to Genesis 5 (**Adam** to **Noah**). Verses 5–23 give the descendants of Noah, as recorded in

Genesis 10. From Genesis 11 comes the genealogy of **Abraham** (vv. 24–27).

B. From Abraham to Israel (1:28–54)

Abraham's natural descendants, listed in Genesis 25, are given in verses 28–33. The descendants of Isaac, the son of promise, are dealt with next. Esau, from Genesis 36, is mentioned in verses 35–54, thus clearing the way for the descendants of Jacob (Israel). Chapters 2 through 9 trace the posterity of Israel.

Here in the first chapter the chronicler is narrowing the focus from Adam, the father of the human race, to Jacob, the father of the twelve tribes of Israel. He quickly clears the stage of all but the chosen nation. Here we also have the beginning of the messianic line (cf. Luke 3:34–38).

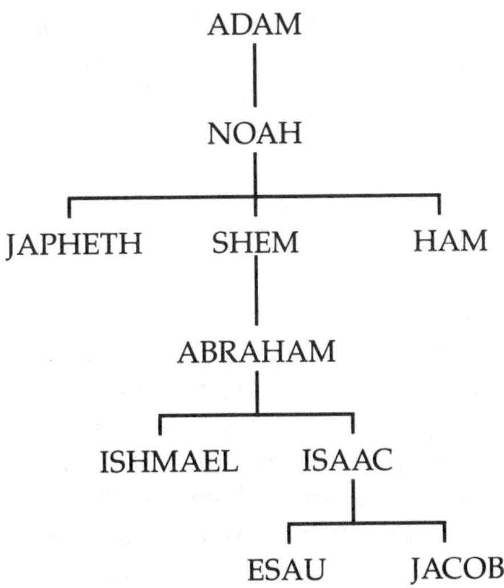

C. Descendants of Israel (Chaps. 2—8)

1. Judah (2:1—4:23)

Judah was the head of the largest tribe and the foremost in blessing and promise, and thus his genealogy is the first and the longest to be taken up (2:3—4:23). The genealogies of two descendants **of Judah** are developed more fully—**Caleb**: 2:18–20, 42–55 (this is not the Caleb of Num. 13; see 4:15), and **David**: 3:1–24.

Several historical notes are sprinkled throughout the genealogies. These are things to which the Holy Spirit would draw our attention, points of interest in this panoramic sweep of the history of Israel. In the genealogies of Judah, God's dealings with two wicked men and His blessing of one righteous man are brought to our attention.

"Er, the firstborn of Judah, was wicked in the sight of the Lord, so He killed him" (2:3). He was the offspring of Judah's marriage to **Shua**, a Canaanite woman (Gen. 38:1, 10). We are not told what he did, but only that he was evil **in the sight of the Lord.** His wickedness cost him his privileges as the firstborn, his place in the messianic line, and his life. His name became a blot on the family record for all generations to view. Men would do well to ponder the consequences of evil before it is too late. "For evildoers shall be cut off; but those who wait on the Lord, they shall inherit the earth" (Ps. 37:9).

The story of **Achar** (Achan) (2:7) is found in Joshua 7. He "saw," "coveted," and "took" (Josh. 7:21) the things under the ban in Jericho. He troubled **Israel** in that, because of his sin, thirty-six men died in the unsuccessful attack on Ai. He was singled out by the Lord, and he and his family were executed.

"Now Jabez was more honorable than his brothers" (4:9). Here was a man who had a large concept of God and honored Him by seeking His blessing. Jabez was a man of faith, and the Lord took note of it. "But without faith it is impossible to please Him, for he who comes to God must believe that He is, and that He is a rewarder of those who diligently seek Him" (Heb. 11:6). Ironside comments:

> His prayer is fourfold. "Bless me indeed." That is, "Give me true happiness." This is only found as one prevails and walks with God. "Enlarge my coast." He was not content to go on only with what he had. He would enter into and enjoy more of the inheritance of the Lord. "That Thine hand may be with me!" He counted on God's protecting care. And lastly, he prayed, "Keep me from evil that it may not make me sorrowful." Sin is the only thing that can rob a child of God of his joy in the Lord.[9]

Jabez sought and was rewarded. May God strengthen us to follow his example!

Bithia (4:18) is one of the few women mentioned in these genealogies. She was a **daughter of Pharaoh** but was now living with the chosen people. Her name means *daughter of Jehovah*.

One apparent discrepancy should be mentioned before we move on. In 2:15 **David** is called **the seventh** son of Jesse while in 1 Samuel 16:10, 11 and 17:12 he is the eighth son. One of Jesse's sons probably died childless or before he married and so is not included by the chronicler.

2. Simeon (4:24–43)

4:24–43 Simeon, Jacob's second born, is taken up next, probably because of the close association of his tribe with Judah. Simeon's portion in the Promised Land was within the territory of Judah (Josh. 19:9). The **cities** listed in 4:28–33 were **their** inheritance. However, later in history they acquired additional land through conquest.

3. Reuben, Gad, and the Half-tribe of Manasseh East of the Jordan (Chap. 5)

Chapter 5 deals with the transjordanian tribes of **Reuben, Gad**, and the half-tribe **of Manasseh**. Very little space is devoted to these tribes. They were among the first to go into captivity (5:26).

Verses 1 and 2 explain why the blessing of the **birthright was given to** other tribes instead of to the Reubenites. When Jacob blessed his children before his death (Gen. 49), he took note of Reuben's wickedness (Gen. 35:22) and removed him from having preeminence. The double portion of land due the firstborn went to **Joseph** (through Ephraim and Manasseh), and the double portion (as far as leadership was concerned) went to **Judah**.

The Gadites are listed in verses 11–17, and the leaders of **the half-tribe of Manasseh** are given in verses 23 and 24.

The rest of chapter 5 gives a brief account of the fate of these tribes. Together they had fought successfully against **the Hagrites** (Ishmaelites) (vv. 10, 19–22). With a small army of 44,760 men, they defeated a much bigger enemy force. They had trusted **in** their **God** (v. 20), and He gave them victory and abundant spoils (v. 21).

Being constantly exposed to the idolatrous nations around them, they soon **played the harlot after the gods of the peoples of the land, whom God had destroyed before them** (v. 25). They turned to **the gods** who could not save the Ishmaelites and forsook the one true **God** in whose strength they had conquered. So God gave them into the hand of the Assyrian **king** and they were **carried** away **into captivity**.

4. Levi (Chap. 6)

6:1–53 This chapter takes up the **sons of Levi**, descendants of Jacob's third-born son. Verses 1–15 and 49–53 deal with the most famous family of this tribe, that of **Aaron**. The high priesthood had been given to Aaron and his sons, and thus the importance of an accurate genealogy from **Aaron** to the **captivity**.

Samuel (v. 28) the **son** of **Elkanah** (v. 27) was a great prophet and the last judge in Israel before Saul became king. His ministry is described in 1 Samuel.

Levi had three sons: **Gershom, Kohath, and Merari**. Their genealogies are given in verses 16–30. Verses 31–48 contain three genealogies: **Heman**, a Kohathite (vv. 33–38); **Asaph**, a Gershomite (vv. 39–43); and **Ethan**, a Merarite (vv. 44–47). These were the "songmasters" **whom David appointed** to minister before **the Lord** (vv. 31, 32).

Heman was probably the author of Psalm 88. He was a descendant of the Prophet **Samuel**. There are psalms which bear Asaph's name—e.g., Psalm 50 and Psalms 73—83. **Ethan** may be the author of Psalm 89.

6:54–81 The rest of the chapter is a listing of **the cities** and **common-lands given to** the Levites by the other tribes. This was in accordance with the Lord's command through Moses (Num. 35:1–8). The command was carried out under the supervision of Joshua (Josh. 21).

5. *Issachar (7:1–5)*

Six tribes are mentioned in chapter 7:

Issachar (vv. 1–5)
Benjamin (vv. 6–12)
Naphtali (v. 13)
Half-tribe of **Manasseh** (west of the Jordan) (vv. 14–19)
Ephraim (vv. 20–29)
Asher (vv. 30–40)

These genealogies are not nearly as complete as those of Judah or Levi, perhaps because neither the throne nor the priesthood is involved.

6. *Benjamin (7:6–12)*

Although the tribe of **Benjamin** had at one time been reduced to 600 men because of their folly (Judg. 20), they seem to have regained their strength and size. Benjamin's descendants are listed again in chapter 8. Here in chapter 7 the emphasis is on Benjamin in relation to the people, whereas in the next chapter it is on Benjamin in relation to Saul and Jerusalem.

7. *Naphtali (7:13)*

The four sons of Naphtali are called **sons of Bilhah** because she was Naphtali's mother. Further descendants of these four are passed over.[10]

8. *Half-tribe of Manasseh West of the Jordan (7:14–19)*

Manasseh's descendants living east of the Jordan in Gilead and Bashan were recorded in 5:23, 24. This passage deals with the half of the tribe that settled in Canaan, west of the Jordan.

A descendant of Manasseh who stands out in the genealogy is Zelophehad, who had all daughters. They are named in Joshua 17:3 and remembered because they spoke up for the inheritance that the Lord had promised women in such cases (see Num. 27:1–11). Jewish women had rights at a time when most pagan women had few.

9. *Ephraim (7:20–29)*

The writer goes into greater depth with the tribe of **Ephraim** in order to trace the lineage of **Joshua**, the most famous Ephraimite of ancient history. Men who do exploits for God are a glory to their families and are lovingly remembered and held forth as examples to succeeding generations.

10. Asher (7:30–40)

The four **sons of Asher** and **their sister Serah** coincide with the listing in Genesis 46:17. Their descendants were **choice men, mighty men of valor, chief leaders**.

11. Benjamin (Chap. 8)

8:1–28 **Benjamin**, Judah, and some of the tribes of Simeon and Levi formed the southern kingdom taken into Babylonian captivity. Most of the Israelites who returned to Judah under Nehemiah were from these tribes; hence the larger space devoted to them in these genealogies.

The Benjamites are discussed here more fully than in 7:6–12. When comparing these two lists, as well as those given in Genesis 46:21 and Numbers 26:38–41, the following principles help us to understand the seeming discrepancies.

1. Some men had more than one name.
2. The spelling of some names changed over the years.
3. Some names are omitted because the men died early or childless.
4. The word translated *son* (*ben*) can mean son, grandson, great-grandson, etc.
5. Some names are left out because they don't serve the chronicler's purpose.

8:29–40 **Saul**, a Benjamite, was Israel's first king. His genealogy is given here and in 9:35–44. Only the descendants of his son **Jonathan**, the friend of David, are given here. **Merib-Baal** (v. 34) is another name for Mephibosheth.[11]

The genealogies of Dan and Zebulun are not given. (Dan is also left out in other portions of Scripture—notably Rev. 7.)

D. Those who Returned from Captivity (9:1–34)

Verses 2–9 mention briefly some of the sons of **Judah** and **Benjamin** who returned to **Jerusalem**, leaders in **their fathers' houses** (v. 10). Verses 10–13 mention **the priests**, while verses 14–34 mention the other **Levites** who returned, describing some of their duties. Another listing of those who returned can be found in Nehemiah 11.

E. The Genealogy of Saul (9:35–44)

The last ten verses of chapter 9, which are virtually the same as 8:29–40, give the lineage of **Saul** and set the stage for the historical part of 1 Chronicles (chaps. 10—29). Saul's history is recorded in 1 Samuel 9—31.

II. THE DEATH OF SAUL (Chap. 10)

10:1–5 A parallel account of the death of Saul and his sons is found in 1 Samuel 31:1–13.

C. H. Spurgeon comments on verse 5:

> While we earnestly condemn the self-destruction, we cannot but admire the faithfulness of the armour-bearer—faithful unto death. He would not survive his master. Shall this man live and die for Saul, and shall we betray our royal master, Jesus the Lord?[12]

10:6–10 In connection with Saul's death several things should be noticed. **"All his house died together"** (v. 6) refers only to those who fought with Saul (1 Sam. 31:6). Saul had other sons not slain by **the Philistines** (vv. 13, 14; 2 Sam. 2:8; 21:1–8). But even these did not finally escape the fate that overtook their father (2 Sam. 21:1–8).

10:11, 12 Upon hearing the news of Saul and his sons, **the valiant men** of **Jabesh Gilead** marched all night to retrieve their **bodies** from **the Philistines** and then **buried their bones** and **fasted seven days**. Earlier Saul had saved their city from Nahash the Ammonite (1 Sam. 11); these **valiant men** did not forget his kindness.

10:13, 14 These verses give two reasons for Saul's death: **He did not keep the word of the LORD** (see 1 Sam. 13 and 15) and **he consulted a medium** (see 1 Sam. 28).

This brief account of Saul clears the way for the history of David, God's choice to rule over His people Israel.

III. THE REIGN OF DAVID (Chaps. 11—29)

A. David's Army (Chaps. 11, 12)

1. David's Valiant Warriors (Chap. 11)

11:1–3 Chronicles does not mention the short and unsuccessful rule of Ishbosheth (2 Sam. 2—4) but moves on to David's coronation **at Hebron** (cf. 2 Sam. 5).

11:4–9 King David's first order of business was to secure a capital for himself. These verses tell how **Jerusalem** was taken (cf. 2 Sam. 5:6–10).

David's nephew, **Joab the son of Zeruiah**, was also commander of his army. He displayed great courage and bravery in the capture of **Jerusalem**. In accordance with David's promise, he was made **chief** of the armies of Israel. Although a valiant warrior, **Joab** was a ruthless man, not named among David's mighty men, perhaps because of his unscrupulous character.

11:10 This list of David's warriors is put at the beginning of his reign. In 2 Samuel 23 a similar list is placed at the end of his reign. These **mighty men** came to **David** at different times in his career. Some came to him when he was in the cave at Adullam (vv. 15–19). Some came when he was at Ziklag (12:1–22). Some came when David was made king in Hebron (12:23–40).

Following is a list of some of David's **"mighty men"** and a few of their "mighty deeds":

11:11 Jashobeam: He single-handedly defeated **three hundred** men with nothing but a **spear**. God gave him a supernatural victory against Israel's enemies. Valiant men can still do extraordinary things for God when they trust Him and press the battle against the enemy of men's souls.

11:12–14 Eleazar the son of Dodo: Note first of all that **he was "with David."** He was loyal to David and stood with him when all others **fled**. And for what was he risking himself? A **field . . . of barley**! Principle, not property, was at stake. That land belonged by promise to Israel, and **the Philistines** were not to have so much as one foot of it. Today Christians need to realize that they belong to God and must not allow Satan a foothold in their lives, even in a seemingly insignificant area.

11:15–19 The **three . . . men** at **Adullam**: They were with **David** in his extremity and knew the **longing** of his heart. They risked **their lives** to bring him **water from the well of Bethlehem** which would refresh his spirit. It was not for the honor they would receive, since their names are not mentioned, but for the pleasure it would afford David. Where are the men and women today who dwell close enough to the Lord Jesus to know the longings of His heart? Where are the men and women who will **risk** all to refresh His soul by bringing Him **a drink** from some needy mission field? Those who do so will certainly be reckoned among His valiant ones.

11:20, 21 Abishai the brother of Joab was the most honored of the second **three**.[13] Scripture tells us that **Abishai** was a man of unwavering devotion to David. He went with David into Saul's camp (1 Sam. 26), he was with David when he fled Jerusalem during Absalom's revolt (2 Sam. 16), he crushed the revolt of Sheba (2 Sam. 20), he saved David from the giant Ishbi-Benob (2 Sam. 21), and in many other ways he gave faithful service to his king (2 Sam. 10, 18; 1 Chron. 18). Selfless bravery linked with devoted faithfulness will make anyone a valued friend and servant of the King of kings.

11:22–25 Benaiah: His father was a priest (1 Chron. 27:5) and **a valiant man**. He was the head of David's personal bodyguard. A few of his exploits are listed here. Later he took Joab's place as commander of the armies of Israel (1 Kgs. 2:34, 35). In his victories we see a picture of the overcoming life, where the world (the **Egyptian** giant), the flesh (**Moab**), and the devil (the roaring **lion**) are all confronted and conquered.

11:26–47 Although no deeds are recorded in verses 26–47, the names of those who served David heroically are duly mentioned. Some of the names are very interesting. For example:

Zelek the Ammonite (v. 39) and **Ithmah the Moabite** (v. 46): They were by birth enemies of Israel. But here they are found in the service of Israel's king. We all were born enemies of God, but by His grace we too can find a place in the King's army.

Uriah the Hittite (v. 41): He was a member of a people who were supposed to have been exterminated by the Israelites when they conquered the Promised Land (Deut. 7:1, 2). But here he is, a warrior for David. David proved unworthy of his loyalty, ordering Uriah to be murdered so that he could have his wife, Bathsheba (2 Sam. 11).

2. David's Loyal Followers (Chap. 12)

Chapter 11 dealt with those *individuals* who identified themselves with David. This chapter deals primarily with the *tribes*, along with their **captains**, who allied themselves with the king. Every tribe is listed here in chapter 12, from those **who came to David** when he was in hiding (vv. 1–22) to those who **came to . . . Hebron** after Ishbosheth's death (vv. 23–40). **". . . and all the rest of Israel were of one mind to make David king. . . . for there was joy in Israel"** (vv. 39, 40).

Many who were in trouble or distress had previously come to David to find protection (1 Sam. 22:1, 2). But now these men came to serve David and assist him in obtaining the throne which was his by divine decree. Today the kingdom of God needs men and women who are equipped by God (v. 2), trained and swift (v. 8), strong in faith, able to prevail against overwhelming odds and put the enemy to flight (vv. 14, 15), full of the Spirit, and selflessly dedicated to Jesus (v. 32)—people who have an undivided heart (v. 33)!

David rightly questioned **the sons of Benjamin and Judah** (v. 17) because earlier he had been betrayed by some of them (1 Sam. 23).

The historical events referred to in verses 19–22 can be found in 1 Samuel 29 and 30. God prevented **David** from fighting against Israel while he was **with the Philistines**. He also gave him victory over the Amalekites who had raided **Ziklag** and captured his family.

The eastern tribes came in large numbers (v. 37), while those closer to Hebron were represented by smaller forces—e.g., **Judah**, **Simeon**, etc. (vv. 24, 25 ff.).

Now that Israel was united around their divinely appointed king, there was much rejoicing, feasting, and blessing (v. 40). Division and strife, caused by Saul's disobedience, were past. Israel would now find new prosperity under their godly shepherd-king.

B. David Brings the Ark to Jerusalem (Chaps. 13—16)

13:1–8 Chapter 13 records David's first attempt to **bring the ark** to his newly acquired royal city.

The ark had been neglected during the reign **of Saul**. The Philistines had captured it and held it for seven months, then returned it to **Kirjath Jearim**, where it was kept in **the house of Abinadab**, a Levite (1 Sam. 4—7). Now, at David's instigation, **Uzza and Ahio** put **the ark . . . on a new cart** for the trip to Jerusalem. **Shihor in Egypt** probably refers to the Brook of Egypt (Wady el Arish).

13:9–12 When **the oxen stumbled, Uzza put out his hand to** steady **the ark**. Immediately **God . . . struck him** dead. The law forbade anyone to touch the ark, even the priests (Num. 4:15). When the Kohathites carried the ark, they placed the poles on their shoulders, but did not come in contact with the ark itself. The **place** was henceforth **called Perez Uzza** (*outburst against Uzza*). **David became angry** and fearful of bringing **the ark** to Jerusalem.

13:13, 14 So **the ark** was taken aside to **the house of Obed-Edom the Gittite**, where it **remained** for **three months**, bringing great blessing to its host.

14:1, 2 After **David** was established as king over all Israel, **Hiram, king of Tyre, sent** men and materials **to build** David **a house**. This was the beginning of a long and close friendship that extended into the reign of Solomon.

14:3–7 **David** sinned against the Lord by "multiplying **wives**"; this was expressly forbidden in Deuteronomy 17:17. Chronicles, while recording the violation, does not mention its sinful implication. The first four **children** mentioned in verse 4 were the sons of Bathsheba (1 Chron. 3:5). 2 Samuel 11 records David's illicit affair with her. However, even here we see the grace of God at work, for the names of two of the **children** of this marriage appear in the genealogy of our Lord: **Nathan** (Luke 3:31), ancestor of Mary, and **Solomon** (Matt. 1:6), ancestor of Joseph.

14:8–17 Upon hearing that **David had been** made **king** in **Israel, the Philistines** came up to attack him. **David inquired of God** (v. 10) and won a spectacular victory. The idols, which could not deliver their worshipers from the living God, were carried away (2 Sam. 5:21) and **burned** (v. 12). When **the Philistines** recovered and returned for a second attack, **David inquired again of** the Lord. He didn't assume that God's guidance would be the same. This time God gave victory through a completely different battle-plan.

These victories struck fear into the hearts of neighboring nations. Note the connection between verses 16 and 17: **"So David did as God commanded him . . . Then the fame of David went out into all lands."**

15:1–3 Three months after the tragedy of Perez Uzza (chap. 13), **David . . . prepared** once again **to bring . . . the ark** to his capital, **Jerusalem**. However, this time he first made diligent search in the law and then proceeded accordingly.

A tent, not a house, was **prepared . . . for the ark** at this time because this was the pattern found in the law. The **tent** was probably made in the same fashion as the one used during Israel's Exodus (Ex. 26). However, **the ark** was the only piece of furniture in David's **tent**, the tabernacle and its furnishings being at Gibeon (16:39) until the days of Solomon.

15:4–15 Then David assembled the heads of the Levitical households. The chief **priests, Zadok and Abiathar** (1 Kgs. 4:4), were also **called** for this occasion (v. 11). The ark was now carried by the right men and in the right way, **as Moses had commanded according to the word of the Lord** (v. 15). Hence, this effort met with success (16:1).

15:16–29 The sweet psalmist of Israel also made elaborate arrangements for joyful **music** of praise to accompany the ark. Some sang, some played musical **instruments**. David was leaping and **making music with stringed instruments and harps**, and all were filled **with joy**. There was one sour note in this happy symphony, however. **Michal**, David's wife, was mocking (v. 29; cf. 2 Sam. 6:16 ff.).

16:1–3 As soon as **the ark** was placed in the tent, sacrifices were **offered**. The **burnt offerings** were the highest expression of worship ceremonially possible (cf. Lev. 1). It was wholly consumed by the flames and it ascended in smoke to be enjoyed by **God** alone.

The other sacrifices offered at this time were the **peace offerings**. These were the only Levitical offerings in which everyone had a part. The fat and the kidneys were offered up to the Lord upon the altar, a portion of the remainder went to the priests, and the rest was given to the offerer to be shared with his family and friends before the Lord (cf. Lev. 3). The peace offering pictured communion with the Lord and a sharing of the good things which came from the Lord. Both **peace** and **burnt offerings** were prominent in the observance of festivals and solemn occasions, and certainly this was a festive day for all Israel. Everyone received a helping of meat before he left for home (v. 3).

16:4–7 David next acted to insure that thanksgiving and rejoicing before the Lord would be carried on daily and not be reserved for special occasions (cf. vv. 37–42). **Levites** were appointed **to commemorate, to thank, and to praise the Lord . . . with . . . instruments** and voices.

16:8–22 The psalm recorded on this occasion has two main parts. Verses 8–22 are addressed to **Israel**, and verses 23–34 are addressed to all **the nations**. Verses 35 and 36 close the psalm. It is a composite of Psalms 105:1–15; 96:1–13; 106:1, 47, 48.

In verses 8–22 the Israelites are exhorted to **sing** the Lord's greatness and to **seek** the Lord's **face**. They are to **remember** His *deeds*, **the marvelous works which He has done** in the past, and they are to **remember His** *covenant*, the unconditional promises He made to their fathers.

16:23–34 Widening the perspectives to **all the earth,** the psalmist urges **all** men to speak of the **glory** of **the Lord**. *Fear* is His due as the God of creation. **Glory** is His due as the God of splendor, **strength**, and **majesty**. *Joy* is His due as the God who sustains and **reigns** over His world.

16:35, 36 This closing prayer is almost identical to Psalm 106:47, 48.

16:37–43 David was careful to appoint Levites to carry on the worship of Jehovah before **the ark** in Jerusalem, and also **at Gibeon** where **the tabernacle** and **the altar of burnt offering** were still located. At Jerusalem he **designated** singers, door-keepers, and trumpeters, all under Abiathar. The priesthood of **Zadok** officiated in **Gibeon**. The chief emphasis in this passage is on the musicians. Two different Obed-Edoms are possibly mentioned in verse 38, and there are two different Jeduthuns in verses 38 and 42. . . . Now that the ark was settled in Zion, all **the people** went home and **David returned** to pronounce a blessing on **his house.**

C. David's Desire to Build the Temple and God's Response (Chap. 17)

Chapter 17 is divided into three parts: David's *desire* to build God a house (vv. 1, 2), God's *determination* to build David a house (vv. 3–15), and David's responsive *prayer* (vv. 16–27). Second Samuel 7 is the parallel passage.

17:1–4 **David** told **Nathan the prophet** that he was unhappy to be living in a luxurious home while **the ark of the covenant** was in a tent. His desire to **build** a house for **the LORD** met with Nathan's hasty approval. But then the Lord corrected **Nathan**: **David** was **not** the man chosen for this task.

17:5, 6 The ark of God had never been **in a** permanent **house**, but in a **tent**. Neither had God **commanded** that such **a house** be built up to this time. David later revealed to his son, Solomon, a fact not mentioned here: He was disqualified from building the temple because he had been involved in so much bloodshed and violence (22:7, 8). It was left for his son, "a man of rest" (22:9), to bring the ark of the Lord to its rest.

17:7–15 As God had spoken in grace to the patriarchs in the past, so now He singles out Israel's shepherd-king for unmerited blessing. These unconditional promises are known as the Davidic covenant. Second Samuel 7:12–16 and Psalm 89 also record the covenant. John Walvoord summarizes its provisions:

> The provisions of the Davidic covenant include . . . the following: (1) David is to have a child, yet to be born, who shall succeed him and establish his kingdom. (2) This son (Solomon) shall build the temple instead of David. (3) The throne of his kingdom shall be established forever. (4) The throne will not be taken away from him (Solomon) even though his sins justify chastisement. (5) David's house, throne, and kingdom shall be established forever.[14]

This covenant, like the other unconditional covenants God made, plays an important part in His dealings with mankind. It is mentioned in several other places in Scripture (e.g., Isa. 9; Jer. 23,33; Ezek. 37; Zech. 14). It will find its complete and total fulfillment in the Lord Jesus Christ, to whom belong the throne and the kingdom forever.

17:16–27 Upon hearing these things, **David** went **before the LORD** and poured out his heart in believing prayer. His response to God shows two of David's outstanding traits: humility and trust in the Lord. Verses 16 and 17 inspired the former slave-trader and later preacher of the gospel, John Newton, to write his famous spiritual song, "Amazing Grace." Like

David he saw his own unworthiness and smallness exalted by God's truly amazing grace.[15]

D. David's Victories (Chaps. 18—20)

The events summarized in the next three chapters (18—20) took place historically after David was made king (chap. 12) and before the ark was brought to Jerusalem (chaps. 13—17).

Many of Israel's hostile neighbors were now brought under her sway as had been originally intended by God. Up till then sin and disobedience had kept her in servitude under those she was meant to conquer. Now, tribute was sent from these Gentile nations to Israel in recognition of her superiority and power.

18:1–6 **The Philistines, Moabites, Syrians**, and Edomites were all defeated because **the Lord preserved** ["helped," NASB] **David wherever he went.**

Verse 4 records another failure on David's part to observe the laws concerning the behavior of Israel's kings (Deut. 17:15–17). First he had multiplied wives for himself (14:3), and now he multiplied horses.

18:7–11 Much wealth was subsequently acquired. For example, **all kinds of articles of gold, silver, and bronze**, taken from Hadadezer's **servants**, he **dedicated . . . to the Lord**, later to be used by **Solomon** in building the temple.

18:12, 13 The **eighteen thousand** who were **killed** by **Abishai** are attributed to David in the parallel passage in 2 Sam. 8:13. See the commentary there for a resolution of this apparent discrepancy.

18:14–17 David's enemies felt his wrath, but his people enjoyed his righteousness **and justice**. He was not only a good general but also an efficient administrator. David's officers and officials are listed here as well as in 2 Samuel 8:16–18. God likes to give recognition for service to Him and His leaders.

19:1–4 **Nahash** had fought against Israel in the days of Saul (1 Samuel 11). Evidently he had also rendered some unrecorded service to **David** during Saul's reign. Because of this, **messengers** were **sent . . . to comfort** his **son, Hanun**, after his father's death. But **Hanun** followed unwise counsel and treated the ambassadors contemptuously.

19:5–7 Fearing reprisal, **the people of Ammon hired** mercenaries and prepared for war.

19:8–15 **Joab** along with **his brother . . . Abishai** defeated the combined forces of the Ammonites **and Syrians**. Joab's exhortation in verse 13 inspired the Israelites and showed that he had the proper perspective as he faced the battle.

19:16–19 **The Syrians . . . sent** for their relatives **beyond the River** and planned to avenge their recent loss. **David** realized the danger, quickly **gathered** his forces, and took up the offensive. The surprised army, under **Shophach**, was no match for Israel, and the proud **Syrians . . . became** David's **servants**.

20:1, 2 **Joab** had been sent against **Rabbah** (modern-day Amman) by King David while David himself **stayed at Jerusalem** (2 Sam. 12:1). The siege probably lasted about two years. During this time David became involved with Bathsheba, the wife of Uriah, one of his thirty "mighty men." Second Samuel 12 tells about David's sin and restoration but, true to the form of Chronicles, the sin is not mentioned here. **Joab** summoned **David** when the city was ready to fall, and the **crown** of the defeated monarch was placed **on David's head**.

20:3 This verse may refer only to the men of war. Since the Hebrew wording is somewhat obscure in this passage, a possible rendering offered by some commentators is that the people were put under forced labor (see notes on 2 Samuel 12).

20:4–8 Three giants were killed in the course of fighting with Israel's constant enemies, **the Philistines. Sibbechai killed Sippai . . . at Gezer, Elhanan . . . killed Lahmi** (referred to as Goliath in 2 Sam. 21), and **David's** nephew **Jonathan** (son of his **brother . . . Shimea**, or Shammah) struck down a **giant** who had **six . . . fingers . . . on each hand and six . . . toes . . . on each foot**. Matthew Henry applies the verse for us:

> The servants of David, though men of ordinary stature, were too hard for the giants of Gath in every encounter because they had God on their side. . . . We need not fear great men against us while we have the great God for us. What will a finger more on each hand do, or a toe more on each foot, in contest with Omnipotence?[16]

E. The Census and the Plague (Chap. 21)

When this chapter is compared with 2 Samuel 24, it is not at first clear who was behind David's sin of numbering the people. Second Samuel says that the Lord moved David to number Israel because His anger was kindled against the nation. Here we are told that Satan incited the action. Both statements are, of course, true. God allowed Satan to tempt David. God is not the author of evil, but He permits it and causes it to serve His appointed ends.

For the differences between the figures given in this chapter and those given in 2 Samuel 24, see Endnotes.[17]

21:1–7 **Joab** was against the census from the start and was not very diligent in carrying out the king's orders. **Levi** was not included perhaps because the tribe was dispersed throughout Israel and Judah, and to number the people would have been difficult. **Benjamin** may have been omitted because the census was interrupted before reaching that tribe (1 Chron. 27:24). In numbering the people no ransom was collected, as commanded in Exodus 30:12. David's disobedience and pride brought grave consequences.

21:8–15 Although **David . . . sinned greatly**, he was quick to confess and humble himself before the Lord. When given a choice as to the penalty of his wrongdoing, he chose to **fall into the hand of the LORD** because he knew that He is merciful. **Seventy thousand men** were slain before the pestilence was stopped.

To us the punishment may seem severe. All of us have weaknesses and besetting sins. David was generally humble, but in this instance he fell into the ancient sin of the devil, pride. Matthew Henry makes application for all of us:

> He was proud of the multitude of his people, but divine Justice took a course to make them fewer. Justly is that taken from us, weakened, or embittered to us, which we are proud of.[18]

21:16, 17 When **David** raised **his eyes** he saw a terrifying sight: **the angel of the LORD** with **drawn sword** stretched **out over** his beloved **Jerusalem**. His response was much better than most believers show when caught in some major sin or disobedience. Henry's four-point summary on how David bore his correction may prove helpful to us all, especially those in a place of leadership.

1. He made a very penitent confession of his sin, and prayed earnestly for the pardon of it, *v.* 8. Now he owned that he had sinned, had sinned greatly, had done foolishly, very foolishly; and he entreated that, however he might be corrected for it, the iniquity of it might be done away. 2. He accepted the punishment of his iniquity: "Let thy hand be *on me, and on my father's house, v.* 17. I submit to the rod, only let me be the sufferer, for I am the sinner; mine is the guilty head at which the sword should be pointed." 3. He cast himself upon the mercy of God (though he knew he was angry with him) and did not entertain any hard thoughts of him. However it be, *Let us fall into the hands of the Lord, for his mercies are great, v.* 13. Good men, even when God frowns upon them, think well of him. *Though he slay me, yet will I trust in him.* 4. He expressed a very tender concern for the people, and it went to his heart to see them plagued for his transgression: *These sheep, what have they done?*[19]

21:18–26 Through **Gad**, the Lord directed David to acquire **the threshing floor of Ornan** (Araunah in 2 Sam.), a **Jebusite**, and to build **an altar** there and offer sacrifices. **Ornan** offered the land **to David** as a gift, but the king insisted on paying for it. Verse 24 is an important spiritual principle: Effective sacrifice is always costly. This **threshing floor** later became the site of the temple (2 Chron. 3:1).

21:27–30 It was on Moriah that Abraham offered up Isaac (Gen. 22). Here the plague was stopped, and when **the LORD commanded the angel,** he **returned his sword to its sheath**, as we read in this chapter. Here the temple stood. And we believe that it was on this same ridge, although not on the same spot, that the Lord Jesus died on the cross for the sins of mankind.

The realization that the site of the **threshing floor** was to be the new center of worship may account for David's fear to go to **Gibeon** for guidance.

F. Preparations for the Temple (Chaps. 22—26)

1. Materials, Men, and Motivation (Chap. 22)

22:1–5 David recognized that the threshing floor (21:28) was the future site of the temple and of **the altar of burnt offering**. Therefore he began to **make preparations** for construction, though he knew that **Solomon** was the one who would have the privilege of building the temple. **The aliens** mentioned in verse 2 were the Canaanites who remained **in the land** (1 Kgs. 9:20, 21). **Israel** was supposed to have destroyed them, but, having failed to do this, the Jews now subjected them to forced labor.

22:6–13 In a rather formal address **to Solomon, David** rehearsed his own desire to **build** the temple, his disqualification because he had been a man of **blood**, and the Lord's promise that his son **Solomon** would **build** the **house** of God. He requested that **the LORD** would **be with** Solomon, giving him **wisdom and understanding**, and urged Solomon to be obedient to **the law of** God.

22:14–16 Finally, David told Solomon about all **the troubles** he had taken to **prepare** materials and **workmen** for the task. He ended with advice that all Christians would do well to heed: **"Arise and begin working, and the LORD be with you."**

22:17–19 Then the king urged **the leaders of Israel** to cooperate with **Solomon**. Notice that building for God is first a matter of the heart, then of the hands: **"Set your heart . . . and build the sanctuary."**

2. *Divisions and Duties of the Levites (Chaps. 23—26)*

23:1–3 Near the end of David's reign, a census was taken of **the Levites from the age of thirty years and above**, the age at which they could begin their active service.

23:4, 5 The **thirty-eight thousand** men were then divided into four general groups: **twenty-four thousand** overseers in the temple, **six thousand . . . officers and judges, four thousand . . . gatekeepers**, and **four thousand** musicians and singers to worship continually before **the Lord**. These instructions were divinely inspired and communicated to David through his prophets (2 Chron. 29:25).

23:6–24 In verses 6–23, the Levitical genealogies are given again: **the Gershonites** (vv. 7–11), Kohathites (vv. 12–20) (including **Moses** and **Aaron**, the most famous Levites of all), and Merarites (vv. 21–23).

Certain priestly functions had been committed exclusively to **Aaron . . . and his sons forever** (v. 13). Burning **incense**, ministry to the Lord in the holy place and Holy of Holies (for the high priest alone), and blessing in the name of Jehovah (Num. 6:23–27) were reserved for the priests.

23:25–27 Next the duties of **the Levites** are spelled out. **They** would **no longer carry the tabernacle** and its furniture as they had been commanded by Moses, since the temple would be a permanent house for God. **David**, with his **last words**, lowered the minimum age to **twenty years old and above** because more manpower would be needed in the service of the temple.

23:28–32 The 6000 judges were probably dispersed throughout Israel while the other Levites served in relation to the temple. The 24,000 overseers of the work in the temple were to **attend to the needs of** the priests in the duties enumerated in verses 28–32.

24:1–19 In chapter 24 we are told how the priestly and Levitical **divisions** were formed. There were twenty-four households or divisions of priests (vv. 1–19) and twenty-four divisions of Levites (vv. 20–31). Each division was assigned a **schedule** on a rotating basis to minister in the temple, thus giving everyone the opportunity of serving approximately two weeks each year. Zacharias (Luke 1:5) belonged to **the eighth** course, the course of **Abijah** (v. 10).

The households of Aaron's two surviving **sons, Eleazar and Ithamar,** comprised the priesthood, **sixteen** divisions belonging to the former and **eight** divisions going to the latter (v. 4). The **lot** was cast in the presence of **David**, the **leaders** of Israel, and **Zadok** and **Ahimelech** the priests; the results were recorded by **Shemaiah . . . the scribe** with meticulous care.

24:20–31 The Levites also cast their lot before David and the princes. The lot apparently determined the division to which each man was assigned.

25:1–7 In chapter 25 other sons of Levi, the singers and musicians, are set in their courses to perform their sacred service. These are **the sons of Asaph** (v. 2), **Jeduthun** (v. 3), and **Heman** (vv. 4, 5). These **two hundred and eighty-eight** men were appointed to sing **in the house of the Lord**, accompanied by **cymbals, stringed instruments, and harps** (vv. 6, 7).

25:8–31 They were assigned to their **twenty-four** courses or shifts by **lot**, as indicated in verses 8–31.

26:1–19 Details concerning **the gatekeepers** and the gates to which they were assigned by **lot** are given next. Here we find **the Korahites** (v. 1), ". . . their duty being to prevent the presumption of which their father was guilty (Num. 16). Such are the ways of God."[20] Here too is **Obed-Edom**, who sheltered the ark, after the death of Uzza (13:14). God had not forgotten his faithfulness.

Verse 18 means that there were **four** gatekeepers or temple guards at a causeway adjoining one of the gates, and **two** more at the other end of the causeway leading to **Parbar**, probably a court or colonnade extending west of the temple.[21]

26:20–28 Some **Levites** were appointed to guard the temple **treasuries, the spoils**, and the freewill offerings that had been **dedicated** to the Lord.

26:29–32 A third group of Levites was set apart **as officials and judges, one thousand seven hundred . . . west . . . of the Jordan** and **two thousand seven hundred** on the east side of the river in **Gilead**.

G. Military and Governmental Leaders (Chap. 27)

27:1–15 The army, like the Levites, served in **divisions**. **Twenty-four thousand** men were on duty each **month**. All the commanders are listed among David's mighty men (chap. 11 and 2 Sam. 23).

27:16–22 **The tribes** are listed in a designed order. First listed are the sons of Leah, in their proper order: **the Reubenites, the Simeonites, the Levites, Judah, Issachar,** and **Zebulun**. Then the sons of Rachel: Joseph (represented by his sons **Ephraim** and **Manasseh**) and **Benjamin**. The children of Bilhah are given (but not in chronological order): **Naphtali** and **Dan**. The sons of Zilpah (Gad and Asher) are not named here.

27:23, 24 **Those twenty years old and under** were **not** recorded in the census that David had ordered. The **census** was never completed because the **wrath** of the Lord fell before **Joab** finished. **David**, perhaps ashamed of his sin, ordered that the result of the ill-fated census should not be put in the public records.

27:25–34 David had twelve officials who had charge of his domestic affairs. He also had counselors and close friends who advised him. Ahithophel's sad story is given in 2 Samuel 15 and 17. He was, like **Joab**, a man of high privilege but low character. How much nobler was **Hushai, the king's companion. Ahithophel** was a self-seeking opportunist, but **Hushai** was a self-effacing servant. Each one reaped what he had sown (see 2 Sam. 15—17). Both served the king, but each had different motives. The opportunist works for his own glory, but the servant for that of his master.

H. David's Last Days (Chaps. 28, 29)

28:1–8 **David assembled at Jerusalem all the leaders** of the various **divisions** and the **officers of the tribes** and **captains**. Once again he explained his desire **to build a house** for **the Lord** and the reasons why he had not been permitted to do so. But he had been chosen and established as **king** in **Israel**, and his **son Solomon** had been **chosen** to succeed him. Since David's **throne** had been firmly established by God, the people were to obey the Lord through **Solomon** as they had through David.

28:9, 10 Next David addressed his **son**. Verse 9 contains a command, a promise, and a warning. *The command:* **"As for you, my son Solomon, know the God of your father, and serve Him with a loyal heart and with a willing mind."** *The promise:* **"If you seek Him, He will be found by you."** The warning: **"But if you forsake Him, He will cast you off forever."** Since **the Lord** had appointed Solomon

to build the temple, he should take courage **and do it**.

28:11–19 But, like Moses before him, **Solomon** must build according to the pattern given **by the Spirit**, perhaps in a vision. There was no room for human imagination or ingenuity, because the temple is a type of Christ. **David gave . . . Solomon the plans** he had drawn up under the inspiration of the **Spirit**. He had even weighed the raw materials to be used for each piece of furniture. (More complete details are given in 2 Chron. 2—4.) **The chariot, that is, the gold cherubim** (v. 18), according to Unger, probably means "the cherubim as the chariot upon which God enters or is throned."[22]

28:20, 21 **Solomon** now had **the plans**; the materials were collected; the temple servants, **the Levites**, had all been assigned their duties. **God** was **with** him and would not fail him; therefore his father urged him again, **"Be strong . . . and do it."**

29:1–9 Although **King David** had **given** so much already to the work of the temple, yet as a final offering and as an example to the people he dedicated more **silver** and **gold** from his private funds and urged **the people** to give liberally. Their generous response brought rejoicing to their own hearts and to the heart of the king.

29:10–19 David then offered a magnificent prayer of worship and thanksgiving. He eulogized the **LORD** as worthy of all **honor**, **exalted as head over all**, and as the Source of all **riches and honor**. He acknowledged that he and his **people** were unworthy to give to God, and that what they gave had **come from** Him anyway. He prayed that the present devotion (an *upright* **heart**, v. 17) of his people would become a permanent trait (a **heart** *fixed* on God, v. 18), and that his **son** would have **a loyal heart** (v. 19) in building **the temple**.

29:20–22a When he called on the congregation to **bless the LORD**, they **bowed** low and **prostrated themselves before the LORD and the king**. **The next day . . . they** sacrificed 3000 animals, and **they ate and drank before the LORD**.

29:22b–25 **Solomon** was **made . . . king** a **second time** (v. 22; cf. 23:1); then, after David's death, he **sat on the throne**, enjoying the blessing of the Lord and the allegiance of the people. His glorious kingdom prepictures the splendor of Christ's millennial reign over the entire earth.

29:26–30 First Chronicles closes with a brief summary of David's **reign**. **He died full of days** (he was seventy), **riches, and honor**.

ENDNOTES

[1](Intro) Thus when our Lord speaks of the blood of Abel (Gen. 4:10, 11) to the blood of Zechariah the son of Berechiah (2 Chron. 24:20, 21), He is saying "from Genesis to Malachi" (or Revelation).

[2](Intro) It would seem to imply that the Chronicler filled in what Samuel and Kings neglected.

[3](Intro) If Chronicles paralleled Samuel and Kings even more it would no doubt be criticized as being redundant.

[4](Intro) William Kelly, *Lectures on the Books of Chronicles*, p. 13.

[5](Intro) *Ibid.*

[6](Intro) The Septuagint translates it *seers*, the Hebrew word for *seers* being close to the name *Hozai*.

[7](Intro) W. Graham Scroggie, *Know Your Bible*, Vol. 1, *The Old Testament*, p. 86.

[8](1:Intro) The New King James Version, which text the *Believers Bible*

Commentary comments upon, footnotes these variations rather fully in most editions, yet the OT editor as well as the executive editor, translators, and review committees, all hold the position of inerrancy of the original text.

[9](2:1—4:23) H. A. Ironside, *The Continual Burnt Offering*, Reading for March 12.

[10](7:13) *Jahzul* and *Shallum* illustrate names that are slightly different from their Genesis spelling (Jahzeel and Shillum in Gen. 46:24; cf. NKJV footnote).

[11](8:29–40) The "bosheth" part of Mephibosheth's name (cf. Ishbosheth) means *"shame."* Rather than say the name of a pagan deity (here, Baal) devout Jews would replace it with this insult to idolatry.

[12](10:1–5) C. H. Spurgeon, *Spurgeon's Devotional Bible*, p. 265.

[13](11:20, 21) The Syriac version reads "thirty" (see NKJV footnote).

[14](17:7–15) John Walvoord, quoted by J. Dwight Pentecost, *Things to Come*, pp. 101, 102.

[15](17:16–27) Samuel Willoughby Duffield, *English Hymns: Their Authors and History*, p. 166.

[16](20:4–8) Matthew Henry, "1 Chronicles," in *Matthew Henry's Commentary on the Whole Bible*, II:887.

[17](21:Intro) The apparent discrepancies in numbers between 2 Samuel 24 and 1 Chronicles 21 can be reconciled as follows:

	2 SAMUEL 24	*1 CHRONICLES 21*
1. *Census figures*		
	800,000 valiant men of Israel who drew the sword (v. 9)	1,100,000—all Israel who drew the sword (v. 5)
	500,000 men of Judah (v. 9)	470,000 men of Judah who drew the sword (v. 5)
	1,300,000 men	1,570,000 men

But note the different classifications: valiant men vs. *all Israel*; men of Judah vs. men of Judah *who drew the sword*. The figures necessarily include different classes.

2. *Years of famine*		
	seven years (v. 13)	three years (v. 12)

The seven years may include the three-year famine caused by Saul's slaying of the Gibeonites (2 Sam. 21:1). If David chose three additional years, any part of an intervening year would count as a year, and thus the total famine would be seven.

3. *Price paid to Araunah (Ornan)*		
	50 shekels (v. 24)	600 shekels (v. 25)

The fifty shekels were for the threshing floor and the oxen. The 600 shekels were for "the place of this threshing floor" (v. 22), the larger area of which the threshing floor was only a part.

[18](21:8–15) Henry, "1 Chronicles," II:889.

[19](21:16, 17) *Ibid.*

[20](26:1–19) George Williams, *The Student's Commentary on the Holy Scriptures*, p. 236.

[21](26:1–19) Another theory is that *Parbar* was a suburb of Jerusalem. The term is uncertain in meaning.

[22](28:11–19) Merrill F. Unger, *Unger's Bible Dictionary*, p. 190.

BIBLIOGRAPHY

Henry, Matthew. "1 Chronicles" and "2 Chronicles." In *Matthew Henry's Commentary on the Whole Bible*. Vol. 2. Reprint. McLean, VA: MacDonald Publishing Company, n.d.

Keil, C. F. "The Books of the Chronicles." In *Biblical Commentary on the Old Testament*. Vol. 9. Grand Rapids: Wm. B. Eerdmans Publishing Co., 1971.

Kelly, William. *Lectures on the Books of Chronicles*. Oak Park, IL: Bible Truth Publishers, 1963.

Payne, J. Barton, "I and II Chronicles." In *The Wycliffe Bible Commentary*. Chicago: Moody Press, 1962.

Sailhamer, John. *First and Second Chronicles. Everyman's Bible Commentary*. Chicago: Moody Press, 1983.

Zöckler, Otto. "The Books of the Chronicles." In *Commentary on the Holy Scriptures, Critical, Doctrinal, and Homiletical*. Vol. 4. Reprint (24 vols. in 12). Grand Rapids: Zondervan Publishing House, 1960.

SECOND CHRONICLES

"The Book of 2 Chronicles outlines God's discipline based on His conditional promises. The period of 427 years covers nineteen kings of Judah. Seven were good kings likened to David; ten were bad kings, likened to Israel or Jeroboam; two were good turning to bad, namely Solomon and Joash. Here we see discipline turning into judgment."

—John Heading

For Introduction see 1 Chronicles.

OUTLINE

I. THE KINGDOM OF SOLOMON (Chaps. 1—9)
   A. Solomon's Worship, Wisdom, and Wealth (Chap. 1)
   B. Solomon's Preparation, Construction, and Dedication of the Temple (Chaps. 2—7)
      Excursus on Apparent Discrepancies
   C. Solomon in All His Splendor (8:1—9:28)
   D. Solomon's Death (9:29–31)

II. THE DIVISION OF THE KINGDOM (Chap. 10)

III. THE KINGDOM OF JUDAH (11:1—36:19)
   A. King Rehoboam (Chaps. 11, 12)
   B. King Abijah (Chap. 13)
   C. King Asa (Chaps. 14—16)
   D. King Jehoshaphat (Chaps. 17—20)
   E. King Jehoram (Chap. 21)
   F. King Ahaziah (22:1–9)
   G. Usurpation of Queen Athaliah (22:10—23:21)
   H. King Joash (Chap. 24)
   I. King Amaziah (Chap. 25)
   J. King Uzziah (Chap. 26)
   K. King Jotham (Chap. 27)
   L. King Ahaz (Chap. 28)
   M. King Hezekiah (Chaps. 29—32)
   N. King Manasseh (33:1–20)
   O. King Amon (33:21–25)
   P. King Josiah (Chaps. 34, 35)

Q. King Jehoahaz (36:1–3)
R. King Jehoiakim (36:4–8)
S. King Jehoiachin (36:9, 10)
T. King Zedekiah (36:11–19)

IV. THE BABYLONIAN CAPTIVITY (36:20, 21)

V. THE DECREE OF CYRUS (36:22, 23)

Commentary

The break between 1 and 2 Chronicles was made strictly for convenience, since they were originally one very large book. Thus 2 Chronicles takes up exactly where 1 Chronicles leaves off. The dividing point is well chosen—between David's and Solomon's reigns.

In 1 Chronicles 29 David established Solomon as his successor. Second Chronicles traces the Davidic line from Solomon to the return of the Jewish remnant from the Babylonian Captivity. First and Second Kings cover basically the same time period, but the emphasis in Chronicles is almost entirely on Judah. The kings of Israel are mentioned only as they relate to the history of Judah. Also, the emphasis of Chronicles is *spiritual* while that of Kings is *historical*. Although much of the material is the same in both books, Chronicles sometimes contains details not found in Kings, Chronicles being written at a later date and for a different purpose. We will comment on some of the differences between the two books, but it will be impossible to go into depth about all of them. (Other books have been written for this purpose.)

I. THE KINGDOM OF SOLOMON (Chaps. 1—9)

A. Solomon's Worship, Wisdom, and Wealth (Chap. 1)

1:1–3 First Kings 1—3 tells what went on between the death of David (1 Chron. 29) and the time when **Solomon** was established as king. Adonijah and Joab were killed in a power struggle as Solomon secured his father's throne in accordance with the word of the Lord (1 Chron. 22:9, 10).

With **his kingdom** secured, **Solomon** called together his subordinates and led them in a solemn procession to **Gibeon**, where **the tabernacle** was located.

1:4–6 **David had** moved **the ark** to **Jerusalem** (1 Chron. 13—15), but the rest of the furniture of **the tabernacle** was at Gibeon, including the **bronze altar**. Upon this **altar . . . Solomon . . . offered a thousand burnt offerings**, a display of his devotion and loyalty to Jehovah, the God of his father.

1:7–12 **God appeared** to him **that** same **night** in a dream and asked him what he most desired (v. 7; 1 Kgs. 3:5). Solomon's request for **wisdom**

and knowledge in ruling the **people** so pleased the Lord that He also promised him unparalleled **riches, wealth, and honor**. In a sense, God appears to every believer and asks him what he wants. What we want in life largely determines what we get.

1:13–17 Solomon returned **to Jerusalem** to a reign of great prosperity. These verses dwell on his **chariots, horsemen, chariot cities, silver, gold**, cedar, and **horses**. But his prosperity contained the seeds of his eventual failure, as is often the case.

B. Solomon's Preparation, Construction, and Dedication of the Temple (Chaps. 2—7)

2:1, 2 In preparation for construction of **the temple, Solomon selected seventy thousand men** to carry the materials, plus **eighty thousand** stonecutters and **three thousand six hundred** supervisors.

2:3–10 Then he **sent** for help to **Hiram, king of Tyre**, who had supplied **cedars** for David's royal palace. After describing the spiritual significance of the project, **Solomon** asked specifically for a skilled craftsman to work with the artisan **whom David** had hired, and also for the necessary **timber**. Solomon promised to pay handsomely for any help given. There seems to be a discrepancy as to the actual amount.[1]

Apparent Discrepancies

In commenting on 2 Chronicles, we must note that there are some seeming discrepancies between this book and the parallel accounts in 1 and 2 Kings. If we overlook these differences, we do a disservice to our readers. On the other hand, if we overemphasize the differences, we run the risk of undermining confidence in the Word, and we certainly do not want to do this. Our solution is this: We have decided to bring the principal differences out into the open, even if we can't solve them all. At the same time we want to make it clear that they in no way affect the inspiration of the Scriptures. We believe that

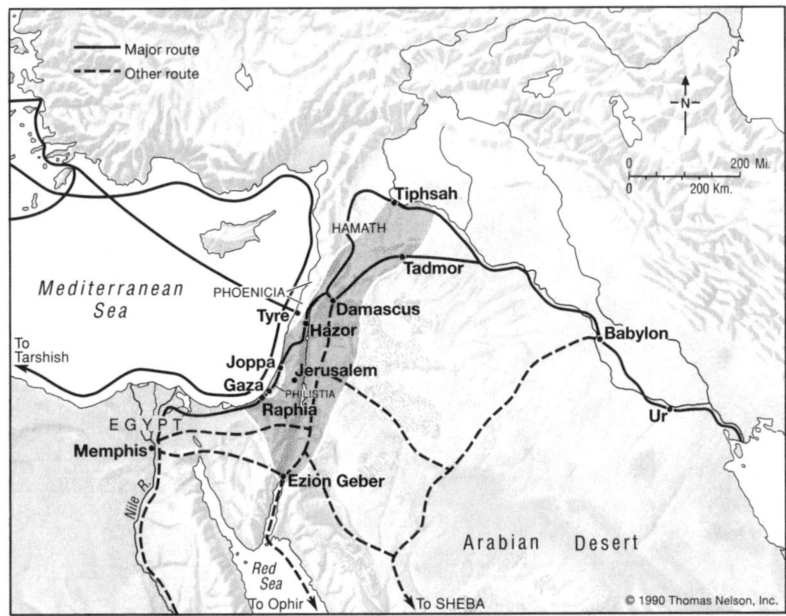

The Spread of Solomon's Fame. Solomon's influence in economic and political affairs was enhanced by the transportation and trade routes that intersected his kingdom.

the Bible, as originally given, is inspired by God, inerrant, and infallible.

We have handled the problems in the Endnotes. In this way the technical discussions of apparently contradictory details will not break up the flow of the commentary. On the other hand, it gives us opportunity to investigate the problems briefly but freely.

Many of the discrepancies are copyists' errors. We should not be surprised if scribes made minor mistakes in copying and recopying the Bible over the course of many centuries. Even today it is almost impossible to publish a book without some typographical errors creeping in.

Someone might ask, "If God could guide the original writers of Scripture to be free from error, why couldn't He cause the scribes to produce error-free copies?" The answer, of course, is that He could have, but in His wisdom He didn't choose to do so. The important point is that, in spite of minor scribal or copyists' errors (mostly in the spelling of names and in numbers), the Bible as we have it today is the Word of God. Any problems have to do with minor details and not with any Bible doctrine. It is reassuring to remember that when the Lord Jesus was on earth, He used an edition of the OT (not the original manuscripts) and He quoted this text as the Word of God. We can use reputable versions of the Bible today with the same confidence that they are the Word of God.‡

2:11–16 Hiram's reply **in writing, which he sent to Solomon**, seemed to indicate a genuine, spiritual recognition that the undertaking was historic. He said he was sending **Huram,** a **craftsman** with impeccable qualifications.[2] He also promised to send **wood from Lebanon** in exchange for

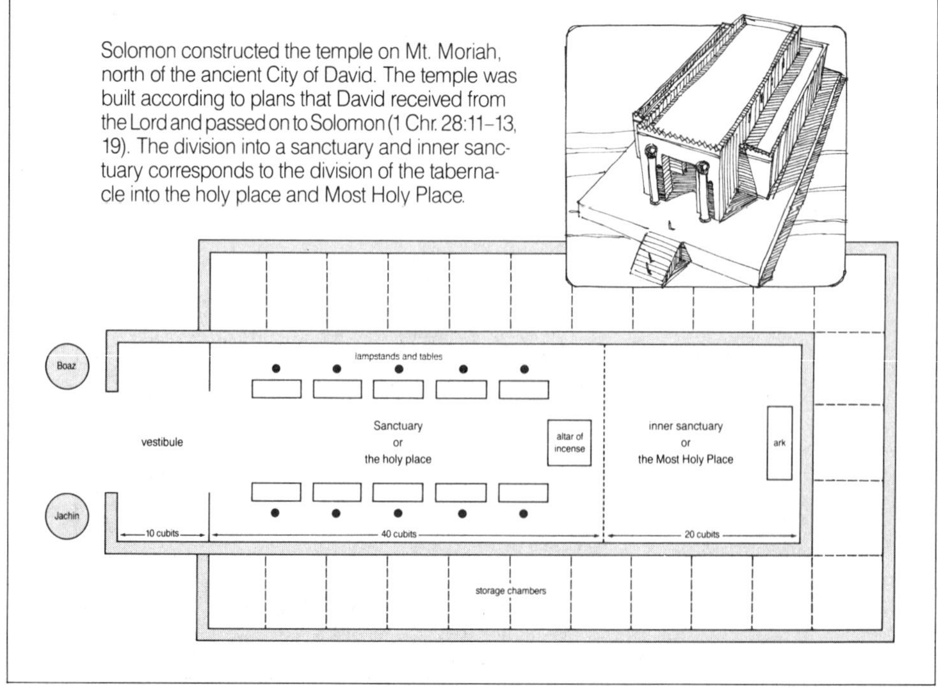

The Plan of Solomon's Temple

wheat, barley, oil, and . . . wine. The timber would be floated on **rafts** down the Mediterranean Sea **to Joppa**, then transported overland **to Jerusalem**.

2:17, 18 The 153,000 **aliens** or strangers were Canaanites whom the Israelites had failed to destroy. Now they were used as forced laborers.[3]

3:1–4 After much planning and preparation, the construction finally began **in the fourth year of** Solomon's **reign**. With over 150,000 workmen and almost limitless resources, it would still take over seven years to complete this mammoth undertaking.

The foundations were laid **on Mount Moriah**. The temple would be ninety feet long, thirty feet wide, and forty-five feet high (see 1 Kgs. 6, where more details are given). It was roughly twice the size of the tabernacle and had a **vestibule** or porch thirty feet long.[4]

3:5–9 The interior of the temple was divided into two rooms on the main floor. The two rooms were **the larger room** (literally **house**, NKJV marg.) and the **Most Holy Place**. The building was of stone. The interior was **paneled with cypress** wood which was **overlaid with pure gold**, ornamented with various designs, and studded **with precious stones**. All that was visible inside the temple was **gold**, the symbol of deity, picturing the glory of the Lord which was to fill the place.

3:10–13 **Two cherubim** were put into the **Most Holy Place** (in addition to the two cherubim which formed part of the mercy seat atop the ark). Their combined wingspans extended the entire width of the **Most Holy Place**. The ark would later be placed under them (5:7). **Cherubim** are spirit-beings which appear often in Scripture. The walls (v. 7) and the veil (v. 14) were decorated with them, symbolizing their continual waiting on God. The temple and the tabernacle were types of the true dwelling place of God—i.e., heaven, where He is worshiped and glorified day and night by myriad hosts (Heb. 8:5). They were also types of Christ (John 1:14, where "dwelt" is literally "tabernacled"; 2:19).

3:14–17 A **veil** separated the two rooms, just as in the tabernacle. There were also doors (v. 7) between the rooms in the temple. **Two pillars** with capitals and **one hundred** ornamental **pomegranates** were placed **in front of the temple**.[5] The pillar **on the right** side was named **Jachin** (*He shall establish*) and **the one on the left** was called **Boaz** (*in Him is strength*).

4:1–22 The two chief metals used in the temple were **bronze** and **gold**. Chapter 4 briefly lists some of the furnishings made from these metals. **Bronze** was used for the **altar** of burnt offering, **the Sea** and supporting **oxen** (vv. 2–5, 10),[6] **ten lavers** or portable basins (v. 6), overlay for the **doors** of the court (v. 9), various utensils (vv. 11, 14–18), and the **two pillars** and **capitals** (vv. 12, 13). These were all **cast in clay molds between Succoth and Zeredah** (v. 17).

Solomon used **gold** for **ten lampstands** for the holy place (vv. 7, 20), **ten tables** for **the showbread** (vv. 8, 19) a golden **altar** (v. 19), various utensils (vv. 8, 21, 22), and overlay for the holy place and Most Holy Place (v. 22). **Gold** was used primarily for items inside the temple while the **bronze** furnishings were mainly employed outside.

All the furnishings for the temple were made by **Solomon** except the ark of the covenant. That was brought from the tabernacle.

5:1–10 Now the temple **was fin-**

ished (v. 1; cf. 1 Kgs. 8). Verses 2–10 tell about the transporting of the furniture from **the tabernacle of meeting** to the temple. **The ark** was placed in the **Most Holy Place**. Perhaps the other items, like the altar of incense and the table of showbread, were put into the treasury at this time, since they were not used in Solomon's temple.

The Levites who carried **the ark** were **priests** (vv. 4, 7). They set **the ark** in **its place . . . under the wings of the** guarding **cherubim** (vv. 7, 8). Exodus 25:15 required that **the poles** stay with the ark. ("Drew out," v. 9 KJV, is inaccurate.) According to 1 Kings 8:8, **the ends of the poles of the ark could be seen from** the holy place. **The two tablets** of the law were **in the ark** at this time.

5:11–14 Verse 11b, **"all the priests . . . without keeping to their divisions,"** means that **all the priests . . . present** that day participated, not just the course that was assigned the duty.

When **the Levites** and **priests** assembled **at the east end of the altar, praising and thanking the Lord** for His goodness and **mercy, the glory of the Lord filled** the temple **so that the priests could not** minister inside.

6:1–11 Before addressing the Lord in his prayer of dedication, Solomon reminded the people how, in Israel's earlier history, the Lord had not **chosen** a **city** as the religious capital or a **man** as **ruler**. (It is true that Samuel and others were leaders, but they did not have the power of a sovereign.) But the time came when God chose **Jerusalem** as His city and **David** as king **over . . . Israel**. **David** desired **to build a temple, but** his good intention was to be carried out by one of his sons. And now here stood **Solomon**, a testimony to the faithfulness of God.

6:12, 13 The central part of chapter 6 is Solomon's prayer of dedication (vv. 12–42). It is the longest prayer recorded in the Bible and is full of praise and petition. Ascending a special **platform** in the temple court, **Solomon . . . spread out his hands** and prayed. He had much for which *to be thankful*. Emboldened by grace, he had much for which *to ask*.

6:14–17 First of all Solomon prayed about **the throne of Israel**. God had **kept** His word thus far concerning His promises to **David**. The king asked that His faithfulness might continue.

6:18–21 These four sentences contain the sum and substance of the entire prayer. All that follows is an expansion of the simple thought expressed by the verbs **hear** and **forgive** (v. 21).

6:22, 23 Next Solomon requests the Lord to **hear . . . and judge** oaths taken **before** His **altar**.

6:24, 25 Then he asks forgiveness for **sin** that might cause **Israel** to be **defeated** by her enemies.

6:26, 27 He requests **rain** after drought caused by **sin**.

6:28–31 He requests deliverance from **famine** or **pestilence** in order that the **people** might learn the **fear** of the Lord.

6:32, 33 He requests that foreigners may see God work when they come to call on His great Name.

6:34, 35 He requests victory in **battle**.

6:36–39 He requests deliverance from **captivity** once the people **repent** and confess their wickedness.

6:40–42 Solomon closed by requesting three things. He asked that his **prayer** might be accepted. He asked for grace and joy for the **priests**, those who serve God in His temple. He prayed for favor for himself based on God's great love for his father **David**.

Lest we think that this prayer consists of petitions only, let us go back through it once more. There is a great deal about the attributes of God here. Solomon mentioned God's: uniqueness (v. 14); lovingkindness (v. 14); transcendence (v. 18); immensity (infinity) (v. 18); omnipresence (v. 18); justice (v. 23); forgiveness (vv. 25, 27, etc.); omniscience (v. 30); grace (v. 33); and mercy (vv. 38, 39).

Besides all these, the Lord's omnipotence and holiness are implied throughout.

7:1–7 As soon as **Solomon had finished praying, fire came down from heaven and consumed the burnt offering** and **the sacrifices, and the glory of the Lord filled the temple**. The people **saw . . . the glory** cloud coming **down . . . on the temple**, and **they bowed . . . on the pavement**, worshiping and praising **the Lord**. **Solomon** then led **the people** in offering thousands of **bulls** and **sheep** as sacrifices to **the Lord**.

The priests took their positions, **the Levites** played the Lord's musical **instruments, which King David had made** for praising **the Lord. Opposite** the Levites, **the priests sounded their trumpets, while all** the Israelites **stood**.

The bronze altar was too small for the enormous number of sacrifices and **offerings**.

7:8–10 The dedication **feast** lasted for **seven days**, including the Day of Atonement. This was followed by the Feast of Tabernacles, after which Solomon dismissed **the people**.

7:11–16 After **Solomon** had **finished** the temple and his own palace, **the Lord appeared to** him at **night** with promises and warnings. In the event that God sent drought, **locusts**, or **pestilence** on the **people**, they should **humble themselves, . . . pray, . . . seek** His **face, and turn from their wicked ways. Then** He would **forgive their sin** and restore them.

Verse 14 may very well be the golden text of this entire book. Though originally addressed to the chosen nation of Israel, it has rightly been *applied* to those nations which have a biblical heritage. It is the sure road to restoration and revival for all times. If the conditions are met, the promises are sure of fulfillment.

J. Barton Payne comments:

> This great verse, the best known in all Chronicles, expresses as does no other in Scripture God's requirement for national blessing, whether in Solomon's land, in Ezra's, or in our own. Those who believe must forsake their sins, turn from the life that is centered in self, and yield to God's word and will. Then, and only then, will heaven send revival.[7]

7:17–22 If Solomon would live in obedience **before** God, He would **establish** his **throne** and allow Solomon's descendants to sit upon it. On the other hand, **if** Solomon and his people forsook the Lord for **other gods**, they would be carried into captivity, and God would reject the temple so that it would be an object of derision and a testimony to the nations that Israel had forsaken **the Lord**.

Verse 16 seems to imply that the temple would endure for all time; yet we know that it was destroyed in 586 B.C. The explanation, of course, is that God's promise was conditioned on Israel's faithfulness and obedience. Verses 19 and 20 specifically warn that if the people became idolaters, God would reject the temple.

C. Solomon in All His Splendor (8:1—9:28)

8:1–6 Here we read of Solomon's accomplishments and successes in various areas. First he undertook a vast urban-development program, rebuilding or capturing **storage cities**, **fortified cities**, **chariot cities**, and settlements.

8:7–10 He conscripted Canaanites for his slave **labor** force but used the Israelites as fighting **men**, commanders, and chief **officials**.[8]

8:11 He would not allow his wife, **the daughter of Pharaoh**, to live in the royal palace, saying that it was **holy** because **the ark of the LORD** had entered there. This does not mean that the ark had actually been taken inside the palace, but rather that the palace was **holy** by reason of its proximity to **the ark** in the temple. Unfortunately, the fact that Solomon restricted her to a special residence did not restrict her from leading him off into idolatry (1 Kgs. 11:1–8).

8:12–16 The king was careful to observe the sacrifices and **offerings** connected with the religious calendar. **He** also **appointed . . . the priests** and **Levites** to **serve . . . according to the** schedules prepared by **David his father**.

Thus **all the work of Solomon was** well-ordered from start to finish.

8:17, 18 Finally, we read of Solomon's maritime ventures in partnership with **Hiram**. The **ships** traveled between **Ezion Geber and Elath**—both on the northern tip of the eastern arm of the Red Sea (Gulf of Aqaba)—and **Ophir**.[9] It has been variously conjectured that Ophir was in southern Arabia, eastern Africa, or India.

9:1–9 When the queen of Sheba heard of the fame of Solomon, she traveled with **a very great** caravan loaded down with gifts to find out for herself. After seeing the splendor of his kingdom and testing his wisdom with hard **questions**, she was overwhelmed. She confessed that **the half** had **not** been **told**. She realized that Solomon's prosperity was due to the favor of his **God**.

9:10–12 Verses 10 and 11 interrupt the narrative to explain the source of some of Solomon's wealth and the uniquely beautiful uses to which he put it. When **the queen of Sheba** left, **Solomon gave** her gifts **much** greater in number and value **than** those **she had brought to** him.

9:13–28 Solomon received over **six hundred and sixty-six talents of gold** each year and used some of it to make **shields**, to overlay his **throne of ivory**, and to make goblets and tableware. His greatness brought him honor and wealth from **all the kings of the earth**. His trade went all the way to Tarshish, which may have been in Spain.[10] He was rich in the abundance of **horses**,[11] territory, **silver**, and **cedar**. Although he reigned over the territory from **the River** Euphrates westward, it was not incorporated as part of Israel but consisted of vassal states that paid tribute to him.

D. Solomon's Death (9:29–31)

Solomon died after he had **reigned** for **forty years**, and was succeeded by **his son . . . Rehoboam**. The noncanonical books mentioned in verse 29 were probably used as resource materials by the chronicler, but they have since been lost.

II. THE DIVISION OF THE KINGDOM (Chap. 10)

10:1–5 Perhaps to conciliate the northern tribes, **Rehoboam** decided to go **to Shechem** for his inauguration. The people promised to **serve** him if he would **lighten the heavy yoke** which Solomon had placed on them. **"All Israel"** (v. 3) means representatives from all the northern tribes. **Rehoboam** asked for **three days** to consider the people's request.

10:6–11 First **King Rehoboam** checked with **the elders who** had served **his father Solomon**. They told him to listen **to "these" people**. He next turned to **the young men** for **advice**, rejecting the elders' counsel, and heard what was more appealing to him. They urged him to speak roughly to the people.

10:12–19 When **the people** returned after three days and heard the king's threats, they rebelled, under the leadership of **Jeroboam**. The kingdom was divided, fulfilling the word of the Lord through Ahijah (1 Kgs. 11:29 ff.). After the murder of **Hadoram** the tax collector, **Rehoboam** retreated **to Jerusalem**, where he reigned over **Judah** and Benjamin. Williams comments:

> This fulfillment of the prediction of Ahijah affords an instance, similar to many others in the Scriptures, of prophecies being accomplished by the operation of human passions, and in the natural course of events. Men think that they are obeying their own wills and carrying out their own plans, unconscious that the matter is of God, and permitted and overruled by Him for the performance of His Word.[12]

III. THE KINGDOM OF JUDAH (11:1—36:19)

A. King Rehoboam (Chaps. 11, 12)

11:1–4 When Rehoboam returned **to Jerusalem, the Lord** intervened through the prophet **Shemaiah** to prevent a civil war. He told Rehoboam to accept the status quo because **"this thing is done from Me."** Rehoboam had not listened to wise counsel before, but he did this time. There was constant strife between the two kingdoms (12:15), but all-out war was avoided. The expression **"all Israel in Judah and Benjamin"** (v. 3) refers to all in the southern kingdom who were loyal to David's dynasty.

11:5–12 Much of the king's time was spent in building **cities** of **defense** for **Judah**. The **fortified cities**, located south of Jerusalem, showed that he feared attack from Egypt.

11:13–17 Meanwhile **Jeroboam** plunged the northern kingdom into gross idolatry (1 Kgs. 12), causing those **priests** and **Levites** who were loyal **to the Lord** to flee **to Judah**. They were followed by all those who had hearts for **God**, and in this way Rehoboam's kingdom was strengthened. It cost them everything to come **to Jerusalem**, for they **left their common-lands**, **possessions**, and friends behind.

11:18–23 Rehoboam was a polygamist, although he did not match his father in this regard! **He** had **eighteen wives, sixty concubines, twenty-eight sons, and sixty daughters**. The wives mentioned by name were Israelites from the royal family and not heathen women.

12:1–4 Whereas 1 Kings 14:22–24 mentions some of the details of Rehoboam's apostasy, Chronicles simply says that **"he forsook the law of the Lord"** and "did not prepare his heart to seek the Lord" (v. 14). Now five short years after the powerful monarch Solomon had died, the Egyptians were at Jerusalem's gates to carry away her treasures. Rehoboam's **fortified cities** availed nothing. **Shishak** subdued **Judah** not because of Egypt's military superiority but because of Judah's unfaithfulness to Jehovah.

12:5–8 When **Shemaiah the prophet came to Rehoboam** a second time (see 11:2) and delivered his message of doom, **the king** and the princes of Judah **humbled themselves** before the Lord and acknowledged His righteousness in the coming judgment. Instantly the Lord's mercy and grace provided **deliverance**, but not without a painful lesson on the difference between serving Jehovah and serving their captors.

12:9–12 The people were spared but the kingdom was spoiled. **Rehoboam** tried to adjust as much as possible. He substituted **bronze shields** for **gold**, unwittingly illustrating that God's presence and favor (**gold**) were being replaced by His judgment (**bronze**).[13]

12:13–16 The story of Rehoboam concludes with the statement that **he did evil** and **rested with his fathers**. The difference between Rehoboam and his grandfather David can be seen by comparing Psalm 27:8 with verse 14. David sought the Lord's face. Rehoboam did not.

B. King Abijah (Chap. 13)

13:1–3 Abijah, whose **mother's name was Michaiah,**[14] **became** the next **king** and **reigned three years in Jerusalem**. First Kings 15 mentions his sin in not following after the Lord, as David had done. But Chronicles skips over everything in Abijah's reign except one **battle** with **Jeroboam**.

13:4–12 In his speech before the battle, **Abijah** reminded **Jeroboam** that God had given the kingdom **to David** and to his posterity. **Jeroboam** had **rebelled against** the Davidic dynasty and had mustered a band of **worthless rogues against Rehoboam** when the latter was virtually defenseless. Israel hoped to win the victory because of its superior numbers and **the golden calves**. Israel had set up a counterfeit priesthood which men could enter without divine authorization. Judah, by contrast, clung to the Levitical priesthood, which was still serving the Lord in the prescribed manner. **God** was the Captain of Judah's army, **and His priests** used their **trumpets to sound the alarm against** Israel. It was folly, therefore, for the northern tribes to **fight against the LORD God**.

13:13–18 Instead of listening to Abijah, **Jeroboam** set **an ambush**. When the trap closed on **Judah**, the men **cried out to the LORD** and **the priests** blew **the trumpets**. The Lord answered by giving Judah a great victory. **Five hundred thousand choice men of Israel fell**—a staggering price to pay for turning away from God!

13:19–22 Abijah acquired additional territory, although he didn't completely subdue Israel. The loss was devastating for **Jeroboam**, who was later **struck** down by **the LORD**. But **Abijah** became powerful and prosperous.

C. King Asa (Chaps. 14—16)

14:1, 2 The next three chapters give us a brief report of **Asa** and his forty-one year reign. First Kings 15:9–24 should be read along with these chapters. Verse 1 is a bridge from the previous chapter. The Hebrew Bible starts chap. 14 with v. 2.

14:3–8 The source of Asa's peaceful reign was his heart's attitude toward Jehovah. He put away many of the sins of his fathers and urged his people **to seek the LORD**, leading the way himself by zealously purging his kingdom of idolatry.[15] During this time of rest, Asa **fortified** his **cities** and gathered a large **army**.

14:9–15 Judah's peace was shattered by an **Ethiopian . . . army of a million men** with **three hundred chariots**. Judah's smaller force was victorious because of their trust in Jehovah. The enemy was routed decisively.

Asa's prayer in verse 11 is short and to the point. There is no time **in battle** to be eloquent, but prayers born out of desperate need are very effective if the person praying is in a right relationship with God, as **Asa** was. Because he followed the Lord in peace, he knew the Lord would care for him in war. The fight began in **Mareshah**, a city in Judah, and ended **around Gerar**, a city belonging to the Philistines. Many were slain, including those who owned **livestock**, and huge amounts of **spoil** and animals were **carried** back **to Jerusalem**.

15:1–6 **Asa** and his men were jubilant over their recent success against overwhelming odds. As they returned to Jerusalem, the Lord had a lesson for them. First, **Azariah** reminded them that **the Lord** was **with** them because they had sought Him. **But . . . He** would **forsake** them **if** they forsook **Him**. And history proved more times than not that Israel had forsaken their God. Consequently they had **no peace**, and they were continually beaten by their enemies. **But when** the nation **sought . . . the Lord**, they found Him always ready to forgive and restore.

15:7 Since Asa was seeking after Jehovah, Azariah encouraged him to keep up the good work. Tucked away in this historical narrative, verse 7 is well worth memorizing: **"But you, be strong and do not let your hands be weak, for your work shall be rewarded!"** The parallel for believers today is 1 Corinthians 15:58.

15:8–15 **"Oded"** (v. 8) probably refers to Oded's son, Azariah (see NKJV marg.). The king responded to the word of **the prophet** with real enthusiasm. He stepped up his reformation program immediately, removing more **idols** (cf. 14:3), not only **from** his own **land of Judah** but **from the cities . . . of Ephraim** which he had taken in battle. He restored the altar in the temple and consecrated it with sacrifices. He called a solemn assembly **at Jerusalem**, **offered** part of the Ethiopian **spoil . . . to the Lord** on the altar, and bound the people with **an oath . . . to seek the Lord**. He left no room for dissenters—all who did not obey the covenant were to be executed (v. 13).

15:16–19 **Also** Asa **removed** his grandmother (not his **mother**[16]) from her position as **queen** mother and destroyed her **obscene image**. For comment on verse 17 see the note on 14:3–8. Treasures were **brought into** the temple instead of being taken out. His work was rewarded as the Lord had promised through Azariah, and he had peace.

16:1 Late **in the reign of Asa**,[17] **Baasha king of Israel** attempted to prevent his own people from defecting **to Asa** by fortifying **Ramah**, a town not far from Jerusalem.

16:2–6 **Asa** turned to the assistance of man instead of trusting in the arm of the Lord, as he had done earlier when invaded by the Ethiopians. He sent the Lord's treasure to purchase the help of **Ben-Hadad**. The Syrian **king** then **attacked . . . Israel** from the north and forced **Baasha** to withdraw from **Ramah** in order to defend his northern border. Asa's scheme apparently worked, but God was displeased.

16:7–10 The end certainly did not justify the means in Jehovah's eyes, so He sent His prophet **Hanani** to speak **to Asa**. **Hanani** boldly accused the king of acting **foolishly**. Had not **the Lord . . . delivered** him from **the Ethiopians**? Was not God continually looking for men through whom He could work? Since Asa had chosen to fight according to the flesh, he would **have wars** from then on. **Asa . . . was enraged**. Instead of heeding the word of the Lord, as he had done earlier (15:8), he **put** Hanani **in prison**.

16:11–14 Asa chose to work contrary to the way of the Lord, so the Lord afflicted him with a foot **disease**. But he still refused to repent and turn back to Jehovah. He tried **the physicians** instead, and shortly thereafter **died**. Some think that **the physicians** may have been magicians or spiritistic healers.

Despite his sad end, Asa was one of the best kings Judah had (15:17). The people greatly mourned his death. The **very great burning** of verse 14 refers to burning incense, not to the cremation of his body.

D. King Jehoshaphat (Chaps. 17—20)

17:1–5 **Jehoshaphat** succeeded his father and reigned twenty-five years (20:31). Much more space is devoted to him in 2 Chronicles (chaps. 17—20) than in Kings. The material in chapter 17 has no parallel in 1 Kings.

Upon ascending the throne, **Jehoshaphat . . . strengthened** his kingdom **against Israel**. He *fortified* his **kingdom**, but the secret of his successful reign was that he *followed* **the Lord**, as **David** had done. It is interesting how **David** is constantly used as the standard by which kings were measured. If they **walked** after his example, they prospered and were blessed. If they did not, they failed. The land was at peace under **Jehoshaphat**, and his enemies paid tribute (vv. 10–12).

17:6–9 The Word of God had high priority in Jehoshaphat's life. He was zealous in following its precepts and **took delight** in obeying it. He also made it the rule of his kingdom, sending a special commission of princes, **Levites**, and **priests** to educate the people **in the ways of the Lord**, thus obeying God's commands in Deuteronomy 6:6ff.

17:10–19 Under Jehovah's blessing, **Jehoshaphat became increasingly powerful**. And what an army he had! Rehoboam started out over sixty years earlier with 180,000 men. Now Judah's militia numbered 1,160,000 men, not counting those stationed **in the fortified cities**. Many of these men had no doubt defected from Israel because they saw that the Lord was with Judah. It is too bad that Jehoshaphat did not use his manpower more wisely, as we shall see in chapter 18.

18:1 Up to this point Israel and Judah had been hostile toward each other. But Jehoshaphat's son married Ahab's daughter (21:5, 6), thus forming an alliance between the two kingdoms.

18:2–7 **Ahab** asked **Jehoshaphat** to help him attack the Syrians, who held some of Israel's territory (cf. 1 Kgs. 22:3, 4). Jehoshaphat immediately consented to help Ahab, but he suggested that they first **inquire for the word of the Lord**. Accordingly Ahab sent for **the prophets**, who with one voice predicted success. However, they must not have been too convincing, because Jehoshaphat, who possessed a measure of spiritual discernment, asked for **"a prophet of the Lord,"** as if to imply that the **four hundred men** already assembled were not in touch with Jehovah. It appears that even Ahab knew the difference between his **prophets** and a real **prophet**. But **Micaiah**, the **one man** through whom they could get the word of the Lord, was hated by Ahab because he **always** prophesied **evil** about the king.

18:8–11 When **Micaiah** was being

summoned, **Zedekiah** dramatically portrayed how **the Syrians** would be **destroyed** (perhaps the two **horns** he put on signified the two Jewish kings), while all the king's other prophets chimed in their assent. D. L. Moody comments:

> Ahab had his preachers and prophets. No man is so corrupt, but he will find some one who preaches to suit him.[18]

18:12, 13 Micaiah meanwhile was being pressured by the king's **messenger** to agree with the other **prophets** in forecasting victory, but **Micaiah** promised only to deliver the word of the Lord. Verse 13 should be the motto of every preacher and every Christian: **"As the LORD lives, whatever my God says, that I will speak."**

18:14–17 At first **Micaiah** pretended to go along with the others, but it was soon apparent that he was not serious. When Ahab made him **swear** to speak **the truth**, he told of Israel's coming defeat and of Ahab's death.

18:18–22 Micaiah also explained why Ahab's prophets were giving him false information: They were under the influence of **a lying spirit** which **the LORD** sent because of Ahab's wickedness. Ahab was now the object of judgment, as had been prophesied earlier by Elijah (1 Kgs. 21:19–24). Matthew Henry comments:

> It is not without the divine permission that the devil deceives men, and even thereby God serves his own purposes.... Thus Micaiah gave Ahab fair warning, not only of the danger of proceeding in this war, but of the danger of believing those that encouraged him to proceed.[19]

18:23–26 Micaiah suffered for his honesty. **Zedekiah... struck** him **on the cheek** and Ahab imprisoned him with only **bread** and **water**, probably intending to kill him. To both men Micaiah responded by saying that the Lord would prove that he was telling the truth. Scripture does not tell us what happened to Zedekiah, but we do know that Ahab was slain in battle, according to the word of Jehovah.

18:27–29 The prophet's words must have had some impact on Ahab, because he tried to **disguise** himself and thus escape God's judgment. He suggested that **Jehoshaphat** wear his kingly **robes** while he (Ahab) donned a soldier's uniform.

18:30–34 But the word of the Lord came to pass. **Jehoshaphat** was delivered from the Syrians, after learning a lesson about the dangers of unholy alliances (2 Cor. 6:14). Ahab was not delivered. God directed a seemingly **random** arrow **between the joints of his armor**, and **about the time of sunset he died**.

19:1–5 When **Jehu, the son of Hanani, the seer**, who was also a prophet, rebuked **Jehoshaphat** for his alliance with Ahab, he responded by repenting.

His relationship with the idolatrous Ahab had set a poor example for his subjects. So the king **went** throughout his kingdom to bring **the people... back to the LORD**. He also established a judicial system in accordance with the Mosaic Law (Deut. 16:18–20). This, along with his earlier dispersal of teachers throughout the land (17:7–9), showed Jehoshaphat's tremendous respect for the Scriptures. These actions also displayed his concern for his subjects and his desire to act faithfully as Jehovah's regent.

19:6–11 The king's exhortations were taken from the **law** (v. 10). He reinforced the Lord's original commands to those who would act as

judges among His people. Since they were judging God's covenant people and since He was watching all that was done, the judges were to **fear . . . the Lord** and **"take heed."** Judges were also **appointed** in the capital city of **Jerusalem**, where difficult cases could be brought. **Amariah the chief priest** was in charge of religious cases, **and Zebadiah** the head of the tribe **of Judah** was responsible to handle civil **matters**. **The Levites** served as **officials**.

20:1–6 A huge army from across the Dead Sea declared war on Judah. (Some Hebrew manuscripts read "Edom" for "Syria" in v. 2.[20]) **Jehoshaphat** was justifiably alarmed. He **proclaimed a fast** and called the people to the temple, where he prayed to **the Lord**. This is the third "king's prayer" in 2 Chronicles (see also Solomon's prayer, chap. 6, and Asa's prayer, 14:11).

20:7–13 Jehoshaphat reminded the Lord that the Jews were His covenant **people**. The **temple**, where Jehoshaphat was praying, was God's **sanctuary** and the place where He promised to **hear** and answer prayer. Those to whom **Israel** had once shown kindness were now coming to destroy her and take away her land. Jehoshaphat closed his impassioned appeal, and with **all Judah . . . stood before the Lord**, awaiting His answer.

20:14–17 The Spirit of the Lord spoke through **Jahaziel**, dispelling the fear that had gripped the nation. **The battle** was **God's**; the people had only to **go** out the next day and **see** what He had done.

20:18–21 By faith the people rejoiced in their victory even before it came to pass. The next **morning** they were up at dawn to see what **the Lord** had done. They marched to the battlefield as though they were going to a festival, the singers leading the way.

20:22–30 God confounded the enemy when He heard His people singing their song of faith. He stirred up the opposition so that they fought and destroyed **one another**. **When Judah** arrived, the only thing left to do was to collect the **spoil**, a task requiring **three days**. **With** unbounded **joy** they praised **the Lord** and returned **to Jerusalem** singing. The neighboring **countries** took notice, and Judah enjoyed peace.

20:31–34 As is customary, a summary of the reign of **Jehoshaphat** is given. Despite his efforts he was unable to stamp out idolatry. But on the whole his had been a good reign. He sought to do good and, even though he was not perfect, he usually did **what was right** in God's **sight**.

20:35–37 This is a postscript concerning Jehoshaphat's partnership **with Ahaziah**, the wicked **king of Israel**. **They made . . . ships** at **Ezion Geber** to travel **to Tarshish**, but **the Lord** wrecked the project, as announced by a prophet named **Eliezer**.

Jehoshaphat was sixty years old when he died. His son Jehoram, who had been his co-regent, succeeded him on the throne of Judah (21:1).

E. King Jehoram (Chap. 21)

21:1–3 Beginning with the reign of **Jehoram**, the history recorded in 2 Chronicles is downhill all the way, ending in calamity and captivity.

Two Azariahs are listed in verse 2 as brothers of Jehoram. The NKJV uses the alternate spelling of one (**Azaryahu**).

21:4–6 Judah's fifth king chose to walk **in the way of the kings of Israel** instead of in the way of **David**. **Jehoram** was a murderer and an idolater. He ruthlessly **killed all his** own

brothers to strengthen his hold on the throne. Scripture leaves us in no doubt as to the evil influence that caused Jehoram to act so wickedly: His **wife** was Ahab's **daughter** (v. 6). Earlier Jehoshaphat had arranged the marriage between the two kingdoms, and now Judah was infected with the same wickedness that was ruining Israel. Ahab's daughter Athaliah was a tool in Satan's hands to bring judgment on God's people.

21:7 But **the LORD** remembered the Davidic **covenant** and so He did not deal as sternly with Jehoram and Judah as He had dealt with Ahab and Israel. (**"A lamp"** means a descendant to serve as king.) Still, Judah was to suffer much because of this unholy union.

21:8–15 The Edomites, who had feared Judah during the days of Jehoshaphat (17:10), now **revolted**. **Libnah**, a city in Judah, also rebelled. **Jehoram** made matters worse by leading his people further and further into idolatry. Even the prophecy of **Elijah**, contained in **a letter** to the king, failed to turn him from his course of evil. Jehoram certainly knew of the prophet's powerful ministry in Israel, but he proved as unresponsive to it as **Ahab** had been.

Elijah was taken to heaven sometime during the reign of Jehoshaphat (2 Kgs. 2:11). Since Jehoram reigned with his father for about five years, Elijah may have been alive when this message was delivered. Or the prophet might have written the letter by divine instruction and given it to Elisha to deliver at the appropriate time.

21:16, 17 **The Philistines and the Arabians carried away** Jehoram's **possessions** and his family, **except Jehoahaz, the youngest of his sons** (usually called Ahaziah). Since he had murdered his father's family this punishment would seem to fit his own crime.

21:18–20 Jehoram **died in severe pain** from **an incurable disease** of the **intestines**. He **departed** this life **to no one's** sorrow. Since he had not walked as the other **kings** had in life, he was not **buried** with them in death.

F. King Ahaziah (22:1–9)

22:1–9 The trouble caused by association with the house of Ahab now reached to the third generation. **Ahaziah** (same as Jehoahaz, 21:17, and Azariah, v. 6) became **king** after Jehoram's death. He was twenty-two[21] (NKJV marg.) **years old** at the time.

His mother, **Athaliah**, a **granddaughter of Omri**, continued her pernicious influence in Judah after the death of her husband. She was her son's chief counselor to do **evil—"to his destruction." Ahaziah** had been spared (v. 1) so as to leave a son of David on the throne, but he proved himself ungrateful by repeating his father's sins. He joined **with Jehoram (Joram) to war against . . . Syria**. **Jehu** and his men found Ahaziah **hiding in Samaria** and **killed him**. The king's servants gave him a decent burial (2 Kgs. 9:28) because he was a grandson of the godly Jehoshaphat. Ahaziah left no son old enough to carry on the kingdom.

G. Usurpation of Queen Athaliah (22:10—23:21)

22:10–12 Having lost her husband and now her son, **Athaliah** seized the throne for herself by killing *her own grandchildren!* Satan was the unseen motivator behind this ruthless slaughter of the **royal** family, attempting to cut off the messianic line as he had tried to do earlier and would try to do again. But since the promise of Genesis 3:15 guaranteed the Lord's preserving the line through which the Lord Jesus would eventually come, Jehovah moved **Jehoshabeath** to hide her nephew **Joash**. **He was hidden** in the temple, where Jehoshabeath's husband, **Jehoiada the priest**, took care of him **for six years**.

Second Kings 8—11 gives more details concerning these events and also relates what was going on in Israel at the same time.

23:1–7 Until he felt that Joash was old enough, **Jehoiada** had to bide his time while the usurper sat on David's throne. But **in the seventh year** he called together the princes and **Levites** and plotted Athaliah's overthrow. Word **went** out **throughout** the kingdom and many entered into **a covenant** to set Joash on his father's throne. The words in verse 6b **"all the people shall keep the watch of the LORD"** mean that they were to observe the law forbidding entrance into the temple (see v. 6a). **The Levites** and princes were given their assignments, and a **Sabbath** was chosen as the fateful day.

23:8–11 As new **divisions** came to the temple, the old divisions were **not dismissed**; thus **Jehoiada** was able to gather a large number of men without drawing suspicion. The men were equipped with David's weapons, which **were in the temple**, and when all the preparations were complete, seven-year-old Joash was **brought out** of the temple and crowned. He was given a copy of the law (**the Testimony**) in accordance with the word of Moses (Deut. 17:18–20). Some think this was the original copy of the law which had been placed in the ark (Ex. 25:21; 2 Chron. 5:10).

23:12–15 Queen **Athaliah came to the people in the temple** to investigate the cheering and shouting, only to find a child rival she thought long dead now wearing a royal crown. But what must have alarmed her even more was the realization that **the people** were solidly behind him. No one listened to her charge of **treason**. After all, she was the usurper, not Joash. **Jehoiada** ordered her killed, but not inside the temple. **She** was taken to **the Horse Gate**, where she was put to death for the atrocities she had committed in Judah.

23:16–19 With Athaliah out of the way, reform was swift. **Jehoiada** and **the people** covenanted to **be the LORD's**. To demonstrate their commitment, they destroyed **the temple of Baal** and **killed Mattan, the priest of Baal**. As a priest, **Jehoiada** was sensitive concerning the temple and divine worship. One of the first things he did was to set the temple service in order, as had been commanded by **Moses** and **David**. **The Levites** and **priests** were **assigned** to their duties. The holiness of the temple was no longer to be treated as a light thing; **gatekeepers** were to keep out ceremonially **unclean** people. Jehoiada knew that reform must begin in **the house of the LORD**.

23:20, 21 Joash was taken **to the king's house**. **The people** looked forward with expectancy to life under Joash, thankful that a son of David sat **on** Judah's **throne** once more.

H. King Joash (Chap. 24)

24:1–3 **Joash was** only **seven years old when he became king, and he reigned forty years**. Joash **did what was right** as long as **Jehoiada the priest** was alive. Even Joash's **two wives** were chosen **for him** by this influential priest of God.

24:4–14 In order to restore the temple, **Joash** ordered **the Levites** to expedite **the collection** of funds from **all Israel**. When **the Levites** failed to respond **quickly**, he became upset with **Jehoiada**. Finally **a** special **chest** was **set** before the temple, and the people were commanded to come and deposit their "temple tax."[22] This was then taken and distributed to **the workmen** who **restored the house of God to its original condition and reinforced it**.[23]

24:15–19 When **Jehoiada . . . died**, after a long and fruitful life, he was honored by being **buried** with **the kings**, an unusual honor for one who was not of royalty. But with his godly influence gone, Joash turned to idolaters for advice, to the ruin of his kingdom. Jehovah *sent prophets* to warn him, but rather than repent, the leader of Judah rebelled.

24:20–27 **Zechariah** spoke God's warning to the people, and **the king** ordered him **stoned** for it. **Joash . . . did not remember the kindness which Jehoiada**, the father (or grandfather) of Zechariah,[24] **had done to him**. Perhaps in answer to Zechariah's dying prayer, the Lord sent a **small . . . army** from **Syria** to plunder **Judah** and to slay the officials and princes. Those who had given wicked counsel to Joash were killed, and Joash himself, **severely wounded**, was then murdered by **his own servants**. Like wicked Jehoram before him, he was denied burial with **the kings** of Judah.

Because Joash forsook the Lord in the latter part of his life, all that he had done earlier was for nothing. He had repaired the temple and had refurnished it, only to hand over its treasures to Hazael the Syrian (2 Kgs. 12:17, 18). It is good to *start* well, but it is far more important to *finish* well. The Apostle John, knowing the tendency people have to "fade in the stretch," warns us to "Look to yourselves, that we do not lose those things we worked for, but that we may receive a full reward" (2 John 8).

Second Kings 12 gives more details about the life and reign of Joash (there called Jehoash); see comments on that chapter.

I. King Amaziah (Chap. 25)

25:1–10 After establishing his throne and dealing with his father's murderers according to **the law**, Amaziah turned his attention to foreign affairs. The Edomites had rebelled against Judah during the reign of Jehoram (21:10), and now perhaps **Amaziah** wanted to bring them back under his rule. So **he . . . hired** mercenaries **from Israel**. However, after being warned by **a man of God**, he sent the Israelites home. Although he was concerned about losing the money he had already paid the mercenaries, he accepted the prophet's assurance that **the Lord** was **able to give** him **much more** to make up for his foolish investment.

25:11–13 **Amaziah** and his men **killed ten thousand** Edomites, then **took ten thousand** others **captive**, only to kill them later by hurling them over a precipice. The latter victims may have been guilty of unusual cruelty, or Amaziah may have been following an accepted wartime policy of that day. The mercenaries whom **Amaziah** had sent home to Ephraim angrily **raided the cities of Judah**, killing **three thousand** people and taking **much spoil**.

25:14–21 When **Amaziah** began worshiping idols which he had brought back from Edom, **a prophet** reproved him for thinking that **gods** which could not deliver **their own people** could help *him!* Amaziah interrupted the prophet with a threat, perhaps a veiled allusion to Zechariah, who had lost his life by prophesying against

Amaziah's father (24:20–22). The prophet responded to the king's warning by saying in effect, "I am not going to be struck down. Since you have refused my advice, you are the one who is going to be destroyed." Amaziah did not listen to God's counsel but instead **asked advice** of his own staff. Foolishly he made war with **Joash of Israel**, refusing to heed the prophet's warning.

25:22–28 **Judah was defeated** and **Amaziah** was humiliated and impoverished. **Jerusalem** was invaded and the temple was pillaged. Amaziah's subjects conspired **against him**, and eventually he **fled** from Jerusalem. He was murdered in **Lachish**, then brought back to Jerusalem and **buried**.

J. King Uzziah (Chap. 26)

26:1–5 The reason for Uzziah's success is given early in the chapter. **He did what was right** and **sought God**. **Zechariah** (not the same as the Prophet Zechariah) was his godly counselor, a man of **understanding**.

26:6–15 Everywhere **Uzziah** turned, he was blessed. He warred successfully **against the Philistines** and **the Ammonites**, and he increased Judah's defenses as well. He assembled **an** elite **army** and built up a powerful armory to equip it. He also **built cities** and encouraged agricultural development (v. 10). The **"devices"** (v. 15) were a form of catapult.

26:16–23 But Uzziah was **lifted up** with pride. He entered **the temple . . . to burn incense** before **the LORD**, something which only the priests were authorized to do. **Azariah** and **eighty** other **priests**, all **valiant men**, **went in after** the king. The priests' rebukes angered **Uzziah**, but before he could do anything **the LORD struck him** with **leprosy**. He was **hurried . . . out** of the temple, to which he never returned. He remained **a leper** from that day on, living **in an isolated house** while **Jotham his son** ruled. **Uzziah** was not **buried** in the graves of **the kings**, because he was **a leper**; he was interred **in the field** adjacent to the royal graves.

K. King Jotham (Chap. 27)

27:1–4 Like his father Uzziah, **Jotham** enjoyed peace so that he was able to build and improve his capital and the surrounding **cities**. He followed his father's example, except in the matter of Uzziah's sin. However, the high places were not removed, and Jotham does not appear to have been much of a reformer. He did little to prevent his **people** from acting **corruptly**.

27:5–9 **The Ammonites** had been subdued by Uzziah (26:8), but perhaps his death prompted them to withhold their tribute. **Jotham . . . fought** against them and they were forced to pay tribute once again. His strength lay in the fact that he considered **God** in all he did. They **buried** Jotham **in the city of David** and **Ahaz his son** became Judah's next king.

L. King Ahaz (Chap. 28)

28:1–4 To get the full story of **Ahaz**, one should read 2 Kings 16 and Isaiah 7. He was the most wicked king that Judah had yet known, reigning **sixteen years in Jerusalem.**[25]

After Ahaz became king, he wasted no time plunging into idolatry. He chose **the** evil **kings of Israel** as his pattern instead of **David**. Ahaz revived the abominable ritual of child sacrifice **in the Valley of the Son of Hinnom**, outside Jerusalem. The worship of Molech, of which this was a part, had not been practiced since the days of Solomon (1 Kgs. 11:7), but now all forms of idolatry and **abomi-**

nations were widely practiced and encouraged.

28:5–8 Because of this **the LORD** brought many adversaries against Judah. Isaiah tells us that Rezin, **king of Syria**, and **Pekah**, king of Israel, were allies against Jerusalem. They did not succeed in overthrowing the capital city but they did great damage to **Judah**. The Israelites **killed one hundred and twenty thousand... men... in one day** and **carried** off **two hundred thousand** people **captive**. Many noblemen were slain at this time. It was when Ahaz was threatened by Rezin and Pekah that God in grace gave to the house of Israel through him the promise of the virgin-born Immanuel (Isa. 7:14).

28:9–15 The Israelites intended to enslave their brethren from Judah, which was forbidden in the Law of Moses, **but** the Lord sent **a prophet** to warn them not to do so, for the **fierce wrath of the LORD** was against them. True, Israel had been God's instrument of judgment, but their cruelty had been unwarranted. **Some of the heads of Ephraim** had enough sense to heed **Oded** the prophet and secure the release of **the captives**, who were then fully equipped and fed **from the spoil**, and **returned to** their land.

28:16–27 At this **same time King Ahaz** was also troubled by those nations which his father had subdued, Edom and Philistia. But rather than turn to the Lord in his extremity, Ahaz turned to **the** king **of Assyria, Tiglath-Pileser**. He hired the Assyrians with gold from the temple and the king's **house**. **The king of Assyria** then attacked Syria and killed Rezin in Damascus (2 Kgs. 16:9). When Ahaz went to Damascus to meet Tiglath-Pileser, he became enamored with the gods of the Syrians (2 Kgs. 16:8–10). Ahaz's alliance with the king of Assyria proved costly, since Assyria deceived him and exacted heavy tribute. But his alliance with the idols **of Syria** proved fatal because it provoked Jehovah to great anger. **King Ahaz** established idolatry so strongly in **Judah** that not even good Hezekiah, his son, would be able to root it out. When Ahaz died, he was **not... buried** in **the tombs of the kings**.[26] **Ahaz** is called the **king of Israel** in verse 19. Sometimes the kings of Judah were given this name (see 2 Chron. 21:2).

M. King Hezekiah (Chaps. 29—32)

29:1–11 The Bible accords several chapters to Hezekiah's reign. Three chapters are devoted to him in 2 Kings (18—20), four in the Book of Isaiah (36—39), and four here. Second Chronicles mentions primarily his religious dealings while 2 Kings relates more of his political and foreign accomplishments. Both books bring out his outstanding character and devotion to the Lord.

Hezekiah started his reformation with the religious leaders. He called together **the priests** and **Levites** and ordered them to consecrate themselves and the temple. Because of unfaithfulness on the part of their fathers, **the wrath of the LORD** was on the land and many people had already been slain or taken captive. The king wanted to get right with God, and he urged the priests and Levites to do the same.

29:12–24 The Levites listed by name in verses 12–14 led their brothers in obeying the king's command. They **cleansed** (v. 18) the courts for eight days, then the temple itself for **eight days** (v. 17). They set the utensils in order for temple-service, then informed **King Hezekiah** that all had been carried out according to his word. Hezekiah offered **a sin-offering** on behalf of **the kingdom**. The blood from the **sin** and **burnt** offerings was used to purge **the altar**.

29:25–36 The priests and **Levites** were stationed in their places as appointed in the time **of David**, and they **sang** and played the holy **instruments** while the **burnt offering** was being offered. **All** those present **bowed** in worship along with **the Levites**, and those who were so inclined brought **burnt** and **thank offerings**. So much was brought for this freewill gift that **the Levites** had to help **the priests** slaughter the animals because not enough **priests had sanctified themselves. The people rejoiced** because of the suddenness of the revival and because it produced a glimmer of hope for a better future for Judah. But this was only the beginning of Hezekiah's reforms.

30:1–5 Chapter 30 is wholly taken up with Hezekiah's reinstatement of **the Passover** Feast, which **had not** been observed in such fashion since before the kingdom was divided (2 Chron. 8:13).

In the first month the king had purified the temple and reestablished its services. **In the second month** he prepared to **keep the Passover** and the Feast of Unleavened Bread. According to Numbers 9:11, **the Passover** could be celebrated **in the second month** if a dead corpse resulted in somebody's uncleanness, or if they were far away on a journey. In Hezekiah's case, observance during the first month, **the regular time**, was not possible **because a sufficient number of priests had not consecrated themselves** (v. 3). Since it was a national feast, the whole nation must be invited. So messengers were sent **throughout** Judah and **Israel** to ask the people to come to **Jerusalem**. Israel was an Assyrian province at this time, the bulk of the people having been taken into captivity. However, Hezekiah was able to invite the remaining Israelites without opposition from the Assyrians.

30:6–12 Most of the Israelites ridiculed the couriers who exhorted them to **return to the Lord**. However, a small remnant did repent and travel **to Jerusalem** to observe the Passover in the first year of Hezekiah's reign, 716–715 B.C. (2 Chron. 29:3).

30:13–15 The zeal of the **people** shamed **the priests and . . . Levites** and awakened them to a more serious consideration of their duties. The city was cleansed of its heathen filth, and every vestige of idolatry was thrown **into the Brook Kidron**.

30:16–27 The Levites aided those who were ceremonially unclean and **Hezekiah prayed** that the Lord would overlook the irregularities and accept the **heart** attitude of the people. **And the Lord** did. **The Feast of Unleavened Bread** was such a joy to all that they decided to celebrate an extra **seven days**. The king and **the leaders** contributed animals for this extended **feast** and **there was great joy in Jerusalem. The whole assembly** was blessed; things were as they had been in Israel's golden age, and once more the prayers of Jehovah's priests were heard in **heaven**.

31:1 The first verse of chapter 31 is linked to the closing verse of the previous chapter. **When** the men of **Israel** left Jerusalem, they thoroughly destroyed the idols and idol shrines in **Judah, Benjamin, Ephraim, and Manasseh, then . . . returned to** their homes.

31:2–10 Hezekiah now **appointed the priests and the Levites . . . to their** respective duties, then provided for their **support** through tithes. The people responded so generously that there was **enough to eat and plenty left**.

31:11–19 Special **rooms** had to be set aside in the temple to store the surplus, and capable men were appointed as overseers. These are listed by name, showing how God takes note of each individual who serves His cause.

While the principle of tithing (giving one-tenth) is not commanded in the NT, the practice of systematic, proportionate giving *is* taught.

31:20, 21 Chapter 31 closes with a commendation of **Hezekiah**. Whatever he did for God, **he did . . . with all his heart**. No wonder **he prospered**!

32:1–8 Having carried the northern tribes into captivity (2 Kgs. 17), the Assyrians were now threatening to do the same to **Judah**. **Hezekiah**, who had earlier paid tribute to **Sennacherib** (2 Kgs. 18:13–16), was hard-pressed by the Assyrians to surrender his kingdom as well.

When **Sennacherib** invaded **Judah**, **Hezekiah** responded by cutting off **the water** supply **outside the city**, rebuilding and repairing **the wall** of Jerusalem, providing **weapons** and officers, and encouraging the people to look to Jehovah instead of fearing the army of the Assyrians. G. Campbell Morgan writes:

> It would seem to be a strange answer of God to the faithfulness of His servant that a strong foe should at this moment invade the kingdom. The story needs more details than are found in this record. They may be found in 2 Kings 18:7–16. From that passage we find that Hezekiah had flung off the yoke of the king of Assyria which his father Ahaz had consented to wear. Then Sennacherib had invaded Judah; and in a moment of weakness Hezekiah had paid him a heavy tribute, and again yielded to his rule in order to buy him off. The result was not what he desired, for Sennacherib now demanded an unconditional surrender. In this hour of crisis, resulting from his own vacillation, his faith and courage were renewed. He took immediate action to embarrass the foe by stopping the supply of water, by strengthening the fortifications, by mobilizing his army, and finally by assuring the people: "There is a Greater with us than with him."[27]

32:9–19 While besieging **Lachish**, the **king of Assyria** taunted Hezekiah and the people, implying that Jehovah was no more powerful than the other **gods** he had already conquered, and suggesting that the wise thing to do was to stop listening to **Hezekiah** and to surrender. Verse 12 shows that even the Assyrians had heard about Hezekiah's reforms. But Sennacherib had not counted on two things: the loyalty of the people to King Hezekiah and the power of Jehovah.

32:20–23 After Sennacherib derided the Lord, **Hezekiah and . . . Isaiah** devoted themselves to prayer, and **the LORD sent an angel who cut down** the Assyrian army. Sennacherib **returned** home in humiliation and was later murdered by **his own** sons in **the temple of his god**.

32:24–26 Hezekiah's illness and recovery probably took place before the siege of Sennacherib. In his sickness he called on **the LORD** and was promised an extension of life, confirmed by **a sign** in which the sun seemed to go backward. When he failed to respond properly to this mercy, the Lord was angry with him, but because he **humbled himself** the punishment **did not come upon** Judah until after his death.

32:27–30 Special mention is made

of his **riches and honor**, and of the **tunnel** he built to bring **water** from a spring in the Kidron Valley to a reservoir inside Jerusalem. (See 2 Kings 20:20 for more details on this water tunnel.)

32:31 **Ambassadors** came from **Babylon**, intrigued by the celestial **wonder** that God had given Hezekiah. They would be especially interested in this since they worshiped the sun and stars. The king foolishly showed them his treasures, arousing their desire to possess them, a desire that was soon to be fulfilled.

32:32, 33 **The rest of the acts of Hezekiah . . . are written . . . in Isaiah**. When **Hezekiah** died, he was buried with full honors. **Manasseh his son reigned in his place**.

N. King Manasseh (33:1–20)

33:1–11 In spite of having such a devout father, **Manasseh** had the most **evil** reign in Judah. It was also the longest, **fifty-five** years. The list of Manasseh's sins is also very lengthy. He polluted God's city and temple with his idols and revived the practice of burning children to Molech **in the Valley of the Son of Hinnom**. He was an inveterate murderer (2 Kgs. 21:16); Josephus states that daily executions were ordered by him. Tradition says that he murdered Isaiah the prophet by having him sawn in two (the reference in Heb. 11:37 to being "sawn in two" may include this tradition). When **Manasseh** refused to **listen** to **the LORD** and turn from his wickedness, **the LORD** moved **the king of Assyria** to take him away **to Babylon**, which was then under Assyrian control.

33:12–20 Only 2 Chronicles mentions Manasseh's repentance (the reference in verse 18 is not to the canonical books of Kings but to a lost secular chronicle). After serving every kind of detestable idol for years, Manasseh learned that the ***LORD*** is **God**, and he was converted. He did what he could to lead the people back to faithfulness to Jehovah and to purge idolatry from his realm. **The high places** mentioned in verse 17 were used for sacrificing **to the LORD** away from Jerusalem. This was forbidden by the law, but went on anyway.

O. King Amon (33:21–25)

After Manasseh's death his son did not follow his reforms but rather his earlier sins. Young King **Amon** lasted only **two years** before he was **killed** by **his** own **servants in his own house**. Then **the people of the land** executed Amon's killers and replaced him with **his son Josiah**.

P. King Josiah (Chaps. 34, 35)

34:1–7 The idolatrous **altars** which Manasseh had removed from the city (33:15) had been brought back by Amon and the people. **In the eighth year of his reign** the teenage King **Josiah . . . began to seek the God of his father David**. Four years later he started his reforms. **Josiah** made sure that the same mistake would not be made again, so he completely destroyed everything connected with idolatry and burned it or ground it to **powder**. He extended his reforms to the farthest reaches of Israel.

34:8–18 Like the great reformers before him, he soon turned his attention to repairing **the temple**. A copy of **the Book of the Law** was subsequently **found** and **read . . . before the king**. Every major or minor revival of true faith has involved a rediscovery of the teaching of the Word of God. The great Reformation of the sixteenth century was no exception.

34:19–28 Josiah took its warnings

The lush Esdraelon Valley as viewed from the site of the ancient city of Megiddo. (Photo by Howard Vos)

seriously and sent **to Huldah the prophetess** to see if there was still a chance for mercy. Her words only confirmed that God's **wrath** was on the way. However, Josiah would be spared from seeing Judah's day of **calamity because his heart was tender and** he **humbled** himself and believed the Word of the Lord.

34:29–32 Even though Josiah knew that judgment was inevitable, he still **gathered . . . the people** and entered into **a covenant** with **the Lord**. He set the Word of God before the people so that they might understand how grave their situation was and see the deep need for repentance.

34:33 Because of his strong leadership, he was able to promote fidelity to **the Lord** throughout his lifetime. The contents of verse 33 are treated in much greater detail in 2 Kings 23:4–20. The reform that followed the finding of the law and the making of the covenant was even more thorough than Josiah's first purge of his kingdom.

35:1–6 Like Hezekiah before him, **Josiah** encouraged **the priests** and **Levites** to carry out their appointed **service**. They were to **put the holy ark** back in the temple, organize themselves in their respective **divisions**, take up their station in the temple, and be cleansed and ready to celebrate **the Passover**. There are several suggestions as to why **the ark** had been removed from the temple, and was now to be returned. The priests may have carried it **on** their **shoulders** from place to place to protect it from being profaned. Manasseh or some other idolatrous king may have ordered it to be removed. Josiah may have had it removed elsewhere while the temple was being restored.

35:7–19 Since the land was impoverished by the Assyrians, **Josiah** provided most of the animals for the feast, with other **leaders** and **priests** providing what they could. The Mosaic ordinances **for the Passover** and **the Feast of Unleavened Bread** were followed to the letter. Amid songs of praise, the king and the people celebrated the most notable **Passover . . . since the days of Samuel**. It was not the largest or most elaborate, but it was the most pleasing to Jehovah, perhaps because of the quality of the worship. This **Passover** was held in the same year as the great temple restoration (v. 19; cf. 34:8ff).

35:20–24 Nothing is mentioned about the next thirteen years of Josiah's reign. When he was thirty-nine he went out to fight against **Necho king of Egypt**. The Egyptian army was on its way **to fight** alongside the Assyrians **against** the Babylonians (2 Kgs. 23:29). Josiah could not imagine that God's hand was behind Necho's movements and did not inquire of the Lord to see if the Pharaoh's words were true. Although he **disguised himself**, he was killed in the battle.[28] His people greatly **mourned** his loss, and those who believed the word of the Lord knew that with **Josiah** gone, divine wrath was imminent (34:22–28).

John Whitcomb comments on these events.

> Now came one of the strangest episodes in Old Testament history. The heathen king, Necho II of Egypt, informed Josiah that "God hath commanded me to make haste" and that if Josiah interfered with God's plan, God would destroy him (2 Chron. 35:21). We would immediately dismiss such a statement as propaganda, of course, were it not for the explanation by the Chronicler that Josiah "hearkened not unto the words of Necho from the mouth of God"! Furthermore, Necho must be believed, for Josiah was killed. What does this mean? Did Josiah lose his salvation because of disobedience? No, for Huldah had said he would die "in peace" (2 Chron. 34:28). Was Pharaoh-necho a prophet of Jehovah? No, for God had spoken to pagan kings directly at various times without necessarily transforming their hearts (see Gen. 12:17–20; 20:3–7). We may conclude that God wanted to maneuver the Egyptian army to the Euphrates so that Nebuchadnezzar could destroy it as well as the Assyrian army, and thus fulfill His warning that the Babylonians would conquer and chasten Judah (see Jer. 25:8–11).[29]

35:25–27 Jeremiah . . . lamented Josiah's death. The singers remembered him even after the captivity. **Josiah** was a man of one Book; he lived by **the Law of the Lord**, and his faithfulness is forever recorded in the Word of the Lord. In Jeremiah 22:16 we read, "'He judged the cause of the poor and needy; then it was well. Was not this knowing Me?' says the Lord." Josiah evidenced by his life that he knew God. He started early to seek the Lord (34:3) and carefully obeyed the subsequent light he received. "Now before him there was no king like him, who turned to the Lord with all his heart, with all his soul, and with all his might, according to all the Law of Moses; nor after him did any rise like him" (2 Kgs. 23:25).

Q. King Jehoahaz (36:1–3)

The captivity of Judah took place in stages. In 605 B.C., Nebuchadnezzar entered Jerusalem, made Jehoiakim a vassal, and took captives to Babylon, including Daniel (2 Kgs. 24:1). In 597 B.C., Nebuchadnezzar again invaded Jerusalem, deported Jehoiachin, and took additional captives, including Ezekiel (2 Kgs. 24:10). Finally, in 586 B.C., Nebuchadnezzar destroyed the temple and took captive all but the poorest of the people (2 Kgs. 25:1–10).

Jehoahaz . . . reigned only **three months**, then was **deposed** by **the** Egyptian **king** and forced to pay heavy **tribute**. He was an evil man, not at all like his father Josiah (cf. 2 Kgs. 23:31–34). He was taken **to Egypt**, where he died.

R. King Jehoiakim (36:4–8)

Eliakim, also called **Jehoiakim**, was **Jehoahaz's** older **brother**. He was placed on the throne by **Necho**. His **eleven**-year reign was characterized by wickedness and was ended by **Nebuchadnezzar**, who looted the temple in 605 B.C. Nebuchadnezzar intended **to carry** Jehoiakim **to Babylon** but did not succeed. Although Chronicles does not record the fact, we know that he died ignominiously while still in Jerusalem, as Jeremiah had prophesied (Jer. 22:19; 36:30).

S. King Jehoiachin (36:9, 10)

Jehoiachin was eighteen (NKJV marg.[30]) **when he became king**. After a short reign of **three months and ten days**, **Jehoiachin** surrendered Jerusalem and spent the next thirty-seven years of his life in prison in **Babylon**. After the death of Nebuchadnezzar, he was released and elevated to a place of honor (2 Kgs. 25:27–30).

T. King Zedekiah (36:11–19)

Zedekiah, whose other name was Mattaniah, was yet another son of Josiah. When Jehoiachin proved unfaithful to the Babylonians, they chose Zedekiah as his successor. **He did evil** and refused to **humble himself before Jeremiah the prophet**. **He also** broke his oath to **Nebuchadnezzar** and **rebelled**. **Jerusalem** underwent a terrible siege lasting eighteen months. When **the Chaldeans** (Babylonians) took the city in 586 B.C., they **destroyed** it and the temple. Then they took all but the poorest of the land into exile.

IV. THE BABYLONIAN CAPTIVITY (36:20, 21)

The Jewish people had refused to keep the sabbatic year for 490 years; now their **land** would keep an enforced **Sabbath** for **seventy years**. For different ways of computing the seventy-year captivity, see the Introduction to the Commentary on Ezra.

V. THE DECREE OF CYRUS (36:22, 23)

While the people of Judah were in captivity, Babylon was conquered by Medo-Persia. Seventy years after the captivity began, **Cyrus, king of Persia**, issued **a proclamation** permitting the Jews to return to their land.

It is noteworthy that in the Hebrew order of the OT books, Chronicles stands last. Instead of ending "with a curse" (Mal. 4:6), the Jewish Bible ends on this positive and encouraging note:

> Thus says Cyrus king of Persia: All the kingdoms of the earth the LORD God of heaven has given me. And He has commanded me to build Him a house at Jerusalem which is in Judah. Who is among you of all His people? May the LORD his God be with him, and let him go up!

ENDNOTES

[1](2:3–10) How much did Solomon pay Hiram? First Kings 5:11 states one amount while 2 Chron. 2:10 gives another. First Kings refers to a personal gift given to Hiram's household while verse 10 refers to the supplies given to Hiram's workmen who were cutting lumber for Solomon.

[2](2:11–16) Who was Huram's mother? Second Chronicles 2:14 says she was a Danite while 1 Kings says she was a widow from the tribe of Naphtali. The answer is that she was a Danite whose first husband was from the tribe of Naphtali; hence she

was a widow of Naphtali. Her second husband was a man of Tyre.

[3](2:17, 18) How many overseers were there on the temple project: 3,600 (2:18) or 3,300 (1 Kgs. 5:16)? There are two other important passages to consider in resolving this problem. Second Chronicles 8:10 says that Solomon had 250 officers who ruled over the work. Add this number to the 3,600 overseers (2:18), and you get 3,850. First Kings 9:23 numbers Solomon's officers at 550. Add this number to the 3,300 overseers mentioned in 1 Kings 5:16 and you get 3,850. The total number of officers and overseers is therefore the same in both books; the proportion is just enumerated differently. The term "officers" refers to military or political personnel, while the term "overseers" refers to industrial personnel (i.e., superintendants or foremen).

[4](3:1–4) Was the porch 120 cubits high (3:4) or 30 cubits (1 Kgs. 6:2) high? Some say this is a copyist's error. Others, like Josephus, maintain that 120 cubits was the actual height. Matthew Poole thinks the 120 cubits refers to a kind of turret.

[5](3:14–17) Were the pillars in front of the temple thirty-five cubits tall (3:15) or eighteen cubits (1 Kgs. 7:15; Jer. 52:21)? Notice that 1 Kings specifically refers to the *height* of one pillar, while the margin of verse 15 says the pillars were thirty-five cubits *long* (i.e., together). In other words, thirty-five cubits was the *total* length of the pillars, which were probably cast in one piece and then cut in two. This would make the two pillars eighteen cubits each (to the nearest cubit).

[6](4:1–22) The measurements given for the Laver in 4:2 are sometimes used to show that the Bible contains error. If the diameter was ten cubits (180″), the circumference would be 180 times pi (π = 3.14), or 565.49 inches, instead of thirty cubits (540″). The difficulty is solved by noting that the Laver was a handbreadth thick (4″). Verse 2 gives the outside diameter and the inside circumference. The inside diameter would have been 180 inches minus two handbreadths (8″), or 172 inches. Multiplying 172 times pi (3.14), we get 540.36 inches, which to the nearest inch equals the thirty cubits of the text.

How much water did the Laver hold—2,000 baths (1 Kgs. 7:26), or 3,000 baths (4:5)? The answer—both. Two thousand baths was probably what the Sea held *normally*, but its brimful capacity was 3,000 baths.

[7](7:11–16) J. Barton Payne, "II Chronicles," *The Wycliffe Bible Commentary*, p. 397.

[8](8:7–10) How many officers were in Solomon's administration—250 (8:10) or 550 (1 Kgs. 9:23)? See Endnotes on 2 Chron. 2:17, 18.

[9](8:17, 18) Did Solomon receive 450 talents of gold from Ophir (8:18), or 420 (1 Kgs. 9:28)? The Hebrew numbers 2 and 5 could very easily be confused by later copyists. Some suggest that the thirty-talent difference went to pay for supplies and wages for the trip.

[10](9:13–28) The name *Tarshish* is used in a generic sense for areas connected with the refining of metals. In the OT it is used for a distant country rich in metals. "Most scholars identify the name with Tartessus, a city in SW Spain, . . . rich in silver, copper, and lead" (*The Revell Bible Dictionary*, p. 1136). "The ships of Tarshish" may have simply referred to deep-sea vessels used to transport refined metals, not necessarily doing business with Spain.

[11](9:13–28) Did Solomon have 4,000 stalls for his horses (v. 25), or 40,000

(1 Kgs. 4:26)? The NASB margin points out that 1 Kings 4:26 reads 4,000 in one ancient manuscript. Since there were only 12,000 horsemen, the very high figure in 1 Kings may well be a copyist's error.

[12](10:12–19) George Williams, *The Student's Commentary on the Holy Scriptures*, p. 246.

[13](12:9–12) Gold is widely recognized by Bible students as symbolic of deity, and bronze (KJV, brass) as symbolic of judgment.

[14](13:1–3) Abijah's mother, Michaiah, was the daughter of Uriel (13:2). But 2 Chronicles 11:20 says she was Maachah the daughter of Absalom. The Jewish historian Flavius Josephus tells us that Uriel was Absalom's son-in-law and the father of Michaiah or Maachah (two names for the same person). This makes Michaiah the daughter of Uriel and the granddaughter of Absalom. (The Hebrew word for *daughter* can also mean *granddaughter*.)

[15](14:3–8) Second Chronicles 14:3 and 14:5 state that Asa removed the high places, but 15:17 says that he did not. Which is right? Both statements are true. Some high places were dedicated to idols, while others were dedicated to Jehovah (e.g., 1 Kings 3:2). Some scholars think that Asa destroyed only the idolatrous shrines.

Keil believes that the second text merely implies that the king did not succeed in carrying his reforms out thoroughly. Rawlinson suggests that the above texts refer to different times; Asa in the early part of his reign, putting down idolatry with a strong hand, but in his later years, when his character had deteriorated, allowing idol-worship to creep in again. See John Haley, *Alleged Discrepancies of the Bible*, p. 323.

[16](15:16–19) The Hebrew word for *mother* can mean *grandmother* in some contexts, as here.

[17](16:1) According to 1 Kings 15:33, Baasha, the third king of the northern tribes, died in Asa's *twenty-seventh* year. But 2 Chronicles 15:19 and 16:1 speak of war between Baasha and Asa in Asa's *thirty-sixth* year. Thiele, an expert in the chronology of the Hebrew kings, maintains that Judah's history and not Asa's sole reign is meant here. The thirty-fifth year of Judah's kingdom, dating from Rehoboam's rebellion, would have been the fifteenth year of Asa's personal reign. This explanation is not without problems, too detailed to go into here. Many simply suggest that a copyist's error is the cause of the discrepancy.

[18](18:8–11) D. L. Moody, *Notes from My Bible*, p. 59.

[19](18:18–22) Matthew Henry, "1 Kings," *Matthew Henry's Commentary on the Whole Bible*, II:703.

[20](20:1–6) In Hebrew the word for *Syria* looks much like the spelling of *Edom*. A copyist's error would be easy to make here.

[21](22:1–9) The Masoretic Text of 2 Chronicles 22:2 says that Ahaziah was *forty*-two years old when he began to reign. However, 2 Kings 8:26 says he was *twenty*-two. This younger age seems likely because his father was only forty when he died. "Forty-two years old" is almost certainly a copyist's error.

[22](24:4–14) Was the chest for the collection of the money placed outside the gate (24:8), or was it located beside the altar (2 Kgs. 12:9)? Some commentators think there were two chests, one outside and one beside the altar. Others think that there was only one box but that it was moved.

[23](24:4–14) Second Kings 12:13 says that no temple vessels were made out of the money collected, but 2 Chroni-

cles 24:14 says that vessels were made with the surplus. Second Kings refers to what went to the workmen for repairing the house, while Chronicles refers to what was done with the surplus afterward.

[24](24:20–27) In 24:20 Zechariah is said to be the son of Jehoiada. However, our Lord referred to him as the son of Berechiah (Matt. 23:25). A different Zechariah, the author of the book by that name, is also said to be the son of Berechiah (Zech. 1:1, 7). A probable explanation is as follows: The Zechariah mentioned in 2 Chronicles 24 was the grandson of Jehoiada and the son of Berechiah; in Hebrew usage, *son* can also mean *grandson*. The Zechariah who wrote the book that bears his name was also the son of Berechiah, but a different Berechiah, of course. Both names were common in OT times.

[25](28:1–4) If Ahaz was thirty-six years old when he died (28:1), that would make him only eleven when Hezekiah was born (29:1), or according to another reconstruction of the data, fifteen. Some think that Ahaz could possibly father a child at eleven; he certainly could at fifteen. Others suggest that a copyist's error may be involved. The simple fact is that we do not have enough information to solve the problem of Ahaz's chronology.

[26](28:16–27) Second Kings 16:20 says that Ahaz was buried with his fathers while 2 Chronicles 28:27 says he was not buried in the tombs of the kings. Both statements are true. He rested with his fathers and was buried with them (i.e., in the city of Jerusalem), although not in the actual royal tombs.

[27](32:1–8) G. Campbell Morgan, *Searchlights from the Word*, p. 127.

[28](35:20–24) Did Josiah die in Jerusalem (35:24), or in Megiddo (2 Kgs. 23:29)? He was mortally wounded in the battle at Megiddo, and Kings speaks of him as dying there because that is where he received his death wound. Chronicles more specifically states he actually died in Jerusalem. Today we might say a person died in an automobile accident even though he actually died in a hospital a little later. What we mean is that the accident was the cause of death even if it was not the location of the person's last breath.

[29](35:20–24) John C. Whitcomb, Jr., *Solomon to the Exile*, p. 141.

[30](36:9, 10) Verse 9 says Jehoiachin was *eight* years old when he became king while 2 Kings 24:8 says he was *eighteen*. Doubtless verse 9 contains a copyist's error, because Jehoiachin had wives when he surrendered to the Babylonians, only a few months after his ascension to the throne (2 Kgs. 24:15). Some Hebrew manuscripts and the Septuagint and Syriac versions also read *eighteen*.

BIBLIOGRAPHY

See Bibliography at the end of 1 Chronicles.

EZRA

Introduction

"The Book of Ezra is a work of so simple a character as scarcely to require an 'Introduction'. . . . It is a plain and straightforward account of one of the most important events in Jewish history—the return of the people of God from the Babylonian captivity . . . . Very little that is directly didactic occurs in it: the writer tells his story as plainly as he can, and leaves his story to teach its own lesson."

—George Rawlinson

I. Unique Place in the Canon

At one point in history Ezra and Nehemiah were one book in the Hebrew Bible, but being separate books (as in modern Bibles) was no doubt even earlier because Ezra 2 and Nehemiah 7 are virtually the same. Such a repetition would never occur in one book.

Ezra is spiritual, or religious history. It shows that a book which includes many documents from secular sources can by the Holy Spirit's selection and arrangement make them a part of the inspired record.

Of the 280 verses in Ezra we have the following most unusual breakdown for a Bible book:

111 verses: registers
109 verses: narrative
44 verses: letters
10 verses: prayer
3 verses: proclamation
3 verses: excerpt

280 total verses[1]

II. Authorship

Although the book is anonymous, the inspired compilation of first person memoirs (see 7:27—9:15), genealogies, and documents is probably the work of Ezra. The official documents, logically enough, are in Aramaic, the official Gentile language used as a *lingua franca* during Ezra and Nehemiah's time. About one fourth of Ezra is in this language.[2] The beautiful *form* of the alphabet that we call "Hebrew" was actually borrowed from this semitic sister-tongue, Aramaic.

III. Date

A fifth century B.C. Jewish community living at Elephantine, on the Egyptian Nile, left behind papyri in Aramaic similar to that of Ezra and Nehemiah. This supports the traditional fifth century date of these books rather than the liberal notion of the era of Alexander the Great (about 330 B.C.).

Ezra is believed to have penned his book between the events at the end of chapter 10 (456 B.C.) and Nehemiah's arrival in Jerusalem (444 B.C.). The following chronological chart will aid in understanding the Books of Ezra, Nehemiah, and Esther:

Chronology of Ezra, Nehemiah, and Esther
(Dates are approximate)

538 BC	The decree of Cyrus to rebuild the temple.
538/7 BC	Zerubbabel's expedition to Jerusalem.
536 BC	Foundation of the temple laid.
535 BC	Work on the temple halted.
520 BC	Ministry of Haggai and Zechariah.
520 BC	Decree of Darius to resume work on the temple.
516 BC	Temple completed.
486 BC	Reign of Ahasuerus (Xerxes) begins.
479/8 BC	Esther crowned queen.
464 BC	Reign of Artaxerxes begins.
458 BC	Ezra's expedition to Jerusalem.
444 BC	Nehemiah arrives in Jerusalem.
444 BC	Walls of Jerusalem completed.
420 BC	Nehemiah's second journey to Jerusalem.

IV. Background and Themes

As the book of Ezra opens the Neo-Babylonian Empire is passing away and Jeremiah's prophecy of restoration of the Jews to their land is being fulfilled (Jer. 29:10–14).

In chapters 1—6 the first expedition back to Palestine takes place under Zerubbabel. The first thing the returned exiles do is to build the altar of burnt offering, followed by the house of the Lord. The latter goes up against much opposition from the enemies of God's people, but also with the encouragement of the Prophets Haggai and Zechariah.

Between chapters 6 and 7 there is a period of about fifty-eight years. During that era occur the dramatic story of Queen Esther in sacred history and the famous battles of Marathon, Thermopylae, and Salamis in secular history.[3]

Chapters 7—10 recount Ezra's journey to Jerusalem in about 458 B.C. with a commission from King Artaxerxes Longimanus. Ezra's personal attempts to reform the people are detailed in these chapters.

OUTLINE

I. THE RETURN OF CAPTIVES TO JERUSALEM UNDER ZERUBBABEL (Chaps. 1—6)
  A. The Decree of Cyrus (1:1–4)
  B. Preparations and Provisions (1:5–11)
  C. Register of Those Who Returned (Chap. 2)
  D. Construction of the Altar and the Temple Foundations (Chap. 3)
  E. Opposition to Rebuilding the Temple (Chap. 4)
    1. In the Reign of Cyrus (4:1–5, 24)
    2. In the Reign of Ahasuerus (4:6)
    3. In the Reign of Artaxerxes (4:7–23)
  F. Haggai and Zechariah's Encouragement to Rebuild (5:1, 2)
  G. Opposition During the Reign of Darius (5:3–17)
  H. Completion of the Temple through a Favorable Decree of Darius (Chap. 6)

II. THE RETURN OF CAPTIVES UNDER EZRA (Chaps. 7—10)
  A. Generous Authorization by Artaxerxes (Chap. 7)

B. Register of Those Who Returned (8:1–14)
C. Account of the Trip to Jerusalem (8:15–36)
D. Mixed Marriages and Ezra's Prayer of Confession (Chap. 9)
E. The Jews' Covenant to Put Away Foreign Wives and Children (Chap. 10)

Commentary

I. THE RETURN OF CAPTIVES TO JERUSALEM UNDER ZERUBBABEL (Chaps. 1—6)

A. The Decree of Cyrus (1:1–4)

The first three verses duplicate the last two verses of 2 Chronicles. God used **Cyrus, king of Persia**, to issue **a proclamation** permitting the Jews to return to **Judah** and to rebuild the temple **in Jerusalem**. In addition, he commanded their neighbors to contribute generously to the returning remnant. Many years before his birth, **Cyrus** had been named by God and set apart for this high destiny (Isa. 44:28—45:13). He illustrates the truth of Proverbs 21:1: "The king's heart is in the hand of the LORD, like the rivers of water; He turns it wherever He wishes."

The decree ended seventy years of captivity for the Jews. The seventy-year period can be calculated in two ways: from 605 B.C., when Nebuchadnezzar attacked Jerusalem and led off the first deportation, to 535

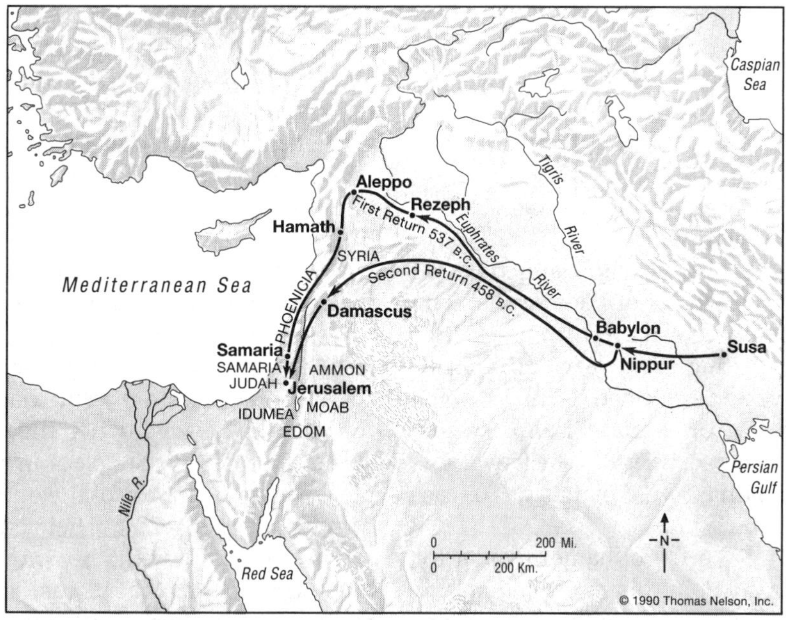

The Return from Exile. When Cyrus the Persian captured Babylon in 539 B.C., the way was opened for captive Judah to begin the return to her homeland. Two major expeditions made the journey, one in 537 B.C. and another in 458 B.C.

B.C., when the foundation of the temple was laid; or from the fall of Jerusalem, in 586 B.C., to the completion of the temple, in 516 B.C.

B. Preparations and Provisions (1:5–11)

In addition to the wealth donated by the neighbors of the Jews, **King Cyrus** gave them **five thousand four hundred** vessels **of gold and silver** that **Nebuchadnezzar had taken from** the temple in **Jerusalem**. **Sheshbazzar** (v. 8) may be the Persian name for Zerubbabel; he may be a totally different person. Notice the mention of **twenty-nine knives** in verse 9. If God cares for such details, how much more does He care for His people!

C. Register of Those Who Returned (Chap. 2)

2:1–58 In verses 1–61 we have a list of those **who returned to . . . Judah** under **Zerubbabel**. Some are recorded according to parentage (vv. 3–19) and some according to hometown (vv. 20–35). Special mention is made of **the priests** (vv. 36–39), **the Levites** (vv. 40–42), and **the Nethinim** or temple-servants (vv. 43–54). They would occupy important roles in the reconstructed temple.

2:59–63 Some who claimed to be **priests** but who **could not** prove their **genealogy** were barred from serving or from eating the priests' food until they were authorized through consulting **the Urim and Thummim**, or *"lights and perfections."*[4] The **governor** (or Tirshatha, NKJV marg., v. 63) was Zerubbabel.

2:64–67 A list of names similar to the one given in this chapter is found in Nehemiah 7. While there are some minor differences in tabulations, both give the total number of Jews returning to Judah as **forty-two thousand three hundred and sixty** plus **seven thousand three hundred and thirty-seven** servants. Ezra adds 245 singers and Nehemiah adds 200. So the total of the returning remnant was about 50,000—a small fraction of those who had been carried away.

2:68–70 When the Jews reached **Jerusalem, some of the heads of the fathers' houses** contributed **gold** and **silver** for the construction of **the house of God** and **garments** for the priests. Then the **people** settled **in their** respective **cities**.

D. Construction of the Altar and the Temple Foundations (Chap. 3)

3:1–7 In **the seventh month**, which was the beginning of the civil year, the repatriated Jews **gathered** in **Jerusalem** to celebrate **the Feast of Tabernacles**. Under the leadership of **Jeshua**[5] and **Zerubbabel**, they **built an altar** and **offered burnt offerings**, as required by **the Law of Moses**. They felt that by thus honoring Jehovah He would protect them from their enemies. Then they moved ahead with preparations for building **the temple**, using help from **Tyre** and **Sidon**.

3:8–13 The actual construction began fourteen months after the return. As soon as the **foundation . . . was laid, the priests** and **Levites** led in a service of dedication. But many of the **old men . . . wept** when they compared the splendor of Solomon's temple with the plainness of the one now being built (Hag. 2:3). Their cries of sorrow mingled with the shouts of **joy** and praise so that it was difficult to distinguish them, **and the sound was heard afar off**.

E. Opposition to Rebuilding the Temple (Chap. 4)

1. *In the Reign of Cyrus (4:1–5, 24)*

4:1–3 The adversaries of Judah and Benjamin mentioned in verse 1 were descendants of colonists from other countries who had been planted in the land when Assyria took the northern kingdom into captivity. These colonists had intermarried with the Jews who remained in the land, and their offspring became known as Samaritans. **They came to Zerubbabel** and pretended that they wanted to assist in the rebuilding of the temple. They too worshiped Jehovah, but He was only one of many gods in their idolatrous system of religion. So their offer was refused by Israel's leaders.

4:4–5, 24 The Samaritans then changed their strategy. First they **tried to discourage the people** of Judah. Then **they troubled them in building**. They also **hired counselors** to lobby against Israel at the royal court **to frustrate** the Jews through the use of scare tactics. The work on the temple thus came to a halt.

Verse 24 follows verse 5 chronologically. The enemies of Judah succeeded in having **work** on the temple stopped **until the second year of** Darius's **reign**.

2. *In the Reign of Ahasuerus (4:6)*[6]

Verse 6 mentions a letter that was written during **the reign of Ahasuerus**, bringing **an accusation against** the Jews. Verses 7–23 describe another letter, written in the days of Artaxerxes, accusing the Jews of rebuilding the city and its walls as an act of rebellion. The king thereupon ordered the work to stop.

3. *In the Reign of Artaxerxes (4:7–23)*

The rebuilding of the temple was completed during the reign of Darius, who ruled before Ahasuerus (v. 6) and **Artaxerxes** (v. 7). Therefore, the letters described in verses 6–23 were written *after* the temple was rebuilt. They have to do with attempts to rebuild **the walls** of Jerusalem, not *the temple*. But they are placed here, out of their chronological order, as further illustrations of attempts made to obstruct the work of the returned exiles.

From 4:6 to 6:8, the **language** used is **Aramaic**[7] instead of Hebrew. This was the language used by **Persia** in official decrees.

F. Haggai and Zechariah's Encouragement to Rebuild (5:1, 2)

From **Haggai** 1:1 **and Zechariah** 1:1 we learn that this chapter belongs to the second year of Darius's reign (v. 1, cf. 4:24). These two **prophets** urged the Israelites to resume work on the temple instead of building expensive houses for themselves (Hag. 1:4). **Zerubbabel . . . and Jeshua** obeyed the Lord and ordered construction to begin immediately. Notice here that it was not by the power of the king's decree that the work was resumed, but by the power of *the Holy Spirit* speaking through **the prophets of God** (cf. Zech. 4:6).

G. Opposition During the Reign of Darius (5:3–17)

5:3–5 Opposition arose quickly. The Persian **governor** and his associates **came to** Jerusalem and asked what authority the Jews had to start building and what **the names of the men** were (see vv. 9, 10). They were given **the names** of the Jewish leaders. These Persian officials were more reasonable than those mentioned in chapter 4. They did not stop the work, but sent a **letter . . . to Darius**

to determine its legality. Because the Jews had started to obey God's word, His **eye . . . was upon** them to fulfill it.

5:6–17 In their **letter . . . to Darius, Tattenai . . . and Shethar-Boznai** told of their conversation with the Jews and the latter's reply. The **elders** of the people first of all gave their divine authority. They were **servants of** the one true **God**, but they had been delivered up to the Babylonians because of their sins. Now that Jehovah had brought them back to their land, they were to rebuild His temple. As to human authority, they had the **decree** of **Cyrus** which gave them permission to rebuild the temple. **Cyrus** himself had contributed generously to the project. The governor requested that **a search be made** to determine if **King Cyrus** had made such **a decree** and asked Darius to notify him what action should be taken **concerning this matter**.

H. Completion of the Temple through a Favorable Decree of Darius (Chap. 6)

6:1–5 After diligent search, the **decree** of Cyrus **was found** in what used to be his capital city, **Achmetha** (or Ecbatana, NKJV marg.). (The edict was much more detailed than is summarized in chap. 1.) In it, the specifications of **the temple** were given along with an order to return all **the gold and silver articles** taken by **Nebuchadnezzar**.

6:6–12 **Darius** then spelled out to **Tattenai** and his colleagues their responsibilities toward the Jews. They were not to hinder **the work** but were to pay for **the cost** of the temple out of the royal treasury from collected **taxes**. Provisions for the temple service were to be supplied upon **request of the priests** (v. 9) so that the Jews might find favor in the eyes of **God** and hence be effectual in their prayers **for the . . . king and his** family. Darius put some teeth into his **edict** by making it a capital offense to hinder the work. He called on **God** to deal with anyone, kings included, who might try to **destroy this house of God** in the future.

6:13–15 The king's orders were quickly obeyed and the work on the temple surged ahead. With encouragement from God's prophets and provisions from Darius's treasury, the temple was completed four years later, but nineteen or twenty years after the laying of the foundation. **Artaxerxes** actually lived later; he contributed to the maintenance of the temple, not to its building.

6:16 The Israelites and their leaders **celebrated the dedication of the** temple with joy. Dennett observes:

> It was but natural that they should rejoice at such a moment, for the house of their God was the expression of all the blessings of the covenant in which they stood. And at length, after weary years of failure, difficulties, disappointments, and sorrow, it stood completed before their eyes. It was for this that they had been brought up out of Babylon, and if any of them had sown in tears they now reaped in joy.[8]

6:17–22 They **offered sacrifices**. If we compare this dedication with Solomon's: 22,000 oxen and 120,000 sheep plus innumerable oxen and sheep sacrificed before the ark (2 Chron. 7:5; 5:6), it pales into a poor and feeble event. Fortunately they did not dwell on this.

Today in many churches, fellowships, denominations, schools, and even whole countries of Christendom, a comparison not unlike the decline from Solomon's time to Ezra's is apparent. Dennett has an encouraging application that is worth quoting at length:

> Faith, however, has to do with unseen things, and it could thus recall to the mind of this feeble remnant that Jehovah was no less mighty and no less merciful for them than for Solomon.
>
> The house might be less glorious, and they themselves but poor subjects of a Gentile monarch, but if God was for them, as He was, the resources available to faith were as unbounded as ever. This truth cannot be too deeply impressed on our minds, that Christ remains the same for His people in a day of difficulty as in a season of prosperity. To be in the power of this raises us, as nothing else can, above our circumstances, and gives us courage to press on, whatever the perils of the path.[9]

Afterward **the Passover** was observed and **the Feast of Unleavened Bread** was **kept . . . with** great **joy**, for the people clearly saw God's hand behind the favors they had obtained from Darius. Darius is called **the king of Assyria** here because he was ruling over the old Assyrian empire.

II. THE RETURN OF CAPTIVES UNDER EZRA (Chaps. 7—10)

A. Generous Authorization by Artaxerxes (Chap. 7)

7:1–5 There is about a fifty-eight-year gap between chapters 6 and 7. (See the chart "CHRONOLOGY OF EZRA, NEHEMIAH, AND ESTHER" in the Introduction.) During that time Darius was succeeded by Ahasuerus (Xerxes). His reign covered the events recorded in the book of Esther. After him, **Artaxerxes** (Longimanus), mentioned in verse 1, came to the throne.

A brief genealogy of **Ezra** is given in verses 1–5 to show his priestly ancestry. G. Campbell Morgan comments:

> As messengers of the will of God, the scribes took the place of the prophets, with this difference: instead of receiving new revelations, they explained and applied the old. Of this new order Ezra was at once the founder and type. . . . He was expert in exposition and application of the Law. The qualifications for such work are very clearly set out in the statement made concerning him in the tenth verse of this chapter. He "set his heart to seek . . . to do . . . to teach."[10]

7:6–10 Besides possessing a distinguished pedigree, **Ezra was . . . a skilled scribe in the Law of Moses.** Certainly **Ezra** was a man of the Book and a living illustration of the first three verses of Psalm 1.[11] Because he meditated on **the Law of the Lord** day and night, he prospered in what he sought to do for God. Jehovah once more directed the heart of a heathen king to carry out His counsels. A decree was issued which made possible a second return **to Jerusalem**, this one under **Ezra**.

7:11–26 **King Artaxerxes** of Persia granted sweeping powers **to Ezra** in this **letter** recorded here. Any Israelites who desired could accompany him **to Jerusalem**, where he was **to inquire** if everything was being done in accordance with **the Law** of Moses. Generous gifts had been donated by **the king and his counselors**. These, along with any temple vessels which were still left **in . . . Babylon**, were committed to his charge. The gifts were to be used to maintain the temple services, and any surplus was to be distributed at Ezra's discretion. If that was not enough, **silver**, **wheat**, **wine**, **oil**, **and salt** were to be supplied **without prescribed limit** from the royal treasury. The last four items were essential ingredients in the Jewish sacrificial system. Those who served in the temple were granted exemption from taxes. Finally, the edict gave Ezra the political power to appoint **magistrates and judges** for the Jews living west of **the** Euphrates **River**. These **judges** were to **teach** and enforce **the laws of . . . God**.

7:27, 28 In his thanksgiving prayer, Ezra **blessed . . . God** for directing **the king's heart to beautify** the temple and humbly thanked Him for the enabling strength He gave to undertake such an important work. **Encouraged** by the Lord's **hand** on him, Ezra **gathered chief men of Israel to go up with** him to Jerusalem.[12]

B. Register of Those Who Returned (8:1–14)

8:1–14 This first paragraph lists those who went back to Jerusalem **with** Ezra **from Babylon**. Several from these same families had returned under Zerubbabel years earlier (chap. 2). Almost 1500 **males** made up this second expedition.

C. Account of the Trip to Jerusalem (8:15–36)

8:15–20 While stopped **by the river** near **Ahava** (location unknown), Ezra noticed that there were no Levites in his company, so he commissioned eleven of the leading **brethren** to go to **Casiphia**, where he evidently knew that some Levites had settled, to encourage the Levites and temple **servants** to join him. Thirty-eight **Levites** and **two hundred and twenty Nethinim** (servants) responded.

8:21–23 Before the Jews began their 900-mile journey, they camped **at the river of Ahava**, and there Ezra proclaimed **a fast**. He had previously testified of God's goodness and power to the king. **To request** a military escort now would be to deny his words by his actions. Instead he put his faith on the line, trusting in the God who delights to save those who lean hard on Him. He would not be disappointed. **He answered** their **prayer**.

8:24–34 The money and utensils that had been given to Ezra **were weighed** out to **twelve of the leaders of the priests** and twelve **Levites**. Since these things were holy (set apart for sacred use), they had to be kept by men who were holy. After a three-and-a-half-month trek, the entire party reached **Jerusalem** without incident. Upon arrival in Jerusalem **the silver and the gold and the articles** were **weighed** again and given to those in charge of the temple.

8:35, 36 The first order of business for the exiles was to offer **burnt** and **sin** offerings on Jehovah's altar for all Israel. When they had taken care of their spiritual obligations, **they delivered the king's orders** to his officials in the western provinces, who in turn supplied them accordingly.

D. Mixed Marriages and Ezra's Prayer of Confession (Chap. 9)

9:1, 2 Ezra had not been in Jerusalem long when some of **the leaders** approached him with the disturbing news that **the rulers** and **the people** were intermarrying with the heathen. This was one of the sins for which Israel had been punished in days past. The law was clear (Ex. 34:16; Deut. 7:3); God's people must be **holy**. He wants them to separate themselves from the world and every other form of evil.

9:3, 4 Ezra was **astonished** when he **heard** about these mixed marriages. He was plunged into deep mourning **until the evening sacri-**

fice. With **robe** torn and patches of **hair** missing from his **head and beard**, he **sat** in silence while others who feared the Lord gathered around him.

9:5–15 As the blood of **the evening sacrifice** was being poured out before Jehovah for the **iniquities** of the people, Ezra **fell** to his **knees** and lifted his voice in confession. Making the people's sin his own, he was **humiliated** that they had responded so wickedly to the **grace** which had preserved them **as a remnant** through past judgments **and** had given **them a peg in His holy place** (v. 8). This "peg" speaks of the security of anyone or anything that depends on God. Some, such as Ironside, believe that ultimately it refers to Christ Himself:

> The reference to the "nail" [**peg**, NKJV] is doubtless a recognition of Isaiah's prophecy of the "nail in a sure place," upon which Jehovah's glory was to hang, which is, in the full sense, Christ Himself (Isa. 22:21–25).[13]

The prophets had spoken clearly on mixed marriages. So the men were without excuse, especially in light of the recent favors God had granted them. **"Here we are before You, in our guilt."** There was nothing else to say.

E. The Jews' Covenant to Put Away Foreign Wives and Children (Chap. 10)

10:1–5 Ezra's prayer of confession caused **the people** to weep **bitterly**. Acting as a spokesman, **Shechaniah** confessed their guilt but reminded **Ezra** that there was yet **hope**, if their confession was followed by forsaking the unequal yoke. He suggested that Ezra lead them in making **a covenant . . . to put away** the foreign **wives and** children. **The priests, the Levites, and all Israel** responded to this plea for national repentance and **so they swore an oath**.

10:6–8 All the exiles were summoned to **gather at Jerusalem** for a solemn time of public confession. Those who refused to come **within three days** and face the issues were threatened with loss of **property** and excommunication.

10:9–11 With only **three days** to respond to the command, **all the men of Judah and Benjamin** hurried to **Jerusalem** from the surrounding cities. Adverse weather did not deter them, for the matter to be settled was very grave and caused more consternation than did the rainy weather. **Ezra** spoke to the gathering, pointing out their transgressions.

10:12–17 **All the assembly** was quick to acknowledge that they had disobeyed God's law. But because of the **heavy rain** and the large number of cases involved, they suggested that the individual cases be examined city by city. Four men tried to oppose the plan but were unsuccessful. Judges were appointed, and in less than two weeks the inquiry began. Within three months the probe was complete.

10:18–44 Those indicted are listed in verses 18–43: **priests** first (vv. 18–22), then **Levites** (vv. 23, 24), and finally **others of Israel** (vv. 25–43). Verse 44 reads: **All these had taken pagan wives, and some of them had wives by whom they had children.** Though it is not stated, it is likely that adequate provision was made for the support of these **wives** and **children**. The sorrow created by the disruption of these families must be weighed against the importance of maintaining the solidarity of the nation destined to produce the Messiah.

The unequal yoke is still forbidden (2 Cor. 6:14–18). It should not be found among the children of God. But 1 Corinthians 7:12, 13 is the NT rule for those already bound to an unbeliever at conversion. Under grace, the believer is not required to put away the unbeliever or the children. The latter are set apart in a position of external privilege by the believer.

The book of Ezra is a study in revival. When men read the Word of God and apply its truths to their lives, when intercessory prayers flow for the saints, and when there is confession and separation from known sin, there will be power in the church to do great things for God.

ENDNOTES

[1](Intro) This breakdown is from W. Graham Scroggie, *Know Your Bible*, Vol. I, Old Testament, p. 90. (His total, "880," is no doubt a typographical error.)

[2](Intro) 4:8—6:18 and 7:12–26 are in Aramaic.

[3](Intro) Scroggie, *Know Your Bible*, Vol. I, p. 91.

[4](2:59–63) We do not know for certain exactly what the Urim and Thummim were: "Possibly two precious stones, which were put inside the pouch. They may have been used, like lots, to determine God's will" (*Ryrie Study Bible*, New King James Version, p. 135). See also Ex. 28:30; Lev. 8:8; Num. 27:21; Deut. 33:8; 1 Sam. 28:6; Neh. 7:65.

[5](3:1–7) Jeshua (or "Yeshua") is the Hebrew form of *Jesus*.

[6](4:6) Verses 6–23 belong later in the outline chronologically. See the chart "Chronology of Ezra, Nehemiah, and Esther."

[7](4:7–23) Older books in English often called this language "Chaldee."

[8](6:16) Edward Dennett, *Exposition of the Book of Ezra: Restoration from Babylon*, p. 55.

[9](6:17–22) *Ibid.*, pp. 55, 56.

[10](7:1–5) G. Campbell Morgan, *Searchlights from the Word*, p. 131.

[11](7:6–10) Although Psalm 1 is anonymous, many Bible scholars believe that Ezra is the human author (likewise of Psalm 119, which is about the Word of God).

[12](7:27, 28) In the Bible, going to Jerusalem is always "up," no matter from which direction one is coming. This is partly because the city is up in the mountains of Judea. It probably also has a spiritual application: Going to *God's* house is always "up."

[13](9:5–15) H. A. Ironside, "Notes on the Book of Ezra," in *Notes on Ezra, Nehemiah and Esther*, p. 90.

BIBLIOGRAPHY

Dennett, Edward. *Exposition of the Book of Ezra: Restoration from Babylon*. Oak Park, IL: Bible Truth Publishers, 1956.

Ironside, H. A. "Ezra." In *Notes on Ezra, Nehemiah and Esther*. Neptune, NJ: Loizeaux Brothers, 1972.

Jensen, Irving L. *Ezra/Nehemiah/Esther*. Chicago: Moody Press, 1970.

Keil, C. F. "Ezra." In *Biblical Commentary on the Old Testament*. Vol. 10. Grand Rapids: Wm. B. Eerdmans Publishing Co., 1971.

Kidner, Derek. *Ezra and Nehemiah*. The Tyndale Old Testament Commentaries. Downers Grove, IL: InterVarsity Press, 1979.

Rawlinson, George. "Ezra." In *The Pulpit Commentary*. Vol. 15. Ed. by H.D.M. Spence. New York: Funk and Wagnalls, 1909.

NEHEMIAH

Introduction

"More than half this book is a personal record, punctuated with 'asides' and frank comments which make it (in such parts) one of the liveliest pieces of writing in the Bible. Much of Ezra's story was also told in the first person (Ezra 8:15—9:15), but Ezra was a quieter personality than the formidable, practical Nehemiah; he does not leap out of the page as this man does."

—Derek Kidner

I. Unique Place in the Canon

If you are having any sort of a building program and are having trouble getting people involved, Nehemiah is the book to read, study, teach, or preach. The leadership qualities needed to get a nearly impossible job done are wonderfully exemplified in this 5th century B.C. Hebrew leader.

Whitcomb writes:

> No portion of the Old Testament provides us with a greater incentive to dedicated, discerning zeal for the work of God than the book of Nehemiah. The example of Nehemiah's passion for the truth of God's Word—whatever the cost or consequences, is an example sorely needed in the present hour.[1]

II. Authorship

Nehemiah, whose name appropriately means *Jehovah consoles*, writes his memoirs in the first person, but he also includes state documents to which he had access. The Elephantine papyri witness to the historical truth of the book, mentioning Johanan the high priest (see Neh. 12:22, 23) and the sons of Nehemiah's arch-foe, Sanballat.

All of this supports the traditional authorship by Nehemiah the son of Hachaliah and brother of Hanani (1:1, 2). We know little of Nehemiah's background, but he was probably born in Persia.

The tact, drive, and leadership qualities shown in this book are the type that would be demanded by Nehemiah's position as king's cupbearer, a very important position.

III. Date

Nehemiah probably wrote soon after the events recorded, or about 430 B.C. This would be during the reign of Artaxerxes I (464–424 B.C.).

Josephus says that Jaddua was high priest when Alexander the Great came through Palestine. Since Nehemiah 12:22 mentions a Jaddua, some use this to date the book later than Nehemiah's time. It may be that Jaddua was a very young man when Nehemiah mentioned him (because he was in the priestly line) and was about ninety in Alexander's time. Or, there may have been two high priests with this name. A third possibility is that Josephus, who often was wrong on his chronology of this era, was mistaken here as well!

IV. Background and Theme

Nehemiah was the *third* great leader in the Jewish restoration. Zerubbabel led the *first* group of exiles back to Jerusalem in 538–537 B.C. (Ezra 2) and supervised the building of the temple. Almost eighty years later, Ezra the scribe came to the holy city with a *second* group of Jews, bringing sweeping reforms through his ministry of God's Word. But in time things degenerated in Jerusalem.

Thirteen years after Ezra's expedition, Nehemiah was burdened by God about conditions in Jerusalem. After receiving permission to rectify the situation, he provided the kind of quality leadership the Israelites desperately needed. His roots were deep in God (notice the numerous references to his prayer life); this enabled him to weather the storm of opposition that buffeted him from the outset of his mission. It has been well said that "there are three kinds of people in the world—those who don't know what's happening, those who watch what's happening, and those who make things happen." Nehemiah was a man who made things happen. Whereas the book of Ezra deals with the temple and worship, Nehemiah deals with the walls and everyday work. The book of Nehemiah brings God into the everyday affairs of life.

OUTLINE

I. NEHEMIAH'S FIRST VISIT: RESTORATION OF JERUSALEM (Chaps. 1—12)
   A. Consternation over Jerusalem's Condition (Chap. 1)
   B. Authorization for Jerusalem's Restoration (2:1–8)
   C. Reconstruction of Jerusalem's Wall (2:9—6:19)
      1. Private Inspection and Public Opposition (2:9–20)
      2. The Workers and Their Work (Chap. 3)
      3. External Hindrances and Special Precautions (Chap. 4)
      4. Internal Problems and Social Reformation (Chaps. 5, 6)
   D. Organization of Jerusalem's Guards (7:1–4)
   E. Registration of Jerusalem's Population (7:5–73)
   F. Revitalization of Jerusalem's Religion (Chaps. 8—10)
   G. Repopulation of Jerusalem's Precincts (Chap. 11)
   H. Tabulation of Jerusalem's Priests and Levites (12:1–26)
   I. Dedication of Jerusalem's Wall (12:27–47)

II. NEHEMIAH'S SECOND VISIT: REFORMATION OF JERUSALEM (Chap. 13)
   A. Expulsion of Tobiah from the Temple (13:1–9)
   B. Restoration of Tithes for the Levites (13:10–14)

C. Elimination of Illegal Activity on the Sabbath (13:15–22)
D. Dissolution of Interracial Marriages (13:23–31)

Commentary

I. NEHEMIAH'S FIRST VISIT: RESTORATION OF JERUSALEM (Chaps. 1—12)

A. Consternation over Jerusalem's Condition (Chap. 1)

1:1–3 Little is given by way of introduction in this first chapter. We are told only two things about **Nehemiah**: his father's name was **Hachaliah** and he himself was the cupbearer to King Artaxerxes, a very influential position. His reaction to the news **concerning Jerusalem** shows that he was a man of spiritual character. J. Alec Motyer comments:

> It is rather an uncertain time of history, but it seems very likely that some of the enthusiasm engendered by the mission of Ezra took a political or nationalistic direction; enthusiasm was so roused that it began to flow out into an unauthorized rebuilding of the walls of Jerusalem. Some of the enemies of God's people in the area reported this matter back to . . . Artaxerxes, and he commanded that the building work should cease. The enemies of God capitalized on this by going up to Jerusalem with the royal mandate in their hands, causing the work to cease, and tearing down the city walls. It is very likely that it was the news of this action which came to Nehemiah.[2]

1:4–11 Nehemiah had a burden for the remnant in Judah. Even though he had not experienced their hardships, he identified with them, denying himself the luxuries of the palace in order to fast, mourn, and pray. He confessed their **sins** as his own and asked God to **remember** His Word and to be faithful in regathering His people as He had been righteous in scattering them. He also asked the Lord to **grant him** favor **in the sight** of the king, for a bold plan to aid his brethren was taking shape in his mind. For days he pleaded his case before the Most High.

Nehemiah is often used as an example of effective leadership. First, he had a vision of a goal to be achieved. After analyzing the problem, he decided on a proper course of action. Then he motivated others to share his vision and to become actively involved. Next we see him delegating authority and assigning tasks. He supervised the work and checked on performance until the project was satisfactorily completed.

B. Authorization for Jerusalem's Restoration (2:1–8)

2:1–3 It was three or four months before Nehemiah's faith was rewarded in a most unexpected way. One day when he was serving **wine . . . to the king**, his **face** betrayed his **sorrow of heart**. The king's question brought on a wave of fear, for sadness was not allowed in the royal presence (Est. 4:2). George Williams notes:

> Eastern monarchs being in daily dread of poison, any appearance of agita-

tion in the cup-bearer would be regarded as especially suspicious.[3]

But Nehemiah meant no harm to the king. The cause of his sorrow was the desolation of Jerusalem, his ancestral home.

2:4, 5 Nehemiah's prayerful dependence upon the Lord was not in vain. Not only did **the king** give him what he requested, he also made him governor of **Judah** (5:14). Artaxerxes' decree fulfilled the word of the Lord to Daniel (Dan. 9:25), even as the earlier decree of Cyrus had fulfilled the prophecy of Jeremiah (Jer. 29:10; Ezra 1).

2:6–8 In answer to the king's question, Nehemiah told him how long he expected to be away. As it turned out, Nehemiah was away from Persia for at least twelve years (5:14). In all of this Nehemiah acknowledged the **good hand of God upon** him.

C. Reconstruction of Jerusalem's Wall (2:9—6:19)

1. *Private Inspection and Public Opposition (2:9–20)*

2:9–16 Along with the **king's** official **letters**, Artaxerxes sent an armed escort with Nehemiah. Shortly after he **came to Jerusalem**, the new governor surveyed his capital under cover of darkness in order to attract as little attention as possible and to keep his plans secret. He knew it was imperative that **the walls** be repaired if the city was to survive. At one place the rubble was so deep that his mount could not **pass**.

2:17–20 Later he called the leaders together, told them what needed to be done, and encouraged them by relating how **the hand** of the Lord **had been** with him so far, **and also of the king's words**. The Jews were excited and ready to begin. Their enemies, **Sanballat**, **Tobiah**, and **Geshem**, scoffed and tried to stop the building project by raising the false cry of "rebellion **against the king**." But Nehemiah was not intimidated; the **God** of **heaven** had promised success. The people were united, and that is necessary if God is going to bless (Ps. 133:1–3).

2. *The Workers and Their Work (Chap. 3)*

The priests were the first to begin the task by repairing **the Sheep Gate**. This gate, located in the northeastern corner of the city, was so named because the sheep destined for the temple altar were brought through it. The gates are mentioned counterclockwise: **the Sheep Gate** (vv. 1, 2); **the Fish Gate** (vv. 3–5); **the Old Gate** (or Corner Gate) (vv. 6–12); **the Valley Gate** (v. 13); **the Refuse** (or Dung) **Gate** (v. 14); **the Fountain Gate** (vv. 15–25); **the Water Gate** (v. 26); **the Horse Gate** (v. 28); **the East Gate** (v. 29); and **the Miphkad Gate** (Inspection Gate, NASB) (v. 31). Verse 32 brings us back full circle to **the Sheep Gate**. Two other gates are mentioned in the book—the Gate of Ephraim (8:16) and the Prison Gate (Gate of the Guard, NASB) (12:39). There were twelve gates in all, even as there will be twelve gates in the New Jerusalem (Rev. 21:12). It is significant that God keeps a careful record of all those who serve Him; this is seen in the listing of those who repaired the walls and gates.

The House of the Mighty (v. 16) may originally have been the headquarters for David's mighty men.

Men and women, artisans and laborers, princes and commoners, all labored side by side. There was only one case of disunity—the **nobles** of

Photo: Levant Photo Service

Excavated section of the wall built by Nehemiah in Jerusalem after the Jewish people returned from the Captivity in Babylonia.

Tekoa shirked their responsibility (v. 5). Some who finished their assigned task took on an additional portion of the wall (cf. vv. 4, 21; 5, 27). God has given different work assignments to believers today. He has equipped us with various gifts and abilities appropriate to our calling, and He knows who is not really involved and who is doing double duty. "Each one's work will become clear; for the Day will declare it, because it will be revealed by fire; and the fire will test each one's work, of what sort it is" (1 Cor. 3:13).

3. *External Hindrances and Special Precautions (Chap. 4)*

4:1–6 **When Sanballat** and **Tobiah . . . mocked** the early rebuilding efforts, Nehemiah responded by prayer and went on with the work. While the imprecatory language of verses 4 and 5 was acceptable in the Dispensation of Law, it would not be suitable for Christians in this Age of Grace (Rom. 12:19–21). Soon the wall reached **half its** intended **height**.

4:7–14 External pressure from the **Arabs**, the **Ammonites, and the Ashdodites** was not the only threat; at times the immensity of the job almost crushed the Jews. The seemingly unending piles of rubble sapped their **strength** and drive (v. 10). When their countrymen living outside Jerusalem warned of imminent attack, Nehemiah **positioned men behind the lower parts of the wall** and armed the workers, encouraging them to **"Remember the Lord . . . and fight."**

4:15–23 With the element of surprise lost, Judah's **enemies** abandoned their plan for a direct attack. **From that time on, half** the Jews **worked at construction, while the other half** stood guard. Even **the builders** carried weapons. Nehemiah kept a trumpeter with him at all times to sound the alarm in case of attack and **rally** the men who were spread out along **the wall**. Those who came from outside the city were ordered to spend the **night in Jerusalem** so as to be readily available if needed. Their strategy was to *pray, watch,* and *work*. The people emulated the courage and resoluteness of their indomitable leader. Nehemiah, his relatives, his **servants**, and **the** Persian **guard** that accompanied him gave themselves no leisure as they kept vigil over the city.

4. *Internal Problems and Social Reformation (Chaps. 5, 6)*

5:1–7 In the midst of rebuilding, an ugly internal problem arose. Food was evidently scarce and expensive. Inflation, plus **the . . . tax** burden placed on the Jews by the king, had reduced many of them to poverty. They were forced to borrow **money** from their wealthier brothers and to mortgage their property. Some even had to sell their **sons** and **daughters** as slaves. And since their land was owned by others, they were left without means to buy back the children. When they told Nehemiah of their sad plight, he called the wealthy to a solemn assembly and **rebuked** them.

5:8–10 Was it not inconsistent to drive their **Jewish brethren . . . into slavery** when Nehemiah and others had been redeeming them from bondage to their heathen neighbors? Was it not imperative for their safety that they maintain a right relationship with **God**? How could they afford to alienate Jehovah by breaking His holy law by charging **usury** (v. 9; cf. Ex. 22:25)? Even as their leader, Nehemiah, had set an example by not charging interest on loans he made, should they not do the same?

5:11, 12 After Nehemiah urged the rich to return the property gained by usury and to **restore** a measure of the interest exacted on loans of **money, grain, new wine**, and **oil**, they promised to do so. The **priests** were **called** and they sealed their pledge with **an oath**.

5:13 A vivid warning was then given of what would happen to anyone who reneged. He would **be shaken** off the good land like the dust off a **garment**. With a hearty **"Amen"** the men left the meeting and performed their vow.

5:14–19 A short account of Nehemiah's **twelve**-year tenure as **governor** closes chapter 5. He supported himself rather than charge the people with his maintenance. He did not take advantage of his position to acquire **land** or feather his nest for the future. His time was devoted to making Jerusalem safe for his **brothers**, not to building his own personal fortune. He supplied his own **table** and welcomed strangers to share his hospitality. He did all this because he feared **God**. If **God** kept track of his sacrifices, that was sufficient for Nehemiah.

6:1–4 Having failed to obstruct the Jews by other means, the enemy next tried to destroy Nehemiah. Four times **Sanballat** and **Geshem the Arab** tried to get Nehemiah to leave his work and meet with them **in the plain of Ono**. **Four times** Nehemiah refused, knowing that they were plotting **to do** him **harm**. Such a **great work** must not be stopped.

6:5–9 Still pretending to be his ally, **Sanballat** accused Nehemiah in a **letter** of planning to make himself **king** of **Judah** in rebellion against **the king** of Persia. Sanballat said he wanted to help Nehemiah avoid trouble with the king and suggested that they get **together** to discuss the matter. But Nehemiah refused, knowing all too well that Sanballat did not have his best interests at heart. Besides, the slanderous charges were false. Nehemiah's loyalty spoke for itself.

6:10–14 It was no secret that Nehemiah was a devout **man** and one who feared the Word of the Lord. So false prophets were hired to trick him into sinning and incurring God's displeasure. A Jew named **Shemaiah,** who **was a secret informer** for the enemy, warned Nehemiah about a supposed plot on his life and suggested that the governor accompany him into **the temple** for safety. Nehemiah saw through the prophet's ruse. God's Word forbade any but the priests to enter the temple. Nehemiah would rather lose his life than violate the law. And so Sanballat's third scheme fell harmlessly to the ground.

Verses 9 and 14 are examples of the "arrow prayers"[4] that characterized Nehemiah's life (see also 2:4; 4:9; 5:19). He habitually turned to God in times of crisis. Matthew Henry comments:

> In the midst of his complaint of their malice, in endeavouring to frighten him, and so weaken his hands, he lifts up his heart to Heaven in this short prayer: *Now therefore, O God! strengthen my hands.* It is the great support and relief of good people that in all their straits and difficulties they have a good God to go to, from whom, by faith and prayer, they may fetch in grace to silence their fears and *strengthen their hands* when their enemies are endeavouring to fill them with fears and weaken their hands. When, in our Christian work and warfare, we are entering upon any particular services or conflicts, this is a good prayer for us to put up: "I have such a duty to do, such a temptation to grapple with; *now therefore, O God! strengthen my hands.*"[5]

6:15–19 Despite continued opposition, **the wall was** completed **in fifty-two days**, a remarkable feat. This evidence of divine blessing demoralized Judah's **enemies**. One further grief Nehemiah endured while the walls were going up is added in verses 17–19. Many of **the nobles** in Jerusalem stayed on friendly terms with the wicked **Tobiah** because they were related to him by marriage. (Tobiah was governor of the Ammonites—2:10.) The nobles **reported** Nehemiah's **words to** Tobiah on the one hand and praised Tobiah in Nehemiah's hearing on the other. We meet Tobiah again in chapter 13.

Although it took only **fifty-two days** to finish the walls, Nehemiah had plenty of other duties to fill up his twelve or more years as governor.

D. Organization of Jerusalem's Guards (7:1–4)

7:1, 2 As soon as the walls and gates were finished and **the gatekeepers, singers, and . . . Levites** were **appointed** to their posts, Nehemiah turned **the charge of** the city over **to** his **brother Hanani and** to **Hananiah**. Both were godly men, well-suited for the responsibility. Hananiah had a deep reverence for **God**, which made him of kindred spirit with Nehemiah.

7:3, 4 Instructions were given to insure Jerusalem's security. **The gates** were to **be opened** only during daylight hours, and **guards** were to be posted around the city, with each man serving by **his own house**. By faith Nehemiah had built the walls where they used to be, even though the enclosed area was too **large** for so **few** inhabitants.

E. Registration of Jerusalem's Population (7:5–73)

7:5, 6 As he planned to repopulate the city with those whose **genealogy** proved their descent as Jews, he **found a register** of those **who** had **returned to Jerusalem and Judah** under Zerubbabel.

7:7–65 This list in verses 7–65 is almost identical with the one given in Ezra 2. The duplication argues against the theory that Ezra and Nehemiah were *originally* one book, even if Jewish tradition put them together at one point.

7:66–69 In these verses we have a recapitulation **of the whole assembly**, **besides** the **servants**, **singers**, and animals used for transport.

7:70–72 Donors and their contributions to the work are listed. Verses 70–72 differ significantly from Ezra 2:68, 69. The accounts may refer to two different but overlapping collections. The governor's plan for Jerusalem was not fully carried out until chapter 11.

7:73 The chapter closes peacefully with the **cities** of **the children of Israel** populated and secure.

F. Revitalization of Jerusalem's Religion (Chaps. 8—10)

8:1–8 This important chapter tells of spiritual revival among God's people through the public reading of the Scriptures. Notice that Nehemiah is now referred to in the third person (until 12:31). Ezra is the main character in the next few chapters.

On **the first day of the seventh month**, **the people gathered together** for a holy convocation, the Feast of Trumpets (Lev. 23:24, 25), typifying the regathering of Israel from among the Gentile nations. Standing **on a** special **platform** and flanked by thirteen Levites, **Ezra read from . . . the Law of Moses** for several hours. **The people** showed deep respect for God's Word as **the Levites**, mentioned in verse 7, **helped them to understand** (v. 8) what was being read. Since the Aramaic language replaced Hebrew after the captivity, it was necessary to explain many words of the Hebrew Scriptures.[6]

Today, many centuries later, in an entirely different culture and language, preachers and Bible teachers must explain a great deal more. Dr. Donald Campbell emphasizes the importance of this ministry:

> Ezra and his helpers were the first in a long line of expository preachers who explained the Bible. This method of preaching has been blessed by God down through the centuries and continues to be an effective instrument for bringing Christians to spiritual maturity. Topical and textual preaching may often be inspiring and helpful but the spiritual benefits do not compare with those resulting from a preaching ministry like Ezra's. Blessed indeed are the believers who are privileged to sit under expository preaching of the Scriptures.[7]

8:9–12 Their tears showed that the message was taken seriously (v. 9). They were right in taking the Word of God seriously, but they did not need to be overwhelmed by grief. The feast was not for weeping but for rejoicing. Only one occasion for mourning and fasting was found among Israel's feasts, and that was the Day of Atonement. The rest of the feasts were to be kept with joy and celebration. The fruit of the Spirit was to be visible: love, in sharing with the less fortunate; joy, in eating and drinking before the Lord; peace, in calming their fears and putting their hearts at rest. Their sadness was turned to joy, and **the joy of the LORD** was their **strength**.

8:13–15 The next **day** a special time for Bible study was held for the leaders, **the priests, and** the **Levites**. They discovered the ordinances concerning the Feast of Booths (Tabernacles), which was to be observed later that **month**.

8:16–18 This holiday foreshadowed the time when Israel would dwell securely in the Promised Land. They quickly made provisions to keep **the feast**, the first time it had been done by the entire assembly **since the days of Joshua**. (A partial observance of the feast had been kept by the first exiles who returned to Jerusalem under Zerubbabel—Ezra 3:4.) **Booths** were built on rooftops, in courtyards, and in the streets. Joy ran high as the Word **of God** was daily opened to hungry hearts. The feast lasted from the fifteenth through the twenty-second of the month.

9:1–3 After the feast the people **assembled** for a great day of national confession. They **separated themselves from** the **foreigners** in their midst and humbled themselves before **the LORD. With fasting** and mourning, **they . . . read** the Scriptures for three hours. Then for three more hours, **they confessed and worshiped**. Confession is the road to revival.

9:4–38 Afterward the **Levites** mentioned in verses 4 and 5 led the people in a great prayer of confession (vv. 6–37) and dedication (v. 38). Some think Ezra led the prayer, although his name is not specifically mentioned. It is one of the longest prayers in the Bible, and its roots go deep into sacred history.

The overriding theme of the prayer is God's faithfulness despite Israel's waywardness. The prayer can be outlined as follows: Creation (v. 6); the call of **Abraham** and the **covenant** God **made . . . with him** (vv. 7, 8); the exodus from **Egypt** (vv. 9–12); the giving of the law at **Mount Sinai** (vv. 13, 14); God's miraculous provision during the wilderness journey (v. 15); Israel's frequent rebellions **in the wilderness** contrasted with God's unfailing kindness (vv. 16–21); the conquest of Canaan (vv. 22–25); the era of the judges (vv. 26–28); unheeded warnings and ultimate captivity (vv. 29–31); appeal for forgiveness and deliverance from the consequences of the captivity (vv. 32–37); the people's desire to **make a . . . covenant** with God (v. 38).

Another way to outline the prayer is to follow its progress through the books of the Bible: vv. 6–8, Genesis; vv. 9–13, Exodus; v. 14, Leviticus; vv. 15–20, Numbers (except v. 18); vv. 21–23, Numbers and Deuteronomy; vv. 24, 25, Joshua; vv. 26–29, Judges; vv. 30–37, 1 Samuel through 2 Chronicles. That is biblical praying! Events are seen from God's point of view. His faithfulness is acknowledged throughout, and **mercy** and grace are recognized as the only foundation upon which the nation can stand.

In many ways the last verse (38) is the most significant part of the prayer. The Jews realized that the problem was with them, not with the Lord, and they determined to do something about it (see chap. 10 for the details of the **covenant**). Prayer and confession, important as they are, are no substitutes for obedience.

10:1–27 These verses list the men who signed the covenant on behalf of the people (9:38b). Nehemiah's name heads the list (v. 1), followed by **the priests** (vv. 2–8), **the Levites** (vv. 9–13), and **the leaders of the people** (vv. 14–27).

10:28, 29 These two verses form

a preamble to the covenant, stating that the entire population agreed **to observe and do all the *commandments* of the LORD** their **Lord, and His *ordinances* and His *statutes*.**

10:30–38 More specifically, the Jews bound themselves to refrain from foreign marriages (v. 30), to observe **the Sabbath day** and the sabbatical year (v. 31), to make an annual contribution for the temple services (vv. 32, 33), to provide **wood** for **the altar of the LORD** (v. 34), and to bring the redemption money for their **firstborn** and the **firstfruits of** their crops to the temple for the support of **the priests** and **Levites**—i.e., to restore **the tithes** (vv. 35–39).

Concern for their religious life was central in this covenant. With the exception of verses 30 and 31, the covenant deals exclusively with the maintenance of the temple and its servants.

10:39 The words **"we will not neglect the house of our God"** expressed the overriding concern of the postexilic Jews. Out of this genuine care for the externals of their faith would grow the corrupt pharisaical system which so violently opposed the Lord Jesus because He stressed the weightier issues of the law—obedience, mercy, etc. But in its original innocence such devotion must certainly have pleased Jehovah.

G. Repopulation of Jerusalem's Precincts (Chap. 11)

11:1, 2 Chapter 11 is closely related to the last verse of chapter 7. Nehemiah was concerned about the sparse population in **Jerusalem**; more **people** should have been living there to defend the city in case of attack. But fear kept many Jews in the country. Finally, **lots** were **cast** to bring **in one out of** every **ten** residents of the small towns **to dwell in Jerusalem.** Others who volunteered joined them in the city.

11:3–36 Having been enrolled earlier (chap. 7), the families living in Jerusalem are named here (vv. 3–24). There were **four hundred and sixty-eight** men **of Judah**, each the head of a household (vv. 4–6). The Benjamites were **nine hundred and twenty-eight** families strong (vv. 7, 8); **Joel . . . and Judah** were their overseers (v. 9). Three divisions of **priests** are listed in verses 10–14; **Zabdiel** was their leader. The Levites in **the holy city**[8] numbered four hundred and fifty-six, **one hundred and seventy-two** of them being gatekeepers (vv. 15–19). The temple servants, under **Ziha and Gishpa**, lived **in Ophel**, a section of Jerusalem close to the temple (v. 21). A man named **Uzzi** had overall charge **of the Levites**, and **Pethahiah** was **the king's** agent in the city, under Nehemiah, of course (vv. 22–24). The rest of the Jews lived in the neighboring **villages**: **Judah** lived in the **villages** listed in verses 25–30, and **Benjamin** in the **villages** listed in verses 31–35. Some **divisions of Levites** that formerly lived in Judah now moved over to the territory of **Benjamin** (v. 36).

H. Tabulation of Jerusalem's Priests and Levites (12:1–26)

The priests . . . who returned **with Zerubbabel** are named in verses 1–7. **The Levites** who came back are listed in verses 8 and 9. Verses 10 and 11 name the high priests from **Jeshua** (in the days of **Zerubbabel**, v. 1), until **Jaddua**. In verses 12–21 we have **the priests** who served **in the days of Joiakim**, whose son **Eliashib** was the high priest in Nehemiah's day (3:1). Most of them were probably still alive.

The Levites were registered under succeeding high priests from Eliashib until Jaddua. The men mentioned by name in verses 24–26 served before and during Nehemiah's administration as governor.

I. Dedication of Jerusalem's Wall (12:27–47)

12:27–30 For **the dedication of the wall, the Levites** (particularly **the singers**) from the surrounding areas were brought **to Jerusalem. The priests and Levites** ceremonially **purified themselves** along with **the people, the wall**, and **the gates**.

12:31–42 Then Nehemiah assembled the princes **of Judah . . . on the wall** and divided them into **two large thanksgiving choirs**. They headed in different directions around the wall, with the singers in front and the people following behind their **leaders** until they met again at the temple.

12:43–46 Great sacrifices were **offered** amid loud rejoicing. **At the same time some** men **were appointed** to oversee the collection of **the offerings, the firstfruits, and the tithes** for the support of **the priests and Levites**, as required by **the law**. The people contributed joyfully because they were happy to have the divine services resumed. **The priests and Levites** performed their duties of worship and purification. **The singers and . . . gatekeepers** also carried on their assigned tasks, tasks that, as far as **the singers** were concerned, dated back to the time of **David and Asaph**.

12:47 In the days of Zerubbabel and . . . Nehemiah, the people provided all that was necessary for the support of **the singers, gatekeepers, Levites**, and priests.

II. NEHEMIAH'S SECOND VISIT: REFORMATION OF JERUSALEM (Chap. 13)

A. Expulsion of Tobiah from the Temple (13:1–9)

13:1–3 After serving for twelve years in Jerusalem, in 433 B.C. Nehemiah returned to Babylon for an unspecified time. Then he obtained permission to visit Jerusalem again, a visit that dealt with the correcting of abuses. **"On that day"** (v. 1) may refer back to the last chapter, or it may refer to another day during Nehemiah's absence (v. 6). In either case, the Word was **read**, including the part barring Moabites and Ammonites from the congregation. These Canaanites had not only refused bread and water to God's people, but had hired Balaam to curse them. But God had turned the curse into a blessing. What a wonderful God He is! The people responded by separating **the mixed multitude from Israel**.

13:4, 5 In expelling the foreigners, they were finishing the job they started in 9:2. **Eliashib the priest** had made a home for the wicked **Tobiah** in the forecourt of **the house of God**, using a storeroom which should have been full of **tithes** for **the Levites** and **priests**.

13:6–9 Upon his return it did not take Nehemiah long to remedy the situation. Other problems had also appeared in his absence, and Nehemiah indignantly campaigned to halt these evils.

B. Restoration of Tithes for the Levites (13:10–14)

Nehemiah rebuked the officials in charge of such matters for their irresponsibility in neglecting **the Levites**. The Levites who had been forced to work in the fields to make a living were regathered, and **faithful** men were **appointed . . . to distribute** the tithes among them. For this good deed Nehemiah asked his **God** to **remember** him (v. 14).

C. Elimination of Illegal Activity on the Sabbath (13:15–22)

Nehemiah had to rebuke the rulers who allowed the people to work **on the Sabbath**. The foreigners who lived among them tried to make it a market day. But the Sabbath must be kept holy, by force if necessary. Men were sent to secure **the gates**, and **the** greedy **merchants** camping **outside** the city were run off under threat of violence. Illicit activity came to an abrupt halt. For this too Nehemiah asked to be remembered (v. 22).

D. Dissolution of Interracial Marriages (13:23–31)

Several years earlier the foreign **wives** had been put away at the command of Ezra (Ezra 10). The people had since then made a covenant to separate themselves from the heathen (chap. 10) and had done so to a certain extent. But in time the practice of **Jews** marrying **women of Ashdod, Ammon, and Moab** flourished once more, even in the priesthood. Some of the malefactors were physically punished; others were excommunicated. A grandson of **the high priest** was sent away.[9] The heathen were driven away and the Lord was asked to deal with those who had **defiled** their holy offices. Once more Nehemiah asked the Lord that he be remembered (v. 31).

In the church there is no ban on marriage between different ethnic groups, because Christianity is a faith embracing all peoples and tribes. But even in OT times the main reason for the ban was no doubt the corrupt, false religions of the Gentile nations.

Campbell comments on the type of mixed marriages that are destructive to Christianity:

> The New Testament adds its consistent witness against marriages between believers and unbelievers. Paul directed believers to marry "only in the Lord" (1 Cor. 7:39). Yet today as in previous ages, some believers rationalize that they will lead the unsaved mate to the Lord—but it rarely works that way and children more often than not follow the ways of the unregenerate parent.[10]

Throughout his rule Nehemiah was a man of action. Nowhere is that more evident than here, as zeal for the things of God consumed him (Ps. 69:9). Because he was no respecter of persons, his anger was felt equally by all who transgressed the law of the Lord. He warned, admonished, reprimanded, **contended**, **struck**, **pulled out hair**, and generally made things difficult for the ungodly! He was a courageous man and a tenacious general in the front lines of the fight against evil. He was a tireless worker and a great builder for God.

This chapter brings *OT history* to a close. The books that follow Nehemiah fit *chronologically before* this time (except for Malachi, which is contemporary with Nehemiah).[11]

Charles Swindoll closes his commentary on Nehemiah, *Hand Me Another Brick*, with a challenge to us all:

> I think it is significant that the final scene in Nehemiah's book portrays him on his knees asking God for grace. He had fought hard for the right, but he had kept his heart soft before the Lord. What a magnifi-

cent model of leadership! He was a man of honesty, conviction, and devotion.

Can you handle another brick?[12]

ENDNOTES

[1](Intro) John C. Whitcomb, "Nehemiah," *The Wycliffe Bible Commentary*, p. 435.

[2](1:1–3) J. Alec Motyer, *Toward the Mark*, further documentation unavailable.

[3](2:1–3) George Williams, *The Student's Commentary on the Holy Scriptures*, p. 264.

[4](6:10–14) In the terminology of devotion, such are called "arrow prayers," since they are shot swiftly to God's throne.

[5](6:10–14) Matthew Henry, "Nehemiah," in *Matthew Henry's Commentary on the Whole Bible*, II:1087.

[6](8:1–8) Hebrew and Aramaic are closely related Semitic languages. The oral Aramaic "paraphrases" of the Hebrew original text were later written down and called the *Targums*.

[7](8:1–8) Donald Campbell, *Nehemiah: Man in Charge*, p. 75.

[8](11:3–36) This is the first time Jerusalem is called "the holy city."

[9](13:23–31) Josephus says that the exiled rebel went to Samaria, where Sanballat built him a temple which became a refuge for apostate Jews.

[10](13:23–31) Campbell, *Nehemiah*, pp. 116, 117.

[11](13:23–31) The period following Nehemiah is sometimes known as "The Four Hundred Silent Years," although this term is not strictly accurate. Daniel 11, for example, gives a detailed history of the Grecian era, except that it is pre-written history, that is, prophecy. In fact, this section is so accurate in its detail (for those who know the history of the Ptolemies and the Seleucids) that most liberals and their admirers reject Daniel as an actual prophecy. The OT Apocrypha, though uninspired, contains valuable historical information concerning this period.

[12](13:23–31) Charles R. Swindoll, *Hand Me Another Brick*, p. 205.

BIBLIOGRAPHY

Campbell, Donald K. *Nehemiah: Man in Charge*. Wheaton, IL: Victor Books, 1979.

Henry, Matthew. "Nehemiah." In *Matthew Henry's Commentary on the Whole Bible*. Vol. 2. Joshua to Esther. McLean, VA: MacDonald Publishing Company, n.d.

Ironside, H. A. *Notes on Ezra, Nehemiah, Esther*. Neptune, NJ: Loizeaux Brothers, 1972.

Jensen, Irving L. *Ezra/Nehemiah/Esther*. Chicago: Moody Press, 1970.

Keil, C. F. "Nehemiah." In *Biblical Commentary on the Old Testament*. Vol. 10. Grand Rapids: Wm. B. Eerdmans Publishing Company, 1971.

Swindoll, Charles R. *Hand Me Another Brick*. Nashville: Thomas Nelson Publishers, 1978.

ESTHER

Introduction

"The book of Esther gives us a segment of the history of the Jews which is not supplied elsewhere in the Bible. For instance, it is here that we learn about the origin of the Feast of Purim *which, as we all know, is celebrated by the Jewish people to this very day."*

—Carl Armerding

I. Unique Place in the Canon

A Soviet Jew was recently asked by a Westerner what he thought would be the outcome if the USSR stepped up its anti-Semitic policies. "Oh, probably a feast!" Asked for an explanation, the Jewish man said, "Pharaoh tried to wipe out the Hebrews and the result was Passover; Haman tried to exterminate our people and the result was Purim; Antiochus Epiphanes tried to do us in, and the result was Hanukkah!"

Esther explains the origin of the Feast of Purim, a colorful Jewish holiday that today features noisemakers sounding off every time Haman's name occurs in the annual public reading of the book.

Esther is unique in several ways. It tells the story of non-observant[1] Jews who preferred prosperity in Persia[2] to the rigors of the small remnant that returned to Jerusalem under Zerubbabel (Ezra 2). All reference to religion other than fasting is lacking in Esther.

Another remarkable feature of the book is that the name of God[3] is not found in it, a fact that has caused some to question its right to a place in Scripture. But J. Sidlow Baxter points out that the name *Jehovah* is hidden four times as an acrostic (1:20; 5:4; 5:13; 7:7), always at a crucial point in the story. Also the name *Ehyeh* (I am who I am) is found once in acrostic form (7:5). "This cannot be of chance," writes Scroggie, "and the difficulty of constructing such forms will be apparent to anyone who attempts it."[4]

Since few Christians know Hebrew, and this is a difficult literary form to grasp without examples, we quote two of Arthur T. Pierson's artistic and ingenious attempts to illustrate the acrostics in rhymed English couplets. He uses the word LORD for YHWH. Notice that, as in the original, one example uses *initial* letters and one uses *final* letters. Also, in Pierson's first example, the hidden name "L-O-R-D" is spelled backwards, and in the second example it is in normal order. This parallels the original Hebrew:

Due **R**espect **O**ur **L**adies, all
Shall give their husbands, great and small (i. 20).
Il**L** t**O** fea**R** decree**D** I find,
Toward me in the monarch's mind (vii. 7).[5]

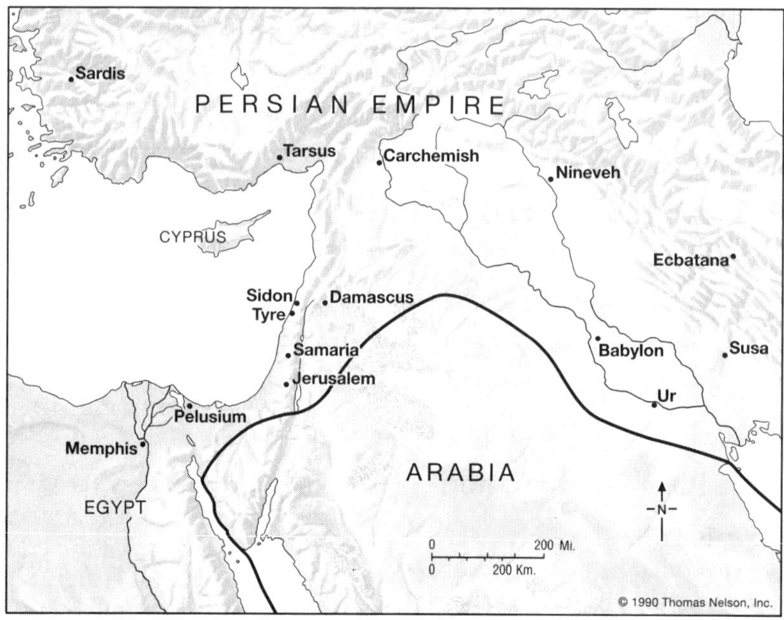

The Persian Empire, c. 500 B.C.

Although God's name is not found explicitly, His presence and power are clearly manifested throughout as He provides deliverance for His people through a series of designed "coincidences." Even if Jehovah's name is not explicitly associated with those who voluntarily stayed in Babylon instead of returning to their own city and land, His care for them cannot be questioned. They were still His people, and He would protect them from the anti-Semitism (inspired by the devil) which sought to exterminate them. God is the Author of all history, even if He does not sign His name at the bottom of every page.

The poetry of James Russell Lowell is a fitting commentary on the Book of Esther:

Careless seems the great avenger:
History's pages but record
One death grapple in the darkness,
'twixt old systems and the Word.
Truth for ever on the scaffold;
Wrong for ever on the throne:
But that scaffold sways the future;
and behind the dim unknown
Standeth God, within the shadow,
keeping watch above His own.

Esther is not quoted in the NT, and so far no fragment has been found in the Dead Sea Scrolls. For these and other reasons, some (even a few Jews) have questioned the canonicity of Esther. However, the book has wonderful lessons on the faithfulness of God even when His people are dis obedient.

II. Authorship

The writer of this book was no doubt a Jew who knew Persian customs and the details of the palace. (Archaeology has confirmed some of these special features.) He writes as an eyewitness, using the type of Hebrew of the post-exilic era. Some have suggested Ezra or Nehemiah as author. Jewish tradition points to Mordecai as author. Actually we have no idea who wrote Esther; perhaps the human writer was an unimportant figure historically. Whoever it was, as the Pulpit Commentary put it, "no disbeliever in God could have written it; and no believer in God can read it without finding his faith strengthened thereby."

III. Date

Esther 10:2 implies that King Ahasuerus (Xerxes) was already dead; since he died in 465 B.C., this would date the book after that year. The Persian cultural details, access to court records, and eyewitness vividness all support a date soon after Xerxes' death, sometime during the reign of Artaxerxes I (464–424 B.C.). As usual, unbelieving critics date the book much later (third or second century B.C.).

IV. Background and Theme

The events in this book took place between the sixth and seventh chapters of Ezra, during the reign of Ahasuerus (Xerxes), king of Persia. The book is concerned with those Jews who decided to remain in Babylon rather than go back to Jerusalem with the small remnant that returned to Jerusalem under Zerubbabel (Ezra 2). It derives its name from its principal character, Esther, the orphan girl who became queen. Esther, her Persian name, means "star" and may have been derived from the goddess Ishtar. Hadassah, her Hebrew name, means "myrtle."

Ahasuerus held court in Shushan (Susa, NKJV marg.), one of three principal capital cities in Persia, the others being Achmetha (Ecbatana, NASB), and Babylon. Shushan is the Hebrew name and means "lily."[6] The Prophet Daniel spent time there (Dan. 8). Nehemiah served there after Esther's day (Neh. 1). It is there that our story takes place, beginning in the year 483 BC. (Xerxes came to power in 486 BC; chapter 1 opens in the third year of his reign—v. 3.)

OUTLINE

I. THE EXPULSION OF VASHTI DECREED (Chap. 1)

II. THE ELEVATION OF ESTHER ACCOMPLISHED (Chap. 2)

III. THE EXTERMINATION OF THE JEWS PLANNED (Chaps. 3, 4)
- A. Haman's Talk with the King (Chap. 3)
- B. Mordecai's Talk with the Queen (Chap. 4)

IV. THE EXTERMINATION OF THE JEWS THWARTED (Chaps. 5—9)
- A. Esther's Supplication and Haman's Rage (Chap. 5)
- B. Haman's Humiliation and Mordecai's Honor (Chap. 6)
- C. Esther's Accusation and Haman's Execution (Chap. 7)
- D. Mordecai's Promotion and the Jews' Deliverance (Chap. 8)
- E. The Enemy's Destruction and the Inauguration of the Feast of Purim (Chap. 9)

V. THE EXALTATION OF MORDECAI (Chap. 10)

Commentary

I. THE EXPULSION OF VASHTI DECREED (Chap. 1)

1:1–4 Although not all scholars agree as to the identity of **Ahasuerus**, most modern commentators believe him to be Xerxes (see NKJV, marg.), the son of Darius the Great. Xerxes reigned from 486 to 465 BC.

The first **feast** did not necessarily last *uninterrupted* for **one hundred and eighty days**. Rather, this was the time required to display **the riches of his glorious kingdom**. Probably different nobles came at different times throughout this period since the empire was so vast.

1:5–8 The second **feast** lasted **seven days** and was open to **all the people** of **Shushan**. **Royal wine** flowed freely from **golden vessels** in the elegantly furnished garden court (v. 6 is surely the most colorful verse in the Bible!). Guests were permitted to drink as much or as little as they chose.

1:9–12 The inebriated Xerxes ordered his chamberlains **to bring Queen Vashti**, who was hosting **the women** at a separate banquet. He wanted her at the public celebration so that he could **show her beauty**. Since Persian modesty required women to be veiled in public, it appears that the king was asking her to degrade herself to satisfy his drunken whim. She refused to be displayed, thus greatly angering **the king**.

1:13–20 When **the king** consulted his **wise men**, they told him that Vashti's **behavior** would prove a bad example to the **women** throughout the realm. **Memucan** therefore suggested that Vashti be deposed by **a royal decree** and that the **decree** be circulated in every part of the **empire**. Knowing that the law of the Medes and Persians was unalterable, the wise men might have suggested such a drastic step to ensure that Vashti would not return to power and punish them.

1:21, 22 **The king** rashly signed their advice into law and ordered it published in every **province** in the **language** of **every people**. Included was the law that every **man should be master in his own house** and that his **language** should be the one used there. Dr. J. Vernon McGee has suggested that Memucan *at home* was a hen-pecked husband, and that he was getting back at his wife with this **decree**.[7]

II. THE ELEVATION OF ESTHER ACCOMPLISHED (Chap. 2)

2:1–4 When the king seemed to have second thoughts over what he had done to **Vashti**, his counselors proposed that a search be made **among all the beautiful young virgins** for a **young woman** to become **queen** in her place.

2:5–7 As potential young women were brought to **Shushan**, **Esther**, one of the capital's maidens, joined them. She had been adopted by her cousin **Mordecai** after the death of her parents. Mordecai was **a Benjamite**, whose ancestor, **Kish**, had been carried into captivity **with Jeconiah** (2 Kgs. 24:14–16).

2:8–11 **Hegai**, the keeper of the harem, showed special favor to **Esther** by **readily** supplying her and her attendants with **beauty preparations, besides her allowance**, and also by giving her **the best place in the house of the women**. In obedience to **Mordecai**, she did not yet reveal her ethnic origin. Although Mordecai could not contact her directly, he had ways of getting news of her progress every day.

2:12–14 The course preparing the young ladies to be brought into the king's bedchamber lasted for **twelve** months. They went through a ceremonial purification program with ointments, spices, and cosmetics. Then, when the **turn** of **each** one **came**, she could request anything in the way of apparel, adornments, or jewels. She then spent one night with **the king**, and would never be with him **again unless** she so pleased him that he asked **for her by name**.

For the Christian, lifetime is training time for reigning time. Soon the Lord will present the church to Himself without spot or wrinkle or any such thing (Eph. 5:27).

2:15–18 Instead of making lavish requests for outward adornments, **Esther** followed Hegai's advice. Perhaps he suggested that she depend on her natural beauty. In any event, **the king loved Esther more than** any of the others, chose **her** as his **queen**, and **made a great feast** in her honor. The **holiday** he made in **the provinces** may have included an amnesty, or a remission of taxes, or it may have been simply a holiday. He also **gave gifts** in keeping with his wealth.

2:19–23 **A second** gathering of **virgins** took place, perhaps to add to the king's harem. **Esther** was still keeping her nationality secret, and **Mordecai** was still positioning himself strategically **at the king's gate**. It was at this time that he overheard a plot to assassinate **King Ahasuerus**. He reported it to **Esther**, who in turn notified **the king**. The assassins were apprehended, tried, and **hanged**.

The incident was routinely recorded in the official **chronicles** of the kingdom. Mordecai was not rewarded immediately. He had to wait, but it was sure to come. God keeps good records. The ancient Greek historian Herodotus says that hanging was the standard punishment for traitors and rebels in Persia at that time.[8]

III. THE EXTERMINATION OF THE JEWS PLANNED (Chaps. 3, 4)

A. Haman's Talk with the King (Chap. 3)

3:1 The words **"After these things"** indicate a five-year interval between chapters 2 and 3. The last important figure in the drama of Esther comes on stage in verse 1, **Haman, the son of Hammedatha**. We are not told why he was **promoted**, but subsequent history makes it clear that the hand behind the hand of the king was Satan's. Haman was an **Agagite**, a descendant of the kings of the Amalekites (Agag was a royal title). The Lord had declared perpetual war against Amalek (Ex. 17:8–16). The Book of Esther relates the last recorded battle in that war (see also 1 Sam. 15:32; 30:1–10; 1 Chron. 4:43).

3:2–6 By official order **Haman** was now to be **paid homage** as one second only to the king. But **Mordecai** refused to **bow** to a mere man, especially to an Amalekite. The fear of God overcame any fear of man. The law of Moses did not forbid showing due respect to those in authority, but it did forbid the worship of any but God. Eastern monarchs often demanded such worship. Mordecai's fellow workers sought to gain favor in Haman's eyes by pointing out his refusal. Haman was a very egotistical man, and the sight of Mordecai's blatant disrespect infuriated him beyond reason. Instead of dealing with Mordecai alone, he set in motion a plan to annihilate **all the Jews** in **the kingdom**!

3:7–11 Haman's first step was to cast lots **to determine** a suitable date for the mass execution. By a seeming coincidence the date indicated was nearly a year away. As someone has said, "Even superstition was chained to the divine chariot-wheels." God overruled to allow sufficient time to thwart Haman's plan. "The lot is cast into the lap, but its every decision is from the LORD" (Prov. 16:33). **Haman** next approached the king with an inflammatory report about **the Jews**, misrepresenting them as a danger to the **kingdom**. He urged that **a decree** be issued ordering their extinction. According to the law of the Medes and Persians, this decree, once issued, could never be changed or withdrawn. As added incentive, Haman offered to **pay ten thousand talents of silver** into the royal **treasuries**, now badly depleted by the king's losses in Greece. Ahasuerus sealed the death writ **with his signet ring**, sentencing thousands of innocent men, women, and children to be sacrificed at the altar of Haman's pride. Verse 11 might mean that **the money** taken from the slain would belong to Haman.

3:12–15 Copies of the execution order were sent out with great thoroughness, setting **the thirteenth day of the twelfth month** aside for the atrocity. In the palace Ahasuerus and Haman complacently **sat down to drink, but** in **the city** there was great perplexity. Irving Jensen comments on this:

> The last phrase of chapter 3 is significant: "But the city Shushan was perplexed" (KJV). Not only the Jews, but non-Jews reacted to this outrageous example of violent despotism. Sometimes the masses are wrong, but not always. Here was a situation where a king and his high minister were an erring minority with extensive authority. But all people—nations and individuals alike—must reckon with the highest Authority—God. The king's decree was issued and posted, but the King of kings would have the last word.[9]

B. Mordecai's Talk with the Queen (Chap. 4)

4:1–3 The Jewish population was stunned as the news broke throughout the land. There is always sadness where evil reigns. **Mordecai** put on mourner's garb and lamented through **the city** until he came to **the king's gate**, beyond which he could not go because **sackcloth** was not allowed in his majesty's presence. He knew that he was the main object of Haman's hatred. The fate awaiting his nation had been unwittingly prompted by him.

4:4–9 Since custom forbade **Esther** to leave her confinement in the palace, **she sent** a servant to take some **garments to clothe Mordecai** so that he might not be seen in **sackcloth** by the king and lose his life. But Mordecai refused to disguise his anguish. When **Hathach**, Esther's personal servant, came to find out why he continued in mourning, Mordecai told him the whole story. **A copy of the written decree** was sent back to the queen along with an order to use her office to intercede **for her people**.

4:10–12 **Esther** responded to **Mordecai** by reminding him that it was a capital offense to appear before **the king** uninvited, unless he spared the intruder's life by extending **the golden scepter**. She told of a further complication which would make such action doubly dangerous: She had not been summoned by Ahasuerus for **thirty days**, indicating that she may have somehow incurred his displeasure.

4:13, 14 Mordecai's reply to Esther's rationale was to the point: She would not **escape**, when the rest of **the Jews** were slain, even if she was queen. If she refused to act now, someone else would **arise** to deliver His people, but she would be destroyed. And perhaps this opportunity to save her people was the reason she had been exalted to the throne. The words of verse 14 should challenge each of us: **"Yet who knows whether you have come to the kingdom for such a time as this?"** Though few of us will ever be in such a position as Esther's, each believer has an essential role to play in the ongoing plan of God.

4:15–17 Making her decision, **Esther** instructed **all the Jews** to **fast** with her **for three days**. Then she would **go** before **the king**.

Matthew Poole comments on Esther's famous and heroic words, **"If I perish, I perish"**:

> Although my danger be great and evident, considering the expressness of that law, and the uncertainty of the king's mind, and that severity which he showed to my predecessor Vashti, yet rather than neglect my duty to God and to His people, I will go to the king and cast myself cheerfully and resolutely upon God's providence for my safety and success.[10]

The Christian's attitude in difficult and trying circumstances should not be one of fatalism but of optimism, especially when it comes to approaching the heavenly throne for grace to help in time of need. We have bold and confident access; the scepter of God's forgiveness has been stretched out to us at Calvary. "Let us therefore come boldly to the throne of grace, that we may obtain mercy and find grace to help in time of need" (Heb. 4:16).

IV. THE EXTERMINATION OF THE JEWS THWARTED (Chaps. 5—9)

A. Esther's Supplication and Haman's Rage (Chap. 5)

5:1–3 On the third day, when the fast was completed, **Esther put on her royal robes**, summoned her courage, and appeared before Ahasuerus uninvited. Recognizing that only a very important matter would cause his queen to risk her life, **the king held out to Esther the golden scepter** and granted her safety. He also promised to grant her **request**, **up to half** his **kingdom** (a figure of speech meaning that he would give her anything at all within reason). Christ holds out His scepter of grace to any unbeliever who comes to Him in repentance and faith (see John 6:37b). For the believer the golden scepter is always extended (see Heb. 10:22).

5:4–8 At this point **Esther** simply invited **the king** and his favorite minister, **Haman, to the banquet** (the fourth banquet in the book). During the meal the king again tried to find out what the queen wanted. Once more Esther procrastinated and asked Ahasuerus and Haman to return the following day for yet another **banquet**. Then she would make her matter known. Opinions vary as to why Esther planned these two delays before making her request: (1) She wanted time to ingratiate herself with the king, having apparently been out of favor with him (see notes on 4:10–12); (2) her courage failed her both times; (3) she wanted to build up an element of suspense and impress upon the king that her business was vitally important and no mere whim; (4) she wanted to inflate Haman's pride and take him off guard before she exposed him as a vicious murderer. Perhaps elements of all these ideas entered into her strategy.

5:9–14 Filled with pride, **Haman** left the banquet in good spirits. When he met **Mordecai** on the way out of the palace, **he was filled with indignation** but **restrained himself** from violence. Calling **his friends** and **his wife Zeresh** together, he recited all the favorable things that had happened to him. The only cloud on his horizon was that stubborn **Jew**! **His wife** advised him to make **a gallows** seventy-five feet **high**, then get permission from **the king** to hang **Mordecai . . . on it**. This pleased Haman; **so he had the gallows made**.

B. Haman's Humiliation and Mordecai's Honor (Chap. 6)

6:1–3 While Haman was sleeping, God kept Ahasuerus awake to thwart the evil scheme. In trying to make the best of his insomnia, **the king** had **the chronicles** of his reign **read** to him. By divine "coincidence" the portion that was read contained the account of the attempt on his life which had been foiled by **Mordecai**. Upon inquiry it was learned that **nothing** had ever **been done** to reward **him** for this service.

It is good to notice what J. G. Bellett calls

> . . . the wonderful interweaving of circumstances which we get in this history. There is plot and underplot, "wheels within wheels," circumstances hanging upon circumstances, all formed together to work out the wonderful plans of God.[11]

The Lord is in perfect control.

6:4–11 Probably it was in the morning that **Haman** came **to suggest that the king hang Mordecai**. Strangely enough, it was at the very same time that the king had an impulse to reward the man who had saved him from the assassins. When Haman entered, Ahasuerus asked the general question, **"What shall be done for the man whom the king delights to honor?"** Thinking that *his own* great moment had come, Haman suggested the most elaborate **parade** and the bestowing of honors second only to those of the king himself. Haman further suggested that a public announcement be made as the **parade** moved **through the city**: **"Thus shall it be done to the man whom the king delights to honor!"** Thereupon **the king** ordered **Haman** to **hurry** and bestow all these honors not on Haman, but on **Mordecai the Jew**! Haman went out to proclaim his worst enemy as the man whom the king delighted to honor. Pride went before destruction and a haughty spirit before a fall (Prov. 16:18).

In our day there is a Man whom the King delights to honor—the Lord Jesus Christ. God has decreed that every knee shall bow to Him and every tongue confess Him Lord to the glory of God the Father (Phil. 2:10, 11).

6:12–14 Crestfallen, **Haman** retreated **to his house** and reported these strange developments. **His wife** and **wise . . . friends** saw in the day's events an omen of victory for the Jew and defeat for Haman. But by then it was time for **Haman** to hurry off to Esther's **banquet**.

C. Esther's Accusation and Haman's Execution (Chap. 7)

7:1–4 Esther's second **banquet** turned out to have ramifications which would shake the entire kingdom, starting with Haman's house. At the king's bidding she finally made her appeal. She asked for her own **life** and the lives of her **people**, who had been sentenced to death. If they had only been **sold as . . . slaves** she would **have held** her peace, "for the trouble would not be commensurate with the annoyance to the king" (v. 4b NASB). But the seriousness of their plight impelled her to act.

7:5–7a The king indignantly asked **who** had instigated such a heinous plot against Esther's people. The queen had wisely invited Haman for just this moment. To his face she charged **"this wicked Haman!"** Haman's true character was now fully revealed. Ahasuerus stalked out to **the palace garden** like a raging panther. His conscience might have been bothering him too as he remembered his part in approving the terrible scheme. It was hitting much closer to home than he had anticipated.

7:7b–10 In mortal fear Haman threw himself **before Queen Esther, pleading for his life**. **The king**, returning to the room, interpreted this as an attempt to assault his wife sexually. Haman's fate was now sealed. Without an express word from the king, the servants **covered** his **face**, a preliminary to execution. **One of** them told **the king** about **the gallows . . . Haman** had built, and Ahasuerus ordered the villain to be hanged **on it**. Thus **Haman** took Mordecai's place **on the gallows**. He reaped what he had sown. **Then the king's wrath subsided**.

D. Mordecai's Promotion and the Jews' Deliverance (Chap. 8)

8:1, 2 Haman's **house** was given to **Esther** and his position was given **to Mordecai**.

8:3–8 Haman was out of the way, but his destructive plot was still in motion. Once again **Esther** appeared before **the king** uninvited, careless of her own life, and tearfully pled for her people. Again **the golden scepter** of grace was extended to her. Verse 3 gives the gist of her plea, verses 5 and 6 the exact words. She asked that the first decree be revoked. But according to the law, no edict signed and sealed by a Persian king could be altered. However, after reminding Esther of what he had already done on her behalf, the king permitted her and Mordecai to **write** another **decree** *counteracting* the first one.

8:9–14 **The king's scribes were called** and Mordecai dictated an edict which gave **the Jews** the right to **protect their lives**. With great speed the new law was carried to the utmost parts of the kingdom on royal **swift steeds**. How much more should the news of man's redemption from the power of evil be disseminated through Satan's realm with thoroughness and speed!

8:15–17 Having discarded his sackcloth, **Mordecai** left the palace in robes of splendor. **The Jews** were filled with **gladness** when they heard of the sudden turn of events, while the rest of the people were filled with dread. Not wanting to be numbered among their enemies, **many** Gentiles **became** proselytes to the Jewish faith at this time.

E. The Enemy's Destruction and the Inauguration of the Feast of Purim (Chap. 9)

9:1–5 When the fateful **day** arrived—**the thirteenth day** of **the twelfth month—the Jews gathered together in their** respective **cities** and destroyed their enemies. Even the princes and rulers **helped the Jews** because they feared **Mordecai**, now the second-most-powerful man in the kingdom.

9:6–15 In the capital alone **five hundred men** were **killed**, along with **the ten sons of Haman**. When it was reported to the king, he realized that the slaughter in the rest of the land must be great as well. **Esther** requested that an additional day be given **the Jews** in **Shushan** to wipe out any remaining pockets of anti-Semitism. As a result **three hundred** more **men** were executed. She also asked that the bodies of **Haman's ten sons be** publicly **hanged**.

9:16 In the king's provinces the Jews killed seventy-five thousand, but had **not** taken any of their foes' **plunder**. This would make it clear to all that they were interested only in protecting themselves, not in growing rich.

9:17–28 The Jews in the provinces held a great feast **on the fourteenth of the month** while those **at Shushan** celebrated **on the fifteenth**. This was the beginning of the feast of Purim. The name **Purim**[12] comes from **"Pur"**—the lot which Haman had cast (3:7). Later Mordecai decreed that both **the fourteenth** and **the fifteenth** should **be observed** by all the Jewish people. Like the feasts of old, it was to be celebrated annually as a reminder to succeeding generations of this marvelous deliverance.

9:29–32 Apparently two **letters** went out **to all the Jews**, charging them to keep the Feast **of Purim**—the first one in verse 20, and the second in verses 29–32. **The book** referred to in verse 32 was probably the chronicles of the kingdom (cf. 2:23; 6:1; 10:2).

V. THE EXALTATION OF MORDECAI (Chap. 10)

10:1, 2 The Book of Esther closes with the exaltation **of Mordecai**. His advancements were recorded alongside the accomplishments of **Ahasuerus . . . in the book of the chronicles of the kings of Media and Persia**. Carl Armerding closes his book on Esther with these words:

> The fact that we have no record of his death is quite remarkable, because the history of most men concludes with some sort of obituary. Not so with Mordecai. Thus the impression is left in our minds of one who lives on and on. "He that doeth the will of God abideth forever" (I John 2:17).[13]

10:3 Mordecai sought the **good of his people**. Spurgeon applies his ministry to Christians:

> Mordecai was a true patriot, and therefore, being exalted to the highest position under Ahasuerus, he used his eminence to promote the prosperity of Israel. In this he was a type of Jesus, who, upon His throne of glory, seeks not His own, but spends His power for His people. It were well if every Christian would be a Mordecai to the church, striving according to his ability for its prosperity. Some are placed in stations of affluence and influence, let them honour their Lord in the high places of the earth, and testify for Jesus before great men. Others have what is far better, namely, close fellowship with the King of kings, let them be sure to plead daily for the weak of the Lord's people, the doubting, the tempted, and the comfortless.[14]

ENDNOTES

[1](Intro) A non-observant Jew is one who is part of the Jewish ethnic community but does not practice his religion or try to keep the Mosaic

Law, such as the dietary rules and traditions.

[2](Intro) Today Persia is called Iran. Their language, Farsi (=Persian) is not related to Arabic but uses a modified Arabic script and many Arabic words from the Muslim religion and culture.

[3](Intro) Thinking to "remedy" this situation, some Jews added many passages (in Greek) to the canonical text of Esther. They did not realize that they were actually ruining the very message of the book—God working in the shadows for His people, even for those who chose to live far from His temple in Jerusalem. These additions will be found in the Apocrypha, and are of a very different character from the Hebrew original. They add a great deal of religious activity along with some almost soap-opera-style content. Jews and Protestants have rightly rejected these apocryphal additions to God's Word.

[4](Intro) W. Graham Scroggie, *Know Your Bible, Vol. I, The Old Testament*, p. 96.

[5](Intro) Quoted by Scroggie, *ibid*.

[6](Intro) Our English names *Susan* and *Susannah* come from this Hebrew word for *lily*.

[7](1:13–20) J. Vernon, McGee, *Ruth and Esther: Women of Faith*, pp. 232, 33.

[8](2:19–23) Cited by Carl Armerding, *Esther: For Such a Time as This*, p. 35.

[9](3:12–15) Irving L. Jensen, *Ezra/Nehemiah/Esther*, p. 88.

[10](4:15–17) Matthew Poole, *Matthew Poole's Commentary on the Holy Bible*, p. 913.

[11](6:1–3) J. G. Bellett, further documentation unavailable.

[12](9:17–28) *Pûrîm* is the Hebrew plural, meaning "lots."

[13](10:1, 2) Armerding, *Esther*, p. 128.

[14](10:3) Charles Haddon Spurgeon, *Morning and Evening*, p. 667, reading for November 28, Evening.

BIBLIOGRAPHY

Armerding, Carl. *Esther: For Such a Time as This*. Chicago: Moody Press, 1955.

Baldwin, Joyce G. *Esther*. Tyndale Old Testament Commentaries. Downers Grove, IL: InterVarsity Press, 1984.

Ironside, H. A. "Esther." In *Notes on Ezra, Nehemiah, and Esther*. Neptune, N.J.: Loizeaux Brothers, 1972.

Keil, C. F. "Esther." In *Commentary on the Old Testament in Ten Volumes*. Vol 10. Grand Rapids: Wm. B. Eerdmans Publishing Co., 1982.

McGee, J. Vernon *Ruth and Esther: Women of Faith*. Nashville: Thomas Nelson Publishers, 1988

INTRODUCTION TO THE POETICAL BOOKS

"Poetry," someone has said, "is that which is lost in translation." Fortunately for us, this is not true, or at best it is a great exaggeration when speaking of OT Hebrew poetry. Classic English or French poetry, on the other hand, being so dependent as a rule on rhyme, strict meter, and special forms, is most difficult to translate into other languages with real success.

Hebrew poetry has meter to a certain extent, uses the techniques of alliteration (words beginning with the same sound), and other devices common to our own poetry.

Though much of the Prophets are written in poetic form, five books in the OT are considered poetical as such: Job, Psalms, Proverbs, Ecclesiastes, and the Song of Songs.[1]

I. The Poetical Books

A. Job

This may be the oldest book in the Bible, since in all its discussions of right and wrong no reference is made to the Law. In dramatic dialogues the greatly suffering yet righteous Job contends with his "friends" about the reason for his affliction, only to be taught at last by the Lord to accept His sovereign will for him. This is Wisdom Literature at its best, recognized even by unbelievers as truly majestic poetry.

B. Psalms

The most popular book in the OT for Christians is the book of Psalms. We often see it bound together with the NT for convenience when a complete Bible is too unwieldy to carry. Many who love the Psalms are not even aware that it is all poetry.[2]

Psalms is the hymnbook of ancient Israel, consisting of a collection of five books written over a period of about a thousand years, from about 1400 B.C. (Moses) to about 400 B.C. (Ezra).

C. Proverbs

The second most likely OT book to be used by believers on a regular basis is the Book of Proverbs. It is absolutely chock full of wise sayings on how to live a successful life from God's viewpoint (which in the final analysis, is the only one that really counts). It is a marvelous example of Wisdom Literature.

D. Ecclesiastes

This book is the hardest for most people to fit into the framework of Bible teaching. The key to Ecclesiastes is the expression "under the sun," since "the Preacher" is reasoning from the viewpoint of a person without God's revelation. Here is another good example of Wisdom Literature.

E. Song of Songs

All Bible lovers are agreed that this is a beautiful poem of true and pure love, though the interpretations of the story are diverse. The title "Song

The Setting of the Books of Wisdom & Poetry

of Songs" is a Hebrew idiom meaning "the most exquisite song." Solomon wrote 1,005 songs (1 Kgs. 4:32); this was his finest.

II. Enjoying OT Poetry

Unfortunately, many people get "turned off" to poetry in school, either by being forced to memorize poems they don't like or don't understand, or by having had teachers who made them dissect poems till all the beauty and freshness was gone. It is somewhat like growing a rose, which anyone can do with little knowledge at all except a desire to experience beauty. A biology class assignment that takes the rose to pieces part by part is no doubt educational, but hardly helpful from an artistic or aesthetic viewpoint.

Enjoying OT poetry is somewhat like a middle ground between experiencing a rose with no knowledge of roses on the one hand, and doing a scientific study on the other. You will enjoy roses more if you know the difference between a tea rose and a floribunda, if you can tell red from pink and pink from coral and red-orange.

Likewise if you can notice the forms and techniques that lend "color" to poetry, and the techniques of the psalmist or other biblical poet, you will get a great deal more out of Bible poetry. This is true not only in the five books considered poetic, but in the rest of the OT as well—not to mention in the NT.

III. Parallelism

Bible poetry's greatest technique is not to *rhyme sounds*, as in much English poetry, but to "rhyme" *ideas*—that is, to put two or more lines together that somehow match each other. We should be grateful to God that this is the mainstay of biblical poetry because it translates nicely into nearly all languages, and not too much beauty is lost in the translation process. Our Lord Himself also frequently spoke in parallelism. (Carefully reread, e.g., Matthew 5—7 and John 13—17 after studying the following notes.)

We would like to present some examples of the main types of Hebrew parallelism so that the reader can look for similar structures, not only while studying the OT with the help of the *Believers Bible Commentary*, but also while having daily devotions and listening to sermons.

1. Synonymous Parallelism

As the name implies, this type has the second or parallel line saying about the same thing as the first—for emphasis. Proverbs is especially full of these:

In the way of righteousness is life,
And in its pathway there is no death (Prov. 12:28).

I am the rose of Sharon,
And the lily of the valleys (Song 2:1).

2. Antithetic Parallelism

This type puts two lines "against" each other that form a *contrast:*

For the LORD knows the way of the righteous,
But the way of the ungodly shall perish (Ps. 1:6).[3]

Hatred stirs up strife,
But love covers all sins (Prov. 10:12).

3. Formal Parallelism

This type is parallel in *form* only; the two (or more) lines don't contrast, expand, or emphasize. It is just two lines of poetry put together to express a thought or theme:

Yet I have set My King
On My holy hill of Zion (Ps. 2:6).

4. Synthetic Parallelism

The second line of poetry builds up (*synthesis* is Greek for "putting together") the thought in the first line:

The LORD is my shepherd;
I shall not want (Ps. 23:1).

Keep your heart with all diligence,
For out of it spring the issues of life (Prov. 4:23).

5. Emblematic Parallelism

A figure of speech in the first *line* of poetry illustrates the content of the second line:

As the deer pants for the water brooks,
So pants my soul for You, O God (Ps. 42:1).

As a ring of gold in a swine's snout,
So is a lovely woman who lacks discretion (Prov. 11:22).

IV. Literary Figures

We use these every day without realizing it. Such expressions as "She's a real angel" or "He eats like a pig" are figures of speech.

1. Comparisons

Vivid comparisons are often made between one thing and another in the Bible, especially in the five poetical books.

a. Simile

When the comparison uses the word *like* or *as* it is called a *simile:*

For You, O LORD, will bless the righteous;
With favor You will surround him **as** with a shield (Ps. 5:12).

Like an apple tree among the trees of the woods,
So is my beloved among the sons (Song 2:3a).

b. Metaphor

When the comparison is direct, and one thing is called another, without *like* or *as*, it is a *metaphor*. This is a very popular device[4]:

For the LORD God is a sun and shield;
The LORD will give grace and glory;
No good thing will He withhold
From those who walk uprightly
(Ps. 84:11).

A garden enclosed is my sister, my spouse,
A spring shut up, a fountain sealed
(Song 4:12).

2. Alliteration

Several words in close proximity beginning with the same letter—often a consonant—give us "apt alliteration's artful aid."[5] For example, the opening verses of the Song of Solomon have many words beginning with the "sh" sound (the letter *shîn* in Hebrew), including the name of the book and the Hebrew form of Solomon.

Obviously the alliteration in translation will not and indeed cannot match or be in the same place as in the original language.[6] Nevertheless the KJV and the NKJV have many striking illustrations in translation:

He frustrates the devices of the **c**rafty,
So that their hands **c**annot **c**arry out their plans.
He **c**atches the wise in their own **c**raftiness,
And the **c**ounsel of the **c**unning comes **q**uickly upon them
(Job 5:12, 13).

Man who is born of woman
is of **f**ew days and **f**ull of trouble.
He comes **f**orth like a **f**lower and **f**ades away;
He **f**lees like a shadow and does not continue (Job 14:1, 2).

He **h**as sent redemption to **H**is people;
He **h**as commanded **H**is covenant forever:
Holy and awesome is **H**is name
(Ps. 111:9).

A **p**resent is a **p**recious stone
in the eyes of its **p**ossessor;
Wherever he turns, he **p**rospers
(Prov. 17:8).

The words of a **t**alebearer are like **t**asty **t**rifles,
And **t**hey go down into the inmost body (Prov. 18:8).

3. Anthropomorphism

This means "human form," and describes God, who is spirit, as having human parts:

The LORD is in His holy temple,
The LORD's throne is in heaven;
His **eyes** behold,
His **eyelids** test the sons of men
(Ps. 11:4).

4. Zoomorphism

Similarly, God's attributes are compared to *animal forms:*

He shall cover you with His **feathers**,
And under His **wings** you shall take refuge;
His truth shall be your shield and buckler (Ps. 91:4).

5. Personification

An object or abstract quality is treated as a person:

Let the heavens rejoice, and let the earth be glad;
Let the sea roar, and all its fullness;
Let the field be joyful, and all that is in it.

Then all the trees of the woods will
rejoice before the LORD
(Ps. 96:11, 12).

I, wisdom, dwell with prudence,
And find out knowledge and
discretion (Prov. 8:12).

6. Acrostic

This is one device that is almost impossible to translate,[7] because the poem is based on the Hebrew alphabet, and successive lines of poetry are in alphabetical order. Well-known examples are Psalm 119 and four of the five chapters in Lamentations. The book of Proverbs ends with the twenty-two-verse tribute to the ideal woman based on the letters of the Hebrew alphabet (Prov. 31:10–31).

There are other figures of speech as well, some of them overlapping a bit with those we have presented, but these will be enough for most believers.

If the reader will be on the lookout for some of these poetic devices while studying these five books (and much of the rest of the Bible as well), a great deal of fresh interest may be found in the sacred text—not to mention a deeper appreciation of its beauty. (See Eccl. 3:11a.)

ENDNOTES

[1]Three of these—Job, Proverbs, and Ecclesiastes—are also called Wisdom Literature. While poetic in form their contents stress wisdom, or the art and skill of living according to the fear of God.

[2]Part of the reason for this is that the KJV traditionally has printed all forms of Bible literature—laws, history, poetry, epistles—in exactly the same format. More modern versions seek to show by the format itself the type of writing being presented.

[3]The entire first psalm is an antithetical parallelism between the righteous and the ungodly, a masterpiece of what in art is called "dark against light and light against dark."

[4]Our Lord used metaphors when He called Himself "the Door," "the Vine," "the Bread of Life," and "the Good Shepherd."

[5]Preachers are especially fond of this device for sermon outlines, and when not forced, fanciful, or overdone, alliteration is a real help to the memory.

[6]In the NT the book of Hebrews opens with a cluster of words beginning with the "p" sound (Greek *pi*) in the original.

[7]Ronald Knox's translation of the Bible makes a rather impressive attempt to do so, but necessarily dropping four lesser-used letters from the English alphabet, since Hebrew has only twenty-two letters.

THE BOOK OF JOB

Introduction

'It is our first, oldest statement of the never-ending Problem—man's destiny, and God's way with him here in this earth . . . . Sublime sorrow, sublime reconciliation; oldest choral melody as of the heart of mankind—so soft, and great; as the summer midnight, as the world with its seas and stars! There is nothing written I think, in the Bible or out of it, of equal literary merit.''

—Thomas Carlyle

I. Unique Place in the Canon

Job is the only book of its kind in the whole Word of God: a long, dramatic dialogue in poetic form set like a large multi-faceted diamond in between a prose historical prologue and epilogue. As originally written in the Hebrew language, the book was entirely in poetry, with the exception of chapters 1, 2, 32:1–6a, and 42:7–17.

Samuel Ridout comments about its place in Holy Scripture:

> From its size, and a rapid glance at its contents, we would judge that the book of Job is a very important part of the word of God. Yet how much it is neglected by most; an intimate familiarity even with its contents is the exception rather than the rule.[1]

The majesty of the language is recognized even (and sometimes especially) by unbelievers. Of course, the rationalists are ever ready with their theories of "sources," "redactions," and "interpolations"—usually with no manuscript evidence whatever to support their destructive theories.

The great Reformer, Martin Luther, who was himself a gifted writer and translator, said that Job was "more magnificent and sublime than any other book of Scripture." Alfred Lord Tennyson, who as poet laureate of England could be expected to recognize great poetry, called Job "the greatest poem whether of ancient or modern literature."

In light of the book of Job's great style and insight into the human condition, it should prove no surprise that our everyday speech has been greatly enriched by this book. The following expressions are some of the rather clear borrowings. Most of these are direct quotations from the book of Job that have become a part of our everyday speech:

The hair on my body stood up (4:15b). (My hair stood on end.)

My life is a breath (7:7a).

Put my life in my hands (13:14b). (Take my life in my hands.)

"Job's comforters." (These *exact* words are not found, but in 16:2 Job calls his friends "Miserable comforters.")

There is no justice (19:7).

I have escaped by the skin of my teeth (19:20b).

The root of the matter (19:28b).

Put your hand over your mouth (21:5b).

The land of the living (28:13b).

Eyes to the blind . . . feet to the lame (29:15).

Spit in my face (30:10b).

Great men are not always wise (32:9).

Words without knowledge (35:16b).

This far. . . but no farther, and here your proud waves must stop (38:11).

The gates of death (38:17a).

He smells the battle from afar (39:25). (We say: "The smell of battle.")

Repent in dust and ashes (42:6b).

The expression "I know that my Redeemer lives . . ." (19:25) is well-known partly because of Handel's marvelous musical setting of the words in his *Messiah*.

The expression "the patience of Job" (Jas. 5:11, KJV) though not in the book of Job, has become a part of everyday conversation.

As to the content of the book, it has been pointed out that the deep questions that Job poses about life, death, suffering, and life after death are all met in the Mediator he longed for, the Lord Jesus Christ.

II. Authorship

The book of Job is anonymous, though Jewish tradition chooses Moses as the author. Other suggestions are Elihu, Solomon, Hezekiah, Ezra, a nameless Jew living somewhere between 500 and 200 B.C., or Job himself. Since Job lived 140 additional years after the events in the book and experienced all of the events and speeches, perhaps he is the most likely choice.

III. Date

As to the events in the book, it is widely believed that Job lived prior to the birth of Abraham. Thus, the events in the book of Job would fall somewhere in the latter part of Genesis 11. There are several reasons why Job is assigned to this period in history. First of all, there is no undisputable mention in the book of his being a Jew. There is no mention of the Exodus or Law of Moses. In fact, it is clear that Job was the priest for his own family (1:5), and this type of family priesthood belonged to the patriarchal period. The lifestyle characterized by wealth being determined by cattle and other animals is also largely patriarchal. Job lived for more than two hundred years, and this age span was characteristic of the era immediately preceding Abraham. Scholars also notice the musical instruments (21:12) and the forms of money (42:11) which are mentioned in the book of Job, and they assign these to the early part of Genesis chronologically.[2]

As to the time of writing, scholars range all the way from the patriarchal era (c. 2100–1900 B.C.) to the second century B.C.! (This last view is held by extreme liberals, and is virtually impossible to reconcile with Dead Sea Scroll portions of Job coming from the same era.)

The two most likely eras are the patriarchal and Solomonic. It would seem to modern Westerners that such long and complex speeches would be best preserved if written down soon after they were delivered. However, Eastern and Semitic oral transmission is known to be remarkable for its accuracy.

The best argument for the Solomonic age is the content and style of the book: it is Wisdom Literature, not unlike the works of King Solomon. Such conservative OT scholars as Franz Delitzsch and Merrill F. Unger held a Solomonic date for the actual writing of the book, but obviously allowing for a long and accurate oral tradition. Such a literary phenomenon is widely understood in the East but hard for Westerners to relate to.

IV. Background and Theme

Although the author of the book of Job is unknown, there is no question as to its inspiration or historical accuracy. The apostle Paul quotes from Job 5:13 in 1 Corinthians 3:19: "He catches the wise in their own craftiness." In Ezekiel 14:14, Job is spoken of as a historical person, not a fictional character. He is also named in James 5:11: "You have heard of the perseverance of Job and seen the end intended by the Lord—that the Lord is very compassionate and merciful."

The subject of the book is the mystery of human suffering and the problem of pain. Why do all people suffer some, and especially why do the righteous suffer? In Job we see a man who was probably exposed to more catastrophes in one day than any other person who has ever lived, with the exception of the Lord Jesus. The Lord allowed these sufferings to come into Job's life in order to enlarge his capacity for communion with God. Perhaps in a special way, the book is also intended to shadow forth the sufferings of the Jewish people.

If the Jews were to accept a *suffering* Messiah (as over against a heroic "Maccabean" type), it was necessary to show that suffering is not necessarily in return for individual sins. Christ suffered for us, the just for the unjust.

Several passages in this book can be applied to the Lord Jesus:

1. 9:33—"Nor is there any mediator between us, who may lay his hand on us both." (Christ is the Mediator who can bridge the gap between God and man.)
2. 16:8–19—The sufferings of Job. Many of the expressions in this passage are applied in the Psalms to the sufferings of the Messiah.
3. 16:21—"Oh, that one might plead for a man with God, as a man pleads for his neighbor!" (The Lord Jesus Christ is our Advocate who pleads our case before the Father.)
4. 19:25, 26—"For I know that my Redeemer lives." (Christ's role as Redeemer and coming King are clearly described.)
5. 33:24—" 'Deliver him from going down to the Pit; I have found a ransom.' " (The word "ransom" here is the same word as "atonement." Through the atonement of Christ, believers are delivered from the pit of hell.)

Several statements in the book of Job are often said to reveal an advanced knowledge of science:

1. The evaporation-precipitation cycle (36:27, 28).
2. Wind and weather directions (37:9, 17).
3. Composition of the human body (33:6).
4. Suspension of the earth (26:7).
5. Ocean-bottom phenomena (38:16).
6. Cloud-lightning relationship (37:11).
7. The orbits of heavenly bodies and their influence upon the earth (38:32, 33).

OUTLINE

I. THE PROLOGUE: THE TESTING OF JOB (Chaps. 1, 2)
   A. Scene I: The Land of Uz (1:1–5)
   B. Scene II: Heaven—The Lord's Presence (1:6–12)
   C. Scene III: The Land of Uz—Calamity to Job's Property and Posterity (1:13–22)
   D. Scene IV: Heaven—The Lord's Presence Again (2:1–6)
   E. Scene V: Uz—Calamity to Job's Person (2:7–13)

II. THE DEBATE BETWEEN JOB AND HIS FRIENDS (Chaps. 3—31)
   A. The First Round of Speeches (Chaps. 3—14)
      1. Job's Opening Lament (Chap. 3)
      2. Eliphaz's First Speech (Chaps. 4, 5)
      3. Job's Response (Chaps. 6, 7)
      4. Bildad's First Speech (Chap. 8)
      5. Job's Response (Chaps. 9, 10)
      6. Zophar's First Speech (Chap. 11)
      7. Job's Response (Chaps. 12—14)
   B. The Second Round of Speeches (Chaps. 15—21)
      1. Eliphaz's Second Speech (Chap. 15)
      2. Job's Response (Chaps. 16, 17)
      3. Bildad's Second Speech (Chap. 18)
      4. Job's Response (Chap. 19)
      5. Zophar's Second Speech (Chap. 20)
      6. Job's Response (Chap. 21)
   C. The Third Round of Speeches (Chaps. 22—31)
      1. Eliphaz's Third Speech (Chap. 22)
      2. Job's Response (Chaps. 23, 24)
      3. Bildad's Third Speech (Chap. 25)
      4. Job's Response (Chap. 26)
      5. Job's Closing Monologue (Chaps. 27—31)

III. THE INTERVENTION OF ELIHU (Chaps. 32—37)
   A. Elihu's Speech to Job's Three Friends (Chap. 32)
   B. Elihu's Speech to Job (Chap. 33)
   C. Elihu's Second Speech to Job's Three Friends (Chap. 34)
   D. Elihu's Second Speech to Job (Chaps. 35—37)

IV. THE REVELATION OF THE LORD (38:1—42:6)
   A. The Lord's First Challenge to Job (38:1—40:2)
      1. Introductory (38:1–3)
      2. The Challenge of the Wonders of Inanimate Creation (38:4–38)
      3. The Challenge of the Wonders of Animate Creation (38:39—40:2)
   B. Job's Response (40:3–5)
   C. The Lord's Second Challenge to Job (40:6—41:34)
      1. Job Challenged to Respond Like a Man (40:6–14)

2. Job Challenged to Consider Behemoth (40:15–24)
3. Job Challenged to Consider Leviathan (Chap. 41)

D. Job's Humble Response (42:1–6)

V. EPILOGUE: THE TRIUMPH OF JOB (42:7–17)

A. Job's Friends Rebuked and Restored (42:7–9)

B. Job's Prosperity Restored (42:10–17)

VI. CONCLUSION: LESSONS FROM THE BOOK OF JOB

Commentary

I. THE PROLOGUE: THE TESTING OF JOB (Chaps. 1, 2)

A. Scene I: The Land of Uz (1:1–5)

1:1–3 **Job** was a wealthy **man** who lived **in the land of Uz**. From Lamentations 4:21 it appears that Uz was located in Edom, southeast of Palestine.[3] The **upright** and God-fearing Job had **seven sons and three daughters**. So vast were his holdings of livestock that he **was the greatest** man in **the East**.

1:4, 5 One of the strong arguments that the events of Job took place in the patriarchal era is the fact that Job, as father of the family, acted as priest and sacrificed **burnt offerings** for his sons. The danger of frivolous and even sacrilegious talk when even generally devout people are **feasting** and making merry is ever present. In his evening meditation for Christmas Day, C. H. Spurgeon makes a good application for us in the Christian dispensation:

> What the patriarch did early in the morning, after the family festivities, it will be well for the believer to do for himself ere he rests tonight. Amid the cheerfulness of household gatherings it is easy to slide into sinful levities, and to forget our avowed character as Christians. It ought not to be so, but so it is, that our days of feasting are very seldom days of sanctified enjoyment, but too frequently degenerate into unhallowed mirth. . . . Holy gratitude should be quite as purifying an element as grief. Alas! for our poor hearts, that facts prove that the house of mourning is better than the house of feasting. Come, believer, in what have you sinned to-day? Have you been even as others in idle words and loose speeches? Then confess the sin, and fly to the sacrifice. The sacrifice sanctifies. The precious blood of the Lamb slain removes the guilt, and purges away the defilement of our sins of ignorance and carelessness.[4]

B. Scene II: Heaven—The Lord's Presence (1:6–12)

As the story unfolds we are told of a scene in heaven when **the sons of God**[5] (angels) appeared **before the Lord. Satan** (the word is Hebrew for "Accuser") **also** was present. When God spoke to Satan concerning the uprightness of His **servant Job**, Satan implied that the only reason Job feared God was that He had been so good to him. According to Satan, if the Lord had not put **a** protective **hedge around** Job, then he would have cursed his Creator **to** His **face**.

C. Scene III: The Land of Uz—Calamity to Job's Property and Prosperity (1:13–22)

1:13–19 The Lord, thereupon, granted **Satan** permission to test Job by robbing him of his possessions. However, the devil was *not* permitted to touch Job's **person**.

Then followed a series of dreadful calamities in rapid succession:

1. **The Sabeans** stole **five hundred yoke of oxen** and **five hundred female donkeys**, and **killed the** servants who were in charge of these animals.
2. Lightning destroyed **seven thousand sheep**, as well as **the servants** who were tending them.
3. **The Chaldeans** stole **three thousand camels** and **killed the servants** who cared for them.
4. **A great wind** caused the collapse of **the house** in which Job's **sons and daughters were eating and drinking wine**, killing all of them.

1:20–22 In spite of these terrible losses, **Job** was enabled to worship God, saying, **"Naked I came from my mother's womb, and naked shall I return there. The Lord gave, and the Lord has taken away; blessed be the name of the Lord."**

D. Scene IV: Heaven—The Lord's Presence Again (2:1–6)

In chapter 2, we find **Satan** appearing **before the Lord** once again. This time **Satan** implies that Job's faithfulness to God would soon vanish if he were allowed to **touch his** body. Permission to do so is granted.

E. Scene V: Uz—Calamity to Job's Person (2:7–13)

2:7–10 Job, thereupon, breaks out with **painful boils** from **the sole of his foot to the crown of his head**. So great is his misery that even his **wife** urges him to **"Curse God and die!"** But Job answers her, **"Shall we indeed accept good from God, and shall we not accept adversity?"** Regarding Job's wife, Harold St. John quotes the following paragraph:

> I think of all the cruel and one-sided things that masculine commentators have written about Job's wife, and I almost despair of my sex; it takes a woman to understand a woman, and it is reserved for a lady writer (I think that her name was Louise Haughton) to discern that as long as Job's wife could share in his sorrows she bore up bravely, but as soon as he enters a fresh chamber of suffering and leaves her outside, then she breaks down: for her the one intolerable woe is that which she is forbidden to share with him.[6]

2:11–13 Shortly after this, **three** of **Job's friends** hear of his **adversity** and determine to visit him with words of comfort. The friends are **Eliphaz, Bildad, and Zophar**.

However, when they see Job's pitiful and wretched condition, they are so shocked that they are unable to speak to him for **seven days and seven nights**!

II. THE DEBATE BETWEEN JOB AND HIS FRIENDS (Chaps. 3—31)

Chapter 3 begins a series of discourses by Job and his friends, the largest and most complex section of the book. Ridout describes it well:

> It has been well named *The Entangle-*

ment, for it is a mass of argument, denunciation, accusation, suspicion, partly correct theories, and withal flashes of faith and hope—all in the language of loftiest poetry, with magnificent luxuriance of Oriental metaphor. To the casual reader there may seem to be no progress, and but little clarity in the controversy. And it must be confessed that God's people at large seem to have gained little from these chapters beyond a few familiar, beautiful and oft-quoted verses.[7]

These discourses may be divided into three series: Job first speaks, then is answered by one of his friends; Job replies to him, only to be answered by another; poor Job seeks to defend himself again—only to be rebuked by the third friend!

The three series of discourses may be shown as follows:

First Round
Job: Chap. 3
Eliphaz: Chaps. 4, 5
Job: Chaps. 6, 7
Bildad: Chap. 8
Job: Chaps. 9, 10
Zophar: Chap. 11

Second Round
Job: Chaps. 12—14
Eliphaz: Chap. 15
Job: Chaps. 16, 17
Bildad: Chap. 18
Job: Chap. 19
Zophar: Chap. 20

Third Round
Job: Chap. 21
Eliphaz: Chap. 22
Job: Chaps. 23, 24
Bildad: Chap. 25
Job: Chaps. 26—31
(Zophar does not speak again.)

The arguments of the three friends may be summarized as follows:

Eliphaz stresses experience or general observation: "I have seen. . . ." (4:8, 15; 5:3; 15:7; 22:19).

Bildad is the voice of tradition and the authority of antiquity (8:8). "His discourses abound in proverbs and pious platitudes which, though true enough, are known to everyone (9:1–3; 13:2)."[8]

Zophar counsels legalism and religiosity (11:14, 15). "He presumes to know what God will do in any given case, why He will do it, and what His thoughts about it are."[9] His ideas are mere assumptions, pure dogmatism.

The remaining portion of the book is taken up with a long speech by a young man named Elihu (Chaps. 32—37), and then by a conversation between God and Job (Chaps. 38—42). Job ends with a prose epilogue that matches the prologue.

A. The First Round of Speeches (Chaps. 3—14)

1. *Job's Opening Lament (Chap. 3)*

3:1–9 This chapter has been well titled "Unhappy Birthday," because in it Job curses **the day of his birth**, extols the blessings of death, and yet complains that he cannot die! He assigns total **darkness** to the day **a male child**—himself— was **conceived**.

3:10–12 Since he was conceived and born, **why** couldn't he have died **at birth**? (It is worth noting that even in his tremendous bitterness and grief Job does not suggest either abortion or infanticide, which were common evils in the ancient world, and are now so again today in the West.)

3:13–19 Job praises death as a situation where **the weary are at rest, small and great are there, and the servant is free from his master**.

3:20–26 Next he questions why the **light** of life is given to those who are **in misery** (as he was) and **long for death** as if for **hidden treasures**.

Verse 25 is very famous:

For the thing I greatly feared has come upon me,
And what I dreaded has happened to me.

Could this indicate that even in Job's happy and prosperous days he had fears of losing what he had? This is a common characteristic of the very rich: extreme fear of losing wealth and having to live a frugal life. Riches give no real security; only *God* can give that.

2. *Eliphaz's First Speech (Chaps. 4, 5)*

Chapter four commences the cycle of speeches of Job's friends and his responses to them. Ridout summarizes the gist of their message as follows:

> In the controversy of the three friends we have a unity of thought, based on a common principle. That principle is that all suffering is of a *punitive* rather than of an instructive nature; that it is based on God's justice rather than on His love—though these are ever combined in all His ways. Such a principle necessarily fails to distinguish between the sufferings of the righteous and those of the wicked.[10]

In chapters 4 and 5, Eliphaz speaks. Eliphaz (his name may mean *God is strength* or *God is fine gold*) was a pious and prominent person, orthodox in his views of God's greatness, but sadly lacking in compassion. He becomes harsher as the series of speeches progress. It is worth noting that while the three friends become *less and less* understanding (in both senses of that word) throughout the book, Job becomes *more and more* understanding of God's ways, until, after speeches by Elihu and a true encounter with Jehovah, he accepts God's will with true humility.

4:1–11 **Eliphaz** says in effect, "You helped others ('Your words have kept men on their feet' 4:4, James Moffatt), but now you cannot help yourself." (These words are reminiscent of Christ's mockers at the Crucifixion: "He saved others; He cannot save Himself.") The reason he gives for this is Job's self-righteousness. "Hath not thy piety been thy confidence, and the perfection of thy ways thy hope?" (4:6, JND). Since people suffer for wickedness, it must be that Job has sinned (vv. 7–9).

4:12–21 Then Eliphaz tells of a vision which was **secretly brought to** him at **night**. In this vision **a spirit** asks the question, **"Can a mortal be more righteous than God? Can a man be more pure than his Maker?"** (v. 17). The meaning of this seems to be that man has no right to reply against God. If a person suffers, it is his own fault, not God's. After all, God is so great that He cannot trust **His** own **servants**, and when compared to Him, **His angels** are guilty of **error**. Since this is so, **how much more** untrustworthy and fallible are mortal men who are as transient as **a moth**!

5:1–7 Eliphaz challenges Job to summon men or angels (the **holy ones**) to disprove that sin is followed by judgment. The speaker himself has observed the unalterable link between wickedness and punishment. Trouble is never causeless. **Man**, being sinful, is destined **to trouble**, as sure **as the sparks fly upward**.

5:8–16 The thing to do is to **seek God** and to **commit** one's **cause** to Him, because He is all-wise and all-powerful. This is seen in His control of nature and in His providential dealings with mankind. Verse 13 is quoted by Paul in 1 Corinthians 3:19 to unmask the false wisdom of this world.

5:17–27 By submitting to **the chastening of the Almighty**, says Eliphaz, people experience divine deliverance from **famine**, **war**, slander, civil strife, peril, drought, wild **beasts**, and crop damage. They enjoy domestic **peace**, security, fruitfulness, and longevity.

3. Job's Response (Chaps. 6, 7)

6:1–13 **Job** admits that his **words** have been **rash**, but *there is a reason!* His **grief** and **calamity** are **heavier than the sand of the sea**, and his **spirit** is drinking in the **poison** of **the arrows of the Almighty**. In spite of all the negative and awful things that are expressed in this book, especially by Job, they are so beautifully worded that the sensitive reader is struck by their potency. Job protests that he would not complain so bitterly without cause, any more than animals would **bray** without a reason. Suffering and weeping are linked just like **flavorless food** and seasoning. He wishes he could die because he has no **strength** to endure and no **hope** for the future. Prolonging **life** is useless.

6:14–23 Job's friends (he calls them **brothers**) have failed him and disappointed him when he needed them most. He compares them to brooks or wadis that **vanish** completely when you need them. Though he had sought nothing from them, they had criticized him vaguely without telling him how he had sinned.

6:24–30 Job maintains his integrity in spite of the implications of Eliphaz's speech that he is a secret sinner. He wants to know specifically *where* he has **erred** and desires proof of **injustice on** his **tongue**. Verse 27 is a counter-accusation to the friends; perhaps the **friend** they are undermining is Job himself!

7:1–10 Now Job addresses the Lord directly. It is as natural for him to have the death-wish as for **a servant** to long for rest after a hard day's work. However in Job's case the **night** hours bring no relief to his tortured body, as he tosses **till dawn**. **Like a weaver's shuttle** his life is passing swiftly **without hope**, vanishing from sight like a **cloud**.

7:11–21 He asks the Lord why He should pay so much attention to an insignificant human being, hemming him in, terrifying him with nightmares, until he would rather be strangled. **Is man** so great that God should cause him to suffer continually? Even if Job had **sinned**, is there no **pardon**, since he is going to die soon anyway?

4. Bildad's First Speech (Chap. 8)

The name Bildad may mean *son of contention*, which would be a very appropriate meaning, since this friend of Job seems to love controversy. Ridout compares Bildad to Eliphaz in style and knowledge as follows:

> There is perhaps less of the courtesy and dignity which marked the speech of Eliphaz, together with some harshness toward Job, caused apparently by the bitter charge of the latter against God. With all his ignorance of divine principles, Bildad is jealous of the honor of God, and cannot allow Him to be accused. In this he is surely right, but he fails to convince Job because of the root error in the thoughts, indeed, of them all: God must punish sin, and Job must be a sinner for he is being punished.[11]

8:1–7 Accusing Job of irresponsible and blustery speech, **Bildad** defends the justice of **God** in punishing the wicked and rewarding the **upright**. He says unkindly that Job's **sons** were destroyed because of **their**

transgression. There is no indication of this, and even had there been, it was a cruel thing to say to a man in great sorrow and suffering. But **if** Job would **earnestly** turn **to God**, says Bildad, there was still hope for divine favor.

8:8–22 He next appeals to history to prove the link between evil and retribution. Just as **reeds** wither when there is no **water**, so is the doom of the irreligious and **the hypocrite**. (Verse 16a may be an allusion to the absorption of chlorophyll from sunlight.) God delights to replace **the wicked** with **the blameless**, whom He then proceeds to bless.

5. Job's Response (Chaps. 9, 10)

9:1–13 When **Job** asks, **"How can a man be righteous before God?"**, he is not inquiring as to the way of salvation, but expressing the hopelessness of ever proving his innocence before One who is so great. It is folly **to contend** with **God** since **one could not answer Him one time out of a thousand**. He is sovereign, all-**wise**, and all-powerful, as seen in His control of **mountains, earth, sun, stars, sea, yes, wonders without number**.

9:14–31 What chance would Job have of defending himself? Could he be sure that God is listening? The Lord is merciless, arbitrary, and unjust, Job says, and therefore a fair trial is impossible. In his despair, Job accuses God of undiscriminatingly destroying the **blameless and the wicked**, of laughing **at the plight of the innocent**, and of causing earth's **judges** to act unrighteously. He says, "I am innocent, but I no longer care. I am sick of living. Nothing matters; innocent or guilty, God will destroy us" (vv. 21, 22 TEV). As his life runs out, he finds no hope in careless self-forgetfulness or self-improvement.

9:32–35 Job sighs for a **mediator between** God and himself, but finds none. We know that the Mediator who could meet his (and our) deepest need is the Lord Jesus Christ (1 Tim. 2:5). Matthew Henry comments:

> Job would gladly refer the matter, but no creature was capable of being a referee, and therefore he must even refer it still to God himself and resolve to acquiesce in his judgment. Our Lord Jesus is the blessed daysman, who has mediated between heaven and earth, has laid his hand upon us both; to him the Father has committed all judgment, and we must. But this matter was not then brought to so clear a light as it is now by the gospel, which leaves no room for such a complaint as this.[12]

10:1–7 In exasperation, Job complains bitterly, asking God to explain His unreasonable behavior to one He had created. Does He act like a mere **man** in judging uncharitably, even when He knows that Job is **not wicked**?

10:8–12 Harold St. John comments on this paragraph as follows:

> We must not miss this amazing passage in which the Clay expostulates with the Potter and reminds God that in creating man He has assumed responsibilities from which he cannot honorably escape. 10:8 Thy hands made and fashioned me. 10:10 The formation of the physical embryo. 10:11 The growth of skin and flesh and the development of bones and sinews. 10:12 (a) The gift of "soul" with its many-sided expressions and (b) The visitation of God by which man's highest part, the "spirit," is conferred and preserved.[13]

10:13–22 **Why** does the Lord inflict severe calamities on Job? Seemingly it makes no difference whether he is **righteous** or **wicked**; his life is filled with divine **indignation**. **Why** did God allow him to be born? But now why not let him have **a little comfort before** he passes off into oblivion, **where even the light is like darkness**?

6. Zophar's First Speech (Chap. 11)

11:1–12 Zophar the Naamathite insists that such empty, arrogant **talk** should not go unanswered. Regarding the meaning of Job's third friend's name, Ridout writes:

> Zophar, "a sparrow," from the root verb "to twitter," is the masculine form of Zipporah, Moses' wife, and like her he was an unconscious opponent of God's judgment on the flesh, though he was very zealous in condemning the fancied works of the flesh in Job. His vehement denunciations being utterly out of place, were as harmless as the "twitterings" of the bird for which he was named.[14]

If Job could only see things as *God* does, Zophar contends, he would realize that he is not suffering as much as he really deserves! His ignorance of God's greatness disqualifies him to question His justice. Verse 12 is an especially unkind cut, aimed obviously at Job: **"For an empty-headed man will be wise, when a wild donkey's colt is born a man."**

11:13–20 The best thing for Job to do is **put . . . away** his sins; **then** God will give him security, rest, and comfort. If not, there is no escape from destruction.

7. Job's Response (Chaps. 12—14)

12:1–6 In biting (and now famous) sarcasm, **Job** accuses his friends of intellectual conceit:

> **No doubt you are the people,**
> **And wisdom will die with you!**

Anyone knows that **God** is wise and powerful, but how do they explain the excruciating sufferings of a man who once received answers to his prayers, and the contrasting prosperity of the ungodly? "You have no troubles, and yet you make fun of me; you hit a man who is about to fall" (v. 5 TEV).

12:7–12 Even the world of nature—**the beasts** and **the birds** and **the fish**—shows God's arbitrariness in destroying some and protecting others. If Job's critics tested **words** as carefully as they tasted **food**, they would agree with the ancients, who uniformly agreed with what Job had said.

12:13–25 Now Job launches into a majestic recital of the Lord's sovereignty, **wisdom, and strength**, and how they often produce inexplicable and paradoxical results.

13:1–19 Job scolds his critics. They have not said anything new. He wants to plead his case with God, not with these forgers of lies and worthless physicians. If they kept **silent**, people would think they were wise. Their explanation of God's action was not true; they would be accountable to Him for it. Their arguments were weak and useless. If they would just be quiet, he would plead his **case . . . before** God and commit his **life** to Him. He is confident he will be vindicated, but even if God were to **slay** him he **will** *still* **trust** the Lord.

13:20–28 From 13:20 through 14:22, Job addresses God directly. He begs relief from suffering and demands an explanation of why God is treating him so severely. He wastes away like a rotten thing, a **moth-eaten garment**—scarcely worthy of such notice by God.

Francis Andersen evaluates Job's words as follows:

> Here Job shows himself to be a more honest observer, a more exuberant thinker, than the friends. The mind reels at the immensity of his conception of God. The little deity in the theology of Eliphaz, Bildad and Zophar is easily thought and easily believed. But a faith like Job's puts the human spirit to strenuous work.[15]

14:1–6 Job continues to ask why God is so unrelenting with one who is so fleeting, frail, and faulty. Verse 1 is very widely quoted, perhaps because it seems to fit so many occasions:

> **Man who is born of woman**
> **is of few days and full of trouble.**

Why not let him live out the rest of his short life with some measure of peace?

14:7–12 **There is** more **hope for a tree** that has been **cut down** than there is for him. There is a terrible finality about human death; a dead person is like a dried-up **river**.

14:13–17 Job wishes that God would **hide** him **in the grave . . . until** His anger subsides. Then if the Almighty calls him forth, he will vindicate himself. In the meantime, God takes note of his every sin.

Job does four things in this section: (1) He asks for a revelation of what his sins are; (2) He describes the transitoriness of human life; (3) He despairs over the finality of death (longing for a mediator and grasping at the hope of life beyond); (4) He complains of his present plight.

Verse 14a asks a most important question: **If a man dies, shall he live again?** Our Lord answers the question in John 11:25, 26:

> I am the resurrection and the life. He who believes in Me, though he may die, he shall live. And whoever lives and believes in Me shall never die.

Harold St. John comments on verses 14 and 15:

> In 14:14,15 light dawns on a silent sea, light breaks in, and in a passage of almost incredible daring, Job declares that man is more than matter, that though the heavens will pass and decay, the everlasting hills will crumble, he himself may lie in the grasp of the grave for millennia, yet a day must break when God will feel a hunger round His heart for His friend and will have a desire for the work of His hands.
>
> Then from the deeps of the underworld, Job will answer and, more abiding than the hills, more permanent than the heavens, he will be reunited with the God who had become homesick for His servant.[16]

14:18–22 As inevitable as erosion in nature is man's decay under trials. **His** body returns to dust and **his soul** goes to a place of sadness.

This ends the first round of speeches. The logic of Job's friends has been: God is righteous; He punishes the wicked; if Job is being punished it proves he is wicked. But Job has steadily maintained that he is *not* a wicked person at all.

B. The Second Round of Speeches (Chaps. 15—21)

In the second round of speeches Job's "comforters," no longer appealing for repentance, become more condemning and vehement. Job, meanwhile, becomes more stubborn.

1. Eliphaz's Second Speech (Chap. 15)

15:1–6 It is now the turn of **Eliphaz the Temanite** to reproach Job again for his vanity and his impious, **unprofitable talk**. In a series of rapid-fire questions, **the Temanite** ridicules Job's supposed **knowledge**, calling it **empty**. While Job's bold words challenging God did lay him open to the charge of "casting **off fear**," it was not fair to accuse him of choosing **the tongue of the crafty**. If anything, Job was too open and self-revealing. A hypocrite he was *not!* It is vain for him or for any person to profess righteousness.

15:7–13 Next Eliphaz challenges what he considers Job's arrogance in thinking so highly of his own thoughts: **"Do you limit wisdom to yourself?"** he asks. By Eliphaz's calling the three comforters' words "the **consolations** of God" and "gentle," he shows a complete lack of a heart for genuine compassionate counseling.

15:14–16 Eliphaz repeats his remarks of 4:17–19 on the holiness of **God** and the sinfulness of **man**. But how is Job any more sinful than Eliphaz? Ridout asks:

> Why then apply it to Job as though it proved *him* a sinner above all others? This, surely, is more like crafty speech than all the hot utterances of Job. Let Eliphaz take his place beside Job and confess that he too is "abominable and filthy." The poor sufferer might have responded to that.[17]

15:17–26 Turning to the ancient wisdom **from the fathers**, Eliphaz describes the **pain** that a **wicked man** experiences in life.

15:27–35 A terrible catalog of troubles overtakes **the wicked**, and these calamities are proportionate to the guilt.

2. *Job's Response (Chaps. 16, 17)*

16:1–5 **Job** rejects Eliphaz's analysis of the situation and fights back by calling his critics **"miserable comforters." If** they were in his **place**, he would at least try to **comfort** them!

16:6–14 But now God has turned against him and tortures him by turning him over **to . . . ungodly** men and persecuting him beyond endurance, **with wound upon wound**. All this is in spite of the fact that he is guilty of no unrighteousness.

16:15–22 The fact that Job had **sewn** (not merely *put* on) **sackcloth** over his **skin** shows he is in permanent mourning. Without **friends** to comfort, or anyone to plead his case, he will soon **go the way of no return**.

Some of the language in verses 9–19 is employed in the Psalms to refer to the Messiah. Therefore we are justified in making an *application* of them to the sufferings of Christ, even if that is not the *primary* meaning.

17:1–12 As Job, **broken** in **spirit**, teeters on the edge of **the grave**, his friends mock him. He wants God alone to try his case because his critics have proven themselves of no use. The Lord has made him an object of contempt. **Upright men** who see his condition will rise **up against** his critics, while he continues to protest his integrity. He cannot find **one wise man among** his three antagonists.

17:13–16 There is nothing left for Job but **the grave** with its **darkness**, **corruption**, and worms.

3. *Bildad's Second Speech (Chap. 18)*

18:1–4 **Bildad the Shuhite** denounces Job for very strongly scorning the **words** of wisdom spoken by his friends and himself. One good thing that can be said about Bildad: he is *briefer* in his reproaches than his two fellow-comforters. Perhaps his awareness of this virtue of conciseness gave him boldness to suggest that Job **should put an end to words**.

18:5–21 He repeats the now-familiar refrain that **the wicked** person gets caught in the **net** of his own sins.

Then he gives a dreadful list of the calamities that come upon a sinner's house. Bildad was *right* in saying that men suffer for their sins, but he was *wrong* in giving this as an explanation of *Job's* sufferings. Not all suffering is a direct result of sin in one's life.

4. Job's Response (Chap. 19)

19:1–22 **Job** tells his friends that they ought to be **ashamed** of the way they have **wronged** him. He has been mistreated by **God** and by **relatives, friends**, and servants. His body has wasted away and he has barely **escaped** death. Yet his **friends** join **God** in attacking him pitilessly.

19:23, 24 He wishes that his **words** of defense were **inscribed in a book** and **engraved on a rock with an iron pen and lead, forever**, so that sometime in the future he might obtain justice.

19:25–27 In a rare burst of light, he believes that there is a **Redeemer** who will one day vindicate him and then restore him, even though death and decay intervene.

The great English preacher, Spurgeon, whose own style is not unlike that of the Book of Job, makes a fine application of verse 25:

> The marrow of Job's comfort lies in that little word "My"—"My Redeemer," and in the fact that the Redeemer lives. Oh! to get hold of a living Christ. We must get a property in Him before we can enjoy Him . . . So a Redeemer who does not redeem *me*, an avenger who will never stand up for *my* blood, of what avail were such? Rest not content until by faith you can say, "Yes, I cast myself upon my living Lord; and He is mine." It may be you hold Him with a feeble hand; you half think it presumption to say, "He lives as *my* Redeemer;" yet, remember if you have but faith as a grain of mustard seed, that little faith *entitles* you to say it. But there is also another word here, expressive of Job's strong confidence, "*I know*." To say, "I hope so, I trust so," is comfortable; and there are thousands in the fold of Jesus who hardly ever get much further. But to reach the essence of consolation you *must* say, "I know."[18]

The fact that Job has faith to **see God in** his **flesh after** his **skin is destroyed**, strongly suggests the physical resurrection, a doctrine not widely taught in the OT, but accepted as standard in the time of our Lord by OT—believing Jews.

Again Spurgeon comments in a beautiful way on verse 26:

> Mark the subject of Job's devout anticipation—"I shall see God." He does not say, "I shall see the saints"—though doubtless that will be untold felicity—but, "I shall see *God*." It is not—"I shall see the pearly gates, I shall behold the walls of jasper, I shall gaze upon the crowns of gold," but "I shall see God." This is the sum and substance of heaven, this is the joyful hope of all believers.[19]

19:28, 29 In view of this coming vindication, his friends should not **persecute him**, or they will be punished.

5. Zophar's Second Speech (Chap. 20)

20:1–19 Apparently Job's confession of faith fell on deaf ears. **Zophar** was not listening. He says that human history demonstrates that the proud **man . . . will perish** out of sight **forever. His children will** beg from **the poor**, and return what he has taken unjustly. Though still in **youthful vigor**, he will be cut off. No matter how luxuriously he has lived, he will suddenly lose everything he has gained through oppressing **the poor**.

20:20–29 Almost every imaginable calamity will come upon him, including hunger, **distress**, **misery**, armed attack, **fire**, and loss of tranquility. Heaven **and . . . earth** will conspire **against him**, and his possessions will disappear. This is **the heritage appointed to** the wicked **by God**.

G. Campbell Morgan says concerning this:

> In a passage thrilling with passion, Zophar describes the instability of evil gains. There is a triumph, but it is short. There is a mounting up, but it is followed by swift vanishing. There is a sense of youth, but it bends to dust. There is a sweetness but it becomes remorse; a swallowing down, which issues in vomiting; a getting without rejoicing. The final nemesis of the wicked is that God turns upon him, and pursues him with instruments of judgment. Darkness enwraps him. His sin is set in the light of the heavens, and earth turns against him. Let the history of wickedness be considered and it will be seen how true this is.[20]

6. *Job's Response (Chap. 21)*

21:1–22 **Job** now asks for strict attention. His **complaint** is not primarily **against man**, although his pathetic condition should awaken human sympathy. He counters their arguments with the true observation that **the wicked** often prosper in every area of life and die without suffering, even if they have had no place for **God** in their life. **How often**, he asks, do the wicked reap the reward of their sins in their own lifetime? How often are they driven away **like chaff** in **the wind**?

> You claim God punishes a child for the sins of his father. No! Let God punish the sinners themselves; let Him show that He does it because of their sins. Let sinners bear their own punishment; let them feel the wrath of the Almighty God. When a man's life is over, does he really care whether his children are happy? Can a man teach God who judges even those in high places? (vv. 19–22 TEV).

21:23–34 **One** person **dies** at peace and **in** full **strength**, prosperous. **Another** passes away **in . . . bitterness** and poverty. In death all are alike. If Job's friends insist that the wicked are always punished in this life, he will appeal to those **who travel** extensively to testify that although the wicked may be punished in the afterlife, he often lives quite happily here. No one condemns or punishes him, and he dies just like all others. As a parting shot Job says, "And you! You try to comfort me with nonsense. Every answer you give is a lie!" (v. 34 TEV).

With these words Job ends the second round of speeches between himself and his friends. These "comforters" have about reached the end of their attempts to "convict" Job of sin; they will attempt one more round—minus Zophar.

The problem of the book of Job is still unsolved. Why do the righteous suffer? Job, however, has made some progress and little glimmers of light have begun to shine through the dark enigma of his suffering.

C. The Third Round of Speeches (Chaps. 22—31)

1. *Eliphaz's Third Speech (Chap. 22)*

In the third round Eliphaz and Bildad conclude their arguments, using a great deal of repetition. Zophar remains silent. Job answers them and is apparently unaffected by their arguments since he knows that he is not a secret sinner nor a hypocrite, but, as chapter one reveals, a blameless man (but not sinless or humble). Eliphaz's last speech is full of dignity and literary beauty; he is slightly more polite to the poor sufferer, but unjust nevertheless.

22:1–11 Eliphaz's questions are designed to show that **God** doesn't need Job or anything he has or does, including his **blameless . . . ways**. Then he launches into a prolonged tirade in which he accuses Job of gross **wickedness**— taking wrongful **pledges from** the poor, refusing **water** to **the weary**, **bread** to **the hungry**, taking **land** by force, and oppressing **widows** and orphans. That, according to Eliphaz, accounts for Job's present dilemma. The facts, however, were otherwise; Job had shown great social consciousness and had been generous in his charity.

22:12–20 Job should not think that **God in the height of heaven** doesn't **see** what is going on. If he continues in sin, he will share the fate of the people of Noah's day, when the earth's **foundations were swept away by a flood**—people whom God had previously prospered. **The righteous** rejoice whenever the wicked are punished.

22:21–30 Eliphaz truly has some exquisite words for Job in this his final appeal: **"Now acquaint yourself with Him, and be at peace"** (v. 21a); **"Yes, the Almighty will be your gold and your precious silver"** (v. 25); and **"so light will shine on your ways"** (v. 28b). These words are not only beautiful, but also *true*—for a repentant sinner "returning **to the Almighty**" and "removing **iniquity far from** his **tents"** (v. 23)! The only problem is one of application: Job has not been living in sin! Barnes summarizes Eliphaz's final appeal to Job:

> The Almighty would be his defense; he would find happiness in God; his prayer would be heard; light would shine upon his ways; and when others were humbled, he would be exalted.[21]

2. *Job's Response (Chaps. 23, 24)*

Chapters 23 and 24 are all one speech, merely divided for convenience by the ancient Bible scholars. Job develops three main themes in chapter 23: his longing to present his case at God's throne (vv. 1–9); his defense of his own righteous lifestyle (vv. 10–12); and his fear of God as if He were his adversary (vv. 13–17).

23:1–9 Job's **complaint** is bitter. If only he could **come to** God's throne and **find Him**! Spurgeon comments:

> His first prayer is not "O that I might be healed of the disease which now festers in every part of my body!" nor even "O that I might see my children restored from the jaws of the grave, and my property once more brought from the hand of the spoiler!" but the first and uppermost cry is, "O that I knew where I might find HIM, who is my God! that I might come even to His seat!" God's children run home when the storm comes on. It is the heaven-born instinct of a gracious soul to seek shelter from all ills beneath the wings of Jehovah.[22]

Job is confident that if he could approach the Lord He would have to admit that Job was righteous and so he **would be delivered forever from** his **Judge**.

23:10–12 Verse 10 is often quoted to prove the sanctifying effects of trials, but in context it is really Job's confidence in a "not-guilty" verdict. In the meantime God acts in an arbitrary manner, and His fearful judgments leave Job **terrified**. In spite of this, Job believes that if his case were to ever come to trial at God's judgment seat, he would be found to be as pure **as gold** and to have been always obedient to God's **words**, which he has **treasured . . . more than** his **necessary food**. The lovely words of verse 10 are well worth learning by heart for our own lives:

But He knows the way that I take;
When He has tested me,
I shall come forth as gold.

23:13–17 Meanwhile **the unique** and apparently arbitrary God does **whatever His soul desires** and Job **is afraid of Him**, and even **terrified**, because **God** has **made** Job's **heart weak**.

24:1–12 Since nothing is **hidden from the Almighty**, Job can't understand why He doesn't give the solution to the problem of the wicked's prosperity to **those who know Him**. He enumerates in detail the horrible injustice in this world—the crimes of the oppressors and the sufferings of the oppressed.

Ridout comments:

> It is an awful picture of facts only too well-known to them—and to us. How can Eliphaz make such facts fit in with his theory that evil is always punished in this life? But, oh, how can *God* close His eyes to these things, and afflict a faithful man instead of these wrong doers? This is Job's great trouble, and for this he has found no solution.[23]

Job complains of the apparent failure of God's governing of the world (v. 12):

The dying groan in the city,
And the souls of the wounded cry out;
Yet God does not charge them with wrong.

24:13–17 Next Job describes the rebellious **murderer, adulterer**, and burglar. All three favor **the night** for their activities; the **morning is the same to them as the shadow of death**.

24:18–25 In spite of the fact that these wicked sinners **should be cursed** in the **earth** and they **should be remembered no more, God** apparently **gives them security**. Job maintains that the wicked don't die any more violently than anyone else. He defies anyone to disprove this.

Since Bildad's speech is so short, Zophar has none, and Job's response is so long, some Bible scholars have suggested that verses 18–25 are not really Job at all. Some modern versions even rearrange the text here (and elsewhere) in a very conjectural way. Andersen, who is "not convinced that Job could not have uttered these words,"[24] describes what some have done with them:

> We should not too hastily remove these words from Job's lips, just because they don't sound like what we think he should say. This has been done in three ways: to remove them altogether as a pious gloss which makes Job sound more orthodox than he is; to transfer them to one of the friends, either Bildad (NAB), or Zophar (Pope); to take them as a quotation by Job of what his friends say (RSV, which adds *You say*, and identifies verses 21–24 as Job's rejoinder; or Gordis, who takes all of verses 18–24 as the quotation).[25]

3. *Bildad's Third Speech (Chap. 25)*

The last of the speeches of Job's comforters turns out to be not by Zophar, but by **Bildad the Shuhite**. Apparently Zophar has depleted his fund of rhetoric. Even Bildad's speech is very short—the briefest in the book of Job:

> Judging from the brevity of Bildad's address, and the fact that it contains practically nothing new, it would seem that the friends have exhausted all the arguments that their position permitted them to advance. And this is saying a great deal, for they were men of sober thoughtfulness, with abilities for expression rarely excelled. Their language is noble and elevated, their metaphors of rare beauty and force, but their position and contention were wrong, narrow, and untenable.[26]

Since Bildad has apparently finally comprehended that a multitude of words will not help, he only tries to communicate two themes: the greatness of God (vv. 1–3) and the nothingness of man (vv. 4–6).

25:1–3 God possesses **dominion and fear**, and **His armies** are without **number**.

25:4–6 When even **the moon and the stars are not pure in** God's **sight**, what hope is there for man, a mere **maggot** and **worm**? Bildad's words are true and beautifully stated, but they are spoken without love and comfort, and so they have not ministered to Job's needs.

4. *Job's Response (Chap. 26)*

26:1–4 First of all Job counters Bildad's argument. Even granting that Job is **without power** and **has no strength** or **wisdom, how** has Bildad helped? His words have been futile, insensitive, and a total failure as an answer to Job's arguments.

26:5–13 The rest of the chapter gives a marvelous description of God's power in the universe: the evaporation/precipitation cycle; the density of the **clouds**; the cycle of **light and darkness; the storm** at **sea**; and the stars and constellations **by** which **His Spirit** has **adorned the heavens**.

While Bildad stressed God's glory in the heavens, Job here dwells on His power in the depths: **under the waters, Sheol,** and destruction.

Job describes—centuries before science taught it—that God **hangs the earth on nothing** (which is a poetic depiction of the earth's position and movement in the solar system).

> How immeasurably above the cosmogonies of the heathen philosophers are these few grand words! In them we have as in germ the discoveries of a Newton and a Keppler. It is a great mistake to think Scripture does not teach scientific truth. It teaches all needed truth, even if not in scientific language, yet with scientific accuracy.[27]

26:14 If these wonders are only the **edges of His ways**, and a mere **whisper we hear of Him**, Job asks, what must the full **thunder of His power** be if not incomprehensible?

5. *Job's Closing Monologue (Chaps. 27—31)*

Job's "comforters" have not proved their cases—but then neither has Job solved his problem! He is, however, on the right road, and seems to be growing in faith.

Job's monologue has three main themes: Job contrasts his integrity with *the doom of the wicked* (chap. 27); he lauds *the priceless quality of wisdom* (chap. 28); and finally he dwells on *himself* (chaps. 29—31).

27:1–5 The opening words of this chapter, **"Moreover Job continued his discourse, and said,"** suggests a major break. No longer is he merely *answering* Bildad (26:1); he is addressing all, and he is getting many things "off his chest," as we would say. **Job** continues to insist on his own honesty, **integrity**, and **righteousness**. He refuses to admit that his critics might conceivably be right in accusing him of suffering as a result of secret sin.

27:6–23 Job does not defend **the wicked**, **the unrighteous**, and **the hypocrite**; their calamity is deserved. He **will teach** his three friends about God's dealings with the unrighteous man—truths that they themselves have observed. Disaster will often (but not always) strike his family, his possessions, **his house**, and himself. He will perish while good people rejoice.

28:1–11 This lovely chapter is built around the question voiced in both verses 12 and 20:

> **But where can wisdom be found? And where is the place of understanding?**

Man shows great skill and perseverance in digging for **precious** metals and jewels. Here in the first section of the chapter human cleverness (seen in mining) has been unable *to find wisdom*. In verses 13–19 human riches are incapable *of buying wisdom*, and in verses 21–28 God alone is seen as *the giver of wisdom*.

The description of mining in ancient times is very fascinating, but contains some difficulties for translators. Verse 4 is especially hard: nearly every English version has a different understanding of the text here. Andersen comments that "it is hard to believe that they all had the same Hebrew text in front of them."[28]

Unlike Bildad, who calls man "a maggot," Job admits man's cleverness in mining:

> Man's remarkable success as a miner shows how clever and intelligent he is; but, for all that, he has failed completely to unearth wisdom.[29]

28:12–19 The path of **wisdom** is not found so easily. It cannot be discovered **in the land** or **the sea**, it cannot **be purchased**, nor can an adequate **price** be placed on it, because its **price . . . is above rubies** and **topaz**, and **cannot** be **valued in pure gold**.

28:20–28 Wisdom and **understanding** are **hidden from the eyes of all living** creatures. **Destruction and Death have** only **heard . . . about** them. The same **God** who designed the patterns of nature is the source of wisdom, because **He . . . declared** and **prepared it**. To **fear** Him **is wisdom** and **to depart from evil is understanding**.

This chapter seems to imply that we should submit to God's providential dealings even if we don't always understand them.

29:1–17 Job now gives a masterful and nostalgic account of the good old days of his prosperity and honor, and yearns for their return. He enjoyed God's favor and guidance. His **children were** with him. He lived in luxury and was respected in **the city** by **young** and old, by **princes** and **nobles**, because of his deeds of charity, his **righteousness**, and **justice**.

29:18–25 He anticipated long life and a peaceful death **"in** his **nest,"** as he enjoyed prosperity, vigor, and strength, pictured by **the dew . . . all night on** his **branch**, his **glory . . . fresh within** him, and his **renewed . . . bow**. Others welcomed his advice as a farmer welcomes **the spring rain**. His smiling **countenance** renewed their confidence. His leadership made him like a **chief**, or as a **king in the army**, **as one who comforts mourners**. It is hard to understand why God would punish such a man as this!

30:1–8 Now, sad to say, Job is scorned by **younger . . . men . . . whose fathers** were outcasts of society, unfitted even to help Job's **dogs** watch the sheep; worn out, weak, and poor; so hungry they fed on desert shrubs; **driven out from among men**; homeless nomads; driven **from the land**.

30:9–15 It is these dregs of humanity who now treat Job with utter contempt. Notice the phrases descriptive of their scorn—**"taunting song," "I am their byword," "they abhor me,"** "they **spit in my face," "they push away my feet"** (trip him?), **"they break up** (or block) **my path,"** etc. Job's **honor** and **prosperity** have totally vanished.

30:16–23 He is racked with **pains**, disfigured with agony, reduced to **dust and ashes**, and ready to die. God won't **answer** his prayers, cruelly opposes him, tosses him around, and is about to kill him.

30:24–31 **Surely** He will not afflict in the grave one who has prayed to Him **when** dying. Job had shown mercy to others but he himself was shown no mercy. His intense suffering is compounded by loneliness and rejection. His physical and emotional condition are appalling. Why would a righteous man like Job have to become **a brother of jackals and a companion of ostriches**?

31:1–12 Job insists that he has not been guilty of lustful looks at **a young woman**. He knows that God sees and punishes such sin. He has not acted deceitfully; an **honest** examination would convince **God** of this. He has not strayed **from the way** of righteousness; otherwise he would deserve to lose his **harvest**. He has not coveted his **neighbor's** wife; otherwise his own **wife** should become another man's, and his possessions and life be destroyed.

31:13–37 Job had been merciful to his servants; charitable to **the poor**, to **the widow**, and to the **fatherless**. He had been free from greed for **gold**; he had not **been secretly enticed** by idolatry (kissing his **hand** toward **the sun** or **the moon**); he was without malice toward his enemies; hospitable to all; free from secret sin; and honest in his real estate dealings. If any charges against him were **written in a book**, he would be proud to **carry it** around and wear it **like a crown**!

31:38–40 At the end of chapter 31 **the words of Job are ended**. Samuel Ridout, for one, is not yet satisfied with Job's finale:

> Job's words will be rightly ended when he is ready to give praise to the One who alone is worthy of it. We are glad to be through with Job's words as uttered here.[30]

III. THE INTERVENTION OF ELIHU (Chaps. 32—37)

A. Elihu's Speech to Job's Three Friends (Chap. 32)

32:1–6 Here the conversation between **Job** and his **three** friends ceases. Normally, as we noted above, it would have been Zophar's turn to speak, but for some reason he chooses not to do so.

A **young** man named **Elihu, the son of Barachel the Buzite**, had been listening to the heated debate between **Job** and **his three** critics. Many Bible students see him as a picture of Christ, our Mediator. He seems the perfect bridge between Job's friends' analysis of his situation and the solution of Jehovah. In short, he is a middleman between men and God, a mediator to prepare for the Lord's coming on the scene.

Other commentators have less favorable views of him, viewing him as a conceited young upstart!

At any rate, Elihu (his name means *my God is He*) became incensed with **Job** for justifying **himself rather than God**. He was also angry with **his three friends** for failing to **answer** Job adequately. In these few opening verses he summarizes twenty-nine chapters of discussions.

32:7–22 In deference to their **age**, he had kept quiet and **paid close attention to** their **words**, but now he can restrain himself no longer.

He says that **great men** (or **men of many years**, NKJV marg.) are **not always wise**, and that God can give insight to a younger man like himself. He blames Job's critics for not coming up with convincing arguments. Because of their failure, he is compelled from **within** to **speak** and he will do so without **partiality** or flattery.

B. Elihu's Speech to Job (Chap. 33)

33:1–7 Elihu, using the word **"please,"** calls for Job's attention because he is going to speak **words** of sincerity and truth. Job had desired the opportunity to vindicate himself before God. Now Elihu, though a mortal **formed out of clay** like himself, is serving as Job's **spokesman before God**, and Job can make his defense, if he wishes, without **fear** of divine wrath.

33:8–18 Elihu rebukes Job for the way in which he had professed absolute innocence, and for blaming God for unjust treatment. **God is greater than man**, and **does not** have to **give an accounting of . . . His** dealings with man. However, **God** does **speak** to people through dreams and nocturnal visions to warn them against evil and **pride** and to save them from violent death.

33:19–30 The Lord also speaks through **pain** and serious illness, when even **succulent food** seems revolting. **If . . . a messenger** or **a mediator** explains God's way of **uprightness** (and if the sufferer responds in faith), **God** saves **him from going down to the Pit** on the basis of an acceptable **ransom**. Elihu does not explain what he means by a **ransom**, but we are justified in linking it with the One "who gave Himself a ransom for all" (1 Tim. 2:6). When a person responds to the Lord's voice, says Elihu, then he is restored to physical health and spiritual well-being. It is the one who confesses his sin who is redeemed from spiritual and/or physical death.

33:31–33 **If . . . Job** wants to **speak**, he should do so. **If not**, he should continue to **listen** carefully, holding his **peace** while Elihu teaches him **wisdom**.

C. Elihu's Second Speech to Job's Three Friends (Chap. 34)

34:1–15 **Elihu** next asks the three friends to test his **words** as they would taste **food**. He quotes Job's claim that God was unfair in causing a **righteous** man like him to suffer, and that there is no use being pious in order to please God. He then insists that **God** is never guilty of injustice. **If He** were to withdraw **Himself**, His creatures **would** utterly **perish**.

34:16–30 If it is inappropriate to tell **a king** or a noble that he is **wicked** or **worthless**, how much more unthinkable to condemn the Sovereign of the universe who is completely impartial! No wickedness can be hidden from God; **He strikes** down the evil and delivers the oppressed.

34:31–37 Apparently addressing Job, Elihu next counsels him to confess and forsake his sin, and to stop demanding God to do what he wants. **Job** has been talking ignorance, speaking evil, spewing forth **rebellion**, **sin**, and a multitude of **words against God**.

D. Elihu's Second Speech to Job (Chaps. 35—37)

35:1–8 **Elihu** then reproves Job for claiming to act **more** righteously **than** God and for saying that **righteousness** does not pay. Man's **sin** does not harm the sovereign God, neither does his righteousness benefit God.

35:9–16 Proud oppressors **cry out** in trouble, but they do not acknowledge the **God** who gave them wisdom above that of animals and **birds**; therefore their prayers are **not** answered. Even if we **do not see Him**, God does see *us*, and we should trust Him and not be arrogant.

36:1–12 In Elihu's fourth speech, he professes to draw from deep truths to defend the **justice** of God and to explain suffering. The Lord is eminently just in dealing with the wicked and the oppressed as well as **the righteous** (vv. 7–9), whether they are **kings . . . on the throne** or prisoners **in fetters**. If **righteous** men **have acted defiantly, He seeks to bring them to repentance by convincing them** of **their . . . transgressions**. **If they obey and serve Him**, He prospers them. **If they** don't, **they . . . perish by the sword** and **without** the **knowledge** of God.

36:13–21 If Job had been submissive and contrite, the Lord **would have** delivered him **out of** his **dire distress**, but because he was stubbornly self-righteous, he suffers **the** same **judgment** as **the hypocrites**. Elihu warns him that if he continues, he will suffer a fate from which **a large ransom** will **not** deliver him. (Verse 18 is a needed warning for sinners in all ages.)

36:22–33 Because **God** is all-wise, Job should **magnify** Him. His greatness is seen in His control of the **rain**, **clouds**, **thunder**, and **lightning**. We cannot fully **understand** the magnitude of His providential dealings, but we know that they portend grace to His people. Andreae wrote long ago:

> The same storm which on the one side is sent upon the lands for punishment and destruction is at the same time appointed on the other side to bless them abundantly, and to make them fruitful. Thus even the severest judgments of God are ever to be regarded as at the same time a source out of which divine grace distils forth.[31]

37:1–13 Elihu continues to delve into various realms of nature to show the wisdom, power, awesome majesty, and golden splendor of **God**. His descriptions of nature, of a thunderstorm with its **heavy rain**, or of the **whirlwind**, **snow**, **gentle rain**, **cold . . . winds of the north**, **thick** and **bright clouds**, or **bright** sunlight, are classic.

37:14–23 Elihu ends with a direct appeal: **"Listen to this, O Job, stand still and consider the wondrous works of God."** He goes on to challenge Job's knowledge of nature: how **the clouds** are **balanced** and why he gets **hot** when the **southwind blows**. These lead up to the similar, but even more challenging, nature questions that the Creator Himself will pose to Job in the next main section of the book. Such **excellent . . . power** surpasses our feeble comprehension. It is best to **fear** the Lord and to submit to His discipline, and not to be like Job, criticizing Him as unfair.

37:24 Elihu's last verse is the application to Job, a concise conclusion to the whole matter. The first line of verse 24 is easy to understand; the second is difficult in the NKJV (and other versions). Francis Andersen translates the second line differently by taking the negative word in Hebrew in this construction as an assertion rather than a negation:

Therefore men fear Him;
Surely all wise of heart fear Him![32]

IV. THE REVELATION OF THE LORD (38:1—42:6)

A. The Lord's First Challenge to Job (38:1—40:2)

1. *Introductory (38:1–3)*

The Lord Himself now answers **Job out of the whirlwind**, a not uncommon vehicle for an appearance of God in the OT. God's words are a welcome relief after the strife of words in the previous chapters. Job had been darkening **counsel by words without knowledge**, that is, he had been foolishly questioning the justice of God's dealings with him. Now the Lord will do the questioning, and it is time for Job to get ready to **answer**!

In the questions that follow, God does not give a detailed explanation of the mystery of suffering. Instead He ranges through the universe to give glimpses of His majesty, glory, wisdom, and power. He is saying, in effect, "Before you take it on yourself to criticize My ways, you should ask yourself if you could manage the creation as well as I do." This, of course, can only show Job how powerless, ignorant, insignificant, inadequate, incompetent, and finite he is.

We have here, as Ridout points out, the voice of the Lord:

> We are no longer listening to the gropings of the natural mind, as in the discourses of the friends; nor to the wild cries of a wounded faith, as in Job; nor even to the clear, sober language of Elihu—we are in the presence of Jehovah Himself, who speaks to us.[33]

As we listen to the Lord's questions, we have a recurring suspicion that they might be *allegorical*, that is, that they might have a deeper spiritual meaning, and that even the order of the questions might have significance. In the meantime, we see through a glass darkly.

Some might proudly say that, thanks to modern science, we know the answers to many of the questions that God asks. In response to that, Baron Alexander Humboldt acknowledged that

> what Job could not answer, the men of science cannot answer yet. It is overwhelming to them; because although men of science are very clever about secondary causes, they are always stopped by primary causes. They never can arrive at the great cause, and they do not want the great cause.[34]

2. *The Challenge of the Wonders of Inanimate Creation (38:4–38)*

38:4–7 In poetic words of unsurpassed beauty, the Lord mentions the creation of the world when He **laid the foundations of the earth**, its measurements, its survey, its support (suspended in space, of course), and the angelic celebration. Then He asks, **"Where were you when** all this took place?"

38:8–11 Moving from cosmology to geography and oceanography, He describes how He restricted **the sea** to its assigned shores, forbade further intrusion, and clothed the waters, as if they were a baby, **with clouds** and **thick darkness**.

38:12–18 Next He vividly pictures His control of **the morning**—the light of **dawn** streaking across the heavens, illuminating everywhere it goes; unmasking **the wicked** who operate in darkness, as if by shaking them out; revealing the configuration of earth's surface, as if it had been stamped out **like clay under a seal**; and bringing out the colors of the landscape as if it were a beautiful garment. Darkness, which is the preferred **"light"** of **the wicked, is withheld from** them and their evil plots are frustrated. He challenges Job to tell what he knows about the depths of the ocean, the realm **of death**, and **the breadth** of **the earth**.

38:19–24 God now cross-examines Job on the origin and nature of **light**. The sun is not a sufficient answer, because there was light (Gen. 1:3) before the sun was put in place (Gen. 1:16). Was Job old enough to know the answer? And what does he know about **snow** and **hail**, which God sometimes harnesses in times of trouble and war? How do **light** and **the east wind**, which seem to come from a point, spread **over the** surface of **the earth**?

38:25–30 Next, in a class on weather, Job is quizzed on rainfall and thunder, on how water falls on a desert, causing it to produce luxuriant growth, and on the source of **rain**, **dew**, ice, and **frost**. How is it that water freezes hard as **stone** and solidifies **the surface of the deep**?

38:31–33 No science is so calculated to show man his insignificance as astronomy. So God questions Job on his ability to control the stars and constellations, or keep them in their orbits, or determine their influence **over the earth**.

In light of modern man's supposedly great control over nature through science, Spurgeon's words, based on the KJV text of verse 31, are a healthful counterbalance:

> "Canst thou bind the sweet influences of Pleiades, or loose the bands of Orion?"—Job xxxviii. 31.
>
> If inclined to boast of our abilities, the grandeur of nature may soon show us how puny we are. We cannot move the least of all the twinkling stars, or quench so much as one of the beams of the morning. We speak of power, but the heavens laugh us to scorn. When the Pleiades shine forth in spring with vernal joy we cannot restrain their influences, and when Orion reigns aloft, and the year is bound in winter's fetters, we cannot relax the icy bands. The seasons revolve according to the divine appointment, neither can the whole race of men effect a change therein. Lord, what is man?[35]

38:34–38 Obviously, anyone who can question the wisdom and power of God should be able to bring down rain by shouting **to the clouds**, and command lightning so that it obeys instantly! Can Job tell God how **the mind** operates, how man gets **wisdom** and **understanding** in all these areas?[36] No man has the **wisdom** to **number the clouds**, to say nothing of the particles of moisture by which they are formed. And no one can determine the time when the rain falls on arid ground that has been hardened into **clumps** and **clods**.

3. *The Challenge of the Wonders of Animate Creation (38:39—40:2)*

38:39–41 God now moves from the *inanimate creation* to the *animate*. By continued questions, He reminds Job of His providence—how He opens His hand and satisfies **the appetite** of every living thing, from kingly **lions in their dens** and **lairs** to the unprepossessing **raven** and **its young ones**.

39:1–8 Job is reminded that no one but God knows fully the gestation periods, the birth habits, and the instincts of **the wild mountain goats** and **the deer. The wild donkey** (also called **onager**) scorns restraint, **city** life, and harness, but roams at will over the desert and mountain ranges searching for **every green thing**.

39:9–18 The wild ox also rejects a life of service in plowing or transporting. And what about **the ostrich** with her unusual **wings**? In some ways she acts foolishly, laying **her eggs** in places where they are vulnerable, and treating **her young harshly**. Yet she can outrun the race **horse and its rider**!

39:19–25 God next asks Job if he gave **strength** to the war **horse**, or **clothed his neck with thunder** (or **a mane**, NKJV marg.). Majestic and unafraid, devouring **distance with fierceness and rage**, this proud animal eagerly **gallops into** the **battle** in utter disregard of **shouting, trumpet**, or **glittering spears and javelin**.

39:26–30 Did Job give **wisdom** to **the hawk** to migrate **south**? And was he the one who taught **the eagle** to fly, to nest on the high rocky **crag**, to spy out carrion from a great distance, and to train **its young ones** to find their food?

40:1, 2 Again **the Lord** rebukes **Job** for his impertinence in finding fault with **the Almighty**. If he is so wise and powerful, surely he should be able to answer the catalog of questions that he has just heard!

B. Job's Response (40:3–5)

The Lord asks **Job** if he has any right to **correct** or rebuke Him in the realm of providence when he knows so little about the natural creation. With this, **Job** at last takes his proper place, saying, **"Behold, I am vile; what shall I answer You? I lay my hand over my mouth."** Overwhelmed by the wide-ranging knowledge of the Lord, he determines to say no more.

C. The Lord's Second Challenge to Job (40:6—41:34)

1. Job Challenged to Respond Like a Man (40:6–14)

But Job's response comes somewhat short of repentance, so **the Lord** continues to remonstrate with him **out of the whirlwind**. He challenges Job to speak up **like a man**. After all, Job had accused God of injustice, and condemned Him in order to justify himself. Now then, let him play the part of deity by displaying omnipotence and by speaking **in thunder**. Let him take the throne, clothing himself with **majesty, splendor, glory, and beauty**. Let him pour out his **wrath** on the guilty and humble the **proud**. If he can do all these things, then the Lord will acknowledge his power to be his own deliverer.

2. Job Challenged to Consider Behemoth (40:15–24)

Next the Lord challenges Job to consider **behemoth, which** He **made along with** Job. This rules out the notion of some commentators that behemoth and Leviathan are *mythological* creatures well known in ancient time. What challenge can a nonexistent creature be to a created being such as man?

The word behemoth is simply the plural form of the common Hebrew word for cattle (*behēmah*). Meredith Kline explains:

> The designation **behemoth**, taken as a plural intensive, "the beast par excellence," would be an epithet like chief of the ways of God (v. 19a). Note the similar supreme claims made for leviathan (41:33, 34).[37]

God presents **the behemoth** as **the first of** His **ways**, that is, as Exhibit A in the animal kingdom. Although we cannot identify it with certainty, we know that it is herbivorous, amphibian, and exceedingly powerful. It rests in shady, marshy areas and is not easily intimidated. The lesson is that if Job can't even control this brute, how can he control the world?

The behemoth is sometimes identified with the hippopotamus,[38] and some translations, such as the Louis Segond translation in French, actually put that animal in the text. But by no stretch of the imagination can the hippopotamus be called "the first of the ways of God"—an elephant or a mammoth might merit that epithet perhaps, but hardly a hippo! When children go to the zoo they squeal with glee at the cute, stubby tail of the hippo—hardly **a tail like a cedar**!

Some Christian scientists are now convinced that the behemoth must be an animal now extinct, or perhaps found in some remote parts of the African jungle. In fact, a reptile of the dinosaur type does fit the description very closely.[39]

3. Job Challenged to Consider Leviathan (Chap. 41)

God has not answered Job's complaints directly. Rather, He has just been saying in effect, "You should be able to trust the wisdom, love, and power of One who is so great, so majestic, so glorious."

41:1–9 Another awesome amphibious creature is **Leviathan**, unique in the creation of God. Can Job harness him? God wants to know. "Touch him once and you'll never try it again; you will never forget the fight" (v. 8 TEV). The term **Leviathan** in ancient Canaanite literature referred to "a seven-headed sea dragon," but as Andersen points out, this "does not prove that Leviathan is still a mythological monster in this poem."[40]

In English we use words like *Thursday, January*, and *hell* with no belief whatever in the pagan literary origins of the *words themselves*. Usage must determine meaning, and here God clearly challenges Job to consider a real creature, even if we can't be positive today which one it was. A popular choice is the Nile crocodile, and several parts of the description do fit that reptile well.

While the behemoth is primarily a *land* creature, Leviathan is primarily *aquatic*. Man cannot catch him with **hook** and **line**. Or domesticate him or make him a family pet. He is not considered a **banquet** delicacy. His armor-like exterior resists **harpoons** and **spears**, and **the sight of him** discourages meddling with him.

41:10, 11 God interrupts the description to ask a pertinent question: If men stand in such awe of a mere creature, how much more should they fear Him who created the creature, who is eternal, who is obligated to no one, and who is Owner and Creator of all? Kline comments:

> Here indeed is the point of the passage: Job is to discover from his inability to vanquish even a fellow creature the folly of aspiring to the Creator's throne.[41]

41:12–34 Back to Leviathan. His build is massive and **his mighty power** is enormous. His hide is a tough, protective covering. He cannot be bridled. His mouth and **teeth** are viselike. His skin and **scales** resemble armor with overlapping plates. In poetic terms, the Lord describes his sneezes, **eyes**, **mouth**, and **nostrils** as terrifying when he is aroused. Leviathan's strength is tremendous and his flesh compacted. While he himself is fearless, he fills the stoutest hearts with fear as he thrashes around, and normal weapons bounce off his hide. When he crawls through the mud, he leaves a trail of pointed marks, as if his underside was broken glass. He whips the water into a boiling **pot**, leaving a white phosphorescent **wake**. Even making ample allowance for the Oriental use of great poetic exaggeration (hyperbole), it is hard to see how even the largest crocodile could be called **"king over all the children of pride."**[42]

The descriptions of the wild animals and possibly dinosaurs in these chapters *reflect* the glory, power, and majesty of God Himself. They are His creation, and He purposely uses them to illustrate His own splendor and strength. Therefore, it is not surprising that He begins with harmless creatures such as the deer and the raven and gradually increases in size to the greatest of all creatures, the *behemoth* on land, and the king of all beasts—Leviathan of the sea, which was unbelievably awesome in its reputation.

D. Job's Humble Response (42:1–6)

Job is overwhelmed. He has had enough! He acknowledes the sovereignty of God. He confesses that he has spoken unadvisedly with his lips. Now that he has not only **heard** the Lord but his **eye** has seen Him, he hates himself and repents **in dust and ashes**. He did not see God visually,[43] of course, but he had such a vivid revelation of His wisdom, power, providence, and sovereignty that it was tantamount to a sight of the great God.

In Job 1:1 Job is called "blameless." Here at the end of the book he abhors himself. This has been the experience of the choicest of God's saints through the ages.[44] The more one grows in grace, writes D. L. Moody, "the meaner he is in his own eyes."[45]

V. EPILOGUE: THE TRIUMPH OF JOB (42:7–17)

A. Job's Friends Rebuked and Restored (42:7–9)

The Lord then reprimands **Eliphaz** and his **two friends**[46] for misrepresenting Him. They had insisted that all suffering is punishment for sin. That was not true in Job's case. In obedience to the divine command, they then offered a huge **burnt offering (seven bulls and seven rams)**. Job served as mediator by praying **for his friends**, and as a result judgment on them was averted and Job was accepted.

B. Job's Prosperity Restored (42:10–17)

42:10–12 As soon as Job prayed for them, the Lord restored in inverse order twice as much as Job **had before**: **twice as** many **sheep**, **camels**, **oxen**, and **female donkeys**.

42:13–17 **He also** received **seven sons and three daughters**, which doubled his family, since he presumably still *had* the first ones in heaven. **Job lived** an additional **one hundred and forty years**. **The Lord blessed the latter days of Job more than his beginning**. So **Job died, old and full of days**. And in all this, Job had not cursed God as Satan said he would.

It is a lovely touch of God's grace

that Job, who had been so hideously disfigured by his disease, after his restoration had **daughters** who were exceptionally **beautiful** (fathers love to boast of their lovely daughters!). The meanings of their names are instructive[47]: **Jemimah** (*dove*); **Keziah** (*cassia*, a fragrant *cinnamon bark*); and **Keren-Happuch** (*horn of eye-makeup*[48]). Job also gave them an inheritance with their *brothers*, probably not a common practice in the patriarchal era.

VI. CONCLUSION: LESSONS FROM THE BOOK OF JOB

Actually, the mystery of human suffering is not fully explained. As Wesley Baker puts it:

> When the end of the Book of Job comes, there is no answer written out. There is nothing there that would satisfy the logical mind![49]

However, we can be sure of these two facts:

First of all, Job's suffering was not a direct result of his personal sin. God testified that he was a perfect and an upright man (1:8). Also, God said that the reasoning of Job's three friends—that God was punishing him because of his sins—was not right (42:8).

Secondly, although Job was not suffering because he had sinned, yet his trials *did reveal* pride, self-justification, and animosity in his heart. He was not delivered until he had a vision of his own nothingness and of God's greatness (42:1–6), and until he prayed for his friends (42:10).

Some of the lessons we learn about suffering from the book of Job are:

1. The righteous are not exempt from suffering.
2. Suffering is not necessarily a result of sin.
3. God has set a protective hedge around the righteous.
4. God does not send sickness or suffering. It comes from Satan (Luke 13:16; 2 Cor. 12:7).
5. Satan has some control in the realm of wicked men (the Sabeans and Chaldeans), supernatural disasters (fire from heaven), weather (a great wind), sickness (the boils on Job), death.
6. Satan can bring these things on a believer *only by God's permission*.
7. What God permits, He often is said to do. "Shall we receive good at the hands of the Lord and shall we not receive evil (adversity)."
8. We should *view* things as coming from the Lord, by His permission, and not from Satan. "The Lord gave, and the Lord has taken away."
9. God does not always explain the reason for our suffering.
10. Suffering develops endurance.
11. In visiting suffering saints, we should not be judgmental.
12. We should make our visits brief.
13. Human reasonings aren't helpful. Only God can comfort perfectly.
14. At the end of the book of Job we see that "the Lord is very compassionate and merciful" (Jas. 5:11). We also learn that *sometimes*, at least, wrongs are made right in this life.
15. Job's patience in suffering vindicated God.
16. Job's patience proved Satan to be a false accuser and liar.
17. "A man is greater than the things that surround him and,

whatever may befall his possessions or his family, God is just as truly to be praised and trusted as before."

18. We should be careful about making blanket statements that do not allow for exceptions.
19. Satan is neither omnipresent, omnipotent, nor omniscient.
20. In spite of God's allowing unmerited suffering, He is still just and good.

From other parts of the Bible, we get further light on some of the reasons why God allows His saints to suffer:

1. Sometimes it is a result of unjudged sin in the life (1 Cor. 11:32).
2. It is a means by which God develops spiritual graces, such as patience, longsuffering, humility (Rom. 5:3, 4; John 15:2).
3. It purges dross or impurities from the believer's life so that the Lord can see His image reflected more perfectly (Isa. 1:25).
4. It enables the child of God to comfort others with the same type of comfort with which God comforted him or her (2 Cor. 1:4).
5. It enables the saint to share in the non-atoning sufferings of the Savior and thus to be more grateful to Him (Phil. 3:10).
6. It is an object lesson to beings in heaven and on earth (2 Thess. 1:4–6). It shows them that God can be *loved for Himself alone*, and not just because of the favors He bestows.
7. It is an assurance of sonship since God only chastens those whom He loves (Heb. 12:7–11).
8. It causes saints to trust in God alone and not in our own strength (2 Cor. 1:9).
9. It keeps God's people close to Himself (Ps. 119:67).
10. It is a pledge of future glory (Rom. 8:17, 18).
11. God never allows us to be tempted above what we are able to bear (1 Cor. 10:13).

"You have heard of the perseverance of Job and seen the end intended by the Lord—that the Lord is very compassionate and merciful" (Jas. 5:11b).

ENDNOTES

[1](Intro) Samuel Ridout, *Job: An Exposition*, p. 5.

[2](Intro) Genesis 1—11 is generally dated from about 2000 B.C. and much earlier as one traces back through the genealogies.

[3](1:1–3) "Others support an identification with the region E. of Edom in N. Arabia" (*The Revell Bible Dictionary*, ed. by Lawrence O. Richards, p. 1138).

[4](1:4, 5) Charles Haddon Spurgeon, *Morning and Evening*, p. 721.

[5](1:6–12) In the Semitic languages "sons of God" was a standard term for angels.

[6](2:1–10) Harold St. John, *Job, The Lights and Shadows of Eternity*, p. 9.

[7](Chaps. 3—31:Intro) Ridout, *Job*, p. 33.

[8](Chaps. 3—31:Intro) The *New Scofield Study Bible, New King James Version*, p. 595.

[9](Chaps. 3—31:Intro) *Ibid.*, p. 598.

[10](Chaps. 4,5:Intro) Ridout, *Job*, pp. 43, 44.

[11](Chap. 8:Intro) *Ibid.*, p. 64.

[12](9:32–35) Matthew Henry, "Job," in *Matthew Henry's Commentary on the Whole Bible*, III:59.

[13](10:8–12) St. John, *Job*, p. 17.

[14](11:1–12) Ridout, *Job*, p. 31.

[15](13:20–28) Francis I. Andersen, *Job: An Introduction and Commentary*, p. 163.

[16](14:13–17) St. John, *Job*, pp. 17, 18.

[17](15:14–16) Ridout, *Job*, p. 84.

[18](19:25–27) Spurgeon, *Morning and Evening*, Devotion for April 21, Morning.

[19](19:25–27) *Ibid.*, p. 21.

[20](20:20–29) G. Campbell Morgan, *Searchlights from the Word*, p. 145.

[21](22:21–30) Albert Barnes, "Job," in *Notes on the Old Testament*, II:3.

[22](23:1–9) Spurgeon, *Morning and Evening*, Devotion for November 19, Evening.

[23](24:1–12) Ridout, *Job*, p. 124.

[24](24:18–25) Andersen, *Job*, p. 213.

[25](24:18–25) *Ibid.*

[26](Chap. 25:Intro) Ridout, *Job*, p. 127.

[27](26:5–13) *Ibid.*, pp. 133, 134.

[2]8 (28:1–11) Andersen, *Job*, p. 225.

[29](28:1–11) *Ibid.*

[30](31:38–40) Ridout, *Job*, p. 169.

[31](36:22–33) Quoted by Otto Zöckler, "The Book of Job," in *Lange's Commentary on the Holy Scriptures*, IV:596.

[32](37:24) Andersen, *Job*, p. 268.

[33](38:1–3) Ridout, *Job*, pp. 210, 211.

[34](38:1–3) Cited by William Kelly in *Eleven Lectures on the Book of Job*, p. 278.

[35](38:31–33) Spurgeon, *Morning and Evening*, Devotion for March 21, Evening.

[36](38:34–38) Because verse 36 seems to interrupt the discussion of weather phenomena in verses 34–38, many other translations have been suggested. The Hebrew is admittedly difficult.

[37](40:15–24) Meredith G. Kline, "Job," in *Wycliffe Bible Commentary*, p. 488.

[38](40:15–24) For example, Barnes used the following description to make the text fit a hippopotamus: "The huge head of the animal, from the prominency of its eyes, the great breadth of its muzzle, and the singular way in which the jaw is placed in the head, is almost grotesque in its ugliness. When it opens its jaws, its enormously large mouth and tongue, pinkish and fleshly, and armed with tusks of most formidable character, is particularly striking" ("Job," II:247, 248). The problem with this depiction is that while Barnes's description of the *hippopotamus* is good, the tusks, fleshy pink mouth, etc., are not found in *Job!* Also, neither the jaw, head, nor muzzle of the behemoth (ch. 40) is described in Scripture.

[39](40:15–24) See Ken Ham, "What Happened to the Dinosaurs?" *ANSWERS to Some of the Most Asked Questions on Creation/Evolution* (Sunnybank, Australia: Creation Science Foundation Ltd., 1986). See also Henry Morris, *The Remarkable Record of Job* (Grand Rapids: Baker Book House, 1990).

[40](41:1–9) Andersen, *Job*, p. 289.

[41](41:10, 11) Kline, "Job," p. 488.

[42](41:12–34) *Leviathan* may have been an ocean-dwelling dinosaur. The description of the reptile with its four giant flippers and a very long neck could be the "plesiosaurus," an enormous aquatic but believed-to-be extinct reptile. The descriptions in Job 41 are consistent with this creature or similar sea-dinosaur. The famous "Loch Ness Monster" description also fits the *plesiosaurus*.

[43](42:1–6) It is possible that God appeared in a *theophany* to Job, a visible manifestation of God's glory.

[44](42:1–6) Some other biblical figures who sensed their own wretched sinfulness in God's presence include

Moses (Ex. 3:6); Isaiah (Isa. 6:5); Peter (Luke 5:8); Paul (Acts 9:4); and John (Rev. 1:17).

[45](42:1–6) Moody, *Notes from My Bible*, p. 62.

[46](42:7–9) It is interesting to notice that Elihu, the fourth man to address Job, is not rebuked. Furthermore he is not mentioned again in the book. His advice was apparently correct, and perhaps was used as a "transition" between the friends' bad advice and God's majestic answer to Job. This may also fit in with the afore-mentioned theory that Elihu was a type of Christ.

[47](42:13–17) Ridout believes that the names have "divine significance. . . . These are the fruit of Job's trials. The dove, suggesting the gentleness and love of the bird of sorrow. Cassia, telling of the fragrance that has come from his bruising; and the horn of cosmetic, of the 'beauty for ashes' that is now his. Love, fragrance, beauty—these come of our sorrows. Truly there are no daughters so fair as these" (*Job*, pp. 263, 264).

[48](42:13–17) The ancient women emphasized their eyes with makeup more than their lips. All this illustrates Solomon's words that "There is nothing new under the sun"!

[49](Conclu) Wesley C. Baker, *More Than a Man Can Take: A Study of Job*, p. 128.

BIBLIOGRAPHY

Andersen, Francis I. *Job: An Introduction and Commentary*. London: Inter-Varsity Press, 1976.

Baker, Wesley C. *More Than a Man Can Take: A Study of Job*. Philadelphia: The Westminster Press, 1966.

Delitzsch, F. "The Book of Job." In *Biblical Commentary on the Old Testament*. Vol. 9, 10. Reprint. Grand Rapids: Eerdmans Publishing Co., 1971.

Green, William Henry. *The Argument of the Book of Job*. Reprint. Minneapolis, MN: James & Klock Christian Publishers, 1977.

Ham, Ken. "What Happened to the Dinosaurs?" *Answers to Some of the Most Asked Questions on Creation/ Evolution*. Sunnybank, Australia: Creation Science Foundation Ltd., 1986.

Kelly, William. *Eleven Lectures on the Book of Job*. Reprint. Denver: Wilson Foundation, n.d.

Kline, Meredith G. "Job." In *Wycliffe Bible Commentary*. Chicago: Moody Press, 1962.

Minn, H. R. *The Burden of this Unintelligible World* or *The Mystery of Suffering*. Auckland, New Zealand: Whitcombe & Tombs Limited, 1942.

Morris, Henry. *The Remarkable Record of Job*. Grand Rapids: Baker Book House, 1990.

Ridout, Samuel. *The Book of Job: An Exposition*. Seventh Printing. Neptune, NJ: Loizeaux Brothers, 1976.

St. John, Harold. *Job, The Lights and Shadows of Eternity* (pamphlet). New York: Bible Scholar, n.d.

Zöckler, Otto. "The Book of Job." In *Lange's Commentary on the Holy Scriptures*. Vol. 4. Grand Rapids: Zondervan Publishing House, Reprint, 1960.

THE BOOK OF PSALMS

Introduction

"I may truly call this book an anatomy of all parts of the soul, for no one can feel a movement of the spirit which is not reflected in this mirror. All the sorrows, troubles, fears, doubts, hopes, pains, perplexities and stormy outbreaks by which the hearts of men are tossed have been depicted here to the very life."

—John Calvin

I. Unique Place in the Canon

If you were to be marooned on a desert island with only one book of the Bible, which one would you choose?

Frankly, I hope I never have to make this choice, but if I had to, I think I would choose the Psalms! Their range of subjects is so vast, their catalog of life's experiences so full and their worship so exalted that I would be well supplied with rich spiritual food and powerful fuel for praise and prayer for a long time to come.

Our opening quotation shows that Calvin would probably have chosen the Psalms, too.

Graham Scroggie would probably also have cast his vote for the Psalms. He said:

> How full of praise to God are these Psalms! The Keyboard of Creation, Providence and Redemption are all swept by the ecstatic soul; and heaven and earth, sea and sky, things animate and things inanimate are summoned to praise the Lord.[1]

When first studying the Psalms we are often frustrated at our inability to find an orderly flow of thought in certain Psalms. It seems that the continuity is sometimes erratic, sometimes veiled and sometimes completely missing. Two observations by Albert Barnes and C. S. Lewis may help us. Barnes said:

> The Psalms are mostly lyrical poetry, that is, poetry adapted to the harp or lyre; to be used in connection with instrumental music; to be *sung*, not *read*.[2]

Lewis similarly explained:

> Most emphatically the Psalms must be read as poems; as lyrics, with all the licenses and all the formalities, the hyperboles, the emotional rather than logical connections, which are proper to lyric poetry.[3]

These insights can open up a whole new window of understanding for us.

II. Authorship

The Psalms are often called "The Psalms of David," but only about half (seventy-three) are directly attributed to the "sweet singer of Israel." Twelve are attributed to Asaph, ten to the sons of Korah, two to Solomon, and one each to Moses, Ethan, Heman, and Ezra. Forty-nine, or nearly one third, of the Psalms are anonymous.

When we think of the Psalms,

Psalm	Portrayal	Fulfilled
2:7	The Son of God	Matthew 3:17
8:2	Praised by children	Matthew 21:15, 16
8:6	Ruler of all	Hebrews 2:8
16:10	Rises from death	Matthew 28:7
22:1	Forsaken by God	Matthew 27:46
22:7, 8	Derided by enemies	Luke 23:35
22:16	Hands and feet pierced	John 20:27
22:18	Lots cast for clothes	Matthew 27:35, 36
34:20	Bones unbroken	John 19:32, 33, 36
35:11	Accused by false witnesses	Mark 14:57
35:19	Hated without cause	John 15:25
40:7, 8	Delights in God's will	Hebrews 10:7
41:9	Betrayed by a friend	Luke 22:47
45:6	The eternal King	Hebrews 1:8
68:18	Ascends to heaven	Acts 1:9–11
69:9	Zealous for God's house	John 2:17
69:21	Given vinegar and gall	Matthew 27:34
109:4	Prays for enemies	Luke 23:34
109:8	His betrayer replaced	Acts 1:20
110:1	Rules over His enemies	Matthew 22:44
110:4	A priest forever	Hebrews 5:6
118:22	The chief stone of God's building	Matthew 21:42
118:26	Comes in the name of the Lord	Matthew 21:9

The Messianic Psalms

however, we usually do so in connection with the life of David. An unknown author expresses this beautifully:

> The harp of David still sounds in our ears, and the Holy Ghost has crystallized for us the prayers and praises of the son of Jesse. Someone said that architecture was music frosted. The Psalms are the music of the heart, sometimes plaintive and sad, sometimes joyous and jubilant, sometimes full of darkness and anguish, sometimes tranquil and happy, the music of David's soul, preserved by the Spirit that, hearing it, we may feel encouraged to draw nigh to God.

III. Date

The Psalms were written over a period of about a thousand years, from Moses to Ezra (about 1400–400 B.C.). However, most of them were written during the three hundred years from David to Hezekiah (about 1000–700 B.C.). Thus, the Psalter was written over the same period of time as the whole OT (although Job may pre-date Moses).

IV. Background and Themes

The Psalms are divided into five books, each of which closes with a doxology. The doxology for Book 5 is the entire 150th Psalm.

F. W. Grant suggests that the Psalms are grouped according to subject matter.[4] He summarizes each of the five books of the Psalms, found in the Hebrew Bible, as follows:

1. Christ in the counsel of God, the source of all blessing for His people Israel (Pss. 1—41).
2. Their ruin, but redemption in the latter days (Pss. 42—72).
3. The holiness of God in His dealings with them (Pss. 73—89).
4. The failed first man replaced by the Second, and the world established under His hand (Pss. 90—106).
5. The moral conclusion as to the divine ways in which God and man are found at last together (Pss. 107—150).

There may also be a parallel between these five divisions and the books of the Pentateuch. For example, the second division fits the redemption from Egypt; the third matches Leviticus in its emphasis on holiness.

The Psalms themselves may be divided into classifications, although certain Psalms may fit more than one of these classes:

1. Historical—connected with some definite event or events in Israel's history or in the life of the psalmist.
2. Messianic—dealing with the sufferings of Christ and the glories that should follow.
3. Prophetic or Millennial—pointing forward to Israel's future tribulation and the subsequent era of peace and prosperity.
4. Penitential—recording the psalmist's deep confession of sins and his broken-hearted cries for forgiveness.
5. Imprecatory—imploring God to take vengeance on the enemies of His people.

Many other Psalms are expressions of individual or communal praise and worship to God, and still others are

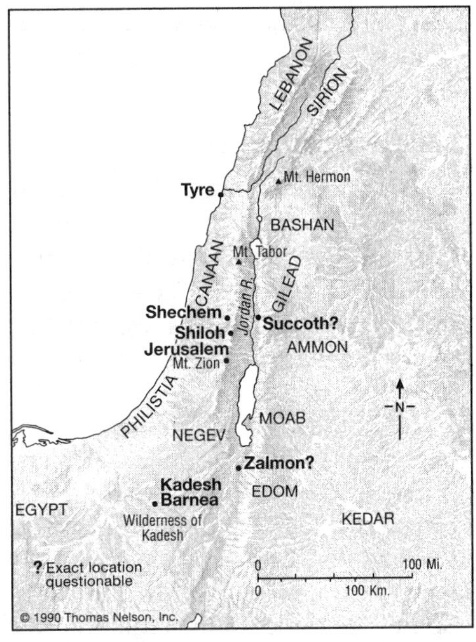

Places Named in the Psalms

narratives of the Lord's dealings with His people.

Interpreting the Psalms

The distinction between Israel and the church is maintained throughout the *Believers Bible Commentary*. Many of the Psalms, especially the ones which call down curses on the wicked, were entirely appropriate for Jews living under the law but are not suitable language for believers of the Church Age. In this age, we are urged to *love* our enemies and to *do good* to those who despitefully use us. Unless we recognize this important dispensational difference, we will encounter severe problems in interpreting the Psalms.

Every careful reader of the Psalms quickly notices that there is a close parallel between the experiences of the psalmist, the nation of Israel, and the Lord Jesus Christ. All three experienced persecution, suffering, sorrow, hatred and abandonment—as well as exaltation, glory and jubilation. We point out these similarities frequently in the *BBC*.

Applying the Psalms

While not all of the Bible is written directly *to* the church, all Scripture is profitable *for* the church. We can find comfort, teaching, rebuke and exhortation in the Psalms as we see our own experiences mirrored in those of the psalmist.

We in the church can learn important lessons from teachings which are primarily Jewish. The Jewish temple can be considered a prefigurement of the body of Christ, made up of all believers and indwelt by the Holy Spirit. The battles in the Psalms speak to us of our spiritual warfare against principalities and powers, against the forces of darkness in the heavenly places. The material blessings of Israel on earth point us to our spiritual blessings in the heavenlies in Christ—and so forth.

If we use these keys, the Psalms become richly meaningful to us, and many of the problems in interpretation disappear.

Psalm Titles

The titles to the Psalms are very ancient and are probably part of the sacred text. However, the meaning and purpose of many of them are very obscure, and for this reason, we have omitted commenting on most of them. It would not be helpful simply to keep repeating "We do not know what this means!"

OUTLINE

I. BOOK 1 (Psalms 1—41)

II. BOOK 2 (Psalms 42—72)

III. BOOK 3 (Psalms 73—89)

IV. BOOK 4 (Psalms 90—106)

V. BOOK 5 (Psalms 107—150)

Commentary

I. BOOK 1 (PSALMS 1—41)

Psalm 1: The Good Life

The book of Psalms opens by dispelling the common illusion that the sinful life is the good life. Daily the world is being brainwashed into thinking that true and lasting satisfaction is found by indulging the lusts of the flesh. Television, radio, movies, and magazines all suggest that permissiveness is the road to fulfillment. The life of purity is dismissed as "puritanical." But the psalmist sets the record straight.

1:1 The truly **blessed** person is the one who steers clear of the lifestyle **of the ungodly**. In his contacts with them he avoids complicity with them or even tacit approval of their sin and scoffing. This does not mean that the happy man isolates himself completely from the wicked. Instead he witnesses to them of "sin, righteousness, and judgment," and seeks to introduce them to Christ, the one source of lasting pleasure. The happy man is a real friend to the ungodly, but he is not a partner with them.

1:2 It is impossible to visualize a happy man who is not also a man of God's Book. He has an insatiable hunger for the Word **of the LORD**. He loves the Bible and **meditates** on it **day and night**. By this means his own life is enriched and he becomes a channel of blessing to others.

1:3 The man who is separated from sin and separated to the Scriptures has all the qualities of a strong, healthy, fruitful **tree**:

> **Planted**[5] **by the rivers of water**—he has a never-failing supply of nourishment and refreshment.
>
> It **brings forth its fruit in its season**—he displays the graces of the Spirit, and his words and actions are always timely and appropriate.
>
> Its **leaf also shall not wither**—his spiritual life is not subject to cyclical changes but is characterized by continuous inner renewal. As D. L. Moody put it, "All the Lord's trees are evergreen."[6]

This kind of man **shall prosper** in everything he undertakes. The reason, of course, is that he is living in fellowship with the Lord, and all his service is therefore guided by the Holy Spirit. The only way to be efficient and successful in the Christian life is to be led by the Spirit of God. Self-directed activity is an enormous waste of time, money, and effort!

1:4 **The ungodly are not so**; that is, they are neither well-planted, fruitful, enduring nor prosperous. **Like chaff**, they lack body or substance. When the storms of life blow, they prove unstable. A strong **wind drives** them **away**.

1:5 **The ungodly shall not stand in the judgment**. They will, of course, appear before God at the Judgment of the Great White Throne. But the meaning here is that they will have no adequate defense. In idiomatic language, they won't have a leg to stand on! Furthermore, they will never stand **in the congregation of the righteous**; they will be forever excluded from the company of those who are saved by grace through faith in the Lord Jesus Christ.

1:6 What is the reason for all this? **The LORD knows the way of the righteous**. He is not only *aware* of their lives, but He *approves* them as well. What a contrast with the termination of a sinful life—eternal death!

We cannot emphasize too often, however, that a person's destiny is *not* determined by the way he lives. The determining factor is whether he has ever been born again by faith in Jesus Christ. The righteous person is the one who has confessed his sin and received the Lord Jesus Christ as his personal Savior. His righteous life is the *result* of his new life in Christ. **The ungodly** person is the one who refuses to acknowledge his need and to bow his knee to the Lord Jesus. He would rather keep his sin than have the Savior, and thus he seals his doom.

Psalm 2: The Unchanging Decree

To place this Psalm in its proper setting, we must look ahead to the close of the Great Tribulation, immediately prior to the glorious return and reign of our Lord Jesus Christ. At this time a vast federation of rulers and nations will unite in a passionate determination to prevent Christ from taking the reigns of world government.[7]

2:1–3 But such a federation will prove to be an exercise in futility. "**Why**," asks the psalmist, "**do the** Gentile **nations** and the Jewish **people** enter such a hopeless conspiracy? How do the Gentile **kings** and Jewish rulers think they can ever succeed in rebelling **against** the authority of **the Lord and** of **His Anointed**?"

2:4–6 God **in the heavens shall laugh** at their stupid insolence. He will mock their clenched fists and fiery slogans. Their boasts and threats are the squeaks of a mouse against a lion!

Eventually God will break His silence. When He speaks it will be in such **wrath** and fury that His enemies will be terrified. They will hear His irrevocable decision: "**I have** installed **My King on My holy hill of Zion**." Once God pronounces this decision, its fulfillment will be as certain as if it had already taken place.

2:7 Then Christ Himself will add His testimony. He will reveal that in private conversation, the Father had **said** first of all **to** Him, **"You are My Son, today I have begotten You."** This **decree** may be understood in at least four ways. First, there is a real sense in which Christ was the Son of God *from all eternity*. In Acts 13:33, however, the verse is quoted in reference to Christ's *Incarnation*. In a third sense, Christ was begotten in *Resurrection*—"the first-born from the dead" (Col. 1:18). Finally, some suggest that "this day" refers to the *future day* when Christ will be crowned as King.

2:8 But the Father also added, **"Ask of Me, and I will give You the nations for Your inheritance, and the ends of the earth for Your possession."** In other words, God the Father has promised universal dominion to His Son. All the earth will submit to His authority, and His rule will extend from shore to shore.

2:9 Finally, God has given Christ the authority to deal with all insubordination and rebellion. He **shall break . . . with a rod of iron** those who rise up against Him, shattering them **like a potter's vessel**. From other Scriptures we learn that Christ will exercise this authority both when He returns to earth and throughout His thousand-year reign. Prior to His inauguration as King, He will destroy those who do not know God and who do not obey the gospel. Then, in the Millennium, Christ will rule with a rod of iron, punishing rebellion wherever it raises its ugly head.

2:10, 11 The voice of the Holy Spirit is heard next. In a moving evangelistic appeal, He urges **kings** and rulers to love and **serve the Lord**. To refuse Him means destruction, whereas to trust Him brings safety and true happiness.

2:12 For man to trust his Creator is the most sane, logical, reasonable thing he can do. On the other hand, to disbelieve and defy the Almighty is about as irrational a thing as a person can do.

Psalm 3: A Study In Moods

If we are subject to rapidly changing moods, we can take courage from the fact that David was too! In this Psalm he sweeps the scale from dark despair to calm confidence.

3:1, 2 At the outset **David** is overawed by his enemies. Their superior numbers strike terror to his heart. What is one among so many? Then too, he is stung by their taunting jibes. They insinuate that his sin has cut him off from any hope of divine **help**.

Verse 2 closes with the enigmatical word **Selah**. Since this is the first of its seventy-one occurrences in the Psalms, we pause to comment on it. Unfortunately, our remarks will be less an explanation than a confession of ignorance! The simple fact is that *we do not know* what the word means. All we can do is list some of the meanings that have been suggested and let the reader decide which seems best.

> *Selah* may mean to intensify voices or instrumental accompaniment; that is, to sing or play louder. Crescendo!
>
> It may indicate a pause or a rest, as if to say, "Stop and think about that."
>
> "It is rendered in the Septuagint by *diapsalmos*, which either means louder playing, *forte*, or more probably, an instrumental interlude."[8]
>
> Some think it means a repetition, like *da capo*.
>
> It may mean the end of a strophe (a musical section).
>
> It may even mean the bending of the body as an act of reverence or respect.

3:3 The mood of the Psalm changes in verse 3. David gets his eyes off his enemies and on the LORD, and that changes his whole outlook. Immediately he realizes that he has in Jehovah **a shield**, a source of **glory, and the One who lifts up** his **head**. As his **shield**, the Lord gives him complete protection from enemy assaults. As his glory, the Lord gives him honor, dignity and vindication in place of the shame, reproach and slander that were being heaped upon him. As the lifter of his head, the Lord encourages and exalts him.

3:4 Inspired by these great and true thoughts of God, David goes to **the LORD** in prayer and receives immediate assurance that his petition has been heard and answered. God answers **from His holy hill**, that is, from the site of the temple in Jerusalem, the place where He dwelt among His people.

3:5, 6 Assured of Jehovah's protection, the psalmist lies down and goes to sleep. It is the sweetest kind of sleep, a gift of God to those who trust Him in the midst of life's most distressing circumstances.

After a restful night, David awakes with the consciousness that it was the Lord who had calmed the nerves that were taut with fear and foreboding. Now he has courage to face his foes unafraid, even if he is surrounded by **ten thousands of** them!

3:7 But this does not mean that prayer is no longer necessary. The grace that sustained us last night will not do for today. We need a fresh supply of God's grace every day. So David comes to the Lord for continuing deliverance, believing that God will strike his **enemies on the cheekbone** and break their **teeth**.

3:8 As far as David is concerned, Jehovah is the only One who can deliver anyone; **salvation belongs to the LORD** alone. So he asks that God will bless His **people** by continuing to show them His marvelous deliverance.

The swirling emotions of this man of God can perhaps be better understood if we look at the heading of the Psalm once more:

> "A Psalm of David, when he fled from Absalom his son."

The commander of David's enemies was *his own son*! It would have been bad enough if the adversaries were foreign invaders, but because they were led by David's rebel son, his grief and bitterness were compounded.

Psalm 4: God's Secret Tranquilizer

4:1 As David enters the Lord's presence, he addresses Him as **God of my righteousness**. This conveys the thought that the God of justice could be depended on to judge David righteously. Men may defame and blackball but God knows the true facts and will see that justice triumphs!

Then David adds, **"You have relieved me in my distress."** In Darby's *New Translation* this reads, "In pressure thou hast enlarged me." Ordinarily we think of pressure as reducing the compass or volume of its object, but God uses pressure to produce spiritual enlargement! Prosperity does little for us, but adversity produces growth and maturity. Spurgeon once said:

> I am afraid that all the grace I have got out of my comfortable and easy times and happy hours might almost lie on a penny. But the good that I have received from my sorrows and pains and griefs is altogether incalculable. What do I not owe to the hammer and the anvil, the fire and the file! Affliction is the best bit of furniture in my house.[9]

Remembering how God had answered his prayers in the past when he was under pressure, David feels free to ask God to **hear** him again.

4:2, 3 The immediate occasion for David's appeal can be deduced from verses 2–5. He was being maligned and slandered by unprincipled men. These carping critics were dragging his name in the mud, assassinating his character, and besmirching his reputation with baseless accusations and downright **falsehood**.

David asks them **how long** their mindless rage against him will continue, then reminds them that their efforts to overthrow him are futile because God Himself is on his side: **"The LORD has set apart for Himself him who is godly."** Those who trust in the Lord are as "the apple of His eye" (Zech. 2:8). Their names are engraved on the palms of His hands (Isa. 49:16). He hears them when they call and hastens to their assistance. David is thus anticipating Paul's argument in Romans 8:31: If God is for us, who can be successfully against us?

4:4 David's enemies should let their passions cool. If they must **be angry**, it should be in a righteous cause. The clause **"Be angry and do not sin"** is quoted in Ephesians 4:26, but there it is addressed to believers, reminding them that it is right to be angry *in God's cause* but never in one's own. Here in Psalm 4, of course, the words are spoken to wicked men to warn them against the overflow of anger into violent action. As they lie awake in the quietness of the night hours, they should search their own hearts and consider the stupidity of fighting against God. Such sober reflections would silence their slanderings and terminate their wicked plans.

4:5 In a bold evangelistic thrust, David counsels the wicked to combine practical **righteousness** with faith **in the LORD**. "Make justice your sacrifice" (Gelineau). But this can only be done by those who have **put** their **trust in the LORD**.

4:6 There are many who want prosperity and happiness. They are continually yearning to see some **good**. But the trouble is that they want blessing without the Blesser, and good without God. They want all the benefits of a Christ-filled life but they don't want the Benefactor.

In contrast to them, David goes straight to the Fountainhead of all good with the words, **"LORD, lift up the light of Your countenance upon us."**

4:7 His **gladness** in the Lord far exceeds the joy of the ungodly when their silos bulge with grain and their casks overflow with wine. "Never did rich harvests of corn and wine bring gladness like the gladness Thou puttest into my heart" (Knox).

4:8 Reassured of the Lord's all-sufficiency, the psalmist's inner agitation subsides. He can now **lie down in peace and sleep**, knowing that it is the **LORD** who makes him **dwell in safety**. What a change prayer has produced in only eight short verses!

Psalm 5: Morning Prayer

The heading of Psalm 5 reads:
To the chief musician; with flutes. A Psalm of David.

Since many of the Psalms have titles somewhat similar to this, we should mention again that many scholars believe that these superscriptions are part of the inspired text. In some versions of the Bible (following the original Hebrew), the titles are included as verse one. Some scholars think the headings actually belong at the end of each preceding Psalm, but the evidence for this is not convincing. The big problem with these titles is that the meanings are often obscure. In Psalm 5, they indicate the instrumental accompaniment, but in other cases they might indicate the tune of another song to which the Psalm can be sung. Psalm 57, for example, reads in the superscription, "Set to *Do Not Destroy*." This may have been the name of a well-known song at that time. Occasionally, the meaning is so doubtful that the NKJ translators decided to transliterate the Hebrew words. Psalm 16, for instance, reads "A *Michtam*[10] of David." Fortunately for us, our enjoyment of a Psalm does not depend on our full understanding of its title.

Psalm 5 is a morning prayer in which David reflects on God's contrasting attitudes toward the righteous and the wicked.

5:1, 2 At the outset he asks God to hear not only **his words** but **consider** his **meditation** as well. It is a valid request. The Holy Spirit can interpret our meditations just as easily as the words we speak.

The psalmist asks God to hear not only his meditations, but also the sound of his **cry**. This may mean more than the mere words; it suggests the very intonation, the deep, earnest pitch of the voice.

In addressing the Lord as **"my King and my God,"** David reveals the warm, personal, intimate relationship he enjoyed with the Lord. In the words, **"for to You I will pray,"** he shows that the true God was the only One to whom he prayed—"to You and to You alone." The relationship was not only possessive, but exclusive as well.

5:3 David's prayers were not spasmodic but regular. Every **morning** the Lord heard his voice. Every **morning** the man of God prepared a sacrifice of praise and prayer and watched for the Lord to reveal Himself during the day. Too often we do not watch for God's responses. "We miss many answers," said F. B. Meyer, "because we get tired of waiting on the docks for the returning ships."

5:4–6 Always aware of his enemies, David's confidence in prayer is strengthened by remembering God's holiness and righteousness. Believers have an inside track to the throne of grace. Not so the ungodly. **God** cannot be tolerantly pleased with any form of **wickedness. Evil** cannot be His overnight guest. **The boastful** are not favored with an audience before this King. He hates all evildoers—a truth that punctures the prevalent myth that God is all love and therefore incapable of hatred! God's holiness demands that He punish all liars and abhor all murderers and deceivers.

5:7 In contrast to his wicked adversaries, David had instant access into the presence of the Lord through **the multitude of** God's unfailing **mercy** or grace. In a spirit of deep reverence, David worshiped, like all godly Jews, facing the **holy temple**. Since the actual temple was not built until after David's death, the word here must refer to the tabernacle, as it does in 1 Samuel 1:9; 3:3 and 2 Samuel 22:7.

5:8 Harassed as he is by **enemies**, David asks the Lord to display His justice by leading him safely through the surrounding danger and making his pathway crystal clear.

5:9 Next the psalmist introduces strong reasons why God should vindicate His righteous servant and punish the wicked enemies. You can't believe a word they say. **Their inward** lives, their thoughts and motives, are utterly corrupt and bent on **destruction. Their throat is** like **an open tomb**, stinking with corruption and ready to devour their victims. They are inveterate and insincere flatterers.

5:10 Their doom is just. They should be made to bear their guilt. Their evil schemes should be made to boomerang on themselves. Their innumerable **transgressions** demand their eviction. Their crowning sin is that **they have rebelled against** the Lord God.

5:11, 12 But while God deals with His enemies in judgment, may His friends always have reason to **rejoice** and **shout for joy** as they find Him to be their Refuge, strong and sure. May all who love Jehovah magnify Him as their unfailing Defender! No question about it—God does favor the righteous man; He **will surround him** with grace like a protective **shield**.

Psalm 6: Double Trouble

It was bad enough to be racked with a serious illness, but David's grief was compounded by the tormenting pressure of his opponents. Perhaps they were gloating that his condition was hopeless.

6:1 David interpreted his sickness as a stroke of God brought on by some sin. We commonly do this ourselves; often it is the first thought that crosses our mind. And this diagnosis is sometimes correct: some illnesses *are* indeed caused by unconfessed sin in the believer's life (1 Cor. 11:30). But this is by no means always the case. God often permits illness as a springboard for the display of His power and glory (John 9:3; 11:4), or as a means of producing spiritual fruit (Rom. 5:3), or to prevent sin (2 Cor. 12:7), or as a natural result of overwork (Phil. 2:30) or old age (Eccl. 12:3–6).

Whenever sickness strikes, the first thing we should do is to make sure that we have no unconfessed sin in our life. Then we should ask the Lord to work out His purpose in the illness and to heal us. After that it is proper to resort to a physician and to the use of medicine, but we must be careful that our trust is in the Lord and not in the means that He uses (2 Chron.

16:12). All healing is from the Lord, whether miraculous or ordinary. If in any particular case He does not choose to heal, then He will give grace for suffering or for dying. Ordinarily we do not get dying grace until we need it.

6:2, 3 The psalmist was vocal and articulate in his plea for healing. He was wasting away. His **bones** pained him continually. Even his whole inner life—his emotions, intellect and will—were affected. But it seemed that the **Lord** was slow in responding. **How long** would it be before He would graciously heal the sufferer?

6:4 David asks the **Lord** to turn from what seems to be an attitude of indifference, and to **save** his life from sickness and death. His only claim to deliverance from misery is the steadfast mercy of Jehovah.

6:5 Then follows an unusual argument for healing, namely, that if David should die, it would be no advantage to God. As long as he is alive, he can remember the Lord and praise Him. But if he dies, God would be forgotten. The body without the spirit would not be able to **give** Him **thanks.**

The argument has a certain validity as far as the body is concerned, for a corpse is devoid of memory and of the power to praise. But as far as the spirit and soul are concerned, the argument reflects the limited knowledge which OT saints possessed of life beyond death. Thanks to the fuller revelation which Christ brought, we now know that when a believer dies, he leaves his earthly body and departs to be with Christ, which is far better (Phil. 1:23). He is away from the body and at home with the Lord (2 Cor. 5:8). So the believer does not go into a limbo of soul-sleep, but is consciously in the presence of the Lord, praising and worshiping Him.

It must be said in David's favor that he made wonderful use of the light that he had, weaving it into the fabric of his prayers. If our prayers made as good use of the superior light we have, what paragons of praise and petition they would be!

6:6, 7 We get some idea of the depth of the psalmist's misery by his description of his condition. He was utterly worn out **with** moaning and **groaning. All night** he soaked his pillow **with** his crying and drenched his **couch with** his **tears**. His eyes had become sunken due to his profound **grief**, and vision was fading because of the oppression **of all** his **enemies**. It seemed that his life was filled to overflowing with trouble and that he could stand no more.

6:8–10 But prayer changes things. By the secret, mysterious communication of the Spirit, the assurance comes to him that **the Lord has heard** the sound **of** his **weeping** and that his **prayer** has been answered. Strengthened by this assurance, he orders his **enemies** to disperse. He is no longer cowed by their threat because he realizes that they will go **suddenly** down to shameful defeat when the Lord rises up to punish them.

Lord, what a change within us one
  short hour
Spent in Thy presence will avail
  to make!
What heavy burdens from our
  bosoms take!
What parched grounds refresh as with
  a shower!
We kneel, and all around us seems
  to lower;
We rise, and all—the distant and the
  near—
Stands forth in sunny outline, brave
  and clear;

We kneel, how weak; we rise, how full of power!
Why, therefore, should we do ourselves this wrong
Or others—that we are not always strong,
That we are sometimes overborne with care,
That we should ever weak or heartless be,
Anxious or troubled, when with us in prayer,
And joy and strength and courage are with Thee?

—*Richard Chenevix Trench*

Psalm 7: The Cry of the Oppressed

The Hebrew title identifies this as **a** *Shiggaion* **of David, which he sang to the LORD concerning the words of Cush, a Benjamite**. F. W. Grant writes that the word *shiggaion* implies a wandering ode or a loud, enthusiastic hymn, in which the writer is carried away with his enthusiasm. **Cush**, the subject of the ode, was from the same tribe as Saul and was probably one of his lieutenants. In any case he was a malicious foe of David. The NKJV translates *shiggaion* as **a meditation**.

7:1, 2 In a passionate appeal David prays for deliverance from his pursuers. Otherwise he will be like a helpless lamb, attacked by **a lion** and dragged off, limp and lifeless.

7:3–5 Cush was obviously accusing David of a long list of crimes, probably including attempts on Saul's life and raids on the king's supply bases. But David protests his innocence. He was not guilty of the charges. His **hands** had not **plundered**. He had not taken vengeance on the king, even when he had had the opportunity to do so. If he had actually done these things, then he was willing to face the music— to be hunted, captured, struck down and killed.

7:6–8 But since it wasn't so, he boldly calls on the **LORD** to **arise in** His **anger**, punish the **enemies** and vindicate the innocent. He pictures God calling a great trial to order. A huge throng of people are gathered in the courtroom. Jehovah sits on the bench and judges **the peoples**. All David asks is that he be judged **according to** his own **righteousness** and **integrity**. This may sound like the height of conceit, but we must remember that David is not claiming absolute righteousness in every area of his life—only in regard to those accusations that were being hurled against him.

7:9–11 Verse 9 voices the age-long cry of God's oppressed people. Every devout heart pants for the day when the reign of evil will be ended and **the just** will inherit the earth. That day will come when Christ returns to set up His kingdom. In the meantime, the righteous God who knows man's thoughts and motives is the shield or protector of **the upright** and the righteous **judge** who **is angry with the wicked every day**.

7:12, 13 God has a well-stocked armory. Unless the wicked repents, **He will sharpen His sword** and tighten **His bow** to shoot **arrows** barbed with fire. All God's weapons are deadly ones!

7:14–16 In the end, David is confident that his enemy will reap what he has sowed. His sin will follow the familiar course of conception, pregnancy, birth, and death. The enemy first **conceives** a plot to destroy the psalmist. Soon he is bulging with wicked ideas. Then he brings to birth his treacherous scheme. But it backfires on himself. He falls into his own trap, and all the **trouble** and violence he had mapped out for the psalmist recoils **on his own crown** (head) by an inexplicable irony of circumstances.

7:17 This even-handed justice prompts David to lift his heart to **the LORD** in thanksgiving and to **sing praise to the name of the LORD Most High**.

Psalm 8: What Is Man?

God is indescribably great. Man, by contrast, is pathetically tiny. Yet God has conferred tremendous glory and honor upon man. The wonder of this fact brings forth an eloquent gasp from David.

8:1 The majesty of the **LORD** is evident in all creation, if a person only has eyes to see it. Every area of natural science teems with evidences of the wisdom and power of the Creator. God's **glory** is higher than **the heavens**. The planets, the stars, the limitless universe give only a partial view of how very great God really is. Yet sophisticated men shrug off the evidence as if it didn't exist.

8:2 But **infants** in their innocent faith chant God's greatness in their simple hymns. It is exactly as Christ Himself declared: God has hidden these things from the wise and understanding and has revealed them to babes (Matt. 11:25).

Whether we think of **babes** in a literal way or as those disciples of the Lord who have childlike faith in Him, it is still true that they form a bulwark for the Lord **because of** His **enemies**. They can often silence an enemy of God through an innocent question or a naive observation. Just as it takes only a small pin to prick a large balloon, so these homespun followers of the Lamb often bring low the lofty pretensions of those who deny God's hand in creation and providence!

8:3 No branch of science proclaims God's greatness and man's insignificance more eloquently than astronomy. The simple fact that distances must be reckoned in light-years (the distance that light travels in a year) illustrates the point. Light travels 186,000 miles per second, and there are 31.5 million seconds in a year, so light travels roughly six trillion miles in a single year! Yet some stars are billions of light-years from the earth. No wonder we call such computation astronomical.

To gaze into **the heavens** at night should give us great thoughts about God. **The moon and the stars** are **the work** of His **fingers**! When we think of the numberless myriads of **stars**, of the vast distances in the universe, and of the power that holds the planets in orbit with mathematical precision, it boggles the mind.

8:4 Relatively speaking, the planet earth is a speck of dust in the universe. If this is so, what is a single **man** perched upon this planet? Yet God is interested in every individual! He has a personal, intimate concern for every human being.

8:5 God **made** man in His own image and after His own likeness. Though **lower** than God,[11] man shares with Him some faculties that are not shared by any other order of creation on earth. Everything God made was pronounced to be good, but the verdict on the Creation of man was "*very* good."

8:6–8 As God's representative on earth, man was given **dominion over** all kinds of animals, **birds, fish**, and reptiles. There was nothing that was not put under him.

But the writer to the Hebrews reminds us that we do not see man enjoying this undisputed sway at the present time (Heb. 2:5–9). Dogs bark at man, snakes bite him, birds and fish elude him. The explanation is that when sin entered the world through Adam, man lost his unqualified sovereignty over the lower creation.

Yet God's purpose still stands. He has decreed that man shall indeed have dominion, and nothing can block God's purposes. So while we do not see all things subject to man right now, we do see Jesus—the one Person by whom man's dominion will eventually be restored. When Christ came to earth, He became temporarily lower than the angels so that as Man He could die for the human race. Now He is crowned with glory and honor at God's right hand. Someday Christ the Son of man will return to earth to reign as King of kings and Lord of lords. In the Millennium, the dominion that was forfeited by the first Adam will be restored by the Last Adam.

8:9 Then God's redeemed people will join to sing with new appreciation, **"O Lord, our Lord, how excellent is Your name in all the earth!"**

Psalm 9: The Day of Retribution

If the inscription in the Chaldee version is correct, **David** is here celebrating his victory over Goliath. But he is obviously looking beyond this triumph to God's final victory over His enemies. The Psalm is an acrostic, based on the first half of the Hebrew alphabet.[12]

9:1, 2 The sweet singer of Israel is ecstatic over **all** God's **marvelous works**. Here he is not thinking so much of His deeds in creation or redemption but of His spectacular feats in crushing the nation's foes. David gives all the glory to God—none to himself and none to man's weapons or skill. With every fiber of his being he honors and magnifies the **name** of the **Most High**. The example of his love and devotion to the Lord makes many of us realize how cold and unresponsive we often are.

9:3, 4 Then he reminisces about God's epic battle, though the final fulfillment of his words will not come to pass until the Second Coming of our Lord Jesus Christ. One sight of Him will cause the **enemies** to **turn back** and flee. **They shall fall** in panicky disarray **and perish** before they can escape. The righteous will be vindicated in that day by the King on His glorious **throne**. Finally the earth will taste what righteous judgment is really like.

9:5, 6 Gentile oppressors will be sharply **rebuked**, and all Israel's enemies will sink into perpetual oblivion. They will be buried in the ruins of their vaunted civilization. Cities that now seem to be timeless will be completely uprooted. Names like Washington, Moscow, or Ottawa will be forgotten forever.

9:7, 8 The adversaries will all be gone, **but the Lord shall endure forever**, as righteous and trustworthy as He has always been. Resplendent in glory on **His throne**, He will rule **the world** in absolute **righteousness**. Everyone will get a square deal from Him. Paul used the first part of verse 8 in his message at Athens, explaining that the active agent in this future judgment will be the risen Lord Jesus Christ:

> Truly, these times of ignorance God overlooked, but now commands all men everywhere to repent, because He has appointed a day on which He will judge the world in righteousness by the Man whom He has ordained. He has given assurance of this to all by raising

Him from the dead (Acts 17:30, 31).

9:9, 10 Earth's **oppressed** masses will find Him to be their high tower and unfailing **refuge**. All **who know** Him **will put their trust in** Him, realizing that He has never disappointed the confidence of His people.

9:11, 12 Israel will not only **sing praises to the LORD** but she will also fulfill a missionary role to the Gentile **people**, rehearsing the wonderful deliverances of the Lord and pointing out that **He** who **avenges** the **blood** of His people was not indifferent to their sufferings after all—that their prayers did not go unanswered.

9:13, 14 But millennial conditions have not yet come. Verses 13 and 14 bring us back with a jolt to the distressing present! David still needs God's **mercy** to protect him from the enemy, so that **the gates** of **Zion** will again echo to his happy songs of praise.

9:15 Then he leaps forward once more to the time when **the** anti-Semitic **nations** will fall into **the pit which they** dug for the Jews and be trampled **in the net which they** intended for God's ancient people. It is history repeating itself—another instance of Haman being hanged on the gallows he made for Mordecai.

9:16 Once again **the LORD** will reveal Himself as the One who evens the score by causing the ungodly to reap what they have sown. God is not mocked. The meaning of **"Selah"** is uncertain. It may mean an intensification (see notes on Psalm 3).

9:17 When David says that **the wicked shall be turned into hell** (Heb., *Sheol*), he does not restrict the word to the disembodied state or to the grave. Here the context demands that it mean **hell** itself. This is the fate of **all the nations that forget God**.

9:18 Equally certain is the fact that **the needy shall not always be forgotten**. As Knox translates, "The patience of the afflicted will not go for nothing." All that they hoped for will be fulfilled in that millennial day.

9:19, 20 David's thoughts of the coming reign of righteousness arouse longings for its arrival. The prayer is born that the **LORD** will **arise** to foil man's plans and to judge **the nations**. As they stand in the presence of the Almighty Judge, they will realize in terror what puny, mortal **men** they really are.

Psalm 10: Public Enemy Number One

Here the psalmist employs an acrostic based on the second half of the Hebrew alphabet[13] to describe the supreme villain. Since this "Public Enemy Number One" seems to be the very embodiment of sin, we naturally link him with the "Man of Sin" who will arise at the beginning of the seven-year Tribulation. This "son of perdition" will oppose and exalt himself against every so-called god or object of worship. Taking his seat in the temple of God in Jerusalem, he will proclaim himself to be God (2 Thess. 2:3, 4). Those who refuse to worship him will suffer economic sanctions, persecution and even death.

The Silence of God (10:1)

As the Psalm opens we find the question that comes to all of us sooner or later: **Why** does the **LORD** remain silent while the innocent suffer and the wicked reign unchallenged? It is mysteries like this that call our faith into action, that encourage us to trust when we cannot understand, and that challenge us to endure to the end.

The Prayer of the Oppressed (10:2)

In their insufferable arrogance, **wicked** men relentlessly hunt down the helpless saints. What could be more fitting for them than to suffer the very fate **they** had **devised** for the righteous?

The Profile of the Enemy (10:3–11)

10:3, 4 It is typical for **the wicked** to boast about all the things he plans to do. In his mad craze to get rich he blasphemes **and renounces the LORD,** for to worship gold is to repudiate God. His lifestyle is one of self-sufficiency. He feels no need for **God** and lives as if He never existed.

10:5, 6 Everything seems to go his way; somehow he escapes the troubles that dog the rest of mankind. The guidelines which God has established for His own people are **far** beyond the wicked man; he cannot understand spiritual truths or divine principles. **He** sneers at **all his enemies** with utter contempt; nothing is ever going to disturb his security, he thinks. As long as he lives he will enjoy a trouble-free existence.

10:7, 8 Whenever he is around, you can expect the air to be blue with profanity. If he's not deceiving someone, he's probably browbeating someone else! He never seems to talk about anything constructive; it's always about crime and destruction. Like the other gangsters, he waits in unpatrolled, **lurking places** to ambush **the innocent**; when they walk past, he guns them down. He is always on the lookout for the unsuspecting and the **helpless**.

10:9–11 Like **a lion in his den**, he is poised ready to pounce on his prey. Like a hunter, he lures the victims **into his net**, whether for blackmail, extortion, bribery, servitude, or death. The unfortunate victim is overwhelmed—felled by the enormous power of the criminal. In his despair he feels that **God has forgotten** him, that He is looking in another direction and **will never see** the predicament of His child.

The Cry of the Faithful (10:12–18)

10:12, 13 But now it is time for the LORD to act by lifting His **hand** in judgment on the oppressor and in mercy on the afflicted. Why should the forces of evil be allowed to continue in their godlessness and irreligion? Why should they be encouraged to think that God will never demand **an account** for their crimes?

10:14, 15 God *does* see. He keeps a careful score of every act of injustice and wrong, so that He can **repay** in full in a coming day. So it is not in vain that **the helpless commits himself to** God. Has God not proved Himself to be the orphan's friend? The Lord will hear the cry of the faithful by breaking **the arm of the wicked** and by exposing **his wickedness until** every last vestige is punished.

10:16 That day of vengeance will arrive when the kingdoms of this world become the kingdom of our LORD and of His Christ. Then the wicked and persecuting **nations** will **have perished**, as foretold by Isaiah:

> Behold, all those who were incensed against you shall be ashamed and disgraced; they shall be as nothing, and those who strive with you shall perish. You shall seek them and not find them—those who contended with you. Those who war against you shall be as nothing, as a nonexistent thing. For I, the Lord your God, will hold your right hand, saying to you, "Fear not, I will help you" (Isa. 41:11–13).

10:17, 18 We can be fully assured that the LORD will hear and answer the prayers of the **humble**. He will give them grace for every trial and will bend low to see that **justice** is the lot of **the fatherless and the oppressed**. The day is coming, praise God, when **the man of the earth** will **oppress** the poor and defenseless **no more**!

Psalm 11: Why Flee When You Can Trust?

Psalm 11 is an antidote for gloomy headlines. When the news is all bad—wars, violence, crime, corruption and political unrest—**David** reminds us that we can rise above the circumstances of life by keeping our eyes on the Lord.

It seems that when David had opened his front door, a frenzied visitor had burst in. His face was pale and drawn, his eyes were popping with excitement and his lips were quivering. In jerky, breathless gasps he told of imminent disaster and advised David to head for the hills. This Psalm is David's answer to the pessimistic visitor's counsel of despair and discouragement.

11:1–3 David first states his simple **trust in the LORD** as his refuge: "Why *flee* when you can *trust?*" Then he reproaches Calamity Charlie for seeking to disturb his peace. Notice that the text from verse 1b through verse 3 contains the words of the gloom peddler. It begins with **"Flee as a bird to your mountain."** He had said to David, in effect, "You are as insignificant and defenseless as a little bird. The best thing you can do is escape. Criminals now have the upper hand, and they are armed to the teeth, ready to gun down decent, law-abiding citizens. Law and order have vanished and **the foundations** of society are crumbling. This being so, what hope do you think there is for a **righteous** person like you?"

11:4–6 What hope? Why, **the LORD**, or course! **The LORD is in His holy temple**, and nothing can stop the fulfillment of His plans! His **throne is in heaven**, unmoved and unmovable, no matter what kingdoms on earth may rise or fall. Though nothing can disturb God's poise and serenity, He is nevertheless concerned about the doings of **the sons of men**. He not only sees what happens but constantly makes value judgments about **the righteous** and **the wicked**. Although God is infinite love, **His soul hates** men who practice **violence**. He will **rain** down a storm of judgment on them; the rain will be **coals** of **fire and brimstone** and the **wind** will be scorching heat.

11:7 Just as God hates the violent man, so He loves the righteous. God Himself **is righteous** and **He loves righteousness**. The ultimate reward of **the upright** will be to stand in God's presence.

So we need not get all upset over the headlines. The waves of adverse circumstances may seem to be against us at any particular time, but the tide of God's irresistible purpose is sure to win in the end.

> He everywhere hath sway, and all
> things serve His might;
> His every act pure blessing is, His
> path unsullied light.
> We comprehend Him not, yet earth
> and heaven tell
> God sits as sovereign on the throne
> and ruleth all things well.
> —*Author unknown*

Psalm 12: The Words of Men—and of God

12:1 The general decline of faithfulness among men, especially in their speech, evokes the prayer of verse 1:

> Lord, come to my rescue; piety is dead; in a base world, true hearts have gone rare (Knox).

12:2 Three specific charges are then leveled against the faithless generation:

> **Lies**—They are guilty not only of blatant forms of deceit, but of white lies, half-truths, exaggerations and broken promises.
>
> **Flattery**—They heap insincere compliments on others. Praise is not the same as flattery; it only becomes flattery when it ascribes virtues to a person which he is known not to possess. And flattery usually has some sinister or selfish motive.
>
> **Two-facedness**—They think one thing and say something quite different. Like Machiavelli, they practice duplicity and intrigue.

12:3, 4 The age-long sigh of God's true saints is that **the Lord** Himself will silence the ungodly's **flattering lips**—that He will immobilize the tongues of those who boast that their principles **will prevail**, that they have full freedom to say whatever they want, regardless of what anybody thinks.

12:5, 6 In response to the groan of the **poor** and **needy, the Lord** promises to **arise** and "grant them the salvation for which they thirst" (Gelineau). And what He has promised He will surely perform. His promises are **pure . . . , like silver tried in a furnace of earth, purified seven times**—in other words, like the purest **silver** known. There is no deceit, no flattery, no double meaning, no error in God's words. They can be fully trusted.

12:7 So the believer instinctively turns to the **Lord** for protection from **this generation**—protection not only from its attacks but from any form of compromise or complicity with it.

12:8 The last verse is a description of "this generation"—**the wicked** generation which is continually on the prowl, exalting **vileness** and scoffing at virtue. It is the same generation described in Proverbs 30:11–14:

> There is a generation that curses its father, and does not bless its mother. There is a generation that is pure in its own eyes, yet is not washed from its filthiness. There is a generation—oh, how lofty are their eyes! And their eyelids are lifted up. There is a generation whose teeth are like swords, and whose fangs are like knives, to devour the poor from off the earth, and the needy from among men.

Psalm 13: How Long?

Four times the words formed on David's lips—"How long?" Pursued hotly by the enemy (perhaps Saul), **David** wondered what was delaying the chariot of God. Would help never come to free him from the four terrible burdens that were crushing him?

> He felt as if God had forgotten him.
>
> He considered himself cut off from the Lord's favor.
>
> He experienced deep depression in his soul daily.
>
> He suffered the constant humiliation of being on the losing side.

13:1–4 God must take note of David's plight and send help quickly in order to avert two disasters. The first would be David's death and the second would be the jubilant boasting of his **enemy**. Unless the Lord acted quickly to restore the sparkle to David's eyes, they would soon be closed forever in **death**. Unless Jehovah turned the tide, the enemies would soon be boasting that they had won—that David was thoroughly trounced.

13:5, 6 Now there is no doubt as to the outcome. The psalmist believes that the answer is on the way. Trusting in the **mercy** of the Lord, he knows that he will live to celebrate deliverance from his adversary. In anticipation of this **salvation**, he can **sing** praises **to the LORD** for His boundless lovingkindness.

This Psalm is like many of our God-sent testings: they begin with a sigh but end with a song!

Psalm 14: The Fool's Creed

14:1 The creed of the fool is **"There is no God."** He does not *want* there to be a God, therefore he denies the existence of God. It is an irrational position to take. First of all, it is a claim to omniscience; it says, "I know everything. It is not possible that a God could exist beyond the boundaries of my knowledge." Second, this attitude claims omnipresence; it says, "I am present in all places at one and the same time, and it is not possible that God could exist any place in the universe without my knowing it." Again, this position ignores the wonders of God in creation—the immensity of the universe, the amazingly precise movement of the planets, the marvelous suitability of the earth to sustain life, the intricate design of the human body, the fantastic complexity of the human brain and the extraordinary properties of water and soil.

Take for instance the suitability of the earth to sustain life. Henry Bosch has pointed out the following instances of God's careful and marvelous design:

> The earth rotates on its axis at approximately 1000 miles per hour. If that had been 100 miles per hour, our days and nights would be ten times longer, and our planet would alternately burn and freeze. Under such circumstances vegetation could not live!
>
> If the earth were as small as the moon, the power of gravity would be too weak to retain sufficient atmosphere for man's needs; but if it were as large as Jupiter, Saturn, or Uranus, extreme gravitation would make human movement almost impossible. If we were as near to the sun as Venus, the heat would be unbearable; if we were as far away as Mars, we would experience snow and ice every night, even in the warmest regions. If the oceans were half their present dimensions, we would receive only one-fourth the rainfall we do now. If they were one-eighth larger, our annual precipitation would increase fourfold, and this earth would become a vast, uninhabitable swamp.
>
> Water solidifies at 32 degrees above zero [°F]. It would be disastrous if the oceans froze at that temperature, however, for then the amount of thawing in the polar regions would not balance out, and ice would accumulate throughout the centuries! To prevent such a catastrophe, the Lord put salt in the sea to alter its freezing point.[14]

The possibility that all this happened by chance is too small to warrant consideration. That is why the Bible says that atheists are fools. They are *moral* fools. It is not a question of their intelligence quotient but of their morality quotient.

God's verdict on these fools is that **they are corrupt** in themselves and that they act abominably. There is a close connection between a man's creed and his conduct. The lower his conception of God, the lower his morals are apt to be. Either as cause or consequence, atheism and agnosticism are linked with a corrupt life. Barnes writes:

> The belief that there is no God is commonly founded on the desire to lead a wicked life, or is embraced by those who in fact live such a life, with a desire to sustain themselves in their depravity and to avoid the fear of future retribution.[15]

14:2, 3 When **the LORD looks down from heaven** to see if any of Adam's descendants act wisely by seeking after **God**, His findings are dismal. By nature and by practice, man is a sinner. If left to himself, he would never seek after God. It is only through the ministry of the Holy Spirit that men become aware of their need for God and His salvation.

Paul quotes from the first three verses of this Psalm in Romans 3:10–12 to show that sin has affected all mankind and every part of everyone's being. Here in the Psalm, David is not thinking of the whole human race, although the description would certainly be true; rather, he is thinking of outright God-deniers in contrast to the righteous. It is these infidels who have apostatized from the true and living God. They are morally corrupt. God Himself cannot find one of them **who does good, no, not one**.

14:4 Their ignorance is apparent in the way they treat God's **people**. If they realized how God defends the poor and punishes sin, they would never devour believers as if it were a legitimate, everyday thing, like eating **bread**! If they knew the goodness and severity of God, they would not go through life without praying.

14:5, 6 When the Lord takes the part of the innocent, the unrighteous will be greatly terrified. They had always mocked **the poor** for their simple faith, but now they will see that the God they denied is the **refuge** of His own.

14:7 It will be a great day when the Messiah comes **out of Zion** to deliver His people. Israel's joy will be unbounded when Christ's Jewish saints are fully and finally rescued from **captivity** among the nations that deny the only true God.

Psalm 15: The Man God Chooses

15:1 The individual God chooses as His companion is the subject of Psalm 15. Although it does not say so in this Psalm, the basic qualification for entrance into God's kingdom is to be born again. Apart from the new birth, no one can see or enter the kingdom. This birth from above is experienced by grace, through faith, and takes place completely apart from any meritorious works on man's part.

Taken by itself, the Psalm seems to imply that salvation is somehow connected with a man's righteous character or noble deeds. But taken with the rest of Scripture, it can only mean that the kind of faith that saves is the same kind of faith that results in a life of holiness. Like James in his epistle, David is here saying that genuine faith in the Lord results in the kind of good works described in this Psalm.

Incidentally, the Psalm does not profess to give a complete catalog of the virtues of the citizen of Zion. The portrait is suggestive but certainly not exhaustive.

15:2 First of all, the citizen of Zion **walks** with integrity. The man of integrity is a man of moral soundness. He is complete, well-rounded, and balanced.

Second, the citizen of Zion does what is right. He is careful to maintain a conscience that is void of offense. He would rather go to heaven with a good conscience than stay on earth with a bad one.

You can depend on this man to tell **the truth** from **his heart**. He would rather die than lie. His word is his bond. His yes means yes and his no means no.

15:3 He . . . does not backbite with his tongue. You won't find him gossiping about others. Slander and mud-slinging never get past his lips. He disciplines his tongue to edify instead of assassinate!

He does no **evil to his neighbor**. His whole desire is to help, to encourage and to instruct. When he hears some juicy tidbit of scandal about **his friend**, he lets it die right there. Depend on him not to repeat it to anyone.

15:4 Moral distinctions are not blurred in his vision. He discerns between sin and righteousness, darkness and light, evil and good. He despises **a vile person** in the sense that he outspokenly witnesses against his ungodliness. On the other hand, he identifies himself in open approval with everyone in the household of faith.

Once he has made a promise, he stands by it, even if it results in financial loss. A believer, for example, might agree to sell his house for $85,000. But before the papers are signed, he finds he could have sold the house to a large development company for $90,000. But he has given his word to the first buyer—and he keeps his contract.

15:5 The friend of God **does not put out his money at** interest, that is, to another member of God's family. Under the law of Moses, an Israelite could lend to Gentiles at interest (Deut. 23:19, 20) but was forbidden to do so to a fellow Jew (Ex. 22:25; Lev. 25:35–37).

If Jews living under law were guided by this principle, how much more so should Christians living under grace!

Finally, the righteous man does not **take a bribe against the innocent**. He hates the perversion of justice, and disproves the old saying that "everybody has his price."

This then is the type of person who lives for God in time and for eternity. Come to think of it, no one else would be comfortable in God's presence!

Psalm 16: Christ Arose!

The key to understanding Psalm 16 is found in Acts 2:25–28 where Peter quotes verses 8–11a as referring to the resurrection of Christ. Let us put the key in the door, then, and listen as our wonderful Savior prays to His Father immediately prior to His death.

16:1, 2 As the perfect Man, completely dependent on **God**, Christ cries out for preservation to the One who is His only refuge. Throughout His thirty years of life on earth, the Savior not only acknowledged God as His Lord but joyfully confessed God as the absorbing passion of His life. The words **"My goodness is nothing apart from You"** are not a denial of the Savior's sinlessness, but are simply a moving testimony that Christ found all His sufficiency in God. This testimony is comparable to the worship of Psalm 73:25: "Whom have I in heaven but You? And there is none upon earth that I desire besides You."

16:3 The centrality of God in Messiah's life does not, however, exclude a deep regard for **the saints** in the land. In fact, the two are vitally connected: to love God is to love His people (1 John 5:1, 2). The Lord Jesus considers His saints the nobility of **the earth**, the people **in whom** He finds **all** His **delight**. Consider a similar testimony by an old saint of God:

> From the first day I set off until the present hour, I have been as highly favored as a mortal and sinful being can well be. My fellowship has been with the excellent of the earth, and every one of them striving to the utmost of his power to show me kindness for the Lord's sake.[16]

16:4 Standing in stark contrast to the true worshipers of God are people who worship **another god**. Idolatry inevitably brings a train of **sorrows** into the lives of its devotees. Perhaps one of the greatest judgments on idolaters is that they become like the thing they worship. The holy Son of God disavows any fellowship with **their drink offerings of blood**. He will, in fact, not even mention **their names** in any way that might suggest tolerance toward them or toward their heathen rites.

16:5, 6 As for His personal life, Christ's chosen **portion** and **cup** is the **Lord**. All His wealth and enjoyment rest in God. It is the Lord who guards the boundaries of His **inheritance**. As He thinks of how wisely and wonderfully the Father has planned every detail of His life, He compares it to a **pleasant** estate in a magnificent setting, and to an **inheritance** that is comprised entirely of **good** things. If we are living in fellowship with God, we too can praise Him for the ordering of our lives. When we complain, we betray a lack of confidence in God's wisdom, love and power.

16:7 Here Christ praises **the Lord** for the faithful way He has provided guidance and **counsel** throughout all His life. Even during hours of sleeplessness, as He prayed and meditated on God's Word, His **heart** had instructed Him. Far from being wasted, the time was sanctified to His comfort and blessing. How often has Christ's experience been duplicated in the lives of God's people!

> For many a rapturous minstrel
> Among those sons of light
> Will say of his sweetest music,
> "I learned it in the night."
> And many a rolling anthem
> That fills the Father's home
> Sobbed out its first rehearsal
> In the shade of a darkened room.
> —*Author unknown*

The remaining verses of Psalm 16 were quoted by Peter on the Day of Pentecost as referring to the resurrection of Christ:

> For David says concerning Him: "I foresaw the Lord always before my face, for He is at my right hand, that I may not be shaken. Therefore my heart rejoiced, and my tongue was glad; moreover my flesh also will rest in hope. For You will not leave my soul in Hades, nor will You allow Your Holy One to see corruption. You have made known to me the ways of life; You will make me full of joy in Your presence."
>
> Men and brethren, let me speak freely to you of the patriarch David, that he is both dead and buried, and his tomb is with us to this day. Therefore, being a prophet, and knowing that God had sworn with an oath to him that of the fruit of his body, according to the flesh, He would raise up the Christ to sit on his throne, he, foreseeing this, spoke concerning the resurrection

of the Christ, that His soul was not left in Hades, nor did His flesh see corruption. This Jesus God has raised up, of which we are all witnesses. Therefore being exalted to the right hand of God, and having received from the Father the promise of the Holy Spirit, He poured out this which you now see and hear (Acts 2:25–33).

Now notice the points that Peter made (most of which we ourselves would never have gathered from the passage):

1. David was speaking of Christ (v. 25). David could not have been speaking about himself, since his body is still in a tomb in Jerusalem.
2. As a prophet, the psalmist knew that God would raise up Christ prior to the time He would reign upon His throne.
3. David therefore predicted that God would not allow Christ's soul to remain in Hades, nor would He allow Christ's body to decompose.
4. God did indeed raise up Christ, and what happened on the Day of Pentecost was the result of His glorification at God's right hand.

With this introduction in mind, let us now look at the closing verses of this Psalm.

16:8 First of all, Messiah asserts without any equivocation that He has kept **the Lord always before** Him. Jehovah has been the One for whom He lived. He has never done anything in self-will; everything has been done in obedience to His Father's will.

Because He is at my right hand, I shall not be moved. In Scripture the **right hand** speaks of:

Power (Ps. 89:13)
Safety (Ps. 20:6)
Honor (Ps. 45:9; 110:1)
Pleasure (Ps. 16:11)
Favor (Ps. 80:17)
Support (Ps. 18:35).

Here it speaks of safety and security.

16:9, 10 Assured of God's constant care and protection, the Savior faces the future with confidence. His **heart is glad**. His soul **rejoices** and His body is safe. He knows that God **will not leave** His **soul in Sheol** or **allow** His body **to see corruption**. In other words, Christ will be raised from the dead.

The reference to **Sheol** needs a word of explanation. It is the word used in the OT for the grave, for the "netherworld," and to describe the disembodied state. It is equivalent to the NT Greek word "Hades." Sheol did not so much indicate a geographical location as the *condition* of the dead—the separation of the personality from the body. It was used to describe the condition of everyone who died, whether believer or unbeliever. On the other hand the NT equivalent, Hades, is used only of *unbelievers*. Sheol was a very indefinite, imprecise word. It did not convey a clear picture of life after death. In fact, it expressed more of uncertainty than of knowledge.

In the NT, all that is changed. Christ has brought life and immortality to light through the gospel (2 Tim. 1:10). Today we know that when an unbeliever dies, his spirit and soul are in a state of suffering called Hades (Luke 16:23), while his body goes to the grave. The spirit and soul of the believer go to be with Christ in heaven (2 Cor. 5:8; Phil. 1:23), while his earthly body goes to the grave.

When the Savior said **". . . You will not leave my soul in Sheol,"** He revealed His foreknowledge that God would not allow Him to remain in the disembodied state. Though He *entered* Sheol, He did not remain there.

God did not allow the usual process of decomposition to take place. By a miracle of preservation, Christ's lifeless body was kept from **corruption** for three days and nights.

16:11 In the final verse, our blessed Lord has complete confidence that God **will show** Him **the path of life—the path** from death back to **life** again. This **path** would ultimately lead Him back to heaven, to God's **presence**. There He would experience **fullness of joy** and **pleasures forevermore**.

Psalm 17: The Perennial Puzzle

When we do wrong and suffer for it, our own consciences tell us that our punishment is just. But it's another story when our suffering is unrelated to any wrong we have done! This kind of suffering—the "suffering for righteousness sake," as Peter calls it—is a perennial puzzle to the child of God.

David knew his share of it. But he also knew what to do about it. He took his case to the Righteous Judge. There he was confident of a fair trial.

At times David seems to be defending himself in a giant ego-trip. He loudly protests his righteousness, integrity and obedience. It almost sounds as if he has reached a state of sinless perfection. But this is really not the case at all. David is not claiming guiltlessness in *all* areas of his life, but simply in *the present circumstances*. He is saying that he did not do anything to provoke the current hostility of his foes.

We might paraphrase David's case as follows:

17:1, 2 "**LORD**, I ask you to **hear** my **cause** because it is a **just** one. Listen attentively to what I say, for I am being unjustly persecuted. In my plea for justice I am 'telling it like it is'—no deceit or shading of the truth. Before your tribunal I seek acquittal. **Let your eyes** see every aspect of the case and then decide in favor of the right.

17:3–5 "If **You** test **my heart**, if You check me out in the darkness as well as in the light—no matter how thoroughly you examine me—you will find that the opposition has no valid reason for harassing me the way they do. Honestly—I am telling the truth. As far as the usual wickedness of men is concerned, I have been able to steer clear of violence by staying close to Your **word**, the Bible. Not by depending on my own strength but by Your commands and promises, I have walked in paths of obedience to You. My **footsteps** haven't slipped; I haven't resorted to violence against my enemies when I had plenty of chance to do so.

17:6, 7 "Now I'm committing my cause to You. **I** appeal to **You** for justice, confident that You'll **hear** and answer **me**. You are the Savior of those who seek sanctuary from their enemies at **Your right hand**. As I come running to You now, **show Your marvelous lovingkindness** to me in a spectacular way.

17:8–12 "Protect **me as the apple of Your eye**—I'm thinking of the pupil of the eye and how it is 'protected by the eyelash, lid, brow, bony socket and the swiftly uplifted hand' (F. B. Meyer). **Hide me** in the protective and affectionate **shadow of Your wings**. Then I will be safe **from the wicked who** rob me of everything I have and seek to take my life itself. As You know so well, **their fat hearts** are incapable of pity, and **their mouths** spew out the most frightening boasts of what they are going to do to me. They stealthily track me down. **They have now** hemmed me in. **Their eyes** are intent on the final knockout blow. Savage **as a lion** that is ravenously hungry, and sly as **a young lion lurking** in the bush, they are ready **to tear** me to shreds.

17:13, 14 "LORD, You simply *must* come to my defense. Meet them head on and topple them. **With Your sword** rescue me from the clutches of these **wicked** men who are only concerned with what they can get **in this life**. You have given them more than enough of material things. Even their **children** have an oversupply—enough to **leave** to **their babes**.

17:15 "Well, they can have it all as far as I'm concerned. My interest lies in spiritual rather than material treasures. It is enough for me that I will look upon **Your face** as one who has been declared righteous and not as a guilty sinner. **I shall be satisfied when I awake in Your likeness.**"

E. Bendor Samuel has pointed out that verse 15 contains every element of 1 John 3:2:

Supreme satisfaction:	1 Jn.—It has not yet been revealed . . . but Ps.—**I shall be satisfied.**
A great transformation:	1 Jn.—We shall be like Him. Ps.—I shall **awake in Your likeness.**
An enlarged vision:	1 Jn.—We shall see Him as He is. Ps.—**I will see Your face.**[17]

See also 1 Corinthians 15:51–55 and Revelation 22:4.

Psalm 18: The Power That Raised Christ From the Dead

We get a clue that this Psalm may be about the Lord Jesus Christ from the fact that verse 49 is quoted in Romans 15:9 as referring to Him.

> For this reason I will confess to You among the Gentiles, and I will sing to Your name.

As we investigate more closely, we find that we were right. The Psalm is indeed all about the Lord Jesus Christ. It describes graphically His death, resurrection, exaltation, Second Coming and glorious kingdom.

Nowhere else in the Bible are we given such a vivid account of the tremendous battle that took place in the unseen world at the time of our Savior's resurrection. But more of that later.

18:1–3 The song opens with praise to **the LORD** for hearing and answering the prayers of His beloved Son. Notice the figures of speech that are used to describe the **strength**, safety, security, and **salvation** that are found in **God: my strength . . . my rock . . . my fortress . . . my deliverer . . . my shield and the horn of my salvation, my stronghold**.

18:4–6 **Death** is rapidly closing in on the suffering Savior. In quickly changing pictures, He describes Himself as being bound with ropes, being gradually overwhelmed with waves, being entangled by cords, and being confronted with a host of inescapable **snares**. In such a desperate situation, there is only one resource: prayer to **God**. Christ did not ask to be delivered from dying; that, after all, was His purpose in coming into the world (John 12:27). What He requested was to be delivered out of death. "Who in the days of His flesh, having offered up both supplications and entreaties to Him who was able to save Him out of death, with strong crying and tears . . ." (Heb. 5:7, JND).

In His deep **distress** Christ had the assurance that His prayer was heard and answered. The rest of the Psalm reveals how Immanuel's plaintive cries from Gethsemane and Golgotha mobilized all the forces of Omnipotence on His behalf. "The voice is thin and solitary," wrote F. B. Meyer, "but the answer shakes creation."

18:7–15 When you come to verses 7–19, it sounds as if a war has broken out. And that is exactly what happened at the resurrection of Christ. The battle was between God and the hosts of hell. Satan and all his demons encamped at the tomb outside Jerusalem, determined that the Lord Christ would never rise again. Their success in having the Son of God crucified would be completely nullified if He were to rise from the dead. So they massed themselves at the sealed tomb of the Savior.

Then God lowered the heavens and came down in the greatest display of power the world has ever known. The Apostle Paul later spoke of it as "the working of His mighty power which He worked in Christ when He raised Him from the dead" (Eph. 1:19, 20). Greater than the might that created the universe, greater than the strength that delivered Israel from Egypt, God's resurrection power drove back the hosts of principalities, powers, and wicked spirits on that first Easter morning.

At the approach of God **the earth** is convulsed. His rage is fierce, pictured by **smoke** billowing forth **from His nostrils**, intense **fire** issuing in torrents **from His mouth**, and great **coals** of flame hurtling against His enemies. As He descends, riding upon a cloud that resembles **a cherub**, the world is shaken by a violent storm of **darkness**, thunder, **lightnings** and **hailstones** pummeling the enemy in a massive bombing attack. Just as in the crossing of the Red Sea, the waters **of the sea** and rivers recoil in fear at the titanic display of the wrath of the Almighty.

18:16–19 In striking symbolism God smashes, bruises, crushes, wounds and maims the foe until he retreats in utter defeat. Then He reaches down and takes Christ from the still-sealed tomb. Hallelujah! Christ is risen! Not only does God raise Him from the dead but He gives Him a triumphant ascension through the enemy's realm and glorifies Him at His own right hand. Thus, as Paul says, "Having disarmed principalities and powers, He made a public spectacle of them, triumphing over them in it" (Col. 2:15).

18:20–30 Here we have the rationale or mystique of the Resurrection. There was a certain moral necessity for God to raise the Lord Jesus. This necessity arose from Christ's sinless, spotless life, from His undeviating devotion to the will of His Father, and from the perfection of His work at Calvary's cross. All the righteous attributes of God demanded that He bring the Savior up from the grave in the power of an endless life. This is what is meant by the majestic utterance, "Christ was raised from the dead by the glory of the Father" (Rom. 6:4). The glorious character of God made the Resurrection a moral necessity, the reward of Christ's perfect, personal righteousness.

While David did write verses 20–30, they are really not completely true of him. Instead, he was speaking prophetically through the inspiration of the Holy Spirit about the One who would be both his Son and his Lord (Matt. 22:41–46).

18:31–42 These verses describe Christ's Second Advent. He will come from heaven "with His mighty angels, in flaming fire taking vengeance on those who do not know God, and on those who do not obey the gospel of our Lord Jesus Christ" (2 Thess. 1:7, 8). He will be "clothed with a robe dipped in blood . . . out of His mouth goes a sharp sword, that with it He should strike the nations . . . He Himself treads the winepress of the fierceness and wrath of Almighty God" (Rev. 19:13, 15).

Christ is pictured primarily as a man of war here. This is consistent with the other Scriptures that teach that when He comes back to earth, He will come first of all "to execute judgment on all, to convict all who are ungodly among them of all their ungodly deeds which they have committed in an ungodly way, and of all the harsh things which ungodly sinners have spoken against Him" (Jude 15).

After being equipped for war by **God** the Father (vv. 31–37), Christ pursues and utterly destroys His **enemies** (vv. 37–42).

18:43–45 Following the crushing of His foes, Christ sets up His kingdom on earth and reigns as King of kings and Lord of lords. He is now the **head of** all **the nations** on earth. Both redeemed Israel and redeemed Gentiles serve in willing submission to the righteous rule of the glorified Christ. **Foreigners** yield feigned obedience.

18:46–50 The Psalm closes as it began—with a hymn of praise to **God** for His wonderful vindication of the Lord Jesus. He has given **great** victories to **His king,** and **shown mercy to His anointed,** His Son.

Because of what He has done, we too should extol Him **among the Gentiles, and sing praises to** His **Name.**

Psalm 19: God's Two Books

19:1, 2 "The heavens declare the glory of God; and the firmament shows His handiwork." And what a story they tell! Think, first of all, what they tell about the immensity of the universe. If we traveled at the speed of light—186,000 miles a *second* or roughly six trillion miles a *year*—it would take us ten billion *years* to reach the farthest point we can see with a telescope. But this would still be far from the outermost limits of space. Now astronomers think that space may have no bounds at all! Our earth is nothing but a tiny speck in a limitless expanse!

Think too of the number of stars and other heavenly bodies. With the naked eye we can see about five thousand stars. With a small telescope we can see about two million. But with the Palomar telescope we can see billions of *galaxies,* to say nothing of individual stars.

Then think about the distances of the heavenly bodies from the earth and from each other. Someone has pictured the distances as follows: if it cost a penny to ride 1000 miles, a trip to the moon would cost $2.38, a trip to the sun would cost $930, but a trip to the *nearest* star would cost $260 million.

It takes light from the most remote stars which can be seen with telescopes ten billion years to reach the earth. So when we look out into space, we are really looking backward in time. For example, we do not see the Andromeda galaxy where it is now but where it was two million years ago!

Although the stars may appear to be crowded in the firmament, the distances between them are so great that they have been likened to lonely lightships a million miles apart, floating in an empty sea.

If creation is so great, how much greater is the Creator! Day and night the heavens are telling the greatness of His power and wisdom. **The firmament** unceasingly proclaims the marvels of His **handiwork**. (In Bible usage "firmament" refers to the expanse of the heavens.) As Isaac Watts wrote, "Nature with open volume stands to spread her Maker's praise abroad."

19:3, 4a There is no speech, no words, no audible voice, yet the sermon of the stars goes **out through all the earth**, and its message **to the end of the world**. Simply by looking up into the heavens man can know that there is a God and can perceive His eternal power (Rom. 1:20). The terrifying dimensions and complexity of the universe confirm Lord Kelvin's observation that "if you think strongly enough, you will be forced by science to believe in God." Kant wrote:

> It is impossible to contemplate the fabric of the world without recognizing the admirable order of its arrangement and the certain manifestation of the hand of God in the perfection of its correlations. Reason, when once it has considered and admired so much beauty and so much perfection, feels a just indignation at the dauntless folly which dares ascribe all this to chance and a happy accident. It must be that the Highest wisdom conceived the plan and Infinite power carried it into execution.[18]

19:4b–6 The psalmist sees the vaulted arch of heaven as a vast tent which God prepared **for the sun**. As the sun rises in the morning, it is **like a bridegroom coming out of his chamber**. The sun moves through the arc of the heavens like a **strong man** joyfully running a **race**. The course begins at the eastern end of the heavens and continues on down to the western horizon. We know, of course, that the sun does not actually rise and set, but that the earth moves in relation to the sun, creating this illusion. But in poetic passages the Bible often uses the language of human appearance, just as we do in our everyday speech.

There is nothing hidden from the **heat** of the sun. It enjoys universal exposure, pervading every remote corner and crevice of the world.

19:7–9 But creation is only *one* of God's volumes of self-revelation. Verse 7 introduces us to Volume Two of God's revelation—**"the law of the LORD."** Both volumes glorify God and inspire the worship of thoughtful persons. Few commentators on the Psalms can resist quoting Kant's famous dictum:

> The starry sky above me and the moral law in me, are two things which fill the soul with ever increasing admiration and reverence.[19]

But there is a difference between the two books of God. Creation reveals God as the Mighty One, the God of Power. But His Word reveals Him as the One who enters into covenant relationship with His people. God's *works* reveal His knowledge and power but His *Word* reveals His love and grace. Scientific truth may stimulate our intellect but spiritual truth convicts our heart and conscience!

In his eulogy of God's Word, David describes it not only as **the law of the LORD** but also as **the testimony of the LORD, the statutes of the LORD, the commandment of the LORD, the fear of the LORD**, and **the judgments of the LORD**. The psalmist attributes eight excellent qualities to the Word of God; it is **perfect, sure, right, pure, clean, enduring, true**, and **righteous**. Then he lists five of its wonderful ministries: it converts **the soul**, makes **wise the simple**, rejoices **the heart**, enlightens **the eyes**, and warns the servant of God.

19:10 The values of the Word cannot be computed in terms of **gold**. But it does have this one thing in common with gold: persons must dig for its treasures. Great wealth is hidden in the pages of God's Book, and our best interests are served by searching for them.

> It is the glory of God to conceal a matter,
> But the glory of kings is to search out a matter (Prov. 25:2).

I can truly say that no prospector is ever more delighted with the discovery of gold than I am to find nuggets of spiritual treasure in the Bible! Much as I like **honey**, its taste is never as sweet to me as the taste of the good Word of God! No words can ever describe the enrichment and satisfaction I have found in my Bible.

> This old book is my guide;
> 'Tis a friend by my side.
> It will lighten and brighten my way.
> And each promise I find
> Soothes and gladdens my mind
> As I read it and heed it each day.
> —*Edmund Pillifant*

Incidentally, there is a beautiful touch in the expression **"sweeter also than honey and the** drippings of the **honeycomb."** The purest honey is that which drips from the comb rather than being pressed out.

19:11 Morever, by them Your servant is warned. By the Scriptures the believer is taught to resist the devil, flee from temptation, hate sin and avoid the very appearance of evil. In obeying the precepts of the Word, the Christian finds true fulfillment in life. Spiritually, physically, and mentally he enjoys the good life! On top of all this, he accumulates **reward** to be bestowed at the Judgment Seat of Christ. "Godliness is profitable for all things, having promise of the life that now is and of that which is to come" (1 Tim. 4:8).

19:12 But when we think of how holy, just and perfect the law of the Lord is, we realize what failures we are, and we exclaim with David, **"Who can understand his errors?"** Barnes writes:

> In view of a law so pure, so holy, so strict in its demands, and so extended in its requirements—asserting jurisdiction over the thoughts, the words and the whole life—who can recall the number of times he has departed from such a law? A somewhat similar sentiment is found in Psalm 119:96: "I have seen an end of all perfection; Thy commandment is exceeding broad."[20]

As the Scriptures expose us to ourselves and convict us of sins we were previously unaware of, we are prompted to pray for forgiveness from **secret faults**—faults hidden to ourselves and even to others but not to God. Sin is sin, even if we are ignorant of it. So our confession should always cover hidden sins.

19:13 But the Psalm teaches us to pray not only for clearing from unknown sins, but for preservation **from presumptuous sins**, that is, from **sins** that are born of pride and self-confidence. Pride was the parent sin of the universe. It led to Lucifer's original rebellion against God. More than anything else, the psalmist feared the dominion of such **presumptuous sins** in his own life. If he can escape their domination, he writes, he **shall be innocent of great transgression**—

specifically, the **great transgression** of departing from God and revolting against Him.

19:14 The eulogy is finished. David has extolled the book of creation and the book of revelation. Now he lifts a parting prayer for his **words** and **meditation** to **be acceptable** in the **sight** of the LORD, his **strength** (lit. "Rock") and his **Redeemer**. When God is referred to as a rock, the figure is designed to express **strength**, security, and salvation. As our **Redeemer**, God in Christ is the One who buys us back from sin, servitude, and shame.

Psalm 20: The Name of the God of Jacob

The nation is on the brink of war. Before leading his troops off into battle, King **David** has come to offer sacrifices. A multitude of loyal subjects are there to wish him success. In verses 1–5 we hear them praying that the Lord will protect him and give him victory. Encouraged by his people's prayers, the king expresses confidence that Jehovah will intervene on his behalf (v. 6). His confidence overflows to the people, and their prayers are now mixed with assurance of deliverance (vv. 7–9).

The People's Prayer (20:1–5)

20:1 On the eve of battle the people look to **the LORD** to **answer** the king in the approaching battle by turning back the enemy in crushing defeat. When they chant **"May the name of the God of Jacob defend you,"** they remind us that the name of God stands for the Person Himself. Three times in this Psalm we find references to that wonderful name:

> **May the name of the God of Jacob** set you securely on high (v. 1).
> In the name of our God we will set up our banners (v. 5).
> We will remember the name of the LORD our God (v. 7).

Williams aptly alliterates these allusions as:

> The Defending Name.
> The Displayed Name.
> The Delivering Name.

20:2 The source of the desired aid is specified. The **sanctuary** in **Zion** was the dwelling place of God on earth, and so it was reasonable to expect **help from the sanctuary** and support **out of Zion.**

20:3 The king's faithful obedience in bringing **offerings** and **burnt sacrifice** is presented as a special reason why the Lord should **remember** him with favor.

20:4, 5 The king's **desire** was that the Lord should crown his plans and **purpose** with success. Here his loving people pray that this will indeed be the outcome of the battle. They are already thinking of a great victory celebration, with hilarious joy and excitement as the news is announced and with **banners** whipping and snapping in the breeze in tribute **to the name of** their **God.**

There is a question whether the words "**May the LORD fulfill all your petitions**" are spoken by the people, the priest, or the king. In any case it is a worthy prayer.

The King's Response (20:6)

Buoyed by the prayerful interest of his people, the king rejoices in the knowledge that **the LORD** will indeed send all needed help from **His holy heaven** and intervene with marvelous displays of His infinite **strength.**

The People's Confident Prayer (20:7–9)

20:7, 8 Such confidence is contagious. The devoted people, inspired by the assurance of their leader, are no longer awed by the vaunted military might of the enemy. Let him boast of his invulnerable **chariots** and battle-tested **horses**; Israel will boast in **the name of the LORD**! It is better to trust in Him than in arsenals of stockpiled weapons. At the glance of the Lord even the mightiest armies will crumple to the ground! But those who are on the Lord's side will still **stand upright** when the smoke of battle has cleared away.

20:9 With this peace of mind, the people once again ask the **LORD** to give victory to **the King**, thereby answering their prayers for deliverance.

Application

The historical application of the Psalm may be found in David's defeat of the Ammonites and Syrians (2 Sam. 10:14–19).

But the Psalm may also be applied to the Lord Jesus as a prayer for His Resurrection. His believing people pray that God will indicate His own complete satisfaction with Christ's sacrifice at Calvary by raising Him from the dead. As Messiah engages in conflict with Satan and his armies, He is confident of the final outcome. Psalm 20 anticipates the exultation of the first Easter morning.

The Psalm can also be applied to missionaries moving out into Satan's territory, or to any Christian striving to gain new ground for the Lord.

Psalm 21: Thanksgiving for Victory

There is a close link between this Psalm and the preceding one. There we heard the people praying for victory for the king as he went off to war. Here the prayer has been answered, and these same people rehearse the victory with the Lord. First they review the thrilling way in which God gave success (vv. 1–7). Then they anticipate the final subjugation of all the king's foes (vv. 8–12). Finally they extol the strength and power of Jehovah (v. 13).

The Sweet Taste of Victory (21:1–7)

21:1–4 **The king** rejoices in the way the **LORD** has just revealed His **strength** as the God of battle. He overflows with exultation when he thinks of Jehovah's timely intervention. God has given him the victory he craved, the success for which he prayed. Jehovah went out to **meet him with the blessings** of triumph and prosperity. The Most High **set** an imperishable **crown of pure gold upon his head**. In response to the king's request for preservation God **gave** him **life**—yes, **length of days forever and ever**. This latter expression probably means long life in David's case, but it is literally true of the endless resurrection life of the Messiah.

21:5–7 This passage takes on added beauty when we see them as referring to the Lord Jesus Christ. God's saving help has given Him great **honor**. By raising Him from the dead and seating Him at His own right hand, God has crowned Him with **glory** and **honor** (Heb. 2:9). Yes, the Lord has **made him most blessed forever** and a blessing to all the world! Seated in the highest place, Christ is filled with joy in the presence of His Father. It was His undivided trust **in the LORD** that brought Him to this place of honor. And it is **the mercy of the Most High** that will insure His perpetual exaltation.

The Doom of the King's Enemies (21:8–12)

21:8–10 At this point the people address the king directly. (In the previous section they had been speaking to the Lord.) If we identify the king as the Messiah, the passage describes the doom of Christ's enemies at the time of His Second Advent.

His **right hand will** ferret out **all** His **enemies**; none of those who **hate** Him will escape. The instrument of their destruction will be fire; He will be "revealed from heaven . . . in flaming fire taking vengeance on those who do not know God, and on those who do not obey the gospel of our Lord Jesus Christ" (2 Thess. 1:7, 8). He will also destroy **their offspring from** off the face of **the earth, and their descendants** from the human race.

21:11, 12 This **plot** to thwart Christ from taking the reins of universal government (also described in Ps. 2:2, 3) will fail dismally. The rebels will retreat in terror when God fires at them point-blank!

Praise the Lord (21:13)

In the closing stanza, the **LORD** is **exalted** because of the way He has revealed His **own strength**. Songs of praise burst forth because of God's **power** unleashed to deliver His own and to put down all His enemies. It is the song of Israel's remnant, praying for the exaltation of the Messiah and acknowledging Him at last as Lord of all.

Psalm 22: Christ in Suffering and Glory

Deserted! God could separate from
His own essence rather;
And Adam's sins have swept
between the righteous Son and
Father;
Yea, once, Immanuel's orphaned
cry His universe hath shaken—
It went up single, echoless, "My
God, I am forsaken!"
It went up from His holy lips,
amid His lost creation
That no believer e'er should use
those words of desolation.
—*Elizabeth Barrett Browning*

22:1, 2 Approach this Psalm with the utmost solemnity and reverence, because you have probably never stood on holier ground before. You have come to Golgotha where the Good Shepherd is giving His life for the sheep. For three hours the earth has been enveloped in thick darkness. Now "Immanuel's orphaned cry" echoes through the universe: **"My God, My God, why have You forsaken Me?"**

Behind the poignant question lies an awful reality—the suffering Savior actually *was,* literally and completely, **forsaken** by **God**. The eternal Son who had always been the object of His Father's delight was now abandoned. The Perfect Man who unfailingly did the will of God experienced the terrible desolation of being cut off from God.

The question is, "Why?" Why should the holy, sinless Son of God suffer the concentrated horror of eternal hell in those three long hours of darkness? Scripture gives us the answer. First of all, God is holy, righteous and just, and this means that He must punish sin wherever He finds it. To wink at sin or to overlook it is impossible for God. That brings us to the second point. Although the Lord Jesus had no sins of His own, He took our sins upon Himself. He voluntarily assumed responsibility to pay the penalty of all our iniquities. The debt we owed was charged to

His account, and He willingly became surety for it all. But now what can God do? All His righteous attributes demand that sin be punished. Yet here He looks down and sees His only begotten Son becoming the scapegoat for others. The Son of His love has become our sin-bearer. What will God do when He sees our sins laid on His own beloved Son?

There was never any doubt as to what God would do! He deliberately unleashed all the fury of His righteous wrath on His own beloved Son. The fierce torrent of divine judgment broke upon the innocent Victim. For our sakes, Christ was **forsaken** by **God** so that we might *never* be forsaken.

Thus when we read of Christ's deep, deep suffering, it should always be with the keen awareness that He bore it all for us. We should punctuate each statement with the words *for me.* He was forsaken—*for me.* When I hear Him cry, **"Why are You so far from helping Me, and from the words of My groaning?"** I know that it was for *me.* And it was for my sake that the heavens were silent to Him by day and by **night**.

22:3 In a sense the Savior explained His forsakenness in the words, **"But You are holy, enthroned in the praises of Israel."** The love of God demanded that sin's wages be paid. God's love provided what His holiness demanded. He sent His Son to die as a substitutionary sacrifice. Now "stern justice can demand no more, and mercy can dispense her store."

22:4, 5 But listen again! The Savior is still speaking to His Father, reminding Him that the patriarchs were never forsaken. Their believing cries for help never went unanswered. Not once were they disappointed when **they cried** for deliverance. In spite of their sin and waywardness, God never had occasion to forsake them. *That* sentence was reserved for the spotless Lamb of God!

22:6, 7 Not only was He forsaken by God, but He was **despised** and rejected **by the people**. To the creatures whom His hands had made Christ was hardly even a **man**—just **a worm**. He knew the bitterness of scorn and rejection by the very people He had come to save. Even as Christ hung on the cross, the watching throng ridiculed and mocked the Eternal Lover of their souls! Incredible as it seems, they sang a taunt song in which they mocked His apparent helplessness and the seeming futility of His trust in God.

22:8 **"He trusted in the LORD, let Him rescue Him; let Him deliver Him, since He delights in Him!"** This is exactly what the jeering crowd said at the cross (Matt. 27:39, 43).

22:9–11 **But** now the Son of Man turns away from man to God, and remembers Bethlehem. It was God who had brought Him forth from the virgin's **womb**. It was God who had preserved Him during the fragile days of His infancy. It was God who had sustained Him in His boyhood and young manhood. On the basis of this past relationship of love Christ now appeals to God to draw near in this hour of His crushing, solitary trial.

22:12, 13 **Many** of the hate-filled crowd at Calvary were Israelites. Christ likens them here to **strong bulls of Bashan** and to **a raging and roaring lion**. The district of **Bashan**, east of the Jordan, was known for its rich pasture-land and for its strong, well-fattened animals. Amos later referred to the luxury-loving Israelites as cows of Bashan (Amos 4:1). When Christ speaks here of **bulls of Bashan**, He is referring to His own fellow countrymen, who were even then waiting to close in for the kill. They were not only like goring **bulls** but also like ravening and roaring lions. The Messiah of Israel had come, and they were pouncing on Him like lions on a lamb!

22:14, 15 Christ's physical sufferings were excruciating beyond description. There was His exhaustion; He was **poured out like water**. There was the agony of bone dislocation by hanging on the cross; **all** His **bones** were **out of joint**. There was violent disorder of His internal organs; His **heart**, for instance, was **melted like wax within** His breast. There was His unendurable weakness; His **strength** was **dried up like** a fragment of pottery. There was His unremitting thirst; His **tongue** was clinging **to** His **jaws**. It could only mean that God was laying Him in **the dust of death**.

22:16, 17 Just as He had spoken of His *Jewish* tormentors under the figure of *bulls* and *lions,* so He now compares His *Gentile* executioners to **dogs**. It was a common name for Jews to use in referring to Gentiles (Matt. 15:21–28). Here it refers particularly to the Roman soldiers who **surrounded** Him like a pack of vicious, snarling curs. It was this company of evil-doers who had **pierced** His **hands and** His **feet**. As they gazed upon His half-naked form, they could see His **bones** pressing out against His shrunken skin. This gave them keen pleasure and satisfaction.

22:18 Then, in one of the several wonderful prophecies of this Psalm, the Lord Jesus foresees that the soldiers would **divide** His **garments among them** and **cast lots** for His **clothing**. Here is how it happened hundreds of years later:

> Then the soldiers, when they had crucified Jesus, took His garments and made four parts, to each soldier a part, and also the tunic. Now the tunic was without seam, woven from the top in one piece. They said therefore among themselves, "Let us not tear it, but cast lots for it, whose it shall be" (John 19:23, 24).

22:19–21 For the last time in this Psalm the Savior implores God for His presence and assistance. He asks to be delivered **from the sword** and **from the power of the dog**, both references to the Gentiles. **The sword** is the symbol of governmental power (Rom. 13:4). Here, it refers to the Roman government with its power of capital punishment. **The dog**, as explained above, refers to the Gentile soldiers. Then, in verse 21, Christ asks to be saved **from the lion's mouth and from the horns of the wild oxen**. As we saw in verses 12 and 13, this refers to the Jewish people who said to Pilate, "We have a law, and according to our law He ought to die . . ." (John 19:7).

"You have answered Me" makes a distinct and triumphant break between verses 21 and 22. It is the hinge which unites the two sections of the Psalm. The poetry now obviously moves from plaintive pleading to jubilant song. The sufferings of the Lord Jesus are now forever past. His redeeming work has been finished. The cross has been exchanged for the crown!

Between these two verses the psalmist transports us in a moment of time from Christ's First Advent to His Second—from Calvary to Olivet! Although the Psalm does not mention it, we know that the intervening period includes the Savior's death, burial, Resurrection, and Ascension as well as the entire Church Age in which we live.

22:22 By this point in the Psalm Christ has returned to earth to reign as King. The faithful remnant of the nation of Israel has entered the kingdom with all its millennial glories. The Messiah of Israel is ready to testify to His Jewish **brethren** about the faithfulness of God in answering His prayers in the first part of the Psalm. Now Christ praises God **in the midst of the assembly**.

22:23, 24 The next two verses give the substance of what Christ will say to redeemed Israel in that future millennial day. In three majestic parallelisms Christ addresses them as **"you who fear the LORD," "you descendants of Jacob,"** and **"you offspring of Israel."** Then He exhorts them to **praise** the Lord, to **glorify Him** and to **fear Him**. The reason for this reverent response is that God has heard and answered those anguished cries that went up from dark Calvary. God did not despise the sufferings endured by His beloved Son, nor did He permanently hide His face from Him. Instead, "God . . . has highly exalted Him and given Him the name which is above every name, that at the name of Jesus every knee should bow . . . and that every tongue should confess that Jesus Christ is Lord, to the glory of God the Father" (Phil. 2:9–11).

22:25 God is the object of Messiah's **praise**: **"My praise shall be of You in the great assembly. . . ."** In His distress Christ had vowed to praise the Lord publicly, and now He **will pay** those **vows before those who fear** the Lord.

22:26 In the last six verses of the Psalm there is a change of speaker. Now the Holy Spirit speaks, describing the ideal conditions that will prevail during the peace and prosperity of the Millennium.

Poverty will then be banished; **the poor shall eat and be satisfied**.

The earth will be full of God's **praise. All who seek Him will praise the LORD.** On all these worshipers the Spirit pronounces the blessing, **"Let your heart live forever!"**

22:27 There will be worldwide revival. **All the ends of the world shall remember** what Christ did at Calvary **and shall turn to the LORD. All the families of the nations** will unite in one great act of homage and **worship**.

22:28, 29 The Lord Himself will exercise worldwide dominion. The throne rights are His, and He will rule **over the nations**. All the great men of the earth will submit to His rule, and every mortal man **shall bow** down **before Him—all those who go down to the dust** and **who cannot keep** themselves **alive.**

22:30, 31 Christ's fame will endure. One generation after another will **serve Him** and proclaim His excellencies. A special message will be passed down from one **generation** to the next: that Christ has righteously finished the great work of redemption. Psalm 22 begins with the *fourth word* from the cross—the atonement cry. It ends with the words **"that He has done this,"** which have exactly the same meaning as Christ's *seventh word* from the cross: "It is finished!" (John 19:30). Down through the centuries of time the good news will be passed from one generation to another with grateful wonder that Christ **has done** it all.

Psalm 23: The Great Shepherd

The Twenty-Third Psalm is probably the best-loved poem in all literature. Whether sung to the stately measures of Crimond or recited in a Sunday School program, it has a charm that is perennial and a message that is deathless. "Blessed is the day," wrote an old theologian, "when Psalm 23 was born!"

J. R. Littleproud's outline is hard to improve upon:

> The secret of a happy life—every need supplied.
> **The LORD is my shepherd; I shall not want.**
>
> The secret of a happy death—every fear removed.
> **Yea though I walk through the valley of the shadow of death, I shall fear no evil; for You are with me.**
>
> The secret of a happy eternity—every desire fulfilled.
> **Surely goodness and mercy shall follow me all the days of my life, and I will dwell in the house of the LORD forever.**[21]

23:1 Despite its worldwide popularity, the Psalm is not for everyone. It is applicable only to those who are entitled to say, **"The LORD is my Shepherd."** It is true that the Good Shepherd died for all, but only those who actually receive Him by a definite act of faith are His sheep. His saving work is *sufficient* for all, but it is *effective* only for those who actually believe on Him. Everything therefore hinges on the personal pronoun *my.* Unless He is *my* Shepherd, then the rest of the Psalm does not belong to me. On the other hand, if He is really mine and I am really His, then I have everything in Him!

23:2 I shall not lack food for my soul or body because **He makes me to lie down in green pastures**.

I shall not lack refreshment either because **He leads me beside the still waters**.

23:3 I shall not lack vitality because **He restores my soul**.

I shall not lack moral direction because **He leads me in the paths of righteousness for His name's sake**.

We smile at the youngster who panicked when reciting this Psalm and came up with the novel version, "The Lord is my shepherd: I should not worry." But he was more right than wrong. He missed the exact words but caught the exact sense. If the Lord is our Shepherd, we need not worry!

23:4 And we need not be afraid of death. In **the valley of the shadow of death** there is no need to **fear**, because the Shepherd is right there **with** us. The sting of death is sin—sin unconfessed and unforgiven. But Christ has robbed death of its sting for the believer. He has put away our sins once for all. Now the *worst* thing that death can do to us is really the *best* thing that can happen to us! Thus we can sing:

> O death, O grave, I do not fear your power;
> The debt is paid.
> On Jesus in that dark and dreadful hour
> Our sins were laid.
>
> —*Margaret L. Carson*

It is true that Christians may have a certain foreboding about the suffering that so often accompanies death. As one old saint was overheard to say, "I don't mind the Lord taking down my tent, but I hope He takes it down gently!"

It is also true that we usually do not get dying grace until we need it. But the fact still remains that death has lost its terror for us because we know that dying means going to be with Christ—and this is far better. "To die is gain."

The Shepherd's **rod** and **staff** are sources of **comfort**, protection, and guidance. Whenever necessary He may use the rod for correction also. Most sheep need this ministry from time to time.

23:5 In the meantime, the Shepherd prepares **a table before** us **in the presence of** our **enemies**. On the **table** are spread all the spiritual blessings which He purchased for us with His precious blood. The **table** pictures everything that is ours in Christ. Though surrounded by **enemies**, we enjoy these blessings in peace and security.

J. H. Jowett illustrates:

> Eastern hospitality guarantees the security of the guest. "All the hallowed sanctions of hospitality gather around him for his defense. He is taken into the tent, food is placed before him, while his evaded pursuers stand frowningly at the door."

He also anoints our heads **with oil**. Shepherds anoint the heads of their sheep to soothe the scratches and wounds. For priests the anointing oil speaks of consecration to their work. For kings the anointing oil is associated with coronation. Every believer is anointed with the Holy Spirit the moment he receives the Savior. This anointing guarantees him the teaching ministry of God the Spirit.

When we think of all the riches of grace which we have in Christ Jesus, we burst forth with the grateful acknowledgment, **"My cup runs over!"**

> His love has no limit,
> His grace has no measure,
> His power has no boundary known
> unto men:
> For out of His infinite riches in Jesus
> He giveth, and giveth, and giveth
> again.
>
> —*Annie Johnson Flint*

23:6 Finally there is the secret of a happy eternity. Escorted through **all** of **life** by God's **goodness and mercy**, we reach the Father's **house** at last, our eternal dwelling place. As we think of it all, we have to agree with Guy King when he said, "What lucky beggars we are!"

Psalm 24: Who Is the King of Glory?

The Twenty-Fourth Psalm looks forward to a glorious event which occurs at the end of the Great Tribulation. The thunders of God's judgments have ceased, the Lord Jesus has returned to earth and has put down all His foes, and Christ is now marching to Jerusalem to reign as King of kings and Lord of lords. This is a triumphal procession such as the world has never seen. Even as onlookers were once startled by the depths of the Savior's suffering, so they are now speechless at the height of His glory.

24:1, 2 As the throng nears the city, the announcement rings out that **the earth** and everything in it belong to God. It is a statement of divine ownership and of Christ's full right to reign. Then the reason is given. Christ is the One who made **the world**. It was He who gathered **the waters** together in one place and made the dry land appear. It was He who formed the rivers, some on the surface of the earth and some beneath the ground. So now He is coming to claim what is really His own but has been denied to Him for centuries.

24:3–6 The next four verses describe the kind of people who will enter the kingdom and enjoy the thousand-year reign of peace and prosperity. These are the believing remnant of Israel and the redeemed Gentiles who will go up to the temple in Jerusalem to worship. It might seem that these people qualify for the kingdom by their good character, but this is not the case. Their character is the *result* of their new birth from above, for unless a man is born again he can neither see nor enter the kingdom of God (John 3:3, 5). These people, then, are the noble saints who have come through great tribulation and have made their robes white in the blood of the Lamb.

Four traits of character are specified. They have **clean hands**; in other words, their actions are righteous and blameless. They have **a pure heart**; that is, their motives are sincere and their minds uncorrupted. They do not subscribe to falsehood in any form. And finally, they do not pervert justice by testifying to what is not true. Their **hands**, their **heart**, their **soul**, their lips are all righteous.

These are the kind of people who will be subjects in Christ's Millennial Kingdom. Though formerly ridiculed and despised by the ungodly, they will now be vindicated by the God of their salvation. Yes, these are the citizens of the Millennium—people who seek God's face, people who have received grace from the God who loves the unworthy.

24:7, 8 I like to think that the procession has been singing the words of verses 1–6 as they cross the Valley of the Kidron. But now their singing is interrupted by the clarion call of the herald at the head of the parade. He calls out to the watchmen at the gates of Jerusalem: **"Lift up your heads, O you gates! And be lifted up, you everlasting doors! And the King of glory shall come in."** A sentry on the wall of the city calls back in loud, impressive tones, **"Who is this King of glory?"** The answer comes back in clear, stentorian words, **"The LORD strong and mighty, the LORD mighty in battle."**

24:9, 10 They are closer to the city now, and the **gates** are still hesitating. So the herald commands again that the doors be opened to **the King of glory**. Again he is asked to identify the King. He responds, **"The LORD of hosts, He is the King of glory."**

Then the King enters the city with His loyal subjects to take the scepter of universal dominion in His nail-pierced hand.

F. B. Meyer says:

> This Psalm is accomplished in us when Jesus enters our hearts as our King to reign, and it will have its full realization when the earth and its population welcome Him as its Lord.[22]

Psalm 25: The Secret of the Lord

This is an acrostic Psalm, though one letter of the Hebrew alphabet is omitted, and one is used twice.[23] It is difficult to find a unified theme; instead, the Psalm seems to be a potpourri of prayers and meditations with the only apparent link being the alphabetical one.

25:1–3 First comes a prayer for protection. David's enemies are never far away, it seems. So he looks to the **LORD** for help, acknowledging **God** as the sole object of his **trust**. David's dual supplication is that he will never be disappointed for having trusted in Jehovah and that his **enemies** will never have occasion to gloat because God has failed His child. This is his prayer for *all* who depend on the Lord. As for those who deliberately deal falsely, he wishes them a full dose of shame.

25:4, 5 In the next section, the psalmist portrays a disciple seeking instruction. He wants to know the

ways of the LORD, to walk in His **paths**, and to grow in His **truth**. His motivation arises from love for **the God of** his **salvation**, the One in whom all his expectations are bound up.

25:6, 7 Then David appears as a sinner seeking forgiveness. He appeals to the long-standing **mercies** and **lovingkindness** of the Lord and asks the Lord to remember that He has demonstrated such grace in the past— as if He could ever forget! If such requests betray an imperfect apprehension of God's grace on David's part, we must remember that he lived in an age of shadows while we enjoy the full light of the gospel era. . . . **The sins** of David's **youth** were bedeviling him; they have a way of doing that. The psalmist succinctly asks the Lord to forget these sins but to **remember** him **according to** His **lovingkindness** and for His **goodness' sake**. Such a prayer is irresistible. . . . What release there is in knowing that our sins are under the blood, removed as far as the east is from the west, buried in the sea of God's forgetfulness, forgiven forever!

25:8–10 David now moves from prayer to contemplation. He is lost in admiration as he thinks of the teaching ministry of Jehovah. Because **the LORD** is essentially **good and upright, He teaches sinners in the way of** truth, **justice**, and salvation. The single most important quality which we need to learn from Him is humility—we must be meek enough to admit our ignorance and our need for further instruction. If we are teachable we soon learn what is right, that is, what the will of God is. Far from having to endure an unpleasant life, those who obey the Word of the Lord find that life is filled with tokens of God's steadfast love and faithfulness.

25:11 David now returns briefly to prayer for forgiveness. Thoroughly convicted of the vastness of his guilt, he bases his appeal on **"Your name's sake, O LORD."** Since a person's name often stands for the person himself, the psalmist is here pleading God's own character—and especially His mercy and grace—as his only claim to **pardon**. There is not a word about David's own merit!

25:12, 13 Once again he interrupts his prayer to engage in a spiritual soliloquy. He envisions **the man that fears the LORD** as the one who enjoys God's best. This kind of person will experience:

Unmistakable guidance—God will show him the way to go.
Personal prosperity—he will enjoy abundant provision.
Family security—his children will possess the land.
Divine fellowship—he will be in the inner circle of friends to whom the Lord reveals His mind and ways in an intimate manner.

25:14 This is undoubtedly the golden verse of the Psalm:

The secret of the LORD is with those who fear Him;
And He will show them His covenant.

It was to Daniel, "a man greatly beloved," that God revealed the wonderful visions of Gentile governments superseded by the final kingdom of our Lord and Savior Jesus Christ. And it was to John, the disciple who leaned on Jesus' bosom, that the glorious revelation of Patmos was given.

25:15 David includes himself in this God-fearing group. His **eyes are** looking continually heavenward in trust and expectation, and he is confident that **the LORD** will extricate him from **the net** of trouble and affliction in which he is presently entangled.

25:16–21 The mention of a net causes David to cut short his spiritual reveries and to utter a prayer about his present plight. He is lonely **and afflicted. The troubles of** his **heart** are compounded. So he implores God to turn to him in **mercy**, to relieve his overburdened heart, to **deliver** him from his **distresses**, to take inventory of his afflictions and to **forgive all** his **sins**. David also asks the Lord to protect him from his **enemies** and their vitriolic **hatred**, thereby vindicating him for having trusted in Jehovah. When he prays **"Let integrity and uprightness preserve me"** he is not referring to his own rectitude, but is instead asking God to show His righteousness by delivering the one who put his trust in Him.

25:22 In the final verse, David identifies himself with **Israel** and prays for the nation's redemption. This suggests that a Psalm like this will become the language of the godly Jewish remnant during the coming days of the Tribulation.

Psalm 26: A Psalm of Separation

When we first read Psalm 26 we might conclude that it is the product of a surpassing egotist. More sober consideration, however, will show us that it is really just a factual description of a life that has been separated to God from the world. Reading between the lines, we find that David had been accused of fraternizing with ungodly men and of thus being untrue to Jehovah. Here he pleads his own defense. Nowhere is he claiming sinlessness, but he certainly does plead "not guilty" to the specific charges that were being made against him.

26:1–3 He rests his case with the LORD, asking for divine vindication. Contrary to what his accusers were saying, David had indeed conducted himself with moral **integrity**. He *had* consistently walked in dependence on the Lord. In language borrowed from metallurgy, he submits himself to God to be tested for genuineness and sincerity, to be proved in the smelting furnace for the presence of dross. Both as to his **heart** (affections) and his **mind** (motives), he was confident of acquittal because he had always kept the Lord's **lovingkindness** before him and had walked in paths of faithfulness to God's Word.

26:4, 5 To sit **with idolatrous mortals** means to have approving fellowship with them; this David had not done. To consort **with hypocrites** means to be a willing partner with deceivers and pretenders; David had not been this either. On the contrary, he had **hated** the companionship of criminals and had shown a holy determination to avoid fraternizing **with the wicked**.

26:6–8 But his separation was not merely *from wicked men*; it was *to God*. Before approaching the **altar** of the LORD, David had made sure that his **hands** were cleansed from sin and defilement. Then, as a purged worshiper, he sang a hearty **thanksgiving** and recounted the **wondrous works** of Jehovah. To him worship was not a dreary ritual to be endured stoically; he actually loved the **house** of the Lord where the **glory** cloud symbolized the glorious Presence of God Himself.

26:9–11 Because he had refused to join the gang in this world, David prays to escape their fate in the next. He had shunned the practices of **sinners**, murderers, and payoff men in life; now he pleads to escape their company in death. Because he had lived a righteous life, he now asks to be saved from the doom of the wicked, and to be handled with all the grace of God.

26:12 Standing on the level ground of an unblemished history, David vows to **bless the LORD ... in the congregations**.

We should note that there is an aspect of separation that is not brought out in this Psalm. Though we should be separate from sinners as far as silent assent or complicity with their evil is concerned, we should not be isolated from them when it comes to telling them about their need of Christ. The Lord Jesus Himself was a friend of sinners; He not only received them but ate and drank with them. But He never compromised His loyalty to God or failed to tell them about their sin and their need of forgiveness. When He visited the house of Simon, says Bishop Ryle:

> He carried His "Father's business" with Him to the Pharisee's table. He testified against the Pharisee's besetting sin. He explained to the Pharisee the nature of free forgiveness of sins, and the secret of true love to Himself. He declared the saving nature of faith. If Christians who argue in favor of intimacy with unconverted people will visit their houses in the spirit of our Lord, and speak and behave as He did, let them by all means continue the practice. But do they speak and behave at the tables of their unconverted acquaintances as Jesus did at Simon's table? That is a question they would do well to answer.[24]

This is a question that all of us should ponder.

Psalm 27: The Arrest and Trial of Jesus

Psalm 27 is beautiful in any setting, but it takes on a special attraction if we think of it as expressing our Lord's innermost thoughts during those fateful hours immediately preceding Calvary.

27:1 For example, when the chief priests, the captains of the temple and the elders came to the Garden of Gethsemane to capture Christ, He said to them, "This is your hour, and the power of darkness" (Luke 22:53). But at this very moment He may have been consoling Himself with the thought:

> **The LORD is my light and my salvation;**
> **Whom shall I fear?**
> **The LORD is the strength of my life;**
> **Of whom shall I be afraid?**

God was His **light** as the darkness settled in. God was His **salvation**, that is, His Deliverer from earthly enemies. God was the stronghold of His **life**, a refuge in the time of storm. With such protection, He need not **be afraid** of anyone!

27:2 When men came to arrest the Lord Jesus, He asked them, "Whom are you seeking?" They answered Him, "Jesus of Nazareth." As soon as He said "I am He," they recoiled and fell to the ground (John 18:6). At that moment Christ could well have been meditating on these words:

> **When the wicked came against me**
> **To eat up my flesh**
> **My enemies and foes,**
> **They stumbled and fell.**

They pounced on Him like birds of prey, but the glory of His deity as the Great I AM shone through His garb of humanity, and His captors were knocked to the ground.

27:3 John tells us that the gang

who came to arrest Jesus in the Garden consisted of a detachment of troops, several officers from the chief priests, and numerous Pharisees. They came with lanterns, torches, and weapons (John 18:3). As He watched them approaching, He could say with perfect composure:

Though an army may encamp against me,
My heart shall not fear;
Though war may rise against me,
In this I will be confident.

27:4 Poor Peter tried to defend his Master by cutting off the ear of the high priest's slave. But Jesus replied to Peter, "Shall I not drink the cup which My Father has given Me?" His one desire was to dwell with God, and since the pathway to glory led first to the cross, He was prepared to endure its suffering and shame. His language was:

One thing I have desired of the LORD,
That will I seek:
That I may dwell in the house of the LORD
All the days of my life,
To behold the beauty of the LORD,
And to inquire in His temple.

There is something indomitable about "one-thing" people. They know what they want and are determined to get it. Nothing can stand in their way.

27:5 Finally the band of soldiers with their captain and the officers of the Jews seized Jesus and tied Him up (John 18:12). To the onlookers it must have seemed like a lost cause for the Lord Jesus. But at this very moment He may well have been saying:

For in the time of trouble
He shall hide me in His pavilion;
In the secret place of His tabernacle
He shall hide me,
He shall set me high upon a rock.

His heart was resting on the protection which God has promised to all those who love Him.

27:6 The soldiers took Christ to Caiaphas, the high priest (Matt. 26:57). It was Caiaphas who had previously given counsel to the Jews that it was expedient for one man to die for the people (John 18:14). Though Christ's enemies planned to have Him lifted up on a cross between heaven and earth, our Lord Himself was anticipating another kind of lifting up:

And now my head shall be lifted up above my enemies all around me;
Therefore I will offer sacrifices of joy in His tabernacle;
I will sing, yes, I will sing praises to the LORD.

Strange optimism, this, for a man on trial for His life and knowing that the outcome would be His execution! Yet even now He was delighting Himself with anticipations of glory. Did He not say to Caiaphas, "Hereafter you will see the Son of Man sitting at the right hand of the Power, and coming on the clouds of heaven" (Matt. 26:64)?

27:7, 8 At this, the high priest exploded with charges of blasphemy. "What do you think?" he demanded of his onlookers. "He is deserving of death," was their reply. Here I can picture the Savior praying silently:

Hear, O LORD, when I cry with my voice!
Have mercy also upon me, and answer me.
When You said, "Seek My face,"
My heart said to You,
"Your face, LORD, I will seek."

27:9 By this time the disciples had all forsaken Him and fled (Matt. 26:56). But God had been His help in the past, and now He pleads that God would not forsake Him at this crucial moment either.

Do not hide Your face from me;
Do not turn Your servant away in anger;
You have been my help;
Do not leave me nor forsake me,
O God of my salvation.

27:10 As far as we know, David's parents never forsook him, and neither did our Lord's. J. N. Darby probably translates the verse more accurately as follows:

> For had my father and my mother forsaken me, then had Jehovah taken me up.

27:11, 12 At Christ's religious trial the chief priests and the whole council had solicited false testimony against Jesus in a determined effort to put Him to death. But they couldn't seem to concoct anything damaging until two witnesses appeared with the accusation, "This fellow said, 'I am able to destroy the temple of God and to build it in three days'" (Matt. 26:59–61). What Jesus had actually said (referring to the temple of His body) was, "Destroy this temple, and in three days I will raise it up" (John 2:19, 21). But since the whole trial was a sham anyway, the testimony was accepted. Now we can hear the Savior praying:

Teach me Your way, O LORD,
And lead me in a smooth path, because of my enemies.
Do not deliver me to the will of my adversaries;
For false witnesses have risen against me,
And such as breathe out violence.

27:13 Next we hear the frenzied mob outside Pilate's judgment hall screaming, "Let Him be crucified" (Matt. 27:22, 23). The blessed Lord Jesus heard the shouts too, and He knew what they meant. Yet He could have truly said at this very time:

I would have lost heart, unless I had believed
That I would see the goodness of the LORD
In the land of the living.

27:14 But how about the last verse of the Psalm? How does it fit into our interpretation? Well, I like to think that this verse is His parting word to each of us—a little personal advice from heaven based on the Lord's own experiences in trusting His Father.

Wait on the LORD;
Be of good courage,
He shall strengthen your heart;
Wait, I say, on the LORD!

Psalm 28: The Silence of God

28:1, 2 It's **to You** and You alone that I call, **O LORD**. You are **my Rock**, with all that that name implies of security, strength and stability. I beg You **not** to turn a deaf ear **to me—if** You do, it will be like being united with the wicked in death—utter separation from Yourself. **Hear** my pleading **voice** as I storm Your throne for help—as **I lift up my hands toward Your** inner **sanctuary**, the most **holy** place.

28:3 Never, never abandon **me** to the fate of **the wicked**, who ruthlessly plot **iniquity** against others, **who speak** so smoothly and peaceably **to their neighbors** while planning to do them in.

28:4 Lord, deal with them **according to** what they deserve, taking into account **their deeds** and the exceeding **wickedness of** what they do. Reward **them according to the work of their hands**—that which **they** richly **deserve**.

28:5 And not just because of *their* works, and the work of *their* hands, but because they have no appreciation for *Your* **works** and the **operation** of *Your* **hands**. That is why You will demolish them like a building that can never be rebuilt.

28:6 Lord, while I have been praying, Your Holy Spirit has given me that wonderful, inner assurance that **my supplications** have been **heard** and answered, and I bless You for it. Now I have a song to sing.

28:7, 8 Someone has made a beautiful metrical paraphrase of these verses:

> The Lord's my strength; He is my shield
> On Him my heart relies.
> So I am helped, my heart exults,
> To Him my thanks arise.
> For all His chosen people too,
> The source of strength is He.
> And for His blest anointed Son
> His saving strength shall be.

28:9 Lord, now that You have promised to deliver me, I ask one more thing. **Save Your people. Bless** Israel, **Your** heritage. Like the kind and tender Shepherd that You are, feed them well **and bear them up** in Your arms **forever**.

Thank You, Lord!

Psalm 29: The Voice of the Lord

29:1, 2 Do you ever complain about the weather? As David watched a thunderstorm sweep down over Israel it inspired him to praise rather than grumble. In fact he calls upon all the hosts of heaven to **worship the Lord** in full recognition of His **glory and strength** as revealed in the storm.

> Oh, worship the Lord in the beauty of holiness,
> Bow down before Him, His glory proclaim;
> With gold of obedience, and incense of lowliness,
> Kneel and adore Him; the Lord is His Name.
>
> —*J. S. B. Monsell*

29:3, 4 The expression "**the voice of the Lord**" is used seven times. It seems to be applied to the storm in general and to the thunder in particular.

At first the storm **is over the** Mediterranean, moving inland to Lebanon. The thunder reverberates **over many waters** like an advancing cannonade. It is a sound of awesome power and **majesty**.

29:5,6 Now the mountains of **Lebanon** are being bombarded. Tall **cedars** go crashing under the lightning assault. As the wind passes over the forest in sudden, violent gusts, the trees bend in rhythmic waves, creating the impression that the Lebanese range is skipping **like a calf** and Mount **Sirion** (Hermon) **like a young wild ox.**

29:7, 8 The lightning is streaking southward. **The Wilderness of Kadesh** is shaken by the ferocity of nature's onslaught.

29:9 As David sees the storm fade away in the south, he summarizes his admiration in three observations. First he says that **the voice of the Lord makes the deer give birth**. It is a scientific fact that weather disturbances have a direct influence on animals that are about to deliver their young.

The psalmist sees the **forests** denuded of leaves. The trees stand gaunt and bare, robbed of their foliage in a matter of minutes.

Then the sweet singer of Israel reminds us that **in** God's **temple everyone** cries **"Glory!" His temple** here quite clearly means the world of nature, especially the area that is being convulsed by the storm. The arrows of lightning, the peals of thunder, the winds of gale velocity, the forests, the wilderness—all join in telling forth the power, **glory** and majesty of God.

29:10, 11 The storm has gone; **the Lord** remains. His throne is unmoved by earth's violent upheavals, including **the** great **Flood**. His sovereignty remains undisturbed by natural cataclysms. In all the tumults of life He is able to **give strength** and **peace** to **His people**. May He be pleased to do so!

Some Bible students believe that this Psalm prefigures a military storm that will sweep down from the north on the nation of Israel during the Tribulation (vv. 3–9). Following that troubled time, the Lord Jesus Christ will reign as King over all the earth and bless His earthly people with strength and peace (vv. 10, 11). The idea deserves serious consideration.

W. E. Vine sees the Psalm as picturing Christ in His Second Advent, appearing first at Har-Magedon (Rev. 16:16), then sweeping down to the wilderness of Kadesh, the center of which is Bozrah (Isa. 63:1).[25] The Psalm thus describes poetically the complete overthrow of the nations that will have invaded Israel at that time.

But then there is always the practical application for today and every day. God's voice is heard in the storms of life as well as in the sunshine. He is working out His purposes. Nothing is beyond His control. For those who know and love Him, He is working all things together for good. Ironside says:

> It is a wonderful picture of the soul that has gone through its exercises, its stress, its trouble, but has learned that God is over all, that He is strong to save. And so the heart rests in Him and is at peace.[26]

Psalm 30: A Song of Healing

Most of us have at one time or another experienced the delicious relief of recovery from a serious illness. We have said goodbye to the sterile world of surgery, anesthesia, intensive care, intravenous feedings, hypodermic injections and the interminable pill parade! It is too easy to think that our recovery was "thanks to modern medicine!" We forget to sing a psalm of thanksgiving to the One who is ultimately responsible for *all* our healing.

But **David** did not forget. It may be that he had just gotten over a critical illness when it came time to dedicate his **house**. In any case, the dedication was the occasion for this hymn of praise to Jehovah, his Healer.

30:1–4 It teaches us first of all to **extol** the **Lord** with undiluted thanksgiving for the return of good health. David had sunk very low. His life signs were feeble. His **foes** were all but gloating over his imminent demise. Then **he cried out to** the **Lord** in his extremity and the Lord answered by bringing him back from the brink. It was a narrow escape from the dissolution of Sheol, a close call from going **down to the** grave.

Psalm 30 teaches us that we should not only thank God ourselves, but that we should share our exuberance by inviting the **saints** to join us in **praise**; let the solo become a choir!

The sweet singer of Israel called on all God's people to **sing praises to the Lord** and to **give thanks** to **His holy name**.

30:5 Then he gives the reason for this praise in the form of two extraordinarily beautiful contrasts. Knox's translation of this verse is priceless:

> For a moment lasts His anger,
> for a life-time His love;
> sorrow is but the guest of a night,
> and joy comes in the morning.

Let me pause here with a personal story. There was a time when the MacDonald family was plunged into deep sorrow. Friends trooped in to express their condolences, but nothing seemed to assuage the grief. Their words were well-intentioned but inadequate. Then Dr. H. A. Ironside sent a brief note in which he quoted Psalm 30:5:

> **Weeping may endure for a night,**
> **But joy comes in the morning.**

That did it. The bands of sorrow were snapped!

Since then I have had occasion to share this verse with many other believers who were passing through the dark tunnel of grief, and always the verse has evoked a nod of gratitude.

30:6, 7 The next lesson in the Psalm is that we should not rest in material **prosperity** but in God. Before his illness David was prosperous and self-reliant. He thought he was immune from trial and trouble. He was apparently immovable—like a great **mountain**. He had cushioned himself with every conceivable form of protection and security. It seemed he had nothing to fear.

But then something happened. As if overnight, the Lord seemed to hide His **face**; it seemed as if He were angry and had withdrawn His favor. Life became a nightmare.

30:8–10 But the nightmare produced a sudden change in David's prayer life. In his prosperity his prayers had been dull and listless. But now in his illness he prayed intently and sincerely. He reasoned with God that if he died, this would not benefit the Almighty. The lifeless remains of the psalmist could not **praise** Him, nor could his **dust declare** God's faithfulness.

> **What profit is there in my blood,**
> **When I go down to the pit?**
> **Will the dust praise You?**
> **Will it declare Your truth?**

To us such an argument does not carry much weight. In fact, it seems grossly deficient from a doctrinal standpoint. But we must be careful not to be too severe on the OT saints. In many ways they saw through a glass darkly. We have two illustrations of this in the Psalm before us.

In verse 5 David had interpreted his illness as a sign of God's anger. We know that God's chastening is a sign of His love, not of His anger (Heb. 12:6). Yet even we ourselves often slip into the fallacious thinking that sickness and suffering are marks of His displeasure.

Then in verse 9 David speaks as though death ends all praise on the part of the believer. As far as praise and witness on this earth are concerned, he is of course correct. But we know from NT teaching that a believer's spirit departs to be with Christ at the time of his death while his body goes into the grave (2 Cor. 5:8; Phil. 1:23). The believer himself is in the conscious presence of the Lord, worshiping Him in a way he never could on earth. The OT saints could not have known this. Christ is the One who brought life and immortality to light through the gospel (2 Tim. 1:10).

But the remarkable thing is this: with their more limited knowledge in many areas, many OT saints seem to have outstripped us in faith, prayer, zeal and devotion!

30:11 Now back to David. Verses 9 and 10 give us his prayer to God when he was in the throes of his illness. Then between verses 10 and 11 the answer comes. He is healed by the Lord. The last two verses of the Psalm celebrate his recovery. For David it was like the difference between the **mourning** of a funeral and the joy of a wedding. Or to change the figure, it was like a new suit of clothes. God had removed his **sackcloth** and dressed him up in garments of **gladness**.

30:12 One result of David's healing was that he could now **praise** the Lord in life rather than lying **silent** in the grave. And that is exactly what he intended to do—to **give thanks to** the Lord **forever**. He says, in effect, "I can never forget what the Lord has done for me, and I'll never cease to praise Him for it."

I don't know what this Psalm does to you, but it makes me feel ashamed. I think of all the times I've been sick, and of the urgent, desperate prayers with which I stormed the gates of heaven, and of how the Lord graciously answered. But then I forgot to come before Him with a thank-offering of praise. I took the healing too much for granted. I neglected to express my thanks.

God has given us David's example not only for us to admire but to follow as well!

Psalm 31: Into Thy Hand

The fifth verse of Psalm 31 alerts us that it has a definite association with the suffering, dying Lamb of God, for these words formed His final cry from the cross:

> "Father, 'into Your hands I commit My spirit' " (Luke 23:46).

Of course, the fact that one verse in a Psalm is definitely associated with the Messiah does not require that all the other verses must be. However, in this particular Psalm every verse does seem to have at least some connection with Him.

There is a problem, though, in analyzing this Psalm. Instead of tracing the suffering, death, burial, and resurrection of the Lord Jesus in chronological order, the Psalm alternates back and forth between suffering and resurrection. But we must remember, as C. S. Lewis pointed out, that "the Psalms are poems, and poems intended to be sung; not doctrinal treatises, nor even sermons."[27]

Prayer for Deliverance (31:1–5a)

31:1 In the opening verses the Lord Jesus is praying to His Father from the cross. As the perfect man He has always lived in total dependence on God. Now, in the hour of His deepest anguish, He reaffirms His **trust** in the LORD as His sole and sufficient sanctuary. He asks that He might **never be ashamed** for having relied on God the Father. It is a very powerful prayer, reminding God that the honor of His name is inseparably connected with the Resurrection of His Son. It would be an act of **righteousness** for the Father to raise the Lord Jesus from among the dead. Were He not to do so, the Savior would be exposed as a victim of misplaced confidence and would thus be humiliated.

31:2, 3 In an elegant anthropomorphism, the lonely sufferer asks

God to lean over with His **ear** facing Calvary; then He asks God to hear His urgent plea and to run to His rescue **speedily**. He further asks the Lord to **be** His **rock of refuge**, steadfast and unmovable, and to be a strong bastion in which He can be safe from every peril.

Of course God already *was* His **rock** and **fortress**, His only **defense** and security.

Other refuge have I none;
Hangs my helpless soul on Thee.
Leave, O leave me not alone,
Still support and comfort me.
—*Charles Wesley*

Once again Christ bases His appeal on the fact that the honor of God is at stake. **"For Your name's sake lead me and guide me."** Had not God promised to deliver the righteous? Indeed He had! Now He is asked to honor His name by delivering the Lord Jesus Christ out of death to Resurrection and glory.

31:4 A **net** of death had been carefully **laid** to capture and hold the Savior. Here Christ cries to God to **pull** Him **out of** this **net**, to rescue Him from the grave, for Jehovah is His refuge, safe and strong.

31:5a Luke writes that Jesus quoted the words of verse 5a with *a loud voice.* No man took Christ's life from Him; He laid it down voluntarily and in full possession of His faculties. These words have been repeated by dying saints of God down through the centuries since that time—by men like Luther, Knox, Hus and scores of others.

Praise for Resurrection (31:5b–8)

31:5b, 6 There is a distinct break in the middle of verse 5, a transition from death to Resurrection, a change from prayer to praise. True to His Word, God had **redeemed** His Holy One from death and the grave. It was a glorious vindication of His Son for trusting in the living **God**; those who trust in **useless idols** earn nothing but Jehovah's contempt!

31:7, 8 A song of praise now wings its way heavenward for the changeless love that hovered over God's beloved Son in His affliction. This was a love that took full account of all His **adversities**, that refused to abandon Him finally to the power of the enemy, that pulled the Savior out of the pit and **set** His **feet** on the **wide place** which is "Resurrection ground."

Deep Distress (31:9–13)

31:9, 10 But now we are brought back to the life of our Lord prior to His trial and Crucifixion. We are allowed to hear the prayers of the Man of Sorrows as He endured the bitter hatred of sinners. Despised and rejected by men, He turned to Jehovah in His distress and appealed for gracious consideration. His eyes were sunken through excessive grief, and His **soul** and body wasted away with weeping. He was worn out with **grief** and exhausted **with sighing**. His misery had sapped away His strength, and His very **bones** seemed fragile.

The only way **"My strength fails because of my iniquity"** can be applied to the sinless Savior is by understanding it to mean *our* **iniquity**, which He took upon Himself as our Sin-bearer. Otherwise the verse cannot have a Messianic connotation.

31:11–13 The patient Sufferer next speaks of Himself as an object of scornful contempt **among all** His **enemies** and a terrifying sight to His **neighbors**. They would cross the street to avoid Him or duck down an alley if they saw Him coming. He was quickly lost to their memory, discarded **like a**

broken dish. He heard the slander campaign that was being carried on against Him. Terror stalked Him day and night as men hatched plots to kill Him.

This picture of abject pathos and misery is sad enough for any man. But what shall we say when we learn that it was written to describe the Maker of the universe, the Lord of life and glory!

Prayer for Deliverance (31:14–18)

31:14–17a Sorrow and sighing give way to believing prayer. The One whom men reject confesses Jehovah as His Hope and the **God** of His life. He finds unspeakable comfort in the fact that His **times are in** the Father's **hand**. This comfort has been shared by God's trusting people as they have sung in sunshine and sorrow:

> Our times are in Thy hand;
> Father, we wish them there!
> Our life, our souls, our all, we leave
> Entirely to Thy care.
>
> —*William F. Lloyd*

Following this affirmation of trust and submission, the Lord Jesus prays specifically that God will **deliver** Him **from the** clutches of His persecuting **enemies**. He asks that the Father might look down upon Him in favor. He pleads for salvation out of death, a plea based on the steadfast love of the Lord. Again He asks that He might never be disappointed as He looks to Jehovah alone as His Deliverer. The language is rhetorical, of course, emphasizing style at the expense of literalness. There was no possibility that Christ could ever have been put to shame for trusting in Jehovah. He knew that, and we know it. But we lose something if we insist on strict literalness when we read impassioned prayer or lyrical poetry.

31:17b, 18 Turning to **the wicked**, Christ prays that *they* might be the ones who are put to shame, who go speechless to Sheol. He asks that their **lying lips** might be silenced for their slander of the Holy Son of God. Some sincere people consider these verses sub-Christian in their tone, but the more you think of the ruthlessness of the criminals, the vileness of their crime, and the innocence of the Victim, the more you conclude that the language is not too strong!

God, the Great Refuge (31:19, 20)

Once again the Psalm moves from distress to delight, from petition to praise. In majestic cadence, the Lord Jesus extols His Father as the incomparable Hiding Place. He pictures God as the administrator of an inexhaustible storehouse of **goodness** treasured up for His believing people. To all who seek shelter in Him He waits to pour out these treasures abundantly in the presence of the sons of men. God's presence is a place where His chosen saints can hide from the malicious **plots of man**; He is adequate shelter from what Knox calls "the world's noisy debate."

Personal Gratitude (31:21, 22)

The Lord Jesus had experienced a wonderful demonstration of God's goodness when He was completely surrounded by foes, like a besieged city. In His alarm it seemed to Him as if He had been completely deserted by Jehovah. But though He was forsaken during those three awful hours on the cross, yet God heard His cry and raised Him from the dead.

Love the Lord! (31:23, 24)

Having tasted the love of God, Christ loves Him in return and rightly feels that everyone else should too.

Jehovah can be depended on to protect His believing ones and to mete out adequate punishment to arrogant rebels!

Any believer who is up against seemingly impossible odds can thus be strong and courageous in the assurance that no one can **hope in the Lord** in vain—ever!

Psalm 32: Forgiven!

Happiness is to be forgiven! It is an emotion that defies description. It is the relief of an enormous burden lifted, of a debt canceled, of a conscience at rest. Guilt is gone, warfare is ended, peace is enjoyed. To David it meant the forgiveness of his great transgression, the covering of his sin, the non-imputation of his iniquity, and the cleansing of his spirit from deceit. To the believer today it means more than the mere covering of his sin; that was the OT concept of atonement. In this age the believer knows that his sins have been put away completely and buried forever in the sea of God's forgetfulness.

32:1, 2 In Romans 4:7, 8 the apostle Paul quotes Psalm 32:1, 2 to show that justification was by faith apart from works even in the OT period. But the proof lies not so much in what David says as in what he does not say. He is not speaking about a righteous man who earns or deserves salvation. He is talking about a sinner who has been forgiven. And he makes no mention of works in describing the blessedness of the **forgiven** man. Through the Holy Spirit Paul deduces from this that David is describing the happiness of the one to whom God imputes righteousness apart from works altogether (Rom. 4:6).

32:3, 4 Next David switches to a minor key. After he had committed adultery with Bathsheba and plotted the death of Uriah, he steadfastly refused to confess his sin. He tried to sweep it all under the rug. Perhaps he rationalized that "time heals all things." But in his stubborn refusal to break, he was fighting against God and against his own best interests. He became a physical wreck, and it was all caused by his unrelieved anguish of spirit. He realized that God's **hand was heavy upon** him, blocking him, thwarting him, frustrating him at every turn. Nothing worked out right anymore. The gears of life never meshed. The carefree days had vanished, and continued existence was as unappealing as an arid wilderness.

32:5 After a year of this impenitence, David finally came to the place where he was willing to utter the three words that God had been waiting for—"I have sinned." Then the whole shameful story came out like pus from an abscess. Now there is no attempt to gloss over, to mitigate or to excuse. David finally calls sin by its real name—**"my sin . . . my iniquity . . . my transgressions."** As soon as he confesses, he receives the instant assurance that the Lord has forgiven **the iniquity of** his **sin**.

32:6 His experience of answered prayer moves him to pray that all God's people would prove their Lord in the same way. Those who live in fellowship with the Lord will be delivered in a time of distress. The rush **of great waters** will never reach them.

32:7 The one who had been so hard and impenitent is now contrite and broken. With keen gratitude He acknowledges that God is his **hiding place**, his protection from trouble, and the One who surrounds him **with songs of deliverance**.

32:8, 9 There is a question as to

whether verses 8 and 9 are the words of David or of the Lord. If we interpret them as David's language, then they remind us, in Jay Adam's words, that "the natural response of forgiveness is to help others by sharing one's own experience and specifically by counseling others in trouble."[28] If we adopt the other view, then it is the Lord replying to David's worship with a promise of guidance and a lesson on the need for constant yieldedness. It is the Father spreading a feast for the returned backslider. He offers supervised instruction about the pathway ahead and personal counsel in all the decisions of life. But there is also a word of caution. **Do not be like the horse**, restless to move ahead without command, **or like the mule**, obstinately refusing to go even when directed. Both animals need the bit and bridle in order to make them submissive and obedient. The believer should be so sensitive to the Lord's leading that he does not need the harsher disciplines of life to bring him into line.

32:10, 11 As far as David is concerned, the righteous man has it all over the wicked. There is no comparison. **Many sorrows** are the heritage of **the wicked**. But the humble believer is surrounded by the **mercy** of the Lord. So it is only fitting that the **righteous** should **be glad in the LORD and** should **shout for joy**.

Psalm 33: A New Song

There appears to be an unmistakable link between the first verse of this Psalm and the last verse of the preceding one. In both, the writer urges the righteous to rejoice in the Lord. But this Psalm elaborates the theme by telling why it is appropriate for the righteous to praise Him.

We should note that there is no mention here of active enemies, of persecution, of tribulation. It is rather a peaceful scene, with Israel dwelling in safety and the Lord acknowledged as the universal Sovereign. The Psalm thus belongs to the beginning of Christ's kingdom, when Gentile oppression has been smashed and the time of Jacob's trouble is past.

33:1, 2 The call to worship goes out to Israel in the first seven verses, then to the Gentiles as well in verse 8. **Praise** is so **beautiful** and so compelling that the sweetest and finest possible instrumental accompaniment should be utilized—**the harp** and **an instrument of ten strings**.

33:3 The **new song** is the song of redemption. It follows the forgiveness of sins (Ps. 32) and belongs to all who have been cleansed by the precious blood of Christ. But this **song** will be sung in a very special way by redeemed Israel at the outset of the Millennium (Rev. 14:3).

33:4 The new song celebrates **the word of the LORD** and **all His work.** His **word** is absolutely true and righteous, unchanging and trustworthy. **All His works** are **done in** faithfulness. This is seen in creation—"seedtime and harvest, cold and heat, winter and summer, and day and night" (Gen. 8:22). It is seen in providence. "All things work together for good to those who love God, to those who are the called according to His purpose" (Rom. 8:28). And it is seen in redemption—"If we confess our sins, He is faithful and just to forgive us our sins and to cleanse us from all unrighteousness" (1 John 1:9).

33:5 God is not only upright and faithful, upholding **righteousness and justice**, but the evidences **of the goodness of the LORD** are everywhere.

33:6, 7 The greatness of God is

seen in that He created **the heavens** and their starry **host** by no greater expenditure of energy than by speaking the energizing word. Just this easily did He confine the oceans within appointed limits. Some see these two utterances as a poetic veiled reference to Israel as the stars of the heavens (Gen. 15:5) and to the Gentile nations as the raging seas, bottled up at last by the Lord Jesus at His Second Advent.

33:8, 9 In any case, God is so great that all mankind should reverence Him and show Him the deepest respect. His word was the sound energy which became matter. By His command all creation came into being.

33:10, 11 Throughout human history the ungodly **nations** have collaborated to thwart God and to ruin His people. But, as Burns said, "The best-laid schemes o' mice an' men gang aft agley," or, as we would say, they often go haywire! God ultimately frustrates the cleverest plots hatched by His opponents. And nothing can hinder the accomplishment of His purposes. He will always have the last word, and whatever He plans will come to pass.

33:12 So the pathway of blessing lies in cooperating with God. Happy **is the nation** that acknowledges Jehovah as its **God**. This is **the people He has chosen as His own inheritance**.

33:13–17 As **the Lord looks** down **from heaven, He** has a perfect view of all mankind. Nothing escapes Him. He sees all that is done and, what is more, He knows the thoughts and intents of every heart. He sees some who fight with carnal weapons—and He chuckles at their folly. They depend on **army**, navy, and air force rather than on the living God. When will they learn that the finest cavalry can't bring them victory?

33:18, 19 God also sees those who trust in Him for salvation and who depend on His **mercy** for provision. These are the ones who please Him. He looks down on them with keenest favor.

33:20–22 There is no question which class the psalmist and his people belong to. They trust Jehovah as their Helper and Protector. They have found true happiness by putting all their confidence **in His holy name**. All they ask is that they might continue to bask in the sunshine of His steadfast love as they continue to depend on Him alone.

Psalm 34: Psalm of the New Birth

The historical background of this Psalm is found in 1 Samuel 21. In his flight from Saul, **David** had sought refuge with the Philistine king of Gath whose name was Achish, **or Abimelech**, according to the heading of the Psalm. (**Abimelech** may have been a title rather than a personal name.) Fearing that this enemy king might kill him, David had **pretended** to be crazy by making marks on the doors of the gate and letting his saliva drool down over his beard. The trick worked. The king didn't need any more madmen and so he dismissed David, who then escaped to the cave of Adullam. This episode was certainly not one of the more heroic or brilliant chapters in the psalmist's checkered career, but he nevertheless looked back upon it as a dramatic deliverance by the Lord, and so he wrote this Psalm to celebrate that event.

Believers down through the centuries have loved Psalm 34 because it expresses so eloquently their own testimony of salvation by grace through faith in the Lord. Let's look at the Psalm in this light.

34:1 Salvation from sin is a gift of such tremendous value that it should draw unceasing thanks from our hearts to the Giver. If we were to **bless the Lord at all times**, it could hardly be too much. If **His praise** were to **be continually** on our lips, we couldn't begin to exhaust the subject. No human tongue will ever be able to thank God adequately throughout all eternity.

34:2 The converted person boasts **in the Lord**—not in his own character or achievements. When we understand the gospel of grace we realize that *we* did all the sinning and *Christ* did all the saving. So our **boast** must be in Him alone. If those who are still in the grip of sin will hear and heed our testimony of full and free salvation, they too will joyfully awaken to realize that there is hope for them as well.

34:3 The well-saved soul isn't content to enjoy his redemption in isolation. The subject is so superlative that he calls on all his brotherhood to **magnify the Lord with** him **and** to **exalt His name** collectively. Some couples have this reference inscribed on their wedding rings.

34:4 When the Spirit of God begins to brood over the soul of the sinner, He implants in it a divine instinct to seek **the Lord**. Only later does the saved sinner realize that it was the *Lord* who was the original Seeker! It is as the hymn says:

> I sought the Lord, and afterward I knew
> He moved my soul to seek Him, seeking me;
> It was not I that found, O Savior true.
> No, I was found of Thee.
>
> —*Anonymous*

Still, when we seek Him He answers, delivering us **from all** our **fears**—the fear of the unknown future, the fear of dying with our sins unconfessed and unforgiven, the fear of standing before the Judgment of the Great White Throne. When we trust Christ as Lord and Savior we hear His words of absolution: "Your sins are forgiven; go in peace!"

34:5 But this is not a private salvation—it is available to all. All those who look to Christ in faith become **radiant**. Frowns are transmuted to smiles of joy, and depression and despair give way to delight. No one who commits his life to the Lord will ever be disappointed; He cannot fail the trusting heart.

34:6 We come to Him in our poverty and rags, our humiliation and helplessness, and gladly confess our inability to procure our own salvation. We put our whole trust in Him. Our language is:

> In my hand no price I bring,
> Simply to Thy cross I cling.

The Lord hears our cry. Our poverty appeals to His unlimited resources. He stoops down and saves us **out of all** our **troubles**—out of the tangled web of sin which we had woven by our own hands.

34:7 The believer is not only saved, but kept as well. **The angel of the Lord**, that is, the Lord Jesus Christ Himself, serves as an encircling garrison for **those who fear Him**, delivering them from dangers seen and unseen. No sheep of His can ever perish (John 10:28).

34:8, 9 Those who know the Savior long to share Him with others. Like the four lepers in Samaria, they say, "We are not doing right. This is a day of good news, and we are silent and do not speak up" (2 Kings 7:9,

Amplified Bible). And so the evangel rings out, **"Oh, taste and see that the LORD is good; blessed is the man who trusts in Him!"**

This is the authentic, urgent invitation to the unconverted. We may reason, argue, resort to logic and marshal Christian evidences, but when all is said and done, a man must taste and see for himself. G. Campbell Murdoch writes:

> We may argue about God, His existence, and the external evidences which the universe and providence provide. But only when His love and presence touch our hearts can we really know Him in His unspeakable goodness.[29]

Then follows the invitation to the converted. It is the call to the life of faith. The **saints** are invited to walk by faith and not by sight, and to experience God's marvelous, miraculous, and abundant provision. It is the message of Matthew 6:33:

> But seek first the kingdom of God and His righteousness, and all these things shall be added to you.

34:10 While **young lions**[30] sometimes **lack** food and **suffer hunger, those who seek the LORD shall not lack any good thing**, for our Lord Jesus Christ is our great, all-sufficient Provider!

34:11 The grace of God not only saves, keeps, and provides but it instructs as well.

> For the grace of God that brings salvation has appeared to all men, teaching us that, denying ungodliness and worldly lusts, we should live soberly, righteously, and godly in the present age, looking for the blessed hope and glorious appearing of our great God and Savior Jesus Christ, who gave Himself for us, that He might redeem us from every lawless deed and purify for Himself His own special people, zealous for good works (Tit. 2:11–14).

So here the psalmist offers practical instruction to his sons on what constitutes the true **fear of the LORD.**

34:12–15:

1. A controlled **tongue**—one that is free **from evil** and **deceit**.
2. A separated walk—separated **from evil** and separated to **good** works.
3. A peaceable disposition—as Paul said, "If it is possible, as much as depends on you, live peaceably with all men" (Rom. 12:18).

Peter states in 1 Peter 3:9, "Knowing that you were called to this [blessing others], for the very purpose that you might inherit a blessing." He then quotes verses 12–16a of this Psalm to reinforce his teaching that we should not return evil for evil or reviling for reviling, but that we should rather bless. The blessing is the favor of the Lord; His **eyes are on the righteous, and His ears are open to their cry** (Ps. 34:15).

34:16 In quoting verse 16, Peter confined himself to the first half:

> **The face of the LORD is against those who do evil.**

He did not quote the rest, which says: **To cut off the remembrance of them from the earth.**

The first part of the verse is true in any age. The second half will be fulfilled when the Lord Jesus Christ returns to the earth as King of kings.

34:17 **The righteous** have the unspeakable privilege of instant audience with **the Lord**. He **hears** them every time they cry and **delivers them out of all their troubles**. Barnes comments here, "No one has ever fully appreciated the privilege of being permitted to call upon God, the privilege of prayer."

Before leaving verse 17 we should note that the Lord does not deliver us *from troubles;* He delivers us *out of them*. Believers are not immune to troubles, but they do have a Mighty Deliverer! That's the crucial difference.

34:18 **The Lord** knows how to resist the proud, but He cannot resist a **broken** and contrite **heart**. He keeps Himself accessible to the brokenhearted, and is always on hand to rescue the crushed in **spirit**.

34:19 As already mentioned, the righteous do have **many afflictions**. Perhaps we will find someday that we have had more than the ungodly. But at least all our troubles are confined to *this* life. What is more, we do not have to bear them alone, for our eternal Friend is by our side. We have the assurance of complete and final deliverance from afflictions through the Resurrection of the Lord Jesus. Because He has risen from the dead, we too shall rise someday, forever free from sin, sickness, sorrow, suffering, and death!

34:20 But even in death, the Lord protects the bodies of His saints:

> **He guards all his bones;**
> **Not one of them is broken.**

This verse was fulfilled literally at our Lord's death:

> But when they came to Jesus and saw that He was already dead, they did not break His legs. For these things were done that the Scripture should be fulfilled, "Not one of His bones shall be broken" (John 19:33, 36).

In this, of course, our Lord was the perfect antitype of the paschal lamb, about which it was written:

> Nor shall you break one of its bones (Ex. 12:46).

34:21, 22 The last two verses of the Psalm hinge on the word "**condemned**." As for **the wicked**, calamity shall bring them down in death, and they **shall be condemned**. But the **servants of** Jehovah have One who redeems their soul, **and none of those who trust in Him shall be condemned**. Praise God, there is no condemnation for those who are in Christ Jesus! (See Rom. 8:1.)

> Who shall condemn us now?
> Since Christ has died, and ris'n, and gone above,
> For us to plead at the right hand of Love,
> Who shall condemn us now?
> —*Horatius Bonar*

And so the believer is saved, kept, and abundantly satisfied for time and eternity. It's a wonderful thing to be born again! That is the message of this Psalm.

Psalm 35: Friends Turned Traitors

35:1–3 In an innocent use of his imagination, **David** calls on God to arm Himself with a generous supply of weapons and to thereby deal summarily with those professed friends of the psalmist who turned out to be his cruel adversaries. The psalmist wants to see the **Lord** reach over for His **shield and buckler** and move into action, hurling His well-aimed **spear**, then saying to David in an aside, "I'll take care of them and be your Savior."

35:4–6 It would be even-handed justice for these would-be murderers to be ashamed and disgraced, and for their devilish plots to be repulsed and foiled. It would be a righteous thing for them to become as helpless and weightless as **chaff** in **the wind**, driven relentlessly by **the angel of the LORD** (the Lord Jesus Christ in one of His pre-incarnate appearances). Yes, it would be fitting retribution for **their way** to **be** as **dark and slippery** as ice, with the **angel of the LORD** in hot pursuit.

35:7, 8 They had no good reason for plotting against the psalmist as they did, for trying to capture him as if he were a wild animal. So now let the Lord lower the boom on them unexpectedly, and let them be caught in their own **net**!

35:9, 10 Then David will **be joyful in the LORD**, celebrating **His salvation. All** his being will join in acknowledging the **LORD as** the incomparable One who saves the defenseless from the superior power of his opponent, the helpless and needy from the spoiler.

35:11–14 To understand the psalmist's deep emotional involvement, we must realize that these people who are now testifying against him were once his friends. Now they malign him and accuse him of things of which he has no knowledge. For all the kindness he has shown to them, he is getting paid with hatred. No wonder he is disconsolate! **When** these same people **were sick**, it was another story. David had grieved over them sympathetically. He couldn't even eat. With his head bowed down in sorrow, he had prayed for them continually—just as he would for an intimate **friend or brother**. His mourning was as deep **as** when **one mourns** the death of **his** own **mother**.

35:15, 16 But when calamity and **adversity** struck David, they were elated. They rose up in a body to accuse him. They brought along railing derelicts from the street to defame him with a continuous tirade. Impertinently they taunted him in a rising crescendo, at the same time baring **their teeth** in hatred. The psalmist's experience makes us think of the Lord Jesus before Pontius Pilate or before Herod; much of the language here applies forcefully to what He endured.

35:17, 18 How long can the **Lord look** down **on** the injustice of it all before being moved to action? The time has come to **rescue** the innocent one from the havoc of his foes and to save his **precious life from** these human **lions**.

35:19–21 What a travesty it would be if those who are David's **enemies** for no good reason should have occasion to gloat over his downfall and wink their eyes in apparent triumph. They don't want peace—all they want is to concoct false charges against decent, law-abiding citizens. Whenever they see the slightest slip they say, **"Aha, aha!** Just as we predicted! We saw you do it."

35:22–25 But **You have seen** too, **LORD**. You've seen the whole miserable mess. Don't shut Yourself up in silent seclusion. Don't stay so **far from me**. It's time to **awake** and take resolute action to defend me and my righteous cause. I long for You to vindicate me—You always do what is right—and to thwart their desire to celebrate my collapse. Don't ever **let them** exult that they have seen their desires fulfilled, that they have succeeded in devouring me.

35:26 O Lord, see to it that those **who rejoice** to see me fall will be thoroughly disgraced. Dress them with ignominy **and dishonor** for the insolent way they have treated me.

35:27, 28 But may all those who

are hoping for my ultimate acquittal have reason to **shout for joy and be glad**. Let them bear witness that You are truly a great Lord because You take such a keen delight in the welfare of those who serve You. And **my tongue** won't be silent, either; it will be continually telling others about Your justice and Your praiseworthiness!

Psalm 36: Great Sin, Greater God

36:1–4 An **oracle** in the **heart** of David gives a vivid picture of **the transgression of the wicked**. The sinner abandons any **fear of God** that he might have had. **He flatters himself** that his crimes cannot be proved against him and punished. His speech is saturated with **wickedness** and deceit. He scorns a respectable, law-abiding life. When he ought to be sleeping, **he devises** new misdeeds, then deliberately embarks on an evil course, gladly saying "yes" to sinful solicitations.

36:5 In stark contrast to the depravity of such a sinner are the perfections of the LORD. His **mercy**, for instance, extends to **the heavens**. Barnes writes:

> It is very exalted: to the very heavens, as high as the highest object of which man can conceive. The idea is not that the mercy of God is manifested in heaven . . . nor that it has its origin in heaven (though that is true) but that it is of the most exalted nature, it is as high as men can conceive.[31]

God's **faithfulness reaches to the clouds**, that is, it is limitless in its dimensions. A. W. Pink says:

> What a word is this! "Thy faithfulness extends to the clouds." Far above all finite comprehension is the unchanging faithfulness of God. Everything about God is great, vast, incomparable. He never forgets, never fails, never falters, never forfeits His word. To every declaration of promise or prophecy the Lord has exactly adhered, every engagement of covenant or threatening He will make good, for "God is not a man, that He should lie; neither the son of man, that He should repent: hath He said, and shall He not do it? or hath He spoken, and shall He not make it good?" (Num. 23:19, AV). Therefore does the believer exclaim, "His compassions fail not, they are new every morning: great is Thy faithfulness" (Lam. 3:22, 23, AV).[32]

36:6 God's **righteousness is like the great mountains** He has made—stable, steadfast, immovable, thoroughly dependable. He can always be depended on to do the thing that is right. This was perfectly manifested at the cross. God's righteousness demands that sin be punished. If we were to be punished for our sins we would perish eternally. This is why God's blessed Son took our sins upon Himself. So unbending is God's righteousness that when He saw our sins on His sinless Son, He poured out the torrents of His judgment upon Him. Now God has a righteous basis upon which He can save ungodly sinners—the penalty has been paid by a worthy Substitute.

> The perfect righteousness of God
> Is witnessed in the Savior's blood.
> 'Tis in the cross of Christ we trace
> His righteousness, yet wondrous grace.
>
> —*Albert Midlane*

God's **judgments are** like the **great deep**. This means that His decrees, decisions, thoughts and plans are wonderfully profound, complex, and wise. When contemplating this attribute of God, Paul exclaimed: "Oh, the depth of the riches both of the wisdom and knowledge of God! How unsearchable are His judgments and His ways past finding out!" (Rom. 11:33).

"O LORD, You preserve man and beast." Here it is a matter of temporal salvation—of the providence of God preserving His creatures. And what a great mercy this is. Think of all that is involved in caring for so many human beings and so many animals, birds, and fish. As for man, God numbers the very hairs of his head; as for the insignificant sparrow, not a single one falls to the ground without your heavenly Father!

36:7 Nothing that enters human life is more precious than the **lovingkindness of God**. It is eternal, sovereign, infinite, causeless, and unchanging. And nothing can ever separate the child of God from it. In 1743 John Brine wrote:

> No tongue can fully express the infinitude of God's love, or any mind comprehend it: it "passeth knowledge" (Eph. 3:19). The most extensive ideas that a finite mind can frame about Divine love are infinitely below its true nature. The heaven is not so far above the earth as the goodness of God is beyond the most raised conceptions which we are able to form of it. It is an ocean which swells higher than all the mountains of opposition in such as are the object of it. It is a fountain from which flows all necessary good to all those who are interested in it.[33]

This is why **the children of men** find refuge **under the shadow of** His **wings**. Unfortunately, not all men choose to enjoy God's loving protection. But the privilege is available to all, and people from every nation, class, and culture have found rest, refreshment, and safety under those incomparable wings.

36:8 Not only is there protection, but abundant provision as well. **"They are abundantly satisfied with the fullness of Your house, and You give them drink from the river of Your pleasures."** What food can match that of the house of the Lord for quality and for quantity? And what pleasures also? As F. B. Meyer pointed out, God gives sorrows by cupfuls but pleasure by riverfuls!

36:9 In Christ is **the fountain** or source **of life**. "In Him was life, and the life was the light of men" (John 1:4). **In** that **light we see light**. Just as natural light reveals things in their true form, so the light of God enables us to see things as He does. It enables us to form correct estimates of spiritual realities, of the world, of others, and of ourselves.

> Corot, the great landscape painter once said, "When I find myself in one of Nature's beautiful places, I grow angry with my pictures." Pleased with them in his studio, the artist was humbled in sight of Nature's glory. Judging ourselves in the light of the world, we may easily find grounds for personal satisfaction; but to judge ourselves in the light of the Lord, to measure ourselves by the Divine standard, is to put our pride to shame. (*Choice Gleanings*)

36:10, 11 After scaling the Himalayan peaks of the perfections of God, the son of Jesse returns to the valley of human need and prays for continued protection from **the wicked**. Verse 11 explains verse 10. The way in which David asks God to continue His **lovingkindness** and deliverance is by restraining the foot of arrogant men from trampling him down and

the hand of the wicked from driving him far **away**.

36:12 His prayer is answered. Faith enables the psalmist to see the wicked **fallen** down and powerless **to rise** again.

Psalm 37: True Peace

David had suffered plenty at the hands of ungodly, unscrupulous men during his lifetime. Now an old man, he shares some advice on how to react when we become a victim of wicked schemes and venomous tongues.

37:1, 2 First, we must **not** allow ourselves to **fret because of evildoers**. The danger is that we will lie in bed at night and rehearse the whole outrageous episode. First we think of all they said and did, then we go over how we answered them, then we wish we had thought of some other choice brickbats to hurl at them! Soon our digestive juices have turned to sulfuric acid and we lie and toss and turn, wondering when sleep will ever come! Our fretting is hurting no one but ourselves and accomplishes nothing. We must not do it!

Whatever else we do, we must not **be envious of** the unrighteous! This earth is the only heaven they're ever going to have. The scythe of retribution will **soon** mow them **down**, and their spectacular careers will fade and **wither**.

37:3 That's the negative side of the picture—don't be agitated over them and don't wish you were like them. On the positive side, the first thing to do is to **trust in the Lord, and do good**. This trust does not mean an unfounded, breezy optimism that everything will turn out right. Instead, it means a deep, abiding reliance on the God who has promised to punish the ungodly and to reward the righteous. His Word can never fail. The upright will indeed **dwell in the land** and enjoy security. Despite the fiercest attacks of demons or men, no sheep of Christ will ever perish (John 10:27–29). A dwelling place in the Father's house is guaranteed to all who trust Christ (John 14:1–6).

John Wesley once sent financial help to a preacher-friend named Samuel Bradburn. Enclosing a five-pound note, he wrote: "Dear Sammy: 'Trust in the Lord, and do good; so shalt thou dwell in the land, and verily thou shalt be fed.' " In expressing his thanks, Bradburn said, "I have often been struck with the beauty of the passage of Scripture quoted in your letter, but I must confess that I never saw such a useful expository note on it before."

37:4 But suppose you have had great desires to carry on a certain ministry for the Lord. You feel confident that He has been leading you, and your only desire is to glorify Him. Yet a powerful adversary has opposed, blocked, and thwarted you at every bend in the road. What do you do in a case like this? The answer is that you **delight yourself also in the Lord**, knowing that in His own time **He shall give you the desires of your heart**. It is not necessary for you to fight back. "The battle is not yours, but God's" (2 Chron. 20:15). "The Lord will fight for you, and you shall hold your peace" (Ex. 14:14).

37:5, 6 Or it may be that you have been misquoted, falsely accused or slandered. If there were some shred of truth to the charges they wouldn't be so hard to take. But they are absolutely untrue and malicious. What should you do? **Commit** the entire matter **to the Lord**. Roll the whole weight of it onto Him. Let Him act on your behalf, and then you will be completely vindicated. It will become clear for all to see that you were innocent after all. Barnes says:

> If you are slandered, if your character is assailed and seems for the time to be under a cloud, if reproach comes upon you from the devices of wicked men in such a way that you cannot meet it—then, if you will commit the case to God, He will protect your character, and will cause the clouds to disperse, and all to be as clear in reference to your character and the motives of your conduct as the sun without a cloud.[34]

37:7, 8 Having committed your way to the Lord, the next step is to **rest in** Him. Since He is carrying your burden, it is not necessary for you to bear it also. Too often that is exactly what we do. We cast our care hesitatingly on Him, then promptly take it back on ourselves.

> It is God's will that I should cast
> On Him my care each day.
> He also bids me not to cast
> My confidence away.
> But oh, I am so foolish
> That when taken unawares,
> I cast away my confidence
> And carry all my cares.
>
> —*T. Baird*

"And wait patiently for Him." Notice how the believer's resource is repeatedly said to be in the Lord:

> Trust in *the* L*ORD* *(v. 3).*
> Delight in *the* L*ORD* *(v. 4).*
> Commit your way to *the* L*ORD* *(v. 5).*
> **Rest in *the* L*ORD*** (v. 7a).
> **Wait patiently for *Him*** (v. 7b).

Sometimes this is the hardest thing for us to do. Waiting is the thing we do least well! But true faith waits, confident that God is able to do what He has promised (Rom. 4:21).

A second time David says, **"Do not fret . . . ."** Why the repetition? For needed emphasis, of course. Even after determining not to get upset over the way we are treated, we often go back and stir up the mud all over again in our minds. But this is both self-defeating and hazardous. Even if the evil person **prospers in his way**—even if he succeeds in carrying out **wicked schemes**—the Christian should not become emotionally disturbed or build up anger, resentment, malice, and hatred. If we allow ourselves to indulge in these attitudes, they can eventually lead to violent words and acts. Then we become offenders ourselves.

37:9–11 The day is coming when all the wrongs of earth will be righted. At that time the **evildoers shall be cut off** and the trusting saints will possess all the blessings He has promised. It will not be very long until **the wicked** vanish from the scene. If you **look carefully for** them in their usual hangouts your search will be in vain! In that day **the meek shall inherit the earth** and thoroughly enjoy its unprecedented prosperity. When will that day come? For the church it will begin when the Savior descends into the clouds to catch away His waiting people and take them to their heavenly home. For the believing remnant of Israel and the nations it will begin when the Lord Jesus returns to earth to decimate His foes and to reign for a thousand years **of peace**. In the Sermon on the Mount, Jesus looked forward to this glorious day in these words:

> "Blessed are the meek; for they shall inherit the earth" (Matt. 5:5).

37:12, 13 In the meantime the cheats, the extortioners and the oppressors lay their plans against God's children. They express the bitterest hostility toward those who love the Lord. But Jehovah is not agitated by the sound of their grinding **teeth**. He knows that the **day** of reckoning is not far away. It is good for us when we can look upon our foes with that same detached nonchalance, when, as someone has suggested, we can leave behind us the world of little men.

37:14, 15 It often seems that "truth is forever on the scaffold, wrong forever on the throne." **The wicked** are well-armed and well-trained. The righteous, by comparison, seem ill-equipped and continually outwitted. But there are certain inflexible laws at work in the moral realm. The way of the transgressor is hard in the end. Sins are sure to come home to roost some day. Men can't get away with their sins forever. The boomerang effect is always at work: **Their sword shall enter their own heart.** When they need them most their weapons will fail: their **bows shall be broken.**

37:16 The few possessions of the **righteous** are **better than the** enormous **riches** of **many wicked** since the saint has the Lord while the sinner does not. The writer of the letter to the Hebrews, after documenting all the incomparable wealth that the believer enjoys in Christ, adds rather wryly: "Being content with what you have, for He Himself has said, 'I will never leave you nor forsake you'" (Heb. 13:5).

37:17, 18 The arms of the wicked (that is, their strength) **shall be broken**. But not so **the righteous**. They will be upheld by **the LORD** of infinite power. He **knows** the number of **the days of the upright**, all that those days contain, and where they will lead at last. He knows that the heritage of the just will last **forever**—an **inheritance** which is incorruptible, undefiled and unfading, reserved in heaven for all those who by God's power are guarded through faith for a salvation ready to be revealed in the last time (1 Pet. 1:4, 5).

37:19 The saints **shall not be ashamed** of their faith when hard times come. They have the hidden spiritual resources to see them through. In **days of** scarcity they enjoy a special kind of abundance. First of all, they have learned to live sacrificially, so that they do not feel deprived when the meal barrel is low. But also they have the Lord, who is able to spread a table in the wilderness. They have the privilege of seeing God provide for them in miraculous ways, and there is a special, secret-sweet flavor to all such manna from heaven.

37:20 But the wicked shall perish. Throughout the Psalm this death bell tolls for **the enemies of the LORD**. They are called **wicked**, wrongdoers, those who prosper in their way, men who carry out evil devices, enemies of the Lord, those cursed by the Lord, children of the wicked, and transgressors. The word "wicked" is mentioned fourteen times in this Psalm and constitutes one of its keynotes.

The Lord's foes are **like the splendor of the** pastures or **meadows**. One day they luxuriate in wild flowers and verdure; the next day they are mowed down by the reaper or withered with the change of season. Insubstantial as **smoke, they shall vanish away**.

37:21 The wicked borrows and does not pay back. This may mean that he is *careless* about paying back *or cannot*. But with all his money, why can't he **pay back**? The answer is that he is always over-extended. In his greed for money he speculates. When he loses, he borrows to cover his losses. It's the old story of borrowing from Peter to pay Paul. He builds his empire on credit and then, when reverses come, he grows desperate to prop up his sagging fortunes. Behind the outward veneer of prosperity lies financial chaos.

Though **the righteous** are often far from affluent, yet they are incredibly generous, always finding it more blessed to give than to receive. They have proved that if a believer really wants to give, he will never lack the means to do it. As Paul taught:

> And God is able to make all grace abound to you, that always having all sufficiency in everything, you may have an abundance for every good deed (2 Cor. 9:8).

37:22 The destiny of the righteous and the wicked hinges on their relationship to the Lord. Those who have been justified by faith are **blessed by** the Lord; they will possess the land. Those who have refused God's offer of salvation have put themselves in the unenviable position of standing under His curse; they will be destroyed.

37:23, 24 The steps of a *good* man are ordered by the LORD . . . . Although the word *good* is not in the original text, the idea is certainly included in verses 23 and 24. God plans and orders the pathways of the man who lives in fellowship with Him. He **upholds** the one whose ways please Him. Though such a man may fall into trials and tribulations, he will never be engulfed by them, for the Lord holds him securely by **His hand**. It is also true that if a righteous man falls into sin, he will not be abandoned by the Lord, though this is not the specific kind of fall that this verse is referring to.

37:25 Throughout David's life—and he was an **old** man when he wrote this—he had never **seen the righteous forsaken** or **his descendants begging bread**. If someone objects that he has known instances where these things have actually happened, we would make two comments. First, David may have meant that he never knew of the righteous man to be *finally* forsaken. Or second, he may have been stating a general principle, without barring the possibility of isolated exceptions. Scripture often does this. It makes sweeping statements describing the normal outworking of spiritual laws. Exceptions do not disprove the overall principles.

37:26 Far from having to send out his children to beg, the righteous man is a generous donor **and lends frequently**. By following God's Word he practices industriousness, thrift and conservation. By working hard, shopping carefully, eliminating waste, and avoiding extravagance, he is able to stretch his funds and thereby to help others who are in need. **His descendants** become a blessing because they have learned these lessons thoroughly at home and follow them throughout their own lives.

37:27 This verse is one of several in the Bible that seem to teach salvation by good works. We know from passages such as Ephesians 2:8–10 and Titus 3:5 that this is not the case. We must conclude that if a man is saved he will produce **good** works, and that such faithful saints are the only ones who will abide forever.

37:28 The LORD loves justice, and it is in keeping with His justice to make **His saints** eternally secure. It is not that the saints deserve eternal life, but that Christ died to purchase it for them, and that God must honor the terms of the purchase.

The psalmist loves to meditate on the security of the believer (see vv. 18, 24, 28 and 33). All who have been born again through faith in the Lord Jesus Christ can know on the authority of the Word of God that they are saved forever. F. W. Dixon wrote:

> If you lack assurance there is only one way to gain it or regain it—take the Word of God. Take it and believe it. God says you are His; that you are safe and absolutely secure, and that He will never let you go; take a large dose of that.[35]

But while the righteous will be **preserved forever**, the children **of the wicked shall be cut off**. It is a melancholy business to contemplate the doom of the unsaved. What will it mean to be separated from God, from Christ, and from hope for all eternity?

37:29 Israel's prime hope was to live in **the land** under the reign of the Messiah. Devout Jews admittedly had a heavenly hope as well (Heb. 11:10), but the emphasis in the OT era was upon material blessings in the land of Israel during the golden age of peace and prosperity. When we read that the righteous will dwell upon the land *forever*, we must understand that the earthly kingdom of Christ will last for one thousand years, then merge into His everlasting kingdom. It may be that in the eternal state redeemed Israel will inhabit the new earth mentioned in Revelation 21:1; if that is the case then the promise of possessing the land **forever** can be taken literally.

The contrast between the righteous and the wicked continues.

37:30, 31 The just man's speech is brimful of **wisdom**. What he says is sound, scriptural, and solid. He speaks **justice**—not crookedness and deceit. He meditates continually on the Word of God, and this keeps **his steps** from slipping into sin and shame. As Spurgeon has mentioned, he has:

> the best thing—the law of his God,
> in the best place—in his heart,
> producing the best result—his steps
> do not slip.

37:32, 33 The wicked watches for an opportunity to pounce on the innocent and destroy him. But Jehovah will neither abandon the innocent to the power of the foe nor allow him to be declared guilty if a case against him comes to a trial. God is the Guardian and Advocate of all His own people.

37:34 Our best policy is therefore to *trust* (**wait on the LORD**) and *obey* (**keep His way**). There's no other way to be happy in Jesus!

But that is not all. For the sixth time the psalmist promises that all such will **inherit the land**. Then he adds a further assurance. **When the wicked are** destroyed, the believers' only involvement will be that of spectators. They will not take pleasure in this awful event, but will themselves stand free from any form of judgment.

37:35 David was keen and perceptive in observing human life. He had once observed a **wicked**, overbearing man **spreading himself like a** luxuriating **tree** in its **native** soil. Apparently the thought is that this tree had never suffered the setback caused by transplanting. It was still in its **native** soil and thus vigorous and large. The wicked man was correspondingly prosperous and powerful.

37:36 But the next time David was passing through that place, the man was gone. He **sought him but** couldn't find him anywhere. The man prospered for awhile. His power lasted for a short time, but then he himself was gone, and so were his prosperity and power.

37:37, 38 The psalmist counsels us to notice the contrast between the **blameless**, upright **man** and **the transgressors**. There is a posterity for the man of **peace**, whereas **the future** of the **wicked shall be cut off**. *Both the righteous and the unrighteous produce long lines of physical descendants.* Tholuck says of the man of **peace**, "It shall go well at last to such a man." But the wicked has no such promising tomorrow.

37:39, 40 The greatest thing about **the righteous** is their connection with God. He is their Savior and their strength in time of trouble. No wonder Christians turn instinctively to Him in time of need! They find that He helps them, delivers them, and saves them **because they** depend on **Him** completely. Are you in trouble right now? **Trust in Him**. He will see you through!

Psalm 38: Sorrow for Sin

We might think that this Psalm describes the suffering of the Savior were it not for the references to "my sin" (v. 3), "my iniquities" (v. 4), "my foolishness" (v. 5) and "my plague" (v. 11). It might be valid to apply much of the rest of the language to the Lord Jesus as He suffered at the hands of God and of man, but the basic interpretation certainly belongs to David at a time in his life when intense physical and mental distress were admittedly connected to some sin he had committed.

38:1–4 First David thinks of his sufferings as the **rebuke** of an angry God and the chastening of His **hot displeasure**, and he asks the **Lord** to lift the siege. The **arrows** of the Almighty have found their mark in the psalmist's mind and body, and God's **hand** has come down with crushing pressure upon him. As a result of divine wrath his whole body is sick. The illness has seeped into his very **bones**—and all because of his **sin**. There is no excusing his **iniquities**—he is thoroughly convicted of them. Like gigantic waves, they have dashed over him. Like an enormous weight, they have broken his strength.

38:5–8 **Foul and festering wounds** have broken out over his body, and he has no doubt why this has happened. He is doubled over in pain, laid low with weakness—a living specter of grief. His body is racked with a high fever, and there is no part of his anatomy that has escaped. He has no more fight left in him. Thoroughly whipped, he can do nothing but **groan** to express how he feels.

38:9–11 It is some comfort to David to realize that the **Lord** knows the anguish of his heart and the emotions he feels but cannot express. But still his **heart** is palpitating wildly, his **strength** rapidly draining away, and all sparkle vanishing from his **eyes**. His **loved ones and** his **friends** avoid him as if he were a leper, and even his **relatives** are reluctant to visit him.

38:12–14 Nor have his would-be assassins given up their plots, threats, and villainy. **But** David is **deaf** to all their threats and remains silent as far as defense, self-vindication, or rebukes are concerned.

38:15–17 Yet no matter how dark the present situation is, he is not without **hope**. He still has the confidence that **God** will answer him. He asks that his adversaries might not have the pleasure of celebrating his complete calamity. But right now he is continually racked with pain and near the limit of human endurance.

38:18 With refreshing candor and brokenness and with no attempt to gloss over his **sin**, David confesses his **iniquity** and says "I'm sorry!" Any man who sincerely takes this position before God will never be denied forgiveness. The Lord has gone on record to state that He will grant mercy to the one who confesses and forsakes his sin (Prov. 28:13). If this were not so, all men would be hopelessly doomed.

38:19, 20 David's thoughts go back to his **enemies** once more. Though he is weak and sickly, they are **vigorous** and **strong**. He then acknowledges the justice of God's chastenings but protests that his **adversaries** have no valid cause for their malice. He has been kind to them but gets only hatred in return. At the bottom of their hostility is the fact that David is a follower of God and of **good**.

38:21, 22 So he appeals to **God** not to **forsake** him, but to stay close by and to hurry to his rescue—to truly be the psalmist's Savior-God!

Psalm 39: Inner Fire

39:1–3 "I was fiercely determined to keep myself from rebelling or complaining against the Lord in spite of the extremity of my plight. I vowed to muzzle my mouth as long as I was in earshot of unbelievers; I didn't want to give them any excuse for questioning the providence of God. So there I was, dumb and silent, with no outlet for my suppressed emotions. But it was of no use. **My heart was** red **hot** with indignation and perplexity. I couldn't understand why the Lord was allowing me to endure such overwhelming grief. The more I nursed my bitterness of soul, the greater the inward pressure became. Finally all my pent up feelings burst forth in questioning prayer.

39:4–6 "LORD, how long is this nightmare going to last? Tell me how much time I have left, and when it is going to run out. At best the span of my life is only about the width of my palm; compared to Your eternity, my lifetime isn't worth mentioning. All of us humans are as unsubstantial as a **vapor**. We go through life like phantoms. We rush around in frenzied activity—but what does it all amount to after all? We spend our lives scrimping and saving, and leave it all behind to be enjoyed by ingrates or fools or strangers!

39:7, 8 "So what hope do I have, **Lord? My** only **hope is in You**. Apart from You I have nothing. **Deliver me from all my transgressions**—particularly those sins that might have brought this awful trouble into my life. I can't stand the thought of **foolish** people gloating over my calamity.

39:9, 10 "You know how I have kept quiet since this trouble struck—because I knew it came by Your permissive will. But now I am asking You to **remove Your** chastening hand from me; I am exhausted under Your recurring blows.

39:11 "**When**, Lord, **You correct a man** for his sins with various forms of discipline, he wastes away like a prized garment when it is eaten by moths. It is clear that we are all as transient as a **vapor**!

39:12, 13 "So I come to You, LORD, and ask You to **hear my prayer**. Hear and answer my urgent appeal. Don't be unmoved by my tears. After all, I am like an overnight guest in this world of Yours, a nomad like my ancestors. All I ask is that You stop frowning on me in judgment and let me enjoy a brief period of health and happiness **before I** make my exit from the stage of life, never to be seen on earth again."

Psalm 40: Rescued!

The well-known words "Sacrifice and offering You did not desire" (vv. 6–8) identify this as a Psalm of the Messiah; the words are applied to the Lord Jesus in Hebrews 10:5. But the Psalm poses a difficulty in that the first part deals with His Resurrection while the last part seems to revert to His agony on the cross. To explain this introversion is not easy. Some suggest that in the early verses the Savior is looking forward to His Resurrection and speaking of it as if it had already taken place. Others apply the anguished prayer at the close of the Psalm to the Jewish remnant during the Great Tribulation. In our study we will apply the entire Psalm to the Lord Jesus—first to His Resurrection and then to His sufferings on the cross. If this violation of the chronological order offends our western minds, we may take comfort in the fact that people from the East do not always consider time order to be supremely important.

40:1 The speaker is Messiah Jesus. He **waited patiently for the Lord** to hear His prayer and to deliver Him out of death. Even our blessed Lord did not always receive instant answers to prayer. But He realized that *delays* do not necessarily mean *denials*. God answers prayer at the time that is best suited to the accomplishment of His purposes in our lives.

God's help comes, not too soon,
  lest we should not know
the blessedness of trusting in the
  dark, and not too late,
lest we should know the misery of
  trusting in vain.

40:2 The Savior likens His glorious deliverance out of death to being rescued **out of a horrible pit** and from a **miry** bog. Who can imagine what it meant to the Giver of life to step forth from the tomb as the Victor over sin, Satan, death, and the grave—alive forevermore!

Though Christ's deliverance was unique, in a lesser sense we can all experience the power of God in saving us out of the pits and bogs of life. As we all know, life is full of these deep holes. The unconverted person who is being convicted of his sins by the Holy Spirit is in a particularly **horrible pit**. The backslidden believer also finds himself in a treacherous quagmire. There are the bogs of sickness, suffering and sorrow. Often when we are seeking guidance, we seem to be in a dark dungeon. And of course we sometimes founder in the morass of bereavement, loneliness, or discouragement. These are unforgettable experiences, times when we pray and cry and groan but nothing seems to happen. We need to learn from our Savior's example to wait patiently for the Lord. In God's own time and way He will come to our side, pulling us **up out of** the **pit**, setting our **feet upon a rock** and making our **steps** secure.

40:3 Notice that God is the *source* of our **praise** as well as its *object*. **He** puts the **new song in** our **mouth**—and it is a song of **praise *to our God.***

Our deliverance results not only in praise to God but in testimony to others: **"Many will see it and fear, and will trust in the Lord."** This was never more true than in connection with the Resurrection of the Lord Jesus. Think of the endless line of faith's pilgrims who have been won to the Living God through the miracle of the empty tomb!

40:4 As He thinks of those who have tasted and seen that the Lord is good, the Risen Redeemer utters one of the greatest, most basic truths in all spiritual life: **"Blessed is that man who makes the LORD his trust. . . ."** True happiness and fulfillment in life come only through faith in God. It could not be otherwise. We have been created in such a way that we can realize our destiny only when we acknowledge God as our Lord and Master. Pascal said it well: "There is a God-shaped vacuum in the human heart!" And Augustine put it this way: "Thou has made us, O Lord, for Thyself, and our heart shall find no rest till it rest in Thee!"

The blessed man not only turns *to* God but he turns *away from* **proud** men and followers of false gods. He is not tricked by two of the greatest delusions of life—the idea that the honor of proud men is important and the concept that the false gods of materialism, pleasure, and sexual indulgence can satisfy the human heart. The blessed man is more concerned with God's approval than with man's, realizing that fullness of joy is found only in God's presence—not in the company of those who worship at idol shrines.

40:5 This leads the Messiah to think of how numberless are the mercies of God. His **works** and His **thoughts** of grace **toward** His people are beyond computation. Who can fully describe the infinite details of His natural creation? Who can exhaust the remarkable interventions of His providence? Who can comprehend the magnitude of His spiritual blessings—election, predestination, justification, redemption, propitiation, pardon, forgiveness, salvation, the new birth, the indwelling Spirit, the seal of the Spirit, the earnest of the Spirit, the anointing, sanctification, sonship, heirship, glorification—**"if I would declare and speak of them, they are more than can be numbered."**

> When all Thy mercies, O my God,
> My rising soul surveys,
> Transported with the view, I'm lost
> In wonder, love and praise!
>
> —*Joseph Addison*

40:6 As was mentioned, verses 6–8 identify the Psalm as being distinctly Messianic. In Hebrews 10:5–9 we learn that these words were the language of the Son of God when He came into the world. He was saying, in effect, that although God had instituted **sacrifice and offering** for the nation of Israel, they never represented His ultimate intention. They were designed as types and shadows of something better to come. As temporary stop-gaps, they had their place. But God was never really satisfied with them; to Him they were less than ideal because they did not provide a final solution to the sin problem. Recognizing the inherent weakness of burnt offerings and sin offerings, God instead **opened** the **ears** of His Beloved Son. This simply means that the Savior's ears were open to hear and to obey the will of His Father. It was with this attitude of willing and ready obedience that Christ came into the world.

In the margin of the ERV, the expression **"My ears You have opened"** is rendered "Ears thou hast digged (or pierced) for me." Some interpreters think this refers to the Hebrew slave of Exodus 21:5, 6. If a slave did not desire to be freed in the seventh year, his ear was pierced with an awl at the doorpost and he became indentured to his master forever. Christ, the Antitype, became a willing bondslave in His Incarnation (Phil. 2:7) and will continue to serve His people when He comes again (Luke 12:37).

When the clause **"My ears You have opened"** is quoted in Hebrews 10:5, it is changed to "a body You have prepared for Me." As to the authority for making such a change, the same Holy Spirit who first inspired the words in Psalm 40 certainly has the right to clarify them when He quotes it in the NT. The literal rendering of the Hebrew expression "to dig an ear" is probably a figure of speech in which a part (here, the ear) is given for the whole (here, the body). (This is called synecdoche.) The NT expands and explains the meaning as a reference to the Incarnation.

40:7, 8 When Christ became Man, it was not with meek resignation but with wholehearted delight. He said at this time, **"Behold, I come; in the scroll of the book it is written of me. I delight to do Your will, O my God, and Your Law is within my heart."** From cover to cover of the OT it was foretold not only that Christ would come into the world but that He would come with an eager, ready spirit to do the will of God. The **will** of God was not just in His head—it was inscribed in His very **heart**.

40:9, 10 These verses describe His earthly ministry. He had **proclaimed the good news** of deliverance **in the great assembly**, that is, to the house of Israel. He had not held back anything that God had given Him to declare. He had not hoarded the great truths of God's saving help, enduring faithfulness, or steadfast love.

40:11 The remaining verses of the Psalm (11—17) seem to carry us back to the cross. We hear the Savior issuing a most compelling and poignant distress call. There is a close link with what He had just said in verse 10. The connection is this: "I have told the people of Your salvation, Your faithfulness and Your steadfast love. Now do not negate My testimony by withholding these **tender mercies from me. Let** them **continually preserve me!**"

40:12 The immediate occasion of His desperate plea was that the calamitous tortures of Calvary were crashing down upon Him. These **innumerable evils** were linked with innumerable sins, as effect is linked with cause. But when He says, **"My iniquities . . ."** we must be sure to remember that they were actually *our* iniquities—those sins for which He had contracted to pay the awful penalty. So intense were His sufferings that His **heart** was failing. Who of us can ever imagine the depths of agony which He endured that we might be pardoned and forgiven!

40:13 In His extremity, Christ stormed the gates of heaven for help—for immediate help. It is as if He pled, "Please **deliver me** and please *do it now!*" That is the kind of prayer that wins. Divine Omnipotence is moved into action by it.

40:14, 15 As for His enemies, He asks that their punishment be suited to their crimes. For their attempts on His **life** He wishes them disgrace and **confusion**. For wishing Him **evil** He hopes they will be repelled and shamed. For gloating over His misfortune He would like to see them shocked by the depth of their own humiliation. If someone objects that these sentiments are incompatible with a God of love, I would only remind him that in refusing love, man deliberately chooses his own punishment.

40:16 As for the friends of God, Christ prays that they might always find their enjoyment in the Lord. He hopes that **all those who seek** God will **rejoice and be glad in** Him, and that **such as love** His **salvation** will **say continually, "The LORD be magnified!"**

40:17 As for Himself, His strength is small and His need is desperate. But He takes comfort in the fact that the Lord takes thought for Him. As someone has said, "Poverty and need are not barriers to the thoughts of God."

As for God Himself, He is the **help** and **deliverer** of His beloved Son. And so in a final salvo of supplication the Lord Jesus prays, **"Do not delay, O my God."** The answer is not long in coming. On the third day the Father reaches down and delivers Him from the desolate pit, as we saw in the first part of the Psalm.

It seems, then, that in this Psalm we have first the *answer* to prayer and then the *prayer itself*. This vividly suggests the promise, "Before they call, I will answer; and while they are still speaking, I will hear" (Isa. 65:24).

Psalm 41: Prayer From a Sickroom

David was sick, and his enemies hoped it was nothing trivial. They were already rejoicing among themselves that his illness was undoubtedly terminal. An added grief to David was that one of the traitors had been his own close friend at one time.

41:1–3 But the patient is not without comfort. First he remembers that the Lord blesses the person **who considers the poor**. Here **"the poor"** probably means not so much poor financially as poor in health, weakened by sickness. David consoles himself with the thought that he had done just what the Lord did for people in distress—he had assisted, comforted, and cheered all who were in the grip of disease. Now he claims the promise that **the LORD will deliver** him too **in time of trouble**. Yes, the Lord will keep a protective vigil over him, preserving his life. Because David has earned a good reputation for his consideration of the sick and the suffering, he is confident that God will not desert him to the malicious will of his foes. He will instead give David all needed grace for his time in the sickroom, then raise him up to health and strength once more. The Lord is pictured as a nurse, adjusting the patient's bed so as to make him comfortable.

41:4 But the psalmist did not depend solely on his own past consideration of the ill and infirm. He wisely took his illness to the Lord in prayer, confessing his sin and pleading for healing as something he didn't deserve. Not all sickness is a direct result of sin in a believer's life. Many of the ailments of older people, for example, are part of the normal process of deterioration due to age. Sometimes, however, there is a direct link between sin and sickness, and where the faintest possibility of this exists, the believer should rush into the Lord's presence in heartfelt confession. In all such cases, the Great Physician's forgiveness should precede the local doctor's remedies.

41:5 In the meantime, the psalmist's **enemies** were waiting hopefully for a bulletin from the hospital stating that David had died. **"When will he die?"** they asked each other, "and when will we hear the last of this fellow?"

41:6 Occasionally one of these evil-wishers would show up during visiting hours, but he had no comfort to offer, no words of hope or encouragement. He talked without saying anything. Actually, it seemed he was just looking for some information to use against

David. After he left he broadcast every negative report he could imagine.

41:7, 8 A whispering campaign was going on against the sick man, and the prophets of doom were outthinking themselves in conceiving calamities for David. They spread the word that a fatal **disease** had attacked him and that his next stop would be the morgue.

41:9 Perhaps the "unkindest cut of all" was the treachery of one who had been an intimate **friend**. Of all the sorrows of life, this is certainly one of the bitterest—to be betrayed by one who has had close associations with you. It is a sorrow the Savior experienced in the betrayal of Judas, and a not-uncommon experience in the lives of those who follow this Captain.

The Lord Jesus quoted verse 9 in connection with Judas. However, it is significant that He omitted the words **"my own familiar friend in whom I trusted."** Knowing in advance that Judas would betray Him, the Lord had never trusted him, so He simply said, "He who eats My bread has lifted up his heel against Me" (John 13:18).

41:10 David turns away from the one who had, as it were, stabbed him in the back, and looks instead to the LORD for mercy. When others were deserting him, he counts on the Lord to stand by faithfully. He then makes what might seem to be a strange request: **"and raise me up, that I may repay them."** If at first this seems unworthy of a man of David's stature, we must remember that he was the Lord's anointed ruler of Israel, and it was his duty as king to deal with sedition and betrayal. While as an individual he might have chosen to tolerate villainy and treachery against himself, as the king he was obliged to suppress any attempts to overthrow the government.

41:11, 12 David sees in the failure of his enemies' plots an indication of the Lord's favor toward him. Then he adds:

> **You uphold me in my integrity,**
> **And set me before Your face**
> **forever.**

If we prefer this translation, it may sound as if David is boasting excessively. But he actually *was* a man of **integrity** in spite of his sins and failures. And compared to his foes he was a paragon of virtue. It is entirely possible that the Lord did **uphold** him because He saw sincerity and righteousness in his life.

Gelineau's translation of the verse presents less difficulty:

> If you uphold me I shall be unharmed
> and set in your presence for evermore.

In this version everything is dependent on the Lord rather than on David's integrity. The Lord's sustaining grace assures safety in this life and a standing in the presence of the heavenly King forever.

41:13 Confident and serene, the psalmist now raises his voice in a parting burst of praise. Jehovah, the covenant-keeping **God of Israel**, is worthy to be worshiped **from everlasting to everlasting**. David could add a double **Amen** to this tribute, and so can we!

II. BOOK 2 (PSALMS 42—72)

Psalm 42: Thirsting for God

Some people hear the voice of David in this Psalm as he wandered in exile during the rebellion of his own son, Absalom.

Others recognize the voice of the Messiah during the time of His rejection and suffering.

Still others detect the plaintive sob of the Jewish remnant during the future Tribulation Period.

Then there are those who like to apply it to the believer as he looks back on the days of his first love and longs for the renewal of that kind of fellowship with the Lord.

Fortunately, it is not necessary to isolate one view, since all of them are legitimate applications. This is typical of the versatility of the Psalms.

42:1 Our inner longing for fellowship with **God** can be compared to the vehement craving of **the deer** as it wanders through the parched countryside, its sides throbbing and its breathing quickened as it longs **for the brooks**. Gamaliel Bradford transferred the picture to himself when he said:

> My one unchanged ambition
> Wheresoe'er my feet have trod
> Is a keen, enormous, haunting,
> Never-sated thirst for God.

42:2 Our thirst is **for God** alone; no one else will do. And it is **for the living God**—not for a dead idol. It is a desire that will only be fully satisfied by a personal appearance before the Lord and the privilege of gazing on His face.

> Show me Thy face, one transient gleam of loveliness divine,
> And I shall never think or dream of other love than thine;
> All lesser lights shall darken quite, all lower glories dim,
> The beautiful of earth will ne'er seem beautiful again.
>
> —*Author unknown*

42:3 Who can describe the bitterness of separation from the Lord? It is like a continual diet of **tears**, a life of unalleviated misery. As if that were not enough, there is the added grief of the enemies' taunts, **"Where is your God?"** This is what Shimei meant when he said to David, "So now you are caught in your own evil, because you are a bloodthirsty man!" (2 Sam. 16:8). And this is what the chief priests meant when they said of the crucified Messiah, "He trusted in God; let Him deliver Him now if He will have pleasure in Him . . ." (Matt. 27:43).

42:4 Then, of course, there is the memory of better days. It is the remembrance of how wonderful it was to walk in unbroken fellowship with **God** that makes the absence of this fellowship so intolerable. Knox wonderfully captures the mood in his translation of verse 4:

> Memories come back to me yet, melting the heart; how once I would join with the throng, leading the way to God's house, amid cries of joy and thanksgiving, and all the bustle of holiday.

42:5 The thought of the happy past leads to spiritual depression and activates a ping-pong struggle between pessimism and faith. The **soul** becomes downcast and **disquieted**, but faith challenges the tension of this burdened state of mind.

> **Hope in God; for I shall yet praise Him for the help of His countenance.**

If this were just a pious optimism that "everything will turn out all right," it would be an utterly worthless sentiment. What makes this hope 100% valid is that it is based on the promise of God's Word that His people will see His face (Ps. 17:15; Rev. 22:4).

42:6 The depression recurs in cycles. But faith strikes back with the confident assertion that it **will remember** God **from the land of the Jordan** and **of Hermon** and **from the Hill Mizar**. Perhaps these three places symbolize three spiritual experiences; we do not know. What does seem clear is that they represent the land of exile, far removed from the house of God in Jerusalem. And the thought seems to be that even when we cannot visit the house of God, we can still remember the God of the house!

42:7 When we come to the seventh verse, our spiritual instincts tell us that in a very special way we are at Calvary, hearing the cries of the Lord Jesus as the **waves and billows** of God's judgment rolled over Him. The cataracts of divine wrath cascaded down upon Him with resounding thunder as He bore our sins in His own body on the cross.

> View that closing scene of anguish:
> All God's waves and billows roll
> Over Him, there left to languish
> On the Cross, to save my soul.
> Matchless love! how vast! how free!
> Jesus gave Himself for me.
>
> —*J. J. Hopkins*

42:8 Yet, as George Mller said, "Trials are food for faith to feed on." So we hear the confident believer affirm:

> **The LORD will command His lovingkindness in the daytime, and in the night His song shall be with me—a prayer to the God of my life.**

This is the answer to the day-and-night sequence in verse 3. There the psalmist had said, "My tears have been my food day and night. . . ." But now the day is filled with God's steadfast love and the night is filled with song and prayer. So by day and by **night** God's goodness is proven.

42:9, 10 Once again discouragement returns, this time because of the relentless oppression of the enemy. It seems that God has **forgotten** His child. The forlorn believer wanders about like a mourner. He says, "With cries that pierce me to the heart, my enemies revile me" (Gelineau). From all outward appearances it would seem that God has forsaken His child. So the **enemies** taunt him continually with the question, **"Where is your God?"**

42:11 But faith always has the last word. Don't be discouraged. Don't be unsettled. **Hope in God**; you will be delivered from your enemies and from your depression as well. And you'll **praise Him** once again as your Savior and your God. As someone has said:

> The remedy—challenge depression, look up, hope. The Christian life is alertness, upward striving, activity, the running of a race. It is never downcast eyes, folded hands and the acceptance of defeat.

Psalm 43: Send Out Your Light and Your Truth

This is a twin to the preceding Psalm. The connection is so great that the NEB links them together as if they were one composition.

43:1, 2 Here we have the continued prayer of an exile who wants to worship in Zion but is opposed by an apostate **nation** and an **unjust man**. This may picture the oppression of the godly Jewish remnant during the Tribulation by the unbelieving nation of Israel and the Antichrist.

First comes the plea for vindication and for help. The psalmist asks God to defend the **cause** of His people against their unbelieving brethren and the man of sin. It is one of faith's agonies to take refuge in God and yet feel **cast off** by Him; it is one of faith's puzzles to be on the winning side and yet suffer under the heel **of the enemy**.

43:3 Then follows a positive and specific prayer for the return to Zion. The beauty of the language is incomparable:

> **Oh, send out Your light and Your truth!**
> **Let them lead me;**
> **Let them bring me to Your holy hill**
> **And to Your tabernacle.**

The psalmist wanted an escort consisting of the **light** of God's presence and the **truth** of God's promise. With these to lead him and with goodness and mercy following him (Ps. 23:6), he was assured of a glad return to God's **holy hill**.

43:4 Notice the progression in verses 3 and 4:

> To Your holy hill;
> To Your tabernacle;
> **To the altar of God;**
> **To God my exceeding joy.**

The true worshiper is satisfied with neither a geographical location nor a building nor an altar. He must get through **to God** Himself!

43:5 Brightened by the prospect of appearing before God, the writer once again remonstrates with himself for being disheartened and troubled. Have faith **in God**, he urges, and He will surely bring you to your desired end.

> Be still, my soul: thy best, thy heavenly Friend
> Through thorny ways leads to a joyful end!
> —*Katharina von Schlegel*

Psalm 44: Sheep for the Slaughter

The pain of defeat is made more bitter by the memory of former victories, and we never value our fellowship with God so much as when His face seems to be hidden from us.

44:1–3 Israel's history was replete with soul-thrilling instances of God's intervention on their behalf. He had driven the heathen out of the land of Canaan and had given it to His own people. By subduing the Canaanites He had set Israel free in a country of their own. It certainly wasn't because of any military superiority that the Jews won possession of the pleasant land, nor was it by **their own** strength that they came off victorious. It was by God's powerful **right hand**, by His omnipotent **arm**, by His loving favor showered down on them.

44:4–8 The memory of what the Lord has done inspires our own hearts to praise Him. He is the great **King** and mighty **God** who gives **victories** to the unworthy sons of unworthy **Jacob**. It is through Him that Israel has been able to bulldoze through the ranks of her **enemies** and to walk triumphantly over her attackers. She has learned that the battlebow is not to be trusted for success, nor is the **sword** a sufficient savior. *God* is the One who has delivered His people and thoroughly confused their foes! No wonder the people kept boasting of their connection with Him, kept saying they would never cease to thank Him!

44:9–12 But something has happened in the meantime to change their song to a lament. It seems that the Lord has forsaken His people and made them suffer dishonor. The armies marched out without God's presence and help, and soon they were retreating in panic, with the enemies looting all Israel's wealth. The Lord has abandoned His **sheep** to the butchers and scattered the survivors among the Gentile nations. It all happened like a business deal in which God sold His **people for next to nothing**. And the enemy apparently got away with it all without having to pay the consequences.

44:13–16 Poor Israel became the laughingstock of the other nations, an object of ridicule and **scorn**. Traditional bywords and epithets of **derision** were used to defame these Jews. God's ancient people became the butt of crude jokes **among the nations**. Theirs was a shame from which they could not escape. Their faces were constantly crimsoned by the reproaches and jeers of their enemies, by the very sight of the vengeful foe.

44:17 The puzzling thing about all this defeat and shame was that it was not brought on by any conscious backsliding on Israel's part. At other times in history there *was* a definite connection between suffering and sin. But in this particular case it was not so. It seemed instead that the people's plight was due to the fact that they were God's chosen people. It was a case of suffering for God and for His **covenant**.

44:18, 19 The calamities had come to a people who had **not turned** their backs on God or violated His covenant. They had not abandoned their love for Him or the pathway He had marked out for them. Yet the Lord had shattered them **in the** forsaken land **of jackals, and covered** them **with the shadow of death**.

44:20–22 **If** they **had forgotten the name of** their **God** or worshiped idols, wouldn't God have known it? He knows the innermost thoughts and motives. No, that was not the cause. The people were suffering because of their connection with Jehovah. It was for *His* **sake** that they were enduring a living death, abused like animals destined for the slaughterhouse.

Centuries later the apostle Paul found himself in the same situation, and quoted Psalm 44:22 to describe the sufferings of God's people in every age (Rom. 8:36).

44:23–26 The Psalm reaches a peak of bold urgency in verse 23, when the **Lord** is roused from His apparent slumber and asked to intervene for His people. It is more than the psalmist can understand—how God can **hide** His **face** in neglect and indifference while His people lie prostrate in **the dust**. And so he sounds reveille once again:

> **Arise for our help,**
> **And redeem us for Your mercies' sake.**

Psalm 45: The King of Kings

45:1 It was easy for the psalmist to write this Psalm. In fact, his **heart** was bursting to put in writing the poem he had composed **concerning the King**. The words flowed freely from his pen; he felt himself being literally borne along. His **tongue** was like **the pen of a ready** scribe, and we are not stretching matters if we identify the ready scribe as the Holy Spirit Himself.

45:2 First we are introduced to the King Himself. His beauty is surpassing. He is the chiefest among ten thousand, the altogether lovely One. **Grace is poured upon** His **lips**; His speech is most sweet. Because of His personal excellence, **God has blessed** Him **forever**.

> Fairest of all the earth-born race,
> Perfect in comeliness Thou art;

Replenished are Thy lips with grace,
And full of love Thy tender heart.
God ever-blest, we bow the knee,
And own all fullness dwells in Thee.
—*Author unknown*

45:3–5 Then almost immediately we are carried forward to Christ's Second Advent, to the time when He returns to earth in power and great glory. This time He comes as a conquering warrior, not as the humble carpenter of Nazareth. With **sword upon** His **thigh**, the **Mighty One** descends in **glory** and **majesty**. In dazzling splendor He rides forth in triumph in the cause of **truth, humility, and righteousness.** His nail-scarred **right hand** is adept in wielding the sword in frightening power against His foes. His **arrows** find their mark **in the heart of the King's enemies; the peoples fall** in waves before Him.

45:6, 7a Now the smoke of battle has passed and the King is seated on the **throne** of His glory in Jerusalem. The voice of God is heard from heaven addressing Him as **God** and certifying His reign as an eternal one. We know it is the voice of God, because Hebrews 1:8, 9 tells us so:

> But to the Son He says: "Your throne, O God, is forever and ever; a scepter of righteousness is the scepter of Your kingdom. You have loved righteousness and hated lawlessness; therefore God, Your God, has anointed You with the oil of gladness more than Your companions."

Notice that God addresses His Son as **God,** one of the clearest proofs of the deity of Christ in the entire Bible. It is true that some translators of Psalm 45:6 render this phrase "Your divine throne endures for ever and ever" instead of "Your throne, O God, is forever and ever." But when they quote this verse in the Hebrews passage, it becomes "Your throne, O God, is forever and ever." So it is not only true that Christ's throne is divine, but also that He Himself is God.

Christ's kingdom will last **forever.** After His reign of one thousand years on earth, His earthly kingdom will merge into "the everlasting kingdom of our Lord and Savior Jesus Christ" (2 Pet. 1:11).

Christ's royal **scepter** is a scepter of equity. A scepter is a staff which symbolizes royal authority. Here the meaning is that the Messiah will rule with absolute justice. And the reign will also be absolutely holy, for the King loves **righteousness** and hates **wickedness.**

45:7b, 8 Because of His righteousness and integrity, God has **anointed** the Lord Jesus **with the oil of gladness more than** all other rulers. **The oil of** joy or **gladness** refers to the holy anointing oil with which priests were inducted into their office (Ex. 30:22–25). Since our Lord is to be a Priest-King, this is the oil to be used. **Myrrh** and **cassia** were the two principal ingredients in this oil, and **aloes** was one of the "chief spices" mentioned in Song of Solomon 4:14. All of these speak of the surpassing fragrance of the Person and work of our Lord. The **myrrh** and **aloes** may have special reference to His sufferings and death, since they were used in preparing His body for burial (John 19:39).

Out of the ivory palaces they make Him **glad.** It is the royal symphony, sounding forth the world's jubilation that man's day of sobbing and sighing has ended and that the golden age has dawned at last!

45:9 The King is not alone in the day of His power. The **daughters** of earth's monarchs are among His royal attendants. **At** His **right** side is **the queen**, decked with jewelry of **gold from Ophir**. And who is **the queen**? Here we must resist the temptation to identify her with the church, since the church is not the subject of OT revelation (Eph. 3:5–9; Col. 1:26). We believe that the queen is the redeemed remnant of the nation of Israel (Ezek. 16:10–14) and that the attendants may represent Gentile nations won to Christ through Israel's testimony.

45:10, 11 The queen is counseled by an unidentified voice, perhaps that of the Holy Spirit, to **forget** her **own people** and her **father's house**. The meaning, of course, is that she should sever the ties which bind her to her pre-conversion life and be totally committed to the King as her Lord. This advice anticipates the words of our Savior in Luke 14:26:

> If anyone come to Me and does not hate his father and mother, wife and children, brothers and sisters, yes, and his own life also, he cannot be My disciple.

Our love for Christ must be so great that all other loves are hatred *by comparison*. The beauty of wholeheartedness is pleasing to Him. Since He is Lord, He deserves all that we are and have.

45:12 The wealthy **daughter of Tyre will come** to the queen **with a gift**. Yes, the richest people in the world will travel to Jerusalem with the choicest presents.

45:13 Then **the royal daughter** is seen in her **palace**, dressed in regal splendor preparatory to her presentation to the King. Once the wearied drudge of sin, she is now seen in her chamber dressed in garments embroidered with **gold**.

45:14, 15 And now **she** is **brought to the King**, arrayed in multi-colored **robes** and accompanied by a retinue of virgin companions. There is great rejoicing as they move along, eventually entering the **palace** of the King Himself.

> Who can tell of that joy, the joy of the Father, and of the Son, and of the Holy Spirit, and of the holy angels, not to mention their own joy as they enter into the joy of their Lord! Comely in all comeliness, beautiful in all beauty, graceful in all grace, charming in every charm, attractive in every attractiveness, conformed to the image of God's Son (source unknown).

45:16, 17 In the last two verses God the Father is speaking to Christ the King. He promises Him **sons** who will be worthy successors of the patriarchs, who will "divide a world between them for their domain" (Knox).

As for the King Himself, His **name** will be praised **in all generations**. There never will come a time when **the people** will cease to adore Him.

Psalm 46: God With Us

During the First World War in an island community in the highlands of Scotland, young men were being called up in increasing numbers for military service. Each time contingents of them gathered at the pier to sail to the mainland, their relatives and friends assembled there and sang:

> God is our refuge and our strength,
> in straits a present aid;
> Therefore, although the earth remove,
> we will not be afraid:
> Though hills amidst the seas be cast;
> Though waters roaring make,
> And troubled be; yea, though the
> hills by swelling seas do shake.
>
> A river is, whose streams make glad
> the city of our God;

The holy place, wherein the Lord
most high hath his abode.
God in the midst of her doth dwell;
nothing shall her remove:
The Lord to her an helper will,
and that right early prove.

Be still and know that I am God:
among the heathen I
Will be exalted; I on earth
will be exalted high.
Our God, who is the Lord of hosts,
is still upon our side:
The God of Jacob our refuge
for ever will abide.
—*from the Scottish Psalter*

This scene is one of thousands in which God's saints have been comforted by this Psalm in times of great crisis. No one can know the hearts that have been lifted as these majestic lines have been read in the sickroom, the house of mourning, the dungeon of persecution and the narrow chamber of suffering and tragedy. It was this Psalm that led a tried and harried former Augustinian monk named Martin Luther to pen his famous Reformation hymn, "A Mighty Fortress Is Our God." Its message is timeless and its encouragement unceasing.

There are three distinct sections to the Psalm, which G. Campbell Morgan has titled as follows:

1–3 Nothing to fear. God is with us.
The challenge of confidence.

4–7 The Lord enthroned in Jerusalem.
The secret of confidence.

8–11 Peace on earth and worldwide dominion.
The vindication of confidence.

It is generally thought that the historical background of the Psalm is the miraculous deliverance of Jerusalem when it was besieged by the Assyrian wolf, Sennacherib (2 Kgs. 18:13—19:35; Isa. 36:1—37:36). At this time the people of Judah were tremendously conscious of God's presence with them in a unique way. And so the Psalm celebrates the praises of Him who is Immanuel—God with us.

46:1–3 God is our refuge and strength, a very present help in trouble. He is also "abundantly available for help in tight places" (NASB marg.). Blessed are we when we realize that our safety and protection lie not in riches or armies but in Jehovah alone!

Imagine the worst that can happen! Suppose **the earth** itself should melt as if caught in the flow of a gigantic volcano. Suppose an earthquake should toss **the mountains into the midst of the sea**. Suppose a flood of water should **roar** and foam over the land, or that **the mountains** should stagger with wild convulsions of nature.

Or think of **the mountains** as symbols of empires or cities, and the **waters** as nations. The very foundations of society are crumbling; kingdoms are toppling and disintegrating. The nations of the world are churning with political, economic and social confusion and trouble of unprecedented intensity is enveloping the world.

But God . . . ! The worst that can happen is no cause for fear. God Himself is still with us!

46:4 He Himself is the **river whose streams shall make glad the city of God.** Actually the city of Jerusalem has no river. But everything that a river is to an ordinary city, God is to His holy habitation—and more, for He is the fountain of life and refreshment, the river of mercy and goodness!

There the majestic Lord will be for us a place of broad rivers and streams, in which no galley with oars will sail, nor majestic ships pass by (Isa. 33:21).

46:5 It is because **God** is enthroned in Jerusalem that **she shall** never **be moved. God shall help her, just at the break of dawn.** It has been a long dark night for God's people, but soon the morning will dawn and Christ will take His rightful place, showing Himself strong on behalf of His own.

46:6 **The nations** of the earth may rage in fury; **the kingdoms** may totter. When God speaks in His wrath, **the earth** will melt in subservience to Him.

46:7 These words look forward in a special way to the Great Tribulation when the earth will be racked with violent disturbances of nature, with political upheaval, with wars and pestilences, and with inconceivable distress. Then the Lord will appear from heaven to crush all insubordination and rebellion and reign in righteousness and peace. At that time the believing remnant of the nation of Israel will say, **"The LORD of hosts is with us; the God of Jacob is our refuge."**

The assurance of this verse is inexpressibly sweet. **The LORD of hosts is with us**, that is, **the LORD of** the angelic armies of heaven. But He is also **the God of Jacob**. Now Jacob means "cheat" or "supplanter." Yet God speaks of Himself as **the God of Jacob**. Put the two thoughts together and you learn that the God of the angelic hosts is also the God of the unworthy sinner. The One who is infinitely high is also intimately nigh. He is with us in every step of our way, our unfailing **refuge** in all the storms of life.

46:8 By the time we get to verse 8 the tumult and cataclysms have ended. Man's day is over. Now the King is seated upon His throne in Jerusalem. We are invited to go out and examine the field of His victory. Everywhere we look we see the wreckage of His defeated foes. Everywhere lies the evidence of the awful judgments which have descended on the world during the Tribulation and at His glorious appearing.

46:9 But now that the Prince of Peace is enthroned, **wars** have ceased throughout the world. What councils and leagues and summits have been helpless to achieve, the Lord Jesus brings about by His iron rod. Disarmament has passed from discussion to actuality. Weaponry is scrapped, and the funds formerly spent on munitions are now diverted into agriculture and other productive channels.

46:10 The voice of God rings out to all the inhabitants of the earth in accents of assurance and supremacy. **"Be still, and know that I am God; I will be exalted among the nations, I will be exalted in the earth!"** Every fear is stilled, every anxiety quieted. His people can relax. He is God. His cause is victorious. He is supreme **among the nations**, supreme over all **the earth**.

It is from verse 10 that Katharina von Schlegel, the author of the hymn "Be Still, My Soul" drew inspiration.

Be still, my soul; thy God doth undertake
To guide the future as He has the past.
Thy hope, thy confidence let nothing shake;
All now mysterious shall be bright at last.
Be still, my soul: the winds and waves still know
His voice who ruled them while He dwelt below.

46:11 No matter what may happen or how dark the hour may be, the believer can still say with confidence and fearlessness, **"The LORD of hosts is with us; the God of Jacob is our refuge."** If the One who directs the armies of heaven is on our side, who can be successfully against us? The God of the unworthy worm **Jacob** is a fortress in which we can all take **refuge** from the storms of this uncertain life!

> Be still, the morning comes,
> The night will end;
> Trust thou in Christ thy Light,
> Thy faithful Friend.
> And know that He is God,
> Whose perfect will
> Works all things for thy good:
> Look up—Be still.
>
> —*Florence Wills*

Psalm 47: Happy New Year!

Jerusalem: The first New Year of the Golden Age of the Messiah was greeted at sundown by a sacred concert in the National Auditorium. Central in the program were the jubilant strains of Psalm 47, which acquired new meaning in view of recent international developments.

47:1–4 As the Psalm began, the audience realized that the Gentile nations which survived the recent global Tribulation were being summoned to **clap** their **hands** and **shout to God** with loud songs of joy. In an unprecedented display of emotion, the choir itself clapped rhythmically as if to lead the way. When the singers came to the words **"For the LORD Most High is awesome"** the people spontaneously rose to their feet. They remembered the recent coronation of the Lord Jesus Christ, when He was publicly acclaimed **"a great King over all the earth."** Gratitude welled up as the people remembered how He subdued "the goat nations" **under our feet**, those nations which had been implacably hostile to Israel during our time of trouble. Ripples of applause swept through the auditorium as the choir sang:

> **He will choose our inheritance for us,**
> **The excellence of Jacob whom He loves. Selah.**

47:5 The Messiah who had come down as a man of war to subdue His foes was now hailed as having **gone up** to His throne in Jerusalem amid the delirious shouts of His people and the trumpets announcing His overwhelming victory.

47:6, 7 It was a moving moment when the choir called Israel to **sing praises to God**, to **sing praises to our King**. No longer was there any hesitancy in acknowledging that King Jesus is God, and that the hands that were pierced on Calvary now hold the reins of universal government! Everyone felt the appropriateness of singing to Him with a skillful Psalm—a *maskil* of **understanding** and contemplation.

47:8 Repeatedly the choir emphasized the deity of the Messiah-King. He is the One who now **reigns over the nations** and whose throne is established on holiness.

47:9 Perhaps a tinge of apprehension was felt by some as the words were sung.

> **The princes of the people have gathered together . . .**

So often in the past the princes had gathered to drive Israel into the sea. But as the choir continued, it became clear that they were now assembling as **the people of the God**

of Abraham. They were joining with the Israelites in bringing tribute to the King of kings and Lord of lords.

Not everyone might have understood that **the shields of the earth** meant the rulers, who were appointed as protectors of the people. Now they all **belong to God; He is greatly exalted** high above all earth's potentates.

At the conclusion of the concert, critics agreed that there had never been such a meaningful Rosh Hashanah in the entire history of the nation!

Psalm 48: What Did They See?

A foreign invader had come up to the very gates of Jerusalem. Inside, the people were expecting the agonies of a long siege. Humanly speaking, the prospects were bleak. Then the Lord worked a miracle. The enemy saw something that threw them into utter panic. They retreated in terror. Jerusalem was preserved from destruction, and a great wave of praise went up to God. Psalm 48 captures something of the ecstasy of that moment.

48:1, 2 **The Lord** is inexpressibly **great**. He is great in power, in knowledge, in glory, in grace. His love is great, and His mercy, and His compassion. He is great in wisdom and in knowledge. His judgments are unsearchable and His ways inscrutable.

Because God is so **great**, He is **greatly to be praised**. He is worthy to be praised as the great Creator, the great Sustainer, the great Prophet, the great High Priest, the King of all kings, the great Redeemer, and the great Deliverer of His people. Here in Psalm 48 it is His greatness as the Savior and Protector of His city and His people that is especially in view.

The people speak of God and **the city of God** in the same breath. They associate the city with the God who dwelt there in the inner shrine of the temple. To them Jerusalem is the most **beautiful** city in the world, situated on the summit **of His holy mountain**. Like a gem in a handsome crown, it is **beautiful in** its **elevation**—the jewel **of the whole earth**.

Sometimes known as **Mount Zion** (after one of the eminences in the city) Jerusalem is described as being "in the far north" or **"on the sides of the north."** Both Knox and Gelineau translate this phrase as "the true pole of the earth." Jerusalem is truly this in the eyes of God's ancient people; it is the center of magnetic attraction, the place toward which they gravitate as the religious, political and cultural capital of the world. And it is **the city of the great King**, the future capital of the Lord Jesus Christ when He returns to earth to reign as King of kings.

48:3 Inside her walls **God** has proved Himself a trustworthy Defender. Everyone knows how He miraculously rescued the city when her destruction seemed momentary. Here is what happened:

48:4 The enemy forces had massed their troops outside the city. In overwhelming hordes they took up their positions in preparation for the assault. Militarily the city had little hope of holding out against such a concentration of armed strength.

48:5 Then the attackers **saw** something that unnerved them. What did they see?

Was it the city of Jerusalem, as seems indicated in the text? It seems unlikely that the mere sight of such a small city would cause professional military men to panic.

It may be that the curtain between them and the invisible world was drawn back, and that they saw an army of angels poised to defend the city. Or was the mountain filled with horses and chariots of fire (see 2 Kgs. 6:17)? Or did they see the angel of the Lord—the Lord Jesus Christ in one of His preincarnate appearances? (See Isa. 37:36.)

48:6, 7 Frankly, we do not know. But whatever it was, it was an apparition of such terrifying nature that the stout-hearted warriors lost their courage. The sight threw them into panic. Pandemonium broke out in the camp. They beat a hasty retreat, trembling as they went. Their anguish was comparable to that of a **woman in** the **pangs** of childbirth. The chaos and disorder among the enemy invaders was like the scattering of an ocean-going fleet when struck by a hurricane.

48:8 The people inside **the city** are now delirious with joy. What seemed like imminent disaster for them has been turned to miraculous victory. They had always **heard** in the past that God was the Founder and Defender of Jerusalem; now they **have seen** with their own eyes. "We have proved what long has been told us—that God upholds the city forever" (Knox).

48:9–11 So they lift their hearts in praise to **God**. They have had abundant reason to meditate on the **loving-kindness** of the Lord as they went up to the **temple** with their thank-offerings. They reflect that wherever God's **name** is known in **the earth**, there He is praised as the One whose **right hand** is filled with righteous victory. They call on Jerusalem to celebrate and on the lesser cities of **Judah** to **be glad**.

48:12–14 Now they are walking around the city in a sort of post-victory tour. They encourage one another to count the number of **towers** (every one of them is still there), to consider her **bulwarks** (they are all intact), and to walk through the now-deserted **palaces** (just as undamaged as they were before the enemy arrived). It will be a wonderful story to share with their children and grandchildren—how God supernaturally preserved Jerusalem from the slightest damage! They will teach the new **generation** that the **God** who did this is **"our God for ever and ever. He will be our guide even to death."**

Someone has beautifully suggested that verse 14 could be rendered:

> This God is our God from eternity to eternity. He will be our guide even unto death, over death, and beyond death.

Psalm 49: The Wicked and Their Wealth

One of the great riddles of life is how the wicked so often enjoy material prosperity while believers are often poor and dispossessed. But this is not the whole story. The wealth in which the ungodly trust so devoutly will fail them in their hour of greatest need. It cannot save them from dying. They cannot enjoy it forever, nor can it prevent corruption in the grave. They can neither take it with them nor come back to enjoy it. In the long run it is stupid to trust in money rather than in the Lord! That is the gist of David's message in Psalm 49.

49:1–4 The message is for **all peoples** and individuals, for small and great, for **rich and poor** alike. It is a message of distilled wisdom that comes from a heart that is full of insight. David turns his attention to probe into this common inequality of life; then, when he comes up with the answer, he sings it to the accompaniment of the **harp**.

49:5–9 Really, there is no reason for God's people to worry in those dark **days** when oppressors are dogging their heels, when persecutors are surrounding them with their iniquitous plots. Their enemies trust in their gold and in the power it gives; they boast about how affluent they are. But—and this is a very big BUT— all their money cannot save their brother from death (KJV) or their own selves either. The **redemption** of a man's life is tremendously **costly**; attempts to stave off the day of death through financial negotiations must be abandoned **forever**. No one has the means to purchase endless life on earth or to escape the grave.

As the dashes before and after verse 8 indicate, it is parenthetical. Putting verses 7 and 9 together, they read:

> **None of them can by any means redeem his brother, nor give to God a ransom for him . . . that he should continue to live eternally, and not see the Pit.**

49:10 Sooner or later even **wise men die**. Likewise **the** rich **fool** and the unthinking man of affluence die **and leave their wealth to others**. Notice that it does not say that the *wise man* leaves his wealth to other people. It is more probable that his last will and testament reads:

> Being of sound mind, I put my money to work for the Lord while I was still alive.

49:11, 12 It is a strange fact of life that men who are intelligent enough to build up a fortune in this world do not seem to realize that they are mortal. Their inward thoughts tell them **that their houses will last forever**, that they are going to live on here indefinitely. They name estates and streets and towns after themselves. But the inescapable truth is that **man** with all his **honor** must **perish**. In that respect **he is like the beasts**. In other respects, of course, man is quite different from the animals. For example, though man's body goes to the grave, his spirit and soul do not perish. And his body will be raised from the grave, either for eternal judgment or for eternal blessing. Man has endless being while the animals do not.

49:13, 14 This is the fate **of those who** unwisely trust in their wealth rather than in God—they foolishly live as if they were never going to die. But die they must, and when they do their relatives and friends quote them for their profound wisdom. Destined inevitably to be disembodied, they are **like sheep** being led relentlessly by the shepherd of death to **the grave**. **"The upright shall have dominion over them in the morning"**; that is, the tables will be turned, as with the rich man and Lazarus. Remember that Abraham said to the rich man:

> Son, remember that in your lifetime you received your good things, and likewise Lazarus evil things; but now he is comforted and you are tormented (Luke 16:25).

All the magnificence and **beauty** of the rich man wastes away, and he has no home but Sheol—a striking contrast to the home he enjoyed on earth!

49:15 Here we have one of the few flashes of light about the resurrection found in the OT. Generally speaking, the OT writers reveal very indistinct views of death and beyond. But here the psalmist voices the confidence that **God will redeem** his **soul from the power of the grave,**

that is, that God will deliver his **soul** from the disembodied state and reunite it with his resurrected body. When he says **"for He shall receive me,"** he uses the same word that is used in connection with God's receiving Enoch and Elijah.

49:16–19 So there is really no need for a believer to be disturbed when the ungodly man **becomes rich** and **his house** becomes more and more ornate and lavish. This earth is the only heaven he is ever going to enjoy! **When he dies he shall carry** none of his wealth with him. Empty-handed he will go to the grave, with none of his splendor to accompany him. As long as **he lives** he thinks he can never be robbed of his happiness, and people applaud him for feathering his own nest. But sooner or later he will die like his forefathers and share their long dark night with them.

49:20 There is simply no way that **a man** can hold on to earthly wealth and **honor**. Death is as inevitable for him as for **the beasts that perish**.

Of course someone could object that the righteous die as well as the wicked. This is true. We will all die if the Lord does not come in the meantime. But the point of the Psalm is that the wicked leave all their wealth behind while the righteous go to their eternal reward of infinite wealth.

One final observation. Very often in Scripture a rich man is synonymous with a wicked man. This ought to sober us. While the Bible doesn't say that it is a sin to be rich, it does condemn trusting in riches rather than in the living God (and it is hard to have riches without trusting in them!). The Bible condemns the love of money. It condemns the accumulation of wealth through oppression and dishonesty. And it condemns the hoarding of riches in callous disregard of the needs of a lost and suffering world.

Psalm 50: God's Ongoing Judgment

The setting of this Psalm is a courtroom with God Himself the Judge, Israel the defendant, and heaven and earth the witnesses.

But we should not think of this courtroom scene as some obscure trial that took place long ago in Israel's history; it is instead God's continuing evaluation of His saints throughout the world.

The Court in Session (50:1–6)

50:1 First the Judge is *heard* as He summons all the people in the entire land[36] of Israel—from east to west—to stand before His tribunal. What gives authority to the Judge's voice is the fact that He is **the Mighty One, God the LORD**.

50:2, 3 Next the Judge is *seen* as He leaves His chamber in the temple on Mount **Zion** in the form of a dazzling, brilliant glory cloud—the Shekinah. He will no longer **keep silent** about His people's sin. He comes down as He did at Mount Sinai, with a great jet of **fire** sweeping **before Him** and a great storm with thunder and lightning **all around Him**. But this time He comes not to *present* the law, but to *interpret* its inward, spiritual meaning.

50:4, 5 As He takes His place on the judgment seat He subpoenas **the heavens** and **the earth** to stand by in the witness box. Then He commands His attendants to bring in the defendants. First He is going to try the **saints** of the nation of Israel, whom He describes as **those who have made a covenant with** Him **by sacrifice**. (This refers to the covenant of the law made at Mount Horeb and ratified by the blood of sacrifices—Ex. 24:3–8.) The trial of His faithful ones is found in verses 7–15. Later He has a special session with the wicked (vv. 16–19).

50:6 **The heavens** are called to bear witness to the **righteousness** of God's judgments. The fact that **God Himself is** the **Judge** means that He has perfect knowledge of all the facts, that He is absolutely impartial, and that all His verdicts are wise and equitable.

The Sin of Ritualism (50:7–15)

50:7 God now assumes the position of prosecuting attorney, testifying against His **people, Israel**. In human affairs it would be unthinkable for the judge to also serve as prosecutor, but in this case it is altogether proper, for the Judge is none other than **God** the Most High.

50:8 God makes it clear at the outset that Israel has not been remiss in bringing **sacrifices** to Him. They had been faithful in bringing their **burnt offerings**. But the trouble was that they thought these rituals completely discharged their obligations to Jehovah. They were like girls who treat their mother indifferently throughout the year, then smother her with chocolates on her birthday! Or like sons who never thank their father for all he does for them, then give him a gift tie on Father's Day!

So Jehovah protests that while they had loaded His altar with sacrificial animals, they had treated Him personally with cold neglect. As to the technical details of the offerings, His people had been punctilious. But when it came to a warm, personal relationship with the Lord Himself, they were seriously lacking. F. B. Meyer writes:

> The Psalm is a severe rebuke of the hypocrite who contents himself with giving a mere outward obedience to the ritual of God's house, but withholds the love and homage of his heart.[37]

50:9 That is why God says that **He will not take a bull from** their **house, nor goats out of** their **folds**. He is not a ritualist, satisfied with religious ceremonies. In instituting the sacrificial system, God had never intended right outward action to serve as a cover for wrong inward attitudes.

50:10–13 If they would only stop to think, God's people would realize that God owns all the creatures in the world anyway—**every beast of the forest . . . the cattle on a thousand hills, . . . the birds** of the air, and everything that moves in **the field**. They would quickly realize that God doesn't need a single thing from men. He doesn't suffer hunger; if He did, He wouldn't have to ask us for anything, because He has a well-stocked pantry! Nor does He derive nourishment or satisfaction from **bulls'** meat or **goats'** blood. In that sense, God is totally self-sufficient.

50:14, 15 What then *does* **God** want from His people? Three things:

> ***Thanksgiving.*** No gift can ever take the place of simple gratitude. Too often we are like the family that took their queenly mother for granted, then after her death attempted to atone for their thanklessness by dressing her body in a two-thousand-dollar Dior original!
>
> *Fulfilled* ***vows.*** **"Pay your vows to the Most High"**—vows of love, worship, service, and devotion.
>
> *Fellowship in prayer.* **"Call upon Me in the day of trouble; I will deliver you, and you shall glorify Me."** Here we have a wonderful

insight into the heart of God. He loves to hear His people pray, and He loves to answer those prayers. He cherishes an intimate, tender relationship between His people and Himself.

But to the Wicked . . . (50:16–21)

50:16, 17 It seems clear that the Judge now turns to address a different portion of the nation, those who profess to be religious but whose lives openly contradict the truth. He denies that they have any right to piously quote the Scriptures or to claim the blessings of the Covenant for themselves. Then He levels a series of charges against them.

They hated discipline. Apparently they considered themselves above correction. Instead of welcoming or at least tolerating constructive criticism, these hypocrites resented it bitterly and attacked anyone who tried to offer it—even if it was the Lord.

They treated God's Word with contempt. Instead of profound reverence for the Scriptures, they **cast** God's **words behind** them as a worthless thing.

50:18 *They refused to walk in a path of separation.* By fraternizing with thieves and **adulterers**, they disobeyed the Lord and brought reproach on His name.

50:19, 20 *Their speech was wicked.* Their mouths spewed out **evil** without restraint. They had become experts in lying and **deceit**. Even their closest relatives were not safe from their vicious slander.

50:21 Because God had not punished them immediately, they **thought** He was as careless as they were. They failed to realize that His patience was designed to give them time to repent. But now the Lord breaks His silence and rebukes them for the charges listed above.

Warning and Promise (50:22, 23)

The Psalm closes with a warning and a promise. The warning is to those **who forget God**, living as if He doesn't matter. If they do not repent, God will pounce on them like a lion and utterly destroy them. But those who come to Him with sacrifices of thanksgiving glorify Him; all who walk in this pathway of obedience will experience God's marvelous deliverances in times of peril.

Psalm 51: Sweet Perfumes of Penitence

Alexander Maclaren once said, "The alchemy of divine love can extract sweet perfumes of penitence and praise out of the filth of sin." We have an illustration of this in Psalm 51. As the heading explains, it was written by **David** after **Nathan the prophet** had boldly exposed him for committing adultery with **Bathsheba** and for murdering Uriah. Utterly convicted of his sin, David pours out this torrent of penitence from his broken and contrite heart.

We might paraphrase his confession as follows:

51:1 Mercy, . . . O God! I ask for Your **mercy**! I deserve to be punished. But You are a God of **lovingkindness** and on that basis I ask that You not treat me the way I deserve. Your **mercies** are super-abounding and because of that I dare to ask that You erase my awful violations of Your holy law.

51:2 Wash me through and through from every instance where I have departed from Your straight line, **and cleanse me from** the frightful ways in which I have missed the mark.

51:3 Oh my God, **I** publicly **acknowledge** that I have broken Your law. My sin was public and my repentance is public, too. The guilt of **my sin** has been haunting me day and night, and I cannot stand it any more.

51:4 I now see clearly that it was **against You**, and **You** alone that **I sinned**. Oh, I realize that I also sinned against Bathsheba and against her faithful husband, Uriah—God forgive me for my treachery to this valiant general. But I realize that all sin is first and foremost **against You**. Your law has been broken. Your will has been flouted. Your name has been dishonored. So I take sides with You against myself. You are absolutely justified in any sentence You hand down, and no one can find fault with Your decisions.

51:5 Lord, I am no good. **I was** born **in iniquity**, and going back even farther, I was **conceived in sin**. In saying this I don't mean to cast any shame on my mother, or even to extenuate my own guilt. What I mean is that not only have I committed sins but that I am sinful in my very nature.

51:6 But You hate sin and You love faithfulness in a man's **inward** being, so now I am coming to You and asking You to teach me **wisdom** deep in my heart.

51:7 You directed that **hyssop** and running water should be used in the ceremony for cleansing a leper (Lev. 14:1–8). Well, Lord, I take the place of a moral leper. **Purge me with hyssop, and I shall be clean; wash me, and I shall be whiter than snow.**

51:8 When I sinned, I lost my song. It has been so long since I have known what real **joy and gladness** are. Let me hear the music of rejoicing once again. In my backslidden condition, it seemed that You had crippled me by breaking my **bones**. I could no longer dance before You in the holy festivals. Now heal those fractures so that I may join Your people in praising Your name in the dance.

51:9 Oh, my God, I beg You to turn away **Your face** from looking on **my sins** in judgment and punishment. **Blot out** the last vestige of **my** enormous **iniquities**. How they stab me every time I think of them!

51:10 Looking back, I realize that the trouble all started in my mind. My thought-life was polluted. I entertained evil thoughts until at last I committed the sins. So now I ask that You **create in me a clean** mind. I know that if the fountain is clean, the stream flowing from it will be clean as well. Yes, Lord, **renew** my entire inner self so it will be **steadfast** in guarding against future outbreaks of sin.

51:11 Don't give up on me, Lord, or banish me from Your presence. I can't stand the thought of being away from You, or of having **Your Holy Spirit** taken **from me**. In this age in which I live, You do take Your Holy Spirit from men when they walk in disobedience to You. You did it to Saul (1 Sam. 16:14)—I shudder to think of the consequences. Please, Lord, spare me from this fate.

51:12 As I said before, I have lost my song. Not my soul, but my song. Not Your salvation, but **the joy of Your salvation**. Now that I have come to You in repentance, confession, and forsaking of sin, I pray that the "chords that are broken may vibrate once more." And not only do I pray that You will restore to me **the joy of Your salvation**, but also that You will **uphold me by Your generous Spirit**. In other words, I want Your Spirit to make me willing to obey You and to please You in all things. Then I will be maintained in paths of righteousness.

51:13 One by-product of my forgiveness will be that I will aggressively witness to other **transgressors** and tell them **Your ways** of pardon and peace. When they hear of what You have done for me, they will want to return **to You** also.

51:14 Then, too, if You **deliver me from the guilt of bloodshed, O God,** the whole world will hear my testimony of Your deliverance. The guilt of Uriah's blood is heavy upon me, O **God of my salvation**. Wipe the slate clean and I'll praise You forever.

51:15 **My lips** have been sealed shut by my sin. **Open** them by Your forgiveness and **my mouth** will be dedicated to speaking and singing **Your praise**.

51:16, 17 Lord, I am not depending on rituals or ceremonies for forgiveness. I know that You are not a ritualist. If I thought You wanted animal **sacrifice, I would** bring them. But **burnt offering** does **not delight** Your heart. It is true that You instituted sacrifices and offerings, but they never represented Your ultimate ideal. And so I come to You with **a broken heart**—that is the sacrifice You require. **You will not despise** this shattered and **contrite heart** that I bring to You.

51:18 And now, Lord, I want to pray for Your dear people as well as for myself. Be pleased to shower them with good things. Rebuild **the walls of Jerusalem**. My sins have doubtless hindered the progress of Your work. I have brought reproach upon Your name. Now may Your cause move forward without hindrance.

51:19 When we all walk in fellowship with You, confessing and forsaking our sins, **then You shall be pleased with** our **sacrifices of righteousness**. **Offerings** that speak of complete dedication to Yourself will gladden Your heart. We will **offer bulls on Your altar**—in praise to the God who forgives sin and pardons iniquity.

Psalm 52: The Traitor Unmasked

The historical background of this Psalm is found in 1 Samuel 21, 22. **Doeg the Edomite** was King Saul's chief herdsman. He was present when the fugitive David received food and Goliath's sword from **Ahimelech** the priest. Soon afterward he went and tattled to **Saul**, and was rewarded by being delegated to kill Ahimelech and eighty-four other priests of the Lord. Subsequently he massacred the women and children at Nob and destroyed the village and even the animals.

Doeg's character is delineated in verses 1–4 and his doom in verses 5–7. The psalmist's contrasting character is seen in verses 8 and 9.

52:1–4 David's opening question assails the traitor for taking pride in his extreme **evil** and for "forging wild lies all day against God's loyal servant" (NEB). This treacherous prototype of the Antichrist had a razor-sharp **tongue** that cut people down with its slander. He had a strong bent for **evil more than good**, and would rather lie than tell the truth. The personification of deceit, he reveled in speech that wrecked other lives.

52:5 Divine and human justice agree on the fate which the psalmist foretells for Doeg and all his counterparts. God will break him down to the ground like a building reduced to rubble. The Most High will snatch him out of His tent, and completely **uproot** him **from the** world of **living** men.

52:6, 7 God-fearing people will live to **see** that day, will be struck by the awesome judgment of God, and will chuckle at his reversal, saying:

> **Here is the man who did not make God his strength, but trusted in the abundance of his riches, and strengthened himself in his wickedness.**

52:8, 9 The psalmist's character is in glaring contrast. He compares himself to **a green olive tree in the house of God**—a picture of prosperity and fruitfulness. The olive is, according to F. W. Grant:

> . . . the tree in which abides that (oil) which typifies the Spirit of God, green in its freshness of life eternal. It is in the house of God (in contrast to) that "tent" out of which the wicked one is cast.[38]

In contrast to Doeg who would not make God his refuge, David is determined that he will **trust in the mercy of the Lord forever and ever**.

Something else he will do forever is to thank the Lord for what He has done—namely, for punishing the wicked and vindicating the righteous.

Finally, he will magnify the **name of** the Lord in **the presence of** His loyal **saints**, because His name **is good** and all that He is is good.

Psalm 53: The Folly of Atheism

The main difference between Psalm 14 and this one is that the name of God is changed from Jehovah (or Yahweh) to Elohim.[39] In Psalm 14 the fool denies the existence of the covenant-keeping God (Jehovah, Lord) who is deeply interested and involved in the welfare of His people. Here the fool denies the existence of an almighty, sovereign God (Elohim) who sustains and governs the universe.

> God can be denied in both senses: some deny that the Creator has any special interest in any particular race or group of men; others repudiate any possibility of there being a God at all (Daily Notes of the Scripture Union).

53:1 The fool is not necessarily a dunce or stupid. He may be intellectually brilliant as far as contemporary education is concerned, but he does not want to face the evidence as to the person, power and providence of God. He is willfully ignorant. "The Hebrew word has in it the idea of a malicious refusal to acknowledge the truth."

Atheism is linked with depravity and degradation, sometimes as cause, sometimes as effect. Therefore it is not surprising that those who say **"There is no** Elohim" **are corrupt**, doing **abominable iniquity. There is none** of them **who does good.**

53:2 Now the subject seems to glide from atheists in particular to mankind in general. Paul quotes snatches from these verses in Romans 3 to establish the total depravity of all mankind. The indictment is true, of course. As **God looks down from heaven upon the** race **of men,** He cannot find one who, left to himself, would have the wisdom to fear the Lord. Apart from the prior ministry of the Holy Spirit, no one would **seek God**.

53:3 They have all **turned aside** from the living God. **They have** all **become** depraved. Not one **does good** in the sense of something that can gain favor or merit with the Lord.

53:4, 5 Again, there seems to be a switch to a particular class of sinners, namely, those apostates who persecute God's **people**. How can they be so short-sighted? They are cruel and prayerless. They think no more of destroying the faithful remnant than of eating **bread**. And they never feel the need of speaking to **God** in prayer. They seem completely insensible to the fact that one day they will be seized with unprecedented terror. God will scatter **the bones** of those who wage war against His loyal followers.

53:6 In the last verse, David prays for the coming of the Messiah. He is the Deliverer who will **come out of Zion** (Rom. 11:26) and save all believing Israel. In that day Israel will be restored, **Jacob** will **rejoice and Israel** will **be glad**.

Psalm 54: God Is My Helper

When **David** was fleeing from Saul, **the Ziphites** twice revealed his whereabouts to the king (1 Sam. 23:19; 26:1). These betrayals gave rise to the words of this Psalm, a suitable prayer for God's people in any age when suffering at the hands of men.

54:1 The opening cry for help asks for salvation by God's **name** and vindication **by** His **strength**. His **name** stands for His nature or character and His **strength** for His omnipotence. Salvation here means temporal deliverance from enemies.

54:2, 3 The now-or-never urgency of the psalmist is seen in the importunate plea for **God** to **hear**, to listen to the hissing-hot **words of** his **mouth**.

What had happened was that these **strangers** had conspired to double-cross David; bloodthirsty men were out to get him—apostates who cared nothing about **God**.

54:4, 5 **God** is the answer. **The Lord is with those who uphold** the believer's **life.** One day **He will repay** the **enemies** of His people with calamity and ruin.

The knowledge of what God will do turns quickly into the prayer, "Do it, Lord. In proof of Your faithfulness, bring their wicked careers to an end."

54:6 The saving name of verse 1 will then become the worshiped name. David will bring a freewill **sacrifice** to the Lord, and offer thanksgivings to the **name** of the **Lord**—the precious name in which all **good** is enshrined.

54:7 In the final verse David speaks as if **all** his **trouble** was past, and as if he had already witnessed the demise of his **enemies**. "Already," writes Morgan, "though perhaps yet in the midst of the peril, he sings the song of deliverance, as though it were already realized."[40] Faith thus "gives substance to our hopes, and makes us certain of realities we do not see" (Heb. 11:1, NEB).

Psalm 55: Cast Your Burden

Ahithophel was one of David's most trusted advisers who later led a defection to the usurping Absalom. In this Psalm, we sense the extreme anguish of David's heart over this bitter blow. We can also read here something of the deep tides of emotion which surged through the Savior's soul in connection with His betrayal by Judas. And the Psalm foreshadows the prayer of the remnant as they suffer under the conspiracy of the coming Antichrist.

55:1, 2a In deep distress the soul does not lack variety or originality in attracting the attention of God. Positively, there is the request to **give ear**. Negatively, the word is **"do not hide Yourself."** There is the appeal for audience, **"Attend to me,"** and the appeal for action, **"and hear me."**

55:2b–5 Then follows a heart-rending catalog of personal grief and of desperate need.

> **Restless** in complaining and moaning.
> Distracted by the shouts **of the enemy**.
> Oppressed by **the wicked**.
> Buried by them under heaps of **trouble**.
> Exposed to furious assaults.
> Heartbroken with anguish.
> Terrified by impending doom.
> Afflicted by uncontrollable **trembling**.
> **Overwhelmed** with **horror**.

55:6–8 His first impulse is to **fly away** from all his troubles. If he **had wings**, he would take off for some quiet spot **in the wilderness**. He would waste no time in escaping from the **tempest** that was swirling around him.

55:9a But now his terror gives way to burning indignation. He is so revolted by the treachery of the conspirators that he calls on the Lord to **destroy**—without specifying whether He should **destroy** the people or their plans. Also he asks God to **divide their tongues**—which may be an allusion to David's prayer at this time that the Lord would turn the counsel of Ahithophel into foolishness (2 Sam. 15:31).

55:9b–11 As the son of Jesse looks at **the city** of Jerusalem which he conquered and chose, he sees it filled with **violence and strife; day and night** these twin evils stalk around **it on its walls**. The city of peace is now a city of mischief and trouble. Ruin is resident. **Oppression and** fraud never leave the marketplace, where there ought to be justice and equity.

55:12–15 At the heart of David's complaint, of course, is his cruel betrayal. The pain would have been more endurable if the culprit had been **an** avowed **enemy**. If the taunts and insults had come from an out-and-out adversary, then the psalmist could have kept out of his way. But it was one of his own, a **companion**, a loved and trusted friend who had knifed him in the back. It was one with whom the psalmist used to have **sweet** fellowship as they **walked** together in the courts of the tabernacle. The perfidy of this man and his followers deserves sudden death, a quick trip to Sheol, "for wickedness dwells in their homes and deep in their hearts" (Gelineau).

55:16–21 Yet in all his emotional turmoil, David is assured of help in answer to prayer. The sobs and moans that ascend to God **evening and morning and at noon** will reach the Savior's ear. In spite of the numerical superiority of those arrayed against him, David will emerge from **the battle** with **peace** as his portion. Yes, **God will hear, and afflict them**, even **He who** sits eternally enthroned. This is the condemnation of those with whom there is no **change**, i.e., repentance, and who **do not fear God**. This is the condemnation of the traitor—the bosom companion who stretched out his hand to harm his friends and who broke the covenant of friendship and allegiance. His **words** seemed **smoother than butter, . . . yet they were drawn swords**.

55:22 The golden peak of Psalm 55 is reached in verse 22:

> **Cast your burden on the Lord,**
> **And He shall sustain you;**
> **He shall never permit**
> **the righteous to be moved.**

The psalmist came to realize that the best course in time of troubles is not to run away from them, but to **cast** the **burden** of them **on the Lord**. May we learn the lovely lesson set forth by Bishop Horne: "He who once bore the burden of our sins and sorrows requests that we should now and ever permit Him to bear the burden of our cares."

55:23 Men of murder and treachery will die violently and prematurely. Ahithophel did (2 Sam. 17:14, 23) and so did Judas (Matt. 27:5). But God's people can depend on Him to save them.

Psalm 56: God Is For Me!

It was a bitter pill for **David** to have to seek refuge from his own countrymen among the **Philistines** in **Gath** (1 Sam. 21:10–15; 27:4; 29:2–11), but the fierce hostility of King Saul drove him to it—or so he felt. Psalm 56 describes some of the alternating waves of fear and faith which swept over him at that time.

56:1, 2 He begins with a prayer for God's gracious help in view of the constant harassment of his pursuers. Notice the three kinds of terror which were coming upon him **all day** from hostile men:

> . . . **he oppresses me** (v. 1)
> **My enemies . . . hound me** (v. 2)
> . . . they twist my words (v. 5)

His foes were arrogantly attacking him, constantly plotting evil **against** him, federating for greater strength, lurking to pounce upon him, continually spying on him (vv. 2, 5, 6). It seemed like a clear case of overkill.

56:3 But faith breaks through the gloom with the confident declaration, **"Whenever I am afraid, I will trust in You."** This "cheerful courage of a fugitive," as Delitzsch calls it, is based on the character of God and on the faithfulness of His promises. He is more powerful than all our foes combined, and He has promised to protect us from harm. Nothing can penetrate the protective hedge which He sets up around us except by His permissive will. This is why we can trust in God without a fear.

56:4–6 To the bold challenge **"What can** mere man **do to me?"** reason might answer, "Plenty. Man can persecute, injure, maim, shoot, and kill." But the fact is that the child of God is immortal until his work is done. Also we should understand David's fearlessness in the light of our Savior's words:

> And do not fear those who kill the body but cannot kill the soul. But rather fear Him who is able to destroy both soul and body in hell (Matt. 10:28).

56:7 After rehearsing the studied attempts of his enemies to wipe him out, David calls **on God** to requite them for their treachery by casting them **down in** His **anger**.

56:8 Here is an exquisite description of the tender, personalized care of our Lord. He keeps a count of our **wanderings** or restless tossings during the night, of our fevered turnings from one side to another. He cares so much about the details of our **tears** of sorrow that He can be asked to keep our **tears** in His **bottle**. This may be an allusion to an ancient custom of mourners, namely, preserving their falling tears in a small bottle, which was placed in the tomb of deceased friends, as a memorial of the survivors' affection. In any event, God does keep a record of our **tears in** His **book**, just as Jesus later taught us that He numbers the very hairs of our heads.

56:9 With David we can be confident that God will turn back our **enemies** in answer to our prayers. We know this because God is for us. And if God is for us, who can successfully be against us (Rom. 8:31)?

There is, ultimately, only one question which matters in life; everything else is secondary to this—'Is God *for* us?' David, at *last*, was sure of God; and the man who is sure of God is beyond fear (11) (*Daily Notes of the Scripture Union*).

56:10, 11 The refrain of verse 4 is repeated in verses 10 and 11 but this time using two different names of God:

In God [Elohim] **(I will praise His word),**
in the LORD [YHWH, Jehovah] **(I will praise His word),**
in God [Elohim] **I have put my trust;**
I will not be afraid.
What can man do to me?

The psalmist praises the promise of the Almighty One and of the covenant-keeping One, in utter assurance of His protecting care, and in cool contempt of frail man's ability to harm him.

56:12, 13 The present assurance of future deliverance puts David under constraint to fulfill the **vows** he **made** to the Lord, and to pay his debt of gratitude to Him. Though still in enemy territory, he is enjoying the blessing of full salvation. His life has been saved, and his **feet** kept from stumbling so that he might continue to **walk** in the presence of **God in the light of** life.

Psalm 57: In the Shadow of His Wings

David was hiding from **Saul** in a **cave** when he wrote this Psalm—either the cave of Adullam or the one at Engedi. There are two ever-present realities before him—the gracious God and the formidable foe. The Psalm see-saws between the two, but faith in the former is greater than fear of the latter and tilts the see-saw in that direction.

The Ever-Present God (57:1–3)

The psalmist does not demand deliverance, as if he had a right to expect it. He asks it as a mercy from **God**, an undeserved blessing stemming from His kindness. Oblivious of his dank, dark surroundings, he reckons himself as sheltered **in the shadow of** God's **wings**, like a chicken snuggled under the wings of the mother hen. And there he will stay **until** the storms of life **have passed by**. From this privileged place of conscious nearness, he cries **to God Most High** with the confidence that no one and nothing can hinder Him from accomplishing His purposes in the lives of His people. When the answer comes **from heaven**, it will mean deliverance for the trusting heart and dishonor for those who walk all over him. It will be an unforgettable demonstration of God's love and dependability.

The Ever-Present Enemy (57:4)

The enemies are formidable—like savage, fiery **lions** that tear and devour; these **sons of men** have **teeth** like **spears and arrows**, and tongues like **sharp** swords. Yet David lies down to rest in the middle of such danger—a truly remarkable feat of faith.

The Ever-Present God (57:5)

In a refrain that is repeated in verse 11, David longs to see God's **glory** manifested in the crushing of His foes and the vindication of His cause. Nothing will do but that His **glory** be astral and global in its dimensions.

The Ever-Present Enemy (57:6)

The adversaries laid careful plans to trap the son of Jesse: his **soul** was bent over with heaviness. Yes, **they** had **dug a pit** to trap him, but **they themselves** fell into it.

The Ever-Present God (57:7–11)

No wonder the psalmist's **heart** is steadfastly determined to **sing** with melody to the **Lord**. No wonder he rouses his soul, and dusts off **the lute and harp**. No wonder he is determined to greet **the dawn** with songs of praise.

Nor will it be a private, provincial songfest. He will thank the Lord **among the peoples**, and **sing** psalms **among the nations**, because God's **mercy** is as infinite as **the heavens** and His **truth** as limitless as **the clouds**.

F. B. Meyer notes that just as David "rose above personal grief in a desire for God's glory" so we should subordinate our own petty griefs in a great passion to see Him **exalted**.

Psalm 58: The Judges Judged

58:1, 2 As the Psalm opens, it is a vigorous protest against unjust judges or rulers. The mighty lords of the earth are put on the spot. Have they been fair in their decisions? Have they dispensed justice to the common people? The obvious answer is **"No."** In their hearts they have concocted all sorts of crookedness. Then their **hands** have dealt out **the violence** that their hearts had planned. The land is filled with perversion of justice.

58:3 The subject broadens from dishonest magistrates to the wider class of **wicked** people to which they belong. Their corruption is not a development of later life; it can be traced right back to their birth. Their lawlessness and rebellion are inborn; as soon as they begin to talk, they begin to lie.

58:4, 5 Their speech is slanderous and malignant **like the** deadly **poison of a serpent**. Their ears are deaf to the voice of God **like the deaf cobra** that will not listen to the charmer, no matter how **skillfully** he plays.

58:6, 7 Just as David drew from the world of nature to describe their wickedness, so he now dips into natural science for fitting metaphors of judgment. Let the **teeth** of these fierce lions be broken, their cruel **fangs** extracted. Let them vanish like **waters** that quickly disappear into the ground, or a stream that mysteriously vanishes underground.

The Hebrew of verse 7b is uncertain. It may mean, "May they be as **arrows** with the heads **cut** off—blunt and harmless."

58:8 Then the world of snails and slugs is invaded. Just as a **snail "melts away"** in a trail of slime, so let these criminals disappear from the haunts of men. Whether snails actually dissolve in slime is an unimportant technicality. No one objects when we say that a burning house "goes up in smoke." Then why quibble over a figurative expression in the Bible?

The next imprecation is that these evildoers might die prematurely, **like a stillborn child** that never sees **the sun**. "The eyes of the wicked have never been opened," says Scroggie, "and their possibilities have never unfolded; the sinner is an abortion, a promise never fulfilled."[41]

58:9 Finally the psalmist asks that they may be suddenly swept **away**, like **burning thorns** are scattered by **a whirlwind** before the pot above them feels the heat. Maclaren says:

> The picture before the psalmist seems to be that of a company of travellers

> round their camp, preparing their meal. They heap brushwood under the pot, and expect to satisfy their hunger; but before the pot is warmed through, not to say before the water boils or the meal is cooked, down comes a whirlwind, which sweeps away fire, pot and all.[42]

58:10 There is nothing uncertain about the Hebrew here. It states unmistakably that the people of God will be elated when **the wicked** are punished, that **he shall wash his feet in the blood of the wicked**. If this sounds vindictive and loveless to our Christian ears, we may justify it by saying, with J. G. Bellett, that while we cannot rejoice in judgment in this age of grace, believers will do so when the Lord vindicates His divine glory by **vengeance**. Or we may consider the words of Morgan that "it is a sickly sentimentality and a wicked weakness that has more sympathy with the corrupt oppressors than with the anger of God."[43]

58:11 In the ongoing judgment of the ungodly, men realize that **the righteous** are rewarded, and that **God** actually does judge men here on **earth**.

Psalm 59: The God Who Comes to Meet Us

Here **David** storms the throne of God in almost breathless haste because Saul has **sent men** to surround **the house** and tighten the noose.

59:1–4 The words come gushing out like a hot torrent—**"Deliver me . . . defend me . . . save me."** The language is vehement, abrupt, urgent. These ungodly men are thirsting for his blood. Relentlessly they wait for their chance to kill him; they unite in a common effort to eliminate him. And yet it is all so unprovoked. The psalmist is not guilty of the treason and disloyalty with which they charge him. Their feverish preparations were provoked **through no fault of** his. If only God would awaken and come to David's rescue!

59:5 For a moment, the son of Jesse seems to look beyond his immediate foes to all the enemies of **Israel** and calls on God to do a thorough work of punishment. Here he addresses God as *Jehovah, Elohim Sabaoth, Elohe Israel,* a reduplication of the names of God that is intended to express all He is in His essential being and in His special relation to **Israel**.

59:6, 7 Like a pack of wild alley dogs, they return to besiege the psalmist, howling and prowling. Their incessant barking, their snarling growls fill the air. They arrogantly suppose themselves to be immune from detection.

59:8, 9 But they are known to the LORD—and He laughs at their insensate folly, the same God who looks down on the boasting **nations** with cool **derision**. This great **God** is David's **Strength**, the One for whom he watches and his sure **defense**.

59:10 Someone has given us this unforgettable paraphrase of verse 10a: "**My God**, with His lovingkindness, **shall come to meet me** at every corner." What a comfort for storm-tossed souls of every age! Linked with this assurance is the knowledge that **God** will preserve us to **see** this defeat of our **enemies**.

59:11–13 The prayer of verse 11 is unique. David asks the Lord **not** to **slay** the enemy suddenly **lest** the **people** of Israel entertain light thoughts of the seriousness of sin. If the punishment is gradual, the severity of God will be more indelibly impressed on them. But it is clear from what follows that ultimate destruction is included in the catalog of dire judgments which the psalmist specifies for his persecutors. He prays that they be scattered by God's **power, and** brought **down** by the Lord who guards Israel. He asks that they might be captured while they are showing off their consummate **pride** and brought to account for their sinful, wicked **words**. Finally he prays that they might be utterly destroyed for their **cursing and lying** speech. Then at last the world will **know** from east to west that **God** really does care for the descendants of **Jacob**.

59:14, 15 In the meantime the human dogs **return** to **the city** searching for the psalmist, growling, prowling, and howling for his life, and angry when they don't get it.

59:16, 17 The dogs are growling in the evening, but the son of Jesse is singing **in the morning**. He is extolling the **power** and **mercy** of the Lord because He has proved Himself a **defense and refuge in the day of** deep need. **The morning** is coming for all God's people when their enemies will be gone and when the **power** and love of the Savior will be the theme of endless song.

Psalm 60: Our Hope Is in the Lord

According to the heading, the historical background of this Psalm is **when** David **fought against Mesopotamia and Syria of Zobah, and Joab returned and killed twelve thousand Edomites in the Valley of Salt**. It seems that there was a temporary setback in this war with Syria and Edom (2 Sam. 8:3–14), causing David to storm the gates of heaven with this importunate plea for help.

The outline of the Psalm is as follows:

1. Israel's Defeat Is from the Lord, vv. 1–4.
2. Israel's Hope Is in the Lord, v. 5.
3. Eventual Victory is Promised by the Lord, vv. 6–8.
4. Israel's Need Is for the Lord, vv. 9–11.
5. Israel's Confidence Is in the Lord, v. 12.

Israel's Defeat Is from the Lord (60:1–4)

60:1–3 As he studies reports of casualties inflicted by the Edomite-Syrian alliance, David interprets the disaster as an indication of the Lord's desertion of His people. It can only mean that **God** has rejected Israel. In His anger, He has smashed down the nation's defenses, leaving it helplessly exposed to enemy attack. Now is it not time for the Lord to turn in mercy and restore His battered forces?

It is as if the country has been torn apart by an enormous earthquake. The economic, political, and social foundations of the nation have been **broken** up. The walls of society, weakened by gaping holes, are tottering. If only the Lord would repair the **breaches** and return His people to a measure of normality!

The population has passed through a fiery ordeal. **The wine of** suffering and defeat has caused them to reel like a drunkard.

60:4 This verse is somewhat obscure in the original. It may mean, as in the NKJV, that the Lord unfurls **a banner** for **those who fear** Him, **that it may be displayed because of the truth**. But the margin of the RV gives quite an opposite sense:

> Thou hast given a banner to them that fear thee, that they may flee from before the bow.

David would then be complaining, with undisguised sarcasm, that the **banner** God has raised for Israel is not one of victory but of defeat, a flag that signals retreat from before the forces of the enemy.

Israel's Hope Is in the Lord (60:5)

Prayer is born from the ashes of humiliating defeat. Speaking both for himself and his people as **"Your beloved,"** the psalmist implores the Lord for deliverance, victory and the renewal of communion. "O come and deliver Your friends, help with Your right hand and reply" (Gelineau).

Eventual Victory Is Promised by the Lord (60:6–8)

60:6, 7 Verses 6–8 form a divine oracle in which the voice of **God**, heard in the sanctuary, expresses His determination to reoccupy all the land of Israel and to conquer His Gentile foes.

Shechem, Succoth, Gilead, Manasseh, Ephraim, and **Judah** are all Jewish territory. God claims them as His own. He will subdivide **Shechem**, on the west of the Jordan, and the **Valley of Succoth** on the east. He will possess the trans-Jordan land of **Gilead**, and the two territories of **Manasseh**, one on either side of the Jordan.

Ephraim, located centrally in Israel, is His **helmet**, the tribe that will take the lead in national defense. And **Judah** is His scepter; according to Jacob's dying prophecy (Gen. 49:10), it will be the governmental seat.

60:8 Then turning to three of the surrounding nations, the Lord asserts His dominion over them. **Moab**, situated on the southeastern shore of the Dead Sea, will be His **washpot**. He will **cast** His **shoe** upon **Edom**, a figure signifying forcible possession and servitude and perhaps also contempt. **Philistia** will **shout in triumph because of** God's judgments.

Israel's Need Is for the Lord (60:9–11)

60:9 It seems clear that the speaker changes at this point.[44] It could scarcely be the Lord's voice because He would not need anyone to **bring** Him **to the strong city**. So we understand these to be the words of David, longing for the day when the capital city of Edom (variously called Bozrah, Sela and Petra) will fall into the hands of the Israelites. Of course, the city here stands for the whole country of **Edom**. David wishes that he could be instrumental in fulfilling God's intention to cast His shoe upon it.

60:10 But it is a vain hope at the moment because **God** has hidden His face from His people. He has **cast** them **off**. He no longer accompanies Israel's **armies** as a guarantee of victory.

60:11 So David pleads for God to fight once again on behalf of His troubled people. Divine help is indispensable; **the help of man is useless.**

Israel's Confidence Is in the Lord (60:12)

The Psalm closes on a note of confidence. Given God's aid, Israel's army is assured of an illustrious record. Their **enemies** will be crushed under His heel.

Application

The believer's enemies are the world, the flesh and the devil. In himself he is powerless to conquer them. And the help of other men is insufficient, no matter how well-meaning they might be. But there is victory through the Lord Jesus Christ. Those who trust in Him for deliverance will never be disappointed.

Psalm 60 will have a final fulfillment in the last days when the Jewish remnant, harried and dispirited, looks to the Messiah for salvation and triumph. Then the land of Israel will be apportioned among the tribes and the nation's foes will be brought to bay.

Psalm 61: The Rock That Is Higher Than I

David had a wonderful relationship with the Lord. To him God was:

> . . . a living bright Reality,
> More present to faith's vision keen
> Than any earthly object seen.
> More dear, more intimately nigh
> Than e'en the closest earthly tie.
> —*Author unknown*

Especially in times of danger, when the situation seemed utterly hopeless, he had learned to cast his burden on the Lord and leave it there.

Here he is in another of those cliff-hanging predicaments. The pressure of circumstances wrings from his heart a prayer that has seldom been surpassed for sheer poignancy and articulateness. It has become the timeless language of thousands of God's people as they have passed through persecution, heartache and suffering because it says what they feel but could never express so well.

61:1 Into the throne room of the universe comes the familiar voice of David:

Hear my cry, O God; attend to my prayer.

God's heart is delighted. The childlike faith of His servant assures instant audience with the Sovereign.

61:2 From the end of the earth I will cry to You,
When my heart is overwhelmed.

The psalmist is not literally **at the end of the earth**, but he is literally in a place of extremity where safety and deliverance seem remote, where life ends and death begins. Physically and emotionally he is spent, but he knows that the throne of grace is only a breath away, so he draws near to receive mercy and find grace to help in time of need. "Distance," someone has said, "is meaningless and no extremity of life effective in blocking prayer."

Lead me to the rock that is higher than I.

A true spiritual instinct teaches David that he needs **a rock** for protection, that **the rock** must be **higher than** himself, and that he needs divine guidance to reach it. The Lord, of course, is the Rock (2 Sam. 22:32); the metaphor is never used of any mere man in the Bible.[45] **The rock** must be someone greater than man; otherwise man can never find shelter in it. This points to the deity of Christ. (And incidentally the rock must be cleft to provide a hiding place from the enemy.) Finally, David acknowledges that he does not have the wisdom or strength to direct his own steps, so he asks the Lord to lead him to Himself—the Rock of ages.

61:3 For You have been a shelter for me,
A strong tower from the enemy.

These words confirm that God is the Rock. David had proved Him to be his trustworthy refuge and a **tower** of strength into which the righteous can run for safety (Prov. 18:10). What He has been, He will be.

61:4 I will abide in Your tabernacle forever;

I will trust in the shelter of Your wings. Selah

Prayers like this cannot fail to touch the throne of God! Such tender affection and simple trust could never be refused. No wonder that God called David a man after His own heart (1 Sam. 13:14). The expression **"the shelter of Your wings"** may be an allusion to the wings of the cherubim which overshadowed the blood-sprinkled mercy seat.

61:5 For You, O God, have heard my vows;
You have given me the heritage of those who fear Your name.

The word **heritage** or *inheritance* is applied in the OT to the land of Canaan (Ex. 6:8), the people of Israel (Ps. 94:5), the Word of God (Ps. 119:111), children in a family (Ps. 127:3), immunity from harm (Isa. 54:17), and finally to the tabernacle or temple (Jer. 12:7). The last named is probably the primary meaning here since the preceding verse mentioned God's tent and alluded to the cherubim. Today, we would think of the heritage of those **who fear** God's **name** as eternal life (Col. 1:12).

61:6, 7 You will prolong the king's life,
His years as many generations.
He shall abide before God forever.
Oh, prepare mercy and truth, which may preserve him!

It is interesting that in these two verses, David slips from the first person to the third. Interesting—because while he was still no doubt referring to himself and to the covenant God made with him (2 Sam. 7), his words are more appropriate for another King. If we apply the words to David, they can only be understood as requesting long life for himself and the perpetuation of his kingdom. But applied to the Lord Jesus, they are literally fulfilled:

- His life was prolonged endlessly, in spite of persecution (Heb. 7:16).
- His years will endure to all generations (Heb. 1:12).
- He will be enthroned forever before God (Heb. 1:8).
- Steadfast love and faithfulness will watch over Him, like bodyguards (Ps. 91:1–16).

Even the ancient Jewish comment in the Targum says that the King Messiah is in view here.

61:8 So I will sing praise to Your name forever,
That I may daily perform my vows.

And so the Psalm that opened in extremity closes in serenity. David has reached the Rock that is higher than himself, and is so grateful that he determines to sing the praises of the Lord continually, paying his **vows** of worship, love, and service. He will not be like those who make extravagant vows when the pressure is on, then quickly forget them when the crisis is past. He will not be one who "leaps in prayer but limps in praise."

Psalm 61 inspired this lovely hymn:

O sometimes the shadows are deep,
And rough seems the path to the goal;
And sorrows, sometimes how they sweep
Like tempests down over the soul!

Refrain:
O then to the Rock let me fly,

To the Rock that is higher than I;
O then to the Rock let me fly,
To the Rock that is higher than I.

O sometimes how long seems the day,
And sometimes how weary my feet;
But toiling in life's dusty way,
The Rock's blessed shadow, how sweet!

O near to the Rock let me keep,
If blessings or sorrows prevail,
Or climbing the mountain way steep,
Or walking the shadowy vale.
—*Erastus Johnson*

Psalm 62: God Alone!

The message of Psalm 62 is that God is the only true refuge. The repetition of the words **only** and **alone** emphasize His exclusive right to our full and undivided trust.

Among the many beautiful ways in which He is presented are:

the source of our **salvation** (vv. 1b, 2a, 6a, 7a)
our **rock** (vv. 2a, 6a, 7b)
our **defense** (vv. 2c, 6c)
the basis of our **expectation** (v. 5b)
our **glory** (v. 7a)
our **refuge** (vv. 7b, 8b)
the source of **power** (v. 11b)
the fountain of **mercy** (v. 12a)

Anyone who makes God the ground of his confidence and strength has the following confidences:

he **shall not be greatly moved** (v. 2b)
he has boldness to rebuke his enemies (v. 3)
he can see through their plans and strategies (v. 4)
he **shall not be moved** (v. 6b)
he will want others to know the joy of trusting **God** (v. 8)

There are five other objects in which people often trust, but such trust is sure to be disappointed. (1) **Men of low degree**, that is, common people, are as substantial and transitory as a **vapor**. (2) **Men of high degree**, whether rulers or wealthy people, are a delusion in that they seem to offer help and security but they are not dependable. Put the rabble or the elite in the scales and they are weightless as far as trustworthiness is concerned. (3) **Oppression** is a foolish method to depend on; "it reeks with God's curse." (4) **Robbery** might seem to be a quick route to power and wealth, but ill-gotten gain is doomed to the judgment of God. (5) *Even **riches*** gained through honest industry should never take the Lord's place in our affections and service. F. B. Meyer wrote: "How often have we looked for help from men and money in vain—but God has never failed us."

It seems probable that this Psalm was inspired by Absalom's rebellion. The rebels were out to shatter David as if he were a **leaning wall and a tottering fence**. Their goal was to **cast him down from his high position**, that is, from his throne. While pretending loyalty, they were plotting treachery. The fugitive king urges his loyal subjects to maintain their unwavering confidence in the Lord. His enemies were trusting in men and in money, but there was no salvation in either of these. His own trust was in the Lord. Repeatedly the Lord had assured him that He is the fountainhead of power and love; that His power is used to deliver the faithful and to punish the foes; that His love is used to comfort and bless His people. He will see that justice is meted out to all who refuse His grace.

John Donne's comment on the Psalm is memorable:

He is my rock, and my salvation, and
my defense, and my refuge and my
glory.
If my refuge, what enemy can
pursue me?
If my defense, what temptation shall
wound me?
If my rock, what storm shall shake
me?
If my salvation, what melancholy shall
deject me?
If my glory, what calumny shall defame me?

Psalm 63: Better Than Life

Temporarily deposed, **David** is trekking across **the wilderness of Judah** to his enforced exile east of the Jordan (2 Sam. 15:23–28; 16:2; 17:16). Even though the king's political fortunes are at a low ebb, his spiritual vitality is high.

63:1 It is magnificent to hear him claiming God as his own: **"O, God, You are my God."** The words in themselves are simple and childlike, but they contain a world of meaning. **My God**—an intimate, personal relationship. **My God**—an abiding treasure when all else is gone. **My God**—a sufficient resource in every crisis.

And it is humbling to notice the psalmist's passion for God, especially when we remember how cold and diffident we often are. He sought the Lord **early—early** in life and **early** every day. And he sought him with a fervor that would not be denied. His **soul** thirsted for God, his **flesh** fainted for God—which means that his entire being cried out for fellowship with the Eternal. His longing was as intense as the thirst of a traveler in a **dry**, weary, waterless **land**. This, incidentally, is not a bad description of the world—an arid wasteland.

63:2 In memory he goes back to those times when he worshiped at the **sanctuary** in Jerusalem, to those ineffable moments when, caught up in an ecstasy of sacred contemplation, he saw God in all His **power** and **glory**. Now his soul cannot be satisfied with anything less than a new unveiling of the Lord in splendor and might. Some call it the beatific vision—this view of God in His divine glory. Whatever it is called, it is an experience that makes all other glory seem jaded and dull.

Be Thou my vision, O Lord of my
heart—
Nought be all else to me, save that
Thou art;
Thou my best thought, by day
or by night—
Waking or sleeping, Thy presence
my light.

—*8th century Irish hymn*
Trans. by Mary E. Byrne
Versified by Eleanor H. Hill

63:3, 4 Then up from the unlikely wilderness of Judah rises one of the great rhapsodies of adoration.

Because Your lovingkindness is better than life,
My lips shall praise You.
Thus I will bless You while I live;
I will lift up my hands in Your name.

The **lovingkindness** of the Lord is **better than** anything that **life** can afford. Human **lips** are best employed in praising Him. All of life is not too long to spend in blessing Him. Our **hands** pulsate with fulfillment when lifted **up** to Him in praise and prayer.

63:5–8 No banquet is like this sacred communion. Our souls are fed with the choicest delights, and **joyful lips** respond with overflowing thanks as we redeem the sleepless hours of **night** by meditating on our glorious Lord. What a help He has been to us—who can ever measure all He has done for us? Shadowed by His **wings**, we raise our joyful song. And as we cling to Him in loving dependence and in conscious need, He preserves us from dangers seen and unseen, and empowers us to press on toward the mark for the prize.

63:9, 10 "Enemies?" did you say. "O yes, I do have enemies, men who are determined to obliterate me. But they are destined to destruction. They will die a violent death and will suffer the disgrace of not having a decent burial.

63:11 "But I will go on enjoying **God**. In fact, **everyone who swears** allegiance to **Him** will share in the jubilation, whereas those who love to lie will be silenced."

Psalm 64: Bows and Arrows

Two archery contests emerge in Psalm 64. The preliminary event is between the wicked and the righteous (vv. 1–6). The main event is between God and the wicked (vv. 7–10).

64:1–6 The first battle seems to be completely one-sided. The righteous **David** is opposed by a multitude of villains. He has no arrows; their quivers are full. But he has the secret weapon of prayer and he uses it to enlist the help of his unseen Partner. First, he raises his **voice** to **God** for preservation **from fear** and for protection **from the secret plots of the wicked**. Then he gives God an intelligence report about **the enemy**. Their tongues are finely honed, as sharp as **a sword**. They **bend their bows to shoot their arrows** of accusation—**bitter words** of reproach. Their attacks come unexpectedly from **secret** hide-outs and without fear of a counterattack. They are inflexible in their determination to destroy the innocent. As they conspire to trap the psalmist secretly, they imagine that they are immune from detection. "They have thought their plan out well, each with a cunning heart, each in his deep craft" (v. 6, Moffatt).

64:7 Everything seems to be on the side of the villains so far. But the righteous cling to the promise, "The Lord will fight for you while you keep silent" (Ex. 14:14). "For the battle is not yours but God's" (2 Chron. 20:15).

64:8 So in the second contest we see **God** shooting His **arrow** (singular) at them. It's a bull's-eye. **They** fall **wounded** to the ground. God causes their evil words to recoil on themselves, and all the spectators **flee away** in terror.

64:9, 10 The result is that a sense of awe comes over the populace. Word spreads quickly, and men realize that righteousness has triumphed. This causes **righteous** people to **be glad**, of course, and to **trust in** Jehovah. All those who love what is right will celebrate.

Psalm 65: Millennial Harvest Song

While Psalm 65 is generally used as a classic song of "harvest home," there can be little doubt that its primary interpretation deals with conditions at the Second Advent of the Lord.

65:1 During the long centuries of Israel's estrangement from God, **Zion** was barren as far as **praise** to **God** was concerned. But when God's ancient people are restored to Him, **praise** will await Him there in the silence of awe and reverence. **To** Him **the vow shall** at last **be performed**. This may mean His own vow that every knee will bow to Him (Isa.

45:23). It may refer to the Messiah's vow of Psalm 22:22: "In the midst of the assembly I will praise You." Or it may mean the vow of love, worship, and service that the persecuted remnant will make during the terrible suffering of the Tribulation.

65:2 Whereas Israel was primarily in view in verse 1, here the subject broadens to include **all** mankind. God is known by the grand and noble title, **"You who hear prayer."** The converted nations will lay hold of Him in believing **prayer**.

65:3 It is important to notice the change of speakers here. In the first clause, the Messiah is rehearsing His vicarious work at Calvary when He was crushed beneath sin's awful load. But the Jewish remnant quickly acknowledges that it was not His sins but **"our transgressions."** They say, "He was wounded for our transgressions, He was bruised for our iniquities; the chastisement for our peace was upon Him; and by His stripes we are healed" (Isa. 53:5). And as soon as Israel makes this confession of guilt, they will have the assurance that their transgressions are all forgiven.

65:4 Again we are aware that the first part of the verse speaks of the Messiah Jesus, whereas the second part is the language of redeemed Israel. God's blessed Son is the One whom God chose, as we read in Isaiah 42:1: "... My elect One in whom My soul delights." Also He is the One whom God caused to **approach** Him—a priest forever according to the order of Melchizedek. He shall **dwell** in the **courts** of the Lord, in the place of special nearness to Him.

Then the remnant expresses its confidence of complete satisfaction **with the goodness** of God's **house**, that is, His **holy temple**. This reference to **the temple** causes some to question the Davidic authorship of the Psalm since the temple was not built until after David's death. However the difficulty vanishes when we realize that the word *temple* was sometimes used to describe the tabernacle before Solomon's temple was erected (1 Sam. 1:9; 3:3; 2 Sam. 22:7).

65:5–7 The remnant is still speaking. In answer to their prayers, the Lord righteously punishes their enemies with **awesome** judgments. Thus He reveals Himself as the **God of** their **salvation** and **the confidence** of people throughout **the earth and** in **far-off seas**. What a great God He is! With omnipotence as His belt, He **established the mountains** firm in their place by an act of super-power. It's nothing for Him to pacify the raging **seas**, the fury of **their waves** (on the Sea of Galilee, for instance). Or to suppress the fury of the Gentile **peoples**, for that matter.

65:8 No wonder that unbelievers **in the farthest** lands **are afraid** of the **signs** and wonders which God visits upon them. Or that believers in the lands of sunrise and sunset **rejoice**.

65:9 While verses 9–13 describe the harvest year from seedtime to harvest, they apply especially to conditions in the Millennium when the curse will be lifted and bumper crops will be the rule.

Springtime is like a visit from God. He sends the showers from His overhead river—the clouds that scud across the sky. Then when the ground has been prepared, He provides the seed to be planted.

65:10 During the growing season, the plowed furrows are irrigated, the rain melting the clods and keeping the ground **soft**. Soon the crops are shooting up in profusion.

65:11–13 God crowns the growth

cycle **with** His **goodness**. Wherever His feet have passed, the stream of plenty flows (Knox). **The pastures** yield rich supplies of fodder. **The little hills** are covered with lush vegetation, as if hilarious with joy. **The pastures** wear a sheepskin coat, **clothed** as they are **with** innumerable **flocks**. Ripened **grain** bends in rhythmic cadence across the floors of **the valleys**. It seems that all nature is celebrating the arrival of the age of the Messiah.

Psalm 66: Come, See, and Hear!

66:1–4 In the first four verses, the psalmist calls on the whole **earth** to join in singing the praises of **God**. It should be a **joyful** song and one that celebrates the excellencies **of His name**. The **praise** should be **glorious** because the Subject is glorious. The very words of the song of universal worship are given. We might paraphrase them as follows:

> Lord, Your accomplishments are tremendous. Your power is so devastating that Your enemies cringe before You. At last the whole earth bows before You in worship. Everywhere people praise Your name in song.

This song will no doubt be a favorite when the kingdom age arrives.

66:5–7 The recurrence of *our* and *us* in verses 5–12 leads us to believe that these are the evangelistic sentiments of the Jewish remnant in the last days as they invite the nations to ponder the astounding things that **God** has done for Israel. Two terrific displays of His might come to mind. He made a highway of **dry** land through the Red **Sea**. And when the Israelites came to **the** Jordan **River** forty years later, they were able to cross dry-shod. What rejoicing exploded in Israel then! The people exulted in their God whose mighty dominion never ends and whose **eyes** keep close watch on **the nations**. It's foolish for anyone to rebel against a God like this.

66:8–12 The Gentiles should also **bless God** for the miraculous way in which He preserved the people of Israel. In a rapidly changing succession of figures Israel is pictured as:

> being **tested** like **silver** when it is subjected to intense heat by the smelter (v. 10).
> being imprisoned as if in a **net** (v. 11a).
> being forced to slave labor (v. 11b).
> being downtrodden by wretched men (v. 12a).
> being exposed to frightful dangers, as if going **through fire and through water** (v. 12b).

Yet God did not allow them to be finally overthrown. Rather He **brought** them into **rich fulfillment**—a reference to Israel's superabundant prosperity in the Millennium. As Williams puts it:

> In spite of the unceasing efforts of Satan and man to utterly destroy Israel, her twelve tribes will appear at Mt. Sion upon the Millennial morn, and so demonstrate the truth of the ninth verse. They will testify that the chastisements justly laid upon them (vv. 10–12) were designed in love and executed in wisdom.[46]

66:13–15 In verses 13–20, the **I** and **my** indicate that the chorus has become a solo. Several sober commentators believe that the speaker is the Lord Jesus, Israel's King and Great High Priest. He comes to God with **burnt offerings** of a life totally devoted to the will of His Father. He pays the **vows** of praise which He had promised when in trouble. This may refer to His own sufferings on the cross, or to the sufferings which He felt in the sufferings of His people, for "In all their affliction He was afflicted" (Isa. 63:9).

When we read here of **burnt offerings**, of the sacrifice of **rams** and of an offering of **bulls** and **goats**, we need not take them with exact literalness, except as the psalmist spoke of his own experience. In association with His people, the Messiah uses these as figures of the spiritual worship which He and the remnant will bring. However, this does not deny that a modified sacrificial system may be reinstituted in the Kingdom.

66:16–19 In verse 5, the invitation was "Come and see." Here in verse 16 it is **"Come and hear."** The works of **God** in history can be seen, but His dealing with the soul can only be heard. The Messiah invites all God-fearing people to hear His testimony of answered prayer. He had **cried to Him** in supplication and in exaltation. The reference is to the days of His flesh when He "offered up both supplications and entreaties to Him who was able to save Him out of death, with strong crying and tears" (Heb. 5:7, JND). If He had regarded **iniquity** in His **heart, the Lord** would not have heard Him. But He was without sin, and so He was heard "because of His piety" (Heb. 5:7, JND).

66:20 And this inspired the closing burst of praise:

Blessed be God,
Who has not turned away my prayer,
Nor His mercy from me!

Psalm 67: Israel's Missionary Call

When God called the nation of Israel, He intended that the nation should have a missionary character. It was to be a witness and a testimony to the surrounding nations of two important truths.

1. The truth of monotheism—that there is only one God (Ex. 20:2, 3; Deut. 6:4; Isa. 43:10–12).
2. The truth that a people living in obedience under the government of Jehovah would be happy and prosperous (Lev. 26:3–12; Deut. 33:26–29; 1 Chron. 17:20; Jer. 33:9).

It was not God's will that Israel should be the *terminal* of His *blessing*, but a *channel*. There are numerous indications throughout the OT that God's salvation was for the Gentiles as well as for the Jews, and that Israel as a kingdom of priests was to serve as mediator between God and the nations.

Unfortunately Israel failed in this aspect of its mission. By lapsing into idolatry, it denied the very truths it was called on to proclaim.

But God's purposes are not so easily defeated. During the Tribulation, a remnant of believing Jews will carry the gospel of the kingdom to all the world (Matt. 24:14). And in the ensuing kingdom, Israel will be the channel of blessing to the nations (Isa. 61:6; Zech. 8:23).

67:1, 2 This Psalm anticipates that time. In it we hear believing Jews praying that **God** will **bless** them so that they can be the means of evangelizing the Gentiles. When we read the words, **"that Your way may be known on the earth,"** we should remember that Christ is the way (John 14:6). Only through Him can God's saving power be experienced by **nations** or individuals.

67:3, 4 In an extraordinary burst of missionary enthusiasm, Israel then prays that great torrents of praise will ascend to God from the Gentiles, that **the nations** will enjoy a gala time of celebration as they enjoy Christ's beneficent and equitable rule and His tender, shepherd care.

67:5 Just as Israel yearns to hear **God** praised by **all the peoples** of the world, as F. B. Meyer reminds us, so should "we want crowns for the brow of Christ."

67:6, 7 The last two verses picture the Millennium as having already arrived. The crops have been harvested, and the barns and silos are bursting. This proof of God's blessing to Israel will be a powerful testimony to the nations. The Hebrew scholar Franz Delitzsch summarized: "For it is the way of God, that all the good that He manifests toward Israel shall be for the well-being of mankind."[47]

Psalm 68: Our God Is Marching On!

This is Israel's national processional, in which the journey of the ark of the covenant from Mount Sinai to Mount Zion is seen as symbolizing the march of God to ultimate victory. To the Jewish mind, the ark rightly represented the presence of God; when the ark moved, God moved.

It is quite generally believed that the song was composed to celebrate one particular incident in the history of the ark—the return to Mount Zion after its inglorious capture by the Philistines and after its stay in the house of Obed-Edom (2 Sam. 6:2–18).

We can better enter into the spirit of this marching song if we see that it is divided into the following seven sections:

1. Introductory hymn of praise to God (vv. 1–6).
2. The ark moving from Sinai through the wilderness (vv. 7, 8).
3. The entrance and conquest of the land of Canaan (vv. 9–14).
4. The capture of Jerusalem by David (vv. 15–18).
5. Song praising God for victory over the Jebusites (vv. 19–23).
6. The procession carrying the ark to the sanctuary in Jerusalem (vv. 24–27).
7. The jubilant throng anticipating the final victory of God (vv. 28–35).

In its Messianic setting, the Psalm pictures Christ's Incarnation, His conquest at Calvary, His Ascension, and His Second Advent.

Introductory Hymn (68:1–6)

68:1–3 The first verse gives us a clue that the movements of the ark are the main subject; these are almost the same words which Moses used when the ark first started off from Sinai (Num. 10:35). The sight of the sacred chest under way suggested the time when **God** arises and moves into action. For **His enemies** it means disaster and dispersal; for the righteous, deep-seated joy. His enemies scatter in every direction. They **flee** in pandemonium. As insubstantial as smoke, as unresisting as melting **wax,** they stagger to their doom. But for the righteous it is a time of vindication and reward, of joy and jubilation.

68:4–6 It is a time to **sing** praises **to God** and to clear a way for the Lord in the deserts (MT, see NKJV margin, cf. Isa. 40:3; 62:10). **His name** is **YAH,** the covenant-keeping Jehovah; He is worthy of endless praise. Though He is infinitely high, yet He is intimately near to the friendless and the dispossessed. As the **God** of all grace, He is **father of the fatherless, defender of widows**. He provides the warmth and fellowship of a happy home for the lonely, and as for those who have been unjustly condemned to prison, He leads them **into prosperity** with shouts of joy.

With **the rebellious**, it's a different story; they are consigned to a desolate wilderness.

These introductory verses, then, say in the words of the "Battle Hymn of the Republic," "Our God is marching on," and contrast the results of His march on the righteous and on rebels.

Although it is not noticeable in the English version, seven names of God are woven into the texture of this Psalm: *Elohim* (v. 1), *Yah* (v. 4), *Jehovah* (v. 10), *El Shaddai* (v. 14), *Yah Elohim* (v. 18), *Adonai* (v. 19), and *Jehovah Adonai* (v. 20).

The Ark Moves from Sinai through the Wilderness (68:7, 8)

When the Israelites broke camp at Sinai and started the trip toward the Promised Land with the ark in the vanguard, it was an emotion-packed moment. Nature itself seemed to enter into the awesomeness of the event. **The earth** quaked, the **heavens** broke loose with **rain**, and Mount **Sinai** shuddered at the sight.

The Entrance and Conquest of the Land (68:9–14)

68:9, 10 By verse 9, Israel is in Canaan and **God** has produced changes in the weather so that the land is abundantly supplied with **rain**—a welcome change from the irrigation of Egypt and the wilderness drought. The countryside has taken a new lease on life as the drooping vegetation revives and flourishes. The people are at home, richly provisioned by the Lord.

68:11–13 The narrative moves quickly to the conquest of the land. **The Lord** gives **the word**, that is, the command to march against the enemy. Implicit in His word is the assurance of victory. The next thing you know, a great company of women[48] are spreading the news at home: **"Kings of armies flee, they flee!"** In language strongly reminiscent of the Song of Deborah (Judg. 5), we see the women dividing **the spoil** of battle, though they themselves never left **the sheepfolds**. As they try on the beautiful clothes and jewelry, they resemble **the wings of a dove covered with silver**, or, when the light hits at a different angle, they gleam like **feathers of yellow gold**.

68:14 For the enemy it was a disastrous rout. God **scattered kings** like **snow in Zalmon**.

The Capture of Jerusalem by David (68:15–18)

68:15, 16 Jerusalem was still held securely by the pagan Jebusites. The first thing David did after he had been anointed king over all Israel was to move against the city. The defenders were smugly satisfied that it was so impregnable that it could be defended by the blind and lame. But David and his men captured the stronghold and called it the City of David (2 Sam. 5:1–9).

This is what the psalmist is referring to here. As the citadel's capture reveals Jerusalem as the chosen city, the high snow-summit of Hermon, located north of **Bashan**, looks enviously at Mount Zion. Hermon is a majestic mountain range with **many** majestic **peaks**, yet **God** passed it by and chose Zion for His permanent dwelling. That is why it looks jealously at Zion.

68:17 David recalls the capture of Jerusalem from the Jebusites. But he has no illusions as to the real source of victory. It was not his clever strategy or the valor of his men. It was **the** numberless **chariots of God** assaulting the city. The march of God that had begun at **Sinai** had now reached a glorious finale at Zion.

68:18 As David remembered how his soldiers had stormed the heights of Jerusalem, he looked beyond flesh and blood to see God ascending the **high** mount, taking captives in His train and winning spoils of victory for those who were former rebels so that He could **dwell** among these people as their Lord and Savior.

Paul applies verse 18 to the Ascension of Christ (Eph. 4:8–10). When Christ ascended from earth to heaven, **He led captivity captive**, that is, He triumphed gloriously over His foes and gave gifts to men. The **gifts** He **received** *among* men as reward for His finished work on the cross (Ps. 68:18), He turned around and gave these same gifts *to* men for the establishment and expansion of His church (Eph. 4:8).

Song Praising God for Victory over the Jebusites (68:19–23)

68:19, 20 Memories of the capture of Zion inevitably awaken praise to God. The song presents God as both Deliverer and Destroyer. As Deliverer, He "bears our burdens and wins us the victory" (Knox). He is **the God of our salvation**, and He has the power to deliver **from death**.

68:21–23 As Destroyer, He will crush His foes, those rebels whose long hair symbolizes their lawless, wicked careers. He has promised to track them down in the wilds **of Bashan** and from the coasts of the high seas so that Israel can wash its feet **in** their **blood**, and so that Israel's **dogs** can feed on their carcasses.

Verse 22 does not refer to the regathering of Israel, but to the hunting down of Israel's enemies.

The Procession Carrying the Ark to the Sanctuary in Jerusalem (68:24–27)

Not long after David captured Jerusalem, he arranged for the ark to be brought to a tent which had been erected to house it (2 Sam. 6:12–19). The **procession** is described here. As it moves toward **the sanctuary**, "the psalmist says, in effect, 'Look, here He comes.'"[49] The choir is leading, the band brings up the rear, and in between are young women **playing timbrels**. Listen to the words of the song:

> **Bless God in the congregations,**
> **The LORD, from the fountain of Israel.**

The tribes are all represented, from those in the south—**little Benjamin** and **Judah**—to those in the north—**Zebulun** and **Naphtali**.

The Jubilant Throng Anticipating the Final Victory of God (68:28–35)

As the ark disappears inside the tabernacle, the people outside join in a final prayer (vv. 28–31) and in a song urging all the earth to praise the Lord (vv. 32–35).

68:28, 29 The prayer first of all calls on **God** to summon His might, to show His **strength** again on behalf of His people, to complete what He has begun for them. This prayer will be finally answered in the Millennium when **the temple** will be the glory of **Jerusalem**, and when **kings will bring presents** of gold and frankincense (Isa. 60:6) to the Great King.

68:30 The Hebrew of verse 30 is obscure, but the overall thought seems to be this: The people call on God to **rebuke the beasts** and **the herd of bulls. The beasts** that live among **the**

reeds, probably crocodiles and hippopotami, represent the leaders of Egypt. The bulls represent the other rulers who "lord it over the peaceful herd of nations" (Knox).

The clause translated **"Till everyone submits himself with pieces of silver,"** may mean "until those nations bow down to You with **silver** as tribute" or "vanquishing those nations that have thrived on **silver** tribute." The sense is good in either case. And in the same vein the prayer goes up, **"Scatter the peoples who delight in war."** These requests will be fully answered at the Second Advent of Christ when aggressors and warmongers will be destroyed.

68:31 In that day, **envoys** from **Egypt** will bring tribute, and **Ethiopia will stretch out her hands** imploringly and adoringly to the King of all the earth.

68:32–35 The closing verses call on the **kingdoms of the earth** to acknowledge the **God** of Israel as worthy of homage and praise. The words carry a tremendous sense of the grandeur and greatness of God. He is the transcendent One, **who rides** in the ancient **heavens**. He is the God of revelation, speaking with **a mighty voice**. He is the omnipotent one, strong on behalf of **Israel**, but almighty beyond **the clouds**.

Awesome as He is in His **holy places**, yet He stoops to give **strength and power to His people.**

There is only one thing left to say—**Blessed be God!**

Psalm 69: Save Me, O God!

Our blessed Redeemer's sufferings and death were, for Him, an immersion in the ocean of God's wrath. He Himself spoke of His approaching passion as a baptism:

> I have a baptism to be baptized with, and how distressed I am till it is accomplished! (Luke 12:50).

And in Psalm 42:7 we hear Him crying:

> Deep calls unto deep at the noise
> of Your waterfalls;
> All Your waves and billows have
> gone over me.

In His death of bitterest woe, He plumbed the depths of God's judgment against our sin.

69:1–3 Here in Psalm 69 we are privileged to hear the deepest exercises of His holy soul as He sinks into death. **The waters have come up to** His **neck** and are about to engulf Him completely. There is nothing to support Him—nothing but **deep mire** under His feet. Now the **floods** are dashing over His head. The waters are very deep—deeper than any of the ransomed will ever know. In a real sense God has gathered all **the waters** together in one place—Calvary—and the Son of His love is enduring that mighty ocean of judgment in order to pay the penalty for our sins.

Above the trackless waste of water reverberates His continuous urgent appeal, **"Save me, O God!"** It seems as if He has been pleading for an eternity. His throat is hoarse and parched—worn out **with** His **crying**. His **eyes** are swollen shut, ceaselessly scanning the horizon for some sight of help from **God**. But no help is near.

69:4 The angry mob is milling before the cross, a seething collage of venom, hatred, bitterness and cruelty. What a scene! The Creator and Sustainer of the universe is hanging on a criminal's cross. His guilty murderers are gathered before Him. Who are they? They are men and women who owe their very breath to Him, yet they **hate** Him **without a cause**. They are out to **destroy** Him; they attack Him with lies.

Why? What hath my Lord done?
What makes this rage and spite?
He made the lame to run,
He gave the blind their sight.
Sweet injuries!
Yet they at these
Themselves displease,
And 'gainst Him rise.
—*Samuel Crossman*

Now the poignant sentence crosses the Savior's lips: "What I did not steal, **I still must restore**." Through man's sin, God was robbed of service, worship, obedience, and glory, and man himself was robbed of life, peace, gladness and fellowship with God. In a very real sense Christ came to **restore** what He did not steal.

Aside He threw His most divine array,
And veiled His Godhead in a robe of clay
And in that garb didst wondrous love display,
Restoring what He never took away.
—*Author unknown*

In this respect He reminds us of the trespass offering (Lev. 5). The prominent feature of this offering was that restitution had to be made for any loss that the offerer had caused, and an additional fifth part had to be added. As our trespass offering, the Lord Jesus not only restored what had been stolen through man's sin, but He added more. For God has received more glory through the finished work of Christ than if sin had never entered. Through sin He *lost creatures;* through grace He *gained sons*. And we are better off in Christ than we ever could have been in unfallen Adam.

In Him the sons of Adam boast
More blessings than their father lost.

69:5 We must understand verse 5 as referring to *our* **sins** which Jesus voluntarily took upon Himself. He had no folly or wrongs, but "He took our sins and our sorrows, and made them His very own." It was wonderful grace that He would identify Himself so closely with us that He could speak of our sins as His sins.

69:6 Then a fear casts a shadow across His holy mind. He fears that some earnest believers might be stumbled by the fact that His prayers to God go unanswered. He prays that it may not happen—that no one who hopes in **God** might be **ashamed because of** what was happening to Him, and that no one who seeks the God of Israel might be brought to dishonor through His humiliation and abandonment.

69:7, 8 It was, after all, **because** of His obedience to the Father's will that He was bearing **reproach**. It was His delight in pleasing God that allowed men to cover His **face** with unmentionable **shame** and spitting. Part of the cost of obedience was the sorrow of alienation from His own **mother's children**: His own half-brothers looked upon Him as being out of His mind.

69:9 The Lord Jesus was consumed with a **zeal for** His Father's **house**. Whenever He heard men speak insultingly about God, He took it as a personal insult. On that day in Jerusalem when He drove the money changers from the temple courts, His disciples remembered that it was written of Him here in Psalm 69, **"Zeal for Your house has eaten me up"** (John 2:17).

69:10–12 Nothing that He ever did as a perfect man here on earth seemed to please His critics. If He humbled His **soul with fasting**, they found fault with Him—perhaps suggesting, for instance, that He was only trying to appear pious. When He was plunged in the deepest mourning, He **became a byword to them** instead of an object of sympathy. In all strata of society, He was spoken against—from the rulers who sat at **the gate** of the city to **the drunkards** in the local taverns, bawling their coarse songs of derision. This is indeed a strange thing—the Lord of life and glory has come into the world and He is **the song of the drunkards!**

69:13–18 And so once again He retreats into **God**, His only resource. What fervency, what importunity there is in His **prayer**! He storms the bastions of heaven with successive pleas for help. But even then He reserves to God the right to answer at an **acceptable time**. As He sinks into **the mire**, He implores God to rescue Him with His faithful help, to **deliver** Him from His enemies, and to save Him **out of the deep waters, . . . the floodwater** and **the pit**. In His deep extremity, He bases His pleas on God's **lovingkindness** and His abundant **mercies**. His petitions are short and specific. **Hear me, . . . turn to me, . . . do not hide** from me, **draw near to** me, **redeem** me, and **deliver** me. **"Deliver me because of my enemies"** doubtless means "lest they gloat over my unalleviated distress."

69:19, 20 That mention of His enemies recalls all that He has suffered at the hands of men. His pathway through life was strewn with **reproach, shame** and **dishonor**. From the time of His infancy, He was pursued by **adversaries**: God knew how numerous they were. His **heart** was **broken** by insults—that **heart** that desires only good for the sons of men. The grief and **heaviness** of it all plunged Him into despair. There was no one who took **pity** on Him in His sorrow and suffering. He **looked** in vain **for comforters**. Even His disciples forsook Him and fled. He was *all alone.*

69:21 Then in another of those startling prophecies spoken by David but fulfilled only in Jesus, we read:

> **They also gave me gall for my food,**
> **And for my thirst they gave me vinegar to drink.**

The fulfillment is found in Matthew 27:34, 48:

> They gave Him sour wine mingled with gall to drink. But when He had tasted it, He would not drink. . . . Immediately one of them ran and took a sponge, filled it with sour wine and put it on a reed, and offered it to Him to drink.

Gall was a bitter and perhaps poisonous substance which in small quantity might have acted as a sedative. The Lord would not take it because He must suffer as our Substitute in full consciousness. The **vinegar** was a sour wine which might have accentuated His thirst rather than alleviating it.

69:22 The tone of the Psalm changes abruptly at verse 22, and for the next seven verses we hear the dying Savior calling on God to punish the nation which condemned Him to die. At first this seems surprising when we remember that the Lord Jesus also prayed, "Father, forgive them, for they do not know what they do" (Luke 23:34). But actually there is no conflict between the two prayers. Forgiveness was available if they would have repented. But, in the absence of any change of heart, there was nothing left but the judgment described here.

It is important to see that these verses apply particularly to the nation of Israel. Paul applies verses 22 and 23 to Israel in Romans 11:9, 10. Also the mention of "their tents," signifying encampment (v. 25), is a distinctly Jewish allusion.

The verses predict the judgments which would come upon the race of people who had rejected their Messiah and brought about His execution.

Their table would **become a snare**. The **table** speaks of the sum total of the privileges which were conferred on Israel as God's chosen, earthly people. Instead of being a blessing, these privileges would determine the measure of their condemnation.

When they experience **well-being** (*peace*, Heb. *shālôm*), it would become **a trap**. Tribulation would spring forth just as the people think that all is well.

69:23 **Their eyes** would **be darkened, so that they** would **not** be able to **see**. This refers to the judicial blindness which has actually come on Israel nationally (2 Cor. 3:14). Because they rejected the Light, they have been denied the Light.

Their loins would **shake continually**. Dispersed among the nations, they would find no rest for the sole of their feet, but the Lord would give them "a trembling heart, failing eyes, and anguish of soul" (Deut. 28:65).

69:24 God's **indignation** would be poured out **upon them** and His **wrathful anger** would overtake **them**. We remember with deep, deep sorrow how this has been fulfilled in the awful anti-semitic pogroms, the concentration camps, the gas chambers and the ovens. Though these atrocities were perpetrated by wicked men, there can be no doubt that they were *not prevented* by God from coming upon descendants of the people who said, "His blood be on us and on our children" (Matt. 27:25).

69:25 Their **dwelling place** would become **desolate** and **no one** would **live in their tents**. Here we are reminded of the Messiah's words in Matthew 23:38, "See! Your house is left to you desolate." The words were amply fulfilled in A.D. 70 when Titus and the Roman army sacked Jerusalem and destroyed the temple.

69:26 If the punishment seems severe, think of the crime that provoked it.

> **For they persecute the ones** [or *one*] **You have struck,**
> **And talk of the grief of those You have wounded.**

In the parable of the vineyard, the tenants are quoted as saying concerning the son of the householder, "This is the heir. Come, let us kill him and seize his inheritance" (Matt. 21:38). They *knew* He was the Son, and they killed Him nonetheless. The latter part of verse 26 described those followers of the Messiah who would be martyred.

69:27, 28 In view of this, there is no need to apologize for the severity of the Savior's words:

> **Add iniquity to their iniquity,**
> **And let them not come into Your righteousness.**
> **Let them be blotted out of the book of the living,**
> **And not be written with the righteous.**

And yet we should not forget that even after the crucifixion of God's Son, the Spirit of God still pleaded with the nation of Israel to repent and to turn to Jesus as the Messiah. All through the period of the Acts, you hear the heartbeat of God as He yearns over the nation He loves and tenderly invites to accept His mercy and grace. Even today the gospel goes out to the Jewish people as to the Gentiles. And the only ones who ever have to suffer the judgments described in verses 22–28 are those who deliberately choose that fate by rejecting the Christ of God.

69:29 Now there is a final word from the dying sinner's Friend. Afflicted and in indescribable pain, He asks that the **salvation** of **God** might **set** Him securely **on high**.

And that is exactly what happened. God raised Him from the dead on the third day and set Him at His own right hand, a Prince and a Savior. His sufferings for sin are over forever. And we are glad!

> Never more shall God Jehovah
> Smite the Shepherd with the sword;
> N'er again shall cruel sinners
> Set at nought our glorious Lord.
> —*Robert C. Chapman*

And now we sing:

> The storm that bowed Thy blessed Head
> Is hushed forever now,
> And rest divine is ours instead,
> Whilst glory crowns Thy brow.
> —*H. Rossier*

69:30–33 The speaker in the final seven verses is the risen Redeemer. First He vows to extol God for delivering Him from death and the grave. He **will praise the name of God with a song and will magnify Him with thanksgiving.** This will mean far more to **the Lord** than the most costly sacrifices. And oppressed people everywhere will take heart when they realize that just as **the Lord** heard the Savior's prayers and delivered Him, so He will hear the needy and free the **prisoners** who call on Him.

69:34–36 And what about the nation of Israel? The last three verses predict a bright tomorrow. Though set aside temporarily, Israel will be restored to the place of blessing. When they look on Him whom they pierced and mourn for Him as one mourns for an only son, when they say, "Blessed is He who comes in the name of the Lord," **God will save Zion and** rebuild **the cities of Judah**. No longer dispersed among the nations, **His servants** shall **dwell** in the land, and their children shall **possess** it. This looks forward, of course, to the Millennium when the Lord Jesus will reign as Messiah-King, and Israel will **dwell** securely in the land.

Psalm 70: Help Quickly!

For the most part, Psalm 70 is a repetition of Psalm 40:13–17. The heading states that it is a **Psalm of David, to bring to remembrance**. Four distinct movements appear.

Help Quickly (70:1)

Morgan calls it "a rushing sob of anxious solicitude." This is certainly the impression we get in verse 1 where David is urging the Lord to **make haste to deliver** him.

Punish Thoroughly (70:2, 3)

The defeat and rout of his foes is of major concern at the moment. He accuses them of trying to kill him, of taking pleasure in harming him, and of jeering at his calamity. He, in turn, asks that they might be thoroughly nonplussed, that they might be **turned back and confused**, and that they might be startled or appalled by the depth of **their** own **shame**.

Be Praised Continually (70:4)

The flow of thought here is that if God comes to the psalmist's rescue, this will result in a great wave of praise to Him. **All those who seek** the Lord will have occasion to exult in His help, and to worship Him as the great **God** of **salvation**.

Help Quickly (70:5)

Again the cry for speedy rescue goes up from the destitute. Although David cannot be said to be soaring in confidence, yet his faith is in the LORD as his **help and** his **deliverer**, and such faith will never go unrewarded.

Psalm 71: Old Age

As is so often the case, we can trace a close parallel between the experiences of the psalmist and those of the nation of Israel. Thus, as Bellett suggests, this Psalm can be studied as a prayer of the afflicted remnant in Israel's old age.[50]

71:1–3 The first three verses are similar to Psalm 31:1–3. The LORD is praised as **refuge, rock** and **fortress**, and is entreated for vindication of the psalmist's **trust**, for deliverance, rescue, salvation, and for His saving help as a **rock** of refuge and a **fortress**.

71:4 As the prayer continues, it is pervaded by a strong sense of gratitude for God's help in the past and confidence in His continued mercy in old age.

If we apply the Psalm to Israel, the **wicked**, unjust and **cruel** man of verse 4 is the Antichrist. His dictatorship of horror will tax the endurance of the saints and wring out from them the most importunate pleas.

71:5, 6 Happy is the man who can say that **God** has been his **hope** and **trust from** childhood. If he has leaned on Jehovah **from** his **birth**, he will not lack support in the sunset years of life. If he can trace God's marvelous grace back to the moment of his **birth**, he will not lack material for **praise** in later years.

71:7, 8 The psalmist had been **a wonder to many** by the depth of his rejection and suffering, and perhaps also by his marvelous deliverances. But through all the changing circumstances of life, God had been his **strong refuge**. And so he wanted every **day** to be crammed with His praise and **glory**.

71:9 Do not cast me off in the time of old age;
Do not forsake me when my strength fails.

To grow old gracefully calls for more Grace than Nature can provide. Old age is a new world of strange conflicts and secret fears; the fear of being left alone, the fear of being a burden to loved ones, the fear of becoming a helpless invalid, the fear of losing one's grip, the fear of being imposed upon. These fears are not new. The psalmist is here thinking aloud for the encouragement of all who are in the autumn of life (*Daily Notes of the Scripture Union*).

71:10, 11 Of course, he had the added fear of **enemies** who vilified him and who conspired to kill him. Mistakenly supposing that **God** had **forsaken him**, they prepared their final assault with no fear of opposition.

71:12, 13 This crisis prompted a distress call in which he urges **God** to come to his side and **help**. With no additional trouble, God could also swamp the foes with shame and defeat, **reproach and dishonor**.

71:14–16 But **hope** quickly rises above fear, and praise begins its mighty crescendo. The lyrics recount God's righteous acts and the numberless times He has rescued His beleaguered child. With holy determination the psalmist says, "I will come with the inexhaustible narration of the mighty acts of Jehovah Elohim."[51]

71:17, 18 Once again, as in verses 5–11, he runs the gamut from youth to old age (vv. 17–21) and finds nothing but the faithfulness of **God**. God had **taught** him **from** the days of his **youth** and, as Knox continues, "still I am found telling the tale of Thy wonders." Now he is **old and grayheaded**, but he doesn't feel his work is done. He pleads for time to tell the new **generation** and those **to come** about the mighty miracles of the Lord. This prayer was answered, of course, by the Psalm's being preserved in the sacred Scriptures.

71:19–21 God is really wonderful! His power and His **righteousness** are higher than the heavens. No one can hold a candle to Him, especially when you think of the **great things** He has **done**.

Sometimes God is said to have done what He has permitted. So here, He made the psalmist (and Israel) experience many bitter troubles. For Israel, this suggests the Tribulation Period. But He is the God of recovery, and He will revive His people, and snatch them from the jaws of the grave. That isn't all! He will give them honor in place of reproach and surround them with comfort.

71:22 **The lute** will be pressed into service to sing the **faithfulness** of **God**, and the **harp** enlisted to magnify the **Holy One of Israel**. This name of God—the **Holy One of Israel**—is used two other times in the Psalms—in 78:41 and 89:18.

71:23, 24 But lute and harp will be joined in the chorus by the psalmist's **lips, soul** and **tongue**. His **lips** will be effervescently joyful in song. His **soul, redeemed** by the blood of the Lamb, will also **greatly rejoice** in song. His **tongue also shall** be unwearied in talking about God's dependability, for all his enemies have been thoroughly **confounded**.

Psalm 72: Messiah's Glorious Reign

This Psalm starts out as a prayer for an earthly monarch, possibly **Solomon**, but before long we realize that the writer is looking beyond Solomon to the glories of the reign of the Lord Jesus Christ. It will be a wonderful time for this weary, warring world. The golden era for which mankind has yearned will then be ushered in. Creation's groan will be hushed, and peace and prosperity will flourish.

72:1 In the first verse, we hear the prayer that rises from the holy convocation as the King is invested. Knox translates it, "Grant to the King Thy own skill in judgment; the inheritor of the throne, may He be just as Thou art just."

Every one of the "He will's" or "He shall's" in the rest of Psalm 72 will become fact when the Redeemer sets up His resplendent reign.

72:2 **He will judge** the **people with righteousness and** the **poor with justice**. Corruption, bribery and oppression will have ceased. Trials will be conducted with strict impartiality, and the **poor** will no longer be disadvantaged.

72:3 **The mountains will** bear a harvest of **peace** and prosperity for **the people**, and justice will cover **the little hills**. **Mountains** are often used in Scripture to signify governmental authorities. So the thought here may be that the subjects of Christ's kingdom can expect equity and justice from all the courts in the land—from the supreme court all the way down to the local magistrate.

72:4 Down through the centuries the poor and needy have been oppressed, underpaid, persecuted and even killed. In the Millennium, the King Himself will be their Advocate. He will emancipate them once for all and punish those who took advantage of them.

72:5, 6 His subjects will respect and **fear** Him **as long as the sun and moon endure, throughout all generations.** His presence shall prove beneficial and refreshing—just **like rain upon the grass** and **showers** on the parched **earth.**

72:7 He will be the true Melchizedek—King of righteousness and King of **peace**. During His reign justice will flourish, and **peace** will abound, **until the moon** ceases to exist. Notice that righteousness precedes peace. "The work of righteousness will be peace, and the effect of righteousness, quietness and assurance forever" (Isa. 32:17). By His righteous work for us on the cross, He bequeathed peace to us. And by His righteous rule He will one day bring peace to the war-torn world.

72:8 The boast of the United Kingdom used to be, "The sun never sets on the British Empire." British colonies were interspersed among the other nations of the world. But Christ's kingdom will be universal. It will not be a matter of scattered colonies. *All* nations will be included. His **dominion** will extend from one **sea to** another **and from the** Euphrates **River to the ends of the earth**.

72:9 The ungovernable nomads of the desert **will bow before Him** at last, and **His enemies** will go down to defeat. To **lick the dust** means to suffer ignoble and shameful subjugation.

72:10, 11 Gentile **kings** will come to Jerusalem with tribute and with **presents** for the King of kings. Here comes the ruler of Spain, there are the heads of states from various island countries, and now you see the rulers of the sheikdoms of Southern Arabia. The airport is crowded with visiting dignitaries because all acknowledge His sway and **all nations** without exception **serve Him**.

"Kings of wealth, and thought, and music, and art have already acknowledged Him, and shall," said Meyer.

72:12–14 The King's tremendous compassion for **the needy** is seen here. **The poor**, the downtrodden and the underdogs will have a Mighty Deliverer. Poverty will vanish and social injustice will be a thing of the past. The weak and **the needy** will have instant access to Him, and will be certain of considerate attention and prompt action. He will rescue them from unjust and cruel treatment, and He will show the world how **precious** their lives are to Him.

72:15 The shout, "Long **live** the King," will rise from His loyal subjects. In their gratitude they will give Him **gold** from the treasures **of Sheba**. Never-ceasing **prayer** will ascend from all over the world **for Him**, and people will bless Him from dawn to dusk.

72:16 The fertility of the land will be indescribable. Barns and silos will bulge with **grain**. Even places never previously cultivated, like **the top of the mountains**, will **wave** with fields of ripened grain, undulating in the breeze **like** the forests of **Lebanon**.

The cities will be richly inhabited with people, as the fields are filled with **grass**. It will be a population explosion of epic proportions, yet there will be no scarcity of food.

72:17 His name shall endure,

loved and revered **forever. As long as the sun** exists, **His** fame **shall continue**. In accordance with the promise God made to Abraham, all **men shall** bless themselves **in Him**, and **all nations shall call Him blessed**.

72:18, 19 The Psalm closes with a doxology. The glorious reign of the Lord Jesus is God's achievement. It is He who brings about these wonderful conditions, as no one else could do. And so it is fitting that **His glorious name** be praised forever, and that **His glory** fill the **whole earth**.

72:20 The prayers of David the son of Jesse are ended. This cannot mean that David's prayers are ended as far as the Book of Psalm is concerned, for many more follow. It might mean that his **prayers are ended** as far as Book II of the Psalms is concerned, Psalm 72 being the last in Book II. But a more plausible explanation is that the predicted reign of the Lord Jesus Christ represents the ultimate fulfillment of his **prayers**. The kingdom described in the preceding verses was the subject of his last words (2 Sam. 23:1–4), and was the event toward which his **prayers** *were directed*. When the Messiah would take His place upon the throne and rule, David's desires would be fully met.

III. BOOK 3 (PSALMS 73—89)

Psalm 73: Faith's Dilemma

73:1 This is **Asaph** speaking. And let me make one point clear at the outset. I know for a fact that **God is good to Israel, to such as are pure in heart**. The truth is so obvious that you'd think no one would ever question it.

73:2, 3 But there *was* a time when I actually began to wonder. My stance on the subject became very wobbly, and my faith **almost** took a temporary tumble. You see, I began to think how well off **the wicked** are—lots of money, plenty of pleasure, no troubles—and soon I was wishing I was like them.

73:4–9 Everything seems to be going their way. They don't have as much physical suffering as believers do. Their bodies are healthy and sleek (naturally—they can afford the best of everything). They escape many of the troubles and tragedies of decent people like ourselves. And even if trouble should strike them, they are heavily insured against every conceivable form of loss. No wonder they are so self-confident. They are as proud as a peacock and ruthless as a tiger. Just as their bodies seem to overflow with fatness, so their minds are spilling over with crooked schemes. And are they ever arrogant! They scoff and curse at their underlings and treat them as if they were dirt, threatening them continually. Even God Himself does not escape their malice. Their speech is punctuated with profanity, and they brazenly blaspheme Him. **Their tongue** swaggers and struts **through the earth**, as if to say, "Here I come; get out of my way."

73:10–12 Most of the ordinary **people** think they are great. They bow and scrape and show utmost respect. No matter what the wicked do, the people find no fault with them. And this only confirms the oppressors in their arrogance. They figure that if there is a God, He certainly doesn't **know** what's going on. So they feel safe in pursuing their careers of crookedness. And there they are—cushioned in luxury and getting richer all the time.

73:13, 14 Well, I began to think,

"What good has it done me to live a decent, honest, respectable life?" The hours I've spent in prayer. The time spent in the Word. The distribution of funds to the work of the Lord. The active testimony for the Lord, both public and private. All I've got for it has been a daily dose of suffering and punishment. I wondered if the life of faith was worth the cost.

73:15 Of course, I never shared my doubts and misgivings with other believers. I knew better than to do that. I often thought of the man who said, "Tell me of your certainties; I have doubts enough of my own." So I kept all my doubts to myself, lest I should offend or stumble some simple, trusting soul.

73:16 But still the whole business was a riddle to me: the wicked prosper while the righteous suffer. It seemed so hard to understand. In fact, it wore me out trying to solve the problem.

73:17 Then something wonderful happened. One day **I went into the sanctuary of God**—not the literal temple in Jerusalem but the *heavenly* one. I entered there by faith. As I was complaining to the Lord about the prosperity of the wicked in this life, the question suddenly flashed across my mind, "Yes, but what about the life to come?" The more I thought about their eternal destiny, the more everything came into focus.

73:18–20 So I spoke to the Lord something like this: Lord, now I realize that, despite all appearances, the life of the wicked is a precarious existence. They are walking on the **slippery** edge of a vast precipice. Sooner or later they fall over to their **destruction**. **In a moment** they are cut off—swept away by a wave of **terrors** too horrible to contemplate. They are to me like **a dream when one awakes** in the morning—the things that disturbed the dreamer are seen to be nothing but phantoms.

73:21, 22 I see now that the things that were causing me to be envious were mere shadows. It was stupid of me to become bitter and agitated over the seeming prosperity of the ungodly. In questioning Your justice I was acting more **like a beast** than a man. (Excuse me for behaving as I did.)

73:23, 24 Yet in spite of my ignorant behavior, You have not forsaken me. **I am continually with You**, and **You hold** on to me, like a father holds his child **by** the **hand**. Throughout all my life, **You** guide me **with Your counsel**, and then at last You will **receive me to glory**.

73:25, 26 It is enough that I have *You* **in heaven**; that makes me fabulously wealthy. And now I have no desire for anything **on earth** apart from Yourself. Let the ungodly have their wealth. I am satisfied with **You** and find my all-sufficiency in You. My body may waste away and my **heart** may **fail, but God is the strength of my** life and all I'll ever need or want throughout eternity.

73:27, 28 **Those who** try to keep as **far** away **from You** as possible **shall perish** without You. **And all those who desert You** for false gods will be destroyed. As far as I am concerned, I want to be as **near to** You as possible. I have committed myself to You for protection, and I want to **declare all Your** wonderful **works** to anyone who will listen.

Psalm 74: Remember!

This moving lament looks back to the destruction of the temple by the Babylonians under Nebuchadnezzar.

But it also looks forward to three other similar tragedies in Israel:

The desecration of the sanctuary by Antiochus Epiphanes, 170–168 B.C.
The leveling of the temple by Titus and his Roman legions, A.D. 70.
The still-future desolation of the temple, as prophesied in Matthew 24:15.

When the Babylonian wreckers were finished, it seemed that God had forsaken His people once for all. As they watch smoke arising from the debris, they correctly interpret the catastrophe as a smoking of His anger. But even then they remind the Lord with telling pathos that they are still:

the sheep of His pasture (v. 1).
His congregation (v. 2).
the tribe of His inheritance (v. 2).
His poor turtledove (v. 19).
the oppressed (v. 21).
the afflicted and needy (v. 21).

They also ring the changes on the word "Remember":

Remember Your congregation (v. 2).
Remember Mount Zion (v. 2).
Remember the scoffing of the enemy (v. 18).
Remember how an impious man sneers and reviles God's name (v. 22).

74:1–4 As if He didn't know what had happened, they call **God** to come and see how completely the Chaldean soldiers had razed the sacred building. Then they give an eyewitness account of how it happened. The foreign invaders stormed right into the middle of the holy place. **They set up their** own **banners for signs**, which means that they introduced heathen rites and idolatrous symbols in place of the scriptural worship of Jehovah.

74:5–8 Just as **thick trees** go down in swift succession under the deft blows of the woodsmen, so the costly **carved work** and wood paneling of the temple was shattered by the **axes and** sledge **hammers** of the pagan warriors. As soon as the place was in shambles, they **set** the ruins on **fire** and thus utterly desecrated God's **sanctuary**. Intent on making complete havoc of Israel and its worship, **they burned up all the meeting places of God in the land**.

74:9 The extreme plight of the nation is summed up in three vacuums and four questions. The vacuums are:

No **signs**. The miraculous interventions of God which Israel had experienced in the past were conspicuously absent.

No **prophet**. The prophetic voice was silenced at this time (Ezek. 3:26).

No hope of respite. There was no one **who** knew **how long** the misery would continue.

74:10, 11 The four questions are:

How long will **God** allow **the adversary** to ridicule?

Will God allow His **name** to be reviled indefinitely?

Why is His **hand** restrained from stopping the destruction?

Why does He keep His **right hand** idly hidden in the folds of His robe?

74:12–17 But the psalmist finds hope and comfort in rehearsing God's mighty power in the past on behalf of His people. As Israel's **King** of long standing, He has distinguished Himself by the fantastic deliverances He wrought in various places. For instance, He **divided the** Red **Sea by** His **strength** to make an easy route for the Jews escaping from Egypt. Then when the Egyptian **sea serpents**, that is, Pharaoh's soldiers, tried to follow, He caused the waters to return to normal and drowned the hosts of the enemy. He crushed **the heads of Leviathan**, the monstrous crocodile that symbolized Egyptian power, and the corpses of the soldiers, washed up on the shores of the sea, became food for the vultures and beasts of the desert. He **broke open** springs and brooks in the wilderness, and **dried up** the Jordan so the people could enter the promised land. **Day** and **night** are under His control, and the **sun**, moon, and stars serve by His appointment. It was He who arranged the geography and topography **of the earth**, and the seasons are controlled by Him.

74:18–21 The psalmist reminds God that He too is involved in the disaster. **The enemy has reproached** His **name**; yes, a vile, **foolish people has** heaped contempt on Him.

But His people's plight is desperate. They implore Him not to abandon them, His **turtledove, to the wild** Babylonian **beast**, or to **forget** His afflicted ones **forever**. They beg Him to **respect the covenant** which He made with Abraham now when **the dark places of the** land of Israel harbored violence and **cruelty**. They beg Him to bring back His **oppressed** people in honor, not in shame, and thus give them ample cause to **praise** His **name** afresh for answered prayer.

74:22, 23 Ultimately it is *God's* **cause** that is at stake. He must defend the honor of His name, because the impious are mocking Him **daily**. He must **not forget** the swelling derision of His **enemies** which fills the air **continually** with challenges.

Psalm 75: The Source of Exaltation

The prayer of Psalm 74 is answered in Psalm 75. The Lord *will* arise to plead His own cause (Ps. 74:22) and to quell all insubjection. Ultimately the Psalm looks forward to that moment in history when the Lord Jesus returns to earth to reign in righteousness.

75:1 In anticipation of that event, the Savior leads His people in giving **thanks to God**. All God's **wondrous works declare that** He **is near** to deliver His chosen ones and to punish His foes. All His mighty miracles give proof that He cares (LB).

75:2 The same Speaker says, **"When I choose the proper time, I will judge uprightly."** The time has been set by God the Father (Mark 13:32). When it arrives, He will seize it and fulfill Isaiah's prophecy, "A king will reign in righteousness" (32:1).

75:3 At that crucial time when the foundations of human government will be disintegrating, He will **set up** a kingdom that shall never be moved. Though human society becomes utterly corrupt spiritually, politically, and morally, the **pillars** of His government are solid and secure.

75:4, 5 He says **to the boastful**, "Quit your bragging," **and to the wicked**, "Who do you think you are? Don't be so proud, self-confident, and unbending. Don't exalt yourself with conceit."

75:6, 7 "True **exaltation** doesn't come in that way. It doesn't come **from the east** or **west**, or from the wilderness in **the south**. . . ." The fact that the north is not mentioned may be because the invader usually came from the north, and that meant conquest rather than exaltation. Or it may be because the north is sometimes associated with God's dwelling place (Isa. 14:13; Ps. 48:2). In either case, the thought is clear that "lifting up" does not come from any human or earthly source but from the Lord alone. He is the Supreme Ruler, abasing **one** and exalting **another**.

75:8 As the Abaser, He holds **a cup in** His **hand**. The cup contains **the wine** of judgment. It is foaming, **red**, and **fully mixed**, that is, in restive motion and highly potent. When **He pours it out**, the **wicked** inhabitants of the earth will be compelled to **drink** all of it—**down** to the **dregs**.

75:9, 10 In the last two verses, the Lord Jesus is still the Speaker. He **will sing praises** forever **to the God of Jacob**, the God who has exalted His unworthy people. **The horns of the wicked**, that is, their strength and honor, He will cut off, but the power and glory **of the righteous shall be** increased.

Psalm 76: The Wrath of Man Praising God

In 701 B.C. the Assyrian army under Sennacherib threatened to destroy Jerusalem. But before they could even get near the city, the Angel of the Lord visited their encampment by night and slew 185,000 troops.

This Assyrian disaster is memorialized in Byron's epic poem, "The Destruction of Sennacherib," which is quoted in full at the commentary on Isaiah 37:36. If we see Psalm 76 against this historical backdrop, it will come alive in a new and exciting way. It is well worth reading along with this psalm.

76:1 **God** is famous **in Judah** because of His spectacular overthrow of the army that threatened the city and the sanctuary. **His name** is illustrious **in Israel** for this unforgettable chapter in the history of the nation.

76:2–4 He designated Jerusalem, the city of peace, as His capital, the hill of **Zion** as **His dwelling place**. And that is where He smashed the armaments of the foe—the glistening **arrows, the shield, and sword of battle**, and all the other weapons.

This city set upon a hill is **more** majestic **than the mountains of prey**, that is, than the great Gentile governments that have plundered her. And by metonymy this means that the God of Jerusalem is **more glorious** than any power that might lift its hand against Judah.

76:5, 6 This is seen in what happened to the Assyrian army. **The stouthearted** warriors suddenly dropped their weapons. In a moment they became powerless. One word from the **God of Jacob** and **both** riders and horses sank **into** the **sleep** of death.

76:7–9 What a God He is! And how greatly He should **be feared**! All opposition is futile when once His anger has been ignited. As soon as He pronounces **judgment to** come **from heaven, the earth** trembles and becomes **still**—like the lull before the storm. Then God steps forth to make right the wrongs of earth and **to deliver** its **oppressed** people.

76:10 He has a wonderful way of making **the wrath of man** to **praise** Him. And what won't praise Him, He girds on Him like a sword of a conquered general.

The wrath of men shall praise Thee,
The rest shalt Thou restrain,
And out of earth's disasters
Will bring eternal gain.
The purpose of man's evil heart
Works out Thy sovereign will.
Our God is still upon the throne,
Therefore, believe, be still.

Be still and know that I am God,
This banishes our fears,
While passing through this scene of strife,
Of sorrow and of tears.
The One who rules the heavenly hosts
Holds all within His hand,
And none can say, "What doest Thou?"
Or can His arm withstand.
—*Author unknown*

76:11a In view of the inexpressible greatness and glory of the Lord, the people of Judah are exhorted to **make vows to the LORD** their **God, and** to **pay them**.

76:11b, 12 Then the Gentile nations surrounding Israel are counseled to **bring presents** as tribute to the Supreme Ruler—this Mighty One who can reduce earth's **princes** to size and cause **awesome** things to happen to the most powerful rulers.

Psalm 77: The Cure for Introspection

In the first ten verses, **Asaph** has a king-sized case of introspection. The personal pronouns *I, me,* and *my* are found *over twenty* times, while the names of God are found only *seven* times, and pronouns referring to God *seven* times. But there is a distinct change at verse 10. In the last ten verses the personal pronouns are found only *three* times whereas nouns and pronouns referring to Deity are used *over twenty* times. "The ministry of Christ through the Holy Spirit does away with *I, me,* and *my.*"

Someone has described the flow of thought here in four words:

Sighing (vv. 1–4)
Sinking (vv. 7–10)
Singing (vv. 11–15)
Soaring (vv. 16–20)

77:1–3 First, Asaph pours out his tale of woe **to God**. Some unnamed trouble has come to camp on his doorstep. In his misery, he can think of no one and nothing but himself. In spite of unceasing prayer, he complains that comfort eludes him. He finds himself in the anomalous situation where thoughts of **God** cause him to moan instead of rejoice. The more he meditates, the more melancholy he becomes.

77:4–6 He blames his acute case of insomnia on God alone. Words fail him to express the anguish of his spirit. He seeks comfort in remembering the good old **days** when things went smoothly with him. But the more he is occupied with himself and looks for victory within, the more he begins to doubt the kindness of the Lord. He is assailed by doubts that find expression *in five unbelieving questions*.

77:7–10 *The first* raises the frightening suggestion that perhaps **the Lord** is finished with him for good. The *second* asks if God has **ceased** to love. *Next* he wonders if the Lord has scrapped His promises. *Again,* the impertinent thought crosses his mind that perhaps **God has forgotten to be gracious**. And *finally,* he asks if God's **anger** has cut off the flow of **His** compassion. And he answers himself that this is the case. **The right hand of the Most High** has changed. All his grief can be traced to a change in God's attitude toward him.

77:11–13 But in verse 11 there is a spiritual turning point comparable to the transition from Romans 7 to Romans 8. After introspection had plunged him into the depths of despondency, Asaph turns his eyes heavenward and determines to reflect on God's past interventions for His people when they were in tight spots.

This leads him at once to the acknowledgment that God is holy, that everything He does is perfect, righteous, and good. He makes no mistakes.

77:14, 15 Specifically the psalmist thinks of the marvelous and miraculous display of the **strength** of God that delivered the people of Israel from the bondage of Egypt. By this time he is soaring. The personal pronouns have disappeared entirely from his vocabulary. Self-centeredness has given way to God-centeredness.

77:16–18 With superb literary skill, he pictures **the waters** of the Red Sea as looking up and seeing their Creator, then retreating in terror. All nature exploded in a violent storm. Torrents of rain poured down. Shattering crashes of **thunder** burst overhead. Lightning zigzagged across the sky, lighting up the landscape. A furious whirlwind blitzed the area, and the countryside shook under the fierce assault.

77:19, 20 God Himself made a highway through **the sea**. It was He who opened a **path** so His people could cross dry-shod. Yet no one saw His footprints. As is so often the case, there were abundant evidences of His presence and power, though He Himself was concealed in the shadows.

The Psalm closes on a peaceful note—the Shepherd-God leading Israel through the wilderness to Canaan in the care of **Moses and Aaron**. At the outset, Asaph was a likely prospect for a psychiatric clinic. At the end he is calm and serene. And so the Psalm is an illustration of the well-known saying:

> Occupation with self brings distress;
> Occupation with others brings discouragement;
> Occupation with Christ brings delight.

Psalm 78: A Parable From History

"God's ways in grace and Israel's ways in perverseness"—that is how Bellett sums up the message of this Psalm. It is one of the great songs of Israel's history. Its purpose is to teach us to learn from the past, so that we will not be condemned to relive it.

The Psalmist's Invitation to Learn from History (78:1–4)

The psalmist calls for the attention of his **people** (and of all of us) because he is going to speak **in a parable**, that is, there is going to be a deeper meaning beneath the surface of what he recounts. As he rehearses various chapters from the history of his nation, there will be hidden lessons which he calls **"dark sayings of old."** Just as our parents passed down to us a record of the past, so we are obligated to pass on to the next **generation** an account of the Lord's dealings with His people in grace and government.

God's Gracious Intention in Giving the Law (78:5–8)

Asaph begins his parabolic teaching with the institution of the **law**. God gave it to **Israel** with instructions that it be faithfully transmitted to succeeding **generations**. God's desire in all this was fourfold:

> **That** His people would **set their hope in** Him.
> That they would **not forget** His glorious **works**.
> That they would be obedient.
> That they would learn from the past and not repeat the rebellions of their forefathers.

The People's Disobedience, Rebellion, and Ingratitude (78:9–11)

But what happened? Under the leadership of the tribe of **Ephraim**, the Israelites failed the Lord. **Armed** with **bows**, they **turned back in the day of battle**. This may refer to their dismal cowardice at Kadesh Barnea when they accepted the pessimistic report of the spies. Or it may allude to their failure in utterly driving out the Canaanites from the land. More probably it is a general description of their characteristic behavior. They repeatedly and willfully broke the **law** of God. They habitually **forgot** all the mighty **wonders that He had** performed for their benefit.

The People's Forgetfulness of Their Deliverance from Egypt (78:12–14)

They forgot **Egypt**—and the marvel of their deliverance from the forced slave-labor in the fields of **Zoan** (Tanis). How could they forget the crossing of the Red **Sea**—when the **waters** stood at attention on both sides of them so they could cross on dry land? There was the miracle of **the** glory **cloud** that led them **in the daytime** and the fiery **light** that went before them at **night**.

The People's Forgetfulness of God's Miraculous Supply of Water in the Wilderness (78:15, 16)

They quickly forgot how God provided water **in abundance** by splitting **rocks in the wilderness**—it came gushing out as if there were a huge fountain. **Rivers** of water in the desert—but their memories were short.

The People's Insolent Demand for Bread and Meat (78:17–22)

They began to provoke the Lord about their diet. Dissatisfied and grumbling, they presented new demands to **the Most High**. They insinuated that God had led them out into **the wilderness** to die of starvation. They doubted His ability to provide. Grudgingly admitting that He had provided **water**, they questioned His willingness and ability to provide **bread** and **meat**.

It really infuriated **the Lord** that His people did not trust Him. He was understandably **furious** that **they did not trust** His saving power. He caused the **fire** of His **anger** to blaze forth **against Israel**.

God's Gracious Supply of Manna (78:23–25)

They wanted bread. But there were no supermarkets in the wilderness. Neither were there the ingredients for making bread. So God **opened the doors** of His heavenly granary and **rained down** unfailing supplies of **manna**. The people feasted on something better than bread; it was **angels' food, the bread of heaven**.

God's Gracious Supply of Quail (78:26–31)

They also wanted **meat**. But where could they find meat to feed a multitude in the desert? God solved the problem by harnessing the **east wind** to deliver flocks of quail right into the **camp** of the Israelites. These birds certainly weren't native to the wilderness; they had to be brought from some distance. But they were provided abundantly and freely.

While the people were still gorging themselves, **the wrath of God** blazed out **against them**. He sent a plague that killed off the finest specimens of Israel's manhood.

The People's Continued Sin and God's Unfailing Mercy (78:32–39)

In spite of all the proofs of His love, their hearts were **still** unfaithful. Nothing God did pleased them. Despite His miracles, they were compulsive grumblers. So from time to time Jehovah visited the nation with death and destruction. This seemed to speak to the survivors for a while; they turned to the Lord, repented of their wickedness, and became earnest seekers. They realized what a refuge He had been to them, how He had redeemed them from the terrors of Egypt. But soon again they were living a lie, speaking piously and acting perversely. They were fickle and disobedient.

The Lord showed tremendous restraint. Because of His super-abounding **compassion**, He **forgave** their chronic backsliding and withheld the disaster they deserved. **He remembered that they were** mere men, here today and gone tomorrow.

The People's Rebellions, Provocations, and Ingratitude (78:40, 41)

The psalmist is going to go over the whole sorry history again (vv. 40–58). If *we* as readers grow weary of the repetition, think of how irritating it was to *the Lord!*

Their repeated rebellions **in the desert grieved Him** to the heart. Over and over again they put Him to the test and pained **the Holy One of Israel** by limiting Him.

The People's Forgetfulness of Their Deliverance from Egypt (78:42–53)

78:42 They did not remember how He had proved Himself strong on their behalf, how **He** had rescued **them from the enemy**. Their deliverance from Egypt was the greatest display of divine power in human history up to that time. But they took it for granted.

78:43 In verses 43–53 **Egypt** is in retrospect again, this time with emphasis on six of the plagues in the following order:

First plague—*rivers turned to blood* (v.44).
Fourth plague—*flies* (v. 45a).
Second plague—*frogs* (v. 45b).
Eighth plague—*locusts* (v. 46).
Seventh plague—*hail* (vv. 47, 48).
Tenth plague—*death of the firstborn* (vv. 49–51).

78:44 God **turned their rivers into blood**, so **that** the Egyptians **could not drink** from them. The Nile, which they regarded as sacred, suddenly became polluted. But the water supply of the Israelites remained uncontaminated.

78:45 He sent swarms of flies into all the houses of the Egyptians. They had worshiped Beelzebub, the "lord of flies," and now this god turned on them to devour them. Interestingly enough, the flies did not invade the land of Goshen where the Israelites were living.

He sent a plague of **frogs** into Egypt. Respected as a symbol of fertility, the frogs **destroyed** the people in the sense that they brought normal life to a standstill. But the plague affected only Egyptians; the Hebrews were protected by the hand of God.

78:46 God sent locusts to cover the land of Egypt. The god Serapis was supposed to protect the people from these destructive insects. But Serapis was powerless. The **crops** were ruined; the harvest wiped out. During all this the Israelites saw neither **caterpillar** nor **locust**.

78:47, 48 The seventh plague involved **hail**, **frost** and **fiery lightning**. It wrought tremendous havoc on man, **cattle**, **flocks**, **vines**, and **trees**. But it was a discriminating judgment. ". . . In the land of Goshen, where the children of Israel were, there was no hail" (Ex. 9:26).

78:49 Then there was the culminating stroke of God—the death of the **firstborn**. The psalmist speaks of it as a loosing of God's fierce **wrath, indignation, and trouble**, the work of a company of **angels of destruction**. In some Scriptures the Lord Himself is described as passing through the land of Egypt to destroy the firstborn (Ex. 11:4; 12:12, 23, 29), but in Exodus 12:23, there is a reference to a destroyer whom He used as His active agent. The psalmist suggests that it was a band of destroying **angels**.

78:50–53 He made a path for His anger so that it could blaze forth without restraint. In every Egyptian home the firstborn son was struck down by an otherwise unnamed **plague** or pestilence. The flower of Egypt's manhood died that night. But the homes of the Israelites were protected by the blood of the passover lamb, and not one Hebrew son was killed.

All the plagues were so discriminating that no natural explanation could ever account for them. How could the Jews ever cease to be thankful for the wonderful way God had worked in their behalf?

He led them out of Egypt **like a flock** of **sheep, and guided them** through a trackless **wilderness**. "He led them in safety with nothing to fear, while the sea engulfed their foes" (Gelineau). It was a marvelous exhibition of His love and power!

The People's Forgetfulness of God's Kindness in Bringing Them to the Promised Land (78:54, 55)

He brought them to the **border** of the **holy** land, to the **mountain** range **which His right hand had acquired** for them. Of course, it was inhabited by idolatrous pagans at the time, so **He also drove out the nations** and divided the land among **the tribes of Israel**. No shepherd ever cared as tenderly for his sheep as Jehovah did for His!

The People's Treachery and Idolatry in the Land (78:56–58)

Were they grateful to Him? No! During the time of the Judges **they tested** Him to the limit, they rebelled against Him, they disregarded His commandments. **Like fathers**—like sons, they proved utterly faithless and unreliable, just like a warped **bow** that the archer cannot depend on. **They provoked** the Lord by their idolatrous hilltop shrines, and made Him exceedingly jealous **with their carved images**.

God's Wrath, and His Rejection of Israel (78:59–67)

78:59, 60 In poetic language, the psalmist pictures **God** as hearing of their dark ingratitude and exploding in a storm of wrath. Actually it came as no surprise to Jehovah; it was only the last straw in a long series of rebellions. But this time He lowered the boom on Israel, that is, on the northern tribes who were the ringleaders in the provocations and rebellions. He abandoned **Shiloh** as the site of **the tabernacle**—the spot on earth where He had previously chosen to dwell among His people.

78:61–64 At this time God allowed **His strength**, that is, the ark of the covenant, to be taken **into captivity** by the Philistines. The gold-covered symbol of His glory passed into enemy hands (1 Sam. 4:11a). There was a great slaughter among the people of Israel; 30,000 foot soldiers fell in the battle (1 Sam. 4:10). With so many **young men** devoured by war, there were no **marriage** songs, no wedding bells for **their maidens**. The **priests** who **fell by the sword** were Hophni and Phinehas, the corrupt sons of Eli (1 Sam. 4:11b). **Their widows** did not mourn their passing, probably because of their overriding grief that the ark had been captured by the Philistines. They realized that the glory had departed from Israel (1 Sam. 4:19–22).

78:65, 66 For a while it seemed that Jehovah was indifferent to His people's plight. But then He **awoke** with blazing indignation, shouting like a man who has been aroused with **wine**. And what a rout it was for the Philistines! **He beat** them **back** as they turned to flee—a shameful way for them to suffer defeat (1 Sam. 7:10, 11; 13:3, 4; 14:23).

78:67 Yet God stood firm in His decision to reject **the tent of Joseph**; He would **not choose the tribe of Ephraim**. Here both **Joseph** and **Ephraim** are used to signify the ten northern tribes. After Reuben had forfeited the birthright, Joseph inherited the double portion as far as territory was concerned, through his sons, Ephraim and Manasseh.

God's Choice of Judah, Mt. Zion, and David (78:68–72)

78:68, 69 But Ephraim was the leader in rebellion; therefore God bypassed him as far as rule was concerned and gave that honor to **Judah**. It was in Judah's territory that He chose **Mount Zion** as the place to build **His sanctuary**—towering like the high heavens and immoveable as **the earth**.

78:70, 71 And it was from Judah that **He also chose David His servant**. This shepherd-king served his apprenticeship among the **sheepfolds**, caring for **the ewes that had young** and learning spiritual truths from the natural realm. Then Jehovah **brought him to shepherd Jacob His people, and Israel His inheritance**. And David did this.

78:72 So he shepherded them according to the integrity of his heart, And guided them by the skillfulness of his hands.

And so the Psalm closes on this peaceful, pastoral note. But before leaving it, we must remind ourselves that Israel's history is only a mirror of our own. And if anything, we are more culpable than they because our privileges are so much greater. Living in the full blaze of Calvary's love, why should we ever complain, or rebel, or limit the Lord, or fail to be thankful? Yet we stand condemned. We have provoked the Holy One of Israel times without number. We have grieved Him by a thousand falls. We have murmured and grumbled in spite of countless blessings.

God's patience is not inexhaustible. There comes a time when He allows us to taste the bitterness of our backsliding. If we despise His grace, we will experience His government. If we refuse to serve Him faithfully and loyally, He will find others to do it. We will miss the blessing, and will never find a better master to serve.

Psalm 79: The Groans of the Prisoners

Psalm 79 is a partner to Psalm 74. That one dealt primarily with the destruction of God's real estate—the temple. Although this one refers briefly to the bulldozing of the temple, it is mostly concerned with the ravaging of God's people—the Israelites. The psalmist pleads the cause of the Jews with rare eloquence and asks for respite and revival.

79:1 The pagan aggressors have invaded the land of Israel and have swept, like panzer units, into the capital. The sacred shrine has been defiled by their unsanctified feet, and the beloved city is now reduced to rubble.

79:2–4 The carnage is terrible. The air reeks with the smell of rotting flesh. Jewish **bodies** lie everywhere, suffering the final indignity of being left unburied. The vultures swoop down on them, and the carnivorous **beasts** greedily gobble their prey. **Blood** has flowed **like water all around Jerusalem**, and the invaders haven't bothered to arrange for burial of the slain. Israel's Gentile **neighbors** are gloating over the national calamity.

79:5–7 It is obviously a sign of the Lord's fierce anger and jealous wrath, but how long will His **jealousy burn like fire** against Israel? Isn't it time to turn against the Gentiles for a change? After all, these **nations** do not *want* to **know** Jehovah; they willfully refuse to **call on** His **name**. And now they have crowned their sins with the slaughter of God's people and the devastation of the land.

79:8–10 Everything up to this point has been introductory. The psalmist comes to the crux of the matter now when he recognizes that the nation's sin is the root cause of the disaster. "**Do not remember** the **iniquities** of our forefathers **against us**!" Once that confession has surfaced, he brings out irresistible arguments to move the Almighty to mercy. First he appeals to the compassion of God; the people never needed it more than now. Then he bases his plea on **the glory of** God's own **name**. The Lord has promised forgiveness and deliverance to those who are broken and contrite; now the honor of His name is at stake. And finally, it is important to silence the jeers of the enemy. They are saying that Israel's **God** doesn't exist. This is His grand opportunity to prove His existence by raining down vengeance upon them to requite **the** outpoured **blood of** His loyal **servants**.

79:11, 12 The psalmist then asks God to listen to the doleful **groaning of the prisoner**, and to rescue **those who are** abandoned **to die** in a way that is worthy of His great **power**. And He asks that the enemies will reap **sevenfold** for all the sacrilegious taunts which they hurled at the **Lord**.

79:13 All this will mean peace for Israel and praise to God. His loving flock will never cease to thank Him. Generation after generation will rise to sing His **praise**.

Psalm 80: The Man of God's Right Hand

The sorrow and sighing which permeate so many of the Psalms are continued here also. First under the figure of a flock, then of a vine, Israel pleads for forgiveness and restoration.

80:1–3 The appeal is addressed to the **Shepherd of Israel**, a name of God which appeared in Jacob's blessing of **Joseph**—"the Shepherd, the Stone of Israel" (Gen. 49:24). It was He who led **Joseph like a flock** from Egypt to Canaan. It was He who in the glory cloud was enthroned **between the cherubim** which overshadowed the mercy seat in the most holy place. But now it seems that He has deserted Israel, and the sanctuary has been destroyed, thus the prayer for Him to **shine forth** in mercy and favor before **Ephraim, Benjamin, and Manasseh**. These were the three tribes that were in the vanguard of the procession when the Kohathites carried the ark. Here they represent all of Israel. They desperately desire God to **stir up** His **strength** (perhaps we would say "to flex His muscles") and to move in to their rescue. They appeal that He **restore** them from captivity. If only His **face** would **shine** on them in compassion, their deliverance would be assured.

80:4–7 Terrible distance has come in between Israel and the **LORD God of hosts** (*Jehovah Elohim Sabaoth*). He is **angry** not only with their sins but even with their prayers. For food He has given them a diet of weeping, and for drink a torrent of **tears**. He has **made** them **a** cause of **strife** and contention to their Gentile **neighbors**, and they are the butt of cruel jokes among their **enemies**. There is only one solution—that is for the **God of hosts** (*Elohim Sabaoth*) to look down in grace and salvation upon them.

80:8–11 God **brought** Israel **out of Egypt** like a tender **vine**. In order to plant it in the promised land, He **cast out the** Canaanites. As the owner of a vineyard clears the ground and cultivates it, so the Lord took great pains with His people. The transplant was successful. The vine took **deep root** and the population multiplied and **filled the land**. The vine became luxuriant, higher than **the hills** in glory and stronger than **the mighty cedars**. Its tendrils reached out **to the** Mediterranean **Sea** on one side and to **the River** Euphrates on the other. Under the reign of Solomon Israel occupied land as far east as the Euphrates (1 Kgs. 4:21, 24), but this was very temporary.

80:12, 13 But then God lowered His protective wall and allowed the marauding nations to pick away at the vine. **The boar** and other **wild** animals came in and laid it waste—first Egypt, Assyria, and Babylonia, then in later years Persia, Greece, and Rome. In using the figure of a **boar**, the psalmist wrote beyond his knowledge because centuries later Israel was ravaged by the Roman army with the **boar** proudly displayed as its military ensign.

80:14, 15 Once more the people implore the **God of hosts** to **return** to them in blessing. They want Him to **look down from** the ramparts of **heaven** and take pity on **this vine** which they describe as **"the vineyard which Your right hand has planted, and the branch that You made strong for Yourself."** The Targum, interestingly enough, renders this "and upon the King Messiah, whom You have established for Yourself." In verse 15 it seems more consistent to regard **the vineyard** and **the branch** as referring to Israel. Two verses later the Messiah is unmistakably introduced.

80:16 The vine has been **cut down** and **burned** by the invading armies. **They** deserve to **perish** by a condemning frown from the Lord.

80:17, 18 **"Let Your hand be upon the man of Your right hand, upon the son of man *whom* You made strong for Yourself."** The Man of God's right hand is the Lord Jesus Christ (Ps. 110:1; Heb. 1:3; 8:1; 10:12). **The Son of Man** is the title by which He most frequently spoke of Himself in the Gospels. Full and complete blessing will only come to Israel when He is given His proper place. Then Israel will never backslide again. Revived by the Lord, they **will call upon** the **name** of the Lord.

80:19 The familiar refrain closes the Psalm. The Shepherd is urged to **restore** His wandering sheep. One smile from the **LORD God of hosts** and Israel **shall be saved**.

Psalm 81: The Feast of Trumpets

Unger describes this Jewish holiday as follows:

> [The Feast of Trumpets] was observed as a feast day, in the strict sense, by resting from all work, and as a memorial of blowing of horns, by a holy convocation. In later times, while the drink offering of the sacrifice was being poured out, the priests and Levites chanted Psalm 81, while at the evening sacrifice they sang Psalm 29. Throughout the day trumpets were blown at Jerusalem from morning to evening. . . . The rabbins [rabbis] believed that on this day God judges all men, and that they pass before him as a flock of sheep pass before a shepherd.[52]

The Feast of Trumpets is a type of the regathering of Israel to its homeland after the out-gathering of the Church.

81:1–5a In the opening verses, the people of Israel are called to join in singing the praises of **God** who is the source of their **strength**, and to **make a joyful shout to the God of Jacob**, that is, the God of all grace. The Levites are invited to join the happy chorus with their musical instruments, and the priests mark the arrival of the seventh **New Moon** by blowing the shophar. It is a holiday instituted by God for the nation of Israel (Lev. 23:23–25; Num. 29:1). **He established** it **in Joseph** (here **Joseph** stands for all Israel) **when He went throughout the land of Egypt**. Here the meaning seems to be that God ordained this feast after the confrontation with **Egypt** and after His people came out of that **land**.

81:5b At the end of verse 5, we read, **"I heard a language I did not understand,"** and we must consider whether the speaker is the psalmist, Israel, or God.

If it is the psalmist or Israel speaking, the language may refer to:

1. The foreign **language** of the Egyptians (Ps. 114:1).
2. God speaking to Israel in the redemption from Egypt, a new revelation of God to their souls.
3. The oracle of God which is found in the remaining verses of the Psalm.

If God is the Speaker, then the thought may be:

> **I heard a language** (of the Egyptians) that **I did not** know (in the sense of "acknowledge"). As Williams puts it, "He did not acknowledge the Egyptians as His sheep."

In favor of the latter is the fact that the pronoun "I" in the rest of the Psalm always refers to God.

81:6, 7 God had relieved the shoulders of the people **from the burden** of servile work under the Egyptians. Their **hands were freed from** having to carry **baskets** filled with clay and bricks. From all their **trouble** He **delivered** them when they **called**. He **answered** them **in the secret place of thunder**—a reference to the cloud which guided and protected them, or to the giving of the law at Mt. Sinai. He **tested** them **at the waters of Meribah** where Moses struck the rock and incurred God's displeasure.

81:8–10 He had warned them that the pathway of blessing lay in faithfulness to Him as the one true God. His prohibition of idolatry was unmistakable. After reminding them how He had **brought** them **out of the land of Egypt**, He made the marvelous promise that if they would **open** their **mouth wide**, He would **fill it**. This promise has sometimes been wrongly used by lazy preachers to justify any lack of preparation; all they have to do is open their mouth and the Lord will give them a message. But that is not the meaning at all! The thought is that if they came to God with great petitions, He would grant them. There is nothing good that He would not do for an obedient people. Gaebelein puts it well:

> Who is able to grasp the full meaning of the sentence! He is the omnipotent Lord; there is nothing too hard for the Lord. Open thy mouth, He says, as wide as you can, and I will fill it. Ask anything in My Name, He says in the New Testament, and I will do it. All He asks is obedience to Him, the yielding of the heart and will.[53]

81:11–16 **But** God's **people** turned a deaf ear to His **voice, and Israel would** not obey Him. So He let them have their own way, and **gave them over to** the misery of following **their own** advice. But this abandonment was not without a pang in the heart of God. He mourns their continued folly and stubbornness. If only they **would listen** to Him, He **would soon subdue their enemies. Their adversaries** would come cringing in fear before Him, and Israel's prosperity would know no interruption (AV). **He would** feed His people **with the finest of wheat**—that is, the best spiritual and physical nourishment, **and with** the delicious **honey** that comes **from** beehives in the rocks of Palestine.

Psalm 82: Earth's Rulers on Trial

82:1 The court is called to order. The Judge has taken His place at the bench. It is **God** Himself. He has called a special session of the divine council in order to reprove the rulers and judges of the earth. They are called **gods** because they are representatives of God, ordained by Him as His servants in order to maintain an ordered society. Actually, of course, they are only men like ourselves. But because of their position, they are the anointed of the Lord. Even if they do not know God personally, yet they are God's agents officially and therefore dignified here with the name of **gods**. The basic meaning of the name is *mighty ones.*

82:2 First God rebukes them for malfeasance in office. They have been guilty of graft and corruption. Under their administration, the rich have been favored while the poor have been oppressed. Criminals have escaped unpunished, and the innocent have had to suffer loss without recourse. The scales of justice have become scales of oppression.

82:3, 4 Then the Judge of all the earth reminds them once more of their responsibilities in the area of social justice. They are to champion the rights of **the poor and fatherless, . . . the afflicted and needy**. They should be the helpers of all who are dispossessed and downtrodden.

82:5 But despite all the Lord's warnings, there seems to be no hope of improvement. As if in an aside, He sighs that they fail to act with knowledge and understanding. Since they themselves are groping **about in darkness**, there is scant hope of their helping others who need direction. And as a result of their failure to act righteously and wisely, **the foundations of** society **are unstable**. Law and order have all but vanished.

82:6, 7 Though exalted to heaven in privilege, they shall be cast down in punishment. The fact that God calls them **gods** and **children of the Most High** does not grant them immunity from judgment. They will be subject to the same treatment as other **men, and fall like one of the princes**. Actually the *degree* of their punishment will be greater because of their greater privilege.

Our Lord quoted verse six in one of His confrontations with His foes (John 10:32–36). They had just accused Him of blaspheming because He claimed equality with God.

> Jesus answered them, "Is it not written in your law, 'I said, "You are gods"'? If He called them gods, to whom the word of God came (and the Scripture cannot be broken), do you say of Him whom the Father sanctified and sent into the world, 'You are blaspheming,' because I said, 'I am the Son of God'?"

To the western mind, the argument might not seem clear or convincing, but it obviously had compelling power on His hearers. They understood that Jesus was arguing from the lesser to the greater. The force of the argument is as follows:

In Psalm 82, rulers and judges are addressed by God as gods. Actually they are not divine, but because of their position as God's ministers, they are dignified with the name of gods. Their greatest distinction is that the word of God came to them, that is, they were officially ordained by God as higher powers concerned with government and justice (Rom. 13:1).

If the name *gods* could thus be loosely applied to men like them, how much more fully and accurately can the name God be applied to the Lord Jesus. He had been sanctified and sent into the world by God the Father. This implies that He had lived with God the Father in heaven from all eternity. Then the Father had set Him apart to a mission on earth and had sent Him to be born in Bethlehem.

The Jews understood perfectly that He was claiming equality with God, and they sought to apprehend Him but He eluded them (John 10:39).

82:8 But now back to the last verse of the Psalm:

> **Arise, O God, judge the earth;**
> **For You shall inherit all nations.**

It is Asaph calling on the Lord to intervene in the affairs of men, bringing righteousness and justice to replace corruption and inequity. The prayer will be answered when the Lord Jesus returns to reign over the earth. At that time, as the prophets predicted, "justice will dwell in the wilderness, and righteousness remain in the fruitful field" (Isa. 32:16). The earth will enjoy a time of social justice and freedom from graft and deceit.

Psalm 83: Psalm of the Six-Day War

On May 28, 1967, Gamal Abdel Nasser, President of the United Arab Republic, said, "We plan to open a general assault on Israel. This will be total war. Our basic aim is the destruction of Israel." When war broke out on June 5, the United Arab Republic was joined by Jordan, Syria, Iraq, Algeria, Sudan, Kuwait, Saudi Arabia, and Morocco. The attempt of this confederacy to drive Israel into the sea was unsuccessful. In six days the war was over. Israel was the undisputed victor.

For many Bible lovers, Psalm 83 took on new meaning after the Six-Day War. And perhaps it will have further fulfillments before Israel's claim to the land is irrevocably settled by the coming of the Lord Jesus to reign as King.

83:1–5 The language is obviously that of besieged Israel, calling on **God** to break His silence and to act decisively. Although the people are pleading for their own safety and preservation, they present their case as if it were God's cause as much as their own: **"Your enemies . . . those who hate You . . . Your people . . . Your sheltered ones . . . They form a confederacy against You."** They will not let Him forget that Israel's enemies are His enemies.

The details are true to life. The enemies are in tumult—a vivid description of the blustering threats of the opposition. They lay crafty plans—assisted behind the scenes by advisors from Soviet Russia. They consult together—in what have now become known as Arab summit meetings. They threaten the annihilation of Israel—as witnessed by the quotation above. They form a formidable federation of nations—mostly of people who are near relatives of the Israelites.

83:6–8 When we try to identify these nations with modern counterparts, we run into difficulty. We do know that **Assyria** is the same as modern-day Iraq, and that **the Ishmaelites**, descended from Abraham and Hagar, were the progenitors of the Arabs. We know that the Edomites and the Amalekites were descended from Esau, and the Moabites and Ammonites from **Lot**, but to trace them today is well-nigh impossible. The Philistines inhabited the area now known as the Gaza strip. The city of **Tyre** was located in what is now Lebanon. **Gebal** is the same as ancient Gubla or Byblos, located in Phoenicia. Some sources list the **Hagrites** as descendants of Hagar, and therefore a segment of the Ishmaelites, but the identification is not positive. Since so much obscurity surrounds these names, it is best not to try to link them with modern countries in the Middle East, but simply to see them as representing Gentile foes of Israel.

How could little Israel stand against such an overwhelming confederacy? Part of the answer is found in the fact that God's people are His "sheltered ones" (v. 3), His "hidden ones" (AV), His "precious ones" (LB), or "those He loves" (Gelineau). In the hour of danger, He miraculously shields them, and makes His strength perfect in their weakness. When the odds are all against them, He sends a victory that defies all human explanations.

83:9, 10 Now the beleaguered people call on Jehovah to **deal with** the current threat as He did with His enemies on three different occasions in the past.

Jabin, king of Canaan, and **Sisera**, his commander in chief, were killed ingloriously at **En Dor** after a disastrous defeat at the **Brook Kishon** (Judg. 4). Their decaying carcasses became fertilizer for Israel's soil.

83:11, 12 **Oreb** and **Zeeb**, two princes of Midian were killed and decapitated (Judges 7:23–25). According to Isaiah (10:26), it was an epic slaughter.

Two kings of Midian, **Zebah and Zalmunna**, had threatened to occupy **"the pastures of God."** They managed to escape from the Israelites when Oreb and Zeeb were slain, but they were subsequently overtaken and executed by Gideon (Judg. 8).

83:13–18 In its bold plea for God's judgment on His foes, Israel leaves nothing to the divine imagination. The details of the punishment are specified. Let **them** be **like the whirling dust**, or as some translate it, like a tumbleweed. Let them be **like the chaff** driven **before the wind**. Let them be pursued **as** if by a **fire** sweeping through **the woods**, and consumed as if by a raging holocaust. Let them be terrified by the Lord's **storm**. Let them be thoroughly put to **shame** so that men might **seek** the **LORD**. Let them **perish** in disgrace so that men might learn that Jehovah **alone** is the Sovereign Ruler **over all the earth**.

Strong language? Yes, strong but not unjustified. When the honor of God is at stake, love can be firm. Morgan explains:

> These singers of the ancient people were all inspired supremely with a passion for the honor of God. With them, as with the prophets, selfish motives were unknown. Selfishness sings no song, and sees no visions. On the other hand, a passion for the glory of God is capable of great sternness as well as great tenderness.[54]

Psalm 84: Homesick for Heaven!

There is no question as to the primary *interpretation* of Psalm 84. It breathes out the deep longings of exiled Jews to be back at the temple in Jerusalem once again.

It can also be *applied*, of course, to the Christian today who is somehow prevented from attending the meetings of the local fellowship. He eats his heart out to be back with God's people as they meet to worship the Lord.

But the application I like best is that of a godly pilgrim who is downright homesick for heaven. Let us look at the Psalm from this viewpoint.

84:1, 2 What place can be compared in loveliness to the dwelling place of God! It is a place of unparalleled beauty, unique splendor and unutterable glory. But let us be clear on this point. The *place* is used, by a figure of speech known as metonymy, for the *Person* who lives there. And so when the psalmist says, **"My soul longs, yes, even faints for the courts of the Lord,"** he was really yearning to be with the Lord Himself. He says as much in the next sentence, **". . . my heart and my flesh cry out for the living God."**

84:3 The pilgrim compares himself to a **sparrow** and a **swallow**. In another Psalm, the sparrow is used as a picture of utter loneliness, ". . . a sparrow alone on the housetop" (102:7). And anyone who has ever watched a **swallow** knows what a restless creature it is, darting and soaring on the air currents. Both are apt descriptions of God's people sojourning in this wilderness; they are lonely and restless. The only place where they find rest and security for themselves and their families is at the **altars** of the **Lord**.

There were two **altars** in the tabernacle and the temple. One was the brazen altar and the other the golden altar. The first typified Christ's death and the second His resurrection. Taken together they represent the finished work of our Savior. Here is the place where our souls, like the swallow, can rest, and here we can bring our children to find rest also. "Believe on the Lord Jesus Christ, and you will be saved, *you and your household*" (Acts 16:31).

84:4 Then in an outburst of what we might call sanctified jealousy, the exile says, **"Blessed *are* those who dwell in Your house; they will still be praising You."** When we thus think of the happiness of loved ones who have gone home to be with the Lord, we cannot grieve over them. For us it is loss, but for them eternal gain. They are better off than we are.

84:5 In verses 5–7 we switch back from the blessedness of those who are already in heaven to the lesser blessedness of those who are en route. Several things are mentioned about them. First of all, their **strength is in** the Lord, not in themselves. They are "strong in the Lord and in the power of His might" (Eph. 6:10). Then in their heart are the highways to Zion. The world is not their home. Though *in* it, they are not *of* it. Their **heart *is* set on pilgrimage.**

84:6, 7 The third thing is that **as they pass through the Valley of** weeping, for that is what **Baca** means, **they** convert it into **a spring**. These indomitable souls can sing in the midst of sorrow and trace the rainbow through their tears. They transform tragedies into triumphs and use misfortunes as stepping stones to greater things. The secret of their victory over circumstances is found in the next statement, **"the rain also covers it with pools."** The **rain** is commonly taken as a type of the Holy Spirit, and here He is seen in His ministry of refreshment, providing **pools** of cool, clear water for the desert travelers. We take the water to stand for the Word of God (as in Eph. 5:26). This explains how **they go from strength to strength**. Instead of getting weaker as the journey progresses, they get stronger all the time. Though the outer nature is wasting away, the inner nature is being renewed every day (2 Cor. 4:16). And then a wonderful note of assurance: **Each one appears before God in Zion**. No question about it, the trek through the desert will be crowned at last with the joy of seeing the King in His beauty.

84:8 Now the psalmist breaks out into impassioned prayer. It is addressed first to the **LORD God of hosts**, then in the next breath to the **God of Jacob**. As **LORD God of hosts**, He is the sovereign over the vast multitude of angelic beings. As the **God of Jacob**, He is the God of the unworthy one, the God of the cheat. Just think! The God of innumerable angels in festal gathering is also the God of the worm Jacob. The One who is infinitely high is also intimately nigh. And that is the only reason why you and I will ever enter His presence.

84:9 And what is our title to be there? **O God, behold our shield, and look upon the face of Your anointed.** Our only acceptance is through the Person and work of the Lord Jesus.

> God sees my Savior and then He
> sees me
> In the Beloved, accepted and free.

84:10 And what is it like, being in heaven? Well, **a day in** His **courts** is **better than a thousand** elsewhere. Which is just another way of saying that there is no comparison. We simply cannot conceive the glory, the joy, the beauty, the freedom of being where Jesus is. And it's a good thing we can't. Otherwise we would probably be unhappy to remain here and to get on with our work.

Better to **be a doorkeeper in the house of** your **God than** to **dwell in the tents of wickedness.** As Spurgeon said, "God's worst is better than the devil's best." And not only better but more enduring. Note the contrast between **the house of our God** and **the tents of wickedness**. One is a permanent dwelling, the other is pitched for a relatively short while.

84:11 The LORD God is a sun providing illumination through the darkness, and **a shield** for protection against the scorching heat along the way. **The LORD will give grace** along the way for every time of need, and then He **will give glory** at the end of the journey as He welcomes His redeemed children into His eternal home. As a matter of fact the pilgrim has the assurance that he will lack nothing between here and heaven for **no good thing will He withhold from those who walk uprightly.** If it's **good**

for us, He won't **withhold** it; if He withholds it, it isn't good. "He who did not spare His own Son, but delivered Him up for us all, how shall He not with Him also freely give us all things?" (Rom. 8:32).

84:12 No wonder the psalmist ends with the heartfelt exclamation, **"O LORD of hosts, blessed is the man who trusts in You!"** To which my own heart responds, "Yes, Lord, I'm eternally grateful to be a Christian."

Psalm 85: Revive Us Again!

This prayer for revival is divided into four easily discernible sections:

A past instance of revival in Israel (vv. 1–3).
A plea for God to do it again (vv. 4–7).
A pause to hear how the Lord will answer (vv. 8, 9).
A promise of future restoration (vv. 10–13).

It is impossible to pinpoint the particular restoration of Israel that is described here. It could not be the restoration after the Babylonian captivity since this is **a Psalm of the sons of Korah**, and they lived long before that time. But the identification of the event is not important. What really matters is that God had done it. And if He did it once, He can certainly do it again.

85:1–3 The revival is described as a time when the **LORD** was **favorable to** the **land** and when He restored the fortunes **of Jacob**. Three actions led up to it. The first was confession of **sin**. Though this is not explicitly stated, confession is an invariable moral necessity before the others can take place. The second was forgiveness of **the iniquity of** His **people** and the third an averting of God's **wrath**.

85:4 This former demonstration of God's pardoning mercy is the basis for a plea that He repeat it. Faith is not satisfied with history; it wants to see God in current events. Although the psalmist does not engage in confession, it is implicit in the prayer, **"Restore us. . . ."** When **God** restores, He first brings His people to repentance, then He forgives their sins, and then He terminates the punishment that resulted from His indignation.

85:5 Any time spent away from the Lord seems like an eternity of misery. But the poignant plea of verse 5 takes on special meaning in the lips of the nation of Israel with its centuries of persecution and dispersion: **"Will You be angry with us forever? Will You prolong Your anger to all generations?"**

85:6 Spiritual declension results inevitably in a loss of joy. Broken fellowship means that the believer's song is gone. Rejoicing cannot coexist with unconfessed sin. So here the prayer goes winging up to heaven. **"Will You not revive us again, that Your people may rejoice in You?"** The Spirit's renewal sets the joy-bells ringing once again. Every great revival has been accompanied by song.

85:7 When God restores His people it is a gracious demonstration of His **mercy**. But no more than any of His other dealings with us. It is love that chastens us, that disciplines us, that corrects us, and that brings us back at last. And how steadfast is that love that bears with us in all our wanderings, our backslidings, and our disobedience. There is no love like the love of the Lord.

And revival is a granting of **salvation** from the Lord—here not salvation of the soul but deliverance from all the consequences of unfaithfulness—dispersion, captivity, affliction, powerlessness, and unhappiness.

85:8, 9 Having brought His plea for restoration to the throne of grace, the psalmist waits for the answer, confident that it will be an answer of **peace**, and that it will come quickly. His confidence is based on the fact that the covenant-keeping God always speaks **peace** to those who turn to Him in their hearts, and delivers those who fear Him, not turning **back to folly**. And the inevitable result is **that glory** will **dwell in** the **land. Glory** here is used to signify the *God* of **glory**, and the thought is that the Lord can be depended on to **dwell** in the midst of His people when they are in fellowship with Him.

85:10 The answer to the prayer for revival is given in the closing verses. They describe the idyllic conditions which will prevail when the Lord Jesus reigns over restored Israel in the coming age of glory. But in a broader poetic sense they tell what it is always like when revival fires are burning.

Mercy and truth have met together. In human affairs strict adherence to the claims of **truth** usually prevent the display of love and **mercy**. But God can shower His steadfast love on His people because all the claims of **truth** were fully met by the Lord Jesus on the cross. In the same sense, **righteousness and peace have kissed.** Believers enjoy peace with God because all the claims of divine justice were met by the substitutionary work of the Savior.

> Our sins were placed on Jesus' head.
> 'Twas in His blood our debt was
> paid.
> Stern justice can demand no more,
> And mercy can dispense her store.
> —*Albert Midlane*

85:11–13 Truth, or faithfulness, **shall spring out of the earth, and righteousness shall look down from** the sky. As the believer is true to His Eternal Lover, the heavens respond righteously with multiplied blessing. **The Lord**, ever faithful to His Word, gives **what is good**. He withholds no good thing from those who walk uprightly (Ps. 84:11). Drought and famine conditions cease and **the land** produces a bumper crop. As the Lord visits His land, His route takes Him among a people whose righteous lives are morally prepared for His presence.

Psalm 86: Prayer with Reasons Attached

One of the noteworthy things about this Psalm is that David gives a reason for almost everything he says, whether in petition or adoration. We may illustrate this by the following arrangement:

PETITION	*REASON*
86:1 For audience with the **Lord**.	The psalmist's helplessness and need.
86:2a For preservation. (Note the recurrence of the title "servant" in vv. 4 and 16.)	His position as a **holy** person.
86:2b For temporal salvation.	No explicit reason is given but it may be implied in the clause **"You are my God."**
86:3 For gracious consideration.	David's persistence in prayer **all day long**.
86:4 For joy and gladness.	His hope is in the **Lord** and in no one else.

86:5

This verse may give an additional reason for the preceding requests. Or it may be mated to the prayer in verse 6.

The goodness, readiness **to forgive**, and **mercy** of the Lord are poured out on **all those who call upon** Him.

86:6 For audience with the Lord.

86:7 For help **in the day of** his **trouble**.

The fact that God does hear and **will answer** prayer.

The psalmist turns to praise in the next verses.

PRAISE	*REASON*
86:8 For the matchlessness of the Lord's Person and **works**.	
86:9 For His worthiness to be adored by **all nations**. (This will be fulfilled in the Millennium.)	
86:10	God is **great**. His works are **wondrous**. There is no other **God**.

PETITION	*REASON*
86:11 For instruction in the **way** of the LORD.	In order that the psalmist might **walk** in obedience to God's **truth**. For a **heart** that is completely dedicated to revere and obey the Lord.

PRAISE	*REASON*
86:12, 13 Here David simply expresses his determination to **praise** the Lord **with all** his being, and to **glorify** His **name forevermore**.	For God's **great mercy** in delivering him **from the depths of Sheol**. If we apply the Psalm to the Messiah, then this is a reference to His resurrection.

86:14–16 The remaining verses describe the imminent peril of the psalmist. **A mob** of arrogant, **violent** men have conspired to take his **life**. These men have no time for God. **But** David knows the **Lord** and in this crucial moment he comforts himself in the knowledge that **God** is **full of compassion, gracious, longsuffering and abundant in mercy and truth**. Therefore he is confident in asking the Lord to **turn to** him in pity, to strengthen him and to **save** him—**the son of** God's **maidservant**. Some understand the expression **"the son of Your maidservant"** to be a figure of speech meaning "your property" as was the case with the son of a female slave. Those who take the Psalm as Messianic see it as a possible reference to the Virgin Mary.

86:17 Finally, the psalmist asks that that the Lord will give him some definite **sign** of His favor. Then his enemies will realize that they have been on the wrong side when they see how God has **helped** David **and comforted** him.

We mentioned at the outset that the Psalm was notable in that it gave reasons for most of its prayers or praises. There are two other unique features that should be mentioned. First, David has quoted prolifically from other Scriptures; he is actually praying or praising with almost a scissors-and-paste collection of Bible verses. Second, the divine name "Adonai" is used seven times (it is translated "Lord" in vv. 3, 4, 5, 8, 9, 12 and 15). God-fearing Jews often used this title rather than Jehovah.

The Sopherim, or ancient custodians of the Sacred Text, changed the name Jehovah to Adonai 134 times when reading aloud, out of what they considered extreme reverence for the ineffable Name "Jehovah."[55]

Regarding *uniting* our hearts to fear God's name (v. 11b) F. W. Grant writes:

> This is indeed what is everywhere the great lack among the people of God. How much of our lives is not spent in positive evil, but frittered away and lost in countless petty diversions which spoil effectually the positiveness of their testimony for God! How few can say with the apostle, "This *one* thing I do!" We are on the road . . . but we stop to chase butterflies among the flowers, and make no serious progress. How Satan must wonder when he sees us turn away from the "kingdoms of the world and the glory of them" . . . and yet yield ourselves with scarce a thought to endless trifles, lighter than the thistle-down which the child spends all his strength for, and we laugh at him. Would we examine our lives carefully . . . , how should we realize the multitude of needless anxieties, of self-imagined duties, of permitted relaxations, of "innocent" trifles, which incessantly divert us from that alone in which there is profit! How few, perhaps, would care to face such an examination of the day by day unwritten history of their lives![56]

Psalm 87: Psalm of the Royal Census

The mayor of Jerusalem, Teddy Kollek, and his co-author express natural wonder at the surprising greatness of their 4,000 year old city:

> Archaeologists and historians have long wondered why Jerusalem should have been established where it was, and why it should have become great. It enjoys none of the physical features which favored the advancement and prosperity of other important cities in the world. It stands at the head of no great river. It overlooks no great harbour. It commands no great highway and no cross-roads. It is not close to abundant sources of water, often the major reason for the establishment of a settlement, though one main natural spring offered a modest supply. It possesses no mineral riches. It was off the main trade routes. It held no strategic key to the conquest of vast areas prized by the ancient warring empires. Indeed it was blessed with neither special economic nor topographic virtues which might explain why it should have ever become more than a small, anonymous mountain village with a fate any different from that of most contemporary villages which have long since vanished.[57]

87:1–3 The reason for its greatness, of course, is that it was chosen by God. He founded it **in the holy mountains**, and He **loves** its **gates** more than all the other cities or towns in the land. And its greatest glory is still future—when it will be the capital of the Messianic Kingdom, the royal city of the long-awaited King. This Psalm looks forward to that day when **glorious things** will be **spoken** of **Zion**, the **city of God**.

There is a sense in which it will be the spiritual birthplace of many nations:

> Now it shall come to pass in the latter days *that* the mountain of the Lord's house shall be established on the top of the mountains, and shall be exalted above the hills; and all nations shall flow to it. Many people shall come and say, "Come, and let us go up to the mountain of the Lord, to the house of the God of Jacob; He will teach us His ways, and we shall walk in His paths (Isa. 2:2, 3).

87:4 That is what seems to be in

view in verse 4. Zion is personified as saying that among those nations that know her as mother, she can mention **Rahab** (that is, Egypt) to the south and **Babylon** to the north. Also people will speak of **Philistia, Tyre,** and **Ethiopia** as having been **born** in Jerusalem. These will be among the nations that recognize Zion as the spiritual, political, and economic capital of the world, and will go up to worship there and bring their tribute to the Great King (Isa. 60:5–7). The nations that refuse to go up to keep the Feast of Booths will suffer drought and plague (Zech. 14:16–19).

87:5 **Zion** therefore will be reckoned as the place where the nations experience spiritual rebirth, because the **Most High Himself shall establish her** in that place of universal sovereignty.

87:6 And when **the LORD** takes a census of **the peoples**, He will note carefully that certain nations realized their true destiny in becoming citizens of Zion. They visit the capital:

> not to admire its architecture, or gaze upon its battlements, or envy the tribes who had come up to worship in the city which is compact together, but to claim its municipal immunities, experience its protection, obey its laws, live and love in its happy society, and hold communion with its glorious Founder and Guardian.[58]

Gaebelein writes:

> Jehovah keeps a record as one after another of the nations are brought into the Kingdom through Zion's exaltation and blessing. Then Zion becomes the glorious metropolis of the whole world.[59]

87:7 It will be a time of festival and holiday. **Singers** and **players on instruments** will join in the chorus, **"All my springs are in you."** No longer the place of tears and trouble, Jerusalem will be a fountain of blessing, a source of refreshment, and a spiritual home to all the nations of the earth.

But before leaving the Psalm, there is a personal application that should be made. It is this. A time is coming when God is going to register the people. It will be the census of heaven's inhabitants. The great, single qualifying factor will be the new birth. Only those who have been born again will see or enter the kingdom of God (John 3:3–5). So when God writes up the people, He will say, "This man was born again in such and such a place."

Will He be able to say that concerning you?

There is a way in which you can qualify for heavenly citizenship. That way is set forth in John 1:12:

> But as many as received Him, to them He gave the right to become children of God, to those who believe in His name.

Psalm 88: The Saddest Psalm

When we come to Psalm 88 we have reached the nadir of human sorrow and suffering. It seems that the psalmist here ransacks the vocabulary of gloom and bitterness to describe his hopeless plight. His is definitely a terminal case, he feels—as if he were on the critical list in the isolation ward of a hospital for incurables. The only thing left is the morgue, and it is only a matter of time before the sheet will be drawn over his face and he will be carted away.

88:1, 2 The only bright spot in the Psalm is the name of **God** with which it begins—**"O LORD, God of my salvation."** Gaebelein calls it the one ray of light that struggles through the gloom, the star that pierces the thick midnight darkness.

But immediately the writer launches into a mournful description of his desperate predicament. **Day and night** he has been crying to the Lord, but still no relief. When will God break the impasse by hearing his **prayer** and doing something about it?

88:3–7 His life is one seething mass **of troubles**, and he is moving irresistibly toward death and **the grave**. He has been given up for dead—already **counted** as a casualty. Any strength he had has ebbed away. Now he is **adrift among the dead**, like an unconscious soldier on a corpse-strewn battlefield, or like a war victim buried with others in a common **grave**. He feels that he is forgotten by God and thus **cut off from** any hope of divine help. Like a captive consigned to a dungeon, so he has been abandoned by God to **the lowest pit**, to the chamber of horrors, dark and ominous. There can be only one explanation, he feels: God is angry with him and he is being submerged by the mountainous **waves** of divine judgment.

88:8, 9 His **acquaintances** have forsaken him as if he were a leper. They treat him as if he were some hideous apparition or "as a thing accursed" (Knox). He is **shut up** in a cell from which there is no escape. His eyes, once bright and full of expression, have lost all their sparkle. And prayer seems unavailing. **Daily** he cries to the Lord with his **hands** raised in earnest entreaty, but nothing happens.

88:10 Then in a series of questions he challenges God to tell what good would come to Him from the psalmist's death. The questions reveal the imperfect knowledge which OT saints had concerning death and the hereafter, and make us unceasingly grateful for the assurance that to die is to be with Christ which is far better (Phil. 1:23). Here then are the questions:

Does God **work wonders for** those who have died? The implied answer is "No." To a Jew living under law, death was a perplexing region of oblivion where nothing constructive ever happens.

Do the "shades" **arise** to **praise** Him? Those who have departed are regarded as ghost-like shadows that have no way of praising the Lord.

88:11, 12 Is God's steadfast love **declared in the grave** or His **faithfulness in** Abaddon, **the place of destruction**?

> Since it was believed that no action or speech was possible in the grey, grim, dusty halls of Sheol, it was surely in God's own interests to keep alive as long as possible those whose earnest praises were always pleasing to Himself.[60]

88:13–18 As if with renewed intensity, the psalmist pleads with the Lord. As surely as he lives, every **morning** hears his passionate **prayer**. He expresses utter perplexity that God should so completely abandon him and hold back any look of pity or of favor. **From** his **youth** his life had been an uninterrupted story of suffering and dying. Now in the vortex of the divine **terrors**, he is **distraught** and helpless. God's **fierce wrath has** overwhelmed him like a tidal wave, and His **terrors** have left him speechless. The furious flood is encircling and unremitting; the waves close in on him in one united assault. It is as if God has caused **loved one and friend** to forsake him. His only companion is **darkness**.

And so ends the saddest Psalm. If we wonder why it is in the Bible, we might listen to the testimony of J. N. Darby. He said that at one time this was the only Scripture that was any help to him because he saw that someone had been as low as that before him. Clarke quotes an unknown source:

> "There is only one Psalm like this in the Bible to intimate the rareness of the experience, but there is one to assure the most desperately afflicted that God will not forsake him."[61]

Psalm 89: God's Covenant with David

89:1, 2 At the outset, **Ethan** declares his personal delight in the steadfast love and **faithfulness** of Jehovah as expressed in the Davidic covenant. He is determined to **sing of the mercies of the LORD forever** because they endure **forever**.

89:3, 4 Faith reverently reminds God of the **covenant** He had made with **David**. Because David was His chosen **servant**, He had **sworn** that he would never lack heirs to sit on his **throne** and that his kingdom would endure **to all generations**. An unbroken dynasty sitting on an everlasting **throne**!

89:5 Then faith rehearses the **wonders** of the **LORD** who had made the covenant. It is almost as if Ethan is reminding the Lord that the honor of His name is at stake.

89:6–8 He is greater than all the angelic hosts **in the heavens**. The myriads above are called to praise His wonders and His **faithfulness**. No angel **can be compared** to Him; He is supreme above all the heavenly beings. The greatest of them stand in reverential awe of Him; they recognize that He is greater in every way. No one is as mighty as the **LORD God of hosts**, resplendent in robes of **faithfulness**.

89:9, 10 But that is not all. God is great in creation, in providence and in moral perfections (vv. 9–15). One dramatic instance of His greatness in creation is the way in which He rules **the raging of the sea** and makes its **waves** cease. He did this on blue Galilee many years ago, and He does it continually in the storm-tossed lives of His people. As to His greatness in providence, what better example could be adduced than His conquest of Egypt (**Rahab**) at the time of the exodus? He crushed that proud nation like a lion crushes the carcass of its victim; He **scattered** His **enemies** like leaves in the wind.

89:11–13 **The heavens** and **the earth** are His by creatorial right; **the world** and everything in it belongs to Him because it was He who **founded them. The north and the south** owe their origin to Him. Mount **Tabor and** Mount **Hermon** lift up their heads as if joyfully acknowledging Him as their Maker. His **arm** is enormously **mighty** and His **hand** is **strong**. His **right hand** is **high** over all, supreme in the world of power.

89:14 As for His moral perfections, His **throne** is founded on the twin principles of **righteousness and justice. Mercy and truth** are shed abroad wherever He goes.

89:15–18 Having rehearsed the greatness of the covenant-making God, Ethan now describes the blessedness of His **people: "Blessed are the people who know the joyful sound!"** To the pious Jew the **joyful sound** was the festive shouts of the people as they walked to Jerusalem for the high holy days of the religious calendar. To us, it will always be the **joyful sound** of the gospel. Several things are delineated concerning these happy **people. They walk . . . in the light of** His **countenance**; that is, **they walk**

in His favor and are guided by His presence. They find in Him the spring of all their joy and never stop rejoicing **in** His **righteousness**. They do not boast in their own power but in His alone. It is only through His **favor** that their **horn is exalted**, in other words, that they are made strong. **For our shield belongs to the Lord, and our king to the Holy One of Israel.**

89:19 And that brings Ethan to the covenant which Jehovah made with **David** (vv. 19–37). Many years before, God had spoken to his faithful one **in a vision**. The **holy one** may refer to Samuel (1 Sam. 16:1–12), to Nathan (2 Sam. 7:1–17) or perhaps to the Servant of Jehovah, the Lord Jesus Christ. He made an unconditional covenant of free grace, setting the crown upon a **mighty** one, and exalting **one chosen from the people**. In many of these descriptions of David, we feel almost instinctively that we are seeing beyond David to the coming Messiah-King.

89:20–24 Jehovah had selected **David** from among his brothers and, through Samuel, had **anointed him** with the **holy oil** reserved for king-making. The covenant guaranteed that God's **hand** would forever be upon David and the inheritors of his throne in preservation and protection, and His **arm** would provide all needed strength. The king's enemies would not be able to outfox him, neither would the wicked be able to **afflict him**. The Lord guaranteed to crush **his foes** and **plague those who hate him**. The **faithfulness** and **mercy** of the Lord would never leave him, and the house of David would derive its strength from Him.

89:25 In accordance with the promise made to Abram (Gen. 15:18), the eventual borders of the kingdom would stretch from the Mediterranean to the Euphrates river. In Genesis 15, it says from the river of Egypt to the river Euphrates, but since the river of Egypt flows into the Mediterranean, the boundaries are the same.

89:26, 27 David would acknowledge Jehovah as his **Father**, his **God, and** his **rock** of refuge. God in turn would **make him** His **firstborn, the highest of the kings of the earth**. The phrase **"the firstborn"** sometimes means first in time, as when Mary brought forth her first-born Son (Luke 2:7). But it could not mean that in David's case because he was the *last-born* son of Jesse. Here it means first in rank or honor, as explained in the rest of the verse, **"the highest of the kings of the earth."** This is also what Paul means when he refers to the Lord Jesus as "the firstborn over all creation" (Col. 1:15). It does not mean that Jesus was the first created being, as some cults teach, but that He is preeminent *over all creation*.

89:28, 29 Nothing will ever alter God's love for David, and nothing will affect the **covenant** He has made. There will always be a **throne** of David, and the royal line will be perpetuated **forever**.

89:30–32 The covenant would not exempt David's **sons** from punishment when they sinned. Any infractions of the **law** would be dealt with righteously. Historically, this is what had happened. David's descendants had been unfaithful to Jehovah, and He had chastised them **with the** rod and scourges of Babylonian captivity.

89:33 Nevertheless the covenant still stood, and although the kingdom was in eclipse for a time, and there was no king reigning in Jerusalem, yet God was still miraculously preserving the royal seed and He would re-institute the kingdom in His own time.

89:34–37 In the strongest possible language, God repeats the inviolability of the **covenant** and His determination to keep His promise **to David**. David's line would **endure forever, and his throne** as long as **the sun** and **the moon . . . in the sky**.

89:38, 39 To outward appearances it may have seemed that God had forgotten the Davidic covenant. Judah was invaded by the Babylonians and carried off into exile. No one has sat on the throne of David from that day to this. But God had not forgotten. Almost two thousand years ago, the Lord Jesus was born in David's royal city. He was the adopted son of Joseph, and since Joseph was in the direct line of the kings of Judah, Jesus inherited the *legal right* to the throne of David through him (Matt. 1). Jesus was the *real son* of Mary, and since Mary was a lineal descendant of David through Nathan, our Lord is of the seed of David (Luke 3:23–38). So the covenant is thus fulfilled in the Lord Jesus Christ. David's throne is perpet uated through Him, and since He lives in the power of an endless life, there will always be a descendant of David to sit upon the throne. One day, perhaps soon, He will return to earth to take His rightful place on the throne of David and reign as David's greatest Son.

Ethan could not have seen this, of course. To him it looked as if the covenant had been scrapped. Listen to him as he complains that God has cast off and rejected the royal line, that He has been **furious** against the king whom He had **anointed**. To Ethan there was no other explanation than that God had gone back on His promise to David, and dragged **his crown** in the dust. Ethan knew deep in his heart that God couldn't renege on His promise, and yet from all appearances it had happened.

89:40–45 The walls of Jerusalem had gaping holes in them, and the **strongholds** were shattered. Travelers passing the city helped themselves to the unprotected loot, and unfriendly Gentile **neighbors** sneered at Judah's plight. Israel's **adversaries** held the upper **hand** and chortled over their victory. The weapons of God's people proved useless in **battle**; the soldiers simply were not able to stand against the foe. The king was deposed and **his throne** vandalized. Humiliated and **covered . . . with shame**, he became an old man prematurely.

89:46–48 The LORD who had made the covenant seemed to be hiding from His people. His **wrath** against them was burning **like fire**. The plaintive **"How long?"** goes winging its way to heaven. Ethan asks God to remember **how short** He has made human life anyway, how frail man is, and how insignificant as well. In his day, every **man** could be sure of **death**; **the power of the grave** would at last win over him. We have a better hope than Ethan; we know that not all will die but that all will be changed when the Lord Jesus returns to take His church home to heaven (1 Cor. 15:51; 1 Thess. 4:13–18). But all this was a secret as far as OT saints were concerned.

89:49–51 Ethan's pleading is very bold and clamant. He asks what has happened to the **lovingkindnesses** which God had guaranteed **to David** in the strongest possible terms. He is keenly sensitive to the taunts and jeers of Israel's enemies, how they insult Ethan himself and mock the exiled king as he moves about.

89:52 But in the closing verse faith triumphs. Though Ethan cannot see the answer to his perplexity, he can still bless Jehovah. It is as if he is saying, "Lord, I can't understand but

I will still trust." So he ends his prayer on the rapturous note, **"Blessed be the Lord forevermore! Amen and Amen."**

IV. BOOK 4 (PSALMS 90—106)

Psalm 90: Tolling of the Death Bell

Permit me to use a little sanctified imagination in explaining this Psalm. The scene is the Wilderness of Sinai. It is years since the spies returned to Kadesh-Barnea with their evil report. Now the people are still trekking around the desert but getting nowhere in the process. It is an exercise in futility.

Every morning a reporter comes to Moses' tent with a fresh report of casualties. Deaths, deaths, deaths, and more deaths. Obituaries are the commonest item of news, and the desert seems to be an expanding cemetery. Every time the people break camp, they leave another field of graves behind.

On this particular day, **Moses the man of God** has had all he can take. Overwhelmed by the mounting toll, he retreats into his tent, prostrates himself on the ground and pours out this **prayer** to God.

90:1, 2 In the midst of so much transience and mortality, he first finds relief in the eternity of the Lord. While all else fades and vanishes, God is unchanging, a home and refuge for His people. From all eternity and to all eternity, He is **God**, "infinite, eternal and unchangeable in His being, wisdom, power, holiness, justice, goodness, and truth."

90:3, 4 In stark contrast to God's agelessness is the brevity of human life. It seems that God is constantly issuing the order, **"Return** to dust," and a never-ending line trudges down to the grave. To One who is eternal, fallen man's original life-span of about **a thousand years** is no more than a **past** memory or a fraction of a **night**.

90:5, 6 Even to Moses, human life seems as evanescent as **sleep**. You sleep, you dream, you awake, and yet you are scarcely conscious of the passing of time. Or to change the figure, life is **like grass**—fresh and green in the morning, then faded and withered by **evening**. As Spurgeon said, it is "sown, grown, blown, mown, gone."

90:7–10 While all death is a result of the entrance of sin, Moses realizes that what is happening in the desert is a special visitation from God. All the soldiers who were twenty years or older when they left Egypt will die before they reach Canaan. The tolling of the death bell is a sign that God is angry with His people because they took sides with the unbelieving spies instead of marching into Canaan as Caleb and Joshua had encouraged. Their **iniquities** and **secret sins** are ever **before** Him, a constant irritation and rankling. As a result, the Israelites are living under the somber cloud of His anger, and overwhelmed in the churning waves of His **wrath**. Some, it is true, live their allotted span of **seventy years**, and some even as much as **eighty**. But even in their case, life is a weariness. One ailment follows another. The smallest tasks are an effort. And soon the pulse beat has stopped, and another one becomes "the missing face."

90:11, 12 The man of God stands in awe of **the power** of God that has been awakened in **anger**. Who, he wonders, can reverence Him adequately when one considers the immensity of His **wrath**? This much is sure: it should make us value every day of our lives and spend each one in obedience to Him, and in such a way that it will count for eternity.

90:13, 14 Moses pleads with the **LORD** to **return** to His people in **mercy**. Will His anger burn forever? Won't He please **have compassion** on them and **satisfy** them **early with** His **mercy** that they might live out their remaining **days** in a measure of tranquility and happiness?

90:15, 16 Now Moses pleads for "equal time," that is, he asks for as many years of gladness for Israel as the years of affliction and trouble they had **seen**. They had already seen His power displayed in works of judgment; now he asks that the Lord show the other side of His countenance; that is, acts of grace.

90:17 Finally, the intercessor asks the Lord to look in favor on His chosen earthly people and to make them fruitful in all their endeavors: **"Yes, establish the work of our hands."**

Traditionally Psalm 90 has been a favorite reading at Christian funerals. And not without reason, because it reminds us of the shortness of life and the need to redeem the time or buy up the opportunities. But the Psalm does not breathe out the comfort and assurance of the NT era. Christ has brought "life and immortality to light through the gospel." We know that to die is gain; it is to be absent from the body and to be at home with the Lord. And so the somber and dark outlook of the Psalm should be replaced by the joy and triumph of the believer's hope in Christ, for now death has lost its sting and the grave has been robbed of its victory. The believer can sing:

> Death is vanquished! Tell it with joy, ye faithful;
> Where is now the victory, boasting grave?
> Jesus lives! no longer thy portals are cheerless;
> Jesus lives, the mighty and strong to save.
>
> —*Fanny J. Crosby*

Psalm 91: My Psalm

In 1922, in the Western Hebrides, a five-year-old lad was dying of diphtheria. A mucous membrane was forming across his throat, and breathing was becoming increasingly difficult. His Christian mother turned her back so she would not see him take his last breath. At that very moment there was a knock at the door. It was her brother-in-law from an adjoining village. He said, "I've just come to tell you that you don't have to worry about the child. He is going to recover, and one day God is going to save his soul." She was distracted and incredulous: "Whatever makes you say that?" Then he explained he had been sitting at his fire reading Psalm 91 when God distinctly spoke to him through the last three verses:

> Because on me he set his love,
> I'll save and set him free;
> Because my great name he hath known,
> I will set him on high.
>
> He'll call on me, I'll answer him;
> I will be with him still,
> In trouble to deliver him,
> And honour him I will.
>
> With length of days unto his mind
> I will him satisfy;
> I also my salvation
> Will cause his eyes to see.
>
> —from *The Scottish Psalms In Metre.*

I was that boy. God delivered me from death that night; He saved my soul thirteen years later, and He has satisfied me with long life. So you will understand why I refer to Psalm

91 as *my Psalm.* I usually add, with tongue in cheek, that I am willing to share it with others—but it is definitely *my* Psalm!

Most theologians don't agree with me at all. They say that this is a Messianic Psalm. And of course they are right. Its primary *interpretation* concerns our wonderful Lord Jesus Christ. And we are going to study it from that perspective, but all the while remembering that in a lesser way, we may *appropriate* its precious promises to ourselves:

> All the rivers of Thy grace, I claim;
> Over every promise write my name.

91:1, 2 Jesus is the One who in a preeminent way dwelt in **the secret place of the Most High**, and abode **under the shadow of the Almighty**. There never was a life like His. He lived in absolute, unbroken fellowship with God, His Father. He never acted in self-will but did only those things that the Father directed. Though He was perfect God, He was also perfect Man, and He lived His life on earth in utter and complete dependence on God. Without equivocation He could look up and say, **"My refuge and my fortress, my God, in Him I will trust."**

91:3 It seems that the Holy Spirit's voice is heard in verses 3–13, assuring the Lord Jesus of the tremendous security that was His because of His life of perfect trust. What are the guarantees of security? There are nine:

Deliverance from hidden dangers. **The snare of the** bird-trapper speaks of the enemy's evil plot to trap the unwary.

Immunity from fatal disease. In our Lord's case, there is no reason to believe that He was ever sick at all.

91:4 *Shelter and **refuge** in the Almighty.* God's tender, personal care is likened to that of a mother bird with her young.

Protection in the faithfulness of God. His promises are sure. What He has said, He will do. This is the believer's **shield and buckler**.

91:5 *Freedom from fear.* Four types of danger are mentioned that commonly cause apprehension:

> Attacks made by an enemy under the cover of **night** are especially terrifying because the source is hard to identify.
>
> **The arrow that flies by day** may be understood as a literal missile or as a figure for "the evil plots and slanders of the wicked" (Amplified Version).

91:6 The pestilence that walks in darkness may also be taken literally or figuratively. Physical disease thrives where it is shielded from the sun's rays, and moral evil also breeds in the dark.

> **The destruction that lays waste at noonday** is unspecified, and perhaps it is best to leave it that way, so that the promise may have a more widespread application.

91:7, 8 *Safety even in the midst of massacre.* Even where there is slaughter on a wholesale basis, the Beloved of the Lord is absolutely safe. When **the wicked** are punished, He will be a spectator only, free from the possibility of harm.

91:9, 10 *Insurance against calamity.* **Because** the Savior made **the Most High** His **refuge** and His **dwelling place**, no disaster would strike Him, no calamity would get near Him.

91:11, 12 *Guarded by angelic escort.* This is the passage which Satan quoted to the Lord Jesus when tempting Him to throw Himself down from the pinnacle of the temple (Luke 4:10, 11). Jesus did not deny that the verses applied to Him, but He did deny that they could be used as a pretext for tempting God. God had not told Him to jump down from the temple. If the Savior had jumped, He would have been acting outside the divine will, and then the promise of protection would not have been valid.

91:13 *Victory over* ***the lion and cobra.*** It is interesting that Satan stopped before coming to this verse. If he had quoted it, he would have been describing *his own doom!* The devil is presented in Scripture as a roaring lion (1 Pet. 5:8) and as an ancient serpent (Rev. 12:9). As a lion, he is the loud, horrendous persecutor using physical violence. As a serpent, he employs wily stratagems to deceive and to destroy.

And so the Holy Spirit has given nine guarantees of safe-conduct to the Son of Man during His life of perfect trust and obedience on earth. At this point God the Father confirms the guarantees by six tremendous "I wills." In these perhaps there is a suggestion of the entire career of the man Christ Jesus:

91:14 *His spotless life on earth.* **"Because he has set his love upon Me, therefore I will deliver him; I will set him on high, because he has known My name."**

91:15 *His suffering for sins.* **"He shall call upon Me, and I will answer him; I will be with him in trouble."**

His resurrection and ascension. **"I will deliver him and honor him."**

91:16 *His present session at God's right hand and His coming kingdom.* **"With long life I will satisfy him, and show him My salvation."**

So much for what the Psalm says! But wait! You are probably thinking of what it does not say, of important questions that it does not answer. For example, how can we reconcile all these promises of safe-keeping for the Messiah with the fact that men ultimately *did* put Him to death? And if we apply the Psalm to believers today, how does it square with the fact that some of them do succumb to disease, or fall in battle, or die in plane crashes?

Part of the answer, at least, lies in this: The one who trusts in Jehovah is immortal until his work is done. Jesus said as much to His disciples. When He suggested returning to Judea, the disciples said:

> "Rabbi, lately the Jews sought to stone You, and are You going there again?" Jesus answered, "Are there not twelve hours in the day? If anyone walks in the day, he does not stumble, because he sees the light of this world. But if one walks in the night, he stumbles, because the light is not in him" (John 11:7–10).

The Lord knew that the Jews could not touch Him until He had finished His work. And this is true of every believer; he is kept by the power of God through faith.

Then the Lord may speak to a believer in a special, personal way through some verse of this Psalm. If He does, the person can claim the promise and rely on it. The personal incident at the beginning illustrates this.

And finally, it is true in a general way that those who trust the Lord are sure of His protection. We may tend to overemphasize the exceptions. The general rule is still true: there is safety in the Lord.

Psalm 92: A Lesson in Spiritual Botany

92:1–5 No one can deny the fact that **it is** downright **good to give thanks to the Lord**. It **is good** in the sense that the Lord deserves such gratitude, and it **is good** also for the one who offers the **thanks** and for those who hear it. **To sing praises to** the **name** of the **Most High** is about as appropriate an activity as anyone can engage in. And there is no lack of subject matter for praise. His **loving kindness** is an unending theme for **the morning and** His **faithfulness** is sufficient to occupy the nighttime hours—and then some. Enhance the beauty of the song with **an instrument of ten strings, the lute**, and **the harp**, and **with harmonious sound**. No amount of sweet music is enough to praise the Lord for His wonderful **works** of creation, providence, and redemption. Just to think of all He has done makes the heart sing with joy. The marvelous, intricate plans of God, His **deep** designs and wise plans add fuel to the flame of praise.

92:6–9 But don't expect the natural **man** to **understand** the deep things of God. He can't understand them, "because they are spiritually discerned" (1 Cor. 2:14). As far as divine realities are concerned, he is dull and stupid though he may be an intellectual giant as far as the world is concerned. He never comes to grip with the fact that fixed moral laws in the universe prescribe destruction for **the wicked**. Though he may seem to prosper for a while, still his success is as short-lived as **grass**. Just as sure as **the Lord** is enthroned **forevermore**, so surely will His **enemies** be **scattered** and **perish**.

92:10, 11 The other side of the coin is that God exalts the **horn** of the righteous **like** that of the **wild ox**, that is, He gives strength and honor to His people. And He anoints the faithful ones **with fresh oil**, which typifies the gracious ministry of the Holy Spirit. When the last chapter is written, the saints of God will have witnessed the demise of their **enemies**, and will have heard the long, low wail of their doom.

92:12–15 The prosperity of the **righteous** is comparable to that of **a palm tree** and **a cedar** of **Lebanon**. The **palm tree** symbolizes beauty and fruitfulness while the **cedar** is an emblem of strength and permanence. The reason for the luxuriant growth of believers is that they **are planted in the house of the Lord** and **flourish in the courts of our God**. In other words, they live in daily fellowship with the Lord, drawing their strength and sustenance from Him. Age does not impair their fruit-bearing capabilities. They continue to pulsate with vigorous spiritual life (the sap) and their testimony remains ever green. Their prosperity is an evidence **that the Lord is upright** in fulfilling His promises. **He is** the dependable **rock, and there** is nothing unreliable about **Him**.

The wicked are compared to grass (v. 7), the righteous to an evergreen (v. 14). The wicked wither and fade away, but the righteous go on from strength to strength. This is the order in spiritual botany.

Psalm 93:
The Eternal King and His Eternal Throne

93:1, 2 The songs that will be sung when Jesus is crowned **Lord** are all ready—and this is one of them. It anticipates the glorious day when Israel's Messiah proclaims Himself King. He will be **clothed with majesty**, in contrast to the lowly grace which characterized Him at His First Advent. He will openly clothe Himself **with** the **strength** that is needed to reign over **the world**. And world conditions will then be established on a firm, stable basis, no longer subject to vast moral and political convulsions.

Of course, the **throne** of Jehovah has always existed, but it has not been as clearly manifest as it will be when the Millennium dawns. The King Himself too is eternal, and as His authority had no beginning, so it will have no end.

93:3, 4 When the psalmist speaks of **floods** and **mighty waves**, it seems clear that he is thinking of the Gentile nations which have oppressed His people through the ages and which will conspire against Him when He comes to reign. But their efforts will be futile and short-lived. Though they will **lift up** their voices in terrifying threats and awesome boasts, they will learn that the enthroned Jehovah **is mightier than** all their federations, than all the armed might they can assemble.

93:5 And so it will be seen that God's Word is true after all, and all the promises He made concerning the defeat of His foes and the establishment of His righteous reign will be fulfilled. The temple in Jerusalem will be cleansed from evil, an appropriate purity for the One whose **house** it is.

> All will be holy when He reigns; and everything will be characterized by holiness, as predicted in Isaiah 23:18; Zechariah 14:20, 21; Revelation 4:8.[62]

Psalm 94: God of Vengeance

In his splendid work on *The Attributes of God,* A. W. Pink writes:

> It is sad to find so many professing Christians who appear to regard the wrath of God as something for which they need to make an apology, or at least they wish there were no such thing. . . . Others harbor the delusion that God's wrath is not consistent with His goodness, and so seek to banish it from their thoughts. . . . But God is not ashamed to make it known that vengeance and fury belong to Him. . . . The wrath of God is as much a Divine perfection as His faithfulness, power or mercy. . . . The very nature of God makes Hell as real a necessity as Heaven is.[63]

94:1–3 In Psalm 94 we hear the faithful remnant of Israel in the last days appealing to the **God** of **vengeance** to reveal Himself in His hatred of evil. The time has come for the righteous **Judge of** all **the earth** to avenge the crimes of evil rulers against His beloved people. The cry **"How long?"** is about to be hushed. The gloating of **the wicked** will soon be silenced.

94:4–7 The condemnation of the proud persecutors is itemized. "Hear their insolence! See their arrogance! How these men of evil boast!" (LB). They grind Jehovah's **people** under their heels; they are unremitting in their harassment of His loyal **heritage**. They victimize the defenseless **widow**, the unsuspecting guests, the helpless orphans. And their attitude is that **the God of Jacob does not understand** or care what is happening.

94:8–11 What stupid **fools** they are to think that God is unaware! If He had the skill to plant **the ear in** man's body, does He **not** have the power also to **hear** what the wicked are saying? Can the Creator of **the eye** be blind Himself as to what is going on? If He has power to chasten **the nations**, as history demonstrates, is He incapable of chastising the Mafia that is oppressing His beloved ones? How can He have less **knowledge** than He imparts to mankind? The fact is that **the LORD knows** everything, He knows what these crooked men are thinking, and He knows that their thoughts are empty wisps of breath.

94:12–15 Faith enables the afflicted psalmist to see his troubles as part of God's education for him. It is a great thing to be thus taught by the **LORD**, and to be trained **out of** His **law**. God gives **him rest from the days of adversity, until the pit** is being **dug for the wicked**. He can be confident that Jehovah will never forsake **His people** or abandon the **inheritance** He loves. Inevitably justice will be restored to its proper place and honest people will show it to others and receive it in return.

94:16–19 There were times when the psalmist wondered **who** would defend him against the overwhelming power of **evildoers**. But he was never left alone. **The LORD** always came to his **help**; otherwise he would have soon been ushered into the **silence** of the cemetery. Whenever he thought he was about to fall before the onslaughts of men, he found himself wonderfully sustained by the **mercy** of the **LORD**. When **anxieties** and doubts began to rise in his mind, the Lord soothed and caressed his soul with all kinds of consolations.

94:20–23 Can there by any fellowship between Jehovah and these wicked rulers? Can there be partnership between Christ and Antichrist? Can the Lord approve men who enact ordinances to legalize sin? To ask the question is to answer it. The power-drunk rulers slay **the righteous and condemn** the **innocent. But the LORD** is a fortress for His own, and **the rock** in which they can hide. He will repay the unjust in full measure. He will wipe them out for all their **iniquity**. Yes, sir, He will wipe them out.

Sic semper tyrannis!
(Thus ever to tyrants!)

Psalm 95: Worship and Warning

The Psalm opens with an exuberant call to worship, and it is difficult to read it without being caught up in the enthusiasm of the writer. (In Heb. 4:7 the Psalm seems to be attributed to David, but the expression "in David" (JND) may simply mean in the book of Psalms, since so many of them were written by him.)

95:1, 2 No doubt we hear the voice of the Holy Spirit in these verses calling Israel back to the worship of Jehovah at the close of her dark days of tribulation. But we must not miss His voice calling to us as well "from each idol that would keep us."

It is interesting to notice the variety of expressions used to describe true worship. It is singing **to the LORD**. It is making a joyful **shout to the Rock of our salvation**, that is, to the cleft Rock of Ages in whom we find eternal refuge. It is coming into **His presence**, confessing with thanksgiving all that He has done for us. It is making the rafters ring with **psalms** of praise to Him.

95:3–5 And just as there is great variety in the manner of our praise, so there is infinite scope in its matter. **The LORD** is to be praised because He **is the great God** (Heb., *El*, i.e., the Omnipotent One). He is a **great King above all** the idolatrous **gods** of the heathen. The **deep places of the earth** are **in His hand** in the sense that He owns them. The mountain peaks **are**

His also because He formed them. He created the mighty oceans, and it was His hands that shaped the continents and the islands.

95:6, 7a But now a second invitation to **worship** rings out, and it becomes even more personal and intimate. We should **worship** and **kneel before the LORD our Maker**, because **He is our God**. He is our God by creation and then by redemption. He is the Good Shepherd who gave His life for us. Now **we are the people of His pasture, and the sheep** who are led, guided, and protected by **His** nail-pierced **hand**.

95:7b–9 In the middle of verse 7 there is an abrupt change from worship to warning. It is the longing, eloquent sighing of the Holy Spirit:

> **Today, if you will hear His voice. . . .**

In the remaining verses we hear the voice of Jehovah Himself warning His people against an evil heart of unbelief. At Meribah near Rephidim the Israelites provoked God by their complaints about the lack of water (this was the same place as Massah—Ex. 17:7). At another Meribah near Kadesh, Moses offended God by smiting the rock instead of speaking to it (Num. 20:10–12). The two events, one at the beginning of the desert journey and the other near the close, form significant terminals expressing in their names (Meribah = **rebellion**; Massah = **trial**) the faithlessness of the people during that time. Even though they had seen God's marvelous **work** in delivering them from Egypt, they **tested** Him and **tried** Him.

95:10 This provocative conduct spanned **forty years**. Finally God said, in effect, "I've had enough. These tiresome **people** have **hearts** that are bent on wandering. They are determined to disregard the pathway that I have mapped for them. So I have made a solemn oath that **they shall not enter** the **rest** that I had planned for them in Canaan."

This poignant appeal, once directed to Israel, is quoted in Hebrews 3:7–11 and directed to any who might be tempted to forsake Christ in order to return to the law. And it will be a warning to Israel in the last days that unbelief will keep them out of God's millennial rest.

Unbelief excludes men from God's rest in every dispensation.

Psalm 96: The King Is Coming

At least seventeen different ways of praising the Lord, given in the form of crisp commands, are found in Psalm 96. Notice the repetition of "sing" (vv. 1, 2), "give" (vv. 7, 8), and "let" (vv. 11, 12).

96:1, 2 The **new song** is the anthem that will swell when the Lord Jesus returns to earth to begin His glorious reign. It will not only be a *new song* but a *universal* one as well; people from all over the earth will blend their voices in it. Men will **bless** the **name** of the Lord and continually bear testimony to His power to save. "Each day (they will) tell someone that he saves" (LB).

96:3–6 What they will do in the future, we should be doing now, namely, declaring **His glory among the nations** and **His wonders among all peoples**. **The LORD** is **great**, infinitely superior to **all gods**. False **gods** made of wood or stone are powerless; the true God is Jehovah, who **made the heavens**. His attributes are like inseparable attendants, accompanying Him everywhere. Thus **honor and majesty** precede **Him**, and

strength and beauty wait on Him in **His sanctuary**. "Honor and beauty are his escort; worship and magnificence the attendants of his shrine" (Knox).

96:7–9 If we really appreciate the greatness and goodness of **the Lord**, we will want others to magnify His name too. Thus the psalmist calls on the **families of the peoples** to join in telling **the Lord** how majestic and stately and mighty He is. They should ascribe to Him **the glory** that is **due His name**. They should **bring an offering** to lay at His feet. They should **worship** Him **in the beauty of holiness**, or in holy garments (NASB). All the world should pay Him obeisance.

The mention of holy garments reminds us that even the clothes we wear when we worship the Lord should be appropriate to the occasion. While it may be true that reverence is primarily a matter of the heart, it is also true that we can express our reverence by our attire. Slovenly clothes at the communion service, for instance, betray a casualness that is seldom seen at weddings or funerals.

96:10 This verse identifies the occasion of the new song as the investiture of Messiah-King. **The Lord** has begun His reign! The world-system is established on a sound basis so that **it shall not be moved** by wars, depressions, poverty, injustice, catastrophes, or other crises. The clause **"it shall not be moved"** must be understood as meaning "never during the thousand-year reign of Christ." We know that at the end of that time, the heavens and the earth will be destroyed by fire (2 Pet. 3:7–12). The point here is that the Lord will rule over **the peoples righteously**, and will protect them from unsettling influences.

96:11–13 All creation is invited to join in the festal joy as the **Lord** (Jehovah, or Yahweh)[64] arrives to rule **the world**. **The heavens** will be happy. **The earth** will **be glad**. "The sea and all within it will thunder praise" (Gelineau). No field will be silent, and "no tree in the forest but will rejoice to greet its Lord's coming" (Knox). **For He is coming to** rule over the world. He will rule in perfect **righteousness and** in absolute honesty.

"Now therefore, why do you say nothing about bringing back the king?" (2 Sam. 19:10).

Psalm 97: Light Is Sown for the Righteous!

97:1 As the Psalm opens, **the Lord**, Jesus Christ, has taken His throne. The crowning day has come. And there is worldwide rejoicing. The distant **isles** and coastlands have never known such gladness.

97:2 The King's arrival is described in symbolical terms that inspire the deepest reverential awe. First of all, He is swathed in **clouds and darkness**—a reminder that our Lord is often mysteriously hidden from the eyes of men and majestically inscrutable as to His ways. How little we know of Him! Then **righteousness and justice are the foundation of His throne**. His is the ideal government—a beneficent monarchy—where there are no miscarriages of justice, no perversions of the truth.

97:3–5 Great sheets of **fire** sweep **before Him**, consuming those who do not know God and who do not obey the gospel of our Lord Jesus (2 Thess. 1:8). The **lightnings** of His judgments illuminate the countryside. People look on in terror. This is the time when "every mountain and hill shall be brought low" (Isa. 40:4), in other words, when everything that lifts itself against the knowledge of God shall be humbled.

97:6a The heavens declare His righteousness. As He comes in the clouds of heaven (Rev. 1:7) with all His blood-bought saints (1 Thess. 3:13), the world sees that He was righteous after all in restoring Israel as He promised. Also, as Gaebelein explains:

> The many sons He brings with Him to glory make known His righteousness, that great work of righteousness on Calvary's cross by which the redeemed were saved and are now glorified.[65]

97:6b And all the peoples see His glory.

> The King there in His beauty
> Without a veil is seen.
> It were a well-spent journey
> Though seven deaths lay between.
> The Lamb with His fair army
> Doth on Mount Zion stand;
> And glory, glory dwelleth
> In Immanuel's land.
> —*Anne Ross Cousin*

97:7 What will idolaters think then? They will be completely nonplussed, realizing that they had been worshiping empty nothings.

"Worship Him, all you gods" in the Septuagint reads, "Let all God's angels worship him," and it is quoted that way in Hebrews 1:6. The Hebrew word here (Elohim) usually means God but it may also refer to angels, judges, rulers, or even to heathen gods or deities.

97:8, 9 The city of **Zion hears** the news of the King's victories against rebels and idolaters, **and is glad**. The hamlets **of Judah** join in the jubilation. "Glad news for Sion, rejoicing for Judah's townships, when thy judgments, Lord, are made known" (Knox). At last **the Lord** is seen to be what He always was—**most high above all the earth**, and **exalted far above all** other potentates, real or manufactured.

97:10 You who love the Lord, hate evil. The two are moral correlatives—*love* for Jehovah and *hatred* of all that is contrary to Him. Those who pass this test are special objects of His preserving care.

97:11 Light is sown like seed **for the righteous**, that is, the coming of Christ means the diffusion of **light** for the man who does what is right and joy unspeakable for all those whose hearts are honest and sincere.

97:12 So the happy summons rings out to all God's righteous people to join in the rejoicing and **give thanks at the remembrance of His holiness** (NKJV margin). This is a surprise ending for the Psalm. We would have expected it to say "Give thanks at the remembrance of His love—or mercy—or grace—or glory." But no, it is **His holiness**. Once **His holiness** excluded us from His presence. But now, through the redemption accomplished by the Lord Jesus, **His holiness** is on our side instead of being against us, and we can rejoice when we remember it.

Psalm 98: Creation's New Symphony

98:1, 2 The Second Coming of Christ means the final deliverance of Israel from the oppression of the Gentile nations. That glorious emancipation gives rise to this **new song**, celebrating the victory of Messiah over His foes. **"Marvelous"** is the word for all that the Lord **has done** with **His right hand** of power **and His holy arm**.

The Psalm pictures the Kingdom as

having already come. His victory is by now well known. **The nations** have seen the faithful fulfillment of His covenant with Israel.

When Jesus came the first time, Mary sang, "He has helped His servant Israel, in remembrance of His mercy, as He spoke to our fathers . . ." (Luke 1:54, 55). And Zacharias prophesied that He would "perform the mercy promised to our fathers and . . . remember His holy covenant" (Luke 1:72).

98:3 When He comes the second time, Israel will sing:

> **He has remembered His mercy and His faithfulness to the house of Israel;**
> **All the ends of the earth have seen the salvation of our God.**

It was the **mercy** of the Lord that prompted Him to make the promises to Israel, and it is His **faithfulness** that now fulfills them.

98:4–6 At first glance it appears that all the Gentile world is being called to rejoice with Israel in verses 4–6. But the **earth** in verse 4 probably means the "land" of Israel, as in F. W. Grant's translation.[66] The saved Israelites are exhorted to break forth in rapturous song. The Levites are encouraged to join with the accompaniment of **the harp**. And in verse 6 the priests complete the harmony **with** their **trumpets and the sound of a horn**.

98:7–9 Then nature and the nations are welcomed to join the symphony. **The sea** and its numberless inhabitants are imaginatively pictured as roaring with delight. **The world** and its occupants are deliriously happy too. **The rivers clap their hands** as they break upon the rocks. **The hills** lift up their heads as if in songs of ecstasy. All creation reacts with spontaneous transport when the King comes to rule over (**judge**) **the earth**—to give this poor, sick, sobbing world a reign of righteousness and of equity. Who wouldn't be happy?

Psalm 99: Holy, Holy, Holy

99:1 The King's *holiness* is the threefold cord that runs through this Psalm (vv. 3, 5, 9). The psalmist sees the Messiah as already having established His kingdom. **He** sits enthroned "above **the cherubim**" (FWG), which probably means that His throne is supported by symbolical cherubs. These are angelic beings with a human body and also with wings. They are assigned to vindicate the holiness of God against the sin of man. The sight of the enthroned Monarch is so moving that the nations might well tremble and the earth quake with fear.

99:2, 3 **The LORD is great** in power and magnificence as He rules from His throne **in Zion**. He is the exalted Ruler over **all the peoples** on earth. They should honor His **great and awesome name** in acknowledgment of the fact that **He is** unimpeachably **holy**.

99:4, 5 This King of power is **also** a lover of **justice**, a rare combination among earth's rulers and great men. "Might and right are wedded at last" (FWG). In His kingdom, graft and corruption are unknown. **Equity, . . . justice, and righteousness** are the rule rather than the exception. How His people should extol Him, prostrating themselves at **His footstool**. In other Scriptures God's footstool is variously defined as the ark of the covenant (1 Chron. 28:2), the sanctuary (Ps. 132:7), Zion (Lam. 2:1), the earth (Isa. 66:1), or even God's enemies (Ps. 110:1). The reference here is probably to the sanctuary in Zion.

99:6, 7 This is the same King who faithfully guided His people in the past. **Moses and Aaron were among His priests, and Samuel was** one of His great intercessors. (Technically neither Moses nor Samuel was a priest, but both performed priestly functions under divine permission.) The point is that when they cried to the Lord, **He answered them**. He communicated with **Moses and Aaron** in the **pillar** of cloud, delivering the law to them at Mt. Sinai. They obeyed His voice, though imperfectly, and **kept** the law, though only partially.

99:8 But **God . . . answered** their prayers then, and the implied assurance is that He will continue to do so now. He was the **God-Who-Forgives**, though He didn't overlook their evil **deeds**. Though the penalty was forgiven, the consequences in this life remained. God's grace, for instance, forgave Moses for his sin at the waters of Meribah, but God's government kept him out of the Promised Land.

It is not improbable that these three heroes represent the believing portion of the nation of Israel, and that what was true of them was true of all God's faithful covenant people. They called upon the Name of the Lord and were saved, and whoever will call upon Him now will also be saved.

99:9 The threefold reference to the holiness of **God** reminds us of Isaiah 6:3 and Revelation 4:8. Also it brings to mind the stately lines of Heber:

> Holy, Holy, Holy, Lord God Almighty!
> Early in the morning our song shall rise to Thee;
> Holy, Holy, Holy, Merciful and mighty!
> God in three persons, Blessed Trinity.
> —*Reginald Heber*

Psalm 100: Old Hundredth

Affectionately known as "Old Hundredth," from its tune in the Geneva Psalter (1551), this Psalm is a call to all the earth to worship Jehovah. Its summons goes beyond the narrow confines of Israel to **all** the Gentile **lands**. Barnes writes:

> The idea is that praise did not pertain to one nation only; that it was not appropriate for one people merely; that it should not be confined to the Hebrew people; but that there was a proper ground of praise for all, there was that in which all nations, of all languages and conditions could unite. The ground of that was the fact that they had one Creator (v. 3).[67]

We learn from these five short verses that worship is simple. The longest words are **thanksgiving**, **everlasting**, and **generations**. The language is neither involved nor flowery. We learn too that the simple recital of facts about God is worship. The words themselves carry cargoes of wonder. The plain facts are more wonderful than fiction.

There is a definite pattern in the Psalm, as follows:

Call to worship (vv, 1, 2).
  Why God should be worshiped (v. 3).
Call to worship (v. 4).
  Why God should be worshiped (v. 5).

Seven elements of worship are suggested:

Shout joyfully (v. 1).
Serve the Lord with gladness (v. 2a).
Come before Him **with singing** (v. 2b).

Enter into His gates with thanksgiving (v. 4a).
Enter **His courts with praise** (v. 4b).
Be thankful to Him (v. 4c).
Bless His name (v. 4d).

We should praise Him because of who He is. He is our:

LORD (v. 1).
God (v. 3a).
Creator (v. 3b).
Owner (v. 3c).
Shepherd (v. 3d).

We should praise Him because of His attributes:

He **is good** (v. 5).
His mercy is everlasting (v. 5).
His truth endures to all generations (v. 5).

In the first three verses, God is worshiped as Creator. But in the last two verses, it is not hard to read Calvary into the text because nowhere else do we see so clearly His goodness, His mercy, and His faithfulness.

All worlds His glorious power confess,
His wisdom all His works express;
But O His love!—what tongue can tell?
Our Jesus hath done all things well!
—*Samuel Medley*

There is a wonderful conjunction of thoughts in verse 3 that we should not miss. There we learn that **the LORD is God**; this means that He is unapproachably high. But we also read that **we are His**; and this tells us that He is intimately nigh. It is because He is so near to us that the Psalm breathes gladness and singing instead of dread and fear.

The Psalm is a joyful song for the happy God, and its message has been preserved in our hymnology in the well-known paraphrase:

All people that on earth do dwell,
Sing to the Lord with cheerful voice;
Him serve with mirth, His praise forth tell!
Come ye before Him and rejoice.

Know that the Lord is God indeed;
Without our aid He did us make;
We are His flock, He doth us feed,
And for His sheep, He doth us take.

Oh, enter then His gates with praise
Approach with joy His courts unto;
Praise, laud, and bless His name always,
For it is seemly so to do.

For why? the Lord our God is good,
His mercy is forever sure;
His truth at all times firmly stood,
And shall from age to age endure.
—*Scottish Psalter*

Psalm 101: Royal Resolutions

David's aspirations for his private and public life were beyond his own achievements. But the goals he set for his house and kingdom will be fully realized by the Lord Jesus when He comes to sit on David's throne. This Psalm is David's manifesto as he entered upon his reign; in it he hitches his wagon to a star.

101:1 He begins by extolling **mercy and justice**, both as they are found in the Lord and as he would like them to be reproduced in himself. Perhaps he is thinking primarily of the *Godward* side—of God's **mercy** toward Israel and of His just judgment on His foes—because he quickly adds, **"To You, O LORD, I will sing praises."**

101:2 Then he turns to some of the features which he desires for his personal life. He is resolved to give heed to the **way** that is blameless, that is, to conduct himself so closely to the teachings of the Lord that there will be no justifiable grounds of reproach. His desires are so ardent and sincere that he interjects the longing sigh, **"Oh, when will You come to me?"** This has been variously interpreted as meaning:

> he longs for God to come and to find him living in this upright way;
>
> he yearns for the fulfillment of the covenant which God made with him (2 Samuel 7), the final establishment of God's kingdom on the earth;
>
> he "feels that his resolves require the presence of God Himself to carry them out."[68]

He is determined to walk with integrity of **heart** within his **house**. In his domestic life, he will act righteously and sincerely. No hanky-panky and no two-facedness for him!

101:3, 4 When he says he **will** not **set before** his **eyes** anything that is **wicked**, he means that he will not look with approval on any base person, plan or activity.

As far as **the work of** apostates is concerned, he hates it and is determined to keep free from its contamination. **Those who fall away** from the truth and from righteousness shall have no fellowship with him.

Another characteristic which he intends to stay far away from is **a perverse heart**—one that is inclined to falsehood and depravity. He will not indulge this evil in himself, and he will not have that kind of person among his trusted advisors. The worthy resolve **"I will not know wickedness"** may also refer to his own life or to persons in his court. Thus the KJV renders it, "I will not know a wicked person." The word "know" here means to accept with favor or encourage.

101:5 Anyone who **slanders his neighbor** will be cut off. It scarcely means that he will be put to death, as in the RSV, but excluded from a position in the king's administration, or put to silence (NASB Margin).

The same goes for the snobbish, **proud** person. He will not be an office-holder in the royal palace.

101:6 The great qualification for service in the kingdom will be moral and spiritual integrity. **The faithful of the land** will be the king's assistants, and those whose lives are clean will be his servants.

101:7, 8 As for crooks, cheats and liars, they will not be found on the king's payroll. He will have no truck with charlatans and shysters.

Finally, the king is determined to see that all forms of wickedness are dealt with promptly and sternly. Again the word **"destroy"** may mean to punish or to expel them from Jerusalem, **the city of the Lord**. "Wickedness of all kinds must be rooted out of the land, and all vain-doers cut off from the city of Jehovah."[69]

Psalm 102: The Trinity at Calvary

The key to understanding this Psalm lies in detecting the change in speakers.

> The Lord Jesus, hanging on the cross, is speaking to God. (vv. 1–11)
>
> The Father replies to His beloved Son; we know this by comparing verse 12 with Hebrews 1:8. (vv. 12–15)
>
> The speaker is unidentified, but we are safe in assuming that it is the Holy Spirit, describing the future restoration of Israel under the Messiah. (vv. 16–22)
>
> The Savior is heard once more as He suffers at the hands of God for our sins. (vv. 23, 24a)

> Again by comparing this section with Hebrews 1:10–12, we know that the Father is speaking to His Son. (vv. 24b–28)

Here as nowhere else in the Bible we are enabled to listen in on a conversation that took place between the three Persons of the Trinity when the Lord Jesus was making expiation for the sins of the world.

102:1, 2 As we read the prayer of the afflicted one in verses 1 and 2, we should never lose a sense of wonder that the eternal Son of God would ever humble Himself so low that He would become obedient to death, even death on a cross.

> Jesus, the Helper, the Healer, the
> Friend;
> Why, tell me why was He there?

We hear Him imploring the **Lord** to **hear** His **prayer**, to be near Him in distress, and to **answer** Him **speedily**.

102:3–7 Then He describes some of the sufferings which He was called upon to endure as the Man of Sorrows. He was conscious that life was ebbing; His **days** were vanishing **like smoke**. His body was burning with fever. It was as if His vital organs were dried up and **withered**, so much so that appetite had vanished. His torture had been so prolonged that He was now reduced to **skin** and **bones**. **Like a** bird in the **wilderness** or **an owl** in deserted ruins, He was a picture of desolation and melancholia. Sleep was, of course, impossible. Forsaken by God and by man, He was **alone**, **like a sparrow** on a rooftop.

102:8–11 His **enemies** were unremitting in their insults. They used His name for a curse. (Even today the Hebrew name for Jesus, *Yeshua,* is shortened by His foes to *Yeshu,* a curse word meaning "May His name be banished from the earth.") The **ashes** of sorrow were His **bread**, and His **drink** was diluted by tears of grief.

In it all, He realized that He was suffering because of God's **indignation** and **wrath**. Not that God was angry with Him personally, but with our sins which the Lamb of God was bearing in His body on the tree. Forsaken by God, He felt as if He had been picked **up and** thrown **away**. His days were declining like the evening shadows, and His life was withered **like grass**.

102:12–15 God now replies to the Lord Jesus in words of reassurance and encouragement. Addressing the Son as **Lord**, He reminds Him that He would **endure forever**, and His **name to all generations**. Though He would die, it is true, yet He would **arise** and ascend to heaven. Then He would return to earth as Lion of the tribe of Judah and **have** pity **on Zion**. This would be the time when the nation, now set aside, would be brought back into **favor** again. While waiting for this restoration, the people of Israel hold the **stones** of Zion dear **and show favor to her dust**. This is seen, for example, in the deep regard they have for the Western Wall, formerly called the Wailing Wall, and their tremendous sentimental attachment for the old city of Jerusalem. When Zion welcomes back her King, the Gentile **nations shall fear the name of the Lord, and all** earth's rulers shall pay homage to Him.

102:16–22 In verses 16–22, the first and second personal pronouns are dropped; only the third person is used. And so, as we have suggested, it may be the voice of the Holy Spirit describing the future restoration of Israel under the reign of Christ. The Messiah will return **in** power and great **glory** and will rebuild **Zion**. The prayers of His scattered people will be answered in that day. It will then be seen that their supplications were not in vain. Future generations will be able to read the wonderful saga of how **the Lord** looked down **from heaven**, how He heard the cries of His persecuted, scattered people, and how He brought them back to the land of Israel. When the nations gather **in Jerusalem** to worship **the Lord**, they will rehearse the way in which He freed **the prisoner** and the condemned, and they will **praise** the Lord for His gracious dealings with Israel.

102:23–28 Now the Psalm switches back to the Lord as He expires on the cross. He was a young man at the time—in His early thirties. But already His **strength** was broken in the prime of life. His life was about to end prematurely. And so He prays, **"O my God, do not take me away in the midst of my days."**

The answer comes back from God immediately (v. 24b), "Lord, you live forever" (TEV). We know it is God speaking here, because the words that follow are attributed to God the Father in Hebrews 1:10–12. Notice what God testifies concerning His Son:

> He was the Active Agent in creation: He **laid the foundation of the earth, and the heavens are the work of** His **hands**.
>
> Creation **will perish, but** He **will endure**. Creation will wear out and, **like a garment**, be exchanged for something better. But Christ is unchanging and eternal.
>
> And not only is His eternity secure, but also that of His people and of their posterity. **The children of** His **servants** will dwell safely, **and their descendants** in turn will live under His protection.

Psalm 103: Call to Thanksgiving

103:1 One of the reasons we love the Psalms so much is that they verbalize so beautifully what we often feel but cannot find words to express. Nowhere is this more true than in the case of the 103rd. In its majestic cadences of thanksgiving, we read sentiments that mirror our own deepest emotions of gratitude. Here we call on our **soul** to **bless the Lord**—and by our **soul** we mean not just the non-material part of our nature but the entire person. Spirit, soul, and body are cued in to bless the **holy name** of Jehovah.

103:2 The call to worship rings out a second time, with the significant added reminder that we should **forget not all His benefits**. It is a needed reminder because all too often we do forget. We forget to thank Him for soundness of body, soundness of mind, sight, hearing, speech, appetite, and a host of other mercies. We take them too much for granted.

103:3 But above all else, we should be thankful to Him for forgiving **all** our **iniquities**. It is an unspeakable miracle of divine grace that crimson sins can be made whiter than snow. I can empathize with the man who chose one word for his tombstone—FORGIVEN. And also with the Irishman who said, "The Lord Jesus has forgiven me all my sins, and He's never going to hear the end of it." To know that our sins have been put away forever by the precious blood of Christ—well, it's just too much to take in. The second benefit to be remembered is the healing of **all** our **diseases**. Before we get into the problem that this raises, let us notice that healing comes after forgiveness. The physical is closely related to the spiritual. While not *all* sickness is a direct result of sin, *some* of it is. Where the connection exists, forgiveness must precede healing.

But the obvious problem is still there. The verse says "**. . . who heals all your diseases.**" Yet as a matter of practical experience we know that not all diseases are healed, that we will all die sooner or later if the Lord does not come in the meantime. So what does the verse mean? In seeking an answer, we would make the following observations.

First, all genuine healing is from God. If you have been sick, and then have recovered, you can thank God for your recovery because He is the source of all healing. One of the names of God in the Old Testament is *Jehovah Rophi*—the Lord your Healer. Every instance of true healing comes from Him.

Second, the Lord is able to heal *all kinds of diseases*. There is no such thing with Him as an incurable disease.

Third, the Lord can heal by the use of natural means over a period of time or He can heal miraculously and instantly. No limit can be placed on His power to heal.

Fourth, when He was on earth the Lord actually healed all that were brought to Him (Matt. 8:16).

Fifth, during the Millennium He will actually heal all diseases (Isa. 33:24; Jer. 30:17) except in the case of those who rebel against Him (Isa. 65:20b).

But whatever else the verse means, it cannot mean that the believer can claim healing for every disease, because in other verses of the Psalm we are reminded of the shortness of life and of the certainty of its coming to an end (see vv. 15, 16). What the verse says to me is that whenever a believer is healed, this is a mercy from God, and He should be acknowledged and thanked as the Healer.

103:4 Not only does He heal diseases, He also **redeems** our lives from the Pit, or **destruction**. Of course, this can be applied to His saving us from going down to hell. But I think that the meaning here is rather that He continually delivers us from dangers, accidents, tragedies and thus from going down to the grave. Only when we get to heaven will we realize how often we were protected by the personal intervention of our God from premature death.

The fourth benefit is that He **crowns** us **with lovingkindness and tender mercies**. It is a wonderful diadem for those who were once the loveless and guilty. We are loved with everlasting love and showered day by day with His mercy.

103:5 Then again He **satisfies** us with **good things** as long as we live. The Hebrew here is a bit uncertain. The literal translation is He "satisfies your ornament with good things." From there it is rendered "your prime," "your years" or "as long as you live." But even if we can't agree on the exact words, the truth is there that the Lord **satisfies** the longing heart, and that He does not withhold any good thing from those who walk uprightly.

The result of these five benefits—forgiveness, healing, preservation, coronation, and satisfaction—is that our **youth** is **renewed like the eagle's**. Sickness and violence may affect the body but they cannot touch the spirit.

"Though our outer man is decaying, yet our inner man is being renewed day by day" (2 Cor. 4:16). On earth there is no fountain of eternal youth as far as the body is concerned, but the spirit can go from one degree of strength to another.

> Those who wait on the Lord
> shall renew their strength;
> They shall mount up with wings like eagles,
> They shall run and not be weary,
> They shall walk and not faint (Isa. 40:31).

The eagle has a reputation for long life and superior strength. Its life is not one of continuous vitality and renewed youth; it too grows old and dies. But what the psalmist is saying is that the man who dwells in God enjoys continuous revival, and goes from strength to strength, like the eagle soaring from one height to the next.

103:6 The mercy and kindness of **the Lord** are demonstrated in His dealings with the Hebrew people, especially in the exodus from Egypt. That was typical of the way He works vindication **and justice for all who are oppressed**.

103:7, 8 In the trek from Egypt to the Promised Land, God revealed **His ways to Moses** and **His acts to the** people **of Israel**. He took **Moses** into His inner counsels and shared His plans and purposes with him. The people of Israel saw the practical outworking of these plans. The difference between **His ways** and **His acts** is that **His ways** are learned by revelation whereas **His acts** are a matter of observation.

In all His dealings with His people **the Lord** has shown Himself to be **merciful and gracious**. He guides, protects, and provides for every step of the way. His people are wayward, complaining, rebellious and disobedient, yet He puts up with a great deal before His **anger** flares. His **mercy** is steadfast in spite of the ingratitude it meets.

> How utterly unworthy I am, dear Lord, of Thee,
> Yet Thou art always showering Thy wondrous love on me.
> Though oftentimes I wander and fail to do Thy will,
> Thy gracious love constraining abideth with me still.
>
> —*Author unknown*

103:9, 10 There comes a time when the Lord has to chasten His children, but even then His discipline does not last indefinitely. Judgment is His strange work. His mercy rejoices against judgment. If we received what we deserve to receive, we would be in hell forever. But God's mercy is demonstrated in that He does not give us what we deserve. The penalty of **our sins** was paid by another at the cross of Calvary. When we trust the Savior, God can righteously pardon us. And there can be no double jeopardy; Christ has paid the debt once for all, and so we will never be required to pay it.

103:11, 12 God's love in providing this wonderful plan of salvation is immeasurable. It beggars human imagination. If we could measure the distance of **the heavens** from **the earth**, we could get some idea of the magnitude of His love. But we can't. We can't even determine the size of the universe we live in. And talking about infinite distance, that is exactly how **far He has removed our transgressions from us**. Just as "east is east, and west is west, and never the twain shall meet," so the believer and his sins will never meet. Those sins have been put out of God's sight forever by a miracle of love.

103:13, 14 Someone has said that "man's weakness appeals to God's compassion." Just **as a** human **father** watches with loving understanding as his little fellow struggles with some man-sized load, **so the LORD** looks down in pity on us in our weakness. He knows what we are—**that we are** made of **dust**—that we are frail and helpless. Too often we forget what God remembers—**that we are dust**. This leads to pride, self-confidence, independence, and breakdowns.

103:15, 16 Not only is man dust, but he soon returns to dust. The primeval edict, "You are dust, and to dust you shall return," finds its inexorable fulfillment. Man is born for one brief day, then like the **flower of the field** he passes away, and his old haunts never see him again.

103:17, 18 With God's **mercy** there is a vivid contrast. It lasts **from everlasting to everlasting** to **those who fear Him**. In duration, as in volume, it is limitless. **And His righteousness** extends **to children's children**. There is great comfort in this. Christian parents often feel concern about their children and grandchildren growing up in a world of mounting wickedness. But we can safely entrust our little ones to One whose love is infinite and whose righteousness is sufficient not only for us but for succeeding generations as well. Of course, the promises necessarily have a condition attached. They are valid for those who **keep His covenant** and **remember His commandments to do them**. But that is only reasonable.

103:19–22 The LORD is King. **His throne** is **in** the heavens. And His authority is universal. As such He should be the object of praise by everyone and everything; so David steps up to the dais of the universe to lead the massed choir of creation in a mighty diapason of worship. First, he motions to the **angels**, mighty and obedient, to start the rolling anthem. Then he calls on all created beings who serve the Lord to come in with their harmonies of praise. Next he signals all the **works** of God to join the glorious crescendo. And while this great Hallelujah chorus is ringing throughout God's dominion, the choir leader himself adds his voice to **bless the LORD**. Someone has imagined David as saying here:

> "Amidst the praises of creation, let my voice sing His praise."

Psalm 104: Creator and Sustainer

Think of what must be involved in running cities like New York or London or Tokyo with their millions of inhabitants. Complex organizations administer the water department, the housing department, the food supplies and all the other essential services.

But then think how infinitely more complex is God's task of managing the world in which we live. There is the problem of supplying water for all His creatures. There is the immense logistical task of providing food for men, beasts, birds and fish. There is the matter of housing and shelter. It can only give us great thoughts of God to meditate on Him as the Creator and Sustainer of this vast world of nature.

104:1–3 After summoning every part of his being to extol **the LORD**, the unnamed psalmist gives one of those great descriptions of God that must have inspired Michelangelo. It has to be understood as figurative language, because how else can you describe the invisible God or capture His infinite greatness with finite words?

As he stands and gazes and wonders, the psalmist exclaims, **"O LORD my God, You are very great!"** Then the details of the theophany (an appearance of God) pour forth. God has robed Himself in garments of inexpressible splendor **and majesty**. He has covered Himself **with light as with a garment**, a symbol of His absolute purity and righteousness. He spreads the stellar and atmospheric **heavens** over the earth **like a curtain**—a work that boggles the mind by its immensity. The watery cloud-cover over the earth forms the foundation on which the pillars of the heavens were set. Scudding across the sky, **the clouds** are the **chariot** of Jehovah, borne along **on the wings of the wind**.

104:4 Who makes His angels spirits, His ministers a flame of fire. Since the Hebrew uses the same word for *wind* and *spirit* and another word means both *angel* and *messenger,* this may be translated: "Who makes winds His messengers, a flame of fire His ministers." This fits the nature context nicely, but the quotation of this verse in the context of Hebrews 1:7 requires the traditional translation. (The Greek language has the same sets of double meanings, so it applies in both Testaments.)

104:5–9 It becomes evident as we move through the Psalm that we are re-living the days of creation in Genesis 1, although some of the days are not as distinctly referred to as others. The psalmist marvels at the providential arrangements of God for His creatures and especially for man.

First, he recalls how God formed the earth on invisible **foundations** so that it would provide a stable, unshakable surface for habitation. At the outset, the entire earth was covered with **waters** so **deep** that even the **mountains** were submerged. On the third day God said, "Let the waters under the heavens be gathered together into one place, and let the dry land appear" (Gen. 1:9). Immediately the waters beat a hasty retreat. The **mountains** and **valleys** appeared in the locations which God had prearranged for them. The seas and oceans were formed with distinct boundaries so that they would not invade the dry land.

104:10–13 Then God's marvelous water system began operating. **Springs** began pumping out water in abundance. The streams fought their way downhill to the valleys and lowlands and eventually to the seas. Ever since then the **wild** animals have been quenching **their thirst** in these streams, rivers and lakes. And the **birds have** found nesting places in the trees that grow beside these water courses. Another part of the water department is the rain. As Elihu pointed out, God "draws up drops of water, which distill as rain from the mist, which the clouds drop down and pour abundantly upon man" (Job 36:27, 28). And as the great sprinkling system waters the mountains, **the earth is satisfied with** the results of God's irrigation program.

104:14, 15 Next is the commissary department. He provides **vegetation** in abundance and variety **for the cattle,** and grains for **man** to cultivate, both for himself and as fodder for his livestock. By a slow, silent miracle, **food** comes out of **the earth**. The juice of the grapes is turned into **wine** by a marvelous chemical process, and man is cheered as he drinks it. The olive yields its golden **oil** with a wide variety of uses, both healthful and tasty. And from the grain comes **bread**, the staff of life, to give man strength for his labors.

104:16–18 The great **trees of the** forest suck up tons of water from the ground; **the cedars of Lebanon** grow naturally without human planting. These in turn provide housing facilities for **the birds. The stork**, for instance, nests in the **fir trees** (which may mean junipers or cypresses). The **high** mountains provide ideal sanctuary for **the wild goats**, and the rocks a home for the **badgers**.

104:19–23 Since life moves along in cycles and on schedule, there must be some way to measure time. So God set **the moon** in place to mark the months, and **the sun**, as if conscious, **knows** when to set and thus to mark the end of another day. The regular alternation of day and night is providential for animals and man. Under the cover of **darkness** the **beasts of the forest** go prowling after their food. When morning comes, they slink back to the safety of **their dens**. But **man goes** off **to his work** and utilizes the hours of daylight for productive **labor**.

104:24–26 The variety of God's **works** is staggering. "What wisdom has designed them all" (Knox). **The earth is full of** His creatures, and He cares for each one with amazing attention to detail. The **sea** swarms with life **both small and great,** ranging all the way from the minute plankton to the whales.

The mention of **ships** in verse 26 seems somewhat out of place in a discussion of living creatures. Some understand it to mean sea monsters (Gen. 1:21), but **ships** is the correct reading. **Leviathan** (in the same verse) may refer to the whales or porpoises which find the sea an ideal playground for their sporting antics. (But see comments and endnotes on Job 41.)

104:27–30 Though they may not be conscious of it, all living organisms depend on God for **their food**. As He supplies it, **they gather** it **in**. He opens His **hand** and **they are** abundantly **filled**. In verse 13, the earth is satisfied with the results of God's work in sending the rain. In verse 16 the trees are full of sap. And now **all** creatures are **filled**.

An inescapable fact of God's economy is that death strikes down one generation, and a new one is raised up to take its place. When animals die, either by violence or through age, it is as if God were hiding His **face**. But at the same time that these fall and **return to . . . dust**, God sends **forth** His **Spirit** and repopulates **the earth** with what seems like a fresh creation. On the one hand there is a constant wasting away, on the other hand a continual renewal of **the face of the earth**.

104:31, 32 Just as the Psalm opened with the original creation, now it closes with a passionate prayer for the golden age when the ravages of sin will be suppressed and when **the Lord** will be honored and glorified for His greatness and goodness:

> He (the psalmist) longs to see it all brought back, restored, to find himself and all God's creatures, parts of the mighty harmony, that a new sabbath of creation may dawn, a rest of God, in which He shall rejoice in His works and they in Him, and the universe becomes a temple filled with the anthem of praise.[70]

As for **the Lord**, the psalmist prays that His **glory** will **endure forever,** that He will **rejoice in His works**—this great God whose glance produces an earthquake, whose touch causes volcanic eruptions.

104:33–35 As for himself, the sacred writer is determined to **sing**

forth the excellencies of his God **as long as** he lives. He prays that his **meditation** might **be sweet to** Jehovah in whom he finds his true joy.

As for **sinners** who spoil God's creation, he sees a moral fitness in their being banished **from the earth**. God has already decreed that it shall be so, and thus his prayer is in accord with the divine will.

As for ourselves, we can surely join him in his final doxology:

Bless the Lord, O my soul.
Praise the Lord!

Psalm 105: The Covenant with Abraham

In His covenant with Abraham, God promised to his descendants the land from the river of Egypt to the river Euphrates (Gen. 15:18–21; Ex. 23:31; Deut. 1:7, 8; Josh. 1:4). It was an unconditional promise, a covenant of pure grace. Everything depended on God, nothing on man.

This Psalm rehearses with great enthusiasm all that God did from the giving of the covenant to the time when He led the children of Israel into the promised land. The entire emphasis is on what God did. Nothing is said about Israel's sins and backslidings, as in most of the historical Psalms.

Actually Israel has never yet fully occupied all the territory that was promised. The closest she came to it was during the reign of Solomon. Although he ruled over all the kingdoms from the Euphrates to the border of Egypt, the people of Judah and Israel dwelt in the land from Dan to Beersheba (1 Kgs. 4:21–25). But when her Messiah returns in power and glory, Israel's borders will then extend to include all the land which God deeded to Abraham. When that day arrives, believing Israel will sing this song with new spirit and understanding.

Give Thanks and Praise (105:1–6)

Many of the Psalms open on a low-key, then build up to a crescendo of worship. But this one begins with a veritable explosion of praise that catches up the reader in its eloquent appeal. Notice the variety of imperative verbs that are employed to encourage adoration:

Oh give thanks **to the Lord,**
Call **upon His name;**
Make known **His deeds among the peoples!**
Sing **to Him,** ***Sing*** **psalms to Him;**
Talk **of all His wondrous works!**
Glory **in His holy name:**
Let **the heart of those** ***rejoice*** **who seek the Lord.**
Seek **the Lord and His strength;**
Seek **His face evermore!**
Remember **His marvelous works which He has done,**
His wonders, and the judgments of His mouth,
O seed of Abraham His servant,
You children of Jacob, His chosen ones!

His Covenant With Abraham (105:7–11)

105:7, 8 The immediate cause of the psalmist's exhilaration is the Abrahamic **covenant** (Gen. 12:7; 13:14–17; 15:7, 18–21; 17:8; 22:17, 18; Ex. 32:13). It was made by **the Lord our God** whose righteous acts are seen throughout **the earth**. He will never forget His promise, though its fulfillment is delayed **a thousand generations**. Whatever He promises is as certain as if it had already taken place.

105:9–11 **The covenant** was **made** originally **with Abraham** (Gen. 12:1–20), later confirmed **to Isaac** (Gen. 26:3,4), and then still later **confirmed to Jacob** (Gen. 28:13–15). It was the word of God who cannot lie, guaranteeing **the land of Canaan as the . . . inheritance** of His earthly people.

In the ensuing history of Israel, we see how God removed roadblocks and conquered enemies to bring His word to pass.

The Nation's Infancy (105:12–15)

When they first came to Canaan from Mesopotamia, they were a handful of defenseless immigrants. Those early days were marked by considerable moving about, both within the land and in other countries (Gen. 12:1–13; 20:1–18; 28:1—29:35). But God protected them from danger and oppression, and **rebuked** rulers like Pharaoh (Gen. 12:17–20) and Abimelech (Gen. 20:1–18; 26:6–11), saying, in effect, to these heathen kings, "Don't you dare **touch My** chosen ones, or **do My prophets** any **harm**—these patriarchs to whom I have given direct revelations."

Joseph's Rise to Power in Egypt (105:16–22)

In the process of time, **a** severe **famine** descended on **the land** of Canaan. **Bread** supplies vanished; the main support of life was gone. It was God who summoned the famine and who **destroyed all the provision of bread**, but only in the sense that He permitted these things to happen. God never originates evil, but He does permit it at times and then overrules it for His glory and His people's good. God's man for the crisis was **Joseph**. Hated by his brothers, he **was sold** into Egypt **as a slave**. There he was falsely accused by a seductive woman and thrown into prison (Gen. 39:20). In verse 18, we have some otherwise unrecorded details concerning his imprisonment: **"They hurt his feet with fetters, he was laid in iron."** During his two years in jail, **the word of the Lord tested** his skill in interpreting dreams and predicting the future. Finally his ability was brought to Pharaoh's attention and he not only **released him**, but promoted him to second in command. He had authority **to bind** Egyptian **princes**, if necessary, and **wisdom** to instruct men who were much older than himself.

Migration of Jacob and Family (105:23–25)

Eventually Joseph's family moved **into Egypt**, and over the years they became numerous, prosperous and strong militarily. But in the providence of God, the Egyptians were allowed to become rabidly anti-semitic and to oppress and cheat the Jews.

Moses and the Plagues in Egypt (105:26–31)

105:26, 27 This time God raised up **Moses and** his lieutenant, **Aaron**, to stand before Pharaoh and demand the release of His enslaved people. Their demands were punctuated with a series of plagues designed to break down the monarch's resistance.

Here the plagues are itemized, not in chronological order, and with two unmentioned—the fifth and the sixth.

105:28 God **sent darkness** over all the land (Plague #9). The psalmist adds the puzzling comment, **"And they did not rebel against His word."** Because of the obvious difficulty, the RSV translators changed it to read, "they rebelled against His words," but they had no manuscript authority to make this change. Barnes explains it as meaning that Moses and Aaron **did not rebel against** the Lord's words, but did as He commanded them. Or it may mean that the darkness was so oppressive that the Egyptians were powerless to resist it.

105:29–31 God **turned their waters into blood** and wiped out the supply of **fish** (Plague #1). It was pollution of the worst kind.

The next mentioned was the plague of **frogs** (Plague #2). There were **frogs** everywhere—**frogs** in the ovens and **frogs** in the beds. Not even the royal suite was proof against these leaping, croaking, slimy creatures!

One word from the Lord and the land was ruined by **swarms of flies** (Plague #4) and by clouds of pesky gnats or **lice** (Plague #3).

105:32–36 Instead of **rain**, He sent destructive **hail** and lightning (Plague #7). As great balls of **fire** careened across the landscape, the **vines**, the **fig trees** and other **trees** were shattered. This plague brought injury and death to men as well (Ex. 9:25).

Then **came** the **locusts**, like an invading army, consuming **all the vegetation** as they advanced, and leaving a wasteland behind (Plague #8).

When none of these plagues succeeded, God **destroyed all the firstborn** of the Egyptians, both of man and beast (Plague #10). That was a night to be remembered—when the pride of every Egyptian home was slain.

The Exodus (105:37, 38)

The Jews left Egypt **with** more **silver and gold** than they had when they arrived; the Egyptians were **glad** to give them anything they wanted just to get rid of them (Ex. 12:33–36). And in spite of the havoc the plagues had wrought on the Egyptians, the Israelites were unaffected. They were all in good condition for travel. Not one staggered or fell behind.

It was a great relief for the Egyptians **when they departed**; they had developed a deep-seated dread of them.

Wilderness Journey (105:39–42)

God's provision for His people in the wilderness was fantastic. **A cloud** not only kept them on course (Ex. 13:21) but served as a sort of smoke screen to hide them from the enemy (Ex. 14:19, 20). It became a pillar of **fire** at **night** to provide illumination for travel. When they wanted food, He gave them the best—**quails** in great abundance and manna, that wonder **bread** from **heaven**. They needed **water**, so **He** split **the rock, and water gushed out**. After they had used all they wanted, there was still enough to make **a river** in the desert. Why all this painstaking provision by Jehovah? Because He could not forget the **holy promise** which He had made to **Abraham His servant.**

In the Land at Last (105:43–45)

It was a great deliverance, accompanied by indescribable **joy** and singing. Jehovah **brought** them into the land of Canaan and dispossessed **the Gentiles** who were living there. Everything was ready made for them; **they** reaped **the labor of the nations**.

And of course the divine objective was that they might obey Him and **keep His laws**. Actually their tenure of the land was conditional on their obedience (Lev. 26:27–33; Deut. 28:63–68; 30:19, 20).

The last verse of the Psalm forms the intended climax. This was what God had been working toward all the time.

And it is true for us as well. God claimed us for His people in order that we might be living in that last verse:

That they might observe His statutes, and keep His laws.
Praise the LORD!

Psalm 106: Lessons from History

Cromwell asked, "What is history but God's unfolding of Himself?" The psalmist would have readily agreed because in the history of his people, he saw Jehovah unfolded as a God of goodness, patience and steadfast love.

Although we cannot name the psalmist, we do know that he was a godly Jew who wrote while his people were in captivity (v. 47). The Psalm is primarily a confession of national sin (vv. 6–46) but it also contains elements of praise (vv. 1–3, 48) and petition (vv. 4, 5, 47).

Praise (106:1–3)

106:1 In his approach to God, he begins with worship; he enters the divine gates with thanksgiving, and the sacred courts with praise. **"Praise the LORD,"** the translation of the Hebrew word "Hallelujah," is the first and last note of the song.

Ceaseless thanksgiving should arise **to the LORD**, because **He** has been so **good** to every one of us. **His mercy endures forever**—our continued survival is proof of that. If we received what we deserve, we would be lost forever.

106:2, 3 No human tongue will ever be able to recount all the miraculous interventions of God on behalf of His people. Eternity itself will not be long enough to praise Him adequately for all that He is and all that He has done.

Lord, Remember Me! (106:4, 5)

Praise is followed by personal petition. Looking forward to the restoration of Israel and the glorious reign of the Messiah-King, the writer prays that he might share in the blessedness of that day when God shows favor to His ransomed saints. He longs to see Israel enjoying unbroken prosperity and rejoicing after its long night of sorrow. He desires to share in the glory of God's ancient earthly people. His prayer is not dissimilar to that of the dying thief, "Lord, remember me when You come into Your kingdom" (Luke 23:42).

Red Sea Rebellion (106:6–12)

The Psalm now turns to confession, following much the same order as the Lord's prayer. Both begin with worship, move on to petition ("Give us this day our daily bread") and then ask for forgiveness ("Forgive us our debts . . .").

It is a mark of true spiritual maturity when a man not only confesses his own sins but the sins of his people as well. How hard it is to say from the heart:

We have sinned with our fathers,
We have committed iniquity, we have done wickedly.

As we consider the sins of the Israelites, we must not look down our theological noses at them. If anything, we are worse than they! Let their backslidings remind us of our own and drive us to our knees in repentance.

Their ingratitude—they did not fully appreciate the **wonders** God performed **in Egypt** to purchase their freedom.

Their forgetfulness—too quickly the memory of God's innumerable **mercies** faded from their minds.

Their rebellion—when they came to **the Red Sea**, they complained that God had led them to die in the wilderness, and that it would have been better to have stayed in Egypt (Ex. 14:11, 12).

But their sin did not quench the Lord's love. He found in their rebellion an opportunity to reveal Himself as their Servant and Savior. True to His name, He delivered them—and what a gigantic exhibition of **power** it was! At the word of His rebuke, the waters of **the Red Sea** parted, leaving a bone-dry causeway for the Jews to cross on. When they were safely on the east side, free from the pursuing enemy, **the waters** returned to their place, conveniently drowning the Egyptian hosts. When they saw this marvelous converging of events, how could the Jews help believing Him and singing **His praise**?

Complaints in the Desert (106:13–15)

But it wasn't long before another cycle of sin began.

Their short memory—**they soon forgot His** miracles for them.

Their self-will—**they** would **not wait for His** guidance.

Their lust—they abandoned self-control in their craving for food (Num. 11:1–35).

Their provocation—they **tested God**.

Well, this time God **gave them** what they wanted, **but sent** a loathsome disease among them (Num. 11:20). Their history teaches us to be careful to pray always in the will of God because, as Matthew Henry said, "What is asked in passion is often given in wrath."

Dathan and Abiram, the Rebels (106:16–18)

Their rejection of God's leadership—**Dathan and Abiram**, together with Korah and On, were leaders of a rebellion against **Moses and Aaron** (Num. 16:1–30). They **envied** these two men of God. Also they wanted to intrude into the office of the priesthood. In rebelling against God's holy ones, that is, against men who were set apart as God's representatives, they were rebelling against God's rule. As a result, **the earth opened up and swallowed** the leaders and their families. And **fire** burst forth to devour the two hundred and fifty other men who offered incense to the Lord (Num. 16:31–35).

The Golden Calf (106:19–23)

Their idolatry—Before Moses had come down from Mount Sinai with the law of God, the people **made a** golden **calf and worshiped** it (Ex. 32:4). **They** exchanged the **glory** of God for the likeness **of an ox that eats grass**. Instead of acknowledging **God** as their **Savior** from Egypt, they gave all the honor to the lifeless calf. God would have destroyed them in a moment if Moses had not interceded. Like a soldier who covers a break in a wall with his body, so **Moses . . . stood before Him in the breach to turn away** God's **wrath**.

The Evil Report of the Spies (106:24–27)

Their faithlessness at Kadesh Barnea (Num. 14:2, 27, 28)—God had promised them **the pleasant land**, a land that was ideal for location, climate and resources. The promise contained all that was necessary to enter and occupy the land. But they did not believe His promise, and turned up their noses at (**despised**) **the land**. Instead of marching forward in faith, they sulked **in their tents**. **Therefore** God **raised His** hand in an oath to destroy that generation **in the wilderness** and to disperse **their descendants among the nations** of the world.

Sin with People of Moab (106:28–31)

Their sinful worship of the Baal of Peor—The men of Israel not only committed fornication with the daughters of Moab, they also joined in sacrificing **to the dead** and in other pagan ceremonies involved in the worship of the **Baal of Peor** (Num. 25:3–8). God was so infuriated that He sent a **plague** to slay the people by the thousands. When **Phinehas** saw an Israelite taking a heathen woman to his tent, he slew both of them with his spear. This **stopped** the **plague**, but only after twenty-four thousand had died. This act was a positive proof of his **righteousness**, and was rewarded by a covenant of peace. The Lord said:

> Behold, I give to him My covenant of peace; and it shall be to him and his descendants after him a covenant of an everlasting priesthood, because he was zealous for his God, and made atonement for the children of Israel (Num. 25:12, 13).

Trouble at Meribah (106:32, 33)

The sin of Moses (Num. 20:2–13)—**At the waters of** Meribah (**strife**), the people were blatantly unbelieving. They accused **Moses** of leading them into the wilderness to die of thirst. Instead of speaking to the rock, as God said, Moses struck it twice with his rod. He also **spoke rashly** against the people for their rebellion. As a result God decreed that he would be denied the privilege of leading the people of Israel into the land of promise.

In Canaan—Same Old Story (106:34–39)

The new environment of Canaan did not change the nature of the Israelites, as seen by:

106:34 *Their failure to exterminate the pagan inhabitants.* The debased Canaanites were a gangrenous limb of the human race. After bearing with them for hundreds of years, God decided that the only solution was amputation, and committed the surgery to Israel. But they failed to obey Him (Judg. 1:27–36).

106:35 *Their intermingling with the heathen.* By fraternizing and intermarrying with the pagans, Israel corrupted its own religion and morals.

106:36 *Their idolatry.* Soon the Jews were worshiping **idols** instead of the true and living God.

106:37–39 *Their human sacrifices.* Particularly revolting to the Lord was the sacrifice of **their sons and daughters** to appease the **demons** (2 Kgs. 3:27; 21:6; Ezek. 16:20, 21). Sons and daughters of God's chosen people were sacrificed to the filthy idols of Canaan, **and the land was polluted with** murder.

The Times of the Judges (106:40–46)

"Offended with His people," writes Barnes, "the Lord treated them as if they were an abomination to Him." **He** turned **them** over to **the Gentiles**—Mesopotamians, the Midianites, the Philistines, the Moabites and others. These ungodly nations lorded it **over** the Jews, oppressing them and persecuting them. In spite of this treatment, the people persisted in their sin and rebellion against Jehovah. But whenever they turned to Him in repentance, He looked down on them in mercy. Mindful of **His covenant**, He turned from judgment to display His steadfast love. Even during the darkest hours of their captivity, the Lord caused **them to be pitied by** their captors—a touching example of mercy triumphing over judgment.—

Save and Regather (106:47)

The psalmist prays for the regathering of his people, scattered throughout the nations of the world. This will result in great **thanks** ascending **to** God's **holy name**; His people will make it their glory to **praise** Him. The prayer anticipates the petitions of the remnant of Israel in the future time of the Tribulation, prior to the inauguration of Christ's glorious kingdom.

Doxology (106:48)

With this rapturous note we come not only to the end of the Psalm but to the end of the fourth book of the Psalms. But in coming to the end we must resist the temptation to put this Psalm in a dispensational pigeon-hole, limiting its message to the wicked nation of Israel and failing to see our own history reflected in it. In 1 Corinthians 10:11 we distinctly read:

> Now all these things happened to them as examples, and they were written for our admonition, upon whom the ends of the ages have come.

It warns us against *ingratitude.* If Israel should have been grateful for redemption by power from Egypt, how much more grateful should we be for redemption by the blood of Christ from sin and from Satan!

It warns us against *forgetfulness.* How easily we forget the suffering and death of the Lord Jesus. How guilty we are of "the curse of dry-eyed Christianity."

It warns us against *complaining.* It becomes a way of life to complain about the weather, about our living conditions, about minor inconveniences, and even about lumps in the gravy.

It warns us against *self-will,* against putting our will above the will of God. "He gave them their request, but sent leanness into their soul" (v. 15).

It warns us against *criticizing* God's leadership, whether governmental officials, elders in the assembly, or parents in the home.

It warns us against *idolatry*—the worship of money, home, cars, education, pleasure, or worldly success.

It warns us against *disbelief* in the promises of God. This sin caused Israel to wander in the wilderness for thirty-eight years and barred the guilty ones from entering the promised land.

It warns us against *immorality.* The worship of the Baal of Peor involved gross sexual sin. God's attitude toward it is seen in the disaster which He visited upon the culprits.

It warns us against what might seem to be *"trivial" disobedience.* Moses struck the rock instead of speaking to it. That may not seem very serious to us, but no disobedience is trivial.

It warns us against *marrying unbelievers.* God is a God of separation. He hates to see the corruption of His people through the formation of unequal yokes.

Finally, it warns us against the *sacrifice of our children.* Too seldom do Christian parents hold the work of the Lord before their children as a desirable way in which to spend their lives. Too often our children are raised with the ambition to make a name for themselves in business or the professions. We raise them for the world—and for hell.

V. BOOK 5 (PSALMS 107—150)

Psalm 107: Let the Redeemed Say So

There is a common behavior pattern in the lives of God's people which can be summarized by two word series:

Sin	or	Rebellion
Servitude		Retribution
Supplication		Repentance
Salvation		Restoration

First of all the people stray from the Lord, walking in disobedience to His Word. Then they suffer the bitter consequences of their backsliding. When they come to themselves, they cry out to the Lord in confession of sin. He then forgives their sin and brings them back into the place of blessing once more. It is the old story of the prodigal son and surely no story is more familiar, more relevant and true to life.

Two basic facts emerge from the contemplation of this ever-recurring cycle. One is the perpetual proneness of the human heart to wander away from the living God. The other is the seemingly inexhaustible mercy of the Lord in restoring His people when they come to Him in repentance.

Here in Psalm 107, the merciful deliverance of the Lord is presented in four different pictures:

Rescue for those lost in the desert (vv. 4–9).
Rescue for those in prison (vv. 10–16).
Recovery for those who are seriously ill (vv. 17–22).
Deliverance for seamen in a terrible storm (vv. 23–32).

Introduction (107:1–3)

First, however, there is an introduction which sounds the theme. It is a call to **give thanks to the Lord**. Two reasons are given—the Lord **is good**, and **His mercy endures forever**. Either reason would be more than enough cause for ceaseless gratitude.

A special class of people is now singled out as particular recipients of His goodness and love, namely, those **whom He has redeemed** from persecution, slavery, oppression and trouble, and brought back to the land from worldwide dispersion. While it is clear that the psalmist has Israel in view, we will not surrender these verses to that nation exclusively because we too have been bought back from the slave market of sin, and as **the redeemed of the Lord** we want to join in the anthem of thanksgiving.

Rescue for Those Lost in the Desert (107:4–9)

This first picture seems clearly to allude to Israel's forty-year trek through the waste, howling **wilderness**. The people were lost. They were **hungry**. They were **thirsty**. They were disheartened and discouraged. **Then they cried out to the Lord.** Suddenly their meanderings ended. The Lord **led them** by a direct route to the Plains of Moab. This proved the jumping-off place for their entrance into Canaan. And there they found **a city** where they could feel at home at last. How they (and all of us) should **give thanks to the Lord** continually for His undying love, and for the **wonderful** care He bestows on His people. For in the Promised Land **He satisfies** the thirsty, and provides the finest food for **the hungry**.

Release for Those in Prison (107:10–16)

107:10–12 The second vignette of Israel's history concerns the Babylonian captivity. The psalmist likens the seventy years to confinement in prison.

Babylon was like a dark, gloomy dungeon. The Israelites felt like chained prisoners condemned to penal servitude (although conditions in Babylon were not as severe as they had been in Egypt). It was because of their rebellion **against the words of God**, their spurning of His Word that they were sent off into exile. Crushed and beaten by hard **labor, they fell down** under the load, and no one took sides with them.

107:13–16 But when they **cried out to the LORD, . . . He saved** them from the land of darkness **and broke** the chains of their captivity. Now the only decent thing for them to do is to **give thanks to the LORD** for His unchanging love and for all the **wonderful works** He has done for them.

> **For He has broken the gates of bronze,**
> **And cut bars of iron in two.**

This is the verse that leads us to believe that the psalmist is referring to the Babylonian captivity in this section. The identifying link is found in Isaiah 45:2 where the Lord used almost identical words to describe the way in which He would bring the exile to a close. Speaking to Cyrus, He said:

> I will go before you and make the crooked places straight; I will break in pieces the gates of bronze, and cut the bars of iron.

The context makes it clear that He was referring to the termination of the exile in Babylon.

Recovery for Those Who Are Seriously Ill (107:17–22)

107:17–20 This third section may refer to the nation of Israel at the time of Christ's First Advent. The nation was sick at the time. They had just been through the trying days of the Maccabees. Some were **fools**, suffering God's judgment **because of their iniquities**. They had lost appetite for **food**, and were rapidly drawing **near to the gates of death**. A godly remnant of the nation was praying and waiting for the hope of Israel. God **sent** forth **His word and healed them**. His Word here may refer to the Lord Jesus Christ, the Logos, who came with a healing ministry to the house of Israel. How many times we read in the Gospel records "and He healed them all." Matthew reminds us that in His healing of the sick, the Savior fulfilled what was spoken by the prophet Isaiah, "He Himself took our infirmities and bore our sicknesses" (Matt. 8:17). If it be objected that not all the Israelites were healed, we should remember that not all entered the promised land and not all returned from captivity in Babylon either.

107:21, 22 Again the psalmist calls on men to praise the Lord for His **goodness and for His wonderful works**. The gift of His Son is special cause for sacrifices of thanksgiving and for recital of His deeds in songs of joy.

Deliverance for Seamen in a Terrible Storm (107:23–32)

107:23–27 The last picture is most graphic. It is about seamen who worked on ocean-going **ships**. They knew something about the power of **the LORD** whenever they ran into a storm at sea. First the **wind** would arise to alarming proportions. Then **the waves** would form gargantuan mountains of water. The ship would rise up on the wave, its timbers creaking. At the crest, it would shudder, then crash into the trough. The stoutest ship would be like a matchbox in a swirling, foaming cauldron.

In a storm like that, the toughest sailors lose courage. It is all they can do to **stagger like a drunken man** around the ship to perform their duties. They feel a terrible sense of their own insignificance and **are at their wits' end**.

107:28–30 It is not surprising that cursing, irreligious sailors pray at a time like this. And the Lord is gracious enough to hear those prayers of desperation. **He calms the storm** and the **waves** become **still**. What a relief! The men can navigate once more, and soon they are entering the port toward which they were sailing.

107:31, 32 The relieved seamen should not forget to thank **the LORD** for His unfailing **goodness** and all the **wonderful** answers to prayer He gives. They should pay their vows by joining with His faithful people in extolling Him, by praising **Him in the company of the elders**.

Are we stretching matters by saying that this depicts Israel's final storm and her subsequent entrance into the kingdom of peace? The storm suggests the Great Tribulation. The sea typifies the seething, restless Gentile nations. The seamen represent the nation of Israel, tossed about by the other nations during the Time of Jacob's Trouble. A believing remnant of the nation calls upon the Lord. He then personally intervenes, returning to earth to set up His reign of peace and prosperity.

The Government and Grace of God (107:33–43)

107:33, 34 The remaining verses of the Psalm explain how God reacts when His people are disobedient and then again when they are obedient. By His almighty power, **He** makes **rivers** bone-dry and causes bubbling springs to evaporate. It is nothing for Him to cause **fruitful land** to turn into salty wasteland when the people turn their backs on Him.

107:35–38 But He can also reverse the process, and this is exactly what will happen when the Prince of Peace returns to rule over the millennial earth. The Negev will be dotted with plentiful **pools of water**. The Sahara and the Mojave will be well-irrigated gardens. Housing settlements will spring up in places that have been uninhabitable for centuries. Modern cities will dot the landscape. The wilderness will suddenly become arable. Grain, vegetables, fruit and berries will grow in profusion. By His blessing there will be bumper crops everywhere, and the **cattle** will be disease-resistant.

107:39–43 The other side of the picture is seen in the way He deals with wicked rulers.

> Tyrants lose their strength and are brought low in the grip of misfortune and sorrow; He brings princes into contempt and leaves them wandering in a trackless waste (vv. 39, 40, NEB).

This was the fate of Pharaoh, Herod, and Hitler, and it will be the termination of the evil triumvirate during the Tribulation.

Yet God lifts **the poor** out of their troubles and blesses them with large families. When good men **see** this, they are profoundly glad. When the ungodly see it, they don't have a word to say (which is unusual for them).

Whoever is wise will see the hand of God behind the changing fortunes of men and of nations and will learn lessons from history and current events. Especially will they consider **the lovingkindness of the LORD** in His dealings with those who obey His Word.

Psalm 108: Help! Quick!

It is not surprising if this Psalm has a familiar ring to it. The first five verses are much the same as Psalm 57:7–11, and the last eight verses are almost identical with Psalm 60:5–12. The Psalm moves successively from praise, to prayer, to promise, to a problem, to prayer again and finally to a bright prospect.

Praise (108:1–5)

108:1, 2 The psalmist **is steadfast** in his determination to **praise** the Lord for His ceaseless love and faithfulness. He is ready and eager to **sing** and make melody to the Most High. While it is still dark, he calls his soul to wake up, and rouses his **lute and harp** from their silent rest in order to greet **the dawn** with songs of thanksgiving. Not a bad idea—to start the day with praise!

108:3 Nor will he confine his song to the privacy of his home or to his own little neighborhood. Wherever he goes, **the peoples** will hear him worshiping the LORD, **the nations** will echo to his songs of praise. This determination should be ours as well.

108:4, 5 Why was David so enthusiastic about the Lord? Because His **mercy** towers in its immensity **above the heavens**, and His **truth** is sky-high. His praise should correspond to His greatness. So may He **be exalted . . . above the heavens**, and may His **glory** be **above all the earth**.

As we listen to David's rapturous songs of adoration, we understand better why someone wrote:

> Praise is more divine than prayer;
> Prayer points the happy road to heaven.
> Praise is already there.

Prayer (108:6)

Now he turns to petition. The country was under attack by enemy forces; the outlook was ominous. The supernatural strokes of success that Israel had so often experienced were strangely absent, therefore he implores the Lord to deliver His **beloved** ones by sending help to turn back the invaders.

Promise (108:7–9)

108:7, 8 Unruffled and majestic in His sanctuary, **God** asserts His sovereign rights over Israel and over the Gentile nations as well. He promises that the Messiah's dominion will include the district of **Shechem**, where Jacob's well is located; **the Valley of Succoth**, where Jacob built booths for his cattle (Gen. 33:17); the lofty plateau of **Gilead**, famous alike for its pastures and medicinal balm; and **Manasseh**, with territory on both sides of the Jordan. **Ephraim** will be His **helmet**, leading the tribes in defending the realm. **Judah** will be His **lawgiver**, the seat of government, as promised in Genesis 49:10.

108:9 Three Gentile nations are mentioned—**Moab, Edom** and **Philistia**—as representative of the foreign territory which will also be included in the kingdom. **Moab** will be His **washpot**, a figure expressing contempt and control. He will **cast** His **shoe . . . over Edom**, implying ownership, servitude, and scorn. While **Moab** and **Edom** will be tributary vassals, **Philistia** will be crushed. **"Over Philistia I will triumph."**

Problem (108:10, 11)

The promise of victory over Edom makes David restless to see its fulfillment. Sela, the capital city (also known as Petra), was renowned as being inaccessible and impregnable. He longs for someone to **lead** him **to Edom** that he might shout in triumph over it. But there is a problem—**God** has hidden His face from Israel. His help has been missing, with disastrous results. Israel's **armies** have been marching on to war—and defeat, because the Lord is not with them.

Prayer (108:12)

Without the Lord the situation is hopeless, no one else will do, David had lived long enough to know that man's **help is useless**. He asks the Mighty God to take up Israel's cause again by giving **help** on the battlefield.

Prospect (108:13)

As soon as he leaves the place of prayer, the psalmist is singing a note of triumph. **"Through God we will do valiantly," for it is He who will** crush the opposition and give victory to His beloved ones. This is the confidence, born of faith, that Paul Gerhardt expressed so eloquently:

> Is God for me? I fear not,
> Though all against me rise;
> When I call on Christ my Savior,
> The host of evil flies.
> My Friend, the Lord Almighty,
> And He who loves me, God;
> What enemy can harm me,
> Though coming like a flood?
>
> The world may pass and perish,
> Thou, God, wilt not remove;
> No hatred of all devils
> Can part me from Thy love;
> No hungering nor thirsting,
> No poverty nor care,
> No wrath of mighty princes
> Can reach my shelter there.
>
> My heart with joy upleapeth,
> Grief cannot linger there,
> She singeth high in glory,
> Amidst the sunshine fair.
> The sun that shines upon me
> Is Jesus and His love,
> The fountain of my singing
> Is deep in heaven above.

Psalm 109: The Fate of God's Enemies

Of all the Psalms of imprecation, this one is unrivaled for first place. No other calls down the judgment of God with such distilled vitriol or with such comprehensive detail. The reader cannot fail to be intrigued and fascinated by the sheer ingenuity of the psalmist in the variety of punishments he invokes on his foes!

109:1–3 The Psalm opens with disarming mildness. David pleads for help from the **God of** his **praise**, that is, the God whom he praises. His enemies have been conducting a vicious verbal assault on him, hurling all manner of **lying** charges against him. **Words of hatred** come zeroing in at him from every direction. What makes it especially hard to take is that the attacks are wholly unjustified.

109:4, 5 David has shown **love** and kindness to his assailants, and what does he receive in return? A barrage of false accusations. And all the while he is praying for them. For every kindness, they repay him with insult, and **for love**, they reward him with **hatred**.

109:6, 7 It is at this point that he seems to dip his pen in acid. From now on the imprecations, hot and lethal, shoot out from his wounded soul. From the many foes of verses 1–5, he now turns to concentrate on one in particular.

Eventually this man will be caught and brought to trial. When that happens, let the Lord arrange the circumstances so that **a wicked man** will be his **accuser**, a satanic man his plaintiff. At the conclusion of the trial let the verdict be **"Guilty!"** And if he appeals the sentence, let his request be counted as contempt of court and the penalty increased.

109:8–10 As for his life, may it be

a short one and may someone else **take his office**. This particular imprecation is quoted of Judas and of his office as treasurer of the band of disciples in Acts 1:20:

> For it is written in the book of Psalms, "Let his dwelling place be desolate, and let no one live in it"; and, "Let another take his office."

It will help us to understand the severity of this Psalm if we remember that it refers not only to David and his foe, but also to Messiah and His betrayer, and also perhaps to Israel and the Anti-Christ in a day still future.

As for the foe's family, let **his children** become **fatherless and his wife** be widowed. **Let his children continually be vagabonds** and beggars, evicted from the ruins that used to be their home.

109:11–13 As for his estate, **let the creditor** step in and **seize all that he has**, and let all that he has earned be shared by **strangers**.

Since he showed no mercy, **let** no **mercy** be shown **to him**, no pity to his **fatherless children**. Let the family name go into oblivion before a **generation** passes. (In eastern reckoning, this is one of the most shameful punishments that could be inflicted.)

109:14, 15 Even his predecessors are not blameless. Let **the Lord** remember **the iniquity of his fathers . . . and let not the sin of his mother be blotted out**. The exact nature of their crimes is not given, but their guilt must have been aggravated since the psalmist goes on to ask that their sins might never be forgotten by the Lord and that **the memory of them** be **cut off . . . from the earth**.

109:16–20 In verse 16 we read the stinging indictment of the wicked man. It was his lifestyle to refrain from showing kindness. Instead he actively and aggressively hunted down **the poor and needy**, and drove the brokenhearted to their death. It is not hard to find Judas in this verse, maliciously hounding the sinless Savior to the cross.

But there is an inexorable law of retribution in the moral realm. Whatever a man sows, that is what he reaps. The harvest is inescapable. There is no getting away with sin. Here the psalmist asks that the law of cause and effect take its full course. This man **loved** to curse others; now may his curses boomerang on himself. He never wanted others to enjoy blessings; now **let** blessings stay **far** away **from him**. He swaggered about **with cursing** as his coat; now let those curses penetrate his life **like water** penetrates a sponge; let them soak into every part of his being, even into the marrow of **his bones**. May cursing cover him like the clothes that he wears, "cling to him like a girdle he can never take off" (Knox).

This then is David's desire for his **accusers** and his calumniators. He has scarcely overlooked one detail in the catalog of judgment. As someone has said, "All is in fact invoked on the wicked that any man could ever desire to see inflicted on an enemy."

109:21–25 The psalmist closes with two prayers and a burst of praise. First, he prays for deliverance from his troubles. He wants **the Lord** to take his part **for** His **name's sake**, that is, in order to glorify Himself as the God of power and justice. In dealing on David's behalf, the Lord will demonstrate once more that His **mercy is good**.

The psalmist's plight is grave. Not only is he **poor and needy**, his **heart** is **wounded within** him. His life is ebbing out **like a** lengthening **shadow**.

He is being **shaken off** from life as easily as a man shakes **a locust** off his hand. **Through** prolonged **fasting**, his **knees** are buckling and his body is reduced to skin and bones. His enemies laugh at him in his pitiable state; they tauntingly **shake their heads** at him.

109:26–29 In his second prayer, he asks the Lord to vindicate him before the foes. When Jehovah comes to his help and rescues him, then the assailants will **know that** it was an act of divine intervention—the **hand** of the Lord. What difference will it make if they **curse**, as long as the Lord blesses. The enemies will **be ashamed**, but the psalmist will **rejoice** at that time. May they be **clothed with shame** and confusion, yes, wrapped in **disgrace as with** a full-cut **mantle**.

109:30, 31 Finally, we hear David planning the **praise** he will offer to **the LORD** when his prayers are answered. It will not be ordinary praise but great thanks. It will not be private but in the midst of the **multitude**. And the theme will be that Jehovah stands **at the right hand of the poor**, delivering **him from those who** have marked him for execution. It gives great confidence to have the Lord as one's defender. As F. B. Meyer says:

> How brave is the accused if he enters court leaning on the arm of the noblest in the land. How futile is it to condemn when the Judge of all stands beside to justify?[71]

IMPRECATORY PSALMS

So much for what Psalm 109 actually says. But it would not be intellectually honest to pass on without facing up to the problem that is implicit in the imprecatory Psalms. The problem, of course, is how to reconcile the vindictive, judgmental spirit of these Psalms with the spirit of forgiveness and love that is elsewhere enjoined upon God's people. Since the 109th is the king of the imprecatory Psalms, this seems to be the place to face the problem.

First, I will list some of the explanations which have been put forward but which do not seem entirely convincing to me. Then I will give what I understand to be the true explanation, although it too is not without difficulties.

It is pointed out that these imprecations are not so much invocations of vengeance or of punishment on the wicked as they are predictions of what will happen to God's enemies. Thus Unger says:

> Curses delivered against individuals by holy men are not the expressions of revenge, passion, or impatience; they are predictions and therefore not such as God condemns.[72]

Many of these passages could just as correctly be translated in the future tense as in the imperative.

A second explanation is that David was speaking as God's anointed. Because of his position, he was God's representative. Therefore, he was permitted to pronounce these severe judgments. (Here it should be noted, however, that not all the imprecatory Psalms were written by David.)

Then again some view these passages as a historical record of how these men felt, without approving of their harshness. Concerning this view Barnes writes:

> These expressions are a mere record of what actually occurred in the mind of the psalmist, and are preserved to us as an illustration of human nature when partially sanctified. According to this view the Spirit of inspiration is no more responsible for these feelings on the part of the psalmist than He is for the acts of David, Abraham,

> Jacob or Peter. . . . The proper notion of inspiration does not require us to hold that the men who were inspired were absolutely sinless. . . . According to this view the expressions which are used in this record are not presented for our imitation.[73]

And there are other explanations. The imprecatory Psalms are defended by reminding us that because Israel was God's chosen nation, therefore Israel's enemies were God's enemies. That there is something in each one of us which righteously approves of proper punishment for crimes. That the psalmists describe what sinners deserve and do not express any personal desire for revenge.

As I said before, I do not find any of these explanations completely satisfying. The explanation that appeals to me most is that the imprecatory Psalms express a spirit that was *proper for a Jew living under the law, but not proper for a Christian living under grace.* The reason these Psalms seem harsh to us is because we are viewing them in the light of the New Testament revelation. David and the other psalmists did not have the New Testament. As Scroggie points out:

> . . . it will be well to recognize at once the fact that the previous dispensation was inferior to the present one, that while the Law is not contrary to the Gospel it is not equal to it, that while Christ came to fulfill the Law He came also to transcend it. We must be careful not to judge expressions in the Psalter which savor of vindictiveness and vengeance by the standards of the Pauline Epistles.[74]

While the inclusion of a man's family in his judgment seems rather extreme to us, it was justified to the psalmist by the fact that God had threatened to visit the iniquity of the fathers upon the children to the third and fourth generation (Ex. 20:5; 34:7; Num. 14:18; Deut. 5:9). Whether we like it or not, there are laws in the spiritual realm under which sins have a way of working themselves out in a man's family. No man is an island; the consequences of his acts reach out to others as well as affecting himself.

We live today in the acceptable year of the Lord. When this age passes and the day of vengeance of our God begins, language such as that of the imprecatory Psalms will once again be on the lips of God's people. For instance, the Tribulation martyrs will say, "How long, O Lord, holy and true, until You judge and avenge our blood on those who dwell on the earth?" (Rev. 6:10).

One final consideration! The severity of the imprecations in the Psalms prepare our hearts in a feeble way to appreciate the One who bore every curse in His body on the cross so that we might be eternally free from the curse and from cursing. Not all the punishments described in the Psalms put together give a feeble, faint reflection of the avalanche of judgment which He endured as our Substitute.‡

Psalm 110: David's Son and David's Lord

This **Psalm of David** enjoys the distinction of being quoted or referred to more frequently in the NT than any other passage in the OT. It is quite clearly a Psalm of the Messiah—first as the glorified One at God's right hand, then as the King of glory returning to earth to take the scepter of universal government, and also as the eternal Priest according to the order of Melchizedek.

110:1 In the first verse David

quotes **the LORD** as saying **to** his **Lord**:

> **"Sit at My right hand, till I make Your enemies Your footstool."**

The key to understanding this lies in identifying the two distinct persons referred to by the name of "Lord." The first use of the word refers unmistakably to Jehovah.[75] The other word "Lord" is the Hebrew *adon* and means "master" or "ruler." It was sometimes used as a name of God and sometimes applied to a human master. Although the word itself does not always indicate a divine person, the words that follow show that David's Lord (*Adon*) was equal with God.

One day when Jesus was speaking to the Pharisees in Jerusalem, He asked them what they believed concerning the identity of the Messiah. From whom would the Promised One be descended? They answered correctly that He would be the son of David. But Jesus showed them that according to Psalm 110 (which they acknowledged to be messianic) the Messiah would also be David's Lord. How could He be David's son and David's Lord at the same time? And how could David, the king, have someone who was his Lord on earth?

The answer of course was that the Messiah would be both God and man. *As God,* He would be *David's Lord. As man,* He would be *David's son.* And Jesus Himself, combining in His Person both deity and humanity, was David's Master and David's son.

It was the moment of truth for the Pharisees. Yet in spite of all the evidence, they were unwilling to acknowledge Jesus as the long-awaited Messiah. So we read:

> And no one was able to answer Him a word, nor from that day on did anyone dare question Him anymore (Matt. 22:41–46; cf. Mark 12:35–37; Luke 20:41–44).

The NT writers leave no room for doubt that the One who is seated at God's **right hand** is none other than Jesus of Nazareth (Matt. 26:64; Mark 14:62; 16:19; Luke 22:69; Acts 2:34, 35; 5:31; 7:55, 56; Rom. 8:34; 1 Cor. 15:24ff; Eph. 1:20; Col. 3:1; Heb. 1:3, 13; 8:1; 10:12, 13; 12:2; 1 Pet. 3:22; Rev. 3:21). Therefore verse 1 tells what Jehovah **said to** the **LORD** Jesus on the latter's ascension day when He sat down **at** God's **right hand**. But He is only there **till** His **enemies** are made His **footstool**.

110:2 Between verses 1 and 2 we have what H. A. Ironside called "the great parenthesis"[76]—the Church Age which extends from the enthronement of Christ to His Second Coming. In verse 2 we see Jehovah sending forth Messiah's royal **rod** from **Zion**; in other words, the Lord establishes Christ as King with Jerusalem as His capital. This scepter is the symbol of royal authority. Christ is given authority to reign over all the earth in the midst of His enemies. **"Rule in the midst of Your enemies."** Prior to this time the Lord Jesus will have destroyed His unreconstructed foes. Here it is not a matter of destroying His foes but of ruling over those foes who have become His friends and who gladly submit to His **rule**.

110:3 This is confirmed by verse 3. His **people** offer themselves willingly on **the day** He leads His army upon the holy mountain. Or as the NKJV states it:

> **Your people shall be volunteers in the day of Your power; in the beauties of holiness. . . .**

Here a willing people greet the King in holy array. "In their lives and conduct," writes Barnes, "they will manifest all the beauty or attractiveness which there is in a holy and pure character."

The last part of verse 3 has been the torture of translators and commentators. Scroggie paraphrases as follows: "... as dew is born of its mother the morning, so Thy army shall come to Thee numerous, fresh, bright and powerful."[77]

110:4 One of the extraordinary features of the Kingdom is that the Lord Jesus will combine in His person the dual offices of king and **priest**. It is a combination that is highly dangerous in the case of mere human rulers; the loud, long cry for separation of church and state has not been without valid cause. But the combination is ideal when Jesus is the Ruler. Uncorrupted kingship and spiritual priesthood will give the world an administration such as it has longed for but has never known.

In verse 4 we learn four things concerning the priesthood of the Messiah:

He was made **a priest** by the oath of Jehovah.
This appointment was irrevocable.
His priesthood is eternal.

It is **according to the order of Melchizedek**.

The phrase **"according to the order of Melchizedek"** is interpreted for us in Hebrews 5—7. There the priesthood of Melchizedek is compared and contrasted with the Aaronic or Levitical priesthood.

Under the law God designated the men of the tribe of Levi and the family of Aaron to be priests. Their priesthood was a matter of parentage and it terminated with their death.

The priesthood of that mysterious personage Melchizedek was by sovereign appointment of God. It was not inherited from his parents ("without father, without mother, without genealogy," Heb. 7:3a) and there is no mention of his priesthood ever beginning or ending ("having neither beginning of days nor end of life," Heb. 7:3b). In these and other ways, the Melchizedek priesthood was superior to that of Levi. Melchizedek was a prototype of the Lord Jesus. Our Lord's priesthood was not a matter of parentage; He was of the tribe of Judah, not Levi. His priesthood was established by the sovereign eternal decree of God, and since He lives in the power of an endless life, His priesthood will never end.

Another way in which **Melchizedek** foreshadowed the Messiah is that he was both king and priest. His name and title signify that he was king of righteousness and king of peace (Heb. 7:2). He was also priest of God Most High (Gen. 14:18).

110:5 The last three verses of the Psalm picture the Lord Jesus as a mighty Conqueror, putting down all lawlessness and rebellion prior to the inauguration of His kingdom. The problem of identifying the personages in these verses is largely solved if we think of them as being addressed to Jehovah and as referring to the Messiah-King. Thus verse 5 would read:

> **The Lord** (Adonai—here the Lord Jesus) **is at Your** (Jehovah's) **right hand; He** (Messiah) **shall execute kings in the day of His wrath**.

110:6 It is the Lord Jesus marching forth against the Gentile nations, as foreseen in Joel 3:9–17; Zechariah 14:3; and Revelation 19:11–21. He executes judgment **among the nations**, strewing the landscape with their corpses. The further statement **"He shall execute the heads of many countries"** could also be translated "He shall strike through the head over a wide land." This could be a reference to the doom of the Man of Sin, "whom the Lord will consume with the breath of His mouth and destroy with the brightness of His coming" (2 Thess. 2:8).

110:7 As He goes forth to deal with His foes, the King **shall drink of the brook by the wayside**. Since water is often a type of the Holy Spirit (John 7:38, 39), this suggests that the Lord is refreshed and reinvigorated by the ministry of the Spirit, and this explains why He subsequently lifts up His **head** in victory.

Psalm 111: The Wonderful Works of the Lord

There are three threads that run through Psalm 111:

- the works of Jehovah (vv. 2–4, 6–7).
- the words of Jehovah, under such synonyms as covenant (vv. 5, 9), precepts (v . 7).
- the everlasting character of all that He is and does (vv. 3, 5, 8–10).

In the Hebrew it is an acrostic Psalm. Each of the first eight verses has two lines. The last two have three lines each. Each of the twenty-two lines begins with a letter of the Hebrew alphabet in proper order.

The subject of the Psalm is the excellencies of the enthroned Christ. Israel is singing the praises of the One who called them out of the darkness of Egypt and of the Babylonian captivity into His marvelous light.

111:1 The song opens with a call to the faithful to **praise the LORD** (Heb., "Hallelujah"), and with the psalmist's own determination to **praise the LORD** without inhibition or distraction. He will do this both in small assemblies of believers and in the great gatherings of the people, or as we might say, both in private and in public.

111:2, 3 The four descriptions of **the works of the LORD** here are true of all He does, but the "Mt. Everest" of all God's works to the OT Jew was the deliverance from Egypt. **The works of the LORD are great**; they form a fruitful study **by all who have pleasure in them**. They are stupendous displays of His glory and majesty, **and His righteousness endures forever**.

111:4, 5 He established the Passover as an enduring memorial of Israel's salvation by the blood of the lamb, a lasting remembrance of His grace and mercy. In the Lord's Supper, He left a memorial of our salvation by the blood of a better Lamb, the unforgettable reminder that He is **gracious and full of compassion**. Perhaps verse 5 refers especially to God's miraculous provision of **food** (lit. "prey") for the Israelites during their wilderness journeys. He never forgot that they were His covenant people. But it is *always* true that He is faithful to the promises He has made.

111:6 He gave His people another demonstration of His mighty works by dispossessing the Canaanite nations and bringing His people safely into the Promised Land, which the psalmist here calls **"the heritage of the nations."**

111:7–9 All God's **works** demonstrate that He is always faithful and just. **All His precepts** are absolutely dependable. He keeps His promises forever, and fulfills them faithfully and honorably. **He sent redemption to His people** at the time of the exodus, then later when He brought them back from the captivity in Babylon. He will do it again when He brings the twelve tribes back to the land of Israel prior to His glorious reign. It is all part of **His covenant,**

and it can never fail. **His name** is **holy and awesome**, or reverend, and as His name is, so is He!

111:10 Only the man who reverences Him has started on the road to **wisdom**. The more we obey Him, the more light He gives us. "Obedience is the organ of spiritual knowledge."

He is worthy to be praised **forever**!

Psalm 112: Rewards of the Righteous

112:1 There is a close correspondence between this Psalm and the preceding one, both in its acrostic form and in its spiritual teaching. It takes up where Psalm 111 leaves off—with **the man who fears the LORD** and who practices wisdom. Several of the things that are said about the Lord in the first are applied to the godly man in the second. We see the Sun of Righteousness shining in all His glory in the 111th; here we see the believer, like the moon, reflecting that glory. By beholding the beauty of the Lord, the believer is changed into the same beauty by the Holy Spirit (2 Cor. 3:18).

"Praise the LORD!" These words frequently expressed the psalmist's sentiments, and he has left a good example for the rest of us.

Who is the happy man? It is the one who reverences and submits to **the LORD, who delights greatly in His commandments**, and proves it by obeying them. He reaps the benefits that flow from a life of practical godliness. Such as—

112:2 *Distinguished Posterity.* **His descendants will** occupy positions of power and prestige; they will be honored because of their godly heritage. (In interpreting these blessings for the Church Age, we are wise to transfer them from their earthly, material meaning to the spiritual counterpart.)

112:3 *Prosperity.* It is generally true that obedience to the Word of God saves men from waste and poverty. The results of his righteousness, that is, of his honesty, diligence, and frugality continue to distant generations.

112:4 *Assured illumination.* There is no guarantee of immunity from darkness, but there is the promise that **light** will rise **in the darkness**. In all the dark times of life the Lord shows Himself to be **gracious, and full of compassion**.

112:5, 6 *Generosity.* Things go better for the man who is generous and who doesn't refuse to lend to others who are in genuine need. This man manages his business **with discretion** and justice. His life is built on a stable foundation, and he will be remembered long after he is gone.

112:7 *Freedom from Fear.* He doesn't have to live in constant fear of bad news, of business reverses, of natural calamities. He is **trusting in the LORD**, and knows that nothing can happen to him apart from God's will.

112:8 *Confidence under Attack.* Even **his enemies** do not upset his poise or calm. He is confident that though they might seem to have the upper hand at the moment, yet their downfall is certain, and he is on the winning side.

112:9 *Lasting Fruitfulness and Honor.* Because he has been generous, the results of his kindness **to the poor** will never cease to be remembered. He won't have to hang **his horn** (symbol of strength) in shame. Rather his head will be crowned with plaudits. Paul quotes this verse in 2 Corinthians 9:9 to show the lasting benefits of generosity.

112:10 *The Envy of the Wicked.* When **the wicked** shall **see** the eventual vindication and permanent honor of the godly, they will be chagrined and envious. They **will gnash** their **teeth** in fury, then become unhinged and evaporate. All that they lived for **shall perish** with them. Barnes notes:

This is in strong contrast to what is said in the Psalm would occur to the righteous. They would be prospered and happy; they would be able to carry out their plans; they would be respected while living, and remembered when dead; they would find God interposing in their behalf in the darkest hours; they would be firm and calm in the day of danger and of trouble; they would put their trust in the Lord, and all would be well. Surely there is an advantage . . . in being a friend of God.[78]

Psalm 113: So Great, Yet So Gracious

113:1–6 The first five verses present God as the One who is *infinitely high,* the last four as the One who is *intimately nigh.*

Our God is infinitely high. As such He is worthy to be praised.

By whom?	By all His **servants** (v. 1).
How?	By blessing His **name**, which means by thanking Him for all that He is (v. 2a).
How often?	Continually—now and **forevermore** (v. 2b).
Where?	Everywhere—from lands of sunrise to lands of sunset (v. 3a).
For what?	*For His Greatness.* He **is high above all nations, His glory above the heavens** (v. 4).
	For His matchlessness. No one can be compared to Him, seated on His throne **on high** (v. 5).
	For His limitless vision. There is nothing in heaven or earth that He does not see (v. 6). The text suggests that He has to humble Himself even **to behold the things** in heaven!

But, praise His name, the One who is infinitely high is also intimately nigh.

113:7–9 **The poor** can know this! He **lifts** them from **the dust**.

The **needy** can know this! He elevates them from their low estate and seats them **with princes**, with the excellent of the earth.

The barren woman can know this! **He grants** her **a home** and makes her **like a joyful mother of children**. Barrenness was a fearsome reproach among Jewish women. To be delivered from this curse was the occasion of the most extravagant joy, according to the Prayer Book Commentary.

Application

I was *poor,* but through faith in Christ I have become fantastically wealthy in spiritual things.

I was *needy,* but the Lord Jesus took this beggar from the dunghill and gave him wonderful Christian brothers and sisters, a fellowship that beats anything the world has to offer.

I was *barren,* with no fruit in my life for God. But He has delivered me from empty, wasteful existence to meaningful, productive life.

No wonder I sing with the psalmist: **Praise the Lord!**

He fills the throne, the throne above,
He fills it without wrong;
The object of His Father's love,
Theme of the ransomed's song.

Though high, yet He accepts the praise
His people offer here;
The faintest, feeblest cry they raise
Will reach the Savior's ear.
—*Thomas Kelly*

Psalm 114: The Powerful Presence of Lord

114:1 The saga of Israel's redemption from **Egypt**, her wilderness experiences, and her arrival in the land of promise was a tremendous display of the power of God from beginning to end. In fact, to the Jewish mind it was the greatest demonstration of divine power that had ever taken place.

What a historic time that was **when Israel went out of Egypt**, the long years of bondage and oppression over! Who can measure the ecstasy of the people to be emancipated from the Egyptians? No more would they cringe under threats and curses barked out at them in an alien tongue!

114:2 In time the territory assigned to the tribe of **Judah became** God's **sanctuary**. The temple was erected there in Jerusalem. And the entire land of **Israel** became **His dominion**—an area He tended with unwearied care. What was true in a geographic sense of Judah and Israel then is true in a spiritual sense of the church today.

114:3 When the people of Israel came to the Red Sea, the waters took one look and retreated in panic. But be assured that it was not the sight of this ragtag mob of refugees that caused the terror. **The sea** looked up and **saw** its Creator, then quickly **turned back** so that Israel could pass over without even getting their feet wet.

It was the same thing forty years later when they entered the Promised Land. The **Jordan** River halted its flow at the city of Adam, and the last barrier to entering the land became a causeway.

The Red Sea and the Jordan crossings are the two termini of this epic chapter in the nation's history. The Red Sea passage typifies our redemption from the world by God's power through identification with Christ in His death, burial and resurrection. The crossing of the Jordan speaks of deliverance from wilderness wandering and entering into our spiritual inheritance, again through Christ's death, burial and resurrection.

114:4 Between these two events there were other awesome examples of God's power. One of the most spectacular was the giving of the law at Mt. Sinai. Nature was so convulsed that **the mountains skipped like rams, the little hills like lambs**. It seems that the glory of God was so overpowering that the entire area was rocked as if by a cataclysm. So terrifying was the sight that Moses, the man of God, said, "I am exceedingly afraid and trembling" (Heb. 12:21). The writer of the Letter to the Hebrews reminds us that we have not come to that fearful mount of the law but to the throne of grace.

The terrors of law and of God
With me can have nothing to do;
My Savior's obedience and blood
Hide all my transgressions from view.
—*Augustus M. Toplady*

114:5, 6 The psalmist is so delighted by these exhibitions of God's power that he teases the **sea**, the **Jordan**, the **mountains** and the **little hills** to explain why they acted as they did. The questions form a mild taunt song, smiling at some of the greatest symbols of power and stability in nature for recoiling at a glance from the Lord.

114:7, 8 The argument follows that the whole **earth** should have the profoundest reverence and respect for such a God. He is the ever-great I AM and at the same time He is the **God of Jacob**, the unworthy one. He **turned the rock into a pool of water, the flint into a fountain of waters.** It happened twice (Ex. 17:6; Num. 20:11). The people of Israel were completely disheartened by thirst. They complained bitterly and even wished they were back in Egypt. God miraculously provided **a pool of water** for them out of a rock, first at Horeb, then at Meribah. Paul tells us that the *rock* was a type of *Christ*, struck for us on Calvary and yielding life-giving water to all who come to Him in faith (1 Cor. 10:4).

Psalm 115: Israel Renounces Idols

The Jews have now returned from their exile in Babylon; they are back in their own land. But they do not take any credit for it to themselves. Their restoration is due solely to Jehovah. He did it because of His unfailing love for His people and because of His faithfulness to His promise.

115:1, 2 For too long the heathen have been taunting the Israelites. **"So where is** your **God?** He doesn't seem to be very interested in you when He leaves you to languish in captivity for seventy years!" But now they can't say this any more. Their scorn and ridicule have been silenced. God has vindicated His name.

115:3 It should be apparent now to all the world that the true **God** is transcendent—**"Our God is in heaven"** and He is sovereign—**"He does whatever He pleases."** The transcendence of God means that He is exalted above the universe, and has His being apart from it. The sovereignty of God means that He is free to do **whatever He pleases**, and what He pleases is always good, just and wise.

115:4–7 It was because of their idolatry that God allowed the Jews to be taken captive by the Babylonians. But now that they have learned the impotence and worthlessness of **idols**, they taunt the heathen for their graven images.

The **idols** are made of **silver and gold**, and therefore their value is determined by conditions in the market place. They are manufactured by men and thus they are inferior to the ones who worship them. **They have mouths but they** cannot teach or predict the future. They have **eyes . . . but they do not see** the problems of their people. **They have ears but** no power to **hear** prayer. They have **noses . . . but they do not smell** the incense that is offered to them. **They have hands but** no power to feel. They have **feet . . . but they do not** move off their pedestal. They can't even **mutter through their throat**.

115:8 Those who make them are like them. It is a settled principle in the spiritual realm that men become like the object of their worship. Their moral standards are shaped by their god. **Everyone who trusts in** images becomes impure, feeble, obtuse and uncomprehending.

115:9 Only Jehovah is worthy of trust. So now a soloist steps forward and calls **Israel** to a life of unswerving **trust in the Lord**. The choir responds with the confession—**He is their help and their shield.**

115:10, 11 Next the priestly **house of Aaron** is exhorted to put its faith unreservedly **in the Lord**; the choir again responds with the acknowledgment that **He is their** tested and proven **help** and Defender. The third time the precentor widens his appeal to all **who fear the Lord**, possibly including Gentile converts as well. They too know that **He is their** true **help and their shield**.

115:12–15 It sounds as if the priests take up the song next, assuring the people that **the** same **Lord** who **has been mindful** of the nation in restoring their fortunes **will bless** them—the people, the priests, the proselytes, those of every age, rank, class and condition. They pray that God **will bless** His people and their descendants with **increase**—probably thinking of numerical increase for a nation whose ranks were depleted. But the prayer could also include spiritual and material prosperity. In addition they invoke the general blessing of **the Lord**, the One **who made heaven and earth**.

115:16 God made **the heavens** as His own dwelling place, but He assigned **the earth** as a place for **men** to live. And in this place man can worship and serve Him.

115:17, 18 Verse 17 mirrors the common view of OT saints that death ends a man's ability to **praise the LORD**. As far as they knew, **the dead** are in a condition of stony silence. We now know that those who die in faith pass immediately into the presence of the Lord. Though their bodies lie silent in the grave, yet their spirits are unfettered in worship and adoration of the Lord. But the climax of their argument is valid for us—that is, that we should bless the Lord while we are alive. And that is the vow with which the Psalm closes:

> **We will bless the LORD from this**
> **time forth and forevermore.**
> **Praise the LORD!**

Psalm 116: I Love the Lord!

The joy and gladness of the first Easter morning are singing throughout the Psalm. The garden tomb is empty. Christ has been raised from the dead by the glory of His Father. And now He bursts forth in a song of thanksgiving to God for answered prayer in connection with His Resurrection.

116:1–4 Notice how He begins: **"I love the LORD."** Only four monosyllables, yet the purest worship. To timid souls who mistakenly think that God can only be approached in grandiose language, it should be a tremendous encouragement to know that the simplest statement of love for the Lord is genuine worship.

But we need not stop there. Like the Savior, we can go on to recite the great things that God has done for us. This too is worship. The Lord Jesus overflowed with ceaseless thanks because His Father had **heard** His anguished **supplications** from Gethsemane and Golgotha. When **death** was tightening its ropes around Him, and **the pangs** of physical dissolution were laying **hold of** Him, when He was enduring agony beyond description, then He called to **the LORD** to **deliver** Him. And the Lord did. He did not save Him from dying, but He did save Him out of death.

116:5, 6 A third element of worship is found in telling out the excellencies of the Lord. The risen Christ here lists some of the virtues of God which were displayed in His Resurrection. God is **gracious**, that is, kind and good. God is **righteous**; all He does is just and fair. **God is merciful**; He is of great compassion. **The LORD preserves the simple**, which in the case of the Lord Jesus on the cross meant that He preserved the sincere, the guileless or the helpless. God saves His people when they are in danger.

116:7 Finally God deals **bountifully** with those who trust in Him—He is not miserly in His benefits. And so the Lord Jesus says, **"Return to your rest, O my soul."** His agitation, His anguish, His agony are over. God has heard Him and delivered Him. Now He enters into well-earned **rest**.

116:8–11 Our Lord next returns to a review of what His Father had done for Him. We learn from this that we need not fear to repeat ourselves in worship. God never tires to hear His children's praise. And the subject is worthy of endless repetition. Christ's heart was full of gratitude to the Father for His threefold deliverance: His **soul** was **delivered from** death; His **eyes** were delivered **from tears**; and His **feet** were delivered **from falling** or defeat. Now He walked **before the LORD in the land of the living**—a victor over sin, death, the grave, and Sheol.

The continuity of thought in verses 10, 11 is admittedly difficult. Perhaps the TEV catches the general meaning:

I kept on believing, even when I said, "I am completely crushed," even when I was afraid and said, "No one can be trusted."

His faith did not falter, even in the moment of His deepest agony, or when men proved how untrustworthy they were. What He said was not born out of distrust but out of deep conviction.

116:12, 13 And then there is a final element of worship, as expressed by the question, **"What shall I render to the LORD for all His benefits toward me?"** In our case, there can be no thought of repaying Him; any repayment we might make would be an insult to His grace. But there is an inborn desire to respond to His grace in some appropriate way. That way is to **take up the cup of salvation and call upon the name of the LORD.** To lift **up the cup of salvation** means to express thanksgiving to the Lord for saving us. Calling **upon the name of the LORD** means to make a special act of devotion in recognition of the greatness of His salvation.

116:14 The risen Savior was determined to **pay** His **vows to the LORD . . . in the presence of all His people**. These were **vows** of praise, worship and thanksgiving which He made before and during His passion. He **now** fulfills those **vows**.

116:15 Once again the flow of thought seems suddenly interrupted by the Lord's observation, **"Precious in the sight of the LORD is the death of His saints."** Even if we have difficulty fitting it into the context, we can still enjoy it as an isolated text. It is true of all **saints**—their death is **precious** to our God because it means they are with Him in glory. But it was never more true than in the case of the Lord Jesus. His death was **precious** to His Father because it provided a righteous basis upon which He could justify ungodly sinners.

116:16, 17 In verse 16, Jesus, the Risen One, is still "the Servant of Jehovah." It is as if He is saying, "I love my master . . . I will not go out free" (Ex. 21:5). And so He indentures Himself as a **servant** forever. As the Son of God's **maidservant**, He vows to serve God just as His mother Mary did, because Jehovah has **loosed** His **bonds**.

116:18, 19 Again He vows to **offer to** the Father **the sacrifice of thanksgiving, and . . . call upon the name of the LORD**. In the congregation of God's **people**, assembled at the temple in Jerusalem, the Lord Jesus **will** yet **pay** His **vows** as He leads them in a resounding chorus of praise **to the LORD**. This will take place when He returns to earth, the great Immanuel, to take the scepter of the universe in His nail-scarred hand.

Psalm 117: The Gentiles Glorify God

In this shortest chapter of the Bible, the **Gentiles** are called to **praise the LORD . . . for His merciful kindness** and enduring **truth**. The Apostle Paul grasped its significance and quoted verse 1 in Romans 15:11 to show that the Gentile nations share with Israel in the mercy of the Messiah. He came not only to confirm the promises given to the patriarchs but also that "the Gentiles might glorify God for His mercy."

The stately paraphrase gives us the message of the Psalm in lines of unusual beauty:

From all that dwell below the skies,
Let the Creator's praise arise;
Let the Redeemer's name be sung
Through every land, by every tongue.

Eternal are Thy mercies, Lord;
Eternal truth attends Thy word;
Thy praise shall sound from shore to shore,
Till suns shall rise and set no more.

—*Isaac Watts*

Psalm 118: Behold Your King!

The occasion of this magnificent chorus of praise is the Second Coming of our Lord and Savior, Jesus Christ. The scene is Jerusalem where the crowds have gathered to celebrate the Advent of Israel's long-awaited Messiah. In the shadow of the temple, a soloist takes his place at the microphone, the choir standing behind him. A hush comes over the audience.

118:1 SOLOIST: **Oh, give thanks to the LORD, for He is good!**
CHOIR: **For His mercy endures forever.**
(All over the audience heads are nodding in hearty assent.)

118:2 SOLOIST: **Let Israel now say,**
CHOIR: **"His mercy endures forever."**

118:3 SOLOIST: **Let the house of Aaron now say,**
CHOIR: **"His mercy endures forever."**
(Deep-throated "Amens" rise from the priests who are standing at the temple door.)

118:4 SOLOIST: **Let those who fear the LORD now say,**
CHOIR: **"His mercy endures forever."**
(At this, a company of God-fearing Gentiles bite their lips and fight back tears of gratitude for the grace that enables them to share in the glory of this moment.)

118:5–9 SOLOIST: **I called on the LORD in distress;**
The LORD answered me and set me in a broad place.
The LORD is on my side; I will not fear.
What can man do to me?
The LORD is for me among those who help me;
Therefore I shall see my desire on those who hate me.
It is better to trust in the LORD
Than to put confidence in man.
It is better to trust in the LORD
Than to put confidence in princes.
(The crowd understands that this is the language of the faithful remnant of Israel, marvelously preserved by God during the Tribulation Period. They have learned to trust in God alone, and have lost their fear of men. At last they realize that **it is better to trust in the LORD than** even **in princes**, that is, the best of men.)

118:10 SOLOIST: **All nations surrounded me,**
CHOIR: **But in the name of the LORD I will destroy them.**

118:11 SOLOIST: **They surrounded me, yes, they surrounded me;**
CHOIR: **But in the name of the LORD I will destroy them.**

118:12 SOLOIST: **They surrounded me like bees;**
They were quenched like a fire of thorns;
(Thornbushes make a spectacular blaze but die down quickly.)
CHOIR: **For in the name of the LORD I will destroy them.**

118:13, 14 SOLOIST: **You pushed me violently, that I might fall, But the LORD helped me.**
The LORD is my strength and song.
And He has become my salvation.
(The soloist is referring in verse 13 to the Antichrist and to his bestial treatment of the remnant for their refusal to buckle under to his demands. In the nick of time the Lord intervened and cast the false messiah into the lake of fire [Rev. 19:19, 20].)

118:15, 16 SOLOIST: **The voice of rejoicing and salvation**
Is in the tents of the righteous;
(All over Israel there is unrestrained jubilation over the triumph of the Messiah. In every home the people are singing the following song of victory.)

CHOIR: **The right hand of the LORD does valiantly.**
The right hand of the LORD is exalted;
The right hand of the LORD does valiantly.

118:17, 18 SOLOIST: **I shall not die, but live,**
And declare the works of the LORD.
The LORD has chastened me severely,
But He has not given me over to death.
(Speaking as the remnant, the soloist recalls the many pogroms against the Jews and their close calls with extinction. But the Lord miraculously rescued them from the mouth of the lion, and now they face the future with confidence and security.)

118:19, 20 SOLOIST: **Open to me the gates of righteousness;**
I will go through them,
And I will praise the LORD.
(Redeemed Israel seeks admission to the temple courts in order to offer sacrifices of thanksgiving to the Lord. The sacrificial system will be partially reinstituted during Christ's reign with the sacrifices looking back to Calvary, that is, they will be commemorative.)

CHOIR: **This is the gate of the LORD;**
Through which the righteous shall enter.
(These are the words of those Levites who are doorkeepers at the temple. They explain that **this gate** belongs to Jehovah and is for the use of those godly ones who wish to draw near to Him.)

118:21, 22 SOLOIST: **I will praise You,**
For You have answered me,
And have become my salvation.
(Israel acclaims the Lord Jesus Christ as her Savior.)

CHOIR: **The stone which the builders rejected**
Has become the chief cornerstone.
(The Lord Jesus is **the stone**. **The builders** were the

Jewish people, and especially their leaders, who rejected Him at His First Advent. Now the people of Israel confess what Parker calls "the stupidity of the specialists" as they see the despised Nazarene crowned with glory and honor. The rejected stone has become the Headstone of the corner [ASV]. There is some question as to whether the headstone is:

1. the cornerstone of a building.
2. the keystone of an arch.
3. the topmost stone of a pyramid.

Whichever is the correct view, the context demands the thought of highest honor.)

118:23 **This was the LORD's doing;**
It is marvelous in our eyes.
(The choir represents Israel as acknowledging that it is Jehovah who has given the Lord Jesus His proper place in the hearts and affections of His people. The crowning day has come at last!)

118:24 **This is the day the LORD has made;**
We will rejoice and be glad in it.
(Barnes writes: "As if it were a new day, made for this very occasion, a day which the people did not expect to see, and which seemed therefore to have been created out of the ordinary course, and added to the other days."[79])

118:25 **Save now, I pray, O LORD;**
O LORD, I pray, send now prosperity!
(This is the verse which the people of Jerusalem quoted at the time of Christ's so-called triumphal entry; "Hosanna" is the original word for "Save now" [Matt. 21:9]. But they soon changed their welcome to a call for His execution. Now, however, Israel is welcoming the Lord in the day of His power, and their sentiments are both sincere and lasting.)

118:26 SOLOIST: **Blessed is he who comes in the name of the LORD;**
(As the Lord approaches the temple area, the chief singer chants the blessing of the people in clarion tones. It is an historic moment. Centuries before, Jesus had warned the people of Israel that they would not see Him again until they said, "Blessed is he who comes in the name of the LORD" [Matt. 23:39]. Now at last they gladly acknowledge Him as their Messiah and King.)

CHOIR: **We have blessed you from the house of the LORD.**
(Perhaps this is the blessing of the priests, standing inside the door of the temple.)

118:27 **God is the Lord, and He has given us light;**
Bind the sacrifice with cords to the horns of the altar.
(The congregation of Israel worships Jesus as God and as the One who has brought light to their darkened hearts. As the procession moves toward the brazen altar, with Him at the forefront, they call for **cords** to **bind the sacrifice**.)

118:28, 29 SOLOIST: **You are my God, and I will praise You;**
You are my God, I will exalt You.
(The Lord Jesus Christ is confessed as God by a people who formerly used His name as a by-word.)
Oh, give thanks to the Lord, for He is good;

CHOIR: **For His mercy endures forever.**
(The song has risen to a crescendo of deep, deep praise and worship. The music reverberates through the surrounding streets of old Jerusalem. Then as it dies away, the people return to their dwellings to enjoy the wonderful thousand-year kingdom of the glorious Lord whose right it is to reign.)

Psalm 119: All About the Bible

This has been called the golden alphabet of the Bible. The reason is that it is divided into twenty-two sections, one for each letter of the Hebrew alphabet. Each section has eight verses and every verse in a section begins with the corresponding Hebrew letter. Thus in the Hebrew, every verse in the first section begins with Aleph; in the second section every verse begins with Beth; and so on.

In the NKJV, all but four verses in this longest Psalm contain some title or description of the Word of God. The four exceptions are verses 84, 121, 122 and 132. The names used to describe God's Word are: law, testimonies, ways, precepts, statutes, commandments, ordinances, word(s), promise, judgments, faithfulness, appointment, justice and commands.

By using the alphabet in this acrostic form, Ridout feels that the writer may have been suggesting that "all the possibilities of human language are exhausted in setting forth the fullness and perfection of the Word of God."[80] We have a similar suggestion in the NT. Our Lord speaks of Himself as the Alpha and Omega (Rev. 1:8). These are, of course, the first and last words of the Greek alphabet. The thought is that He is everything of goodness and perfection that can be expressed by every letter of the alphabet, arranged in every possible combination.

No two verses in the Psalm say exactly the same thing. There is some different shade of meaning in every one.

Concerning the 119th Psalm, C. S. Lewis said:

> The poem is not, and does not pretend to be, a sudden outpouring of the heart like, say Psalm 18. It is a pattern, a thing done like embroidery, stitch by stitch, through long, quiet hours, for love of the subject and for the delight in leisurely, disciplined craftsmanship.[81]

The following subject headings for the various sections of the Psalm are based primarily on F. W. Grant's notes:

vv. 1–8	The Blessedness of Obeying the Word
vv. 9–16	Cleansing By the Word
vv. 17–24	Discernment By the Word
vv. 25–32	Sense of Personal Insufficiency Through the Word
vv. 33–40	The Power of the Word
vv. 41–48	Victory Through the Word
vv. 49–56	Rest and Comfort Through the Word
vv. 57–64	Perseverance in the Word
vv. 65–72	The Pricelessness of the Word in Good and Evil Times
vv. 73–80	Insights Through the Word
vv. 81–88	The Afflicted One Sustained By the Word
vv. 89–96	Eternity of the Word
vv. 97–104	Wisdom Through the Word
vv. 105–112	The Word a Lamp and Light For All Occasions
vv. 113–120	The Wicked and the Word
vv. 121–128	Separation and Deliverance Through the Word
vv. 129–136	Joy and Communion Through the Word
vv. 137–144	Zeal For the Word
vv. 145–152	Experience Through the Word
vv. 153–160	Salvation Through the Word
vv. 161–168	Perfection of the Word
vv. 169–176	Prayer and Praise Through the Word

In an eminent sense, the Psalm expresses the love for the Word of God which our Savior experienced as a Man here on earth. Also Bellett suggests that "in its full prophetic character [this Psalm] will be the language of the true Israel on their return to God and His long neglected oracles."[82]

119:1 The **blessed** or happy man is the one whose life is conformed to the Word of **the LORD**. Even if he sins and fails, there is provision in the Word for confession and restoration, and this keeps him in an **undefiled** condition.

119:2 It is obedience to **His testimonies** that counts—not a reluctant, half-hearted, feet-dragging obedience, but a deep, enormous desire to please **Him with the whole heart**!

119:3 Negatively, happiness is found in separation from every form of **iniquity**. Positively it is following the route He has mapped out for us in the Scriptures. The surest way to abstain from evil is to be completely occupied with doing good.

119:4 God's **precepts** are not options but *commandments*, and they are not to be kept haphazardly but **diligently**.

119:5 The psalmist now moves from what is true in general to what he wants to be true in his own life. In moving insensibly from precept to prayer, he acknowledges that the desire as well as the power to be steadfast in obedience must come ultimately from God.

119:6 As long as he keeps all the statutes of the Lord, he will be spared from the shame that tortures the mind, crimsons the cheek and even at times makes the body squirm.

119:7 "From prayer to praise is not a long or difficult journey." Those who **learn** to obey **God's righteous** ordinances have fullness of joy and this leads to spontaneous adoration.

119:8 Firm resolve is coupled with humble dependence. The psalmist is determined to follow hard after the Lord. But he realizes his own inadequacy. The prayer **"Do not forsake me utterly"** is not so much a possible actuality as a statement of what the writer feels he might deserve.

119:9 One of the most crucial problems in the life of every **young man** is how to keep pure. The answer is by practical obedience to the words of the Bible.

119:10 In the matter of holiness, there is a curious merging of human desire (**With my whole heart I have sought You**), and divine empowering (**Oh, let me not wander from Your commandments**).

119:11 He does not make us holy against our will or without our cooperation. Someone has wisely said, "The best book in the world is the Bible. The best place to put it is **in** the **heart**. The best reason for putting it there is that it saves us from sinning **against** God."

119:12 Because God is so great and so gracious, the renewed nature desires to learn His **statutes** and be molded by them. The love of Christ constrains us!

119:13 Deep delight in the treasures of the Word leads inevitably to the desire to share them with others. It is a law of life that when we really believe something, we want to pass it on.

119:14 No prospector was ever more pleased with his nuggets of gold than the one who searches out the hidden wealth of the Scriptures.

119:15 God's Word provides endless resource material for the most satisfying meditation, but this should never be divorced from the determination to be doers of the Word.

119:16 "His commandments are not burdensome" (1 Jn. 5:3). Whoever is born of God **will delight** in the **statutes** of the Lord and determine to keep them in constant remembrance.

119:17 Without Him we can do nothing. We need His grace for living and also for obeying His **word**. Let us ask for plenteous grace since our need is so great.

119:18 The Bible abounds with **wondrous**, spiritual goodies which are hidden from the casual glance. Our **eyes** need to be opened to see them.

119:19 The Bible is a road map that guides the pilgrim unerringly to his destination.

119:20 It is good when our thirst for the Scriptures is enormous and unflagging. The psalmist's **soul** was eaten up with longing for the Word, and he had this ardent, intense longing **at all times**.

119:21 History teems with instances of how **the proud** and insolent have defied the Lord's **commandments** and soon were brought down by the mighty hand of God.

119:22 The believer is scorned and ridiculed by the world. "They think it strange that you do not run with them in the same flood of dissipation, speaking evil of you" (1 Pet. 4:4). But integrity will be rewarded, and His "well done" will more than compensate for **reproach and contempt**.

119:23 Even when those in positions of authority collaborate in vilifying the Christian, he can find strength and solace in meditating on the Bible, "answering his traducers by not answering them at all."

119:24 Matthew Henry comments:

> Was David at a loss what to do when the princes spoke against him? God's statutes were his counsellors, and they counselled him to bear it patiently and commit his cause to God.[83]

119:25 Life has its valleys as well as its mountaintops. Even when we are cast down in sorrow, we can call on the Lord to **revive** us through the restoring power of the **word**.

119:26 When we tell of our **ways**, that is, make open confession of our sins, the Lord answers us by forgiving. This leads to a renewed desire for holiness, as expressed in the prayer, **"Teach me Your statutes!"**

119:27 We need to understand the meaning of God's **precepts** and how to apply them practically in our lives. This will lead to meditation on God's **wonderful works**.

119:28 In the dark spots of life, when our **soul melts** in tears, the God of all comfort bends low and often with a single verse of Scripture lifts us and strengthens us to go on.

119:29 By the Spirit of God and through the Word of God, we can distinguish between truth and error. The Bible inculcates a holy hatred for every form of **lying**. It also teaches us that truth is what God says about a thing (John 17:17).

119:30 No one drifts into holiness. It requires a deliberate choice of **the way of truth** as revealed in the sacred Scriptures. Spurgeon says, "The commands of God must be set before us as the mark to aim at, the model to work by, and the road to walk in."

119:31 The psalmist had adhered to the **testimonies** of God as if he had been glued to them. But he still realizes his proneness to wander, and cries to the LORD in conscious dependence.

119:32 It is when God gives us big hearts, not big heads, that we hasten to keep His commandments. It is more a matter of the affections than of the intellect.

119:33 We should pray for instruction. As students in the school of God, we should be eager to learn how to translate precept into practice, and determine to obey His Word **to the end** of our lives.

119:34 We should pray for **understanding**. It is important to have right views of the Scriptures, of their meaning and obligations. How else can we follow Him with undivided devotedness?

119:35 We should pray for guidance. The spirit is willing but the flesh is weak. So we want the Lord to guide our feet in **the path of** His will, because that is the only way in which we are truly happy.

119:36 We should pray for spiritual rather than material enrichment. "Godliness with contentment is great gain" (1 Tim. 6:6). It is a miracle of grace that takes the love of money from a man and replaces it with a love for the Bible.

119:37 We should pray for divine realities, not shadows. Here is God's commentary on TV: **"Turn away my eyes from looking at worthless things."** TV depicts a never-never land, a world that doesn't exist. God's Word deals with life as it really is.

119:38 We should pray for God to **establish** His promise. "All the rivers of Thy grace I claim; over every promise write my name." Our claim to His promises lies in the fact that we fear Him.

119:39 We should pray to be kept from **reproach**, from anything that would bring shame or dishonor on the name of the Lord Jesus. His **judgments are good**; we need to follow them faithfully.

119:40 We should pray for personal revival. "The parched ground shall become a pool, and the thirsty land springs of water" (Isa. 35:7). As we burn and **long for** His **precepts**, He will **revive** us **in** His **righteousness**.

119:41 We must not take God's **mercies** and **salvation** for granted. We are as dependent on His compassion and protection as when we were first saved. So we claim His promise to care for and keep us day by day.

119:42 Undeniable proofs of the Lord's answers to prayer serve to silence the **reproaches** of unbelievers. Our faith is based on the **word** of God which can never fail.

119:43 May we never be afraid or ashamed to speak **the word of truth**. If we **have hoped in** God's **ordinances**, He will provide continuing opportunities to witness for Him.

119:44 Our response to His love and grace should be an inflexible resolve to **keep** His Word as long as we live. "How can I do less than give Him my best and live for Him completely after all He's done for me?"

119:45 Those who are set free by the Son of God are free indeed (John 8:36). The world thinks of the Christian life as a system of bondage. But those who **seek** His **precepts** are the ones who enjoy perfect **liberty**.

119:46 Faith gives boldness to **speak** for Jesus in the presence of **kings**. How many potentates have heard the Good News from humble and often despised subjects!

119:47 Those who love the Bible find deep personal enjoyment in its pages. It is a fountain of **delight**, a river of pleasure, a never-failing source of satisfaction.

119:48 We revere the Bible in the sense that we stand in awe of its scope, its depths, its power, its treasures and its infinity. We **love** it for what it is and for what it has done. And we **meditate** in it by day and by night.

119:49 It is not possible that God could ever forget His promise, but in the furnace of affliction, when faith has its lapses, we are permitted to pray, "Lord, **remember**..." "He cannot have taught us to trust in His name, and thus far have led us to put us to shame."

119:50 Those who have experienced the quickening powers of the **word** find it an unfailing source of **comfort**. The words of well-meaning men are often empty and unavailing but God's Word is always living, relevant and effective.

119:51 If we are faithful to the Lord, we can expect to receive our share of mocking and sneering **derision**, but when we have found divine principles, we should stick with them.

119:52 We are encouraged by the memory of how the Lord has intervened for us in the past. The same mercy that has brought us this far will certainly take us the rest of the way. "His love in times past forbids us to think He'll leave us at last in darkness to sink."

119:53 It causes the believer burning **indignation** to see God's law being dishonored and disobeyed. It was true of the Lord Jesus, "The reproaches of those who reproached You fell on Me" (Rom. 15:3). Any dishonor to the Father was taken as a personal insult by the Son.

119:54 Thanks to the wonderful Word of God, the pilgrim can sing **in the house of** his **pilgrimage**, or, as Knox put it, "in a land of exile." The way may be rough but it cannot be long. The night may be dark but God gives a song.

119:55 The seemingly interminable hours of a sleepless **night** can be redeemed by musing on the Lord as He is revealed in the Word. The more we get to know Him, the more we love Him, and loving Him, we want to **keep** His **law**.

119:56 Obedience is a blessing. "Godliness is profitable for all things, since it holds promise for the present life and also for the life to come" (1 Tim. 4:8).

119:57 The realization of what an incomparable treasure we have in the Lord should make us vow to **keep** His **words**. He is the All-sufficient One. To have Him is to be fabulously wealthy.

119:58 Though He is all-sufficient, we are not. "Our sufficiency is from

God" (2 Cor. 3:5). So we must be people of prayer, entreating God's **favor** and claiming His promise of mercy.

119:59 Guidance is a perennial problem. Which way should we go? Frankly, we don't have the wisdom in ourselves to know. All right, then. Let us turn our **feet** to the paths outlined in the Scriptures.

119:60 We live in a day of instant foods, instant service and instant this and that. Instant obedience to the revealed will of God is something to ponder—and to produce.

119:61 **Wicked** men may conspire to trip up the innocent believer, but that is all the more reason for him to remember the Word for guidance and protection.

119:62 "At midnight Paul and Silas were praying and singing hymns to God" (Acts 16:25). They were being unjustly treated by men but they could still sing about God's **righteous judgments**.

119:63 Those who love God love His people. And those who love the Bible love all Bible-lovers. It is a worldwide fellowship that transcends national, social, and racial distinctions.

119:64 God's steadfast love can be found anywhere in the world, but more than that, **the earth . . . is *full* of** it. Our grateful hearts respond by saying, "Lord, keep me teachable by Your Holy Spirit."

119:65 How long is it since I have thanked the **LORD** for the wonderful way He has treated me **according to** the promise of His **word**? "Count your blessings: name them one by one; and it will surprise you what the Lord has done!"

119:66 We all need to pray for **good judgment** as well as **knowledge**. It is possible to have knowledge without discernment and without balance. From the Word and from the disciplines of life we learn sound judgment.

119:67 God's discipline "yields the peaceable fruit of righteousness to those who have been trained by it" (Heb. 12:11). The memory of what our wanderings cost us serves as a healthy deterrent against repeating them.

119:68 The English words "God" and **"good"** may have a common derivation. God is **good** and everything He does is **good**. To become good we must take His yoke upon us and learn of Him.

119:69 When ungodly men try to ruin our reputation with lies, we can find protection in faithful, unfaltering obedience to the Bible.

119:70 Let the worldling wallow in luxury and pleasure. We find our satisfaction in spiritual instruction rather than in sensual indulgence.

119:71 Sufferings are only for a moment but the benefits of suffering are forever. Men intend their persecution to harm us; God overrules it for good.

119:72 The Bible is the most valuable material possession we have in the world. A computer can add up fantastically large figures but it cannot record the value of the Scriptures.

119:73 Since God has **made** us by such marvelous skill, what is more reasonable than that He should be our Teacher as well. We should find out His purpose in creating us and fulfill it to the hilt.

119:74 There is keen spiritual refreshment in meeting a Christian who is on fire for the Lord Jesus. Those who hope in God's Word become radioactive with the Holy Spirit.

119:75 Sickness, suffering and affliction do not come directly from God, but He permits them under certain circumstances and then harnesses them for His own goals. It is a mark of spiritual maturity when we vindicate Him for His justice and **faithfulness** in them all.

119:76 And yet in ourselves we are weak as dust, and we need His compassionate love to sustain us. "Let us therefore come boldly to the throne of grace, that we may obtain mercy and find grace to help in time of need" (Heb. 4:16).

119:77 Every display of the **tender mercies** of God is like a fresh transfusion of life to the hard-pressed saint. Those who **delight** in His **law** may have confidence that He will **come** alongside to help.

119:78 Gelineau translates verse 78, "Shame the **proud** who harm me with lies, while I ponder **your precepts**." God allows sin to work itself out and the psalmist is merely praying for God to do as He has said He would.

119:79 It is a spiritual instinct to seek the fellowship of **those who know** and love the Word of God. But how often do we ask the Lord to lead **those who fear God** across our pathway?

119:80 There are many reasons why we should desire to **be blameless** in obeying the **statutes** of the Lord. The one singled out by the psalmist here is that we might avoid the searing, scorching shame of falling into sin.

119:81 The believer may be afflicted but not crushed; perplexed but not driven to despair; persecuted but not forsaken; struck down but not destroyed (2 Cor. 4:8, 9). Here he languishes for God's saving help but **hope** is still alive.

119:82 Even though his **eyes** grow dim with **searching** for the fulfillment of God's promise of deliverance, he does not pray "Will you comfort me?" but rather **"When will you comfort me?"**

119:83 **A wineskin in** the **smoke** is shriveled and blackened. The simile explains itself. The harassed believer is wizened, parched, and unsightly through waiting, but he is not hopeless as long as He has the Word to fall back on.

119:84 Life at best is very brief. The **days** of affliction seem to occupy a disproportionate share. It is time for the Lord to act by punishing the oppressors.

119:85 The villains of this verse are godless and lawless; these two characteristics go together. They plot the downfall of the righteous and innocent—it is an evidence that they refuse to conform to God's **law**.

119:86 There is nothing as dependable as God's Word. He has promised to rescue His persecuted people. So when we are attacked by lying accusers, we can confidently use the "golden prayer," **"Help me!"**

119:87 Spurgeon said, "If we stick to the **precepts** we will be rescued by the promises." Even if we reach the place where we despair of life, we should never falter in our obedience. Help will come. Only believe!

119:88 The best prayer comes from a strong, inward necessity. Here the psalmist prays that the Lord will spare his life so that he can go forth to glorify God by obeying His Word.

119:89 Faith is not a leap in the dark. It is based upon the surest thing in the universe—the Bible. There is no risk in believing a word that is fixed firmly and **forever** in **heaven**.

119:90 The **faithfulness** of God is displayed not only in His Word but also in His works. It extends to all generations and is seen in the order and precision of nature.

119:91 Heaven and earth obey His laws. Seedtime and harvest, cold and heat, summer and winter, day and night **are all** God's **servants**. And all are regulated and sustained by His word of power.

119:92 Barnes comments:

> "I should have sunk a thousand times," said a most excellent, but much afflicted man to me, "if it had not been for one declaration in the Word of God, 'The Eternal God is thy refuge, and underneath are the everlasting arms.'"[84]

119:93 Those who have experienced the power of the Scriptures in their lives are not likely to **forget** them, We were "born again, not of corruptible seed but incorruptible, through the word of God which lives and abides forever" (1 Pet. 1:23).

119:94 Even after we have been saved from the penalty of sin, we still need to be saved day by day from defilement and damage. Acquaintance with God's **precepts** and with our own hearts makes us aware of the need of this present-tense salvation.

119:95 The only way to avoid the attacks of **the wicked** is to lead a petty, inconsequential life. As long as our lives are effective for Him, we can expect opposition. But we find strength and solace when we **consider** God's **testimonies**.

119:96 The very best things in this world fall short of **perfection** and come to an end, but the Word of God is perfect and infinite. The more we get to know the Bible, the more we realize how far short we ourselves come.

119:97 Those who **love** the Lord will certainly love His Word as well. And this love will be manifested in musing on the Bible at every opportunity. It is in moments of meditation that we suddenly discover new beauties and wonders in the Scriptures.

119:98 The humble believer, equipped with the wisdom of the Word, can see more on his knees than his **enemies** can on their tiptoes.

119:99 If the teacher becomes complacent and rests on his laurels, he will soon be surpassed by a younger man who constantly meditates on the Word.

119:100 This may sound like irresponsible boasting, but not so. It is not a person's age or intelligence that matters, but his obedience. So the youth may outstrip the aged if he has a higher OQ (Obedience Quotient).

119:101 Here we have obedience in action. The psalmist restrains his **feet from** paths of sin in order that he might obey to his utmost.

119:102 The sanctifying influence of the Bible is great. **Taught** by the Lord through its pages, we develop a hatred for sin and a love for holiness.

119:103 And then, of course, the Bible is a source of sheer enjoyment.No other book in the world is as pleasurable. **Honey** is **sweet** but God's Word is **sweeter**.

119:104 In order to detect counterfeit money, people study genuine bills. So a deep acquaintance with the truth enables us to detect and despise **every false way**.

119:105 The **word** guides negatively by forbidding certain behavior patterns. And it guides positively by showing the right way. How much we owe to the friendly beams of this **lamp**!

119:106 Here is a holy determination to obey the Holy Scriptures. This is for the glory of God, for the blessing of others, and for our own good as well.

119:107 Spurgeon says:

> In the previous verse the psalmist had been sworn in as a soldier of the Lord, and in this verse he is called to suffer hardness in that capacity. The service of the Lord does not screen us from trial, but rather secures it for us.[85]

119:108 We come before the Lord as priests and as pupils. As priests we "offer the sacrifice of praise to God, that is, the fruit of lips, giving thanks to his name" (Heb.13:15). As pupils, we open our hearts and minds to His divine instruction.

119:109 When our **life** is constantly in danger, there is safety and security in remembering the **law** of the Lord. The tendency to panic, to become hysterical, and to forget God's Word must be avoided at any cost.

119:110 Those who are instructed in the Word are not ignorant of Satan's designs. By simple obedience to the Bible, they avoid his booby-traps.

119:111 The Scriptures are to be chosen as a prized possession, as a **heritage** of vast value. Think of the joy that comes to an heir when he inherits a fortune. How much greater joy should be ours in possessing the Book of books.

119:112 All who realize its worth should determine to obey it **to the very end** of life's day. There should be no vacations, no time off in the school of obedience.

119:113 Moffat translates this verse, "I hate men who are half and half. I love thy law." **Double-minded** people are for God one minute and for the world the next. They can speak out of both corners of their mouth and are traitors to the **law** of God.

119:114 The Lord is our **hiding place** when we are pursued and our **shield** when we are being directly attacked. Those who **hope in** His promise will never be disappointed because He cannot deceive or be deceived.

119:115 We part company with those who do not **keep the commandments of** our **God**. But while we separate from their sinful ways, we still maintain contact with men of the world in order to share the Good News with them.

119:116 The argument of this prayer is: "You have promised to uphold me. Now do as You have said, Otherwise people would say that You have failed me, and I would be disappointed in **my hope**."

119:117 We are no more able to keep ourselves **safe** than we were to save ourselves in the first place. If God holds us **up**, we **shall be safe**. But our part is to keep His **statutes continually**.

119:118 The Lord spurns those who **stray from** His **statutes**. Their cleverness will one day appear in its true light as stupidity.

119:119 The Word clearly teaches that God will cast **away all the wicked of the earth** like a refiner casts off the scum that rises to the surface of the molten metal. If He did not deal righteously with sin, we could not respect His written Word.

119:120 When we think of God's **judgments** on the wicked, we might well tremble. But also as Barnes says, we are "filled with awe at the strictness, the spirituality, the severity of His law."

119:121 The psalmist's plea that he had done what was just and right must be understood as a general rule and not an invariable one. His righteous life was the fruit of His salvation and therefore a proper basis to ask the Lord **not** to abandon him **to** his **oppressors**.

119:122 A **surety** is one who stands for another, who represents him. He who was our surety at Calvary pleads our cause successfully through all of life and restrains the arrogant oppressor.

119:123 Here is a man who looked for God's deliverance till his **eyes** were sore. He waited till exhausted for the fulfillment of the **righteous** promise that the Lord would intervene for him.

119:124 In spite of what might seem like a plea for justice in verse 121, he here casts himself on the **mercy** or grace of the Lord. One form of His **mercy** is His gracious teaching ministry. **"Teach me Your statutes."**

119:125 The more a **servant** knows about his master, the more useful and effective he can be. So we need **understanding** to **know** the mind of God as it is revealed in His **testimonies**.

119:126 This is an about-face. The servant is now indirectly calling on the Master to **act**, for His **law** has been broken. And this is the cry of God's people in every time of darkness, **"It is time for You to act, O LORD!"**

119:127 One index of how precious the Bible is to us is the amount of time we spend reading it. If we value it above **fine gold**, its cover will be worn and its pages frayed.

119:128 Another proof of our esteem for the Book will be the degree to which we obey it. Unless we do what it says and **hate every false way**, we are deceiving ourselves.

119:129 God's Word is **wonderful** in its timelessness, its purity, its accuracy, its harmony, its universal relevance, its power and its sufficiency. Such a book deserves to be read and heeded.

119:130 **The entrance of** the Word **gives light**, whether to nations, families, or individuals. We little realize the sanctifying influence it has had throughout the world. **It gives understanding to** those who acknowledge themselves to be **simple** and therefore in need of help.

119:131 A deep, enormous thirst for the Word of God is what we all need. "As newborn babes, desire the pure milk of the Word" (1 Pet. 2:2).

119:132 We may tire of these repeated pleas for mercy, but the psalmist didn't, and neither does God. We never get to the place in this life where we are beyond the need of His grace.

119:133 Here are the two sides of the coin of holiness—to be kept going on steadily for the Lord in accordance with His **word**, and to be delivered from the power of indwelling sin.

119:134 The first part of this prayer is not unusual; any of us would want to be delivered from man's **oppression**. But notice the unusual purpose, **"that I may keep Your precepts."**

119:135 In our service for the Lord, we may ask Him for some token of His favor, presence, and power. He knows how to drop encouraging bonuses in answer to our prayer. And we should never lose the desire to be taught more and more.

119:136 Tears flowing like **rivers of water**—a dramatic expression for the deepest anguish and sorrow! And for what? For injustice to the psalmist himself? No, for man's disregard of God's **law** and thus dishonor to His name.

> Bendetti, . . . author of "Stabat Mater," one day was found weeping, and when asked the reason of his tears, replied, "I weep because Love goes about unloved."[86]

119:137 The Author of the Book is **righteous**, so it is not surprising that the Book is **upright** too. Most of us know this, but how few of us turn it into an act of praise and worship by thanking the LORD.

119:138 Everything God says is **righteous** and **faithful**, and His Word is completely trustworthy. To believe God's Word is not a meritorious act. It is just common sense.

119:139 Barnes comments with insight:

> It is a great triumph in a man's soul when, in looking on the conduct of persecutors, calumniators and slanderers, he is more grieved because they violate the law of God than because they injure him.[87]

119:140 The Bible has been well tried. Thousands have tested its promises and found them true. "It has survived the hatred of men, the fires of spurious priesthood, the sneers of infidels, and the carnal wisdom of modern critics" (Scripture Union).

119:141 In the estimation of his enemies, the psalmist was **small and despised**. But man's scorn did not scare him away from clinging to the Bible.

119:142 God's **righteousness** is not a passing mood but an **everlasting** virtue. It is not enough to say that the Bible contains truth; the Bible **is truth**. Every utterance of God is true.

119:143 The writer had a full cup of **trouble and anguish**, but with the Word of God, he could trace the rainbow through his tears.

119:144 It is not only that God's **testimonies** are righteous now; they always will be. The more we understand them, the greater is our capacity for enjoying life, both now and in heaven.

119:145 The word **"cry"** is the key of this section.[88] Here we have an appeal for help from a trusting heart. Almighty God cannot resist prayers that come from a whole heart and that express a desire to do His will.

119:146 When, like Peter, we begin to sink beneath the waves, we can always send up that short prayer **"Save me."** The Lord then raises us up to go forth and live for Him again.

119:147 Weigle writes, "This is a description of the devotional habits of a pious (man) who rises before dawn to begin his day with meditation and prayer." Our motto should be, "No Bible, no breakfast."

119:148 Even the sleepless hours of the **night** can be utilized for meditation on the Word. Not uncommonly, that is when the Lord gives us "the treasures of darkness."

119:149 We should never get over the wonderful fact that we have instant access to the presence of God in prayer. Like the psalmist, we can plead God's **lovingkindness** and **justice** to preserve our lives.

119:150 The enemy is **near**. They are intent on harm for God's servant. Having rejected the authority of God's **law** over their lives, they will seemingly stop at nothing.

119:151 But the LORD is **near**, and one with God is a majority. "No foe can harm us, no fear alarm us, on the victory side." God's word is true, and He will never forsake His own.

119:152 It is a tremendous comfort to know that God's Word stands forever. "Standing on the promises that cannot fail, when the howling storms of doubt and fear assail; by the living Word of God we shall prevail; standing on the promises of God."

119:153 The Lord really does look on our **affliction**. "In every pang that rends the heart, the Man of Sorrows has a part." And He comes to **deliver** those who cling to Him and to His Word.

119:154 The writer asks God to serve as His advocate and His lifegiver. Grievous charges have been made against him; he needs a defender. He has been persecuted to the point of exhaustion; he needs a new infusion of life.

119:155 God does not save men against their will. He will not populate heaven with people who don't want to be there. There is no **salvation** for those who refuse to listen to the Word.

119:156 No human language could ever be adequate to describe the mercy of God. His **tender mercies** can never be exhausted by our requests. The persecuted psalmist asks for the mercy of life, that is, deliverance from his would-be slayers.

119:157 Many of these verses find their true fulfillment in the Lord Jesus, of course. Surrounded by **persecutors and enemies**, still He remained faithful to the **testimonies** of His Father.

119:158 It is a mark of spiritual maturity to grieve more over insults to God than over wrongs to oneself. Oh, to be thus consumed with zeal for the Lord!

119:159 In verse 153, the psalmist wrote, "Consider my affliction." Here, as Spurgeon points out, he says, in effect, "Consider my affection," that is, affection for the precepts. Also he asks, for the third time in this section, for the preservation of his life (vv. 154, 156).

119:160 God's **word is truth** in its **entirety**. Every promise in it is sure of fulfillment. "Till heaven and earth pass away, one jot or one tittle will by no means pass from the Law till all is fulfilled" (Matt. 5:18).

119:161 Men in places of authority have often oppressed God's servants. But a deep respect and **awe** for the **word** of God preserves the faithful from turning traitor to the Lord.

119:162 The thrill of discovering a hidden cache of **treasure** is experienced by the one who delves into the Bible and finds wonderful spiritual riches.

119:163 Acquaintance with the Word teaches us to **love** what God loves (the **law**) and **hate** what He hates (**lying**). We come to think God's thoughts after Him.

119:164 Since **seven** is the number of perfection or completeness, we understand the psalmist to mean that he praised the Lord continually and wholeheartedly for His **righteous** ordinances.

119:165 The Word gives **peace** in a world of turmoil and safety from the power of temptation. The verse doesn't mean that believers are immune from sorrow or trouble, but rather that by obeying the law, they avoid the pitfalls of sin.

119:166 Psalm 37:3 says, "Trust in the Lord, and do good." Here the psalmist says he had followed that advice. Faith comes first, then works are the fruit of faith.

119:167 The people in Malachi's day found obedience to be a weariness (Mal. 1:13). Not so the writer. He obeyed the Word and grew to **love** it more and more.

119:168 These last three verses in this section speak of practical obedience to the Bible. If it seems to be stretching a point to attribute them to the average believer, just think of them as the Words of our Savior and the problem vanishes.

119:169 As the Psalm comes to a close, it seems to rise to a crescendo of fervent petition. The word **"let"** is found seven times. First there is the urgent appeal for audience and then for true spiritual **understanding**.

119:170 The enemy never seems far away in these verses, and hence there is the reiterated plea for deliverance in accordance with the promise of the **word**.

119:171 Increased knowledge of God's **statutes** should not lead to pride and exaggerated self-esteem, but to **praise** and adoration of the Lord.

119:172 Instead of talking about trivia and matters of no lasting importance, we should discipline ourselves to talk about spiritual matters. **All** God's **commandments** are **righteousness** and tremendously worthwhile.

119:173 It is a lovely picture—the nail-scarred **hand** of Omnipotence reaching down from heaven to rescue a mere man but one who had deliberately chosen the Lord's **precepts** as his rule of life.

119:174 While enjoying the **salvation** of our souls as an accomplished fact, we long for salvation from the presence of sin when Jesus comes again. In the meantime we find great **delight** in reading and obeying the Bible.

119:175 We are not only saved to serve, but even more directly to **praise**. Every deliverance from sickness or accident should give new momentum to our worship, and new urgency to our prayers for **help**.

119:176 This is one of the few confessions of sin in the Psalm. "The loftiest flights of holy rapture must ever come back to a lowly confession of sin and unworthiness."

Psalm 120: The Helpless Victim of Slander

One of the bitter experiences of a believer's life is to be the victim of lies and slander. It is then he helplessly realizes the truth of Spurgeon's observation that "a lie can go around the world while truth is putting its boots on." He can easily become a twisted mass of humiliation and frustration.

120:1, 2 That was the kind of **distress** that sent the psalmist racing to **the Lord** in this first **"Song of Ascents."**[89] His request was short, simple and specific. He wanted to be delivered from the **lying lips** of his enemies, from the **deceitful tongue** of the pagans.

120:3, 4 Then just as quickly, he turns aside to one particular culprit and predicts severe punishment for him. **What** sentence **shall be** handed down **to** him? **Sharp arrows** shot from the bow of the Master Archer. And what will be done to that deceitful tongue? Will it be washed with soap? No, it will be cauterized **with** glowing **coals of the broom tree**! The root of this desert shrub is used to produce burning charcoal, noted for its intense heat.

120:5 In a moment of self-pity, the peace-loving psalmist laments his enforced stay among the tribes of **Meshech** and **Kedar**. **Meshech** was a son of Japheth (Gen. 10:2), and his descendants became noted as savage, uncivilized people. **Kedar** was the second son of Ishmael (Gen. 25:13), and his posterity was also cruel and merciless. According to the International Standard Bible Encyclopedia, "it is through Kedar that Muslim genealogists trace the descent of Mohammed from Ishmael."

120:6, 7 The psalmist's enforced exile among barbarians who hated **peace** had been **too long** to suit him. His efforts to bring about peaceful co-existence had been repulsed by new acts of war.

Had he lived in NT times, he would have been more prepared to expect slander and strife, and would have been better able to cope with it. He would have the example of the Lord Jesus:

> Who, when He was reviled, did not revile in return; when He suffered, He did not threaten, but committed Himself to Him who judges righteously (1 Pet. 2:23).

He would have the teaching of Peter:

> But when you do good and suffer, if you take it patiently, this is commendable before God (1 Pet. 2:20b).

> Not returning evil for evil or reviling for reviling, but on the contrary blessing, knowing that you were called to this, that you may inherit a blessing (1 Pet. 3:9).

And finally he would have the word of the Lord Jesus:

> Blessed are you when they revile and persecute you, and say all kinds of evil against you falsely for My sake. Rejoice and be exceedingly glad, for great is your reward in heaven, for so they persecuted the prophets who were before you (Matt. 5:11, 12).

Psalm 121: Kept!

121:1, 2 In the KJV, this Psalm begins:

> I will lift up mine eyes unto the hills, from whence cometh my help.
> My help cometh from the LORD, which made heaven and earth.

Later translators thought they detected a pagan heresy here, namely, the idea that help comes from the hills rather than from the Lord (Jer. 3:23). So they punctuated the second clause of verse 1 as a question. The NKJV, for instance, reads:

> **I will lift up my eyes to the hills—**
> **From whence comes my help?**
> **My help comes from the LORD,**
> **who made heaven and earth.**

I still prefer the KJV here, and I'll tell you why. The temple in Jerusalem was the dwelling place of God on earth. The glory cloud in the Holy of Holies signified the Lord's presence among His people. The city of Jerusalem is situated on a mountain and is surrounded by mountains. So when a Jew in other parts of Israel needed divine **help**, he looked toward the **hills**. To him this was the same as looking to the Lord. Since the Creator's dwelling was in the Jerusalem hills, there was a poetic sense in which **all help** came from **the hills**.

In the first two verses, the speaker is the psalmist, expressing his complete reliance on the Maker of **heaven and earth**.

121:3 Beginning with verse 3, there is a change of speaker. In the remaining verses, we hear the Holy Spirit guaranteeing the eternal security of those whose trust is in the Lord. There is the guarantee of unassailable stability. The believer's **foot** will be preserved from being **moved**. Since the foot speaks of foundation or standing, it means that God will keep His trusting child from slipping or failing.

121:4 There is the guarantee of a Guardian who **shall neither slumber nor sleep**. Alexander the Great told his soldiers, "I wake that you may sleep."[90] Throughout the night hours, when we are no longer conscious of the world around us, there is One greater than Alexander who watches over us with constant, unwearied care.

121:5, 6 There is the guarantee that our **keeper** is none other than **the LORD** Himself. The great Sovereign of the universe is personally involved in the security of the most obscure saint.

There is the guarantee that He will protect from every evil influence. When it says that He is **"your shade at your right hand,"** it means that He is alongside as a bodyguard to shield His own from harm day or night. **The sun shall not strike you by day** is usually interpreted by modern day literalists as sunstroke.[91] The allusion to **the moon** is often condescendingly treated as a biblical accommodation to ancient superstition and folklore. To those, however, who have been delivered from demonism, and who realize the important role of the sun and moon in the realm of spiritism, these verses promise welcome protection and freedom from the chains of demon possession.

121:7, 8 There is the guarantee of deliverance **from all evil**. It is a solid fact that nothing can come into the life of a believer apart from God's permissive will. There are no random circumstances, no purposeless accidents, no fatalistic tragedies. Though He is not the author of sickness, suffering, or death, He overrules and harnesses them for the accomplishment of His purposes. In the meantime His trusting child can know that God is working all things together for good to those who love Him, who are called according to His purpose (Rom. 8:28).

Finally there is the guarantee of God's watch-care over all our movements in time and throughout all eternity. He will keep our **going out and** our **coming in from this time forth and even forevermore**.

The words "keep" and "keeper" occur three times in the space of these eight verses. **Preserve** occurs three times.[92] They join to declare that no one is as secure as the person who has received the Lord as his only hope.

> The soul that on Jesus hath leaned for repose,
> He'll never, no never desert to his foes.
> That soul, though all hell should endeavor to shake,
> He'll never, no never, no never forsake!
> —*Richard Keen (1787)*

Psalm 122: The City of Peace

> Oh, the pure delight of a single hour
> That before Thy throne I spend,
> When I kneel in prayer, and with Thee, my God,
> I commune as friend with friend!
> —*Fanny J. Crosby*

122:1 David caught the scent of that pure delight when the reminder was passed to him by God-fearing Jews that it was time to **go** to the feast in Jerusalem. He **was glad**. It was no burdensome duty or dreary routine. In going to the temple to worship he found fulfillment and gladness.

122:2 And now faith's pilgrims were actually **standing** inside the city. **"Our feet have been standing within your gates, O Jerusalem!"** As if by a divine homing instinct, they had returned to the place which God had chosen. It was wonderful to be there!

122:3, 4 They stand back to admire the ocher-tinted **city**, built compactly **together**. Within its sun-drenched walls, one mile square, were domed and flat-roofed houses and cluttered alleys. But the one building for which the people had a fierce sentimental attraction was the temple of the Lord. In a real sense it was the temple that made the city for them.

That was the place to which **the tribes of the Lord** made their pilgrimages. It was the one spot on earth where God had decreed for His people to gather and give thanks to His **name**.

122:5 Jerusalem also was the political capital of Israel, of course. It was the seat of the royal **house of David**, and therefore it was the appointed place for the administration of justice.

122:6 Though its name means "the city of peace," the name has been a misnomer so far. Few cities have known the strife, the suffering, the carnage that this city has:

> Jerusalem's stones bear the stigmata of her sanctity and her walls the memory of the crimes committed within them in the name of religion. David and Pharaoh, Sen-

nacherib and Nebuchadnezzar, Ptolemy and Herod, Titus and the Crusaders of Godefrey de Bouillon, Tamerlane and the Saracens of Saladin, all fought and killed there.[93]

In prophecy as well as in history, there is an ocean of meaning in the poignant plea, **"Pray for the peace of Jerusalem!"** Dark days lie ahead. The narrow streets of the city will echo to the tread of Gentile invaders until the Prince of Peace, Israel's Messiah, returns to assume the reins of government (Luke 21:24).

F. B. Meyer notes that there is a graceful alliteration here in verse 6:

> Peace in the City of Peace.
> May those be at peace who love her.

The benediction of peace rests upon all who love the city of the Great King.

122:7–9 This love is expressed in praying for and promoting tranquility **within** its **walls** and safety within its towers. What the godly Jew desired for Jerusalem, we should desire for the church. How we should endeavor to keep the unity of the Spirit in the bond of peace (Eph. 4:3)! It is through the peace and prosperity of the church that blessing will flow out to the world.

That is the thought in verse 8. **For the sake of** relatives and friends, we should long to see the internal wounds of the church healed, its strifes and divisions ended. Barnes explains:

> This expresses the true feelings of piety all over the world; this is one of the grounds of the strong love which the friends of God have for the Church—because they hope and desire that through the Church those most near to their hearts will find salvation.[94]

As already mentioned, the greatest glory of the city is that the house of the Lord is there. Not the city's location, nor its misshapen buildings nor its sad history—no, the central fact is that God chose this city as the site for the temple. The presence of the Lord casts an aura of glory about all that He touches in grace.

Centuries later Jesus was to remind the Pharisees and scribes of this truth. They valued the gold of the temple more than the temple itself, the gift on the altar more than the altar. Jesus pointed out that it is the temple that makes the gold sacred, and the altar that sanctifies the gift (Matt. 23:16–22). And so it is the Lord Himself who set Jerusalem apart from all other cities in the world.

Psalm 123: Eyes that Look for Mercy

There are two key words in this **Song of Ascents**, "eyes" and "mercy." The first is found four times, the second three. The scene is the land of captivity—an all-too-familiar setting for the oppressed people of Israel. They found themselves there in Egypt, in Babylon, in Nazi Germany, in the Warsaw ghetto and more recently in Siberian slave-labor camps. Though the name is not mentioned, the country here is probably Babylon.

123:1 With **eyes** upturned to **the heavens** and straining for some sight of divine mercy, the captives plead with the Lord to end their long, dark night of persecution.

123:2 They compare themselves to **servants** looking **to the hand of their masters**, and **as . . . a maid** looking **to the hand of her mistress**. This is usually interpreted to mean a readiness to perceive and to obey the will of the master. But that is not the picture here. Rather it indicates the attentiveness and expectancy of the Jews for Jehovah to have **mercy** upon them. And the particular **mercy** which they have in mind is a speedy end to their exile and a return to the land of heart's desire. They are looking to His **hand** for salvation from their oppressors.

123:3, 4 Twice the urgent plea for **mercy** ascends to the throne of God from a people who have had more than their fill of **contempt**. Day after day they have had a diet of **scorn** and hatred, dished out by their Gentile overlords. Too long they have endured the cutting, snide remarks **of those who are at ease** (Zech. 1:15). Too long they have suffered under the arrogance of their **proud** Babylonian captors (Jer. 50:31, 32). Now they are surfeited. Enough is enough! They feel that the breaking time has come.

And so they pour out this compelling prayer to the One who is their only refuge and security in a world of anti-Semitism and discrimination—to the Friend of the oppressed and downtrodden.

Psalm 124: The All—Important *"If"*

124:1 "If it had not been the LORD who was on our side . . ."

Everything depended on that *if*. It spelled the difference between deliverance and disaster. But the Lord *was* there, and that made all the difference.

Probably no people have had as many narrow escapes as the Jews. According to all natural laws, they should have been extinct long ago. When you think of the sieges, the massacres, the pogroms, the gas chambers, the ovens, the bombs, it is a miracle they have survived. But survive they did—and that for one compelling reason—the **LORD was on** their **side**.

Unfortunately the nation has not always been willing to acknowledge that fact. Too often they have chalked up their victories to their own cleverness and power. But there have always been those godly Jews who realized that apart from the Lord, they would have been exterminated.

124:2–5 The psalmist thinks of times when enemies **rose up against** Israel in overwhelming numbers and with superior armaments. Food supplies dwindled to precarious levels. Medical supplies were gone. Communications were cut off. Necessities had to be improvised out of whatever was available. They were completely surrounded. Their enemies were threatening to drive them into the sea. The outlook was grim.

124:6, 7 Like ferocious beasts, the foe was about to swallow them alive. Or to change the figure, they were about to be engulfed in a great tidal wave of Gentile military might.

But then the unexpected happened. **The LORD** caused the enemy to quarrel among themselves over strategy. Or to get faulty intelligence reports concerning the Jews. Or to panic over the death of a leader. Or to agree to a cease-fire when victory was in their clutch.

On the other hand, the Lord may have led the Jews to unexpected food reserves. Or to hidden caches of weapons. Or He may have brought outside help from the most unlikely source. In either case, the converging of circumstances was so marvelous that it could only be brought about by the hand of God.

Those who have spiritual intelligence give all the glory to the Lord for their mysterious, miraculous deliverance. The carnivorous Gentile beasts have not succeeded in devouring little Israel. God's people have escaped from the trap that was set for them by Gentile summitry. **The snare** has been **broken**, the ring of steel surrounding the Jews has been snapped, and once again they have **escaped**.

124:8 Their humble and grateful confession is this:

> **Our help is in the name of the Lord,**
> **Who made heaven and earth.**

However, Israel has no monopoly on the God of miracles. The church can appropriate the words of this Psalm in celebrating God's nick-of-time deliverances. And individual believers know that if the Lord had not been on their side, they would have been completely subdued by the world, the flesh and the devil.

Psalm 125: The Way of Peace

125:1 **Mount Zion** is one of the promontories in the city of Jerusalem, and is sometimes used as a figure of speech for the city itself. Here it signifies the ultimate in stability and strength, a citadel that cannot be moved.

The man of faith is like that. His life is built on the solid rock. When the rains fall, and the floods come, and the winds blow and beat upon his house, it does not fall, because it has been built on the rock (Matt. 7:25).

The psalmist says that **Mount Zion . . . abides forever**. As far as the earthly city is concerned, this must be understood as the way it appeared to believers at that time. We know from the NT that the earth will some day be destroyed by fire (2 Pet. 3:7, 10, 12). However, we ourselves use similar expressions. We speak of the everlasting hills and the eternal city (Rome).

The important point is that although Mt. Zion will one day be destroyed, the believer in Christ will never perish. Because he is positionally in Christ, he is as safe as God can make him.

125:2 The psalmist saw another spiritual truth in the topography of **Jerusalem**. It is surrounded by **mountains** from which its army can guard every approach to the city. So **the Lord** Himself forms a protective ring around His children **"from this time forth and forever."** This is the hedge which Satan spoke of as encircling Job.

> Have You not made a hedge around him, around his household, and around all that he has on every side? (Job 1:10).

Which means, of course, that nothing can reach the trusting saint except by the permissive will of God.

125:3 Another gigantic claim is made in verse 3:

> **For the scepter of wickedness shall not rest on the land allotted to the righteous, lest the righteous reach out their hands to iniquity.**

Some might take exception to the first part of this verse by pointing out that the land of Israel has often been invaded and conquered by wicked men. This is true. But the verse must be interpreted in its context. The Psalm is dealing with people who trust in the Lord; its promises are only for that kind of people. It was only when Israel was away from the Lord that its borders were violated and its walls breached. As long as they obeyed the Lord and trusted in Him, **the scepter of wickedness**, that is, the rule of wicked Gentile monarchs was not allowed to come near them.

An interesting reason is given why God kept back the menacing enemies of Israel during times when the people walked with Him. The reason was that the **righteous** Israelites might be tempted to **reach out their hands to** do wrong. God saves us not only from outside foes but from the inner self and its tendency to sin when unjustly treated.

125:4 The fourth verse must also be understood in the context: **Do good, O LORD, to those who are good, and to those who are upright in their hearts**. The **good** people here are those who have been saved by faith and who walk in obedience to the Lord. Their uprightness is not the basis of their salvation, but is the fruit of their trust and obedience.

125:5 There are others who profess to be members of God's people but who **turn aside to their crooked ways. The LORD shall lead them away** into captivity and dispersion **with the workers of iniquity**.

Peace be upon Israel! The Psalm itself gives the formula for **peace**, both for Israel and everyone else. It is found through trust in the Lord Jesus. When Israel turns to Him whom they pierced and mourns for Him as for an only Son, then the peace that has eluded them for centuries will be theirs at last.

Shalom, shalom!

Psalm 126: Tearful Sowing, Joyful Reaping

126:1 When the announcement reached the Jewish communities in exile, the people were electrified and ecstatic. The Persian King Cyrus had decreed that the captives could return to their land. It seemed almost too good to be true. During the long years in exile, many of them had wondered if they would ever see Jerusalem again. But now at last the news had come. As they gathered their few pitiful belongings together, they were like people walking around in a trance.

126:2 The excited gabble of a normally demonstrative and talkative people was even louder than usual, For the first time in about seventy years, they had something to bring keenest pleasure to them. Something to make them hilarious. They were going home. As their preparations moved into high gear, they laughed and sang—something new for them.

126:3 It was a tremendous testimony to the non-Jewish people. They seemed to sense that things happened for the Jews that could not be explained on the natural level. They acknowledged that the God of the Hebrews had intervened for them in miraculous ways. Above the other nations of the earth, Israel appeared to be the special object of Jehovah's love and care.

And the grateful exiles joyfully concurred with the Gentiles in attributing their deliverance to the Lord alone.

> **The LORD has done great things for us, and we are glad.**

126:4 But they were going back to the land a pathetic remnant with little more than the clothes they wore. They needed manpower, finances and protection. This accounts for their prayer:

> **Bring back our captivity, O LORD, as the streams in the South.**

The South (Heb., Negev) was the desert in the south. Ordinarily it was arid and barren. But after heavy rains, the dry waterbeds became torrential **streams** that made the wilderness blossom. So the returning exiles pray that what is now only a trickle of people may become a multitude until all twelve tribes have been brought back. They pray that the Lord will provide them the means to rebuild and restore. And they ask for everything else that would be needed to make them a happy, fruitful people in the land.

126:5, 6 The first year after their return would be especially difficult. There would be no crops to harvest right away. They would have to make a fresh start by planting their crops and waiting for harvest time. It would be a period of austerity, of doling out the meager food supplies as frugally as possible.

There would be a certain sorrow or frustration about sowing the seed for that first crop. Here is a farmer whose barrel of grain is low. He can use the grain to feed his family now or he can sow most of it in hope of an abundant supply in days to come. He decides to **sow** it, but as he dips his hand into his apron and scatters the seed over the plowed land, his **tears** fall into the apron. He is thinking of his wife and children, of the skimpy bowls of porridge, of how sacrificially they will have to live in the days till harvest. He feels as if he is taking food out of their mouths.

But a cheering word goes out to the returned exiles:

> **He who continually goes forth weeping, bearing seed for sowing, shall doubtless come again with rejoicing, bringing his sheaves with him.**

So they go forth and sow the seed. Their present anguish will be more than compensated by the **joy** of **bringing** their **sheaves** of ripened grain to the barn.

The principle applies also, of course, in the spiritual realm. Those who live sacrificially for the spread of the gospel may endure present privation, but what is that compared to the joy of seeing souls saved and in heaven worshiping the Lamb of God forever and forever?

It is true also in the matter of soul winning. Someone has wisely said, "Winners of souls are first weepers for souls." So our prayer should be:

> Let me look on the crowd as my Savior did,
> Till my eyes with tears grow dim.
> Let me view with pity the wandering sheep
> And love them for love of Him.
>
> —*Author unknown*

Psalm 127: God in Everything

There is a saying, "Little is much if God is in it," but the reverse is also true, "Much is nothing if God is not in it." And that's what this Psalm says: unless our activity is ordered and directed by the Lord, it is a waste of time and energy. We can set out on projects of our own, even in Christian service; we can build vast organizational empires; we can amass statistics to show phenomenal results; but if the projects are not vines planted by the Lord, they are worse than worthless. "Man proposes but God disposes."

The psalmist chooses four common activities of life to illustrate his point. They are house construction, civil defense, general employment, and family building.

127:1 There are two ways to build a **house**. One is to move ahead with plans based on one's own knowledge, skill and financial resources, then ask God's blessing on the completed structure. The other is to wait until the LORD has given unmistakable guidance, then move ahead in conscious dependence on Him. In the first case, the project never rises above flesh and blood. In the second, there is the thrill of seeing God working through the marvelous provision of needed supplies, through the miraculous timing and sequence of events, and through the converging of circumstances that would never happen according to the laws of chance. It makes all the difference in the world to be building with God.

The second illustration of the futility of human effort without God is in the area of security: **Unless the LORD guards the city, the watchman stays awake in vain.** This does not mean we should not have a police force or other protective agencies. Rather it means that ultimately our security lies in the Lord, and unless we are really depending on Him, our ordinary precautions are not enough to keep us safe.

127:2 In our everyday employment, it is futile to work long hours, earning one's living through anxious toil, unless we are in the place of God's choosing. Please don't misunderstand. Throughout the Bible we are taught to work diligently to supply our own needs, the needs of our family, and the needs of others. This Psalm does not encourage people to sit around all day drinking colas and sponging off friends. But the point is this—if we are working in independence of God, we don't really get anywhere. Haggai describes the situation very well:

> You have sown much, and bring in little; you eat, but do not have enough; you drink, but you are not filled with drink; you clothe yourselves, but no one is warm; and he who earns wages, earns wages to put into a bag with holes (Hag. 1:6).

On the other hand, if we are really yielded to the Lord and living for His glory, He can give us gifts while we are sleeping which we could never obtain through long, weary hours of labor without Him. That seems to be the meaning of the clause, **"For so He gives His beloved sleep,"** or as Moffatt translates it, "God's gifts come to His loved ones, as they sleep."

127:3 The fourth and final illustration has to do with building a family. And children are one of the gifts of God. **"Behold, children are a heritage from the LORD; the fruit of the womb is a reward."**

What is said about children presupposes that they have been brought up in a home where the Lord has been honored and obeyed. They have been brought up in the discipline and instruction of the Lord.

127:4 "Like arrows in the hand of a warrior, so are the children of one's youth." When parents become old, they can depend on godly children to fight for them as a **warrior**, and also to provide for them as a hunter does with his bow and **arrows**.

127:5 "Happy is the man who has his quiver full of them!" In spite of the torrent of modern propaganda against large families, God pronounces a blessing on **the man who has** a **quiver full of** children. But once again it is assumed that they are believing children, members of the household of faith. Otherwise they could be an enormous heartache rather than a blessing.

"They shall not be ashamed, but shall speak with their enemies in the gate." F. B. Meyer reminds us that contending armies of a besieged city would meet at the gate. So the thought here is that a man's children defend him in civil or legal matters so that he does not suffer loss or injury. They see that justice is done.

The Psalm is a tremendous unfolding of the word of the Lord through Zechariah, "Not by might nor by power, but by My Spirit, says the Lord of hosts" (Zech. 4:6). There is such a danger that we depend on the power of the dollar or on human ingenuity. But the Lord's will is not accomplished in that way. It is by His Spirit that we build for eternity. It is not what we do for God through our own resources, but what He does through us by His mighty power. All we can produce is wood, hay, stubble. He can use us to produce gold, silver, precious stones. When we act in our own strength, we are spinning our wheels. When we bring God into everything, our lives become truly efficient. Carnal weapons produce carnal results. Spiritual weapons produce spiritual results.

Psalm 128: The Blessing of the Lord

128:1 The believer who really enjoys life to the hilt is the one who acknowledges **the Lord** in every area of life and **who walks** in practical obedience to the Word of God.

Under the law of Moses this man was rewarded with natural blessings.

128:2 *Longevity.* He did not die prematurely but lived to enjoy the material wealth for which he had labored.

Happiness. He enjoyed freedom from discord and strife, and the joyful contentment of having God's countenance shining upon him.

Prosperity. Things went **well with** him. He was protected from calamity, blight, drought, pestilence and defeat.

128:3 *Productivity.* Like a fruitful vine, his **wife** bore many **children**. There they are, clustered **around** his **table**, like tender **olive plants**—full of vim, vigor and vitality.

128:4 In the Dispensation of Grace, the believer is already blessed in Christ with every spiritual blessing in the heavenly places (Eph. 1:3). But as Williams says, "faith can spiritualize the material blessings of this song and make them real and present." Better than long life on earth is the life of the Lord Jesus energizing us. No happiness can compare with that of the soul set free. Soul prosperity is the best prosperity. And spiritual reproduction surpasses the joys of physical fertility.

128:5, 6 The last two verses of the Psalm may be read as a promise or a prayer. Following the latter, they ask that **the Lord** will **bless** His believing people from His dwelling place in the sanctuary in **Zion** or from His throne in **Jerusalem**. They ask that the godly might **see the** prosperity **of Jerusalem** as long as they live. They ask for long life to enjoy the second generation of offspring. And they pray for **peace upon Israel**.

The Psalm joyfully anticipates the future blessedness of the individual and the nation when Israel's King returns and reigns in righteousness.

Psalm 129: The Harvest of Anti-Semitism

This **Song of Ascents** rehearses Israel's past treatment at the hands of her many foes, then asks the Lord to insure an unpromising future for these cruel aggressors.

129:1, 2 From the early days of nationhood, Israel had been sorely **afflicted**. Their oppression in Egypt, for example, was an unforgettable chapter of servitude and suffering in the nation's **youth**. **Yet** the enemy never succeeded in exterminating the Jews. God's people were always delivered from captivity. Their survival has been one of the great miracles of history.

129:3 Their sufferings were deep and prolonged. The Gentile taskmasters rode over them like a farmer plowing a field. The **furrows** on their **back** were long welts caused by the lash.

129:4 But **the Lord**, who is **righteous**, intervened in the nick of time by cutting **the cords** or chains with which His people were held captive by their merciless assailants.

129:5–7 May it always be the case that anti-Semites are disgraced and routed. May they never experience a harvest of blessing. Rather let them be like the few odd clumps of **grass** that grow on the flat rooftops in the Middle East. Because they have no depth of soil, these tufts cannot take good root, and they are soon scorched by the blazing sun. Actually the grass **withers before it** has a chance to produce any sizable growth. A **reaper** would never get a handful to cut, let alone **sheaves** to hold in **his arms**.

129:8 Rooftop grass could never produce the happy harvest scene in which onlookers say to the reapers, **"The blessing of the Lord be upon you"** and the reapers call back, **"We bless you in the name of the Lord"** (see Ruth 2:4). So may the enemies of Israel be denied any happy outcome to all the cruel plowing they have done down through the centuries. Rather let them reap what they have sown.

Psalm 130: Out of the Depths

Someone has said that the best prayer comes from a strong, inward necessity. In pleasant, prosperous times of life, meaningful prayer is often the first casualty. But when we are being tossed around by the storms of life, then we really know how to touch the throne of grace in fervent, insistent pleading.

130:1, 2 I am often amazed at the depths of sorrow and suffering that can be endured by the human frame. The psalmist is in one of those dark troughs of life. There is no way to look but up. And so his clamant call goes winging up from **out of the depths** to the throne of heaven.

He urgently pleads that his thin, solitary **voice** be heard, that the **Lord** will grant him audience. The plea is, of course, answered. Always!

In the suppliant's mind, his trouble was somehow connected with some sin. This may or may not have been true. But in any case it is always a good idea to eliminate unconfessed sin as a possible cause of our calamities.

130:3, 4 If the **Lord should mark iniquities** in the sense of keeping an itemized account and making each of us pay on the line, then the situation would be positively hopeless. But we can be eternally grateful that there is a way in which sins can be forgiven. **There is forgiveness** for the guilty sinner and **there is forgiveness** for the sinning saint.

The first is *judicial* forgiveness, that is, forgiveness from God, the Judge. It is obtained by faith in the Lord Jesus Christ. It covers the penalty of all sins—past, present, and future. It is possible because of the finished work of Christ at Calvary; in His death He paid the penalty for all our sins and God can freely forgive us because all His righteous claims have been met by our Substitute.

The second is *parental* forgiveness—the forgiveness of God, our Father. It is obtained by confessing our sins to Him. It results in a restoration of fellowship with God and with His family. It too is purchased for us by the blood of Jesus, shed on the cross.

One result of His forgiveness is that He should **be feared**. When I think what it cost Him to forgive my sins, and when I realize that His **forgiveness** is full, free, and eternal, it causes me to reverence, trust, love and worship Him forever.

130:5,6 Although the psalmist hasn't asked directly for forgiveness, it is certainly implied in verses 3, 4. But when he says in verse 5 that he **waits for the LORD**, *he does not mean for forgiveness*. That is assured as soon as he confesses. Rather he **waits** for the Lord to deliver him from the depths. Sometimes God answers prayer immediately. Sometimes He teaches us to wait.

God answers prayer; sometimes when
  hearts are weak,
He gives the very gifts His children
  seek,
But often faith must learn a deeper
  rest,
And trust God's silence when He
  cannot speak;
For He whose name is love, will send
  the best;
Stars may burn out, nor mountain
  walls endure,
But God is true, His promises are
  sure
To those who seek.

—*Author unknown*

So here he has learned to **wait for the LORD** and to **hope in His word**, that is, in His promise to hear and to answer. **More than** the watchmen wait for the light of dawn, he longs to see the Lord bring light into his darkness.

But verses 5, 6 have a wider application that we must not miss. They express the earnest longing of the believer today as he looks for the coming of Christ to translate His church to heaven. This blessed hope will not be disappointed.

130:7, 8 The last two verses of the Psalm may be thought of as the psalmist's testimony after his prayer for deliverance had been answered. Having proved God's faithfulness for himself, he wants others to share the experience also. It is always this way: if a person really believes something, he is anxious to communicate it to others.

So **Israel** is encouraged to **hope in the LORD**. Three reasons are given. First, His **mercy** is unchanging. Then, His **redemption** is **abundant** in its supply. And finally His willingness to **redeem Israel from all his iniquities** is assured.

The Psalm opened in the depths of gloom. It closes with a vibrant call to trust in the God for whom no problem is too mountainous, no dilemma too complex.

Psalm 131: Intellectual Humility

There are some problems in life that defy explanation. Mysteries too deep to fathom. Strange circumstances that puzzle the keenest intellect.

Who, for example, can say the last word on the problem of human suffering?

Who can answer all the questions that surface in the area of unanswered prayer?

Who can reconcile God's sovereign election and man's free will?

131:1 David didn't profess to know all the answers. His **heart** was not lifted up like that of an insufferable know-it-all. His **eyes** were not raised too high, as if he were the finished intellectual egotist. He recognized his limitations and was not ashamed to say, "I don't know." He was content to know what he could know and leave the mysteries with God. Why occupy himself with things that were too **great** and **too profound** for him? No, he gave God credit for understanding things that he could never understand.

131:2 This attitude of trust in the wisdom, love, and power of God brought peace and quietness to his **soul**. He was **like a weaned child** who is **quieted** at his mother's breasts. At the outset a child may be squalling, restless, impatient. But then feeding time comes and the baby is suddenly silent, relaxed in his mother's arms. And so we can work ourselves into a dither of frustration, trying to understand things that are too high for us. But as soon as we leave the unanswerable questions with God, our souls are loosed from tension.

131:3 The psalmist recommends this attitude of confidence in the Lord to all of **Israel**. So did A. W. Tozer. He wrote: "Never forget that it is a privilege to wonder, to stand in delighted silence before the Supreme Mystery and whisper, 'O Lord God, thou knowest.' "

Psalm 132: Prayer and Promise

There is considerable disagreement as to the author and occasion of this Psalm. One of the possible viewpoints is that it was composed by Solomon when he brought the ark of the covenant to its proper place in the newly-constructed temple in Jerusalem. In that case, the first ten verses are Solomon's prayer that the Lord will descend in the Shekinah (the glory cloud) and dwell above the ark. Verses 11 and 12 reaffirm the covenant God made with David. And the last six verses contain specific promises from God corresponding to Solomon's specific requests.

132:1–5 The opening request that the LORD should **remember** in David's favor **all** the **afflictions** that he endured does not refer to the general hardships which dogged his steps throughout his life, but rather to the deep emotional and physical experiences he passed through in order to have the temple erected as God's dwelling place on earth. This is explained in the next three verses. On an occasion not otherwise recorded in the Scriptures, David had made a solemn contract with Jehovah that he would **not** enter his own **house**, lie down in his own **bed**, or go to sleep **until** he had arranged a house **for the LORD, a place** where **the Mighty One of Jacob** might dwell. The vow must not be understood with precise literalness. It is David's figurative way of saying that he would not rest contentedly until he had established a permanent place for the ark of God. We know that David was not permitted to build the temple because he was a man of war, but he was enabled to make important contributions of materials to Solomon, and God rewarded him for his desire.

132:6 These verses seem to be a reminiscence concerning the location of the ark in Kirjath, and the expressed determination of David's men to bring it to Jerusalem. Verse 6 is especially difficult because it seems to connect the ark with **Ephrathah** (Bethlehem), yet there is no record of the ark's ever having been there. The following are the common attempts to solve the difficulty.

1. The king and his men first heard of the ark's whereabouts when they were in Bethlehem, but they

finally located it in Jaar, i.e., Kirjath-Jearim.

2. Ephrathah may stand for Ephraim, and refer to the residence of the ark in Shiloh.
3. Ephrathah may mean Caleb Ephrathah (see 1 Chron. 2:24) and not Bethlehem. According to this view, Caleb Ephrathah is the same as Jaar (wood) of Kirjath-Jearim, which means "the city **of the woods**." If this is so, then the two clauses of verse 6 form a parallelism in which the meaning of both is the same.

Behold, we heard of it in Ephrathah;
We found it in the fields of the woods.

132:7 As the procession moves with the sacred chest to Jerusalem, the people rejoice that they are going to God's **tabernacle** to **worship at His footstool**. The ark itself is conceived as being God's **footstool** since His presence was in the glory cloud above it.

132:8–10 Next we hear Solomon's prayer when he was dedicating the temple (vv. 8–10; cf. 2 Chron. 6:41, 42). He is asking God to come to dwell in the Sanctuary and thus make real the symbolism of the **ark**. Also he asks for a godly line of **priests**, for a people who are overflowing with **joy**, and for God's continued favor on the king. The phrase **"Your Anointed"** may be understood to refer to Solomon himself, but also ultimately to the Messiah.

132:11–13 **The Lord** answers the prayer first by making brief reference to the Davidic **covenant**. This covenant was unconditional as far as **David** was concerned; it promised him a **throne forevermore** and a descendant to sit upon it forever. But it was conditional as far as David's offspring were concerned; it depended on their obedience. Thus although the Lord Jesus is a descendant of David, He is not physically a descendant of Solomon but of another son of David, Nathan (Luke 3:31).

132:14–18 Then specific answers are given to Solomon's specific requests. This may be seen from the following comparisons:

Arise, O Lord, to Your resting place; You and the ark of Your strength (v. 8).	**This is My resting place forever; here I will dwell, for I have desired it** (v. 14).
Let Your priests be clothed with righteousness (v. 9a).	**I will also clothe her priests with salvation** (v. 16a).
And let Your saints shout for joy (v. 9b).	**And her saints shall shout aloud for joy** (v. 16b).
For Your servant David's sake, do not turn away the face of Your Anointed (v. 10).	**There I will make the horn of David grow; I will prepare a lamp for My Anointed . . . But upon Himself His crown shall flourish** (vv. 17, 18b).

Actually the Lord answers abundantly above all that Solomon requests. There is the added promise of plentiful provisions and of **bread** for the **poor** (v. 15). There is the promise that the **priests** will be clothed **with salvation**, not just with righteousness (v. 16a). There is the promise that **the saints** will **shout aloud for joy** (v. 16b). There is the promise that the **enemies** will be clothed **with shame** (v. 18a).

The meaning of verse 17 is that in Jerusalem God will make a powerful King to come forth from **David** (see Luke 1:69) and has prepared a **lamp** or Son (see 1 Kgs. 15:4) for David, His **Anointed**. These promises of a perpetual dynasty are fulfilled in the Lord Jesus Christ.

The **enemies** of Christ will be covered **with shame**, but His head will be crowned with glory and honor.

The head that once was crowned
with thorns
Is crowned with glory now!
Heaven's royal diadem adorns
The mighty Victor's brow!
—*Thomas Kelly*

Psalm 133: In Praise of Unity

Great things come in small packages. This Psalm is short but it is a literary and spiritual gem that makes up in quality what it lacks in quantity.

The psalmist has four main points. First, it is good and pleasant when brothers dwell together in unity. Second, it is fragrant. Third, it is refreshing. Finally, it is the sure guarantee of God's blessing.

133:1 Unity among **brethren** is a sight to **behold**. However, **unity** does not require that they see eye to eye on everything. On matters of fundamental importance they agree. On subordinate matters there is liberty for differing viewpoints. In all things there should be a spirit of love. There can be unity without uniformity; we are all different but that does not prevent our working together. All the members of the human body are different, but as they function in obedience to the head, there is a glorious unity. There can be unity without unanimity; God never intended that everyone should agree on matters of minor importance. It is enough to agree on the basics. On everything else we may disagree as long as we can do it without being disagreeable. The real enemies of unity are jealousy, gossip, backbiting, censoriousness and lovelessness.

133:2 Unity is **like the** fragrant perfume that was used in anointing **Aaron** the priest (Ex. 30:22–30). It was poured on his **head**, then ran **down** on his **beard**, and from there to the **edge of his** robe. The pleasing scent was enjoyed not only by the priest himself but by everyone in the vicinity. The holy anointing **oil** pictures the ministry of the Holy Spirit, descending as a sweet-smelling savor on God's people when they live happily together, and diffusing the aroma of their testimony to the surrounding areas.

133:3 Then again unity brings refreshment. **"It is like the dew of Hermon, descending upon the mountains of Zion."** The psalmist sees Mt. **Hermon** as the source of cool, invigorating moisture for distant mountains. Again the dew typifies the Holy Spirit, carrying refreshment from united brethren to the ends of the earth. No one can measure how far-reaching is the influence of believers who walk in fellowship with God and with one another.

The final point is that the LORD commands **the blessing** where brothers and sisters live together in unity. Take Pentecost as an illustration. The disciples were living in harmony and peace, united in prayer and waiting for the promised Holy Spirit. Suddenly the Spirit of God descended upon them in all His fullness and they went forth with the fragrance and refreshment of the gospel to Jerusalem, Judea, Samaria, and the uttermost parts of the earth.

The blessing is explained as being **life forevermore**. This may be understood in two ways. When there is unity among God's people, *they* themselves enjoy **life** in its truest sense. And not only so, they become the channels through which **life** flows out to *others*.

Psalm 134: Come, Bless the Lord!

134:1, 2 After the usual daily schedule of activities at the temple in Jerusalem, the people returned to their homes, but there were priests and Levites who stood watch during the **night** (1 Chron. 9:33), burning incense, giving thanks, and praising the Lord (2 Chron. 29:11; 31:2).

It may be that as the people withdrew, they sang the first two verses of this song to the priests. It is certainly clear that the verses are addressed to **servants of the Lord** on **night** duty in the temple, and that the ministry of these men was to **bless the Lord** and **lift up** their **hands** toward **the sanctuary** in a posture of prayer.

134:3 The response of verse 3 is the blessing of the priests invoking God's blessing on the people individually. Notice four things about the blessing.

The Blesser—**the Lord**, Jehovah, the covenant-keeping God.
His Greatness—He . . . **made heaven and earth**.
The One Blessed—May **the Lord . . . bless you** ("you" here is singular).
The Locale of the Blesser—**Zion**, the place of the sanctuary.

Psalm 135: The Why of Praise

135:1, 2 The first two verses sound out a rather general summons to **"Praise the Lord!"** It is directed quite clearly to the priests and Levites, but probably also to all the people of Israel and to all that fear the Lord (see vv. 19, 20).

135:3 Notice the many reasons that are adduced for praising His name. He **is good**. No created tongue, in time or in eternity, will ever be able to tell how good He is. All we can do is state the fact and adore.

His name is lovely, or **pleasant**. It is amazing grace that saves sinful wretches and destines them to eternal glory.

135:4 The Lord chose **Israel** as His own possession. The sovereign election of God leaves the wondering soul asking the perpetual question "Why me?" It is this that makes us worshipers!

135:5 The Lord is great. When we contemplate Him as Creator, Sustainer and Redeemer, we sing with deep appreciation "How **great** Thou art!"

Our Lord is supreme **above all gods**, that is, above all rulers and potentates and above all idols. "On His robe and on His thigh He has a name written, *KING OF KINGS, AND LORD OF LORDS*" (Rev. 19:16).

135:6 He is the universal sovereign (v. 6). He does as He **pleases** in every imaginable realm. As Arthur Pink wrote:

> Divine sovereignty means that God is God in fact, as well as in name, that He is on the Throne of the universe, directing all things, working all things "after the counsel of His own will."[95]

135:7 He holds absolute power over nature. The clouds, the **lightning** and the **wind**—formidable as they are—are directed by His mighty hand. Stephen Charnock says, "God's power is like Himself: infinite, eternal, incomprehensible; it can neither be checked, restrained, nor frustrated by the creature."

135:8, 9 He delivered Israel from **Egypt**. The greatest display of power in Israel's history was the crushing of Pharaoh through the plagues (that were climaxed by the death of **the**

firstborn) and by the parting of the Red Sea.

135:10, 11 He defeated Israel's foes. God graciously gave victory to His people over **Sihon, Og,** and the heathen nations inhabiting **Canaan**.

135:12 He gave Canaan **to Israel**. The land of Canaan was given **as a heritage to** the escapees from Egypt.

135:13 He is eternal. His **name endures forever**, and His name, of course, stands for all that He is.

He has eternal **fame**. He will be lovingly remembered **throughout** eternity.

135:14 He is just and compassionate. We can depend on this—that God will vindicate **His people** and **will have compassion on His servants**. Moses sang it first in Deuteronomy 32:36 but the song will never end.

135:15–18 He is superior to **idols**. The mere description of these false gods is enough to expose their worthlessness. They are **silver and gold**, therefore perishable. They are created by man, therefore inferior to man. They are dumb, blind, deaf and lifeless. And sad to say, **those who make them are like them**—spiritually blind, deaf, dumb, and dead.

135:19, 20 Such a consideration of the greatness of God leads to the desire to **bless** Him, that is, to shower Him with honor, praise, homage, worship and thanksgiving. All the **house of Israel** should **bless** Him. All who minister as priests (**house of Aaron**) should **bless** Him. Those who serve as Levites should **bless** Him. All **who** revere **the Lord** should **bless** Him, which is another way of saying that all classes of men should praise Him. This is what Israel will sing when the Messiah returns to Zion and reigns from Jerusalem.

135:21 Blessed be the Lord out of Zion,
Who dwells in Jerusalem!
Praise the Lord!

That is what we should be saying and doing now.

Psalm 136: The Great Hallel!

What makes this Psalm unique is that the second member of each of the twenty-six verses is the same antiphonal response, "for His mercy endures forever." "If one everlasting is not enough," wrote Thomas Goodwin, "there are twenty-six everlastings in this one psalm."

It is known as the Great Hallel, the singing of which was a regular part of the observance of both Pesach and Rosh Hashanah—the Jewish Passover and New Year celebrations. It was also used in their daily worship.

The repetition of the theme is not tiresome; it says to us that the steadfast love of the Lord needs to be constantly before us and that the subject can never be exhausted. His kindness, loyalty and fidelity never fail.

Call to Worship (136:1–3)

The introduction summons us to **give thanks to the Lord** because of who He is, and because of His intrinsic goodness. He is Jehovah—the covenant-keeping Lord. He is **the God of gods**—supreme over all the mighty rulers in the universe. He is **the Lord of lords**—the sovereign over all who hold places of leadership, whether angelic or human. But He is not only great; **He is good** as well—**good** as Creator, Redeemer, Guide, Champion, and Provider for His people.

Creator (136:4–9)

His goodness and mercy are seen first of all in the **great wonders** of creation. **By** His **wisdom** He **made the** marvelous expanse of **the heavens**. He brought forth the continents as if they were enormous floating islands. He placed gigantic light fixtures in the sky—**the sun** providing daylight, and **the moon and stars** as subdued lights for man's bedroom hours.

Redeemer (136:10–15)

The Great Creator is also the Mighty Redeemer. In order to rescue His people from Egyptian tyranny, He cut down the flower of Egypt's manhood, then took His people by His **strong hand** and led them out to freedom. To do this, He had to divide **the Red Sea** into **two** parts with a dry strip of land in between. **Israel** got **through** safely, but the soldiers of **Pharaoh** were engulfed when the waters returned to their place. It was a never-to-be-forgotten display of the steadfast love of Jehovah for His people.

Guide (136:16)

For forty years, God **led** the Israelites **through the** waste, howling **wilderness**. There were no paved highways, no road signs, no maps, but the Lord was all they needed—the Incomparable Guide.

Champion (136:17–22)

He even fought their battles for them. When King **Sihon** and King **Og** blocked their way, He soundly defeated them, **and gave their land** as part of Israel's domain.

Helper, Savior, Provider (136:23–25)

As a sort of summary, the psalmist extols Jehovah for being the wonderful Helper, Savior, and Provider that He is. **He remembered** Israel when the people were few in number, defenseless, and oppressed. He **rescued** them out of the clutches of their **enemies**. He unfailingly provides **food** for **all** living things.

The God of Heaven (136:26)

We take Him too much for granted. Constant awareness of His personal greatness and His ceaseless **mercy** would cause us to **give thanks** to Him more and more.

Psalm 137: If I Forget You, O Jerusalem!

In April, 1948, the Jewish sector of Jerusalem was practically in a state of siege. Food supplies were almost exhausted. The people were existing on a weekly ration of two ounces of margarine, a quarter of a pound of potatoes and a quarter of a pound of dried meat. Then the news spread that a convoy of trucks was arriving from Tel Aviv with supplies. Hundreds of people ran out to welcome the dozens of trucks. They will never forget the first sight they had of the convoy. On the front bumper of the blue Ford leading the procession, someone had painted the words:

If I forget you, O Jerusalem. . . .

And so these words of Psalm 137:5 have become a rallying cry for the Jewish people down through their tumultuous history of captivity and dispersion.

137:1 Written after the return from Babylonian bondage, the Psalm looks back to the bitterness of being exiled from Zion.

Whenever they had free time, perhaps on the Sabbath, they gathered **by the rivers of Babylon** to pray.

Memories would come crowding back and the tears would flow. They **remembered Zion**. To them it was the spiritual center of the whole earth and the center of their lives. They remembered the spiritual joy and exhilaration of being there during the great holy convocations. And now they could no longer go up there to worship, and the holy places were in the unclean hands of the uncircumcised heathen. As they looked into **the rivers of Babylon**, they saw in them a picture of their own rivers of tears and anguish. As Jeremiah had prayed, "My eyes overflow with rivers of water for the destruction of the daughter of my people" (Lam. 3:48). And again:

> O that my head were waters, and my eyes a fountain of tears, that I might weep day and night for the slain of the daughter of my people! (Jer. 9:1).

137:2 They had **hung** their **harps upon the willows**, or as we would say, they had put them on the shelf. And why not? There was no use for musical instruments. From the human standpoint, at least, there was nothing to sing about. And without a song to sing, there was no need of accompaniment.

137:3 It often happened that the Babylonian captors **asked** them to sing one of the Hebrew folk songs. As if to rub salt into the wounds, they would say, "**Sing us one of** those happy **songs** you used to sing in your homeland!"

137:4 Ridiculous! The Jews wouldn't sing. Not just because their hearts were breaking, but even more because it would be utterly incongruous to **sing the LORD's song** in a land of heathen idolaters. It would be like forgetting Jerusalem. They saw a moral impropriety about mixing the things of the Lord and the things of the world. "The land of the stranger and the song of the Lord can never be found together," wrote F. B. Meyer.

137:5, 6 Now that he is back in the land the psalmist expresses the enormous determination of his people to have **Jerusalem** at the center of their life—and we remember here that **Jerusalem** stands for the Lord who dwelt there. Should the time ever come when he no longer has that inexplicable, instinctive attachment to Zion, then a fitting retribution would be that his **right hand** should wither and never again be able to sweep the strings of the harp. Yes, if it should ever happen that Jerusalem doesn't have first place in his heart, then he concurs that his **tongue** should **cling to the roof of** his **mouth** so that he could never sing the sweet old songs of Zion again.

137:7 Having first pronounced these conditional curses on himself, he finds it an easy transition to think next of those who had had a part in the destruction of the Holy City.

Take the **sons of Edom**, for example. They formed a sort of cheering squad, egging the invaders to wreck it completely. "**Raze** it, tear it down!" they yelled, **"to its very foundation!"** May the Lord remember their vicious satisfaction in seeing the city laid low!

137:8 And then there was **Babylon**, of course, the cruel devastator. Though this nation was the instrument in God's hands to punish His people, yet He did not excuse the Babylonians for their merciless atrocities.

> I was angry with My people, I have profaned My inheritance, and given them into your hand. You

> showed them no mercy; on the elderly you laid your yoke very heavily (Isa. 47:6).

> I am exceedingly angry with the nations at ease; for I was a little angry, and they helped—but with evil intent (Zech. 1:15).

There was no question in the psalmist's mind as to Babylon's destruction. It had been foretold by the prophets (Isa. 13:1–22; Jer. 50:15, 28; 51:6, 36). Those who accomplished the destruction would have the satisfaction to be used by God as instruments of His judgment.

137:9 The last verse of the Psalm is the one that gives most difficulty:

> **Happy the one who takes and dashes your little ones against the rock!**

To those who have been raised on the non-violent teachings of the NT it seems unusually harsh, vindictive, and unloving. Why should innocent, defenseless children be treated so inhumanely? In answer to the question, we would suggest the following:

First, we begin with the premise that this verse is part of the Word of God, verbally and plenarily inspired. Therefore any problem lies in our understanding rather than in the Word itself. Second, the destruction of Babylon's little ones was clearly predicted by Isaiah:

> Their little children also will be dashed to pieces before their eyes; their houses will be plundered and their wives ravished (Isa. 13:16).

So the psalmist is only saying what God had already foretold (except for the part about the happiness of the ones who execute God's sentence).

Then again we know that innocent children are often involved in the consequences of their parents' sin (see Ex. 20:5; 34:7; Num. 14:18; Deut. 5:9). No man is an island. What he does affects others, either for good or for evil. Part of the bitterness of sin is that, in being allowed to work itself out, it engulfs others in its tragic retribution.

In these imprecatory passages, we keep coming back to the fact that conduct and attitudes that were suitable for a person living under the law of Moses are not necessarily suitable for a Christian living under grace. The Lord Jesus said as much in the Sermon on the Mount (see Matt. 5:21–48).

No matter how you interpret the verse, the spiritual application is clear. We must deal radically with little sins in our lives. The little darlings must be destroyed or they will destroy us. C. S. Lewis says, in this connection:

> I know things in the inner world which are like babies; the infantile beginnings of small indulgences, small resentments, which may one day become dipsomania, or settled hatred, but which woo us and wheedle us with special pleadings, and seem so tiny, so helpless that in resisting them, we feel we are being cruel to animals. They begin whimpering to us, "I don't ask much, but," or "I had at least hoped," or "you owe yourself *some* consideration." Against all of such pretty infants (the dears have such winning ways) the advice of the Psalm is the best. Knock the little brats' brains out. And "blessed" he who can, for it's easier said than done.[96]

Psalm 138: God's Faithful Word

David was exuberantly thankful for some great answer to prayer. In this expression of his gratitude, he has left us all a worthy example of how we should respond to God's wonderful deliverances. Without doubt this Psalm will realize its fullest application when Israel is finally restored under the aegis of Jesus, the Messiah.

138:1 There is nothing half-hearted about David's thanks. All his powers are employed in blessing Jehovah.

And there is nothing timid or private about his worship. He sings unashamedly **before the gods**, that is, before the kings of the earth. The word "gods" here could also mean angels or idols but the context seems to limit it to the surrounding rulers.

138:2 In accordance with the custom of godly Jews, David bowed down **toward** the **holy** tabernacle when worshiping (the temple had not yet been erected).[97] He extolled the name of Jehovah for His steadfast love and faithfulness. It is His love that prompts Him to give us "His precious and very great promises" and it is His faithfulness that insures that every one of them is fulfilled.

"For You have magnified Your word above all Your name." The context has to do with the faithfulness of God in keeping His **word**, and the meaning seems to be that He has not only done what He said He would, but has done much more in addition. Also there may be the thought that "in the abundant fulfilment of His promise (to David) God had surpassed all previous revelation of Himself."[98] If the verse is applied to the Incarnate Word, then it means, of course, that God has magnified the Lord Jesus above every other manifestation of Himself.

138:3 Verse 3 reveals the immediate occasion for the psalmist's outburst of praise. In a day of desperate need he had **cried out** to the Lord and the answer came immediately. A vast supply of **strength** was poured into his **soul**, casting out fear and emboldening him to meet danger.

138:4–6 God's faithfulness in answering David's prayer is a powerful testimony to **the kings of the earth**. They know what God had promised, and now they see how the prophecy has been fulfilled. So they too acknowledge how **great is the glory of** Jehovah. They realize that though God is the exalted One, yet He takes a special interest in **the lowly** (like David) and keeps tabs on the **proud** (like David's enemies).

138:7 It is a beautiful picture—David is surrounded by all kinds of foes, all kinds of hazards, all kinds of distresses, yet the Lord enables him to **walk** safely through them as if they didn't exist. The same **hand** that strikes out against his adversaries **will save** him from disaster.

138:8 With justified confidence, David affirms, **"The LORD will perfect that which concerns me."** It is the same confidence that Paul expressed in Philippians 1:6, "Being confident of this very thing, that He who began a good work in you will complete it until the day of Christ Jesus."

The work which His goodness began,
The arm of His strength will complete;
His promise is Yea and Amen,
And never was forfeited yet:
Things future, nor things that are
now,
Nor all things below nor above,
Can make Him His purpose forego,
Or sever our souls from His love.
—*Augustus M. Toplady*

Yes, His steadfast love endures for ever, and though we are permitted to pray with David, **"Do not forsake the works of Your hands,"** the fact is that He never can or will.

Psalm 139: God Is So Great!

God is so great!
There is nothing He does not know.
There is nowhere He is not present.
There is nothing He cannot do.

If men insist on being the enemies of such a great God, they richly deserve their fate.

That, in brief, is the flow of David's meditation in this magnificent Psalm.

139:1, 2 First, he begins with *the omniscience of God*. God knows everything.

There is nothing He does not know.
Though limitless the universe and
gloriously grand,
He knows the eternal story of
every grain of sand.

But here it is His knowledge of the individual life that is particularly in view. In 1988 it was estimated that there were 5,000,000,000 people in the world. Yet God is intimately acquainted with each one. He knows all about every one of us.

He has **searched** us **and known** us! Words and deeds, thoughts and motives, He knows us inside out. He knows when we sit **down** to relax and when we rise **up** to engage in the varied activities of life. He can tell what we are thinking, and even anticipates our thoughts.

139:3 He sees us when we walk and when we lie **down**; in other words, He keeps a constant watch on us. None of our **ways** is hidden from Him.

139:4 He knows what we are going to say before we ever say it. The future as well as the past and present is completely open to Him.

139:5 "And there is no creature hidden from His sight, but all things are naked and open to the eyes of Him to whom we must give account" (Heb. 4:13). And because His knowledge of us is so inconceivably absolute, He can guard us **behind and before**. Ever and always His **hand** is **laid** protectingly **upon** us.

139:6 God's infinite **knowledge** boggles the mind. Our human brains strain under the weight of the idea. It is **too** exalted for us to comprehend. But when we come to the frontier of our capacity to understand and can go no farther, we can still bow in worship at the immensity of the knowledge of God!

139:7, 8 Not only is God omniscient; *He is omnipresent as well*. He is in all places at one and the same time. However, the all-presence of God is not the same as pantheism. The latter teaches that the creation *is* God. The Bible teaches that God is a Person who is separate and distinct from His creation. Is there any place where man can evade the Holy **Spirit** of God? Is there any place **where** he **can** hide from the **presence** of the Lord? Suppose man should **ascend into heaven**, would he elude God there? Of course not; heaven is the throne of God (Matt. 5:34). Even if he made his **bed in** Sheol, the disembodied state, he would find the Lord **there** as well.

139:9, 10 **"If I take the wings of the morning, and dwell in the uttermost parts of the sea, even there Your hand shall lead me, and Your right hand shall hold me." The wings of the morning** are an allusion to the rays of the **morning** sun that streak across the heavens from east to west at 186,000 miles per second. Even if we could travel to some remote corner of the universe at the speed of light, we would find the Lord there, waiting to guide and uphold us.

Incidentally verses 9 and 10 are

fantastically appropriate for the age of jet travel in which we live. I shall never forget how the Lord spoke to me through this precious promise as I was about to embark on an extended ministry trip in 1969. The many jet aircraft in which I flew were like the wings of the morning, taking me literally to **the uttermost parts of the** earth. But always there was the sense of the Lord's presence and protection, regardless of speed or distance. So claim this promise for yourself, and share it with Christian friends who travel by air.

139:11, 12 If a person wanted **the darkness** to **hide** him **from** God, he would be trusting a false refuge. **Night** cannot shut out the presence of the Lord. **Darkness** is not dark to Him. **"The night shines as the day; the darkness and the light are both alike to You."**

God is absolutely inescapable. As Pascal said, "His center is everywhere; His circumference is nowhere."

139:13, 14 So much then for the omnipresence of God. David now turns to consider *His power and skill.* And the particular phase of divine omnipotence he chooses is the marvelous development of a baby in his mother's womb. In a speck of watery material smaller than the dot over this i, all the future characteristics of the child are programmed—the color of his skin, eyes and hair, the shape of his facial features, the natural abilities he will have. All that the child will be physically and mentally is contained in germ form in that fertilized egg. From it will develop:

> . . . 60 trillion cells, 100 thousand miles of nerve fiber, 60 thousand miles of vessels carrying blood around the body, 250 bones, to say nothing of joints, ligaments and muscles.[99]

David describes the formation of the fetus with exquisite delicacy and beauty. **"You formed my inward parts; You covered me in my mother's womb."** Yes, God **formed** our **inward parts**; each one a marvel of divine engineering. Think of the brain, for instance, with its capacity for recording facts, sounds, odors, sights, touch, pain; with its ability to recall; with its power to make computations; with its seemingly endless flair for making decisions and solving problems.

And God knit us together in our **mother's womb**. This aptly describes the marvelous weaving of the muscles, sinews, ligaments, nerves, blood vessels and bones of the human frame.

David bursts forth in **praise** to the Lord. As he thinks of man, the crown of God's creation, he can only confess that he is **fearfully and wonderfully made**. The more we think of the marvels of the human body, its orderliness, its complexity, its beauty, its instincts and inherited factors—the more we wonder how anyone trained in natural science can fail to be a believer in an infinite Creator.

139:15 Again the psalmist reverts to the time when his body was being formed in his mother's womb. Notice here that he uses the personal pronouns *I, my, me* to refer to the embryo or fetus. The scriptural view is that human personality exists before birth and that abortion therefore, except in cases of extreme medical necessity, is murder.

David was aware that God knew him through and through from the very beginning. His **frame**, that is, his skeletal structure was **not hidden from** God **when** David **was** being **made in secret, and skillfully wrought in the lowest parts of the earth.** It cannot mean below the surface of the earth; no one is formed there. In the context it can only mean "inside the mother's womb." A similar expression is found in Ephesians 4:9, which speaks of Christ as having descended into the *lower parts of the earth*. Once again in the context it refers to His entering the world through the ante-chamber of the virgin's womb. It is His Incarnation that is in view.

139:16 When the psalmist speaks of his **unformed... substance**, he uses a word that means something rolled or wrapped together. Barnes and others think that the word most aptly denotes the embryo, or the fetus, "where all the members of the body are as yet folded up, or undeveloped; that is, before they have assumed their distinct form and proportions." Even in that preliminary phase of his existence, God's **eyes** beheld the sweet singer of Israel.

And in God's **book, all the days** of David's life were recorded by the divine Architect before that historic moment when David announced his arrival by that first lusty cry.

139:17, 18a The psalmist thinks of God's careful planning in the creation of his spirit, soul, and body. **How precious . . . are** His **thoughts**—His attention to the minutest details. Andrew Ivy says, "Each cell almost without exception 'knows' its role in carrying out design or purpose for the welfare of the body as a whole."

139:18b "When I awake, I am still with You." It seems to me that the psalmist is here referring to the moment of his birth. In the preceding verses (13–18a) he has been emphasizing God's closeness to him during the nine months prior to his birth. But even after he is born the picture does not change; he is still with the Lord as his Sustainer, Protector, and Guide. He speaks of his birth as an *awaking* just as we speak of it as "first seeing the light of day."

139:19–22 After contemplating the *omniscience*, the *omnipresence* and the *omnipotence* of God, the psalmist thinks of those puny men who dare to turn against Him, and he concludes that their punishment is well-deserved. Inevitably some will raise their eyebrows at David's prayer in verses 19–22 as being something less than Christian in its tone. They will protest that the psalmist's sentiments are judgmental and incompatible with divine love. For my own part I feel that the love of God has been emphasized all out of proportion to His holiness and righteousness. It is *true* that God is love but it is not *all* the truth. That is only *one* of His attributes. And His love can never be exercised at the expense of any other attribute. Furthermore, the fact that God is love does not mean that He is incapable of hating; "the one who loves violence His soul hates" (Ps. 11:5); He hates all evildoers (Ps. 5:5); He hates haughty eyes, a lying tongue, hands that shed innocent blood, a heart that devises wicked plans, feet that make haste to run to evil, a false witness who breathes out lies, and a man who sows discord among brothers (Prov. 6:16–19).

Edward J. Young reminds us:

> Before we proceed to condemn David for this prayer, it is well to note that we ourselves pray for the same thing, whenever we pray the words of the Lord's prayer, "Thy kingdom come, Thy will be done."[100]

The coming of Christ's kingdom will be preceded by the destruction of His foes, so to pray for the one is to pray for the other. David unashamedly longs for the time when God will slay the wicked, and when men of blood will have ceased their harassment of him forever (v. 19). These are the men who maliciously defy the Lord God and who lift themselves up against God with evil intent.

David's hatred of these men was not a matter of personal pique. Rather it was because they hated God and rebelled against the Most High. It was his zeal for the Lord's honor that made him **hate them with perfect hatred** and **count them** as his own **enemies**. In this he reminds us of the Lord Jesus whose zeal for His Father's house prompted Him to drive out the money changers. "The strings of David's harp were the chords of the heart of Jesus." Young explains:

> David hated, but his hatred was like God's hatred; it proceeded from no evil emotion, but rather from the earnest and thoroughly sincere desire that the purposes of God must stand and that wickedness must perish. Had David not hated, he would have desired the success of evil and the downfall of God Himself. It is well to keep these thoughts in mind when we consider the nature of David's hatred.[101]

139:23, 24 The Psalm closes with a prayer that has perennial suitability for all God's people, a prayer that will never die as long as there are sinning saints on earth. It asks the Mighty God to thoroughly **search** and **know** the **heart**, to carefully test and **know** the thoughts or **anxieties**. It asks Him to expose every **wicked way** in order that it might be confessed and forsaken. And finally it asks Him to **lead** him **in the way everlasting**.

It is not the challenge of a person protesting his innocence or righteousness. Rather it is the confession of one who has been in the presence of the Lord and is convicted of his own sinfulness. He realizes that he is not cognizant of all his iniquities and wants the Lord to point them out so they can be dealt with effectively.

Psalm 140: From the Hands of the Wicked

140:1–3 **David** begins with a prayer for deliverance from the defamation of the foe. **Evil men** were slandering him and **violent men** were hatching horrendous plans against him. They weren't happy unless they were stirring up **war**. They had honed **their tongues** to a fine edge, and deadly **poison** came shooting out from **under their lips**.

140:4, 5 But the psalmist also needed protection from the snares of the enemy. These **wicked** men were masters in the art of trapping. They planted devices to trip him up. They put hidden booby-traps in his path. They **spread a net** to get him all fouled up. They dangled baits and lures all along the way.

140:6–8 And then too, he needed protection from their murderous scheming. So he draws near to God.

In commitment—**"You are my God."**

In petition—**"Hear the voice of my supplications."**

In dependence—**"O God the Lord, the strength of my salvation."**

In gratitude—**"You have covered my head"** (as with a helmet) **"in the day of battle."**

In supplication—**"Do not grant, O Lord, the desires of the wicked; do not further his wicked scheme."**

This last supplication means, "Do not let him do the things he wants to do against me. Do not seem to be an accomplice to his evil plot by even allowing it." We know that God would never aid and abet any wickedness, but the thought here is that the mere toleration of it might seem to indicate His approval.

140:9–11 Next the psalmist prays that the tables will be turned on the wicked, that the dire things they had mapped out for him might come crashing down on their own proud heads, that **burning coals** might rain **upon them**, that they might be cast into dungeons without any means of escape. He asks that **a slanderer** might never get a foothold in the land, and that disaster will track down the **violent man** without delay.

140:12, 13 The Psalm closes with quiet confidence in the righteous Lord. Whatever happens, David knows that right will prevail—that **the LORD** is on the side of **the afflicted** and **the poor**. And **the righteous shall** always have reason to thank the Lord for His help. **The upright shall dwell in** His **presence** forever, and that makes all the sufferings of this life seem like pin-pricks.

Psalm 141: Prayer Counted as Incense

141:1 At the outset of the Psalm **David** prays for audience and acceptance. As his plaintive cry wings its way heavenward, he asks that the **LORD** will come to him quickly and listen attentively.

141:2 This verse is extraordinarily beautiful. He asks that his **prayer** might be as pleasing and fragrant to God **as incense**, and that **the lifting up of** his **hands** in supplication might have the same impact with the Lord as **the evening sacrifice**.

141:3, 4 But then he moves from generalities to specifics. His first main concern is that he might be kept from partnership with ungodly men in word or in deed. He asks for **a guard** to be stationed at his **mouth** to prevent the escape of any wrong word, to keep **the door of** his **lips** from speech that would not be honoring to the Lord. Then too, he asks for a **heart** that is free from any hankering to collaborate with the corrupt men in their **wicked** practices. He does not want to partake of their advantages, however attractive or tempting they might seem.

141:5 The suggestions, criticisms, and rebukes of godly friends are welcomed by sensible people. We often cannot see faults in ourselves as clearly as we can see them in others. Only those who really care for us are willing to point out our defects and "blind spots." It is **a kindness** on their part and should be welcomed like medicine by us.

For still my prayer is against the deeds of the wicked.

The connection here is abrupt, but the meaning seems to be that David continues to pray that the criminal plans of the wicked men mentioned in verse 4 will fail. Darby translates this clause "for yet my prayer also is [for them] in their calamities." Here the thought is that he prays for those who rebuke him in kindness when trouble comes into their lives. Some take it to mean that he prays for his enemies in their calamities, but such a magnanimous Christian attitude seems to be contradicted by verse 10.

141:6 Their judges are overthrown by the sides of the cliff, and they hear my words, for they are sweet.

Their judges here probably refers to the ring-leaders of the evil Mafia. When they meet their inevitable doom, the rest of the sinners will realize that David's words were true after all.

141:7 Our bones are scattered at

the mouth of the grave, as when one plows and breaks up the earth.

Here the subject seems to shift from the enemies of Israel to the Jewish people themselves. Their persecutions have been as thorough as the plowing of a field. Now it is as if nothing is left but their skeletons, and Sheol waits with open **mouth** to devour the **bones**. This makes us think of Ezekiel's vision of the dry bones, referring, of course, to Israel (Ezek. 37:1–14).

141:8–10 In the last three verses, the psalmist prays for deliverance for himself and retribution for his enemies. His expectation is solely from **the Lord**, and his hope for refuge and defense is in **God** alone. Therefore he asks that he might be delivered from the well-laid traps of the ungodly, and that they themselves may be caught in them.

Psalm 142: No Man Cares

Pursued by his enemies, deserted by his friends, holed up **in** a **cave**—that is where we find **David** now.

142:1, 2 He is praying out loud—even if he is alone. The cries and supplications of a forsaken man reverberate through the cavern. He pours out his **complaint before** the Lord—not that he is angry or resentful but simply that he wants to tell the Lord all about his **trouble** and grief. It is comforting for him to know that when his strength is all but gone, Jehovah knows what he is going through.

142:3, 4 One major factor in his tale of woe is the constant threat of his enemies; they are always setting a trap where they think he will walk. When he looks to the right, that is, to the place of an advocate or helper, there is no one. Everyone seems indifferent to his desperate need. No one cares for his life. It is really a haunting cry, **"No one cares for my soul,"** a terrible indictment against a selfish, depersonalized society—and perhaps today against a sleeping church.

142:5–7 But if there is no refuge on the human level, he can turn to the **Lord**, an unfailing **refuge** and a blessed **portion in the land of the living**. So David asks the Lord to come to his rescue quickly because he is at the end of his rope. Those who are out after him hold the balance of power, so he needs the Lord to tip the scales in his favor. When Jehovah delivers him from this **prison** of exile and trouble, David will show how thankful he is.

Also the believers will crowd around to congratulate him and join in thanksgiving because the Lord has been so good to him. As Clarke says, "Those who cannot protect us in our trouble may yet participate in our triumph."[102]

Psalm 143: The Wide Spectrum of Prayer

It is amazing how many different subjects and moods can be touched in a Psalm of twelve verses. Here we have:

143:1 *General request for audience.* **"Hear . . . give ear . . . answer."** There is no poverty of expression but rather emphatic diversity. David asks God to **answer** him **in** His **faithfulness** (to His promises) and **in** His **righteousness** (i.e., because it is right for Him to defend His defenseless servant).

143:2 *Penitence.* He does **not** want God to give him justice. That would be disastrous. All are sinners. No one is able to produce by himself the perfect righteousness that God demands. So man must cast himself on the grace of God.

When we come to Him as undeserving penitents, acknowledging our sins and accepting Christ as our Savior from sin, then God imputes His own righteousness to us, and in Christ we are made fit for heaven.

143:3 *Acute crisis*. The situation is grim. **The enemy** has been pursuing him relentlessly. He feels as if he has been pummeled **to the ground**. His tormentors have forced him to live in isolation, **darkness**, and hiding, cut off and forgotten like ancient corpses in the tombs.

143:4 *Desperation*. He fears that he can't take much more. His **spirit** is ready to give up, and his **heart** is numb.

143:5 *Reminiscence*. He thinks back to **the days** when God worked mighty deliverances for him, and also for the nation of Israel. Where are those times now?

143:6 *Fervency*. The sincerity and ardor of his prayer is indicated by his **hands** pleadingly **spread out** toward God.

Intensity. He **longs for** God, **like** parched, weary ground thirsts for the refreshing rain.

143:7 *Urgency*. The **LORD** must hurry to his rescue or he is sure he won't survive much longer.

Request for favor. The hiding of God's **face**, either in anger or disinterest, would be tantamount to death.

143:8 *Plea for* ***lovingkindness***. He longs to hear God speak soon to him in words and tones of steadfast love. **". . . In the morning"** means early or without delay.

Prayer for guidance. Someone has said that this is a verse that everyone could take as a life motto, **"Cause me to know the way in which I should walk, for I lift up my soul to You."** Divine guidance is indispensable. We simply do not **know the way**, or what would be best for ourselves. Only the God-directed life is effective and enjoyable.

143:9 *Petition for deliverance*. The threat of his **enemies** causes David to cry to the Lord for rescue and relief. He has not depended on anyone else for protection—only on the **LORD**, and this singleness of trust now forms the basis of his entreaty.

143:10 *Appeal for instruction*. The psalmist not only wanted to know the will of God (v. 8b), he also wanted a heart trained to obey that **will**. God, after all, was his **God**, and what could be more proper than for the creature to obey his Creator?

Prayer for a level path. Everyone has his ups and downs in life, but not everyone has as rocky a road as David. His desire here is that the Lord's **good Spirit** will **lead** him over smoother terrain, free from the extreme forms of danger and disaster to which he had been exposed.

143:11 *Plea for preservation*. In linking his own continued preservation with the glory of God (**"For Your name's sake"**), the psalmist employs one of the strongest levers to move the hand and heart of Omnipotence. In the same way he pleads the **righteousness** of God as the reason why he should be delivered from **trouble**. This is powerful prayer.

143:12 *Retribution on enemies*. Finally he asks that God search out and destroy his **enemies** as a display of His **mercy**. If these things—destruction and **mercy**—sound irreconcilable to us, we should remember that:

> the destruction of the wicked is a favor to the universe; just as the arrest and punishment of a robber is a mercy to society, to mankind, just as every prison is a display of mercy as well as justice:—mercy to society at large; justice to the offenders.[103]

David's last appeal is based on the fact that he is Jehovah's **servant**. He is on the Lord's side. He is serving the Lord. Only through the removal of his foes does he feel he can continue.

Psalm 144: The Happy People

Although this Psalm is largely made up of excerpts from other Psalms, it is not pieced together haphazardly. There is real continuity.

144:1, 2 First, **David** honors God as all he needs in the battles of life. It is the Lord who imparts skill and dexterity to him in his confrontations with the enemy. **The Lord** is his **Rock**, his **lovingkindness**, his **fortress**, his **high tower**, his **deliverer**, his **shield**, his **refuge** and his victory. What more could he need or desire?

144:3, 4 In the light of the greatness of God, **man** is utterly insignificant. It's a wonder that God ever takes notice of him. He is as evanescent as **a breath** on a cold day, as transient as **a passing shadow**. This is true of all mankind, but perhaps David is thinking especially of his adversaries here.

144:5–8 This leads David to pray for the moment when the invincible God marches forth against His puny enemies. But how can you describe the arrival of the invisible God? The only way is by sketching out one of those majestic theophanies in which all nature is convulsed and the universe is shaken. The **heavens . . . bow down** as God descends. He touches **the mountains** and they become smoking volcanoes. **Lightning** rips across the sky like **arrows** from the Almighty. Then when the enemy has been thoroughly disorganized and repulsed, God reaches down and rescues David from the raging billows of trouble. He delivers him **from the hand of** foreign invaders who are inveterate liars, who raise their **right hand** to lie rather than to confirm the truth.

144:9–11 As a result of his rescue, the psalmist **will sing a new song** to the Lord. With the ten-stringed **harp** he will extol the One who rescued him **from the deadly sword** of the alien adversaries—these men who are habitual liars even when under oath to tell the truth.

144:12 When the king has been delivered from these subversive elements, then his kingdom will enjoy the ideal conditions described here. Actually these conditions will not be fully realized until the Lord returns, crushes all rebellion, and establishes His Millennial Reign.

First, there will be the blessing of family vitality. The **sons** will be healthy, wholesome and handsome, like strong, vigorous **plants**. The girls will be statuesque and beautiful, like the sculptured **pillars** of a **palace**.

144:13–15 Then there will be agricultural abundance. The **barns** and silos will be filled with **all kinds of** grain and **produce**. The **sheep** will reproduce prolifically till there are herds of **ten thousands in** the **fields**. The cattle will bear without mishap, or it may mean that the **oxen** will be weighted down with immense loads. The expressions **"no breaking in or going out"** and **"no outcry in our streets"** may mean that the country will be free from foreign invaders, that there will be no forced migrations into exile, and no noisy demonstrations or riots **in** the **streets**.

It is a picture of unparalleled happiness, the happiness that belongs to **people** who acknowledge Jehovah as their **God**.

Psalm 145: The Missing Nun

David's "Psalm of Praise" is an acrostic, each verse beginning with a successive letter of the Hebrew alphabet. However, in the traditional (Masoretic) Hebrew text, the letter "nun," corresponding to our "n," is missing between verses 13 and 14. The ancient Greek, Syriac, and Latin versions add the following:

> "The Lord is faithful in all His words, and gracious in all His works."

In the twentieth century this same line—the missing "nun" line—was also found in Hebrew in the Dead Sea Scrolls.

145:1–3 The theme of the Psalm is the greatness of the Lord. The psalmist is consumed with a holy determination to **extol, bless** and—elpraise his **God** and **King** both in time (**every day**) and in eternity (**forever and ever**). The gist of his endless song will be that God is **great**, that his greatness is worthy of great praise, and that **His greatness** is infinite in its dimensions.

145:4 The **works** and **mighty acts** of God will be extolled from **one generation . . . to another**. The song will never die.

145:5 The psalmist himself **will** gratefully **meditate on the glorious splendor of** God's **majesty** as revealed in His **wondrous works** of deliverance.

145:6 Men shall rehearse the power of God's **awesome acts** of judgment, and David **will** continue to **declare** the Lord's **greatness**.

145:7 People everywhere will enthusiastically pour out the fame of the Lord's **great goodness**. And the greatness of His **righteousness** will be the theme of joyful singing.

145:8 The Lord's greatness extends to His grace and **compassion**. He is great in His self-control and **great in mercy**.

145:9, 10 His goodness extends **to all**, without discrimination, and He is compassionate toward **all His** creatures, without exception.

All His **works** give thanks to Him, though inaudibly. Their very existence demonstrates His wisdom and power. **And** His **saints** join in blessing Him for His infinite perfections.

145:11–13 Then there is the greatness of His **kingdom**. His is the **power** and **glory**. His own people tell the rest of mankind the greatness of His deeds and the bright-shining perfections of His rule. The **kingdom** is **everlasting**, enduring **throughout all generations**.

145:14 The LORD is great in His preservation of those who are going **down** under the burdens of life. And He **raises up** those who have buckled under the pressures and problems.

145:15, 16 Then too, He is great in His provision. All creatures look to Him in dependence and in expectation, and He provides **them their food** as it is needed—a marvelous organizational feat of growth, preparation and distribution. With no greater effort than opening His **hand**, He feeds His numberless creatures throughout the universe. What a great God He is!

145:17 He is great in His righteousness and kindness. Nothing He does is wrong or unmerciful. Only in God do these virtues perfectly unite.

145:18 He is great in His condescension and availability—always **near** those who sincerely seek Him.

145:19 He is great in His salvation. No one who approaches Him in contrition and faith is ever turned away.

145:20 He is great in His watch-care over **all who love Him**, He invites them to cast all their cares on Him.

Finally, He is great in His wrath. Eventually, **all the wicked** will be destroyed.

145:21 David's mind was made up—He would **praise** this great God **forever**, and He would exhort everyone else to do the same.

Which leads me to say this about the missing "nun": While all the rest of the universe is praising the Lord, don't you be the missing one!

Psalm 146: Glories of the God of Jacob

146:1 The first verse contains two imperatives in which the psalmist calls upon himself to **"Praise the LORD!"**

146:2 The second verse contains two declaratives in which he responds, in effect, **"While I live I will praise the LORD; I will sing praises to my God while I have my being."** It is a lovely dialogue between a man and his best self.

146:3, 4 The rest of the Psalm explains why God and not man is worthy of our full, confiding trust. It isn't long before most of us learn **not** to **trust in man**—not even **in princes** who are supposed to be superior. The best of men are men at best. They cannot save themselves, let alone others. When man's heart stops beating, he dies, is buried, and his body **returns** to dust. All his grandiose **plans perish**. So we might say of man that he is unreliable, impotent, mortal and fleeting.

146:5 The way of happiness, help and hope is to rely on **the God of Jacob**, that is, the God of the undeserving. Here are some of the reasons why He is worthy of all our confidence:

146:6 *Omnipotent Creator*. He **made** the heavens, the **earth, the sea, and all** the creatures in the universe. If He can do that, what can't He do?

Dependable One. **He keeps truth forever**. It is impossible for Him to lie or to go back on His word. There is no risk involved in trusting Him. He cannot fail.

146:7 *Advocate of the helpless*. He sees to it that the righteous are vindicated, that their cause eventually triumphs. The waves may seem to be against them but the tide is sure to win.

Provider. He **gives food to the hungry**, both in a spiritual and physical sense. He brings us into His banqueting house, and what a table He spreads!

Emancipator. He sets the captives free—from human oppression, from the chains of sin, from the grip of the world, from the bondage of the devil, and from selfish living.

146:8 *Sight-Giver*. **The LORD opens the eyes of the blind,** some are **blind** physically, some mentally and spiritually, some by birth, some by accident, and some by choice. No case is too hard for Him.

Uplifter. He lifts the flagging spirits of **those who are bowed down** beneath the burdens of worry, affliction, trouble and sorrow.

Lover of good men. Barnes writes, "It is a characteristic of God, and a foundation for praise, that He loves those who obey law; who do that which is right."

146:9 *Protector of exiles*. He is interested in the welfare of **strangers**, sojourners, and exiles. Pilgrims find a true paraclete in Jehovah.

Friend of the bereft. He upholds **the fatherless** and the **widow**, and all others who have no human helper.

Judge of the evil. He thwarts the best laid plans of ungodly men and makes **the way of the wicked** end in ruin.

146:10 *Eternal King*. In contrast to man's transiency is the eternity of God. **The LORD shall reign forever—to all generations. Praise the LORD!**

Aren't you glad you know Him?

Psalm 147: Jerusalem Restored—Praise God!

It is generally thought that this song celebrates the restoration of Jerusalem after the Babylonian exile. If it was appropriate then, it will have even fuller meaning when the King comes back and finally restores the fortunes of the city and of the nation.

The continuity of the Psalm is as follows:

The appropriateness of praise (v. 1).
For the restoration of Israel (vv. 2–6).
For God's providence in nature (vv. 7–9).
For His delight in the spiritual rather than in the physical (vv. 10, 11).
For His goodness to Jerusalem (vv. 12–14).
For His control of the elements (vv. 15–18).
For His special favor to Israel (vv. 19, 20).

147:1 The renewed nature of man shows instinctively that **it is good to . . . praise the LORD. It is pleasant** as well and eminently appropriate.

147:2–4 He is the God of restoration. Here He is praised for rebuilding **Jerusalem** and regathering Israel's émigrés from their captivity. The fact that a nation or individual has failed does not mean that God is finished with them. In His gracious ministry of restoring, **He heals the brokenhearted and binds up their wounds.** And since He numbers **the stars** and **calls** each of **them . . . by name**, it must follow that He numbers His people and knows each one individually and intimately.

The way in which the tender compassion of the Lord is placed beside His infinite knowledge in verses 3 and 4 caused Archibald G. Brown to exclaim:

> O Holy Spirit, with lowly reverence we venture yet to say that never hast Thou collected and put side by side two more exquisite statements than these: "He healeth the broken in heart, and knoweth the number of the stars."[104]

> With His healing hand on a broken heart,
> And the other on a star,
> Our wonderful God views the miles apart,
> And they seem not very far.
> —*M. P. Ferguson*

147:5, 6 He is a **great** Lord—**mighty in power**, and **infinite** in **understanding**. He revives and perks up the oppressed, and throws **down** their **wicked** oppressors.

147:7–9 Then **God** should be thanked and praised for His providence in nature. We should **sing** our gratitude to Him for the **clouds** spread across **the heavens**. We should make melody to Him for the **rain** and all it means to **the earth**. We should praise Him for the **grass** that covers the hills. Whole books could be written about the essential roles played by the **clouds**, the **rain**, and the **grass**.

Though He is so great, yet He is concerned to see that the wild animals get their **food**, and He responds to the plaintive caw of the hungry **young ravens**.

147:10, 11 He should be worshiped for the priority He gives to the spiritual over the physical. He is not awed by the horses in the cavalry unit, or for the strong, muscular **legs** of the infantrymen. Or to change the figure, He doesn't take pleasure in the horses as they race, or the athletes as they contend in the Olympics. But **the LORD** is delighted with **those who** reverence **Him** and **who hope in His mercy**.

147:12–14 Then again He should be adored for His goodness to **Jerusalem**. Four distinct blessings come into view.

Civil security—He makes strong cross-bars to secure the city **gates** against invasion.

Domestic felicity—The inhabitants enjoy a happy, full life.

National tranquility—**He makes peace** along the frontiers.

Agricultural prosperity—He satisfies the people with the **finest** foods.

147:15–18 His control over the elements should not be forgotten when praising Jehovah. When **He sends out His** orders, they produce prompt and dramatic results. The earth becomes covered with **snow**, as if it were a woolen blanket. He dusts the ground with **frost** that looks like white **ashes**. When the **hail** stones come crashing down, who can refrain from scurrying for shelter? Then He changes His orders and the snow and ice melt. The south wind causes the temperature to rise and the spring thaw begins. And so it is in human affairs that the dark, cold winters are followed by the warmth and revival of spring.

147:19, 20 Finally, He is to be honored for His special favor **to Israel**. It was to this nation alone that He delivered His laws and covenants. No other **nation** has been so favored. The Gentiles were not the recipients of His regulations. Williams writes:

> His election of Israel as the depository of His Word, and as the channel of its communication to the world (vv. 19 and 20) moved both Moses and Paul to wonder and worship (Deut. 4:8; Rom. 3:2; 11:33).[105]

Psalm 148: Creation's Choir

I have seen and heard many different choirs but never one like this. It is made up of all creation, animate and inanimate. The universe is the choir loft, endless rows of chairs, tier upon tier.

148:1–6 In the topmost section are the **angels**, praising **the LORD from the heavens**, the **hosts** of heaven singing out the glories of Jehovah. **The sun, moon** and **stars** are next; their part is the music of the spheres. The highest **heavens** and the water-laden clouds are singing "Glory to God in the highest. . . ." All are honoring God as their Creator, the One who spoke and brought the worlds into being. It is He who gave permanence and stability to His creation, and who built into it certain laws and principles which are unvarying.

148:7, 8 Next in descending order are the **great sea creatures** and all the swarming life of the oceans. They too testify that the Hand that made them is divine. **Fire, hail, snow, clouds**, and the **stormy** gale, quick to obey His orders, remind us that Jehovah controls the seasons and the weather and harnesses them to do His will.

148:9, 10 Then there are the **mountains and all** the **hills**, lifting their heads in adoration. **All** the **trees** are there, those that bear fruit and those that yield lumber; they are lifting up their branches to His name. Wild **beasts** and domestic animals, **creeping things** and birds—all are chanting the wisdom and power of the Lord.

148:11, 12 As we come toward the front rows, we see the great assemblage of mankind—**kings, princes, all** governmental officials, and all the common people. Fellows and girls, **old men and children**—all with heads tilted back and mouths opened wide in worship of Jehovah.

148:13, 14 The massed choir is praising **the name of the LORD** as the **name** above every name and as the One whose **glory** is unsurpassable. And there is a particular theme in the song of the choir—they are magnifying the Lord for what He has done for **Israel**. He has raised up a **horn** for **His people**, that is, the Messiah. In the Second Advent of the Lord Jesus, He has given special occasion for **His saints** to **praise** Him. **The children of Israel**, there at the front of the choir, stand in a place of special nearness **to Him**. Through the restored nation, blessing flows out to all the world. That is why the choir is joining in one grand Hallelujah—**"Praise the LORD!"**

Psalm 149: The High Praises of God

There are two parts to this Psalm. In the first (vv. 1–6a) the saints are singing. In the second (vv. 6b–9) they are reigning. The time in question is when the Lord Jesus returns to the earth and ushers in His long-awaited kingdom.

149:1–3 The **new song** which Israel sings is the song of creation, redemption, and reign. They rejoice in Jehovah as the Author of their natural and spiritual creation and as their glorious Monarch.

They praise Him not only in song but in **the dance** as well. What is this? Believers dancing? Yes, dancing in holy and pure delight before the Lord. As an expression of true spiritual joy and worship, **the dance** is acceptable to God. But to use this verse to justify dancing as it is practiced today is something else. There is a difference between the use of the dance and its abuse. The psalmist is only speaking about its divinely sanctioned use. The same is true of instrumental music. If timbrels and harps had emotions, they would all aspire to make melody to the Lord. Too often they are debased to sensual employment. Their proper use is good; their abuse is horrendous.

149:4–6a Why all the fuss, all the jubilant music? Because **the LORD takes pleasure in His** restored **people**; He has awarded a garland of victory to the loyal remnant. The Great Tribulation is past, and it is a day of clear shining after rain.

The people have much reason to rejoice **in** the **glory** which is theirs as they are associated with the King of Glory. They have every reason to raise the rafters with **joyful** song as they sit on their thrones by day or lie **on their beds** at night (the word "beds" in verse 5 may refer to either). It is really appropriate that all their vocal chords be filled with the **high praises of God**.

149:6b–8 As you see, there is an abrupt change in the middle of verse 6. From this point to the end Israel is found in the role of judges, dispensing justice. This may refer to the destruction of her foes at the return of the Messiah. That judgment will be executed by the Lord, but the nation may, in a figure, be thought of as sharing in it. But I rather think it refers to Israel's role as head of the nations during the Millennium. The Lord Jesus will rule with a rod of iron during that period (Rev. 2:27). The apostles will sit on thrones judging the twelve tribes of Israel (Matt. 19:28). And Israel herself will share in the rule over the Gentiles (Dan. 7:22).

So the saints have **two-edged** swords **in their** hands, administering **vengeance and punishments on the peoples** whenever necessary. Rebellious **kings** and **their nobles** will be bound **with chains** and **fetters of iron**. It will be a reign of absolute righteousness, of undeviating justice.

149:9 This is the honored role of Israel in that day—to see that all insubordination and subversion are punished promptly.

It is also true that the *NT* **saints** will share in the coming reign of Christ. We read about that in 1 Corinthians 6:2, 3.

Psalm 150: Praise the Lord!

We have reached the grand finale. And what could be more appropriate than to find a short, pointed appeal for creation to find its true destiny in the worship of God? The Psalm answers four key questions on the subject of praise: Where, What, How, and Who?

The glory of God was the purpose of creation. Therefore man finds the central reason for his existence in praising the Lord. As it is so tersely stated in the Shorter Catechism, "The chief end of man is to glorify God and to enjoy Him forever."

150:1 But *where?* We should **praise** Him **in His sanctuary** and **in His mighty firmament**, which is another way of saying *everywhere*—on earth and in heaven. There is no place where worship is out of place.

150:2 And for *what?* **For His mighty acts** and **according to His excellent greatness**. In other words, we should praise Him for what He has done for us, and for who He is. But not only *for* His exceeding greatness—also *according to* His exceeding greatness. It is a sin to be unenthusiastic in rehearsing the excellencies of our Creator and Redeemer.

150:3–5 *How?* With an orchestra of every kind of instrument. **The trumpet** with its martial, commanding notes. The **lute** with its dulcet, pastoral tones. The **harp**, gentle and sweet in its strains. **The timbrel,** festive and uninhibited in its accompaniment of the **dance**. **Stringed instruments** of all sorts, the cello, the bass viol, the violin, the mandolin, the guitar—capture every note and chord in the world of music to honor the Great King. Wind instruments—the flute, the oboe, the clarinet—don't miss one in this great philharmonic extravaganza. And the percussion instruments, bless them—especially the crashing, **clashing**, ear-splitting **cymbals**, punctuating the anthem with loud amens.

150:6 But that brings us to the last question. *Who?* And the answer, of course, is, **"Let everything that has breath praise the LORD."** The massed choir of all the voices of earth are given the cue to join in the loud, eternal burst of praise to God. *Hallelujah!* **Praise the LORD!**

ENDNOTES

[1](Intro) Graham Scroggie, *Daily Notes of the Scripture Union*.

[2](Intro) Albert Barnes, *Notes on the Book of Psalms*, I:xix.

[3](Intro) C. S. Lewis, *Reflections on the Psalms*, p. 10.

[4](Intro) F. W. Grant, "Psalms," in *The Numerical Bible*, III:10.

[5](1:3) The word translated "planted"

(*shātûl*) literally means *transplanted* (Koehler-Baumgartner, *Lexicon in Veteris Testamenti Libros*, p. 1015), a fitting image of the born-again person.

[6](1:3) D. L. Moody, *Notes from My Bible*, p. 64.

[7](2:Intro) In Acts 4:25–28, Peter and Paul connected Psalm 2 with the rejection of Christ. It is true that it had a partial fulfillment when Herod, Pontius Pilate, the Gentiles, and the people of Israel united to kill Christ. But the final fulfillment is still future.

[8](3:1, 2) *International Standard Bible Encyclopedia*, III:2096.

[9](4:1) Charles H. Spurgeon, quoted in "Choice Gleanings Calendar."

[10](5:Intro) Koehler and Baumgartner conjecture that *michtām* may be related to the Akkadian word for *cover* and thus may mean "expiation psalm."

[11](8:5) Hebrew has *Elohim* here; see NKJV footnote.

[12](9:Intro) Psalm 10 is built on the second half of the Hebrew alphabet, hence some believe Psalms 9 and 10 were originally one psalm.

[13](10:Intro) See previous note.

[14](14:1) Henry Bosch, *Our Daily Bread*.

[15](14:1) Barnes, *Psalms*, I:114.

[16](16:3) Documentation unavailable.

[17](17:15) E. Bendor Samuel, *The Prophetic Character of the Psalms*, p. 26

[18](19:3, 4a) Immanuel Kant, *General History of Nature*, further documentation unavailable.

[19](19:7–9) Quoted from Wallace's *Kant*, by Alexander Wright in *The Psalms of David and the Higher Criticism, Or Was David "The Sweet Psalmist of Israel"?*, p. 109.

[20](19:12) Barnes, *Psalms*, I:175.

[21](23:Intro) J. R. Littleproud, further documentation unavailable.

[22](24:9, 10) F. B. Meyer, *F. B. Meyer on the Psalms*, p. 35.

[23](25:Intro) The letter for "r" (*resh*) occurs in both verses 18 and 19 whereas as one would expect a "q" (*qoph*) in verse 18.

[24](26:12) J. C. Ryle, *Expository Thoughts on the Gospels, Luke*, II:239.

[25](29:10, 11) W. E. Vine, *Isaiah*, p. 205.

[26](29:10, 11) H. A. Ironside, *Studies on the Psalms*, p. 173.

[27](31:Intro) Lewis, *Reflections*, p. 10.

[28](32:8, 9) Jay Adams, *Competent to Counsel*, p. 124.

[29](34:8, 9) G. Campbell Murdoch, *From Grace to Glory*, p. 66.

[30](34:10) Some scholars believe that "young lions" should be read "deniers of God," but the meaning of the verse remains the same.

[31](36:5) Albert Barnes, further documentation unavailable.

[32](36:5) Arthur W. Pink, *The Attributes of God*, p. 47.

[33](36:7) John Brine, quoted in *The Attributes of God*, Arthur W. Pink, p. 80.

[34](37:5, 6) Barnes, *Psalms*, I:320.

[35](37:28) F. W. Dixon, further documentation unavailable.

[36](50:1) The same Hebrew word (*eretz*) means both *earth* and *land*.

[37](50:8) Meyer, *Psalms*, p. 63.

[38](52:8, 9) Grant, "Psalms," III:212.

[39](53:Intro) In Psalm 14 the name Jehovah is used four times and Elohim three times. Here the name Elohim is found seven times.

[40](54:7) G. Campbell Morgan, *An Exposition of the Whole Bible*, p. 240.

[41](58:8) W. Graham Scroggie, *Psalms*, p. 50.

[42](58:9) A. Maclaren, quoted in *Psalms* by W. Graham Scroggie, II:49.

[43](58:10) Morgan, *Exposition*, p. 242.

[44](60:9) The NKJV editors show that they agree by ending v. 8 with quotation marks.

[45](61:2) Concerning Matthew 16:18, G. Campbell Morgan says: "Remember,

He was talking to Jews. If we trace the figurative use of the word through Hebrew Scriptures, we find that it is never used symbolically of man but always of God. So here at Caesarea Philippi, it is not upon Peter that the Church is built. Jesus did not trifle with figures of speech. He took up their old Hebrew illustration—rock, always the symbol of Deity, and said, 'Upon God Himself, Christ, the Son of the living God—I will build my church.' " Perhaps the one exception to Morgan's statement is found in Deuteronomy 32:31: "their rock is not as our Rock." But even here, "rock" is a symbol of deity (although a false god).

[46](66:8–12) Williams, *Student's Commentary on the Holy Scriptures*, p. 67.

[47](67:6, 7) Franz Delitzsch, "Psalms," in *Biblical Commentary on the Old Testament*, XII:240.

[48](68:11–13) The Hebrew word for "those who proclaimed it" (*hamebasserôt*) is feminine plural.

[49](68:24) Lewis, *Reflections*, p. 45.

[50](71:Intro) John G. Bellett, *Short Meditations on the Psalms*, p. 76.

[51](71:14–16) Williams, *Commentary*, p. 72.

[52](81:Intro) Merrill F. Unger, *Unger's Bible Dictionary*, p. 350.

[53](81:8–10) Gaebelein, *Psalms*, p. 316.

[54](83:13–18) Morgan, *Exposition*, p. 252.

[55](86:17) E. W. Bullinger, *The Companion Bible*, Appendix 32, p. 31.

[56](86:17) Grant, "Psalms," III:330.

[57](87:Intro) Teddy Kollek and Moshe Pearlman, *Jerusalem, A History of Forty Centuries*, p. 12.

[58](87:6) Documentation unavailable.

[59](87:6) Gaebelein, *Psalms*, p. 332.

[60](88:11, 12) *The New Bible Commentary*, p. 474.

[61](88:13–18) Quoted by A. G. Clarke, *Analytical Studies in the Psalms*, p. 219.

[62](93:5) Williams, *Student's Commentary*, p. 372.

[63](94:Intro) Pink, *Attributes*, p. 75.

[64](96:11–13) *Jehovah* is the traditional pronunciation of a combination of the consonants *JHWH* (or *YHWH*) and the vowels of *Adonai* (Lord). The Hebrew name was probably originally pronounced *Yahweh*. For fear of profaning the Name of God the Jews said their word for "Lord" (*Adonai*) whenever the sacred letters YHWH appeared in the text. It is noteworthy that the initial letters of the four Hebrew words in the first clause of verse eleven spell out the personal name of God, Yahweh (YHWH). KJV and NKJV indicate the name of God by "LORD" in all capitals, but *quotations* from the Bible generally do not use all capitals.

[65](97:6a) Gaebelein, *Psalms*, p. 363.

[66](98:4–6) See F. W. Grant, "Psalms," III:363. See also previous one on this word. This expression also has been found in the Dead Sea Scrolls of Deuteronomy 32:43 and the LXX there as well. Conceivably the Masoretes (preservers of Jewish tradition) deleted it there because Christians used the verse to support the deity of Christ (as in Heb. 1:6).

[67](100:Intro) Barnes, *Psalms*, III:56.

[68](101:2) Clarke, *Psalms*, p. 247.

[69](101:7, 8) Grant, "Psalms," III:368.

[70](104:31, 32) J. J. Stewart Perowne, *The Book of Psalms*, II:234.

[71](109:30, 31) Meyer, *Psalms*, p. 133.

[72](Essay) Unger, *Bible Dictionary*, p. 231.

[73](Essay) Barnes, *Psalms*, I:xxxvii.

[74](Essay) Scroggie, *The Psalms*, p. 32.

[75](110:1) In the KJV and NKJV "LORD" in all capitals always stands for Jehovah (= *Yahweh*), the personal, covenant name of God. See note 64.

[76](110:2) Ironside used this expres-

sion as a book title: *The Great Parenthesis,* that is, the current dispensation of the Christian church.

[77](110:3) Scroggie, *The Psalms,* p. 85.

[78](112:10) Barnes, *Psalms,* III:149.

[79](118:24) *Ibid.,* pp. 173, 174.

[80](119:Intro) Samuel Ridout, *How to Study the Bible,* p. 73.

[81](119:Intro) Lewis, *Reflections,* p. 52.

[82](119:Intro) Bellett, *Short Meditations,* p. 131.

[83](119:24) Matthew Henry, *Commentary in One Volume,* p. 706.

[84](119:92) Barnes, *Psalms,* III:204.

[85](119:107) Charles H. Spurgeon, *The Treasury of David,* VI:244.

[86](119:136) Quoted by Moody, *Notes,* p. 79.

[87](119:139) Barnes, *Psalms,* III:217.

[88](119:145) Verses 145–152 begin with the letter "qoph," the first letter of the Hebrew word for "cry."

[89](120:1, 2) Psalms 120–134 are called "Songs of Ascents" because the pilgrims sang them as they *went up* to Jerusalem for the annual feasts of the Lord (Passover, etc.).

[90](121:4) Moody, *Notes,* p. 79.

[91](121:5, 6) It must be remembered that this is *poetry,* and it may be a figure of speech that gives both extremes and means everything in between. This is called a *merism.* Another example is "your going out and your coming in" (v. 8), i.e., your whole lifestyle.

[92](121:7, 8) All these forms translate one Hebrew verb, *shāmar.*

[93](122:6) Collins and Lapierre, *O Jerusalem!,* p. 33.

[94](122:7–9) Barnes, *Psalms,* III:238.

[95](135:6) Pink, *Attributes,* p. 27.

[96](137:9) Lewis, *Reflections,* pp. 113, 114.

[97](138:2) The word translated *temple* (*hêkāl*) can also mean a palace or other building, including the tabernacle; the Jewish temple is not always meant.

[98](138:2) Clarke, *Psalms,* p. 337.

[99](139:13, 14) Radmacher, further documentation unavailable.

[100](139:19–22) Edward J. Young, *Psalm 139,* p. 95.

[101](139:19–22) *Ibid.,* p. 105.

[102](142:5–7) Clarke, *Psalms,* p. 343.

[103](143:12) Barnes, *Psalms,* III:314.

[104](147:2–4) Archibald G. Brown, further documentation unavailable.

[105](147:19, 20) Williams, *Student's Commentary,* p. 148.

BIBLIOGRAPHY

Alexander, Joseph A. *The Psalms Translated and Explained.* Grand Rapids, Baker Book House, Reprinted from 1873 Edinburgh edition, 1977.

Barnes, Albert. *Notes on the Books of Psalms.* 3 vols. New York: Harper Bros. Publishers, 1868.

Bellett, J. G. *Short Meditations on the Psalms.* Oak Park, IL: Bible Truth Publishers, 1961.

Bridges, Charles. *Psalm 119.* Edinburgh: The Banner of Truth Trust, Reprinted from 1827 edition, 1977.

Clarke, A. G. *Analytical Studies in the Psalms.* Kilmarnock: John Ritchie, Ltd., 1949.

Delitzsch, Franz. "Psalms." In *Biblical Commentary on the Old Testament.* Vols. 11—13. Grand Rapids: Wm. B. Eerdmans Publishing Co., 1970.

Gaebelein, A. C. *The Book of Psalms.* Neptune, N.J.: Loizeaux Bros., 1939.

Grant, F. W. "Psalms." In *The Numerical Bible.* New York: Loizeaux Bros., 1897.

Ironside, H. A. *Studies on Book One of the Psalms.* Neptune, N.J.: Loizeaux Bros., 1952.

Kidner, Derek. *Psalms 1–72.* Downers Grove, IL: InterVarsity Press, 1973.

———. *Psalms 73—150.* Downers

Grove, IL: InterVarsity Press, 1975.

Lewis, C. S. *Reflections on the Psalms*. London: Collins, Fontana Books, 1969.

Maclaren, A. *The Book of Psalms*. London: Hodder & Stoughton, 1908.

Meyer, F. B. *F. B. Meyer on the Psalms*. Grand Rapids: Zondervan Publishing House, n.d.

Morgan, G. Campbell. *Notes on the Psalms*. Westwood, N.J.: Revell Co., 1947.

Perowne, J. J. Stewart. *The Book of Psalms*. 2 vols. Grand Rapids: Zondervan Publishing House, Reprinted from 1878 edition, 1966.

Samuel, E. Bendor, *The Prophetic Character of the Psalms*. London: Pickering & Inglis, n.d.

Scroggie, W. Graham. *Psalms*. Vol. 2. London: Pickering & Inglis, 1949.

———. *The Psalms*. Old Tappan, N.J.: Fleming H. Revell Co., 1948.

Spence, H.D.M. and Exell, Joseph S., Editors. *Pulpit Commentary*, Vol. 8. Grand Rapids: Wm. B. Eerdmans Publishing Co., 1950.

Spurgeon, C. H. *The Treasury of David*. Grand Rapids: Baker Book House, 1983.

Wright, *The Psalms of David and the Higher Criticism, Or Was David "The Sweet Psalmist of Israel"?* Edinburgh and London: Oliphant Anderson & Ferrier, 1900.

Young, E. J. *Psalm 139*. London: The Banner of Truth Trust, 1965.

PROVERBS

Introduction

"It is not a portrait-album or a book of manners: it offers a key to life. The samples of behaviour which it holds up to view are all assessed by one criterion, which could be summed up in the question, 'Is this wisdom or folly?' "

—Derek Kidner

I. Unique Place in the Canon

The Book of Proverbs is as modern as today. It deals with the problems of life that each of us has to face.

If any book in the Bible could be said to be beamed especially to young people, this one could.

> When a young man said to Carlyle that there was nothing in the Book of Proverbs, he replied: "Make a few proverbs and you will think differently of the book."[1]

Proverbs is the world's finest collection of sound, sanctified common sense, written so that young people might not have to make some of the dreary mistakes their elders have made.

The purpose of Proverbs is stated in 1:1–7. In brief, it is to give wisdom and understanding to a young man so that he will find true blessedness in life and escape the snares and pitfalls of sin. The key verse is 9:10, "The fear of the Lord is the beginning of wisdom, and the knowledge of the Holy One is understanding."

Arnot calls the book, "Laws from heaven for life on earth."[2] That describes its contents very concisely.

A proverb is a pithy statement of wisdom, often worded in a clever way to make it easy to remember. Most of the proverbs consist of two clauses, presenting either similarities or contrasts.

There are several varieties of proverbs, as will be seen from the following:

1. Some are single statements, expressing a simple fact:

   When a man's ways please
   the Lord,
   He makes even his enemies to
   be at peace with him (16:7).

2. Some consist of two clauses or phrases, in which one thing is compared to another:

   As cold water to a weary
   soul,
   So is good news from a far
   country (25:25).

3. Still others have two clauses or phrases, usually connected by *but*, and describing things that are opposite to each other:

   The memory of the righteous
   is blessed,
   But the name of the wicked
   will rot (10:7).

   This type of proverb is found mostly in Chapters 10—15.

4. There are proverbs with two clauses or phrases in which the same thought is repeated in a slightly different way:

For a harlot is a deep pit,
And a seductress is a narrow
well (23:27).

II. Authorship

This book is sometimes called "The Proverbs of Solomon," since most of these sayings were written by that very wise king (1:1; 10:1; 25:1). 1 Kings 4:32 tells us that Solomon composed 3,000 Proverbs, so these are the several hundred the Spirit of God inspired to be Holy Scripture.

Chapter 30 is said to contain "the words of Agur the son of Jakeh" (30:1). Chapter 31 is introduced as "the words of king Lemuel" (31:1). We have no knowledge today as to the identity of these two men. Some think that these were other names used by Solomon.

III. Date

Since Proverbs 25:1 tells us that the men of Hezekiah copied out a section of the Proverbs of Solomon the final form of the book has to be at least as late as 700 B.C. Solomon's original contributions would be from the 900's B.C. If Agur and Lemuel are not poetic names for Solomon himself, and they lived either before 900 B.C. or after 700 B.C., that would expand the possible period of compilation still further.

IV. Background and Themes

Written by Solomon and others, the colorfully poetic book of Proverbs provides a liberal education. It covers a wide range of subjects—from spanking a child to ruling a kingdom. One sometimes wonders if there is any truth that is not found here, at least in germ form. It speaks of the liquor problem, installment buying, juvenile delinquency, and labor management. You will meet all kinds of people here—the brawling woman, the proud fool, the man who does not like to be told his faults, and the ideal wife. And best of all, the Lord Jesus is here, speaking to us as Wisdom personified. "The ideal elements in the book speak of Him; the actual shortcomings cry out for Him" (quoted in Daily Notes).

Proverbs is difficult to outline. Instead of presenting a continuity of thought, like a motion picture, it presents individual pictures, like colored slides.

As you study it, you will find that it resembles the book of James in many ways.

Another valuable study device is to find illustrations of individual proverbs from:

1. The Bible Itself
2. History
3. Biography
4. Literature
5. Nature
6. Newspapers and Periodicals
7. Radio and Television
8. Your own Experience

It will be helpful to remember that while some of the proverbs are statements of *absolute truth,* some are statements that are *generally true* but that might have an exception here and there. For instance, it is always true that "the name of the Lord is a strong tower" (18:10), but there may be exceptions to the statement that "a friend loves at all times" (17:17).

In studying *The Believers Bible Commentary*, it is essential to read the corresponding verse or verses first. Many of the explanations will be meaningless unless you have read the proverb in question.

Classification of Some of the Subjects in the Book of Proverbs

The Lord

The blessing of (10:22)
Confidence in (3:25, 26)
Creation by (3:19, 20; 16:4; 20:12; 22:2b; 29:13b)
Discipline of (3:11, 12)
The fear of the Lord (1:7, 29; 2:5; 8:13; 9:10; 10:27; 14:26, 27; 15:16, 33; 16:6; 19:23; 22:4; 23:17; 24:21; 28:14)
Guidance of (3:5, 6; 16:3, 9)
Judgment and justice by (15:25a; 17:3; 21:2; 29:26)
Omnipresence of (15:3)
Omniscience of (15:11; 16:2)
Prayer answered by (15:8, 29)
Protection by (15:25b; 18:10)
The rich man and the poor man (10:15; 13:7, 8; 14:20, 21, 31; 15:16; 17:1, 5; 18:23; 19:1, 4, 17; 21:13; 22:2, 7, 16, 22, 23; 28:3, 6, 11, 27; 29:7, 13)
Source of wisdom (2:6–8)
Sovereignty and power of (16:1, 7, 9, 33; 19:21; 20:24; 21:30, 31; 22:12)
To be trusted (29:25b)

Parenting

Instruction in child training (13:24; 19:18; 22:6, 22:15; 23:13, 14; 29:15, 17)
Obedience and disobedience to parents (1:8, 9; 6:20, 22; 13:1, 19–26; 20:20; 23:22; 30:17)
Words of parental advice (1:8–19; 2:1–22; 3:1–35; 4:1–27; 5:1–23; 6:1–35; 7:1–27; 23:19–35; 24:4–22; 31:1–9)

Speech

Appropriate (15:23; 25:11)
Backbiting (25:23)
Belittling (11:12a)
Disturbing (27:14)
Evil (12:13a; 15:28b)
Excessive (10:19a; 13:3b)
Flattering (20:19; 26:28b; 28:23; 29:5)
Foolish (12:23b; 14:3a, 7; 15:2b; 18:6, 7)
Gentle (15:1a, 4a)
Good (10:20a, 21a; 16:21, 23, 24; 23:16)
Harmful (11:9, 11; 12:18a; 15:4b; 16:27; 18:21; 26:18, 19)
Harsh (15:1b)
Hasty (18:13; 29:20)
Healing (12:18b; 15:4a; 16:24; 18:21)
Honest (12:19a; 13:5)
Inappropriate (17:7)
Lying, deceitful (6:17; 10:18a; 12:19b, 22a; 14:25b; 17:4; 26:18, 19, 23–26, 28a)
Perverse (4:24; 10:31b, 32b; 15:4b; 17:20b)
Restrained (10:19b; 11:12b, 13b; 12:23a; 13:3a; 17:27a, 28; 21:23)
Satisfying (12:14; 18:20)
Slanderous (10:18b; 30:10)
Talebearing, gossiping (11:13a; 16:28; 17:9b; 18:8; 20:19; 22:11a; 26:10, 22–26, 28)
Thoughtful (15:28a)
True and false witness (6:19; 12:17; 14:5, 25; 19:5, 9, 28; 21:28; 25:18)
Wise (10:31a; 14:3b; 15:2a; 18:4)
Worthless (14:23b)

Various Themes

Abominations
—to the Lord (3:32; 6:16; 8:7; 11:1, 20; 12:22; 15:8, 9, 26; 16:5; 17:15; 20:10, 23; 21:27; 28:9)
—to others (13:19; 16:12; 24:9; 26:25; 29:27)
Ancient landmarks (22:28; 23:10, 11)
Borrowing and lending (22:7b)
The diligent man (21:5; 22:29; 27:18, 23–27; 28:19a)
The diligent man and the sluggard contrasted (10:4, 5; 12:24, 27; 13:4)
Enemy (16:7; 24:17, 18; 25:21; 27:6)
Envy (3:31; 14:30; 23:17; 24:1, 19; 27:4)
False balances and weights (11:1; 16:11; 20:10, 23)

Friends, neighbors, and friendship (3:27–29; 6:1–5; 11:12; 12:26; 14:21; 16:28; 17:9, 17; 18:17, 24; 21:10; 22:24, 25; 24:17, 19; 25:8, 9, 17, 20, 21, 22; 26:18, 19; 27:6, 9, 10, 14, 17; 28:23; 29:5)

Honey (16:24; 24:13; 25:16, 27; 27:7)

Industriousness (12:9, 11; 14:4, 23a)

The interrelationship between physical, mental, and spiritual health (3:1, 2, 7, 8, 16; 4:10, 22; 9:11; 13:12; 14:30; 15:13, 30; 16:24; 17:22; 18:14; 27:9)

Justice and injustice (13:23; 17:15, 26; 18:5; 21:15; 22:8, 16; 24:23, 24)

The king or ruler (14:28, 35; 16:10, 12–15; 19:12; 20:2, 8, 26, 28; 21:1; 22:11, 29; 23:1; 24:21, 22; 25:2–7, 15; 28:15, 16; 29:2, 4, 12, 14, 26; 30:31; 31:4, 5)

The lot (16:33; 18:18)

Old age (16:31; 17:6; 20:29)

Partiality (18:5; 24:23b–25; 28:21)

Pride and humility (3:34b; 8:13; 11:2; 15:33; 16:5,18, 19; 18:12; 22:4; 29:23)

Reputation (10:7; 22:1)

The righteous man and the wicked man contrasted (3:32, 33; 10:3, 6, 7, 9, 11, 16, 24, 25, 28, 29–32; 11:3–11, 17–21, 23, 27, 31; 12:2, 3, 5–8, 12–14, 20, 21, 26, 28; 13:2, 5, 6, 9, 21, 25; 14:2, 9, 11, 14, 22, 32; 15:8, 9, 26; 24:15, 16; 28:1, 12)

The scorner or scoffer (3:34a; 9:7, 8, 12; 13:1; 14:6; 15:12; 19:25; 21:11, 24; 22:10; 24:9; 29:8a)

Servants and slaves (14:35; 17:2; 19:10; 29:19, 21)

The sluggard (6:6–11; 10:26; 15:19; 18:9; 19:15, 24; 20:4, 13; 21:25; 22:13; 24:30–34; 26:13–16)

Soul-winning (11:30; 24:11, 12)

Strife and contention (10:12; 12:18; 13:10; 15:1–4, 18; 16:27, 28; 18:6–8; 21:9, 19; 28:25)

Suretyship (6:1–5; 11:15; 17:18; 20:16; 22:26, 27; 27:13)

Teachableness (willingness to accept instruction and correction): (1:5; 9:7–9; 10:17; 12:1, 15; 13:1, 10, 18; 15:5, 10, 12, 31, 32; 17:10; 19:20, 25; 21:11; 25:12; 27:5, 6; 28:23; 29:1)

Temper and patience (14:17, 29; 15:18; 16:32; 19:11)

Temperance and self-control (23:1–3; 25:28)

Wine (20:1; 21:17; 23:20, 21, 29–35; 31:4–7)

The wisdom of getting guidance or advice from others (11:14; 12:15; 15:22; 20:18; 24:6)

Wisdom personified (1:20–33; 8:1–36; 9:1–6; 14:1a; 16:16, 22; 19:23)

The wise man and foolish man contrasted (3:35; 10:8, 13, 14, 23; 12:15, 16, 23; 13:16; 14:3, 8, 15, 16, 18, 19, 24, 33; 15:7, 14, 20, 21; 17:11, 12, 16, 21, 24, 25, 28; 18:2, 6–8; 29:8, 9, 11)

The Word and obedience to it (13:13, 14; 16:20; 19:16; 28:4, 7, 9; 29:18; 30:5, 6)

Wealth

Accompanied by trouble (15:6, 16, 17; 16:8; 17:1)

Brings friends (19:4, 6)

Gained by violence (11:16)

Gained dishonestly (10:2; 13:22b; 15:6b; 20:17; 21:6; 22:16; 28:8)

Gained hastily (13:11; 20:21; 28:20b, 22)

Gained honestly (10:16)

Gifts and bribes (15:27; 17:8, 23; 18:16; 19:6; 21:14; 25:14; 29:4)

Inherited (19:14)

Its limited value (11:4)

Less valuable than wisdom (16:16)

Not to be trusted (11:28)

Pretended (13:7)

Protection of (10:15a; 13:8; 18:11)

Stewardship and generosity (3:9, 10, 27, 28; 11:24–26; 19:6; 21:26b; 22:9; 28:27)

Transient (23:4, 5; 27:24)

The Wicked Woman

The wicked woman or harlot (2:16–19; 5:3–23; 6:24–35; 7:5–27; 9:13–18; 22:14; 23:27, 28; 30:20)

Other women

A beautiful woman without discretion (11:22)

A contentious woman (19:13; 21:9, 19; 25:24; 27:15, 16)

A good wife (12:4; 18:22; 31:10–31)

A gracious woman (11:16)

A prudent wife (19:14)

An unloved woman (30:23)

The wife of one's youth (5:18, 19)

OUTLINE

I. INTRODUCTION (1:1–7)

II. PROVERBS OF SOLOMON ON WISDOM AND FOLLY (1:8—9:18)
- A. Wisdom's Admonition (1:8–33)
- B. Wisdom's Ways (Chap. 2)
- C. Wisdom's Rewards (3:1–10)
- D. Wisdom as the Prize (3:11–20)
- E. Wisdom Practiced (3:21–35)
- F. Wisdom as a Family Treasure (4:1–9)
- G. Wisdom and the Two Paths (4:10–27)
- H. The Folly of Immorality (Chap. 5)
- I. The Folly of Suretyship, Laziness, and Deception (6:1–19)
- J. The Folly of Adultery and Harlotry (6:20—7:27)
- K. Wisdom Personified (Chap. 8)
- L. Invitations from Wisdom and Folly (9:1–18)

III. PROVERBS OF SOLOMON ON PRACTICAL MORALITY (10:1—22:16)
- A. Righteous and Wicked Lifestyles Contrasted (10:1—15:33)
- B. The Righteous Lifestyle Exalted (16:1—22:16)

IV. PROVERBS OF THE WISE MEN (22:17—24:34)
- A. Words of the Wise (22:17—24:22)
- B. Further Sayings of the Wise (24:23–34)

V. PROVERBS OF SOLOMON COMPILED BY HEZEKIAH'S MEN (25:1—29:27)

VI. THE WORDS OF AGUR (Chap. 30)

VII. THE WORDS KING LEMUEL'S MOTHER TAUGHT HIM (31:1–9)

VIII. THE IDEAL WIFE AND MOTHER (31:10–31)

Commentary

I. INTRODUCTION (1:1–7)

1:1 Solomon the son of David was the wisest, richest, and most honored of the kings **of Israel** (1 Kgs. 3:12, 13; 4:30, 31). He spoke three thousand **proverbs**, but only some of them are preserved in this book. These extend from 1:1 to 29:27.

1:2, 3 Verses 2–6 tell us why he wrote these proverbs. In brief, they provide practical **wisdom** for the living and management of life.

Here people may learn shrewdness and receive the kind of **instruction** that provides know-how. Here they may learn to **perceive the words of understanding**, to discern between what is good and evil, profitable and worthless, helpful and harmful. Here men are schooled in what is wise, righteous, proper, and honorable.

1:4 By listening to these proverbs **the simple** develop **prudence** or "savvy," and **young** people gain insight and sanctified common sense.

1:5 Wise men will grow wiser by heeding these proverbs, and **a man of understanding** will learn how to guide himself and to advise others as well. Is it not significant that a book addressed primarily to youth should announce at the very outset, **"A wise man will hear"**? That is what is meant by a wise person in the book of Proverbs. It is one who is teachable. He is willing to listen and not do all the talking. He is not an insufferable know-it-all.

1:6 The book is designed to enable a person **to understand a proverb and an enigma**, i.e., the lesson which often lies beneath the surface. It helps him to grasp the meaning of **wise** sayings and the hidden truths contained in them.

1:7 Now we come to the key verse of the book (see also 9:10). **The fear of the Lord is the beginning** or chief part **of knowledge**. If a man wants to be wise, the place to begin is in reverencing God and in trusting and obeying Him. What is more reasonable than that the creature should trust his Creator? On the other hand, what is more illogical than for a man to reject God's Word and to live by his own hunches? The wise thing to do is to repent of one's sins, trust Jesus Christ as Lord and Savior, and then live for Him wholeheartedly and devotedly.

Fools despise wisdom and instruction. Just as a wise man in this book is one who is willing and anxious to learn, a fool is one who cannot be told anything. He is intractable and conceited, and only learns lessons the hard way, if at all.

II. PROVERBS OF SOLOMON ON WISDOM AND FOLLY (1:8—9:18)

A. Wisdom's Admonition (1:8–33)

1:8 The first seven chapters are largely addressed to **"My son"**; the expression occurs about 15 times. In these chapters, we hear the heartbeat of a parent who wants the best in life for his child. By heeding this parental advice, a young person will avoid life's booby traps and develop expertise in practical, everyday affairs.

How much we owe to the influence of godly parents, and especially godly mothers! Henry Bosch reminds us:

> Many great men of the past have been richly blessed by what they

learned at their mother's knee. Consider Moses, Samuel, and Timothy. The maternal care and godly influence experienced by these spiritual leaders bore rich fruit in their lives. Think too of Augustine, John Newton, and the zealous Wesley brothers. Their names would probably never have lighted the pages of history if it hadn't been for the godly women who raised them in homes where the law of love and Christian witness was their daily guide and inspiration.[3]

1:9 When parental advice is followed, it becomes a **graceful** wreath **on** the **head** and ornamental **chains about** the **neck**, which is a poetic way of saying that obedience brings honor and moral beauty to the life of a wise son.

1:10 Often when a young man ruins his life, the explanation is given that he "got in with the wrong crowd." The process is described in verses 10–19 in living color.

First, however, the warning flag is flown. Life is full of enticements to evil. We must have the courage and backbone to say "No" a thousand times a week.

1:11 Here the street-corner gang invites our young friend to participate in an armed robbery. If necessary they will "bump off" the victim. Our friend may be flattered that these toughs would accept him as one of the gang. **"Come with us," they say**. And he may be lured by the excitement of anything so daring.

1:12–14 Perhaps he is bored by a sheltered life, and wants to do something "for kicks." Well, here it is! The perfect crime! Sudden and violent death, then a quick disposal of any tell-tale evidence. And the great incentive, of course, is that they will all be rich overnight. There will be enough loot to **fill** the **houses** of all the accomplices. So the word is, "Get with it, and you'll make a bundle. Everyone shares equally. You can't lose."

1:15, 16 But a wiser voice says, "**My son**, don't do it. Stay as far away from them as possible. Have nothing to do with their plans for instant wealth. You can't win."

"What you must realize is that these guys constantly pursue lives of crime, and are quick on the trigger. They commit one murder after another in rapid succession."

1:17, 18 A **bird** has enough sense to avoid any **net** or snare that can be clearly seen. But these men make a trap for **their own lives**, then walk straight into it.

1:19 There is a moral to the story. Those who try to get rich quick pay for their greed with their own lives. **So are the ways of everyone who is greedy for gain; it takes away the life of its owners.**

This particular passage deals with the attempt to get rich through violence. But the application is wider. Any get-rich-quick scheme is included, whether it be gambling, sweepstakes, or stock market speculation.

Next we hear two voices calling out to men as they pass by. One is the voice of Wisdom, the other the voice of the strange woman. Wisdom, though presented here as a woman, actually symbolizes the Lord Jesus Christ.[4] The strange woman is a type of sinful temptation and of the ungodly world.

In verses 20–33 wisdom pleads with those who foolishly think they can get along without her.

1:20 Notice that **Wisdom** stands and **calls aloud** in strategic places so that everyone may hear her message. **She raises her voice in the** city **squares**.

1:21 Now **she** is at the noisy intersections, and now at the entrances

of the gates of the city. And so it is that our Lord calls to the race of men wherever they pass by:

> Where cross the crowded ways of life,
> Where sound the cries of race and clan,
> Above the noise of selfish strife,
> We hear Thy voice, O Son of Man!
> —*Frank Mason North*

1:22 Wisdom cries to the **simple**, the **scorners**, and **fools**. The **simple** are naive, impressionable people who are open to all kinds of influences, both good and bad; here their instability seems to be leading them in the wrong direction. **Scorners** are those who treat wise counsel with contempt; nothing is sacred or serious to them. **Fools** are those who senselessly refuse instruction; they are conceited and opinionated in their ignorance.

1:23 This verse may be understood in two ways. First, it may mean,

> Since you won't listen to my invitation, now **turn** and listen to **my rebuke. I will pour out my spirit** in words of judgment, and will tell you what lies ahead for **you**.

According to this interpretation, verses 24–27 are the words which describe their fate.

The second possible meaning is this:

> **Turn** and repent when I reprove you. If you do, then **I will pour out my spirit on you** in blessing, and **make my words** of wisdom **known to you**.

The word **"spirit"** here probably means "thoughts" or "mind." While it is true that Christ pours out the Holy Spirit on those who answer His call, this truth was not as clearly stated in the OT as it is in the NT.

1:24 One of the greatest tragedies of life is the crass rejection of wisdom's gracious entreaties. It **called** forth the lament of lost opportunity from the summit of Olivet, "I would… but you would not."

1:25 Wisdom sorrows over men who brush aside **all** her **counsel** and who will have nothing to do with her constructive criticism.

What makes man's stubborn refusal so irrational is that God's commandments and warnings are for man's good, not for God's. This is illustrated in a story which D. G. Barnhouse told. A small child squeezed past the metal railing that kept spectators six feet from the lions' cage at the Washington Zoo. When her grandfather ordered her to come out, she backed away teasingly. A waiting lion grabbed her, dragged her into the cage, and mangled her to death. According to Barnhouse the lesson is this:

> God has given us commandments and principles that are for our good; God never gives us a commandment because He is arbitrary or because He doesn't want us to have fun. God says, "Thou shalt have no other gods before Me," not because He is jealous of His own position and prerogatives, but because He knows that if we put anything, anything before Him, it will hurt us. If we understand the principle behind this fact, we can also understand why God chastens us. "Whom the Lord loves, he chastens" (Heb. 12:6). He doesn't want us to back into a lion, for there is a lion, the devil, seeking whom he may devour.[5]

1:26 If man persists in his refusal to listen, that rejection will inevitably bring disaster and ruin. Then it will be wisdom's turn to **laugh**. **"I also**

will laugh at your calamity; I will mock when your terror comes."

Does this mean that the Lord will actually **laugh** when disaster falls on the ungodly, as suggested here and in Psalm 2:4? If we think of the laughter as containing any trace of cruelty, malice, or vindictiveness, then the answer is clearly "No." Rather we should think of this laughter in a figurative way. In idiomatic language, it expresses how ludicrous and ridiculous it is for a mere man to defy the Omnipotent Sovereign, as if a gnat should defy a blast furnace. And there may also be this thought: A man may laugh at Wisdom's commandments or treat them as if they didn't exist; but when that man is reaping the harvest of his folly, the commandments still stand unmoved, and to the scorner, at least, they seem to be having the last laugh—the **laugh** of poetic justice.

1:27 Payday will surely come. The judgment men feared will descend on them **like a storm**. Calamity will roar down like a tornado. **Distress, anguish**, shock, and despair will seize them.

1:28 **Then** men **will call on** Wisdom in vain. They will be desperate to find her, but won't be able to. They will realize too late that light rejected is light denied. They *would not* see; now they *cannot* see. God's Spirit will not always strive with man (Gen. 6:3). This is what gives urgency to the Gospel appeal:

> Be in time! Be in time!
> While the voice of Jesus calls you,
> Be in time!
> If in sin you longer wait,
> You may find no open gate,
> And your cry be just too late.
> Be in time!
> —*Author unknown, 19th Century*

1:29 The condemnation of these scorners is that they **hated** Wisdom's instructions, and stubbornly refused to reverence Jehovah. Perhaps they sneered that the gospel was all right for women and children, but not for them. "Professing to be wise, they became fools" (Rom. 1:22). The hatred of wisdom is also treated in John 3:19–21.

1:30 **They** had no place in their lives for the good **counsel** contained in the Word of God, and laughed when the Scriptures condemned their ungodly words and works. They weren't afraid of God or of His **rebuke**.

1:31 Now they must pay the staggering price of their willfulness, and be glutted with **the** bad **fruit of their own** schemes. It is their own fault, not Wisdom's. They simply would not listen.

1:32 "For heedless folk fall by their own self-will, the senseless are destroyed by their indifference" (Moffatt). Every man is free to make his own choices in life, but he is not free to choose the *consequences* of his choices. God has established certain moral principles in the world. These principles dictate the consequences for every choice. There is no way to put asunder what God has thus joined together.

1:33 On the plus side, the one who heeds Wisdom will live in safety and in freedom from **fear**. Those who are Wisdom's disciples enjoy the good life, escaping the sufferings, sorrows, and shame that dog the footsteps of the willful and the wicked.

B. Wisdom's Ways (Chap. 2)

In chapter 2, Solomon urges his son to walk in the ways of wisdom. The first four verses give the conditions for receiving the knowledge of God; a person must be earnest and sincere in seeking it with all his heart. The rest of the chapter promises that wisdom and discernment will be given. The 22 verses correspond to the 22 letters of the Hebrew alphabet.

2:1 First, the **son** is urged to take to heart his father's teaching and **treasure** up his **commands**. The proverbs were intended to be treasured up **"within you,"** or memorized.

2:2 There must be an open **ear** and an open **heart** or mind. The son must be an attentive listener, not a compulsive talker. He is not told to talk out his problems, as in much of modern counseling; rather he should listen to the wise advice of others.

2:3,4 If he really means business, let him **cry out for discernment**, and send out an appeal for **understanding**. Seriousness of purpose is of primary importance. It is a law of life that we get what we go after.

What we need is the same kind of drive that men have in mining for **silver** or in searching for **hidden treasures**. The tragedy is that too often men show more zeal in acquiring material wealth than spiritual riches.

2:5 But those who seek inevitably **find**. Those who are anxious to come into a right relationship with the Lord and to really know **God** are never disappointed. That is why one of the early church fathers said that the man who seeks God has already found Him. Christ reveals the Father to all who believe on Him. To know Christ is to know God.

2:6 After we have been saved through faith in Christ, we are then in a position to learn divine **wisdom** from the LORD. He teaches us how to think straight, how to evaluate, how to discern truth and error and how to develop divine insight.

2:7 He provides rich stores of **sound wisdom for the upright**, and a special **shield** of protection for **those who walk** in integrity.

2:8 **He guards the paths of** those who live clean, moral lives. **His saints** escape the pain and bitterness that sin leaves in its trail. "Safe and sound the chosen friends of God come and go" (Knox).

2:9 This verse parallels verse 5. Both begin with **"Then"** and list the benefits of seriously seeking the knowledge of God.

The person who keenly desires to know and do God's will learns how to behave righteously, to act fairly, to conduct himself honestly—in short, to choose the right way **and every good path**.

2:10 The reason this happens is that **wisdom** takes control of one's mind or **heart**, and the **knowledge** of what is right becomes **pleasant** rather than distasteful. To the true believer, God's commands are not irksome. Christ's yoke is easy and His burden is light.

2:11 **Discretion**, or the ability to make wise decisions, saves a person from many a "bad trip." Sound judgment delivers us from involvement with wicked men. None of us realizes the extent to which we are daily preserved from spiritual, moral, and physical perils. The Christian enjoys a well-guarded life, having escaped the corruption that is in the world through lust.

2:12 We are saved from the partnership of **evil** *men* (vv. 12–15) and from the embrace of the loose *woman* (vv. 16–19).

First we are saved from the world of ungodly men who misrepresent facts and distort the truth. Their speech is utterly untrustworthy.

2:13–15 These are men **who leave** the well-lighted streets of **uprightness**

to slink in the dark alleys of crime and crookedness.

They take savage pleasure in **doing evil** and **delight in** the way their sin turns everything topsy-turvy.

They follow **crooked** routes and **their** behavior is sly and **devious**.

2:16 Wisdom saves not only from the company of men like these but also from the clutches of the **immoral woman**. We may understand this woman as a literal prostitute or we may see her as a figure of false religion or of the ungodly world.

Her method is flattery: "You aren't appreciated at home as you should be. You are so handsome, so talented. You have so much to offer. You need love and sympathetic understanding, and I'm the one to give it to you."

2:17 She is unfaithful to **the companion of her youth**, that is, her husband. She **forgets the covenant of her God**, that is, the marriage vows that she made before God. Or "the covenant of her God" may refer to the Ten Commandments and specifically to the seventh commandment, which forbids adultery.

2:18 The first clause of verse 18 may be translated **"For her house leads down to death"** or "she sinketh down unto death, which is her house" (RV margin). The parallel second clause of the verse seems to support the NKJV translation. Putting them together, the thought is: **her house leads down to death**, and therefore those who enter it are sliding toward the grave. Her **paths** lead **to the dead**, and therefore those who follow her will soon be in the realm of departed spirits. Since everybody will die some day, death must be more here than the common lot of all mortals; it must mean moral death leading to eternal death.

2:19 Once a man is ensnared by her, it is almost impossible to escape. The verse actually seems to rule out any hope of a comeback at all. But many statements in the Bible must be understood as general rules, to which there may be a few exceptions. That is the point here. Once a man is initiated into her secrets, it is extremely hard to **regain** the right road.

2:20 Link verse 20 with verse 11. Wisdom preserves not only from evil men and the strange woman, but, on the positive side, it encourages companionship with those who are worthwhile and upright.

2:21, 22 Under the Law of Moses, men of integrity—**the upright** and **the blameless**—were rewarded with a secure place **in the land** of Canaan. When we come over to the NT, these material blessings in earthly places give way to spiritual blessings in the heavenlies. But the fact remains that righteousness and decency are rewarded in this life as well as in the life to come.

It is equally true that **the wicked will be cut off from the** land of blessing. There is no lasting inheritance there for the treacherous.

C. Wisdom's Rewards (3:1–10)

3:1 Like all good parents, Wisdom wants the best for her children. She knows that that can come only through obedience to her teachings, which is another way of saying obedience to the sacred Scriptures. So here she pleads with her **son** to remember with the mind and obey with the **heart**.

3:2 In general, those who are subject to their parents live longer and better lives. Those who kick up their heels against parental discipline invite illness, accidents, tragedies, and premature death. This verse thus corresponds to the fifth commandment (Ex. 20:12) which promises **long life** to those who honor their parents. Jay Adams writes:

> The Bible teaches that a peace of mind which leads to longer, happier living comes from keeping God's commandments. A guilty conscience is a body-breaking load. A good conscience is one significant factor which leads to longevity and physical health. And so, in a measure, one's somatic (bodily) welfare stems from the welfare of his soul. A close psychosomatic connection between one's behavior before God and his physical condition is an established physical principle.[6]

3:3, 4 **Mercy** and **truth** should be seen in the outward behavior (**bind them around your neck**) and should be true of the inward life as well (**write them on the tablet of your heart**).

This is the way to **find favor and high esteem** (or success, AV margin) **in the sight of God and man**. What it boils down to is that the satisfying life is the one that is lived in the center of God's will. But that brings up the question, "How can I know God's will in my life?" A classic answer is given in the next two verses.

3:5 First, there must be a full commitment of ourselves—spirit, soul, and body—to **the Lord**. We must **trust** Him not only for the salvation of our souls but also for the direction of our lives. It must be a commitment without reserve.

Next, there must be a healthy distrust of self, an acknowledgment that we do not know what is best for us, that we are not capable of guiding ourselves. Jeremiah expressed it pointedly: "O Lord, I know the way of man is not in himself; it is not in man who walks to direct his own steps" (Jer. 10:23).

3:6 Finally, there must be an acknowledgment of the Lordship of Christ: **"In all your ways acknowledge Him."** Every area of our lives must be turned over to His control. We must have no will of our own, only a single pure desire to know His will and to do it.

If these conditions are met, the promise is that God **shall direct** our **paths**. He may do it through the Bible, through the advice of godly Christians, through the marvelous converging of circumstances, through the inward peace of the Spirit, or through a combination of these. But if we wait, He will make the guidance so clear that to refuse would be positive disobedience.

3:7, 8 Conceit puts us on "hold" as far as divine guidance is concerned. When we **fear the Lord** and **depart from evil**, it means "all systems go." It spells **health to** the body and **strength** (lit. *drink* or *refreshment*) **to** the **bones**. Here again we are brought face to face with the close connection between man's moral and spiritual condition and his physical health.

It has been estimated that fear, sorrow, envy, resentment, hatred, guilt, and other emotional stresses account for over 60% of our illness. Add to that the terrible toll taken by alcohol (cirrhosis of the liver); tobacco (emphysema, cancer, heart disease); immorality (venereal diseases, AIDS). Then we realize that "he shall direct your paths" is more literally "he shall make your paths smooth" or "straight," but guidance is surely included in the promise. Solomon, by divine inspiration, was way ahead of his times in the field of medical science.

3:9 One way in which we can **honor** the lordship of Christ is in our stewardship of **possessions**. All we have belongs to Him. We are stewards, responsible for its management. It is our privilege to choose a modest standard of living for ourselves, put everything above that to work for God, and trust God for the future. Like David Livingston, we should determine not to look upon anything we possess except in relation to the Kingdom of God.

3:10 The generous Jew in the OT was promised bulging **barns** and overflowing **vats** of **wine**. Even though our blessings may be of a more spiritual nature, it is still true that we cannot outgive the Lord.

D. Wisdom as the Prize (3:11–20)

3:11, 12 We can also acknowledge the Lord by submitting to His discipline. Too often we tend to think of discipline as meaning punishment, but it actually includes all that is involved in the proper training of a child, i.e., instruction, warning, encouragement, advice, **correction**, and **chastening**. Everything that God allows to come into our lives is purposeful. We should not **detest** it or **despise** it. Neither should we shrink from it or give up under it. Rather we should be concerned that God's purpose is achieved through the discipline, and thus we reap the maximum profit from it. God's ultimate purpose in the disciplines of life is that we become partakers of His holiness.

Discipline is a proof of love, not anger. **Correction** is a proof of sonship (see Heb. 12:6–8).

Thought: A gardener prunes grapevines but not thistles.

3:13 The **happy** individual is the one **who finds wisdom**, and especially so when we remember that Wisdom here is a veiled presentation of Christ Himself. Let us put Christ into the following verses and see what happens.

3:14 The benefit of knowing the Lord Jesus far surpasses any **profits** a man might get from **silver** and **gold**. He gives what money can never buy.

> I'd rather have Jesus than silver or
> gold.
> I'd rather be His than have riches
> untold,
> I'd rather have Jesus than houses or
> land,
> I'd rather be led by His nail-pierced
> hand
> Than to be the king of a vast domain
> And be held in sin's dread sway.
> I'd rather have Jesus than anything
> This world affords today.
>
> —*George Beverly Shea*

3:15 He is **more precious than rubies**, or any other jewels, more to be desired than any earthly prize.

3:16 With one **hand** He offers long life, in fact, eternal life. With the other, spiritual **riches and honor**.

3:17 All His **ways are ways of pleasantness**, and **all** His **paths are peace**. "Where He guides, journeying is pleasant, where He points the way, all is peace" (Knox, alt.).

3:18 To those who take hold of Him, He is like **a tree** whose fruit is **life** worth living. Those who remain close to Him are the **happy** ones.

3:19, 20 These two verses describe the **wisdom** of God in creation, in judgment, and in providence. In creation He **founded the earth** and **established the heavens**. With **understanding**, He opened up the fountains of the great deep at the time of the Flood. By providence, He lifts the water from the ocean into the **clouds**, then distributes it again as rain upon the earth.

And who is the active agent of the Godhead in doing all this? It is Christ, the Wisdom of God (John 1:3; Col. 1:16; Heb. 1:2).

E. Wisdom Practiced (3:21–35)

3:21 The privilege of being instructed by the Wisdom that created and sustains the universe is too great to miss. We shouldn't let **sound wisdom and discretion** out of our sight.

3:22–24 They provide inward vitality (**life to your soul**) and outward beauty (**grace to your neck**).

They enable us to **walk safely in** our **way**, free from danger of tripping or slipping.

They guarantee a good night's **sleep**, with no guilt on the conscience and no fear on the mind.

3:25 They preserve a man from the kind of **sudden terror** that overtakes **the wicked**. Those who envy the apparent prosperity of the ungodly fail to realize the built-in hazards of that kind of life—such as extortion, theft, revenge, payoffs, blackmail, kidnapping, and murder.

3:26 **The Lord** guards those who walk in His ways. He won't let our **foot** get **caught** in a trap. We are often conscious of God's marvelous interventions and rescues in our lives. But these are only the tip of the iceberg. Some day we will realize more fully all we have been saved from as well as saved to.

3:27 Notice the negatives in verses 27–31: **"Do not withhold** . . . do not say . . . do not devise . . . do not strive . . . do not envy . . . do not choose. . . ."

First, never **withhold** anything **good from those to whom it is due** when you are in a position to give it. This might refer to wages that have been earned, to a debt that is due, to tools that have been borrowed.

But in a wider sense it may mean, "Never withhold a kindness or a good deed from someone who is entitled to it." This injunction may be introduced here to warn the righteous against becoming so occupied with their proper relationship with God as to neglect their responsibility towards others (see Jas. 4:17).

3:28 Don't put **your neighbor** off till **tomorrow** when you can meet his need today.

Who is my neighbor? Anyone who needs my help.

What does my neighbor need? He needs to hear the good news of salvation.

If the Holy Spirit burdens my heart to witness to someone, I should do it today. Never refuse any prompting of the Spirit.

3:29 Love to our **neighbor** forbids us to **devise evil against** him as he **dwells** trustingly and unsuspectingly in the house next door. This rules out all the mean, sarcastic, and cruel revenge that too often follows neighborhood squabbles.

3:30 Here we are warned against picking a fight **with a man** when he has done nothing to provoke it. There is already enough strife in the world without needlessly going around to stir up more!

3:31, 32 **The oppressor** may seem to have instant success. But we should **not envy** his prosperity or follow **his ways**. **The Lord** hates, loathes, despises, and abominates **the perverse person**, but takes the upright into His intimate confidence (see John 14:23).

3:33 God's condemnation or His confidence, His **curse** or His blessing—that is the choice! A dark cloud hovers over **the house of the wicked**. The sunshine of God's favor beams down on **the home of the just**.

3:34 Again the choice is between God's scorn and His **grace**. **He scorns the** scoffer **but gives grace to the humble**. The importance of this choice is seen in that the verse is quoted twice in the NT (Jas. 4:6; 1 Pet. 5:5).

3:35 Finally the choice is between honor and disgrace. **Wise** men **inherit glory**; **fools** become well-known by falling into disgrace.

F. Wisdom as a Family Treasure (4:1–9)

4:1 In the first nine verses, Solomon rehearses the sound teaching which his father had passed on to him, and urges his **children** to spare no effort in gaining true insight. The book of Proverbs teems with earnest exhortations to the young to listen to **instruction** from a wise **father**.

4:2 It pays to cultivate the friendship of godly, older people. You can learn a lot from them and benefit from their years of experience. Their **doctrine** is **good**, and **not** to be disregarded.

4:3 Here Solomon refers to the time when he was a **son** to his father and **"the only one" in the sight of** his **mother**. Actually he was not an only son, but perhaps the expression **"the only one in the sight of my mother"** means "my mother's darling" (Knox).

4:4 Solomon's father, David, had **taught** his son to **retain** his sound advice and thus **live** a life that counts. A summary of David's instruction is given in verses 4b–9.

4:5, 6 His major concern was for his son to **get wisdom** and **understanding**—which really means to live for the Lord. Whatever else Solomon did, he should never **forget** this, because only the life that's lived for God really counts.

4:7 The first step in getting **wisdom** is to have motivation or determination. We get in life what we go after. We should **get wisdom** at all cost, and in the process **get** good **understanding** and discernment. This means, among other things, that we will learn to choose between the evil and the good, the good and the best, the soulish and the spiritual, the temporal and the eternal.

4:8 If we give wisdom first place in our priorities, **she will promote** us handsomely. If we **embrace her** lovingly, **she will bring** us to places of **honor**.

4:9 "She will adorn you with charm and crown you with glory" (Moffatt). Wisdom confers a moral beauty on her children. Contrast, for instance, the repulsiveness of a life abandoned to dissipation and immorality.

G. Wisdom and the Two Paths (4:10–27)

4:10 Having finished quoting his father's counsel, Solomon now resumes his appeal to his own **son**. It is a general rule, though not without exceptions, that a clean life is conducive to a long **life**. Think how tobacco, alcohol, drugs, and sexual sin are directly linked with disease and death.

4:11, 12 A father can be gratified when he has **taught** his son **the way of wisdom** and has been a good example to him. However, the teaching must be combined with the example. A father's actions speak louder than his words.

A son who walks in the **right paths** will **walk** unimpeded and will **run** without stumbling.

The Syriac version reads: "As thou goest step by step, I will open up the way before thee." This teaches two important principles: First, God guides us step by step, rather than revealing the whole plan at once. Second, God guides people when they are moving forward for Him. A ship must be in motion before the skipper can steer it. So must a bicycle; you can only guide it when it is moving. The same is true of us; God guides us when we are in motion for Him.

4:13 We should **take firm hold** of good **instruction**, and **not let** it slip from us. We should guard wisdom as we would guard our life—because it **is** our **life**, especially when we think of Wisdom Incarnate in the person of the Lord Jesus.

4:14 Verses 14–19 warn against evil companions and contrast **the way of** darkness with the way of light.

These exhortations against joining up with unrighteous men do not forbid our witnessing to them but they do forbid any partnership in their plans.

4:15 There is a note of urgent warning in these short, staccato commands. **Avoid** a life of sin. Don't pass by to investigate. **Turn** the other way. Keep going. It might seem interesting, intriguing, and thrilling, but it eventually will destroy you.

4:16, 17 The henchmen of sin **do not sleep** well **unless they have** pulled some shady deal. They get a king-sized case of insomnia **unless they** have lured **someone** to ruin and disaster.

Their diet is **the bread of wickedness** and **the wine of violence**. Or we might say that **wickedness** is their meat and drink.

These verses give a very drastic picture of the sinful nature of man. Since his nature is sin, sinning is for him as meat and drink for the body. This passage does not apply only to criminals. (See *BBC* on Jer. 17:9).

4:18, 19 Not so the life of the righteous person. It is **like the** dawning light which **shines ever brighter** until it reaches the full blaze of noonday. In other words, **the path of the just** grows better and **brighter** all the time.

The wicked stagger on in deep **darkness**, with no idea as to what they're stumbling over.

4:20 Solomon continues to plead with his **son** to pay close **attention to** his instruction in wisdom. In a verse like this, we should hear the voice of the Lord speaking to us.

4:21 It is for our own good that we should **not let** wisdom's teachings out of our sight, but should rather treasure them **in** our **heart**.

4:22 Wisdom's words **are** life-giving and creative. As Jesus said, "The words that I speak to you are spirit, and they are life" (John 6:63).

And they are **health to** the whole body because they deliver a person from the sins and stresses that cause so much illness.

4:23 Verses 23–27 are the OT counterpart of Romans 12:1. They beseech us to present our entire beings to God—heart, mouth, lips, eyes, and feet. God begins with the inner man, then works outward.

The **heart** is first. It speaks of the inner **life**, the mind, the thoughts, the motives, the desires. The mind is the fountain from which the actions spring. If the fountain is pure, the stream that flows from it will be pure. As a man thinks, so is he. So this verse emphasizes the importance of a clean thought life.

4:24, 25 A **deceitful mouth** signifies dishonest and devious speech. **Perverse lips** refer to conversation that is not straightforward and aboveboard.

Eyes and **eyelids** that **look straight ahead** suggest a walk with singleness of purpose, one that does not turn aside for sin or for anything that is unworthy. In a day when the mass media bombard us with publicity designed to arouse our animal appetites, we must learn to keep our eyes on Jesus (Heb. 12:2).

4:26, 27 If we are careful to **ponder the path** of holiness, **all** our **ways** will be well-ordered and safe.

All along the highway, **to the right** and **to the left**, there are side streets and alleys which lead to the haunts of sin. "Let's be true to Jesus, though a thousand voices from the world may call."

When tempted to go to a questionable place, ask yourself, "Would I like to be found there when Jesus comes back?" **Remove your foot from evil**.

H. The Folly of Immorality (Chap.5)

5:1, 2 Solomon is anxious to warn his **son** against one of the besetting sins of youth. Those who **pay attention** to sound advice and learn from the experience of others develop true **discretion**. Because their speech is pure and true, it protects them from getting into trouble. Nothing but the Word of God is an adequate safeguard against the seduction and delusion running rampant in our day. Therefore, Paul exhorts Timothy to stick to the Word when surrounded by apostasy (2 Tim. 3:13–17).

5:3 The rest of chapter 5 deals with what has been called "the oldest profession"—prostitution. The **immoral woman** is a prostitute, one who hires herself out for debased purposes. She may be thought of as a symbol of sin, of the evil world, of false religion, of idolatry, or of any other seductive temptation that the sons of men meet. Her **lips . . . drip honey**—sweet, smooth, and specious. She is a flatterer, a slick, clever talker.

5:4 At first she seems pleasant and desirable, **but in the end she is bitter as wormwood**. It is the old story—sin is attractive as a prospect but hideous in retrospect.

The price of going to bed with her is enormous—guilty conscience, remorse, scandal, venereal disease, wrecked marriage, broken home, mental disturbance, and a host of other ills.

5:5, 6 She leads her victims down a one-way street **to death** and **hell**. Abandoned woman, she cares nothing for the good life. **Her** character is **unstable** and shifty, and she doesn't realize how low she has fallen. "The high road of Life is not for her, shifty and slippery are her tracks" (Moffatt).

5:7 As he considers all that is at stake, Solomon injects a solemn warning to his **children**, to **hear** him and **not depart from** what he has to say.

5:8 One great safeguard is to stay as **far** away **from** the temptation as possible. There is no use asking God for deliverance if we insist on toying with objects or places that are associated with sin.

In some cases, it is necessary to actually flee. Joseph did this, and although he lost his coat, he maintained his purity and gained a crown.

In order to obey verse 8 we may have to get a new job, move to a different location, or take some other equally decided step.

5:9, 10 Those who visit the brothel squander their manly vigor, and **give** the best of their golden **years to** a **cruel** temptress.

In addition, "respectable" citizens who have secret immoral liaisons—whether literally or through pornography, "x-rated" films and videotapes—often find themselves the victims of blackmail. If they don't pay "hush money," they are threatened with public exposure.

5:11 The end of such a life is punctuated with a protracted groan, as the **body** is racked with gonorrhea, syphilis, blindness, locomotor ataxia, AIDS, and emotional disturbances.

5:12, 13 There is the added grief of regret and remorse. The burned out wreck reproaches himself for not having **obeyed** his parents, his Sunday School **teachers**, his Christian friends. He could have avoided oceans of misery, but he was too pig-headed to be warned.

5:14 And there is the possibility of being brought to public disgrace. That seems to be the thought in this verse, although it might also include the idea of being sentenced for his misdeeds.

5:15, 16 In figurative language, Solomon counsels his son to find all his sexual satisfaction with his **own** wife in a life of pure married love.

If we follow the KJV, this verse describes the blessings of a faithful marriage relationship reaching out to family and friends.

The NKJV changes the verse to a question: **"Should your fountains be dispersed abroad, streams of water in the streets?"** This is a picturesque description of the utter waste of one's reproductive powers that is involved in going in to a prostitute.

Knox translates the verse, "Thence let thy offspring abound, like waters from thy own fountain flowing through the public streets." The wife here is the fountain, and the waters are the children, tearing out of the house and playing happily in the streets.

5:17 The true marriage relationship is an exclusive one, and the children enjoy the security of "belonging." So this verse warns against the tragedy of illegitimate children or the doubtful parentage of those who are born as a result of promiscuous sexual union.

5:18 The **fountain** here again refers to a man's own wife. Let him find his joy and companionship in **the wife of** his **youth**. In "forsaking all others" a man finds, as Michael Griffiths expressed it, that "there is no end to the richness that springs out of that exclusive relationship, and the warmth of the welcome that reaches out from his home to bless others."[7]

5:19, 20 Let a man reserve the intimacies of marital union for his wife, treating her as the **loving, graceful** woman she is. **Let her breasts** be his satisfying portion, and may he **always be enraptured with her love**.

For **why should** he be **enraptured** by the false charms of **an immoral woman**? Or why fold a **seductress** into his arms?

5:21, 22 Though no human eye may follow him to the brothel, the motel room, or the secret rendezvous, yet God sees **all** that takes place. "Secret sin on earth is open scandal in heaven."

Man cannot **sin** and get away with it. Sin's built-in consequences are inescapable. As Jay Adams counsels:

> Sinful habits are hard to break, but if they are not broken, they will bind the client ever more tightly. He is held fast by these ropes of his own sin. He finds that sin spirals in a downward cycle, pulling him along. He is captured and tied up by sin's ever-tightening cords. At length he becomes sin's slave.[8]

5:23 Ellicott calls this verse the final scene in the life of the profligate. He would not exercise self-control. Now he dies as a result. "For lack of sense he dies; his utter folly ruins him" (Moffatt).

The poet Shelley is an illustration of this passage. In his conceit, he ridiculed the idea of monogamous marriage, as if it were a matter of marrying one and disappointing thousands. The results of his approach, according to Griffiths, were desertions, suicides, illegitimate children, and jealousy. G. Sampson questioned "whether in the life of any poet there is such a trail of disasters as that which this 'beautiful but ineffectual' angel left behind him."

I. The Folly of Suretyship, Laziness, and Deception (6:1–19)

6:1 The first five verses are a warning against becoming **surety**, that is, making oneself liable for someone else's debt in case that other person is unable to pay. Suppose **your friend** wants to buy a car on the installment plan but doesn't have much of a credit rating. The loan company demands the signature of someone who can pay in case the borrower defaults. The neighbor comes to you and asks you to cosign the note with him. This means that you will pay if he doesn't.

The **friend** in this verse is your neighbor. The **stranger** is the loan company to which you give your guarantee.

6:2 **You are snared by the words of your mouth; you are taken by the words of your mouth.** In other words, if you have made a rash promise, you have fallen into a trap. It was a great mistake.

6:3 Now the best thing to do is to get **yourself** released from the agreement. Try to persuade **your friend** to get your signature removed from the note you have been trapped into signing.

6:4, 5 The matter is of such importance that you shouldn't rest until you are released from this liability. You should squirm free **like a gazelle from** its captor, or like **a bird from . . . the fowler**.

But why does the Bible warn against suretyship so sternly? Isn't it a kindness to do this for a friend or neighbor? It might seem to be a kindness, but it might not be at all.

1. You might be helping him to buy something which it is not God's will for him to have.
2. You might be encouraging him to be a spendthrift or even a gambler.
3. If he defaults and you have to pay for something that is not your own, friendship will end and bitterness begin.

It would be better to give money outright if there is a legitimate need. In any case, you should not become surety for him.

6:6, 7 Verses 6–11 are a protest against laziness. **The ant** is an object lesson to us as it scurries back and forth, keeps on the move, and often carries oversized loads. It gets a lot accomplished without benefit of a boss, foreman, or superintendent. When we watch a swarm of ants, they seem to move crazily in every direction, but their activity is purposeful and directed, even though there is no apparent chain of command.

6:8 This little creature diligently and industriously works **in the summer** and **gathers her food in the harvest**. The emphasis here is not on making provision for the future but on hard work now.

This passage should not be used to teach that Christians should make provision for a rainy day. We are forbidden to lay up treasures on earth (Matt. 6:19). It is true that ants do provide for their future, and it is also true that Christians should provide for theirs. But the difference is that an ant's future is in this world, whereas the believer's future is in heaven. Wise Christians, therefore, lay up their treasures in heaven, not on earth.

6:9 The lazy fellow seems to have an endless capacity for **sleep**. His philosophy is, "It's nice to get up in the morning, but it's nicer to lie in bed." He seems to have an infinite deafness to alarm clocks.

6:10, 11 When finally roused, he says, "Just let me have a few more winks, **a little** more **sleep**, a short nap, a quick beauty rest."

Others in the household may wait, but the day of **poverty** won't. **So shall your poverty come on you like a prowler, and your need like an armed man.**

6:12 Verses 12–15 are a classic description of a con man. He is a malicious swindler whose cunning smile masks a treacherous heart. He goes around with falsehood on his lips.

6:13, 14 He uses all kinds of suggestive gestures and sinister motions to signal to his accomplice or to take his victims off guard. He **winks with his eyes**, **shuffles** or scrapes with **his feet**, and beckons **with his fingers**.

His heart is filled with malice and **perversity** as he incessantly plots mischief and **sows discord**.

6:15 "Such men will be overtaken by their doom ere long, crushed all of a sudden beyond hope of remedy" (Knox). If you look hard enough, you can probably find an illustration of this in today's newspaper.

6:16 The **things** which characterize this wicked man (vv. 12–15) are hated by God (vv. 16–19), especially the sowing of discord (compare vv. 14 and 19).

The formula **"six things . . . yes, seven . . ."** may mean that the list is specific but not exhaustive. Or it may indicate that the seventh is worst of all.[9]

6:17 A proud look. Pride is dust deifying itself. The valet of an emperor said:

> I cannot deny that my master was vain. He had to be the central figure in everything. If he went to a christening, he wanted to be the baby. If he went to a wedding, he wanted to be the bride. If he went to a funeral, he wanted to be the corpse.[10]

A lying tongue. The tongue was created to glorify the Lord. To lie is to pervert its use for that which is ignoble. Is it ever right for a believer to lie? The answer is that God cannot lie, and He cannot give the privilege to anyone else.

Hands that shed innocent blood. Every human life is of infinite value to God. He proved this by paying an infinite price at Calvary for our redemption. The institution of capital punishment (Gen. 9:6) reflects God's attitude toward murder.

6:18 A heart that devises wicked plans. This, of course, refers to the mind that is always plotting some evil. The Lord Jesus listed some of these wicked imaginations in Mark 7:21, 22.

Feet that are swift in running to evil—God hates not only the mind that plans the evil but the **feet** that are eager to carry it out.

6:19 A false witness who speaks lies. Here it is a matter of public testimony in a court of law. In verse 17b it was more a matter of everyday conversation.

One who sows discord among brethren. The striking thing here is that God ranks the one who causes divisions among **brethren** with murderers, liars, and perjurers!

How many of the seven sins listed above can you associate with the trial and crucifixion of our Lord?

J. The Folly of Adultery and Harlotry (6:20—7:27)

6:20 The subject of adultery or unfaithfulness is taken up again here.

The frequency with which it recurs is not accidental. The words of verse 20 are a sort of formula used to introduce important instruction.

6:21 Some extreme literalists in Jesus' day thought they obeyed this verse by wearing phylacteries, that is, small leather boxes containing Scripture portions. During prayer, these Jews wore one on the left arm (near the **heart**) and one on the head (near the **neck**). Some Jews still use them today.

But what this verse *really* means is that we should make the Word of God so much a part of our lives that it will accompany and direct us wherever we go. It is not just a question of honoring the Scriptures outwardly but of obeying them from the heart.

6:22 Obedience to God's Word affords:

guidance—**When you roam, they will lead you.**
protection—**When you sleep, they will keep** (guard) **you.**
instruction—***When* you awake, they will speak with you.**

6:23 This verse amplifies the previous one:

the commandment is a lamp—for guidance
the law is **a light**—for protection
reproofs of instruction are the way of life—for teaching.

6:24, 25 One particular ministry of the Word is to save men from the **seductress** with the glib, **flattering tongue**.

No one should be taken in by **her** natural **beauty** or by the come-hither flickers of her eyelashes.

6:26 The interpretation of this verse differs according to different translations.

The thought in the NKJV and the NASB is that a man is **reduced** to poverty (**a crust of bread**) by **a harlot**, and may lose **his precious life** to **an adulteress**. Both kinds of entanglement are costly.

The RSV says, "for a harlot may be hired for a loaf of bread, but an adulteress stalks a man's very life." Here a distinction is made between a harlot, who can be hired, and an adulteress who is not satisfied until she controls the man completely.

6:27, 28 To have illicit relations with another man's wife is like carrying **fire** in one's **bosom**. You can't do it without being **burned**. It is like walking **on hot coals**; you can't do it without burning your **feet**. Griffiths warns:

> It is utter folly for all that will commit adultery, for the result will be self-destruction, wounds and dishonor, disgrace, and the unappeased anger of the wronged parties.[11]

6:29 As sure as a man **goes in to his neighbor's wife**, he will be caught and punished. There is a principle in the moral universe by which such sin is generally brought to light. Even, if by some remote chance, his sin is not discovered in this life, it will have to be accounted for in the next.

6:30, 31 These verses may be understood in one of two ways. According to the KJV and the NKJV, **people** have a measure of sympathy **if** a man **steals to** feed **himself** and his hungry family, but even then, **when he is** caught, he has to make restitution, even if it means losing everything he owns.

The RSV, by translating verse 30 as a question, implies that men *do* despise a thief, even if he steals to satisfy his hunger, and that he has to make complete restitution.

In either case, the point is that a thief can make restitution for his crime whereas an adulterer can never fully erase the damage he incurs.

6:32 **Whoever commits adultery lacks** sense because he **destroys** himself socially, spiritually, and morally, and perhaps even physically (Deut. 22:22).

6:33 For one moment of passion, he gets **wounds and dishonor**, perhaps from the enraged husband. He also gets shame and disgrace that will dog him the rest of his life. (Thank God, however, there is forgiveness with the Lord if the man will repent, confess, and forsake his sin.)

6:34 Here we see the **fury** of the jealous husband who returns unexpectedly and finds his wife in the arms of another man. When he starts to take revenge, **he will not** be conciliated by any pleas or excuses.

6:35 Nothing that the offender could pay would appease the husband; no bribe would be sufficient satisfaction for the violation of his marriage.

7:1 Chapter 7 continues to warn young people against ruining their lives by immorality. They should **treasure** these inspired **commands** as more valuable than earthly, material riches.

7:2 Obedience to God's Word is the pathway to abundant living. Therefore, it should be kept **as the apple of** the **eye**. With regard to this expression, the *International Standard Bible Encyclopedia* says:

> The eyeball, or globe of the eye, with pupil in center, is called "apple" from its round shape. Its great value and careful protection by the eyelids' automatically closing when there is the least possibility of danger made it the emblem of that which was most precious and jealously protected.[12]

7:3 In poetic language, this verse says to let the Word of God control all that we do (**bind them on your fingers**) and become a matter of unquestioning obedience (**write them on the tablet of your heart**).

7:4 We should treat **wisdom** with the honor and respect due to a **sister**, and make **understanding** one of our **nearest kin**. **Wisdom** in this passage is contrasted with the evil woman, who is to be carefully avoided.

7:5 Those who follow wisdom and her instructions are preserved from **the immoral woman** and from the flattery of **the seductress**. Two different words are used here to describe this evil woman. **Immoral** means loose and faithless to her marriage vows. **Seductress** means foreigner and adventuress.

7:6 Verses 6–23 give a vivid account of a prostitute plying her trade and of a young man being "taken in" by her. The tragic drama unfolded as the writer **looked through** the venetian blinds on his **window**.

7:7 An empty-headed, aimless **young man** is out on the town. Perhaps he is from a decent home, but now he is out to have a good time. It could be that he is a G.I. who isn't going to be outdone by his boasting pals. He isn't really a hardened sinner, just an inexperienced small-town guy.

7:8 Now he wanders into the red-light district. He crosses **the street near her corner**. He slowly saunters on with the gait of idleness. That's the whole trouble. If he were busy in some constructive, worthwhile activity, he wouldn't be here. If his feet were shod with the preparation of the gospel of peace, he wouldn't have time to waste! There is real protection from sin in a life sold out to God. On the other hand, as Isaac Watts said,

"Satan finds some mischief still, for idle hands to do."

7:9 He has been wandering around all **evening**—from sunset to dusk to midnight blackness—"There is a certain symbolic meaning," writes Barnes, "in the picture of the gathering gloom. Night is falling over the young man's life as the shadows deepen."

He is like a moth flying to the flame. The awful moment of danger approaches when the temptation to sin and the opportunity to sin coincide. We should pray constantly that these two should never come together in our lives.

7:10 The prostitute now makes her appearance, dressed to kill in the latest Hollywood styles, painted, powdered, and perfumed. Beneath her charming exterior lies a sensuous, secretive, subtle **heart**.

7:11, 12 No gracious, modest lady this! She is brash, **loud**, and aggressive. Not for her to be a homemaker! She must prowl the streets for clients.

She is almost ubiquitous. **At times she was outside, at times in the open square, lurking at every corner.** Sin is like that; it is easy to find. The Gospel should be easy to find, but unfortunately we fail to make it widely available.

7:13 The first step in her technique is the shock treatment. She rushes up to him, throws her arms around him and kisses him. Wow! He is swept off his feet by this tremendous display of love. He doesn't know it is lust, not love.

7:14 Next comes the religious pose. She says, **"I have peace offerings with me; today I have paid my vows."** He remembers his mother and the Bible on the living room table, then says to himself, "This woman must be all right. She's religious. I can't go wrong with anyone who has peace offerings and who pays her vows." The noose is tightening.

There is an added lure in the **peace offerings**. Those who offered them had to eat them that day or the next (Lev. 7:15ff), so she has plenty of good food with which to regale him. She believes that at least one way to a man's heart is through his stomach.

7:15 Then she pretends that he is the one she has been looking for. What a lie! She would have taken the first man who came along. But he is elated to think that he is important; someone really appreciates him, someone really cares.

7:16, 17 She gives more than a hint of her proposal by describing her bed: **"I have spread my bed with tapestry, colored coverings of Egyptian linen. I have perfumed my bed with myrrh, aloes, and cinnamon."** Everything here is designed to appeal to his sensual nature. Even his sense of smell is to be captivated by exotic perfumes.

7:18 Now the mask is torn away. She openly invites him to go to bed with her. With carefully chosen words, she makes it all sound very pleasurable.

7:19, 20 She disarms him by explaining that the man of the house **is not at home** and won't be home for a long time, because **he has gone on a long journey**. He expected to be away for an extended time because he took a good supply of cash **with him**. He wouldn't come home till full moon (v. 20b NASB). The darkness described in verse 9 indicates that the moon wouldn't be full for some time.

7:21 The more she talks, the more his resistance melts. **With** a little more flattery, **she caused him to yield**.

7:22 He makes a snap decision to follow **her** to her house.

As he saunters along with her,

there is all the pathos of **an ox** going unwittingly **to the slaughter**.

The Hebrew text of the last line is very obscure, as will be seen by the variety of translations:

> **"or as a fool to the correction of the stocks"** (KJV, NKJV).
> "or as one in fetters to the correction of the fool" (ASV).
> "or as a stag is caught fast" (RSV).
> "like a dog cajoled to the muzzle" (Moffatt).
> "or as a frisky lamb" (Knox).
> "as in fetters a fool to his punishment" (Berkeley).

But the general sense is clearly that the victim is moving irresistibly toward shackles and punishment.

7:23 The expression **"till an arrow struck his liver"** may mean:

1. The method by which the ox in the preceding verse is killed, i.e., a knife pierces its entrails.
2. The thorough inflaming of the man's passions.
3. The consequences of immorality in the man's body. The young man goes in to the harlot like a bird flies into a net, little realizing what it is going to cost him (e.g., VD or AIDS).

7:24, 25 No wonder then that the writer pleads for an attentive ear from his **children**! They should guard their **heart** against any desire to associate with this type of woman. They should guard their feet from straying **into her paths**.

7:26, 27 Her list of victims is a long one. She has ruined or **slain** a great army.

Anyone who enters **her house** is on the broad road **to hell**. He is marching down **to the chambers of death**.

K. Wisdom Personified (Chap. 8)

8:1 Chapter 8 is in sharp contrast to chapter 7. There the adulteress called out to the sons of men. Here **wisdom** invites them to follow her, and gives strong reasons for doing so. A parallel passage in the NT is John 7:37 where Christ calls men to come to Him and drink.

8:2, 3 These verses tell where Wisdom is found. The list of places indicates that she is readily available to the race of men in their daily travels.

8:4, 5 She issues her **call** to all types of **men**, to those of distinction and those of inferior rank. She calls to the **simple** and the **fools**. She is "the would-be guide of Everyman," says Kidner.

8:6–9 The character of Wisdom's teaching is next described. She speaks **of excellent things, . . . right things, . . . truth,** and **righteousness**. From her **lips** come no evil, **crooked** or **perverse** things. Anyone who has a measure of discernment and understanding will find them straight and just.

8:10, 11 The value of Wisdom's **instruction** is incomparable. It is to be desired above **silver, . . . choice gold, . . . rubies**, or anything else that men prize highly.

8:12, 13 **Wisdom** lives in the same house with **prudence**. They go together, so that, if you have Wisdom, you also have insight. Wisdom gives **knowledge and discretion** for the management of the affairs of life.

There are things that Wisdom does *not* live with. They are moral opposites, and she despises them, namely, all forms of **evil**, whether **pride, arrogance**, wicked behavior, or lying speech.

8:14–21 Some of the rewards or benefits of Wisdom are:

Good **counsel** (v. 14a)
Sound judgment (v. 14b)
Understanding (v. 14c)
Moral **strength** to do what is right and to resist evil (v. 14d)
Leadership ability (vv. 15a, 16a)
Judicial skill (vv. 15b, 16b)
Affection and companionship (see John 14:21) (v. 17a)
Ready access to those who mean business (v. 17b)
Enduring riches coupled with **honor** and **righteousness** (v. 18)
Character that is worth more **than fine gold** or **choice silver** (v. 19)
Guidance in paths **of righteousness** and **of justice**, bringing **wealth** in abundance (vv. 20, 21).

We have already mentioned that these passages dealing with Wisdom can be fittingly applied to the Lord Jesus, since the NT refers to Him as Wisdom (Matt. 11:19; Luke 11:49; 1 Cor. 1:24,30; Col. 2:3). Nowhere is the application more clear and beautiful than in the following verses. The Christian Church has consistently regarded this paragraph as referring to the Lord Jesus Christ.

What then do we learn about Christ in "this noble specimen of sacred eloquence?"

8:22 His eternal generation: **"The Lord possessed me at the beginning of His way."** We must not understand the word "possessed" as implying that Christ ever had a beginning. God never existed without the quality or attribute of wisdom, and neither did He ever exist without the Person of His Son. The meaning here is exactly the same as in John 1:1: "In the beginning . . . the Word was with God. . . ."

8:23 His appointment from eternity. **"Established"** means anointed or appointed. Long before creation took place, He was appointed to be the Messiah of Israel and the Savior of the world.

8:24–26 His pre-existence. The words **"brought forth"** must not be taken to mean that He was ever created and thus had a beginning. They are poetic language describing the Son's eternal existence and His personality as being distinct from that of God the Father.

The primal dust refers to the beginnings of the world.

8:27–29 His presence at creation. He was there when **the heavens** were stretched over the land and sea, when **clouds** were formed, and **fountains** and springs began gushing forth. He was there when the boundaries of the oceans were decided upon, **the waters** being commanded not to pass beyond the limits set. He was there when **the foundations of the earth** were made, including the internal structure that supports the outer crust.

8:30a His activity in creation. Here we learn that the Lord Jesus was the active Agent in creation. The NKJV correctly renders the first part of verse 30, **"Then I was beside Him as a master craftsman. . . ."** This agrees, of course, with John 1:3; Colossians 1:16; and Hebrews 1:2.

8:30b His position of affection and **delight . . . before** God. The eternal and infinite love of the Father for His Son increases the marvel that He would ever send that Son to die for sinners.

8:30c His personal delight before God. This magnifies the grace of our Lord Jesus Christ—that He would ever leave that scene of pure and perfect joy to come to this jungle of shame, sorrow, and suffering.

8:31 His **rejoicing in** the **inhabited world**. It is amazing that out of all the vast universe, He should be especially interested in this speck of a planet.

His special **delight** in **the sons of men**. The final wonder is that He should set His affection upon the rebel race of men.

William Cowper left us this magnificent hymn based on verses 22–31:

Ere God had built the mountains,
Or raised the fruitful hills;
Before He filled the fountains
that feed the running rills;
In Thee, from everlasting
The wonderful I AM
Found pleasures never wasting,
And Wisdom is Thy Name.

When like a tent to dwell in,
He spread the skies abroad,
And swathed about the swelling
Of ocean's mighty flood,
He wrought by weight and measure;
And Thou wast with Him then:
Thyself the Father's pleasure,
And Thine, the sons of men.

And could'st Thou be delighted
With creatures such as we,
Who, when we saw Thee, slighted
And nailed Thee to a tree?
Unfathomable wonder?
And mystery divine?
The voice that speaks in thunder
Says, "Sinner, I am thine!"

8:32–36 This final paragraph sets forth the eternal issues involved in man's response to Wisdom's call. It pronounces a blessing on those who **listen to** her instruction, walking in her **ways**. It promises happiness to those who wait **daily at** her **gates**, who keep faithful vigil **at** her **doors**. It holds out **life** and divine **favor** to those who find her, but personal loss and death to those who miss her.

Apply these last two verses to Christ. Whoever finds Him receives eternal life and stands in full favor with God (see John 8:51; 17:3; Eph. 1:6; 1 John 5:12). But those who miss Him injure themselves, and **those who hate** Him **love death** (cf. John 3:36b).

L. Invitations from Wisdom and Folly (9:1–18)

9:1 Here Wisdom is seen building **her house** and preparing a great feast for those who will answer her invitation. A feast is especially appropriate as a picture of the joy, fellowship and satisfaction which she provides for her guests.

Various interpretations have been given for the **seven pillars**. Some commentators refer us to Isaiah 11:2, the sevenfold gifts of the Holy Spirit which rested on the Messiah; but actually only six are clearly listed. An alternative interpretation is found in James 3:17 where the wisdom from above is described as (1) pure, (2) peaceable, (3) gentle, (4) willing to yield, (5) full of mercy and good fruits, (6) without partiality and (7) without hypocrisy.

9:2, 3 **Meat** and **wine** are served in abundance. The **table** is richly **furnished**. The regal hostess sends forth **her maidens** to issue the invitation **from the highest places of the city**. The commission of the maidens should remind us who have come to know the Wisdom of God, i.e., the Lord Jesus, to share this Wisdom with others, inviting them to come, find, and enjoy it for themselves.

9:4–6 The actual words of the invitation are given. It is issued to the **simple**, that is, to impressionable people who are prone to go astray and therefore need help and guidance. It is not issued to the wise because they are already inside the palace.

The menu includes the finest foods and the most exquisite **wine**, **mixed** by Wisdom herself.

Those who come are expected to part company with **foolishness**, and show that a moral change has taken place in their own lives.

9:7–9 The continuity here seems to be broken, but perhaps these verses explain either why the invitation is not sent to scorners, or why Wisdom's guests must forsake them.

If you **correct a scoffer**, you get only abuse for it. If you rebuke **a wicked man**, he will turn on you and assault you.

The way in which a man receives rebuke is an index of his character. **A scoffer** hates you, whereas **a wise man** will thank you. How do you react when parent, teacher, employer, or friend corrects you?

Instead of resenting criticism, a wise man takes it to heart and thus becomes **still wiser. A just man** benefits by increasing his store of useful **learning**.

9:10 Once again we are reminded that the starting point for all true **wisdom** is in **the fear of the LORD**. "To know the Deity is what knowledge means" (Moffatt). Because he knows the Holy, a true believer can see more on his knees than others can see on their tiptoes.

The Holy One (plural) may be the plural of majesty, excellence, and comprehensiveness, or it may modify Elohim (understood), a plural word for God.

9:11 Wisdom leads to **multiplied . . . days** and increased **years. . . .** It provides not only for long **life**, but for good and productive living, and then—beyond that—for the life that never ends.

9:12 It is **for** a man's own best advantage to be **wise**; he benefits himself more than anyone else. On the other hand, **if** he chooses to **scoff**, he will suffer the penalty of his choice, though others may be dragged in as well, of course. In the long run, he **alone** is the winner or loser.

9:13 Those who reject Wisdom's feast are prime prospects for Folly's fast. Notice the obvious contrast between Wisdom's elegant offer (vv. 1–6) and Folly's tawdry proposition (vv. 13–18).

The **foolish woman** is loudmouthed, empty-headed and brazenfaced.

9:14–16 She sits outside her front **door** or on conspicuous heights **of the city**, not as a gracious lady, but as the shameless harlot she is.

She is out to seduce men who are easily led, **simple** fellows **who** have no sense.

9:17 Her line is, **"Stolen water is sweet, and bread eaten in secret is pleasant."** Basically she means that illicit intercourse is attractive because it is forbidden and because there is the intrigue of secrecy about it.

When fallen human nature is forbidden to do a certain thing, that prohibition stirs up the desire to do it all the more (see Rom. 7:7, 8). The harlot appeals to this depraved instinct in man. She invites the gullible and the "easy touches" in for a visit.

9:18 But she doesn't tell them the other side of the story. Following the moment of pleasure and passion is the lifetime of remorse and the eternity in the **depths of hell**.

Even the world sometimes recognizes the truth of this verse. A very popular French song of the past century, speaking of the world's idea of "love," put it well:

> Love's pleasure lasts only for a night;
> Love's chagrin lasts for a lifetime.[13]

III. PROVERBS OF SOLOMON ON PRACTICAL MORALITY (10:1—22:16)

Up to this point in the book of Proverbs, there has been a definite continuity of thought and a connection between the verses. Subjects have been dealt with in paragraph form. From 10:1—22:16 we have a series of 375 proverbs, each distinct in itself. Most of them present contrasting statements, separated by the word "but." It may be no coincidence that the numerical value of the letters of Solomon's name in Hebrew is 375, corresponding to the number of proverbs in this section entitled **"The proverbs of Solomon."**

A. Righteous and Wicked Lifestyles Contrasted (10:1—15:33)

10:1 The behavior of **a . . . son** has a direct effect on the emotional health of his parents. Every son may turn out to be a Paul (**a wise son**) or a Judas (**a foolish son**), with all that means by way of joy or grief.

10:2 Wealth obtained illegally doesn't last; it has a way of disappearing. And in the hour of death, it cannot win a moment's reprieve. **Righteousness**, on the other hand, **delivers from death** in at least two ways. It preserves a man from the perils of a sinful life, and, as the outward evidence of the new birth, it shows that he has eternal life.

10:3 It is a general rule that God **will not allow the righteous soul to famish**. David said, "I have been young, and now am old; yet I have not seen the righteous forsaken, nor his descendants begging bread" (Ps. 37:25). But it is equally true that the Lord "thwarts the craving of the wicked" (RSV). Just as they reach out to grasp satisfaction and fulfillment, it eludes them.

10:4 The lazy, careless person reaps poverty. The one who is **diligent** and aggressive succeeds.

10:5 Summertime is reaping time. It is senseless to go to all the labor of plowing, planting, and cultivating, only to sleep when the time comes to **harvest** the crop. Jesus says to all His disciples, "Lift up your eyes and look at the fields, for they are already white for harvest" (John 4:35).

10:6 The law of harvest is that we reap what we sow. If we sow an upright life, we will receive the **blessings** of God and the praise of our fellow men. If we sow the wild oats of sin, our mouth will be covered with **violence**. This is what happened to Haman: his **mouth** was covered and he was led out to a violent death (Est. 7:8–10).

10:7 A holy life lingers long after the person is gone. The **name of the wicked** evokes a stench, not a fragrance. Men still call their sons Paul—but not Judas!

10:8 A wise-hearted person **will receive commands** in the sense that he is willing to listen to sound advice. The loudmouthed **fool**, because of his unwillingness to learn and obey, is hurled down to his ruin.

10:9 There is safety and security in an upright life, but the life that is built on deception will be found out and exposed.

10:10 The contrast in this verse is clearer if we follow the RSV: "He who winks with the eye causes trouble, but he who boldly reproves makes peace." The winking eye indicates subterfuge and cunning. When this form of deceit is frankly rebuked, peace is exchanged for sorrow.

10:11 The mouth of a **righteous** person **is a well of life** flowing with words of edification, comfort, and counsel. **The mouth of the wicked** is silenced by his **violence** and malice.

10:12 A hateful spirit isn't satisfied to forgive and forget; it insists on raking up old grudges and quarrels. A heart of **love** draws a curtain of secrecy over the faults and failures of others. These faults and failures must, of course, be confessed and forsaken, but love does not gossip about them or keep the pot boiling.

10:13 The conversation of an intelligent man is helpful to others. A fool helps no one, but only succeeds in bringing punishment on himself.

10:14 **Wise people** value **knowledge** and **store** it **up** for the appropriate moment. "He reserves what he has to say for the right time, place, and persons (cf. Matt. 7:6)," writes Barnes. But you never know what a **foolish** blabbermouth will say next. He is always bringing trouble to others and to himself.

10:15 The **rich** get richer and the **poor** get poorer. Those who have money can make money. The poor man can't get started; his **poverty** is his undoing. The rich can buy quality merchandise that lasts longer. The poor buy worn out, second-hand things that keep them poor with repair bills. This is the way things are in life, but not the way they should be.

10:16 Wealth obtained by reputable employment is a blessing. Profit from dishonorable work leads **to sin**. Compare a Christian carpenter and a non-Christian bartender. The income of the carpenter represents positive, productive work and is used for beneficial purposes. The work of the barkeeper is destructive. The more he works, the more he sins. The more he sins, the more he makes.

10:17 The one who makes it a practice to listen to godly **instruction** stays on the road **of life**. The one who turns his back on good advice **goes astray** himself and leads others astray.

10:18 This proverb contrasts the man who **hides** his **hatred** by insincere words and the man who openly reveals it by slandering his neighbor. The first is a hypocrite, the second **is a fool**, and there is not much to choose between them. A third alternative, and one that believers should learn to practice, is not to harbor any hatred at all.

10:19 The more we talk, the greater is the probability of saying something wrong. Compulsive talkers should beware! The lust for incessant conversation often leads to exaggeration, breaking of confidences, and associated sins. Trying to top someone else's joke often mushrooms into off-color stories.

The man who exercises self-control in his speech **is wise**. He saves himself from embarrassment, apologies, and outright sin.

10:20 What a good man says is a reflection of what he is. Because his character is sterling, so is his speech. Since **the heart** (or mind) **of the wicked** man is not worthwhile, neither is the conversation that flows from it.

10:21 Someone has aptly paraphrased this proverb, "Good feeds itself and others. Evil cannot keep itself alive."

Fools here are stubborn, intractable people.

10:22 It is only **the blessing of the LORD** that truly enriches a life.

But is it true that **He adds no sorrow with it**? How does this reconcile with the fact that the most godly people pass through times of deep sorrow?

There are several possible explanations for this second part of the proverb:

1. God doesn't send sorrow. All sorrow, sickness, and suffering come from Satan. God often permits them in the lives of His children but He is not the source.
2. Sorrow is not an ingredient of God's blessing as it is of prosperity apart from God.
3. Another possible translation is "and toil adds nothing to it" (margin of RV and RSV). Here the thought is that toil, apart from God, adds nothing to the blessing. Toil is good, but unless it is God-directed, it is futile (see Ps. 127:1, 2).

10:23 A fool amuses himself by getting into trouble; it's his favorite **sport**. **A man of understanding** gets his pleasure in conducting himself wisely.

10:24 The calamity which the wrongdoer fears will descend on him. **The desire of the righteous**—the will of God in this life and the presence of God in the next—**will be granted**. In this vein, C. S. Lewis says:

> In the end, that Face which is the delight or the terror of the universe must be turned upon each of us either with one expression or the other, either conferring glory inexpressible or inflicting shame that can never be cured or disguised.[14]

10:25 When the whirlwind of God's judgment **passes by, the wicked is** nowhere to be found. **But the righteous** person is established on the Rock of Ages; nothing can ever move him.

10:26 Vinegar sets the **teeth** on edge, and **smoke** irritates the **eyes**. In the same way, a **lazy** messenger who dillydallies on the way proves exasperating, frustrating, and annoying **to those who send him**.

10:27 A devout life leads to longevity. **Wicked** men are cut off prematurely, e.g., gangland slayings, reprisal killings, deaths caused by drunkenness, drugs, and dissipation.

10:28 The things **the righteous** look forward to **will be** realized with **gladness**. Not so **the wicked**—their hopes will be thoroughly disappointed. G. S. Bowes illustrates:

> Alexander the Great was not satisfied, even when he had completely subdued the nations. He wept because there were no more worlds to conquer, and he died at an early age in a state of debauchery. Hannibal, who filled three bushels with the gold rings taken from the knights he had slaughtered, committed suicide by swallowing poison. Few noted his passing, and he left this earth completely unmourned. Julius Caesar, "dyeing his garments in the blood of one million of his foes," conquered 800 cities, only to be stabbed by his best friends at the scene of his greatest triumph. Napoleon, the feared conqueror, after being the scourge of Europe, spent his last years in banishment.[15]

Surely **the expectation of the wicked** perishes!

10:29 In His providential dealings **the LORD** proves to be a tower of **strength for the upright, but destruction . . . to** evildoers.

10:30 God guarantees a dwelling place to **the righteous, but the wicked** will be exiles and vagabonds.

The captivity of Israel illustrates this.

10:31 A good man's **mouth** is like a tree that **brings forth** blossoms of **wisdom**. Speech that is crooked and **perverse** will be **cut out**.

10:32 You can depend on a good man to say **what is acceptable**. **The wicked** man knows only how to distort the facts and to speak **what is perverse**.

11:1 Crooked merchants sometimes had two sets of weights, one for buying and one for selling. The buying weights were heavier than they should have been, so that he got more merchandise than he paid for. The selling weights were lighter than the standard, so that the customer got less than he paid for.

There are dishonest practices in business today that come under this ban on **dishonest scales**, as well as applications in school life, social life, home life, and church life.

11:2 First, **pride**; then a fall; **then comes shame** connected with the fall. But to be **humble** and down-to-earth reduces the danger of stumbling.

11:3 Honesty is the best policy. The **integrity** of **upright** people **will guide them** on the right track; the experience of Joseph is an example. The crookedness **of the unfaithful** is their downfall; Balaam's life testifies to this.

11:4 **Riches** cannot avert the wrath of God in time or in eternity. **Righteousness** is a safeguard against premature **death** in the here and now. And only those who are clothed in the righteousness of God will escape the second death.

11:5 The **blameless** man is directed by **righteousness**, the ideal guide. **The wicked** man **will fall**, a victim of **his own wickedness**.

11:6 **Righteousness** not only guides good men; it **will deliver them** from perils seen and unseen. Apostates, like Judas, **will be caught** in the meshes of **their** own **lust** and greed.

11:7 It has been said that a fool is a man, all of whose plans end at the grave. When the coffin lid closes, all his hopes are ended. The things he lived for are no longer his, and **his expectation** of prosperity is gone forever.

11:8 God delivers **the righteous** from **trouble** and sends it upon **the wicked instead**. Thus the three Hebrews were delivered out of the fiery furnace, but their would-be executioners were consumed by the fire (Dan. 3:22–26).

11:9 An apostate or **hypocrite** seeks to undermine the faith of **his neighbor** with doubts and denials. **Knowledge** of the truth enables **the righteous** to detect the counterfeit, and to save himself and others from subversion.

11:10 Two occasions when a **city** breaks out in joyful celebration are **when the righteous** prosper and **when the wicked perish**.

11:11 **The blessing of the upright** may refer to their prayers for **the city** (1 Tim. 2:1, 2), or to the benefits which their presence and godly influence bring to the city (cf. Jesus' description of His followers as the salt of the earth in Matt. 5:13).

The deceit, broken promises, fraud, and profanity of the wicked are enough to ruin any local government.

11:12 **He who is devoid of wisdom despises his neighbor, but a man of understanding holds his peace.** To belittle another man is to insult God, to hurt the man, to invite strife, and to help no one. **A man of understanding** knows that it is better to say nothing if he can't praise or edify.

11:13 **A talebearer** seems to take a malicious delight in spreading scandal, informing on others, and breaking confidences. He doesn't hold anything back, but tells everything he knows.

A **faithful** friend knows how to maintain a confidence and to refrain from talking.

11:14 Without wise leadership and

statesmanship, **the people** are bound to **fall** into trouble. On the other hand, **there is safety** in having the combined judgment of many good **counselors**.

11:15 To be **surety for a stranger** means to guarantee his debt or his promissory note. The person who does this **will suffer** for it, that is, he will pay a stinging penalty. The man who **hates** suretyship saves himself a lot of headaches. See notes on 6:1–5.

11:16 **A gracious woman retains** respect and **honor**, as is seen in the case of Abigail (1 Sam. 25). **Ruthless men** may **retain riches** but they never get a good name.

11:17 A man's disposition affects his own health. The kind person avoids the dyspepsia, apoplexy, gastrointestinal ulcers, and heart trouble which the **cruel** one brings on himself. He **does good for his own soul**.

The *British Medical Journal* once said that there is not a tissue in the human body that is wholly removed from the spirit. A **cruel** disposition takes its toll on the body. One having such a temperament **troubles his own flesh**.

11:18 **The wicked man does deceptive work, but he who sows righteousness will have a sure reward.** It is true that evil people often seem to grow rich overnight, but their wealth is unsatisfying, unenduring, and unable to help them when they need it most. The rewards of a righteous life are real and permanent.

11:19 All conduct leads in one of two directions—either **to life** or **to . . . death**. This proverb does not teach salvation by good works, however. No one can be steadfast in **righteousness** unless he is in right relationship to God. He must first have been born again. A man **who pursues evil** proves thereby that he never was converted.

11:20 As far as **the Lord** is concerned, a **heart** that is false is hateful and loathsome. He really likes the person who is straightforward. No view of God is complete unless it sees that He is capable of hatred as well as of love.

A heart that is **blameless**, on the other hand, is **His delight**.

11:21 **"Though they join forces"** is literally "hand in hand" (NKJV margin). It may refer to two things that are certain in this uncertain world—the punishment of **the wicked** and the deliverance of **the posterity of the righteous**.

11:22 **A ring of gold in a** pig's **snout** is incongruous. The **snout** is as unattractive as the **ring** is lovely. **A lovely woman who lacks discretion** also combines two opposites—physical attractiveness and moral deficiency.

11:23 **Righteous** people aspire **only** for **good** and they get it. **The wicked** seek for evil and they get it in the form of **wrath** or judgment.

This proverb emphasizes the importance of having worthy goals, because ultimately we get what we go after in life. That is why Emerson said, "Hitch your wagon to a star." A British statesman urged his cabinet, "Whatever else you do, buy big maps!"

11:24 Here is a glorious paradox. We enrich ourselves by being generous. We impoverish ourselves by laying up treasures on earth.

What we save, we lose. What we give, we have.

Jim Elliot said, "He is no fool who gives what he cannot keep to gain what he cannot lose." And Dr. Barnhouse observed that everybody tithes, either to the Lord or to the doctor, the dentist, and the garage mechanic.

11:25 **The generous** person reaps dividends that the miser can never know. Whatever we do for others returns to us in blessing.

When a Sunday school teacher prepares diligently and then teaches her class, who do you think benefits from it most—the students or herself?

11:26 The selfish man keeps his **grain** off the market in a time of famine, hoping for greater return as the price is forced up. He is a profiteer, enriching himself by impoverishing and starving others. No wonder **the people will curse** him! They want someone who will meet their desperate need now.

The world is perishing for the bread of life. The bread is free, and always will be. We have it to share with others. What are we waiting for? **Blessing will be on** the one **who sells** the grain, that is, who spreads the good news of the gospel.

11:27 When a man's motives are pure and unselfish, he wins the esteem of others. But the man who is out to cause **trouble** for others will get it for himself.

11:28 The NT counterpart of this proverb is 1 Timothy 6:17–19. **Riches** are uncertain and therefore not worthy of trust. Our confidence should be in the living God who gives us richly all things to enjoy.

"The lust of gold," said Samuel Johnson, "unfeeling and remorseless, is the last corruption of degenerate man."

The righteous, that is, those whose trust is in the Lord, **will flourish** with life and vitality **like foliage**.

11:29 There are several types of men who trouble their **own house**—the drunkard, the crank, and the adulterer, for instance. But here it is probably the man who is greedy of gain (see 15:27), and who loses sight of the worthwhile values of life in his mad quest for wealth. He **will inherit the wind**, that is, end up with nothing tangible to satisfy his greed. His penalty for thus playing **the fool** will be servitude to a man who acts more wisely.

11:30 A **righteous** life is like a fruit-bearing **tree** that brings nourishment and refreshment to others. The **wise** man **wins** others to a life of wisdom and righteousness.

This is one of the great texts for soul winners in the Bible. It reminds us of the promise which Jesus made to Peter, "You will catch men" (Luke 5:10). What an unspeakable privilege it is to be used of God in doing a work in human lives that will result in eternal blessing! Every soul won to the Lord will be a worshiper of the Lamb of God forever and ever!

11:31 Even **righteous** people are **recompensed** in this life for their misdeeds. Moses was excluded from the Promised Land and David had to restore fourfold. If the righteous reap what they sow, **how much more** do **the ungodly**! Or, as Peter put it, "If the righteous one is scarcely saved, where will the ungodly and the sinner appear?" (1 Pet. 4:18).

12:1 Anyone who is open to discipline and **instruction** shows that he really wants to learn. The man who resents being told anything and refuses **correction is stupid**.

12:2 A moral, ethical person can be sure of the Lord's **favor**. A **man of wicked intentions** can be equally sure of His condemnation. "Think—" wrote Foreman, "the supreme Power in the universe against what a wicked man is doing, determined that he shall fail! The supreme Power leaving man to himself in silent scorn."

12:3 Lives that are dominated by **wickedness** have no stability. They are like the seed which fell on the rocky places (Matt. 13:5, 6); the earth was shallow and because they had no root, the seeds quickly withered away.

A **righteous** man has his **root** deep in God. He is able to stand when the storms of life blow. This man is described in Psalm 1:3.

12:4 An **excellent wife** brings joy and gladness to **her husband**. The one who disgraces her husband gives him a terrible letdown—as if **his bones** rotted away.

12:5 The goals **of the righteous** are honorable, and, just as surely, the plans **of the wicked are deceitful**. In other words, a man's aims are a mirror of his character.

12:6 By their speech sinners seek to lay fatal traps for the innocent and unwary. **Upright** men **deliver** themselves and others by speaking the truth.

12:7 When justice catches up with **the wicked**, that's the end of them. Godly people have a good foundation; they are not swept away by calamity.

12:8 People speak well of one who has insight and acts wisely, but they have nothing but contempt for one who has no principles.

12:9 Better is the one who is slighted but has a servant, than he who honors himself but lacks bread. The combination of low rank and food on the table is better than pretended status with starvation.

12:10 A righteous man's kindness extends even to dumb animals, but a **wicked** man is **cruel**, even when he thinks he is being most gentle.

Although God is transcendent, He is not too high to care for animals, but legislates concerning them (Ex. 20:10; 23:4, 5). He even legislates concerning a bird's nest (Deut. 22:6).

12:11 A man who engages in positive, constructive work, like farming, **will** have his needs supplied. But the man who spends his time in worthless pursuits not only has an empty cupboard but also an empty head.

12:12 The **catch of evil men** means, by metonymy, what is caught in the net of evil, or what is taken from others unjustly. In other words, **the wicked covet** what belongs to others.

In contrast, **the righteous** are satisfied to provide quietly for their own needs.

12:13 Ungodly people are often trapped by their own words. By failing to tell a consistent story, they trip themselves up. A liar has to have a good memory; otherwise his accounts won't mesh. And to support a lie, he has to build a structure of other lies.

The righteous will come through trouble. God does not promise His people freedom from *all* trouble, but rather that they will **come through** it.

12:14 Good speech and **good** behavior carry their own reward with them. Wise, gentle, pure speech is rewarded with love, favor, and respect. **Good** deeds come back to a man in blessing.

12:15 You can't tell **a fool** anything. He knows everything, and will not listen. But a **wise** man will welcome advice. He recognizes that it is impossible for one person to see all sides of a question.

12:16 A fool doesn't restrain his **wrath**. He blows up at the slightest provocation. **A prudent man** knows how to ignore insult and to exercise self-control.

12:17 A witness who tells the **truth** in court gives righteous evidence. **A false witness** tells lies.

12:18 Some people use their tongues like **a sword**; slashing away at others, cutting and causing pain. **The wise** person speaks words of **health** and healing, that is, healing the wounds inflicted by the prattler.

12:19 Truth is eternal. Why? Because truth is what God says about a thing; therefore, it never changes.

A lying tongue lasts as long as a wink.

12:20 Treachery fills **the heart of those who** plan wickedness. **Joy** fills the heart of those who pursue **peace**.

12:21 It is true in a general sense that **no grave trouble** happens to **the righteous**. However, this is not a rule without exception. What is true without exception is that the just are preserved from the evil consequences that follow the behavior of the wicked.

The wicked get plenty of this type of trouble.

12:22 God hates liars. How careful we should be about shading of the truth, white lies, exaggerations, and half-truths! A sure way of bringing **delight** to His heart is by being absolutely honest and trustworthy.

12:23 A **prudent man** doesn't go around showing off how much he knows. He modestly **conceals** his learning. But you aren't long in the presence **of fools** before they reveal their **foolishness**.

12:24 In the ordinary course of life, dedicated, **diligent** people rise to positions of leadership just as cream rises to the surface. Laziness leads to poverty, and poverty reduces man to the level of **forced labor**.

Oswald Chambers said that slovenliness is an insult to the Holy Spirit; he could have said the same thing about laziness.

12:25 **Anxiety . . . causes depression**. A **good**, encouraging, or sympathetic **word** works wonders in perking someone up again.

12:26 Contrary to appearances, **the righteous** man is actually better off than his unrighteous neighbor. It doesn't seem that way. The sinner seems to have everything going his own way, and this seduces people into believing that forbidden fruit really is sweeter. Therefore the Christian **should choose his friends carefully**.

12:27 This **lazy** loafer either doesn't hunt or he **does not roast what he** has taken **in hunting**. In the first place he lacks the inertia to get started; in the second, he lacks the drive to finish what he began.

The Hebrew of the latter part of the proverb is also obscure, like the first part, but the sense almost surely is that a diligent person values what he has worked for and uses it to the best advantage. Ruth was like that; she beat out what she had gleaned (Ruth 2:17). In our Bible study, we should improve on what we have learned and we can do it through meditation, prayer, and practical obedience:

> Thus on Thy Holy Word we'd feed
> and live and grow,
> Go on to know the Lord, and
> practice what we know.

12:28 In the narrow path of **righteousness**, there **is life** along **the way** and life at the close of the journey. **There is no death** in it, as there is on the broad road that leads to destruction. **"Life"** here looks to a future beyond death, to eternal life. The NIV translates the verse, "In the way of righteousness there is life; along that path is immortality."

13:1 Both in physical and spiritual development, there is a normal process of development. A baby, for instance, must crawl before he walks or talks. In the spiritual realm, a convert must listen and learn before he launches forth in service. **A wise son** submits to the discipline of **instruction**. The **scoffer** won't have it; he thinks he has all the answers, and refuses to be corrected.

13:2 Here is **a man** whose speech is edifying, encouraging, and comforting; he himself is rewarded when he sees the beneficial results of the spoken word. By way of contrast, the **unfaithful** man plans **violence** for others, and he is paid in his own coin.

13:3 The man who **guards his** speech controls **his** whole **life** (see Jas. 3:2b). The one who exercises no self-control is in for trouble. The lesson is: be careful what you say—it might be used against you.

13:4 "If wishes were horses, beggars would ride." The **lazy man** has great **desires**, but that isn't enough. "The wish without the exertion is useless." **The diligent** man applies himself to his work and carries home the bacon. This is true in spiritual matters as well as in temporal. Bosch illustrates:

> Adam Clark is reported to have spent 40 years writing his commentary on the Scriptures. Noah Webster labored 36 years forming his dictionary; in fact, he crossed the ocean twice to gather material needed to make the book absolutely accurate. Milton rose at 4 o'clock every morning in order to have sufficient hours to compose and rewrite his poetry which stands among the best of the world's literature. Gibbon spent 26 years on his book *The Decline and Fall of the Roman Empire*, but it towers as a monument to careful research and untiring dedication to his task. Bryant rewrote one of his poetic masterpieces 100 times before publication, just to attain complete beauty and perfection of expression. These men enjoyed what they were doing, and each one threw all of his energy into his effort no matter how difficult the job.
>
> The most happy and productive people are those who are diligent in their labors for the betterment of mankind and the glory of God.[16]

13:5 A righteous man hates any kind of dishonesty, **but a wicked man** "acts shamefully and disgracefully" (RSV). J. Allen Blair illustrates from the life of a great American:

> It is said of Abraham Lincoln that he would accept no case in which the client did not have justice on his side. One time a man came to employ him. Lincoln stared at the ceiling, yet listened intently as the facts were given. Abruptly, he swung around in his chair.
>
> "You have a pretty good case in technical law," he said, "but a pretty bad one in equity and justice. You will have to get someone else to win the case for you. I could not do it. All the time while pleading before the jury, I'd be thinking, Lincoln you're a liar! I might forget myself and say it out loud."
>
> Lying and all forms of guilt grieve the heart of God. No Christian should lie or deceive, regardless of consequences to himself. If he does, he will never advance in the things of God.[17]

13:6 A righteous life is a protected life. God undertakes to guard the **blameless**. But **the sinner** walks in constant peril, for their **wickedness overthrows** them sooner or later.

13:7 There are two ways of looking at this proverb. First, a man who has nothing in the way of material possessions may try to create the impression that he is wealthy, while one who actually has lots of money may give the appearance of being **poor**.

Or it may mean this. The godless millionaire actually is a spiritual pauper, whereas the humblest believer, though financially poor, is an heir of God and a joint heir with Jesus Christ. Morgan illustrates:

> Our age abounds with men who have made themselves rich, and yet have

> nothing. They have amassed great wealth, and yet it has no purchasing power in the true things of life. It cannot insure health, it brings no happiness, it often destroys peace. On the other hand, there are those who have impoverished themselves, and have by so doing become wealthy in all the highest senses of the word. How is this to be explained? Is not the solution found by laying the emphasis in each of the contrastive declarations, upon the word self. To make self rich, is to destroy the capacity for life. To make self poor, by enriching others is to live. It is impossible to consider this saying of Hebrew wisdom, without thinking of the One who became incarnate Wisdom.[18]

13:8 A rich man is often threatened by those who want his money. He faces robbery, blackmail, and kidnapping for **ransom**, and he has to guard his **life** by hiring protection or by meeting extortionate demands. **The poor** person never has to listen to this kind of threat.

13:9 The testimony **of the righteous** is like a **light** that burns brightly and cheerily. The life and hopes **of the wicked** are a **lamp** that **will be put out**.

13:10 There may be two thoughts in the first line. One is that when contentions come, **pride** is the invariable cause. Or second, "by pride there only cometh contention" (JND), that is, nothing good ever comes from pride: only bitter feuding. C. S. Lewis writes:

> It is Pride which has been the chief cause of misery in every nation and every family since the world began. Other vices may sometimes bring people together; you may find good fellowship and jokes and friendliness among drunken people or unchaste people. But Pride always means enmity—it is enmity. And not only enmity between man and man, but enmity to God.[19]

Those who are willing to listen to good advice are wise; they avoid pride and the personality conflicts that go with it.

13:11 **Wealth gained by dishonesty** comes in haste or without exertion. This would include the money won by gambling, sweepstakes, or stock market speculation. This kind of wealth has a way of leaking out of a man's hands.

Wealth gained **by** honest **labor** accumulates instead of dwindling.

13:12 Repeated postponement of one's expectations is disheartening; **but when the desire** is at last fulfilled, it is a source of tremendous satisfaction. Apply this to the coming of the Lord.

13:13 **The "word"** here is the Word of God. Our attitude toward it is a matter of life and death. Whoever **despises** it pushes the self-destruct button. Whoever trusts and obeys **the commandment** is abundantly **rewarded**.

13:14 The counsel and instruction **of the wise** are a **fountain of life** and refreshment to those who heed. They deliver a person from deadly **snares** along life's pathway.

13:15 **Good understanding** brings a person into **favor** with God and man. "A man with good sense is appreciated" (LB).

In the second part of the proverb, the word translated **"hard"** basically means permanent, enduring, or perennial. But to make good sense it has been taken to mean **hard** or rugged. If it meant permanent, there would have to be a negative, that is, "the way of the unfaithful is not permanent." Perhaps we are best to stick to the traditional text: **"the way of the unfaithful is hard."** Each day's newspaper provides illustrations of that truth!

13:16 A man's conduct reveals his character. If a **man** is **prudent**, it comes out in the responsible way he **acts**. **A fool** displays **his folly** for everyone to see.

13:17 An unreliable **messenger** brings **trouble** to everyone concerned. Better to send **a faithful ambassador**; he accomplishes his mission to the satisfaction of all.

"Now then, we are ambassadors for Christ . . ." (2 Cor. 5:20).

13:18 The one **who disdains correction** and discipline earns **poverty and shame** by his stubbornness. The man **who** listens to **a rebuke will be honored**.

13:19 Good men are pleased when they achieve their goals, but **fools** hate to give up their sin. The contrast seems to be between good men pursuing worthy objects, and sinners unwilling to **depart from evil**.

13:20 We should seek out the companionship of **wise men**; they will lift us up. "Evil company corrupts good habits" (1 Cor. 15:33). A man is often known by the company he keeps. A **companion of fools** is brought to ruin.

13:21 Sinners are dogged by the hounds of misfortune, physical harm, bad reputation, loss of possessions. **The righteous** enjoy a **good** reputation, a **good** life, and a **good** reward.

13:22 A good man leaves an inheritance not only **to his** children but to his grandchildren. In the OT, this probably meant that he left *material* wealth for them. But a Christian today is better advised to leave a rich *spiritual* heritage to his descendants.

The wealth of the sinner is stored up for the righteous; "ill-gotten gain has a way of finding better hands."

13:23 Poor people cultivate their land intensively and get **much** produce from a small area. They use what they have to the best advantage.

The second part of the verse may mean that: (1) rich men, with bigger farms, often come to ruin because of their injustice, or (2) the tillage of the poor is often swept away by injustice.

13:24 The Bible teaches corporal punishment, whether the modern "experts"agree or not. To withhold punishment from a child when it is deserved is to encourage the child in sin and thus to contribute to his eventual ruin. The parent **who spares his rod** might think he is manifesting love, but God says it is hatred.

For years Dr. Benjamin Spock encouraged parents to be permissive. After living to see a generation of bratty, pesky children, he admitted that he had been wrong. He said, "Inability to be firm is, to my mind, the commonest problem of parents in America today." He placed the blame, at least in part, on the experts—"the child psychiatrists, psychologists, teachers, social workers, and pediatricians, like myself."[20]

The parent **who** genuinely **loves** his child does not condone naughtiness, but **disciplines** the child **promptly**.

13:25 God insures that the needs of **the righteous** will be supplied, but **wicked** men are equally assured of an empty **stomach**.

14:1 A sensible housewife attends to **her house** and her family. **The foolish** woman neglects her husband and children, and wonders why her family goes to ruin.

Is it possible for a woman to tear **down** her home by too much religious activity too?

14:2 A man's conduct is a reflection of his attitude toward **the LORD**. The righteous man is guided by what he knows will please God. The **perverse** man doesn't care what God thinks, and thus reveals his contempt of **Him**. Kidner writes:

> Every departure from God's path is a pitting of one's will, and a backing of one's judgment, against His; but the contempt which it spells is too irrational to acknowledge.[21]

14:3 In the mouth of a fool is a rod of pride. He will have to take a beating for his arrogant talk. **Wise** people's speech **will preserve them** from any such punishment.

14:4 A barn can be kept cleanly swept **where** there are **no oxen**, but isn't it better to have some dust and dirt around, knowing that the labor **of an ox** will lead to a bountiful harvest? The rewards of toil more than compensate for its disagreeable aspects.

This proverb is not intended to encourage homes or chapels that look like disaster areas. But it does discourage that passion for order and dustlessness that puts the brakes on progress and productiveness.

14:5 C. H. Mackintosh once said that it is better to go to heaven with a good conscience than stay on earth with a bad one. How careful we should be to be utterly truthful at all times!

14:6 By continued refusal to listen, **a scoffer** loses the capacity to hear. He can never **find** true **wisdom** as long as he rejects the Lord.

The man of understanding perceives the right thing quickly. "For whoever has, to him more will be given, and he will have abundance..." (Matt. 13:12).

14:7 Don't cultivate the friendship **of a foolish man**, "for there you do not meet words of knowledge" (RSV), or "you will not find a word of sense in him" (Moffatt).

14:8 For a **prudent** man **wisdom** means knowing how to behave honestly, conscientiously, and obediently. What a fool considers to be wisdom is actually **folly**, and the essence of that folly is deceiving others, which eventually results in self-inflicted **deceit**.

14:9 Although the Hebrew here is obscure, the NKJV makes good sense.

> Fools make a mock of sin, will not
> believe;
> It has a fearful dagger up its sleeve;
> "How can it be," they say, "that such
> a thing,
> So full of sweetness, e'er should wear
> a sting?"
>
> They know not that it is the very
> spell
> Of sin, to make them laugh
> themselves to hell.
> Look to thyself then, deal with sin
> no more.
> Lest He who saves, against thee shuts
> the door.
>
> —*John Bunyan*

The upright enjoy the Lord's **favor**, free from the guilt and condemnation of sin.

14:10 There are sorrows in the human **heart** that no other human being can share (though the Lord can and does). There is also **joy** that can be enjoyed only by the person directly involved.

14:11 Notice the contrast between **house** and **tent**. We think of a *house* as permanent and a *tent* as temporary. But it is **the tent of the upright** pilgrim that survives, while **the house of the wicked** earth dweller tumbles.

14:12 The **way** which **seems right**

to men is salvation by good works or good character. More people go down to hell laboring under that misconception than under any other. (See also 16:25.)

In a broader sense, the **way** which **seems right to a man** is his own way, the path of self-will that scorns divine guidance or human counsel. It can **end** only in disaster and spiritual **death**.

14:13 There is no such thing in life as pure, unadulterated joy. **Sorrow** is always mixed to some extent. Knox says, "Joy blends with grief, and laughter marches with tears."

14:14 The backslider in heart will be filled with his own ways, but a good man will be satisfied from above. A person who wanders away from the Lord reaps the consequences of his waywardness. Thus Naomi said, "The Almighty has dealt very bitterly with me. I went out full, and the Lord has brought me home again empty" (Ruth 1:20b, 21a). And the prodigal son said, "How many of my father's hired servants have bread enough and to spare, and I perish with hunger!" (Luke 15:17).

The upright man is satisfied with his ways, because they are the Lord's ways. He can say with David, "My cup runs over" (Ps. 23:5c). Or with Paul, "I have fought a good fight, I have finished the race, I have kept the faith" (2 Tim. 4:7).

14:15 A naive, gullible person is susceptible to **every** new idea or fad. **The prudent** man takes a second look and thus preserves **his steps** from error. Faith demands the surest evidence, and finds it in the Word of God. Credulity believes what every passing scientist, philosopher, or psychologist has to say.

14:16 A wise man fears in the sense that he is careful and cautious. Of course, the verse may also mean that he fears the Lord.

The **fool** is arrogant and careless, throws off restraint, and is obviously **self-confident**.

14:17 A quick-tempered man acts foolishly. In anger, he does things without stopping to consider the consequences. He slams doors, throws whatever is handy, yells curses and insults, breaks furniture, and walks out in a rage. But if we had to choose, we could tolerate him more easily than **the man of wicked intentions**. Everyone hates this man for his cold-blooded treachery.

14:18 The simple inherit folly. If they refuse to listen to sound teaching, they thereby choose to become more stupid.

The prudent are honored and rewarded by acquiring more and more **knowledge**.

14:19 This proverb points to the eventual triumph of good over evil. God will vindicate the cause of the righteous. The day came when Haman had to **bow before** Mordecai. And the day will come when every knee in the universe **will bow before** Jesus Christ as King of kings and Lord of lords.

14:20 The poor man is hated even by his own neighbor. It shouldn't be this way, but it often is. Many people form friendships on the basis of self-interest. They avoid the poor and cultivate the rich for selfish ends. We should be interested in people for what we can do for them, not what we can get from them.

In one sense **the rich** man **has many friends**, but in another sense he never knows how many true friends he has, that is, friends who love him for who he is rather than for what he has.

14:21 This verse is obviously connected with the preceding one. It is sin to despise the poor because God has chosen them (Jas. 2:5). The man **who has mercy on the poor** is blessed in the act.

We should never forget that the Lord Jesus came into the world as a poor man. Someone referred to Him as "my penniless friend from Nazareth."

14:22 Those who plot mischief and **devise evil** plans are destined to **go astray. Those who devise** the **good** of others are rewarded with **mercy and truth**. This means that God shows kindness to them and is true to His promises of protection and reward. It also means that people repay them with loyalty and faithfulness.

14:23 **All** honorable work is profitable. Nothing but talk **leads only to poverty**. We all know people who talk by the hour about their problems but never lift a little finger to solve them. They talk up a storm about world evangelism but never move from their reclining chair to witness to their neighbor. Without coming up for air, they tell you what they plan to do in the future, but they never do it.

14:24 The glory **of** the **wise is their riches**. They have something to show for their wisdom, whether we think of that wealth as spiritual or material. **Fools** have nothing but **folly** to show for their lives and labors.

14:25 **A true witness** in a court of law **delivers** innocent people from being "framed." **A deceitful witness** misrepresents the facts, with all the ruinous results that flow from such deceit.

The gospel preacher is **a true witness** who **delivers souls** from eternal death. The "liberals" and "cultists" are **deceitful** witnesses who speak **lies** and lead souls astray.

14:26 The man who fears **the Lord** has every reason to have **strong confidence**. If God is for him, no one can be successfully against him (Rom. 8:31). That man's **children will have a place of refuge** under God's wings when evil attacks.

14:27 Trust in God is a source of spiritual strength and vitality, enabling one to avoid **the snares of death**.

14:28 The size, contentment, and loyalty of the populace determine **a king's honor**. There is little prestige for **a prince** to hold the title if he has few or no **people** over whom to rule.

14:29 A man who is patient under provocation shows **great** insight. **He who is impulsive** promotes **folly** and holds it up to public view.

14:30 **A sound heart** here means a satisfied mind. Thus Knox translates, "Peace of mind is health of body."

Envy and passion are bad for a person's health. Dr. Paul Adolph confirms this:

> Some of the most important causes of so-called nervous diseases which psychiatrists recognize are guilt, resentment (an unforgiving spirit), fear, anxiety, frustration, indecision, doubt, jealousy, selfishness, and boredom. Unfortunately, many psychiatrists, while definitely effective in tracing the causes of emotional disturbances which cause disease, have significantly failed in their methods of dealing with these disturbances because they omit faith in God as their approach.[22]

14:31 Whoever takes advantage of **the poor** insults **his** Creator. George Herbert said that man is God's image, but a poor man is Christ's stamp as well.

The second line means that those who have compassion **on the needy** honor God in the process.

14:32 "When the wicked is paid in his own coin, there is an end of him; at death's door, the just still hope" (Knox). Judas is an illustration of the first line, and Paul, of the second.

14:33 The clause, **"Wisdom rests in the heart of him who has understanding"** may mean (1) that wisdom is at home there, or (2) that the man doesn't needlessly parade everything he knows.

The second line is more difficult. It may mean (1) you will soon find out **what is in the heart of fools**; (2) wisdom is not known in the heart of fools (RSV); (3) "wisdom must clamor loudly before being recognized by fools" (Berkeley margin).

14:34 In order for **a nation** to be great, its leaders and people must have upright, moral characters known for their **righteousness**. Corruption, graft, bribery, "dirty tricks," scandal, and all forms of civil unrighteousness bring disgrace to a country.

14:35 A ruler looks with **favor** on a **servant** who acts wisely (compare Joseph, Mordecai, Daniel). **His wrath is** directed **against him who** acts shamefully. "The king favors an able minister; his anger is for the incompetent" (Moffatt).

15:1 Much of chapter 15 is devoted to the subject of speech. A gentle or conciliating **answer** prevents **wrath** from bursting forth or from increasing. If you answer a man with **a harsh word**, it **stirs up** his fleshly nature, and pretty soon you have a violent quarrel on your hands. Spurgeon gives a charming illustration:

> I once lived where my neighbor's garden was divided from me only by a very imperfect hedge. He kept a dog, and his dog was a shockingly bad gardener, and did not improve my plants. So, one evening, while I walked alone, I saw this dog doing mischief and being a long way off, I threw a stick at him, with some earnest advice as to his going home. This dog, instead of going home, picked up my stick, and came to me with it in his mouth, wagging his tail. He dropped the stick at my feet and looked up to me most kindly. What could I do but pat him and call him a good dog, and regret that I had ever spoken roughly to him?[23]

15:2 A **wise** man's **tongue** pours forth helpful information. He knows what, when, where, and how to speak. **Foolishness** gushes like a torrent from **the mouth of fools**.

15:3 God is omniscient, that is, He knows everything. His **eyes** are **in every place**. Nothing is hidden from Him. He is **keeping watch** over every word, act, thought, and motive, both on **the evil and the good**. This caused David to exclaim, "Such knowledge is too wonderful for me; it is high, I cannot attain it" (Ps. 139:6).

15:4 **Wholesome**, gracious speech refreshes, soothes, and revives. Perverse, malicious talk **breaks the spirit**.

15:5 We have met this **fool** before. He considers his father outdated, his ideas old-fashioned, and his **instruction** worthless. The wise son **receives** parental **correction** and benefits by it. He is **prudent** and becomes even more so.

15:6 Those who were reared in a godly home can testify to the truth of the first line. Even though the parents might not have been affluent, they left their children a spiritual heritage of immense value.

The ill-gotten gain of the unscrupulous man brings **trouble** on himself and his family. A good illustration of this is Achan (Josh. 7).

15:7 A **wise** man's conversation is full of helpful **knowledge**. The foolish man can't edify anyone else because his own mind is empty.

15:8 The first line teaches the worthlessness of ritual without reality. A **wicked** man may bring costly offerings **to the LORD** but God despises them. He wants the man's life to be clean first. "To obey is better than sacrifice" (1 Sam. 15:22). God delights in the humble **prayer of the upright** person; "The sacrifices of God are a broken spirit, a broken and a contrite heart—these, O God, You will not despise" (Ps. 51:17).

15:9 **The way of the wicked** displeases **the LORD** greatly. **He loves** the person **who** lives in obedience to His Word.

15:10 There are two ways of looking at this proverb. It may be describing two different men—the wayward (**him who forsakes the way**) and the unteachable (**he who hates correction**), and the punishment they earn—**harsh discipline** and death respectively. Or it may be describing the same man in both lines. At first his waywardness brings him severe **harsh discipline**. But he refuses to learn from it and so plunges on to death. Hebrew poetic structure (parallelism) favors the second interpretation.

15:11 **Hell and Destruction** (Heb., *Sheol* and *Abaddon*) are symbolic of the unseen world beyond the grave. If God knows all about what transpires in death and in the hereafter, **how much more** does He know the thoughts and secrets **of the sons of men** on earth? "All things are naked and open to the eyes of Him to whom we must give account" (Heb. 4:13).

15:12 **A scoffer** resents being corrected. **Nor will he go to the wise** person for advice, but to someone who he thinks will tell him what he wants to hear. Such a policy is self-defeating; it only confirms him in his obstinacy and leaves him in the grave of stagnation.

15:13 **A merry heart** is reflected in a smiling face, but a broken **heart** has deeper effects. It causes despondency and despair.

15:14 The most knowledgeable people never stop in their pursuit of **knowledge**. **The mouths of fools** chew vacantly **on foolishness**. "The wise grow wiser, the foolish more dense."

15:15 This seems to contrast the pessimist and the optimist. The first is always down-in-the-mouth. He is gloomy, fearful, and negative. The optimist always seems to be on top. He enjoys life to the full.

15:16 A poor believer is **better** off than a wealthy worrywart. Wealth has **trouble** attached. The life of faith is the carefree life.

15:17 A plate of vegetables in an atmosphere of **love is . . . better** than a filet mignon roast where there is strife. Moffatt says, "Better is a dish of vegetables, than the best beef served with hatred."

A fatted calf is one that has been raised in a stall and given the best feed; its meat is tender and delicious.

Joseph R. Sizoo says:

> In a nearby city I visited one of the most luxurious estates I've ever seen in America. Within the house were Italian fireplaces, Belgian tapestries, Oriental rugs, and rare paintings. I said to a friend, "How happy the people must have been who lived here!" "But they weren't," he replied. "Although they were millionaires, the husband and wife never spoke to each other. This place was a hotbed of hatred! They had no love for God or for one another." (*Our Daily Bread*)

15:18 A hot-tempered **man** is always spreading **strife**. A wiser man knows how to avoid **contention** or cool it down after it has started.

15:19 The way of the lazy man is beset with all kinds of difficulties. Maybe he tries to use these as an excuse for doing nothing. **The way of the upright is a** smooth, well-paved **highway**.

15:20 A clean-living **son** brings great satisfaction to his dad. But the wayward son treats **his mother** with contempt by disobeying her will and disregarding her tears.

15:21 A stupid man enjoys his stupidity. He has never known anything better. The wise man gets his joy out of a life of sobriety and morality.

A pig enjoys wallowing in the mire, whereas a sheep wants the clean pasture.

15:22 When men act singly, **without counsel** of others, their programs often **go awry**. It is safer to get a broad range of information and advice. Men who have had experience can warn against dangers to be avoided, can suggest the best methods, etc.

15:23 There is genuine satisfaction in being able to give an honest, helpful **answer**. Also a timely **word**—**spoken** at just the right time to meet a particular need—**how good it is!** Compare Isaiah 50:4, ". . . a word in season to him who is weary." Jesus knows how to speak that word.

15:24 The wise person's pathway **winds upward** toward **life, that he may** avoid the pathway that leads downward to death and destruction. Once again we are reminded of the two roads and two destinies of the human race.

15:25 The LORD will destroy the estate **of the** haughty and highhanded, **but He will** protect **the boundary of the** oppressed widow's little farm.

15:26 The LORD detests **the wicked** plans of unscrupulous men, but He is pleased with **the words of the pure**.

15:27 This proverb may refer primarily to a judge or other public officer who swells his bank account by accepting bribes. In so doing he perverts judgment and corrupts his conduct. But even worse—he brings trouble unlimited on **his own** household. The man who refuses to have anything to do with **bribes** is the one who enjoys life.

15:28 A good man thinks before he speaks. He meditates on **how to answer**. An ungodly man opens his **mouth** and out comes a torrent of profanity, filth, and vileness.

15:29 The LORD is far from the wicked in the sense that He does not enjoy fellowship with them, and they are not in touch with Him by prayer. Believers have instant audience with the Sovereign of the universe in the throne room of heaven by prayer. "Now we know that God does not hear sinners; but if anyone is a worshiper of God and does His will, He hears him" (John 9:31).

15:30 A person's beaming countenance is contagious. It gladdens **the heart** of everyone he meets. Also, good news **makes** a man's whole being feel good.

15:31 The man who heeds counsel that leads to the true way **of life** takes his place **among the wise** of the earth. The teaching of the Bible in general and the gospel in particular is life-giving counsel.

15:32 If a man won't listen to godly **instruction**, it means that he **despises** himself because he is plunging over the cataract to ruin. **He who heeds rebuke** promotes his own best interests.

15:33 The fear of the LORD is the discipline that leads to **wisdom**. **Humility** is the way to **honor**.

B. The Righteous Lifestyle Exalted (16:1—22:16)

16:1 The name Jehovah (LORD) occurs nine times in the first eleven verses of chapter 16. Man may plan his thoughts in advance, but **the LORD** is sovereign and overrules all man's words for the accomplishment of His purposes. "Man proposes but God disposes."

Balaam, for instance, wanted to curse the people of Israel, but the words came out as a blessing (Num. 22:38; 23:7–10).

Or think of Caiaphas, who spoke beyond his own wisdom (John 11:49–52). Herod and Pilate conspired to do to Jesus what God had already appointed to be done (Acts 4:27, 28).

It may also mean that though God's persecuted people often plan in advance what to say at their trial, God gives the proper words at the suited time (Matt. 10:19).

16:2 A man's **ways** are his outward acts; he judges himself by them and pronounces himself **pure**. But God sees the motives and intentions of the heart. "Who can understand his errors? Cleanse me from secret faults" (Ps. 19:12).

16:3 The best way to insure that our dreams and goals will be achieved is to dedicate our **works to the LORD**. J. Allen Blair advises:

> Occasionally we find ourselves disturbed and depressed, even in trying to do the Lord's work. Could anything be further from what God desires? God cannot work through anxious hearts. Whenever a Christian reaches this state, he should stop at once and ask himself, "Whose work is it?" If it's God's work, never forget the burden of it is His, too. You are not the important person. Christ is! He is at work through us. What should we do then when things do not go well? Go to Him! Anything less than this is disobedience.[24]

Prayer: "Give me the eye which sees God in all, and the hand which can serve Him in all, and the heart which can bless Him for all" (Daily Notes).

16:4 This verse does not suggest that God has created certain men to be damned. The Bible nowhere teaches the doctrine of reprobation. Men are damned by their own deliberate choice, not by God's decree.

The proverb means that God has an end, object, or purpose for everything. There is a result for every cause, a reward or punishment for every act. He has ordained a **day** of trouble or evil for **the wicked**, just as He has prepared heaven for those who love Him. "Everything the Lord has made has its destiny; and the destiny of the wicked man is destruction" (TEV).

16:5 Human pride is hateful **to the LORD**. As explained previously, **"though they join forces"** literally reads "hand in hand." In this context it probably suggests the certainty of the proud's being punished.

16:6 The doctrine of this verse must be studied in the light of all other Scriptures on the subject. It cannot mean that a man is saved by being merciful and truthful; salvation is by grace through faith in the Lord. Only to the extent that **mercy and truth** are the signs of saving faith can they be said to purge **iniquity**.

The second part of the proverb is clear on the face of it. By trusting **the LORD**, men escape misfortune and calamity.

16:7 Like so many of the proverbs, this is a general rule, but it does have exceptions. "A righteous life disarms opposition." Or, as Barnes put it, "Goodness has power to charm and win even enemies to itself."

Stanton treated Lincoln with utter contempt. He called him a "low cunning clown" and "the original gorilla." He said there was no need to go to Africa to capture a gorilla when one was available in Springfield, Illinois. Lincoln never retaliated. Instead he made Stanton his war minister, believing that he was the best qualified for the office.

Years later when Lincoln was killed by an assassin's bullet, Stanton looked down on his rugged face and said tearfully, "There lies the greatest ruler of men the world has ever seen."

16:8 It is **better** to have a modest income, which is earned honestly than to have **vast revenues without justice** or with fraud.

16:9 As we were reminded in verse 1, man goes to great length to plan his career, **but the LORD** alone determines whether these plans ever come to pass. Saul of Tarsus planned to persecute the Christian saints in Damascus but ended up becoming one of them! Onesimus planned to leave Philemon forever but God brought him back on better terms than ever.

16:10 Because a **king** is a representative of God (Rom. 13:1), his edicts and decisions carry authority and finality. Therefore **his mouth must not transgress in judgment.**

16:11 God maintains a Bureau of Standards. He determines **honest weights and scales**. When men deal in accordance with His standards, He approves and blesses them.

16:12 Actually **it is an abomination for** *anyone* **to commit wickedness**, but especially for **kings**. They represent God in their position, and therefore have greater responsibility. The **throne is established** on a foundation of doing right.

It should be added that the verse may mean that **it is an abomination** to kings for *their subjects* **to commit wickedness**. Lawful, orderly government must be sustained **by righteousness**. Where moral standards are abandoned, anarchy prevails.

16:13 Good **kings** don't appreciate those who flatter and speak hypocritically. They want men whose word is trustworthy, who are frank and sincere.

16:14 Once enraged, a king can quickly sentence offenders to **death. A wise man** will not provoke the ruler needlessly but **will** seek to pacify him.

16:15 When the king is joyful, the happiness of his **face** spreads gladness through the realm. **His favor** is as refreshing as the clouds that bring **the latter rain**.

16:16 Earthly riches are not to be compared to **wisdom** and knowledge. Riches often disappear overnight but divine wisdom remains throughout eternity.

16:17 The righteous follow **the highway of** holiness without turning off on the tangents of sin. The one **who keeps** straight on this highway **preserves his** life from damage and misfortune.

16:18 A tall tree attracts lightning. So God puts down those who are conceited. Stuck-up people usually suffer some humiliating experience, designed to deflate their ego. It takes only a small pin to prick a large balloon.

It was **pride** that caused the **fall** of Lucifer—as Marlowe described him, "aspiring pride and insolence for which God threw him from the face of heaven."

16:19 It's **better to be of a humble spirit** yourself and to be a companion of **the lowly, than to** share the seeming advantages of **the proud**.

Would'st thou be chief—then lowly
  serve;
Would'st thou go up—go down;
But go as low as e'er you will,
The Highest has been lower still.
—*Author unknown*

16:20 He who heeds the word wisely will find good, and whoever trusts in the LORD, happy is he. So the proverb says, "Read your Bible; heed it; and trust the One who wrote it."

16:21 A man who is truly **wise . . . will be** acknowledged for his discernment and insight. In addition, the pleasant manner in which he speaks will make others more willing to listen to him and to learn. "Sweetness of speech increases persuasiveness" (NASB).

16:22 Understanding serves as a **wellspring of life** and refreshment **to** its possessor, whereas **folly** is like a whiplash to **fools**. They are punished by their own **folly**. "Folly is the chastisement of fools" (Berkeley).

16:23 The speech of a **wise** man is an index of what is in his **heart**. He displays his knowledge by what he says. And there is a certain persuasiveness about his statements. He speaks with authority.

16:24 Kind, **pleasant words** have the qualities of a **honeycomb**—sweet to the taste **and health to the bones**. As Kidner puts it, "To say nice things when we can is a simple benefit we may bring a person, in mind and thence in body."

Watchman Nee told of a woman whose husband never expressed appreciation for anything she had ever done. She worried constantly that she had failed as a wife and mother. Possibly this is what caused her to develop tuberculosis. When she was dying, her husband said to her, "I don't know what we are going to do. You have done so much and done it well." "Why didn't you say that sooner?" she asked, "I have been blaming myself all along, because you never once said 'Well done.'"[25]

16:25 This repeats 14:12 for emphasis. It seems logical and reasonable that the way to heaven is by being good and doing good. But the true fact is that the only people who will ever get to heaven are sinners saved by grace.

16:26 The person who labors, labors for himself, for his hungry mouth drives him on. He knows that if he doesn't work, he won't collect his paycheck, and without money he can't go to the supermarket to buy food. So if he is ever tempted to stop working, his appetite urges him on.

This is also true in the spiritual realm. A realization of our deep spiritual need drives us to the Word and to prayer.

16:27 Verses 27–30 give different portraits of wickedness. First we see **an ungodly man** as one who **digs up evil**, and whose speech is **like a burning fire**, scorching and injuring.

16:28 A perverse man is one who distorts the truth. By lying, shading the truth, or withholding the facts, he spreads **strife**. A talebearer **separates** close **friends**.

16:29 A violent man seeks to lead **his neighbor** astray, encouraging **him** to be a partner in crime (see Rom. 1:32).

16:30 Facial expressions can have evil connotations. A wink can hint at connivance **to devise** some **perverse things**. Compressed **lips** can express the determination to see it through.

16:31 The "if" should be omitted. **The silver-haired head** stands for long life. It **is a crown of glory** or beauty because it is looked on here as a reward for a righteous life. So this verse is the opposite of Psalm 55:23, "Bloodthirsty and deceitful men shall not live out half their days."

16:32 A man who can control his temper is a greater hero than a military conqueror. Victory in this area is more difficult than in capturing a city. If you don't believe it, try it!

> Peter the Great, although one of the mightiest of the Czars of Russia, failed here. In a fit of temper he struck his gardener, and a few days afterwards the gardener died. "Alas," said Peter, sadly, "I have conquered other nations, but I have not been able to conquer myself!"[26]

16:33 In the OT and even up to the time of Pentecost, the casting of **the lot** was a legitimate way of determining the will of God. The whole process seemed very much a matter of chance, but **the Lord** overruled to reveal His guidance.

Today the complete Word of God gives us a general outline of God's will. When we need specific guidance in matters not covered in the Word, we learn His will through waiting on Him in prayer. Then we find that **every decision is from the Lord**.

17:1 A piece of zwieback or **dry** toast eaten in a relaxed setting is **better** than a sumptuous meal in an elegant **house full of feasting** where there is bickering and unhappiness.

17:2 A capable **servant** often rises higher than **a son who causes shame**. Thus Solomon's servant, Jeroboam, gained control over ten of the tribes of Israel, leaving Solomon's son, Rehoboam, with only two.

The servant often shares the **inheritance** with the sons on an equal basis. In Abram's case it looked for a while as if his servant would be his only heir (Gen. 15:2, 3).

17:3 God can do what no crucible or **furnace** can do. They can test **silver** and **gold** but **the Lord** can test the human heart. In the process of testing, He removes the dross and purifies the life until He sees His own image reflected.

> When thro' fiery trials thy pathway
> shall lie,
> My grace, all sufficient, shall be thy
> supply;
> The flame shall not hurt thee; I only
> design
> Thy dross to consume, and thy gold
> to refine.
>
> *—George Keith*

17:4 An evildoer . . . gives heed to people with **false lips**. They welcome lies, unfounded rumors, false accusations. Liars, in turn, like to listen to scandal, slander, and **a spiteful tongue**. In that sense, the kind of talk a man feeds on is a barometer of what he is at heart.

17:5 We have already seen in 14:31 that whoever **mocks the poor** insults **his Maker** (see Jas. 5:1–4). Whoever takes a heartless satisfaction in **calamity** (which almost invariably makes people poor) **will not go unpunished** by the Lord. The book of Obadiah pronounces doom on Edom for rejoicing when Jerusalem fell.

17:6 A numerous and godly posterity brings honor to **old men** (see Ps. 127:3–5; 128:3). **Children** likewise can be grateful for **their father**. There is no reason for a generation gap here.

17:7 Noble and **excellent speech** seems out of place in the mouth of **a** boorish **fool**. Even more unsuitable are **lying lips to a prince**. You expect more from a prince. The world expects more from those of us who are children of God. They have higher standards for us than they do for themselves.

17:8 A bribe serves like a good luck charm, or so its owner thinks. **Wherever he** uses it, it performs wonders for him, opening doors, obtaining favors and privileges, or getting him out of trouble.

17:9 The man who refuses to remember an offense against him **seeks love** and friendship. The one who insists on digging up past grievances only succeeds in alienating **friends**.

"When we learn to love," Adams writes, "we also learn to cover, to forget, and to overlook many faults in others."

One woman to another: "Don't you remember the mean thing she said about you?"

The other woman: "I not only don't remember; I distinctly remember forgetting!"

George Washington Carver was refused admission to a college because he was black. Years later, when someone asked him for the name of the college, he answered, "It doesn't matter!" Love had conquered.

17:10 A simple **rebuke** makes a deeper impression on **a wise man than a** severe beating **on a fool**. Usually people who are sensitive do not need harsh forms of discipline. But those who are unfeeling and indifferent require the sledgehammer treatment. It is hard for them to think that they are ever wrong.

17:11 An evil man seeks only rebellion. He is unwilling to submit to lawful authority. He is determined to have his own way. The **cruel messenger** who **will be sent against** the rebel may be the arresting officer sent by the king, or it may be the messenger of death sent by God.

17:12 A bear robbed of her cubs is fierce and unmanageable. But she is not nearly as dangerous **as a fool in** a fit of temper. Once he gets some crazy idea into his head, nothing will stop him.

17:13 A curse rests upon the house of any man who repays a kindness with an injury. David repaid his loyal general, Uriah, with treachery, and, as a result, brought misery upon his house (2 Sam. 12:9, 10).

17:14 When a hole develops in a dike, the water rushing through it enlarges the hole rapidly. It is the same with quarrels. Minor disputes have a way of growing to major proportions. So it is better to **stop** while a dispute is still insignificant. Otherwise you may be plunged into a great war soon.

17:15 God hates miscarriages of justice. To acquit the guilty or to condemn the innocent is equally abhorrent to Him. Our law courts are filled with this today, but men will give an account for it all when they stand before God. The dictum "Justice, justice you shall follow" echoes down through the corridors of history.

17:16 A person is **a fool** to go to great expense to get an education if he doesn't really mean business. To be a good learner, one must be highly motivated. He must have "a mind to learn" (Moffatt).

A second and more probable meaning of the proverb is this: a fool should not spend money for wisdom when he doesn't have the ability to grasp things in the first place. "Why is this—a price in the hand of a fool to buy wisdom, when he has no capacity?" (Berkeley). He thinks he can buy wisdom as if it were a loaf of bread. He doesn't realize that he must have an understanding heart.

17:17 A true **friend loves** in adversity as well as in prosperity. Often it takes hard times to show which friends are genuinely loyal. A quaint note from D. L. Moody's Bible says, "A true friend is like ivy—the greater the ruin, the closer he clings.[27]

A brother is born for adversity, that is, one of the great privileges of brotherhood is to be at your side when you need him most.

It is not hard to find the Lord Jesus in this verse.

There's not an hour that He is not
near us,
No, not one! No, not one!
No night so dark but His love can
cheer us,
No, not one! No, not one!
—Johnson Oatman

17:18 This verse modifies the previous one by showing that love should not be without discernment. It would be a case of bad judgment to agree to guarantee a friend's debts in the event that he should default. Any man who needs a **surety** is a bad credit risk. Why be **surety** for a bad credit risk?

17:19 The man **who loves transgression loves strife**, and vice versa. The man **who exalts his gate** is one who (1) talks arrogantly (Moffatt); (2) loudly proclaims his wealth; or (3) lives luxuriously and perhaps beyond his means. This man courts destruction.

17:20 **A deceitful heart** never wins, and **a perverse tongue** never prospers. They invite mischief and prevent happiness.

17:21 The parent of a senseless dolt (**scoffer**) lives with **sorrow**. There is **no joy** in being **the father** of a "dull thud."

17:22 Here again we learn that a person's mental outlook has a lot to do with recovery from sickness or accident. A cheerful disposition is a powerful aid to healing. **A broken**, disconsolate **spirit** saps a person's vitality.

In a footnote on this verse, the Berkeley Version comments: "Up-to-date therapy, unsurpassed."

> Today's doctors tell us that a hearty laugh is great exercise. When you emit an explosive guffaw, they say, your diaphragm descends deep into your body and your lungs expand, greatly increasing the amount of oxygen being taken into them. At the same time, as it expands sideways, the diaphragm gives your heart a gentle, rhythmic massage. That noble organ responds by beating faster and harder. Circulation speeds up. Liver, stomach, pancreas, spleen, and gall bladder are all stimulated—your entire system gets an invigorating lift. All of which confirms what that sage old Greek, Aristotle, said about laughter more than 2000 years ago: "It is a bodily exercise precious to health."[28]

But not all laughter is healthful. Howard Pollis, a psychology professor at the University of Tennessee, reports that when laughter and smiling are used in an aggressive way—to sneer at, to ridicule, to embarrass—they are "nonhealthy" and can really do more harm to the laugher than the one who is laughed at.

A broken spirit dries the bones. Blake Clark agrees:

> Emotions can make you ill. They can make hair fall out by the handful, bring on splitting headaches, clog nasal passages, make eyes and nose water with asthma and allergies, tighten the throat with laryngitis, make skin break out in a rash, even cause teeth to drop out. Emotions can plague one's insides with ulcers and itises, give wives miscarriages, make husbands impotent—and much more. Emotions can kill.[29]

17:23 **A wicked man accepts a bribe behind the back** to influence the decision of the judge in his favor.

17:24 A man of **understanding** sets **wisdom** as the goal before his eyes and goes right toward it. **A fool** has no definite ambition. Rather than search for wisdom, which requires discipline, his **eyes** wander in fantasy all over the world.

17:25 One of the great sorrows of

parenthood is to have a child who causes nothing but **grief . . . and bitterness**.

17:26 Also, to punish the righteous is not good, nor to strike princes for their uprightness. Yet this perversion of justice takes place every day.

17:27 He who has knowledge spares his words, and a man of understanding is of a calm spirit. Rash speech and quick temper betray a shallow character.

17:28 You can't tell **a fool** by his facial appearance; he might look ever so wise. "With closed lips he may be counted sensible" (Moffatt).

"At times," writes James G. Sinclair, "it is better to keep your mouth shut and let people wonder if you're a fool than to open it and remove all doubt."

18:1 The difficulty of this proverb is evident from the widely different interpretations that are given.

A man who isolates himself seeks his own desire; he rages against all wise judgment. This is the nonconformist who is going to have his own way even if it conflicts with tested knowledge or approved methods. He flies in the face of sound wisdom by his self-assertion.

The RSV is quite different: "He who is estranged seeks pretexts to break out against all sound judgment." In other words, the man who becomes alienated looks for excuses to justify all kinds of irresponsible conduct.

Knox's translation is somewhat similar and needs no explanation: "None so quick to find pretexts, as he that would break with a friend; he is in fault continually."

Jewish commentators understand the proverb to commend the life of separation from sin and folly. The man who does this desires his own higher interests and mingles himself with all true wisdom. But this interpretation is improbable, though true.

18:2 A fool refuses to listen to people with **understanding**; he is interested only **in expressing his own heart**, or in displaying what he is.

18:3 When the wicked comes, contempt comes also; and with dishonor comes reproach. This is another way of saying that outward shame and reproach come on the heels of inward wickedness and baseness.

18:4 Generally speaking, **the words of a man's mouth** don't give him away. They **are deep waters** hiding his true thoughts and motives.

By way of contrast, the fountain **of wisdom is a** gushing, **flowing brook**. In other words, wisdom's message is clear and transparent.

Moffatt understands the verses as saying that the words of a wise man are a deep pool, a flowing stream, and a fountain of life. They are profound, not shallow; flowing, not brackish; refreshing, not insipid.

18:5 God here condemns the reversal of moral judgments. **To show partiality to the wicked** is, in effect, condoning their wickedness. To deprive **the righteous** of justice is what Lowell called putting Truth on the scaffold and Wrong on the throne.

18:6 A loudmouthed fool is always trying to pick a fight or start trouble. A drunkard excels at this, but all he succeeds in doing is bringing black eyes, contusions, and abrasions on himself.

18:7 A fool's speech **is his** downfall. His reckless and foul language bring about his eventual ruin.

18:8 The words of a talebearer are like delicious tidbits; they are eagerly devoured by the listeners. It is almost as if the listeners say, "Yum, yum. I like that. Tell me more!"

18:9 The lazy or **slothful** man has

much in common with **a destroyer**; they both cause great havoc or devastation. Griffiths warns:

> We know today that it is shoddy workmanship in cars, airplanes, buildings, and the like which is the cause of fatal accidents. This is also true in some offices and leadership in the church, where negligence of responsibility may lead to a breakdown of fellowship. A church may be disintegrated through foolish negligence and laziness as well as by Satanic attack.[30]

18:10 **The name of the LORD** stands for the Lord Himself. The Lord **is a** place of refuge and protection for those who trust in Him. Therefore, in the moment of fierce temptation, call upon the name of the Lord, and He will preserve you from sinning.

18:11 The **rich** man trusts his **wealth** to protect him. **In his own esteem**, he thinks it will serve **like a high wall** to guard him from danger of every kind. But his riches fail him when he needs them most.

Verse 10 is fact: verse 11 is fiction. The righteous man of verse 10 trusts in fact, the rich man of verse 11 in fiction.

18:12 Pride has one foot in the grave and another on a banana skin. Humility walks securely toward honor. William Law draws the contrast sharply: "Look not at pride only as an unbecoming temper, nor at humility as a decent virtue—one is all hell and the other all heaven."

18:13 A man should get all the facts before giving his opinion. Otherwise he will be embarrassed when the full details are made known. There are two sides to every question: every divorce, every quarrel, etc. Don't agree with a person if you have not heard the other person's side.

18:14 A man's **spirit** can bear up under all kinds of physical infirmities, **but a broken spirit** is far more difficult to endure. Emotional problems are often more serious than physical ailments.

Dr. Paul Adolph tells of an elderly patient who was recovering satisfactorily in the hospital from a broken hip. At her release, she was transferred to an old people's home. Within a few hours, the patient showed general physical deterioration and she died in less than a day—"not of a broken hip but of a broken heart."[31]

A man who had faced the horrors of concentration camp with gallantry discovered after his release that it was his own son who had informed on him. "The discovery beat him to his knees and he died. He could bear the attack of an enemy, but the attack of one whom he loved killed him."

18:15 The wise man never comes to the place where he ceases to learn. His mind is always open to instruction, and his **ear** is receptive to **knowledge**.

18:16 **A man's** bribe or gratuity buys his way into the presence of those whom he wishes to influence.

It is also true, as the proverb is sometimes used, that a man's spiritual gift provides opportunities for him to exercise it. If he can teach or preach the Word, for instance, he will have plenty of openings. But that is not the meaning of this verse.

18:17 When a man tells his side of the story, it seems very convincing and you are apt to believe him. But when **his neighbor comes and** asks him a few leading questions, then it may appear that he was not so right after all.

18:18 When believers in the OT cast **lots**, they were actually appealing to the Lord to settle matters for which they felt themselves inadequate. The lot provided a just and peaceful settlement of matters between powerful contenders who might otherwise have resorted to force.

We too should let the Lord be the final Judge when difficulties arise with others. We can do this, not by casting lots, but by reading and obeying the Bible, by confessing our faults one to another, by prayer, and by the inward witness of the Spirit.

18:19 Quarrels between close relatives are often the hardest to mend. It is easier to conquer a fortified **city** than to effect reconciliation between **offended** brothers. Their **contentions are like the bars of a castle**—cold, straight, and immovable. Civil wars are always the bitterest.

18:20 We sometimes say that a man has to eat his words. If they have been good words, they will yield satisfaction to him. He will be rewarded according to the nature of his speech.

18:21 **The tongue** has great potential for good or evil. **Those who love** to use **it** a lot must be prepared to take the consequences.

18:22 The word "good" is implied before **wife.** A man **who finds a** good **wife finds a** treasure. It is a token of the Lord's favor when he finds a godly, helpful bride.

18:23 **Poor** people often speak softly, humbly, pleadingly. **Rich** people, on the other hand, can respond **roughly** and be overbearing, but not all rich people have bad manners!

18:24 Here again we have a proverb with many interpretations.

A man who has friends must himself be friendly. If we follow the KJV and NKJV, the thought is that friendliness wins friends, and that some friends are closer than others.

The NASB, ASV, NKJV margin, and JND say that a man who has many friends will come to ruin, **but** that **there is a friend who sticks closer than a brother**. This means that it is better to have one true friend than a host of friends who will lead you astray.

The RSV reads, "There are friends who pretend to be friends, but there is a friend who sticks closer than a brother." This presents a contrast between fair-weather friends and those who are loyal through thick and thin.

Happily, most versions agree on the second line—that **there is a friend who sticks closer than a brother**. G. Campbell Morgan writes:

> All consideration of this great verse leads us at last to one place, to One Person. He is the Friend of sinners. There comment ceases. Let the heart wonder and worship.[32]

19:1 The contrast is between a **poor** person **who** is honest and a devious (and perhaps rich) **fool** who distorts the truth. The **poor** person has it all over the **fool**; he is better off.

19:2 **Also, it is not good for a soul to be without knowledge.** This man knows what he wants to do, but he doesn't know how to do it, so he goes off "half-cocked."

Haste only adds to his misery. He is in too much of a hurry to ask for directions or to follow them if given, so he misses the way and goes around in circles.

19:3 When men make a mess of their lives, they turn around and blame the Lord. Thus, Adam tried to put the blame on God with the words "The woman whom You gave to be with me . . ." (Gen. 3:12).

More than we know, apostasy has its seeds in moral failure. A man engages in some form of immorality, then instead of confessing and forsaking the sin, he turns away from the Christian faith and rages **against the LORD**. W. F. Adeney comments, "It is monstrous to charge the providence of God with the consequences of actions that He has forbidden."

19:4 The fact that **wealth makes many friends** is a proof of the innate selfishness of the human heart. **The poor** man is **separated from his friend** because the latter wants only those friendships that will benefit him.

19:5 One who gives **false** testimony or engages in other forms of dishonesty will surely be punished by the Lord, even if he is never caught in this life.

19:6 **The nobility** here means a generous or powerful person. **Many** try to cultivate his friendship with the hope of getting favors. People tend to befriend those from whom they hope to benefit.

19:7 The relatives **of** a **poor** man often desert **him**. **Much more do his friends** give him the cold shoulder. **He** appeals to them pathetically for help and sympathy, **yet they abandon him**.

19:8 It is a form of enlightened self-interest to seek **wisdom** and common sense. And to hold on to **understanding** and insight is a sure road to success.

19:9 We should not be surprised at the frequency with which this is repeated. After all, one of the Ten Commandments deals with perjury (Ex. 20:16).

19:10 **Luxury is not fitting for a fool.** He doesn't know how to act in the midst of culture and refinement. Neither does a slave know how to act in a position of authority. He treats his former superiors arrogantly.

19:11 A man of good sense knows how to control his temper. He can graciously **overlook** it when somebody wrongs him. The big-heartedness which David frequently displayed toward Saul illustrates the proverb well.

19:12 **The king's wrath, like** a lion's **roaring**, warns offenders of danger ahead. **His favor** to those who are obedient subjects **is** as gentle and refreshing as **dew on the grass**.

Romans 13:1–7 sets forth these two aspects of governmental authority and cautions, "Therefore, you must be subject, not only because of wrath but also for conscience' sake" (v. 5).

19:13 Two things that make domestic life miserable are a wayward **son** and a nagging **wife**. The former brings grief to **his father**, and the latter is as annoying as **a continual dripping** of water on metal.

19:14 You can inherit real estate **and** money **from fathers**, but only **the LORD** can provide **a prudent wife**. She is a special gift of God.

This reminds us of Isaac and Rebekah's storybook marriage, of which it is said, "The thing comes from the Lord" (Gen. 24:50). It was a marriage that was arranged in heaven.

19:15 **Laziness** is like a drug that **casts one into a deep sleep**. **An idle person** courts poverty and **will suffer hunger**.

This is true in connection with Bible study and prayer.

19:16 The one **who** obeys **the commandment** of the Lord is doing what is best for himself in the long run, both physically and spiritually. The person **who** lives recklessly and carelessly **will die**.

19:17 Giving to **the poor** is lending **to the LORD**. God will not only **pay back** the amount loaned but will pay good interest as well. Even a cup of cold water given in His name will be rewarded (Matt. 10:42). Henry Bosch illustrates:

A father once gave his boy a half dollar, telling him he could do with it as he pleased. Later when he asked about it, the little fellow said he had lent it to someone. "Did you get good security?" inquired his father. "Yes, I gave it to a poor beggar who looked hungry!" "O how foolish you are. You'll never get it back!" "But Dad, I have the best security; for the Bible says, he that giveth to the poor lendeth to the Lord!" Thinking this over, the Christian father was so pleased that he gave his son another half dollar! "See!" said the boy. "I told you I'd get it again, only I didn't think it would come so soon!"[33]

We lose what on ourselves we spend,
We have, as treasures without end,
Whatever, Lord, to Thee we lend,
Who givest all.

—*Christopher Wordsworth*

19:18 Discipline **your son while** he is still young and teachable. Corporal punishment, administered fairly and in an atmosphere of genuine love, will not harm him but, on the contrary, will do him an enormous amount of good.

The second line, **"do not set your heart on his destruction,"** means you should not let his life be ruined by your refusal to punish him. Permissiveness is cruelty. It could *also* mean, of course, "Don't become so angry that you are in danger of overpunishing him."

19:19 A hot-headed **man will suffer punishment** for it. Even **if you rescue him** from the consequences of his vile temper, he will soon be at it again, and **you will have to do it again**.

19:20 Listen to sound advice **and receive instruction** in early life, so **that you may be wise in** later life. As someone has said, "Wisdom is a long-term investment."

19:21 Man makes all kinds of **plans, nevertheless** it is **the LORD's** purposes that come to pass. "Man has his wickedness but God has His way." Ultimately man can do nothing against the truth (2 Cor. 13:8).

19:22 Darby's translation of this verse is priceless: "The charm of a man is his kindness; **and a poor man is better than a liar**." The quality that endears **a man** to you **is kindness**. That's what makes him to be **desired** as a friend. **A poor man** who has nothing but sympathy to offer is better than a rich man who promises help but doesn't deliver it.

19:23 The fear of the LORD is the pathway **to life**. The one **who has it** has every reason to be satisfied. **He will not be** overtaken **with** calamity.

19:24 A lazy man buries his hand in the bowl, and will not so much as bring it to his mouth again. He reaches into the bowl of potato chips but is too **lazy** to lift them to his mouth. They are too heavy.

19:25 Even if you **strike a scoffer**, he won't change, but at least some impressionable onlookers might learn a lesson. This is reminiscent of 1 Timothy 5:20, "Those who are sinning rebuke in the presence of all, that the rest also may fear."

You don't have to strike **one who has understanding**. A word of **rebuke** will make him correct his error and grow wiser in the process.

19:26 A son **who mistreats** or slanders (Berkeley) **his father** and evicts **his mother** from the home is shameful and disgraceful himself **and brings** disgrace and **reproach** to his heartbroken parents. It is small thanks for all his parents have done for him.

19:27 This proverb is like a diamond; every way you turn it, it sparkles with new light. The three most probable interpretations are these:

The KJV means, "Excellent advice for young people in schools and colleges where the Bible is under attack! Better to sacrifice a college career than to subject yourself to a barrage of doubts and denials."

The RSV and Berkeley read: "Cease, my son, to hear instruction only to stray from the words of knowledge." There is no sense in getting good instruction if you are not going to obey it. You are wasting your own time and the teacher's, and increasing your load of guilt. "It is better not to know, than, knowing, to fail to do."

The third interpretation is a warning: **"Cease listening to instruction, my son, and you will stray from the words of knowledge"** (NKJV).

19:28 A disreputable witness scorns justice—except when *he* is on trial! He greedily **devours** or spreads **iniquity**. He resembles Eliphaz's description of man, drinking iniquity like water (Job 15:16).

19:29 While **scoffers** and **fools** play to the balconies from the stage of human history, punishment and **judgments** are waiting in the wings. As soon as the curtain is drawn, the inevitable meeting will take place.

20:1 Wine does mock men but here the thought is that it causes men to become mockers or scoffers. **Strong drink** converts them into **a brawler**.

Wine is made from grapes, **strong drink** from grain. They both lead men astray. First a man becomes a social drinker, then a heavy drinker, then an alcoholic. He tries to shake off the habit, but he is held as if by chains. Christ gives power to break the chains, but first man must want deliverance.

20:2 When **a king** is angry, fear spreads throughout his court. That fear **is like the roaring of a lion**, warning of danger. **Whoever provokes** the king **to anger** takes **his own life** in his hands.

The lesson for us is found in Romans 13:4: "For he (i.e., the ruler) is God's minister to you for good. But if you do evil, be afraid; for he does not bear the sword in vain; for he is God's minister, an avenger to execute wrath on him who practices evil."

20:3 An **honorable** person makes a point of keeping aloof from strife. **A fool** isn't happy unless he's quarreling with someone.

20:4 Plowing time in Israel is in November and December, when the wind commonly blows from the North. **The lazy man** uses the cold weather to excuse his inaction. Without the plowing there can be no planting, and without the planting no harvest. He'll go out looking for grain in his fields and wonder why it isn't there.

20:5 A man's thoughts and intentions are often hidden deeply in his mind. He will not generally bring them to the surface. **But a** person of discernment knows how to **draw** them **out** by wise questions. For example, a good counselor can help a person bring crooked thinking to the light and thus remedy it.

20:6 It is not hard to find those who *profess* to be loyal, but it is another thing to **find** those who really *are* **faithful**. There is a difference between what men are, and what they want others to think they are. It is the difference between "Person" and "Personality."

20:7 The righteous man walks in honesty and **integrity**. **His children** come into a noble heritage and benefit from his life and example.

20:8 A king who sits on the throne of judgment winnows **all evil with his eyes**. When Christ sits upon His throne of judgment, His all-seeing eyes, like flames of fire, will see through pretense and sift all evidence.

20:9 By his own efforts, no one can cleanse himself from sin. **Who can say, "I have made my heart clean, I am pure from my sin"?** If a man thinks he is pure, he is a victim of pure delusion.

But there is cleansing through the precious blood of Christ. True believers have "washed their robes and made them white in the blood of the Lamb" (Rev. 7:14).

> The blood that purchased our release,
> and purged our crimson stains,
> We challenge earth and hell to show
> a sin it cannot cleanse.
> —*Augustus M. Toplady*

20:10 God hates deceitful **weights** and measurements. This includes any dishonest device to benefit self at the expense of others. It includes the butcher's trick of resting his finger on the scales when he is weighing the meat. And it even includes the practice of demanding stricter standards from others than we do from ourselves.

20:11 The basic nature of a person reveals itself early in life. Some children are downright ornery, others are pleasant. "The child is father of the man." He carries his character into adulthood, whether for good or for evil.

20:12 **The Lord created the hearing ear and the seeing eye**. What can this mean but that they belong to Him and should be used for His glory?

20:13 Don't overindulge in **sleep, lest you** land in the poorhouse. Get up and go to work. You'll earn money to pay your rent, buy your groceries, and give to the work of the Lord.

20:14 This is an old buyer's trick. As he looks over the used car, he squawks about its dents, its worn tires, its noisy engine, and its hideous color. **"It is good for nothing."** The seller hadn't realized it was such a junk-heap; he naively lowers the price. The buyer gives him the money, **then he** goes and **boasts** to his friends about his tremendous bargain.

20:15 A person may wear **gold** jewelry and precious gems, but the best adornment is wise speech. Wear this!

20:16 **Take the garment of one who is surety for a stranger, and hold it as a pledge when it is for a seductress.** Any man who is foolish enough to make financial guarantees for people he doesn't know is a bad credit risk. If you have any dealings with him, be sure that he puts up plenty of collateral so that you will be protected in case he reneges or goes bankrupt. The advice is especially true if the stranger is an immoral person.

20:17 Any form of wealth **gained** dishonestly might yield momentary satisfaction, **but** eventually it will prove as unpleasant and aggravating as a mouthful of **gravel**. This condemns falsifying tax returns, fudging on expense accounts, bribing inspectors, labeling dishonestly, and advertising product differences that don't exist.

20:18 A pooling of advice is desirable before making any **plans**. No general makes war without consulting with other military experts.

20:19 **A** gossip betrays confidences. **Therefore, do not associate with** a blabber, because if he talks against others to you, you can be sure that he will talk against you to others.

20:20 Under the law of Moses, cursing one's parents was a capital offense (Ex. 21:17). This should give pause to young people today who are hostile toward their parents. Unless this bitterness is resolved, it will lead to temporal obscurity and eternal perdition.

20:21 The prodigal son got his share of the **inheritance . . . hastily**, but he lost it just as quickly. But this proverb is true also of any get-rich-quick schemes. Easy come, easy go.

20:22 Don't seek vengeance on your enemies. Vengeance is the Lord's. He will repay. **Wait for the LORD. He will** deliver **you** and vindicate you.

20:23 Adam Clarke worked for a silk merchant who suggested that he should stretch the silk when measuring it for a customer. Adam's reply was, "Your silk may stretch, sir, but my conscience won't." God honored Adam Clarke by enabling him years later to write a widely used commentary on the Bible.

20:24 This verse emphasizes God's sovereignty and not man's free will, though both are true. The thought is that God is sovereign over human affairs and He knows what is best for us. Therefore, we ought to look to Him for direction, and not try to be the masters of our fate and manipulate to get our **own way**.

20:25 It is a snare for a man to devote rashly something as holy and afterward to reconsider his vows. It is dangerous to dedicate something to the Lord, and then to have second thoughts about it. Before making a **vow**, a man should be sure that he is able to fulfill it and that he definitely intends to.

20:26 A wise king does not tolerate **the wicked**. He **brings the threshing wheel over them**, that is, he separates them from the righteous, brings them to trial, and punishes them.

20:27 The spirit of a man in this verse is generally taken to refer to the conscience. It is given to us by **the LORD** and serves as a **lamp**, throwing light on our thoughts, motives, affections, and actions. It approves and reproves the innermost thoughts and intents of our lives (see Rom. 2:14, 15).

20:28 A leader who is characterized by **mercy and truth** will have the respect and support of his subjects. He maintains his position of authority **by lovingkindness**, not by tyranny.

20:29 A prominent **glory of young men is their strength**, while the **gray** hair **of old men** is associated with wisdom and experience. Every church needs both strength for service and age for wise counsel.

20:30 "Blows that hurt cleanse away evil, as do stripes the inner depths of the heart."

The thought seems to be that physical punishment has value in dealing with moral **evil**. A child remembers the pain of the last spanking when he is tempted to steal from his mother's purse.

21:1 Just as a channel or canal directs the flow **of water**, so **the LORD** rules and overrules a **king's** thoughts and actions. This is an encouragement to Christians under oppressive governments or to missionaries taking the gospel to hostile lands.

21:2 A man is not a valid judge of his own life or service; he judges by outward appearances. **The LORD weighs** the thoughts and motives of people's **hearts**.

21:3 The LORD is not as pleased with burnt offerings and **sacrifice** as with obedience to His voice (1 Sam. 15:22). God is not a ritualist. What He wants is inward reality.

21:4 This proverb lists three things that are sin in God's sight: **a haughty look**, i.e., the outward expression of conceit; **a proud heart**, i.e., the inward reservoir; and **the plowing of the wicked**, which may mean their prosperity, happiness, life, or hope.

21:5 Those who work diligently for their living are contrasted with those who seek to get rich overnight. The first are assured of **plenty**; the second, of **poverty**.

21:6 Those who seek riches through fraud and **by a lying tongue** are chasing the wind. They are pursuing that which will elude them, and they will perish in the process. Their position is like that of a desert traveler chasing a mirage; it proves to be a snare of **death** for him.

21:7 **The violence of the wicked will destroy them, because they refuse to do justice.** There is a moral principle at work in the universe which guarantees that violence, wickedness, and injustice will never escape unpunished. Never!

21:8 "Very crooked is the way of a guilty man, but as for the pure, his work is upright" (JND). Guilt causes a man to lie, to hide, to masquerade, to fear, and to act deceitfully. The man who has confessed and forsaken his sins has nothing to hide; he can walk in the light.

21:9 Houses in Bible lands had flat roofs. This proverb says that it would be **better to** live alone **in a** cramped **corner of** one of those roofs, exposed to heat, cold, rain, snow, wind, and hail, **than** to live **in a house shared with a** nagging, cantankerous **woman**. The storms from without would be more endurable than the tempest inside.

21:10 **The soul of the wicked** is always plotting some new **evil**, and he shows no mercy to **his neighbor** in perpetrating it. Thus his sin is both deliberate and ruthless. Modern sociological excuses for crime simply won't hold water.

21:11 Even if a **scoffer** might not learn a lesson from the punishment he receives, the naive person will see it and be warned. A **wise** man doesn't need to be punished; he will learn from simple instruction.

21:12 **The righteous God wisely considers the house of the wicked, overthrowing the wicked for their wickedness. God** keeps close watch on all the affairs of ungodly men; at the proper time He throws the switch which brings their doom upon them.

21:13 The rich man of Luke 16:19–31 was quite unconcerned about the desperate need of the beggar at his gate. In the afterlife, he himself cried for relief but his cry went unanswered.

21:14 The Bible often reports facts without approving them. Thus it observes that an angry man will quiet down if the offender slips him **a gift**, and a man who is in a rage is appeased by **a bribe** tucked in his pocket.

21:15 **It is a joy for the just to do justice, but destruction will come to the workers of iniquity.** This is illustrated by the second advent of Christ. It will be a time of ecstasy for the redeemed, but a time of horror for all others (2 Thess. 1:6–9).

21:16 You meet all kinds of people in Proverbs. This **man who wanders** is like a vagrant in the Sahara of sin. When you last see him, he is resting **in the assembly of the dead**.

21:17 Instead of giving the satisfaction and fulfillment they promise, **pleasure** and luxurious living (**wine and oil**) only serve to impoverish **a man**. They drain his financial resources and also reduce him to spiritual poverty.

21:18 In Isaiah 43:3, God says that He gave Egypt as **a ransom for** His people, Israel. The Lord rewarded Cyrus for liberating the Jews by permitting him to possess Egypt and the neighboring kingdoms.

In a broad sense the verse means

that **the wicked** are punished so that the **upright** can go free.

21:19 A touch of sanctified humor! The writer would prefer the discomfort, distance, and loneliness of a desert to being cooped up with an **angry**, quarrelsome **woman**.

21:20 The contrast here is between the cottage **of the wise** man where there is a plentiful supply of all good things, and the home of **a foolish man** where sin, waste, and extravagance lead to scarcity.

We are reminded of the alcoholic who used to sell his furniture and other household goods in order to buy whiskey. After his conversion to Christ, someone said to him, "You don't really believe that stuff about Jesus' turning water into wine, do you?" His answer was, "I don't know about turning water into wine, but I know that in my house He turned whiskey into furniture!"

21:21 The point here seems to be that the one **who** pursues **righteousness and mercy** gets more than he bargained for; in addition to **righteousness** he receives **life** and **honor**.

21:22 The **wise** Christian **brings down the . . . stronghold**, not with artillery and bombs, but with faith, prayer, and the Word of God (see 2 Cor. 10:4). In the spiritual conflict, wisdom can accomplish what armed might is unable to do.

21:23 **Whoever** can control **his mouth** saves himself **from** stacks of trouble. "Even so the tongue is a little member and boasts great things. See how great a forest a little fire kindles! And the tongue is a fire, a world of iniquity. The tongue is so set among our members that it defiles the whole body, and sets on fire the course of nature; and it is set on fire by hell" (Jas. 3:5, 6).

21:24 If you meet **a proud and haughty man**, just call him **"Scoffer."** That's **his name**! The **name**, of course, stands for what a person is. "For as his name is, so is he" (1 Sam. 25:25).

21:25, 26 The **lazy man** is torn apart between his craving for riches on the one hand, and his determination not to exert himself on the other. It's a killing impasse! While he spends his time in a dream-world of unfulfilled hopes, the righteous man works hard and earns money so that he can give unsparingly to worthy causes.

21:27 God is "turned off" by the donations of unrepentant sinners but He hates it even more when a gift is intended to "buy Him off" or induce Him to condone, approve, or bless some wicked scheme.

21:28 "A false witness will perish, but the word of a man who hears will endure" (RSV). The false witness swears before God that he will tell the truth, then deliberately perjures himself. The man who listens carefully and answers honestly gives testimony that can never be shaken.

21:29 The brazen **face** of **a wicked man** shows that he is confirmed in his iniquity. He has a forehead of brass. **The upright** man, by being teachable, is safe and **establishes his** behavior.

21:30 Man is powerless to outwit God in **wisdom**, **understanding**, or strategy. None of his plots can avail **against the LORD**. "Every purpose of the Lord shall be performed" (Jer. 51:29).

21:31 Men may go to elaborate plans to insure military success, but victory on **the day of battle** comes from **the LORD** alone. It is better to trust in Him than in horses—or in nuclear weapons—(see Ps. 20:7).

Plumptre summarizes verses 30 and 31 as follows:

Verse 30: Nothing avails against God.

Verse 31: Nothing avails without God.

22:1 A good name means a **good** reputation. It is the fruit of a good character. It is better **than great riches** because it is more precious, more powerful, and more enduring.

For the same reasons, **loving favor** is better **than silver and gold**.

22:2 Social distinctions are artificial in the sense that we are all of the same human family, and all come from the same Creator. Class distinctions that survive in life are abolished in death.

22:3 A prudent man looks ahead **and hides himself** from coming judgment. The Israelites did this on the Passover night by sprinkling the blood on their door. We do it by finding refuge in Christ.

The thoughtless **pass on** in their folly and "pay for it" (Moffatt).

22:4 Humility and the fear of the Lord may seem very dull and commonplace, but don't knock them till you've tried them. They are rewarded with spiritual **riches**, divine **honor**, and abundant **life**.

22:5 All kinds of difficulties and troubles lie **in the way of the perverse** man. The man who keeps himself clean avoids **them**.

22:6 The usual interpretation of this proverb is that if you **train up a child** properly (**in the way he should go**), he will go on well in later life. Of course there are exceptions, but it stands as a general rule. Henry Ward Beecher observes:

> It is not hard to make a child or a tree grow right if you train them when they're young, but to make them straighten out after you've allowed things to go wrong is not an easy matter.[34]

Susannah Wesley, the mother of Charles, John, and 15 other children, followed these rules in training them: (1) Subdue self-will in a child and thus work together with God to save his soul. (2) Teach him to pray as soon as he can speak. (3) Give him nothing he cries for and only what is good for him if he asks for it politely. (4) To prevent lying, punish no fault which is freely confessed, but never allow a rebellious, sinful act to go unnoticed. (5) Commend and reward good behavior. (6) Strictly observe all promises you have made to your child.

The proverb can also be understood as encouraging parents to train their children along the lines of their natural talents, rather than forcing them into professions or trades for which they have no native inclination. Thus Kidner says that the verse teaches respect for the child's individuality and vocation, though not for his self-will.

And the proverb may be a warning that if you train a child in the way that he himself wants to go, he will continue to be spoiled and self-centered in later life. Jay Adams writes:

> The verse stands not as a promise but as a warning to parents that if they allow a child to train himself after his own wishes (permissively), they should not expect him to want to change these patterns when he matures. Children are born sinners and, when allowed to follow their own wishes, will naturally develop sinful habit responses. The basic thought is that such habit patterns become deep-seated when they have been ingrained in the child from the earliest days.[35]

22:7 Money is power, and it can be used for good or for evil. Too often **the rich** use it for evil, and perhaps that is why it is called the mammon of unrighteousness.

The borrower is a slave **to the lender**. Debt is a form of bondage. It requires the payment of exorbitant interest rates. It keeps a man's nose to the grindstone. It limits his mobility and his ability to take advantage of opportunities.

22:8 One **who sows iniquity** gains nothing substantial or worthwhile. The attempt to beat others into submission by **anger will** be thwarted.

22:9 The **generous** man is **blessed** in showing benevolence to others. By sharing **his** substance with **the poor**, he gains present happiness and future reward.

22:10 When a **scoffer** fails to respond to instruction, correction, and admonition, the next step is eviction. **Cast** him **out**! When Ishmael was put out of the house, **contention**, quarreling, and abuse ceased (Gen. 21:9, 10).

22:11 The man **who loves purity of heart** and whose speech is gracious will enjoy royal friendships. God may be the **King** referred to here.

> A little word in kindness spoken,
> A motion, or a tear
> Has often healed the heart that's broken,
> And made a friend sincere.
>
> —*Author unknown*

22:12 **The LORD** preserves and perpetuates the **knowledge** of the truth so that it will never perish from the earth in spite of the rage of demons and men. The same Lord **overthrows** false teaching and exposes lies.

22:13 If a **lazy man** can't find an excuse for not going to work, he will make one up, no matter how ridiculous it is. Here he says that **there is a lion . . . in the streets** of the city. What would a lion be doing in the city? It's probably nothing more than a cat!

22:14 The seductive words **of an immoral woman** conceal a trap that is difficult to escape from. A man **who** has estranged himself from **the LORD will fall** into that trap. This reminds us that God often abandons men to sin when those men reject the knowledge of God (see Rom. 1:24, 26, 28).

22:15 Mischief and self-will are native to **the heart of a child**, but by applying the board of education to the seat of learning you can rid him of these vices. Matthew Henry counsels:

> Children need to be corrected, and kept under discipline, by their parents; and we all need to be corrected by our heavenly Father (Heb. xii. 6, 7), and under the correction we must stroke down folly and kiss the rod.[36]

22:16 The employer who gets rich by paying starvation wages will himself suffer want. This will also happen to the man **who gives to the rich**, presumably in order to court their favor. We should give to those who can't repay us.

IV. PROVERBS OF THE WISE MEN (22:17—24:34)

A. Words of the Wise (22:17—24:22)

22:17 Verses 17–21 form a section that introduces the proverbs from 22:22 to 24:22. It invites the reader to **incline** his **ear** to **hear the words of the wise**. Perhaps Solomon collected some of these proverbs from others, but the second half of the verse indicates that some of them are his own.

22:18 A person should **keep** these proverbs in his mind (to remember and obey) and **let them all be fixed upon his lips** (to pass them on to others).

22:19 The reason Solomon made known the proverbs was that the readers might truly **trust . . . in the Lord**.

22:20 In the RSV this verse reads, "Have I not written for you thirty sayings of admonition and knowledge?" Some scholars point out that the proverbs that follow (up to 24:22) can be divided into about 30 groupings, as follows:

22:22, 23	23:22–25
24, 25	26–28
26, 27	29–35
28	24:1, 2
29	3, 4
23:1–3	5, 6
23:4, 5	7
6–8	8, 9
9	10
10, 11	24:11, 12
12	13, 14
13, 14	15, 16
23:15, 16	17, 18
17, 18	19, 20
19–21	21, 22

The Berkeley Bible reads, "Have not I written for you previously of counsels and knowledge . . . ?" The word "previously" is in contrast to "this day" in verse 19.

22:21 The writer aimed at imparting **the words of truth** so that his pupils might be able to teach others who sent to him for counsel or so that they might be able to satisfy **those who** sent them for training.

22:22, 23 This begins the section that ends at 24:22. No one should take advantage of **the** defenseless **poor**. Neither should anyone show injustice to **the afflicted at the gate**, that is, at the place of judgment. For God pleads the cause of the poor, and He will punish the rich oppressor and the unjust judge.

22:24, 25 Association with **an angry**, hot-tempered **man** is bad business. It often makes a man become like the company he keeps. This can really be a snare because in a moment of passion, a man can ruin his life and testimony.

22:26, 27 Shaking **hands in a pledge** here means to guarantee someone else's debt. It is foolish to do it. If you can't afford to make full payment of the debt, **why** run the risk of having the furniture taken out of your house, and thus expose yourself to discomfort and shame?

22:28 **The ancient landmark** was a series of stones which indicated the boundaries of a person's property. Dishonest people often moved them during the night to increase the size of their farm at their neighbor's expense.

Spiritually, the ancient landmarks would be "the faith which was once for all delivered to the saints" (Jude 3). The fundamental doctrines of Christianity should not be tampered with.

22:29 A **man who excels in his work . . . will** be promoted to a position of honor. **He will not** serve **unknown men**. This is another reminder that cream rises to the surface. We see it in the lives of Joseph, Moses, Daniel, and Nehemiah.

> The heights by great men reached
> and kept
> Were not attained by sudden flight,
> But that while their companions slept
> Were toiling upward through the
> night.
>
> —*Longfellow*

23:1–3 Here we are warned against gluttony and surfeiting. **When** we **eat with** an influential person, we should consider **what** or *who* (JND) **is before** us. Then we should **put a knife to**

our **throat**, that is, exercise restraint in eating and drinking.

Verse 3 suggests that someone might be wining and dining us in order to influence us in some way. It isn't a case of unselfish hospitality but a means of using us for some subtle purpose.

23:4, 5 The ceaseless struggle **to be rich** is a form of "wisdom" to be avoided. It means that you are spending your life pursuing false values and putting your trust in what doesn't last. **Riches** have a way of sprouting **wings** and flying **away like an eagle**.

23:6–8 Another social situation to avoid! Don't be a guest of a man who has an evil eye, **a miser** who begrudges you every bite of the food you eat. It's what **he thinks**, not what he says, that counts. For while he is saying, "Help yourself . . . Have some more, **Eat and drink!"** he is actually counting every spoonful you take.

The LB paraphrases these verses as follows:

> Don't associate with evil men; don't long for their favors and gifts. Their kindness is a trick; they want to use you as their pawn. The delicious food they serve will turn sour in your stomach and you will vomit it, and have to take back your words of appreciation for their "kindness."

23:9 Don't try to teach a dull, stupid **fool**. You are wasting your time on him. **He will despise** your **words** of **wisdom**.

23:10, 11 Don't dishonestly take the property of someone else by secretly moving the **ancient** boundary stones. Don't take advantage of the defenseless by seizing their fields. **For their** Avenger **is mighty**. You will have to deal with *Him*! **He will plead their cause against you.**

23:12 There is no easy way **to** gain **instruction**. It requires discipline and application. Disregard the ads that promise it in "three easy lessons."

23:13, 14 It is not a kindness to **a child** to allow him to run wild. The Bible does not condone permissiveness but rather encourages **correction** with **a rod**, and promises that the child **will not die**. This may mean that the beating will not kill him, or that the beating will actually save him from premature and reckless death. It will **deliver his soul from** Sheol.

Instead of disciplining his wicked sons, Eli rebuked them with a mild "Why do you do such things?" (1 Sam. 2:22–25). He fostered a permissiveness that brought ruin on his house, on the priesthood, and on the nation.

David failed in the area of parental discipline, too. He never displeased Adonijah by correcting him (1 Kgs. 1:6). After making two treasonable attempts to seize the throne, Adonijah was killed by Solomon.

23:15, 16 A father rejoices when his son has a **heart** that is **wise** and **lips** that **speak** the truth. The teacher experiences this same joy when his pupil receives wisdom and shares it with others. In a similar vein Paul said, "For now we live, if you stand fast in the Lord" (1 Thess. 3:8). And John said, "I have no greater joy than to hear that my children walk in truth" (3 John 4).

23:17, 18 There is something better than envying the prosperity of the wicked; that is to live in constant fellowship with **the Lord**. Occupation with the wicked brings discouragement; occupation with the Lord brings delight. So the lesson is to make communion with God the aim of our life. Also, to remember that **there is a** future day of reckoning for the wicked and a bright hope of reward for the righteous which shall never be disappointed. The **hereafter** looks past death and resurrection to a glorious future in heaven.

23:19 Whatever others may do, an obedient **son** should heed instruction, **be wise, and guide** his **heart in the** right **way**, that is, the way of God.

23:20, 21 There are two kinds of "drunkards"—those who drink too much and those who eat too much. They both make bad company for anyone who wants the good life.

Intemperance takes its toll. **The drunkard and the glutton** are headed for **poverty**. The stupor which results from surfeiting will clothe a man in rags.

23:22 Young people should welcome advice from their **father**, and not treat their **mother** with contempt. Old folks have years of experience behind them. Young people should recognize this and try to benefit as much as possible from their experience.

23:23 We should be willing to pay a great price for **truth**, but unwilling to **sell it** for any consideration. The same goes for **wisdom and instruction and understanding**. We should spare no pains to acquire them, but never surrender them for anything in this world.

23:24, 25 Modern custom says, "Give father a tie on Father's Day, and give mother a box of chocolates on Mother's Day." But more rewarding to parents is a son who lives wisely and prudently. Hence, the exhortation: **"Let your father and your mother be glad, and let her who bore you rejoice."**

23:26–28 The earnest plea, **"My son, give me your heart . . ."** introduces solemn warnings against immorality and drunkenness. The writer is saying, "Listen to me carefully and observe the counsel I give you." A prostitute **is** like **a deep**, concealed **pit**, forming a trap for the careless. She **is a narrow well**—easy to fall into but hard to get out of. **She lies in wait** like a robber. She may have a pathological hatred for men, and wreaks her revenge on them by entangling them through deception, like one hooks a fish with a lure. Daily she adds to the list of unfaithful men whose marriages and families are torn apart.

23:29, 30 The rest of chapter 23 is a classic description of a drunkard. He brings all kinds of **woe** upon himself and staggers from one **sorrow** to another. His life is marked by **contentions**, since he is forever trying to pick a fight. He grumbles and complains incessantly, but it never dawns on him that *he* is the cause of all his troubles! He has bruises, **wounds**, a black eye—all from fights that were unnecessary. His **eyes** are bleary and bloodshot. He sits in the tavern all night, consuming one **mixed** drink after another.

23:31, 32 He is warned against being fascinated by the clear **red wine**, by its brilliant sparkle, by the way **it swirls around smoothly**. But he doesn't listen, and so he suffers the consequences, which are like the bite of **a serpent** and the sting of **a viper**—poisonous and painful.

23:33, 34 His **eyes will see strange things**, a possible reference to the horrors of delirium tremens, the violent mental disturbances caused by excessive and prolonged use of liquor. His conversation is thick, garbled, and vile. He reels to and fro unsteadily, as if he were bobbing back and forth in **the sea**, or perched on **top of the mast** as it rocks crazily from one side to the other.

23:35 Someone has clobbered him,

but when he regains consciousness, he says that he **was not hurt**. They mauled him but he **did not feel it**. As soon as he is completely **awake**, he plans to go back to the bar for **another drink**.

24:1, 2 It is not wise **to be envious** of the success **of evil men** or to **desire** their company. They have a way of dragging others down to their own levels. And what is that level? Their minds are always planning **violence** and their conversation centers on **troublemaking**.

24:3, 4 The **house** here may refer to a man's life. A great life is not **built** by wickedness but by godly **wisdom**. Wickedness wrecks a life but **understanding** gives it solidity. Wickedness leaves it empty; true **knowledge** fits it out with **precious and pleasant** furnishings.

24:5, 6 A wise man can wield greater power than a strong man, and a man of brains is mightier than a man of brawn. **War** can be waged through **wise** counselors, and the more wise **counselors** there are, the better.

24:7 Wisdom seems to be forever beyond the grasp of **a fool**. He can never speak with authority, like the elders at **the gate** of the city do.

24:8, 9 The one who uses his God-given faculties to invent new forms of **evil** earns the title of "master **schemer**." **The devising of foolishness is sin,** and the arrogant **scoffer** who is brazen in his wickedness earns the contempt of others.

24:10 One test of a person's worth is how he behaves under pressure. If he gives up when the going is rough, he doesn't have what it takes.

Christ, if ever my footsteps should
falter,
And I be prepared for retreat;
If desert and thorn cause lamenting,
Lord, show me Thy feet.
Thy bleeding feet, Thy nail-scarred
feet,
My Jesus, show me Thy feet.
O God, dare I show Thee
My hands and my feet?

—*Amy Carmichael*

24:11, 12 When innocent people are being led off to gas chambers, ovens, and other modes of execution—when unborn babies are destroyed in abortion clinics—it is inexcusable to stand by and not seek to rescue them. It is also useless to plead ignorance. As Dante said, "The hottest places in hell are reserved for those who in a time of great moral crisis maintain their neutrality."

Does this have a voice for those of us who are believers and who are entrusted with the good news of salvation? Men and women are dying without Christ. Jesus said, "Lift up your eyes and look at the fields: for they are already white for harvest" (John 4:35). Dare we remain neutral?

See the shadows lengthen round us,
Soon the day-dawn will begin;
Can you leave them lost and lonely?
Christ is coming—call them in!

—*Anna Shipton*

24:13, 14 Honey is used here as a symbol of wisdom. Both are beneficial and **sweet** to the **taste. So shall the knowledge of wisdom be to your soul; if you have found it, there is a prospect, and your hope will not be cut off.** In other words, the man who finds wisdom is assured of a bright future and the realization of all his hopes.

24:15, 16 The unscrupulous person is warned against trying to dispossess a **righteous** man of his home. Maybe the latter has been overtaken by temporary hardship, and the wicked man is ready to pounce on his property.

A righteous man may fall into trouble or calamity **seven times**, but he will recover each time. **The wicked** can stumble to his ruin in a single misfortune.

24:17, 18 A man of good character should never **rejoice when** trouble catches up with his adversary, or be happy to see him stumble. If **the Lord** sees anyone harboring a gloating, vindictive spirit, He will consider that spirit more punishable than the guilt of the enemy.

24:19, 20 Once again we are warned not to get all upset over the apparent success of **evildoers**, and not to envy **the wicked**. This time the reason given is that the prospects of the ungodly are very bad. They have nothing good to look forward to. Instead the light of their life will be extinguished.

24:21, 22 This proverb inculcates reverence and respect for **the Lord and** also for **the king** as His representative. It also warns against **those who** are out to **change** divine institutions or to overthrow civil governments. Both types of rebelliousness will bring sudden and unimaginable **calamity** on the guilty ones.

The Christian is taught to obey human government as long as he can do so without compromising his loyalty to the Lord. If a government orders him to disobey the Lord, then he should refuse and humbly take the consequences. Under no circumstances should he join any plot to overthrow the government.

B. Further Sayings of the Wise (24:23–34)

24:23–26 Here begins a new section of sayings **that belong to the wise**, extending through verse 34.

It is a despicable thing **to show partiality** when judging matters of right and wrong. The judge who blurs moral distinctions by acquitting the guilty will be cursed by the people and hated by nations. On the other hand **those** judges **who rebuke** sin will be rewarded by God and blessed by men. Those who render honest and just verdicts will win the kiss of approval from the people.

24:27 Just as a man must clear away the trees and cultivate the land before building a **house**, so he should get his own life in order before having a family. Thus, the proverb may be a warning against rushing into marriage with all its responsibilities before a person is spiritually, emotionally, and financially prepared.

24:28, 29 Under no circumstance should anyone bring false accusations **against** his **neighbor** or spread lies about him. Even if the neighbor has done those very things, there is no excuse for returning evil for evil.

24:30–34 The writer passed by the sluggard's **vineyard** and saw that **it was all overgrown with thorns**. Plants with stinging hairs or **nettles** were everywhere to be seen. The **stone wall was** in ruins. There was an object lesson in this. When anyone asks for just **a little** more **sleep**, a few more winks, a few more yawns, you can be sure that **poverty** will overtake him like a highwayman and like **an armed** robber.

When we succumb to laziness in spiritual matters, our life (vineyard) becomes infested with the works of the flesh (thistles and nettles). There is no fruit for God. Our spiritual defenses (the wall) are down, and the devil gains a foothold. The result of our coldness and backsliding is poverty of soul.

V. PROVERBS OF SOLOMON COMPILED BY HEZEKIAH'S MEN (25:1—29:27)

25:1 The proverbs contained in chapters 25—29 were composed by Solomon but **copied** years later by the men of **Hezekiah, king of Judah**. There are 140 proverbs, corresponding to the numerical value of the letters in the Hebrew form of the name Hezekiah.

25:2 It is the glory of God to conceal a thing. Think of all the secrets hidden in His natural creation, in His written Word, and in His providential dealings! "He would not be God," said Thomas Cartwright, "if His counsels and works did not transcend human intelligence."

The glory of kings is to search out a matter. In its context, this probably means that a wise king will keep himself informed of important developments affecting his kingdom and will make full investigation in order to render true judgments and formulate sound policies.

The application for us is that we should be diligent in searching out the spiritual treasures that are concealed in the Bible.

25:3 The **height** of **the heavens** seems to be limitless, and the **depth** of **the earth** seem to be **unsearchable**. Likewise there is something inscrutable about the **heart of** noble **kings**; no one knows exactly what they are thinking.

25:4, 5 When **silver** is melted in a crucible, **the dross** or impurities rise to the surface like scum. When this scum is removed, **the silversmith** has molten metal that is suitable for making **jewelry**. The **dross** here symbolizes **wicked** counselors in the king's court. When they are removed, the kingdom is **established** on a righteous basis.

The first thing Christ will do when He returns to reign will be to cleanse His kingdom of rebellion, lawlessness, and everything else that offends.

25:6, 7 It is a wise policy not to push **yourself** to the forefront **in the** royal court, or to seek a place among celebrities. **It is** far **better** to be invited to a place of honor than to seize it and then be publicly humiliated in the king's presence.

This advice is reminiscent of Jeremiah 45:5, "And do you seek great things for yourself? Do not seek them." Also the words of the Lord Jesus in Luke 14:8–10.

The last clause **"whom** (or "what") **your eyes have seen"** should possibly belong to the next verse, as in the RSV, "What your eyes have seen do not hastily bring into court . . . ."

25:8–10 The Bible condemns the litigious spirit, that is, the desire to rush **to** the law **court** to settle every grievance. A person might tell everything he has seen and yet be **put to shame** when his **neighbor** testifies.

It is better to handle grievances privately (see Matt. 18:15), and not to blab about them to others, as an unknown author advises:

> A little disagreement arises with some friends, and you have not the courage to go and speak about it to that friend alone, but mention it to another. The principle laid down in God's Word is forgotten, and mischief follows. Talking about a thing of this kind does no good, and in the end widens the breach. If we would only take such a passage as our guide, and regulate our conduct by it, we would lay aside many trivial "causes" of offense, and spare ourselves many disturbings of mind.

Verse 10 contemplates the third party's rebuking you for not going directly to the offender, and your gaining a **reputation** as a gossip—or worse!

25:11 An appropriate **word . . . is like apples of gold in settings of silver**. The right **word** is as morally beautiful and suitable as the combination of precious and attractive metals.

25:12 **An earring of gold and an ornament of fine gold** enhance physical beauty; so a **wise rebuker** adds moral beauty to the one who is willing to learn.

25:13 Ordinarily **snow** would be a disaster **in** the **time of harvest**. Here it means snow added to a drink of water and given to a reaper in the harvest field.

Just as an iced drink refreshes a man on a hot day, so **a faithful messenger . . . refreshes** those who sent him.

25:14 **Whoever** promises a gift but fails to deliver it is **like clouds and wind** which make people think rain is coming but which pass away **without** bringing **rain**.

Although this proverb does not deal with spiritual gifts, there is a valid application. A man may pretend to be a great teacher or preacher, but it is disappointing when he cannot live up to people's expectations. The Indians used to have a word for it: "Heap big wind—no rain."

25:15 Gentleness and patience will often persuade a prince more than if a person becomes provoked and excited. In the same way, **a gentle tongue** can break **a bone**, that is, it can accomplish more than the crunch of powerful jaws and teeth.

25:16 **Honey** is good when taken in moderation, but too much of a good thing is sickening. We should eat to live, not live to eat. Larry Christenson illustrates:

Some friends of ours have eight children, and they all love ice cream. On a hot summer day, one of the younger ones declared that she wished they could eat nothing but ice cream! The others chimed agreement, and to their surprise the father said, "All right. Tomorrow you can have all the ice cream you want—nothing but ice cream!" The children squealed with delight, and could hardly contain themselves until the next day. They came trooping down to breakfast shouting their orders for chocolate, strawberry, or vanilla ice cream—soup bowls full! Mid-morning snack—ice cream again. Lunch—ice cream, this time slightly smaller portions. When they came in for mid-afternoon snack, their mother was just taking some fresh muffins out of the oven, and the aroma wafted through the whole house.

"Oh goody!" said little Teddy. "Fresh muffins! My favorite!" He made a move for the jam cupboard, but his mother stopped him.

"Don't you remember? It's ice cream day—nothing but ice cream."

"Oh yeah . . . ."

"Want to sit up for a bowl?"

"No thanks. Just give me a one-dip cone."

By suppertime the enthusiasm for an all-ice-cream diet had waned considerably. As they sat staring at fresh bowls of ice cream, Mary—whose suggestion had started this whole adventure—looked up at her daddy and said, "Couldn't we just trade in this ice cream for a crust of bread?"[37]

25:17 Moderation applies not only to honey but to visiting. It is important to know when to leave. You can overstay your welcome.

"How much better is God's friendship than man's!" says Cartwright. "We are the more welcome to God the oftener we come to Him."

25:18 Here are three apt similes for a **man who bears false witness against his neighbor**:

a club—mauling and smashing to pieces.
a sword—with its two sharp cutting edges.
a sharp arrow—piercing and wounding.

25:19 If you bite down hard with a broken tooth, you'll wish you hadn't. If you put your weight on a foot that's out of joint, it will let you down. That's exactly what it's like to put confidence in an unreliable person in time of trouble—painful and disappointing.

25:20 To **sing songs to a heavy heart** is provoking, annoying, unwelcome. It is as unsuitable as taking **away a** man's **garment in cold weather**, or as pouring **vinegar on soda**, causing violent agitation.

Keith Weston told of a fellow minister who was making his first hospital visit. "He found a poor patient with both legs strung up to pulleys, both arms in plaster, and an intravenous in one of them. And he said with his big evangelical smile and taking out his big evangelical Bible, 'Brother, are you rejoicing?' " Weston said, "The minister never told me what the patient said, but it wasn't very polite."[38]

25:21, 22 Paul quotes these verses in Romans 12:20. We can overcome evil with good by repaying every offense or discourtesy with a kindness.

An irate neighbor called a new believer and delivered a violent tirade against the believer's five-year-old daughter for trampled flowers, a broken window, and other offenses. When the neighbor came up for air, the Christian asked her to come over to discuss the matter.

By the time the neighbor arrived, the table had been set for coffee and sweet rolls. "Oh, I'm sorry—you're having company." "No," replied the believer, "I thought we could talk about my daughter over a cup of coffee." The Christian gave thanks for the food and asked for God's wisdom. When she opened her eyes, the visitor was crying. "It's not your daughter, it's mine," blurted the neighbor. "I don't know why I lashed out at you. I just can't cope with my children, my husband, or my home!"

As soon as the neighbor made this admission, the young believer started sharing Christ. Within six weeks the neighbor and her family had been born again.[39]

25:23 **The north wind brings forth rain**; likewise **a backbiting tongue** produces **angry** looks. The angry looks almost surely come from the victim of gossip and they should also come from anyone else who hears it. If people would rebuke the backbiter, he would soon go out of business.

25:24 This is almost identical with 21:9, repeated to emphasize the unpleasantness of living with a nagging woman.

25:25 The gospel is God's **good news from a far country**—heaven. Like **cold water to a** thirsty soul, the gospel is refreshing and thirst quenching.

25:26 When good men bow down **before the wicked**, when they compromise, yield, or fail to stand up for the right, it is like a muddied **spring** or **a polluted well**. You go looking for purity and cleanliness and are disappointed.

25:27 **It is not good to** overindulge in **honey**. "Beyond God's 'enough' lies nausea," writes Kidner, "not ecstasy."

The Hebrew of the second line is obscure, It may mean, as in the NKJV, **to seek one's own glory is not glory** (the "not" is supplied from the first line), or "to search into weighty matters is itself a weight" (JND), or again "to search into weighty matters is glory" (JND margin). All three make good sense.

25:28 A man who has never learned to discipline his life is like an undefended **city**, open to every kind of attack, exposed to every temptation.

26:1 **Snow** is distinctly unseasonable **in summer, and rain in harvest** is injurious as well. It is equally out of place and injurious to honor fools. It is morally unfitting and only encourages them in their folly.

26:2 The **sparrow** and the **swallow** flit and dart in the air but never alight on us. In the same manner, an undeserved **curse** will never land on a person, no matter what superstition says. Balaam tried to curse Israel but couldn't (Num. 23:8; Deut. 23:5).

26:3 Just as it is necessary to use **a whip** on a **horse**, and **a bridle** on **a donkey**, so sharp correction is the only language a fool seems to understand. "Do not be like the horse or like the mule, which have no understanding, which must be harnessed with bit and bridle, else they will not come near you" (Ps. 32:9).

26:4, 5 These two verses present an apparent contradiction. The first says **not** to **answer a fool**, the second says to **answer** him. What is the explanation? The latter part of each verse holds the key.

Do not answer a fool in such a manner that you become a fool in the process. Don't lose your temper, or behave rudely, or speak unadvisedly.

But **answer a fool**. Don't let him off with his folly altogether. Reprove and rebuke him, as **his folly** deserves, so he will not **be wise in his own eyes**.

26:6 To send **a message by the hand of a fool** is to work against your own best interests. It's like cutting **off** your **own** legs or drinking poison. The fool won't deliver the message properly. He will only cause you grief. To cut off the **feet** means to render oneself helpless.

26:7 **The legs of the lame** man **hang limp** and useless. That's the way it is with a **proverb in the mouth of fools**. It is useless to them because they don't know when, where, or how to apply it.

26:8 You shouldn't bind **a stone in a sling**; it should be free for release. It is just as absurd to give **honor to a fool**.

A second possible meaning is that just as a stone is soon parted from a slingshot, so **a fool** will quickly prove himself unworthy of any **honor** that is bestowed upon him.

26:9 When **a drunkard** handles thorns, they are painful and dangerous to himself and others. So a parable **in the mouth of fools** can be misapplied and distorted. He might use it to justify his folly and to draw false conclusions concerning others.

26:10 The Hebrew text of this verse is very obscure, as is seen by the variety of translations:

> "A master roughly worketh everyone: he both hireth the fool and hireth passers-by" (JND).
>
> "Like an archer who wounds everybody is he who hires a passing fool or drunkard" (RSV).
>
> "The law settles quarrels at last, yet silence the fool, and feud there shall be none" (Knox).

"A master performs all things, but he who hires a fool hires a passer-by" (Berkeley).

"Like an archer who wounds everyone, so is he who hires a fool or who hires those who pass by" (NASB).

"An employee who hires any fool that comes along is only hurting everyone concerned" (TEV).

"The great God who formed everything gives the fool his hire and the transgressor his wages" (NKJV).

It is impossible to say which meaning is correct.

26:11 **A dog** is no more revolted by its **own vomit** than **a fool** by **his folly**; they both go back to that which is repulsive and disgusting. This verse is applied in 2 Peter 2:22 to people who experience moral reformation but who are never truly born again. Eventually they revert to their old ways.

26:12 A conceited person is above correction or instruction or rebuke. It is hopeless to try to correct him. An ignorant fool can sometimes be helped by a beating, but the conceited man is impervious to advice.

26:13–16 Here is **the lazy man** again and the imaginary **lion** that prevents his going to work. He **turns,** like **a door on its hinges, . . . on his bed**. Now he lies on his back, now on his front. Back and forth he swings with plenty of motion but no progress toward getting up. Later when he is at the table, he **dips his hand in the bowl** but can't muster up enough energy to lift the food **to his mouth**. Even something as pleasurable as eating is an exhausting effort. He **is wiser in his own eyes than seven men who can** give a proper **answer**; that is, seven intelligent men, unanimous in their insistence that he is wrong, wouldn't change his mind a fraction.

26:17 The passer-by who vexes himself or **meddles in a quarrel** that is none of his business is asking for trouble. It's like grabbing **a dog by the ears**; you don't dare hold on and you don't dare let go.

26:18, 19 Like a **madman** who **throws firebrands** and deadly **arrows** is the man who deals treacherously with **his neighbor** and then, when the harm is done, says, "**I was only** kidding." It is like excusing murder as a joke. This proverb could be applied to irresponsible courtship and engagement.

26:20, 21 Just as fuel feeds a fire, so gossip feeds trouble. Unless a troublemaker keeps adding aggravations and gossip and lies, strife will soon die out.

Some years ago the following appeared in the *Atlanta Journal*:

> I am more deadly than the screaming shell of a howitzer. I win without killing. I tear down homes, break hearts, and wreck lives. I travel on the wings of the wind. No innocence is strong enough to intimidate me, no purity pure enough to daunt me. I have no regard for truth, no respect for justice, no mercy for the defenseless. My victims are as numerous as the sands of the sea, and often as innocent. I never forget and seldom forgive. My name is Gossip![40]

26:22 This is a repetition of 18:8. Fallen human nature eats up gossip as if it were **tasty trifles**.

26:23–26 **Fervent lips with a wicked heart are like earthenware covered with silver dross.** A shining, silvery finish disguises the worthlessness and drabness of the **earthenware** pottery underneath. So lips burning with pretended love often cover a heart full of **hatred**. The pretended affection of Judas, the betrayer, illustrates the point.

The chronic hater tries to hide his enmity with gracious words, at the same time storing **up deceit within**. Though he may speak graciously, you can't trust him. He hides **seven abominations in his heart**, that is, he is full of evil and malice. **Though his hatred** may be hidden for the time **by deceit**, eventually his wickedness will be manifested before all.

26:27 Man's evil recoils upon himself, just as Louis the Strong's workmanship did. He was asked to make chains that would hold the most desperate prisoners during one of the early French wars. He tempered some very fine steel and made chains that were unparalleled for strength.

Later Louis himself was found guilty of treason and sent to prison. He was heard to moan, "These are my own chains! If I had known I was forging them for myself, how differently I would have made them!"

26:28 This proverb castigates the slanderer and the flatterer. The first one **hates** his victims, the second **works ruin** on his.

27:1 No one is sure of **tomorrow**. Therefore, don't **boast** about all you will do, like the rich fool did (Luke 12:16–21). See also Jas. 4:13–15.

27:2 It is in poor taste and very inelegant to **praise** yourself. A truly refined person tries to keep himself in the background, while praising others. "Beware of autobiographies" (Berkeley margin).

27:3 The persistent, provocative remarks of a fool are harder to put up with than a **heavy** physical burden. A man would rather carry **stone** or **sand** than be constantly annoyed by a loud-mouthed fool.

27:4 **Wrath** and anger are **cruel** and overwhelming, yet often they are short-lived. But **jealousy** continually gnaws away at a person and is therefore more grievous. This would apply, for instance, to one whose marriage has been disrupted by a third person.

27:5 A forthright **open rebuke** benefits the recipient but no one benefits from secret **love**, that is, love that refuses to point out a person's failings or is never acknowledged to exist.

27:6 Most people do not want to be honest with you about your faults; they are afraid that you will turn against them. It is a true friend who is willing to risk your goodwill in order to help you by constructive criticism.

The kisses of an enemy are deceitful, or profuse (RSV).

Judas gave a sign to the mob in advance to help them distinguish Jesus from the disciples; the sign was a kiss. The universal symbol of love was to be prostituted to its lowest use.

As he approached the Lord, Judas said, "Hail, Master!" then kissed Him profusely. Two different words for kiss are used (Matt. 26:48,49). The first, in verse 48, is the normal word for kiss. But in verse 49, a stronger word is used, expressing repeated or affectionate kissing.

27:7 A man who is overfed loses his appreciation of the choicest, sweetest foods. A **hungry** person is grateful for the slimmest pickings.

This is true of material possessions and of spiritual privileges.

27:8 **A man who wanders** from his home is one who is discontented and restless. He has the wanderlust. He is **like a bird that** strays **from its nest**, shirking responsibilities and failing to build anything solid and substantial.

27:9 The pleasantness of **ointment and perfume** is compared to the fragrance of loving advice from a **friend**. There is something truly heartwarming about fellowship with a friend.

27:10 Friendships must be cultivated and kept alive. Often the oldest friends are the best. So don't lose touch with your friends or old friends of the family.

"Nor go to your brother's house"—obviously meaning the home of one who has been offended, one who is **far** off. When trouble comes, you will get more help and sympathy from a faithful **neighbor** than from a near relative who is estranged from you.

27:11 A son's behavior reflects on his father's instruction. A disciple brings either joy or shame to his teacher. Berkeley's footnote says it well:

> "The teacher's one defense—the success of his students."

27:12 Noah was **a prudent man**, hiding **himself** and his family in the ark. The rest of the people went on their way carelessly and indifferently and suffered for it. (See notes on 22:3.)

27:13 In modern idiom, the first line means that the man **who is surety for a stranger** will "lose his shirt."

The second line reads, **"and hold it in pledge when he is surety for a seductress."** In other words, be sure you have a legal claim on the property of anyone who will guarantee the debts unworthy of strangers, for if the debtor can't pay, the surety will have to.

27:14 A man doesn't appreciate loud, flattering greetings **early in the morning** when he is trying to sleep. They are more of a nuisance than a blessing.

27:15, 16 The **continual** drip, drip, drip of water through the roof **on a very rainy day** has this in common with a scolding, nagging wife. They are both enough to "drive a person up the wall!"

Whoever restrains her restrains the wind, and grasps oil with his right hand. No matter what you say, she will evade, excuse, blame others—and go right on nagging.

27:17 It used to be common to see the host at a table sharpening the carving knife by drawing each side of the cutting edge against a hardened steel rod with fine ridges. Just as the action of **iron** against **iron sharpens**, so the interchange of ideas among people makes them more acute in their thinking. Sharing each other's opinions gives a helpful breadth of view. Asking questions **sharpens** wits. Friendly intercommunication hones the personality.

27:18 **Whoever** takes good care of a **fig tree** is rewarded by a good crop. Diligence in attending to one's occupation insures food in the pantry or deepfreeze.

It is also true that the one **who** faithfully **waits on his** employer **will be honored**. Jesus said, "If anyone serves Me, him My Father will honor" (John 12:26).

27:19 As you look into a clear pool, you see your **face** reflected **in** the **water**. Even so, as you study other people, you see much that you find in yourself—the same emotions, temptations, ambitions, thoughts, strengths, and weaknesses.

That is why it happens that if a man preaches to himself, he is surprised by how many other people he hits.

27:20 **Hell and Destruction** (Heb. *Sheol* and *Abaddon*), death and the grave never reach the point where they don't claim more victims. **So the eyes of man are never satisfied** by anything the world has to offer. Arthur G. Gish illustrates:

> Tolstoy tells of a farmer who had a lust for more and more land. Finally he heard of cheap land among the Bashkirs. He sold all he had, made a long journey to their territory, and arranged a deal with them. For one thousand rubles he could buy all the land he could walk around in one day. The next morning he set out and walked far in one direction and then turned left. He made many detours to include extra areas of good soil. By the time he made his last turn, he realized he had gone too far. He ran as fast as possible to get back to the starting point before sunset. Faster and faster he ran and finally staggered and fell across the starting point just as the sun set. He lay there dead. They buried him in a small hole, all the land he needed.[41]

Fortunately, the craving of man's heart is fully satisfied in Christ:

> O Christ, He is the fountain,
> The deep sweet well of love!
> The streams on earth I've tasted,
> More deep I'll drink above!
> There, to an ocean fullness,
> His mercy doth expand.
> And glory, glory dwelleth
> In Immanuel's land.
>
> —*Anne Ross Cousin*

27:21 As **a refining pot** or crucible tests **silver**, and **a furnace** tests **gold**, so "a man is tried by his praise." This may mean that **a man** is tested by how he reacts to praise. Does it go to his head and ruin him, or does he accept it calmly and humbly?

Or it may mean that a man is tested by the things that he praises (ASV margin). His standards or sense of values are a reflection of his character.

Or again it might mean, as Barnes suggests, "So let a man be to his praise," that is, "let him purify it from all the alloy of flattery and baseness with which it is too probably mixed up."

27:22 You have probably seen **a mortar** and **pestle** on display in a drug store. The **mortar** is a bowl-shaped object. The **pestle** is a short, thick rod with a globular end and is used for pounding or pulverizing things in the mortar.

Even if you could put **a fool in a mortar** with wheat and pound both **with** the **pestle**, you wouldn't be able to separate the fool and **his foolishness**. In other words, you can separate the wheat from the chaff, but folly is too much a part of **a fool** to take it from him.

27:23–27 This paragraph extols the virtues of agricultural life, but puts ample stress on the importance of the farmer's diligence.

Unwearied and unceasing care must be exercised in tending the **flocks** and **herds**. Pastoral prosperity can only be maintained by constant diligence. This applies with equal force to the shepherding of sheep in a local church.

Riches do not last and the honors of royalty soon pass away unless constant care is exercised in attending to one's affairs.

There is tremendous satisfaction for the farmer in seeing the crops appearing, and in harvesting the vegetation from the hills. **The lambs will provide** wool for **clothing**, and by selling **goats** he can buy additional fields. There is plenty of **food for** his family and for his servants.

28:1 A guilty conscience makes a man jump at the slightest noise. People with a clear conscience don't have to drive with one eye on the rearview mirror; the **righteous are as bold as a lion**.

28:2 When **a land** is guilty of widespread **transgression**, it suffers frequent changes of government. When the ruler is a man of integrity and understanding, the country enjoys a settled, stable condition.

The Northern kingdom (Israel) had 19 kings in the space of about 200 years, or an average of only ten years per reign.

28:3 A poor man who rises to a position of wealth and power is often more oppressive on **the poor** than people from a higher income level would be. He is **like a driving rain** that levels fields of grain, that destroys the crops instead of helping them to grow.

28:4 People who throw off the restraint of God's **law** and of civil law often **praise the wicked**. This, of course, is an attempt to justify themselves.

Those who **keep the law** oppose the transgressors and speak out for the cause of righteousness.

28:5 Evil men do not understand justice; by refusing to practice it, they lose the power to understand it.

Those who seek the Lord's will are given proper powers of discernment. There is a close link between morality and understanding (see Ps. 119:100).

28:6 A **poor** man who lives a clean, honest life is better than a **rich** man who is **perverse in his ways**, who pretends to be living a good life while all the time practicing deceit and treachery.

28:7 A law-abiding **son** is **discerning**. One who associates with **gluttons** and drunkards brings disgrace on **his father**.

28:8 Under the law of Moses, a Hebrew was forbidden to charge **usury** (interest) to another Hebrew. He could charge it to a Gentile but not to a fellow-Jew (Deut. 23:19, 20). Today usury means exorbitant rates of interest.

Those who enrich themselves **by usury** or other forms of illicit revenue will lose their wealth; it will be taken from them and given to someone who knows how to use it better and how to treat **the poor** considerately.

28:9 If **one** will not hear and obey God's **law**, God will not hear **his prayer**. Actually his prayer is hateful to God.

> I may as well kneel down
> And worship gods of stone
> As offer to the Living God
> A prayer of words alone.
>
> —*John Burton*

28:10 Whoever tempts **the upright** to fall into sin **will fall into** a **pit** of punishment. Jesus warned, "Whoever causes one of these little ones who believe in Me to sin, it would be better for him if a millstone were hung around his neck, and he were drowned in the depth of the sea" (Matt. 18:6).

But the blameless will inherit good. Here **the blameless** may mean those who lead others in paths of holiness rather than sin. Or it may mean those who refuse to be victimized by solicitations to sin.

28:11 A **rich man** who glories in his riches thinks he is very clever. Priding himself on his rare financial acumen, he **is wise in his own** conceit. He confuses riches and wisdom.

A **poor** person **who has understanding** can see through such pretension. Charles Lamb once approached one of those swaggering men with the remark, "Excuse me, sire, but are you anybody in particular?"

28:12 When the righteous rise to power, there is great rejoicing. **When the wicked** triumph, **men hide themselves** for fear.

28:13 There are two kinds of forgiveness, judicial and parental. When we trust Christ as Lord and Savior, we receive forgiveness from the penalty of sins; that is judicial forgiveness. When we, as believers, confess our sins, we receive parental forgiveness (1 Jn. 1:9); this maintains fellowship with God our Father.

There is no blessing for the person **who covers his sins**, that is, who refuses to drag them out into the light and to confess them to God and to anyone else who has been wronged. But anyone who **confesses and forsakes** his sins has the assurance that God not only forgives but forgets (Heb. 10:17).

28:14 One element of true happiness is to have a tender heart before the Lord. It is the one who becomes hard and unrepentant who falls into trouble. God can resist the proud and brazen but He cannot resist a broken and contrite heart.

28:15 Beast-like and inhumane describes the tyrant who rides herd **over poor**, weak, and defenseless people. He is **like a roaring lion and a charging bear**.

28:16 Apparently the prince described here is one **who lacks understanding** in the sense that he seeks to enrich himself at all costs. This man **is** also **a great oppressor** because he tramples on others to get richer. The ruler **who hates covetousness** and lives unselfishly for the good of his people **will prolong his days**.

28:17 A man who is burdened with bloodshed will flee into a pit; let no one help him. The willful murderer is a fugitive, racing toward his doom. No one should seek to obstruct or interfere with justice. God has said, "Whoever sheds man's blood, by man his blood shall be shed" (Gen. 9:6).

28:18 The first line refers to salvation from damage in this life, not from damnation in the next. Eternal salvation from the penalty of sin is not obtained by walking uprightly but by faith in the Lord Jesus Christ. The upright walk is a fruit of that salvation, although **whoever walks blamelessly will be saved** from many a snare in this life.

The man who vacillates from one form of crookedness to another will go down in one fell swoop.

28:19 The contrast here is between **plenty of** food and plenty of **poverty**. The diligent farmer has the former. The one who engages in empty, non-productive activities has the latter.

28:20 A faithful man here is one who is honest and who does not covet great wealth. He will be richly blessed. The man who seeks to enrich himself quickly by unscrupulous means will be punished.

28:21 It is rank injustice for a judge **to show partiality**, and yet a man will often do this **for a piece of bread**, that is, for the most trifling consideration.

28:22 A miserly, grudging, ungenerous man races **after riches**, little realizing **that poverty will** soon overtake **him**.

28:23 When a friend lovingly **rebukes** you, it is hard to take at the time. It hurts your pride. But **afterward** you realize that this friend must really have cared for you to point out your faults, and so you are grateful to him.

Flattery may seem pleasant at the time, but eventually you realize that it wasn't true anyway, and that the person was simply trying to gain your favor. **He** probably **flatters** everyone he meets.

28:24 A son who **robs his** parents might excuse it on the grounds that it will be his eventually, or that he has dedicated it to the Lord in the meantime (Mark 7:11). But God is not deceived; He puts that person in the same class as a robber or murderer.

28:25 The proud, grasping person **stirs up strife**, perhaps by pushing everyone else aside in a futile race for riches or power or preeminence (see Jas. 4:1). It is the God-fearing man who succeeds in finding peace and satisfaction.

28:26 **He who trusts in his own** wisdom to guide him through life **is a fool**. He is casting his anchor inside the boat, and thus will drift incessantly. The one who looks to the Lord for guidance acts **wisely** (see Jer. 9:23,24).

28:27 God will reward those who show mercy **to the poor**. The man who turns away **his eyes** from genuine cases of need **will have many** a sorrow.

28:28 **When the wicked** rise to power, the populace **hides** itself for fear. **But when** wicked rulers are overthrown, **the righteous increase**.

29:1 A man who continues in sin, in spite of repeated warnings, **will suddenly be destroyed, . . . without** hope of any further opportunity. The people who lived before the flood refused to listen to Noah. The flood came and they were destroyed.

An acquaintance of mine who had repeatedly rejected the gospel invitation met a Christian lady who had prayed for him often. She said, "Don't you think it's time you turned to the Lord?" He answered, "What has He ever done for me?" That weekend his life was snuffed out in a mysterious mishap. It was one of those accidents that couldn't happen—but did!

29:2 The character of a nation's rulers affects the morale of the country. **When the righteous are in authority**, that is, in numbers and in power, **the people rejoice. A wicked** ruler causes widespread mourning.

29:3 A son who **loves wisdom**, who lives a dedicated, separated Christian life, brings joy to **his father**. But the son who lives in immorality **wastes** his father's money. The prodigal son, you remember, squandered his father's substance in riotous living.

29:4 By acting with **justice**, a **king** brings his country to a position of strength. The one who accepts **bribes** to pervert justice is undermining the stability of the government.

29:5 The flatterer imperils **his neighbor** by refusing to tell him the truth or by praising him for things that are not true. Also he encourages pride which leads to a fall.

29:6 **An evil man** is often **snared** in the net of his own sin. **The righteous** man is happy because he does not have to fear the consequences of transgression. **He sings and rejoices.**

29:7 **Righteous** people take an active interest in **the cause of the poor. The wicked** are not interested in showing any such concern.

29:8 **Scoffers set a city aflame.** They create turmoil by arousing tempers, agitating the people, and creating divisions. **Wise men** seek to avert discord and promote peace.

29:9 This proverb may have two meanings. The more probable is this: When **a wise man** argues **with a foolish man**, the fool will only rage and laugh (NKJV, RSV, Berkeley). He will never be persuaded, and **there** will be **no peace**.

The other interpretation is that when **a wise man** argues **with a foolish man**, whether *the wise man* uses severity **or** humor, it doesn't make any difference. Nothing positive is accomplished.

29:10 Again there are two possible interpretations. One is set forth in the ASV: "The bloodthirsty hate him that is perfect; and, as for the upright, they seek his life." Here the bloodthirsty are the wicked aggressors in each case.

The other meaning is found in the NKJV, JND, and Berkeley. Here **the bloodthirsty** are found destroying life in the first line, **but the upright** are seen seeking to preserve and protect it, in the second line.

29:11 A fool vents all his feelings, but a wise man holds them back. Adams counsels:

> The idea of allowing anger to break out in an undisciplined manner by saying or doing whatever comes into mind without weighing the consequences, without counting ten, without holding it back and quieting it, without hearing the whole story, is totally wrong.[42]

29:12 The thought here seems to be that **if a ruler** wants to be pampered, flattered, and comforted by pleasant news, then **all his servants** will treat him exactly that way. They will lie and flatter.

29:13 There may be a great gulf between **the poor** and **the oppressor** in human society, but they meet on a **common** level before God. It is **the** **Lord** who **gives light** to their **eyes**.

29:14 In judging a ruler, God is especially interested in whether he treats **the poor** considerately and without prejudice. If so, He promises to establish **his throne . . . forever**. Actually we know only one such ruler; His name is Jesus.

29:15 This proverb flatly contradicts many modern specialists who advocate "permissive democracy." **The rod** is corporal punishment; **rebuke** is verbal correction. These two forms of parental discipline impart **wisdom**. They do not inhibit **a child** or warp his personality as the "experts" say.

29:16 When the wicked grow more numerous and powerful, the crime rate rises. **But the righteous will** live to **see their** downfall. Of course there are exceptions, but they are the exceptions that prove the rule.

29:17 A child who has been disciplined properly will bring **delight** and **rest** to his parents instead of anxiety and heartache.

29:18 Where there is no revelation, the people cast off restraint; but happy is he who keeps the law. Here **revelation** means *prophetic* revelation, hence the Word of God (see 1 Sam. 3:1). The thought is that when God's Word is not known and honored, the people run wild. The ones who obey the law, that is, the Word of God, are the truly blessed ones.

29:19 This verse seems to describe the obstinate, intractable attitude of many **a servant**. Oral orders are not always enough. They may understand the master's instructions but they don't always carry them out. They just remain silent and sullen. Jesus said, "Why do you call Me, 'Lord, Lord,' and not do the things which I say?" (Luke 6:46).

29:20 Of all the subjects dealt with in Proverbs, our **words** come in for a lion's share of attention. Here we learn that the man who speaks before he thinks is more hopeless than **a fool**. This puts him in the same class as the man who is wise in his own conceits (26:12).

29:21 If you pamper and spoil a **servant** he will forget his proper position and will soon expect you to treat him like **a son**. Undue familiarity in the employer-employee relationship often breeds contempt.

The word translated **"son"** in the

second line is of very uncertain meaning.

29:22 Most of us have met these two men at one time or another. The **angry man stirs up** all kinds of trouble, and the passionate or **furious man** commits plenty of sins.

29:23 A proud man can be sure of being brought **low**. It is **the humble** man who is elevated to a place of **honor**.

> Professor Smith was climbing the Weisshorn. When near the top the guide stood aside to permit the traveler to have the honor of first reaching the top. Exhilarated by the view, forgetful of the fierce gale that was blowing, he sprang up and stood erect on the summit. The guide pulled him down, exclaiming, "On your knees sir; you are not safe there except on your knees." Life's summits, whether of knowledge, of love, or of worldly success, are full of perils. (*Choice Gleanings*)

> O Lamb of God, still keep me
> Close to Thy pierced side;
> 'Tis only there in safety
> And peace I can abide.
>
> With foes and snares around me,
> And lusts and fears within,
> The grace that sought and found me,
> Alone can keep me clean.
>
> —*James G. Deck*

29:24 An accomplice of **a thief** acts as if he **hates his own life**. Why? Because when **he swears to tell the truth,** that is, when the judge puts him under oath to tell all he knows, he **reveals nothing,** that is, he does not testify, and thus perjures himself. Under the law of Moses, a man who heard the judge putting him under oath and yet refused to testify, was counted guilty and was punished accordingly (see Lev. 5:1). There was no such thing as "pleading the Fifth Amendment."

29:25 **The fear of man** results in yielding to human pressure to commit evil or to refrain from doing what is right. How many have gone to hell because they were afraid of what their friends would say if they trusted Christ!

The man who **trusts in the LORD** is **safe,** come what may. "We fear man so much," wrote William Gurnall, "because we fear God so little."

29:26 **Many** people look to an earthly ruler as if he were the solution to all their problems, **but** it is **from the LORD** that **justice comes**.

29:27 There is no rapport between **an unjust man** and a **righteous** one. The just one looks with disfavor on the ungodly, and the wicked abominates the upright. Just as a straight stick shows up a crooked one, so the contrast between a clean life and a wicked one is glaring.

The proverbs of Solomon end at this point.

VI. THE WORDS OF AGUR (Chap. 30)

30:1 All we know about **Agur** is found in this chapter. He introduces himself as **the son of Jakeh**.

The words **his utterance** (oracle, NIV) may also be translated "of Massa" (RSV). This would identify Agur as a descendant of Ishmael (Gen. 25:14).

The second line may also read, "The man said, 'I have wearied myself, O God, I have wearied myself, O God, and am consumed'" (ASV margin). This leads naturally into what follows—the impossibility of the infinitesimal comprehending the Infinite.

30:2 Agur begins with a confession of his own inability to attain to **understanding**. Apparently it is a statement of genuine humility—a proper attitude for anyone who would inquire into the works and ways of God.

30:3 He does not profess to have **learned wisdom** or to have found God by human searching. He recognizes that he does not have the power in himself to attain to the **knowledge of the Holy One**.

30:4 By a series of questions, he sets forth the greatness of God as He is revealed in nature.

The first describes God as having access to the heights and depths of the universe where no man can follow Him. The second points out His control over the massive power of the **wind**. Third is His might in containing **the waters**, either in clouds above the earth or in the ocean beds. Next is His establishment of the boundaries of the land masses.

What is His name, and what is His Son's name? The thought is, "Who can ever fully know such a great Being, so incomprehensible, so mysterious, so powerful, so omnipresent?" The answer is "No one can ever understand Him fully." But we do know that His name is the Lord (Jehovah) and His Son's name is the Lord Jesus Christ.

This is a text that surprises most Jewish people, who have been taught that God never had a Son. From this verse OT believers could understand that God has a Son.

30:5 Agur now turns from the revelation of God in nature to His revelation in the Word. He asserts the infallibility of the sacred Scriptures—**"every word of God is pure."** Then he speaks of the security of all who **trust in** the God of the Bible—**"He is a shield to those who put their trust in Him."**

30:6 The absolute sufficiency of the Scriptures is asserted next. No man should dare to **add** his thoughts and speculations to what God has spoken.

This verse condemns the cults which give their own writings and traditions the same authority as the Bible.

30:7–9 These verses contain the only prayer in the book of Proverbs. The prayer is short and to the point. It contains two petitions, one covering the spiritual life and the other covering the physical life.

First Agur wanted his life to be worthwhile and honest. He didn't want it to be wasted on trivia. He didn't want to major on minors, And he didn't want to deceive others or to be deceived.

As to the physical, he asked to be delivered from the extremes of **poverty** and **riches**. He would be satisfied with the provision of His daily needs. He was saying, in effect, "Give me this day my daily bread."

He gives reasons for wanting to avoid the twin extremes of affluence and poverty. If he were **full**, he might become independent of the Lord and **deny** Him by not feeling any great need for Him. He might be emboldened to say, **"Who is the LORD?"**—that is, who is He that I should look to Him for what I need or want?

The peril of poverty would be that he might **steal**, and then, to cover up, he might deny under oath that he had done it.

30:10 In what seems to be an abrupt transition, Agur warns against slandering **a servant to his master**. The penalty would be that the **curse** he pronounces against you would come to pass because God is the Defender of the oppressed.

The NT warns us against judging servants of the Lord; to their own Master they stand or fall (Rom. 14:4).

30:11 The **generation** described here bears striking resemblance to the generation living today and to the one which will exist in the last days (2 Tim. 3:1–7). Notice the following features:

Disrespectful to parents. They curse their **father** and show no gratitude to their **mother**, thus breaking the Fifth Commandment. The hostility of young people toward their parents is one of the chief characteristics of our decadent society.

30:12 *Self-righteous.* These people are vile and unclean, yet they have no sense of shame. Outwardly they appear like whitewashed tombs but inwardly they are full of dead men's bones.

30:13 *Pride and arrogance.* They resemble Rabbi Simeon Ben Jochai who said, "If there are only two righteous men in the world, I and my son are the two. If only one, I am he."

30:14 *Fiercely oppressive.* In their insatiable greed for wealth, they rip, tear, and **devour the poor** by long hours, low wages, miserable working conditions, and other forms of social injustice.

30:15, 16 The greed of the oppressors in the preceding verse leads on to other examples of desires that are never satisfied.

1. The **leech** or vampire (ASV margin) is pictured as having **two daughters** who have an endless capacity for sucking blood. They are both named **"Give."**
2. **The grave** never says "No vacancy." Death never takes a holiday, and the tomb never fails to accommodate its victims.
3. **The barren womb** is never willing to accept its sterility but hopes continually for motherhood.
4. **The earth** is **not satisfied with water**, no matter how much rain falls. It can always absorb some more.
5. **The fire never says "Enough!"** It will devour as much fuel as a person wants to feed it.

The expression **"There are three things . . .** yes, **four . . ."** is a literary formula used to produce a sense of climax. Grant indicated that **four** is the number of earthly completeness or universality (as in the four corners of the earth), or of the creature in contrast to the Creator.[43]

30:17 This proverb seems to be isolated from the rest, though similar to verse 11. It teaches that a son who **mocks his father** and disobeys **his mother** will die a violent death and will be denied a decent burial. To the Jewish mind, it was a great tragedy and disgrace for a body to be unburied. The fate of the wayward son is for his carcass to be devoured by vultures.

30:18, 19 Agur lists **four** things that were **too wonderful for** him. As we study them, we have a vague suspicion that there is a spiritual analogy beneath the surface, but what is that analogy and what is the common thread that ties them together? Most commentators suggest that these four things leave no trace behind them. This seems to be confirmed by the way the adulterous woman in verse 20 is able to hide her guilt. Kidner says that the common denominator is "the easy mastery, by the appropriate agent, of elements as difficult to negotiate as air, rock, sea—and young woman."[44]

1. **The way of an eagle in the air.** Here we face the marvel of flight.

The gracefulness and speed of the eagle are proverbial.

2. **The way of a serpent on a rock.** The wonder here is the movement of a reptile without benefit of legs, arms, or wings.
3. **The way of a ship in the midst of the sea.** It is possible that the "ship" here may be a poetic name for fish (see also Ps. 104:26), and that Agur is marveling at the navigational finesse of marine life.
4. **The way of a man with a virgin.** The simplest explanation of this expression refers it to the instinct of courtship. Some, however, take a less idyllic view and apply it to the seduction of a virgin.

30:20 A fifth wonder, apparently thrown in for good measure, is the way **an adulterous woman** can satisfy her lust, then wipe **her mouth** and protest her complete innocence.

30:21–23 Four insufferable things are next listed; they are the kind of things that throw the earth into turmoil.

1. **A servant when he reigns**. He becomes arrogant and overbearing, drunk with his new position.
2. **A fool . . . filled with food**. His prosperity causes him to be more insolent than ever.
3. **A hateful woman** who finally succeeds in getting **married**. Her wretched disposition would normally have kept her single, but by some fluke, she lands a husband. Then she becomes imperious and haughty, taunting those who are still unmarried.
4. **A maidservant who succeeds her mistress**. She doesn't know how to act with refinement and grace, but is coarse, rude, and vulgar.

30:24 Now Agur turns to **four things which** are **wise** out of all proportion to their size.

30:25 1. **The ants** are tiny creatures and seemingly helpless, yet they busy themselves during **the summer** months. Most of the common ant species do not provide for the winter, because, according to the World Book, "Ants cluster together and spend the winter sleeping inside their nests." The harvester ant is an exception, however, since it stores food in warm, dry seasons for later use during cold times. The emphasis in this text, though, is on the ants' busy activity preparing **their food**.

30:26 2. **The rock badgers** are naturally **feeble** and defenseless, yet they have the wisdom to find protection in the rocks. (The **rock badger**, also known as the "hyrax," is not to be confused with the common badger, which is quite a fighter.) Cleft rocks provide the best protection. The spiritual application is found in the hymn, "Rock of Ages, cleft for me."

30:27 3. **The locusts have no** visible ruler, **yet** the order in which they **advance** is remarkable.

30:28 4. **The spider**, or lizard (NASB), is small, yet it succeeds in getting into **king's palaces**. Its access to unlikely and important places is often duplicated by Christians today. God does not leave Himself without a witness, even in courts of royalty.

30:29–31 The final series has to do with **four** examples of stately, **majestic**, or graceful movement.

1. **The lion**, the king of **beasts**, is majestic and unruffled as it walks.

2. There is considerable uncertainty about the second example. It may be a strutting rooster (NIV), a warhorse (JND margin), or **a greyhound**. All these fit the description of lofty dignity, but perhaps the graceful **greyhound** is the best choice.
3. **A** ram or **male goat** is a picture of noble bearing as it strides at the head of a flock.
4. There is also some doubt about the fourth example, whether it should read "a king, against whom there is no rising up" (KJV), "a king striding before his people" (RSV), or **"a king whose troops are with him"** (NKJV). In any case, the point is clear that the king marches with regal dignity.

30:32, 33 The chapter closes with two verses that seem strangely unrelated to what has preceded. Williams paraphrases the verses:

> If feeble man in his folly has lifted up himself against God, or even indulged hard thoughts of Him, let him listen to the voice of wisdom and lay his hand upon his mouth; for otherwise there will be a result as surely as there is a result when milk is churned, the nose wrung, or anger excited.[45]

VII. THE WORDS KING LEMUEL'S MOTHER TAUGHT HIM (31:1–9)

31:1 We have no way of knowing who **King Lemuel** was. His name means "dedicated to God" or "belonging to God." The important thing is that he has preserved for us the wise counsel which **his mother** gave him.

31:2 We might fill in the thought here as follows: "**What** shall I say to you, and **what** gems of wisdom will I pass on to you, **my son**, whom I have dedicated to the Lord?"

31:3 First is a warning to avoid a life of dissipation and sensual lust. *The Speaker's Commentary* points out that "the temptations of the harem were then, as now, the curse of all Eastern kingdoms."

31:4–8 Second is a plea to refrain from the excessive use of **wine** and strong **drink**. The danger for kings is that their ability to judge and to make proper decisions might be impaired by drinking. They might **forget** the standards of **justice** demanded by **the law** and fail to uphold the rights of the downtrodden. The medicinal use of wine is sanctioned as a stimulant for the dying and an anti-depressant for the despondent. It is all right for people like these to **drink**, and to **forget** their need and their **misery**.

31:9 The king should be a responsible spokesman for all who cannot defend themselves, and plead the cause of all who are left **to die**. He should speak up on behalf of **the poor and needy**.

VIII. THE IDEAL WIFE AND MOTHER (31:10–31)

The closing section of the book describes the ideal wife. It is written in the form of an acrostic, each verse beginning with a letter of the Hebrew alphabet in proper order. Knox's translation attempts to reproduce this acrostic style in English, using twenty-two of our twenty-six letters.

31:10–12 **A virtuous** or fine **wife** is one who is capable, diligent, worthy, and good. **Her worth** cannot be measured in terms of costly jewels. **Her husband** can have full confidence in **her**, with no need to fear any **lack of** honest **gain**. Her finest efforts are put forth to help him; she never fails to cooperate.

31:13–15 She is always on the lookout for **wool and flax**, and enjoys converting them into cloth. On her shopping trips, **she is like the merchant ships** that return to port laden with produce **from afar**. See her going to the supermarket, loading her shopping cart with the best bargains. **She also rises** before daybreak to prepare **food for her household**. The **portion** she gives to **her maidservants** may include not only their breakfast but their work assignments for the day.

31:16–18 When she hears that some nearby **field** is for sale, she goes out to see it. It is just what she needs, so she **buys it**, then industriously **plants a vineyard** with money she has earned. She prepares herself for her tasks with great vigor and enthusiasm. She is not afraid of strenuous work. She takes a quiet, humble satisfaction in the results of her labor. After the others have gone to bed, she often works late into the **night**.

31:19–22 She stretches out her hands to the distaff, and her hand holds the spindle, that is, she busies herself spinning wool and flax into yarn and thread. In addition to all this, she finds time to help **the needy**. She unselfishly shares with those who are less fortunate. She does not dread the approach of winter because there is plenty of warm clothing in the closets. **She makes tapestry for herself; her** own **clothing is fine linen and purple**.

31:23 Her husband is a man of prominence in the community. He sits at the **gates** with **the elders**. He can devote himself to public affairs without worrying about conditions at home.

31:24–27 His wife weaves **linen garments and sells them** at the market. She also earns money by **supplying sashes** to **the merchants**. Clothed with industry and dignity, she faces the future with confidence. The instruction she gives to her family is a balance of **wisdom** and **kindness**. She keeps in close touch with the affairs of **her household**, and does not waste time or engage in shallow, unproductive activity.

31:28, 29 Her children realize that she is an outstanding mother, and they tell her so. **Her husband also praises her** as a God-given wife. He says, "There are **many** good wives in the world, **but you excel them all**."

31:30, 31 The writer now adds his *amen* to what the husband has just said. It is true. A woman may have **charm** but no common sense. She may be beautiful but impractical. **But a woman who fears the LORD**, as described above, is the best kind. Let her be honored for her diligence and noble character. When the town fathers meet at the civic center, let them **praise** her outstanding accomplishments.

It is noteworthy and fitting that Proverbs should end on this very positive note about women. Three women have been prominent in this book: the personification of *Wisdom*, seen as a woman inviting learners to her banquet, the immoral woman or *seductress*, and finally, the *"woman* (or wife) *of valor,"* as the literal translation reads in 31:10 (NKJV margin).

ENDNOTES

[1](Intro) Quoted by D. L. Moody in *Notes from My Bible*, p. 81.

[2](Intro) Arnot uses this as the title for his commentary on Proverbs (see Bibliography).

[3](1:8) Henry Bosch, ed., *Our Daily Bread*.

[4](1:19) The Hebrew word for wis-

dom (*ḥokmāh*) is a feminine noun, hence it was natural to personify this virtue as a woman.

[5](1:25) Donald Grey Barnhouse, *Words Fitly Spoken*, p. 239.

[6](3:2) Jay Adams, *Competent to Counsel*, p. 125.

[7](5:18) Michael Griffiths, *Take My Life*, p. 117.

[8](5:22) Adams, *Counsel*, p. 145.

[9](6:16) Derek Kidner, *The Proverbs: An Introduction and Commentary*, p. 73. See similar forms in 30:15, 18.

[10](6:17) J. Oswald Sanders, *On To Maturity*, p. 63.

[11](6:28) Griffiths, *Life*, p. 116.

[12](7:2) *International Standard Bible Encyclopedia*, I:209.

[13](9:18) The French text is as follows:
Plaisir d'amour ne dure qu'une nuit;
Chagrin d'amour dure toute la vie.

[14](10:24) C. S. Lewis, *Weight of Glory*, ed. by Walter Hooper, p. 13.

[15](10:28) G. S. Bowes, quoted in *Our Daily Bread*.

[16](13:4) Bosch, ed., *Daily Bread*,

[17](13:5) J. Allen Blair, further documentation unavailable.

[18](13:7) G. Campbell Morgan, *Searchlights from the Word*, p. 203.

[19](13:10) C. S. Lewis, *Christianity*, pp. 110, 111.

[20](13:24) Benjamin Spock, taken from the Tampa Tribune, Tampa, FL, January 22, 1974.

[21](14:2) Kidner, *Proverbs*, p. 106.

[22](14:30) Paul Adolph, "God in Medical Practice," in *The Evidence of God in an Expanding Universe* by John Clover Monsma, pagination unavailable.

[23](15:1) Charles Haddon Spurgeon, quoted by A. Naismith in *1200 More Notes, Quotes and Anecdotes*, p. 239.

[24](16:3) J. Allen Blair, further documentation unavailable.

[25](16:24) Watchman Nee, *Do All to the Glory of God*, p. 55.

[26](16:32) Henry Durbanville, *Winsome Christianity*, p. 41.

[27](17:17) Moody, *Notes*, p. 83.

[28](17:22) Paul Brock, *Reader's Digest*, September, 1974.

[29](17:22) Blake Clark, *Reader's Digest*, May, 1972.

[30](18:9) Griffiths, *Life*, p. 53.

[31](18:14) Adolph, "God in Medical Practice," pagination unavailable.

[32](18:24) Morgan, *Searchlights*, p. 204.

[33](19:17) Henry Bosch, ed., *Our Daily Bread*.

[34](22:6) Henry Ward Beecher, further documentation unavailable.

[35](22:6) Adams, *Counsel*, p. 158.

[36](22:15) Matthew Henry, *Matthew Henry's Commentary on the Whole Bible*, III:919.

[37](25:16) Larry Christenson, *The Christian Family*, p. 58.

[38](25:20) Keith Weston, further documentation unavailable.

[39](25:21, 22) Sarah Anne Jepson, "Preparing Tables of Forgiveness," *Good News Broadcaster*, June 1975, p. 13.

[40](26:20, 21) *Atlanta Journal*, further documentation unavailable.

[41](27:20) Arthur G. Gish, *Beyond the Rat Race*, p. 91.

[42](29:11) Adams, *Counsel*, p. 221.

[43](30:15, 16) F. W. Grant, *The Numerical Bible*, I:15.

[44](30:18, 19) Kidner, *Proverbs*, p. 180.

[45](30:32, 33) George Williams, *The Student's Commentary on the Holy Scriptures*, p. 437.

BIBLIOGRAPHY

Arnot, William. *Laws for Heaven for Life on Earth*. London: James Nisbet & Co., n.d.

Bridges, Charles. *A Commentary on Proverbs*. Reprint. Edinburgh: The Banner of Truth Trust, 1983.

Delitzsch, Franz. "Proverbs." In *Biblical Commentary on the Old Testament*. Vols. 16, 17. Grand Rapids: Wm. B. Eerdmans Publishing Co., 1971.

Harris, R. Laird. "Proverbs." In *The Wycliffe Bible Commentary*. Chicago: Moody Press, 1962.

Henry, Matthew. "Proverbs." In *Matthew Henry's Commentary on the Whole Bible*. Vol. 3. McLean, VA: MacDonald Publishing Company, n.d.

Ironside, H. A. *Notes on the Book of Proverbs*. Neptune, N.J.: Loizeaux Brothers, 1964.

Jensen, Irving L. *Proverbs*. Everyman's Bible Commentary. Chicago: Moody Press, 1982.

Kidner, Derek. *The Proverbs: An Introduction and Commentary*. Downers Grove, IL: InterVarsity Press, 1964.

MacDonald, William. *Listen, My Son*. Kansas City, KS: Walterick Publishers, 1965.

Plumptre, E. H. "Proverbs." In *Commentary on the Holy Bible* (Speaker's Commentary). London: John Murray, 1873.

Spence, H.D.M., and Joseph S. Exell, eds. "Proverbs." In *The Pulpit Commentary*, Vol. 9. Grand Rapids: Wm. B. Eerdmans Publishing Company, 1909.

ECCLESIASTES

Introduction

"I know nothing grander in its impassioned survey of mortal pain and pleasure, its estimate of failure and success, none of more noble sadness; no poem working more indomitably for spiritual illumination."

—E. C. Stedman

I. Unique Place in the Canon

Ecclesiastes is one book of the Bible whose *uniqueness,* at least, has never been questioned, even though nearly everything else about it *has* been (e.g., its authorship, date, theme, and theology).

The reason this book seems to clash with the rest of the Word of God is that it presents merely human reasoning "under the sun." This phrase, *under the sun,* forms the most important single key to understanding Ecclesiastes. The fact that it occurs twenty-nine times indicates the general perspective of the author. His search is confined to this earth. He ransacks the world to solve the riddle of life. And his whole quest is carried on by his own mind, unaided by God.

If this key—*under the sun*—is not kept constantly in mind, then the book will present mountainous difficulties. It will seem to contradict the rest of Scripture, to set forth strange doctrines, and to advocate a morality that is questionable, to say the least.

But if we remember that Ecclesiastes is a compendium of human, not divine, wisdom, then we will understand why it is that while some of its conclusions are true, some are only half true, and some are not true at all.

Let us take some illustrations. Ecclesiastes 12:1 is true and dependable advice for young people in all ages; they should remember their Creator in the days of their youth. Verse 4 of chapter 1 is only half true; it *is* true that one generation follows another, but it is *not* true that the earth remains forever (see Ps. 102:25–26 and 2 Pet. 3:7, 10). And the following statements, if taken at face value, are not true *at all:* "Nothing is better for a man than that he should eat and drink, and that his soul should enjoy good in his labor" (2:24); "Man has no advantage over animals" (3:19); and "The dead know nothing" (9:5).

However, if we did not have any revelation from God, we would probably arrive at the same conclusions.

Ecclesiastes and Inspiration

When we say that some of the book's conclusions "under the sun" are only half true and that some are not true at all, what does this do to the inspiration of Ecclesiastes? The answer is that it does not affect the question of inspiration in the slightest.

The book is part of the inspired Word of God. It is God-breathed in the sense that the Lord ordained that it should be included in the canon of Scripture. We hold to the verbal, plenary inspiration of Ecclesiastes as we do of the rest of the Bible. (See Introduction to the Old Testament, page 15.)

But the inspired books of the Bible sometimes contain statements by Satan or by men which are not true. In Genesis 3:4, for instance, Satan told Eve that she would not die if she ate the fruit of the tree in the middle of the garden. It was a lie, but it is quoted in the Scripture to teach us that the devil has been a liar from the beginning. As Dr. Chafer observed:

> Inspiration may record the untruth of Satan (or of men) but it does not vindicate the lie or sanctify it. It secures the exact record of what was said—good or bad.[1]

Misuse of Ecclesiastes

For the very reason that it does present human reasoning "under the sun," Ecclesiastes is one of the favorite books of skeptics and of the false cults. They quote it with great enthusiasm to prove their unbelieving or heretical doctrines, especially doctrines dealing with death and the hereafter. For instance, they use verses from this book to teach soul-sleep after death and the annihilation of the wicked dead. They wrench verses out of context to deny the immortality of the soul and the doctrine of eternal punishment.

But they never put the key in the door. They never tell their victims that Ecclesiastes expounds man's wisdom under the sun and therefore is not a valid source of proof texts for doctrines of the Christian faith.

II. Authorship

Until the seventeenth century most Jews and Christians believed Solomon wrote the book of Ecclesiastes. A century before that, the generally conservative Martin Luther rejected Solomonic authorship, but he was an exception.

It will come as a surprise to some to learn that today most Bible scholars—including conservative ones—believe the book was not written by Solomon but was presented in a Solomonic framework, not to deceive, but as a literary device.

The Problem with Solomonic Authorship

The main argument for rejecting the traditional authorship by King Solomon is *linguistic*. That is, many experts say the book contains words and grammatical constructions that did not exist till the Babylonian Captivity or later.

For most evangelicals, the whole idea of putting words into Solomon's mouth seems to be an illegitimate literary device, at least suggesting deception to Western believers.

The arguments pro and con are lengthy and involved, and we cannot go into them here. It is sufficient to say that none of the objections that have been raised against Solomonic authorship are insuperable. Responsible scholars, such as Gleason Archer, show that to believe that Solomon wrote the book is still a live option.[2]

The Arguments for Solomonic Authorship

Since the traditional view has never been really disproved—no matter how unpopular it may be at present—we feel it is safest to maintain the Solomonic authorship.

The *indirect indications* that Solomon wrote this book include the references in 1:1, 12 to the writer as "son of David, king in Jerusalem." While "son" can refer to a later descendant, these phrases, when coupled with the direct details that dovetail with King Solomon's known biography, have real weight.

Since the writer says he "was" king, many take this as proof that the writer no longer was king. Hence, they say, it could not be Solomon, because he died as king. This is not a necessary inference. Writing in his old age it would be quite possible to refer to the distant past in this way.

The *direct historical references* in Ecclesiastes fit Solomon exactly—and really no one else.

Solomon was a king in Jerusalem: (1) of great *wisdom* (1:16); (2) of great *wealth* (2:8); (3) one who denied himself no *pleasure* (2:3); (4) one who had many *servants* (2:7); and (5) one who was noted for a great *building* and *beautification* program (2:4–6).

Jewish tradition[3] ascribes Ecclesiastes to Solomon, and centuries of Christian scholars have followed suit until fairly modern times.

This evidence, coupled with the fact that the linguistic arguments on which non-Solomonic authorship are largely based have been seriously challenged by specialists in Hebrew, makes us opt for the traditional Judeo-Christian view of authorship.

III. Date

If we accept King Solomon as the human author a date of about 930 B.C. is likely, assuming he wrote in old age when he was disillusioned with his self-seeking life.

If Solomon is rejected as "the Preacher" (*Koheleth*), then "dates assigned for the Book range over nearly a thousand years."[4]

Due to what many scholars consider "late" Hebrew (though Archer classifies it as "unique"), Ecclesiastes is generally dated in the *late post-exilic era* (c. 350–250 B.C.). Some evangelicals prefer the immediately preceding *late Persian period* (c. 450–350 B.C.).

The latest possible date for Ecclesiastes is 250–200 B.C., since the apocryphal book of Ecclesiasticus (c. 190 B.C.) definitely makes use of the book, and the Dead Sea Scrolls (late second century B.C.) contain fragments of the book.

IV. Background and Theme

Building a foundation on the Solomonic authorship of Ecclesiastes makes it easier to trace the historical background and theme of the book with some confidence.

Solomon's Search

At one time in his life, Solomon set out to find the true meaning of human existence. He was determined to discover the good life. Richly endowed with wisdom and comfortably cushioned by wealth (1 Kgs. 10:14–25; 2 Chron. 9:22–24), King Solomon thought that if anyone could find lasting satisfaction, he was the one.

But there was a self-imposed condition to Solomon's search. He was going to do this on his own. He hoped that his own intellect would enable him to discover fulfillment in life, quite apart from divine revelation. It would be the exploration of a man without any help from God. He would search "under the sun" for the greatest good in life.

Solomon's Findings

Solomon's search for meaning ended with the dismal conclusion that life is "vanity and grasping for the wind" (1:14). As far as he was able to determine, life under the sun simply wasn't worth the effort. He wasn't able to find fulfillment or lasting satisfaction. In spite of all his wealth and wisdom, he failed to discover the good life.

And of course his conclusion was right. If one never gets *above* the sun, life is an exercise in futility. It is meaningless. Everything that the world has to offer, put together, cannot satisfy the heart of man. It was Pascal who said, "There is a God-shaped vacuum in the human heart." And Augustine observed, "You have made us, O Lord, for Yourself, and our heart will find no rest until it rests in You."

Solomon's experience anticipated the truth of the words of the Lord Jesus, "Whoever drinks of this water will thirst again" (John 4:13). The water of this world cannot provide lasting satisfaction.

Solomon's search for reality was only a temporary phase, a single chapter in his biography. We do not know how old he was when he embarked on this philosophical quest for truth, but apparently he was an older man when he wrote this diary of it (1:12; 11:9). Eventually Solomon did get his sights above the sun; this seems evident from the fact that the greater part of three books of the Bible are attributed to him. However, the sin and failure which clouded the closing years of his life remind us how seriously a believer can backslide, and how imperfect even the most brilliant types[5] of the Lord Jesus are.

Solomon and God

It is obvious that Solomon believed in God, even during the time when he was searching for fulfillment. He makes no less than forty references to Him in Ecclesiastes. But this does not mean that he was a devout believer at that time. The word for "God" which he uses throughout is *Elohim,* the name which reveals Him as the Mighty Creator. Not once does he refer to God as *Jehovah* (LORD, *Yahweh*), the God who enters into covenant relationship with man.

This is an important observation. Man under the sun can know that there is a God. As Paul reminds us in Romans 1:20:

> For since the creation of the world His invisible attributes are clearly seen, being understood by the things that are made, even His eternal power and Godhead, so that they are without excuse.

The existence of God is obvious from creation. Atheism is not a mark of wisdom but of willful blindness. Solomon, the wisest man who ever lived, groping for truth with his own mind, acknowledged the fact of a Supreme Being.

But while anyone can know that there is a God (*Elohim*) who created all things, God as *Jehovah* can only be known by special revelation. So the repeated references to God (*Elohim*) in this book should not be equated with saving faith. All they prove is that creation witnesses to the existence of God, and that people who deny it are fools (Ps. 14:1; 53:1).

The Need for Ecclesiastes

The question inevitably arises, "Why did God ordain that a book which never rises above the sun should be included in the Holy Bible?"

First of all, the book was included so that no one will ever have to live through Solomon's dismal experience, searching for satisfaction where it cannot be found.

Natural man instinctively thinks he can make himself happy through possessions, pleasure, or travel on the one hand, or through drugs, liquor, or sexual indulgence on the other. But the message of this book is that someone wiser and wealthier than any of us will ever be in this life has tried and failed. So we can save ourselves all the expense, heartache, frustration, and disappointment by looking above the sun to the One who alone can satisfy—the Lord Jesus Christ.

But there is a further value to this unique book for those who are not yet ready to accept the gospel. As Dr. W. T. Davison put it:

> There is no need to point at length the contrast between Ecclesiastes and Christ's Gospel. There is perhaps some need to insist on the fact that the appearance of the new Evangel has not made void or useless the Wisdom-Literature of an earlier age. It did its work in its own time, and it has work to do still. There are times in a man's history when he is not ready to sit at the feet of Jesus, and when it is better for him to go to school to Koheleth. The heart must be emptied before it can be truly filled. The modern preacher has often to enforce the lesson, not yet obsolete, nor ever to become obsolete, "Fear God and keep His commandments, for this is the whole duty of man." He must come to Christ to learn how to do this effectively, and to be taught those higher lessons for which this does but prepare the way.[6]

OUTLINE

I. PROLOGUE: ALL IS VANITY UNDER THE SUN (1:1–11)

II. ALL IS VANITY (1:12—6:12)
   - A. The Vanity of Intellectual Pursuits (1:12–18)
   - B. The Vanity of Pleasure, Prestige, and Affluence (Chap. 2)
   - C. The Vanity of the Cycle of Life and Death (Chap. 3)
   - D. The Vanity of Life's Inequalities (Chap. 4)
   - E. The Vanity of Popular Religion and Politics (5:1–9)
   - F. The Vanity of Passing Riches (5:10—6:12)

III. ADVICE FOR LIFE UNDER THE SUN (7:1—12:8)
   - A. The Good and the Better Under the Sun (Chap. 7)
   - B. Wisdom Under the Sun (Chap. 8)
   - C. Enjoying Life Under the Sun (Chap. 9)
   - D. The Wise and the Foolish Under the Sun (Chap. 10)
   - E. Spreading the Good Under the Sun (11:1—12:8)

IV. EPILOGUE: THE BEST THING UNDER THE SUN (12:9–14)

Commentary

I. PROLOGUE: ALL IS VANITY UNDER THE SUN (1:1–11)

1:1 The author introduces himself as **the Preacher, the son of David, king in Jerusalem**. That word *Preacher* is interesting. The Hebrew equivalent is *Koheleth,* and it means "caller" or "congregator." The Greek is *ekklēsiastēs,* meaning, "one who convenes an assembly." From there it has been variously interpreted as meaning "convener, assembler, speaker, debater, spokesman, and preacher."

The Preacher was **the son of David**. While *son* here could admittedly mean a grandson or an even later descendant, the first sense probably makes the best sense. Solomon was the only descendant of David who was **king** over Israel *in Jerusalem* (v. 12). All the rest were kings over Judah. Those of other dynasties who were kings over Israel used Shechem (1 Kgs. 12:25) or Samaria (1 Kgs. 16:24), and not Jerusalem as their capital.

1:2 Solomon comes to the point right away; we don't have to wait till the last chapter. The result of all of Solomon's investigation and research under the sun is that **all is vanity**. Life is transitory, fleeting, useless, empty, and futile. It has no meaning. Nothing on this earth provides a valid goal of existence.

Is that true? Yes, it is absolutely true! If this life is all, if death draws a final curtain on human existence, then life is nothing but a vapor—unsubstantial and evanescent.

The Apostle Paul reminds us that the whole creation was subjected to vanity or futility as a result of the entrance of sin (Rom. 8:20). And it is not without significance that the first parents named their second son Abel, which means "vanity" or "vapor." Solomon is right. **All is vanity** under the sun.

1:3 Frail man's life is filled with **labor** and activity, but where does it get him when all is said and done? He is on a treadmill, a tiresome round of motion without progress. You ask him why he works, and he replies, "To get money, of course." But why does he want money? To buy food. And why does he want food? To maintain his strength. Yes, but why does he want strength? He wants strength so he can work. And so there he is, right back where he began. He works to get money to buy food to get strength to work to get money to buy food to get strength, and so on, ad infinitum. As Henry Thoreau observed, he lives a life of quiet desperation.

Seeing a woman crying at a bus stop, a Christian asked her if he could be of any help. "Oh," she replied, "I'm just weary and bored. My husband is a hard worker, but he doesn't earn as much as I want. So I went to work. I get up early every morning, fix breakfast for our four children, pack lunches, and take a bus to my job. Then I return home for more drudgery, a few hours of sleep, and another day just like the one before. I guess I'm just sick of this endless routine."

It was H. L. Mencken who said:

> The basic fact about human experience is not that it is a tragedy, but that it is a bore. It is not that it is predominantly painful, but that it is lacking in any sense.[7]

1:4 The transience of man stands in stark contrast to the seeming permanence of his natural environment. **Generation** succeeds **generation** with irresistible momentum. This is life under the sun.

> Each one dreams that he will be
> enduring,
> How soon that one becomes the
> missing face![8]
> —*Will H. Houghton*

Apart from revelation, we might think that **the** present **earth** *will* last **for-**

ever. That is what Solomon concludes. But Peter tells us that the earth and the works that are upon it will be burned up in the coming Day of the Lord (2 Pet. 3:10).

1:5 Nature moves in a continuous, inexorable cycle. For instance, **the sun . . . rises** in the east, swings through the heavens to set in the west, then **hastens** around the other side of the world to rise in the east again. This seemingly endless pattern, age after age, makes man realize that he is nothing but a passing shadow.

If any are tempted to accuse Solomon of a scientific blunder for describing the sun as moving when actually it is the earth that moves in relation to the sun, they should hold their fire. He was merely using the language of human appearance. The sun *appears* to rise and set. Even scientists use this language all the time, and it is so readily understood that it should not require explanation.

1:6 Solomon continues the thought into verse 6. **The wind** patterns change with the same regularity as the seasons of the year. In the winter, the north winds sweep down over Israel to the Negev, the desert in **the south**. Then when summer comes, the south winds carry warmth on their northward flights. With almost dreary sameness, they follow this **circuit**, and then, with callous disregard for the world of men, pass off the scene.

1:7 Not only the earth, the sun, and the wind, but the water follows its same monotonous routine throughout the centuries. **All the rivers run into the sea** but never to the point where the ocean overflows, because the sun evaporates enormous quantities of water. Then as air cools, the vapor condenses and forms clouds. The clouds in turn scud across the skies and drop the water over the land areas in the form of rain, snow, or hail. And as the rivers are fed with the surplus, they bear the water back to the ocean. The ceaseless activity of nature reminds man of his own unending labor. Perhaps Kristofferson had this verse in mind when he wrote, "I'm just a river that rolled forever and never got to the sea."

1:8 Thus the life that is confined to this earth is full of weariness. Human language is inadequate to describe the monotony, boredom, and futility of it all. Man is never **satisfied**. No matter how much he sees, he still wants more. And his ears never reach the stage where they don't want to hear something new. He travels incessantly and frenetically for new sensations, new sights, new sounds. He is after what an American sociologist calls the fundamental wish for new experience. But he returns dissatisfied and jaded. Man is so constituted that all the world cannot bring lasting happiness to his heart. This does not mean that his case is hopeless. All he needs to do is get above the sun to the One who "satisfies the longing soul, and fills the hungry soul with goodness" (Ps. 107:9).

> Worldly joy is fleeting—vanity itself;
> Vain the dazzling brightness, vain
> the stores of wealth;
> Vain the pomp and glory; only Thou
> canst give
> Peace and satisfaction while on earth
> we live.
> There is none, Lord Jesus, there is
> none like Thee
> For the soul that thirsteth, there is
> none like Thee.[9]
>
> —*Author unknown*

1:9 An additional feature of Solomon's disillusionment was the discovery that **there is nothing new under the sun**. History is constantly repeating itself. He longed for new thrills, but before long, he found everything was, in its own way, "a bad trip."

1:10 Is it true that there is nothing really **new**? Yes, in a sense. Even the most modern discoveries are developments of principles that were locked into creation at the beginning. Many of man's most boasted achievements have their counterparts in nature. Birds flew long before man did, for instance. Even space travel is not new. Enoch and Elijah were transported through space without even having to carry their own oxygen supplies with them! So those who spend their lives searching for novelties are bound to be disappointed. **It has already** happened **in ancient times**, long **before** we were born.

1:11 Another bitter pill that man has to swallow is the speed with which he forgets and is forgotten. Lasting fame is a mirage. Many of us would have great difficulty in naming our great-grandparents. And fewer, perhaps, could name the last four vice-presidents of the United States. In our self-importance, we think that the world can't get on without us; yet we die and are quickly forgotten, and life on the planet goes on as usual.

II. ALL IS VANITY (1:12—6:12)

A. The Vanity of Intellectual Pursuits (1:12–18)

1:12 So much for Solomon's conclusions. Now he is going to retrace for us the pilgrimage he made in search of the *summum bonum*—the greatest good in life. He reminds us that he **was king over Israel in Jerusalem**, with all that implies of wealth, status, and ability.

When Solomon says **I . . . was king**, he does not mean that his reign had ended. He **was king** and still is king (v. 1).

1:13 Here Solomon begins his search for happiness **under the sun**. First, he decides to travel the intellectual route. He thinks he might be happy if he could just acquire enough knowledge. So he applies himself to get the most comprehensive education possible. He devotes himself to research and exploration, synthesis and analysis, induction and deduction. But he soon becomes disenchanted with learning as an end in itself. In fact, he says that it is an unhappy business with which **God** allows men to occupy themselves—this deep inner drive to find out the meaning of life.

Malcolm Muggeridge, a contemporary sage, reached a similar conclusion:

> Education, the great mumbo-jumbo and fraud of the ages, purports to equip us to live, and is prescribed as a universal remedy for everything from juvenile delinquency to premature senility. For the most part, it only serves to enlarge stupidity, inflate conceit, enhance credulity and put those subjected to it at the mercy of brainwashers with printing presses, radio and television at their disposal.[10]

Recently someone painted this telling graffiti in bold, black letters on the wall of a university library: APATHY RULES. Someone had found what Solomon had learned centuries earlier—that education is not the sure road to fulfillment, but that, taken by itself, it can be a bore.

This does *not* mean that intellectual pursuit cannot play an important role in life. There is a place for it, but that place is at the feet of Christ. It should not be an end in itself but a means of glorifying Him.

The reference to **God** in this verse must not be equated with deep personal faith. The name of *God* is what W. J. Erdman calls His natural name—*Elohim*.[11] As mentioned in the introduction, this name presents Him as the Almighty One who created the universe. But nowhere in this book does Solomon acknowledge Him as the covenant-keeping Jehovah who shows redeeming grace to those who put their trust in Him.

1:14 There can be no doubt that Solomon got the best education that was available in Israel at that time. This is apparent from his unblushing claim to **have seen** everything that is **done under the sun**. What this means is that he became highly knowledgeable in the sciences, philosophy, history, the fine arts, the social sciences, literature, religion, psychology, ethics, languages, and other fields of human learning.

But an alphabet of degrees after his name and a room papered with diplomas didn't give him what he was seeking. On the contrary, he concluded that it was **all** a **grasping for** something as elusive as **the wind**.

1:15 He was frustrated to discover that book learning doesn't solve all the puzzles of life. There are **crooked** things that **cannot be made straight** and missing things that **cannot be numbered**. Robert Laurin observed:

> Life is full of paradoxes and anomalies that cannot be solved; and contrariwise, it is empty of so much that could give it meaning and value.[12]

Man can fly to the moon, but the flight of a bee defies all known laws of aerodynamics. Scientists have delved into the secrets of the atom, but they cannot harness lightning or store its power. Diseases such as polio and tuberculosis have been controlled, but the common cold is still unconquered.

1:16 After he had won all his academic laurels, Solomon took personal inventory. He could boast that he had more **wisdom** than **all** those **who** had ruled **before** him **in Jerusalem** (1 Kgs. 4:29–31; 2 Chron. 1:12). His mind had absorbed an enormous fund of knowledge. And he had **wisdom** as well; he knew how to apply his **knowledge** to the practical, everyday affairs of life, to make sound judgments, and to deal judiciously with others.

1:17 Solomon reminisced about how he had disciplined himself to acquire **wisdom** on the one hand, and to learn about **madness and folly** on the other. In other words, he explored both extremes of human behavior, just in case the true meaning of life was found in either or in both. He ran the gamut of life's experiences, but his disconsolate conclusion was that it was all a **grasping for the wind**.

Centuries later, a young fellow named Henry Martyn sought and won top honors at Cambridge University. Yet in the hour of his academic triumph, he said, "I was surprised to find I had grasped a shadow." It was a blessed disillusionment for, as J. W. Jowett noted, "His eyes were now lifted far above scholastic prizes to the all-satisfying prize of the high calling of God in Christ Jesus our Lord."

1:18 If intellectualism is the key to meaning in life, then our college campuses would be Camelots of peace and contentment. But they are not. Rather they are cauldrons of ferment and unrest. The timeworn caricature of a college student, swathing his head in a turkish towel and washing down aspirin with huge mugs of coffee, fits in well with Solomon's conclusion in verse 18:

> **For in much wisdom is much grief,**
> **And he who increases knowledge**
> **increases sorrow.**

In other words, "The wiser you are the more worries you have; the more you know, the more it hurts." According to this, there is *some* truth to the adages, "Ignorance is bliss," and "What you don't know won't hurt you."

B. The Vanity of Pleasure, Prestige, and Affluence (Chap. 2)

2:1 Having failed to find fulfillment in intellectual pursuit, Solomon turns next to the pursuit of **pleasure**. *It seems reasonable that one would be happy if one could just enjoy enough pleasure,* he thought. Pleasure, by definition, means the enjoyable sensations that come from the gratification of personal desires. So he decided that he would live it up, that he would try to experience every stimulation of the senses known to man. He would drink the cup of fun to the full, and then, at last, his heart would ask no more.

But the search ended in failure. He concludes that pleasures under the sun are **vanity**. His disappointment is echoed in the verse:

> I tried the broken cisterns, Lord,
> But ah, the waters failed,
> E'en as I stooped to drink they fled
> And mocked me as I wailed.[13]
>
> —*B. E.*

Does this mean that God is opposed to His people having pleasure? Not at all! In fact the reverse is true. God wants His people to have a good life. But He wants us to realize that this world cannot provide true pleasure. It can only be found above the sun. In His "presence is fullness of joy"; at His "right hand are pleasures forevermore" (Ps. 16:11). In that sense, God is the greatest hedonist or pleasure-lover of all!

The big lie promulgated by the movies, TV, and the advertising media is that man can make his own heaven down here without God. But Solomon learned that all this world can offer are cesspools and cisterns, whereas God offers the fountain of life.

2:2 As he thinks back on all the empty **laughter**, he sees that it was mad, and all his good times actually accomplished nothing. And so it is. Behind all the laughing there is sorrow, and those who try to entertain others are often in great need of personal help.

Billy Graham tells in *The Secret of Happiness* of the disturbed patient who consulted a psychiatrist for help. He was suffering from deep depression. Nothing he had tried could help. He woke up discouraged and blue, and the condition worsened as the day progressed. Now he was desperate; he couldn't go on this way. Before he left the office, the psychiatrist told him about a show in one of the local theaters. It featured an Italian clown who had the audience convulsed with laughter night after night. The doctor recommended that his patient attend the show, that it would be excellent therapy to laugh for a couple of hours and forget his troubles. Just go and see the Italian clown! With a hangdog expression, the patient muttered, "I am that clown." He too could say **of laughter—"Madness!"; and of mirth, "What does it accomplish?"**

How often in life we look at others

and imagine that they have no problems, no hangups, no needs. But E. A. Robinson shatters the illusion in his poem, "Richard Cory":

Whenever Richard Cory went down
  town,
We people on the pavement looked
  at him:
He was a gentleman from sole to
  crown,
Clean favored, and imperially slim.

And he was always quietly arrayed,
And he was always human when he
  talked;
But still he fluttered pulses when he
  said,
"Good morning," and he glittered
  when he walked.

And he was rich—yes, richer than a
  king—
And admirably schooled in every
  grace;
In fine, we thought that he was
  everything
To make us wish that we were in his
  place.

So on we worked, and waited for the
  light,
And went without the meat, and
  cursed the bread;
And Richard Cory, one calm summer
  night,
Went home and put a bullet through
  his head.[14]

2:3 Next Solomon, the OT prodigal, turns to **wine**. He would become a connoisseur of the choicest vintages. Perhaps if he could experience the most exquisite taste sensations, his whole being would relax satisfied.

He was wise enough to place a bound on his Epicureanism. It is expressed in the words **while guiding my heart with wisdom**. In other words, he would not abandon himself to intemperance or drunkenness. There was no thought of his becoming *addicted* to strong drink. And nowhere in his search for reality did he suggest that he became hooked on drugs. He was too wise for that!

Another thing he tried was **folly**, that is, harmless and enjoyable forms of nonsense. Just in case **wisdom** didn't hold the answer, he decided to explore its opposite. Sometimes people who are clods seem to be happier than those who are very clever. So he didn't want to leave that stone unturned. He turned his attention to trivia, indulgence, and amusement. It was a desperate ploy to discover the best way for man to occupy himself during his few fleeting **days** under the sun. But he didn't find the answer there.

2:4, 5 So Solomon decided to embark on a vast real estate program. If education, pleasure, wine, or folly didn't hold the key, then surely possessions would. He built luxurious **houses, and planted** for himself **vineyards** by the acre. From what we know of Solomon's building programs, we can be sure that he spared no expense.

He built enormous estates with parks and **gardens**—literal paradises. **Orchards** with **all kinds of fruit trees** punctuated the landscape. It's easy to imagine him taking his friends on guided tours and having his ego inflated by their expressions of awe and enthusiasm.

Probably none of his guests had the courage to say to him what Samuel Johnson said to a millionaire who was taking a similar ego trip. After seeing all the luxury and magnificence, Johnson remarked, "These are the things that make it hard for a man to die."

The world still has its share of the deluded millionaires, like the king in Andersen's tale, *The Emperor's Clothes*.

This king went on parade in what he wanted to believe were stunningly beautiful clothes, but a little child could see that he was stark naked.

2:6 Such vast estates needed irrigation during the hot, dry summers. So Solomon constructed aqueducts, lakes, and ponds, with all the necessary canals, ditches, and ducts to transport the **water**.

If the accumulation of possessions could guarantee peace and happiness, then he had arrived. But like the rest of us, he had to learn that true pleasure comes from noble renunciations rather than from frenzied accumulations. He was spending his money for what is not bread and his wages for what does not satisfy (Isa. 55:2).

2:7 Battalions of **servants** were needed to operate and maintain the king's grandiose estates, so he hired **male and female** slaves. What is more, he had slaves that were **born in** his **house**—an exceptionally important status symbol in the culture of that time.

To Solomon, as to most men, one aspect of greatness lay in being served. To sit at the table was greater than to serve. A greater than Solomon came into the world as a Slave of slaves and showed us that true greatness in His kingdom lies in servanthood (Mark 10:43–45; Luke 9:24–27).

The largest **herds and flocks** ever owned by any resident of **Jerusalem** grazed in the pastures of Solomon's ranches. If prestige was the key to a happy life, then he held the key. But it wasn't, and he didn't. Someone has said, "I asked for all things that I might enjoy life; I was given life that I might enjoy all things."

2:8 And what shall we say about his financial resources! He had **silver and gold** in abundance and the **treasure of kings and of the provinces**. This may mean the taxes which he collected from those under him or wealth taken from conquered territories, or it may refer to objects of art which were presented to him by visiting dignitaries, such as the Queen of Sheba.

He tried music. Music has power to charm, they say. So he assembled the finest **singers**, both **male and female**. The Jerusalem News probably carried rave reviews of all the public concerts. But of course the king had private performances too—dinner music, chamber ensembles—you name it. Yet I think his disappointment was well expressed by Samuel Johnson in *The History of Rasselas, The Prince of Abyssinia*:

> I likewise can call the lutanist and the singer, but the sounds that pleased me yesterday weary me today, and will grow yet more wearisome tomorrow. I can discover within me no power of perception which is not glutted with its proper pleasure, yet I do not feel myself delighted. Man has surely some latent sense for which this place affords no gratification, or he has some desires distinct from sense which must be satisfied before he can be happy.[15]

And he tried sex. Not just wine (v. 3) and song (v. 8) but women as well. Wine, women, and song! The meaning of the word translated **musical instruments** in NKJV is actually unknown, and this rendering was chosen chiefly by context. The NASB renders the last clause "the pleasures of men—many concubines." The Bible tells us factually (though not approvingly) that Solomon had 700 wives and 300 concubines (1 Kgs. 11:3). And did he suppose this was the way to happiness? Just think of all the jealousy, gossip, and backbiting possible in such a harem!

And yet the delusion persists in our own sick society that sex is a highway to happiness and fulfillment. Within the God-appointed bounds of monogamous marriage, that can be true. But the abuse of sex leads only to misery and self-destruction.

A victim of today's sex-obsession felt afterward that she had been cheated. She wrote:

> I guess I wanted sex to be some psychedelic jackpot that made the whole world light up like a pinball machine, but when it was all over I felt I had been shortchanged. I remember thinking, "Is that all there is? Is that all there *really* is?"[16]

2:9 So Solomon **became great**. He had the satisfaction of outclimbing **all** his predecessors on the prestige ladder—for whatever that satisfaction is worth. And his natural **wisdom** still **remained with** him after all his experiments and excursions. He hadn't lost his head.

2:10 In his search for satisfaction, he had placed no limits on his expenditures. If he saw something he **desired**, he bought it. If he thought he'd enjoy some pleasure, he treated himself to it. He found a certain sense of gratification in this ceaseless round of getting things and doing things. This fleeting joy was all the **reward** he got for his exertions in pursuing pleasure and possessions.

2:11 **Then** he took stock of all that he had done, and of all the energy he had expended, and what was the result? **All was vanity** and futility, a **grasping for the wind**. He hadn't found lasting satisfaction under the sun. He found, like Luther, that "the empire of the whole world is but a crust to be thrown to a dog." He was bored by it all.

Ralph Barton, a top cartoonist, was bored too. He wrote:

> I have few difficulties, many friends, great successes. I have gone from wife to wife, from house to house, and have visited great countries of the world. But I am fed up with devices to fill up twenty-four hours of the day.[17]

The failure of pleasure and possessions to fill the heart of man was further illustrated by a fictional character who only had to wish for something and he got it instantly:

> He wanted a house and there it was with servants at the door; he wanted a Cadillac, and there it was with chauffeur. He was elated at the beginning, but it soon began to pall on him. He said to an attendant, "I want to get out of this. I want to create something, to suffer something. I would rather be in hell than here." And the attendant answered, "Where do you think you are?"[18]

That is where our contemporary society is—in a hell of materialism, trying to satisfy the human heart with things that cannot bring lasting enjoyment.

2:12 Because of the disheartening outcome of all his research, Solomon began **to consider** whether it's better to be a wise man or a fool. He decided to look into the matter. Since life is such a chase after bubbles, does the man who lives prudently have any advantage over the one who goes to the other extreme, having a good time in **madness and folly**?

Being an absolute monarch, and a wise and wealthy one at that, he was in a good position to find out. If he couldn't find out, what chance did anyone succeeding him have? Anyone **who succeeds the king** could scarcely discover any new light on the subject.

2:13 His general conclusion was that **wisdom** is better than **folly** to the same degree that **light excels darkness**. The wise man walks in the light and can see the dangers in the way. The fool, on the other hand, gropes along in darkness and falls into every ditch and trap.

2:14 But even granting that advantage—that **the wise man's eyes** can see where he's going—what final difference does it make? They both die eventually and no amount of wisdom can delay or cancel that appointment. It is the lot of **them all**.

2:15 When Solomon realized that the same fate was awaiting him as awaited **the fool**, he wondered why he had put such a premium on being **wise** all his life. The only redeeming feature of wisdom is that it sheds light on the way. Apart from that, it is no better. And so the pursuit of wisdom is also a great waste of effort.

2:16, 17 He continues this idea into verses 16 and 17. After the funeral, both the wise man and the fool are quickly forgotten. Within a generation or two, it is as if they had never lived. The names and faces that seem so important today will fade into oblivion. As far as lasting fame is concerned, **the wise** man is no better off than **the fool**.

The chilling realization that fame is ephemeral and that man is quickly **forgotten** made Solomon hate **life**. Instead of finding satisfaction and fulfillment in human activity under the sun, he found only grief. It troubled him to realize that everything was **vanity and grasping for the wind**.

A former athlete who had achieved fame said:

> The greatest thrill of my life was when I first scored the decisive goal in a big game and heard the roar of the cheering crowds. But in the quiet of my room that same night, a sense of the futility of it swept over me. After all, what was it worth? Was there nothing better to live for than to score goals? Such thoughts were the beginning of my search for satisfaction. I knew in my heart that no one could meet my need but God Himself. Soon after, I found in Christ what I could never find in the world.[19]

2:18 One of the greatest injustices that bothered Solomon was that he would not be permitted to enjoy the wealth which he had accumulated. C. E. Stuart wrote:

> Death is a worm at the root of the tree of pleasure. It mars pleasure, it chills enjoyment, for it cuts off man just when he would sit down after years of toil to reap the fruit of his labor.[20]

And he has to **leave it** all to his heir.

2:19 The galling thing is that the heir may not **be wise**. He may be a spendthrift, a dummy, a playboy, a loafer, but he will inherit the estate nevertheless. He will preside over the dissipation of a fortune for which he neither labored nor planned.

This really nettled Solomon. Perhaps he had a premonition that it would happen in his own family. Perhaps Solomon foresaw that his son, Rehoboam, would squander by his folly all that he had **toiled** so hard to accumulate. History tells us that Rehoboam did just that. By refusing to listen to his older counselors, he precipitated the division of the kingdom. When the Egyptians invaded Judah, he bought them off by giving them the temple treasures. The gold shields went to swell the coffers of Egypt, and Rehoboam had to substitute brass shields in their place (see 2 Chron. 12:9–10).

2:20 The prospect of having to leave his life's work and wealth to an unworthy successor plunged the Preacher into gloom and depression. It seemed so senseless and incongruous. It made him feel that all his efforts were for nothing.

2:21 The whole idea distressed him, that a man who builds up financial resources through wise investments, shrewd business decisions, and skillful moves is forced at death to leave it to someone who never did a lick of work for it or expended an ounce of worry. What is this but an absurdity **and a great** calamity?

In spite of Solomon's finding, parents throughout the world still spend the best part of their lives accumulating wealth that will be left to their children. They altruistically describe it as their moral obligation. But Jamieson, Fausset, and Brown suggest, "Selfishness is mostly at the root of worldly parents' alleged providence for their children."[21] Their first thought is to provide luxuriously for their own old age. They are thinking primarily of themselves. That their children inherit what is left is only the result of the parents' death and the laws of inheritance.

From the Christian perspective, there is no reason for parents to work, scrimp, save, and sacrifice in order to leave money to their children. The best heritage to bequeath is spiritual, not financial. Money left in wills has often caused serious jealousy and disunity in otherwise happy and compatible families. Children have been ruined spiritually and morally by suddenly becoming inheritors of large bequests. Other evils almost inevitably follow.

The spiritual approach is to put our money to work for God *now* and not to leave it to children who are sometimes unworthy, ungrateful, and even unsaved. Martin Luther felt he could trust his family to God as he had trusted himself. In his last will and testament he wrote:

> Lord God, I thank You, because You have been pleased to make me a poor and indigent man upon earth. I have neither house nor land nor money to leave behind me. You have given me wife and children, whom I now restore to You. Lord, nourish, teach and preserve them, as You have me.

2:22 Solomon concludes that **man** has nothing of enduring value as a result of **all his labor** and heartache **under the sun**. He strives, he plods, he frets and fumes—but for what? What difference does it all make five minutes after he dies?

Apart from revelation, we would come to the same conclusion. But we know from God's Word that our lives can be lived for God and for eternity. We know that all that is done for Him will be rewarded. Our labor is not in vain in the Lord (1 Cor. 15:58).

2:23 For the man who has no hope beyond the grave, however, it is true that his days are filled with pain and vexatious **work**, and his nights with tossing and turning. Life is a king-sized frustration, filled with worry and heartache.

2:24 This being the case, a logical philosophy of life for the man whose whole existence is under the sun is to find enjoyment in eating, drinking, and **in his labor**. The Preacher is not advocating gluttony and drunkenness but rather finding pleasure wherever possible in the common things of life.

Even this is **from the hand of God**—that men should enjoy the normal mercies of life, the taste of good food, the refreshment of table beverages, and the satisfaction that comes from honest work. Man does not have the power of enjoyment unless it is given to him by **God**.

A later preacher, the Apostle Paul, confirmed Solomon's outlook. He said that if there is no resurrection of the dead then the best policy is, "Let us eat and drink, for tomorrow we die!" (1 Cor. 15:32).

Solomon adds that the ability to eat and find enjoyment in other ways comes from **God**. Without Him, we cannot enjoy the most ordinary pleasures. We depend on Him for food, appetite, digestion, sight, hearing, smell, memory, health, sanity, and all that makes for normal, pleasurable experiences.

2:25 In verse 25, he adds that he was able to enjoy all these things more than anyone.

John D. Rockefeller had an income of about a million dollars a week, yet all his doctors allowed him to eat cost only a few cents. One of his biographers said that he lived on a diet that a pauper would have despised:

> Now less than a hundred pounds in weight, he sampled everything (at breakfast): a drop of coffee, a spoonful of cereal, a forkful of egg, and a bit of chop the size of a pea.[22]

He was the richest man in the world but did not have the ability to enjoy his food.

2:26 Finally, the Preacher felt that he observed a general principle in life that God rewards righteousness and punishes sin. **To a man** who pleases Him, **God gives wisdom and knowledge and joy. But to the** habitual **sinner, He gives the** burden of hard **work**, accumulating and piling up, only to see it taken over by someone who strikes God's fancy. What could be more fruitless and defeating than that?

C. The Vanity of the Cycle of Life and Death (Chap. 3)

3:1 As a research student of life and of human behavior, Solomon observed that there is a predetermined **season** for **everything** and a fixed **time** for **every** happening. This means that God has programmed every activity into a gigantic computer, and, as Hispanics say, *"Que será, será"*: What will be, will be! It also means that history is filled with cyclical patterns, and these recur with unchangeable regularity. So man is locked into a pattern of behavior which is determined by certain inflexible laws or principles. He is a slave to fatalism's clock and calendar.

In verses 1–8, the Preacher enumerates twenty-eight activities which are probably intended to symbolize the whole round of life. This is suggested by the number twenty-eight, which is the number of the world (four) multiplied by the number of completeness (seven).

The list is made up of opposites. Fourteen are positives and fourteen negatives. In some ways, they seem to cancel out each other so that the net result is zero.

3:2 There is **a time to be born.** The person himself has no control over this, and even the parents must wait out the nine months which form the normal birth cycle.

There is also **a time to die**. Man's allotted span is seventy years, according to Psalm 90:10, but even apart from that, it seems that death is a predetermined appointment that must be kept.

It is true that God foreknows the terminus of our life on earth, but for the Christian this is neither morbid nor fatalistic. We know that we are immortal until our work is done. And though death is a possibility, it is not a certainty. The blessed hope of Christ's return inspires the believer to look for the Savior rather than the mortician. As the preacher Peter Pell put it so colorfully, "I'm not waiting for the *undertaker*—I'm waiting for the *uppertaker*!"

A time to plant, and a time to pluck what is planted. With these words, Solomon seems to cover the entire field of agriculture, linked closely as it is with the seasons of the year (Gen. 8:22). Failure to observe these seasons in planting and harvesting can only spell disaster.

3:3 A time to kill, and time to heal. Bible commentators go to great lengths to explain that this cannot refer to murder but only to warfare, capital punishment, or self-defense. But we must remember that Solomon's observations were based on his knowledge under the sun. Without divine revelation, it seemed to him that life was either a slaughterhouse or a hospital, a battlefield or a first-aid station.

A time to break down, and a time to build up. First the wrecking crew appears to demolish buildings that are outdated and no longer serviceable, then the builders move in to erect modern complexes and rehabilitate the area of blight.

3:4 A time to weep, and a time to laugh. Life seems to alternate between tragedy and comedy. Now it wears the black mask of the tragedian, then the painted face of the clown.

A time to mourn, and a time to dance. The funeral procession passes by with its mourners wailing in grief. But before long, these same people are dancing at a wedding reception, quickly removed from their recent sorrow.

3:5 A time to cast away stones, and a time to gather stones. Taken at face value, this means that there is a time to clear land for cultivation (Isa. 5:2), then to gather the stones for building houses, walls, or other projects. If we take the words figuratively, as most modern commentators do, there may be a reference to the marriage act. Thus, TEV paraphrases, "The time for having sex and the time for not having it."

A time to embrace, and a time to refrain from embracing. In the realm of the affections, there is a time for involvement and a time for withdrawal. There is a time when love is pure and a time when it is illicit.

3:6 A time to gain, and a time to lose. This makes us think of business cycles with their fluctuating profits and losses. First the markets are bullish with income soaring. Then they become bearish, and companies find themselves in the red.

A time to keep, and a time to throw away. Most housewives are familiar with this curious pattern. For months or even years, they stash things away in closets, basements, and attics. Then in a burst of housecleaning zeal, they clear them out and call some local charity to cart the gathered items away.

3:7 A time to tear, and a time to sew. Could Solomon have been thinking of the constant changes in clothing fashions? Some noted fashion designer dictates a new trend, and all over the world, hems are let out or shortened. Today the fashions are daring and attention-getting. Tomorrow they revert to the quaint styles of grandmother's day.

A time to keep silence, and a time to speak. The **time to keep silence** is when we are criticized unjustly, when we are tempted to criticize others, or to say things that are untrue, unkind, or unedifying. Because Moses spoke unadvisedly with his lips, he was barred from entering the promised land (Num. 20:10; Ps. 106:33).

The **time to speak** is when some great principle or cause is at stake. Mordecai advised Esther that the **time** had come for her **to speak** (Est. 4:13–14). And he could have added, with Dante, "The hottest places in hell are reserved for those who remain neutral in a time of great moral crisis."

3:8 A time to love, and a time to hate. We must not try to force these words into a Christian context. Solomon was not speaking as a Christian but as a man of the world. It seemed to him that human behavior fluctuated between periods of **love** and periods of **hate**.

A time of war, and a time of peace. What is history if it is not the record of cruel, mindless wars, interspersed with short terms **of peace**?

3:9 The question lingering in Solomon's mind was, "**What** lasting gain **has the worker** for all his toil?" For every constructive activity there is a destructive one. For every plus a minus. The fourteen positive works are cancelled out by fourteen negatives. So the mathematical formula of life is fourteen minus fourteen equals zero. Man has nothing but a zero at the end of it all.

3:10 Solomon had conducted an exhaustive survey of all the activities, employments, and pursuits that God has given to man to occupy his time. He has just given us a catalog of these in verses 2–8.

3:11 He concluded that God **has made everything beautiful in its time**, or, better, that there is an appropriate time for each activity. He is not so much thinking here of the beauty of God's creation as the fact that every action has its own designated time, and that in its time it is eminently fitting.

Also God **has put eternity** in man's mind. Though living in a world of time, man has intimations of **eternity**. Instinctively he thinks of "forever," and though he cannot understand the concept, he realizes that beyond this life there is the possibility of a shoreless ocean of time.

Yet God's works and ways are inscrutable to man. There is no way in which we can solve the riddle of creation, providence, or the consummation of the universe, apart from revelation. In spite of the enormous advances of human knowledge, we still see through a glass darkly. Very often we have to confess with a sigh, "How little we know of Him!"

3:12 Because man's life is governed by certain inexorable laws and because all his activities seem to leave him where he started, Solomon decides that the best policy is to be happy and enjoy life as much as possible.

3:13 He did not mean that life should be an orgy of drunkenness, dissipation, and debauchery, but that **it is the gift of God** for man to enjoy his food and drink and find what pleasure he can in his daily work. It is a low view of life, and completely sub-Christian in its outlook, but we must continually remember that Solomon's viewpoint here was thoroughly earthbound.

3:14 He did accurately perceive that God's decrees are immutable. What God has decided will stand and man cannot alter it, either by addition or subtraction. It is foolish for creatures to fight against the arrangements of their Creator. Much better to respect Him and submit to His control.

3:15 Current events are merely a replay of what has happened previously, and nothing will happen in the future but what **has already been**. God arranges everything on a recurring basis so that things will happen over and over again. He brings back again what is past and thus history repeats itself. The expression **"God requires an account of what is past"** is often used to press home the fact that past sins must be accounted for by unbelievers. While this is true, it is hardly the force of this passage. Here God is rather seen as recalling past events to form another cycle of history. R. C. Sproul calls it the theme of eternal recurrence. "This idea maintains that in infinite time, there are periodic cycles in which all that has been is repeated over again. The drama of human life is a play with one encore after another."[23]

3:16 Among other things that pained the Preacher were injustice and **wickedness**. He found crookedness in the law courts where justice should be dispensed and dishonesty in government circles where **righteousness** should be practiced.

3:17 These inequalities of life led him to believe that there has to be **a time** when God will **judge** men, when the wrongs of earth will be made right. Solomon does not say explicitly that this will be in the next life, but it is a foregone conclusion since so many inequities are unrequited in this world. His conclusion mirrors a common emotion in the hearts of righteous people. Decency and fairness demand a time when accounts are settled and when the right is vindicated.

3:18 In the closing verses of chapter 3, the Preacher turns to the subject of death, and sees it as the grim spoilsport, ending all man's best ambitions, endeavors, and pleasures. He views it exactly as we would if we did not have the Bible to enlighten us.

Notice that he introduces his views with the words, **"I said in my heart."** It is not a question of what God revealed to him but of what he concluded in his own mind. It is his own reasoning under the sun. Therefore, this is not a passage from which we can build an adequate doctrine of death and the hereafter. And yet this is precisely what many of the false cults have done. They use these verses to support their erroneous teachings of soul-sleep and the annihilation of the wicked dead. Actually a careful study of the passage will show that Solomon was not advocating either of these views.

Basically what he is saying is that **God tests** man through his short life on earth to show him how frail and transient he is—just **like animals**. But is he saying that man is no better than an animal?

3:19 No, the point is not that man is an animal, but that in *one respect*, he has no advantage over an animal. As death comes **to animals**, so it comes to man. **All have one breath**, and at the time of death, that breath is cut off. So life is as empty for man as for the lower orders of creation.

3:20 **All** share a common end in the grave. They are both going to the same place—the **dust**. They both came from it; they will both go back to it. Of course, this assumes that the body is all there is to human life. But we know that this is not true. The body is only the tent in which the person lives. But Solomon could not be expected to know the full truth of the future state.

3:21 Solomon's ignorance as to what happens at the time of death is evident from his question, **"Who knows the spirit of the sons of men, which goes upward, and the spirit of the animal, which goes down to the earth?"** This must not be taken as a doctrinal fact. It is human questioning, not divine certainty.

From the NT, we know that the spirit and soul of the believer go to be with Christ at the time of death (2 Cor. 5:8; Phil. 1:23), and his body goes to the grave (Acts 8:2). The spirit and soul of the unbeliever go to Hades, and his body goes to the grave (Luke 16:22b–23). When Christ comes into the air, the bodies of those who have died in faith will be raised in glorified form and reunited with the spirit and soul (Phil. 3:20–21; 1 Thess. 4:16–17). The bodies of the unbelieving dead will be raised at the Great White Throne Judgment, reunited with the spirit and soul, then cast into the lake of fire (Rev. 20:12–14).

Strictly speaking, animals have body and soul but no spirit.[24] Nothing is said in the Bible concerning life after death for animals.

3:22 From what he knew about death, and also from what he didn't know, Solomon figures that the best thing a man can do is enjoy his daily activities. That, after all, is his lot in life, and he might as well cooperate with the inevitable. He should find satisfaction in accepting what cannot be changed. But above all, he should enjoy life as it comes to him, because no one can tell him what **will happen** on earth **after** he has passed on.

D. The Vanity of Life's Inequalities (Chap. 4)

4:1 Robert Burns said, "Man's inhumanity to man makes countless thousands mourn!" Sensitive hearts in every age have been grieved to see the **oppression** that is carried out by men against their fellowmen. It tormented Solomon also. He was grieved to see **the tears of the oppressed**, the **power** of **their oppressors**, and the failure of anyone to defend the downtrodden. **Power** was **on the side of** the **oppressors**, and no one dared to defy that power. From this vantage point, it seemed that "Truth [was] forever on the scaffold, Wrong forever on the throne." He could not see that "behind the dim unknown, standeth God within the shadow, keeping watch above His own."[25]

4:2 So in his dejection, he concluded that **the dead** are better off **than the living**. To him, death provided welcome escape from all the persecutions and cruelties of this life. He was not concerned at the moment with the deeper implications of death—that a person who dies in unbelief is doomed to more severe suffering than the worst oppression on earth. For him the question was not, "Is there life after death?", but rather, "Is there life after birth?"

4:3 Solomon's cynicism touched bottom with the observation that though the dead are better off than the living, the unborn are still more enviable. They have never lived to be driven mad by oppressions **under the sun**. They have never had to endure "that ghastly mockery of happiness called life."

4:4 There was something else that drove him up the wall—the fact that human activity and skill are motivated by the desire to outdo one's

neighbor. He saw that the wheel of life was propelled by the competitive spirit. The desire to have better clothes and a more luxurious home—it all seemed so empty and unworthy of men created in God's image and after His likeness.

When Michelangelo and Raphael were commissioned to use their artistic talents for the adornment of the Vatican, a deep spirit of rivalry broke out between them. "Although each had a different job to do, they became so jealous that at last they would not even speak to one another."[26] Some are more adept at concealing their envy than these geniuses were, but this same attitude of rivalry is at the bottom of much contemporary activity.

A modern cynic has written, "I've tried everything that life has to offer, but all I see is one guy trying to outdo another in a futile attempt at happiness."[27]

4:5 In contrast to the one whose motive and reward is envy is **the fool**—the dull, stupid sluggard. He **folds his hands** and lives off what little food he can get without much exertion. Perhaps he is wiser than his neighbors who are driven relentlessly on by their envy and covetousness.

4:6 While those around him are working themselves into a frenzy of competition, the fool's sentiments are: **Better a handful with quietness than both hands full, together with toil and grasping for the wind.** Or as H. C. Leupold paraphrases it, "Rather would I have my ease, though I possess but little, than acquire more and have all the vexation that goes with it."

4:7, 8 There was another kind of folly which blew the Preacher's mind. It was the mindless craze of the man who is alone, to keep working and accumulating wealth. **He has neither son nor brother,** no close relatives. He already has more money than he will ever need. Yet he wears himself out day after day and denies himself the simple amenities of life. It never occurs to him to ask, **"For whom do I toil and deprive myself of good?"** Charles Bridges in his exposition comments, "The miser—how well he deserves the name—the wretched slave of mammon, grown old as a toiling, scraping, griping drudge!" His name is miser and as his name, so is he—miserable. What an empty, wretched way to live, thought Solomon!

Surely Samuel Johnson was right when he said, "The lust for gold, unfeeling and remorseless, is the last corruption of degenerate man."

4:9 The solitariness of the miser leads Solomon to point out the advantages of fellowship and partnership. He uses four illustrations to press home his thesis. First of all, **two** workers are **better than one**, because by cooperation they can produce more efficiently.

4:10 Also if there is an accident on the job, one can help **his companion.** But pity the man who falls off the ladder when he is alone. There is no one around to call for help.

4:11 **Two** in a bed on a cold night are better than one because they help to keep each other **warm**. We could shoot holes in his argument by mentioning the annoyance caused by the partner who has cold feet or who hogs the covers, or the superior controlled heat that comes from the electric blanket. But the point remains that there are pleasures and benefits from friendship and socializing that are unknowable to the one who lives in isolation.

4:12 The third illustration has to do with protection against attack. A thief can often overpower one victim, but two can usually resist the intruder successfully.

Finally, a rope made with three cords is stronger than a rope with only one or two strands. In fact, three strands twisted together are more than three times as strong as three separate strands.

4:13–16 The follies and vanities of life are not confined to the peons; they are even found in the palaces of kings. Solomon describes **a king** who overcame poverty and a prison record in his rise to the throne; yet now when he is old, he is intractable. He will not listen to his advisers. It would be better to have a young man who is teachable, even though **poor**, to reign in his place. Solomon thought about **all the people** who are subjects of the **king** and about the young man who is second in the chain of command—the heir apparent. Multitudes flock to his banner. They are tired of the **old** ruler and want a change, hoping for a better administration. **Yet** even **those who come afterward will not** be happy with **him**.

This fickleness and craving for novelty made Solomon realize that even the world's highest honors are **vanity**. They too are like **grasping for the wind**.

E. The Vanity of Popular Religion and Politics (5:1–9)

Man is instinctively religious, but that is not necessarily good. In fact, it may be positively bad. His very religiosity may hide from him his need of salvation as a free gift of God's grace. In addition, man's own religion may be nothing more than a charade, an outward show without inward reality. Vanity may seep into religious life just as much as in any other sphere, maybe even more so. So, in chapter 5, Solomon lays down some advice to guard against formalism and externalism in dealing with the Creator.

5:1 First, he advises people to watch their steps **when** they **go to the house of God**. While this may refer to reverence in general, here it is explained to mean being more ready to learn than to engage in a lot of rash talk. Rash promises are the sacrifice of fools. Unthinking people make them without considering that it is **evil**.

5:2 Worshipers should avoid recklessness in prayers, promises, or in professions of devotion to **God**. The presence of the Almighty is no place for precipitate or compulsive talking. The fact that **God is** infinitely high above man, as **heaven** is high above the **earth**, should teach man to curb his speech when drawing near to Him.

5:3 Just as a hyperactive mind often produces wild dreams, so a hyperactive mouth produces a torrent of foolish words, even in a prayer. Alexander Pope wrote that "Words are like leaves, and where they most abound, much fruit of sense beneath is rarely found."

Solomon did not intend verse 3 to be a full, scientific explanation of the origin of dreams; he was merely pointing out what seemed to him to be a connection between the whirring wheels of his mind during the day and the restless dreams that often followed at night.

5:4 In the matter of vows **to God**, simple honesty demands that they be paid promptly. God has no use for the dolt who talks up a storm, then fails to deliver. So the word is, **"Pay what you have vowed."**

5:5 If you don't intend to **pay**, don't **vow** in the first place.

How well the Preacher knew man's propensity to strike a bargain with

God when caught in a tight, desperate situation: "Lord, if you get me out of this, I'll serve you forever." But then the tendency is to forget quickly when the crisis is past.

Even in moments of spiritual exhilaration, it is easy to make a vow of dedication, or celibacy, or poverty, or the like. God has never required such vows of His people. In many cases, such as in the matter of celibacy, it would be better not to make them anyway. But where they are made, they should be kept. Certainly the marriage vow is ratified in heaven and cannot be broken without costly consequences. Vows made before conversion should be kept, except in those cases where they violate the Word of God.

5:6 So the general rule is **not** to **let your mouth** lead you into **sin** through shattered vows. And don't try to excuse yourself before God's **messenger** by saying it was **an error** and that you didn't really mean it. Or don't think that the mechanical offering of a sacrifice before Him will atone for careless breaking of vows.

The messenger of God may refer to the priest, since broken vows were to be confessed before him (Lev. 5:4–6). But this presupposes a knowledge of the Mosaic law, whereas Solomon is speaking here apart from revealed religion. So perhaps we are safer to understand him as meaning anyone who serves as a representative **of God**.

The basic thought is that God is exceedingly displeased by insincerity of speech. Why then say things that are certain to anger Him? This will inevitably cause Him to obstruct, frustrate, and **destroy** everything you try to do.

5:7 Just as there is tremendous unreality **in** a **multitude of dreams**, so in words spoken unadvisedly there is **vanity** and ruin. The thing to do, says Solomon, is to **fear God**. However, he does not mean the loving trust of Jehovah but the actual fear of incurring the displeasure of the Almighty. G. Campbell Morgan reminds us that this is the fear of a slave, not a son. Unless we see this, we give Solomon credit for a greater burst of spiritual insight than is intended here.

5:8 Next Solomon reverts to the subject of **oppression of the poor** and **perversion of justice**. He counsels against complete despair if we see these evils **in a province**. After all, there are chains of command in government, and those in the higher echelons watch their subordinates with an eagle eye.

But do they really? Too often the system of checks and balances breaks down, and every level of officialdom receives its share of graft and payola.

The only satisfaction that righteous people have is in knowing that God is higher than the highest authorities, and He will see that all accounts are settled some day. But it is doubtful if Solomon refers to this here.

5:9 Verse 9 is one of the most obscure verses in Ecclesiastes. The reason is that the original Hebrew is uncertain. This can be seen from the wide variety of translations:

JND: Moreover the earth is every way profitable: the king (himself) is dependent on the field.

NASB: After all, a king who cultivates the field is an advantage to the land.

TEV: Even a king depends on the harvest.

NKJV: **Moreover the profit of the land is for all; even the king is served from the field.**

The general thought seems to be that even the highest official is dependent on the produce of the field and thus on the providence of God. All are accountable to God.

F. The Vanity of Passing Riches (5:10—6:12)

5:10 People who love money are never **satisfied**; they always want more. Wealth does not buy contentment. Profits, dividends, interest payments, and capital gains whet the appetite for more. It all appears rather empty.

5:11 When a man's possessions **increase**, it seems that there is a corresponding increase in the number of parasites who live off his wealth, whether management consultants, tax advisers, accountants, lawyers, household employees, or sponging relatives.

A man can wear only one suit at a time, can only eat so much in a day. So the main benefit of his wealth is to be able to look at his bank books, stocks, and bonds, and to say with other rich fools, "Soul, you have many goods laid up for many years to come; take your ease, eat, drink and be merry" (Luke 12:19).

5:12 When it comes to sound **sleep, a laboring man** has the advantage. Whether he has had a banquet or a snack, he can rest without care or apprehension. Across town, **the rich** man is having a fitful night worrying about the stock market, wondering about thefts and embezzlements, and swallowing antacid to calm the churning sea of dyspepsia that is in his stomach.

5:13 Solomon saw that hoarding **riches** gives rise to disastrous consequences. Here is a man who had vast reserves of wealth, but instead of using them for constructive purposes, he kept them stashed away.

5:14 All of a sudden, there was some calamity such as a market crash, and the money was all gone. Even though the man had **a son**, he had **nothing** to leave to him. He was penniless.

5:15 Empty-handed he had come **from his mother's womb**, and now empty-handed he leaves this world. In spite of all the money he had been able to accumulate during his lifetime, he dies a pauper.

Cecil Rhodes spent years exploiting the natural resources of South Africa. When he was about to die, he cried out in remorse:

> I've found much in Africa. Diamonds, gold and land are mine, but now I must leave them all behind. Not a thing I've gained can be taken with me. I have not sought eternal treasures, therefore I actually have nothing at all.[28]

5:16 Solomon says **this is a severe evil**—a painful calamity—he could have used his money for lasting benefit. Instead of that he leaves as empty as he came, with nothing to show for all his work. He **has labored for the wind**.

5:17 The tragedy is compounded by the fact that the closing days of this man's life are filled with gloom, **sorrow**, worry, **sickness, and anger**. His life has been a reverse Cinderella story—from riches to rags.

Of course, there is a sense in which every man who dies leaves everything. But here the Preacher seems to point up the folly of hoarding money when it could be put to useful purposes, then losing it all, and having nothing to show for a lifetime of work.

5:18 So the best strategy is to enjoy the common activities of daily life—eating, drinking, and working.

Then no matter what happens, nothing can rob one of the pleasures he has already had. **Life** at best is very brief, so why not **enjoy** it while you can?

5:19 Solomon thought that it was ideal when God **gave** a man **riches and wealth** and when at the same time He also gave him the ability to enjoy them, to be satisfied with his lot in life, and to enjoy his work. This combination of circumstances was a special **gift of God**, or as we might say, this was "the real thing."

5:20 Such a man doesn't brood over the shortness **of his life** or its tragedies and inequities because **God keeps** his mind occupied **with the joy of his** present circumstances.

6:1, 2 There is a cruel irony in life that lays a heavy burden on men. It concerns **a man to whom God has given** everything that his heart could desire in the way of **riches and wealth and honor**, but unfortunately **God does not give him the** capacity to enjoy these things. Notice that Solomon blames **God** for depriving him of the enjoyment of his wealth.

Then premature death robs this man of the power to enjoy his riches. He leaves it all to a stranger, not even to a son or a close relative. This certainly makes life look like an empty bubble or a malignant disease.

6:3 Even **if a man** has a big family and lives to a ripe, old age, these superlative mercies mean nothing if he can't enjoy life or if he doesn't have a decent **burial** at the end. In fact, **a stillborn child** is more to be envied than he.

6:4 The untimely birth **comes in vanity and departs in** anonymity. His name is covered in the obscurity of one who was never born and who never died.

6:5 Though the stillborn child never sees **the sun** or gets to know anything, nevertheless he enjoys **more rest** than the miser. He never experiences the maddening perversities of life.

6:6 Even if the miser should live **a thousand years twice** over, what good is it if he **has not** been able to enjoy the good things of life? He shares the same fate as the stillborn child by going to the grave.

6:7 A man's main reason for working is to buy food for himself and his family. But the odd thing is that he is never **satisfied**. The more his income rises, the more he wants to buy. Contentment is the carrot on the stick that forever eludes him.

6:8 So in this futile quest, **the wise man** doesn't have any advantage over **the fool**. And even if a poor man knows how to face life better than the rest of the people, he isn't any further ahead.

6:9 It is far **better** to be content with the meals that are set before one than to be always craving for something additional. This business of always lusting for more is as foolish as **grasping for the wind**. As Leupold said, it's like "lustful straying about from one thing to another in quest of true satisfaction."[29]

6:10, 11 **Whatever one is**, rich or poor, wise or foolish, old or young, **he has already** been given the name of **man**. *Man* here represents the Hebrew word *adam* and means "red clay." How can red clay dispute with the Creator?

6:12 The simple fact, according to the Preacher, is that no one **knows** what is best for him in this **vain life** of shadows. And no one knows **what will happen** on the earth **after** he is gone.

III. ADVICE FOR LIFE UNDER THE SUN (7:1—12:8)

A. The Good and the Better Under the Sun (Chap. 7)

7:1 The sour note at the end of chapter 6 was that man cannot determine what is best for him under the sun. But Solomon does have ideas as to some things that are good and others that are better. That is his subject in chapter 7. In fact, the words *good* and *better* together occur here more times than in any other chapter in the OT.

First, **a good name is better than precious ointment. A good name**, of course, signifies **a good** *character*. **Precious ointment** represents what is costly and fragrant. The thought is that the most expensive perfume can never take the place of an honorable life.

The Preacher says **the day of death is better than the day of one's birth**. This is one of his statements that leaves us guessing. Did he mean this as a general axiom, or was he referring only to a man with **a good name**? When applied to true believers, the observation is quite true. But it is certainly not true of those who die with sins unconfessed and unforgiven.

7:2 Next Solomon decides that it is **better to go to** a funeral parlor than gorge oneself at a banquet. Death **is the end of all men**, and when we come face to face with it, we are brought up short and forced to think about our own departure.

Every thinking person must take into account the fact of death and should have a philosophy of life which enables him or her to confidently face that inevitable appointment. The gospel tells of the Savior, who, through death, destroyed him who has the power of death, that is, the devil, and who delivers all those who, through fear of death, are subject to lifelong bondage (Heb. 2:14–15).

7:3 Another "better": **sorrow is better than laughter**. The Preacher was convinced that seriousness accomplishes more than levity. It sharpens the mind to grapple with the great issues of life, whereas frivolity wastes time and prevents people from coming to grips with what is important.

> I walked a mile with Pleasure;
> She chattered all the way,
> But left me none the wiser
> For all she had to say
>
> I walked a mile with Sorrow,
> And not a word said she;
> But oh, the things I learned from her
> When Sorrow walked with me!
> —*Robert Browning Hamilton*

For by a sad countenance the heart is made better. It is one of the paradoxes of life that joy can coexist with sorrow. Even heathen philosophers have attributed a therapeutic value to suffering and sadness. But what is only moderately true for the unbeliever is more gloriously true for the child of God. Sorrows and sufferings here are the means of developing graces in his life. They give him a new appreciation of the sufferings of Christ. They enable him to comfort others who are experiencing similar trials. And they are a pledge of future glory (Rom. 8:17).

7:4 The mind of a **wise** person maintains poise and serenity in the presence of death. He can cope with sorrow and pressure because his roots are deep. **Fools** can't stand to face serious crises. They try to drown out the sounds of life as it is with laughter and gaiety. They avoid contact with hospitals and mortuaries because their shallow resources do not equip them to stand up under the pressures of life.

7:5 There is something else that is *better*. **It is better to hear the rebuke of the wise than for a man to hear the song of fools.** Constructive criticism instructs, corrects, and warns. The empty mirth of fools accomplishes nothing of lasting value.

7:6 **The laughter of the fool** is **like the crackling of thorns under a pot**—showy and noisy but not productive. Burning thorns may snap, crackle, and pop, but they do not make a good fuel. Little heat is generated, and the fire goes out quickly. It is noise without effectiveness, froth without body.

7:7 Even **a wise** person acts foolishly when he becomes a cheating oppressor. He becomes power-mad and loses his sense of balance and restraint. And all those who indulge in bribery and graft corrupt their own minds. Once they stoop to accept payola, they lose the power to make unprejudiced judgments.

7:8 It seemed to Solomon **that the end of a thing is better than its beginning**. Perhaps he was thinking of the tremendous inertia that must often be overcome to begin a project and of the drudgery and discipline that go into its early stages. Then by contrast there is the sense of achievement and satisfaction that accompanies its completion.

But it doesn't take much insight to realize that the rule does not always hold. The end of *righteous* deeds is better than the beginning, but the end of sin is worse. The latter days of Job were **better than** the **beginning** (Job 42:12), but the end of the wicked is indescribably terrible (Heb. 10:31).

The Preacher was on firmer ground when he said that **the patient in spirit is** superior to **the proud in spirit**. Patience is an attractive virtue, whereas pride is the parent sin. Patience fits a man for God's approval (Rom. 5:4), whereas pride fits him for destruction (Prov. 16:18).

7:9 Next we are warned against the tendency to fly off the handle. Such lack of self-control reveals a decided weakness of character. Someone has said that you can judge the size of a man by the size of what it takes to make him lose his temper. And if we nurse grudges and resentments, we expose ourselves as **fools**. Intelligent people don't spoil their lives by such nonsensical behavior.

7:10 Another foolish activity is living in the past. When we constantly harp on "the good old days" and wish they would return because they were so much better, we are living in a world of unreality. Better to face conditions as they are and live triumphantly in spite of them. Better to light a candle than to curse the darkness.

7:11 Solomon's thought with regard to **wisdom** and **an inheritance** may be understood in several ways. First, **wisdom is good with an inheritance** (NKJV; NASB); it enables the recipient to administer his bequest carefully. Second, wisdom is good *as* an inheritance (JND); if one could choose only one heritage, wisdom would be a good choice. Third, wisdom is *as good as* an inheritance; it is a source of wealth. Also it is an advantage **to those who see the sun**, that is, to those who live on earth. How this is so is explained in verse 12.

7:12 **Wisdom** resembles **money** in that both afford protection and security of sorts. With **money**, one can insure himself against physical and financial losses, whereas **wisdom** provides added protection from moral and spiritual damage. That is why wisdom is superior; it preserves the lives of its possessors, not just their material fortunes.

When we remember that Christ is the wisdom of God and that those who find Him find life, the infinite superiority of wisdom is obvious. In Him are hidden all the treasures of wisdom and knowledge (Col. 2:3).

7:13 One thing a wise person will do is to **consider** God's sovereign control of affairs. If **He has made** something **crooked, who can make** it **straight**? In other words, who can successfully countermand His will? His decrees are immutable and not subject to human manipulation.

7:14 In His ordering of our lives, God has seen fit to permit times of prosperity and times of adversity. When **prosperity** comes, we should be glad and enjoy it. **In the day of adversity**, we should realize that God sends the good and the bad, happiness and trouble, so that man will not know what is going to happen next. This can be both a mercy and a frustration.

There may also be the thought that God mixes the good and the bad so people won't be able to find fault with Him.

In either case, the conclusions are distinctly subsolar. They do not rise above flesh and blood.

7:15 We have an expression "Now I've **seen everything**" when we witness the unexpected, the paradoxical, the ultimate surprise. That seems to be Solomon's meaning here. In the course of his empty life, he had seen every kind of contradiction. He saw **just** people die young and **wicked** ones live to old age.

7:16 Since the Preacher could not detect a fixed relation between righteousness and blessing on the one hand and sin and punishment on the other, he decided that the best policy is to avoid extremes. This shallow, unbiblical conclusion is known as "the law of the golden mean."

By avoiding extreme righteousness and excessive wisdom, one might escape premature destruction. This, of course, is untrue. God's standard for His people is that they should not sin (1 Jn. 2:1). And His guarantee for His people is that they are immortal till their work is done.

7:17 The other danger, in Solomon's reckoning, was extreme wickedness. The foolhardy man can also be cut off **before** his **time**. A middle-of-the-road policy is therefore the ideal toward which we should strive, says the Preacher.

It is clear that these are man's reasonings, not God's revelations. God cannot condone sin at all. His standard is always perfection.

7:18 According to the Preacher, the best policy is to **grasp this** fact—the untimely fate of the overrighteous man—and not to let go of the opposite fact—the self-destruction of the profligate. The one **who fears God** (by walking in the middle) **will escape** from both pitfalls.

This advice wrongly puts God in favor of moderation in sin and in unrighteousness. But it arose from Solomon's observations under the sun. Unless we remember that, we will be puzzled by such a worldly philosophy.

7:19 Solomon believes that **wisdom** gives **more** strength and protection to a man **than ten rulers** give to a **city**, which simply means that wisdom is greater than armed might. God is not necessarily on the side of the biggest battalions.

7:20 The fact that this verse begins with **for** shows that it is vitally connected with what precedes. But what is the connection? The connection is that we all need the benefits of the wisdom that the Preacher has been describing, because we are all imperfect. There is no one who is absolutely righteous in himself, **who** invariably **does good** and who never sins.

Generally verse 20 is taken to teach the universality of sin, and that application is legitimate. But in its context, writes Leupold, the verse tells why we stand in need of a closer alliance with that wisdom which has just been described.[30]

7:21 A healthy sense of our own imperfection will help us to take criticisms in stride. If we **hear** a **servant cursing** us, though he is much lower on the social ladder, we can always be glad he doesn't know us better, because then he would have more to curse!

When Shimei cursed David, Abishai wanted to cut off his head, but David's reply implied that perhaps Shimei's cursing was not entirely causeless (2 Sam. 16:5–14).

7:22 And we should always remember that we have been guilty of the same thing. **Many times** we **have cursed others** in our **heart**. We can scarcely expect others to be perfect when we are so far from perfect ourselves.

That is one of the frustrations of a perfectionist. He wants everything and everyone else to be perfect, but he lives in a world of imperfection, and he himself cannot reach the goal he sets for others.

7:23 The Preacher used his extraordinary **wisdom** to probe into all these areas of life. He wanted to be **wise** enough to solve all mysteries and unravel all the tangled skeins. But because he was making all his investigations apart from God, he found that the ultimate answers eluded him. Without special revelation, life remains an insoluble riddle.

7:24 Explanations of things as they exist are remote, inaccessible, **and exceedingly deep**. The world is filled with enigmas. The realm of the unknown remains unexplored. We are plagued by mysteries and unanswered questions.

7:25 In spite of his failure to come up with the answers, Solomon doggedly persevered in his search for greater wisdom and a solution to the human equation. He wanted to understand **the wickedness of folly, even of foolishness and madness**, that is, why people abandon themselves to debauchery and shame.

7:26 In that connection, he thought especially of a loose **woman** or a prostitute—a woman whose influence is **more bitter than death**. Her mind is filled with subtle ways of snaring men, and those in her clutches are bound as if by chains. Anyone whose desire is to please **God shall escape** her traps, but the man who plays around with sin is sure to cross her path and be hooked **by her**.

It is altogether possible that the woman here may be a type of the world or of the wisdom of the world (Col. 2:8; Jas. 3:15).

7:27, 28 Verses 27–29 seem to express Solomon's general disappointment with his fellow human beings. When he first met anyone, he had great expectations, but after he got to know that person better, his hopes were dashed. No one met his ideal. Perhaps he would see someone who was rather attractive. He would think, *I must get to know that person better. I'd like to develop a close personal friendship.* But the more he got to know this new acquaintance, the more disillusioned he became. He found that there is no such person as the perfect stranger, and that familiarity *does* breed contempt.

Solomon decided to total the number of friendships in which he found a measure of real satisfaction and of fulfilled hopes. Out of all the people he had known, how many did he regard as true "soul brothers"?

He had sought repeatedly for a perfect person, but had never been able to find a single one. Everyone he met had some flaws or weaknesses of character.

All that he discovered was that good men are rare and good women rarer still. He found one man in a thousand who came close to his ideal, that is, a man who was a loyal, dependable, selfless friend.

But he couldn't find one woman in a thousand who impressed him as a reasonable approach to excellence. He did not find **a woman among** all those. Such a shocking outburst of male chauvinism is incomprehensible and offensive to us today, but that is because our judgments are based on Christian principles and values. It would not be shocking to the orthodox Jew who thanks God every day that he was not born a woman. Nor would it be shocking to men of some cultures in which women are looked on as slaves or mere property.

Commentators go through interpretive gymnastics to soften the force of Solomon's harsh words here, but their well-intentioned efforts are misdirected. The fact is that the Preacher probably meant exactly what he said. And his conclusion is still shared by men throughout the world whose outlook is earthbound and carnal.

Solomon's view of women was terribly one-sided. G. Campbell Morgan gave a more balanced view when he wrote:

> The influence of women is most powerful for good or for ill. I once heard one of the keenest of observers say that no great movement for the uplifting of humanity has been generated in human history but that woman's influence had much to do with it. Whether so superlative a statement is capable of substantiation I do not know; but I believe there is a great element of truth in it. It is equally true that the part that women have taken in corrupting the race has been terrible. When the womanhood of a nation is noble, the national life is held in strength. When it is corrupt, the nation is doomed. Woman is the last stronghold of good or of evil. Compassion and cruelty are superlative in her.[31]

Solomon later redeemed himself by writing one of literature's noblest tributes to womanhood—Proverbs 31. In Ecclesiastes he writes from the earthly plane of human prejudice, but in Proverbs 31 he writes from the lofty peak of divine revelation.

With the advent of the Christian faith, woman has reached the summit in her rise to dignity and respect. The Lord Jesus is her truest Friend and Emancipator.

7:29 As the Preacher pondered his unending disappointment in the people he had met, he correctly concluded that man has fallen from his original condition. How true! **God made man** in His own image and after His likeness. But man **sought out many** sinful **schemes** which marred and distorted the divine image in him.

Even in his fallen condition, man still has an intuitive hunger to find perfection. He goes through life looking for the perfect partner, the perfect job, the perfect everything. But he cannot find perfection in others or in himself. The trouble is that his search is confined to the sphere *under the sun*. Only one perfect life has ever been lived on this earth, that is the life of the Lord Jesus Christ. But now He is above the sun, exalted at the right hand of God. And God satisfies man's hunger for perfection with Christ—no one else, no other thing.

B. Wisdom Under the Sun (Chap. 8)

8:1 In spite of the failure of human wisdom to solve all his problems, Solomon still admired the **wise man** above others. No one else is as qualified to search out the hidden meaning of things. As far as the Preacher-King was concerned, **wisdom** is even mirrored in one's physical appearance. **His face** is radiant, and an otherwise stern visage is softened.

8:2 Wisdom teaches one how to act in the presence of the king, whether that king be conceived of as God or as an earthly monarch. It inculcates obedience first of all. The Hebrew of the latter part of this verse is ambiguous, as is seen by the following translations:

> and that in regard of the oath of God (KJV).
> because of the oath before God (NASB).
> **for the sake of your oath to God** (NKJV).

The **oath** here may refer to one's pledge of allegiance to the government or to God's oath by which He authorized kings to rule (e.g., see Ps. 89:35).

8:3 The obscurity continues in verse 3. We may understand this verse to advise leaving the king's presence without delay when unpleasantness develops. Or it may advise *against* making a **hasty** exit, either in anger, disobedience, insolence, or in quitting one's job (KJV, NASB, NKJV).

At any rate the thrust of the passage is that it is unwise to cross a king, since he has wide authority to do **whatever pleases him**.

8:4 Whenever **a king** speaks, his word is backed with **power**. It is supreme and is not subject to challenge by his subjects.

8:5 Those who obey the king's **command** need not fear the royal displeasure. Wisdom teaches a person what is appropriate, both as to **time** and procedure in obeying the royal edicts.

8:6 There's a right and wrong way of doing things, and a right and wrong **time** as well. The trouble that lies heavy upon man is that he cannot always discern these moments of destiny.

8:7 There is so much that **he does not know** or do. He cannot know the future—**what** is going to **happen** or **when it will occur**.

8:8 He cannot prevent his **spirit** from departing or determine the exact time of his **death**. He cannot obtain discharge **from that war**—the war that death is relentlessly waging against him. He cannot win a reprieve by any form of **wickedness** that he may give himself over to.

8:9 These are some of the things that the Preacher observed when he studied life **under the sun**, in a world where one man crushes another under his heel, **in which one man** has exercised authority **over another to his own hurt**.

8:10 So much of life is shallow. The **wicked** dies and is **buried**. He once made trips to **the place of** worship. Now that he is gone, people praise him for his piety **in the** very **city** where he used to carry on his crooked schemes. Religion can be a facade to cover up dishonesty. It is all so empty and meaningless.

8:11 Endless delays in the trial and punishment of criminals only serve to encourage lawlessness and create contempt for the judicial system. While it is important to guarantee that every defendant has a fair trial, it is possible to overprotect the criminal at the expense of his victim. Fair, impartial justice meted out promptly serves as a deterrent to crime. On the other hand, interminable postponements make offenders more fixed in their determination to break the law. They reason that they can get away with it or at least get a light sentence.

8:12 Although Solomon had seen some cases that seemed to be exceptions, he believed that **those who fear God** will fare best in the long run. Even if a habitual criminal lives to an old age, that exception doesn't invalidate the fact that righteousness is rewarded eventually and that the way of the transgressor is hard.

8:13 The Preacher was confident that **the wicked** person is an ultimate loser. By his failure to **fear before God**, he dooms himself to a short life. His life is transient **as a shadow**.

8:14 Solomon seems to alternate between general rules and glaring exceptions. Sometimes **just men** seem to be punished as if they were **wicked**. And sometimes **wicked men** seem to be rewarded as if they were decent, **righteous** citizens. These violations of what ought to be caused the Philosopher-King to be disgusted with the **vanity** of life.

8:15 The only logical policy, as far as he was concerned, is to enjoy life while you can. There is **nothing better under the sun than to eat, drink, and** have a good time. **This will** stand by a person as he toils on throughout **his life which God gives him** in this world. No pie-in-the-sky philosophy for Solomon. He wanted his pie here and now.

8:16 So the Preacher devoted himself to finding all the answers. He trained his mind in the study of philosophy, determined to get to the bottom of the activities of life—a task in which **one sees no sleep day or night**.

8:17 **Then** he found that **God** has so arranged things **that a man cannot** put all the parts of the puzzle together. No matter how hard he tries, he will fail. And no matter how brilliant he is, **he will not be able to find** answers to all the questions.

C. Enjoying Life Under the Sun (Chap. 9)

9:1 In chapter 9, the Preacher **considered** all **this**, taking in as wide and exhaustive a view as possible. He saw that good people and **wise** people and all that they do **are in the hand of God**. But whether what will happen to them is a sign of God's **love** or **hatred**, no one knows. The entire future is unknown and unknowable, and anything can happen.

9:2 What makes it all so enigmatical is that **the righteous and the wicked, the good** and the evil, **the clean and the unclean**, the worshiper and the nonworshiper **all** end in the same place—the grave. As far as escaping death is concerned, **the righteous** person has no advantage over **the wicked**. Those who put themselves under **oath** are in the same predicament as those who shun **an oath**.

9:3 **This is** the great calamity of life—that death eventually claims **all** classes of men. People can live outrageous, insane lives, and after that—death. What is this but gross injustice if death is the end of existence?

9:4 As long as man is alive, **there**

is hope; that is, he has something to look forward to. In that sense, **a living dog is better** off **than a dead lion**. Here the **dog** is spoken of, not as man's best friend, but as one of the lowest, meanest forms of animal life.[32] The **lion** is the king of beasts, powerful and magnificent.

9:5 **The living** at least **know that they will die, but the dead** don't know anything about what's going on in the world.

This verse is constantly used by false teachers to prove that the soul sleeps in death, that consciousness ceases when the last breath is taken. But it is senseless to build a doctrine of the hereafter on this verse, or on this book, for that matter. As has been repeatedly emphasized, Ecclesiastes represents man's best conclusions as he searches for answers "under the sun." It sets forth deductions based on observations and on logic but not on divine revelation. It is what a wise man might think if he did not have a Bible.

What would you think if you saw a person die and watched his body as it was lowered into the grave, knowing that it would eventually return to dust? You might think, *That's the end. My friend knows nothing now; he can't enjoy any activities that are going on; he has forgotten and will soon be* ***forgotten***.

9:6 And so it is, thought Solomon. Once a person has died, there is no more **love, hatred, envy** or any other human emotion. Never again **will** he **have a share** in any of this world's activities and experiences.

9:7 So once again the Preacher comes back to his basic conclusion—live your life, have a good time, enjoy your food, cheer your heart with **wine**. **God has already** approved what you do. It's all right with Him.

9:8 Wear bright clothing, not mourning attire. And put perfume on **your head** rather than ashes. Some people think the world was made for fun and frolic, and so did Solomon.

9:9 The joys of the marriage relationship should also be exploited to the full as long as possible. It's a vain, empty life anyway, so the best thing is to make the most of it. Enjoy every day because that's all you are going to get out of your toil and trouble.

Verses 7–9 are strikingly similar to the following passage in the Gilgamesh Epic, an ancient Babylonian account of immortality and of the great deluge:

> Since the gods created man
> Death they ordained for man,
> Life in their hands they hold,
> Thou, O Gilgamesh, fill indeed thy belly.
> Day and night be thou joyful,
> Daily ordain gladness,
> Day and night rage and be merry,
> Let thy garments be bright,
> Thy head purify, wash with water.
> Desire thy children which thy hand possesses.
> A wife enjoy in thy bosom.[33]

The significance of this is not that one was copied from the other, but that man's wisdom **under the sun** leads to the same conclusion. I was impressed with this fact when I read Denis Alexander's summary of what humanism offers us today:

> The humanist model does seem a very big pill to swallow. As a representative of a late twentieth-century generation of under-thirties, I am first asked to believe that I am the result of a purely random evolutionary process. The only prerequisites for this process are the presence of matter, time and chance. Because by some strange whim of fate, I and other men are the only physical structures which happen to have been bestowed

with a consciousness of their own existence, I am supposed to think of both myself and others as being in some way more valuable than other physical structures such as rabbits, trees or stones, even though in a hundred years time the atoms of my decayed body may well be indistinguishable from theirs. Furthermore the mass of vibrating atoms in my head are supposed to have more ultimate meaning than those in the head of a rabbit.

At the same time I am told that death is the end of the line. In the time-scale of evolution my life is a vapour which soon vanishes. Whatever feelings of justice or injustice I may have in this life, all my strivings, all my greatest decisions, will be ultimately swallowed up in the on-going march of time. In a few million years' time, a mere drop compared with the total history of the earth, the memory of the greatest literature, the greatest art, the greatest lives will be buried in the inexorable decay of the Second Law of Thermodynamics. Hitler and Martin Luther King, James Sewell and Francis of Assisi, Chairman Mao and Robert Kennedy, all will be obliterated in the unthinking void.

So, I am told, I must make the best of a bad job. Even though I have strong feelings of transcendence, a deep sense that I am more than just a blind whim of evolution, I must nevertheless forget such troubling questions, and concern myself with the real problems of trying to live responsibly in society. Even though my job involves studying man's brain as a machine, like any other of nature's machines, I must still believe that man has some special intrinsic worth which is greater than an animal's worth, and while my emotions tell me that it may be true, I am not given any more objective reason for believing it.[34]

9:10 The maxim in verse 10, one of the best known in the book, is often used by believers to encourage zeal and diligence in Christian service, and the advice is sound. But in its context, it really means to seize every possible pleasure and enjoyment while you can, because you won't be able to work, invent, think, or know anything **in the grave, where** you are irreversibly heading.

The advice given in this verse is excellent, but the reason is utterly bad! And even the advice must be restricted to activities that are legitimate, helpful, and edifying in themselves.

9:11 Another thing that the Preacher observed is that luck and chance play a big part in life. **The race is not** always won by the fastest runner. The bravest soldiers don't always win **the battle**. The wisest don't always enjoy the best meals. The cleverest are not always the richest. And the most capable do not always rise to the presidency. Bad luck dogs everyone's steps. **Time and chance** are factors that play an important role in success and failure. When the billionaire J. Paul Getty was asked to explain his success, he replied, "Some people find oil. Others don't."

9:12 And no one knows when bad luck will strike. **Like fish caught in a net** or **birds in a** trap, man is overtaken by bad fortune or even by death. He never knows which bullet has his name on it.

9:13–15 Still another heartache in life is that **wisdom** is not always appreciated. To illustrate: **There was a little city with few** inhabitants and therefore poorly defended. **A** powerful **king** surrounded it with artillery and prepared to break through the walls.

When the situation seemed hopeless, a **man** who was **poor** but very **wise** came forward with a plan that saved **the city**. At the moment he was a hero, but then he was quickly forgotten.

9:16 It grieved the Preacher that though **wisdom is better than** power, yet the **poor man's** advice was subsequently **despised**. As soon as the crisis was past, no one was interested in what he had to say.

This parable has a definite evangelistic ring to it. The city is like man's soul—small and defenseless. The great king is Satan, bent on invasion and destruction (2 Cor. 4:4; Eph. 2:2). The deliverer is the Savior—poor (2 Cor. 8:9) and wise (1 Cor. 1:24; Col. 2:3). Though He provided deliverance, yet how little He is honored and appreciated! Most people of the world live as if He had never died. And even Christians are often careless about remembering Him in His appointed way, that is, in the Lord's Supper.

9:17 Yet in spite of man's ingratitude and indifference it is still true that the **words of the wise, spoken quietly**, are worth more than the shouting tirades of a powerful **ruler of fools**.

9:18 **Wisdom is** superior to **weapons** and munitions. In 2 Samuel 20:14–22 we read how a wise woman delivered the city of Abel of Beth Maachah when Joab besieged it.

But one sinful dolt can undo a lot of **good** that the wise person accomplishes, just as little foxes can spoil the vines.

D. The Wise and the Foolish Under the Sun (Chap. 10)

10:1 When **flies** get caught in the **perfumer's ointment** and die, they cause it **to give off a foul odor**. And in this, there is an analogy to human behavior. A man may build up a reputation for wisdom and honor, yet he can ruin it all by a single misstep. People will remember one little indiscretion and forget years of worthy achievements. Any person can ruin his reputation by speaking just three words of the wrong kind in public.

10:2 **The right hand** is traditionally viewed as more dexterous, the **left** more awkward. **A wise** man knows the right way to do a thing; **a fool** is an awkward bungler.

10:3 **Even when a fool** does something simple, like walking **along the way**, he betrays a lack of common sense. He **shows everyone that he is a fool**, which may mean that he calls everyone else stupid or that he shows his own ignorance in all he does. The latter is probably the thought.

10:4 If a **ruler** explodes in anger at you, it is best not to quit in a huff. It is better to be meek and submissive. This will be more apt to pacify him and atone for serious **offenses**.

10:5, 6 Another inconsistency which bothered Solomon in this mixed-up world proceeded from unwise decisions and injustices **proceeding from the ruler**. Often men are appointed to positions without suitable qualifications, while capable men waste their talents on menial tasks.

10:7 Thus **servants** often ride **on horses, while princes** have to travel by foot. Such inequities exist in politics, in industry, in the military services, and in religious life as well.

10:8 **He** who **digs a pit** to harm others will be the victim of his own malice. Chickens have a way of coming home to roost.

Whoever breaks down a wall of stones, either for unlawful entry, or mischief, or to change a property line can expect to **be bitten by a serpent** or to pay for it in some other unpleasant way.

10:9, 10 Even legitimate activities

have risks attached. The quarryman is in danger of being **hurt by** stones, and the log-splitter is **endangered by** the ax.

It's a good idea to work with sharp tools. Otherwise it takes a lot more labor to get the job done. The time spent sharpening the ax is more than compensated by the time and effort saved. **Wisdom** teaches shortcuts and labor-saving devices. As Leupold renders it, "Wisdom prepares the way for success."[35]

10:11 What good is a charmer if the **serpent** bites before the charm begins? Or as we might say, why lock the barn after the horse is stolen? Things must often be done on time in order to be valuable and effective.

10:12, 13 **The words of a wise man's mouth** bring him favor because they **are gracious**. The words **of a fool** prove to be his downfall.

He may begin with harmless nonsense, but by the time he is through, he is engaging in **raving madness**.

10:14 **A fool** doesn't know when to stop. **Words**, words, words. He talks on and on as if he knew everything, but he doesn't. His endless chatter almost inevitably includes boasts of what he will do in the future. He is like the rich fool who said, "I will do this: I will pull down my barns and build greater, and there I will store all my crops and my goods. And I will say to my soul, 'Soul, you have many goods laid up for many years; take your ease; eat, drink, and be merry'" (Luke 12:18–19). But he does not know what is going to happen next. He would be better advised to say, "If the Lord wills, we shall live and do this or that" (Jas. 4:15).

10:15 He exhausts himself by his inefficient and unproductive work. He can't even see the obvious or find the way to anything as conspicuous as a **city**. Perhaps we could add that he doesn't know enough to come in out of the rain. His ignorance in such simple matters makes his plans for the future all the more ludicrous.

10:16, 17 Pity the **land** whose ruler is immature and impressionable like **a child** and whose legislators carouse **in the morning** instead of attending to their duties.

The fortunate **land** is one in which the **king is** a man of character and nobility, and in which the other leaders manifest propriety and self-control by eating **for strength and not for drunkenness**.

10:18 Continued **laziness** and neglect cause a **house** to fall apart, whether that house represents a government or an individual life. Any roof will leak unless the owner provides regular maintenance.

10:19 Meal time is a happy time. **Wine** adds sparkle to life. **Money answers everything.**

Did Solomon really believe that **money** is the key to all pleasure? Perhaps he simply meant that money can buy whatever man needs in the way of food and drink. Or maybe he was just quoting the drunken rulers of verse 16 when they were warned where their excesses would lead (v. 18). The fact, as someone has said, is that money will buy anything except happiness and is a ticket to everywhere except heaven. A man's life does not consist in the abundance of the things he possesses.

10:20 Be careful **not** to speak evil against **the king** or his **rich** subordinates. You may think that nobody hears. But even the walls have ears, and some unsuspected **bird** will **carry** the message to the royal palace. "Indiscretions have a way of sprouting wings."

E. Spreading the Good Under the Sun (11:1—12:8)

11:1 Bread is used symbolically here for the grain from which it is made. To **cast bread upon the waters** may refer to the practice of sowing in flooded areas, or it may mean carrying on grain trade by sea. In any case, the thought is that a widespread and wholesale distribution of what is good will result in a generous return in the time of harvest.

This verse is true of the gospel. We may not see immediate results as we share the bread of life, but the eventual harvest is sure.

11:2 Giving **a serving to seven,** even **to eight** suggests two things—unrestrained generosity or diversifying of business enterprises. If the first is meant, the idea is that we should show uncalculating kindness while we can, because a time of calamity and misfortune may come when this will not be possible. Most people save for a rainy day; this verse counsels to adopt a spirit of unrestricted liberality because of the uncertainties of life.

Or the thought may be: Don't put all your eggs in one basket. Invest in several interests so that if one fails, you will still be able to carry on with the others. This is known as *diversification*.

11:3 Verse 3 carries on the thought of the previous one, especially with regard to the unknown evil which may happen on earth. It suggests that there is a certain inevitability and finality about the calamities of life. Just as surely as rain-laden clouds **empty themselves upon the earth,** so surely do troubles and trials come to the sons of men. And once **a tree** is felled, it remains a fallen monarch. Its destiny is sealed.

A wider application of the verse is given in the poem:

> As a tree falls, so must it lie,
> As a man lives, so must he die,
> As a man dies, so must he be,
> All through the years of eternity.
> —*John Ray*

11:4 It is possible to be too cautious. If you wait till conditions are perfect, you will accomplish nothing. There are usually some **wind** and some **clouds**. If you wait for zero wind conditions, you will never get the seed into the fields. If you wait until there is no risk of rain, the crops will rot before they are harvested. The man who waits for certainty will wait forever.

11:5 Since we don't know everything, we have to muddle along with what knowledge we do have. We don't understand the movements of **the wind** or **how the bones** are formed **in the womb** of an expectant mother. Neither do we understand all that **God** does or why He does it.

11:6 Since we don't know this, the best policy is to fill the day with all kinds of productive work. We have no way of knowing **which** activities **will prosper**. Maybe they all will.

In spreading the Word of God, success is guaranteed. But it is still true that some methods are more fruitful than others. So we should be untiring, versatile, ingenious, and faithful in Christian service.

Then too we should sow **in the morning** of life and not slack off **in the evening**. We are called to unremitting service.

11:7, 8 The light may refer to the bright and shining days of youth. It's great to be young—to be healthy, strong, and vivacious. But no matter how many years of vigor and prosperity a man enjoys, he should be aware that **days of darkness** are almost sure to come. The aches and pains of old age are inevitable. It's a dreary, empty time of life.

11:9 It is hard to know whether verse 9 is sincere advice or the cynicism of a disillusioned old man. Do what your **heart** desires and see as much as you can. **But** just remember that eventually **God will bring you into judgment**, that is, the **judgment** of old age, which seemed to Solomon like divine retribution for the sins of early life.

11:10 While you have your **youth**, maximize enjoyment and minimize **sorrow** and trouble. (**Evil** here probably means trouble rather than sin.) **Childhood and youth are vanity** because they are so short-lived.

Nowhere in literature is there a more classic description of old age than in the first half of chapter 12. The meaning does not lie on the surface because it is presented as an allegory. But soon the picture emerges of a doddering old man, a walking geriatric museum, shuffling his way irresistibly to the grave.

12:1 The doleful picture of age and senility is a warning to young people to **remember** their **Creator in the days of** their **youth**. Notice Solomon does not say their Lord or Savior or Redeemer but their **Creator**. That is the only way Solomon could know God from his vantage point under the sun. But even at that, the advice is good. Young people *should* **remember** their **Creator . . . before** the sunset time of life, when the days are **difficult** and cruel and the years are totally lacking in **pleasure** and enjoyment. The aspiration of every young person should be that which is expressed in the following lines:

Lord, in the fullness of my might,
  I would for Thee be strong;
While runneth o'er each dear delight,
  To Thee should soar my song.

I would not give the world my heart,
  And then profess Thy love;
I would not feel my strength depart,
  And then Thy service prove.

I would not with swift winged zeal
  On the world's errands go:
And labor up the heav'nly hill
  With weary feet and slow.

O not for Thee my weak desires,
  My poorer baser part!
O not for Thee my fading fires,
  The ashes of my heart.

O choose me in my golden time,
  In my dear joys have part!
For Thee the glory of my prime
  The fullness of my heart.[36]

—*Thomas H. Gill*

12:2 Old age is the time when the lights grow dim, both physically and emotionally. The days are dreary, and the nights are long. Gloom and depression settle in.

Even in earlier years, there was a certain amount of **rain**, that is, trouble and discouragement. But then the sun would emerge and the spirit would quickly bounce back. Now it seems that the sunny days are gone, and after each spell of **rain, the clouds** appear with the promise of more.

Youth is the time to remember the Creator because then the **sun, . . . moon, and . . . stars are not darkened, and the clouds do not return after the rain.**

12:3 Now the body of the old man is presented under the figure of a **house. The keepers of the house** are the arms and hands, once strong and active, now wrinkled, gnarled, and trembling with Parkinson's disease.

The strong men are the legs and thighs, no longer straight and athletic, but bowed like parenthesis marks, as if buckling under the weight of the body.

The grinders cease because they are few, that is, the teeth are no longer able to chew because there are too few uppers to meet the remaining lowers. The dentist would say there is inadequate occlusion.

Those that look through the windows grow dim. The eyes have been failing steadily. First they needed bifocals, then trifocals, then surgery for cataracts. Now they can only read extra large type with the use of a magnifying glass.

12:4 The doors on the street **are shut**. This refers, of course, to the ears. Everything has to be repeated over and over. Loud noises, like the **grinding** of the mill, are very **low** and indistinct.

The old man suffers from insomnia; he **rises up** bright and early, when the first **bird** begins to chirp or the rooster crows.

All the daughters of music are brought low; the vocal chords are seriously impaired. The voice is crackling and unsteady, and song is out of the question.

12:5 They develop *acrophobia*, that is, **they are afraid of height**, whether ladders, views from tall buildings, or plane rides.

And **terrors** are **in the way**. They have lost self-confidence, are afraid to go out alone, or to go out at night.

The blossoming **almond tree** is generally taken to picture the white hair, first in rich profusion, then falling to the ground.

The grasshopper may be interpreted in two ways. First, **the grasshopper is a burden**, that is, even the lightest objects are too heavy for the old person to carry. Or, the grasshopper dragging itself along (NASB) caricatures the old man, bent over and twisted, inching forward in jerky, erratic movements.

Desire fails in the sense that natural appetites diminish or cease altogether. Food no longer has flavor or zest, and other basic drives peter out. Sexual vigor is gone.

This degenerative process takes place because **man** is going to **his** long-lasting **home** of death and the grave, and soon his funeral procession will be moving down the street.

12:6 And so the advice of the wise man is to **remember** the **Creator before the silver cord** is snapped, **or the golden bowl is broken, or the pitcher** is **shattered at the fountain, or the wheel broken at the** cistern. It is difficult to assign precise meanings to all of these figures.

The snapping of **the silver cord** probably refers to the breaking of the tender thread of life when the spirit is released from the body. The blind poet apparently understood it in this way when she wrote:

> Some day the silver cord will break
> And I no more as now shall sing
> But oh the joy when I shall wake
> Within the palace of the King.[37]
>
> —*Fanny J. Crosby*

The golden bowl has been understood to mean the cranial cavity, and its breaking to be a poetic picture of the cessation of the mind at the time of death.

The broken **pitcher** and **wheel** taken together could be a reference to the circulatory system with the breakdown of systolic and diastolic blood pressure.

12:7 Rigor mortis sets in. Then the body begins its return to **dust**, while **the spirit** returns **to God who gave it**. Or so it seemed to Solomon. In the case of a believer, his conclusion is true. But in the case of an unbeliever, the spirit goes to Hades, there to await the Great White Throne Judgment. Then the spirit will be reunited with the body and the entire person cast into the lake of fire (Rev. 20:12–14).

12:8 And so the Preacher comes full-circle to where he began—with the basic tenet that life under the sun is **vanity**, meaningless, futile, and empty. His pathetic refrain reminds us of the little girl who went to the fair and stayed too long.

> I wanted the music to play on forever—
> Have I stayed too long at the fair?
> I wanted the clown to be constantly clever—
> Have I stayed too long at the fair?
> I bought me blue ribbons to tie up my hair,
> But I couldn't find anybody to care.
> The merry-go-round is beginning to slow now,
> Have I stayed too long at the fair?
>
> I wanted to live in a carnival city,
> with laughter and love everywhere.
> I wanted my friends to be thrilling and witty.
> I wanted somebody to care.
> I found my blue ribbons all shiny and new,
> But now I've discovered them no longer blue.
> The merry-go-round is beginning to taunt me—
> Have I stayed too long at the fair?
> There is nothing to win and no one to want me—
> Have I stayed too long at the fair?[38]
>
> —*Billy Barnes*

As we come here to Solomon's last reference to the emptiness of life under the sun, I am reminded of a story which E. Stanley Jones used to tell. On board ship he saw a very corpulent couple, their faces bovine, who lived from meal to meal. They were retired on plenty—and nothing.

> They were angry with the table stewards for not giving them super-service. They seemed to be afraid they might starve between courses. Their physical appetites seemed the one thing that mattered to them. I never saw them reading a book or paper. They sat between meals and stared out, apparently waiting for the next meal. One night I saw them sitting thus and staring blankly, when a bright idea flashed across the dull brain of the man. He went to the mantelpiece and picked up the vases, and looked into them, and then returned to his wife with the news: "They're empty!" I came very near laughing. He was right; "They're empty!" But it wasn't merely the vases! The souls and brains of both of them were empty. They had much in their purses, but nothing in their persons; and that was their punishment. They had security with boredom—no adventure. They had expanding girths and narrowing horizons.[39]

IV. EPILOGUE: THE BEST THING UNDER THE SUN (12:9–14)

12:9 Besides being **wise** himself, **the Preacher** shared his **knowledge** with others. He sought to transmit his wisdom in the form of **proverbs**, after carefully weighing them and testing them for accuracy.

12:10 He chose his **words** carefully, trying to combine what was comforting, pleasant, and true. It was like preparing a nutritious meal, then serving it with a sprig of parsley.

12:11 **The** teachings **of the wise are like** sharp, pointed instruments, plain, direct, and convincing. And the collected sayings from the **one Shepherd are like well-driven nails**

or pins that give stability to a tent. They provide strength and are also pegs on which we may hang our thoughts.

Most Bible versions capitalize the word **Shepherd**, indicating that the translators understood it as referring to God. However, it should also be remembered that in Eastern thought, a king is looked on as a shepherd. Homer said, "All kings are shepherds of the people." So it could be that King Solomon was referring to *himself* as the **one shepherd**. This interpretation fits into the context more smoothly.

12:12 There is no thought that Solomon had exhausted the subject. He could have written more, but he warns his readers that the conclusion would be the same. **There is no end** to the writing and publishing of **books**, and it would be exhausting to read them all. But why bother? All they could reveal would be the vanity of life.

12:13 His final **conclusion** may give the impression that he has at last risen above the sun. He says, "**Fear God and keep His commandments**, because **this is** the whole duty of man, **man's all**." But we must keep in mind that the **fear** of **God** here is not the same as saving faith. It is the slavish terror of a creature before His Creator. And the **commandments** do not necessarily mean the law of God as revealed in the OT. Rather they might mean any commands which God has instinctively written on the hearts of mankind.

In other words, we need not assign a high degree of spiritual insight to Solomon's words. They may be nothing more than what a wise person would conclude from natural intuition and from practical experience.

This is man's all—not just the whole duty but the basic elements that make for a full and happy life.

12:14 The motive for fearing and obeying **God** here is the certainty of coming **judgment**. We can be eternally grateful as believers that the Savior has delivered us from this kind of fear.

"There is no fear in love; but perfect love casts out fear, because fear involves torment. But he who fears has not been made perfect in love" (1 Jn. 4:18).

We do not trust and obey because of fear but because of love. Through His finished work on Calvary, we have the assurance that we will never come into judgment but have passed from death into life (John 5:24). Now we can say:

> There is no condemnation,
> There is no hell for me,
> The torment and the fire
> My eyes shall never see;
> For me there is no sentence,
> For me there is no sting
> Because the Lord who loves me
> Shall shield me with His wing.
> —*Paul Gerhardt*

ENDNOTES

[1](Intro) L. S. Chafer, *Systematic Theology*, I:83.

[2](Intro) See Gleason Archer, *A Survey of Old Testament Introduction*, pp. 478–88.

[3](Intro) *Megillah 7a; Sabbath 30*.

[4](Intro) W. Graham Scroggie, *Know Your Bible*, I:143.

[5](Intro) Solomon is widely held to be a "type" (or picture) of Christ reigning in peace during the Millennial Kingdom.

[6](Intro) Quoted by Scroggie, *Know Your Bible*, I:144.

[7](1:3) H. L. Mencken, quoted by Bill Bright, *Revolution Now*, 1969, p. 15.

[8](1:4) Will Houghton, "By Life or by Death."

[9](1:8) Author unknown. "Thou Alone, Lord Jesus," in *Hymns of Grace and Truth*, no. 220.

[10](1:13) Malcolm Muggeridge, *Jesus Rediscovered*, p. 11.

[11](1:13) For example, this name was used by other Semitic nations, and even in the OT *Elohim* is used for false "gods." It is debated whether Satan's words in Genesis 3:5 should be translated "You shall be like God" (KJV, NKJV) or "You shall be like gods" (NEB, Knox).

[12](1:15) Robert Laurin, "Ecclesiastes," in *The Wycliffe Bible Commentary*, p. 587.

[13](2:1) B. E. "None but Christ Can Satisfy!" in *Hymns of Truth and Praise*, no. 306.

[14](2:2) From *Selected Poems of Edwin Arlington Robinson*. London: The Macmillan Company, 1965, pp. 9, 10.

[15](2:8) Samuel Johnson, *The History of Rasselas, The Prince of Abyssinia*, ed. J. P. Hardy.

[16](2:8) Quoted by David R. Reuben, "Why Wives Cheat on Their Husbands," in *Reader's Digest*, Aug. 1973, p. 123.

[17](2:11) Ralph Barton, quoted by Denis Alexander, *Beyond Science*, p. 123. Used by permission of Lion Publishing.

[18](2:11) E. Stanley Jones, *Growing Spiritually*, p. 4.

[19](2:16, 17) *Choice Gleanings Calendar*. Grand Rapids: Gospel Folio Press.

[20](2:18) C. E. Stuart, further documentation unavailable.

[21](2:21) Robert Jamieson, A. R. Fausset, and David Brown, *Critical and Experimental Commentary on the Old and New Testament*, III:518.

[22](2:25) Jules Abels, *The Rockefeller Billions*, p. 299.

[23]*Table Talk*, Vol. 11, No. 4, August 1987, p. 3.

[24](3:21) The same Hebrew word translated *spirit* can also mean *breath*.

[25](4:1) James Russell Lowell, "The Present Crisis," in *Complete Poetical Works*, p. 67.

[26](4:4) Cited by Henry G. Bosch, *Our Daily Bread*, 24 May 1973.

[27](4:4) Quoted by Bill Bright, *Revolution Now*, p. 37.

[28](5:15) *Choice Gleanings Calendar*.

[29](6:9) H. C. Leupold, *Exposition of Ecclesiastes*, p. 141.

[30](7:20) *Ibid.*, p. 167.

[31](7:27, 28) G. Campbell Morgan, *Searchlights from the Word*, p. 217.

[32](9:4) Dogs in the Middle East are often snarling curs that feed on garbage and run wild through the streets, not the beloved pets of Western homes.

[33](9:9) The Gilgamesh Epic, quoted by Leupold, *Ecclesiastes*, p. 216.

[34](9:9) Denis Alexander, *Beyond Science*, pp. 132–33. Used by permission of Lion Publishing.

[35](10:9, 10) Leupold, *Ecclesiastes*, p. 242.

[36](12:1) Thomas H. Gill, "Lord in the Fullness of My Might," in *Hymns*, no. 26.

[37](12:6) Fanny J. Crosby, "Saved by Grace," in *Hymns of Truth and Praise*, no. 621.

[38](12:8) Billy Barnes, "I Stayed Too Long at the Fair." Used by permission.

[39](12:8) E. Stanley Jones, *Is the Kingdom of God Realism?*, pagination unknown.

BIBLIOGRAPHY

Delitzsch, Franz. "Ecclesiastes." In *Biblical Commentary on the Old Testament*. Vol. 18. Grand Rapids: Wm. B. Eerdmans Publishing Co., 1971.

Eaton, Michael A. *Ecclesiastes*. The Tyndale Old Testament Commentaries. Downers Grove, IL: InterVarsity Press, 1983.

Erdman, W. J. *Ecclesiastes*. Chicago: B.I.C.A., 1969.

Hengstenburg, Ernest W. *A Commentary on Ecclesiastes*. Reprint. Minneapolis: James and Klock Christian Publishing Co., 1977.

Lange, John Peter, ed. "Ecclesiastes." In *Commentary on the Holy Scriptures*. Vol. 7. Reprint (25 vols. in 12). Grand Rapids: Zondervan Publishing House, 1960.

Laurin, Robert. "Ecclesiastes." In *The Wycliffe Bible Commentary*. Chicago: Moody Press, 1962.

Leupold, H. C. *Exposition of Ecclesiastes*. Grand Rapids: Baker Book House, 1952.

MacDonald, William. *Chasing the Wind*. Chicago: Moody Press, 1975.

THE SONG OF SOLOMON

Introduction

"In the glorious temple of revelation, a place which the Lord our God has chosen to cause his name to dwell there, even in brighter glory than in the temple of the material world, does this book stand, like one of the apartments in the temple on Mount Zion, small indeed, but exquisitely finished, the walls and ceiling of something richer than cedar, richer than bright ivory overlaid with sapphires, and filled with specimens of truth brought down from heaven by the Holy Spirit, and here deposited for the comfort and delight of those who love the habitation of God's house, and the place where his glory dwelleth."

—George Burrowes

I. Unique Place in the Canon

The title "the Song of Songs" is a Hebrew idiom meaning *The Most Exquisite Song*. The Jewish Midrash calls it "the most praiseworthy, most excellent, most highly treasured among the songs." This song, also called Canticles, is generally considered the hardest book in the Bible to *understand*. Franz Delitzsch wrote, "The Song is the most obscure book in the Old Testament."[1] It is not hard to *enjoy* it if you appreciate poetry, love, and nature, but what *is* it and what does it *mean*?

Scholars are divided as to whether it is an anthology of unrelated love lyrics, a little drama, or a "unified dramatic lyric dialogue of love."[2] In the light of repeated refrains and the flow of the story, plus the too great brevity of the work to be a real "play," the last named is the best choice.

But still how is one to *interpret* the book? Here the imagination of readers throughout the ages has had a field day. While certain Jews and Christians have prudishly avoided the book as "sensual," some of the most devout saints throughout history have reveled in its pages.

II. Authorship

Jewish tradition has it that Solomon wrote the Song in his youth, Proverbs in his prime, and Ecclesiastes after he had grown weary of this world. This view has much to commend it. Since the author praises marital fidelity, it has been suggested that Solomon dedicated the book to the first of his many wives, before he got entangled in polygamy and concubinage. The present commentary, however, takes quite a different view.

Seven verses in the Song refer to Solomon by name (1:1, 5; 3:7, 9, 11; 8:11, 12). The first one probably ascribed *authorship* to him (though it could also be translated "The Song of Songs which is *about* Solomon"). The allusions to nature fit in with Solomon's interests (1 Kgs. 4:33). Also, references to royal horses, chariots, and the palanquin tend to support Solomonic authorship. The

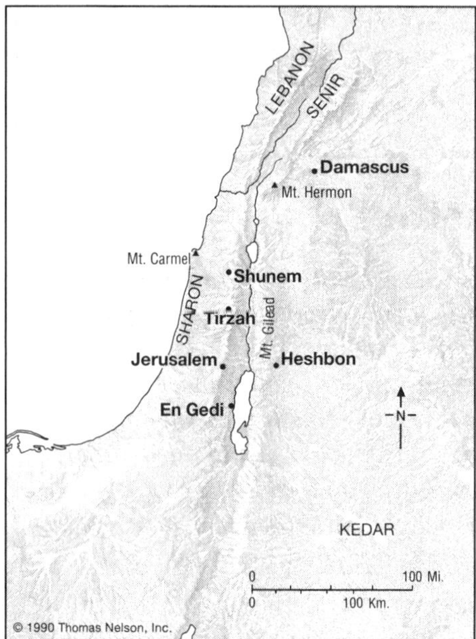

Places Named in the Song of Solomon

geographical references suggest that the places were all in one united kingdom, which was true chiefly during Solomon's reign.

Thus, there is every reason to accept the traditional view of authorship, and contrary arguments are not convincing.

III. Date

King Solomon probably wrote this loveliest of his 1,005 songs (1 Kgs. 4:32) some time during his forty year reign (971–931 BC). The tradition that he was still young and not yet jaded with too many women is logical and attractive.

IV. Background and Theme

The usual Christian interpretation given to this book is that it represents the love of Christ for His church. This interpretation is followed in the chapter headings in many editions of the Bible. According to this view Solomon is a type of Christ and the Shulamite a type of the church. However, the careful student of Scripture will realize that this cannot be the primary interpretation of the book since the church was a secret hidden in God from the foundation of the world and not revealed until the apostles and prophets of the NT (Rom. 16:25, 26; Eph. 3:9). Few Christians will deny that in this song we have a very beautiful picture of the love of Christ for the church, but this is an application and not the interpretation. The primary *interpretation* of the book must be concerned with Jehovah and the nation of Israel.

A second interpretation sees this book as a protest against marital infidelity. Solomon, with his many wives, seeks to woo a young Shulamite maiden. But she has a shepherd-lover to whom she is faithful and true. She does not yield to the blandishments of Solomon. Every time he flatters her, she begins to speak about her own lover. At the close of the book, she is seen united with her shepherd-lover and resting in his love. Those who accept this interpretation point out that most references to Solomon have the city and palace as background whereas references to the shepherd picture him appropriately in a rural setting. This sharp contrast between the city and the country reinforces the idea that there are two male characters in the drama, not just one. This interpretation is not popular because it puts Solomon in an unfavorable light.[3] However, it is true that he was a polygamist whereas God's order for His people was monogamy. The nation of Israel, of course, had been unfaithful to Jehovah, running after other lovers. In this song, they read of the beauty of faithful love.

A third interpretation sees the Shulamite maiden as a type of the believing remnant of the nation of Israel in a coming day. Solomon is a type of the Lord Jesus. The song pictures the loving fellowship which will be enjoyed by the remnant when they look on Him whom they have pierced and mourn for Him as one mourning for an only son. The fact that Solomon was a polygamist does not bar him from being a type of the Lord. The type is imperfect; the Antitype is perfect.

A fourth view, very popular today, is to see the book as an encouragement to true love and purity within the bonds of matrimony. In light of the world's exploitations of sex without married love, this is a viable option, fitting in well with Genesis 1:27 and 2:20–24.

At any rate, no matter which view one holds, the Song of Songs has been widely, and we believe rightly, used by believing couples on their wedding night and to enhance their marriage.

OUTLINE

I. TITLE (1:1)

II. THE SHULAMITE IN SOLOMON'S COURT THINKS OF HER ABSENT SHEPHERD-LOVER AND TELLS THE COURT LADIES ABOUT HIM AND ABOUT HERSELF (1:2–8)

III. SOLOMON WOOS THE SHULAMITE MAIDEN BUT SHE IS DEAF TO HIS FLATTERY (1:9—2:6)

IV. THE MAIDEN'S CHARGE TO THE DAUGHTERS OF JERUSALEM (2:7)

V. THE SHULAMITE REMINISCES ABOUT A VISIT FROM HER SHEPHERD-LOVER, INTERRUPTED BY ORDERS FROM HER BROTHERS TO GET TO WORK (2:8–17)

VI. THE MAIDEN DREAMS OF A RENDEZVOUS WITH HER BELOVED (3:1–4)

VII. REPETITION OF CHARGE TO DAUGHTERS OF JERUSALEM (3:5)

VIII. SOLOMON'S PROCESSION ARRIVES AT JERUSALEM (3:6–11)

IX. AGAIN SOLOMON SEEKS TO WIN THE MAIDEN, BUT SHE IS IMPERVIOUS TO HIS CHARMS (4:1–6)

X. THE YOUNG SHEPHERD ARRIVES AND APPEALS TO THE MAIDEN TO LEAVE JERUSALEM FOR THE HOME THEY HAVE PLANNED IN THE COUNTRY, AND SHE EXPRESSES HER WILLINGNESS (4:7—5:1)

XI. THE SHULAMITE RECALLS A DISTURBING DREAM IN WHICH SHE MISSED SEEING HIM BECAUSE OF HER LETHARGY (5:2–8)

XII. ON INQUIRY BY THE COURT LADIES, SHE EXTOLS THE BEAUTIES OF HER BELOVED, MAKING THEM WANT TO SEE HIM TOO (5:9—6:3)

XIII. SOLOMON RENEWS HIS AMOROUS APPEALS (6:4–10)

XIV. SHE EXPLAINS TO THE COURT LADIES THE UNEXPECTED WAY IN WHICH SHE WAS BROUGHT TO THE PALACE (6:11–13)

XV. SOLOMON'S FINAL APPROACH PROVES TO BE IN VAIN (7:1–10)

XVI. SHE CONVERSES WITH HER SHEPHERD-LOVER WHO HAS ARRIVED TO TAKE HER AWAY (7:11—8:2)

XVII. FINAL CHARGE TO THE DAUGHTERS OF JERUSALEM (8:3, 4)

XVIII. THE COUPLE ARRIVE IN THEIR COUNTRY VILLAGE, EXCHANGE THEIR VOWS, AND LIVE HAPPILY EVER AFTER (8:5–14)

Commentary

I. TITLE (1:1)

The song of songs is introduced as **Solomon's**; it could also mean "concerning Solomon."

II. THE SHULAMITE IN SOLOMON'S COURT THINKS OF HER ABSENT SHEPHERD-LOVER AND TELLS THE COURT LADIES ABOUT HIM AND ABOUT HERSELF (1:2–8)

1:2–4 The Shulamite is longing for **the kisses** of her shepherd-lover; then, imagining that he is present, she tells him that his **love is better than wine**. Comparing his virtues to fragrant **ointment**, she sees this as the reason why he is loved by **the** other **virgins**, but she longs for him to come and claim her as his own. The daughters of Jerusalem **will** try in vain to follow. King Solomon **has brought** the Shulamite **into his chambers**, presumably to add her to his harem, but it was quite against her own will. When the daughters of Jerusalem adopt her sentiments concerning her beloved as their own, she comments that their appreciation of him is justified.

1:5, 6 Unlike the pale court ladies, the rustic Shulamite has spent much time in **the sun** as **a keeper of the vineyards**. Hence she is **tanned** and **dark, but**[4] **lovely**.

1:7, 8 Her thoughts wander to her lover. She wonders **where he** is feeding his **flock, where** he is making **it rest at noon**. And she can't understand **why** she can't be with him instead of being a veiled woman in the presence of others, who were, to her, less worthy men.

The daughters of Jerusalem[5] sarcastically suggest that she could find him by following **the footsteps of the flock**.

III. SOLOMON WOOS THE SHULAMITE MAIDEN BUT SHE IS DEAF TO HIS FLATTERY (1:9—2:6)

1:9, 10 Solomon now begins his courtship of the Shulamite. She reminds him of a caparisoned prize **filly among Pharaoh's chariots**. He sees her **cheeks** adorned with choice **ornaments** and her **neck** draped **with chains of gold**.

1:11 Using the editorial we,[6] he offers to enrich her with golden **ornaments** and **studs of silver**.

1:12–14 The Shulamite is unaffected by the king's flattering words and luring offers. She can think only of her lover. **While the king** sits **at his table**, she has her own source of **fragrance**—a little sachet **of myrrh** that she keeps next to herself as a memento of her shepherd. He is as fragrant to her as **a cluster of henna blooms in the vineyards of En Gedi**.

1:15 Again Solomon tries to woo her, this time extolling her beauty and comparing her **eyes** to those of a dove.

1:16,17 But the Shulamite switches the conversation in her own mind, at least, by telling her lover how **handsome** he is. She pictures the great outdoors as their house, the grass as their **bed**, and the overhanging **cedar** and **fir** branches as their roof. The setting of their romance is uniformly pastoral, not a palace.

2:1 The maiden continues by protesting her own plainness and unworthiness. When she likens herself to **the rose of Sharon** and **the lily of the valleys**,[7] she is not thinking of the cultivated flowers we call "roses" and "lilies" but probably of the common, wild scarlet anemones, or perhaps the crocus.[8]

2:2 Solomon must have heard her protestations of mediocrity because he tells her that she is very special. Compared to other virgins, she is like a **lily among thorns**.

2:3 Switching again to rural scenes, she sees her beloved as a cultivated **apple tree among the** wild **trees of the woods**. To be with him had always been delightful, and fellowship with him was ever so **sweet**.

2:4–6 Just to be with him was like being in a **banqueting house**; always overhead was **his banner** of **love**. Overcome with thoughts of him she calls for **cakes of raisins** and **apples** to **refresh** and strengthen her. It is as if he were actually with her, holding and embracing her.

IV. THE MAIDEN'S CHARGE TO THE DAUGHTERS OF JERUSALEM (2:7)

Turning to the **daughters of Jerusalem**,[9] the Shulamite strikes the keynote of the book. There is a time for love. It should not be aroused by carnal means (as the king was trying to do). She charges them **by the** graceful **gazelles** that they should **not stir up** or **awaken love until it pleases**. In other words, "love is not a thing to be bought or forced or pretended, but a thing to come spontaneously, to be given freely and sincerely."[10] If Israel had followed this simple rule, it would not have been unfaithful to Jehovah.

V. THE SHULAMITE REMINISCES ABOUT A VISIT FROM HER SHEPHERD-LOVER, INTERRUPTED BY ORDERS FROM HER BROTHERS TO GET TO WORK (2:8–17)

2:8–14 Now the maiden recalls a past visit of her **beloved**. He came **leaping** over **the mountains**, **skipping** over **the hills** in his haste to reach her. He had all the grace of **a gazelle or a young stag**. Soon he was standing **behind** the **wall**, **looking through the windows**, **gazing through the lattice**. She heard his voice, calling to her to leave with him. The dark night of **winter** was **past** and the **rain** was **over**. All the signs of spring were appearing—**the flowers**, **the turtledove**, **the fig tree** with **green figs**, and **the vines with . . . tender grapes**. He urged her to "**Rise up, . . . and come away.**" Perhaps there was a delay, because he then asked her to come to the window, so he could **see** her **face** and **hear** her **voice**. Up to now she was hidden from him like a **dove, in the clefts of the rock**, or in the covert of a **cliff**.

2:15 Any possibility of leaving was lost when her brothers appeared and ordered her and her companions (the command is plural in the original)[11] to **catch . . . the little foxes** that were ruining **the vines** at the crucial time when they were bearing **tender grapes**.[12]

2:16,17 This is a great disappointment, but she is consoled by the fact that she and her shepherd-lover belong to each other. So she said to him, in effect, "Come back again sometime in the cool of the evening, when **the shadows** have flown **away**. Return with the speed of **a young stag** over **the mountains of Bether** (or Separation, i.e., the mountains that separate us)."

VI. THE MAIDEN DREAMS OF A RENDEZVOUS WITH HER BELOVED (3:1–4)

Now the maiden is recalling a dream in which she had a rendezvous with her beloved. One **night** she was looking for him, but when she couldn't **find him**, she went into **the city**, searched **the streets** and **squares**, and even asked **the watchmen**. Then almost immediately she **found** him, embraced **him**, and took **him** to her family home.

VII. REPETITION OF CHARGE TO DAUGHTERS OF JERUSALEM (3:5)

She interrupts long enough to repeat her **charge** to the **daughters of Jerusalem**—don't **stir up . . . love until it pleases**.

VIII. SOLOMON'S PROCESSION ARRIVES AT JERUSALEM (3:6–11)

The scene changes. We now watch the colorful and grandiose arrival of **Solomon's** procession at Jerusalem. The question implied is, "Who could resist the romantic overtures of such a glorious king?" The implied answer, of course, is "The Shulamite can." She is faithful to her own lover, and deaf to all other voices.

The spectators along the parade route are awed by the king's arrival, with the attendant clouds of **myrrh and frankincense**. They see the **couch** or **palanquin** of Solomon, guarded by **sixty** fully armed soldiers. Inside are the magnificent **pillars of silver, the support of gold, the seat of purple** upholstery, and the carpeting woven lovingly **by the daughters of Jerusalem**. Zion's citizens are summoned to greet **King Solomon**, wearing **the crown** given to him by **his mother . . . on the day of his wedding**.

IX. AGAIN SOLOMON SEEKS TO WIN THE MAIDEN, BUT SHE IS IMPERVIOUS TO HIS CHARMS (4:1–6)

4:1–5 There is a difference of opinion among those who hold the three-character view of the Song of Songs as to whether the speaker in these verses is Solomon or the shepherd. We shall assume that it is the much-married Solomon who has just returned to Jerusalem and is making another attempt to captivate the Shulamite.

He launches into a detailed description of her beauty. Her **eyes**, looking out from **behind** a **veil**, remind him of **doves' eyes**. The rippled sheen of her **hair** resembles a **flock of goats** moving together **down** the side of **Mount Gilead** in the sunshine. Her gleaming white **teeth** make him think of ewes, newly sheared and freshly washed. The teeth are like twin lambs in that every upper has a corresponding lower; not one is missing. **Her lips are like a strand of scarlet**, and the symmetry of her **mouth** is perfect. Her **temples behind** the **veil are** contoured **like a piece of pomegranate**. Her **neck, like the tower of David**, speaks of strength and dignity. Her **two breasts, like** twin **fawns**, suggest delicate and tender beauty.

4:6 The Shulamite interrupts[13] to let Solomon know that she is impervious to his flattery, and that she is looking forward to reunion with her beloved. When **the day** cools and **the shadows** vanish, she **will go . . . to the mountain of myrrh, and to the hill of frankincense**, that is, to her shepherd-lover.

X. THE YOUNG SHEPHERD ARRIVES AND APPEALS TO THE MAIDEN TO LEAVE JERUSALEM FOR THE HOME THEY HAVE PLANNED IN THE COUNTRY, AND SHE EXPRESSES HER WILLINGNESS (4:7—5:1)

4:7–15 Now the shepherd appears[14] and urges his fiancée to **come with** him **from Lebanon**, at the same time praising her for her beauty, **love, lips, the fragrance of** her **garments**, meaning her life, and her chastity. He likens her to **a** well-watered **garden**, bearing the choicest **fruits** and the most **fragrant . . . spices**.

4:16 In poetic language, she tells him to **come** to the **garden** and claim it as his own.

5:1a Now the shepherd responds to the Shulamite's invitation of 4:16, saying that he is coming **to** the **garden** to gather his spices, to eat **honeycomb**, and to drink **wine** and **milk**.

5:1b The latter part of verse 1 seems to be an anonymous encouragement from interested spectators to these two ardent lovers.[15]

XI. THE SHULAMITE RECALLS A DISTURBING DREAM IN WHICH SHE MISSED SEEING HIM BECAUSE OF HER LETHARGY (5:2–8)

5:2–7 Now the maiden describes a dream in which she heard him knocking at the door, calling for her to **open**. He was wet **with** the **dew** of the evening. When she hesitated to open to him because she had already bathed and retired for the night, he withdrew **his hand** from **the door**. Finally she got up and went to the door. Her **hands** became perfumed **with** the **liquid myrrh** which he had left **on the handles of the lock**. But he **had . . . gone**. She looked for him, **called** for **him, but . . . could not find him. The** city **watchmen**—misunderstanding her character—**struck** her and **took** off her **veil**.

5:8 In her sorrow she charges the **daughters of Jerusalem** to **tell him**, if they should somehow see him, that she still loves him as much as ever.

XII. ON INQUIRY BY THE COURT LADIES, SHE EXTOLS THE BEAUTIES OF HER BELOVED, MAKING THEM WANT TO SEE HIM TOO (5:9—6:3)

5:9 Her constant enthusiasm for a mere shepherd arouses the interest of the daughters of Jerusalem. They can't understand why anyone should refuse the love of a Solomon for some obscure country lad, so they ask her **what** is so special about her **beloved**.

5:10–16 This gives her just the opportunity she wants to extol his physical attractiveness as **"chief among ten thousand."** Using a wealth of poetic metaphors and similes, she raves about **his** complexion, **head, locks, eyes, cheeks, lips, hands, body, legs, countenance**, and **mouth**. In short, her **beloved** and her **friend is altogether lovely**.[16]

6:1 By this time **the daughters of Jerusalem** really want to see this paragon of male beauty. They ask **where they might seek him with** her.[17]

6:2,3 The maiden's answer is purposely vague and evasive—he **"has gone to his garden."** Why should she tell *them?* She belongs to him, he belongs to her, and that's the way she intends it to remain!

XIII. SOLOMON RENEWS HIS AMOROUS APPEALS (6:4–10)

Solomon appears again and tries to woo her. Using middle-eastern imagery, he raves over her facial beauty; much of what he says is a repeat of 4:1–3. In his mind, she surpassed **sixty queens, eighty concubines**, and numberless **virgins**. Not only was she her mother's **favorite**, but **the queens, concubines**, and maidens all **praised her**, saying, **"Who is she who looks forth as the morning, fair as the moon, clear as the sun, awesome as an army with banners?"**

XIV. SHE EXPLAINS TO THE COURT LADIES THE UNEXPECTED WAY IN WHICH SHE WAS BROUGHT TO THE PALACE (6:11–13)

6:11,12 The Shulamite deflects Solomon's overtures with an obscure explanation, perhaps of how the king's chariot came by while she was in the field checking the fruit and **garden of nuts**. The king's subsequent interest, in taking her to the palace in Jerusalem was nothing that she had planned or even desired.

6:13 As she starts to leave, either Solomon and the daughters of Jerusalem or his friends call her back for another **look** at her beauty. But she asks why they would want to look on anyone as ordinary as she. The last line in the verse is difficult. **The two camps** (Heb. *Mahanaim*) that the Shulamite speaks of may well be a dance in which two groups of dancers weave in and out with one another.

XV. SOLOMON'S FINAL APPROACH PROVES TO BE IN VAIN (7:1–10)

7:1–9a Solomon continues his fulsome praise by giving a full-length portrait of her physical charms, comparing her to famous places in his far-flung realm: **Heshbon, Bath Rabbim, Damascus**, and **Mount Carmel**. Then he sees her as a stately **palm tree**, and would like to embrace her. When he does, her **breasts** would **be like clusters of** fruit, her **breath like apples**, and her kisses **like the best wine**—

7:9b–10 The maiden finishes the sentence by letting him know that her **wine** is not for him but **for** her **beloved**. She belongs to her lover and not to the king. Even as she said it, she knew that the shepherd was longing for her.

XVI. SHE CONVERSES WITH HER SHEPHERD-LOVER WHO HAS ARRIVED TO TAKE HER AWAY (7:11—8:2)

7:11–13 Now the shepherd-lover has arrived in Jerusalem and she is free to **go to the field** and **the villages** with him. She anticipates walking in **the field** with him, going out at daybreak **to the vineyards** to check **the vine . . . and the pomegranates**. In that rural setting where **the mandrakes** are fragrant, she will give him her love and all kinds of **pleasant fruits** which she has stored up for him.

8:1, 2 The Shulamite is still speaking. If the shepherd **were** only her **brother**, she could **kiss** him and **not be** reproached. She would take him to her mother's **house** and serve him the choicest **spiced wine** made of **pomegranate**.

XVII. FINAL CHARGE TO THE DAUGHTERS OF JERUSALEM (8:3, 4)

In an aside **to the daughters of Jerusalem**, the Shulamite sees herself in his arms, then charges them for the last time **not** to **stir up** love **until it pleases**.

XVIII. THE COUPLE ARRIVES IN THEIR COUNTRY VILLAGE, EXCHANGE THEIR VOWS, AND LIVE HAPPILY EVER AFTER (8:5–14)

8:5a In her home village, the local people see her returning **from** Jerusalem and ask **who it is, coming up from the wilderness, leaning upon her beloved**.

8:5b Then as the lovers approach, the shepherd points out familiar places—**under the apple tree** where their romance began, and then also her birthplace.

8:6,7 The Shulamite suggests renewing their vows. In words of great beauty that have been widely quoted, she affirms that there is no rival for her **love**. It **is as strong as death,** unquenchable, and beyond price.

8:8, 9 Years ago, when planning the young Shulamite's future, her **brothers** had made this decision. If she proved to be chaste, pure, and faithful, they would give her a **silver** dowry. **If**, however, **she** was promiscuous and accessible as **a door**, they would hide her away in seclusion.

8:10, 11 The maiden assures them that, now of marriageable age, she has been steadfast as **a wall**. Her lover knows that. She tells them of Solomon's **vineyard at Baal Hamon** with its many tenants.

8:12 But she wasn't interested. She had her **own vineyard**—her shepherd-lover. **Solomon** could keep his wealth as far as she was concerned.

8:13 In the presence of witnesses, the shepherd asks her to commit herself to him now in marriage, to say "I do."

8:14 In figurative language, she tells her **beloved** to **make haste** to claim her as his own. And thus the book closes. It has been called

> the Old Testament's endorsement of monogamy in the face of the most glaring example of polygamy to be found in the Scriptures. It is a powerful plea to Israel of Solomon's day to return to the God-given ideal of love and marriage.[18]

ENDNOTES

[1](Intro) Franz Delitzsch, "The Song of Songs," in *Biblical Commentary on the Old Testament*, XVI:1.

[2](Intro) Arthur Farstad, "Literary Genre of the Song of Songs," p. 63.

[3](Intro) Clarke's commentary (see

Bibliography) presents the same view as the *Believers Bible Commentary*.

[4](1:5, 6) The little word translated "but" (*we*) can be (and more often is) translated "and." Then a literal translation would be "black and beautiful."

[5](1:7, 8) The translators of the NKJV take verse 8 to be the words of the Beloved, and hence not sarcastic. The Beloved and Solomon are taken as the same person rather than as rivals for the Shulamite's love. It should be stressed that the headings in the NKJV, New Scofield, or any Bible, are editorial, and not part of the text. However, as the note at 1:1 in the NKJV points out, the Hebrew wording is clearer than the English as to gender and number of persons referred to.

[6](1:11) The NKJV takes the "we" literally as referring to the daughters of Jerusalem.

[7](2:1) In prose, poetry, and hymnody our Lord has been likened to the lily of the valley and the rose of Sharon. That comparison is still valid even if it is not the thought in this passage.

[8](2:1) Farstad, "Literary Genre," p. 79, f.n. 6.

[9](2:7) The NKJV takes the address to the daughters to start at v. 4.

[10](2:7) W. Twyman Williams, "The Song of Solomon," *Moody Monthly*, February 1947, p. 398.

[11](2:15) The plural form of "catch" may be explained by the likelihood that these lines (extremely song-like and full of rhymes in the original) are a "vine-dresser's ditty" (Delitzsch, "Song of Songs," p. 53). Otto Zöckler writes that "this verse is a little vintagers' song or at least a fragment of one" and says that all the commentators of his time who are not allegorists are settled on this ("Song of Songs," in *Lange's Commentary on the Holy Scriptures*, V:71).

[12](2:15) Young foxes (the term includes jackals) come out in the spring and destroy the vines by burrowing passages and holes beneath the roots, thus undermining their support. See Delitzsch, "Song of Songs," p. 54.

[13](4:6) The NKJV editors take this verse as part of the Beloved's speech.

[14](4:7–15) The NKJV editors see no indication of a new speaker here and take these verses as part of the Beloved's speech.

[15](5:1b) The NKJV editors agree, calling these people "His friends."

[16](5:10–16) Based on the Christological interpretation of the book, the phrases "chief among ten thousand" and "altogether lovely" have been applied to our Lord in sermon and song. Especially in the spiritual sense, these applications are well warranted, even if not originally meant by the context.

[17](6:1) In the Christological interpretation the bride's (= church's) "witnessing" to the beauties of her beloved (= Christ) causes others to seek Him too.

[18](8:14) Williams, "Song," p. 422.

BIBLIOGRAPHY

Bellett, J. G. *Meditations upon the Canticles*. London: G. Morrish, n.d.

Burrowes, George. *A Commentary on the Song of Solomon*. Philadelphia: William S. & Alfred Martien, 1860.

Clarke, Arthur G. *The Song of Songs*. Kansas City, KS: Walterick Publishers, n.d.

Delitzsch, Franz. "The Song of Songs." In *Biblical Commentary on the Old Testament*, Vol. 16. Grand Rapids: Wm. B. Eerdmans Publishing Company, 1971.

Zöckler, Otto. "The Song of Solomon." *Lange's Commentary on the Holy Scriptures*. Vol. 5. Grand Rapids: Zondervan Publishing House, 1960.

Periodicals

Williams, W. Twyman. "The Song of Solomon," *Moody Monthly*, February 1947.

Unpublished Materials

Farstad, Arthur L. "Literary Genre of the Song of Songs." Th.M. Thesis, Dallas Theological Seminary, 1967.

INTRODUCTION TO THE PROPHETS

The section of the OT from Isaiah through Malachi is often spoken of as "the Prophets." Isaiah, Jeremiah, Ezekiel, and Daniel are known as the *Major* Prophets, simply because their books are longer than most of the others. The twelve shorter prophets are known as the *Minor* Prophets.

I. The Ministry of the Prophets

In the true biblical sense, a prophet is one who speaks for God. These men[1] were raised up in periods of sin and declension to accuse the people of their sin and predict the judgment of God if they did not repent.

In the OT, the prophetic period began in the time of Samuel (about 1100 B.C.), when the priesthood had failed. The prophets continued their ministry through the end of OT history (about 400 B.C.), including the return from captivity and the rebuilding of Jerusalem and the temple.

However, the *writing* prophets of the OT did not come upon the scene until the time of the divided kingdom (about 930 B.C.). Thus, they fit into the events recorded in 1 and 2 Kings and 1 and 2 Chronicles, and also extend through Ezra and Nehemiah.

II. The Methods of the Prophets

It has often been pointed out that the prophets' messages consisted of both forthtelling and foretelling.

By *forthtelling*, we mean that these prophets told forth the Word of God. They were conscious that they were doing this. They used such expressions as, "Thus says the Lord," or "The word of the Lord came to me" (See Jer. 1:9 and Ezek. 2:7).

As *foretellers*, they peered into the future and told the people what the consequences would be if they obeyed or disobeyed. The prophets did not always understand the messages themselves (Dan. 7:28; 8:15–27; 10:7–15; Rev. 7:13, 14; 17:6). They had particular difficulty when they made prophecies concerning the coming Messiah. When they prophesied of the sufferings of Christ and the glories that should follow (1 Pet. 1:10–13), they could not understand how the Messiah could come as the suffering Servant of Jehovah and at the same time reign as the King over all the earth. They did not realize that there were two distinct comings—His coming to Bethlehem and His coming back again to the Mount of Olives. They did not realize that an interval of time would come between these two comings.

III. The Topics of the Prophets

The topics taken up by the OT prophets may be summarized as follows:

1. The holiness of God.
2. The sin and failure of God's chosen people.
3. A call to repentance.
4. God's judgment on them if they would not repent.

5. God's judgment on the surrounding nations.
6. The return of part of the nation from captivity.
7. The coming of the Messiah and His rejection.
8. The Messiah's coming in power and great glory.
9. The restoration of God's chosen people.
10. Christ's universal reign.

It should be noted at this point that the church is not the subject of OT prophecy. We would not expect the church to be found here since we are distinctly told in the NT that it is a mystery which was hidden in God from the foundation of the world (Eph. 3:4–6).

The law of double reference is a helpful key to understanding certain OT passages. The law of double reference simply means that some of the prophecies of the OT had an immediate and partial fulfillment, and yet would some day have a complete fulfillment. For instance, the prophecy in Joel 2:28–32 had a partial fulfillment on the Day of Pentecost (Acts 2:7–21), but it will have a complete fulfillment when the Lord Jesus returns to set up His kingdom on the earth at the close of the Great Tribulation period.

It is good to remember that while some prophecies are crystal clear from the outset, there are others that will not be clear until they actually take place.

We should avoid fanciful interpretations of prophecy. Great harm has been done by stating that certain individuals and events are fulfillments, when it later becomes obvious that they were not.

IV. The Terminology of the Prophets

Some further key terms to help us understand the Prophets are:

1. The name *Israel* ordinarily refers to the Northern Kingdom, the ten tribes. But it sometimes refers to the entire nation—all who are descendants of Abraham.
2. *Judah*, on the other hand, usually refers to the Southern Kingdom, the two tribes of Judah and Benjamin.
3. *Ephraim* is used, especially in Hosea, to describe the ten tribes, or the Northern Kingdom. The house of Joseph also refers to the Northern Kingdom.
4. *Samaria* was the capital of the Northern Kingdom and is mentioned frequently.
5. *Jerusalem*, on the other hand, was the capital of the Southern Kingdom.
6. *Nineveh* was the capital of Assyria.
7. The city of *Babylon* was the capital of the nation of Babylon (also called Babylonia).
8. *Damascus* was the chief city-state of Syria.

In their denunciation of idolatry, the prophets often used words associated with idolatry, such as "wooden images," "high places," "terebinth trees" or "oaks," and "gardens."

"Judgment" is often used by the prophets to mean justice. They denounced the perverting of "judgment," meaning that they condemned judges who took bribes and thus did not dispense justice.

The thought of a remnant of the nation of Israel is prominent in the Prophets. These books predict the return of a believing remnant of the nation in a latter day, just as a remnant returned after the captivity in Babylon.

V. The Classification of the Prophets

The books of the Prophets may be classified in several ways. We have already seen that they are divided into the Major and Minor Prophets. They can also be classified according to the time in which they lived:

Pre-exilic

Isaiah	Jonah
Jeremiah	Micah
Hosea	Nahum
Joel	Habakkuk
Amos	Zephaniah
Obadiah	

Exilic	**Post-exilic**
Ezekiel	Haggai
Daniel	Zechariah
	Malachi

The pre-exilic prophets were those who ministered *before* the nation was taken into captivity. The exilic prophets were those who spoke for God *during* the time of the Babylonian captivity. The post-exilic prophets returned with the people *after* the captivity and urged them to rebuild the city and the temple and to reform their morals.

Then the prophets may also be classified according to the people to whom their messages were primarily directed:

Israel	**The Nations**
Hosea	Nahum
Amos	Obadiah
Jonah	

Judah

Isaiah	Zephaniah
Jeremiah	Ezekiel
Joel	Daniel
Micah	Haggai
Habakkuk	Zechariah
Malachi	

Some of these prophets ministered to more than one of these groups. For instance, Jonah might also be listed as a prophet to the nations. Micah prophesied to Israel as well as to Judah. Nahum spoke to Judah (1:15) as well as to Nineveh. Habakkuk had much to say about the nations.

In several instances, the name of the prophet is hidden in the text of his prophecy. For instance, the name Isaiah means *Jehovah is salvation*. In Isaiah 12:2 we read, "YAH, the Lord has . . . become salvation."

Jeremiah—*Jehovah establishes* or *exalted of Jehovah*—52:31.
Ezekiel—*God strengthens*—34:16.
Joel—*Jehovah is God*—2:13.
Micah—*who is like Jehovah?*—7:18.
Zephaniah—*hidden by Jehovah*—2:3.
Malachi—*My messenger*—3:1.

VI. The Chronology of the Prophets

The following chronology will help the reader to understand various references in the books of the Prophets.

Kingdom of Israel (Northern Tribes)

Syria was the principal foreign foe of Israel after the division of the Kingdom.

Then Assyria rose to power and menaced Israel. The steps by which Assyria conquered Israel are as follows:

1. Jehu paid tribute to Shalmaneser, King of Assyria (842 B.C.).
2. Menahem paid tribute to Tiglath-Pileser. The latter started taking the Israelites away from the land.
3. In the reign of Pekah, Tiglath-Pileser captured cities of Naphtali and carried off inhabitants to Assyria (2 Kgs. 15:29). He also overran the country east of the Jordan and deported the two and one-

half tribes to Mesopotamia, 740 B.C. (1 Chron. 5:26). By his connivance, Pekah was killed, and Hoshea was put on the throne.

4. Hoshea became Shalmaneser's servant and paid tribute to him, but plotted against him by sending gifts to Egypt and seeking an alliance so that the Assyrian yoke could be broken (2 Kgs. 17:3, 4).
5. Shalmaneser besieged Samaria. The city was taken in the first year of Sargon's reign, 722 B.C. or 721 B.C. Many of the people were deported to Mesopotamia and Media (2 Kgs. 17:5, 6, 18). The rest were placed under tribute.

Kingdom of Judah (Southern Tribes)

After conquering the Northern Kingdom, Assyria began to threaten Judah. God assured the Jews that, though the Assyrians would come against them, they would not succeed, but would be destroyed. This happened when Sennacherib came against Jerusalem during Hezekiah's reign.

Then Babylon rose to power and became the great threat to Judah. The political steps that led to the conquest of Judah by Babylon are as follows:

1. Jehoiakim became the puppet of the King of Egypt.
2. Babylon conquered Egypt and Assyria, and thus Judah came under her power (605 B.C.).
3. In 605 B.C. (third or fourth year of Jehoiakim), Nebuchadnezzar came to Jerusalem, took some of the vessels of the temple to Babylon, and carried off certain members of the royal family as captives. The captives included the king (Jehoiakim) and the prophet Daniel (2 Kgs. 24:1–6; 2 Chron. 36:5–8; Jer. 45:1; Dan. 1:1, 2).
4. In 597 B.C., Nebuchadnezzar carried off Jehoiachin (Jeconiah or Coniah) and many others (2 Kgs. 24:10–16). Ezekiel was taken to Babylon in this deportation.
5. In 586 B.C., the armies of Nebuchadnezzar burned the temple, destroyed Jerusalem, and carried off the bulk of the population, leaving only some of the poorest people in the land (2 Kgs. 25:2–21).
6. The people who remained in the land were ruled by a governor, Gedaliah. Jeremiah was in this group. Then Gedaliah was assassinated, and many of the people fled to Egypt, taking Jeremiah with them (2 Kgs. 25:22–26).

Seventy-Year Captivity and Post-Captivity Period

The Babylonian world empire extended to 539 B.C., when Cyrus captured Babylon. It was he who issued the decree permitting the captives to return to the land of Israel. An expedition under Zerubbabel returned in 538 B.C., and another under Ezra in 458 B.C.

Darius the Mede reigned from 538–536 B.C.

The Medo-Persian empire continued until 333 B.C., when the Grecians, under Alexander the Great, gained world dominion.

The seventy-year captivity extended from the fall of Jerusalem in 586 B.C. to the rebuilding of the temple in 516 B.C.

ENDNOTES

[1]There were also some female prophets, or prophetesses, such as Huldah (2 Kgs. 22:14; 2 Chron. 34:22).

ISAIAH

Introduction

"Isaiah . . . is the greatest of the Hebrew prophets and orators. For splendor of diction, brilliance of imagery, versatility and beauty of style, he is unequalled. Correctly he has been called the 'Prince of Old Testament Prophets.'"

—Merrill F. Unger

I. Unique Place in the Canon

Visitors to Ireland's lovely capital who appreciate Christian culture are often shown a private house where one of the greatest musical compositions had its "world premiere." It was in Dublin on April 13, 1742 that Handel's *Messiah* was first performed.[1] No knowledgeable person has ever questioned the excellence of Handel's composition as to the music, but what about the libretto (words) of this most famous of all oratorios? They are all from God's Word, especially from the OT Messianic prophecies. And the prophet who contributed most to the libretto[2] was a Hebrew writer who lived seven centuries before the incarnation of his Messiah—and Handel's, and yours, and mine. His name is Isaiah and he wrote the longest, loveliest, and most Messianic of OT prophecies.

II. Authorship

Isaiah (Hebrew, *Yesha'yāhû, Jehovah is salvation* or *salvation of Jehovah*), the son of Amoz, had a vision which constitutes the Book of Isaiah. Because of the critical theories that have "sawn it asunder," we will give a somewhat fuller introduction to this book than to most.

The Unity of Isaiah

There are several theories of the so-called "higher critics" that have been taught for a century or so, not as hypotheses, but almost as fact. These are virtually taken for granted in many circles. Among them are: Moses did not write the Pentateuch, Daniel did not write Daniel, Peter did not write 2 Peter, Paul (probably) did not write the Pastoral Epistles,[3] and Isaiah only wrote the first part of the sixty-six chapters attributed to him.

Because Isaiah is such a major work, is so replete with messianic prophecies (especially in the parts the critics attribute to others), and is quoted so often in the NT, we feel it is necessary to spend more space on this critical question than we ordinarily would in a book on a popular level for ordinary believers.

Our approach will be to give the *positive arguments* for Isaiah's authorship of the entire book and then answer one by one the arguments presented against that unity.

1. The witness of history and tradition

Until the late 1700's virtually all Jewish and Christian scholars accepted

Isaiah as one long prophecy by one very gifted writer, Isaiah the son of Amoz.

But in 1795 J. C. Doederlein proposed a "Second Isaiah" (or "Deutero-Isaiah") as the author of chapters 40—66. Of course the difference in content and outlook between Isaiah 1—39 and 40—66 had been noted by all careful readers for centuries, but this does not necessitate different authors. In 1892 B. Duhm denied the unity of chapters 40—66, postulating a "Third Isaiah" (or "Trito-Isaiah") for chapters 55—66. Some carried the thing even further, but two or three "Isaiahs" are generally accepted in liberal circles.

No early tradition ever suggested two or more authors; in fact, belief in the unity of Isaiah is early, uniform, and unchallenged.

2. *The Witness of the NT*

Isaiah is the second most quoted OT book in the NT (after Psalms), and there is always an assumption of unity. Quotations from the second part of the prophecy as being by Isaiah are made by John the Baptist (Matt. 3:3; Luke 3:4; John 1:23); by Matthew (8:17; 12:18–21); by John (12:38–41); and by Paul (Rom. 9:27–33; 10:16–21). This is especially noteworthy in John 12:38–41 because the actual author as a person, and not merely the book, is referred to: "These things Isaiah said when he saw His glory and spoke of Him" (v. 41). The "these things" are Isaiah 53:1, which is from the second part of the book (v. 38) and Isaiah 6:10 (where Isaiah saw Christ's glory) (vv. 39–40) is from the first.

3. *Unity of Plan and Development*

The book of Isaiah displays a consistent plan and order which does not go well with the theory of a collection of fragments by two or more different authors.

4. *The Sheer Grandeur of the Poetry*

The outstanding beauty in the second part of the book makes it hard to believe that such a marvelous writer, alleged to live in the 500's B.C., could be completely forgotten. After all, the very short Minor Prophets are all ascribed to their authors by name.

5. *Dead Sea Scrolls*

The Dead Sea Scrolls of Isaiah (Second Century B.C.) give no hint whatsoever of any split at chapter 40.

Arguments Against Isaianic Unity Answered

Three main arguments are leveled against the unity of the book: Its *historical* viewpoint, the *linguistic* argument, and the *theological* argument.

1. *The Historical Viewpoint*

That Isaiah falls into two main sections is agreed upon by nearly all (1—39 and 40—66). Chapters 36—39 are a sort of historical interlude. It is interesting how chapters 1—39 mirror the OT and 40—66 parallel the NT—even in the numbers: one chapter per OT and NT book. This may be coincidental, however, since the chapter divisions are not part of the inspired text.

The viewpoint of chapters 1—39 is definitely pre-exilic and that of 40—66 is clearly post-exilic. Could Isaiah project himself into the future and write from a viewpoint in the future? Many critics say no. And yet Jeremiah, Daniel, and even our Lord (Matt. 13) did so on occasion.

If chapters 40—66 were written in the 500's B.C., why is the flavor of the book Palestinian and not Babylonian?

2. *Linguistic Argument*

The style of "Second Isaiah" is different from that of Isaiah, critics maintain. All have noted the major break in outlook beginning with "Comfort, yes, comfort My people" (40:1). But this can merely prove the versatility of the writer. Plato, Milton, and Shakespeare also could vary their styles amazingly—according to content. The glorious comfort of the Messiah, prominent in 40—66, is enough to explain the difference.

Also, there are many similarities of style between the two (or three) parts of the book. Many details demand a knowledge of Hebrew, but one of Isaiah's phrases that shows up throughout his work is "the Holy One of God"—a divine title.

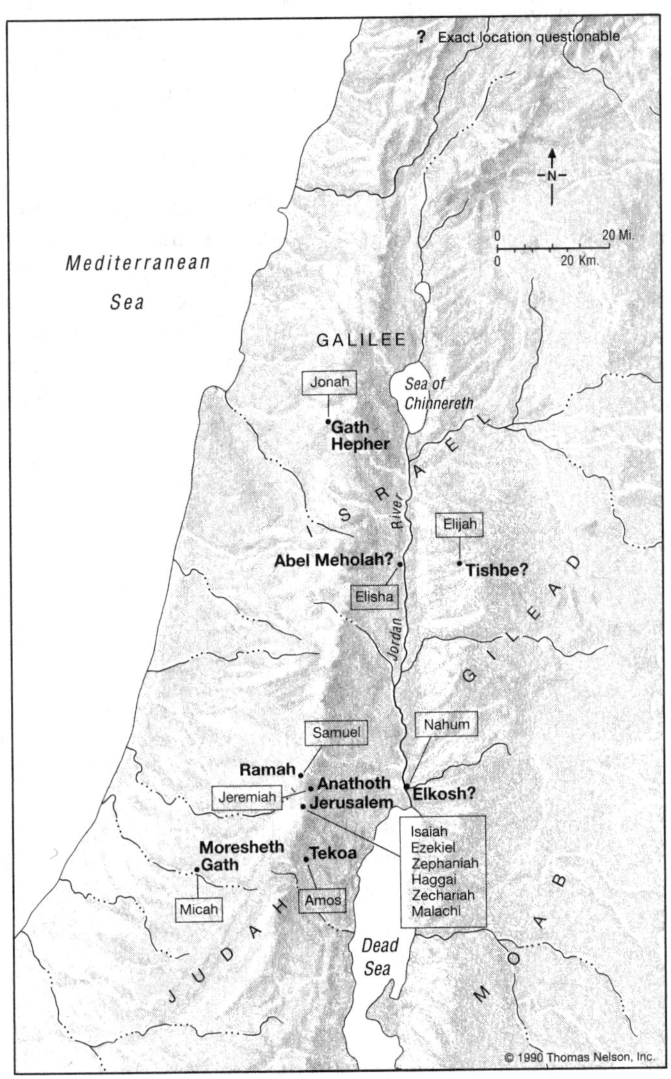

The Prophets of Israel and Judah

3. *Theological Argument*

Critics do not suggest a contradiction between the theology of "First" and "Second" Isaiah, merely that "Second Isaiah" is more "advanced." (This fits in with the whole unsound theory of evolution as applied to everything, and not merely to biology. Isaiah is said to emphasize God's majesty, "Second Isaiah" His infinity. Actually, Micah, who was a contemporary of Isaiah, contains similar ideas to the alleged "Second Isaiah.")

The theological argument is the weakest of the three, but it does suggest the *real* reason for the theories in the first place: anti-supernaturalism.

Isaiah mentions Cyrus by name centuries before he was born—if we accept one Isaiah. Josephus said that Cyrus himself was influenced by reading this in Isaiah 45.[4]

Many of the passages that are generally said to have been added are mostly *specific prophecies that have been fulfilled*. Here again an anti-supernatural bias seems evident in rejecting their early dating.

After all, if God is omniscient, He has no problem predicting the future through His prophets in as great detail as He chooses.

Hence, in spite of all the inroads that these theories have made in supposedly Christian circles, the ancient, uniform, evangelical position is strong and also logical: The entire book was written, as 1:1 says, by Isaiah, the son of Amoz.

III. Date

Isaiah started his ministry "in the year that King Uzziah died" (6:1; c. 740 B.C.). His years of ministry, chiefly to Judah, extended through the reigns of four kings: Uzziah and Jotham, who were largely good kings; Ahaz, a wicked king; Hezekiah, a very good king and a personal friend of the prophet. Since Isaiah records Sennacherib's death (681 B.C.), he likely lived till at least 680, giving a very long ministry indeed—sixty years! According to tradition Isaiah died during wicked King Manasseh's reign.

IV. Background and Theme

The meaning of Isaiah's name also gives the main theme of the book. Salvation is from the Lord. The word *salvation* occurs twenty-six times in this prophecy and only seven times in all the other prophets put together. This theme also illustrates the unity of the book: Chapters 1—39 depict man's tremendous need for salvation and chapters 40—66 give God's gracious provision of it.

Isaiah warned Israel that her wickedness would be punished, and yet God in His grace would one day provide a Savior for both the Jews and the Gentiles.

Politically, the super-powers between whose pincers little Israel was so frequently caught were Assyria to the north, the rising power, and Egypt to the south, the waning power. The latter part of the book projects the prophet in the Spirit 200 years into the future days of the super-power Babylon.

OUTLINE

I. PROPHECIES OF PUNISHMENT AND BLESSING FROM ISAIAH'S TIME (Chaps. 1—35)
   - A. Judgments on Judah and Jerusalem with Glimpses of Glory Shining Through (Chaps. 1—5)
     1. God's Case Against Israel (Chap. 1)
     2. Future Blessing Through Cleansing (Chaps. 2—4)
     3. Israel's Punishment for Sin (Chap. 5)
   - B. Isaiah's Call, Cleansing, and Commission (Chap. 6)
   - C. The Book of Immanuel (Chaps. 7—12)
     1. Messiah's Miraculous Birth (Chap. 7)
     2. Messiah's Marvelous Land (Chaps. 8—10)
     3. Messiah's Millennial Kingdom (Chaps. 11, 12)
   - D. Judgment on the Nations (Chaps. 13—24)
     1. Judgment on Babylon (13:1—14:23)
     2. Judgment on Assyria (14:24–27)
     3. Judgment on Philistia (14:28–32)
     4. Judgment on Moab (Chaps. 15, 16)
     5. Judgment on Damascus (Chap. 17)
     6. Judgment on Unnamed Lands in Africa (Chap. 18)
     7. Judgment on Egypt (Chaps. 19, 20)
     8. Judgment on Babylon (21:1–10)
     9. Judgment on Dumah (Edom) (21:11, 12)
     10. Judgment on Arabia (21:13–17)
     11. Judgment on Jerusalem (Chap. 22)
     12. Judgment on Tyre (Chap. 23)
     13. Judgment on All the Earth (Chap. 24)
   - E. The Book of Songs (Chaps. 25—27)
     1. Israel's Song of Praise for Kingdom Blessings (Chap. 25)
     2. Judah's Song to the Rock of Ages (Chap. 26)
     3. God's Song over Redeemed Israel (Chap. 27)
   - F. The Fall and Rising Again of Israel and Jerusalem (Chaps. 28—35)
     1. Woe to Ephraim/Israel (Chap. 28)
     2. Woe to Ariel/Jerusalem (Chap. 29)
     3. Woe to the Alliance with Egypt (Chaps. 30, 31)
     4. The Reign of the Righteous King (Chap. 32)
     5. Woe to the Plunderer/Assyria (Chap. 33)
     6. Woe to All Nations (Chap. 34)
     7. The Glory of the Coming Kingdom (Chap. 35)

II. HISTORICAL TRANSITION: THE BOOK OF HEZEKIAH (Chaps. 36—39)
   - A. Hezekiah's Deliverance from Assyria (Chaps. 36, 37)
     1. Assyria's Defiance of God (Chap. 36)
     2. God's Destruction of Assyria (Chap. 37)
   - B. Hezekiah's Sickness and Recovery (Chap. 38)
   - C. Hezekiah's Sin (Chap. 39)

III. PROPHECIES OF COMFORT FROM THE VIEWPOINT OF THE FUTURE CAPTIVITY (Chaps. 40—66)

A. The Comfort of Israel's Coming Deliverance (Chaps. 40—48)
   1. Comfort from God's Pardon and Peace (40:1–11)
   2. Comfort from God's Attributes (40:12–31)
   3. Comfort from the Holy One of Israel (Chap. 41)
   4. Comfort from the Servant of the Lord (Chap. 42)
   5. Comfort from Israel's Restoration (Chaps. 43, 44)
   6. Comfort from Cyrus, God's Anointed (Chap. 45)
   7. Comfort from the Fall of Babylon's Idols (Chap. 46)
   8. Comfort from the Fall of Babylon (Chap. 47)
   9. Comfort from Israel's Return after Chastening (Chap. 48)

B. The Messiah and His Rejection by Israel (Chaps. 49—57)
   1. The Messiah as Servant (Chap. 49)
   2. The Messiah as True Disciple (Chap. 50)
   3. The Messiah as Righteous Ruler (51:1—52:12)
   4. The Messiah as Sin-bearing Sacrifice (52:13—53:12)
   5. The Messiah as Redeemer and Restorer (Chap. 54)
   6. The Messiah as World Evangelist (55:1—56:8)
   7. The Messiah as Judge of the Wicked (56:9—57:21)

C. Israel's Sin, Judgment, Repentance, and Restoration (Chaps. 58—66)
   1. The Delights of True Spirituality (Chap. 58)
   2. The Iniquities of Israel (Chap. 59)
   3. The Future Glory of Zion (Chap. 60)
   4. The Messiah's Ministries (Chap. 61)
   5. The Future Delights of Jerusalem (Chap. 62)
   6. The Day of Vengeance (63:1–6)
   7. The Prayer of the Remnant (63:7—64:12)
   8. The Lord's Answer to the Prayer of the Remnant (Chap. 65)
   9. The Consummation: Peace Like a River (Chap. 66)

Commentary

I. PROPHECIES OF PUNISHMENT AND BLESSING FROM ISAIAH'S TIME (Chaps. 1—35)

A. Judgments on Judah and Jerusalem with Glimpses of Glory Shining Through (Chaps. 1—5)

1. God's Case Against Israel (Chap. 1)

1:1 The first verse of Isaiah is much like a title; its historical references are handled in our Introduction.

1:2, 3 The whole universe is summoned to attend a trial with God as the Judge, and with **Judah and Jerusalem** as defendants. The indictment charges the people with being intractible sons who **have rebelled against** God and fail to show the natural gratitude and devotion that could be expected of a domestic animal!

1:4–6 The **people** are guilty of aggravated **iniquity** in turning their backs on **the Holy One**. God's chastenings have not succeeded, even though the body is covered with **wounds and bruises and putrefying sores**.

1:7–9 Beginning with verse 7, the prophet describes the future as if it had already taken place.[5] Enemy invaders have made Judah **desolate**. Jerusalem, **the daughter of Zion**, is like a crude, temporary **hut**, standing gauntly amid the wreckage. But for the grace of God in sparing **a very small remnant**, the destruction **would have** been as complete as that of **Sodom** and **Gomorrah**.

1:10–15 The **rulers** and **people of** Jerusalem (**Sodom** and **Gomorrah**) should realize that God despises rituals without reality, **sacrifices** without obedience, gifts without the givers. As long as people are living in sin, their attendance at the temple services is an insulting trampling of His **courts**. The mixing of **iniquity** and solemn assembly is hateful to Him. He will pay no attention to their outstretched **hands** or **many prayers**.

W. E. Vine warns believers of the same danger today:

> Mere external religion is ever a cloak to cover iniquity. The Lord exposed all that in His strong denunciations in Matt. 23. The guilty combination in Judaism has largely developed in Christendom. The conscience of a believer may become so seared that a person can practise religion while yet living in sin.[6]

1:16, 17 What they should do is **wash** themselves through repentance and forsaking of **evil**, then practice righteousness and social **justice**.

1:18–20 If they follow this line of divine reasoning, they will be cleansed from **sins** of deepest dye and enjoy **the good** things that God has provided for them. It is significant that the first chapter of the evangelical prophet, whose name means "the salvation of Jehovah," should contain the winning gospel invitation:

> **"Come now, and let us reason together," says the LORD, "Though your sins are like scarlet, they shall be as white as snow; though they are red like crimson, they shall be as wool."**

Divine reasoning, accepted by faith, teaches that there is cleansing from sin, that this cleansing is totally apart from human merit or effort, and that it is only through the redemption which the Lord Jesus accomplished by the shedding of His blood on the cross. Who can know the throngs who have answered the invitation of Isaiah 1:18? And it is still sounding out!

But if the people **refuse and rebel**, then war and destruction await them.

1:21–23 Jerusalem is no longer a **city** of faithfulness, **justice**, and **righteousness**. It is now a **harlot** city, a refuge of **murderers**. Its best things have been corrupted and its **princes** are scoundrels. Bribery and injustice are everywhere.

1:24–31 **Therefore**, God **will** vent His wrath on all those who show by their sin that they are His **enemies**. His judgments will **purge** all impurity and restore Jerusalem to its former glory. His **righteousness** will insure the deliverance of those who repent.

The Lord's combined name, **the LORD of hosts**, insures the inevitability of the judgments described.

But **sinners** will be destroyed. Idolaters will **be ashamed** of their shrines (**terebinth trees** and **gardens**). They themselves will be like a **terebinth whose leaf fades** and a parched **garden that has no water**. Leaders who rely on their own strength (**the strong**) will be like highly flammable **tinder**, ignited by the **spark** of their own wicked works.

2. *Future Blessing Through Cleansing (Chaps. 2—4)*

2:1–3 **The son of Amoz** now looks beyond the current chaos to the glorious kingdom of the Messiah. In that day **Jerusalem** will **be established** as the religious and political capital of the world. The Gentile **nations** will make pilgrimages to **Zion** for worship and for divine instruction.

2:4 The King will arbitrate international problems and settle disputes for the **people**. As a result, there will be universal disarmament.[7] The funds formerly spent on munitions will be spent on agricultural equipment. These opening verses resemble Micah 4:1–3, either because they are inspired by the same Holy Spirit or because one prophet could be quoting the other.

2:5 The glorious prospect of Christ's kingdom moves Isaiah to call the people of Judah to repentance immediately.

2:6–9 Then addressing God directly, Isaiah rehearses the sins which led to the nation's calamity. Instead of looking to the Lord, the people consulted diviners from the East and became **soothsayers like the Philistines**. They made forbidden alliances with the heathen. In disobedience to the law of God, they heaped up financial **treasures** and **horses** and **chariots**, trusting in these for security. They worshiped idols which they themselves had made. Those are the reasons God has humbled them, and does **not forgive them**. The expression **"filled with eastern ways"** aptly describes the current popularity of Eastern religion in Western countries.

2:10, 11 Turning now to the people, the seer warns them to seek refuge from the coming **terror of** Jehovah's wrath which will lay low **the lofty looks of man**.

2:12–18 In a sudden transition, Isaiah jumps forward to the judgments of **the day of the LORD** which will precede Christ's reign. **The LORD of hosts** will deal with all human arrogance, whether of individuals (**cedars** and **oaks**), governments (**high mountains** and **hills**), military might (**tower and wall**), or commerce (**ships** and **beautiful sloops**[8]). Man's **loftiness** will be leveled and **the LORD alone will be exalted**. **Idols** will be abandoned.

2:19–22 People will seek for shelter wherever they can hide. It will be clear then that fleeting man is unworthy of trust. Only the Lord is worthy of the undivided confidence of His people.

3:1–5 In that day of which we read in 2:20, **the Lord** will take **away** the responsible leadership that the people had depended on. The loss of **bread and water** may refer to famine conditions, but here **bread and water** probably symbolize essential leaders, as suggested by the following verse. There will be a lack of capable, mature leaders in every walk of life. It will be a time of oppression, anarchy, insolence, disrespect, and insubordination.

3:6–8 People will try to draft a relative to take charge of **"these ruins,"** but the latter will refuse, since he has neither **food nor clothing in** his **house**. And no one is to blame for the calamity, says Isaiah, but the people **themselves**.

3:9–12 In verse 9, the prophet begins a series of eight "woes," two in this chapter and six in chapter 5. The first arraigns the populace for partiality and for shamelessness. The second upbraids them for their wickedness, but promises blessing to **the righteous** remnant. One result of their sin is that they are being led by the inexperienced and immature (**children**), by the weak (**women**), and by deceivers.

3:13–15 In these verses **the LORD** summons Israel to stand trial. The charges are leveled. He takes the rulers to task for enriching themselves at the expense of **the poor** (through bribery and extortion, no doubt). Since the verdict is "guilty," the sentence is announced.

3:16–24 Next comes a scathing denunciation of the women of Judah for their pride, their suggestive mannerisms, and their expensive clothing and jewelry. The faces on which they had spread expensive cosmetics will be encrusted with scabs. Their bodies will be stripped of all the **finery**. Instead of being elegant ladies, they will become bedraggled refugees—reeking of body odor, tied with **rope**, their heads shaved bald, only burlap to wear, branded for identification.

3:25—4:1 An added calamity will be the loss of their **men... in war**. The decimation of the male population will lead **seven women** to aggressively propose to **one man**, promising to support themselves as long as they can carry his **name** and thus escape the awful **reproach** of being unmarried and of dying childless.

4:2–6 The rest of chapter 4 looks forward to the **glorious** kingdom of Christ. He is **the Branch** of verse 2, **beautiful and glorious**. Matthew Henry comments:

> He is the *branch of the Lord,* the man the branch; it is one of his prophetical names, *my servant the branch* (Zech. iii. 8; vi. 12), the *branch of righteousness* (Jer. xxiii. 5; xxxiii. 15), a *rod out of the stem of Jesse and a branch out of his roots* (*ch.* xi. 1), and this, as some think, is alluded to when he is called a *Nazarene,* Matt. ii. 23. Here he is called *the branch of the Lord,* because planted by his power and flourishing to his praise. The ancient Chaldee paraphrase here reads it, *The Christ, or Messiah, of the Lord.*[9]

He is also the first **fruit of the** land, in whom the restored Israelites boast. Unbelievers will have been destroyed by the Lord Jesus at His Second Advent. Saved Jews, **recorded** for life **in Jerusalem, will be called holy**. The cleansing of verse 4 is accomplished **by... judgment** and not by the gospel. **Mount Zion** will be covered by a canopy of **cloud... by day** and **of flaming fire by night**, a symbol of God's care and protection.

3. Israel's Punishment for Sin (Chap. 5)

5:1, 2 In the song which Isaiah sings for his **Well-beloved** (Jehovah, or NKJV LORD), he rehearses the tender care of the Lord for **His vineyard**. God chose the best location, cultivated the land, **planted it with the choicest vine**, protected it, and prepared **a winepress** in hope of a good harvest. Instead of the harvest He expected (obedience, thanksgiving, love, worship, service), He found foul-smelling, **wild grapes** (disobedience, rebellion, idolatry).

5:3–6 Indignantly the Lord asks Judah **what more could** He **have... done**, and **why** did He receive such poor returns. He then announces the punishment impending. He will **take away** Judah's **hedge** of protection. The country will be invaded and laid **waste**. It will return to **briers and thorns** and suffer drought. All this looks forward, of course, to the oncoming captivity.

5:7 The cause is clear: when God **looked for justice** and righteousness from Israel and Judah, He got nothing but murder and the **cry** of the downtrodden.

5:8–10 In verses 8–23 we have six

woes, continued from chapter 3. The woes are pronounced as follows:

First Woe: Covetous landowners who try to corner the real estate market till there is an acute shortage of houses and land, yet the owners **dwell** in solitary splendor. The captivity will leave many **houses** empty, and the land will yield only fractional harvests. The grapevines growing on five acres of land will yield only five gallons of wine. Ten bushels **of seed** will produce only **one** bushel of grain.

5:11–17 *Second Woe:* Confirmed alcoholics who imbibe from **morning . . . until night**. They feast and carouse in total disregard of God and His works.

It is for this kind of unthinking behavior that the exile is drawing near. The **honorable men** and the **multitude** will suffer famine and then death. No class will escape humiliation. But God will be vindicated by His righteous **judgment** when foreign bedouin shepherds feed their flocks in the ruins of Israel.

5:18, 19 *Third Woe:* Brazen liars and God-defiers who are hitched to sin and drag guilt and punishment after them. They challenge God to **hasten** with the punishment He has threatened on them.

5:20 *Fourth Woe:* Those who obliterate moral distinctions, denying the difference between **good** and **evil**.

5:21 *Fifth Woe:* Conceited men who cannot be told anything.

5:22, 23 *Sixth Woe:* Judges who are heroes at **drinking** and who pervert **justice** through accepting bribes.

5:24, 25 These wicked men who have no respect for the Word of God will be devoured like grass in a prairie **fire**. God will deal with **His people** in judgment, causing **the hills** to shake and **the streets** to be littered with **carcasses**. But there is more!

5:26–30 He . . . will whistle for the Babylonians to come. See their troops approaching—in top physical condition, perfectly uniformed, well armed. The horses and chariots approach fast and furiously. The troops pounce **like a lion** upon the populace, then carry the people off into exile. It's a dark **day** for Judah!

B. Isaiah's Call, Cleansing, and Commission (Chap. 6)

6:1 In the year that King Uzziah died,[10] Isaiah had a vision of the King of kings. We learn from John 12:39–41 that the King he saw was none other than the Lord Jesus Christ. F. C. Jennings comments:

> He, like John of Patmos, becomes "in the Spirit," and sees Adohn (the name of God as the supreme Lord of all; and here, as in Romans 9:5, "Christ who is *over all*, God, blessed forever") with every accompaniment of majestic splendor, sitting on a Throne, which is itself "high and exalted," for "His Throne ruleth over all;" yet, while sitting on this lofty Throne the hem of His raiment fills that glorious temple.[11]

6:2–5 Attending Him were celestial beings called **seraphim,**[12] with "four wings for reverence and two for service." These celebrate the holiness of God and require that God's servants be cleansed before serving Him.

The vision produced deep conviction of sin in the prophet, then brought him to the place of confession.

6:6–8 This was immediately followed by cleansing. Only then did Isaiah hear the call **of the Lord**. He quickly consecrated himself to the Lord and was given his commission.

6:9, 10 He was to declare the Word of the Lord to a **people** who would be judicially blinded and hardened through rejection of the message. Verses 9 and 10 do not describe the *goal* of Isaiah's ministry, but its inevitable *result*. These verses are quoted in the NT to explain Israel's rejection of the Messiah. Vine writes:

> The people had so persistently perverted their ways that they had gone beyond the possibility of conversion and healing. A man may so harden himself in evil as to render his condition irremediable, and this by God's retributive judgment upon him.[13]

6:11–13 The question **"How long?"** means how long would God's judgments continue on His people. The answer was **"Until the cities are laid waste and without inhabitant, the houses are without a man, the land is utterly desolate, the LORD has removed men far away."** God will spare a remnant (**a tenth**), but even this remnant will have to pass through deep tribulation. This **holy seed** is like the living **stump** of a great tree that survives after the rest of the tree has been destroyed.

C. The Book of Immanuel (Chaps. 7—12)

1. Messiah's Miraculous Birth (Chap. 7)

7:1, 2 Chapters 7–12 have been called the Book of Immanuel because of their clear prophecies concerning Christ.

Between chapters 6 and 7 Isaiah passes over the reign of Jotham and takes up the narrative during the time **of Ahaz**. It is the time when **Syria and** Israel (**Ephraim**) have made an alliance **against** Judah and are threatening **Jerusalem**.

7:3 Isaiah and his **son Shear-Jashub**[14] go out to meet King **Ahaz . . . at the end of the aqueduct from the upper pool, on the highway to the Fuller's Field**. Perhaps the king had gone there to secure the safety of the city's water supply. The Fuller's Field was where the people spread their freshly-washed clothes to bleach in the sun.

7:4–9 The Lord assures Ahaz through the prophet that he need **not fear**. The kings of Syria and Israel (**Rezin** and **Pekah**) are nothing but the **stubs of smoking firebrands** on the verge of being extinguished. Although the confederacy does plan to attack Judah and **set** up some otherwise unknown **son of Tabel** as puppet **king**, the plan will largely fail. (Syria and Israel did invade Judah, but the pressure lifted when the Assyrians advanced.) As sure as Syria's chief city-state is **Damascus** and its **head is Rezin**, so surely will Israel be conquered **within sixty-five years**. (See 2 Kgs. 17 for fulfillment.) As sure as Israel's capital is **Samaria** and its **head** is Pekah, so **surely** will Ahaz be disestablished if he does **not believe** the Word of the Lord.

7:10–13 The LORD instructs **Ahaz** to **ask** for **a sign**, on earth or in the heavens, that the Syria-Israel alliance will not prevail against Judah. Unwilling to abandon his trust in Assyria for protection, Ahaz refuses, with mock piety and humility. The Lord is displeased with the king's attitude but gives the sign anyway. Vine comments:

> As Ahaz refused to ask for a sign, the Lord would give one of His own choosing, and a sign the range of which would extend to circumstances far beyond those of the time of Ahaz, and would bring to a culmination the prophecies and promises relating to "the house of David". Ahaz and men of that sort would have no share in the blessings and glories of the fulfillment of the sign.[15]

7:14 Like many prophecies, this one seems to have had an early fulfillment (in the days of Ahaz) and later, complete fulfillment (in the First Advent of Christ). Verse 14 points irresistibly to Christ—the **Son** of **the virgin**[16] whose name indicates that He is **Immanuel**, God-with-us. Again we quote Vine:

> "Behold", in Isaiah, always introduces something relating to future circumstances. The choice of the word *almah* is significant, as distinct from *bethulah* (a maiden living with her parents and whose marriage was not impending); it denotes one who is mature and ready for marriage.[17]

7:15–17 Verses 15 and 16 may refer to Isaiah's second son, Maher-Shalal-Hash-Baz, who is said to be a sign in 8:18. This maiden-born son will live in poverty (eating **curds and honey**) until he reaches the age of accountability. But **before** he reaches that age, the lands of Syria and Israel will be **forsaken by . . . their kings** and thus the alliance that Judah feared will come to nothing. But God will also punish Judah through the incursions of **the king of Assyria**. How?

7:18–22 God **will whistle for the fly** (Egypt) **and for the bee** (Assyria) and they will swarm over Judah. **Assyria** will be God's **hired razor**, bringing shame and disgrace. Jennings notes:

> *Poor* indeed shall Judah be in that day, for the sum-total of a man's wealth shall consist in a calf and two sheep, or goats, yet so abundant shall be the pasture afforded by the uncultivated lands that even these three creatures shall give him all the food he needs, or indeed can get.[18]

7:23–25 Land that formerly yielded bumper crops will be covered by **briers and thorns**. No longer arable, it will be fit only for **oxen** and **sheep**.

2. *Messiah's Marvelous Land (Chaps. 8—10)*

8:1–4 The Lord instructs Isaiah to write **"Maher-Shalal-Hash-Baz"** on a tablet in clear letters, and to have two **witnesses, Uriah the priest and Zechariah the son of Jeberechiah,** who will later attest the message. The name means "speed the spoil, hasten the booty," and points to the destruction of Syria and Israel by Assyria. **The Lord** interprets the meaning when he directs Isaiah to give this name to his newborn **child**.

8:5–10 The Lord also has a word about Israel. Because the **people** of the Northern Kingdom had **refused the waters of Shiloah that flow softly**, they will be inundated by **the River**, i.e., the Euphrates. **Shiloah** (called "Siloam" in John 9:7) was the secret water supply of Jerusalem and is here used as a symbol of God's word of grace or of trust in the Lord. The Euphrates typifies **Assyria** which will conquer Israel and Syria. It will also invade **Judah**, covering the breadth of Immanuel's land, but not with complete success—only **up to the neck**. Judah's enemies will eventually **be shattered** in spite of their plans and preparations.

8:11–15 Isaiah is **instructed** by Jehovah **not** to join **this people** in their fear of the **conspiracy** formed against them, but to trust the Lord alone. **He will be as a sanctuary** to all who rely on Him, **but a stone of stumbling** to all others.

8:16–18 Isaiah commands that the word of the Lord be stored up by faithful disciples until history records its fulfillment. The prophet **will wait** for **the Lord, who** is now estranged **from** His people, **and . . . will hope in Him**. Isaiah (*Jehovah saves*), Shear-jashub (*a remnant shall return*), and

Maher-Shalal-Hash-Baz (*speed the spoil, hasten the booty*) are by their very names **signs and wonders** of God's eventual mercy to **Israel** and judgment on their foes.

8:19 The prophet cautions his people against those who advocate consulting spirit **mediums and wizards**. Men should turn to the living God, not to **the dead on behalf of the living**. Today's devotion to the occult is nothing new:

> Before every great crisis in human affairs there has been an outburst of spiritism. So it was in Judah and Israel just before the captivity. So it was at the time of Christ's Incarnation and atoning Death. So it is today. God has provided all that is requisite for our guidance and spiritual needs in the Scriptures of truth (2 Tim. 3:16, 17).[19]

8:20–22 All teachers must be tested by the **word** of God. If their teaching does not agree with the Scriptures, **"there is no light in them."** All who are thus misguided will wander about, **hard pressed and hungry**, cursing **their God** and **their king** for their plight. They will **look** heavenward and earthward for relief, but will find nothing but **darkness** and **gloom of anguish**.

9:1–5 Now we are carried forward to the coming of the Messiah. The northern territory of Israel, called **the land of Naphtali**, which had been brought into contempt by the invaders, will be made glorious. (**Galilee of the Gentiles** was the Savior's boyhood home and the scene of part of His public ministry.) Christ's First Advent brought **light** to Galilee. His Second Coming will bring **joy** to the nation and put an end to slavery and war.

9:6 The First Advent is described in verse 6a: **"For unto us a Child is born, unto us a Son is given."** The first clause speaks of His humanity, the second of His deity. The next part of the verse points forward to the Second Advent:

the government will be upon His shoulder—He will reign as King of kings and Lord of lords. The rest of the verse describes His personal glories:

His name will be called Wonderful— *this name is a noun*, not an adjective, and speaks of His Person and work.

Counselor—His wisdom in government.

Mighty God—the omnipotent, supreme Ruler.

Everlasting Father—or better, the Father (or "Source") of eternity. Eternal Himself, He confers eternal life on those who believe in Him. Vine comments: "There is a twofold revelation in this: (1) He inhabits and possesses eternity (57:15); (2) He is loving, tender, compassionate, an all wise Instructor, Trainer, and Provider."[20]

Prince of Peace (*Sar-Shālôm*)—the One who will at last bring peace to this troubled world.

9:7 **His government** will be far-flung, peaceful, and endless. Sitting **upon the throne of David**, He will rule with **judgment** and **justice**. How will all this be brought about? The Lord's jealous care for His people **will perform this**.

9:8–12 Again the prophet turns back to the thunders of judgment, dividing his message into four stanzas, each ending with the refrain,

"For all this His anger is not turned away, but His hand is stretched out still" (vv. 12, 17, 21, 10:4).

Unmoved by previous punishment, **Israel** threatens **in pride and arrogance** to **rebuild** more gloriously than ever. But the Lord promises that they will be attacked by **the Syrians** from the east and **the Philistines** from the west.

9:13–17 He further warns of the wholesale destruction of the population, from the honored **elder** to the **prophet who teaches lies**. Because ungodliness prevails, the Lord's **anger is not turned away** and **His hand is stretched out still**—in judgment, not in mercy.

9:18–21 Because of general **wickedness**, the land is consumed with **the fire** of civil war, anarchy, famine, looting, and cannibalism.

10:1–4 A **woe** is pronounced on those rulers who **rob the needy**, oppress **the poor**, and write unjust **decrees**. When the judgment of God falls, they will lose all the wealth they gained through graft and extortion.

10:5–11 God will use **Assyria** to punish Judah. But the Assyrian has bigger plans than that! His aim is to build a world empire through conquest. He boasts that his **princes** (or commanders) are all **kings**, that the cities in his pathway are no greater than those he has conquered, and that the **idols** of Israel and Judah are not comparable to those of the kingdoms he has captured, or to himself.

10:12–19 But God will **punish** the pride and arrogance of **the king of Assyria**. The latter ascribes his success to his own **strength** and **wisdom**. The **rod** and **staff** in the hands of the Lord should not boast itself against the hands that hold it. A terrible disaster will strike Assyria's stout warriors, who are also called his glory and **the glory of his forest and of his fruitful field. The light of Israel** is the Lord, and **His thorns and His briers** are the Assyrian troops. The survivors of those troops **will be so few . . . that a child** will be able to count them.

10:20–23 In that day . . . the remnant of Israel never again will depend on the Assyrian, as Ahaz did, **but rather on the LORD**. Much of this prophecy looks forward to the Second Advent.

10:24–27 Though **the Assyrian** king will march against Jerusalem from the north, the people of Judah need **not be afraid**, because **the LORD of hosts will** intervene, as He did against **Midian** and **Egypt**, and Judah will be freed from the fear of Assyrian domination.

10:28–34 In the cities mentioned we have a graphic, animated description of the marching route of the Assyrians. Everywhere there is panic and flight as the invaders approach. Finally they come within sight of **the hill of Jerusalem**. Then **the Lord** intervenes and destroys the army, officers and men, as if He were cutting down a **forest**.

3. Messiah's Millennial Kingdom (Chaps. 11, 12)

11:1 Isaiah 11 is one of the greatest passages on the Millennium in either the OT or the NT. In one of the quick transitions, so frequent in the prophets, we are now carried forward to the Second Coming of Christ.

First we see the lineage of the Son of David, **a Rod from the stem of Jesse**,[21] who was David's father (1 Sam. 17:12).

11:2 Messiah's anointing with **the spirit of the LORD** is expressed in three pairs of spiritual attributes. W. E. Vine explains them clearly and concisely:

The first, **"the spirit of wisdom and understanding"**, relates to powers of mind: wisdom discerns the nature of things, understanding discerns their differences. The second, **"the spirit of counsel and might"**, relates to practical activity: counsel is the ability to adopt right conclusions, might is the power exercised in carrying them out. The third pair, **"the spirit of knowledge and of the fear of the Lord"**, relates to fellowship with Jehovah; knowledge is here a knowledge of Jehovah (both details of this pair go with "of Jehovah"); Christ Himself said "ye have not known Him (*ginōskō*, i.e., ye have not begun to know Him), but I know Him (*oida*, i.e., I know Him intuitively and fully)", John 8:5.[22]

11:3–5 Next the absolute **equity** of Christ's rule is described in majestic poetry; then His punishment of **the wicked**, His personal **righteousness**, and His reign of peace and safety.

11:6–9a Even wild animals will submit to Messiah's rule, making it possible for a **nursing child** to **play by the cobra's hole**.[23]

11:9b One of the most glorious promises in all of Holy Scripture is the second half of v. 9, giving the reason for the ideal conditions during the Millennial Kingdom. Jennings translates it into rhymed English verse, bringing out the poetic name for the Lord (Jah):

> For full of Jah's knowledge shall
> the land be,
> E'en as the waters cover the sea.

11:10–16 The Messiah will be **a banner**, attracting **the Gentiles** to Himself, and the seat of His authority will **be glorious**. The Lord will regather **the remnant of His people** from all directions of the compass. **Judah and** Israel (**Ephraim**) will live together in peace, and will subdue their enemies—the Philistines, Edomites, Moabites, and Ammonites. **The tongue of the Sea of Egypt** (the Red Sea) will be dried up, and **the River** (the Euphrates) will be reduced to **seven streams** so that the Jews can return to the land. **A highway** will connect **Assyria** and **Israel** so that the return from the north will be made easy.

12:1–6 In the glad millennial **day**, Israel will sing songs of thanksgiving and of **trust**. **With joy** the saved remnant will quench its thirst by drawing **water from the wells of salvation**. Israel will also **sing** as God's missionaries to the nations, inviting them to come to Christ for satisfaction.

D. Judgment on the Nations (Chaps. 13—24)

1. *Judgment on Babylon (13:1—14:23)*

13:1–5 The next eleven chapters contain prophecies against Gentile nations. The first is **Babylon**, the world power that crushed Assyria (about 609 B.C.). In Chapter 13, we see Babylon being conquered by the Medes and Persians (539 B.C.). However, some of the prophecies look beyond that event to the final destruction of Babylon at the close of the Great Tribulation (Rev. 17, 18).

God musters the Medo-Persian army (**"My sanctified ones"**) to **enter the gates of the nobles** (the City of Babylon) and **to destroy the whole land**.

13:6–13 The horrors of the disaster are described next—fear **and sorrows**, terrible celestial disturbances, and an awesome reduction in the population. Some of these verses look beyond the Medo-Persian triumph to **the day of the Lord**, which will affect **the** whole **world** and which will actually involve cataclysms in **the heavens**.

13:14–22 There will be a mass exit from Babylon, foreigners returning to their own lands. Those who remain will suffer unspeakable cruelty. Verses 19–22 have had a partial fulfillment,[24] but the complete unfolding is future.

There are certain difficulties connected with the prophecies of the destruction of Babylon, both the city and the country (Isa. 13:6–22) 14:4–23; 21:2–9; 47:1–11; Jer. 25:12–14; 50; 51). For example, the capture of the city by the Medes (Isa. 13:17) in 539 B.C. did not result in a destruction similar to that of Sodom and Gomorrah (Isa. 13:19); did not leave the city uninhabited forever (Isa. 13:20–22); was not accomplished by a nation from the north—Medo-Persia was to the east—(Jer. 50:3); did not result in Israel or more than a remnant of Judah seeking the Lord or returning to Zion (Jer. 50:4, 5); and did not involve the breaking of the walls and burning of the gates (Jer. 51:58).

When we come to a difficulty like this, how do we handle it? First of all, we reaffirm our utter confidence in the Word of God. If there is any difficulty, it is because of our lack of knowledge. But we remember that the prophets often had a way of merging the immediate future and the distant future without always indicating any time signals. In other words, a prophecy could have a local, partial fulfillment and a remote, complete fulfillment. That is the case with Babylon. Not all the prophecies have been fulfilled. Some are still future.

Babylon is slated to play a prominent role in the Tribulation. But its doom is already painted in vivid colors in Revelation 17 and 18. Before the Second Advent of Christ, all the prophecies concerning the destruction of Babylon will be fulfilled to a "T." What is unclear to us today will be crystal clear to those living at that time.

14:1, 2 **The Lord** in His **mercy** will restore Israel to **their own land**. Gentile nations will assist in the return and live peacefully with God's people. Israel's former overlords will be her **servants**.

Jacob and **the house of Israel** represent the Jews in captivity in Babylon. The Lord's choosing them means His delivering them from the country of captivity and settling them back in **their own land**. Those **strangers** who clung to **the house of Jacob** are the proselytes from Babylon. The **people** that **bring them to their place** would consist of the favorable backing of Cyrus and others who helped the Jews in their return.

14:3–11 Free from persecution and **hard bondage**, Israel will sing a taunt song against the **king of Babylon. The Lord has broken** his power and ended his tyranny. Now the earth rejoices—even the forests, which will no longer be denuded by his armies. Peace at last! Sheol's inhabitants are there to greet him, delighted that he too has been stripped of power. The **pomp** and pageantry of Babylon's king has passed away. The palace music is ended. He sleeps on a sheet of maggots, and is covered by a blanket of **worms**.

14:12–17 As the taunt song continues, the theme seems to expand from the fall of the king of Babylon to the fall of the one who energized him, Satan (**Lucifer**[25]) himself. Ryrie writes that this is "evidently a reference to Satan, because of Christ's similar description (Luke 10:18) and because of the inappropriateness of the expressions of Isa. 14:13–14 on the lips of any but Satan (cf. 1 Tim. 3:6)."[26] Because this day star, **son of**

the morning, proudly asserted his **will** above the will of God, he was cast out of heaven. Verses 13, 14 record the notorious "I will's" of Satan in his defiance of God. Eventually he will be consigned **to Sheol**, an object of astonishment. The denizens of Sheol will marvel that one who exercised such power has been brought so low.

14:18–21 Returning to the king of Babylon, the song mentions that while most **kings** lie in magnificent tombs, he is denied a decent burial. He will have no monument, and the royal line (**his children**) will be cut off.

14:22, 23 The city of Babylon will be depopulated and swept clean by **the broom** of God.

2. *Judgment on Assyria (14:24–27)*

The subject now switches to the destruction of **the Assyrian**, which had dominion over Babylon at this time. The armies of Assyria will be crushed on the **mountains** of Israel.[27] The complete fulfillment of this prophecy will be in the Tribulation period when the king of the North is defeated as he attempts to sweep down over Immanuel's land.

3. *Judgment on Philistia (14:28–32)*

14:28–31 Philistia should **not rejoice** in the death of **Ahaz**, the grandson (here called **rod**) of Uzziah, who had **struck** the Philistines (2 Chron. 26:6, 7). Another descendant, Hezekiah, would attack them like **a viper** and **a fiery flying serpent** (see 2 Kgs. 18:8). Then God's **poor** and **needy** would be safe, but the Lord would visit the Philistines **with famine** and **slay** the survivors. The invading Assyrians would come from **the North** like a cloud of **smoke**. However, God's people would be safe in Jerusalem.

14:32 If any Gentile couriers ask what is going on, they will be told that **the Lord** is fulfilling His promises to **Zion**, and protecting the inhabitants of Jerusalem.

4. *Judgment on Moab (Chaps. 15, 16)*

15:1–7 Isaiah sings an eloquent dirge concerning the doom of **Moab**. Its capital, **Ar**, and its proud fortress, **Kir**, are suddenly destroyed. The towns and hamlets are plunged into mourning. Even Isaiah is moved to compassion for the refugees as they **flee** the country. The landscape is **laid waste** and the people stream across the frontier with whatever they can salvage.

15:8, 9 The cry extends to **the borders of Moab**. The name of the town of **Dibon** (pining) in verse 2 becomes **Dimon** in verse 9—perhaps a play on words, since Dimon resembles the Hebrew word *dām* (blood). So **"the waters of Dimon will be full of blood."** Even those who escape will be tracked down as by a lion.

16:1, 2 The description of Moab's devastation continues in chapter 16. The Moabites who have fled to **Sela** (Petra, their capital) for refuge are counseled to send **the** tribute **lamb to the ruler of the land** (the king of Judah) in the mountain **of the daughter of Zion** (Jerusalem) as they had previously sent lambs to Samaria (2 Kgs. 3:4). The people are nervously agitated over their impending calamity.

16:3–5 The Lord counsels **Moab** to **hide** God's Jewish **outcasts**, as if in a dark **shadow**, to provide sanctuary and safety for them. **The spoiler, extortioner**, and oppressor will cease, and the Lord will reign on **the throne . . . of David . . . in mercy, truth, justice**, and **righteousness**.

16:6–12 The downfall of **Moab** is caused by **his pride** and **haughtiness**. There is widespread mourning in the land. **The** fertile **fields of Heshbon**

are bare, and the luxuriant vines **of Sibmah** are ruined. Again the prophet himself mourns over the widespread ruin. When Moab prays to his idols, no help will come.

16:13, 14 To God's previous prophecies concerning the fall of Moab, He now adds the information that it will happen **within three years, as the years of a hired man**—i.e., not a minute longer than the agreed time.

5. Judgment on Damascus (Chap. 17)

17:1–3 The third oracle foretells the leveling of **Damascus**, the chief city-state of Syria, and of its satellite cities. Because of its alliance with **Syria, Ephraim** (Israel) will share a similar downfall. **Ephraim** will be stripped of its defenses, **Damascus** of its **kingdom**, and the surviving Syrians of their **glory**. Damascus was destroyed by the Assyrian armies in 732 B.C., and Samaria fell ten years later.

17:4–6 In the **day** of its judgment, Israel will be disgraced and starved. It will be stripped like harvested fields in **the Valley of Rephaim**—only a small remnant will be left.

17:7–11 Then people will turn **to** the true and living God, their **Maker, the Holy One of Israel**, and will renounce everything that has to do with idolatry. Fortified **cities will** lie waste, like the cities of the Hivites and Amorites after the invading Israelites had conquered them. And why will all this happen? **Because** God's people have **forgotten** Him and have turned to **foreign seedlings**, i.e., foreign alliances, religions, and customs. **The harvest will be** disastrous.

17:12–14 Beginning with verse 12 and continuing throughout chapter 18, we have a short interlude with two movements, each beginning with **"Woe."** The first movement pictures the Gentile nations moving against Israel with the awesome **noise** of modern warfare. But suddenly they are turned back by the Lord, and the threat to Israel is lifted overnight, as in the destruction of the Assyrian army.

6. Judgment on Unnamed Lands in Africa (Chap. 18)

This is not a **"woe"**[28] but a "ho," calling to an unidentified friendly nation that **sends ambassadors** to the people of Israel (vv. 2, 7). The expression **"shadowed with buzzing wings"** may suggest the desire to protect the Jewish people.

At the same time, other Gentile nations will prey upon God's people while He watches silently. But eventually God will destroy them, leaving their carcasses to the **beasts** and **birds of prey**.

Israel will then come **to Mount Zion** as **a present . . . to the LORD**. Verse 7 may read, "In that day shall a present be brought unto Jehovah *of* a people scattered and ravaged . . ." (JND) rather than "*from* a people. . . ." This speaks of the restoration of Israel at the Second Advent of Christ.

7. Judgment on Egypt (Chaps. 19, 20)

19:1–3 When **the LORD** descends in judgment on **Egypt, the idols . . . will totter** and the people will panic. Civil war will break out and the government's best brains will resort in vain to **idols** and various forms of spiritism (**the charmers**).

19:4–10 **A cruel** despot **will rule** the land. Severe drought will dry up the water supplies, causing crop failure, wiping out the fishing industry, closing up the textile mills, and bringing ruin to all segments of the population, whether leaders or common people.

19:11–15 Pharaoh's best **coun-**

selors, who lived in **Zoan** and **Noph**, will have no wisdom to cope with the situation. In fact, their advice has brought disaster on Egypt, so that the situation is now hopeless.

The first fifteen verses have already been fulfilled. Following the death of Tirhakah, who was ruling Egypt at the time of Isaiah's prophecy, the country was torn by civil strife. Egypt was split up into twelve kingdoms, all subject to Assyria. Finally the country was united again under Psammetichus, the "cruel master" of verse 4. The rest of the chapter is still unfulfilled.

19:16, 17 When God shakes His fist, the populace will shake with **fear**. The mere mention **of Judah** will cause the hearts of the Egyptians to sink.

19:18–20 But **the land of Egypt** is promised restoration also. **Five cities** will become centers for the worship of Jehovah, including Heliopolis (city of the Sun), also called **the City of Destruction**. **There will be an altar to the LORD in the midst of the land, and a pillar to the LORD at its border**, both of which will be witnesses **to the Lord**. Josephus tells us that the prophecy of verse 19 was fulfilled in 1 B.C. when Onias, the high priest, fleeing from Jerusalem, obtained permission to build an altar in Egypt. But the full meaning of the prophecy is undoubtedly millennial.

19:21, 22 God's judgments on **Egypt** will succeed in bringing the people to worship Him.

19:23 A highway will pass **from Egypt** (through Israel) **to Assyria** with unrestricted passage. The nations will unite in the worship of Jehovah.

19:24, 25 Then **Israel will be one of three with Egypt and Assyria**, that is, they will form a triple alliance, enjoying the blessings of Christ's kingdom. Note the repetition of **"in that day"** (vv. 16, 18, 19, 21, 23, 24).

20:1–6 In 711 B.C., the **Tartan**, or commander-in-chief of **Sargon the king of Assyria**, conquered the Philistine city of **Ashdod**. **At the same time the LORD** told **Isaiah** to walk **naked** (scantily clad—not completely naked) **and barefoot** as **a sign and a wonder** of the three-year humiliation that would come to **Egypt** and **Ethiopia** when conquered by **Assyria**. Then the people of Judah would see the folly of trusting Egypt for protection against Assyria. (Some commentators suggest that verses 5 and 6 refer to the Philistines or to both Judah and the Philistines, that is, the whole land of Palestine.)[29]

8. Judgment on Babylon (21:1–10)

21:1–4 The three oracles in chapter 21 bring bad news for Babylon, Edom, and Arabia.

The Wilderness of the Sea is Babylon, perhaps that portion of Babylon adjacent to the Persian Gulf. Destruction will roar upon it like **whirlwinds . . . from the desert**. Because it still **plunders** and despoils, it will be laid low by the Persians (**Elam**) and the Medes (**Media**). No more will Babylon cause others, like the Jewish captives, to groan. The vision is so terrible that it causes Isaiah acute anguish.

21:5 While the rulers feast and carouse in supposed security, suddenly the call to arms rings out (**"Anoint the shield!"**). The reference, of course, is to Belshazzar's Feast (Dan. 5).

21:6–10 The **Lord** instructs Isaiah to appoint **a watchman** to describe the attacking hordes, especially the numberless cavalry units. After waiting for days and nights, he reports the advance of riders in pairs. This may suggest the Medes and the Persians. Then, with a lion-like roar, he announces the fall of Babylon and of her idolatrous religion. The announcement is a message of comfort to Israel, a nation that has been threshed and winnowed by Babylon. It is good to remember that this prophecy was made about two hundred years before Babylon's fall.

We too can be watchmen for God's kingdom:

> The watchman is one who stands in God's counsels, knows what is coming and looks out for the event. So now, he who learns from the completed Scriptures what God has foretold, discerning His purposes, not by speculative interpretation, but by comparing Scripture with Scripture, and accepting what is therein made plain, is able to warn and exhort others. He stands upon the watch-tower (verse 7) in fellowship with God.[30]

9. Judgment on Dumah (Edom) (21:11, 12)

Dumah is Idumea, or Edom. An anxious Edomite asks **the watchman** how far gone **the night** is, that is, if the Assyrian menace is almost over. The answer is:

> The night of your present turmoil will end, and a new day will follow, but soon another night will come. If you seek a comforting answer to your anxious inquiries, you must first "return," a word which also means "repent." Only then will the answer be such as you hoped for; the night of your suffering will end, and a new bright morning of deliverance will dawn upon you.[31]

10. Judgment on Arabia (21:13–17)

There is trouble ahead for **Arabia**, too. The caravans **will** hide (**lodge**) **in the forest** from the Assyrian army, and those who escape from the carnage will suffer intense hunger and thirst. **The LORD** has decreed that Arabia's **glory will fail** in **a year**, and only a few of her famous warriors will survive. The expression **"the year of a hired man"** means not one day longer than a year.

11. Judgment on Jerusalem (Chap. 22)

22:1–5 The Valley of Vision refers to Jerusalem (see vv. 9–11). The city is in siege. The people are milling about on **the housetops** to see the enemy at the gates. The streets of the once festive city are littered with victims of plague. The rulers and people who attempt escape **are captured** without a struggle. Isaiah himself is inconsolable as he sees the threatened judgment of God on Jerusalem.

22:6–11 Elam and Kir are the southern and northern units of the Babylonian army. Their **chariots** and cavalry fill the **valleys** surrounding the city. The Jews make elaborate plans to withstand the siege. They ransack the armory (**the House of the Forest**), they demolish **houses** to get stones for repairing **the wall**, they try to devise a makeshift water supply. They do everything but look to their **Maker** who wrought the disaster and planned it **long** before.

22:12–14 At a time when **the Lord** is calling them to repentance, they live riotously and callously. For this they will not be forgiven.

22:15–19 Shebna, the palace administrator in Hezekiah's court, is preparing **himself** an ornate **sepulcher**. God says through Isaiah that his efforts are futile. The Lord **will toss** him into captivity **like a** wadded **ball**, and he will **die** in a foreign land so that he will be long remembered.

Perhaps Shebna led the party that advocated alliance with Egypt.

22:20–24 After Shebna is demoted, **Eliakim** (God will establish) will take his place. A type of the Lord Jesus, Eliakim will be a responsible and compassionate ruler with full authority. He will be given **the key of the house of David,**[32] controlling the royal chambers and choosing the servants in the royal household. (In Rev. 3:7 the Lord Jesus is said to have the key of the house of David.) Eliakim will be firmly established in his position and will have complete authority in his sphere of service.

22:25 Since Eliakim is clearly **the peg that is fastened in the secure place** (v. 23a), his removal and **fall** may refer to the captivity of the house of Judah, of which he was a representative.

12. Judgment on Tyre (Chap. 23)

23:1–5 Returning from **Tarshish** (probably means Spain here), seamen from **Tyre** receive news of the city's fall when they reach **Cyprus**. With their houses destroyed and **no harbor** to return to, they howl in dismay. The **merchants of Sidon** sit in stunned silence as they remember how their Tyrian neighbors had crossed **the sea**, bringing **grain** from the Upper Nile (**Shihor**), how they had been the merchants of **the nations**. **Sidon**, the mother city of Tyre, is **ashamed** as the waves beating against the ruins of Tyre seem to echo the city's lament. It is as if Tyre never had any **children** to inhabit it! **Egypt**, too, is **in agony at the report** of the loss of her best customer.

23:6–9 The Tyrians are told to seek asylum as far away as Spain (**Tarshish**). Once the **inhabitants** of an ancient prosperous **city**, their **feet** now carry them to **far off** lands. And **who** brought this horror on **Tyre**, with all its power, riches, and glory? It was **the Lord of hosts**—determined **to dishonor the pride of all** human **glory**.

23:10–17 In view of Nebuchadnezzar's attack on **Tyre**, the people are told to escape to other countries, spreading out **like the River** (i.e., the Euphrates River which flows through many countries). God has roused Babylon to destroy the merchant city (**Canaan**). Even if the refugees flee **to Cyprus**, they will find **no rest**. The prophet is amazed that an obscure nation with humble beginnings, **founded** by **Assyria**, should bring Tyre **to ruin**. **Tyre will be forgotten** during the **seventy years** of the Chaldean monarchy. At the end of that time, it will joyfully resume its commercial **fornication with all the kingdoms of the world**.

23:18 "Tyre's **gain and her pay"** looks forward to the Second Advent of Christ when "the daughter of Tyre will come with a gift" (Ps. 45:12). Her treasures will be a holy offering to the Lord.

13. Judgment on All the Earth (Chap. 24)

24:1–3 The judgments of God seem to start with the land of Israel, but they widen to include the whole earth and even wicked beings in the heavens. **"The earth"** may also be translated "the land," and the reference to **the priest** in verse 2 suggests that the land of Israel is in view in verses 1–3. Notice how the text alternates between the land and **the people**. The destruction is cataclysmic and affects all classes of the populace.

24:4–13 Mention of **"the world"** in verse 4 suggests that the theater of judgment has widened. The cause of worldwide pollution is that men **have broken the everlasting covenant**. Some take this to refer to the Noahic covenant (Gen. 9:16), but that unconditional covenant depended entirely on God. Others think that the Mosaic law is referred to, but that was given only to Israel, and is not said to be an **everlasting covenant**. *The Bible Knowledge Commentary* says it is "the covenant people implicitly had with God to obey His Word."[33] **The city of confusion** could mean Jerusalem, but in a wider sense could include all urban civilization.

24:14–20 A preserved remnant is heard singing the praises of Jehovah (NKJV, LORD) for His saving grace.

Then the prophet mourns the dread horrors of the Great Tribulation. It will be a time of treachery. Escape will be impossible. **The earth** will careen **like a drunkard**, as if struck by a mammoth quake. It falls to rise no more.

24:21–23 The wicked hosts in heavenly places will also be judged. This corresponds to Revelation 19:19, 20; 20:1–3. **Kings of the earth** who have served as their puppets will share in this judgment at the Second Advent of Christ. The Lord's surpassing glory will put **the sun** and **moon** to shame.

E. The Book of Songs (Chaps. 25—27)

1. *Israel's Song of Praise for Kingdom Blessings (Chap. 25)*

25:1–5 Chapters 25–27 have been called "the Book of Songs." Here the restored Jewish remnant praises the LORD for its deliverance through the Great Tribulation. Enemy cities (not necessarily any particular city) have been pulverized, causing Gentiles to acknowledge Jehovah's power. God has been to His people all that they needed.

25:6–9 On Mount Zion **the Lord** spreads **a feast** of the finest spiritual delights. He removes the covering of ignorance, **the veil** of satanic blindness that has shrouded **all nations**. He conquers **death** (by raising the tribulation saints who have died), abolishes sorrow, and removes the stigma from the Jewish **people**. The remnant will say **"This is our God; we have waited for Him; we will be glad and rejoice in His salvation."**

25:10–12 Israel's enemies, of whom **Moab** is perhaps representative, will be shamefully **trampled**. God is compared to **a swimmer** in verse 11, spreading out **His hands** in judgment in the midst of the Moabites.

2. *Judah's Song to the Rock of Ages (Chap. 26)*

26:1–4 Back in the land, the restored remnant celebrates the life of faith and dependence. The **city** of God is in contrast to man's city (24:10). **The righteous nation** (redeemed Israel) experiences the **perfect peace** that comes from leaning hard on Jehovah. Regarding verse 3 the celebrated American Baptist hymnwriter, Philip P. Bliss, used to say "I love this verse more than any other verse in the Bible, 'Thou wilt keep him in perfect peace whose mind is stayed on Thee: because he trusteth in Thee.' "[34]

Moody tied v. 3 with v. 4 in the following words: "The tree of peace strikes its roots into the crevices of the Rock of Ages."[35] They realize at last that **"in YAH, the LORD** (Heb. YAH, a shortened form of YHWH) **is everlasting strength,"** or **"the Rock of Ages"** (NKJV marg.). It was from this expression that Augustus Toplady got the idea for one of the greatest hymns in the English language, "Rock of Ages." Seeking shelter in a cleft in a rocky crag during a violent thunderstorm, he wrote:

Rock of Ages, cleft for me,
Let me hide myself in Thee;
Let the water and the blood,
From Thy riven side which flowed,
Be of sin the double cure,
Cleanse me from its guilt and power.

While I draw this fleeting breath,
When mine eyes shall close in death,
When I soar to worlds unknown,
See Thee on Thy judgment-throne,
Rock of Ages, cleft for me,
Let me hide myself in Thee.

26:5,6 Man's proud civilization has been brought low to the point where **the feet of the poor** and **needy** trample down **the lofty city**.

26:7–15 Verses 7–19 seem to rehearse the prayers of the remnant when passing through the Tribulation. The Lord has smoothed the path for them and they **have waited** earnestly **for** Him to reveal Himself. Only when God acts in judgment will the wicked **learn righteousness**. God's **hand** has been raised in readiness, but when it descends in fury they will **be ashamed**, and then there will be **peace for** Israel. The remnant has been ruled by many Gentile **masters**, **but** God is their true and **only** Lord. The nations that troubled Israel **will not rise** to trouble God's people again. This verse does not deny the bodily resurrection of the wicked; it merely promises that the Gentile powers will never be restored.

26:16–19 But after Israel goes through travail similar to that of childbirth, which seemingly has accomplished nothing, the nation will enjoy a resurrection. Jehovah answers His people's prayer with a definite promise of national restoration when the refreshing **dew of herbs** (the Holy Spirit) is poured out on the land.

26:20,21 In the meantime, the Lord counsels the faithful remnant of His **people** to **hide** in secret **chambers** while He pours out His wrath on the apostate world.

3. God's Song over Redeemed Israel (Chap. 27)

27:1 In the coming **day** of **the Lord**, Jehovah **will punish Leviathan the fleeing serpent** (Assyria), **Leviathan that twisted serpent** (Babylon), **and He will slay the reptile that is in the sea** (Egypt). Some commentators understand *all three* monsters as symbolizing Babylon. Still others see them as picturing Satan, who energizes world powers; he is called serpent and dragon (Gen. 3:1; Rev. 12:3; 13:2; 16:13).

27:2–6 **In that day** God will rejoice over His redeemed **vineyard of red wine** (Israel) with singing. He will guard **it night and day**. He has no more **fury** against His people. If any hostile powers were to arise against the remnant, He **would burn them** like **briers and thorns**. It would be better for such powers to turn to the Lord for protection and **peace**. In the Millennium **Israel shall blossom and bud, and fill the face of the world with fruit.**

27:7–9 God has not dealt with **Israel** as with her Gentile overlords! No, His chastisement of Israel has been **in measure** and limited. He drove them off into exile to purge them of the **sin** of idolatry. This objective will be achieved when Israel utterly destroys every last vestige of **images**.

27:10, 11 In the meantime, Jerusalem is seen in ruins, as shown by calves grazing on the bushes, and **women** gathering **boughs** for firewood. All this has come because the people showed no spiritual discernment.

27:12, 13 **In** a coming **day, the**

Lord will thresh the true and the false within the land **of Israel**. Then He will regather those Jews who are dispersed in such Gentile nations as **Assyria** and **Egypt**. Back in the land, **they will come** to Jerusalem to **worship the Lord**.

F. The Fall and Rising Again of Israel and Jerusalem (Chaps. 28—35)

1. Woe to Ephraim/Israel (Chap. 28)

28:1–4 Samaria was **the crown of pride**, the **fading flower** of **the drunkards of** Israel (**Ephraim**). The hilltop city was like a crown looking over **the verdant valleys** of people **overcome with wine**, pleasure, materialism, and sex. The Assyrian conquerors stand ready to devour the city as if it were a ripe fig in June.

28:5, 6 The Lord of hosts will be an unfading **crown of glory... to the** faithful **remnant** when He returns to set up His Kingdom. He will empower the leaders to execute **judgment** and to **turn back** the enemy to his own city **gate**.

28:7, 8 The prophet turns to Judah. Like Israel, they are drunken and wallowing in their own **vomit and filth** of the **tables**. Even **the priest and the prophet** have become dissolute.

28:9, 10 The religious leaders mock God, complaining that He uses baby talk in speaking to them. Does the Lord think He is dealing with youngsters, teaching them with monosyllables (in the Hebrew)?[36]

28:11–13 "All right," says God, "since you don't want to listen to my simple, understandable language, I will send a foreign invader (Assyria) into your midst." Their alien **tongue** will be a sign of judgment on a **people** who refused God when He vainly offered rest to them and the ability to administer **rest** to others. As for **the Lord**, He will, as Jennings puts it,

> continue to speak in the simplest, clearest words; but that will be in order that all responsibility for their rejection can only be charged, not to the obscurity of the message, but to those who reject it.[37]

28:14, 15 The rulers of Judah boasted of their **covenant with** Egypt as making them free from Assyrian attack, but their alliance would mean **death... and Sheol** for them. They were trusting **lies** and **falsehood**. (The **covenant with death** and the pact **with Sheol** was not a literal treaty, of course. The thought seems to be that Judah felt that it was on good terms **with death** and **Sheol**, and had nothing to fear, because of its alliance with Egypt. Some commentators see this covenant as picturing the still-future alliance between Israel and the Beast [Dan. 9:27].)

28:16, 17 God has established the Messiah as the only worthy object of trust, **a sure foundation**. Those who rely on Him never need run scared. Under His reign, everything will have to meet the test of **justice** and **righteousness**, and judgment will **sweep away** every false object of trust.

28:18–22 Judah's power politics will fail to protect her **when the** invader comes. Every enemy incursion will succeed. The people will realize too late the truth of what God had been saying. **The bed is too short, the covering** too **narrow**, that is, the **covenant** fails to provide the desired comfort and protection. God **the Lord will rise up** in judgment against His people as He had formerly done against their enemies—a judgment that was utterly foreign to Him. If they scoff, they will only increase their bondage.

28:23–29 As Herbert Vander Lugt points out, the prophet illustrates

> the way God deals with His children by citing three aspects of a farmer's work. First, he declares that the plowman doesn't continue breaking the ground indefinitely, but stops when it is ready for planting (v. 24). Likewise, our trials are brought to an end as soon as they have accomplished His purposes in our lives. Then the prophet says that the farmer sows his seed with discernment, scattering the cummin but putting the wheat in rows (vv. 25, 26). This assures us that the Lord carefully selects the discipline especially suited to our particular need. Finally, Isaiah portrays the laborer threshing his crop. With extreme care he beats out the dill with a light stick, and strikes the cummin with a heavier flail. For the wheat he employs a wheel just heavy enough to avoid crushing the grain (vv. 27, 28). Thus the Almighty uses the gentlest possible touch for our condition, never allowing an affliction to be greater than we can bear.[38]

2. *Woe to Ariel/Jerusalem (Chap. 29)*

29:1–4 **Ariel** is the privileged city of Jerusalem **where David** had his headquarters. The people there may go through their religious motions **year** after **year**, but God will bring **distress** on the city till it is nothing but an Ariel. The name Ariel has two meanings, "lion of God" and "altar" (see Ezek. 43:15, 16 where *ariel* is translated *altar hearth*). The city that was once the "lion of God" is now a *flaming altar*. Its people are the sacrificial victims.

29:5–8 Yet God will intervene **suddenly** and the enemies will be driven back **like fine dust** and **chaff**. Just when the foes think they will completely devour Jerusalem, they will be foiled as if waking out of a dream.

29:9–12 The people's willful blindness had brought judicial blindness upon them, and they **stagger** as if **drunk**. God's word is unintelligible to them. To some it is a **sealed...book**, to others illegible. Everyone has an excuse.

29:13–14 Because their religion is purely external and their only fear of God is a matter of memorized creeds, God will perform a supernatural work of judgment, stripping the keenest minds of wisdom and discernment. The **"marvelous work"** in verse 14 refers to the invasion of Sennacherib. W. E. Vine writes:

> The rulers of Judah sought to rely on Egypt for assistance. That was a piece of political wisdom from the natural point of view; in God's sight it was an act of rebellion; hence God brought the policy to nought, reducing Judah to a condition of helplessness, that they might depend on God alone.[39]

Today the "marvelous work" is accomplished by the gospel (see 1 Cor. 1:18–25).

29:15, 16 A **woe** is pronounced on the deceitful rulers who are making plots with Egypt, as if God does not see them. They have everything topsy-turvy, putting **the clay** in the potter's place and vice versa, thus denying God's power and knowledge.

29:17–21 But a day of deliverance is coming when God will also reverse things. What is now a wild forest (**Lebanon**) will be **a fruitful field**, and what is now counted **a fruitful field** will be looked on as nothing more than an overgrown **forest**. Then **the deaf shall hear, the blind shall see, the humble also shall increase their joy in the Lord**. The oppressor and the scoffer shall be no more—also those nit-pickers who tried to trip up the righteous!

29:22–24 The closing verses describe the believing remnant, here called **Jacob**. Shame and reproach will be a thing of the past. The children of Jacob will realize how God has intervened on their behalf and will honor Him for it. **Those who** misjudged and **complained** will be knowledgeable and teachable.

3. Woe to the Alliance with Egypt (Chaps. 30, 31)

30:1–7 **The rebellious children** are the politicians of Judah who make a league with **Egypt** against Assyria. Since there is no record of such an alliance, we are justified in thinking of this as still future. Judah will learn that **Egypt** is not worthy of trust. Caravans are seen carrying tribute from Judah to Egypt, through dangerous areas in the Negeb (**the South**), but though the Jewish envoys get as far as **Zoan** and **Hanes**, the whole project is doomed to failure. God calls Egypt **"Rahab-Hem-Shebeth"** (Rahab who sits still).

30:8–14 Let it be recorded for posterity that the treaty with Egypt (and all such misplaced trust) is a blatant rejection of **the law of the Lord** through His prophets. Judah will see that Egypt is a poor wall of defense. In fact the **high wall** will **bulge** and crash. It will be smashed as completely as an earthenware vessel, with no **fragments** big enough to use in minor chores.

30:15–17 God has been saying to Judah, "Your salvation lies **in returning** to Me and resting on Me. **Your strength** lies in quiet trust in Me rather than frenzied flight to Egypt." But Judah said, **"No, for we will** fly against the enemy." To which God answers, "You will fly all right, but in retreat and in panic! You will be chased by undermanned forces till you are like a single, scrawny **pole on a hill**."

30:18–25 Still **the Lord will wait** to **be gracious**. "God waits until the disaster of our choice has taught us the foolishness of that choice." When Judah turns to the Lord, He will be their Teacher, Guide, Giver of **rain**, fertility and prosperity, Healer, Rock, and Defender. His people "will throw away their idols like the polluted things they are, shouting after them 'Good riddance!'"

30:26–33 The intensified **light** of verse 26 must be understood as symbolic of glory and righteousness. The godless nations will be sifted in a sieve of destruction. **Assyria will be beaten down** by the Lord, and every stroke **of punishment** will be accompanied by jubilant music from Judah. The burning **fires** of **Topheth** (hell) are ready to welcome **the** wicked **king**.

31:1–3 God is against those who go **to Egypt for help**, who trust in **horses, . . . chariots, . . . and in horsemen** for victory. He **will arise against the house of evildoers** (Judah) **and against the** helpers (Egypt) **of those who work iniquity** (Judah). The helper (Egypt) **will** stumble, **and he who is helped** (Judah) **will fall**.

31:4–9 God is like **a lion** which **a multitude of shepherds** (Assyria) tries to frighten away. Or, to change the figure, He is like a flock of **birds**, hovering over **Jerusalem**; He is ready to defend and **deliver** the city. When **Israel** turns back to the Lord, it will **throw away** its **idols**. The Assyrians will perish by a direct intervention of the Lord. The destruction of Sennacherib did not exhaust the meaning of these verses, so the prophecy has a future fulfillment as well, that is, in the Tribulation.

4. *The Reign of the Righteous King (Chap. 32)*

32:1–8 The first five verses describe the Millennial **reign** of Christ. He is the **king** who reigns **in righteousness**; the **princes** may be the twelve apostles (see Matt. 19:28). **"A man will be as a hiding place from the wind . . ."**—that Man is the Lord Jesus, providing shelter, protection, refreshment, and shade. No longer will judicial blindness afflict the people, nor will **ears** be closed to listening obediently. Those who now make **rash** decisions will have discernment, and those who now stammer will express themselves without hesitation. Moral distinctions will no longer be blurred. The senseless person will not be honored. The coming of Christ will reveal men in their true light. The fool and the knave will be exposed as such (and punished accordingly). The **generous** man also will be manifested and blessed. Verses 6–8 describe life as Isaiah saw it in his day.

32:9–15 But the kingdom hasn't come yet. The **women** of Judah are still living in luxury, **ease**, and complacency. Soon the blow of judgment will fall—crop failure, depopulation, and desolation. Judah's troubles will continue **until the Spirit is poured** out at the Second Advent of Christ. Then the desert will become **a fruitful field**, and what is now considered **a fruitful field** will be as luxuriant **as a forest**.

32:16–20 Social **justice** and **righteousness** will permeate every aspect of life, resulting in **peace**, **quietness**, safety, and confidence. The enemy (**forest**) shall be leveled by the **hail** of God's judgment and **the city** (its capital) shall be laid low. It will be a happy time, when people can safely sow beside all waters and when **the ox and the donkey** can range freely without danger.

5. *Woe to the Plunderer/Assyria (Chap. 33)*

33:1–6 The destructiveness and treachery of the Assyrian come back on him (vv. 1, 2). Then God's people pray to the LORD for deliverance in their time of trouble. When God moves into action, a thunderous **noise** sends the nations scrambling. It is the Jews' turn to pounce on the loot of the fleeing enemy and pick it over thoroughly. Christ is enthroned, filling **Zion with justice and righteousness**, thus making the **times** stable, and enriching His people with spiritual **treasure**.

33:7–9 These verses revert to the time when Hezekiah sent **ambassadors of peace** to Sennacherib and was told to pay a fine of three hundred talents of silver and thirty talents of gold (2 Kgs. 18:13–16). But even this did not succeed in buying off the Assyrian. He marched against Judah, leaving a trail of havoc and suffering.

The envoys from Judah are weeping bitterly because of the failure of their mission. The Assyrian has broken his word by invading Judah. The most scenic places are scenes of desolation.

33:10–12 In the nick of time **the LORD** arises to deal with the foe. In biting sarcasm, He describes the Assyrian as conceiving **chaff** and bringing **forth stubble**. In other words, his schemes are futile. The same kind of wrath he vented on others will backfire and utterly devour himself. Burning **lime** and **thorns** speak of complete judgment.

33:13–16 A word goes out to godless Gentiles (**you who are afar off**) and to apostate Jews in Zion (**you who are near**). In the fire of God's judgment, the burning of His wrath, the only ones who will survive are those who walk **righteously** and separate themselves from every form of **evil**.

33:17 Then secure and satisfied, the believing remnant **will see the King in His beauty** and **the land** whose borders are greatly expanded.

A. J. Gordon adapted this verse for one of his hymns:

> I shall see the King in His beauty,
> In the land that is far away,
> When the shadows at length have lifted,
> And the darkness has turned to day.
>
> I shall see Him in the glory,
> The Lamb that once was slain;
> How I'll then resound the story
> With all the ransomed train!
> Hallelujah, Hallelujah!
> To the Lamb that once was slain;
> Hallelujah, Hallelujah,
> Hallelujah! Amen.

33:18, 19 Only a harmless memory will be those moments of **terror** when the Assyrian weighed out the gold paid in tribute, when his spies counted **the towers** of the city in preparing to attack it, when the Jews heard the foreign language of the Assyrians in their midst.

33:20–22 In the millennial **Zion**, the solemn **appointed feasts** will be held again. The city will be like a tent that is pitched securely and permanently. **The LORD will be** to Zion everything that a river is to a city—protection, refreshment, and beauty. No enemy **galley** or **majestic ships** will ever **pass by**, because **the LORD** is there.

33:23, 24 Commentators are disagreed whether verse 23a refers to Jerusalem or to her enemies. If it refers to Zion's enemies, then it pictures the fate of any ship that would presume to attack the city. If it refers to Jerusalem, verse 23

> speaks of the weakness and inability of the people themselves, pictured whether as unable to guide the ship of state, or, what is more probable, arrange their tent as their dwelling place, with the necessary cord, tent pole and canvas.[40]

In the kingdom, even **the lame** will be able to **take the prey**. Sickness will be over, and the **iniquity** of **the people** will **be forgiven**.

6. Woe to All Nations (Chap. 34)

34:1–4 In chapter 34 we have God's **indignation against all nations** in general, and against Edom in particular. The latter may be representative of all the other nations. When Jehovah judges the Gentiles (**nations**) the air will reek from the decomposing **corpses**, and **the mountains** will melt away from the torrent of **their blood**. Even **the** stellar **heavens** will be convulsed.

34:5–7 The **sword of the LORD**, "intoxicated **with blood**," will fall in fury **on Edom**, both on the common people (**lambs, goats, rams**) and on the nobles or leaders (**wild oxen, young bulls, mighty bulls**).

34:8 It is the day of the Lord's vengeance.

> The word 'vengeance' is of crucial importance. It does not mean getting even with someone, as we use it. It refers to God's action in carrying out the sentence which He as Judge has justly imposed (*Daily Notes of the Scripture Union*).

34:9–17 This passage describes Edom's fate—a blazing inferno, an uninhabited waste, taken over by mysterious birds and **wild beasts**. God will not stop until it is without form and void.[41] There will be no **kingdom**, no king, no **princes** worthy of the name. Its ruins will be overgrown with **thorns** and it will be a sanctuary for strange creatures (which cannot be identified with certainty). Every weird creature will have **a mate**, and thus will reproduce, and God has given them the ruins of Edom to **possess . . . from generation to generation**. **Forever** in this chapter (vv. 10, 17) means **from generation to generation**.

7. *The Glory of the Coming Kingdom (Chap. 35)*

35:1–7 After the rebellious nations are destroyed, the glorious kingdom of our Lord and Savior, Jesus Christ, is introduced. Features of that period include increased fertility of the land and the personal presence of **the Lord** in **glory** and **excellence**. There will be mutual encouragement among the saints. Every type of disability will be removed, and great rejoicing will celebrate the transformation of **the desert** into well-irrigated fields.

35:8–10 The hundreds of miles of desert route from exile back to Jerusalem will become a **"Highway of Holiness,"** exclusive to God's redeemed people. The **return** of Israel from worldwide dispersion prepictures the **joy** and **gladness** that will accompany the translation of believers to the Father's house when Jesus comes again.

In some editions of the Bible, the supplied summary titles at the tops of the pages of Isaiah will read in substance, "Blessings on the church" and "Curses on Israel." In fact, almost all these predictions are directly aimed at Israel—whether blessings or curses, and the church comes in later or by application. Jennings decries this unjust treatment of Israel by many Christians:

> We justly blame those who take all the promises of the Old Testament, and leave only the threatenings for the poor Jew, for in this they do greatly err; yet there is an element of truth in their contention, since "all the promises of God are Yea and Amen in Christ Jesus." Their error is in saying that since God has no further use for Israel, these comforting forecasts apply, and only apply, to Christians, not to Israel as a nation at all! God be thanked that whatever is of a spiritual character does so apply: the material blessings that Israel shall enter into on the basis of the new covenant of grace are, in a spiritual sense, ours by that same grace. But that does not *fulfil* these promises that were given directly to Israel as identified with her Messiah, Jesus, and given her long before the Church of God was revealed at all.[42]

II. HISTORICAL TRANSITION: THE BOOK OF HEZEKIAH (Chaps. 36—39)

Chapters 36 through 39, sometimes called "The Book of Hezekiah," form the historical section of the book of Isaiah. Except for 38:9–20, they are almost an exact repetition of 2 Kings 18:13, 17—20:19.

A. Hezekiah's Deliverance from Assyria (Chaps. 36, 37)

1. *Assyria's Defiance of God (Chap. 36)*

36:1–3 In chapter 36, **the Rabshakeh** (lit. *chief wine-pourer*, but used of a governor or chief of staff), an envoy of the King of Assyria, meets three delegates of **Hezekiah by the aqueduct from the upper pool, on the highway to the Fuller's Field**. This is the same place where Ahaz had stood when he was bent on trusting Assyria rather than Jehovah to save him from the Syrian-Ephraim alliance (7:3).

36:4–10 **The Rabshakeh** warns them that it is folly to **trust** in promises from **Egypt** because that base kingdom will wound anyone who **leans** on it. To any claim that they were trusting in Jehovah, he says that Hezekiah had removed the **high places** and **altars** of Jehovah. This was either ignorance or deliberate misrepresentation; **Hezekiah** had removed the **high places** of the idols and strengthened the worship of Jehovah at the temple. The Rabshakeh further taunts that the King of Judah couldn't provide enough **riders** if Sennacherib were to donate **two thousand horses**. Since Judah is so undermanned, how can they hope to defeat the Assyrians, even with Egypt's help? Finally he falsely claims that **the LORD** has commanded the Assyrians **to destroy** Judah.

36:11–20 Hezekiah's envoys fear that the Rabshakeh's insolent boasts and threats, spoken in Hebrew, will undermine the morale of the men of Judah, so they ask him to **speak . . . in Aramaic**. He not only refuses, but begins another **loud** harangue, charging that **Hezekiah** is deceiving the people into false security. He promises the men of Judah plenty of food if they surrender to him, plus eventual relocation in a land of equal fertility. He lists a series of conquered cities (including **Samaria**) whose **gods** had not been able to save them from the Assyrian juggernaut, and pointedly asks what chance **Jerusalem** has. The Rabshakeh arrogantly decides that God's people should surrender.

36:21, 22 Following their **king's commandment** Hezekiah's men do not try to answer him but go and report his words to the king.

2. *God's Destruction of Assyria (Chap. 37)*

37:1–4 **When King Hezekiah** hears what the Rabshakeh has said, he is plunged into gloom. After going to the temple, he sends a deputation **to Isaiah** saying, **"Children have come to birth, but there is no strength to bring them forth."** As J. A. Alexander points out, this metaphor is "expressive of extreme pain, imminent danger, critical emergency, utter weakness, and entire dependence on the aid of others."[43] In timidity that surpasses faith, Hezekiah suggests that maybe Jehovah **has heard the** mocking **words of the Rabshakeh**, and **will rebuke** him.

37:5–7 **The LORD** then assures the king through Isaiah that there is no reason to fear the king of Assyria. The Lord **will send a spirit** (perhaps of apprehension) **upon** Sennacherib so that, hearing **a rumor**, he will **return to his own land** and be killed there.

37:8–13 When **the Rabshakeh** leaves Jerusalem to rejoin Sennacherib, he finds that the latter has redirected his fighting **from Lachish** to **Libnah**, ten miles to the northwest. Another part of the army, of course, is besieging Jerusalem. Then, frustrated by a rumor that **Tirhakah**, an Ethiopian ruling in Egypt, has set out to attack him, Sennacherib sends **messengers to Hezekiah** with a blasphemous letter similar to the diatribe that Rabshakeh had delivered. He cites the folly of trusting in Jehovah by recounting the historic victories of the kings of Assyria.

37:14–20 **Hezekiah** has the good sense to take **the letter** to the temple **and spread it before the Lord**. In a short but moving prayer that demonstrates the king's great faith, he asks God to **save** Judah from the king **of Assyria** so **"that all the kingdoms of the earth may know that You are the Lord, You alone."**

37:21–29 Jehovah answers through **Isaiah** in a poem that first pictures **Jerusalem** as **a virgin**, taunting **Sennacherib** as he goes down to defeat. Then Jehovah takes the Assyrian to task for mocking **the Lord** Himself and for bragging as if he had already conquered Judah and Egypt. God tells Sennacherib that he is only a pawn in Jehovah's hand, doing what He planned long ago. The same Lord who knows everything about this wicked king will lead him **back** to Assyria like an animal with a **hook in** its **nose**.

37:30–32 Then turning to Hezekiah, the Lord assures him that though food supplies will be limited **this year and the** next because of the Assyrian incursion, crops will return to normal in **the third year**. The people who have holed up in **Jerusalem** in preparation for a siege will emerge and resume normal life. Jehovah's **zeal** for His people will guarantee it.

37:33–35 **The Lord** assures Hezekiah that **the king of Assyria** will not enter Jerusalem or get near enough to attack it. God **will defend** the **city** and send back the invader **the way that he came**.

37:36 And so it happened. **The angel of the Lord killed one hundred and eighty-five thousand** Assyrian soldiers during the night.

One of the great poems in the English language, written in 1815, dramatizes this event. Since many readers do not have access to an extensive library, we make no apology for reproducing it in full:

THE DESTRUCTION OF SENNACHERIB

The Assyrian came down like the wolf on the fold,
And his cohorts were gleaming in purple and gold;
And the sheen of their spears was like stars on the sea,
When the blue wave rolls nightly on deep Galilee.

Like the leaves of the forest when Summer is green,
That host with their banners at sunset were seen:
Like the leaves of the forest when Autumn hath blown,
That host on the morrow lay withered and strown.

For the Angel of Death spread his wings on the blast,
And breathed in the face of the foe as he passed;
And the eyes of the sleepers waxed deadly and chill,
And their hearts but once heaved, and forever grew still!

And there lay the steed with his nostril all wide,
But through it there rolled not the breath of his pride;
And the foam of his gasping lay white on the turf,
And cold as the spray of the rock-beating surf.

And there lay the rider distorted and pale,
With the dew on his brow, and the rust on his mail:
And the tents were all silent—the banners alone—
The lances unlifted—the trumpet unblown.

And the widows of Ashur are loud in their wail,
And the idols are broke in the temple of Baal;

And the might of the Gentile, unsmote
by the sword,
Hath melted like snow in the glance
of the Lord![44]
—*George Gordon, Lord Byron*
(1788–1824)

37:37, 38 **Sennacherib** returned to **Nineveh**, only to be slain by **his sons Adrammelech and Sharezer** in his idol temple.

B. Hezekiah's Sickness and Recovery (Chap. 38)

38:1–8 Chapter 38 does not follow chapter 37 chronologically because in verse 6 Hezekiah is promised deliverance from the Assyrian threat, whereas, at the end of the previous chapter, that threat has already ended.

When **Hezekiah** is taken seriously ill, he earnestly prays for lengthened life, and **the God of David** his **father** grants him **fifteen** more **years**. As a **sign** that he will recover and that Sennacherib will be repulsed, God promises to make **the shadow on the sundial of Ahaz** go **ten degrees backward**. The Hebrew of verse 8 is difficult, but it seems probable that Ahaz had built an obelisk with steps leading up to it for telling time, and that God miraculously caused the shadow to decline **ten degrees** while Hezekiah watched.

38:9–15 To celebrate his recovery, Hezekiah wrote a poem or psalm. This is the unique part of the historical section; it has no parallel in 2 Kings. It opens with the sadness that filled him when he heard that he was going to die **in the prime of** his **life**. He will **not see YAH, the LORD**, that is, experience the goodness of the Lord, and he will be cut off from the rest of mankind. His **life** is ending as if **a shepherd's tent** is being taken down, or a finished fabric **cut off** from the loom. He describes his sense of desolation, his **bitterness**, his earnest supplication, and his helplessness under the stroke of God.

38:16–20 But a change comes in verse 16. Hezekiah acknowledges that **by these** afflictions **men live**, and that they have a beneficial influence on man's character. Now God has delivered him from dying, an indication to the king that the Lord has forgiven his **sins**. Verse 18 reflects the indistinct view of the disembodied state which OT saints had. Now, because he is alive, he can give thanks to the Lord and tell his **children** of the faithfulness of God. He is determined to **praise** Jehovah **all the days of** his **life**.

38:21, 22 These two verses fit chronologically between verses 6 and 7. By placing them here, writes Kelly, "God shows His interest in His own, whatever their infirmity, and explains the means employed, and why the sign was given."[45]

Matthew Henry draws two good lessons on healing from this passage:

> 1. That God's promises are intended not to supersede, but to quicken and encourage, the use of means. Hezekiah is sure to recover, and yet he must *take a lump of figs and lay it on the boil, v.* 21. We do not trust God, but tempt him, if, when we pray to him for help, we do not second our prayers with our endeavours. . . . 2. That the chief end we should aim at, in desiring life and health, is that we may glorify God, and do good, and improve ourselves in knowledge, and grace, and meetness for heaven.[46]

C. Hezekiah's Sin (Chap. 39)

39:1–7 Chapter 39 records Hezekiah's colossal mistake in showing all his resources to a delegation which came from **the king of Babylon**, ostensibly to congratulate him on his recovery. **Hezekiah** probably hoped that the Babylonians would help Judah against the menace of Assyria. When **Isaiah** heard what had happened, he pronounced God's judgment. Judah will be taken into captivity by the Babylonians. The king's **sons** will **be eunuchs in the palace** at **Babylon**. This prediction was made seventy years in advance of the events, when *Assyria,* not Babylon, was the major threat to Judah.

39:8 Hezekiah's response, **"The word of the Lord . . . is good!"** reflects his submission and also his own relief that he personally would not live to see the disaster.

III. PROPHECIES OF COMFORT FROM THE VIEWPOINT OF THE FUTURE CAPTIVITY (Chaps. 40—66)

If the preceding thirty-nine chapters correspond to the books of the OT, then the following twenty-seven chapters, filled with pictures of Jesus the Messiah, certainly correspond to the books of the NT.

In this section of Isaiah (chaps. 40—66), the prophet looks forward to Judah's return from Babylonian captivity and then to the entire nation's future restoration at the Second Advent of Christ.

A. The Comfort of Israel's Coming Deliverance (Chaps. 40—48)

1. Comfort from God's Pardon and Peace (40:1–11)

40:1, 2 Chapter 40 opens with a message of **comfort** for the returning captives. Jerusalem's troubles are over, **her iniquity is pardoned, for she has received . . . double** (that is, full and fitting measure) **for all her sins**. This will be fully realized at the Second Coming of Christ. In the meantime this old earth and even the church is greatly in need of comfort. Each one of us can do his or her bit to comfort God's people:

> Ask God to give thee skill
>   In comforts' art;
> That thou mayst consecrated be
>   And set apart
>   Into a life of sympathy.
> For heavy is the weight of ill
>   In every heart;
> And comforters are needed much
>   Of Christlike touch.
>
> —*A. E. Hamilton*

40:3–5 The call goes out to **"Prepare the way of the Lord."** John the Baptist filled the role of forerunner at Christ's First Advent (Matt. 3:3), and Elijah will fill it at the Second Advent (Mal. 4:5, 6). The preparation for His coming is moral and spiritual, not topographical. Morgan writes:

> The faithful among men prepare His way and make straight His highway when they yield to Him their complete loyalty, and confide in Him alone.[47]

Mountains and hills represent the proud and arrogant among men, valleys the people of low degree. All unevenness and roughness of character must be **made smooth**. **The glory of the Lord** (that is, the Lord Himself) **shall be revealed, and all flesh shall see it together** (see Rev. 1:7).

40:6–8 The Lord instructs the prophet to **"Cry out!"** to men, telling them how transitory they are, and how permanent His **word** is. While these verses describe the transience of all men, they may refer especially to Israel's overlords.

"The word of our God stands forever" has been adopted as the motto of a number of Christian schools, usually in Latin: *Verbum Dei manet in aeternam*. William Kelly wrote that

> as the end draws nearer we do greatly need simplicity to rest upon God's Word. There may be difficulties to such as we are, and the Word seems a weak thing to confide in for eternity, but in truth it is more stable than heaven or earth.[48]

40:9–11 **Zion** herself may be the herald of the **good tidings** of the Messiah's advent or the news may be brought to Zion by some female herald. (The **You** is feminine.) Verses 10 and 11 show the severity and the goodness of God—severity to those who refuse to acknowledge Him, but gentle goodness to His **flock** and **lambs** who have been dispersed among the Gentiles. These verses picture His coming in power and glory.

2. *Comfort from God's Attributes (40:12–31)*

40:12 Here begins a classic passage on the greatness of God in contrast to the utter vanity of idols. Jehovah has **measured the waters** of the sea **in the hollow of His hand**, and **measured heaven with a span**, the distance from the tip of His thumb to the tip of His little finger. He enclosed **the dust of the earth in a measure** (about a peck).

40:13, 14 No one ever **directed the Spirit of the Lord**. All His works of creation and providence were and are performed without outside help.

40:15–17 **The nations are** as insignificant **as a drop in a bucket** to Him. The forests of **Lebanon** are **not sufficient** for fuel and all its animals inadequate for a worthy **burnt offering** to Him.

40:18–26 What man-made **image** could ever portray a **God** so great? The rich man makes his idol with precious metal and the poor man with wood. Utterly ridiculous! **Have** they **not known** or **heard** of the greatness of Jehovah's Person and power? What image could ever capture the **greatness** of the One who made the stars? When He calls them to come out at night, **not one is missing**.

40:27–31 If any of the people of Judah are discouraged and wonder if God still cares for them, let them realize that those **who wait on the Lord** are assured of renewed **strength**. It is absurd to think that He cares less for His people than for the stars which He guides so unerringly.

3. *Comfort from the Holy One of Israel (Chap. 41)*

41:1 God summons the nations to a confrontation with Him; they should **renew their strength**, i.e., produce their strongest arguments.

41:2–4 Jehovah first describes His calling of Cyrus, the **one from the east**. The past tense is used to describe the certainty of what is still future. It should be mentioned here that some commentators believe verses 2 and 3 refer to the call of Abraham, but the military victories of the man described here far overshadow Abraham's achievements. This man (Cyrus, King of Persia) has an unbroken record of victories. In the path of his juggernaut, resistance is as weak as dust and stubble. He advances swiftly into places that are new to him. **Who raised up** Cyrus and calls one generation to succeed another? It is Jehovah—**the first; and with the last**, that is, **with the last** generation, He is still the same.

41:5–7 The nations are terrified as they hear of the conqueror's approach. The people try to encourage one another that there is nothing to fear. Then they hastily fashion an idol to save them from destruction. The poor idol has to be nailed into place so it will **not totter**!

41:8–10 Verses 8–20 describe God's personal love and care for His people. The implied question is, "Have idols ever cared for you so tenderly?" God has called them from Ur of the Chaldees to be His **servant**; they are assured of His presence, His relationship, His help, and His sustaining power in what must be one of the loveliest verses in Isaiah:

> **Fear not, for I am with you; be not dismayed, for I am your God. I will strengthen you, yes, I will help you, I will uphold you with My righteous right hand.**

41:11–16 Their enemies **shall perish** and disappear; God is their Helper and **Redeemer**. The Lord will use Israel as His **threshing sledge** against the nations and Israel will **rejoice in the LORD** alone.

41:17–20 **The poor and needy** will be cared for by the Lord. The millennial earth will have **water** in abundance, and the **wilderness** will flourish with a great variety of trees. It will be a lesson to all that **the LORD** really cares for His own.

41:21–24 In verse 21, God switches back to His controversy with the nations. He challenges them to produce idols which can predict **things to come**, or even account for things that already are. Let them prophesy, or let them do **good** or **evil**—anything to show that they can do *something!* But they cannot. They are a fraction of **nothing**—not even complete nothing.[49]

41:25–28 Cyrus comes into view again in verse 25, this time as **one from the north**. He originally came from Persia (the east, v. 2), then he conquered Media (**the north**), and proceeded on his conquests from there. Cyrus called on God's name in the sense that he acknowledged God as the One who guided and empowered him (Ezra 1:2). No idol had ever predicted the coming of Cyrus. God told it in advance to His people, but He cannot find one among the idols to speak with authority. They are all a delusion, and unworthy of trust.

41:29 The last verse in chapter 41 clearly reveals the contrast between God and worthless "molded images." Vine renders it close to the original as follows:

> Look at them all! Vanity! Their productions are nothingness; wind and desolation are their molten images.[50]

4. Comfort from the Servant of the Lord (Chap. 42)

42:1–4 The name **"Servant"** is applied by Isaiah to the *Messiah,* to the entire *nation of Israel,* to the *godly remnant* of the people (43:10), and to *Cyrus*. Usually the context makes clear which one is intended. In verses 1–4 it is clearly the Lord Jesus—upheld and chosen by God and endued with the Holy **Spirit**. He will **bring forth justice to the Gentiles**, will not be a rabble-rouser, will **not** crush true penitence or **quench** a spark of faith, **will not fail nor be discouraged till He has established** His righteous kingdom.

42:5–9 **God**, the mighty Creator, now addresses the Messiah and tells what He proposes to accomplish through this One whom He has **called . . . in righteousness**. God **will not** share His **glory** with **another**, and least of all with **carved images**. His past predictions **have come to pass**, and now He reveals the future once more.

42:10–13 Israel calls on earth's

remotest nations to join in **praise** to the Messiah as He descends, **a mighty . . . man of war**, to execute vengeance on His **enemies**. The mention of **Kedar** and **Sela** means that Arab voices will join in the **new song**.

42:14–17 Jehovah is speaking here. The time of His self-restraint is past; now He will unloose His fury on His foes, He will deal mercifully with the believing remnant of Israel, and He will utterly shame all idolaters.

42:18–22 In verse 19 the **servant** is no longer the Messiah. It is Israel, **deaf** and **blind** to the words and works of Jehovah. **"Who is blind as he who is perfect?"** may mean **perfect** as to privilege, or may be translated "Who is blind as him whom I have trusted?" (JND), or, "Who is so blind as he that is at peace with Me?" (NASB). Israel was brought into covenant relationship with the Lord, but did not walk worthy of her high calling. The Lord exalted **the law**. It was **honorable** to Him. But Israel despised and disobeyed it, and as a result was given over to robbery, **plunder**, and prison.

42:23–25 The prophet Isaiah asks: **"Who among you will give ear to this? . . . Who gave Jacob for plunder, and Israel to the robbers? Was it not the LORD, He against whom we have sinned?"** God had **poured** out **on** Israel **the fury of His anger** and the **fire** of **battle**, but no one seemed to discern the significance of His chastisement or **take it to heart**.

5. *Comfort from Israel's Restoration (Chap. 43, 44)*

43:1–7 In tones of tender love, Jehovah assures His people that they need **not . . . fear**, because He who created, formed, redeemed, and called them **will be with** them in the flood and **fire**. **The Holy One of Israel** gives **Egypt** as their **ransom**, a promise that was fulfilled after the return of the Jews from captivity. Vine writes:

> The Lord rewarded Cyrus the Persian Monarch for liberating them, by permitting him and his son Cambyses to possess Egypt and the neighbouring kingdoms. Seba was the large district between the White and the Blue Nile, contiguous to Ethiopia. The possession of these lands was not merely a gift, it was a ransom price (a *kopher*, or covering), the people on whose behalf payment was made, being covered by it.[51]

Because Israel is **precious**, **honored**, and **loved**, God **will give men** in exchange **for** her, that is, judgment will fall on the Gentiles in every direction in order that His **sons and** His **daughters** might be restored to the land. Verses 5–7 describe that restoration.

43:8–13 The Lord now summons Israel and **all the nations** to a court test. **Let them bring . . . witnesses** as to the ability of idols to predict future events. Otherwise let them acknowledge that only God is true. **The LORD** calls Israel as His **witnesses**;[52] they should testify that He is the only true **God**, that He is eternal, that **besides** Him **there is no savior** and Deliverer, and that His decrees and acts cannot be thwarted.

43:14–21 **The LORD** is determined to crush **Babylon** for Israel's sake. This will demonstrate that He is **the LORD**, His people's **Holy One**, **Creator**, and **King**. He is the One who brought them through the Red **Sea**, destroying the pursuing Egyptians at the same time. But the Exodus is forgettable compared to what He is now going to do. He will **make a road** through the desert for His **people** as they return from captivity. In the renewed earth, the waste places will enjoy plentiful water supplies so that the creatures of **the wilderness** will be grateful. God's **people**, too, will be grateful and will **praise** His Name.

43:22–24 These verses revert to Israel's pre-captivity days. The people were prayerless and they grew **weary of** God. Although they **brought** Him **offerings** in a perfunctory way, their hearts were far from God, so it was the same as if they brought no sacrifices. They didn't overload God with gifts—only **with** their **iniquities**!

43:25–28 Yet in His grace He **blots out** their **transgressions** and forgives and forgets their **sins**. Can they cite any merit in themselves why He should do this? No. Their entire history has been one unbroken record of sin and failure—from Adam on. That is why His judgment came upon them.

44:1–5 In these verses we hear the heartbeat of the Lord for His people. His love is unextinguished by all their sin. He calls them **Jacob** (supplanter), **Israel** (prince of God), and **Jeshurun** (upright). He **who made** them, **formed** them, and chose them **will help** them. The promise of the **Spirit** was partially fulfilled at Pentecost but it will have its final and complete fulfillment at the Second Advent. Then the thirsty **ground**, both literal and figurative, will experience **floods** of water. Israel's **offspring** will flourish, and they will not be ashamed to identify themselves **by the name of Israel** and **by the name of Jacob** and by **the LORD's** name. (Or verse 5 *may* mean that *Gentiles* will identify themselves with Jehovah and with His people, see Ps. 87:4, 5.)

44:6–8 **The LORD**, the **King of Israel**, is unique—the only true God. He challenges any so-called god to predict the future as He does, especially with regard to **the ancient people**, Israel. His people need **not fear** any challenge to His supremacy. They are His **witnesses** that He has foretold the future, and that He is the only **God**. He Himself does **not know** of any **other** genuine **Rock**; how then could Israel know of any?

44:9–11 **Those who make an image** are doomed to shame and disappointment. The idols are **useless** and powerless.

44:12–17 Here is a **blacksmith** making an idol for a rich man. He works hard, forming it into the desired shape. But then he has to stop for a break—he needs food, drink, and a rest. If the idol maker runs out of **strength** so quickly, what about the inanimate image which he makes?

Or here is a **craftsman**, making a wooden idol for a poor man. He chisels away at the block of wood until the **figure of a man** appears. Maybe he himself had planted the tree. He uses **some of it** as fuel **to warm himself**, some to bake his food, and some to make **a god**. Then he **falls down** and worships a god of his own creation.

44:18–20 Because of their refusal to see, God **has shut** the **eyes** of the idolaters. They never stop to think that the same tree that is their master is also their servant, that they worship part of it and use part for household chores! They feed **on** what is worthless as **ashes**, they are led astray by a delusion, they **cannot deliver** themselves from their bondage, and they never face up to the fact that the god they hold in their **hand** is **a lie**.

44:21–23 **Israel** is called to **remember** that God is their Creator who never forgets them, and that they are His **servant**. He has **blotted out** the **cloud** of **transgressions** that hid His face from them; He has bought them back from bondage and invites them to **return to** Him. All creation is invited to **sing** and **shout**, because **the LORD has redeemed Jacob**.

44:24–27 God presents Himself to the faithful remnant as **Redeemer**, Jehovah (**the LORD**), Creator, Protector, and Restorer. He **frustrates** the predictions of the Chaldean **babblers and . . . diviners** and the wisdom of the **wise**. He **confirms** the predictions of His own prophets that **Jerusalem** and **Judah** will be restored, and that His people will return from captivity under the decree of Cyrus.

44:28 This prophecy concerning **Cyrus** is remarkable in that it mentions him *by name* 150 to 200 years before he was born. It is also amazing that God calls him **"My shepherd."**

Again Cyrus is named as the one whom God will use to deliver His people from Babylon and to authorize the rebuilding of **the temple**. Josephus, the Jewish historian, wrote:

> Now Cyrus learned this (as to building the Temple) by reading the book that Isaiah had left of his own prophecies 210 years before. . . . These things Isaiah foretold 140 years before the Temple was destroyed. When Cyrus, therefore, had read them, and had admired their divine character, an impulse and emulation seized him to do what was written.[53]

6. *Comfort from Cyrus, God's Anointed (Chap. 45)*

45:1–6 **The LORD** calls **Cyrus** His **"anointed"** (the same word as "messiah" in Hebrew) because the Persian monarch was a prototype of the Messiah who would give final deliverance to His people. Jehovah promises to give him victory over **nations**, principally Babylon, to remove all hindrances to his conquests, and to hand over to him tremendous amounts of **hidden riches** in **secret places**. Still addressing Cyrus, **the LORD** speaks of Himself as the only true **God**, who calls Cyrus **by name**, who surnames him as **anointed** and shepherd (44:28), and who equips him for his mission. God does all this for the sake of His people, and so that the whole world may know that He alone is **the LORD**.

45:7 Verse 7 does not mean that God creates moral "evil," as some have claimed, based on the King James Version and other early translations.[54]

Delitzsch points out that the early "Christian" heretic Marcion, and the heretical Valentinians and other Gnostic sects, abused this text to teach that the God of the OT was "a different being from the God of the New."[55]

Addressing the problem of evil (including calamity, no doubt), Delitzsch continues, "Undoubtedly, evil as an act is not the direct working of God, but the spontaneous work of a creature endowed with freedom."[56]

In the present context the contrasts are between **light** and its opposite, **darkness**; between **peace** and its opposite, **calamity**. What God permits, He is often said to **create**. Some think that **light** and **darkness** refer to two principles which the Persians practically revered as two gods who were in perpetual conflict. (Others say that there is no evidence that Cyrus followed this religion.) As Cyrus swept forward in his campaigns, there would be **peace** for Israel and **calamity** for Israel's foes, and God was the One who was supervising the entire operation.

45:8 The ideal conditions of abundant **righteousness** (or justice) and **salvation** (or deliverance) described here are those that would result on a small scale from Cyrus's intervention on behalf of Israel. Their *complete* fulfillment awaits the Millennial Kingdom.

45:9–11 A **woe** is pronounced on any who would question Jehovah's right to use a foreigner in redeeming Judah. That is like **clay** talking back to the **potter** and accusing him of having **no hands**—of being powerless. Verse 11 should possibly be read as a question, "*Do you ask* **Me** what I purpose far in the future **concerning My sons**, or *do you command* **Me concerning the work of My hands?"** In other words, "What right do you have to question Me?"

45:12, 13 The same One who **created man and stretched out the heavens** and **the earth raised up** Cyrus to liberate His **exiles**, and **build** His **city** of Jerusalem. While the rebuilding of the city was actually accomplished later through the decree of Artaxerxes (Neh. 2:8b), it was Cyrus's leadership that first laid the groundwork for this project by allowing the Jews to return from Babylon.

45:14–17 Israel's former enemies will one day **come to** her with gifts and tribute, acknowledging that the **God** of the Jews is the true **God** and that **there is no other**. This promise, as well as all God's dealings, causes the saved remnant to praise God for His inscrutable judgments and His ways past finding out. Makers and worshipers of false gods will **be ashamed**, whereas **Israel, saved by the Lord**, will never have occasion to **be ashamed** after the Second Coming of the Messiah.

45:18, 19 When **the Lord created** the world, it was not as a chaos or **in vain** (*tōhû*, the same word used in Gen. 1:2). He **formed it to be inhabited** by men, and revealed Himself to men in clear, understandable language. He did not create chaotically, nor did He communicate chaotically. Rather He revealed Himself in truth and **righteousness** as the absolute and supreme God.

45:20, 21 He calls on the Gentiles, toting their idols and praying to powerless gods, to produce evidence that their idols can foretell the future as He has done. Only He can do this—and He is the only **just God and a Savior**.

45:22–25 He invites the Gentiles to come to Him for salvation, and decrees that **every knee shall bow** to Him and **every tongue** confess Him (see Rom. 14:11; Phil. 2:9–11). This will find its fulfillment in the Millennium. Then men will acknowledge the Lord Jesus as the only source of **righteousness and strength**. **All** His enemies will come to Him in contrition, and **Israel shall be justified and shall glory** in Him, not in idols.

7. *Comfort from the Fall of Babylon's Idols (Chap. 46)*

46:1, 2 The idols of Babylon, **Bel** and **Nebo**, are being carted away by the Persians. As the weary **beasts** plod on, the **idols** topple. The gods they represent cannot save the load; instead they are carried off **into captivity**.

46:3, 4 In contrast to the idols which are carried by the people, the true God **will carry** His people **even to** their **old age**. James Stewart summarizes concisely:

> Ever since Isaiah, men have been aware that one of the vital distinctions between true religion and false is that whereas the latter is a dead burden for the soul to carry, the former is a living power to carry the soul.[57]

46:5–7 What image could ever represent the absolute and exclusive Deity? Yet, deluded people still pay generous amounts to the goldsmith to make **a god** for them. **They prostrate themselves** in **worship**, . . . **they**

carry it, and when they **set it** down, it stays there, unable to **move**. It can neither hear prayer **nor save**.

46:8–11 Any people who are leaning toward idolatry should stop and **remember** that only the true **God** has revealed events before they came to pass with the determination to accomplish all His plans. He will call Cyrus (**a bird of prey from the east**) to deliver His people from the Chaldeans.

46:12, 13 Those who stubbornly refuse to face the evidence now hear God's established purpose to **place salvation in Zion**.

8. Comfort from the Fall of Babylon (Chap. 47)

47:1–4 The city of **Babylon** is pictured as a beautiful young **virgin** queen who is forced to step down from her **throne** and become a servant, doing menial work and wading **through the rivers** into captivity. She will be stripped bare and exposed to public view. God will **take vengeance** and spare no **man**, because He is acting as the **Redeemer, . . . the Holy One of Israel**.

47:5–15 Babylon will be punished for four sins.

1. Although God did appoint her to carry His people into exile, He did *not* order her to be cruel and merciless. She overplayed her part. Now she says, **"I shall be a lady forever,"** but God says, **"You shall no longer be called the Lady of Kingdoms."**
2. She was proud and arrogant, supposing that nothing could ever destroy her prosperity. She will become widowed and childless **in one day**, and none of her **sorceries** will be able to prevent the calamity.
3. She considered herself immune from detection and punishment. But her smugness and proud self-sufficiency will be rewarded with disaster.
4. She trusted in sorcerers and **astrologers**. Jennings writes, "Jehovah counsels her to call all these powers to her aid, for she will need them sorely."[58] God's punishment will be a blazing inferno, not **a** comfortable **fire** in the fireplace. Those who trafficked with Babylon will go their own way, unable to **save** her.

9. Comfort from Israel's Return after Chastening (Chap. 48)

48:1, 2 God here addresses the captives of **Judah** in Babylon. Most of them are probably apostate; only a few are faithful to Jehovah. He complains that they call themselves by the name of **Israel** (prince of God) but they are not princes. They are descended from **Judah** (praise) but they do not praise Him. They confess the God of Israel but they do not confess their sins. **They call themselves after the holy city** but they are not holy. They **lean on the God of Israel** but they are not godly.

48:3–5 Jehovah had predicted their history well in advance, and it **came to pass** as foretold. Knowing their stubbornness and hardness, God **proclaimed** what He would do so they wouldn't credit it to their idols when it happened.

48:6–8 Now He is going to predict something **new**—the restoration from captivity under Cyrus. He is doing this so that they will not be able to say, **"Of course I knew** it all along."

48:9–11 He will end the exile for Judah, not because of their merit, but **for** His **own sake**. He has **refined**

them, **not** like **silver** in literal fire, but **in the furnace of affliction** (the Babylonian captivity). Now He will restore them for His own **name's sake—a name** that has been **profaned** by them. He will not share the credit for this restoration with their idols.

48:12–16 Presenting Himself as the eternal, absolute God (**the First** and **the Last**), the Creator and Sustainer of the universe, the Arranger of history, the God of prophecy, He announces that He will raise up one whom He loves (Cyrus) to defeat the Babylonians and to deliver the people of Israel. Notice all three Persons of the Trinity in verse 16—**the Lord God and His Spirit**, and **Me** (i.e., Christ). Here the subject turns almost imperceptibly from Cyrus to his Antitype, the Lord Jesus, who will deliver the nation from their worldwide dispersion at His Second Advent.

48:17–19 Again **the Lord** appeals to the people of **Israel** as their **Redeemer**, their **God**, their Teacher, and Guide. If they had obeyed Him, they would have enjoyed **peace, righteousness,** fertility, and uninterrupted fellowship with Him.

48:20–22 He calls on the godly remnant to **go forth from Babylon** and joyfully **proclaim** the Lord as their Redeemer (see Rev. 18:4). Verse 21 was fulfilled in the Exodus from Egypt. If Jehovah did it once, He can do it again. **The wicked** Israelites who refuse to obey the Lord by separating themselves from Babylon and all it stands for can never know **peace**.

B. The Messiah and His Rejection by Israel (Chaps. 49—57)

1. The Messiah as Servant (Chap. 49)

In chapters 49 through 53, God is dealing with His people because of their rejection of the Messiah. This is the book of the Suffering Servant of Jehovah.

49:1–6 The **servant** of Jehovah in chapter 49 may seem to be the nation of Israel in verses 1–3, but only the Lord Jesus fully answers to the text. In verse 3 **Israel** is mentioned by name, but it is Christ, the true "Prince of God," and not the nation. In verses 5 and 6 the Servant is distinguished from Israel. The restorations of Israel merge in these verses, first the return under Cyrus, then the future restoration when the Messiah sets up His kingdom.

The Servant calls on the people of the world to **heed** Him as He recounts His birth, the **name** that was given to Him before His birth (Matt. 1:21), His incisive, authoritative message, and His appointment by God as Servant, a Prince of God (**Israel**) in whom Jehovah would **be glorified**. He further intimates the trouble of soul He experienced over His rejection by Israel (see Matt. 11:16–24), but then His satisfaction that God would **reward** (cf. v. 4 with Matt. 11:25, 26).

God called Him not only to bring about the spiritual rebirth of Israel, but also to bring salvation **to the Gentiles**. Verse 6b is quoted in Acts 13:47 as referring to Christ.

49:7 In His First Advent **the Lord** was deeply despised and abhorred by **the nation** of Israel, lower on the social ladder than the Gentile **kings**. But in His Second Advent, earth's monarchs will pay homage to Him. The phrase **"Servant of rulers"** has been true of Israel as well; compare Joseph, Mordecai, Ezra, Nehemiah, and Daniel.

49:8–13 God answered Christ's prayer by raising Him from the dead, then assigning Him to bring Israel back to the land. The Servant of

Jehovah will summon **the people** to return to the land, and provide ideal travel conditions along the way. They will come **from all** over the world, from as far away as **Sinim** (possibly China). It will be a glad day for the world when Israel experiences His comfort and compassion in this way.

49:14–16 In the meantime, the city of **Zion** is portrayed as feeling that her **Lord has forgotten** her. Jehovah's answer is that a mother may **forget her nursing** baby, but He will never **forget** His city. Zion is **inscribed on the palms of** His **hands**, and her **walls are** never out of His mind. We instinctively compare the reference to **the palms** of Jehovah's hands with the lovewounds borne by Christ for us. A great English Christian poet expressed it beautifully:

> My name from the palms of His hands
> Eternity will not erase;
> Impress on His heart it remains
> In marks of indelible grace.
>
> —*Augustus Toplady*

49:17, 18 Israel's children are hurrying back to Zion, while the wrecking crew is leaving. The assembling crowds, converging on the city, become like jewels on **a bride**.

49:19–21 The **waste and desolate places** of Israel will experience a population explosion. Zion will wonder where so many Jews come from—after all, she has been widowed a long time!

49:22, 23 At a signal **from the Lord God**, the nations will set up an enormous airlift to carry the exiles back to the land. Gentile monarchs will serve God's people, and Israel will realize that it does pay after all to **wait for** the Lord.

49:24–26 If the **captives** in Babylon have any qualms as to the possibility of their being freed from **the mighty** tyrant, let them know that Jehovah **will contend with** their adversaries and **save their children**. When the oppressors reap what they have sown, then the world will know that the Lord is Israel's **Savior and** their **Redeemer, the Mighty One of Jacob**.

2. *The Messiah as True Disciple (Chap. 50)*

50:1–3 In a heart-to-heart talk with Israel, Jehovah reminds them that it was not for some trifling whim that He divorced them (though He did divorce them, Jer. 3:8), nor did He deliver them to the Chaldeans because of any debt to that Gentile nation. The cause was their own **iniquities** and **transgressions**. No one in the nation welcomed Him, and no one answered His call. Did they think He was powerless **to deliver** them? Had He not dried up **the** Red **Sea** and the Jordan River? Had He not **clothed the heavens** in mourning?

50:4–9 The Messiah speaks next. The nation that spurned Jehovah in the OT spurned Jesus in the NT. He came as the True Disciple, taught by God to speak the appropriate **word**. Every **morning** His **ear** was **opened** to receive instructions from His Father for that day. He delighted to do the will of God, even if it meant going to the cross. He did not turn **back** but willingly **gave** Himself over to suffering and **shame**. In full confidence that **God** would vindicate Him, He **set** His **face like a flint** to go to Jerusalem. He was vindicated, of course, by His resurrection. Now he challenges the adversary, Satan, to **condemn** Him. (We too can now throw out the same challenge, Rom. 8:31–39.) All His foes will **grow old like a** moth-eaten **garment**.

50:10 The last two verses describe

two classes of people. The first are those who walk in dependence on **the LORD**. They confess their own need for guidance. For them God's advice is to **trust in the name of the LORD and rely upon** their **God**. Then they will be flooded with illumination.

50:11 The second class are those who try to manufacture their own guidance, feeling no need of divine direction. They can **walk in the light of** their own **sparks** but the Lord will see to it that they will **lie down in torment**.

3. The Messiah as Righteous Ruler (51:1—52:12)

51:1–3 All in Israel who seek deliverance should remember God's care for them since He took them from **the rock** quarry (Mesopotamia). They should be encouraged by the memory of God's gracious dealings with **Abraham . . . and Sarah**, and how He gave them a numerous posterity. And they should be heartened by His promise to **comfort Zion**. Notice three calls to **listen** (vv. 1, 4, 7) and three calls to awake (51:9, 17; 52:1).

51:4–6 The Messiah will rule over **the** Gentile **peoples** as well as Israel during the Millennium. At the close of the kingdom, **the heavens** and **the earth** will be destroyed, and all unbelievers will perish, but God's people will be eternally secure.

51:7, 8 The Lord urges the remnant **not** to **fear** the wrath **of men** during the dark days of the Tribulation period, because the doom of evil men is sealed, and the deliverance of His people is assured.

51:9–11 This prompts the remnant to call on **the LORD** to deliver His people as He delivered them from Egypt (**Rahab**) and from Pharaoh (**the serpent**, his symbol), drying **up the sea** so **the redeemed** could **cross over**. The memory of God's intervention in the past causes them to foresee the **ransomed** captives' **return to Zion**. F. C. Jennings describes the event beautifully:

> Their heads are garlanded with joy and gladness which they have vainly pursued hitherto, but have overtaken at last, while the storm through which they have passed rolls off like a thick cloud, taking with it all their sighs and tears![59]

51:12–16 Jehovah speaks a message of comfort to those who fear the tyrant, whether Nebuchadnezzar in that day or the man of sin in the future. They should fear **the LORD** who **stretched out the heavens and laid the foundations of the earth**; then they would lose their fear of frail **man. The captive exile hastens, that he may be loosed, that he should not die in the pit, and that his bread should not fail.** These captive were **loosed** at that time by Cyrus, and will be **loosed** by the Messiah at His appearing in glory. Jehovah will bring it to pass; He who is infinitely high is also intimately nigh, hiding His people **with the shadow of** His **hand**. He puts His **words in** their **mouth** so that they might be His missionaries to the world. Verse 16 may also be applied to the Lord Jesus. The Father put His **words** in the Messiah's **mouth**, protected and equipped Him that He might **plant the** new **heavens** and new **earth** of the millennial period **and say to Zion, "You are My people."**

51:17–20 **"Awake, awake!"** He bids **Jerusalem** after her dark night of suffering when none of her **sons** could **guide her**, when she was devastated by famine and sword, when her men lay helpless **like an** exhausted **antelope** caught **in a net**.

51:21–23 He will take the **cup of** His **fury** which has made Jerusalem stagger, and He will give it to her enemies who have gone beyond the limits assigned to them by God by being cruel and merciless.

52:1, 2 Again **Zion** is called to **"Awake, awake!"** from its sleep of captivity and **put on** its **beautiful garments**. Never again will it be invaded by the heathen. This, of course, looks forward to the inauguration of the kingdom; only then will it be true.

52:3–6 Israel had not been **sold** as a slave for monetary gain; she will **be redeemed without money** as well. The Israelites **went down at first into Egypt** as guests; but subsequently they were abused. Later **the Assyrian oppressed them without cause**, but not for monetary gain. **Now** once again God's people are being tyrannized by oppressors who make no payment to the Lord. The overlords are delighted, and God's **name is blasphemed**. But He will show Himself strong on behalf of His own, and they will know that **He** is all that He promised to be.

52:7–10 The next verses picture the return of the Jews from their worldwide dispersion. As the exiles travel over **the mountains . . . to Zion** they are preceded by heralds who proclaim the **good news** of the Messiah's reign. The **watchmen** on the walls of Jerusalem **sing** with joy as they **see . . . the Lord** returning at the head of the multitude. **Jerusalem** itself is summoned to celebrate the Lord's mighty deliverance.

52:11, 12 The exiles are urged to leave behind the pollutions of the land of captivity as they **bear** the temple **vessels** back to Jerusalem. They will not leave in panic or fright; **the God of Israel** will be their protection both **before** and behind.

4. The Messiah as Sin-bearing Sacrifice (52:13—53:12)

The closing verses of chapter 52 really belong to chapter 53. They trace the history of the Servant of Jehovah from His earthly life to the cross and then to His glorious appearing. Adolph Saphir, himself a Hebrew Christian, rhapsodizes on this greatest of all prophecies of the cross:

> Blessed, precious chapter, how many of God's ancient covenant people have been led by thee to the foot of Christ's cross!—that cross over which was written, "Jesus Christ, the King of the Jews!" And oh! what a glorious commentary shall be given of thee when, in the latter days, repentant and believing Israel, looking unto Him whom they have pierced, shall exclaim, "Surely He hath borne our griefs, and carried our sorrows; yet we did esteem Him stricken, smitten of God, and afflicted!"[60]

52:13 Jehovah's **Servant** dealt **prudently** throughout His earthly ministry. He was **exalted** in Resurrection, lifted up in Ascension, and made **very high** in glory at God's right hand.

52:14 At His first coming, **many were astonished** at the depths of His suffering. His face and His body were **marred** beyond recognition as a **man**.

52:15 But when **He** comes again men will be startled (NKJV marg.)[61] at the magnificence of His glory. Gentile **kings** will be speechless when they see His unheard of splendor. They will understand then that the humble Man of Calvary is the King of kings and Lord of lords:

> Did Thy God e'en then forsake Thee,
> Hide His face from Thy deep need?
> In Thy face, once marred and smitten,
> All His glory now we read.
>
> —*Miss C. Thompson*

53:1 The repentant remnant of Israel recalls that when the **report** of the Messiah's First Advent went forth, not many **believed**. And consequently the saving power **of the LORD** was not **revealed** to many either.

53:2 The Lord Jesus grew **up before** the delighted gaze of Jehovah like an exotic, **tender plant** in this world of sin. He was like **a root out of dry ground**. Israel was the **dry ground**, a most unlikely soil. The nation of Israel could see **no beauty** in Him, nothing in His appearance to attract them. F. B. Meyer describes the mystery of His humiliation:

> The tender plant; the sucker painfully pushing its way through the crust of the caked ground; the absence of natural attractiveness. Such imagery awaits and receives its full interpretation from the New Testament, with its story of Christ's peasant parentage, his manger-bed, and lowly circumstances—fisherfolk his choice disciples; poverty his constant lot; the common people his devoted admirers; thieves and malefactors on either side of his cross; the lowly and poor the constituents of his Church. This were humiliation indeed, though the irregularities of human lot are scarce distinguishable from the heights whence He came.[62]

53:3 **Despised and rejected**, He was **a Man of sorrows** who knew what **grief** was. To men He was repulsive; even by Israel He was not appreciated.

> "Man of Sorrows," what a name
> For the Son of God who came
> Ruined sinners to reclaim!
> Hallelujah! what a Saviour!
>
> Bearing shame and scoffing rude,
> In my place condemned He stood;
> Sealed my pardon with His blood;
> Hallelujah! what a Saviour!
>
> —*Philip P. Bliss*

53:4–6 The remnant now knows and acknowledges the truth about Him. They confess: "It was *our* griefs He bore, *our* sorrows He **carried**, yet as we saw Him on the cross, we thought He was being punished **by God** for *His own* sins. But no! It was for **our** transgressions, for *our* iniquities, and in order that *we* might have **peace**, in order that we might be **healed**. The truth is that *we* were the ones who went **astray** and who walked in self-will, and Jehovah placed our **iniquity on Him**, the sinless Substitute."

Until that time when the remnant acknowledges Him, we who are Christians can confess:

> He was wounded for our transgressions,
> He bore our sins in His body on the tree;
> For our guilt He gave us peace,
> From our bondage gave release,
> And with His stripes, and with His stripes,
> And with His stripes our souls are healed.
>
> He was numbered among transgressors,
> We did esteem Him forsaken by His God;
> As our sacrifice He died,
> That the law be satisfied,
> And all our sin, and all our sin,
> And all our sin was laid on Him.
>
> We had wandered, we all had wandered,
> Far from the fold of "the Shepherd of the sheep";
> But He sought us where we were,
> On the mountains bleak and bare,
> And brought us home, and brought us home,
> And brought us safely home to God.
>
> —*Thomas O. Chisholm*

Our Lord Jesus suffered all five kinds of wounds known to medical science: *contusions*—blows by a rod; *lacerations*—scourging; *penetrating wounds*—crown of thorns; *perforating wounds*—nails; *incised wounds*—the spear.

53:7, 8 Like **a sheep**, that is, **silent** and uncomplaining **before its shearers**, He endured the cross. He was hurried away **from prison** and a fair trial (or "by oppression and judgment He was taken away"). It seemed impossible that He would have any posterity since **He was cut off** in His prime, slain for the sins of the people.

53:9 **Wicked** men plotted to bury Him with the criminals, but God overruled, and He was **with the rich at His death**—in the new tomb of Joseph of Arimathea. Men plotted a shameful burial for Him although **He had done no** wrong, spoken no lie.

53:10, 11a Yet **the LORD** saw fit **to bruise Him**, to **put Him to grief**. When **His soul** has been made **an offering for sin, He will see His** posterity, that is, all those who believe on Him, **He shall prolong His days**, living in the power of an endless life. All God's purposes shall be realized through Him. Seeing the multitudes of those who have been redeemed by His blood He will **be** amply **satisfied**.

53:11b "By His knowledge My righteous Servant shall justify many." This may mean that **His knowledge** of the Father's will led Him to the cross, and it is by His death and resurrection that He can reckon believers to be righteous. Or it may mean "by the **knowledge** of Him," that is, it is by coming to know Him that men are justified (John 17:3). In either case, it is through His bearing their **iniquities** that justification is possible for the **"many."**

The last stanza of Thomas Chisholm's hymn, quoted above, reads triumphantly:

> Who can number His generation?
> Who shall declare all the triumphs of
> His Cross?
> Millions, dead, now live again,
> Myriads follow in His train!
> Victorious Lord, victorious Lord,
> Victorious Lord and coming King!

53:12 Another result of His finished work is that Jehovah will **divide** Him **a portion with the great**, that is, with the saints, whose only greatness lies in their connection with Him. **And He shall divide the spoil with the strong**; here again **the strong** are those believers who are weak in themselves but strong in the Lord.

Four reasons for His glorious triumph are given. (1) **He poured out His soul unto death**; (2) **He was numbered with the transgressors**, that is, the two thieves; (3) **He bore the sin of many**; (4) He **made intercession for the transgressors**. David Baron comments:

> The verb . . . *yaph'gia'* ("made intercession") is an instance of the imperfect or indefinite future, and expresses a work begun, but not yet ended. Its most striking fulfilment, as Delitzsch observes, was the prayer of the crucified Saviour, "Father, forgive them, for they know not what they do." But this work of intercession which He began on the cross He still continues at the right hand of God, where He is now seated, a Prince and a Saviour, to give repentance unto Israel and the forgiveness of sins.[63]

On the paradoxes of this great passage as a whole, Moody comments:

> Despised, yet accepted and adored. Poor, yet rich. To die, yet to live. The Rabbis said there must be a double Messiah to fulfil this chapter.[64]

5. *The Messiah as Redeemer and Restorer (Chap. 54)*

54:1–3 It is not a coincidence that chapter 54 should begin with the word **"Sing!"** Coming immediately after the 53rd chapter with its presentation of Christ's death, burial, resurrection, and exaltation, no word could be more appropriate.

The first verse contrasts Israel in captivity, **barren** and **desolate**, with the restored and redeemed nation, prolific and rejoicing. Paul applied the verse in Galatians 4:21–31 to the heavenly Jerusalem versus the earthly city. The borders of the land will be considerably enlarged to accommodate the population explosion, Israel will be the leader of the **nations**, and God's people will inhabit **cities** that had been abandoned.

54:4–8 All the shame connected with enslavement in Egypt (**youth**) and captivity in Babylon (**widowhood**) shall be forgotten because Jehovah will bring the nation back into fellowship with Himself. The captivity expressed God's momentary **wrath**; the restoration will demonstrate His great compassion and **everlasting kindness**.

54:9, 10 Just as God made a covenant with **Noah**, so He now promises that when Israel enters the Millennium, she will never experience His rebuke or wrath again.

54:11, 12 Though Jerusalem has been **afflicted** and **tossed** with **tempest**, yet God will restore and beautify her. Her **stones** will be set **with colorful gems**, and her **foundations** will be laid **with sapphires**. Her **pinnacles**, **gates**, and **walls** will be **precious stones**—figurative language expressive of extreme beauty. Dean Alford expressed Jerusalem's future in English verse:

Far o'er yon horizon
  Rise the city towers,
Where our God abideth;
  That fair home is ours!
Flash the streets with jasper,
  Shine the gates with gold,
Flows the gladdening river,
  Shedding joys untold.

54:13–15 Divine education will be given to all, and prosperity will abound. **Righteousness** will prevail. No longer will there be **fear** of invasion, exile, or **oppression**. Anyone who causes trouble with Israel will be tried and punished.

54:16, 17 The God who created the munitions-maker (**blacksmith**) and the conqueror (**spoiler**) is well able to control His creatures. Jehovah has decreed that **no weapon formed against** Israel **shall** succeed, and that Israel herself **shall condemn . . . every** accuser. This freedom from condemnation and certain victory are **the heritage of the servants of the Lord**. This is how God will vindicate them in the golden era of peace and prosperity.

6. *The Messiah as World Evangelist (55:1—56:8)*

55:1 The Spirit of God sends out the evangelistic invitation to Israel to return, and at the same time invites **everyone** everywhere to the gospel feast. All that is necessary is a consciousness of need (thirst). The blessings are the **waters** of the Holy Spirit, the **wine** of joy, and the **milk** of the good Word of God. They are the free gift of grace, **without money and price**.

55:2–5 In its alienation from God, Israel has been wasting its energy and resources. True satisfaction and lasting pleasure are found only in the Lord. If Israel returns to the Lord, they will receive all the **sure mercies**

promised to **David** in the **everlasting covenant** (see Psalm 89:3, 4, 28, 29). These blessings are fulfilled in the Lord Jesus and in His glorious reign. The Gentile **nations**, too, will share in the benefits of the kingdom, and there will be amicable relations between Israel and the nations.

55:6,7 The pathway of blessing lies in seeking **the LORD** and in forsaking sin. Those who thus **return to the Lord** will find Him full of **mercy** and **pardon**.

55:8,9 Men shouldn't judge Jehovah by their own **thoughts** and **ways**. He thinks and acts in **ways** that transcend anything man could ever imagine. This is never more true than in the gospel plan of salvation, which is all of God's grace and allows no glory in self-effort. William Cowper expressed it with his usual elegant English in his poem "Truth":

> O how unlike the complex works of man,
> Heav'n's easy, artless, unencumber'd plan!
> No meretricious graces to beguile,
> No clustering ornaments to clog the pile;
> From ostentation, as from weakness, free,
> It stands like the cerulian arch we see,
> Majestic in its own simplicity.
> Inscribed above the portal, from afar
> Conspicuous as the brightness of a star,
> Legible only by the light they give,
> Stand the soul-quickening words—
> BELIEVE, AND LIVE.

55:10, 11 God's **word** is just as irresistible and effective as **the rain** and **snow**. All the armies in the world cannot stop them, and they **accomplish** their intended purpose. God's Word *never fails* to achieve its aims:

> **So shall My word be that goes forth from My mouth; it shall not return to Me void, but it shall accomplish what I please, and it shall prosper in the thing for which I sent it.**

55:12, 13 Those who seek the Lord will leave the land of captivity **with joy**, and travel home **with peace**. All nature will rejoice in their liberation. The land will enjoy freedom from the curse, with resulting fruitfulness. **Instead of the thorn** and **the brier**, the **cypress**, and **the myrtletree** will **come up**. All the foregoing millennial blessings will bring **the LORD** renown and will **be . . . for an everlasting sign**, that is, an eternal memorial of His grace and goodness.

56:1–8 In anticipation of God's deliverance, the exiles are urged to practice **justice** and **righteousness** and keep **the Sabbath**. Neither **the foreigner** nor **the eunuch** should fear that they will be barred from any of the benefits of Christ's kingdom. In fact, those who obey the Word of the Lord will have preferred positions. The temple will then be **a house of prayer for all nations**, not just Israel. God will gather Gentiles to His fold in addition to the house of Israel.

7. *The Messiah as Judge of the Wicked (56:9—57:21)*

56:9–12 Verse 9 reverts to Israel in her days of rebellion. The nations (**beasts**) are summoned to chastise a people whose watchmen don't see the danger. They are like **dumb dogs** that don't **bark** and warn the people. They are **slumber**-loving dreamers. They are mercenary, self-seeking, **greedy shepherds**. They invite their friends to **drink** and carouse, saying, "Tomorrow shall be as today was, and braver, braver yet" (Ronald Knox).

57:1, 2 The first two verses of chapter 57 are linked with verses 9–12 of the preceding chapter. In the midst of all the sin and oppression, **the righteous** are swept away by persecution. From the human standpoint **no one** cares. But God cares—He delivers the godly **from evil** and ushers them into **peace** and **rest**.

57:3–6 Even in exile, some of the people are continuing with their idolatrous practices. In this sense they are **offspring of** their unfaithful parents, **the adulterer and the harlot**. Mocking the Lord, they are **children of transgression** and **falsehood**. They burn with lust in the worship of trees, they sacrifice **children** to Baal or Molech **in the valleys**.

57:7–10 It is all an adulterous relationship with idols at the **mountain** shrines. Instead of writing the law of God on the **posts . . . of the doors** (Deut, 6:9; 11:20), they hang idolatrous symbols **behind the doors**, and engage in sex orgies. They bring gifts and offerings **to the king** (Molech means king) and send **messengers to Sheol** in search of new abominations. Even when they become exhausted by their dissipation, they do not give up, but seem to get their second wind and press on to further wickedness.

57:11–13 Without fear of Jehovah, they lie and do not give Him a second thought. Because He holds His **peace**, they lose their respect for Him. But He will expose their self-**righteousness** and sin, and their **idols** will not help them. Their gods will utterly fail them, but those **who . . . trust in** the Lord will enter into blessing.

57:14–19 To the faithful ones in exile, God promises that a highway will be constructed for their return, and every obstruction will be removed. For the God who dwells **in the high and holy place** also dwells in the **humble** and **contrite** heart. He **will not contend forever** with **the souls** that He has **made**, otherwise they would perish under His anger. God did send forth His wrath against His covetous, **backsliding** people, but His anger has a limit. He will **restore** those who turn from their idolatry, causing them to bring Him **the fruit of** their **lips**.

57:20, 21 Isaiah's marvelous comparison of **the wicked** to **the troubled sea** is rendered nicely into English verse as follows:

> 20: But as to the wicked—they are as the sea,
> Storm-tossed, nor able to rest,
> But its waters are ever upheaving,
> Upheaving the mire and the dirt![65]

It will be peace to the righteous but **no peace . . . for the wicked**.

C. Israel's Sin, Judgment, Repentance, and Restoration (Chaps. 58—66)

The last nine chapters of the book of Isaiah depict the final outcome of both the faithful and the apostate. Alfred Martin summarizes:

> The closing section of the book describes the glorious consummation which God has in store for Israel, the people of the Servant, and God's channel of blessing to the world. There is a strong contrast throughout the section between the rebellious and the faithful, a contrast which is never entirely absent from any extended portion of the Word of God.[66]

1. *The Delights of True Spirituality (Chap. 58)*

58:1–5 The prophet must loudly proclaim the **transgression** of Judah.

The people seem to take real pleasure in going through the prescribed **daily** rituals, acting as if they are a truly obedient **nation**. In fact they accuse **God** of being indifferent to their fasts and acts of contrition, but God accuses them of self-gratification, of taking advantage of their employees, and of **fist**-fighting in the midst of their fasting. Theirs is not the kind of fasting that counts with God. True fasting is not a matter of physical posture or of outward display of mourning.[67]

58:6–8 God wants **the fast** that is accompanied by the loosing of the shackles **of wickedness**, lifting the **yoke** of oppression, feeding **the hungry**, providing shelter for **the poor**, clothing **the naked**, and helping the needy neighbor. Those who thus practice social justice are assured of guidance, **healing**, and a protective escort. **"Your righteousness"** may mean the abovementioned acts of mercy or it may mean the righteousness of God which is imputed to those who believe. The paraphrase of verses 5–8 in the Scottish Psalter is worth quoting:

> Let such as feel oppression's load thy
> tender pity share:
> And let the helpless, homeless poor
> be thy peculiar care.
> Go, bid the hungry orphan be with
> thy abundance blest;
> Invite the wanderer to thy gate and
> spread the couch of rest.
> Let him who pines with piercing cold
> by thee be warmed and clad;
> Be thine the blissful task to make the
> downcast mourner glad.
> Then, bright as morning, shall come
> forth, in peace and joy, thy days;
> And glory from the Lord above shall
> shine on all thy ways.

58:9–12 The godly one is assured that whenever he calls, **the LORD will answer . . . "Here I am."** If he will eliminate oppression, stop **pointing . . . the finger** in accusation or in scoffing, and cease from mud-slinging and slander, if he will alleviate human need, both spiritual and physical, then God promises that his night will turn to day. He will enjoy guidance, abundant supply of good things, health and strength, beauty and fruitfulness, and national restoration. "Your sons will rebuild the long-deserted ruins of your cities, and you will be known as 'The People who Rebuild their Walls and Cities'" (v. 12, LB).

58:13, 14 If God's people respect **the Sabbath**[68] by abstaining from business or selfish **pleasure**, if they consider it a delight to honor God's **holy day**, **then** they will **delight . . . in the LORD** who gave the day, and He will give them a place of leadership in the earth and **the heritage** that God promised to **Jacob**. Nothing can hinder this because **the mouth of the LORD has spoken**.

2. *The Iniquities of Israel (Chap. 59)*

59:1–8 It is Israel's sin that holds God back from delivering them; the fault cannot be laid at Jehovah's door. Their **hands**, **fingers**, **lips**, and **tongue** are all active in murder and lying. There is widespread perversion of **justice** and dishonesty. People **conceive evil and bring forth** crime. Their activities are as dangerous as **vipers' eggs** and as useless as a **spider's web**. Sin controls every area of their lives—what they do, where they go, what they think. They care nothing for **peace** and **justice**, preferring what is **crooked**. What was true of Israel is also true of the entire human race (Rom. 3:15–17).

59:9–15a Speaking for the believing remnant, Isaiah now confesses their sin as his own. He acknowledges their injustice, unrighteousness, blindness, deadness. They **growl** with impatience and **moan** in despondency. There is no **justice** and no deliverance. Their **transgressions** had **multiplied** in God's sight and testified **against** them. They denied the Lord and wandered far from Him. They spoke in the language of **oppression**, rebellion, and **falsehood**. **Justice is** driven **back**, **righteousness stands afar off**, and **truth** falls a victim **in the street**. Uprightness is refused admission, **truth** is nowhere to be found, and the godly man is assaulted.

59:15b–21 When **the Lord** looks down, He is grieved **that there is no justice**. He marvels that there is **no man** (**intercessor** or mediator) capable of handling the situation, so He steps in and does it Himself. **His own arm** (strength) brings **Him** victory and **His own righteousness** upholds **Him**. He dons the armor and moves out against His foes in **righteousness**, **salvation**, **vengeance**, **zeal**, and **fury**. He gives the Gentiles exactly what they deserve, so that, at last, all the people from east to west are forced to acknowledge that He is Lord, for He (the Messiah) **comes in like a flood**, driven by the breath of Jehovah. He will come as **Redeemer** to the godly remnant in **Zion**. Then God will make a new **covenant with** the house of Israel, as we also read in Jeremiah 31:31–34; Hebrews 8:10–12; 10:16, 17.

3. *The Future Glory of Zion (Chap. 60)*

60:1–3 Zion's time to **arise** and **shine has come**, for **the glory of the Lord**, that is, the Messiah Himself, has appeared. It is the time of His Second Advent. The world is still in spiritual **darkness** and the darkness of the Tribulation, but the Lord shines on Israel and through Israel to the rest of the world. Representatives of **the Gentiles**—including kings—flock to Jerusalem to pay their respect to the reborn nation.

60:4–7 As Jerusalem raises her **eyes**, she sees her **sons** and **daughters** returning to the land. Super-abounding **joy** fills her **heart** as she watches **the Gentiles** bringing their gifts and tribute. Camel caravans from far and near come with **gold and incense**, praising Jehovah's name. Great **flocks** arrive in Jerusalem to be used for the sacrifices at the temple, commemorating the Messiah's finished work on Calvary. Note that myrrh is missing in verse 6. Myrrh speaks of suffering. Christ's atoning sufferings are finished forever! At His Second Advent there will only be **gold** (glory) **and incense** (fragrance).

60:8, 9 Plane-loads of Israel's **sons** and exiles return to Israel like flocks of birds, along with large **ships** bringing their accumulated wealth with them.

60:10 Foreigners serve as construction crews, and **kings** as servants of God's people. The tables are turned. God is now showing **mercy** to the nation that He has punished.

60:11–14 No need to lock the city **gates** because there is no danger. On the contrary, it is important to keep them **open** because **kings** and caravans of **wealth** are arriving **day** and **night**! Destruction awaits any **nation** that does **not serve** Israel in that day. **Lebanon** sends its finest trees **to beautify** the temple area. The descendants **of those** Gentiles who formerly persecuted Israel now acknowledge Jerusalem as **The City of the Lord, Zion of the Holy One of Israel**.

60:15, 16 Formerly **hated** and **for-**

saken, Zion becomes a city of **excellence**, nourished and supported by the rest of the world. Jehovah's ancient people will know then that He is their **Savior and** their **Redeemer, the Mighty One of Jacob**.

60:17–22 The costliest materials—**gold** and **silver** and **bronze** and **iron**—will be used in building the city, with **peace** serving as superintendents and **righteousness** as the police force. In place of **violence** and **destruction** will be **Salvation** and **Praise**. The light of **the sun** and **moon** will no longer be necessary in Jerusalem, since the glory of **the LORD will** provide all necessary **light**. Darkness will vanish and Israel's **mourning shall be ended**. A **righteous . . . people inherit the land**, planted by God for His glory. The humblest of the people will be blessed with numerous posterity, because **the LORD** has decreed it and **will hasten** to do it.

4. The Messiah's Ministries (Chap. 61)

61:1–4 We know that the Lord Jesus is the speaker here because He quoted verses 1–2a in the synagogue at Nazareth (Luke 4:16–21) and added, "Today this Scripture is fulfilled in your hearing" (v. 21). He was **anointed** with the Holy Spirit at His baptism and His earthly ministry was concerned with bringing the **good tidings** of salvation **to the poor**, binding up **the brokenhearted**, proclaiming **liberty** to sin's **captives**, and **opening . . . the prison** (or eyes, RSV marg.) of **those who** were **bound**. He ended the quotation with the words **"to proclaim the acceptable year of the LORD"** because what follows, **"the day of vengeance of our God,"** will not be fulfilled until His Second Advent. At His glorious appearing He will proclaim **the day of** God's judgment. Then He will **comfort** those **who mourn** in Zion, granting to them a garland in place of **ashes** on their heads, **the oil of joy** instead of **mourning**, **praise** instead of a **spirit of heaviness**. His chosen people will then **be called trees of righteousness**, planted by the Lord, and bringing glory to Him. **They** will **rebuild the** cities of the promised land that have lain in **ruins**.

61:5–9 Foreigners will serve the Israelites as farm hands, honoring them as **priests** and **servants of our God**. Gentile **riches** will come to the Jews, and the reproach of the centuries will be ended as the Lord's people enjoy a **double** portion of **honor**. (The **"you"** and **"they"** in verse 7 refer to the same people, that is, the Jews.) Remembering the injustice, **robbery**, and wrong that His chosen ones have suffered, Jehovah will reward them and make **an everlasting covenant . . . with them**, so that the nations will **acknowledge them** as the **blessed** of **the LORD**. This is generally understood to be the new covenant (Jer. 31:31–34; Heb. 8:8–12).

61:10, 11 The Messiah leads the praises of His redeemed remnant. He celebrates the glorious **garments of salvation** and **righteousness** with which God has decked them, and the sprouting forth of practical **righteousness and praise** in Israel before the nations during the Millennium. (The speaker in vv. 10, 11 is variously identified as Isaiah, Zion, or the Messiah Himself. We prefer the last, the same speaker as in vv. 1–3.)

5. The Future Delights of Jerusalem (Chap. 62)

62:1–5 The Lord **will not** keep silent or **rest** satisfied until the blessings promised to Jerusalem are realized. Then **the Gentiles** will **see** Zion vindicated, and Jehovah will give **a new name** to the city. He will handle

Zion admiringly as a king handles his **crown**. The city called **"Forsaken"** will henceforth be called "My delight is in her" (**Hephzibah**) and the land named **"Desolate"** will be renamed **"married"** (**Beulah**). These names tell of God's tender affection and marital delight in His city and land. Jerusalem's citizens will be wedded to her, and the Lord will **rejoice over** Zion like a **bridegroom**.

62:6–9 In the meantime, Jehovah has **set watchmen on** the **walls** of **Jerusalem** and has instructed them not to rest in their intercession or to **give Him . . . rest till Jerusalem** becomes the queen city of the world. Never again will Israel's produce be carried off by **enemies**. Rather it will be enjoyed by those who **labored** for it.

62:10–12 Now the exiles are told to **go through the gates** of Babylon and return to Israel over well-paved highways with ensign waving proudly. The announcement has gone out worldwide that Israel's **salvation** has come in the Person of the Messiah, and He will **reward** His people. They will carry the dignified name **"The** Holy People" and Jerusalem will be called **"Sought Out, A City Not Forsaken."** This paragraph looks beyond the return from Babylon to the final restoration of Israel at the Second Coming of Christ.

6. The Day of Vengeance (63:1–6)

When the Lord returns to set up His kingdom, He must first destroy His enemies. That destruction takes place at different times and in different places. One stage occurs in the Valley of Armageddon (Rev. 16:16), another in the Valley of Jehoshaphat (Joel 3:12), and still another in **Edom**. The latter is what we have here in chapter 63. The Messiah is marching up **from Bozrah**, a metropolis of **Edom**, in glorious **garments** that are **red** with the **blood** of Israel's foes. When asked why His **apparel** is **red**, He uses the figure of a **winepress** to describe His trampling of His enemies. The time had come for Him to wreak **vengeance** on them and to redeem His people. In the absence of any merely human deliverer, He stepped in and won the victory.

7. The Prayer of the Remnant (63:7—64:12)

63:7–10 Next the prophet, speaking for the remnant in captivity, seeks deliverance from their pitiable condition. First he rehearses God's past dealings with the nation. Jehovah has displayed nothing but **loving-kindnesses**, **great goodness**, and **mercies**. God had called them as His **people**. Though He knew in advance exactly what they would do, He is here represented as considering it unthinkable that they would ever forsake Him for other gods. **So He became their Savior.** He also became their partner in all their trials, and particularly **in all their affliction** in Egypt. **The Angel** (same word as *Messenger*) **of His Presence**, that is, the Messiah, **saved them**. **In His love and in His pity He redeemed them** out of Egypt, and cared for them throughout their wilderness journeys. They repaid His love with rebellion, and so He became their Adversary.

63:11–13 But even remembering the **days of old**, of **Moses and his** generation, would raise the questions: "**Where is He who brought** Israel through **the** Red **Sea with** Moses and Aaron and their other shepherds? **Where is He who put His Holy Spirit** in Moses, then divided the sea so that **Moses** could lead them through, thus bringing **everlasting** honor to

His **name**? Where is Jehovah who brought them through the sea, making the way as smooth as a flat desert where **a horse** never needs to **stumble**?"

63:14 As a beast goes down into the valley to find rest and refreshment, **so** God led His **people** into the land of rest, and in so doing, He earned **a glorious name** for Himself. Note the Trinity: the Lord Jehovah (v. 7); the Angel of Jehovah (v. 9); **the Spirit of the Lord** (vv. 10, 11, 14).

63:15, 16 The recital of past mercies leads the prophet to look ahead to the Babylonian captivity and to intercede for the exiles. It seems that God's **zeal**, **strength**, and **mercies** are being withheld from the remnant. Isaiah pleads that God is still their **Father**, even **though Abraham** and **Israel** were to disown them.

63:17–19 In verse 17, the remnant seems to blame **the Lord** for their backsliding, but the truth is that God only hardens men's hearts after they have first **hardened** their own **heart**. Probably the remnant means to say, "Why did you permit us to err from Your ways?" God is often said to do what He permits. In any case, the exiles cry to Jehovah to **return** to them in grace. Israel had **possessed** the land in peace for only a comparatively short time, and now the **sanctuary** lies in ruins, and the Israelites, God's people, are no better off than the other nations who never had a covenant relationship with the Lord.

64:1–5 The prayer which began in 63:15 now continues and turns to confession. The remnant implores God to **rend the heavens** and **come down** in fury on His **adversaries**. They recall previous interventions of God, unique manifestations of the only true God who **acts for the one who waits for Him**. They remember that God shows favor to those who delight in practical **righteousness**, but they have incurred His anger by their long-continued sins, and wonder if there is any hope for people like them **to be saved**.

64:6, 7 They confess to personal uncleanness, and admit that their best deeds (**righteousnesses**) **are like filthy rags**.[69] No wonder that they are fading leaves, driven away by **the wind** of their own **iniquities**. There is spiritual deadness in Israel. Intercessors are nowhere to be found, because Jehovah has abandoned them to the consequences of their sins.

64:8, 9 Yet the **Lord** is still their **Father**, and there is still hope that the **potter** can do something with **the clay**. And so they plead with Him to relax His anger, to forgive and forget their sins, and to acknowledge them as His **people** still.

64:10–12 The devastated condition of the country, and particularly of **Jerusalem** and the **temple**, are strong reasons why God should release His anger and act decisively in behalf of His afflicted people.

8. The Lord's Answer to the Prayer of the Remnant (Chap. 65)

65:1 Here begins Jehovah's answer to the preceding prayer (63:15—64:12).

In context the first verse refers to Israel's failure to **seek** God and her unwillingness to answer His call. But Paul applies it in Romans 10:20 to the call of the Gentiles: "I was found by those who did not seek Me; I was made manifest to those who did not ask for me."

65:2–7 These verses refer unmistakably to Israel. God pleads tirelessly with a **people** who give themselves over to the **abominable things** associated with idolatry and heathenism. Because they have been initiated into secret rites, they consider themselves **holier than** their fellows. Because they are a continual irritation to the Most High, He will **repay** them for all their idolatry and sin.

65:8–12 Jehovah promises to spare a good **cluster** of grapes (the faithful remnant) in an otherwise bad vineyard (the rest of the nation). This preserved remnant will **dwell** in the land. **Flocks** will graze on the Plain of **Sharon** in the west and in **the Valley of Achor** to the east, all for the benefit of the saints. As for the apostate mass, it is a different story. They have forsaken the temple and worship **Gad** (meaning Troop, Fortune) and **Meni** (meaning **number**, Destiny). Therefore God will destine them **for the sword**. Instead of responding to the Lord's entreaties, they **chose** the things that were **evil** and distasteful to the Lord.

65:13–16 The contrast between the lot of the true believers and that of the unbelievers is brought out here. It is the difference between abundant food and hunger, between plentiful drink and thirst, between rejoicing and shame, between singing and wailing, between the curse of an adulteress (Num. 5:21–24) and a blessing. In that day, when the wrongs of earth are righted, people will use the name **"the God of truth"** when they **bless** themselves or when they take an oath. In other words, God will be acknowledged as the One who brings His plans to pass, who does as He says He will do.

65:17 The closing verses of chapter 65 describe millennial conditions. The **new heavens and** the **new earth** here refer to Christ's kingdom on earth; in Revelation 21 they refer to the eternal state. In Isaiah's **new heavens** and **new earth** there is still sin and death; in Revelation 21, these have passed away.

65:18–23 When the kingdom comes, the Lord **will rejoice in Jerusalem** and in the **people** of Israel. The sounds of sorrow and anguish will **no longer be heard**. Infant mortality and premature death will be eradicated. A person who dies at the age of **one hundred years** will be reckoned **a child**. A centenarian who sins outwardly will be cut off. Men will live to enjoy the **fruit** of their labors because the lifespan will extend throughout the Millennium for the faithful. There will be no unproductive **labor**, and young people will not be cut off by war or calamity. Parents and children will enjoy the blessing of **the Lord**.

65:24, 25 There will be no more hindrances to prayer. Wild animals will be domesticated, and poisonous snakes will feed on the **dust** of defeat and humiliation. There will be no more danger in God's **holy mountain** of Zion.

9. The Consummation: Peace Like a River (Chap. 66)

66:1, 2 The opening words of the last chapter of Isaiah were written to the unrepentant people of Israel. They need not think that, in that condition, they can please God by building a temple for Him. After all, He is the universal Creator and Owner, enthroned in **heaven**, with the **earth** as His **footstool**. The dwelling place He desires is the heart of a person who is humble and **contrite**, and **who trembles at** His **word**.

66:3, 4 Those who are impenitent offend God by their religious observances. When divorced from practical holiness, their **sacrifices** and offerings are crimes and **abominations**. They can choose their hypocritical **ways**, but they cannot **choose** the consequences. God will do that.

Those who refuse His call to repentance and who go on in ways that He hates will taste His wrath.

66:5, 6 Those faithful, God-fearing Jews **who tremble at His word** will be persecuted by their own **brethren**. The wicked persecutors will think that they are doing God service, as is evidenced by their pseudo-pious taunt, **"Let the Lord be glorified, that we may see your joy,"** that is, **your joy** at being miraculously delivered. But the Lord will intervene to shame their foes. The work of judgment will begin at **the temple**; there **the voice** of Jehovah will reveal that the time of recompense has come.

66:7–9 In verse 7 Israel brings forth **a male child** (the Messiah) *before* the time of her birth-pangs (the Great Tribulation). In verse 8 she brings forth sons *after* her time of travail. The first birth took place nearly two thousand years ago at Bethlehem. The second is the spiritual rebirth of Israel, which will occur after the Tribulation. Nothing will hinder God from accomplishing this purpose.

66:10–17 The day of Israel's restoration will be a time of great rejoicing in **Jerusalem**. **All . . . who love her** and who have wept with her will share in the ecstasy and jubilation of that moment. Enriched by **the glory of the Gentiles**, she in turn will give prosperity, nourishment, **comfort**, and rejuvenation to all who come to her. Then it will be obvious to all that Jehovah is committed to the welfare of His own and to the punishment of **His enemies**. The Lord's Second Coming will mean the unleashing of His fiery **indignation** against all idolaters and rebels. He sees them going through ceremonies to make themselves ritually clean, only to engage in the most abominable idolatrous practices.

66:18–21 He knows **their works and their thoughts** and when He rains down judgment on them, **they** will **see** His **glory**. He will give them some supernatural **sign**, which we cannot identify at present. Those **who escape** will go to the ends of the earth with the news of the Lord's power and **fame**. Then the Gentiles will mobilize their transportation facilities to carry dispersed Israelites back to the land, as if they were bringing **an offering** to Jehovah. God will reinstitute the priesthood and the Levitical order for service in the millennial temple.

66:22, 23 Israel's status with God will be as permanent and secure as **the new heavens and the new earth**. Pilgrims **from** all nations will come to Jerusalem at the appointed times **to worship**.

66:24 While there they will walk out to the Valley of Hinnom and see **the corpses** of rebels being cremated in the perpetual **fire** of the city dump.

It is worth noting that our Lord quotes from the last verse in Isaiah as a warning to those who would live in sin and offend Christ's little ones. Three times[70] in Mark 9 Jesus uses Isaiah's solemn words: **"Their worm does not die and their fire is not quenched"** (vv. 44, 46, 48).

The good news is that a person can escape these eternal fires of hell by putting his or her faith in the Savior, the Servant of the Lord that Isaiah has described so winsomely in so many of his prophecies.

For most of our readers, who have already received Christ as their Savior, the book of Isaiah is great prophecy and great poetry—certainly among the finest in the OT. But it would be a shame if that were all. We are meant to *apply* this book to our daily lives and practice God's good pleasure.

We close with a practical exhortation from the devout English Bible scholar, W. E. Vine:

> All this brings home the folly, futility and sinfulness of pursuing our own way, carrying out our own designs and turning after that in which God cannot take pleasure, instead of waiting upon Him, listening to His voice and delighting in the fulfilment of His will. Through our walking with God He fulfils, and will fulfil, all the promises of His Word. He responds to delighted confidence in Him, by adding an Amen to His assurance. The peace of an obedient heart and a trusting spirit is that which enjoys the sunshine of His countenance and the calmness of holy communion with Him.[71]

ENDNOTES

[1](Intro) It was a benefit performance "for the relief of Prisoners in the several Gaol's, and for the support of Mercer's Hospital in Stephen Street, and of the Charitable Infirmary on the Inn's Quay." In light of Isaiah's stress of freeing the prisoners, and binding up the wounds of the sick, he no doubt would have been pleased with these charities, which were often associated with early performances of *Messiah*.

[2](Intro) After the Overture, the very beginning of the second part of Isaiah is sung in a tenor solo: "Comfort ye My people" (40:1). Who can read Isaiah 7:14 without hearing the contralto solo of "Behold, a virgin shall conceive," or Isaiah 9:6 without hearing the chorus sing "Unto us a Child a born, unto us a Son is given"? "Surely He hath borne our griefs, and carried our sorrows" is another lesser-known setting with words by Isaiah (53:4). Also with words by Isaiah are: "O thou that tellest good tidings to Zion" (40:9); "Then shall the eyes of the blind be open'd and the ears of the deaf unstopped" (35:5); "He shall feed His flock like a shepherd" (40:11); and the moving "He was despised and rejected of men" (53:3).

Comparatively little of the text of the oratorio is from the NT, which is unusual, especially when we consider that the subject matter is all about the Messiah.

[3](Intro) See the *Believers Bible Commentary* in the Introductions to the books mentioned for a defense of the traditional and orthodox positions on the authorship.

[4](Intro) Josephus, *Antiquities* XI:1:f.

[5](1:7–9) So sure are the prophecies that they are often expressed in the Hebrew perfect tense, suggesting a completed action.

[6](1:10–15) W. E. Vine, *Isaiah: Prophecies, Promises, Warnings*, p. 14.

[7](2:4) This verse—minus the opening words about God—is inscribed on the United Nations Building in New York City.

[8](2:12–18) A sloop is a kind of ship that generally has one mast.

[9](4:2–6) Matthew Henry, "Isaiah," *Matthew Henry's Commentary on the Whole Bible*, IV:27.

[10](6:1) This would be 740 B.C. Moody writes: "Uzziah's reign was a kind of Victorian era in Jewish history. It was when this passed away into shame and disgrace that Isaiah saw the Eternal King on his throne." *Notes from My Bible*, p. 85.

[11](6:1) F. C. Jennings, *Studies in Isaiah*, p. 61.

[12](6:2–5) The word *seraphim* is from the Hebrew verb *sāraph*, "burn," stressing the burning holiness of God, as in "Our God is a consuming fire" (Heb. 12:29, cf. Deut. 4:24).

[13](6:9, 10) Vine, *Isaiah*, p. 32.

[14](7:3) His son's name means *a remnant shall return*.

[15](7:10–13) Vine, *Isaiah*, p. 35.

[16](7:14) The Hebrew word translated *virgin* (*'ālmāh*) in verse 14 may also mean "young woman." The prophecy may have had an early, partial fulfillment when Isaiah's wife gave birth to Maher-Shalal-Hash-Baz (8:1–4). But the ultimate, complete fulfillment was in the birth of Christ. When Matthew quotes verse 7, he uses the Greek word *parthenos*, which can only mean *virgin* (Matt. 1:23).

[17](7:14) Vine, *Isaiah*, p. 35.

[18](7:18–22) Jennings, *Isaiah*, p. 90.

[19](8:19) Vine, *Isaiah*, p. 41.

[20](9:6) *Ibid.*, p. 43.

[21](11:1) The beautiful old German carol, "Lo, How a Rose E'er Blooming," captured Isaiah's thought here so well. Poetically the author chose a rose as the plant which will grow from Jesse's roots.

[22](11:2) Vine, *Isaiah*, p. 49.

[23](11:6–9a) The self-taught American Quaker artist Edward Hicks loved this passage so much that he painted several very literal canvases called "The Peaceable Kingdom." His charming style far outweighed his knowledge of animal anatomy.

[24](13:14–22) Ryrie writes, "The decline of Babylon occurred in stages. By 20 B.C. Strabo described it as 'a vast desolation.' Even the desert wanderer (*the Arabian*) shunned the site because it became an omen of ill fortune" (*Ryrie Study Bible, New King James Version*, p. 1053).

[25](14:12–17) "Lucifer" is the Latin form of "day-star," meaning "light-bearer."

[26](14:12–17) Ryrie, *Study Bible*, p. 1054.

[27](14:24–27) Ryrie writes that "the fulfillment of this prediction of the destruction of Assyria is recorded in 37:21–38," *ibid.*, p. 1055.

[28](18:1–7) The word is the usual one for *woe*, but here "it differs from ch. xvii. 12 and is an expression of compassion (cf. Isa. 1v.1, Zech. ii.10) rather than of anger," Franz Delitzsch, "Isaiah," in *Biblical Commentary on the Old Testament*, XVII:348.

[29](20:1–6) The name "Palestine" is derived from the word Philistine.

[30](21:6–10) Vine, *Isaiah*, p. 62.

[31](21:11, 12) Victor Buksbazen, *The Prophet Isaiah*, p. 224.

[32](22:20–24) D. L. Moody writes, "The Spanish Jews have a silver key of David, bearing the inscription 'God shall open, the King shall enter'" (*Notes*, p. 85).

[33](24:4–13) John A. Martin, "Isaiah," *The Bible Knowledge Commentary, Old Testament*, p. 1072.

[34](26:1–4) Quoted by Moody in *Notes from My Bible*, p. 86.

[35](26:1–4) *Ibid.*

[36](28:9, 10) These verses are often quoted out of context as the proper way to teach (going from the known to the unknown, a little at a time, for example). While this is no doubt good advice, it is certainly not the meaning of the text within the context.

[37](28:11–13) Jennings, *Isaiah*, p. 333.

[38](28:23–29) H. Vander Lugt, *Our Daily Bread*, Radio Bible Class, further documentation unavailable.

[39](29:12–14) Vine, *First Corinthians*, p. 23.

[40](33:23, 24) Vine, *Isaiah*, p. 83.

[41](34:9–17) The Hebrew for "confusion and emptiness" in v. 11 is the same as those words translated "without form and void" in Gen. 1:2.

[42](35:8–10) Jennings, *Isaiah*, p. 417.

[43](37:1–4) J. A. Alexander, *The Prophecies of Isaiah*, p. 289.

[44](37:36) See *The Literature of England, An Anthology and a History*, p. 726.

[45](38:21, 22) Kelly, *Isaiah*, p. 289.

[46]38:21, 22) Henry, "Isaiah," VI:209.

[47](40:3–5) G. Campbell Morgan, *Searchlights from the Word*, p. 229.

[48](40:6–8) Quoted by Jennings, *Isaiah*, p. 467.

[49](41:21–24) Jennings, *Isaiah*, p. 486, f.n.

[50](41:25–29) Vine, *Isaiah*, p. 105.

[51](43:1–7) *Ibid.*, p. 115.

[52](43:8–13) One of the anti-Trinitarian cults uses this passage "You are My witnesses, says Jehovah," as the origin of their name. Since they witness against so much of the Lord's truth, one fears that they must be called *false* witnesses. The context is far removed from their use of the passage.

[53](44:28) Flavius Josephus, *Antiquities*, xi.2.

[54](45:7) English has a much larger vocabulary than Hebrew. The Hebrew word here translated "evil" in the KJV and "calamity" in the NKJV can mean either of those two things—and several more ("disaster," "badness," etc.). It is unfortunate that the English word that suggests *moral* wrong (*evil*) should have been chosen here in 1611. The rendering *calamity* is much better in context.

[55](45:7) Delitzsch, "Isaiah," in *Biblical Commentary on the Old Testament*, XVIII:220, 21.

[56](45:7) *Ibid.*, p. 221.

[57](46:3, 4) James S. Stewart, further documentation unavailable.

[58](47:5–15) Jennings, *Isaiah*, p. 556.

[59](51:9–11) *Ibid.*, p. 593.

[60](52:11, 12) Quoted by David Baron in *The Servant of Jehovah*, pp. 46, 47.

[61](52:15) The parallel expression "shut their mouths" favors the reading "startle." However, the traditional reading "sprinkle" recalls the sprinkling of sacrificial blood of Leviticus and the global outreach of the message of redemption. Noting the similarity between "astonish" and "startle," Vine writes: "In the degradation and disfigurement which man inflicted on Him many were astonished; in the coming manifestation of His glory He will astonish (cause to leap and tremble in astonishment) many nations; 'startle' is the meaning here, not 'sprinkle' (as the grammatical phraseology makes clear)." *Isaiah*, p. 166.

[62](53:2) F. B. Meyer, *Christ in Isaiah*, p. 126.

[63](53:12) David Baron, *The Servant of Jehovah*, p. 140.

[64](53:12) Moody, *Notes*, p. 87.

[65](57:20, 21) Jennings, *Isaiah*, p. 668.

[66](58:Intro) Alfred Martin, *Isaiah*, p. 107.

[67](58:1–5) Literal fasting can also be a good tool for spiritual discipline. While the NT does not *command* fasting, our Lord did say, "*When* you fast . . ." (not "*If* you fast").

[68](58:13, 14) For a discussion of the Sabbath and how it relates to the Christian, see the NT volume of *The Believers Bible Commentary*, p. 64.

[69](64:6, 7) Literally, menstrual cloths.

[70](66:24) Some Greek mss. lack two of these verses; see the NT volume of the *BBC* under Endnotes to Mark 9 for details.

[71](66:24) Vine, *Isaiah*, pp. 214, 215.

BIBLIOGRAPHY

Alexander, Joseph A. *The Prophecies of Isaiah*. Grand Rapids: Zondervan Publishing House, 1974.

Archer, Gleason L. "Isaiah." In *The Wycliffe Bible Commentary*, Chicago: Moody Press, 1962.

Baron, David. *The Servant of Jehovah: The Sufferings of the Messiah and the Glory that Should Follow*. Reprint. Minneapolis: James Family Publishing, 1978.

Buksbazen, Victor. *The Prophet Isaiah.* West Collingswood, N.J.: The Spearhead Press, 1971.

Delitzsch, Franz. "Isaiah." In *Biblical Commentary on the Old Testament.* Vols. 17, 18. Grand Rapids: Wm. B. Eerdmans Publishing Co., 1971.

Jennings, F. C. *Studies in Isaiah.* New York: Loizeaux Bros., 1935.

Henry, Matthew. "Isaiah." In *Matthew Henry's Commentary on the Whole Bible*, Vol. IV.

Kelly, William. *Exposition of Isaiah.* London: Robert L. Allen, 1916.

Martin, Alfred. *Isaiah: The Salvation of Jehovah.* Chicago: Moody Press, 1967.

Meyer, F. B. *Christ in Isaiah.* Grand Rapids: Zondervan Publishing House, 1952.

Vine, W. E. *Isaiah—Prophecies, Promises, Warnings.* London: Oliphants, Ltd., 1947.

Young, Edward. *Who Wrote Isaiah?* Grand Rapids: Wm. B. Eerdmans Publishing Co., 1958.

JEREMIAH

Introduction

"Most impressive of all . . . is the way in which Jesus Christ was associated in the popular mind with Jeremiah. When on one occasion Christ took a sampling of public opinion from His disciples (Matt. 16:13f.), some reports identified Him with the outstanding prophetic figure of the seventh century B.C. It is hardly surprising that some mistook the Man of sorrows for the prophet of the broken heart, for Jeremiah and Christ both lamented and wept over their contemporaries (cf. 9:1 and Luke 19:41)."

—R. K. Harrison

I. Unique Place in the Canon

Jeremiah is best known as "the weeping prophet." This is the key to his writings, for if we remember this and the reason for his weeping, we shall be able to understand his message.

This prophet is unique in that he reveals his heart and personality more than any other OT prophet.[1] By nature he was sensitive and retiring, yet he was divinely called to severely denounce the apostasy of his day. International tension between Babylon, Egypt, and Assyria for world supremacy, severe spiritual decline in Israel after Judah's last revival under Josiah, as well as people who had been raised on God's Word and true religion turning to pagan cults, all remind us of Western Christendom today.

II. Authorship

The prophecy was written by Jeremiah (Heb. *Yirmeyāhû* or *Yirmeyāh*). The name probably means *Jehovah hurls*, or *throws*, perhaps in the sense of laying down a foundation, hence *Jehovah establishes*. Another possible meaning is *exalted of Jehovah*. The prophet was the son of Hilkiah, a priest from Anathoth, a town less than three miles from Jerusalem, in the territory of Benjamin.

Like most preachers who are faithful to God and are willing to endanger their position and financial security by preaching a message that people do not wish to hear, Jeremiah was slandered and misrepresented by his enemies. There is no evidence that Jeremiah himself ever entered the priesthood.

III. Date

Jeremiah gives many chronological notes scattered throughout his book. He started his ministry about 627 B.C. (Josiah's thirteenth year, 1:2). Jeremiah's ministry was long, extending to the eleventh year of Zedekiah. He was prophesying during the last forty years of Judah, right up to the time when Jerusalem fell and the Jews were deported to Babylon (586

B.C.).[2] After Jerusalem's fall Jeremiah was under the protection of Gedaliah, the governor. When Gedaliah was assassinated by fanatics, the prophet went down to Egypt with some Jews. There he lived out the rest of his days. Apparently he was still ministering as late as 582 B.C. (chaps. 40—44).

In studying Jeremiah it is well to remember that the prophecies are not given in chronological order.

IV. Background and Theme

Jeremiah began his ministry to Judah after the Northern Kingdom of Israel had fallen to the Assyrians, and not many years before the end of the Kingdom of Judah. At the time of his prophecy, there was a three-sided power struggle by Assyria, Egypt, and Babylon. Warned by God that Judah would go into Babylonian captivity, Jeremiah spoke out against any alliance with Egypt, which nation would be a loser. Assyria had made Judah pay tribute, but within twenty years Nineveh, her capital, had fallen after a terrible siege. Necho of Egypt marched north through Palestine to Haran, killing King Josiah (609 B.C.). He and the Assyrian remnant met their match in Nebuchadnezzar, who routed his forces at the famous battle of Carchemish. Judah passed into the hands of Babylon automatically. Necho had previously deposed and replaced Josiah's successor, Jehoahaz, with Jehoiakim in hopes that he would be more favorable to Egypt. Nebuchadnezzar ignored Judah for a while, giving Jehoiakim a chance to try to get Egyptian help to bring about independence for Judah. In 598 B.C. Nebuchadnezzar attacked Jerusalem, captured Jehoiachin, the rebel's son and successor, and took some of the people captive. He put Zedekiah on the throne.

It was probably Psamtik II, Necho's successor, who sought to set up an alliance against Babylon. Jeremiah fought strongly against Judah's part in this (e.g., chap. 28). Jeremiah said those who proposed this were false prophets.

Through Egyptian plotting, Zedekiah broke faith with Babylon, bringing that ruler down to besiege Jerusalem. This was in 588, and Egypt lifted the siege with her armies. The siege was resumed soon, however, and Jeremiah was shown to be correct in his view of Egypt as "a broken reed" to lean on. Much to his personal sorrow, Jeremiah saw his prophecies of destruction and captivity fulfilled.

God revealed to the prophet that Judah's sins would result in that nation's being taken into captivity by the Babylonians and held in exile for seventy years. Jeremiah's unwelcome mission was to announce this fact to his fellow-countrymen and to advise them to submit to the Babylonian power. They accused him of being a traitor and made an attack on his life.

When Jerusalem finally fell to the foreign invaders, Jeremiah was one of those who was permitted to stay in the homeland, while the bulk of the nation was carried away. He now advised the remaining people not to flee to Egypt for help, but they disregarded his counsel and carried him off with them. There the prophet died.

In addition to predicting the Babylonian captivity, Jeremiah also foresaw the destruction of that empire at the end of seventy years and the return of the Jews to their land.

OUTLINE

I. INTRODUCTION: THE PROPHET JEREMIAH'S APPOINTMENT AND COMMISSION (Chap. 1)

II. JEREMIAH'S PUBLIC MINISTRY (Chaps. 2—10)

- A. Sermon against Judah's Willful Infidelity (2:1—3:5)
- B. Judah's Future Conditioned upon Repentance (3:6—6:30)
    1. Past Sin and Future Glory (3:6–18)
    2. The Need for Repentance (3:19—4:4)
    3. Woes of the Judgment from the North (4:5–31)
    4. Judah's Sins to Be Judged (Chap. 5)
    5. Jerusalem's Fall Predicted (Chap. 6)
- C. Jeremiah's Ministry at the Temple gate (Chaps. 7—10)
    1. Judah's Hypocritical Religion (Chap. 7)
    2. Judah's Insensitivity to Sin (Chap. 8)
    3. The Weeping Prophet's Lament (Chap. 9)
    4. A Satire on Idolatry (10:1–18)
    5. The Weeping Prophet's Prayer (10:19–25)

III. JEREMIAH'S PERSONAL EXPERIENCES (Chaps. 11—19)

- A. Jeremiah and the Men of Anathoth (Chaps. 11, 12)
- B. Jeremiah and the Ruined Sash (Chap. 13)
- C. Jeremiah's Intercession Concerning the Drought (Chaps. 14, 15)
- D. Jeremiah's Solitary Ministry (16:1–18)
- E. Jeremiah's Steadfast Heart (16:19—17:18)
- F. Jeremiah's Sabbath Sermon (17:19–27)
- G. Jeremiah at the Potter's House (Chap. 18)
- H. Jeremiah and the Earthen Flask (Chap. 19)

IV. PROPHECIES AGAINST THE CIVIL AND RELIGIOUS LEADERS OF JUDAH (Chaps. 20—23)

- A. Prophecy against Pashhur (20:1–6)
- B. Jeremiah's Complaint to God (20:7–18)
- C. Prophecy against King Zedekiah (21:1—22:9)
- D. Prophecy against King Shallum (22:10–12)
- E. Prophecy against King Jehoiakim (22:13–23)
- F. Prophecy against King Jehoiachin (22:24–30)
- G. Prophecy of the Righteous King (23:1–8)
- H. Prophecy against Judah's False Prophets (23:9–40)

V. PROPHECIES CONCERNING THE DESTRUCTION OF JERUSALEM AND THE BABYLONIAN CAPTIVITY (Chaps. 24—29)

A. The Sign of the Figs (Chap. 24)

B. The Seventy-year Captivity in Babylon Predicted (25:1–11)

C. The Babylonian Captors to Be Judged (25:12–38)

D. Jeremiah's Warning to the People (Chap. 26)

E. The Sign of the Yoke (Chap. 27)

F. Hananiah's False Prophecy and Death (Chap. 28)

G. Jeremiah's Message to the Jewish Captives of Babylon (Chap. 29)

VI. PROPHECIES CONCERNING THE RESTORATION (Chaps. 30—33)

A. The Captives to Be Regathered (Chap. 30)

B. The Country to Be Restored (31:1–30)

C. The Covenant Renovated (31:31–40)

D. The City to Be Rebuilt (Chap. 32)

E. The Covenant Recognized (Chap. 33)

VII. HISTORICAL SECTION (Chaps. 34—45)

A. The Downfall of Judah and Jerusalem (Chaps. 34—39)
   1. Zedekiah's Captivity Foretold (Chap. 34)
   2. The Rechabites' Obedience Rewarded (Chap. 35)
   3. King Jehoiakim Burns the Scroll of Jeremiah (Chap. 36)
   4. Jeremiah Imprisoned and Interviewed by Zedekiah (Chaps. 37, 38)
   5. The Fall of Jerusalem (Chap. 39)

B. Events in Judah after the Fall of Jerusalem (Chaps. 40—42)
   1. Jeremiah Dwelling with Governor Gedaliah (Chap. 40)
   2. Governor Gedaliah Assassinated (Chap. 41)
   3. God Forbids Fleeing to Egypt (Chap. 42)

C. Jeremiah and the Remnant in Egypt (Chaps. 43, 44)

D. The Lord's Message to Baruch (Chap. 45)

VIII. PROPHECIES AGAINST THE GENTILE NATIONS (Chaps. 46—51)

A. Prophecies against Egypt (Chap. 46)

B. Prophecies against Philistia (Chap. 47)

C. Prophecies against Moab (Chap. 48)

D. Prophecies against Ammon (49:1–6)

E. Prophecies against Edom (49:7–22)

F. Prophecies against Damascus (49:23–27)

G. Prophecies against Kedar and Hazor (49:28–33)

H. Prophecy against Elam (49:34–39)

I. Prophecies against Babylon (Chaps. 50, 51)

IX. CONCLUSION: THE FALL OF JERUSALEM (Chap. 52)

Commentary

I. INTRODUCTION: THE PROPHET JEREMIAH'S APPOINTMENT AND COMMISSION (Chap. 1)

1:1–10 In the first chapter of the prophecy, **Jeremiah the son of Hilkiah** is presented, called, and instructed. His father is described as one **of the priests of Anathoth**, in **Benjamin**. He was **ordained . . . a prophet . . . before** his birth (v. 5), humanly reluctant (v. 6), divinely empowered (vv. 8, 9), and commissioned to predict destruction and restoration (v. 10). William Kelly nicely summarizes the prophet's person and work:

> The different character and style of Jeremiah as compared with Isaiah must strike any careful reader. Here we have not the magnificent unfoldings of the purposes of God for that earth of which Israel was the centre, but we have the prophecy in its moral dealing with the souls of the people of God. No doubt, judgments are pronounced upon the heathen, still the intention was to act upon the conscience of the Jew, and in order to do this we see how much the Spirit of God makes of Jeremiah's own experience. Of all the prophets we have none who so much analysed his own feelings, his own thoughts, his own ways, his own spirit.[3]

1:11–19 Next Jehovah (NKJV, LORD) teaches His prophet through visual aids, namely **an almond tree** and **a boiling pot**. The **almond tree**, a first sign of spring, indicated the nearness of the fulfillment of God's Word (vv. 11, 12). The **boiling pot . . . facing away from the north** was Babylon, ready to boil over into Judah because the people forsook God for idolatry (vv. 13–16). Jeremiah must prophesy this unpopular message **against the kings of Judah**, her **princes**, her **priests, and** her **people**, but will receive divine help. **They will fight against** him, but God will be **with** him **to deliver** him (vv. 17–19).

II. JEREMIAH'S PUBLIC MINISTRY (Chaps. 2—10)

A. Sermon against Judah's Willful Infidelity (2:1—3:5)

2:1–3 Chapters 2 through 19 give a general denunciation of Judah. Judah was once passionately in **love** with Jehovah. She was holy to Him, and anyone who troubled her experienced **disaster**. Now, however, as Kyle Yates puts it:

> *The honeymoon is over*. God reminds rebellious Israel of the fervor and the warmth and the purity of the love streams in the early days. She was desperately in love with her Lover and the tender love made life full of music and joy and hope. She was pure and clean and holy. No disloyalty or unclean thought marred the beauty of her devotion. But now the picture is heart-rending. God's heart is crushed with grief and disappointment. Israel now is living in open sin. She is unfaithful to the covenant vows. Other gods have stolen her affection. She has ceased to love Yahweh and her conduct is shameful in the extreme.[4]

2:4–19 Now **the LORD** asks why she has changed. The people, **priests, rulers**, and **prophets** have forgotten all God did for them. Unlike such heathen lands as **Cyprus** and **Kedar**, who are loyal to their **gods**, Judah has **forsaken the LORD** her **God** for worthless idols. Why had they forsaken the Lord and thus exchanged their freedom for slavery through alliances with Assyria and Egypt?

2:20–25 Verse 20 reads, **"For of old I have broken your yoke and burst your bonds,"** meaning that God had delivered them from slavery in Egypt. Or it may read, "For long ago you broke your yoke and burst your bonds; and you said, 'I will not serve' " (RSV), in which case the meaning is that Judah threw off the divine restraints imposed by the law. In either case, the passage goes on to describe how degenerate the people became in their idolatry. God had **planted** them as a **noble vine**, but they had become **degenerate** shoots of **an alien vine**; their **iniquity** was ineradicable by **soap**; they were like **a swift dromedary or a wild donkey**, burning for sexual intercourse, hopelessly enamored with **aliens**.

2:26–37 When **the house of Israel's** sin catches up with her and she cries for deliverance, her numberless **gods** will be helpless to save. In the meantime, the Lord remonstrates with her for unresponsiveness to chastening, freedom from divine restraint, forgetfulness of God, exceeding a harlot's skill in sinning, destroying **the poor innocents**, yet all the while protesting innocence. God will punish them with exile for their trust in nations which He has rejected.

3:1–5 According to Deuteronomy 24:1–4, a man could not remarry **his** divorced **wife** if she had married **another** man in the meantime. Judah had had **many lovers, yet** the Lord still invites her to **return**. Her promiscuity had brought pollution and drought on the land, yet she was as shameless as a harlot. She spoke to God in words of pretended repentance but He knew her **evil** words and deeds.

B. Judah's Future Conditioned upon Repentance (3:6—6:30)

1. Past Sin and Future Glory (3:6–18)

3:6–14 **Israel**, the Northern Kingdom, had practiced gross harlotry, and had refused to **return to** the Lord. **Judah saw** her taken captive by the Assyrians, yet persisted in her sin, refusing to return to the Lord. Thus because the **backsliding** ten tribes of **Israel** were **more righteous than treacherous Judah**, God invites them to return to Him in repentance and confession so that He can **bring** them back to Zion.

Note in verse 8 that God divorced Israel and that it was because of adultery. The Savior's words in Matthew 19:9 are consistent with this. He taught that divorce is permissible for an innocent partner when the spouse has been guilty of immorality. When we read in Malachi 2:16 that God hates divorce, it must mean unscriptural divorce, not all divorce.

3:15–18 These verses anticipate the Millennium. God **will give** them **shepherds according to** His **heart, who will feed** them **with knowledge and understanding**. There will then be no need for **the ark of the covenant** because the Messiah Himself will be there. **Jerusalem will be** the world capital and **called The Throne of the LORD**. **Israel** and **Judah** will be restored from worldwide dispersion and reunited.

2. The Need for Repentance (3:19—4:4)

Here we have a future dialogue between Jehovah and His people. He covets the very best for them but their sins have cut them off from blessing. They respond with contrite **weeping**. Once more He calls them to **return**. They confess that idols are a deception, that God **is the** only **salvation**, that their apostasy has cost them dearly and that they are now covered by **shame** and **reproach**.

3. Woes of the Judgment from the North (4:5–31)

4:5–13 To those who would **return** to **the Lord**, the Messiah would come, and **the nations** would **bless themselves in Him**. The Lord now warns **the men of Judah and Jerusalem**, again exhorting them to be contrite and to throw away their idols. Otherwise God will send the invader (Babylon) as a **lion**, **a** hot **dry wind**, **clouds**, **a whirlwind**, and **eagles**. Verse 10 expresses Jeremiah's inability to reconcile God's former promises of **peace** with His present threats of judgment. The prophet knew that God is faithful, but he was making the mistake of doubting in the darkness what he knew in the light. In times of trouble and discouragement, there is a tendency to question our certainties. A better policy for Christians is to believe our beliefs and doubt our doubts, rather than doubting our beliefs and believing our doubts.

4:14–18 Judah should hasten to turn **from** its **wickedness** because warnings of **affliction** are already coming from **Dan** and **Mount Ephraim** in the north. Besiegers are ready to descend on Jerusalem because of Judah's **bitter** sin and rebellion.

4:19–22 The prophet's affection for his people is expressed in verses 19–21: **"O my soul, my soul!"** means "My anguish, my anguish." He is overwhelmed when he thinks of the approaching **war**, **destruction upon destruction**, and devastation. The question in verse 21, **"How long will I see the standard, and hear the sound of the trumpet?"** is answered by the Lord in verse 22, where he says in effect, "Until the people turn from their foolishness and sin."

4:23–31 Jeremiah describes a vision he **beheld** of the coming all-inclusive catastrophe on Judah. **The Lord** warns that the desolation will be thorough, yet it will not be complete and final. God's unalterable purpose to chasten will not be deterred by Jerusalem's cosmetic beauty or by her cry of **anguish** as **of** a woman **who brings forth her first child**.

4. Judah's Sins to Be Judged (Chap. 5)

5:1–9 The Lord would **pardon . . . Jerusalem** if **a** righteous **man** could be found **in** it. Unable to find one among the **poor** and **foolish**, Jeremiah turned to **the great men**, but was equally unsuccessful. **Therefore** judgment, pictured by the rapacious work of **lion**, desert **wolf**, and **leopard**, was inevitable. **How** could the Lord **pardon** a people who had once made a covenant with Him but were now swearing by other **gods** and giving themselves over to **adultery**?

5:10–13 The enemy is ordered to invade and destroy (**but . . . not make a complete end**) because the people were denying **the Lord** and the imminence of danger, and **the prophets** were telling lies.

5:14–19 Jeremiah's **words** were like **fire**, consuming the **people**, who were like **wood**. The Babylonians were coming to devour and to demolish but not completely. Judah's servitude **in a** foreign **land** would be her recompense for serving **foreign gods in** her own **land**.

5:20–31 God marvels at the obtuseness of His **foolish people**. **The sea** obeys Him, but they do not. They show no inclination to **fear** the One **who gives rain**, even when the rain is withheld. How can God withhold punishment from a nation **so defiant**, so **rebellious**, so steeped in sin? Kelly remarks:

> And the worst phase of the national evil was that not merely a certain portion of the people were guilty, but "a wonderful and horrible thing," he says, "is committed in the land; the prophets prophesy falsely, and the priests bear rule by their means; and My people love to have it so: and what will ye do in the end thereof?" (verses 30, 31).
>
> Thus all the springs of moral rectitude were corrupted; and consequently it was plain that nothing but judgment could come to them from the Lord.[5]

5. *Jerusalem's Fall Predicted (Chap. 6)*

6:1–8 A warning **trumpet** and **a signal-fire** tell the **children of Benjamin** to **flee from . . . Jerusalem** because the Babylonian **shepherds** and **their flocks** (military leaders and soldiers) are preparing to attack. The Chaldeans are heard discussing strategy. God has ordered exile for Judea because of the **oppression, violence** and **plundering** of the people. Even at this late hour He warns His people to desist.

6:9–15 **The Lord of hosts** warns that the Babylonians will strip the land as bare as a thorough-going **grape-gatherer** gleans a **vine**. Jeremiah feels frustrated in having to **speak** to people who won't **heed**, but he cannot refrain. Jehovah directs him to **pour . . . out** the message of impending doom because of their **covetousness**, the falsehood of the prophets and priests, and their shamelessness. It is characteristic of false prophets to promise prosperity in a time of spiritual declension.

6:16–21 The people reject God's call for them to **walk in . . . the old paths** of righteousness and refuse to be warned. Therefore **calamity will** come in spite of the sweet-smelling **sacrifices** that they bring. The people will stumble and **perish**.

6:22–26 The enemy invasion **from the north country** would cause great **fear, mourning, and bitter lamentation**.

6:27–30 The Lord appoints Jeremiah **as an assayer** and tester of metals. The people of Judah are the metals, **stubborn** as **bronze and iron**, like **lead** from which the dross cannot be removed, **rejected silver**. Yates comments:

> Perhaps some day we may see clearly how unattractive, how loathsome, how useless sinful men are in the sight of a holy God. How we need to look objectively at ourselves to see the miserable emptiness that is so clearly visible to God! There is no point in keeping refuse silver. It has no worth. Can it be that God has already marked off as valueless many who consider themselves useful?[6]

C. Jeremiah's Ministry at the Templegate (Chaps. 7—10)

1. *Judah's Hypocritical Religion (Chap. 7)*

7:1–4 Chapter 7 has been called "The Temple Sermon." The men **of Judah** thought they were safe because God would never allow **the temple** to be destroyed. Wrong! They were putting false confidence in the building rather than trusting the One who dwelt there.

7:5–15 Their true safety lay in **thoroughly** turning from sin and living righteously. They thought they could get away with their sins as long as they came to the temple and said **"We are delivered."** Our Lord Himself, whose views of outward religion were like Jeremiah's, used the prophet's words in verse 11 about the temple being **"a den of thieves,"** when He cleansed His Father's house (Matt. 21:13; Mark 11:17; Luke 19:46). Because Judah had polluted and desecrated the temple, it would be destroyed just as the sanctuary **in Shiloh** had been. (The destruction of Shiloh is believed to have taken place during Judges or 1 Samuel.)[7]

7:16–26 Jeremiah should **not pray for . . . Judah**—even then they were worshiping **the queen of heaven**[8] and **other gods . . . in the streets**. The people might as well **eat** their **offerings** and **sacrifices**. What God desires is obedience, not rituals. Verse 22 must be read in the light of verse 23: sacrifice without commitment is worthless.

7:27–34 Because of Judah's persistent refusal to **receive correction**, Jeremiah should lament. Because they polluted the temple and offered human sacrifices, they will be overtaken by a terrible slaughter and **the land shall be** left **desolate**.

2. *Judah's Insensitivity to Sin (Chap. 8)*

8:1–7 **The bones** of those who **worshiped** the starry **host of heaven** will be dug up by the Babylonians and exposed to the heavens, and the living will wish they could die. Unlike those who **fall and** rise again, who sin and repent, Judah refused **to return** to Jehovah. As far as the law was concerned, the people compared unfavorably with the **stork, the turtledove, the swift, and the swallow,** which are obedient to **their appointed** laws of migration.

8:8–12 The people thought they were **wise** concerning **the law of the Lord**, but **the scribe, the prophet,** and **the priest** had misinterpreted and **rejected** it. They were covetous and deceitful, and dealt with problems superficially. For their shamelessness they would share in the coming **time** of **punishment**.

8:13–17 God will sweep them away like a fully-picked **vine** or **fig tree**. The people are resigned to perishing in the city. The Babylonian army advances like **vipers which cannot be charmed**.

8:18–22 The brokenhearted prophet seems to hear the exiled Jews asking, "Where is God?" God answers by asking why they had forsaken Him for **images** and **foreign idols**. Again the **people** wail that the deliverance for which they hoped never came. Jeremiah weeps inconsolably over the seemingly hopeless plight of the people. Verse 22 is the source of a well-known spiritual, "There Is a Balm in Gilead":

> There is a balm in Gilead to make
> the wounded whole;
> There is a balm in Gilead to heal
> the sin-sick soul.

3. *The Weeping Prophet's Lament (Chap. 9)*

9:1–11 Jeremiah is the speaker in the first two verses. His title "the weeping prophet" is beautifully expressed in verse 1:

> **Oh, that my head were waters,**
> **And my eyes a fountain of tears,**
> **That I might weep day and night**
> **For the slain of the daughter of my people!**

Many preachers and missionaries can relate to Jeremiah's feelings in v. 2. Kyle Yates writes:

> This verse reveals a glimpse of a tired, worn, discouraged prophet in

> one of his lowest moments. It might be called "a passing shadow on a great soul." In his hour of vexation he imagines he would like to break away from people who do not deserve anything of him. How sweet to be relieved of all responsibility and all irritations! He was literally sick of watching the empty, godless, formal substitute for religion. All his days he prayed, loved, preached and warned, only to find the sort of unresponsiveness that seared his soul.[9]

He laments the sinfulness and consequent punishment of the people. Then he quotes the Lord as cataloging their sins, arguing the inevitability of judgment, yet **weeping** over God's making **Jerusalem a den of jackals** and the **cities of Judah desolate**.

9:12–22 The calamity is directly linked to Judah's idolatry, and for this sin the people will go into exile. **The LORD** directs that **skillful wailing women** (professional mourners) be called to lament the terrible slaughter and destruction. There is no use in the people's boasting **in . . . wisdom, might** or **riches**; what really counts is to know **the LORD**.

9:23, 24 These are two of the most famous verses in Jeremiah. As G. Herbert Livingston remarks, they are

> worthy to be memorized. Humans strive for **wisdom**, **might**, and **riches**, while God delights in **lovingkindness**, **judgment** (justice), and **righteousness**. Blessed is the one who **understands** the Lord so as to delight in what He delights.[10]

9:25, 26 An added bitterness in Judah's cup will be to be punished with Gentile nations, because Judah is **uncircumcised in the heart**. Clipping the hair on the temples [RV and NASB][11] was a heathen practice forbidden to the Jews (Lev. 19:27).

4. A Satire on Idolatry (10:1–18)

10:1–5 This chapter alternates between the vanity of idols and the greatness of God. God's people should **not learn the way of the Gentiles** and their lifeless idols.

Yates comments about the satire on idols:

> Jeremiah is cruel in his treatment of the poor, defenseless idols that men use as substitutes for God. They are unresponsive sticks that have to be decorated so as to conceal the fact that they are only dead wood. Instead of carrying they must be carried. They must be fashioned, God fashions. No speech, no power, no breath, no intelligence, no worth, no influence, and no permanence can be attributed to them. In contrast Yahweh is eternal, living, active, powerful.[12]

10:6–9 God is the **great . . . King of the nations**, worthy of fear. Those who worship idols are **dull-hearted and foolish**, bowing to **the work** of men's **hands**.

10:10–16 **The LORD is the true** and **living God**. Manufactured gods will **perish**. Jehovah is the God of Creation and providence. Idol-makers are **dull-hearted**, and their images **futile**. The God (**Portion**) **of Jacob** is **the Maker, the LORD of hosts**.

10:17, 18 **The inhabitants of the land** are told to **gather up** what they can carry because the Lord is sending them into exile.

5. The Weeping Prophet's Prayer (10:19–25)

Speaking for the nation, Jeremiah laments the horrors of the siege and exile, confesses human ignorance, asks God to discipline His people and to **pour out** His **fury on** their enemies because **they have eaten up** His people.

III. JEREMIAH'S PERSONAL EXPERIENCES (Chaps. 11—19)

A. Jeremiah and the Men of Anathoth (Chaps. 11, 12)

11:1–10 **The Lord** commands **Jeremiah** to remind the people of **the covenant** of the law which He gave at Sinai, of the curse on those who disobeyed and the blessings for those who obeyed. God's unceasing reminders in the past had met with persistent refusal. Now **the men of Judah** are pictured as forming a **conspiracy** to break the **covenant** by forsaking God for **other gods**.

11:11–13 When God's judgment falls, He **will not listen to** their prayers, and Judah's innumerable **gods will** be powerless to **save them at all**.

11:14–17 Three times the prophet was told **not** to **pray for this people** (7:16; 11:14; 14:11). The people have no right to come to the temple with offerings as if to hide their guilt or avert their **doom**. Once called a beautiful **Green Olive Tree** by **the Lord**, Judah is now destined to be burned because of its idolatry.

11:18–23 **The Lord** informs the **docile** and unsuspecting prophet that **the men of Anathoth** have **devised schemes** to kill him. When he prays, he receives assurance that his adversaries **will** be punished.

12:1–6 Jeremiah asks why **the Lord**, who is Himself **righteous**, allows **the wicked** to **prosper**—such as the men of Anathoth—and permits the righteous, like himself, to suffer. God answers that Jeremiah will meet more bitter opposition than this, including treachery from his own **brothers**. If he found it difficult to cope in relatively calm conditions (running **with the footmen**), what would he do in the severe trials that were coming (contending **with horses**)?

12:7–14 Using many words of endearment to describe **Judah**, God expresses grief over the devastation she has brought upon herself. A bird that is markedly different is often attacked by the others, hence the reference to Judah as a **speckled vulture**. God will punish the Gentile nations and restore **Judah** to the land.

12:15–17 But later the Gentiles will be restored to their lands, and if they turn from idols to God, they will share His blessings **in the midst of** His **people**. Otherwise they will be wiped out.

B. Jeremiah and the Ruined Sash (Chap. 13)

13:1–11 **Judah** is compared to a used **sash** (waist-cloth) which Jeremiah was instructed to take **to the Euphrates** and **hide**. Judah once occupied a place of closest intimacy with Jehovah, but like the **sash**, would be carried away and "hidden." Because of her sin, **Judah** was carried away two hundred and fifty miles and "hidden" near **the Euphrates** (Babylon) in captivity. When Jeremiah retrieved the **sash**, it was **ruined**, **profitable for nothing**. As to whether Jeremiah actually went to the Euphrates, Scofield has this helpful footnote:

> Some have questioned the possibility of Jeremiah's having actually buried his girdle, or belt, by the Euphrates, in view of the distance and the war conditions. However, there were periods in Jeremiah's ministry when the whole area was at peace. It is not impossible that Jeremiah may have actually made a visit to Babylon, and if so, this event could easily have taken place at that time, as he might have buried the belt on his way there and might have dug it up on his way back. It is also possible to interpret

the Hebrew word as meaning, not the Euphrates but the Wadi Farah, a few miles north of Jerusalem. In this case he could have buried the belt at any time prior to the final Babylonian attack. Thus there is reason to assume that this passage describes an actual event—not a mere vision or imaginary story. Jeremiah's marred girdle served as a symbol indicating Israel's unsatisfactory life and service.[13]

13:12–14 All the people will **be filled with wine**—not literal wine, as they thought, but the wrath of Almighty God, and they will be smashed like bottles. Harrison comments:

> Jeremiah stresses that just as alcohol affects judgment and impairs mobility, so in the coming crisis men will behave as though inebriated, being unable to distinguish friend from foe or to defend themselves.[14]

13:15–23 Repentance is urged, or exile is inevitable. If the people don't glorify God, they will get **darkness** and **the shadow of death. The king and the queen mother** will be dethroned and **the cities of the South** besieged. The Babylonians will make the land desolate—all because of the iniquity of Judah. Judah and her sins are inseparable.

13:24–27 The words used to describe Judah's apostasy—**adulteries, lustful neighings, lewdness,** and **harlotry**—all have an immoral connotation.

Harrison explains the illustration:

> Like nominal believers in all ages, the people were incredulous that such calamities could overtake them. Jeremiah, however, places the blame firmly on their own shoulders and promises them the shameful public disgracing associated with prostitutes .... The irony of it all is that this will be inflicted by the very people whom Judah once courted. Because of her indulgence in the unfruitful works of darkness Judah would be exposed publicly as the corrupt wanton that she was by the One who had first espoused her in covenant love.[15]

C. Jeremiah's Intercession Concerning the Drought (Chaps. 14, 15)

14:1–6 The messages in chapters 14–39 were given before the fall of Jerusalem. Judah is overtaken by severe **droughts** and famine.

> The significance of a drought at this time was very great. It was one of the signs predicted in the Palestinian Covenant (Deut. 28:23–24), and had already been fulfilled in part in the reign of Ahab (1 Ki. 17:lff.). As that sign had been followed, even though after a long interval, by the Assyrian captivity of the northern kingdom, it should have been received by Judah as a most solemn warning.[16]

14:7–16 The prophet, confessing for the people, asks for relief, but **the LORD** says that there will be no relief; rather, the people will be destroyed **by ... sword, ... famine and ... pestilence**. The false **prophets** promised safety, but they were lying and would **be consumed** along with **the people to whom they** prophesied. Jeremiah was commanded to lament the awful destruction of Judah in **city** and country.

14:17–22 He continues to plead with God for the people, reminding us of the intercessions of Abraham (Gen. 18:23–33), Moses (Ex. 32:11–13), and Samuel (1 Sam. 7:5–9). He acknowledges their **wickedness**, and promises that they **will wail** for the only **God** who can **cause rain** and **showers**.

15:1–4 Intercession for the people is useless; they are destined to **death**, the **sword**, **famine**, and **captivity**. **Even** prime intercessors like **Moses and Samuel** couldn't forestall the judgment. **Manasseh** was the cause; he had promoted gross forms of idolatry **in Jerusalem**, including the worship of Molech (see 2 Kgs. 21:1–16).

15:5–10 The pitiable condition of **Jerusalem** is the result of failure to respond to the chastening of the Lord. A woman with an ideal family would not live to enjoy her children.

15:11–18 Jeremiah is hated by his own people without cause but God promises that he will be vindicated when his adversaries turn to him for help. Judah will not be able to **break iron** from the north (the Chaldeans). Instead the latter will carry off Judah's **treasures**. The prophet is puzzled by his persecution and suffering, especially when he had been so faithful to the Lord. Nevertheless he finds his resource in God's **word, the joy and rejoicing of** his **heart**.

15:19–21 God's answer is that the prophet has entertained wrong thoughts about Him, and has given expression to these unworthy thoughts from time to time. They must be purged, as one removes **vile** dross from **precious** metal. His adversaries might **return to** him **but** he **must not return to them**. G. Campbell Morgan comments:

> Let him purge his heart of such dross, and devote himself only to the gold of truth about God. So and only so would he be fitted to be as the mouth of God in uttering His messages.[17]

God **will make** the prophet **a fortified bronze wall** that his oppressors cannot topple. He **will deliver** and **redeem** His servant.

D. Jeremiah's Solitary Ministry (16:1–18)

16:1–9 Jeremiah is commanded **not** to marry because of the impending destruction. He is the only man in the Bible who was forbidden to marry. **Mourning** and **feasting** are also forbidden because death is so widespread and because the calamity is the Lord's doing.

With reference to v. 6, it was the custom for relatives and friends to gather at the home of one who had died, **break bread** together while rehearsing the admirable qualities of the departed one, and drink a **cup** of wine. In this way they consoled the mourners. Kelly shows how this ancient Jewish tradition was transformed by our Lord:

> This practice of breaking bread in connection with death seems to be the origin of what the Lord Jesus consecrated into the grand memorial of His remembrance. "Neither shall men break bread for them in mourning, to comfort them for the dead; neither shall men give them the cup of desolation." There you have the Supper, in both its parts. It was a familiar custom among the Jews, but the Lord gave a unique significance to it, and stamped new truth upon it. It was connected with the passover, for, as we know, that was the time of its institution. There was a particular reason for its establishment at that and at no other time, because it was to mark the impressive change from the great central and fundamental feast of Israel. A new and different feast was begun for the Christians.[18]

16:10–18 If asked the reason for **all** the **great** disaster God had predicted, Jeremiah should remind them of the disobedience and idolatry of their **fathers** and themselves. God **will bring** the people **back** from captivity some day, but first **fishermen** and **hunters** (the Babylonians) will search them out and carry them into captivity where God will punish them for **their iniquity and their sin**.

E. Jeremiah's Steadfast Heart (16:19—17:18)

16:19–21 The prophet foresees the day when **the Gentiles** will turn from idols to God. In verse 21, the Lord expresses His steadfast determination to make Judah know His **might** through His chastening.

17:1–11 Judah's idolatry, deeply **engraved**, will result in her being sent off into captivity. God's **mountain** is Jerusalem. . . . To trust in **man** brings a curse; to trust **in the LORD** brings blessing. God knows man's **deceitful . . . heart** and will punish **the man who gets riches** dishonestly **"as a partridge[19] that broods but does not hatch,"** and then sees the chicks leave.

Verse 9 is an unpopular (but nonetheless very true) estimate of the natural heart of man. R. K. Harrison comments on what is translated "desperately wicked" in the KJV tradition and "gravely ill" by some:

> Unregenerate human nature is in a desperate condition without divine grace, described by the term *gravely ill* in verse 9 (RSV *desperately corrupt*, NEB *desperately sick*). *Cf.* 15:18 and 30:12, where the meaning "incurable" occurs. Every generation needs regeneration of soul by the Spirit and grace of God (*cf.* Jn. 3:5f.; Tit. 3:5).[20]

To those who may feel that this is too harsh an indictment of *their* heart, we quote an extended but needed exposé by Matthew Henry:

> There is that wickedness in our hearts which we ourselves are not aware of and do not suspect to be there; nay, it is a common mistake among the children of men to think themselves, their own hearts at least, a great deal better than they really are. *The heart*, the conscience of man, in his corrupt and fallen state, *is deceitful above all things*. It is subtle and false; it is apt to *supplant* (so the word properly signifies); it is that from which Jacob had his name, a *supplanter*. It calls evil good and good evil, puts false colours upon things, and cries peace to those to whom peace does not belong. When men say in their hearts (that is, suffer their hearts to whisper to them) that there is no God, or he does not see, or he will not require, or they shall have peace though they go on; in these, and a thousand similar suggestions, the heart is deceitful. It cheats men into their own ruin; and this will be the aggravation of it, that they are self-deceivers, self-destroyers. Herein the heart is *desperately wicked*; it is deadly, it is desperate. The case is bad indeed, and in a manner deplorable and past relief, if the conscience which should rectify the errors of the other faculties is itself a mother of falsehood and a ringleader in the delusion. What will become of a man if that in him which should be *the candle of the Lord* give a false light, if God's deputy in the soul, that is entrusted to support his interests, betrays them? Such is the deceitfulness of the heart that we may truly say, *Who can know it?* Who can describe how bad the heart is.[21]

17:12–18 Jeremiah rejoices that Judah's **place of** security is the **glorious high throne** of God. Then he speaks of the folly of trusting anyone else and prays to **the hope of Israel**, on behalf of the people, for healing and deliverance. The people ask him **where** the judgment is that God had promised. Jeremiah reminds the Lord that he had **not** tried to escape from being **a shepherd** of God, neither had he **desired the woeful day** of Jerusalem's destruction; he had only spoken the words of the Lord. He asks God to vindicate him by punishing those who were scoffing at the word of God.

F. Jeremiah's Sabbath Sermon (17:19–27)

Here the **kings of Judah, and all Judah, and all the inhabitants of Jerusalem** are admonished to **hallow the Sabbath**. They are promised future rulers of David's dynasty and continuance of temple worship if they obey, and are warned of the penalty for refusing to obey (the destruction of **Jerusalem**).

Irving L. Jensen explains why Sabbath observance was so important to Israel:

> The real test of the heart's relation to God is *obedience to His Word*. One of the laws for Israel was the hallowing of the Sabbath by not working on that day (17:21–22). The constant pressure of materialism upon the lives of all, including the people of God, made the keeping of such a commandment difficult, and for this reason this one commandment of the ten was a real test of the priority of the temporal or the eternal in the heart. Was the keeping of the Sabbath law that crucial to Judah? The symbolic action of Jeremiah and the explicit words he was told to speak gave an affirmative answer.[22]

Similar principles apply to the Lord's Day for Christians. It too is for spiritual and physical refreshment, remembrance of the Redeemer and our redemption, worship of the Lord, and commemorating our Lord's first-day-of-the-week Resurrection victory.

G. Jeremiah at the Potter's House (Chap. 18)

18:1–12 The Lord is **the potter**; Judah (here called **Israel**) is **the vessel**. The spoiling of the vessel was not God's fault but Israel's. The **clay** is in God's **hand** to do with it as He wishes—judgment or blessing. God threatens **disaster** if the people don't repent, but their answer is that they will **walk according to** their **own plans**.

18:13–17 The Lord pronounces their behavior as unparalleled and unnatural. By their idolatry they invite destruction that will astonish those who see the **land** made **desolate**. The RSV probably gives the sense of verse 14: "Does the snow of Lebanon leave the crags of Sirion? Do the mountain waters run dry, the cold flowing stream?" You could depend on these things *in nature*, but God couldn't depend on *His people!* "Although the snow does not forsake Lebanon, Israel has forgotten the fountain of living water from which water of life flows to it."[23]

18:18 Hearing this, the people of Jerusalem **devise plans against Jeremiah**, express continued faith in their own priests and prophets, and plot to **attack** him by slander.

18:19–23 Jeremiah expresses regret that he ever asked God to spare them. Such a prayer is scarcely suitable for believers in this age of grace.

H. Jeremiah and the Earthen Flask (Chap. 19)

19:1–9 Jeremiah is told to take an **earthen flask** out to the city dump, and there **proclaim** to the **kings of Judah** and **inhabitants of Jerusalem** that **God** is about to smash Judah because of its idolatry and human sacrifices. **The Valley of the Son of Hinnom** will become **the Valley of**

Slaughter. In **the siege** of Jerusalem cannibalism will be practiced.

19:10–15 In breaking **the flask**, the prophet pictures the havoc and destruction to be caused by the Babylonians. Burial places will be scarce, and the houses where idolatry was practiced will **be defiled**. Jeremiah returns to the temple **court** and repeats the fact that judgment is about to fall because the people refuse to **hear** God's **words** and repent.

IV. PROPHECIES AGAINST THE CIVIL AND RELIGIOUS LEADERS OF JUDAH (Chaps. 20—23)

A. Prophecy against Pashhur (20:1–6)

Pashhur, the **chief** officer in the **house of the LORD**, caused **Jeremiah** to be beaten and **put** into **stocks**. **The next day**, when the prophet was released, he announced to Pashhur his doom, the doom of his family, and the doom of all Jerusalem and **Judah**. **The king of Babylon** would **carry them** into captivity. Pashhur's name was changed to **Magor-Missabib** (**terror** on every side), which is what he would experience.

B. Jeremiah's Complaint to God (20:7–18)

In verses 7–18, Jeremiah regrets his unpopular ministry. The Lord **persuaded** (deceived) him into it. He wanted to stop delivering the unpopular message of Babylonian captivity, but could not. **The word of the LORD** burned like a fire within him. He overheard his friends plotting against him, but committed his cause to **the LORD**. At times, he is confident, praising **the LORD**, but at other times is so discouraged he wishes he had never been **born**.

C. Prophecy against King Zedekiah (21:1—22:9)

21:1–7 When King Zedekiah sent . . . Pashhur (not the same one as in chap. 20) **and Zephaniah** (not the prophet) to **inquire of the LORD** concerning the approaching Babylonians, Jeremiah sent back word that the Lord would help the invaders against Judah. The **king** and the **people** who would survive would be taken into captivity. Regarding this action taken against the king, Kelly comments:

> Royalty was always the last stem of blessing in the history of Israel. If only the king had been right, though the people and the prophets were ever so wrong, God would still send blessing to Israel. Everything depended upon the king, the seed of David. God might have chastised the prophets and priests and people, but He would have held to them for His servant David's sake. But when not only they went astray but the king himself was the leader of the wickedness, it was utterly impossible to hold to them, and it was the sorrowful task of Jeremiah to pronounce this divine decision.[24]

21:8–14 Those who resisted would perish; those who surrendered to the Babylonians (**Chaldeans**) would **live**. The royal **house** was warned to cease its injustice and oppression. The people of Jerusalem, the inhabitants **of the valley**, are forewarned of their destruction. The terms **"inhabitant of the valley, and rock of the plain"** are probably terms of scorn or derision; they do not seem to be literal descriptions of Jerusalem.

22:1–9 Chapter 22 deals with the last four kings of Judah, though not in chronological order. The historical order was: Jehoahaz, Jehoiakim, Jehoiachin, and Zedekiah; in other words the last king is first and the rest are in order.

Zedekiah, the first king, is warned to dispense justice **and righteousness;** otherwise **Judah**, though magnificent as **Gilead** and **Lebanon**, will be stripped bare and depopulated. The warning is enforced by the history of three kings who met dismal ends.

D. Prophecy against King Shallum (22:10–12)

Shallum, the second king, also called Jehoahaz, was **the son of Josiah**. He was carried **captive** into Egypt and died there without seeing his native **land** any **more**.

E. Prophecy against King Jehoiakim (22:13–23)

22:13–19 Jehoiakim, the third king, built his palace with unpaid labor, failed to follow his father's (**Josiah**) example and would therefore be **dragged... out of... Jerusalem**, to die unlamented. He would **be buried with the burial of a donkey**, that is, tossed into a ditch.

22:20–23 The populace is told to **go up to Lebanon** and **Bashan** and mourn the crushing of their **lovers** (foreign allies) and shepherds (**rulers**) by Nebuchadnezzar. They themselves will groan with the labor **pangs** of captivity.

F. Prophecy against King Jehoiachin (22:24–30)

Coniah (also called Jeconiah and Jehoiachin), the fourth king, would be taken captive by the Babylonians and would **die** in Babylon. **None of his descendants** would ever sit **on the throne of David**. No offspring of Jeconiah succeeded him to the throne. His replacement, Zedekiah, the last king of Judah, was his uncle. Charles H. Dyer comments:

> This prophecy also helps explain the genealogies of Christ in Matthew 1 and Luke 3. Matthew presented the legal line of Christ through his stepfather, Joseph. However, Joseph's line came through Shealtiel who was a son of Jehoiachin (Jeconiah, Matt. 1:12; cf. 1 Chron. 3:17). Had Christ been a physical descendant of Joseph and not virgin-born, He would have been disqualified as Israel's King. Luke presented the physical line of Christ through Mary, who was descended from David through the line of his son Nathan (Luke 3:31). In that way Christ was not under the "curse" of Jehoiachin.[25]

G. Prophecy of the Righteous King (23:1–8)

The rulers (**shepherds**) are condemned for failure to care for God's **people**. But God will restore a **remnant** of His people and give them faithful **shepherds**. He **will raise** up the Messiah to be their **King**. A not too popular, but necessary caution, is given to us Christians on this passage by Kelly:

> It is plain this prophecy points to the Messiah, the Lord Jesus. But the Messiah is the Lord Jesus not so much in relation to us as to Israel. This is important to hold fast. We do not lose by doing so. Many persons have the idea that if these prophecies are not applied to Christians and the church we lose something. Honesty is always the best policy. You cannot take something from your neighbour without losing far more than your neighbour loses. No doubt he may have a little loss, but you will have a terrible one. As this is true in natural things so much the more is it true in spiritual things. You cannot defraud Israel of one fraction of their portion, without impoverishing yourself immensely.[26]

In verse 5, the Messiah is called the **Branch** (or Son) of **David**. In Zechariah 3:8, He is "My servant the BRANCH." In Zechariah 6:12, He is presented as "The Man . . . the Branch." And in Isaiah 4:2, He is "The Branch of the Lord." These correspond to the four ways Christ is presented in the Gospels—as King, Servant, Son of Man, and Son of God.

"THE LORD OUR RIGHTEOUSNESS" or *Jehovah-Tsidkenu* (v. 6) is one of seven compound names of Jehovah.[27] M'Cheyne wrote an excellent hymn based on his increasing appreciation of the Lord under this title:

JEHOVAH TSIDKENU—
The Lord Our Righteousness

I once was a stranger to grace and
to God,
I knew not my danger, and felt not
my load;
Though friends spoke in rapture of
Christ on the tree,
Jehovah Tsidkenu was nothing to
me.

I oft read with pleasure, to soothe
or engage,
Isaiah's wild measure and John's
simple page;
But e'en when they pictured the
blood-sprinkled tree,
Jehovah Tsidkenu seemed nothing
to me.

Like tears from the daughters of
Zion that roll,
I wept when the waters went over
His soul;
Yet thought not that my sins had
nailed to the tree
Jehovah Tsidkenu—'twas nothing
to me.

When free grace awoke me, by light
from on high,
Then legal fears shook me, I
trembled to die;
No refuge, no safety in self could I
see—
Jehovah Tsidkenu my Saviour must
be.

My terrors all vanished before the
sweet name;
My guilty fears banished, with
boldness I came
To drink at the fountain, life-giving
and free—
Jehovah Tsidkenu is all things to
me.

Jehovah Tsidkenu! my treasure and
boast,
Jehovah Tsidkenu! I ne'er can be
lost;
In Thee I shall conquer by flood and
by field—
My cable, my anchor, my breastplate and shield!

Even treading the valley, the shadow
of death,
This watchword shall rally my
faltering breath;
For while from life's fever my God
sets me free,
Jehovah Tsidkenu my death-song
shall be.

—*Robert Murray M'Cheyne*

God will be known as the One **who brought** the people back to the **land**.

H. Prophecy against Judah's False Prophets (23:9–40)

23:9–22 The rest of chapter 23 is a solemn denunciation of the lying **prophets**, both of Israel and **of Jerusalem**. The latter continued to promise **peace**, but if they had listened to God's Word, they would have known that His judgment was inevitable and that it would continue until the divine purposes were accomplished. They spoke without a divine commission.

23:23–29 The omnipresent and omniscient God exposes **the prophets**

for **their dreams**, which led **people** into idolatry. Their dreams were **chaff** compared to God's **word**, which is like nutritious **wheat**, and also like **fire and . . . a hammer**.

23:30–32 The LORD is **against** these lying **prophets**. Yates describes them well:

> They were professionals who claimed to be speaking with divine authority but were actually giving utterance to lies and deceit. Jeremiah hurls three charges against them. He says they were actually immoral, that they did not know God, and that they had no message for the people. They were careless of sacred responsibilities and lowered the moral standards of the people by active participation in sin. Their knowledge of God was on a low plane. Not understanding His holy nature they thought and preached that He could not desert Israel.[28]

They are still very much with us.

23:33–40 Apparently the **people** were mocking Jeremiah by asking **"What is the** burden (**oracle**)[29] **of the LORD?"** The prophet should answer that they themselves were His burden and that He was going to cast them off. God forbade them to use the word "burden" (**oracle**) any more in jest. If they disobey, He **will punish** them severely.

V. PROPHECIES CONCERNING THE DESTRUCTION OF JERUSALEM AND THE BABYLONIAN CAPTIVITY (Chaps. 24—29)

A. The Sign of the Figs (Chap. 24)

24:1–7 The LORD showed Jeremiah **two baskets of figs set** in front of **the temple. One basket** contained **very good figs** and **the other** contained **very bad figs**.

The **good figs** pictured the exiles in **Babylon**, who would be brought **back** to the land because they would **return** to God **with their whole heart**.

24:8–10 The bad figs pictured **Zedekiah the king of Judah, his princes**, and the people remaining in the land after the deportation in Jeconiah's reign. The exiles will be brought **back to** the **land**, but the others will be scattered and **consumed** by sword, famine, and pestilence.

B. The Seventy-year Captivity in Babylon Predicted (25:1–11)

Jeremiah had warned **all the people of Judah** for twenty-three years; other men of God had not ceased to call them to repentance. Because they would **not** listen, they would be taken captive by God's **servant, Nebuchadnezzar**, and remain in exile for **seventy years**.

The reason the captivity lasted seventy years and God told the Jews in advance how long it would last is indicated in 2 Chronicles 36:20, 21:

> And those who escaped from the sword he carried away to Babylon, where they became servants to him and his sons until the rule of the kingdom of Persia, to fulfill the word of the LORD by the mouth of Jeremiah, until the land had enjoyed her Sabbaths. As long as she lay desolate she kept Sabbath, to fulfill seventy years.

Leviticus 25:3–5 teaches that the land was to lie fallow every seventh year. The people had disobeyed this law.

C. The Babylonian Captors to Be Judged (25:12–38)

25:12–29 The hope of a speedy return was therefore a lie. After the **seventy years**, God would direct His wrath against the **Chaldeans** (Babylonians). Under the symbol of a **cup** of **wine,** Jeremiah is told to pronounce God's **fury** on **Judah** and on other **nations** to be crushed by Nebuchadnezzar, and finally upon Nebuchadnezzar himself (**king of Sheshach**). By his prophetic utterances, Jeremiah should tell these nations that they *must* **drink . . . the cup** of God's wrath. If God punishes Jerusalem first, the nations can hardly expect to escape.

25:30–38 These verses amplify the terrors of the cup of God's **fierce anger**, using such descriptive and poetic words as **roar, shout,** and **noise** to describe it. **The leaders of the flock** of Jews will wail because **the LORD has plundered their pasture**.

D. Jeremiah's Warning to the People (Chap. 26)

26:1–11 Jeremiah is told to **stand in the** temple **court,** warning the people that if they do not repent, the Lord will forsake the temple as He did **Shiloh**. (Note that the *conditional promises* of God are subject to relenting on God's part if man does not meet the conditions [v. 3]. God can never **relent concerning** His *unconditional promises*.) The priests and false prophets and the people became incensed and threatened the prophet.

26:12–19 Fearlessly Jeremiah repeats his message. Then **the princes and all the people** defend him, and the elders remind the crowd that Micah had prophesied boldly in the days of a good king and had not been put to death.

26:20–24 These verses may be an argument presented by the opposition or they may simply be the record of the fact that **Jehoiakim** ordered the execution of a prophet named **Urijah** who prophesied the same things as Jeremiah. However, **Ahikam the son of Shaphan** prevails to deliver **Jeremiah** from death.

E. The Sign of the Yoke (Chap. 27)

27:1–11 This prophecy is dated in the time of **Jehoiakim** (v. 1) but the rest of the chapter places it in the reign of Zedekiah. Some explain it as a scribal error. The ambassadors of five Gentile kings had come to Jerusalem, perhaps to form an alliance against Babylon. They are told by the object lesson of **bonds and yokes** that the **yoke of . . . Babylon** will come upon them until Babylon is conquered by Medo-Persia, and that if they don't submit to the yoke, they will be destroyed—this in spite of what the seers in these nations were saying.

27:12–22 Ryrie's note on an ancient custom as it applied to the Jewish temple will clarify this passage:

> A conqueror customarily took the idols of a conquered people back to the temple of his own god. Since Judaism was an imageless religion, the vessels of the Temple were taken instead.[30]

Zedekiah is entreated by Jeremiah to submit to the Babylonians and not to believe the lying prophets who predict that **the vessels of the LORD's house will shortly be brought back from Babylon**. Jeremiah suggested that the prophets prove their authority by asking God to prevent **the vessels which are left in** Jerusalem from being taken **to Babylon**. But it would be in vain. These vessels were going to be **carried to Babylon** and remain there till the end of the captivity—seventy years later.

F. Hananiah's False Prophecy and Death (Chap. 28)

28:1–9 Hananiah the son of Azur the prophet makes the false prediction that the Babylonian captivity will end in **two . . . years**. Jeremiah replies that he wishes this were true, but implies that the prophecy will not come to pass. The true prophets invariably predicted **disaster**; the false prophets predicted **peace**.

28:10–17 Hananiah **broke** the wooden **yoke** which had been on **Jeremiah's neck**, and made a lying prophecy. **Jeremiah** walked **away** (v. 11). Kelly commends the prophet for his self-restraint:

> The servant of the Lord shall not strive. The same man, Jeremiah, who had been like a brazen wall, who had resisted kings and prophets and priests to the face, now refuses to contend with the prophet Hananiah.
>
> The reason for his conduct is plain. Jeremiah did remonstrate, and warn while there was hope of repentance or when long-suffering grace called for it, but where there was no conscience at work, where there was a false pretence of the name of the Lord, he simply goes his way. He leaves God to judge between prophet and prophet. If Jeremiah was true, Hananiah was false.[31]

God, however, will put **a yoke of iron on** the **nations** to **serve Nebuchadnezzar king of Babylon. Hananiah** is denounced as a lying **prophet** and told he will **die** that **year**; he died two months later (cf. v. 1, **the fifth month** and v. 17, **the seventh month**).

G. Jeremiah's Message to the Jewish Captives of Babylon (Chap. 29)

29:1–9 This is **the letter that Jeremiah . . . sent** to the captives in **Babylon** advising them to prepare for a long stay, warning them against listening to the false **prophets** and **diviners**.

29:10–14 The LORD promises that the captivity in **Babylon** will end in **seventy years** and that the people will return to the land.

Verse 13 is an encouragement to all who have been seeking the Lord, sometimes without apparent success:

> God's Word to His people in the day of Jeremiah is still His sure word for men who have sinned and lost touch with the Infinite. No perfunctory gesture of interest can procure the rich treasure that is more valuable than all gold. He is always available. His longing is that all men may look to Him and live. His arms are always open in loving invitation to any who will turn to Him. It is just as true, however, that a diligent search is necessary. One who becomes conscious of his need, senses the satisfying gift of God, and sets out to find Him can be sure of victory if he seeks with his whole heart. Cleansing, peace, joy, victory will be his at the hand of a loving God who delights to welcome His children home.[32]

29:15–32 Contrary to what false **prophets . . . in Babylon** were saying, the king and the people remaining in Jerusalem were to suffer by **the sword, the famine, and the pestilence** because they refused to listen to God's **words**. Doom is pronounced on two lying prophets, **Ahab the son of Kolaiah and Zedekiah the son of Maaseiah**, and on another named **Shemaiah the Nehelamite**, who wrote **letters** rebuking the priest in Jerusalem for not fulfilling his duty by casting **Jeremiah . . . in prison. Zephaniah the priest read** the **letter** to **Jeremiah**. The latter then prophesied that Shemaiah's **family** would be destroyed, and he would not live to **see** the end of the captivity.

VI. PROPHECIES CONCERNING THE RESTORATION (Chaps. 30—33)

Chapters 30—33 contain messages of hope and deliverance and are the bright spot in a book majoring on judgment. Clyde T. Francisco characterizes them as follows:

> No more stirring passages ever were written than those found in this section of Jeremiah. Although most of his messages concerned judgment and doom, when he dreamed of the future he could preach the way he really preferred. All his heart went into these sermons.[33]

The return from captivity was only a partial fulfillment; these chapters look forward to the end times and the final restoration.

This is a very important section, as it contains the famous new covenant passage which predicts the revival of the nation of Israel. This can only take place after "the time of Jacob's trouble" (the Great Tribulation) in 30:4–17. God keeps His covenants, contrary to the views of some. Jeremiah is told to buy a field to show the certainty of the restoration.

A. The Captives to Be Regathered (Chap. 30)

30:1–11 Both **Israel and Judah** will be regathered. First there will be **the time of Jacob's trouble** (the Great Tribulation), then God **will break** the power of the Gentiles over His people. The promise that God **will raise up for them David their king** is generally understood to mean the Lord Jesus, the seed of David. However, some take it to mean the literal David, risen from the dead.

30:12–17 Though the nation's **affliction** now seems **incurable**, God **will . . . heal** their **wounds** and plunder their **adversaries**.

30:18–24 These verses describe the idyllic conditions that will prevail in the Millennium. The last two verses of the chapter depict God's judgment on **the wicked**; this precedes His blessing on Israel, as seen in the next chapter.

B. The Country to Be Restored (31:1–30)

31:1–20 In words of endearment, **the Lord** promises to restore **Israel**, the northern tribes; the people will return from all over the world; they will be filled with singing instead of **mourning**; **Rachel weeping** was a figurative expression signifying the sorrow of seeing captives go into exile. It will cease when Israel repents and God pardons. Matthew quotes verse 15 in connection with the massacre of the infants by Herod (Matt. 2:18). Kelly comments:

> It is beautiful to see that the Holy Spirit . . . applies to that event the passage about sorrow but not that about joy. . . He only referred to what was fulfilled. There was bitter sorrow then, even in the birthplace of royalty. Deep anguish was in the place where there ought to have been the greatest joy. The birth of the Messiah ought to have been the signal for universal joy in the land of Israel. And there would have been if there had been faith in God and His promise, but there was not. Moreover, since the state of the people was one of shameful unbelief so there was an Edomite usurper on the throne. Hence violence and deceit ruled in the land, and Rachel wept for her children and could not be comforted because they were not. . . . So the Holy Spirit applied the first part of the prophecy, but there He stops.[34]

31:21, 22 Repentant **Israel** will return by roads marked by **signposts** and **landmarks**. Her days of unfaithfulness will be over, because the Lord has accomplished something **new—a woman** will **encompass** or embrace **a man**. The **woman** here is Israel and the man is Jehovah. "The prediction," writes Williams, "is that the virgin of Israel will cease to go 'hither and thither after idols' and will seek and cleave to Immanuel."[35]

Kelly, a devout scholar of undoubted orthodoxy, explains why a popular interpretation of v. 22b is not valid:

> It has been common among the Fathers as well as the divines . . . to apply this passage to the birth of the Lord of the Virgin Mary, but the prophecy has not the smallest reference to it. A woman compassing a man is not at all the same thing as the Virgin compassing and bearing a son. Compassing a man has no reference whatever to the birth of a child.[36]

31:23–30 Judah also will be restored, and her **cities** rebuilt. At this point Jeremiah **awoke** from a pleasant **sleep**. Both Judah and Israel will be repopulated. Men will be punished for their **own iniquity**, not for their fathers' sin.

C. The Covenant Renovated (31:31–40)

The days are coming when God **will make a new covenant with . . . Israel and . . . Judah, not** like the law, but a covenant of grace. Men will be given a new moral nature, and knowledge of the Lord will be universal (See Heb. 8:8–13; 10:15–17).

God made the new covenant primarily with Israel and Judah (v. 31). Unlike the Mosaic Law, it was unconditional. It emphasized what God will do, not what man must do; notice the occurrences of "I will" in verses 33, 34. Jesus is the Mediator of the new covenant because it is through Him that its blessings are secured (Heb. 9:15). The covenant was ratified by His blood (Luke 22:20). It will not become effective for Israel as a nation until Christ's Second Coming. In the meantime, however, individual believers enjoy some of its benefits; e.g., their obedience is motivated by grace, not law; God is their God and they are His people; God no longer remembers their sins and iniquities. Universal knowledge of the Lord (v. 34a) awaits the Millennium.

Those who would seek to wipe out Israel from the face of the earth would do well to learn verses 35 and 36. **Israel** will **cease from being a nation** only when and if **the ordinances of the sun, moon, stars**, and **sea depart**. Jerusalem will be rebuilt in a future day, and areas now unclean will **be "holy to the Lord."**

D. The City to Be Rebuilt (Chap. 32)

32:1–5 The Babylonians were now besieging the city. **Zedekiah** had imprisoned **Jeremiah . . . in the court of the prison** for predicting success for the Babylonians. In verse 4 is one of three prophecies that were uttered concerning Zedekiah. Here it says that he would **see** the **king of Babylon . . . face to face**. In Ezekiel 12:13 we read that he would not see Babylon and that he would die in Babylon. Here is how these seemingly contradictory prophecies were fulfilled: Nebuchadnezzar put out Zedekiah's eyes in Riblah, in the land of Hamath (2 Kgs. 25:7). Then Zedekiah was taken to Babylon, but he never saw Babylon (his eyes having been put out) and he died there.

32:6–25 In obedience to the Lord, the prophet purchased his cousin

Hanamel's **field . . . in Anathoth** for **seventeen shekels of silver**. (**Hanamel** had come to him with the offer.) This was an assurance to the people that God would bring them back from Babylon. **Both** of the **deeds** were given to **Baruch** for safekeeping in an **earthen vessel.** As he watches the Babylonians besieging Jerusalem, Jeremiah wonders why God told him to **buy the field** in Anathoth.

32:26–44 The Lord's answer **to Jeremiah** is classic: **"Behold, I am the LORD, the God of all flesh. Is there anything too hard for Me?"**

> The Savior can solve every problem,
> The tangles of life can undo.
> There's nothing too hard for Jesus;
> There's nothing that He cannot do.
> —*Author unknown*

Although God will destroy **Jerusalem** because of the idolatry of the people, yet He will later **gather** His own and bless them greatly. Property will be bought and sold again, and thus the deed to the field of Anathoth will still be valid in a coming day.

E. The Covenant Recognized (Chap. 33)

33:1–16 While . . . Jeremiah . . . was still in the court of the prison, the Lord gave further glowing promises of restoration to **Israel** and **Judah**—the land will be repopulated with joyful people; the **mountains** will be enriched with **flocks**; and, best of all, the Messiah, **"A Branch of righteousness"** descended from **David** will come. **Jerusalem . . . will be called THE LORD OUR RIGHTEOUSNESS.** Jehovah gives His name to restored Israel, just as a man does to his bride and just as Christ does to the church (1 Cor. 12:12).

33:17–26 God's promise concerning the perpetuation of the Davidic dynasty and the Levitical priesthood would be as unbreakable as God's **covenant** of **day and night**. Some of the people were accusing God of forsaking His two houses—Israel and Judah, and were thus despising the Jews as being cast-offs, a non-people. The Lord replies that His **covenant** with His **people** is as fixed as the laws of nature. **The descendants of David** would be as innumerable as **the host of heaven** and **the sand of the sea**.

VII. HISTORICAL SECTION (Chaps. 34—45)

A. The Downfall of Judah and Jerusalem (Chaps. 34—39)

1. *Zedekiah's Captivity Foretold (Chap. 34)*

34:1–7 While the Babylonians were besieging **Jerusalem**, Jeremiah was commanded to tell **the king, Zedekiah**, that he would be carried into exile and would **die** in **Babylon**, though **not . . . by the sword**.

34:8–22 At one time during the fighting, **King Zedekiah** made **the people** agree to set at **liberty** all **Jewish** slaves, perhaps so that they would help defend the city. Later, when the enemy withdrew for a while under pressure from the Egyptian army (37:1–10), the people put all the slaves back **in bondage** again! They thus **profaned** God's **name** by breaking a promise made before Him. God therefore decreed that they would experience the **"liberty"** of **the sword, . . . pestilence, and famine**. Those who had ratified **the covenant** to free the slaves (v. 15) by sacrificing a **calf** in the temple area, and then had broken the covenant, would be delivered to their enemies for slaughter. **Zedekiah . . . and his princes** would be taken captive. The Babylonians would return and **burn** the city **with fire**.

2. *The Rechabites' Obedience Rewarded (Chap. 35)*

35:1–11 Jeremiah obeyed the Lord by inviting **the Rechabites . . . into the house of the LORD** and by offering **them wine to drink. The Rechabites** courteously refused to **drink** it because of instructions their **father** had given them. Also, they had refused to **build a house, sow seed, plant a vineyard**, or own vineyards. (They were forced to live in **Jerusalem** by the advance of **the Chaldeans**.) They maintained a true pilgrim character. What an example!

35:12–19 In marked contrast were the people of **Judah**. They were disobedient to God and would be punished. The Rechabites would be rewarded by always having **a man to stand before** God. The Rechabites were named after Rechab whose son Jonadab was active in aiding Jehu in the expulsion of Baal worship in the Northern Kingdom in 841 B.C. They were a nomadic tribe descended from the Kenites (1 Chron. 2:25) who had attached themselves to Judah and continued to be associated with them but did not identify with their manner of life (*Daily Notes of the Scripture Union*).

Some think that the Rechabites were absorbed into the tribe of Levi and that this is how God's promise is fulfilled. Though we cannot identify the Rechabites today, we believe that their identity will become known in the Millennium.

3. *King Jehoiakim Burns the Scroll of Jeremiah (Chap. 36)*

36:1–10 In the fourth year of Jehoiakim, the Lord commanded **Jeremiah** to **write** down **all the** prophecies which he had delivered; these were dictated to **Baruch** and **read** by him publicly at the temple a year later. No explanation is given why Jeremiah was prevented from going. He was not imprisoned at this time, but was certainly a hunted man.

36:11–19 When Michaiah . . . heard the prophecies, he reported immediately to **the princes**. They in turn called for **Baruch** and asked him to **read** the prophecies to them. **Then** they told **Baruch** that he **and Jeremiah** should **go and hide** and **let no one know where** they were.

36:20–26 When the princes reported the matter to **the king** (Jehoiakim) at **court**, he **sent** for **the scroll**. As **Jehudi read** to him, **the king cut** off portions of **the scroll** (God's Word) and threw them **into the fire**, a perfect picture of what liberals and rationalists have been doing with the Word of God ever since. Eventually, **all the scroll was consumed**, although against the protests of three of the princes. The king looked for **Baruch . . . and Jeremiah . . . , but the LORD hid them**.

36:27–32 After the king had burned the scroll, Jeremiah rewrote the prophecies, adding an appropriate section concerning the fearful **doom** of **Jehoiakim**! The fact that Jehoiachin was Jehoiakim's son and his successor (2 Kgs. 24:6) seems to invalidate the curse of verse 30a. The usual explanation is that Jehoiachin reigned for only three months, not long enough to be of significance.

4. *Jeremiah Imprisoned and Interviewed by Zedekiah (Chaps. 37, 38)*

37:1–10 Though **King Zedekiah**, a vassal ruler under Nebuchadnezzar, **gave** no **heed** to Jeremiah's **words**, still he asked the prophet to **pray . . . for**

him and his followers. When the Egyptian **army** came to assist Judah, the **Chaldeans** (Babylonians) left **Jerusalem** to repel them. Jeremiah sent word to Zedekiah that the Babylonians would **come back** to destroy Jerusalem. Even if Zedekiah could reduce the Chaldean army to a remnant of **wounded men**, they would still succeed in burning **the city**.

37:11–21 As **Jeremiah** was leaving **Jerusalem** on a personal errand, he was arrested and imprisoned in a dungeon on a charge of desertion. After many days, **Zedekiah** called for him to hear what **the Lord** had to say. Jeremiah courageously announced that the Babylonians would capture the city and the king. Then he asked for release from **prison** and the request was granted. He was committed to **the court of the prison**.

38:1–13 **Jeremiah** was **cast into** a miry **dungeon** because he advised the people to leave the city and turn themselves over to the Babylonians. Zedekiah openly expressed his weakness: he could not thwart the will of the princes by protecting the prophet. An **Ethiopian** eunuch succeeded in having him **pulled . . . out** with **ropes** and **old clothes and rags** and returned to **the court of the prison**.

38:14–20 When King **Zedekiah** sought **advice** from **Jeremiah**, promising him immunity, he was told to **surrender to the** invaders and was assured that **the Jews** who had **defected** would not **abuse** him.

38:21–23 **If** Zedekiah refused to go over to the invaders, **the** palace **women** would taunt him in the presence of their Babylonian captors, reminding him how his **close friends** had misled him, then had forsaken him. Also the king's **wives, children** and the king himself would **be taken** captive **by the** invaders, and Jerusalem would **be burned**.

38:24–28 **Zedekiah** asked **Jeremiah** not to tell what had been discussed but simply to say that he had requested not to go back to the dungeon. **The princes** did come and ask, and Jeremiah answered as Zedekiah had directed. Obviously there is a question here concerning the ethics of Jeremiah's reply. Was it the truth, a half-truth or a complete falsehood? What he said was probably true, but he did not feel obligated to tell all that he knew. **Jeremiah remained in the court of the prison** until the fall of **Jerusalem**.

5. The Fall of Jerusalem (Chap. 39)

39:1–10 When **Jerusalem** was taken by the Babylonians (586 B.C.), **Zedekiah**, his **sons**, and his **men of war** tried to flee but were **captured** and taken **to Riblah**. The king's **sons** were **killed**, his own **eyes** were **put out**, and he was taken into captivity. The city was destroyed and only **the poor** of the **people** were **left in the land**.

39:11–14 **Nebuchadnezzar**, the **king of Babylon, gave** instructions through **Nebuzaradan the captain of the guard** that Jeremiah should be well-treated. So the prophet was released from **the court of the prison** and entrusted **to Gedaliah**.

39:15–18 **Ebed-Melech,**[37] **the Ethiopian** eunuch, had previously been promised safety by the Lord. Presumably he obtained deliverance at this time. Chronologically verses 15–18 fit after 38:13.

B. Events in Judah After the Fall of Jerusalem (Chaps. 40—42)

1. Jeremiah Dwelling with Governor Gedaliah (Chap. 40)

40:1–6 When **Nebuzaradan** the Chaldean **captain of the guard** gave

Jeremiah the choice of going **to Babylon** or of staying **in the land** under the rule of **Gedaliah**, he hesitated. Noticing this indecision, the captain sent him **back to Gedaliah** and **gave him rations and a gift** for the journey. The captain's use of the name of **"the LORD your God"** may have been a result of his familiarity with Jewish vocabulary, or it may have been by divine dictation.

40:7–10 Then **when all the captains of the armies who were in the fields heard that . . . Gedaliah** had been left in charge of some survivors, **they came to** him **at Mizpah**, which had now become the capital of the Babylonian province of Judah. He urged them to submit to the Chaldean rule and to resume their usual work. He would represent them to **the Chaldeans**.

40:11–16 Other Jewish refugees returned to **Gedaliah** from **Moab**, Ammon, **Edom** and other **countries** and resumed normal activities. **Johanan and** others warned **Gedaliah** that **Ishmael** was deputized by **Baalis the king of the Ammonites**, to **murder** him, and even offered to **kill Ishmael** secretly. Unfortunately for him, **Gedaliah** merely accused **Johanan** of misrepresenting **Ishmael**.

2. *Governor Gedaliah Assassinated (Chap. 41)*

41:1–9 Ishmael and . . . ten of his **men struck Gedaliah** and his followers, perhaps because they resented his negotiating with the Babylonians, or perhaps because they wanted to rule, since Ishmael was **of the royal family**. Ishmael, pretending sympathy, also killed seventy mourners who **came from Shechem** to worship at the site of the destroyed temple, then **cast** their bodies into **a pit**. He spared **ten** who had hoarded food supplies and who bartered them for their lives.

41:10–18 Others, including **the king's daughters**, who were taken **captive** were rescued by **Johanan** and his fighting men, and fled to **Bethlehem**, planning to escape from there **to Egypt** because they feared reprisal by **the Chaldeans**. **Ishmael** and **eight** of his **men . . . escaped to** Ammon.

3. *God Forbids Fleeing to Egypt (Chap. 42)*

42:1–6 Johanan and his fearful companions asked **Jeremiah** to find out from **the LORD** what they **should do**. When **the prophet** consented, they promised to obey, no matter what the guidance was.

42:7–22 Ten days later the answer came: Don't flee **to . . . Egypt** but stay in the land. If they stay, God will prosper them. If they flee, all the perils they **feared** in Judah will **overtake** them **in Egypt**. But it seems that the people were already *determined* to flee to **Egypt**, so Jeremiah told them flatly that they would meet disaster there.

Modern Christians often do the same thing: they ask God for guidance—and they often request counsel from parents, Sunday School teachers, elders, pastors, and others—yet their mind is already made up to do what they want. Unfortunately, such "seeking counsel" is all window dressing.

C. Jeremiah and the Remnant in Egypt (Chaps. 43, 44)

43:1–7 Accusing **Jeremiah** of lying and being misled by **Baruch, Johanan . . . took all** his people, along with **Jeremiah and . . . Baruch**, and **went to the land of Egypt**.

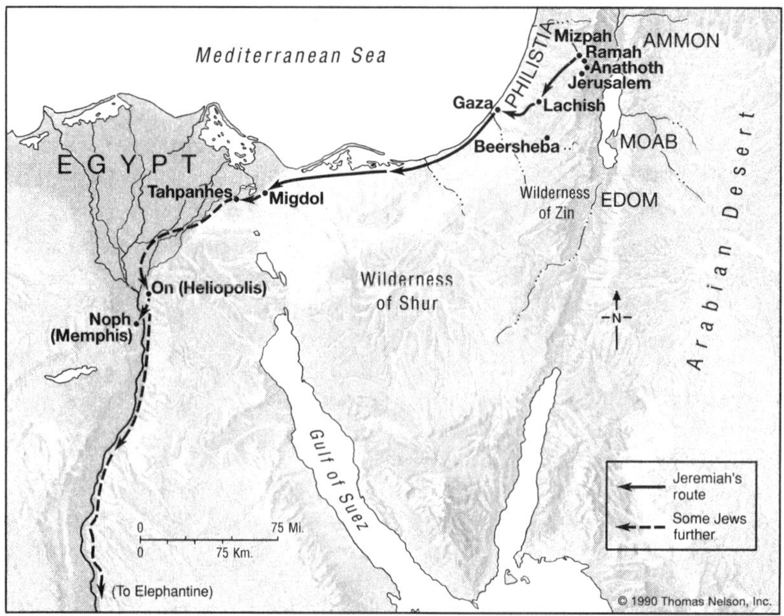

Jeremiah's Journey to Egypt

43:8–13 In Tahpanhes, Egypt, **the Lord** commanded **Jeremiah** to **hide** some **large stones** . . . in the clay of the brick courtyard **at the entrance** to **Pharaoh's** palace. He then predicted that **Nebuchadnezzar** would invade **Egypt** and **set his throne above** the **hidden . . . stones**. Those who did not die by famine, pestilence, or **the sword** would be led off **to captivity**. The **gods of Egypt** would be destroyed **with fire**.

44:1–14 Chapter 44 is the last record we have of Jeremiah in Egypt. It is presumed that he died there.

Jeremiah reminded his countrymen that **all** their **calamity** came as a result of idolatry; yet they were still worshiping false **gods** in **Egypt**. As a result, they would be utterly destroyed; **none** would **return** to Judah **except** a few refugees.

44:15–30 But the people refused to listen to Jeremiah, claiming that they prospered more when they served **the queen of heaven**. **The men** were involved in this false worship as well as **the women**. Again the prophet told them that idolatry was the cause of their trouble and that by their sin, they have forfeited the right to call upon the **Name** of **the Lord**. A terrible judgment! They would be sorely punished, and the **king of Egypt** in whom they trusted would be overcome.

D. The Lord's Message to Baruch (Chap. 45)

This chapter was **written** in the reign **of Jehoiakim** and thus precedes chapter 44 chronologically. Perhaps it follows 36:1–8. It is a message of comfort to **Baruch**, who was clearly discouraged because of the threatened judgments on Judah. Perhaps he was also frustrated because his aspirations for a high position were thwarted. God has a right to build up and to tear down. Baruch should **not seek great things for** himself or for Judah, but should be content to escape with

his life and do whatever task was assigned to him, no matter how lowly. Kelly comments:

> The great lesson for Baruch was that in a day of judgment the proper feeling for a saint and servant of God is an absence of self-seeking . . . . Lowliness of mind always becomes the saint, but in an evil day, it is the only safety. Humility is always morally right, but it is also the only thing that preserves from judgment. I am speaking now not of God's final judgment, but of that which is executed in this world. Now it seems to me plain that Baruch had not learned this lesson. He had now to learn it. This was the word of the prophet to him at an earlier date—the fourth year of Jehoiakim.[38]

VIII. PROPHECIES AGAINST THE GENTILE NATIONS (Chaps. 46—51)

In this section Jeremiah delivers warnings of destruction and judgment—poetically and beautifully. He prophesies against nine nations: Egypt, Philistia, Moab, Ammon, Edom, Damascus, Arabia (Kedar and Hazor), Elam, and Babylon. The nations are listed geographically i.e., from west to east. Topically these prophecies fit after 25:13. They were fulfilled after the destruction of Jerusalem. Babylon will be destroyed and desolate, while Israel will be redeemed. This prophecy of Babylon is probably already fulfilled, though some scholars envisage a rebuilding[39] and subsequent overthrow. The rise of the Medes is taken up in 51:1–24.

A. Prophecies against Egypt (Chap. 46)

46:1–12 Chapter 46, a song dealing with **Egypt**, begins a series of prophecies regarding Gentile nations. An **army** is seen preparing for **battle**, then making a hasty retreat. The army is Egypt's, but it is composed mainly of mercenaries—**Ethiopians, Libyans, and Lydians**. Its defeat took place at Carchemish in 605 B.C.

46:13–19 Next **Egypt** is warned to prepare for invasion and exile. When Nebuchadnezzar invades the land, the **valiant** mercenary soldiers will **fall** against one **another**, then decide to **go back** home. **Pharaoh** will be nicknamed "Empty sound," he is just so much **noise**. The Chaldean's commanding presence, like **Tabor** and **Carmel**, will spell **captivity** for the Egyptians.

46:20–24 The Babylonian gadfly will sting the **very pretty** Egyptian **heifer; her mercenaries, fat** and undisciplined **bulls**, will retreat in disarray. The sound of Egypt "fleeing from the enemy is like the rustling of an escaping **serpent**" (Amplified Version). The invaders approach with battle **axes**. **They cut down** the Egyptians as if they were a thick **forest**. **They are . . . more numerous than** a swarm of **grasshoppers**. **Egypt** is thoroughly disgraced.

46:25–28 **The Lord** will punish **Amon of No** (the sun god of ancient Thebes), **Pharaoh and Egypt with their gods and their kings**. But **afterward** they will **be inhabited** again. **Israel**, too, will be restored to her land, and will enjoy quiet and ease.

B. Prophecies against Philistia (Chap. 47)

The Philistines will be crushed by the Babylonian invasion from **the north**. They will be **cut off from Tyre and Sidon**, and their great cities, **Gaza** and **Ashkelon**, plunged into mourning, will be struck by the **sword of the Lord**.

C. Prophecies against Moab (Chap. 48)

48:1–10 **Moab**, too, is slated for invasion by Babylon. **Her cities** will be destroyed. The **cry of destruction** is **heard** throughout the land. The people are advised to **flee** from **the plunderer**. They **trusted** their **works and . . . treasures** in vain; now their national god **Chemosh** will **go . . . into captivity** with them. Verse 10 is a curse on the invader if he does not do his work thoroughly. It can also be a warning to us against doing the work of the Lord negligently, and failing to declare all the counsel of God, no matter how unpopular it might be.

48:11–27 **Moab** had had an unruffled history and this did not make for a strong character. It was like new wine that had never **been emptied from vessel to vessel** to strain out the **dregs**, and therefore became unpalatable. Now the Chaldeans will destroy all that the nation trusted. **Moab** will be put to shame because **of Chemosh**, just as **Israel was** put to shame because of the golden calf **of Bethel**. Empty boasts are turned to dirges. The **strongholds** are **destroyed**, the people are fleeing, the country is brought low. **The cities** of the **plain** are in ruins. Because Moab mocked **Israel**, it will be made **drunk** with God's fury.

48:28–39 The once-proud people are exhorted to flee to remote hiding places. Their **haughtiness** and **arrogance** were well-known, but now God sincerely mourns over their ruined crops and their loss of **joy and gladness**. A **cry** of despair goes up from **Moab** as God threatens to put an end to this idolatrous nation. Again the Lord mourns **for the men of Kir Heres**, who have lost their wealth. There is **a general lamentation** by the people of **Moab**.

48:40–47 Babylon will swoop down **like an eagle**, causing terror and destruction. Escape will be impossible. Though the people go into exile, they will be restored **in the latter days**.

D. Prophecies against Ammon (49:1–6)

The Ammonites took possession of the territory of Reuben and **Gad** after these tribes went into captivity. They will be punished for their pride and self-sufficiency, but the nation will not be exterminated.

E. Prophecies against Edom (49:7–22)

Edom prided itself in its **wisdom** and its impregnable position (in **the clefts of the rock**), but God has decreed that it will be without inhabitants. Williams comments: "The first part of verse 12 applies to Israel; the second part to Edom. If God's children must be punished for sin, how much more those who are not His children!"[40] No promise of restoration is held out for Edom.

F. Prophecies against Damascus (49:23–27)

Damascus (Syria) is slated for destruction; **her young men** will **fall in her streets**, **all** her soldiers will be destroyed, and **Damascus** will be burned. Verse 25 may be the words of a citizen within the quotation of the Lord, rather than said by Himself, as the capital "M" of the NKJV would indicate.[41]

G. Prophecies against Kedar and Hazor (49:28–33)

49:28, 29 Kedar's nomadic people (the Arabians) will be defeated by the Babylonians.

49:30–33 Unprotected **Hazor** will be invaded by **Nebuchadnezzar**, will be robbed of its treasures, and left **a desolation**.

H. Prophecy against Elam (49:34–39)

The Elamites (Persians) will be scattered throughout the earth, but the Lord **will bring** them **back . . . in the latter days**. God will set His throne in Elam in the sense that He will rule there in judgment.

I. Prophecies against Babylon (Chaps. 50, 51)

50:1–16 This and the following chapter deal with the judgment of God **against Babylon**. The prophecies have partial reference to the capture of Babylon by the Medes. But their complete fulfillment is still future.

Babylon is mentioned 164 times in Jeremiah, more than in the rest of God's Word combined. That country will be conquered **from the north**. Six times, after the prophet speaks of judgment on Babylon, he predicts blessing for Israel and Judah; verses 4–7 form the first. Jews in exile are told to lead the return of captives to their own lands because Babylon will be plundered. There will be elements of several nations in the conquering army. Verse 11 is addressed to the Chaldean army. **"Your mother"** is the nation itself. See the *BBC* on Isaiah 13:14–22 for a discussion of certain problems associated with the destruction of Babylon.

50:17–34 **The scattered sheep** of **Israel** will be restored to a fertile land and pardoned. God's wrath against Babylon is described in verses 21–32, and then His remembrance of **Israel** and **Judah**.

50:35–46 Destruction by the **sword** awaits the people **of Babylon**. The invader will leave the city **desolate**, and the news of its fall will be heard **among the nations**. Verses 41–43, and 44–46, previously applied to Judah and Edom respectively (6:22–24; 49:19–21), are here applied to **Babylon**.

51:1–19 God **will send** a destroyer **to Babylon** (*Leb Kamai* is a code word meaning, "The heart [or midst] of those who rise against me.") who will **not spare**; this will be evidence that He has **not forsaken . . . Israel** and **Judah**. God used Babylon as a golden cup of judgment to make the nations stagger; now it will experience **the vengeance of the LORD**. Jewish exiles in Babylon are speaking in verses 9 and 10 in behalf of all the nations which had been conquered by Babylon. God's greatness is contrasted with idols; the true God is the God of Israel and Judah.

51:20–37 Verses 20–23 are addressed to the Medes; verse 24 is probably intended for Judah. Then verse 25 reverts to Babylon again ("the **destroying mountain**"). It is to be a perpetual waste, **without an inhabitant, a heap** of ruins, the haunt of wild animals. The inhabitants of Judah and **Jerusalem** are speaking in verses 34 and 35.

51:38–44 These verses had a partial fulfillment in 539 B.C. The Medes captured **Babylon** while Belshazzar and his court were feasting and drinking (Dan. 5). However, the city was not sacked at that time. **The sea** refers to future conquering invaders.

51:45–51 The Jewish captives were forewarned to leave the city before the attack and to return to **Jerusalem** as soon as possible.

51:52–58 The proud city will fall, its **carved images** be destroyed, its boastings be stilled, its leaders be slain, and its **walls** leveled.

51:59–64 Jeremiah commands **Seraiah** to carry these written prophecies against Babylon with him into captivity. After **reading** them, he is to **sink** them in **the Euphrates**—a picture of the doom of **Babylon**. Chronologically, these verses belong to chapter 29.

IX. CONCLUSION: THE FALL OF JERUSALEM (Chap. 52)

The last chapter of Jeremiah is historical, recounting the capture of Jerusalem and the captives.

52:1–16 The account of Zedekiah's closing days is repeated in verses 1–11. The destruction of **Jerusalem** is repeated in verses 12–16.

52:17–23 Then a detailed inventory is taken of the temple **articles** which were seized by the Babylonians and **carried . . . away**.

52:24–27 **The captain of the guard** brought seventy-four **men . . . out of** Jerusalem **to the King of Babylon**, who, in turn, killed them **at Riblah**.

52:28–34 Others were taken into captivity in three deportations. **In the thirty-seventh year of** his **captivity**, King **Jehoiachin** was taken **out of prison** by the king of **Babylon** and cared for kindly **until the day of his death**.

And thus, a prophetic book steeped in judgment and tears, ends on a kindly note.

We should not think that this is merely "Hebrew history" pre-written as prophecy in many places. It *is* that, to be sure. But the book of Jeremiah is part of the Word of God, ever fresh, ever relevant. Nearly three centuries ago the English commentator Matthew Henry summarized the spiritual lessons from Jeremiah for us:

> And now, upon the whole matter, comparing the prophecy and the history of this book together, we may learn, in general, (1.) That it is no new thing for churches and persons highly dignified to degenerate, and become very corrupt. (2.) That iniquity tends to the ruin of those that harbour it; and, if it be not repented of and forsaken, will certainly end in their ruin? (3.) That external professions and privileges will not only amount to an excuse for sin and an exemption from ruin, but will be a very great aggravation of both. (4.) That no word of God shall fall to the ground, but the event will fully answer the prediction; and the unbelief of man shall not make God's threatenings, any more than his promises, of no effect. The justice and truth of God are here written in bloody characters, for the conviction or the confusion of all those that make a jest of his threatenings. Let them *not be deceived, God is not mocked*.[42]

ENDNOTES

[1](Intro) See, e.g., 10:23, 24; 11:18—12:6; 15:10–21; 17:9–11, 14–18; 18:18–23; 20:7–18.

[2](Intro) This means that he ministered during the reigns of five kings: Josiah, Jehoahaz, Jehoiakim, Jehoiachin (also called Jeconiah and Coniah), and the puppet king, Zedekiah.

[3](1:1–10) William Kelly, *Jeremiah: The Tender-Hearted Prophet of the Nations*, p. 9.

[4](2:1–3) Kyle M. Yates, *Preaching from the Prophets*, p. 139.

[5](5:20–31) Kelly, *Jeremiah*, p. 20.

[6](6:27–30) Yates, *Preaching*, p. 141.

[7](7:5–15) "Excavations reveal that Shiloh was destroyed about 1050 B.C. This would have been at the time when the Philistines captured the ark (1 Sam. 4:11)." (*The Wesley Bible*, New King James Version, ed. by Albert F. Harper, et al., p. 1095). The Mosaic tabernacle survived Shiloh and was later located at Gibeon (2 Chron. 1:2, 3).

[8](7:16–26) After Christendom became the state religion of the Roman Empire, hordes of unconverted heathens flooded into the churches, bringing in their pagan ideas. The application of this pagan title "queen of heaven" to the virgin mother of our Lord, while no doubt thought to be a great honor, would be totally rejected by the lowly "maidservant of the Lord" (Luke 1:38).

[9](9:1–11) Yates, *Preaching*, p. 143.

[10](9:23, 24) G. Herbert Livingston, "Jeremiah," *Wesley Bible*, p. 1100.

[11](9:25, 26) This is an alternative translation of the phrase "all who are in the farthest corners."

[12](10:1–5) Yates, *Preaching*, p. 144.

[13](13:1–11) *New Scofield Reference Bible, New King James Version*, pp. 784, 785.

[14](13:12–14) R. K. Harrison, *Jeremiah and Lamentations*, pp. 99, 100.

[15](13:24–27) *Ibid.*, p. 101.

[16](14:1–6) *New Scofield, NKJV*, p. 785.

[17](15:19–21) G. Campbell Morgan, *Searchlights from the Word*, p. 243.

[18](16:1–9) Kelly, *Jeremiah*, pp. 43, 44.

[19](17:1–11) "The reference to *the partridge* is to the popular belief that it would hatch the eggs of other birds" (Harrison, *Jeremiah*, p. 107). However, in a footnote on the same page Harrison says that it "could refer to some variety of sand grouse."

[20](17:1–11) *Ibid.*, p. 106.

[21](17:1–11) Matthew Henry, "Jeremiah," in *Matthew Henry's Commentary on the Whole Bible*, IV:519, 520.

[22](17:19–27) Irving L. Jensen, *Jeremiah, Prophet of Judgment*, p. 59.

[23](18:13–17) C. F. Keil. "Jeremiah," in *Biblical Commentary on the Old Testament*, XIX:300.

[24](21:1–7) Kelly, *Jeremiah*, p. 47.

[25](22:24–30) Charles H. Dyer, "Jeremiah," in *Bible Knowledge Commentary*, I:1158.

[26](23:1–8) Kelly, *Jeremiah*, p. 48, 49.

[27](23:1–8) The others are: *Jehovah-Jireh* (The-LORD-will-provide—Gen. 22:13, 14); *Jehovah-Ropheka* (The LORD who heals you—Ex. 15:26); *Jehovah-Nissi* (The Lord, my banner—Ex. 17:8–15); *Jehovah-Shalom* (The-LORD-*is*-peace—Judg. 6:24); *Jehovah-Ro'i* (The Lord, my shepherd—Ps. 23:1); and *Jehovah-Shammah* (THE LORD *IS* THERE—Ezek. 48:35).

[28](23:30–32) Yates, *Preaching*, p. 146.

[29](23:33–40) The same Hebrew word (*massā'*) can mean either "burden" or "oracle." Ryrie calls it "a customary word for a weighty, prophetic message" (cf. Nah. 1:1; Hab. 1:1) in the *Ryrie Study Bible, New King James Version*, p. 1182.

[30](27:12–22) Charles C. Ryrie, ed., *The Ryrie Study Bible, New King James Version*, p. 1187.

[31](28:10–17) Kelly, *Jeremiah*, p. 67.

[32] (29:10–14) Yates, *Preaching*, pp. 146, 147.

[33](Chaps. 30—33:Intro) Clyde T. Francisco, *Studies in Jeremiah*, p. 107.

[34](31:1–20) Kelly, *Jeremiah*, pp. 75, 76.

[35](31:21, 22) George Williams, *The Student's Commentary on the Holy Scriptures*, p. 552.

[36](31:21, 22) Kelly, *Jeremiah*, p. 77.

[37](39:15–18) His name means "servant of the king."

[38](Chap. 45) Kelly, *Jeremiah*, p. 94.

[39](Chaps. 46—51:Intro) At the time of substantive editing of this commentary (1990), Iraq, where ancient Babylon was located, had actually begun the rebuilding of Babylon under Saddam Hussein. Now, however, (1991) that rebuilding has surely been set back by the Allied bombing of Iraq during the UN-sponsored liberation of Kuwait.

[40](49:7–22) Williams, *Student's Commentary*, p. 563.

[41](49:23–27) Since Hebrew does not have capital and lower case letters, all capitalization in English versions must necessarily be decided upon by the translators.

[42](52:28–34) Henry, "Jeremiah," IV:711.

BIBLIOGRAPHY

Dyer, Charles A. "Jeremiah" and "Lamentations." In *The Bible Knowledge Commentary. Old Testament*. Wheaton, IL: Victor Books, 1985.

Feinberg, Charles L. *Jeremiah: A Commentary*. Grand Rapids: Zondervan Publishing House, 1982.

Francisco, Clyde T. *Studies in Jeremiah*. Nashville: Convention Press, 1961.

Harrison, R. K. *Jeremiah and Lamentations*. The Tyndale Old Testament Commentaries. Downers Grove, IL: InterVarsity Press, 1973.

Henry, Matthew. "Jeremiah." In *Matthew Henry's Commentary on the Whole Bible*. Vol. 4. McLean, VA: MacDonald Publishing Company, n.d.

Jensen, Irving L. "Jeremiah and Lamentations." In *Everyman's Bible Commentary*. Chicago: Moody Press, 1974.

Keil, C. F. "Jeremiah—Lamentations." In *Biblical Commentary on the Old Testament*. Vols. 19, 20. Grand Rapids: Wm. B. Eerdmans Publishing Company, 1971.

Kelly, William. *Jeremiah: The Tender-Hearted Prophet of the Nations*. Charlotte: Books for Christians, n.d.

von Orelli, Hans Conrad. *The Prophecies of Jeremiah*. Reprint. Minneapolis: Klock & Klock Christian Publishers, 1977.

LAMENTATIONS

Introduction

"It is a mute reminder that sin, in spite of all its allurement and excitement, carries with it heavy weights of sorrow, grief, misery, barrenness, and pain. It is the other side of the 'eat, drink and be merry' coin."

—Charles R. Swindoll

I. Unique Place in the Canon

This little book is called "Lamentations" in the Greek, Latin, and English versions. The Jews refer to it by the first Hebrew word of chapters 1, 2, and 4, which is translated "How" or "Alas." The book consists of five separate poems united by the common *theme* of Jerusalem's destruction by Nebuchadnezzar in 586 B.C. and by the unique acrostic *structure* of the first four chapters.

Probably to facilitate memorization, the lines of the poems are in Hebrew alphabetical order, one verse beginning with each letter, except in chapter 3 where each letter is assigned three verses in a row starting with the same letter. Chapter 5 has the same number of verses as the Hebrew alphabet (twenty-two) but is not in acrostic form.

In spite of the difficulty of writing in such a rigid framework, the book succeeds in passionately expressing patriotic and heartfelt sorrow.

II. Authorship

The book of Lamentations itself does not name its author, but the tradition that Jeremiah wrote it is ancient and was not challenged until the 18th century.

The Greek translation (the Septuagint) of Lamentations actually gives a preface whose style seems to suggest a Hebrew original: "And it came to pass, after Israel was led into captivity and Jerusalem laid waste, that Jeremiah sat weeping and lamented with this lamentation over Jerusalem, and said . . ." (Here chapter one begins).

The style of the book suggests "the weeping prophet" and 2 Chronicles 35:25 also connects Jeremiah with dirge or lament types of composition. The fact that the author was an eyewitness, and that no other logical candidate comes forth as author lends support to the traditional Jewish and Christian view that Jeremiah wrote Lamentations.

III. Date

The first-hand descriptions of the devastation of Zion are so vivid and compelling that it is likely they were penned very shortly after the event itself (about 586 or 585 B.C.), and before Jeremiah went to Egypt.

IV. Background and Theme

The fall of Jerusalem was a time of terrible suffering and anguish. It was this fearful catastrophe that brought forth the book of Lamentations, wrung, we believe, from the heart of the prophet Jeremiah.

This book forms a sort of appendix to the prophecies of Jeremiah. It describes the deep mourning of the prophet at the destruction of Jerusalem and of the temple. Instead of being elated over the fact that his prophecies had been fulfilled, he wept bitterly over the miseries of his people.

In addition to being the words of Jeremiah, the book may also be thought of as expressing:

1. The sorrow of the Jewish remnant, for whom Jeremiah was a spokesman, as they witnessed the Babylonian invasion.
2. The anguish of the Messiah when He came to suffer, bleed, and die on the cross of Calvary (see 1:12, for instance).
3. The sorrow of the Jewish remnant in a future day when they will be called upon to go through the Great Tribulation, the Time of Jacob's Trouble.

Sin ⟶ Suffering (1:8)
Sorrow ⟶ Repentance (1:20)
Prayer ⟶ Hope (3:19–24)
Faith ⟶ Restoration (5:21)

The Road to Renewal

OUTLINE

I. THE AWFUL DESOLATION OF JERUSALEM (1:1–11)

II. THE SAD CRY, CONFESSION, AND PRAYER OF THE PEOPLE (1:12–22)
   A. The Cry (1:12–17)
   B. The Confession (1:18, 19)
   C. The Prayer (1:20–22)

III. THE LORD SEEN AS THE ONE WHO PUNISHED JERUSALEM (Chap. 2)
   A. The Effects of God's Wrath (2:1–13)
   B. The Cause of God's Wrath—the False Prophets' Failure to Warn the People (2:14)
   C. The Ridicule of the Onlookers (2:15, 16)
   D. The Fulfillment of God's Threats (2:17)
   E. The Call to Repentance (2:18, 19)
   F. The Prayer for God's Mercy (2:20–22)

IV. THE PROPHET VOICES THE SORROW AND CONFESSION OF THE REMNANT (Chap. 3)
   A. The Judgments of God (3:1–18)
   B. The Mercies of the Lord (3:19–39)

C. The Call for Spiritual Renewal (3:40–42)
D. The Sorrow of Jeremiah over Jerusalem (3:43–51)
E. The Prophet's Prayer for Deliverance from His Foes (3:52–66)

V. THE PAST AND PRESENT OF JUDAH CONTRASTED (4:1–20)

VI. THE FUTURE PROSPECT—EDOM TO BE DESTROYED AND JUDAH RESTORED (4:21, 22)

VII. THE REMNANT APPEALS TO GOD FOR MERCY AND RESTORATION (Chap. 5)

Commentary

I. THE AWFUL DESOLATION OF JERUSALEM (1:1–11)

Here we see the utter desolation of Jerusalem. Verses 1–11 are the language of an onlooker. **The** once populated **city** is now **a** bereaved **widow**; the **princess has become a slave**, forsaken by her idols, and betrayed by her allies (vv. 1, 2). The people have **gone into captivity** because of their sin, and no pilgrims come to worship in **Zion** (vv. 3–9). The precious vessels of the **sanctuary** have been taken by the Babylonians (v. 10), and the **people** suffer famine (v. 11).

II. THE SAD CRY, CONFESSION, AND PRAYER OF THE PEOPLE (1:12–22)

A. The Cry (1:12–17)

This passage speaks of the unique **sorrow** of Jerusalem. Verse 12 has become "a classic expression of grief"[1] and reminds us of our Lord's lament over the same city for its stiff-necked rejection of Him. The language also fits Christ's condition on the cross, with the hardened soldiers, religious establishment, and general populace callously watching His suffering as a public spectacle.

The Jewish people recognize that it is the LORD (v. 15) who has brought the devastation to pass, and though **Zion spreads out her hands** in appeal for mercy, **no one comforts** her; she has **become an unclean thing** (v. 17).

B. The Confession (1:18, 19)

In the Jews' confession they admit **that the LORD is righteous** in sending them into **captivity**; that they had **rebelled against His commandment**, and that her pagan "lovers"—the Gentile nations—had **deceived** her.

C. The Prayer (1:20–22)

Judea prays that God will repay the **wickedness** of her gloating **enemies**, all the while admitting **her transgressions** amid her many **sighs**.

III. THE LORD SEEN AS THE ONE WHO PUNISHED JERUSALEM (Chap. 2)

A. The Effects of God's Wrath (2:1–13)

2:1–7 These verses describe what God has done to **Judah**—destroyed the temple (**footstool**) (v. 1), **swallowed up** the cities (v. 2), refused to hold back the **enemy**, as if He Himself were Judah's foe (vv. 3–5), treated the temple as if it were a mere **garden**, caused the sacrificial system to cease **in Zion**, and set aside both **king and priest** (vv. 6, 7).

2:8–13 He has laid the city in ruins, the rulers are in exile, the **prophets** receive no word **from the LORD**, **the elders** mourn, and the maidens hang **their heads** in shame (vv. 8–10). **The children . . . faint** from hunger **in the streets**; they fall and die (vv. 11, 12). The people's calamity is greater than anything the prophet can think of with which to **comfort** them (v. 13). **"Virgin daughter of Zion"** is what the people *should* have been, not what they actually *were*.

B. The Cause of God's Wrath—the False Prophets' Failure to Warn the People (2:14)

Judah's **prophets** had **seen false and deceptive visions**. Rather than exposing the people's **iniquity** they had manufactured **false prophecies and delusions**.

C. The Ridicule of the Onlookers (2:15, 16)

Judah's neighbors gloat over Jerusalem's downfall. They **clap their hands**, **hiss**, and **say** with sadistic pleasure, **"This is the day we have waited for; we have found it, we have seen it!"**

D. The Fulfillment of God's Threats (2:17)

The LORD had **fulfilled His word**. He had put His own people **down** and **exalted the** power (**horn**, a Hebrew figure of speech) of Judah's **adversaries**.

E. The Call to Repentance (2:18, 19)

Parents are summoned to **cry . . . out to the LORD** unceasingly for their **young children**, who **faint from hunger at every street** corner.

F. The Prayer for God's Mercy (2:20–22)

Women eat their own **offspring** because of the famine. **The streets** are filled with the **slain** because God has **invited** the Babylonians to come **as** if **to a feast**.

IV. THE PROPHET VOICES THE SORROW AND CONFESSION OF THE REMNANT (Chap. 3)

A. The Judgments of God (3:1–18)

Alternating between **I** and **we**, the prophet draws a parallel between his own experiences and those of his people. God's **wrath** is depicted under the figures of **darkness**, incessant blows from **His hand** (vv. 1–3); premature aging, **broken bones**, confinement in **bitterness**, **woe**, and a living death (vv. 4–6); inescapable imprisonment, unanswered **prayer** (vv. 7–9); animal-like **ambush**, target-like attack (vv. 10–12); deep wounds, derision, a diet of **bitterness** (vv. 13–15); **broken teeth**, **ashes for** clothing (v. 16); loss of memory, **peace**, and prosperity, all **hope** of divine help **perished** (vv. 17, 18).

B. The Mercies of the LORD (3:19–39)

With a prayer to God to **remember** his bitter plight, yet with lingering depression over his misery (vv. 19, 20), the prophet gets his eyes off himself and onto the Lord. Hope is revived when he remembers that **the LORD's mercies** and **compassions . . . are new every morning**, and that His **faithfulness** is **great**[2] (vv. 21–24). He cites lessons learned in the school of affliction: it **is good** to **wait** quietly **for** the Lord's deliverance and to submit to His **yoke** early in life (vv. 25–27); to accept divine chastening and human blows and insults without talking back

(vv. 28–30); God's rejection is neither final nor causeless; His **compassion** and **mercies** will always follow (vv. 31–33); **the LORD does not approve** of oppression, injustice, or the denial of rights (vv. 34–36); He is sovereign, His Word prevails, all things serve His will; to **complain** when He punishes sin is senseless (vv. 37–39).

C. The Call for Spiritual Renewal (3:40–42)

The way of blessing is found in self examination, and turning **back to the LORD**. Unconfessed sin is **not pardoned**.

D. The Sorrow of Jeremiah over Jerusalem (3:43–51)

The subject reverts to the sufferings of Jeremiah and his people. God had **pursued** and **slain** without pity, cut Himself off from their prayers, and made them the scum of the earth (vv. 43–45). All their **enemies** mocked while God's people experienced **fear**, danger, and **destruction**. The devastation of his people caused the prophet to weep **without interruption** (vv. 46–51).

E. The Prophet's Prayer for Deliverance from His Foes (3:52–66)

Hunted down like a bird, stoned in a **pit**, engulfed by water, the prophet thought the end had come (vv. 52–54). He prayed earnestly **from the lowest** depths, and God answered, telling him **not** to **fear** (vv. 55–57). Now he asks the LORD to consider how he has been mistreated—the **vengeance**, **schemes**, **reproach**, insults, gossip, and taunts against him—and to judge his case. Righteousness demands that his enemies be punished, cursed, pursued, and destroyed (vv. 58–66). **"A veiled heart"** (v. 65), as in "when Moses is read, a veil lies on their [the Jews'] heart" (2 Cor. 3:15), probably does not refer to "hardening, but blinding of the heart, which casts into destruction."[3]

V. THE PAST AND PRESENT OF JUDAH CONTRASTED (4:1–20)

The prophet compares the former glory and the present pitiful condition of Jerusalem. The temple is destroyed, mothers desert **their young** (vv. 3, 4), people die of hunger (v. 5), the **punishment** is prolonged (v. 6), the princes are **unrecognized in the streets** (vv. 7, 8), cannibalism prevails even among **compassionate women** (v. 10), and the city that was considered impregnable has fallen (v. 12). It was all caused by **the sins of her prophets, . . . the priests**, and **the people** (vv. 13–16). They looked in vain to Egypt **for** their **help** (v. 17). The Babylonians besieged them suddenly (vv. 18, 19), and King Zedekiah, **the anointed of the LORD**, was captured (v. 20).

VI. THE FUTURE PROSPECT—EDOM TO BE DESTROYED AND JUDAH RESTORED (4:21, 22)

The daughter of Edom rejoiced over the fall of Jerusalem, but she will be punished severely and her **sins** laid bare. **Zion** will be restored.

VII. THE REMNANT APPEALS TO GOD FOR MERCY AND RESTORATION (Chap. 5)

5:1–14 In these verses, the people bewail the terrible conditions that have come upon them—the high cost of necessities (v. 4); the forced **labor**

(v. 5); the oppression (v. 8); the famine and danger (vv. 9, 10); the atrocities committed against **maidens**, **princes**, and **elders** (vv. 11, 12); hardships for **young men**, **boys**, and **elders** (vv. 13, 14).

5:15–18 Because of all these horrors Judah's **joy** had **ceased**, her **dance** had become **mourning**, **the crown** had **fallen from** her **head**, and **Mount Zion** lay **desolate**.

The reason for it all is confessed: **"Woe to us, for we have sinned!"**

5:19–22 Finally the people ask the **LORD** to **turn** them **back** to Himself so they can **be restored** and renewed. It is interesting that in many Hebrew manuscripts, verse 21 is repeated after verse 22, apparently so that the book will end with a note of hope rather than gloom.[4] Actually, as Keil notes, a right understanding of verse 22 makes such a repetition unnecessary:

> This conclusion entirely agrees with the character of the Lamentations, in which complaint and supplication should continue to the end,—not, however, without an element of hope, although the latter may not rise to the heights of joyful victory, but, as Gerlach expresses himself, "merely glimmers from afar, like the morning star through the clouds, which does not indeed itself dispel the shadows of the night, though it announces that the rising of the sun is near, and that it shall obtain the victory."[5]

ENDNOTES

[1](1:12–17) R. K. Harrison, *Jeremiah and Lamentations*, p. 210.

[2](3:19–39) If the reader will pardon a personal recollection, verses 22 and 23 have a special meaning to the editor. My father was fond of quoting "Through the LORD's mercies we are not consumed" (v. 22), and my mother's favorite hymn, "Great Is Thy Faithfulness," is based on v. 23. Only after both had gone to be with the Lord did we realize that their sentiments—each characteristic of their personalities—were fittingly "back to back" in Lamentations chapter 3.

[3](3:52–66) C. F. Keil, "Lamentations," in *Biblical Commentary on the Old Testament*, XX:455.

[4](5:19–22) A similar repetition for more suitable synagogue readings occurs at the end of Ecclesiastes, Isaiah, and Malachi.

[5](5:19–22) Keil, "Lamentations," XX:455.

BIBLIOGRAPHY

For Bibliography see Jeremiah.

EZEKIEL

Introduction

"From the first to the last chapter of Ezekiel one supreme thought runs throughout, that of the sovereignty and glory of the Lord God. He is sovereign in Israel and in the affairs of the nations of the world, though the loud and boisterous claims of men seem to have drowned out this truth. In His sovereign will God has purposed that we should glorify Him in life and witness to the ends of the earth."

—Charles Lee Feinberg

I. Unique Place in the Canon

Thanks largely to the famous spirituals "Ezekiel Saw the Wheel" and "Dry Bones," Ezekiel is known as a biblical character by millions of people. Unfortunately, the level of Bible knowledge of his difficult book often doesn't go too much deeper. Certainly Ezekiel is not the first book Christians should read right after conversion, although at least some literary persons have become captivated by the Bible through this prophet's remarkable style.

The unusual thing about Ezekiel (unlike Jeremiah, and to a lesser extent Isaiah and most of the Minor Prophets) is his emphasis, not on judgment, but on *comforting* God's people. From the Chebar Canal, which may have been a kind of ancient concentration camp near Babylon, Ezekiel wrote his prophecies to encourage the Jewish exiles.

II. Authorship

Ezekiel (God strengthens or strengthened by God) was one of those who was taken to Babylonia with the second group of captives, eleven years before Jerusalem was destroyed.

Until the 1920's, Ezekiel's prophecies had largely escaped the "scissors" of rationalistic critics. This situation was lamented by some liberals, who swiftly went to work spinning theories denying the unity, authorship by Ezekiel, and traditional date of writing.

Actually, the ancient and universal Judeo-Christian position that the book was written by a poetic prophet, "Ezekiel the priest, the son of Buzi," is quite defensible and the critical view has been answered well.[1]

We summarize John B. Taylor's six arguments for the unity of the book as having been written by one author as follows:

1. The book has *continuity*, from start to finish, producing a deliberate effect.
2. The book has a *consistent message*: the fall of Jerusalem and the destruction of the temple.
3. The *style and language* are uniform, including special phrases, repeated throughout the work (such as "son of man," "the word of the LORD came to me," "they

shall know that I am the LORD," and "the glory of the LORD").
4. Ezekiel has a definite *chronological sequence* unique among the Major Prophets (see Isaiah and Jeremiah).
5. The use of the *first person singular* throughout gives a distinctively autobiographical framework to the book. The writer is identified as Ezekiel in 1:3 and 24:24.
6. Ezekiel's *personality and character* are consistent throughout. These are shown by his earnestness, love of symbolism, concern for detail, and awe at God's glory and transcendence.[2]

III. Date

Ezekiel dated his prophecies precisely. His first prophecy (1:2) came in the fifth year of Jehoiachin's exile (593 B.C.); his last dated prophecy was in 571 B.C. (29:17). Hence his ministry lasted at least twenty-two years. If, as a priest, he started his ministry at the age of thirty, he would have been over fifty when he finished his prophesying.

IV. Background and Themes

Ezekiel ministered to his fellow-exiles immediately before and during the first twenty-some years of the captivity. They falsely expected to return to Jerusalem, so he taught them that they must first return to the Lord.

Ezekiel's prophecy is divided into three parts. First, he rehearses the sins of Judah and warns of God's impending judgment in the captivity of the people and the destruction of the capital. This is all vividly announced in unusual visions and symbolic acts. A bright, shining cloud, a figure of God's presence, is seen lingering over the temple, then reluctantly departing. This meant that God could no longer dwell among His people because of their sin, and His sword of judgment must soon descend on the polluted temple. The glory of the Lord is one of the key thoughts running throughout the book of Ezekiel.

In the second section, Judah's neighbors are condemned because of their idolatry and their cruel treatment of God's people. These are the Ammonites, Moabites, Edomites, Philistines, Tyrians, Sidonians, and Egyptians.

Finally, in the last section, Ezekiel tells of the restoration and reunion of the entire nation—both Israel and Judah. When the people repent of their sins, God will put His Holy Spirit within them. The Messiah will come to His people and destroy their last enemies. The temple will be rebuilt, and the glory of the Lord will return to it. These prophecies have not yet been fulfilled, but look forward to Christ's one-thousand-year reign on earth, the Millennium.

Like many other prophetic books, Ezekiel is not entirely chronological, though more so than Isaiah and Jeremiah. We should take notice of the dates or time periods that are given at the beginning of many chapters. Albert Barnes puts the prophecies in chronological order as follows:

> The prophecies are divided into groups by dates prefixed to various chapters, and we may assume that those prophecies which are without date were delivered at the same time as the last given date, or at any rate, they followed closely upon it.

1. The fifth year of Jehoiachin's captivity.
   Chs. 1—7. Ezekiel's call, and prediction of the coming siege of Jerusalem.

2. The sixth year.
   Chs. 8—19. An inspection of the whole condition of the people, with predictions of coming punishment.
3. The seventh year.
   Chs. 20—23. Fresh reproofs and fresh predictions of the coming ruin.
4. The ninth year.
   Ch. 24. The year in which the siege began. The declarations that the city should be overthrown.
5. The same year.
   Ch. 25. Prophecies against Moab, Ammon and the Philistines.
6. The eleventh year.
   Chs. 26—28. Prophecies against Tyre.
   In this year Jerusalem was taken after a siege of eighteen months and the temple destroyed.
7. The tenth year.
   Ch. 29:1–16. Prophecy against Egypt.
8. The twenty-seventh year.
   Chs. 29:17—30:19. Prophecy against Egypt.
9. The eleventh year.
   Chs. 30:20—31:18. Prophecy against Egypt.
10. The twelfth year.
    Ch. 32. Prophecy against Egypt.
11. The same year.
    Chs. 33—34. Reproof of unfaithful rulers.
12. The same year, or some year between the twelfth and twenty-fifth.
    Ch. 35. Judgment of Mount Seir.
13. The same year.
    Chs. 36—39. Visions of Comfort. Overthrow of Gog.
14. The twenty-fifth year.
    Chs. 40—48. The vision of the temple.[3]

Regarding Ezekiel's ability to communicate God's Word across the many miles between Babylonia and Judea, the *Daily Notes of the Scripture Union* say:

> One of the problems of this book is Ezekiel's ministry to those in far off Jerusalem, while he was himself an exile in Babylonia. It must be assumed that those who had been deported were free to maintain communications with the homeland; with the intervening territory unified and pacified by Babylon, this was no doubt more practicable than it had been in earlier times. It was simpler for a messenger to describe in his own words Ezekiel's symbolic act than to bear a verbal message which might have faded in his memory, or a written message which might have invited the attention of the Babylonian authorities.

OUTLINE

I. CALL AND COMMISSION OF EZEKIEL (1:1—3:21)
   A. Ezekiel's Circumstances (1:1–3)
   B. Ezekiel's Vision of God's Glory Riding on a Throne-Chariot (1:4–28a)
   C. Ezekiel's Appointment to Prophesy to the People of Israel (1:28b—3:21)
      1. The Character of the People—Rebellious (1:28b—2:7)
      2. The Nature of the Message—Judgment, as Indicated by the Scroll (2:8—3:3)

3. The Character of the People—Impudent and Hard-hearted (3:4–11)
4. The Role of the Prophet—Watchman (3:12–21)

II. JUDGMENT OF JUDAH AND JERUSALEM DEPICTED (3:22—24:27)

A. Visual Aids Illustrating Coming Judgment (3:22—5:17)
1. Ezekiel Commanded to Pretend to Be Mute until Told by God to Speak (3:22–27)
2. The Siege of Jerusalem Portrayed with a Tile (Chap. 4)
3. The People's Fate Predicted by the Use of a Sharp Sword and Hair (Chap. 5)

The Destruction of Idolatry and Preservation of a Remnant of the People (Chap. 6)

C. The Imminence and Severity of the Babylonian Invasion (Chap. 7)

D. The Vision of Gross Idolatry in the Temple (Chap. 8)

E. The Removal of God's Presence and the Subsequent Destruction of Idolaters (Chap. 9)

F. The Vision of God's Glory Visiting Jerusalem with Judgment (Chap. 10)

G. The Repudiation of the Counsel of Wicked Princes (11:1–13)

H. The Preservation of a Remnant Promised (11:14–21)

I. The Removal of the Glory Cloud to the Mount of Olives (11:22–25)

J. Ezekiel's Signs of the Coming Exile (Chap. 12)
1. His Baggage (12:1–16)
2. His Quaking (12:17–28)

K. The Doom of the False Prophets and Prophetesses (Chap. 13)

L. God's Threat to the Idolatrous Elders (Chap. 14)

M. The Parable of the Fruitless Vine (Chap. 15)

N. The Parable of Jerusalem's Marriage (Chap. 16)

O. The Parable of the Two Eagles (Chap. 17)

P. The Repudiation of the Parable of the Sour Grapes (Chap. 18)

Q. Lamentation for the Last Kings of Judah (Chap. 19)

R. Vindication of God's Dealings with Israel (20:1–32)
1. Idolatry in Egypt (20:1–9)
2. Defiling God's Sabbaths (20:10–17)
3. Rebellion in the Wilderness (20:18–26)
4. Idolatry (20:27–32)

S. God's Promise of Eventual Restoration (20:33–44)

T. Pictures of the Imminent Invasion (20:45—21:32)
1. The Sign of the Forest Fire (20:45–49)
2. The Sign of the Drawn Sword (21:1–17)
3. The Sign of the Fork in the Road (21:18–32)

U. Three Oracles on Jerusalem's Defilement (Chap. 22)

V. The Parable of the Two Harlot Sisters (Chap. 23)
1. Oholah (23:1–10)
2. Oholibah (23:11–21)
3. The Invasion of the Babylonians (23:22–35)
4. The Judgment of Oholah and Oholibah (23:36–49)

- W. The Parable of the Boiling Pot (24:1–14)
- X. The Sign of the Death of Ezekiel's Wife (24:15–27)

III. PROPHECIES AGAINST SEVEN GENTILE NATIONS (Chaps. 25—32)

- A. Prophecy against Ammon (25:1–7)
- B. Prophecy against Moab (25:8–11)
- C. Prophecy against Edom (25:12–14)
- D. Prophecy against Philistia (25:15–17)
- E. Prophecy against Tyre (26:1—28:19)
  1. The Destruction of Tyre (Chap. 26)
  2. The Dirge over Tyre (Chap. 27)
  3. The Downfall of the Prince of Tyre (28:1–19)
- F. Prophecy against Sidon (28:20–26)
- G. Prophecy against Egypt (Chaps. 29—32)
  1. General Threat against Pharaoh and His People (Chap. 29)
  2. Lamentation over the Fall of Egypt (30:1–19)
  3. The Downfall of Pharaoh (30:20—31:18)
  4. Lamentation over Pharaoh and Egypt (Chap. 32)

IV. ISRAEL'S RESTORATION AND THE PUNISHMENT OF HER FOES (Chaps. 33—39)

- A. The Prophet Recommissioned as a Watchman (Chap. 33)
- B. The False Shepherds and the Good Shepherd (Chap. 34)
- C. The Doom of Edom (Chap. 35)
- D. The Restoration of the Land and the People (Chap. 36)
- E. The Vision of the Valley of Dry Bones (37:1–14)
- F. The Reunification of Israel and Judah (37:15–28)
- G. The Destruction of Israel's Future Enemies (Chaps. 38, 39)

V. MILLENNIAL SCENES (Chaps. 40—48)

- A. The Millennial Temple in Jerusalem (Chaps. 40—42)
  1. The Man with the Measuring Rod (40:1–4)
  2. The East Gate of the Outer Court (40:5–16)
  3. The Outer Court (40:17–19)
  4. The Other Two Gates of the Outer Court (40:20–27)
  5. The Three Gates to the Inner Court (40:28–37)
  6. The Equipment for Sacrifice (40:38–43)
  7. The Chambers for the Priests (40:44–47)
  8. The Vestibule of the Temple (40:48, 49)
  9. The Sanctuary and Most Holy Place (41:1–4)
  10. The Side Chambers (41:5–11)
  11. A Building West of the Temple (41:12)
  12. The Measurements of the Temple (41:13–15a)
  13. The Interior Decoration and Furnishing of the Temple (41:15b–26)
  14. The Priests' Quarters (42:1–14)
  15. The Measurements of the Outer Court (42:15–20)
- B. The Millennial Worship (Chaps. 43, 44)

C. The Millennial Administration (Chaps. 45, 46)
D. The Millennial Land (Chaps. 47, 48)
1. The Healing of the Waters (47:1–12)
2. The Boundaries of the Land (47:13–23)
3. The Division of the Land (Chap. 48)

Commentary

I. CALL AND COMMISSION OF EZEKIEL (1:1—3:21)

A. Ezekiel's Circumstances (1:1–3)

As the book opens, **Ezekiel** was already in **captivity**, having been carried off in one of the earlier deportations. But he prophesied about the destruction of Jerusalem six or seven years before it happened. Ezekiel was probably thirty years of age at this time (**"in the thirtieth year"**). The first twenty-four chapters were written *before* the fall of Jerusalem, but *after* the first deportations.

B. Ezekiel's Vision of God's Glory Riding on a Throne-Chariot (1:4–28a)

The first chapter is taken up with a vision of the glory of God among the captives. Ezekiel first saw a fierce **whirlwind coming** from **the north.** Then he saw **four living creatures, each** of which **had four faces (lion, ox, eagle, man),**[4] four **wings,** straight feet, and hands under its wings. The creatures symbolize those attributes of God which are seen in creation: His majesty, power, swiftness, and wisdom. Many nations forget about the God above the cloud, who sits on the throne. They worship the creative attributes rather than the Creator Himself.

Above the firmament was **a throne,** with **the Lord** of **glory** seated upon it. **Beside each** of the living creatures there was **a wheel**, or rather **a wheel** within **a wheel** (perhaps one wheel at right angle to the other like a gyroscope). Thus the vision seems to represent a throne-chariot, with **wheels . . . on the earth**, four living creatures supporting a platform, and the **throne** of God above it. It was this vision of the **glory** of God that preceded Ezekiel's call to the prophetic ministry.

The passage evokes the response in Faber's fine hymn:

My, God, how wonderful Thou art,
Thy majesty how bright,
How beautiful Thy mercy seat,
In depths of burning light!

How dread are Thine eternal years,
O everlasting Lord:
By prostrate spirits day and night
Incessantly adored!

Father of Jesus, love's reward,
What rapture will it be
Prostrate before Thy throne to lie,
And gaze, and gaze on Thee.

—*Frederick William Faber*

Ezekiel explains what he viewed in 43:3 as "the vision which I saw when He[5] [NKJV marg.] came to destroy the city." In other words, the vision depicted God in His glory coming out of the north in judgment on Jerusalem, the Babylonians being the agents of His judgment.

Ezekiel's Throne Car Vision. This drawing portrays the author's conception of the throne car of Ezekiel 1. In one regard it differs from the text's description, namely that *each* creature has *four* faces, while in this drawing, for the purpose of simplicity, each creature shows only one face.

C. Ezekiel's Appointment to Prophesy to the People of Israel (1:28b—3:21)

1. *The Character of the People—Rebellious (1:28b—2:7)*

The Spirit entered Ezekiel, **set** him on his **feet**, and told him to prophesy to a rebellious nation, Judah, regardless of the results. He was to be fearless and obedient.

The Lord commissioned Ezekiel, whom He calls **"son of man."**[6] This important expression occurs ninety times in Ezekiel. Taylor explains the usage:

> The first words that God addresses to Ezekiel appropriately put the prophet in his rightful place before the majesty which he has been seeing in his vision. The phrase *son of man* is a Hebraism which emphasizes Ezekiel's insignificance or mere humanity. "Son of" indicates "partaking of the nature of" and so when combined with *'adām*, "man," it means nothing more than "human being." In the plural it is a common phrase for "mankind".[7]

By the time of Daniel (7:13, 14) this title had taken on near messianic implications, and in the first century it had become a term for the Messiah:

> Our Lord's use of the title seems to have taken advantage of the ambiguity between the simple and the technical meanings, so that in one sense He could not be accused of making any overt claim to Messiahship, while in the other sense He did not debar those with the requisite spiritual insight from accepting the fuller significance of His person.[8]

2. *The Nature of the Message—Judgment, as Indicated by the Scroll (2:8—3:3)*

2:8–10 Ezekiel was then commanded to **eat . . . a scroll** on which were written the sorrowful judgments that were to fall on the nation.

He was forewarned that his ministry would not be popular. We too are forewarned that a true presentation of the gospel will be offensive to the unsaved. It is known as the offense of the cross. To some people we are a savor of death.

3:1–3 Ezekiel **ate** the **scroll**, as commanded. A later prophet, "John the Revelator," would do the same thing (Rev. 10:8–10). Every prophet or preacher needs to internalize the message, making it a part of his own life (cf. 3:10).

3. *The Character of the People—Impudent and Hard-hearted (3:4–11)*

Then God repeated that Ezekiel was being **sent to a people** who would **not listen** (Judah is here called **Israel**). Language barriers can be overcome, as many missionaries tell us. But the barrier of a **rebellious** heart cannot be overcome. He was to be fearless . . . in speaking to the Jews in the land and to those in captivity.

True servants of Christ must be tough-minded but not hard-hearted.

4. *The Role of the Prophet—Watchman (3:12–21)*

3:12–15 The Lord then **took** Ezekiel **to the captives** at **the River Chebar**, and he **sat** with them in silence for **seven days**. Kyle Yates describes Ezekiel's situation:

> The call of Ezekiel to leave his comfortable home and go to preach to the captives at Tel-Abib came as an unwelcome interruption. He felt the hand of God upon him and realized a divine compulsion that could not be resisted, but he went in bitterness of spirit to a distasteful task. Fortunately for him and for the people he did not begin preaching immediately but sat among the distraught people for a whole week. That experience gave him a clear understanding of their problems, their miseries and their crying needs. The preacher who is able to see life through the window of his people will be able to help them and provide the leadership so sorely needed.[9]

3:16–21 Ezekiel was appointed **a watchman**, responsible to **speak** God's Word and to **warn the** people solemnly. The solemn fact of bloodguiltiness is taught not only in the OT (vv. 18–20) but in the NT as well (Acts 20:26). However high the responsibility of God's messenger is, Christians should not take this as teaching that they ought to cram the gospel down every throat, or witness in every elevator. Despite his great responsibility, Ezekiel was shut up by God and had to wait for God-given opportunities. We also need to be sensitive to His leading in witnessing. *Sometimes* we need to be silent. However, most of us are silent when we ought to be witnessing.

II. JUDGMENT OF JUDAH AND JERUSALEM DEPICTED (3:22—24:27)

A. Visual Aids Illustrating Coming Judgment (3:22—5:17)

Judgment, wrote Peter, must begin at the house of God (1 Pet. 4:17). And so God starts with the center of revealed religion, the temple at Jerusalem.

1. Ezekiel Commanded to Pretend to Be Mute until Told by God to Speak (3:22–27)

First Ezekiel **went out into the plain** where he beheld **the glory of the Lord**. Then he was commanded to **go** to his **house** where he would be bound and **mute** until God revealed to him what to say.

2. The Siege of Jerusalem Portrayed with a Tile (Chap. 4)

4:1–8 Jerusalem was built with stones on a rock foundation. Brick (made of **clay** like tile) is a symbol of Babylon (cf. Gen. 11:3,9). Now Jerusalem has become even worse than Babylon in her morals and idolatry (see 5:7). God therefore commanded Ezekiel to **portray** the **siege** of **Jerusalem**, using a **clay tablet** (tile) to represent the **city** and **an iron plate** (or pan) to picture the **wall** of **iron** that would cut the city off from help. The prophet is God's representative. This shows that the Lord Himself was besieging Jerusalem. Ezekiel was to **lie . . . on** his **left side . . . three hundred and ninety days** for **Israel** and **on** his **right side . . . forty days** for **Judah**.

Each day represented a year, but no explanation of the totals is completely satisfactory. The Septuagint seeks to solve the problem by changing 390 to 190, but the change lacks Hebrew manuscript support. Another unanswered question is whether Ezekiel actually lay on his side day and night for these two periods of time. Many commentators suggest that he did it only during that part of each day when he would be *seen* by the public, since it was a visual teaching aid.

4:9–17 These verses speak of the famine which resulted from the siege, with **food** and **water** rationed. At first, **human** excrement was to be used as fuel for baking, but later this was changed to the more customary **cow dung**. The chapter is a picture of siege, discomfort, hunger, and defilement—all the result of Judah's sin and departure from God.

3. The People's Fate Predicted by the Use of a Sharp Sword and Hair (Chap. 5)

5:1–9 In an object lesson, Ezekiel showed that **one-third** of the city would die of pestilence (**fire**) or famine (v. 12), **one-third** would fall by **the sword** (knife), and a third would be scattered to other lands (compare v. 2 and v. 12). A remnant would be spared, but even some of these would later perish (vv. 3, 4), perhaps those who were killed at the time Ishmael assassinated Gedaliah. These calamities would come upon **Jerusalem** because the people acted **more** wickedly **than the** surrounding **nations**, in spite of their greater privileges.

We as Christians have even higher privileges than the Jews. May the Lord give us grace not to misuse them and thus bring about our own temporal judgment and loss of eternal rewards!

5:10–17 Cannibalism would be prevalent (v. 10). Because the temple had been **defiled**, God would not **have . . . pity** (vv. 11–13). The Jews would be despised **among the nations** and would suffer violence and **destruction** (vv. 14–17).

B. The Destruction of Idolatry and Preservation of a Remnant of the People (Chap. 6)

6:1–7 **The mountains of Israel** are used here to refer to idolatry, since idol shrines (**high places**) were commonly built on mountains. The land would be punished for its idolatry.

6:8–14 **A remnant** would be spared; these would **remember** the Lord in their captivity and **loathe themselves for . . . their abominations** (vv. 8–10). Idolatry would be punished by **pestilence**, warfare, and **famine** (vv. 11–14).

In every age, God maintains a remnant testimony for Himself—not the moral majority but the *despised minority*.

C. The Imminence and Severity of the Babylonian Invasion (Chap. 7)

7:1–18 The time for God's judgment to fall had **come**, and there would be no question that it was **the Lord** who was striking (vv. 1–13). **No one** would answer the call **to battle**; courage and strength would fail because of the awful destruction (vv. 14–18).

7:19–22 Material possessions would be useless (v. 19). Because the temple (**"the beauty of his ornaments"**) had been polluted with idols, it would be given to **strangers**—the Babylonians. They would **plunder** it and **defile** it (vv. 20–22).

7:23–27 All classes would be affected by the **desolation—the king**, princes, prophets, priests, **elders**, and **common people**. The **common people** should have been a testimony to God, but they totally failed. The only testimony that can be given to God now is through judgment. What a solemn thought. The judgment is complete: all classes and all the land. Any nation that rejects the knowledge of God loses its moral fiber, and has no means of support when trouble comes. This is true of individuals, too.

D. The Vision of Gross Idolatry in the Temple (Chap. 8)

8:1–6 The elders had to witness the judgment, which they had failed to help to avert. This often happens today, too. The Lord carried Ezekiel from Babylon **to Jerusalem . . . in visions**. There he saw some terrible examples of the idolatry of the people. He saw an abominable idolatrous **image . . . in the entrance** of the temple—one which provoked the Lord **to jealousy**.

8:7–15 The second thing the prophet **saw** was in **the court** of the temple. **The elders of** Judah were assembled there **each** with **a censer in his hand**, worshiping vile pictures **portrayed all around on the walls**.

The third sight was at the north gate—the **women were . . . weeping for Tammuz**, a Babylonian deity. The vegetation supposedly dried up when he died.

8:16–18 The fourth instance of idolatry was in **the inner court of the**

temple, where **about twenty-five men**, representing the priests, **were worshiping the sun** and following the lewd practices of that cult. The reference to **the "branch"** or "twig" (v. 17) is obscure. To put **the branch to** the **nose** may have indicated contempt or scorn for God. The branch may have been an obscene phallic symbol.

It is often unsaved religious leaders who grab the headlines by their ungodly behavior and outrageous heresies; but God sees, and He will have the last word.

E. The Removal of God's Presence and the Subsequent Destruction of Idolaters (Chap. 9)

9:1, 2 In this chapter, **six** executioners are seen coming **from** the **north** (the direction from which the Babylonians were to come) to destroy the idolaters of the previous chapter. The man **clothed with linen** may symbolize grace.

9:3 **The glory** cloud (symbol of God's presence) leaves the holy of holies in the temple, grieved away by the idolatry of the people. **The glory** cloud moves **to the threshold of the temple** where its brightness fills the court.

9:4 Those faithful Jews who opposed the idolatry were sealed by **a mark on** their **foreheads** so that they would **not** be killed. This verse should challenge us. How do we react, if some do not follow the Lord? Do we join them? Will they influence us? Do we justify them? Do we show indifference? These faithful men and women sighed and cried; this reaction showed what was in their heart and kept them from judgment.

The sign—or mark on the forehead—was the last letter of the Hebrew alphabet (*tau*), which the rabbis said suggested completeness. It is also the first letter of *torâ* (law). Feinberg notes a "remarkable similarity between what is stated here and in Revelation 7:1–3."[10] He adds a fascinating parallel from much later times:

> Christian interpreters have seen a somewhat prophetic allusion to the sign of the cross. In the earlier script the last letter of the Hebrew alphabet (*taw*) had the form of a cross. Ezekiel, of course, could not have thought of Christian symbolism nor is the passage a direct prediction of Christ's cross. It is a remarkable coincidence, however.[11]

9:5–7 Then the executioners began to **slay** the idolaters, starting **with the elders** (ancient men). **"Do not come near anyone on whom is the mark,"** says God. We don't know if they were aware of the mark, but believers today can be sure on the basis of the Word that they are safe from judgment. How frightening not to have this assurance!

9:8–11 When Ezekiel interceded for the people, the Lord said that He would **not spare** or **have pity**. The people were saying that because **the** **Lord** God had **forsaken** them and no longer saw their plight, they owed no loyalty to Him. **"The Lord does not see"** sounds like a very modern quotation!

Judging from this and other texts (cf. Noah and the ark, e.g.), it seems to be characteristic of God to deliver true believers before pouring out judgment on the ungodly.

F. The Vision of God's Glory Visiting Jerusalem with Judgment (Chap. 10)

Chapter 10 is closely linked with Chapter 1, giving further information about the throne-chariot, the living creatures (here identified as cherubim), and the glory of the Lord. However, Chapter 1 was addressed to the exiles whereas this is addressed to rebels in Jerusalem.

10:1, 2 The Lord commanded **the man clothed** in **linen** to take burning **coals . . . from** between **the cherubim, and scatter them over** Jerusalem. This signified God's judgment that was to be poured out on **the city**.

10:3–5 These verses are a parenthesis, repeating the movement of the glory cloud described in 9:3.

10:6–17 A detailed description of **the cherubim** and **the wheels** of the throne—chariot is given in these verses, which are admittedly difficult to visualize. The **cherub . . . face** in verse 14 may be the same as the ox face in 1:10.

10:18, 19 The glory cloud next moves **from the threshold** to **the east gate of the LORD's house**.

10:20–22 Ezekiel then emphasized that **the cherubim** were the same as **the living creature** he had seen **by the River Chebar** in chapter 1.

This vision teaches us never to lose a sense of the awesome power, wisdom, and majesty of our God.

G. The Repudiation of the Counsel of Wicked Princes (11:1–13)

11:1–3 The **twenty-five men** (representing the princes) were advising the people of the city that there was nothing to fear. They could carry on their construction projects as usual. They were as secure as **meat** encased in an iron **caldron**. Thus the **twenty-five men** flatly contradicted the word of the Lord, which said: **"The time is not** near to build . . . ." God had given orders through Jeremiah (Jer. 29:4–11) that the captives would build houses in Babylon because Jerusalem would fall. **The men who devise iniquity** tried to awaken false hopes among the captives by letters. Despite the fire of God's judgment, the princes in Jerusalem felt quite safe there.

In the same way many nominal Christians feel safe from God's judgment despite the sin in their lives, but the Lord will tell them, "I never knew you."

11:4–12 Ezekiel was told to reinterpret their symbolism quite differently! The **city** of Jerusalem was the **caldron**, and the **slain** people were **the meat**! They themselves would be taken **out of** the city and judged **at the border of Israel** (see 2 Kgs. 25:18–21; Jer. 5:24–27).

11:13 When **Pelatiah** (perhaps the leader of the twenty-five men) dropped dead, seemingly as a result of his evil counsel, Ezekiel interceded to **GOD** for his people.

H. The Preservation of a Remnant Promised (11:14–21)

11:14, 15 The LORD answered by telling the prophet what **the inhabitants of Jerusalem** had been saying, namely, that the exiles had wandered **far . . . from the LORD** and that the land belonged to those remaining in Judah and **Jerusalem**.

11:16–21 But the **Lord GOD** promised that He would be **a little sanctuary** to the exiles, and that He would regather them to **the land of Israel**, completely cleansed of idolatry and with **a heart** to obey the Lord. Yates comments:

> Ezekiel follows Jeremiah in urging spiritual religion. It is definitely a heart religion that God wants. The heart is beyond repair. A new one will be provided. Formalism must be left behind. The spiritual emphasis will give them touch with Yahweh that will transform their thinking, their worship, their conduct and their

> loyalty. A new spirit will be their special gift from their God (Cf. 18:31; 36:26f).[12]

The real hope for the exiles is based on the Lord's promise. The promise of **one heart** (one **of flesh**), and a **new spirit** are unconditional; they are yet to be fulfilled in the New Covenant.

> Jesus, before Thy face we fall—
> Our Lord, our life, our hope, our all!
> For we have nowhere else to flee—
> No sanctuary, Lord, but Thee!
> —*Samuel Medley*

I. The Removal of the Glory Cloud to the Mount of Olives (11:22–25)

At the close of the chapter, **the glory** cloud rises **from the . . . city** and goes to the Mount of Olives, to **the east side of** Jerusalem. George Williams comments:

> It retired unwillingly. Its throne was the Most Holy Place, 8:4; it then withdrew to the threshold, 9:3; then, above the threshold, 10:4; then it retired to the Eastern Gate, 10:19; and, finally, to the mountain on the east side of the city, 11:23. Thus did the God of Israel in lingering love forsake His city and temple, not to return till 43:2 (still future).[13]

J. Ezekiel's Signs of the Coming Exile (Chap. 12)

1. *His Baggage (12:1–16)*

12:1–12 Ezekiel was commanded to move his household goods from one **place . . . to another**, as a sign to the Jews that they would be moving off **into captivity**. By digging **through the wall** at night with his eyes covered, he predicted that Zedekiah (**the prince**) would flee from the city **at twilight** (when he could not **see the ground**).

12:13–16 However, he would be captured and taken **to Babylon**, though he would never **see it . . . with his eyes** (v. 13). This is exactly what happened. Zedekiah was captured as he fled from Jerusalem, his eyes were put out at Riblah, and then he was carried to Chaldea (2 Kgs. 25:7). The people would be scattered among the nations, and many of them would die from **the sword, famine, and . . . pestilence**.

2. *His Quaking (12:17–28)*

12:17–20 When Ezekiel ate and drank **with trembling** and **quaking**, he gave a pre-picture of the fear **and anxiety** that would precede the exile.

12:21–28 The people had a **proverb** that God's prophecies of doom were never fulfilled. God gave them another proverb, announcing that the day of **fulfillment** was **at hand**, and that **every** prophecy (**vision**) would come to pass. Those who said that the **fulfillment** was yet future would see it in their own day.

The people's tendency to explain the prophecies away or apply them to future generations is still with us. When God speaks to *us* through a message or a book, we immediately seem to know how *our brother or sister* should apply it and change. It is an evil and destructive tendency to apply God's Word to others and not to our own lives.

We should also watch out for glib clichés that contradict God's Word or that deny or postpone His intervention.

K. The Doom of the False Prophets and Prophetesses (Chap. 13)

13:1–3 The subject here is false **prophets** (vv. 1–16) and false prophetesses (vv. 17–23). The former invented prophecies **out of their own heart**;

they would fail the people when most needed. They used the words, **"The LORD says,"** but it was a lie, a **false divination**.

Today we need preachers who don't give us their own thoughts and opinions, but who get their message in the prayer closet, and from God's Word.

Denis Lane gives the following characteristics of the preaching in Ezekiel's day:

> It never rose higher than the preachers' own minds. It deceptively claimed to be God's word. It had no practical or useful effect. It offered cheap grace and a false peace. It simply endorsed the latest world view.[14]

13:4–7 False religious leaders, like **foxes in the deserts**, are always looking for prey in the midst of destruction, filling their own needs and desires. In a situation like this it is the preacher's duty to stand in **the gaps** to intercede and to repair the **wall** by leading people to repentance and a holy life. This is done by preaching God's Word.

13:8–16 They would be destroyed for predicting **peace when there** was **no peace**, for whitewashing **a wall** that was ready to crumble (daubing it **with untempered mortar**). The **wall** represented the rulers' efforts to prevent the divine judgment. Davidson explains the illustration:

> The figure incisively describes the futile projects of the people, and the feeble flattery and approval of the prophets. When a weak man cannot originate anything himself, he acquires a certain credit (at least in his own eyes) by strong approval of the schemes of others, saying, Right! I give it my cordial approval, and indeed would have suggested it. What made the prophets whitewash the wall which the people built was partly the feeling that from the place they occupied they must do something, and maintain their credit as leaders even when being led; and partly perhaps that having no higher wisdom than the mass they quite honestly approved their policy. Being sharers with them in the spirit of the time they readily acquiesced in their enterprises.[15]
>
> Modern apostate religious leaders are exactly the same—whitewashed walls.[16]

13:17–23 The prophetesses practiced witchcraft, putting **magic charms** on people's wrists and **veils** on their **heads**. They doomed some people to death by magic spells and kept others **alive**. **GOD** would **deliver** His **people** and destroy these false prophetesses. The LB paraphrases verses 17–19 as follows:

> Son of dust, speak out against the women prophets too who pretend the Lord has given them his messages. Tell them the Lord says: Woe to these women who are damning the souls of my people, of both young and old alike, by tying magic charms on their wrists and furnishing them with magic veils and selling them indulgences. They refuse to even offer help unless they get a profit from it. For the sake of a few paltry handfuls of barley or a piece of bread will you turn away my people from me? You have led those to death who should not die! And you have promised life to those who should not live, by lying to my people—and how they love it!

L. God's Threat to the Idolatrous Elders (Chap. 14)

14:1–11 When **some of the elders of Israel**—idolaters at heart—visited Ezekiel to get counsel from the Lord, **the LORD** announced that He would

answer idolaters directly, not through a **prophet**. **If a prophet** did answer the idolaters, he would be deceived and would be punished together with the inquirers.

14:12–20 Even if **three** righteous **men** like **Noah, Daniel, and Job** should be **in** the **land**, God would not hearken but would send **famine, wild beasts, the sword**, and **pestilence** on the **land**. Daniel was living at the court of Nebuchadnezzar when Ezekiel wrote, and yet he was reckoned with God's righteous men of old. It is not true that there cannot be heroes and heroines of the faith today as there have been in former times. Will you be one of them?

14:21–23 **If** He would severely judge any **land, how much more . . . Jerusalem**, where His temple was located. But **a remnant** would be saved to testify that **the LORD** was justified in doing what He did.

Judah's guilt was too great to be pardoned, even through the intercession of Noah, Daniel, and Job. What about *our* society with its crime, violence, abortion, immorality, idolatry, drugs, and secular humanism?

M. The Parable of the Fruitless Vine (Chap. 15)

A **vine** is good only for bearing fruit; it is not good for making furniture or even **a** little **peg**. If it has been charred in a **fire**, it is even more useless. In one sense, the **vine** is the people **of Jerusalem** (v. 6). Failing to bear fruit for God, they were charred by the **fire** of the Babylonian invasion. But in a wider sense the vine represents the entire nation, including both Israel and Judah (v. 4). The northern end of the **branch** was charred by the Assyrians. The southern end was charred by the Egyptians. And now the middle, i.e., **Jerusalem**, would be charred by the Babylonians (see 2 Kgs. 25:9). The second **fire** of verse 7 pictures the captivity of those who escaped. God has determined to **make the land desolate** (v. 8).

As believers we have high privileges, but also the responsibility to produce fruit for God's glory. If we don't glorify Him with our life, our existence is vain and useless. It is like the vine without fruit, and our testimony will be destroyed (cf. John 15:6). As branches in Christ, the True Vine, our chief function is to bear fruit for God. Primarily that means the development of Christian character as seen in the fruit of the Spirit.

N. The Parable of Jerusalem's Marriage (Chap. 16)

16:1–7 **The LORD** here traces the history of **Jerusalem**, as a type of the people. It began as a foundling child, unwashed and unwanted. The Lord had pity on her and cared for her lovingly, and she **grew, matured, and became very beautiful**.

16:8–22 When she came to young womanhood, Jehovah (NKJV, LORD) betrothed Himself to her, purified her for marriage, lavished kindnesses upon her, and **adorned** her. But because she **trusted in** her **own beauty**, she turned from Him to idols, becoming a **harlot . . . to everyone who passed by**.

16:23–34 Instead of trusting in the Lord, she played the prostitute to such Gentiles as **the Egyptians, the Assyrians**, and the traders of **Chaldea**. As someone has said, "She outheathened the heathen." She was unlike the usual **harlot** in that *she* **hired** others to sin with her! Who would do something like that? Is it possible that the harlot will pay the man? That she will give her precious possessions away? And yet many who say they follow the Lord, give up their precious rewards and inheritance above, spend their money and time on worldly pleasures instead of laying up treaures in heaven. They compromise with the world and lose eternal reward and blessing. This is called spiritual adultery, and whoever is engaged in it pays a high price.

16:35–43 The judgment on her **filthiness** was that she would be destroyed by the Gentile nations which she solicited as **lovers** for hire. Those who turn from God like an unfaithful lover and make compromises with the world will be destroyed by the world they wanted to befriend. This is a solemn warning to us (cf. Jas. 4:4–10).

16:44–52 The abominations committed by Jerusalem (Judah) were worse than those of her heathen predecessors, the Hittites, Amorites, **Samaria**, or **Sodom**. Sexual perversion was only *one* of Sodom's sins. The **iniquity of Sodom** also included **fullness of food and abundance of idleness**. This reads only too much like a description of modern Christendom! Feinberg comments:

> Notice how pride was singled out as the root of Sodom's sin when her abominations were traced to their source. God had blessed her abun dantly with fullness of bread (Gen. 13:10), but she monopolized these blessings for her own pleasures and basked in prosperous ease. Provision for her own needs made her insensible to the needs of others; she had no social conscience. Then she committed the abominations and enormities which are linked inseparably with her name. God took her away with a final blow when He saw it (Gen. 18:21).[17]

16:53–58 In grace, God will restore **Sodom** and **Samaria** and Jerusalem in a day yet future. Verse 53 describes the restoration of cities but in no way suggests the eventual salvation of the wicked dead.

16:59–63 He **will establish an everlasting covenant with** His people, and Judah will **be ashamed** that she ever forsook the Lord for idols. This is an unconditional covenant of blessing with the patriarchs which the Lord will fulfill in the future.

John Newton was right when he wrote that the bright glories of God's grace above His other wonders shine.

O. The Parable of the Two Eagles (Chap. 17)

17:1–6 The Lord told Ezekiel to **pose a riddle to the house of Israel. A great eagle came to Lebanon**, broke **off the topmost . . . twig** from a **cedar** tree, **and carried it to a** foreign **land.** It also **took . . . the seed of the land and planted it in . . . fertile** soil. There **it grew** into **a spreading vine**.

17:7–10 Then the **vine** began to grow **toward . . . another great eagle**, but it no longer thrived.

17:11–21 The Lord Himself gives the interpretation of the allegory. The first eagle was Nebuchadnezzar, **king of Babylon** (v. 12). He carried off Jehoiachin, **king** of Judah (the topmost twig), from **Jerusalem** (Lebanon) into **Babylon** (land of traffic), and Babylon (city of merchants). He also took Zedekiah, **the king's offspring**, and set him up as his vassal king in Judah (v. 13). For a while, Zedekiah, a **low** spreading vine, flourished in the homeland, but then he turned **to** the king of **Egypt** (another great eagle) for deliverance from Babylon. When Zedekiah broke **the covenant** with Nebuchadnezzar (2 Chron. 36:13), it was the same as if **he broke** it with God (v. 19). As a result, Zedekiah would be carried into **Babylon** and

die there; **Pharaoh**-Hophra would not be able to help him (vv. 16–21).

17:22–24 In these verses the coming of the Messiah (the **tender . . . twig**) is promised; He would be descended from the house of David. He would be a fruitful **tree** and afford safety to the people (v. 23). The God of hope does not leave them hopeless, but directs their eyes towards the Messiah. We also should have the future in view and comfort each other with these truths. Carl F. Keil elaborates:

> The cedar, . . . as rising above the other trees, is the royal house of David, and the tender shoot which Jehovah breaks off and plants is not the Messianic kingdom or sovereignty, . . . but the Messiah Himself. . . . The high mountain, described in ver. 23 as the high mountain of Israel, is Zion, regarded as the seat and centre of the kingdom of God, which is to be exalted by the Messiah above all the mountains of the earth (Isa. ii. 2, etc.). The twig planted by the Lord will grow there into a glorious cedar, under which all the birds will dwell. The Messiah grows into a cedar in the kingdom founded by Him, in which all the inhabitants of the earth will find both food (from the fruits of the tree) and protection (under its shadow).[18]

Politics always proves to be a washout. Only the return of Christ offers any hope to this sin-drugged world.

P. The Repudiation of the Parable of the Sour Grapes (Chap. 18)

18:1–4 The people of Judah had a **proverb** which blamed their sins on the failure of their ancestors:

> **"The fathers have eaten sour grapes,**
> **And the children's teeth are set on edge."**

God refutes the proverb, stating that individuals are held responsible for their own sins.

18:5–24 He then gives several examples of His principles of judgment:

1. **A man** who shuns sin and lives righteously **shall surely live** (vv. 5–9).
2. A righteous man's wicked **son . . . shall surely die** (vv. 10–13). The Jews during the captivity as well as in the Lord Jesus' time prided themselves on having Abraham as their father (Luke 3:8; John 8:39). God points out that it will do no good to have a righteous father, if their own life is wicked. We also have the tendency to rely on the spirituality of others. But the righteous and holy life of our fathers and godly leaders must become a reality in our own lives.
3. An unrighteous man's righteous **son . . . shall surely live** (vv. 14–17), but the unrighteous **father . . . shall die for his iniquities** (v. 18).
4. **A wicked man** who repents and **turns from his sins** will **live** (vv. 21–23).
5. **A righteous man** who **turns away from his righteousness and commits iniquity . . . shall die** (v. 24).

There is no contradiction between verse 20 and Exodus 20:5. It is true, as taught in Exodus, that children are generally involved in the consequences of their parents' misdeeds. It is also true, as taught here, that each one is personally responsible for his or her actions.

In verse 20, the punishment is *temporal*, not eternal. It is *physical* death because of sin now. The principles stated in verses 5–24 are not dealing with *eternal* life; otherwise we would be forced to conclude that salvation is by works (vv. 5–9) and that the righteous may eventually be lost, two doctrines clearly refuted by our Lord in the NT (e.g., Eph. 2:8, 9; John 10:28).

18:25–32 The people continued to accuse God of injustice, but He shows that there is no injustice because even **a wicked man** can be saved by turning from his sins, and that is what the Lord wants them to do.

When God forgives, He forgets (v. 22). This does not indicate a poor memory but the perfect satisfaction of His justice through the atoning work of Christ. For the believer the case is closed.

Q. Lamentation for the Last Kings of Judah (Chap. 19)

19:1–9 This is a lament for the last kings of Judah. Not all are agreed as to the identity of the kings, but probably they are Jehoahaz, Jehoiachin, and Zedekiah. Judah is the **lioness**. The other nations are **the lions**, and their rulers are **the young lions** (v. 2). The whelp who **became a young lion** (v. 3) is perhaps Jehoahaz, who was captured and taken off **to . . . Egypt** (v. 4). The other whelp (v. 5) is possibly Jehoiachin. Judah was no different than all the other nations, a lioness **among the lions**. The leaders of **the nations** are fierce and selfish, "but among you it shall not be so." The Lord expects His people to be different. If not, they are inviting His judgment.

19:10–14 **"Your mother"** (v. 10) is Judah or Jerusalem, a **vine in** their **bloodline** that was **fruitful and full of branches**. At one time, she had strong kings (**strong branches**), but she would be destroyed by Babylon (**the east wind**), and the people carried into captivity (**the wilderness**, vv. 11–13). Zedekiah, the **fire** of verse 14, is regarded as a usurper and the ruin of his people.

Israel had wanted a king like the other nations. Here Ezekiel lowers the curtain on the last act of their monarchy. God wants His people to be different from the world, to be a holy people for Himself, and to acknowledge *Him* as King.

R. Vindication of God's Dealings with Israel (20:1–32)

1. Idolatry in Egypt (20:1–9)

When **the elders . . . came** to Ezekiel **to inquire of the Lord**, He refused to **be inquired of by** them. Instead He recounted their repeated rebellions against Him. The elders were quite conservative and orthodox; they did inquire of the Lord, but their hearts were far from Him. Idols keep us from getting God's answers to our questions. When God recounts our sins and shows us His grace by leading us to repentance, many of us get bored: "We've heard that so often." "The Bible is just full of do's and don'ts." "Is there nothing else but judgment in it?" Instead of reacting properly to God's Word, we are in danger of staying lukewarm.

In spite of their idolatry **in the land of Egypt** (vv. 4–8a), God did not punish them there so that **the Gentiles** would not mock (vv. 8b–9).

2. Defiling God's Sabbaths (20:10–17)

Israel profaned God's **Sabbaths . . . in the wilderness** (vv. 10–13a). Again the Lord restrained His wrath and **spared them from destruction** lest the heathen should laugh (vv. 13b–17).

3. *Rebellion in the Wilderness (20:18–26)*

The rebellion of the **children** of the original generation **in the wilderness** is recalled (vv. 18–21a); again God held back His **anger against them** (vv. 21b–26).

4. *Idolatry (20:27–32)*

Their terrible idolatry in **the land** of promise even included making their **sons pass through the fire**, that is, offering them as human **sacrifices**.

S. God's Promise of Eventual Restoration (20:33–44)

20:33–38 In spite of their efforts, God would **never** let them become *permanently* **like the Gentiles . . . serving wood and stone** (v. 32). He would regather them **from the peoples** of captivity, set them in judgment before Him, receive the righteous (v. 37), and **purge** the **rebels from among them** (v. 38).

20:39–44 When the nation is restored to the land **of Israel**, they will no longer worship **idols**, but they will worship **the LORD** in holiness (vv. 39–44).

The apostle John's admonition is timeless: "Little children, keep yourselves from idols."

T. Pictures of the Imminent Invasion (20:45—21:32)

1. *The Sign of the Forest Fire (20:45–49)*

Verse 45 marks the beginning of chapter 21 in the Hebrew Bible, a more logical place to break, as our outline indicates. In verses 45–49, we have a prophecy **against the South** (Heb. *Negev*, part of Judah); it will be destroyed by the **forest . . . fire** (Babylonian invasion).

2. *The Sign of the Drawn Sword (21:1–17)*

21:1–7 God expresses His determination to lay waste Judah and **Jerusalem** with His sharpened **sword**. Ezekiel's sighing was to warn the people of the fearfulness of God's **coming** judgment.

21:8–17 The **sword** of Babylon is prepared for the **slaughter** (vv. 8–13) and will satisfy the **fury** of Jehovah (vv. 14–17). Verses 10c and 13 are especially difficult. The thought may be this: It was no time for Judah to **make mirth**. They had despised all previous weapons of affliction, which are spoken of in the NKJV as having been made of **wood**. Now they would experience a **sword** made of steel, and there was the possibility that **the scepter** that despises, i.e., Judah, would be no more.

3. *The Sign of the Fork in the Road (21:18–32)*

21:18–24 Next, **the king of Babylon** is seen marching toward the **land**. He comes to a **fork** in **the road**: One branch leads **to . . . Jerusalem**, and the other **to Rabbah** (capital of Ammon). Which city shall he attack first? He uses three means of divination: (1) He marks an arrow **for Jerusalem** and one for Rabbah; (2) **He consults** his household gods; (3) **He looks** into **the liver** of some slaughtered animal. The decision? Attack **Jerusalem** *first!*

21:25–27 Zedekiah is the **profane, wicked prince** of verse 25. His kingship is **overthrown** and he will be the last king over God's people **until** the Messiah comes, **whose right it is** to reign. Matthew Henry comments:

> There *shall be no more* kings of the house of David after Zedekiah, till Christ comes, *whose right the kingdom is*, who is that seed of David in

> whom the promise was to have its full accomplishment, and *I will give it to him*. He shall have *the throne of his father David*, Luke i. 32. . . . And having the right, he shall in due time have the possession: *I will give it to him;* and there shall be a general overturning of all rather than he shall come short of his right, and a certain overturning of all the opposition that stands in his way to make room for him, Dan. ii. 45; 1 Cor. xv. 25. This is mentioned here for the comfort of those who feared that the promise made in David would fail for evermore. "No," says God, "that promise is sure, for the Messiah's kingdom shall last for ever."[19]

21:28–32 The Ammonites will next be attacked by the king of Babylon; they will be utterly destroyed.

History and current events are full of instances of God overturning human governments until Christ comes, whose right it is to reign.

U. Three Oracles on Jerusalem's Defilement (Chap. 22)

22:1–12 Here is presented a catalog of the sins of Jerusalem—**bloodshed** (v. 9) (perhaps meaning human sacrifices in this context) and idolatry (vv. 3, 4); murder (v. 6); contempt of parents, oppression of strangers, orphans and widows (v. 7); desecrating the temple and breaking the **Sabbaths** (v. 8); **slander**, idolatry and **lewdness** (v. 9); immorality (v. 10); adultery, incest (v. 11); bribery, **usury**, **extortion**, and forgetfulness of **the Lord God** (v. 12).

22:13–22 For these sins of **dishonest profit** and **bloodshed**, the people would be scattered **among the nations** (vv. 13–16). Jerusalem would be like a refiner's pot, in which the people, like worthless **dross**, would **be melted** (vv. 17–22).

22:23, 24 The Lord tells Ezekiel to **say to** the land that she is in sad shape. Taylor explains what this means for the land:

> The land is described in this oracle as deprived of the blessings of rain. Most commentators prefer to follow LXX in verse 24, which translates not "cleansed" but "rained upon": thus, "a land without rain and without shower."[20]

22:25–31 All classes of society were guilty before the Lord—rulers (v. 25) [**"prophets"** in the KJV and NKJV reads "princes" in the Septuagint];[21] **priests** (v. 26); magistrates (v. 27); **prophets** (v. 28); **people** (v. 29). Not **a** righteous **man** could be found, not a reformer nor an intercessor to **stand** for God (vv. 30, 31).

God is not looking for new methods or programs; God is always looking for someone to stand in the gap. One person can make a difference.

V. The Parable of the Two Harlot Sisters (Chap. 23)

1. Oholah (23:1–10)

23:1–4 This is the parable of **two** harlot sisters, **Oholah the elder** and **Oholibah her sister**. **Oholah** was **Samaria**, and **Oholibah** was **Jerusalem**.

23:5–10 Oholah means *[she has] her own tent*. Samaria had set up her own center of worship. God's temple was in Jerusalem.[22] **Oholah played the harlot** to the good-looking and macho **horsemen** of Assyria; therefore, she was abandoned to **her lovers** by God, and **they uncovered her nakedness** and **slew her with the sword**.

2. Oholibah (23:11–21)

Oholibah (my tent is in her) went even further in her idolatrous **harlotry**

and immorality. First **she lusted** after the **Assyrians**, just as Israel had done (vv. 12, 13). Then she doted on the **images** of the **men** of Babylon **portrayed in vermilion. She lusted for them and sent messengers to them**, inviting them to her land (2 Kgs. 16:7). Recalling her youthful sins **in the land of Egypt**, she also **multiplied her harlotry** and gave herself over to the Babylonians to commit terrible **immorality**.

3. The Invasion of the Babylonians (23:22–35)

As a result, God would destroy **Oholibah** by her Babylonian **lovers**. Those **desirable young men** she lusted after would treat her **hatefully**. She tried to find satisfaction in the fleshly world, apart from God. Now her sins must be judged. Verses 33 and 34 describe the symptoms of depression and despair, which we find all over today. Only if we drink of God's living water, will we never thirst again.

4. The Judgment of Oholah and Oholibah (23:36–49)

Both sisters were guilty of the same sins: **adultery** (literal and spiritual), murder, offering human sacrifices (v. 37); desecration of the temple, Sabbath-breaking (v. 38); mixing idolatry with worship of God (v. 39); committing spiritual adultery with foreign nations (vv. 40–44). **Righteous men** (nations chosen by God) would **repay** the sisters **for** their **lewdness** with well-deserved destruction (vv. 45–49).

Judah's religion was syncretistic, that is, it combined the worship of Jehovah with idolatry and paganism. Much of modern Christendom, sad to say, combines elements of the Bible with Judaism, paganism, eastern religion, humanism, and psychology.

W. The Parable of the Boiling Pot (24:1–14)

On **the day** the **siege** of **Jerusalem** began, Ezekiel spoke the **parable** of the boiling **pot**. The pot was Jerusalem; the **pieces of meat** were the people. The pot was about to **boil**. It had **scum**, or rust, **in it**—the **lewdness** of idolatry. After the pot was thoroughly emptied, it would be burned to remove the scum. Thus would **the Lord** seek to purge His people of idolatry.

X. The Sign of the Death of Ezekiel's Wife (24:15–27)

24:15–18 Ezekiel was warned that his wife, **the desire of** his **eyes**, would die. She **died** on the **evening** of that day, and, contrary to all normal reactions, he was commanded not to **mourn**.

24:19–24 When **the people** asked the meaning of his strange behavior, he told them that when **the desire of** *their* **eyes** (the temple) would be destroyed and their **sons and daughters** would be killed, they were not to **mourn**.

One purpose of fulfilled prophecy is to let the world **know** who is **the Lord God** (v. 24).

24:25–27 Ezekiel was not to utter any more prophecies to Judah until a fugitive brought him the news that **their stronghold** had fallen. That event is recorded in 33:21, 22. The intervening chapters, 25—32, are prophecies to *Gentile* nations, not to Judah.

III. PROPHECIES AGAINST SEVEN GENTILE NATIONS (Chaps. 25—32)

In these chapters we read of God's judgment on seven heathen nations. These nations are judged for various forms of rebellion against God. They had contact with God's people, knew about Him, but were unwilling to turn to Him. Let us observe this closely, for God's ways always reveal His thoughts, whether in judgment or in grace.

A. Prophecy against Ammon (25:1–7)

The first nation upon which judgment is pronounced is Ammon. Because **the Ammonites rejoiced** at the fall of God's **sanctuary**, **Israel** and **Judah**, and the Babylonian captivity, they would be destroyed by the Babylonians (**men of the East**). **Rabbah** would become a **stable for camels and Ammon a resting place for flocks**.

B. Prophecy against Moab (25:8–11)

The second nation is **Moab**, which shared with **Seir** a hostile attitude toward **Judah**. The land of Moab would be opened to the Babylonians and would suffer the same fate as Ammon. The **territory** would be cleared of its **cities**, and Moab would know that God is **the Lord**.

C. Prophecy against Edom (25:12–14)

The third nation is **Edom**. Because it took **vengeance** against the **house of Judah**, **the Lord God** said, it would know *His* **vengeance**.

D. Prophecy against Philistia (25:15–17)

The Philistines are the fourth people. Their never-ending **hatred** of Judah would bring upon them **the vengeance of the Lord**.

Just as these nations would learn that if you touch God's people, you touch Him, so those who engage in "Christian-bashing" today will one day learn that believers are the apple of God's eye. This is even true when God's people fall into sin and are judged for it. We should beware of all malicious joy, gloating, or revengeful thoughts. Rather, like Ezekiel, we should mourn, intercede, and confess the sins of other believers as our own.

E. Prophecy against Tyre (26:1—28:19)

1. The Destruction of Tyre (Chap. 26)

26:1, 2 The fifth object of God's judgment is the seacoast city of **Tyre**. Its punishment extends from 26:1 to 28:19. Super-commercial Tyre rejoiced when it heard that its rival city, **Jerusalem**, had fallen, thinking that it would now get *all* the business! Jerusalem had controlled all the overland trade routes, and its fall meant freer traffic for Tyre with Egypt and other southern countries.

26:3–11 God would use **many nations to** chastise this city—state. The predictions of verses 4–6 have been literally fulfilled. First **Nebuchadnezzar** king of **Babylon, king of kings,**[23] marched **against Tyre from the north** and attacked it (vv. 7–11). The siege was extremely long—about 587 B.C.—574 B.C. Feinberg gives a vivid picture of the type of siege this renowned city endured:

> The forts, the mound and the buckler were all familiar features. The buckler or the testudo or roof of shields was used to protect against missiles thrown from the walls. The battering engines were the battering rams employed to breach the walls. The axes, literally, swords, were used in a figurative manner for all the weapons of warfare. Some have considered the first part of verse 10 a hyperbole, but it is not beyond the range of literal fulfillment. Because of the multitude of the enemy's cavalry, they would cover the city with dust upon entering, at the same time shaking the walls with the noise of the horsemen and chariots. Every street was to be commandeered and the

people slain with the sword. The pillars spoken of were actually obelisks, and were probably those mentioned by the historian Herodotus as erected in the temple of Heracles at Tyre. One was of gold and the other of emerald, which shone brilliantly at night, and were dedicated to Melkarth, god of Tyre (cf. I Kings 7:15). These impressive pillars would be demolished by the invader.[24]

26:12–14 But the people fled with their possessions to an offshore island, also called Tyre. They remained secure there for 250 years. Then Alexander the Great built a causeway to the island by scraping clean the original city and throwing the rubble into the sea. This action by Alexander's soldiers (332 B.C.) is described in this paragraph. Over a hundred years ago a traveler described the ruins of Tyre as being exactly as predicted:

> The island, as such, is not more than a mile in length. The part which projects south beyond the isthmus is perhaps a quarter of a mile broad, and is rocky and uneven. It is now unoccupied except by fishermen, as "a place to spread nets upon."[25]

26:15–21 News of the fall of Tyre would cause consternation among other nations. All her beauty which they had so admired would be destroyed. But God **shall establish** an everlasting **glory in the land of the living,** which is a part of the same kingdom we belong to.

Tyre has never been rebuilt—a fulfillment of verse 21. In his book, *Science Speaks,* Peter Stoner says that this entire prophecy concerning Tyre, considering all the details, using the principle of probability, had a one-in-four hundred million chance of fulfillment.[26]

2. *The Dirge over Tyre (Chap. 27)*

27:1–9 **Tyre** is likened to a beautiful ship, luxurious in its construction, with materials in it from all over the world. Tyre was not a military force which conquered the world; the Tyrians were merchants. All kinds of **merchandise** and knowledge were exchanged for the sake of personal gain. This is commonly accepted, but all beauty and knowledge apart from the Lord Jesus is empty. If you gain the whole world, and lose your own soul, what will you give for your soul?

27:10–36 Tyre's army, including soldiers from **Persia, Lydia, and Libya,** is described in verses 10 and 11. The vastness of its commerce in **luxury goods** is seen in verses 12–27a. But it was to be wrecked by an **east wind** (the Babylonians, vv. 26b, 27). The other nations would be convulsed by the fall of the city (vv. 28–36).

3. *The Downfall of the Prince of Tyre (28:1–19)*

28:1–10 The pride, **wisdom,** and wealth of **the prince of Tyre** are described in verses 1–6, and then his destruction by the Babylonians (vv. 7–10). No doubt this prince foreshadows the Antichrist.

28:11–19 In verse 11 there is a change from the prince of Tyre to **the king of Tyre.** The latter is the spirit that animated the prince. The king of Tyre was noted for his **beauty,** but because of his pride he was destroyed.

The description of the **king of Tyre** as **the seal of perfection, full of wisdom and perfect in beauty,** as having been **in Eden, the garden of God,** as having **every precious stone as a covering,** as being **the anointed cherub,** and as having been **on the holy mountain of God,** taken together seem too impressive for *any* great ruler, even allowing for great use of hyperbole, or literary exaggeration.

For this reason many Bible students see in verses 11–19 a description of Satan and of his fall from heaven. Feinberg explains:

> Ezekiel . . . appeared to have the situation of his day in mind with his attention riveted upon the ruler of Tyre, the embodiment of the people's pride and godlessness. But as he viewed the thoughts and ways of that monarch, he clearly discerned behind him the motivating force and personality who was impelling him in his opposition to God. In short, he saw the work and activity of Satan, whom the king of Tyre was emulating in so many ways. Recall the incident in Matthew 16:21–23 where Peter was rebuked by our Lord Jesus. No sterner words were spoken to anyone in Christ's earthly ministry. But He did not mean that Peter had somehow become Satan himself; He was indicating that the motivation behind Peter's opposition to His going to Calvary was none other than the prince of the demons. This appears to be a similar situation. Some liberal expositors admit that it would appear that Ezekiel had in mind some spirit or genius of Tyre comparable to the angelic powers and princes in the book of Daniel who are entrusted with the affairs of nations.[27]

If pride is deadly enough to destroy a most powerful and wise being, how much more should we mortals take heed not to walk independently of the Lord!

F. Prophecy against Sidon (28:20–26)

28:20–23 The sixth object of God's judgment is **Sidon**. It was a seacoast city near Tyre. God warned that it would be subjected to **pestilence** and **sword**, but He did not say it would be destroyed forever. Sidon still stands today as a town in Lebanon, though biblical Tyre has been wiped out completely (see 26:21).

28:24–26 These verses predict the restoration of Israel when **the Lord GOD** sets up His kingdom on the earth.

G. Prophecy against Egypt (Chaps. 29—32)

The seventh and last nation in this catalog of judgments is Egypt (Chaps. 29—32). These seem to be the most unsparing judgments of all. Without the River Nile, Egypt would be dead, and one would expect its people to cherish life. But no, Egypt is the land of death. Its most famous book is the *Book of the Dead*. Its greatest monuments are the pyramids, which are huge *tombs*. Its kings built small palaces but huge *sepulchers*, and they were embalmed to enjoy their time in the *grave!* The heart of the Egyptian is quite unimpressed facing death, full of self-assertion. Therefore judgment had to come over Egypt, which nation in the Bible is a picture of the world, especially as being without God.

1. General Threat against Pharaoh and His People (Chap. 29)

29:1–12 In verses 1–5, **Pharaoh** is compared to a crocodile in the great **River** Nile. This crocodile is proud, but short-sighted. **The fish** are the people of Egypt. All are to be punished by God. In looking to Egypt for help, Israel had **leaned on** a broken **reed** (vv. 6–9a). Egypt receives the most severe judgment because it was unreliable and untrustworthy. If we as believers have this character flaw, with the Lord's help we need to change. He is in the character-changing business.

Because of Pharaoh's pride, **the land of Egypt** would be **desolate** for **forty years** (vv. 9b–12).

29:13–21 Then God would **gather** the people, but **Egypt** would never be a great **kingdom** again, and **Israel** would **no longer** look to it for help (vv. 13–16). **Nebuchadnezzar** had worked hard besieging **Tyre,** but **received** no **wages** for it (because the people fled to the island fortress with their possessions). Therefore God would **give** him **Egypt** as his **wages** (vv. 17–20). **In** the **day** that Nebuchadnezzar received Egypt as his pay, God caused **the horn of the house of Israel to** bud **forth** (a revival of power of which we have no other mention) and Ezekiel declared God's message to the people (v. 21).

2. *Lamentation over the Fall of Egypt (30:1–19)*

30:1–12 Egypt and **all** her allies—**Ethiopia, Libya,** and **Lydia**—would **fall . . . by the sword** of the Babylonians (vv. 1–9). **Nebuchadnezzar king of Babylon** is named as the one who would **destroy the land** (vv. 10–12).

30:13–19 The leading cities of Egypt are listed as doomed to destruction with their **idols** and **images: Noph** (Memphis), **Pathros** (perhaps in the upper southern part of Egypt), **Zoan** (Tanis), **No** (Thebes), **Sin** (Pelusium), **Aven** (Heliopolis), **Pi Beseth** (perhaps Bubastis), **Tehaphnehes**[28] (probably the ancient Daphne, vv. 13–19). The prophecy, **"there shall no longer be princes from the land of Egypt"** (v. 13), has been literally fulfilled. No full-blooded Egyptian of the royal family has reigned in Egypt since that time. King Farouk belonged to a dynasty that was founded by an Albanian in the early 1800's. Farouk was the first member of the dynasty to have even a complete mastery of the Arabic language!

3. *The Downfall of Pharaoh (30:20—31:18)*

30:20–26 Here the downfall of Egypt is seen in two stages. **One** of Pharaoh's **arms . . . was broken** figuratively when he was defeated in the battle of Carchemish (605 B.C.). The other **was broken** when the Babylonians invaded Egypt and conquered it.

31:1–9 Whom was **Pharaoh . . . like in** his **greatness**? He was like the king of **Assyria, a** lofty **cedar**. That king grew powerful, so that there was no one else as great as he, a veritable giant tree in whose **shadow all great nations make their home.**

31:10–14 But because his **heart was** lifted up with arrogance, God delivered him over to the Babylonians.

31:15–18 The Assyrian was dashed **down to hell** (Heb., *Sheol*), while other **nations** looked on (vv. 15–17). **The nations . . . were comforted** (v. 16) in the sense that they were gratified to see the humiliation of Assyria, the nation that had formerly despised them. Pharaoh is like the Assyrian in that, although he became great, he too, would be delivered **to the depths of the Pit** (v. 18).

4. *Lamentation over Pharaoh and Egypt (Chap. 32)*

32:1–16 Pharaoh thought himself **a young lion**, but God looked upon him as **a monster**, which He would catch in His **net** and destroy. **The king of Babylon** would bring to nothing the **pomp of Egypt**, and **the land** would be left **desolate** and quiet. The nations lamented with tears. **The Lord** ordered Ezekiel to utter **a lamentation** over **Egypt for all her multitude.**

The Lord Jesus also shed tears for a city of murderers that would not accept Him and come under His protective wings. God cares for His creatures and does not enjoy judging them. O Lord, give us tears of compassion for the lost!

32:17–32 In verses 17–31, we have a view of Sheol (**the Pit**) where **Egypt** is sent. **Assyria is there** (vv. 22, 23) and **Elam** (vv. 24, 25), **Meshech and Tubal** (vv. 26, 27), **Edom** (v. 29), and **the Sidonians** (v. 30). Egypt had been great in this world, but in Sheol she is reduced to the same shame as the other nations (vv. 28, 31, 32). This finishes Ezekiel's oracles against seven nations (and city-states).

IV. ISRAEL'S RESTORATION AND THE PUNISHMENT OF HER FOES (Chaps. 33—39)

From chapter 33 to the end of the book, Ezekiel deals primarily with the restoration of Israel and the rebuilding of the temple.

A. The Prophet Recommissioned as a Watchman (Chap. 33)

33:1–9 In this chapter, Ezekiel is compared to a **watchman**. If he warns **the people** faithfully, but they do not hear, then they will be responsible for their own destruction. If he fails to **warn** the people, and they perish, God **will require** their **blood** at the watchman's **hand**.

God held Ezekiel responsible for **the house of Israel**. The question arises for every believer: For whom will God hold us responsible? To whom shall we witness? Whom shall we warn? Our relatives, fellow workers, neighbors, friends? It is a solemn responsibility, and we do harm to our own soul if we do not fulfill it faithfully.

33:10–20 The people ask in despair: **"How can we then live?"** How many people today have lost all hope and are in depression and despair. The Lord's answer is: Repent! There is hope for the worst sinner, but the only hope is in turning from sin, and not in condoning it. The people complained that God's dealings with them were not just, but He denies this, reminding them that He will pardon a **wicked** man who confesses and forsakes **his sin**; also, He will punish a **righteous man** who turns to **wickedness**.

33:21, 22 Ezekiel's **mouth** was **opened**, and he **was no longer mute** when an escapee **from Jerusalem** came and announced, **"The city has been captured!"** (see 24:27).

33:23–29 These verses apparently refer to the few Jews who were left **in the land of Israel** after the fall of Jerusalem. They argued that if **one** man—**Abraham**—had **inherited the land**, how much more right did such a group as they have to it. But God was interested in quality, not quantity. They were even then committing various forms of idolatry, and **the land** would have to be cleansed from such **abominations**, which testified against them. They were not true (spiritual) descendants of Abraham. Their outward profession would not save them from judgment because God was not interested in mere words, but in life (cf. Jas. 2:14).

33:30–33 The people liked to *listen to* Ezekiel, but they had no intention of *obeying* his **words**! **When** his prophecies were fulfilled, **they** would **know that a prophet** had been in their midst.

We should come to the Word of God with the intention of obeying, and constantly checking our hearts, lest we fail to apply what we hear. The best response to a sermon is not, "That was a fine message," but "God has spoken to me; I must do something."

B. The False Shepherds and the Good Shepherd (Chap. 34)

34:1–6 The shepherds (rulers) were interested in **themselves** and not in the welfare of the **sheep** (the people). They **ruled** harshly, and the **sheep** became **scattered**.

To this day many religious leaders have not learned the lesson of *serving* the sheep. They confuse their "service" with a means of *gain*. We can praise God for leaders who serve eagerly, as examples to the flock.

The Lord allowed **the flock** to be **scattered** first in order to prevent further damage (v. 10). Yates describes the situation well:

> A heart-rending picture is painted of the unfaithful preachers of Ezekiel's day. The flock are scattered, untended and hungry while selfish shepherds pamper themselves and loll in idleness and luxury without any thought of their responsibility. They are careful to look out for their own food and clothing and comfort but no one else is to be considered for a minute.[29]

34:7–10 Therefore God is determined to rescue His **sheep** from these false **shepherds**. But all the time He has blessing in mind, and so He will gather the sheep and take care of individual needs. The greatest blessing will be the relation between the Lord and His sheep, an intimate fellowship between God and man.

34:11–16 He will be their Shepherd and **will . . . gather them to** the **land** and rule over them (during the Millennium). Evangelist D. L. Moody nicely outlines God's ministry to His sheep:

> Notice the "I will's" of the Lord God on behalf of his sheep.
> The Shepherd and the sheep:—
> v. 11. I will search them and seek them out.
> v. 12. I will deliver them.
> v. 13. I will bring them out.
> v. 13. I will gather them together.
> v. 13. I will bring them in.
> v. 14. I will feed them.
> v. 15. I will cause them to lie down.
> v. 16. I will bind up the broken.
> v. 16. I will strengthen the sick.
>
> There are a good many lean sheep in God's fold, but none in his pasture.[30]

Some people, including a certain type of preacher, try to suggest that the God of the OT is a harsh and unloving Deity, in contrast to God as He is presented in the NT.[31] John Taylor beautifully ties together the revelations of God as Shepherd in both Testaments for us:

> The picture of the shepherd searching out the wanderer, in verse 12, is a remarkable foreshadowing of the parable of the lost sheep (Lk. 15:4ff.), which our Lord doubtless based on this passage in Ezekiel. It illustrates as clearly as anything can do the tender, loving qualities of the God of the Old Testament, and strikes a deathblow at those who try to drive a wedge between Yahweh, God of Israel, and the God and Father of our Lord Jesus Christ. Nor is it the only passage that speaks of the tender shepherd (*cf.* Pss. 78:52f.; 79:13; 80:1; Is. 40:11; 49:9f.; Je. 31:10).[32]

34:17–24 The Lord GOD will also save His true **sheep** from the false shepherds, which are selfish and cruel. **"My servant David"** in verses 23 and 24 refers to the Lord Jesus, who is descended from David. The Hebrew Christian, David Baron, explains:

> Even the Jews explained the name "David" in these passages as applying to the Messiah—the great Son of David in whom all the promises to the Davidic house are centered. Thus Kimchi, in his comment on Ezekiel

> 34:23, says: "My servant David—that is, the Messiah who shall spring from his seed in the time of salvation": and in the 24th verse of chapter 37 he observes: "The King Messiah—His name shall be called David because He shall be of the seed of David." And so practically all the Jewish commentators.[33]

34:25–31 The security and prosperity of God's **flock** during the future reign of Christ are described here. Under **a covenant of peace** (v. 25) **there shall be showers of blessing** (v. 26) and **a garden of renown** (v. 29).

The *ideal* form of government is a beneficent, absolute monarchy with Christ as King.

C. The Doom of Edom (Chap. 35)

35:1–7 Mount Seir is **Edom**. That country is here denounced by the Lord because of its perpetual **hatred** of the Jews, its rejoicing when Jerusalem fell, its cruelty to the fugitives, and its plan to seize the land **of Israel**. Edom wanted *the blessing*, but they did not want *the Lord*. Apart from the Lord Jesus we cannot be blessed, and this still holds true today. Edom is doomed to perpetual desolation, with all trade cut off (v. 7).

35:8–15 Edom blasphemed the Jews and treated them as enemies. But the Lord still identified Himself with His people. They were under discipline, but not rejected. Edom failed to notice the difference.

As Edom **rejoiced** over the desolation **of Israel**, so **the whole earth will rejoice** over Edom's destruction.

God is displeased when believers secretly rejoice over the downfall of enemies of the faith. Love that is real does not feel even a quiet satisfaction when others are hurt, whether friends or foes.

D. The Restoration of the Land and the People (Chap. 36)

Chapter 36 has been called "the Gospel according to Ezekiel," largely because of verses 25–30.

36:1–7 The nations that seized **the land of Israel** and scorned God's people, especially the nation of **Edom**, would be punished by Jehovah.

36:8–15 Israel's **cities** and country places would be **inhabited**, the land would be more fertile and prosperous than ever, and the other **nations** would no longer taunt Israel.

36:16–21 Not only would the **land** be restored, but the people would be restored to the land. The reasons for their exile were bloodshed and idolatry; they caused the **name** of God to be **profaned among the nations wherever they went**.

36:22, 23 Paul quotes verse 22 in Romans 2:24 in his indictment of Jewish inconsistencies in relation to the Gentiles and the law. In order to vindicate His own **name**, and not for Israel's **sake**, God would restore the people to their homeland.

36:24–29a Verses 24–29 describe Israel's spiritual regeneration. God would cleanse them, **give** them **a new heart** and **a new spirit** (the new birth), and save them **from . . . uncleanness**. Keil comments on this important passage:

> Cleansing from sins, which corresponds to justification, and is not to be confounded with sanctification . . . , is followed by renewal with the Holy Spirit, which takes away the old heart of stone and puts within a new heart of flesh, so that the man can fulfill the commandments of God, and walk in newness of life.[34]

When our Lord marveled at Nicodemus's ignorance of the new birth, this passage in Ezekiel is surely one of the main texts that He expected him, as a teacher in Israel, to know (John 3:10).

36:29b, 30 Crops of **grain** and **fruit** would be increased, and they would never suffer **famine** again. All this the Lord would do, not because they deserved it, but for the honor of His Name.

36:31–38 **The** surrounding **nations** will **know that** God has repopulated and replanted the land. **Men** will then be as plentiful as the **flocks** of animals in **Jerusalem on its feast days**. These prophecies had a partial fulfillment when the Jews returned to the land from Babylon, but the complete fulfillment awaits the future reign of Christ.

Modern Israel achieved statehood in 1948. Jews are even now trickling back to the land in unbelief. It must soon be time for the Lord to come.

E. The Vision of the Valley of Dry Bones (37:1–14)

37:1–8 In the vision of verses 1 and 2, Ezekiel saw the **dry . . . bones** of Israel and Judah in a **valley**. He was ordered to **prophesy to** the **bones** that they would come to life. Yates makes an application to our own need of the breath of life today:

> With weirdness, realism and dramatic force the prophet presents the heartening news that Israel may hope to live. A revival is possible! Even dry bones, without sinew and flesh and blood, can live. The coming of God's Spirit brings life. The same thrilling truth is still needed in a world that has dry bones everywhere. What we need is to have the Holy Spirit come with His quickening power that a genuine revival may sweep the earth. (Cf. also Gen. 2:7; Rev. 11:11.)[35]

The first time he spoke the Word of God, **the sinews, flesh . . . and . . . skin came upon** the bones.

37:9–14 The next time he prophesied **to the** wind or **breath**, and the **breath came into** the bodies. This pictured the national restoration **of Israel** (vv. 11–14), first the restoration of a people spiritually dead, and then their regeneration.

We should notice the parallel in our own regeneration. There must be the word of the Lord (v. 4) and the Spirit (breath) of God (v. 9).

F. The Reunification of Israel and Judah (37:15–28)

37:15–23 Ezekiel was next commanded to **take** two sticks, one representing **Judah** and the other Israel (**Joseph** or **Ephraim**). By holding them end to end, he joined **them . . . into one stick**. This meant that the **two kingdoms**, torn apart in the days of Rehoboam, would be reunited. **One king** (the Messiah) would reign **over them**, and they would be saved, cleansed, and restored.

37:24–28 **David** (here the Lord Jesus) would be the **king**, and the people would obey Him implicitly. God would make an **everlasting covenant . . . of peace** with them, and the temple would be set **in their midst**. This is still future.

This and the following chapter foretell the destruction of Israel's future enemies. Gog is the leader of the foes, and Magog is his land. Bible students do not agree on the identity of Gog. Apparently the time of the events described here is after Israel will return to the land but before the Millennium. The Gog and Magog described in Revelation 20:8, however, belong to the period *after* the Millennium.

G. The Destruction of Israel's Future Enemies (Chaps. 38, 39)

38:1–16 God will lure **Gog** and his allies to muster their **troops** (vv. 1–6). Gog is said to be the **prince of Rosh,**[36] **Meshech, and Tubal**, which some have taken to be the ancient names from which come Russia, Moscow, and Tobolsk. This is a fascinating possibility, but by no means proven. They will move south against the land **of Israel**. The Jews will be **dwelling** securely in **unwalled villages**. God knows the plans of the enemy even thousands of years ahead of time. He has a plan to deliver His people, which gives great comfort to believers.

38:17–23 Then the forces of **Gog** will swarm over the land. But they will meet the blazing **wrath** and **jealousy** of God. The land will be terribly shaken by **a great earthquake**; Gog's men will be terrified by **pestilence, bloodshed, flooding rain, hailstones, fire, and brimstone** (vv. 17–23).

The destruction of the enemies of God's people reminds us of the Lord's promise in Isaiah 54:17: "No weapon formed against you shall prosper. . . . This is the heritage of the servants of the LORD."

39:1–6 The hordes of **Gog** will meet utter destruction on **the mountains of Israel**. The mention of **bows and arrows** in verse 3 does not necessarily mean that future armies will revert to the use of primitive weapons, although it could mean that. Why would any nation do so?, one may well ask. A possible explanation lies in the fact that for years various military powers have been working on inventions that would totally disable any mechanical weapon, such as a tank, plane, etc. If this is perfected, it would necessitate using horses and non-mechanical weapons in warfare again.

On the other hand, S. Maxwell Coder maintains that the Hebrew words are sufficiently flexible to include modern, sophisticated hardware. Thus, bows and arrows might mean launching devices and missiles. The "horses" in 38:4 (literally "leapers") could be self-propelled vehicles such as tanks or helicopters. The weapons in 39:9, 10 are not necessarily made of wood. The word could mean military equipment such as fuel oil and rocket propellants, many believe.[37]

39:7, 8 **The LORD** will vindicate His **holy name** in that **day**.

39:9, 10 **The weapons** of Gog, strewn on the mountains, will provide fuel **for seven years**. The fact that they will not need **wood from the field** or the **forest** with which to make campfires would seem to support the view that the abundant and abandoned weapons are indeed made of wood.

39:11–16 **Burial** of the dead **bodies** will take place in the **Valley of Hamon Gog** (Gog's multitude), **east of the** Dead **sea**. The task will require **seven months**.

39:17–20 The dead bodies of the **horses and riders** will provide **a great** feast for birds and beasts of prey.

39:21–24 In that day, **the Gentiles shall know that** Israel's captivity was not because God was unable to *prevent* it but **because** their **uncleanness** and **transgressions** *demanded* it.

39:25–29 Israel's restoration will be complete. They will forget **their shame** and acknowledge **the LORD**, who will pour **out** His **Spirit on the house of Israel**.

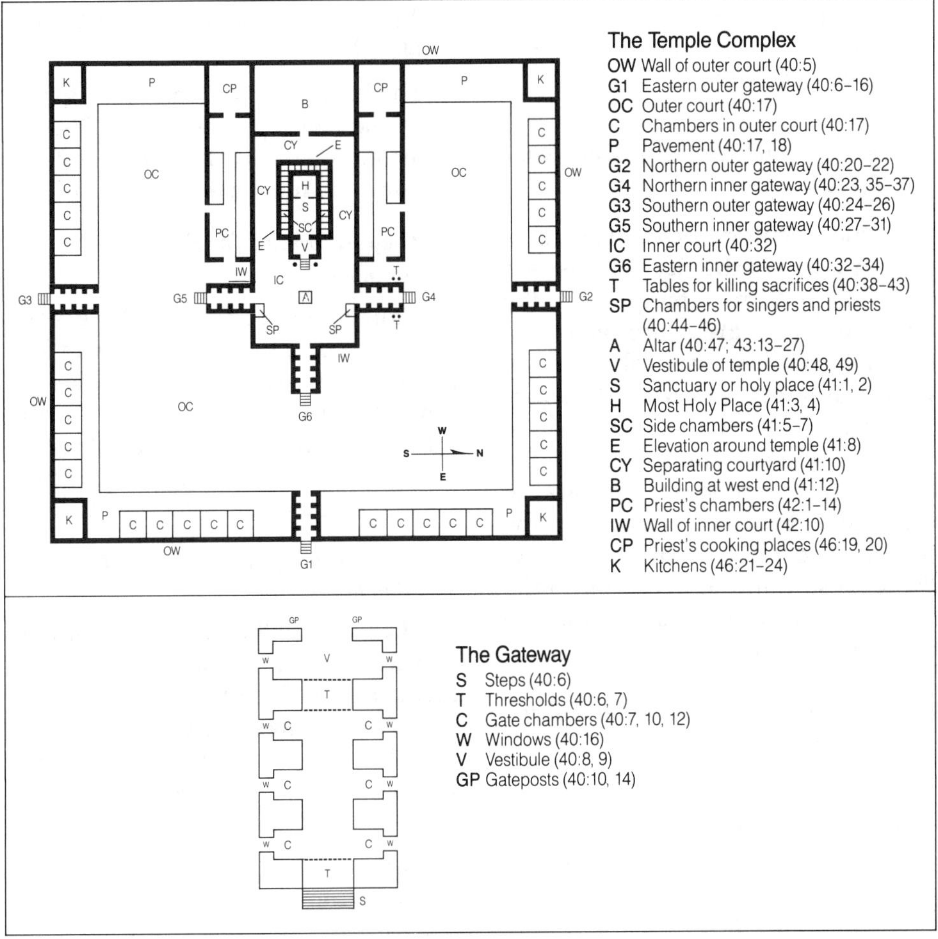

Ezekiel's Temple

V. MILLENNIAL SCENES (Chaps. 40—48)

A. The Millennial Temple in Jerusalem (Chaps. 40—42)

This and the two following chapters give the details of the temple which will be erected in Jerusalem. Many of the descriptions are admittedly difficult to understand, but the general outline can be seen. Paul Lee Tan writes:

> Non-literal interpreters maintain that this prophecy is a symbol of the Christian church. However, this major prophecy in the Book of Ezekiel contains descriptions, specifications, and measurements of the millennial Temple which are so exhaustive that one may actually make a sketch of it, just as one might of Solomon's historic temple. In fact, F. Gardiner in Ellicott's *Commentary on the Whole Bible* succeeds in sketching the layout of the millennial Temple—all the while denying it is possible. This has prompted Alva J. McClain to comment that "if an uninspired commentator can make some sense out of the architectural plan, doubtless the fu-

ture builders working under divine guidance should have no trouble putting up the building."[38]

1. The Man with the Measuring Rod (40:1–4)

In the opening verses, Ezekiel is given a vision of **the city** of Jerusalem and the millennial temple. **In the fourteenth year after** Jerusalem was **captured**, Ezekiel was taken up in **visions** and **set on a very high mountain**. He was shown a vision of **the city** of Jerusalem and the millennial temple by a **man whose appearance was like . . . bronze**. The prophet was commanded to **fix** his **mind** on **everything** he saw and to **declare** it **to the house of Israel**. This he does in the ensuing chapters.

2. The East Gate of the Outer Court (40:5–16)

Since the temple was situated east and west, the natural entrance was the **east gate**, and with this gate the architectural description begins. First, the **wall all around the outside of the temple** is measured (v. 5). Then the **east . . . gate** of this outer court is described (vv. 6–16).

3. The Outer Court (40:17–19)

Facing **the pavement**, which may well be a mosaic, as in 2 Chronicles 7:3 and Esther 1:6, there are to be **thirty chambers**.

4. The Other Two Gates of the Outer Court (40:20–27)

The **gateway facing north** is to be like the eastern one, with **its archways** and **its palm trees**. The **gateway facing south** had **the same measurements** and structure. There is no gateway facing west.

5. The Three Gates to the Inner Court (40:28–37)

The inner court also has three gateways: **the southern gateway** (vv. 28–31); a second gateway **facing east** (vv. 32–34); and a **north gateway** (vv. 35–37).

6. The Equipment for Sacrifice (40:38–43)

Eight tables at the **vestibule** will be provided at the north **gateway** for animal sacrifices. Also, **four tables of hewn stone** will be used **for burnt offering**. Both **instruments** for slaughtering the sacrifices and also **hooks fastened all around** will be provided.

7. The Chambers for the Priests (40:44–47)

Chambers will be provided **for the singers, one** set **facing south** and **one facing north**. The first is to be **for the priests who have charge of** the temple; the one facing **north is for the priests who have charge of the altar** (**the sons of Zadok**).

8. The Vestibule of the Temple (40:48, 49)

The vestibule or porch **of the temple** seems to be planned like the one in Solomon's temple. The pillars remind us of the ones named Jachin and Boaz in that structure (1 Kgs. 7:21).

Chapter 40 deals primarily with the area surrounding the temple; chapter 41 describes the temple itself.

The detailed measurements in chapters 40—43 remind us that in all our service we must build according to God's specifications (see Ex. 25:40). Precise measurements also would seem to be meaningless unless this is to be a literal building. An allegory or type would scarcely be so architecturally precise. Also, no one has given a satisfactory explanation of the several parts if they are merely symbolic.

9. The Sanctuary and Most Holy Place (41:1–4)

The measurements of the sanctuary are to be the same as in Solomon's temple and twice as large as the tabernacle in the wilderness. The man with the appearance of bronze **brought** Ezekiel **into the sanctuary**, but he alone went into the **Most Holy Place**, reminding us of the ancient temple and tabernacle restrictions of entry (see Heb. 9:8, 12; 10:19). The same twofold division of the ancient temple apparently will be continued in the millennial temple.

10. The Side Chambers (41:5–11)

The temple will be very massive and spacious; it will have **three stories** with **thirty chambers in each story**. They will **increase** in size as one ascends, probably by going deeper into the main structure in stair-like fashion (v. 7).

11. A Building West of the Temple (41:12)

Facing the western end of the temple complex is a separate building **seventy** by **ninety cubits**. The purpose of this structure is not given.

12. The Measurements of the Temple (41:13–15a)

Ezekiel's guide to the temple **measured** it at **one hundred cubits long** and **one hundred cubits** wide.

13. The Interior Decoration and Furnishing of the Temple (41:15b–26)

The interior of the temple is to have **galleries** on both sides, **doorposts**, and **beveled window frames**.

Cherubim and **palm trees** will be the decorations, alternating **all around** the building. The cherubim, which speak of God's holiness (see Genesis 3), have **the face of a young lion toward** one **palm tree** and **the face of a man** toward the other **palm tree**. Palm trees are symbolic of victory and righteousness in Scripture.

The altar, which is to be made of **wood**, is called by Ezekiel's guide **"the table that is before the LORD."**

The temple is to have **two doors** of **two panels** each, also **carved** with **cherubim** and **palm trees**.

The vestibule outside will be covered with a **wooden canopy**.

No mention is made of any veil, ark, or high priest. The veil was split apart at Calvary. The symbolism of the ark is fulfilled in Christ. And He is there as Great High Priest.

14. The Priests' Quarters (42:1–14)

The priests will have quarters located both **north** and **south** of the temple. These areas will be where the priests will **eat the most holy offerings**, and in which they will keep their sacred **garments** for ministering.

15. The Measurements of the Outer Court (42:15–20)

The measurements of the outer court are to be **five hundred rods** on each of its four sides. The distinction between **holy** and **common** in verse 20 is the difference between what we might call *sacred* and *secular*. It is the difference between worship and the common affairs of everyday life.

B. The Millennial Worship (Chaps. 43, 44)

43:1–5 Earlier in the book of Ezekiel (11:23) we saw the glory cloud reluctantly leaving the temple at Jerusalem. But **the glory of the God of Israel** will return in the Person of the Lord Jesus when He comes to reign.

43:6–9 He **will dwell . . . forever . . . in the midst of** His people; **no more** will they practice spiritual **harlotry** (idolatry) and related **abominations** in the shadow of the temple.

43:10–12 When **the House of Israel** is **ashamed of all that they have done**, they will see the **pattern, design**, and **arrangement of the** new **temple**. As soon as they repent, God will give them new hope. (We should also react in this way when someone repents.) The people were to be told that **the whole area surrounding the mountaintop** on which **the temple** would be built would be **most holy**.

A true sight of the glory of the Lord makes us ashamed of our iniquities (v. 10):

'Tis the look that melted Peter,
'Tis that face that Stephen saw,
'Tis that heart that wept with Mary,
Can alone from idols draw.
—*Author unknown*

43:13–17 **The measurements of the altar**, apparently like a terraced platform, are given next. The **altar hearth** is the surface of the altar, where the fire is built. It will have **four horns extending upward from the hearth**. An unusual feature of this altar is the fact that it has **steps** leading up to it; this was banned in the previous temples. This one will be so high that it will need a way to mount up to the top.

43:18–27 Next is given the ritual to be followed in consecrating **the altar** by blood. This will take **seven days**, and its importance in Israel's public worship can be seen in several OT texts: Exodus 29:37, Leviticus 8:11, 15, 19, 33; 1 Kings 8:62–65, and 2 Chronicles 7:4–10. After all these rites, **on the eighth day**, the regular **offerings** will begin.

The chapter ends on an encouraging note: not only would God accept the people's offerings, but, **"I will accept you," says the Lord God.**

Note that **the priests** in that day will be the sons **of Zadok** (v. 19), an honor probably stemming from Zadok's unwavering loyalty to David and Solomon.

44:1–3 **The east . . . gate** of the **outer** court must be permanently **shut** because once **the Lord** returns to the temple, He will never leave. Only **the prince** could **sit** in **the vestibule** of the **gate** and **eat** the sacrificial meal there. Some think that the prince is the Messiah Himself, others that he is a descendant of David who will serve as a vice-regent under Christ, the King. However, F. W. Grant points out that he cannot be the Messiah because he has sons (46:16) and he offers a sin offering for himself (45:22).[39]

44:4–9 When the Lord **brought** Ezekiel **to the front of the temple**, the prophet was awestruck by **the glory of the Lord** as it **filled the house**. Verse 4 should create a passionate desire for worship meetings where the glory of the Lord is so manifest that the worshipers are prostrate before Him.

The Lord instructed him to pay close attention to **the** new **ordinances . . . concerning** the temple, its entrance and exits (v. 5), and to warn the people that the use of any **foreigner** in the service of the temple must cease (vv. 6–9).

44:10–16 Henceforth, the menial **work** would be assigned to **the Levites**, who had once fallen into idolatry. Only **the sons of Zadok** could serve as **priests**, drawing **near** and ministering to God. The sons of Zadok were faithful in the times of trouble under David (2 Sam. 15:24; 1 Kgs. 1:32 etc.; 2:26, 27, 35). The Levites might be suspended from priestly service because of the curse on Eli's family or because of unfaithfulness during the times of the kings. We learn from all this that sin often has bitter consequences, and that faithfulness will be rewarded.

44:17–19 The priests would be required to wear **linen garments**, not woolen. The expression **"in their holy garments they shall not sanctify the people"** (v. 19b) refers to a ritual holiness reserved only for the service of the sanctuary and not for the priests' regular duties (Ex. 29:37; 30:29; Lev. 6:18, 27; Hag. 2:10–12).

44:20–22 Regulations are given concerning well-trimmed haircuts, restrictions on **wine**, and suitable marriages for the priests.

44:23, 24 The sons of Zadok would also serve as teachers and **judges**, making God's **people discern between** what is **holy** and **clean** on the one hand, and **unholy** and **unclean** on the other.

44:25–27 Their necessary contact with **a dead person** would require certain rituals of cleansing.

44:28–31 They will be supported by things **dedicated** to the Lord. The Lord wants to be their inheritance, and they will have nothing on earth. This is true for the servants of God today; He wants us to find our full satisfaction in Him, and thus be free to serve unhindered by worldly attachments. Like Paul we can learn to be content in every state (Phil. 4:11), but we do have to *learn* it because it does not come naturally to anyone. A broken man can say, "There is none upon earth that I desire besides You. . . . God is the strength of my heart and my portion forever" (Ps. 73:25, 26).

C. The Millennial Administration (Chaps. 45, 46)

45:1 In the center of **the land** of Israel, a piece of land will be set apart **for the LORD** as **a holy. . . district**. It will be **twenty-five thousand cubits** by **ten thousand**.

45:2–5 It will be divided into two strips. The top half will contain the **sanctuary**, and will also be for **the priests**. The lower half will be for **the Levites**.

45:6 At the bottom of the square will be a third strip, a common place, which will include **the city** of Jerusalem.

45:7, 8 All **the land** to **the east** and **west** of this square, as far as the boundaries of the land, will belong to **the prince**.

45:9–12 The **princes of Israel** are to **execute justice** in their dealings (v. 9), using **honest scales** and measures.

45:13–17 In these verses, **all the people** are required to **offer** a certain percentage of their crops to **the prince in Israel** in order to provide for the regular **offerings** and **appointed seasons**.

45:18–20 **On the first day** of **the first month**, **the sanctuary** is to be cleansed, and **on the seventh day of the** same **month**, the people are to be cleansed of sins committed **unintentionally or in ignorance**.

45:21–25 **The Passover** is to be kept **on the fourteenth day of the** first **month** and the Feast of Tabernacles on **the fifteenth day** of **the seventh month**.

No mention is made of the Feast of Pentecost, the Feast of Trumpets, or the Day of Atonement.

In the light of all these rituals and holy days how grateful we should be for the once-for-all substitutionary work of Christ on our behalf!

Millennial Sacrifices

In Ezekiel 43:20, 26; 45:15, 17 some of the offerings that will be presented during the Millennium are distinctly said to be for the purpose of making atonement. How can this be reconciled with Hebrews 10:12: "But this Man, after He had offered one sacrifice for sins forever, sat down at the right hand of God." Or Hebrews 10:18: "Now where there is remission of these, there is no longer an offering for sin?"

As used in the OT, the word "atonement" (lit., covering) never means the putting away of sins. Hebrews 10:4 reminds us that ". . . it is not possible that the blood of bulls and goats could take away sins." Rather the sacrifices were an annual reminder of sins (Heb. 10:3). What then did *atonement* mean? It meant that the sacrifices produced an outward, ceremonial cleanness. They conferred a ritual purification on people, enabling them to draw near as worshipers in fellowship with God. The sacrifices even made atonement for inanimate things, such as the altar (Ex. 29:37), where there could be no thought of remission of sins. All it means is that the altar was cleansed ceremonially and thus made fit for God's service.

When we read of the forgiveness of unintentional sin in connection with atonement (Lev. 4:20), it can only mean the removal of ceremonial defilement so that the person could draw near in worship.

In our day the word *atonement* has acquired a much wider and deeper meaning. It is used, for instance, to describe the entire sacrificial work of Christ by which our sins are put away and we are reconciled to God. But it never has this meaning in the Bible. (In Rom. 5:11 KJV, the word *atonement* should be *reconciliation*,[40] as in NKJV and other versions.)

The sacrifices in Israel's history looked forward to the perfect and complete sacrifice of Christ. The sacrifices in the Millennium will commemorate His work on Calvary. They will be memorials for Israel just as the Lord's Supper is for us.

The passages in Hebrews do not rule out any sacrificial ceremony in the future. But they insist that no future sacrifices can ever deal effectively with sins, any more than they did in the past.‡

46:1–8 Verses 1–8 tell how **the prince** is to **stand** in **the east** gate **of the inner court** to **worship** when he brings **his . . . offerings** for the Feast of the Sabbath and of **the New Moon** (v. 6). He cannot enter the inner court. **The people** are to stand behind the prince and **worship** as **the priests** sacrifice. Neither the prince nor the people can enter the inner court.

In the Millennium, Israel will see Christ in the offerings, something the nation as a whole never did in the past.

46:9, 10 The people are to leave the outer court by **the opposite gate** to which they entered. They were to follow the movements of the prince.

46:11–18 In verses 11 and 12, the prince's freewill offerings are described; in verses 13–15, the daily sacrifices. Laws with respect to the prince's property prevent him from losing it permanently or from adding to it unjustly.

46:19–24 Kitchens are provided for the **priests** and for **the people**.

D. The Millennial Land (Chaps. 47, 48)

1. *The Healing of the Waters (47:1–12)*

Ezekiel saw in a vision a river **flowing** from the door **of the temple**, past **the altar**, through the wall south of the **east** Gate, and down to **the** Dead **Sea**. **The waters** of **the sea... will be healed**, and **fish** will abound in it. Yates writes:

> The water of life is a favorite figure in the Old Testament. Desert areas need water that life may be possible. This stream which Ezekiel sees flowing from the Temple makes its way toward the arid regions of the Arabah. In an ever deepening stream it goes on its way to bring life and health and abundant fruit wherever it goes. It is the one remedy that is needed. Jesus took that figure as a basis for his sermon to the woman at the well. (Cf. also Ps. 1:3; 46:4; Joel 3:18; Zech. 14:8; John 4:7–15; 7:38; Rev. 22:1, 2.)[41]

This stream (which will be an actual geographical river) is a striking figure of the blessing, widespread yet incomplete (v. 11), that will flow out during the Millennial Reign of Christ. God will dwell in the temple and therefore a stream of blessing, ever increasing, will go forth to other places. Today God does dwell in our bodies (1 Cor. 6:19) and therefore a stream of blessing should be flowing to others around us (John 7:37, 38). "If a man is filled with the Holy Spirit, and his life touches other lives, something happens for God." What a challenge for us to meet the conditions that will produce a blessing!

The river will bring life wherever it flows—a vivid picture of the life-giving ministry of the Holy Spirit.

2. *The Boundaries of the Land (47:13–23)*

47:13–20 The future **borders** and divisions of **the land** are next given. The boundaries are described here.

Ezekiel's mention of the Jordan River as a boundary of the land (v. 18) cannot be a mistake; he certainly knew that the land would stretch east to the Euphrates (Gen. 15:18). Here he may be referring to a preliminary occupation of Palestine itself. Or he may be indicating that the Jordan formed only *part* of the eastern boundary, while the rest reached north-north-east as far as the Euphrates. The second explanation is less popular, but since Ezekiel's description is so detailed and does not mention the Euphrates at all, it merits consideration.

47:21–23 Within each tribal portion, the **land** will be divided **by lot, according to the tribes of Israel**, but **strangers** will not be excluded from **an inheritance**.

3. *The Division of the Land (Chap. 48)*

48:1–7 It seems that the **land** will be divided in horizontal strips, from the Mediterranean to the eastern boundary of the land. The northernmost strip will be **for** the tribe of **Dan** (v. 1). Then below that, **for Asher** (v. 2), **for Naphtali** (v. 3), **for Manasseh** (v. 4), **for Ephraim** (v. 5), **for Reuben** (v. 6), and **for Judah** (v. 7).

48:8–22 **South** of **Judah** will be the portion already assigned to the prince, and including **the sanctuary** and the city of Jerusalem. This **"holy district"** will be a large square area bordering on the northern part of the Dead Sea. It will be divided into three horizontal strips, the northernmost one belonging to the priests, and having the Millennial **temple in** its **center**. The middle strip will be for the Levites, and the southern strip for the common people, with Jerusalem in its center. The remaining territory east and west of the square will belong to **the prince**.

48:23–27 Then south of the holy

district will be **sections** for the tribes of **Benjamin** (v. 23), **Simeon** (v. 24), **Issachar** (v. 25), **Zebulun** (v. 26), and **Gad** (v. 27).

48:28–35 The city of New Jerusalem will have twelve **gates**, three on each **side**, one for each of the twelve tribes of Israel. Its **name** will be: *Jehovah Shammah*—**THE LORD IS THERE.**

This name reminds us of what was always in the heart of God: He loves His creatures so much that He always planned to have them close to Himself. He is ever searching, asking, "Where are you?", calling to repentance and faith. As Son of God He even came down to earth to die for us. His wish will be fulfilled: man will be close to His heart. We can engage in and participate in His search for the lost even now, while living close to His heart here on earth. This is God's desire for us.

We close our commentary on Ezekiel with a summary by the Hebrew Christian OT scholar, Charles L. Feinberg:

> This incomparable prophecy began with a vision of the glory of God and concludes with a description of the glory of the Lord in the glorified city of Jerusalem. Ezekiel concluded, as John in the Revelation, with God dwelling with man in holiness and glory. Beyond this there is no greater goal of history and God's dealings with man.[42]

ENDNOTES

[1](Intro) E.g., by Gleason Archer, in *A Survey of Old Testament Introduction*, under "Ezekiel."

[2](Intro) John B. Taylor, *Ezekiel: An Introduction and Commentary*, Tyndale Old Testament Commentaries, pp. 14–16.

[3](Intro) Albert Barnes, *The Bible Commentary, Proverbs-Ezekiel*, p. 302.

[4](1:4–28a) These four faces have traditionally been linked to the four portraits of our Lord in the Gospels: Matthew—the lion (Christ as King); Mark—the ox (Christ as servant); Luke—man (Christ as the perfect Man); John—eagle (Christ as Son of God). See NT volume of *BBC*, Introduction to the Gospels, p. 13.

[5](1:4–28a) The NKJV, following the Masoretic text, reads "When I came." The New Scofield note on this textual problem reads: "Obviously it was not Ezekiel who came to destroy the city of Jerusalem for her sins, but the LORD Himself. On the basis of the requirements of the context, the reading in some six manuscripts, the version of Theodotion and that of the Vulgate, the best reading is 'when He came to destroy the city.' A possible rendering, and perhaps preferable, would be to read the final letter of the disputed word as a well-known abbreviation for "LORD," thus giving us the reading 'when the LORD came to destroy the city.'" *The New Scofield Study Bible, New King James Version*, p. 995.

[6](1:28b—2:7) The NRSV paraphrases "son of man" as "mortal" to avoid the "masculine-oriented" words *son* and *man*; this obscures the link with Daniel and our Lord's usage.

[7](1:28b—2:7) Taylor, *Ezekiel*, p. 60.

[8](1:28b—2:7) *Ibid*.

[9](3:12–15) Kyle M. Yates, *Preaching from the Prophets*, p. 181.

[10](9:4) Charles Lee Feinberg, *The Prophecy of Ezekiel: The Glory of the Lord*, p. 56.

[11](9:4) *Ibid*.

[12](11:16–21) Yates, *Prophets*, p. 182.

[13](11:22–25) George Williams, *The Student's Commentary on the Holy Scriptures*, p. 579.

[14](13:1–3) Denis Lane, *The Cloud and the Silver Lining*, pp. 53–62.

[15](13:8–16) A. B. Davidson, *The Book of the Prophet Ezekiel*, p. 88.

[16](13:8–16) Our Lord calls the Pharisees by a similar (but worse!) name: "whitewashed tombs" (Matt. 23:27).

[17](16:44–52) Feinberg, *Ezekiel*, p. 91.

[18](17:22–24) Carl F. Keil, "Ezekiel," in *Biblical Commentary on the Old Testament*, XXI:244, 245.

[19](21:25–27) Matthew Henry, "Ezekiel," in *Matthew Henry's Commentary on the Whole Bible*, IV:878, 879.

[20](22:23, 24) Taylor, *Ezekiel*, pp. 168, 169.

[21](22:25–31) *Ibid.*, p. 169. This ancient Greek version sometimes preserves original Hebrew readings other than those in the traditional Hebrew (Masoretic) text. Footnotes to verses 24 and 25 in the NKJV give two examples, as well as readings from other ancient versions.

[22](23:5–10) A rival center of false worship persisted. The Samaritan woman seems to defend their "denominational difference" to our Lord in John 4:20.

[23](26:3–11) Nebuchadnezzar received this title because he had forced many other kings to submit to his rule.

[24](26:3–11) Feinberg, *Ezekiel*, p. 149.

[25](26:12–14) Quoted by W. M. Thomson in *The Land and the Book*, p. 155n.

[26](26:15–21) Peter Stoner, *Science Speaks*, p. 76.

[27](28:11–19) Feinberg, *Ezekiel*, pp. 161, 162.

[28](30:13–19) This is the well-known frontier city to which Jeremiah was taken after Governor Gedaliah's assassination (Jer. 43:7; cf. 44:1).

[29](34:1–6) Yates, *Preaching*, p. 183.

[30](34:11–16) D. L. Moody, *Notes from My Bible*, p. 90.

[31](34:11–16) One liberal Protestant "bishop" of Washington, D.C. in the 1950's blasphemed the God of the OT as a "bully."

[32](34:11–16) Taylor, *Ezekiel*, pp. 220, 221.

[33](34:17–24) David Baron, *The Shepherd of Israel*, pp. 8, 9.

[34](36:24–29a) Keil, "Ezekiel," p. 110.

[35](37:1–8) Yates, *Preaching*, p. 184.

[36](38:1–16) The KJV rendering, which makes the Hebrew *Rosh* an adjective meaning "chief" and modifying "prince," is based on the Latin Vulgate and the Targum, and is not accurate. Surprisingly, this translation was retained in the NIV, perhaps from a fear that people would see Russia in the word *Rosh*. However, taking Rosh as a proper name does not decide the issue as to which area the term will apply. It might refer to Russia, but then again it might not. Most historians and geographers identify Meshech and Tubal as areas in what is now central Turkey.

[37](39:1–6) S. Maxwell Coder, "That Bow and Arrow War," *Moody Monthly*, April 1974, p. 37.

[38](40:Intro) Paul Lee Tan, *The Interpretation of Prophecy*, p. 161.

[39](44:1–3) F. W. Grant, "Ezekiel," in *The Numerical Bible*, IV:273.

[40](Essay) In 1611 *atonement* was "at-one-ment" and *meant* "reconciliation." It was the correct translation in its time, but our language has changed a great deal since the 1600's.

[41](47:1–12) Yates, *Preaching*, p. 184.

[42](48:28–35) Feinberg, *Ezekiel*, p. 239.

BIBLIOGRAPHY

Alexander, Ralph. *Ezekiel*. Everyman's Bible Commentary. Chicago: Moody Press, 1976.

Davidson, A. B. *The Book of the Prophet Ezekiel. The Cambridge Bible for Schools and Colleges*. Cambridge: The University Press, 1900.

Feinberg, Charles Lee. *The Prophecy of Ezekiel: The Glory of the Lord*. Chicago: Moody Press, 1969.

Grant, F. W. "Ezekiel." In *Numerical Bible*. Vol. 4. Neptune, N.J.: Loizeaux Bros., 1977.

Henry, Matthew. "Ezekiel." In *Matthew Henry's Commentary on the Whole Bible*, Vol. IV. McLean, VA: MacDonald Publishing Company, n.d.

Keil, C. F. "Ezekiel." In *Biblical Commentary on the Old Testament*. Vols. 22, 23. Reprint. Grand Rapids: Wm. B. Eerdmans Publishing Co., 1971.

Mills, Montague S. *Ezekiel: An Overview*. Dallas: 3E Ministries, n.d.

Tatford, Frederick A. *Dead Bones Live: An Exposition of the Prophecy of Ezekiel*. Eastbourne, East Sussex: Prophetic Witness Publishing House, 1977.

Taylor, John B. *Ezekiel: An Introduction and Commentary*. The Tyndale Old Testament Commentaries. Downers Grove, IL: InterVarsity Press, 1969.

DANIEL

Introduction

"I wish to stress . . . that none of the prophets has so clearly spoken concerning Christ as has this prophet Daniel. For not only did he assert that He would come, a prediction common to the other prophets as well, but also he set forth the very time at which He would come. Moreover he went through the various kings in order, stated the actual number of years involved, and announced beforehand the clearest signs of events to come."

—Jerome (A.D. 347–420)

I. Unique Place in the Canon

Daniel is one of the most fascinating and also among the most crucial books in the OT. Due no doubt to its precise predictions, messianic prophecies, and inspiring example of clean-cut separation from apostate world religion, Daniel has come under attacks from rationalist and unbelieving scholarship. No wonder that conservative Bible scholar Sir Robert Anderson titled one of his books *Daniel in the Critic's Den.*

The main thrust of the assault has been as to whether the book was actually written by a *prophet* named Daniel in the sixth century B.C., as conservative Jews and Christians have maintained, or by an unknown second century author writing *history* (especially chap. 11) *as though it were prophecy*.

II. Authorship

Since the traditional authorship of Daniel is so widely rejected and it is very important for a believer to be well grounded in this great book, we give a fuller treatment here than for most other books.

The first salvo against the orthodox position that Daniel was a real prophet who was divinely endowed with detailed visions of Gentile world empires and the coming of the Messiah was fired in the third century A.D. by the anti-Christian philosopher, Porphyry.

His ideas were later taken up by a handful of Jews in the seventeenth century and then in Christendom in the eighteenth and following centuries. With the spread of rationalism these ideas were further expanded and accepted in liberal and semi-liberal circles.

Merrill F. Unger writes:

> Modern criticism views the establishment of a Maccabean date (about 167 B.C.) and the rejection of the traditional Danielic authorship as one of its assured achievements. These views, however, are erected upon a series of

> highly plausible fallacies, and unsound assumptions.[1]

Before examining the main charges *against* Danielic authorship, let us note several positive evidences *for* this position.

1. Our Lord Jesus Christ specifically quotes the book as by Daniel (Matt. 24:15). This alone is proof enough for the devout Christian.
2. The book sparkles with the local color and customs of ancient Babylon and Medo-Persia, not Maccabean Palestine.
3. Jews and Christians have been edified and blessed for centuries by this book. While this is true of a number of uninspired writings, the Holy Spirit's powerful illumination of the book of Daniel scarcely comports with its being a forgery.
4. A manuscript of Daniel found in Qumran Cave 1 is believed to have been copied during or before the Maccabean era, which fact demands that the original has to be older yet.

The arguments against the authenticity of Daniel are threefold: linguistic, historical, and theological.

The linguistic argument is that Daniel could *not* have been written in the sixth century because the book contains Persian and even Greek words, and the Aramaic is alleged to be a variety from a later date.

Since, however, Daniel lived and served into the Medo-*Persian* period (530's B.C.) the presence of Persian words indicates quite the opposite of the liberal contention. The chances of a second century forger in Palestine knowing Persian are dim.

As to the *Greek* words, most Bible students are shocked when they find out that there are only *three*—and all names for musical instruments! It is a well-known fact that the names of *objects* from a culture often go into another language long before there is heavy intercultural involvement. While the Greek *Empire* was still in the future when Daniel wrote, Greek culture and inventiveness were already spreading in the ancient world.

As to the *Aramaic,* Kitchen and Kutscher have demonstrated that it does indeed fit the Imperial Period of Daniel.

The historical arguments against the orthodox position on authorship include the contention that the Jews put Daniel in the third section of the OT ("The Writings") and not among the Prophets because that section of the canon was already closed when "Daniel" wrote. It is simpler to realize that Daniel was a prophet not by calling, but by ministry. By vocation he was a statesman. Hence, he was not put with the professional prophets —Isaiah, Jeremiah, etc.

Various alleged historical problems have been raised against the authenticity of Daniel—but all have intelligent answers by conservative scholars of undoubted integrity. For those who wish to pursue this, authors recommended, in chronological order, are: Robert Dick Wilson, Charles Boutflower, John F. Walvoord, R. K. Harrison, and Gleason Archer.

The theological argument against Daniel is that the book has too "advanced" views on angels, the life hereafter (resurrection), and the Messiah. This notion stems from applying the theory of evolution to religion. The *real* protest against Daniel, as a few liberal scholars, such as R. Pfeiffer (*Old Testament Introduction,* p. 755), are honest enough to admit, is prejudice against the supernatural. There are too many miracles, too much precise prediction in Daniel to suit rationalistic criticism. Just as Daniel the prophet escaped unscathed from the lions' den, so does Daniel the prophecy escape from the "critics' den" in the minds and hearts of intelligent believers.

III. Date

Scholars range all the way from the sixth century to the second century B.C. in dating Daniel. Liberals and their admirers nearly all date the book in its present form as being from the Maccabean era. They generally view it as an attempt to encourage the Jews during the horrible anti-Semitic excesses of Antiochus Epiphanes.

Those who believe that God can inspire not only general prophecies of kingdoms not as yet well-known (Greece and Rome) but also minute details of the Grecian period several centuries before they happen (chap. 11), have no trouble accepting the conservative teaching that Daniel wrote his prophecy in the sixth century, probably about 530 B.C.

Even with their "late" date, as Unger points out, the critics have not escaped God's omniscient insight into the future:

> It must be remembered that even if the latest date assigned to the composition of the book of Daniel were proved correct, the prophecy yet displays a knowledge of the future which can only be ascribed to divine inspiration.[2]

IV. Background and Theme

Accepting then the orthodox view of authorship and date, we believe Daniel was one of the intelligent and attractive young Jewish captives carried off to Babylon by Nebuchadnezzar when Jehoiakim was king of Judah (about 604 B.C.). His name means "God is my Judge." His character and behavior show that he lived in the light of that fact.

As to office, Daniel was a statesman high up in the administration of Nebuchadnezzar's and Belshazzar's courts. When Medo-Persia conquered Babylon, Daniel was made the first of three presidents under Darius. He also served under Cyrus. As noted, this is probably why the Hebrew OT has Daniel in the section known as "The Writings," and not with "The Prophets," as in English.

Daniel's *ministry*, however, was that of a prophet, and our Lord so labeled him (Matt. 24:15 and Mark 13:14). Daniel is not unlike those who hold a "secular" job and still give much time to Bible study and preaching. For example, Sir Robert Anderson, himself a scholar of Daniel's prophecy, headed up Scotland Yard's Criminal Investigation Division in the late Victorian era, and yet had a widely blessed biblical ministry.[3]

Since so much of the book has to do with Gentile world powers, it should not surprise us that Daniel 2:4 through chapter 7 is in Aramaic. This is a Gentile tongue related to Hebrew but widely used in international communication in Daniel's time in much the same way that English is today. Some scholars outline Daniel's prophecy by these changes in language.

As to context, Daniel's first six chapters are largely *narrative* with prophetic themes subordinated. The last six chapters are largely *prophetic* with narrative subordinated.

OUTLINE

I. THE STEADFAST FIDELITY OF DANIEL AND HIS COMPANIONS (Chap. 1)

II. NEBUCHADNEZZAR'S VISION OF THE IMAGE MADE OF FOUR METALS (Chap. 2)

III. NEBUCHADNEZZAR'S GOLDEN IDOL AND THE FIERY FURNACE (Chap. 3)

IV. NEBUCHADNEZZAR'S DREAM OF THE RUINED TREE AND ITS MEANING (Chap. 4)

V. BELSHAZZAR'S DOOM ANNOUNCED BY THE HANDWRITING ON THE WALL (Chap. 5)

VI. DECREE OF DARIUS AND THE DEN OF LIONS (Chap. 6)

VII. DANIEL'S DREAM OF FOUR BEASTS DEPICTING FOUR WORLD EMPIRES (Chap. 7)

VIII. DANIEL'S VISION OF THE RAM AND GOAT NATIONS (Chap. 8)

IX. DANIEL'S VISION OF THE SEVENTY WEEKS OF GENTILE SUPREMACY (Chap. 9)

X. VISION OF GOD'S GLORY INTRODUCING OUTLINE OF COMING EVENTS (Chap. 10)

XI. PROPHECIES OF THE IMMEDIATE FUTURE (11:1–35)
   A. Greece's Conquest of Medo-Persia (11:1–3)
   B. The Decay of the Grecian Empire (11:4–35)
      1. The Wars Between Egypt and Syria (11:4–20)
      2. The Reign of Wicked Antiochus Epiphanes (11:21–35)

XII. PROPHECIES OF THE DISTANT FUTURE (11:36—12:13)
   A. The Antichrist (11:36–45)
   B. The Great Tribulation (Chap. 12)

Commentary

I. THE STEADFAST FIDELITY OF DANIEL AND HIS COMPANIONS (Chap. 1)

1:1–7 The scene is the court of **Nebuchadnezzar** in **Babylon** following his attack on **Jerusalem** in **the third year of** Jehoiakim's **reign**. Nebuchadnezzar ordered several Jewish **young men** to be prepared **to serve** him as **men** of **wisdom** and **knowledge**. Among these were **Daniel, Hananiah, Mishael, and Azariah**. Their Chaldean **names** were **Belteshazzar, Shadrach, Meshach,** and **Abed-Nego**. As part of their preparation, they were to eat of **the king's delicacies** and drink of his **wine**. These foods probably included meats that were unclean, according to the OT law or perhaps they were connected with idol worship.

There is a seeming discrepancy between verse 1 and Jeremiah 25:1. Here Nebuchadnezzar is said to have besieged **Jerusalem in the third year of** Jehoiakim's **reign**. The Jeremiah passage says that the fourth year of Jehoiakim was the first year of Nebuchadnezzar. This may be explained by the difference between Jewish and Babylonian reckoning.

1:8–12 Daniel nobly refused to eat them. He asked if he and his friends could eat **vegetables** and **drink . . . water** instead. Ashpenaz, **the chief of the eunuchs** (not understanding Jewish customs nor their God), was horrified at this idea, noting that his own **head** would be endangered if the plan didn't work! God honors those who honor Him.

1:13–21 Daniel's request was nonetheless granted. At the end of the probationary period of **ten days**, they stood **before . . . the king** and proved to be **ten times better than all** the wise men of Babylon. They were therefore accepted by the king. **God** graciously gifted **them** with **knowledge and skill in all literature and wisdom**, and to **Daniel** he granted **understanding in all visions and dreams**.

II. NEBUCHADNEZZAR'S VISION OF THE IMAGE MADE OF FOUR METALS (Chap. 2)

2:1–13 Nebuchadnezzar had a dream for which he demanded not merely the interpretation, but the contents of the dream itself—a much harder demand, not to say impossible. His own wise men, **the Chaldeans**, were not able to tell him **the dream** or its meaning, so he made the sweeping **decision** that **all** the wise men (including **Daniel and his companions**) should be destroyed!

2:14–30 In answer to prayer, **Daniel** learned from the Lord **in a night vision** the nature of the **dream** and **the interpretation** of it. In thanks Daniel **blessed the God of heaven** with a beautiful prayer of praise. Then he **went to Arioch** to prevent further killing **of the wise men of Babylon**. Brought by **Arioch** into **the presence of the king**, Daniel revealed the source of his divinely revealed **secret**.

2:31–35 Daniel made known that the **king** had seen **a great image**, both splendid and **awesome**. **This image's head was of fine gold, its chest and arms of silver, its belly and thighs of bronze, its legs of iron, its feet partly of iron and partly of clay.** Nebuchadnezzar **watched while a stone . . . cut out without hands** destroyed **the image** and **became a great mountain**, filling **the whole earth**.

2:36–45 The image represented the four Gentile powers that would exercise world dominion, ruling over the Jewish people. Nebuchadnezzar, an absolute monarch (Babylon), was the **head of gold** (v. 38). Persia was the arms of silver, one arm representing Media and the other Persia. Greece, the **third kingdom**, was **the belly and thighs of bronze**. The Roman Empire was the two legs and feet of **iron**, the legs representing the eastern and western wings of the **kingdom**. **The feet** of **iron** and baked **clay** depict the revived Roman Empire, the toes representing ten kingdoms. Note the decreasing value of the metals and the increasing strength (except in the feet of iron and clay). Note also that man pictures his empires as valuable metals whereas God pictures those same kingdoms as wild beasts (chap. 7). The Lord Jesus is the **stone . . . cut out . . . without hands**. He will destroy the four kingdoms and rule over the whole earth, his **kingdom** standing **forever**.

2:46–49 When **King Nebuchadnezzar** heard Daniel's wisdom, **he made him ruler over the whole province of Babylon, and chief administrator over all the wise men of Babylon**. The three other Jewish youths were made deputies or assistants.

III. NEBUCHADNEZZAR'S GOLDEN IDOL AND THE FIERY FURNACE (Chap. 3)

3:1–7 Nebuchadnezzar . . . made an idolatrous **image of gold** ninety feet high **and set it up in the plain of Dura**. He then commanded that when they heard **horn, flute, harp, lyre, and psaltery, in symphony with all kinds of music**, all men were to **fall down** to **worship** it. Any who refused would **be cast . . . into** a **fiery furnace**.

3:8–12 Shadrach, Meshach, and Abed-Nego, as faithful Jews, refused to **worship** the idol and were reported by **certain Chaldeans** to the **king**.

3:13–21 He gave them a chance to change their minds, but they would not. Their confidence in deliverance was magnificent. But even **"if not,"** they would still be true to the Lord. So the king ordered **the** fiery **furnace** heated **seven times** hotter than usual, and then **commanded** that the three Jews be thrown **into** it fully clothed.

3:22–25 The **furnace** was so **hot** that the **men** who threw them in were killed, but when the astonished **Nebuchadnezzar** looked into the furnace, he saw **four** men—the **three** Jews and a **fourth** whose **form** was **like the Son of God** (NKJV) or *a son of the gods* (NKJV marg.). We believe that it was indeed **the Son of God**, no matter how the king viewed Him. The Lord either saves us out of troubles or He is with us in the troubles.

3:26–30 The Jews were unharmed. **The fire** had burned only the cords that bound them. Afflictions succeed in accomplishing God's purposes and setting us free from the things that bind us. **The king** was so impressed that he forbade anyone to speak **against the God of** the Jews and **promoted** the three young men **in the province of Babylon**. All this in spite of the fact that they had **frustrated** his **word**!

IV. NEBUCHADNEZZAR'S DREAM OF THE RUINED TREE AND ITS MEANING (Chap. 4)

4:1–9 Here **Nebuchadnezzar the king** witnesses to the greatness of **the Most High God** and to an experience in his life which led to his conversion (vv. 1–3). He had **a dream** which his own **wise men** were unable to interpret, so he sent for **Daniel** and **told** him **the dream**.

4:10–15b He had seen **a tree**, high, beautiful, and fruitful. **The tree . . . reached to the heavens** and spread out **to the ends of all the earth. A watcher, a holy one coming down from heaven**, ordered **the tree** to be chopped **down**, leaving only a **stump and roots in the** ground.

4:15c–18 Then the holy one described **a man** losing his senses and becoming like **a** wild **beast** of the earth for **seven** years.

4:19–26 Daniel told the king that **the tree** represented him and his worldwide empire. He would lose his throne, and he would become insane for **seven** years, living like an animal in **the field**. (The medical name for his condition is boanthropy.[4]) But **the stump** signified that Nebuchadnezzar would not be destroyed but would be restored.

4:27–37 Daniel also counseled the king to change his ways. However, after **twelve months** of impenitence on the king's part, the vision came to pass. For **seven** years he lived like a beast. **At the end of** that **time**, he turned to God and acknowledged that He is **the Most High . . . who lives forever**. He was then **restored to the the glory of** his **kingdom**.

V. BELSHAZZAR'S DOOM ANNOUNCED BY THE HANDWRITING ON THE WALL (Chap. 5)

5:1–4 **Belshazzar** was the son of Nabonidus and the grandson of **Nebuchadnezzar** (**"father"** in v. 2 may also mean "grandfather"). He **made a great feast**, using the sacred **gold and silver vessels which . . . Nebuchadnezzar had** stolen **from the temple . . . in Jerusalem** for an idolatrous carnival. The king and his entourage drank themselves drunk on wine, and **praised the gods of gold and silver, bronze and iron, wood and stone**.

5:5–9 While he and his lords became drunken and riotous, **the fingers of a man's hand appeared**, writing **on the . . . wall**. The terrified king offered a **purple** robe, a **chain of gold**, and promotion to be one of three rulers (probably with Nabonidus and Belshazzar), to anyone who could interpret the writing.

5:10–16 At the queen's suggestion, **Daniel** was summoned to interpret the **writing**.[5] Even after all these

Ishtar Gate. A procession moves along Marduk's Way and enters Nebuchadnezzar's palace through the massive Ishtar Gate in this painting by Maurice Bardin. The famous hanging gardens are pictured in the upper righthand corner, and the city's Ziggurat appears behind them.

years and the changes in government, the **excellent wisdom** and spirituality of Daniel were remembered at least by someone. So **Daniel was brought in before the king**.

5:17–24 After reviewing the experience of **Nebuchadnezzar** and boldly rebuking **Belshazzar** for desecrating **the vessels** of the temple by using them in a drunken, idolatrous feast, Daniel proceeded to reveal the **writing** and its meaning.

5:25–31 The writing was **MENE, MENE, TEKEL, UPHARSIN. MENE** means **"numbered." God** had **numbered** the Babylonian Empire **and fin-**

ished it. **TEKEL**[6] means **"weighed."** Belshazzar was **weighed in the balances, and found wanting. UPHARSIN** means **"divided"** or divisions. (PHARSIN is the plural of **PERES**. The **"U"** means "and.") Belshazzar's **kingdom** was **divided, and given to the Medes and Persians. That** same **night**, the Medo-Persian armies marched into Babylon, slew **Belshazzar**, and seized world dominion. **Darius the Mede** was the new king.

VI. DECREE OF DARIUS AND THE DEN OF LIONS (Chap. 6)

6:1–3 In this chapter, one of the best known in the whole Bible, Daniel is living under Persian rule. He has been promoted by **Darius** the king to become **one** of **three governors** to be **over** the **one hundred and twenty satraps**. Due to the **excellent spirit** in **Daniel**, Darius **gave thought to setting him over the whole realm**.

6:4–8 Officials who were jealous of **Daniel** and who knew that they would never **find** him guilty of any real crime persuaded the **king** to pass a law forbidding prayer to anyone but Darius **for thirty days**. Once the **decree** became **law**, it could not **be changed**. Daniel's steadfastness is a challenge to us (1 Pet. 3:15, 16).

6:9–13 King Darius signed the written decree, but **Daniel** continued to pray to **God . . . three times** daily, and his enemies quickly reported him to **the king.**[7]

6:14–17 Darius **labored till** sunset to free **Daniel**, but the **decree** was unalterable, so he was compelled to have Daniel **cast . . . into the den of lions**. Nevertheless, this pagan king encouraged Daniel that the God whom Daniel served **continually** would **deliver** him. It is beautiful to see how even unbelievers will sometimes pick up on the faith and morals of consistent believers whom they observe at close hand. Only too often Christians fail their unsaved friends and relatives by *not* having as high standards of faith and practice as the world expects from God's people.

6:18–28 Rejecting his usual nightly entertainment, Darius **spent the night fasting. Very early in the morning, the** worried **king . . . went in haste to the den** and found the Jewish prophet unharmed by **the lions.**

In typical fashion the devout prophet gave the Lord the glory: **"My God sent His angel and shut the lions' mouths, so that they have not hurt me."**

Then Daniel's accusers were **cast** to the **lions** and devoured. The result of all this was that **King Darius** issued a decree **to all peoples, nations, and languages** honoring **the God of Daniel.**

VII. DANIEL'S DREAM OF FOUR BEASTS DEPICTING FOUR WORLD EMPIRES (Chap. 7)

The first six chapters of Daniel are mainly historical; the last six are prophetical. Daniel's **dream and visions** in chapters 7 and 8 occurred during the reign of Belshazzar, king of Babylon, before the Medes and Persians rose to power.

7:1–4 In chapter 7, we have Daniel's vision of **four great beasts** coming **up from the sea**. (The **Great Sea** is the Mediterranean.) These represent the four world empires.

The **lion** represents *Babylon*. The **eagle's wings** suggest swiftness of conquest.[8] **The wings . . . plucked** may refer to Nebuchadnezzar's insanity, and the rest of verse 4 to his recovery and conversion.

7:5 The **bear** pictures *Medo-Persia*. The Persian section was raised up to greater importance than the Median. The **three ribs** which it held **in its mouth** perhaps represent the three sections of the Babylonian Empire which were sacked by the Medes and Persians under Cyrus—Babylon in the east; Egypt in the south; and the Lydian kingdom in Asia Minor.

7:6 The **leopard** is a type of *Greece*. Its **four wings of a bird** speak of the rapid expansion of the Grecian Empire. **Four** is the number of the world. **Wings** speak of speed. Within thirteen years Alexander conquered the world, marching as far east as India. Then he died at thirty-three—empty handed. The leopard's **four heads** apparently set forth the division of the empire to four of Alexander's generals after his death.

7:7, 8 The **fourth beast**, powerful and destructive, was different from the others but had some of their bestial characteristics. It is described as **dreadful and terrible, exceedingly strong**, with **huge iron teeth**. It speaks of the *Roman Empire*, which would follow the Grecian Empire, would cease, and then, after a considerable space of time would be revived. It is in this revived form that it would have **ten horns**, that is, ten kings, and a **little . . . horn**, i.e., the future head of the Revived Roman Empire—the Antichrist.

7:9–14 In verse 9, Daniel pictures the fifth and final world empire—the glorious kingdom of the Lord Jesus Christ; He will be given universal dominion. The description of **the Ancient of Days** here resembles that of Christ in Revelation 1. But this identification is somewhat obscured in verse 13 by **One like the Son of Man coming** before **the Ancient of Days**. Then it would read as if Christ were coming before Himself. Perhaps it is best to think of **the Ancient of Days** here as being God the Father. **One like the Son of Man** would then be the Lord Jesus, coming before the Father to be invested with the kingdom.

The Ancient of Days sits as a Judge in **court** (vv. 10, 26). The little **horn** and his empire are **destroyed** (v. 11). The other world empires also cease, but the nations and people continue (v. 12). The Lord Jesus is **given** universal **dominion, a kingdom, the one which shall** never **be** superseded (v. 14).

7:15–18 When **Daniel** expressed anxious perplexity, an unidentified interpreter explained that the **four . . . great beasts** represented **four** world rulers who would **arise out of the earth**, but who would be succeeded by **the kingdom** of **the Most High** and of His **saints**. Whereas this world's kingdoms will all pass away, **the saints of the Most High** will have an everlasting **kingdom**. In verse 3 the beasts come out of the sea, which usually typifies the Gentile nations. Here in verse 17 they come **out of the earth**; this refers to their moral outlook as being earthbound and their character as being nonspiritual.

7:19–22 Daniel made special inquiry concerning **the fourth beast** which surpassed the others in cruelty and ferocity. He also wanted **to know** about **the ten horns and the other horn before which three fell**. He saw the little **horn . . . making war** with **the saints** of the Tribulation Period **until the Ancient of Days came**, ended their sufferings, and gave them **the kingdom**.

7:23–28 The unnamed interpreter explained **the fourth beast, the ten horns**, and the **pompous** little horn. The latter will blaspheme **the Most High, persecute the saints**, and **in-**

tend to change the Jewish calendar for three and a half years. (This is the Great Tribulation referred to by the Lord Jesus in Matt. 24:21.) But he will be stripped of his power and the glorious, **everlasting kingdom** of our Lord will be ushered in. Daniel responded with alarm and wonderment.

VIII. DANIEL'S VISION OF THE RAM AND GOAT NATIONS (Chap. 8)

8:1–4 Two years later **Daniel** had **a vision** of **a ram** and a male goat. The **ram** was Persia, and the **two horns** the kings of Media and Persia. **One** horn **was higher than the other**, the Persian king being the more powerful. **The ram** was on a rampage of conquest, **westward, northward, and southward**. Seemingly he was irresistible.

8:5–8 Then **a male goat** (Greece) **came from the west** on a blitzkrieg. It **had** one conspicuous **horn** (Alexander the Great). **The goat** defeated **the ram** and went on to tremendous conquests. When Alexander died, his kingdom was divided into **four** parts, depicted by the **four notable** horns which **came up toward the four winds of heaven**.

8:9–14 **One of** these was later ruled by **a little horn** (Antiochus Epiphanes), whose military success took him **south, east**, and into Palestine (**the Glorious Land**). Verse 10 describes his persecution of the Jews.[9] He blasphemed the Lord, caused the **sacrifices** to cease in Jerusalem, and desecrated the temple (vv. 11, 12). Daniel learned that this desecration would continue **two thousand three hundred** days. This took place between 171 B.C. and 165 B.C.

8:15–17 **Gabriel** was ordered to explain **the vision** to **Daniel**.

8:18–26 Daniel, although a godly and courageous man, was so overcome by fear in the angel's presence that he fell on his **face** into **a deep sleep**. Perhaps this is to emphasize God's power and holiness which is felt even in the presence of His angels. The explanation of the vision begins in verses 19–22, but at verse 23 we seem to see beyond Antiochus Epiphanes to his future counterpart—**a king** with **fierce features** who will ruthlessly persecute **the holy people** in the Tribulation Period. He will be **cunning**, proud, and deceitful, and **even rise against the Prince of princes** (the Lord Jesus Christ), but he will be destroyed by divine intervention. Daniel **was told** that **the vision** referred to the **future**.

8:27 Daniel became ill **for days, astonished** and perplexed.

IX. DANIEL'S VISION OF THE SEVENTY WEEKS OF GENTILE SUPREMACY (Chap. 9)

9:1, 2 This chapter takes place during the reign **of Darius** the Mede. By studying the book of **Jeremiah**, Daniel realized that the **seventy years** of captivity were almost at an end.

9:3–19 He confessed his **sins** and the **sins** of his people (he used the word **our**) and asked the Lord to fulfill His promises concerning **Jerusalem** and the people **of Judah**. In answer to his prayers God granted the prophet the very important revelation of the "seventy weeks," which has been called "the backbone of Bible prophecy."

Daniel's petitions were based on the character of God (His greatness, awesomeness, faithfulness, **righteousness**, forgiveness, **mercies**) and on His interests (**Your people, Your city, Your holy mountain, Your sanctuary**).

9:20–23 While he was . . . praying, Gabriel, being caused to fly swiftly, reached Daniel **about the time of the evening sacrifice**. He told him that he was **greatly beloved**, a tremendous tribute, coming as it did from God Himself. He then gave him an outline of the future history of the Jewish nation under the figure of seventy weeks. Each "week"[10] represents seven years. Since the prophecy is so crucial to understanding God's program, we will examine it phrase by phrase.

9:24 Seventy weeks have been decreed **for your people** (Israel) **and for your holy city** (Jerusalem). The historical fulfillment of the first part of the prophecy shows that the weeks are weeks of years. Thus seventy weeks equal 490 years. We will see that the seventy weeks are divided into seven weeks plus sixty-two weeks, and then, after a time gap, one final week. At the end of these **seventy weeks**, the following six things will happen:

To finish the transgression, to make an end of sins. While this may refer in a general sense to all Israel's sinful ways, it has special reference to the nation's rejection of the Messiah. At the Second Advent of Christ, a remnant will turn to Him in faith and the nation's **transgression** and **sins** will be forgiven.

To make reconciliation for iniquity. The basis for **reconciliation** was laid at Calvary, but this refers to the time, still future, when the believing portion of the nation of Israel will come into the benefit and enjoyment of the finished work of Christ.

To bring in everlasting righteousness. This, too, points forward to the Second Advent and the Millennium, when the King will reign in **righteousness**. It is **everlasting righteousness** in the sense that it will continue on into the eternal state.

To seal up vision and prophecy. The main body of OT **prophecy** centers on the glorious return of Christ to earth, and His subsequent kingdom. Therefore, the bulk of prophecies will be fulfilled at the end of the seventy weeks.

And to anoint the Most Holy Place. At the beginning of the thousand-year reign, the temple described in Ezekiel 40–44 will be anointed or consecrated in Jerusalem. The glory will return in the Person of the Lord (Ezek. 43:1–5).

9:25 So you are to **know and understand that from the** issuing of **the command to restore and** rebuild **Jerusalem**. This was the decree of Artaxerxes in 445 B.C. (Neh. 2:1–8).

Until Messiah the Prince. This refers not merely to the First Advent of Christ, but more particularly to His death (see v. 26a).

There shall be seven weeks (forty-nine years) **and sixty-two weeks** (434 years). The sixty-nine weeks are divided into two periods, **seven weeks** and **sixty-two weeks**.

The city **shall be built again,** with plaza and moat, **even in troublesome times**. Jerusalem would be rebuilt (during the first seven weeks) with public square and protective channel, but not without opposition and turmoil.

9:26 Then **after the sixty-two weeks**—that is, **after the sixty-two** week portion of time, which is really at the end of the sixty-ninth week, **The Messiah shall be cut off**. Here we have an unmistakable reference to the Savior's death on the cross.

A century ago in his book *The*

Coming Prince, Sir Robert Anderson gave detailed calculations of the sixty-nine weeks, using "prophetic years," allowing for leap years, errors in the calendar, the change from B.C. to A.D., etc., and figured that the sixty-nine weeks ended on the very day of Jesus' triumphal entry into Jerusalem, five days before his death.[11]

But not for Himself, or literally *and have nothing*. This may mean that He had received nothing from the nation of Israel, to which He had come. Or it may mean that He died without apparent posterity (Isa. 53:8). Or it may be a general statement of His utter poverty; He left nothing but the clothes that He wore.

And the people of the prince who is to come. This **prince who is to come** is the head of the revived Roman Empire, identified by some as the Antichrist. He will come to power during the Tribulation. His **people**, of course, are the Romans.

Shall destroy the city and the sanctuary. The Romans, under Titus, destroyed Jerusalem and its magnificent gold-trimmed white marble temple in A.D. 70.

The end of it shall be with a flood. The city was leveled as if by a flood. Not one stone of the temple, for instance, was left on another. Titus forbade his soldiers to put Herod's temple to the torch, but in order to get the gold they disobeyed, thus melting down the gold. To retrieve the melted gold successfully from between the stones they had to pry loose the great stones, thus fulfilling Christ's words in Matthew 24:1, 2, as well as Daniel's prophecy.

And till the end of the war desolations are determined. From that time on, the history of the city would be one of war and destruction. **The end** here means the end of the times of the Gentiles.

9:27 We now come to the seventieth week. As mentioned previously, there is a time gap between the sixty-ninth and seventieth weeks. This parenthetical period is the Church Age, which extends from Pentecost to the Rapture. It is never mentioned specifically in the OT; it was a secret hidden in God from the foundation of the world but revealed by the apostles and prophets of the NT period. However, the principle of a gap is nicely illustrated by our Lord in the synagogue at Nazareth (Luke 4:18, 19). Jesus quoted Isaiah 61:1, 2a but cut it short at "the acceptable year of the LORD" (His First Advent), and left off the judgment of His Second Advent: "and the day of vengeance of our God" (Isa. 61:2b). In between was to occur the whole Church Age.

Then he (the Roman prince) **shall confirm a covenant with many** (the unbelieving majority of the nation of Israel) **for one week** (the seven-year Tribulation Period). It may be a friendship treaty, a non-aggression treaty, or a guarantee of military assistance against any nation attacking Israel.

But in the middle of the week he shall bring an end to sacrifice and offering. The Roman prince will turn hostile toward Israel, forbidding further sacrifices and offerings to Jehovah.

And on the wing of abominations. We learn from Matthew 24:15 that he will set up an abominable idolatrous image in the temple and presumably he will command that it be worshiped. Some think that **wing** here refers to a wing of the temple.

Shall be one who makes desolate. He will persecute and destroy those who refuse to worship the image.

Even until the consummation, which is determined, is poured out on the desolate. Terrible persecution of the Jews will continue for the last half of the seventieth week, a period known as the Great Tribulation. Then the Roman prince, "the **one who makes desolate**," will himself be destroyed, as decreed by God, by being cast into the lake of fire (Rev. 19:20).

X. VISION OF GOD'S GLORY INTRODUCING OUTLINE OF COMING EVENTS (Chap. 10)

10:1–9 The events of this chapter took place **in the third year of Cyrus, king of Persia**. Some captives had already gone back to Jerusalem, as permitted by Cyrus's decree, but **Daniel** had remained in exile. After **mourning** for **three weeks**, perhaps because of discouraging reports from those who had returned (the work on the temple had stopped), because of the poor spiritual condition of those still in exile, or because he wanted to know the future of his people, Daniel was standing **by the** banks **of the Tigris** (Heb., *Hiddekel*). There he **saw** a **vision** of a glorious **man clothed in linen**. This description resembles that of the Lord Jesus in Revelation 1:13–16.

10:10–14 Then a voice explained why Daniel's prayers had been delayed. **The prince of the kingdom of Persia** had opposed for **twenty-one days**. Who is this **prince** (or ruler) who **withstood** the answering of Daniel's prayer for so long? Since **Michael** the archangel and protector of Israel is called into the fray, it must be an evil angelic power, one stronger than a merely human "prince." Leon Wood, in his excellent commentary on Daniel, explains:

> Because Greece also would have a similar "prince" assigned to her in due time (cf. v. 20), and God's people would be under Greece's jurisdiction following Persia's fall to Greece, the suggestion seems reasonable that Satan often assigns special emissaries to influence governments against the people of God. Certainly this chapter has much to contribute regarding the nature of struggles between the higher powers in reference to God's program on earth (cf. Eph. 6:11, 12).[12]

But how could the Prince of Persia successfully resist the Lord for twenty-one days, and why would the omnipotent Lord need the help of Michael (v. 13)?[13] One suggestion is that "the certain man" in verses 5 and 6 is *not* the Lord but an angelic being, perhaps Gabriel.

In either case, the voice explained why Daniel's prayers had been hindered; as already mentioned, **the prince of the kingdom of Persia** was responsible. The voice also promised to reveal the things which would **happen to** Daniel's **people**, the Jews, **in the latter days**.

10:15–19 This is done in chapters 11 and 12. There is a question whether the voice was that of the man in linen or the voice of an angelic messenger. Daniel **became** weak and **speechless** by this experience, but was **strengthened** by one with human appearance.

10:20, 21 **Then** this one whom Daniel addressed as "my lord" **said** that he **must** first **fight with the prince of Persia**, then encounter **the prince of Greece**. He would reveal further to Daniel what is written in **the Scripture of Truth**. **Michael**, **"your"** (Daniel's and his people's) **prince**, was the only one who stood firmly with him in these battles.

XI. PROPHECIES OF THE IMMEDIATE FUTURE (11:1–35)

A. Greece's Conquest of Medo-Persia (11:1–3)

Though still in the future when written, verses 1–35 are now past history. Verses 36 to 45 are still future. The **him** in verse 1 may refer to Michael, mentioned in the preceding verse, or **Darius**. Verse 2 tells of the power of four **kings** of Persia and the opposition of the last one to **Greece**. The four **kings** were Cambyses, Pseudo-Smerdis, Darius I (Hystaspes), and Xerxes I (Ahasuerus). Alexander the Great was the **mighty king** who wrested world power from Persia to Greece.

B. The Decay of the Grecian Empire (11:4–35)

1. *The Wars Between Egypt and Syria (11:4–20)*

11:4 When Alexander died, **his kingdom** was **divided** into **four** parts—Egypt, Syria-Babylon, Asia Minor, and Greece. The ruler of Egypt was the king of the south, while the ruler of Syria-Babylon was the king of the north. Not one of Alexander's successors was from **among his posterity**, but rather they were his generals.

11:5, 6 Verses 5–35 describe warfare lasting about two centuries between these latter two kingdoms. The *first* **king of the South** was Ptolemy I, and the **one** who **shall gain power over him** was Seleucus I of Syria. These two were allies at first, then antagonists.[14] Later Berenice, **the daughter** of Ptolemy II, married Antiochus II, king of Syria, to bring rapprochement between the two nations, but the strategem failed in a torrent of intrigue and murder.

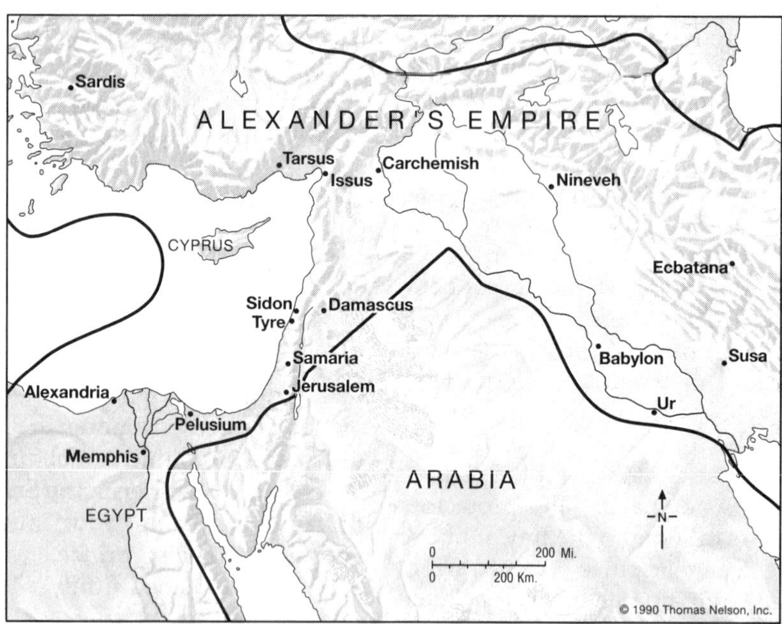

Alexander's Greek Empire

11:7–9 Ptolemy III, a brother of Berenice, successfully attacked the realm of Seleucus Callinicus, returning **to Egypt** with captives and great spoil. Two years later Seleucus launched an unsuccessful attack against Egypt.

11:10–17 **His sons** proved to be more successful, especially Antiochus III. Verses 10–20 describe how the tide of battle seesawed between **the North** and **the South**. Verse 17b tells how Antiochus III made a pact with

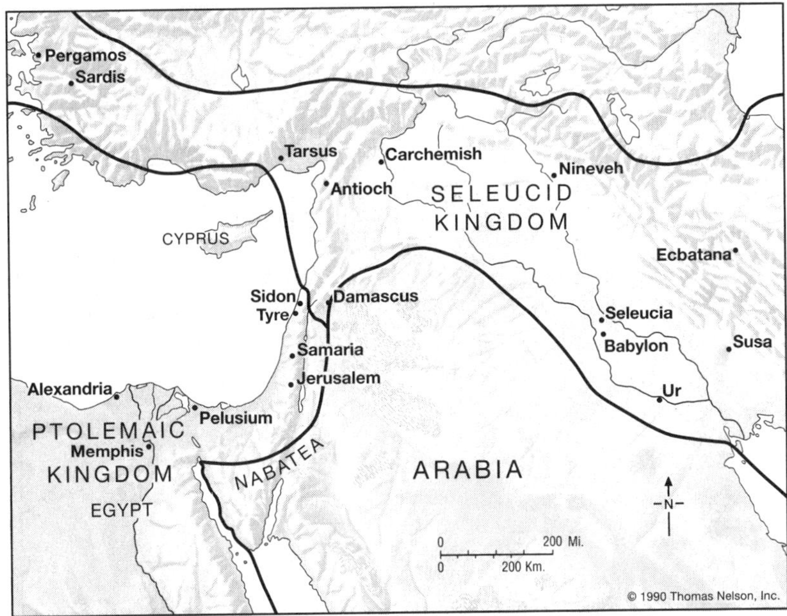

Ptolemaic Control of Palestine

Egypt, giving his **daughter** Cleopatra (not the famous—or notorious—queen of Egypt) in marriage to Ptolemy V, but she defected to side with Egypt.

11:18–20 When Antiochus III attempted to conquer Greece, he was defeated by the Romans at Thermopylae and Magnesia, and returned to his own land to die in an insurrection. His successor, Seleucus Philopater, became infamous for his oppressive **taxes on the glorious kingdom**, Israel. He died mysteriously, perhaps by poisoning.

2. *The Reign of Wicked Antiochus Epiphanes (11:21–35)*

11:21, 22 Verse 21 brings us to the rise of Antiochus Epiphanes, the "little horn" of Daniel 8. This **vile person** gained by **intrigue** the throne that rightfully belonged to his nephew. Kingdoms were inundated by his military might, and the Jewish high priest, Onias, **the prince of the covenant,** was murdered.

11:23, 24 Antiochus made treaties with various nations, especially Egypt, but always to his own advantage. When he plundered a conquered **province**, he used the wealth to extend his own power.

11:25, 26 His campaign **against** Egypt receives special mention; **the king of the South** was not able to withstand him, partly because of treachery among his own followers.

11:27, 28 Subsequently **both** the kings of Syria and of Egypt engaged in hypocritical and deceitful conferences. When Antiochus was **returning to his** own **land**, he began to direct his hostility against Israel, inflicting great slaughter and destruction.

11:29–31 The next time Antiochus marched against Egypt, he was repulsed by the Romans (**ships** of **Cyprus**) near Alexandria. Returning through Palestine, he took out his anger against Israel. Some apostate Jews collaborated with him. He discontinued **the daily sacrifices** and

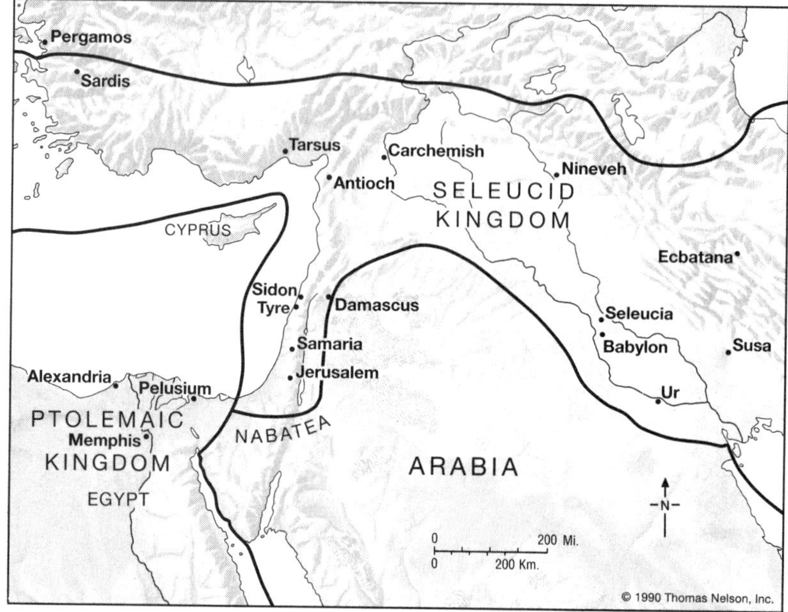

Seleucid Control of Palestine, c. 190 B.C.

ordered an idol to be erected in **the sanctuary**. According to secular history, he polluted the temple by offering a sow upon the altar. **The holy covenant** (vv. 28, 30, 32) refers to the Jewish faith, with particular emphasis on the sacrifical system.

11:32–35 These outrages brought on the Maccabean revolt, led by Judas Maccabaeus ("the hammer") and his

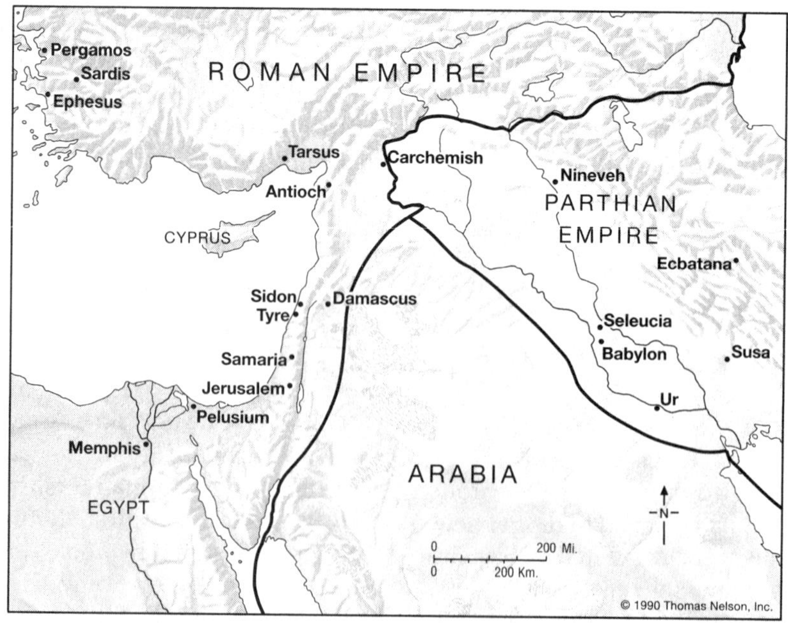

Roman Control of Palestine

family. Apostate Jews sided with Antiochus, but the faithful ones were **strong** and did **great exploits**. It was a terrible time of slaughter on one hand, but of spiritual brilliance and revival on the other.

XII. PROPHECIES OF THE DISTANT FUTURE (11:36—12:13)

A. The Antichrist (11:36–45)

11:36–39 As mentioned, verses 36–45 are still future. Verse 36 introduces the willful **king**, whose description makes him sound very much like the Antichrist. He will **prosper till** God's **wrath** against Israel is **accomplished**. Many believe that he will be a Jew, judging from such expressions as **"the God of his fathers"** and **"the desire of women"** (i.e., the Messiah). The Jews would hardly be deceived by a Gentile messiah. At any rate, he will greatly extend his sway through aggressive militarism.

11:40–45 There is a problem in verses 40–45 as to who is intended by **he** and **him.** One interpretation is as follows: **The king of the South** collides with the willful king in battle. **The king of the North** then swoops down through Palestine and on into Egypt. **But** disturbing **news from the east and** from **the north** causes him to return to Palestine where he encamps between **the seas** (Mediterranean and Dead Seas) and Jerusalem. He will be destroyed, with **no one** coming to **help him**.

B. The Great Tribulation (Chap. 12)

12:1–3 Verse 1 describes the Great Tribulation, the three and one-half years preceding Christ's Second Advent. Some will be raised to enter the Millennium with Christ; the wicked dead will be raised at the end of the Millennium (v. 2; see Rev. 20:5). **Those** tribulation saints **who** proved themselves **wise** by obeying the Lord and by leading others to faith and **righteousness** will be resplendent in eternal glory.

Some commentators see verse 2 as referring not to *physical resurrection* but to the *national and moral revival* of Israel. After God's ancient people are regathered to the land in unbelief, a remnant will respond to the gospel and will enter the Millennium. These are the ones who awake **to everlasting life**. All the others, who worship the Antichrist, will be condemned **to shame and everlasting contempt**. Buried among the Gentiles for centuries, Israel will be restored nationally, and then the believing remnant will experience the spiritual resurrection described in Isaiah 26:19 and Ezekiel 37.

12:4 Daniel was instructed to preserve the prophecies in a **book**. Verse 4b is commonly taken to speak of advances in transportation and scientific knowledge. But it probably doesn't mean this. Darby translates: "many shall diligently investigate." Tregelles renders it, "many shall scrutinize the book from end to end."[15] It teaches that many will study the prophetic Word and **knowledge** of it **shall increase** in the Great Tribulation.

12:5–10 These verses record a discussion between **two** unidentified individuals and a **man clothed in linen** as to **how long** it would be to the time of the end. The time given is three and a half years (**time, times, and half a time**). When Daniel expresses continued failure to **understand**, he is told that the vision will not be completely clear until it occurs. But he can be assured that the righteous will **be purified**, **the wicked** will manifest themselves as such, and only **the wise** will **understand**. From the beginning of the Great Tribulation to its end would be **time, times, half a time** (three and a half years or 1,260 days).

12:11 Perhaps **the abomination of desolation** will be set up in the temple of Jerusalem thirty days before the Great Tribulation begins; this would explain the **one thousand two hundred and ninety days** here.

12:12 As for the **one thousand three hundred and thirty five days**, this has been explained as taking us past the Coming of Christ and the judgment of His foes to the beginning of His reign.

12:13 Daniel would **rest** (in death) and **arise** in resurrection to enjoy his **inheritance**—millennial blessings with his Messiah, the Lord Jesus Christ.

ENDNOTES

[1](Intro) Merrill F. Unger, *Introductory Guide to the Old Testament*, p. 396.

[2](Intro) *Ibid.*, p. 399.

[3](Intro) Anderson first worked out the minutely detailed chronology of Daniel's Seventy Weeks in his classic, *The Coming Prince*.

[4](4:19–26) *Boanthropy* (ox-man), is a rare form of *monomania*. Dr. R. K. Harrison narrates in some detail his meeting a man in a London mental institution with this disease (*Introduction to the Old Testament*, pp. 1114–17).

[5](5:10–16) This probably refers not to Belshazzar's wife, but what we would call the *queen mother*.

[6](5:25–31) *Tekel* is related to the Hebrew word *shekel*. The *words* are in the language of the people present (Aramaic), but the meaning was so cryptic they could not understand the *message*. Also, perhaps the words were in a script other than that used for Aramaic.

[7](6:9–13) In Esther, King Ahasuerus was *also* duped by *his subjects* into making an "unalterable" law condemning God's people. Daniel, threatened by the lion's den, and Esther, facing Ahasuerus, both were in danger of losing their lives. Both depended on their God to save them, facing danger heroically. Both were foreigners in the Persian empire. In each case, a Persian king regretted signing a decree into an irrevocable law. In both accounts, God's people were saved from their enemies.

[8](7:1–4) The winged lion was Babylon's symbol just as a lion is the United Kingdom's and the eagle is the United States' emblem.

[9](8:9–14) Antiochus is in that long line of Jew-haters that includes Haman and Adolf Hitler. He is probably a type of the coming Antichrist. Antiochus liked to be called Epiphanes (Illustrious), but the Jews had another name for him: Epimanes (Madman)! His story is told in the apocryphal books of Maccabees.

[10](9:20–23) The Hebrew word for *week* merely means a unit of seven, and so some prefer to translate with the word *heptad*, a little-used word from the Greek for *seven*.

[11](9:26) April 6, A.D. 32, according to Anderson. In our time, Dr. Harold Hoehner, using a slightly different beginning date (444 B.C.) and ending date (A.D. 33), also comes up with a perfect set of dates for this prophecy. See *Bibliotheca Sacra*, January-March, 1975, pp. 62–64.

[12](10:10–14) Leon Wood, *A Commentary on Daniel*, pp. 272, 273.

[13](10:10–14) Some, like William Kelly, answer these objections by suggesting that the speaker in verse 13 is a person other than the Lord.

[14](11:5, 6) It is important to recognize that the titles "king of the North"

and "king of the South" refer to the leaders of Syria and Egypt ruling at the time of the events described in any verse, and not to the same set of rulers all the way through the text.

[15](12:4) S. P. Tregelles, *The Prophetic Visions in the Book of Daniel*, p. 158.

BIBLIOGRAPHY

Anderson, Sir Robert. *The Coming Prince*. London: Hodder & Stoughton, 1881. Reprint. Grand Rapids: Kregel Publications, 1975.

Baldwin, Joyce G. *Daniel: An Introduction and Commentary*. The Tyndale Old Testament Commentaries. Downers Grove, IL: InterVarsity Press, 1978.

Campbell, Donald K. *Daniel: Decoder of Dreams*. Wheaton, IL: SP Publications, Victor Books, 1977.

Dennett, Edward. *Daniel the Prophet: And the Times of the Gentiles*. Reprint. Denver: Wilson Foundation, 1967.

Gaebelein, Arno C. *The Prophet Daniel. A Key to the Visions and Prophecies of the Book of Daniel*. New York: "Our Hope," 1911.

Keil, C. F. *Biblical Commentary on the Old Testament*. Vol. 24. Grand Rapids: Wm. B. Eerdmans Publishing Company, 1971.

Luck, G. Coleman. *Daniel*. Chicago: Moody Press, 1958.

Pentecost, J. Dwight. "Daniel." In *The Bible Knowledge Commentary*. Wheaton: Victor Books, 1985.

Tregelles, S. P. *The Prophetic Visions in the Book of Daniel*. London: Samuel Bagster & Sons, 1864.

Walvoord, John F. *Daniel: The Key to Prophetic Revelation*. Chicago: Moody Press, 1971.

Wilson, Robert Dick. *Studies in the Book of Daniel*. Grand Rapids: Baker Book House, 1979.

Wiseman, D. J., et. al. *Notes on Some Problems in the Book of Daniel*. London: Tyndale Press, 1965.

Wood, Leon. *A Commentary on Daniel*. Grand Rapids: Zondervan Publishing House, 1973.

HOSEA

Introduction

"We have in the Book of Hosea one of the most arresting revelations of the real nature of sin, and one of the clearest interpretations of the strength of the Divine love. No one can read the story of Hosea without realizing the agony of his heart. Then, lift the human to the level of the Infinite, and know this, that sin wounds the heart of God."

—G. Campbell Morgan

I. Unique Place in the Canon

While the book of Hosea is not in narrative or story form, it does contain a story, although it is interwoven with the text.[1] Briefly, the story is that Hosea married Gomer and she bore three children—Jezreel, Lo-ruhamah, and Lo-ammi. Gomer was unfaithful, and in spite of this, Hosea sought her in great love, and bought her back from slavery and degradation.

The usual translation of Hosea 1:2 says that God apparently commanded the prophet to marry a woman who was already a harlot.[2]

Many Bible readers see a moral problem here. Would a holy God ask one of his prophets to marry a "wife of harlotry"? And would a morally sensitive prophet obey? At least three solutions have been proposed:

1. The first is that it is a *parable* to illustrate God's love for sinful Israel, and is not to be taken literally. However the style is *narrative*, as in Isaiah 7:3 and Jeremiah 13:11, which also are direct commands from God to prophets—and no one takes them as mere parables. The truth in this view is that the story does beautifully illustrate God's love for sinful Israel; the error lies in saying it was just a story.

2. A second view says, Yes, God did command it and Hosea obeyed. This certainly seems to be the normal reading of the text. (However, see Endnote 2.) The goal—in this case, salvation— justified the sorrowful means that Hosea had to experience.

Against this view is the fact that if Gomer were a harlot *before* her marriage, this would be a poor type of Israel.

3. A third solution says that Hosea married a pure woman who *later* became an adulteress. This view fits well with the prophet and his wife as being types of Jehovah and His unfaithful wife Israel. It also fits in with the prophet's (and the Bible's) high ideals of marriage. People who hold this view often find it hard to conceive of Hosea suffering so much grief over his wrecked marriage if Gomer had been immoral *to start with*.

A strong argument against this is that Hosea 1:2 calls her "a wife of harlotry" in the very command to take her as wife!

Perhaps our very repugnance against marrying an immoral woman is a further illustration of God's grace in putting up with Israel's sins (and the church's!) when He is much holier than any prophet or preacher ever could be.

Whichever view we may take, the story behind the prophecy vividly illustrates, as words alone could not, the amazing grace of God toward sinful, straying Israel, and by application, to all sinners who turn from their evil ways to a God of love.

II. Authorship

Hosea was the son of Beeri. His name means *salvation* and is basically the same as the name *Joshua* and its Greek form, *Jesus*. Living up to his name, Hosea prophesied concerning the salvation of Jehovah which will come when Christ returns to set up His kingdom. Hosea was a prophet chiefly to Israel, but there are passages that reflect a Judean interest as well.

III. Date

Hosea prophesied when Jeroboam II, the son of Joash, was king of Israel, and also when Uzziah, Jotham, Ahaz, and Hezekiah were kings of Judah. This would be a period of several decades in the eighth century B.C. R. K. Harrison believes Hosea's ministry "extended from about 753 B.C. to a time just before the fall of Samaria in 722 B.C."[3]

IV. Background and Theme

Hosea foretold the Assyrian invasion of the Northern Kingdom and the fall of Samaria.

When his wife Gomer left him to live shamefully in sin, God instructed His servant to buy her on the public market and bring her back in blessing. The purpose of all this, of course, was to picture God's relationship with Israel, (also called Ephraim, Jacob, and Samaria). The nation had proved unfaithful, living in idolatry and moral wickedness. For many years it would be without a king, a sacrifice, or idols. That is its present status.

In the future, however, when Israel returns to the Lord in repentance, He will have mercy. Ephraim will then be forever cured of her idolatrous backsliding and converted to God. Henry Gehman writes:

> Hosea presents the exhaustless mercy of God which no sin of man can bar or wear out. The master thought of Hosea's message is that God's mighty and inextinguishable love for Israel will not rest satisfied until it has brought all Israel into harmony with itself.[4]

Behind the chastening, as G. Campbell Morgan points out, there is a God of love:

> The supreme thing in every one of the prophecies is that the God with Whom these men were intimate was known by them to be a God of tender love, of infinite compassion, angry because He loves, dealing in wrath upon the basis of His love, and proceeding through judgment to the ultimate purpose of His heart. It is the heartbeat of God that throbs through these passages.[5]

OUTLINE

I. THE REJECTION OF ISRAEL PICTURED BY THE NAMES OF HOSEA'S THREE CHILDREN (1:1–9)

II. THE RESTORATION OF ISRAEL PROMISED (1:10—2:1)

III. GOD'S WARNING AGAINST ISRAEL'S UNFAITHFULNESS AND HIS THREATENED JUDGMENT (2:2–13)

IV. A FUTURE OF BLESSING FORETOLD FOR ISRAEL (2:14–23)

V. THE REDEMPTION OF HOSEA'S WIFE A TYPE OF ISRAEL'S ULTIMATE RETURN TO JEHOVAH (Chap. 3)

VI. GOD'S CONTROVERSY WITH HIS PEOPLE (Chaps. 4—10)
   A. The Sins of the People (4:1–6)
   B. The Sins of the Priests (4:7–11)
   C. The Idolatry of the People (4:12–14)
   D. A Special Appeal to Judah (4:15–19)
   E. The Evil Behavior of the Priests, the People, and the Royal Family (5:1–7)
   F. The Promised Judgments of Israel and Judah and God's Intention to Await Their Repentance (5:8–15)
   G. An Appeal to Israel to Repent (6:1–3)
   H. The Sinfulness of Both Israel and Judah (6:4–11)
   I. The Wickedness of Israel Unveiled (7:1–16)
   J. A Warning to Prepare for Foreign Invasion Because of Idolatry and Foreign Alliances (8:1–14)
   K. The Captivity of Israel Predicted as a Result of Its Iniquity (9:1—10:15)

VII. IN WRATH, GOD REMEMBERS MERCY (Chaps. 11—13)

VIII. ISRAEL URGED TO REPENT AND ENJOY GOD'S BLESSING (Chap. 14)

Commentary

I. THE REJECTION OF ISRAEL PICTURED BY THE NAMES OF HOSEA'S THREE CHILDREN (1:1–9)

1:1–5 The LORD directed the prophet **Hosea the son of Beeri** to marry an unfaithful woman. (See Introduction, "Unique Place in the Canon," for a discussion of the ethical question involved in such a marriage.) **He** married **Gomer, the daughter of Diblaim.**

Their first child was named **Jezreel** (God will scatter), an indication of what the Lord was about to do to the nation of Israel. The Assyrian army would **break** the power **of Israel in the Valley of Jezreel.**

1:6, 7 The second child was named **Lo-Ruhamah** (unpitied). This signified that **Israel** would **no longer** be pitied but would be sent into captivity, while **Judah** would be spared from the assaults of the Assyrians.

1:8, 9 The third child was named **Lo-Ammi** (**not My people**). **God** no longer recognized Israel as His own. Some also feel the prophet was questioning whether or not this child was *his own*.

II. THE RESTORATION OF ISRAEL PROMISED (1:10—2:1)

1:10, 11 But this judgment on **Israel** was only temporary. God would regather Israel and Judah and acknowledge them as His own. This will take place at the Second Coming of Christ.

In context the latter part of verse 10 clearly applies to *Israel*. But Paul quotes these words in Romans 9:26 and applies them to the call of the *Gentiles*. This illustrates the truth that when the Holy Spirit quotes OT verses in the NT, He is a law unto Himself.

2:1 In chapter 2 Hosea is told to speak to a faithful remnant of the nation. These **brethren** are spoken of as Ammi (**My people**) and Ruhamah (she who has obtained **mercy**).

III. GOD'S WARNING AGAINST ISRAEL'S UNFAITHFULNESS AND HIS THREATENED JUDGMENT (2:2–13)

2:2, 3 The faithful remnant should plead with the mass of the nation of Israel to put away her idolatry and **harlotries** or God will **strip her naked** and bring drought upon **her**.

2:4, 5 The **children** of the sinful nation will also be unpitied because **they are children of** a **harlot** who went **after** false gods and gave these idols credit for supplying her with food, clothing, and luxuries.

2:6, 7 God will put all kinds of roadblocks and obstructions in her way, and cut her off from her idols until she decides to **return** to Him (her **first husband**).

2:8 **She did not** give God credit for supplying her with necessities and luxuries, including the **gold** and **silver** which she used to make an idol of **Baal**.

2:9, 10 So God **will** cut off from her the food and clothing, and **will** thoroughly **uncover her lewdness**.

2:11–13 **Her mirth** and her **appointed** religious holidays will be canceled and **her vines and . . . fig trees** will be destroyed (**she** thought **these** were her pay from her idol **lovers**), and she will be punished **for** all **the days . . . she** served Baal.

IV. A FUTURE OF BLESSING FORETOLD FOR ISRAEL (2:14–23)

2:14–17 After that, He will restore and **comfort** Israel. God **will give her her vineyards** and **she** will **sing** as in the time **when she came up from the land of Egypt**. **She** will then call Him *Ishi* (**My Husband**), not *Baali* (**My Master**). The people will be cleansed from Baal-worship, even to the degree of forgetting the **names of the Baals**.

2:18–20 The nation will dwell in safety and peace because of the **covenant** God will make **with the beasts of the field** and other animals, rendering all wild animals harmless. Warfare will also be ended. Israel will be married to **the LORD forever**, under terms of **righteousness and justice, in lovingkindness and mercy**, bound by God's **faithfulness**.

2:21–23 **In that day, Jezreel** (Israel) will no longer mean *scattered*, but *sown*. The people will be sown in their own land; heaven and **earth** will join in blessing them and making them fruitful. Williams helpfully explains this paragraph as follows:

> Jezreel (Israel), as sown by God in the land (v. 23), will cry to the corn, the wine, and the oil to supply her needs; they will cry to the earth to

fructify them; the earth will cry to the heavens for the needed rain in order to produce the fruit; and the heavens will cry to Jehovah to fill them with the required water, and from Him there will be no further appeal, for He is the Great First Cause! In response to the appeal He will fill the heavens with moisture, the heavens will discharge it upon the earth, the earth will produce, as a result, the corn, the wine and the oil, Israel will have ample provision, and the heaven and earth will be bound together with a chain of love. Then God will have pity on Israel, will acknowledge her as His people, and Israel will acknowledge Him as her God.[6]

V. THE REDEMPTION OF HOSEA'S WIFE A TYPE OF ISRAEL'S ULTIMATE RETURN TO JEHOVAH (Chap. 3)

3:1–3 **Then the Lord** told Hosea to go to the public market and buy back his faithless wife from her sin. The purchase price, **fifteen shekels of silver** and **one and one-half homers of barley**, was that of a female slave. For **many days** after that, there were to be no marital relations; later she would be restored to her full marital status. This pictures the past, present, and future of the nation of Israel. Unfaithful to Jehovah (NKJV, Lord), she ran after other lovers (idols). But God brought her back.

3:4, 5 Her present condition is given in verse 4—**without** a **king**, without a **prince** (or royal family), **without a sacrifice** (that is, the Levitical sacrifices have been suspended), without **a sacred pillar** (idol), **without** an **ephod** (symbol of the Levitical priesthood), and without **teraphim** (household gods). Israel's future is given in verse 5—she will **return** to **the Lord** and will love and **fear** Him in faithfulness.

VI. GOD'S CONTROVERSY WITH HIS PEOPLE (Chaps. 4—10)

A. The Sins of the People (4:1–6)

4:1–3 God contends with Israel because of the people's unfaithfulness, unkindness, irreligion, **swearing, lying, killing, stealing, adultery**, and murder. Five of the Ten Commandments are summarized in verse 2. Violations of these commands were the reasons for the condition of **the land**. Even the wildlife would **waste away** because of the coming judgment.

4:4–6 Both **priest** and **prophet** are blamed because of their willful **lack of knowledge**. God's **people** were **destroyed for lack of knowledge**; they had **forgotten the law of** their **God**.

B. The Sins of the Priests (4:7–11)

The more the people **sinned**, the more sin offerings the priests greedily received. So, **like people, like priest**, they were both corrupt. Their punishment would be their enslavement to **harlotry, wine, and new wine**, indulging and never becoming satisfied.

C. The Idolatry of the People (4:12–14)

The idolatry of the people is described next. They sought guidance from **wooden idols**. They worshiped at mountain shrines, in the **shade** of trees. The men set the example, and the women followed.

D. A Special Appeal to Judah (4:15–19)

Judah is warned not to follow Israel's wicked example. Israel is stubborn, refusing to be separated from its idols and loving shame more than glory. In the RSV, verse 16 reads, "Like a stubborn heifer, Israel is stubborn; can the Lord now feed them like a lamb in a broad pasture?"

E. The Evil Behavior of the Priests, the People, and the Royal Family (5:1–7)

The **priests**, the people, and the **king** are alike guilty of idolatry and **Israel is defiled. Ephraim** has become a harlot. Both **Israel** and **Judah** shall be punished for their guilt because **they have dealt treacherously with the LORD**; they will take **flocks and herds** as offerings for **the LORD** but will **not** be able to **find Him**.

F. The Promised Judgments of Israel and Judah and God's Intention to Await Their Repentance (5:8–15)

5:8–12 The historical background for this section is found in 2 Kings 16. Israel (**Ephraim**) and Syria had invaded Judah. With the help of Assyria, Judah had counterattacked and captured territory. Three cities of **Benjamin** are warned to prepare for punishment with the words: **"Blow the ram's horn in** Gibeah, the trumpet in Ramah! Cry aloud at Beth Aven (v. 8). God **will be . . . like a moth** to Israel and dry rot **to the house of Judah**.

5:13–15 When Ephraim saw his sickness he sought help from **Assyria**. But he was not cured because Assyria was hired by Judah (and utilized by God) to fight against him. God determined to **return** to His **place** and wait for Israel and Judah to confess their sins and **seek** His **face**.

G. An Appeal to Israel to Repent (6:1–3)

Verses 1–3 are Israel's response to God's call to repentance (5:15). At first it seems genuine and heartfelt, but upon closer examination, we see that no sin is specifically confessed. The repentance is shallow and insincere. This is apparent from God's continued remonstrance with the nation in the rest of the chapter. True repentance does not come until the last chapter. There the nation repudiates its idolatry and acknowledges its need of God's grace.

Verse 2 may contain an allusion to the resurrection of Christ, which took place **after two days** and **on the third day**. If so, the national restoration of Israel is founded on and foreshadowed by the resurrection of Christ. Or the reference may be to the last three "days" of the Tribulation Period. Israel's repentance and mourning extend over the first two days. Then the nation is reborn on the third day and the Messiah appears.

H. The Sinfulness of Both Israel and Judah (6:4–11)

6:4–6 Because Israel and **Judah** have been faithless, God has condemned **them by the prophets**; He wanted love more than **sacrifice**, and **knowledge of** Himself **more than burnt offerings**.

6:7–11 "But they, like Adam (RV),[7] had **transgressed the covenant**." The wickedness of Israel is pictured in verses 7–10 as **a city of evildoers, bands of robbers**, and a murdering **company of priests. Judah**, too, is **appointed** to **a harvest** of suffering (v. 11) before God restores the fortunes of His people. (Some think the harvest here is one of blessing, not judgment.)

I. The Wickedness of Israel Unveiled (7:1–16)

7:1–7 The corruption of **Ephraim** was great, including **fraud**, robbery,

lies, wicked **deeds**, adultery, and drunkenness. The people and the royal **princes** were inflamed with lustful passions.

7:8–10 They **mixed** with foreigners, wasting their substance, and they would not listen to rebuke. The metaphor of Ephraim being **a cake unturned** suggests a lack of balance. On one side the cake is burnt and overdone; on the other side it is doughy and underdone. In short, Ephraim is completely spoiled.

7:11, 12 **Ephraim** flew **like a silly dove . . . to Egypt** and **Assyria** for help, but God would catch the dove in a **net** and punish the people.

7:13, 14 **They** had **fled from** the Lord and showed no genuine repentance. They **wailed** to God with their voice but **not with their heart**. It wasn't the soft sobs of repentance but the howling with pain of a wounded animal.

7:15, 16 The Lord had taught them how to win victories by being **disciplined and strengthened**; yet they trusted in idols, and so would meet defeat and **derision**.

J. A Warning to Prepare for Foreign Invasion Because of Idolatry and Foreign Alliances (8:1–14)

8:1–3 The Assyrian invader is likened to **an eagle** or a vulture, hovering over Israel. The people had broken the **law**, and therefore their doom was near. Though they professed to **know** the Lord, they had spurned Him.

8:4–6 The division of the kingdom into Israel and Judah was without His approval. Their idolatry caused God's **anger** to burn. God asks, **"How long until they attain to innocence?"** or, in modern terms, "When will they ever learn?"

8:7–10 The grain crops would fail, and the nation would be scattered **among the Gentiles**. Because Ephraim sought help from **Assyria** and its allies **among the nations**, God would punish him. This is poetically expressed by **"they shall sorrow a little"** (or "begin to diminish," NKJV marg.)

8:11–14 Israel's idolatry and Judah's trust in **multiplied fortified cities** would bring suffering and destruction.

K. The Captivity of Israel Predicted as a Result of Its Iniquity (9:1—10:15)

9:1, 2 **Israel** should **not rejoice**. Their idols would not give them the rich harvests they expected. Idolatry is *spiritual adultery*. Francis Shaeffer explains:

> Notice the form of speech God uses. A woman is out harvesting, and there is a freedom in the midst of the harvest. She takes a gift of money from some man to sleep with him on the corn floor in the midst of the harvesting. That is what those who had been God's people had become. The wife of the living God is this in her apostasy.[8]

9:3, 4 Because of their adultery, the people would go into captivity—not literally **to Egypt**, but to captivity **in Assyria** similar to the bondage in Egypt. Theirs was a mixed worship—idolatry mixed with the worship of Jehovah, pleasing neither Him nor themselves.

9:5–9 They would not be in the land to observe the appointed feasts; rather, they would be taken into captivity. **The tents** of Ephraim would be inhabited by **nettles** and **thorns** instead of by the people themselves. The exile was near, as well as the doom of false **prophets**.

9:10–17 **Israel** had been such

promising fruit at the outset, like **the firstfruits on the fig tree**, but it lapsed into terrible idolatry, and so is appointed to barrenness and loss of **children**. The expression **"to the last man"** (v. 12) must be understood relatively, not absolutely (see v. 17c). The male population would be drastically reduced. Because of exchanging their **glory** for **abomination**, **Ephraim** was given the sentence—**"No birth, no pregnancy, and no conception!"**

10:1, 2 Israel, once a luxuriant **vine**, is now empty, because it only used its prosperity to increase its idolatry. God now accuses them of being double-minded, holding them **guilty** for allowing **their heart** to be **divided**.

10:3, 4 The people disclaimed any need of God or of a **king**. In this we see how far the nation of Israel had fallen. Originally at Mt. Sinai they had pledged themselves to God's rule through Moses and Aaron. A long, continuous, downward apostasy followed, finally leading to a point where they could not even accept a king's rule over them. The progression of their spiritual demise is shown by the successive forms of government they had rebelled against: (1) God (theocracy); (2) Moses (prophet-lawgiver); (3) Joshua (spiritual/military general); (4) judges (judicial government); (5) kings (monarchy); (6) no king (anarchy—no government). They made covenants with empty oaths; therefore **judgment** would cover the land **like** poisonous **hemlock**.

10:5–8 The golden **calf** of **Beth Aven** (Bethel)[9] would **be** captured and **carried** away by the Assyrians. Instead of loving their God, who had saved them many times, the following words suggest with divine sarcasm that Israel was in love with the golden calf: **"Because of the calf . . . its people mourn for it . . . and its priests shriek for it—because its glory has departed."** No wonder God was about to punish them! Samaria's king would perish, the idol shrines would be destroyed, and men would call on **the mountains** and **hills** to fall on them.

10:9, 10 At **Gibeah** the tribes stood together in punishing the tribe of Benjamin for its sin (Judg. 20). But since then, the history of **Israel** has been a record of sin. Now God will use the nations to **chasten** a people united in sin.

10:11 **Ephraim** was once **a trained heifer**, reserved for the light work of threshing **grain**, but now it will be put under the yoke of captivity, and **Judah**, too, will be put to hard labor.

10:12–15 Their only hope of escape would be in repentance and seeking **the Lord**. But Israel must **reap** the fruit of its sinful dependence on chariots and soldiers. The land would be plunged into war, **all** their **fortresses** would **be plundered**, Samaria would be destroyed, and the king killed. **Shalman** (v. 14) is Shalmaneser III, although some think the name refers to a king of Moab named Salamanu.

VII. IN WRATH, GOD REMEMBERS MERCY (Chaps. 11—13)

It is helpful to distinguish the speakers in the next four chapters—whether it is the Lord or Hosea.

The Lord:	11:1—12:1
Hosea:	12:2–6
The Lord:	12:7–11
Hosea:	12:12—13:1
The Lord:	13:2–14
Hosea:	13:15—14:3
The Lord:	14:4–8

11:1–4 In love, God **called . . . Israel . . . out of Egypt** (Ex. 12). (This is also applied to the Lord Jesus in Matt. 2:15.) The more He **called**, the more **they went** after idols. He dealt tenderly and lovingly with **Ephraim**, but the latter **did not know that** the Lord had **healed** him.

11:5–8 Because of their turning from God, His people would **not** be sent to **Egypt** but would be exiled to Assyria. God's **heart** churned to think of making Israel as desolate as the cities of the plain, **Admah** and **Zeboiim**.

11:9–12 These verses are future. God has planned restoration and blessing for His people, and He will no more **destroy Ephraim**. In the Hebrew Bible, verse 12 is the first verse of chapter 12. It may mean, as in the KJV and NKJV, that while Israel was full of **lies** and **deceit**, **Judah** was **still** trusting in the Lord in Hosea's time. Or it may mean, as in the NASB, that Judah resembled Israel in its unruliness.

12:1, 2 Ephraim fed **on the wind** in the sense that he depended for survival on treaties **with the Assyrians** and **Egypt**. God has a controversy with Judah, and although Ephraim's sin was greater, He would **punish Jacob** as well.

12:3 The patriarch Jacob is in view here. Though in some other places he is seen in an unfavorable light, here he is held out as an example of one who won victories through turning to God.

12:4–6 The Angel in verse 4 is identified as the **LORD God of hosts** and **the LORD** in verse 5. He is the same as the angel of the Lord who appeared to Hagar (Gen. 16:7–11); Abraham (Gen. 18:1–33; 22:11, 15, 16) and Jacob (Gen. 31:11–13; 48:16). See also Exodus 3:2, 6–15 and Numbers 22:22–35. Evangelicals generally believe that He is the Second Person of the Trinity in a preincarnate appearance.

Ephraim is admonished to imitate Jacob by depending on God's strength rather than his own (see Gen. 32:28).

12:7, 8 But Ephraim is **a cunning Canaanite**[10] (merchantman), a cheater, a self-reliant boaster, who thought himself immune from detection.

12:9 The LORD reminds him that he owes all his prosperity to the One who brought him out **of Egypt**. If he would only obey, God would still **make** him **dwell in tents, as in the days of the . . . Feast** (of Tabernacles).

12:10–12 Jehovah had **spoken** repeatedly through **the prophets**, but in vain. **Gilead** and **Gilgal**, the two parts of the Northern Kingdom, divided by the Jordan, will be brought to nothing because of their idolatry. The nation's ancestor, **Jacob**, was a fugitive in **Syria** and a lowly tender of **sheep** in Mesopotamia.

12:13 But God graciously led his descendants **out of** servitude in **Egypt** by Moses the **prophet**.

12:14 Unmindful of this, **Ephraim** has **provoked** the Lord **to anger** by his idolatry and has brought **the guilt of his bloodshed** on himself. God will bring back **his** shame and **reproach upon him**.

13:1 Before Ephraim's idolatrous career, **he exalted himself in Israel when** he **spoke, but when he** turned to **Baal worship, he died**.

13:2, 3 Now the people plunge deeper and deeper into idolatry, telling **men** to **kiss the calves**. For this they will be as transient as **the morning** cloud **or the early dew**. They will be **blown** away **like chaff** or **smoke from a chimney**.

13:4–8 It was **the LORD** who saved them from **Egypt** and provided for them **in the wilderness**. But **they**

forgot Him and turned to idols. Now God will turn on them **like a . . . wild beast**.

13:9–13 When the Lord does this, who **will** then **save** them? Ephraim's sin was **bound up** and kept for the day of judgment. The pains of **childbirth** would **come upon him**, but he did not present himself **where children are born**, that is, at the mouth of the womb for birth. This means that Ephraim did not repent in spite of God's judgments.

13:14 The RSV translates the first part of this verse as questions: "Shall I ransom them from the power of Sheol? Shall I redeem them from death?" The implied answer is "No." Instead, He will call to **Death** for its **plagues**, and to the **Grave** (Sheol) for its **destruction**, because **pity is hidden from** His **eyes**. This verse, however, is quoted in a different sense in 1 Corinthians 15:55.

13:15, 16 The dreadful destruction of Israel and **Samaria** by the cruel Assyrians (**"an east wind"**) is then predicted.

VIII. ISRAEL URGED TO REPENT AND ENJOY GOD'S BLESSING (Chap. 14)

14:1–3 Israel is called to repentance and even given the **words** of confession to use in a day still future. Reliance on **Assyria**, trust in the **horses** of Egypt, and idolatry are the sins mentioned. They acknowledge that God is their only hope.

14:4–7 In truly exquisite nature poetry, the Lord promises healing, **love**, refreshment, attractiveness, revival, and growth.

14:8 The Lord is still speaking in verse 8.[11] He wants the **idols** of His people to be a thing of the past. He reminds them that He is their Protector and Provider.

14:9 The prophet Hosea closes his prophecy by emphasizing that wisdom and prudence lie in obedience to **the ways of the Lord**.

ENDNOTES

[1](Intro) Jonah is the only prophecy in narrative form.

[2](Intro) Morgan, following Ewald and the margin of the ERV and ASV, translates, "When Jehovah spake at the first with (not "by") Hosea." He maintains that the prophet was looking back to his early communion *with* God. Hosea was saying, "in effect: When away back there my ministry began, when, before the tragedy came into my life, Jehovah spoke with me, it was He Who commanded me to marry Gomer. The statement distinctly calls her a woman of whoredom, but it does not tell us that she was that at the time. It certainly does mean that God knew the possibilities in the heart of Gomer, and that presently they would be manifested in her conduct, and knowing, He commanded Hosea to marry her, knowing also what his experience would do for him in his prophetic work. When Hosea married Gomer, she was not openly a sinning woman, and the children antedated her infidelity" (G. Campbell Morgan, *Hosea: The Heart and Holiness of God*, p. 9).

[3](Intro) R. K. Harrison, *Introduction to the Old Testament*, p. 860.

[4](Intro) Henry Snyder Gehman, Editor, *The New Westminster Dictionary of the Bible*, p. 410.

[5](Intro) G. Campbell Morgan, *The Minor Prophets*, p. 6.

[6](2:21–23) George Williams, *The Student's Commentary on the Holy Scriptures*, p. 633.

[7](6:7–11) In Hebrew the same letters spell *man* and *Adam*.

[8](9:1, 2) Francis A. Schaeffer, *The Church at the End of the 20th Century*, p. 124.

[9](10:5–8) *Bethel* means *house of God;* the name *Beth Aven* is a parody of this name, meaning *house of wickedness*.

[10](12:7, 8) The Canaanites were such avid "traffickers" (ERV, ASV) that their name became synonymous with huckstering.

[11](14:8) The punctuation is not part of the original, but most translations agree on this.

BIBLIOGRAPHY

Feinberg, Charles Lee. *The Minor Prophets*. Chicago: Moody Press, 1976.

Keil, C. F. "Hosea." In *Commentary on the Old Testament*. Vol. 25. Grand Rapids: Wm. B. Eerdmans Publishing Co., 1971.

Kelly, William. *Lectures Introductory to the Study of the Minor Prophets*. London: C. A. Hammond Trust Bible Depot, n.d.

Kidner, Derek. *Love to the Loveless: The Message of Hosea. The Bible Speaks Today*. Downers Grove, IL: Inter-Varsity Press, 1981.

Logsdon, S. Franklin. *Hosea: People Who Forgot God*. Chicago: Moody Press, 1959.

Morgan, G. Campbell. *The Heart and Holiness of God*. Old Tappan, NJ: Fleming H. Revell, 1967.

———. *The Minor Prophets*. Old Tappan, NJ: Fleming H. Revell Company, 1960.

Pfeiffer, Charles F. "Hosea." In *The Wycliffe Bible Commentary*. Chicago: Moody Press, 1962.

Stevenson, Herbert F. *Three Prophetic Voices. Studies in Joel, Amos and Hosea*. Old Tappan, NJ: Fleming H. Revell, 1971.

Tatford, Frederick A. *The Minor Prophets*. Vol. 1. Reprint (3 vols.). Minneapolis: Klock & Klock Christian Publishers, 1982.

JOEL

Introduction

"Joel, . . . was probably the first of the so called writing prophets; so this book provides a valuable insight into the history of prophecy, particularly as it furnishes a framework for the end times which is faithfully followed by all subsequent Scripture. God started a new work with the writing of Joel, that of preparing the human race for the end of this temporal era, and thus gave an outline of His total plan. Later prophets, including even our Lord, would only flesh out this outline, but in keeping with the divine nature of true Scripture, never found it necessary to deviate from this, the initial revelation."

—Montague S. Mills

I. Unique Place in the Canon

The prophecy of Joel is short but certainly not lacking in beauty or interest. The prophet uses many literary devices to produce his vivid style: alliteration, metaphors, similes, and both synonymous and contrasting parallelism (see Introduction to the Psalms for a discussion of parallelism). W. Graham Scroggie praises Joel's literary impact as follows:

> The style is elegant, clear, and impassioned, and must be given a high place in Hebrew literature.[1]

A most unusual feature of the Book of Joel is the plague of locusts (Chap. 1). Are they to be taken literally or is this symbolic of invading armies? Probably both. Sometime during the prophet's lifetime—and the date is very much controverted—an all-pervasive plague of locusts invaded Judah and completely devastates the land. This natural phenomenon is a vivid picture of the coming invasion of troops and the great and dreadful Day of the LORD.

A third remarkable feature of the prophecy is the prediction of the outpouring of God's Spirit on all flesh (2:28–32) and the wonders that would follow. Since Peter quotes this passage in his sermon in Acts 2, Joel has also become known as "the prophet of Pentecost."

II. Authorship

Joel is introduced as the son of Pethuel. Apart from that, little is known of him. His name means *Jehovah is God*. He has been called the John the Baptist of the OT.

III. Date

No king is mentioned by Joel and there are few chronological hints in his short prophecy to help place the book in its proper time frame. Dates as varied as the tenth century to the fifth century B.C. have been suggested.

Joel's position in the "Book of the Twelve," as the Jews call the Minor Prophets, indicates that Jewish tradition considered Joel to be an early book. Its style fits the earlier classical period better than the post-exilic era of Haggai, Zechariah, and Malachi. The fact that no king is mentioned may be due to the book having been written when Jehoiada the high priest was regent (in the boyhood years of Joash, who reigned between 835–796 B.C.). Also, Judah's enemies are the Phoenicians and Philistines (3:4) as well as the Egyptians and Edomites (3:19), not her later foes—the Syrians, Assyrians, and Babylonians.

IV. Background and Theme

If we accept the early date, Joel spoke to the nation of Judah from the reign of Joash to that of Ahaz. This would make him the earliest of the *writing* prophets.

The key phrase of the book is "the Day of the Lord," found five times (1:15; 2:1, 11, 31; 3:14).

There is a distinct break or turning point in the book at 2:18. Up to that verse, *Joel* has been speaking of the *desolation* that would come on Judah. From then on, God tells of the *deliverance* which He will bring to the nation.

OUTLINE

I. DESCRIPTION OF THE LOCUST PLAGUE (Chap. 1)
   A. Its Unprecedented Severity (1:1–4)
   B. Its Effect Upon:
      1. Drunkards (1:5–7)
      2. Priests (1:8–10, 13–16)
      3. Farmers (1:11, 12, 17, 18)
      4. The Prophet Joel (1:19, 20)

II. DESCRIPTION OF THE ENEMY INVASION (2:1–11)

III. DIVINE APPEAL TO JUDAH TO REPENT (2:12–14)

IV. DECLARATION OF A FAST (2:15–17)

V. DIVINE DELIVERANCE PROMISED (2:18—3:21)
   A. Material Prosperity (2:18, 19, 21–27)
   B. Destruction of the Enemy (2:20)
   C. Pouring out of God's Spirit (2:28, 29)
   D. Signs Preceding Christ's Second Advent (2:30–32)
   E. Judgment of Gentile Nations (3:1–16a)
   F. Restoration and Future Blessing of the Jews (3:16b–21)

Commentary

I. DESCRIPTION OF THE LOCUST PLAGUE (1:1–20)

A. Its Unprecedented Severity (1:1–4)

1:1–4 Under the figure of a locust plague, **Joel the son of Pethuel** here describes the impending invasion of Judah by an army from the north. This prophecy received a partial fulfillment in the Babylonian invasion, but in the future, the invader will be the king of the North (Assyria).

The severity of the locust plague was such that the elders could not remember **anything like** it. The plague was in four stages, the four stages in the growth of the locust: **the chewing locust, the swarming locust, the crawling locust**, and **the consuming locust.**[2] These may refer to the four world empires which ruled over God's people—Babylon, Medo-Persia, Greece, and Rome.

B. Its Effect Upon:

(1) Drunkards (1:5–7);
(2) Priests (1:8–10, 13–16);
(3) Farmers (1:11, 12, 17, 18); and
(4) The Prophet Joel (1:19,20)

The nation is called upon to repent, fast, and pray—from the **drunkards** to the **farmers** (vv. 11, 12, 17, 18), and the **priests** (vv. 8–10, 13–16).

The locusts had so **stripped** the **land** that there was nothing left with which to make offerings and sacrifices to **the LORD** (vv. 8–10).

The prophet saw this as **the day of the Lord and destruction from the Almighty** (v. 15). This expression refers to any time when God steps forth in judgment, putting down evil and rebellion, and triumphing gloriously. In the future, the Day of the Lord include the Tribulation Period, the Second Advent, the Millennial Reign of Christ, and the final destruction of the heavens and earth with fire.

The prophet, speaking for the people, cries to the LORD for mercy, because **fire has devoured** both **pastures** and **trees**. Even the **beasts of the field cry out to** God because the **brooks are dried up**.

II. DESCRIPTION OF THE ENEMY INVASION (2:1–11)

2:1–3 The people are called to battle by a **trumpet** sounding the **alarm**, for **the day of the Lord . . . is at hand**. The immediate reference was to the Babylonian captivity, but the complete fulfillment is still future. Before the invaders come, **the land** of Judah is like **the Garden of Eden**; afterwards it is a **desolate wilderness**.

2:4–11 The comparison of the locusts to **swift steeds**, climbing **the wall like men of war** marching **in formation**, entering everywhere **like a thief** and blackening the skies with their immense numbers, constitutes some of the most graphic, poetic description in the prophets.

This unendurable invasion is all at the beck and call of **the LORD**, whose **camp is very great**.

III. DIVINE APPEAL TO JUDAH TO REPENT (2:12–14)

Even now, **the LORD** calls the people to repentance. It is not too late to **return to** Him. But it must be more than outward ritual. Their turning was to be

with all their **heart, with fasting, with weeping, and with mourning.**

IV. DECLARATION OF A FAST (2:15–17)

All classes of people are summoned to **a sacred assembly** and to **consecrate a fast**. In a future day, **the priests** will cry to the **Lord** in a solemn penitential **assembly**.

V. DIVINE DELIVERANCE PROMISED (2:18—3:21)

A. Material Prosperity (2:18, 19, 21–27)

Then the Lord will be zealous for His land and pity His people. He will **send** them **grain, new wine, and oil** to their satisfaction, in addition to removing their **reproach** from **among the nations**. The land will be restored to fertility and productiveness. Abundant **rain** will result in **vats** overflowing and **threshing floors . . . full of wheat. The people** will be restored and will **never** again **be put to shame**. All **the years that the swarming locust** had **eaten** would be restored as well (2:25).

B. Destruction of the Enemy (2:20)

In the remainder of Joel, the Lord tells what He will do for Judah. He will destroy **the northern army** (the Assyrian) from **the eastern sea** (Dead Sea) to **the western sea** (Mediterranean).

C. Pouring out of God's Spirit (2:28, 29)

God **will pour out** His **Spirit on all flesh** in that day. The younger generation **shall prophesy** and **see visions** and the **old men shall dream dreams**. This latter prophecy was partially fulfilled in Acts 2:16–21, but Pentecost did not exhaust it. Its complete fulfillment will take place at the outset of Christ's one-thousand year reign.

D. Signs Preceding Christ's Second Advent (2:30–32)

The outpouring of the Spirit will be preceded by **wonders in the heavens**. Some of these predicted signs are: **Blood, fire, pillars of smoke, the sun** turning **into darkness and the moon into blood**. All who turn to Jesus as Messiah, calling **on** His **name**, will **be saved** to enter the Millennium with Him.

E. Judgment of Gentile Nations (3:1–16a)

3:1–8[3] God will gather the Gentile nations **to the Valley of Jehoshaphat** and will judge them there for their treatment of the Jews. **Tyre, Sidon**, and **Philistia** will be recompensed for plundering and enslaving God's **people**. The people in those cities would in turn be **sold** as slaves—a fitting punishment for their crime.

3:9–16a The Gentiles are told to **"Prepare for war!"**, for the Lord will fight with them **in the valley of decision**. In **the Valley of Jehoshaphat** the Lord **will sit to judge all the surrounding nations**. The sovereign God is currently testing all men and nations, as unfashionable as that concept may be to today's worldly thinkers. Stevenson remarks:

> Men dismiss the Biblical teaching concerning judgment to come, for individuals and nations, as a now outmoded concept. But the people of God have held fast through all the generations to the assurance that, in the "day of the Lord," the Judge of all the earth will do right. That is our confidence, based upon the rock of Holy Scripture.[4]

F. Restoration and Future Blessing of the Jews (3:16b–21)

But **the Lord** will bless **His people** with deliverance, safety from invaders, and abundant supplies. The land of Israel would become fruitful and well-watered: **the mountains shall drip with new wine, the hills shall flow with milk, and all the brooks of Judah shall be flooded with water. Egypt** and **Edom** will become **a desolate wilderness, . . . but Judah** will be inhabited **forever**. God will also **acquit** her of her **guilt of bloodshed**.

The book ends on a secure note with a reason: **For the LORD dwells in Zion**.

ENDNOTES

[1](Intro) W. Graham Scroggie, *Know Your Bible*, Vol. I, p. 155.

[2](1:1–4) The KJV's "palmerworm, locust, cankerworm, and caterpillar" would suggest four different species of insect. This is not a likely meaning.

[3](3:1–8) In the Hebrew Bible, 2:28–32 constitute chapter 3 and our chapter 3 becomes chapter 4.

[4](3:9–16a) Herbert F. Stevenson, *Three Prophetic Voices. Studies in Joel, Amos and Hosea*, p. 40.

BIBLIOGRAPHY

Feinberg, Charles Lee. *The Minor Prophets*. Chicago: Moody Press, 1976.

Keil, C. F. "Joel." In *Commentary on the Old Testament*. Vol. 25, 26. Grand Rapids: Wm. B. Eerdmans Publishing Co., 1971.

Kelly, William. *Lectures Introductory to the Study of the Minor Prophets*. London: C. A. Hammond Trust Bible Depot, n.d.

Morgan, G. Campbell. *The Minor Prophets*. Old Tappan, NJ: Fleming H. Revell Company, 1960.

Stevenson, Herbert F. *Three Prophetic Voices. Studies in Joel, Amos and Hosea*. Old Tappan, NJ: Fleming H. Revell Company, 1971.

Tatford, Frederick A. *The Minor Prophets*. Vol. 1. Reprint (3 vols.). Minneapolis: Klock & Klock Christian Publishers, 1982.

AMOS

Introduction

"Unlike other prophets, Amos was not a man whose life was devoted to hearing and speaking the Word of the Lord. He was no product of the "schools of prophets," nor a professional "seer." He left his flock for a limited period, at the command of God, to deliver a specific message at Bethel. That done, he presumably returned to his sheep-tending at Tekoa."

—Herbert F. Stevenson

I. Unique Place in the Canon

The book of Amos is written in some of the finest OT Hebrew style. Amos was a sheep-breeder and tender of sycamore trees. Perhaps he illustrates the appearance of God-ordained men throughout history who speak very effectively and even beautifully for the Lord without the traditional "school of the prophets" background or formal education so much sought after today.

II. Authorship

Amos, whose name means *burden*, gives no family pedigree, hence we can assume he was not of noble or prominent stock, like Isaiah or Zephaniah. It has been common for preachers to paint Amos's "country" background too strongly. The word used to describe his regular livelihood is not the usual Hebrew word for "shepherd" but is used elsewhere only of King Mesha, who had a successful sheep-breeding business (2 Kgs. 3:4).[1] Although he belonged to the kingdom of Judah, he was commissioned to go north to Samaria and prophesy against the kingdom of Israel. Amos was a stern prophet of righteousness and uncompromising justice.

III. Date

Amos ministered during the reigns of Uzziah in Judah (790–739 B.C.) and Jeroboam II in Israel (793–753), an age of affluence, luxury, and moral laxity, especially in the Northern Kingdom. Amos mentions that this was "two years before the earthquake." This doesn't necessarily pinpoint the date, but archaeology has unearthed evidence of a violent earthquake in about 760 B.C., which would fit in with the dates of the kings that Amos mentions.

IV. Background and Theme

Assyria under Adad-nirari III had defeated the Syrian confederacy, thus allowing Jehoash and Jeroboam II to appropriate new land. Israel made enormous gains as Samaria became a trade stop-off for caravans. Ivory palaces were built, and businessmen became impatient with Sabbath restrictions. The rich were oppressive and corrupt, the courts were unjust; the religious services were either a sham or consisted of idolatry. Superstition and immorality abounded. Amos saw that such dreadful conditions could not last and that clouds of judgment were looming. Although he belonged to the Southern Kingdom, he was commissioned to go north to Samaria and prophesy against the kingdom of Israel. Israel was a basket of summer fruits whose judgment was on the way.

OUTLINE

I. THE THREATENED JUDGMENTS ON EIGHT NATIONS (Chaps. 1—2)
   A. Introductory (1:1, 2)
   B. Damascus (1:3–5)
   C. Gaza (1:6–8)
   D. Tyre (1:9, 10)
   E. Edom (1:11, 12)
   F. Ammon (1:13–15)
   G. Moab (2:1–3)
   H. Judah (2:4, 5)
   I. Israel (2:6–16)

II. THE GUILT AND PUNISHMENT OF ISRAEL (Chaps. 3—6)
   A. The First Summons to Hear (Chap. 3)
   B. The Second Summons to Hear (Chap. 4)
   C. The Third Summons to Hear (5:1–17)
   D. The First Woe (5:18–27)
   E. The Second Woe (6:1–14)

III. THE SYMBOLS OF APPROACHING JUDGMENT (7:1—9:10)
   A. The Plague of Locusts (7:1–3)
   B. The Devouring Fire (7:4–6)
   C. The Plumb Line (7:7–9)
   D. Parenthesis: Refusal of Amos to Be Intimidated (7:10–17)
   E. The Basket of Summer Fruit (Chap. 8)
   F. The Striking of the Lintel (9:1–10)

IV. THE FUTURE RESTORATION OF ISRAEL (9:11–15)

Commentary

I. THE THREATENED JUDGMENTS ON EIGHT NATIONS (Chaps. 1—2)

A. Introductory (1:1, 2)

In his first two chapters, Amos pronounces judgment against eight nations.

B. Damascus (1:3–5)

Each pronouncement of judgment is introduced by the words, "For three transgressions . . . and for four." J. Sidlow Baxter explains this Hebrew idiom for us:

> The phrase is not to be taken arithmetically, to mean a literal three and then four, but idiomatically, as meaning that the measure was full, and more than full; the sin of these people had overreached itself; or, to put it in an allowable bit of modern slang, they had "gone one too many," they had "tipped the scale."[2]

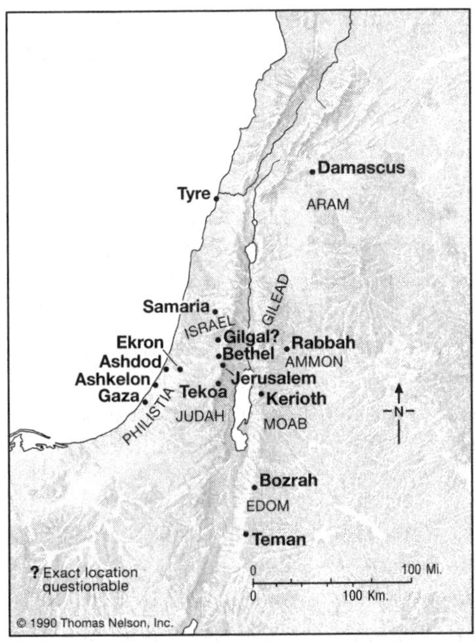

Amos: Places Judged by God

1:3–5 The first is against **Damascus**, the chief city-state of **Syria**. The Syrians had fought against the two and one-half tribes east of the Jordan (**Gilead**), and had apparently been extremely barbarous and cruel (suggested by **implements of iron**). The punishment for **the people of Syria** was to be carried away **captive to Kir**.

C. Gaza (1:6–8)

The second is against **Gaza**, where the Philistines handed over **captive** Israelites **to** the cruel Edomites. Other Philistine centers to be punished are **Ashdod**, **Ashkelon**, and **Ekron**. The result would be that **the remnant of the Philistines** would **perish**.

D. Tyre (1:9, 10)

The third is against **Tyre**. The Tyrians also **delivered up** captives **to Edom** and broke a treaty **of brotherhood** with Israel. **"Fire"** is also predicted for Tyre's **palaces**.

E. Edom (1:11, 12)

The fourth is against **Edom**. The Edomites were perpetual and cruel enemies of their brothers (Esau was a **brother** of Jacob). Because of their merciless dealings and implacable hatred, they would receive a fitting punishment upon the cities of **Teman** and **Bozrah**.

F. Ammon (1:13–15)

The fifth is against **Ammon**. The Ammonites committed terrible atrocities in conquering portions of the land of **Gilead**. **They** even **ripped open** pregnant **women** of **Gilead** in their bloody cruelty. Both **king** and **princes** were destined to **captivity**, **fire**, and a tempestuous battle.

G. Moab (2:1–3)

The sixth judgment is against **Moab**, who deprived **the king of Edom** of a decent burial (See 2 Kgs. 3:26, 27 where "his eldest son" probably refers to the eldest son of the King of Edom, not Moab).

H. Judah (2:4, 5)

Now **the LORD** is getting uncomfortably close to home: The next two nations to be judged are **Judah** and Israel! It is startling that they should be listed along with six Gentile nations. To the Jews of Amos's time, this would have been most degrading! But God points out in this way that, by their sin, Judah and Israel had forfeited all special recognition by Jehovah (NKJV, LORD). Judah would be punished because **they** had **despised the law of the LORD**, they did not keep **His commandments**, and they **followed . . . lies** (idols).

I. Israel (2:6–16)

2:6–8 Up to this point the people of **Israel** would applaud Amos's denunciations. But now he turns to them, and their applause will quickly turn to indignation! Israel would be punished because they oppressed **the righteous** and **the poor**, they committed terrible forms of immorality, they kept pledged **clothes** overnight,[3] and they became drunk in the temple with **wine** purchased with money gained by extortion and bribery.

2:9–12 Next, God recites His past mercies for Israel—He **destroyed the Amorites**, who dwelt like **cedars** and **oaks** in the land of Canaan. He saved Israel out **of the land of Egypt** and **raised up . . . Nazirites** to exhibit to them lives of separation. But they corrupted the **Nazirites** and **commanded the prophets not** to **prophesy**.

2:13–16 As a consequence, God would crush them, prevent their **escape**, and cause their defeat by the Assyrians. Even the **mighty** men will not be able to **deliver** themselves, and **flight shall perish from the swift.**

II. THE GUILT AND PUNISHMENT OF ISRAEL (Chaps. 3—6)

A. The First Summons to Hear (Chap. 3)

3:1, 2 Again **the LORD** threatens judgment on **the children of Israel**. Because they occupied a uniquely close relationship to Jehovah, their sin was all the more serious, and their punishment would be all the more severe. Therefore He would **punish** them **for all** their **iniquities**.

3:3–8 The judgment would not descend without a reason—every effect has a cause. Amos asks seven cause-and-effect questions, culminating with an urban **calamity** caused by **the LORD**. It should not come as a surprise because God had revealed it in advance through His **prophets**.

3:9–12 **Ashdod** (Philistia) and **Egypt** are invited to witness the oppression, injustice, **violence**, and **robbery** in **Samaria**. These sins would bring the Assyrian invader into **the land** of Israel. Only a small remnant, graphically pictured as **remnant** parts of a devoured sheep, would survive.

3:13–15 **The altars** at **Bethel**, where the golden calf was worshiped, would be thoroughly destroyed. The calf itself would be taken to Assyria (Hos. 10:5, 6). The **great houses** of the affluent would **have an end**.

B. The Second Summons to Hear (Chap. 4)

4:1–3 The rich women of Samaria are likened to **cows of Bashan**, well-fed and unmanageable. They were guilty of oppressing **the poor** and living luxuriously. For this they would be carried into Assyrian captivity, leaving the land in confusion and panic. In their exit they and their **posterity** are pictured being led away **with fishhooks** and scrambling **through broken walls**.

Instead of transliterating **Harmon** as a place name (RSV, NASB, NKJV), some versions, including KJV, translate it "palace." Darby notes:

> Some translate "to the mountains"; others, "to the (enemy's) fortress," or "to the palace" [KJV], as in 1:4: the meaning is not ascertained.

4:4–13 God invites them ironically to carry on their idolatrous worship, bringing their **sacrifices** to **Bethel**; there was nothing for Him in it. They had suffered **lack of bread** (v. 6), drought (vv. 7, 8), **blight**, **mildew**, a plague of locusts (v. 9), pestilence, warfare, slaughter (v. 10), and catastrophes (v. 11). Since none of these things caused them to repent, **Israel** should now **prepare to meet . . . God** Himself—**the Lord God of hosts**. Verse 12 is not a gospel appeal, but a message of judgment.[4]

C. The Third Summons to Hear (5:1–17)

5:1–7 The prophet laments over Israel's downfall; only one soldier in ten will be spared. Even yet, the people should **not seek** the cities where the idol shrines were (**Bethel**, **Beersheba**, **Gilgal**); they should **seek the Lord and live**.

5:8–13 Otherwise the Lord who made the constellations **Pleiades and Orion** and rules the universe will pour out His wrath upon them for their lack of **justice** and righteousness. The sinners of Israel hated a righteous man who reproved them and abhorred an honest man. Because they had grown rich dishonestly, they would not be permitted to enjoy their wealth.

5:14–17 A call to righteousness and social justice goes forth: **"Seek good and not evil . . . establish justice."** However, it is clear from the sudden change—**"There shall be wailing in the streets"**—that the people will not listen and so are doomed to punishment.

D. The First Woe (5:18–27)

5:18–20 The people should not **desire the day of the Lord**; it will be a day of **darkness** and calamity, with one evil overtaking another.

5:21–27 Israel was bringing sacrifices and **offerings** to the Lord on their **feast days**, but their lives were corrupt, so their **offerings** were rejected by God. He would rather have **righteousness** than ritual. Even in the wilderness, when professing to worship Jehovah, they had practiced idolatry with Moloch and other **idols**, such as **Sikkuth** and **Chiun**.

E. The Second Woe (Chap. 6)

6:1–8 Their luxury, ease, complacency, and security would be disturbed by violence. **"Woe"** is pronounced on those **who lie on beds of ivory, stretch out on** their **couches**, eating all they want, **sing idly to the sound of stringed instruments, drink wine** abundantly **from bowls, anoint themselves with the** most expensive perfumes and colognes, **recline at banquets**. God's reaction to their attitude of ease and complacency is: **"I abhor the pride of Jacob, and hate his palaces."** Samaria would be delivered up to the Assyrians.

6:9, 10 These tragic verses are well described by Page H. Kelly:

In the pestilence that will sweep across the land there will be so many victims that normal burial practices will have to be set aside and the survivors will resort to the unusual procedure of burning the corpses, When the relative of a deceased man enters his house to take out his body to be burned, he discovers that there is a lone survivor, hidden in some far corner of the house. When the relative calls out to him, he responds with a Hebrew interjection translated "Hush!" and then adds, "We must not mention the name of the Lord." These men have profaned the name of God in the past but now they dare not pronounce it, lest it loosen some fresh avalanche of His wrath. It is significant that even to this day an orthodox Jew will not pronounce the covenant name of Israel's God.[5]

6:11–14 Their behavior was foolish and futile, and it is compared to **oxen** plowing **on rocks**. They perverted **justice** and scorned **righteousness**. They boasted in their military **strength**, though **Lo Debar** and **Karnaim** were insignificant victories. The Assyrians would **afflict** the land **from the** northern **entrance to Hamath** to the southern boundary, **the Valley of Arabah**.

III. THE SYMBOLS OF APPROACHING JUDGMENT (7:1—9:10)

A. The Plague of Locusts (7:1–3)

In verses 1–9, Amos intercedes for his people. Three threats to Israel are described, The first may typify the attack of Pul, king of Assyria, under the figure of a devouring **locust**. In answer to Amos's prayer, the judgment was averted.

B. The Devouring Fire (7:4–6)

The second may have been the invasion of Tiglath-Pileser, under the symbol of a consuming **fire**. Prayer for little **Jacob** again prevented a catastrophe.

C. The Plumb Line (7:7–9)

The third may refer to the destruction of Samaria by Shalmaneser. The **plumb line** speaks of the absolute uprightness of the judgment. God announced that He would **not pass by... Israel** in mercy **anymore**.

D. Parenthesis: Refusal of Amos to Be Intimidated (7:10–17)

7:10–13 **Amaziah**, an idolatrous **priest of Bethel**, forbade Amos to **prophesy** against **the king's sanctuary** of **Bethel**, telling him to go back to his home in **Judah** and earn his **bread . . . there**.

7:14–17 **Amos answered** that God had put him into the ministry and that he would not stop. He **was no prophet** in the technical sense, or the **son of a prophet**, but he must speak **the word of the Lord**. So, he told Amaziah of the fearful doom which would come upon him, his **wife**, his **sons and daughters**, and **his land**.

E. The Basket of Summer Fruit (Chap. 8)

8:1–6 The **basket of summer fruit** signified that Israel was ripe for judgment. God would **not pass by** in mercy **anymore**. The rich were oppressing **the poor**; they could not wait for the feast days to end so they could make more money; their business practices were corrupt; they were guilty of **falsifying the scales**.

8:7–12 For all of this, the Lord will punish **the land** with fearful earthquakes. Darkness will cover the earth during the day, and **mourning** will visit every house. People will long to hear **the word of the Lord**, but it will be withheld from them. **Famine** and drought (of God's **word**) will prevail.

8:13, 14 Idolatry will bring severe drought on Israel's most attractive **young** people and destruction on **those who swear by** false gods. Men will seek for a message from their idols but will not receive it.

F. The Striking of the Lintel (9:1–10)

9:1–4 **The LORD** is seen beginning His judgment at **the altar**, perhaps the false altar at Bethel. The people find no way of ultimate escape; the sword pursues them wherever they try to flee. Even hypothetical places of "refuge" would elude them: **hell, heaven, on top of** Mt. **Carmel, the bottom of the sea, captivity before their enemies**. The seriousness of God's anger against them is seen in the words: **"I will set My eyes on them for harm and not for good."** In no uncertain terms the people of Israel are told that they are in big trouble!

9:5–10 Who can withstand **the Lord GOD of hosts** with His almighty power? The **layers** of earth's atmosphere and the **strata** of rock in the earth itself were **built** and **founded** by the same **LORD**. Israel is compared here to heathen **Ethiopia** and called **"the sinful kingdom"** by God Himself—strong language indeed! They had forfeited any special place of privilege. He would punish **the sinners** but save a remnant **as grain is sifted in a sieve; yet not the smallest grain** would **fall to the ground**. Although most would be destroyed, those found worthy by the Almighty would be spared.

IV. THE FUTURE RESTORATION OF ISRAEL (9:11–15)

9:11, 12 The restoration of Israel is described in verses 11–15. God's promises to **David** will be fulfilled. While some people employ verse 11 to teach that Israel and the church are one and the same, and that the church now is the "repaired" **tabernacle** (lit. "booth," figure of a deposed dynasty, NKJV marg.) it is surely to be taken in context to refer to Israel and **all the Gentiles** in the Millennial Kingdom. Scofield writes:

> The Davidic monarchy, pictured by a tabernacle . . . , was in a degraded condition. Cp. Isa. 11:1. On the basis of this verse the Talmudic rabbis called Messiah *Bar Naphli* ("the son of the fallen"). But He will arise (Mal. 4:2).[6]

9:13–15 Crops such as **grapes, wine**, wheat, olives, and **fruit** will grow up with amazing speed, the **cities** will be rebuilt and re-inhabited, and God **will plant** the people, who will never be driven out of **the land** again.

ENDNOTES

[1](Intro) The word for a shepherd is *rō'eh*; the word for a sheep-breeder is *nōqēd*.

[2](1:3–5) J. Sidlow Baxter, *Explore the Book*, p. 130.

[3](2:6–8) A garment given in pledge that a debt would be paid was not to be kept overnight, since it might well be the only blanket that a poor person had (Deut. 24:12, 13).

[4](4:4–13) However, by application it makes a great gospel warning. The evangelist D. L. Moody, for example, found "four things in this text:—*a*. There is one God. *b*. We are accountable to him. *c*. We must meet him. *d*. We need preparation to meet him" (*Notes from My Bible*, p. 92).

[5](6:9, 10) Page H. Kelly, *Amos, Prophet of Social Justice*, p. 97.

[6](9:11, 12) *The New Scofield Study Bible. New King James Version*, p. 1056.

BIBLIOGRAPHY

Feinberg, Charles. *The Minor Prophets*. Chicago: Moody Press, 1976.

Kelly, Page H. *Amos, Prophet of Social Justice*. Grand Rapids: Baker Book House, 1966.

Mills, Montague S. *The Minor Prophets. A Survey*. Dallas: 3E Ministries, n.d.

Stevenson, Herbert F. *Three Prophetic Voices. Studies in Joel, Amos and Hosea*. Old Tappan, NJ: Fleming H. Revell Company, 1971.

Tatford, Frederick A. *The Minor Prophets*. Vol. 1. Reprint (3 vols.). Minneapolis: Klock & Klock Christian Publishers, 1982.

OBADIAH

Introduction

"The prophecy of Obadiah is unique in the character of its contents. It is a book of unmitigated condemnation, unrelieved by any suggestion of compassion or hope."

—Frederick A. Tatford

I. Unique Place in the Canon

"The vision of Obadiah" (1:1) is the shortest book in the OT and the third shortest in the Bible. It has one theme only: the destruction of the descendants of Jacob's twin brother Esau. Throughout history the Edomites had constantly fought against Israel and demonstrated their contempt for the chosen people.

II. Authorship

There are a dozen men in the OT named Obadiah (servant of Jehovah), but none can be identified with this prophet with any likelihood. Actually, we know absolutely nothing about the writer of the book beyond what is revealed by his words.

III. Date

Since we know nothing about the author, the date must be determined by internal considerations.

Liberals, generally, and many conservatives, prefer a late date, soon after 586 B.C., when Jerusalem was destroyed. While similarities to Jeremiah, Lamentations, Psalm 137, and certain vocabulary[1] suggest a late date, the fact that total destruction of the city and temple are not mentioned probably goes better with an earlier date.

The earlier dates suggested are during Jehoram's reign (848–841 B.C.) or Ahaz's reign (731–715 B.C.). Not many hold to the last named period, but those who do, tie their argument to 2 Chronicles 28:17, which tells of Edomites attacking Jerusalem and taking prisoners.

If the earliest date is correct, Obadiah is the very first of the *writing* prophets and a contemporary of Elisha. Besides the fact that the book does not suggest the total destruction of 586 B.C., Obadiah vv. 12–14 seem to be a warning to the Edomites not to *repeat* what they had done in the past. If Jerusalem were in ashes, such an admonition would be meaningless.

A Bible-believing Christian can hold any of these three views without compromising a high view of inspiration. A date of about 840 B.C. would seem the most likely, however.

IV. Background and Theme

The prophecy is against the Edomites, who were descendants of Esau and bitter enemies of the people of Israel. They are pictured as having rejoiced over the fall of Jerusalem.

Matthew Henry paints the strong emotions that form the backdrop for Obadiah's short prophecy:

> Some have well observed that it could not but be a great temptation to the people of Israel, when they saw themselves, who were the children of beloved Jacob, in trouble, and the Edomites, the seed of hated Esau, not only prospering, but triumphing over them in their troubles; and therefore God gives them a prospect of the destruction of Edom, which should be total and final, and of a happy issue of their own correction.[2]

As we noted, Bible students are not agreed as to whether this refers to the destruction by Nebuchadnezzar or to an earlier downfall of the city.

In the NT, Edom is known as Idumea. Ruined economically by the Arabs and later conquered by the Romans, the Edomites disappeared from the pages of history about A.D. 70.

OUTLINE

I. EDOM'S PRIDE TO BE ABASED (vv. 1–4)

II. DESTRUCTION OF EDOM (vv. 5–9)
   A. The Completeness of the Plunder (vv. 5, 6)
   B. The Betrayal by Edom's Allies (v. 7)
   C. The Destruction of Edom's Leaders (vv. 8, 9)

III. REASONS FOR EDOM'S DOWNFALL (vv. 10–14)

IV. EDOM'S JUDGMENT IS RETRIBUTIVE (vv. 15, 16)

V. RESTORATION OF ISRAEL AND JUDAH AND EXTINCTION OF EDOM (vv. 17–21)

Commentary

I. EDOM'S PRIDE TO BE ABASED (vv. 1–4)

Obadiah opens with a prediction of the downfall of **Edom** by invaders because of its **pride**. An envoy is pictured inciting **the nations** to go to war **against** Edom. Its leading city, Sela or Petra, was carved out of the side of the **high**, rose-red cliffs south of the Dead Sea. It was considered impregnable against attack. However, the Lord would bring them down from their **eagle** heights and their **nest among the stars**.

II. DESTRUCTION OF EDOM (vv. 5–9)

A. The Completeness of the Plunder (vv. 5, 6)

Edom's destruction could not be accounted for as the work of **thieves** or **robbers**; they would only have taken what they wanted. Even marauders **would . . . have left some gleanings** and not stripped it bare. But even Esau's **hidden treasures** would be **sought after**!

B. The Betrayal by Edom's Allies (v. 7)

All the men in Edom's **confederacy** would betray her and **lay a trap for** her.

C. The Destruction of Edom's Leaders (vv. 8, 9)

Her **wise men** and **mighty men**, in whom she gloried, would **be cut off by slaughter**.

III. REASONS FOR EDOM'S DOWNFALL (vv. 10–14)

The Edomites **should not have . . . rejoiced** when they saw **Jerusalem** attacked. They should not have gloated or **spoken proudly** or helped to loot the city or **cut off** the fleeing Jews as they sought to escape or handed over to the enemy **those among them who remained**.

The picture drawn here is one of an utterly cold and heartless lack of restraint in Edom's cruel treatment of God's people. Edom was completely without mercy, showing not one shred of compassion to their **brother Jacob**. Perhaps this betrayed family relationship was one reason why their "doom" was so final.

IV. EDOM'S JUDGMENT IS RETRIBUTIVE (vv. 15, 16)

The day of God's wrath on **the nations** was **near**, and Edom would be punished for her treatment of Judah. Their **reprisal** would bounce back on their **own head**. G. Herbert Livingston explains the illustration of drinking as follows:

> The sorrow attending punishment is sometimes depicted by the prophets as comparable to drinking strong wine. See Jer 25:15–28 for an extended application of this analogy. God would not merely pick out Edom for an example but would equally judge all nations for their sins.[3]

V. RESTORATION OF ISRAEL AND JUDAH AND EXTINCTION OF EDOM (vv. 17–21)

vv. 17, 18 Israel's future **deliverance** is foretold in the last section of Obadiah. Israel and Judah shall be **a flame** to **devour . . . the house of Esau** completely. Tatford summarized the history of Edom's demise:

> The Edomites were expelled from their country by the Nabateans, but took possession of the Negev, which became known as Idumea, and even temporarily occupied part of Judah, until routed by Judas Maccabeus in 185 B.C. Simon of Gerasa later laid Idumea waste and the Edomites seem to have disappeared altogether in the first century A.D. It is true that Petra became the seat of a Christian patriarchate until the country was taken by the Mohammedans in the 7th century A.D. Today there is no trace of any who could be identified as an Edomite. Obadiah's prediction that there would be no survivor has been fulfilled.[4]

vv. 19–21 The land of Edom will be given to the Israelites dwelling in **the South** (the Negev). Those on the coastal plains (*Shephelah*; **the Lowland**) will be given the land of the Philistines. **The captives** will once more **possess** portions of **the land of the Canaanites. Saviors**[5] (or deliverers) will rule **the mountains of Esau**, and the Lord will reign over the entire **kingdom**.

ENDNOTES

[1](Intro) Such as the Hebrew word translated *captives* in v. 20.

[2](Intro) Matthew Henry, "Obadiah," *Matthew Henry's Commentary on the Whole Bible*, IV:1271.

[3](vv. 15, 16) G. Herbert Livingston, "Obadiah," *The Wycliffe Bible Commentary*, p. 841.

[4](vv. 17, 18) Frederick A. Tatford, *Prophet of Edom's Doom*, p. 55.

[5](vv. 19–21) The deliverers or saviors of verse 21 may be the saints who will reign with Christ.

BIBLIOGRAPHY

Feinberg, Charles Lee. *Joel, Amos and Obadiah*. New York: American Board of Missions to the Jews, 1948.

Henry, Matthew. "Obadiah." In *Matthew Henry's Commentary on the Whole Bible*. Vol. IV. McLean, VA: MacDonald Publishing Company, n.d.

Livingston, G. Herbert. "Obadiah." In *The Wycliffe Bible Commentary*. Chicago: Moody Press, 1962.

Mills, Montague S. "Obadiah." In *The Minor Prophets: A Survey*. Dallas: 3E Ministries, n.d.

Tatford, Frederick A. *Prophet of Edom's Doom*. Eastbourne, England: Prophetic Witness Publishing House, 1973.

JONAH

Introduction

"The book is unique in that it is more concerned with the prophet himself than with his prophecy. The condition of his soul, and God's loving discipline of him, instruct and humble the reader."

—George Williams

I. Unique Place in the Canon

Jonah (Heb. for *dove*) is the only one among the prophets whose prophecy does not consist of what he said but rather of his own life and experience. His experience portrays the past, present, and future of the nation of Israel, as follows:

1. Intended to be a witness for God to the Gentiles.
2. Jealous that a message of grace should be extended to the Gentiles.
3. Thrown into the sea (Gentile world) and swallowed by the nations, yet not assimilated by them.
4. Cast upon dry land (restored to the land of Israel) and made a blessing to the nations.

The only part of his experience that does not seem to fit is what is found in chapter 4. Nowhere in the Bible is it ever suggested that Israel will pout and sulk when millennial blessings flow out to the Gentiles!

II. Authorship

Only chapter 2, Jonah's very personal "psalm" from the belly of the great fish, is in the first person (I, me, my). The fact that the other three chapters are *about* Jonah and use the third person (he, him, his), however, does not rule out his having written the whole book (the traditional view). Other Bible writers, including Moses, have done the same from time to time. The authorship of this book should not be made a test of orthodoxy, though, since technically it is anonymous.

III. Date

Jonah's mission to Nineveh took place in the reign of the Northern Kingdom's mightiest monarch, Jeroboam II (2 Kgs. 14:25), who ruled from about 793 to 753 B.C. While Assyrian inscriptions do not mention a great revival during this era, a number of events dovetail with Jonah. It is well known that ancient pagans viewed famines and eclipses as divine portents of coming disaster. The Lord may well have used the Assyrian famines of 765 and 759 B.C. and the total eclipse of June 15, 763 B.C. to prepare the hearts of the Ninevites for Jonah's evangelistic mission. Also, there was a brief swing toward monotheism in the reign of Queen Semiramis and her co-reigning son Adad-Nirari III (810–782 B.C.). This could have been a result of Jonah's ministry.

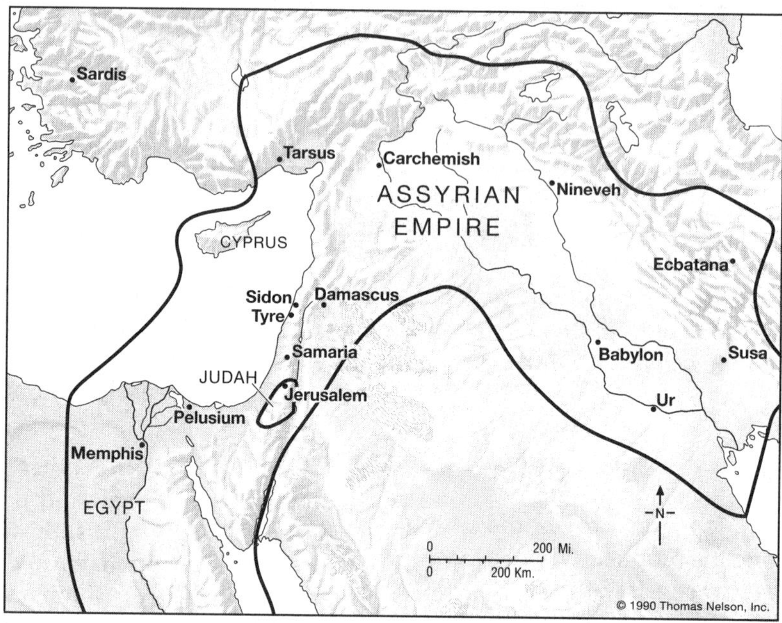

The Assyrian Empire, c. 650 B.C.

IV. Background and Theme

Jonah was the son of Amittai (true [to God]). In 2 Kings 14:25, we learn that his home was in Gath Hepher, in Galilee.

He prophesied during the days when Assyria was threatening the Northern Kingdom, Israel. God sent him to preach repentance to Nineveh, the capital of Assyria. He was reluctant to do this, fearing that the city would repent and be spared. Assyria was an extremely cruel nation. If their inscriptions are to be believed, they flayed their enemies alive, made heaps of their skulls, and did other dreadful deeds. The haughty and blasphemous words of the Rabshakeh, the Assyrian spokesman of Sennacherib, are recorded in 2 Kings 18:17ff.

Therefore, Jonah fled to go to Tarshish and was swallowed by a great fish en route. After his release, he obeyed the Lord's commission by preaching to Nineveh. The city repented and was spared—much to Jonah's displeasure!

The Lord Jesus used Jonah as a sign of His death, burial, and resurrection (Matt. 12:40; 16:4).

The book is a commentary on Romans 3:29:

> Is He the God of the Jews only? Is He not also the God of the Gentiles? Yes, of the Gentiles also.

It is also an illustration of Romans 11:12, 15. When Jonah was cast into the sea, it resulted in the salvation of a boatload of Gentiles. But when he was cast onto dry land, it resulted in the salvation of a city. So the fall of Israel has resulted in riches to the Gentile world, but how much more blessing will flow to the world through the restoration of Israel!

OUTLINE

I. THE DISOBEDIENCE OF THE PROPHET (Chap. 1)
  A. Jonah's Missionary Call (1:1, 2)
  B. Jonah's Flight to Tarshish (1:3)
  C. The Storm at Sea (1:4–10)
  D. Jonah Thrown Overboard and Swallowed by a Great Fish (1:11–17)

II. THE DELIVERANCE OF THE PROPHET (Chap. 2)
  A. Jonah's Prayer (2:1–9)
  B. God's Answer (2:10)

III. THE DECLARATION OF GOD'S MESSAGE THROUGH THE PROPHET (Chap. 3)
  A. The Threat of Judgment (3:1–4)
  B. The City-Wide Repentance (3:5–9)
  C. The Judgment Averted (3:10)

IV. THE DISPLEASURE OF THE PROPHET (Chap. 4)
  A. Jonah's Petulant Prayer (4:1–3)
  B. God's Searching Question (4:4)
  C. Jonah Sulking Outside the City (4:5)
  D. Object Lesson on God's Sovereign Mercy (4:6–11)

Commentary

I. THE DISOBEDIENCE OF THE PROPHET (Chap. 1)

A. Jonah's Missionary Call (1:1, 2)

God sent **Jonah** to preach **to Nineveh**, the capital city of Israel's prime enemy, Assyria. One can understand the prophet's dread of going there from a strictly natural viewpoint (see Background and Theme above).

B. Jonah's Flight to Tarshish (1:3)

In disobedience, **Jonah** took a **ship** for **Tarshish** (probably on the south coast of Spain). H. C. Woodring comments on the prophet's rebellion against his assignment:

God wanted him to go to Nineveh, 500 miles northeast of Palestine. Instead of going east, Jonah went 2000 miles to the west. God wished Jonah to take an overland trip via the Fertile Crescent. Instead he took a distasteful sea voyage (the Jews hated the sea). God sent him to the greatest metropolis of the day. Instead Jonah headed for a remote trading post on the fringes of civilization. The Lord wished to go with His prophet. Instead Jonah tried to flee from the presence and power of God.[1]

C. The Storm at Sea (1:4–10)

The Lord sent out (lit. hurled) **a great wind . . . and a mighty tempest**

that imperiled **the ship** and its occupants. The heathen **mariners**, probably Phoenicians, **cast lots** to see who was responsible for the trouble. **Jonah** the **Hebrew** was revealed as the culprit; he was fleeing **from the presence of the Lord**.

D. Jonah Thrown Overboard and Swallowed by a Great Fish (1:11–17)

1:11–16 The question, **"What shall we do to you that the sea may be calm for us?**, shows a typical human attitude of caring for one's own skin at all costs. However, for pagan old salts they displayed a real sense of fair play. Jonah advised them to **throw** him overboard. They were reluctant to do this and **rowed hard to return to land** instead. But finally they were driven to do it as a last resort because **the sea continued to grow more tempestuous against them**.

1:17 A great fish, prepared by **the Lord**, swallowed **Jonah** and kept him a captive for **three days and three nights**. (The miracle was not that a fish could swallow a man, but that the man was not digested.)

II. THE DELIVERANCE OF THE PROPHET (Chap. 2)

A. Jonah's Prayer (2:1–9)

Jonah's prayer to God from the stomach of the fish celebrates his deliverance from drowning and not his escape from the fish. The escape followed his prayer. His prayer is remarkable in that it contains fragments from the book of Psalms. J. Sidlow Baxter analyzes the prayer as follows:

> There is not one word of petition in Jonah's prayer. It consists of thanksgiving (verses 2–6), contrition (verses 7, 8) and rededication (verse 9). It is really a psalm of praise, a "Te Deum," a "doxology." I know of a man who once sang the Doxology with his head in his empty flour barrel, as an expression of faith that God would send a further supply of flour! But the novelty of singing a doxology with your head—and all the rest of you—inside a great fish in mid-ocean, is absolutely without rival.[2]

Jonah's prayer is a foreshadowing of Israel's future repentance. When the nation acknowledges the Messiah as Savior, it will be restored to a place of blessing under Him.

The mention of **the belly of Sheol** in verse 2 has led some to believe that Jonah actually *died* in the fish and was resurrected. However, the Hebrew word *Sheol* can mean *grave, afterlife,* and other things. Here it is probably a poetic usage for "the depths," or as modern idiom might put it, "the pits."

Even though it is most unlikely that Jonah literally died and was raised again, our Lord Himself used the prophet as a picture of His own death, burial for three days and nights, and His glorious resurrection (Matt. 12:41). Incidentally, this shows that Christ accepted Jonah as a historical character, and not merely as a "parable," as some modern preachers claim.

B. God's Answer (2:10)

As soon as he acknowledged that salvation is of the Lord, **the fish . . . vomited Jonah** out **onto dry land**.

III. THE DECLARATION OF GOD'S MESSAGE THROUGH THE PROPHET (Chap. 3)

A. The Threat of Judgment (3:1–4)

The Lord recommissioned **Jonah** to go **to Nineveh,**[3] and this time he obeyed. After entering that **great city**, he announced that it would **be overthrown** in **forty days**.

B. The City-Wide Repentance (3:5–9)

The Ninevites, who worshiped the fish god Dagon, apparently knew what had happened to Jonah. Other men who have survived similar experiences in history had such mottled skin from the digestive juices that they would stand out in any crowd. He was a sign to them. The entire city repented and **believed God, from the greatest to the least. A fast** was **proclaimed** for **man and beast** alike, and **sackcloth** was put on all, from **king** to cattle.

C. The Judgment Averted (3:10)

As a result, Nineveh was spared **from the disaster**. We know from history, however, that the Assyrians returned to their wicked ways, and after over 150 years of grace their capital was destroyed.

IV. THE DISPLEASURE OF THE PROPHET (Chap. 4)

A. Jonah's Petulant Prayer (4:1–3)

Jonah was **angry** that Israel's Gentile enemies had been spared. In despondency, he asked that he might **die**, perhaps fearing that Assyria might again threaten Israel.

Most of Israel's enemies were severely dealt with by God, and the people of Israel expected their enemies' destruction—not their salvation. Even though Jonah, as a preacher, understood that God was **gracious and merciful**, he also knew that countries like Assyria were usually reserved for annihilation by God. For God to show mercy to Assyria (one of the worst of Israel's enemies in the OT economy) seemed totally wrong to the average Israelite.

B. God's Searching Question (4:4)

The Lord pricked the prophet's conscience with the probing query: **"Is it right for you to be angry?"**

C. Jonah Sulking Outside the City (4:5)

By way of answer, **Jonah** passed through Nineveh **and sat on** the **east side of the city** to **see what would become of** it.

D. Object Lesson on God's Sovereign Mercy (4:6–11)

4:6–8 There **the** Lord **God prepared a** large **plant** to protect him from the sun.[4] Jonah was greatly pleased by this. **The next day**, however, God **prepared a worm** which caused **the plant** to wither. Also, the Lord **prepared a** sultry **east wind** which, together with **the sun**, caused the prophet to **faint** and to **wish** for **death**.

4:9–11 Then God reminded His prophet that if he had **pity on the plant**, how much more reason did the Lord have to show **pity** to a **city** with **more than one hundred and twenty thousand** children alone, to say nothing of **much livestock**.

The lesson of this little book is that God loves the *world*—not just the Jews, but the Gentiles as well.

ENDNOTES

[1](1:3) H. Chester Woodring, "Easter Challenge" Lectures on Jonah, Emmaus Bible School (now College), 1960.

[2](2:1–9) J. Sidlow Baxter, *Explore the Book*, p. 169.

[3](3:1–4) "Nineveh . . . was surrounded by a complex of lesser cities and

villages; so its vast metropolitan area is appropriately described . . . as being so vast that it took three days to journey (50/60 miles) through it." Montague S. Mills, *The Minor Prophets, A Survey*, p. 55.

[4](4:6–8) The Lord *prepared* four things for the unsubmissive prophet: (1) a great fish (1:17); (2) the plant (4:6); (3) a worm (4:7); and (4) a vehement east wind (4:8).

BIBLIOGRAPHY

Banks, William L. *Jonah, the Reluctant Prophet*. Chicago: Moody Press, 1966.

Blair, J. Allen. *Living Obediently: A Devotional Study of the Book of Jonah*. Neptune, N.J.: Loizeaux Brothers, 1963.

Draper, James T., Jr. *Jonah: Living in Rebellion*. Wheaton, IL: Tyndale House Publishers, 1971.

Feinberg, Charles L. *Jonah, Micah, and Nahum*. New York: American Board of Missions to the Jews, 1951.

Gaebelein, Frank E. *Four Minor Prophets: Obadiah, Jonah, Habakkuk, and Haggai*. Chicago: Moody Press, 1977.

Keil, C. F. "Jonah." In *Commentary on the Old Testament*. Vol. 25. Grand Rapids: Wm. B. Eerdmans Publishing Co., 1971.

Kleinert, Paul. "The Book of Jonah." In *Lange's Commentary on the Holy Scriptures*. Reprint (24 vols. in 12). Grand Rapids: Zondervan Publishing House, 1960.

Mills, Montague S. "Jonah." In *The Minor Prophets: A Survey*. Dallas: 3E Ministries, n.d.

Tatford, Frederick A. *The Minor Prophets*. Vol. 2. Reprint (3 vols.). Minneapolis: Klock & Klock Christian Publishers, 1982.

Unpublished Materials

Woodring, H. Chester. "Easter Challenge" Lectures on Jonah. Emmaus Bible School (now College), 1960.

MICAH

Introduction

"It is good to find a worthy champion of the poor who has courage and power to deliver an effective message. Knowing his fellows so intimately Micah was able to present in vivid colors the challenge to justice and consideration. His profound sympathy with the oppressed people came to life in unforgettable words. His spirit burned with righteous indignation as he saw the rank injustice practiced upon his neighbors and friends. The poor peasants of Judah had a strong champion in this powerful young preacher from the country."

—Kyle M. Yates

I. Unique Place in the Canon

Micah is the fourth largest of the minor prophets. It is quoted five times in the NT, once by our Lord. The most famous quotation (Matt. 2:6) is from 5:2, the verse that predicts that the Messiah would be born in Bethlehem Ephrathah (there was another Bethlehem up north).

Another fascinating feature of Micah is the prophet's fondness for "paronomasia," or more popularly, "punning." Many people enjoy making plays on words. In English-speaking cultures this is not generally considered a serious literary form (although Shakespeare used it often). In Hebrew, however, such serious writings as constitute the OT have many plays on words. Micah presents in 1:10–15 a famous example which some have compared with the Latin poet Cicero's oratory. Unfortunately, this is one of the hardest types of literature to translate, since no two languages have the same sets of double meanings. (See footnotes in NKJV and the Moffatt translation quoted below for attempts to express these puns in English.)

II. Authorship

The name Micah—a shorter form of *Mîkāyāh* and *Mîkāyāhû*—(who is like Jehovah) advertises the fact that the prophet was a servant of the one true God, the God of Israel. Like so many prophets he had the name for God (*-el*) or Jehovah (*-yah*) as part of his name. He is probably making a wordplay on his own name in 7:18 when he asks: "Who is a God like You?"

Micah was a contemporary of Isaiah, but from a humbler social class. He came from Moresheth, near Gath, about twenty-five miles southwest of Jerusalem.

III. Date

Micah prophesied from about 740 to about 687 B.C., during the reigns of Jotham, Ahaz, and Hezekiah. Though his main message was to Judah, Micah did predict the captivity of the Northern Kingdom, which occurred in 722/21 B.C. The dates for delivering the messages that constitute his little prophecy may have been some time before he wrote them down.

IV. Background and Theme

By the eighth century B.C. the old agricultural system in Israel and Judah, with its fairly even distribution of wealth, was gradually replaced by a greedy, materialistic, and harsh society that split the people sharply into the "haves" and the "have-nots." The rich land-owners got richer and the poor farmers got poorer. The latter migrated to cities, which were characterized by poverty and vice alongside the upper classes' luxury and also their cruelty to the poor.

Trade with pagan nations also brought in their false religious cults and lower morals.

In short, things were much like Christendom in the Western world today.

Against this dark and worldly background Micah wrote his prophecy, weaving it chiefly around three cities: Samaria, Jerusalem, and Bethlehem.

OUTLINE

I. PREDICTION OF WRATH AGAINST ISRAEL AND JUDAH (Chap. 1)

II. THE DOOM OF THE WEALTHY OPPRESSORS (2:1–11)

III. THE PROMISE OF RESTORATION (2:12, 13)

IV. DENUNCIATION OF RULERS, FALSE PROPHETS, AND PRIESTS (Chap. 3)

V. THE GLORY OF CHRIST'S MILLENNIAL REIGN (Chap. 4)

VI. THE PROMISE OF THE MESSIAH'S COMING (Chap. 5)

VII. ISRAEL ON TRIAL (Chap. 6)

VIII. THE NATION BEWAILS ITS SAD STATE (7:1–10)

IX. FUTURE BLESSING FOR ISRAEL (7:11–20)

Commentary

I. PREDICTION OF WRATH AGAINST ISRAEL AND JUDAH (Chap. 1)

1:1–3 The **peoples** are summoned by **the Lord GOD** to hear His message of judgment as He leaves **His holy temple**, the **place** of blessing, to **witness against** them.

1:4–7 His punishment will be severe on **Samaria** and **Jerusalem** because these cities had become the centers of idolatry. When He arrives in judgment the **mountains will melt under Him, the valley will split like wax before . . . fire, Samaria** will become a **heap of ruins, all her idols** will be **beaten to pieces**, and **her wounds** will be **incurable**.

1:8, 9 Micah's lament that he would **wail and howl** and **go stripped and naked** is the ultimate in extreme **mourning**, like the lonely, nocturnal **jackals** and **the ostriches**.

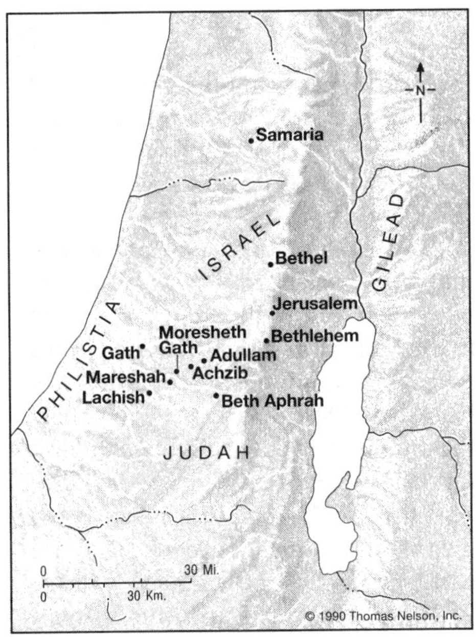

Geographical Puns in Micah

1:10–14 Verses 10–16 are a clever lament, describing the invasion of the land by the Assyrian army. Various cities of Israel and Judah are addressed—**Gath, Beth Aphrah, Shaphir, Zaanan, Beth Ezel, Maroth, Jerusalem, Lachish, Moresheth Gath, Achzib, Mareshah,** and **Adullam**—as the Assyrians draw near. There are many plays on words in this section.[1] Moffatt has translated the passage as follows:

> Weep tears at Teartown (Bochim),
> grovel in the dust at Dustown
> (Beth-ophrah),
> fare forth stripped, O Fairtown
> (Saphir)!
> Stirtown (Zaanan) dare not stir,
> Beth-êsel . . . .
> and Maroth hopes in vain;
> for doom descends from the Eternal
> to the very gates of Jerusalem.
>
> To horse and drive away,
> O Horsetown (Lakhish),
> O source of Sion's sin,
> where the crimes of Israel centre!
> O maiden Sion, you must part with
> Moresheth of Gath;
> and Israel's kings are ever balked
> at Balkton (Achzib).[2]

1:15, 16 A conqueror would descend on Israel, and the people would flee **to Adullam**. Israel should shave its head **bald** in mourning **because** its **precious children**, that is, the people, would be taken from the land **into captivity**.

II. THE DOOM OF THE WEALTHY OPPRESSORS (2:1–11)

2:1–5 The reasons for the judgment are recited here. The rich people dispossessed the poor of their **houses** and land **by violence**. As a result, this property would be taken from the rich by a foreign invader, and they would have nothing left.

2:6, 7 The people told Micah **not** to **prophesy** such unpleasant things because disgrace would not overtake them. But Micah replied that they should not say, **"Is the Spirit of the Lord restricted? Are these** works of judgment **His doings? Do not** His **words do good to him who walks uprightly?"**

2:8–11 By their sins, His **people** had become like **an enemy** of Jehovah—robbing the peaceful of their clothes and driving **women** and **children** out of **their . . . houses**. They should **arise and depart** into exile, for the land they polluted would **destroy** them. Any **false** prophet who advocated **wine and** strong **drink** would be quickly accepted by **this people**.

III. THE PROMISE OF RESTORATION (2:12, 13)

After the judgment, God **would gather the remnant of Israel** back from exile. A breaker (**the Lord**) would break down anything that would hinder their restoration.

IV. DENUNCIATION OF RULERS, FALSE PROPHETS, AND PRIESTS (Chap. 3)

3:1–4 The **rulers of the house of Israel** are condemned for their injustice, unrighteousness, and covetousness. They treated the poor most cruelly. They hated **good** and loved **evil**. Instead of being **shepherds** of the sheep, as rulers are meant to be, these politicians were **wolves**, turning the sheep into **meat for the pot** and **flesh** for **the caldron**. They were the opposite of David, a literal shepherd who came to shepherd a nation (1 Sam. 17:15; 2 Sam. 5:2, 7:7). When their calamity comes, God **will not hear** their cries for help.

3:5–7 **The** false **prophets** would **chant "Peace"** to those who paid them well and predict **war** to those who would not pay. **Therefore** God would withhold from them the knowledge of His will. They would receive **no answer from God**.

3:8–12 In contrast, Micah was empowered **by the Spirit of the Lord** to declare God's message to **Israel** and Judah (**Jacob**). The mercenary rulers, **priests**, and **prophets** thought that they were safe, but Micah announced that **Jerusalem** would be reduced to **heaps of** rubble.

V. THE GLORY OF CHRIST'S MILLENNIAL REIGN (Chap. 4)

4:1–4 The first eight verses speak of the blessings of Christ's Millennial Reign. Jerusalem will **be exalted**, Gentile **nations** will **come** there to learn about **the Lord**, and He will rule over all nations. Worldwide disarmament is vividly and concretely portrayed in the famous words: **"They shall beat their swords into plowshares, and their spears into pruning hooks."**[3] Peace and security will prevail and the Lord will be acknowledged by all His people.

4:5–8 Verse 5 contrasts the idolatry that was practiced in Micah's day with the pure worship that will prevail in the Millennial Kingdom. The people who were crippled by captivity will be restored to the land ("I will collect the stragglers," v. 6, Moffatt), and **the Lord will reign** as King over them. The first or **former dominion** (v. 8) means the highest government on earth, the reign of the Messiah King.

4:9–13 In the meantime, Judah must go into captivity **to Babylon**. Also, before the restoration, the Lord will gather the Gentile **nations** together and judge them; Israel will be His instrument to punish them, and their wealth shall be devoted **to the Lord of the whole earth**.

VI. THE PROMISE OF THE MESSIAH'S COMING (Chap. 5)

5:1 Verse 1 seems to describe the status of the nation at the time that Micah was writing. **Israel**, here meaning Judah, is told to prepare for a **siege** by the Babylonians, who will treat the king insolently and rudely. This may refer to Sennacherib's taunting Hezekiah or Nebuchadnezzar's humiliating Zedekiah.

5:2 Verse 2 looks forward to the birth of **the One** who was **to be Ruler in Israel, whose goings forth are from of old, from everlasting**. These words point to the Messiah's eternity, and therefore His deity. Since there were two Bethlehems in the Holy Land, Micah specifies **Bethlehem**

Ephrathah, six miles south of Jerusalem. This verse is intended as a contrast to verse 1. Although Israel's contemporary situation might be discouraging, yet all would be changed when the Messiah came.

5:3 Three stages in the history of Israel are described here: (1) Because of its rejection of the Lord Jesus, it is given up. That describes its present condition in the Age of Grace. (2) Next, a time of travail awaits the nation, that is, the Tribulation. (3) After these pangs, Israel gives **birth**. This refers to the "believing remnant out of the still unbelieving nation" (Scofield). This **remnant** of **Israel** will be regathered to the land, and Christ will rule over His people.

5:4–6 Christ's shepherd care for Israel and His worldwide dominion are set forth in verse 4. **When the** future **Assyrian** army strikes Jerusalem, the Messiah **will raise** up enough capable leaders to drive them back. The expression **"seven shepherds and eight princely men"** should not be taken to mean there would literally be only fifteen leaders raised up to withstand **"the Assyrian."** When one number is followed by the next highest number in a poetic framework,[4] the meaning is that there is an adequate or complete number of whatever occurs in the context.

5:7–9 **Then** Israel will be a channel of blessing to all. The nation will be as invincible **as a lion**—well able to crush God's **adversaries**.

5:10–15 **In that day**, Israel will have been purified. It will no longer trust in **horses** and **chariots** or fortified **cities**. Sorcerers and **soothsayers** will be abolished. **Carved images** and **sacred pillars**—pagan shrines—will be destroyed. Enemy **nations** will be punished with God's **vengeance**.

VII. ISRAEL ON TRIAL (Chap. 6)

6:1–5 **The mountains** are called to serve as judges while **the LORD** (the Prosecutor) states His **case** against **Israel** (the defendant). He rehearses His kindness to them—delivering them **from . . . Egypt** and preventing **Balak** and **Balaam** from cursing them.

6:6–8 **What** does **the Most High** seek in return for this? Not extravagant animal sacrifices! Certainly not *human* sacrifices! But justice, and **mercy**, and humility. Verse 8 describes what God requires; to obey this a person must have divine life. An unconverted person is totally incapable of producing this kind of righteousness.

6:9–12 **The LORD's voice cries to the city**, recounting its sins as the cause of its calamity. The inhabitants used false **weights** and measures, they practiced **violence**, and they spoke **lies**.

6:13–16 Sin brings its own destruction, and the sins of the violent rich people would incur sickness, desolation, **hunger**, dissatisfaction, and frustration. They would not be permitted to enjoy the things they had obtained through dishonesty. **The statutes of Omri** (v. 16) may well refer to the idolatry which **Omri** encouraged (1 Kings 16:25, 26).

VIII. THE NATION BEWAILS ITS SAD STATE (7:1–10)

7:1, 2 Micah here takes his place with the nation and intercedes to God. The city has been stripped of men who are **faithful** and **upright**; violence and murder abound. The sad situation is compared with gleaning **vintage grapes** and finding **no cluster to eat**.

7:3–6 The rulers and judges ask

for bribes; their **punishment** is near. None can be depended on. Friends, neighbors, even relatives betray one another.

7:7–10 Only **the Lord** can be trusted. The faithful remnant of the nation warns their **enemy... not** to **rejoice** much **over** them. The calamity is a result of the people's sins, but the Lord will yet restore His own, to the dismay of their enemies.

IX. FUTURE BLESSING FOR ISRAEL (7:11–20)

7:11–12 Next Jerusalem is addressed. Her **walls** would be **built** again and her boundaries greatly extended. The exiles would return from the lands of their captivity, and the heathen world would be punished for its wickedness.

7:13 This verse seems strange at first reading. The desolation of **the land** probably refers to the results of the judgment of the Gentiles **for the fruit of their deeds**. This takes place just before the promised restoration. It should be noted that the Hebrew word translated "land" (*eretz*) can also mean "earth."[5] Moffatt paraphrases along these lines also: "though all the world lies desolate in retribution for its pagan ways."

7:14–17 Verse 14 is a prayer addressed to the Lord, asking for food and **shepherd** care. The Lord assures His **people** that He will do such wonderful things for them that the Gentile **nations** will **be ashamed** and will bow low before Him.

7:18–20 Micah closes his prophecy with a song of praise to **God**, extolling His **mercy**, forgiveness, **compassion**, faithfulness, and steadfast love.

ENDNOTES

[1](1:10–14) See the literal renderings in the NKJV margin.

[2](1:10–14) *The Bible: A New Translation*, by James Moffatt, Micah 1:10–14.

[3](4:1–4) Although these words are inscribed on the United Nations building in New York City (from the parallel in Isa. 2:2–4, which see in this commentary), since the Prince of Peace is left out, the world cannot expect any lasting peace till He comes.

[4](5:4–6) This numerical usage is not uncommon in the OT. See, e.g., Job 5:19, Ps. 62:11, 12; Amos 1:3.

[5](7:13) The NIV so translates it here.

BIBLIOGRAPHY

Carlson, E. Leslie. "Micah." In *The Wycliffe Bible Commentary*. Chicago: Moody Press, 1968.

Feinberg, Charles L. *The Minor Prophets*. Chicago: Moody Press, 1976.

Keil, C. F. "Micah." In *Biblical Commentary on the Old Testament*. Vol. 24. Grand Rapids: Wm. B. Eerdmans Publishing Co., 1971.

Mills, Montague S. *The Minor Prophets: A Survey*. Dallas: 3E Ministries, n.d.

Morgan, G. Campbell. *The Minor Prophets*. Old Tappan, NJ: Fleming H. Revell Company, 1960.

Tatford, Frederick A. *The Minor Prophets*. Vol. 2. Reprint (3 vols.). Minneapolis: Klock & Klock Christian Publishers, 1982.

NAHUM

Introduction

"The descriptions given by Nahum are exceedingly fine and vivid, and the book is deservedly classed among the finest productions of Old Testament literature."

—C. H. H. Wright

I. Unique Place in the Canon

The little prophecy of Nahum, while it is written by a Hebrew against the capital of a Gentile world power (Nineveh), is not a nationalistic treatise, but a denunciation of rampant militarism and tyranny, especially as it affects God's people. Although God uses pagans to punish His people's apostasy and sin, the tool itself is also liable to punishment.

As R. K. Harrison puts it:

> In this small prophecy of doom the author demonstrated in vigorous and memorable language that the God of the nation whom the Assyrians had despised was in fact the artificer and controller of all human destiny. To His justice even the greatest world power must submit in humility and shame.[1]

II. Authorship

Nahum was from Elkosh, a town not certainly known, but often identified with Capernaum (Hebrew: *Kāphar Naḥûm,* Nahum's town), near the Sea of Galilee. The prophet's name means "Consoler."

III. Date

Although no date is given, it is possible to pin down the period of writing to within half a century. It had to be written *after* the conquest of No-Amon (Thebes) in 663 B.C. since Nahum mentions that event (3:8). It must have been written *before* 612 B.C. when Nineveh was destroyed. This would put the book within the long reign of idolatrous King Manasseh (696–642), probably between about 663 and 654 B.C.

IV. Background and Theme

Nahum the Elkoshite had a message of consolation to Judah since he foretold the doom of the Assyrians and the restoration of God's people. His prophecy supplements the book of Jonah. In Jonah we see Nineveh's repentance, but in Nahum the Ninevites have returned to their old ways and have incurred God's wrath. Our Lord favorably compares the Ninevites in their repentant mode with the unrepentant Pharisees (Matt. 12:41).

The little book is a classic rebuke of militarism. The Assyrians were ruthless with their enemies. Their inscriptions of military victories gloated over hanging the skins of their conquered enemies on their tents and walls. Whether a common practice or not, it reveals their mentality.

They also despised the God of Israel, the God who controls all things—including Nineveh's fall.

Nahum predicts the destruction of Nineveh, the capital of Assyria and the world's largest city of that day. In the literal sense, the prophecy has been fulfilled, but in another sense, it looks forward to the Assyrian of the future who will threaten God's people.

OUTLINE

I. THE CHARACTER OF GOD, THE JUDGE (1:1–8)
II. CERTAINTY OF THE DOOM OF NINEVEH (1:9–15)
III. DESCRIPTION OF THE SIEGE OF NINEVEH (2:1–12)
IV. GOD'S DETERMINATION TO DESTROY THE CITY (2:13—3:19)

Commentary

I. THE CHARACTER OF GOD, THE JUDGE (1:1–8)

1:1–5 The character of **God** is described as **jealous**, avenging, and wrathful on the one hand, and yet **slow to anger** and **in great power** on the other. He controls the universe and all its inhabitants. His jealousy is the righteous jealousy of a husband for the wife he loves, not an envy of others' happiness. Israel is the "wife" of Jehovah (NKJV, LORD; see Hosea).

1:6–8 When He punishes, no one can withstand Him. Yet He **is good** to **those who trust in Him**. His judgment would sweep like **an overflowing flood** through Assyria, destroying Nineveh, her capital.

II. CERTAINTY OF THE DOOM OF NINEVEH (1:9–15)

1:9–11 These words are addressed to the Assyrians. God was about to destroy them. The **one who** plotted **evil against the LORD** would fall. This probably refers to Sennacherib or to the insolent Rabshakeh.

1:12, 13 **Though** the Assyrians **are** currently **safe**, they **will be cut down**. **Though** Israel had been **afflicted**, it will be afflicted **no more**, for God **will break off** the Assyrians' **yoke from** His people.

1:14 Next, **the LORD** addresses the Assyrian king directly. His **name** would be forgotten, his idol-temple would be pillaged, and the Lord would **dig** his **grave**, because he was **vile**.

1:15 This verse describes the messenger **who brings** the **good tidings** of Assyria's destruction and the resulting **peace** in **Judah**. Paul quotes similar words in Romans 10:15, but there they are used in a *gospel* context (Isa. 52:7).

III. DESCRIPTION OF THE SIEGE OF NINEVEH (2:1–12)

2:1 The first ten verses deal with the siege of Nineveh by the Babylonians. **"He who scatters"** may be interpreted as referring to the Lord or to the Babylonians. The frenzied inhabitants of the city are mockingly told to prepare for battle with four commands: **"Man the fort!" "Watch the road!" "Strengthen your flanks!"** and **"Fortify your power mightily."**

2:2 The LORD will restore His people. There will be some restoration of Israel's **excellence**, but it will not necessarily be soon. The Southern Kingdom had not yet been deported, but was paying tribute.

Another totally different meaning to this text is possible from an alternate translation. In his nearly 400-page commentary on Nahum's short prophecy, Walter A. Maier translates "restore" by a word of opposite meaning, "cut off," and renders "excellence" by its frequent translation, "pride." He writes:

> The statement "Yahweh hath cut off the pride of Jacob" describes a past historic punishment which Yahweh has visited upon Judah, the prophet's home, because of its haughty rejection of the Almighty. Nahum may be thinking of the devastation wrought by Sennacherib, who boasted that he had ravaged Judah.[2]

The reference to Israel as a **ruined** and **emptied** vineyard fits in with several OT images (Ps. 80:8; Isa. 5:13; Jer. 12:10; Hos. 10:1).

2:3–6 The soldiers of Babylon are pictured in verses 3 and 4, clad in their favorite colors: the Babylonians in **red**, and their allies, the Medes, in their **scarlet** tunics. (The Assyrians' military color was blue.) The stumbling officers of verse 5 have been understood as being the Assyrian defenders, but the context points rather to the Babylonian invaders. The **rivers** pour into the city, undermining the foundations so that **the palace is dissolved**.

2:7–10 The queen is **led away captive**. The people **flee** from the city, disregarding the order to **"Halt!"** The **wealth** and **treasure** of **Nineveh** are plundered—the **spoil of silver** and the **spoil of gold**. The city is now desolate. Fear reigns on every face.

2:11, 12 These verses will be much better appreciated when we recall that as Great Britain has the lion, and the United States has the eagle as its emblem, the Assyrians were simply mad about lions. Men's heads with lions' bodies (or vice versa) appear regularly in Assyrian art and sculpture. No doubt they thought of themselves as lions and tried to act the part.

Comparing Nineveh to a lion's den, Nahum pushes his ironical knife in deeply to wound Ninevite arrogance by using the words **lions, young lions, lioness, lion's cub**—seven times in two verses!

IV. GOD'S DETERMINATION TO DESTROY THE CITY (2:13—3:19)

2:13 The LORD of hosts has decreed Nineveh's utter destruction. Since the Lord has made himself her enemy, the city does not stand a chance. Her **chariots** will be burned and her **young lions** (warriors) will be **cut off** by **the sword**. The sound of her armies would **be heard no more** and she would have no more victims.

3:1–3 Chapter 3 continues the picture of the fall of Nineveh and gives the underlying reasons: It is a **bloody city** and **full of lies and robbery**, having seized booty from many others. Now the Babylonian **horsemen** are attacking **with bright sword,**

and the streets are full of **countless corpses**.

3:4–7 The nation is being judged for **her harlotries** and **sorceries**, corrupting others with her idolatry and commerce. Jehovah will expose sinfulness and cover her with **shame**, the punishment befitting **a seductive harlot**.

3:8–10 She will not escape any more **than No Amon** (Thebes)[3] did, that great city which symbolized the concentrated might of **Ethiopia and Egypt**.

As allies or **helpers**, Thebes also counted on Put and Lubim for security. These are territories generally associated with Libya,[4] but we cannot be dogmatic. Put may have been as far south as present-day Somaliland.[5]

3:11–13 Nineveh, **also**, would **be drunk** with the cup of God's wrath. Like **ripened figs**, it was ready for judgment. Its defenses would fail when **the gates of** their **land** would swing **wide open for** their **enemies**.

3:14–17 In spite of Nineveh's most elaborate preparations **for the siege**—acquiring extra **water** and fortifying its **strongholds** with new clay bricks where needed—it would fall. Though the **merchants**, **commanders**, and **generals** were as numerous as **the stars of heaven**, yet they would desert the city **like swarming locusts** flying off at sunrise.

3:18, 19 The **shepherds** (leaders) of **Assyria** now **slumber** in death. The nation has suffered a mortal **wound**. **News of** its fall will cause great rejoicing because many have suffered at its hands. Nineveh fell in 612 B.C.

So thoroughly was Nahum's prophecy fulfilled that, in later times, armies, such as Xenophon's and Alexander the Great's, were totally unaware that they were marching near or over the ruins of great Nineveh.

Not until the nineteenth century was the ancient site of Nineveh even definitely relocated.[6]

ENDNOTES

[1](Intro) R. K. Harrison, *Introduction to the Old Testament*, p. 930.

[2](2:2) Walter A. Maier, *The Book of Nahum, A Commentary*, p. 228.

[3](3:8–10) The Targum and Vulgate read "populous Alexandria" here.

[4](3:8–10) Our word "Libyan" is probably related to "Lubim."

[5](3:8–10) "Put" may be Egyptian "Punt," a country on the Red Sea coast as far south as Somaliland. See Maier, *Nahum*, pp. 321, 322.

[6](3:18, 19) Paul Emile Botta, Austen Henry Layard, and George Smith were pioneer archaeologists among the famed ruins of Nineveh (1840's to 1870's).

BIBLIOGRAPHY

Feinberg, Charles Lee. *The Minor Prophets*. Chicago: Moody Press, 1976.

Keil, C. F. "Nahum." In *Biblical Commentary on the Old Testament*. Vol. 25. Grand Rapids: Wm. B. Eerdmans Publishing Co., 1971.

Maier, Walter A. *The Book of Nahum. A Commentary*. Reprint. Minneapolis: James Family, 1977.

Tatford, Frederick A. *The Minor Prophets*. Vol. 1. Reprint (3 vols.). Minneapolis: Klock & Klock Christian Publishers, 1982.

HABAKKUK

Introduction

"Habakkuk was not a self-centered person concerned only with the comfort and safety of himself and his family. As a true patriot, he was deeply distressed by the moral and spiritual conditions about him. He loved his nation, and knew it was moving ever closer to the precipice of destruction by continuing to break the laws of God. Therefore two anguished questions burst forth form his lips: How long? and Why?"

—Richard W. De Haan

I. Unique Place in the Canon

Habakkuk 2:4 has the distinction of being quoted three times in the NT (see below). In Acts 13:40, 41 the apostle Paul ended his sermon in the synagogue at Antioch, Pisidia by quoting Habakkuk 1:5, another illustration of how an apparently obscure and short OT book can have rich doctrinal content. Also, compare Habakkuk 3:17, 18 with Philippians 4:4, 10–19. Both the prophet and the apostle could rejoice in their God no matter what the outward circumstances of life might be.

As to style, the Hebrew Christian scholar Charles Feinberg writes:

> All concede to Habakkuk a very high place among the Hebrew prophets. The poetry of chapter 3 has been rightly praised on every hand as the most magnificent Hebrew poetry. The language of the book is very beautiful.[1]

II. Authorship

We know virtually nothing about this prophet. The name Habakkuk[2] may mean *embrace* or *wrestle*.

Since he is one of only a handful to call himself a prophet, some scholars believe that he not only had the *gift* of prophecy, but the *office* as well. (Daniel, for example, was a statesman by calling, but a prophet by gift.) Since Habakkuk refers to musical instruments in chapter 3 it has been suggested that he may have been associated with the temple choir, though this is only a conjecture.

III. Date

Because Habakkuk mentions no kings, his little prophecy is hard to date. It is probably from the 600's B.C., though of course, some rationalistic critics date it much later for reasons of their own. Conservative scholars generally place the prophet during the reigns of either Manasseh, Josiah, or Jehoiakim, all kings of the seventh century B.C. The last named king's reign is perhaps the best choice, with a date near the Battle of Carchemish (605 B.C.), at which Babylon was victorious.

IV. Background and Theme

The religious revival under King Josiah did not last long. Public morals, once more influenced by the licentious Baal and Ashtaroth cults, were very low. Injustice was widespread. These were the deplorable conditions with which Habakkuk had to deal.

This prophet spoke to Judah prior to the Babylonian captivity (586 B.C.). Since his name may mean "wrestler," it is fitting that he wrestled with Jehovah over the sin and punishment of the people of Judah.

Preferring the meaning "to embrace," Feinberg quotes Martin Luther with favor as follows:

> Habakkuk signifies an embracer, or one who embraces another, takes him into his arms. He embraces his people, and takes them to his arms, i.e., he comforts them and holds them up, as one embraces a weeping child, to quiet it with the assurance that, if God wills, it shall soon be better.[3]

OUTLINE

I. THE PROPHET IS PERPLEXED THAT GOD DOES NOT PUNISH THE INIQUITY OF JUDAH (1:1–4)

II. THE LORD REPLIES THAT HE WILL USE THE BABYLONIANS TO PUNISH JUDAH (1:5–11)

III. HABAKKUK NOW QUESTIONS GOD'S CHOICE OF A MORE WICKED NATION TO PUNISH JUDAH (1:12–17)

IV. GOD'S ANSWER IS THAT THE JUST PEOPLE OF JUDAH WILL SURVIVE, BUT THE UNJUST CHALDEANS WILL BE DESTROYED (Chap. 2)
- A. Habakkuk Awaits God's Answer (2:1)
- B. Instructions to Record the Answer and Await Its Fulfillment (2:2, 3)
- C. The Just Shall Live by Faith, and the Unjust Chaldeans Will Die (2:4)
- D. Catalog of the Chaldean's Sins (2:5–19)
  1. Endless Appetite for Conquest (2:2–8)
  2. Greed and Pride (2:9–11)
  3. Enrichment through Bloodshed (2:12–14)
  4. Corruption of Neighbors (2:15–17)
  5. Idolatry (2:18, 19)
- E. Silence Enjoined Before the Storm of God's Judgment (2:20)

V. HABAKKUK PRAYS AND TRUSTS (Chap. 3)
- A. He Appeals to God to Act for His People (3:1, 2)
- B. He Reviews God's Care for Israel from Egypt to Canaan (3:3–15)
- C. He Waits for the Enemy to Be Punished (3:16)
- D. No Matter What Happens, He Will Trust in God, His Strength (3:17–19)

Commentary

I. THE PROPHET IS PERPLEXED THAT GOD DOES NOT PUNISH THE INIQUITY OF JUDAH (1:1–4)

The burden (or **oracle**, NKJV marg.) **which the prophet Habakkuk saw** is probably a title for the whole book. In verses 2–4, he complained to the Lord about the terrible **violence**, **iniquity**, robbery, **strife**, and injustice in Judah. He asked **the LORD how long** it would be allowed to go unpunished. Because of this and similar questionings of God, Habakkuk has sometimes been called "the doubting Thomas of the OT."

The first eleven verses of the prophecy are a dialogue between Habakkuk and the Lord.

II. THE LORD REPLIES THAT HE WILL USE THE BABYLONIANS TO PUNISH JUDAH (1:5–11)

God's answer is given in verses 5–11. He would raise up the Chaldean army to punish Judah. The enemy would be **hasty**, **bitter**, avaricious, violent, dreadful, and proud. The Babylonians were noted for their cavalry, swift in conquest and fiercer **than evening wolves**. They scoffed at captive **kings and princes**, and their might was their **god**. Feinberg comments:

> The success of the Chaldean will be multiplied; he will carry all before him, as the wind sweeps over vast stretches of land. In doing so, the Chaldean conqueror heaps up guilt before God because of his ungodly ambitions and his subjugation of many helpless peoples.[4]

III. HABAKKUK NOW QUESTIONS GOD'S CHOICE OF A MORE WICKED NATION TO PUNISH JUDAH (1:12–17)

When Habakkuk heard this, he was troubled, and his agitation brought forth the second dialogue (1:12—2:20). How could God punish Judah by a nation that was worse than they were? He argues with God based on his knowledge that God is **of purer eyes than to behold evil, and cannot look on wickedness**. And the Babylonians were undoubtedly wicked! However, Judah's wickedness was greater, since the Jews were sinning against much greater light. How could God **look** upon the **wickedness** of the Babylonians as they took men captive by the netful, even by the **hook** and the **net**? They sacrificed to their idols and grew fat. Would there be no end to their slaughter of the **nations**? J. E. Evans explains:

> An analogy was drawn from the life of a fisherman. The men were like fishes whom the fisherman collected in his net, and then paid divine honors to the net by which he has been so enriched. In this comparison, the world was the sea; the nation was the fishes; Nebuchadnezzar was the fisherman; the net was the military might of the Chaldean by which he was able to gain great wealth through the conquest.[5]

IV. GOD'S ANSWER IS THAT THE JUST PEOPLE OF JUDAH WILL SURVIVE, BUT THE UNJUST CHALDEANS WILL BE DESTROYED (Chap. 2)

A. Habakkuk Awaits God's Answer (2:1)

Habakkuk retired to his watchtower to see how the Lord would answer him. He wanted to get alone in order to gain God's perspective. This is a most important principle for believers today as well. Whether we call it our "quiet time," "devotions," or by some other term, daily communion with God is crucial for every Christian.

B. Instructions to Record the Answer and Await Its Fulfillment (2:2, 3)

2:2 **The LORD** commanded the prophet: **"Write the vision"** (His answer to Habakkuk's question) so that the **one who** read **it** might **run** with the news (of the downfall of Babylon and the restoration of Judah).

2:3 A. J. Pollock says that this verse refers to the hope of the Jew—Christ's coming to earth to subdue His enemies, take out of His kingdom all things that offend, and set up His glorious reign, making Israel the head of the nations because He will be at the head of the Jewish nation.[6] When verse 3 is quoted in Hebrews 10:37, the **"it"** (i.e., **the vision**) becomes "He" (i.e., the Lord), who **will surely come** and **will not tarry**. The NT context refers to the hope of the Christian—the Rapture of the church.

C. The Just Shall Live by Faith, and the Unjust Chaldeans Will Die (2:4)

Because the **soul** of the king of Babylon was lifted up with pride, he would die, but the godly remnant of Israel would **live by... faith**. Verse 4c is quoted three times in the NT. The three parts of the verse—the just—shall live—by faith, go well with the emphases of the three contexts where they appear: Romans 1:17 emphasizes "the just"; Gal. 3:11 emphasizes "faith"; Heb. 10:38 emphasizes "shall live." The literal rendering in Habakkuk's context, is "By his faith the just shall live." It could also be paraphrased "the justified-by-faith-one shall live."

D. Catalog of the Chaldean's Sins (2:5–19)

1. Endless Appetite for Conquest (2:5–8)

2:5 **Wine** drinking was a national sin of Babylon, and, no doubt, of Nebuchadnezzar. Keil writes that this addiction "is attested by ancient writers . . ., and it is well known from Dan. [chap.] v. that Babylon was conquered while Belshazzar and the great men of his kingdom were feasting at a riotous banquet."[7] In addition, the latter had an insatiable thirst for conquest.

2:6–8 Verse 6 begins a taunt song, containing five woes against Babylon. The first **woe** is against lust for empire, or aggression. The **many nations** which Nebuchadnezzar had conquered would taunt him for his ill-gotten gain, and would **oppress** and **plunder** Babylon as he had done to them.

2. Greed and Pride (2:9–11)

A second **woe** is pronounced on Nebuchadnezzar for his covetousness and pride. He tried to make his dynasty safe from the reach of **disaster**, but his dishonest **gain** and cruelty would **cry out** against him.

3. *Enrichment through Bloodshed (2:12–14)*

The third **woe** against the king was for his lust for magnificence and his bloodshedding tactics. The cities of Babylon, built by slave **labor**, would merely end up feeding the insatiable **fire**, and **the earth** would acknowledge Jehovah as the true God.

But a day is coming when the one true God will be globally acknowledged. This glorious time is predicted in a deservedly famous poetic comparison: **"For the earth will be filled with the knowledge of the glory of the LORD, as the waters cover the sea"** (2:14).

4. *Corruption of Neighbors (2:15–17)*

The fourth woe is against Nebuchadnezzar for taking a savage delight in corrupting other nations, for shamelessness, and for his destruction of Jerusalem and Judah. In short, Nebuchadnezzar was guilty of promoting two main ingredients of modern television, movies, and "literature"—shameless sexual lifestyles (including forms of perversion) and inordinate **violence**.

5. *Idolatry (2:18, 19)*

The fifth and final **woe** condemns the king for the idolatry of Babylon in vividly sarcastic lines. What good is a **gold** or **silver**-plated idol when **there is no breath** in it **at all**?

E. Silence Enjoined Before the Storm of God's Judgment (2:20)

A beautiful musical setting of this verse is used in some churches to subdue the congregation to quiet contemplation of the sermon. Unfortunately, while the words fit, the context of the text is that **the LORD** is about to demonstrate His power in *judgment*. For that reason **all the earth** should **keep silence before Him**.

V. HABAKKUK PRAYS AND TRUSTS (Chap. 3)[8]

A. He Appeals to God to Act for His People (3:1, 2)

Habakkuk now prays to the LORD. He had heard of the Lord's dealings in the past with the enemies of His people; now he asks Him to **revive** His **work** by punishing His foes and saving His people.

B. He Reviews God's Care for Israel from Egypt to Canaan (3:3–15)

3:3–7 In a splendid vision of God's sovereignty that Scroggie calls a "Theophanic Ode"[9] (song about God's manifestation), Habakkuk pictures **God** marching forth against His foes, crushing them by His power and triumphing gloriously. He makes frequent allusions to the Lord's past punishment of Israel's enemies, the judgment of Egypt at the time of the Exodus, the countries that opposed Israel on the way to the promised land, and the nations that had to be driven out of Canaan by Joshua.

In the first section of the prayer God's **glory** and **brightness** are seen in both **the** *heavens* and **the earth**.

The geographical details—**Teman**, **Mount Paran**, **Cushan**, and **Midian**, all speak of enemies of Israel. For example, Teman, a large city in Edom, stands for all of Idumea, and Cushan is probably the same as "Cush," or Ethiopia.

3:8–11 God's power is stressed in these words, especially as manifested over **the rivers**, **the seas**, and **the mountains**.

Verse 11 refers to the famous event at Gibeon during which the Lord worked a mighty miracle in the sky to help Joshua win the battle (Josh. 10:12).

3:12–15 Here God is seen marching **through the land** for Israel and trampling their **enemies** in anger.

The reference in v. 15 is to the crossing of the Red Sea (Ex. 14) when there was a **heap of great waters** on either side of the people of God as they marched through as if on dry land. Habakkuk envisions God as moving **through the sea with** His **horses**.

C. He Waits for the Enemy to Be Punished (3:16)

When the prophet **heard** of the judgment of the Babylonian invaders, he **trembled** and determined to wait quietly for the event to come to pass.

D. No Matter What Happens, He Will Trust in God, His Strength (3:17–19)

In the meantime, whatever trials the prophet Habakkuk and his people might be called upon to endure as a result of the Babylonian invasion—**Though the fig tree may not blossom, . . . and the fields yield no food; . . . and there be no herd in the stalls**—he would **rejoice in the Lord** and **joy in the God of** his **salvation**. Baxter exclaims:

> The literal is "I will jump for joy in the Lord; I will spin around for delight in God." Here is the hilarity of faith!—joy at its best with circumstances at their worst! What a victory! May it be ours![10]

ENDNOTES

[1](Intro) Charles Lee Feinberg, *Habakkuk, Zephaniah, Haggai and Malachi*, p. 12.

[2](Intro) Most people accent the name on the first syllable, but accenting the second syllable is preferred in English. In Hebrew the last syllable is accented (*Ha-ba-KOOK*).

[3](Intro) Feinberg, *Habakkuk*, p. 11.

[4](1:5–11) *Ibid.*, p. 17.

[5](1:12–17) J. E. Evans, further documentation unavailable.

[6](2:3) A. J. Pollock, further documentation unavailable.

[7](2:5) C. F. Keil, "Habakkuk," in *Biblical Commentary on the Old Testament*, Vol. 25, pp. 74, 75.

[8](Chap. 3) This lovely chapter was set to music by the Jews and used in their worship service.

[9](3:3–7) Scroggie, "Habakkuk," in *Know Your Bible*, Vol. 1, The Old Testament, p. 196.

[10](3:17–19) J. Sidlow Baxter, *Explore the Book*, p. 212.

BIBLIOGRAPHY

De Haan, Richard W. *Song in the Night*. Grand Rapids: Radio Bible Class (booklet), 1969.

Feinberg, Charles Lee. *Habakkuk, Zephaniah, Haggai and Malachi*. New York: American Board of Missions to the Jews, 1951.

Kelly, William. *Lectures Introductory to the Study of the Minor Prophets*. London: C. A. Hammond Trust Bible Depot, n.d.

Keil, C. F. "Habakkuk." In *Biblical Commentary on the Old Testament*. Vol. 25. Grand Rapids: Wm. B. Eerdmans Publishing Company, 1971.

Scroggie, W. Graham. "Habakkuk." In *Know Your Bible*. Vol. 1. The Old Testament. London: Pickering & Inglis Ltd., n.d.

Tatford, Frederick A. *The Minor Prophets*. Vol. 3. Reprint (3 vols.). Minneapolis: Klock & Klock Christian Publishers, 1982.

ZEPHANIAH

Introduction

"If anyone wishes all the secret oracles of the prophets to be given in a brief compendium, let him read through this brief Zephaniah."
—Martin Bucer (1528)

I. Unique Place in the Canon

Many people are "royalty-watchers" and enjoy following the nobility. As a great grandson of good King Hezekiah,[1] and thus a distant cousin of the currently reigning godly King Josiah, Zephaniah may have been a member of this set. Sad to say, between the reigns of these two righteous kings there had been over half a century of evil rule by Amon and Manasseh. Zephaniah probably had access to the royal court in the capital of the Southern Kingdom, Judah.

II. Authorship

We know very little about Zephaniah the son of Cushi. His name means *Jehovah hides*, i.e., "protects" or "treasures." His genealogy, as noted, traces back to a royal forebear. He liked to put dark against light and light against dark, painting a very gloomy picture of the Day of the Lord, yet giving a very bright foreglimpse of Israel's coming glory and the conversion of the Gentiles to the Lord. As Hewitt points out, the Prophet Zephaniah minced no words:

> There is no compromise in the language used. He denounces sin and announces judgment with perfect fearlessness and closes his book with a song full of inspiration and hope looking forward to the inauguration of the Millennial Kingdom.[2]

III. Date

Zephaniah ministered during the reign of Josiah (640–609 B.C.). Believing scholars are divided as to whether he wrote before or after the great revival of 621 B.C. If before, his prophecy likely helped bring about the spiritual awakening. But several details, such as quoting the newly rediscovered law, would suggest a date after 621. Since Zephaniah 2:13 shows that Nineveh was still standing, a date before that city's destruction in 612 B.C. is called for. Hence the book was probably written between 621 and 612 B.C.

IV. Background and Theme

Zephaniah probably prophesied from Jerusalem ("this place," 1:4). The historical background of his prophecy will be found in 2 Kings 21—23 and the early chapters of Jeremiah:

> Zephaniah saw the menacing hordes of Scythians, rising over the horizon, swift and terrible in their movements . . . . The position of Judah was delicate and difficult, for with its small resources it could not hope to prevail

over the great powers. When the greater nations to the north and south of Judah strove for the mastery of the world, the weak nations that lay between became involved and were often ravaged. Aware of the seething unrest all around, Zephaniah became a preacher of righteousness and denounced the evils of his age in unsparing terms.[3]

He uses the expression "the Day of the Lord" seven times in his little book. This gives the theme of the book: God's judgment is coming on Judah for disobedience. Other key expressions are "jealousy" and "in the midst." God is jealous in the sense that He resents the idolatry of His people. He is "in the midst" first as a righteous Judge (3:5) and then as Conqueror of their foes (3:15).

OUTLINE

I. GOD'S DETERMINATION TO EXECUTE JUDGMENT (1:1–18)
  A. On All the Earth (1:1–3)
  B. On Judah and Jerusalem because of Idolatry (1:4–6)
  C. The Day of the Lord under the Figure of a Sacrifice (1:7–13)
    1. Guests—Judah's Enemies (1:7)
    2. Victims—Wicked People of Judah (1:8–13)
  D. The Terror of the Day of the Lord (1:14–18)

II. JUDAH IS CALLED TO REPENT (2:1–3)

III. THE DOOM OF GENTILE NATIONS (2:4–15)
  A. The Philistines (2:4–7)
  B. The Moabites and Ammonites (2:8–11)
  C. The Ethiopians (2:12)
  D. The Assyrians and Especially the City of Nineveh (2:13–15)

IV. WOE PRONOUNCED ON JERUSALEM (3:1–7)
  A. Disobedience, Unresponsiveness, Unbelief, Impenitence (3:1, 2)
  B. Greed of the Princes and the Judges (3:3)
  C. Levity and Treachery of the Prophets and Sacrilege of the Priests (3:4)
  D. The Lord's Presence in Judgment (3:5–7)

V. MESSAGE OF COMFORT TO THE FAITHFUL REMNANT (3:8–20)
  A. Destruction of Wicked Gentiles (3:8)
  B. Conversion of the Remaining Nations (3:9)
  C. Restoration of Dispersed Israel (3:10–13)
  D. Rejoicing over the Second Advent of Christ (3:14–17)
  E. What God Will Do for His People (3:18–20)

Commentary

I. GOD'S DETERMINATION TO EXECUTE JUDGMENT (1:1–18)

A. On All the Earth (1:1–3)

It is usual for prophets to name their father, and sometimes their grandfather, as the Jews were very "roots"-oriented, as we would say today. But **Zephaniah the son of Cushi** traces back four generations of his ancestors, doubtless to let us know of his regal forebear, King **Hezekiah**.

The chapter as a whole describes the destruction of **the** whole **land,** then specifically of Jerusalem and Judah. God will make **the whole land . . . utterly** desolate.

B. On Judah and Jerusalem because of Idolatry (1:4–6)

The inhabitants of **Judah** will be punished for their idolatry—their **Baal**-worship, their star-**worship**, and their worship of **Milcom**, the god of the Ammonites.

C. The Day of the Lord under the Figure of a Sacrifice (1:7–13)

1. Guests—Judah's Enemies (1:7)

The Lord has prepared a sacrifice; Judah is the victim, and the Babylonians are the **guests**.

2. Victims—Wicked People of Judah (1:8–13)

God **will punish** Judah for their idolatrous **apparel** and practices, and for their **violence and deceit**. Howls will go up from such various sections of the capital as **the Fish Gate**, **the Second Quarter**, and **the hills**, as the invaders slaughter and take **booty**.

D. The Terror of the Day of the Lord (1:14–18)

The most vivid picture in the Bible of **the day of the Lord** is given here; it is **the day of** God's **wrath** on men because of their wickedness, the men of Judah in particular. It is **a day of** war, **distress**, and slaughter. A classic Latin hymn is based on verses 15 and 16:

> Thomas of Celano in 1250 wrote his famous judgment hymn from verse 15, *Dies irae, dies illa,* meaning "That day is a day of wrath." The day is one of wrath, trouble, distress, wasteness, desolation (the Hebrew words for wasteness and desolation—*sho'ah* and *umesho'ah*—are alike in sound to convey the monotony of the destruction), darkness, gloominess, clouds, thick darkness, trumpet, alarm against fortified cities and high towers.[4]

God is jealous of the affections of His people and will punish all rivals.

II. JUDAH IS CALLED TO REPENT (2:1–3)

God calls on the **undesirable** (or shameless, NKJV marg.) **nation** to repent. Verse 3 seems to point to a remnant of righteous Jews. If they **seek the Lord**, they **will be hidden in the day of** His fierce **anger**.

III. THE DOOM OF GENTILE NATIONS (2:4–15)

A. The Philistines (2:4–7)

Verses 4–15 foretell judgment on surrounding nations to the west, east, south, and north. First are **the Philistines**, who are also identified by their other name—**the Cherethites**. Their cities—**Gaza**, **Ashkelon**, **Ashdod**—will be **forsaken** and **desolate**. They will be destroyed, and their **land** will be used by **Judah** for pasture.

B. The Moabites and Ammonites (2:8–11)

Next come **Moab** and **Ammon**. God had heard their insolent words and boasts **against** His **people**. They will be left desolate, and the **residue** of God's **people** will dwell there. Verse 11 anticipates millennial conditions, when **the Lord** has reduced **to nothing all the gods of the earth**.

C. The Ethiopians (2:12)

Ethiopia will be punished **by** God's **sword** (the king of Babylon). Some, such as Feinberg, link **"Ethiopians"** here with Egypt:

> The fortunes of Ethiopia were bound up with those of Egypt which was subject to Ethiopic dynasties. Note Jeremiah 46:9 and Ezekiel 30:5, 9. There is reason to believe that Egypt itself is meant under the term Ethiopians.[5]

D. The Assyrians and Especially the City of Nineveh (2:13–15)

Nebuchadnezzar will also **destroy Assyria**. **Nineveh** will be a refuge for animals and birds, and **everyone who passes by her shall hiss and shake his fist**.

IV. WOE PRONOUNCED ON JERUSALEM (3:1–7)

A. Disobedience, Unresponsiveness, Unbelief, Impenitence (3:1, 2)

The city of Jerusalem, personified as a woman, is condemned as being **rebellious, polluted**, and **oppressing**. She has been disobedient and has **not trusted in the Lord** or **drawn near to her God**.

B. Greed of the Princes and the Judges (3:3)

Her princes . . . are like **roaring lions**, and **her judges** are as greedy as **evening wolves**.

C. Levity and Treachery of the Prophets and Sacrilege of the Priests (3:4)

Her prophets are faithless, and **her priests** profane. Feinberg comments:

> In verse 4 we have the only denunciation of the prophets in this book. They were guilty of levity, trifling with the weightiest matters. There was no gravity or steadfastness in their life or teaching. They were treacherous because unfaithful to Him whom they claimed to represent, rather encouraging the people in their apostasy from the Lord. By their unholy deeds they profaned the sanctuary; they made the sacred profane. They did violence to the law by distorting its plain intent and meaning when they were teaching the people.[6]

D. The Lord's Presence in Judgment (3:5–7)

In spite of all this sin and corruption, **the Lord** is **in her midst** to judge righteously. He had punished other **nations**, thinking that this would **surely** cause Judah to **fear** Him, but the people became even more corrupt.

V. MESSAGE OF COMFORT TO THE FAITHFUL REMNANT (3:8–20)

A. Destruction of Wicked Gentiles (3:8)

The faithful remnant of Judah is exhorted to **wait for** God **until** He destroys **all** His foes **with the fire of** His **jealousy**.[7]

B. Conversion of the Remaining Nations (3:9)

The **pure language** of verse 9 probably does not refer to a universal tongue but rather to lips that are undefiled by idolatry, or to speech that is pure with praise to Jehovah. **All peoples** will **serve Him with one accord**.

C. Restoration of Dispersed Israel (3:10–13)

In that Millennial Day the Gentiles will **bring** the dispersed Jews back to the land as an **offering** to the Lord. Wicked men **who rejoice in** their **pride** will be destroyed from Judah, and therefore will no longer cause the believing **remnant of Israel** to be

afraid. Those who are left will be **humble** and **meek**, trusting **in the name of the** **Lord** and living righteously.

D. Rejoicing over the Second Advent of Christ (3:14–17)

Verses 14–20 give the song of restored Israel, praising Jehovah (NKJV, Lord) for His mighty deliverance and celebrating His love for His own. The **daughter of Zion** has much to **sing, shout**, and **rejoice** about! Not only have her enemies been thrown out, but the Messiah-**King**, the **Lord** Himself, is right **in** her **midst**. There is no need to **be weak** or **fear**, because **God** the **Mighty One will quiet** her **with His love**.

E. What God Will Do for His People (3:18–20)

Since judgment was soon to be upon the people, **the Lord** ends the prophecy with a strong promise of a complete turnabout for the godly remnant. Instead of the **reproach** and **sorrow** of missing **the appointed assembly**, the exiles will be granted **praise and fame in every land where they were put to shame**.

ENDNOTES

[1](Intro) The "Hizkiah" in 1:1 of KJV is exactly the same spelling as Hezekiah in the original Hebrew.

[2](Intro) J. B. Hewitt, *Outline Studies in the Minor Prophets*, p. 45.

[3](Intro) *Ibid*., p. 44.

[4](1:14–18) Charles Lee Feinberg, *Habakkuk, Zephaniah, Haggai, Malachi*, p. 50.

[5](2:12) *Ibid*., p. 59.

[6](3:4) *Ibid*., p. 64.

[7](3:8) Zephaniah 3:8 is the only verse in the original text of the OT which contains all the letters of the Hebrew alphabet.

BIBLIOGRAPHY

Feinberg, Charles Lee. *Habakkuk, Zephaniah, Haggai and Malachi*. New York: American Board of Missions to the Jews, Inc., 1951.

———. *The Minor Prophets*. Chicago: Moody Press, 1976.

Hewitt, J. B. *Outline Studies in the Minor Prophets*. West Glamorgan, U.K.: Precious Seed Publications, n.d.

Keil, C. F. "Zephaniah." In *Biblical Commentary on the Old Testament*. Vol. 26. Grand Rapids: Wm. B. Eerdmans Publishing Co., 1971.

Kelly, William. *Lectures Introductory to the Study of the Minor Prophets*. London: C. A. Hammond Trust Bible Depot, n.d.

Morgan, G. Campbell. *The Minor Prophets*. Old Tappan, N.J.: Fleming H. Revell Company, 1960.

Tatford, Frederick A. *The Minor Prophets*. Vol. 3. Reprint (3 vols.). Minneapolis: Klock & Klock Christian Publishers, 1982.

C. Encouraged by Haggai, the People Resumed Work on the Temple (1:12–15)

II. SECOND PROPHECY—TWENTY-FIRST DAY OF SEVENTH MONTH (2:1–9)
  A. The Prophet Again Encouraged the People with Assurance of the Lord's Presence (2:1–5)
  B. The Glory of the Future Temple Would Exceed that of the Past (2:6–9)

III. THIRD PROPHECY—TWENTY-FOURTH DAY OF NINTH MONTH (2:10–19)
  A. Sacrifices Offered on the Altar Were Unclean as Long as the Temple Was in Ruins (2:10–14)
  B. Before the Foundation of the Temple Was Laid, the People Suffered from Scarcity (2:15–17)
  C. If They Would Resume Work on the Temple, the Lord Would Bless Them (2:18, 19)

IV. FOURTH PROPHECY—TWENTY-FOURTH DAY OF NINTH MONTH (2:20–23)
  The People Encouraged by Promise of the Overthrow of Gentile Kingdoms and Establishment of the Messiah's Reign

Commentary

I. FIRST PROPHECY—FIRST DAY OF SIXTH MONTH (Chap. 1)

A. Rebuke for Neglect in Rebuilding the Temple (1:1–4)

This prophecy is dated as being **in the second year of King Darius**, the Medo-Persian king. **The LORD** reproved the people of Judah for delay in rebuilding the **temple**, while they themselves were living comfortably **in** their **paneled houses**.

B. Failure to Rebuild Resulted in Scarcity and Drought (1:5–11)

They should have been warned by their recent history. When they neglected the Lord's house, they suffered hunger, thirst, and poverty. Now **the LORD** commanded them to start work on **the temple**. As long as God's **house** lay **in ruins**, they could expect nothing but **drought**.

C. Encouraged by Haggai, the People Resumed Work on the Temple (1:12–15)

Zerubbabel the **governor of Judah**, and **Joshua . . . , the high priest**, together **with all the remnant of the people, obeyed** the Word of **the LORD** and began rebuilding twenty-three days after the command to rebuild.

II. SECOND PROPHECY—TWENTY-FIRST DAY OF SEVENTH MONTH (2:1–9)

A. The Prophet Again Encouraged the People with Assurance of the Lord's Presence (2:1–5)

About a month later, **in the seventh month**, the people had become discouraged with the new building, when they thought of the **glory** of the **former . . . temple**. The leaders were told to **"Be strong"** and **not** to **fear** because God's **Spirit** remained **among** them.

B. The Glory of the Future Temple Would Exceed that of the Past (2:6–9)

God encouraged the leaders with the assurance that **the glory of** the **temple** of the future (millennial) would **be greater than** any of its predecessors. **"The Desire of All Nations"** is often taken to refer to the Messiah and His return to the **temple**. However, the context suggests that it might mean the *treasures of the nations* (NKJV marg.).[2] Their **silver** and **gold** would flow into Jerusalem to beautify the temple. Verse 9a reads: **"The glory of this latter temple shall be greater than the former . . . ."** The two temples were viewed as one house. In addition to **glory, peace** is also promised for that future time.

III. THIRD PROPHECY—TWENTY-FOURTH DAY OF NINTH MONTH (2:10–19)

A. Sacrifices Offered on the Altar Were Unclean as Long as the Temple Was in Ruins (2:10–14)

The third prophecy was given **on the twenty-fourth day of the ninth month**. The people were told to **ask the priests** two questions: (1) **If . . . holy meat** carried **in the fold of** a **garment** should touch other foods, would those other foods **become holy? The priests** correctly **answered . . . "No."** (2) **If one who** has become **unclean** through touching **a dead body** should touch these foods, would they become **unclean? The priests** correctly **answered** "Yes."

In other words the following was understood: "He that is holy imparts no holiness to anything else, but he that is defiled communicates defilement."[3] Or, to put it another way, "Work and worship do not sanctify sin, but sin contaminates work and worship."[4] This was a reminder to the **people** that their offerings to God were polluted and that they themselves, were **unclean** as long as the temple was in ruins.

B. Before the Foundation of the Temple Was Laid, the People Suffered from Scarcity (2:15–17)

Before they had started building **the temple**, they had experienced shortages of grain and **wine**, and their crops had suffered **blight, mildew**, and **hail**. Even since then, their interminable delays in rebuilding had brought the chastisement of God in hardship and deprivation.

C. If They Would Resume Work on the Temple, the Lord Would Bless Them (2:18, 19)

But **from** the **day** on which they would lay **the foundation of the LORD's temple**, God would **bless** them.

IV. FOURTH PROPHECY—TWENTY-FOURTH DAY OF NINTH MONTH (2:20–23)

The People Encouraged by Promise of the Overthrow of Gentile Kingdoms and Establishment of the Messiah's Reign

Zerubbabel is here a type of the Lord Jesus Christ. God would **overthrow** and **destroy** this world's **Gentile kingdoms** and set up Christ's Millennial Kingdom. The **signet ring** indicates that divine authority to rule is committed to the Messiah.

ENDNOTES

[1](Intro) Dr. Howard Hendricks has a colorful phrase for this all-too-common disposition to gush over successful preachers after a sermon: "The glorification of the worm ceremony."

[2](2:6–9) The capitalization in the NKJV goes with this traditional interpretation but the lower case "the desire of all nations" in the margin suggests the alternative view.

[3](2:10–14) William Kelly, *Lectures Introductory to the Study of the Minor Prophets*, p. 427.

[4](2:10–14) Donald Campbell, further documentation unavailable.

BIBLIOGRAPHY

Baldwin, Joyce G. *Haggai, Zechariah, Malachi: An Introduction and Commentary*. The Tyndale Old Testament Commentaries. Downers Grove, IL: InterVarsity Press, 1972.

Feinberg, Charles Lee. *The Minor Prophets*. Chicago: Moody Press, 1976.

Kelly, William. *Lectures Introductory to the Study of the Minor Prophets*. London: C. A. Hammond Trust Bible Depot, n.d.

Keil, C. F. "Haggai." In *Biblical Commentary on the Old Testament*. Vol. 26. Grand Rapids: Wm. B. Eerdmans Publishing Co., 1971.

Tatford, Frederick A. *The Minor Prophets*. Vol. 3. Reprint (3 vols.). Minneapolis: Klock & Klock Christian Publishers, 1982.

ZECHARIAH

Introduction

"The prophecy of Zechariah is profoundly precious to the Christian because of its unique Messianic emphasis and its panoramic unfolding of the events connected with the first and especially the second advent of Christ and the consequent millennial restoration of the nation Israel."

—Merrill F. Unger

I. Unique Place in the Canon

Genesis, Psalms, and Isaiah are the most quoted books in the NT, which, considering their length and crucial contents, is not surprising. Most would be amazed to learn that Zechariah, with only fourteen chapters, is quoted about forty times in the NT. Doubtless this is due especially to the fact that the book is so messianic, certainly the most Christ-centered of the Minor Prophets.

Zechariah's fascinating symbolic visions, plus his messages and revelations, all enhance the importance and interest of this post-exilic book.

II. Authorship

There are about thirty men in the OT named Zechariah (Jehovah remembers), the same name as the NT (Greek) Zacharias and English Zachary.

This prophet and priest was born probably in Babylon during the exile. Nehemiah mentions his arrival at Jerusalem (12:4, 16) and Ezra mentions his ministry (5:1; 6:14). Zechariah took over the short public ministry of the older Haggai to encourage the remnant.

Zechariah had a long ministry and wrote chapters 9–14 probably much later than the dated sections.

III. Date

Zechariah started his prophecies in 520 B.C., the same year that Haggai ministered, but he continued for at least three years.

IV. Background and Theme

Zechariah was the son of Berechiah. Like Haggai, he was a prophet to the people of Judah who had returned to the land after the captivity. He joined with Haggai in encouraging them to rebuild the temple (Ezra 5:1). Zechariah's prophecy began half-way between Haggai's second and third messages.

In eight visions, using highly symbolic language, he predicted the overthrow of Gentile world powers; the judgment of apostate Jews because of their rejection of Christ; the cleansing, restoration and glory of a remnant; and the future prosperity of Jerusalem. The first five visions are messages of grace; the last three, of judgment.

Zechariah's notable prophecies

concerning the Messiah foretell His entry into Jerusalem (9:9); His betrayal for thirty pieces of silver (11:12, 13); His death as the stricken Shepherd (13:7); His coming again to the Mount of Olives (14:4); and His Millennial Reign as High Priest and King (14:9).

While many of the prophecies had a partial application or fulfillment in Zechariah's day, there are many that are still future.

OUTLINE

I. EXHORTATION TO REPENTANCE AND OBEDIENCE, AND WARNING TO PROFIT FROM MISTAKES OF FATHERS (1:1–6)

II. SERIES OF EIGHT VISIONS, DESIGNED TO ENCOURAGE PEOPLE TO REBUILD THE TEMPLE (1:7—6:8)
- A. Man Riding on a Red Horse (1:7–17)
- B. Four Horns and Four Craftsmen (1:18–21)
- C. Man with a Measuring Line (2:1–13)
- D. Joshua the High Priest (Chap. 3)
- E. The Golden Lampstand and the Two Olive Trees (Chap. 4)
- F. The Flying Scroll (5:1–4)
- G. The Woman in a Basket (5:5–11)
- H. The Four Chariots (6:1–8)

III. JOSHUA CROWNED AS HIGH PRIEST (6:9–15)

IV. JEWS FROM BETHEL INQUIRE CONCERNING CONTINUANCE OF FAST (Chaps. 7, 8)
- A. The Question Concerning the Fast (7:1–3)
- B. First Message (7:4–7)
- C. Second Message (7:8–14)
- D. Third Message (8:1–17)
- E. Fourth Message (8:18–23)

V. THE FIRST ORACLE OR BURDEN, EMPHASIZING MESSIAH'S FIRST ADVENT (Chaps. 9—11)
- A. Gentile Nations Will Be Judged (9:1–8)
- B. First Coming of Messiah to Zion (9:9)
- C. Disarmament and Universal Peace at the Second Coming of Christ (9:10)
- D. Return of Captives to Jerusalem from Exile (9:11, 12)
- E. Triumph of All Israel over Greece (9:13)
- F. Intervention of Jehovah to Protect His People (9:14–17)
- G. People Exhorted to Ask for Rain from the Lord, Not from Idols (10:1, 2)
- H. God Will Punish the Leaders of Judah, Raise Up the Messiah, and Give Victory to the People (10:3–5)
- I. Israel and Judah Will Be Regathered and Restored (10:6–12)

J. Unfaithful Rulers Will Be Punished (11:1–3)
K. Messiah Becomes True Shepherd of the Flock (11:4–8a)
L. Messiah Is Rejected by His People (11:8b–14)
M. God Delivers Them Over to the Idol Shepherd (Antichrist) (11:15–17)

VI. THE SECOND ORACLE OR BURDEN, EMPHASIZING MESSIAH'S SECOND ADVENT (Chaps. 12—14)
A. Jerusalem Will Be a Source of Trouble to the Nations (12:1–3)
B. The Lord Will Destroy the Enemies of Judah (12:4)
C. The Jews Will Acknowledge God as Their Strength (12:5)
D. Outlying Judah Will Devour Its Enemies and Will Be First to Gain the Victory (12:6–9)
E. The Nation Will Mourn Over Its Rejection of the Messiah (12:10–14)
F. Provision Will Be Made for Cleansing from Sin (13:1)
G. Idols and False Prophets Will Be Banished (13:2–6)
H. Messiah Will Be Slain and Israel Scattered (13:7)
I. A Remnant of the Nation Will Return to the Lord (13:8, 9)
J. Gentiles Will Gather Against Jerusalem (14:1, 2)
K. The Lord Himself Will Intervene (14:3–5)
L. Cosmic Changes in Weather and in Illumination (14:6, 7)
M. River of Living Water (14:8)
N. Christ Will Reign as King (14:9)
O. Geographical Changes in the Land (14:10)
P. Jerusalem Inhabited and Secure (14:11)
Q. Plague and Panic Will Afflict the Gentile Foes (14:12–15)
R. Gentile Survivors Will Worship at Jerusalem Or Be Under Penalty of the Plague (14:16–19)
S. Even Common Utensils and Objects Will Be Sacred to the Lord, and Merchants Will Not Trade in the House of the Lord (14:20–21)

Commentary

I. EXHORTATION TO REPENTANCE AND OBEDIENCE, AND WARNING TO PROFIT FROM MISTAKES OF FATHERS (1:1–6)

The first six verses are introductory. They convey a message from **the Lord** through **Zechariah the son of Berechiah** to the people, urging them to **return to** the Lord. Verse 3 strikes the keynote of the book: **"Thus says the Lord of hosts: 'Return to Me,' says the Lord of hosts, 'and I will return to you,' says the Lord of hosts."** He urges the people to profit from the mistakes of their **fathers**, who refused to listen to **the former prophets**, such as Isaiah, Jeremiah, and Hosea. Judgment overtook the people, as the Lord had warned, and then they realized that **the Lord** was dealing with them because of their evil ways.

II. SERIES OF EIGHT VISIONS, DESIGNED TO ENCOURAGE PEOPLE TO REBUILD THE TEMPLE (1:7—6:8)

Zechariah begins his book with a prophetic panorama from his own time to the Millennial Kingdom.

A. Man Riding on a Red Horse (1:7–17)

Meaning: God is displeased with the Gentiles who are at rest while His people suffer. He will punish the nations and restore His people.

1:7–11 In verse 7, the prophet begins his series of eight visions.

In the first vision, the Lord is seen (**man** on the **red horse**, compare **"the Angel of the LORD,"** v. 11) with His agents (probably angels) who patrol **the earth** on **red, sorrel, and white ... horses. The myrtle trees in the hollow** or low place represent Israel under Gentile subjugation. When the prophet asks the meaning of the riders, an interpreting **angel** promises to explain, but the Lord (**the man** standing **among the myrtle trees**) answers that their function is to patrol **the earth**. The patrols report to the Lord that **all the earth** is **quietly** at rest, probably meaning that the Gentile nations, especially Babylon, are at ease while God's people are being oppressed.

1:12–17 The Angel of the LORD intercedes to **the LORD of hosts** for **Jerusalem and ... Judah**, which have been desolate for **seventy years**. Given an encouraging reply, **the** interpreting **angel** tells the prophet to **proclaim** that God will intervene for His people. **The nations** had angered God by their cruelty to Judah. God would return **to Jerusalem**, and the temple would be rebuilt. The **surveyor's line** here speaks of reconstruction whereas in 2 Kings 21:13, it signifies destruction. . . . The prophet should tell the people that God will prosper the **cities** of Judah, **comfort Zion, and will again choose Jerusalem**.

B. Four Horns and Four Craftsmen (1:18–21)

Meaning: Destruction of four Gentile world empires.

The complete fulfillment of this second vision is still future. The **four horns** are identified as the four nations which have **scattered Judah**, Israel, and Jerusalem—in other words, the four Gentile world empires: Babylon, Medo-Persia, Greece, and Rome.[1] The **four craftsmen** are not identified, but they are obviously agencies raised up by God to destroy the Gentile powers which had **scattered Judah**. G. Coleman Luck explains:

> What are these four agents of God? It has been suggested that they may represent the four judgments of God mentioned in Ezekiel 14:21 and Revelation 6:1–8, these being war, famine, wild animals, and pestilence. Another suggestion which seems more probable is that they represent four successive powers that overthrow the four empires pictured in the previous vision: that is, Media-Persia overthrew Babylon, Greece overthrew Media-Persia, Rome overthrew Greece, and the Revived Roman Empire of the last days will be overthrown by the great Messianic kingdom. Certainly the general truth is clearly brought out that every evil power that rises up against the people of God will eventually be overthrown and judged.[2]

C. Man with a Measuring Line (2:1–13)

Meaning: Future prosperity, populousness, and security of Jerusalem.

2:1–5 The third vision reveals **a man with a measuring line**. When the prophet asked him **where** he was **going**, he answered that he was going **to measure** the site of **Jerusalem**, that is, where the city would be rebuilt. **The** interpreting **angel** met **another angel** who told him to assure the **young man** (either Zechariah or the man with the measuring line) that **Jerusalem** would yet be thickly populated, and that it would not need **walls** because **the LORD** would protect it. This refers ultimately, of course, to Jerusalem during the Millennial Reign of Christ.

2:6–12 Here the Jewish captives remaining in exile are summoned to return to Jerusalem **from the land of the north**. (Though Babylon is northeast of Jerusalem, yet the captives would come via the route of the Fertile Crescent and thus enter Israel **from the . . . north**.) This will also have a fulfillment **"after glory"** has been revealed and established, that is, after the Second Coming of Christ. God will punish the enemies of His people because the latter are what he describes as **"the apple of** His **eye."** Singing will break out when Christ comes to the millennial temple, and Gentile **nations** will join themselves to Him **in that day**. The term **the Holy Land** for Palestine is used only here in the entire Bible.

2:13 All flesh is commanded to **be silent** while **the LORD** rouses Himself to punish the nations.

D. Joshua the High Priest (Chap. 3)

Meaning: The priesthood, representative of the nation, cleansed and restored.

3:1–3 Joshua the high priest, clothed in **filthy garments**, pictures the priesthood as representative of Israel. **Satan** (Heb. for *adversary*) accuses Israel of being unfit to carry out its priestly function. God answers **Satan** that He has **plucked** the nation as **a brand . . . from the fire**, i.e., the captivity.

3:4–7 The Angel promises that the nation will be cleansed and invested **with rich robes**. At Zechariah's request, **a clean turban** is placed **on** Joshua's **head**, and he is invested while **the Angel of the LORD** stands **by. If** the people are faithful and obedient to the Lord, they will rule God's **house, and have charge of** His **courts**, and have the right of access **among** those standing there.

3:8, 9 Joshua and his fellow-priests were **a wondrous sign** ("men wondered at," that is, men that are for a **sign**). Unger elaborates:

> . . . men of prophetic portent, men who in their official position shadow forth coming events. . . . Through Christ, Israel will be redeemed and restored and constituted a high-priestly nation, which Joshua and his associate priests prefigure.[3]

In verse 8 Christ is spoken of as **"My Servant the BRANCH"**; in verse 9 He is referred to under the figure of an engraved **stone** (cf. Dan. 2:34, 35). Some have suggested that **"the Branch"** applies to the First Advent, **the stone** to the Second. Gaebelein says that **the** engraved **stone** with **seven eyes** on it must also mean the redeemed nation, the foundation of the kingdom, filled with His Spirit, for we read in connection with it, "I will remove the iniquity of that land in one day." He speaks of it as "restored Israel as the nucleus of the kingdom of God."[4]

3:10 The chapter closes with a deservedly famous glimpse of the peaceful nature of pastoral life in the Millennium:

"In that day," says the LORD of hosts, "everyone will invite his neighbor under his vine and under his fig tree."

E. The Golden Lampstand and the Two Olive Trees (Chap. 4)

Meaning: Israel, God's lightbearer, will rebuild the temple by the Spirit of God (pictured by the oil).

4:1–6 The fifth vision describes a **lampstand of solid gold** with **two olive trees** beside it. It seems that the golden **lampstand** had a base with a stem coming up out of it. At the top of the stem was **a bowl** which served as a reservoir for oil. Reaching upward out of the stem were **seven pipes** with **seven** small oil-burning **lamps** on top of each. On either side of the golden lampstand was an olive tree, apparently supplying oil directly to **the bowl** of the golden stand, and then through the **pipes** from **the bowl** to the **seven lamps**.

The golden **lampstand** may possibly be a picture of Israel as God's witness in the world. It can only fulfill its function as a light to the world by the oil, i.e., by the Holy **Spirit**. The immediate interpretation of the vision is that the temple would be rebuilt, not by human energy or power, **but by** the **Spirit** of the Lord. Difficulties would be removed, and the hands of Zerubbabel would finish the rebuilding of the temple, just as they had laid the foundation. Unger comments:

> The spiritual principle here stated (v. 6) is beautifully illustrated by the imagery of the vision in which the automatic and spontaneous supply of oil for lighting totally apart from human agency prefigures Israel's millennial testimony conducted in the fullness of the outpoured Spirit. But in its context, the promise has direct application to Zerubbabel, then faced with the colossal task of completing the temple.[5]

4:7–10 In spite of mountainous opposition, the **temple** would be completed and would bring forth exclamations **of "Grace, grace . . . !"** to its beauty. Those **who** have **despised the day of small things**, that is, those who mocked the possibility of God's doing some great thing would see **the plumb line in the hand of Zerubbabel**, that is, would **see . . . the day** when Zerubbabel would **finish** the structure.

The seven lamps are **the** seven **eyes of the LORD**, signifying His watchful care over the rebuilding and over **the whole earth**.

4:11–14 When Zechariah asks about the **two olive trees** and the **two olive branches**, the angel explains that they are **the two anointed ones** standing by **the LORD**. This is commonly taken to refer to Zerubbabel and Joshua, representing the offices of king and priest.

This vision teaches that spiritual power was necessary for the restoration, just as the previous vision taught that cleansing was necessary.

F. The Flying Scroll (5:1–4)

Meaning: The curse of God pronounced against perjury and theft in the land.

5:1, 2 The vision of the **flying scroll** is the first in a series of three having to do with administration and judgment. The **scroll** measured thirty feet long by fifteen feet wide, the same size as the portico of Solomon's temple.

5:3, 4 It pronounced a curse on **every thief** and **every perjurer**. As part of this **curse**, the very **house** of the ones who stole or who swore **falsely** would be destroyed, both **tim-**

ber and stones. Perhaps this vision has to do with the worldwide judgments that will precede the setting up of Christ's kingdom. Sins against man (theft) and sins against God (false swearing) will be dealt with at that time. (These may also represent the two tables of the law.)

G. The Woman in a Basket (5:5–11)

Meaning: Idolatry and mercenary religion removed from the land to its ancient home base in Babylon.

The seventh vision shows **a woman** in **a basket** (Heb. *ephah*). The ephah was the largest unit of measure used in business, somewhat like a bushel basket. The woman is the personification of **"Wickedness."** In the land, the **lead cover** was kept on the ephah, meaning that wickedness was restricted. But **two** other **women** flew with the ephah to **Shinar** (Babylon). This seems to signify the removal of idolatrous and mercenary religion from Israel to its base in Babylon where it originated. Such a removal would, of course, be preparatory to the judgment of Babylon and to the setting up of the kingdom. **"House"** in verse 11 means "heathen temple."

Israel was cleansed of idolatry after the Babylonian captivity, but it will embrace a worse form of idolatry in the future when it worships the Antichrist as God.

H. The Four Chariots (6:1–8)

Meaning: God's patrols indicate Israel's enemies have been put down.

6:1–4 Zechariah next sees **four** sets of **horses** and **chariots . . . coming** out **from between two mountains of bronze**. The **horses** are **red, black, white**, and **dappled** or grisled—all **strong steeds**.

6:5–7 **The** interpreting **angel** identifies the four sets of horses and chariots as the **four spirits of heaven**, God's agents to bring the Gentile world into subjection to the Messiah. **The black horses** go **to the north**, and **the dappled** ones, to **the south**. These two directions in the prophetic Scriptures are commonly associated with enemies of Israel (for example, king of the North and king of the South). **The white** horses go forth **after** the black ones and apparently the red horses patrol in undesignated areas.

6:8 The interpreting angel points out that the horses which went **toward the north country** had **given rest to** His **Spirit**. This may imply the destruction of the northern army (Babylon) which was a constant source of danger to the land of Israel. Taking the vision as a whole, it seems to indicate the destruction of Israel's enemies by messengers of the Lord. Once again, this is an event that will precede Christ's kingdom on earth.

III. JOSHUA CROWNED AS HIGH PRIEST (6:9–15)

Meaning: A picture of Christ coming as King and High Priest, the ideal combination of church and state.

6:9–13 Now that the visions of judgment are ended, a highly symbolic act takes place. Zechariah was commanded to get **gold** and **silver . . . from** three of the returned exiles—**from Heldai, Tobijah, and Jedaiah**—and to **make an elaborate crown** for **Joshua**[6] **. . . the high priest**, in **the house of Josiah**. Ordinarily, a **crown** is made for a ruler, not for a high priest. But this action points forward to the coming of Christ as King and Priest. He is spoken of in verse 12 as **the BRANCH** who will **build the** millennial **temple**, **bear** royal honor,

and . . . sit and rule on His throne. David Baron notes:

> Surely it is in keeping with the Royal Priesthood of Messiah, that the Hebrew word used here (for temple) means both palace and sanctuary. As King He has entered into His palace, and as Priest into His sanctuary.[7]

"The counsel of peace shall be between them both," that is, peaceful understanding will exist between King and Priest (in one Person).

6:14 The . . . crown was to be kept **in the temple** as **a memorial. Helem** is the same as Heldai and **Hen** is Joshua.

6:15 The restoration of dispersed Israel and the fulfillment of the messianic promise are set before the people as an encouragement to obedience.

IV. JEWS FROM BETHEL INQUIRE CONCERNING CONTINUANCE OF FAST (Chaps. 7, 8)

A. The Question Concerning the Fast (7:1–3)

Chapters 7 and 8 form a division by themselves, dealing with the subject of fasting. A delegation from Bethel (NKJV marg.)[8] came to inquire if they **should** continue to **fast** on the anniversary of the fall of Jerusalem. They had been doing this for over seventy **years.**

B. First Message (7:4–7)

Meaning: The fasts were *their* idea, not *God's*. The Lord wants reality, not just ritual.

The answer to the above question is given in four distinct messages (7:4–7; 7:8–14; 8:1–17; 8:18–23). In the first, God reminds them that the fast **in** both **the fifth and seventh months** had been instituted by themselves, not by Him. Both their fasting and their feasting were for themselves, not for God. Before the destruction of **Jerusalem, the former prophets** had warned the people that God wants righteousness and reality rather than ritual.

C. Second Message (7:8–14)

Meaning: Judgment had come upon the people because they had refused to practice justice, righteousness, and mercy.

In the second message, God explains why judgment came upon the nation. He had called the people to practice **justice, mercy, and compassion**. But **they refused to heed**. Notice the results of their disobedience: divine **wrath**; unanswered prayer; scattering of the people **among . . . the nations**; desolation of **the land**. In other words, the fast about which they were inquiring was a result of their own sinfulness and disobedience. As William Kelly warns:

> Ordinances, whatever they may do, never take the place of practical righteousness, and still less of faith, in the sight of God.[9]

D. Third Message (8:1–17)

Meaning: The Lord will yet pour out His blessings on Judah.

8:1–5 The third message to the delegation from Bethel promises future blessing to Judah. **Great** wrath will go out against the enemies of Judah (v. 2). **Jerusalem** will be restored and **called "the City of Truth,"** its **streets** transformed into a playground for **boys and girls** and a social center for old folks.

8:6–8 If this seemed **marvelous** to **the** numerically tiny **remnant,** was it therefore so hard for *God* to do? He is the One who **will bring . . . back**

the exiles and **dwell in** their **midst** as **their God**.

While these verses had an immediate application to the people in Zechariah's time, their complete fulfillment awaits our Lord's Second Advent.

8:9–13 The people who had been hearing the encouragements of Haggai and Zechariah were exhorted to continue building. **Before** they started work on the temple, there had been widespread unemployment, and violence stalked the streets. But now God promises them **peace** and prosperity, and they would **be a blessing** to the Gentiles instead of **a curse**.

8:14–17 **Just as** surely as God had promised calamity to His people in the day of their disobedience, so now He purposes to **do good to** them. In view of that, they are exhorted to live truthfully, justly, and peacefully, avoiding the **things that the LORD** hates (thinking **evil . . . against** one's **neighbor** and loving **a false oath**—dishonesty).

E. Fourth Message (8:18–23)

Meaning: Israel's fasts will be turned to feasts, and Jerusalem will be the world center of worship.

8:18 As an encouragement to the delegation from Bethel, the Lord promises that the mournful fasts would be turned into seasons of **joy and gladness and cheerful feasts**. **The fast of the tenth** month mourned the siege of Jerusalem (2 Kgs. 25:1); **the fourth** month marked its capture (2 Kgs. 25:3); **the fifth** month, its destruction (2 Kgs. 25:8–10); **the seventh** month, the murder of Gedaliah (2 Kgs. 25:25).

8:19–23 The closing verses of the chapter picture **many** Gentile **peoples and strong nations** flocking to **Jerusalem** from all over the world **to seek the LORD of hosts**. In that day, the Jews will be the channel of blessing to the world. Notice the frequent use of the expression **"Thus says the LORD"** or **"Thus says the LORD of hosts"** in this chapter: vv. 2, 3, 4, 6, 7, 9, 14, 19, 20, 23.

V. THE FIRST ORACLE OR BURDEN, EMPHASIZING MESSIAH'S FIRST ADVENT (Chaps. 9—11)

The remaining chapters contain two oracles or burdens. The first, in chapters 9—11, emphasizes the First Advent of the Messiah, while the second one, chapters 12—14, looks forward to Christ's glorious appearing.

A. Gentile Nations Will Be Judged (9:1–8)

9:1–7 Here in chapter 9, God's judgment is first pronounced **against** Syria (**Hadrach**, **Damascus**, **Hamath**—vv. 1, 2a), **Tyre and Sidon** (vv. 2b–4), and Philistia (**Ashkelon**, **Gaza**, **Ekron**, **Ashdod**—vv. 5–7). **Tyre** was proud of its riches and its fortress city, but **the LORD** would **cast her** into the sea. The Philistine cities would be dismayed to **see** the fall of Tyre; they thought it was impregnable. **The Philistines** themselves would be cleansed from idolatry, and they would dwell as a clan in Israel. **Ekron** would be **like** the Jebusites in the sense that they would live among the people of Israel as loyal, peaceful citizens.

9:8 Foreign invaders would no longer threaten the temple or the people. Actually, verses 1–8 had a partial fulfillment when these Gentile powers were conquered by Alexander the Great (see reference to Greece in v. 13).

B. First Coming of Messiah to Zion (9:9)

God's people are next encouraged by the promise of the **coming** of the

Messiah (**King**). Verse 9 describes His First Coming, in **lowly** grace, **on a donkey**. Both Matthew, the most Jewish of the four Gospels, and John, the most universal, quote this verse as referring to the so-called "Triumphal Entry" of our Lord into Jerusalem.

C. Disarmament and Universal Peace at the Second Coming of Christ (9:10)

Verse 10, however, looks forward to His Second Advent, when He will come in power and great glory. Weapons of war will be abolished, and Christ will reign **"from sea to sea, and from the River to the ends of the earth"** (Zechariah is quoting Ps. 72:8). The present Age of Grace is hidden between verses 9 and 10.

D. Return of Captives to Jerusalem from Exile (9:11, 12)

"The blood of your covenant" refers to the **blood** by which a **covenant** was sealed. This expression could refer to the covenant of the law (Ex. 24:8), the covenant guaranteeing the land to Israel (Deut. 30:1–10), the Davidic Covenant (2 Sam. 7:4–17), or the general covenantal relationship of Israel with Jehovah (NKJV, LORD).

Israel's captives will be set **free from the waterless pit** of foreign countries and returned to **the stronghold**, which may mean Jerusalem, Palestine, or God Himself.

E. Triumph of All Israel over Greece (9:13)

Judah and Israel (**Ephraim**) will be conquering nations in that day, subduing **Greece**. This prophecy was partially fulfilled in the War of the Maccabees, 175–163 B.C. It also anticipates the final restoration of Israel from worldwide dispersion.

F. Intervention of Jehovah to Protect His People (9:14–17)

An unknown commentator vividly describes what amounts to a "holy war":

> Not only will God's victors drink full of the blood of their vanquished enemies and be like the sacrificial bowls filled with blood to be sprinkled upon the sides of the altar and its horns, but they shall come through gory triumph bespattered with blood like the corners of the altar.

Merrill Unger depicts the contrast between Israel and her enemies:

> In apparent antithesis to Israel's enemies as *sling-stones* trodden in the mire, in the preceding verse, Zechariah compares Zion's victorious sons (the saved remnant) to *precious stones* of a crown which sparkle over the Lord's land. The figure is evidently of the reward of the faithful martyrs and valiant saints of Israel who enter the kingdom of Messiah.[10]

G. People Exhorted to Ask for Rain from the Lord, Not from Idols (10:1, 2)

The people are exhorted to **ask the LORD for rain** and not to pray to worthless **idols**. Idolatry causes **people** to wander **like sheep** without a **shepherd**.

H. God Will Punish the Leaders of Judah, Raise Up the Messiah, and Give Victory to the People (10:3–5)

10:3 God's **anger is kindled against the shepherds** and leaders (**goatherds**) for leading the people astray. **The LORD . . . will visit** the **flock . . . of Judah** and transform it into a war **horse**.

10:4, 5 Many commentators interpret verse 4 as a promise of the Messiah. Coming out of **Judah**, He would be the chief **cornerstone, the tent peg, the battle bow**, and the **ruler**. Others believe that this is a picture of restored Israel. Feinberg says that the last line describes what the Messiah will do, namely, cast foreign oppressors out of the land[11] (see KJV). In any case, the men of Judah will gloriously triumph over **their enemies**.

I. Israel and Judah Will Be Regathered and Restored (10:6–12)

Verses 6–12 predict the regathering of both Israel (**Joseph**) and **Judah** from worldwide dispersion. Israel (**Ephraim**) will **be like a mighty warrior**.

The Lord **will whistle for** His people **and gather them** back **into the land of Gilead and Lebanon . . . from . . . Egypt** and **from Assyria** where He had sown or scattered them. The nations that formerly enslaved them will be punished, and Judah and Israel will glory **in** the **name** of the Lord. The **"He"** in verse 11 is **the Lord**. The **affliction** with which He strikes **the waves of the sea** may well stand for anything that hinders the return, as the Red Sea seemed to hinder the Exodus.

J. Unfaithful Rulers Will Be Punished (11:1–3)

Chapter 11 deals with the rejection of the Messiah and the destruction of Jerusalem by the Romans, and also with the rise of the Antichrist.

The first three verses may be a literal description of the destruction wrought in the forests of Israel (**Lebanon**), both in the highlands and in the lowlands. The **shepherds** howl because the pastures along **the Jordan** are ruined and their sheep have nothing to eat. Some think this points forward to the devastation of the land by the Romans in A.D. 70.

K. Messiah Becomes True Shepherd of the Flock (11:4–8a)

11:4–6 The Lord instructs Zechariah to assume the role of a shepherd whose **flock** is doomed to **slaughter**. In this, Zechariah is a type of the Lord Jesus. The sheep (the Jewish remnant) have been cruelly exploited by their previous **shepherds** (rulers). God has determined to deliver the wicked **inhabitants of the land** into the hands of the Roman emperor whom they will acknowledge as their **king** (John 19:15).

11:7, 8a In carrying out the role of shepherd, Zechariah **took . . . two staffs**—grace (**Beauty**) and union (**Bonds**). They represent God's desire to show grace to His people, and to unite Judah and Israel. Zechariah had to dismiss **three** false **shepherds**, generally taken to refer to the three offices of king, priest and prophet, in order to do his work. (Unger suggests that the three shepherds picture three orders of rulers in the Jewish state—priests, teachers of the law, and civil magistrates. He explains the **one month** as the period of culminating unbelief just before Israel's leaders crucified our Lord.)[12]

L. Messiah Is Rejected by His People (11:8b–14)

11:8b–11 When the people reject the shepherd, he leaves them to their fate. Zechariah then breaks the first **staff (Beauty) . . . in two**, annulling the covenant that restrained the Gentiles from oppressing God's people. Only **the poor of the flock** understood what God was doing and why.

11:12, 13 When Zechariah asks for his **wages**, they give him **thirty pieces of silver**—the redemption price of a slave who has been gored by an ox. This payment is cast **to the potter**, a prophecy of what Judas would do after his betrayal of the Lord.

11:14 Then Zechariah cuts **in two** his **other staff**, (**Bonds**), indicating that **the brotherhood between Judah and Israel** was broken, and that there would be disunity and internal strife among the Jews.

M. God Delivers Them Over to the Idol Shepherd (Antichrist) (11:15–17)

Feinberg points out that the Church Age is hidden between verses 14 and 15.[13]

Because Israel rejected the *Good* Shepherd, they would be given a *false* **shepherd**. Zechariah acts this out by taking **the implements of a** worthless **shepherd**. This points to the future Antichrist, who will not care for the sheep but will rob and slay them. **His arm** will be withered **and his right eye . . . blinded** in battle.

VI. THE SECOND ORACLE OR BURDEN, EMPHASIZING MESSIAH'S SECOND ADVENT (Chaps.12—14)

A. Jerusalem Will Be a Source of Trouble to the Nations (12:1–3)

Here the Gentile **nations** are seen marching **against . . . Jerusalem** in a future **day**. All who trouble the city will be greatly troubled. They will hurt themselves in trying to lift this **very heavy** millstone.

B. The Lord Will Destroy the Enemies of Judah (12:4)

In that day God **will strike** the invaders, both **horse** and **rider**, **with madness** and panic.

C. The Jews Will Acknowledge God as Their Strength (12:5)

The **governors of Judah** outside of Jerusalem **shall say in their heart** that **the inhabitants of Jerusalem** have **strength** from **the Lord**.

D. Outlying Judah Will Devour Its Enemies and Will Be First to Gain the Victory (12:6–9)

In that day, . . . the governors of Judah will be like a devouring fire, burning everything they touch. Victory will come **first** to the inhabitants of outlying **Judah** so that the men **of Jerusalem** will **not** be exalted above them. **The inhabitants of Jerusalem** will be protected and strengthened, and **the** invading Gentile **nations** will be destroyed.

E. The Nation Will Mourn Over Its Rejection of the Messiah (12:10–14)

The people **will mourn** bitterly when they **look on** the Messiah **whom they** had **pierced**. **"Then they shall look on Me whom they pierced. Yes, they will mourn for Him as one mourns for his only son"** (v. 10b). Notice **"on Me."** The One **whom they pierced** was the Lord Jesus Christ, Jehovah. Mourning for an **only son** was the deepest form of sorrow for an Israelite. Concerning **"the mourning at Hadad Rimmon"** (v. 11), see 2 Chronicles 35:20–24. The mourners will include the royal **family**, the prophets (**Nathan**), the priests (**Levi**), the teachers (**Shimei**), and the people. Some think that Shimei should be Simeon,[14] who, with Levi, was cruel to the men of Shechem (Gen. 34:25). . . . Notice the repetition of the words **by themselves** (vv. 12–14); true confession requires us to be alone with God.

F. Provision Will Be Made for Cleansing from Sin (13:1)

The first verse of chapter 13 is closely connected with the preceding chapter. After the people of Judah and Israel have been brought to the place of repentance for their rejection of the Messiah, then will follow a great national day of atonement. The **fountain** for cleansing was opened at Calvary, but Israel nationally will not enter into the good of it until the Second Advent.

G. Idols and False Prophets Will Be Banished (13:2–6)

13:2 The land will be purged of **idols**, and false **prophets** and **unclean** spirits will be banished.

13:3–5 These verses apparently describe the wrath which will come upon false prophets in the day of Israel's restoration. If a man falsely poses as a **prophet**, his own parents will threaten him and stab him. Men will not lightly claim to be prophets if they are not truly sent by God but will rather identify themselves as farmers, or whatever occupation they actually hold.

13:6 If a false prophet has been stabbed or if he has **wounds** which were self-inflicted as part of the cultic practices of the false prophets, he will not give the real reason when asked about them. Rather, he will give some ambiguous answer, such as, **"Those with which I was wounded in the house of my friends."**

Many devout preachers have used verse 6 to refer to our Lord Jesus Christ and to the nail wounds which He received at Calvary. However, it seems difficult to fit such a meaning into the context when a false prophet is clearly in view.[15] In our zeal to protect messianic OT passages from the unbelief of rationalistic critics we must be careful not to press a verse out of its setting.

Such a conservative Bible teacher as G. Coleman Luck agrees with the non-messianic interpretation:

> The man being questioned has denied that he ever was a false prophet. His questioner, however, is suspicious and persists in the examination. It was customary for false prophets to inflict cuttings or wounds on themselves (see 1 Kings 18:28; Jer. 16:6, etc.).[16]

Further details in the verse itself fit the false prophet better. In Hebrew the word for *hands* (KJV) refers to the forearms. **These wounds between your arms**, as the NKJV more precisely translates it, could refer to any wounds on one's torso, front or back, such as could be administered in cultic cuttings (or by one's "friends," if the false prophet was telling the truth). Also, our Lord was not wounded in the house of His *friends*, but in that of His cruelest enemies.

H. Messiah Will Be Slain and Israel Scattered (13:7)

Verse 7 starts a section that all believing Bible students consider messianic. Jehovah orders His **sword** to **awake . . . against** the Lord Jesus. **The Shepherd** was struck at Calvary, and **the** Jewish **sheep** have been **scattered** ever since.

I. A Remnant of the Nation Will Return to the Lord (13:8, 9)

Because of their rejection of the Lord Jesus, **two-thirds** of the nation will **die** during the Great Tribulation, yet a remnant of **one-third** will be preserved. This remnant will be refined like **silver** and **gold**. They will acknowledge **God**, and He will acknowledge them as **"My people."**

J. Gentiles Will Gather Against Jerusalem (14:1, 2)

The day of the Lord here refers to the final siege of **Jerusalem** by the nations. The invading armies will divide the **spoil** they have taken inside **the city. Half of the** people will be taken **into captivity** and the other half will remain.

K. The Lord Himself Will Intervene (14:3–5)

Then the Lord Himself will come to **the Mount of Olives. The Mount** will **be split in two, half** to **the north** and **half** to **the south**, with **a very large valley** between. **"Thus the Lord my God will come, and all the saints with You."** Unger explains:

> To demonstrate his ecstasy, the seer passes from indirect to direct address, a phenomenon often met with in animated Hebrew style.[17]

L. Cosmic Changes in Weather and in Illumination (14:6, 7)

The *precise* meaning of this passage is so obscure that many modern versions (such as Moffatt, RSV, NEB, NIV) have adapted one or more of the ancient translations, which convey the idea "that all extremes of temperature will cease."[18] Baldwin gives as an alternative translation of the last clause of verse 6 in the Hebrew text, " 'the splendid ones (stars), congeal,' that is, lose their brightness."[19]

The *general* meaning of the text is clear: the changes predicted will be *cosmic* in scope.

Unger, who rejects the readings supported by the early versions as "obviously wrong," sees the day as a period (the Day of the Lord), not a twenty-four hour interval. He ties this passage in with Isaiah 30:26:

> Moreover the light of the moon will be as the light of the sun, and the light of the sun will be sevenfold, as the light of seven days, in the day that the Lord binds up the bruise of His people and heals the stroke of their wound.[20]

M. River of Living Water (14:8)

Living waters shall flow from Jerusalem, half to the Dead Sea (**eastern sea**) **and half** to the Mediterranean (**the western sea**) in all seasons.

N. Christ Will Reign as King (14:9)

The Lord shall be King over all the earth and He shall be acknowledged as the only true God.

O. Geographical Changes in the Land (14:10)

All the land shall be turned into a plain, with **Jerusalem** elevated above the rest.

P. Jerusalem Inhabited and Secure (14:11)

Jerusalem shall be safely inhabited, and **the people** who **dwell in it** will **no longer** be under the threat of enemy invasion and **utter destruction**.

Q. Plague and Panic Will Afflict the Gentile Foes (14:12–15)

Chronologically these verses belong with 14:3, which describes Christ conquering the enemies of Israel. These enemies will be struck with a terrible plague[21]—**"their flesh shall dissolve while they stand on their feet, their eyes shall dissolve in their sockets, and their tongues shall dissolve in their mouths."** There will be a **great panic from the Lord**. Rural **Judah** will assist in the defense of **Jerusalem**, and the spoil shall be **great**.

R. Gentile Survivors Will Worship at Jerusalem Or Be Under Penalty of the Plague (14:16–19)

Surviving Gentile **nations** will come to **Jerusalem** annually **to worship the King, the Lord of hosts, and to keep**

the Feast of Tabernacles. Unger explains why:

> The Feast of Tabernacles is the only one of the seven Jewish festivals which is represented in this prophecy as being observed in the kingdom age. Why? It is the only one which at that time will be unfulfilled typically and the only one which will be in process of fulfillment by the kingdom itself.[22]

Those refusing to come and worship will suffer drought. **Egypt** is mentioned specifically as one of the countries that will have **no rain** if they are disobedient.

S. Even Common Utensils and Objects Will Be Sacred to the Lord, and Merchants Will Not Trade in the House of the Lord (14:20–21)

In that day everything will be **"HOLINESS TO THE LORD."** There will be no difference between "secular" and "sacred." Even **the bells** on **the horses** and the common pots **in Jerusalem and Judah** will be sacred! The **Canaanite**—a derisive term for a huckster or an unclean person—will be banished from the temple, **the house of the LORD of hosts**.

ENDNOTES

[1](1:18–21) Some see the *four* only as representing "the totality of opposition, just as it represents all directions in the eighth vision" (Joyce G. Baldwin, *Haggai, Zechariah, Malachi*, p. 407). However, the specific reference to individual nations is an ancient interpretation.

[2](1:18–21) G. Coleman Luck, *Zechariah*, pp. 26, 27.

[3](3:8, 9) Merrill F. Unger, *Zechariah: Prophet of Messiah's Glory*, pp. 64, 65.

[4](3:8, 9) Arno C. Gaebelein, *Studies in Zechariah*, p. 42.

[5](4:1–6) Unger, *Zechariah*, p. 75.

[6](6:9–13) It is worth noting that *Joshua* and *Jeshua* (Heb. form of Jesus) are really the same name.

[7](6:9–13) David Baron, *The Visions and Prophecies of Zechariah*.

[8](7:1–3) *Bethel* is Hebrew for *house of God*, but the temple is called *the house of the LORD (Jehovah)*, so the city of Bethel is probably meant, contrary to KJV/NKJV tradition. Notice also that *to* is in italics (v. 2), meaning that it is not in the Hebrew (but then neither is *from*). As Baldwin remarks, "The correct way to translate this verse is far from evident." (See Joyce G. Baldwin, *Haggai, Zechariah, Malachi*, pp. 141–143.)

[9](7:8–14) William Kelly, *Lectures Introductory to the Study of the Minor Prophets*, p. 467.

[10](9:14–17) Unger, *Zechariah*, p. 170.

[11](10:4, 5) Charles Lee Feinberg, *God Remembers*, p. 188.

[12](11:7, 8a) Unger, *Zechariah*, p. 195.

[13](11:15–17) Feinberg, *God Remembers*, p. 211.

[14](12:10–14) In Hebrew Simeon is *Shimon*. In the ancient, consonantal text, before the vowels were added, this could very easily be miscopied as *Shimei*.

[15](13:6) Unger, an eminent OT scholar, applies the verse to Christ, but admits that few Bible scholars agree with him:

> The boldness and daring of this Messianic prophecy and the *dramatic abruptness* with which it is introduced have frightened most expositors away from its true import on the supposition that it is inseparably connected with verses 2–5, and therefore, still has the false prophet in mind, and to in-

troduce the Messiah is flagrantly to ignore the context.

Dr. Unger goes on for five columns of his commentary to defend his view (pp. 228–230).

[16](13:6) G. Coleman Luck, *Zechariah*, p. 113.

[17](14:3–5) Unger, *Zechariah*, p. 250.

[18](14:6, 7) Baldwin, *Haggai, Zechariah, Malachi*, p. 203.

[19](14:6, 7) *Ibid*.

[20](14:6, 7) Unger, *Zechariah*, pp. 252, 253.

[21](14:12–15) Many modern readers have noticed how closely this passage resembles the dreadful results of a nuclear attack.

[22](14:16–19) Unger, *Zechariah*, p. 265.

BIBLIOGRAPHY

Baldwin, Joyce G. *Haggai, Zechariah, Malachi: An Introduction and Commentary*. Downers Grove, Ill: Inter Varsity Press, 1972.

Feinberg, Charles Lee. *God Remembers*. New York: American Board of Missions to the Jews, Inc., 1965.

Gaebelein, Arno C. *Studies in Zechariah*. New York: Our Hope Publishers, 1904.

Laney, J. Carl. "Zechariah." In *Everyman's Bible Commentary*. Chicago: Moody Press, 1984.

Lindsey, F. Duane. "Zechariah." In *The Bible Knowledge Commentary*. Wheaton: Victor Books, 1985.

Luck, G. Coleman. *Zechariah*. Chicago: Moody Press, 1969.

Mills, Montague S. "Zechariah." In *The Minor Prophets: A Survey*. Distributed by 3E Ministries. Dallas: n.d.

Tatford, Frederick A. *The Minor Prophets*. Vol. 3. Reprint (3 vols.). Minneapolis: Klock & Klock Christian Publishers, 1982.

———. *Prophet of the Myrtle Grove*. Eastbourne, England: Prophetic Witness Publishing House, 1971.

Unger, Merrill F. *Zechariah: Prophet of Messiah's Glory*. Grand Rapids: Zondervan Publishing House, 1962.

MALACHI

Introduction

"Malachi is like a late evening, which brings a long day to a close; but he is also the morning dawn, which bears a glorious day in its womb."

—Nagelsbach

I. Unique Place in the Canon

Malachi (My messenger, possibly a shortened form of *Malā'k-îyyāh*, messenger of Jehovah), has the distinction of being the last of the prophets and the bridge between the two Testaments, looking forward both to John the Baptist and the Lord Jesus Himself.

Strangely enough, some believe the prophecy of Malachi is anonymous, and that the name is merely a title for Ezra or some other writer. Some church fathers even thought the writer was an angel, since in Greek (and Hebrew) the same word can mean *angel* or *messenger*![1]

Malachi also has a special dialectic (question and answer) style that has caused some to call him "the Hebrew Socrates."

II. Authorship

Although Jewish tradition says that Malachi belonged to the "Great Synagogue," and was a Levite from Supha, in Zebulun, we know nothing definite about the prophet apart from his book. There is every reason to accept him as a bold, often severe writer, who with Haggai and Zechariah called the post-exilic Jews back to their covenantal relationship with God.

III. Date

It is clear that Malachi wrote after 538 B.C., since he used an almost exclusively post-exilic word for *governor*.[2] It is also obvious that he wrote later than the other two post-exilic "minor" prophets, Haggai and Zechariah, since in Malachi the temple is finished, the rituals have been reinstituted, and in fact, enough time had elapsed for spiritual declension to set in. Also, the walls of Jerusalem had been rebuilt.

Malachi probably should be dated between about 470 and 460 B.C.

IV. Background and Theme

The problems in Malachi are the same as those in Nehemiah—mixed marriages with pagans, unjust financial practices, withholding of tithes from God's house, and general spiritual apathy. Either they are the identical problems mentioned in Nehemiah or a repetition or continuation of them not too long after his time.

Because of the lackluster religious life of the post-exilic Jews, Malachi sought to stir them up by using his vivid method of dialogue with an unfaithful people.

It has been pointed out that Malachi

is well named "My messenger" or "messenger of Jehovah" (NKJV, LORD), because in these four short chapters, the prophet describes three messengers—the priest of the Lord (2:2); John the Baptist (3:1a); and our Lord Himself (3:16).

Malachi records Jehovah's last pleading with His people in the OT period. After this, the prophetic voice will be silent for four centuries until the coming of John the Baptist.

It is worth noting that no matter how "late" some critics may date Malachi or other prophecies, these writings were definitely written long before the advents of John and the Lord Jesus. Thus they are true *prophecies*, and not "history written *as* prophecy," as some destructive critics claim.

OUTLINE

I. THE LORD'S CHARGES AGAINST ISRAEL, THEIR REPLIES, AND HIS THREATENED JUDGMENTS (1:1—3:15)
   A. Ingratitude (1:1–5)
   B. Sacrilege by the Priests (1:6–14)
   C. Condemnation of the Priests (2:1–9)
   D. Divorce and Mixed Marriages (2:10–16)
   E. Denial of God's Holiness and Justice (2:17)
   F. Parenthesis: Messiah's Coming in Judgment (3:1–6)
   G. The Backsliding of the People (3:7)
   H. Robbing God of Tithes and Offerings (3:8–12)
   I. False Charges Against God (3:13–15)

II. THE BLESSING OF THE REMNANT AND THE JUDGMENT OF THE WICKED (3:16—4:6)
   A. The Restoration of the Faithful Remnant (3:16–18)
   B. The Judgment of the Wicked (4:1)
   C. The Coming of the Messiah to the Remnant (4:2, 3)
   D. Closing Exhortation to Obedience, with Promise of the Coming of Elijah the Prophet (4:4–6)

Commentary

I. THE LORD'S CHARGES AGAINST ISRAEL, THEIR REPLIES, AND HIS THREATENED JUDGMENTS (1:1—3:15)

A. Ingratitude (1:1–5)

In the first chapter, we find the Lord making certain charges against the people, and the people replying with strong denials. First, **the LORD** pleads His love for them, and they ask Him to prove it: **"In what way have You loved us?"** He does so by reminding them of His love for **Jacob** (from whom they were descended), His rejection of **Esau**, and His judgments on Esau's descendants, the Edomites. The **eyes** of **the people** of **Israel** would **see** the desolation of **Edom**, and they would acknowledge the greatness of God.

B. Sacrilege by the Priests (1:6–14)

1:6 Next the Lord charges the **priests** with despising His **name** and failing to **honor** and **reverence** Him. They ask for evidence of their profane behavior.

1:7, 8 The Lord accuses them of bringing **defiled** offerings. They deny this, too, but He reminds them that they acted as if anything was good enough for the Lord. They brought **blind** and **lame** sacrifices, which they would not dare **offer . . . to** their **governor**.

1:9 The prophet urges them to repent of their sins so that God's wrath might be averted.

1:10 **The Lord of hosts** wishes that someone would **shut the doors** of the temple so that the sacrifices might stop, because the sacrifices were utterly unacceptable to Him.

1:11 But **the Lord** will vindicate His **name . . . among the Gentiles** even though His own people will not honor Him.

1:12–14 The Jews despised the sacred things of the temple and were wearied of serving God. A curse would rest upon all who brought their **blemished** odds and ends to God for **sacrifices**. The reason is that **the Lord of hosts** is **a great King**, and His **name is to be feared among the nations**.

C. Condemnation of the Priests (2:1–9)

The **priests** are solemnly warned of dreadful judgment if they do not repent and change their ways. They are reminded that the priests of old were faithful to God's **covenant with Levi**, but now the priests had become utterly corrupt, and so God had **made** them **contemptible and base before all the people**.

D. Divorce and Mixed Marriages (2:10–16)

2:10–12 Next the subject of divorce and marriage to idolatrous heathen wives is dealt with. The people of **Judah had dealt treacherously** by marrying foreigners, thus destroying their national solidarity. Those who entered mixed marriages would be **cut off**.

2:13–16 The people wept at **the altar** because the Lord no longer accepted their offerings with favor. And why not? **Because the Lord** had **been** a **witness** at their marriages, which they were now breaking so readily. He had intended them to be one pure people, producing **godly offspring** and separated from the corruptions of the heathen. **God . . . hates** unscriptural **divorce** and its resulting **violence**. The link between **divorce** and **violence** is explained by Baldwin as follows:

> He sees divorce to be like *covering one's garment with violence*, a figurative expression for all kinds of gross injustice which, like the blood of a murdered victim, leave their mark for all to see.[3]

E. Denial of God's Holiness and Justice (2:17)

They had **wearied the Lord** by saying that He did not care about the behavior of **everyone who did evil**. Hypocritically, they challenged Him to intervene, saying, **"Where is the God of justice?"**

F. Parenthesis: Messiah's Coming in Judgment (3:1–6)

3:1 God next answers the impious challenge of the previous verse. He will **send** His **messenger**, a promise that had an early and partial fulfillment in John the Baptist, but awaits a later and complete fulfillment when Elijah (4:5) will prepare the way of **the Lord, . . . the Messenger of the covenant** whom they desired (irony). The irony here is that when He later arrived (His First Advent), the nation of Israel did *not* **delight in** Him but crucified Him instead.

3:2–4 **The day of His coming** will be the Second Advent. The Lord will come in judgment on sin, and **who** will be able to **stand**? This purifying ministry, pictured by Christ's cleansing of the temple, awaits final fulfillment at His Second Coming. **The sons of Levi** (priests) will be purified so that they can make offerings of holiness and **righteousness** that are **pleasant to the LORD, as in the days of old**.

3:5 The Lord will also punish **sorcerers, adulterers, perjurers**, oppressors of **wage earners, widows, and orphans**, as well as **those who turn away an alien**.

3:6 The fact that **the LORD** is the unchanging One accounts for the preservation of the **sons of Jacob** from destruction.

G. The Backsliding of the People (3:7)

The LORD invites the people to **return to** Him, but they deny having **gone away**, asking hypocritically, **"In what way shall we return?"**

H. Robbing God of Tithes and Offerings (3:8–12)

Under the Mosaic Law, the Israelites were required to give a tenth of all produce and livestock to the Lord (or they could redeem it with money and add a fifth part). The tithes were in addition to numerous offerings, and were an acknowledgment that everything belonged to God and that He was the Giver of all possessions.

The NT teaches believers to give systematically, liberally, cheerfully, and as the Lord has prospered them, that is, proportionately. But no mention is made of tithing. Rather, the suggestion is that if a Jew living under law gave a tenth, how much more should a Christian living under grace give!

The reward for faithful tithing in the OT was material wealth; the reward for faithful stewardship in the present age is spiritual riches.

So He reminds them of their failure to bring their **tithes and offerings**, thus robbing **God** and bringing **a curse** on themselves. If they will be faithful with their **tithes**, He will bless them with incredible plenty, so much so **that there will not be room enough to receive it**. He will deliver them from drought, plague, enemies, and locusts, and make them a blessing in the earth.

I. False Charges Against God (3:13–15)

Again **the LORD** charges that they have spoken **harsh** things **against** Him, saying that it does not pay **to serve God** or obey Him. They taught that **the proud**, the wicked, and those who **tempt God** not only prosper but get away with it scot-**free**.

II. THE BLESSING OF THE REMNANT AND THE JUDGMENT OF THE WICKED (3:16—4:6)

A. The Restoration of the Faithful Remnant (3:16–18)

But there was a remnant of people true to Jehovah. These shall be spared and blessed, and acknowledged as God's own possession, being made into His **jewels**.

William Kelly comments:

> The Jews themselves will no longer take the ground of being mere Jews. They will see the vanity of an outward place; they will value what is of God, they will abhor the more those who are wicked because they are Jews (v. 18).[4]

B. The Judgment of the Wicked (4:1)

The day is coming, burning like an oven, when **all the proud** and the wicked shall be destroyed, **root** and **branch**.

C. The Coming of the Messiah to the Remnant (4:2, 3)

The faithful will welcome **the Sun of Righteousness,** who will **arise with healing in His wings**. Those **who fear** God's **name** will triumph over their foes like **ashes under** their **feet**.

D. Closing Exhortation to Obedience, with Promise of the Coming of Elijah the Prophet (4:4–6)

The book closes with an *exhortation* to **remember the Law of Moses** and with a *promise* to **send . . . Elijah** to Israel **before the . . . day of the Lord. He will** bring about reform in the lives of the people, making them resemble their godly forefathers. Otherwise God will have to visit the land[5] (or **earth**) **with a curse**. In reading Malachi in the synagogue the Jews repeat verse 5 after verse 6 so that the book will not end with a curse. However, as Wolf observes, "This attempt to soften the message does not alter the grim reality."[6]

Since we read the Old Covenant in the fuller light of the New, what better way to end the OT volume of the *Believers Bible Commentary* than by quoting the last paragraph of Keil and Delitzsch's devout and scholarly OT commentary,[7] which nicely binds the two together:

> Law and prophets bore witness of Christ, and Christ came not to destroy the law or the prophets, but to fulfil them. Upon the Mount of Christ's Transfiguration, therefore, there appeared both Moses, the founder of the law and mediator of the old covenant, and Elijah the prophet, as the restorer of the law in Israel, to talk with Jesus of His decease which He was to accomplish in Jerusalem . . . for a practical testimony to the apostles and to us all, that Jesus Christ, who laid down His life for us, to bear our sin and redeem us from the curse of the law, was the beloved Son of the Father, whom we are to hear, that by believing in His name we may become children of God and heirs of everlasting life.[8]

ENDNOTES

[1](Intro) Our English word *angel* comes from the Greek word *angelos* (messenger or angel). The name of the book is from the Hebrew word *māla'k*, with the same meanings.

[2](Intro) Joyce Baldwin, *Haggai, Zechariah, Malachi*, p. 241.

[3](2:13–16) *Ibid.*, p. 241.

[4](3:16–18) William Kelly, *Lectures Introductory to the Study of the Minor Prophets*, p. 536.

[5](4:4–6) The same Hebrew word (*eretz*) can mean *land* or *earth*.

[6](4:4–6) Herbert Wolf, *Haggai and Malachi*, p. 126.

[7](4:4–6) It is well worth noting that Keil and Delitzsch's multi-volume work, while over a century old, is still in print and widely used. Whereas rationalistic commentaries are constantly being replaced by ever more

radical unbelief, doctrinally sound and well-written ones can prove valuable for decades and even centuries to come.

[8](4:4–6) C. F. Keil, "Malachi," *Biblical Commentary on the Old Testament*, XXVI:475.

BIBLIOGRAPHY

Baldwin, Joyce G. *Haggai, Zechariah, Malachi: An Introduction and Commentary*. The Tyndale Old Testament Commentaries. Downers Grove, IL: InterVarsity Press, 1972.

Feinberg, Charles Lee. *Habakkuk, Zephaniah, Haggai and Malachi*. New York: American Board of Mission to the Jews, Inc., 1951.

———. *The Minor Prophets*. Chicago: Moody Press, 1976.

Keil, C. F. "Malachi." In *Biblical Commentary on the Old Testament*. Vol. 26. Grand Rapids: Wm. B. Eerdmans Publishing Co., 1971.

Kelly, William. *Lectures Introductory to the Study of the Minor Prophets*. London: C. A. Hammond Trust Bible Depot, n.d.

Logsdon, S. Franklin. *Malachi* or *Will a Man Rob God?* Chicago: Moody Press, 1961.

Morgan, G. Campbell. *The Minor Prophets*. Old Tappan, N.J.: Fleming H. Revell Company, 1960.

Tatford, Frederick A. *The Minor Prophets*. Vol. 3. Reprint (3 vols.). Minneapolis: Klock & Klock Christian Publishers, 1982.

Wolf, Herbert. *Haggai and Malachi*. Chicago: Moody Press, 1976.

GENERAL BIBLIOGRAPHY

Abels, Jules. *The Rockefeller Billions.* New York: Macmillan, 1965.

Adams, J. *Competent to Counsel.* Grand Rapids: Baker Book House, 1970.

Adolph, Paul Ernest. "God in Medical Practice," a chapter in *The Evidence of God in an Expanding Universe* by John Clover Monsma. Bangalore, India: Thomas Samuel, 1968.

Alexander, Denis. *Beyond Science.* Philadelphia: Holman, 1972.

The Apocrypha. Revised Standard Version. New York: Thomas Nelson & Sons, 1957.

Archer, Gleason. *A Survey of Old Testament Introduction.* Chicago: Moody Press, 1974.

Armerding, Carl. *The Fight for Palestine.* Wheaton, IL: Van Kampen Press, 1949.

Barnes, Albert. *The Bible Commentary, Proverbs-Ezekiel.* Grand Rapids: Baker Book House, 1953.

Barnhouse, Donald Grey. *Words Fitly Spoken.* Wheaton, IL: Tyndale House, 1969.

Baron, David. *The Shepherd of Israel.* London: Morgan and Scott, Ltd., n.d.

Baxter, J. Sidlow. *Explore the Book.* London: Marshall, Morgan and Scott, Ltd., 1958.

Bermant, Chaim, and Michael Weitzman. *Ebla: A Revelation in Archaeology.* New York: Times Books, 1979.

Borland, James A. *Christ in the Old Testament.* Chicago: Moody Press, 1978.

Bright, Bill. *Revolution Now.* San Bernardino, CA: Campus Crusade, 1969.

Bullinger, E. W. *The Companion Bible.* London: Lamp Press, n.d.

Campbell, M. *From Grace to Glory.* London: Banner of Truth Trust, 1970.

Chafer, L. S. *Systematic Theology.* 8 vols. Dallas: Dallas Seminary Press, 1947.

Christenson, Larry. *The Christian Family.* Minneapolis: Bethany Fellowship, 1970.

Collins, Larry, and Dominique Lapierre, *O Jerusalem!* New York: Simon and Schuster, 1972.

Cook, F. C., ed. *Barnes' Notes on the Old and New Testaments.* Reprint. Grand Rapids: Baker Book House, 1973.

Crockett, William D. *A Harmony of Samuel, Kings and Chronicles.* Grand Rapids: Baker Book House, 1961.

Darby, J. N. *The Collected Writings of J. N. Darby.* 34 vols. plus Index. Reprint. Oak Park, IL: Bible Truth Publishers, 1972.

———. *Synopsis of the Books of the Bible.* 5 vols. Reprint. Winschoten, Netherlands: H. L. Heijkoop, 1970.

Davidson, Stibbs and Kevan, eds. *The New Bible Commentary.* Chicago: Inter-Varsity Christian Fellowship, 1953.

Durbanville, Henry. *Winsome Christianity.* Edinburgh: B. McCall Barbour, n.d.

Edersheim, Alfred. *Bible History. Old Testament.* Reprint (7 vols. in 1). Grand Rapids: William B. Eerdmans Publishing Company, 1982.

Falwell, Jerry, ed. *Liberty Bible Commentary. Vol. 1. Old Testament.* Lynchburg, VA: The Old Time Gospel Hour, 1982.

Flynn, Leslie B. *Your God and Your Gold.* Williamsport, PA: Hearthstone Publishers, Inc., 1961.

Gehman, Henry Snyder, ed. *The New Westminster Dictionary of the Bible.* Philadelphia: The Westminster Press, 1976.

Gish, Arthur. *Beyond the Rat Race.* Scottsdale, PA: Herald Press, 1973.

Grant, F. W. *The Numerical Bible.* 7 vols. Neptune, NJ: Loizeaux Bros., 1977.

Gray, James M. *Christian Workers' Commentary on the Whole Bible.* Westwood, NJ: Fleming H. Revell Co., 1953.

Griffiths, Michael. *Take My Life.* Downers Grove, IL: InterVarsity Press, 1967.

Griffith Thomas, W. H. *The Pentateuch.* Grand Rapids: Kregel Publications, 1985.

Haley, John W. *Alleged Discrepancies of the Bible.* Nashville: Gospel Advocate Company, 1967.

Halley, Henry H. *Halley's Bible Handbook.* 24th ed. Grand Rapids: Zondervan Publishing House, 1965.

Harrison, Roland K. *Introduction to the Old Testament.* Grand Rapids: William B. Eerdmans Publishing Company, 1969.

———. Ed. *Major Cities of the Biblical World.* Nashville: Thomas Nelson Publishers, 1985.

Henry, Matthew. *The Matthew Henry Commentary on the Whole Bible. 6 vols.* Grand Rapids: Zondervan, 1974.

Henry, Scott and others. *The Pocket Bible Commentary.* Vol. 4. Chicago: Moody Press, n.d.

Hoste, William, and William Rodgers. *Bible Problems and Answers.* Kilmarnock, Scotland: John Ritchie Ltd., 1957.

Ironside, H. A. *The Continual Burnt Offering.* New York: Loizeaux Bros., 1941.

Jamieson, Fausset, and Brown. *A Commentary, Critical, Experimental, and Practical on the Old and New Testaments.* 6 vols. London: Wm. Collins and Co. Ltd., n.d.

Johnson, Samuel. *The History of Rasselas, Prince of Abyssinia.* ed. J. P. Hardy. London: Oxford University, 1968.

Jones, E. Stanley, *Is the Kingdom of God Realism?* Nashville: Abingdon-Cokesbury, 1940.

———. *Growing Spiritually.* Nashville: Abingdon Press, 1953.

Josephus, Flavius. *The Works of Flavius Josephus.* Trans. William Whiston. Hartford, CT: The S. S. Scranton Co., 1905.

Kautzsch, E. ed. *Gesenius' Hebrew Grammar.* Revised by A. E. Cowley. Reprint. Oxford: Clarendon Press, 1976.

Keil, C. F. *Manual of Historico-Critical Introduction to the Canonical Scriptures of the Old Testament.* 2 vols. Grand Rapids: Wm. B. Eerdmans Publishing Co., 1952.

Keil, C. F. and Franz Delitzsch. *Biblical Commentary on the Old Testament.* 26 vols. Grand Rapids: Wm. B. Eerdmans Publishing Company, 1971.

———. *Lectures Introductory to the Study of the Minor Prophets.* Fifth Edition. London: C. A. Hammond Trust Bible Depot, n.d.

Kitchen, J. Howard. *Holy Fields. An Introduction to the Historical Geography of the Holy Land.* Grand Rapids: Wm. B. Eerdmans Publishing Company, 1955.

Kollek, Teddy and Moshe Pearlman. *Jerusalem, a History of Forty Centuries.* London: Weidenfeld and Nicholson, 1968.

Lange, John Peter. *A Commentary on the Holy Scriptures*. 25 vols. Reprint. Grand Rapids: Zondervan Publishing House, 1960.

Lewis, C. S. *Weight of Glory*. Ed. by Walter Hooper. New York: MacMillan Publishing Company, 1980.

Lockyer, Herbert, Sr., ed. *Nelson's Illustrated Bible Dictionary*. Nashville: Thomas Nelson Publishers, 1986.

MacDonald, William. *Kingdom Divided: A Study of the Books of the Old Testament from Kings to Esther*. Toronto: Everyday Publications, 1974.

———. *16 Men with a Message: The Old Testament Prophets*. Toronto: Everyday Publications, 1972.

Mackintosh, C. H. *Genesis to Deuteronomy*. Neptune, NJ: Loizeaux Bros, 1972.

———. *The Mackintosh Treasury*. Neptune: NJ: Loizeaux Bros., 1976.

Mantle, J. G. *Better Things*. New York: Christian Alliance Publishing Co., 1921.

McMillen, S. I. *None of These Diseases*. Old Tappan, NJ: Fleming H. Revell Co., 1972.

Meyer, F. B. *Through the Bible Day by Day*. 7 vols. Philadelphia: American Sunday-School Union, 1917.

Miller, Rev. H. S. *General Biblical Introduction*. Houghton, NY: The Word-Bearer Press, 1956.

Moody, D. L. *Notes From My Bible*. New York: Fleming H. Revell Company, 1895.

Morgan, G. Campbell. *An Exposition of the Whole Bible*. Westwood, NJ: Fleming H. Revell Company, 1959.

———. *Living Messages from the Books of the Bible, Genesis—Malachi*. New York: Fleming H. Revell Company, 1912.

———. *Searchlights from the Word*. London: Oliphants, 1970.

Muggeridge, Malcolm. *Jesus Rediscovered*. Garden City, NY: Doubleday, 1969.

Naismith, *1200 More Notes, Quotes and Anecdotes*. London: Pickering & Inglis, 1975.

Nee, Watchman. *Do All To The Glory of God*. New York: Christian Fellowship Publishers, Inc., 1974.

A New and Concise Bible Dictionary. London: Central Bible Hammond Trust, 1973.

Orr, James, ed. *International Standard Bible Encyclopedia*. 5 vols. Grand Rapids: Wm. B. Eerdmans Publishing Co., 1939.

Packer, J. I. *Knowing God*. Downers Grove: InterVarsity Press, 1977.

Pentecost, J. D. *Things to Come*. Grand Rapids: Zondervan Publishing House, 1974.

Pfeiffer, Charles F. *Baker's Bible Atlas*. Grand Rapids: Baker Book House, 1966.

———. ed. *The Biblical World*. Grand Rapids: Baker Book House, 1966.

———. *An Outline of Old Testament History*. Chicago: Moody Press, 1960.

Pfeiffer, Charles F., and Everett F. Harrison, eds. *The Wycliffe Bible Commentary*. Chicago: Moody Press, 1962.

Pierson, Arthur T. *Knowing the Scriptures*. Fincastle, VA: Scripture Truth Book Company, 1975.

———. *An Outline of Old Testament History*. Chicago: Moody Press, 1960.

Pilkey, John. *Origin of the Nations*. San Diego, CA: Master Book Publishers, 1984.

Pink, A. W. *The Attributes of God*. Grand Rapids: Baker Book House, 1975.

Poole, Matthew. *Matthew Poole's Commentary on the Holy Bible*. Edinburgh: The Banner of Truth Trust, 1974.

Pritchard, James A. *Archaeology and the Old Testament*. Princeton, NJ: Princeton University Press, 1958.

Reid, John. *The Chief Meeting of the Church*. Waynesboro, GA: Christian Missions Press, 1978.

The Revell Bible Dictionary. Ed. by Lawrence O. Richards. Old Tappan, NJ: Fleming H. Revell Company, 1990.

Ridout, Samuel. *How to Study the Bible*. New York: Loizeaux Brothers, 1947.

Ryrie, Charles C., *The Grace of God*. Chicago: Moody Press, 1975.

———., ed. *The Ryrie Study Bible, New King James Version*. Chicago: Moody Press, 1985.

Sanders, J. Oswald. *On to Maturity*. Chicago: Moody Press, 1969.

Schaeffer, Francis A. *The Church at the End of the 20th Century*. Downers Grove, IL: Inter-Varsity Press, 1970.

Schultz, Samuel J. *The Old Testament Speaks*. New York: Harper & Brothers, Publishers, 1960.

Scofield, C. I., E. Schuyler English, et al., eds. *The New Scofield Study Bible*. New King James Version. Nashville: Thomas Nelson Publishers, 1989.

Scott, Walter. *Handbook to the Bible. Old Testament*. Reprint. Charlotte, NC: Books for Christians, 1977.

Scroggie, W. Graham. *Know Your Bible. A Brief Introduction to the Scriptures. Vol. 1, The Old Testament*. London: Pickering & Inglis Ltd., n.d.

The Serious Christian. Series I. Reprints in 22 vols. Charlotte, NC: Books for Christians, n.d.

The Serious Christian. Series II. Reprints in 13 vols. to date. Charlotte, NC: Books for Christians, n.d.

Sider, Ronald J. *Rich Christians in an Age of Hunger*. Downers Grove: InterVarsity Press, 1978.

Sparks, T. Austin. *What Is Man?* Indianapolis: Pratt Printing Co., n.d.

Spurgeon, C. H. *Morning and Evening*. Grand Rapids: Zondervan Publishing House, 1980.

———. *Spurgeon's Devotional Bible*. Grand Rapids: Baker Book House, 1974.

———. *Spurgeon's Sermons*. Vol. 1. Reprinted. Grand Rapids: Baker Book House, 1984.

Stevenson, Herbert F. *Three Prophetic Voices*. Old Tappan, NJ: Fleming H. Revell Company, 1971.

Stoner, Peter W. *Science Speaks*. Chicago: Moody Press, n.d.

Tan, Paul Lee. *The Interpretation of Prophecy*. Winona Lake, IN: BMH Books, Inc., 1974.

Tenney, Merrill C., gen. ed. and Steven Barabas, assoc. ed. *The Zondervan Pictorial Encyclopedia of the Bible*. 5 Vols. Grand Rapids: Zondervan, 1975.

Thiele, Edwin R. *The Mysterious Numbers of the Hebrew Kings*. 1st ed. Chicago: University of Chicago Press, 1951.

Thomson, W. M. *The Land and the Book; or, Biblical Illustrations Drawn from the Manners and Customs, the Scenes and Scenery of The Holy Land*. London: T. Nelson and Sons, Paternoster Row, 1884.

Unger, M. F. *Introductory Guide to the Old Testament*. Grand Rapids: Zondervan Publishing House, 1951.

———. *Unger's Bible Dictionary*. Chicago: Moody Press, 1965.

———. *Unger's Bible Handbook*. Chicago: Moody Press, 1966.

Vine, W. E. *First Corinthians*. London: Oliphants, Ltd., 1951.

Walvoord, John F. and Roy B. Zuck, eds. *The Bible Knowledge Commentary. Old Testament*. Wheaton, IL: Victor Books, 1985.

Weston, Keith. *Living in the Light*. Bromley, Kent, England: STL Books, 1983.

Westwood, Tom. *Meditations on Elijah and Elisha*. Glendale, CA: The Bible Treasury Hour, Inc., n.d.

Williams, George. *The Student's Commentary on the Holy Scriptures*. 6th ed. Grand Rapids: Kregel Publications, 1971.

Wilson, Robert Dick. *A Scientific Investigation of the Old Testament*. Philadelphia: The Sunday School Times Company, 1926.

Wood, Leon. *A Survey of Israel's History*. Grand Rapids: Zondervan Publishing House, 1970.

Yates, Kyle M. *Preaching from the Prophets*. Nashville: Broadman Press, 1942.

Young, Edward J. *Thy Word Is Truth*. Reprint. Grand Rapids: Wm. B. Eerdmans Publishing Co., 1957, 1970.

Articles and Periodicals

Brock, Paul. "Your Emotions Can Make You Ill." Reader's Digest, Sept. 1974.

Choice Gleanings Calendar. Grand Rapids: Gospel Folio Press, n.d.

Coder, S. Maxwell. "That Bow and Arrow War." *Moody Monthly,* April 1974.

Daily Notes of the Scripture Union. London: C.S.S.M., various dates.

Houghton, Will. "By Life or by Death." Copyright by Hope Publishing Co.

Our Daily Bread. Grand Rapids, Radio Bible Class, various dates.

Reuben, David R. "Why Wives Cheat on Their Husbands," *Reader's Digest,* August 1973.

Sims, Bennett J. "Sex and Homosexuality." *Christianity Today,* February 24, 1978, p. 29.

Toward the Mark. Weston-super-Mare, England: various dates.

Westwood, Tom. *Meditations on David and Joseph*. Denver: Wilson Foundation, n.d.

Unpublished Materials

Gibson, O. J. Unpublished notes, Discipleship Intern Training Program. San Leandro, CA.

Woodring, H. C. Unpublished notes, Emmaus Bible School, Oak Park, IL.

Poetry, Hymns, and Music

Barnes, Billy. "I Stayed Too Long at the Fair." Hollywood: Tylerson Music, 1957. Copyright 1957, Tylerson Music Co.

The Children of the Night.

Duffield, Samuel Willoughby. *English Hymns: Their Authors and History.* New York: Funk & Wagnalls Company, 1886.

Eliot, T. S. "East Coker," *Four Quartets.* New York: Harcourt Brace Jovanovich.

Hymns. Chicago: InterVarsity Press, 1947.

Hymns of Grace and Truth. Neptune: NJ: Loizeaux Bros., n.d.

Hymns of Truth and Praise. Fort Dodge, IA: Gospel Perpetuating Publ., 1971.

Lowell, James R. "The Present Crisis," *Complete Poetical Works.* Boston: Houghton Mifflin, 1897.

Selected Poems of Edwin Arlington Robinson. London: The Macmillan Company, 1965.

Tozer, A. W. *The Christian Book of Mystical Verse.* Harrisburg, PA: Christian Publications, 1963.

SUPPLEMENTS

THE INTERTESTAMENTAL PERIOD

When God delivered His final message through Malachi, He paused in His communications through man for nearly four hundred years. A deafening silence in divine revelation resulted.

No doubt the silence of God gave rise to many theories about His nature. Some might have demanded that He act as He had always acted. Others might have surmised that man was too sinful to hear from God (this is always an absurdity since *any* sin is an affront to God and apart from grace He would not have communed with any person or generation *before* Malachi's time, let alone after). Still others might have suggested, and quite strongly so, that man's lack of faith was the cause of God's silence and apparent inactivity.

None of these theories would have taken into account the omniscience and sovereignty of Jehovah God. His determined, covenantal love (Hebrew *hesed*) had already set His course. This long silence was part of His eternal plan. He had spoken on numerous occasions and through various people, but He was now preparing to speak His greatest and most powerful Word to mankind: Jesus. A pause—a long and distinct pause—would add emphasis to that monumental revelation.

The ways of God are certainly beyond the complete grasp of man. "For as the heavens are higher than the earth, so are My ways higher than your ways, and My thoughts than your thoughts" (Is. 55:9). But the Architect of this universe is not without order and symmetry in His work, even in His dealings with finite, fickle human beings. Occasionally that order may be discerned.

A brief review of the way God ministered to man during the years chronicled in the Old Testament is very instructive. A consistent pattern of action emerges from the accounts recorded through the Holy Spirit's inspiration. Such consistency in the past sheds light upon the workings of God during what may be called the Intertestamental Period.

Two things stand out. First, God generally designed or allowed a *desperate situation* to arise before presenting His message or providing His deliverance. Secondly, He always called upon a *faithful servant* to "stand in the gap," making intercession to Him on behalf of the people (Ezek. 22:30), and to be His agent through whom He performed His work.

Consider the terrible conditions that prevailed in antediluvian society. God expressed regret that He had even created man (Gen. 6:6). Against the backdrop of this dark, dismal scene, the Bible declares: "But Noah found grace in the eyes of the LORD" (Gen. 6:8). Thus we have a desperate situation, and God's faithful servant.

This pattern was repeated with Abraham in God's calling of a chosen people out of a human race enmeshed in pride and idolatry. It appeared again with Joseph in the sparing of Israel from famine. Moses was another deliverer, who came just in time to rescue God's people from apparently impossible circumstances. The same theme runs through the book of Judges, and continues to appear in such lives as Esther and Nehemiah.

In each of these examples, and others like them, the efforts of man had to be frustrated before divine intervention ensued. The recorded history of the Intertestamental Period points to a similar experience. It seems that God allowed His people to exhaust their resources and to be reduced to another desperate situation before He brought to the scene His most faithful and only perfect Servant, His Son Jesus Christ.

THE PERIOD IN QUESTION

If the book of Malachi was completed in 397 B.C., then the period under consideration begins at that point and continues until the angel's announcement of the birth of John the Baptist (Luke 1:11–17). Throughout this four-hundred-year span of time there were no prophets and no inspired writers of divine revelation.

Six historical divisions are observable. The Persian Era, which actually dates all the way back to 536 B.C. but coincides with the Intertestamental Period from 397 to 336 B.C.; the Greek Era (336–323 B.C.); the Egyptian Era (323–198 B.C.); the Syrian Era (198–165 B.C.); the Maccabean Era

(165–63 B.C.); and the Roman Era (63–4 B.C.). This study will be presented chronologically according to these six divisions. Attention will be given to the historical situation and the religious developments within each segment.

The Persian Era (397–336 B.C.)

Historical Situation

As has already been noted, the Persians were the dominating power in the Middle East as far back as 536 B.C. God had used the Persians to deliver Israel from the Babylonian captivity (Dan. 5:30, 31).

Persia's attitude was tolerant toward the Jewish remnant in Palestine, until internal rivalry over the politically powerful office of high priest resulted in partial destruction of Jerusalem by the Persian governor. Otherwise the Jewish people were left undisturbed during this period.

Religious Developments

The Babylonian captivity was used by God to purge idolatry from His people. They returned to Jerusalem with a new reverence for the Scriptures, especially the law of Moses. They also had a firm grasp on the theological concept of monotheism. These two influences carried over into the Intertestamental Period.

The rise of the *synagogue* as the local center of worship can be traced back to this period. *Scribes* became very important for the interpretation of the Scriptures in the synagogue services. By the time Jesus was born, the synagogue was well developed in organization and was widely spread throughout the Jewish communities of the world.

Another development that affected the spread of the gospel during New Testament times had its origin toward the end of the Persian rule. A temple was founded in Samaria, establishing a form of worship that rivaled Judaism. That event encouraged the ultimate social and religious separation between Jew and Samaritan.

The Greek Era (336–323 B.C.)

Historical Situation

Alexander the Great, in many respects the greatest conqueror of all time, was the central figure of this brief period. He conquered Persia, Babylon, Palestine, Syria, Egypt, and western India. Although he died at the age of thirty-three, having reigned over Greece only thirteen years, his influence lived long after him.

Religious Developments

The cherished desire of Alexander was to found a worldwide empire united by language, custom, and civilization. Under his influence the world began to speak and study the Greek language. This process, called Hellenization, included the adoption of Greek culture and religion in all parts of the world. Hellenism became so popular that it persisted and was encouraged even into New Testament times by the Romans.

The struggle that developed between the Jews and Hellenism's influence upon their culture and religion was long and bitter. Although the Greek language was sufficiently widespread by 270 B.C. to bring about a Greek translation of the Old Testament (the Septuagint), faithful Jews staunchly resisted pagan polytheism.

The Egyptian Era (323–198 B.C.)

Historical Situation

With the death of Alexander in 323 B.C., the Greek empire became divided into four segments under as many generals: Ptolemy, Lysimachus, Cassander, and Selenus. These were Daniel's "four kingdoms" which took the place of the "large horn" (Dan. 8:21, 22).

Ptolemy Soter, the first of the Ptolemaic dynasty, received Egypt and soon dominated nearby Israel. He dealt severely with the Jews at first, but toward the end of his reign and on into the rule of Ptolemy Philadelphus, his successor, the Jews were treated favorably. It was during this time that the Septuagint was authorized.

The Jews prospered until near the end of the Ptolemaic dynasty when conflicts between Egypt and Syria escalated. Israel was again caught in the middle. When the Syrians defeated Egypt in the Battle of Panion in 198 B.C., Judea was annexed to Syria.

Religious Developments

The policy of toleration followed by the Ptolemies, by which Judaism and Hellenism coexisted peacefully, was very dangerous for the Jewish faith. A gradual infiltration of Greek influence and an almost unnoticed assimilation of the Greek way of life took place.

Hellenism's emphasis on beauty, shape, and movement encouraged Jews to neglect Jewish religious rites which were aesthetically unappealing. Thus worship was influenced to become more external than internal, a notion that had a lasting impact upon Judaism.

Two religious parties emerged: the Hellenizing party, which was pro-Syrian, and the orthodox Jews, in particular the Hasidim or "Pious Ones" (predecessors of the Pharisees). A struggle for power between these two groups resulted in a polarization of the Jews along political, cultural, and religious lines. It was this same conflict that brought about the attack of Antiochus Epiphanes in 168 B.C.

THE SYRIAN ERA (198–165 B.C.)

Historical Situation

Under the rule of Antiochus the Great and his successor Seleucus Philopater, the Jews, though treated harshly, were nonetheless allowed to maintain local rule under their high priest. All went well until the Hellenizing party decided to have their favorite, Jason, appointed to replace Onias III, the high priest favored by the orthodox Jews, and to bring this about by bribing Seleucus's successor, Antiochus Epiphanes. This set off a political conflict that finally brought Antiochus to Jerusalem in a fit of rage.

In 168 B.C. Antiochus set about destroying every distinctive characteristic of the Jewish faith. He forbade all sacrifices, outlawed the rite of circumcision, and canceled observance of the Sabbath and feast days. The Scriptures were mutilated or destroyed. Jews were forced to eat pork and to sacrifice to idols. His final act of sacrilege, and the one that spelled his ultimate ruin, was to desecrate the Most Holy Place by building an altar and offering a sacrifice to the god Zeus. Many Jews died in the ensuing persecutions.

Perhaps a reminder of God's way of working with man is needed at this point. He creates or allows a desperate situation, then calls upon a special, faithful servant. However, man often attempts to rescue himself and seems to be almost at the point of success only to wind up in worse shape than before. This was about to happen in the life of God's people the Jews. God was simply setting the stage for the coming of the true Deliverer.

Religious Developments

As can be seen by the historical developments of this period, the Jewish religion was divided over the issue of Hellenism. The groundwork was laid for an orthodox party, generally led by the scribes and later called the Pharisees, and for what we may call a more pragmatic faction of Jews which became more or less associated with the office of high priest. The pattern of thinking upon which the latter group was based fostered the rise of the Sadducees at a later date.

THE MACCABEAN ERA (165–63 B.C.)

Historical Situation

An elderly priest named Mattathias, of the house of Hasmon, lived with his five sons in the village of Modein, northwest of Jerusalem. When a Syrian official tried to enforce heathen sacrifice in Modein, Mattathias revolted, killed a renegade Jew who did offer sacrifice, slew the Syrian official, and fled to the mountains with his family. Thousands of faithful Jews joined him, and history records one of the most noble demonstrations of holy jealousy for the honor of God.

After the death of Mattathias three of his sons carried on the revolt in succession: Judas surnamed Maccabaeus (166–160 B.C.), Jonathan (160–142 B.C.), and Simon (143–134 B.C.). These men had such success that by December 25, 165 B.C., they had retaken Jerusalem, cleansed the temple, and restored worship. This event is commemorated even today as the Feast of Hanukkah (Dedication).

Fighting continued in the outlying areas of Judea with several futile attempts by Syria to defeat the Maccabeans. Finally, under the leadership of Simon, the Jews received their independence (142 B.C.). They experienced almost seventy years of independence under the reign of the Hasmonaean dynasty, the most notable leaders of which were John Hyrcanus (134–104 B.C.) and Alexander Jannaeus (102–76 B.C.).

Religious Developments

The most significant religious development of this period resulted from a strong difference of opinion concerning the kingship and high priesthood of Judea. For hundreds of years the position of high priest had taken on some very obvious political overtones. Emphasis had not been upon the Aaronite line but upon political strength. Orthodox Jews resented and resisted this development. When John Hyrcanus became governor and high priest of Israel, he conquered Transjordan and Idumaea and destroyed the Samaritan temple. His power and popularity led him to refer to himself as a king. This flew in the face of the orthodox Jews, who by this time were called Pharisees. They recognized no king unless he was of the lineage of David, and the Hasmonaeans were not.

Those who opposed the Pharisees and supported the Hasmonaeans were called Sadducees. These names appeared for the first time during the reign of John Hyrcanus who himself became a Sadducee.

THE ROMAN ERA (63–4 B.C.)

Historical Situation

The independence of the Jews ended in 63 B.C., when Pompey of Rome took Syria and entered Israel. Aristobulus II, claiming to be the king of Israel, locked Pompey out of Jerusalem. The Roman leader in anger took the city by force and reduced the size of Judea. Israel's attempt at freedom from oppression had paid off for a while, but now all hope seemed to be lost.

Antipater the Idumaean was appointed procurator of Judea by Julius Caesar in 47 B.C. Herod, the son of Antipater, eventually became the king of the Jews around 40 B.C.

Although Herod the Great, as he was called, planned and carried out the building of the new temple in Jerusalem, he was a devoted Hellenist and hated the Hasmonaean family. He killed every descendant of the Hasmonaeans, even his own wife Marianne, the granddaughter of John Hyrcanus. Then he proceeded to murder his own two sons by Marianne, Aristobulus and Alexander. This is the man on the throne when Jesus was born in Bethlehem. What a dark and desperate situation for God's people!

Religious Developments

The rise of the Pharisees and Sadducees has already been mentioned. Before moving on to a discussion of three other important parties, some attention needs to be given to these two major groups.

(1) *The Pharisees* were so named early in the reign of John Hyrcanus. The name means "Separatists." They depended heavily upon the scribes and were loyal to the law and religion of Jehovah. Their emphasis upon the strict adherence to the Scriptures led to a strong attachment to the "oral law," or Mishnah, which sought to apply the written law to everyday life.

During the earthly ministry of Jesus, the "oral law" was so rigid with legalistic expansions that it usually had little to do with the original intent of Scripture. What started out to be a very wholesome and much-needed dependence on the Word of God deteriorated to a formalism and legalism that denied the spirit of the Word.

(2) *The Sadducees* derived their name from the word *Zadokites* or maybe from the Hebrew word *tsaddik*, meaning "righteous." Whereas the Pharisees were strongly connected with the scribes, the Sadducees were related to the high priest. The priests seem to have tended toward the more social, political, and earthly aspects of their position. This pattern of thinking was attractive to many of the more socially minded Jewish leaders.

Numerically a much smaller party than the Pharisees, the Sadducees belonged mostly to the wealthy influential priestly families who formed the social aristocracy of the Jewish nation. They felt that God's law and a nation's politics were totally separate. In other words, they saw no relationship between the need for holiness and the destiny of their nation. Religion was religion; politics was politics. They were therefore very skeptical of the Pharisees and seemingly concluded that the latter were old-fashioned, irrelevant, and fanatical.

(3) *The Herodians* emerged during the Roman Era (Matt. 22:16). This was a politi-

cal party whose major aim was to further the cause of Herod's government. They were perhaps motivated by a fear of the Roman government and the possibility of total destruction that could result from an act of rebellion on the part of the Jews. They were strongly inclined toward Hellenism and were opposed to the Pharisees and their constant emphasis on separation.

(4) *The Zealots* (or "Cananaeans," from the Aramaic *kanna'ah*, "zealous"—"Canaanites" in the NKJV New Testament) were also a political party but were in direct opposition to the Herodians. They would not conform to Roman rule, and they did not believe in waiting submissively like the Pharisees until Israel's Messiah would come and overthrow the Romans. In their opinion God only helped those who helped themselves. The Jews must be ready to fight for independence.

To a Pharisee-like fanaticism for the letter of the law, the Zealots added a fiery nationalistic spirit. The teachings of this group stressed a type of man-made, military deliverance rather than divine intervention.

(5) *The Essenes* were also a product of the Roman Era. They are not mentioned in the New Testament but have received considerable attention since the discovery of the Dead Sea Scrolls.

This group of people was religious, not political. They were a type of pseudospiritual cult which felt that they must withdraw from ordinary human society and practice a monastic kind of life and a mystical kind of Judaism.

With a passion for the spirit of the law and a separation to God, the Essenes lost all consciousness of the evangelistic mission of Israel. They were content to lock out the world, ignore its problems, and let it die without hope.

Conclusion

The stage was set. Man's futile attempts to deal with the shifting tide of political power and religious belief had produced very little. Israel was in a kind of spiritual bondage that was even worse than her political bondage. The rise of the various parties and movements discussed above was evidence of a sincere search for some final solution to her problem. All seemed to have failed. The stage of history was dark. The situation was indeed desperate.

Amid this setting God broke four hundred years of silence with the announcement of the coming of Christ, the faithful Servant of the Lord, and the Intertestamental Period came to an end.

People and Places of the Bible

This article identifies the most outstanding people and places whose proper names occur in the Bible, excluding the deuterocanonical books. The names are set out alphabetically as they are spelled in the New King James Version. People and places bearing the same name in Scripture are treated under separate entries with personal names listed first. Variant spellings are enclosed in brackets [ ], and the meaning of the name is then given in parentheses ( ). Under each entry, various individuals or places bearing this name are differentiated by boldface brackets, like this: **[1]**; **[2]**; and so on. Then follows a description of the entry with several Bible verses listed where the name occurs. (Not all verses are given. If the reader is considering a passage that is not cited in the section, he must choose the name that would most likely be identical with the person or place in his passage.)

No attempt has been made to designate each person as a Palite, Harodite, Gileadite, and so on. Many of these designations refer to the ancestor of an individual. In other cases, they refer to the person's city, district, or distinctive clan. It is often a guess as to which meaning is intended.

The meanings of the names are not infallibly accurate. They are simply interesting possibilities.

Many people and places in Scripture bear the same name. In dozens of cases, it cannot be determined whether an individual or place in one book is identical with the same use of the name in another book. In the ancient world, a person was often called by more than one name. Many of the place names are pre-Israelite, and their history is obscure and uncertain. Different names were used to refer to certain sites in different periods of history (e.g. Ararat and Armenia). These are grouped under the most familiar biblical name with the other names cross referenced to it. Modern place names are given under most of the biblical names.

In the transmission of Scripture, copyists occasionally made errors. Surely Enoch was not called Hanoc, nor Imna called Jimna, and so on. Yet which is original? Only in a few cases do we have any clues.

We find variant forms and contractions of names throughout the Bible. They probably presented little difficulty to an ancient reader. But this further complicates the identification problem for us. Often a Hebrew name refers to both a person and a place.

The Hebrew genealogies are abbreviated at many points. At times it is difficult to distinguish a man from his ancestor. Consider also the problem of trying to match an abbreviated list with a fuller list. Either the names in the abbreviated list are independent of the longer list or they are already included in it. In other words, we may find the same person included in two lists or two different people in two lists.

In a few cases, our English versions use the same word to transliterate several similar Hebrew names. In these instances, we have recorded a separate entry for each Hebrew name (e.g., Joash).

A

Aaron ("enlightened, rich, mountaineer"), the brother of Moses. He became the first high priest of Israel (Ex. 4:14, 30; 7:2, 19; 17:9–12; 29; Num. 12; 17).

Abdon ("service, servile"). **[1]** A judge of Israel for eight years (Judg. 12:13, 15). *See* Bedan. **[2]** A descendant of Benjamin who dwelt in Jerusalem (1 Chr. 8:23). **[3]** Firstborn son of Jehiel, mentioned in Chronicles (1 Chr. 8:30; 9:36). **[4]** One sent to Huldah to inquire of the meaning of the Law (2 Chr. 34:20). He is called Achbor in Second Kings 22:12. Possibly he is identical with **[2]**.

Abdon ("servile"), a city belonging to the tribe of Asher, located at the present site of Khirbet Abdeh (Josh. 21:30; 1 Chr. 6:74). It was once called Hebron; *see* Hebron **[2]**, the city.

Abed-Nego ("servant of Nebo; servant of Ishtar"), name given to Azariah, one of the three friends of Daniel who were carried captive to Babylon. He was thrown into a fiery furnace (Dan. 1:7; 2:49; 3:12–30).

Abel ("a breath, vapor; shepherd"), second son of Adam and Eve, slain by his brother Cain (Gen. 4:1–10; Heb. 11:4; 12:24).

Abel Keramim, a place east of the Jordan River, site of the battle in which Jephthah defeated the forces led by Ammon (Judg. 11:33).

Abez ("lofty"), a town in northern Palestine apportioned to the tribe of Issachar (Josh. 19:20).

Abi-Albon ("father of strength"), one of David's "valiant men" (2 Sam. 23:31). Also called Abiel (1 Chr. 11:32).

Abiasaph [Ebiasaph] ("my father has gathered"), a Levite whose descendants were gatekeepers of the tabernacle (Ex. 6:24; 1 Chr. 6:23; 9:19).

Abiathar ("father of super-excellence or preeminence"), the only priest to escape Saul's massacre at Nob, he was a high priest in David's time. He was deposed by Solomon (1 Sam. 22:20–23; 1 Kin. 2:27; 1 Chr. 15:11, 12). First Samuel 21 says that Ahimelech **[1]** was the high priest when David ate the showbread, yet Mark 2:26 states this occurred in the days of Abiathar the high priest. Abiathar may have been assisting his father as high priest and thus could be so designated. Or, since Abiathar was more prominent in history than was his father Ahimelech, he is so mentioned here instead of Ahimelech. If this is so (and it seems to be), then Abiathar is called the "high priest" before he actually assumed that office.

Abigail ("father [i.e., cause] of delight"). **[1]** A wife of Nabal and afterward of David (1 Sam. 25:3, 14–44). **[2]** Mother of Amasa, whom Absalom made captain (2 Sam. 17:25; 1 Chr. 2:16, 17).

Abihu ("he is my father"), a son of Aaron, destroyed with his brother for offering strange fire to God (Ex. 6:23; Lev. 10:1).

Abijah [Abijam] ("Jehovah is my father"). **[1]** A son of Samuel and wicked judge of Israel (1 Sam. 8:2; 1 Chr. 6:28). **[2]** The wife of Hezron (1 Chr. 2:24). **[3]** Son of Rehoboam and successor to the throne of Judah, an ancestor of Christ (1 Chr. 3:10; 2 Chr. 11:20—14:1; Matt. 1:7). He was also known as Abijam (1 Kin. 15:1). **[4]** The seventh son of Becher the son of Benjamin (1 Chr. 7:8). **[5]** A descendant of Aaron appointed by David in connection with the priestly courses (1 Chr. 24:10; cf. Luke 1:5). **[6]** A son of Jeroboam I of Israel (1 Kin. 14:1–8). **[7]** A priest of Nehemiah's time who sealed the covenant (Neh. 10:7). Possibly the same as the priest mentioned in Nehemiah 12:1, 4, 17.

Abijam ("father of the sea [or west]"). *See* Abijah **[3]**.

Abimelech ("father of the king"). **[1]** Many scholars believe the King(s) Abimelech(s) of Gerar in Genesis 20, 21, and 26 are not proper names but a royal title borne by the Philistine kings. The Psalm 34 title mentions Abimelech where Achish should occur. Since the story of Achish was well known, it seems improbable to regard this as a mistake, but rather a royal title of Achish, king of Gath. **[2]** A son of Gideon who tried to become king of Israel, and did reign for three years (Judg. 8:30—10:1). **[3]** *See* Ahimelech **[2]**.

Abinadab ("father or source of liberality or willingness"). **[1]** A man of Judah in whose house the ark was placed (1 Sam. 7:1; 2 Sam. 6:3, 4; 1 Chr. 13:7). **[2]** A brother of David (1 Sam. 16:8; 17:13; 1 Chr. 2:13). **[3]** Son of Saul slain by the Philistines (1 Sam. 31:2; 1 Chr. 8:33; 9:39; 10:2). **[4]** Father of one of Solomon's officers (1 Kin. 4:11).

Abiram ("father of elevation"). **[1]** One who conspired against Moses and was destroyed (Num. 16:27; Ps. 106:17). **[2]** Firstborn son of Hiel who died when his father began to rebuild Jericho (1 Kin. 16:34; cf. Josh. 6:26).

Abishag ("my father was a wanderer"), a beautiful woman chosen to nurse the aged David (1 Kin. 1:3, 15; 2:17, 21, 22). This woman may also be the heroine of the Song of Solomon, where she is simply called "the Shulamite."

Abishai ("my father is Jesse; source of wealth"), a son of David's sister, Zeruiah. He was one of David's mighty men (1 Sam. 26:6–9; 2 Sam. 2:18; 10:10; 23:18).

Abner [Abiner] ("my father of light"), a shortened form of *Abiner;* the captain of the host under Saul and Ishbosheth (1 Sam. 14:50, 51; 26:5, 7; 2 Sam. 2; 3).

Abraham [Abram]. The founder of the Jewish nation and an ancestor of Christ. His name was changed from Abram ("the father is exalted") to Abraham ("father of multitudes") (Gen. 11—26; Matt. 1:1, 2).

Absalom ("father of peace"), a son of David who tried to usurp the throne from his father (2 Sam. 3:3; 13—19).

Achan [Achar] ("trouble"), one who stole part of the spoil of Jericho and brought "trouble" on his people. He was killed for this (Josh. 7:1-24). In First Chronicles 2:7, he is called *Achar*.

Achim ("woes"), ancestor of Christ (Matt. 1:14).

Achish ("serpent-charmer"). **[1]** A king of Gath to whom David fled for safety (1 Sam. 21; 27-29). **[2]** Another king of Gath who bore the same name but reigned during Solomon's time (1 Kin. 2:39, 40). However, many believe the kings to be identical.

Achor ("trouble"), a valley south of Jericho, in which Achan was stoned (Josh. 7:24); and which formed the northern boundary of Judah (Josh. 15:7).

Achzib [Chezib] ("false"). **[1]** A Canaanite city in the lowlands of Judah, captured by Joshua (Gen. 38:5; Josh. 15:44). **[2]** A seashore town on the northern side of Galilee near the Lebanon border (Josh. 19:29; Judg. 1:31).

Adam ("of the ground; firm"), the first man. His sin caused a curse to fall upon all the race (Gen. 2—3; 1 Cor. 15:22, 45). He is listed in the genealogy of Christ (Luke 3:38).

Adam ("red; of the earth"), a city on the east bank of the Jordan River that was given to the tribe of Reuben (Josh. 3:16).

Adino ("ornament"), a chief of David's mighty men (2 Sam. 23:8). Some identify him with Jashobeam **[1]**; others deny this.

Admah ("redness"), one of the Cities of the Plain that God destroyed with Sodom and Gomorrah (Gen. 19:25-29); its location may now be submerged by the southern end of the Dead Sea.

Adnah ("pleasure"). **[1]** A captain who joined David at Ziklag (1 Chr. 12:20). **[2]** A chief captain of Jehoshaphat (2 Chr. 17:14).

Adonijah ("Jehovah is my Lord"). **[1]** A son of David, executed by Solomon for trying to usurp the throne (2 Sam. 3:4; 1 Kin. 1:2). **[2]** One sent by Jehoshaphat to teach the law (2 Chr. 17:8). **[3]** One who sealed the new covenant with God after the Exile (Neh. 10:14-16).

Adoni-Zedek ("lord of justice or righteousness"), a king of Jerusalem defeated by Joshua (Josh. 10:1-27).

Adramyttium ("from Adramys, brother of Craesus"), a port city of Mysia in the northwestern part of the Roman province of Asia (Acts 27:2; cf. 16:7).

Adriatic ("from [the city] Adria of Italy"), originally a name referring to the sea east of Italy. In later times, the term included the Mediterranean between Greece and Sicily (Acts 27:27).

Adullam ("refuge"), a town of Judah near Succoth. David made the headquarters of his rebellion against Saul in a cave near this town (Josh. 12:7-15; 1 Sam. 22; 2 Sam. 23:13).

Aenon ("fountains"), a place noted for its abundant supply of water, where John baptized his converts. Most likely this site was at the head of the Valley of Shechem (John 3:23).

Agabus ("locust"), a prophet of Jerusalem who foretold suffering for Paul if he went to Jerusalem (Acts 11:28; 21:10).

Agrippa. *See* Herod.

Ahab ("father's brother [uncle]"). **[1]** The seventh king of Israel. He was wicked and idolatrous and married a woman of the same character—Jezebel (1 Kin. 16:28—22:40). **[2]** A false prophet killed by Nebuchadnezzar (Jer. 29:21, 22).

Ahasuerus. **[1]** The king of Persia whom Esther married. He is known as Xerxes to historians (Esth. 1:1; 2:16; 10:3). **[2]** The father of Darius the Mede (Dan. 9:1). **[3]** Another name for Cambyses, king of Persia (Ezra 4:6).

Ahaz ("he holds"). **[1]** The eleventh king of Judah and an ancestor of Christ (2 Kin. 15:38—16:20; Matt. 1:9). **[2]** A descendant of Benjamin (1 Chr. 8:35, 36; 9:41, 42).

Ahaziah [Azariah] ("Jehovah holds or sustains"). **[1]** The eighth king of Israel. He was weak and idolatrous (1 Kin. 22:51—2 Kin. 1:18). **[2]** The sixth king of Judah; he reigned only one year (2 Kin. 8:24-29; 9:16ff.). He was also known as Jehoahaz (2 Chr. 21:17; 25:23). His being called Azariah in Second Chronicles 22:6 is an error; over fifteen Hebrew manuscripts and all recent versions read Ahaziah. *See* Jehoahaz.

Ahihud ("brother of honor"). **[1]** A prince of Asher (Num. 34:27). **[2]** A member of the family of Ehud, descended from Benjamin (1 Chr. 8:7).

Ahijah ("Jehovah is brother; my brother is Jehovah"). **[1]** A prophet who prophesied the splitting away of the ten tribes (1 Kin. 11:29, 30; 14:2, 4, 5). **[2]** Father of Baasha who conspired against Nadab (1 Kin. 15:27, 33; 21:22). **[3]** A son of Jerahmeel (1 Chr. 2:25). **[4]** One of David's mighty men (1 Chr. 11:36). **[5]** One who sealed the new covenant with

God after the Exile (Neh. 10:26). **[6]** One set over the temple treasures (1 Chr. 26:20). *See also* Ahimelech.

Ahimaaz ("powerful brother"). **[1]** Father of Ahinoam, wife of Saul (1 Sam. 14:50). **[2]** One of Solomon's officers (1 Kin. 4:15). **[3]** Son of Zadok who remained loyal to David (2 Sam. 15:27, 36; 17:17, 20; 18:19–29).

Ahimelech ("brother of the king; my brother is king"). **[1]** A Hittite friend of David (1 Sam. 26:6). **[2]** A priest, son of Abiathar and grandson of **[3]** (2 Sam. 8:17; 1 Chr. 24:6). Some think the readings in these passages have been transposed (i.e., they speak of Ahimelech the son of Abiathar instead of Abiathar the son of Ahimelech). But this seems unlikely, especially in First Chronicles 24. He is called Abimelech in First Chronicles 18:16. The Septuagint has Ahimelech here also. **[3]** One of the priests of Nob slain for helping David (1 Sam. 21:1–8; 22:9–20). *See also* Abimelech; Ahijah.

Ahinoam ("pleasant brother"). **[1]** Wife of King Saul (1 Sam. 14:50). **[2]** A woman of Jezreel who married David (1 Sam. 25:43; 27:3; 1 Chr. 3:1).

Ahithophel ("brother of foolishness"), the real leader of Absalom's rebellion against David. When he saw that victory was impossible, he committed suicide (2 Sam. 15—17).

Ahitub ("a good brother; my brother is goodness"). **[1]** A son of Phinehas (1 Sam. 14:3; 22:9, 11, 12, 20). **[2]** Father of Zadok the high priest (2 Sam. 8:17; 15:27; 1 Chr. 6:7, 8). **[3]** A high priest of the same family who served during Nehemiah's time (1 Chr. 6:11; 9:11; Neh. 11:11).

Ai [Aiath; Aija] ("heap of ruins"). **[1]** One of the strongest Canaanite cities, located east of Bethel (Josh. 7:2; Neh. 11:31). In Isaiah 10:28 the Hebrew feminine form of the name (Aiath) occurs. **[2]** A city of the Ammonites, probably located near Heshbon (Jer. 49:3).

Aijalon [Ajalon] ("place of harts"). **[1]** A town located 22.5 km. (14 mi.) northwest of Jerusalem, designated as a Levitical city (Josh. 19:42; 21:24; 2 Chr. 28:18). **[2]** A site belonging to the tribe of Zebulun west of the Sea of Galilee, where the judge Elon was buried (Judg. 12:12). Its exact location is unknown.

Ain ("eye"). **[1]** A town of Judah near Rimmon, assigned to the Levites serving the tribe of Simeon (Josh. 15:32; 19:7; 21:16; 1 Chr. 4:32). **[2]** A site on the boundary line of the Promised Land, west of Riblah (Num. 34:11). Its exact location is unknown.

Akel Dama [Potter's Field] ("field of blood"), a field purchased by the priests of Jerusalem with the 30 pieces of silver that bought the betrayal of Jesus (Acts 1:19); also called Potter's Field (Matt. 27:7).

Alexander ("helper of man"). **[1]** A son of the Simon who bore Christ's cross (Mark 15:21). **[2]** A kinsman of Annas and a leading man in Jerusalem (Acts 4:6). **[3]** A Christian with Paul when the Ephesians had a riot (Acts 19:33). Perhaps the same as **[1]**. **[4]** A convert who apostatized (1 Tim. 1:20). **[5]** A person who did much harm to Paul (2 Tim. 4:14). Perhaps the same as **[4]**.

Alexandria ("city of Alexander the Great"), a city on the Mediterranean coast of Egypt, which served as Egypt's capital city for many years (Acts 27:6; 28:11–13).

Almon Diblathaim ("hiding place of two fig sacks"), a site between the Arnon River and Shittim where the Israelites camped during their wandering in the wilderness (Num. 33:46).

Alphaeus ("leader; chief"). **[1]** The father of Levi (Matthew) (Mark 2:14). **[2]** The father of the apostle James (Matt. 10:3; Mark 3:18; Acts 1:13). Some identify him with Clopas.

Alush ("crowd"), a site where the Israelites camped on their journey from Egypt to Mount Sinai (Num. 33:14).

Amana ("forth"), a range of mountains in Lebanon, probably south of the Amana [Abana] River (Song 4:8).

Amasa ("burden-bearer; people of Jesse"). **[1]** A nephew of David who became the commander of Absalom's army (2 Sam. 17:25; 19:13; 20:4–12). **[2]** One who opposed making slaves of captured Jews (2 Chr. 28:12).

Amaziah ("Jehovah has strength"). **[1]** Son and successor of Joash to the throne of Judah. He was murdered at Lachish (2 Kin. 12:21—14:20). **[2]** A man of the tribe of Simeon (1 Chr. 4:34). **[3]** A Levite descendant from Merari (1 Chr. 6:45). **[4]** An idolatrous priest of Bethel (Amos 7:10, 12, 14).

Amittai ("truthful"), father of the prophet Jonah (2 Kin. 14:25; Jon. 1:1).

Ammiel ("my people are strong; my kinsman is God"). **[1]** One of those who spied out the Promised Land (Num. 13:12). **[2]** Father of Machir, David's friend (2 Sam. 9:4, 5; 17:27). **[3]** A porter of the tabernacle in the time of David (1 Chr. 26:5).

Amminadab [Aminadab] ("my people are willing or noble"). **[1]** Aaron's father-in-law (Ex. 6:23). **[2]** A prince of Judah and ancestor of Christ (Num. 1:7; 2:3; Ruth 4:19, 20; Matt. 1:4). **[3]** A son of Kohath (1 Chr. 6:22). **[4]** One who helped to bring the ark of the covenant from the house of Obed-Edom (1 Chr. 15:10, 11).

Ammon. *See* Ben-Ammi.

Amnon ("upbringing; faithful"). **[1]** Eldest son of David, by Ahinoam, slain by Absalom

(2 Sam. 3:2; 13:1–39). **[2]** A son of Shimon of the family of Caleb (1 Chr. 4:20).

Amon ("workman" or "trustworthy"). **[1]** Governor of Samaria in Ahab's time (1 Kin. 22:26; 2 Chr. 18:25). **[2]** Son and successor of Manasseh to the throne of Judah; an ancestor of Christ (2 Kin. 21:19–25; Jer. 1:2; Zeph. 1:1; Matt. 1:10).

Amos ("burden-bearer; burdensome"). **[1]** A prophet during the reigns of Uzziah and Jeroboam (Amos 1:1; 7:10–12, 14). **[2]** An ancestor of Christ (Luke 3:25).

Amoz ("strong"), father of the prophet Isaiah (2 Kin. 19:2, 20; Is. 1:1; 2:1; 13:1).

Amram ("people exalted; red"). **[1]** A descendant of Levi and father or ancestor of Aaron, Moses, and Miriam (Ex. 6:18, 20; Num. 3:19; 26:58, 59). **[2]** One who had taken a foreign wife (Ezra 10:34).

Ananiah ("Jehovah has covered"), a town inhabited by the tribe of Benjamin after the Exile (Neh. 11:32).

Ananias ("Jehovah is gracious"). **[1]** A disciple struck dead for trying to deceive the apostles (Acts 5:1, 3, 5). **[2]** A disciple of Damascus who helped Paul after receiving a vision (Acts 9:10–17; 22:12). **[3]** A high priest in Jerusalem who opposed Paul (Acts 23:2; 24:1).

Anathoth ("answer"), a town of the tribe of Benjamin, located about 4 km. (2.5 mi.) northeast of Jerusalem (Josh. 21:18; Ezra 2:23); the birthplace of the prophet Jeremiah (Jer. 1:1; 11:21).

Andrew ("manly; conqueror"), the brother of Peter and one of the twelve apostles (Matt. 4:18; 10:2; John 1:40, 44; 6:8).

Anna ("grace"), a prophetess of the tribe of Asher in Christ's time (Luke 2:36).

Annas ("grace of Jehovah"), high priest of the Jews who first tried Christ (Luke 3:2; John 18:13, 24; Acts 4:6).

Antioch ("speedy as a chariot"). **[1]** A Syrian city on the south side of the Orontes River, where the followers of Jesus were first called Christians (Acts 11:19–26). **[2]** A city of Phrygia near the border of Pisidia, visited by Paul and Barnabas on their missionary journey (Acts 13:14).

Antipas, a Christian martyr of Pergamos (Rev. 2:13).

Aphek [Aphik] ("strength"). **[1]** A city north of Sidon (Josh. 13:4). **[2]** A town assigned to the tribe of Asher but never captured from the Canaanites; located just southeast of Acco (Josh. 19:30; Judg. 1:31). **[3]** A town on the Plain of Sharon northeast of Joppa, whose king was killed by Joshua (Josh. 12:18). **[4]** A town between Shunem and Jezreel, whose soldiers fought in the war between Saul and the Philistines (1 Sam. 28:4; 29:1, 11; 31:1).

Apollonia ("city of Apollo"), a Macedonian town visited by Paul on his way to Thessalonica (Acts 17:1).

Apollos ("a destroyer"), a Jewish Christian, mighty in the Scriptures, who came to Ephesus and was instructed by Aquila and Priscilla (Acts 18:24; 19:1; 1 Cor. 1:12; 3:4–6; Titus 3:13).

Appii Forum ("marketplace of Appius"), a town in Italy about 64 km. (40 mi.) from Rome. Roman Christians met Paul here when he was brought to plead his case before Caesar (Acts 28:15).

Aquila ("eagle"), a pious Jewish Christian, husband of Priscilla and friend of Paul (Acts 18:2, 18, 26; Rom. 16:3; 1 Cor. 16:19).

Arabah ("steppe"), the depression of land holding the Sea of Galilee and the Dead Sea (Josh. 18:18). The "valley" of Joshua 11:2 probably refers to the Arabah.

Arabia ("desert"), a large peninsula bounded on the east by the Persian Gulf and the Gulf of Oman, on the west by the Red Sea, and on the south by the Indian Ocean. It was the home of many nomadic tribes, and was sometimes called the "East Country" (2 Chr. 21:16; Is. 13:20).

Ararat ("high land"), a mountainous, hilly land in western Asia (Jer. 51:27) later known as Armenia (Is. 37:38; 2 Kin. 19:37). Noah's ark rested on mountains in this area (Gen. 8:4).

Araunah ("Jehovah is firm"). *See* Ornan.

Archelaus ("people's chief"), the son of Herod the Great who succeeded his father as the ruler of Idumea, Judea, and Samaria (Matt. 2:22).

Archippus ("chief groom"), a "fellow-soldier" whom Paul addresses (Col. 4:17; Philem. 2).

Areopagus ("hill of Ares [Mars]"), a hill west of the acropolis in Athens, where Paul addressed several Greek philosophers; also known as Mars's Hill (Acts 17:19–34).

Aretas ("pleasing; virtuous"), Aretas IV, Philopatris. King of the Nabataeans whose deputy tried to seize Paul (2 Cor. 11:32).

Arimathea ("heights"), the home of a businessman named Joseph, who gained permission to bury the body of Jesus (Matt. 27:57; Luke 23:51).

Aristarchus ("the best ruler"), a faithful companion who accompanied Paul on his third missionary journey (Acts 19:29; 20:4; Col. 4:10).

Aristobulus ("best counselor"), a person in Rome whose household Paul saluted (Rom. 16:10).

Armageddon (Hebrew, *Har Megiddo*—"hill

of Megiddo"), the site of the final battle between Christ and Satan (Rev. 16:16).

Armenia. *See* Ararat.

Arnon ("rushing water"), a river that pours into the Dead Sea (Num. 21:13; Josh. 13:16).

Artaxerxes ("fervent to spoil"). **[1]** A king of Persia, Artaxerxes I Longimanus, at whose court Ezra and Nehemiah were officials (Ezra 7:1, 7, 11, 12; Neh. 2:1; 5:14). **[2]** Some suppose that Ezra 4:7 uses "Artaxerxes" to refer to the pseudo-Smerdis king of Persia, but the reference is probably to **[1]**.

Asa ("physician; healer"). **[1]** The third king of Judah and an ancestor of Christ (1 Kin. 15:8—16:29; Matt. 1:7, 8). **[2]** Head of a Levite family (1 Chr. 9:16).

Asahel ("God is doer; God has made"). **[1]** A son of David's sister, Zeruiah. He was slain by Abner (2 Sam. 2:18–32; 3:27, 30). **[2]** A Levite sent to teach the Law (2 Chr. 17:8). **[3]** A Levite employed as an officer of the offerings and tithes (2 Chr. 31:13). **[4]** Father of Jonathan, appointed to take a census of foreign wives (Ezra 10:15).

Asaph ("collector; gatherer"). **[1]** One of David's three chief musicians (1 Chr. 6:39; 15:17, 19). Author of Psalms 50, 73—83. **[2]** Father of Joah the recorder to Hezekiah (2 Kin. 18:18, 37; 2 Chr. 29:13). **[3]** A Levite whose descendants lived in Jerusalem (1 Chr. 9:15). **[4]** One whose descendants were porters in David's time (1 Chr. 26:1). The text should possibly read Abiasaph (q.v.). **[5]** A keeper of the royal forests in Judah (Neh. 2:8).

Asenath ("dedicated to [the deity] Neit"), the Egyptian wife of Joseph (Gen. 41:45, 50; 46:20).

Ashdod ("stronghold"), one of the five chief Canaanite cities; the seat of the worship of the fish god Dagon; located halfway between present-day Jaffa and Gaza (Josh. 11:22; 1 Sam. 5:1). In the N.T. the city is called Azotus (Acts 8:40).

Asher ("happy"), a town on the southern border of Manasseh (Josh. 17:7).

Ashkelon [Askelon] ("wandering"), one of the five chief Canaanite cities, the seat of the worship of the goddess Derceto; located about 19 km. (12 mi.) north of the present-day city of Gaza (Josh. 13:3; Jer. 47:5).

Ashpenaz, prince of Nebuchadnezzar's eunuchs who had charge of the captives from Judah (Dan. 1:3).

Asia ("eastern"), the term used by the Bible to refer to Asia Minor (1 Cor. 16:19; Acts 2:9). It is sometimes used to refer to a Roman province in Asia Minor (Acts 19:10; Rev. 1:4).

Askelon. *See* Ashkelon.

Asshur [Assur] ("level plain"). **[1]** A son of Shem (Gen. 10:22; 1 Chr. 1:17). Possibly the people of Assyria are intended. **[2]** Genesis 10:11, if denoting a person, refers to a son of Ham or to **[1]**. However, many scholars translate: "From that land he **[Nimrod]** went into Assyria **[Asshur]**."

Asshur [Assur] ("level plain"), a city in Assyria which was sometimes the capital, or the nation itself may be referred to (Num. 24:22, 24).

Assur. *See* Asshur.

Assyria ("country of Assur"), a Semitic nation on the Tigris River, whose capital was Nineveh (Gen. 2:14; 2 Kin. 15:10, 20).

Atad ("a thorn"), the campsite near Hebron used by Joseph and his brothers as they prepared to take Jacob's body back to Canaan (Gen. 50:11). The new name given the site was a pun: the Canaanites saw the mourning [Hebrew, *ēbhel*] of the Egyptians and called the place *Abel* [Hebrew, *ābhel*]—"meadow"; *Mizraim*—"of the Egyptians."

Ataroth Addar [Ataroth Adar] ("crown of Addar"), a village on the southern frontier of Ephraim (Josh. 16:5; 18:13). The town is probably to be identified with Ataroth (Josh. 16:2).

Athaliah ("whom Jehovah has afflicted; Jehovah is strong"). **[1]** The daughter of Jezebel, wife of King Jehoram, and afterwards ruler of Israel for six years (2 Kin. 8:26; 11:1–20; 2 Chr. 22:2—23:21). **[2]** A son of Jeroham (1 Chr. 8:26). **[3]** Father of a returned exile (Ezra 8:7).

Athens ("city of Athena"), the greatest city of classical Greece, capital of the Greek city-state of Attica, where Paul founded a Christian church (Acts 17:15–18).

Attai ("seasonable; timely"). **[1]** One who joined David at Ziklag (1 Chr. 12:11). **[2]** A son of King Rehoboam (2 Chr. 11:20). **[3]** Descendant of Pharez (1 Chr. 2:35, 36).

Augustus (i.e., "consecrated" or "holy"). Acts 25:21, 25; 27:1 use the Greek rendering of the title "reverend" in this fashion, since Augustus had been dead many years.

Augustus Caesar, the imperial name of Octavian, a nephew of Julius Caesar who became emperor of Rome. During his reign, Christ was born (Luke 2:1).

Azarel [Azareel] ("God is helper"). **[1]** One who joined David at Ziklag (1 Chr. 12:6). **[2]** One who ministered in the song service of the temple (1 Chr. 25:18). **[3]** A prince of Dan (1 Chr. 27:22). **[4]** One who took a foreign wife (Ezra 10:41). **[5]** A priest of the family of Immer (Neh. 11:13). **[6]** One who played the trumpet at the dedication of the new temple (Neh. 12:36).

Azariah ("Jehovah has helped"). **[1]** *See* Uzziah. **[2]** A ruler of Solomon's officers (1

Crete ("carnal"), a large island southeast of Greece (Titus 1:5).

Crispus ("curled"), a ruler of the Jewish synagogue at Corinth who was converted to Christ (Acts 18:7, 8; 1 Cor. 1:14).

Cyprus ("fairness"), an island in the northeastern Mediterranean Sea about 96 km. (60 mi.) east of Syria (Acts 13:4; 15:39).

Cyrus, founder of the Persian Empire; he returned the Jews to their land (Ezra 1:1–4, 7; 3:7; Is. 44:28; 45:1–4; Dan. 6:28).

D

Dalmanutha ("bucket"), a fishing village on the western coast of the Sea of Galilee (Mark 8:10).

Damascus ("sackful of blood"), an important Syrian trade center; Paul was converted on the road from Jerusalem to this city (Gen. 14:15; Acts 9:2).

Dan ("judge"), the fifth son of Jacob and ancestor of one of the twelve tribes of Israel (Gen. 30:6; 49:16, 17).

Dan ("judge"), a town of the tribe of Dan in the northwest portion of Palestine (Josh. 19:47; Judg. 20:1).

Daniel ("God is my judge"). **[1]** A prophet at the time of Nebuchadnezzar and Cyrus. His wisdom and faith earned him a position of esteem under Nebuchadnezzar and Darius (Dan. 1:1–6; 2; 6:1, 2). **[2]** One of the sons of David (1 Chr. 3:1). *See* Chileab. **[3]** A Levite of the line of Ithamar (Ezra 8:2; Neh. 10:6).

Darius ("he that informs himself"). **[1]** The sub-king of Cyrus who received the kingdom of Belshazzar (Dan. 5:30—6:28); also known as Darius the Mede. **[2]** The fourth king of Persia (Ezra 4:5; Hag. 1:1; Zech. 1:1); also called Hystaspis. **[3]** Darius II (Nothus) who ruled Persia and Babylon (Neh. 12:22).

Dathan ("fount"), a chief of the tribe of Reuben who tried to overthrow Moses and Aaron (Num. 16; 26:9; Deut. 11:6).

David ("beloved"), the great statesman, general, and king of Israel. He united the divided tribes of Israel and made many preparations for the temple, which his son Solomon would complete (1 Sam. 16—1 Kin. 2:11). He was an ancestor of Christ (Matt. 1:6).

Dead Sea. *See* Salt Sea.

Deborah ("bee"). **[1]** The nurse of Rebekah (Gen. 24:59; 35:8). **[2]** Prophetess and judge of Israel who helped to deliver her people from Jabin and Sisera (Judg. 4:4–14; 5).

Decapolis ("ten cities"), a league of ten cities forming a Roman district on the Plain of Esdraelon and the Upper Jordan Valley (Matt. 4:25).

Delaiah ("Jehovah has raised; Jehovah is deliverer"). **[1]** One of David's priests (1 Chr. 24:18). **[2]** A prince who urged Jehoiakim not to destroy the roll containing Jeremiah's prophecies (Jer. 36:12, 25).

Delilah ("longing; dainty one"), a woman whom the Philistines paid to find Samson's source of strength (Judg. 16).

Demetrius ("belonging to Demeter"). **[1]** A Christian praised by John (3 John 12). **[2]** A silversmith who led the opposition against Paul at Ephesus (Acts 19:24–41).

Derbe ("sting"), a city of southeastern Asia Minor, where Paul sought refuge after being stoned at Lystra (Acts 14:6–20).

Didymus. *See* Thomas.

Dinah ("justice"), the daughter of Jacob and Leah who was violated by Shechem; this resulted in a tribal war (Gen. 34).

Dionysius ("Bacchus"), a member of the supreme court at Athens converted by Paul (Acts 17:34).

Dorcas. *See* Tabitha.

Dothan ("two wells"), a city of the tribe of Manasseh west of the Jordan River and northeast of Samaria, near Mount Gilboa; here Joseph was sold into slavery (Gen. 37:17; 2 Kin. 6:13).

Drusilla ("watered by dew"), a Jewess, the daughter of Herod Agrippa I and wife of Felix; she and Felix heard a powerful message of Paul's (Acts 24:24, 25).

Dura ("fortress"), the Babylonian plain where King Nebuchadnezzar set up a golden idol (Dan. 3:1).

E

Ebenezer ("stone of help"). **[1]** The site of the defeat of Israel by the Philistines (1 Sam. 4:1–22). It was in the north of Sharon near Aphek. **[2]** Name of a stone Samuel erected to commemorate his victory over the Philistines (1 Sam. 7:12). The stone was possibly named after **[1]** to give the idea that Israel's defeat there had been reversed.

Eden ("pleasure"). **[1]** The garden that God created as the first residence of man (Gen. 2:15); its exact location is unknown. It may have been between the Tigris and Euphrates Rivers near the head of the Persian Gulf. **[2]** A region in Mesopotamia (2 Kin. 19:12; Is. 37:12).

Edom ("red"), name given to Esau, the elder son of Isaac, because of the red stew for which he sold his birthright (Gen. 25:30). *See* Esau; Obed-Edom.

Edom ("red"), a mountainous region south of Moab, which stretches from the Dead Sea to the Gulf of 'Aqabah. It was settled by the descendants of Esau, the Edomites (Gen. 32:3; Ex. 15:15).

Eglah ("calf"), one of David's wives (2 Sam. 3:5; 1 Chr. 3:3).

Eglon ("of a calf"), a town in the lowlands of Judah (Josh. 15:39); its exact location is unknown.

Egypt ("land of the soul of Ptah"), northeast corner of Africa where the Israelites were held in bondage until Moses led them to the Promised Land (Gen. 45:9; 47:6).

Ehud ("strong"). **[1]** A judge who delivered Israel from the oppression of Eglon of Moab (Judg. 3:15–30). **[2]** Great-grandson of Benjamin (1 Chr. 7:10; 8:6); perhaps the same as **[1]**.

Elah ("oak"). **[1]** A chieftain of Edom (Gen. 36:41; 1 Chr. 1:52). **[2]** Father of a commissary officer under Solomon (1 Kin. 4:18). **[3]** The son and successor of Baasha, king of Israel. He was murdered by Zimri (1 Kin. 16:6–14). **[4]** The father of Hoshea, last king of Israel (2 Kin. 15:30; 17:1). **[5]** A son of Caleb, son of Jephunneh (1 Chr. 4:15). **[6]** A descendant of Benjamin (1 Chr. 9:8).

El Bethel ("God of Bethel"), name Jacob gave the scene of his vision at Luz (Bethel) (Gen. 35:7).

Eldad ("God is a friend"), one of two elders who received the prophetic powers of Moses (Num. 11:26, 27).

Eleazar ("God is helper"). **[1]** Third son of Aaron and successor to the high priest's office (Ex. 6:23; Num. 3:32; 20:28). **[2]** One sanctified to keep the ark of the covenant (1 Sam. 7:1). **[3]** One of David's mighty men (2 Sam. 23:9; 1 Chr. 11:12). **[4]** A descendant of Merari who had no sons (1 Chr. 23:21, 22; 24:28). **[5]** A priest who accompanied Ezra when he returned to Jerusalem (Ezra 8:33). **[6]** A priest who assisted at the dedication of the walls of Jerusalem (Neh. 12:42); possibly the same as **[5]**. **[7]** An ancestor of Jesus (Matt. 1:15).

Eliakim ("God is setting up"). **[1]** Successor of Shebna as master of Hezekiah's household (2 Kin. 18:18, 26; Is. 22:20). **[2]** Original name of King Jehoiakim (q.v.).

Eliezer ("God is help"). **[1]** Abraham's chief servant (Gen. 15:2). **[2]** The second son of Moses and Zipporah (Ex. 18:4; 1 Chr. 23:15, 17). **[3]** A descendant of Benjamin (1 Chr. 7:8). **[4]** A priest who assisted with bringing the ark of the covenant to Jerusalem (1 Chr. 15:24). **[5]** A prince of Reuben in the time of David (1 Chr. 27:16). **[6]** A prophet who rebuked Jehoshaphat (2 Chr. 20:37). **[7]** A leader who induced others to return to Jerusalem (Ezra 8:16).

Elihu ("God himself"). **[1]** One who joined David at Ziklag (1 Chr. 12:20). **[2]** A porter at the tabernacle at the time of David (1 Chr. 26:7). **[3]** The youngest "friend" of Job (Job 32:2, 4–6).

Elijah ("Jehovah is my God"). **[1]** A great prophet of God, he strenuously opposed idolatry. He was caught up in a chariot of fire to heaven (1 Kin. 17:1—2 Kin. 2:11; Matt. 17:3). **[2]** A chief of the tribe of Benjamin (1 Chr. 8:27). **[3]** One who married a foreign wife during the Exile (Ezra 10:26). **[4]** Another who took a foreign wife during the Exile (Ezra 10:21).

Elimelech ("my God is King"), the husband of Naomi and father-in-law of Ruth. He died in Moab (Ruth 1:2, 3; 2:1, 3; 4:3, 9).

Eliphaz ("God is dispenser"). **[1]** The leader of Job's three "friends" who confronted him (Job 2:11; 4:1; 15:1). **[2]** A son of Esau (Gen. 36:4, 10–12; 1 Chr. 1:35, 36).

Eliphelet [Elpelet] ("God is escape"). **[1]** The last of David's thirteen sons (2 Sam. 5:16; 1 Chr. 3:8; 14:7). **[2]** Another of David's sons (1 Chr. 3:6); called Elpelet in First Chronicles 14:5. **[3]** One of David's mighty men (2 Sam. 23:34).

Elisha [Elishah] ("God is Savior"). **[1]** The disciple and successor of Elijah; he held the prophetic office for 55 years (1 Kin. 19:16, 17, 19; 2 Kin. 2—6; Luke 4:27). **[2]** Eldest son of Javan and grandson of Noah (Gen. 10:4). Possibly the people of Cyprus or the inhabitants of Alasiya, a country near Cilicia. Others suggest it includes the Italians and Peloponnesians.

Elishama ("God is hearer"). **[1]** Grandfather of Joshua (Num. 1:10; 2:18; 1 Chr. 7:26). **[2]** A son of King David (2 Sam. 5:16; 1 Chr. 3:8). **[3]** Another son of David (1 Chr. 3:6); also called Elishua in Second Samuel 5:15 and First Chronicles 14:5. **[4]** A descendant of Judah (1 Chr. 2:41). **[5]** One of the "royal seed" and grandfather of Gedaliah (Jer. 41:1; 2 Kin. 25:25). **[6]** A scribe or secretary of Jehoiakim (Jer. 36:12, 20, 21). **[7]** A priest sent by Jehoshaphat to teach the Law (2 Chr. 17:8).

Elizabeth ("God is swearer; oath of God"), the wife of Zacharias and mother of John the Baptist (Luke 1:5–57).

Elkanah [Elkonah] ("God is possessing"). **[1]** Grandson of Korah (Ex. 6:24; 1 Chr. 6:23). **[2]** Father of the prophet Samuel and a descendant of **[1]** (1 Sam. 1:1–23; 2:11, 20). **[3]** A descendant of Levi (1 Chr. 6:25, 36). **[4]** A descendant of Levi (1 Chr. 6:26, 35); perhaps the same as **[3]**. **[5]** A Levite ancestor of Berechiah (1 Chr. 9:16). **[6]** One who joined David at Ziklag (1 Chr. 12:6). **[7]** A gatekeeper of the ark of the covenant (1 Chr. 15:23); perhaps the same as **[6]**. **[8]** An officer of King Ahaz (2 Chr. 28:7).

Elymas ("a sorcerer"), a false prophet who

opposed Saul and Barnabas at Paphos (Acts 13:8); he was also called Bar-Jesus (v. 6).

En Dor ("fountain of habitation"), a town of the tribe of Manasseh where Saul consulted a witch about his future (Josh. 17:11); probably modern Indur on the northeastern shoulder of the Little Hermon Mountain, 10 km. (6 mi.) southeast of Nazareth.

En Gedi ("fountain of the goat"), a town on the western shore of the Dead Sea assigned to the tribe of Judah; originally called Hazazon Tamar (2 Chr. 20:2; Josh. 15:62).

Enoch ("teacher"). **[1]** The eldest son of Cain (Gen. 4:17, 18). **[2]** A son of Jared and an ancestor of Christ (Gen. 5:18, 19, 21; 1 Chr. 1:3; Luke 3:37; Heb. 11:5).

Enoch ("initiated"), a city built by Cain (Gen. 4:17).

Enos [Enosh] ("mortal"), son of Seth and ancestor of Christ (Gen. 4:26; 5:6–11; 1 Chr. 1:1; Luke 3:38).

Enosh. *See* Enos.

Epaphras (shortened form of *Epaphroditus*—"lovely"), a Christian worker with Paul who served as missionary to Colosse (Col. 1:7; 4:12; Philem. 23).

Epaphroditus ("lovely"), a Philippian Christian who worked so strenuously that he lost his health (Phil. 2:25; 4:18).

Ephesus ("desirable"), a town on the western coast of Asia Minor between Miletus and Smyrna; an important trading center (Acts 19:1).

Ephod ("oracular"), father of a prince of the tribe of Manasseh (Num. 34:23).

Ephraim ("doubly fruitful"), the second son of Joseph by Asenath. Although Ephraim was the younger of the two sons of Joseph, he received the firstborn's blessing. He was an ancestor of one of the twelve tribes of Israel (Gen. 41:52; 46:20; 48; 50:23).

Ephrathah [Ephrath] ("fertility"), the second wife of Caleb (1 Chr. 2:19, 50; 4:4).

Ephron ("strong"), a Hittite from whom Abraham bought a field with a cave, which became Sarah's burial place (Gen. 23:8, 10, 13, 14; 49:30).

Erastus ("beloved"). **[1]** Christian sent with Timothy into Macedonia while Paul stayed in Asia (Acts 19:22). **[2]** An important person in Corinth sending greetings to Rome (Rom. 16:23). **[3]** One who remained at Corinth (2 Tim. 4:20). Perhaps some or all of the above are identical.

Esarhaddon ("Ashur has given a brother"), the son of Sennacherib and a powerful king of Assyria (2 Kin. 19:37; Ezra 4:2; Is. 37:38).

Esau ("hairy"), eldest son of Isaac and twin brother of Jacob. He is the progenitor of the tribe of Edom (Gen. 25:25). He sold his birthright to Jacob (Gen. 25:26–34; 27; 36).

Esther ("star; [the goddess] Ishtar"), the Persian name of Hadassah, who was chosen by Ahasuerus to be his queen. The book of Esther tells her story.

Ethan ("ancient"). **[1]** A wise man in the days of Solomon (1 Kin. 4:31; Ps. 89, title). **[2]** A descendant of Judah (1 Chr. 2:6, 8). He is possibly identical with **[1]**. **[3]** *See* Jeduthun. **[4]** A descendant of Levi (1 Chr. 6:42).

Ethbaal ("Baal's man; with Baal"), king of Sidon and father of Ahab's wife Jezebel (1 Kin. 16:31).

Ethiopia [Cush?] ("burnt face"), a nation located in the upper region of the Nile River (Ps. 68:31; Is. 18:1). It is not the same as modern Ethiopia.

Eubulus ("of good counsel"), one of the Roman Christians that remained loyal to Paul (2 Tim. 4:21).

Eunice ("conquering well"), the pious mother of Timothy (2 Tim. 1:5; cf. Acts 16:1).

Euphrates (meaning unknown), a major river of western Asia, which begins in Armenia and joins the Tigris River before flowing into the Persian Gulf. It formed the western boundary of Mesopotamia (Gen. 2:14; 15:18).

Eutychus ("fortunate"), a young man at Troas whom Paul restored to life (Acts 20:6–12).

Eve ("life; life-giving"), the first woman, Adam's wife (Gen. 3:20; 4:1; 2 Chr. 11:3).

Evil-Merodach (Babylonian, Arvil-Marduk—"the man of [the god] Marduk"), the king of Babylon who released Jehoiachin from imprisonment. He succeeded his father, Nebuchadnezzar (2 Kin. 25:27–30; Jer. 52:31).

Ezekiel ("God strengthens"), a prophet of a priestly family carried captive to Babylon. He prophesied to the exiles in Mesopotamia by the river Chebar, and is the author of the book bearing his name (Ezek. 1:3; 24:24).

Ezra ("help"). **[1]** Head of one of the courses of priests that returned from the Exile (Neh. 12:1). The full form of his name, *Azariah*, occurs in Nehemiah 10:2. **[2]** A descendant of Judah through Caleb (1 Chr. 4:17). **[3]** A prominent scribe and priest descended from Hilkiah the high priest (Ezra 7:1–12; 10:1; Neh. 8:1–13). *See* Azariah.

F

Felix ("happy"), Roman governor of Judea that presided over the trial of Paul at Caesarea (Acts 23:23–27; 24:22–27).

Festus ("swine-like"), successor of Felix to the governorship of Judea. He continued the trial of Paul begun under Felix (Acts 25; 26).

Fortunatus ("fortunate"), a Corinthian

Christian who cheered and comforted Paul at Ephesus (1 Cor. 16:17, 18).

G

Gad ("fortune"). **[1]** The seventh son of Jacob and an ancestor of one of the twelve tribes (Gen. 30:11; 49:19). **[2]** David's seer who frequently advised him (1 Sam. 22:5; 1 Chr. 21:9–19).

Gad ("lot; fortune"), the territory settled by the tribe of Gad, east of the Jordan River (1 Sam. 13:7; Josh. 13:24).

Gadara ("walls"), a town located east of the Jordan River, 11 km. (7 mi.) south of the Sea of Galilee (Mark 5:1; Luke 8:26). It was one of the Decapolis cities (q.v.). *See also* Gergesa.

Gaius ("lord"). **[1]** One to whom John's third epistle is addressed (3 John 1). **[2]** A native of Macedonia and a companion of Paul (Acts 19:29). **[3]** A man of Derbe who accompanied Paul as far as Asia (Acts 20:4). **[4]** The host to Paul when he wrote to the Romans (Rom. 16:23). **[5]** A convert whom Paul baptized at Corinth (1 Cor. 1:14); some think he is identical with **[4]**.

Galilee ("circle"), one of the largest Roman districts of Palestine; the primary region of Jesus' ministry (Luke 3:1; 23:6).

Galilee, Sea of, a large lake in northern Palestine, fed by the Jordan River; several of Jesus' disciples worked as fishermen on this lake (John 6:1). The lake was also known as the Sea of Chinnereth, the Sea of Tiberias, and the Sea of Gennesaret. *See also* Chinnereth **[1]** and Gennesaret **[2]**.

Gallio (meaning unknown), Roman proconsul of Achaia before whom Paul was tried in Corinth (Acts 18:12–17).

Gamaliel ("reward or recompense of God"). **[1]** A prince of the tribe of Manasseh (Num. 1:10; 2:20). **[2]** A great Jewish teacher of the Law. He persuaded his fellow Jews to let the apostles go free (Acts 5:33–40; 22:3).

Gath ("winepress"), one of the five chief Philistine cities; home of the giant Goliath (1 Sam. 17:4; 2 Kin. 12:17; 2 Chr. 26:6). Its exact location is not known.

Gaza ("strong"). **[1]** The southernmost of the five chief Philistine cities, located 72 km. (44.5 mi.) south of modern Jaffa and 4 km. (2.4 mi.) from the Mediterranean Sea. It was the scene of Samson's exploits (Josh. 11:22; Judg. 16:1–3; 2 Kin. 18:8; Jer. 25:20). **[2]** A town of the tribe of Ephraim located on a small plain near Shiloh (1 Chr. 7:28).

Gehazi ("valley of vision; diminisher"), the dishonest servant of Elisha (2 Kin. 4:12–37; 5:20–27; 8:4).

Gennesaret ("garden of the prince"). **[1]** The region on the northwest shore of the Sea of Galilee (Matt. 14:34). **[2]** Another name for the Sea of Galilee (Luke 5:1).

Gergesa ("pilgrims"), a town or district which would have been located on the eastern side of the Sea of Galilee. Its location is not certain, but some have suggested modern-day Kersa (Matt. 8:28).

Gershon [Gershom] ("exile"), an important priest, the eldest son of Levi (Gen. 46:11; Ex. 6:16; 1 Chr. 6:1). He is also called Gershom (1 Chr. 6:16, 17, 20; 15:7).

Gethsemane ("oil press"), a garden east of Jerusalem, beyond the Brook Kidron at the foot of Mount Olivet; the site of Christ's betrayal (Matt. 26:36–56).

Geuel ("salvation of God"), the spy sent out from Gad to bring back word about Canaan (Num. 13:15).

Gibeah ("hill"). **[1]** A Judean town about 16 km. (10 mi.) northwest of Hebron (Josh. 15:57). **[2]** A town midway between Jerusalem and Ramah; home and capital of King Saul (1 Sam. 10:26; 15:34). The town is called Gibeath in Joshua 18:28. **[3]** A town or hill in the territory of Ephraim (Josh. 24:33); probably near Timnah **[1]**. **[4]** A hill in Kirjath Jearim on which was located the house of Abinadab (2 Sam. 6:3, 4).

Gibeon ("hill height"), the chief city of the Hivites, assigned to the tribe of Benjamin; located 9 km. (5.5 mi.) north-northwest of Jerusalem (Josh. 11:19; 2 Sam. 20:1–9). Its modern name is El-Jib.

Gideon ("feller [i.e., great warrior]"), the great judge of Israel who delivered his people from Midian (Judg. 6—8); he was given the name Jerubbaal (q.v.).

Gihon ("stream; bursting forth"). **[1]** One of the four rivers of Eden **[1]** (Gen. 2:13). **[2]** An intermittent spring outside the walls of Jerusalem, south of the temple area (1 Kin. 1:38–45; 2 Chr. 32:30).

Gilgal ("rolling"). **[1]** The first campsite of the Israelites after they crossed the Jordan River into Canaan, probably near Jericho (Josh. 4:19–24). **[2]** A village 11 km. (7 mi.) northeast of Bethel, from which Elijah and Elisha began their journey (2 Kin. 2:1–4; 4:38); present-day Jiljilia.

Gog ("high; mountain") (. **[1]** A descendant of Reuben (1 Chr. 5:4). **[2]** A prince of Rosh, Meshech, and Tubal (Ezek. 38:2; 39:1, 11). In Revelation 20:8 Gog appears to have become a nation as is Magog, thus indicating the name is to be understood symbolically.

Golan ("passage"), a city of Bashan east of the Jordan River, assigned to the Levites as a city of refuge (Deut. 4:43; Josh. 21:27). It is probably the site of modern Sahem el-Jaulan, 27 km. (17 mi.) east of the Sea of Galilee.

Golgotha [Calvary] ("skull"), a hill just outside the walls of ancient Jerusalem; the site of Jesus' crucifixion (Matt. 27:33; John 19:17). Its exact location is unknown, but it was probably inside the walls of what is now called the "old city."

Goliath ("an exile or soothsayer"). **[1]** The Philistine giant who was slain by David (1 Sam. 17:4-54). **[2]** Another giant, possibly the son of **[1]** (2 Sam. 21:19).

Gomer. [1] Eldest son of Japheth (Gen. 10:2, 3; 1 Chr. 1:5, 6). Possibly a people inhabiting the north, probably including or identical with the Cimmerians of classical history. **[2]** The immoral wife of Hosea (Hos. 1:3; 3:1-4).

Gomorrah ("submersion"), one of the five Cities of the Plain destroyed along with Sodom (Gen. 18:20; 19:24, 28). Many scholars believe it was submerged by the southeastern tip of the Dead Sea.

Goshen ("drawing near"). **[1]** A cattle-raising district of the Nile delta assigned to the Israelites before they were placed in bondage (Gen. 46:28). **[2]** A town in the hill country of Judah (Josh. 15:51); probably modern Dahariyeh, about 21 km. (13 mi.) southwest of Hebron. **[3]** A region of Judah that probably derived its name from the town of Goshen (Josh. 10:41; 11:16).

Greece (meaning uncertain), a country of Southern Europe between Italy and Asia Minor; one of the most powerful nations of the ancient world (Dan. 8:21; Zech. 9:13; Acts 20:2).

H

Habakkuk ("love's embrace"), A prophet during the reigns of Jehoiakim and Josiah (Hab. 1:1; 3:1).

Hadassah ("myrtle"), the Hebrew name of Esther (q.v.).

Hagar ("wandering"), an Egyptian servant of Sarah; she became the mother of Ishmael by Abraham (Gen. 16:1-16; 21:14-17).

Haggai ("festive"), the first of the prophets who prophesied after the Babylonian Captivity (Ezra 5:1; Hag. 1:1, 3, 12).

Haggith ("festal"), the fifth wife of David and mother of Adonijah (2 Sam. 3:4; 1 Kin. 1:5, 11).

Ham, the youngest son of Noah. Because of his wickedness, his son Canaan was cursed (Gen. 5:32; 9:22-27).

Ham. [1] A name for Egypt used only in poetry (Ps. 78:51). **[2]** A place between Ashteroth Karnaim in Bashan and the Moabite country (Gen. 14:5). Possibly modern Ham about 5 mi. south of Irbid in the 'Ajlūn district.

Haman ("celebrated Human [Humban]"), the prime minister of Ahasuerus who plotted against the Jews (Esth. 3—9).

Hamath ("anger"). **[1]** A Hittite city on the Orontes River about 200 km. (125 mi.) north of Damascus; a supply base for Solomon's armies (2 Chr. 8:4). **[2]** The ideal northern boundary of Israel (Num. 13:21; 34:8).

Hamon Gog ("multitude of Gog"), the valley where Gog and his armies will be defeated in their final struggle against God's people (Ezek. 39:11-15).

Hanani ("gracious"). **[1]** A musician and head of one of the courses of the temple services (1 Chr. 25:4, 25). **[2]** The father of the prophet Jehu; cast into prison by Asa (1 Kin. 16:1, 7; 2 Chr. 16:7-10). **[3]** A priest who married a foreign wife (Ezra 10:20). **[4]** A brother of Nehemiah and a governor of Jerusalem under him (Neh. 1:2; 7:2). **[5]** A priest and musician who helped to purify the walls of Jerusalem (Neh. 12:36).

Hananiah ("Jehovah is gracious"). **[1]** A descendant of Benjamin (1 Chr. 8:24). **[2]** An officer of Uzziah (2 Chr. 26:11). **[3]** The father of a prince under Jehoiakim (Jer. 36:12). **[4]** The leader of the sixteenth division of David's musicians (1 Chr. 25:4, 23). **[5]** The grandfather of Irijah (Jer. 37:13). **[6]** A false prophet who opposed Jeremiah (Jer. 28). **[7]** One of Daniel's friends at Babylon (Dan. 1:7, 11, 19). *See also* Shadrach. **[8]** A son of Zerubbabel (1 Chr. 3:19, 21). **[9]** A Levite who married a foreign wife during the Exile (Ezra 10:28). **[10]** A druggist and priest who helped to rebuild the wall of Jerusalem (Neh. 3:8). **[11]** One who helped to rebuild the gate of Jerusalem (Neh. 3:30); perhaps the same as **[10]**. **[12]** A faithful Israelite placed in charge of Jerusalem (Neh. 7:2). **[13]** One who sealed the new covenant with God after the Exile (Neh. 10:23). **[14]** A priest present at the dedication of the walls of Jerusalem (Neh. 12:12, 41).

Hannah ("grace"), a prophetess, the mother of Samuel (1 Sam. 1).

Hanoch [Enoch] ("dedicated"). **[1]** A grandson of Abraham (Gen. 25:4). **[2]** The eldest son of Reuben, and founder of the Hanochite clan (Gen. 46:9; 1 Chr. 5:3). **[3]** Enoch, the son of Jared (1 Chr. 1:3).

Haran ("strong; enlightened"). **[1]** A brother of Abraham who died before his father (Gen. 11:26-31). **[2]** A descendant of Levi (1 Chr. 23:9). **[3]** A son of Caleb (1 Chr. 2:46).

Haran ("mountains"), a Mesopotamian city located 386 km. (240 mi.) northwest of Nineveh and 450 km. (280 mi.) north-northeast of Damascus (Gen. 11:31; 12:4, 5).

Hashabiah ("Jehovah is associated"). **[1]** A

descendant of Levi (1 Chr. 6:45). **[2]** Another descendant of Levi (1 Chr. 9:14). **[3]** A son of Jeduthun (1 Chr. 25:3). **[4]** A descendant of Kohath (1 Chr. 26:30). **[5]** A son of Kemuel who was a prince of the Levites (1 Chr. 27:17). **[6]** A chief of a Levite clan (2 Chr. 35:9). **[7]** A Levite who returned with Ezra from Babylon (Ezra 8:19). **[8]** A chief of the family of Kohath (Ezra 8:24). **[9]** One who repaired the wall of Jerusalem (Neh. 3:17). **[10]** One who sealed the covenant with Nehemiah (Neh. 10:11). **[11]** A Levite in charge of certain temple functions (Neh. 11:15). **[12]** An attendant of the temple (Neh. 11:22). **[13]** A priest in the days of Jeshua (Neh. 12:21). **[14]** A chief Levite (Neh. 12:24). [Note: It is quite possible that **[9]**, **[12]**, and **[14]** refer to the same person.]

Hattush ("contender"). **[1]** Descendant of the kings of Judah, perhaps of Shechaniah (1 Chr. 3:22). **[2]** A descendant of David who returned fro the Exile with Ezra (Ezra 8:2). **[3]** A priest who returned from the Exile with Zerubbabel (Neh. 12:2). **[4]** One who helped to rebuild the wall of Jerusalem (Neh. 3:10). **[5]** A priest who signed the covenant (Neh. 10:1, 4). [Note: Entries **[1]**, **[2]**, **[3]**, and **[5]** may refer to the same person.]

Hazael ("God sees"), the murderer of Ben-Hadad II who usurped the throne of Syria (1 Kin. 19:15, 17; 2 Kin. 8:8-29).

Hazor ("enclosure"). **[1]** The capital of the Canaanite kingdom, later included in the territory of Naphtali in northern Palestine (Josh. 11:1, 10, 13); site of a major archaeological excavation. **[2]** A place in extreme southern Judah (Josh. 15:23); possibly modern el-Jebariyeh. **[3]** Another city in southern Judah (Josh. 15:25). Hezron was a district or region of the city or another name for the city itself (verse 25). **[4]** A village of the tribe of Benjamin, to which the Jewish exiles returned (Neh. 11:33); modern Khirbet Hazzur, 6 km. (4 mi.) north-northwest of Jerusalem. **[5]** A region of the Arabian Desert east of Palestine (Jer. 49:28, 30, 33).

Heber ("companion"). **[1]** A descendant of Asher (Gen. 46:17; 1 Chr. 7:31, 32). **[2]** The husband of Jael, who killed Sisera (Judg. 4:11, 17, 21; 5:24). **[3]** Head of a clan of Judah (1 Chr. 4:18). **[4]** A descendant of Benjamin (1 Chr. 8:17). **[5]** Used in Luke 3:35 to refer to Eber **[1]**.

Hebron ("friendship"). **[1]** A city in the hills of Judah, 32 km. (20 mi.) south of Jerusalem (Gen. 13:18; Num. 13:22). **[2]** A town of the tribe of Asher, more frequently called Abdon (Josh. 21:30).

Hell ("conceal"), the place of woe for the departed. "Hades" is the New Testament name for "Sheol," which was conceived as a place where the souls of all dead resided (Ps. 16:10; Matt. 11:23; Acts 2:27). The KJV also has *hell* as its translation of *Gehenna*, a valley outside Jerusalem that Jesus used as a symbol of woe for lost souls. For believers, He said that Hades would be Paradise (Luke 23:43); for the godless, it would be "Gehenna" (cf. Luke 16:22, 23).

Heman ("faithful"). **[1]** A musician and seer appointed by David as a leader in the temple's vocal and instrumental music (1 Chr. 6:33; 15:17; 2 Chr. 5:12; 35:15). **[2]** A wise man with whom Solomon was compared (1 Kin. 4:31; 1 Chr. 2:6). He composed a meditative Psalm (Ps. 88, title).

Hermon ("devoted to destruction"), the highest mountain of the Anti-Lebanon range, marking the northeast boundary of Palestine (Deut. 3:8; Josh. 11:17; 1 Chr. 5:23).

Herod ("heroic"). **[1]** Herod the Great, the sly king of Judea when Christ was born. In order to maintain power, he murdered the children of Bethlehem, thinking that he would be killing the Messiah (Matt. 2:1-22; Luke 1:5). **[2]** Herod Antipas, son of the former, was tetrarch of Galilee and Perea. He was the murderer of John the Baptist (Matt. 14:1-10; Luke 13:31, 32; 23:7-12). **[3]** Herod Philip, son of Herod the Great, was tetrarch of Iturea and Trachonitis (Luke 3:1). **[4]** Herod Philip, another son of Herod the Great, is the Philip whose wife Herod Antipas lured away (Matt. 14:3). **[5]** Herod Agrippa I, tetrarch of Galilee and eventual ruler of his grandfather's (i.e., Herod the Great's) old realm. He bitterly persecuted Christians (Acts 12:1-23). **[6]** Herod Agrippa II, son of Agrippa I and king of various domains, witnessed the preaching of Paul (Acts 25:13-26; 26:1-32). *See also* Archelaus; Bernice; Drusilla.

Herodias ("heroic"), granddaughter of Herod the Great, wife of Antipas, and ultimate cause of John the Baptist's death (Matt. 14:3-9; Luke 3:19).

Hezekiah ("Jehovah is strength"). **[1]** One who returned from Babylon (Ezra 2:16; Neh. 7:21). He, or his representative, is called Hizkijah (a form of Hezekiah) in Nehemiah 10:17. **[2]** The twelfth king of Judah; an ancestor of Christ. He instituted religious reform and improved the overall safety and prosperity of the nation (2 Kin. 18—20; 2 Chr. 29—32; Matt. 1:9, 10). **[3]** A son of Neariah, a descendant of the royal family of Judah (1 Chr. 3:23).

Hiddekel ("sound"), an archaic name for the Tigris River (Gen. 2:14; Dan. 10:4). It is narrower than the Euphrates, but carries more water. It joins the Euphrates 100 miles from the Persian Gulf at Al Qurna.

Hiel ("God is living"), a man who rebuilt Jericho (1 Kin. 16:34) and sacrificed his sons, in fulfillment of Joshua's curse (Josh. 6:26).

Hilkiah ("Jehovah is protection" or "my portion"). **[1]** One who stood with Ezra at the reading of the Law (Neh. 8:4). **[2]** A Levite who kept the children of the temple officials (1 Chr. 6:45). **[3]** A gatekeeper of the tabernacle (1 Chr. 26:11). **[4]** Master of the household of King Hezekiah (2 Kin. 18:18, 26; Is. 22:20; 36:3). **[5]** A priest of Anathoth and father of Jeremiah (Jer. 1:1). **[6]** High priest and the discoverer of the Book of the Law in the days of Josiah (2 Kin. 22:4, 8; 23:4). **[7]** The father of Gemariah (Jer. 29:3). **[8]** A chief of priests who returned from captivity (Neh. 12:7) and his later descendants (Neh. 12:12, 21).

Hinnom, an unknown person who had a son(s) after whom a valley near Jerusalem was named. Human sacrifices took place there in Jeremiah's day, and garbage was later incinerated in this defiled place (Josh. 15:8; 18:16; Neh. 11:30; Jer. 7:31, 32).

Hinnom ("their riches"), a narrow valley southwest of Jerusalem (Josh. 15:8; 18:16; 2 Chr. 28:3).

Hiram [Huram] (abbreviated form of Ahiram, "My brother is the exalted"). **[1]** A king of Tyre who befriended David and Solomon (2 Sam. 5:11; 1 Kin. 5; 9:11; 10:11). **[2]** The skillful worker in brass whom Solomon secured from King Hiram (1 Kin. 7:13, 40, 45; 2 Chr. 4:11, 16). **[3]** A descendant of Benjamin (1 Chr. 8:5).

Hobab ("beloved"), the father-in-law or brother-in-law of Moses (Num. 10:29; Judg. 4:11). The phrase "father-in-law" in Judges 4:11 may possibly mean nothing more than "in-law," or perhaps Jethro was also named Hobab; but the identity is uncertain. *See also* Jethro.

Horeb ("desert"), a range of mountains on the Sinai Peninsula, of which Mount Sinai is the highest (Ex. 17:6); now called the Serbal range.

Hosea ("help; i.e., Jehovah is help"), a prophet of Israel; he denounced the idolatries of Israel and Samaria (Hos. 1:1, 2).

Hoshea [Hosea] ("Jehovah is help or salvation"). **[1]** A chief of the tribe of Ephraim in the days of David (1 Chr. 27:20). **[2]** The last king of Israel; he was imprisoned by Sargon of Assyria (2 Kin. 15:30; 17:1, 4, 6; 18:1). **[3]** One who sealed the covenant with Nehemiah (Neh. 10:23). **[3]** The original name of Joshua (q.v.).

Hur ("free; noble"). **[1]** One of the men who held up Moses' arms during the battle with Amalek (Ex. 17:10, 12; 24:14). **[2]** A son of Caleb (Ex. 31:2; 35:30; 38:22; 1 Chr. 2:19, 50; 4:1, 4). **[3]** A Midianite king slain by Israel (Num. 31:8; Josh. 13:21). **[4]** An officer of Solomon on Mount Ephraim (1 Kin. 4:8). **[5]** The ruler of half of Jerusalem under Nehemiah (Neh. 3:9).

Huram. *See* Hiram.

Hushai ("quick"), a friend and counselor of David (2 Sam. 15:32, 37; 16:16–18; 17:5–15).

I

Ibzan ("famous; splendid"), a Bethlehemite who judged Israel for seven years (Judg. 12:8–10).

Iconium ("coming"), capital of the province of Lycaonia in Asia Minor (Acts 13:51; 14:1).

Iddo ("adorned"). **[1]** A prophet who wrote about the kings of Israel (2 Chr. 9:29; 2 Chr. 12:15). **[2]** A priest who returned to Jerusalem with Zerubbabel (Neh. 12:4); perhaps the same as **[1]**.

Igal ("Jehovah redeems") **[1]** One of the twelve spies sent to search out Canaan (Num. 13:7). **[2]** One of David's heroes (2 Sam. 23:36). **[3]** A descendant of the royal house of Judah (1 Chr. 3:22).

Illyricum ("joy"), a Roman province on the east coast of the Adriatic Sea, stretching from Italy on the north to Macedonia on the south (Rom. 15:19). It was later renamed Dalmatia.

Immer ("lamb"), a person or place in Babylonia (Ezra 2:59; Neh. 7:61); its exact location is unknown.

Imna [Jimna; Jimnah; Imnah] ("lugging") **[1]** A descendant of Asher (Gen. 46:17; 1 Chr. 7:35). **[2]** A son of Asher (Num. 26:44; 1 Chr. 7:30). **[3]** Father of Kore in Hezekiah's reign (2 Chr. 31:14).

Imnah. *See* Imna.

India (meaning unknown), a land on the eastern limit of the Persian Empire, surrounding the Indus River (Esth. 1:1; 8:9).

Ira ("watchful"). **[1]** A priest of David (2 Sam. 20:26). **[2]** One of David's thirty mighty men (1 Chr. 11:28; 2 Sam. 23:38) and a captain of the temple guard (1 Chr. 27:9). **[3]** Another of David's thirty (1 Chr. 11:40; 2 Sam. 23:26).

Isaac ("laughter"), the son of Abraham and Sarah, born to them in their old age. He was the father of Jacob and Esau and an ancestor of Christ (Gen. 21— 25; Matt. 1:2).

Isaiah ("salvation of Jehovah"), called the "prince of prophets"; his career lasted over sixty years. He foretold the coming of Christ (Is. 1:1; 7:14; 9:6; 52:12–53).

Iscariot. *See* Judah **[8]**.

Ishbosheth ("man of shame"), son and successor of King Saul. He reigned two years before being defeated by David (2 Sam. 2:8–15;

3:8, 14, 15; 4:5–12). He also was known as Esh-Baal (1 Chr. 8:33; 9:39).

Ishmael ("God hears"). **[1]** Son of Abraham and Hagar; his descendants are the Arabian nomads (Gen. 16:11–16; 17:18–26; 25:9–17; 28:9; 36:3). **[2]** The cunning son of Nethaniah and traitor of Israel (Jer. 40:8—41:18). **[3]** A descendant of Benjamin (1 Chr. 8:38). **[4]** Father of Zebadiah (2 Chr. 19:11). **[5]** A captain in the time of Jehoiada and Joash (2 Chr. 23:1). **[6]** A Levite who married a foreign wife during the Exile (Ezra 10:22).

Israel. *See* Jacob.

Israel ("who prevails with God"), the northern kingdom of the Hebrews in Palestine, inhabited by the ten tribes that followed Ishbosheth and Jeroboam. The cities of Jericho and Gezer marked its southern boundary (2 Chr. 35:18; cf. Gen. 32:32).

Issachar ("reward"). **[1]** Ninth son of Jacob and ancestor of one of the twelve tribes of Israel (Gen. 30:17, 18; 49:14, 15). **[2]** A tabernacle porter (1 Chr. 26:5).

Italy ("abounding with calves"), the peninsula jutting from the Alps into the Mediterranean Sea, bounded on the south by the straits of Messina (Acts 18:2; 27:1).

Ittai ("timely"), a Philistine friend and general of David (2 Sam. 15:11–22; 18:2, 4, 12).

J

Jabesh ("dry place"), father of Shallum, who killed Zechariah and reigned in his place (2 Kin. 15:10–14). *See also* Jabesh Gilead.

Jabesh Gilead ("dry"), a city of Gilead (Judg. 21:8; 1 Sam. 11:1). It may have been located at a site now called Wadi Yabis, about 32 km. (20 mi.) south of the Sea of Galilee.

Jabin ("intelligent; observed"). **[1]** A king of Hazor defeated by Joshua (Josh. 11:1). **[2]** Another king of Hazor who oppressed Israel and was defeated by Deborah (Judg. 4).

Jachin ("founding" or "he will establish"). **[1]** A son of Simeon (Gen. 46:10; Ex. 6:15; Num. 26:12). He is called Jarib in First Chronicles 4:24. **[2]** A priest in Jerusalem after the Babylonian Captivity (1 Chr. 9:10; Neh. 11:10). **[3]** Head of a family of Aaron (1 Chr. 24:17).

Jachin ("God establishes"), the right hand pillar of Solomon's porch on the temple of Jerusalem (1 Kin. 7:21).

Jacob ("supplanter; following after"). **[1]** Son of Isaac, twin of Esau, and an ancestor of Christ. He bought Esau's birthright and became the father of the Jewish nation (Gen. 25—50; Matt. 1:2). God changed his name from Jacob to Israel ("God strives"; Gen. 32:28; 35:10). **[2]** The father of Joseph, the husband of Mary (Matt. 1:15, 16).

Jaddua ("very knowing; known"). **[1]** One who sealed the covenant (Neh. 10:21). **[2]** The last high priest mentioned in the Old Testament (Neh. 12:11, 22).

Jael ("a wild goat"), wife of Heber who killed Sisera (Judg. 4:17–22; 5:6, 24).

Jahaziel ("God reveals"). **[1]** One who joined David at Ziklag (1 Chr. 12:4). **[2]** A priest who helped bring the ark of the covenant into Jerusalem (1 Chr. 16:6). **[3]** Son of Hebron (1 Chr. 23:19; 24:23). **[4]** A Levite who encouraged Jehoshaphat's army against the Moabites (2 Chr. 20:14). **[5]** A chief man whose son returned from Babylon (Ezra 8:5).

Jair ("Jehovah enlightens"). **[1]** A descendant of Judah through his father and of Manasseh through his mother (Num. 32:41; Deut. 3:14; 1 Kin. 4:13; 1 Chr. 2:22). **[2]** Judge of Israel for twenty-two years (Judg. 10:3–5). **[3]** The father of Mordecai, Esther's cousin (Esth. 2:5).

Jairus ("enlightened"), a ruler of a synagogue near Capernaum whose daughter Jesus raised from the dead (Luke 8:41).

James (Greek form of Jacob). **[1]** The son of Zebedee and brother of John called to be one of the Twelve. He was slain by Herod Agrippa I (Matt. 4:21; Mark 5:37; Luke 9:54; Acts 12:2). **[2]** The son of Alphaeus, another of the twelve apostles. He is probably the same as James "the less," the son of Mary. By "the less" is meant his age or height in relation to James the son of Zebedee (Matt. 10:3; Mark 15:40; Acts 1:13). **[3]** The brother of Jesus (Matt. 13:55). After Christ's resurrection, he became a believer (1 Cor. 15:7) and a leader of the church at Jerusalem (Acts 12:17; Gal. 1:19; 2:9). He wrote the epistle of James (James 1:1). **[4]** Unknown person mentioned as "the brother of Judas." Most view this as an incorrect translation and would render "Judas, the son of James" (Luke 6:16; Acts 1:13).

Japheth ("the extender; fair; enlarged"), second son of Noah, considered the father of the Indo-European races (Gen. 5:32; 6:10; 7:13; 9:18, 23, 27; 1 Chr. 1:4, 5).

Jason ("healing"). **[1]** Paul's host during his stay at Thessalonica (Acts 17:5–9). **[2]** A Jewish Christian kinsman of Paul who sent salutations to Rome (Rom. 16:21). Both are possibly identical.

Jebus ("manager"), another name for Jerusalem (Judg. 19:10, 11).

Jeconiah. *See* Jehoiachin.

Jedaiah ("Jehovah is knowing"). **[1]** A priest of Jerusalem (1 Chr. 9:10; 24:7; Ezra 2:36; Neh. 7:39). **[2]** A priest who returned with Zerubbabel (Neh. 11:10; 12:6, 19). **[3]** Another priest who came up with Zerubbabel (Neh. 12:7, 21). **[4]** One who brought gifts to the temple (Zech. 6:10, 14).

Jediael ("God knows"). **[1]** A son of Benjamin (1 Chr. 7:6, 10, 11). Possibly the same as Ashbel (1 Chr. 8:1). **[2]** One of David's mighty men (1 Chr. 11:45). **[3]** One who joined David at Ziklag (1 Chr. 12:20). **[4]** A descendant of Korah, son of Meshelemiah (1 Chr. 26:2).

Jedidiah ("beloved of Jehovah"), the name God gave Solomon through Nathan (2 Sam. 12:25).

Jeduthun ("a choir of praise"). **[1]** One of the three chief musicians of the service of song (1 Chr. 9:16; 25:1-6; Neh. 11:17). He was also named Ethan (1 Chr. 6:44; 15:17, 19). **[2]** The father of Obed-Edom (1 Chr. 16:38). Some believe him identical with **[1]**.

Jehoahaz ("Jehovah upholds"). **[1]** Son and successor of Jehu on the throne of Israel. His reign was one of disaster (2 Kin. 10:35; 13:2-25). **[2]** The son of Josiah and ruler of Judah for three months before he was deposed by Pharaoh Necho (2 Kin. 23:30-34; 2 Chr. 36:1-4). He was also called Shallum before becoming king (1 Chr. 3:15; Jer. 22:11). **[3]** *See* Ahaziah **[2]**.

Jehoash [Joash] ("Jehovah has given; Jehovah supports"). **[1]** The ninth king of Judah. Until the time of Jehoiada the priest's death Jehoash followed God; afterward, he brought idolatry and disaster to his country (2 Kin. 11:21—12:21). He is more frequently called by the shortened form of his name, Joash. **[2]** The twelfth king of Israel; he was successful in many military campaigns (2 Kin. 13:9—14:16). He is most frequently called Joash, an abbreviated form of his name.

Jehoiachin ("Jehovah establishes"), ruler of Judah when it was captured by Nebuchadnezzar. He was an ancestor of Christ (2 Kin. 24:8-16; 2 Chr. 36:9, 10; Matt. 1:11, 12). Jeconiah ("Jehovah is able") is an altered form of his name (1 Chr. 3:16, 17; Jer. 24:1) as is Coniah ("Jehovah is creating"; Jer. 22:24, 28; 37:1).

Jehoiada ("Jehovah knows"). **[1]** The father of one of David's officers (2 Sam. 8:18; 1 Kin. 1:8, 26). **[2]** The chief priest of the temple for many years of the monarchy. He hid Joash from Athaliah for 6 years (2 Kin. 11—12:9). **[3]** One who joined David at Ziklag (1 Chr. 12:27). **[4]** A counselor of David (1 Chr. 27:34). **[5]** One who helped to repair a gate of Jerusalem (Neh. 3:6). **[6]** A priest replaced by Zephaniah (Jer. 29:26).

Jehoiakim ("Jehovah sets up" or "Jehovah has established"), the name given to Eliakim by Pharaoh Necho when he made him king of Judah. The name probably means that Necho claimed Jehovah had authorized him to put Eliakim on the throne (2 Kin. 23:34—24:6). Not to be confused with Joiakim.

Jehonadab [Jonadab] ("Jehovah is liberal"). **[1]** Descendant of Rechab, who forbade his followers and descendants to drink wine and live in houses (Jer. 35:6-19; 2 Kin. 10:15, 23). **[2]** The sly son of David's brother, Shimeah (2 Sam. 13:3, 5, 32, 35).

Jehoram [Joram] ("Jehovah is high"), Joram is a shortened form of the name. **[1]** Son and successor of Jehoshaphat to the throne of Judah and an ancestor of Christ (2 Kin. 8:16-24; Matt. 1:8). **[2]** The ninth king of Israel, slain by Jehu (2 Kin. 1:17; 3:1-6; 9:24). **[3]** A priest commissioned to teach the people (2 Chr. 17:8).

Jehoshaphat [Joshaphat] ("Jehovah is judge"). **[1]** The recorder of David (2 Sam. 8:16; 20:24; 1 Kin. 4:3). **[2]** An officer of Solomon (1 Kin. 4:17). **[3]** Father of Jehu, who conspired against Joram (2 Kin. 9:2, 14). **[4]** A priest who helped to bring the ark of the covenant from Obed-Edom (1 Chr. 15:24). **[5]** Faithful king of Judah and an ancestor of Christ (1 Kin. 22:41-50; Matt. 1:8).

Jehoshaphat ("judged of God"), the valley where the Last Judgment will take place (Joel 3:2); tradition identifies it as the Kidron Valley (q.v.).

Jehu ("Jehovah is he"). **[1]** The prophet who brought tidings of disaster to Baasha of Israel (1 Kin. 16:1-12; 2 Chr. 19:2). **[2]** The tenth king of Israel (1 Kin. 19:16, 17; 2 Kin. 9; 10). His corrupt leadership weakened the nation. **[3]** A descendant of Hezron (1 Chr. 2:38). **[4]** A descendant of Simeon (1 Chr. 4:35). **[5]** One who joined David at Ziklag (1 Chr. 12:3).

Jeiel [Jehiel] ("God snatches away"). **[1]** A chief of the tribe of Reuben (1 Chr. 5:7). **[2]** An ancestor of Saul (1 Chr. 9:35). **[3]** One of David's mighty men (1 Chr. 11:44). **[4]** A singer and gatekeeper of the tabernacle (1 Chr. 15:18, 21; 16:5). **[5]** A descendant of Asaph (2 Chr. 20:14). **[6]** A scribe or recorder of Uzziah (2 Chr. 26:11). **[7]** A Levite in Hezekiah's time (2 Chr. 29:13). **[8]** A chief Levite in the days of Josiah (2 Chr. 35:9). **[9]** One who returned to Jerusalem with Ezra (Ezra 8:13). **[10]** One who married a foreign wife during the Exile (Ezra 10:43).

Jephthah ("an opposer"), a judge of Israel who delivered his people from Ammon (Judg. 11—12:7).

Jeremiah ("Jehovah is high"). **[1]** A woman of Libnah whose daughter married King Josiah (2 Kin. 23:31; Jer. 52:1). **[2]** Head of a family of the tribe of Manasseh (1 Chr. 5:24). **[3]** One who joined David at Ziklag (1 Chr. 12:4). **[4]** A man of Gad who joined David at Ziklag (1 Chr. 12:10). **[5]** Another who joined

David at Ziklag (1 Chr. 12:13). **[6]** A priest who sealed the new covenant with God after the Exile (Neh. 10:2; 12:1, 12). **[7]** A descendant of Jonadab (Jer. 35:3). **[8]** A prophet whose activity covered the reigns of the last five kings of Judah. He denounced the policies and idolatries of his nation (Jer. 1; 20; 26; 36).

Jericho ("his sweet smell"), a fortified city of Canaan located about 8 km. (5 mi.) from the north end of the Dead Sea and 27 km. (17 mi.) west of the Jordan River (Num. 22:1; Deut. 32:49). Today it is the oldest continually inhabited city in the world.

Jeroboam ("enlarger; he pleads the people's cause"). **[1]** The first king of Israel after the division of the kingdom. He reigned for 22 years (1 Kin. 11:26-40; 12:1—14:20). **[2]** The thirteenth king of Israel; his Israel was strong but overtly idolatrous (2 Kin. 14:23-29).

Jeroham ("loved"). **[1]** A Levite, the grandfather of Samuel (1 Sam. 1:1; 1 Chr. 6:27). **[2]** A descendant of Benjamin (1 Chr. 9:8). **[3]** Head of a family of Benjamin (1 Chr. 8:27). **[4]** A priest whose son lived in Jerusalem after the Exile (1 Chr. 9:12; Neh. 11:12). **[5]** Father of two who joined David at Ziklag (1 Chr. 12:7). **[6]** Father of Azareel, prince of Dan (1 Chr. 27:22). **[7]** Father of one who helped Jehoiada to set Joash on the throne of Judah (2 Chr. 23:1).

Jerubbaal ("let Baal contend" or possibly "let Baal show himself great"), the name given to Gideon by his father (Judg. 6:32; 7:1; 8:29).

Jerubbesheth ("contender with the idol"), name given to Jerubbaal (Gideon) by those who wanted to avoid pronouncing Baal (2 Sam. 11:21).

Jerusalem ("possession of peace"), capital of the southern kingdom of Judah, located 48 km. (30 mi.) from the Mediterranean Sea and 29 km. (18 mi.) west of the Jordan River (Josh. 10:1; 2 Sam. 5:5).

Jeshurun ("blessed"), a symbolic name for Israel (Deut. 32:15; Is. 44:2).

Jesse ("Jehovah exists; wealthy"), father of David and an ancestor of Christ (Ruth 4:17, 22; 1 Sam. 17:17; Matt. 1:5, 6).

Jesus (Greek form of Joshua). **[1]** A Christian who, with Paul, sent greetings to the Colossians (Col. 4:11); he was also called Justus. **[2]** *See* Joshua.

Jesus Christ (*Jesus*—"Jehovah is salvation," *Christ*—"the anointed one"), the son of the Virgin Mary who came to earth to fulfill the prophecies of the King who would die for the sins of His people. The account of His ministry is found in the Gospels of Matthew, Mark, Luke, and John.

Jethro ("preeminence"), the father-in-law of Moses. He advised Moses to delegate the time-consuming administration of justice (Ex. 3:1; 4:18; 18:1-12). He is called Reuel in Exodus 2:18. In Numbers 10:29, the KJV calls him Raguel; but the Hebrew text reads Reuel.

Jezebel ("unexalted; unhusbanded"). **[1]** The wicked, idolatrous queen of Israel (1 Kin. 16:31; 18:4—21:25; 2 Kin. 9:7-37). **[2]** A false prophetess at Thyatira (Rev. 2:20). Possibly the name is symbolic and not the prophetess's real name.

Jezreel ("God sows"). **[1]** A descendant of Etam (1 Chr. 4:3). **[2]** The symbolic name of a son of Hosea (Hos. 1:4).

Jimna. *See* Imna.

Joab ("Jehovah is father"). **[1]** A son of Zeruiah, David's sister. He was captain of David's army (2 Sam. 2:13-32; 3:23-31; 18; 1 Kin. 2:22, 23). **[2]** A descendant of Judah (1 Chr. 2:54). Some scholars believe a city of Judah is referred to here. The name would include the four words that follow in the KJV and be written: Atroth beth joab. **[3]** One of the tribe of Judah (1 Chr. 4:14). **[4]** An ancestor of returned captives (Ezra 2:6; 8:9; Neh. 7:11).

Joanna [Joannas] ("God-given"). **[1]** An ancestor of Christ (Luke 3:27). **[2]** The wife of Chuza, Herod's steward, who ministered to Christ and the apostles (Luke 8:3; 24:10).

Joash (abbreviated form of Jehoash). **[1]** A man of Judah (1 Chr. 4:22). **[2]** Father of Gideon the judge (Judg. 6:11-32). **[3]** A son of Ahab (1 Kin. 22:26; 2 Chr. 18:25). **[4]** One who joined David at Ziklag (1 Chr. 12:3). **[5]** *See* Jehoash **[1]**. **[6]** *See* Jehoash **[2]**.

Joash ("Jehovah has aided"). **[1]** A son of Becher, a descendant of Benjamin (1 Chr. 7:8). **[2]** The keeper of David's stores of oil (1 Chr. 27:28).

Job ("hated; persecuted"). **[1]** A pious man of Uz. His endurance in fierce trial resulted in marvelous blessing (Job 1—3; 42; Ezek. 14:14, 20). **[2]** The third son of Issachar (Gen. 46:13); he is also called Jashub (Num. 26:24; 1 Chr. 7:1).

Jochebed ("Jehovah is honor or glory"), a descendant of Levi and mother of Moses (Ex. 6:20; Num. 26:59).

Joel ("Jehovah is God"). **[1]** The firstborn son of Samuel the prophet (1 Sam. 8:2; 1 Chr. 6:33; 15:17). **[2]** A descendant of Simeon (1 Chr. 4:35). **[3]** The father of Shemaiah, a descendant of Reuben (1 Chr. 5:4, 8). **[4]** A chief of the tribe of Gad (1 Chr. 5:12). **[5]** An ancestor of the prophet Samuel (1 Chr. 6:36). **[6]** A descendant of Tola (1 Chr. 7:3). **[7]** One of David's mighty men (1 Chr. 11:38). **[8]** A Levite in David's time (1 Chr. 15:7, 11; 23:8). **[9]**

A keeper of the treasures of the Lord's house (1 Chr. 6:22). **[10]** A prince of Manasseh west of the Jordan (1 Chr. 27:20). **[11]** A Levite who aided in cleansing the temple (2 Chr. 29:12). **[12]** One who married a foreign wife during the Exile (Ezra 10:43). **[13]** An overseer of the descendants of Benjamin in Jerusalem (Neh. 11:9). **[14]** A prophet in the days of Uzziah (Joel 1:1; Acts 2:16).

Johanan ("Jehovah is gracious"). **[1]** A captain who allied with Gedaliah after the fall of Jerusalem (2 Kin. 25:23; Jer. 40:8, 13). **[2]** Eldest son of Josiah, king of Judah (1 Chr. 3:15). **[3]** A son of Elioenai (1 Chr. 3:24). **[4]** Father of a priest in Solomon's time (1 Chr. 6:9, 10). **[5], [6]** Two valiant men who joined David at Ziklag (1 Chr. 12:4, 12). **[7]** One who opposed making slaves of Judean captives in Ahaz's time (2 Chr. 28:12). **[8]** A returned exile (Ezra 8:12). **[9]** A priest who beckoned the exiles to Jerusalem (Ezra 10:6). **[10]** A son of Tobiah the Ammonite (Neh. 6:18). **[11]** A priest in the days of Joiakim (Neh. 12:22, 23).

John (a contraction of Jehohanan, "gift of God"). **[1]** The son of Zacharias and Elizabeth who came to prepare the way for the Messiah. He was called John the Baptist and was beheaded by Herod (Matt. 3; 11:7–18; 14:1–10; Luke 1:13–17). **[2]** A son of Zebedee and one of the twelve apostles. He is traditionally accorded the authorship of the Revelation, the Fourth Gospel, and the three epistles bearing his name (Matt. 4:21; 10:2; Acts 1:13; Gal. 2:9; Rev. 1:1). **[3]** A relative of the high priest Annas, who sat in judgment on Peter (Acts 4:6). **[4]** A missionary better known by his surname, Mark (q.v.). *See also* Johanan.

Joiakim ("Jehovah sets up"), the son of Jeshua who returned from the Babylonian Captivity (Neh. 12:10, 12, 26). Not to be confused with Jehoiakim.

Joiarib ("Jehovah knows"). **[1]** One whom Ezra sent to persuade ministers to return to the land of Israel (Ezra 8:16). **[2]** An ancestor of a family living in Jerusalem (Neh. 11:5). **[3]** A priest who returned from captivity (Neh. 11:10; 12:6, 19). He is called Jehoiarib in First Chronicles 9:10.

Joktan, a son of Eber of Shem's line (Gen. 10:25, 26; 1 Chr. 1:19, 20, 23). Perhaps the reference is to an Arabian tribe from whom many other Arabian groups sprang.

Jonadab. *See* Jehonadab.

Jonah [Jonas] ("a dove"). **[1]** The father of Simon Peter (John 1:42; 21:15–17). **[2]** A Hebrew prophet sent to preach to Nineveh in the days of Jeroboam II. He was the first Hebrew prophet sent to a heathen nation (2 Kin. 14:25; Jon. 1:1, 3, 5, 17; 2:10; Matt. 12:39–41).

Jonathan ("Jehovah is given"). **[1]** A priest of an idol shrine in the territory of Ephraim (Judg. 18:30). **[2]** A son of Abiathar the high priest (2 Sam. 15:27, 36; 17:17; 1 Kin. 1:42). **[3]** A son of Shimea, David's brother (2 Sam. 21:21; 1 Chr. 20:7). **[4]** One of David's mighty men (2 Sam. 23:32; 1 Chr. 11:34). **[5]** A grandson of Onam (1 Chr. 2:32, 33). **[6]** An uncle of David (1 Chr. 27:32). **[7]** Father of one who returned with Ezra (Ezra 8:6). **[8]** One involved with the foreign wife controversy (Ezra 10:15). **[9]** A descendant of Jeshua the high priest (Neh. 12:11). **[10]** A priest (Neh. 12:14). **[11]** A scribe in whose house Jeremiah was kept prisoner (Jer. 37:15, 20; 38:26). **[12]** One who joined Gedaliah after the fall of Jerusalem (Jer. 40:8). **[13]** A son of Saul and close friend of David (1 Sam. 14; 18:1–4; 31:2).

Joppa ("beauty"), a town on the coast of Palestine (2 Chr. 2:16; Acts 9:36).

Jordan (meaning uncertain), the major river of Palestine. It rises in a valley between Mount Lebanon and Hermon. It follows a twisting route to enter the north end of the Dead Sea (Gen. 13:10; Josh. 2:7).

Jose, an ancestor of Christ (Luke 3:29). Not to be confused with Joses.

Joseph ("increaser"). **[1]** The son of Jacob and Rachel. He was sold into slavery but became the prime minister of Egypt (Gen. 37; 39—50). **[2]** Father of one of the spies sent into Canaan (Num. 13:7). **[3]** A son of Asaph (1 Chr. 25:2, 9). **[4]** One who married a foreign wife during the Exile (Ezra 10:42). **[5]** A priest of the family of Shebaniah (Neh. 12:14). **[6]** The husband of Mary, mother of Jesus (Matt. 1:16–24; 2:13; Luke 1:27; 2:4). **[7]** A converted Jew of Arimathea in whose tomb Jesus was laid (Matt. 27:57, 59; Luke 15:43). **[8]** An ancestor of Christ (Luke 3:24). **[9]** Another ancestor of Christ (Luke 3:26). **[10]** Yet another ancestor of Christ (Luke 3:30). **[11]** A disciple considered to take the place of Judas Iscariot (Acts 1:23). He was also known as Barsabas and Justus.

Joses ("helped"). **[1]** One of the brothers of Christ (Matt. 13:55; Mark 6:3). **[2]** The son of Mary, the wife of Clopas (Matt. 27:56; Mark 15:40, 47). Not to be confused with Jose.

Joshaphat. *See* Jehoshaphat.

Joshua [Hoshea] ("Jehovah is salvation"). **[1]** The successor of Moses; the general who led the conquest of the Promised Land (Ex. 17:9–14; 24:13; Deut. 31:1–23; 34:9). Moses changed his name from Hoshea ("Jehovah is help"), to Joshua. **[2]** A native of Beth Shemeth in the days of Eli (1 Sam. 6:14, 18). **[3]** The governor of Jerusalem under Josiah (2 Kin. 23:8). **[4]** High priest at the rebuilding of the temple (Hag. 1:1, 12, 14; 2:2, 4; Zech. 3:1, 3, 6).

Josiah ("Jehovah supports"). **[1]** Godly king of Judah during whose reign the Book of the Law was found (1 Kin. 13:2; 2 Kin. 22:1—23:30). He was an ancestor of Christ (Matt. 1:10, 11). **[2]** A son of Zephaniah living in Jerusalem (Zech. 6:10).

Jotham ("Jehovah is perfect"). **[1]** The son of Gideon who managed to escape from Abimelech (Judg. 9:5, 7, 21, 57). **[2]** A son of Jahdai (1 Chr. 2:47). **[3]** The twelfth king of Judah and an ancestor of Christ (2 Kin. 15:5-38; Is. 1:1; 7:1; Matt. 1:9).

Judah [Judas; Jude] ("praise"). **[1]** A son of Jacob by Leah and an ancestor of Christ. He acquired the birthright Reuben lost. His descendants became one of the twelve tribes of Israel (Gen. 29:35; 37:26-28; 43:3-10; Matt. 1:2, 3; Luke 3:33). **[2]** An ancestor of one who helped to rebuild the temple (Ezra 3:9). **[3]** One who married a foreign wife during the Exile (Ezra 10:23). **[4]** Second in authority over Jerusalem after the Exile (Neh. 11:9). **[5]** One who came up to Jerusalem with Zerubbabel (Neh. 12:8). **[6]** A prince of Judah (Neh. 12:34). **[7]** A priest and musician (Neh. 12:36). **[8]** One of the twelve apostles. He betrayed his Lord and hanged himself (Matt. 10:4; 26:14, 25, 47; 27:3; Luke 6:16; 22:3, 47, 48). He was called Iscariot, apparently meaning "a man of Kerioth," a town 19 km. (12 mi.) from Hebron. **[9]** One of the brothers of Jesus (Matt. 13:55; Mark 6:3). He wrote the epistle bearing his name (Jude 1). **[10]** A Galilean who caused a rebellion against Rome (Acts 5:37). **[11]** One with whom Paul stayed at Damascus (Acts 9:11). **[12]** A prophet sent to Antioch with Silas (Acts 15:22, 27); he was surnamed Barsabas. **[13]** *See* Thaddaeus. **[14], [15]** Two ancestors of Christ (Luke 3:26, 30).

Judah ("the praise of the Lord"), the territory of one of the original twelve tribes. Judah, along with Benjamin, formed the southern kingdom after Solomon's death. The uncertain border between Israel and Judah ran between Bethel in Israel and Ramah in Judah. Jerusalem was its capital (2 Chr. 13:18; 15:8).

Judea ("the praise of the Lord"), first mentioned as a Persian province (Ezra 5:8). Later it became a Roman province (Matt. 2:1). Its northern boundary was Joppa on the west to a point 16.1 km. (10 mi.) north of the Dead Sea on the east. Its southern boundary was about 7 miles southwest of Gaza, through Beersheba, to the southern end of the Dead Sea.

Justus ("just"). **[1]** A believer in Corinth with whom Paul lodged (Acts 18:7). **[2]** *See* Jesus **[2]**. **[3]** *See* Joseph **[11]**.

K

Kadesh. *See* Kadesh Barnea; also Meribah **[2]**.

Kadesh Barnea ("holy"), a wilderness on Palestine's southern frontier. It was on the border between the wilderness of Paran on the south and the wilderness of Zin on the north of the Sinai Peninsula (Num. 32:8; 34:4). It is also called simply Kadesh (Num. 13:26; 20:1). In Genesis 14:7 the region is called En Mishpat.

Kedesh ("holy"). **[1]** A city of the Canaanites near the northern border, defeated by Joshua (Josh. 12:22; 19:37). **[2]** Levitical city of refuge in Naphtali. It was sometimes called Kedesh Naphtali (Josh. 20:7; Judg. 4:6, 9). It is probably modern Kades, about 7.2 km. (4.5 mi.) northwest of Lake Huleh. **[3]** A Levitical city in Issachar (1 Chr. 6:72). **[4]** A city of Judah near Hazor and Ithan (Josh. 15:23).

Keilah ("fortress"), a town in the lowlands of Judah (1 Sam. 23:1, 13; Josh. 15:44). It is 8.5 mi. north of Hebron at Khirbet Kila.

Kemuel ("God stands" or "God's mound"). **[1]** A son of Nahor and a nephew of Abraham (Gen. 22:21). **[2]** A prince of Ephraim (Num. 34:24). **[3]** A Levite (1 Chr. 27:17).

Kenaz [Kenez] ("side" or "hunting"). **[1]** A duke of Edom (Gen. 36:42; 1 Chr. 1:53). **[2]** The fourth son of Eliphaz (Gen. 36:11, 15; 1 Chr. 1:36); perhaps the same as **[1]**. **[3]** Father of Othniel the judge (Josh. 15:17; Judg. 1:13). **[4]** A grandson of Caleb (1 Chr. 4:15).

Kidron ("obscure; making black or sad"), a valley in Jerusalem between the Mount of Ophel and the Mount of Olives (2 Sam. 15:23; John 18:1). Today it is called Wadi Sitti Maryan.

Kirjath Jearim ("city of woods"), originally one of the cities of the Gibeonites located at the northwestern boundary of Judah (Josh. 9:17; Judg. 18:12). It is identical with Baalah (Josh. 15:9); Kirjath Arim (Ezra 2:25), Kirjath Baal (Josh. 18:12), and Baale Judah (2 Sam. 6:2). It is thought to be modern Deir el-Azhar, about 13.4 km. (8.3 mi.) northwest of Jerusalem.

Kish [Cis] ("bow; power"). **[1]** A son of Gibeon (1 Chr. 8:30; 9:36). **[2]** A Levite in David's time (1 Chr. 23:21; 24:29). **[3]** A descendant of Levi who assisted in the cleansing of the temple under Hezekiah (2 Chr. 29:12). **[4]** Great-grandfather of Mordecai (Esth. 2:5). **[5]** The father of King Saul (1 Sam. 9:1, 3; 14:51; Acts 13:21).

Kishon [Kison] ("bending; crooked"), a river in central Palestine which rises in Mount Tabor and, flowing westward, drains the valley of Esdraelon [Jezreel] (Judg. 4:7,

13; 1 Kin. 18:40; Ps. 83:9). Next to the Jordan, it is the most important river in Palestine.

Korah ("baldness"). **[1]** A son of Esau by Aholibamah (Gen. 36:5, 14, 18; 1 Chr. 1:35). **[2]** A son of Eliphaz (Gen. 36:16). **[3]** A son of Hebron (1 Chr. 2:43). **[4]** Grandson of Kohath and ancestor of some sacred musicians (1 Chr. 6:22; Ps. 42; 45—46 titles). He was one of the leaders of the rebellion against Moses and Aaron; the earth swallowed them up (Num. 16:1-35).

Kore ("one who proclaims; quail"). **[1]** A Levite in charge of the freewill offerings in Hezekiah's time (2 Chr. 31:14). **[2]** A son of Asaph whose descendants were gatekeepers at the tabernacle (1 Chr. 9:19; 26:1, 19).

L

Laban ("white; glorious"), the brother of Rebekah and father of Rachel and Leah. Jacob served him for seven years in order to marry Rachel, but Laban tricked him by substituting Leah at the wedding festivals (Gen. 24—31).

Lamech ("strong youth; overthrower"). **[1]** Father of Noah and ancestor of Christ (Gen. 5:25-31; Luke 3:36). **[2]** Father of Jabal and Jubal; he is the first recorded polygamist (Gen. 4:18-26).

Laodicea ("just people"), a chief city of Phrygia in Asia Minor (Col. 2:1; 4:15; Rev. 1:11). It is located on the Lycos River, a tributary of the Meander.

Lazarus (abridged form of Eleazar, "God has helped"). **[1]** The brother of Mary and Martha whom Jesus raised from the dead (John 11:1—12:17). **[2]** A believing beggar who was carried to Abraham's bosom (Luke 16:19-31).

Leah ("weary"), Jacob's wife through the deception of her father, Laban (Gen. 29—31).

Lebbaeus. *See* Thaddaeus.

Lebanon ("white"), one of two ranges of mountains in northern Palestine (Deut. 1:7; Josh. 1:4). The second is called the Anti-Lebanons; Mount Hermon is its highest peak. Running for about 161 km. (100 mi.), the chain begins about 24.1 km. (15 mi.) southeast of Sidon and runs north to about 19.3 km. (12 mi.) north-northeast of Tripolis in Syria.

Lemuel ("Godward; dedicated"), an unknown king often supposed to be Solomon or Hezekiah, whose words are recorded in Proverbs 31:1-9.

Levi ("joined"). **[1]** The third son of Jacob who avenged Dinah's wrong (Gen. 34:25-31), and went to Egypt with his father (Gen. 29:34; Ex. 6:16). His descendants became the priests of Israel. **[2]** An ancestor of Christ (Luke 3:24). **[3]** An ancestor of Christ (Luke 3:29). **[4]** Another name of Matthew (q.v.).

Libya ("heart of the sea"), the Greek name for the continent of Africa, west of Egypt (Acts 2:10). The Hebrews called this region Phut [Put]. Even though the Hebrew text of Ezekiel 30:5 and 38:5 read Phut, the KJV rendered the word *Libya*.

Lois ("pleasing; better"), the pious grandmother of Timothy (2 Tim. 1:5).

Lot ("veiled"), Abraham's nephew who escaped from wicked Sodom (Gen. 13:1-14; Gen. 19).

Lucifer (Latin, "light-bearer"), an epithet for the king of Babylon (Is. 14:12). Lucifer translates a Hebrew word meaning "light-bearer." The title came to be applied to Satan.

Lucius ("morning born; of light"). **[1]** A prophet or teacher from Cyrene ministering at Antioch (Acts 13:1). **[2]** A Jewish Christian who saluted the community at Rome (Rom. 16:21). Perhaps the same as **[1]**.

Luke ("light-giving"), evangelist, physician, and author of the Third Gospel and Acts (Col. 4:14; 2 Tim. 4:11; Philem. 24).

Lycaonia ("she-wolf"), an inland district of Asia Minor. Paul twice visited in the cities of Derbe and Lystra here (Acts 14:6-11). It was bordered on the north by Galatia and on the south by Cilicia.

Lydda ("a standing pool"), a town located on the plains of Sharon (Acts 9:32). It is identical with Lod (q.v.).

Lydia ("native of Lydia"), a woman convert of Thyatira (Acts 16:14, 15).

Lydia ("Lydus land"), a country and people in Northern Africa, west of Egypt (Ezek. 30:5).

Lysias. *See* Claudius Lysias.

Lystra ("that dissolves"), a city of Lycaonia in central Asia Minor. Paul was stoned here (Acts 14:6-21).

M

Maachah [Maacah] ("depression"). **[1]** The son of Nahor, Abraham's brother (Gen. 22:24). **[2]** One of David's wives and mother of Absalom (2 Sam. 3:3; 1 Chr. 3:2). **[3]** A king of Maachah (2 Sam. 10:6). Some translate "the king of Maacah." **[4]** Father of Achish, king of Gath (1 Kin. 2:39). He is called Maoch in First Samuel 27:2. **[5]** The mother of Asa, king of Judah (1 Kin. 15:10, 13; 2 Chr. 15:16). She is called Michaiah (2 Chr. 13:2). **[6]** Concubine of Caleb (1 Chr. 2:48). **[7]** Wife of Machir, son of Manasseh (1 Chr. 7:15, 16). **[8]** Wife of Jehiel (1 Chr. 8:29; 9:35). **[9]** Father of one of David's warriors (1 Chr. 11:43).

[10] Father of Shephatiah, ruler of Simeon (1 Chr. 27:16).

Macedonia (meaning unknown), a nation lying to the north of Greece proper (Acts 16:9; 18:5).

Magdala ("tower"), a village located on the western edge of the Sea of Galilee (Matt. 15:39). It is present-day el-Mejdel, 4.8 km. (3 mi.) north-northwest of Tiberias.

Mahalaleel [Mahalalel] ("God is splendor"). **[1]** Son of Cainan and an ancestor of Christ (Gen. 5:12, 13, 15; Luke 3:37). **[2]** One whose descendants lived at Jerusalem (Neh. 11:4).

Maher-Shalal-Hash-Baz ("the spoil hastens, the prey speeds"), symbolic name of Isaiah's son (Is. 8:1–4).

Mahlon ("mild; sickly"), the first husband of Ruth who died in Moab (Ruth 1:2–5).

Malachi ("messenger of Jehovah" or "my messenger"), the last of the prophets recorded in the Old Testament; he was contemporary with Nehemiah (Mal. 1:1).

Malchiah [Malchijah; Melchiah] ("Jehovah is king"). **[1]** A leader of singing under David's reign (1 Chr. 6:40). **[2]** An Aaronite whose descendants dwelt in Jerusalem after the Captivity (1 Chr. 9:12; Neh. 11:12). **[3]** Head of a priestly family (1 Chr. 24:9). **[4], [5], [6]** Three who married foreign wives during the Exile (Ezra 10:25, 31). **[7], [8], [9]** Three who helped to rebuild the wall of Jerusalem (Neh. 3:11, 14, 31). **[10]** A prince or Levite who stood beside Ezra as he read the Law (Neh. 8:4). **[11]** A priest who helped to purify the wall of Jerusalem (Neh. 10:3; 12:42). **[12]** Father of Pashhur (Jer. 21:1; 38:1).

Malchijah. *See* Malchiah.

Malchishua. *See* Melchishua.

Malluch ("counselor; ruling"). **[1]** A descendant of Levi (1 Chr. 6:44). **[2], [3]** Two who took foreign wives during the Exile (Ezra 10:29, 32). **[4]** A priest who sealed the covenant (Neh. 10:4). **[5]** A leader who sealed the new covenant with God after the Exile (Neh. 10:27). **[6]** One of the priests who returned with Zerubbabel (Neh. 12:2); he is called Melichu in verse 14.

Malta ("affording honey"), an island located in the Mediterranean Sea (Acts 28:1). It is 96.5 km. (60 mi.) south of Sicily.

Mamre ("firmness; vigor"), an Amorite chief who allied with Abraham (Gen. 14:13, 24).

Manahath ("resting place; rest"), a city of Benjamin (1 Chr. 8:6).

Manasseh ("causing forgetfulness"). **[1]** The first son of Joseph (Gen. 41:51). His descendants became one of the twelve tribes of Israel and occupied both sides of the Jordan (Josh. 16:4–9; 17). **[2]** The idolatrous successor of Hezekiah to the throne of Israel. He was an ancestor of Christ (2 Kin. 21:1–18; Matt. 1:10). **[3]** One whose descendants set up graven images at Laish (Judg. 18:30). Most scholars suggest that we should read Moses here instead. Perhaps a scribe felt an idolatrous descendant would cast reproach on the great lawgiver. A few manuscripts of the Septuagint, Old Latin, and the Vulgate read Moses here. **[4], [5]** Two who had taken foreign wives (Ezra 10:30, 33).

Manoah ("rest"), the father of Samson the judge (Judg. 13:1–23).

Marah ("bitter"), the fountain of bitter water in the wilderness of Shur where the Israelites first halted after crossing the Red Sea (Ex. 15:23; Num. 33:8). The traditional site is 'Ain Hawarah, about 75.6 km. (47 mi.) from Suez.

Mark ("polite; shining"), a Christian convert and missionary companion of Paul (Acts 12:12, 25; 15:37, 39; Col. 4:10). Mark is his Latin name, John his Hebrew name. He wrote the Gospel bearing his name.

Martha ("lady"), sister of Mary and Lazarus in Bethany (Luke 10:38, 40, 41; John 11:1–39).

Mary (Greek form of Miriam, "strong"). **[1]** The mother of Jesus Christ; her song of faith (Luke 1:46–55) reveals her deep faith (Matt. 1:16–20; cf. John 2:1–11). **[2]** Mary the sister of Martha. She anointed the Lord with ointment and received His approval (Luke 10:39, 42; John 11:1–45). **[3]** A woman of Magdala in Galilee. She had been converted after having "seven devils" cast out of her (Matt. 27:56, 61; 28:1; Luke 8:2; John 19:25). **[4]** The mother of John Mark (Acts 12:12). **[5]** A Roman Christian to whom Paul sent greetings (Rom. 16:6). **[6]** Mary, the mother of Joses (Mark 15:47) and James (Luke 24:10), the "other Mary" (Matt. 28:1), and the Mary, wife of Clopas (John 19:25), are possibly to be identified as the same person (Mark 15:40).

Massah ("temptation"), the name of a spot in the vicinity of Horeb where the Israelites tempted God (Ex. 17:7; Deut. 6:16). *See also* Meribah **[1]**.

Mattaniah ("gift of Jehovah"). **[1]** The original name of King Zedekiah (2 Kin. 24:17). **[2]** A descendant of Asaph whose family dwelt at Jerusalem (1 Chr. 9:15; 2 Chr. 20:14; Neh. 11:17, 22; 13:13). **[3]** A son of Heman the singer (1 Chr. 25:4, 16). **[4]** One who helped to cleanse the temple (2 Chr. 29:13). **[5], [6], [7], [8]** Four who married foreign wives during the Exile (Ezra 10:26, 27, 30, 37). **[9]** One of the gatekeepers (Neh. 12:25).

Matthat ("gift"). **[1]** Grandfather of Joseph

and ancestor of Jesus (Luke 3:24). **[2]** Another ancestor of Jesus (Luke 3:29).

Matthew ("gift of God"), one of the twelve apostles; he was a tax collector before his call. He was also known as Levi (Matt. 9:9; 10:3; Mark 2:14). He wrote the Gospel bearing his name.

Matthias ("God's gift"), a Christian chosen to become an apostle to fill the place of Judas (Acts 1:23, 26). He was surnamed Justus.

Mattithiah ("gift of Jehovah"). **[1]** A Levite in charge of "things that were baked in the pans" (1 Chr. 9:31). **[2]** A Levite singer and gatekeeper (1 Chr. 15:18, 21; 16:5). **[3]** A son of Jeduthun (1 Chr. 25:3, 21). **[4]** One who took a foreign wife during the Exile (Ezra 10:43). **[5]** One who stood with Ezra when he read the Law (Neh. 8:4).

Medad ("love"), one of the elders of the Hebrews on whom the Spirit fell (Num. 11:26, 27).

Media ("middle land"), a country of Asia located south of the Caspian Sea, west of Parthia, north of Elam, and east of the Yagros Mountains. During the 400s B.C. the Persians and Medes had a powerful empire here (Esth. 1:3, 14, 18; Dan. 8:20).

Melchishua [Malchishua], the third son of King Saul (1 Sam. 14:49; 31:2; 1 Chr. 8:33).

Melchizedek [Melchisedec] ("king of righteousness"), king and high priest of Salem. He was a prophetic symbol or "type" of Christ (Gen. 14:18–20; Ps. 110:4; Heb. 5—7).

Memphis ("abode of the good"), an ancient Egyptian city located on the western bank of the Nile in the central portion of the country (Hos. 9:6). It was also called Noph (Jer. 2:16).

Menahem ("comforter"), the idolatrous and cruel usurper of the throne of Israel who killed Shallum (2 Kin. 15:14–23).

Mephibosheth ("idol breaker"). **[1]** Son of Saul by his concubine Rizpah (2 Sam. 21:8). **[2]** A grandson of Saul. He was loyal to David, even though Ziba told David he was a traitor (2 Sam. 4:4; 9:6–13). He was also called Merib-Baal ("Baal contends") (1 Chr. 8:34; 9:40).

Merab ("increase"), daughter of Saul promised to David but given to Adriel (1 Sam. 14:49; 18:17, 19). Apparently she was a sister of Michal.

Meremoth ("strong; firm"). **[1]** A priest who weighed the gold and silver vessels of the temple (Ezra 8:33; Neh. 3:4, 21). **[2]** One who took a foreign wife during the Exile (Ezra 10:36). **[3]** One who sealed the new covenant with God after the Exile (Neh. 10:5; 12:3).

Meribah ("quarrel"). **[1]** The desert location where Moses smote the rock (Ex. 17:7). **[2]** Another name for Kadesh Barnea in the Wilderness of Zin, where the Hebrew people rebelled against Moses (Num. 20:13). In Deuteronomy 32:51 the place is called Meribah Kadesh.

Meribah Kadesh. *See* Meribah **[2].**

Mesha ("freedom"). **[1]** A king of Moab who rebelled against Ahaziah (2 Kin. 3:4). **[2]** Eldest son of Caleb (1 Chr. 2:42). **[3]** A descendant of Benjamin (1 Chr. 8:9).

Meshach ("the shadow of the prince; who is this?"), the name given to Mishael after he went into Babylonian captivity. He was delivered from the fiery furnace (Dan. 1:7; 3:12–30).

Meshullam ("associate; friend"). **[1]** Grandfather of Shaphan, a scribe (2 Kin. 22:3). **[2]** A descendant of King Jehoiakim (1 Chr. 3:19). **[3]** Head of a family of Gad (1 Chr. 5:13). **[4]** A descendant of Ben-jamin (1 Chr. 8:17). **[5]** One whose son lived in Jerusalem (1 Chr. 9:7). **[6]** One who lived in Jerusalem (1 Chr. 9:8). **[7]** A descendant of Aaron and an ancestor of Ezra (1 Chr. 9:11; Neh. 11:11). He is also called Shallum (Ezra 7:2; 1 Chr. 6:12, 13). **[8]** A priest (1 Chr. 9:12). **[9]** An overseer of the temple work (2 Chr. 34:12). **[10]** A chief man who returned with Ezra to Jerusalem (Ezra 8:16). **[11]** One who assisted in taking account of those who had foreign wives after the Exile (Ezra 10:15). **[12]** One who took a foreign wife during the Exile (Ezra 10:29). **[13], [14]** Two who rebuilt part of the wall of Jerusalem (Neh. 3:4, 6, 30; 6:18). **[15]** A prince or priest who stood with Ezra while he read the Law (Neh. 8:4). **[16]** A priest who sealed the new covenant with God after the Exile (Neh. 10:7). **[17]** One who sealed the new covenant with God after the Exile (Neh. 10:20). **[18]** One whose descendants lived in Jerusalem (Neh. 11:7). **[19]** A priest who assisted in the dedication of the wall of Jerusalem (Neh. 12:13, 33). **[20]** A descendant of Ginnethon (Neh. 12:16). **[21]** A Levite and gatekeeper after the Exile (Neh. 12:25).

Mesopotamia ("between two rivers"), a region located between the Tigris and Euphrates Rivers (Gen. 24:10; Deut. 23:4), excluding the mountain regions where the rivers take their rise and the low-lying plains of Babylon.

Methuselah, the longest living human recorded in the Bible, the grandfather of Noah and an ancestor of Christ (Gen. 5:21–27; Luke 3:37).

Micah [Micha, Michah—all probably contractions of Micaiah]. **[1]** Owner of a small private sanctuary (Judg. 17:1–5). **[2]** A descendant of Reuben (1 Chr. 5:5). **[3]** A son of Merib-Baal, Mephibosheth in Second Samuel 4:4 (1 Chr. 8:34). **[4]** A descendant of Kohath, son of Levi (1 Chr. 23:20; 24:24). **[5]**

The father of Abdon (2 Chr. 34:20). He is called Michaiah in Second Kings 22:12. **[6]** A prophet (Jer. 26:18; Mic. 1:1). **[7]** The son of Zichri (1 Chr. 9:15; Neh. 11:17). **[8]** One who signed the covenant (Neh. 10:11).

Michael ("who is like God?"). **[1]** One sent to spy out the land of Canaan (Num. 13:13). **[2]** A descendant of Gad (1 Chr. 5:13). **[3]** Another descendant of Gad (1 Chr. 5:14). **[4]** An ancestor of Asaph (1 Chr. 6:40). **[5]** A chief of the tribe of Issachar (1 Chr. 7:3). **[6]** One residing in Jerusalem (1 Chr. 8:16). **[7]** A warrior who joined David at Ziklag (1 Chr. 12:20). **[8]** Father of Omri, a prince of Issachar (1 Chr. 27:18). **[9]** A son of Jehoshaphat (2 Chr. 21:2). **[10]** An ancestor of one who returned from the Exile (Ezra 8:8).

Michaiah [Micaiah] ("who is like Jehovah?"). **[1]** Wife of Rehoboam (2 Chr. 13:2). She is also called Maachah (1 Kin. 15:2; 2 Chr. 11:20). *See* Maachah **[5]**. **[2]** *See* Micah **[5]**. **[3]** A prince of Judah (2 Chr. 17:7). **[4]** The son of Zaccur (Neh. 12:35). **[5]** One present at the dedication of the wall (Neh. 12:41). **[6]** A prophet who predicted Ahab's downfall (1 Kin. 22:8–28; 2 Chr. 18:7–27).

Michal ("who is like God?"), a daughter of Saul whom David married (1 Sam. 14:49). Michal "had no child unto the day of her death" (2 Sam. 6:23). Yet Second Samuel 21:8 states she had five sons. The KJV rendering, "whom she brought up for Adriel," is not a permissible translation—the Hebrew text states she bore them. A few Hebrew, Greek, and Syriac manuscripts read: "the five sons of Merab" instead of Michal, which seems a plausible solution to the problem. See First Samuel 18:19.

Midian ("contention"), a son of Abraham by Keturah and founder of the Midianites (Gen. 25:2, 4; 36:35; 1 Chr. 1:32).

Midian ("contention"), the land of the descendants of Midian beyond the Jordan. It included Edom, the Sinai Peninsula, and Arabian Petra (Ex. 2:15, 16; Judg. 6:1; Acts 7:29).

Miletus ("scarlet"), a coastal city of Ionia (Acts 20:15; 2 Tim. 4:20). It was 57.9 km. (36 mi.) south of Ephesus.

Miriam ("fat; thick; strong"). **[1]** The sister of Moses and Aaron. She rebelled against Moses with Aaron at Hazeroth (Ex. 2:4–10; Num. 12:1–15; 20:1). **[2]** A woman descendant of Judah (1 Chr. 4:17).

Mishael ("who is what God is?"). **[1]** One who carried away the dead Nadab and Abihu (Ex. 6:22; Lev. 10:4). **[2]** One who stood with Ezra at the reading of the Law (Neh. 8:4). **[3]** One of the companions of Daniel in Babylon (Dan. 1:6, 7, 11, 19). *See* Meshach.

Mithredath ("given by [the god] Mithra"). **[1]** The treasurer of Cyrus through whom he restored the temple vessels (Ezra 1:8). **[2]** One who wrote to the king of Persia protesting the restoration of Jerusalem (Ezra 4:7).

Mitylene ("purity"), the principal city of the Island of Lesbos off the western coast of Asia Minor (Acts 20:14).

Mizpah ("a watchtower"). **[1]** A mound of stones on Mount Gilead (Gen. 31:49). **[2]** A Hivite settlement in northern Palestine at the foot of Mount Hermon (Josh. 11:3). **[3]** A city in the lowlands of Judah (Josh. 15:38). It was just north of Eleutheropolis [Beit Jibrin]. **[4]** A town in Gilead east of the Jordan (Judg. 11:34). It is possibly identical with Ramath Mizpah. **[5]** A town of Benjamin just north of Jerusalem (Josh. 18:26; 1 Kin. 15:22). The exact site is uncertain. **[6]** A place in Moab (1 Sam. 22:3); perhaps modern Rujm el-Meshrefeh west-southwest of Madaba.

Mizraim. The second son of Ham (Gen. 10:6, 13; 1 Chr. 1:8, 11). Possibly the Egyptian people are intended.

Mnason ("remembering"), a Cyprian convert who accompanied Paul from Caesarea on Paul's last visit to Jerusalem (Acts 21:16).

Moab ("from my father"), the son of Lot by his daughter and an ancestor of the Moabites (Gen. 19:34–37).

Moab. A land that consisted of the plateau east of the Dead Sea between the wadis Arnon and Zered, though at certain periods extending to the north of the Arnon (Deut. 1:5; Num. 22—25).

Mordecai ("dedicated to Mars"). **[1]** A Jewish exile who became a vizier of Persia. He helped save the Jews from destruction (Esth. 2—10). **[2]** A leader who returned from the Babylonian Captivity (Ezra 2:2; Neh. 7:7).

Moreh ("stretching"). **[1]** The first stopping place of Abraham after he entered Canaan (Gen. 12:6). It was near Shechem. **[2]** A hill lying at the foot of the valley of Jezreel (Judg. 7:1). It is probably modern Jebel Dahy or Little Hermon about 12.9 km. (8 mi.) northwest of Mount Gilboa.

Moriah ("bitterness of the Lord"). **[1]** An elevation in Jerusalem on which Solomon built the temple (2 Chr. 3:1). Probably the same hilltop was used as the threshing floor of Araunah. The name Moriah was possibly ascribed by the Chronicler because of its traditional meaning (2 Sam. 24:18; 2 Chr. 3:1). **[2]** The hill on which Abraham was prepared to sacrifice Isaac (Gen. 22:2). The site is uncertain, but Samaritans identify Moriah with Moreh **[1]**. This seems unlikely.

Moses ("drawer-out; child; one-born"), the great prophet and lawgiver of Israel. He led his people from Egyptian bondage. The book of Exodus tells his story. He wrote the first five books of the Bible.

N

Naamah ("pleasant"). **[1]** Daughter of Lamech and Zillah (Gen. 4:22). **[2]** A wife of Solomon and mother of Rehoboam (1 Kin. 14:21; 2 Chr. 12:13).

Naaman ("pleasantness"). **[1]** A Syrian general who was healed of leprosy by bathing in the Jordan (2 Kin. 5; Luke 4:27). **[2]** Grandson of Benjamin (Gen. 26:38, 40). **[3]** A son of Benjamin and founder of a tribal family (Gen. 46:21).

Nabal ("foolish; wicked"), a wealthy Carmelite who refused David and his men food (1 Sam. 25).

Naboth ("a sprout"), the owner whom Jezebel had killed in order to obtain his vineyard (1 Kin. 21:1–18).

Nachon. *See* Chidon.

Nadab ("liberal"). **[1]** Firstborn son of Aaron, struck dead for offering "strange fire" to God (Ex. 6:23; Lev. 10:1–3). **[2]** A descendant of Jerahmeel (1 Chr. 2:28, 30). **[3]** A brother of Gibeon (1 Chr. 8:30). **[4]** Son of Jeroboam I; he ruled Israel for two years (1 Kin. 15:25–31).

Nahash ("oracle" or "serpent"). **[1]** The father of Abigail and Zeruiah (2 Sam. 17:25). **[2]** An Ammonite king that was defeated by Saul (1 Sam. 11:1, 2; 12:12). **[3]** Another king of Ammon (2 Sam. 10:2; 17:27; 1 Chr. 19:1, 2). Not to be confused with Ir-Nahash.

Nahor ("piercer"). **[1]** Grandfather of Abraham and ancestor of Christ (Gen. 11:22–25; Luke 3:34). **[2]** A brother of Abraham (Gen. 11:26, 27, 29; 22:20, 23; Josh. 24:2).

Nahum ("comforter"), one of the later prophets; he prophesied against Nineveh (Nah. 1:1). Not to be confused with Naum.

Nain ("beauty"), a village in Galilee where Christ resurrected a widow's son (Luke 7:11). It is located 3.2 km. (2 mi.) south of Mount Tabor and a little southwest of the Sea of Galilee.

Naioth ("habitation"), the place in Ramah where a community of prophets gathered around Samuel (1 Sam. 19:18–23; 20:1). Its location is not clearly identified. *See also* Ramah **[2]**.

Naomi ("pleasantness; my joy"), mother-in-law to Ruth (Ruth 1:2—4:17).

Naphtali ("wrestling"), the sixth son of Jacob (Gen. 30:7, 8). His descendants became one of the twelve tribes.

Naphtali [Nephthalim] ("that struggles"), a territory assigned to the tribe of Naphtali, located in mountainous northern Palestine (Josh. 19:32–39; Matt. 4:13). It was bounded on the east by the Upper Jordan River and the Sea of Galilee and on the west by the territories of Zebulun and Asher.

Nathan ("gift"). **[1]** Prophet and royal advisor to David (2 Sam. 7:2–17; 12:1–25). **[2]** A son of King David and ancestor of Christ (2 Sam. 5:14; 1 Chr. 3:5; Luke 3:31). **[3]** Father of Igal (2 Sam. 23:36). **[4]** A descendant of Jerahmeel (1 Chr. 2:36). **[5]** A companion of Ezra (Ezra 8:16). **[6]** One of those who had married a foreign wife (Ezra 10:39). **[7]** Brother of Joel, one of David's valiant men (1 Chr. 11:38). **[8]** Father of Solomon's chief officer (1 Kin. 4:5). **[9]** A chief man of Israel (Zech. 12:12).

Nathanael ("God has given"), a Galilean called by Christ to be a disciple. He is probably to be identified with Bartholomew (John 1:45–49; 21:2; Acts 1:13). *See also* Bartholomew.

Nazareth ("sanctified"), the hometown of Jesus in lower Galilee, north of the Plain of Esdraelon [Jezreel] (Matt. 4:13; Mark 1:9). It is 8 km. (5 mi.) west-southwest of Tiberias, 32.2 km. (20 mi.) southwest of modern Tell Hum [Capernaum] and 141.6 km. (88 mi.) north of Jerusalem.

Nebo ("that prophesies"). **[1]** The mountain from which Moses saw the Promised Land (Deut. 32:49; 34:1). It is a peak in the Abarim Mountains east of the Jordan, opposite Jericho; probably modern Jebel en Neba 12.9 km. (8 mi.) east of the mouth of the Jordan. On a clear day, all of Palestine can be seen from this peak. **[2]** A city of Reuben that fell again to the Moabites (Num. 32:3, 38; 33:47). It is probably modern Khirbet el-Mekhayyet, south of Mount Nebo. **[3]** A city in Judah (Ezra 2:29; Neh. 7:33), probably modern Beth-Nube, near Lydda.

Nebuchadnezzar [Nebuchadrezzar](Babylonian, *Nabur-kudurri-utsur*—"may [the god] Nabu guard my boundary stones"), great king of the Babylonian Empire; he captured Jerusalem three times and carried Judah into captivity (2 Kin. 24:1, 10, 11; 25:1, 8, 22; Dan. 1—4).

Nehemiah ("Jehovah is consolation"). **[1]** Governor of Jerusalem; he helped rebuild the fallen city (Neh. 1:1; 8:9; 12:47). **[2]** A chief man who returned from the Exile (Ezra 2:2; Neh. 7:7). **[3]** One who repaired the wall of Jerusalem (Neh. 3:16).

Nepheg ("sprout; shoot"). **[1]** A brother of Korah (Ex. 6:21). **[2]** A son of David (2 Sam. 5:15; 1 Chr. 3:7; 14:6).

Ner ("light"). **[1]** An uncle (?) of Saul, father of Abner (1 Sam. 14:50). **[2]** Grandfather of Saul (1 Chr. 8:33; 9:39). These relationships are unclear. Abner may have been Saul's uncle. If so, Ner **[1]** and **[2]** are the same. He is also called Abiel (1 Sam. 9:1). It is also possible that Ner [2] (Abiel) had sons names Ner [1] and Kish, the father of Saul.

Nethanel ("God gives"). [1] Chief of Issachar whom Moses sent to spy out the land of Canaan (Num. 1:8; 2:5; 7:18, 23; 10:15). [2] Fourth son of Jesse (1 Chr. 2:14). [3] One of the trumpet blowers when the ark of the covenant was brought up (1 Chr. 15:24). [4] A Levite (1 Chr. 24:6). [5] A son of Obed-Edom and gatekeeper of the tabernacle (1 Chr. 26:4). [6] A prince commissioned by Jehoshaphat to teach the people (2 Chr. 17:7). [7] A Levite in the days of Josiah (2 Chr. 35:9). [8] A priest who married a foreign wife (Ezra 10:22). [9] A priest in the days of Joiakim (Neh. 12:21). [10] Levite musician at the purification ceremony (Neh. 12:36).

Nicanor ("conqueror"), one of the seven chosen in the ministry to the poor (Acts 6:5).

Nicodemus ("innocent blood"), a Pharisee and ruler of the Jews who assisted in Christ's burial (John 3:1–15; 7:50–52; 19:39–42).

Nicolas ("conqueror of the people"), one of the seven chosen to aid in the ministration to the poor (Acts 6:5).

Nile ("dark blue"), the greatest river of Egypt and the world's longest. It is simply referred to in Scripture as "the river" (Gen. 13:1; Ex. 2:3; 7:21). The Nile is about 6,669.3 km. (4,145 mi.) long.

Nimrah. *See* Beth Nimrah.

Nimrod ("valiant; strong"), a son of Cush (Gen. 10:8, 9; 1 Chr. 1:10). His kingdom included Babel, Erech, Accad, and Calneh, cities in Shinar, but also included Assyria.

Nineveh [Nineve] (meaning unknown), the capital of the Kingdom of Assyria (Nah. 1:1; cf. 3:1; Luke 11:32; Zeph. 2:13). It was located east of the Tigris River in the area north of the point the Tigris joins the Upper Zab. The ruins are now called Tell Kuyunjik and Tell Nebi Yunus.

Noah ("rest"), son of Lamech; the patriarch chosen to build the ark. Only his family survived the flood (Gen. 5:28–32; 6:8–22; 7—10). He was an ancestor of Christ (Luke 3:36).

Nod ("vagabond"), an unidentified land east of Eden to which Cain fled after the murder of Abel (Gen. 4:16). Some suppose it to be China, but this is speculation.

Noph. *See* Memphis.

Nun [Non] ("continuation; fish"). [1] A descendant of Ephraim (1 Chr. 7:27); possibly the same as [2]. [2] The father of Joshua (Ex. 33:11; 1 Kin. 16:34).

O

Obadiah ("servant of Jehovah"). [1] The governor or prime minister of Ahab who tried to protect the prophets against Jezebel (1 Kin. 18:3–16). [2] A descendant of David (1 Chr. 3:21). [3] A chief of the tribe of Issachar (1 Chr. 7:3). [4] A descendant of King Saul (1 Chr. 8:38; 9:44). [5] A man of the tribe of Zebulun (1 Chr. 27:19). [6] A chief of the Gadites who joined David at Ziklag (1 Chr. 12:9). [7] One of the princes whom Jehoshaphat commissioned to teach the Law (2 Chr. 17:7–9). [8] A Levite overseer in work done on the temple (2 Chr. 34:12). [9] The chief of a family that returned to Jerusalem (Ezra 8:9). [10] One who sealed the covenant with Nehemiah (Neh. 10:5). [11] A gatekeeper for the sanctuary of the temple (Neh. 12:25). [12] The fourth of the "minor prophets." His message was directed against Edom (Obad. 1).

Obed ("servant"). [1] A son of Boaz and Ruth, father of Jesse, and ancestor of Christ (Ruth 4:17; Matt. 1:5; Luke 3:32). [2] A descendant of Judah (1 Chr. 2:37, 38). [3] One of David's warriors (1 Chr. 11:47). [4] A Levite gatekeeper in David's time (1 Chr. 26:7). [5] Father of Azariah, who helped make Joash king of Judah (2 Chr. 23:1).

Obed-Edom ("servant of [the god] Edom"). [1] A man who housed the ark for three months (2 Sam. 6:10–12; 1 Chr. 13:13, 14). [2] One of the chief Levitical singers and doorkeepers (1 Chr. 15:18, 21, 24; 16:5, 38; 26:4, 8, 15). [3] A temple treasurer or official, or perhaps the tribe that sprang from [2] (2 Chr. 25:24).

Oded ("aiding" or "restorer"). [1] Father of Azariah the prophet (2 Chr. 15:1). [2] A prophet of Samaria who persuaded the northern army to free their Judean slaves (2 Chr. 28:9- 5).

Olives, Mount of [Mount of Corruption; Olivet], a ridge east of Jerusalem and separated from Jerusalem by the Kidron Valley (2 Sam. 15:30; Mark 11:1; Acts 1:12). It is called the Mount of Corruption in Second Kings 23:13.

Omri ("Jehovah apportions; pupil"). [1] The sixth king of Israel and founder of the third dynasty. He founded Samaria and made it Israel's capital (1 Kin. 16:15–28). [2] A descendant of Benjamin, the son of Becher (1 Chr. 7:8). [3] A descendant of Perez living at Jerusalem (1 Chr. 9:4). [4] A prince of Issachar in the days of David (1 Chr. 27:18).

Onan ("vigorous"), the second son of Judah. He was slain by God for disobedience (Gen. 38:4–10; Num. 26:19).

Onesimus ("useful"), a slave on whose behalf Paul wrote an epistle to his master, Philemon (Col. 4:9; Philem. 10, 15).

Onesiphorus ("profit-bringer"), a loyal friend of Paul's who often refreshed him in prison (2 Tim. 1:16; 4:19).

Ophir ("fruitful region"), a region where Solomon mined gold (1 Kin. 9:28; 1 Chr. 29:4). The location is highly uncertain. Josephus thought it was India, but the African coast in modern Somaliland is more probable.

Ornan ("active"), a Jebusite from whom David bought a piece of land, on which Solomon's temple was erected (1 Chr. 21:15–25). He is called Araunah in Second Samuel 24:16.

Orpah ("fawn; youthful freshness"), daughter-in-law of Naomi (Ruth 1:4–14).

Othniel ("God is power"), Caleb's younger brother who liberated Israel from foreign rule (Judg. 1:13; 3:8–11; 1 Chr. 27:15).

Ozem ("strength"). **[1]** A brother of David (1 Chr. 2:15). **[2]** A son of Jerahmeel of Judah (1 Chr. 2:25).

P

Padan Aram [Padan] ("plain [tableland] of Aram"), the plain region of Mesopotamia from the Lebanon Mountains to beyond the Euphrates, and from the Taurus Mountains on the north to beyond Damascus on the south (Gen. 25:20; 28:2; 31:18). It is called simply Padan in Genesis 48:7.

Palestine [Palestina] ("which is covered"), an ill-defined region between the Jordan River and the Dead Sea on the east and the Mediterranean on the west (Ex. 15:14; Joel 3:4; Gen. 15:18). Its northern border is roughly the Lebanon Mountain range. It stretches in a southwesterly triangle to the Gulf of Aqaba on the Red Sea.

Paltiel ("God delivers"). **[1]** A prince of the tribe of Issachar (Num. 34:26). **[2]** The man who married David's wife (2 Sam. 3:15). He is called Phalti in First Samuel 25:44.

Pamphylia ("a nation made up of every tribe"), a southern coastal area in Asia Minor; its main city is Perga (Acts 13:13; 14:24; 27:5).

Paphos ("that which boils"), a town on the southwest extremity of Cyprus; it was visited by Paul and Barnabas (Acts 13:6–13). It is modern Baffa.

Paradise ("pleasure ground; park"), figurative name for the place where God dwells (2 Cor. 12:3) and the abode of the righteous (Luke 23:43; Rev. 2:7).

Paran ("beauty"), a wilderness seven days' march from Mount Sinai (Gen. 21:21; Num. 10:12; 1 Sam. 25:1). It is located east of the wilderness of Beersheba and Shurj, and it merges with the Wilderness of Sin with no clearly marked boundary. The area borders on Edom and Midian; it is sometimes called Mount Paran (Hab. 3:3) and El Paran (Gen. 14:6).

Parmenas ("steadfast"), one of the seven deacons (Acts 6:5).

Pashhur ("splitter; cleaver"). **[1]** Head of a priestly family (Ezra 2:38; 10:22; Neh. 7:41). **[2]** A priest who sealed the covenant with God after the Exile (Neh. 10:1, 3). Possibly identical with **[1]**. **[3]** A priest, the "chief governor in the house of the Lord," who persecuted Jeremiah (Jer. 20:1–6). **[4]** Son of Melchiah, whose family returned to Jerusalem (1 Chr. 9:12; Neh. 11:12; Jer. 21:1; 38:1).

Patmos ("mortal"), a barren island to which John was banished (Rev. 1:9). It is in the Greek archipelagos and is now called Patino.

Paul (Latin, *Paulus*—"little"), the Roman name of Saul of Tarsus, a Pharisee who studied Jewish law under Gamaliel (Acts 21:39). He was converted and made an apostle to the Gentiles (Acts 26:12–20). Perhaps he used his Roman name in humility. The Book of Acts tells of his missionary journeys.

Pedaiah ("Jehovah delivers"). **[1]** Father of Joel (1 Chr. 27:20). **[2]** Grandfather of King Josiah (2 Kin. 23:36). **[3]** Son or grandson of Jeconiah (1 Chr. 3:18, 19). **[4]** One who helped to rebuild the wall of Jerusalem (Neh. 3:25). **[5]** One who stood with Ezra when he read the Law (Neh. 8:4; 13:13). **[6]** A descendant of Benjamin (Neh. 11:7).

Pelatiah ("Jehovah delivers"). **[1]** One who sealed the new covenant with God after the Exile (Neh. 10:22). **[2]** A descendant of David (1 Chr. 3:21). **[3]** A captain of Simeon (1 Chr. 4:42, 43). **[4]** A wicked prince seen in Ezekiel's vision (Ezek. 11:1, 13).

Peniel. *See* Penuel.

Penuel [Peniel] ("face of God"), an encampment of the Hebrews east of Jordan (Gen. 32:30, 31; Judg. 8:8, 17). It derived its name from the fact that Jacob had seen God face-to-face there.

Perga ("very earthy"), the capital of Pamphylia in Asia Minor during the Roman period (Acts 13:13).

Pergamos ("elevation"), a city of Mysia in northwest Asia Minor and the site of one of the seven churches of Asia (Rev. 2:12–17).

Persia ("cuts or divides"), a great empire including all of western Asia and parts of Europe and Africa (Ezek. 38:5; Ezra 1:8). Persia proper corresponded to what is now the province of Fars in Iran.

Peter ("stone; rock"), a fisherman called to be an apostle of Christ. He became one of the leaders of the early church (Matt. 4:18–20; 16:15–19; Acts 2). Christ changed this man's name from Simon to a name meaning "rock" (*Cephas* in Aramaic, *Peter* in Greek).

Pharaoh ("inhabitant of the palace"), royal title of Egyptian kings, equivalent to our word *king* (Gen. 12:15; 37:36; Ex. 2:15; 1 Kin. 3:1; Is. 19:11).

Philadelphia ("love of a brother"), a town of Lydia in Asia Minor. It was the site of one of the seven churches of Asia (Rev. 1:11; 3:7–13). It was 45.5 km. (28.3 mi.) southeast of Sardis.

Philemon ("friendship"), a convert at Colosse to whom Paul wrote an epistle on behalf of his runaway servant, Onesimus (Philem. 1, 5–7).

Philetus ("amiable"), a convert who was condemned by Paul because of his stand on the Resurrection (2 Tim. 2:17).

Philip ("lover of horses"). **[1]** One of the twelve apostles of Christ (Matt. 10:3; John 1:44–48; 6:5–9). **[2]** An evangelist mentioned several times in Acts (Acts 6:5; 8:5–13). **[3]** *See* Herod **[3], [4].**

Philippi ("pertaining to Philip"), a city of Macedonia founded by Philip the Great and named for him (Acts 16:12; 20:3–6). It lies inland about 16.1 km. (10 mi.) northwest of its seaport, Neapolis.

Philistia ("land of sojourners"), an area on the southwest coast of Palestine (Ps. 60:8; 87:4; 108:9). This land, which was the home of traditional enemies of Israel, was 80 km. (50 mi.) long and only 24 km. (15 mi.) wide.

Phinehas ("mouth of brass"). **[1]** Grandson of Aaron and high priest (Ex. 6:25; Num. 25:6–18; 1 Chr. 6:4; 9:20). **[2]** Younger son of Eli; he was a priest who abused his office (1 Sam. 1:3; 2:22–24, 34). **[3]** Father of Eleazar (Ezra 8:33).

Phoebe ("shining"), a servant of the church at Corinth or Cenchrea who helped Paul (Rom. 16:1).

Phoenicia ("land of palm trees"), a thin strip of territory between the Mediterranean Sea on the west and on the east the mountains of Lebanon (Acts 21:2; 11:19; 15:3). It included the hills running south from those mountains.

Phoenix ("land of palm trees"). **[1]** A harbor in southern Crete (Acts 27:12). **[2]** *See* Phoenicia.

Phrygia ("barren"), a large and important inland province of Asia Minor (Acts 2:10; 16:6).

Phut. *See* Libya.

Pilate. *See* Pontius Pilate.

Pisgah ("fortress"), the mountain ranges from which Moses viewed the Promised Land (Num. 21:20; Deut. 3:27). This part of the Abarim Range is near the northeast end of the Dead Sea.

Pisidia ("pitch"), an inland district of Asia Minor with Antioch as its capital (Acts 13:14).

Pontius Pilate (Latin, *Pontius Pilatus*—"marine dart-carrier"), a Roman procurator of Judea. When Christ was brought before him for judgment, Pilate, fearing the Jews, turned Him over to the people even though he found Him not guilty (Matt. 27:2–24; John 18:28–40).

Pontus ("the sea"), a district in northeastern Asia Minor on the Pontus Euxinus (Acts 2:9; 1 Pet. 1:1).

Porcius Festus. *See* Festus.

Potiphar ("belonging to the sun-god"), Egyptian captain of the guard who became the master of Joseph (Gen. 37:36; 39:1).

Poti-Pherah ("given of the sun-god"), a priest of On; father-in-law of Joseph (Gen. 41:45, 50).

Potter's Field. *See* Akel Dama.

Praetorium. The Praetorium was originally the headquarters of a Roman camp, but in the provinces the name was used to designate the official residence. Jesus was brought to Pilate's Praetorium in Jerusalem (Mark 15:16).

Priscilla [Prisca] ("ancient one"), the wife of Aquila; a Jewish Christian deeply loyal to her faith (Acts 18:2, 18, 26; Rom. 16:3).

Prochorus ("choir leader"), one of the seven deacons (Acts 6:5).

Publius ("common; first"), governor of Malta who courteously received Paul and his company when they were shipwrecked (Acts 28:1–10).

Pul. *See* Tiglath-Pileser.

Put. *See* Libya.

R

Rabmag. This is not a proper name, but an official position of some sort. It is unclear whether it is a high religious or governmental position (Jer. 39:3, 13). Nergal-Sharezer of Babylonia bore this title.

Rabsaris, not a proper name, but an official position in the Babylonian and Assyrian governments. Its precise nature is unknown (Jer. 39:3, 13; 1 Kin. 18:17).

Rabshakeh, the title of an office in the Assyrian government. Its precise function is unknown, but suggestions include that of a field marshal or governor of the Assyrian provinces east of Haran (2 Kin. 18:17- 8; 19:4, 8).

Rachel ("ewe"), daughter of Laban, wife of Jacob, and mother of Joseph and Benjamin (Gen. 29—35).

Raguel. *See* Jethro.

Rahab ("broad"), the harlot of Jericho who helped the Hebrew spies and who became an ancestor of Christ (Josh. 2:1–21; 6:17–25; Matt. 1:5).

Ram [Aram] ("exalted"). **[1]** An ancestor of David and of Christ (Ruth 4:19; Matt. 1:3, 4; Luke 3:33). **[2]** Son of Jerahmeel of Judah (1 Chr. 2:27). **[3]** Head of the family of Elihu (Job 32:2).

Ramah ("elevated"). **[1]** A town in Benjamin near Gibeah, Geba, and Bethel (Josh. 18:25; Judg. 4:5; Is. 10:29; Matt. 2:18). It has been identified as modern Er-Ram 8 km. (5 mi.) north of Jerusalem. **[2]** The town where Samuel was born (1 Sam. 1:1). It is also called Ramathaim Zophim (1 Sam. 1:1). Its location is uncertain but has been identified with Ramah **[1]** and modern-day Rentis, about 14.5 km. (9 mi.) northeast of Lydda. It may be Arimathea. **[3]** A frontier town of Asher (Josh. 19:29). If not the same as Ramah **[4]** it may be Rameh, about 20.9 km. (13 mi.) south-southeast of Tyre. **[4]** A fortified city of Naphtali (Josh. 19:36). The site may be modern Rameh 27.4 km. (17 mi.) east-northeast of Acco. **[5]** *See* Ramoth Gilead.

Ramathaim Zophim. *See* Ramah **[2]**.

Rameses ("child of the sun"), a fertile district of Egypt where the Israelites settled (Gen. 47:11; Ex. 12:37). It was possibly the Land of Goshen.

Ramoth Gilead [Ramoth] ("heights of Gilead"), the chief city of Gad. It was a city of refuge ascribed to the Levites (1 Kin. 4:13; 22:4). Sometimes it is called simply Ramoth (Deut. 4:43; Josh. 20:8). It has been identified with both Tell Ramith and Tell el-Hush.

Rapha ("fearful"). **[1]** The fifth son of Benjamin (1 Chr. 8:2). He is called Rephaiah in First Chronicles 9:43. **[2]** A descendant of King Saul (1 Chr. 8:37).

Rebecca. Greek form of Rebekah (q.v.).

Rebekah [Rebecca] ("flattering"), wife of Isaac and mother of Jacob and Esau (Gen. 22:23; 24—28).

Rechab ("companionship"). **[1]** A descendant of Benjamin who murdered Ishbosheth (2 Sam. 4:2, 5–9). **[2]** Founder of a tribe called Rechabites (2 Kin. 10:15; Jer. 35). **[3]** A descendant of Hemath (1 Chr. 2:55). **[4]** One who helped to build the wall of Jerusalem (Neh. 3:14).

Red Sea, a sea that divides Egypt and Arabia. It was across this body of water that the Israelites escaped from Egypt (Ex. 10:19). The Hebrews called it the Sea of Deliverance; others called it the Sea of Reeds.

Refuge, Cities of. *See* Cities of Refuge.

Refuse Gate. A gate in the southwest wall of Jerusalem (Neh. 2:13; 12:31).

Rehoboam ("freer of the people"), the son of Solomon; when he was king, ten tribes revolted from him and he set up the southern kingdom of Judah (1 Kin. 11:43; 12; 14). He was an ancestor of Christ (Matt. 1:7).

Rehoboth ("spaces"). **[1]** A well dug by Isaac in the Valley of Gerar (Gen. 26:22). It is probably modern Wadi Ruheibeh, 30.6 km. (19 mi.) southwest of Beersheba. **[2]** A suburb of Nineveh (Gen. 10:11). **[3]** A city somewhere in northern Edom (Gen. 36:37; 1 Chr. 1:48). Its location is unidentified.

Rephaim, Valley of ("valley of the giants"), the site in Judah where David defeated the Philistines (Is. 17:5; 2 Sam. 5:18). It lies between Jerusalem and Bethlehem, southwest of Jerusalem and the Valley of Hinnom. It is probably the present-day Valley el-Bukaa.

Reuben ("behold, a son"), eldest son of Jacob and Leah; he lost his birthright through sin against his father (Gen. 29:32; 35:22; 37:29). His descendants became one of the twelve tribes of Israel.

Reuel ("God is his friend"). **[1]** A son of Esau by Basemath (Gen. 36:4; 1 Chr. 1:35, 37). **[2]** Descendant of Benjamin (1 Chr. 9:8). **[3]** *See* Jethro.

Rezin ("dominion"). **[1]** The last king of Syria who, along with Pekah, fought Judah (2 Kin. 15:37; 16:5–10). **[2]** One whose descendants returned from the Babylonian Captivity (Ezra 2:48; Neh. 7:50).

Rhoda ("rose"), a maid in the house of Mary (Acts 12:12–15).

Riblah ("quarrel"). **[1]** A city on the Orontes where the sons of Zedekiah were slain (Jer. 39:5–7; 2 Kin. 23:33). It was 80 km. (50 mi.) south of Hamath. It may be modern Ribleh in the Plain of Coelesyria. **[2]** A border city of the Promised Land (Num. 34:11). It is perhaps modern Harmel northeast of the source of the Orontes.

Rimmon. **[1]** A town in southern Judah (Josh. 15:32; 1 Chr. 4:32; Zech. 14:10). It is identified with Khirbet Umm er-Ramāmīn, about 9 mi. from Beersheba. **[2]** A rock near Gibeah (Judg. 20:45–47; 21:13). It is possibly a limestone projection 3½ mi. east of Bethel. **[3]** A border town of Zebulun (1 Chr. 6:77). The town is called Dimnah in Joshua 21:35, a reading many scholars consider a corruption of Rimmon. The site is referred to in Joshua 19:13 as Remmon-methoar. Many translate verse 13: "[the border] goes out to Ittah-Kazin and goes to Kemmon and bends [methoar] to Neah."

Rome ("city of Romulus"), the capital of the great Roman Empire (Acts 23:11). It is located in Italy on the Tiber River.

Rufus ("red"). **[1]** A son of Simon of Cyrene (Mark 15:21). He was probably well-known to those to whom Mark wrote his Gospel. **[2]** A

Roman Christian (Rom. 16:13); some identify him with **[1]**.

Ruth ("friendship; companion"), Moabite wife of Mahlon and Boaz; she was the great-grandmother of David and an ancestor of Christ (Ruth 1:4, 5, 14-16; 4:10; Matt. 1:5).

S

Salamis ("shaken"), a town located on the east end of Cyprus (Acts 13:5). It is 4.8 km. (3 mi.) northwest of modern Famagusta.

Salem ("perfect peace"), the city of Melchizedek (Gen. 14:18; Ps. 76:2). It is possibly modern Salim; however, many believe it to be Jerusalem.

Salim ("path"), the place where John baptized (John 3:23). It is near the waters of Aenon, which were probably north of Shechem, although the site is uncertain.

Salome ("clothing; strength"). **[1]** One of the women who saw the Crucifixion (Mark 15:40; 16:1). Matthew 27:56 mentions that the mother of the sons of Zebedee was present; she is probably to be identified with Salome. John 19:25 lists the sister of Jesus' mother among those near the cross; some scholars identify her with Salome, but others deny this. **[2]** The daughter of Herodias who danced before Herod (Matt. 14:6; Mark 6:22).

Salt, City of. *See* City of Salt.

Salt Sea [Dead Sea; East Sea], the body of water at the southern end of the Jordan Valley, which contains no marine life because of its heavy mineral contents (Gen. 14:3; Num. 34:12). Its modern name is the Dead Sea.

Samaria ("watch mountain"). **[1]** The capital of the northern kingdom of Israel (1 Kin. 20:1; 2 Chr. 18:2; Jer. 41:5). It was 67.6 km. (42 mi.) north of Jerusalem. **[2]** Another name for the kingdom of Israel (1 Kin. 13:32; 2 Kin. 17:24). **[3]** A district of Palestine in Christ's time (Luke 17:11-19). Galilee was on its north and Judea on the south.

Samson ("distinguished; strong"), judge of Israel for 20 years. His great strength and moral weakness have made him famous (Judg. 13:24; 14—16).

Samuel [Shemuel] ("asked of God; heard of God"), prophet and last judge of Israel. He anointed Saul and later David as king (1 Sam. 1:20; 3—13; 15—16; 19; 25:1; Heb. 11:32).

Sanballat ("strong"), a leading opponent of the Jews at the time they were rebuilding the walls of Jerusalem (Neh. 2:10; 4:1, 7; 6:1-14).

Sapphira ("beautiful; sapphire"), the dishonest wife of Ananias, who was struck dead by God (Acts 5:1-10).

Sarah [Sarai] ("princess"), the wife of Abraham and mother of Isaac (Gen. 17—18; 20—21; Heb. 11:11; 1 Pet. 3:6). Her name was changed from Sarai ("Jehovah is prince") to Sarah ("princess") because she would be the progenitor of a great nation (Gen. 17:15).

Sarai. *See* Sarah.

Sardis ("prince of joy"), the capital city of Lydia where a church was located (Rev. 1:11; 3:1, 4). It was on the east bank of the Pactolus River about 80.5 km. (50 mi.) east of Smyrna.

Sargon ("[the god] has established the king [ship]"), an important king of Assyria who finished the siege of Samaria and carried away Israel. He is called by name only once in Scripture (Is. 20:1).

Saul [Shaul] ("asked"). **[1]** The first king of Israel; God eventually gave him up. He tried several times to slay David, but was killed himself at Gilboa (1 Sam. 9—31). **[2]** The original name of Paul (q.v.). **[3]** The sixth king of Edom (Gen. 36:37, 38; 1 Chr. 1:48, 49).

Seir ("tempest"). **[1]** The valley and mountains of Arabah from the Dead Sea south to the Elanitic Gulf (Gen. 14:6; 32:3). Seir was the name of the mountain range in Edom and the name came to include the entire territory. **[2]** A ridge on Judah's border west of Kirjath Jearim (Josh. 15:10).

Sela ("a rock"). **[1]** The capital of Edom, located between the Dead Sea and the Gulf of 'Aqaba (2 Kin. 14:7; Is. 16:1). It is also called Petra. **[2]** A rock formation about 1,160 m. (3,800 ft.) above sea level, which dominates the city of Petra (cf. Judg. 1:36). It is now called Ummel-Bizarah.

Sennacherib (Babylonian, *Sin-ahi-eriba*—"[the god] Sin has substituted for my brother"), an Assyrian king who killed his brother to usurp the throne. He unsuccessfully invaded Judah. The amazing story of the destruction of his army is told in Second Kings 19 (2 Kin. 18:13; Is. 36:1; 37:17, 21, 37).

Seraiah ("Jehovah is prince; Jehovah has prevailed"). **[1]** A scribe of David (2 Sam. 8:17). In Second Samuel 20:25, he is called Sheva and Shavsha in First Chronicles 18:16. He is also called Shisha in First Kings 4:3. **[2]** Chief priest of Jerusalem (2 Kin. 25:18; 1 Chr. 6:14; Ezra 7:1). **[3]** One whom Gedaliah advised to submit to Chaldea (2 Kin. 25:23; Jer. 40:8). **[4]** The brother of Othniel (1 Chr. 4:13, 14). **[5]** A descendant of Simeon (1 Chr. 4:35). **[6]** A priest that returned to Jerusalem with Zerubbabel (Ezra 2:2). **[7]** A leader sent to capture Jeremiah (Jer. 36:26). **[8]** A prince of Judah who went to Babylon (Jer. 51:59, 61). **[9]** A son of Hilkiah dwelling in Jerusalem after the Exile (Neh. 11:11). **[10]** A chief of the priests who returned from Babylon (Neh. 12:1, 7).

Sergius Paulus. The Roman deputy of Cyprus who was converted because Elymas was struck blind (Acts 13:7).

Seth [Sheth] ("compensation; sprout"), son of Adam and Eve, and an ancestor of Christ (Gen. 4:25, 26; 1 Chr. 1:1; Luke 3:38).

Shabbethai ("sabbath-born"). **[1]** An assistant to Ezra (Ezra 10:15). **[2]** One who explained the Law to the people (Neh. 8:7). **[3]** A chief Levite in Jerusalem (Neh. 11:16). All three may be identical.

Shadrach ("servant of [the god] Sin"), the name given to Hananiah at Babylon. He was cast into a fiery furnace and rescued (Dan. 1:7; 3).

Shallum [Shallun] ("recompenser"). **[1]** The youngest son of Naphtali (1 Chr. 7:13). He is also called Shillem (Gen. 46:24; Num. 26:49). **[2]** A descendant of Simeon (1 Chr. 4:25). **[3]** A descendant of Judah (1 Chr. 2:40, 41). **[4]** One who usurped the throne of Israel and reigned for one month (2 Kin. 15:10–15). **[5]** Husband of Huldah the prophetess (2 Kin. 22:14; 2 Chr. 34:22). **[6]** *See* Jehoahaz **[2]**. **[7]** *See* Meshullam **[7]**. **[8]** A gatekeeper of the tabernacle (1 Chr. 9:17–19, 31; Ezra 2:42; Neh. 7:45). **[9]** Father of Jehizkiah (2 Chr. 28:12). **[10], [11]** Two who married foreign wives during the Exile (Ezra 10:24, 42). **[12]** One who helped to repair the wall of Jerusalem (Neh. 3:12). **[13]** One who helped to repair the gate of Jerusalem (Neh. 3:15). **[14]** An uncle of Jeremiah (Jer. 32:7). **[15]** Father of one who was a temple officer in the days of Jehoiakim (Jer. 35:4).

Shammah ("fame; renown"). **[1]** A grandson of Esau (Gen. 36:13, 17; 1 Chr. 1:37). **[2]** A son of Jesse (1 Sam. 16:9; 17:13). He is also called Shimeah or Shimea (2 Sam. 13:3; 21:21; 1 Chr. 20:7; 2:13). **[3]** One of David's mighty men or the father of one of David's mighty men (2 Sam. 23:11). **[4]** Another of David's mighty men (2 Sam. 23:33), called Shammoth in First Chronicles 11:27. **[5]** Yet another of David's mighty men (2 Sam. 23:25).

Shammua ("famous"). **[1]** One sent to spy out the land of Canaan (Num. 13:4). **[2]** One of David's sons (2 Sam. 5:14; 1 Chr. 14:4). In First Chronicles 3:5, he is called Shimea. **[3]** A Levite who led the temple worship after the Exile (Neh. 11:17). He is also called Shemaiah (1 Chr. 9:16). **[4]** The head of a priestly family in Nehemiah's day (Neh. 12:18).

Shaphan ("prudent; sly"). **[1]** A scribe of Josiah who read him the Law (2 Kin. 22:3; 2 Chr. 34:8–21). **[2]** Father of a chief officer under Josiah (2 Kin. 22:12; 2 Chr. 34:20). **[3]** Father of Elasah (Jer. 29:3). **[4]** Father of Jaazaniah whom Ezekiel saw in a vision (Ezek. 8:11). Many scholars consider all of the above to be identical.

Shaphat ("judge"). **[1]** One sent to spy out the land of Canaan (Num. 13:5). **[2]** Father of Elisha the prophet (1 Kin. 19:16, 19; 2 Kin. 3:11; 6:31). **[3]** One of the family of David (1 Chr. 3:22). **[4]** A chief of Gad (1 Chr. 5:12). **[5]** One over David's herds in the valley (1 Chr. 27:29).

Sharon ("his song"). **[1]** A region that lies between the Mediterranean Sea from Joppa to Carmel and the central portion of Palestine (1 Chr. 27:29; Acts 9:35). **[2]** A district east of the Jordan occupied by the tribe of Gad (1 Chr. 5:16).

Shear-Jashub ("a remnant returns"), symbolic name given a son of Isaiah (Is. 7:3).

Sheba ("oath; covenant"). **[1]** A chief of Gad (1 Chr. 5:13). **[2]** One who rebelled against David and was beheaded for it (2 Sam. 20). **[3]** A grandson of Abraham (Gen. 25:3; 1 Chr. 1:32). **[4]** A descendant of Shem (Gen. 10:28; 1 Chr. 1:22). Some scholars identify **[5]** with **[4]**. They believe Sheba is a tribe or people and stress that close genealogical ties account for the occurrence of the name in both Ham's and Shem's genealogy. **[5]** A descendant of Ham (Gen. 10:7; 1 Chr. 1:9).

Sheba ("oath"). **[1]** A country in southwest Arabia (1 Kin. 10:1–13; 2 Chr. 9:1–12). Its capital was Ma'rib, which was about 60 miles east-northeast of San'a, the present capital of Yemen. **[2]** A town of Simeon mentioned after Beersheba (Josh. 19:2). Its location is uncertain.

Shechaniah [Shecaniah] ("Jehovah is a neighbor"). **[1]** Head of a family of the house of David (1 Chr. 3:21, 22). **[2], [3]** Two whose descendants returned from the Babylonian Captivity (Ezra 8:3, 5). **[4]** One who took a foreign wife during the Exile (Ezra 10:2). **[5]** Father of one who repaired the wall of Jerusalem (Neh. 3:29). **[6]** Father-in-law to one who opposed Nehemiah (Neh. 6:18). **[7]** A priest who returned from the Exile (Neh. 12:3). **[8]** A priest in the time of David (1 Chr. 24:11). **[9]** A priest in Hezekiah's day (2 Chr. 31:15).

Shechem ("shoulder"). **[1]** Son of Hamor who defiled Dinah; he and his family were soon destroyed for that act (Gen. 33:19; 34). **[2]** A descendant of Manasseh (Num. 26:31; Josh. 17:2). **[3]** Another descendant of Manasseh (1 Chr. 7:19).

Shechem ("portion"), an ancient city in central Palestine (Gen. 12:6; 33:18; Josh. 24:32; Acts 7:16), in the hill country of Ephraim. It is present-day Nablus, located about 66 km. (41 mi.) north of Jerusalem between Mount Ebal and Mount Gerizim.

Shelomith ("peacefulness"). **[1]** Mother of one stoned for blasphemy in the wilderness (Lev. 24:11). **[2]** Daughter of Zerubbabel (1 Chr. 3:19). **[3]** A descendant of Gershon (1 Chr. 23:9). **[4]** A descendant of Levi and Kohath (1 Chr. 23:18). **[5]** One over the treasures in the days of David (1 Chr. 26:25–28). **[6]** Child of Rehoboam (2 Chr. 11:20). **[7]** An ancestor of a family that returned from the Exile (Ezra 8:10). Not to be confused with Shelomoth.

Shem ("name; renown"), son of Noah and ancestor of Christ (Gen. 5:32; 6:10; 10:1; Luke 3:36).

Shemaiah ("Jehovah is fame" or "Jehovah hears"). **[1]** A prophet who warned Rehoboam against war (1 Kin. 12:22; 2 Chr. 11:2). **[2]** A descendant of David (1 Chr. 3:22). **[3]** Head of a family of Simeon (1 Chr. 4:37). **[4]** Son of Joel (1 Chr. 5:4). **[5]** A descendant of Merari (1 Chr. 9:14; Neh. 11:15). **[6]** One who helped to bring the ark of the covenant to the temple (1 Chr. 15:8, 11). **[7]** A Levite who recorded the allotment in David's day (1 Chr. 24:6). **[8]** A gatekeeper for the tabernacle (1 Chr. 26:4, 6, 7). **[9]** A Levite whom Jehoshaphat sent to teach the people (2 Chr. 17:8). **[10]** One who helped to cleanse the temple (2 Chr. 29:14). **[11]** A Levite in Hezekiah's day (2 Chr. 31:15). **[12]** A chief Levite in Josiah's day (2 Chr. 35:9). **[13]** One who returned with Ezra (Ezra 8:13). **[14]** A person sent to Iddo to enlist ministers (Ezra 8:16). **[15], [16]** Two who married foreign wives during the Exile (Ezra 10:21, 31). **[17]** One who helped to repair the wall of Jerusalem (Neh. 3:29). **[18]** One who tried to intimidate Nehemiah (Neh. 6:10). **[19]** One who sealed the new covenant with God after the Exile (Neh. 10:8). **[20]** One who helped to purify the wall of Jerusalem (Neh. 12:36). **[21]** One at the dedication of the wall of Jerusalem (Neh. 12:42). **[22]** Father of the prophet Urijah (Jer. 26:20). **[23]** One who wanted the priests to reprimand Jeremiah (Jer. 29:24, 31). **[24]** Father of a prince of the Jews (Jer. 36:12). **[25]** *See* Shammua **[3]**. **[26]** A prince of Judah who took part in the dedication of the wall (Neh. 12:34). **[27]** A Levite of the line of Asaph (Neh. 12:35). **[28]** A chief of the priests who returned with Zerubbabel (Neh. 12:6, 7).

Shemariah [Shamariah] ("whom Jehovah guards"). **[1]** One who joined David at Ziklag (1 Chr. 12:5). **[2]** A son of King Rehoboam (2 Chr. 11:19). **[3], [4]** Two who married foreign wives during the Exile (Ezra 10:32, 41).

Shemuel (variant form of Samuel—"asked of God"). **[1]** One appointed to divide the land of Canaan (Num. 34:20). **[2]** Head of a family of Issachar (1 Chr. 7:2). **[3]** *See* Samuel.

Shephatiah ("Jehovah is judge"). **[1]** A son of David by Abital (2 Sam. 3:4; 1 Chr. 3:3). **[2]** Father of Meshullam who dwelt in Jerusalem (1 Chr. 9:8). **[3]** A valiant man who joined David at Ziklag (1 Chr. 12:5). **[4]** A prince of Simeon (1 Chr. 27:16). **[5]** A son of Jehoshaphat (2 Chr. 21:2). **[6]** An ancestor of returned captives (Ezra 2:4; Neh. 7:9). **[7]** One of Solomon's servants whose descendants returned from the Babylonian Captivity (Ezra 2:57; Neh. 7:59). **[8]** An ancestor of returned captives (Ezra 8:8). He is possibly identical with **[6]**. **[9]** A descendant of Perez whose descendants dwelt in Jerusalem (Neh. 11:4). **[10]** A prince of Judah in Zedekiah's time (Jer. 38:1).

Sheshbazzar ("O Shamash [the god], protect the father"), the prince of Judah into whose hands Cyrus placed the temple vessels. Many believe he is the same as Zerubbabel, but others deny this. They claim Sheshbazzar was governor under Cyrus and Zerubbabel under Darius (Ezra 1:8, 11; 5:14–16).

Shihor [Sihor] ("blackness"), the east branch of the Nile River (1 Chr. 13:5; Jer. 2:18). Ideally, this was to be Israel's southern boundary.

Shiloh ("peace"), a town in Ephraim (Josh. 18:1–10; Judg. 21:19). It is halfway between Shechem and Bethel.

Shimea [Shimeah] ("[God] has heard [a prayer]"). **[1]** A descendant of Merari (1 Chr. 6:30). **[2]** Father of Berachiah (1 Chr. 6:39). **[3]** *See* Shammah **[2]**. **[4]** *See* Shammua **[2]**. **[5]** One of the family of King Saul whose descendants dwelt in Jerusalem (1 Chr. 8:32; 9:38). In the latter passage he is called Shimeam.

Shimei [Shimi] ("Jehovah is fame; Jehovah hear me"). **[1]** A son of Gershon and a grandson of Gershon (Ex. 6:17; Num. 3:18, 21; Zech. 12:13). **[2]** A descendant of Benjamin who cursed David when he was fleeing from Absalom (2 Sam. 16:5–13; 19:16–23). **[3]** A loyal officer of David (1 Kin. 1:8). **[4]** An officer of Solomon (1 Kin. 4:18). **[5]** Grandson of King Jeconiah (1 Chr. 3:19). **[6]** A man who had sixteen sons and six daughters (1 Chr. 4:26, 27). **[7]** A descendant of Reuben (1 Chr. 5:4). **[8]** A son of Libni (1 Chr. 6:29). **[9]** Father of a chief of Judah (1 Chr. 8:21). **[10]** A Levite (1 Chr. 23:9). **[11]** A Levite in the temple song service in the days of David (1 Chr. 25:17). **[12]** One in charge of many vineyards (1 Chr. 27:27). **[13]** One who helped to cleanse the temple (2 Chr. 29:14). **[14]** A Levite in charge of the temple offerings under Hezekiah (2 Chr. 31:12, 13). **[15], [16], [17]** Three men who took foreign wives during the Exile (Ezra 10:23, 33, 38). **[18]** Grandfather of Mordecai (Esth. 2:5).

Shimri ("Jehovah is watching"). **[1]** Head of a family of Simeon (1 Chr. 4:37). **[2]** Father of one of David's mighty men (1 Chr. 11:45). **[3]** Gatekeeper of the tabernacle in David's day (1 Chr. 26:10). **[4]** One who helped to cleanse the temple (2 Chr. 29:13).

Shinar ("watch of him that sleeps"), the plains later known as Babylonia or Chaldea, through which the Tigris and Euphrates Rivers flow (Gen. 10:10; Is. 11:11).

Shittim [Acacia Grove] ("thorns"). **[1]** The final Israelite encampment before crossing the Jordan. Here Moses bade farewell and the Law was completed (Num. 25:1; Josh. 2:1). It was in Moab, east of Jordan, opposite Jericho. **[2]** A dry and unfruitful valley (Joel 3:18). The name may not denote any particular valley, but it may refer to the Kidron Wadi which starts northwest of Jerusalem, moves toward the east and runs toward the Dead Sea. It may also be a portion of the Arabah around the Dead Sea.

Shur ("wall"), a desert in the northwest part of the Sinai Peninsula (Gen. 16:7; 25:18). It was outside the eastern border of Egypt and was probably a caravan route between Egypt and Beersheba.

Shushan [Susa] ("a lily"), the capital of Elam inhabited by the Babylonians; later a royal residence and capital of the Persian Empire (Neh. 1:1; Dan. 8:2). The city was also known as Susa. The site is modern Shush on the Ulai River.

Sidon ("hunting"), an ancient city of Canaan (Gen. 10:15, 19; Josh. 11:8; Luke 4:26).

Sihon ("great; bold"), an Amorite king that was defeated by Israel (Num. 21:21–31; Deut. 1:4; 2:24–32; Josh. 13:15–28).

Sihor. *See* Shihor.

Silas [Silvanus] ("forest; woody; third; asked"), an eminent member of the early church who traveled with Paul through Asia Minor and Greece and was imprisoned with him at Philippi (Acts 15:22, 32–34; 2 Cor. 1:19; 1 Thess. 1:1).

Siloam ("sent"). **[1]** A famous pool of Jerusalem at the south end of Hezekiah's tunnel (John 9:7). It is identical with Shiloah. **[2]** A tower on the Ophel ridge near Siloam (Luke 13:4).

Silvanus. *See* Silas.

Simeon [Simon] ("hearing"). **[1]** The second son of Jacob by Leah (Gen. 29:33; 34:25; 48:5; 49:5). His descendants became one of the twelve tribes of Israel. **[2]** A devout Jew who blessed the Christ child in the temple (Luke 2:25–34). **[3]** An ancestor of Jesus (Luke 3:30). **[4]** A disciple and prophet at Antioch (Acts 13:1); he was surnamed Niger ("black"). **[5]** Original name of Peter (q.v.). Simon is but another form of Simeon. Not to be confused with Shimeon.

Simon ("hearing"). **[1]** Original name of the apostle Peter (Matt. 4:18; 16:16, 17; Luke 4:38; Acts 10:18). **[2]** Another of the twelve apostles, called Simon the Canaanite, indicating his fierce loyalty either to Israel or to his faith (Matt. 10:4; Mark 3:18; Luke 6:15; Acts 1:13). **[3]** One of Christ's brothers (Matt. 13:55; Mark 6:3). **[4]** A leper of Bethany in whose house Christ was anointed (Matt. 26:6; Mark 14:3). **[5]** A Cyrenian who was forced to bear the cross of Christ (Matt. 27:32; Mark 15:21). **[6]** A Pharisee in whose house the feet of Christ were anointed (Luke 7:40, 43, 44). **[7]** The father of Judas Iscariot (John 6:71; 12:4; 13:2). **[8]** A sorcerer who tried to buy the gifts of the Holy Spirit (Acts 8:9, 13, 18, 24). **[9]** A tanner of Joppa with whom Peter lodged (Acts 9:43; 10:6, 17, 32).

Sin ("bush"). **[1]** A city on the eastern side of the Nile (Ezek. 30:15, 16). It is possibly Pelusium; but is also identified with Syene, which is present-day Aswan at the first cataract of the Nile. **[2]** A wilderness area located between the Gulf of Suez and Sinai (Ex. 16:1; Num. 33:11, 12).

Sinai ("a bush"). **[1]** An area in the center of the peninsula that lies between the horns of the Red Sea, the Gulf of Suez, and the Gulf of 'Aqaba (Ex. 16:1; Acts 7:30–38). **[2]** A mountain, called also Horeb, where the Israelites received the Ten Commandments (Ex. 19:18). The location of the site is uncertain, although it is generally agreed to be in central Sinai. The traditional site is Jebel Musa, but other possibilities are Mount Serbal and Ras es-Safsafeh.

Sion ("breastplate"). **[1]** Another name for Mount Hermon (Deut. 4:48). **[2]** *See* Zion.

Sirion ("breastplate"), the name given to Mount Hermon by the Sidonians (Deut. 3:9; Ps. 29:6).

Sisera ("mediation; array"). **[1]** Captain of the army of Jabin who was murdered by Jael (Judg. 4:1–22; 5:26, 28). **[2]** One whose descendants returned (Ezra 2:53; Neh. 7:55).

Smyrna ("myrrh"), a city on the western coast of Asia Minor (Rev. 2:8–11). It is 64.4 km. (40 mi.) north of Ephesus.

Sodom ("their secret"), one of the five Cities of the Plain (Gen. 10:19; Rom. 9:29), destroyed because of its wickedness. The exact location of the site is unknown, but it is in the Dead Sea area.

Solomon ("peace"), son of David by Bathsheba and king of a united, strong Israel for forty years. His wisdom and carnal sin stand out in his multi-faceted character (1 Kin.

1:11; 2:11). He was an ancestor of Christ (Matt. 1:6, 7).

Solomon's Pools. A repository of water built by Solomon near Bethlehem (Eccl. 2:6).

Solomon's Porch. A colonnade built by Solomon on the east side of the temple (John 10:23; Acts 3:11).

Sosthenes ("strong; powerful"). **[1]** Chief ruler of the synagogue at Corinth, beaten by the Greeks (Acts 18:17). **[2]** A believer who united with Paul in addressing the Corinthian church (1 Cor. 1:1). Some believe he was [1] after conversion.

Stephanas ("crown"), one of the first believers of Achaia (1 Cor. 1:16; 16:15–17).

Stephen ("crown"), one of the seven deacons. He became the first martyr of the church after Christ (Acts 6:5–9; 7:59; 8:2).

Succoth ("tents"). **[1]** A town where Jacob built himself a house (Gen. 33:17; Josh. 13:27). It was east of the Jordan between Peniel and Shechem. Its probable location is Deir 'Alla, about 1.6 km. (1 mi.) west of where the Jabbok bulges and turns south. **[2]** The first camping ground of the Israelites after leaving Egypt (Ex. 12:37; 13:20).

Supply Cities [Treasure House]. Designated cities at which the kings of the ancient world kept their treasures and tithes (Ex. 1:11; Ezra 5:17).

Susa. *See* Shushan.

Susanna ("lily"), one of the women who ministered to Christ and was His follower (Luke 8:3).

Sychar ("end"), a town of Samaria near Jacob's well (John 4:5).

Syria (a form of the word *Assyria*), the country lying north and east of Palestine (Judg. 10:6; 1 Kin. 10:29; Acts 15:23). It stretched far inland from the Mediterranean and was bounded by the Taurus Mountains to the north.

Syrtis Sands ("shallows"), two shoals off the coast of Africa between Carthage and Cyrene (Acts 27:17). The greater Syrtis is now called the Gulf of Sidra, the lesser Syrtis the Gulf of Gabes.

T

Tabel ("God is good"). **[1]** Father of a man the kings of Israel and Damascus planned to make king of Judah (Is. 7:6). **[2]** A Persian official who tried to hinder the rebuilding of the wall of Jerusalem (Ezra 4:7).

Taberah ("burning"), a place three days north of Mount Sinai where Israel was punished for murmuring against God (Num. 11:3; Deut. 9:22).

Tabitha ("gazelle"), the Christian woman of Joppa whom Peter raised from the dead (Acts 9:36–42). Dorcas is the Greek form of the name.

Tabor ("purity"). **[1]** A mountain located in the northern part of the Valley of Jezreel (Judg. 4:6, 12, 14; Ps. 89:12). It is now called Jebel el-Tur and is 8.8 km. (5.5 mi.) southeast of Nazareth. **[2]** A town of Zebulun given to the Levites (1 Chr. 6:77). Its location is uncertain. It may be the Chisloth Tabor of Joshua 19:12 or Khirbet Dabural, which is on a hill between Tabor and Nazareth. **[3]** An oak (not a plain as in KJV) in Benjamin (1 Sam. 10:3).

Tahpenes. An Egyptian queen, wife of the pharaoh, who received the fleeing Hadad, an enemy of Solomon (1 Kin. 11:18–20).

Talmai ("bold; spirited"). **[1]** A man or clan defeated by Caleb (Num. 13:22; Josh. 15:14; Judg. 1:10). **[2]** King of Geshur and father-in-law of David (2 Sam. 3:3; 13:27).

Tamar ("palm"). **[1]** The wife of Er, mother of Perez, and an ancestor of Christ (Gen. 38:6, 11, 13; Ruth 4:12; Matt. 1:3). **[2]** The daughter of David violated by Amnon (2 Sam. 13:1–32). **[3]** A daughter of Absalom (2 Sam. 14:27).

Tarshish [Tarshishah] ("hard"). **[1]** A son of Javan and grandson of Noah (Gen. 10:4; 1 Chr. 1:7). Possibly a people who inhabited a region in Spain (Tartessus), near Gibraltar. **[2]** One of the seven princes of Persia (Esth. 1:14). **[3]** A descendant of Benjamin (1 Chr. 7:10).

Tarsus ("winged"), the most prominent city of Cilicia located on the river Cydnus in Asia Minor; it was the birthplace of Paul (Acts 9:11).

Tartan (meaning unknown), the title of a high Assyrian officer. There is evidence that the office was second only to the king. There are two Tartans mentioned in Scripture (2 Kin. 18:17; Is. 20:1).

Tattenai ("gift"), a Persian governor of Samaria in the days of Zerubbabel (Ezra 5:3; 6:6, 13).

Temple. The structure in which the Israelites worshiped and offered sacrifices to God. There were three temples: Solomon's, Zerubbabel's, and Herod's.

Terah ("turning; duration"), the father of Abraham and ancestor of Christ (Gen. 11:27–32; Luke 3:34).

Tertius ("third"), the scribe to whom the epistle to the Romans was dictated (Rom. 16:22). Some conjecture that he is Silas (q.v.).

Tertullus ("third"), an orator hired by the Jews to state skillfully their case against Paul before Felix (Acts 24:1–8).

Thaddaeus (a name derived from an Aramaic word for the female breast), one of the twelve apostles (Matt. 10:3; Mark 3:18). He is the same as Judas, the brother of James

(Luke 6:16; John 14:22; Acts 1:13). He was also named Lebbaeus ("heart").

Theophilus ("loved by God"), an unknown person, possibly a Roman official, to whom Luke addressed his Gospel and Acts (Luke 1:3; Acts 1:1).

Thessalonica ("victory at sea"), a city situated on the Macedonian coast at the head of the Thermaic Gulf (Acts 17:1, 11, 13; 27:2). It is known as Salonika today.

Thomas ("twin"), one of the twelve apostles of Jesus. When Christ rose from the dead, Thomas was most skeptical (Matt. 10:3; Mark 3:18; John 20:24–29). His Aramaic name is Didymus in Greek.

Three Inns. A station on the Appian Way near the modern city of Cisterna (Acts 28:15).

Thyatira ("sacrifice of labor"), a city between Pergamos and Sardis (Acts 16:14; Rev. 2:18–29). It was in Lydia in Asia Minor.

Tiberias ("good vision"), a city on the west coast of the Sea of Galilee (John 6:1; 21:1).

Tiberius ("son of [the river] Tiber"), third emperor of the Roman Empire (Luke 3:1).

Tibni ("intelligent"), one who rivaled Omri for the throne of Israel (1 Kin. 16:21, 22).

Tiglath-Pileser (Babylonian, *Tukulti-apil-Esharra*—"my trust is in the son of Asharra"), a king of Assyria who invaded Naphtali during the time of Pekah of Israel. He conquered northern Palestine and deported many from Naphtali (2 Kin. 15:29; 16:7, 10; 1 Chr. 5:6, 26). His native name was Pul (2 Kin. 15:19). Realizing he bore two names, we should translate First Chronicles 5:26, " ...God...stirred...Pul king of Assyria, that is, [not *and*] Tiglath-Pileser king of Assyria."

Timon ("honorable"), one of the seven deacons (Acts 6:1–6).

Timothy ("honored of God"), a young friend and convert of Paul; he traveled extensively with the apostle. He was from Lystra and was the son of Eunice, a Jewess, and a Greek father (Acts 16:1; 17:14, 15; 1 Tim. 1:2, 18; 6:20).

Titus ("pleasant"), a converted Grecian entrusted with a mission to Crete (2 Cor. 2:13; Gal. 2:1; Titus 1:4).

Tobiah [Tobijah] ("Jehovah is good"). **[1]** A Levite sent by Jehoshaphat to teach the Law (2 Chr. 17:8). **[2]** An ancestor of returning captives who had lost their genealogy (Ezra 2:60; Neh. 7:62). **[3]** An Ammonite servant of Sanballat who opposed Nehemiah (Neh. 2:10–20). **[4]** A leader who returned from the Babylonian Captivity (Zech. 6:10, 14).

Tobijah. *See* Tobiah.

Tophet [Topheth] ("a drum"), once a part of a king's garden in Hinnom; it became a place where people in Jerusalem sacrificed their children (Is. 30:33; Jer. 19:6, 11–14; 2 Kin. 23:10).

Troas ("penetrated"), an important city on the coast of Mysia (Acts 16:8; 2 Tim. 4:13). It was in northern Asia Minor and is also called Alexandria.

Trophimus ("a foster child"), a Christian convert and afterward a companion-in-travel with Paul (Acts 20:4; 21:29; 2 Tim. 4:20).

Tychicus ("fortunate"), a disciple and messenger of Paul (Acts 20:4; Eph. 6:21; 2 Tim. 4:12).

Tyrannus ("tyrant"), a Greek rhetorician or Jewish rabbi in whose school Paul taught at Ephesus (Acts 19:9).

Tyre ("rock"), a city on the central coast of Phoenicia noted for its commercial activity (Josh. 19:29; 2 Sam. 5:11; Jer. 25:22). It is located halfway between Acco and Sidon.

U

Ur. The city which Abram left to go to Haran (Gen. 11:28, 31). Ur is generally identified as ancient Ur (Uri), modern Tell el-Muqayyar located on the Euphrates in south Iraq.

Uriah [Urijah] ("Jehovah is my light"). **[1]** A Hittite soldier in David's army. He was killed in a fierce battle, for David, desiring to marry his wife, Bathsheba, had placed him on the front battle line (2 Sam. 11). **[2]** A priest under Ahaz who built a pagan altar on the king's command; then placed it in the temple (2 Kin. 16:10–16). **[3]** A prophet whose message of judgment so offended Jehoiakim that he murdered him (Jer. 26:20–23). **[4]** A priest, the father of Meremoth (Ezra 8:33; Neh. 3:4, 21). **[5]** A man who stood by Ezra when he read the Law (Neh. 8:4). Possibly the same as **[4]**. **[6]** A priest whom Isaiah took as a witness (Is. 8:2).

Urijah. *See* Uriah.

Uz [Huz] ("counsel; firmness"). **[1]** Eldest son of Aram (Gen. 10:23). Possibly the name refers to an Aramean tribe or people. **[2]** A son of Shem (1 Chr. 1:17). The Septuagint makes this Uz identical with [1] naming Aram as his father. It is also possible the Hebrew text was abbreviated here. **[3]** A son of Dishan, son of Seir (Gen. 36:28). **[4]** The son of Nahor by Milcah (Gen. 22:21).

Uz ("counsel; firmness"). **[1]** The country where Job lived (Job 1:1). The two most likely locations are Hauran, south of Damascus, and the area between Edom and north Arabia. **[2]** A kingdom not far from Edom (Jer. 25:20; Lam. 4:21). Perhaps identical with **[1]**.

Uzza [Uzzah] ("strength"). **[1]** A man who

was struck dead by God when he touched the ark of the covenant (2 Sam. 6:2–7; 1 Chr. 13:6–10). **[2]** A descendant of Merari (1 Chr. 6:29). **[3]** A descendant of Ehud (1 Chr. 8:7). **[4]** An ancestor of a Nethinim family that returned from Babylon (Ezra 2:49; Neh. 7:51).

Uzziah ("Jehovah is strong" or "my strength is Jehovah"). **[1]** The eleventh king of Judah. When he attempted to offer incense unlawfully, God struck him with leprosy. He was also called Azariah (2 Kin. 15:1–8; 2 Chr. 26). He was an ancestor of Christ (Matt. 1:8, 9). **[2]** A Levite descended from Kohath and ancestor of Samuel (1 Chr. 6:24). **[3]** Father of Jehonathan (1 Chr. 27:25). **[4]** A priest who had married a foreign wife (Ezra 10:21). **[5]** A descendant of Judah (Neh. 11:4).

Uzziel ("God is my strength" or "God is strong"). **[1]** The ancestor of the Uzzielites; the son of Kohath (Ex. 6:18). **[2]** Captain of the sons of Simeon (1 Chr. 4:42). **[3]** A son of Bela and grandson to Benjamin (1 Chr. 7:7). **[4]** An assistant wall-builder (Neh. 3:8). **[5]** A Levite, son of Jeduthun, who helped to cleanse the temple (2 Chr. 29:14). **[6]** A musician set by David over the service of song in the temple (1 Chr. 25:4). Uzziel is the same as Azarel in verse 18.

V

Valley Gate. A gate in the southwest wall of Jerusalem leading to the Hinnom Valley (Neh. 2:13).

Vashti ("beautiful woman; best"), the queen of Persia who was divorced by King Ahasuerus because she refused to come to his great feast (Esth. 1:10–22).

W

Water Gate. A gate on the east side of Jerusalem, above the spring of Gihon (Neh. 8:1, 3).

Wilderness. The area in which the Israelites wandered for 40 years before entering Canaan (Deut. 1:1; Josh. 5:6). Several places are encompassed in the designation Wilderness; these are listed under their individual names (e.g., Paran, Zin. etc.).

Z

Zacchaeus ("pure"), a publican with whom Jesus lodged during His stay at Jericho (Luke 19:1–10).

Zacharias (Greek form of Zechariah—"memory of the Lord"). **[1]** The prophet whom the Jews stoned (Matt. 23:35; Luke 11:51). Some believe this prophet to be identical with Zechariah **[11]** or **[16]**, though it is possible the reference is to an unknown prophet. **[2]** A priest, father of John the Baptist (Luke 1).

Zadok ("righteous"). **[1]** A high priest in the time of David (2 Sam. 8:17; 15:24–36; 1 Kin. 1:8–45). **[2]** Father of Jerusha, wife of Uzziah and mother of Jotham, both kings of Israel (2 Kin. 15:33; 2 Chr. 27:1). **[3]** Son of Ahitub and father of Shallum or Meshullam (1 Chr. 6:12, 13; Ezra 7:2). **[4]** A young man of valor (1 Chr. 12:28). **[5], [6]** Two who repaired the wall of Jerusalem (Neh. 3:4, 29). **[7]** One who sealed the covenant with Nehemiah (Neh. 10:21). **[8]** A scribe under Nehemiah (Neh. 13:13). **[9]** An ancestor of Christ (Matt. 1:14).

Zalmunna ("withdrawn from protection"), a Midianite king slain by Gideon (Judg. 8:5–21).

Zaphnath-Paaneah ("savior of the world; revealer of secrets"), name given to Joseph by Pharaoh (Gen. 41:45).

Zarephath ("smelting place"), a town located near Zidon (Sidon) that was the residence of Elijah (1 Kin. 17:9).

Zealot, The. *See* Simon **[2]**.

Zebedee ("the gift of Jehovah"), a fisherman of Galilee, husband of Salome, and father of the apostles James and John (Matt. 4:21; 27:56; Mark 1:19, 20).

Zebulun ("dwelling"), tenth son of Jacob and ancestor of one of the twelve tribes (Gen. 30:20; 49:13; 1 Chr. 2:1).

Zebulun ("dwelling"), the territory given to the tribe of Zebulun (Josh. 19:27, 34). It was north of Issachar, east of Asher, and southwest of Naphtali.

Zechariah ("Jehovah my righteousness"). **[1]** A chief of the tribe of Reuben (1 Chr. 5:7). **[2]** A Levite gatekeeper in the days of David (1 Chr. 9:21; 26:2, 14). **[3]** A Levite set over the service of song in the days of David (1 Chr. 15:18, 20; 16:5). **[4]** A priest in the days of David (1 Chr. 15:24). **[5]** A descendant of Levi through Kohath (1 Chr. 24:25). **[6]** A descendant of Levi through Merari (1 Chr. 26:11). **[7]** Father of Iddo (1 Chr. 27:21). **[8]** A prince of Jehoshaphat sent to teach the people (2 Chr. 17:7). **[9]** A Levite who encouraged Jehoshaphat against Moab (2 Chr. 20:14). **[10]** A son of Jehoshaphat (2 Chr. 21:2). **[11]** A son of Jehoiada who was stoned (2 Chr. 24:20). Also mentioned in Matthew 23:35 and Luke 11:51. **[12]** Prophet in the days of Uzziah (2 Chr. 26:5). **[13]** A Levite who helped to cleanse the temple (2 Chr. 29:13). **[14]** A descendant of Levi (2 Chr. 34:12). **[15]** A prince of Judah in the days of Josiah (2 Chr. 35:8). **[16]** A prophet in the days of Ezra. His book still exists (Ezra 5:1; 6:14; Zech. 1:1, 7; 7:1, 8). **[17]** A chief man of Israel (Ezra 8:3). **[18]** One who returned from the Exile

(Ezra 8:11). The chief man in Ezra 8:16 was probably **[17]** or **[18]**. **[19]** One who took a foreign wife during the Exile (Ezra 10:26). **[20]** A prince with Ezra (Neh. 8:4). **[21]** A descendant of Perez (Neh. 11:4). **[22]** One whose descendants dwelt in Jerusalem (Neh. 11:5). **[23]** A priest (Neh. 11:12). **[24]** A Levite trumpeter (Neh. 12:35, 36). **[25]** A priest who took part in the dedication ceremony (Neh. 12:41). **[26]** One whom Isaiah took as a witness (Is. 8:2). **[27]** Father of Abi or Abijah, mother of Hezekiah (2 Kin. 18:2). **[28]** Son and successor of Jeroboam II. He reigned only six months (2 Kin. 18:2).

Zedekiah ("Jehovah my righteousness; Jehovah is might"). **[1]** A false prophet who encouraged Ahab to attack the Syrians at Ramoth Gilead (1 Kin. 22:11, 24; 2 Chr. 18: 10, 23). **[2]** A false prophet (Jer. 29:21–23). **[3]** A prince of Judah in the days of Jehoiakim (Jer. 36:12). **[4]** The last king of Judah; his rebellion spelled the doom of Judah (2 Kin. 24:18—25:7; 2 Chr. 36:11–21). He is probably referred to in First Chronicles 3:16 as a "son" or successor of Jeconiah. *See* Mattaniah **[1]**.

Zephaniah ("Jehovah is darkness; Jehovah has treasured"). **[1]** A prophet in the days of Josiah (Zeph. 1:1). **[2]** A Levite or priest, ancestor of Samuel (1 Chr. 6:36). Possibly the same as Uriel **[1]**. **[3]** Son of Josiah the priest (Zech. 6:10, 14). **[4]** A priest who opposed Babylonian rule (2 Kin. 25:18; Jer. 21:1; 37:3).

Zered ("brook"), a brook and valley that marks the greatest limit of the Hebrews wandering in the wilderness (Num. 21:12; Deut. 2:13, 14). It was south of the Arnon, probably Wadi el-Hesa.

Zerubbabel ("seed of Babylon"). **[1]** The leader of a group who returned from Exile; he began the rebuilding of the temple (Ezra 3—5; Neh. 7:7; 12:1, 47). He was an ancestor of Christ (Matt. 1:12, 13). **[2]** An ancestor of Christ (Luke 3:27); perhaps the same as **[1]**.

Zimri ("celebrated"). **[1]** A disobedient Israelite slain by Phinehas (Num. 25:14). **[2]** A captain who slew Elah (1 Kin. 16:9–20). **[3]** A son of Zerah of Judah (1 Chr. 2:6). **[4]** A descendant of Benjamin (1 Chr. 8:36; 9:42).

Zin ("swelling"), a wilderness on the southern border of Canaan, not to be confused with the wilderness of Sin. It was either a part of the Wilderness of Paran or bordered on the wilderness which contained Kadesh Barnea (Num. 20:1; 27:14; Josh. 15:1–3).

Zion [Sion] ("monument; fortress; set up"), one of the hills on which Jerusalem stood. It came to be applied to the temple and the whole of Jerusalem and its people as a community whose destiny depends on God (2 Sam. 5:7; Is. 8:18; Ps. 48:11; Joel 2:23). Zion also is a symbol of heaven (Rev. 14:1).

Ziphron ("rejoicing"), a place specified by Moses as the northern boundary of the Promised Land (Num. 34:9). It is probably Za'feranh southeast of Restan.

Zipporah ("little bird"), the wife of Moses and daughter of Reuel (Ex. 2:21; 4:25; 18:2).